Financial Accounting The Impact on Decision Makers

Fourth Edition

Gary A. Porter and Curtis L. Norton

Managerial Accounting A Focus on Decision Making

Second Edition

Steve Jackson and Roby Sawyers

SOUTH-WESTERN
THOMSON LEARNING™

Printed in the United States of America

South-Western College Publishing
5191 Natorp Blvd
Mason, Ohio 45040
USA

For information about our products, contact us:
Thomson Learning Academic Resource Center
1-800-423-0563
http://www.swcollege.com

International Headquarters
Thomson Learning
International Division
290 Harbor Drive, 2nd Floor
Stamford, CT 06902-7477
USA

UK/Europe/Middle East/South Africa
Thomson Learning
Berkshire House
168-173 High Holborn
London WCIV 7AA

Asia
Thomson Learning
60 Albert Street, #15-01
Albert Complex
Singapore 189969

Canada
Nelson Thomson Learning
1120 Birchmount Road
Toronto, Ontario MIK 5G4
Canada
United Kingdom

ISBN 0-324-28485-3

The Adaptable Courseware Program consists of products and additions to existing South-Western College Publishing products that are produced from camera-ready copy. Peer review, class testing, and accuracy are primarily the responsibility of the author(s).

Financial Accounting
The Impact on Decision Makers

Fourth Edition

Gary A. Porter
University of St. Thomas - Minnesota

Curtis L. Norton
Northern Illinois University

SOUTH-WESTERN
THOMSON LEARNING

Preface

WELCOME ABOARD THE FOURTH EDITION!

Follow our Roadmap to Success! As you and your students take the "trip" though our text, you will experience a "journey" that will reveal the primary information needed for understanding the business environment and the important role of financial accounting in that environment. You will venture through the process of transforming the information from transactions to financial reports, deciphering the important information contained in those reports, and then analyzing it to make financial decisions.

Follow Our Well-Developed, Balanced Road

Throughout the development of our first three editions, we found that most instructors want the best of both worlds: a *decision-making focus* featuring streamlined topics and special elements to capture student interest along with rock-solid coverage and materials for teaching the *preparation of financial statements from transactions.* By striking *the right balance* with the best combination of topical coverage and pedagogical features for both of these valid approaches, we have led the way for successfully teaching financial accounting with this balanced approach. The present edition builds upon the success of its predecessors to provide the best of both.

We continue to provide *many choices* for coverage in order to meet the needs of your course and your students. As reflected in the table of contents, there are several appendices that provide additional procedural and decision-focused coverage. Any one of these can be included or excluded as desired. In addition, there is a large selection of pedagogical elements and assignments to allow *flexibility* and *variety.*

TRAVEL ON A FIRM FOUNDATION

For the fourth edition, we remain committed to four principles that have been instrumental to the success of the earlier editions:

- An emphasis on *pedagogy* and *student appeal that accommodates most learning styles.*
- A focus on *financial statements.*
- A focus on *actual public companies.*
- A *decision-making* emphasis.

Our adherence to these principles has meant that thousands of business majors and accounting majors alike are prepared for future business success. We have continued and further enhanced and expanded those elements that have proven to be most effective.

Rely on the Text's Solid Infrastructure

Supporting the balance within the text is a basic internal structure, developed around the balance sheet. Assisting in tying that structure together is the flagship company, to which students return many times as they develop their understanding of financial information. A roadmap provides a recurring visual to assist students in understanding where they are in their journey through the text.

NEW! Our **Roadmap to Success** guides students as they move through the text. The master roadmap appears at the beginning of the text, across from the title page, and provides an overview of the text. Each signpost displays one or more key questions for each chapter.

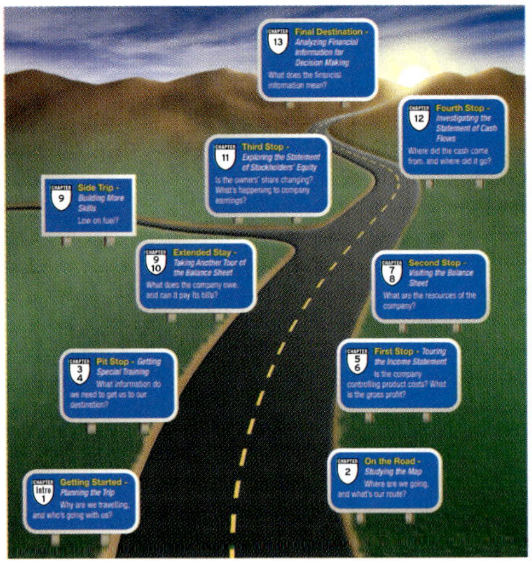

The roadmap reappears at the beginning of each chapter, where its sign expands to include a statement of the core focus of the chapter and serves as a continuing reminder of the text's direction and decision-making coverage.

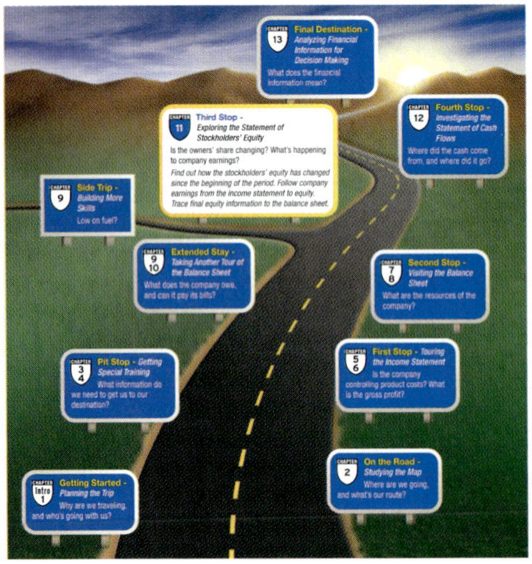

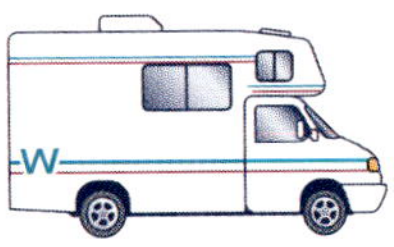

NEW! Information about **Winnebago Industries**, the new flagship company, is interwoven through every chapter in the text. Students are introduced to the company in the Introduction section and Chapter 1. In subsequent chapters, the flagship company is revisited many times with the coverage identified by a feature icon. The entire Winnebago Industries 2001 annual report is reproduced in Appendix A at the end of the text. Subsequent annual reports will be linked to the text's Web site (http://porter.swlearning.com) or may be accessed directly through the company site (http://www.winnebagoind.com).

Part Openers. Each part is introduced by **A Word to Students**, which provides an overview of the coverage to come, the title of the chapters and appendices contained within the part, and a photo introducing the featured companies.

Part I

The Accounting Model

A Word to Students About This Course

Knowing accounting is just plain smart for everyone in today's job market. This book is therefore not just for accounting majors—it's for anyone who wants to learn how to read and understand financial information. You'll work with numbers in this course. But at every turn, this book and its study aids—not to mention your instructor—will walk you through the details. You'll write some memoranda backing up your calculations, pitting your analytical skills against real financial statements and problems. And you'll have the chance to put yourself in different business roles.

In fact, this book will help you think, talk, and write skillfully about accounting information.

- **Part I—The Accounting Model**—begins with **Getting Started in Business.** This introduction is designed to help students orient themselves to the business world so that all members of the class will have basic information about the structure of businesses, the importance of financial accounting, and the decision makers in the business environment. The story of Winnebago Industries begins its path through the text in this introduction. From there, students move through Chapters 1–4. These chapters describe the four main financial statements and supporting information found in annual reports, GAAP, accrual accounting, and the basic processing of transactions through the accounting cycle.
- **Part II—Accounting for Assets**—and **Part III—Accounting for Liabilities and Owners' Equity**—"tour" the balance sheet, going from assets through liabilities to equity. We present the essential explanations of the statement's core content and clearly tie the balance sheet accounts to the other financial statements and disclosures.
- **Part IV—Additional Topics in Financial Accounting**—provides an in-depth explanation of the statement of cash flows with descriptions of both the direct and indirect methods. This section also brings together and expands on all of the analysis coverage presented earlier in the text.

Tools. Supporting several chapters are appendices that contain special "tools" for students. These include coverage of *work sheets* (Ch. 4 appendix), *internal controls* (Ch. 5 appendix), *perpetual inventory costing method* (Ch. 6 appendix), *payroll accounting* (Ch. 9 appendix A), *using Excel for interest calculations* (Ch.9 appendix B), and *statement of cash flows preparation using a work-sheet approach* (Ch. 12 appendix).

Integrative Problem. We have strategically placed a comprehensive problem at the end of each part. Each assignment challenges the student to think through a multi-faceted problem that requires knowledge learned throughout that section of the text.

Complete Glossary. For quick reference, a comprehensive glossary of key terms is located at the end of the text. Also included is the page number where each term was originally defined.

Company and Subject Indexes. Because we provide many examples and references to actual companies and other entities throughout the text, we have provided a separate company index for your convenience. This is followed by a complete subject index for quick referencing.

Navigate Our New Features

In addition to our new roadmap and new flagship company, we have further enriched our text features to assist students with understanding financial accounting.

NEW! Comparing Two Companies in the Same Industry: Winnebago Industries and Monaco Coach Corporation. Each chapter contains a new comparative case. By completing these cases, students gain a greater understanding of two competitors in the same industry. They discover differences in approaches to reporting financial information and analyze the annual reports to get a better understanding of how financial information is used by decision makers. Appendix B, at the end of the text, contains the complete Monaco Coach Corporation 2001 Annual Report. Subsequent annual reports will be linked to the text's Web site (http://porter.swlearning.com) or may be accessed directly through the company site (http://monacocoach.com)

Cases

Reading and Interpreting Financial Statements

http://www.winnebagoind.com
http://www.monacocoach.com

***Case 4-1 Comparing Two Companies in the Same Industry: Winnebago Industries and Monaco Coach Corporation* LO 3, 4, 5**

Refer to the financial information for Winnebago Industries and Monaco Coach Corporation in Appendices A and B at the end of the book.

Required

1. Neither company reports on its balance sheet an account titled "Accounts Receivable." Identify the account or accounts on each company's balance sheet that is equivalent to Accounts Receivable.
2. What dollar amount does each company report in Prepaid Expenses on its balance sheet at the end of 2001? When the benefits from this asset expire in the future this account will be credited and an expense account will be debited. For each company, identify the account or accounts on its income statement that you would expect to be debited.

NEW! Updates for the Latest Pronouncements. Chapters 8 and 10 have been revised to reflect the impact of FASB Statements 141, 142, and 145. As new pronouncements arise that impact on text coverage, additional updates will be posted on our Web site (http://porter.swlearning.com).

- Chapter 8 includes discussion of the impact of the new rules for amortizing intangibles with finite lives and the impairment rules for intangible, such as goodwill. Care is taken throughout to focus attention on how these changes affect the financial statements rather than on the specifics of the authoritative standards, something better left to an intermediate accounting course.
- Chapter 10 reflects the recent change in the classification of any gain or loss on the early retirement of bonds. The new financial accounting standard reverses an earlier pronouncement, which required extraordinary treatment for these gains and losses.

NEW! Ratios for Decision Making. The purpose of this presentation, which appears in chapters where ratios and other key calculations are introduced, is to briefly review the core reason for use of the ratio(s) for decision making. The ratios are restated along with their formulas. In addition, the financial statement or note source of each ratio component is identified. This consolidated review of the chapters ratios provide students with a quick reference and reinforcement.

Ratios for Decision Making

Long-term assets are used to produce the products and services that allow a company to operate profitably. Therefore, it is important for investors and creditors to analyze whether the long-term assets are sufficient to support the company's activities. Investors and creditors should analyze the average life of the assets, the average age of the assets, and the asset turnover. The asset turnover is a measure of how many dollars of assets are necessary to generate a dollar of sales. The following ratios can be used to calculate the life, age, and turnover of the long-term assets (assuming the company is using the straight-line method of depreciation):

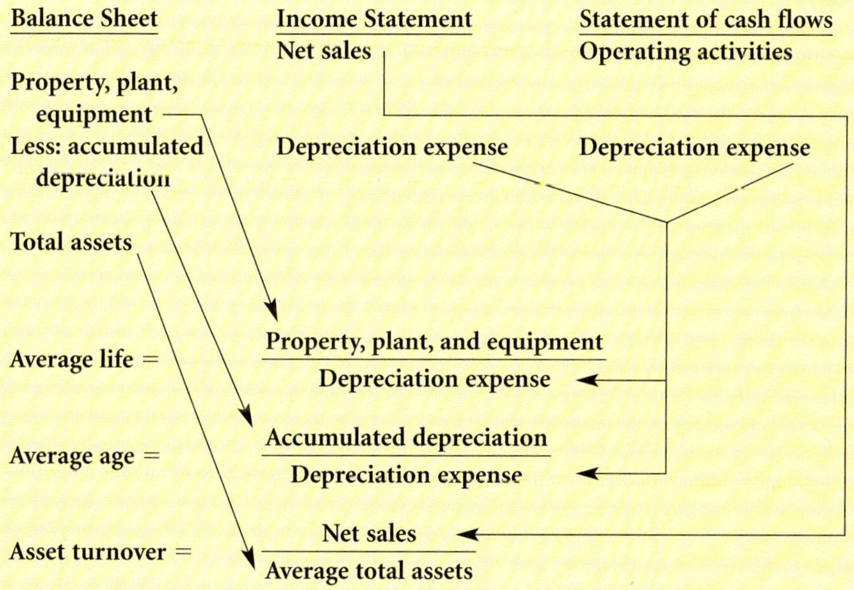

NEW! **Impact on the Financial Reports.** The purpose of this presentation is to show, in one place, the impact of the chapter's topical coverage on one or more of the four financial statements and the notes. This also reinforces how interconnected these reports are and where decision makers should expect to see impact and disclosure.

Impact on the Financial Reports

Impact on the Financial Reports

BALANCE SHEET

Current Assets
Noncurrent Assets
Property, plant, and equipment
Less: accumulated depreciation of property, plant, and equipment
Intangible assets, net of accumulated amortization
Current Liabilities
Noncurrent Liabilities
Equity

INCOME STATEMENT

Revenues
Expenses
Depreciation expense
Amortization expense
Other
Losses on sale of assets
Gains on sale of assets

STATEMENT OF STOCKHOLDERS' EQUITY

Contributed Capital
Retained Earnings

STATEMENT OF CASH FLOWS

Operating Activities
Depreciation expense
Amortization expense
Loss on sale of asset
Gain on sale of asset
Investing Activities
Purchase of asset
Sale of asset
Financing Activities
Noncash Transactions

NOTES

The methods used to depreciate long-term assets and the life of the assets should be presented in the accounting policies footnote.

NEW! **Assistance with Calculations.** As instructors, we realize the varied approaches used to teach students time value of money concepts. In Chapter 9, as either an alternative or an addition to the use of tables to perform future and present value calculations, students are introduced to the use of financial calculators to aid the process. One of the most popular of these, a Texas Instrument model, is illustrated in the examples in the chapter. The use of a financial calculator is also reinforced in Chapter 10.

NEW! **Excel as a Tool.** A new appendix to Chapter 9, "Accounting Tools: Using Excel for Problems Involving Interest Calculations," illustrates for the student how one of the most widely used spreadsheets can serve as a tool in solving time value of money problems.

NEW! **Expanded Coverage of Income Statement Items.** It is not unusual to find an income statement that include the impact of a discontinued segment, an extraordinary item, or cumulative effect of a change in an accounting principle. To better prepare students for understanding these disclosures, we have added coverage of these topics in a new Chapter 13 appendix, "Reporting and Analyzing Other Income Statement Items."

NEW! **Which Way to Go?** In accounting, there are many decisions that must be made regarding how a transaction should be handled and what its effect will be on reported financial information. We have added this feature to allow you and your students to discuss some of those choices and their impact. Suggested solutions are provided in the Instructor's Resource Manual.

Which Way To Go?

R&D Expense or Long-Term Asset?

For the past six months, Taz Industries has been struggling with a problem in its production line. The number of units produced each day has been steadily dropping. The company believes worn-out equipment is partly the cause. Three months ago, the plant manager put an engineer and the senior machinist to work, full time, to solve the problem. They created a new, electronic tool that, when used in the assembly process, significantly improves production. It is expected that this tool will be useful for at least the next five years.

The total cost of the salaries for the engineer and machinist for three months, plus the cost of materials used in the development process, is $35,000. This includes the cost of time and materials for creating early models that did not solve the problem.

Even though the company plans to use the new tool only for internal production and has no intention of selling it, management believes obtaining a patent is a good idea. The various fees involved in obtaining the patent are expected to total $10,000.

How should the company record the costs? Why should they be recorded in this manner?

Explore the Real World

Coverage of well-known companies greatly enhances student interest. We have *fully updated* all of the financial and other relevant information related to the large number of publicly traded companies that we feature.

Focus on Financial Results. As each chapter opens, students are introduced to its focus company. This feature provides up-to-date background and key financial data that create an interest-generating, real-world setting for the reader. This company and its pertinent financial information thread throughout the chapter. All companies are well-known and publicly traded. In addition to Winnebago Industries, examples of chapter-focus companies are Gateway, PepsiCo, and McDonald's.

You're in the Driver's Seat. This chapter-opening section contains questions relating to the focus company. Directives assist the reader in thinking about how the chapter's coverage provide answers to decision makers.

From Concept to Practice. Throughout the text, these elements invite students to apply what they have learned to answer questions related to Winnebago Industries and other featured companies.

From Concept to Practice 8.1

What amount did Winnebago Industries report as depreciation in fiscal year 2001? Where is it disclosed? What depreciation method was used?

FOCUS ON FINANCIAL RESULTS

- Chapter-opening introduction illustrates a key financial issue related to the chapter.

Focus on Financial Results

What groups of people care about the financial performance of Winnebago Industries, one of the leading manufacturers of motor homes and recreational vehicles (RVs) in the United States? Since its founding over 40 years ago, the company's managers, investors, employees, dealers, and suppliers have all had a vested interest in the financial health of the company whose name is synonymous with RVs.

To communicate its financial performance, Winnebago Industries uses the language of accounting. The *selected financial data* that follow here summarize key measures including revenues, income, and assets. This information shows that *beginning with September 1, 1997,* both revenues and net income rose in *the next three* fiscal years, 1998, 1999, and 2000, although the company experienced a decline in both of these measures in *fiscal year 2001*. As explained in the annual report, the drop in revenues corresponds to a decline in consumer confidence levels and a slowdown in the economy. Beginning in fiscal year 1997 the company refocused on its core motor home business and is encouraged by what it sees: an increase in market share of 10 percent calendar year-to-date through September 2001 versus one year earlier.

What will be the future of Winnebago Industries? In its 2001 message to its shareholders, Winnebago Industries sounded quite optimistic about its future. This optimism likely contributed to the company's decision to continue to pay the $0.20 per share dividend to shareholders that it had paid in each of the previous four years. A series of graphs[1] show that the company leads the RV industry in return on shareholders' equity, return on assets, operating margin, and net profit margin. This standing among its competitors, along with six consecutive quality awards from its dealers association, does indeed give Winnebago Industries and its shareholders reason to be optimistic about the future.

Company net income rose in fiscal years 1998, 1999, and 2000

Company revenues rose in fiscal years 1998, 1999, and 2000

Selected Financial Data

(dollars in thousands, except per share data)	Aug. 25, 2001(1)	Aug. 26, 2000	Aug. 28, 1999	Aug. 29, 1998	Aug. 30, 1997
For the Year:					
Net revenues (2)	$681,834	$753,382	$677,011	$533,385	$445,621
Income before taxes	59,228	73,992	66,609	35,927	6,992
Pretax profit % of revenue	8.7%	9.8%	9.8%	6.7%	1.6%
Provision for income taxes	$ 15,474	$ 25,593	$ 22,349	$ 11,543	$ 416
Income tax rate	26.1%	34.6%	33.6%	32.1%	5.9%
Income from continuing operations	$ 47,704	$ 48,399	$ 44,260	$ 24,384	$ 6,576
Gain on sale of Cycle-Sat subsidiary	...	...	...	...	16,472
Net income	$ 42,704	$ 48,399	$ 44,260	$ 24,384	$ 23,048
Income per share:					
Continuing operations:					
Basic	$ 2.06	$ 2.23	$ 1.99	$ 1.01	$ .26
Diluted	2.03	2.20	1.96	1.00	.26
Discontinued operations:					
Basic	...	...	...	...	.65
Diluted	...	...	...	...	.64
Net income per share:					
Basic	$ 2.06	$ 2.23	$ 1.99	$ 1.01	$ .91
Diluted	2.03	2.20	1.96	1.00	.90
Weighted average common shares outstanding (in thousands):					
Basic	20,735	21,680	22,209	24,106	25,435
Diluted	21,040	22,011	22,537	24,314	25,550
Cash dividends per share	$ .20	$ .20	$ .20	$ .20	$ .20
Book value	9.99	8.22	6.70	5.11	4.86
Return on assets (ROA)	12.5%	15.7%	15.5%	10.6%	10.8%
Return on equity (ROE)	20.6%	27.7%	29.6%	20.9%	18.6%
Unit Sales:					
Class A	5,666	6,819	6,054	5,381	4,834
Class C	3,410	3,697	4,222	3,390	2,724
Total Class A & C Motor Homes	9,076	10,516	10,276	8,771	7,558
Class B Conversions (EuroVan Campers)	703	854	600	978	1,205
At Year End:					
Total assets	$307,095	$307,095	$285,889	$230,612	$213,475
Stockholders' equity	174,909	174,909	149,384	116,523	123,882
Working capital	143,274	143,274	123,720	92,800	100,772
Long-term debt	...	...	...	...	...
Current ratio	3.0 to 1	3.0 to 1	2.5 to 1	2.5 to 1	3.4 to 1
Number of employees	3,325	3,300	3,400	3,010	2,830

(1) Includes a noncash after tax cumulative effect of change in accounting principle of $1.1 million expense or $.05 per share due to the adoption of SAB No. 101.
(2) Net revenues have been restated for the adoption of a new accounting principle related to shipping and handling fees and costs.

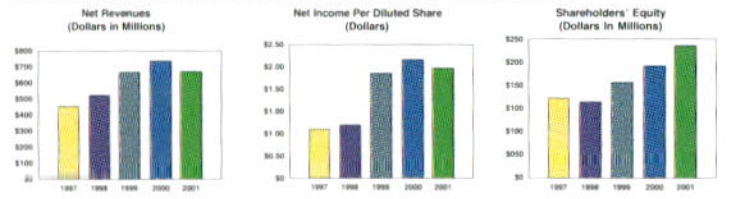

- A financial statement or excerpt from the company's annual report.

http://www.winnebagoind.com

- The company's Web site.

You're in the Driver's Seat

If you were considering a marketing job with Winnebago Industries, how would your decision be affected by the company's decision to refocus its attention on its core business? Have the company's sales continued to rise? If so, have they risen at a slower or faster pace than in the previous five years? Use this chapter and the succeeding ones to help you better understand the financial performance of Winnebago Industries.

[1] *The complete Winnebago Industries 2001 Annual Report is provided in the Appendix at the end of the text. The series of graphs appear on page 1 of that report.*

- Thought-provoking questions relate the company back to the chapter.

Business Strategy. The current business environment can be very challenging to companies as many of them try to turn around declining positions and grow their businesses. What is the company doing to maintain a strong competitive edge in the marketplace? What are the management strategies? Where is the company placing most of its effort? Often including a global perspective, the information in these boxes answers these and other questions and brings to life the strategic viewpoint of each chapter's focus company. Students find this information to be very interesting and to add an in-depth understanding of the role of financial accounting in the business environment.

Instructors can use these strategy boxes as additional research topics by challenging their students to find out whether the goals of the company's strategy are being reached and what, if any, new strategies have been reported by management in the most recent annual report or other communications.

Business Strategy

To Build or Not to Build?

What should a company's strategy be when it has recently reported a decline in net revenues of nearly 10 percent from the prior year and over 10 percent in net income? Winnebago Industries explained in its 2001 annual report that the decrease in revenues was a reflection of the decline in consumer confidence levels and a slowdown in the economy. However, at the same time, the RV manufacturer feels that, in the long term, demographics are in its favor. Supporting this positive outlook is the anticipated increase over the next 30 years of the number of people 50 years and older, which is a key target market for Winnebago Industries.

So what was Winnebago Industries' reaction to what could be construed as conflicting signals: a decline in revenues but some favorable demographics regarding its market? On April 1, 2002, the company left little doubt in the minds of its stockholders about its optimism for the future. On this day, it announced plans to build a new manufacturing facility, an expansion that would be the company's largest to date. Once the new plant in Charles City, Iowa, is operating at full capacity, it will increase Winnebago Industries' motor home production by about 30 percent. The company expects production at the new plant to begin in early 2003.

Other Featured Companies. *Financial Accounting: The Impact on Decision Makers, 4e,* is rich with *recent financial information* about other public companies. Some of these are direct competitors of the chapter's focus company, such as AMR Corp. in Chapter 11 where Delta Air Lines, Inc., is the featured company, and some are from other industries, such as Nike, Inc., in Chapter 6 where Circuit City Stores, Inc., is the chapter focus company.

Identifying the Components of the Stockholders' Equity Section of the Balance Sheet

The liabilities and stockholders' equity portion of the balance sheet of **AMR Corporation** (American Airlines) is provided in Exhibit 11-3. We will focus on the Stockholders' (Shareholders') Equity category of the balance sheet. All corporations, including AMR, begin the Stockholders' Equity category with a list of the firm's contributed capital. In some cases, there are two categories of stock: common stock and preferred stock (the latter is discussed later in this chapter). Common stock normally carries voting rights. The common stockholders elect the officers of the corporation and establish its by-laws and governing rules. It is not unusual for corporations to have more than one type of common stock, each with different rights or terms. For example, **Continental Airlines, Inc.**, one of AMR's competitors, has two classes of common stock listed on its 2001 balance sheet.

http://www.amrcorp.com

http://www.continental.com

Information from many public companies is included in assignments, as well. Throughout the text, the *URL* of each company is provided for easy access to its Web site.

Reading and Interpreting Financial Statements. These cases require students to study the financial statement information of publicly traded companies, analyze that information, and prepare their responses. At least one of the cases in each chapter involves financial information for the text's flagship company, Winnebago Industries or a close competitor.

Internet Research Case. Each case ties to the chapter's focus company and requires students to research additional, up-to-date information using resources available on the Internet.

Which Way to Go: Make Decisions

In addition to the many decision-making challenges involving real company information, *Financial Accounting: The Impact on Decision Makers, 4e,* provides students with the opportunity to place themselves in an important business role and apply reasoning to determine their responses.

Accounting for Your Decisions. Students assume the positions of user of financial information, decision maker, and business person, and are asked to respond to questions about realistic situations they may encounter in the future. Answers are offered to provide guidance to the students.

Accounting for Your Decisions

You Are the Sole Owner

Your accountant has presented you with three sets of financial statements—each with a different depreciation method—and asks you which depreciation method you prefer. You answer that other than for tax purposes, you don't really care. Should you?

ANS: For tax purposes you would prefer to use the accelerated depreciation method, which minimizes your net income so that you can pay the minimum allowable taxes. For financial statement purposes you may use a different method. As a sole owner, you may believe that the depreciation method chosen does not matter because you are more concerned with the cash flow of the firm and depreciation is a noncash item. However, the depreciation method is important if you are going to show your statements to external parties—for example, if you must present your statements to a banker in order to get a loan.

Making Financial Decisions. These cases feature financial information that students must analyze and use to make decisions. Students draw from the chapter content but must also think beyond it to determine their responses.

Accounting and Ethics Cases. As is very obvious in the current business environment, everyone engaged in the financial reporting and decision making must maintain a high level of ethical standards. Thus, is it essential for students throughout their academic studies to practice the process of reasoning through challenging ethical questions.

Learn from Dynamic Guides

On any new adventure, it is very helpful to have experienced guides. When the guide is one that provides dynamic ways to learn, the trip is more successful. Students will find many pedagogical elements in each chapter that create interest, challenge thinking, and strengthen understanding.

Learning Objectives. Students can concentrate on the important information by reviewing the learning objectives, which provide measurable goals. These objectives, which contain the page numbers where the relevant coverage begins, are repeated in the margins at the beginning of that coverage and are indicated by number next to reinforcing assignments.

LEARNING OBJECTIVES

After studying this chapter, you should be able to:

LO 1 Identify the primary users of accounting information and their needs. (p. 14)

LO 2 Explain the purpose of each of the financial statements and the relationships among them, and prepare a set of simple statements. (p. 16)

LO 3 Identify and explain the primary assumptions made in preparing financial statements. (p. 22)

LO 4 Describe the various roles of accountants in organizations. (p. 24)

Straight-line method A method by which the same dollar amount of depreciation is recorded in each year of asset use.

Study Tip

When interest rates increase, present values decrease. This is called an *inverse relationship.*

Marginal Glossaries. The definitions of key terms appear in the margin near their initial use in the text. (Student knowledge of these terms and their definitions is tested in the Key Terms Quiz at the end of the chapter.)

Study Tips. As students move through a chapter, these tips appear in the margin to help students focus on important concepts and provide a useful study tool when reviewing the chapter.

Two-Minute Review. How well do the students understand what they just read? This quick review helps them answer that question. Each chapter contains one or more reviews with the answers provided at the end of the chapter, just before the Warmup Exercises.

Two-Minute Review

1. *What items should be included when calculating the acquisition cost of an asset?*
2. *Which will be higher in the early years of an asset's life—straight-line depreciation or accelerated depreciation? Which will be higher in the later years? Which will be higher in total over the entire life of the asset?*

Answers—p. 408

Answers to the Two-Minute Reviews

Two-Minute Review on Page 393

1. *The general rule for calculating the acquisition cost of an asset is to include all of the costs that were necessary to acquire the asset and prepare it for use. Normally, that would include the purchase price but would also include costs such as freight costs, taxes, and installation costs if they were necessary to prepare the asset for use.*
2. *Accelerated depreciation will be higher in the early years of the asset, and straight-line will be higher in the later years. Over the life of the asset, the total amount of depreciation will be the same under all of the methods, assuming that the same amount of salvage value is estimated for each of the methods.*

Warmup Exercises with Suggested Solutions. These simple exercises preview the assignments to come and help students move from reading the text to doing the end-of-chapter assignments. Suggested solutions are provided as a self-check learning tool.

Warmup Exercises

Warmup Exercise 10-1

A bond due in 10 years, with face value of $1,000 and face rate of interest of 8%, is issued when the market rate of interest is 6%.

Required

1. What is the issue price of the bond?
2. What is the amount of premium or discount on the bond at the time of issuance?
3. What amount of interest expense will be shown on the income statement for the first year of the bond?

Solutions to Warmup Exercises

Warmup Exercise 10-1

1. The issue price of the bond would be calculated at the present value:

$80 (7.360) =	$ 588.80	using Table 9-4, where i = 6% and n = 10
$1,000 (0.558) =	558.00	using Table 9-2, where i = 6% and n = 10
Issue price	$1,146.80	

You should perform the following steps when using a calculator to determine the present value:

ENTER	DISPLAY
10 N	N = 10
6 I/Y	I/Y = 8
80 PMT	PMT = 80
1000 FV	FV = 1000
CPT PV	PV = 1,147*
*(rounded)	

2. The amount of the premium is the difference between the issue price and the face value:

Premium = $1,146.80 − $1,000
= $146.80

Review Problem with Suggested Solution. Located at the end of every chapter, this problem and suggested solution tests student understanding of some of the major ideas in the chapter. These problems also serve as a walk-through demonstration with audio explanation in WebTutor Advantage.

A Large Number of EOC Choices. Assignments in the end-of-chapter section are numerous. These include:

- *Key Terms Quiz*—to test vocabulary knowledge (solutions are provided at the very end of the assignment material); an Alternate Terms list further enriches knowledge.
- *Questions*—to stimulate thinking and class discussion; these can be used for writing assignments to assist students in the practice of expressing and supporting their ideas.
- *Exercises*—to provide reinforcement of chapter content and prepare students for the challenge of the problem and case assignments; the first set of exercises is focused on a single learning objective, followed by a section of "multi-concept exercises;" exercises are primarily focused on application.
- *Problems*—to provide reinforcement of chapter content and focus on analysis and decision making; the first set of problems is tied to single learning objectives, followed by a section of "multi-concept problems;" a set of "alternate problems" provides additional assignment opportunities.
- *Cases*—to further reinforce analysis, decision making, professionalism, and research skills.

Icons for Quick Identification. Icons are like signposts that help you and your students identify key places along the way. For the fourth edition, we provide the following icons for the specific purposes indicated

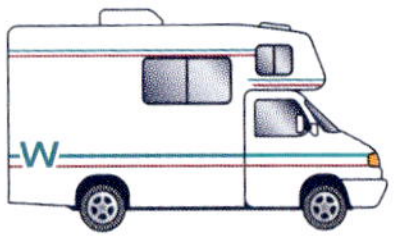

Winnebago Industries—After Chapter 1, this image will identify those places where key information relating to our flagship company appears.

Global—Most corporations operate in an international environment and, therefore, have global accounting and strategic concerns. This icon serves as an indicator of where global coverage is provided.

DECISION MAKING

GENERAL LEDGER

Decision Making—Many assignments involve decision-making opportunities. These are identified by this image.

General Ledger—Those assignments that may be solved using the general ledger software have this icon in the margin next to them.

SPREADSHEET

INTERNET

Spreadsheet—Assignments that are included in the Excel spreadsheet templates or that can easily be answered using spreadsheet software are identified by this image.

Internet—This image indicates assignments for which the resources of the Internet are recommended.

Personal Trainer—Assignments identified by PT, after their learning objective numbers, may be completed using the Personal Trainer® homework tutor described below.

ADD POWER TO YOUR COURSE

With its many, quality options for you and your students, *Financial Accounting: The Impact on Decision Makers, 4e,* provides extra power to help pave the way to financial accounting excellence!

At the beginning of each chapter's assignment section, there is the following box that serves as a reminder to students to look at the technology information in this preface. In addition, students may want to refer to the inside front cover where resource information is also presented.

http://

http://porter.swlearning.com

Technology and other resources for your success

If you need additional help, visit the text's Web site. Also, see pages xv–xvii in this text's preface for a description of available technology and other resources. If your instructor is using PERSONAL Trainer in this course, you may complete, on line, the assignments identified by PT.

Ahead of the Curve: Our Top-of-the-Line Technology

Personal Trainer®. This *Homework Tutor* is an Internet-based assistant designed specifically for students taking the introductory course in financial accounting. With the help of warm-ups and hints, students can complete assigned homework or practice by completing unassigned homework on-line. Instructors receive the results, which can be automatically entered into a grade book for the assigned homework, and can view the efforts of the unassigned work completed by students. Unlike any other tutorial on the market, students receive the pedagogical benefits of the completion of homework assignments and instructors have more time to devote to other classroom activities.

WebTutor® Advantage with Personal Trainer. Available in either WebCT™ or Blackboard® platforms, this rich course management product is a specially designed extension of the classroom experience that enlivens the course by leveraging the power of the Internet with comprehensive educational content. WebTutor Advantage on WebCT™ or Blackboard® includes Personal Trainer to provide both students and instructors an unprecedented real-time, guided, self-correcting study outside the classroom. Instructors or students can use these resources along with those on the Product Web site to supplement the classroom experience. Use this effective resource as an integrated solution for your distance learning or web-enhanced course! This powerful, turnkey solution provides the following content customized for this edition:

- **E-Lectures**—PowerPoint® slides of the key topical coverage accompanied by audio explanations provide additional learning support.
- **Interactive Quizzes**—Multiple choice, true/false, matching, and sentence completion questions, which test the knowledge of the chapter content, provide immediate feedback on the accuracy of the response. These quizzes help students pinpoint areas needing more study.
- **Problem Demonstrations**—The chapter review problem is presented, and an audio step-by-step explanation of the solution is provided to guide student understanding.
- **Videos**—Short, high-interest segments focus on chapter-related topics.
- **Reviews of Key Concepts—**Tied to each learning objective, these chapter reviews reinforce important concepts from each chapter.
- **Flashcards**—A terminology quiz helps students gain a complete understanding of the key terms from the chapter.
- **Spanish Dictionary—**To aid Spanish-speaking students, a Spanish dictionary of key financial accounting terms is provided.
- **Crossword Puzzles**—These interactive puzzles provide an alternative tool for students to test their understanding of terminology.
- **Quiz Bowl Game**—Students can review chapter content using this on-line game, which is similar to Jeopardy!®.
- **Personal Trainer**—This Internet-based homework tutor, described fully in the preceding section, is a rich tool for students and instructors.

Xtreme! With Personal Trainer. This hybrid CD-ROM and Internet-based product provides the same content as WebTutor Advantage but without the platform. You can leverage technology to take your students to the outer limits of mastering the introductory financial accounting course! Features include:

- Learning Objectives that summarize key concepts from each chapter
- Quizzing that reinforces concepts and helps your students better focus their study efforts
- Quiz Bowl Game, an innovative and fun way for students to review concepts
- Crossword puzzles to test student knowledge of the glossary and make learning "the language of business" more fun
- E-Lectures that provide a PowerPoint® lecture-style with audio voiceovers to help students review chapter content or work on difficult topics
- Problem demonstrations to guide students through the review problems and save you time
- Video clips that provide real-world examples of applications so students can make the connection between the accounting concept and its use in the business world
- Personal Trainer, an on-line self-grading homework tutorial with a gradebook for monitoring student progress and reporting the details to help you better target your teaching efforts!

Xtra! for Financial Accounting. This CD-ROM provides lecture replacement resources and access to games and interactive quizzes so that students can test their understanding of the content of the fourth edition. *Free when bundled with a new text,* students receive an access code so that they can receive Xtra! reinforcement in financial accounting.

General Ledger & Spreadsheet CD-ROM. Developed for the learning market, this resource helps students understand the use of general ledger software and spreadsheet templates in an accounting environment. Selected assignments, identified by icons in the text, may be completed using the general ledger software or the spreadsheet templates provided.

Text Web Site. (http://porter.swlearning.com) The Web site for the fourth edition has expanded to offer you and your student even more resources for teaching and learning than the third edition.

Among the many elements available to ***Students*** are:

- *Quizzes with feedback*
- *Hotlinks* to many resources on the Web, including all of the Web sites listed in the text; this provides a quick connection to key information
- *PowerPoint® presentation slides* for review of chapter coverage
- *Excel templates* for selected assignments in the text
- *Crossword puzzles* for fun testing of vocabulary knowledge
- *Check figures* to selected assignments
- *Learning objectives* from the chapter provided as a study aid to keep clear focus on the core goals
- *Updates* for the latest information about changes in GAAP and any new, important information related to the text

For Instructors, in addition to full access to the student resources listed above, a password-protected section of the Web site contains a number of resource files, including:

- *Solutions Manual*
- *Instructor's Manual*
- *Solutions to Excel templates*

- *Solution transparencies*
- Additional *updates* pertinent to instructors

Select from Other Helpful Support Materials

For Students:

- *Study Guide*—Use the Study Guide to review the chapter's main focus, key concepts, and key terms and brush up your homework and test-taking skills. Solutions are provided.
- *Working Papers*—Why use notebook paper for your homework when you can save time by simply entering the answers in the format preferred by your instructor? This handy book provides all the forms you'll need when your instructor asks you to manually prepare the homework assignments from the text.

For Instructors:

- *Instructor's Resource Manual*, composed of the Instructor's Manual and the Solutions Manual, this ancillary's content is also available in electronic form on the Instructor's Resource CD-ROM and (restricted) on the product support Web site.
- *Test Bank* is a complete and plentiful set of newly revised test items that is also available in electronic form (using ExamView® software, provided) on the Instructor's Resource CD-ROM.
- *Solution Transparencies* consist of acetate transparencies of the numerical solutions to the exercises, problems, and cases.
- *Instructor's Resource CD-ROM with ExamView®* contains key instructor ancillaries (solutions manual, instructor's manual, test bank, and PowerPoint® presentation slides)—giving instructors the ultimate tool for customizing lectures and presentations. The testbank files on the CD-Rom are provided in ExamView® format. This program is an easy-to-use test-creation software compatible with Microsoft® Windows. Instructors can add or edit questions, instructions, and answers and select questions (randomly or numerically) by previewing them on the screen. Instructors can also create and administer quizzes online, whether over the Internet, a local area network (LAN), or a wide area network (WAN).
- *PowerPoint® Presentation Slides* are located on the Instructor's Resource CD-ROM and on the text's Web site. These colorful slides reinforce chapter content and provide a rich tool for in-class lectures and out-of-class reviewing.

Additional Financial Accounting Resources

INSIDE LOOK: *Analysis From All Angles* Accounting is in the news *and* the classroom with access to this new Web site from Thomson/South-Western. The *Access Card* allows the instructor and the student to utilize information related to the Enron, Andersen, and other "names in the news" that involve accounting-related concerns. Well-known, popular news sources provide the background for the selected current events. Teaching tools are available to the instructor to implement class discussions, while analysis and questions are available to the student to utilize in many accounting discipline areas. This site is intended to help instructors teach and students to learn about critical current issues and understand them in the context of their accounting studies. **For a Demo, go to:** http://insidelook.swcollege.com.

Business & Professional Ethics for Accountants, 3e (by Leonard J. Brooks, Rotman School of Management, University of Toronto). Cases, readings, and textual material are blended to provide a concise, practical understanding of how to behave ethically in a post-Enron world for accounting and business students. This text provides a complete business and professional ethics guide to working in the age of accounting scandals. Issues and cases in this new edition cover: Enron and Enron-triggered changes in governance for corporations and the accounting profession;

increased ethical sensitivity to ethical issues; calls for increased accountability to stakeholders, ethical decision making and behavior, and the development of ethical organization cultures domestically and internationally.

Accounting Ethics in the Post—Enron Age, 1e (by Iris Stuart and Bruce Stuart, of California State University—Fullerton). With the Enron/Andersen debacle, ethics is becoming an increasingly important (and interesting) part of accounting education. Ethics coverage is also required by the AACSB for accreditation purposes. Most texts include some limited ethics coverage, but many instructors would like to include more. This timely supplement contains ethics cases based on real situations in the business world. Examples include cases tied to Enron, Global Crossing, and Boston Chicken. Identifying ethical dilemmas and projecting their resolution will allow students to develop essential skills for success in their future careers. In each section of the textbook, the problems will be labeled according to subject matter (e.g., bad debt expense, revenue recognition). This allows the instructor to select problems consistent with the needs of the course.

The Financial Reporting Project and Readings, 3e (by Bruce A. Baldwin, of Arizona State University—West, and Clayton A. Hock, of Miami University). This project book requires students to obtain and analyze "live" financial statement from publicly traded firms. Also included in the book are several high-interest articles from popular publications, such as *The Wall Street Journal* and *Business Week*. The project has a flexible format and accommodates individual or team-based learning. Students are encouraged to compose short written responses to explain their analysis and to express their ideas based on the readings.

An Introduction to Accounting, Business Processes, and ERP (by Phil Reckers, Julie Smith David, and Harriet Maccracken, all of Arizona State University). Utilizing JD Edwards software demos, an industry leading ERP company, your students will learn an overview of the use of ERP software for accounting and business processes. Unlike any other product on the market, they will not only learn the advantages of technology in accessing business information but will also learn to apply it in three different business models. After each module, student learning is reinforced by quizzing. Equip your students with this class-tested and easy-to-use experience to help them meet the ever-changing challenges of business and technology!

InfoTrac® College Edition With this resource, your students can receive anytime, anywhere on-line access to a database of full-text articles from hundreds of popular and scholarly periodicals, such as *Newsweek, Fortune, Entrepreneur, Journal of Accountancy*, and *Nation's Business*, among others. Students can use its fast and easy search tools to find relevant news and analytical information among the tens of thousands of articles in the database—updated daily and going back as far as four years—all at a single Web site. InfoTrac is a great way to expose students to online research techniques, with the security that the content is academically based and reliable. An InfoTrac College Edition subscription card can be packaged free with new copies of our financial accounting texts. For more information, visit http://www.swcollege.com/infotrac/infotrac.html.

INTAACT Financial Accounting (by D.V. Rama and K. Raghunandan, both of Texas A&M International University). This Internet-based tutorial at http://rama.swcollege.com was designed for use in a financial accounting course or in any course where a review of the key financial concepts and terminology is needed. The program offers a visual, user-friendly way to reinforce accounting principles and includes tutorials, demonstration problems, exercises, and an interactive glossary. Users will receive an access certificate that will allow them to do the on-line tutorial over the full term of a course.

Accounting Career Consultant: Financial Accounting (by Charles Davis and Eric Sandburg). This resource is an online, interactive, tutored simulation. It is designed to complement both the classroom instruction and the text presentations.

Each module includes links to review questions with customized feedback (approximately 20 questions), links to resources to further augment learning, and company profiles for the businesses discussed.

The Monopoly Game Practice Set (by Robert Knechel, of University of Florida). This fun practice set, based on the Monopoly game, helps students understand accounting information transaction as triggered by real business events. Each student's solution is unique but easily graded.

ACKNOWLEDGEMENTS

In preparing for this new edition of our text and the supporting materials, a number of individuals provided very helpful comments and suggestions. Among those are:

Thomas J. Brady, University of Dayton
Sarah Brown, University of North Alabama
John M. Coulter, Western New England College
Marcia Agee Croteau, University of Maryland Baltimore County
M. Taylor Ernst, Lehigh University
Susan Coomer Galbreath, Lipscomb University
Gloria Grayless, Sam Houston State University
John W. Hatcher, Purdue University
Herbert Hunt, California State University—Long Beach
Beth Kern, Indiana University—South Bend
Cathy Larson, Middlesex Community College
Douglas Larson, Salem State College
Elliott Levy, Bentley College
Larry Logan, University of Massachusetts—Dartmouth
Lois Mahoney, University of Central Florida
Linda Nichols, Texas Tech University
Betty S. Nolen, Floyd College
Elizabeth Plummer, Southern Methodist University
Angela Sandberg, Jacksonville State University
Cindy Seipel, New Mexico State University
Kathy Sevigny, Bridgewater State College
Diane Tanner, University of North Florida
Martin Taylor, University of Texas—Arlington
James Williamson, San Diego State University
Thomas L. Zeller, Loyola University—Chicago

We wish to thank those individuals for their contribution and Richard Friary, who provided valuable guidance to our ongoing effort to have the best teaching resources available for financial accounting.

Throughout the first three editions, many individuals have contributed helpful suggestions, which have resulted in several features that we have continued in the new fourth edition. We acknowledge these colleagues for their assistance.

Sheila Ammons, Austin Community College
David Angelovich, San Francisco State University
Alana Baier, Marquette University
Ray Bainbridge, Lehigh University
Amelia A. Baldwin-Morgan, Eastern Michigan University
Bobbe M. Barnes, University of Colorado at Denver

Maj. Curt Barry, U.S. Military Academy
Peter Battell, University of Vermont
Paul Bayes, East Tennessee State University
Angela Bell, Jacksonville University
Dorcas Berg, Wingate University
Mark Bettner, Bucknell University
Frank Biegbeder, Rancho Santiago Community College
Francis Bird, University of Richmond
Karen Bird, University of Michigan
Eddy Birrer, Gonzaga University
Michelle Bissonnette, California State University—Fresno
John Blahnik, Lorain County Community College
Bruce Bolick, University of Mary Hardin Baylor
Frank Bouchlers, North Carolina State University
Thomas Brady, University of Dayton
Ed Bresnahan, American River College
Bob Brill, St. Bonaventure University
Sarah Brown, University of North Alabama
David Brunn, Carthage College
Philip Buchanan, George Washington University
Rosie Bukics, Lafayette College
Gary Bulmash, American University
Bryan Burks, Harding University
Ronnie Burrows, University of Dayton
Judith Cadle, Tarleton State University
Carolyn Callahan, University of Notre Dame
Linda Campbell, University of Toledo
Jim Cashell, Miami University
Charles Caufield, Loyola University Chicago
David N. Champagne, Antelope Valley College
Gyan Chandra, Miami University
Mayer Chapman, California State University at Long Beach
Alan Cherry, Loyola Marymount University
Mike Claire, College of San Mateo
David C. Coffee, Western Carolina University
John E. Coleman, University of Massachusetts at Boston
David Collins, Eastern Kentucky University
Gail Cook, University of Wisconsin, Parkside
Judith Cook, Grossmont Community College
Susan Coomer Galbreath, Tennessee Tech University
John C. Corless, California State University—Sacramento
Rosalind Cranor, Virginia Polytechnic Institute
Dean Crawford, University of Toledo
Carrie Cristea, Augustana College, South Dakota
Fred Current, Furman University
Shirley J. Daniel, University of Hawaii at Manoa
Alan Davis, Community College of Philadelphia
Jim Davis, Clemson University
Henry H. Davis, Eastern Illinois University
Lyle E. Dehning, Metropolitan State College—Denver
Les Dlabay, Lake Forest College
Patricia Doherty, Boston University
Jaime Doran, Muhlenberg College
Margaret Douglas, University of Arkansas
Patricia Douglas, Loyola Marymount University
Alan Doyle, Pima Community College East
Alan Drebin, Northwestern University
Betty Driver, Murray State University
Kathy Dunne, Rider College
Dean Edmiston, Emporia State University
Kenneth Elvik, Iowa State University
Anette Estrada, Grand Valley State University
Ed Etter, Syracuse University
Alan Falcon, Loyola Marymount University
Charles Fazzi, Robert Morris College
Anita Feller, University of Illinois
Howard Felt, Temple University
David Fetyko, Kent State University
Richard File, University of Nebraska—Omaha
Ed Finkhauser, University of Utah
Jeannie M. Folk, College of DuPage
J. Patrick Forrest, Western Michigan University
Patrick Fort, University of Alaska—Fairbanks
Diana Franz, University of Toledo
Tom Frecka, University of Notre Dame
Gary Freeman, University of Tulsa
Paquita Y. Friday, University of Notre Dame
Joan Friedman, Illinois Wesleyan University
Veronique Frucot, Rutgers University—Camden
Leo Gabriel, Bethel College
Joe Gallo, Cuyahoga Community College
Michelle Gannon, Western Connecticut State University
Will Garland, Coastal Carolina University
John Gartska, Loyola Marymount University
Sharon Garvin, Wayne State College
Roger Gee, San Diego Mesa College
Cynthia Van Gelderen, Aquinas College
Linda Genduso, Nova University
Don E. Giacomino, Marquette University
Claudia Gilbertston, Anoka Ramsey Community College
Hubert Gill, University of North Florida

Lorraine Glasscock, University of North Alabama
Larry Godwin, University of Montana
Art Goldman, University of Kentucky
Lynn Grace, Edison Community College
Bud Granger, Minnesota State University—Mankato
Marilyn Greenstein, Lehigh University
Paul Griffin, University of California—Davis
Jack Grinnell, University of Vermont
Bonnie Hairrell, Birmingham Southern
Jeanne Hamilton, Cypress College
Al Hannan, College of Notre Dame
Leon Hanouille, Syracuse University
Joseph Hargadon, Widener University
Suzanne Hartley, Franklin University
Robert Hartwig, Worcester State College
Jean Hatcher, University of South Carolina at Sumner
Donna Sue Hetzel, Western Michigan University
Thomas F. Hilgeman, St. Louis Community College—Meramec
Nathan Hindi, Shippensburgh University of Pennsylvania
Robert E. Holtfreter, Ft. Hays State University
Betty Horn, Southern Connecticut State University
Kathy Horton, University of Illinois, Chicago
Fred Ihrke, Winona State University
Bruce Ikawa, Loyola Marymount University
Danny Ivancevich, University of Nevada—Las Vegas
Janet Jackson, Wichita State University
Sharon Jackson, Auburn University at Montgomery
Stanley Jenne, University of Montana
Patricia Johnson, Canisius College
Randy Johnston, Pennsylvania State University
Becky Jones, Baylor University
Christopher Jones, George Washington University
William Jones, Seton Hall University
Naida Kaen, University of New Hampshire
Manu Kai'ama, University of Hawaii at Manoa
Jane Kapral, Clark University
Mary Keim, California State University—Bakersfield
Anne Marie Keinath, Indiana University Northwest
Don Kellogg, Rock Valley College
Robert Kelly, Corning Community College
Marcia Kertz, San Jose State University
Jean Killey, Midlands Technical College
Ronald King, Washington University
Rita Kingery, University of Delaware
William Kinsella, Loyola Marymount University
Paul Kleichman, University of Richmond
George Klersey, Birmingham Southern College
Charles Konkol, University of Wisconsin—Milwaukee
Greg Krippel, Coastal Carolina University
Frank Korman, Mountain View College
Lynn Koshiyama, University of Alaska
Bobby Kuhlmann, Chaffey College
James Kurtenbach, Iowa State University
Jay LaGregs, Tyler Junior College
Michael Lagrone, Clemson University
Lucille E. Lammers, Illinois State University
Ellen Landgraf, Loyola University Chicago
Horace Landry, Syracuse University
Laurie Larson, Valencia Community College
Kristine Lawyer, North Carolina State University
Terry Lease, Loyola Marymount University
Tom Lee, Winona State University
Susan Lightle, Wright State University
Tom Linsmeier, University of Iowa
Chao Liu, Tarleton State University
Chao-Shin Liu, University of Notre Dame
Alan Lord, Bowling Green State University
Gina Lord, Santa Rosa Junior College
Don Loster, University of California, Santa Barbara
Bruce Lubich, American University
Catherine Lumbattis, Southern Illinois University
Patsy Lund, Lakewood Community College
Raymond D. MacFee, Jr., University of Colorado
George Macklin, Susquehanna University
David Malone, University of Idaho
Janice Mardon, Green River Community College
Jim Martin, University of Montevallo
Spencer Martin, University of Rhode Island
Mary D. Maury, St. John's University
Al Maypers, University of North Texas
John C. McCabe, Ball State University
Nancy McClure, Lock Haven University
Margaret McCrory, Marist College
Christine McKeag, University of Evansville
Thomas D. McLaughlin, Monmouth College
Laura McNally, Black Hills State College
Mallory McWilliams, San Jose State University
Laurie McWhorter, University of Kentucky
E. James Meddaugh, Ohio University
Paul Mihalek, University of Hartford
Cynthia Miller, GM Institute

Charles Milliner, Glendale Community College
William Mister, Colorado State University
Tami Mittelstaedt, University of Notre Dame
Perry Moore, David Lipscomb University
Barbara Morris, Angelo State University
Mike Morris, University of Notre Dame
Theodore D. Morrison, Valparaiso University
Howard E. Mount, Seattle Pacific University
Rafael Munoz, University of Notre Dame
Muroki Mwaura, William Paterson University
Marcia Niles, University of Idaho
Mary J. Nisbet, University of California—Santa Barbara
Priscilla O'Clock, Xavier University
Mary Ellen O'Grady, Ramapo College
Phil Olds, Virginia Commonwealth University
Bruce Oliver, Rochester Institute of Technology
Daniel O'Mara, Quinnipiac College
Michael O'Neill, Gannon University
John Osborn, California State University—Fresno
Janet O'tousa, University of Notre Dame
Prakash Pai, Kent State University
Rimona Palas, William Paterson College of New Jersey
Beau Parent, Tulane University
Jane Park, California State University, Los Angeles
Paul Parkison, Ball State University
Victor Pastena, SUNY Buffalo
Sue Pattillo, University of Notre Dame
Charles A. Pauley, Gannon University
Ron Pawliczek, Boston College
Kathy Petroni, Michigan State University
Chris Pew, Galivan College
Donna Philbrick, Portland State University
Harry V. Poynter, Central Missouri State University
Joseph Ragan, St. Joseph's University
Mitchell Raiborn, Bradley University
Al Rainford, Greenfield Community College
John Rhode, University of San Francisco
Keith Richardson, Indiana State University
Ann Riley, American University
Mary Rolfes, Minnesota State University—Mankato
Robert Rouse, College of Charleston
Donna Rudderow, Franklin University
Joseph Rue, Syracuse University
Leo A. Ruggle, Minnesota State University—Mankato
Victoria Rymer, University of Maryland
Judith Sage, University of Southern Colorado
Marilyn Sagrillo, University of Wisconsin—Green Bay
Rick Samuelson, San Diego State University
Gail Sanderson, Lebanon Valley College
George Sanderson, Moorhead State University
Richard Sathe, University of St. Thomas
Karen Saurlander, University of Toledo
Warren Schlesinger, Ithaca College
Edward S. Schwan, Susquehanna University
Don Schwartz, National University
Richard Scott, University of Virginia
Karen Sedatole, Stephen F. Austin
John Sherman, University of Texas, Dallas
Richard Sherman, St. Joseph's University
Richard Silkoff, Quinnipiac College
Ron Singer, University of Wisconsin—Parkside
Ray Slager, Calvin College
David Smith, Metropolitan State University
David Smith, University of Dayton
Jill Smith, Idaho State University
Kim Sorenson, Eastern Oregon State University
Amy Spielbauer, St. Norbert College
Charles Stanley, Baylor University
Catherine Staples, Virginia Commonwealth University
Anita Stellenwerf, Ramapo College
Jens Stephan, University of Cincinnati
Stephen Strange, Indiana University at Kokomo
Donna Street, James Madison University
David Strupeck, Indiana University NW
Linda Sugarman, University of Akron
Kathy Sullivan, George Washington University
Jeanie Sumner, Pacific Lutheran University
Judy Swingen, Rochester Institute of Technology
Tim Tancy, University of Notre Dame
Larry Tartaglino, Cabrillo College
Martha Turner, Bowling Green State University
Bente Villadsen, Washington University
Alan K. Vogel, Cuyahoga Community College—Western
Vicki Vorell, Cuyahoga Community College—Western
Phil Walter, Bellevue Community College
Ann Watkins, Louisiana State University
Karen Walton, John Carroll University
Dewey Ward, Michigan State University
David P. Weiner, University of San Francisco
Michael Welker, Drexel University
Jane Wells, University of Kentucky
Jennifer Wells, University of San Francisco

Judy Wenzel, Gustavus Adolphus College
Charles Werner, Loyola University Chicago
Michael Werner, University of Miami
Paul Wertheim, Pepperdine University
Shari Wescott, Houston Baptist University
T. Sterling Wetzel, Oklahoma State University
Steven D. White, Western Kentucky University
Jill Whitley, Sioux Falls College
Jane Wiese, Valencia Community College
Samuel Wild, Loyola Marymount University
Jack Wilkerson, Wake Forest University
Michael Williams, Century College
David Willis, Illinois Wesleyan University
Lyle Wimmergren, Worcester Polytechnic Institute
Carol Wolk, University of Tennessee
Betty Wolterman, St. John's University, MN
Steven Wong, San Jose City College
Gail Wright, Bryant College
Robert Zahary, California State University at Los Angeles
Thomas L. Zeller, Loyola University Chicago

Gary Porter
Curt Norton

Meet the Authors

Gary A. Porter; CPA, is Professor of Accounting at the University of St. Thomas—Minnesota. He earned Ph.D. and M.B.A. degrees from the University of Colorado and his B.S.B.A. from Drake University. He has published in the *Journal of Accounting Education, Journal of Accounting, Auditing & Finance,* and *Journal of Accountancy*, among others and has conducted numerous workshops on the subjects of introductory accounting education and corporate financial reporting.

Dr. Porter's professional activities include experience as a staff accountant with Deloitte & Touche in Denver, a participant in KPMG Peat Marwick Foundation's Faculty Development program and as a leader in numerous bank training programs. He has won an Excellence in Teaching Award from the University of Colorado and Outstanding Professor Awards from both San Diego State University and the University of Montana.

He served on the Illinois CPA Society's Innovations in Accounting Education Grants Committee, the steering committee of the Midwest region of the American Accounting Association, and the board of directors of the Chicago chapter of the Financial Executives Institute.

Curtis L. Norton; is Deloitte & Touche Professor of Accountancy at Northern Illinois University. He earned his Ph.D. from Arizona State University, his M.B.A. from the University of South Dakota, and his B.S. from Jamestown College, North Dakota. His extensive list of publications include articles in *Accounting Horizons, The Journal of Accounting Education, Journal of Accountancy, Journal of Corporate Accounting, Journal of the American Taxation Association, Real Estate Review, The Accounting Review, CPA Journal*, and many others. In 1988-89, Dr. Norton received the University Excellence in Teaching Award, the highest university-wide teaching recognition at NIU. He is also a consultant and has conducted training programs for governmental authorities, bank, utilities, and other entities.

Dr. Norton is a member of the American Accounting Association and a member and officer of the Financial Executives Institute.

Brief Contents

Contents

Honey Nut Chex
Betty Crocker
Banana Nut
Muffin Mix
Chocolate
Cookie Mix
Yoplait
Ready to Bake!

Drive-Thru

GAP
GAP

CIRCUIT
CITY

PEPSI

AOL Time Warner

JCPenney

Coca-Cola
BOTTLING CO.
US DOT 155950

IBM

WRIGLEY'S
SPEARMINT
JUICY FRUIT
DOUBLEMINT

To those who really "count":
Melissa
Kathy, Amy, Andrew

Part I

The Accounting Model

A Word to Students About This Course

Knowing accounting is just plain smart for everyone in today's job market. This book is therefore not just for accounting majors—it's for anyone who wants to learn how to read and understand financial information. You'll work with numbers in this course. But at every turn, this book and its study aids—not to mention your instructor—will walk you through the details. You'll write some memoranda backing up your calculations, pitting your analytical skills against real financial statements and problems. And you'll have the chance to put yourself in different business roles.

In fact, this book will help you think, talk, and write skillfully about accounting information.

Introduction

WINNEBAGO INDUSTRIES

Getting Started in Business

Roadmap to Success

*See the full road map at the front of the text.

LEARNING OBJECTIVES

After studying this module, you should be able to:

LO 1 Explain why financial information is important in making decisions. (p. 2)

LO 2 Understand what business is about. (p. 3)

LO 3 Distinguish among the forms of organization. (p. 4)

LO 4 Describe the various types of business activities. (p. 6)

Pick your favorite company. Maybe it is The Gap, because you buy all of your clothes there. Or maybe it is The Tribune Company because it owns your favorite team, the Chicago Cubs. Or is it Gateway because you like its commercials? At any rate, have you ever wondered how the company got started? Here is the abbreviated story of the birth of a well-known recreational vehicle manufacturer as told on its Web site:

In the mid-1950s, Forest City, Iowa, was looking at a bleak future. The farm economy was down and young people were leaving this rural area. Forward-looking members of the community set about bringing industry to town. In 1958, businessman John K. Hanson and others convinced a California company to open a travel trailer factory in Forest City. After a rough start, the operation was purchased by five Forest City residents, and John K. Hanson became president. In 1960 the name of the company was changed to Winnebago Industries.[1]

WINNEBAGO INDUSTRIES: THE NEED TO MAKE FINANCIAL DECISIONS

LO 1 Explain why financial information is important in making decisions.

From its humble beginnings, **Winnebago Industries** has made tremendous strides in its first 40 years. Revenues in 2001 exceeded $681 million. Numerous reasons account for the company's success, not the least of which is the strong desire people in the United States have for travel and leisure activities. However, any company owes a major part of its success to its ability to make *financial decisions.* Initially, John Hanson and his fellow investors made a crucial decision to invest their own money and buy the company. Would *you* have been willing to risk your savings to enter a new business? This was a financial decision these five Forest City residents had to make.

During the 1960s, the investors made significant strides to get the young company off the ground and on solid financial footing. For example, they introduced an assembly line to the motor home industry in an effort to reduce costs. That allowed Winnebago Industries to cut its costs to better compete against other companies. One of the most pivotal financial decisions in the life of Winnebago Industries was made in 1966. Many successful companies reach a point in their existence when it becomes necessary to consider "going public." January 25, 1966, marked the first time Winnebago Industries sold its stock to the public. The initial price was $12.50 per share. As is the case for many companies, a public offering of its stock provided the additional resources it needed to continue to grow and become a leader in its industry.

In 1970, the company was faced with another crucial financial decision. Should it move its operation to a larger manufacturing facility? Although this would certainly be a costly decision, the investors decided the move was in the best interests of their company. Did it prove to be a good decision? Apparently so, since a series of positive mile-

In the mid-1950s, this early Winnebago was the primary product for the company. As reflected in both its annual report, at the end of this text, and its Web site, Winnebago Industries has greatly changed and expanded it product line. By providing investors and creditors with reliable financial information, the company has been able to get the resources it has needed to help it grow.

[1]This information, and that in the following section, is provided in more detail on Winnebago Industries' Web site in the section titled "The Winnebago Story."

stones in the following decades certainly support the decision made. In the same year as the expansion, Winnebago Industries' stock was first listed on the New York Stock Exchange, and in the following year, the stock had appreciated in price more than any other company's stock on the exchange. This significant increase reflected the confidence investors had in the future growth of the company. In 1977, Winnebago Industries became the first recreational vehicle (RV) manufacturer to build 100,000 units. Another milestone occurred in 1984 when sales topped $400 million for the first time in the company's history. Two years later, Winnebago Industries first appeared on *Fortune Magazine's* list of the top 500 U.S. corporations. Not bad for a company that less than 30 years earlier got its start when five residents in a small Iowa town made a decision to take a chance on not only a new business but on a whole new industry!

All the major events to date in the history of Winnebago Industries involved a need to take risks and make decisions. And in each of these decisions, the decision makers needed to rely on financial information. We all use financial information in making decisions. For example, when you were deciding whether to enroll at your present school, you needed information on the tuition and, in some cases, the room-and-board costs at the different schools you were considering. When a stockbroker decides whether to recommend to a client the purchase of stock in a company, the broker needs information on the company's profits and whether it pays dividends. When trying to decide whether to lend money to a company, a banker must consider the company's current debts.

In this book, we explore how accounting can help all of us in making informed financial decisions. Before we turn to the role played by accounting in decision making, we need to explore business in more detail. What *is* business? What forms of organization carry on business activities? In what types of business activities do those organizations engage?

WHAT IS BUSINESS?

LO 2 Understand what business is about.

Business All the activities necessary to provide the members of an economic system with goods and services.

Just as Winnebago Industries got its start in Forest City, Iowa, your study of accounting has to start somewhere. All disciplines have a foundation on which they rest. For accounting, that foundation is business.

Broadly defined, **business** consists of all the activities necessary to provide the members of an economic system with goods and services. Certain business activities focus on the providing of goods or products, such as ice cream, automobiles, and computers. Some of these companies produce or manufacture the products. Others are involved in the distribution of the goods, either as wholesalers (who sell to retail outlets) or retailers (who sell to consumers). Other business activities by their nature are service oriented. Corporate giants such as Citicorp, Walt Disney, AOL Time Warner, and United Airlines remind us of the prominence of service activities in the world today. The relatively recent phenomenon of various "service providers," such as health-care organizations and Internet companies, are a testimony to the growing importance of the service sector in the U.S. economy.

To appreciate the kinds of business enterprises in our economy, consider the various types of companies that have a stake in the delivery of a pint of ice cream to the grocery store. We will use as an example the case of Ben & Jerry's, a Vermont-based producer of super-premium ice cream. First, Ben & Jerry's must contract with a local milk *supplier,* St. Albans Cooperative Creamery. As a *manufacturer* or *producer,* Ben & Jerry's takes the milk and other various raw materials, such as sugar and chocolate, and transforms them into a finished product. At this stage, a *distributor* or *wholesaler* gets involved. For example, Ben & Jerry's sells a considerable amount of its ice cream to Dreyer's Grand Ice Cream. Dreyer's, in turn, sells the products to many different *retailers,* such as Albertsons' and Safeway. Although maybe less obvious, any number of *service* companies are also involved in the process. For example, various trucking companies transport the milk to Ben & Jerry's for production, and others move the ice cream along to Dreyer's. Still others get it to supermarkets and other retail outlets. Exhibit I-1 summarizes the process.

Exhibit I-1 Types of Businesses

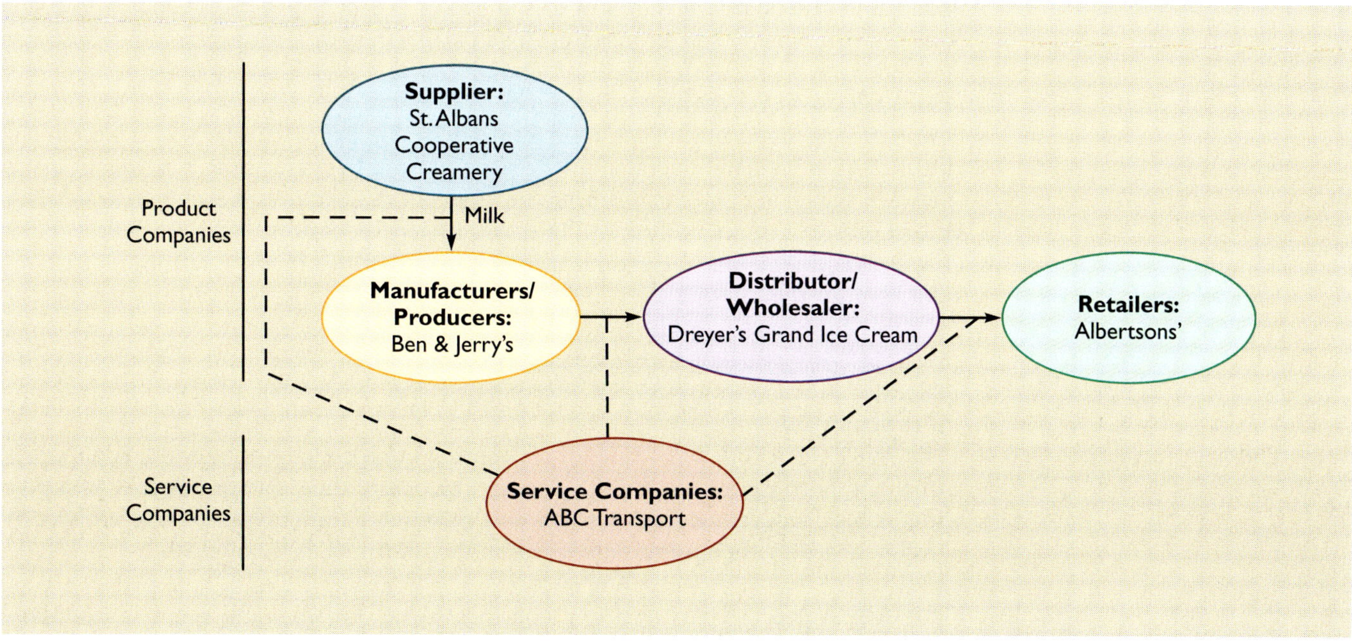

FORMS OF ORGANIZATION

LO 3 Distinguish among the forms of organization.

There are many different types of organizations in our society. One convenient way to categorize the myriad types is to distinguish between those that are organized to earn money and those that exist for some other purpose. Although the lines can become blurred *business entities* generally are organized to earn a profit, whereas *nonbusiness entities* generally exist to serve various segments of society. Both types are summarized in Exhibit I-2.

Exhibit I-2 Forms of Organization

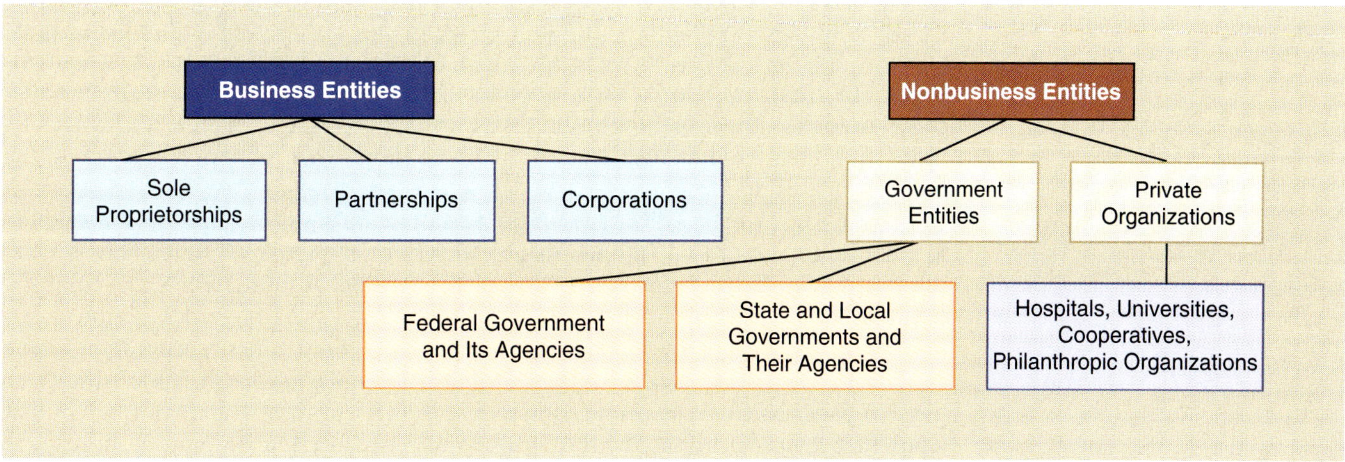

Business Entities

Business entities are organized to earn a profit. Legally, a profit-oriented company is one of three types: a sole proprietorship, a partnership, or a corporation.

Sole Proprietorships This form of organizaion is characterized by a single owner. Many small businesses are organized as **sole proprietorships.** Very often the business is owned and operated by the same person. Because of the close relationship between the owner and the business, the affairs of the two must be kept separate. This is one example in accounting of the **economic entity concept,** which requires that a single, identifiable unit of organization be accounted for in all situations. For example, assume that Bernie Berg owns a neighborhood grocery store. In paying the monthly bills, such as utilities and supplies, Bernie must separate his personal costs from the costs associated with the grocery business. In turn, financial statements prepared for the business must not intermingle Bernie's personal affairs with the affairs of the company.

Unlike the distinction made for accounting purposes between an individual's personal and business affairs, the IRS does not recognize the separate existence of a proprietorship from its owner. That is, a sole proprietorship is not a taxable entity; any profits earned by the business are taxed on the return of the individual.

Partnerships A **partnership** is a business owned by two or more individuals. Many small businesses begin as partnerships. When two or more partners start out, they need some sort of agreement as to how much each will contribute to the business and how they will divide any profits. In many small partnerships, the agreement is often just an oral understanding between the partners. In large businesses, the partnership agreement is formalized in a written document.

Although a partnership may involve just two owners, some have thousands of partners. Public accounting firms, law firms, and other types of service companies are often organized as partnerships. Like a sole proprietorship, a partnership is not a taxable entity. The individual partners pay taxes on their proportionate shares of the profits of the business.

Corporations Although sole proprietorships and partnerships dominate in sheer number, corporations control an overwhelming majority of the private resources in this country. A **corporation** is an entity organized under the laws of a particular state. Each of the 50 states is empowered to regulate the creation and operation of businesses organized as corporations in it.

To start a corporation, one must file articles of incorporation with the state. If the articles are approved by the state, a corporate charter is issued, and the corporation can begin to issue stock. A **share of stock** is a certificate that acts as evidence of ownership in a corporation. Although not always the case, stocks of many corporations are traded on organized stock exchanges, such as the New York and American Stock Exchanges.

What are the advantages of running a business as a corporation rather than a partnership? This was the question the owners of Winnebago Industries had to ask themselves. The company enjoyed early success in the market, and to capitalize on that success, it needed to grow. To grow meant that it would need a larger manufacturing facility, more equipment, and a larger staff. All of these things cost money. Where would the money come from?

One of the primary advantages of the corporate form of organization is the ability to raise large amounts of money in a relatively brief period of time. This is what prompted Winnebago Industries to "go public" in 1966. To raise money, the company sold a specific type of security: stock. As stated earlier, a share of stock is simply a certificate that evidences ownership in a corporation. Sometimes, corporations issue another type of security called a bond. A **bond** is similar in that it is a certificate or piece of paper issued to someone. However, it is different from a share of stock in that a bond represents a promise by the company to repay a certain amount of money at a future date. In other words, if you were to buy a bond from a company, you would be lending it money. Interest on the bond is usually paid semiannually. We will have more to say about stocks and bonds when we discuss financing activities later.

The ease of transfer of ownership in a corporation is another advantage of this form of organization. If you hold shares of stock in a corporation whose stock is actively traded and you decide that you want out, you simply call your broker and put in an order to sell. Another distinct advantage is the limited liability of the stockholder. Generally speaking, a stockholder is liable only for the amount contributed to the business. That is, if a company goes out of business, the most the stockholder stands to lose is the amount invested. On the other hand, both proprietors and general partners usually can be held personally liable for the debts of the business.

Nonbusiness Entities

Most **nonbusiness entities** are organized for a purpose other than to earn a profit. They exist to serve the needs of various segments of society. For example, a hospital is organized to provide health care to its patients. A municipal government is operated for the benefit of its citizens. A local school district exists to meet the educational needs of the youth in the community.

All these entities are distinguished by the lack of an identifiable owner. The lack of an identifiable owner and of the profit motive changes to some extent the type of accounting used by nonbusiness entities. This type, called *fund accounting,* is discussed in advanced accounting courses. Regardless of the lack of a profit motive in nonbusiness entities, there is still a demand for the information provided by an accounting system. For example, a local government needs detailed cost breakdowns in order to levy taxes. A hospital may want to borrow money and will need financial statements to present to the prospective lender.

Organizations and Social Responsibility

Although nonbusiness entities are organized specifically to serve members of society, U.S. business entities also have become more sensitive to their broader social responsibilities. Because they touch the lives of so many members of society, most large corporations recognize the societal aspects of their overall mission and have established programs to meet their social responsibilities. Some companies focus their efforts on local charities, while others donate to national or international causes. Certainly all of the companies showcased in the chapter openers of this book have programs in place to meet their objectives in the area of corporate giving.

THE NATURE OF BUSINESS ACTIVITY

LO 4 Describe the various types of business activities.

Because corporations dominate business activity in the United States, in this book we will focus on this form of organization. Corporations engage in a multitude of different types of activities. It is possible to categorize all of them into one of three types, however: financing, investing, and operating.

Financing Activities

All businesses must start with financing. Simply put, money is needed to start a business. John Hanson and his fellow investors needed money in the late 1950s to buy the travel trailer factory and get their business off the ground. As described earlier, Winnebago Industries found itself in need of additional financing in 1966 and thus made the decision to sell stock to the public. Some companies not only sell stock to raise money but also borrow from various sources to finance their operations.

As you will see throughout this book, accounting has its own unique terminology. In fact, accounting is often referred to as *the language of business.* The discussion of financing activities brings up two important accounting terms: liabilities and capital stock. A **liability** is an obligation of a business; it can take many different forms. When a company borrows money at a bank, the liability is called a *note payable.* When a company sells bonds, the obligation is termed *bonds payable.* Amounts owed to the government for taxes are called *taxes payable.* Assume Winnebago Industries buys from Clear Glass Company the glass for the windows in its RVs. Assume that Clear Glass gives Winnebago Industries 30 days to pay for purchases. During this 30-day period, Winnebago Industries has an obligation called *accounts payable.*

Capital stock is the term used by accountants to indicate the dollar amount of stock sold to the public. Capital stock differs from liabilities in one very important respect. Those who buy stock in a corporation are not lending money to the business, as are those who buy bonds in the company or make a loan in some other form to the company. Someone who buys stock in a company is called a **stockholder,** and that person is providing a permanent form of financing to the business. In other words, there is not a due date at which time the stockholder will be repaid. Normally, the only way for a stockholder to get back his or her original investment from buying stock is to sell it to someone else. Someone who buys bonds in a company or in some other way makes a loan to it is called a **creditor.** A creditor does *not* provide a permanent form of financing to the business. That is, the creditor expects repayment of the amount loaned and, in many instances, payment of interest for the use of the money as well.

Investing Activities

There is a natural progression in a business from financing activities to investing activities. That is, once funds are generated from creditors and stockholders, money is available to invest. Winnebago Industries used the money it received from selling stock to grow and eventually open a new manufacturing facility.

An **asset** is a future economic benefit to a business. For example, cash is an asset to a company. To Winnebago Industries, its land, buildings, and machinery are assets. At any point in time, Winnebago Industries has a supply of materials to be used in building RVs. It also has RVs that are in the process of being manufactured and others that are ready to be sold to dealers. The finished RVs and the materials are called *inventory* and are another valuable asset of a company.

An asset represents the right to receive some sort of benefit in the future. The point is that not all assets are tangible in nature, as are inventories and plant and equipment. For example, assume that Winnebago Industries sells RVs to one of its dealers and allows this dealer to pay for its purchase at the end of 30 days. At the time of the sale, Winnebago Industries doesn't have cash yet, but it has another valuable asset. The right to collect the amount due from the customer in 30 days is an asset called an *account receivable.* As a second example, assume that a company acquires from an inventor a patent that will allow the company the exclusive right to manufacture a certain product. The right to the future economic benefits from the patent is an asset. In summary, an asset is a valuable resource to the company that controls it.

At this point, you should notice the inherent tie between assets and liabilities. How does a company satisfy its liabilities, that is, its obligations? Although there are some exceptions, most liabilities are settled by transferring assets. The asset most often used to settle a liability is cash.

Operating Activities

Once funds are obtained from financing activities and investments are made in productive assets, a business is ready to begin operations. Every business is organized with a purpose in mind. The purpose of some businesses is to sell a *product.* Winnebago Industries was organized to manufacture and sell RVs. Other companies provide *services.* Service-oriented businesses are becoming an increasingly important sector of the U.S. economy. Some of the largest corporations in this country, such as banks and airlines, sell services rather than products. Some companies sell both products and services.

Accountants have a name for the sale of products and services. **Revenue** is the inflow of assets resulting from the sale of products and services. When a company makes a cash sale, the asset it receives is cash. When a sale is made on credit, the asset received is an account receivable. For now, you should understand that revenue represents the dollar amount of sales of products and services for a specific period of time.

We have thus far identified one important operating activity: the sale of products and services. However, costs must be incurred to operate a business. Employees must be paid salaries and wages. Suppliers must be paid for purchases of inventory, and the utility company has to be paid for heat and electricity. The government must be paid the taxes owed it. All of these are examples of important operating activities of a business. As you might expect by now, accountants use a specific name for the costs incurred in operating a business. An **expense** is the outflow of assets resulting from the sale of goods and services.

Exhibit I-3 summarizes the three types of activities conducted by a business. Our discussion and the exhibit present a simplification of business activity, but actual businesses are in a constant state of motion with many different financing, investing, and operating activities going on at any one time. The model as portrayed in Exhibit I-3 should be helpful as you begin the study of accounting, however. To summarize, a company obtains money from various types of financing activities, uses the money raised to invest in productive assets, and then provides goods and services to its customers.

Exhibit I-3 A Model of Business Activities

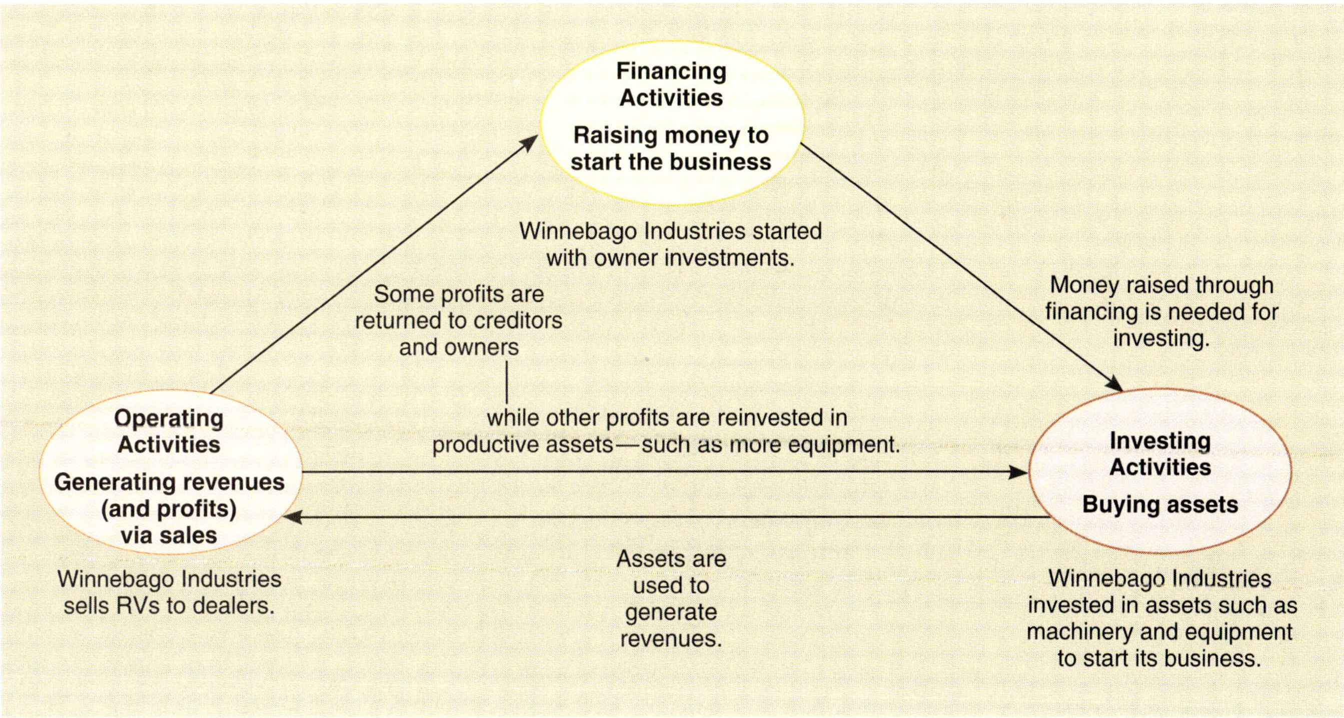

STARTING THE STUDY OF ACCOUNTING

The purpose of this module was to introduce you to business and help you to understand why it is the foundation on which accounting is based. Now that you have a basic understanding of what business is, the types of organizations that engage in business, and the various activities they conduct, you are ready to begin the study of accounting itself.

This module introduced you to business and decision making by telling a brief story of how Winnebago Industries got started. You will learn more about the company and its financial statements in Chapter 1. Beginning in Chapter 2, another new feature company will start off each chapter as a way of introducing the material in that chapter.

If you do not own stock in one of these companies, how can you get access to its financial statements and other information about it? One way is by calling or writing to the company's investor relations department. A much more efficient and timely approach to gathering this information, however, is to use the Internet. Nearly all major corporations, as well as many smaller ones, now post financial statements and other information on their Web sites. To help in your search, each chapter contains the URLs of the companies discussed there.

http://

http://porter.swlearning.com

Technology and other resources for your success

If you need additional help, visit the text's Web site. Also, see pages xv–xvii in this text's preface for a description of available technology and other resources. If your instructor is using PERSONAL Trainer in this course, you may complete, on line, the assignments identified by PT.

Key Terms Quiz

Note to the student: We conclude each chapter with a quiz on the key terms, which are in bold where they appear in the chapter. We have included a quiz for the numerous important terms introduced in this getting started module.

Read each definition below and then write the number of that definition in the blank beside the appropriate term it defines. The first one has been done for you. The solution appears at the end of this module. When reviewing terminology, come back to your completed key terms quiz. Study tip: Also check the glossary in the margin or at the end of the book.

_____	Business	_____	Nonbusiness entity
_____	Business entity	_____	Liability
_____	Economic entity concept	_____	Capital stock
_____	Sole proprietorship	_____	Stockholder
_____	Partnership	_____	Creditor
_____	Corporation	1	Asset
_____	Share of stock	_____	Revenue
_____	Bond	_____	Expense

1. A future economic benefit.
2. A business owned by two or more individuals; organization form often used by accounting firms and law firms.
3. An inflow of assets resulting from the sale of goods and services.
4. A form of entity organized under the laws of a particular state; ownership evidenced by shares of stock.
5. Organization operated for some purpose other than to earn a profit.
6. An outflow of assets resulting from the sale of goods and services.
7. An obligation of a business.
8. A certificate that acts as ownership in a corporation.
9. A certificate that represents a corporation's promise to repay a certain amount of money and interest in the future.
10. One of the owners of a corporation.
11. Someone to whom a company or person has a debt.
12. The assumption that a single, identifiable unit must be accounted for in all situations.
13. Form of organization with a single owner.
14. Indicates the owners' contributions to a corporation.
15. All the activities necessary to provide the members of an economic system with goods and services.
16. Organization operated to earn a profit.

Questions

1. What is business about? What do all businesses have in common?
2. What is an asset? Give three examples.
3. What is a liability? How does the definition of *liability* relate to the definition of *asset*?
4. Business entities are organized as one of three distinct forms. What are these three forms?
5. What are the three distinct types of business activity in which companies engage? Assume you start your own company to rent bicycles in the summer and skis in the winter. Give an example of at least one of each of the three types of business activities in which you would engage.

Solutions to Key Terms Quiz

15	Business (p. 4)	5	Nonbusiness entity (p. 7)
16	Business entity (p. 6)	7	Liability (p. 8)
13	Sole proprietorship (p. 6)	14	Capital stock (p. 8)
12	Economic entity concept (p. 6)	10	Stockholder (p. 8)
2	Partnership (p. 6)	11	Creditor (p. 8)
4	Corporation (p. 6)	1	Asset (p. 8)
8	Share of stock (p. 6)	3	Revenue (p. 9)
9	Bond (p. 6)	6	Expense (p. 9)

Chapter 1

Accounting as a Form of Communication

Focus on Financial Results

What groups of people care about the financial performance of Winnebago Industries, one of the leading manufacturers of motor homes and recreational vehicles (RVs) in the United States? Since its founding over 40 years ago, the company's managers, investors, employees, dealers, and suppliers have all had a vested interest in the financial health of the company whose name is synonymous with RVs.

To communicate its financial performance, Winnebago Industries uses the language of accounting. The *selected financial data* that follow here summarize key measures including revenues, income, and assets. This information shows that *beginning with September 1, 1997,* both revenues and net income rose in *the next three* years, 1998, 1999, and 2000, although the company experienced a decline in both of these measures in *fiscal year* 2001. As explained in the annual report, the drop in revenues corresponds to a decline in consumer confidence levels and a slowdown in the economy. Beginning in fiscal year 1997 the company refocused on its core motor home business and is encouraged by what it sees: an increase in market share of 10 percent calendar year-to-date through September 2001 versus one year earlier.

What will be the future of Winnebago Industries? In its 2001 message to its shareholders, Winnebago Industries sounded quite optimistic about its future. This optimism likely contributed to the company's decision to continue to pay the $0.20 per share dividend to shareholders that it had paid in each of the previous four years. A series of graphs[1] show that the company leads the RV industry in return on shareholders' equity, return on assets, operating margin, and net profit margin. This standing among its competitors, along with six consecutive quality awards from its dealers association, does indeed give Winnebago Industries and its shareholders reason to be optimistic about the future.

Company net income rose in fiscal years 1998, 1999, and 2000

Company revenues rose in fiscal years 1998, 1999, and 2000

Selected Financial Data

(dollars in thousands, except per share data)	Aug. 25, 2001(1)	Aug. 26, 2000	Aug. 28, 1999	Aug. 29, 1998	Aug. 30, 1997
For the Year:					
Net revenues (2)	$681,834	$753,382	$677,011	$533,385	$445,621
Income before taxes	59,228	73,992	66,609	35,927	6,992
Pretax profit % of revenue	8.7%	9.8%	9.8%	6.7%	1.6%
Provision for income taxes	$ 15,474	$ 25,593	$ 22,349	$ 11,543	$ 416
Income tax rate	26.1%	34.6%	33.6%	32.1%	5.9%
Income from continuing operations	$ 42,704	$ 48,399	$ 44,260	$ 24,384	$ 6,576
Gain on sale of Cycle-Sat subsidiary	---	---	---	---	16,472
Net income	$ 42,704	$ 48,399	$ 44,260	$ 24,384	$ 23,048
Income per share:					
Continuing operations:					
Basic	$ 2.06	$ 2.23	$ 1.99	$ 1.01	$ .26
Diluted	2.03	2.20	1.96	1.00	.26
Discontinued operations:					
Basic	---	---	---	---	.65
Diluted	---	---	---	---	.64
Net income per share:					
Basic	$ 2.06	$ 2.23	$ 1.99	$ 1.01	$ .91
Diluted	2.03	2.20	1.96	1.00	.90
Weighted average common shares outstanding (in thousands):					
Basic	20,735	21,680	22,209	24,106	25,435
Diluted	21,040	22,011	22,537	24,314	25,550
Cash dividends per share	$ .20	$ .20	$ .20	$ .20	$ .20
Book value	9.99	8.22	6.70	5.11	4.86
Return on assets (ROA)	12.5%	15.7%	15.5%	10.6%	10.8%
Return on equity (ROE)	20.6%	27.7%	29.6%	20.9%	18.6%
Unit Sales:					
Class A	5,666	6,819	6,054	5,381	4,834
Class C	3,410	3,697	4,222	3,390	2,724
Total Class A & C Motor Homes	9,076	10,516	10,276	8,771	7,558
Class B Conversions (EuroVan Campers)	703	854	600	978	1,205
At Year End:					
Total assets	$307,095	$307,095	$285,889	$230,612	$213,475
Stockholders' equity	174,909	174,909	149,384	116,523	123,882
Working capital	143,274	143,274	123,720	92,800	100,772
Long-term debt	---	---	---	---	---
Current ratio	3.0 to 1	3.0 to 1	2.5 to 1	2.5 to 1	3.4 to 1
Number of employees	3,325	3,300	3,400	3,010	2,830

(1) Includes a noncash after tax cumulative effect of change in accounting principle of $1.1 million expense or $.05 per share due to the adoption of SAB No. 101.
(2) Net revenues have been restated for the adoption of a new accounting principle related to shipping and handling fees and costs.

Net Revenues (Dollars in Millions)

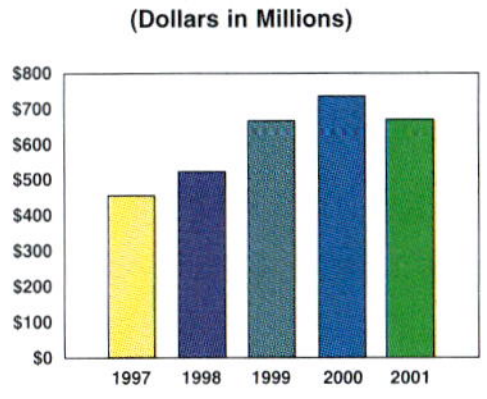

Net Income Per Diluted Share (Dollars)

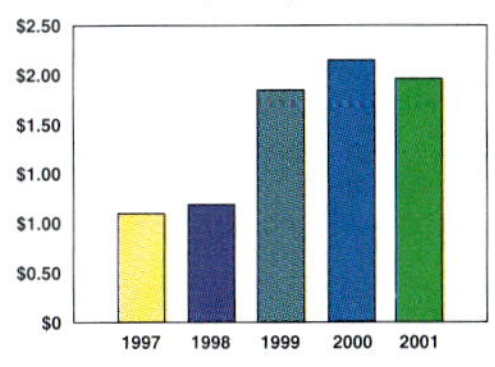

Shareholders' Equity (Dollars In Millions)

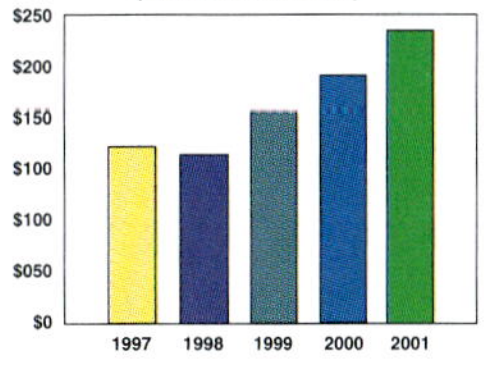

http://www.winnebagoind.com

You're in the Driver's Seat

If you were considering a marketing job with Winnebago Industries, how would your decision be affected by the company's decision to refocus its attention on its core business? Have the company's sales continued to rise? If so, have they risen at a slower or faster pace than in the previous five years? Use this chapter and the succeeding ones to help you better understand the financial performance of Winnebago Industries.

[1]*The complete Winnebago Industries 2001 Annual Report is provided in Appendix A at the end of the text. The series of graphs appear on page 1 of that report.*

LEARNING OBJECTIVES

After studying this chapter, you should be able to:

LO 1 Identify the primary users of accounting information and their needs. (p. 14)

LO 2 Explain the purpose of each of the financial statements and the relationships among them, and prepare a set of simple statements. (p. 16)

LO 3 Identify and explain the primary assumptions made in preparing financial statements. (p. 22)

LO 4 Describe the various roles of accountants in organizations. (p. 24)

WHAT IS ACCOUNTING?

Accounting The process of identifying, measuring, and communicating economic information to various users.

Many people have preconceived notions about what accounting is. They think of it as a highly procedural activity practiced by people who are "good in math." This notion of accounting is very narrow and focuses only on the record-keeping or bookkeeping aspects of the discipline. Accounting is in fact much broader than this in its scope. Specifically, **accounting** is "the process of identifying, measuring, and communicating economic information to permit informed judgments and decisions by users of the information.[1]

Each of the three activities in this definition—*identifying, measuring,* and *communicating*—requires the judgment of a trained professional. We will return later in this chapter to acccounting as a profession and the various roles of accountants in our society. Note that the definition refers to the users of economic information and the decisions they make. Who *are* the users of accounting information? We turn now to this important question.

USERS OF ACCOUNTING INFORMATION AND THEIR NEEDS

LO 1 Identify the primary users of accounting information and their needs.

It is helpful to categorize users of accounting information on the basis of their relationship to the organization. Internal users, primarily the managers of a company, are involved in the daily affairs of the business. All other groups are external users.

Internal Users

Management accounting The branch of accounting concerned with providing management with information to facilitate planning and control.

The management of a company is in a position to obtain financial information in a way that best suits its needs. For example, if a plant manager at Winnebago Industries needs to know how much it costs to build a Winnebago Adventurer, the best selling motor home of its type on the market, this information exists in the accounting system and can be reported. If the same manager wants to find out if the monthly payroll is more or less than the budgeted amount, a report can be generated to provide the answer. **Management accounting** is the branch of accounting concerned with providing internal users (management) with information to facilitate planning and control. The ability to produce management accounting reports is limited only by the extent of the data available and the cost involved in generating the relevant information.

External Users

External users, those not involved directly in the operations of a business, need information that differs from that needed by internal users. In addition, the ability of exter-

[1]American Accounting Association, *A Statement of Basic Accounting Theory* (Evanston, Ill.: American Accounting Association, 1966), p. 1.

nal users to obtain the information is more limited. Without the day-to-day contact with the affairs of the business, outsiders must rely on the information presented to them by the management of the company.

Certain external users, such as the Internal Revenue Service, require that information be presented in a very specific manner, and they have the authority of the law to ensure that they get the required information. Stockholders, bondholders, and other creditors must rely on *financial statements* for their information.[2] **Financial accounting** is the branch of accounting concerned with communication with outsiders through financial statements.

Financial accounting The branch of accounting concerned with the preparation of financial statements for outsider use.

Stockholders and Potential Stockholders Both existing and potential stockholders need financial information about a business. If you currently own stock in a company, you need information that will aid in your decision either to continue to hold the stock or to sell it. If you are considering buying stock in a company, you need financial information that will help in choosing among competing alternative investments. What has been the recent performance of the company in the stock market? What were its profits for the most recent year? How do these profits compare with those of the prior year? How much did the company pay in dividends? One source for much of this information is the company's financial statements.

Business Strategy

To Build or Not to Build?

What should a company's strategy be when it has recently reported a decline in net revenues of nearly 10 percent from the prior year and over 10 percent in net income? Winnebago Industries explained in its 2001 annual report that the decrease in revenues was a reflection of the decline in consumer confidence levels and a slowdown in the economy. However, at the same time, the RV manufacturer feels that, in the long term, demographics are in its favor. Supporting this positive outlook is the anticipated increase over the next 30 years of the number of people 50 years and older, which is a key target market for Winnebago Industries.

So what was Winnebago Industries' reaction to what could be construed as conflicting signals: a decline in revenues but some favorable demographics regarding its market? On April 1, 2002, the company left little doubt in the minds of its stockholders about its optimism for the future. On this day, it announced plans to build a new manufacturing facility, an expansion that would be the company's largest to date. Once the new plant in Charles City, Iowa, is operating at full capacity, it will increase Winnebago Industries' motor home production by about 30 percent. The company expects production at the new plant to begin in early 2003.

Winnebago Industries' investors did not have to wait long to have their confidence boosted in the company's management. Less than three months later, on June 19, 2002, the company released its results for the third quarter of its 2002 fiscal year. Revenues had already begun to rebound from the declines in the earlier year, with a 26 percent increase compared to the revenues in the same quarter of the prior year. Net income for the quarter was up even more, showing a 45 percent increase from the comparable quarter in 2001. Management attributed the encouraging third-quarter results to a variety of factors, including improvements in consumer confidence levels and sustained low interest rates. Only time will tell whether Winnebago Industries' strategic decision to build a new plant after just reporting a decline in revenues was the right decision. But third-quarter results certainly should help the company reassure its investors that it is on the right road. ■

Source: Winnebago Industries' 2001 Annual Report and Web site.

[2]Technically, stockholders are insiders because they own stock in the business. In most large corporations, however, it is not practical for stockholders to be involved in the daily affairs of the business. Thus, they are better categorized here as external users because they normally rely on general-purpose financial statements, as do creditors.

Bondholders, Bankers, and Other Creditors Before buying a bond in a company (remember you are lending money to the company), you need to feel comfortable that the company will be able to pay you the amount owed at maturity and the periodic interest payments. Financial statements can help you to decide whether to purchase a bond. Similarly, before lending money, a bank needs information that will help it to determine the company's ability to repay both the amount of the loan and interest. Therefore, a set of financial statements is a key ingredient in a loan proposal.

http://www.irs.gov

http://www.sec.gov

Government Agencies Numerous government agencies have information needs specified by law. For example, the Internal Revenue Service (IRS) is empowered to collect a tax on income from both individuals and corporations. Every year a company prepares a tax return to report to the IRS the amount of income it earned. Another government agency, the Securities and Exchange Commission (SEC), was created in the aftermath of the Great Depression. This regulatory agency sets the rules under which financial statements must be prepared for corporations that sell their stock to the public on organized stock exchanges. Similar to the IRS, the SEC prescribes the manner in which financial information is presented to it. Companies operating in specialized industries submit financial reports to other regulatory agencies, such as the Interstate Commerce Commission and the Federal Trade Commission.

Other External Users Many other individuals and groups rely on financial information given to them by businesses. A supplier of raw material needs to know the creditworthiness of a company before selling it a product on credit. To promote its industry, a trade association must gather financial information on the various companies in the industry. Other important users are stockbrokers and financial analysts. They use financial reports in advising their clients on investment decisions. In reaching their decisions, all of these users rely to a large extent on accounting information provided by management. Exhibit 1-1 summarizes the various users of financial information and the types of decisions they must make.

Exhibit 1-1 Users of Accounting Information

CATEGORIES OF USERS	EXAMPLES OF USERS	COMMON DECISION	RELEVANT QUESTION
Internal	Management	Should we build another new manufacturing facility?	What will be the cost to construct the new plant?
External	Stockholder	Should I buy shares of Winnebago Industries stock?	How much did the company earn last year?
	Banker	Should I lend money to Winnebago Industries?	What existing debts or liabilities does the company have?
	Employee	Should I ask for a raise?	How much are the company's sales, and how much is it paying out in salaries and wages? Is it paying out too much in compensation compared to its sales?
	Supplier	Should I allow Winnebago Industries to buy milk from me and pay me later?	What is the current amount of the company's accounts payable?

FINANCIAL STATEMENTS: HOW ACCOUNTANTS COMMUNICATE

LO 2 Explain the purpose of each of the financial statements and the relationships among them, and prepare a set of simple statements.

The primary focus of this book is financial accounting. This branch of accounting is concerned with informing management and outsiders about a company through financial statements. We turn our attention now to the composition of three of the major statements: the balance sheet, the income statement, and the statement of retained earnings.[3]

The Accounting Equation and the Balance Sheet

The accounting equation is the foundation for the entire accounting system:

Assets = Liabilities + Owners' Equity

The left side of the accounting equation refers to the *assets* of the company. Those items that are valuable economic resources and will provide future benefit to the company should appear on the left side of the equation. The right side of the equation indicates who provided, or has a claim to, those assets. Some of the assets were provided by creditors, and they have a claim to them. For example, if a company has a delivery truck, the dealer that provided the truck to the company has a claim to the assets until the dealer is paid. The delivery truck would appear on the left side of the equation as an asset to the company; the company's *liability* to the dealer would appear on the right side of the equation. Other assets are provided by the owners of the business. Their claims to these assets are represented by the portion of the right side of the equation called **owners' equity.**

The term *stockholders' equity* is used to refer to the owners' equity of a corporation. **Stockholders' equity** is the mathematical difference between a corporation's assets and its obligations or liabilities. That is, after the amounts owed to bondholders, banks, suppliers, and other creditors are subtracted from the assets, the amount remaining is the stockholders' equity, the amount of interest or claim that the owners have on the assets of the business.

Stockholders' equity arises in two distinct ways. First, it is created when a company issues stock to an investor. As we noted earlier, capital stock reflects ownership in a corporation in the form of a certificate. It represents the amounts contributed by the owners to the company. Second, as owners of shares in a corporation, stockholders have a claim on the assets of a business when it is profitable. **Retained earnings** represents the owners' claims to the company's assets that result from its earnings that have not been paid out in dividends. It is the earnings accumulated or retained by the company.

The **balance sheet** (sometimes called the *statement of financial position*) is the financial statement that summarizes the assets, liabilities, and owners' equity of a company. It is a "snapshot" of the business at a certain date. A balance sheet can be prepared on any day of the year, although it is most commonly prepared on the last day of a month, quarter, or year. At any point in time, the balance sheet must be "in balance." That is, assets must equal liabilities and owners' equity.

Balance sheets for Winnebago Industries at the end of two recent years are shown in Exhibit 1-2. Note the headings on the two columns of the balance sheet: August 25, 2001, and August 26, 2000. Winnebago Industries chooses to end its fiscal or accounting year on the last Saturday in August, which was August 25 in 2001 and August 26 in 2000. Although December 31 is the most common year-end, some companies such as Winnebago Industries use a date other than December 31 to end their year. Often this choice is based on when a company's peak selling season ends. For Winnebago Industries, most of its sales occur in spring and early summer. Thus, a year-end date near the end of August makes sense.

As the exhibit makes clear, there are the three main sections of the balance sheet corresponding to the three elements of the accounting equation: Assets, Liabilities, and Stockholders' Equity.

In the following table, note some of the main types of items that appear on the balance sheet:

1 Cash and Cash Equivalents: Includes cash on hand as well as cash in various checking and savings accounts

Study Tip

The accounting equation and the financial statements are at the heart of this course. Memorize the accounting equation, and make sure you study this introduction to how the financial statements should look, how to read them, and what they say about a company.

Owners' equity The owners' claims on the assets of an entity.

Stockholders' equity The owners' equity in a corporation.

Retained earnings The part of owners' equity that represents the income earned less dividends paid over the life of an entity.

Balance sheet The financial statement that summarizes the assets, liabilities, and owners' equity at a specific point in time.

[3] The fourth major financial statement is the statement of cash flows. This important statement will be introduced in Chapter 2.

Exhibit 1-2 Winnebago Industries Balance Sheets

Consolidated Balance Sheets

(dollars in thousands)

	Assets A = L + SE	August 25, 2001	August 26, 2000
A	Current assets:		
1	Cash and cash equivalents	$ 93,779	$ 51,443
2	Receivables, less allowance for doubtful accounts ($244 and $1,168, respectively)	20,183	32,045
	Dealer financing receivables, less allowance for doubtful accounts ($117 and $27, respectively)	40,263	32,696
3	Inventories	79,815	85,707
	Prepaid expenses	3,604	3,952
	Deferred income taxes	6,723	7,675
	Total current assets	244,367	213,518
4	Property and equipment, at cost:		
	Land	1,029	1,138
	Buildings	45,992	45,219
	Machinery and equipment	82,182	78,099
	Transportation equipment	5,482	5,414
		134,685	129,870
	Less accumulated depreciation	88,149	84,415
	Total property and equipment, net	46,536	45,455
	Investment in life insurance	22,223	21,028
	Deferred income taxes	21,495	19,044
	Other assets	7,412	8,050
	Total assets	$342,033	$307,095
=			
L	**Liabilities and Stockholders' Equity**		
	Current liabilities:		
5	Accounts payable, trade	$ 30,789	$ 26,212
	Income taxes payable	4,938	8,790
	Accrued expenses:		
	Accrued compensation	13,730	13,924
	Product warranties	8,072	8,114
	Insurance	4,567	5,384
	Promotional	3,181	3,145
	Other	4,842	4,675
	Total current liabilities	70,119	70,244
	Postretirement health care and deferred compensation benefits	64,450	61,942
+			
SE	Stockholders' equity:		
	Capital stock common, par value $.50; authorized 60,000,000 shares, issued 25,886,000 and 25,878,000 shares, respectively	12,943	12,939
	Additional paid-in capital	22,261	21,994
6	Reinvested earnings	234,139	195,556
		269,343	230,489
	Less treasury stock, at cost	61,879	55,580
	Total stockholders' equity	207,464	174,909
	Total liabilities and stockholders' equity	$342,033	$307,095

See notes to consolidated finanial statements.

2 Receivables: Arises from selling RVs to dealers and allowing them to pay later

3 Inventories: Refers to the RVs and related products that the company sells

4 Property and Equipment: Includes land, buildings, machinery, and transportation equipment that are all needed to build and transport RVs

5 Accounts Payable, Trade: Arises from buying supplies and other materials and being allowed to pay later

6 Reinvested (or Retained) Earnings: Amount of income earned less dividends distributed over life of the company

Exhibit 1-3 summarizes the relationship between the accounting equation and the items that appear on a balance sheet.

Exhibit 1-3

The Relationship between the Accounting Equation and the Balance Sheet

Assets	=	Liabilities	+	Owners' Equity
Economic resources Examples: • Cash • Accounts receivable • Inventory		**Creditors' claims to the assets** Examples: • Accounts payable • Notes payable		**Owners' claims to the assets** Examples: • Capital stock • Retained earnings

Exhibit 1-3 refers to Owners' Equity, while Exhibit 1-2 refers to Stockholders' Equity. Remember, both are correct! "Owners' equity" is the general term by which we refer to ownership. "Stockholders' equity" refers only to ownership of a corporation by shareholders.

The Income Statement

An **income statement,** or statement of income, as it is sometimes called, summarizes the revenues and expenses of a company for a period of time. Comparative income statements for Winnebago Industries for three recent years are shown in Exhibit 1-4. Unlike the balance sheet, an income statement is a *flow* statement. That is, it summarizes the flow of revenues and expenses for the year. As was the case for the balance sheet, you are not expected at this point to understand fully all of the complexities involved in preparing an income statement. However, note the two largest items on the income statement—Revenues: Manufactured products and Cost of manufactured products. For now, it is sufficient to understand that the former is Winnebago Industries' primary source of revenue and the latter is its most significant expense.

Income statement A statement that summarizes revenues and expenses.

From Concept to Practice 1.1

Reading Winnebago Industries' Income Statement

Winnebago Industries' income statement states that its "Revenues from manufactured products" decreased in 2001 from the prior year. Does it seem logical that the "Cost of manufactured products" shown under "Costs and expenses" would also decrease? Explain your answer and give some examples of the types of costs that would be included in "Cost of manufactured products" for Winnebago Industries.

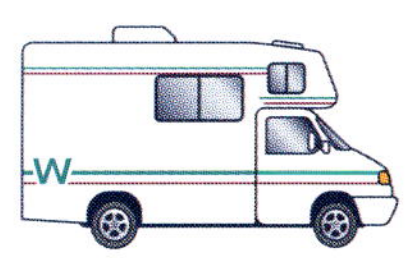

The Statement of Retained Earnings

As discussed earlier, Retained Earnings represents the accumulated earnings of a corporation less the amount paid in dividends to stockholders. **Dividends** are distributions of the net income or profits of a business to its stockholders. Not all businesses pay cash

Dividends A distribution of the net income of a business to its owners.

Exhibit 1-4 Winnebago Industries Income Statements

Winnebago Industries primary source of revenue

Winnebago Industries most significant expense

Consolidated Statements of Income

(in thousands, except per share data)	August 25, 2001	Year Ended August 26, 2000	August 28, 1999
Revenues:			
Manufactured products	$677,593	$749,474	$674,016
Dealer financing	4,241	3,908	2,995
Total net revenues	$681,834	$753,382	$677,011
Costs and expenses:			
Cost of manufactured products	$587,330	$640,488	$574,603
Selling	25,423	25,118	24,321
General and administrative	13,607	17,122	14,105
Total costs and expenses	$626,360	$682,728	$613,029
Operating income	$ 55,474	$ 70,654	$ 63,982
Financial income	3,754	3,338	2,627
Income before income taxes	$ 59,228	$ 73,992	$ 66,609
Provision for taxes	15,474	25,593	22,349
Income before cumulative effect of change in accounting principle	$ 43,754	$ 48,399	$ 44,260
Cumulative effect of change in accounting principle, net of taxes	(1,050)	—	—
Net income	$ 42,704	$ 48,399	$ 44,260

See notes to consolidated financial statements.

dividends. Among those companies that do pay dividends, the frequency with which they pay differs. For example, Winnebago Industries currently pays a cash dividend of $0.10 per share twice each year.

Statement of retained earnings The statement that summarizes the income earned and dividends paid over the life of a business.

A **statement of retained earnings** explains the change in retained earnings during the period. The basic format for the statement is as follows:

Beginning balance	$xxx,xxx
Add: Net income for the period	xxx,xxx
Deduct: Dividends for the period	xxx,xxx
Ending balance	$xxx,xxx

Revenues minus expenses, or net income, is an increase in retained earnings, and dividends are a decrease in the balance. Why are dividends shown on a statement of retained earnings instead of on an income statement? Dividends are not an expense and thus are not a component of net income, as are expenses. Instead, they are a *distribution* of the income of the business to its stockholders.

Recall that stockholders' equity consists of two parts: capital stock and retained earnings. In lieu of a separate statement of retained earnings, many corporations prepare a comprehensive statement to explain the changes both in the various capital stock accounts and in retained earnings during the period. Winnebago Industries, for example, presents the more comprehensive statement of changes in stockholders' equity. (It is not shown here, but you will find it in the printed annual report or online with Winnebago Industries' other financial statements.)

Accounting for Your Decisions

You Are a Potential Stockholder

You are deciding whether to invest in a company's stock. Which financial statement would you want to see, and which areas would you be most interested in?

ANS: All of them. The balance sheet will show the relative size of the assets and liabilities, and the stockholders' equity section should state how many shares of stock have been sold (outstanding shares) and how many more are available (authorized but not yet issued). The income statement's net sales, gross profit, operating income, and net income are important, not only for the most current year but also for previous years to determine trends. The statement of retained earnings will report whether dividends were paid and, if so, the amount.

Relationships Among Winnebago Industries' Financial Statements

Because the statements of a company such as Winnebago Industries are complex, it may not be easy at this point to see the important links among them. The relationships among the statements are summarized for you in Exhibit 1-5. Recall that in its annual report, Winnebago Industries does not present a separate statement of retained earnings. The information for the statement of retained earnings in Exhibit 1-5 appears as one of the columns in Winnebago Industries' statement of changes in stockholders' equity. Three important relationships are seen by examining the exhibit (NOTE: Here

Exhibit 1-5
Relationships among Financial Statements: Winnebago Industries Example

INCOME STATEMENT FOR 2001

Revenues	$ xxx
Less: Expenses	xxx
Net income	$42,704 (1)

STATEMENT OF RETAINED EARNINGS FOR 2001

Beginning balance, retained earnings	$195,556
Add: Net income	42,704 ◄ (1)
Deduct: Cash dividends	(4,121) ◄ (2)
Ending balance, retained earnings	$234,139 (3)

BALANCE SHEETS

	END OF 2001	END OF 2000
Total assets	$ xxx	$ xxx
Liabilities	$ xxx	$ xxx
Capital stock	xxx	xxx
Retained earnings	(3) ► 234,139	195,556
Total liabilities and stockholders' equity	$ xxx	$ xxx

and throughout the book, the numbers that follow correspond to the highlighted numbers in the exhibit; numbers in this exhibit are stated in thousands of dollars):

1 The 2001 income statement reports net income of $42,704. Net income increases retained earnings, as reported on the statement of retained earnings.

2 Cash dividends in the amount of $4,121 decrease retained earnings and, therefore, are shown as a deduction on the statement of retained earnings.

3 The ending balance of $234,139 in retained earnings, as reported on the statement of retained earnings for 2001, is transferred to the balance sheet at the end of 2001.

Two-Minute Review

1. *State the accounting equation, and indicate what each term means.*
2. *What are the three financial statements presented in this chapter?*
3. *How do amounts in the three statements interrelate?*

Answers on p. 29

THE CONCEPTUAL FRAMEWORK: FOUNDATION FOR FINANCIAL STATEMENTS

LO 3 Identify and explain the primary assumptions made in preparing financial statements.

Study Tip

The concepts in this section underlie everything you will learn throughout the course. You'll encounter them later in the context of specific topics.

Many people perceive the work of an accountant as being routine. In reality, accounting is anything but routine and requires a great deal of judgment on the part of the accountant. The record-keeping aspect of accounting—what we normally think of as bookkeeping—is the routine part of the accountant's work and only a small part of it. Most of the job deals with communicating relevant information to financial statement users.

The accounting profession has developed a *conceptual framework for accounting* that aids accountants in their role as interpreters and communicators of relevant information. The purpose of the framework is to act as a foundation for the specific principles and standards needed by the profession. An important part of the conceptual framework is a set of assumptions accountants make in preparing financial statements. We will briefly consider these assumptions, returning to a more detailed discussion of them in later chapters.

The *economic entity concept* was introduced in "Getting Started" when we first discussed different types of business entities. This assumption requires that an identifiable, specific entity be the subject of a set of financial statements. For example, even though some of Winnebago Industries' employees are stockholders and therefore own part of Winnebago Industries, their personal affairs must be kept separate from the business affairs. When we look at a balance sheet for the RV business, we need assurance that it shows the financial position of that entity only and does not intermingle the personal assets and liabilities of the employees or any of the other stockholders.

Cost principle Assets are recorded at the cost to acquire them.

The **cost principle** requires that accountants record assets at the cost paid to acquire them and continue to show this amount on all balance sheets until the company disposes of them. With a few exceptions, companies do not carry assets at their market value (how much they could sell the asset for today) but at original cost. Accountants use the term historical cost to refer to the original cost of an asset. Why not show an asset such as land at market value? The *subjectivity* inherent in determining market values supports the practice of carrying assets at their historical cost. The cost of an asset is verifiable by an independent observer and is much more *objective* than market value.

Going concern The assumption that an entity is not in the process of liquidation and that it will continue indefinitely.

Accountants assume that the entity being accounted for is a **going concern.** That is, they assume that Winnebago Industries is not in the process of liquidation and that it will continue indefinitely into the future. Another important reason for using historical cost rather than market value to report assets is the going concern assumption. If we assume that a business is *not* a going concern, then we assume that it is in the process of liquidation. If this is the case, market value might be more relevant than cost as a basis for recognizing the assets. But if we are able to assume that a business will continue indefinitely, cost can be more easily justified as a basis for valuation. The **monetary unit** used in preparing the statements of Winnebago Industries was the dollar. The reason for using the dollar as the monetary unit is that it is the recognized medium of exchange in the United States. It provides a convenient yardstick to measure the position and earnings of the business. As a yardstick, however, the dollar, like the currencies of all other countries, is subject to instability. We are all well aware that a dollar will not buy as much today as it did 10 years ago.

Monetary unit The yardstick used to measure amounts in financial statements; the dollar in the United States.

Inflation is evidenced by a general rise in the level of prices in an economy. Its effect on the measuring unit used in preparing financial statements is an important concern to the accounting profession. Although accountants have experimented with financial statements adjusted for the changing value of the measuring unit, the financial statements now prepared by corporations are prepared under the assumption that the monetary unit is relatively stable. At various times in the past, this has been a reasonable assumption and at other times not so reasonable.

Under the **time period** assumption, accountants assume that it is possible to prepare an income statement that accurately reflects net income or earnings for a specific time period. In the case of Winnebago Industries, this time period was one year. It is somewhat artificial to measure the earnings of a business for a period of time indicated on a calendar, whether it be a month, a quarter, or a year. Of course, the most accurate point in time to measure the earnings of a business would be at the end of its life. Accountants prepare periodic statements, however, because the users of the statements demand information about the entity on a regular basis.

Time period Artificial segment on the calendar, used as the basis for preparing financial statements.

Financial statements prepared by accountants must conform to **generally accepted accounting principles (GAAP).** This term refers to the various methods, rules, practices, and other procedures that have evolved over time in response to the need for some form of regulation over the preparation of financial statements. As changes have taken place in the business environment over time, GAAP have developed in response to these changes.

Generally accepted accounting principles (GAAP) The various methods, rules, practices, and other procedures that have evolved over time in response to the need to regulate the preparation of financial statements.

Accounting as a Social Science

Accounting is a service activity. As we have seen, its purpose is to provide financial information to decision makers. Thus, accounting is a *social* science. Accounting principles are much different from the rules that govern the *physical* sciences. For example, it is a rule of nature that an object dropped from your hand will eventually hit the ground rather than be suspended in air. There are no rules comparable to this in accounting. The principles that govern financial reporting are not governed by nature but instead develop in response to changing business conditions. For example, consider the lease of an office building. Leasing has developed in response to the need to have access to valuable assets, such as office space, without spending the large sum necessary to buy the asset. As leasing has increased in popularity, it has been left to the accounting profession to develop guidelines, some of which are quite complex, to be followed in accounting for leases. Those guidelines are now part of GAAP.

Enron's demise is a prime example of the downward spiral a company can take when investors question whether the company adhered to the rules of GAAP.

Two-Minute Review

1. *Name the four concepts (other than the economic entity concept) in the conceptual framework presented in this section.*
2. *Give a brief example of each concept.*
3. *What is "GAAP"?*

Answers on p. 29

Who Determines the Rules of the Game?

Who determines the rules to be followed in preparing an income statement or a balance sheet? No one group is totally responsible for setting the standards or principles to be followed in preparing financial statements. The process is a joint effort among the following groups.

Securities and Exchange Commission (SEC) The federal agency with ultimate authority to determine the rules in preparing statements for companies whose stock is sold to the public.

http://www.sec.gov

The federal government, through the **Securities and Exchange Commission (SEC),** has the ultimate authority to determine the rules for preparing financial statements by companies whose securities are sold to the general public. However, for the most part, the SEC has allowed the accounting profession to establish its own rules.

Financial Accounting Standards Board (FASB) The group in the private sector with authority to set accounting standards.

http://www.fasb.org

The **Financial Accounting Standards Board (FASB)** sets these accounting standards in the United States. A small independent group with a large staff, the board has issued more than 140 financial accounting standards, and seven statements of financial accounting concepts, since its creation in the early 1970s. These standards deal with a variety of financial reporting issues, such as the proper accounting for lease arrangements and pension plans, and the concepts are used to guide the board in setting accounting standards.

American Institute of Certified Public Accountants (AICPA) The professional organization for certified public accountants.

http://www.aicpa.org

The **American Institute of Certified Public Accountants (AICPA)** is the professional organization of certified public accountants. It advises the FASB but actually sets the auditing standards to be followed by public accounting firms.

International Accounting Standards Board (IASB) The organization formed to develop worldwide accounting standards.

http://www.iasc.org.uk

Finally, if you are considering buying stock in Porsche, the German-based car manufacturer, you'll want to be sure that the rules Porsche followed in preparing the statements are similar to those the FASB requires for U.S. companies. Unfortunately, accounting standards can differ considerably from one country to another. The **International Accounting Standards Board (IASB)** was created in 2001. Prior to that time, the organization was known as the International Accounting Standards Committee (IASC), which was formed in 1973 to develop worldwide accounting standards. Organizations from many different countries, including the FASB in this country, participate in the IASB's efforts to develop international reporting standards. Although the group has made considerable progress, compliance with the standards of the IASB is strictly voluntary, and much work remains to be done in developing international accounting standards.

THE ACCOUNTING PROFESSION

LO 4 Describe the various roles of accountants in organizations.

Accountants play many different roles in society. Understanding the various roles will help you to appreciate more fully the importance of accounting in organizations.

Employment by Private Business

Many accountants work for business entities. Regardless of the types of activities companies engage in, accountants perform a number of important functions for them. A partial organization chart for a corporation is shown in Exhibit 1-6. The chart indicates that three individuals report directly to the chief financial officer: the controller, the treasurer, and the director of internal auditing.

Controller The chief accounting officer for a company.

The **controller** is the chief accounting officer for a company and typically has responsibility for the overall operation of the accounting system. Accountants working for the controller record the company's activities and prepare periodic financial statements. In this organization, the payroll function is assigned to the controller's office, as well as responsibility for the preparation of budgets.

Treasurer The officer responsible in an organization for the safeguarding and efficient use of a company's liquid assets.

The **treasurer** of an organization is typically responsible for the safeguarding, as well as the efficient use, of the company's liquid resources, such as cash. Note that the director of the tax department in this corporation reports to the treasurer. Accountants in the tax department are responsible for both preparing the company's tax returns and planning transactions in such a way that the company pays the least amount of taxes possible within the laws of the Internal Revenue Code.

Exhibit 1-6 Partial Organization Chart

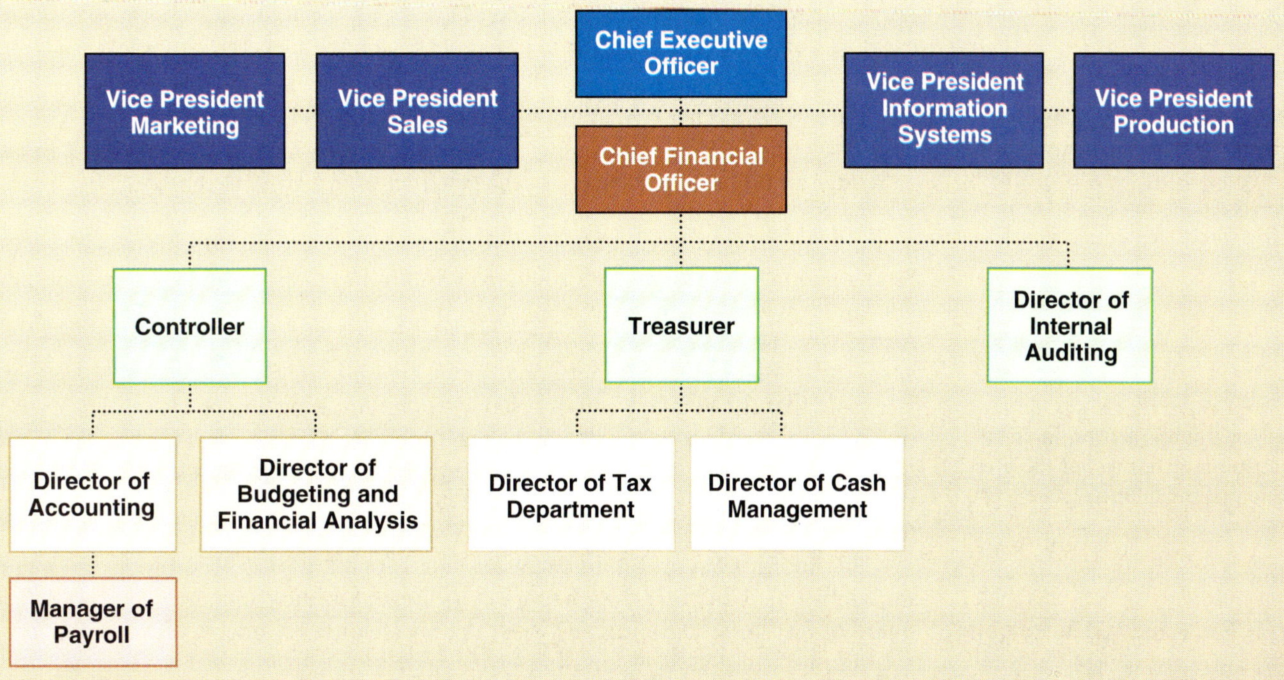

This partial organization chart does not show details of the other departments in the company—such as marketing, sales, production, and so on. That does not mean they are unimportant to the flow of accounting information. In fact, accounting information for internal decision making forms a complex system of reporting, responsibility, and control collectively known as management accounting.

Internal auditing is the department responsible in a company for the review and appraisal of accounting and administrative controls. The department must determine whether the company's assets are properly accounted for and protected from losses. Recommendations are made periodically to management for improvements in the various controls.

Internal auditing The department responsible in a company for the review and appraisal of its accounting and administrative controls.

Employment by Nonbusiness Entities

Nonbusiness organizations, such as hospitals, universities, and various branches of the government, have as much need for accountants as do companies organized to earn a profit. Although the profit motive is not paramount to nonbusiness entities, all organizations must have financial information to operate efficiently. A county government needs detailed cost information in determining the taxes to levy on its constituents. A university must pay close attention to its various operating costs in setting the annual tuition rates. Accountants working for nonbusiness entities perform most of the same tasks as their counterparts in the business sector. In fact, many of the job titles in business entities, such as controller and treasurer, are also used by nonbusiness entities.

Employment in Public Accounting

Public accounting firms provide valuable services in much the same way as do law firms or architectural firms. They provide a professional service for their clients in return for a fee. The usual services provided by public accounting firms include auditing and tax and management consulting services.

Auditing The process of examining the financial statements and the underlying records of a company in order to render an opinion as to whether the statements are fairly presented.

Auditors' report The opinion rendered by a public accounting firm concerning the fairness of the presentation of the financial statements.

http://www.deloitte.com

Auditing Services The auditing services rendered by public accountants are similar in certain respects to the work performed by internal auditors. However, there are key differences between the two types of auditing. Internal auditors are more concerned with the efficient operation of the various segments of the business, and therefore, the work they do is often called *operational auditing.* On the other hand, the primary objective of the external auditor, or public accountant, is to assure stockholders and other users that the statements are fairly presented. In this respect, **auditing** is the process of examining the financial statements and the underlying records of a company in order to render an opinion as to whether the statements are fairly presented.

As we discussed earlier, the financial statements are prepared by the company's accountants. The external auditor performs various tests and procedures to be able to render his or her opinion. The public accountant has a responsibility to the company's stockholders and any other users of the statements. Because most stockholders are not actively involved in the daily affairs of the business, they must rely on the auditors to ensure that management is fairly presenting the financial statements of the business.

Note that the **auditors' report** is an *opinion,* not a statement of fact. For example, one important procedure performed by the auditor to obtain assurance as to the validity of a company's inventory is to observe the year-end physical count of inventory by the company's employees. However, this is done on a sample basis. It would be too costly for the auditors to make an independent count of every single item of inventory.

The auditors' report on the financial statements for Winnebago Industries is shown in Exhibit 1-7. Note first that the report is directed to the company's shareholders and board of directors. The company is audited by Deloitte & Touche, a large international accounting firm. Public accounting firms range in size from those with a single owner to others, such as Deloitte & Touche, that have thousands of partners. The opinion given by Deloitte & Touche on the company's financial statements is the *standard auditors' report.* The first paragraph indicates that the firm has examined the company's balance sheet and the related statements of income, changes in stockholders' equity, and cash flows. Note that the second paragraph of the report indicates that evidence supporting the amounts and disclosures in the statements was examined on a *test* basis. The third paragraph states the firm's *opinion* that the financial statements are fairly presented in conformity with GAAP. (We have highlighted these paragraphs for clarity.)

From Concept to Practice 1.2

Reading Winnebago Industries' Auditors' Report

Note the date at the bottom of the report. Why do you think it takes more than one month after the end of the fiscal year to issue this report?

Tax Services In addition to auditing, public accounting firms provide a variety of tax services. Firms often prepare the tax returns for the companies they audit. They also usually work throughout the year with management to plan acquisitions and other transactions to take full advantage of the tax laws. For example, if tax rates are scheduled to decline next year, a public accounting firm would advise its client to accelerate certain expenditures this year as much as possible to receive a higher tax deduction than would be possible by waiting until next year.

Management Consulting Services By working closely with management to provide auditing and tax services, a public accounting firm becomes very familiar with various aspects of a company's business. This vantage point allows the firm to provide expert advice to the company to improve its operations. The management consulting services rendered by public accounting firms to their clients take a variety of forms. For example, the firm might advise the company on the design and installation of a computer system to fill its needs. The services provided in this area have grown dramatically to include such diverse activities as advice on selection of a new plant site or an investment opportunity.

Exhibit 1-7 Winnebago Industries' Auditors' Report

REPORT OF INDEPENDENT AUDITORS

To the Board of Directors and Shareholders
Winnebago Industries, Inc.
Forest City, Iowa

We have audited the consolidated balance sheets of Winnebago Industries, Inc. and subsidiaries (the Company) as of August 25, 2001 and August 26, 2000 and the related consolidated statements of income, cash flows and changes in stockholders' equity for each of the three years in the period ended August 25, 2001. These consolidated financial statements are the responsibility of the Company's management. Our responsibility is to express an opinion on these consolidated financial statements based on our audits.

We conducted our audits in accordance with auditing standards generally accepted in the United States of America. Those standards require that we plan and perform the audit to obtain reasonable assurance about whether the consolidated financial statements are free of material misstatement. An audit includes examining, on a test basis, evidence supporting the amounts and disclosures in the consolidated financial statements. An audit also includes assessing the accounting principles used and significant estimates made by management, as well as evaluating the overall financial statement presentation. We believe that our audits provide a reasonable basis for our opinion.

In our opinion, the consolidated financial statements present fairly, in all material respects, the financial position of the Company as of August 25, 2001 and August 26, 2000, and the results of their operations and their cash flows for each of the three years in the period ended August 25, 2001 in conformity with accounting principles generally accepted in the United States of America.

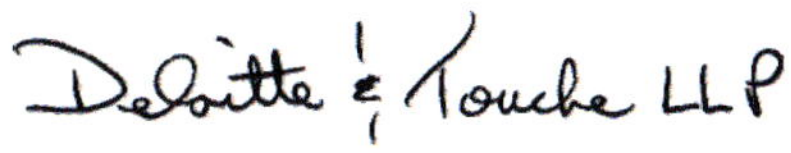

Deloitte & Touche LLP
Minneapolis, Minnesota
October 3, 2001

Standard Auditor's Report

First Paragraph says that the auditor has examined the statements.

Second Paragraph indicates that evidence was gathered on a test basis.

Third Paragraph states the auditor's opinion.

Accountants in Education

Some accountants choose a career in education. As the demand for accountants in business entities, nonbusiness organizations, and public accounting has increased, so has the need for qualified professors to teach this discipline. Accounting programs range from two years of study at community colleges to doctoral programs at some universities. All these programs require the services of knowledgeable instructors. In addition to their teaching duties, many accounting educators are actively involved in research. The **American Accounting Association** is a professional organization of accounting educators and others interested in the future of the profession. The group advances its ideas through its many committees and the publication of a number of journals.

American Accounting Association The professional organization for accounting educators.

http://www.aaa-edu.org

Accounting as a Career

As you can see, a number of different career paths in accounting are possible. The stereotypical view of the accountant as a "numbers person and not a people person" is a seriously outdated notion. Various specialties are now emerging, including tax accounting, environmental accounting, forensic accounting, software development, and accounting in the entertainment and telecommunications industries. Some of these opportunities exist in both the business and the nonbusiness sectors. For example, forensic accounting has become an exciting career field as both corporations and various agencies of the federal government, such as the FBI, concern themselves with fraud and white-collar crime.

As in any profession, salaries in accounting vary considerably depending on numerous factors, including educational background and other credentials, number of years of experience, and size of the employer. For example, most employers pay a premium for candidates with a master's degree and professional certification, such as the CPA. Exhibit 1-8 indicates salaries for various positions within the accounting field.[4]

Exhibit 1-8

Salaries in the Accounting Profession

Position	Salary Range	
Public Accounting		
→ Staff Auditors (1–3 years' experience)	\$34,000–\$49,000	\$
Managers/Directors	\$62,250–\$110,000	\$\$
Partners	\$150,000+	\$\$\$
Industry		
→ Staff Accountants (1–3 years' experience)	\$35,000–\$53,750	\$
Corporate Controllers	\$54,000–\$138,750	\$\$–\$\$\$
Chief Financial Officers	\$83,250–\$360,250	\$\$–\$\$\$\$
→ **Government (entry-level)**		
Federal	\$32,788 average	\$
State/Local	\$33,595 average	\$

Accounting graduates start here.

Accountants and Ethical Judgments

Remember the primary goal of accounting: to provide useful information to aid in the decision-making process. As we discussed, the work of the accountant in providing useful information is anything but routine and requires the accountant to make subjective judgments about what information to present and how to present it. The latitude given accountants in this respect is one of the major reasons accounting is a profession and its members are considered professionals. Along with this designation as a professional,

[4]The information in this section regarding career opportunities and salaries was drawn primarily from the AICPA's Web site (http://www.aicpa.org).

Accounting for Your Decisions

You Are a Student

As a student, you decide to go into the accounting profession. However, you are not sure which area to focus on: private, nonbusiness, public, or education. What information would you seek to help you make this decision?

ANS: You may want to consider the following (not necessarily in this order): (1) both starting and potential increases in salaries; (2) education requirements; (3) advancement opportunities; (4) fringe benefits; and (5) challenging work.

however, comes a serious responsibility. As we noted, financial statements are prepared for external parties who must rely on these statements to provide information on which to base important decisions.

At the end of each chapter are cases titled "Accounting and Ethics: What Would You Do?" The cases require you to evaluate difficult issues and make a decision. Judgment is needed in deciding which accounting method to select or how to report a certain item in the statements. As you are faced with these decisions, keep in mind the trust placed in the accountant by various financial statement users. This is central to reaching an ethical decision.

A FINAL NOTE ABOUT WINNEBAGO INDUSTRIES

As you have seen in this chapter, accounting is a practical discipline. Financial statements of real companies, including Winnebago Industries, are used throughout the remainder of the book to help you learn more about this practical discipline. For example, some of the From Concept to Practice sidebars in future chapters will require you to return to the financial statements of Winnebago Industries, as will some of the cases at the end of the chapters. Because no two sets of financial statements look the same, however, you will be introduced to the financial statements of many other real companies as well. Use this opportunity to learn more not only about accounting but also about each of these companies.

Answers to the Two-Minute Reviews

Two-Minute Review on Page 22

1. *Assets = Liabilities + Owners' Equity*
   Assets are economic resources. Liabilities are creditors' claims against assets. Owners' Equity is owners' claims against assets. See Exhibit 1-3.
2. *The three financial statements are the balance sheet, the income statement, and the statement of retained earnings.*
3. *Net income on the income statement increases retained earnings on the statement of retained earnings. The ending balance in retained earnings is transferred to the balance sheet. See Exhibit 1-5.*

Two-Minute Review on Page 23

1. *Cost principle, going concern, monetary unit, and time period assumption.*
2. *Under the cost principle, we record assets at their cost rather than at market value. Example: Winnebago Industries would record a new machine at its purchase price. Under going concern, we assume that the company will continue existing indefinitely. Example: Winnebago Industries will continue to operate rather than begin liquidating its assets. The monetary unit, such as the dollar, is the company's recognized medium of exchange. Example: Winnebago*

continued

Answers to the Two-Minute Reviews (continued)

Industries uses the dollar as the monetary unit. The time period assumption imposes, for reporting purposes, an arbitrary time period (such as a year) that is shorter than the company's life span. Example: Winnebago Industries' income statement is for the fiscal year ended August 25, 2001.

3. *GAAP is the methods, rules, practices, and other procedures that have evolved to govern the preparation of financial statements.*

Warmup Exercises

Study Tip

Use these exercises to get accustomed to the assignments that follow.

Warmup Exercise 1-1 *Your Assets and Liabilities* **LO 2**

Consider your own situation in terms of assets and liabilities.

Required

1. Name three of your financial assets.
2. Name three of your financial liabilities.

Key to the Solution

Refer to Exhibit 1-3 for definitions of assets and liabilities.

Warmup Exercise 1-2 *Winnebago Industries' Assets and Liabilities* **LO 2**

http://www.winnebagoind.co

Think about Winnebago Industries' business in balance sheet terms.

Required

1. Name three of Winnebago Industries' assets.
2. Name three of Winnebago Industries' liabilities.

Key to the Solution

Refer to Exhibit 1-2 if you need to see Winnebago Industries' balance sheet. Also consult the list on pages 17 and 19.

Warmup Exercise 1-3 *Winnebago Industries and the Accounting Equation* **LO 2**

http://www.winnebagoind.co

Place Winnebago Industries' total assets, total liabilities, and total stockholders' equity in the form of the accounting equation.

Key to the Solution

Refer to Exhibit 1-2. You will have to add up the liabilities since they are not totaled for you.

Solutions to Warmup Exercises

Warmup Exercise 1-1

1. Possible personal financial assets might include checking accounts, savings accounts, certificates of deposit, money market accounts, stocks, bonds, and mutual funds.
2. Possible personal financial liabilities might include student loans, car loans, home mortgages, and amounts borrowed from relatives.

Warmup Exercise 1-2

1. Winnebago Industries' assets are Cash and cash equivalents, Receivables, Inventories, Prepaid expenses, Deferred income taxes, Property and equipment, Investment in life insurance, and Other assets.

2. Winnebago Industries' liabilities are Accounts payable—Trade, Income taxes payable, Accrued expenses, and Postretirement health care and deferred compensation benefits.

Warmup Exercise 1-3

Assets	=	Liabilities	+	Owners' Equity
$342,033	=	$134,569	+	$207,464

Review Problem

WebTUTOR Advantage

Study Tip

Note to the student: At the end of each chapter is a problem to test your understanding of some of the major ideas presented in the chapter. Try to solve the problem before turning to the solution that follows it.

Greenway Corporation is organized on June 1, 2004. The company will provide lawn-care and tree-trimming services on a contract basis. Following is an alphabetical list of the items that should appear on its income statement for the first month and on its balance sheet at the end of the first month (you will need to determine on which statement each should appear).

Accounts payable	$ 800
Accounts receivable	500
Building	2,000
Capital stock	5,000
Cash	3,300
Gas, utilities, and other expenses	300
Land	4,000
Lawn-care revenue	1,500
Notes payable	6,000
Retained earnings (beginning balance)	–0–
Salaries and wages expense	900
Tools	800
Tree-trimming revenue	500
Truck	2,000

DECISION MAKING

Required

1. Prepare an income statement for the month of June.
2. Prepare a balance sheet at June 30, 2004. *Note:* You will need to determine the balance in Retained Earnings at the end of the month.
3. The financial statements you have just prepared are helpful, but in many ways they are a starting point. Assuming this is your business, what additional questions do they raise that you need to consider?

Solution to Review Problem

1.

GREENWAY CORPORATION
INCOME STATEMENT
FOR THE MONTH ENDED JUNE 30, 2004

Revenues:		
Lawn care	$1,500	
Tree trimming	500	$2,000
Expenses:		
Salaries and wages	$ 900	
Gas, utilities, and other expenses	300	1,200
Net income		$ 800

2.

GREENWAY CORPORATION
BALANCE SHEET
JUNE 30, 2004

Assets		**Liabilities and Stockholders' Equity**	
Cash	$ 3,300	Accounts payable	$ 800
Accounts receivable	500	Notes payable	6,000
Truck	2,000	Capital stock	5,000
Tools	800	Retained earnings	800
Building	2,000		
Land	4,000		
Total assets	$12,600	Total liabilities and stockholders' equity	$12,600

3. Following are examples of questions that the financial statements raise:
   - During June, 75% of the revenue was from lawn care and the other 25% from trimming trees. Will this relationship hold in future months?
   - Are the expenses representative of those that will be incurred in the future? Will any other expenses arise, such as advertising and income taxes?
   - When can we expect to collect the accounts receivable? Is there a chance that not all will be collected?
   - How soon will the accounts payable need to be paid?
   - What is the interest rate on the note payable? When is interest paid? When is the note itself due?

Chapter Highlights

1. **LO 1** Both individuals external to a business and those involved in the internal management of the company use accounting information. External users include present and potential stockholders, bankers and other creditors, government agencies, suppliers, trade associations, labor unions, and other interested groups.
2. **LO 2** The accounting equation is the basis for the entire accounting system: **Assets = Liabilities + Owners' Equity.** Assets are valuable economic resources. Liabilities are the claims of outsiders to the assets of a business. Owners' equity is the residual interest that remains after deducting liabilities from assets.
3. **LO 2** A balance sheet summarizes the financial position of a company at a *specific point in time.* An income statement reports on its revenues and expenses for a *period of time.* A statement of retained earnings explains the changes in retained earnings *during a particular period.*
4. **LO 3** A number of assumptions are made in preparing financial statements. Accounting is not an exact science, and judgment must be used in deciding what to report on financial statements and how to report the information. Generally accepted accounting principles (GAAP) have evolved over time and are based on a conceptual framework. The *Securities and Exchange Commission* in the public sector and the *Financial Accounting Standards Board* in the private sector have the most responsibility for developing GAAP at the present time.
5. **LO 4** Accountants are employed by business entities, nonbusiness entities, public accounting firms, and educational institutions. Public accounting firms provide audit services for their clients, as well as tax and management consulting services.

http://

http://porter.swlearning.com

Technology and other resources for your success

If you need additional help, visit the text's Web site. Also, see pages xv–xvii in this text's preface for a description of available technology and other resources. If your instructor is using PERSONAL*Trainer* in this course, you may complete, on line, the assignments identified by PT.

Key Terms Quiz

Read each definition below and then write the number of that definition in the blank beside the appropriate term it defines. The quiz solutions appear at the end of the chapter.

_____ **Accounting**
_____ **Management accounting**
_____ **Financial accounting**
_____ **Owners' equity**
_____ **Stockholders' equity**
_____ **Retained earnings**
_____ **Balance sheet**
_____ **Income statement**
_____ **Dividends**
_____ **Statement of retained earnings**
_____ **Cost principle**
_____ **Going concern**
_____ **Monetary unit**
_____ **Time period**
_____ **Generally accepted accounting principles (GAAP)**
_____ **Securities and Exchange Commission (SEC)**
_____ **Financial Accounting Standards Board (FASB)**
_____ **American Institute of Certified Public Accountants (AICPA)**

_____ International Accounting Standards Board (IASB)

_____ Controller

_____ Treasurer

_____ Internal auditing

_____ Auditing

_____ Auditors' report

_____ American Accounting Association

1. A statement that summarizes revenues and expenses for a period of time.
2. The statement that summarizes the income earned and dividends paid over the life of a business.
3. The owners' equity of a corporation.
4. The process of identifying, measuring, and communicating economic information to various users.
5. The branch of accounting concerned with communication with outsiders through financial statements.
6. The owners' claims to the assets of an entity.
7. The financial statement that summarizes the assets, liabilities, and owners' equity at a specific point in time.
8. The part of owners' equity that represents the income earned less dividends paid over the life of an entity.
9. The branch of accounting concerned with providing management with information to facilitate the planning and control functions.
10. A distribution of the net income of a business to its stockholders.
11. The various methods, rules, practices, and other procedures that have evolved over time in response to the need to regulate the preparation of financial statements.
12. Assets are recorded and reported at the cost paid to acquire them.
13. The federal agency with ultimate authority to determine the rules in preparing statements for companies whose stock is sold to the public.
14. The professional organization for accounting educators.
15. The officer of an organization who is responsible for the safeguarding and efficient use of the company's liquid assets.
16. The assumption that an entity is not in the process of liquidation and that it will continue indefinitely.
17. The group in the private sector with authority to set accounting standards.
18. The yardstick used to measure amounts in financial statements; the dollar in the United States.
19. The professional organization for certified public accountants.
20. The department in a company responsible for the review and appraisal of a company's accounting and administrative controls.
21. A length of time on the calendar used as the basis for preparing financial statements.
22. The chief accounting officer for a company.
23. The process of examining the financial statements and the underlying records of a company in order to render an opinion as to whether the statements are fairly presented.
24. The organization formed to develop worldwide accounting standards.
25. The opinion rendered by a public accounting firm concerning the fairness of the presentation of the financial statements.

Answers on p. 50.

Alternate Terms

Auditors' report Report of independent accountants

Balance sheet Statement of financial position

Cost principle Original cost; historical cost

Creditor Lender

Income statement Statement of income

Net income Profits or earnings

Stockholder Shareholder

Questions

1. What is accounting? Define it in terms understandable to someone without a business background.
2. How do financial accounting and management accounting differ?
3. What are five different groups of users of accounting information? Briefly describe the types of decisions each group must make.
4. How does owners' equity fit into the accounting equation?
5. What are the two distinct elements of owners' equity in a corporation? Define each element.
6. What is the purpose of a balance sheet?
7. How should a balance sheet be dated: as of a particular day or for a particular period of time? Explain your answer.
8. What does the term *cost principle* mean?
9. What is the purpose of an income statement?
10. How should an income statement be dated: as of a particular day or for a particular period of time? Explain your answer.
11. Rogers Corporation starts the year with a Retained Earnings balance of $55,000. Net income for the year is $27,000. The ending balance in Retained Earnings is $70,000. What was the amount of dividends for the year?

12. How do the duties of the controller of a corporation typically differ from those of the treasurer?
13. What are the three basic types of services performed by public accounting firms?
14. How would you evaluate the following statement: "The auditors are in the best position to evaluate a company because they have prepared the financial statements"?
15. What is the relationship between the cost principle and the going concern assumption?
16. Why does inflation present a challenge to the accountant? Relate your answer to the monetary unit assumption.
17. What is meant by the phrase *generally accepted accounting principles*?
18. What role has the Securities and Exchange Commission played in setting accounting standards? Contrast its role with that played by the Financial Accounting Standards Board.

Exercises

Exercise 1-1 ***Users of Accounting Information and Their Needs*** **LO 1**

Listed below are a number of the important users of accounting information. Below the list are descriptions of a major need of each of these various users. Fill in the blank with the one user group that is most likely to have the need described to the right of the blank.

Company management	**Banker**
Stockholder	**Supplier**
Securities and Exchange Commission	**Labor union**
Internal Revenue Service	

User Group	Needs Information About
______________	1. The profitability of each division in the company
______________	2. The prospects for future dividend payments
______________	3. The profitability of the company since the last contract with the work force was signed
______________	4. The financial status of a company issuing securities to the public for the first time
______________	5. The prospects that a company will be able to meet its interest payments on time
______________	6. The prospects that a company will be able to pay for its purchases on time
______________	7. The profitability of the company based on the tax code

Exercise 1-2 ***The Accounting Equation*** **LO 2**

For each of the following independent cases, fill in the blank with the appropriate dollar amount.

	Assets	=	Liabilities	+	Owners' Equity
Case 1	$125,000		$ 75,000		$______
Case 2	400,000		______		100,000
Case 3	______		320,000		95,000

Exercise 1-3 ***The Accounting Equation*** **LO 2**

Ginger Enterprises began the year with total assets of $500,000 and total liabilities of $250,000. Using this information and the accounting equation, answer each of the following independent questions.

1. What was the amount of Ginger's owners' equity at the beginning of the year?
2. If Ginger's total assets increased by $100,000 and its total liabilities increased by $77,000 during the year, what was the amount of Ginger's owners' equity at the end of the year?
3. If Ginger's total liabilities increased by $33,000 and its owners' equity decreased by $58,000 during the year, what was the amount of its total assets at the end of the year?
4. If Ginger's total assets doubled to $1,000,000 and its owners' equity remained the same during the year, what was the amount of its total liabilities at the end of the year?

Exercise 1-4 ***The Accounting Equation*** **LO 2**

Using the accounting equation, answer each of the following independent questions.

1. Burlin Company starts the year with $100,000 in assets and $80,000 in liabilities. Net income for the year is $25,000, and no dividends are paid. How much is owners' equity at the end of the year?
2. Chapman Inc. doubles the amount of its assets from the beginning to the end of the year. Liabilities at the end of the year amount to $40,000, and owners' equity is $20,000. What is the amount of Chapman's assets at the beginning of the year?
3. During the year, the liabilities of Dixon Enterprises triple in amount. Assets at the beginning of the year amount to $30,000, and owners' equity is $10,000. What is the amount of liabilities at the end of the year?

Exercise 1-5 ***Changes in Owners' Equity*** **LO 2**

The following amounts are available from the records of Coaches and Carriages Inc. at the end of the years indicated:

December 31	Total Assets	Total Liabilities
2002	$ 25,000	$ 12,000
2003	79,000	67,000
2004	184,000	137,000

Required

1. Compute the changes in Coaches and Carriages' owners' equity during 2003 and 2004.
2. Compute the amount of Coaches and Carriages' net income (or loss) for 2003 assuming that no dividends were paid during the year.
3. Compute the amount of Coaches and Carriages' net income (or loss) for 2004 assuming that dividends paid during the year amounted to $10,000.

Exercise 1-6 ***The Accounting Equation*** **LO 2**

For each of the following independent cases, fill in the blank with the appropriate dollar amount.

SPREADSHEET

	Case 1	Case 2	Case 3	Case 4
Total assets, end of period	$40,000	$______	$75,000	$50,000
Total liabilities, end of period	______	15,000	25,000	10,000
Capital stock, end of period	10,000	5,000	20,000	15,000
Retained earnings, beginning of period	15,000	8,000	10,000	20,000
Net income for the period	8,000	7,000	______	9,000
Dividends for the period	2,000	1,000	3,000	______

Exercise 1-7 ***Classification of Financial Statement Items*** **LO 2**

Classify each of the following items according to (1) whether it belongs on the income statement (IS) or balance sheet (BS) and (2) whether it is a revenue (R), expense (E), asset (A), liability (L), or owners' equity (OE) item.

Item	Appears on the	Classified as
Example: Cash	BS	A
1. Salaries expense	______	______
2. Equipment	______	______
3. Accounts payable	______	______
4. Membership fees earned	______	______
5. Capital stock	______	______
6. Accounts receivable	______	______
7. Buildings	______	______
8. Advertising expense	______	______
9. Retained earnings	______	______

Exercise 1-8 ***Net Income (or Loss) and Retained Earnings*** **LO 2**

The following information is available from the records of Prestige Landscape Design Inc. at the end of the 2004 calendar year:

(continued)

Accounts payable	$ 5,000	Office equipment	$ 7,500
Accounts receivable	4,000	Rent expense	6,500
Capital stock	8,000	Retained earnings, beginning of year	8,500
Cash	13,000	Salary and wage expense	12,000
Dividends paid during the year	3,000	Supplies	500
Landscaping revenues	25,000		

Required

Use the information above to answer the following questions:

1. What is Prestige's net income for the year ended December 31, 2004?
2. What is Prestige's retained earnings balance at the end of the year?
3. What is the total amount of Prestige's assets at the end of the year?
4. What is the total amount of Prestige's liabilities at the end of the year?
5. How much owners' equity does Prestige have at the end of the year?
6. What is Prestige's accounting equation at December 31, 2004?

Exercise 1-9 *Statement of Retained Earnings* LO 2

Ace Corporation has been in business for many years. Retained earnings on January 1, 2004, is $235,800. The following information is available for the first two months of 2004:

	January	February
Revenues	$83,000	$96,000
Expenses	89,000	82,000
Dividends paid	–0–	5,000

Required

Prepare a statement of retained earnings for the month ended February 28, 2004.

Exercise 1-10 *Accounting Principles and Assumptions* LO 3

The following basic accounting principles and assumptions were discussed in the chapter:

Economic entity
Monetary unit
Cost principle
Going concern
Time period

Fill in each of the blanks with the accounting principle or assumption that is relevant to the situation described.

______________ 1. Genesis Corporation is now in its 30th year of business. The founder of the company is planning to retire at the end of the year and turn the business over to his daughter.

______________ 2. Nordic Company purchased a 20-acre parcel of property on which to build a new factory. The company recorded the property on the records at the amount of cash given to acquire it.

______________ 3. Jim Bailey enters into an agreement to operate a new law firm in partnership with a friend. Each partner will make an initial cash investment of $10,000. Jim opens a checking account in the name of the partnership and transfers $10,000 from his personal account into the new account.

______________ 4. Multinational Corp. has a division in Japan. Prior to preparing the financial statements for the company and all its foreign divisions, Multinational translates the financial statements of its Japanese division from yen to U.S. dollars.

______________ 5. Camden Company has always prepared financial statements annually, with a year-end of June 30. Because the company is going to sell its stock to the public for the first time, quarterly financial reports will also be required by the Securities and Exchange Commission.

Exercise 1-11 *Organizations and Accounting* **LO 4**

Match each of the organizations listed below with the statement that most adequately describes the role of the group.

Securities and Exchange Commission
International Accounting Standards Board
Financial Accounting Standards Board
American Institute of Certified Public Accountants
American Accounting Association

______________ 1. Federal agency with ultimate authority to determine rules used in preparing financial statements for companies whose stock is sold to the public

______________ 2. Professional organization for accounting educators

______________ 3. Group in the private sector with authority to set accounting standards

______________ 4. Professional organization for certified public accountants

______________ 5. Organization formed to develop worldwide accounting standards

Multi-Concept Exercises

Exercise 1-12 *Users of Accounting Information and the Financial Statements* **LO 1, 2**

Listed below are a number of users of accounting information and examples of questions they need answered before making decisions. Fill in each blank to indicate whether the user is most likely to find the answer by looking at the income statement (IS), the balance sheet (BS), or the statement of retained earnings (RE).

User	Question	Financial Statement
Stockholder	How did this year's sales compare to last year's?	______________
Banker	How much debt does the company already have on its books?	______________
Supplier	How much does the company currently owe to its suppliers?	______________
Stockholder	How much did the company pay in dividends this past year?	______________
Advertising account manager	How much did the company spend this past year to generate sales?	______________
Banker	What collateral or security can the company provide to ensure that any loan I make will be repaid?	______________

Exercise 1-13 *Winnebago Industries' Inventories* **LO 2, 3**

Refer to Winnebago Industries' balance sheet reproduced in the chapter.

Required

What was the amount of Inventories at August 25, 2001? What does this amount represent (i.e., cost, market value)? Why does Winnebago Industries carry its inventories at one or the other?

Exercise 1-14 *Roles of Accountants* **LO 1, 4**

One day on campus, you overhear two nonbusiness majors discussing the reasons each did not major in accounting. "Accountants are bean counters. They just sit in a room and play with the books all day. They do not have people skills, but I suppose it really doesn't matter because no one ever looks at the statements they prepare," said the first student. The second student replied, "Oh, they are very intelligent, though, because they must know all about the tax laws, and that's too complicated for me."

Required

Comment on the students' perceptions of the roles of accountants in society. Do you agree that no one ever looks at the statements they prepare? If not, identify who the primary users are.

Problems

Problem 1-1 ***You Won the Lottery*** **LO 1**

You have won a lottery! You will receive $200,000, after taxes, each year for the next five years.

Required

Describe the process you will go through in determining how to invest your winnings. Consider at least two options and make a choice. You may consider the stock of a certain company, bonds, real estate investments, bank deposits, and so on. Be specific. What information did you need to make a final decision? How was your decision affected by the fact that you will receive the winnings over a five-year period rather than in one lump sum? Would you prefer one payment? Explain.

Problem 1-2 ***Users of Accounting Information and Their Needs*** **LO 1**

Havre Company would like to buy a building and equipment to produce a new product line. Some information about Havre is more useful to some people involved in the project than to others.

Required

Complete the following chart by identifying the information listed on the right with the user's need to know the information. Identify the information as

a. *need* to know;

b. *helpful* to know; or

c. *not necessary* to know.

User of the Information			
Management	**Stockholders**	**Banker**	**Information**
______	______	______	**1.** Amount of current debt, repayment schedule, and interest rate
______	______	______	**2.** Fair market value of the building
______	______	______	**3.** Condition of the roof and heating and cooling, electrical, and plumbing systems
______	______	______	**4.** Total cost of the building, improvements, and equipment to set up production
______	______	______	**5.** Expected sales from the new product, variable production costs, related selling costs

Problem 1-3 ***Balance Sheet*** **LO 2**

The following items are available from records of Freescia Corporation at the end of the 2004 calendar year:

Accounts payable	$12,550
Accounts receivable	23,920
Advertising expense	2,100
Buildings	85,000
Capital stock	25,000
Cash	4,220
Notes payable	50,000
Office equipment	12,000
Retained earnings, end of year	37,590
Salary and wage expense	8,230
Sales revenue	14,220

Required

Prepare a balance sheet. *Hint:* Not all the items listed should appear on a balance sheet. For each of these items, indicate where it should appear.

Problem 1-4 ***Corrected Balance Sheet*** **LO 2**

Dave is the president of Avon Consulting Inc. Avon began business on January 1, 2004. The company's controller is out of the country on business. Dave needs a copy of the company's balance sheet for a meeting tomorrow and asked his assistant to obtain the required information from the company's records. She presented Dave with the following balance sheet. He asks you to review it for accuracy.

AVON CONSULTING INC.
BALANCE SHEET
FOR THE YEAR ENDED DECEMBER 31, 2004

Assets		Liabilities and Stockholders' Equity	
Accounts payable	$13,000	Accounts receivable	$16,000
Cash	21,000	Capital stock	20,000
Cash dividends paid	16,000	Net income for 2004	72,000
Furniture and equipment	43,000	Supplies	9,000

Required

1. Prepare a corrected balance sheet.
2. Draft a memo explaining the major differences between the balance sheet Dave's assistant prepared and the one you prepared.

Problem 1-5 ***Income Statement, Statement of Retained Earnings, and Balance Sheet***
LO 2

SPREADSHEET

Shown below, in alphabetical order, is a list of the various items that regularly appear on the financial statements of Maple Park Theatres Corp. The amounts shown for balance sheet items are balances as of September 30, 2004 (with the exception of Retained Earnings, which is the balance on September 1, 2004), and the amounts shown for income statement items are balances for the month ended September 30, 2004:

Accounts payable	$17,600
Accounts receivable	6,410
Advertising expense	14,500
Buildings	60,000
Capital stock	50,000
Cash	15,230
Concessions revenue	60,300
Cost of concessions sold	23,450
Dividends paid during the month	8,400
Furniture and fixtures	34,000
Land	26,000
Notes payable	20,000
Projection equipment	25,000
Rent expense-movies	50,600
Retained earnings	73,780
Salaries and wages expense	46,490
Ticket sales	95,100
Water, gas, and electricity	6,700

Required

1. Prepare an income statement for the month ended September 30, 2004.
2. Prepare a statement of retained earnings for the month ended September 30, 2004.
3. Prepare a balance sheet at September 30, 2004.
4. You have $1,000 to invest. On the basis of the statements you prepared, would you use it to buy stock in Maple Park? What other information would you want before making a final decision?

Problem 1-6 ***Income Statement and Balance Sheet*** **LO 2**

DECISION MAKING

Green Bay Corporation began business in July 2004 as a commercial fishing operation and passenger service between islands. Shares of stock were issued to the owners in exchange for cash. Boats were purchased by making a down payment in cash and signing a note payable for the balance. Fish are sold to local restaurants on open account, and customers are given 15 days to pay their account. Cash fares are collected for all passenger traffic. Rent for the dock facilities is paid at the beginning of each month. Salaries and wages are paid at the end of the month. The following amounts are from the records of Green Bay Corporation at the end of its first month of operations:

Accounts receivable	$18,500
Boats	80,000
Capital stock	40,000
Cash	7,730

(continued)

Dividends	$ 5,400
Fishing revenue	21,300
Notes payable	60,000
Passenger service revenue	12,560
Rent expense	4,000
Retained earnings	???
Salary and wage expense	18,230

Required

1. Prepare an income statement for the month ended July 31, 2004.
2. Prepare a balance sheet at July 31, 2004.
3. What information would you need about Notes Payable to assess fully Green Bay's long-term viability? Explain your answer.

Problem 1-7 *Corrected Financial Statements* LO 2

Hometown Cleaners Inc. operates a small dry-cleaning business. The company has always maintained a complete and accurate set of records. Unfortunately, the company's accountant left in a dispute with the president and took the 2004 financial statements with him. The balance sheet and the income statement shown below were prepared by the company's president.

HOMETOWN CLEANERS INC.
INCOME STATEMENT
FOR THE YEAR ENDED DECEMBER 31, 2004

Revenues:		
Accounts receivable	$15,200	
Cleaning revenue—cash sales	32,500	$47,700
Expenses:		
Dividends	$ 4,000	
Accounts payable	4,500	
Utilities	12,200	
Salaries and wages	17,100	37,800
Net income		$ 9,900

HOMETOWN CLEANERS INC.
BALANCE SHEET
DECEMBER 31, 2004

Assets		Liabilities and Stockholders' Equity	
Cash	$ 7,400	Cleaning revenue—credit sales	$26,200
Building and equipment	80,000	Capital stock	20,000
Less: Notes payable	(50,000)	Net income	9,900
Land	40,000	Retained earnings	21,300
Total assets	$77,400	Total liabilities and stockholders' equity	$77,400

The president is very disappointed with the net income for the year because it has averaged $25,000 over the last 10 years. She has asked for your help in determining whether the reported net income accurately reflects the profitability of the company and whether the balance sheet is prepared correctly.

Required

1. Prepare a corrected income statement for the year ended December 31, 2004.
2. Prepare a statement of retained earnings for the year ended December 31, 2004. (The actual balance of retained earnings on January 1, 2004, was $42,700. Note that the December 31, 2004, retained earnings balance shown above is incorrect. The president simply "plugged" this amount in to make the balance sheet balance.)
3. Prepare a corrected balance sheet at December 31, 2004.
4. Draft a memo to the president explaining the major differences between the income statement she prepared and the one you prepared.

Problem 1-8 ***Statement of Retained Earnings for the Walt Disney Company*** **LO 2**

The Walt Disney Company reported the following amounts in various statements included in its 2001 annual report (all amounts are stated in millions of dollars):

http://disney.go.com

Net loss for 2001	$ (158)
Dividends declared and paid in 2001	438
Retained earnings, September 30, 2000	12,767
Retained earnings, September 30, 2001	12,171

Required

1. Prepare a statement of retained earnings for the Walt Disney Company for the year ended September 30, 2001.
2. The Walt Disney Company does not actually present a statement of retained earnings in its annual report. Instead, it presents a broader statement of stockholders' equity. Describe the information that would be included on this statement and that is not included on a statement of retained earnings.

Problem 1-9 ***Role of the Accountant in Various Organizations*** **LO 4**

The following positions in various entities require a knowledge of accounting practices:

1. Chief financial officer for the subsidiary of a large company
2. Tax adviser to a consolidated group of entities
3. Independent computer consultant
4. Financial planner in a bank
5. Real estate broker in an independent office
6. Production planner in a manufacturing facility
7. Quality control adviser
8. Superintendent of a school district
9. Manager of one store in a retail clothing chain
10. Salesperson for a company that offers subcontract services, such as food service and maintenance to hospitals

Required

For each position listed above, identify the entity in which it occurs as business or nonbusiness and describe the kind of accounting knowledge (such as financial, managerial, taxes, not-for-profit) required by each position.

Problem 1-10 ***Information Needs and Setting Accounting Standards*** **LO 1**

The Financial Accounting Standards Board requires companies to supplement their consolidated financial statements with disclosures about segments of their businesses. To comply with this standard, AOL Time Warner's 2001 annual report provides various disclosures for the six segments in which it operates: AOL, Cable, Filmed Entertainment, Networks, Music, and Publishing.

http://www.aoltimewarner.com

Required

Which users of accounting information do you think the Financial Accounting Standards Board had in mind when it set this standard? What types of disclosures do you think these users would find helpful?

Multi-Concept Problem

Problem 1-11 ***Primary Assumptions Made in Preparing Financial Statements*** **LO 2, 3**

Joe Hale opened a machine repair business in leased retail space, paying the first month's rent of $300 and a $1,000 security deposit with a check on his personal account. He took the tools worth about $7,500, from his garage to the shop. He also bought some equipment to get started. The new equipment had a list price of $5,000, but Joe was able to purchase it on sale at Sears for only $4,200. He charged the new equipment on his personal Sears charge card. Joe's first customer paid $400 for services rendered, so Joe opened a checking account for the company. He completed a second job, but the customer has not paid Joe the $2,500 for his work. At the end of the first month, Joe prepared the following balance sheet and income statement.

(continued)

JOE'S MACHINE REPAIR SHOP
BALANCE SHEET
JULY 31, 2004

Cash	$ 400		
Equipment	5,000	Equity	$5,400
Total	$5,400	Total	$5,400

JOE'S MACHINE REPAIR SHOP
INCOME STATEMENT
FOR MONTH ENDED JULY 31, 2004

Sales		$ 2,900
Rent	$ 300	
Tools	4,200	4,500
Net loss		$(1,600)

Joe believes that he should show a greater profit next month because he won't have large expenses for items such as tools.

Required

Identify the assumptions that Joe has violated and explain how each event should have been handled. Prepare a corrected balance sheet and income statement.

Alternate Problems

Problem 1-1A *What to Do with a Million Dollars* LO 1

You have inherited $1 million!

Required

Describe the process you will go through in determining how to invest your inheritance. Consider at least two options and choose one. You may consider the stock of a certain company, bonds, real estate investments, bank deposits, and so on. Be specific. What information did you need to make a final decision? Where did you find the information you needed? What additional information will you need to consider if you want to make a change in your investment?

Problem 1-2A *Users of Accounting Information and Their Needs* LO 1

Billings Inc. would like to buy a franchise to provide a specialized service. Some information about Billings is more useful to some people involved in the project than to others.

Required

Complete the following chart by identifying the information listed on the right with the user's need to know the information. Identify the information as

a. *need* to know;

b. *helpful* to know; or

c. *not necessary* to know.

User of the Information			
Manager	**Stockholders**	**Franchisor**	**Information**
____	____	____	**1.** Expected revenue from the new service.
____	____	____	**2.** Cost of the franchise fee and recurring fees to be paid to the franchisor.
____	____	____	**3.** Cash available to Billings, the franchisee, to operate the business after the franchise is purchased.
____	____	____	**4.** Expected overhead costs of the service outlet.
____	____	____	**5.** Billings' required return on its investment.

Problem 1-3A *Balance Sheet* LO 2

The following items are available from the records of Victor Corporation at the end of its fiscal year, July 31, 2004:

Accounts payable	$16,900
Accounts receivable	5,700
Buildings	35,000

Butter and cheese inventory	$12,100
Capital stock	25,000
Cash	21,800
Computerized mixers	25,800
Delivery expense	4,600
Notes payable	50,000
Office equipment	12,000
Retained earnings, end of year	26,300
Salary and wage expense	8,230
Sales revenue	14,220
Tools	5,800

Required

Prepare a balance sheet. *Hint:* Not all the items listed should appear on a balance sheet. For each of these items, indicate where it should appear.

Problem 1-4A *Corrected Balance Sheet* LO 2

Pete is the president of Island Enterprises. Island Enterprises began business on January 1, 2004. The company's controller is out of the country on business. Pete needs a copy of the company's balance sheet for a meeting tomorrow and asked his assistant to obtain the required information from the company's records. She presented Pete with the following balance sheet. He asks you to review it for accuracy.

ISLAND ENTERPRISES
BALANCE SHEET
FOR THE YEAR ENDED DECEMBER 31, 2004

Assets		Liabilities and Stockholders' Equity	
Accounts payable	$ 29,600	Accounts receivable	$ 23,200
Cash	14,750	Capital stock	100,000
Cash dividends paid	16,000	Net income for 2004	113,850
Building and equipment	177,300	Supplies	12,200

Required

1. Prepare a corrected balance sheet.
2. Draft a memo explaining the major differences between the balance sheet Pete's assistant prepared and the one you prepared.

Problem 1-5A *Income Statement, Statement of Retained Earnings, and Balance Sheet* LO 2

SPREADSHEET

Shown below, in alphabetical order, is a list of the various items that regularly appear on the financial statements of Sterns Audio Book Rental Corp. The amounts shown for balance sheet items are balances as of December 31, 2004 (with the exception of retained earnings, which is the balance on January 1, 2004), and the amounts shown for income statement items are balances for the year ended December 31, 2004:

Accounts payable	$ 4,500
Accounts receivable	300
Advertising expense	14,500
Audio tape inventory	70,000
Capital stock	50,000
Cash	2,490
Display fixtures	45,000
Dividends paid during the year	12,000
Notes payable	10,000
Rental revenue	125,900
Rent paid on building	60,000
Retained earnings	35,390
Salaries and wages expense	17,900
Water, gas, and electricity	3,600

Required

1. Prepare an income statement for the year ended December 31, 2004.

(continued)

2. Prepare a statement of retained earnings for the year ended December 31, 2004.
3. Prepare a balance sheet at December 31, 2004.
4. You have $1,000 to invest. On the basis of the statements you prepared, would you use it to buy stock in this company? What other information would you want before deciding?

Problem 1-6A *Income Statement and Balance Sheet* LO 2

DECISION MAKING

Fort Worth Corporation began business in January 2004 as a commercial carpet cleaning and drying service. Shares of stock were issued to the owners in exchange for cash. Equipment was purchased by making a down payment in cash and signing a note payable for the balance. Services are performed for local restaurants and office buildings on open account, and customers are given 15 days to pay their account. Rent for office and storage facilities is paid at the beginning of each month. Salaries and wages are paid at the end of the month. The following amounts are from the records of Fort Worth Corporation at the end of its first month of operations:

Accounts receivable	$24,750
Capital stock	80,000
Cash	51,650
Cleaning revenue	45,900
Dividends	5,500
Equipment	62,000
Notes payable	30,000
Rent expense	3,600
Retained earnings	???
Salary and wage expense	8,400

Required

1. Prepare an income statement for the month ended January 31, 2004.
2. Prepare a balance sheet at January 31, 2004.
3. What information would you need about Notes Payable to fully assess Fort Worth's long-term viability? Explain your answer.

Problem 1-7A *Corrected Financial Statements* LO 2

Heidi's Bakery Inc. operates a small pastry business. The company has always maintained a complete and accurate set of records. Unfortunately, the company's accountant left in a dispute with the president and took the 2004 financial statements with her. The balance sheet and the income statement shown below were prepared by the company's president.

HEIDI'S BAKERY INC.
INCOME STATEMENT
FOR THE YEAR ENDED DECEMBER 31, 2004

Revenues:		
Accounts receivable	$15,500	
Pastry revenue—cash sales	23,700	$39,200
Expenses:		
Dividends	$ 5,600	
Accounts payable	6,800	
Utilities	9,500	
Salaries and wages	18,200	40,100
Net loss		$ (900)

HEIDI'S BAKERY INC.
BALANCE SHEET
DECEMBER 31, 2004

Assets		**Liabilities and Stockholders' Equity**	
Cash	$ 3,700	Pastry revenue—	
Building and equipment	60,000	credit sales	$22,100
Less: Notes payable	(40,000)	Capital stock	30,000
Land	50,000	Net loss	(900)
		Retained earnings	22,500
		Total liabilities and	
Total assets	$73,700	stockholders' equity	$73,700

The president is very disappointed with the net loss for the year because net income has averaged $21,000 over the last 10 years. He has asked for your help in determining whether the reported net loss accurately reflects the profitability of the company and whether the balance sheet is prepared correctly.

Required

1. Prepare a corrected income statement for the year ended December 31, 2004.
2. Prepare a statement of retained earnings for the year ended December 31, 2004. (The actual amount of Retained Earnings on January 1, 2004, was $39,900. The December 31, 2004, retained earnings balance shown above is incorrect. The president simply "plugged" this amount in to make the balance sheet balance.)
3. Prepare a corrected balance sheet at December 31, 2004.
4. Draft a memo to the president explaining the major differences between the income statement he prepared and the one you prepared.

Problem 1-8A ***Statement of Retained Earnings for Brunswick Corporation*** **LO 2**

Brunswick Corporation reported the following amounts in various statements included in its 2001 annual report (all amounts are stated in millions of dollars):

http://www.brunswickcorp.com

Net earnings for 2001	$ 81.8
Cash dividends declared and paid in 2001	43.8
Retained earnings, December 31, 2000	1,041.4
Retained earnings, December 31, 2001	1,079.4

Required

1. Prepare a statement of retained earnings for Brunswick Corporation for the year ended December 31, 2001.
2. Brunswick does not actually present a statement of retained earnings in its annual report. Instead, it presents a broader statement of shareholders' (stockholders') equity. Describe the information that would be included on this statement and that is not included on a statement of retained earnings.

Problem 1-9A ***Role of the Accountant in Various Organizations*** **LO 4**

The following positions in various entities require a knowledge of accounting practices:

__________ 1. Chief financial officer for the subsidiary of a large company
__________ 2. Tax adviser to a consolidated group of entities
__________ 3. Accounts receivable computer analyst
__________ 4. Financial planner in a bank
__________ 5. Budget analyst in a real estate office
__________ 6. Production planner in a manufacturing facility
__________ 7. Quality control adviser
__________ 8. Manager of the team conducting an audit on a state lottery
__________ 9. Assistant superintendent of a school district
__________ 10. Manager of one store in a retail clothing chain
__________ 11. Controller in a company that offers subcontract services, such as food service and maintenance to hospitals
__________ 12. Staff accountant in a large audit firm

Required

For each position listed above, fill in the blank to classify the position as one of the general categories of accountants listed below.

Financial accountant	**Accountant for not-for-profit organization**
Managerial accountant	**Auditor**
Tax accountant	**Not an accounting position**

Problem 1-10A ***Information Needs and Setting Accounting Standards*** **LO 1**

http://www.marriott.com

The Financial Accounting Standards Board requires companies to supplement their consolidated financial statements with disclosures about segments of their businesses. To comply with this standard, **Marriott International's** 2001 annual report provides various disclosures for the six segments in which it operates: Full-Service Lodging, Select-Service Lodging, Extended-Stay Lodging, Timeshare, Senior Living Services, and Distribution Services (includes a wholesale food-distribution business).

Required

Which users of accounting information do you think the Financial Accounting Standards Board had in mind when it set this standard? What types of disclosures do you think these users would find helpful?

Alternate Multi-Concept Problem

Problem 1-11A ***Primary Assumptions Made in Preparing Financial Statements*** **LO 2, 3**

Millie Abrams opened a ceramic studio in leased retail space, paying the first month's rent of $300 and a $1,000 security deposit with a check on her personal account. She took molds and paint, worth about $7,500, from her home to the studio. She also bought a new firing kiln to start the business. The new kiln had a list price of $5,000, but Millie was able to trade in her old kiln, worth $500 at the time of trade, on the new kiln, and therefore she paid only $4,500 cash. She wrote a check on her personal checking account. Millie's first customers paid a total of $1,400 to attend classes for the next two months. She opened a checking account in the company's name with the $1,400. She has conducted classes for one month and has sold for $3,000 unfinished ceramic pieces called *greenware.* Greenware sales are all cash. Millie incurred $1,000 of personal cost in making the greenware. At the end of the first month, Millie prepared the following balance sheet and income statement.

MILLIE'S CERAMIC STUDIO
BALANCE SHEET
JULY 31, 2004

Cash	$1,400		
Kiln	5,000	Equity	$6,400
Total	$6,400	Total	$6,400

MILLIE'S CERAMIC STUDIO
INCOME STATEMENT
FOR THE MONTH ENDED JULY 31, 2004

Sales		$4,400
Rent	$300	
Supplies	600	900
Net income		$3,500

Millie needs to earn at least $3,000 each month for the business to be worth her time. She is pleased with the results.

Required

Identify the assumptions that Millie has violated and explain how each event should have been handled. Prepare a corrected balance sheet and income statement.

Cases

Reading and Interpreting Financial Statements

Case 1-1 ***An Annual Report as Ready Reference*** **LO 1, 2**

http://www.winnebagoind.com

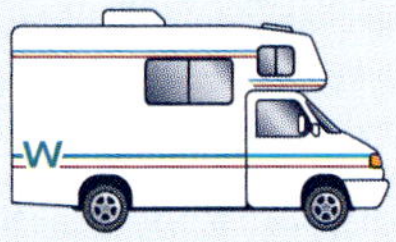

Refer to the **Winnebago Industries** annual report, and identify where each of the following users of accounting information would first look to answer their respective questions about Winnebago Industries:

1. Investors: How much did the company earn for each share of stock I own? How much of those earnings did I receive, and how much was reinvested in the company?
2. Potential investors: What amount of earnings can I expect to see from Winnebago Industries in the near future?

3. Bankers and creditors: Should I extend the short-term borrowing limit to Winnebago Industries? Does it have sufficient cash or cash-like assets to repay short-term loans?
4. IRS: How much does Winnebago Industries owe for taxes?
5. Employees: How much money did the president and vice presidents earn? Should I ask for a raise?

Case 1-2 ***Reading and Interpreting Winnebago Industries' Financial Statements*** **LO 2**

http://www.winnebagoind.com

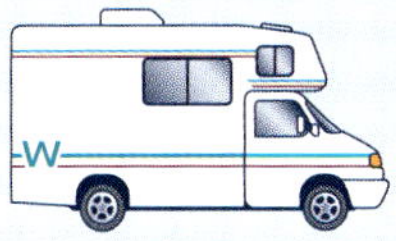

Refer to the financial statements for **Winnebago Industries** reproduced in the chapter and answer the following questions:

1. What was the company's net income for 2001?
2. State Winnebago Industries' financial position on August 25, 2001, in terms of the accounting equation.
3. Explain the reasons for the change in retained (or reinvested) earnings from a balance of \$195,556,000 on August 26, 2000, to a balance of \$234,139,000 on August 25, 2001. Also, what amount of dividends did the company pay in 2001?

Case 1-3 ***Comparing Two Companies in the Same Industry: Winnebago Industries and Monaco Coach Corporation*** **LO 2, 4**

http://www.winnebagoind.com
http://www.monacocoach.com

Refer to the financial information for **Winnebago Industries** and **Monaco Coach Corporation** reproduced in Appendices A and B at the end of the book and answer the following questions:

1. What was the total revenue amount for each company for 2001? (Note that Monaco Coach Corporaton uses the term "net sales" rather than revenues.) Did each company's revenues increase or decrease from its total amount in 2000?
2. What was each company's net income for 2001? Did each company's net income increase or decrease from its net income for 2000?
3. What was the total asset balance for each company at the end of its 2001 fiscal year? Among its assets, what was the largest asset each reported on its 2001 fiscal year-end balance sheet?
4. Did either company pay its stockholders any dividends during 2001? Explain how you can tell whether they did or did not pay any dividends.
5. Compare the auditors' report for the two companies. Is the format of the reports the same? If not, how do they differ? Do they contain the same basic information?

Making Financial Decisions

Case 1-4 ***An Investment Opportunity*** **LO 1**

DECISION MAKING

You have saved enough money to pay for your college tuition for the next three years when a high school friend comes to you with a deal. He is an artist who has spent most of the past two years drawing on the walls of old buildings. The buildings are about to be demolished and your friend thinks you should buy the walls before the buildings are demolished and open a gallery featuring his work. Of course, you are levelheaded and would normally say "No!" Recently, however, your friend has been featured on several local radio and television shows and is talking to some national networks about doing a feature on a well-known news show. To set up the gallery would take all your savings, but your friend feels that you will be able to sell his artwork for 10 times the cost of your investment. What kinds of information about the business do you need before deciding to invest all your savings? What kind of profit split would you suggest to your friend if you decide to open the gallery?

Case 1-5 ***Preparation of Projected Statements for a New Business*** **LO 2**

DECISION MAKING

Upon graduation from MegaState University, you and your roommate decide to start your respective careers in accounting and salmon fishing in Remote, Alaska. Your career as a CPA in Remote is going well, as is your roommate's job as a commercial fisherman. After one year in Remote, he approaches you with a business opportunity.

> As we are well aware, the video rental business has yet to reach Remote, and the nearest rental facility is 250 miles away. We each put up our first year's savings of \$5,000 and file for articles of incorporation with the state of Alaska to do business as Remote Video World. In return for our investment of \$5,000, we will each receive equal shares of capital stock in the corporation. Then we go to the Corner National Bank and apply for a \$10,000 loan. We take the total cash of \$20,000 we have now raised and buy 2,000 videos at \$10 each from a mail-order supplier. We rent the movies for \$3 per title and sell monthly memberships for \$25, allowing a member to check out an unlimited

number of movies during the month. Individual rentals would be a cash-and-carry business, but we would give customers until the 10th of the following month to pay for a monthly membership. My most conservative estimate is that during the first month alone, we will rent 800 movies and sell 200 memberships. As I see it, we will have only two expenses. First, we will hire four high school students to run the store for 15 hours each per week and pay them $5 per hour. Second, the landlord of a vacant store in town will rent us space in the building for $1,000 per month.

Required

1. Prepare a projected income statement for the first month of operations.
2. Prepare a balance sheet as it would appear at the end of the first month of operations.
3. Assume that the bank is willing to make the $10,000 loan. Would you be willing to join your roommate in this business? Explain your response. Also, indicate any information other than what he has provided that you would like to have before making a final decision.

Accounting and Ethics: What Would You Do?

Case 1-6 *Identification of Errors in Financial Statements and Preparation of Revised Statements* LO 1, 2

Lakeside Slammers Inc. is a minor-league baseball organization that has just completed its first season. You and three other investors organized the corporation; each put up $10,000 in cash for shares of capital stock. Because you live out of state, you have not been actively involved in the daily affairs of the club. However, you are thrilled to receive a dividend check for $10,000 at the end of the season—an amount equal to your original investment! Included with the check are the following financial statements, along with supporting explanations.

LAKESIDE SLAMMERS INC.
INCOME STATEMENT
FOR THE YEAR ENDED DECEMBER 31, 2004

Revenues:		
Single-game ticket revenue	$420,000	
Season-ticket revenue	140,000	
Concessions revenue	280,000	
Advertising revenue	100,000	$940,000
Expenses:		
Cost of concessions sold	$110,000	
Salary expense—players	225,000	
Salary and wage expense—staff	150,000	
Rent expense	210,000	695,000
Net income		$245,000

LAKESIDE SLAMMERS INC.
STATEMENT OF RETAINED EARNINGS
FOR THE YEAR ENDED DECEMBER 31, 2004

Beginning balance, January 1, 2004	$ 0
Add: Net income for 2004	245,000
Deduct: Cash dividends paid in 2004	(40,000)
Ending balance, December 31, 2004	$205,000

LAKESIDE SLAMMERS INC.
BALANCE SHEET
DECEMBER 31, 2004

Assets		Liabilities and Stockholders' Equity	
Cash	$ 5,000	Notes payable	$ 50,000
Accounts receivable:		Capital stock	40,000
Season tickets	140,000	Additional owners' capital	80,000
Advertisers	100,000	Parent club's equity	125,000
Auxiliary assets	80,000	Retained earnings	205,000
Equipment	50,000		
Player contracts	125,000	Total liabilities and	
Total assets	$500,000	stockholders' equity	$500,000

Additional information:

a. Single-game tickets sold for $4 per game. The team averaged 1,500 fans per game. With 70 home games × $4 per game × 1,500 fans, single-game ticket revenue amounted to $420,000.

b. No season tickets were sold during the first season. During the last three months of 2004, however, an aggressive sales campaign resulted in the sale of 500 season tickets for the 2005 season. Therefore, the controller (who is also one of the owners) chose to record an Account Receivable—Season Tickets and corresponding revenue for 500 tickets × $4 per game × 70 games, or $140,000.

c. Advertising revenue of $100,000 resulted from the sale of the 40 signs on the outfield wall at $2,500 each for the season. However, none of the advertisers have paid their bills yet (thus, an account receivable of $100,000 on the balance sheet) because the contract with Lakeside required them to pay only if the team averaged 2,000 fans per game during the 2004 season. The controller believes that the advertisers will be sympathetic to the difficulties of starting a new franchise and be willing to overlook the slight deficiency in the attendance requirement.

d. Lakeside has a working agreement with one of the major-league franchises. The minor-league team is required to pay $5,000 *every* year to the major-league team for each of the 25 players on its roster. The controller believes that each of the players is certainly an asset to the organization and has therefore recorded $5,000 × 25, or $125,000, as an asset called Player Contracts. The item on the right side of the balance sheet entitled Parent Club's Equity is the amount owed to the major league team by February 1, 2005, as payment for the players for the 2004 season.

e. In addition to the cost described in **d**, Lakeside directly pays each of its 25 players a $9,000 salary for the season. This amount—$225,000—has already been paid for the 2004 season and is reported on the income statement.

f. The items on the balance sheet entitled Auxiliary Assets on the left side and Additional Owners' Capital on the right side represent the value of the controller's personal residence. She has a mortgage with the bank for the full value of the house.

g. The $50,000 note payable resulted from a loan that was taken out at the beginning of the year to finance the purchase of bats, balls, uniforms, lawn mowers, and other miscellaneous supplies needed to operate the team (equipment is reported as an asset for the same amount). The loan, with interest, is due on April 15, 2005. Even though the team had a very successful first year, Lakeside is a little short of cash at the end of 2004 and has therefore asked the bank for a three-month extension of the loan. The controller reasons, "By the due date of April 15, 2005, the cash due from the new season ticket holders will be available, things will be cleared up with the advertisers, and the loan can be easily repaid."

Required

1. Identify any errors that you think the controller has made in preparing the financial statements.
2. On the basis of your answer in **1**, prepare a revised income statement, statement of retained earnings, and balance sheet.
3. On the basis of your revised financial statements, identify any ethical dilemma you now face. Do you have a responsibility to share these revisions with the other three owners? What is your responsibility to the bank?

Internet Research Case

Case 1-7 Winnebago Industries

Winnebago Industries is a name synonymous with RVs. Although the company has been a leader in the manufacture of recreational vehicles for many years, it did see a decline in its fiscal year 2001 in both sales and net income.

INTERNET

http://www.winnebagoind.com

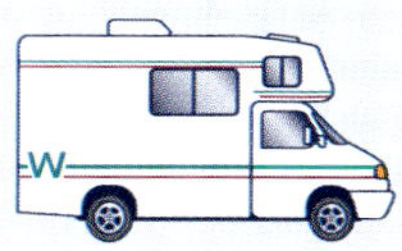

1. What was the amount of Winnebago Industries' revenues and cost of manufactured products for the 2002 fiscal year as reported on its income statement? Was there an increase or a decrease in each of these amounts in 2002? What was the percentage increase or decrease in each amount from the prior year?
2. What was the amount of cash dividends paid, both in total and per share, for the 2002 fiscal year as reported on Winnebago Industries' statement of changes in stockholders' equity? Was there any change in the dividends paid per share from the prior year?

(continued)

3. What was the amount of total assets as reported on Winnebago Industries' balance sheet at the end of the 2002 fiscal year? Did total assets increase or decrease during the year? What was the percentage increase or decrease?

Solutions to Key Terms Quiz

4 Accounting (p. 14)
9 Management accounting (p. 14)
5 Financial accounting (p. 15)
6 Owners' equity (p. 17)
3 Stockholders' equity (p. 17)
8 Retained earnings (p. 17)
7 Balance sheet (p. 17)
1 Income statement (p. 19)
10 Dividends (p. 19)
2 Statement of retained earnings (p. 20)
12 Cost principle (p. 22)
16 Going concern (p. 22)
18 Monetary unit (p. 23)
21 Time period (p. 23)
11 Generally accepted accounting principles (GAAP) (p. 23)
13 Securities and Exchange Commission (SEC) (p. 24)
17 Financial Accounting Standards Board (FASB) (p. 24)
19 American Institute of Certified Public Accountants (AICPA) (p. 24)
24 International Accounting Standards Board (IASB) (p. 24)
22 Controller (p. 24)
15 Treasurer (p. 24)
20 Internal auditing (p. 25)
23 Auditing (p. 26)
25 Auditors' report (p. 26)
14 American Accounting Association (p. 28)

Chapter 2

Financial Statements and the Annual Report

© TERRI MILLER/E-VISUAL COMMUNICATIONS, INC

Focus on Financial Results

Gateway, a manufacturer of personal computers (PCs), has developed a business model over the years that involves selling its products directly to the ultimate consumer and, in some instances, to those consumers in company-operated retail outlets. This model has worked exceedingly well for the company in the past. Throughout its short corporate life (Gateway was founded in 1985), it has continually grown, with sales reaching a record level of $9.6 billion in 2000.

Like many technology companies, however, Gateway found 2001 to be the most challenging year in its existence, with sales dropping to just over $6 billion. The company attributes this decline in part to an overall maturation in the demand for computers and also to a downturn in the economy. At the same time, Gateway realizes the intense competitive nature of the PC market, where price and the availability of new technology seem to be what drives sales. With this in mind, the company laid out a plan, in its 2001 annual report, that focused on investing in the company's core PC business with a more aggressive pricing and marketing strategy in 2002.

Ted Waitt, the founder of Gateway and its current president and CEO, commented on the company's financial position: "Finally, we worked very hard to restore health to our balance sheet, exiting the year with more than a billion dollars in cash and marketable securities, about twice the level we had at the beginning of the year." Indeed, as the accompanying balance sheet shows, Gateway ended the year with nearly $731 million in cash and another $435 million in marketable securities. The future will show whether Gateway is able to use these financial resources to its advantage and return to record-setting years of sales performance.

Gateway 2001 Annual Report

GATEWAY, INC.
CONSOLIDATED BALANCE SHEETS
DECEMBER 31, 2001 AND 2000
(in thousands, except per share amounts)

	2001	2000
ASSETS		
Current assets:		
Cash and cash equivalents	$ 730,999	$ 483,997
Marketable securities	435,055	130,073
Accounts receivable, net	219,974	544,755
Inventory	120,270	315,069
Other, net	616,626	793,166
Total current assets	2,122,924	2,267,060
Property, plant and equipment, net	608,429	897,414
Intangibles, net	36,304	165,914
Other assets, net	219,200	850,257
	$2,986,857	$4,180,645
LIABILITIES AND EQUITY		
Current liabilities:		
Accounts payable	$ 341,122	$ 785,345
Accrued liabilities	468,609	556,323
Accrued royalties	135,698	138,446
Other current liabilities	200,599	179,021
Total current liabilities	1,146,028	1,659,135
Other long-term liabilities	82,636	141,171
Total liabilities	1,228,664	1,800,306
Commitments and contingencies (Note 5)		
Series C redeemable convertible preferred stock, $.01 par value, $200,000 liquidation value, 50 shares authorized, issued and outstanding in 2001	193,109	—
Stockholders' equity:		
Series A convertible preferred stock, $.01 par value, $200,000 liquidation value, 50 shares authorized, issued and outstanding in 2001	200,000	—
Preferred stock, $.01 par value, 4,900 shares authorized; none issued and outstanding	—	—
Class A common stock, nonvoting, $.01 par value, 1,000 shares authorized; none issued and outstanding	—	—
Common stock, $.01 par value, 1,000,000 shares authorized; 323,973 shares and 323,955 shares issued in 2001 and 2000, respectively	3,239	3,239
Additional paid-in capital	731,623	741,646
Common stock in treasury, at cost, 552 shares in 2000	—	(21,948)
Retained earnings	616,420	1,650,335
Accumulated other comprehensive income	13,802	7,067
Total stockholders' equity	1,565,084	2,380,339
	$2,986,857	$4,180,645

The accompanying notes are an integral part of the consolidated financial statements.

Gateway 2001 Annual Report, p. 2.

http://www.gateway.com

You're in the Driver's Seat

If you were thinking of buying shares of Gateway stock, what questions about Gateway's future plans would you want answered? Use this chapter, Gateway's annual report, and its Web site to help you identify and evaluate information about the company's financial performance and management's plans for use of the firm's resources.

LEARNING OBJECTIVES

After studying this chapter, you should be able to:

LO 1 Describe the objectives of financial reporting. (p. 54)

LO 2 Describe the qualitative characteristics of accounting information. (p. 56)

LO 3 Explain the concept and purpose of a classified balance sheet and prepare the statement. (p. 60)

LO 4 Use a classified balance sheet to analyze a company's financial position. (p. 65)

LO 5 Explain the difference between a single-step and a multiple-step income statement and prepare each type of income statement. (p. 67)

LO 6 Use a multiple-step income statement to analyze a company's operations. (p. 69)

LO 7 Identify the components of the statement of retained earnings and prepare the statement. (p. 70)

LO 8 Identify the components of the statement of cash flows and prepare the statement. (p. 70)

LO 9 Read and use the financial statements and other elements in the annual report of a publicly held company. (p. 71)

WHY DOES ACCOUNTING INFORMATION NEED TO BE USEFUL? OBJECTIVES OF FINANCIAL REPORTING

LO 1 Describe the objectives of financial reporting.

The users of financial information are the main reason financial statements are prepared. After all, it is the investors, creditors, and other groups and individuals outside and inside the company who must make economic decisions based on these statements. Therefore, as we learned in Chapter 1, financial statements must be based on agreed-upon assumptions like time-period, going concern, and other generally accepted accounting principles.

Moreover, when the accountants for companies like **Winnebago Industries** and Gateway prepare their financial statements, they must keep in mind financial reporting objectives, which are focused on providing the most understandable and useful information possible. Financial reporting has one overall objective and a set of related objectives, all of them concerned with how the information may be most useful to the readers.

The Primary Objective: Provide Information for Decision Making

The primary objective of financial reporting is *to provide economic information to permit users of the information to make informed decisions.* Users include both the management of a company (internal users) and others not involved in the daily operations of the business (external users). Without access to the detailed records of the business and without the benefit of daily involvement in the affairs of the company, external users make their decisions based on *financial statements* prepared by management. According to the Financial Accounting Standards Board (FASB), "Financial reporting should provide information that is useful to present and potential investors and creditors and other users in making rational investment, credit, and similar decisions".[1]

We see from this statement how closely the objective of financial reporting is tied to decision making. *The purpose of financial reporting is to help the users reach their decisions in an informed manner.*

[1]*Statement of Financial Accounting Concepts [SFAC] No. 1,* "Objectives of Financial Reporting by Business Enterprises" (Stamford, Conn.: Financial Accounting Standards Board, November 1978), par. 34.

Secondary Objective: Reflect Prospective Cash Receipts to Investors and Creditors

Present stockholders must decide whether to hold their stock in a company or sell it. For potential stockholders, the decision is whether to buy the stock in the first place. Bankers, suppliers, and other types of creditors must decide whether to lend money to a company. In making their decisions, all these groups rely partially on the information provided in financial statements. (Other sources of information are sometimes as important, or more important, in reaching a decision. For example, the most recent income statement may report the highest profits in the history of a company. However, a potential investor may choose not to buy stock in a company if *The Wall Street Journal* or *Business Week* reports that a strike is likely to shut down operations for an indeterminable period of time.)

http://www.wsj.com
http://www.businessweek.com

If you buy stock in a company, your primary concern is the *future cash to be received from the investment.* First, how much, if anything, will you periodically receive in *cash dividends?* Second, how much cash will you receive from the *sale of the stock?* The interests of a creditor, such as a banker, are similar. The banker is concerned with receiving the original amount of money lent and the interest on the loan. In summary, another objective of financial reporting is to "provide information to help present and potential investors and creditors and other users in assessing the amounts, timing, and uncertainty of prospective cash receipts from dividends or interest and the proceeds from the sale, redemption, or maturity of securities or loans."[2]

Secondary Objective: Reflect Prospective Cash Flows to the Enterprise

As an investor your ultimate concern is not the company's cash flows—how much comes in and goes out in the course of doing business—but the cash you receive from your investment. But since your investment depends to some extent on the company's business skills in managing its cash flows, another objective of accounting is to provide information that will allow users to make decisions about the cash flows of a company. (We will discuss cash flows briefly later in the chapter and will return to them in Chapter 12.)

Secondary Objective: Reflect the Enterprise's Resources and Claims to Its Resources

The FASB emphasizes the roles of the balance sheet and the income statement in providing useful information. These financial statements should reflect what *resources* (or assets) the company or enterprise has, what *claims to these resources* (liabilities and stockholders' equity) there are, and the effects of transactions and events that change these resources and claims.[3] Thus, another objective of financial reporting is to show the effect of transactions on the entity's "accounting equation."

Exhibit 2-1 summarizes the objectives of financial reporting as they pertain to someone considering whether to buy stock in Gateway. The exhibit should help you to understand how something as abstract as a set of financial reporting objectives can be applied to a decision-making situation.

[2] *SFAC No. 1,* par. 37.
[3] *SFAC No. 1,* par. 40.

Exhibit 2-1 The Application of Financial Reporting Objectives

FINANCIAL REPORTING OBJECTIVE	POTENTIAL INVESTOR'S QUESTIONS
1. The primary objective: Provide information for decision making.	"Based on the financial information, should I buy shares of stock in Gateway?"
2. Secondary objective: Reflect prospective cash receipts to investors and creditors.	"How much cash will I receive in dividends each year and from the sale of the stock of Gateway in the future?"
3. Secondary objective: Reflect prospective cash flows to an enterprise.	"After paying its suppliers and employees, and meeting all of its obligations, how much cash will Gateway take in during the time I own the stock?"
4. Secondary objective: Reflect resources and claims to resources.	"How much has Gateway invested in new plant and equipment?"

WHAT MAKES ACCOUNTING INFORMATION USEFUL? QUALITATIVE CHARACTERISTICS

LO 2 Describe the qualitative characteristics of accounting information.

Since accounting information must be useful for decision making, what makes this information useful? This section focuses on the qualities that accountants strive for in their financial reporting and on some of the challenges they face in making reporting judgments. It also reveals what users of financial information expect from financial statements.

Quantitative considerations, such as tuition costs, certainly were a concern when you chose your current school. In addition, your decision required you to make subjective judgments about the *qualitative* characteristics you were looking for in a college. Similarly, there are certain qualities that make accounting information useful.

Understandability

Understandability The quality of accounting information that makes it comprehensible to those willing to spend the necessary time.

For anything to be useful, it must be understandable. Usefulness and understandability go hand in hand. However, **understandability** of financial information varies considerably, depending on the background of the user. For example, should financial statements be prepared so that they are understandable by anyone with a college education? Or should it be assumed that all readers of financial statements have completed at least one accounting course? Is a background in business necessary for a good understanding of financial reports, regardless of one's formal training? As you might expect, there are no simple answers to these questions. However, the FASB believes that financial information should be comprehensible to *those who are willing to spend the time to understand it:* "Financial information is a tool and, like most tools, cannot be of much direct help to those who are unable or unwilling to use it or who misuse it. Its use can be learned, however, and financial reporting should provide information that can be used by all—nonprofessionals as well as professionals—who are willing to learn to use it properly."[4]

Relevance

Relevance The capacity of information to make a difference in a decision.

Understandability alone is certainly not enough to render information useful. To be useful, information must be relevant. **Relevance** is the capacity of information to make a difference in a decision.[5] For example, assume that you are a banker evaluating the financial statements of a company that has come to you for a loan. All of the financial

[4]*SFAC No. 1,* par. 36.

[5]*Statement of Financial Accounting Concepts [SFAC] No. 2,* "Qualitative Characteristics of Accounting Information" (Stamford, Conn.: Financial Accounting Standards Board, May 1980), par. 47.

statements point to a strong and profitable company. However, today's newspaper revealed that the company has been named in a multimillion-dollar lawsuit. Undoubtedly, this information would be relevant to your talks with the company, and disclosure of the lawsuit in the financial statements would make them even more relevant to your lending decision.

Accounting for Your Decisions

You Are the Stockholder

ABC Technology produces a highly technical product used in the computer industry. You are a stockholder and are currently in the process of reading this year's annual report. You find that you can't understand the report because it contains so much accounting jargon. But the annual report contains a 1-800 number for shareholder inquiries. You call the number and complain about the annual report, but the corporate spokesman politely tells you that "that's the way people talk in accounting." Is your complaint valid?

ANS: One of the purposes of an annual report is to interest potential stockholders in the company. A small percentage of those potential investors are professional money managers who are familiar with the accounting terminology. However, most readers are individual investors who probably don't have a sophisticated accounting background. It is true that the report must assume a minimum level of formal education; accountants expect those who read the report to take the time to understand it. Technicalities aside, however, it is important to write an annual report for as broad an audience as possible.

Reliability

What makes accounting information reliable? According to the FASB, "Accounting information is reliable to the extent that users can depend on it to represent the economic conditions or events that it purports to represent."[6]

Reliability has three basic characteristics:

Reliability The quality that makes accounting information dependable in representing the events that it purports to represent.

- *Verifiability* Information is verifiable when we can make sure that it is free from error—for example, by looking up the cost paid for an asset in a contract or an invoice.
- *Representational faithfulness* Information is representationally faithful when it corresponds to an actual event—such as when the purchase of land corresponds to a transaction in the company's records.
- *Neutrality* Information is neutral when it is not slanted to portray a company's position in a better or worse light than the actual circumstances would dictate—such as when the probable losses from a major lawsuit are disclosed accurately in the notes to the financial statements, with all its potential effects on the company, rather than minimized as a very remote possible loss.

Comparability and Consistency

Comparability allows comparisons to be made *between or among companies.* Generally accepted accounting principles (GAAP) allow a certain amount of freedom in choosing among competing alternative treatments for certain transactions.

Comparability For accounting information, the quality that allows a user to analyze two or more companies and look for similarities and differences.

For example, under GAAP, companies may choose from a number of methods of accounting for the depreciation of certain long-term assets. **Depreciation** is the *process of allocating* the cost of a long-term tangible asset, such as a building or equipment, over

Depreciation The process of allocating the cost of a long-term tangible asset over its useful life.

[6] *SFAC No. 2,* par. 62.

its useful life. Each method may affect the value of the assets differently. (We discuss depreciation in Chapter 8.) How does this freedom of choice affect the ability of investors to make comparisons between companies?

Assume you were considering buying stock in one of three companies. As their annual reports indicate, two of the companies use what is called the "accelerated" depreciation method, and the other company uses what is called the "straight-line" depreciation method. (We'll learn about these methods in a later chapter.) Does this lack of a common depreciation method make it impossible for you to compare the performance of the three companies?

Obviously, comparisons among the companies would be easier and more meaningful if all three used the same depreciation method. However, comparisons are not impossible just because companies use different methods. Certainly, the more alike—that is, uniform—statements are in terms of the principles used to prepare them, the more comparable they will be. However, the profession allows a certain freedom of choice in selecting from among alternative generally accepted accounting principles.

To render statements of companies using different methods more meaningful, *disclosure* assumes a very important role. For example, as we will see later in this chapter, the first note in the annual report of a publicly traded company is the disclosure of its accounting policies. The reader of this note for each of the three companies is made aware that the companies do not use the same depreciation method. Disclosure of accounting policies allows the reader to make some sort of subjective adjustment to the statements of one or more of the companies and thus to compensate for the different depreciation method being used.

Consistency For accounting information, the quality that allows a user to compare two or more accounting periods for a single company.

Consistency is closely related to the concept of comparability. Both involve the relationship between two numbers. *However, whereas financial statements are comparable when they can be compared between one company and another, statements are* consistent *when they can be compared within a single company from one accounting period to the next.*

Occasionally, companies decide to change from one accounting method to another. Will it be possible to compare a company's earnings in a period in which it switches

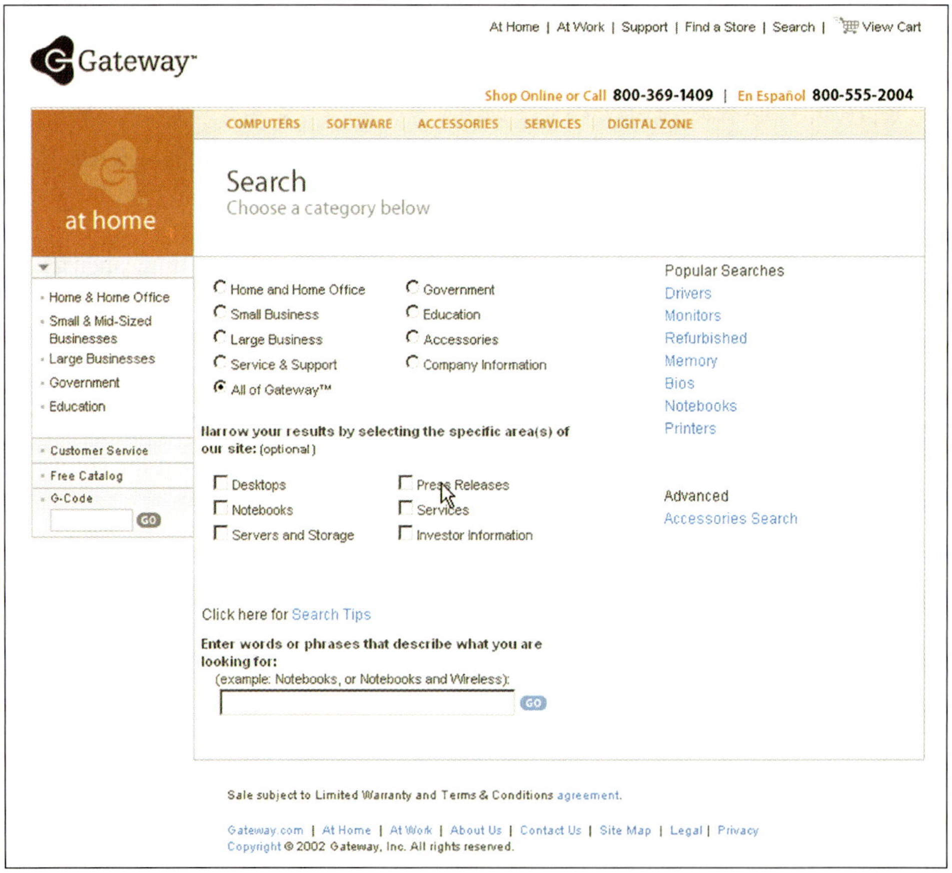

Companies still produce printed annual reports as a way to summarize the past year's business activities, discuss the firm's performance, preview upcoming products and business trends, and give investors and other users of financial information a format for analyzing the financial information. But most companies also provide annual report information—along with news reports and current information—at the Investor Relations *page on their Web site. You can search for Gateway's at http://www.gateway.com/search/index.shtml.*

methods with its earnings in prior years if the methods differ? Like the different methods used by different companies, changes in accounting methods from one period to the next do not make comparisons impossible, only more difficult. When a company makes an accounting change, accounting standards require various disclosures to help the reader evaluate the impact of the change.

Materiality

For accounting information to be useful, it must be relevant to a decision. The concept of **materiality** is closely related to relevance and deals with the size of an error in accounting information. The issue is whether the error is large enough to affect the judgment of someone relying on the information. Consider the following example. A company pays cash for two separate purchases: one for a $5 pencil sharpener and the other for a $50,000 computer. Theoretically, each expenditure results in the acquisition of an asset that should be depreciated over its useful life. However, what if the company decides to account for the $5 as an expense of the period rather than treat it in the theoretically correct manner by depreciating it over the life of the pencil sharpener? *Will this error in any way affect the judgment of someone relying on the financial statements?* Because such a slight error will *not* affect any decisions, minor expenditures of this nature are considered *immaterial* and are accounted for as an expense of the period.

Materiality The magnitude of an accounting information omission or misstatement that will affect the judgment of someone relying on the information.

The *threshold* for determining materiality will vary from one company to the next, depending to a large extent on the size of the company. Many companies establish policies that *any* expenditure under a certain dollar amount should be accounted for as an expense of the period. The threshold might be $50 for the corner grocery store but $1,000 for a large corporation. Finally, in some instances the amount of a transaction may be immaterial by company standards but may still be considered significant by financial statement users. For example, a transaction involving either illegal or unethical behavior by a company officer would be of concern, regardless of the dollar amounts involved.

Conservatism

The concept of **conservatism** is a holdover from earlier days when the primary financial statement was the balance sheet and the primary user of this statement was the banker. It was customary to deliberately understate assets on the balance sheet because this resulted in an even larger margin of safety that the assets being provided as collateral for a loan were sufficient.

Conservatism The practice of using the least optimistic estimate when two estimates of amounts are about equally likely.

Today the balance sheet is not the only financial statement, and deliberate understatement of assets is no longer considered desirable. The practice of conservatism is reserved for those situations in which there is *uncertainty* about how to account for a particular item or transaction: "Thus, if two estimates of amounts to be received or paid in the future are about equally likely, conservatism dictates using the less optimistic estimate; however, if two amounts are not equally likely, conservatism does not necessarily dictate using the more pessimistic amount rather than the more likely one."[7]

Various accounting rules are based on the concept of conservatism. For example, inventory held for resale is reported on the balance sheet at *the lower-of-cost-or-market value.* This rule requires a company to compare the cost of its inventory with the market price, or current cost to replace that inventory, and report the lower of the two amounts on the balance sheet at the end of the year. In Chapter 6 we will more fully explore the lower-of-cost-or-market rule as it pertains to inventory.

Exhibit 2-2 summarizes the qualities that make accounting information useful as these characteristics pertain to a banker's decision regarding whether to lend money to a company.

[7]*SFAC No. 2,* par. 95.

Exhibit 2-2 Qualitative Characteristics of Accounting Information

SITUATION A bank is trying to decide whether to extend a $1 million loan to Russell Corporation. Russell presents the bank with its most recent balance sheet, showing its financial position on a historical cost basis. Each quality of the information is summarized in the form of a question.

QUALITY	QUESTION
Understandability	Can the information be used by those willing to learn to use it properly?
Relevance	Would the information be useful in deciding whether or not to loan money to Russell?
Reliability	
Verifiability	Can the information be verified? Is the information free from error?
Representational faithfulness	Is there agreement between the information and the events represented?
Neutrality	Is the information slanted in any way to present the company more favorably than is warranted?
Comparability	Are the methods used in assigning amounts to assets the same as those used by other companies?
Consistency	Are the methods used in assigning amounts to assets the same as those used in prior years?
Materiality	Will a specific error in any way affect the judgment of someone relying on the financial statements?
Conservatism	If there is any uncertainty about any of the amounts assigned to items on the balance sheet, are they recognized using the least optimistic estimate?

FINANCIAL REPORTING: AN INTERNATIONAL PERSPECTIVE

In Chapter 1 we introduced the International Accounting Standards Board (IASB) and its efforts to improve the development of accounting standards around the world. Interestingly, four of the most influential members of this group, representing the standard-setting bodies in the United States, the United Kingdom, Canada, and Australia, agree on the primary objective of financial reporting. All recognize that the primary objective is to provide information useful in making economic decisions.

The standard-setting body in the United Kingdom distinguishes between qualitative characteristics that relate to *content* of the information presented and those that relate to *presentation.* Similar to the FASB, this group recognizes relevance and reliability as the primary characteristics related to content. Comparability and understandability are the primary qualities related to the presentation of the information.

The concept of conservatism is also recognized in other countries. For example, both the IASB and the standard-setting body in the United Kingdom list "prudence" among their qualitative characteristics. Prudence requires the use of caution in making the various estimates required in accounting. Like the U.S. standard-setting body, these groups recognize that prudence does not justify the deliberate understatement of assets or revenues or the deliberate overstatement of liabilities or expenses.

THE CLASSIFIED BALANCE SHEET

LO 3 Explain the concept and purpose of a classified balance sheet and prepare the statement.

Now that we have learned about the conceptual framework of accounting, we turn to the outputs of the system: the financial statements. First, we will consider the significance of a *classified balance sheet.* We will then examine the *income statement,* the *statement of retained earnings,* and the *statement of cash flows.* The chapter concludes with a brief look at the financial statements of a real company, Gateway, and at the other elements in an annual report.

What Are the Parts of the Balance Sheet? Understanding the Operating Cycle

In the first part of this chapter, we stressed the importance of *cash flow*. For a company that sells a product, the **operating cycle** begins when cash is invested in inventory and ends when cash is collected by the enterprise from its customers.

Operating cycle The period of time between the purchase of inventory and the collection of any receivable from the sale of the inventory.

Assume that on August 1 a retailer, Laptop Computer Sales, buys a computer for $5,000 from the manufacturer, BIM Corp. At this point, Laptop has merely substituted one asset, cash, for another, inventory. On August 20, twenty days after buying the computer, Laptop sells it to an accounting firm, Price & Company, for $6,000. Under the purchase agreement, Price will pay for the computer within the next 30 days. At this point, both the form of the asset and the amount have changed. The form of the asset held by Laptop has changed from inventory to accounts receivable. Also, because the inventory has been sold for $1,000 more than its cost of $5,000, the size of the asset held, the account receivable, is now $6,000. Finally, on September 20, Price pays $6,000 to Laptop, and the operating cycle is complete. As we will explore more fully in later chapters, Laptop has earned $1,000, the difference between what it sold the computer for and what it initially paid for the computer. The cycle starts again when Laptop buys another computer for resale.

Laptop's operating cycle is summarized in Exhibit 2-3. The length of the company's operating cycle was 50 days. The operating cycle consisted of two distinct parts. From the time Laptop purchased the inventory, 20 days elapsed before it sold the computer. Another 30 days passed before the account receivable was collected. The length of the operating cycle depends to a large extent on the nature of a company's business. For

Study Tip

The operating cycle of a business is the basis for deciding which assets are current and which are noncurrent. When you look at a company's balance sheet, be sure you understand the length of its operating cycle so you are clear about how it classifies its assets.

Exhibit 2-3 The Operating Cycle for a Retailer

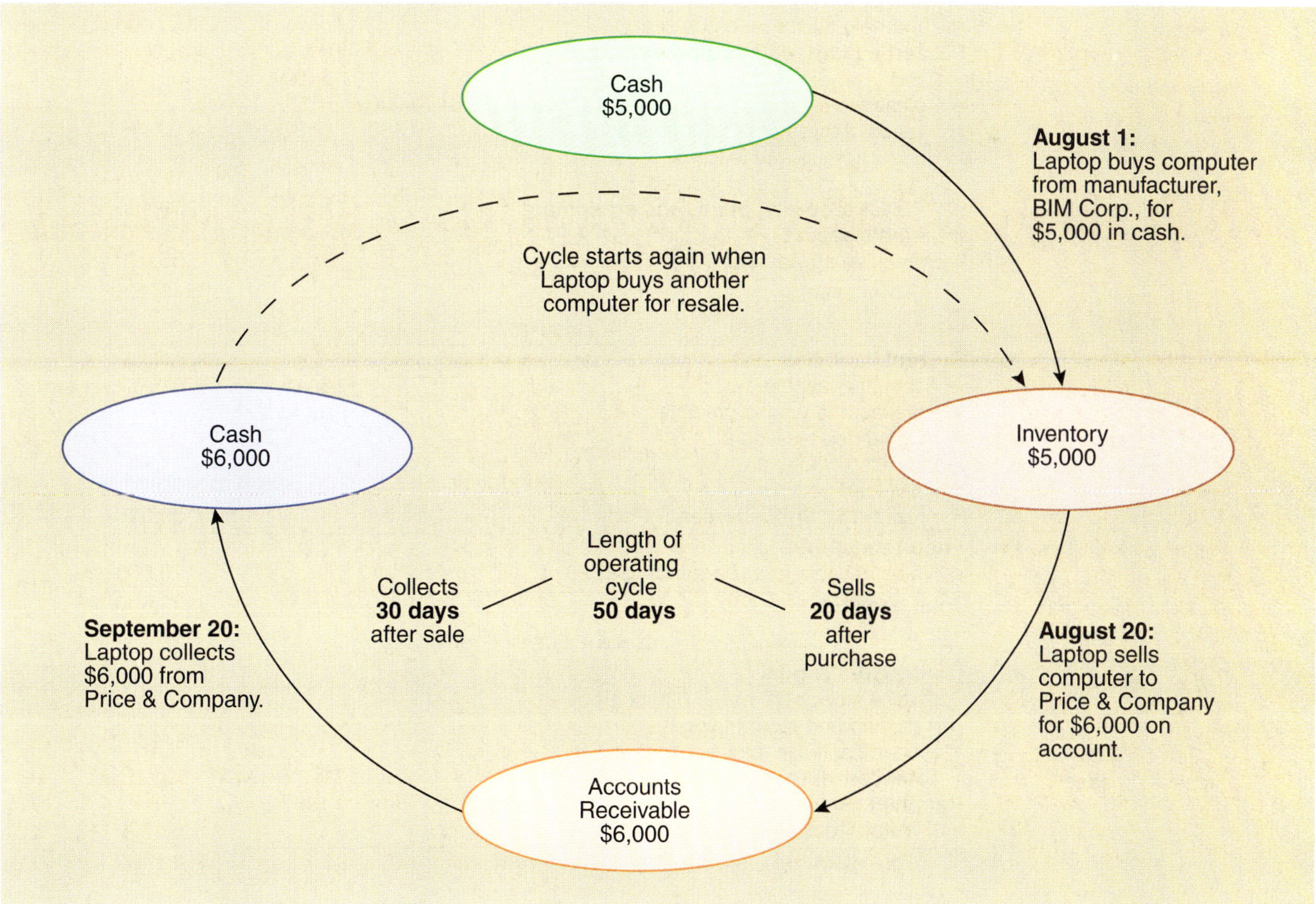

example, in our illustration, the manufacturer of the computer, BIM Corp., received cash immediately from Laptop and did not have to wait to collect a receivable. However, additional time is added to the operating cycle of BIM Corp. to *manufacture* the computer.

The operating cycle of the accounting firm in our example, Price & Company, differs from that of either the manufacturer or the retailer. Price sells a service rather than a product. Its operating cycle is determined by two factors: the length of time involved in providing a service to the client and the amount of time required to collect any account receivable.

A classified balance sheet for a hypothetical company, Dixon Sporting Goods Inc., is shown in Exhibit 2-4. You will want to refer to it as you learn about the different categories on a classified balance sheet. (The bulleted numbers below refer to Exhibit 2-4.)

Exhibit 2-4 Balance Sheet for Dixon Sporting Goods

DIXON SPORTING GOODS INC.
BALANCE SHEET
AT DECEMBER 31, 2004

ASSETS

1 These assets are realizable, sold, or consumed in one year or operating cycle.	**Current assets**			
	Cash		$ 5,000	
	Marketable securities		11,000	
	Accounts receivable		23,000	
	Merchandise inventory		73,500	
	Prepaid insurance		4,800	
	Store supplies		700	
	Total current assets			$118,000
2 These assets will not be realizable, sold, or consumed within one year or operating cycle.	**Investments**			
	Land held for future office site			150,000
	Property, plant, and equipment			
	Land		$100,000	
	Buildings	$150,000		
	Less: Accumulated depreciation	60,000	90,000	
	Store furniture and fixtures	$ 42,000		
	Less: Accumulated depreciation	12,600	29,400	
	Total property, plant, and equipment			219,400
	Intangible assets			
	Franchise agreement			55,000
	Total assets			$542,400

LIABILITIES

3 These are liabilities that will be satisfied within one year or operating cycle.	**Current liabilities**		
	Accounts payable	$ 15,700	
	Salaries and wages payable	9,500	
	Income taxes payable	7,200	
	Interest payable	2,500	
	Bank loan payable	25,000	
	Total current liabilities		$ 59,900
4 These are liabilities that will not be satisfied within one year or operating cycle.	**Long-term debt**		
	Notes payable, due December 31, 2014		120,000
	Total liabilities		$179,900

STOCKHOLDERS' EQUITY

5 These are owners' claims on assets.	**Contributed capital**		
	Capital stock, $10 par, 5,000 shares issued and outstanding	$ 50,000	
	Paid-in capital in excess of par value	25,000	
	Total contributed capital	$ 75,000	
	Retained earnings	287,500	
	Total stockholders' equity		362,500
	Total liabilities and stockholders' equity		$542,400

Current Assets 1

The basic distinction on a classified balance sheet is between current and noncurrent items. **Current assets** are "cash and other assets that are reasonably expected to be realized in cash or sold or consumed during the normal operating cycle of a business or within one year if the operating cycle is shorter than one year."[8]

Current asset An asset that is expected to be realized in cash or sold or consumed during the operating cycle or within one year if the cycle is shorter than one year.

Most businesses have an operating cycle shorter than one year. The operating cycle for Laptop Computer Sales in our illustration was 50 days. Therefore cash, accounts receivable, and inventory are classified as current assets because they *are* cash, will be *realized* in (converted to) cash (accounts receivable), or will be *sold* (inventory) within one year.

Can you think of a situation in which a company's operating cycle is longer than one year? A construction company is a good example. A construction company essentially builds an item of inventory, such as an office building, to a customer's specifications. The entire process, including constructing the building and collecting the sales amount from the customer, may take three years to complete. According to our earlier definition, because the inventory will be sold and the account receivable will be collected within the operating cycle, they will still qualify as current assets.

In addition to cash, accounts receivable, and inventory, the two other most common types of current assets are marketable securities and prepaid expenses. Excess cash is often invested in the stocks and bonds of other companies, as well as in various government instruments. If the investments are made for the short term, they are classified as current and are typically called either *short-term investments* or *marketable securities.* (Alternatively, some investments are made for the purpose of exercising influence over another company and thus are made for the long term. These investments are classified as noncurrent assets.) Various prepayments, such as office supplies, rent, and insurance, are classified as *prepaid expenses* and thus are current assets. These assets qualify as current because they will usually be *consumed* within one year.

© SKIP NALL/GETTYIMAGES/PHOTODISC

Compare the length of the operating cycle of a builder of an office building (or of communications equipment for the Internet) to that of a computer retailer. From the time a construction project "launches" to cash collection may be years, not weeks or months.

Noncurrent Assets 2

Any assets that do not meet the definition of a current asset are classified as *long-term* or *noncurrent assets.* Three common categories of long-term assets are: investments; property, plant, and equipment; and intangibles.

Investments Recall, from the discussion of current assets, that stocks and bonds expected to be sold within the next year are classified as current assets. Securities that are not expected to be sold within the next year are classified as *investments.* In many cases, the investment is in the common stock of another company. Sometimes companies invest in another company either to exercise some influence or actually to control the operation of the other company. Other types of assets classified as investments are land held for future use and buildings and equipment not currently used in operations. Finally, a special fund held for the retirement of debt or for the construction of new facilities is also classified as an investment.

Property, Plant, and Equipment This category consists of the various *tangible, productive assets* used in the operation of a business. Land, buildings, equipment, machinery, furniture and fixtures, trucks, and tools are all examples of assets held for use in the *operation* of a business rather than for *resale.* The distinction between inventory and equipment, for example, depends on the company's *intent* in acquiring the asset. For example, IBM classifies a computer system as inventory because its intent in manufacturing the asset is to offer it for resale. However, this same computer in the hands of a law firm would be classified as equipment because its intent in buying the asset from IBM is to use it in the long-term operation of the business.

http://www.ibm.com

[8]Accounting Principles Board, *Statement of the Accounting Principles Board, No. 4,* "Basic Concepts and Accounting Principles Underlying Financial Statements of Business Enterprises" (New York: American Institute of Certified Public Accountants, 1970), par. 198.

http://www.xcelenergy.com

http://www.microsoft.com

The relative size of property, plant, and equipment depends largely on a company's business. Consider Xcel Energy, a utility company with over $28 billion in total assets at the end of 2001. Over 73% of the total assets was invested in property, plant, and equipment. On the other hand, property and equipment represented less than 4% of the total assets of Microsoft, the highly successful software company. Regardless of the relative size of property, plant, and equipment, all assets in this category are subject to depreciation, with the exception of land. A separate accumulated depreciation account is used to account for the depreciation recorded on each of these assets over its life.

Intangibles Intangible assets are similar to property, plant, and equipment in that they provide benefits to the firm over the long term. The distinction, however, is in the *form* of the asset. *Intangible assets lack physical substance.* Trademarks, copyrights, franchise rights, patents, and goodwill are examples of intangible assets. The cost principle governs the accounting for intangibles, just as it does for tangible assets. For example, the amount paid to an inventor for the patent rights to a new project is recorded as an intangible asset. Similarly, the amount paid to purchase a franchise for a fast-food restaurant for the exclusive right to operate in a certain geographic area is recorded as an intangible asset. Like tangible assets, intangibles are written off to expense over their useful lives. *Depreciation* is the name given to the process of writing off tangible assets; the same process for intangible assets is called *amortization.* Depreciation and amortization are both explained more fully in Chapter 8.

Two-Minute Review

1. *Give at least three examples of current assets.*
2. *Give the three common categories of noncurrent assets.*

Answers on page 79.

Accounting for Your Decisions

You Are a Student

Identify any assets you currently have, and then categorize them as either current or noncurrent.

ANS: Among your current assets would be cash and any investments you expect to sell in the near future. Your car would be a noncurrent asset.

Current Liabilities 3

Current liability An obligation that will be satisfied within the next operating cycle or within one year if the cycle is shorter than one year.

The definition of a current liability is closely tied to that of a current asset. A **current liability** is an obligation that will be satisfied within the next operating cycle or within one year, if the cycle is shorter than one year. For example, the classification of a note payable on the balance sheet depends on its maturity date. If the note will be paid within the next year, it is classified as current; otherwise, it is classified as a long-term liability. On the other hand, accounts payable, wages payable, and income taxes payable are all short-term or current liabilities.

Most liabilities, such as those for purchases of merchandise on credit, are satisfied by the payment of cash. However, certain liabilities are eliminated from the balance sheet when the company performs services. For example, the liability Subscriptions Received in Advance, which would appear on the balance sheet of a magazine publisher, is satisfied not by the payment of any cash but by the delivery of the magazine to the customers. Finally, it is possible to satisfy one liability by substituting another in its place. For example, a supplier might ask a customer to sign a written promissory note to replace an existing account payable if the customer is unable to pay at the present time.

Long-Term Liabilities 4

Any obligation that will not be paid or otherwise satisfied within the next year or the operating cycle, whichever is longer, is classified as a long-term liability, or long-term debt. Notes payable and bonds payable, both promises to pay money in the future, are two common forms of long-term debt. Some bonds have a life as long as 25 or 30 years.

Stockholders' Equity 5

Recall that stockholders' equity represents the owners' claims on the assets of the business. These claims arise from two sources: *contributed capital* and *earned capital.* Contributed capital appears on the balance sheet in the form of capital stock, and earned capital takes the form of retained earnings. *Capital stock* indicates the owners' investment in the business. *Retained earnings* represents the accumulated earnings, or net income, of the business since its inception less all dividends paid during that time.

Most companies have a single class of capital stock called *common stock.* This is the most basic form of ownership in a business. All other claims against the company, such as those of *creditors* and *preferred stockholders,* take priority. *Preferred stock* is a form of capital stock that, as the name implies, carries with it certain preferences. For example, the company must pay dividends on preferred stock before it makes any distribution of dividends on common stock. In the event of liquidation, preferred stockholders have priority over common stockholders in the distribution of the entity's assets.

Capital stock may appear as two separate items on the balance sheet: *Par Value* and *Paid-in Capital in Excess of Par Value.* The total of these two items tells us the amount that has been paid by the owners for the stock. We will take a closer look at these items in Chapter 11.

USING A CLASSIFIED BALANCE SHEET

LO 4 Use a classified balance sheet to analyze a company's financial position.

As we have now seen, a classified balance sheet separates both assets and liabilities into those that are current and those that are noncurrent. This distinction is very useful in any analysis of a company's financial position.

Working Capital

Liquidity The ability of a company to pay its debts as they come due.

Working capital Current assets minus current liabilities.

Investors, bankers, and other interested readers use the balance sheet to evaluate the liquidity of a business. **Liquidity** is a relative term and deals with the ability of a company to pay its debts as they come due. As you might expect, bankers and other creditors are particularly interested in the liquidity of businesses to which they have lent money. A comparison of current assets and current liabilities is a starting point in evaluating the ability of a company to meet its obligations. **Working capital** is the difference between current assets and current liabilities at a point in time. Referring back to Exhibit 2-4, we see that the working capital for Dixon Sporting Goods on December 31, 2004, is as follows:

WORKING CAPITAL

FORMULA	FOR DIXON SPORTING GOODS
Current Assets − Current Liabilities	\$118,000 − \$59,900 = \$58,100

The management of working capital is an important task for any business. A company must continually strive for a *balance* in managing its working capital. For example, too little working capital—or in the extreme, negative working capital—may signal the inability to pay creditors on a timely basis. However, an overabundance of working capital could indicate that the company is not investing enough of its available funds in productive resources, such as new machinery and equipment.

Current Ratio

Current ratio Current assets divided by current liabilities.

Because it is an absolute dollar amount, working capital is limited in its informational value. For example, $1 million may be an inadequate amount of working capital for a large corporation but far too much for a smaller company. In addition, a certain dollar amount of working capital may have been adequate for a company earlier in its life but is inadequate now. However, a related measure of liquidity, the **current ratio,** allows us to *compare* the liquidity of companies of different sizes and of a single company over time. The ratio is computed by dividing current assets by current liabilities. Dixon Sporting Goods has a current ratio of just under 2 to 1:

CURRENT RATIO

FORMULA	FOR DIXON SPORTING GOODS
$\frac{\textbf{Current Assets}}{\textbf{Current Liabilities}}$	$\frac{\$118{,}000}{\$59{,}900} = \underline{\underline{1.97 \text{ to } 1}}$

Some analysts use a rule of thumb of 2 to 1 for the current ratio as a sign of short-term financial health. However, as is always the case, rules of thumb can be dangerous. Historically, companies in certain industries have operated quite efficiently with a current ratio of less than 2 to 1, whereas a ratio much higher than this is necessary to survive in other industries. Consider Tommy Hilfiger Corp., the popular clothing company. At the end of the fiscal year 2001, it had a current ratio of 3.27 to 1. On the other hand, companies in the telephone communication business routinely have current ratios from well under 1 to 1. Sprint's current ratio at the end of 2001 was only 0.49 to 1.

http://www.tommy.com

http://www.sprint.com

Unfortunately, neither the amount of working capital nor the current ratio tells us anything about the *composition* of current assets and current liabilities. For example, assume two companies both have total current assets equal to $100,000. Company A has cash of $10,000, accounts receivable of $50,000, and inventory of $40,000. Company B also has cash of $10,000 but accounts receivable of $20,000 and inventory of $70,000. All other things being equal, Company A is more liquid than Company B because more of its total current assets are in receivables than inventory. Receivables are only one step away from being cash, whereas inventory must be sold and then the receivable collected. Note that Dixon's inventory of $73,500 makes up a large portion of its total current assets of $118,000. An examination of the *relative* size of the various current assets for a company may reveal certain strengths and weaknesses not evident in the current ratio.

In addition to the composition of the current assets, the *frequency* with which they are "turned over" is important. For instance, how long does it take to sell an item of inventory? How long is required to collect an account receivable? Many companies could not exist with the current ratio of 0.81 reported by the McDonald's Corporation at the end of 2001. However, think about the nature of the fast-food business. The frequency of its sales and thus the numerous operating cycles within a single year mean that it can operate with a much lower current ratio than a manufacturing company, for example.

http://www.mcdonalds.com

THE INCOME STATEMENT

The income statement is used to summarize the results of operations of an entity for a *period of time.* At a minimum, all companies prepare income statements at least once a year. Companies that must report to the Securities and Exchange Commission prepare financial statements, including an income statement, every three months. Monthly income statements are usually prepared for internal use by management.

http://www.sec.gov

What Appears on the Income Statement?

From an accounting perspective, it is important to understand what transactions of an entity should appear on the income statement. In general, the income statement reports the excess of *revenue over expense,* that is, the *net income,* or in the event of an excess of *expense over revenue,* the *net loss* of the period. As a reference to the "bottom line" on an income statement, it is common to use the terms *profits* or *earnings* as synonyms for *net income.*

As discussed in Chapter 1, *revenue* is the inflow of assets resulting from the sale of products and services. It represents the dollar amount of sales of products and services for a period of time. An *expense* is the outflow of assets resulting from the sale of goods and services for a period of time. The cost of products sold, wages and salaries, and taxes are all examples of expenses.

Certain special types of revenues, called *gains,* are sometimes reported on the income statement, as are certain special types of expenses, called *losses.* For example, assume that Sanders Company holds a parcel of land for a future building site. The company paid $50,000 for the land 10 years ago. The state pays Sanders $60,000 for the property to use in a new highway project. Sanders has a special type of revenue from the condemnation of its property. It will recognize a *gain* of $10,000: the excess of the cash received from the state, $60,000, over the cost of the land, $50,000.

Format of the Income Statement

LO 5 Explain the difference between a single-step and a multiple-step income statement and prepare each type of income statement.

Different formats are used by corporations to present their results. The major choice a company makes is whether to prepare the income statement in a single-step or a multiple-step form. Both forms are generally accepted. According to the AICPA's annual survey of 600 companies, over three times as many use the multiple-step form than the single-step form. Next, we'll explain the differences between the two forms and their variations.

Single-step income statement An income statement in which all expenses are added together and subtracted from all revenues.

Single-Step Format for the Income Statement

In a **single-step income statement,** all expenses and losses are added together and then are deducted *in a single step* from all revenues and gains to arrive at net income. A single-step format for the income statement of Dixon Sporting Goods is presented in Exhibit 2-5. The primary advantage of the single-step form is its simplicity. No attempt is made to classify either revenues or expenses or to associate any of the expenses with any of the revenues.

Exhibit 2-5 Income Statement (Single-Step Format) for Dixon Sporting Goods Inc.

DIXON SPORTING GOODS INC.
INCOME STATEMENT (SINGLE-STEP FORMAT)
FOR THE YEAR ENDED DECEMBER 31, 2004

Revenues		
Sales	$357,500	
Interest	1,500	
Total revenues		$359,000
Expenses		
Cost of goods sold	$218,300	
Depreciation on store furniture and fixtures	4,200	
Advertising	13,750	
Salaries and wages for sales staff	22,000	
Depreciation on buildings and amortization of trademark	6,000	
Salaries and wages for office staff	15,000	
Insurance	3,600	
Supplies	1,050	
Interest	16,900	
Income taxes	17,200	
Total expenses		318,000
Net income		$ 41,000

In a **single-step** income statement, expenses are deducted from revenues in one step.

Multiple-step income statement An income statement that shows classifications of revenues and expenses as well as important subtotals.

Multiple-Step Format for the Income Statement The purpose of the **multiple-step income statement** is to subdivide the income statement into specific sections and provide the reader with important subtotals. This format is illustrated for Dixon Sporting Goods in Exhibit 2-6.

Exhibit 2-6 Income Statement (Multiple-Step Format) for Dixon Sporting Goods

In a **multiple-step** income statement:

- Sales and the **costs** of sales are compared. 1
- Expenses of the business are detailed.
- Isolating expenses and revenues by type is useful in analyzing a business.
- Operating income is highlighted. 2
- "Nonoperating" revenues and expenses are included here. 3
- 4

DIXON SPORTING GOODS INC.
INCOME STATEMENT (MULTIPLE-STEP FORMAT)
FOR THE YEAR ENDED DECEMBER 31, 2004

Sales		$357,500	
Cost of goods sold		218,300	
Gross profit			$139,200
Operating expenses			
Selling expenses			
Depreciation on store furniture and fixtures	$ 4,200		
Advertising	13,750		
Salaries and wages	22,000		
Total selling expenses		$ 39,950	
General and administrative expenses			
Depreciation on buildings and amortization of trademark	$ 6,000		
Salaries and wages	15,000		
Insurance	3,600		
Supplies	1,050		
Total general and administrative expenses		25,650	
Total operating expenses			65,600
Income from operations			$ 73,600
Other revenues and expenses			
Interest revenue		$ 1,500	
Interest expense		16,900	
Excess of other expenses over other revenue			15,400
Income before income taxes			$ 58,200
Income tax expense			17,200
Net income			$ 41,000

Gross profit Sales less cost of goods sold.

The multiple-step income statement for Dixon indicates three important subtotals. First, 1 cost of goods sold is deducted from sales to arrive at **gross profit:**

Gross Profit = Sales − Cost of Goods Sold

Sales	$357,500
Cost of goods sold	218,300
Gross profit	$139,200

Cost of goods sold, as the name implies, is the cost of the units of inventory sold during the year. It is logical to associate cost of goods sold with the sales revenue for the year because the latter represents the *selling price* of the inventory sold during the period.

The second important subtotal on Dixon's income statement is 2 *income from operations* of $73,600. This is found by subtracting *total operating expenses* of $65,600 from the gross profit of $139,200. Operating expenses are further subdivided between *selling expenses* and *general and administrative expenses.* For example, note that two depreciation amounts are included in operating expenses. Depreciation on store furniture and fixtures is classified as a selling expense because the store is where sales take place. On the other hand, we will assume that the buildings are offices for the administrative staff and thus depreciation on the buildings is classified as a general and administrative expense.

The third important subtotal on the income statement is **3** *income before income taxes* of $58,200. Interest revenue and interest expense, neither of which is an operating item, are included in *other revenues and expenses.* The excess of interest expense of $16,900 over interest revenue of $1,500, which equals $15,400, is subtracted from income from operations to arrive at income before income taxes. Finally, **4** *income tax expense* of $17,200 is deducted to arrive at *net income* of $41,000.

Two-Minute Review

1. *Give at least two examples of items that would appear on a multiple-step income statement but not a single-step statement.*
2. *Classify each of the following expenses as either selling or general and administrative: advertising, depreciation on office building, salespersons' commissions and office salaries.*

Answers on page 79.

Using a Multiple-Step Income Statement

LO 6 Use a multiple-step income statement to analyze a company's operations.

An important advantage of the multiple-step income statement is that it provides additional information to the reader. Although all the amounts needed to calculate certain ratios are available on a single-step statement, such calculations are easier to figure with a multiple-step statement. For example, the deduction of cost of goods sold from sales to arrive at gross profit, or *gross margin* as it is sometimes called, allows us to quickly calculate the **gross profit ratio.** The ratio of Dixon's gross profit to its sales, rounded to the nearest percent, is as follows:

Gross profit ratio Gross profit divided by sales.

GROSS PROFIT RATIO

FORMULA	FOR DIXON SPORTING GOODS
$\dfrac{\text{Gross Profit}}{\text{Sales}}$	$\dfrac{\$139{,}200}{\$357{,}500} = 39\%$

The gross profit ratio tells us that after paying for the product, for every dollar of sales, 39¢ is available to cover other expenses and earn a profit. The complement of the gross profit ratio is the ratio of cost of goods sold to sales. For Dixon, this ratio is $1 - 0.39 = 0.61$, or 61%. For every dollar of sales, Dixon spends $0.61 on the cost of the product.

From Concept to Practice 2.1

Note that Winnebago Industries' income statement does not report gross profit. However, what two items on the statement can be used to determine its gross profit? Calculate the company's gross profit ratio for 2001 and 2000. By what percentage did it go up or down between the two years?

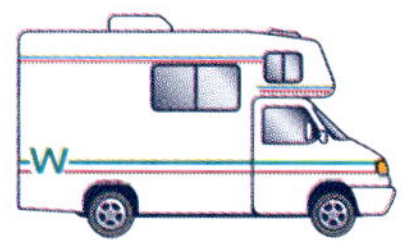

An important use of the income statement is to evaluate the *profitability* of a business. For example, a company's **profit margin** is the ratio of its net income to its sales. Some analysts refer to a company's profit margin as its *return on sales.* Dixon's profit margin is as follows:

Profit margin Net income divided by sales.

PROFIT MARGIN

FORMULA	FOR DIXON SPORTING GOODS
$\dfrac{\text{Net Income}}{\text{Sales}}$	$\dfrac{\$41{,}000}{\$357{,}500} = 11\%$

For every dollar of sales, Dixon has $0.11 in net income.

Two important factors should be kept in mind in evaluating any financial statement ratio. First, how does this year's ratio differ from ratios of prior years? For example, a decrease in the profit margin may indicate that the company is having trouble this year controlling certain costs. Second, how does the ratio compare with industry norms? For example, in some industries the profit margin is considerably lower than in many others, such as in mass merchandising (**Wal-Mart's** profit margin was only 3.3% for the year ended January 31, 2001). It is always helpful to compare key ratios, such as the profit margin, with an industry average or with the same ratio for a close competitor of the company.

http://www.walmart.com

THE STATEMENT OF RETAINED EARNINGS

LO 7 Identify the components of the statement of retained earnings and prepare the statement.

The purpose of a statement of stockholders' equity is to explain the changes in the components of owners' equity during the period. Retained earnings and capital stock are the two primary components of stockholders' equity. If there are no changes during the period in a company's capital stock, it may choose to present a statement of retained earnings instead of a statement of stockholders' equity.[9] A statement of retained earnings for Dixon Sporting Goods is shown in Exhibit 2-7.

Exhibit 2-7

Statement of Retained Earnings for Dixon Sporting Goods Inc.

DIXON SPORTING GOODS INC.
STATEMENT OF RETAINED EARNINGS
FOR THE YEAR ENDED DECEMBER 31, 2004

Retained earnings, January 1, 2004	$271,500
Add: Net income for 2004	41,000
	$312,500
Less: Dividends declared and paid in 2004	(25,000)
Retained earnings, December 31, 2004	$287,500

The statement of retained earnings provides an important link between the income statement and the balance sheet. Dixon's net income of $41,000, as detailed on the income statement, is an *addition* to retained earnings. Note that the dividends declared and paid of $25,000 do not appear on the income statement because they are a payout, or *distribution,* of net income to stockholders rather than one of the expenses deducted to arrive at net income. Accordingly, they appear as a direct deduction on the statement of retained earnings. The beginning balance in retained earnings is carried forward from last year's statement of retained earnings.

THE STATEMENT OF CASH FLOWS

LO 8 Identify the components of the statement of cash flows and prepare the statement.

All publicly held corporations are required to present a statement of cash flows in their annual reports. The purpose of the statement is to summarize the cash flow effects of a company's operating, investing, and financing activities for the period.

The Cash Flow Statement for Dixon Sporting Goods

The statement for Dixon Sporting Goods is shown in Exhibit 2-8. The statement consists of three categories: operating activities, investing activities, and financing activities. Each of these three categories can result in a net inflow of cash or a net outflow of cash.

[9]According to the AICPA's annual survey, most corporations (over 96%) present a statement of stockholders' equity. A separate statement of retained earnings, or a combined statement of income and retained earnings, is used by a small minority of companies.

Exhibit 2-8 Statement of Cash Flows for Dixon Sporting Goods Inc.

DIXON SPORTING GOODS INC.
STATEMENT OF CASH FLOWS
FOR THE YEAR ENDED DECEMBER 31, 2004

CASH FLOWS FROM OPERATING ACTIVITIES		
Cash collected from customers	$362,500	
Cash collected in interest	1,500	
Total cash collections		$364,000
Cash payments for:		
Inventory	$217,200	
Insurance	4,800	
Store supplies	850	
Salaries and wages	38,500	
Income taxes	15,900	
Interest	16,900	
Advertising	13,750	
Total cash payments		307,900
Net cash provided by operating activities		$ 56,100
CASH FLOWS FROM INVESTING ACTIVITIES		
Purchase of land for future office site		(150,000)
CASH FLOWS FROM FINANCING ACTIVITIES		
Dividends declared and paid	$ (25,000)	
Proceeds from issuance of long-term note	120,000	
Net cash provided by financing activities		95,000
Net increase in cash		$ 1,100
Cash at beginning of year		3,900
Cash at end of year		$ 5,000

1 Operating activities involve the purchase and sale of products or services.

2 Investing activities involve the acquisition and sale of long-term assets.

3 Financing activities involve the issuance and repayment of long-term liabilities and stock.

Dixon's *operating activities* generated $56,100 of cash during the period. Operating activities 1 concern the purchase and sale of a product, in this case the acquisition of sporting goods from distributors and the subsequent sale of those goods. As we can readily see, Dixon had one major source of cash, the collection from its customers of $362,500. Similarly, Dixon's largest use of cash was the $217,200 it paid for inventory. In Chapter 12, we will discuss the statement of cash flows in detail and the preparation of this section of the statement.

Financing and investing activities were described in "Getting Started." *Investing activities* 2 involve the acquisition and sale of long-term or noncurrent assets, such as long-term investments, property, plant, and equipment, and intangible assets. *Financing activities* 3 result from the issuance and repayment, or retirement, of long-term liabilities and capital stock. The one investing activity on Dixon's statement of cash flows, the purchase of land for a future office site, required the use of cash and thus is shown as a net outflow of $150,000. Dixon had two financing activities: dividends of $25,000 required the use of cash, and the issuance of a long-term note generated cash of $120,000. The balance in cash on the bottom of the statement of $5,000 must agree with the balance for this item as shown on the balance sheet in Exhibit 2-4.

THE FINANCIAL STATEMENTS FOR GATEWAY

LO 9 Read and use the financial statements and other elements in the annual report of a publicly held company.

The financial statements for our hypothetical company, Dixon Sporting Goods Inc., introduced the major categories on each of the statements. We now turn to the financial statements of an actual company, Gateway. These statements are more complex and require additional analysis and a better understanding of accounting to fully appreciate them. However, we will concentrate on certain elements of the statements. At this stage in your study, look for the similarities rather than the differences between these statements and those of Dixon.

Gateway was founded by Ted Waitt in 1985 in an empty farmhouse near Sioux City, Iowa. What began as a mail-order business has grown to the point that sales in 2000 reached $9.6 billion, although they dropped to about $6.1 billion in 2001. Early on, Gateway adopted a cow as its mascot and began to ship all its products in boxes that looked like the markings on a Holstein cow.[10]

As we will see later, the notes to a set of financial statements give the reader a variety of information about a company. Like the statements of many other companies, Gateway's financials include a note that describes its business:

> Gateway, Inc. (the "Company") is a direct marketer of personal computers ("PCs") and PC-related products and services. The Company develops, manufactures, markets and supports a broad line of desktop and portable PCs, servers, and PC-related products used by individuals, families, businesses, government agencies and educational institutions. The Company also offers and supports PC-related services including training, financing, and Internet service.[11]

Gateway's Balance Sheet

The balance sheets for Gateway at the end of each of two years are shown in Exhibit 2-9. Like most other companies, Gateway chose an accounting or fiscal year that corresponds to the calendar, that is, beginning on January 1 and ending on December 31. However, some companies choose a fiscal year that ends at a point when sales are at their lowest in the annual cycle. For example, Wal-Mart ends its fiscal year on January 31, after the busy holiday season.

Gateway releases what are called *consolidated financial statements,* which reflect the position and results of all operations that are controlled by a single entity. Like most other large corporations, Gateway owns other companies. Often these companies are legally separate and are called *subsidiaries.* How a company accounts for its investment in a subsidiary is covered in advanced accounting courses.

Gateway presents comparative balance sheets to indicate its financial position at the end of each of the last two years. As a minimum standard, the Securities and Exchange Commission requires that the annual report include balance sheets as of the two most recent years and income statements for each of the three most recent years. Note that all amounts on the balance sheet are stated in thousands of dollars. This type of rounding is a common practice in the financial statements of large corporations and is justified under the materiality concept. Knowing the exact dollar amount of each asset would not change a decision made by an investor.

The presentation of comparative balance sheets allows the reader to make comparisons between years. For example, Gateway's *working capital* increased significantly during 2001:

WORKING CAPITAL

	DECEMBER 31, 2000	DECEMBER 31, 2001
Current Assets − Current Liabilities	$2,267,060 − $1,659,135 = $607,925	$2,122,924 − $1,146,028 = $976,896

Gateway's *current ratio* at each of the two dates follows:

CURRENT RATIO

	DECEMBER 31, 2000	DECEMBER 31, 2001
Current Assets / Current Liabilities	$2,267,060 / $1,659,135 = 1.37 to 1	$2,122,924 / $1,146,028 = 1.85 to 1

[10] *International Directory of Company Histories,* vol. 10 (St. James Press, 1995), p. 308.
[11] *Gateway 2001 Annual Report,* p. 31.

Exhibit 2-9 Comparative Balance Sheets for Gateway

GATEWAY, INC.

CONSOLIDATED BALANCE SHEETS
DECEMBER 31, 2001 AND 2000
(in thousands, except per share amounts)

	2001	2000
ASSETS		
Current assets:		
Cash and cash equivalents	$ 730,999	$ 483,997
Marketable securities	435,055	130,073
Accounts receivable, net	219,974	544,755
Inventory	120,270	315,069
Other, net	616,626	793,166
Total current assets	2,122,924	2,267,060
Property, plant and equipment, net	608,429	897,414
Intangibles, net	36,304	165,914
Other assets, net	219,200	850,257
	$2,986,857	$4,180,645
LIABILITIES AND EQUITY		
Current liabilities:		
Accounts payable	$ 341,122	$ 785,345
Accrued liabilities	468,609	556,323
Accrued royalties	135,698	138,446
Other current liabilities	200,599	179,021
Total current liabilities	1,146,028	1,659,135
Other long-term liabilities	82,636	141,171
Total liabilities	1,228,664	1,800,306
Commitments and contingencies (Note 5)		
Series C redeemable convertible preferred stock, $.01 par value, $200,000 liquidation value, 50 shares authorized, issued and outstanding in 2001	193,109	—
Stockholders' equity:		
Series A convertible preferred stock, $.01 par value, $200,000 liquidation value, 50 shares authorized, issued and outstanding in 2001	200,000	—
Preferred stock, $.01 par value, 4,900 shares authorized; none issued and outstanding	—	—
Class A common stock, nonvoting, $.01 par value, 1,000 shares authorized; none issued and outstanding	—	—
Common stock, $.01 par value, 1,000,000 shares authorized; 323,973 shares and 323,955 shares issued in 2001 and 2000, respectively	3,239	3,239
Additional paid-in capital	731,623	741,646
Common stock in treasury, at cost, 552 shares in 2000	—	(21,948)
Retained earnings	616,420	1,650,335
Accumulated other comprehensive income	13,802	7,067
Total stockholders' equity	1,565,084	2,380,339
	$2,986,857	$4,180,645

Use these to find:
- Working capital
- Current ratio

The accompanying notes are an integral part of the consolidated financial statements.

Note that both the amount of working capital and the current ratio increased between 2000 and 2001. Both cash and cash equivalents and marketable securities increased significantly, while accounts receivable and inventory experienced significant declines. Finally, note on the liability side of the balance sheet the sizable decline in accounts payable.

Gateway's Income Statement

We have examined two basic formats for the income statement: the single-step format and the multiple-step format. In practice, numerous variations on these two basic formats exist, depending to a large extent on the nature of a company's business. For example, the multiple-step form, with its presentation of gross profit, is not used by service businesses because they do not sell a product. (Remember that gross profit is sales less cost of goods sold.) As we will see for Gateway, the form of the income statement is a reflection of a company's operations.

Multiple-step income statements for Gateway for a three-year period are presented in Exhibit 2-10. Note the significant decrease in Gateway's *gross profit ratio* from 2000 to 2001:

GROSS PROFIT RATIO

	2000	2001
$\frac{\text{Gross Profit}}{\text{Net Sales}}$	$\frac{\$2,058,994}{\$9,600,600} = 21\%$	$\frac{\$838,192}{\$6,079,524} = 14\%$

Both Gateway's management and its stockholders should be concerned with this decline in both the amount of gross profit and the gross profit ratio. Also, note the inclusion of net income per share information at the bottom of the statement. The per share information helps users of the statement in various ways and is discussed in more detail in Chapter 13.

From Concept to Practice 2.2

Reading Gateway's Income Statement

Compute Gateway's profit margin for the past two years. Did it go up or down from the prior year to the current year?

Other Elements of an Annual Report

No two annual reports look the same. The appearance of an annual report depends not only on the size of a company but also on the budget devoted to the preparation of the report. Some companies publish "bare-bones" annual reports, whereas others issue a glossy report complete with pictures of company products and employees. In recent years, many companies, as a cost-cutting measure, have scaled back the amount spent on the annual report. The creativity in annual reports varies as well. For example, a recent annual report for Reader's Digest gave the appearance in size of the well-recognized publication itself.

http://www.rd.com

Privately held companies tend to distribute only financial statements, without the additional information normally included in the annual reports of public companies. For the annual reports of public companies, however, certain basic elements are considered standard. A letter to the stockholders from either the president or the chairman of the board of directors appears in the first few pages of most annual reports. A section describing the company's products and markets is usually included. At the heart of any annual report is the financial report or review, which consists of the financial statements accompanied by notes to explain various items on the statements. We will now consider these other elements as presented in the 2001 annual report of Gateway.

Exhibit 2-10 Consolidated Income Statements for Gateway

GATEWAY, INC.

CONSOLIDATED STATEMENTS OF OPERATIONS
FOR THE YEARS ENDED DECEMBER 31, 2001, 2000 AND 1999
(in thousands, except per share amounts)

	2001	2000	1999
Net sales	$ 6,079,524	$9,600,600	$8,964,900
Cost of goods sold	5,241,332	7,541,606	7,127,678
Gross profit	838,192	2,058,994	1,837,222
Selling, general and administrative expenses	2,022,122	1,547,701	1,241,552
Operating income (loss)	(1,183,930)	511,293	595,670
Other income (loss), net	(106,383)	(102,693)	67,809
Income (loss) before income taxes, extraordinary item and cumulative effect of change in accounting principle	(1,290,313)	408,600	663,479
Provision (benefit) for income taxes	(275,908)	155,266	235,535
Income (loss) before extraordinary item and cumulative effect of change in accounting principle	(1,014,405)	253,334	427,944
Extraordinary gain on early extinguishment of debt, net of tax	4,341	—	—
Cumulative effect of change in accounting principle, net of tax	(23,851)	(11,851)	—
Net income (loss)	$(1,033,915)	$ 241,483	$ 427,944
Basic net income (loss) per share:			
Income (loss) per share before extraordinary item and cumulative effect of change in accounting principle	$ (3.14)	$ 0.79	$ 1.36
Extraordinary item	0.01	—	—
Cumulative effect of change in accounting principle	(0.07)	(0.04)	—
Net income (loss) per basic share	$ (3.20)	$ 0.75	$ 1.36
Diluted net income (loss) per share:			
Income (loss) per share before extraordinary item and cumulative effect of change in accounting principle	$ (3.14)	$ 0.76	$ 1.32
Extraordinary item	0.01	—	—
Cumulative effect of change in accounting principle	(0.07)	(0.03)	—
Net income (loss) per diluted share	$ (3.20)	$ 0.73	$ 1.32
Weighted average shares outstanding:			
Basic	323,289	321,742	313,974
Diluted	323,289	331,320	324,421

The accompanying notes are an integral part of the consolidated financial statements.

Use these to find:
• Gross profit ratio

Report of Independent Accountants As you see in Exhibit 2-11, Gateway is audited by PricewaterhouseCoopers LLP, one of the largest international accounting firms. Two key phrases should be noted in the first sentence of the independent accountants' report: *in our opinion* and *presents fairly.* The report indicates that responsibility for the statements rests with Gateway and that the auditors' job is to *express an opinion* on the statements, based on certain tests. It would be impossible for an auditing firm to spend the time or money to retrace and verify every single transaction entered

http://www.pwcglobal.com

Business Strategy

Focused on Growth

As pointed out in the chapter opener, Gateway found 2001 to be the most challenging year in its relatively short existence. Sales dropped by over one-third from their level in the previous year. To counteract what the company sees as a maturing of the demand for computers and an economic downturn, Gateway laid out in its 2001 annual report a plan that is squarely focused on growth. As Ted Waitt, the founder as well as current president and CEO, proclaimed, "For 2002, it's grow time, and here's our plan."

Waitt's growth strategy consists of two distinct parts. First, Gateway plans to return to its roots, focusing clearly on its core PC business. Waitt firmly believes that the company must reclaim its leadership position in PCs and plans to do this with a combination of value, price, quality, and service. Key to this part of the strategy is an aggressive new pricing strategy. Second, Gateway is well aware of the tremendous potential for digital solutions and offerings and plans to deliver these in the form of products that incorporate digital photography, music, and video.

The first quarter report of 2002 showed some encouraging signs. Although net sales declined considerably from the comparable period in 2001, the gross profit percentage showed signs of improvement, increasing by almost three percentage points to 12.6%. Also encouraging was a 4% decline in the ratio of selling, general, and administrative expenses to net sales. While improvements in the gross profit ratio and declines in the ratio of expenses to sales will help the "bottom line," Gateway will need to stay focused on improvements to its top line—sales—the lifeblood of all businesses.

Sources: Gateway's 2001 annual report and Web site.

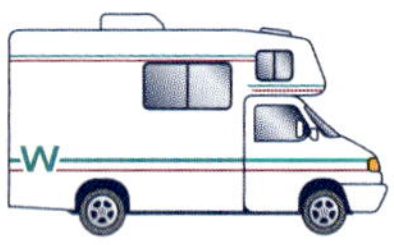

into during the year by Gateway. Instead, the auditing firm performs various tests of the accounting records to be able to assure itself that the statements are free of *material misstatement.* Auditors do not "certify" the total accuracy of a set of financial statements but render an opinion as to the reasonableness of those statements. Finally, note that this format for the auditors' report differs from the one for **Winnebago Industries** presented in Chapter 1. However, both formats contain the same basic information.

The Ethical Responsibility of Management and the Auditors The management of a company and its auditors share a common purpose: to protect the interests of stockholders. In large corporations, the stockholders are normally removed from the daily affairs of the business. The need for a professional management team to run the business is a practical necessity, as is the need for a periodic audit of the company's records. Because stockholders cannot run the business themselves, they need assurances that the business is being operated effectively and efficiently and that the financial statements presented by management are a fair representation of the company's operations and financial position. The management and the auditors have a very important ethical responsibility to their constituents, the stockholders of the company.

Management Discussion and Analysis Preceding the financial statements is a section of Gateway's annual report titled "Management's Discussion and Analysis of Financial Condition and Results of Operations." This report gives management the opportunity to discuss the financial statements and provide the stockholders with explanations for certain amounts reported in the statements. For example, management explains the decrease in sales as follows:

> The Company's net sales were adversely impacted by approximately $200 million per quarter related to a number of strategic actions taken beginning in the second quarter of 2001 to discontinue certain nonprofitable revenue streams, which included, among other things, the closure of certain retail locations, restructuring international markets, discontinuing lower-quality consumer lending, modifying its ISP[12] business model, and

[12]Internet service provider (ISP).

Exhibit 2-11 Report of Independent Accountants for Gateway

Report of Independent Accountants

To the Stockholders and Board of Directors of Gateway, Inc.

In our opinion, the consolidated financial statements listed in the accompanying index present fairly, in all material respects, the financial position of Gateway, Inc. and its subsidiaries at December 31, 2001 and 2000, and the results of their operations and their cash flows for each of the three years in the period ended December 31, 2001, in conformity with accounting principles generally accepted in the United States of America. In addition, in our opinion, the financial statement schedule listed in the accompanying index presents fairly, in all material respects, the information set forth therein when read in conjunction with the related consolidated financial statements. These financial statements and the financial statement schedule are the responsibility of the Company's management; our responsibility is to express an opinion on these financial statements and financial statement schedule based on our audits. We conducted our audits of these statements in accordance with auditing standards generally accepted in the United States of America, which require that we plan and perform the audit to obtain reasonable assurance about whether the financial statements are free of material misstatement. An audit includes examining, on a test basis, evidence supporting amounts and disclosures in the financial statements, assessing the accounting principles used and significant estimates made by management, and evaluating the overall financial statement presentation. We believe that our audits provide a reasonable basis for our opinion.

As discussed in Note 1 to the Consolidated Financial Statements, effective January 1, 2001, the Company adopted Statement of Financial Accounting Standards No. 133, Accounting for Derivative Instruments and Hedging Activities. As discussed in Note 1 to the Consolidated Financial Statements, effective January 1, 2000, the Company changed its revenue recognition policy relating to product shipments.

PricewaterhouseCoopers LLP

PricewaterhouseCoopers LLP

San Diego, California
January 24, 2002, except for the second paragraph of Note 5—Contingencies, as to which the date is February 1, 2002.

exiting certain indirect sales activities. During the third quarter of 2001, the Company exited substantially all of its Company-owned international operations. International net sales were 9% of total Company net sales in 2001.[13]

Notes to Consolidated Financial Statements The sentence "The accompanying notes are an integral part of the consolidated financial statements" appears at the bottom of each of Gateway's four financial statements. These comments, or *notes*, as they are commonly called, are necessary to satisfy the need for *full disclosure* of all the facts relevant to a company's results and financial position. The first note in all annual reports is a summary of *significant accounting policies*. A company's policies for valuing inventories, depreciating assets, and recognizing revenue are among the important items contained in this note. For example, Gateway describes its policy for recognizing advertising costs as follows: "Advertising costs are charged to expense as incurred. Advertising expenses were $239.6 million, $328.0 million, and $256.8 million for 2001, 2000, and 1999, respectively."[14] In addition to the summary of significant accounting policies, other notes discuss such topics as income taxes and financing arrangements.

---

[13]*Gateway 2001 Annual Report.*
[14]*Gateway 2001 Annual Report,* p. 33.

This completes our discussion of the makeup of the annual report. By now you should appreciate the flexibility that companies have in assembling the report, aside from the need to follow generally accepted accounting principles in preparing the statements. The accounting standards followed in preparing the statements, as well as the appearance of the annual report itself, differ in other countries. As has been noted elsewhere, although many corporations operate internationally, accounting principles are far from being standardized.

Ratios for Decision Making

The purpose of this presentation, which will appear in chapters where ratios and other key calculations are introduced, is to briefly review the core reason for use of the ratio(s) for decision making.

Reporting and Analyzing Financial Statement Information Related to a Company's Liquidity and Profitability In order to continue operating, a company must be able to pay its bills when they come due. Checking the working capital information on the balance sheet to make sure there are enough current assets to cover the current liabilities is a simple way to get an idea about the company's liquidity. Then, calculating the current ratio provides decision makers with information about how adequate that coverage is.

The income statement provides important profitability information. The proportion of each sales dollar available after covering the cost of the products sold gives decision makers a better idea of how well the company is operating. The greater the gross profit percentage, the greater the amount of sales dollars available to cover costs and to provide a profit. Also, knowing how the profit margin (or return on sales) has changed from year to year helps decision makers assess the direction the company is going and use that information to help predict future profitability.

In this chapter, you have learned about three new ratios and another calculation that are used for decision making. These four items and the sources of information needed for their analysis are as follows:

Balance Sheet
Current Assets
Current Liabilities

Income Statement
Sales
Gross Profit
Net Income

$$\text{Working Capital} = \text{Current Assets} - \text{Current Liabilities}$$

$$\text{Current Ratio} = \frac{\text{Current Assets}}{\text{Current Liabilities}}$$

$$\text{Gross Profit Ratio} = \frac{\text{Gross Profit}}{\text{Sales}}$$

$$\text{Profit Margin} = \frac{\text{Net Income}}{\text{Sales}}$$

Impact on the Financial Reports

Impact on the Financial Reports

BALANCE SHEET	INCOME STATEMENT
Current Assets *Noncurrent Assets* *Current Liabilities* *Noncurrent Liabilities* *Stockholders' Equity*	*Revenues* *Expenses* *Other*

STATEMENT OF STOCKHOLDERS' EQUITY	STATEMENT OF CASH FLOWS	NOTES
Contributed Capital *Retained Earnings*	*Operating Activities* *Investing Activities* *Financing Activities* *Noncash Transactions*	*Summary of Significant Accounting Policies*

The purpose of this presentation is to show, in one place, the impact of the chapter's topical coverage on one or more of the four financial statements and the notes. This also reinforces how interconnected these reports are and shows where decision makers should expect to see impact and disclosure. The primary sections of each statement are as illustrated.

Answers to the Two-Minute Reviews

Two-Minute Review on Page 64

1. *Cash, accounts receivable, inventory, short-term investments, and prepaid expenses.*
2. *Investments; property, plant, and equipment; and intangibles.*

Two-Minute Review on Page 69

1. *Gross profit, income from operations and income before income taxes.*
2. *Advertising: selling; Depreciation on office building: general and administrative; Salespersons' commissions: selling; Office salaries: general and administrative*

Warmup Exercises

Warmup Exercise 2-1 ***Identifying Ratios*** **LO 4, 6**

State the equation for each of the following ratios:

1. Current ratio
2. Gross profit ratio
3. Profit margin

Key to the Solution

Review the various ratios as discussed in the chapter.

Warmup Exercise 2-2 ***Calculating Ratios*** **LO 6**

Bridger reported net income of $150,000, sales of $1,000,000 and cost of goods sold of $800,000.

Required

Compute each of the following ratios for Bridger:

1. Gross profit ratio
2. Profit margin

Key to the Solution

Recall the equation for each of these ratios as presented in the chapter.

Warmup Exercise 2-3 ***Determining Liquidity*** **LO 4**

Big has current assets of $500,000 and current liabilities of $400,000. Small reports current assets of $80,000 and current liabilities of $20,000.

Required

Which company is more liquid? Why?

Key to the Solution

Calculate the current ratio for each company and compare them.

Solutions to Warmup Exercises

Warmup Exercise 2-1

1. $\text{Current ratio} = \dfrac{\text{Current Assets}}{\text{Current Liabilities}}$

2. $\text{Gross profit ratio} = \dfrac{\text{Gross Profit}}{\text{Sales}}$

3. $\text{Profit margin} = \dfrac{\text{Net income}}{\text{Sales}}$

Warmup Exercise 2-2

1. $\dfrac{\$1{,}000{,}000 - \$800{,}000}{\$1{,}000{,}000} = \dfrac{\$200{,}000}{\$1{,}000{,}000} = \underline{\underline{20\%}}$

2. $\dfrac{\$150{,}000}{\$1{,}000{,}000} = \underline{\underline{15\%}}$

Warmup Exercise 2-3

Small Company appears on the surface to be more liquid. Its current ratio of $80,000/$20,000, or 4 to 1, is significantly higher than Big's current ratio of $500,000/$400,000, or 1.25 to 1.

The following review problem will give you the opportunity to apply what you have learned by preparing both an income statement and a balance sheet.

Review Problem

WebTUTOR™ Advantage

Shown below, in alphabetical order, are items taken from the records of Grizzly Inc., a chain of outdoor recreational stores in the Northwest. Use the items to prepare two statements. First, prepare an income statement for the year ended December 31, 2004. The income statement should be in multiple-step form. Second, prepare a classified balance sheet at December 31, 2004. All amounts are in thousands of dollars.

Accounts payable	$ 6,500
Accounts receivable	8,200
Accumulated depreciation—buildings	25,000
Accumulated depreciation—furniture and fixtures	15,000
Advertising expense	3,100
Buildings	80,000
Capital stock, $1 par, 10,000 shares issued and outstanding	10,000
Cash	2,400
Commissions expense	8,600
Cost of goods sold	110,000
Depreciation on buildings	2,500
Depreciation on furniture and fixtures	1,200
Furniture and fixtures	68,000
Income taxes payable	2,200

Income tax expense	$ 13,000
Insurance expense	2,000
Interest expense	12,000
Interest payable	1,000
Interest revenue	2,000
Land	100,000
Long-term notes payable, due December 31, 2012	120,000
Merchandise inventories	6,000
Office supplies	900
Paid-in capital in excess of par value	40,000
Prepaid rent	3,000
Rent expense for salespersons' autos	9,000
Retained earnings	48,800
Salaries and wages for office staff	11,000
Sales revenue	190,000

Solution to Review Problem

1. Multiple-step income statement:

GRIZZLY INC.
INCOME STATEMENT
FOR THE YEAR ENDED DECEMBER 31, 2004
(IN THOUSANDS OF DOLLARS)

Sales revenue		$190,000	
Cost of goods sold		110,000	
Gross profit			$ 80,000
Operating expenses:			
Selling expenses:			
Advertising expense	$ 3,100		
Depreciation on furniture and fixtures	1,200		
Rent expense for salespersons' autos	9,000		
Commissions expense	8,600		
Total selling expenses		$ 21,900	
General and administrative expenses:			
Depreciation on buildings	$ 2,500		
Insurance expense	2,000		
Salaries and wages for office staff	11,000		
Total general and administrative expenses		15,500	
Total operating expenses			37,400
Income from operations			$ 42,600
Other revenues and expenses:			
Interest revenue		$ 2,000	
Interest expense		12,000	
Excess of other expenses over other revenue			10,000
Income before income taxes			$ 32,600
Income tax expense			13,000
Net income			$ 19,600

2. Classified balance sheet:

GRIZZLY INC.
BALANCE SHEET
AT DECEMBER 31, 2004
(IN THOUSANDS OF DOLLARS)

Assets

Current assets:		
Cash	$ 2,400	
Accounts receivable	8,200	
Merchandise inventories	6,000	
Office supplies	900	
Prepaid rent	3,000	
Total current assets		$ 20,500

(continued)

Property, plant, and equipment:			
Land		$100,000	
Buildings	$ 80,000		
Less: Accumulated depreciation	25,000	55,000	
Furniture and fixtures	$ 68,000		
Less: Accumulated depreciation	15,000	53,000	
Total property, plant, and equipment			208,000
Total assets			$228,500
Liabilities			
Current liabilities:			
Accounts payable		$ 6,500	
Income taxes payable		2,200	
Interest payable		1,000	
Total current liabilities			$ 9,700
Long-term notes payable, due December 31, 2012			120,000
Total liabilities			$129,700
Stockholders' Equity			
Contributed capital:			
Capital stock, $1 par, 10,000 shares issued and outstanding		$ 10,000	
Paid-in capital in excess of par value		40,000	
Total contributed capital		$ 50,000	
Retained earnings		48,800	
Total stockholders' equity			98,800
Total liabilities and stockholders' equity			$228,500

Chapter Highlights

1. **LO 1** The primary objective of financial reporting is to provide information that is useful in making investment, credit, and similar decisions.
2. **LO 1** Investors and creditors are ultimately interested in their own prospective cash receipts from dividends or interest and the proceeds from the sale, redemption, or maturity of securities or loans. Because these expected cash flows are related to the expected cash flows to the company, its cash flows are of interest to investors and creditors. The entity's economic resources, claims to them, and the effects of transactions that change resources and claims to those resources are also of interest.
3. **LO 2** Financial information should be understandable to those who are willing to spend the time to understand it. To be useful, the information should be relevant and reliable. Relevant information has the capacity to make a difference in a decision. Reliable information can be depended on to represent the economic events that it purports to represent.
4. **LO 2** *Comparability* is the quality that allows for comparisons to be made between two or more companies, whereas *consistency* is the quality that allows for comparisons to be made within a single company from one period to the next. These two qualities of useful accounting information are aided by full disclosure—in the notes to the financial statements—of all relevant information.
5. **LO 3** The operating cycle depends to a large extent on the nature of a company's business. For a retailer, it encompasses the period of time from the investment of cash in inventory to the collection of any account receivable from sale of the product. The operating cycle for a manufacturer is expanded to include the period of time required to convert raw materials into finished products.
6. **LO 3** Current assets will be realized in cash or sold or consumed during the operating cycle or within one year if the cycle is shorter than one year. Because most businesses have numerous operating cycles within a year, the cutoff for classification as a current asset is usually one year. Cash, accounts receivable, inventory, and prepaid expenses are all examples of current assets.
7. **LO 3** The definition of *current liability* is related to that of *current asset.* A current liability is an obligation that will be satisfied within the operating cycle or within one year if the cycle is shorter than one year. Many liabilities are satisfied by making a cash payment. However, some obligations are settled by rendering a service.
8. **LO 4** A classified balance sheet is helpful in evaluating the liquidity of a business. Working capital, the difference between current assets and current liabilities, indicates the buffer of protection for creditors. The current ratio, current assets divided by current liabilities, provides the reader with a relative measure of liquidity.
9. **LO 5, 6** All expenses are added together and subtracted from all revenues in a single-step income statement. The multiple-step income statement provides the reader with classifications of revenues and expenses as well as with important subtotals. Cost of goods sold is subtracted from sales revenue on a

multiple-step statement, with the result reported as gross profit. Profitability analysis includes such measures as the gross profit ratio (the ratio of gross profit to sales) and the profit margin (the ratio of net income to sales).

10. **LO 7, 8** If there are no changes in the capital stock accounts, some companies present a statement of retained earnings or a combined statement of income and retained earnings in lieu of a statement of stockholders' equity. The statement of cash flows summarizes the operating, investing, and financing activities of an entity for the period.

11. **LO 9** No two annual reports are the same. However, certain basic elements are included in most of them. In addition to the financial statements, annual reports include, among other items, the independent accountants' report, management's discussion of the amounts appearing in the statements, and notes to the statements.

http://

Technology and other resources for your success

http://porter.swlearning.com

If you need additional help, visit the text's Web site. Also, see pages xv–xvii in this text's preface for a description of available technology and other resources. If your instructor is using PERSONAL Trainer in this course, you may complete, on line, the assignments identified by PT.

Key Terms Quiz

Read each definition below and then write the number of that definition in the blank beside the appropriate term it defines. The quiz solutions appear at the end of the chapter.

_____ Understandability
_____ Relevance
_____ Reliability
_____ Comparability
_____ Depreciation
_____ Consistency
_____ Materiality
_____ Conservatism
_____ Operating cycle
_____ Current asset
_____ Current liability
_____ Liquidity
_____ Working capital
_____ Current ratio
_____ Single-step income statement
_____ Multiple-step income statement
_____ Gross profit
_____ Gross profit ratio
_____ Profit margin

1. An income statement in which all expenses are added together and subtracted from all revenues.
2. The magnitude of an omission or misstatement in accounting information that will affect the judgment of someone relying on the information.
3. The capacity of information to make a difference in a decision.
4. An income statement that provides the reader with classifications of revenues and expenses as well as with important subtotals.
5. The practice of using the least optimistic estimate when two estimates of amounts are about equally likely.
6. The quality of accounting information that makes it comprehensible to those willing to spend the necessary time.
7. Gross profit divided by sales.
8. Current assets divided by current liabilities.
9. The quality of accounting information that makes it dependable in representing the events that it purports to represent.
10. An obligation that will be satisfied within the next operating cycle or within one year if the cycle is shorter than one year.
11. The period of time between the purchase of inventory and the collection of any receivable from the sale of the inventory.
12. Current assets minus current liabilities.
13. Net income divided by sales.
14. The quality of accounting information that allows a user to analyze two or more companies and look for similarities and differences.
15. An asset that is expected to be realized in cash or sold or consumed during the operating cycle or within one year if the cycle is shorter than one year.
16. The ability of a company to pay its debts as they come due.
17. The quality of accounting information that allows a user to compare two or more accounting periods for a single company.
18. Sales less cost of goods sold.
19. The allocation of the cost of a tangible, long-term asset over its useful life.

Answers on p. 100.

Alternate Terms

Balance sheet Statement of financial position or condition

Capital stock Contributed capital

Cost of goods sold Cost of sales

Gross profit Gross margin

Income statement Statement of income

Income tax expense Provision for income taxes

Long-term assets Noncurrent assets

Long-term liability Long-term debt

Net income Profits or earnings

Report of independent accountants Auditors' report

Retained earnings Earned capital

Stockholders' equity Shareholders' equity

Questions

1. How would you evaluate the following statement: "The cash flows to a company are irrelevant to an investor; all the investor cares about is the potential for receiving dividends on the investment"?
2. A key characteristic of useful financial information is understandability. How does this qualitative characteristic relate to the background of the user of the information?
3. What does *relevance* mean with regard to the use of accounting information?
4. What is the qualitative characteristic of comparability, and why is it important in preparing financial statements?
5. What is the difference between comparability and consistency as they relate to the use of accounting information?
6. How does the concept of materiality relate to the size of a company?
7. How does the operating cycle of a retailer differ from that of a service company?
8. How does the concept of the operating cycle relate to the definition of a current asset?
9. What are two examples of the way a company's intent in using an asset affects classification of the asset on the balance sheet?
10. How would you evaluate the following statement: "A note payable with an original maturity of five years will be classified on the balance sheet as a long-term liability until it matures"?
11. How do the two basic forms of owners' equity items for a corporation—capital stock and retained earnings—differ?
12. What are the limitations of working capital as a measure of the liquidity of a business as opposed to the current ratio?
13. What is meant by a company's capital structure?
14. What is the major weakness of the single-step form for the income statement?
15. Why might a company's gross profit ratio increase from one year to the next but its profit margin ratio decrease?
16. How does a statement of retained earnings act as a link between an income statement and a balance sheet?
17. In auditing the financial statements of a company, does the auditor *certify* that the statements are totally accurate and without errors of any size or variety?
18. What is the first note in the annual report of all publicly held companies, and what is its purpose?

Exercises

Exercise 2-1 ***Characteristics of Useful Accounting Information*** **LO 2**

Fill in the blank with the qualitative characteristic for each of the following descriptions:

______________ 1. Information that users can depend on to represent the events that it purports to represent

______________ 2. Information that has the capacity to make a difference in a decision

______________ 3. Information that is valid, that indicates an agreement between the underlying data and the events represented

______________ 4. Information that allows for comparisons to be made from one accounting period to the next

______________ 5. Information that is free from error

______________ 6. Information that is meaningful to those who are willing to learn to use it properly

______________ 7. Information that is not slanted to portray a company's position any better or worse than the circumstances warrant

______________ 8. Information that allows for comparisons to be made between or among companies

Exercise 2-2 ***Classification of Assets and Liabilities*** **LO 3**

Indicate the appropriate classification of each of the following as a current asset (CA), noncurrent asset (NCA), current liability (CL), or long-term liability (LTL):

________ **1.** Inventory
________ **2.** Accounts payable
________ **3.** Cash
________ **4.** Patents
________ **5.** Notes payable, due in six months
________ **6.** Taxes payable
________ **7.** Prepaid rent (for the next nine months)
________ **8.** Bonds payable, due in 10 years
________ **9.** Machinery

Exercise 2-3 ***Selling Expenses and General and Administrative Expenses*** **LO 5**

Operating expenses are subdivided between selling expenses and general and administrative expenses when a multiple-step income statement is prepared. From the following list, identify each item as a selling expense (S) or general and administrative expense (G&A):

________ **1.** Advertising expense
________ **2.** Depreciation expense—store furniture and fixtures
________ **3.** Office rent expense
________ **4.** Office salaries expense
________ **5.** Store rent expense
________ **6.** Store salaries expense
________ **7.** Insurance expense
________ **8.** Supplies expense
________ **9.** Utilities expense

Exercise 2-4 ***Missing Income Statement Amounts*** **LO 5**

For each of the following independent cases, fill in the blank with the appropriate dollar amount:

	Sara's Coffee Shop	Amy's Deli	Jane's Bagels
Net sales	$35,000	$ ______	$78,000
Cost of goods sold	______	45,000	______
Gross profit	7,000	18,000	______
Selling expenses	3,000	______	9,000
General and administrative expenses	1,500	2,800	______
Total operating expenses	______	8,800	13,600
Net income	$ 2,500	$ 9,200	$25,400

Exercise 2-5 ***Income Statement Ratios*** **LO 6**

The 2004 income statement of Holly Enterprises shows net income of $45,000, comprising net sales of $134,800, cost of goods sold of $53,920, selling expenses of $18,310, general and administrative expenses of $16,990, and interest expense of $580. Holly's stockholders' equity was $280,000 at the beginning of the year and $320,000 at the end of the year. The company has 20,000 shares of stock outstanding at December 31, 2004.

Required

Compute Holly's (1) gross profit ratio and (2) profit margin. What other information would you need to be able to comment on whether these ratios are favorable?

Exercise 2-6 ***Statement of Retained Earnings*** **LO 7**

Landon Corporation was organized on January 2, 2002, with the investment of $100,000 by each of its two stockholders. Net income for its first year of business was $85,200. Net income increased during 2003 to $125,320 and to $145,480 during 2004. Landon paid $20,000 in dividends to each of the two stockholders in each of the three years.

(continued)

Required

Prepare a statement of retained earnings for the year ended December 31, 2004.

Exercise 2-7 ***Components of the Statement of Cash Flows*** **LO 8**

From the following list, identify each item as operating (O), investing (I), financing (F), or not on the statement of cash flows (N):

_______ **1.** Paid for supplies
_______ **2.** Collected cash from customers
_______ **3.** Purchased land (held for resale)
_______ **4.** Purchased land (for construction of new building)
_______ **5.** Paid dividend
_______ **6.** Issued stock
_______ **7.** Purchased computers (for use in the business)
_______ **8.** Sold old equipment

Exercise 2-8 ***Basic Elements of Financial Statements*** **LO 9**

Most financial reports contain the following list of basic elements. For each element, identify the person(s) who prepared the element and describe the information a user would expect to find in each element. Some information is verifiable; other information is subjectively chosen by management. Comment on the verifiability of information in each element.

1. Management's report
2. Product/markets of company
3. Financial statements
4. Notes to financial statements
5. Independent accountants' report

Multi-Concept Exercises

Exercise 2-9 ***Financial Statement Classification*** **LO 3, 5, 7**

Potential stockholders and lenders are interested in a company's financial statements. For the list below, identify the statement—balance sheet (BS), income statement (IS), retained earnings statement (RE)—on which each item would appear.

_______ **1.** Accounts payable
_______ **2.** Accounts receivable
_______ **3.** Advertising expense
_______ **4.** Bad debt expense
_______ **5.** Bonds payable
_______ **6.** Buildings
_______ **7.** Cash
_______ **8.** Common stock
_______ **9.** Deferred income taxes
_______ **10.** Depreciation expense
_______ **11.** Dividends
_______ **12.** Land held for future expansion
_______ **13.** Loss on the sale of equipment
_______ **14.** Office supplies
_______ **15.** Organizational costs
_______ **16.** Patent amortization expense
_______ **17.** Retained earnings
_______ **18.** Sales
_______ **19.** Unearned revenue
_______ **20.** Utilities expense

Exercise 2-10 ***Single- and Multiple-Step Income Statement*** **LO 5, 6**

Some headings and/or items are used on either the single-step or the multiple-step income statement. Some are used on both. For the list below, indicate the following: single-step (S), multiple-step (M), both formats (B), or not used on either income statement (N).

_______ **1.** Sales
_______ **2.** Cost of goods sold
_______ **3.** Selling expenses
_______ **4.** Total revenues
_______ **5.** Utilities expense
_______ **6.** Administrative expense
_______ **7.** Net loss
_______ **8.** Supplies on hand
_______ **9.** Accumulated depreciation
_______ **10.** Gross profit

Exercise 2-11 ***Multiple-Step Income Statement*** **LO 5, 6**

Gaynor Corporation's partial income statement follows:

Sales	$1,200,000
Cost of sales	450,000
Selling expenses	60,800
General and administrative expenses	75,000

Required

Determine the gross profit ratio and profit margin. Would you consider investing in Gaynor Corporation? Explain your answer.

Problems

Problem 2-1 ***Materiality*** **LO 2**

Joseph Knapp, a newly hired accountant, wanted to impress his boss, so he stayed late one night to analyze the office supplies expense. He determined the cost by month, for the past 12 months, of each of the following: computer paper, copy paper, fax paper, pencils and pens, note pads, postage, stationery, and miscellaneous items.

1. What did Joseph think his boss would learn from this information? What action might be taken as a result of knowing it?
2. Would this information be more relevant if Joseph worked for a hardware store or for a real estate company? Discuss.

Problem 2-2 ***Costs and Expenses*** **LO 2**

The following costs are incurred by a retailer:

1. Display fixtures in a retail store
2. Advertising
3. Merchandise for sale
4. Incorporation (i.e., legal costs, stock issue costs)
5. Cost of a franchise
6. Office supplies
7. Wages in a restaurant
8. Computer software
9. Computer hardware

Required

For each of these costs, explain whether all of the cost or only a portion of the cost would appear as an expense on the income statement for the period in which the cost was incurred. If not all of the cost would appear on the income statement for that period, explain why not.

Problem 2-3 ***Classified Balance Sheet*** **LO 3**

The following balance sheet items, listed in alphabetical order, are available from the records of Ruth Corporation at December 31, 2004:

Accounts payable	$ 18,255
Accounts receivable	23,450
Accumulated depreciation—automobiles	22,500
Accumulated depreciation—buildings	40,000
Automobiles	112,500
Bonds payable, due December 31, 2008	160,000
Buildings	200,000
Capital stock, $10 par value	150,000
Cash	13,230
Income taxes payable	6,200

(continued)

Interest payable	$ 1,500
Inventory	45,730
Land	250,000
Long-term investments	85,000
Notes payable, due June 30, 2005	10,000
Office supplies	2,340
Paid-in capital in excess of par value	50,000
Patents	40,000
Prepaid rent	1,500
Retained earnings	311,095
Salaries and wages payable	4,200

Required

1. Prepare in good form a classified balance sheet as of December 31, 2004.
2. Compute Ruth's current ratio.
3. On the basis of your answer to requirement **2,** does Ruth appear to be *liquid?* What other information do you need to fully answer this question?

Problem 2-4 ***Financial Statement Ratios*** **LO 4**

The following items, in alphabetical order, are available from the records of Walker Corporation as of December 31, 2004 and 2003:

	December 31, 2004	December 31, 2003
Accounts payable	$ 8,400	$ 5,200
Accounts receivable	13,230	19,570
Cash	10,200	9,450
Cleaning supplies	450	700
Interest payable	–0–	1,200
Inventory	24,600	26,200
Marketable securities	6,250	5,020
Note payable, due in six months	–0–	12,000
Prepaid rent	3,600	4,800
Taxes payable	1,450	1,230
Wages payable	1,200	1,600

Required

1. Calculate the following, as of December 31, 2004, and December 31, 2003:
   - **a.** Working capital
   - **b.** Current ratio
2. On the basis of your answers to **1,** comment on the relative liquidity of the company at the beginning and the end of the year. As part of your answer, explain the change in the company's liquidity from the beginning to the end of 2004.

Problem 2-5 ***Working Capital and Current Ratio*** **LO 4**

The balance sheet of Stevenson Inc. includes the following items:

Cash	$ 23,000
Accounts receivable	13,000
Inventory	45,000
Prepaid insurance	800
Land	80,000
Accounts payable	54,900
Salaries payable	1,200
Capital stock	100,000
Retained earnings	5,700

Required

1. Determine the current ratio and working capital.
2. Beyond the information provided in your answers to **1,** what does the composition of the current assets tell you about Stevenson's liquidity?
3. What other information do you need to fully assess Stevenson's liquidity?

Problem 2-6 *Single-Step Income Statement* **LO 5**

The following income statement items, arranged in alphabetical order, are taken from the records of Shaw Corporation for the year ended December 31, 2004:

Advertising expense	$ 1,500
Commissions expense	2,415
Cost of goods sold	29,200
Depreciation expense—office building	2,900
Income tax expense	1,540
Insurance expense—salesperson's auto	2,250
Interest expense	1,400
Interest revenue	1,340
Rent revenue	6,700
Salaries and wages expense—office	12,560
Sales revenue	48,300
Supplies expense—office	890

Required

1. Prepare a single-step income statement for the year ended December 31, 2004.
2. What weaknesses do you see in this form for the income statement?

Problem 2-7 *Multiple-Step Income Statement* **LO 5**

Refer to the list of income statement items in Problem 2-6. Assume that Shaw Corporation classifies all operating expenses into two categories: (1) selling and (2) general and administrative.

1. Prepare a multiple-step income statement for the year ended December 31, 2004.
2. Compute Shaw's gross profit ratio.
3. What does this ratio tell you about Shaw's markup on its products?

Problem 2-8 *Albertsons' Gross Profit Ratio* **LO 6**

Albertsons Inc. is a large, retail food and drug chain, with 2,300 stores throughout the western, midwestern, and southern states. The following items appeared in the company's 2001 annual report (all amounts are in millions of dollars):

http://www.albertsons.com

	52 Weeks January 31, 2002	52 Weeks February 1, 2001	53 Weeks February 3, 2000
Sales	$37,931	$36,762	$37,478
Cost of goods sold	27,155	26,329	27,164

Required

1. Note that Albertsons' fiscal year ends toward the end of January (actually, on the Thursday nearest to January 31 each year). Why do you think this particular company would choose this time, rather than December 31, to end its accounting year?
2. Compute Albertsons' gross profit and its gross profit ratio for each of the three years.
3. Comment on the *change* in the gross profit ratio over the three-year period. What possible explanations are there for the change?

Problem 2-9 *Statement of Cash Flows* **LO 8**

Colorado Corporation was organized on January 1, 2004, with the investment of $250,000 in cash by its stockholders. The company immediately purchased an office building for $300,000, paying $210,000 in cash and signing a three-year promissory note for the balance. Colorado signed a five-year, $60,000 promissory note at a local bank during 2004 and received cash in the same amount. During its first year, Colorado collected $93,970 from its customers. It paid $65,600 for inventory, $20,400 in salaries and wages, and another $3,100 in taxes. Colorado paid $5,600 in cash dividends.

1. Prepare a statement of cash flows for the year ended December 31, 2004.
2. What does this statement tell you that an income statement does not?

Problem 2-10 *Basic Elements of Financial Reports* **LO 9**

Comparative income statements for Grammar Inc. are presented on the following page.

(continued)

	2004	2003
Sales	$1,000,000	$500,000
Cost of sales	500,000	300,000
Gross margin	$ 500,000	$200,000
Operating expenses	120,000	100,000
Operating income	$ 380,000	$100,000
Loss on sale of subsidiary	(400,000)	—
Net income	$ (20,000)	$100,000

Required

The president and management believe that the company performed better in 2004 than it did in 2003. Write the president's letter to be included in the 2004 annual report. Explain why the company is financially sound and why shareholders should not be alarmed by the $20,000 loss in a year when sales have doubled.

Multi-Concept Problems

Problem 2-11 ***Comparing Coca-Cola and PepsiCo*** **LO 2, 4**

http://www.cocacola.com
http://www.pepsico.com

SPREADSHEET

The following current items, listed in alphabetical order, are taken from the consolidated balance sheets of Coca-Cola and PepsiCo as of December 31, 2001, and December 29, 2001, respectively (all amounts are in millions of dollars):

Coca-Cola

Accounts payable and accrued expenses	$3,679
Accrued income taxes	851
Cash and cash equivalents	1,866
Current maturities of long-term debt	156
Inventories	1,055
Loans and notes payable	3,743
Marketable securities	68
Prepaid expenses and other assets	2,300
Trade accounts receivable, less allowance of $59	1,882

PepsiCo

Accounts and notes receivable, net	$2,142
Accounts payable and other current liabilities	4,461
Cash and cash equivalents	683
Income taxes payable	183
Inventories	1,310
Prepaid expenses and other current assets	752
Short-term borrowings	354
Short-term investments, at cost	966

Required

1. Compute working capital and the current ratio for both companies.
2. On the basis of your answers to 1 above, which company appears to be more liquid?
3. As you know, other factors affect a company's liquidity in addition to its working capital and current ratio. Comment on the *composition* of each company's current assets and how this composition affects its liquidity.

Problem 2-12 ***Comparability and Consistency in Income Statements*** **LO 2, 5**

The following income statements were provided by Gleeson Company, a retailer:

2004 Income Statement		2003 Income Statement	
Sales	$1,700,000	Sales	$1,500,000
Cost of sales	520,000	Cost of sales	$ 450,000
Gross profit	$1,180,000	Sales salaries	398,000
Selling expense	$ 702,000	Advertising	175,000
Administrative expense	95,000	Office supplies	54,000
Total selling and administrative expense	$ 797,000	Depreciation—building	40,000
		Delivery expense	20,000
		Total expenses	$1,137,000
Net income	$ 383,000	Net income	$ 363,000

Required

1. Identify each income statement as either single-step or multiple-step format.
2. Convert the 2003 income statement to the same format as the 2004 income statement.

Problem 2-13 *Classified Balance Sheet, Multiple-Step Income Statement, and Statement of Retained Earnings for Kellogg's* LO 3, 5, 7

In alphabetical order, the following items are taken from Kellogg's 2000 consolidated financial statements:

http://www.kelloggs.com

SPREADSHEET

(millions, except per share data)	2000
Accounts payable	$ 388.2
Accounts receivable, net	685.3
Accumulated other comprehensive income (reduction of owners' equity listed after treasury stock)	(435.3)
Capital in excess of par value	102.0
Cash and cash equivalents	204.4
Cash dividends	(403.9)
Common stock	103.8
Cost of goods sold	3,327.0
Current maturities of long-term debt	901.1
Income taxes (expense)	280.0
Interest expense	137.5
Inventories	443.8
Long-term debt	709.2
Net sales	6,954.7
Notes payable (current liability)	485.2
Other assets (long-term assets)	762.6
Other current assets	273.3
Other current liabilities	718.1
Other income (expense), net	15.4
Other liabilities (long-term liabilities)	797.0
Property, net	2,526.9
Restructuring charges (operating expense)	86.5
Retained earnings, beginning of year	1,317.2
Selling, general, and administrative expense	2,551.4
Treasury stock at cost (reduction of owners' equity listed after retained earnings)	(374.0)

(NOTE: The descriptions in parentheses are not part of the items but have been added to provide you with hints as you complete this problem.)

Required

1. Prepare a multiple-step income statement for Kellogg's for the year ended December 31, 2000.
2. Prepare a statement of retained earnings for Kellogg's for the year ended December 31, 2000.
3. Prepare a classified balance sheet for Kellogg's at December 31, 2000.

Problem 2-14 *Using Kellogg's Classified Balance Sheet and Multiple-Step Income Statement* LO 4, 6

(Note: Consider completing this problem after Problem 2-13 to ensure that you have the various items on the financial statements properly classified.)

SPREADSHEET

Refer to the information set forth in Problem 2-13.

Required

1. Compute Kellogg's working capital and its current ratio at December 31, 2000.
2. Does Kellogg's appear to be liquid? What other factors need to be considered in answering this question?
3. Compute Kellogg's gross profit ratio and its profit margin for 2000.
4. As a Kellogg's stockholder, would you be satisfied with the company's gross profit ratio and its profit margin? What other factors need to be considered in answering this question?

Problem 2-15 ***Cash Flow*** **LO 1, 4, 8**

DECISION MAKING

Franklin Co., a specialty retailer, has a history of paying quarterly dividends of $0.50 per share. Management is trying to determine whether the company will have adequate cash on December 31, 2004, to pay a dividend if one is declared by the board of directors. The following additional information is available:

- All sales are on account, and accounts receivable are collected one month after the sale. Sales volume has been increasing 5% each month.
- All purchases of merchandise are on account, and accounts payable are paid one month after the purchase. Cost of sales is 40% of the sales price. Inventory levels are maintained at $75,000.
- Operating expenses in addition to the mortgage are paid in cash. They amount to $3,000 per month and are paid as they are incurred.

FRANKLIN CO.
BALANCE SHEET
SEPTEMBER 30, 2004

Cash	$ 5,000	Accounts payable	$ 5,000
Accounts receivable	12,500	Mortgage note†	150,000
Inventory	75,000	Common stock—$1 par	50,000
Note receivable*	10,000	Retained earnings	66,500
Building/Land	169,000	Total liabilities	
Total assets	$271,500	and stockholders' equity	$271,500

**Note receivable represents a one-year, 5% interest-bearing note, due November 1, 2004.*

†Mortgage note is a 30-year, 7% note due in monthly installments of $1,200.

Required

Determine the cash that Franklin will have available to pay a dividend on December 31, 2004. Round all amounts to the nearest dollar. What can Franklin's management do to increase the cash available? Should management recommend that the board of directors declare a dividend?

Alternate Problems

Problem 2-1A ***Materiality*** **LO 2**

Jane Erving, a newly hired accountant, wanted to impress her boss, so she stayed late one night to analyze the long-distance calls by area code and time of day placed. She determined the monthly cost, for the past 12 months, by hour and area code called.

Required

1. What did Jane think her boss would learn from this information? What action might be taken as a result of knowing it?
2. Would this information be more relevant if Jane worked for a hardware store or for a real estate company? Discuss.

Problem 2-2A ***Costs and Expenses*** **LO 2**

The following costs are incurred by a retailer:

1. Point-of-sale systems in a retail store
2. An ad in the yellow pages
3. An inventory-control computer software system
4. Shipping merchandise for resale to chain outlets

For each of these costs, explain whether all of the cost or only a portion of the cost would appear as an expense on the income statement for the period in which the cost is incurred. If not all of the cost would appear on the income statement for that period, explain why not.

Problem 2-3A ***Classified Balance Sheet*** **LO 3**

The following balance sheet items, listed in alphabetical order, are available from the records of Singer Company at December 31, 2004:

Accounts payable	$ 34,280
Accounts receivable	26,700
Accumulated depreciation—buildings	40,000
Accumulated depreciation—equipment	12,500
Bonds payable, due December 31, 2010	250,000
Buildings	150,000
Capital stock, $1 par value	200,000
Cash	60,790
Equipment	84,500
Income taxes payable	7,500
Interest payable	2,200
Land	250,000
Marketable securities	15,000
Merchandise inventory	112,900
Notes payable, due April 15, 2005	6,500
Office supplies	400
Paid-in capital in excess of par value	75,000
Patents	45,000
Prepaid rent	3,600
Retained earnings	113,510
Salaries payable	7,400

Required

1. Prepare a classified balance sheet as of December 31, 2004.
2. Compute Singer's current ratio.
3. On the basis of your answer to **2**, does Singer appear to be *liquid?* What other information do you need to fully answer this question?

Problem 2-4A ***Financial Statement Ratios*** **LO 4**

The following items, in alphabetical order, are available from the records of Quinn Corporation as of December 31, 2004 and 2003:

	December 31, 2004	December 31, 2003
Accounts payable	$10,500	$ 6,500
Accounts receivable	16,500	26,000
Cash	12,750	11,800
Interest receivable	200	–0–
Note receivable, due 12/31/2006	12,000	12,000
Office supplies	900	1,100
Prepaid insurance	400	250
Salaries payable	1,800	800
Taxes payable	10,000	5,800

Required

1. Calculate the following, as of December 31, 2004, and December 31, 2003:
   a. Working capital
   b. Current ratio
2. On the basis of your answers to **1**, comment on the relative liquidity of the company at the beginning and the end of the year. As part of your answer, explain the change in the company's liquidity from the beginning to the end of 2004.

Problem 2-5A ***Working Capital and Current Ratio*** **LO 4**

The balance sheet of Kapinski Inc. includes the following items:

Cash	$ 23,000
Accounts receivable	43,000
Inventory	75,000
Prepaid insurance	2,800
Land	80,000

(continued)

Accounts payable	$ 84,900
Salaries payable	3,200
Capital stock	100,000
Retained earnings	35,700

Required

1. Determine the current ratio and working capital.
2. Kapinski appears to have a positive current ratio and a large net working capital. Why would it have trouble paying bills as they come due?
3. Suggest three things that Kapinski can do to help pay its bills on time.

Problem 2-6A *Single-Step Income Statement* LO 5

The following income statement items, arranged in alphabetical order, are taken from the records of Corbin Enterprises, a software sales firm, for the year ended December 31, 2004:

Advertising expense	$ 9,000
Cost of goods sold	150,000
Depreciation expense—computer	4,500
Dividend revenue	2,700
Income tax expense	30,700
Interest expense	1,900
Rent expense—office	26,400
Rent expense—salesperson's car	18,000
Sales revenue	350,000
Supplies expense—office	1,300
Utilities expense	6,750
Wages expense—office	45,600

Required

1. Prepare a single-step income statement for the year ended December 31, 2004.
2. What weaknesses do you see in this form for the income statement?

Problem 2-7A *Multiple-Step Income Statement* LO 5

Refer to the list of income statement items in Problem 2-6A. Assume that Corbin Enterprises classifies all operating expenses into two categories: (1) selling and (2) general and administrative.

Required

1. Prepare a multiple-step income statement for the year ended December 31, 2004.
2. Compute Corbin's gross profit ratio.
3. What does this ratio tell you about Corbin's markup on its products?

Problem 2-8A *Saks' Gross Profit Ratio* LO 6

http://www.saksincorporated.com

Saks Incorporated is a national retailer operating department stores under various names, with the most recognizable being Saks Fifth Avenue. The following items appeared in the company's 2001 annual report (all amounts are in thousands of dollars):

	February 2, 2002	February 3, 2001	January 29, 2000
Net sales	$6,070,568	$6,581,236	$6,434,167
Cost of goods sold	3,960,129	4,211,707	4,028,779

Required

1. Note that Saks' fiscal year ends toward the end of January (actually, on the Saturday closest to January 31 each year). Why do you think this particular company would choose this time to end its accounting year rather than December 31?
2. Compute Saks' gross profit and its gross profit ratio for each of the three years.
3. Comment on any *change* in the gross profit ratio over the three-year period. What possible explanations are there for the change?

Problem 2-9A ***Statement of Cash Flows*** **LO 8**

Wisconsin Corporation was organized on January 1, 2004, with the investment of $400,000 in cash by its stockholders. The company immediately purchased a manufacturing facility for $300,000, paying $150,000 in cash and signing a five-year promissory note for the balance. Wisconsin signed another five-year note at the bank for $50,000 during 2004 and received cash for the same amount. During its first year, Wisconsin collected $310,000 from its customers. It paid $185,000 for inventory, $30,100 in salaries and wages, and another $40,000 in taxes. Wisconsin paid $4,000 in cash dividends.

Required

1. Prepare a statement of cash flows for the year ended December 31, 2004.
2. What does this statement tell you that an income statement does not?

Problem 2-10A ***Basic Elements of Financial Reports*** **LO 9**

Comparative income statements for Thesaurus Inc. are presented below:

	2004	2003
Sales	$1,000,000	$500,000
Cost of sales	500,000	300,000
Gross margin	$ 500,000	$200,000
Operating expenses	120,000	100,000
Operating income	$ 380,000	$100,000
Gain on the sale of subsidiary	—	400,000
Net income	$ 380,000	$500,000

Required

The president and management believe that the company performed better in 2004 than it did in 2003. Write the president's letter to be included in the 2004 annual report. Explain why the company is financially sound and why shareholders should not be alarmed by the reduction in income in a year when sales have doubled.

Alternate Multi-Concept Problems

Problem 2-11A ***Comparing Compaq and Dell*** **LO 2, 4**

The following current items, listed in alphabetical order, are taken from the consolidated balance sheets of Compaq Computer Corporation and Dell Computer Corporation as of December 31, 2001, and February 1, 2002, respectively (all amounts are in millions of dollars):

http://www.hp.com
http://www.dell.com

Compaq

Accounts payable	$3,881
Cash and cash equivalents	3,874
Deferred income (current liability)	1,181
Inventories	1,402
Leases and other accounts receivable	1,881
Other assets (current)	1,498
Other liabilities (current)	4,379
Short-term borrowings	1,692
Trade accounts receivable, net	4,623

Dell

Accounts payable	$5,075
Accounts receivable, net	2,269
Accrued and other (current liabilities)	2,444
Cash and cash equivalents	3,641
Inventories	278
Other (current assets)	1,416
Short-term investments	273

(NOTE: the descriptions in parentheses are not part of the items but have been added to provide you with assistance as you complete this problem.)

(continued)

Required

1. Compute working capital and the current ratio for both companies.
2. On the basis of your answers to 1 above, which company appears to be more liquid?
3. As you know, other factors affect a company's liquidity in addition to its working capital and current ratio. Comment on the *composition* of each company's current assets and how this composition affects its liquidity.

Problem 2-12A ***Comparability and Consistency in Income Statements*** **LO 2, 5**

The following income statements were provided by Chisholm Company, a wholesale food distributor:

	2004	2003
Sales	$1,700,000	$1,500,000
Cost of sales	$ 612,000	$ 450,000
Sales salaries	427,000	398,000
Delivery expense	180,000	175,000
Office supplies	55,000	54,000
Depreciation—truck	40,000	40,000
Computer line expense	23,000	20,000
Total expenses	$1,337,000	$1,137,000
Net income	$ 363,000	$ 363,000

Required

1. Identify each income statement as either single-step or multiple-step format.
2. Restate each item in the income statements as a percentage of sales. Why did net income remain unchanged when sales increased in 2004?

Problem 2-13A ***Classified Balance Sheet, Multiple-Step Income Statement, and Statement of Retained Earnings for Walgreens*** **LO 3, 5, 7**

http://www.walgreens.com

Shown below, in alphabetical order, are items taken from Walgreens' 2001 consolidated financial statements. Walgreen Co. has a fiscal year ending August 31.

	(dollars in millions)
Accounts receivable, net	$ 798.3
Accrued expenses and other liabilities	937.5
Cash and cash equivalents	16.9
Cash dividends declared	142.5
Common stock	79.6
Cost of sales	18,048.9
Deferred income taxes (noncurrent liability)	137.0
Income taxes (current liability)	86.6
Income tax provision (expense)	537.1
Interest expense	3.1
Interest income	5.4
Inventories	3,482.4
Net sales	24,623.0
Other current assets	96.3
Other income	22.1
Other noncurrent assets	94.6
Other noncurrent liabilities	478.0
Paid-in capital	596.7
Property and equipment, at cost, less accumulated depreciation and amortization	4,345.3
Retained earnings, beginning of year	3,787.8
Selling, occupancy, and administration (expense)	5,175.8
Short-term borrowings	440.7
Trade accounts payable	1,546.8

(NOTE: The descriptions in parentheses are not part of the items but have been added to provide you with hints as you complete this problem.)

Required

1. Prepare a multiple-step income statement for Walgreens for the year ended August 31, 2001.
2. Prepare a statement of retained earnings for Walgreens for the year ended August 31, 2001.
3. Prepare a classified balance sheet for Walgreens at August 31, 2001.

Problem 2-14A *Using Walgreens' Classified Balance Sheet and Multiple-Step Income Statement* **LO 4, 6**

(Note: Consider completing this problem after Problem 2-13A to ensure that you have the various items on the financial statements properly classified.)

Refer to the information set forth in Problem 2-13A.

Required

1. Compute Walgreens' working capital and its current ratio at August 31, 2001.
2. Does Walgreens appear to be liquid? What other factors need to be considered in answering this question?
3. Compute Walgreens' gross profit ratio and its profit margin for the year ended August 31, 2001.
4. As a Walgreens stockholder, would you be satisfied with the company's gross profit ratio and its profit margin? What other factors need to be considered in answering this question?

Problem 2-15A *Cash Flow* **LO 1, 4, 8**

Roosevelt Inc., a consulting service, has a history of paying annual dividends of $1 per share. Management is trying to determine whether the company will have adequate cash on December 31, 2004, to pay a dividend if one is declared by the board of directors. The following additional information is available:

- All sales are on account, and accounts receivable are collected one month after the sale. Sales volume has been decreasing 5% each month.
- Operating expenses are paid in cash in the month incurred. Average monthly expenses are $10,000 (excluding the biweekly payroll).
- Biweekly payroll is $4,500, and it will be paid December 15 and December 31.
- Unearned revenue is expected to be earned in December. This amount was taken into consideration in the expected sales volume.

ROOSEVELT INC.
BALANCE SHEET
DECEMBER 1, 2004

Cash	$ 15,000	Unearned revenue	$ 2,000
Accounts receivable	40,000	Note payable*	30,000
Computer equipment	120,000	Common stock—$2 par	50,000
		Retained earnings	93,000
Total assets	$175,000	Total liabilities and stockholder's equity	$175,000

**The note payable plus 3% interest for six months is due January 15, 2005.*

Required

Determine the cash that Roosevelt will have available to pay a dividend on December 31, 2004. Round all amounts to the nearest dollar. Should management recommend that the board of directors declare a dividend?

Cases

Reading and Interpreting Financial Statements

Case 2-1 *Boeing's Operating Cycle* **LO 3**

In Boeing's annual report, note 1, "Summary of Significant Accounting Policies," includes the following explanation of Boeing's inventories:

http://www.boeing.com

(continued)

Inventories

Inventoried costs on commercial aircraft programs and long-term contracts include direct engineering, production and tooling costs, and applicable overhead, not in excess of estimated realizable value. In accordance with industry practice, inventoried costs include amounts relating to programs and contracts with long production cycles, a portion of which is not expected to be realized within one year. Commercial spare parts and general stock materials are stated at average cost not in excess of realizable cost.[15]

Required

1. Based on the note above, describe Boeing's inventory. That is, what types of items would you expect to find in the inventory of this type of company?
2. Why would Boeing expect that a portion of its inventoried costs would *not* be realized within one year?
3. Based on your answer to 2 above, should Boeing classify its inventories as current or as non-current assets? Explain your answer.

http://www.winnebagoind.com
http://www.monacocoach.com

Case 2-2 *Comparing Two Companies in the Same Industry: Winnebago Industries and Monaco Coach Corporation* LO 4

Refer to the financial information for Winnebago Industries and Monaco Coach Corporation reproduced in Appendices A and B at the end of the book for the information needed to answer the following questions.

DECISION MAKING

Required

1. Compute each company's working capital at the end of 2001 and 2000. Also, for each company, compute the change in working capital from the end of 2000 to the end of 2001.
2. Compute each company's current ratio at the end of 2001 and 2000. Compute the percentage change in the ratio from the end of 2000 to the end of 2001.
3. How do Winnebago Industries and Monaco Coach differ in terms of the accounts that made up their current assets at the end of 2001? What is the largest current asset each reports on the balance sheet at the end of 2001?
4. On the basis of your answers to questions 2 and 3 above, which company appears to be the most liquid at the end of 2001? Explain your answer.

Case 2-3 *Interpreting Gateway's Inventory* LO 3, 4

Refer to Gateway's balance sheet as of December 31, 2001.

Required

1. What is the amount of Gateway's inventory at December 31, 2001? Has this amount increased or decreased during 2001?
2. Give some examples of the types of costs you would expect to be included in Gateway's inventory account.

Making Financial Decisions

Case 2-4 *Analysis of Cash Flow for a Small Business* LO 8

DECISION MAKING

Charles, a financial consultant, has been self-employed for two years. His list of clients has grown, and he is earning a reputation as a shrewd investor. Charles rents a small office, uses the pool secretarial services, and has purchased a car that he is depreciating over three years. The following income statements cover Charles's first two years of business:

	Year 1	Year 2
Commissions revenue	$ 25,000	$65,000
Rent	$ 12,000	$12,000
Secretarial services	3,000	9,000
Car expenses, gas, insurance	6,000	6,500
Depreciation	15,000	15,000
Net income	$(11,000)	$22,500

[15] *Boeing Company 2001 Annual Report.*

Charles believes that he should earn more than $11,500 for working very hard for two years. He is thinking about going to work for an investment firm where he can earn $40,000 per year. What would you advise Charles to do?

Case 2-5 ***Factors Involved in an Investment Decision*** **LO 9**

DECISION MAKING

As an investor, you are considering purchasing stock in a fast-food restaurant chain. The annual reports of several companies are available for comparison.

Required

Prepare an outline of the steps you would follow to make your comparison. Start by listing the first section that you would read in the financial reports. What would you expect to find there, and why did you choose that section to read first? Continue with the other sections of the financial report.

Many fast-food chains are owned by large conglomerates. What limitation does this create in your comparison? How would you solve it?

Accounting and Ethics: What Would You Do?

Case 2-6 ***The Expenditure Approval Process*** **LO 2**

Roberto is the plant superintendent of a small manufacturing company that is owned by a large corporation. The corporation has a policy that any expenditure over $1,000 must be approved by the chief financial officer in the corporate headquarters. The approval process takes a minimum of three weeks. Roberto would like to order a new labeling machine that is expected to reduce costs and pay for itself in six months. The machine costs $2,200, but Roberto can buy the sales rep's demo for $1,800. Roberto has asked the sales rep to send two separate bills for $900 each.

What would you do if you were the sales rep? Do you agree or disagree with Roberto's actions? What do you think about the corporate policy?

Case 2-7 ***Barbara Applies For a Loan*** **LO 4, 6**

Barbara Bites, owner of Bites of Bagels, a drive-through bagel shop, would like to expand her business from its current one location to a chain of bagel shops. Sales in the bagel shop have been increasing an average of 8% each quarter. Profits have been increasing accordingly. Barbara is conservative in spending and a very hard worker. She has an appointment with a banker to apply for a loan to expand the business. To prepare for the appointment, she instructs you, as the chief financial officer and payroll clerk, to copy the quarterly income statements for the past two years but not to include a balance sheet. Barbara already has a substantial loan from another bank. In fact, she has very little of her own money invested in the business.

What should you do? Do you think the banker will lend Barbara more money?

Internet Research Case

Case 2-8 ***Gateway***

INTERNET

You can probably do this from your everyday knowledge, but this is good practice in researching a company using the Internet. Find a Web site or a source of information that will list the competitors to Gateway. Choose the top two competitors and answer the following questions:

1. Looking at their balance sheets, what are their total current assets and their total current liabilities? From these numbers, calculate each company's working capital and current ratio. How do they compare to these ratios for Gateway, shown on page 72?
2. From their income statements, calculate their profit margins for the latest year available. How do they compare to those of Gateway, which you were asked to calculate in the From Concept to Practice box on page 74?

Optional Research: From the financial information available on their Web sites, what other comparisons can you make about these companies? Based on your research, are the companies them-

Fill in your source for industry information:
http://www.________________.com

Gateway and its main competitors:
http://www.gateway.com
http://www.________________.com
http://www.________________.com

selves comparable, in such areas as size, products, assets, liabilities, net income? If not, explain five ways in which they differ. Is the financial information itself comparable for the three companies? Explain.

Solutions to Key Terms Quiz

6	Understandability (p. 56)	10	Current liability (p. 64)
3	Relevance (p. 56)	16	Liquidity (p. 65)
9	Reliability (p. 57)	12	Working capital (p. 65)
14	Comparability (p. 57)	8	Current ratio (p. 66)
19	Depreciation (p. 57)	1	Single-step income statement (p. 67)
17	Consistency (p. 58)	4	Multiple-step income statement (p. 68)
2	Materiality (p. 59)	18	Gross profit (p. 68)
5	Conservatism (p. 59)	7	Gross profit ratio (p. 69)
11	Operating cycle (p. 61)	13	Profit margin (p. 69)
15	Current asset (p. 63)		

Chapter 3

Processing Accounting Information

Focus on Financial Results

Being a successful company requires growth, and General Mills is no exception to this rule. Sales, as shown on the accompanying income statement (or statement of earnings), exceeded $7 billion in the 2001 fiscal year. This reflected a nearly 6% increase from the prior year and kept the growth in sales at a 6% annual compound rate over a four-year period. The income statement also shows that General Mills was able to control its costs while increasing its sales, as evidenced by a growth in net earnings of over 8% in 2001.

Brand names are the lifeblood of any consumer product company, and General Mills boasts some of the most recognizable names in the world. Who cannot identify with Cheerios® and Wheaties® in General Mills' Big G division? Or is there anyone who is not familiar with the name Betty Crocker®? Finally, the company leads the $2.3 billion U.S. yogurt category with products such as Yoplait® and Colombo®.

According to its annual report, General Mills' growth formula has four key components: product innovation, channel expansion, international expansion, and margin expansion. This formula has proven to be successful for the company, as evidenced by its leading market position in no less than seven categories, including ready-to-eat cereals, dessert mixes, and family flour. But, as you will read more about later in the chapter, General Mills made the most significant decision in its corporate history in July 2000 when it announced plans to acquire the worldwide Pillsbury businesses from Diageo plc. Growth seems inevitable with the combination of the highly successful brand names of Pillsbury and those of General Mills. What remains to be seen is whether this consumer foods powerhouse can control costs and translate sales growth to its bottom line.

General Mills' 2001 Annual Report

Consolidated Statements of Earnings

In Millions, Except per Share Data; Fiscal Year Ended	May 27, 2001	May 28, 2000	May 30, 1999
Sales	**$7,077.7**	$6,700.2	$6,246.1
Costs and Expenses:			
Cost of sales	**2,841.2**	2,697.6	2,593.5
Selling, general and administrative	**3,067.2**	2,903.7	2,634.9
Interest, net	**206.1**	151.9	119.4
Unusual items—(income) expense	**(35.1)**	—	40.7
Total Costs and Expenses	**6,079.4**	5,753.2	5,388.5
Earnings before Taxes and Earnings (Losses) from Joint Ventures	**998.3**	947.0	857.6
Income Taxes	**349.9**	335.9	307.8
Earnings (Losses) from Joint Ventures	**16.7**	3.3	(15.3)
Net Earnings	**$ 665.1**	$ 614.4	$ 534.5
Earnings per Share—Basic	**$ 2.34**	$ 2.05	$ 1.74
Average Number of Common Shares	**283.9**	299.1	306.5
Earnings per Share—Diluted	**$ 2.28**	$ 2.00	$ 1.70
Average Number of Common Shares—Assuming Dilution	**292.0**	307.3	314.7

See accompanying notes to consolidated financial statements.

http://www.generalmills.com

You're in the Driver's Seat

General Mills' income statement, pictured here, tells a story of the need for generating growth while at the same time keeping a watchful eye over costs. How can the accounting system help you process the information needed to measure sales and various costs and expenses? As you study the accounting process introduced in this chapter, think about how the tools you are learning would be used to record the purchase of Pillsbury.

LEARNING OBJECTIVES

After studying this chapter, you should be able to:

- **LO 1** Explain the difference between an external and an internal event. (p. 104)
- **LO 2** Explain the role of source documents in an accounting system. (p. 105)
- **LO 3** Analyze the effects of transactions on the accounting equation. (p. 105)
- **LO 4** Define the concept of a general ledger and understand the use of the T account as a method for analyzing transactions. (p. 112)
- **LO 5** Explain the rules of debits and credits. (p. 113)
- **LO 6** Explain the purposes of a journal and the posting process. (p. 118)
- **LO 7** Explain the purpose of a trial balance. (p. 121)

ECONOMIC EVENTS: THE BASIS FOR RECORDING TRANSACTIONS

LO 1 Explain the difference between an external and an internal event.

Event A happening of consequence to an entity.

Many different types of economic events affect an entity during the year. A sale is made to a customer. Inventory is purchased from a supplier. A loan is taken out at the bank. A fire destroys a warehouse. A new contract is signed with the union. In short, "An **event** is a happening of consequence to an entity."[1]

External and Internal Events

External event An event involving interaction between an entity and its environment.

Internal event An event occurring entirely within an entity.

Transaction Any event that is recognized in a set of financial statements.

Two types of events affect an entity: internal and external. An **external event** "involves interaction between the entity and its environment."[2] For example, the *purchase* of raw material from a supplier is an external event, as is the *sale* of inventory to a customer. An **internal event** occurs entirely within the entity. The *transfer* of raw material into production is an internal event, as is the use of a piece of equipment. We will use the term **transaction** to refer to any event, external or internal, that is recognized in a set of financial statements.[3]

What is necessary to recognize an event in the records? Are all economic events recognized as transactions by the accountant? The answers to these questions involve the concept of *measurement.* An event must be measured to be recognized. Certain events are relatively easy to measure: the payroll for the week, the amount of inventory destroyed by an earthquake, or the sales for the day. Not all events that affect an entity can be measured *reliably,* however. For example, how does a manufacturer of breakfast cereal measure the effect of a drought on the price of wheat? A company hires a new chief executive. How can it reliably measure the value of the new officer to the company? There is no definitive answer to the measurement problem in accounting. It is a continuing challenge to the accounting profession and something we will return to throughout the text.

From Concept to Practice 3.1

Reading General Mills' Financial Statements

General Mills uses a variety of ingredients in making its products. Is the purchase of oats an internal or external event? The company subsequently uses oats to make Cheerios®. Is this an internal or external event?

[1] *Statement of Financial Accounting Concepts (SFAC) No. 3,* "Elements of Financial Statements of Business Enterprises" (Stamford, Conn.: Financial Accounting Standards Board, 1982), par. 65.

[2] *SFAC No. 3.*

[3] Technically, a *transaction* is defined by the Financial Accounting Standards Board as a special kind of external event in which the entity exchanges something of value with an outsider. Because the term *transaction* is used in practice to refer to any event that is recognized in the statements, we will use this broader definition.

© PHOTODISC

Source documents like these receipts are records that document transactions that the business engages in. Shown here are an employee's travel expense receipts, which will be turned in to the company for reimbursement. Other source documents may be contracts, lease agreements, invoices, delivery vouchers, check stubs, and deposit slips.

The Role of Source Documents in Recording Transactions

LO 2 Explain the role of source documents in an accounting system.

The first step in the recording process is *identification.* A business needs a systematic method for recognizing events as transactions. A **source document** provides the evidence needed in an accounting system to record a transaction. Source documents take many different forms. An invoice received from a supplier is the source document for a purchase of inventory on credit. A cash register tape is the source document used by a retailer to recognize a cash sale. The payroll department sends the accountant the time cards for the week as the necessary documentation to record wages.

Source document A piece of paper that is used as evidence to record a transaction.

Not all recognizable events are supported by a standard source document. For certain events, some form of documentation must be generated. For example, no standard source document exists to recognize the financial consequences from a fire or the settlement of a lawsuit. Documentation is just as important for these types of events as it is for standard, recurring transactions.

Analyzing the Effects of Transactions on the Accounting Equation

LO 3 Analyze the effects of transactions on the accounting equation.

Economic events are the basis for recording transactions in an accounting system. For every transaction, it is essential to analyze its effect on the accounting equation:

Assets = Liabilities + Owners' Equity

We will now consider a series of events and their recognition as transactions for a hypothetical corporation, Glengarry Health Club. The transactions are for the month of January 2004, the first month of operations for the new business.

(1) *Issuance of capital stock.* The company is started when Mary Jo Kovach and Irene McGuinness file articles of incorporation with the state to obtain a charter. Each invests $50,000 in the business. In return, each receives 5,000 shares of capital stock. Thus, at this point, each of them owns 50% of the outstanding stock of the company and has a claim to 50% of its assets. The effect of this transaction on the accounting equation is to increase both assets and owners' equity:

	Assets					= Liabilities		+ Owners' Equity	
TRANSACTION NUMBER	CASH	ACCOUNTS RECEIVABLE	EQUIPMENT	BUILDING	LAND	ACCOUNTS PAYABLE	NOTES PAYABLE	CAPITAL STOCK	RETAINED EARNINGS
1	$100,000							$100,000	
Totals			$100,000				$100,000		

As you see, each side of the accounting equation increases by $100,000. Cash is increased, and because the owners contributed this amount, their claim to the assets is increased in the form of Capital Stock.

(2) *Acquisition of property in exchange for a note.* The company buys a piece of property for $200,000. The seller agrees to accept a five-year promissory note. The note is given by the health club to the seller and is a written promise to repay the principal amount of the loan at the end of five years. To the company, the promissory note is a liability. The property consists of land valued at $50,000 and a newly constructed building valued at $150,000. The effect of this transaction on the accounting equation is to increase both assets and liabilities by $200,000:

	Assets					= Liabilities		+ Owners' Equity	
TRANSACTION NUMBER	CASH	ACCOUNTS RECEIVABLE	EQUIPMENT	BUILDING	LAND	ACCOUNTS PAYABLE	NOTES PAYABLE	CAPITAL STOCK	RETAINED EARNINGS
Bal.	$100,000							$100,000	
2				$150,000	$50,000		$200,000		
Bal.	$100,000			$150,000	$50,000		$200,000	$100,000	
Totals			$300,000				$300,000		

(3) *Acquisition of equipment on an open account.* Mary Jo and Irene contact an equipment supplier and buy $20,000 of exercise equipment: treadmills, barbells, and stationary bicycles. The supplier agrees to accept payment in full in 30 days. The health club has acquired an asset and at the same time incurred a liability:

	Assets					= Liabilities		+ Owners' Equity	
TRANSACTION NUMBER	CASH	ACCOUNTS RECEIVABLE	EQUIPMENT	BUILDING	LAND	ACCOUNTS PAYABLE	NOTES PAYABLE	CAPITAL STOCK	RETAINED EARNINGS
Bal.	$100,000			$150,000	$50,000		$200,000	$100,000	
3			$20,000			$20,000			
Bal.	$100,000		$20,000	$150,000	$50,000	$20,000	$200,000	$100,000	
Totals			$320,000				$320,000		

(4) *Sale of monthly memberships on account.* The owners open their doors for business. During January, they sell 300 monthly club memberships for $50 each, or a total of $15,000. The members have until the 10th of the following month to pay. Glengarry does not have cash from the new members but instead has a promise from each member to pay cash in the future. The promise from a customer to pay an amount owed is an asset called an *account receivable.* The other side of this transaction is an increase in the owners' equity (specifically, Retained Earnings) in the business. In other words, the assets have increased by $15,000 without any increase in a liability or decrease in another asset. The increase in owners' equity indicates that the owners' residual interest in the assets of the business has increased by this amount. More specifically, an inflow of assets resulting from the sale of goods and services by a business is called *revenue.* The change in the accounting equation follows:

	Assets					= Liabilities		+ Owners' Equity	
TRANSACTION NUMBER	CASH	ACCOUNTS RECEIVABLE	EQUIPMENT	BUILDING	LAND	ACCOUNTS PAYABLE	NOTES PAYABLE	CAPITAL STOCK	RETAINED EARNINGS
Bal.	$100,000		$20,000	$150,000	$50,000	$20,000	$200,000	$100,000	
4		$15,000							$15,000
Bal.	$100,000	$15,000	$20,000	$150,000	$50,000	$20,000	$200,000	$100,000	$15,000
Totals			$335,000				$335,000		

(5) *Sale of court time for cash.* In addition to memberships, Glengarry sells court time. Court fees are paid at the time of use and amount to $5,000 for the first month:

	Assets					= Liabilities		+ Owners' Equity	
TRANSACTION NUMBER	CASH	ACCOUNTS RECEIVABLE	EQUIPMENT	BUILDING	LAND	ACCOUNTS PAYABLE	NOTES PAYABLE	CAPITAL STOCK	RETAINED EARNINGS
Bal.	$100,000	$15,000	$20,000	$150,000	$50,000	$20,000	$200,000	$100,000	$15,000
5	5,000								5,000
Bal.	$105,000	$15,000	$20,000	$150,000	$50,000	$20,000	$200,000	$100,000	$20,000
Totals			$340,000				$340,000		

The only difference between this transaction and (4) is that cash is received rather than a promise to pay at a later date. Both transactions result in an increase in an asset and an increase in the owners' claim to the assets. In both cases, there is an inflow of assets, in the form of either Accounts Receivable or Cash. Thus, in both cases, the company has earned revenue.

(6) *Payment of wages and salaries.* The wages and salaries for the first month amount to $10,000. The payment of this amount results in a decrease in Cash and a decrease in the owners' claim on the assets, that is, a decrease in Retained Earnings. More specifically, an outflow of assets resulting from the sale of goods or services is called an *expense.* The effect of this transaction is to decrease both sides of the accounting equation:

	Assets					= Liabilities		+ Owners' Equity	
TRANSACTION NUMBER	CASH	ACCOUNTS RECEIVABLE	EQUIPMENT	BUILDING	LAND	ACCOUNTS PAYABLE	NOTES PAYABLE	CAPITAL STOCK	RETAINED EARNINGS
Bal.	$105,000	$15,000	$20,000	$150,000	$50,000	$20,000	$200,000	$100,000	$20,000
6	−10,000								−10,000
Bal.	$ 95,000	$15,000	$20,000	$150,000	$50,000	$20,000	$200,000	$100,000	$10,000
Totals			$330,000				$330,000		

(7) *Payment of utilities.* The cost of utilities for the first month is $3,000. Glengarry pays this amount in cash. Both the utilities and the salaries and wages are expenses, and they have the same effect on the accounting equation. Cash is decreased, accompanied by a corresponding decrease in the owners' claim on the assets of the business:

	Assets					= Liabilities		+ Owners' Equity	
TRANSACTION NUMBER	CASH	ACCOUNTS RECEIVABLE	EQUIPMENT	BUILDING	LAND	ACCOUNTS PAYABLE	NOTES PAYABLE	CAPITAL STOCK	RETAINED EARNINGS
Bal.	$95,000	$15,000	$20,000	$150,000	$50,000	$20,000	$200,000	$100,000	$10,000
7	−3,000								−3,000
Bal.	$92,000	$15,000	$20,000	$150,000	$50,000	$20,000	$200,000	$100,000	$ 7,000
Totals			$327,000				$327,000		

(**8**) *Collection of accounts receivable.* Even though the January monthly memberships are not due until the 10th of the following month, some of the members pay their bills by the end of January. The amount received from members in payment of their accounts is $4,000. The effect of the collection of an open account is to increase Cash and decrease Accounts Receivable:

	Assets					=	Liabilities		+	Owners' Equity	
TRANSACTION NUMBER	CASH	ACCOUNTS RECEIVABLE	EQUIPMENT	BUILDING	LAND		ACCOUNTS PAYABLE	NOTES PAYABLE		CAPITAL STOCK	RETAINED EARNINGS
Bal.	$92,000	$15,000	$20,000	$150,000	$50,000		$20,000	$200,000		$100,000	$7,000
8	4,000	−4,000									
Bal.	$96,000	$11,000	$20,000	$150,000	$50,000		$20,000	$200,000		$100,000	$7,000
Totals			$327,000							$327,000	

This is the first transaction we have seen that affects only one side of the accounting equation. In fact, the company simply traded assets: Accounts Receivable for Cash. Thus, note that the totals for the accounting equation remain at $327,000. Also note that Retained Earnings is not affected by this transaction because revenue was recognized earlier, in (**4**), when Accounts Receivable was increased.

(**9**) *Payment of dividends.* At the end of the month, Mary Jo and Irene, acting on behalf of Glengarry Health Club, decide to pay a dividend of $1,000 on the shares of stock owned by each of them, or $2,000 in total. The effect of this dividend is to decrease both Cash and Retained Earnings. That is, the company is returning cash to the owners, based on the profitable operations of the business for the first month. The transaction not only reduces Cash but also decreases the owners' claims on the assets of the company. Dividends are not an expense but rather a direct reduction of Retained Earnings. The effect on the accounting equation follows:

	Assets					=	Liabilities		+	Owners' Equity	
TRANSACTION NUMBER	CASH	ACCOUNTS RECEIVABLE	EQUIPMENT	BUILDING	LAND		ACCOUNTS PAYABLE	NOTES PAYABLE		CAPITAL STOCK	RETAINED EARNINGS
Bal.	$96,000	$11,000	$20,000	$150,000	$50,000		$20,000	$200,000		$100,000	$7,000
9	−2,000										−2,000
Bal.	$94,000	$11,000	$20,000	$150,000	$50,000		$20,000	$200,000		$100,000	$5,000
Totals			$325,000							$325,000	

The Cost Principle An important principle governs the accounting for both the exercise equipment in (**3**) and the building and land in (**2**). The *cost principle* requires that we record an asset at the cost to acquire it and continue to show this amount on all balance sheets until we dispose of the asset. With a few exceptions, an asset is not carried at its market value but at its original cost. Why not show the land on future balance sheets at its market value? Although this might seem more appropriate in certain instances, the subjectivity inherent in determining market values is a major reason behind the practice of carrying assets at their historical cost. The cost of an asset can be verified by an independent observer and is much more *objective* than market value.

Two-Minute Review

Assume that on February 1 Glengarry buys additional exercise equipment for $10,000 in cash.

1. *Indicate which two accounts are affected and the increase or decrease in each.*
2. *What will be the total dollar amount of each of the two sides of the accounting equation after this transaction is recorded?*

Answers on page 122.

Balance Sheet and Income Statement for the Health Club

To summarize, Exhibit 3-1 indicates the effect of each transaction on the accounting equation, specifically the individual items increased or decreased by each transaction. Note the *dual* effect of each transaction. At least two items were involved in each transaction. For example, the initial investment by the owners resulted in an increase in an asset and an increase in Capital Stock. The payment of the utility bill caused a decrease in an asset and a decrease in Retained Earnings.

You can now see the central idea behind the accounting equation: Even though individual transactions may change the amount and composition of the assets and liabilities, the *equation* must always balance *for* each transaction, and the *balance sheet* must balance *after* each transaction.

A balance sheet for Glengarry Health Club appears in Exhibit 3-2. All of the information needed to prepare this statement is available in Exhibit 3-1. The balances at the bottom of this exhibit are entered on the balance sheet, with assets on the left side and liabilities and owners' equity on the right side.

An income statement for Glengarry is shown in Exhibit 3-3. An income statement summarizes the revenues and expenses of a company for a period of time. In our example, the statement is for the month of January, as indicated on the third line of the heading of the statement. Glengarry earned revenues from two sources: (1) memberships and (2) court fees. Two types of expenses were incurred: (1) salaries and wages and (2) utilities. The difference between the total revenues of $20,000 and the total expenses of $13,000 is the net income for the month of $7,000. Finally, remember that dividends appear on a statement of retained earnings rather than on the income statement. They are a *distribution* of net income of the period, not a *determinant* of net income as are expenses.

We have seen how transactions are analyzed and how they affect the accounting equation and ultimately the financial statements. While the approach we took in analyzing the nine transactions of the Glengarry Health Club was manageable, can you

© PETER BECK/CORBIS

Companies engage in transactions in many ways. The company from whom this woman is ordering supports sales transactions over the phone using a credit card number. A sales representative may be inputting the card number and the order information into an order database. The company links its order-processing system and other business systems to this customer input.

Exhibit 3-1 Glengarry Health Club Transactions for the Month of January

	Assets					=	Liabilities		+ Owners' Equity	
TRANS. NO.	CASH	ACCOUNTS RECEIVABLE	EQUIPMENT	BUILDING	LAND		ACCOUNTS PAYABLE	NOTES PAYABLE	CAPITAL STOCK	RETAINED EARNINGS
1	$100,000								$100,000	
2				$150,000	$50,000			$200,000		
Bal.	$100,000			$150,000	$50,000			$200,000	$100,000	
3			$20,000				$20,000			
Bal.	$100,000		$20,000	$150,000	$50,000		$20,000	$200,000	$100,000	
4		$15,000								$ 15,000
Bal.	$100,000	$15,000	$20,000	$150,000	$50,000		$20,000	$200,000	$100,000	$ 15,000
5	5,000									5,000
Bal.	$105,000	$15,000	$20,000	$150,000	$50,000		$20,000	$200,000	$100,000	$ 20,000
6	− 10,000									−10,000
Bal.	$ 95,000	$15,000	$20,000	$150,000	$50,000		$20,000	$200,000	$100,000	$ 10,000
7	− 3,000									− 3,000
Bal.	$ 92,000	$15,000	$20,000	$150,000	$50,000		$20,000	$200,000	$100,000	$ 7,000
8	4,000	− 4,000								
Bal.	$ 96,000	$11,000	$20,000	$150,000	$50,000		$20,000	$200,000	$100,000	$ 7,000
9	− 2,000									− 2,000
Bal.	$ 94,000	$11,000	$20,000	$150,000	$50,000		$20,000	$200,000	$100,000	$ 5,000

Total assets: $325,000 | Total liabilities and owners' equity: $325,000

Exhibit 3-2

Balance Sheet for Glengarry Health Club

GLENGARRY HEALTH CLUB
BALANCE SHEET
JANUARY 31, 2004

Assets		Liabilities and Owners' Equity	
Cash	$ 94,000	Accounts payable	$ 20,000
Accounts receivable	11,000	Notes payable	200,000
Equipment	20,000	Capital stock	100,000
Building	150,000	Retained earnings	5,000
Land	50,000	Total liabilities	
Total assets	$325,000	and owners' equity	$325,000

Exhibit 3-3

Income Statement for Glengarry Health Club

GLENGARRY HEALTH CLUB
INCOME STATEMENT
FOR THE MONTH ENDED JANUARY 31, 2004

Revenues:		
Memberships	$15,000	
Court fees	5,000	$20,000
Expenses:		
Salaries and wages	$10,000	
Utilities	3,000	13,000
Net income		$ 7,000

imagine using this type of analysis for a company with *thousands* of transactions in any one month? We now turn our attention to various *tools* used by the accountant to process a large volume of transactions effectively and efficiently.

Business Strategy

As mentioned in the chapter opener, General Mills agreed in July 2000 to acquire Pillsbury, another leading consumer food company. The transaction was completed barely a year later and was celebrated at the New York Stock Exchange on November 1, 2001, when the CEO of the new global General Mills was invited to ring the opening bell. The Pillsbury Doughboy™, the Trix Rabbit™ and other company mascots handed out "blue chip" cookies to traders on the floor.

To its existing list of highly recognizable brand names, General Mills picked up some equally impressive names—including Pillsbury®, Green Giant®, Old El Paso®, and Häagen-Dazs®—and in the process immediately added more than $1 billion to its sales base outside the United States. Management is confident that the company will accelerate its growth with the acquisition of Pillsbury. In fact, the company expects sales to grow at an annual rate of 7%, rather than the 6% achieved over the past four years.

Growth in sales is not the only target for the Pillsbury acquisition. General Mills also expects to achieve significant cost savings from the pairing of the two consumer food giants: an estimated $400 million pretax annually by the end of the second full year of integration. Combining this with sales growth, the company fully expects the bottom line to grow as well. In fact, management has optimistically targeted 11%–15% annual growth in earnings per share over the remainder of this decade. The next few annual reports will tell the story as to whether General Mills was successful in reaching its targeted goals.

Sources: General Mills' 2001 annual report and Web site.

THE ACCOUNT: THE BASIC UNIT FOR RECORDING TRANSACTIONS

An **account** is the record used to accumulate monetary amounts for each asset, liability, and component of owners' equity, such as Capital Stock, Retained Earnings, and Dividends. It is the basic recording unit for each element in the financial statements. Each revenue and expense has its own account. In the Glengarry Health Club example, nine accounts were used: Cash, Accounts Receivable, Equipment, Building, Land, Accounts Payable, Notes Payable, Capital Stock, and Retained Earnings. (Recall that revenues, expenses, and dividends were recorded directly in the Retained Earnings account. Later in the chapter we will see that normally each revenue and expense is recorded in a separate account.) In the real world, a company might have hundreds, or even thousands, of individual accounts.

Account Record used to accumulate amounts for each individual asset, liability, revenue, expense, and component of owners' equity.

No two entities have exactly the same set of accounts. To a certain extent, the accounts used by a company depend on its business. For example, a manufacturer normally has three inventory accounts: Raw Materials, Work in Process, and Finished Goods. A retailer uses just one account for inventory, a Merchandise Inventory account. A service business has no need for an inventory account.

From Concept to Practice 3.2

Reading Winnebago Industries' Balance Sheet

How many current asset accounts does the company report on its balance sheet? What is the dollar amount of the largest of these?

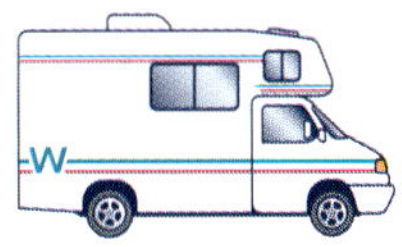

Chart of Accounts

Companies need a way to organize the large number of accounts they use to record transactions. A **chart of accounts** is a numerical list of all of the accounts an entity uses. The numbering system is a convenient way to identify accounts. For example, all asset accounts might be numbered from 100 to 199, liability accounts from 200 to 299, equity accounts from 300 to 399, revenues from 400 to 499, and expenses from 500 to 599. A chart of accounts for a hypothetical company, Widescreen Theaters Corporation, is shown in Exhibit 3-4. Note the division of account numbers within each of the financial statement categories. Within the asset category, the various cash accounts are numbered from 100 to 109, receivables from 110 to 119, etc. Not all of the numbers are currently assigned. For example, only three of the available nine numbers are currently utilized for cash accounts. This allows the company to add accounts as needed.

Chart of accounts A numerical list of all the accounts used by a company.

Exhibit 3-4
Chart of Accounts for a Theater

100–199:	ASSETS
100–109:	Cash
101:	Cash, Checking, Second National Bank
102:	Cash, Savings, Third State Bank
103:	Cash, Change, or Petty Cash Fund (coin and currency)
110–119:	Receivables
111:	Accounts Receivable
112:	Due from Employees
113:	Notes Receivable
120–129:	Prepaid Assets
121:	Cleaning Supplies
122:	Prepaid Insurance
130–139:	Property, Plant, and Equipment
131:	Land
132:	Theater Buildings
133:	Projection Equipment
134:	Furniture and Fixtures

(continued)

Exhibit 3-4

Chart of Accounts for a Theater (*continued*)

200–299:	LIABILITIES
200–209:	Short-Term Liabilities
201:	Accounts Payable
202:	Wages and Salaries Payable
203:	Taxes Payable
203.1:	Income Taxes Payable
203.2:	Sales Taxes Payable
203.3:	Unemployment Taxes Payable
204:	Short-Term Notes Payable
204.1:	Six-Month Note Payable to First State Bank
210–219:	Long-Term Liabilities
211:	Bonds Payable, due in 2013
300–399:	STOCKHOLDERS' EQUITY
301:	Preferred Stock
302:	Common Stock
303:	Retained Earnings
400–499:	REVENUES
401:	Tickets
402:	Video Rentals
403:	Concessions
404:	Interest
500–599:	EXPENSES
500–509:	Rentals
501:	Films
502:	Videos
510–519:	Concessions
511:	Candy
512:	Soda
513:	Popcorn
520–529:	Wages and Salaries
521:	Hourly Employees
522:	Salaries
530–539:	Utilities
531:	Heat
532:	Electric
533:	Water
540–549:	Advertising
541:	Newspaper
542:	Radio
550–559:	Taxes
551:	Income Taxes
552:	Unemployment Taxes

The General Ledger

LO 4 Define the concept of a general ledger and understand the use of the T account as a method for analyzing transactions.

General ledger A book, file, hard drive, or other device containing all the accounts.

Companies store their accounts in different ways, depending on their accounting system. In a manual system, a separate card or sheet is used to record the activity in each account. A **general ledger** is simply the file or book that contains the accounts.[4] For example, the general ledger for Widescreen Theaters Corporation might consist of a file of cards in a cabinet, with a card for each of the accounts listed in the chart of accounts.

[4]In addition to a general ledger, many companies maintain subsidiary ledgers. For example, an accounts receivable subsidiary ledger contains a separate account for each customer. The use of a subsidiary ledger for Accounts Receivable is discussed further in Chapter 7.

In today's business world, most companies have an automated accounting system. The computer is ideally suited for the job of processing vast amounts of data rapidly. *All of the tools discussed in this chapter are as applicable to computerized systems as they are to manual systems. It is merely the appearance of the tools that differs between manual and computerized systems.* For example, the ledger in an automated system might be contained on a computer file server rather than stored in a file cabinet. Throughout the book, we will use a manual system to explain the various tools, such as ledger accounts. The reason is that it is easier to illustrate and visualize the tools in a manual system. However, all of the ideas apply just as well to a computerized system of accounting.

THE DOUBLE-ENTRY SYSTEM

The origin of the double-entry system of accounting can be traced to Venice, Italy, in 1494. In that year, Fra Luca Pacioli, a Franciscan monk, wrote a mathematical treatise. Included in his book was the concept of debits and credits that is still used almost universally today.

The T Account

The form for a general ledger account will be illustrated later in the chapter. However, the form of account often used to analyze transactions is called the *T account,* so named because it resembles the capital letter T. The name of the account appears across the horizontal line. One side is used to record increases and the other side decreases, but as you will see, the same side is not used for increases for every account. As a matter of convention, the *left* side of an *asset* account is used to record *increases* and the *right* side to record *decreases.* To illustrate a T account, we will look at the Cash account for Glengarry Health Club. The transactions recorded in the account can be traced to Exhibit 3-1.

CASH			
INCREASES		**DECREASES**	
Investment by owners	100,000	Wages and salaries	10,000
Court fees collected	5,000	Utilities	3,000
Accounts collected	4,000	Dividends	2,000
	109,000		15,000
Bal.	94,000		

The amounts $109,000 and $15,000 are called *footings.* They represent the totals of the amounts on each side of the account. Neither these amounts nor the balance of $94,000 represents transactions. They are simply shown to indicate the totals and the balance in the account.

Debits and Credits

LO 5 Explain the rules of debits and credits.

Debit An entry on the left side of an account.

Credit An entry on the right side of an account.

Rather than refer to the left or right side of an account, accountants use specific labels for each side. The *left* side of any account is the **debit** side, and the *right* side of any account is the **credit** side. We will also use the terms *debit* and *credit* as verbs. If we *debit* the Cash account, we enter an amount on the left side. Similarly, if we want to enter an amount on the right side of an account, we *credit* the account. To *charge* an account has the same meaning as to *debit* it. No such synonym exists for the act of crediting an account.

Note that *debit* and *credit* are *locational* terms. They simply refer to the left or right side of a T account. They do *not* represent increases or decreases. As we will see, when one type of account is increased (for example, the Cash account), the increase is on the left or *debit* side. When certain other types of accounts are increased, however, the entry will be on the right or *credit* side.

Study Tip

Once you know the rule to increase an asset with a debit, the rules for the other increases and decreases follow logically. For example, because a liability is the opposite of an asset, it is increased with a credit. And it follows logically that it would be decreased with a debit.

As you would expect from your understanding of the accounting equation, the conventions for using T accounts for assets and liabilities are opposite. Assets are future economic benefits, and liabilities are obligations to transfer economic benefits in the future. If an asset is *increased* with a *debit,* how do you think a liability would be increased? *Because assets and liabilities are opposites, if an asset is increased with a debit, a liability is increased with a credit.* Thus, the right side, or credit side, of a liability account is used to record an increase. Like liabilities, owners' equity accounts are on the opposite side of the accounting equation from assets. *Thus, like a liability, an owners' equity account is increased with a credit.* We can summarize the logic of debits and credits, increases and decreases, and the accounting equation in the following way:

ASSETS		=	LIABILITIES		+	OWNERS' EQUITY	
Debits Increases +	Credits Decreases −		Debits Decreases −	Credits Increases +		Debits Decreases −	Credits Increases +

Note again that debits and credits are location-oriented. Debits are always on the left side of an account and credits on the right side.

Accounting for Your Decisions

You Are a Student

A classmate comes to you with a question about the bank statement she has received. Why does the bank credit her account when she makes a deposit to her account, but accounting rules state that cash is increased with a debit?

ANS: The bank is looking at customer deposits from its perspective and not the customers'. Checking account deposits represent liabilities to the bank, such as "Deposits Payable." Thus, when customers make deposits, the bank has increased its liability to those customers, with a credit to its "Deposits Payable."

Debits and Credits for Revenues, Expenses, and Dividends

In our Glengarry Health Club example, revenues were an increase in Retained Earnings. The sale of memberships was not only an increase in the asset Accounts Receivable but also an increase in the owners' equity account Retained Earnings. The transaction resulted in an increase in the owners' claim on the assets of the business. Rather than being recorded directly in Retained Earnings, however, each revenue item is maintained in a separate account. The following logic is used to arrive at the rules for increasing and decreasing revenues:[5]

1. Retained Earnings is increased with a credit.
2. Revenue is an increase in Retained Earnings.
3. Revenue is increased with a credit.
4. Because revenue is increased with a credit, it is decreased with a debit.

The same logic is applied to the rules for increasing and decreasing expense accounts:

1. Retained Earnings is decreased with a debit.
2. Expense is a decrease in Retained Earnings.

[5]We normally think of both revenues and expenses as being only increased, not decreased. Because we will need to decrease them as part of the closing procedure, it is important to know how to reduce these accounts as well as increase them.

3. Expense is increased with a debit.
4. Because expense is increased with a debit, it is decreased with a credit.

Recall that dividends reduce cash. But they also reduce the owners' claim on the assets of the business. Earlier we recognized this decrease in the owners' claim as a reduction of Retained Earnings. As we do for revenue and expense accounts, we will use a separate Dividends account:

1. Retained Earnings is decreased with a debit.
2. Dividends are a decrease in Retained Earnings.
3. Dividends are increased with a debit.
4. Because dividends are increased with a debit, they are decreased with a credit.

Summary of the Rules for Increasing and Decreasing Accounts

The rules for increasing and decreasing the various types of accounts are summarized as follows:

Type of Account	Debit	Credit
Asset	Increase	Decrease
Liability	Decrease	Increase
Owners' Equity	Decrease	Increase
Revenue	Decrease	Increase
Expense	Increase	Decrease
Dividends	Increase	Decrease

Normal Account Balances

Each account has a "normal" balance. For example, assets normally have debit balances. Would it be possible for an asset such as Cash to have a credit balance? Assume that a company has a checking account with a bank. A credit balance in the account would indicate that the decreases in the account, from checks written and other bank charges, were more than the deposits into the account. If this were the case, however, the company would no longer have an asset, Cash, but instead would have a liability to the bank. The normal balances for the accounts we have looked at are as follows:

Type of Account	Normal Balance
Asset	Debit
Liability	Credit
Owners' Equity	Credit
Revenue	Credit
Expense	Debit
Dividends	Debit

Debits Aren't Bad, and Credits Aren't Good

Students often approach their first encounter with debits and credits with preconceived notions. The use of the terms *debit* and *credit* in everyday language leads to many of these notions. "Joe is a real credit to his team." "Nancy should be credited with saving Mary's career." These both appear to be very positive statements. You must resist the temptation to associate the term *credit* with something good or positive and the term *debit* with something bad or negative. *In accounting, debit means one thing: an entry made on the left side of an account. A credit means an entry made on the right side of an account.*

Debits and Credits Applied to Transactions

Recall the first transaction recorded by Glengarry Health Club earlier in the chapter: the owners invested $100,000 cash in the business. The transaction resulted in an increase in the Cash account and an increase in the Capital Stock account. Applying the rules of debits and credits, we would *debit* the Cash account for $100,000 and *credit* the Capital Stock account for the same amount:[6]

CASH	
(1) 100,000	

CAPITAL STOCK	
	100,000 (1)

Double-entry system A system of accounting in which every transaction is recorded with equal debits and credits and the accounting equation is kept in balance.

You now can see why we refer to the **double-entry system** of accounting. Every transaction is recorded so that the equality of debits and credits is maintained, and in the process, the accounting equation is kept in balance. *Every transaction is entered in at least two accounts on opposite sides of T accounts. Our first transaction resulted in an increase in an asset account and an increase in an owners' equity account. For every transaction, the debit side must equal the credit side. The debit of $100,000 to the Cash account equals the credit of $100,000 to the Capital Stock account.* It naturally follows that if the debit side must equal the credit side for every transaction, at any point in time the total of all debits recorded must equal the total of all credits recorded. Thus, the fundamental accounting equation remains in balance.

Transactions for Glengarry Health Club

Three distinct steps are involved in recording a transaction in the accounts.

1. First, we *analyze* the transaction. That is, we decide what accounts are increased or decreased and by how much.
2. Second, we *recall* the rules of debits and credits as they apply to the transaction we are analyzing.
3. Finally, we *record* the transaction using the rules of debits and credits.

We return to the transactions of the health club. We have already explained the logic for the debit to the Cash account and the credit to the Capital Stock account for the initial investment by the owners. We will now analyze the remaining eight transactions for the month. Refer to Exhibit 3-1 for a summary of the transactions.

(2) A building and land are exchanged for a promissory note.
- (a) *Analyze:* Two asset accounts are increased: Building and Land. The liability account Notes Payable is also increased.
- (b) *Recall the rules of debits and credits:* An asset is increased with a debit, and a liability is increased with a credit.
- (c) *Record the transaction:*

BUILDING	
(2) 150,000	

LAND	
(2) 50,000	

NOTES PAYABLE	
	200,000 (2)

(3) Exercise equipment is purchased from a supplier on open account. The purchase price is $20,000.
- (a) *Analyze:* An asset account, Equipment, is increased. A liability account, Accounts Payable, is also increased. Thus, the transaction is identical to the last transaction in that an asset or assets are increased and a liability is increased.

[6]We will use the numbers of each transaction, as they were labeled earlier in the chapter, to identify the transactions. In practice, a formal ledger account is used, and transactions are entered according to their date.

(b) *Recall the rules of debits and credits:* An asset is increased with a debit, and a liability is increased with a credit.

(c) *Record the transaction:*

EQUIPMENT	
(3) **20,000**	

ACCOUNTS PAYABLE	
	20,000 (3)

(4) Three hundred club memberships are sold for $50 each. The members have until the 10th of the following month to pay.

(a) *Analyze:* The asset account Accounts Receivable is increased by $15,000. This amount is an asset because the company has the right to collect it in the future. The owners' claim to the assets is increased by the same amount. Recall, however, that we do not record these claims—revenues—directly in an owners' equity account but instead use a separate revenue account. We will call the account Membership Revenue.

(b) *Recall the rules of debits and credits:* An asset is increased with a debit. Owners' equity is increased with a credit. Because revenue is an increase in owners' equity, it is increased with a credit.

(c) *Record the transaction:*

ACCOUNTS RECEIVABLE	
(4) **15,000**	

MEMBERSHIP REVENUE	
	15,000 (4)

(5) Court fees are paid at the time of use and amount to $5,000 for the first month.

(a) *Analyze:* The asset account Cash is increased by $5,000. The owners' claim to the assets is increased by the same amount. The account used to record the increase in the owners' claim is Court Fee Revenue.

(b) *Recall the rules of debits and credits:* An asset is increased with a debit. Owners' equity is increased with a credit. Because revenue is an increase in owners' equity, it is increased with a credit.

(c) *Record the transaction:*

CASH	
(1) 100,000	
(5) **5,000**	

COURT FEE REVENUE	
	5,000 (5)

(6) Wages and salaries amount to $10,000, and they are paid in cash.

(a) *Analyze:* The asset account, Cash, is decreased by $10,000. At the same time, the owners' claim to the assets is decreased by this amount. However, rather than record a decrease directly to Retained Earnings, we set up an expense account, Wage and Salary Expense.

(b) *Recall the rules of debits and credits:* An asset is decreased with a credit. Owners' equity is decreased with a debit. Because expense is a decrease in owners' equity, it is increased with a debit.

(c) *Record the transaction:*

CASH	
(1) 100,000	**10,000** (6)
(5) 5,000	

WAGE AND SALARY EXPENSE	
(6) **10,000**	

(7) The utility bill of $3,000 for the first month is paid in cash.

(a) *Analyze:* The asset account Cash is decreased by $3,000. At the same time, the owners' claim to the assets is decreased by this amount. However, rather than record a decrease directly to Retained Earnings, we set up an expense account, Utility Expense.

(b) *Recall the rules of debits and credits:* An asset is decreased with a credit. Owners' equity is decreased with a debit. Because expense is a decrease in owners' equity, it is increased with a debit.

(c) *Record the transaction:*

CASH			UTILITIES EXPENSE	
(1) 100,000	10,000 (6)		**(7) 3,000**	
(5) 5,000	**3,000 (7)**			

(8) Cash of $4,000 is collected from members for their January dues.

(a) *Analyze:* Cash is increased by the amount collected from the members. Another asset, Accounts Receivable, is decreased by the same amount. Glengarry has simply traded one asset for another.

(b) *Recall the rules of debits and credits:* An asset is increased with a debit and decreased with a credit. Thus, one asset is debited, and another is credited.

(c) *Record the transaction:*

CASH			ACCOUNTS RECEIVABLE	
(1) 100,000	10,000 (6)		(4) 15,000	**4,000 (8)**
(5) 5,000	3,000 (7)			
(8) 4,000				

(9) Dividends of $2,000 are distributed to the owners.

(a) *Analyze:* The asset account Cash is decreased by $2,000. At the same time, the owners' claim to the assets is decreased by this amount. Earlier in the chapter, we decreased Retained Earnings for dividends paid to the owners. Now we will use a separate account, Dividends, to record these distributions.

(b) *Recall the rules of debits and credits:* An asset is decreased with a credit. Retained earnings is decreased with a debit. Because dividends are a decrease in retained earnings, they are increased with a debit.

(c) *Record the transaction:*

CASH			DIVIDENDS	
(1) 100,000	10,000 (6)		**(9) 2,000**	
(5) 5,000	3,000 (7)			
(8) 4,000	**2,000 (9)**			

Two-Minute Review

1. *Assume Glengarry pays the supplier the amount owed on open account. Record this transaction in the appropriate T accounts.*
2. *Assume Glengarry collects the remaining amount owed by members for dues. Record this transaction in the appropriate T accounts.*

Answers on page 122.

THE JOURNAL: THE FIRM'S CHRONOLOGICAL RECORD OF TRANSACTIONS

LO 6 Explain the purposes of a journal and the posting process.

Journal A chronological record of transactions, also known as the book of original entry.

Posting The process of transferring amounts from a journal to the ledger accounts.

Each of the nine transactions was entered directly in the ledger accounts. By looking at the Cash account, we see that it increased by $5,000 in transaction (5). But what was the other side of this transaction? That is, what account was credited? To have a record of *each entry,* transactions are recorded first in a journal. A **journal** is a chronological record of transactions entered into by a business. Because a journal lists transactions in the order in which they took place, it is called the *book of original entry.* Transactions are recorded first in a journal and then are posted to the ledger accounts. **Posting** is the process of transferring a journal entry to the ledger accounts:

Note that posting does not result in any change in the amounts recorded. It is simply a process of re-sorting the transactions from a chronological order to a topical arrangement.

A journal entry is recorded for each transaction. **Journalizing** is the process of recording entries in a journal. A standard format is normally used for recording journal entries. Consider the original investment by the owners of Glengarry Health Club. The format of the journal entry is as follows:

Journalizing The act of recording journal entries.

		DEBIT	CREDIT
Jan. xx	Cash	100,000	
	Capital Stock		100,000
	To record the issuance of 10,000 shares of stock for cash.		

Each journal entry contains a date with columns for the amounts debited and credited. Accounts credited are indented to distinguish them from accounts debited. A brief explanation normally appears on the line below the entry.

Transactions are normally recorded in a **general journal.** Specialized journals may be used to record repetitive transactions. For example, a cash receipts journal may be used to record all transactions in which cash is received. Special journals accomplish the same purpose as a general journal, but they save time in recording similar transactions. In this chapter, we will use a general journal to record all transactions.

General journal The journal used in place of a specialized journal.

An excerpt from Glengarry Health Club's general journal appears in the top portion of Exhibit 3-5. One column needs further explanation. *Post. Ref.* is an abbreviation for *Posting Reference.* As part of the posting process explained below, the debit and credit amounts are posted to the appropriate accounts, and this column is filled in with the number assigned to the account.

From Concept to Practice 3.3

Reading Winnebago Industries' Financial Statements

Refer to **Winnebago Industries'** *income statement and its balance sheet. Using the appropriate accounts from these statements, prepare the journal entry Winnebago Industries would record if it sold an RV to a dealer for $100,000 and gave the dealer 30 days to pay.*

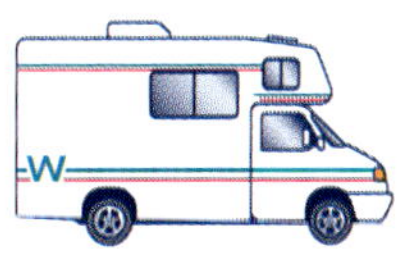

Journal entries and ledger accounts are both *tools* used by the accountant. The end result, a set of financial statements, is the most important part of the process. Journalizing provides us with a chronological record of each transaction. So why not just prepare financial statements directly from the journal entries? Isn't it just extra work to *post* the entries to the ledger accounts? In our simple example of Glengarry Health Club, it would be possible to prepare the statements directly from the journal entries. In real-world situations, however, the number of transactions in any given period is so large that it would be virtually impossible, if not terribly inefficient, to bypass the accounts. Accounts provide us with a convenient summary of the activity, as well as the balance, for a specific financial statement item.

The posting process for Glengarry Health Club is illustrated in Exhibit 3-5 for the health club's fifth transaction, in which cash is collected for court fees. Rather than a

Exhibit 3-5 Posting from the Journal to the Ledger

General Journal — Page No. 1

Date		Account Titles and Explanation	Post. Ref.	Debit	Credit
2004 Jan.	XX	Accounts Receivable	5	15000	
		Membership Revenue	40		15000
		Sold 300 memberships at $50 each.			
	XX	Cash	1	5000	
		Court Fee Revenue	44		5000
		Collected court fees.			

General Ledger

Cash — Account No. 1

Date		Explanation	Post. Ref.	Debit	Credit	Balance
2004 Jan.	XX		GJ1	100000		100000
	XX		GJ1	5000		105000

Court Fee Revenue — Account No. 44

Date		Explanation	Post. Ref.	Debit	Credit	Balance
2004 Jan.	XX		GJ1		5000	5000

T-account format for the general ledger accounts, the *running balance form* is illustrated. A separate column indicates the balance in the ledger account after each transaction. The use of the explanation column in a ledger account is optional. Because an explanation of the entry in the account can be found by referring to the journal, this column is often left blank.

Note the cross-referencing between the journal and the ledger. As amounts are entered in the ledger accounts, the Posting Reference column is filled in with the page number of the journal. (For example, GJ1 to indicate page 1 from the general journal). At the same time, the Posting Reference column of the journal is filled in with the appropriate account number.

The frequency of posting differs among companies, partly based on the degree to which their accounting system is automated. For example, in some computerized systems, amounts are posted to the ledger accounts at the time an entry is recorded in the journal. In a manual system, posting is normally done periodically, for example, daily, weekly, or monthly. Regardless of when performed, the posting process changes nothing. It simply reorganizes the transactions by account.

Accounting for Your Decisions

You Are the Manager

You are the community relations manager for a company. You need to determine whether the company is spending its money wisely in promoting its image in the local community.

1. What types of accounts would you examine? Give examples of the possible names for some of these accounts.
2. Would a general journal or a general ledger be more useful to you in making your determination? Explain your answer.

ANS: 1. Among the possible accounts that you want to examine are Entertainment, Travel, Promotions, Advertising, and Miscellaneous, in addition to any accounts that might contain expenditures related to community relations.

2. You may want to examine the general ledger for each of the accounts listed in part 1. The ledger contains a record for each of the accounts and the activity in them during the period.

THE TRIAL BALANCE

LO 7 Explain the purpose of a trial balance.

Trial balance A list of each account and its balance; used to prove equality of debits and credits.

Accountants use one other tool to facilitate the preparation of a set of financial statements. A **trial balance** is a list of each account and its balance at a specific point in time. The trial balance is *not* a financial statement but merely a convenient device to prove the equality of the debit and credit balances in the accounts. It can be as informal as an adding-machine tape with the account titles penciled in next to the debit and credit amounts. A trial balance for Glengarry Health Club as of January 31, 2004, is shown in Exhibit 3-6. The balance in each account was determined by adding the increases and subtracting the decreases for the account for the transactions detailed earlier.

Exhibit 3-6

Trial Balance for Glengarry Health Club

GLENGARRY HEALTH CLUB
TRIAL BALANCE
JANUARY 31, 2004

Account Titles	Debits	Credits
Cash	$ 94,000	
Accounts Receivable	11,000	
Equipment	20,000	
Building	150,000	
Land	50,000	
Accounts Payable		$ 20,000
Notes Payable		200,000
Capital Stock		100,000
Membership Revenue		15,000
Court Fee Revenue		5,000
Wage and Salary Expense	10,000	
Utility Expense	3,000	
Dividends	2,000	
Totals	$340,000	$340,000

Study Tip

Remember from p. 115 that every account has a normal balance, either debit or credit. Note the normal balances for each account on this trial balance.

Certain types of errors are detectable from a trial balance. For example, if the balance of an account is incorrectly computed, the total of the debits and credits in the trial balance will not equal. If a debit is posted to an account as a credit, or vice versa, the trial balance will be out of balance. The omission of part of a journal entry in the posting process will also be detected by the preparation of a trial balance.

Do not attribute more significance to a trial balance, however, than is warranted. It does provide a convenient summary of account balances for preparing financial statements. It also assures us that the balances of all the debit accounts equal the balances of all the credit accounts. But an equality of debits and credits does not necessarily mean that the *correct* accounts were debited and credited in an entry. For example, the entry to record the purchase of land by signing a promissory note *should* result in a debit to Land and a credit to Notes Payable. If the accountant incorrectly debited Cash instead of Land, the trial balance would still show an equality of debits and credits. A trial balance can be prepared at any time; it is usually prepared before the release of a set of financial statements.

Accounting for Your Decisions

You Are the Stockholder

You own 100 shares of stock in **General Motors.** Every year you receive GM's annual report, which includes a chairman's letter, a description of new models, a financial section, and notes to financial statements. Nowhere in the report do you see a general ledger or a trial balance. Is General Motors hiding something?

ANS: GM's balance sheet, income statement, and statement of cash flows are derived from the company's journal entries, general ledgers, trial balances, and so on. These documents are the building blocks of the final statements. There could literally be millions of transactions during the year—which even the most diehard accounting fan would tire of reading.

Answers to the Two-Minute Reviews

Two-Minute Review on Page 108

1. *Equipment will increase by $10,000, and Cash will decrease by $10,000.*
2. *$325,000 (the effect of the transaction is to increase and decrease assets by the same amount).*

Two-Minute Review on Page 118

1.

CASH	
	20,000

ACCOUNTS PAYABLE	
20,000	

2.

CASH	
11,000	

ACCOUNTS RECEIVABLE	
	11,000

Warmup Exercises

Warmup Exercise 3-1 *Your Debits and Credits* **LO 3, 5**

Assume that you borrow $1,000 from your roommate by signing an agreement to repay the amount borrowed in six months.

Required

1. What is the effect of this transaction on your own accounting equation?
2. Prepare the journal entry to record this transaction in your own records.

Key to the Solution

Recall Exhibit 3-1 for the effects of transactions on the accounting equation, and refer to the summary of the rules for increasing and decreasing accounts on p. 115.

Warmup Exercise 3-2 ***A Bank's Debits and Credits*** **LO 3, 5**

The Third State Bank loans a customer $5,000 in exchange for a promissory note.

Required

1. What is the effect of this transaction on the bank's accounting equation?
2. Prepare the journal entry to record this transaction in the bank's records.

Key to the Solution

Recall Exhibit 3-1 for the effects of the transaction on the accounting equation, and refer to the summary of the rules for increasing and decreasing accounts on p. 115.

Warmup Exercise 3-3 ***Debits and Credits for Winnebago Industries*** **LO 3, 5**

Assume Winnebago Industries goes to its bank and borrows $50,000 by signing a promissory note. The next day the company uses the money to buy a piece of machinery for use in its manufacturing facility.

Required

1. What is the effect of each of these two transactions on Winnebago Industries' accounting equation?
2. Prepare the journal entries to record both transactions in Winnebago Industries' records.

Key to the Solution

Recall Exhibit 3-1 for the effects of transactions on the accounting equation, and refer to the summary of the rules for increasing and decreasing accounts on p. 115.

Solutions to Warmup Exercises

Warmup Exercise 3-1

1. If you borrow $1,000 from your roommate, assets in the form of cash, increase $1,000, and liabilities in the form of a note payable, increase $1,000.
2. Journal entry:

	Debit	Credit
Cash	1,000	
Notes Payable		1,000

Warmup Exercise 3-2

1. If a bank loans a customer $5,000, the bank's assets, in the form of a note receivable, increase $5,000, and its assets, in the form of cash, decrease $5,000.
2. Journal entry:

	Debit	Credit
Notes Receivable	5,000	
Cash		5,000

Warmup Exercise 3-3

1. If Winnebago Industries borrows $50,000 from its bank, assets, in the form of cash, increase $50,000, and liabilities, in the form of a note payable, increase $50,000. If the company uses the money to buy a machine, assets, in the form of machinery, increase $50,000, and assets, in the form of cash, decrease $50,000.
2. Journal entries:

	Debit	Credit
Cash	50,000	
Notes Payable		50,000
Machinery	50,000	
Cash		50,000

Review Problem

WebTUTOR™ Advantage

The following transactions are entered into by Sparkle Car Wash during its first month of operations:

a. Articles of incorporation are filed with the state, and 20,000 shares of capital stock are issued. Cash of $40,000 is received from the new owners for the shares.

b. A five-year promissory note is signed at the local bank. The cash received from the loan is $120,000.

c. An existing car wash is purchased for $150,000 in cash. The values assigned to the land, building, and equipment are $25,000, $75,000, and $50,000, respectively.

d. Cleaning supplies are purchased on account for $2,500 from a distributor. All of the supplies are used in the first month.

e. During the first month, $1,500 is paid to the distributor for the cleaning supplies. The remaining $1,000 will be paid next month.

f. Gross receipts from car washes during the first month of operations amount to $7,000.

g. Wages and salaries paid in the first month amount to $2,000.

h. The utility bill of $800 for the month is paid.

i. A total of $1,000 in dividends is paid to the owners.

Required

1. Prepare a table to summarize the preceding transactions as they affect the accounting equation. Use the format in Exhibit 3-1. Identify each transaction by letter.
2. Prepare an income statement for the month.
3. Prepare a balance sheet at the end of the month.

Solution to Review Problem

1.

SPARKLE CAR WASH
TRANSACTIONS FOR THE MONTH

	Assets				=	Liabilities		+	Owners' Equity	
TRANS.	**CASH**	**LAND**	**BUILDING**	**EQUIPMENT**		**ACCOUNTS PAYABLE**	**NOTES PAYABLE**		**CAPITAL STOCK**	**RETAINED EARNINGS**
a.	$ 40,000								$40,000	
b.	120,000						$120,000			
Bal.	$160,000						$120,000		$40,000	
c.	–150,000	$25,000	$75,000	$50,000						
Bal.	$ 10,000	$25,000	$75,000	$50,000			$120,000		$40,000	
d.						$2,500				$–2,500
Bal.	$ 10,000	$25,000	$75,000	$50,000		$2,500	$120,000		$40,000	$–2,500
e.	–1,500					–1,500				
Bal.	$ 8,500	$25,000	$75,000	$50,000		$1,000	$120,000		$40,000	$–2,500
f.	7,000									7,000
Bal.	$ 15,500	$25,000	$75,000	$50,000		$1,000	$120,000		$40,000	$ 4,500
g.	–2,000									–2,000
Bal.	$ 13,500	$25,000	$75,000	$50,000		$1,000	$120,000		$40,000	$ 2,500
h.	–800									– 800
Bal.	$ 12,700	$25,000	$75,000	$50,000		$1,000	$120,000		$40,000	$ 1,700
i.	–1,000									– 1,000
Bal.	$ 11,700	$25,000	$75,000	$50,000		$1,000	$120,000		$40,000	$ 700

Total assets: $161,700

Total liabilities and owners' equity: $161,700

2.

SPARKLE CAR WASH
INCOME STATEMENT
FOR THE MONTH ENDED XX/XX/XX

Car wash revenue		$7,000
Expenses:		
Supplies	$2,500	
Wages and salaries	2,000	
Utilities	800	5,300
Net income		$1,700

3.

SPARKLE CAR WASH
BALANCE SHEET
XX/XX/XX

Assets		**Liabilities and Owners' Equity**	
Cash	$ 11,700	Accounts payable	$ 1,000
Land	25,000	Notes payable	120,000
Building	75,000	Capital stock	40,000
Equipment	50,000	Retained earnings	700
Total assets	$161,700	Total liabilities and owners' equity	$161,700

Chapter Highlights

1. **LO 1** Both internal and external events affect an entity. External events, such as the purchase of materials, involve the entity and its environment. Internal events, such as the placement of the materials into production, do not involve an outside entity. For any event to be recorded, it must be measurable.
2. **LO 2** Source documents are used as the basis for recording events as transactions. For certain repetitive transactions, a standard source document is used, such as a time card to document the payroll for the week. For other nonrepetitive transactions, a source document has to be generated for the specific event.
3. **LO 3** Economic events are the basis for recording transactions. These transactions result in changes in the company's financial position. Transactions change the amount of individual items on the balance sheet, but the statement must balance after each transaction is recorded.
4. **LO 4** A separate account is used for each identifiable asset, liability, revenue, expense, and component of owners' equity. No standard set of accounts exists, and the types of accounts used depend to a certain extent on the nature of a company's business. A chart of accounts is a numerical list of all the accounts used by an entity. The general ledger in a manual system might consist of a set of cards, one for each account, in a file cabinet. In a computerized system, a magnetic tape or diskette might be used to store the accounts.
5. **LO 4** Accountants use T accounts as the basic form of analysis of transactions. The left side of an account is used for debits, and the right side is for credits. Transactions are recorded in the ledger in more formal accounts than the typical T account.
6. **LO 5** By convention, the left side of an asset account is used to record increases. Thus, an asset account is increased with a debit. Because liabilities are on the opposite side of the accounting equation, they are increased with a credit. Similarly, owners' equity accounts are increased with a credit. Because revenue is an increase in owners' equity, it is increased with a credit. Thus, an expense, as well as a dividend, is increased with a debit. According to the double-entry system, there are two sides to every transaction. For each transaction, the debit or debits must equal the credit or credits.
7. **LO 6** Transactions are not recorded directly in the accounts but are recorded initially in a journal. A separate entry is recorded in the journal for each transaction. The account(s) debited appears first in the entry, with the account(s) credited listed next and indented. Separate columns for debits and credits are used to indicate the amounts for each. A general journal is used in lieu of any specialized journals.
8. **LO 6** Amounts appearing in journal entries are posted to the ledger accounts. Posting can be done either at the time the entry is recorded or periodically. The Post. Ref. column in a journal indicates the account number to which the amount is posted, and a similar column in the account acts as a convenient reference back to the particular page number in the journal.
9. **LO 7** A trial balance proves the equality of the debits and credits in the accounts. If only one side of a transaction is posted to the accounts, the trial balance will not balance. Other types of errors are detectable from the process of preparing a trial balance. It cannot, however, detect all errors. A trial balance could be in balance even though the wrong asset account is debited in an entry.

http://

http://porter.swlearning.com

Technology and other resources for your success

If you need additional help, visit the text's Web site. Also, see pages xv–xvii in this text's preface for a description of available technology and other resources. If your instructor is using PERSONAL Trainer in this course, you may complete, on line, the assignments identified by PT.

Key Terms Quiz

Read each definition below, and then write the number of the definition in the blank beside the appropriate term it defines. The quiz solutions appear at the end of the chapter.

_____ Event
_____ External event
_____ Internal event
_____ Transaction
_____ Source document
_____ Account
_____ Chart of accounts
_____ General ledger
_____ Debit
_____ Credit
_____ Double-entry system
_____ Journal
_____ Posting
_____ Journalizing
_____ General journal
_____ Trial balance

1. A numerical list of all the accounts used by a company.
2. A list of each account and its balance at a specific point in time; used to prove the equality of debits and credits.
3. A happening of consequence to an entity.
4. An entry on the right side of an account.
5. An event occurring entirely within an entity.
6. A piece of paper, such as a sales invoice, that is used as the evidence to record a transaction.
7. The act of recording journal entries.
8. An entry on the left side of an account.
9. The process of transferring amounts from a journal to the appropriate ledger accounts.
10. An event involving interaction between an entity and its environment.
11. The record used to accumulate monetary amounts for each individual asset, liability, revenue, expense, and component of owners' equity.
12. A book, file, hard drive, or other device containing all of a company's accounts.
13. A chronological record of transactions, also known as the *book of original entry.*
14. Any event, external or internal, that is recognized in a set of financial statements.
15. The journal used in place of a specialized journal.
16. A system of accounting in which every transaction is recorded with equal debits and credits and the accounting equation is kept in balance.

Answers on p. 146.

Alternate Terms

Credit side of an account Right side of an account

Debit an account Charge an account

Debit side of an account Left side of an account

General ledger Set of accounts

Journal Book of original entry

Journalize an entry Record an entry

Posting an account Transferring an amount from the journal to the ledger

Questions

1. What are the two types of events that affect an entity? Describe each.
2. What is the significance of source documents to the recording process? Give two examples of source documents.
3. What are four different forms of cash?
4. How does an account receivable differ from a note receivable?
5. What is meant by the statement "One company's account receivable is another company's account payable"?
6. What do accountants mean when they refer to the "double-entry system" of accounting?
7. Owners' equity represents the claim of the owners on the assets of the business. What is the distinction relative to the owners' claim between the Capital Stock account and the Retained Earnings account?
8. If an asset account is increased with a debit, what is the logic for increasing a liability account with a credit?
9. A friend comes to you with the following plight: "I'm confused. An asset is something positive, and it is increased with a debit. However, an expense is something negative, and it is also increased with a debit. I don't get it." How can you straighten your friend out?
10. The payment of dividends reduces cash. If the Cash account is reduced with a credit, why is the Dividends account debited when dividends are paid?
11. If Cash is increased with a debit, why does the bank credit your account when you make a deposit?
12. Your friend presents the following criticism of the accounting system: "Accounting involves so much duplication of effort.

First, entries are recorded in a journal, and then the same information is recorded in a ledger. No wonder accountants work such long hours!" Do you agree with this criticism?

13. How does the T account differ from the running balance form for an account? How are they similar?

14. What is the benefit of using a cross-referencing system between a ledger and a journal?

15. How often should a company post entries from the journal to the ledger?

16. What is the purpose of a trial balance?

Exercises

Exercise 3-1 ***Types of Events*** **LO 1**

For each of the following events, identify whether it is an external event that would be recorded as a transaction (E), an internal event that would be recorded as a transaction (I), or not recorded (NR):

_______ 1. A supplier of a company's raw material is paid an amount owed on account.

_______ 2. A customer pays its open account.

_______ 3. A new chief executive officer is hired.

_______ 4. The biweekly payroll is paid.

_______ 5. Raw materials are entered into production.

_______ 6. A new advertising agency is hired to develop a series of newspaper ads for the company.

_______ 7. The advertising bill for the first month is paid.

_______ 8. The accountant determines the federal income taxes owed based on the income earned during the period.

Exercise 3-2 ***Source Documents Matched with Transactions*** **LO 2**

Following are a list of source documents and a list of transactions. Indicate by letter next to each transaction the source document that would serve as evidence for the recording of the transaction.

Source Documents

a. Purchase invoice
b. Sales invoice
c. Cash register tape
d. Time cards
e. Promissory note
f. Stock certificates
g. Monthly statement from utility company
h. No standard source document would normally be available

Transactions

_______ 1. Utilities expense for the month is recorded.

_______ 2. A cash settlement is received from a pending lawsuit.

_______ 3. Owners contribute cash to start a new corporation.

_______ 4. The biweekly payroll is paid.

_______ 5. Cash sales for the day are recorded.

_______ 6. Equipment is acquired on a 30-day open account.

_______ 7. A sale is made on open account.

_______ 8. A building is acquired by signing an agreement to repay a stated amount plus interest in six months.

(continued)

Exercise 3-3 ***The Effect of Transactions on the Accounting Equation*** **LO 3**

For each of the following transactions, indicate whether it increases (I), decreases (D), or has no effect (NE) on the total dollar amount of each of the elements of the accounting equation.

Transactions	Assets	= Liabilities	+ Owners' Equity
Example: Common stock is issued in exchange for cash.	I	NE	I
1. Equipment is purchased for cash.			
2. Sales are made on account.			
3. Cash sales are made.			
4. An account payable is paid off.			
5. Cash is collected on an account receivable.			
6. Buildings are purchased in exchange for a three-year note payable.			
7. Advertising bill for the month is paid.			
8. Dividends are paid to stockholders.			
9. Land is acquired by issuing shares of stock to the owner of the land.			

Exercise 3-4 ***Types of Transactions*** **LO 3**

As you found out in reading the chapter, there are three elements to the accounting equation: assets, liabilities, and owners' equity. You also learned that every transaction affects at least two of these elements. Although other possibilities exist, five types of transactions are described below. For *each* of these five types, write out descriptions of at least *two* transactions that illustrate these types of transactions.

Type of Transaction	Assets	= Liabilities	+ Owners' Equity
1.	Increase	Increase	
2.	Increase		Increase
3.	Decrease	Decrease	
4.	Decrease		Decrease
5.	Increase Decrease		

Exercise 3-5 ***Balance Sheet Accounts and Their Use*** **LO 4**

Choose from the following list of account titles the one that most accurately fits the description of that account or is an example of that account. An account title may be used more than once or not at all.

Cash	**Accounts Receivable**	**Notes Receivable**
Prepaid Asset	**Land**	**Buildings**
Investments	**Accounts Payable**	**Notes Payable**
Taxes Payable	**Retained Earnings**	**Common Stock**
Preferred Stock		

_______________ 1. A written obligation to repay a fixed amount, with interest, at some time in the future

_______________ 2. Twenty acres of land held for speculation

_______________ 3. An amount owed by a customer

_______________ 4. Corporate income taxes owed to the federal government

_______________ 5. Ownership in a company that allows the owner to receive dividends before common shareholders receive any distributions

_______________ 6. Five acres of land used as the site for a factory

_______________ 7. Amounts owed on an open account to a supplier of raw materials, due in 90 days

__________ 8. A checking account at the bank

__________ 9. A warehouse used to store merchandise

__________ 10. Claims by the owners on the undistributed net income of a business

__________ 11. Rent paid on an office building in advance of use of the facility

Exercise 3-6 ***Normal Account Balances*** **LO 5**

Each account has a normal balance. For the following list of accounts, indicate whether the normal balance of each is a debit or a credit.

Account	Normal Balance
1. Cash	________
2. Prepaid Insurance	________
3. Retained Earnings	________
4. Bonds Payable	________
5. Investments	________
6. Capital Stock	________
7. Advertising Fees Earned	________
8. Wages and Salaries Expense	________
9. Wages and Salaries Payable	________
10. Office Supplies	________
11. Dividends	________

Exercise 3-7 ***Debits and Credits*** **LO 5**

The new bookkeeper for Darby Corporation is getting ready to mail the daily cash receipts to the bank for deposit. Because his previous job was at a bank, he is aware that the bank "credits" your account for all deposits and "debits" your account for all checks written. Therefore, he makes the following entry before sending the daily receipts to the bank:

June 5	Accounts Receivable	10,000	
	Sales Revenue	2,450	
	Cash		12,450
	To record cash received on June 5: $10,000 collections on account and $2,450 in cash sales.		

Required

Explain why this entry is wrong, and prepare the correct journal entry. Why does the bank refer to cash received from a customer as a *credit* to that customer's account?

Exercise 3-8 ***Trial Balance*** **LO 7**

The following list of accounts was taken from the general ledger of Spencer Corporation on December 31, 2004. The bookkeeper thought it would be helpful if the accounts were arranged in alphabetical order. Each account contains the balance normal for that type of account (for example, Cash normally has a debit balance). Prepare a trial balance as of this date, with the accounts arranged in the following order: (1) assets, (2) liabilities, (3) owners' equity, (4) revenues, (5) expenses, and (6) dividends.

Account	Balance
Accounts Payable	$ 7,650
Accounts Receivable	5,325
Automobiles	9,200
Buildings	150,000
Capital Stock	100,000
Cash	10,500
Commissions Expense	2,600
Commissions Revenue	12,750
Dividends	2,000
Equipment	85,000
Heat, Light, and Water Expense	1,400
Income Tax Expense	1,700

(continued)

Account	Balance
Income Taxes Payable	$ 2,500
Interest Revenue	1,300
Land	50,000
Notes Payable	90,000
Office Salaries Expense	6,000
Office Supplies	500
Retained Earnings	110,025

Multi-Concept Exercises

Exercise 3-9 ***Journal Entries Recorded Directly in T Accounts*** **LO 3, 4 , 5**

Record each transaction shown below directly in T accounts, using the numbers preceding the transactions to identify them in the accounts. Each account involved needs a separate T account.

1. Received contribution of $6,500 from each of the three principal owners of the We-Go Delivery Service in exchange for shares of stock.
2. Purchased office supplies for cash of $130.
3. Purchased a van for $15,000 on an open account. The company has 25 days to pay for the van.
4. Provided delivery services to residential customers for cash of $125.
5. Billed a local business $200 for delivery services. The customer is to pay the bill within 15 days.
6. Paid the amount due on the van.
7. Received the amount due from the local business billed in transaction (5) above.

Exercise 3-10 ***Trial Balance*** **LO 4, 7**

Refer to the transactions recorded directly in T accounts for the We-Go Delivery Service in Exercise 3-9. Assume that the transactions all took place during December 2004. Prepare a trial balance at December 31, 2004.

Exercise 3-11 ***Determining an Ending Account Balance*** **LO 3, 4, 5**

Jessie's Bead Shop was organized on June 1, 2004. The company received a contribution of $1,000 from each of the two principal owners. During the month, Jessie's Bead Shop had cash sales of $1,400, had sales on account of $450, received $250 from customers in payment of their accounts, purchased supplies on account for $600 and equipment on account for $1,350, received a utility bill for $250 which will not be paid until July, and paid the full amount due on the equipment. Use a T account to determine the company's Cash balance on June 30, 2004.

Exercise 3-12 ***Reconstructing a Beginning Account Balance*** **LO 3, 4, 5**

During the month, services performed for customers on account amounted to $7,500, and collections from customers in payment of their accounts totaled $6,000. At the end of the month, the Accounts Receivable account had a balance of $2,500. What was the Accounts Receivable balance at the beginning of the month?

Exercise 3-13 ***Journal Entries*** **LO 3, 5, 6**

GENERAL LEDGER

Prepare the journal entry to record each of the following independent transactions (use the number of the transaction in lieu of a date for identification purposes):

1. Sales on account of $1,530
2. Purchases of supplies on account for $1,365
3. Cash sales of $750
4. Purchase of equipment for cash of $4,240
5. Issuance of a promissory note for $2,500
6. Collections on account for $890
7. Sale of capital stock in exchange for a parcel of land; the land is appraised at $50,000
8. Payment of $4,000 in salaries and wages
9. Payment of open account in the amount of $500

Exercise 3-14 ***Journal Entries*** **LO 3, 5, 6**

Following is a list of transactions entered into during the first month of operations of Gardener Corporation, a new landscape service. Prepare in journal form the entry to record each transaction.

April 1: Articles of incorporation are filed with the state, and 100,000 shares of common stock are issued for $100,000 in cash.

April 4: A six-month promissory note is signed at the bank. Interest at 9% per annum will be repaid in six months along with the principal amount of the loan of $50,000.

April 8: Land and a storage shed are acquired for a lump sum of $80,000. On the basis of an appraisal, 25% of the value is assigned to the land and the remainder to the building.

April 10: Mowing equipment is purchased from a supplier at a total cost of $25,000. A down payment of $10,000 is made, with the remainder due by the end of the month.

April 18: Customers are billed for services provided during the first half of the month. The total amount billed of $5,500 is due within 10 days.

April 27: The remaining balance due on the mowing equipment is paid to the supplier.

April 28: The total amount of $5,500 due from customers is received.

April 30: Customers are billed for services provided during the second half of the month. The total amount billed is $9,850.

April 30: Salaries and wages of $4,650 for the month of April are paid.

Exercise 3-15 ***The Process of Posting Journal Entries to General Ledger Accounts***
LO 5, 6

On June 1, Campbell Corporation purchased 10 acres of land in exchange for a promissory note in the amount of $50,000. Using the formats shown in Exhibit 3-5, prepare the journal entry to record this transaction in a general journal, and post it to the appropriate general ledger accounts. The entry will be recorded on page 7 of the general journal. Use whatever account numbers you would like in the general ledger. Assume that none of the accounts to be debited or credited currently contain a balance.

If at a later date you wanted to review this transaction, would you examine the general ledger or the general journal? Explain your answer.

Problems

Problem 3-1 ***Events to Be Recorded in Accounts*** **LO 1**

The following events take place at Dillon's Drive-In:

1. Food is ordered from vendors, who will deliver the food within the week.
2. Vendors deliver food on account, payment due in 30 days.
3. Employees take frozen food from the freezers and prepare it for customers.
4. Food is served to customers, and sales are rung up on the cash register; sales will be totaled at the end of the day.
5. Trash is taken to dumpsters, and the floors are cleaned.
6. Cash registers are cleared at the end of the day.
7. Cash is deposited in the bank night depository.
8. Employees are paid weekly paychecks.
9. Vendors noted in item 2 are paid for the food delivered.

Required

Identify each event as internal (I) or external (E), and indicate whether each event would be recorded in the *accounts* of the company. For each event that is to be recorded, identify the names of at least two accounts that would be affected.

Problem 3-2 ***Transaction Analysis and Financial Statements*** **LO 3**

GENERAL LEDGER

Just Rolling Along Inc. was organized on May 1, 2004, by two college students who recognized an opportunity to make money while spending their days at a beach along Lake Michigan. The two entrepreneurs plan to rent bicycles and in-line skates to weekend visitors to the lakefront. The following transactions occurred during the first month of operations:

May 1: Received contribution of $9,000 from each of the two principal owners of the new business in exchange for shares of stock.

(continued)

May 1: Purchased 10 bicycles for $300 each on an open account. The company has 30 days to pay for the bicycles.

May 5: Registered as a vendor with the city and paid the $15 monthly fee.

May 9: Purchased 20 pairs of in-line skates at $125 per pair, 20 helmets at $50 each, and 20 sets of protective gear (knee and elbow pads and wrist guards) at $45 per set for cash.

May 10: Purchased $100 in miscellaneous supplies on account. The company has 30 days to pay for the supplies.

May 15: Paid $125 bill from local radio station for advertising for the last two weeks of May.

May 17: Customers rented in-line skates and bicycles for cash of $1,800.

May 24: Billed the local park district $1,200 for in-line skating lessons provided to neighborhood kids. The park district is to pay one-half of the bill within five working days and the rest within 30 days.

May 29: Received 50% of the amount billed to the park district.

May 30: Customers rented in-line skates and bicycles for cash of $3,000.

May 30: Paid wages of $160 to a friend who helped out over the weekend.

May 31: Paid the balance due on the bicycles.

Required

1. Prepare a table to summarize the preceding transactions as they affect the accounting equation. Use the format in Exhibit 3-1. Identify each transaction with the date.
2. Prepare an income statement for the month ended May 31, 2004.
3. Prepare a classified balance sheet at May 31, 2004.
4. Why do you think the two college students decided to incorporate their business rather than operate it as a partnership?

Problem 3-3 ***Transaction Analysis and Financial Statements*** **LO 3**

GENERAL LEDGER

SPREADSHEET

Expert Consulting Services Inc. was organized on March 1, 2004, by two former college roommates. The corporation will provide computer consulting services to small businesses. The following transactions occurred during the first month of operations:

March 2: Received contributions of $20,000 from each of the two principal owners of the new business in exchange for shares of stock.

March 7: Signed a two-year promissory note at the bank and received cash of $15,000. Interest, along with the $15,000, will be repaid at the end of the two years.

March 12: Purchased $700 in miscellaneous supplies on account. The company has 30 days to pay for the supplies.

March 19: Billed a client $4,000 for services rendered by Expert in helping to install a new computer system. The client is to pay 25% of the bill upon its receipt and the remaining balance within 30 days.

March 20: Paid $1,300 bill from the local newspaper for advertising for the month of March.

March 22: Received 25% of the amount billed the client on March 19.

March 26: Received cash of $2,800 for services provided in assisting a client in selecting software for its computer.

March 29: Purchased a computer system for $8,000 in cash.

March 30: Paid $3,300 of salaries and wages for March.

March 31: Received and paid $1,400 in gas, electric, and water bills.

Required

1. Prepare a table to summarize the preceding transactions as they affect the accounting equation. Use the format in Exhibit 3-1. Identify each transaction with the date.
2. Prepare an income statement for the month ended March 31, 2004.
3. Prepare a classified balance sheet at March 31, 2004.
4. From reading the balance sheet you prepared in part **3**, what events would you expect to take place in April? Explain your answer.

Problem 3-4 *Transactions Reconstructed from Financial Statements* **LO 3**

The following financial statements are available for Elm Corporation for its first month of operations:

ELM CORPORATION
INCOME STATEMENT
FOR THE MONTH ENDED JUNE 30, 2004

Service revenue		$93,600
Expenses:		
Rent	$ 9,000	
Salaries and wages	27,900	
Utilities	13,800	50,700
Net income		$42,900

ELM CORPORATION
BALANCE SHEET
JUNE 30, 2004

Assets		Liabilities and Owners' Equity	
Cash	$ 22,800	Accounts payable	$ 18,000
Accounts receivable	21,600	Notes payable	90,000
Equipment	18,000	Capital stock	30,000
Building	90,000	Retained earnings	38,400
Land	24,000	Total liabilities and	
Total assets	$176,400	owners' equity	$176,400

Required

Using the format illustrated in Exhibit 3-1, prepare a table to summarize the transactions entered into by Elm Corporation during its first month of business. State any assumptions you believe are necessary in reconstructing the transactions.

Multi-Concept Problems

Problem 3-5 *Identification of Events with Source Documents* **LO 1, 2**

Many events are linked to a source document. The following is a list of events that occurred in an entity:

a. Paid a one-year insurance policy.
b. Paid employee payroll.
c. Sold merchandise to a customer on account.
d. Identified supplies in the storeroom destroyed by fire.
e. Received payment of bills from customers.
f. Purchased land for future expansion.
g. Calculated taxes due.
h. Entered into a car lease agreement and paid the tax, title, and license.

Required

For each item **a** through **h,** indicate whether the event should or should not be recorded in the entity's accounts. For each item that should be recorded in the entity's books:

1. Identify one or more source documents that are generated from the event.
2. Identify which source document would be used to record an event when it produces more than one source document.
3. For each document, identify the information that is most useful in recording the event in the accounts.

Problem 3-6 *Accounts Used to Record Transactions* **LO 3, 5** P/T

A list of accounts, with an identifying number for each, is shown below. Following the list of accounts is a series of transactions entered into by a company during its first year of operations.

(continued)

Required

For each transaction, indicate the account or accounts that should be debited and credited.

1. Cash	**9.** Notes Payable
2. Accounts Receivable	**10.** Capital Stock
3. Office Supplies	**11.** Retained Earnings
4. Buildings	**12.** Service Revenue
5. Automobiles	**13.** Wage and Salary Expense
6. Land	**14.** Selling Expense
7. Accounts Payable	**15.** Utilities Expense
8. Income Tax Payable	**16.** Income Tax Expense

Transactions	Accounts Debited	Accounts Credited
Example: Purchased land and building in exchange for a three-year promissory note.	4, 6	9
a. Issued capital stock for cash.		
b. Purchased 10 automobiles; paid part in cash and signed a 60-day note for the balance.		
c. Purchased land in exchange for a note due in six months.		
d. Purchased office supplies; agreed to pay total bill by the 10th of the following month.		
e. Billed clients for services performed during the month, and gave them until the 15th of the following month to pay.		
f. Received cash on account from clients for services rendered to them in past months.		
g. Paid employees salaries and wages earned during the month.		
h. Paid newspaper for company ads appearing during the month.		
i. Received monthly gas and electric bill from the utility company; payment is due anytime within the first 10 days of the following month.		
j. Computed amount of taxes due based on the income of the period; amount will be paid in the following month.		

Problem 3-7 *Transaction Analysis and Journal Entries Recorded Directly in T Accounts*

LO 3, 4, 5

GENERAL LEDGER

Four brothers organized Beverly Entertainment Enterprises on October 1, 2004. The following transactions occurred during the first month of operations:

October 1: Received contribution of $10,000 from each of the four principal owners of the new business in exchange for shares of stock.

October 2: Purchased the Arcada Theater for $125,000. The seller agreed to accept a down payment of $12,500 and a seven-year promissory note for the balance. The Arcada property consists of land valued at $35,000 and a building valued at $90,000.

October 3: Purchased new seats for the theater at a cost of $5,000, paying $2,500 down and agreeing to pay the remainder in 60 days.

October 12: Purchased candy, popcorn, cups, and napkins for $3,700 on an open account. The company has 30 days to pay for the concession supplies.

October 13: Sold tickets for the opening-night movie for cash of $1,800, and took in $2,400 at the concession stand.

October 17: Rented out the theater to a local community group for $1,500. The community group is to pay one-half of the bill within five working days and has 30 days to pay the remainder.

October 23: Received 50% of the amount billed to the community group.

October 24: Sold movie tickets for cash of $2,000, and took in $2,800 at the concession stand.

October 26: The four brothers, acting on behalf of Beverly Entertainment, paid a dividend of $750 on the shares of stock owned by each of them, or $3,000 in total.

October 27: Paid $500 for utilities.

October 30: Paid wages and salaries of $2,400 total to the ushers, the projectionist, concession stand workers, and the maintenance crew.

October 31: Sold movie tickets for cash of $1,800, and took in $2,500 at the concession stand.

Required

1. Prepare a table to summarize the preceding transactions as they affect the accounting equation. Use the format in Exhibit 3-1. Identify each transaction with a date.
2. Record each transaction directly in T accounts, using the dates preceding the transactions to identify them in the accounts. Each account involved in the problem needs a separate T account.

Problem 3-8 *Trial Balance and Financial Statements* LO 4, 7

Refer to the table for Beverly Entertainment Enterprises in part **1** of Problem 3-7.

Required

1. Prepare a trial balance at October 31, 2004.
2. Prepare an income statement for the month ended October 31, 2004.
3. Prepare a statement of retained earnings for the month ended October 31, 2004.
4. Prepare a classified balance sheet at October 31, 2004.

Problem 3-9 *Journal Entries* LO 3, 5, 6

Atkins Advertising Agency began business on January 2, 2004. Listed below are the transactions entered into by Atkins during its first month of operations.

GENERAL LEDGER

a. Acquired its articles of incorporation from the state, and issued 100,000 shares of capital stock in exchange for $200,000 in cash.

b. Purchased an office building for $150,000 in cash. The building is valued at $110,000, and the remainder of the value is assigned to the land.

c. Signed a three-year promissory note at the bank for $125,000.

d. Purchased office equipment at a cost of $50,000, paying $10,000 down and agreeing to pay the remainder in 10 days.

e. Paid wages and salaries of $13,000 for the first half of the month. Office employees are paid twice a month.

f. Paid the balance due on the office equipment.

g. Sold $24,000 of advertising during the first month. Customers have until the 15th of the following month to pay their bills.

h. Paid wages and salaries of $15,000 for the second half of the month.

i. Recorded $3,500 in commissions earned by the salespeople during the month. They will be paid on the fifth of the following month.

Required

Prepare in journal form the entry to record each transaction.

Problem 3-10 *Journal Entries Recorded Directly in T Accounts* LO 3, 4, 5

Refer to the transactions for Atkins Advertising Agency in Problem 3-9.

Required

1. Record each transaction directly in T accounts, using the letters preceding the transactions to identify them in the accounts. Each account involved in the problem needs a separate T account.
2. Prepare a trial balance at January 31, 2004.

Problem 3-11 *The Detection of Errors in a Trial Balance and Preparation of a Corrected Trial Balance* LO 3, 5, 7

Malcolm Inc. was incorporated on January 1, 2004, with the issuance of capital stock in return for $90,000 of cash contributed by the owners. The only other transaction entered into prior to beginning operations was the issuance of a $75,300 note payable in exchange for building and equipment. The following trial balance was prepared at the end of the first month by the bookkeeper for Malcolm Inc.

(continued)

MALCOLM INC.
TRIAL BALANCE
JANUARY 31, 2004

Account Titles	Debits	Credits
Cash	$ 9,980	
Accounts Receivable	8,640	
Land	80,000	
Building	50,000	
Equipment	23,500	
Notes Payable		75,300
Capital Stock		90,000
Service Revenue		50,340
Wage and Salary Expense	23,700	
Advertising Expense	4,600	
Utilities Expense	8,420	
Dividends		5,000
Totals	$208,840	$220,640

Required

1. Identify the *two* errors in the trial balance. Ignore depreciation expense and interest expense.
2. Prepare a corrected trial balance.

Problem 3-12 ***Journal Entries, Trial Balance, and Financial Statements*** **LO 3, 5, 6, 7**

Blue Jay Delivery Service is incorporated on January 2, 2004, and enters into the following transactions during its first month of operations:

GENERAL LEDGER

SPREADSHEET

January 2: Filed articles of incorporation with the state, and issued 100,000 shares of capital stock. Cash of $100,000 is received from the new owners for the shares.

January 3: Purchased a warehouse and land for $80,000 in cash. An appraiser values the land at $20,000 and the warehouse at $60,000.

January 4: Signed a three-year promissory note at the Third State Bank in the amount of $50,000.

January 6: Purchased five new delivery trucks for a total of $45,000 in cash.

January 31: Performed services on account that amounted to $15,900 during the month. Cash amounting to $7,490 was received from customers on account during the month.

January 31: Established an open account at a local service station at the beginning of the month. Purchases of gas and oil during January amounted to $3,230. Blue Jay has until the 10th of the following month to pay its bill.

Required

1. Prepare journal entries on the books of Blue Jay to record the transactions entered into during the month.
2. Prepare a trial balance at January 31, 2004.
3. Prepare an income statement for the month ended January 31, 2004.
4. Prepare a classified balance sheet at January 31, 2004.
5. Assume that you are considering buying stock in this company. Beginning with the transaction to record the purchase of the property on January 3, list any additional information you would like to have about each of the transactions during the remainder of the month.

Problem 3-13 ***Journal Entries, Trial Balance, and Financial Statements*** **LO 3, 5, 6, 7**

Neveranerror Inc. was organized on June 2, 2004, by a group of accountants to provide accounting and tax services to small businesses. The following transactions occurred during the first month of business:

GENERAL LEDGER

June 2: Received contributions of $10,000 from each of the three owners of the business in exchange for shares of stock.

June 5: Purchased a computer system for $12,000. The agreement with the vendor requires a down payment of $2,500 with the balance due in 60 days.

June 8: Signed a two-year promissory note at the bank and received cash of $20,000.

June 15: Billed $12,350 to clients for the first half of June. Clients are billed twice a month for services performed during the month, and the bills are payable within 10 days.

June 17: Paid a $900 bill from the local newspaper for advertising for the month of June.

June 23: Received the amounts billed to clients for services performed during the first half of the month.

June 28: Received and paid gas, electric, and water bills. The total amount is $2,700.

June 29: Received the landlord's bill for $2,200 for rent on the office space that Neveranerror leases. The bill is payable by the 10th of the following month.

June 30: Paid salaries and wages for June. The total amount is $5,670.

June 30: Billed $18,400 to clients for the second half of June.

June 30: Declared and paid dividends in the amount of $6,000.

Required

1. Prepare journal entries on the books of Neveranerror Inc. to record the transactions entered into during the month. Ignore depreciation expense and interest expense.
2. Prepare a trial balance at June 30, 2004.
3. Prepare the following financial statements:
   a. Income statement for the month ended June 30, 2004.
   b. Statement of retained earnings for the month ended June 30, 2004.
   c. Classified balance sheet at June 30, 2004.
4. Assume that you have just graduated from college and have been approached to join this company as an accountant. From your reading of the financial statements for the first month, would you consider joining the company? Explain your answer. Limit your answer to financial considerations only.

DECISION MAKING

Alternate Problems

Problem 3-1A ***Events to Be Recorded in Accounts*** **LO 1**

The following events take place at Anaconda Accountants Inc.:

1. Supplies are ordered from vendors, who will deliver the supplies within the week.
2. Vendors deliver supplies on account, payment due in 30 days.
3. New computer system is ordered.
4. Old computer system is sold for cash.
5. Services are rendered to customers on account. The invoices are mailed and due in 30 days.
6. Cash received from customer payments is deposited in the bank night depository.
7. Employees are paid weekly paychecks.
8. Vendors noted in item 2 are paid for the supplies delivered.

Required

Identify each event as internal (I) or external (E), and indicate whether each event would be recorded in the *accounts* of the company. For each event that is to be recorded, identify the names of at least two accounts that would be affected.

Problem 3-2A ***Transaction Analysis and Financial Statements*** **LO 3**

GENERAL LEDGER

Beachway Enterprises was organized on June 1, 2004, by two college students who recognized an opportunity to make money while spending their days at a beach in Florida. The two entrepreneurs plan to rent beach umbrellas. The following transactions occurred during the first month of operations:

June 1: Received contribution of $2,000 from each of the two principal owners of the new business in exchange for shares of stock.

June 1: Purchased 25 beach umbrellas for $250 each on account. The company has 30 days to pay for the beach umbrellas.

June 5: Registered as a vendor with the city and paid the $35 monthly fee.

June 10: Purchased $50 in miscellaneous supplies on an open account. The company has 30 days to pay for the supplies.

(continued)

June 15: Paid $70 bill from a local radio station for advertising for the last two weeks of June.

June 17: Customers rented beach umbrellas for cash of $1,000.

June 24: Billed a local hotel $2,000 for beach umbrellas provided for use during a convention being held at the hotel. The hotel is to pay one-half of the bill in five days and the rest within 30 days.

June 29: Received 50% of the amount billed to the hotel.

June 30: Customers rented beach umbrellas for cash of $1,500.

June 30: Paid wages of $90 to a friend who helped out over the weekend.

June 30: Paid the balance due on the beach umbrellas.

Required

1. Prepare a table to summarize the preceding transactions as they affect the accounting equation. Use the format in Exhibit 3-1. Identify each transaction with a date.
2. Prepare an income statement for the month ended June 30, 2004.
3. Prepare a classified balance sheet at June 30, 2004.

Problem 3-3A *Transaction Analysis and Financial Statements* LO 3

GENERAL LEDGER

SPREADSHEET

Dynamic Services Inc. was organized on March 1, 2004, by two former college roommates. The corporation will provide computer tax services to small businesses. The following transactions occurred during the first month of operations:

March 2: Received contributions of $10,000 from each of the two principal owners in exchange for shares of stock.

March 7: Signed a two-year promissory note at the bank and received cash of $7,500. Interest, along with the $7,500, will be repaid at the end of the two years.

March 12: Purchased miscellaneous supplies on account for $350, payment due in 30 days.

March 19: Billed a client $2,000 for tax-preparation services. According to an agreement between the two companies, the client is to pay 25% of the bill upon its receipt and the remaining balance within 30 days.

March 20: Paid a $650 bill from the local newspaper for advertising for the month of March.

March 22: Received 25% of the amount billed the client on March 19.

March 26: Received cash of $1,400 for services provided in assisting a client in preparing its tax return.

March 29: Purchased a computer system for $4,000 in cash.

March 30: Paid $1,650 in salaries and wages for March.

March 31: Received and paid $700 of gas, electric, and water bills.

Required

1. Prepare a table to summarize the preceding transactions as they affect the accounting equation. Use the format in Exhibit 3-1. Identify each transaction with the date.
2. Prepare an income statement for the month ended March 31, 2004.
3. Prepare a classified balance sheet at March 31, 2004.
4. From reading the balance sheet you prepared in part **3,** what events would you expect to take place in April? Explain your answer.

Problem 3-4A *Transactions Reconstructed from Financial Statements* LO 3

The following financial statements are available for Oak Corporation for its first month of operations:

OAK CORPORATION
INCOME STATEMENT
FOR THE MONTH ENDED JULY 31, 2004

Service revenue		$75,400
Expenses:		
Rent	$ 6,000	
Salaries and wages	24,600	
Utilities	12,700	43,300
Net income		$32,100

OAK CORPORATION
BALANCE SHEET
JULY 31, 2004

Assets		Liabilities and Owners' Equity	
Cash	$ 13,700	Wages payable	$ 6,000
Accounts receivable	25,700	Notes payable	50,000
Equipment	32,000	Unearned service revenue	4,500
Furniture	14,700	Capital stock	30,000
Land	24,000	Retained earnings	19,600
Total assets	$110,100	Total liabilities and owners' equity	$110,100

Required

Describe as many transactions as you can that were entered into by Oak Corporation during the first month of business.

Alternate Multi-Concept Problems

Problem 3-5A *Identification of Events with Source Documents* LO 1, 2

Many events are linked to a source document. The following is a list of events that occurred in an entity:

a. Paid a security deposit and six months' rent on a building.

b. Hired three employees and agreed to pay them $400 per week.

c. Sold merchandise to a customer for cash.

d. Reported a fire that destroyed a billboard that is on the entity's property and is owned and maintained by another entity.

e. Received payment of bills from customers.

f. Purchased stock in another entity to gain some control over it.

g. Signed a note at the bank and received cash.

h. Contracted with a cleaning service to maintain the interior of the building in good repair. No money is paid at this time.

Required

For each item **a** through **h,** indicate whether the event should or should not be recorded in the entity's accounts. For each item that should be recorded in the entity's books:

1. Identify one or more source documents that are generated from the event.
2. Identify which source document would be used to record an event when it produces more than one source document.
3. For each document, identify the information that is most useful in recording the event in the accounts.

Problem 3-6A *Accounts Used to Record Transactions* LO 3, 5

A list of accounts, with an identifying number for each, is shown below. Following the list of accounts is a series of transactions entered into by a company during its first year of operations.

Required

For each transaction, indicate the account or accounts that should be debited and credited.

1. Cash
2. Accounts Receivable
3. Prepaid Insurance
4. Office Supplies
5. Automobiles
6. Land
7. Accounts Payable
8. Income Tax Payable
9. Notes Payable
10. Capital Stock
11. Retained Earnings
12. Service Revenue
13. Wage and Salary Expense
14. Utilities Expense
15. Income Tax Expense

(continued)

Transactions	Accounts Debited	Accounts Credited
Example: Purchased office supplies for cash.	4	1
a. Issued capital stock for cash.		
b. Purchased an automobile and signed a 60-day note for the total amount.		
c. Acquired land in exchange for capital stock.		
d. Received cash from clients for services performed during the month.		
e. Paid employees salaries and wages earned during the month.		
f. Purchased flyers and signs from a printer, payment due in 10 days.		
g. Paid for the flyers and signs purchased in part **f.**		
h. Received monthly telephone bill; payment is due within 10 days of receipt.		
i. Paid for a six-month liability insurance policy.		
j. Paid monthly telephone bill.		
k. Computed amount of taxes due based on the income of the period and paid the amount.		

Problem 3-7A *Transaction Analysis and Journal Entries Recorded Directly in T Accounts* LO 3, 4, 5

GENERAL LEDGER

Three friends organized Rapid City Roller Rink on October 1, 2004. The following transactions occurred during the first month of operations:

October 1: Received contribution of $22,000 from each of the three principal owners of the new business in exchange for shares of stock.

October 2: Purchased land valued at $15,000 and a building valued at $75,000. The seller agreed to accept a down payment of $9,000 and a five-year promissory note for the balance.

October 3: Purchased new tables and chairs for the lounge at the roller rink at a cost of $25,000, paying $5,000 down and agreeing to pay for the remainder in 60 days.

October 9: Purchased 100 pairs of roller skates for cash at $35 per pair.

October 12: Purchased food and drinks for $2,500 on an open account. The company has 30 days to pay for the concession supplies.

October 13: Sold tickets for cash of $400 and took in $750 at the concession stand.

October 17: Rented out the roller rink to a local community group for $750. The community group is to pay one-half of the bill within five working days and has 30 days to pay the remainder.

October 23: Received 50% of the amount billed to the community group.

October 24: Sold tickets for cash of $500, and took in $1,200 at the concession stand.

October 26: The three friends, acting on behalf of Rapid City Roller Rink, paid a dividend of $250 on the shares of stock owned by each of them, or $750 in total.

October 27: Paid $1,275 for utilities.

October 30: Paid wages and salaries of $2,250.

October 31: Sold tickets for cash of $700, and took in $1,300 at the concession stand.

Required

1. Prepare a table to summarize the preceding transactions as they affect the accounting equation. Use the format in Exhibit 3-1. Identify each transaction with a date.
2. Record each transaction directly in T accounts, using the dates preceding the transactions to identify them in the accounts. Each account involved in the problem needs a separate T account.

Problem 3-8A *Trial Balance and Financial Statements* LO 4, 7

Refer to the table for Rapid City Roller Rink in part 1 of Problem 3-7A.

Required

1. Prepare a trial balance at October 31, 2004.

2. Prepare an income statement for the month ended October 31, 2004.
3. Prepare a statement of retained earnings for the month ended October 31, 2004.
4. Prepare a classified balance sheet at October 31, 2004.

Problem 3-9A ***Journal Entries*** **LO 3, 5, 6**

Castle Consulting Agency began business in February 2004. Listed below are the transactions entered into by Castle during its first month of operations.

GENERAL LEDGER

a. Acquired articles of incorporation from the state, and issued 10,000 shares of capital stock in exchange for $150,000 in cash.
b. Paid monthly rent of $400.
c. Signed a five-year promissory note for $100,000 at the bank.
d. Received $5,000 cash from a customer for services to be performed over the next two months.
e. Purchased software to be used on future jobs. The software costs $950 and is expected to be used on five to eight jobs over the next two years.
f. Billed customers $12,500 for work performed during the month.
g. Paid office personnel $3,000 for the month of February.
h. Received a utility bill of $100. The total amount is due in 30 days.

Required

Prepare in journal form the entry to record each transaction.

Problem 3-10A ***Journal Entries Recorded Directly in T Accounts*** **LO 3, 4, 5, 7**

Refer to the transactions for Castle Consulting Agency in Problem 3-9A.

Required

1. Record each transaction directly in T accounts, using the letters preceding the transactions to identify them in the accounts. Each account involved in the problem needs a separate T account.
2. Prepare a trial balance at February 28, 2004.

Problem 3-11A ***Entries Prepared from a Trial Balance and Proof of the Cash Balance*** **LO 3, 4, 5, 7**

Russell Company was incorporated on January 1, 2004, with the issuance of capital stock in return for $120,000 of cash contributed by the owners. The only other transaction entered into prior to beginning operations was the issuance of a $50,000 note payable in exchange for equipment and fixtures. The following trial balance was prepared at the end of the first month by the bookkeeper for Russell Company:

RUSSELL COMPANY
TRIAL BALANCE
JANUARY 31, 2004

Account Titles	Debits	Credits
Cash	$???	
Accounts Receivable	30,500	
Equipment and Fixtures	50,000	
Wages Payable		$ 10,000
Notes Payable		50,000
Capital Stock		120,000
Service Revenue		60,500
Wage and Salary Expense	24,600	
Advertising Expense	12,500	
Rent Expense	5,200	

Required

1. Determine the balance in the Cash account.
2. Identify all of the transactions that affected the Cash account during the month. Use a T account to prove what the balance in Cash would be after all transactions are recorded.

Problem 3-12A ***Journal Entries*** **LO 3, 5, 6**

GENERAL LEDGER

Overnight Delivery Inc. is incorporated on January 2, 2004, and enters into the following transactions during its second month of operations:

February 2: Paid $400 for wages earned by employees for the week ending January 31.

February 3: Paid $3,230 for gas and oil billed on an open account in January.

February 4: Declared and paid $2,000 cash dividends to stockholders.

February 15: Received $8,000 cash from customer accounts.

February 26: Provided $16,800 of services on account during the month.

February 27: Received a $3,400 bill from the local service station for gas and oil used during February.

Required

1. Prepare journal entries on the books of Overnight to record the transactions entered into during February.
2. For the transactions on February 2, 3, 4, and 27, indicate whether the amount is an expense of operating in the month of January or February or is not an expense in either month.

Problem 3-13A ***Journal Entries and a Balance Sheet*** **LO 3, 5, 6**

GENERAL LEDGER

Krittersbegone Inc. was organized on July 1, 2004, by a group of technicians to provide termite inspections and treatment to homeowners and small businesses. The following transactions occurred during the first month of business:

July 2: Received contributions of $3,000 from each of the six owners in exchange for shares of stock.

July 3: Paid $1,000 rent for the month of July.

July 5: Purchased flashlights, tools, spray equipment, and ladders for $18,000, with a down payment of $5,000 and the balance due in 30 days.

July 17: Paid a $200 bill for the distribution of door-to-door advertising.

July 28: Paid August rent and July utilities to the landlord in the amounts of $1,000 and $450, respectively.

July 30: Received $8,000 in cash from homeowners for services performed during the month. In addition, billed $7,500 to other customers for services performed during the month. Billings are due in 30 days.

July 30: Paid commissions of $9,500 to the technicians for July.

July 31: Received $600 from a business client to perform services over the next two months.

Required

1. Prepare journal entries on the books of Krittersbegone to record the transactions entered into during the month. Ignore depreciation expense.
2. Prepare a classified balance sheet dated July 31, 2004. From the balance sheet, what cash inflow and what cash outflow can you predict in the month of August? Who would be interested in the cash flow information and why?

Cases

Reading and Interpreting Financial Statements

http://www.winnebagoind.com
http://www.monacocoach.com

Case 3-1 ***Comparing Two Companies in the Same Industry: Winnebago Industries and Monaco Coach Corporation*** **LO 4**

Refer to the income statements for Winnebago Industries and Monaco Coach Corporation in Appendices A and B at the end of the book.

Required

1. How many accounts does each company report on its income statement? (Do not include in your answer any of the subtotals reported, such as operating income.)
2. Winnebago Industries reports an account on its income statement titled "Revenues: Manufactured products." What account is equivalent to this account on Monaco Coach's income statement?

3. One of the accounts on Monaco Coach's income statement is "Selling, general and administrative expenses." How are these expenses reported on Winnebago Industries' income statement?

4. Winnebago Industries reports taxes on its income statement on the line titled "Provision for taxes." Monaco Coach uses the account "Provision for income taxes." What is the dollar amount of taxes each reports on its income statement? Compute the ratio of taxes to income before income taxes for 2000 and for 2001 for each company. Is Winnebago Industries' ratio the same for both years? Is Monaco Coach's ratio the same for both years? Which company has the higher ratio for 2000? Which company has the higher ratio for 2001? What does this ratio information tell you?

Case 3-2 *Reading and Interpreting Winnebago Industries' Statement of Cash Flows* LO 3, 5, 6

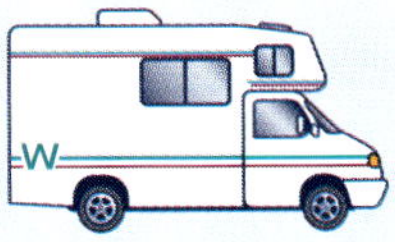

Refer to Winnebago Industries' statement of cash flows for the year ended August 25, 2001.

Required

1. What amount did the company spend on purchases of property and equipment during 2001? Prepare the journal entry to record these purchases, assuming cash was paid.
2. What amount did the company pay to stockholders in cash dividends during 2001? Prepare the journal entry to record the payment.

Case 3-3 *Reading and Interpreting General Mills' Income Statement* LO 4

http://www.generalmills.com

Refer to the chapter opener and General Mills' income statement as shown there.

Required

1. General Mills' income statement does not provide a subtotal for gross profit. Compute gross profit and the gross profit percentage for the years 2000 and 2001. Did each of these increase or decrease in 2001?
2. What is General Mills' largest expense? Compute the ratio of this expense to sales for 2000 and 2001. Did the ratio increase, decrease, or stay the same?
3. Compute General Mills' profit margin for 2000 and 2001. Did the ratio increase, decrease, or stay the same?

Case 3-4 *Reading and Interpreting Delta's Balance Sheet* LO 1, 3, 5, 6

http://www.delta.com

The following item appears in the current liabilities section of Delta Air Lines' balance sheet at December 31, 2001.

Air traffic liability	$1,224 million

In addition, one of Delta's notes states: "We record sales of passenger tickets as air traffic liability on our Consolidated Balance Sheets. Passenger revenues are recognized, and the related air traffic liability is reduced, when we provide the transportation."

Required

1. What economic event caused Delta to incur this liability? Was it an external or an internal event?
2. Describe the effect on the accounting equation from the transaction to record the air traffic liability.
3. Assume that one customer purchases a $500 ticket in advance. Prepare the journal entry on Delta's books to record this transaction.
4. What economic event will cause Delta to reduce its air traffic liability? Is this an external or an internal event?

Making Financial Decisions

Case 3-5 *Cash Flow versus Net Income* LO 2, 3

DECISION MAKING

Shelia Young started a real estate business at the beginning of January. After approval by the state for a charter to incorporate, she issued 1,000 shares of stock to herself and deposited

(continued)

$20,000 in a bank account under the name Young Properties. Because business was "booming," she spent all of her time during the first month selling properties rather than keeping financial records.

At the end of January, Shelia comes to you with the following plight:

> I put $20,000 in to start this business at the beginning of the month. My January 31 bank statement shows a balance of $17,000. After all of my efforts, it appears as if I'm "in the hole" already! On the other hand, that seems impossible—we sold five properties for clients during the month. The total sales value of these properties was $600,000, and I receive a commission of 5% on each sale. Granted, one of the five sellers still owes me an $8,000 commission on the sale, but the other four have been collected in full. Three of the sales, totaling $400,000, were actually made by my assistants. I pay them 4% of the sales value of a property. Sure, I have a few office expenses for my car, utilities, and a secretary, but that's about it. How can I have possibly lost $3,000 this month?

You agree to help Shelia figure out how she really did this month. The bank statement is helpful. The total deposits during the month amount to $22,000. Shelia explains that this amount represents the commissions on the four sales collected so far. The canceled checks reveal the following expenditures:

Check No.	Payee—Memo at Bottom of Check	Amount
101	Stevens Office Supply	$ 2,000
102	Why Walk, Let's Talk Motor Co.—new car	3,000
103	City of Westbrook—heat and lights	500
104	Alice Hill—secretary	2,200
105	Ace Property Management—office rent for month	1,200
106	Jerry Hayes (sales assistant)	10,000
107	Joan Harper (sales assistant)	6,000
108	Don's Fillitup—gas and oil for car	100

According to Shelia, the $2,000 check to Stevens Office Supply represents the down payment on a word processor and a copier for the office. The remaining balance is $3,000 and it must be paid to Stevens by February 15. Similarly, the $3,000 check is the down payment on a car for the business. A $12,000 note was given to the car dealer and is due along with interest in one year.

1. Prepare an income statement for the month of January for Young Properties.
2. Prepare a statement of cash flows for the month of January for Young Properties.
3. Draft a memorandum to Shelia Young explaining as simply and as clearly as possible why she *did* in fact have a profitable first month in business but experienced a decrease in her cash account. Support your explanation with any necessary figures.
4. The down payments on the car and the office equipment are reflected on the statement of cash flows. They are assets that will benefit the business for a number of years. Do you think that *any* of the cost associated with the acquisition of these assets should be recognized in some way on the income statement? Explain your answer.

Case 3-6 *Loan Request* LO 3, 5, 6, 7

DECISION MAKING

Simon Fraser started a landscaping and lawn-care business in April 2004 by investing $20,000 cash in the business in exchange for capital stock. Because his business is in the Midwest, the season begins in April and concludes in September. He prepared the following trial balance (with accounts in alphabetical order) at the end of the first season in business.

FRASER LANDSCAPING
TRIAL BALANCE
SEPTEMBER 30, 2004

	Debits	Credits
Accounts Payable		$13,000
Accounts Receivable	$23,000	
Capital Stock		20,000
Cash	1,200	
Gas and Oil Expense	15,700	
Insurance Expense	2,500	

Landscaping Revenue		33,400
Lawn Care Revenue		24,000
Mowing Equipment	5,000	
Rent Expense	6,000	
Salaries Expense	22,000	
Truck	15,000	
Totals	$90,400	$90,400

Simon is pleased with his first year in business. "I paid myself a salary of $22,000 during the year and still have $1,200 in the bank. Sure, I have a few bills outstanding, but my accounts receivable will more than cover those." In fact, Simon is so happy with the first year, that he has come to you in your role as a lending officer at the local bank to ask for a $20,000 loan to allow him to add another truck and mowing equipment for the second season.

Required

1. From your reading of the trial balance, what does it appear to you that Simon did with the $20,000 in cash he originally contributed to the business? Reconstruct the journal entry to record the transaction you think took place.
2. Prepare an income statement for the six months ended September 30, 2004.
3. The mowing equipment and truck are assets that will benefit the business for a number of years. Do you think that any of the costs associated with the purchase of these assets should have been recognized as expenses in the first year? How would this have affected the income statement?
4. Prepare a classified balance sheet as of September 30, 2004. As a banker, what two items on the balance sheet concern you the most? Explain your answer.
5. As a banker, would you loan Simon $20,000 to expand his business during the second year? Draft a memo to respond to Simon's request for the loan, indicating whether you will make the loan.

Accounting and Ethics: What Would You Do?

Case 3-7 ***Delay in the Posting of a Journal Entry*** **LO 3, 5, 6**

As assistant controller for a small consulting firm, you are responsible for recording and posting the daily cash receipts and disbursements to the ledger accounts. After you have posted the entries, your boss, the controller, prepares a trial balance and the financial statements. You make the following entries on June 30, 2004:

2004			
June 30	Cash	1,430	
	Accounts Receivable	1,950	
	Service Revenue		3,380
	To record daily cash receipts.		
June 30	Advertising Expense	12,500	
	Utilities Expense	22,600	
	Rent Expense	24,000	
	Salary and Wage Expense	17,400	
	Cash		76,500
	To record daily cash disbursements.		

The daily cash disbursements are much larger on June 30 than any other day because many of the company's major bills are paid on the last day of the month. After you have recorded these two transactions and *before* you have posted them to the ledger accounts, your boss comes to you with the following request:

> As you are aware, the first half of the year has been a tough one for the consulting industry and for our business in particular. With first-half bonuses based on net income, I am concerned whether you or I will get any bonus this time around. However, I have a suggestion that should allow us to receive something for our hard work and at the same time will not hurt anyone. Go ahead and post the June 30 cash receipts to the ledger but don't bother to post that day's cash disbursements. Even though the treasurer writes the checks

(continued)

on the last day of the month and you normally journalize the transaction on the same day, it is pretty silly to bother posting the entry to the ledger, since it takes at least a week for the checks to clear the bank.

Required

1. Explain *why* the controller's request will result in an increase in net income.
2. Do you agree with the controller that the omission of the entry on June 30 "will not hurt anyone"? If not, be explicit as to why you don't agree. Whom could it hurt?
3. What would you do? Whom should you talk to about this issue?

Case 3-8 *Debits and Credits* LO 5, 6

You are controller for an architectural firm whose accounting year ends on December 31. As part of the management team, you receive a year-end bonus directly related to the firm's earnings for the year. One of your duties is to review the journal entries recorded by the bookkeepers. A new bookkeeper prepared the following journal entry:

Dec. 3	Cash	10,000	
	Service Revenue		10,000
	To record deposit from client.		

You notice that the explanation for the journal entry refers to the amount as a deposit, and the bookkeeper explains to you that the firm plans to provide the services to the client in March of the following year.

1. Did the bookkeeper prepare the correct journal entry to account for the client's deposit? Explain your answer.
2. What would you do as controller for the firm? Do you have a responsibility to do anything to correct the books?

Internet Research Case

Case 3-9 *General Mills*

http://www.generalmills.com

The acquisition of **Pillsbury** by **General Mills** immediately transformed the company into a global consumer foods giant. Like General Mills before the merger, Pillsbury maintained a leading market position in no less than four food categories. Access the General Mills' Web site and locate its most recent annual report. Review the report to see how successful the company has been in reaching its goals after the Pillsbury acquisition.

1. The company expected sales to grow at an annual rate of 7%, in contrast to the 6% growth rate in the four years preceding the merger. For the most recent year available, compute the increase in sales from the prior year. Did General Mills achieve its targeted growth in sales?
2. With the expected growth in sales and cost savings from the acquisition, General Mills targeted annual earnings per share growth to be between 11% and 15%. For the most recent year available, compute the increase in earnings per share from the prior year. Did the company achieve its targeted growth for this measure?

Source: General Mills' 2001 annual report.

Solutions to Key Terms Quiz

3	Event (p. 104)	8	Debit (p. 113)
10	External event (p. 104)	4	Credit (p. 113)
5	Internal event (p. 104)	16	Double-entry system (p. 116)
14	Transaction (p. 104)	13	Journal (p. 118)
6	Source document (p. 105)	9	Posting (p. 118)
11	Account (p. 111)	7	Journalizing (p. 119)
1	Chart of accounts (p. 111)	15	General journal (p. 119)
12	General ledger (p. 112)	2	Trial balance (p. 121)

Chapter 4

Income Measurement and Accrual Accounting

Focus on Financial Results

McDonald's operates more than 30,000 restaurants in 121 countries and in 2001 served an astounding 46 million customers per day. However, as CEO Jack M. Greenberg proclaims in the annual report, 2001 "was a year in which the resourcefulness of many of the world's best-known companies, including McDonald's, was tested."

As shown on the consolidated statement of income excerpted here, although net income decreased in 2001, total revenues did show a small increase over the prior year. Two kinds of revenue are shown—*sales by company-operated restaurants* and *revenues from franchised and affiliated restaurants.* Operators of the franchised and affiliated restaurants pay McDonald's a fee plus a share of their income for the right to operate as part of the chain. Thus, only a portion of the franchisee's revenue appears in the second line of the income statement, whereas *all* the revenue of company-operated restaurants appears in the first line.

Will McDonald's be able to continue its steady growth in revenue and at the same time rebound from the decline in net income in 2001? The growth in revenue should continue with the company's plans to add between 1,300 and 1,400 restaurants in 2002. Whether or not the planned revenue growth will translate into an improved bottom line (i.e., net income) will be the challenge management of the golden arches faces in the future.

McDonald's 2001 Annual Report

Consolidated Statement of Income

(In millions, except per share data) Years ended December 31,	2001	2000	1999
Revenues			
Sales by company-operated restaurants	$11,040.7	$10,467.0	$ 9,512.5
Revenues from franchised and affiliated restaurants	3,829.3	3,776.0	3,746.8
Total revenues	14,870.0	14,243.0	13,259.3
Operating costs and expenses			
Food and packaging	3,802.1	3,557.1	3,204.6
Payroll and employee benefits	2,901.2	2,690.2	2,418.3
Occupancy and other operating expenses	2,750.4	2,502.8	2,206.7
Total company-operated restaurant expenses	9,453.7	8,750.1	7,829.6
Franchised restaurants—occupancy expenses	800.2	772.3	737.7
Selling, general & administrative expenses	1,661.7	1,587.3	1,477.6
Special charge—global change initiatives	200.0		
Other operating (income) expense, net	57.4	(196.4)	(105.2)
Total operating costs and expenses	12,173.0	10,913.3	9,939.7
Operating income	2,697.0	3,329.7	3,319.6
Interest expense—net of capitalized interest of $15.2, $16.3 and $14.3	452.4	429.9	396.3
McDonald's Japan IPO gain	(137.1)		
Nonoperating expense, net	52.0	17.5	39.2
Income before provision for income taxes	2,329.7	2,882.3	2,884.1
Provision for income taxes	693.1	905.0	936.2
Net income	$ 1,636.6	$ 1,977.3	$ 1,947.9
Net income per common share	$ 1.27	$ 1.49	$ 1.44
Net income per common share—diluted	$ 1.25	$ 1.46	1.39
Dividends per common share	$ .23	$ .22	$ .20
Weighted-average shares	1,289.7	1,323.2	1,355.3
Weighted-average shares—diluted	1,309.3	1,356.5	1,404.2

Maintaining growth in revenues will require global strategies.

See notes to consolidated financial statements.

http://www.mcdonalds.com

You're in the Driver's Seat

How long can McDonald's continue to surpass its past performance, and how will its two types of revenue affect profits? Will it matter that less than 30% of its restaurants are company operated? As you study this chapter, you will begin to understand the effect of the timing of revenues and expenses and their impact on reported profits.

LEARNING OBJECTIVES

After studying this chapter, you should be able to:

LO 1 Explain the significance of recognition and measurement in the preparation and use of financial statements. (p. 150)

LO 2 Explain the differences between the cash and accrual bases of accounting. (p. 152)

LO 3 Describe the revenue recognition principle and explain its application in various situations. (p. 156)

LO 4 Describe the matching principle and the various methods for recognizing expenses. (p. 158)

LO 5 Identify the four major types of adjusting entries and prepare them for a variety of situations. (p. 160)

LO 6 Explain the steps in the accounting cycle and the significance of each step. (p. 173)

LO 7 Explain why and how closing entries are made at the end of an accounting period. (p. 174)

LO 8 Understand how to use a work sheet as a basis for preparing financial statements (Appendix). (p. 181)

RECOGNITION AND MEASUREMENT IN FINANCIAL STATEMENTS

LO 1 Explain the significance of recognition and measurement in the preparation and use of financial statements.

Accounting is a communication process. To successfully communicate information to the users of financial statements, accountants and managers must answer two questions:

1. What economic events should be communicated, or *recognized,* in the statements?
2. How should the effects of these events be *measured* in the statements?

The dual concepts of recognition and measurement are crucial to the success of accounting as a form of communication.

Recognition

Recognition The process of recording an item in the financial statements as an asset, liability, revenue, expense, or the like.

"**Recognition** is the process of formally recording or incorporating an item into the financial statements of an entity as an asset, liability, revenue, expense, or the like. Recognition includes depiction of an item in both words and numbers, with the amount included in the totals of the financial statements."[1] We see in this definition the central idea behind general-purpose financial statements. They are a form of communication between the entity and external users. Stockholders, bankers, and other creditors have limited access to relevant information about a company. They depend on the periodic financial statements issued by management to provide the necessary information to make their decisions. Acting on behalf of management, accountants have a moral and ethical responsibility to provide users with financial information that will be useful in making their decisions. The process by which the accountant depicts, or describes, the effects of economic events on the entity is called *recognition.*

The items, such as assets, liabilities, revenues, and expenses, depicted in financial statements are *representations.* Simply stated, the accountant cannot show a stockholder or other user the company's assets, such as cash and buildings. What the user sees in a set of financial statements is a depiction of the real thing. That is, the accountant describes, with words and numbers, the various items in a set of financial statements. The system is imperfect at best and, for that reason, is always in the process of change. As society and the business environment have become more complex, the accounting profession has striven for ways to improve financial statements as a means of communicating with statement users.

[1] *Statement of Financial Accounting Concepts No. 5,* "Recognition and Measurement in Financial Statements of Business Enterprises" (Stamford, Conn.: Financial Accounting Standards Board, December 1984), par. 6.

Measurement

Accountants depict a financial statement item in both words and *numbers*. The accountant must *quantify* the effects of economic events on the entity. It is not enough to decide that an event is important and thus warrants recognition in the financial statements. To be able to recognize it, the statement preparer must measure the financial effects of the event on the company.

Measurement of an item in financial statements requires that two choices be made. First, the accountant must decide on the *attribute* to be measured. Second, a scale of measurement, or *unit of measure*, must be chosen.

The Attribute to Be Measured Assume that a company holds a parcel of real estate as an investment. What attribute—that is, *characteristic*—of the property should be used to measure and thus recognize it as an asset on the balance sheet? The cost of the asset at the time it is acquired is the most logical choice. *Cost* is the amount of cash, or its equivalent, paid to acquire the asset. But how do we report the property on a balance sheet a year from now?

- The simplest approach is to show the property on the balance sheet at its original cost, thus the designation **historical cost.** The use of historical cost is not only simple but also *verifiable*. Assume that two accountants are asked to independently measure the cost of the asset. After examining the sales contract for the land, they should arrive at the same amount.
- An alternative to historical cost as the attribute to be measured is **current value.** Current value is the amount of cash, or its equivalent, that could be received currently from the sale of the asset. For the company's piece of property, current value is the *estimated* selling price of the land, reduced by any commissions or other fees involved in making the sale. But the amount is only an estimate, not an actual amount. If the company has not yet sold the property, how can we know for certain its selling price? We have to compare it to similar properties that *have* sold recently.

Historical cost The amount paid for an asset and used as a basis for recognizing it on the balance sheet and carrying it on later balance sheets.

Current value The amount of cash, or its equivalent, that could be received by selling an asset currently.

The choice between current value and historical cost as the attribute to be measured is a good example of the trade-off between *relevance* and *reliability*. As indicated earlier, historical cost is verifiable and is thus to a large extent a reliable measure. But is it as relevant to the needs of the decision makers as current value? Put yourself in the position of a banker trying to decide whether to lend money to the company. In evaluating the company's assets as collateral for the loan, is it more relevant to your decision to know what the firm paid for a piece of land 20 years ago or what it could be sold for today? But what *could* the property be sold for today? Two accountants might not necessarily arrive at the same current value for the land. Whereas value or selling price may be more relevant to your decision on the loan, the reliability of this amount is often questionable.

Because of its objective nature, historical cost is the attribute used to measure many of the assets recognized on the balance sheet. However, certain other attributes, such as current value, have increased in popularity in recent years. In other chapters of the book, we will discuss some of the alternatives to historical cost.

What events have economic consequences to a business? The destructive effects of a warehouse fire, for example, will result in losses to buildings and other business assets. These losses will surely be reflected in the next year's financial statements of the affected companies—possibly in the income statement, as a downturn in revenues due to lost sales. What other financial statements would be affected by a big fire?

The Unit of Measure Regardless of the attribute of an item to be measured, it is still necessary to choose a yardstick or unit of measure. The yardstick we currently use is units of money. *Money* is something accepted as a medium of exchange or as a means of payment. The unit of money in the United States is the dollar. In Japan the medium of exchange is the yen, and in Great Britain it is the pound.

The use of the dollar as a unit of measure for financial transactions is widely accepted. The *stability* of the dollar as a yardstick is subject to considerable debate, however. Consider an example. You are thinking about buying a certain parcel of land. As part of your decision process, you measure the dimensions of the property and determine that the lot is 80 feet wide and 120 feet deep. Thus, the unit of measure used to determine the lot's size is the square foot. The company that owns the land offers to sell it for $10,000. Although the offer sounds attractive, you decide against the purchase today.

You return in one year to take a second look at the lot. You measure the lot again and, not surprisingly, find the width to still be 80 feet and the depth 120 feet. The owner is still willing to sell the lot for $10,000. This may appear to be the same price as last year. But the *purchasing power* of the unit of measure, the dollar, may very possibly have changed since last year. Even though the foot is a stable measuring unit, the dollar often is not. A *decline* in the purchasing power of the dollar is evidenced by a continuing *rise* in the general level of prices in an economy. For example, rather than paying $10,000 last year to buy the lot, you could have spent the $10,000 on other goods or services. However, a year later, the same $10,000 may very well not buy the same amount of goods and services.

Inflation, or a rise in the general level of prices in the economy, results in a decrease in purchasing power. In the past, the accounting profession has experimented with financial statements adjusted for the changing value of the dollar. As inflation has declined in recent years in the United States, the debate over the use of the dollar as a stable measuring unit has somewhat subsided.[2] It is still important to recognize the inherent weakness in the use of a measuring unit that is subject to change, however.

Summary of Recognition and Measurement in Financial Statements

The purpose of financial statements is to communicate various types of economic information about a company. The job of the accountant is to decide which information should be recognized in the financial statements and how the effects of that information on the entity should be measured. Exhibit 4-1 summarizes the role of recognition and measurement in the preparation of financial statements.

Exhibit 4-1
Recognition and Measurement in Financial Statements

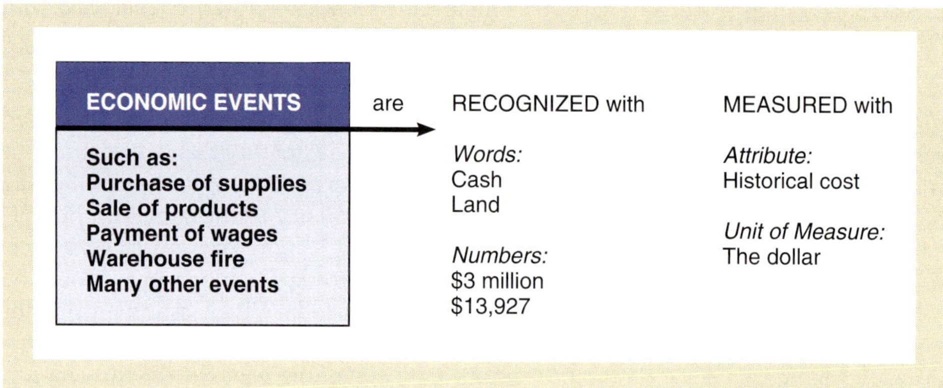

THE ACCRUAL BASIS OF ACCOUNTING

LO 2 Explain the differences between the cash and accrual bases of accounting.

The accrual basis of accounting is the foundation for the measurement of income in our modern system of accounting. The best way to understand the accrual basis is to compare it with the simpler cash approach.

Comparing the Cash and Accrual Bases of Accounting

The cash and accrual bases of accounting differ with respect to the *timing* of the recognition of revenues and expenses. For example, assume that on July 24, Barbara White,

[2]The rate of inflation in some countries, most noticeably those in South America, has far exceeded the rate in the United States. Companies operating in some of these countries with hyperinflationary economies are required to make adjustments to their statements.

a salesperson for Spiffy House Painters, contracts with a homeowner to repaint a house for $1,000. A large crew comes in and paints the house the next day, July 25. The customer has 30 days from the day of completion of the job to pay and does, in fact, pay Spiffy on August 25. *When* should Spiffy recognize the $1,000 as revenue? As soon as the contract is signed on July 24? Or on July 25, when the work is done? Or on August 25, when the customer pays the bill?

In an income statement prepared on the **cash basis,** revenues are recognized when cash is *received.* Thus, on a cash basis, the $1,000 would not be recognized as revenue until the cash is collected, on August 25. On an **accrual basis,** revenue is recognized when it is *earned.* On this basis, the $1,000 would be recognized as revenue on July 25, when the house is painted. This is the point at which the revenue is earned.

Cash basis A system of accounting in which revenues are recognized when cash is received and expenses when cash is paid.

Accrual basis A system of accounting in which revenues are recognized when earned and expenses when incurred.

Recall from Chapter 3 the journal entry to recognize revenue before cash is received. Although cash has not yet been received, another account, Accounts Receivable, is recognized as an asset. This asset represents the right to receive cash in the future. The entry on completion of the job is as follows:

July 25	Accounts Receivable	1,000	
	Service Revenue		1,000
	To recognize revenue from house painting.		

Recall from Chapter 3 that the accounting equation must balance after each transaction is recorded. Throughout the remainder of the book, each time we record a journal entry, we illustrate the effect of the entry on the equation. The effect of the preceding entry on the equation is as follows:

Assets	=	Liabilities	+	Owners' Equity
+1,000				+1,000

At the time cash is collected, accounts receivable is reduced and cash is increased:

Aug. 25	Cash	1,000	
	Accounts Receivable		1,000
	To record cash received from house painting.		

Assets	=	Liabilities	+	Owners' Equity
+1,000				
−1,000				

Assume that Barbara White is paid a 10% commission for all contracts and is paid on the 15th of the month following the month a house is painted. Thus, for this job, she will receive a $100 commission check on August 15. When should Spiffy recognize her commission of $100 as an expense? On July 24, when White gets the homeowner to sign a contract? When the work is completed, on July 25? Or on August 15, when she receives the commission check? Again, on a cash basis, commission expense would be recognized on August 15, when cash is *paid* to the salesperson. But on an accrual basis, expenses are recognized when they are *incurred.* In our example, the commission expense is incurred when the house is painted, on July 25.

Exhibit 4-2 summarizes the essential differences between recognition of revenues and expenses on a cash basis and recognition on an accrual basis.

Exhibit 4-2

Comparing the Cash and Accrual Bases of Accounting

	Cash Basis	Accrual Basis
Revenue is recognized	**When Received**	**When Earned**
Expense is recognized	**When Paid**	**When Incurred**

Business Strategy

http://www.mcdonalds.com

Controlling Costs under the Golden Arches

McDonald's has experienced a long run of rapid and continuous growth, both at home and abroad. Stockholders have been rewarded with an enviable compound annual total return of 12% for the 10 years ended December 31, 2001. The company's vision is "to be the world's best quick service restaurant experience," and it works hard to make that vision a reality. The key is not just to offer food and service that meet customers' needs and corporate quality standards but also to dominate the market, both domestic and foreign, through the sheer number of its outlets.

Management expects to open between 1,300 and 1,400 restaurants in 2002 alone. The company has already put into place a number of initiatives to ensure that both these new restaurants as well as the 30,000 already in existence continue to be profitable. In fact, the 2001 letter to shareholders states that these initiatives are expected to generate ongoing annual savings of about $100 million in selling, general, and administrative expenses, starting in 2001.

Internationally, McDonald's remains concerned about the weak economic conditions in Asia and Latin America. However, given the huge long-term potential of international markets, the company remains committed to finding ways to grow these markets and at the same time contain costs. Attractive pricing is even more critical in countries with significant economic problems. Given the need to be so price sensitive, McDonald's must focus on improving its cost structures in these markets. The ability to control costs will be crucial to the long-term viability of the golden arches outside the United States. ■

Sources: McDonald's 2001 annual report and corporate Web site.

What the Income Statement and the Statement of Cash Flows Reveal

Most business entities, other than the very smallest, use the accrual basis of accounting. Thus, the income statement reflects the accrual basis. Revenues are recognized when they are earned and expenses when they are incurred. At the same time, however, stockholders and creditors are also interested in information concerning the cash flows of an entity. The purpose of a statement of cash flows is to provide this information. Keep in mind that even though we present a statement of cash flows in a complete set of financial statements, the accrual basis is used for recording transactions and for preparing a balance sheet and an income statement.

Recall the example of Glengarry Health Club in Chapter 3. The club earned revenue from two sources, memberships and court fees. Both of these forms of revenue were recognized on the income statement presented in that chapter and are reproduced in the top portion of Exhibit 4-3. Recall, however, that members have 30 days to pay and that, at the end of the first month of operation, only $4,000 of the membership fees of $15,000 had been collected.

Now consider the statement of cash flows for the first month of operation, partially reproduced in the bottom portion of Exhibit 4-3. Because we want to compare the income statement to the statement of cash flows, only the Operating Activities section of the statement is shown. (The Investing and Financing Activities sections have been omitted from the statement.) Why is net income for the month a *positive* $7,000 but cash from operating activities a *negative* $4,000? Of the membership revenue of $15,000 reflected on the income statement, only $4,000 was collected in cash. Glengarry has accounts receivable for the other $11,000. Thus, cash from operating activities, as reflected on a statement of cash flows, is $11,000 *less* than net income of $7,000, or a negative $4,000.

Each of these two financial statements serves a useful purpose. The income statement reflects the revenues actually earned by the business, regardless of whether cash has been collected. The statement of cash flows tells the reader about the actual cash

Exhibit 4-3 Comparing the Income Statement and the Statement of Cash Flows

Membership revenue is $15,000 but only $4,000 was collected in cash. This $11,000 difference explains why net income is different from cash used by operating activities.

Net income and cash used by operating activities differ by $11,000.

The **income statement** for Glengarry Health Club shows the following:

Revenues:		
Memberships	$15,000	
Court fees	5,000	$ 20,000
Expenses:		
Salaries and wages	$10,000	
Utilities	3,000	(13,000)
Net income		$ 7,000

A **partial statement of cash flows** for Glengarry Health Club shows the following:

Cash received from:		
Membership fees	$ 4,000	
Court fees	5,000	$ 9,000
Cash paid for:		
Salaries and wages	$10,000	(13,000)
Utilities	3,000	$ (4,000)
Cash used by operating activities		

inflows during a period of time. The need for the information provided by both statements is summarized by the Financial Accounting Standards Board as follows:

> Statements of cash flows commonly show a great deal about an entity's current cash receipts and payments, but a cash flow statement provides an incomplete basis for assessing prospects for future cash flows because it cannot show interperiod relationships. Many current cash receipts, especially from operations, stem from activities of earlier periods, and many current cash payments are intended or expected to result in future, not current, cash receipts. Statements of earnings and comprehensive income, especially if used in conjunction with statements of financial position, usually provide a better basis for assessing future cash flow prospects of an entity than do cash flow statements alone.[3]

Accrual Accounting and Time Periods

The *time period* assumption was introduced in Chapter 1. We assume that it is possible to prepare an income statement that fairly reflects the earnings of a business for a specific period of time, such as a month or a year. It is somewhat artificial to divide the operations of a business into periods of time as indicated on a calendar. The conflict arises because earning income is a *process* that takes place *over a period of time* rather than *at any one point in time.*

Consider an alternative to our present system of reporting on the operations of a business on a periodic basis. A new business begins operations with an investment of $50,000. The business operates for 10 years, during which time no records are kept other than a checkbook for the cash on deposit at the bank. At the end of the 10 years, the owners decide to go their separate ways and convert all of their assets to cash. They split among them the balance of $80,000 in the bank account. What is the profit of the business for the 10-year period? The answer is $30,000, the difference between the original cash of $50,000 contributed and the cash of $80,000 available at liquidation.

The point of this simple example is that we could be very precise and accurate in our measurement of the income of a business if it were not necessary to artificially divide operations according to a calendar. Stockholders, bankers, and other interested parties cannot wait until a business liquidates to make decisions, however. They need information on a periodic basis. Thus, the justification for the accrual basis of account-

[3] *SFAC No. 5,* par. 24c.

ing lies in the needs of financial statement users for periodic information on the financial position as well as the profitability of the entity.

The Revenue Recognition Principle

LO 3 Describe the revenue recognition principle and explain its application in various situations.

Revenues Inflows of assets or settlements of liabilities from delivering or producing goods, rendering services, or conducting other activities.

Revenue recognition principle Revenues are recognized in the income statement when they are realized, or realizable, and earned.

"**Revenues** are inflows or other enhancements of assets of an entity or settlements of its liabilities (or a combination of both) from delivering or producing goods, rendering services, or other activities that constitute the entity's ongoing major or central operations."[4] Two points should be noted about this formal definition of revenues. First, an asset is not always involved when revenue is recognized. The recognition of revenue may result from the settlement of a liability rather than from the acquisition of an asset. Second, entities generate revenue in different ways: some companies produce goods, others distribute or deliver the goods to users, and still others provide some type of service.

On the accrual basis, revenues are recognized when earned. However, the **revenue recognition principle** involves two factors. Revenues are recognized in the income statement when they are both *realized* and *earned.*[5] Revenues are *realized* when goods or services are exchanged for cash or claims to cash.

Accounting for Your Decisions

You Are the Marketing Manager

The end of the year is fast approaching, and your department has not sold its quota of computers. As you understand the company's accounting policies, revenues are recorded when computers are ordered and shipped to customers. You know that if your department does not make its quota, then your job could be in jeopardy. So you get an idea. You call up some friends and tell them to order computers that they don't really need yet. In return, you'll get them a great price on the machines. Besides, if they don't want the computers, they can send them back in January and get a full refund. Meanwhile, you'll make your quota. Do you think there is anything wrong with this idea?

ANS: Yes, there is something wrong with the idea. For one thing, it is very poor business judgment to push products on customers if you believe they will be returned. Although many customers will say no to your idea, others will go along to get a lower price, only to later regret buying something they don't need. And if the computers are indeed returned in January, then the company's auditors will be obliged to indicate that the company has not followed generally accepted accounting principles, because the intent of the transaction was merely to boost sales in the current year. This shortcut is not only unethical but in violation of the revenue recognition principle.

Other Applications of the Revenue Recognition Principle

At what point are revenues realized and earned by an entity? As a practical rule, revenue is usually recognized at the time of sale. This is normally interpreted to mean at the time of delivery of the product or service to the customer. However, consider the following examples in which it is necessary either to modify or to interpret the meaning of the revenue recognition principle.

[4] *Statement of Financial Accounting Concepts No. 6,* "Elements of Financial Statements" (Stamford, Conn.: Financial Accounting Standards Board, December 1985), par. 78.

[5] An alternative is to recognize revenues when they are *realizable* and earned. *Realizable* has a slightly different meaning, which will be explained later when we look at commodities.

Accounting For Your Decisions

You Are the Stockholder

Assume that a construction company starts two projects during the year. One is a $5 million contract for a bridge. The other is a $4 million contract for a dam. Based on actual costs incurred to date and estimates of costs yet to be incurred, the contractor estimates that at the end of the year the bridge is 20% complete and the dam is 50% complete. Which would be more informative to you as a stockholder of the construction company: (1) an end-of-the-year report that indicates no revenue because no contracts are finished yet or (2) an end-of-the-year report that indicates revenue of $1 million on the bridge (20% of $5 million) and $2 million on the dam (50% of $4 million), both based on the extent of completion?

ANS: As a stockholder, you need information on a timely basis to evaluate your various investments. The percentage-of-completion method will allow you to assess the profitability of your investment in the construction company on a regular basis rather than only at the point when projects are completed.

Long-Term Contracts The **percentage-of-completion method** allows a contractor to recognize revenue over the life of a project rather than at its completion. For long-term contracts in which the sales price is fixed by contract and in which the realization of revenue depends only on production, such as constructing the bridge or the dam (see the box above), the method is a reasonable alternative to deferring the recognition of revenue until the project is completed. The following excerpt from the 2001 annual report of **Foster Wheeler Inc.** is an example of how revenue is recognized by most companies in the construction industry:

Percentage-of-completion method The method used by contractors to recognize revenue before the completion of a long-term contract.

http://www.fwc.com

> The Engineering and Construction Group records profits on long-term contracts on a percentage-of-completion basis on the cost to cost method. Contracts in process are valued at cost plus accrued profits less earned revenues and progress payments on uncompleted contracts.

Franchises Over the last 30 years, franchising has achieved enormous popularity as a way to conduct business. It has been especially prevalent in retail sales, including the fast-food (**McDonald's**), motel (**Holiday Inn**), and car rental (**Hertz**) businesses. Typically, the franchisor grants the exclusive right to sell a product or service in a specific geographic area to the franchisee. As discussed in the chapter opener, a franchisor such as McDonald's generates revenues from one or both of two sources: (1) from the sale of the franchise and related services, such as help in selecting a site and hiring employees and (2) from continuing fees based on performance, for example, a fixed percentage of sales by the franchisee.

At what point should the revenue from the sale of a franchise be recognized? An FASB standard allows a franchisor such as McDonald's to recognize initial franchise fees as revenue only when it has made "substantial performance" of its obligations and when collection of the fee is reasonably assured.[6] An excerpt from McDonald's 2001 annual report indicates how it recognizes both the initial and continuing fees:

> *Revenue Recognition*
> Sales by Company-operated restaurants are recognized on a cash basis. Revenues from franchised and affiliated restaurants include continuing rent and service fees as well as initial fees. Continuing fees are recognized in the period earned. Initial fees are recognized upon opening of a restaurant, which is when the Company has performed substantially all initial services required by the franchise arrangement.

[6]*Statement of Financial Accounting Standards No. 45*, "Accounting for Franchise Fee Revenue" (Stamford, Conn.: Financial Accounting Standards Board, December 1981), par. 5.

> **From Concept to Practice 4.1**
>
> **Reading McDonald's Income Statement**
>
> *Refer to McDonald's comparative income statements for 2001, 2000, and 1999 in the chapter opener. What percentage of total revenues was derived from franchised restaurants? Has this percentage changed over the three-year period?*

Commodities Corn, wheat, gold, silver, and other agricultural and mining products trade on the open market at established prices. Readily convertible assets such as these are interchangeable and can be sold at a quoted price in an active market that can absorb the quantity being sold without significantly affecting the price.[7] Earlier, we mentioned that to be recognized, revenues must be realized. An acceptable alternative is to recognize revenues when they are realizable. Revenues are *realizable* when assets received or held are readily convertible to known amounts of cash or claims to cash.

Assume that a company mines gold. Revenues are realizable by the company at the time the product is mined because each ounce of gold is interchangeable with another ounce of gold and the commodities market can absorb all of the gold the company sells without having an effect on the price. This is one of the few instances in which it is considered acceptable to recognize revenue *prior* to the point of sale. The exception is justified because the important event in the revenue-generation process is the *production* of the gold, not the sale of it. The **production method** of recognizing revenue is used for precious metals, as well as certain agricultural products and marketable securities.

Production method The method in which revenue is recognized when a commodity is produced rather than when it is sold.

Installment Sales Various consumer items, such as automobiles, appliances, and even vacation properties, are sold on an installment basis. A down payment is followed by a series of monthly payments over a period of years. Default on the payments and repossession of the item by the seller are more common in these types of sales than with most other arrangements. For this reason, it is considered acceptable, in limited circumstances, to defer the recognition of revenue on an installment sale until cash is actually collected. The **installment method,** which is essentially a cash basis of accounting, is acceptable only when the seller has no reasonable basis for estimating the degree of collectibility. Note that the production and installment methods are at opposite ends of the spectrum. Under the production method, revenue is recognized *before* a sale takes place; with the installment method, revenue is recognized *after* the sale.

Installment method The method in which revenue is recognized at the time cash is collected.

Rent and Interest In some cases, revenue is earned *continuously* over time. In these cases, a product or service is not delivered at a specific point in time; instead, the earnings process takes place with the passage of time. Rent and interest are two examples. Interest is the cost associated with the use of someone else's money. When should a bank recognize the interest earned from granting a 90-day loan? Even though the interest may not be received until the loan itself is repaid, interest is earned every day the loan is outstanding. Later in the chapter, we will look at the process for recognizing interest earned but not yet received. The same procedure is used to recognize revenue from rent that is earned but uncollected.

Long-term contracts, franchises, commodities, installment sales, rent, and interest are not the only situations in which the revenue recognition principle must be interpreted. The intent in examining these particular examples was to help you think about the variety of ways in which businesses generate revenue and about the need to apply judgment in deciding when to recognize revenue. These examples should help you to realize the subjective nature of the work of an accountant and to understand that the discipline is not as precise as it may sometimes seem.

Expense Recognition and the Matching Principle

LO 4 Describe the matching principle and the various methods for recognizing expenses.

Companies incur a variety of costs. A new office building is constructed. Inventory is purchased. Employees perform services. The electric meter is read. In each of these situations, the company incurs a cost, regardless of when it pays cash. Conceptually, *any*

[7] *SFAC No. 5,* par. 83a.

time a cost is incurred, an asset is acquired. However, according to the definition in Chapter 1, an asset represents a future economic benefit. An asset ceases being an asset and becomes an expense when the economic benefits from having incurred the cost have expired. Assets are unexpired costs, and expenses are expired costs.

At what point do costs expire and become expenses? The expense recognition principle requires that we recognize expenses in different ways, depending on the nature of the cost. The ideal approach to recognizing expenses is to match them with revenues. Under the **matching principle,** the accountant attempts to associate revenues of a period with the costs necessary to generate those revenues. For certain types of expenses, a direct form of matching is possible; for others, it is necessary to associate costs with a particular period. The classic example of direct matching is cost of goods sold expense with sales revenue. Cost of goods sold is the cost of the inventory associated with a particular sale. A cost is incurred and an asset is recorded when the inventory is purchased. The asset, inventory, becomes an expense when it is sold. Another example of a cost that can be matched directly with revenue is commissions. The commission paid to a salesperson can be matched directly with the sale.

Matching principle The association of revenue of a period with all of the costs necessary to generate that revenue.

An indirect form of matching is used to recognize the benefits associated with certain types of costs, most noticeably long-term assets, such as buildings and equipment. These costs benefit many periods, but usually it is not possible to match them directly with a specific sale of a product. Instead, they are matched with the periods during which they will provide benefits. For example, an office building may be useful to a company for 30 years. *Depreciation* is the process of allocating the cost of a tangible long-term asset to its useful life. Depreciation Expense is the account used to recognize this type of expense.

The benefits associated with the incurrence of certain other costs are treated in accounting as expiring simultaneously with their acquisition. The justification for this treatment is that no future benefits from the incurrence of the cost are discernible. This is true of most selling and administrative costs. For example, the costs of heat and light in a building benefit only the current period and therefore are recognized as expenses as soon as the costs are incurred. Likewise, income taxes incurred during the period do not benefit any period other than the current period and are thus written off as an expense in the period incurred.

The relationships among costs, assets, and expenses are depicted in Exhibit 4-4 using three examples. First, costs incurred for purchases of merchandise result in an asset,

Exhibit 4-4

Relationships among Costs, Assets, and Expenses

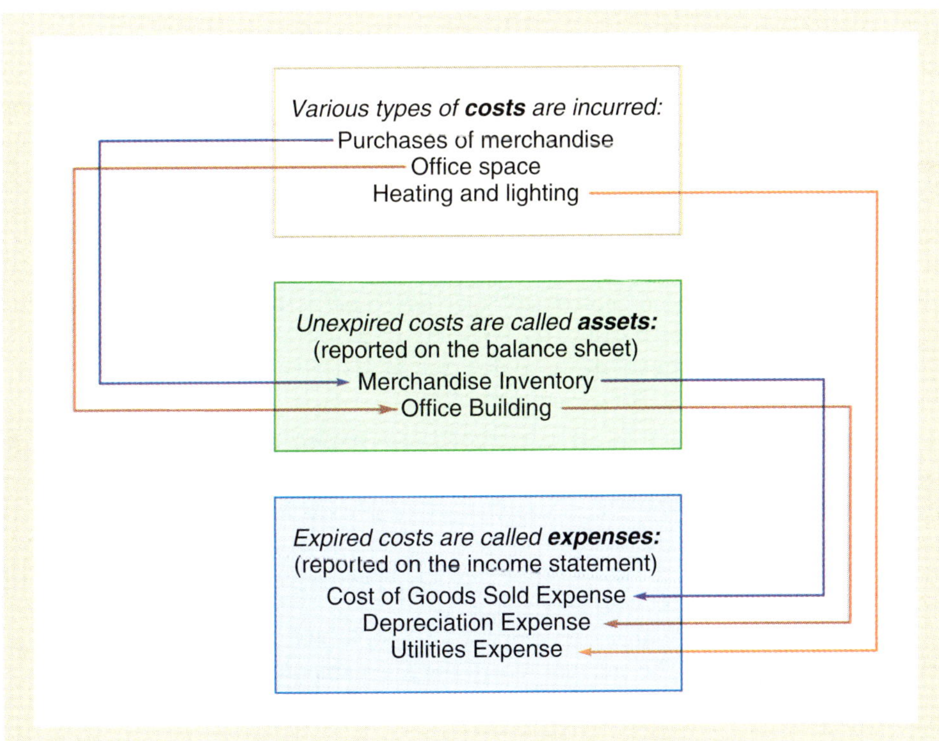

Merchandise Inventory, and are eventually matched with revenue at the time the product is sold. Second, costs incurred for office space result in an asset, Office Building, which is recognized as Depreciation Expense over the useful life of the building. Third, the cost of heating and lighting benefits only the current period and is thus recognized immediately as Utilities Expense.

Expenses Outflows of assets or incurrences of liabilities resulting from delivering goods, rendering services, or carrying out other activities.

According to the FASB, **expenses** are "outflows or other using up of assets or incurrences of liabilities (or a combination of both) from delivering or producing goods, rendering services, or carrying out other activities that constitute the entity's ongoing major or central operations."[8] The key point to note about expenses is that they come about in two different ways: from the use of an asset or from the recognition of a liability. For example, when a retailer sells a product, the asset sacrificed is Inventory. Cost of Goods Sold is the expense account that is debited when the Inventory account is credited. As we will see in the next section, the incurrence of an expense may also result in a liability.

Two-Minute Review

1. *Explain the difference between the attribute to be measured and the unit of measure.*
2. *Give at least three examples of situations in which revenues are recognized other than at the time of sale.*
3. *Explain the different ways in which expenses are matched with revenues.*

Answers on pages 177 and 178.

ACCRUAL ACCOUNTING AND ADJUSTING ENTRIES

LO 5 Identify the four major types of adjusting entries and prepare them for a variety of situations.

Adjusting entries Journal entries made at the end of a period by a company using the accrual basis of accounting.

The accrual basis of accounting necessitates a number of adjusting entries at the end of a period. **Adjusting entries** are the journal entries the accountant makes at the end of a period for a company on the accrual basis of accounting. *Adjusting entries are not needed if a cash basis is used. It is the very nature of the accrual basis that results in the need for adjusting entries.* The frequency of the adjustment process depends on how often financial statements are prepared. Most businesses make adjustments at the end of each month.

Types of Adjusting Entries

Why are there four basic types, or categories, of adjusting entries? The answer lies in the distinction between the cash and the accrual bases of accounting. On an accrual basis, *revenue* can be earned either *before* or *after* cash is received. *Expenses* can be incurred either *before* or *after* cash is paid. Each of these four distinct situations requires a different type of adjustment at the end of the period. We will consider each of the four categories and look at some examples of each.

(1) Cash Paid Before Expense Is Incurred (Deferred Expense) Assets are often acquired before their actual use in the business. Insurance policies typically are prepaid, as often is rent. Office supplies are purchased in advance of their use, as are all types of property and equipment. Recall from our earlier discussion that unexpired costs are assets. As the costs expire and the benefits are used up, the asset must be written off and replaced with an expense.

Assume that on September 1 a company prepays $2,400 in rent on its office space for the next 12 months. The entry to record the prepayment follows:

[8] SFAC No. 6, par. 80.

Sept. 1	Prepaid Rent	2,400	
	Cash		2,400
	To prepay the rent on office space for 12 months.		

Assets	=	Liabilities	+	Owners' Equity
+2,400				
−2,400				

An asset account, Prepaid Rent, is recorded because the company will receive benefits over the next 12 months. Because the rent is for a 12-month period, $200 of benefits from the asset expires at the end of each month. The adjusting entry at the end of September to record this expiration accomplishes two purposes: (1) it recognizes the reduction in the asset Prepaid Rent, and (2) it recognizes the expense associated with using up the benefits for one month. From the last chapter you should recall that an asset is decreased with a credit and that an expense is increased with a debit, as follows:

Sept. 30	Rent Expense	200	
	Prepaid Rent		200
	To recognize $200 of rent expense for the month.		

Assets	=	Liabilities	+	Owners' Equity
−200				−200

T accounts are an invaluable aid in understanding adjusting entries. They allow us to focus on the transactions and balances that will be included in the more formal general ledger accounts. The T accounts for Prepaid Rent and Rent Expense appear as follows after posting the original entry on September 1 and the adjusting entry on September 30:

PREPAID RENT

9/1	2,400		
		200	9/30
Bal.	2,200		

RENT EXPENSE

9/30	200		

The balance in Prepaid Rent represents the unexpired benefits from the prepayment of rent for the remaining 11 months: $200 × 11 = $2,200. The Rent Expense account reflects the expiration of benefits during the month of September.

From Concept to Practice 4.2

Reading Winnebago Industries' Balance Sheet

Refer to the balance sheet in Winnebago Industries' annual report. How does Winnebago Industries classify prepaid expenses? What types of prepaid expenses would you expect the company to have?

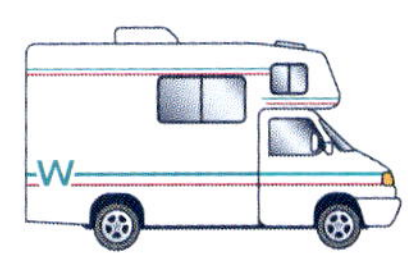

Accounting for Your Decisions

You Are the Store Manager

You are responsible for managing a new running shoe store. The landlord requires a security deposit as well as prepayment of the first year's rent. The security deposit is refundable at the end of the first year. After the first year, rent is payable on a monthly basis. After three months in business, the owner asks you for an income statement. How should the security deposit and the prepayment of the first year's rent be recognized on this income statement?

ANS: The security deposit will not affect the income statement. It is an asset that will be converted to cash at the end of the first year, assuming that you are entitled to a full refund. One-fourth of the prepayment of the first year's rent should be recognized as an expense on the income statement for the first three months.

As discussed earlier in the chapter, depreciation is the process of allocating the cost of a long-term tangible asset over its estimated useful life. The accountant does not attempt to measure the decline in *value* of the asset but simply tries to allocate its cost over its useful life. Thus, the adjustment for depreciation is similar to the one we made for rent expense. Assume that on January 1 a company buys a delivery truck, for which it pays $21,000. The entry to record the purchase is as follows:

Jan. 1	Delivery Truck	21,000	
	Cash		21,000
	To record purchase of delivery truck for cash.		

Assets	=	Liabilities	+	Owners' Equity
+21,000				
−21,000				

Two estimates must be made in depreciating the delivery truck: (1) the useful life of the asset and (2) the salvage value of the truck at the end of its useful life. Estimated salvage value is the amount a company expects to be able to receive when it sells an asset at the end of its estimated useful life. Assume a five-year estimated life for the truck and an estimated salvage value of $3,000 at the end of that time. Thus, the *depreciable cost* of the truck is $21,000 − $3,000, or $18,000. In a later chapter, we will consider alternative methods for allocating the depreciable cost over the useful life of an asset. For now, we will use the simplest approach, called the **straight-line method,** which assigns an equal amount of depreciation to each period. The monthly depreciation is found by dividing the depreciable cost of $18,000 over the estimated useful life of 60 months, which equals $300 per month.

Straight-line method The assignment of an equal amount of depreciation to each period.

The adjustment to recognize depreciation is conceptually the same as the adjustment to write off Prepaid Rent. That is, the asset account is reduced, and an expense is recognized. However, accountants normally use a contra account to reduce the total amount of long-term tangible assets by the amount of depreciation. A **contra account** has a balance that is the opposite of the balance in its related account. For example, Accumulated Depreciation is used to record the decrease in a long-term asset for depreciation, and thus it carries a credit balance. An *increase* in Accumulated Depreciation is recorded with a *credit* because we want to *decrease* the amount of assets and assets are *decreased* by a *credit.* The entry to record depreciation at the end of January is as follows:

Contra account An account with a balance that is opposite that of a related account.

Jan. 31	Depreciation Expense	300	
	Accumulated Depreciation		300
	To record depreciation on delivery truck.		

Assets	=	Liabilities	+	Owners' Equity
−300				−300

Why do companies use a contra account for depreciation rather than simply reducing the long-term asset directly? If the asset account were reduced each time depreciation is recorded, its original cost would not be readily determinable from the accounting records. Businesses need to know the original cost of each asset, for various reasons. One of the most important of these reasons is the need to know historical cost for computation of depreciation for tax purposes.

Study Tip

Think of the Accumulated Depreciation account as simply an extension of the related asset account, in this case the truck. Therefore, although the truck account is not directly reduced for depreciation, a credit to its companion account, Accumulated Depreciation, has the effect of reducing the asset.

The T accounts for Delivery Truck, Accumulated Depreciation, and Depreciation Expense show the following balances at the end of the first month:

DELIVERY TRUCK

	Debit	Credit	
1/1	21,000		

ACCUMULATED DEPRECIATION

	Debit	Credit	
		300	1/31

DEPRECIATION EXPENSE

	Debit	Credit	
1/31	300		

On a balance sheet prepared on January 31, the contra account is shown as a reduction in the carrying value of the truck:

Delivery Truck	$21,000	
Less: Accumulated Depreciation	300	$20,700

(2) Cash Received Before Revenue Is Earned (Deferred Revenue)

You can benefit greatly in your study of accounting by recognizing its *symmetry.* By this we mean that one company's asset is another company's liability. In the earlier example involving the rental of office space, a second company, the landlord, received the cash paid by the first company, the tenant. At the time cash is received, the landlord has a liability because it has taken cash from the tenant but has not yet performed the service to earn the revenue. The revenue will be earned with the passage of time. This is the entry on the books of the landlord on September 1:

		Debit	Credit
Sept. 1	Cash	2,400	
	Rent Collected in Advance		2,400
	To record receipt of rent on office space for 12 months.		

Assets	=	Liabilities	+	Owners' Equity
+2,400		+2,400		

The account Rent Collected in Advance is a liability. The landlord is obligated to provide the tenant uninterrupted use of the office facilities for the next 12 months. With the passage of time, the liability is satisfied as the tenant is provided the use of the space. The adjusting entry at the end of each month accomplishes two purposes: it recognizes (1) the reduction in the liability and (2) the revenue earned each month as the tenant occupies the space. Recall that we decrease a liability with a debit and increase revenue with a credit:

		Debit	Credit
Sept. 30	Rent Collected in Advance	200	
	Rent Revenue		200
	To recognize rent earned for the month.		

Assets	=	Liabilities	+	Owners' Equity
		−200		+200

The balance in Rent Collected in Advance reflects the remaining liability, and the balance in the Rent Revenue account indicates the amount earned for the month:

RENT COLLECTED IN ADVANCE

		2,400	9/1
9/30	200		
		2,200	Bal.

RENT REVENUE

		200	9/30

COURTESY OF AMAZON.COM, INC.

A gift certificate like this is a good example of a deferred revenue. Amazon.com *has received the $25 in payment for the certificate, but because it must wait for the recipient of the gift to pick out a book, it considers the obligation to deliver the book in the future a liability.*

In another example, many magazine subscriptions require the customer to pay in advance. For example, you pay $12 for a one-year subscription to your favorite magazine, and the publisher in turn sends you 12 monthly issues. At the time you send money to the publisher, it incurs a liability. It has taken your money but has not yet done anything to earn it. The publisher has an obligation either to provide you with the magazine over the next 12 months or to refund your $12.

At what point should the publisher recognize revenue from magazine sales? The publisher receives cash at the time the subscription is sold. The revenue has not been *earned* until the company publishes the magazine and mails it to you, however. Thus, a publisher usually recognizes revenue at the time of delivery. An excerpt from the 2001 annual report of AOL Time Warner (which publishes such popular magazines as *Time, People,* and *Sports Illustrated*) reflects this policy:

http://www.aoltimewarner.com

> The unearned portion of paid magazine subscriptions is deferred until magazines are delivered to subscribers. Upon each delivery, a proportionate share of the gross subscription price is included in revenues.

Assume that on March 1 AOL Time Warner sells 500 one-year subscriptions to a monthly magazine at a price of $12 each. The entry to record the receipt of cash from the 500 subscribers is as follows:

Mar. 1	Cash	6,000	
	Subscriptions Collected in Advance		6,000
	To record receipt of cash from sale of 500 one-year subscriptions at $12 each.		

Assets	=	Liabilities	+	Owners' Equity
+6,000		+6,000		

Assuming that each of the subscriptions starts with the March issue of the magazine, AOL Time Warner accountants would make the following entry at the end of the month:

Mar. 31	Subscriptions Collected in Advance	500	
	Subscription Revenue		500
	To recognize subscriptions earned for the month.		

Assets	=	Liabilities	+	Owners' Equity
		−500		+500

The Subscriptions Collected in Advance and Subscription Revenue accounts appear as follows after posting the two entries:

SUBSCRIPTIONS COLLECTED IN ADVANCE

		6,000	3/1
3/31	500		
		5,500	Bal.

SUBSCRIPTION REVENUE

		500	3/31

As you know by now, accounting terminology differs among companies. The account title Subscriptions Collected in Advance is only one of any number of possible titles for the liability related to subscriptions. For example, this same account on AOL Time Warner's balance sheet is called Unearned Portion of Paid Subscriptions.

(3) Expense Incurred Before Cash Is Paid (Accrued Liability) This situation is just the opposite of (1). That is, cash is paid *after* an expense is actually incurred rather than *before* its incurrence, as was the case in (1). Many normal operating costs, such as payroll and utilities, fit this situation. The utility bill is received at the end of the month, but the company has 10 days to pay it. Or consider the biweekly payroll for Jones Corporation. The company pays a total of $28,000 in wages on every other Friday. Assume that the last payday was Friday, May 31. The next two paydays will be Friday, June 14, and Friday, June 28. The journal entry will be the same on each of these paydays:

Accounting for Your Decisions

You Are the Banker

A new midwestern publisher comes to you for a loan. Through an aggressive ad campaign, the company sold a phenomenal number of subscriptions to a new sports magazine in its first six months and needs additional money to go national. The first issue of the magazine is due out next month. The publisher presents you an income statement for its first six months and you notice that it includes all of the revenue from the initial subscriptions sold in the Midwest. What concerns do you have?

ANS: First, the accounting treatment for the magazine revenue is improper. Because the magazine has not yet been delivered to the customer, the subscriptions have not yet been earned, and therefore no revenue should be recognized. As a banker, you should be sufficiently concerned that a potential customer would present improper financial statements, and you should deny the loan on that basis alone. That does not even take into account the fact that the company has yet to establish a sufficient track record to warrant the credit risk.

June 14	Wages Expense	28,000	
(and	Cash		28,000
June 28)	To pay the biweekly payroll.		

Assets	=	Liabilities	+	Owners' Equity
−28,000				−28,000

On a balance sheet prepared as of June 30, a liability must be recognized. Even though the next payment is not until July 12, Jones *owes* employees wages for the last two days of June and must recognize an expense for the wages earned by employees for these two days. We will assume that the company operates seven days a week and that the daily cost is 1/14th of the biweekly amount of $28,000, or $2,000. In addition to recognizing a liability on June 30, Jones must adjust the records to reflect an expense associated with the cost of wages for the last two days of the month:

June 30	Wages Expense	4,000	
	Wages Payable		4,000
	To record wages for last two days of the month.		

Assets	=	Liabilities	+	Owners' Equity
		+4,000		−4,000

What entry will be made on the next payday, July 12? Jones will need to eliminate the liability of $4,000 for the last two days of wages recorded on June 30 because the amount has now been paid. An additional $24,000 of expense has been incurred for the $2,000 cost per day associated with the first 12 days in July. Finally, cash is reduced for $28,000, which represents the biweekly payroll. The entry recorded is:

July 12	Wages Payable	4,000	
	Wages Expense	24,000	
	Cash		28,000
	To pay the biweekly payroll.		

Assets	=	Liabilities	+	Owners' Equity
−28,000		−4,000		−24,000

The following time line illustrates the amount of expense incurred in each of the two months, June and July, for the biweekly payroll:

2 days' expense in June: $4,000		12 days' expense in July: $24,000
Friday, June 28: Last payday	Friday, June 30: End of accounting period	Friday, July 12: Next payday

Another typical expense incurred before the payment of cash is interest. In many cases, the interest on a short-term loan is repaid with the amount of the loan, called the *principal,* on the maturity date. For example, Granger Company takes out a 9%, 90-day, $20,000 loan with its bank on March 1. The principal and interest will be repaid on May 30. The entry on Granger's books on March 1 follows:

Mar. 1	Cash	20,000	
	Notes Payable		20,000
	To record issuance of 9%, 90-day, $20,000 note.		

Assets	=	Liabilities	+	Owners' Equity
+20,000		+20,000		

The basic formula for computing interest follows:

$$I = P \times R \times T$$

where I = the dollar amount of interest
P = the principal amount of the loan
R = the annual rate of interest as a percentage
T = time in years (often stated as a fraction of a year).

The total interest on Granger's loan is as follows:

$$\$20{,}000 \times .09 \times 3/12 = \underline{\underline{\$450}}$$

Therefore, the amount of interest that must be recognized as expense at the end of March is one-third of $450 because one month of a total of three has passed. Alternatively, the formula for finding the total interest on the loan can be modified to compute the interest for one month:[9]

$$\$20{,}000 \times .09 \times 1/12 = \underline{\underline{\$150}}$$

The adjusting entry for the month of March is as follows:

Mar. 31	Interest Expense	150	
	Interest Payable		150
	To record interest for one month on a 9%, $20,000 loan.		

Assets	=	Liabilities	+	Owners' Equity
		+150		−150

The same adjusting entry is also made at the end of April:

Apr. 30	Interest Expense	150	
	Interest Payable		150
	To record interest for one month on a 9%, $20,000 loan.		

Assets	=	Liabilities	+	Owners' Equity
		+150		−150

The entry on Granger's books on May 30 when it repays the principal and interest is as follows:

[9] In practice, interest is calculated on the basis of days rather than months. For example, the interest for March would be $20,000 × .09 × 30/365, or $147.95, to reflect 30 days in the month out of a total of 365 days in the year. The reason the number of days in March is 30 rather than 31 is because in computing interest, businesses normally count the day a note matures but not the day it is signed. To simplify the calculations, we will use months, even though the result is slightly inaccurate.

May 30	Interest Payable	300	
	Interest Expense	150	
	Notes Payable	20,000	
	Cash		20,450
	To record payment of a 9%, 90-day, $20,000 loan with interest.		

Assets	=	Liabilities	+	Owners' Equity
−20,450		−20,300		−150

The reduction in Interest Payable eliminates the liability recorded at the end of March and April. The recognition of $150 in Interest Expense is the cost associated with the month of May.[10] The reduction in Cash represents the $20,000 of principal and the total interest of $450 for three months.

From Concept to Practice 4.3

Reading Winnebago Industries' Balance Sheet

Refer to the balance sheet in Winnebago Industries' annual report. What name does Winnebago Industries use for its accrued liabilities? What are the individual accounts on its balance sheet that are included in accrued liabilities? Which is the largest of those?

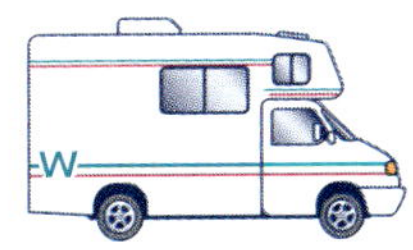

(4) Revenue Earned Before Cash Is Received (Accrued Asset)

Revenue is sometimes earned before the receipt of cash. Rent and interest are both earned with the passage of time and require an adjustment if cash has not yet been received. For example, assume that Grand Management Company rents warehouse space to a number of tenants. Most of its contracts call for prepayment of rent for six months at a time. Its agreement with one tenant, however, allows the tenant to pay Grand $2,500 in monthly rent anytime within the first 10 days of the following month. The adjusting entry on Grand's books at the end of April, the first month of the agreement, is as follows:

Apr. 30	Rent Receivable	2,500	
	Rent Revenue		2,500
	To record rent earned for the month of April.		

Assets	=	Liabilities	+	Owners' Equity
+2,500				+2,500

When the tenant pays its rent on May 7, the effect on Grand's books is as follows:

May 7	Cash	2,500	
	Rent Receivable		2,500
	To record rent collected for the month of April.		

Assets	=	Liabilities	+	Owners' Equity
+2,500				
−2,500				

Study Tip

Now that we have seen examples of all four types of adjusting entries, think about a key difference between deferrals (the first two categories) and accruals (the last two categories). When we make adjusting entries involving deferrals, we must consider any existing balance in a deferred account. Conversely, there is no existing account when making an accrual.

Although we used the example of rent to illustrate this category, the membership revenue of Glengarry Health Club in Chapter 3 also could be used as an example. Whenever a company records revenue before cash is received, some type of receivable is increased and revenue is also increased. In that chapter, the health club earned membership revenue even though members had until the following month to pay their dues.

Accruals and Deferrals

One of the challenges in learning accounting concepts is to gain an understanding of the terminology. Part of the difficulty stems from the alternative terms used by differ-

[10]This assumes that Granger did not make a separate entry prior to this to recognize interest expense for the month of May. If a separate entry had been made, a debit of $450 would be made to Interest Payable.

ent accountants to mean the same thing. For example, the asset created when insurance is paid for in advance is termed a *prepaid asset* by some and a *prepaid expense* by others. Someone else might refer to it as a *deferred expense.*

Deferral Cash has either been paid or received, but expense or revenue has not yet been recognized.

Deferred expense An asset resulting from the payment of cash before the incurrence of expense.

Deferred revenue A liability resulting from the receipt of cash before the recognition of revenue.

We will use the term **deferral** to refer to a situation in which cash has been either paid or received but the expense or revenue has been deferred to a later time. A **deferred expense** indicates that cash has been paid but the recognition of expense has been deferred. Because a deferred expense represents a *future benefit* to a company, it is an *asset.* An alternative name for deferred expense is *prepaid expense.* Prepaid insurance and office supplies are deferred expenses. An adjusting entry is made periodically to record the portion of the deferred expense that has expired. A **deferred revenue** means that cash has been received but the recognition of any revenue has been deferred until a later time. Because a deferred revenue represents an *obligation* to a company, it is a *liability.* An alternative name for deferred revenue is *unearned revenue.* Rent collected in advance is deferred revenue. The periodic adjusting entry recognizes the portion of the deferred revenue that is earned in that period.

Accrual Cash has not yet been paid or received, but expense has been incurred or revenue earned.

Accrued liability A liability resulting from the recognition of an expense before the payment of cash.

Accrued asset An asset resulting from the recognition of a revenue before the receipt of cash.

In this chapter, we have discussed in detail the accrual basis of accounting, which involves recognizing changes in resources and obligations as they occur, not simply when cash changes hands. More specifically, we will use the term **accrual** to refer to a situation in which no cash has been paid or received yet but it is necessary to recognize, or accrue, an expense or a revenue. An **accrued liability** is recognized at the end of the period in cases in which an expense has been incurred but cash has not yet been paid. Wages payable and interest payable are examples of accrued liabilities. An **accrued asset** is recorded when revenue has been earned but cash has not yet been collected. Rent receivable is an accrued asset.

Summary of Adjusting Entries

The four types of adjusting entries are summarized in Exhibit 4-5. Common examples of each are shown, along with the structure of the entries associated with the four categories. Finally, the following generalizations should help you in gaining a better understanding of adjusting entries and how they are used:

1. An adjusting entry is an internal transaction. It does not involve another entity.
2. Because it is an internal transaction, an adjusting entry *never* involves an increase or decrease in Cash.

Exhibit 4-5 Accruals and Deferrals

TYPE	SITUATION	EXAMPLES	ENTRY DURING PERIOD	ENTRY AT END OF PERIOD
Deferred expense	Cash paid before expense is incurred	Insurance policy Supplies Rent Buildings, equipment	Asset Cash	Expense Asset
Deferred revenue	Cash received before revenue is earned	Deposits, rent Subscriptions Gift certificates	Cash Liability	Liability Revenue
Accrued liability	Expense incurred before cash is paid	Salaries, wages Interest Taxes Rent	No Entry	Expense Liability
Accrued asset	Revenue earned before cash is received	Interest Rent	No Entry	Asset Revenue

3. At least one balance sheet account and one income statement account are involved in an adjusting entry. It is the nature of the adjustment process that an asset or liability account is adjusted with a corresponding change in either a revenue or an expense account.

Two-Minute Review

Assume a company wants to prepare financial statements at the end of its first month of operations. Each of the following transactions were recorded on the company's books on the first day of the month.

1. *Purchased a 24-month insurance policy for $3,600.*
2. *Collected $4,800 from a tenant for office space that the tenant has rented for the next 12 months.*
3. *Took out a 6%, 180-day, $10,000 loan at the bank.*

Prepare the necessary adjusting journal entries at the end of the month.

Answers on page 178.

Comprehensive Example of Adjusting Entries

We will now consider a comprehensive example involving the transactions for the first month of operations and the end-of-period adjusting entries for a hypothetical business, Duffy Transit Company. The trial balance in Exhibit 4-6 was prepared after posting to the accounts the transactions entered into during the first month of business. As discussed in Chapter 3, a trial balance can be prepared at any point in time. Because the trial balance is prepared *before* taking into account adjusting entries, it is called an *unadjusted* trial balance. This is the first month of operations for Duffy. Thus, the Retained Earnings account does not yet appear on the trial balance. After the first month, this account will have a balance and will appear on subsequent trial balances.

Exhibit 4-6
Unadjusted Trial Balance

DUFFY TRANSIT COMPANY
UNADJUSTED TRIAL BALANCE
JANUARY 31

	Debit	Credit
Cash	$ 50,000	
Prepaid Insurance	48,000	
Land	20,000	
Buildings—Garage	160,000	
Equipment—Buses	300,000	
Discount Tickets Sold in Advance		$ 25,000
Notes Payable		150,000
Capital Stock		400,000
Daily Ticket Revenue		30,000
Gas, Oil, and Maintenance Expense	12,000	
Wage and Salary Expense	10,000	
Dividends	5,000	
Totals	$605,000	$605,000

Duffy wants to prepare a balance sheet at the end of January and an income statement for its first month of operations. Use of the accrual basis necessitates a number of adjusting entries to update certain asset and liability accounts and to recognize the correct amounts for the various revenues and expenses.

Using a Trial Balance to Prepare Adjusting Entries

A trial balance is an important tool to use in preparing adjusting entries. The deferred expenses on Duffy's trial balance, such as Prepaid Insurance, must be reduced with a corresponding increase in expense. Similarly, any deferred revenues, such as Discount Tickets Sold in Advance, must be adjusted and a corresponding amount of revenue recognized. In addition, any accrued assets, such as Rent Receivable, and accrued liabilities, such as Interest Payable, which do not currently appear on the trial balance, must be recognized.

Adjusting Entries at the End of January

At the beginning of January, Duffy issued an 18-month, 12%, $150,000 promissory note for cash. Although interest will not be repaid until the loan's maturity date, Duffy must accrue interest for the first month. The calculation of interest for one month is $150,000 × .12 × 1/12. The adjusting entry is as follows:

		Debit	Credit
(a)	Interest Expense	1,500	
	Interest Payable		1,500
	To record interest for one month on 12%, $150,000 promissory note.		

Assets	=	Liabilities	+	Owners' Equity
		+1,500		−1,500

The wages and salaries on the trial balance were paid in cash. At the end of the month, Duffy owes employees an additional $2,800 in salaries and wages:

		Debit	Credit
(b)	Wage and Salary Expense	2,800	
	Wages and Salaries Payable		2,800
	To record wages and salaries owed.		

Assets	=	Liabilities	+	Owners' Equity
		+2,800		−2,800

At the beginning of January, Duffy acquired a garage to house the buses at a cost of $160,000. Land is not subject to depreciation. The cost of the land acquired in connection with the purchase of the building will remain on the books until the property is sold. The garage has an estimated useful life of 20 years and an estimated salvage value of $16,000 at the end of its life. The monthly depreciation is found by dividing the depreciable cost of $144,000 by the useful life of 240 months:

$$\frac{\$160{,}000 - \$16{,}000}{20 \text{ years} \times 12 \text{ months}} = \frac{\$144{,}000}{240 \text{ months}} = \underline{\underline{\$600}} \text{ per month}$$

The entry to record the depreciation on the garage for January for a full month is as follows:

		Debit	Credit
(c)	Depreciation Expense—Garage	600	
	Accumulated Depreciation—Garage		600
	To record depreciation for the month.		

Assets	=	Liabilities	+	Owners' Equity
−600				−600

Duffy purchased 10 buses for $30,000 each at the beginning of January. The buses have an estimated useful life of five years, at which time the company plans to sell them for $6,000 each. The monthly depreciation on the 10 buses is:

$$10 \times \frac{\$30{,}000 - \$6{,}000}{5 \text{ years} \times 12 \text{ months}} = 10 \times \frac{\$24{,}000}{60 \text{ months}} = \underline{\underline{\$4{,}000}} \text{ per month}$$

The entry to recognize the depreciation on the buses for the first month is as follows:

(d)	Depreciation Expense—Buses	4,000	
	Accumulated Depreciation—Buses		4,000
	To record depreciation for the month.		

Assets	=	Liabilities	+	Owners' Equity
−4,000				−4,000

Prepaid Insurance on the trial balance represents an insurance policy purchased for $48,000 on January 1. The policy provides property and liability protection for a 24-month period. The adjusting entry to allocate the cost to expense for the first month is as follows:

(e)	Insurance Expense	2,000	
	Prepaid Insurance		2,000
	To record expiration of insurance benefits.		

Assets	=	Liabilities	+	Owners' Equity
−2,000				−2,000

In addition to selling tickets on the bus, Duffy sells discount tickets at the terminal. The tickets are good for a ride anytime within 12 months of purchase. Thus, as these tickets are sold, Duffy debits Cash and credits a liability account, Discount Tickets Sold in Advance. The sale of $25,000 worth of these tickets was recorded during January and is thus reflected on the trial balance. At the end of the first month, Duffy counts the number of tickets that have been redeemed. Because $20,400 worth of tickets has been turned in, this is the amount by which the company reduces its liability and recognizes revenue for the month:

(f)	Discount Tickets Sold in Advance	20,400	
	Discount Ticket Revenue		20,400
	To record redemption of discount tickets.		

Assets	=	Liabilities	+	Owners' Equity
		−20,400		+20,400

Duffy does not need all of the space in its garage and rents a section of it to another company for $2,500 per month. The tenant has until the 10th day of the following month to pay its rent. The adjusting entry on Duffy's books on the last day of the month is as follows:

(g)	Rent Receivable	2,500	
	Rent Revenue		2,500
	To record rent earned but not yet received.		

Assets	=	Liabilities	+	Owners' Equity
+2,500				+2,500

Corporations pay estimated taxes on a quarterly basis. Because Duffy is preparing an income statement for the month of January, it must estimate its taxes for the month. We will assume a corporate tax rate of 34% on income before tax. The computation of Income Tax Expense is as follows (the amounts shown for the revenues and expenses reflect the effect of the adjusting entries):

Revenues:		
Daily Ticket Revenue	$30,000	
Discount Ticket Revenue	20,400	
Rent Revenue	2,500	$52,900
Expenses:		
Gas, Oil, and Maintenance Expense	$12,000	
Wage and Salary Expense	12,800	
Depreciation Expense	4,600	
Insurance Expense	2,000	
Interest Expense	1,500	32,900
Net Income before Tax		$20,000
Times the Corporate Tax Rate		× .34
Income Tax Expense		$ 6,800

Based on this estimate of taxes, the final adjusting entry recorded on Duffy's books for the month is:

(h)	Income Tax Expense	6,800	
	Income Tax Payable		6,800
	To record estimated income taxes for the month.		

Assets	=	Liabilities	+	Owners' Equity
		+6,800		−6,800

An *adjusted* trial balance, shown in Exhibit 4-7, indicates the equality of debits and credits after the adjusting entries have been recorded. Note the addition of a number of new accounts that did not appear on the unadjusted trial balance in Exhibit 4-6. The new trial balance includes the accounts that were added when adjusting entries were recorded.

Exhibit 4-7
Adjusted Trial Balance

DUFFY TRANSIT COMPANY
ADJUSTED TRIAL BALANCE
JANUARY 31

	Debit	Credit
Cash	$ 50,000	
Prepaid Insurance	46,000	
Land	20,000	
Buildings—Garage	160,000	
Accumulated Depreciation—Garage		$ 600
Equipment—Buses	300,000	
Accumulated Depreciation—Buses		4,000
Gas, Oil, and Maintenance Expense	12,000	
Wage and Salary Expense	12,800	
Dividends	5,000	
Discount Tickets Sold in Advance		4,600
Notes Payable		150,000
Capital Stock		400,000
Daily Ticket Revenue		30,000
Rent Receivable	2,500	
Interest Expense	1,500	
Income Tax Expense	6,800	
Depreciation Expense—Garage	600	
Depreciation Expense—Buses	4,000	
Insurance Expense	2,000	
Interest Payable		1,500
Wages and Salaries Payable		2,800
Income Tax Payable		6,800
Discount Ticket Revenue		20,400
Rent Revenue		2,500
Totals	$623,200	$623,200

Ethical Considerations for a Company on the Accrual Basis

As you have seen, the accrual basis requires the recognition of revenues when earned and expenses when incurred, regardless of when cash is received or paid. It was also noted earlier that adjusting entries are *internal* transactions in that they do not involve an exchange with an outside entity. Because adjustments do not involve another company, accountants may at times feel pressure from others within the organization to either speed or delay the recognition of certain adjustments.

Consider the following two examples for a construction company that is concerned about its "bottom line," that is, its net income. A number of jobs are in progress, but because of inclement weather, none of them are very far along. Management asks the accountant to recognize 50% of the revenue from a job in progress even though by the most liberal estimates it is only 25% complete. Further, the accountant has been asked to delay the recognition of various short-term accrued liabilities (and, of course, the accompanying expenses) until the beginning of the new year.

The "correct" response of the accountant to each of these requests may seem obvious: only 25% of the revenue on the one job should be recognized, and all accrued liabilities should be expensed at year-end. The pressures of the daily work environment make these decisions difficult for the accountant, however. The accountant must always remember that his or her primary responsibility in preparing financial statements is to accurately portray the affairs of the company to the various outside users. Bankers, stockholders, and others rely on the accountant to serve their best interests.

THE ACCOUNTING CYCLE

We have focused our attention in this chapter on accrual accounting and the adjusting entries it necessitates. Adjusting entries are one key component in the **accounting cycle.** The accountant for a business follows a series of steps each period. The objective is always the same: *collect the necessary information to prepare a set of financial statements.* Together, these steps make up the accounting cycle. The name comes from the fact that the steps are repeated each period.

LO 6 Explain the steps in the accounting cycle and the significance of each step.

Accounting cycle A series of steps performed each period and culminating with the preparation of a set of financial statements.

The steps in the accounting cycle are shown in Exhibit 4-8. Note that step 1 involves not only *collecting* information but also *analyzing* it. Transaction analysis is probably the most challenging of all the steps in the accounting cycle. It requires the ability to think logically about an event and its effect on the financial position of the entity. Once the transaction is analyzed, it is recorded in the journal, as indicated by the second step in the exhibit. The first two steps in the cycle take place continuously.

Journal entries are posted to the accounts on a periodic basis. The frequency of posting to the accounts depends on two factors: the type of accounting system used by a company and the volume of transactions. In a manual system, entries might be posted daily, weekly, or even monthly, depending on the amount of activity. The larger the number of transactions a company records, the more often it posts. In an automated accounting system, posting is likely done automatically by the computer each time a transaction is recorded.

The Use of a Work Sheet

Step 4 in Exhibit 4-8 calls for the preparation of a work sheet. The end of an accounting period is a busy time. In addition to recording daily recurring transactions, the accountant must record adjusting entries as the basis for preparing financial statements. The time available to prepare the statements is usually very limited. The use of a **work sheet** allows the accountant to gather and organize the information required to adjust the accounts without actually recording and posting the adjusting entries to the accounts. Actually recording adjusting entries and posting them to the accounts can be done after the financial statements are prepared. *A work sheet itself is not a financial statement.* Instead, it is a useful device to *organize* the information needed to prepare the financial statements at the end of the period.

Work sheet A device used at the end of the period to gather the information needed to prepare financial statements without actually recording and posting adjusting entries.

It is not essential that a work sheet be used before preparing financial statements. If it is not used, step 6, recording and posting adjusting entries, comes before step 5, preparing the financial statements. This chapter's appendix illustrates how a work sheet is used to facilitate the preparation of financial statements.

Exhibit 4-8 Steps in the Accounting Cycle

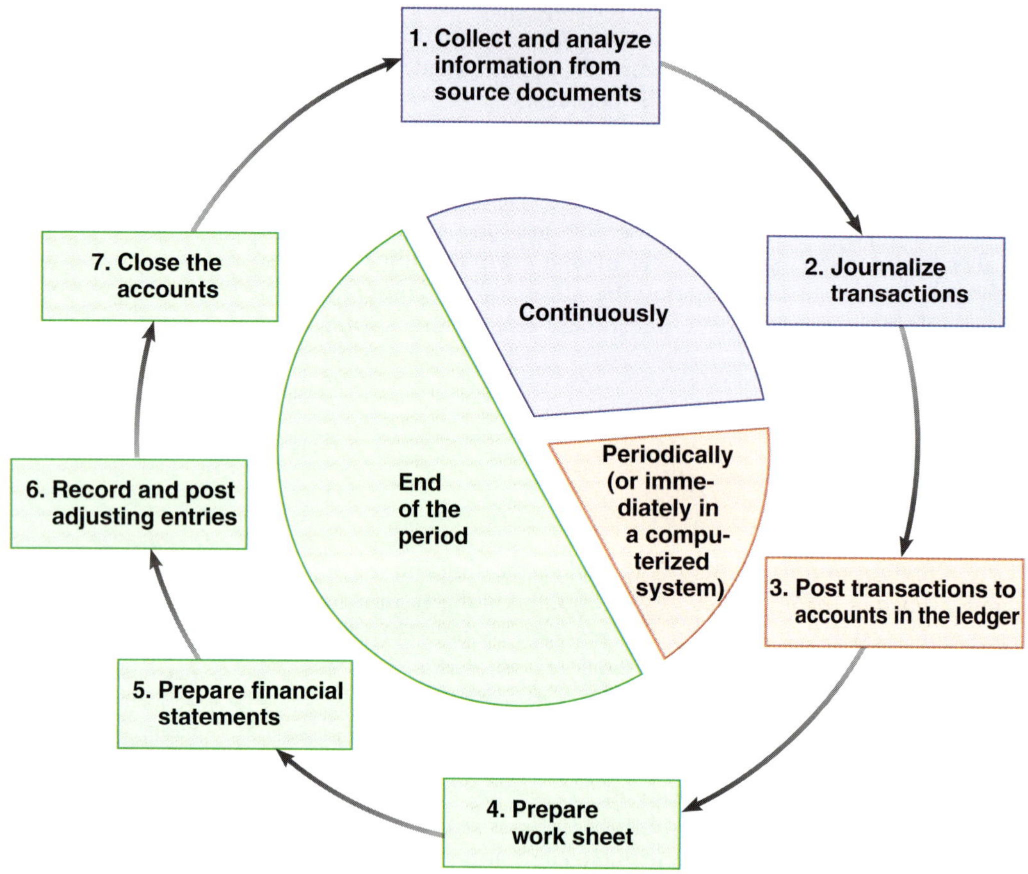

The Closing Process

LO 7 Explain why and how closing entries are made at the end of an accounting period.

Real accounts The name given to balance sheet accounts because they are permanent and are not closed at the end of the period.

Nominal accounts The name given to revenue, expense, and dividend accounts because they are temporary and are closed at the end of the period.

Closing entries Journal entries made at the end of the period to return the balance in all nominal accounts to zero and transfer the net income or loss and the dividends to Retained Earnings.

Two types of accounts appear on an adjusted trial balance. Balance sheet accounts are called **real accounts** because they are permanent in nature. For this reason, they are never closed. The balance in each of these accounts is carried over from one period to the next. In contrast, revenue, expense, and dividend accounts are *temporary* or **nominal accounts.** The balances in the income statement accounts and the Dividends account are *not* carried forward from one accounting period to the next. For this reason, these accounts are closed at the end of the period.

Closing entries serve two important purposes: (1) to return the balances in all temporary or nominal accounts to zero to start the next accounting period and (2) to transfer the net income (or net loss) and the dividends of the period to the Retained Earnings account.

An account with a debit balance is closed by crediting the account for the amount of the balance. An account with a credit balance is closed by debiting the account for the amount of the balance. Thus, revenue accounts are debited in the closing process. Expense accounts are credited to close them. In this way, the balance of each income statement account is restored to zero to start the next accounting period.

Various approaches are used to accomplish the same two purposes: restore the temporary accounts to zero and update the Retained Earnings account. We will use a holding account called Income Summary to facilitate the closing process. A single entry is made to close all of the revenue accounts. The total amount debited to the revenue accounts is credited to Income Summary. Similarly, a single entry is made to close all of the expense accounts, and the offsetting debit is made to Income Summary. This account acts as a temporary storage account. After closing the revenue and expense accounts, Income Summary has a *credit* balance *if revenues exceed expenses.* Finally, the credit balance in Income Summary is itself closed by debiting the account and crediting Retained Earnings for the same amount. The net result of the process is that all of the revenues less expenses, that is, net income, have been transferred to Retained Earnings.

The Dividends account is closed directly to Retained Earnings. Because dividends are *not* an expense, the Dividends account is not closed first to the Income Summary account, as are expense accounts. A credit is made to close the Dividends account with an offsetting debit to Retained Earnings.

The closing process for Duffy Transit Company is illustrated with the use of T accounts in Exhibit 4-9. Rather than show each individual revenue and expense account, a single revenue account and a single expense account are used in the exhibit to illustrate the flow in the closing process.

Exhibit 4-9 The Closing Process

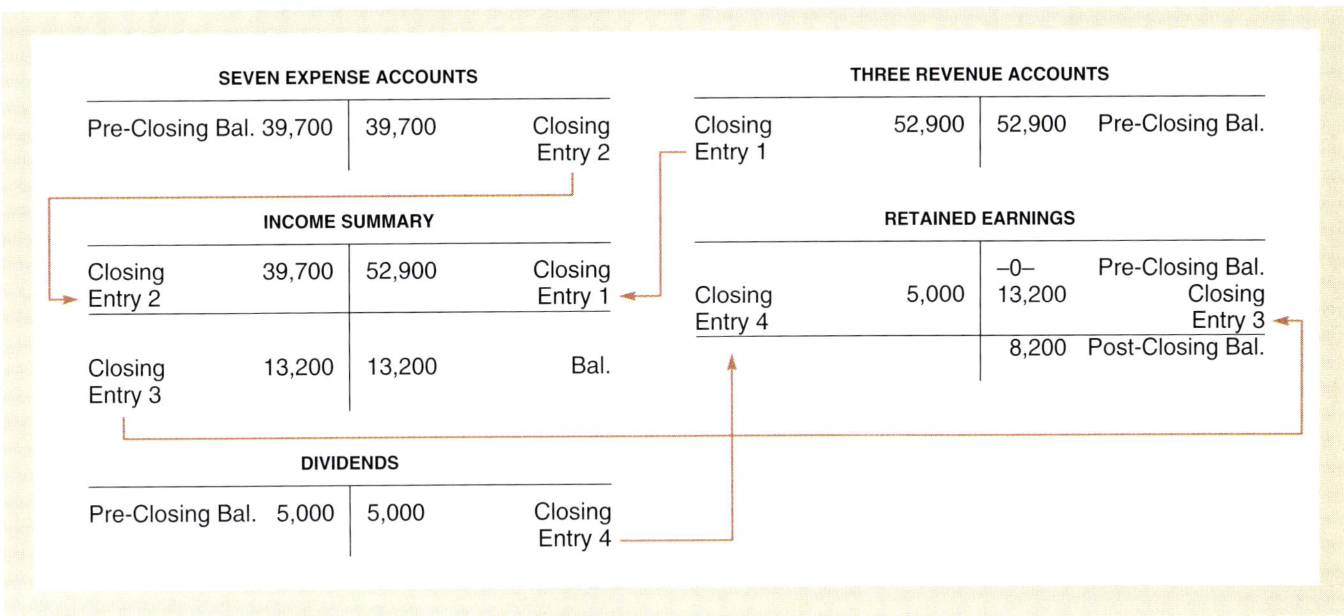

The first closing entry results in a zero balance in each of the three revenue accounts, and the total of the three amounts, $52,900, which represents all of the revenue of the period, is transferred to the Income Summary account. The second entry closes each of the seven expense accounts and transfers the total expenses of $39,700 as a debit to the Income Summary account. At this point, the Income Summary account has a credit balance of $13,200, which represents the net income of the period. The third entry closes this temporary holding account and transfers the net income to the Retained Earnings account. Finally, the fourth entry closes the Dividends account and transfers the $5,000 to the debit side of the Retained Earnings account. The Retained Earnings account is now updated to its correct ending balance of $8,200.

The four closing entries in journal form are shown in Exhibit 4-10. Note that each individual revenue and expense account is closed. Keep in mind that the Post. Ref. column will be filled in with the appropriate account numbers when the entries are posted to the ledger accounts.

Interim Financial Statements

We mentioned earlier in this chapter that certain steps in the accounting cycle are sometimes carried out only once a year rather than each month as in our example. For ease of illustration, we assumed a monthly accounting cycle. Many companies adjust and

Exhibit 4-10

Closing Entries Recorded in the Journal

DATE		ACCOUNT TITLES AND EXPLANATION	POST. REF.	DEBIT	CREDIT
Jan.	31	Daily Ticket Revenue		30,000	
		Discount Ticket Revenue		20,400	
		Rent Revenue		2,500	
		Income Summary			52,900
		To close revenue accounts to Income Summary.			
	31	Income Summary		39,700	
		Gas, Oil, and Maintenance Expense			12,000
		Wage and Salary Expense			12,800
		Interest Expense			1,500
		Depreciation Expense—Garage			600
		Depreciation Expense—Buses			4,000
		Insurance Expense			2,000
		Income Tax Expense			6,800
		To close expense accounts to Income Summary.			
	31	Income Summary		13,200	
		Retained Earnings			13,200
		To close Income Summary to Retained Earnings.			
	31	Retained Earnings		5,000	
		Dividends			5,000
		To close Dividends to Retained Earnings.			

Interim statements Financial statements prepared monthly, quarterly, or at other intervals less than a year in duration.

close the accounts only once a year, however. They use a work sheet more frequently than this as the basis for preparing interim statements. Statements prepared monthly, quarterly, or at other intervals less than a year in duration are called **interim statements.** Many companies prepare monthly financial statements for their own internal use. Similarly, corporations whose shares are publicly traded on one of the stock exchanges are required to file quarterly financial statements with the Securities and Exchange Commission.

Suppose that a company prepares monthly financial statements for internal use and completes the accounting cycle in its entirety only once a year. In this case, a work sheet is prepared each month as the basis for interim financial statements. Formal adjusting and closing entries are prepared only at the end of each year. The adjusting entries that appear on the monthly work sheet are not posted to the accounts. They are entered on the work sheet simply as a basis for preparing the monthly financial statements.

Impact on the Financial Reports

Impact on the Financial Reports

BALANCE SHEET

Current Assets
Rent receivable
Prepaid rent
Prepaid insurance
Supplies
Noncurrent Assets
Property, plant, and equipment
Less accumulated depreciation of property, plant, and equipment
Current Liabilities
Unearned revenue[a]
Wages (salaries) payable
Notes payable
Interest payable
Income tax payable
Noncurrent Liabilities
Stockholders' Equity

INCOME STATEMENT

Revenues
Revenue from long-term construction contracts
Franchise revenue
Revenue from commodities
Revenue from installment sales[b]
Rent revenue
Subscription revenue
Discount ticket revenue
Daily ticket revenue
Expenses
Cost of goods sold
Depreciation expense
Rent expense
Wage (salary) expense
Insurance expense
Utility expense
Oil, gas, and maintenance expense
Income tax expense
Other
Interest income
Interest expense

STATEMENT OF STOCKHOLDERS' EQUITY

Contributed Capital
Retained Earnings
Dividends

STATEMENT OF CASH FLOWS[c]

Operating Activities
Investing Activities
Financing Activities
Noncash Transactions

NOTES

[a]For example, rent or subscriptions collected in advance, gift certificates, deposits, and discount tickets sold in advance.
[b]Rarely used.
[c]Future chapters will provide information about the impact on the statement of cash flows and the notes to the financial statements.

Answers to the Two-Minute Reviews

Two-Minute Review on Page 160

1. *Accountants must decide whether to use historical cost or another attribute or characteristic of an asset, such as its current value, to measure it. Regardless of the attribute measured, it is necessary to choose a yardstick, or unit of measure. In this country, accountants use the dollar to measure assets and other financial statement items.*
2. *The percentage-of-completion method, the production method, and the installment method are all alternatives to recognizing revenue at the point of sale. Also, franchisors normally recognize revenue when they have made substantial performance of their obligations.*
3. *For certain costs, such as cost of goods sold, it is possible to directly match the expense with revenue generated. For other costs, such as depreciation, an indirect form of matching is necessary in which expenses are allocated to the periods benefited, rather than matched with specific revenues. Finally, the*

(continued)

Answers to the Two-Minute Reviews (continued)

benefits associated with the incurrence of certain costs, such as utilities, expire immediately and therefore expense is recognized as soon as the cost is incurred.

Two-Minute Review on Page 169

1. *Insurance Expense*	*150*	
Prepaid Insurance		*150*
To recognize $150 of insurance expense for the month.		

Assets	=	*Liabilities*	+	*Owners' Equity*
−150				*−150*

2. *Rent Collected in Advance*	*400*	
Rent Revenue		*400*
To recognize $400 of rent earned for the month.		

Assets	=	*Liabilities*	+	*Owners' Equity*
		−400		*+400*

3. *Interest Expense*	*50*	
Interest Payable		*50*
To record interest for one month on a 6%, $10,000 loan.		

Assets	=	*Liabilities*	+	*Owners' Equity*
		+50		*−50*

Warmup Exercises

Warmup Exercise 4-1 ***Prepaid Insurance*** **LO 5**

ABC Corp. purchases a 24-month fire insurance policy on January 1, 2004, for $5,400.

Required

Prepare the necessary adjusting journal entry on January 31, 2004.

Key to the Solution

Determine what proportion and therefore what dollar amount of the policy has expired after one month.

Warmup Exercise 4-2 ***Depreciation*** **LO 5**

DEF Corp. purchased a new car for one of its salespeople on March 1, 2004, for $25,000. The estimated useful life of the car is four years with an estimated salvage value of $1,000.

Required

Prepare the necessary adjusting journal entry on March 31, 2004.

Key to the Solution

Determine what dollar amount of the cost of the car should be depreciated and then how much should be depreciated each month.

Warmup Exercise 4-3 ***Interest on a Note*** **LO 5**

On April 1, 2004, GHI Corp. took out a 12%, 120-day, $10,000 loan at its bank.

Required

Prepare the necessary adjusting journal entry on April 30, 2004.

Key to the Solution

Determine the monthly interest cost on a loan that accrues interest at the rate of 12% per year.

Solutions to Warmup Exercises

Warmup Exercise 4-1

Jan. 31	Insurance Expense	225	
	Prepaid Insurance		225
	To recognize $225 of insurance expense for the month.		

Assets	=	Liabilities	+	Owners' Equity
−225				−225

Warmup Exercise 4-2

Mar. 31	Depreciation Expense	500	
	Accumulated Depreciation		500
	To recognize depreciation on car.		

Assets	=	Liabilities	+	Owners' Equity
−500				−500

Warmup Exercise 4-3

Apr. 30	Interest Expense	100	
	Interest Payable		100
	To record interest for one month on a 12%, $10,000 loan.		

Assets	=	Liabilities	+	Owners' Equity
		+100		−100

Review Problem

WebTUTOR Advantage

The trial balance of Northern Airlines at January 31 is shown below. It was prepared after posting the recurring transactions for the month of January, but it does not reflect any month-end adjustments.

NORTHERN AIRLINES
UNADJUSTED TRIAL BALANCE
JANUARY 31

Cash	$ 75,000	
Parts Inventory	45,000	
Land	80,000	
Buildings—Hangars	250,000	
Accumulated Depreciation—Hangars		$ 24,000
Equipment—Aircraft	650,000	
Accumulated Depreciation—Aircraft		120,000
Tickets Sold in Advance		85,000
Capital Stock		500,000
Retained Earnings		368,000
Ticket Revenue		52,000
Maintenance Expense	19,000	
Wage and Salary Expense	30,000	
Totals	$1,149,000	$1,149,000

The following additional information is available:

a. Airplane parts needed for repairs and maintenance are purchased regularly, and the amounts paid are added to the asset account Parts Inventory. At the end of each month, the inventory is counted. At the end of January, the amount of parts on hand is $36,100. *Hint:* What adjusting entry is needed to reduce the asset account to its proper carrying value? Any expense involved should be included in Maintenance Expense.

b. The estimated useful life of the hangar is 20 years with an estimated salvage value of $10,000 at the end of its life. The original cost of the hangar was $250,000.

(continued)

c. The estimated useful life of the aircraft is 10 years with an estimated salvage value of $50,000. The original cost of the aircraft was $650,000.

d. As tickets are sold in advance, the amounts are added to Cash and to the liability account Tickets Sold in Advance. A count of the redeemed tickets reveals that $47,000 worth of tickets were used during January.

e. Wages and salaries owed to employees, but unpaid, at the end of January total $7,600.

f. Northern rents excess hangar space to other companies. The amount owed to Northern but unpaid at the end of January is $2,500.

g. Assume a corporate income tax rate of 34%.

Required

1. Set up T accounts for each of the accounts listed on the trial balance. Set up any other T accounts that will be needed to prepare adjusting entries.
2. Post the month-end adjusting entries directly to the T accounts; do not take the time to put the entries in journal format first. Use the letters **(a)** through **(g)** from the additional information to identify each entry.
3. Prepare a trial balance to prove the equality of debits and credits after posting the adjusting entries.

Solution to Review Problem

1. and 2.

CASH

	Debit	Credit	
Bal.	75,000		

PARTS INVENTORY

	Debit	Credit	
Bal.	45,000		
		8,900	(a)
Bal.	36,100		

LAND

	Debit	Credit	
Bal.	80,000		

BUILDINGS—HANGARS

	Debit	Credit	
Bal.	250,000		

ACCUMULATED DEPRECIATION—HANGARS

	Debit	Credit	
		24,000	Bal.
		1,000	(b)
		25,000	Bal.

EQUIPMENT—AIRCRAFT

	Debit	Credit	
Bal.	650,000		

ACCUMULATED DEPRECIATION—AIRCRAFT

	Debit	Credit	
		120,000	Bal.
		5,000	(c)
		125,000	Bal.

TICKETS SOLD IN ADVANCE

	Debit	Credit	
		85,000	Bal.
(d)	47,000		
		38,000	Bal.

CAPITAL STOCK

	Debit	Credit	
		500,000	Bal.

RETAINED EARNINGS

	Debit	Credit	
		368,000	Bal.

TICKET REVENUE

	Debit	Credit	
		52,000	Bal.
		47,000	(d)
		99,000	Bal.

MAINTENANCE EXPENSE

	Debit	Credit	
Bal.	19,000		
(a)	8,900		
Bal.	27,900		

WAGE AND SALARY EXPENSE

	Debit	Credit	
Bal.	30,000		
(e)	7,600		
Bal.	37,600		

DEPRECIATION EXPENSE—HANGARS

	Debit	Credit	
(b)	1,000		

DEPRECIATION EXPENSE—AIRCRAFT

	Debit	Credit	
(c)	5,000		

RENT RECEIVABLE

	Debit	Credit	
(f)	2,500		

RENT REVENUE	
	2,500 (f)

WAGES AND SALARIES PAYABLE	
	7,600 (e)

INCOME TAX EXPENSE	
(g) 10,200	

INCOME TAXES PAYABLE	
	10,200 (g)

3.

NORTHERN AIRLINES
ADJUSTED TRIAL BALANCE
JANUARY 31

Cash	$ 75,000	
Parts Inventory	36,100	
Land	80,000	
Buildings—Hangars	250,000	
Accumulated Depreciation—Hangars		$ 25,000
Equipment—Aircraft	650,000	
Accumulated Depreciation—Aircraft		125,000
Tickets Sold in Advance		38,000
Capital Stock		500,000
Retained Earnings		368,000
Ticket Revenue		99,000
Maintenance Expense	27,900	
Wage and Salary Expense	37,600	
Depreciation Expense—Hangars	1,000	
Depreciation Expense—Aircraft	5,000	
Rent Receivable	2,500	
Rent Revenue		2,500
Wages and Salaries Payable		7,600
Income Tax Expense	10,200	
Income Taxes Payable		10,200
Totals	$1,175,300	$1,175,300

Appendix: Accounting Tools: Work Sheets

Work sheets were introduced in the chapter as useful tools to aid the accountant. In this appendix we present a detailed discussion of these.

WORK SHEETS

LO 8 Understand how to use a work sheet as a basis for preparing financial statements.

A work sheet is used to organize the information needed to prepare financial statements without recording and posting formal adjusting entries. There is no one single format for a work sheet. We will illustrate a 10-column work sheet by using the information in the chapter for the Duffy Transit Company example. The format for a 10-column work sheet appears in Exhibit 4-11. We will concentrate on the *steps* to complete the work sheet, which has already been completed.

Step 1: The Unadjusted Trial Balance Columns

The starting point for the work sheet is the first two columns, which must be filled in with the appropriate amounts from the unadjusted trial balance of Duffy Transit Company as shown in Exhibit 4-6. The trial balance is labeled *unadjusted* because it does not reflect the adjusting entries at the end of the period.

Exhibit 4-11 The Work Sheet

DUFFY TRANSIT COMPANY
WORK SHEET
FOR THE MONTH ENDED JANUARY 31

	Unadjusted Trial Balance		Adjusting Entries		Adjusted Trial Balance		Income Statement		Balance Sheet	
Account Titles	**Debit**	**Credit**	**Debit**	**Credit**	**Debit**	**Credit**	**Debit**	**Credit**	**Debit**	**Credit**
Cash	50,000				50,000				50,000	
Prepaid Insurance	48,000			(e) 2,000	46,000				46,000	
Land	20,000				20,000				20,000	
Buildings—Garage	160,000				160,000				160,000	
Accumulated Depreciation—Garage		–0–		(c) 600		600				600
Equipment—Buses	300,000				300,000				300,000	
Accumulated Depreciation—Buses		–0–		(d) 4,000		4,000				4,000
Discount Tickets Sold in Advance		25,000	(f) 20,400			4,600				4,600
Notes Payable		150,000				150,000				150,000
Capital Stock		400,000				400,000				400,000
Retained Earnings		–0–				–0–				–0–
Daily Ticket Revenue		30,000				30,000		30,000		
Gas, Oil, and Maintenance Expense	12,000				12,000		12,000			
Wage and Salary Expense	10,000		(b) 2,800		12,800		12,800			
Dividends	5,000				5,000				5,000	
	605,000	605,000								
Interest Expense			(a) 1,500		1,500		1,500			
Depreciation Expense—Garage			(c) 600		600		600			
Depreciation Expense—Buses			(d) 4,000		4,000		4,000			
Insurance Expense			(e) 2,000		2,000		2,000			
Discount Ticket Revenue				(f) 20,400		20,400		20,400		
Rent Receivable			(g) 2,500		2,500				2,500	
Rent Revenue				(g) 2,500		2,500		2,500		
Interest Payable				(a) 1,500		1,500				1,500
Wages and Salaries Payable				(b) 2,800		2,800				2,800
Income Tax Expense			(h) 6,800		6,800		6,800			
Income Tax Payable				(h) 6,800		6,800				6,800
			40,600	40,600	623,200	623,200	39,700	52,900	583,500	570,300
Net Income							13,200			13,200
							52,900	52,900	583,500	583,500

At this point, only the accounts used during the period are entered on the work sheet. Any accounts that are used for the first time during the period because of the adjusting entries will be added in the next step. All but the first two columns of the work sheet should be ignored at this time. Three accounts are included on the work sheet even though they do not have a balance: (1) Accumulated Depreciation—Garage, (2) Accumulated Depreciation—Buses, and (3) Retained Earnings. After this first month of operations, these accounts will always have a balance and will appear on an unadjusted trial balance.

Step 2: The Adjusting Entries Columns

The third and fourth columns of the work sheet have been completed in Exhibit 4-11. Rather than take the time now to prepare adjusting entries and post them to their respective accounts, the accountant makes the entries in these two columns of the work sheet. Formal entries can be made after the financial statements have been prepared. The addition of these two columns to the work sheet requires that we add the accounts used for the first time in the period because of the adjustment process. Letters are typically used on a work sheet to identify the adjusting entries and are therefore used here. In practice, the work sheet can be many pages long, and the use of identifying letters makes it easier to locate and match the debit and credit sides of each adjusting entry.

The two columns are totaled to ensure the equality of debits and credits for the adjusting entries. Keep in mind that the entries made in these two columns of the work sheet are *not* the actual adjusting entries; those will be recorded in the journal at a later time, after the financial statements have been prepared.

Step 3: The Adjusted Trial Balance Columns

Columns 5 and 6 of the work sheet represent an adjusted trial balance. The amounts entered in these two columns are found by adding or subtracting any debits or credits in the adjusting entries columns to or from the unadjusted balances. For example, Cash is not adjusted, and thus the $50,000 unadjusted amount is carried over to the Debit column of the adjusted trial balance. The $2,000 credit adjustment to Prepaid Insurance is subtracted from the unadjusted debit balance of $48,000, resulting in a debit balance of $46,000 on the adjusted trial balance. Finally, note the equality of the debits and credits on the new trial balance, $623,200.

Step 4: The Income Statement Columns

An adjusted trial balance is the basis for preparing the financial statements. The purpose of the last four columns of the work sheet is to separate the accounts into those that will appear on the income statement and those that will appear on the balance sheet. The income statement columns will be completed next.

The three revenue accounts appear in the credit column, and the seven expense accounts appear in the debit column. These amounts are simply carried over, or extended, from the adjusted trial balance. Because Duffy's revenues exceed its expenses, the total of the credit column, $52,900, exceeds the total of the debit column, $39,700. The difference between the two columns, the net income of the period of $13,200, is entered in the debit column. One purpose for showing the net income in this column is to balance the two columns. In addition, the entry in the debit column will be matched with an entry in the balance sheet credit column to represent the transfer of net income to retained earnings. If revenues were *less* than expenses, the *net loss* would be entered in the income statement *credit* column.

Step 5: The Balance Sheet Columns

Why do the income statement columns appear *before* the balance sheet columns on the work sheet? The income statement is in fact a *subset* of the balance sheet, and information from the income statement columns flows into the balance sheet columns. Recall that net income causes an increase in the owners' claim to the assets, that is, an increase in owners' equity, through the Retained Earnings account and, thus, is entered in the balance sheet credit column of the work sheet. In Exhibit 4-11, the amount of *net income*, $13,200, is carried over from the debit column of the income statement to the credit column of the balance sheet. If a company experiences a *net loss* for the period, the amount of the loss is entered in the credit column of the income statement and in the debit column of the balance sheet.

You will note that the Retained Earnings account has a zero balance in the last column of the work sheet, because this is the first month of operations for Duffy Transit Company. On future work sheets, the account will reflect the balance from the *end* of the *previous* month. Dividends appear in the debit column, and net income appears in the credit column. Thus, the ending balance of Retained Earnings can be found by taking its beginning balance, adding the net income of the period, and deducting the dividends. The completed work sheet provides all the necessary information to prepare an income statement, a statement of retained earnings, and a balance sheet.

Appendix Review Problem

Note to the Student: The following problem is based on the information for the Northern Airlines review problem at the end of this chapter. Try to prepare the work sheet without referring to the adjusting entries you prepared in solving that problem.

Required

Refer to the unadjusted trial balance and the additional information for Northern Airlines as presented previously. Prepare a 10-column work sheet for the month of January.

Solution to Review Problem

NORTHERN AIRLINES
WORK SHEET
FOR THE MONTH ENDED JANUARY 31

Account Titles	Unadjusted Trial Balance		Adjusting Entries		Adjusted Trial Balance		Income Statement		Balance Sheet	
	Debit	Credit	Debit	Credit	Debit	Credit	Debit	Credit	Debit	Credit
Cash	75,000				75,000				75,000	
Parts Inventory	45,000			(a) 8,900	36,100				36,100	
Land	80,000				80,000				80,000	
Buildings—Hangars	250,000				250,000				250,000	
Accumulated Depreciation—Hangars		24,000		(b) 1,000		25,000				25,000
Equipment—Aircraft	650,000				650,000				650,000	
Accumulated Depreciation—Aircraft		120,000		(c) 5,000		125,000				125,000
Tickets Sold in Advance		85,000	(d) 47,000			38,000				38,000
Capital Stock		500,000				500,000				500,000
Retained Earnings		368,000				368,000				368,000
Ticket Revenue		52,000		(d) 47,000		99,000		99,000		
Maintenance Expense	19,000		(a) 8,900		27,900		27,900			
Wage and Salary Expense	30,000		(e) 7,600		37,600		37,600			
	1,149,000	1,149,000								
Depreciation Expense—Hangars			(b) 1,000		1,000		1,000			
Depreciation Expense—Aircraft			(c) 5,000		5,000		5,000			
Rent Receivable			(f) 2,500		2,500				2,500	
Income Tax Expense			(g) 10,200		10,200		10,200			
Wages and Salaries Payable				(e) 7,600		7,600				7,600
Rent Revenue				(f) 2,500		2,500		2,500		
Income Taxes Payable				(g) 10,200		10,200				10,200
			82,200	82,200	1,175,300	1,175,300	81,700	101,500	1,093,600	1,073,800
Net Income							19,800			19,800
							101,500	101,500	1,093,600	1,093,600

Chapter Highlights

1. **LO 1** The success of accounting as a form of communication depends on two concepts: recognition and measurement. The items depicted in financial statements are representations. The accountant cannot show the reader an asset but instead depicts it with words and numbers.
2. **LO 1** Measurement in accounting requires choosing an attribute and a unit of measure. Historical cost is the attribute used for many of the assets included in financial statements. One alternative to historical cost is current value. The dollar as a unit of measure is subject to instability, depending on the level of inflation.
3. **LO 2** Under the accrual basis of accounting, revenues are recognized when earned and expenses when incurred. The income statement is prepared on an accrual basis, and the statement of cash flows complements it by providing valuable information about the operating, financing, and investing cash flows of a business.
4. **LO 3** According to the revenue recognition principle, revenues are recognized when they are realized or realizable and earned. On a practical basis, revenue is normally recognized at the time a product or service is delivered to the customer. Certain types of sales arrangements, such as long-term contracts and franchises, present special problems in applying the principle.
5. **LO 4** The matching principle attempts to associate with the revenue of the period all costs necessary to generate that revenue. A direct form of matching is possible for certain types of costs, such as cost of goods sold and commissions. Costs, such as depreciation, are recognized as expenses on an indirect basis. Depreciation is the allocation of the cost of a tangible, long-term asset over its useful life. The benefits from most selling and administrative expenses expire immediately and are recognized as expenses in the period the costs are incurred.
6. **LO 5** The accrual basis necessitates adjusting entries at the end of a period. The four types of adjusting entries result from differences between the recognition of revenues and expenses on an accrual basis and the receipt or payment of cash.
7. **LO 5** Cash paid before expense is incurred results in a deferred expense, which is recognized as an asset on the balance sheet. The adjusting entry reduces the asset and recognizes a corresponding amount of expense. Cash received before revenue is earned requires the recognition of a liability, a deferred revenue. The adjusting entry reduces the liability and recognizes a corresponding amount of revenue.
8. **LO 5** If cash is paid after an expense is incurred, an adjusting entry is needed to recognize the accrued liability and the related expense. Similarly, if cash is received after the revenue is earned, the adjusting entry recognizes the accrued asset and the corresponding revenue. The liability or asset is eliminated in a later period when cash is either paid or received.
9. **LO 5** Adjusting entries are prepared by reference to a trial balance and certain additional information. A trial balance prepared after posting the adjustments to the accounts ensures the equality of debits and credits in the ledger.
10. **LO 6** Steps in the accounting cycle are carried out each period as a basis for the preparation of financial statements. Some of the steps, such as journalizing transactions, are performed continuously, while others, such as recording adjusting entries, are performed only at the end of the period.
11. **LO 7** After adjusting entries are recorded and posted to the accounts, closing entries are made. They have two important purposes: (1) to return the balances in all revenue, expense, and dividend accounts to zero to start the following accounting period and (2) to transfer the net income (or net loss) and the dividends of the period to the Retained Earnings account.
12. **LO 7** A revenue account is closed by debiting it for the credit balance in the account and crediting Income Summary. An expense account is closed by crediting it and debiting Income Summary. If revenues exceed expenses, Income Summary will have a credit balance at this point, representing the net income of the period. Income Summary is closed by debiting it and crediting Retained Earnings. Finally, the Dividends account is closed with a credit and a corresponding debit to Retained Earnings.
13. **LO 8** A work sheet is not itself a financial statement. It is a useful device for organizing the necessary information to prepare financial statements without going through the formal process of recording and posting adjusting entries. The format for a 10-column work sheet includes two columns each (debits and credits) for the unadjusted trial balance, the adjustments, the adjusted trial balance, the income statement, and the balance sheet. (Appendix)

http://

http://porter.swlearning.com

Technology and other resources for your success

If you need additional help, visit the text's Web site. Also, see pages xv–xvii in this text's preface for a description of available technology and other resources. If your instructor is using PERSONAL*Trainer* in this course, you may complete, on line, the assignments identified by PT.

Key Terms Quiz

Read each definition below and then write the number of that definition in the blank beside the appropriate term it defines. The quiz solutions appear at the end of the chapter.

_____ Recognition
_____ Historical cost
_____ Current value
_____ Cash basis
_____ Accrual basis
_____ Revenues
_____ Revenue recognition principle
_____ Percentage-of-completion method
_____ Production method
_____ Installment method
_____ Matching principle
_____ Expenses
_____ Adjusting entries
_____ Straight-line method
_____ Contra account
_____ Deferral
_____ Deferred expense
_____ Deferred revenue
_____ Accrual
_____ Accrued liability
_____ Accrued asset
_____ Accounting cycle
_____ Work sheet
_____ Real accounts
_____ Nominal accounts
_____ Closing entries
_____ Interim statements

1. A device used at the end of the period to gather the information needed to prepare financial statements without actually recording and posting adjusting entries.
2. Inflows or other enhancements of assets or settlements of liabilities from delivering or producing goods, rendering services, or other activities.
3. The method in which revenue is recognized when a commodity is produced rather than when it is sold.
4. Journal entries made at the end of a period by a company using the accrual basis of accounting.
5. Journal entries made at the end of the period to return the balance in all nominal accounts to zero and transfer the net income or loss and the dividends of the period to Retained Earnings.
6. The method used by contractors to recognize revenue before the completion of a long-term contract.
7. A liability resulting from the receipt of cash before the recognition of revenue.
8. The method in which revenue is recognized at the time cash is collected; used for various types of consumer items, such as automobiles and appliances.
9. The name given to balance sheet accounts because they are permanent and are not closed at the end of the period.
10. An asset resulting from the recognition of a revenue before the receipt of cash.
11. The amount of cash, or its equivalent, that could be received by selling an asset currently.
12. The assignment of an equal amount of depreciation to each period.
13. Cash has either been paid or received, but expense or revenue has not yet been recognized.
14. A system of accounting in which revenues are recognized when earned and expenses when incurred.
15. Cash has not yet been paid or received, but expense has been incurred or revenue earned.
16. Financial statements prepared monthly, quarterly, or at other intervals less than a year in duration.
17. Revenues are recognized in the income statement when they are realized, or realizable, and earned.
18. The process of recording an item in the financial statements as an asset, liability, revenue, expense, or the like.
19. An asset resulting from the payment of cash before the incurrence of expense.
20. The name given to revenue, expense, and dividend accounts because they are temporary and are closed at the end of the period.
21. A system of accounting in which revenues are recognized when cash is received and expenses when cash is paid.
22. A liability resulting from the recognition of an expense before the payment of cash.
23. The association of revenue of a period with all of the costs necessary to generate that revenue.
24. An account with a balance that is opposite that of a related account.
25. The amount that is paid for an asset and that is used as a basis for recognizing it on the balance sheet and carrying it on later balance sheets.
26. Outflows or other using up of assets or incurrences of liabilities resulting from delivering goods, rendering services, or carrying out other activities.
27. A series of steps performed each period and culminating with the preparation of a set of financial statements.

Answers on p. 217.

Alternate Terms

Historical cost Original cost

Asset Unexpired cost

Deferred expense Prepaid expense, prepaid asset

Deferred revenue Unearned revenue

Expense Expired cost

Nominal account Temporary account

Real account Permanent account

Questions

1. What is meant by the following statement? "The items depicted in financial statements are merely *representations* of the real thing."
2. What is the meaning of the following statement? "The choice between historical cost and current value is a good example of the trade-off in accounting between relevance and reliability."
3. A realtor earns a 10% commission on the sale of a $150,000 home. The realtor lists the home on June 5, the sale occurs on June 12, and the seller pays the realtor the $15,000 commission on July 8. When should the realtor recognize revenue from the sale, assuming (a) the cash basis of accounting and (b) the accrual basis of accounting?
4. What does the following statement mean? "If I want to assess the cash flow prospects for a company down the road, I look at the company's most recent statement of cash flows. An income statement prepared under the accrual basis of accounting is useless for this purpose."
5. What is the relationship between the time period assumption and accrual accounting?
6. Is it necessary for an asset to be acquired when revenue is recognized? Explain your answer.
7. What is the justification for recognizing revenue on a long-term contract by the percentage-of-completion method?
8. Illinois Fried Chicken sells franchises granting the franchisee in a specific geographic area the exclusive right to use the company name and sell chicken using its secret recipe. An initial franchise fee of $50,000 is charged by Illinois, along with a continuing fee of 3% of sales. The initial fee is for Illinois' assistance in selecting a site and training personnel. When should Illinois recognize the $50,000 as revenue?
9. When should a publisher of magazines recognize revenue?
10. What is the justification for recognizing revenue in certain industries at the time the product is *produced* rather than when it is *sold?*
11. A friend says to you: "I just don't get it. Assets cost money. Expenses reduce income. There must be some relationship among *assets, costs,* and *expenses*—I'm just not sure what it is!" What is the relationship? Can you give an example of it?
12. What is the meaning of *depreciation* to the accountant?
13. What are the four basic types of adjusting entries? Give an example of each.
14. What are the rules of debit and credit as they apply to the contra asset account Accumulated Depreciation?
15. Which of the following steps in the accounting cycle requires the most thought and judgment by the accountant: (a) preparing a trial balance, (b) posting adjusting and closing entries, or (c) analyzing and recording transactions? Explain your answer.
16. What is the difference between a real account and a nominal account?
17. What two purposes are served in making closing entries?
18. Why is the Dividends account closed directly to Retained Earnings rather than to the Income Summary account?
19. Assuming the use of a work sheet, are the formal adjusting entries recorded and posted to the accounts before or after the financial statements are prepared? Explain your answer. Would your answer change if a work sheet is not prepared? (Appendix)
20. Some companies use an eight-column work sheet rather than the ten-column format illustrated in the chapter. Which two columns would you think are not used in the eight-column format? Why could these two columns be eliminated? (Appendix)
21. Why do the income statement columns appear before the balance sheet columns on a work sheet? (Appendix)
22. Does the Retained Earnings account that appears in the balance sheet credit column of a work sheet reflect the beginning or the ending balance in the account? Explain your answer. (Appendix)
23. One asset account will always be carried over from the unadjusted trial balance columns of a work sheet to the balance sheet columns of the work sheet without any adjustment. What account is this? (Appendix)

Exercises

Exercise 4-1 ***Revenue Recognition*** **LO 3** P/T

The highway department contracted with a private company to collect tolls and maintain facilities on a turnpike. Users of the turnpike can pay cash as they approach the toll booth, or they can purchase a pass. The pass is equipped with an electronic sensor that subtracts the toll fee from the pass balance as the motorist slowly approaches a special toll booth. The passes are issued in $10 increments. Refunds are available to motorists who do not use the pass balance, but these are issued very infrequently. Last year $3,000,000 was collected at the traditional toll booths, $2,000,000 of passes were issued, and $1,700,000 of passes were used at the special toll booth. How much should the company recognize as revenue for the year? Explain how the revenue recognition rule should be applied in this case.

Exercise 4-2 ***The Matching Principle*** **LO 4**

Three methods of matching costs with revenue were described in the chapter: (a) directly match a specific form of revenue with a cost incurred in generating that revenue, (b) indirectly match a cost with the periods during which it will provide benefits or revenue, and (c) immediately recognize a cost incurred as an expense because no future benefits are expected. For each of the following costs, indicate how it is normally recognized as expense by indicating either *a, b,* or *c*. If you think there is more than one possible answer for any of the situations, explain why.

1. New office copier
2. Monthly bill from the utility company for electricity
3. Office supplies
4. Biweekly payroll for office employees
5. Commissions earned by salespeople
6. Interest incurred on a six-month loan from the bank
7. Cost of inventory sold during the current period
8. Taxes owed on income earned during current period
9. Cost of three-year insurance policy

Exercise 4-3 ***Accruals and Deferrals*** **LO 5**

For the following situations, indicate whether each involves a deferred expense (DE), a deferred revenue (DR), an accrued liability (AL), or an accrued asset (AA).

Example: __DE__ Office supplies purchased in advance of their use.

________ 1. Wages earned by employees but not yet paid

________ 2. Cash collected from subscriptions in advance of publishing a magazine

________ 3. Interest earned on a customer loan for which principal and interest have not yet been collected

________ 4. One year's premium on life insurance policy paid in advance

________ 5. Office building purchased for cash

________ 6. Rent collected in advance from a tenant

________ 7. State income taxes owed at the end of the year

________ 8. Rent owed by a tenant but not yet collected

Exercise 4-4 ***Office Supplies*** **LO 5**

Somerville Corp. purchases office supplies once a month and prepares monthly financial statements. The asset account Office Supplies on Hand has a balance of $1,450 on May 1. Purchases of supplies during May amount to $1,100. Supplies on hand at May 31 amount to $920. Prepare the necessary adjusting entry on Somerville's books on May 31. What would be the effect on net income for May if this entry is *not* recorded?

Exercise 4-5 ***Prepaid Rent—Quarterly Adjustments*** **LO 5**

On September 1, Northhampton Industries signed a six-month lease, effective September 1, for office space. Northhampton agreed to prepay the rent and mailed a check for $12,000 to the landlord on September 1. Assume that Northhampton prepares adjusting entries only four times a year, on March 31, June 30, September 30, and December 31.

Required

1. Compute the rental cost for each full month.
2. Prepare the journal entry to record the payment of rent on September 1.
3. Prepare the adjusting entry on September 30.

(continued)

4. Assume that the accountant prepares the adjusting entry on September 30 but forgets to record an adjusting entry on December 31. Will net income for the year be understated or overstated? By what amount?

Exercise 4-6 ***Depreciation*** **LO 5**

On July 1, 2004, Red Gate Farm buys a combine for $100,000 in cash. Assume that the combine is expected to have a seven-year life and an estimated salvage value of $16,000 at the end of that time.

Required

1. Prepare the journal entry to record the purchase of the combine on July 1, 2004.
2. Compute the depreciable cost of the combine.
3. Using the straight-line method, compute the monthly depreciation.
4. Prepare the adjusting entry to record depreciation at the end of July 2004.
5. Compute the combine's carrying value that will be shown on Red Gate's balance sheet prepared on December 31, 2004.

Exercise 4-7 ***Prepaid Insurance—Annual Adjustments*** **LO 5**

On April 1, 2004, Briggs Corp. purchases a 24-month property insurance policy for $72,000. The policy is effective immediately. Assume that Briggs prepares adjusting entries only once a year, on December 31.

Required

1. Compute the monthly cost of the insurance policy.
2. Prepare the journal entry to record the purchase of the policy on April 1, 2004.
3. Prepare the adjusting entry on December 31, 2004.
4. Assume that the accountant forgets to record an adjusting entry on December 31, 2004. Will net income for the year ended December 31, 2004, be understated or overstated? Explain your answer.

Exercise 4-8 ***Subscriptions*** **LO 5**

Horse Country Living publishes a monthly magazine for which a 12-month subscription costs $30. All subscriptions require payment of the full $30 in advance. On August 1, 2004, the balance in the Subscriptions Received in Advance account was $40,500. During the month of August, the company sold 900 yearly subscriptions. After the adjusting entry at the end of August, the balance in the Subscriptions Received in Advance account is $60,000.

Required

1. Prepare the journal entry to record the sale of the 900 yearly subscriptions during the month of August.
2. Prepare the adjusting journal entry on August 31.
3. Assume that the accountant made the correct entry during August to record the sale of the 900 subscriptions but forgot to make the adjusting entry on August 31. Would net income for August be overstated or understated? Explain your answer.

Exercise 4-9 ***Customer Deposits*** **LO 5**

Wolfe & Wolfe collected $9,000 from a customer on April 1 and agreed to provide legal services during the next three months. Wolfe & Wolfe expects to provide an equal amount of services each month.

Required

1. Prepare the journal entry for the receipt of the customer deposit on April 1.
2. Prepare the adjusting entry on April 30.
3. What would be the effect on net income for April if the entry in (2) is not recorded?

Exercise 4-10 ***Wages Payable*** **LO 5**

Denton Corporation employs 50 workers in its plant. Each employee is paid $10 per hour and works seven hours per day, Monday through Friday. Employees are paid every Friday. The last payday was Friday, October 20.

Required

1. Compute the dollar amount of the weekly payroll.
2. Prepare the journal entry on Friday, October 27, for the payment of the weekly payroll.
3. Denton prepares monthly financial statements. Prepare the adjusting journal entry on Tuesday, October 31, the last day of the month.
4. Prepare the journal entry on Friday, November 3, for the payment of the weekly payroll.
5. Would net income for the month of October be understated or overstated if Denton doesn't bother with an adjusting entry on October 31? Explain your answer.

Exercise 4-11 *Interest Payable* **LO 5**

Billings Company takes out a 12%, 90-day, $100,000 loan with First National Bank on March 1, 2004.

Required

1. Prepare the journal entry on March 1, 2004.
2. Prepare the adjusting entries for the months of March and April 2004.
3. Prepare the entry on May 30, 2004, when Billings repays the principal and interest to First National.

Exercise 4-12 *Property Taxes Payable—Annual Adjustments* **LO 5**

Lexington Builders owns property in Kaneland County. Lexington's 2003 property taxes amounted to $50,000. Kaneland County will send out the 2004 property tax bills to property owners during April 2005. Taxes must be paid by June 1, 2005. Assume that Lexington prepares adjusting entries only once a year, on December 31, and that property taxes for 2004 are expected to increase by 5% over those for 2003.

Required

1. Prepare the adjusting entry required to record the property taxes payable on December 31, 2004.
2. Prepare the journal entry to record the payment of the 2004 property taxes on June 1, 2005.

Exercise 4-13 *Interest Receivable* **LO 5**

On June 1, 2004, MicroTel Enterprises lends $60,000 to MaxiDriver Inc. The loan will be repaid in 60 days with interest at 10%.

Required

1. Prepare the journal entry on MicroTel's books on June 1, 2004.
2. Prepare the adjusting entry on MicroTel's books on June 30, 2004.
3. Prepare the entry on MicroTel's books on July 31, 2004, when MaxiDriver repays the principal and interest.

Exercise 4-14 *Unbilled Accounts Receivable* **LO 5**

Mike and Cary repair computers for small local businesses. Heavy thunderstorms during the last week of June resulted in a record number of service calls. Eager to review the results of operations for the month of June, Mike prepared an income statement and was puzzled by the lower-than-expected amount of revenues. Cary explained that he had not yet billed the company's customers for $40,000 of work performed during the last week of the month.

Required

1. Should revenue be recorded when services are performed or when customers are billed? Explain your answer.
2. Prepare the adjusting entry required on June 30.

Exercise 4-15 *The Effect of Ignoring Adjusting Entries on Net Income* **LO 5**

For each of the following independent situations, determine whether the effect of ignoring the required adjusting entry will result in an understatement (U), an overstatement (O), or no effect (NE) on net income for the period.

(continued)

Situation	Effect on Net Income
Example: Taxes owed but not yet paid are ignored.	O
1. A company fails to record depreciation on equipment.	_______
2. Sales made during the last week of the period are not recorded.	_______
3. A company neglects to record the expired portion of a prepaid insurance policy (its cost was originally debited to an asset account).	_______
4. Interest due but not yet paid on a long-term note payable is ignored.	_______
5. Commissions earned by salespeople but not payable until the 10th of the following month are ignored.	_______
6. A landlord receives cash on the date a lease is signed for the rent for the first six months and credits Unearned Rent Revenue. The landlord fails to make any adjustment at the end of the first month.	_______

Exercise 4-16 *The Effect of Adjusting Entries on the Accounting Equation* LO 5

Determine whether recording each of the following adjusting entries will increase (I), decrease (D), or have no effect (NE) on each of the three elements of the accounting equation.

	Assets	= Liabilities	+ Owners' Equity
Example: Wages earned during the period but not yet paid are accrued.	NE	I	D
1. Prepaid insurance is reduced for the portion of the policy that has expired during the period.	_______	_______	_______
2. Interest incurred during the period but not yet paid is accrued.	_______	_______	_______
3. Depreciation for the period is recorded.	_______	_______	_______
4. Revenue is recorded for the earned portion of a liability for amounts collected in advance from customers.	_______	_______	_______
5. Rent revenue is recorded for amounts owed by a tenant but not yet received.	_______	_______	_______
6. Income taxes owed but not yet paid are accrued.	_______	_______	_______

Exercise 4-17 *Reconstruction of Adjusting Entries from Unadjusted and Adjusted Trial Balances* LO 5

Following are the unadjusted and adjusted trial balances for Power Corp. on May 31, 2004:

	Unadjusted Trial Balance		Adjusted Trial Balance	
	Debit	Credit	Debit	Credit
Cash	$ 3,160		$ 3,160	
Accounts Receivable	7,300		9,650	
Supplies on Hand	400		160	
Prepaid Rent	2,400		2,200	
Equipment	9,000		9,000	
Accumulated Depreciation		$ 2,800		$ 3,200
Accounts Payable		2,600		2,600
Capital Stock		5,000		5,000
Retained Earnings		8,990		8,990
Service Revenue		6,170		8,520
Promotions Expense	2,050		2,050	
Wage Expense	1,250		2,350	
Wages Payable				1,100
Supplies Expense			240	
Depreciation Expense			400	
Rent Expense			200	
Totals	$25,560	$25,560	$29,410	$29,410

Required

1. Reconstruct the adjusting entries that were made on Power's books at the end of May.
2. By how much would Power's net income for May have been overstated or understated (indicate which) if these adjusting entries had not been recorded?

Exercise 4-18 ***The Accounting Cycle*** **LO 6**

The steps in the accounting cycle are listed below in random order. Fill in the blank next to each step to indicate its *order* in the cycle. The first step in the cycle is filled in as an example.

Order	Procedure
______	Prepare a work sheet.
______	Close the accounts.
1	Collect and analyze information from source documents.
______	Prepare financial statements.
______	Post transactions to accounts in the ledger.
______	Record and post adjusting entries.
______	Journalize daily transactions.

Exercise 4-19 ***Trial Balance*** **LO 6**

The following account titles, arranged in alphabetical order, are from the records of Hadley Realty Corporation. The balance in each account is the normal balance for that account. The balances are as of December 31, after adjusting entries have been made. Prepare an adjusted trial balance, listing the accounts in the following order: (1) assets, (2) liabilities, (3) owners' equity accounts, including dividends, (4) revenues, and (5) expenses.

Accounts Payable	$12,300
Accounts Receivable	21,230
Accumulated Depreciation—Automobiles	12,000
Accumulated Depreciation—Buildings	15,000
Automobiles	48,000
Buildings	60,000
Capital Stock	25,000
Cash	2,460
Commissions Earned	17,420
Commissions Expense	2,300
Dividends	1,500
Insurance Expense	300
Interest Expense	200
Interest Payable	200
Land	40,000
Notes Payable	20,000
Office Supplies	1,680
Office Supplies Expense	5,320
Prepaid Insurance	1,200
Rent Expense	2,400
Retained Earnings	85,445
Wages and Salaries Expense	1,245
Wages and Salaries Payable	470

Exercise 4-20 ***Closing Entries*** **LO 7**

At the end of the year, the adjusted trial balance for Devonshire Corporation contains the following amounts for the income statement accounts (the balance in each account is the normal balance for that type of account).

Account	Balance
Advertising Fees Earned	$58,500
Interest Revenue	2,700
Wage and Salary Expense	14,300
Utilities Expense	12,500

(continued)

Account	Balance
Insurance Expense	$ 7,300
Depreciation Expense	16,250
Interest Expense	2,600
Income Tax Expense	3,300
Dividends	2,000

Required

1. Prepare all necessary journal entries to close Devonshire Corporation's accounts at the end of the year.
2. Assume that the accountant for Devonshire forgets to record the closing entries. What will be the effect on net income for the *following* year? Explain your answer.

Exercise 4-21 ***Preparation of a Statement of Retained Earnings from Closing Entries*** **LO 7**

Fisher Corporation reported a Retained Earnings balance of $125,780 on January 1, 2004. Fisher Corporation made the following three closing entries on December 31, 2004 (the entry to transfer net income to Retained Earnings has been intentionally left out). Prepare a statement of retained earnings for Fisher for the year.

Dec.	31	Service Revenue	65,400	
		Interest Revenue	20,270	
		Income Summary		85,670
	31	Income Summary	62,345	
		Salary and Wage Expense		23,450
		Rent Expense		20,120
		Interest Expense		4,500
		Utilities Expense		10,900
		Insurance Expense		3,375
	31	Retained Earnings	6,400	
		Dividends		6,400

Exercise 4-22 ***Reconstruction of Closing Entries*** **LO 7**

The T accounts shown below summarize entries made to selected general ledger accounts of Cooper & Company. Certain entries, dated December 31, are closing entries. Prepare the closing entries that were made on December 31.

MAINTENANCE REVENUE

12/31	90,000	64,000	12/1 bal.
		13,000	12/15
		13,000	12/30

WAGES EXPENSE

12/1 bal.	11,000	12,000	12/31
12/15	500		
12/30	500		

SUPPLIES EXPENSE

12/1 bal.	2,500	2,750	12/31
12/31	250		

RETAINED EARNINGS

12/31	5,000	45,600	12/1 bal.
		75,250	12/31

DIVIDENDS

12/1 bal.	5,000	5,000	12/31

INCOME SUMMARY

12/31	14,750	90,000	12/31
12/31	75,250		

Exercise 4-23 ***Closing Entries for Winnebago Industries*** **LO 7**

http://www.winnebagoind.com

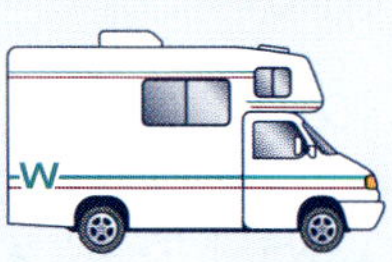

The following accounts appear on Winnebago Industries' 2001 income statement. The accounts are listed in alphabetical order, and the balance in each account is the normal balance for that account. All amounts are in thousands of dollars. Prepare closing entries for Winnebago Industries for 2001.

Cost of manufactured products	$587,330
Cumulative effect of change in accounting principle, net of taxes (same effect on income as an expense or a loss)	1,050
Financial income	3,754
General and administrative (expense)	13,607

Provision for taxes (expense)	$ 15,474
Revenues—dealer financing	4,241
Revenues—manufactured products	677,593
Selling (expense)	25,423

(*Note:* The descriptions in parentheses are not part of the items but have been added to provide you with hints as you complete this exercise.)

Exercise 4-24 *Closing Entries* LO 7

Royston Realty reported the following accounts on its income statement:

Commissions Earned	$54,000
Real Estate Board Fees Paid	5,000
Computer Line Charge	864
Depreciation on Computer	450
Car Expenses	2,200
Travel and Entertainment	4,500
Insurance Expired	780
Advertising Expense	1,460
Office Supplies Used	940

Required

1. Prepare the necessary entries to close the temporary accounts.
2. Explain why the closing entries are necessary and when they should be recorded.

Exercise 4-25 *The Difference between a Financial Statement and a Work Sheet (Appendix)* LO 8

The balance sheet columns of the work sheet for Jones Corporation show total debits and total credits of $255,000 each. Dividends for the period are $3,000. Accumulated depreciation is $14,000 at the end of the period. Compute the amount that should appear on the balance sheet (i.e., the formal financial statement) for *total assets.* How do you explain the difference between this amount and the amount that appears as the total debits and total credits on the work sheet?

Exercise 4-26 *Ten-Column Work Sheet (Appendix)* LO 8

Indicate whether amounts in each of the following accounts should be carried over from the adjusted trial balance columns of the work sheet to the income statement (IS) columns or to the balance sheet (BS) columns. Also indicate whether the account normally has a debit (D) balance or a credit (C) balance.

BS-D **Example:** Cash

______ **1.** Accumulated Depreciation—Trucks
______ **2.** Subscriptions Sold in Advance
______ **3.** Accounts Receivable
______ **4.** Dividends
______ **5.** Capital Stock
______ **6.** Prepaid Insurance
______ **7.** Depreciation Expense—Trucks
______ **8.** Office Supplies
______ **9.** Office Supplies Expense
______ **10.** Subscription Revenue
______ **11.** Interest Receivable
______ **12.** Interest Revenue
______ **13.** Interest Expense
______ **14.** Interest Payable
______ **15.** Retained Earnings

Multi-Concept Exercises

Exercise 4-27 ***Revenue Recognition, Cash and Accrual Basis*** **LO 1, 2, 3**

Hathaway Health Club sold three-year memberships at a reduced rate during its opening promotion. It sold 1,000 three-year, nonrefundable memberships for $366 each. The club expects to sell 100 additional three-year memberships for $900 each over each of the next two years. Membership fees are paid when clients sign up. The club's bookkeeper has prepared the following income statement for the first year of business and projected income statements for Years 2 and 3.

Cash-basis income statements:

	Year 1	Year 2	Year 3
Sales	$366,000	$ 90,000	$ 90,000
Equipment*	$100,000	$ 0	$ 0
Salaries and Wages	50,000	50,000	50,000
Advertising	5,000	5,000	5,000
Rent and Utilities	36,000	36,000	36,000
Net income (loss)	$175,000	$ (1,000)	$ (1,000)

*Equipment was purchased at the beginning of Year 1 for $100,000 and is expected to last for three years and then to be worth $1,000.

Required

1. Convert the income statements for each of the three years to the accrual basis.
2. Describe how the revenue recognition principle applies. Do you believe that the cash-basis or the accrual-basis income statements are more useful to management? to investors? Why?

Exercise 4-28 ***The Effect of the Percentage-of-Completion Method on Financial Statements*** **LO 1, 2, 3**

Fox Valley Inc. is building a bridge. During the first year of the three-year project, Fox Valley incurred construction costs of $1.2 million. The company expects to spend an additional $600,000 in each of the next two years of the project. The state has agreed to pay Fox Valley $4 million for the bridge, $2 million in the first year and $2 million on completion. The company would like to use the percentage-of-completion method to report revenue and income.

Required

1. Complete the following table, comparing the percentage-of-completion method with the cash basis. Use the percentage of costs incurred to date to estimated total costs to determine the percentage of completion.

	Income Recognized under	
Year	**Percentage-of-Completion**	**Cash Basis**
1		
2		
3		
Total		

2. Explain how the revenue recognition principle applies to the percentage-of-completion method.

Exercise 4-29 ***Depreciation Expense*** **LO 4, 5**

During 2004, Carter Company acquired three assets with the following costs, estimated useful lives, and estimated salvage values:

Date	Asset	Cost	Estimated Useful Life	Estimated Salvage Value
March 28	Truck	$ 18,000	5 years	$ 3,000
June 22	Computer	55,000	10 years	5,000
October 3	Building	250,000	30 years	10,000

The company uses the straight-line method to depreciate all assets and computes depreciation to the nearest month. For example, the computer system will be depreciated for six months in 2004.

Required

1. Compute the depreciation expense that Carter will record on each of the three assets for 2004.
2. Comment on the following statement: "Accountants could save time and money by simply expensing the cost of long-term assets when they are purchased. In addition, this would be more accurate because depreciation requires estimates of useful life and salvage value."

Exercise 4-30 ***Accrual of Interest on a Loan*** **LO 4, 5**

On July 1, 2004, Paxson Corporation takes out a 12%, two-month, $50,000 loan at Friendly National Bank. Principal and interest are to be repaid on August 31.

Required

1. Prepare the journal entries for July 1 to record the borrowing, for July 31 to record the accrual of interest, and for August 31 to record repayment of the principal and interest.
2. Evaluate the following statement: "It would be much easier not to bother with an adjusting entry on July 31 and simply record interest expense on August 31 when the loan is repaid."

Problems

Problem 4-1 ***The Revenue Recognition Principle*** **LO 3**

Each of the following paragraphs describes a situation involving revenue recognition.

a. ABC Realty receives a 6% commission for every house it sells. It lists a house for a client on April 3 at a selling price of $150,000. ABC receives an offer from a buyer on April 28 to purchase the house at the asking price. The realtor's client accepts the offer on May 1. ABC will receive its 6% commission at a closing scheduled for May 16.

b. Chicken King is a fast-food franchisor on the West Coast. It charges all franchisees $10,000 to open an outlet in a designated city. In return for this fee, the franchisee receives the exclusive right to operate in the area, as well as assistance from Chicken King in selecting a site. On January 5, Chicken King signs an agreement with a franchisee and receives a down payment of $4,000, with the balance of $6,000 due in three months. On March 13, Chicken King meets with the new franchisee, and the two parties agree on a suitable site for the business. On April 5, the franchisee pays Chicken King the remaining $6,000.

c. Refer to part **b.** In addition to the initial fee, Chicken King charges a continuing fee equal to 2% of the franchisee's sales each month. Each month's fee is payable by the 10th of the following month. The franchisee opens for business on June 1. On July 3, Chicken King receives a report from the franchisee indicating its sales for the month of June amount to $60,000. On July 8, Chicken King receives its 2% fee for June sales.

d. Goldstar Mining Corporation mines and sells gold and other precious commodities on the open market. During August, the company mines 50 ounces of gold. The market price throughout August is $300 per ounce. The 50 ounces are eventually sold on the open market on September 5 for $310 per ounce.

e. Whatadeal Inc. sells used cars. Because of the uncertainties involved in collecting from customers, Whatadeal uses the installment basis of accounting. On December 2, Whatadeal sells a car for $10,000 with a 25% down payment and the balance due in 60 days. The company's accounting year ends on December 31. Whatadeal receives the balance of $7,500 on February 1.

Required

For each situation, indicate when revenue should be recognized, as well as the dollar amount. Give a brief explanation for each answer.

Problem 4-2 ***Adjusting Entries*** **LO 5**

Water Corporation prepares monthly financial statements and therefore adjusts its accounts at the end of every month. The following information is available for March 2004:

GENERAL LEDGER

a. Water Corporation takes out a 90-day, 8%, $15,000 note on March 1, 2004, with interest and principal to be paid at maturity.

b. The asset account Office Supplies on Hand has a balance of $1,280 on March 1, 2004. During March, Water adds $750 to the account for the purchases of the period. A count of the supplies on hand at the end of March indicates a balance of $1,370.

(continued)

c. The company purchased office equipment last year for $62,600. The equipment has an estimated useful life of six years and an estimated salvage value of $5,000.

d. The company's plant operates seven days per week with a daily payroll of $950. Wage earners are paid every Sunday. The last day of the month is Saturday, March 31.

e. The company rented an idle warehouse to a neighboring business on February 1, 2004, at a rate of $2,500 per month. On this date, Water Corporation credited Rent Collected in Advance for six months' rent received in advance.

f. On March 1, 2004, Water Corporation credited a liability account, Customer Deposits, for $4,800. This sum represents an amount that a customer paid in advance and that will be earned evenly by Water over a four-month period.

g. Based on its income for the month, Water Corporation estimates that federal income taxes for March amount to $3,900.

Required

For each of the preceding situations, prepare in general journal form the appropriate adjusting entry to be recorded on March 31, 2004.

Problem 4-3 *Effects of Adjusting Entries on the Accounting Equation* LO 5

Refer to the information provided for Water Corporation in Problem 4-2.

Required

1. Prepare a table to summarize the required adjusting entries as they affect the accounting equation. Use the format in Exhibit 3-1. Identify each adjustment by letter.
2. Assume that Water reports income of $23,000 before any of the adjusting entries. What net income will Water report for March?

Problem 4-4 *Adjusting Entries—Annual Adjustments* LO 5

GENERAL LEDGER

Palmer Industries prepares annual financial statements and adjusts its accounts only at the end of the year. The following information is available for the year ended December 31, 2004:

a. Palmer purchased computer equipment two years ago for $15,000. The equipment has an estimated useful life of five years and an estimated salvage value of $250.

b. The Office Supplies account had a balance of $3,600 on January 1, 2004. During 2004, Palmer added $17,600 to the account for purchases of office supplies during the year. A count of the supplies on hand at the end of December 2004 indicates a balance of $1,850.

c. On August 1, 2004, Palmer credited a liability account, Customer Deposits, for $24,000. This sum represents an amount that a customer paid in advance and that will be earned evenly by Palmer over a six-month period.

d. Palmer rented some office space on November 1, 2004, at a rate of $2,700 per month. On that date, Palmer debited Prepaid Rent for three months' rent paid in advance.

e. Palmer took out a 120-day, 9%, $200,000 note on November 1, 2004, with interest and principal to be paid at maturity.

f. Palmer operates five days per week with an average daily payroll of $500. Palmer pays its employees every Thursday. December 31, 2004, is a Friday.

Required

1. For each of the preceding situations, prepare in general journal form the appropriate adjusting entry to be recorded on December 31, 2004.
2. Assume that Palmer's accountant forgets to record the adjusting entries on December 31, 2004. Will net income for the year be understated or overstated? By what amount? (Ignore the effect of income taxes.)

Problem 4-5 *Recurring and Adjusting Entries* LO 5

The following are Butler Realty Corporation's accounts, identified by number. The company has been in the real estate business for 10 years and prepares financial statements monthly. Following the list of accounts is a series of transactions entered into by Butler. For each transaction, enter the number(s) of the account(s) to be debited and credited.

Accounts

1. Cash	11. Notes Payable
2. Accounts Receivable	12. Capital Stock, $10 par
3. Prepaid Rent	13. Paid-In Capital in Excess of Par
4. Office Supplies	14. Commissions Revenue
5. Automobiles	15. Office Supply Expense
6. Accumulated Depreciation	16. Rent Expense
7. Land	17. Salaries and Wages Expense
8. Accounts Payable	18. Depreciation Expense
9. Salaries and Wages Payable	19. Interest Expense
10. Income Tax Payable	20. Income Tax Expense

Transaction	Debit	Credit
a. **Example:** Issued additional shares of stock to owners at amount in excess of par.	1	12, 13
b. Purchased automobiles for cash.	____	____
c. Purchased land; made cash down payment and signed a promissory note for the balance.	____	____
d. Paid cash to landlord for rent for next 12 months.	____	____
e. Purchased office supplies on account.	____	____
f. Collected cash for commissions from clients for the properties sold during the month.	____	____
g. Collected cash for commissions from clients for the properties sold in the prior month.	____	____
h. During the month, sold properties for which cash for commissions will be collected from clients next month.	____	____
i. Paid for office supplies purchased on account in an earlier month.	____	____
j. Recorded an adjustment to recognize wages and salaries incurred but not yet paid.	____	____
k. Recorded an adjustment for office supplies used during the month.	____	____
l. Recorded an adjusting entry for the portion of prepaid rent that expired during the month.	____	____
m. Made required month-end payment on note taken out in (c); payment is part principal and part interest.	____	____
n. Recorded adjusting entry for monthly depreciation on the autos.	____	____
o. Recorded adjusting entry for income taxes.	____	____

Problem 4-6 *Use of Account Balances as a Basis for Adjusting Entries—Annual Adjustments* LO 5

The following account balances are taken from the records of Chauncey Company at December 31, 2004. The Prepaid Insurance account represents the cost of a three-year policy purchased on August 1, 2004. The Rent Collected in Advance account represents the cash received from a tenant on June 1, 2004, for 12 months' rent, beginning on that date. The Note Receivable represents a nine-month promissory note received from a customer on September 1, 2004. Principal and interest at an annual rate of 9% will be received on June 1, 2005.

Prepaid Insurance	$ 7,200 debit	
Rent Collected in Advance		$6,000 credit
Note Receivable	50,000 debit	

(continued)

Required

1. Prepare the three necessary adjusting entries on the books of Chauncey on December 31, 2004. Assume that Chauncey prepares adjusting entries only once a year, on December 31.
2. Assume that adjusting entries are made at the end of each month rather than only at the end of the year. What would be the balance in Prepaid Insurance *before* the December adjusting entry is made? Explain your answer.

Problem 4-7 *Use of a Trial Balance as a Basis for Adjusting Entries* LO 5

Bob Reynolds operates a real estate business. A trial balance on April 30, 2004, *before* recording any adjusting entries, appears as follows:

GENERAL LEDGER

REYNOLDS REALTY COMPANY
UNADJUSTED TRIAL BALANCE
APRIL 30, 2004

	Debit	Credit
Cash	$15,700	
Prepaid Insurance	450	
Office Supplies	250	
Office Equipment	50,000	
Accumulated Depreciation—Office Equipment		$ 5,000
Automobile	12,000	
Accumulated Depreciation—Automobile		1,400
Accounts Payable		6,500
Unearned Commissions		9,500
Notes Payable		2,000
Capital Stock		10,000
Retained Earnings		40,000
Dividends	2,500	
Commissions Earned		17,650
Utilities Expense	2,300	
Salaries Expense	7,400	
Advertising Expense	1,450	
Totals	$92,050	$92,050

Other Data

a. The monthly insurance cost is $50.

b. Office supplies on hand on April 30, 2004, amount to $180.

c. The office equipment was purchased on April 1, 2003. On that date, it had an estimated useful life of 10 years.

d. On September 1, 2003, the automobile was purchased; it had an estimated useful life of five years.

e. A deposit is received in advance of providing any services for first-time customers. Amounts received in advance are recorded initially in the account Unearned Commissions. Based on services provided to these first-time customers, the balance in this account at the end of April should be $5,000.

f. Repeat customers are allowed to pay for services one month after the date of the sale of their property. Services rendered during the month but not yet collected or billed to these customers amount to $1,500.

g. Interest owed on the note payable but not yet paid amounts to $20.

h. Salaries owed to employees but unpaid at the end of the month amount to $2,500.

Required

1. Prepare in general journal form the necessary adjusting entries at April 30, 2004. Label the entries **a** through **h** to correspond to the other data.
2. Note that the unadjusted trial balance reports a credit balance in Accumulated Depreciation—Office Equipment of $5,000. Explain *why* the account contains a balance of $5,000 on April 30, 2004.

Problem 4-8 ***Effects of Adjusting Entries on the Accounting Equation*** **LO 5**

Refer to the information provided for Reynolds Realty Company in Problem 4-7.

Required

1. Prepare a table to summarize the required adjusting entries as they affect the accounting equation. Use the format in Exhibit 3-1. Identify each adjustment by letter.
2. Compute the net increase or decrease in net income for the month from the recognition of the adjusting entries you prepared in part **1.** (Ignore income taxes.)

Problem 4-9 ***Reconstruction of Adjusting Entries from Account Balances*** **LO 5**

Taggart Corp. records adjusting entries each month before preparing monthly financial statements. The following selected account balances are taken from its trial balances on June 30, 2004. The "unadjusted" columns set forth the general ledger balances before the adjusting entries were posted. The "adjusted" columns reflect the month-end adjusting entries.

	Unadjusted		Adjusted	
Account Title	**Debit**	**Credit**	**Debit**	**Credit**
Prepaid Insurance	$3,600		$3,450	
Equipment	9,600		9,600	
Accumulated Depreciation		$1,280		$1,360
Notes Payable		9,600		9,600
Interest Payable		2,304		2,448

Required

1. The company purchased a 36-month insurance policy on June 1, 2003. Reconstruct the adjusting journal entry for insurance on June 30, 2004.
2. What was the original cost of the insurance policy? Explain your answer.
3. The equipment was purchased on February 1, 2003, for $9,600. Taggart uses straight-line depreciation and estimates that the equipment will have no salvage value. Reconstruct the adjusting journal entry for depreciation on June 30, 2004.
4. What is the equipment's estimated useful life in months? Explain your answer.
5. Taggart signed a two-year note payable on February 1, 2003, for the purchase of the equipment. Interest on the note accrues on a monthly basis and will be paid at maturity along with the principal amount of $9,600. Reconstruct the adjusting journal entry for interest on June 30, 2004.
6. What is the *monthly* interest rate on the loan? Explain your answer.

Problem 4-10 ***Use of a Trial Balance to Record Adjusting Entries in T Accounts*** **LO 5**

Four Star Video has been in the video rental business for five years. An unadjusted trial balance at May 31, 2004, follows.

GENERAL LEDGER

FOUR STAR VIDEO
UNADJUSTED TRIAL BALANCE
MAY 31, 2004

	Debit	**Credit**
Cash	$ 4,000	
Prepaid Rent	6,600	
Video Inventory	25,600	
Display Stands	8,900	
Accumulated Depreciation		$ 5,180
Accounts Payable		3,260
Customer Subscriptions		4,450
Capital Stock		5,000
Retained Earnings		22,170
Rental Revenue		9,200
Wage and Salary Expense	2,320	
Utilities Expense	1,240	
Advertising Expense	600	
Totals	$49,260	$49,260

(continued)

The following additional information is available:

a. Four Star rents a store in a shopping mall and prepays the annual rent of $7,200 on April 1 of each year.

b. The asset account Video Inventory represents the cost of videos purchased from suppliers. When a new title is purchased from a supplier, its cost is debited to this account. When a title has served its useful life and can no longer be rented (even at a reduced price), it is removed from the inventory in the store. Based on the monthly count, the cost of titles on hand at the end of May is $23,140.

c. The display stands have an estimated useful life of five years and an estimated salvage value of $500.

d. Wages and salaries owed to employees but unpaid at the end of May amount to $1,450.

e. In addition to individual rentals, Four Star operates a popular discount subscription program. Customers pay an annual fee of $120 for an unlimited number of rentals. Based on the $10 per month earned on each of these subscriptions, the amount earned for the month of May is $2,440.

f. Four Star accrues income taxes using an estimated tax rate equal to 30% of the income for the month.

Required

1. Set up T accounts for each of the accounts listed in the trial balance. Based on the additional information given, set up any other T accounts that will be needed to prepare adjusting entries.
2. Post the month-end adjusting entries directly to the T accounts but do not bother to put the entries in journal format first. Use the letters **a** through **f** from the additional information to identify the entries.
3. Prepare a trial balance to prove the equality of debits and credits after posting the adjusting entries.
4. On the basis of the information you have, does Four Star appear to be a profitable business? Explain your answer.

Problem 4-11 ***Effects of Adjusting Entries on the Accounting Equation*** **LO 5**

Refer to the information provided for Four Star Video in Problem 4-10.

Required

Prepare a table to summarize the required adjusting entries as they affect the accounting equation. Use the format in Exhibit 3-1. Identify each adjustment by letter.

Multi-Concept Problems

Problem 4-12 ***Cash and Accrual Income Statements for a Manufacturer*** **LO 2, 3**

Drysdale Company was established to manufacture components for the auto industry. The components are shipped the same day they are produced. The following events took place during the first year of operations.

a. Issued common stock for a $50,000 cash investment.

b. Purchased delivery truck at the beginning of the year at a cost of $10,000 cash. The truck is expected to last five years and will be worthless at the end of that time.

c. Manufactured and sold 500,000 components the first year. The costs incurred to manufacture the components are (1) $1,000 monthly rent on a facility that included utilities and insurance, (2) $400,000 of raw materials purchased on account ($100,000 is still unpaid as of year-end, but all materials were used in manufacturing), and (3) $190,000 paid in salaries and wages to employees and supervisors.

d. Paid $100,000 to sales and office staff for salaries and wages.

e. Sold all components on account for $2 each. As of year-end, $150,000 is due from customers.

Required

1. How much revenue will Drysdale recognize under the cash basis and under the accrual basis?
2. Describe how Drysdale should apply the matching principle to recognize expenses.
3. Prepare an income statement under the accrual basis. Ignore income taxes.

Problem 4-13 ***Revenue Recognition on Installment Sales*** **LO 3, 4**

John Deare, an Illinois corn farmer, retired in South Carolina. While retired, he volunteered his time at the Small Business Administration office. One day, Frances Hirise, a condominium builder, came in with a question about the amount of sales she should recognize on her income statement. She had constructed a complex of 200 units. Half of the units sell for $50,000 each, and the other half sell for $60,000. The developer agreed to finance the sale of all units, and by the end of the year, 40 units at $50,000 and 30 units at $60,000 had been sold. Each buyer made a down payment of 10% cash and agreed to pay the remainder in equal annual payments plus interest on the unpaid balance over the next nine years. No payments have been received other than the down payments. John advised Frances that she should recognize sales of $11 million [(100 × $50,000) + (100 × $60,000)].

Required

Do you agree with John? Why did he suggest this amount? What amount of revenue would you suggest that Frances recognize in the current and subsequent years as a result of these sales? When should the costs to build the condos (lumber, labor, etc.) be recognized as expenses?

Problem 4-14 ***Revenue and Expense Recognition and Closing Entries*** **LO 3, 4, 7**

Two years ago, Darlene Darby opened a delivery service. Darby reports the following accounts on her income statement:

Sales	$69,000
Advertising expense	3,500
Salaries expense	39,000
Rent expense	10,000

These amounts represent two years of revenue and expenses. Darby has asked you how she can tell how much of the income is from the first year of business and how much is from the second year. She provides the following additional data:

a. Sales in the second year were double those of the first year.

b. Advertising expense is for a $500 opening promotion and weekly ads in the newspaper.

c. Salaries represent one employee for the first nine months and then two employees for the remainder of the time. Each is paid the same salary. No raises have been granted.

d. Rent has not changed since the business opened.

Required

1. Prepare income statements for Years 1 and 2.
2. Prepare the closing entries for each year. Prepare a short explanation for Darby about the purpose of closing temporary accounts.

Problem 4-15 ***Ten-Column Work Sheet (Appendix)*** **LO 5, 6, 8**

The following unadjusted trial balance is available for Ace Consulting Inc. on June 30, 2004.

GENERAL LEDGER

SPREADSHEET

ACE CONSULTING INC.
UNADJUSTED TRIAL BALANCE
JUNE 30, 2004

Cash	$ 6,320	
Accounts Receivable	14,600	
Supplies on Hand	800	
Prepaid Rent	4,800	
Furniture and Fixtures	18,000	
Accumulated Depreciation		$ 5,625
Accounts Payable		5,200
Capital Stock		10,000
Retained Earnings		17,955
Consulting Revenue		12,340
Utilities Expense	4,100	
Wage and Salary Expense	2,500	
Totals	$51,120	$51,120

Required

1. Enter the unadjusted trial balance in the first two columns of a 10-column work sheet.

(continued)

2. Enter the necessary adjustments in the appropriate columns of the work sheet for each of the following:
   a. Wages and salaries earned by employees at the end of June but not yet paid amount to $2,380.
   b. Supplies on hand at the end of June amount to $550.
   c. Depreciation on furniture and fixtures for June is $375.
   d. Ace prepays the rent on its office space on June 1 of each year. The rent amounts to $400 per month.
   e. Consulting services rendered and billed for which cash has not yet been received amount to $4,600.
3. Complete the remaining columns of the work sheet.

Problem 4-16 ***Monthly Transactions, 10-Column Work Sheet, and Financial Statements (Appendix)*** **LO 5, 6, 8**

GENERAL LEDGER

Moonlight Bay Inn is incorporated on January 2, 2004, by its three owners, each of whom contributes $20,000 in cash in exchange for shares of stock in the business. In addition to the sale of stock, the following transactions are entered into during the month of January:

January 2: A Victorian inn is purchased for $50,000 in cash. An appraisal performed on this date indicates that the land is worth $15,000 and the remaining balance of the purchase price is attributable to the house. The owners estimate that the house will have an estimated useful life of 25 years and an estimated salvage value of $5,000.

January 3: A two-year, 12%, $30,000 promissory note was signed at the Second State Bank. Interest and principal will be repaid on the maturity date of January 3, 2006.

January 4: New furniture for the inn is purchased at a cost of $15,000 in cash. The furniture has an estimated useful life of 10 years and no salvage value.

January 5: A 24-month property insurance policy is purchased for $6,000 in cash.

January 6: An advertisement for the inn is placed in the local newspaper. Moonlight Bay pays $450 cash for the ad, which will run in the paper throughout January.

January 7: Cleaning supplies are purchased on account for $950. The bill is payable within 30 days.

January 15: Wages of $4,230 for the first half of the month are paid in cash.

January 16: A guest mails the business $980 in cash as a deposit for a room to be rented for two weeks. The guest plans to stay at the inn during the last week of January and the first week of February.

January 31: Cash receipts from rentals of rooms for the month amount to $8,300.

January 31: Cash receipts from operation of the restaurant for the month amount to $6,600.

January 31: Each stockholder is paid $200 in cash dividends.

Required

1. Prepare journal entries to record each of the preceding transactions.
2. Post each of the journal entries to T accounts.
3. Place the balance in each of the T accounts in the unadjusted trial balance columns of a 10-column work sheet.
4. Enter the appropriate adjustments in the next two columns of the work sheet for each of the following:
   a. Depreciation of the house
   b. Depreciation of the furniture
   c. Interest on the promissory note
   d. Recognition of the expired portion of the insurance
   e. Recognition of the earned portion of the guest's deposit
   f. Wages earned during the second half of January amount to $5,120 and will be paid on February 3.
   g. Cleaning supplies on hand on January 31 amount to $230.
   h. A gas and electric bill that is received from the city amounts to $740 and is payable by February 5.
   i. Income taxes are to be accrued at a rate of 30% of income before taxes.

5. Complete the remaining columns of the work sheet.
6. Prepare in good form the following financial statements:
   a. Income statement for the month ended January 31, 2004
   b. Statement of retained earnings for the month ended January 31, 2004
   c. Balance sheet at January 31, 2004
7. Assume that you are the loan officer at Second State Bank (refer to the transaction on January 3). What are your reactions to Moonlight's first month of operations? Are you comfortable with the loan you made?

Alternate Problems

Problem 4-1A *The Revenue Recognition Principle* LO 3

Each of the following paragraphs describes a situation involving revenue recognition.

a. Zee Zitter Inc. paints and decorates office buildings. On September 30, 2004, it received $5,750 for work to be completed over the next six months.

b. Tan Us is a tanning salon franchisor in the Midwest. It charges all franchisees a fee of $2,500 to open a salon and an ongoing fee equal to 5% of all revenue during the first five years. The $2,500 is for training and accounting systems to be used in each salon. During January 2004, Tan Us signed an agreement with five individuals to open salons over the next three months.

c. On June 1, 2004, Dan Diver Bridge Building Inc. entered into a contract with the county to renovate an old covered bridge. The county gives Dan an advance of $500,000 and agrees to pay Dan $75,000 each month for 20 months, at which time the project should be completed.

d. Joe Cropper, a wheat grower, harvested the current year's crop and delivered it to the elevator for storage on October 1, 2004, until it is sold to one of several foreign countries. The expected sales value of the wheat is $450,000.

e. Shop-n-Here, a convenience store chain, constructed a strip shopping center next to one of its stores. The spaces are being sold to individuals who will open auto parts and repair facilities. One person is planning to open a brake-repair shop, another will set up a transmission-repair shop, a third will do 10-minute oil changes, and so on. The store spaces sell for $25,000 each. There are six spaces, four of which are sold in May of 2004.

Required

For each of the preceding situations, indicate when in 2004 revenue should be recognized, as well as the dollar amount. Give a brief explanation for each answer.

Problem 4-2A *Adjusting Entries* LO 5

GENERAL LEDGER

Flood Relief Inc. prepares monthly financial statements and therefore adjusts its accounts at the end of every month. The following information is available for June 2004:

a. Flood received a $10,000, 4%, two-year note receivable from a customer for services rendered. The principal and interest are due on June 1, 2006. Flood expects to be able to collect the note and interest in full at that time.

b. Office supplies totaling $5,600 were purchased during the month. The asset account Supplies is debited whenever a purchase is made. A count in the storeroom on June 30, 2004, indicated that supplies on hand amount to $507. The supplies on hand at the beginning of the month total $475.

c. The company purchased machines last year for $170,000. The machines are expected to be used for four years and have an estimated salvage value of $2,000.

d. On June 1, the company paid $4,650 for rent for June, July, and August. The asset Prepaid Rent was debited; it did not have a balance on June 1.

e. The company operates seven days per week with a weekly payroll of $7,000. Wage earners are paid every Sunday. The last day of the month is Saturday, June 30.

f. Based on its income for the month, Flood estimates that federal income taxes for June amount to $2,900.

(continued)

Required

For each of the preceding situations, prepare in general journal form the appropriate adjusting entry to be recorded on June 30, 2004.

Problem 4-3A ***Effects of Adjusting Entries on the Accounting Equation*** **LO 5**

Refer to the information provided for Flood Relief Inc. in Problem 4-2A.

Required

1. Prepare a table to summarize the required adjusting entries as they affect the accounting equation. Use the format in Exhibit 3-1. Identify each adjustment by letter.
2. Assume that Flood Relief reports income of $35,000 before any of the adjusting entries. What net income will Flood Relief report for June?

Problem 4-4A ***Adjusting Entries—Annual Adjustments*** **LO 5**

GENERAL LEDGER

Ogonquit Enterprises prepares annual financial statements and adjusts its accounts only at the end of the year. The following information is available for the year ended December 31, 2004:

a. Ogonquit purchased office furniture last year for $25,000. The furniture has an estimated useful life of seven years and an estimated salvage value of $4,000.

b. The Supplies account had a balance of $1,200 on January 1, 2004. During 2004, Ogonquit added $12,900 to the account for purchases of supplies during the year. A count of the supplies on hand at the end of December 2004 indicates a balance of $900.

c. On July 1, 2004, Ogonquit credited a liability account, Customer Deposits, for $8,800. This sum represents an amount that a customer paid in advance and that will be earned evenly by Ogonquit over an eight-month period.

d. Ogonquit rented some warehouse space on September 1, 2004, at a rate of $4,000 per month. On that date, Ogonquit debited Prepaid Rent for six months' rent paid in advance.

e. Ogonquit took out a 90-day, 6%, $30,000 note on November 1, 2004, with interest and principal to be paid at maturity.

f. Ogonquit operates five days per week with an average weekly payroll of $4,150. Ogonquit pays its employees every Thursday. December 31, 2004, is a Friday.

Required

1. For each of the preceding situations, prepare in general journal form the appropriate adjusting entry to be recorded on December 31, 2004.
2. Assume that Ogonquit's accountant forgets to record the adjusting entries on December 31, 2004. Will net income for the year be understated or overstated? By what amount? (Ignore the effect of income taxes.)

Problem 4-5A ***Recurring and Adjusting Entries*** **LO 5**

The following are the accounts of Dominique Inc., an interior decorator. The company has been in the decorating business for 10 years and prepares quarterly financial statements. Following the list of accounts is a series of transactions entered into by Dominique. For each transaction, enter the number(s) of the account(s) to be debited and credited.

Accounts

1. Cash
2. Accounts Receivable
3. Prepaid Rent
4. Office Supplies
5. Office Equipment
6. Accumulated Depreciation
7. Accounts Payable
8. Salaries and Wages Payable
9. Income Tax Payable
10. Interim Financing Notes Payable
11. Capital Stock, $1 par
12. Paid-In Capital in Excess of Par
13. Consulting Revenue
14. Office Supply Expense
15. Rent Expense
16. Salaries and Wages Expense
17. Depreciation Expense
18. Interest Expense
19. Income Tax Expense

Transaction	Debit	Credit
a. **Example:** Issued additional shares of stock to owners; shares issued at greater than par.	1	11, 12
b. Purchased office equipment for cash.	______	______
c. Collected open accounts receivable from customer.	______	______
d. Purchased office supplies on account.	______	______
e. Paid office rent for the next six months.	______	______
f. Paid interest on an interim financing note.	______	______
g. Paid salaries and wages.	______	______
h. Purchased office equipment; made a down payment in cash and signed an interim financing note.	______	______
i. Provided services on account.	______	______
j. Recorded depreciation on equipment.	______	______
k. Recorded income taxes due next month.	______	______
l. Recorded the used office supplies.	______	______
m. Recorded the used portion of prepaid rent.	______	______

Problem 4-6A *Use of Account Balances as a Basis for Adjusting Entries—Annual Adjustments* LO 5

The following account balances are taken from the records of Laugherty Inc. at December 31, 2004. The Supplies account represents the cost of supplies on hand at the beginning of the year plus all purchases. A physical count on December 31, 2004, shows only $1,520 of supplies on hand. The Unearned Revenue account represents the cash received from a customer on May 1, 2004, for 12 months of service, beginning on that date. The Note Payable represents a six-month promissory note signed with a supplier on September 1, 2004. Principal and interest at an annual rate of 10% will be paid on March 1, 2005.

Supplies	$5,790 debit	
Unearned Revenue		$ 1,800 credit
Note Payable		60,000 credit

Required

1. Prepare the three necessary adjusting entries on the books of Laugherty on December 31, 2004. Assume that Laugherty prepares adjusting entries only once a year, on December 31.
2. Assume that adjusting entries are made at the end of each month rather than only at the end of the year. What would be the balance in Unearned Revenue *before* the December adjusting entry is made? Explain your answer.

Problem 4-7A *Use of a Trial Balance as a Basis for Adjusting Entries* LO 5

Lori Matlock operates a graphic arts business. A trial balance on June 30, 2004, *before* recording any adjusting entries, appears as follows:

GENERAL LEDGER

MATLOCK GRAPHIC ARTS STUDIO
UNADJUSTED TRIAL BALANCE
JUNE 30, 2004

	Debit	Credit
Cash	$ 7,000	
Prepaid Rent	18,000	
Supplies	15,210	
Office Equipment	46,120	
Accumulated Depreciation—Equipment		$ 4,000
Accounts Payable		1,800
Notes Payable		2,000
Capital Stock		50,000
Retained Earnings		24,350
Dividends	8,400	
Revenue		46,850

(continued)

	Debit	Credit
Utilities Expense	$ 2,850	
Salaries Expense	19,420	
Advertising Expense	12,000	
Totals	$129,000	$129,000

Other Data

a. The monthly rent cost is $600.

b. Supplies on hand on June 30, 2004, amount to $1,290.

c. The office equipment was purchased on June 1, 2003. On that date, it had an estimated useful life of 10 years and a salvage value of $6,120.

d. Interest owed on the note payable but not yet paid amounts to $50.

e. Salaries of $620 are owed to employees but unpaid at the end of the month.

Required

1. Prepare in general journal form the necessary adjusting entries at June 30, 2004. Label the entries **a** through **e** to correspond to the other data.
2. Note that the unadjusted trial balance reports a credit balance in Accumulated Depreciation—Equipment of $4,000. Explain *why* the account contains a balance of $4,000 on June 30, 2004.

Problem 4-8A ***Effects of Adjusting Entries on the Accounting Equation*** **LO 5**

Refer to the information provided for Matlock Graphic Arts Studio in Problem 4-7A.

Required

1. Prepare a table to summarize the required adjusting entries as they affect the accounting equation. Use the format in Exhibit 3-1. Identify each adjustment by letter.
2. Compute the net increase or decrease in net income for the month from the recognition of the adjusting entries you prepared in part 1 (ignore income taxes).

Problem 4-9A ***Reconstruction of Adjusting Entries from Account Balances*** **LO 5**

Zola Corporation records adjusting entries each month before preparing monthly financial statements. The following selected account balances are taken from its trial balances on June 30, 2004. The "unadjusted" columns set forth the general ledger balances before the adjusting entries were posted. The "adjusted" columns reflect the month-end adjusting entries.

	Unadjusted		Adjusted	
Account Title	**Debit**	**Credit**	**Debit**	**Credit**
Prepaid Rent	$4,000		$3,000	
Equipment	9,600		9,600	
Accumulated Depreciation		$ 800		$ 900
Notes Payable		9,600		9,600
Interest Payable		768		864

Required

1. The company paid for a six-month lease on April 1, 2004. Reconstruct the adjusting journal entry for rent on June 30, 2004.
2. What amount was prepaid on April 1, 2004? Explain your answer.
3. The equipment was purchased on September 30, 2003, for $9,600. Zola uses straight-line depreciation and estimates that the equipment will have no salvage value. Reconstruct the adjusting journal entry for depreciation on June 30, 2004.
4. What is the equipment's estimated useful life in months? Explain your answer.
5. Zola signed a two-year note on September 30, 2003, for the purchase of the equipment. Interest on the note accrues on a monthly basis and will be paid at maturity along with the principal amount of $9,600. Reconstruct the adjusting journal entry for interest expense on June 30, 2004.
6. What is the *monthly* interest rate on the loan? Explain your answer.

GENERAL LEDGER

Problem 4-10A ***Use of a Trial Balance to Record Adjusting Entries in T Accounts*** **LO 5**

Lewis and Associates has been in the termite inspection and treatment business for five years. An unadjusted trial balance at June 30, 2004, follows:

LEWIS AND ASSOCIATES
UNADJUSTED TRIAL BALANCE
JUNE 30, 2004

	Debit	Credit
Cash	$ 6,200	
Accounts Receivable	10,400	
Prepaid Rent	4,400	
Chemical Inventory	9,400	
Equipment	18,200	
Accumulated Depreciation		$ 1,050
Accounts Payable		1,180
Capital Stock		5,000
Retained Earnings		25,370
Treatment Revenue		40,600
Wages and Salary Expense	22,500	
Utilities Expense	1,240	
Advertising Expense	860	
Totals	$73,200	$73,200

The following additional information is available:

a. Lewis rents a warehouse with office space and prepays the annual rent of $4,800 on May 1 of each year.

b. The asset account Equipment represents the cost of treatment equipment, which has an estimated useful life of 10 years and an estimated salvage value of $200.

c. Chemical inventory on hand equals $1,300.

d. Wages and salaries owed to employees but unpaid at the end of the month amount to $1,080.

e. Lewis accrues income taxes using an estimated tax rate equal to 30% of the income for the month.

Required

1. Set up T accounts for each of the accounts listed in the trial balance. Based on the additional information given, set up any other T accounts that will be needed to prepare adjusting entries.
2. Post the month-end adjusting entries directly to the T accounts but do not bother to put the entries in journal format first. Use the letters **a** through **e** from the additional information to identify the entries.
3. Prepare a trial balance to prove the equality of debits and credits after posting the adjusting entries.
4. On the basis of the information you have, does Lewis appear to be a profitable business? Explain your answer.

Problem 4-11A ***Effects of Adjusting Entries on the Accounting Equation*** **LO 5**
Refer to the information provided for Lewis and Associates in Problem 4-10A.

Required

Prepare a table to summarize the required adjusting entries as they affect the accounting equation. Use the format in Exhibit 3-1. Identify each adjustment by letter.

Alternate Multi-Concept Problems

Problem 4-12A ***Cash and Accrual Income Statements for a Manufacturer*** **LO 2, 3**
Marie's Catering makes sandwiches for vending machines. The sandwiches are delivered to the vendor on the same day that they are made. The following events took place during the first year of operations.

a. On the first day of the year, issued common stock for a $20,000 cash investment and a $10,000 investment of equipment. The equipment is expected to last 10 years and will be worthless at the end of that time.

b. Purchased a delivery truck at the beginning of the year at a cost of $14,000 cash. The truck is expected to last five years and will be worthless at the end of that time.

(continued)

c. Made and sold 50,000 sandwiches during the first year of operations. The costs incurred to make the sandwiches are (1) $800 monthly rent on a facility that included utilities and insurance, (2) $25,000 of meat, cheese, bread, and condiments (all food was purchased on account, and $4,000 is still unpaid at year-end even though all of the food has been used), and (3) $35,000 paid in salaries and wages to employees and supervisors.

d. Paid $12,000 for part-time office staff salaries.

e. Sold all sandwiches on account for $2 each. As of year-end, $25,000 is still due from the vendors.

Required

1. How much revenue will Marie's Catering recognize under the cash basis and under the accrual basis?
2. Explain how accountants apply the revenue recognition principle to Marie's small business. What conditions would allow Marie's to use the cash method to recognize revenue?
3. Prepare an income statement according to the accrual method. Ignore income taxes.

Problem 4-13A *Revenue Recognition on the Percentage-of-Completion and Production Methods* LO 3, 4

Judy Darling owns a diamond mine in South Africa. While vacationing on an island in the Caribbean, she discussed with Marty Jones a recent dig that yielded $1.5 million of raw diamonds. The product is stored with an agent until a buyer is located. The agent expects it to take about two and a half years to sell all of the diamonds. Judy's company spent $1 million to extract the diamonds in 2004.

Marty's company constructs airplane runways and hangars. He is in the process of building a runway for the island and expects to incur the following costs over the next two and one-half years:

2004	$400,000
2005	500,000
2006	100,000

Local residents and the government have already paid Marty $1 million in 2004 and will pay another $500,000 when the project is completed in 2006.

Required

Explain the difference between revenue and cash flow for Judy and Marty. How much revenue will each recognize in 2004, 2005, and 2006?

Problem 4-14A *Revenue and Expense Recognition and Closing Entries* LO 3, 4, 7

Two years ago, Sue Stern opened an audio book rental shop. Sue reports the following accounts on her income statement:

Sales	$84,000
Advertising expense	10,500
Salaries expense	12,000
Depreciation on tapes	5,000
Rent expense	18,000

These amounts represent two years of revenue and expenses. Sue has asked you how she can tell how much of the income is from the first year and how much is from the second year of business. She provides the following additional data:

a. Sales in the second year are triple those of the first year.

b. Advertising expense is for a $1,500 opening promotion and weekly ads in the newspaper.

c. Salaries represent one employee who was hired eight months ago. No raises have been granted.

d. Rent has not changed since the shop opened.

Required

1. Prepare income statements for Years 1 and 2.
2. Prepare the closing entries for each year. Prepare a short explanation for Sue about the purpose of closing temporary accounts.

Problem 4-15A ***Ten-Column Work Sheet and Closing Entries (Appendix)*** **LO 5, 7, 8**

The unadjusted trial balance for Forever Green Landscaping on August 31, 2004, follows:

GENERAL LEDGER

SPREADSHEET

FOREVER GREEN LANDSCAPING
UNADJUSTED TRIAL BALANCE
AUGUST 31, 2004

Cash	$ 6,460	
Accounts Receivable	23,400	
Supplies on Hand	1,260	
Prepaid Insurance	3,675	
Equipment	28,800	
Accumulated Depreciation—Equipment		$ 9,200
Buildings	72,000	
Accumulated Depreciation—Buildings		16,800
Accounts Payable		10,500
Notes Payable		10,000
Capital Stock		40,000
Retained Earnings		42,100
Service Revenue		14,200
Advertising Expense	1,200	
Gasoline and Oil Expense	1,775	
Wage and Salary Expense	4,230	
Totals	$142,800	$142,800

Required

1. Enter the unadjusted trial balance in the first two columns of a 10-column work sheet.
2. Enter the necessary adjustments in the appropriate columns of the work sheet for each of the following:
   a. A count of the supplies on hand at the end of August reveals a balance of $730.
   b. The company paid $4,200 in cash on May 1, 2004, for a two-year insurance policy.
   c. The equipment has a four-year estimated useful life and no salvage value.
   d. The buildings have an estimated useful life of 30 years and no salvage value.
   e. The company leases space in its building to another company. The agreement requires the tenant to pay Forever Green $700 on the 10th of each month for the previous month's rent.
   f. Wages and salaries earned by employees at the end of August but not yet paid amount to $3,320.
   g. The company signed a six-month promissory note on August 1, 2004. Interest at an annual rate of 12% and the principal amount of $10,000 are due on February 1, 2005.
3. Complete the remaining columns of the work sheet.
4. Assume that Forever Green closes its books at the end of each month before preparing financial statements. Prepare the necessary closing entries at August 31, 2004.

Problem 4-16A ***Ten-Column Work Sheet and Financial Statements (Appendix)*** **LO 5, 6, 8**

The following unadjusted trial balance is available for Tenfour Trucking Company on January 31, 2004:

GENERAL LEDGER

TENFOUR TRUCKING COMPANY
UNADJUSTED TRIAL BALANCE
JANUARY 31, 2004

Cash	$ 27,340	
Accounts Receivable	41,500	
Prepaid Insurance	18,000	
Warehouse	40,000	
Accumulated Depreciation—Warehouse		$ 21,600
Truck Fleet	240,000	
Accumulated Depreciation—Truck Fleet		112,500
Land	20,000	

(continued)

Accounts Payable		$ 32,880
Notes Payable		50,000
Interest Payable		4,500
Customer Deposits		6,000
Capital Stock		100,000
Retained Earnings		40,470
Freight Revenue		165,670
Gas and Oil Expense	$ 57,330	
Maintenance Expense	26,400	
Wage and Salary Expense	43,050	
Dividends	20,000	
Totals	$533,620	$533,620

Required

1. Enter the unadjusted trial balance in the first two columns of a 10-column work sheet.
2. Enter the necessary adjustments in the appropriate columns of the work sheet for each of the following:
   - **a.** Prepaid insurance represents the cost of a 24-month policy purchased on January 1, 2004.
   - **b.** The warehouse has an estimated useful life of 20 years and an estimated salvage value of $4,000.
   - **c.** The truck fleet has an estimated useful life of six years and an estimated salvage value of $15,000.
   - **d.** The promissory note was signed on January 1, 2003. Interest at an annual rate of 9% and the principal of $50,000 are due on December 31, 2004.
   - **e.** The customer deposits represent amounts paid in advance by new customers. A total of $4,500 of the balance in Customer Deposits was earned during January 2004.
   - **f.** Wages and salaries earned by employees at the end of January but not yet paid amount to $8,200.
   - **g.** Income taxes are accrued at a rate of 30% at the end of each month.
3. Complete the remaining columns of the work sheet.
4. Prepare in good form the following financial statements:
   - **a.** Income statement for the month ended January 31, 2004
   - **b.** Statement of retained earnings for the month ended January 31, 2004
   - **c.** Balance sheet at January 31, 2004
5. Compute Tenfour's current ratio. What does this ratio tell you about the company's liquidity?
6. Explain why it is not possible to compute a gross profit ratio for Tenfour. Describe a ratio that you believe would be a meaningful measure of profitability for a trucking company. Feel free to "invent" a ratio if you think it would be a meaningful measure of profitability.

Cases

Reading and Interpreting Financial Statements

http://www.winnebagoind.com
http://www.monacocoach.com

Case 4-1 ***Comparing Two Companies in the Same Industry: Winnebago Industries and Monaco Coach Corporation*** **LO 3, 4, 5**

Refer to the financial information for Winnebago Industries and Monaco Coach Corporation in Appendices A and B at the end of the book.

Required

1. Neither company reports on its balance sheet an account titled "Accounts Receivable." Identify the account or accounts on each company's balance sheet that is equivalent to Accounts Receivable.
2. What dollar amount does each company report in Prepaid Expenses on its balance sheet at the end of 2001? When the benefits from this asset expire in the future this account will be credited and an expense account will be debited. For each company, identify the account or accounts on its income statement that you would expect to be debited.

3. On its balance sheet, Winnebago Industries reports a "Property and Equipment" account and deducts from it "Accumulated Depreciation." How does this way of presenting the long-term tangible assets differ from the approach used by Monaco Coach on its balance sheet? Does Monaco Coach disclose the same type of information elsewhere in the annual report? If so, where? Why do you think these companies use different approaches to report this information?

Case 4-2 *Reading and Interpreting McDonald's Notes—Revenue Recognition* LO 3

http://www.mcdonalds.com

Refer to the excerpt on page 158 where McDonald's explains how it recognizes franchise fees as revenue.

Required

1. At what points in time does McDonald's recognize revenue from its franchised restaurants?
2. When are continuing fees recognized as revenue by McDonald's? Does the way in which McDonald's recognizes these fees as revenue seem to be in agreement with the revenue recognition principle?
3. When are initial fees recognized as revenue by McDonald's? Does the way in which McDonald's recognizes these fees as revenue seem to be in agreement with the revenue recognition principle?
4. Refer to McDonald's income statement on page 149. How important are franchise fees as a form of revenue for the company? Support your answer with any necessary computations.

Case 4-3 *Reading and Interpreting Winnebago Industries' Notes—Revenue Recognition* LO 3

http://www.winnebagoind.com

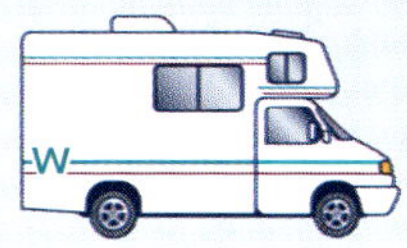

Refer to Winnebago Industries' first note, "Nature of Business and Significant Accounting Policies," and specifically the section that discusses revenue recognition.

Required

1. At what point in time does Winnebago Industries recognize revenue?
2. Explain what "dealer floor plan receivables" are to Winnebago Industries.
3. How and when does Winnebago Industries recognize revenue from dealer floor plan receivables?

Case 4-4 *Reading and Interpreting Sears, Roebuck's Notes—Revenue Recognition* LO 3

http://www.sears.com

The following excerpt is taken from the Sears, Roebuck and Co. 2001 annual report: "Additionally, the Company sells extended service contracts with terms of coverage between 12 and 60 months. Revenue from the sale of these contracts is deferred and amortized over the lives of the contracts while the service costs are expensed as incurred."

Required

1. Why do retailers recognize the revenue over the life of the service contract even though cash is received at the time of the sale?
2. If a product is sold in Year 1 for $2,500, including a $180 service contract that will cover three years, how much revenue is recognized in Years 1, 2, and 3? (Assume a straight-line approach.) What corresponding account can you look for in the financial statements to determine the amount of service contract revenue that will be recognized in the future?

Making Financial Decisions

Case 4-5 *The Use of Net Income and Cash Flow to Evaluate a Company* LO 2, 3, 4

DECISION MAKING

After you have gained five years of experience with a large CPA firm, one of your clients, Duke Inc., asks you to take over as chief financial officer for the business. Duke advises its clients on the purchase of software products and assists them in installing the programs on their computer systems. Because the business is relatively new (it began servicing clients in January 2004), its accounting records are somewhat limited. In fact, the only statement available is an income statement for the first year:

(continued)

DUKE INC.
STATEMENT OF INCOME
FOR THE YEAR ENDED DECEMBER 31, 2004

Revenues		$1,250,000
Expenses:		
Salaries and wages	$480,000	
Supplies	65,000	
Utilities	30,000	
Rent	120,000	
Depreciation	345,000	
Interest	138,000	
Total expenses		1,178,000
Net income		$ 72,000

Based on its relatively modest profit margin of 5.76% (net income of $72,000 divided by revenues of $1,250,000), you are concerned about joining the new business. To alleviate your concerns, the president of the company is able to give you the following additional information:

a. Clients are given 90 days to pay their bills for consulting services provided by Duke. On December 31, 2004, $230,000 of the revenues is yet to be collected in cash.

b. Employees are paid on a monthly basis. Salaries and wages of $480,000 include the December payroll of $40,000, which will be paid on January 5, 2005.

c. The company purchased $100,000 of operating supplies when it began operations in January. The balance of supplies on hand at December 31 amounts to $35,000.

d. Office space is rented in a downtown high-rise building at a monthly rental of $10,000. When the company moved into the office in January, it prepaid its rent for the next 18 months, beginning January 1, 2004.

e. On January 1, 2004, Duke purchased its own computer system and related accessories at a cost of $1,725,000. The estimated useful life of the system is five years.

f. The computer system was purchased by signing a three-year, 8% note payable for $1,725,000 on the date of purchase. The principal amount of the note and interest for the three years are due on January 1, 2007.

Required

1. Based on the income statement and the additional information given, prepare a statement of cash flows for Duke for 2004. (*Hint:* Simply list all of the cash inflows and outflows that relate to operations.)

2. On the basis of the income statement given and the statement of cash flows prepared in part 1, do you think it would be a wise decision on your part to join the company as its chief financial officer? Include in your response any additional questions that you believe are appropriate to ask before joining the company.

Case 4-6 *Depreciation* LO 4

DECISION MAKING

Jenner Inc., a graphic arts studio, is considering the purchase of computer equipment and software for a total cost of $18,000. Jenner can pay for the equipment and software over three years at the rate of $6,000 per year. The equipment is expected to last 10 to 20 years, but because of changing technology, Jenner believes it may need to replace the system as soon as three to five years. A three-year lease of similar equipment and software is available for $6,000 per year. Jenner's accountant has asked you to recommend whether the company should purchase or lease the equipment and software and to suggest the length of the period over which to depreciate the software and equipment if the company makes the purchase.

Required

Ignoring the effect of taxes, would you recommend the purchase or the lease? Why? Referring to the definition of *depreciation,* what is the appropriate useful life to use for the equipment and software?

Accounting and Ethics: What Would You Do?

Case 4-7 *Revenue Recognition and the Matching Principle* LO 2, 3, 4, 5

Listum & Sellum Inc. is a medium-size midwestern real estate company. It was founded five years ago by its two principal stockholders, Willie Listum and Dewey Sellum. Willie is president of the company, and Dewey is vice-president of sales. Listum & Sellum has enjoyed tremendous growth since its inception by aggressively seeking out listings for residential real estate and paying a very generous commission to the selling agent.

The company receives a 6% commission for selling a client's property and gives two thirds of this, or 4% of the selling price, to the selling agent. For example, if a house sells for $100,000, Listum & Sellum receives $6,000 and pays $4,000 of this to the selling agent. At the time of the sale, the company records a debit of $6,000 to Accounts Receivable and a credit of $6,000 to Sales Revenue. The accounts receivable is normally collected within 30 days. Also at the time of sale, the company debits $4,000 to Commissions Expense and credits Commissions Payable for the same amount. Sales agents are paid by the 15th of the month following the month of the sale. In addition to the commissions expense, Listum & Sellum's other two major expenses are advertising of listings in local newspapers and depreciation of the company fleet of Cadillacs (Dewey has always believed that all of the sales agents should drive Cadillacs). The newspaper ads are taken for one month, and the company has until the 10th of the following month to pay that month's bill. The automobiles are depreciated over four years (Dewey doesn't believe that any salesperson should drive a car that is more than four years old).

Due to a downturn in the economy in the Midwest, sales have been sluggish for the first 11 months of the current year, which ends on June 30. Willie is very disturbed by the slow sales this particular year because a large note payable to the local bank is due in July and the company plans to ask the bank to renew the note for another three years. Dewey seems less concerned by the unfortunate timing of the recession and has some suggestions as to how they can "paint the rosiest possible picture for the banker" when they go for the loan extension in July. In fact, he has some very specific recommendations for you as to how to account for transactions during June, the last month in the fiscal year.

You are the controller for Listum & Sellum and have been treated very well by Willie and Dewey since joining the company two years ago. In fact, Dewey insists that you personally drive the top-of-the-line Cadillac. Following are his suggestions:

> First, for any sales made in June, we can record the 6% commission revenue immediately but delay recording the 4% commission expense until July, when the sales agent is paid. We record the sales at the same time we always have, the sales agents get paid when they always have, the bank sees how profitable we have been, we get our loan, and everybody is happy!
>
> Second, since we won't be paying our advertising bills for the month of June until July 10, we can just wait until then to record the expense. The timing seems perfect, given that we are to meet with the bank for the loan extension on July 8.
>
> Third, since we will be depreciating the fleet of Caddys for the year ending June 30, how about just changing the estimated useful life on them to eight years instead of four years? We won't say anything to the sales agents; no need to rile them up about having to drive their cars for eight years. Anyhow, the change to eight years would just be for accounting purposes. In fact, we could even switch back to four years for accounting purposes next year. Likewise, the changes in recognizing commission expense and advertising expense don't need to be permanent either; these are just slight bookkeeping changes to help us get over the hump!

Required

1. Explain why each of the three proposed changes in accounting will result in an increase in net income for the year ending June 30.
2. Identify any concerns you have with each of the three proposed changes in accounting from the perspective of generally accepted accounting principles.
3. Identify any concerns you have with each of the three proposed changes in accounting from an ethical perspective.
4. What would you do? Draft your response to Willie and Dewey in the form of a business memo.

Case 4-8 *Advice to a Potential Investor* LO 4

Century Company was organized 15 months ago as a management consulting firm. At that time, the owners invested a total of $50,000 cash in exchange for stock. Century purchased equipment for $35,000 cash and supplies to be used in the business. The equipment is expected to last seven years with no salvage value. Supplies are purchased on account and paid for in the month after the purchase. Century normally has about $1,000 of supplies on hand. Its client base has increased

(continued)

so dramatically that the president and chief financial officer have approached an investor to provide additional cash for expansion. The balance sheet and income statement for the first year of business are presented below:

CENTURY COMPANY
BALANCE SHEET
DECEMBER 31, 2004

Assets		Liabilities and Owners' Equity	
Cash	$10,100	Accounts payable	$ 2,300
Accounts receivable	1,200	Common stock	50,000
Supplies	16,500	Retained earnings	10,500
Equipment	35,000		
Total	$62,800	Total	$62,800

CENTURY COMPANY
INCOME STATEMENT
FOR THE YEAR ENDED DECEMBER 31, 2004

Revenues		$82,500
Wages and salaries	$60,000	
Utilities	12,000	72,000
Net income		$10,500

Required

The investor has asked you to look at these financial statements and give an opinion about Century's future profitability. Are the statements prepared in accordance with generally accepted accounting principles? If not, explain why. Based on only these two statements, what would you advise? What additional information would you need in order to give an educated opinion?

Internet Research Case

Case 4-9 *McDonald's*

http://www.mcdonalds.com

INTERNET

McDonald's is the largest and best known fast-food supplier in the world, with worldwide (systemwide) sales of over $40 billion in 2001. Even with operations in 121 countries, the company continues to pursue almost limitless opportunities internationally.

Review the chapter-opening introduction to McDonald's and the Business Strategy box. Then go to McDonald's Web site, examine its most recent annual report, and research how this company can fulfill management's goals of ever greater market share, higher customer satisfaction, and increased profitability.

1. McDonald's total revenues include all the revenues from company-operated restaurants and a portion of the revenues of franchisees' restaurants.
   - **a.** Looking at the latest year's income statement, what are McDonald's total revenues for the current year?
   - **b.** McDonald's also refers to total "systemwide" sales in the management section of its annual report. By looking at the current year's annual report, find its systemwide sales for the current year and indicate what that term refers to.
   - **c.** Why is total revenue reported in the income statement and systemwide revenue not reported there? That is, why can't McDonald's place systemwide sales on its income statement?
2. Look at McDonald's Web site and its latest annual report carefully. How is the company working to achieve its strategic goals mentioned above? In what financial statements and line items might you see these goals reflected?

Solutions to Key Terms Quiz

- 18 Recognition (p. 150)
- 25 Historical cost (p. 151)
- 11 Current value (p. 151)
- 21 Cash basis (p. 153)
- 14 Accrual basis (p. 153)
- 2 Revenues (p. 156)
- 17 Revenue recognition principle (p. 156)
- 6 Percentage-of-completion method (p. 157)
- 3 Production method (p. 158)
- 8 Installment method (p. 158)
- 23 Matching principle (p. 159)
- 26 Expenses (p. 160)
- 4 Adjusting entries (p. 160)
- 12 Straight-line method (p. 162)
- 24 Contra account (p. 162)
- 13 Deferral (p. 168)
- 19 Deferred expense (p. 168)
- 7 Deferred revenue (p. 168)
- 15 Accrual (p. 168)
- 22 Accrued liability (p. 168)
- 10 Accrued asset (p. 168)
- 27 Accounting cycle (p. 173)
- 1 Work sheet (p. 173)
- 9 Real accounts (p. 174)
- 20 Nominal accounts (p. 174)
- 5 Closing entries (p. 174)
- 16 Interim statements (p. 176)

Part I

Integrative Problem

Completing Financial Statements, Computing Ratios, Comparing Accrual vs. Cash Income, and Evaluating the Company's Cash Needs

SPREADSHEET

Mountain Home Health Inc. provides home nursing services in the Great Smoky Mountains of Tennessee. When contacted by a client or referred by a physician, nurses visit with the patient and discuss needed services with the physician.

Mountain Home Health earns revenue from patient services. Most of the revenue comes from billing either insurance companies, the state of Tennessee, or the Medicare program. Amounts billed are recorded in the Billings Receivable account. Insurance companies, states, and the federal government do not fully fund all procedures. For example, the state of Tennessee pays an average 78% of billed amounts. Mountain Home Health has already removed the uncollectible amounts from the Billings Receivable account and reports it and Medical Services Revenue at the net amount. Services provided but not yet recorded totaled $16,000, net of allowances for uncollectible amounts. The firm earns a minor portion of its total revenue directly from patients in the form of cash.

Employee salaries, medical supplies, depreciation, and gasoline are the major expenses. Employees are paid every Friday for work performed during the Saturday-to-Friday pay period. Salaries amount to $800 per day. In 2003, December 31 falls on a Wednesday. Medical supplies (average use of $1,500 per week) are purchased periodically to support health care coverage. The inventory of supplies on hand on December 31 amounted to $8,653.

The firm owns five automobiles (all purchased at the same time) that average 50,000 miles per year and are replaced every three years. They typically have no residual value. The building has an expected life of 20 years with no residual value. Straight-line depreciation is used on all firm assets. Gasoline costs, which are a cash expenditure, average \$375 per day. The firm purchases a three-year, extended warranty contract to cover maintenance costs. The contract costs \$9,000 (assume equal use each year).

On December 29, 2003, Mountain Home Health declared a dividend of \$10,000, payable on January 15, 2004. The firm makes annual payments of principal and interest each June 30 on the mortgage. The interest rate on the mortgage is 6%.

The following unadjusted trial balance is available for Mountain Home Health on December 31, 2003.

MOUNTAIN HOME HEALTH, INC.
UNADJUSTED TRIAL BALANCE
DECEMBER 31, 2003

	Debit	Credit
Cash	\$ 77,400	
Billings Receivable (net)	151,000	
Medical Supplies	73,000	
Extended Warranty	3,000	
Automobiles	90,000	
Accumulated Depreciation—Automobiles		\$ 60,000
Building	200,000	
Accumulated Depreciation—Building		50,000
Accounts Payable		22,000
Dividend Payable		10,000
Mortgage Payable		100,000
Capital Stock		100,000
Additional Paid-In Capital		50,000
Retained Earnings		99,900
Medical Services Revenue		550,000
Salary and Wages Expense	\$ 288,000	
Gasoline Expense	137,500	
Utilities Expense	12,000	
Dividends	10,000	
Totals	\$1,041,900	\$1,041,900

Required

1. Set up T accounts for each of the accounts listed on the trial balance. Based on the information provided, set up any other T accounts that will be needed to prepare adjusting entries.
2. Post the year-end adjusting entries directly to the T accounts, but do not bother to put the entries in journal format first.
3. Prepare a statement of income and a statement of retained earnings for Mountain Home Health for the year ended December 31, 2003.
4. Prepare a balance sheet for Mountain Home Health as of December 31, 2003.
5. Compute the following as of December 31, 2003: **a.** Working capital **b.** Current ratio
6. Which of the adjusting entries might cause a difference between cash and accrual based income?
7. Mary Francis, controller of Mountain Home, became concerned about the company's cash flow after talking to a local bank loan officer. The firm tries to maintain a 7-week supply of cash to meet the demands of payroll, medical supply purchases, and gasoline. Determine the amount of cash Mountain Home needs to meet the 7-week supply.

Focus on Financial Results

With over 4,200 stores in the United States, Canada, France, Germany, Japan, and the United Kingdom, Gap Inc. has become a global success story. This youth-oriented retailer of casual fashions, accessories, and personal care products encompasses three distinct brands—Gap®, Banana Republic®, and Old Navy®, in addition to its popular GapKids® and babyGap® lines. The company, like various other retailers, has found the Internet to be a highly efficient and economical alternative to selling its products in stores.

Also, like many of its competitors, Gap Inc. found 2001 to be a most challenging year. Although net sales continued to grow and reach record levels, the company reported a net loss for the year, as pictured on the accompanying income statement, or consolidated statement of operations as it is called. As a retailer, Gap Inc. measures its success in terms of what it earns from buying and selling merchandise. To understand how a company could increase its sales and yet incur a loss, one needs to look no further than the second line on the income statement: cost of goods sold. Two years earlier, this key expense was only 58% of net sales, meaning that only 58 cents of every sales dollar went to cover the cost of the products sold. However, in 2001, over 70 cents of every sales dollar was needed to cover cost of goods sold. With only minor increases in the percentage of each sales dollar spent on operating expenses and interest expense, it is clear that Gap Inc. will need to find ways to lower its product costs if it is to return to profitability.

Gap Inc.'s 2001 Annual Report

Consolidated Statements of Operations

($ in thousands except share and per share amounts)	52 Weeks Ended Feb. 2, 2002	Percentage to Sales	53 Weeks Ended Feb. 3, 2001	Percentage to Sales	52 Weeks Ended Jan. 29, 2000	Percentage to Sales
Net sales	$ 13,847,873	100.0%	$ 13,673,460	100.0%	$ 11,635,398	100.0%
Costs and expenses						
Cost of goods sold and occupancy expenses	9,704,389	70.1	8,599,442	62.9	6,775,262	58.2
Operating expenses	3,805,968	27.5	3,629,257	26.5	3,043,432	26.2
Interest expense	109,190	0.8	74,891	0.5	44,966	0.4
Interest income	(13,315)	(0.1)	(12,015)	0.0	(13,211)	(0.1)
Earnings before income taxes	241,641	1.7	1,381,885	10.1	1,784,949	15.3
Income taxes	249,405	1.8	504,388	3.7	657,884	5.6
Net earnings (loss)	$ (7,764)	(0.1%)	$ 877,497	6.4%	$ 1,127,065	9.7%
Weighted-average number of shares—basic	860,255,419		849,810,658		853,804,924	
Weighted-average number of shares—diluted	860,255,419		879,137,194		895,029,176	
Earnings (loss) per share—basic	$ (0.01)		$ 1.03		$ 1.32	
Earnings (loss) per share—diluted (a)	(0.01)		1.00		1.26	

See Notes to Consolidated Financial Statements.

(a) Diluted losses per share for the 52 weeks ended February 2, 2002, are computed using the basic weighted average number of shares outstanding and exclude 13,395,045 dilutive shares as their effects are antidilutive when applied to losses.

Net sales have increased by slightly more than 19% from fiscal years 1999 to 2001.

Cost of goods sold and occupancy expenses have increased by more than 43% from fiscal years 1999 to 2001.

You're in the Driver's Seat

http://www.gap.com

If you were a manager for Gap Inc., you would want the cost of goods sold percentage to decrease and sales to continue to increase. How would the use of the company's Web site to market its products be likely to affect Gap Inc.'s sales and cost of goods sold and the relationship between them?

LEARNING OBJECTIVES

After studying this chapter, you should be able to:

LO 1 Demonstrate an understanding of how wholesalers and retailers account for sales of merchandise. (p. 223)

LO 2 Explain the differences between periodic and perpetual inventory systems. (p. 228)

LO 3 Demonstrate an understanding of how wholesalers and retailers account for cost of goods sold. (p. 230)

LO 4 Explain the importance of internal control to a business. (p. 234)

LO 5 Describe the basic internal control procedures. (p. 237)

LO 6 Describe the various documents used in recording purchases of merchandise and their role in controlling cash disbursements (Appendix). (p. 246)

THE INCOME STATEMENT FOR A MERCHANDISER

To this point, we have concentrated on the accounting for businesses that sell *services.* Banks, hotels, airlines, health clubs, real estate offices, law firms, and accounting firms are all examples of service companies. In this chapter we turn to accounting by merchandisers. Both retailers and wholesalers are merchandisers. They purchase inventory in finished form and hold it for resale. This is in contrast to manufacturers' inventory, which takes three different forms: raw materials, work in process, and finished goods. (Accounting for the three different forms of inventory for a manufacturer is more complex and is covered in a follow-up course to this one.) We focus in this chapter on accounting for merchandise, that is, inventory held by either a wholesaler or a retailer.

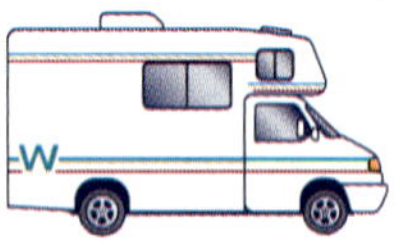

From Concept to Practice 5.1

Reading Winnebago Industries' Annual Report

Is **Winnebago Industries** *a manufacturer, a wholesaler, or a retailer? What items in the annual report can you cite to support your answer?*

A *condensed* multiple-step income statement for Grizzly Hardware Stores is presented in Exhibit 5-1. First note the period covered by the statement: for the year ended December 31, 2004. Grizzly ends its fiscal year on December 31; however, many merchandisers end their *fiscal year* on a date other than December 31. Retailers often choose a date toward the end of January because the busy holiday shopping season is over and time can be devoted to closing the records and preparing financial statements. For example, **Gap Inc.** ends its fiscal year on the Saturday closest to January 31, and **Circuit City** closes its books on the last day of February each year.

http://www.gap.com
http://www.circuitcity.com

We will concentrate on the first two items on Grizzly's statement: net sales and cost of goods sold. The major difference between this income statement and that for a serv-

Exhibit 5-1
Condensed Income Statement for a Merchandiser

GRIZZLY HARDWARE STORES
INCOME STATEMENT
FOR THE YEAR ENDED DECEMBER 31, 2004

Net sales	$100,000
Cost of goods sold	60,000
Gross margin	$ 40,000
Selling and administrative expenses	29,300
Net income before tax	$ 10,700
Income tax expense	4,280
Net income	$ 6,420

ice company is the inclusion of cost of goods sold. Because a service company does not sell a product, it does not report cost of goods sold. On the income statement of a merchandising company, cost of goods sold is deducted from net sales to arrive at gross margin or gross profit.

Gross margin as a percentage of net sales is a common analytical tool for merchandise companies. Analysts compare the gross margin percentages for various periods or for several companies and express concern if a company's gross margin is dropping. Every industry in the retail sector tracks its average gross margin ratio, and its average sales per square foot of retail space. Analysts can use these facts to see how one company is performing in comparison with others in the same industry. If analysts looked at Gap Inc.'s 10-year summary in its annual report, they would find that sales per square foot have ranged from a high of $548 in 1999 to a low of $394 in 2001.

http://www.gap.com

NET SALES OF MERCHANDISE

The first section of Grizzly's income statement is presented in Exhibit 5-2. Two deductions—for sales returns and allowances and sales discounts—are made from sales revenue to arrive at **net sales.** Sales revenue, or simply sales, is a *representation of the inflow of assets,* either cash or accounts receivable, from the sale of merchandise during the period:

LO 1 Demonstrate an understanding of how wholesalers and retailers account for sales of merchandise.

Exhibit 5-2

Net Sales Section of the Income Statement

GRIZZLY HARDWARE STORES
PARTIAL INCOME STATEMENT
FOR THE YEAR ENDED DECEMBER 31, 2004

Sales revenue	$103,500	
Less: Sales returns and allowances	2,000	
Sales discounts	1,500	
Net sales		$100,000

- In a merchandising business, *cash sales* are recorded daily in the journal and are based on the total amount shown on the cash register tape. For example, suppose that the cash register tape in the paint department of Grizzly Hardware Stores shows sales on March 31, 2004, of $350. The transaction is recorded in the journal as follows:

Net sales Sales revenue less sales returns and allowances and sales discounts.

Mar. 31	Cash	350	
	Sales Revenue		350
	To record daily cash receipts in paint department.		

Assets	=	Liabilities	+	Owners' Equity
+350				+350

- *Sales on credit* do not result in the immediate inflow of cash but in an increase in accounts receivable, a promise by the customer to pay cash at a later date. The entry to record a May 4 sale of tools on credit for $125 is recorded as follows:

May 4	Accounts Receivable	125	
	Sales Revenue		125
	To record sale on credit in tools department.		

Assets	=	Liabilities	+	Owners' Equity
+125				+125

Sales Returns and Allowances

The cornerstone of marketing is to satisfy the customer. Most companies have standard policies that allow the customer to *return* merchandise within a stipulated period of http://www.nordstrom.com

time. Nordstrom, the Seattle-based retailer, has a very liberal policy regarding returns. That policy has, in large measure, fueled its growth. A company's policy might be that a customer who is not completely satisfied can return the merchandise anytime within 30 days of purchase for a full refund. Alternatively, the customer may be given an *allowance* for spoiled or damaged merchandise—that is, the customer keeps the merchandise but receives a credit for a certain amount in the account balance. Typically, a single account, **Sales Returns and Allowances,** is used to account both for returns and for allowances. If the customer has already paid for the merchandise, either a cash refund is given or the credit amount is applied to future purchases.

Sales Returns and Allowances Contra-revenue account used to record both refunds to customers and reductions of their accounts.

The accounting for a return or allowance depends on whether the customer is given a cash refund or credit on an account. Assume that Grizzly's paint department gives a $25 cash refund on spoiled paint returned by a customer. The entry follows:

Apr. 25	Sales Returns and Allowances	25	
	Cash		25
	To record return of spoiled paint by customer for a cash refund.		

Assets	=	Liabilities	+	Owners' Equity
−25				−25

Study Tip

Recall Accumulated Depreciation, a contra account introduced in Chapter 4. It reduces a long-term asset. In other cases, such as this one involving sales, a contra account reduces an income statement account.

Sales Returns and Allowances is a *contra-revenue* account. A contra account has a balance opposite to its related account and is deducted from that account on the statement. Thus, the effect of the debit to this account is the same as if Sales Revenue had been reduced (debited) directly.

The purpose of this entry is to reduce the amount of previously recorded sales. So why didn't we simply reduce Sales Revenue for $25? The reason is that management needs to be able to *monitor* the amount of returns and allowances. If Sales Revenue is reduced for returns and at some point we need to determine the total dollars of returns for the period, we would need to add up all of the individual decreases to this account. A much more efficient method is to split the sales revenue into two accounts, one that includes only sales and another that includes only returns. Thus, the total amount of returns is readily available, and decision making is more efficient and effective.

The previous entry illustrates the accounting for a return of merchandise. The same account is normally used when a credit is given and the customer keeps the merchandise. Assume that on May 7 the customer that made the $125 purchase from Grizzly on May 4 notifies it that one of the purchased tools is defective. Grizzly agrees to reduce the customer's unpaid account by $10 because of the defect. The entry to record the allowance follows:

May 7	Sales Returns and Allowances	10	
	Accounts Receivable		10
	To record allowance given for defective merchandise.		

Assets	=	Liabilities	+	Owners' Equity
−10				−10

The Sales Returns and Allowances account gives management and stockholders an important piece of data: that merchandise is being returned or is not completely acceptable. It does not answer the following questions, however. Why is the merchandise being returned? Why are customers getting partial refunds? Is the merchandise shoddy? Are salespeople too aggressive? Should the store's liberal policy regarding returns be changed? Answers to these questions require management to look beyond the accounting data.

Trade Discounts and Quantity Discounts

Trade discount Selling price reduction offered to a special class of customers.

Various types of discounts to the list price are given to customers. A **trade discount** is a selling price reduction offered to a special class of customers. For example, Grizzly's plumbing department might offer a special price to building contractors. The difference between normal selling price and this special price is called a *trade discount.* A **quantity discount** is sometimes offered to customers who are willing to buy in large quantities.

Quantity discount Reduction in selling price for buying a large number of units of a product.

Trade discounts and quantity discounts are *not* recorded in the accounts. Although a company might track the amount of these discounts for control purposes, the reason for ignoring the quantity and trade discounts in the accounting records is that the list price is not the actual selling price. The *net* amount is a more accurate reflection of the amount of a sale. For example, assume that Grizzly gives a 20% discount from the normal selling price to any single customer who buys between 10 and 25 kitchen sinks, and a 30% discount on purchases of more than 25 sinks. The list price for each unit is $200. The selling price and the related journal entry for a customer's purchase of 40 sinks on July 2 are as follows:

List price	$ 200
Less: 30% quantity discount	60
Selling price	$ 140
× Number of sinks sold	× 40
Sales revenue	$5,600

July 2	Accounts Receivable	5,600	
	Sales Revenue		5,600
	To record sale of 40 kitchen sinks at list price less 30% quantity discount.		

Assets	=	Liabilities	+	Owners' Equity
+5,600				+5,600

Credit Terms and Sales Discounts

Most companies have a standard credit policy. Special notation is normally used to indicate a particular firm's policy for granting credit. For example, credit terms of *n/30* mean that the *net* amount of the selling price, that is, the amount determined after deducting any returns or allowances, is due within 30 days of the date of the invoice. *Net, 10 EOM* means that the net amount is due anytime within 10 days after the end of the month in which the sale took place.

Study Tip

To help you calculate amounts to enter in the end-of-chapter transactions, remember how to interpret these terms.

Another common element of the credit terms offered to customers is sales discounts, a reduction from the selling price given for early payment. For example, assume that Grizzly offers a building contractor credit terms of *1/10, n/30.* This means that the customer may deduct 1% from the selling price if the bill is paid within 10 days of the date of the invoice. Normally the discount period begins with the day *after* the invoice date. If the customer does not pay within the first 10 days, the full invoice amount is due within 30 days. Finally, note that the use of *n* for *net* in this notation is really a misnomer. Although the amount due is net of any returns and allowances, it is the *gross* amount that is due within 30 days. That is, no discount is given if the customer does not pay early.

How valuable to the customer is a 1% discount for payment within the first 10 days? Assume that a $1,000 sale is made. If the customer pays at the end of 10 days, the cash paid will be $990, rather than $1,000, a net savings of $10. The customer has saved $10 by paying 20 days earlier than required by the 30-day term. If we assume 360 days in a year, there are 360/20 or 18 periods of 20 days each in a year. Thus, a savings of $10 for 20 days is equivalent to a savings of $10 times 18, or $180 for the year. An annual return of $180/$990, or 18.2%, would be difficult to match with any other type of investment. In fact, a customer might want to consider borrowing the money to pay off the account early.

Some companies record sales *net* of any discounts for early payment; others record the *gross* amount of sales and then track sales discounts separately. Because the effect on the accounting equation does not differ between the two methods, we will concern ourselves only with the *gross method,* which assumes that customers will not necessarily take advantage of the discount offered for early payment. Sales discounts are rarely material, and companies do not normally disclose the method used on their financial statements.

Assume a sale on June 10 of $1,000 with credit terms of 2/10, net 30. The entry at the time of the sale is as follows:

June 10	Accounts Receivable	1,000	
	Sales Revenue		1,000
	To record sale on account, terms 2/10, net 30.		

Assets	=	Liabilities	+	Owners' Equity
+1,000				+1,000

If the customer pays after the discount period, the accountant simply makes an entry to record the receipt of $1,000 cash and the reduction of accounts receivable. However, assume the customer pays its account on June 20, within the discount period. The following entry would be made:

June 20	Cash	980	
	Sales Discounts	20	
	Accounts Receivable		1,000
	To record collection on account.		

Assets	=	Liabilities	+	Owners' Equity
+ 980				−20
−1,000				

Sales Discounts Contra-revenue account used to record discounts given customers for early payment of their accounts.

The **Sales Discounts** account is a *contra-revenue* account and thus reduces owners' equity, as shown in the accounting equation above. Also note in Exhibit 5-2 that sales discounts are deducted from sales on the income statement.

THE COST OF GOODS SOLD

The cost of goods sold section of the income statement for Grizzly is shown in Exhibit 5-3. We will soon turn to each line item in this section. First let us take a look at the basic model for cost of goods sold.

Business Strategy

Returning to the Fundamentals

By its own admission in the 2001 annual report, Gap Inc. strayed from three fundamental principles that had made it successful in the past: offering the right products in the right assortments, staying consistent in what it does, and keeping things simple. In that same report, the company's management vowed to return to the fundamentals of merchandising in all three of its flagship operations: Gap®, Old Navy®, and Banana Republic®.

At the end of fiscal 2001, management felt that it had laid the groundwork to support each of its brands financially. Part of its strategy involved measures designed to manage its costs and cash more wisely. Certainly, improvement was warranted in the control of product costs, given the 7% increase in the ratio of cost of sales to net sales during 2001. Stockholders could look optimistically to the cash on hand at the end of the year: a 250% increase to a balance of over $1 billion at year-end. This was coupled with a reduction in forecasted capital spending during 2002 to a manageable $400 million.

Management concludes its message to stockholders with the reassuring thought that Gap, Old Navy, and Banana Republic are three of the most well-known brands in retail. Time will tell whether a return to fundamentals will put the company back on course and satisfy its customers and stockholders in the process.

Source: Gap Inc. 2001 annual report.

Exhibit 5-3

Cost of Goods Sold Section of the Income Statement

GRIZZLY HARDWARE STORES PARTIAL INCOME STATEMENT FOR THE YEAR ENDED DECEMBER 31, 2004			
Cost of goods sold:			
Inventory, January 1, 2004		$15,000	
Purchases	$65,000		
Less: Purchase returns and allowances	1,800		
Purchase discounts	3,700		
Net purchases	$59,500		
Add: Transportation-in	3,500		
Cost of goods purchased		63,000	
Cost of goods available for sale		$78,000	
Less: Inventory, December 31, 2004		18,000	
Cost of goods sold			$60,000

The Cost of Goods Sold Model

The recognition of cost of goods sold as an expense is an excellent example of the *matching principle.* Sales revenue represents the *inflow* of assets, in the form of cash and accounts receivable, from the sale of products during the period. Likewise, cost of goods sold represents the *outflow* of an asset, inventory, from the sale of those same products. The company needs to match the revenue of the period with one of the most important costs necessary to generate the revenue, the *cost* of the merchandise sold.

It may be helpful in understanding cost of goods sold to realize what it is *not. Cost of goods sold is not necessarily equal to the cost of purchases of merchandise during the period.* Except in the case of a new business, a merchandiser starts the year with a certain stock of inventory on hand, called *beginning inventory.* For Grizzly, beginning inventory is the dollar cost of merchandise on hand on January 1, 2004. During the year, Grizzly purchases merchandise. When the cost of goods purchased is added to beginning inventory, the result is **cost of goods available for sale.** Just as the merchandiser starts the period with an inventory of merchandise on hand, a certain amount of *ending inventory* is usually on hand at the end of the year. For Grizzly, this is its inventory on December 31, 2004.

Cost of goods available for sale Beginning inventory plus cost of goods purchased.

As shown in Exhibit 5-4, think of cost of goods available for sale as a "pool" of costs to be distributed between what we sold and what we did not sell. If we subtract from

Exhibit 5-4

The Cost of Goods Sold Model

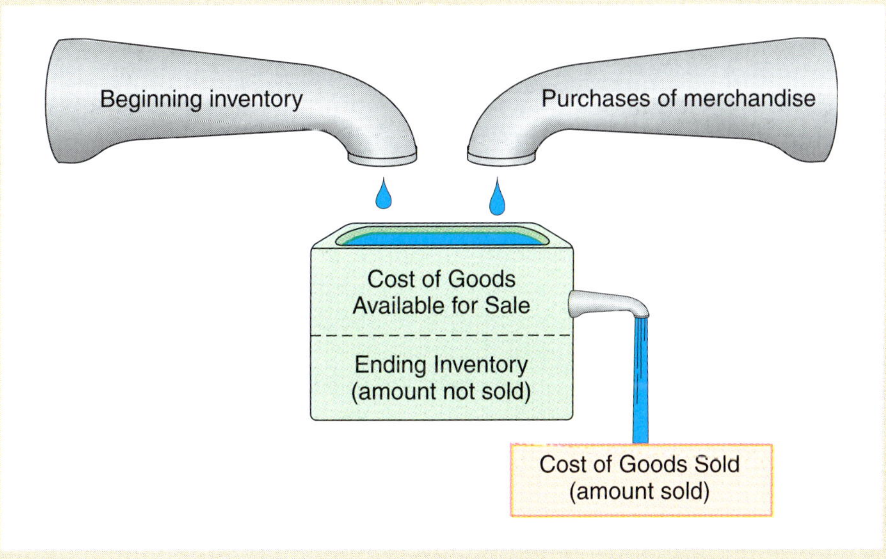

Cost of goods sold Cost of goods available for sale minus ending inventory.

the pool the cost of what we did *not* sell, the *ending inventory,* we will have the amount we *did* sell, the **cost of goods sold.** Cost of goods sold is simply the difference between the cost of goods available for sale and the ending inventory:

Beginning inventory	What is on hand to start the period
+ Purchases	What was acquired for resale during the period
= Cost of goods available for sale	The "pool" of costs to be distributed
− Ending inventory	What was not sold during the period and therefore is on hand to start the next period
= Cost of goods sold	What was sold during the period

The cost of goods sold model for a merchandiser is illustrated in Exhibit 5-5. The amounts used for the illustration are taken from the cost of goods sold section of Grizzly's income statement as shown in Exhibit 5-3. Notice that ending inventory exceeds beginning inventory by $3,000. That means that the cost of goods purchased exceeds cost of goods sold by that same amount. Indeed, a key point for stockholders, bankers, and other users is whether inventory is building up, that is, whether a company is not selling as much inventory during the period as it is buying. A buildup may indicate that the company's products are becoming less desirable or that prices are becoming uncompetitive.

Exhibit 5-5 The Cost of Goods Sold Model: Example for a Merchandiser

Description	Item	Amount
Merchandise on hand to start the period	Beginning inventory	$15,000
Acquisitions of merchandise during the period	+ Cost of goods purchased	63,000
The pool of merchandise available for sale during the period	= Cost of goods available for sale	$78,000
Merchandise on hand at end of period	− Ending inventory	(18,000)
The expense recognized on the income statement	= Cost of goods sold	$60,000

A $3,000 excess of ending inventory over beginning inventory means the company bought $3,000 more than it sold ($63,000 bought versus $60,000 sold).

Inventory Systems: Perpetual and Periodic

LO 2 Explain the differences between periodic and perpetual inventory systems.

Perpetual system System in which the Inventory account is increased at the time of each purchase and decreased at the time of each sale.

Periodic system System in which the Inventory account is updated only at the end of the period.

Before we look at the journal entries to account for cost of goods sold, it is necessary to understand the difference between the periodic and the perpetual inventory systems. All businesses use one of these two distinct approaches to account for inventory. With the **perpetual system,** the Inventory account is updated *perpetually,* or after each sale or purchase of merchandise. Conversely, with the **periodic system,** the Inventory account is updated only at the end of the *period.*

In a perpetual system, every time goods are purchased, the Inventory account is increased, with a corresponding increase in Accounts Payable for a credit purchase or a decrease in the Cash account for a cash purchase. In addition to recognizing the increases in Accounts Receivable or Cash and in Sales Revenue when goods are sold, the accountant also records an entry to recognize the *cost* of the goods sold and the decrease in the cost of inventory on hand:

Cost of Goods Sold	xxx	
Inventory		xxx
To record the sale of inventory under perpetual system.		

Assets	=	Liabilities	+	Owners' Equity
−xxx				−xxx

Thus, at any point during the period, the inventory account is up to date. It has been increased for the cost of purchases during the period and reduced for the cost of the sales.

Why don't all companies use the procedure we just described, the perpetual system? Depending on the volume of inventory transactions, that is, purchases and sales of merchandise, a perpetual system can be extremely costly to maintain. Historically, businesses that have a relatively small volume of sales at a high unit price have used perpetual systems. For example, dealers in automobiles, furniture, appliances, and jewelry normally use a perpetual system. Each purchase of a unit of merchandise, such as an automobile, can be easily identified and an increase recorded in the Inventory account. When the auto is sold, the dealer can easily determine the cost of the particular car sold by looking at a perpetual inventory record.

Can you imagine, however, a similar system for a supermarket or a hardware store? Consider a checkout stand in a grocery store. Through the use of a cash register tape, the sales revenue for that particular stand is recorded at the end of the day. Because of the tremendous volume of sales of various items of inventory, from cans of vegetables to boxes of soap, it may not be feasible to record the cost of goods sold every time a sale takes place. This illustrates a key point in financial information: the cost of the information should never exceed its benefit. If a store manager had to stop and update the records each time a can of Campbell's soup was sold, the retailer's business would obviously be disrupted.

To a certain extent, the ability of mass merchandisers to maintain perpetual inventory records has improved with the advent of point-of-sale terminals. When a cashier runs a can of corn over the sensing glass at the checkout stand and the bar code is read, the company's computer receives a message that a can of corn has been sold. In some companies, however, updating the inventory record is in units only and is used as a means to determine when a product needs to be reordered. The company still relies on a periodic system to maintain the *dollar* amount of inventory. In the remainder of this chapter, we limit our discussion to the periodic system. We discuss the perpetual system in detail in Chapter 6.

Accounting for Your Decisions

You Are the Entrepreneur

A year ago, you and your brother launched a running shoe company in your garage. You buy shoes from four of the major manufacturers and sell them over the phone. Your accountant suggests that you use a perpetual inventory system. Should you?

ANS: The periodic inventory system has the following advantages: The Inventory account is updated only once per year, not after every purchase; the inventory is physically counted on the last day of each period to determine ending inventory; and its cost is low. By operating out of your garage, you are focusing on keeping administrative costs down. A perpetual inventory system would be more costly and would not provide enough extra benefits at low volume. Your decision may change as your business grows, particularly if you began taking orders over the Internet.

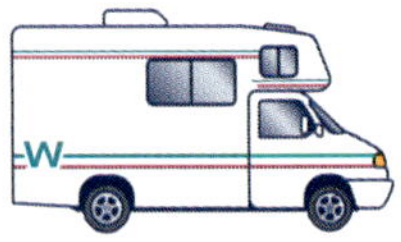

From Concept to Practice 5.2

Understanding Winnebago Industries' Inventory System

Given the nature of its products, would you expect that **Winnebago Industries** *uses a perpetual or a periodic inventory system? Explain your answer.*

Beginning and Ending Inventories in a Periodic System

In a periodic system, the Inventory account is *not* updated each time a sale or purchase is made. Throughout the year, the Inventory account contains the amount of merchandise on hand at the beginning of the year. The account is adjusted only at the end of the year. A company using the periodic system must physically *count* the units of inventory on hand at the end of the period. The number of units of each product is then multiplied by the cost per unit, to determine the dollar amount of ending inventory. Refer to Exhibit 5-3 for Grizzly Hardware Stores. The procedure just described was used to determine its ending inventory of $18,000. Because one period's ending inventory is the next period's beginning inventory, the beginning inventory of $15,000 was based on the count at the end of the prior year.

In summary, the ending inventory in a periodic system is determined by counting the merchandise, not by looking at the Inventory account at the end of the period. The periodic system results in a trade-off. Use of the periodic system reduces record keeping but at the expense of a certain degree of control. Losses of merchandise due to theft, breakage, spoilage, or other reasons may go undetected in a periodic system because management may assume that all merchandise not on hand at the end of the year was sold. In a retail store, some of the merchandise may have been shoplifted rather than sold. In contrast, with a perpetual inventory system, a count of inventory at the end of the period serves as a *control device.* For example, if the Inventory account shows a balance of $45,000 at the end of the year but only $42,000 of merchandise is counted, management is able to investigate the discrepancy. No such control feature exists in a periodic system.

In addition to the loss of control, the use of a periodic system presents a dilemma when a company wants to prepare *interim* financial statements. Because most companies that use a periodic system find it cost-prohibitive to count the entire inventory more than once a year, they use estimation techniques to determine inventory for monthly or quarterly statements. (These techniques are discussed in Chapter 6.)

The Cost of Goods Purchased

LO 3 Demonstrate an understanding of how wholesalers and retailers account for cost of goods sold.

Transportation-in Adjunct account used to record freight costs paid by the buyer.

The cost of goods purchased section of Grizzly's income statement is shown in Exhibit 5-6. The company purchased $65,000 of merchandise during the period. Two amounts are deducted from purchases to arrive at net purchases: purchase returns and allowances of $1,800 and purchase discounts of $3,700. The cost of $3,500 incurred by Grizzly to ship the goods to its place of business is called **transportation-in** and is added to net purchases of $59,500 to arrive at the cost of goods purchased of $63,000. Another name for transportation-in is *freight-in.*

Exhibit 5-6

Cost of Goods Purchased

GRIZZLY HARDWARE STORES
PARTIAL INCOME STATEMENT
FOR THE YEAR ENDED DECEMBER 31, 2004

Purchases	$65,000	
Less: Purchase returns and allowances	1,800	
Purchase discounts	3,700	
Net purchases	$59,500	
Add: Transportation-in	3,500	
Cost of goods purchased		$63,000

Purchases Assume that Grizzly buys merchandise on account from one of its wholesalers at a cost of $4,000. **Purchases** is the temporary account used in a periodic inventory system to record acquisitions of merchandise. The journal entry to record the purchase follows:

Purchases Account used in a periodic inventory system to record acquisitions of merchandise.

Feb. 8	Purchases	4,000	
	Accounts Payable		4,000
	To record the purchase of merchandise on account.		

Assets	=	Liabilities	+	Owners' Equity
		+4,000		−4,000

It is important to understand that Purchases is *not* an asset account. It is included in the income statement as an integral part of the calculation of cost of goods sold and is therefore shown as a reduction of owners' equity in the accounting equation. Because Purchases is a temporary account, it is closed at the end of the period.

Purchase Returns and Allowances We discussed returns and allowances earlier in the chapter from the seller's point of view. From the standpoint of the buyer, purchase returns and allowances are reductions in the cost to purchase merchandise. Rather than record these reductions directly in the Purchases account, the accountant uses a separate account. The account, **Purchase Returns and Allowances,** is a *contra account* to Purchases. Because Purchases has a normal debit balance, the normal balance in Purchase Returns and Allowances is a credit balance. The use of a contra account allows management to monitor the amount of returns and allowances. For example, a large number of returns during the period relative to the amount purchased may signal that the purchasing department is not buying from reputable sources.

Purchase Returns and Allowances Contra-purchases account used in a periodic inventory system when a refund is received from a supplier or a reduction given in the balance owed to a supplier.

Suppose that Grizzly returns $850 of merchandise to a wholesaler for credit on its account. The return decreases both liabilities and purchases. Note that because a return reduces purchases, it actually *increases* net income and thus also increases owners' equity. The journal entry follows:

Sept. 6	Accounts Payable	850	
	Purchase Returns and Allowances		850
	To record the return of merchandise for credit to account.		

Assets	=	Liabilities	+	Owners' Equity
		−850		+850

The entry to record an allowance for merchandise retained rather than returned is the same as the entry for a return.

Study Tip

Earlier in the chapter we saw that the normal balance for the Sales Returns and Allowances account is a debit. Because sales and purchases are opposites, it stands to reason that the normal balance for Purchase Returns and Allowances is a credit.

Purchase Discounts Discounts were discussed earlier in the chapter, from the seller's viewpoint. Merchandising companies often purchase inventory on terms that allow for a cash discount for early payment, such as 2/10, net 30. To the buyer, a cash discount is called a *purchase discount* and results in a reduction of the cost to purchase

Accounting for Your Decisions

You Are the President

You are the president of a mail-order computer business. Your company buys computers and related parts directly from manufacturers and sells them to consumers via direct mail. Recently, you have noticed an increase in the amount of purchase returns and allowances relative to the amount of purchases. What are some possible explanations for this increase?

ANS: Any number of explanations are possible. It is possible that the products are being damaged while in transit. Or it may be that the company has changed suppliers and the merchandise is not of the quality expected. Or the employees are becoming more demanding in what they accept than they used to be.

merchandise. The same two methods that are used to account for sales discounts are used to account for purchase discounts. Regardless of the method used, management must monitor the amount of purchase discounts taken as well as those opportunities missed by not taking advantage of the discounts for early payment. Because the effect on the accounting equation does not differ between the gross and the net methods, we will limit our discussion to the use of the *gross method.*

Assume a purchase of merchandise on March 13 for $500, with credit terms of 1/10, net 30. The entry at the time of the purchase is as follows:

Mar. 13	Purchases	500	
	Accounts Payable		500
	To record purchase on account, terms 1/10, net 30.		

Assets	=	Liabilities	+	Owners' Equity
		+500		−500

If the company does not pay within the discount period, the accountant simply makes an entry to record the payment of $500 cash and the reduction of accounts payable. However, assume the company does pay its account on March 23, within the discount period. The following entry would be made:

Mar. 23	Accounts Payable	500	
	Cash		495
	Purchase Discounts		5
	To record payment on account.		

Assets	=	Liabilities	+	Owners' Equity
−495		−500		+5

Purchase Discounts Contra-purchases account used to record reductions in purchase price for early payment to a supplier.

The **Purchase Discounts** account is contra to the Purchases account and thus increases owners' equity, as shown in the accounting equation above. Also note in Exhibit 5-6 that purchase discounts are deducted from purchases on the income statement. Finally, note that the effect on the income statement is the same as illustrated earlier for a purchase return: because purchases are reduced, net income is increased.

FOB destination point Terms that require the seller to pay for the cost of shipping the merchandise to the buyer.

FOB shipping point Terms that require the buyer to pay for the shipping costs.

Shipping Terms and Transportation Costs The *cost principle* governs the recording of all assets. All costs necessary to prepare an asset for its intended use should be included in its cost. The cost of an item to a merchandising company is not necessarily limited to its invoice price. For example, any sales tax paid should be included in computing total cost. Any transportation costs incurred by the buyer should likewise be included in the cost of the merchandise.

The buyer does not always pay to ship the merchandise. This depends on the terms of shipment. Goods are normally shipped either **FOB destination point** or **FOB shipping point;** *FOB* stands for *free on board.* When merchandise is shipped FOB destination point, it is the responsibility of the seller to deliver the products to the buyer. Thus, the seller either delivers the product to the customer or pays a trucking firm, railroad, or other carrier to transport it. Alternatively, the agreement between the buyer and the seller may provide for the goods to be shipped FOB shipping point. In this case, the merchandise is the responsibility of the buyer as soon as it leaves the seller's premises. When the terms of shipment are FOB shipping point, the buyer incurs transportation costs.

Refer to Exhibit 5-6. Transportation-in represents the freight costs Grizzly paid for in-bound merchandise. These costs are added to net purchases, as shown in the exhibit, and increase the cost of goods purchased. Assume that on delivery of a shipment of goods, Grizzly pays an invoice for $300 from the Rocky Mountain Railroad. The terms of shipment are FOB shipping point. The entry on the books of Grizzly follows:

May 10	Transportation-in	300	
	Cash		300
	To record the payment of freight costs.		

Assets	=	Liabilities	+	Owners' Equity
−300				−300

The total of net purchases and transportation-in is called the *cost of goods purchased.* Transportation-in will be closed at the end of the period. In summary, cost of goods purchased consists of the following:

Purchases
Less: Purchase returns and allowances
        Purchase discounts
Equals: Net purchases
Add: Transportation-in
Equals: Cost of goods purchased

How should the *seller* account for the freight costs it pays when the goods are shipped FOB destination point? This cost, sometimes called *transportation-out,* is not an addition to the cost of purchases of the seller but is instead one of the costs necessary to *sell* the merchandise. Transportation-out is classified as a *selling expense* on the income statement.

Shipping Terms and Transfer of Title to Inventory Terms of shipment take on additional significance at the end of an accounting period. It is essential that a company establish a proper cutoff at year-end. For example, what if Grizzly purchases merchandise that is in transit at the end of the year? To whom does the inventory belong, Grizzly or the seller? The answer depends on the terms of shipment. If goods are shipped FOB destination point, they remain the legal property of the seller until they reach their destination. Alternatively, legal title to goods shipped FOB shipping point passes to the buyer as soon as the seller turns the goods over to the carrier.

The example in Exhibit 5-7 is intended to summarize our discussion about shipping terms and ownership of merchandise. The example involves a shipment of merchandise in transit at the end of the year. Horton, the seller of the goods, pays the transportation charges only if the terms are FOB destination point. Horton records a sale for goods in transit at year-end, however, only if the terms of shipment are FOB shipping point. If Horton does not record a sale, because the goods are shipped FOB destination point, the inventory appears on its December 31 balance sheet. Grizzly, the buyer, pays freight costs only if the goods are shipped FOB shipping point. Only in this situation does Grizzly record a purchase of the merchandise and include it as an asset on its December 31 balance sheet.

The Closing Process for a Merchandiser

The closing process serves two purposes. First, all income statement accounts are returned to a zero balance to start the next accounting period. Second, net income and

Exhibit 5-7

Shipping Terms and Transfer of Title to Inventory

FACTS On December 28, 2004, Horton Wholesale ships merchandise to Grizzly Hardware Stores. The trucking company delivers the merchandise to Grizzly on January 2, 2005. Grizzly's fiscal year-end is December 31.

		If Merchandise Is Shipped FOB	
COMPANY		DESTINATION POINT	SHIPPING POINT
Horton (seller)	Pay freight costs?	Yes	No
	Record sale in 2004?	No	Yes
	Include inventory on balance sheet at December 31, 2004?	Yes	No
Grizzly (buyer)	Pay freight costs?	No	Yes
	Record purchase in 2004?	No	Yes
	Include inventory on balance sheet at December 31, 2004?	No	Yes

Accounting for Your Decisions

You Are the Manager

You manage the student bookstore. To get ready for the spring term, in December you order a large shipment of books from a publisher, with terms of FOB shipping point. On December 31, the books have not yet arrived. Should this shipment be included in the year-end inventory count even though it is not on hand to count? Assume a periodic inventory system.

ANS: Because the books were shipped FOB shipping point, they should be included in the year-end count even though they are not on hand to count. You should review the purchase invoice to determine the number of books ordered and the unit costs.

dividends of the period are transferred to the Retained Earnings account. Many different procedural approaches may be used to close the accounts of a merchandising company. The following list indicates the normal balance in each of the accounts used in a periodic system and whether the account is closed with a debit or a credit:

ACCOUNT	NORMAL BALANCE	CLOSED WITH A
Sales Revenue	Credit	Debit
Sales Returns and Allowances	Debit	Credit
Sales Discounts	Debit	Credit
Purchases	Debit	Credit
Purchase Returns and Allowances	Credit	Debit
Purchase Discounts	Credit	Debit
Transportation-in	Debit	Credit

Two-Minute Review

On April 13, 2004, Bitterroot Distributing sells merchandise to Darby Corp. for $1,000 with credit terms of 2/10, net 30. On April 19, Darby returns $150 of defective merchandise and receives a credit on account from Bitterroot. On April 23, Darby pays the amount due.

1. *Prepare the necessary entries on Bitterroot's books from April 13 through April 23. Assume Bitterroot uses a periodic inventory system.*
2. *Prepare the necessary entries on Darby's books from April 13 through April 23. Assume Darby uses a periodic inventory system.*

Answers on page 241.

AN INTRODUCTION TO INTERNAL CONTROL

LO 4 Explain the importance of internal control to a business.

Internal control system Policies and procedures necessary to ensure the safeguarding of an entity's assets, the reliability of its accounting records, and the accomplishment of overall company objectives.

An employee of a large auto parts warehouse routinely takes spare parts home for personal use. A payroll clerk writes and signs two checks for an employee and then splits the amount of the second check with the worker. Through human error, an invoice is paid for merchandise never received from the supplier. These cases sound quite different from one another, but they share one important characteristic. They all point to a deficiency in a company's internal control system. An **internal control system** consists of the policies and procedures necessary to ensure the safeguarding of an entity's assets, the reliability of its accounting records, and the accomplishment of its overall objectives.

Three assets are especially critical to the operation of a merchandising company: cash, accounts receivable, and inventory. Activities related to these three assets compose the operating cycle of a business. Cash is used to buy inventory, the inventory is eventually sold, and assuming a sale on credit, the account receivable from the customer is collected. We turn now to the ways in which a company attempts to *control* the assets at its disposal. This section serves as an introduction to the important topic of internal control, which is explored further at appropriate points in the book. For example, controls to safeguard cash are discussed in Chapter 7.

The Report of Management: Showing Responsibility for Control

Modern business is characterized by absentee ownership. In most large corporations, it is impossible for the owners—the stockholders—to be actively involved in the daily affairs of the business. Professional managers have the primary responsibility for the business's smooth operation. They are also responsible for the content of the financial statements.

Most annual reports now include a **report of management** to the stockholders. A typical management report, in this case for **Gap Inc.,** is shown in Exhibit 5-8. The first paragraph of the report clearly spells out management's responsibility for the financial information presented in the annual report. The second paragraph refers to the system

Report of management Written statement in the annual report indicating the responsibility of management for the financial statements.

Exhibit 5-8 Report of Management—Gap Inc.

Management's Report on Financial Information

Management is responsible for the integrity and consistency of all financial information presented in the Annual Report. The financial statements have been prepared in accordance with generally accepted accounting principles in the United States of America and necessarily include certain amounts based on Management's best estimates and judgments.

In fulfilling its responsibility for the reliability of financial information, Management has established and maintains accounting systems and procedures appropriately supported by internal accounting controls. Such controls include the selection and training of qualified personnel, an organizational structure providing for division of responsibility, communication of requirement for compliance with approved accounting control and business practices and a program of internal audit. The extent of the Company's system of internal accounting control recognizes that the cost should not exceed the benefits derived and that the evaluation of those factors requires estimates and judgments by Management. Although no system can ensure that all errors or irregularities have been eliminated, Management believes that the internal accounting controls in use provide reasonable assurance, at reasonable cost, that assets are safeguarded against loss from unauthorized use or disposition, that transactions are executed in accordance with Management's authorization and that the financial records are reliable for preparing financial statements and maintaining accountability for assets. The financial statements of the Company have been audited by Deloitte & Touche LLP, independent auditors whose report appears below.

The Audit and Finance Committee (the "Committee") of the Board of Directors is comprised solely of directors who are not officers or employees of the Company. The Committee is responsible for recommending to the Board of Directors the selection of independent auditors. It meets periodically with Management, the independent auditors and the internal auditors to ensure that they are carrying out their responsibilities. The Committee also reviews and monitors the financial, accounting and auditing procedures of the Company in addition to reviewing the Company's financial reports. Deloitte & Touche LLP and the internal auditors have full and free access to the Committee, with and without Management's presence.

First Paragraph
Management's responsibility for the financial information

Second Paragraph
System of internal controls

Third Paragraph
Role of the Audit and Finance Committee

Which Way to Go?
Whose Inventory Is It?

On June 30, its fiscal year end, Taz Industries is notified that a very large shipment of raw materials was sent that day and is expected to arrive at the Taz plant in Springfield, Illinois, on July 8. The supplier has shipped the goods FOB shipping point. Taz's management would like to avoid recording the inventory because they would also have to record the payable. They are concerned about the already high level of liabilities on the year-end balance sheet and the impact on the debt-to-equity ratio (Total debt/Total equity).

Generally, at Taz Industries, the liability is not recognized until the invoice is received, which is usually three days after the seller ships the materials. Since the invoice will not arrive until July 3, management has decided not to include the inventory and the related liability on its June 30 balance sheet.

Do you agree with management's decision in this situation? Who owns the inventory? Who should recognize it on its balance sheet—Taz Industries or the supplier?

of internal controls within the company. One of the features of Gap Inc.'s internal control system is the use of an **internal audit staff.** Most large corporations today have a full-time staff of internal auditors who have the responsibility for evaluating the entity's internal control system.

The primary concern of the independent public accountants, or external auditors, is whether the financial statements have been presented fairly. Internal auditors focus more on the efficiency with which the organization is run. They are responsible for periodically reviewing both accounting and administrative controls, which we discuss later in this chapter. The internal audit staff also helps to ensure that the company's policies and procedures are followed.

The second paragraph of the report states that the company's independent public accountants have audited the company's financial statements. The management of most corporations would consider it cost-prohibitive for the auditors to verify the millions of transactions recorded in a single year. Instead, the auditors rely to a certain degree on the system of internal control as assurance that transactions are properly recorded and reported. The degree of reliance that they are able to place on the company's internal controls is a significant factor in determining the extent of their testing. The stronger the system of internal control, the less testing is necessary. A weak system of internal control requires that the auditors extend their tests of the records.

Internal audit staff Department responsible for monitoring and evaluating the internal control system.

Board of directors Group composed of key officers of a corporation and outside members responsible for general oversight of the affairs of the entity.

Audit committee Board of directors subset that acts as a direct contact between stockholders and the independent accounting firm.

Foreign Corrupt Practices Act Legislation intended to increase the accountability of management for accurate records and reliable financial statements.

The **board of directors** of a corporation usually consists of key officers of the corporation as well as a number of directors whom it does not directly employ. For example, Gap Inc.'s board of 11 directors consists of 5 insiders and 6 outsiders. The outsiders often include presidents and key executive officers of other corporations and sometimes business school faculty. The board of directors is elected by the stockholders.

As referred to in the third paragraph of Exhibit 5-8, the **audit committee** (or the Audit and Finance Committee for Gap Inc.) of the board of directors provides direct contact between the stockholders and the independent accounting firm. Audit committees have assumed a much more active role since the passage of the **Foreign Corrupt Practices Act** in 1977. This legislation was passed in response to a growing concern over various types of improprieties by top management, such as kickbacks to politicians and bribes of foreign officials. The act includes a number of provisions intended to increase the accountability of management and the board of directors to stockholders. According to the act, management is responsible for keeping accurate records, and various provisions deal with the system of internal controls necessary to ensure the safeguarding of assets and the reliability of the financial statements. Audit committees have become much more involved in the oversight of the financial reporting system since the enactment of the act.

From Concept to Practice 5.3

Reading Gap Inc.'s Management Report

Refer to management's report for Gap Inc. in Exhibit 5-8. What is the composition of its Audit and Finance Committee? Why do you think it is composed in this way?

The Control Environment

The success of an internal control system begins with the competence of the people in charge of it. Management's operating style will have a determinable impact on the effectiveness of various policies. An autocratic style in which a few key officers tightly control operations will result in an environment different from that of a decentralized organization in which departments have more freedom to make decisions. Personnel policies and practices form another factor in the internal control of a business. An appropriate system for hiring competent employees and firing incompetent ones is crucial to an efficient operation. After all, no internal control system will work very well if employees who are dishonest or poorly trained are on the payroll. On the other hand, too few people doing too many tasks defeats the purpose of an internal control system. Finally, the effectiveness of internal control in a business is influenced by the board of directors, particularly its audit committee.

© KEN REID/GETTY IMAGES/TAXIS

This woman is using the paper source document in her hand as a reference for entering data into the accounting system. From the standpoint of internal control, should she be the one who is ordering inventory, receiving it, and entering the information into the system? Is she authorized to make journal entries? If so, does her laptop have safeguards that prevent access by unauthorized personnel? These and other internal control procedures are part of the control environment within every company.

The Accounting System

An **accounting system** consists of all the methods and records used to accurately report an entity's transactions and to maintain accountability for its assets and liabilities. Regardless of the degree of computer automation, the use of a journal to record transactions is an integral part of all accounting systems. Refinements are sometimes made to the basic components of the system, depending on the company's needs. For example, most companies use specialized journals to record recurring transactions, such as sales of merchandise on credit.

An accounting system can be completely manual, fully computerized, or as is often the case, a mixture of the two. Internal controls are important to all businesses, regardless of the degree of automation of the accounting system. The system must be capable of handling both the volume and the complexity of transactions entered into by a business. Most businesses use computers because of the sheer volume of transactions. The computer is ideally suited to the task of processing large numbers of repetitive transactions efficiently and quickly.

The cost of computing has dropped so substantially that virtually every business can now afford a system. Today some computer software programs that are designed for home-based businesses cost under $100 and are meant to run on machines that cost less than $1,000. Inexpensive software programs that categorize expenses and print checks, produce financial statements, and analyze financial ratios are available.

Internal Control Procedures

LO 5 Describe the basic internal control procedures.

Accounting system Methods and records used to accurately report an entity's transactions and to maintain accountability for its assets and liabilities.

Administrative controls Procedures concerned with efficient operation of the business and adherence to managerial policies.

Accounting controls Procedures concerned with safeguarding the assets or the reliability of the financial statements.

Management establishes policies and procedures on a number of different levels to ensure that corporate objectives will be met. Some procedures are formalized in writing. Others may not be written but are just as important. Certain **administrative controls** within a company are more concerned with the efficient operation of the business and adherence to managerial policies than with the accurate reporting of financial information. For example, a company policy that requires all prospective employees to be interviewed by the personnel department is an administrative control. Other **accounting controls** primarily concern safeguarding assets and ensuring the reliability of the financial statements. We now turn to a discussion of some of the most important internal control procedures:

- Proper authorizations
- Segregation of duties
- Independent verification
- Safeguarding assets and records
- Independent review and appraisal
- The design and use of business documents

Proper Authorizations

Management grants specific departments the authority to perform various activities. Along with the *authority* goes *responsibility.* Most large organizations give the authority to hire new employees to the personnel department. Management authorizes the purchasing department to order goods and services for the company and the credit department to establish specific policies for granting credit to customers. By specifically authorizing certain individuals to carry out specific tasks for the business, management is able to hold these same people responsible for the outcome of their actions.

The authorizations for some transactions are general in nature; others are specific. For example, a cashier authorizes the sale of a book in a bookstore by ringing up the transaction (a general authorization). It is likely, however, that the bookstore manager's approval is required before a book can be returned (a specific authorization).

Segregation of Duties What might happen if one employee is given the authority both to prepare checks and to sign them? What could happen if a single employee is allowed to order inventory and receive it from the shipper? Or what if the cashier at a checkout stand also records the daily receipts in the journal? If the employee in each of these situations is honest and never makes mistakes, nothing bad will happen. However, if the employee is dishonest or makes human errors, the company can experience losses. These situations all point to the need for the segregation of duties, which is one of the most fundamental of all internal control procedures. Without segregation of duties, an employee is able not only to perpetrate a fraud but also to conceal it. A good system of internal control requires that the *physical custody* of assets be separated from the *accounting* for those same assets.

Like most internal control principles, the concept of segregation of duties is an ideal that is not always completely attainable. For example, many smaller businesses simply do not have adequate personnel to achieve complete segregation of key functions. In certain instances, these businesses need to rely on the direct involvement of the owners in the business and on independent verification.

Accounting for Your Decisions

You Are the Chief Financial Officer

You have been hired by the owner of Mt. Rainier Broom Company to come in and replace the out-of-date accounting systems with a system that uses modern technology. The first thing you notice is that the company's bookkeeper, Mavis, is in charge of collecting receivables, recording payments, ordering and receiving inventory, and preparing and signing checks. When you suggest to her that she has too many duties, she gets angry and appeals to the owner. The owner backs up Mavis and tells you to focus entirely on new accounting technology. What should you do?

ANS: Ever so politely, you should inform the owner and Mavis in a three-way meeting that your suggestion that Mavis not do all the accounting functions is not meant as an insult but is simply good internal control. Even if Mavis is as honest as they come, there is a good chance that she will make errors, which could result in losses to the company. By having at least two people involved in a transaction, the chances are excellent that an error will be caught by one or the other.

Independent Verification Related to the principle of segregation of duties is the idea of independent verification. The work of one department should act as a check on the work of another. For example, the physical count of the inventory in a perpetual inventory system provides such a check. The accounting department maintains the general ledger card for inventory and updates it as sales and purchases are made. The physical count of the inventory by an independent department acts as a check on the work of the accounting department. As another example, consider a bank reconciliation as a control device. The reconciliation of a company's bank account with the bank statement by someone not responsible for either the physical custody of cash or the cash records acts as an independent check on the work of these parties. (We will take a closer look at the use of a bank reconciliation as a control device in Chapter 7.)

Safeguarding Assets and Records Adequate safeguards must be in place to protect assets and the accounting records from losses of various kinds. Cash registers, safes, and lockboxes are important safeguards for cash. Secured storage areas with limited access are essential for the safekeeping of inventory. Protection of the accounting records against misuse is equally important. For example, access to a computerized accounting record should be limited to those employees authorized to prepare journal entries. This can be done with the use of a personal identification number and a password to access the system.

Independent Review and Appraisal A well-designed system of internal control provides for periodic review and appraisal of the accounting system as well as the people operating it. The group primarily responsible for review and appraisal of the system is the internal audit staff. Internal auditors provide management with periodic reports on the effectiveness of the control system and the efficiency of operations.

The Design and Use of Business Documents *Business documents* are the crucial link between economic transactions entered into by an entity and the accounting record of these events. They are often called *source documents.* Many of these are generated by the computer, but a few may be completed manually. The source document for the recognition of the expense of an employee's wages is the time card. The source documents for a sale include the sales order, the sales invoice, and the related shipping document. Business documents must be designed so that they capture all relevant information about an economic event. They are also designed to ensure that related transactions are properly classified.

Business documents themselves must be properly controlled. For example, a key feature for documents is a *sequential numbering system* just like you have for your personal checks. This system results in a complete accounting for all documents in the series and negates the opportunity for an employee to misdirect one. Another key feature of well-designed business documents is the use of *multiple copies.* The various departments involved in a particular activity, such as sales or purchasing, are kept informed of the status of outstanding orders through the use of copies of documents. This chapter's appendix provides an example of the use of business documents for a merchandiser.

Limitations on Internal Control

Internal control is a relative term. No system of internal control is totally foolproof. An entity's size affects the degree of control that it can obtain. In general, large organizations are able to devote a substantial amount of resources to safeguarding assets and records because these companies have the assets to justify the cost. Because the installation and maintenance of controls can be costly, an internal audit staff is a luxury that many small businesses cannot afford. The mere segregation of duties can result in added costs if two employees must be involved in a task previously performed by only one.

Segregation of duties can be effective in preventing collusion, but no system of internal control can ensure that it will not happen. It does no good to have one employee count the cash at the end of the day and another to record it if the two act in concert to steal from the company. Rotation of duties can help to lessen the likelihood for problems of this sort. An employee is less likely to collude with someone to steal if the assignment is a temporary one. Another control feature, a system of authorizations, is meaningless if management continually overrides it. Management must believe in a system of internal control enough to support it.

Intentional acts to misappropriate company assets are not the only problem. All sorts of human errors can weaken a system of internal control. Misunderstood instructions, carelessness, fatigue, and distraction can all lead to errors. A well-designed system of internal control should result in the best-possible people being hired to perform the various tasks, but no one is perfect.

Two-Minute Review

1. *Explain why an internal control system is important to the operation of a merchandising company.*
2. *Explain the difference between administrative controls and accounting controls.*
3. *Explain how the concept of segregation of duties involves an evaluation of costs versus benefits.*

Answers on page 242.

Ratios for Decision Making

By comparing the gross margin as a percentage of net sales (gross margin percentage) from one year to the next as shown below, positive or negative changes become apparent. When the percentage decreases, it indicates that a greater amount of each net sales dollar is needed to cover the cost of the merchandise sold, which leaves fewer dollars to cover the cost of other operating expenses.

When a company has a high (or an increasing) average sales per square foot of retail space ratio, it indicates more efficient use of the retail space available. A decreasing ratio or a ratio significantly lower than others in the industry indicates inefficient use of the retail space.

Reporting and Analyzing Financial Statement Information Related to a Company's Retail Sales

Balance Sheet	Income Statement	Statement of Cash Flows	Notes*

$$\text{Gross Margin Percentage} = \frac{\text{Gross Margin}}{\text{Net Sales}}$$

$$\text{Average Sales Per Square Foot of Retail Space} = \frac{\text{Net Sales}}{\text{Total Square Feet of Retail Space*}}$$

*This information may be found in the multi-year comparison provided in the annual report. Such comparisons may appear in the Financial Highlights section rather than in the Notes section.

Impact on the Financial Reports

Impact on the Financial Reports

BALANCE SHEET

Current Assets
Cash
Accounts receivable
Inventory
Noncurrent Assets
Current Liabilities
Accounts payable
Noncurrent Liabilities
Stockholders' Equity

INCOME STATEMENT

Revenues[a]
Sales revenue
(Sales returns and allowances)
(Sales discounts)
Expenses
Cost of goods sold[b]
Selling and administrative expenses (including transportation-out expenses)
Income tax expenses
Other
Net income

[a]Sales revenue − (Sales returns and allowances + Sales discounts) = Net sales; Net sales − Cost of goods sold = Gross margin.

[b]Purchases − (Purchase returns and allowances + Purchase discounts) = Net purchases; Beginning inventory + Net purchases + Transportation-in − Ending inventory = Cost of goods sold under the periodic inventory system.

(continued)

STATEMENT OF STOCKHOLDERS' EQUITY	STATEMENT OF CASH FLOWS	NOTES
Contributed Capital *Retained Earnings* Net income	*Operating Activities* Cash from sales and for purchases Cash received for accounts receivable Cash paid for accounts payable Cash paid for transportation-in and/or transportation-out Cash paid for selling and administrative expenses Cash paid for income taxes *Investing Activities* *Financing Activities* *Noncash Transactions*	

Answers to the Two-Minute Reviews

Two-Minute Review on Page 234

1.

Date	Account	Debit	Credit
Apr. 13	Accounts Receivable	1,000	
	Sales Revenue		1,000
	To record sale on credit.		

Assets	=	Liabilities	+	Owners' Equity
+1,000				+1,000

Date	Account	Debit	Credit
Apr. 19	Sales Returns and Allowances	150	
	Accounts Receivable		150
	To record return of defective merchandise for a credit on account.		

Assets	=	Liabilities	+	Owners' Equity
−150				−150

Date	Account	Debit	Credit
Apr. 23	Cash	833	
	Sales Discounts	17	
	Accounts Receivable		850
	To record collection on account.		

Assets	=	Liabilities	+	Owners' Equity
+833				−17
−850				

2.

Date	Account	Debit	Credit
Apr. 13	Purchases	1,000	
	Accounts Payable		1,000
	To record the purchase of merchandise on account.		

Assets	=	Liabilities	+	Owners' Equity
		+1,000		−1,000

Date	Account	Debit	Credit
Apr. 19	Accounts Payable	150	
	Purchase Returns and Allowances		150
	To record the return of merchandise for credit to account.		

Assets	=	Liabilities	+	Owners' Equity
		−150		+150

Date	Account	Debit	Credit
Apr. 23	Accounts Payable	850	
	Cash		833
	Purchases Discounts		17
	To record payment on account.		

Assets	=	Liabilities	+	Owners' Equity
−833		−850		+17

(continued)

Answers to the Two-Minute Reviews *(continued)*

Two-Minute Review on Page 240

1. *An effective system of internal controls is critical to protecting a merchandiser's investment in three of its major assets: cash, accounts receivable, and inventory. Without an effective system, these assets are subject to misuse.*
2. *Administrative controls are concerned with the efficient operation of a business and adherence to managerial policies. Alternatively, accounting controls deal with safeguarding assets and ensuring the reliability of the financial statements.*
3. *Involving more than one employee in a specific function reduces the likelihood of theft or other misuse of company assets. However, all businesses must decide whether the benefit of segregation of duties outweighs the additional cost of involving more than one employee in a specific function such as the preparation and distribution of the payroll.*

Warmup Exercises

Warmup Exercise 5-1 ***Net Sales*** **LO 1**

Victor Merchandising reported sales revenue, sales returns and allowances, and sales discounts of $57,000, $1500, and $900, respectively, in 2004.

Required

Prepare the net sales section of Victor's 2004 income statement.

Key to the Solution

Refer to Exhibit 5-2.

Warmup Exercise 5-2 ***Cost of Goods Sold*** **LO 3**

The following amounts are taken from Redfield Inc.'s records (all amounts are for 2004):

Inventory, January 1	$14,200
Inventory, December 31	10,300
Purchases	87,500
Purchase Discounts	4,200
Purchase Returns and Allowances	1,800
Transportation-in	4,500

Required

Prepare the cost of goods sold section of Redfield's 2004 income statement.

Key to the Solution

Refer to Exhibit 5-3.

Warmup Exercise 5-3 ***Internal Control*** **LO 5**

List the internal control procedures discussed in the text.

Key to the Solution

Refer to the section in the chapter that discusses internal control procedures.

Solutions to Warmup Exercises

Warmup Exercise 5-1

VICTOR MERCHANDISING
PARTIAL INCOME STATEMENT
FOR THE YEAR ENDED DECEMBER 31, 2004

Sales revenue	$57,000	
Less: Sales returns and allowances	1,500	
Sales discounts	900	
Net sales		$54,600

Warmup Exercise 5-2

REDFIELD INC.
PARTIAL INCOME STATEMENT
FOR THE YEAR ENDED DECEMBER 31, 2004

Inventory, January 1, 2004		$ 14,200	
Purchases	$87,500		
Less: Purchase returns and allowances	1,800		
Purchase discounts	4,200		
Net purchases	$81,500		
Add: Transportation-in	4,500		
Cost of goods purchased		86,000	
Cost of goods available for sale		$100,200	
Less: Inventory, December 31, 2004		10,300	
Cost of goods sold			$ 89,900

Warmup Exercise 5-3

1. Proper authorizations
2. Segregation of duties
3. Independent verification
4. Safeguarding assets and records
5. Independent review and appraisal
6. Design and use of business documents

Review Problem

WebTUTOR™ Advantage

Mickey's Marts, which operates a chain of department stores, uses the periodic inventory system. The cost of inventory on hand at January 1 amounts to $12,000, and on January 31, it is $9,500. The following transactions are entered into by Mickey's during January:

a. Purchased merchandise on account from various vendors for $25,000. All merchandise is bought with terms of 1/10, net 30. All purchases are recorded initially at the gross amount.

b. Reduced the total amount owed to vendors by $20,000. This is *not* the amount paid but the amount before taking the 1% discount. All accounts are paid within 10 days of the date of the invoice.

c. Recognized purchase returns and allowances of $1,900 during the month.

d. Recognized total sales of $42,000 for the month, of which $28,000 is cash sales and the remainder is on account.

e. Made collections on account of $17,000 for the month.

f. Applied $3,200 of sales returns and allowances for the month to customers' account balances.

g. Paid the freight cost of $2,700 on *incoming* purchases of merchandise.

Required

1. Prepare the necessary journal entries to record each of the transactions **a** through **g.**
2. Prepare a *partial* income statement for the month of January. The last line on the partial statement should be gross margin.

Solution to Review Problem

1. Journal entries:

		Debit	Credit
a.	Purchases	25,000	
	Accounts Payable		25,000
	To record purchases on account.		

Assets	=	Liabilities	+	Owners' Equity
		+25,000		−25,000

		Debit	Credit
b.	Accounts Payable	20,000	
	Purchase Discounts		200
	Cash		19,800
	To record payment of amounts owed on account, less 1% discount for early payment.		

Assets	=	Liabilities	+	Owners' Equity
−19,800		−20,000		+200

		Debit	Credit
c.	Accounts Payable	1,900	
	Purchase Returns and Allowances		1,900
	To record purchase returns and allowances for the month.		

Assets	=	Liabilities	+	Owners' Equity
		−1,900		+1,900

		Debit	Credit
d.	Cash	28,000	
	Accounts Receivable	14,000	
	Sales Revenue		42,000
	To record sales for the month.		

Assets	=	Liabilities	+	Owners' Equity
+28,000				+42,000
+14,000				

		Debit	Credit
e.	Cash	17,000	
	Accounts Receivable		17,000
	To record collections on account for the month.		

Assets	=	Liabilities	+	Owners' Equity
+17,000				
−17,000				

		Debit	Credit
f.	Sales Returns and Allowances	3,200	
	Accounts Receivable		3,200
	To record sales returns and allowances for the month.		

Assets	=	Liabilities	+	Owners' Equity
−3,200				−3,200

		Debit	Credit
g.	Transportation-in	2,700	
	Cash		2,700
	To record payment of freight bill on incoming merchandise.		

Assets	=	Liabilities	+	Owners' Equity
−2,700				−2,700

2. Partial income statement:

MICKEY'S MARTS
PARTIAL INCOME STATEMENT
FOR THE MONTH OF JANUARY

Sales revenue	$42,000
Less: Sales returns and allowances	3,200
Net sales	$38,800

Cost of goods sold:			
Inventory, January 1		$12,000	
Purchases	$25,000		
Less: Purchase discounts	200		
Purchase returns and allowances	1,900		
Net purchases	$22,900		
Add: Transportation-in	2,700		
Cost of goods purchased		25,600	
Cost of goods available for sale		$37,600	
Less: Inventory, January 31		9,500	
Cost of goods sold			28,100
Gross margin			$10,700

Appendix: Accounting Tools: Internal Control for a Merchandising Company

LO 6 Describe the various documents used in recording purchases of merchandise and their role in controlling cash disbursements.

Specific internal controls are necessary to control cash receipts and cash disbursements in a merchandising company. In addition to the separation of the custodianship of cash from the recording of it in the accounts, two other fundamental principles apply to its control. First, all cash receipts should be deposited *intact* in the bank on a *daily* basis. *Intact* means that no disbursements should be made from the cash received from customers. The second basic principle is related to the first: all cash disbursements should be made by check. The use of sequentially numbered checks results in a clear record of all disbursements. The only exception to this rule is the use of a petty cash fund to make cash disbursements for minor expenditures such as postage stamps and repairs. (The use of such a fund is explained in Chapter 7.)

Control over Cash Receipts

Most merchandisers receive checks and currency from customers in two distinct ways: (1) cash received over the counter, that is, from cash sales and (2) cash received in the mail, that is, cash collections from credit sales. Each of these types of cash receipts poses its own particular control problems.

Cash Received over the Counter Several control mechanisms are used to handle these cash payments. First, cash registers allow the customer to see the display, which deters the salesclerk from ringing up a sale for less than the amount received from the customer and pocketing the difference. A locked-in cash register tape is another control feature. At various times during the day, an employee other than the clerk unlocks the register, removes the tape, and forwards it to the accounting department. At the end of the shift, the salesclerk remits the coin and currency from the register to a central cashier. Any difference between the amount of cash remitted to the cashier and the amount on the tape submitted to the accounting department is investigated.

Finally, prenumbered customer receipts, prepared in duplicate, are a useful control mechanism. The customer is given a copy, and the salesclerk retains another. The salesclerk is accountable for all numbers in a specific series of receipts and must be able to explain any differences between the amount of cash remitted to the cashier and the amount collected per the receipts.

Cash Received in the Mail Most customers send checks rather than currency through the mail. Any form of cash received in the mail from customers should be applied to their account balances. The customer wants assurance that the account is appropriately reduced for the amount of the payment. The company must be assured that all cash received is deposited in the bank and that the account receivable is reduced accordingly.

To achieve a reasonable degree of control, two employees should be present when the mail is opened.[1] The first employee opens the mail in the presence of the second employee, counts the money received, and prepares a control list of the amount received on that particular day. The list is often called a *prelist* and is prepared in triplicate. The second employee takes the original to the cashier along with the total cash received on that day. The cashier is the person who makes the bank deposit. One copy of the prelist is forwarded to the accounting department to be used as the basis for recording the increase in Cash and the decrease in Accounts Receivable. The other copy is retained by one of the two persons opening the mail. A comparison of the prelist to the bank deposit slip is a timely way to detect receipts that do not make it to the bank. Because the two employees acting in concert could circumvent the control process, rotation of duties is important.

Monthly customer statements act as an additional control device for customer payments received in the mail. Assume that the two employees responsible for opening the mail and remitting checks to the cashier decide to pocket a check received from a customer. Checks made payable to a company *can* be stolen and cashed. The customer provides the control element. Because the check is not remitted to the cashier, the accounting department will not be notified to reduce the customer's account for the payment. The monthly statement, however, should alert the customer to the problem. The amount the customer thought was owed will be smaller than the balance due on the statement. At this point, the customer should ask the company to investigate the discrepancy. As evidence of its payment on account, the customer will be able to point to a canceled check—which was cashed by the unscrupulous employees.

Finally, keep in mind that the use of customer statements as a control device will be effective only if the employees responsible for the custody of cash received through the mail, for record keeping, and for authorization of adjustments to customers' accounts are not allowed to prepare and mail statements to customers. Employees allowed to do so are in a position to alter customers' statements.

Cash Discrepancies Discrepancies occur occasionally due to theft by dishonest employees and to human error. For example, if a salesclerk either intentionally or unintentionally gives the wrong amount of change, the amount remitted to the cashier will not agree with the cash register tape. Any material differences should be investigated. Of particular significance are *recurring* differences between the amount remitted by any one cashier and the amount on the cash register tape.

The Role of Computerized Business Documents in Controlling Cash Disbursements

A company makes cash payments for a variety of purposes: to purchase merchandise, supplies, plant, and equipment; to pay operating expenditures; and to cover payroll expenses, to name a few. We will concentrate on the disbursement of cash to purchase goods for resale, focusing particularly on the role of business documents in the process. Merchandising companies rely on a smooth and orderly inflow of quality goods for resale to customers. It is imperative that suppliers be paid on time so that they will continue to make goods available.

Business documents play a vital role in the purchasing function. The example that follows begins with a requisition for merchandise by the tool department of Grizzly Hardware Stores. The example continues through the receipt of the goods and the eventual payment to the supplier. The entire process is summarized in Exhibit 5-9. You will want to refer to this exhibit throughout the remainder of this appendix.

Purchase Requisition The tool department at Grizzly Hardware Stores weekly reviews its stock to determine whether any items need replenishing. On the basis of its

---

[1]In some companies, this control procedure may be omitted because of the cost of having two employees present when the mail is opened.

Exhibit 5-9 Document Flow for the Purchasing Function

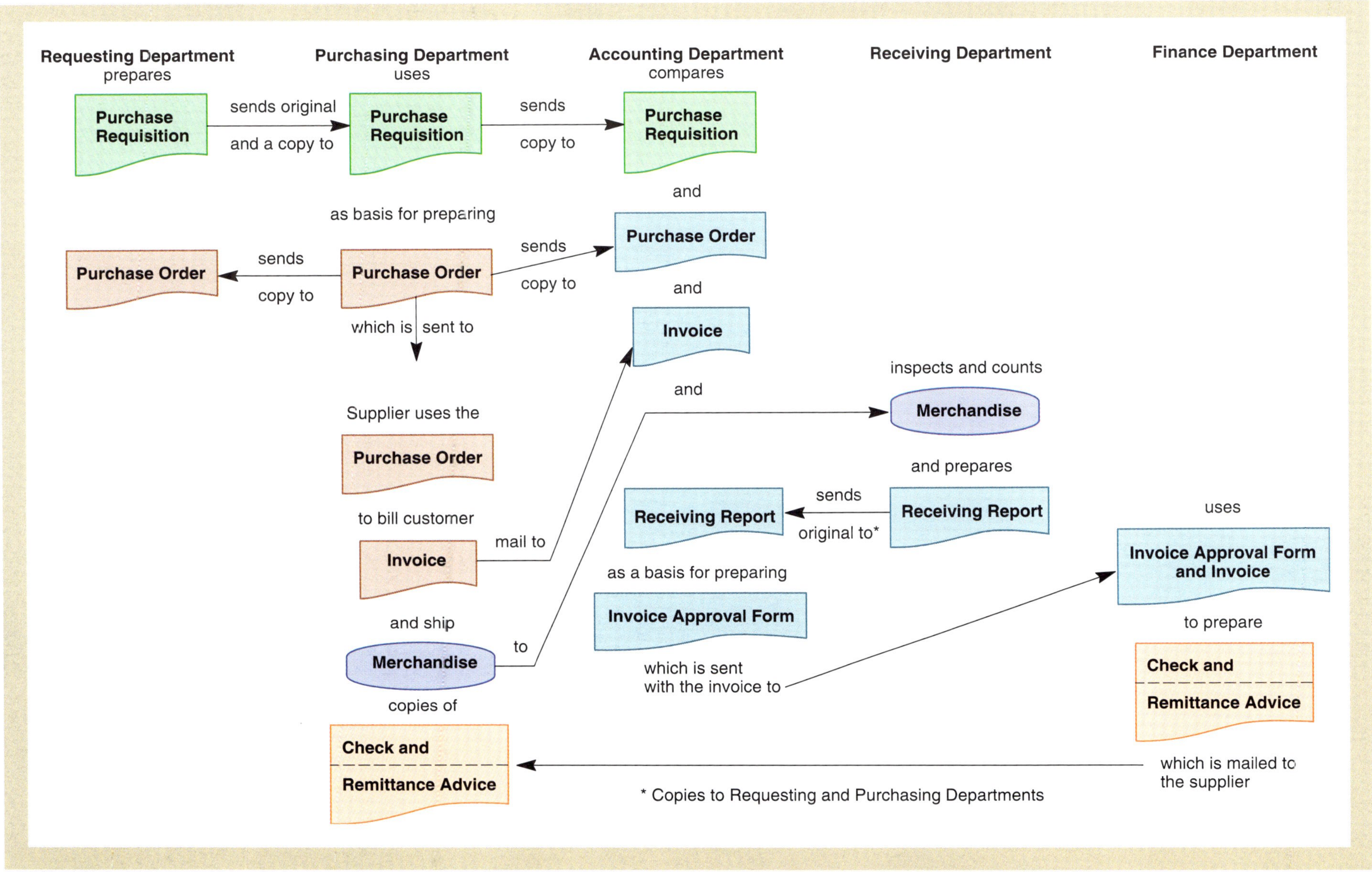

Purchase requisition form Form a department uses to initiate a request to order merchandise.

needs, the supervisor of the tool department fills out the **purchase requisition form** shown in Exhibit 5-10. The form indicates the preferred supplier or vendor, A-1 Tool.

Exhibit 5-10

Purchase Requisition

Grizzly Hardware Stores
676 Sentinel St.
Missoula, MT

PURCHASE REQUISITION

Date 5/28/04 **PR 75638**

Preferred vendor A-1 Tool Co.

Date needed by 6/5/04

The following items are requested for weekly dept. order

Item No.	Quantity	Description/Vendor No.
314627	24 ST	Hobby tool set/5265
323515	12 CD	Hobby blades 5 pk/7512
323682	6 ST	Screwdriver set 5/PC/1589

Requested by Joe Smith **Department** Tool department

The purchasing department has the responsibility for making the final decision on a vendor. Giving the purchasing department this responsibility means that it is held accountable for acquiring the goods at the lowest price, given certain standards for merchandise quality. Grizzly assigns a separate item number to each of the thousands of individual items of merchandise it stocks. Note that the requisition also indicates the vendor's number for each item. The unit of measure for each item is indicated in the quantity column. For example, "24 ST" means 24 sets, and "12 CD" means 12 cards. The original and a copy of the purchase requisition are sent to the purchasing department. The tool department keeps one copy for its records.

Purchase Order Like many other businesses, Grizzly uses a computerized purchasing system. Most companies either have purchased software or have developed software internally to perform such functions as purchasing, sales, and payroll. The software is capable not only of increasing the speed and accuracy of the process but also of generating the necessary documents.

Purchase order Form sent by the purchasing department to the supplier.

A computer-generated **purchase order** is shown in Exhibit 5-11. Purchase orders are usually prenumbered; a company should periodically investigate any missing numbers. The purchasing department uses its copy of the purchase requisition as a basis for preparing the purchase order. An employee in the purchasing department keys in the relevant information from the purchase requisition and adds the unit cost for each item gathered from the vendor's price guide. The software program generates the purchase order as shown in Exhibit 5-11. You should trace all of the information for at least one of the three items ordered from the purchase requisition to the purchase order. The purchase order indicates the instructions for shipping, FOB destination point, and the terms for payment, 2/10, net 30.

The system generates the original purchase order and three copies. As indicated in Exhibit 5-9, the original is sent to the supplier after a supervisor in the purchasing department approves it. One copy is sent to the accounting department, where it will be matched with the original requisition. A second copy is sent to the tool department as confirmation that its request for the items has been attended to by the purchasing department. The purchasing department keeps the third copy for its records.

Exhibit 5-11

Computer-Generated Purchase Order

Grizzly Hardware Stores
676 Sentinel St.
Missoula, MT

PURCHASE ORDER

TO: **PO 54296**

A-1 Tool Co.
590 West St.
Milwaukee, WI

Date 5/30/04 **Ship by** Best Express **Instructions** FOB destination point
Terms 2/10, net 30 **Date required** 6/5/04

Item No.	Quantity	Description/Vendor No.	Unit price	Amount
314627	24 ST	Hobby tool set/5265	$28.59	$686.16
323515	12 CD	Hobby blades 5 pk/7512	0.69	8.28
323682	6 ST	Screwdriver set 5/PC/1589	4.49	26.94
				$721.38

Approved by Mary Jones

A purchase order is not the basis for recording a purchase and a liability. Legally, the order is merely an offer by the company to purchase goods from the supplier. Technically, the receipt of goods from the supplier is the basis for the purchaser's recognition of a liability. As a matter of practice, however, most companies record the payable upon receipt of the invoice.

Invoice When A-1 Tool ships the merchandise, it also mails an invoice to Grizzly, requesting payment according to the agreed-upon terms, in this case 2/10, net 30. The **invoice** may be mailed separately or included with the shipment of merchandise. A-1 Tool, the seller, calls this document a *sales invoice;* it is the basis for recording a sale and an account receivable. Grizzly, the buyer, calls the same document a *purchase invoice,* which is the basis for recording a purchase and an account payable. The invoice that A-1 sent to Grizzly's accounting department is shown in Exhibit 5-12.

Invoice Form sent by the seller to the buyer as evidence of a sale.

Receiving Report The accounting department receives the invoice for the three items ordered. Within a few days before or after the receipt of the invoice, the merchandise arrives at Grizzly's warehouse. As soon as the items are unpacked, the receiving department inspects and counts them. The same software program that generated the purchase order also generates a receiving report, as shown in Exhibit 5-13.

Grizzly uses a **blind receiving report.** The column for the quantity received is left blank and is filled in by the receiving department. Rather than being able simply to indicate that the number ordered was received, an employee must count the items to determine that the number ordered is actually received. You should trace all of the relevant information for one of the three items ordered from the purchase order to the receiving report. The accounting system generates an original receiving report and three copies. The receiving department keeps one copy for its records and sends the original to the accounting department. One copy is sent to the purchasing department to be matched with the purchase order, and the other copy is sent to the tool department as verification that the items it originally requested have been received.

Blind receiving report Form used by the receiving department to account for the quantity and condition of merchandise received from a supplier.

Invoice Approval Form At this point, Grizzly's accounting department has copies of the purchase requisition from the tool department, the purchase order from the purchasing department, the invoice from the supplier, and the receiving report from the warehouse. The accounting department uses an **invoice approval form** to docu-

Invoice approval form Form the accounting department uses before making payment to document the accuracy of all the information about a purchase.

Exhibit 5-12
Invoice

NO. 427953

A-1 Tool Co.
590 West St.
Milwaukee, WI

INVOICE

Sold to Grizzly Hardware Stores
676 Sentinel St.
Missoula, MT
Ship to Same
Terms 2/10, net 30

Date 6/2/04
Order No. 54296
Shipped via Best Express
Date shipped 6/2/04
Ship terms FOB destination

Quantity	Description/No.	Price	Amount
24 ST	Hobby tool set/5265	$28.59	$686.16
12 CD	Hobby blades 5 pk/7512	0.69	8.28
6 ST	Screwdriver set 5 PC/1589	4.49	26.94
			$721.38

ment the accuracy of the information on each of these other forms. The invoice approval form for Grizzly Hardware is shown in Exhibit 5-14.

The invoice is compared to the purchase requisition to ensure that the company is billed for goods that it requested. A comparison of the invoice with the purchase order ensures that the goods were in fact ordered. Finally, the receiving report is compared with the invoice to verify that all goods it is being billed for were received. An accounting department employee must also verify the mathematical accuracy of the amounts that appear on the invoice. The date the invoice must be paid to take advantage of the

Exhibit 5-13
Computer-Generated Receiving Report

Grizzly Hardware Stores
676 Sentinel St.
Missoula, MT

Receiving Report

RR 23637

Purchase Order No. 54296
Vendor A-1 Tool Co.
Ship via Best Express
Terms 2/10, net 30

Date ordered 5/30/04
Date required 6/5/04
Instructions FOB Destination

Quantity received	Our Item No.	Description/Item No.	Remarks
24 ST	314627	Hobby tool set/5265	Box damaged but merchandise ok
12 CD	323515	Hobby blades 5 pk/7512	
6 ST	323682	Screwdriver set 5/PC/1589	

Received by Bob Reed

Date 6/4/04

Exhibit 5-14

Invoice Approval Form

Grizzly Hardware Stores
676 Sentinel St.
Missoula, MT

Invoice Approval Form

	No.	Check
Purchase Requisition	PR 75638	✓
Purchase Order	PO 54296	✓
Receiving Report	RR 23637	✓

Invoice:

- **No.** 427953
- **Date** 6/2/04
- **Price** ✓
- **Extensions** ✓
- **Footings** ✓

Last Day to Pay for Discount 6/12/04

Approved for Payment by Alice Johnson

discount is noted so that the finance department will be sure to send the check by this date. At this point, the accounting department prepares the journal entry to increase Purchases and Accounts Payable. The invoice approval form and the invoice are then sent to the finance department. Some businesses call the invoice approval form a *voucher;* it is used for all expenditures, not just for purchases of merchandise. Finally, it is worth noting that some businesses do not use a separate invoice approval form but simply note approval directly on the invoice itself.

Check with Remittance Advice Grizzly's finance department is responsible for issuing checks. This results from the need to segregate custody of cash (the signed check) from record keeping (the updating of the ledger). On receipt of the invoice approval form from the accounting department, a clerk in the finance department types a check with a remittance advice attached, as shown in Exhibit 5-15.[2]

Before the check is signed, the documents referred to on the invoice approval form are reviewed and canceled to prevent reuse. The clerk then forwards the check to one of the company officers authorized to sign checks. According to one of Grizzly's internal control policies, only the treasurer and the assistant treasurer are authorized to sign checks. Both officers must sign check amounts above a specified dollar limit. To maintain separation of duties, the finance department should mail the check. The remittance advice informs the supplier as to the nature of the payment and is torn off by the supplier before cashing the check.

[2]In some companies, an employee in the accounting department prepares checks and sends them to the finance department for review and signature. Also, many companies use computer-generated checks, rather than manually typed ones.

Exhibit 5-15

Check with Remittance Advice

3690

Grizzly Hardware Stores
676 Sentinel St.
Missoula, MT

June 12 20 04

PAY TO THE ORDER OF A-1 Tool Co. $706.95

Seven hundred six and 95/100 DOLLARS

Second National Bank
Missoula, MT

3690 035932 9321

John B. Martin

Purchase Order No.	Invoice No.	Invoice Date	Description	Amount
PO 54296	427953	6/2/04	24 ST Hobby tool set	$686.16
			12 CD Hobby blades 5pk	8.28
			6 ST Screwdriver set 5PC	26.94
			Total	$721.38
			Less: 2% discount	14.43
			Net remitted	$706.95

Chapter Highlights

1. **LO 1** Merchandise is inventory purchased in finished form and held for resale. Both wholesalers and retailers sell merchandise. Sales revenue is a representation of the inflow of assets from the sale of merchandise during the period. Two deductions are made from sales revenue on the income statement. Sales returns and allowances and sales discounts are both subtracted from sales revenue to arrive at net sales.
2. **LO 2** A perpetual inventory system requires the updating of the Inventory account at the time of each purchase and each sale of merchandise. With the periodic system, the Inventory account is updated only at the end of the year. Separate accounts are used during the period to record purchases, purchase returns and allowances, purchase discounts, and transportation-in. The periodic system relies on a count of the inventory on the last day of the period to determine ending inventory.
3. **LO 3** Cost of goods sold is recognized as an expense under the matching principle. It represents the cost associated with the merchandise sold during the period and is matched with the revenue of the period.
4. **LO 3** The purchases of the period are reduced by purchase returns and allowances and by purchase discounts. Any freight costs paid to acquire the merchandise, called *transportation-in,* are added. The result, cost of goods purchased, is added to the beginning inventory to determine cost of goods available for sale. Cost of goods sold is found by deducting ending inventory from cost of goods available for sale.
5. **LO 3** *FOB destination point* means that the seller is responsible for the cost of delivering the merchandise to the buyer. Title to the goods does not transfer to the buyer until the buyer receives the merchandise from the carrier. *FOB shipping point* means that the buyer pays shipping costs. Title to the goods transfers to the buyer as soon as the seller turns them over to the carrier.
6. **LO 4** The purpose of an internal control system is to provide assurance that overall company objectives are met. Specifically, accounting controls are designed to safeguard the entity's assets and provide the company with reliable accounting records. Management has the primary responsibility for the reliability of the financial statements. Many companies employ a full-time internal audit staff to monitor and evaluate the internal control system.
7. **LO 5** Segregation of duties is the most fundamental of all internal control procedures. Possession of assets must be kept separate from the record-keeping function. Other important control procedures include a system of independent verifications, proper authorizations, adequate safeguards for assets and their records, independent review and appraisal of the accounting system, and the design and use of business documents.
8. **LO 6** Control over cash requires that all receipts be deposited intact on a daily basis and that all disbursements be made by

check. Control procedures are important for cash received over the counter as well as for cash received in the mail. Any material discrepancies between the cash actually on hand and the amount that should be on hand need to be investigated. (Appendix)

9. **LO 6** Business documents play a vital role in various business activities such as the purchase of merchandise. The requesting department fills out a purchase requisition form and sends it to the purchasing department. The purchasing department uses the requisition to complete a purchase order, which it sends to the supplier. The supplier mails an invoice to the buyer's accounting department. The accounting department also gets a receiving report from the warehouse to indicate the quantity and condition of the goods delivered. The accounting department fills out an invoice approval form, which it sends with the invoice to the finance department, which uses them as the basis for preparing and sending a check to the supplier. (Appendix)

http://

http://porter.swlearning.com

Technology and other resources for your success

If you need additional help, visit the text's Web site. Also, see pages xv–xvii in this text's preface for a description of available technology and other resources. If your instructor is using PERSONAL Trainer in this course, you may complete, on line, the assignments identified by PT.

Key Terms Quiz

Because of the large number of terms introduced in this chapter, there are two key terms quizzes. Read each definition below and then write the number of the definition in the blank beside the appropriate term it defines. The quiz solutions appear at the end of the chapter.

Quiz 1: Merchandise Accounting

_____ Net sales
_____ Sales Returns and Allowances
_____ Trade discount
_____ Quantity discount
_____ Sales Discounts
_____ Cost of goods available for sale
_____ Cost of goods sold
_____ Perpetual system
_____ Periodic system
_____ Transportation-in
_____ Purchases
_____ Purchase Returns and Allowances
_____ Purchase Discounts
_____ FOB destination point
_____ FOB shipping point

1. A reduction in selling price for buying a large number of units of a product.
2. The contra-revenue account used to record both refunds to customers and reductions of their accounts.
3. The adjunct account used to record freight costs paid by the buyer.
4. A selling price reduction offered to a special class of customers.
5. The system in which the Inventory account is increased at the time of each purchase of merchandise and decreased at the time of each sale.
6. The contra-purchases account used in a periodic inventory system when a refund is received from a supplier or a reduction given in the balance owed to the supplier.
7. The contra-revenue account used to record discounts given customers for early payment of their accounts.
8. Terms that require the seller to pay for the cost of shipping the merchandise to the buyer.
9. Terms that require the buyer to pay the shipping costs.
10. The system in which the Inventory account is updated only at the end of the period.
11. Beginning inventory plus cost of goods purchased.
12. The contra-purchases account used to record reductions in purchase price for early payment to the supplier.
13. The account used in a periodic inventory system to record acquisitions of merchandise.
14. Sales revenue less sales returns and allowances and sales discounts.
15. Cost of goods available for sale minus ending inventory.

(continued)

Quiz 2: Internal Control

_____ Internal control system
_____ Report of management
_____ Internal audit staff
_____ Board of directors
_____ Audit committee
_____ Foreign Corrupt Practices Act
_____ Accounting system
_____ Administrative controls
_____ Accounting controls
_____ Purchase requisition form (Appendix)
_____ Purchase order (Appendix)
_____ Invoice (Appendix)
_____ Blind receiving report (Appendix)
_____ Invoice approval form (Appendix)

1. The form sent by the seller to the buyer as evidence of a sale.
2. The group composed of key officers of a corporation and outside members responsible for the general oversight of the affairs of the entity.
3. The methods and records used to accurately report an entity's transactions and to maintain accountability for its assets and liabilities.
4. The board of directors subset that acts as a direct contact between the stockholders and the independent accounting firm.
5. Procedures concerned with safeguarding the assets or the reliability of the financial statements.
6. The form a department uses to initiate a request to order merchandise.
7. A form the accounting department uses before making payment to document the accuracy of all the information about a purchase.
8. A written statement in the annual report indicating the responsibility of management for the financial statements.
9. A form used by the receiving department to account for the quantity and condition of merchandise received from a supplier.
10. Legislation intended to increase the accountability of management for accurate records and reliable financial statements.
11. Procedures concerned with efficient operation of the business and adherence to managerial policies.
12. The form sent by the purchasing department to the supplier.
13. The department responsible for monitoring and evaluating the internal control system.
14. Policies and procedures necessary to ensure the safeguarding of an entity's assets, the reliability of its accounting records, and the accomplishment of overall company objectives.

Answers on p. 269.

Alternate Terms

Gross margin Gross profit

Invoice Purchase invoice, sales invoice

Invoice approval form Voucher

Merchandiser Wholesaler, retailer

Report of management Management's report

Sales revenue Sales

Transportation-in Freight-in

Questions

1. When a company gives a cash refund on returned merchandise, why doesn't it just reduce Sales Revenue instead of using a contra-revenue account?
2. Why are trade discounts and quantity discounts not accorded accounting recognition? (The sale is simply recorded net of either of these types of discounts.)
3. What do credit terms of *3/20, n/60* mean? How valuable to the customer is the discount offered in these terms?
4. What is the difference between a periodic inventory system and a perpetual inventory system?
5. How have point-of-sale terminals improved the ability of mass merchandisers to use a perpetual inventory system?
6. In a periodic inventory system, what kind of account is Purchases? Is it an asset or an expense or neither?
7. Why are shipping terms, such as FOB shipping point or FOB destination point, important in deciding ownership of inventory at the end of the year?
8. How and why are transportation-in and transportation-out recorded differently?
9. How do the duties of an internal audit staff differ from those of the external auditors?
10. What is the typical composition of a board of directors of a publicly held corporation?
11. An order clerk fills out a purchase requisition for an expensive item of inventory and the receiving report when the merchandise arrives. The clerk takes the inventory home and then sends the invoice to the accounting department so that the supplier will be paid. What basic internal control procedure could have prevented this misuse of company assets?
12. What are some of the limitations on a company's effective system of internal control?
13. What two basic procedures are essential to an effective system of internal control over cash? (Appendix)

14. How would you evaluate the following statement? "The only reason a company positions its cash register so that the customers can see the display is so that they feel comfortable they are being charged the correct amount for a purchase." (Appendix)

15. Which document, a purchase order or an invoice, is the basis for recording a purchase and a corresponding liability? Explain your answer. (Appendix)

16. What is a blind receiving report, and how does it act as a control device? (Appendix)

17. What is the purpose in comparing a purchase invoice with a purchase order? in comparing a receiving report with a purchase invoice? (Appendix)

Exercises

Exercise 5-1 *Journal Entries to Record Sales* LO 1

Prepare the journal entries to record the following transactions on the books of Ace Corporation for March 3, 2004:

a. Sold merchandise on credit for $500 with terms of 2/10, net 30. Ace records all sales at the gross amount.

b. Recorded cash sales for the day of $1,250 from the cash register tape.

c. Granted a cash refund of $135 to a customer for spoiled merchandise returned.

d. Granted a customer a credit of $190 on its outstanding bill and allowed the customer to keep a defective product.

e. Applied cash of $2,300, received through the mail, to customers' accounts. All amounts received qualify for the discount for early payment.

Exercise 5-2 *Credit Terms* LO 1

Ling Company sold merchandise on credit for $800 on September 10, 2004, to Letson Inc. For each of the following terms, indicate the last day Letson could take the discount, the amount Letson would pay if it took the discount, and the date full payment is due.

a. 2/10, n/30

b. 3/15, n/45

c. 1/7, n/21

d. 5/15, n/30

Exercise 5-3 *Journal Entries for Sales Discounts* LO 1

Prepare the journal entries on the books of Rambler Corporation for the following transactions, using the gross method to record sales discounts (all sales on credit are made with terms of 2/10, net 30).

June 2: Sold merchandise on credit to Huskie Corp. for $1,200.

June 4: Sold merchandise on credit to Hawkeye Company for $2,000.

June 13: Collected cash from Hawkeye Company.

June 30: Collected cash from Huskie Corp.

Exercise 5-4 *Perpetual and Periodic Inventory Systems* LO 2

Following is a partial list of account balances for two different merchandising companies. The amounts in the accounts represent the balances at the end of the year *before* any adjusting or closing entries are made.

Company A		Company B	
Sales revenue	$50,000	Sales revenue	$85,000
Sales discounts	3,000	Sales discounts	2,000
Merchandise inventory	12,000	Merchandise inventory	9,000
Cost of goods sold	38,000	Purchases	41,000
		Purchase discounts	4,000
		Purchases returns and allowances	1,000

(continued)

Required

1. Identify which inventory system, perpetual or periodic, each of the two companies uses. Explain how you know which system each uses by looking at the types of accounts on their books.
2. How much inventory does Company A have on hand at the end of the year? What is its cost of goods sold for the year?
3. Explain why you cannot determine Company B's cost of goods sold for the year from the information available.

Exercise 5-5 ***Perpetual and Periodic Inventory Systems*** **LO 2**

From the following list, identify whether the merchandisers described would most likely use a perpetual or periodic inventory system.

_______________ Appliance store
_______________ Car dealership
_______________ Drugstore
_______________ Furniture store
_______________ Grocery store
_______________ Hardware store
_______________ Jewelry store

How might changes in technology affect the ability of merchandisers to use perpetual inventory systems?

Exercise 5-6 ***Missing Amounts in Cost of Goods Sold Model*** **LO 3**

For each of the following independent cases, fill in the missing amounts:

	Case 1	Case 2	Case 3
Beginning inventory	$ (a)	$2,350	$1,890
Purchases (gross)	6,230	5,720	(e)
Purchase returns and allowances	470	800	550
Purchase discounts	200	(c)	310
Transportation-in	150	500	420
Cost of goods available for sale	7,110	(d)	8,790
Ending inventory	(b)	1,750	1,200
Cost of goods sold	5,220	5,570	(f)

Exercise 5-7 ***Journal Entries for Purchase Discounts*** **LO 3**

Prepare the journal entries on the books of Buckeye Corporation for the following transactions, using the gross method to record purchase discounts (all purchases on credit are made with terms of 1/10, net 30, and Buckeye uses the periodic system of inventory):

July 3: Purchased merchandise on credit from Wildcat Corp. for $3,500.

July 6: Purchased merchandise on credit from Cyclone Company for $7,000.

July 12: Paid amount owed to Wildcat Corp.

August 5: Paid amount owed to Cyclone Company.

Exercise 5-8 ***Journal Entries for Purchases—Periodic System*** **LO 3**

Prepare journal entries for the following transactions entered into by Wolverine Corporation. The company uses the periodic system and the gross method to record purchase discounts.

March 3: Purchased merchandise from Spartan Corp. for $2,500 with terms of 2/10, net/30. Shipping costs of $250 were paid to Neverlate Transit Company.

March 7: Purchased merchandise from Boilermaker Company for $1,400 with terms of net/30.

March 12: Paid amount owed to Spartan Corp.

March 15: Received a credit of $500 on defective merchandise purchased from Boilermaker Company. The merchandise was kept.

March 18: Purchased merchandise from Gopher Corp. for $1,600 with terms of 2/10, net 30.

March 22: Received a credit of $400 from Gopher Corp. for spoiled merchandise returned to them. This is the amount of credit exclusive of any discount.

April 6: Paid amount owed to Boilermaker Company.

April 18: Paid amount owed to Gopher Corp.

Exercise 5-9 *Shipping Terms and Transfer of Title* **LO 3**

On December 23, 2004, Miller Wholesalers ships merchandise to Michael Retailers with terms of FOB destination point. The merchandise arrives at Michael's warehouse on January 3, 2005.

Required

1. Identify who pays to ship the merchandise.
2. Determine whether the inventory should be included as an asset on Michael's December 31, 2004, balance sheet. Should the sale be included on Miller's 2004 income statement?
3. Explain how your answers to part **2** would have been different if the terms of shipment had been FOB shipping point.

Exercise 5-10 *Transfer of Title to Inventory* **LO 3**

From the following list, identify whether the transactions described should be recorded by Cameron Companies during December 2004 or January 2005.

Purchases of merchandise that are in transit from vendors to Cameron Companies on December 31, 2004:

______________ Shipped FOB shipping point
______________ Shipped FOB destination point

Sales of merchandise that are in transit to customers of Cameron Companies on December 31, 2004:

______________ Shipped FOB shipping point
______________ Shipped FOB destination point

Exercise 5-11 *Internal Control* **LO 5**

The university drama club is planning a raffle. The president overheard you talking about internal control to another accounting student, so she has asked you to set up some guidelines to "be sure" that all money collected for the raffle is accounted for by the club.

Required

1. Describe guidelines that the club should follow to achieve an acceptable level of internal control.
2. Comment on the president's request that she "be sure" all money is collected and recorded.

Exercise 5-12 *Segregation of Duties* **LO 5**

The following tasks are performed by three employees, each of whom is capable of performing all of them. Do not concern yourself with the time required to perform the tasks but with the need to provide for segregation of duties. Assign the duties by using a check mark to indicate which employee should perform each task. Remember that you may assign any one of the tasks to any of the employees.

	Employee		
Task	**Mary**	**Sue**	**John**
Prepare invoices			
Mail invoices			
Pick up mail from post office			
Open mail, separate checks			
List checks on deposit slip in triplicate			
Post payment to customer's account			
Deposit checks			
Prepare monthly schedule of accounts receivable			
Reconcile bank statements			

Multi-Concept Exercises

SPREADSHEET

Exercise 5-13 ***Income Statement for a Merchandiser*** **LO 1, 3**

Fill in the missing amounts in the following income statement for Carpenters Department Store Inc.:

Sales revenue		$125,600	
Less: Sales returns and allowances		(a)	
Net sales			$122,040
Cost of goods sold:			
Beginning inventory		$ 23,400	
Purchases	$ (b)		
Less: Purchase discounts	1,300		
Net purchases	$ (c)		
Add: Transportation-in	6,550		
Cost of goods purchased		81,150	
Cost of goods available for sale		$104,550	
Less: Ending inventory		(e)	
Cost of goods sold			(d)
Gross margin			$ 38,600
Operating expenses			(f)
Income before tax			$ 26,300
Income tax expense			10,300
Net income			$ (g)

Exercise 5-14 ***Partial Income Statement—Periodic System*** **LO 1, 3**

LaPine Company has the following account balances as of December 31, 2004:

Purchase returns and allowances	$ 400
Inventory, January 1	4,000
Sales	80,000
Transportation-in	1,000
Sales returns and allowances	500
Purchase discounts	800
Inventory, December 31	3,800
Purchases	30,000
Sales discounts	1,200

Required

Prepare a partial income statement for LaPine Company for 2004 through gross margin. Calculate LaPine's gross margin (gross profit) ratio for 2004.

Problems

Problem 5-1 ***Trade Discounts*** **LO 1**

Essex Inc. offers the following discounts to customers who purchase large quantities:

10% discount: 10–25 units
20% discount: >25 units

Mr. Essex, the president, would like to record all sales at the list price and record the discount as an expense.

Required

1. Explain to Mr. Essex why trade discounts do not enter into the accounting records.
2. Even though trade discounts do not enter into the accounting records, is it still important to have some record of these? Explain your answer.

Problem 5-2 ***Calculation of Gross Margins for Wal-Mart and Kmart*** **LO 1**

http://www.walmart.com
http://www.kmart.com

The following information was summarized from the consolidated statements of income of Wal-Mart Stores Inc. and Subsidiaries for the years ended January 31, 2002 and 2001, and the consolidated statements of operations of Kmart Corporation for the years ended January 30, 2002, and January 31, 2001 (for each company, years are labeled as 2001 and 2000, respectively):

	2001		2000	
(in Millions)	Sales	Cost of Sales*	Sales	Cost of Sales*
Wal-Mart	$217,799	$171,562	$191,329	$150,255
Kmart	36,151	29,936	37,028	29,658

*Described as "cost of sales, buying and occupancy" by Kmart Corporation.

Required

1. Calculate the gross margin (gross profit) ratios for Wal-Mart and Kmart for 2001 and 2000.
2. Which company appears to be performing better? What factors might cause the difference in the gross margin ratios of the two companies? What other information should you consider to determine how these companies are performing in this regard?

Problem 5-3 *Internal Control Procedures* LO 5

DECISION MAKING

You are opening a summer business, a chain of three drive-thru snow-cone stands. You have hired other college students to work and have purchased a cash register with locked-in tapes. You retain one key, and the other is available to the lead person on each shift.

Required

1. Write a list of the procedures for all employees to follow when ringing up sales and giving change.
2. Write a list of the procedures for the lead person to follow in closing out at the end of the day. Be as specific as you can so that employees will have few if any questions.
3. What is your main concern in the design of internal control for the snow-cone stands? How did you address that concern? Be specific.

Problem 5-4 *The Design of Internal Control Documents (Appendix)* LO 6

Motel $49.99 has purchased a large warehouse to store all supplies used by housekeeping departments in the company's expanding chain of motels. In the past, each motel bought supplies from local distributors and paid for the supplies from cash receipts.

Required

1. Name some potential problems with the old system.
2. Design a purchase requisition form and a receiving report to be used by the housekeeping departments and the warehouse. Indicate how many copies of each form should be used and who should receive each copy.

Multi-Concept Problems

Problem 5-5 *Journal Entries for a Merchandiser* LO 1, 2, 3

GENERAL LEDGER

The following transactions were entered into by North Coast Tires Inc. during the month of June:

June 2: Purchased 1,000 tires at a cost of $60 per tire. Terms of payment are 1/10, net 45.

June 4: Paid trucking firm $1,200 to ship the tires purchased on June 2.

June 5: Purchased 600 tires at a cost of $60 per tire. Terms of payment are 2/10, net 30.

June 6: Paid trucking firm $800 to ship the tires purchased on June 5.

June 7: Returned 150 of the tires purchased on June 2 because they were defective. Received a credit on open account from the seller.

June 11: Paid for tires purchased on June 2.

June 13: Sold 700 tires from those purchased on June 2. The selling price was $90 per tire. Terms are 1/10, net 30.

June 22: Received cash from sale of tires on June 13.

June 30: Paid for tires purchased on June 5.

(continued)

Required

1. Prepare the journal entries to record these transactions on the books of North Coast Tires Inc. The company uses the gross method of recording purchase and sales discounts. North Coast uses a periodic inventory system.
2. Given the nature of its product, do you think it would be feasible for North Coast to use a perpetual inventory system? Why? If so, what advantages would accrue to the company by using a perpetual system?

DECISION MAKING

GENERAL LEDGER

Problem 5-6 *Journal Entries for a Merchandiser* LO 1, 2, 3

Leisure Time Furniture Store entered into the following transactions in the month of April:

April 3: Purchased 50 lounge chairs at $150 each with terms 2/10, net 45. The chairs were shipped FOB destination.

April 7: Sold 6 chairs for $320 each, terms 2/10, net 30.

April 8: Purchased 20 patio umbrella tables for $120 each, FOB shipping point, terms 1/10, net 30.

April 9: Due to defects, returned 5 lounge chairs purchased on April 3. Received a credit memorandum, indicating that amount due has been reduced.

April 10: Paid the trucking firm $360 for delivery of the tables purchased on April 8.

April 13: Paid for the chairs purchased on April 3.

April 17: Received payment for the chairs sold on April 7.

April 20: Paid for the tables purchased on April 8.

Required

1. Prepare all journal entries needed to record these transactions for the furniture company. Leisure Time uses the gross method of recording purchase and sales discounts. The company uses a periodic inventory system.
2. Do you think Leisure Time should change to a perpetual inventory system, given the nature of its business? Why or why not? What advantages would a company have using the perpetual system instead of the periodic system?

Problem 5-7 *Trade and Cash Discounts* LO 1, 3

Billings Inc. publishes books and offers trade discounts to customers who purchase in large quantities: 30% for purchases of more than 50 units. It also offers credit terms of 2/10, net 30 to induce early payment. The list price of one book is $60. Columbus Company purchased 100 of these books on September 12. Payment was made on September 21.

Required

1. Prepare the journal entries on Billings' books to record the sale and the receipt of cash.
2. Prepare the journal entries on Columbus' books to record the purchase and the payment.

GENERAL LEDGER

Problem 5-8 *Journal Entries and Partial Income Statement for a Merchandiser* LO 1, 3

Weekend Wonders Inc. operates a chain of discount hardware stores. The company uses a periodic inventory system. Inventory on hand on June 1, 2004, amounts to $25,670; on June 30, 2004, it is $30,200. The company uses the gross method to record purchase and sales discounts. The following transactions take place during the month of June:

a. Purchased merchandise from suppliers at a cost of $80,000 with credit terms of 2/10, net 30.

b. Paid freight costs of $4,250 to the common carrier for merchandise purchased.

c. Returned defective merchandise to suppliers and received credits of $2,300, the amount of credit before taking into account any purchase discounts.

d. Realized $92,000 in sales for the month, of which $68,000 is on credit; the remainder was received in cash. The credit sales are made with terms of 2/10, net 45.

e. Gave sales returns and allowances on credit sales of $4,000 during the month.

f. Made cash payments of $62,000 to suppliers for earlier purchases on account. All amounts paid during the month are made within the discount period.

g. Received $56,000 in cash collections on account from customers. All amounts received during the month are within the discount period.

Required

1. Prepare the journal entries on the books of Weekend Wonders Inc. to record each transaction.
2. Prepare a partial income statement for the month of June. The last line on the statement should be gross margin.
3. Assume that Weekend Wonders decides as a matter of policy to forgo the discount for early payment on purchases (credit terms are 2/10, net 30). What return would Weekend Wonders need to earn on the money it invests by not paying early to justify this decision? Provide any necessary calculations to support your answer.

Problem 5-9 *Purchases and Sales of Merchandise, Cash Flows* LO 1, 2, 3

GENERAL LEDGER

Two Wheeler, a bike shop, opened for business on April 1. It uses a periodic inventory system and records purchases at gross. The following transactions occurred during the first month of business:

April 1: Purchased five units from Duhan Co. for $500 total, with terms 3/10, net 30, FOB destination.

April 10: Paid for the April 1 purchase.

April 15: Sold one unit for $200 cash.

April 18: Purchased 10 units from Clinton Inc. for $900 total, with terms 3/10, net/30, FOB destination.

April 25: Sold three units for $200 each, cash.

April 28: Paid for the April 18 purchase.

Required

1. Prepare the journal entries to record the April transactions.
2. Determine net income for the month of April. Two Wheeler incurred and paid $100 for rent and $50 for miscellaneous expenses during April. Ending inventory is $967 (ignore income taxes).
3. Assuming that the only transactions during April are given (including rent and miscellaneous expenses), compute net cash flow from operating activities.
4. Explain why cash outflow is so much larger than expenses on the income statement.

Problem 5-10 *Gap Inc.'s Sales, Cost of Goods Sold, and Gross Margin* LO 1, 3

http://www.gap.com

The consolidated balance sheets of Gap Inc. included merchandise inventory in the amount of $1,677,116,000 as of February 2, 2002 (the end of fiscal year 2001) and $1,904,153,000 as of February 3, 2001 (the end of fiscal year 2000). Refer also to Gap Inc.'s consolidated statements of earnings for fiscal 2001 and 2000, which are set forth in the opening vignette of this chapter.

Required

1. Unlike most other merchandisers, Gap Inc. doesn't include accounts receivable on its balance sheet. Why doesn't Gap Inc.'s balance sheet include this account?
2. Prepare a summary journal entry for sales during the year ended February 2, 2002.
3. Gap Inc. sets forth net sales but not gross sales on its income statement. What type(s) of deduction(s) would be made from gross sales to arrive at the amount of net sales reported? Why might the company decide not to report the amount(s) of the deduction(s) separately?
4. Reconstruct the cost of goods sold section of Gap Inc.'s 2001 income statement.
5. Calculate the gross margin (gross profit) ratios for Gap Inc. for 2001, 2000, and 1999, and comment on the changes noted, if any. Is the company's performance improving? What factors might have caused the change in the gross margin ratio?

Problem 5-11 *Internal Control* LO 4, 5

At Morris Mart Inc. all sales are on account. Mary Morris-Manning is responsible for mailing invoices to customers, recording the amount billed, opening mail, and recording the payment. Mary is very devoted to the family business and never takes off more than one or two days for a long weekend. The customers know Mary and sometimes send personal notes with their payments. Another clerk handles all aspects of accounts payable. Mary's brother, who is president of Morris Mart, has hired an accountant to help with expansion.

(continued)

Required

1. List some problems with the current accounts receivable system.
2. What suggestions would you make to improve internal control?
3. How would you explain to Mary that she personally is not the problem?

SPREADSHEET

Problem 5-12 ***Financial Statements*** **LO 1, 3**

A list of accounts for Maple Inc. at 12/31/04 follows:

Accounts Receivable	$ 2,359
Advertising Expense	4,510
Buildings and Equipment, Net	55,550
Capital Stock	50,000
Cash	590
Depreciation Expense	2,300
Dividends	6,000
Income Tax Expense	3,200
Income Tax Payable	3,200
Interest Receivable	100
Inventory:	
January 1, 2004	6,400
December 31, 2004	7,500
Land	20,000
Purchase Discounts	800
Purchases	40,200
Retained Earnings, January 1, 2004	32,550
Salaries Expense	25,600
Salaries Payable	650
Sales	84,364
Sales Returns	780
Transportation-in	375
Utilities Expense	3,600

Required

1. Determine cost of goods sold for 2004.
2. Determine net income for 2004.
3. Prepare a balance sheet dated December 31, 2004.

Alternate Problems

Problem 5-1A ***Discounts*** **LO 1**

Whitefish Inc., a recording distributor, would like to offer discounts to customers who purchase large quantities. Whitefish is unsure about the terms to use and how to account for discounts extended to customers. The company also wants to consider a cash discount for early payment by customers. Whitefish expects sales of about $3 million this year. All sales are on account to about 100 different outlets located within 500 miles of the warehouse. Deliveries are made by Whitefish's own trucks and cost about $25 per 100 miles driven. A full truck will hold 1,000 units.

Required

1. Explain the difference between a quantity discount and a discount for early payment. How is each accounted for in the accounting records? What are the reasons to extend the different discounts to customers?
2. Set up a quantity discount plan and a sales discount plan for Whitefish to extend to customers. Be able to explain why you chose your bases for the discounts and the amount of discounts.

Problem 5-2A ***Calculation of Gross Margins for Sears and JCPenney*** **LO 1**

http://www.sears.com
http://www.jcpenney.com

The following information was summarized from the 2001 and 2000 consolidated statements of income of Sears, Roebuck and Co. (for the years ended December 29, 2001, and December 30, 2000), and JCPenney Company, Inc. and Subsidiaries (for the years ended January 26, 2002, and January 27, 2001). For each company, years are labeled as 2001 and 2000, respectively.

(in Millions)	2001 Sales*	2001 Cost of Sales**	2000 Sales*	2000 Cost of Sales**
Sears	$35,843	$26,322	$36,366	$26,721
JCPenney	32,004	22,789	31,846	23,031

*Described as "merchandise sales and services" by Sears and "retail sales, net" by JCPenney.
**Described as "cost of sales, buying and occupancy" by Sears and "cost of goods sold" by JCPenney.

Required

1. Calculate the gross margin (gross profit) ratios for Sears and JCPenney for 2001 and 2000.
2. Which company appears to be performing better? What factors might cause the difference in the gross margin ratios of the two companies? What other information should you consider to determine how these companies are performing in this regard?

Problem 5-3A ***Internal Control Procedures*** **LO 5**

The loan department in a bank is subject to regulation. Internal auditors work for the bank to ensure that the loan department complies with requirements. The internal auditors must verify that each car loan file has a note signed by the maker, verification of insurance, and a title issued by the state that names the bank as co-owner.

Required

1. Explain why the bank and the regulatory agency are concerned with these documents.
2. Describe the internal control procedures that should be in place to ensure that these documents are obtained and safeguarded.

Problem 5-4A ***The Design of Internal Control Documents (Appendix)*** **LO 6**

Tiger's Group is a newly formed company that produces and sells children's movies about an imaginary character. The movies are in such great demand that they are shipped to retail outlets as soon as they are produced. The company must pay a royalty to several actors for each movie that it sold to retail outlets.

Required

1. Describe some internal control features that should be in place to ensure that all royalties are paid to the actors.
2. Design the shipping form that Tiger's Group should use for the movies. Be sure to include authorizations and indicate the number of copies and the routing of the copies.

Alternate Multi-Concept Problems

Problem 5-5A ***Journal Entries for a Merchandiser*** **LO 1, 3**

GENERAL LEDGER

The following transactions were entered into by Maxwell Inc. during the month of July:

July 2: Purchased 1,000 pounds of steak at a cost of $3 per pound. Terms of payment are 2/10, net 30.

July 4: Paid trucking firm $500 to ship the steak purchased on July 2.

July 5: Purchased 600 pounds of steak at a cost of $3 per pound. Terms of payment are 2/10, net 45.

July 6: Paid trucking firm $300 to ship the steak purchased on July 5.

July 7: Due to expired dates on some packages, returned 100 pounds of the steak purchased on July 2. Received a credit on open account from the seller.

July 11: Paid for steak purchased on July 2.

July 13: Sold 1,200 pounds of steak from those purchased on July 2 and July 5. The selling price was $7 per pound, cash.

July 30: Paid for steak purchased on July 5.

(continued)

Required

1. Prepare the journal entries to record these transactions on the books of Maxwell Inc. The company uses the gross method of recording purchase discounts. Maxwell uses a periodic inventory system.
2. Maxwell assumes a $3 per pound cost of inventory when planning profit and setting prices. Is this accurate? Explain.

DECISION MAKING

GENERAL LEDGER

Problem 5-6A *Journal Entries for a Merchandiser* LO 1, 2, 3

Deckside Furniture Store entered into the following transactions in the month of April:

April 3: Purchased 50 lounge chairs at $120 each with terms 2/10, net 45. The chairs were shipped FOB destination.

April 7: Sold 6 chairs for $256 each, terms 2/10, net 30.

April 8: Purchased 20 patio umbrella tables for $96 each, FOB shipping point, terms 1/10, net 30.

April 9: Due to defects, returned 5 lounge chairs purchased on April 3. Received a credit memorandum.

April 10: Paid the trucking firm $288 for delivery of the tables purchased on April 8.

April 13: Paid for the chairs purchased on April 3.

April 17: Received payment for the chairs sold on April 7.

April 20: Paid for the tables purchased on April 8.

Required

1. Prepare all journal entries needed to record these transactions for the furniture company. Deckside uses the gross method of recording purchase and sales discounts. The company uses a periodic inventory system.
2. Do you think Deckside should change to a perpetual inventory system, given the nature of their business? Why or why not? What advantages would a company have using the perpetual system instead of the periodic system?

Problem 5-7A *Trade and Cash Discounts* LO 1, 3

Kalispell Inc. publishes books and offers trade discounts to customers who purchase in large quantities: 20% for purchases of more than 50 units. It also offers credit terms of 2/10, net 30 to induce early payment. The list price of one book is $50. Glacier Company purchased 100 of these books on September 12. Payment was made on September 21.

Required

1. Prepare the journal entries on Kalispell's books to record the sale and the receipt of cash.
2. Prepare the journal entries on Glacier's books to record the purchase and the payment.

DECISION MAKING

GENERAL LEDGER

Problem 5-8A *Journal Entries and Partial Income Statement for a Merchandiser* LO 1, 3

Toppsie Turn Inc. operates a chain of T-shirt stores. The company uses a periodic inventory system. Inventories on hand on June 1 and June 30, 2004, amount to $12,840. The company uses the gross method to record purchase discounts. The following transactions take place during the month of June:

a. Purchased merchandise from suppliers at a cost of $62,000 with credit terms of 2/10, net 30.
b. Paid freight cost of $3,400 to the common carrier for merchandise purchased.
c. Realized $124,000 of sales for the month, all of which are cash sales.
d. Paid for merchandise purchased during the month within the discount period.
e. Accepted $500 in returned merchandise during the month.

Required

1. Prepare the journal entries on the books of Toppsie Turn Inc. to record each transaction.
2. Determine the gross margin that Toppsie Turn would report on the income statement for the month of June.
3. Toppsie is thinking about extending credit to some of its major customers to encourage credit customers to pay quickly. Toppsie expects existing sales will increase by 10% and that, at the

new sales level, 60% of sales will be credit sales. Should Toppsie extend credit terms of 2/10, net 30? Explain your answer.

Problem 5-9A *Purchases and Sales of Merchandise, Cash Flows* LO 1, 2, 3

GENERAL LEDGER

Chestnut Corp., a ski shop, opened for business on October 1. It uses a periodic inventory system and the gross method to record purchase discounts. The following transactions occurred during the first month of business:

October 1: Purchased three units from Elm Inc. for $249 total, terms 2/10, net 30, FOB destination.

October 10: Paid for the October 1 purchase.

October 15: Sold one unit for $200 cash.

October 18: Purchased 10 units from Wausau Company for $800 total, with terms 2/10, net/30, FOB destination.

October 25: Sold three units for $200 each, cash.

October 30: Paid for the October 18 purchase.

Required

1. Prepare the journal entries to record the October transactions.
2. Determine the number of units on hand on October 31.
3. If Chestnut started the month with $2,000, determine its balance in cash at the end of the month, assuming that these are the only transactions that occurred during October. Why has the cash balance decreased when the company reported net income?

Problem 5-10A *Walgreen's Sales, Cost of Goods Sold, and Gross Margin* LO 1, 3

http://www.walgreens.com

The following information was summarized from the consolidated balance sheets of Walgreen Co. and Subsidiaries as of August 31, 2001, and August 31, 2000, and the consolidated statements of income for the years ended August 31, 2001, and August 31, 2000.

(in millions)	2001	2000
Accounts receivable, net	$ 798.3	$ 614.5
Cost of sales	18,048.9	15,465.9
Inventories	3,482.4	2,830.8
Net sales	24,623.0	21,206.9

Required

1. Prepare summary journal entries related to the collection of accounts receivable and sales during 2001. Assume hypothetically that all of Walgreen's sales are on account.
2. Walgreen Co. sets forth net sales but not gross sales on its income statement. What type(s) of deduction(s) would be made from gross sales to arrive at the amount of net sales reported? Why might the company decide not to report the amount(s) of the deduction(s) separately?
3. Reconstruct the cost of goods sold section of Walgreen's 2001 income statement.
4. Calculate the gross margin (gross profit) ratios for Walgreen Co. for 2001 and 2000 and comment on the change noted, if any. Is the company's performance improving? What factors might have caused the change in the gross margin ratio?

Problem 5-11A *Internal Control* LO 4, 5

Abbott Inc. is expanding and needs to hire more personnel in the accounting office. Barbara Barker, the chief accounting clerk, knew that her cousin Cheryl was looking for a job. Barbara and Cheryl are also roommates. Barbara offered Cheryl a job as her assistant. Barbara will be responsible for Cheryl's performance reviews and training.

Required

1. List some problems with the proposed personnel situations in the accounting department.
2. Explain why accountants are concerned with the hiring of personnel. What suggestions would you make to improve internal control at Abbott?
3. How would you explain to Barbara and Cheryl that they personally are not the problem?

SPREADSHEET

Problem 5-12A *Financial Statements* **LO 1, 3**

A list of accounts for Lloyd Inc. at December 31, 2004, follows:

Accounts Receivable	$ 56,359
Advertising Expense	12,900
Capital Stock	50,000
Cash	22,340
Dividends	6,000
Income Tax Expense	1,450
Income Tax Payable	1,450
Inventory	
January 1, 2004	6,400
December 31, 2004	5,900
Purchase Discounts	1,237
Purchases	62,845
Retained Earnings, January 1, 2004	28,252
Salaries Payable	650
Sales	112,768
Sales Returns	1,008
Transportation-in	375
Utilities Expense	1,800
Wages and Salaries Expense	23,000
Wages Payable	120

Required

1. Determine cost of goods sold for 2004.
2. Determine net income for 2004.
3. Prepare a balance sheet dated December 31, 2004.

Cases

Reading and Interpreting Financial Statements

Case 5-1 *Comparing Two Companies in the Same Industry: Winnebago Industries and Monaco Coach Corporation* **LO 1, 2**

http://www.winnebagoind.com
http://www.monacocoach.com

Refer to the financial information for Winnebago Industries and Monaco Coach Corporation in Appendices A and B at the end of the book and answer the following questions.

Required

1. Are Winnebago Industries and Monaco Coach merchandisers, manufacturers, or service providers?
2. What is the dollar amount of inventories that each company reports on its balance sheet at the end of 2001? What percentage of total assets do inventories represent for each company?
3. Refer to note 3 in Winnebago Industries' annual report. What components make up the company's inventory? Which is the largest of these components?
4. Refer to the note in Monaco Coach's annual report titled "Inventories." What components make up the company's inventory? Are you able to determine the dollar amount of each of these components?
5. Given the nature of their businesses, which inventory system, periodic or perpetual, would you expect both Winnebago Industries and Monaco Coach to use? Explain your answer.

Case 5-2 *Reading and Interpreting Gap Inc.'s Management Report* **LO 4**

http://www.gap.com

Gap Inc.'s 2001 annual report includes a management's report. Included in the report is the following:

> In fulfilling its responsibility for the reliability of financial information, Management has established and maintains accounting systems and procedures appropriately supported by internal accounting controls. Such controls include the selection and training of qualified personnel, an organizational structure providing for division of responsibility, com-

munication of requirement for compliance with approved accounting control and business practices and a program of internal audit. The extent of the Company's system of internal accounting control recognizes that the cost should not exceed the benefits derived and that the evaluation of those factors requires estimates and judgments by Management.

Required

1. Why did management include this report in the annual report?
2. What types of costs does Gap Inc. have in mind when it states that "the cost should not exceed the benefits derived"?
3. Based on what you know about retail stores, and Gap Inc. stores in particular, list the kinds of accounting and system controls the company may have in place to safeguard assets.

Making Financial Decisions

Case 5-3 *Gross Margin for a Merchandiser* LO 1, 3

DECISION MAKING

Emblems For You sells specialty sweatshirts. The purchase price is $10 per unit, plus 10% tax and a shipping cost of 50¢ per unit. When the units arrive, they must be labeled, at an additional cost of 75¢ per unit. Emblems purchased, received, and labeled 1,500 units, of which 750 units were sold during the month for $20 each. The controller has prepared the following income statement:

Sales	$15,000
Cost of sales ($11 × 750)	8,250
Gross margin	$ 6,750
Shipping expense	750
Labeling expense	1,125
Net income	$ 4,875

Emblems is aware that a gross margin of 40% is standard for the industry. The marketing manager believes that Emblems should lower the price because the gross margin is higher than the industry average.

Required

1. Calculate Emblems' gross margin ratio.
2. Explain why you believe that Emblems should or should not lower its selling price.

Case 5-4 *Pricing Decision* LO 1, 3

DECISION MAKING

Caroline's Candy Corner sells gourmet chocolates. The company buys chocolates, in bulk, for $5.00 per pound plus 5% sales tax. Credit terms are 2/10, net 25, and the company always pays promptly in order to take advantage of the discount. The chocolates are shipped to Caroline FOB shipping point. Shipping costs are $0.05 per pound. When the chocolates arrive at the shop, Caroline's Candy repackages them into one-pound boxes labeled with the store name. Boxes cost $0.70 each. The company pays its employees an hourly wage of $5.25 plus a commission of $0.10 per pound.

Required

1. What is the cost per one-pound box of chocolates?
2. What price must Caroline's Candy charge in order to have a 40% gross margin?
3. Do you believe this is a sufficient margin for this kind of business? What other costs might the company still incur?

Case 5-5 *Use of a Perpetual Inventory System* LO 2

DECISION MAKING

Darrell Keith is starting a new business. He would like to keep a tight control over it. Therefore, he wants to know *exactly* how much gross profit he earns on each unit he sells. Darrell has set up an elaborate numbering system to identify each item as it is purchased and then to match the item with a sales price. Each unit is assigned a number as follows:

0000-000-00-000

a. The first four numbers represent the month and day an item was received.
b. The second set of numbers is the last three numbers of the purchase order that authorized the purchase of the item.

(continued)

c. The third set of numbers is the two-number department code assigned to different types of products.

d. The last three numbers are a chronological code assigned to units as they are received during a given day.

Required

1. Write a short memo to Darrell explaining the benefits and costs involved in a perpetual inventory system in conjunction with his quest to know exactly how much he will earn on each unit.
2. Comment on Darrell's inventory system, assuming that he is selling (a) automobiles or (b) trees, shrubs, and plants.

Accounting and Ethics: What Would You Do?

Case 5-6 *Sales Returns and Allowances* LO 1

You are the controller for a large chain of discount merchandise stores. You receive a memorandum from the sales manager for the midwestern region. He raises an issue regarding the proper treatment of sales returns. The manager urges you to discontinue the "silly practice" of recording Sales Returns and Allowances each time a customer returns a product. In the manager's mind, this is a waste of time and unduly complicates the financial statements. The manager recommends, "Things could be kept a lot simpler by just reducing Sales Revenue when a product is returned."

Required

1. What do you think the sales manager's *motivation* might be for writing you the memo? Is it that he believes the present practice is a waste of time and unduly complicates the financial statements?
2. Do you agree with the sales manager's recommendation? Explain why you agree or disagree.
3. Write a brief memo to the sales manager outlining your position on this matter.

Case 5-7 *Cash Receipts in a Bookstore* LO 4, 5

You were recently hired by a large retail bookstore chain. Your training involved spending a week at the largest and most profitable store in the district. The store manager assigned the head cashier to train you on the cash register and closing procedures required by the company's home office. In the process, the head cashier instructed you to keep an envelope for cash over and short that would include cash or IOUs equal to the net amount of overages or shortages in the cash drawer. "It is impossible to balance exactly, so just put extra cash in this envelope and use the cash when you are short." You studied accounting for one semester in college and remembered your professor saying that "all deposits should be made intact, daily."

Required

Draft a memorandum to the store manager detailing any problems you see with the current system.

Internet Research Case

INTERNET

http://www.gap.com

Case 5-8 *Gap Inc.*

Gap Inc. has over 4,200 stores selling casual clothes worldwide, including its GapKids and babyGap stores and its Old Navy and Banana Republic stores. While its 2001 revenues were the best in its history, the ratio of cost of goods sold and occupancy expenses to net sales increased by over 7% from the prior year.

Go to Gap Inc.'s Web site, explore the site for company-related information, and view its most recent annual report.

1. For the most recent year available, what is Gap Inc.'s net sales? How does this compare to the previous year? What is shown for cost of goods sold and occupancy expenses? How does this compare to the previous year?
2. Based on the latest accounting year available, what percentage of net sales goes for cost of goods sold and occupancy expenses? How does this compare to the percentage calculated

from the Focus on Financial Results chapter opening vignette? What does this tell you about how well Gap Inc. is controlling its costs?

3. As a manager, how might changes in the gross profit percentage influence future actions? What actions might be taken by management to maximize the difference between net sales and cost of goods sold?

4. Find out from a source such as **Hoovers.com** or **finance.yahoo.com** what companies are in Gap Inc.'s industry segment. Conduct an online search for news articles that compare how well these companies are performing. Then compare the sales revenues and cost of goods sold for Gap Inc. plus two of its competitors.

   a. What are each company's sales revenues?

   b. Over three years, how fast is each company growing in terms of revenues?

   c. Compare each company's cost of goods sold as a percentage of sales.

Solutions to Key Terms Quiz

Quiz 1: Merchandise Accounting

14	Net sales (p. 223)
2	Sales Returns and Allowances (p. 224)
4	Trade discount (p. 224)
1	Quantity discount (p. 225)
7	Sales Discounts (p. 226)
11	Cost of goods available for sale (p. 227)
15	Cost of goods sold (p. 228)
5	Perpetual system (p. 228)
10	Periodic system (p. 228)
3	Transportation-in (p. 230)
13	Purchases (p. 231)
6	Purchase Returns and Allowances (p. 231)
12	Purchase Discounts (p. 232)
8	FOB destination point (p. 232)
9	FOB shipping point (p. 232)

Quiz 2: Internal Control

14	Internal control system (p. 234)
8	Report of management (p. 235)
13	Internal audit staff (p. 236)
2	Board of directors (p. 236)
4	Audit committee (p. 236)
10	Foreign Corrupt Practices Act (p. 236)
3	Accounting system (p. 237)
11	Administrative controls (p. 237)
5	Accounting controls (p. 237)
6	Purchase requisition form (Appendix) (p. 248)
12	Purchase order (Appendix) (p. 248)
1	Invoice (Appendix) (p. 249)
9	Blind receiving report (Appendix) (p. 249)
7	Invoice approval form (Appendix) (p. 249)

Chapter 6

Inventories and Cost of Goods Sold

© TERRI MILLER/E-VISUAL COMMUNICATIONS, INC.

Focus on Financial Results

For the last few years the consumer electronics industry has sustained tremendous growth in a fiercely competitive environment. Circuit City remains a top retailer in the U.S. market. In addition to electronics, Circuit City maintains a revolutionary used-car business known as CarMax. High-quality customer service and state-of-the-art merchandise have rewarded Circuit City with sales that reached nearly $13 billion in each of the last three years.

Sales volume is important for any merchandiser but so is managing *inventory* effectively. Inventory is a major issue for Circuit City as it continues to grow; you can see from the accompanying partial balance sheets that merchandise is the largest company asset, representing over one-third of total assets at the end of the 2002 fiscal year.

Although inventory is still the largest of Circuit City's assets, the ratio of inventory to total assets declined significantly at the end of the 2002 fiscal year. Maintaining large stocks of inventory is costly for any business, and the more a retailer can minimize the amounts it has tied up in merchandise and still meet customer demand, the better off it will be. A combination of efforts to continue to grow sales and to control inventory costs will be two of the most critical factors in the future success of this leading consumer products merchandiser.

Circuit City's 2002 Annual Report

CONSOLIDATED BALANCE SHEETS

(Amounts in thousands except share data)	At February 28 2002	2001
ASSETS		
CURRENT ASSETS:		
Cash and cash equivalents [NOTE 2]	$1,251,532	$ 446,131
Net accounts receivable [NOTE 11]	726,541	585,761
Inventory	1,633,327	1,757,664
Prepaid expenses and other current assets	41,311	57,623
TOTAL CURRENT ASSETS	3,652,711	2,847,179
Property and equipment, net [NOTES 3 AND 4]	853,778	988,947
Other assets	32,897	35,207
TOTAL ASSETS	$4,539,386	$3,871,333

Inventory is about one third of Circuit City's total assets.

CONSOLIDATED STATEMENTS OF EARNINGS

(Amounts in thousands except per share data)	Years Ended February 28 or 29 2002	%	2001	%	2000	%
NET SALES AND OPERATING REVENUES	$12,791,468	100.0	$12,959,028	100.0	$12,614,390	100.0
Cost of sales, buying and warehousing	10,049,793	78.6	10,135,380	78.2	9,751,833	77.3
Appliance exit costs [NOTE 14]	10,000	–	28,326	0.2	–	–
GROSS PROFIT	2,731,675	21.4	2,795,322	21.6	2,862,557	22.7
Selling, general and administrative expenses [NOTE 10]	2,372,941	18.6	2,514,912	19.4	2,309,593	18.3
Appliance exit costs [NOTE 14]	–	–	1,670	–	–	–
Interest expense [NOTE 4]	5,839	–	19,383	0.2	24,206	0.2
TOTAL EXPENSES	2,378,780	18.6	2,535,965	19.6	2,333,799	18.5
Earnings from continuing operations before income taxes	352,895	2.8	259,357	2.0	528,758	4.2
Provision for income taxes [NOTE 5]	134,100	1.1	98,555	0.8	200,928	1.6
EARNINGS FROM CONTINUING OPERATIONS	218,795	1.7	160,802	1.2	327,830	2.6
Discontinued operations [NOTE 15]:						
Loss from discontinued operations of Divx, less income tax benefit	–	–	–	–	(16,215)	(0.1)
Loss of disposal of Divx, less income tax benefit	–	–	–	–	(114,025)	(0.9)
Loss from discontinued operations	–	–	–	–	(130,240)	(1.0)
NET EARNINGS	$ 218,795	1.7	$ 160,802	1.2	$ 197,590	1.6

You're in the Driver's Seat

http://www.circuitcity.com

Also critical to the success of Circuit City is its management of "inventory turns"—the number of times it turns over its merchandise each year. What will lower or higher inventory turns say about the company's effectiveness in choosing, pricing, and promoting its products? While studying this chapter, consider these questions and select the annual report items you need to estimate Circuit City's inventory turns each year.

LEARNING OBJECTIVES

After studying this chapter, you should be able to:

LO 1 Identify the forms of inventory held by different types of businesses and the types of costs incurred. (p. 272)

LO 2 Explain the relationship between the valuation of inventory and the measurement of income. (p. 273)

LO 3 Apply the inventory costing methods of specific identification, weighted average, FIFO, and LIFO using a periodic system. (p. 275)

LO 4 Analyze the effects of the different costing methods on inventory, net income, income taxes, and cash flow. (p. 279)

LO 5 Analyze the effects of an inventory error on various financial statement items. (p. 284)

LO 6 Apply the lower-of-cost-or-market rule to the valuation of inventory. (p. 287)

LO 7 Explain why and how the cost of inventory is estimated in certain situations. (p. 290)

LO 8 Analyze the management of inventory turnover. (p. 292)

LO 9 Explain the effects that inventory transactions have on the statement of cash flows. (p. 293)

LO 10 Explain the differences between a periodic and a perpetual inventory system (Appendix). (p. 298)

LO 11 Apply the inventory costing methods using a perpetual system (Appendix). (p. 300)

THE NATURE OF INVENTORY

LO 1 Identify the forms of inventory held by different types of businesses and the types of costs incurred.

Inventory is an asset that is held for *resale* in the normal course of business. The distinction between inventory and an operating asset is the *intent* of the owner. For example, some of the computers that Circuit City owns are operating assets because they are used in various activities of the business such as the payroll and accounting functions. Many more of the computers Circuit City owns are inventory, however, because the company intends to sell them. This chapter is concerned with the proper valuation of inventory and the related effect on cost of goods sold.

It is important to distinguish between the *types* of inventory costs incurred and the *form* the inventory takes. Wholesalers and retailers incur a single type of cost, the *purchase price,* of the inventory they sell. On the balance sheet they use a single account for inventory, titled **Merchandise Inventory.** Wholesalers and retailers buy merchandise in finished form and offer it for resale without transforming the product in any way. Because they do not use factory buildings, assembly lines, or production equipment, merchandise companies have a relatively small dollar amount in operating assets and a large amount in inventory. For example, on its balance sheet, Circuit City reported inventory of approximately $1.6 billion and total assets of $4.5 billion. It is not unusual for inventories to account for half of the total assets of a merchandise company.

Merchandise inventory The account wholesalers and retailers use to report inventory held for resale.

The cost of inventory to a *merchandiser* is limited to the product's purchase price, which may include other costs we will mention soon. Conversely, three distinct *types* of costs are incurred by a *manufacturer:* direct materials, direct labor, and manufacturing overhead. Direct materials, also called **raw materials,** are the ingredients used in making a product. The costs of direct materials used in manufacturing an automobile include the costs of steel, glass, and rubber. Direct labor consists of the amounts paid to workers to manufacture the product. The $20 per hour paid to an assembly line worker is a primary ingredient in the cost to manufacture the automobile. Manufacturing overhead includes all other costs that are related to the manufacturing process but cannot be directly matched to specific units of output. Depreciation of a factory building and the salary of a supervisor are two examples of overhead costs. Accountants have developed various techniques to assign, or allocate, these manufacturing overhead costs to specific products.

Raw materials The inventory of a manufacturer before the addition of any direct labor or manufacturing overhead.

In addition to the three types of costs incurred in a production process, the inventory of a manufacturer takes three distinct *forms.* The three forms or stages in the development of inventory are raw materials, work in process, and finished goods. Direct materials or raw materials enter a production process in which they are transformed into a finished product by the addition of direct labor and manufacturing overhead. At any point in time, including the end of an accounting period, some of the materials have entered the process and some labor costs have been incurred but the product is not finished. The cost of unfinished products is appropriately called **work in process** or *work in progress.* Inventory that has completed the production process and is available for sale is called **finished goods.** Finished goods are the equivalent of merchandise inventory for a retailer or wholesaler in that both represent the inventory of goods held for sale. Many manufacturers disclose the dollar amounts of each of the three forms of inventory in their annual report. For example, Nike disclosed in its 2001 annual report the following amounts, stated in millions of dollars:

Work in process The cost of unfinished products in a manufacturing company.

Finished goods A manufacturer's inventory that is complete and ready for sale.

http://www.nike.com

	MILLIONS
Inventories:	
Finished goods	$1,399.4
Work in progress	15.1
Raw materials	9.6
	$1,424.1

Exhibit 6-1 summarizes the relationships between the types of costs incurred and the forms of inventory for different types of businesses.

From Concept to Practice 6.1

Reading Winnebago Industries' Notes

Note 3 in Winnebago Industries' 2001 annual report includes information about the composition of its inventory. How does Winnebago Industries categorize these elements of its inventory? What percentage of its total inventory at the end of 2001 is made up of finished goods?

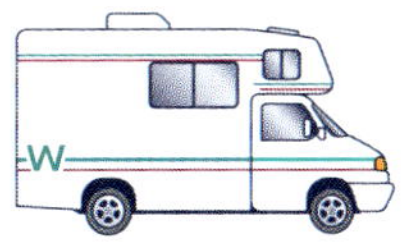

Exhibit 6-1

Relationships between Types of Businesses and Inventory Costs

Type of Business	Inventory	Costs Included in Inventory
Retailer/Wholesaler →	Merchandise inventory	Cost to purchase
	Raw materials	Cost of materials before entered into production
Manufacturer →	Work in process	Costs of direct materials used, direct labor, and overhead in unfinished items
	Finished goods	Cost of completed, but unsold, items

INVENTORY VALUATION AND THE MEASUREMENT OF INCOME

LO 2 Explain the relationship between the valuation of inventory and the measurement of income.

Valuation is the major problem in accounting for inventories. Because of the additional complexities involved in valuing the inventory of a manufacturer, we will concentrate in this chapter on the valuation of *merchandise inventory.* (Accounting for the inventory costs incurred by a manufacturing firm is covered in detail in management accounting textbooks.)

The inventory of a manufacturer consists of raw material, work in process, and finished goods. The electronic device being built here is part of a firm's work in process inventory. The direct materials probably consist of such items as the individual control knobs purchased from another manufacturer. When the manufacturing process is complete, the inventory of finished goods is ready for sale.

One of the most fundamental concepts in accounting is the relationship between *asset valuation* and the *measurement of income.* Recall a point made in Chapter 4: assets are unexpired costs, and expenses are expired costs. Thus, the value assigned to an asset on the balance sheet determines the amount eventually recognized as an expense on the income statement. For example, the amount recorded as the cost of an item of plant and equipment will dictate the amount of depreciation expense recognized on the income statement over the life of the asset. Similarly, the amount recorded as the cost of inventory determines the amount recognized as cost of goods sold on the income statement when the asset is sold. An error in assigning the proper amount to inventory on the balance sheet will affect the amount recognized as cost of goods sold on the income statement. The relationship between inventory as an asset and cost of goods sold can be understood by recalling the cost of goods sold section of the income statement. Assume the following example:

Beginning inventory	$ 500
Add: Purchases	1,200
Cost of goods available for sale	$1,700
Less: Ending inventory	(600)
Cost of goods sold	$1,100

The amount assigned to ending inventory is deducted from cost of goods available for sale to determine cost of goods sold. If the ending inventory amount is incorrect, cost of goods sold will be wrong, and thus the net income of the period will be in error as well. (We will look at inventory errors later in the chapter.)

Inventory Costs: What Should Be Included?

All assets, including inventory, are recorded initially at cost. Cost is defined as "the price paid or consideration given to acquire an asset. As applied to inventories, cost means in principle the sum of the applicable expenditures and charges directly or indirectly incurred in bringing an article to its existing condition and location."[1]

Note the reference to the existing *condition* and *location.* This means that certain costs may also be included in the "price paid." Here are examples:

- Any freight costs incurred by the buyer in shipping inventory to its place of business should be included in the cost of the inventory.
- The cost of insurance taken out during the time that inventory is in transit should be added to the cost of the inventory.
- The cost of storing inventory before the time it is ready to be sold should be included in cost.
- Various types of taxes paid, such as excise and sales taxes, are other examples of costs necessary to put the inventory into a position to be able to sell it.

It is often very difficult, however, to allocate many of these incidental costs among the various items of inventory purchased. For example, consider a $500 freight bill that a supermarket paid on a merchandise shipment that includes 100 different items of inventory. To address the practical difficulty in assigning this type of cost to the different products, many companies have a policy by which transportation costs are charged to expense of the period if they are immaterial in amount. Thus, shipments of merchandise are simply recorded at the net invoice price, that is, after taking any cash discounts for early payment. It is a practical solution to a difficult allocation problem. Once again, the company must apply the cost/benefit test to accounting information.

[1]*Accounting Research Bulletin No. 43,* "Inventory Pricing" (New York: American Institute of Certified Public Accountants, June 1953), Ch. 4, statement 3.

Business Strategy

http://www.circuitcity.com

Capitalizing on the Digital Age

New technology is the lifeblood of all consumer electronics retailers in the new millennium, and Circuit City is no exception. The company fully realizes that it must be on the leading edge in offering the latest innovations to its customers if it is to sustain the growth that has made it successful in this highly competitive environment.

At the heart of the new technology is the revolution that has been taking place in digital products. These products generated significant sales increases for Circuit City in a variety of product lines, including big-screen televisions, imaging products, satellite systems, and wireless phones. The company is especially encouraged by the potential for sustained growth in the sales of big-screen TVs, given that their volume and profits are among the highest in the company's line. Circuit City points to the projections of an industry group that anticipates a growth rate in sales in double-digits in calendar 2002 for big-screen televisions. Certainly a key to the company's success in the next few years will be its ability to take advantage of the move to digital technology and to offer its customers products that will satisfy their appetite for the latest electronic gadgetry. ■

Source: Circuit City 2002 annual report.

INVENTORY COSTING METHODS WITH A PERIODIC SYSTEM

LO 3 Apply the inventory costing methods of specific identification, weighted average, FIFO, and LIFO using a periodic system.

To this point, we have assumed that the cost to purchase an item of inventory is constant. For most merchandisers, however, the unit cost of inventory changes frequently. Consider a simple example. Everett Company purchases merchandise twice during the first year of business. The dates, the number of units purchased, and the costs are as follows:

February 4	200 units purchased at $1.00 per unit	=$200
October 13	200 units purchased at $1.50 per unit	=$300

Everett sells 200 units during the first year. Individual sales of the units take place relatively evenly throughout the year. The question is: *which* 200 units did the company sell, the $1.00 units or the $1.50 units or some combination of each? Recall the earlier discussion of the relationship between asset valuation and income measurement. The question is important because the answer determines not only the value assigned to the 200 units of ending inventory *but also* the amount allocated to cost of goods sold for the 200 units sold.

One possible method of assigning amounts to ending inventory and cost of goods sold is to *specifically identify* which 200 units were sold and which 200 units are on hand. This method is feasible for a few types of businesses in which units can be identified by serial numbers, but it is totally impractical in most situations. As an alternative to specific identification, we could make an *assumption* as to which units were sold and which are on hand. Three different answers are possible:

1. 200 units sold at $1.00 each = $200 cost of goods sold
and 200 units on hand at $1.50 each = $300 ending inventory
or

2. 200 units sold at $1.50 each = $300 cost of goods sold
and 200 units on hand at $1.00 each = $200 ending inventory
or

3. 200 units sold at $1.25 each = $250 cost of goods sold
and 200 units on hand at $1.25 each = $250 ending inventory

The third alternative assumes an *average cost* for the 200 units on hand and the 200 units sold. The average cost is the cost of the two purchases of $200 and $300, or $500, divided by the 400 units available to sell, or $1.25 per unit.

If we are concerned with the actual *physical flow* of the units of inventory, all of the three methods illustrated may be incorrect. The only approach that will yield a "correct" answer in terms of the actual flow of *units* of inventory is the specific identification method. In the absence of a specific identification approach, it is impossible to say which particular units were *actually* sold. In fact, there may have been sales from each of the two purchases, that is, some of the $1.00 units may have been sold and some of the $1.50 units may have been sold. To solve the problem of assigning costs to identical units, accountants have developed inventory costing assumptions or methods. Each of these methods makes a specific *assumption* about the *flow of costs* rather than the physical flow of units. The only approach that uses the actual flow of the units in assigning costs is the specific identification method.

To take a closer look at specific identification as well as three alternative approaches to valuing inventory, we will use the following example:

	UNITS	UNIT COST	TOTAL COST
Beginning inventory			
January 1	500	$10	$ 5,000*
Purchases			
January 20	300	11	$ 3,300
April 8	400	12	4,800
September 5	200	13	2,600
December 12	100	14	1,400
Total purchases	1,000 units		$12,100
Available for sale	1,500 units		$17,100
Units sold	900 units		?
Units in ending inventory	600 units		?

*Beginning inventory of $5,000 is carried over as the ending inventory from the prior period. It is highly unlikely that each of the four methods we will illustrate would result in the same dollar amount of inventory at any point in time. It is helpful when first learning the methods, however, to assume the same amount of beginning inventory.

The question marks indicate the dilemma. What portion of the cost of goods available for sale of $17,100 should be assigned to the 900 units sold? What portion should be assigned to the 600 units remaining in ending inventory? The purpose of an inventory costing method is to provide a reasonable answer to these two questions.

Specific Identification Method

Specific identification method An inventory costing method that relies on matching unit costs with the actual units sold.

It is not always necessary to make an assumption about the flow of costs. In certain situations, it may be possible to specifically identify which units are sold and which units are on hand. A serial number on an automobile allows a dealer to identify a car on hand and thus its unit cost. An appliance dealer with 15 refrigerators on hand at the end of the year can identify the unit cost of each by matching a tag number with the purchase records. To illustrate the use of the **specific identification method** for our example, assume that the merchandiser is able to identify the specific units in the inventory at the end of the year and their costs as follows:

Units on Hand

DATE PURCHASED	UNITS	COST	TOTAL COST
January 20	100	$11	$1,100
April 8	300	12	3,600
September 5	200	13	2,600
Ending inventory	600		$7,300

One of two techniques can be used to find cost of goods sold. We can deduct ending inventory from the cost of goods available for sale:

Cost of goods available for sale		$17,100
Less:	Ending inventory	7,300
Equals:	Cost of goods sold	$ 9,800

Or we can calculate cost of goods sold independently by matching the units sold with their respective unit costs. By eliminating the units in ending inventory from the original acquisition schedule, the units sold and their costs are as follows:

Units Sold

DATE PURCHASED	UNITS	COST	TOTAL COST
Beginning Inventory	500	$10	$5,000
January 20	200	11	2,200
April 8	100	12	1,200
December 12	100	14	1,400
Cost of goods sold	900		$9,800

The practical difficulty in keeping track of individual items of inventory sold is not the only problem with the use of this method. The method also allows management to *manipulate income.* For example, assume that a company is not having a particularly good year. Management may be tempted to do whatever it can to boost net income. One way it can do this is by *selectively selling units with the lowest-possible unit cost.* By doing so, the company can keep cost of goods sold down and net income up. Because of the potential for manipulation with the specific identification method, coupled with the practical difficulty of applying it in most situations, it is not widely used.

Weighted Average Cost Method

The **weighted average cost method** is a relatively easy approach to costing inventory. It assigns the same unit cost to all units available for sale during the period. The weighted average cost is calculated as follows for our example:

Weighted average cost method An inventory costing method that assigns the same unit cost to all units available for sale during the period.

$$\frac{\textbf{Cost of Goods Available for Sale}}{\textbf{Units Available for Sale}} = \textbf{Weighted Average Cost}$$

$$\frac{\$17{,}100}{1{,}500} = \$11.40$$

Ending inventory is found by multiplying the weighted average unit cost by the number of units on hand:

Weighted Average Cost	×	Number of Units in Ending Inventory	=	Ending Inventory
$11.40	×	600	=	$6,840

Cost of goods sold can be calculated in one of two ways:

Cost of goods available for sale		$17,100
Less:	Ending inventory	6,840
Equals:	Cost of goods sold	$10,260

or

Weighted Average Cost	×	Number of Units Sold	=	Cost of Goods Sold
$11.40	×	900	=	$10,260

Note that the computation of the weighted average cost is based on the cost of *all* units available for sale during the period, not just the beginning inventory or purchases. Also note that the method is called the *weighted* average cost method. As the name indicates, each of the individual unit costs is multiplied by the number of units acquired at each price. The simple arithmetic average of the unit costs for the beginning inventory and the four purchases is ($10 + $11 + $12 + $13 + $14)/5 = $12. The weighted average cost is slightly less than $12 ($11.40), however, because more units were acquired at the lower prices than at the higher prices.

First-In, First-Out Method (FIFO)

FIFO method An inventory costing method that assigns the most recent costs to ending inventory.

The **FIFO method** assumes that the first units in, or purchased, are the first units out, or sold. The first units sold during the period are assumed to come from the beginning inventory. After the beginning inventory is sold, the next units sold are assumed to come from the first purchase during the period and so forth. Thus, ending inventory consists of the most recent purchases of the period. In many businesses, this cost-flow assumption is a fairly accurate reflection of the *physical* flow of products. For example, to maintain a fresh stock of products, the physical flow in a grocery store is first-in, first-out.

To calculate *ending inventory,* we start with the *most recent* inventory acquired and work *backward:*

Units on Hand

DATE PURCHASED	UNITS	COST	TOTAL COST
December 12	100	$14	$1,400
September 5	200	13	2,600
April 8	300	12	3,600
Ending inventory	600		$7,600

Cost of goods sold can then be found:

Cost of goods available for sale		$17,100
Less:	Ending inventory	7,600
Equals:	Cost of goods sold	$ 9,500

Or, because the FIFO method assumes that the first units in are the first ones sold, cost of goods sold can be calculated by starting with the *beginning inventory* and working *forward:*

Units Sold

DATE PURCHASED	UNITS	COST	TOTAL COST
Beginning Inventory	500	$10	$5,000
January 20	300	11	3,300
April 8	100	12	1,200
Units sold	900	Cost of goods sold	$9,500

Accounting for Your Decisions

You Are the Controller

Your company, Princeton Systems, is a manufacturer of components for personal computers. The company uses the FIFO method to account for its inventory. The CEO, a stickler for accuracy, asks you why you can't identify each unit of inventory and place a cost on it, instead of making an assumption that the first unit of inventory is the first sold when that is not necessarily the case.

ANS: The CEO is suggesting the specific identification method, which works best when there are fewer pieces of unique inventory, not thousands of units of identical pieces. Because the company makes thousands of identical components each year, it would be impractical to assign specific costs to each unit of inventory. The FIFO method, on the other hand, assumes that the first units in are the first units sold, an appropriate assumption under these circumstances.

Last-In, First-Out Method (LIFO)

The **LIFO method** assumes that the last units in, or purchased, are the first units out, or sold. The first units sold during the period are assumed to come from the latest purchase made during the period and so forth. Can you think of any businesses where the *physical* flow of products is last-in, first-out? Although this situation is not nearly so common as a first-in, first-out physical flow, a stockpiling operation, such as in a rock quarry, operates on this basis.

LIFO method An inventory method that assigns the most recent costs to cost of goods sold.

To calculate *ending inventory* using LIFO, we start with the *beginning inventory* and work *forward:*

Units on Hand

DATE PURCHASED	UNITS	COST	TOTAL COST
Beginning inventory	500	$10	$5,000
January 20	100	11	1,100
Ending inventory	600		$6,100

Cost of goods sold can then be found:

Cost of goods available for sale		$17,100
Less:	Ending inventory	6,100
Equals:	Cost of goods sold	$11,000

Or, because the LIFO method assumes that the last units in are the first ones sold, *cost of goods sold* can be calculated by starting with the *most recent* inventory acquired and working *backward:*

Units Sold

DATE PURCHASED	UNITS	COST	TOTAL COST
December 12	100	$14	$ 1,400
September 5	200	13	2,600
April 8	400	12	4,800
January 20	200	11	2,200
Units sold	900	Cost of goods sold	$11,000

Study Tip

There may be cases, such as this illustration of LIFO, in which it is easier to determine ending inventory and then deduct it from cost of goods available for sale to find cost of goods sold. This approach is easier in this example because there are fewer layers in ending inventory than in cost of goods sold. In other cases, it may be quicker to determine cost of goods sold first and then plug in ending inventory.

SELECTING AN INVENTORY COSTING METHOD

LO 4 Analyze the effects of the different costing methods on inventory, net income, income taxes, and cash flow.

The mechanics of each of the inventory costing methods are straightforward. But how does a company decide on the best method to use to value its inventory? According to the accounting profession, *the primary determinant in selecting an inventory costing method should be the ability of the method to accurately reflect the net income of the period.* But how and why does a particular costing method accurately reflect the net income of the period? Because there is no easy answer to this question, a number of arguments have been raised by accountants to justify the use of one method over the others. We turn now to some of these arguments.

Costing Methods and Cash Flow

Comparative income statements for our example are presented in Exhibit 6-2. Note that with the use of the weighted average method, net income is between the amounts for FIFO and LIFO. Because the weighted average method normally yields results between the other two methods, we concentrate on the two extremes, LIFO and FIFO. The major advantage of using the weighted average method is its simplicity.

The original data for our example involved a situation in which prices were *rising* throughout the period: beginning inventory cost $10 per unit, and the last purchase during the year was at $14. With LIFO, the most recent costs are assigned to cost of goods sold; with FIFO, the older costs are assigned to expense. Thus, in a period of rising prices,

Exhibit 6-2

Income Statements for the Inventory Costing Methods

	WEIGHTED AVERAGE	FIFO	LIFO
Sales revenue—$20 each	$18,000	$18,000	$18,000
Beginning inventory	$ 5,000	$ 5,000	$ 5,000
Purchases	12,100	12,100	12,100
Cost of goods available for sale	$17,100	$17,100	$17,100
Ending inventory	**6,840**	**7,600**	**6,100**
Cost of goods sold	**$10,260**	**$ 9,500**	**$11,000**
Gross margin	**$ 7,740**	**$ 8,500**	**$ 7,000**
Operating expenses	2,000	2,000	2,000
Net income before tax	**$ 5,740**	**$ 6,500**	**$ 5,000**
Income tax expense (40%)	**2,296**	**2,600**	**2,000**
Net income	**$ 3,444**	**$ 3,900**	**$ 3,000**

NOTE: Figures that differ among the three methods are in bold.

the assignment of the *higher* prices to cost of goods sold under LIFO results in a *lower gross margin* under LIFO than under FIFO ($7,000 for LIFO and $8,500 for FIFO). Because operating expenses are not affected by the choice of inventory method, the lower gross margin under LIFO results in lower income before tax, which in turn leads to lower taxes. If we assume a 40% tax rate, income tax expense under LIFO is only $2,000, compared with $2,600 under FIFO, a savings of $600 in taxes. Another way to look at the taxes saved by using LIFO is to focus on the difference in the expense under each method:

	LIFO cost of goods sold	$11,000
−	FIFO cost of goods sold	9,500
	Additional expense from use of LIFO	$ 1,500
×	Tax rate	0.40
	Tax savings from the use of LIFO	$ 600

Study Tip

During a period of falling prices, all of the effects shown here would be just the opposite. For example, cost of goods sold would be lower under LIFO than under FIFO.

To summarize, *during a period of rising prices,* the two methods result in the following:

ITEM	LIFO	RELATIVE TO	FIFO
Cost of goods sold	Higher		Lower
Gross margin	Lower		Higher
Income before taxes	Lower		Higher
Taxes	Lower		Higher

In conclusion, lower taxes with the use of LIFO result in cash savings.

The tax savings available from the use of LIFO during a period of rising prices are largely responsible for its popularity. Keep in mind, however, that the cash saved from a lower tax bill with LIFO is only a temporary savings, or what is normally called a *tax deferral.* At some point in the life of the business, the inventory that is carried at the older, lower-priced amounts will be sold. This will result in a tax bill higher than that under FIFO. Yet even a tax deferral is beneficial; given the opportunity, it is better to pay less tax today and more in the future because today's tax savings can be invested.

Two-Minute Review

1. *Which of the inventory methods will result in the least amount of income before taxes, assuming a period of rising prices?*
2. *What is the easiest way to calculate the tax savings from using one method versus another?*

Answers on page 296.

LIFO Liquidation

Recall the assumption made about which costs remain in inventory when LIFO is used. The costs of the oldest units remain in inventory, and if prices are rising, the costs of these units will be lower than the costs of more recent purchases. Now assume that the company *sells more units than it buys during the period.* When a company using LIFO experiences a liquidation, some of the units assumed to be sold will come from the older layers, with a relatively low unit cost. This situation, called a **LIFO liquidation,** presents a dilemma for the company.

LIFO liquidation The result of selling more units than are purchased during the period, which can have negative tax consequences if a company is using LIFO.

A partial or complete liquidation of the older, lower-priced units will result in a low cost of goods sold figure and a correspondingly high gross margin for the period. In turn, the company faces a large tax bill because of the relatively high gross margin. In fact, a liquidation causes the tax advantages of using LIFO to reverse on the company, which is faced with paying off some of the taxes that were deferred in earlier periods. Should a company facing this situation buy inventory at the end of the year to avoid the consequences of a liquidation? This is a difficult question to answer and depends on many factors, including the company's cash position. At the least, the accountant must be aware of the potential for a large tax bill if a liquidation occurs.

Of course, a LIFO liquidation also benefits—and may even distort—reported earnings if the liquidation is large enough. For this reason and the tax problem, many companies are reluctant to liquidate their LIFO inventory. The problem often festers, and companies find themselves with inventory costed at decade-old price levels.

The LIFO Conformity Rule

Would it be possible for a company to have the best of both worlds? That is, could it use FIFO to report its income to stockholders, thus maximizing the amount of net income reported to this group, and use LIFO to report to the IRS, minimizing its taxable income and the amount paid to the government? Unfortunately, the IRS says that if a company chooses LIFO for reporting cost of goods sold on its tax return, then it must also use LIFO on its books, that is, in preparing its income statement. This is called the **LIFO conformity rule.** Note that the rule applies only to the use of LIFO on the tax return. A company is free to use different methods in preparing its tax return and its income statement as long as the method used for the tax return is *not* LIFO.

LIFO conformity rule The IRS requirement that if LIFO is used on the tax return, it must also be used in reporting income to stockholders.

The LIFO Reserve: Estimating LIFO's Effect on Income and on Taxes Paid for Whirlpool

If a company decides to use LIFO, an investor can still determine how much more income the company would have reported had it used FIFO. In addition, he or she can approximate the tax savings or the additional taxes to the company from the use of LIFO. Consider the following note from the 2001 annual report for Whirlpool Corporation:

http://www.whirlpool.com

(4) Inventories

DECEMBER 31 (MILLIONS OF DOLLARS)	2001	2000
Finished products	$ 949	$ 956
Work in process	58	57
Raw materials	239	257
	$1,246	$1,270
Less excess of FIFO cost over LIFO cost	136	151
Total inventories	$1,110	$1,119

LIFO inventories represent approximately 39% and 33% of total inventories at December 31, 2001 and 2000.

Note that Whirlpool uses more than one inventory method and that at the end of 2001, LIFO inventories accounted for only 39% of the total inventory. It is not unusual for companies to use more than one method to value inventories. For now it is important to understand that Whirlpool reported $1,110,000,000 as its total inventory on the December 31, 2001, balance sheet.

The following steps explain the logic for using the information in the inventory note to estimate LIFO's effect on income and on taxes:

LIFO reserve The excess of the value of a company's inventory stated at FIFO over the value stated at LIFO.

1. The excess of the value of a company's inventory stated at FIFO over the value stated at LIFO is called the **LIFO reserve.** The *cumulative* excess of the value of Whirlpool's inventory on a FIFO basis over the value on a LIFO basis is $136 million at the end of 2001.
2. Because Whirlpool reports inventory at a lower value on its balance sheet using LIFO, it will report a higher cost of goods sold amount on the income statement. Thus, the LIFO reserve not only represents the excess of the inventory balance on a FIFO basis over that on a LIFO basis but also *represents the cumulative amount by which cost of goods sold on a LIFO basis exceeds cost of goods sold on a FIFO basis.*
3. The decrease in Whirlpool's LIFO reserve in 2001 was $15 million ($151 million − $136 million). This means that the decrease in cost of goods sold for 2001 from using LIFO instead of FIFO was also this amount. Thus, income before tax for 2001 was $15 million higher because the company used LIFO.
4. If we assume a corporate tax rate of 35%, the additional taxes from using LIFO amounted to $15 million × 0.35, or $5.25 million.

From Concept to Practice 6.2

Reading Winnebago Industries' Notes

Refer to Note 3 in Winnebago Industries' 2001 annual report. Did the LIFO reserve go up or down in 2001? By how much? Did Winnebago Industries pay more or less taxes in 2001 because it used LIFO?

Costing Methods and Inventory Profits

FIFO, LIFO, and weighted average are all cost-based methods to value inventory. They vary in terms of which costs are assigned to inventory and which to cost of goods sold, but all three assign *historical costs* to inventory. In our previous example, the unit cost for inventory purchases gradually increased during the year from $10 for the beginning inventory to a high of $14 on the date of the last purchase.

Replacement cost The current cost of a unit of inventory.

An alternative to assigning any of the historical costs incurred during the year to ending inventory and cost of goods sold would be to use **replacement cost** to value each of these. Assume that the cost to replace a unit of inventory at the end of the year is $15. Use of a replacement cost system results in the following:

Ending inventory	=	600 units	×	$15 per unit	=	$ 9,000
Cost of goods sold	=	900 units	×	$15 per unit	=	$13,500

Inventory profit The portion of the gross profit that results from holding inventory during a period of rising prices.

A replacement cost approach is not acceptable under the profession's current standards, but many believe that it provides more relevant information to users. Inventory must be replaced if a company is to remain in business. Many accountants argue that the use of historical cost in valuing inventory leads to what is called **inventory profit,** particularly if FIFO is used in a period of rising prices. For example, cost of goods sold in our illustration was only $9,500 on a FIFO basis, compared with $13,500 if the replacement cost of $15 per unit is used. The $4,000 difference between the two cost of goods sold figures is a profit from holding the inventory during a period of rising prices and is called *inventory profit.* To look at this another way, assume that the units are sold for $20 each. The following analysis reconciles the difference between gross margin on a FIFO basis and on a replacement cost basis:

Sales revenue—900 units × $20 =		$18,000
Cost of goods sold—FIFO basis		9,500
Gross margin—FIFO basis		$ 8,500
Cost of goods sold—replacement cost basis	$13,500	
Cost of goods sold—FIFO basis	9,500	
Profit from holding inventory during a period of inflation		4,000
Gross margin on a replacement cost basis		$ 4,500

Those who argue in favor of a replacement cost approach would report only $4,500 of gross margin. They believe that the additional $4,000 of profit reported on a FIFO basis is simply due to holding the inventory during a period of rising prices. According to this viewpoint, if the 900 units sold during the period are to be replaced, a necessity if the company is to continue operating, the use of replacement cost in calculating cost of goods sold results in a better measure of gross margin than if it is calculated using FIFO.

Given that our current standards require the use of historical costs rather than replacement costs, does any one of the costing methods result in a better approximation of replacement cost of goods sold than the others? Because LIFO assigns the cost of the most recent purchases to cost of goods sold, it most nearly approximates the results with a replacement cost system. The other side of the argument, however, is that whereas LIFO results in the best approximation of *replacement cost of goods sold* on the *income statement,* FIFO most nearly approximates replacement cost of the *inventory* on the *balance sheet.* A comparison of the amounts from our example verifies this:

	ENDING INVENTORY	COST OF GOODS SOLD
Weighted average	$6,840	$10,260
FIFO	7,600	9,500
LIFO	6,100	11,000
Replacement cost	9,000	13,500

Accounting for Your Decisions

You Are a Student

The owner/manager of a dairy farm knows that you are an accounting student and has asked your advice about which inventory method to use to measure the cost of both the inventory and the cost of goods sold. Since the inventory of milk and milk byproducts spoils easily, does he have to use the FIFO inventory valuation method? Why or why not?

ANS: No, he does not have to use the FIFO method, just because his products are subject to spoilage. There is a difference between the actual physical flow of the product and the cost flow of that product. From a practical perspective, he would want to sell the milk and milk byproducts on a FIFO basis to minimize spoilage. However, he can keep track of the cost flows for inventory valuation and cost of goods sold purposes using the LIFO method or weighted average cost method.

Changing Inventory Methods

The purpose of each of the inventory costing methods is to *match costs with revenues.* If a company believes that a different method will result in a better matching than that being provided by the method currently being used, it should change methods. A company must be able to justify a change in methods, however. Taking advantage of the tax breaks offered by LIFO is *not* a valid justification for a change in methods.

http://www.goodyear.com

It is very important for a company to *disclose* any change in accounting principle, including a change in the method of costing inventory. For example, some companies use the matching principle to justify a change from LIFO to FIFO, as illustrated by this excerpt from **Goodyear Tire & Rubber Company's** 2000 annual report:

> During the fourth quarter of 2000, the Company changed its method of inventory costing from last-in first-out (LIFO) to first-in first-out (FIFO) for domestic inventories. Prior periods have been restated to reflect this change. The method was changed in part to achieve a better matching of revenues and expenses. The change increased net income in 2000 by $44.4 million ($.28 per basic and diluted share), and increased retained earnings for years prior to 1998 by $218.2 million.

Inventory Valuation in Other Countries

The acceptable methods of valuing inventory differ considerably around the world. Although FIFO is the most popular method in the United States, LIFO continues to be widely used, as is the average cost method. Many countries prohibit the use of LIFO for either tax or financial reporting purposes. Countries in which LIFO is either prohibited or rarely used include the United Kingdom, Canada, New Zealand, Sweden, Denmark, and Brazil. On the other hand, Germany, France, Australia, and Japan allow LIFO for inventory valuation of foreign investments but not for domestic reports.

In Chapter 1 we mentioned the attempts by the International Accounting Standards Board (IASB) to develop worldwide accounting standards. This group favors the use of either FIFO or weighted average when specific identification is not feasible. The IASB recognizes LIFO as an acceptable alternative if a company discloses the lower of the net realizable value of its inventory and cost as determined by either FIFO, weighted average, or current cost.

Two Inventory Systems: Periodic and Perpetual

In the examples presented so far in this chapter, we have assumed a periodic inventory system to concentrate our attention on the various cost-flow assumptions. Recall from Chapter 5 that with this system, a count of the inventory is necessary at the end of the period to determine the number of units sold and the number on hand. The reason is that the Inventory account is not updated each time a purchase is made and each time a sale is made.

For many years, the simplicity of the periodic system resulted in its widespread use. Because of the need in a perpetual system to record the cost of every individual sale when it occurs, use of the perpetual system was limited to businesses that sold products with a relatively high unit cost and low turnover, such as those of an automobile dealer. The ability to computerize the inventory system has resulted, however, in an increase in the use of the perpetual system in all types of businesses. A company can use any one of the costing methods with either a periodic or a perpetual inventory system. The application of the methods when a company maintains a perpetual inventory system is illustrated in the appendix to this chapter.

Inventory Errors

LO 5 Analyze the effects of an inventory error on various financial statement items.

Earlier in the chapter we considered the inherent tie between the valuation of assets, such as inventory, and the measurement of income, such as cost of goods sold. The importance of inventory valuation to the measurement of income can be illustrated by considering inventory errors. Many different types of inventory errors exist. Some errors are mathematical; for example, a bookkeeper may incorrectly add a column total. Other errors relate specifically to the physical count of inventory at year-end. For example, the count might inadvertently omit one section of a warehouse. Other errors arise from cutoff problems at year-end.

For example, assume that merchandise in transit at the end of the year is shipped FOB (free on board) shipping point. Under these shipment terms, the inventory belongs to the buyer at the time it is shipped. Because the shipment has not arrived at the end of the year, however, it cannot be included in the physical count. Unless some type of control is in place, the amount in transit may be erroneously omitted from the valuation of inventory at year-end.

To demonstrate the effect of an inventory error on the income statement, consider the following example. Through a scheduling error, two different inventory teams were assigned to count the inventory in the same warehouse on December 31, 2004. The correct amount of ending inventory is $250,000, but because two different teams counted the same inventory in one warehouse, the amount recorded is $300,000. The effect of this error on net income is analyzed in the left half of Exhibit 6-3.

Exhibit 6-3 Effects of Inventory Error on the Income Statement

	2004			2005		
	REPORTED	CORRECTED	EFFECT OF ERROR	REPORTED	CORRECTED	EFFECT OF ERROR
Sales	$1,000*	$1,000		$1,500	$1,500	
Cost of goods sold:						
Beginning inventory	$ 200	$ 200		**$ 300**	**$ 250**	$50 OS
Add: Purchases	700	700		1,100	1,100	
Cost of goods available for sale	$ 900	$ 900		**$1,400**	**$1,350**	50 OS
Less: Ending inventory	**300**	**250**	$50 OS†	350	350	
Cost of goods sold	**$ 600**	**$ 650**	50 US‡	**$1,050**	**$1,000**	50 OS
Gross margin	**$ 400**	**$ 350**	50 OS	**$ 450**	**$ 500**	50 US
Operating expenses	100	100		120	120	
Net income	**$ 300**	**$ 250**	50 OS	**$ 330**	**$ 380**	50 US

NOTE: Figures that differ as a result of the error are in bold.
*All amounts are in thousands of dollars.

†OS = Overstatement
‡US = Understatement

The *overstatement* of *ending inventory* in 2004 leads to an *understatement* of the 2004 cost of goods sold *expense.* Because cost of goods sold is understated, *gross margin* for the year is *overstated.* Operating expenses are unaffected by an inventory error. Thus, *net income* is *overstated* by the same amount of overstatement of gross margin.[2] The most important conclusion from the exhibit is that an overstatement of ending inventory leads to a corresponding overstatement of net income.

Unfortunately, the effect of a misstatement of the year-end inventory is not limited to the net income for that year. As indicated in the right-hand portion of Exhibit 6-3, the error also affects the income statement for the following year. This happens simply because *the ending inventory of one period is the beginning inventory of the following period.* The *overstatement* of the 2005 *beginning inventory* leads to an *overstatement* of *cost of goods available for sale.* Because cost of goods available for sale is overstated, *cost of goods sold* is also *overstated.* The *overstatement* of cost of goods sold *expense* results in an *understatement* of *gross margin* and thus an *understatement* of *net income.*

Exhibit 6-3 illustrates the nature of a *counterbalancing error.* The effect of the overstatement of net income in the first year, 2004, is offset or counterbalanced by the understatement of net income by the same dollar amount in the following year. If the net incomes of two successive years are misstated in the opposite direction by the same amount, what is the effect on retained earnings? Assume that retained earnings at the beginning of 2004 is correctly stated at $300,000. The counterbalancing nature of the error is seen by analyzing retained earnings. For 2004 the analysis would indicate the following (OS = overstated and US = understated):

[2]An overstatement of gross margin also results in an overstatement of income tax expense. Thus, because tax expense is overstated, the overstatement of net income is not so large as the overstatement of gross margin. For now we will ignore the effect of taxes, however.

	2004 REPORTED	2004 CORRECTED	EFFECT OF ERROR
Beginning retained earnings	$300,000	$300,000	Correct
Add: Net income	300,000	250,000	$50,000 OS
Ending retained earnings	$600,000	$550,000	$50,000 OS

An analysis for 2005 would show the following:

	2005 REPORTED	2005 CORRECTED	EFFECT OF ERROR
Beginning retained earnings	$600,000	$550,000	$50,000 OS
Add: Net income	330,000	380,000	$50,000 US
Ending retained earnings	$930,000	$930,000	Correct

Thus, even though retained earnings is overstated at the end of the first year, it is correctly stated at the end of the second year. This is the nature of a counterbalancing error.

The effect of the error on the balance sheet is shown in Exhibit 6-4. The only accounts affected by the error are Inventory and Retained Earnings. The overstatement of the 2004 ending inventory results in an overstatement of total assets at the end of the first year. Similarly, as our earlier analysis indicates, the overstatement of 2004 net income leads to an overstatement of retained earnings by the same amount. Because the error is counterbalancing, the 2005 year-end balance sheet is correct; that is, ending inventory is not affected by the error, and thus the amount for total assets at the end of 2005 is also correct. The effect of the error on retained earnings is limited to the first year because of the counterbalancing nature of the error.

Exhibit 6-4

Effects of Inventory Error on the Balance Sheet

	2004		2005	
	REPORTED	CORRECTED	REPORTED	CORRECTED
Inventory	**$ 300***	**$ 250**	$ 350	$ 350
All other assets	1,700	1,700	2,080	2,080
Total assets	**$2,000**	**$1,950**	$2,430	$2,430
Total liabilities	$ 400	$ 400	$ 500	$ 500
Capital stock	1,000	1,000	1,000	1,000
Retained earnings	**600**	**550**	930	930
Total liabilities and stockholders' equity	**$2,000**	**$1,950**	$2,430	$2,430

NOTE: Figures that differ as a result of the error are in bold.
*All amounts are in thousands of dollars.

The effects of inventory errors on various financial statement items are summarized in Exhibit 6-5. Our analysis focused on the effects of an overstatement of inventory. The effects of an understatement are just the opposite and are summarized in the bottom portion of the exhibit.

Not all errors are counterbalancing. For example, if a section of a warehouse *continues* to be omitted from the physical count every year, both the beginning and the ending inventory will be incorrect each year and the error will not counterbalance.

Part of the auditor's job is to perform the necessary tests to obtain reasonable assurance that inventory has not been overstated or understated. If there is an error and inventory is wrong, however, the balance sheet and the income statement will both be distorted. For example, if ending inventory is overstated, inflating total assets, then cost of goods sold will be understated, boosting profits. Thus, such an error overstates the financial health of the organization in two ways. A lender or an investor must make a decision based on the current year's statement and cannot wait until the next accounting cycle, when this error is reversed. This is one reason that investors and creditors insist on audited financial statements.

	Effect of Overstatement of Ending Inventory on	
	CURRENT YEAR	FOLLOWING YEAR
Cost of goods sold	Understated	Overstated
Gross margin	Overstated	Understated
Net income	Overstated	Understated
Retained earnings, end of year	Overstated	Correctly stated
Total assets, end of year	Overstated	Correctly stated
	Effect of Understatement of Ending Inventory on	
	CURRENT YEAR	**FOLLOWING YEAR**
Cost of goods sold	Overstated	Understated
Gross margin	Understated	Overstated
Net income	Understated	Overstated
Retained earnings, end of year	Understated	Correctly stated
Total assets, end of year	Understated	Correctly stated

Exhibit 6-5

Summary of the Effects of Inventory Errors

Study Tip

Note the logic behind the notion that an overstatement of ending inventory leads to overstatements of both total assets and retained earnings at the end of the year. This is logical because a balance sheet must balance; that is, the left side must equal the right side. If the left side (inventory) is overstated, then the right side (retained earnings) will also be overstated.

Two-Minute Review

Skipper Corp. omits one section of its warehouse in the year-end inventory count.

1. *Will the omission understate or overstate cost of goods sold on the income statement in the year the error is made?*
2. *Will the omission understate or overstate retained earnings on the balance sheet at the end of the year the error is made?*
3. *Will the omission affect retained earnings on the balance sheet at the end of the following year after the error is made? Explain your answer.*

Answers on page 296.

VALUING INVENTORY AT LOWER OF COST OR MARKET

LO 6 Apply the lower-of-cost-or-market rule to the valuation of inventory.

One of the components sold by an electronics firm has become economically obsolete. A particular style of suit sold by a retailer is outdated and can no longer be sold at regular price. In each of these instances, it is likely that the retailer will have to sell the merchandise for less than the normal selling price. In these situations, a departure from the cost basis of accounting may be necessary because the *market value* of the inventory may be less than its *cost* to the company. The departure is called the **lower-of-cost-or-market (LCM) rule.**

Lower-of-cost-or-market (LCM) rule A conservative inventory valuation approach that is an attempt to anticipate declines in the value of inventory before its actual sale.

At the end of each accounting period, the original cost, as determined using one of the costing methods such as FIFO, is compared with the market price of the inventory. If market is less than cost, the inventory is written down to the lower amount.

For example, if cost is $100,000 and market value is $85,000, the accountant would make the following entry:

Dec. 31	Loss on Decline in Value of Inventory	15,000	
	Inventory		15,000
	To record decline in value of inventory.		

Assets	=	Liabilities	+	Owners' Equity
−15,000				−15,000

Note that the entry reduces both assets, in the form of inventory, and owners' equity. The reduction in owners' equity is the result of reporting the Loss on Decline in Value of Inventory on the income statement as an item of Other Expense.

Why Replacement Cost Is Used as a Measure of Market

A better name for the lower-of-cost-or-market rule would be the lower-of-cost-or-replacement-cost rule because accountants define *market* as *replacement cost.*[3] To understand why replacement cost is used as a basis to compare with original cost, consider the following example. A clothier pays $150 for a man's double-breasted suit and normally sells it for $200. Thus, the normal markup on selling price is $50/$200, or 25%, as indicated in the column Before Price Change in Exhibit 6-6. Now assume that double-breasted suits fall out of favor with the fashion world. The retailer checks with the distributor and finds that because of the style change, the cost to the retailer to replace a double-breasted suit is now only $120. The retailer realizes that if double-breasted suits are to be sold at all, they will have to be offered at a reduced price. The selling price is dropped from $200 to $160. If the retailer now buys a suit for $120 and sells it for $160, the gross margin will be $40 and the gross margin percentage will be maintained at 25%, as indicated in the right-hand column of Exhibit 6-6.

Exhibit 6-6
Gross Margin Percentage before and after Price Change

	BEFORE PRICE CHANGE	AFTER PRICE CHANGE
Selling price	$200	$160
Cost	150	120
Gross margin	$ 50	$ 40
Gross margin percentage	25%	25%

To compare the results with and without the use of the LCM rule, assume that the facts are the same as before and that the retailer has 10 double-breasted suits in inventory on December 31, 2004. In addition, assume that all 10 suits are sold at a clearance sale in January 2005 at the reduced price of $160 each. If the lower-of-cost-or-market rule is not used, the results for the two years will be as follows:

LCM RULE NOT USED	2004	2005	TOTAL
Sales revenue ($160 per unit)	$ 0	$1,600	$1,600
Cost of goods sold			
(original cost of $150 per unit)	0	(1,500)	(1,500)
Gross margin	$ 0	$ 100	$ 100

If the LCM rule is not applied, the gross margin is distorted. Instead of the normal 25%, a gross margin percentage of $100/$1,600, or 6.25%, is reported in 2005 when the 10 suits are sold. If the LCM rule is applied, however, the results for the two years are as follows:

LCM RULE USED	2004	2005	TOTAL
Sales revenue ($160 per unit)	$ 0	$1,600	$1,600
Cost of goods sold			
(replacement cost of $120 per unit)	0	(1,200)	(1,200)
Loss on decline in value of			
inventory: 10 units ×			
($150 − $120)	(300)	0	(300)
Gross margin	$(300)	$ 400	$ 100

[3]Technically, the use of replacement cost as a measure of market value is subject to two constraints. First, market cannot be more than the net realizable value of the inventory. Second, inventory should not be recorded at less than net realizable value less a normal profit margin. The rationale for these two constraints is covered in intermediate accounting texts. For our purposes, we assume that replacement cost falls between the two constraints.

The use of the LCM rule serves two important functions: (1) to report the loss in value of the inventory, $30 per suit or $300 in total, in the year the loss occurs and (2) to report in the year the suits are actually sold the normal gross margin of $400/$1,600, or 25%, which is not affected by a change in the selling price.

Conservatism Is the Basis for the Lower-of-Cost-or-Market Rule

The departure from the cost basis is normally justified on the basis of *conservatism*. According to the accounting profession, conservatism is "a prudent reaction to uncertainties to try to insure that uncertainties and risks inherent in business situations are adequately considered."[4] In our example, the future selling price of a suit is uncertain because of the style changes. The use of the LCM rule serves two purposes. First, the inventory of suits is written down from $150 to $120 each. Second, the decline in value of the inventory is recognized at the time it is first observed rather than waiting until the suits are sold. An investor in a company with deteriorating inventory has good reason to be alarmed. Merchandisers who do not make the proper adjustments to their product lines go out of business as they compete with the lower prices of warehouse clubs and the lower overhead of e-business and home shopping networks.

You should realize that the write-down of the suits violates the historical cost principle, which says that assets should be carried on the balance sheet at their original cost. But the LCM rule is considered a valid exception to the principle because it is a prudent reaction to the uncertainty involved and, thus, an application of conservatism in accounting.

Which Way to Go?
Cost or Lower Market?

It's October, and the accountants at Taz Industries are beginning to prepare the annual financial statements for the fiscal year that ended September 30. One of the staff members, Hudson Clark, is responsible for determining the inventory valuation. Since Taz is a manufacturing company, its inventory includes raw materials, work in process, and finished goods. The inventory costing method used at Taz is LIFO.

In the current economic downturn, the depressed economy has greatly reduced the company's current replacement cost for its ending inventory. While he understands that inventory should be valued at the lower of cost or market, Hudson is quite concerned about writing down ending inventory because that will reduce the income reported to creditors and investors. It also will mean total assets will be much lower in value on the September 30 balance sheet.

In a recent discussion with his manager, Hudson stressed the need to report the inventory at cost. After all, he reasoned, the leading economists are saying that the recovery is beginning. Already, by late October, the company is seeing a slight rise in the cost of raw materials. Certainly, by the end of the new fiscal year, the market will have recovered. Reducing the inventory to the lower market value will make the analysis of the current year's financial information appear significantly worse off than prior years. Yet, once the economy recovers, the numbers will return to "normal." Wouldn't it be best to leave the inventory at cost?

Is Hudson correct in his reasoning? Should Taz Industries report its September 30 inventory at cost or at the lower market value? Explain your reasoning.

From Concept to Practice 6.3

Reading Circuit City's Notes

A note to Circuit City's financial statements states "Circuit City inventory is comprised of finished goods held for sale and is stated at the lower of cost or market." Why do you think the application of the lower-of-cost-or-market rule would be important to a business like Circuit City?

Application of the LCM Rule

We have yet to consider how the LCM rule is applied to the entire inventory of a company. Three different interpretations of the rule are possible:

1. The lower of total cost or total market value for the entire inventory could be reported.
2. The lower of cost or market value for each individual product or item could be reported.
3. The lower of cost or market value for groups of items could be reported. A company is free to choose any one of these approaches in applying the lower-of-cost-or-market rule. Three different answers are possible, depending on the approach selected.

[4]*Statement of Financial Accounting Concepts No. 2,* "Qualitative Characteristics of Accounting Information" (Stamford, Conn.: Financial Accounting Standards Board, May 1980), par. 95.

The item-by-item (No. 2 above) approach is the most popular of the three approaches, for two reasons. First, it produces the most conservative result. The reason is that with either a group-by-group or a total approach, increases in the values of some items of inventory will offset declines in the values of other items. The item-by-item approach, however, ignores increases in value and recognizes all declines in value. Second, the item-by-item approach is the method required for tax purposes, although unlike LIFO, it is not required for book purposes merely because it is used for tax computations.

Consistency is important in deciding which of these approaches to use in applying the LCM rule. As is the case with the selection of one of the inventory costing methods discussed earlier in the chapter, the approach chosen to apply the rule should be used consistently from one period to the next.

METHODS FOR ESTIMATING INVENTORY VALUE

LO 7 Explain why and how the cost of inventory is estimated in certain situations.

Situations arise in which it may not be practicable or even possible to measure inventory at cost. At times it may be necessary to *estimate* the amount of inventory. Two similar methods are used for very different purposes to estimate the amount of inventory. They are the gross profit method and the retail inventory method.

Gross Profit Method

Gross profit method A technique used to establish an estimate of the cost of inventory stolen, destroyed, or otherwise damaged or of the amount of inventory on hand at an interim date.

A company that uses a periodic inventory system may experience a problem if inventory is stolen or destroyed by fire, flooding, or some other type of damage. Without a perpetual inventory record, what is the cost of the inventory stolen or destroyed? The **gross profit method** is a useful technique to estimate the cost of inventory lost in these situations. The method relies *entirely* on the ability to reliably estimate the *ratio of gross profit to sales.*[5]

Exhibit 6-7 illustrates how the normal income statement model that we use to find cost of goods sold can be rearranged to estimate inventory. The model on the left shows the components of cost of goods sold as they appear on the income statement. Assuming a periodic system, the inventory on hand at the end of the period is counted and is subtracted from cost of goods available for sale to determine cost of goods sold. The model is rearranged on the right as a basis for estimating inventory under the gross profit method. The only difference in the two models is in the reversal of the last two components: ending inventory and cost of goods sold. Rather than attempting to estimate *ending* inventory, we are trying to estimate the amount of inventory that should be on hand at a specific date, such as the date of a fire or flood. The estimate of cost of goods sold is found by estimating gross profit and deducting this estimate from sales revenue.

Exhibit 6-7

The Gross Profit Method for Estimating Inventory

INCOME STATEMENT MODEL	GROSS PROFIT METHOD MODEL
Beginning Inventory	Beginning Inventory
+ Purchases	+ Purchases
= Cost of Goods Available for Sale	= Cost of Goods Available for Sale
− Ending Inventory (per count)	− Estimated Cost of Goods Sold
= Cost of Goods Sold	= Estimated Inventory

To understand this method, assume that on March 12, 2004, a portion of Hardluck Company's inventory is destroyed in a fire. The company determines, by a physical count, that the cost of the merchandise not destroyed is $200. Hardluck needs to estimate the

[5]The terms *gross profit* and *gross margin* are synonymous in this context. Although we have used *gross margin* in referring to the excess of sales over cost of goods sold, the method is typically called the *gross profit method.*

cost of the inventory lost for purposes of insurance reimbursement. If the insurance company pays Hardluck an amount equivalent to the cost of the inventory destroyed, no loss will be recognized. If the cost of the inventory destroyed exceeds the amount reimbursed by the insurance company, a loss will be recorded for the excess amount.

Assume that the insurance company agrees to pay Hardluck $250 as full settlement for the inventory lost in the fire. From its records, Hardluck is able to determine the following amounts for the period from January 1 to the date of the fire, March 12:

Net sales from January 1 to March 12	$6,000
Beginning inventory—January 1	1,200
Purchases from January 1 to March 12	3,500

Assume that based on recent years' experience, Hardluck estimates its gross profit ratio as 30% of net sales. The steps it will take to estimate the lost inventory follow:

1. Determine gross profit:

Net Sales	×	**Gross Profit Ratio**	=	**Gross Profit**
$6,000	×	30%	=	$1,800

2. Determine cost of goods sold:

Net Sales	−	**Gross Profit**	=	**Cost of Goods Sold**
$6,000	−	$1,800	=	$4,200

3. Determine cost of goods available for sale at time of fire:

Beginning Inventory	+	**Purchases**	=	**Cost of Goods Available for Sale**
$1,200	+	$3,500	=	$4,700

4. Determine inventory at time of the fire:

Cost of Goods Available for Sale	−	**Cost of Goods Sold**	=	**Inventory**
$4,700	−	$4,200	=	$500

5. Determine amount of inventory destroyed:

Inventory at Time of Fire	−	**Inventory Not Destroyed**	=	**Inventory Destroyed**
$500	−	$200	=	$300

Hardluck would record the following journal entry to recognize a loss for the excess of the cost of the lost inventory over the amount of reimbursement from the insurance company:

Mar. 12	Loss on Insurance Settlement	50	
	Cash (from insurance company)	250	
	Inventory		300
	To record the insurance settlement from fire.		

Assets	=	**Liabilities**	+	**Owners' Equity**
+250				−50
−300				

Another situation in which the gross profit method is used is for *interim financial statements.* Most companies prepare financial statements at least once every three months. In fact, the **Securities and Exchange Commission** requires a quarterly report from corporations whose stock is publicly traded. Companies using the periodic inventory system, however, find it cost-prohibitive to count the inventory every three months. The gross profit method is used to estimate the cost of the inventory at these interim dates. A company is allowed to use the method only in interim reports. Inventory reported in the annual report must be based on actual, not estimated, cost.

http://www.sec.gov

Retail Inventory Method

Retail inventory method A technique used by retailers to convert the retail value of inventory to a cost basis.

The counting of inventory in most retail businesses is an enormous undertaking. Imagine the time involved to count all of the various items stocked in a hardware store. Because of the time and cost involved in counting inventory, most retail businesses take a physical inventory only once a year. The **retail inventory method** is used to estimate inventory for interim statements, typically prepared monthly.

The retail inventory method has another important use. Consider the year-end inventory count in a large supermarket. One employee counts the number of tubes of toothpaste on the shelf and relays the relevant information either to another employee or to a tape-recording device: "16 tubes of 8-ounce ABC brand toothpaste at $1.69." The key is that the price recorded is the *selling price* or *retail price* of the product, not its cost. It is much quicker to count the inventory at retail than it would be to trace the cost of each item to purchase invoices. The retail method can then be used to convert the inventory from retail to cost. The methodology used with the retail inventory method, whether for interim statements or at year-end, is similar to the approach used with the gross profit method and is covered in detail in intermediate accounting textbooks.

ANALYZING THE MANAGEMENT OF INVENTORY TURNOVER

LO 8 Analyze the management of inventory turnover.

Inventory turnover ratio A measure of the number of times inventory is sold during a period.

Managers must strike a balance between maintaining enough inventory to meet customers' needs and incurring the high cost of carrying inventory. The cost of storage and the lost income from the money tied up to own inventory make it very expensive to keep on hand. Investors are also concerned with a company's inventory management. They pay particular attention to a company's **inventory turnover ratio:**

$$\textbf{Inventory Turnover Ratio} = \frac{\textbf{Cost of Goods Sold}}{\textbf{Average Inventory}}$$

http://www.circuitcity.com

Refer to Circuit City's financial statements as displayed in the chapter opener. From the information presented, we can compute the company's inventory turnover ratio for fiscal year 2002 (amounts are in thousands of dollars):

$$\text{Inventory Turnover Ratio} = \frac{\text{Cost of Goods Sold}}{\text{Average Inventory}} = \frac{\$10{,}049{,}793}{(\underbrace{\$1{,}633{,}327}_{\text{(2/28/02 balance sheet)}} + \underbrace{\$1{,}757{,}664}_{\text{(2/28/01 balance sheet)}})/2}$$

$$= \frac{\$10{,}049{,}793}{\$1{,}695{,}496}$$

$$= 5.9 \text{ times}$$

Number of days' sales in inventory A measure of how long it takes to sell inventory.

This ratio tells us that in fiscal year 2002, Circuit City turned over its inventory 5.9 times. An alternative way to look at a company's efficiency in managing inventory is to calculate the number of days, on average, that inventory is on hand before it is sold. This measure is called the **number of days' sales in inventory** and is calculated as follows (we will assume 360 days in a year):

$$\textbf{Number of Days' Sales in Inventory} = \frac{\textbf{Number of Days in the Period}}{\textbf{Inventory Turnover Ratio}}$$

$$= \frac{360}{5.9}$$

$$= 61 \text{ days}$$

How efficient was Circuit City in managing its inventory if it took an average of 61 days, or about two months, to sell an item of inventory in fiscal year 2002? There are no easy answers to this question, but a starting point would be to compare this statistic with the same measure for prior years. Another basis for evaluation is to compare the measure with that for other companies in the same industry or business, in this case consumer electronics. As you can imagine, inventory turnover varies considerably from one industry to the next because of the differences in products. For example, consider **Safeway**, a large regional grocery chain. Safeway's average inventory turnover ratio in 2001 was approximately 9.3 times. This means that on average it takes Safeway only about 360/9.3, or 39 days, to sell its inventory. Given the perishable nature of its products, we would expect Safeway to turn over its inventory more rapidly than a consumer electronics company such as Circuit City. Exhibit 6-8 summarizes the differences in inventory turnover between the two companies.

http://www.safeway.com

Exhibit 6-8

Inventory Turnover for Different Types of Companies

COMPANY	TYPES OF PRODUCTS SOLD	INVENTORY TURNOVER	NUMBER OF DAYS' SALES IN INVENTORY
Circuit City	Televisions, VCRs, personal computers	5.9 times	61 days
Safeway	Grocery items	9.3 times	39 days

From Concept to Practice 6.4

Reading Winnebago Industries' Financial Statements

Compute Winnebago Industries' inventory turnover ratio for 2001. What is the average length of time it takes to sell its inventory? Does this seem reasonable for the type of business the company is in?

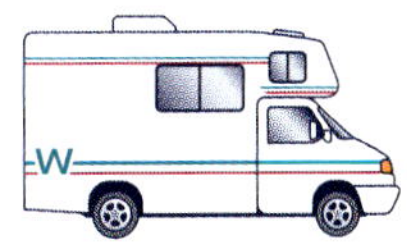

HOW INVENTORIES AFFECT THE CASH FLOWS STATEMENT

LO 9 Explain the effects that inventory transactions have on the statement of cash flows.

The effects on the income statement and the statement of cash flows from inventory-related transactions differ significantly. We have focused our attention in the last two chapters on how the purchase and the sale of inventory are reported on the income statement. We found that the cost of the inventory sold during the period is deducted on the income statement as cost of goods sold.

The appropriate reporting on a statement of cash flows for inventory transactions depends on whether the direct or indirect method is used. If the direct method is used to prepare the Operating Activities category of the statement, the amount of cash paid to suppliers of inventory is shown as a deduction in this section of the statement.

If the more popular indirect method is used, it is necessary to make adjustments to net income for the changes in two accounts: Inventories and Accounts Payable. These adjustments are summarized in Exhibit 6-9. An increase in inventory is deducted because

Exhibit 6-9

Inventories and the Statement of Cash Flows

Item	Cash Flow Statement	
	Operating Activities	
	Net income	XXX
Increase in inventory	→	−
Decrease in inventory	→	+
Increase in accounts payable	→	+
Decrease in accounts payable	→	−
	Investing Activities	
	Financing Activities	

it indicates that the company is building up its stock of inventory and thus expending cash. A decrease in inventory is added to net income. An increase in accounts payable is added because it indicates that during the period, the company has increased the amount it owes suppliers and has therefore conserved its cash. A decrease in accounts payable is deducted because the company actually reduced the amount owed suppliers during the period.

The Operating Activities category of the statement of cash flows for Circuit City is presented in Exhibit 6-10. Note that the company groups prepaid expenses and other current assets for purposes of presentation on the statement of cash flows. Similarly, accounts payable, accrued expenses, and other current liabilities and accrued income taxes are included as one item on the statement.

The decreases in inventory as well as prepaid expenses and other current assets in 2002 are added because the reductions in these assets conserve the company's cash. A buildup of accounts payable, accrued expenses, and other current liabilities and accrued income taxes also conserves Circuit City's cash. Thus, the increase in these items in 2002 is added to net earnings.

Exhibit 6-10 Partial Consolidated Statement of Cash Flows for Circuit City

CONSOLIDATED STATEMENTS OF CASH FLOWS

(Amounts in thousands)	Years Ended February 28 or 29 2002	2001	2000
OPERATING ACTIVITIES:			
Net earnings	$ 218,795	$ 160,802	$ 197,590
Adjustments to reconcile net earnings to net cash provided by operating activities of continuing operations:			
Loss from discontinued operations [NOTE 15]	–	–	16,215
Loss on disposal of discontinued operations [NOTE 15]	–	–	114,025
Depreciation and amortization	150,711	153,090	148,164
Unearned compensation amortization of restricted stock	15,678	11,365	12,096
Loss on disposition of property and equipment	13,735	4,674	17
Provision for deferred income taxes	31,166	19,765	43,053
Changes in operating assets and liabilities, net of effects from business acquisitions:			
(Increase) decrease in net accounts receivable	(140,766)	7,541	(18,922)
Decrease (increase) in inventory	124,337	(67,655)	(184,507)
Decrease (increase) in prepaid expenses and other current assets	16,312	(41,426)	81,316
(Increase) decrease in other assets	(720)	1,012	240
Increase (decrease) in accounts payable, accrued expenses and other current liabilities and accrued income taxes	336,774	(64,193)	244,559
Increase (decrease) in deferred revenue and other liabilities	71,186	(17,855)	(15,565)
NET CASH PROVIDED BY OPERATING ACTIVITIES OF CONTINUING OPERATIONS	837,208	167,120	638,281

Decrease here conserves cash and thus is added.

Increase here conserves cash and thus is added.

Ratios for Decision Making

Reporting and analyzing financial statement information related to a company's inventory:
The inventory turnover ratio and the number of days sales in inventory provide a good estimate of how many times throughout the period the inventory was replaced with new goods and how long products remained in inventory before they were sold. A high inventory turnover ratio indicates inventory is coming in and being sold relatively quickly. A lower ratio means inventory is sitting on the shelf or in the warehouse and is not selling very well. A high number of days will result from a low turnover ratio and indicates the business probably does not need to reorder or manufacture much inventory very soon.

Balance Sheet	Income Statement	Statement of Cash Flows	Notes
Current Assets	Cost of Goods Sold		
Inventory			

$$\text{Inventory Turnover Ratio} = \frac{\text{Cost of Goods Sold}}{\text{Average Inventory}^{*}}$$

$$\text{Number of Days Sales in Inventory} = \frac{\text{Number of Days in the Period}^{**}}{\text{Inventory Turnover Ratio}}$$

*Average inventory can be estimated using the following calculation:

$$\frac{\text{Beginning Inventory} + \text{Ending Inventory}}{2}$$

**Generally, 360 days is a good estimate unless the period is more or less than one year in length.

Impact on the Financial Reports

Impact on the Financial Reports

BALANCE SHEET

Current Assets
Inventory[1]
Noncurrent Assets
Current Liabilities
Accounts payable
Noncurrent Liabilities
Stockholders' Equity

INCOME STATEMENT

Revenues
Sales revenue[2]
Expenses
Cost of goods sold[2]
Selling and administrative expenses (including transportation-out expenses)
Income tax expenses
Other
Loss on declines in value of inventory
Loss on insurance settlement

STATEMENT OF STOCKHOLDERS' EQUITY

Contributed Capital
Retained Earnings

STATEMENT OF CASH FLOWS

Operating Activities[3]
Cash received from sales and paid for purchases
Cash received for accounts receivable
Cash paid for accounts payable
Investing Activities
Financing Activities
Noncash Transactions

NOTES

The basis (cost or LCM) and the method (FIFO, LIFO, average cost, etc.) used to determine cost are disclosed.

[1]For retailer/wholesaler companies, this would be merchandise inventory; for manufacturing companies, this would be made up of raw materials inventory, work in process inventory, and finished goods inventory.
[2]As indicated in Chapter 5, Sales revenue − (Sales returns and allowances + Sales discounts) = Net sales; Net sales − Cost of goods sold = Gross margin; Purchases − (Purchase returns and allowances + Purchase discounts) = Net purchases; Beginning inventory + Net purchases + Transportation-in − Ending inventory = Cost of goods sold under the periodic inventory system.
[3]Under the indirect method (explained in detail in Chapter 12), any increase or decrease in inventory and in accounts payable would be reflected in this section and would replace the items listed above under "Operating Activities."

Answers to the Two-Minute Reviews

Two-Minute Review on Page 280

1. *LIFO*
2. *The easiest approach to calculating the tax savings is to multiply the tax rate times the difference in cost of goods sold between the two methods.*

Two-Minute Review on Page 287

1. *Cost of goods sold will be overstated because the ending inventory is understated.*
2. *Retained earnings at the end of the year in which the error is made will be understated because cost of goods sold is overstated, and thus net income, which goes into retained earnings, is understated.*
3. *Retained earnings at the end of the following year will not be affected because of the counterbalancing nature of this error. Net income in the year of the error is understated, as described above. However, net income of the following year is overstated because cost of goods sold is understated as the result of an understatement of that year's beginning inventory.*

Warmup Exercises

Warmup Exercise 6-1 ***Inventory Valuation*** **LO 3**

Busby Corp. began the year with 75 units of inventory that it paid $2 each to acquire. During the year it purchased an additional 100 units for $3 each. Busby sold 150 units during the year.

Required

1. Compute cost of goods sold and ending inventory assuming Busby uses FIFO.
2. Compute cost of goods sold and ending inventory assuming Busby uses LIFO.

Key to the Solution

Review the mechanics of the methods, beginning on page 278.

Warmup Exercise 6-2 ***Lower of Cost or Market*** **LO 6**

Glendive reports its inventory on a FIFO basis and has inventory with a cost of $78,000 on December 31. The cost to replace the inventory on this date would be only $71,000.

Required

Prepare the necessary journal entry on Glendive's books on December 31.

Key to the Solution

Recall the need to write down inventory when market is less than cost.

Warmup Exercise 6-3 ***Inventory Turnover*** **LO 8**

Sidney began the year with $130,000 in merchandise inventory and ended the year with $190,000. Sales and cost of goods sold for the year were $900,000 and $640,000, respectively.

Required

1. Compute Sidney's inventory turnover ratio.
2. Compute the number of days' sales in inventory.

Key to the Solution

Review how these two statistics are computed on page 292.

Solutions to Warmup Exercises

Warmup Exercise 6-1

1. Cost of goods sold: $(75 \times \$2) + (75 \times \$3) = \$375$

   Ending inventory: $25 \times \$3 = \$\ 75$

2. Cost of goods sold: $(100 \times \$3) + (50 \times \$2) = \$400$

   Ending inventory: $25 \times \$2 = \$\ 50$

Warmup Exercise 6-2

Dec. 31	Loss on Decline in Value of Inventory	7,000	
	Inventory		7,000
	To record decline in value of inventory.		

Assets	=	Liabilities	+	Owners' Equity
−7,000				−7,000

Warmup Exercise 6-3

1. $$\text{Inventory Turnover Ratio} = \frac{\text{Cost of Goods Sold}}{\text{Average Inventory}}$$

   $$= \frac{\$640{,}000}{(\$130{,}000 + \$190{,}000)/2}$$

   $$= \frac{\$640{,}000}{\$160{,}000} = 4 \text{ times}$$

2. $$\textbf{Number of Days' Sales in Inventory} = \frac{\text{Number of Days in the Period}}{\text{Inventory Turnover Ratio}}$$

   $$= \frac{360}{4} = 90 \text{ days}$$

Review Problem

WebTUTOR™ Advantage

Stewart Distributing Company sells a single product for $2 per unit and uses a periodic inventory system. The following data are available for the year:

Date	Transaction	Number of Units	Unit Cost	Total
1/1	Beginning inventory	500	$1.00	$500.00
2/5	Purchase	350	1.10	385.00
4/12	Sale	(550)		
7/17	Sale	(200)		
9/23	Purchase	400	1.30	520.00
11/5	Sale	(300)		

Required

1. Compute cost of goods sold, assuming the use of the weighted average costing method.
2. Compute the dollar amount of ending inventory, assuming the FIFO costing method.
3. Compute gross margin, assuming the LIFO costing method.
4. Assume a 40% tax rate. Compute the amount of taxes saved if Stewart uses the LIFO method rather than the FIFO method.

Solution to Review Problem

1. Cost of goods sold, weighted average cost method:

Cost of goods available for sale		
$500 + $385 + $520 =	$1,405	
Divided by:		
Units available for sale:		
500 + 350 + 400 =	÷ 1,250	units
Weighted average cost	$1.124	per unit
× Number of units sold:		
550 + 200 + 300 =	× 1,050	units
Cost of goods sold	$1,180.20	

2. Ending inventory, FIFO cost method:

Units available for sale	1,250
− Units sold	− 1,050
= Units in ending inventory	200
× Most recent purchase price of	× $ 1.30
= Ending inventory	$ 260

3. Gross margin, LIFO cost method:

Sales revenue: 1,050 units × $2 each		$2,100
Cost of goods sold		
400 units × $1.30 =	$520	
350 units × $1.10 =	385	
300 units × $1.00 =	300	− 1,205
Gross margin		$ 895

4. Taxes saved from using LIFO instead of FIFO:

LIFO Cost of goods sold		$1,205
− FIFO Cost of goods sold:		
Cost of goods available for sale	$1,405	
Ending inventory from part 2	260	
Cost of goods sold		− 1,145
Additional expense from use of LIFO		$ 60
× Tax rate		× 0.40
Tax savings from the use of LIFO		$ 24

Appendix: Accounting Tools: Inventory Costing Methods with the Use of a Perpetual Inventory System

LO 10 Explain the differences between a periodic and a perpetual inventory system.

The illustrations of the inventory costing methods in the chapter assumed the use of a periodic inventory system. In this appendix, we will see how the methods are applied when a company maintains a perpetual inventory system. Before doing so, however, it is useful to look closer at the differences between the two systems.

JOURNAL ENTRIES FOR THE TWO SYSTEMS

To highlight the differences between the two systems, consider the following three transactions:

1. Purchased on account 500 units at $8 each.

2. Returned for credit 100 units damaged in transit.
3. Sold on account 200 units at $10 each.

Exhibit 6-11 shows the journal entries for the three transactions under each of the two inventory systems. Because the inventory account is updated only *periodically* with the periodic system, the purchase of 500 units of merchandise is accumulated in the temporary account Purchases. The cost of the 100 units returned in the second transaction increases the contra-purchases account Purchase Returns and Allowances. The only entry made at the time of a sale records the revenue earned. Because the inventory account has not been updated for purchases and sales during the period, a *physical count* of the merchandise is required at year-end. This establishes the amount to be shown on the balance sheet as the cost of the inventory and helps determine the amount to appear on the income statement for cost of goods sold. Cost of goods sold is in fact a calculated figure determined in the following way:

Beginning inventory	The inventory at the end of the prior period
+ Cost of goods purchased	The balance in the Purchases account, plus any freight-in, less any purchase returns and allowances and any purchase discounts
= Cost of goods available for sale	
− Ending inventory	Based on a physical count
= Cost of goods sold	

As you see in the right-hand side of Exhibit 6-11, in a perpetual system, purchases of merchandise increase the Inventory account directly, and any returns of merchandise reduce it. Unlike the periodic system, the perpetual system requires that *two* entries be made at the time of sale. The first entry is the same as the entry made under the periodic system: to record the sales revenue. Because the inventory account is kept *per-*

Exhibit 6-11 Comparison of the Periodic and Perpetual Inventory Systems

PERIODIC SYSTEM	DR.	CR.	PERPETUAL SYSTEM	DR.	CR.
1. Purchases	4,000		Inventory	4,000	
Accounts Payable		4,000	Accounts Payable		4,000
To record purchase of 500 units.			To record purchase of 500 units.		
A = L + OE			A = L + OE		
+4,000 −4,000 (L, OE)			+4,000 (A) +4,000 (L)		
2. Accounts Payable	800		Accounts Payable	800	
Purchase Returns and Allowances		800	Inventory		800
To record return of 100 damaged units.			To record return of 100 damaged units.		
A = L + OE			A = L + OE		
−800 (L) +800 (OE)			−800 (A) −800 (L)		
3. Accounts Receivable	2,000		Accounts Receivable	2,000	
Sales Revenue		2,000	Sales Revenue		2,000
To record sale of 200 units at $10 each.			To record sale of 200 units at $10 each.		
A = L + OE			A = L + OE		
+2,000 (A) +2,000 (OE)			+2,000 (A) +2,000 (OE)		
			Cost of Goods Sold	1,600	
			Inventory		1,600
			To record 200 units sold at a cost of $8 each.		
			A = L + OE		
			−1,600 (A) −1,600 (OE)		

petually up to date, however, a second entry is made to reduce the Inventory account, with a corresponding increase in expense for the cost of the merchandise sold. Finally, because the Inventory account has been updated for each purchase and sale of merchandise, a physical count is not the basis for valuing the inventory at the end of the period in a perpetual system. For control purposes, however, most businesses that use a perpetual system count the inventory once a year. Any differences between the amount on hand per the count and the amount appearing in the Inventory account require an adjusting entry in the records and should be investigated.

INVENTORY COSTING METHODS WITH A PERPETUAL SYSTEM

LO 11 Apply the inventory costing methods using a perpetual system.

It is important to understand the difference between inventory *costing systems* and inventory *methods.* The two inventory systems differ in terms of how often the inventory account is updated: periodically or perpetually. However, when a company sells identical units of product and the cost to purchase each unit is subject to change, it also must choose an inventory costing method, such as FIFO, LIFO, or weighted average.

Earlier in the chapter, we illustrated the various costing methods with a periodic system. We now use the same data to illustrate how the methods differ when a perpetual system is used. Keep in mind that if a company uses specific identification, the results will be the same regardless of whether it uses the periodic or the perpetual system. To compare the periodic and perpetual systems for the other methods, we must add one important piece of information: the date of each of the sales. The original data as well as number of units sold on the various dates are summarized below:

DATE	PURCHASES	SALES	BALANCE
Beginning inventory			500 units @ $10
January 20	300 units @ $11		800 units
February 18		450 units	350 units
April 8	400 units @ $12		750 units
June 19		300 units	450 units
September 5	200 units @ $13		650 units
October 20		150 units	500 units
December 12	100 units @ $14		600 units

FIFO COSTING WITH A PERPETUAL SYSTEM

Exhibit 6-12 illustrates the FIFO method on a perpetual basis. The basic premise of FIFO applies whether a periodic or a perpetual system is used: the first units purchased are assumed to be the first units sold. With a perpetual system, however, this concept is applied *at the time of each sale.* For example, note in the exhibit which 450 units are assumed to be sold on February 18. The 450 units sold are taken from the beginning inventory of 500 units with a unit cost of $10. Thus, the inventory or balance after this sale as shown in the last three columns is 50 units at $10 and 300 units at $11, for a total of $3,800. The purchase on April 8 of 400 units at $12 is added to the running balance. On a FIFO basis, the sale of 300 units on June 19 comes from the remainder of the beginning inventory of 50 units and another 250 units from the first purchase at $11 on January 20. The balance after this sale is 50 units at $11 and 400 units at $12. You should follow through the last three transactions in the exhibit to make sure that you understand the application of FIFO on a perpetual basis. An important point to note about the ending inventory of $7,600 is that it is the same amount that we calculated for FIFO periodic earlier in the chapter:

FIFO periodic (Exhibit 6-2)	$7,600
FIFO perpetual (Exhibit 6-12)	$7,600

Exhibit 6-12 Perpetual System: FIFO Cost-Flow Assumption

	Purchases			Sales			Balance		
DATE	UNITS	UNIT COST	TOTAL COST	UNITS	UNIT COST	TOTAL COST	UNITS	UNIT COST	BALANCE
1/1							500	$10	$5,000
1/20	300	$11	$3,300				500	10	
							300	11	8,300
2/18				450	$10	$4,500	50	10	
							300	11	3,800
4/8	400	12	4,800				50	10	
							300	11	
							400	12	8,600
6/19				50	10	500	50	11	
				250	11	2,750	400	12	5,350
9/5	200	13	2,600				50	11	
							400	12	
							200	13	7,950
10/20				50	11	550	300	12	
				100	12	1,200	200	13	6,200
12/12	100	14	1,400				300	12	
							200	13	
							100	14	7,600

Whether the method is applied each time a sale is made or only at the end of the period, the earliest units in are the first units out, and the two systems will yield the same ending inventory under FIFO.

LIFO COSTING WITH A PERPETUAL SYSTEM

A LIFO cost flow with the use of a perpetual system is illustrated in Exhibit 6-13. First, note which 450 units are assumed to be sold on February 18. The sale consists of the most recent units acquired, 300 units at $11, and then 150 units from the beginning inventory at $10. Thus, the balance after this sale is simply the remaining 350 units from the beginning inventory priced at $10. The purchase on April 8 results in a balance of 350 units at $10 and 400 units at $12.

Note what happens with LIFO when it is applied on a perpetual basis. In essence, a gap is created. Units acquired at the earliest price of $10 and units acquired at the most recent price of $12 are on hand, but none of those at the middle price of $11 remain. This situation arises because LIFO is applied every time a sale is made rather than only at the end of the year. Because of this difference, the amount of ending inventory differs, depending on which system is used:

LIFO periodic (Exhibit 6-2)	$6,100
LIFO perpetual (Exhibit 6-13)	$6,750

MOVING AVERAGE WITH A PERPETUAL SYSTEM

When a weighted average cost assumption is applied with a perpetual system, it is sometimes called a **moving average.** As indicated in Exhibit 6-14, each time a purchase is made, a new weighted average cost must be computed, thus the name *moving average.* For example, the goods available for sale after the January 20 purchase consist of 500

Moving average The name given to an average cost method when it is used with a perpetual inventory system.

Exhibit 6-13 Perpetual System: LIFO Cost-Flow Assumption

	Purchases			Sales			Balance		
DATE	UNITS	UNIT COST	TOTAL COST	UNITS	UNIT COST	TOTAL COST	UNITS	UNIT COST	BALANCE
1/1							500	$10	$5,000
1/20	300	$11	$3,300				500	10	
							300	11	8,300
2/18				300	$11	$3,300			
				150	10	1,500	350	10	3,500
4/8	400	12	4,800				350	10	
							400	12	8,300
6/19				300	12	3,600	350	10	
							100	12	4,700
9/5	200	13	2,600				350	10	
							100	12	
							200	13	7,300
10/20				150	13	1,950	350	10	
							100	12	
							50	13	5,350
12/12	100	14	1,400				350	10	
							100	12	
							50	13	
							100	14	6,750

units at $10 and 300 units at $11, which results in an average cost of $10.38. This is the unit cost applied to the 450 units sold on February 18. The 400 units purchased on April 8 require the computation of a new unit cost, as indicated in the second footnote to the exhibit. As you might have suspected, the ending inventory with an average cost flow differs, depending on whether a periodic or a perpetual system is used:

Weighted average periodic (Exhibit 6-2)	$6,840
Moving average perpetual (Exhibit 6-14)	$7,290

Exhibit 6-14 Perpetual System: Moving Average Cost-Flow Assumption

	Purchases			Sales			Balance		
DATE	UNITS	UNIT COST	TOTAL COST	UNITS	UNIT COST	TOTAL COST	UNITS	UNIT COST	BALANCE
1/1							500	$10.00	$5,000
1/20	300	$11	$3,300				800	10.38*	8,304
2/18				450	$10.38	$4,671	350	10.38	3,633
4/8	400	12	4,800				750	11.24†	8,430
6/19				300	11.24	3,372	450	11.24	5,058
9/5	200	13	2,600				650	11.78‡	7,657
10/20				150	11.78	1,767	500	11.78	5,890
12/12	100	14	1,400				600	12.15§	7,290

The moving average prices per unit are calculated as follows:

*($5,000 + $3,300) / 800 units = $10.38 (rounded to nearest cent)

†($3,633 + $4,800) / 750 units = $11.24

‡($5,058 + $2,600) / 650 units = $11.78

§($5,890 + $1,400) / 600 units = $12.15

Chapter Highlights

1. **LO 1** A manufacturer's inventory consists of raw materials, work in process, and finished goods. The inventory of a retailer or wholesaler is in a single form called *merchandise inventory.*

2. **LO 2** The amount of cost of goods sold reported on the income statement is inherently tied to the value assigned to ending inventory on the balance sheet. All costs necessary to put inventory into a condition and location for sale should be included in its cost. Freight costs, storage costs, excise and sales taxes, and insurance during the time the merchandise is in transit are all candidates for inclusion in the cost of the asset. As a practical matter, however, some of these costs are very difficult to allocate to individual products and are therefore accounted for as expenses of the period.

3. **LO 3** The purchase of identical units of a product at varying prices necessitates the use of a costing method to assign a dollar amount to ending inventory and cost of goods sold. As alternatives to the use of a specific identification method, which is impractical in many instances as well as subject to manipulation, accountants have devised cost-flow assumptions.

4. **LO 3** The weighted average method assigns the same average unit cost to all units available for sale during the period. It is widely used because of its simplicity.

5. **LO 3** The FIFO method assigns the most recent costs to ending inventory. The older costs are assigned to cost of goods sold. A first-in, first-out approach does tend to parallel the physical flow of products in many businesses, although the actual flow is not our primary concern in choosing a costing method.

6. **LO 3** LIFO assigns the most recent costs to cost of goods sold, and the older costs remain in inventory. In a period of rising prices, this method results in a relatively higher amount assigned to cost of goods sold and, thus, a lower amount of reported net income. Lower net income results in a lower amount of taxes due, and the tax advantages have resulted in the widespread use of the LIFO method.

   A company that chooses to take advantage of the tax break from using LIFO on its tax return must also use the method in preparing the income statement. A concern with the use of LIFO is the possibility of a liquidation. If more units are sold than are bought in any one period, some of the units sold will come from the older, lower-priced units, resulting in a low cost of goods sold and a high gross margin. The high gross margin will necessitate a larger tax amount due.

7. **LO 4** Many accountants favor LIFO because it results in the nearest approximation to the current cost of goods sold. On the other hand, under LIFO, the inventory amount on the balance sheet is, in many cases, very outdated. FIFO gives a much closer approximation to current cost on the balance sheet. It leads, however, to what accountants describe as inventory profit: the portion of the gross margin that is due simply to holding the inventory during an inflationary period.

8. **LO 5** Errors in valuing inventory affect cost of goods sold and thus affect the amount of income reported for the period. An understatement of ending inventory will result in an understatement of net income; an overstatement of ending inventory will result in an overstatement of net income.

9. **LO 6** As used in the lower-of-cost-or-market rule, *market* means *replacement cost.* The purpose of valuing inventory at original cost or replacement cost, whichever is lower, is to anticipate declines in the selling price of goods subject to obsolescence, spoilage, and other types of loss. By being conservative and reducing the carrying value of the inventory at the end of the year, a company is more likely to report its normal gross margin when the units are sold at a reduced price in the next period. The rule can be applied to each item, to a group of items, or to the entire inventory.

10. **LO 7** The gross profit method is used to estimate the cost of inventory lost by theft, fire, flooding, and other types of damage. The method is also useful to estimate the amount of inventory on hand for interim reports, such as quarterly financial statements. It relies on a trustworthy estimate of the gross profit ratio.

11. **LO 7** Retailers use the retail inventory method to estimate the cost of inventory for interim financial statements and to convert the year-end inventory, per a physical count, from retail to cost.

12. **LO 8** Different measures are available to analyze how well a company is managing its inventory levels. The inventory turnover ratio indicates how many times during a period a company sells or turns over its inventory, and the number of days' sales in inventory indicates how long it takes, on average, to sell inventory.

13. **LO 9** The payment of cash to suppliers of inventory represents a cash outflow from operating activities on the statement of cash flows. If a company uses the indirect method, however, adjustments are made to net income for the increase or decrease in the Inventory and Accounts Payable accounts.

14. **LO 10** The periodic system relies on a count of inventory on hand at the end of the year to allocate costs between ending inventory and cost of goods sold. No entry is made in a periodic system to record the cost of inventory sold at the time of sale. Acquisitions of inventory during the period are recorded in the temporary account Purchases. (Appendix)

15. **LO 10** In a perpetual system, the Inventory account is updated at the time of each sale and purchase of merchandise. The computer has made the perpetual system much more feasible for many businesses. (Appendix)

16. **LO 11** Ending inventory costed at FIFO will be the same whether the periodic system or the perpetual system is used. This is not the case when the LIFO method is used: the results under the periodic and the perpetual systems differ. Likewise, ending inventory differs in the periodic system and the perpetual system when a weighted average approach is applied. The average method with a perpetual system is really a moving average approach. (Appendix)

http://

http://porter.swlearning.com

Technology and other resources for your success

If you need additional help, visit the text's Web site. Also, see pages xv–xvii in this text's preface for a description of available technology and other resources. If your instructor is using PERSONAL Trainer in this course, you may complete, on line, the assignments identified by PT.

Key Terms Quiz

Read each definition below and then write the number of the definition in the blank beside the appropriate term it defines. The quiz solutions appear at the end of the chapter.

_____ Merchandise Inventory
_____ Raw materials
_____ Work in process
_____ Finished goods
_____ Specific identification method
_____ Weighted average cost method
_____ FIFO method
_____ LIFO method
_____ LIFO liquidation
_____ LIFO conformity rule
_____ LIFO reserve
_____ Inventory profit
_____ Replacement cost
_____ Lower-of-cost-or-market (LCM) rule
_____ Gross profit method
_____ Retail inventory method
_____ Inventory turnover ratio
_____ Number of days' sales in inventory
_____ Moving average (Appendix)

1. The name given to an average cost method when it is used with a perpetual inventory system.
2. The cost of unfinished products in a manufacturing company.
3. An inventory costing method that assigns the same unit cost to all units available for sale during the period.
4. The account that wholesalers and retailers use to report inventory held for sale.
5. A conservative inventory valuation approach that is an attempt to anticipate declines in the value of inventory before its actual sale.
6. An inventory costing method that assigns the most recent costs to ending inventory.
7. The inventory of a manufacturer before the addition of any direct labor or manufacturing overhead.
8. The current cost of a unit of inventory.
9. An inventory costing method that assigns the most recent costs to cost of goods sold.
10. A measure of how long it takes to sell inventory.
11. A technique used to establish an estimate of the cost of inventory stolen, destroyed, or otherwise damaged or of the amount of inventory on hand at an interim date.
12. A manufacturer's inventory that is complete and ready for sale.
13. A technique used by retailers to convert the retail value of inventory to a cost basis.
14. The IRS requirement that if LIFO is used on the tax return, it must also be used in reporting income to stockholders.
15. An inventory costing method that relies on matching unit costs with the actual units sold.
16. The portion of the gross profit that results from holding inventory during a period of rising prices.
17. The result of selling more units than are purchased during the period, which can have negative tax consequences if a company is using LIFO.
18. The excess of the value of a company's inventory stated at FIFO over the value stated at LIFO.
19. A measure of the number of times inventory is sold during a period.

Answers on p. 321.

Alternate Terms

Gross margin Gross profit

Interim statements Quarterly or monthly statements

Market (value for inventory) Replacement cost

Raw materials Direct materials

Retail price Selling price

Work in process Work in progress

Questions

1. What are three distinct types of costs that manufacturers incur? Describe each of them.
2. What is the relationship between the valuation of inventory as an asset on the balance sheet and the measurement of income?
3. What is the justification for including freight costs incurred in acquiring incoming goods in the cost of the inventory rather than simply treating the cost as an expense of the period? What is the significance of this decision for accounting purposes?
4. What are the inventory characteristics that would allow a company to use the specific identification method? Give at least two examples of inventory for which the method is appropriate.
5. How can the specific identification method allow management to manipulate income?
6. What is the significance of the adjective *weighted* in the weighted average cost method? Use an example to illustrate your answer.
7. Which inventory method, FIFO or LIFO, more nearly approximates the physical flow of products in most businesses? Explain your answer.
8. York Inc. manufactures notebook computers and has experienced noticeable declines in the purchase price of many of the components it uses, including computer chips. Which inventory costing method should York use if it wants to maximize net income? Explain your answer.
9. Which inventory costing method should a company use if it wants to minimize taxes? Does your response depend on whether prices are rising or falling? Explain your answers.
10. The president of Ace Retail is commenting on the company's new controller: "The woman is brilliant! She has shown us how we can maximize our income and at the same time minimize the amount of taxes we have to pay the government. Because the cost to purchase our inventory constantly goes up, we will use FIFO to calculate cost of goods sold on the income statement to minimize the amount charged to cost of goods sold and thus maximize net income. For tax purposes, however, we will use LIFO because this will minimize taxable income and thus minimize the amount we have to pay in taxes." Should the president be enthralled with the new controller? Explain your answer.
11. What does the term *LIFO liquidation* mean? How can it lead to poor buying habits?
12. Historical-based costing methods are sometimes criticized for leading to inventory profits. In a period of rising prices, which inventory costing method will lead to the most "inventory profit"? Explain your answer.
13. Is it acceptable for a company to disclose, in its annual report, that it is switching from some other inventory costing method to LIFO *to save on taxes?*
14. Delevan Corp. uses a periodic inventory system and is counting its year-end inventory. Due to a lack of communication, two different teams count the same section of the warehouse. What effect will this error have on net income?
15. What is the rationale for valuing inventory at the lower of cost or market?
16. Why is it likely that the result from applying the lower-of-cost-or-market rule using a total approach, that is, by comparing total cost to total market value, and the result from applying the rule on an item-by-item basis will differ?
17. Patterson's controller makes the following suggestion: "I have a brilliant way to save us money. Because we are already using the gross profit method for our quarterly statements, we start using it to estimate the year-end inventory for the annual report and save the money normally spent to have the inventory counted on December 31." What do you think of his suggestion?
18. Why does a company save time and money by using the retail inventory method at the end of the year?
19. Ralston Corp.'s cost of sales has remained steady over the last two years. During this same time period, however, its inventory has increased considerably. What does this information tell you about the company's inventory turnover? Explain your answer.
20. In simple terms, how do the inventory costing methods, such as FIFO and LIFO, and the inventory systems, such as periodic and perpetual, differ? (Appendix)
21. Why is the weighted average cost method called a *moving* average when a company uses a perpetual inventory system? (Appendix)

Exercises

Exercise 6-1 ***Classification of Inventory Costs*** **LO 1**

Put an X in the appropriate column next to the inventory item to indicate its most likely classification on the books of a company that manufactures furniture and then sells it in retail company stores.

(continued)

Inventory Item	Classification: Raw Material	Work in Process	Finished Goods	Merchandise Inventory
Fabric				
Lumber				
Unvarnished tables				
Chairs on the showroom floor				
Cushions				
Decorative knobs				
Drawers				
Sofa frames				
Chairs in the plant warehouse				
Chairs in the retail storeroom				

Exercise 6-2 ***Inventoriable Costs*** **LO 1**

During the first month of operations, ABC Company incurred the following costs in ordering and receiving merchandise for resale. No inventory has been sold.

List price, $100, 200 units purchased
Volume discount, 10% off list price
Paid freight costs, $56
Insurance cost while goods were in transit, $32
Long-distance phone charge to place orders, $4.35
Purchasing department salary, $1,000
Supplies used to label goods at retail price, $9.75
Interest paid to supplier, $46

Required

What amount do you recommend the company record as merchandise inventory on its balance sheet? Explain your answer. For any items not to be included in inventory, indicate their appropriate treatment in the financial statements.

Exercise 6-3 ***Inventory and Income Manipulation*** **LO 2**

The president of SOS Inc. is concerned that the net income at year-end will not reach the expected figure. When the sales manager receives a large order on the last day of the fiscal year, the president tells the accountant to record the sale but to ignore any inventory adjustment because the physical inventory has already been taken. How will this affect the current year's net income? next year's income? What would you do if you were the accountant? Assume that SOS uses a periodic inventory system.

Exercise 6-4 ***Inventory Costing Methods*** **LO 3**

VanderMeer Inc. reported the following information for the month of February:

Inventory, February 1	65 units @ $20
Purchases:	
February 7	50 units @ $22
February 18	60 units @ $23
February 27	45 units @ $24

During February, VanderMeer sold 140 units. The company uses a periodic inventory system.

Required

What is the value of ending inventory and cost of goods sold for February under the following assumptions:

1. Of the 140 units sold, 55 cost $20, 35 cost $22, 45 cost $23, and 5 cost $24.
2. FIFO
3. LIFO
4. Weighted average

Exercise 6-5 ***Evaluation of Inventory Costing Methods*** **LO 4**

Write the letter of the method that is most applicable to each statement.

a. Specific identification
b. Average cost
c. First-in, first-out (FIFO)
d. Last-in, first-out (LIFO)

_______ 1. Is the most realistic ending inventory.
_______ 2. Results in cost of goods sold being closest to current product costs.
_______ 3. Results in highest income during periods of inflation.
_______ 4. Results in highest ending inventory during periods of inflation.
_______ 5. Smooths out costs during periods of inflation.
_______ 6. Is not practical for most businesses.
_______ 7. Puts more weight on the cost of the larger number of units purchased.
_______ 8. Is an assumption that most closely reflects the physical flow of goods for most businesses.

Exercise 6-6 ***Inventory Errors*** **LO 5**

For each of the following independent situations, fill in the blanks to indicate the effect of the error on each of the various financial statement items. Indicate an understatement (U), an overstatement (O), or no effect (NE). Assume that each of the companies uses a periodic inventory system.

	Balance Sheet		Income Statement	
Error	**Inventory**	**Retained Earnings**	**Cost of Goods Sold**	**Net Income**
1. Goods in transit at year end are not included in the physical count: they were shipped FOB shipping point.	_______	_______	_______	_______
2. One section of a warehouse is counted twice during the year-end count of inventory.	_______	_______	_______	_______
3. During the count at year-end, the inventory sheets for one of the stores of a discount retailer are lost.	_______	_______	_______	_______

Exercise 6-7 ***Transfer of Title to Inventory*** **LO 5**

For each of the following transactions, indicate which company should include the inventory on its December 31, 2004 balance sheet:

1. Michelson Supplies Inc. shipped merchandise to PJ Sales on December 28, 2004, terms FOB destination. The merchandise arrives at PJ's on January 4, 2005.
2. Quarton Inc. shipped merchandise to Filbrandt on December 25, 2004, FOB destination. Filbrandt received the merchandise on December 31, 2004.
3. James Bros. Inc. shipped merchandise to Randall Company on December 27, 2004, FOB shipping point. Randall Company received the merchandise on January 3, 2005.
4. Hinz Company shipped merchandise to Barner Inc. on December 24, 2004, FOB shipping point. The merchandise arrived at Barner's on December 29, 2004.

Exercise 6-8 ***Gross Profit Method*** **LO 7**

On February 12, a hurricane destroys the entire inventory of Suncoast Corporation. An estimate of the amount of inventory lost is needed for insurance purposes. The following information is available:

Inventory on January 1	$ 15,400
Net sales from January 1 to February 12	105,300
Purchases from January 1 to February 12	84,230

Suncoast estimates its gross profit ratio as 25% of net sales. The insurance company has agreed to pay Suncoast $10,000 as a settlement for the inventory destroyed.

(continued)

Required

Prepare the journal entry on Suncoast's books to recognize the inventory lost and the insurance reimbursement.

Exercise 6-9 *Inventory Turnover for Sears* LO 8

http://www.sears.com

The following amounts are available from the 2001 annual report of Sears, Roebuck & Co. (all amounts are in millions of dollars):

Cost of sales, buying, and occupancy	$26,322
Merchandise inventories, end of 2001	4,912
Merchandise inventories, end of 2000	5,618

Required

1. Compute Sears' inventory turnover ratio for 2001.
2. What is the average length of time it takes to sell an item of inventory? Explain your answer.
3. Do you think the average length of time it took Sears to sell inventory in 2001 is reasonable? What other information do you need to fully answer this question?

Exercise 6-10 *Impact of Transactions Involving Inventories on Statement of Cash Flows* LO 9

From the following list, identify whether the change in the account balance during the year would be added to (A) or deducted from (D) net income when the indirect method is used to determine cash flows from operating activities.

_______ Increase in accounts payable
_______ Decrease in accounts payable
_______ Increase in inventories
_______ Decrease in inventories

Exercise 6-11 *Effects of Transactions Involving Inventories on the Statement of Cash Flows—Direct Method* LO 9

Masthead Company's comparative balance sheets included inventory of $180,400 at December 31, 2003, and $241,200 at December 31, 2004. Masthead's comparative balance sheets also included accounts payable of $85,400 at December 31, 2003, and $78,400 at December 31, 2004. Masthead's accounts payable balances are composed solely of amounts due to suppliers for purchases of inventory on account. Cost of goods sold, as reported by Masthead on its 2004 income statement, amounted to $1,200,000.

Required

What is the amount of cash payments for inventory that Masthead will report in the Operating Activities category of its 2004 statement of cash flows assuming that the direct method is used?

Exercise 6-12 *Effects of Transactions Involving Inventories on the Statement of Cash Flows—Indirect Method* LO 9

Refer to all of the facts in Exercise 6-11.

Required

Assume instead that Masthead uses the indirect method to prepare its statement of cash flows. Indicate how each item will be reflected as an adjustment to net income in the Operating Activities category of the statement of cash flows.

Exercise 6-13 *Periodic and Perpetual Journal Entries (Appendix)* LO 10

Record the journal entries to reflect the following transactions, assuming (a) a periodic system and (b) a perpetual system. Arrange your entries in parallel columns for comparison purposes.

October 1:	Purchased 100 units on account for $7 each.
October 3:	Returned 5 defective units for full credit.
October 8:	Paid $16 freight charges on the October 1 shipment.
October 20:	Sold 75 units on account for $10 each.

Multi-Concept Exercises

SPREADSHEET

Exercise 6-14 *Inventory Costing Methods—Periodic System* LO 3, 4

The following information is available concerning the inventory of Carter Inc.:

	Units	Unit Cost
Beginning inventory	200	$10
Purchases:		
March 5	300	11
June 12	400	12
August 23	250	13
October 2	150	15

During the year, Carter sold 1,000 units. It uses a periodic inventory system.

Required

1. Calculate ending inventory and cost of goods sold for each of the following three methods:
   a. Weighted average
   b. FIFO
   c. LIFO
2. Assume an estimated tax rate of 30%. How much more or less (indicate which) will Carter pay in taxes by using FIFO instead of LIFO? Explain your answer.

Exercise 6-15 *Lower-of-Cost-or-Market Rule* LO 2, 6

Awards Etc. carries an inventory of trophies and ribbons for local sports teams and school clubs. The cost of trophies has dropped in the past year, which pleases the company except for the fact that it has on hand considerable inventory that was purchased at the higher prices. The president is not pleased with the lower profit margin the company is earning. "The lower profit margin will continue until we sell all of this old inventory," he grumbled to the new staff accountant. "Not really," replied the accountant. "Let's write down the inventory to the replacement cost this year, and then next year our profit margin will be in line with the competition."

Required

Explain why the inventory can be carried at an amount less than its cost. Which accounts will be affected by the write-down? What will be the effect on income in the current year and future years?

Exercise 6-16 *Inventory Costing Methods—Perpetual System (Appendix)* LO 4, 11

The following information is available concerning Stillwater Inc.:

	Units	Unit Cost
Beginning inventory	200	$10
Purchases:		
March 5	300	11
June 12	400	12
August 23	250	13
October 2	150	15

Stillwater, which uses a perpetual system, sold 1,000 units for $22 each during the year. Sales occurred on the following dates:

	Units
February 12	150
April 30	200
July 7	200
September 6	300
December 3	150

Required

1. Calculate ending inventory and cost of goods sold for each of the following three methods:
   a. Moving average
   b. FIFO
   c. LIFO

(continued)

2. For each of the three methods, compare the results with those for Carter in Exercise 6-14. Which of the methods gives a different answer depending on whether a company uses a periodic or a perpetual inventory system?
3. Assume the use of the perpetual system and an estimated tax rate of 30%. How much more or less (indicate which) will Stillwater pay in taxes by using LIFO instead of FIFO? Explain your answer.

Problems

Problem 6-1 ***Inventory Costs in Various Businesses*** **LO 1**

Businesses incur various costs in selling goods and services. Each business must decide which costs are expenses of the period and which should be included in the cost of the inventory. Various types of businesses are listed below, along with certain types of costs they incur:

		Accounting Treatment		
Business	**Types of Costs**	**Expense of the Period**	**Inventory Cost**	**Other Treatment**
Retail shoe store	Shoes for sale			
	Shoe boxes			
	Advertising signs			
Grocery store	Canned goods on the shelves			
	Produce			
	Cleaning supplies			
	Cash registers			
Frame shop	Wooden frame supplies			
	Nails			
	Glass			
Walk-in print shop	Paper			
	Copy machines			
	Toner cartridges			
Restaurant	Frozen food			
	China and silverware			
	Prepared food			
	Spices			

Required

Fill in the table to indicate the correct accounting for each of these types of costs by placing an X in the appropriate column. For any costs that receive other treatment, explain what the appropriate treatment is for accounting purposes.

Problem 6-2 ***Evaluation of Inventory Costing Methods*** **LO 4**

Users of financial statements rely on the information available to them to decide whether to invest in a company or lend it money. As an investor, you are comparing three companies in the same industry. The cost to purchase inventory is rising in the industry. Assume that all expenses incurred by the three companies are the same except for cost of goods sold. The companies use the following methods to value ending inventory:

Company A—weighted average cost
Company B—first-in, first-out (FIFO)
Company C—last-in, first-out (LIFO)

Required

1. Which of the three companies will report the highest net income? Explain your answer.
2. Which of the three companies will pay the least in income taxes? Explain your answer.
3. Which method of inventory costing do you believe is superior to the others in providing information to potential investors? Explain.
4. Explain how your answers to **1, 2,** and **3** would change if the costs to purchase inventory had been falling instead of rising.

Problem 6-3 ***Inventory Error*** **LO 5**

The following highly condensed income statements and balance sheets are available for Budget Stores for a two-year period (all amounts are stated in thousands of dollars):

Income Statements	2004	2003
Revenues	$20,000	$15,000
Cost of goods sold	13,000	10,000
Gross profit	$ 7,000	$ 5,000
Operating expenses	3,000	2,000
Net income	$ 4,000	$ 3,000

Balance Sheets	December 31, 2004	December 31, 2003
Cash	$ 1,700	$ 1,500
Inventory	4,200	3,500
Other current assets	2,500	2,000
Long-term assets	15,000	14,000
Total assets	$23,400	$21,000
Liabilities	$ 8,500	$ 7,000
Capital stock	5,000	5,000
Retained earnings	9,900	9,000
Total liabilities and owners' equity	$23,400	$21,000

Before releasing the 2004 annual report, Budget's controller learns that the inventory of one of the stores (amounting to $600,000) was inadvertently omitted from the count on December 31, 2003. The inventory of the store was correctly included in the December 31, 2004, count.

Required

1. Prepare revised income statements and balance sheets for Budget Stores for each of the two years. Ignore the effect of income taxes.
2. If Budget did not prepare revised statements before releasing the 2004 annual report, what would be the amount of overstatement or understatement of net income for the two-year period? What would be the overstatement or understatement of retained earnings at December 31, 2004, if revised statements were not prepared?
3. Given your answers in **2**, does it matter if Budget bothers to restate the financial statements of the two years to rectify the error? Explain your answer.

Problem 6-4 ***Gross Profit Method of Estimating Inventory Losses*** **LO 7**

On August 1, an office supply store was destroyed by an explosion in its basement. A small amount of inventory valued at $4,500 was saved. An estimate of the amount of inventory lost is needed for insurance purposes. The following information is available:

Inventory, January 1	$ 3,200
Purchases, January–July	164,000
Sales, January–July	113,500

The normal gross profit ratio is 40%. The insurance company will pay the store $65,000.

Required

1. Using the gross profit method, estimate the amount of inventory lost in the explosion.
2. Prepare the journal entry to record the inventory loss and the insurance reimbursement.

Problem 6-5 ***Inventory Turnover for Apple Computer and Gateway*** **LO 8**

The following information was summarized from the 2001 annual report of Apple Computer Inc.:

http://www.apple.com

	(in millions)
Cost of sales for the year ended:	
September 29, 2001	$4,128
September 30, 2000	5,817

(continued)

(Continued)	(in millions)
Inventories:	
September 29, 2001	$ 11
September 30, 2000	33
Net sales for the year ended:	
September 29, 2001	5,363
September 30, 2000	7,983

http://www.gateway.com The following information was summarized from the 2001 annual report of Gateway, Inc.:

	(in thousands)
Cost of goods sold for the year ended December 31:	
2001	$5,241,332
2000	7,541,606
Inventory, December 31:	
2001	120,270
2000	315,069
Net sales for the year ended December 31:	
2001	6,079,524
2000	9,600,600

Required

1. Calculate the gross margin (gross profit) ratios for Apple Computer and Gateway for 2001 and 2000.
2. Calculate the inventory turnover ratios for both companies for 2001.
3. Which company appears to be performing better? What other information should you consider to determine how these companies are performing in this regard?

Problem 6-6 ***Effects of Changes in Inventory and Accounts Payable Balances on Statement of Cash Flows*** **LO 9**

Copeland Antiques reported a net loss of $33,200 for the year ended December 31, 2004. The following items were included on Copeland's balance sheets at December 31, 2004 and 2003:

	12/31/04	12/31/03
Cash	$ 65,300	$ 46,100
Trade accounts payable	123,900	93,700
Inventories	192,600	214,800

Copeland uses the indirect method to prepare its statement of cash flows. Copeland does not have any other current assets or current liabilities and did not enter into any investing or financing activities during 2004.

Required

1. Prepare Copeland's 2004 statement of cash flows.
2. Draft a brief memo to the president to explain why cash increased during such an unprofitable year.

Multi-Concept Problems

Problem 6-7 ***Comparison of Inventory Costing Methods—Periodic System*** **LO 2, 3, 4**

Bitten Company's inventory records show 600 units on hand on October 1 with a unit cost of $5 each. The following transactions occurred during the month of October:

Date	Unit Purchases	Unit Sales
October 4		500 @ $10.00
8	800 @ $5.40	
9		700 @ $10.00
18	700 @ $5.76	
20		800 @ $11.00
29	800 @ $5.90	

All expenses other than cost of goods sold amount to $3,000 for the month. The company uses an estimated tax rate of 30% to accrue monthly income taxes.

Required

1. Prepare a chart comparing cost of goods sold and ending inventory using the periodic system and the following costing methods:

	Cost of Goods Sold	Ending Inventory	Total
Weighted average			
FIFO			
LIFO			

2. What does the Total column represent?
3. Prepare income statements for each of the three methods.
4. Will the company pay more or less tax if it uses FIFO rather than LIFO? How much more or less?

Problem 6-8 ***Comparison of Inventory Costing Methods—Perpetual System (Appendix)*** **LO 2, 4, 11**

Repeat Problem 6-7 using the perpetual system.

Problem 6-9 ***Inventory Costing Methods—Periodic System*** **LO 2, 3, 4**

SPREADSHEET

Oxendine Company's inventory records for the month of November reveal the following:

Inventory, November 1	200 units @ $18.00
November 4, purchase	250 units @ $18.50
November 7, sale	300 units @ $42.00
November 13, purchase	220 units @ $18.90
November 18, purchase	150 units @ $19.00
November 22, sale	380 units @ $42.50
November 24, purchase	200 units @ $19.20
November 28, sale	110 units @ $43.00

Selling and administrative expenses for the month were $10,800. Depreciation expense was $4,000. Oxendine's tax rate is 35%.

Required

1. Calculate the cost of goods sold and ending inventory under each of the following three methods (assume a periodic inventory system): (a) FIFO, (b) LIFO, and (c) weighted average.
2. Calculate the gross margin and net income under each costing assumption.
3. Under which costing method will Oxendine pay the least taxes? Explain your answer.

Problem 6-10 ***Inventory Costing Methods—Periodic System*** **LO 2, 3, 4**

DECISION MAKING

Following is an inventory acquisition schedule for Weaver Corp. for 2004:

	Units	Unit Cost
Beginning inventory	5,000	$10
Purchases:		
February 4	3,000	9
April 12	4,000	8
September 10	2,000	7
December 5	1,000	6

During the year, Weaver sold 12,500 units at $12 each. All expenses except cost of goods sold and taxes amounted to $20,000. The tax rate is 30%.

Required

1. Compute cost of goods sold and ending inventory under each of the following three methods (assume a periodic inventory system): (a) weighted average, (b) FIFO, and (c) LIFO.
2. Prepare income statements under each of the three methods.

(continued)

3. Which method do you recommend so that Weaver pays the least amount of taxes during 2004? Explain your answer.
4. Weaver anticipates that unit costs for inventory will increase throughout 2005. Will it be able to switch from the method you recommended it use in 2004 to another method to take advantage for tax purposes of the increase in prices? Explain your answer.

Problem 6-11 ***Interpreting Tribune Company's Inventory Accounting Policy*** **LO 1, 4**

http://www.tribune.com

The 2001 annual report of **Tribune Company and Subsidiaries** includes the following in the note that summarizes its accounting policies:

> **Inventories** Inventories are stated at the lower of cost or market. Cost is determined on the last-in, first-out ("LIFO") basis for newsprint and on the first-in, first-out ("FIFO") or average basis for all other inventories.

Required

1. What *types* of inventory cost does Tribune Company carry? What about newspapers? Are newspapers considered inventory?
2. Why would the company choose three different methods to value its inventory?

Problem 6-12 ***Interpreting Sears' Inventory Accounting Policy*** **LO 3, 7**

http://www.sears.com

The 2001 annual report of **Sears, Roebuck and Co.** includes the following information in the note that describes its accounting policies relating to merchandise inventories:

> Approximately 88% of merchandise inventories are valued at the lower of cost or market, with cost determined using the retail inventory method ("RIM") under the last-in, first-out ("LIFO") cost flow assumption. To estimate the effects of inflation on inventories, the Company utilizes internally developed price indices.

The note also includes the following information about the company's international operations:

> Merchandise inventories of Sears Canada operations, operations in Puerto Rico and NTB stores, which in total represent approximately 12% of merchandise inventories, are recorded at the lower of cost or market based on the FIFO method.

Your grandfather knows you are studying accounting and asks you what this information means.

Required

1. Sears uses the last-in, first-out method for its domestic merchandise inventories and the first-in, first-out method for its international merchandise inventories. Does this mean it sells its newest merchandise first in the United States and its oldest merchandise first overseas? Explain your answer.
2. Does Sears report merchandise inventories on its balance sheet at their retail value? Explain your answer.

Alternate Problems

DECISION MAKING

Problem 6-1A ***Inventory Costs in Various Businesses*** **LO 1**

Sound Traxs Inc. sells and rents videos to retail customers. The accountant is aware that at the end of the year she must account for inventory but is unsure what videos are considered inventory and how to value them. Videos purchased by the company are placed on the shelf for rental. Every three weeks the company performs a detailed analysis of the rental income from each video and decides whether to keep it as a rental or to offer it for sale in the resale section of the store. Resale videos sell for $10 each regardless of the price Sound Traxs paid for the tape.

Required

1. How should Sound Traxs account for each of the two types of tapes—rentals and resales—on its balance sheet?
2. How would you suggest Sound Traxs account for the videos as they are transferred from one department to another?

Problem 6-2A ***Evaluation of Inventory Costing Methods*** **LO 4**

Three large mass merchandisers use the following methods to value ending inventory:

Company X—weighted average cost
Company Y—first-in, first-out (FIFO)
Company Z—last-in, first-out (LIFO)

The cost of inventory has steadily increased over the past 10 years of the product life. Recently, however, prices have started to decline slightly due to foreign competition.

Required

1. Will the effect on net income of the decline in cost of goods sold be the same for all three companies? Explain your answer.
2. Company Z would like to change its inventory costing method from LIFO to FIFO. Write an acceptable note for its annual report to justify the change.

Problem 6-3A *Inventory Error* LO 5

The following condensed income statements and balance sheets are available for Planter Stores for a two-year period (all amounts are stated in thousands of dollars):

Income Statements	2004	2003
Revenues	$35,982	$26,890
Cost of goods sold	12,594	9,912
Gross profit	$23,388	$16,978
Operating expenses	13,488	10,578
Net income	$ 9,900	$ 6,400

Balance Sheets	December 31, 2004	December 31, 2003
Cash	$ 9,400	$ 4,100
Inventory	4,500	5,400
Other current assets	1,600	1,250
Long-term assets, net	24,500	24,600
Total assets	$40,000	$35,350
Current liabilities	$ 9,380	$10,600
Capital stock	18,000	18,000
Retained earnings	12,620	6,750
Total liabilities and owners' equity	$40,000	$35,350

Before releasing the 2004 annual report, Planter's controller learns that the inventory of one of the stores (amounting to $500,000) was counted twice in the December 31, 2003, inventory. The inventory was correctly counted in the December 31, 2004, inventory count.

Required

1. Prepare revised income statements and balance sheets for Planter Stores for each of the two years. Ignore the effect of income taxes.
2. Compute the current ratio at December 31, 2003, before the statements are revised, and then compute the current ratio at the same date after the statements are revised. If Planter applied for a loan in early 2004 and the lender required a current ratio of at least 1-to-1, would the error have affected the loan? Explain your answer.
3. If Planter did not prepare revised statements before releasing the 2004 annual report, what would be the amount of overstatement or understatement of net income for the two-year period? What would be the overstatement or understatement of retained earnings at December 31, 2004, if revised statements were not prepared?
4. Given your answers to **2** and **3**, does it matter if Planter bothers to restate the financial statements of the two years to correct the error? Explain your answer.

Problem 6-4A *Gross Profit Method of Estimating Inventory Losses* LO 7

On July 1, an explosion destroyed a fireworks supply company. A small amount of inventory valued at $4,500 was saved. An estimate of the amount of inventory lost is needed for insurance purposes. The following information is available:

Inventory, January 1	$14,200
Purchases, January–June	77,000
Sales, January–June	93,500

(continued)

The normal gross profit ratio is 70%. The insurance company will pay the supply company $50,000.

Required

1. Using the gross profit method, estimate the amount of inventory lost in the explosion.
2. Prepare the journal entry to record the inventory loss and the insurance reimbursement.

Problem 6-5A ***Inventory Turnover for Wal-Mart and Kmart*** **LO 8**

http://www.walmart.com

The following information was summarized from the 2002 annual report of Wal-Mart Stores, Inc.:

	(in millions)
Cost of sales for the year ended January 31:	
2002	$171,562
2001	150,255
Inventories, January 31:	
2002	22,614
2001	21,442

http://www.kmart.com

The following information was summarized from the fiscal year 2001 annual report of Kmart Corporation:

	(in millions)
Cost of sales, buying, and occupancy for the year ended:	
January 30, 2002	$29,936
January 31, 2001	29,658
Merchandise inventories:	
January 30, 2002	5,822
January 31, 2001	6,412

Required

1. Calculate the inventory turnover ratios for Wal-Mart for the year ending January 31, 2002, and Kmart for the year ending January 30, 2002.
2. Which company appears to be performing better? What other information should you consider to determine how these companies are performing in this regard?

Problem 6-6A ***Effects of Changes in Inventory and Accounts Payable Balances on Statement of Cash Flows*** **LO 9**

Carpetland City reported net income of $78,500 for the year ended December 31, 2004. The following items were included on Carpetland's balance sheet at December 31, 2004 and 2003:

	12/31/04	12/31/03
Cash	$ 14,400	$26,300
Trade accounts payable	23,900	93,700
Inventories	105,500	84,900

Carpetland uses the indirect method to prepare its statement of cash flows. Carpetland does not have any other current assets or current liabilities and did not enter into any investing or financing activities during 2004.

Required

1. Prepare Carpetland's 2004 statement of cash flows.
2. Draft a brief memo to the president to explain why cash decreased during a profitable year.

Alternate Multi-Concept Problems

Problem 6-7A ***Comparison of Inventory Costing Methods—Periodic System*** **LO 2, 3, 4**

Stellar Inc.'s inventory records show 300 units on hand on November 1 with a unit cost of $4 each. The following transactions occurred during the month of November:

Date		Unit Purchases	Unit Sales
November	4		200 @ $9.00
	8	500 @ $4.50	
	9		500 @ $9.00
	18	700 @ $4.75	
	20		400 @ $9.50
	29	600 @ $5.00	

All expenses other than cost of goods sold amount to $2,000 for the month. The company uses an estimated tax rate of 25% to accrue monthly income taxes.

Required

1. Prepare a chart comparing cost of goods sold and ending inventory using the periodic system and the following costing methods:

	Cost of Goods Sold	Ending Inventory	Total
Weighted average			
FIFO			
LIFO			

2. What does the Total column represent?
3. Prepare income statements for each of the three methods.
4. Will the company pay more or less tax if it uses FIFO rather than LIFO? How much more or less?

Problem 6-8A ***Comparison of Inventory Costing Methods—Perpetual System*** **LO 2, 4, 11**

Repeat Problem 6-7A, using the perpetual system.

Problem 6-9A ***Inventory Costing Methods—Periodic System*** **LO 2, 3, 4**

SPREADSHEET

Story Company's inventory records for the month of November reveal the following:

Inventory, November 1	300 units @ $27.00
November 4, purchase	375 units @ $26.50
November 7, sale	450 units @ $63.00
November 13, purchase	330 units @ $26.00
November 18, purchase	225 units @ $25.40
November 22, sale	570 units @ $63.75
November 24, purchase	300 units @ $25.00
November 28, sale	165 units @ $64.50

Selling and administrative expenses for the month were $16,200. Depreciation expense was $6,000. Story's tax rate is 35%.

Required

1. Calculate the cost of goods sold and ending inventory under each of the following three methods (assume a periodic inventory system): (a) FIFO, (b) LIFO, and (c) weighted average.
2. Calculate the gross margin and net income under each costing assumption.
3. Under which costing method will Story pay the least taxes? Explain your answer.

Problem 6-10A ***Inventory Costing Methods—Periodic System*** **LO 2, 3, 4**

DECISION MAKING

Following is an inventory acquisition schedule for Fees Corp. for 2004:

	Units	Unit Cost
Beginning inventory	4,000	$20
Purchases:		
February 4	2,000	18
April 12	3,000	16
September 10	1,000	14
December 5	2,500	12

(continued)

During the year, Fees sold 11,000 units at $30 each. All expenses except cost of goods sold and taxes amounted to $60,000. The tax rate is 30%.

Required

1. Compute cost of goods sold and ending inventory under each of the following three methods (assume a periodic inventory system): (a) weighted average, (b) FIFO, and (c) LIFO.
2. Prepare income statements under each of the three methods.
3. Which method do you recommend so that Fees pays the least amount of taxes during 2004? Explain your answer.
4. Fees anticipates that unit costs for inventory will increase throughout 2005. Will it be able to switch from the method you recommended it use in 2004 to another method to take advantage for tax purposes of the increase in prices? Explain your answer.

Problem 6-11A ***Interpreting the New York Times Company's Financial Statements*** **LO 1, 4**

http://www.nytimes.com

The 2001 annual report of the New York Times Company includes the following note:

> Inventories. Inventories are stated at the lower of cost or current market value. Inventory cost is generally based on the last-in, first-out ("LIFO") method for newsprint and magazine paper and the first-in, first-out ("FIFO") method for other inventories.

Required

1. What *types* of inventory costs does the New York Times Company have? What about newspapers? Aren't these considered inventory?
2. Why did the company choose two different methods to value its inventory?

Problem 6-12A ***Interpreting Home Depot's Financial Statements*** **LO 3, 7**

http://www.homedepot.com

The 2001 annual report for Home Depot includes the following in the note that summarizes its accounting policies:

> Merchandise Inventories. The majority of the company's inventory is stated at the lower of cost (first-in, first-out) or market, as determined by the retail inventory method.

A friend knows that you are studying accounting and asks you what this note means.

Required

1. Home Depot uses the first-in, first-out method. Does this mean that it always sells its oldest merchandise first?
2. Does Home Depot report inventories on its balance sheet at their retail value?

Cases

Reading and Interpreting Financial Statements

Case 6-1 ***Comparing Two Companies in the Same Industry: Winnebago Industries and Monaco Coach Corporation*** **LO 4, 8**

http://www.winnebagoind.com
http://www.monacocoach.com

Refer to the financial information for Winnebago Industries and Monaco Coach Corporation reproduced in Appendices A and B at the end of the book.

Required

1. Compute the inventory turnover ratio for each company for 2001. Which company turned over its inventory more often during the year?
2. Compute the number of days' sales in inventory for each company for 2001. Which company had a fewer number of days' sales in inventory during the year? Is this consistent with your answer in question **1** above? Explain your answer.
3. Locate the note in each company's annual report in which they describe the inventory costing method they use. What inventory method does each company use? Should you be concerned if you are trying to compare Winnebago Industries and Monaco Coach that they do not use the same inventory method? Explain your answer.

Case 6-2 *Reading and Interpreting Winnebago Industries' Annual Report* LO 1, 3

Refer to **Winnebago Industries'** financial statements included in its annual report. http://www.winnebagoind.com

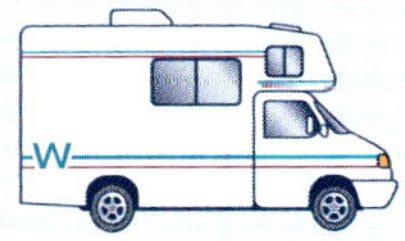

Required

1. Before you look at Winnebago Industries' annual report, what types of inventory accounts do you expect? What types of inventory accounts does Winnebago Industries actually report? (Refer to the note on inventories.)
2. What inventory costing method does Winnebago Industries use? Look in the notes to the financial statements.
3. What portion of total assets is represented by inventory at the end of 2000? at the end of 2001? Do these portions seem reasonable for a company in this business? Explain your answer.
4. Look at the statement of cash flows. Under the operating activities, you will find an adjustment for depreciation, yet there is no mention of depreciation on the income statement. Depreciation on equipment and buildings used in the manufacturing process is included in cost of sales. Make a list of other expenses that you would expect to be included in Winnebago Industries' cost of sales rather than listed separately on the income statement.

Case 6-3 *Reading Winnebago Industries' Statement of Cash Flows* LO 9

Refer to the statement of cash flows in **Winnebago Industries'** 2001 annual report and answer the following questions: http://www.winnebagoind.com

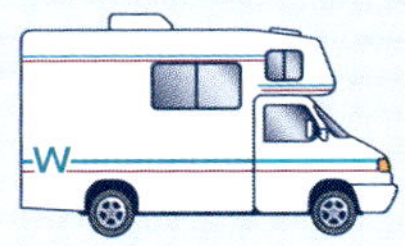

1. Did inventories increase or decrease during 2001? Why was the change in the Inventory account added to net income in the Operating Activities category of the statement?
2. Comment on the size of change in inventories over the last three years. Does the level of inventory at the end of 2001 seem appropriate?
3. Did accounts payable and accrued expenses increase or decrease during 2001? Why was the change in the accounts added to net income in the Operating Activities category of the statement?

Case 6-4 *Reading and Interpreting JCPenney's Financial Statements* LO 4

JCPenney reports merchandise inventory in the Current Assets section of the balance sheet in its 2001 annual report as follows (amounts in millions of dollars): http://www.jcpenney.com

	2001	2000
Merchandise inventory (net of LIFO reserves of $377 and $339)	$4,930	$5,269

Required

1. What method does JCPenney use to report the value of its inventory?
2. What is the amount of the LIFO reserve at the end of each of the two years?
3. Explain the meaning of the increase or decrease in the LIFO reserve during 2001. What does this tell you about inventory costs for the company? Are they rising or falling? Explain your answer.

Case 6-5 *Reading and Interpreting Circuit City's Inventory Note* LO 1, 3

Note 1F in **Circuit City's** 2001 annual report is titled "Inventory" and reads as follows: http://www.circuitcity.com

> Circuit City inventory is comprised of finished goods held for sale and is stated at the lower of cost or market. CarMax inventory is comprised primarily of vehicles held for sale or for reconditioning and is stated at the lower of cost or market. Cost is determined by the average cost method for Circuit City's inventory and by specific identification for CarMax's vehicle inventory. Parts and labor used to recondition vehicles, as well as transportation and other incremental expenses associated with acquiring and reconditioning vehicles, are included in CarMax's inventory.

Required

1. What type(s) of inventory do Circuit City and CarMax report?
2. What inventory costing method(s) do Circuit City and CarMax use? Do the methods seem appropriate for the type of business each operates? Explain your answer.
3. How does CarMax account for transportation costs to acquire its inventory? What is the rationale for accounting for these costs in this manner?

Making Financial Decisions

DECISION MAKING

Case 6-6 *Inventory Costing Methods* LO 3, 4

You are the controller for Georgetown Company. At the end of its first year of operations, the company is experiencing cash flow problems. The following information has been accumulated during the year:

Purchases	
January	1,000 units @ $8
March	1,200 units @ 8
October	1,500 units @ 9

During the year, Georgetown sold 3,000 units at $15 each. The expected tax rate is 35%. The president doesn't understand how to report inventory in the financial statements because no record of the cost of the units sold was kept as each sale was made.

Required

1. What inventory *system* must Georgetown use?
2. Determine the number of units on hand at the end of the year.
3. Explain cost-flow assumptions to the president and the method you recommend. Prepare income statements to justify your position, comparing your recommended method with at least one other method.

DECISION MAKING

Case 6-7 *Inventory Errors* LO 5

You are the controller of a rapidly growing mass merchandiser. The company uses a periodic inventory system. As the company has grown and accounting systems have developed, errors have occurred in both the physical count of inventory and the valuation of inventory on the balance sheet. You have been able to identify the following errors as of December 2004:

- In 2002 one section of the warehouse was counted twice. The error resulted in inventory overstated on December 31, 2002, by approximately $45,600.
- In 2003 the replacement cost of some inventory was less than the FIFO value used on the balance sheet. The inventory would have been $6,000 less on the balance sheet dated December 31, 2003.
- In 2004 the company used the gross profit method to estimate inventory for its quarterly financial statements. At the end of the second quarter, the controller made a math error and understated the inventory by $20,000 on the quarterly report. The error was not discovered until the end of the year.

Required

What, if anything, should you do to correct each of these errors? Explain your answers.

Accounting and Ethics: What Would You Do?

Case 6-8 *Write-Down of Obsolete Inventory* LO 6

As a newly hired staff accountant, you are assigned the responsibility of physically counting inventory at the end of the year. The inventory count proceeds in a timely fashion. The inventory is outdated, however. You suggest that the inventory could not be sold for the cost at which it is carried and that the inventory should be written down to a much lower level. The controller replies that experience has taught her how the market changes and she knows that the units in the warehouse will be more marketable again. The company plans to keep the goods until they are back in style.

Required

1. What effect will writing off the inventory have on the current year's income?
2. What effect does not writing off the inventory have on the year-end balance sheet?
3. What factors should you consider in deciding whether to persist in your argument that the inventory should be written down?

Case 6-9 *Selection of an Inventory Method* **LO 4**

As controller of a widely held public company, you are concerned with making the best decisions for the stockholders. At the end of its first year of operations, you are faced with the choice of method to value inventory. Specific identification is out of the question because the company sells a large quantity of diversified products. You are trying to decide between FIFO and LIFO. Inventory costs have increased 33% over the year. The chief executive officer has instructed you to do whatever it takes in all areas to report the highest income possible.

Required

1. Which method will satisfy the CEO?
2. Which method do you believe is in the best interest of the stockholders? Explain your answer.
3. Write a brief memo to the CEO to convince him that reporting the highest income is not always the best approach for the shareholders.

Internet Research Case

Case 6-10 Circuit City

INTERNET

http://www.circuitcity.com

Circuit City Stores Inc. is a top retailer in the consumer electronics industry (its Circuit City Group), and it is also a significant retailer of autos and trucks (its CarMax Group). Read the chapter opening text and the Business Strategy box, research the company and its financial information available on its web site, and answer the following questions.

1. What is the inventory amount shown for the most current year?
2. What is the inventory turnover for the CarMax Group? For the entire company as a whole? Is this information significant for evaluating each of the two groups in the company against competition? Is it significant for evaluating the company as a whole? Why or why not?
3. What inventory system would you expect Circuit City to use, perpetual or periodic? What makes you think so?
4. How could Circuit City reduce its costs for carrying inventory?

Solutions to Key Terms Quiz

4	Merchandise Inventory (p. 272)
7	Raw materials (p. 272)
2	Work in process (p. 273)
12	Finished goods (p. 273)
15	Specific identification method (p. 276)
3	Weighted average cost method (p. 277)
6	FIFO method (p. 278)
9	LIFO method (p. 279)
17	LIFO liquidation (p. 281)
14	LIFO conformity rule (p. 281)
18	LIFO reserve (p. 282)
16	Inventory profit (p. 282)
8	Replacement cost (p. 282)
5	Lower-of-cost-or-market (LCM) rule (p. 287)
11	Gross profit method (p. 290)
13	Retail inventory method (p. 292)
19	Inventory turnover ratio (p. 292)
10	Number of days' sales in inventory (p. 292)
1	Moving average (Appendix) (p. 301)

Chapter 7

Cash, Investments, and Receivables

Focus on Financial Results

For the last few years PepsiCo, one of the world's fastest growing consumer products companies, has been in the business of revamping itself. In the late 1990s, the company sold off some highly recognizable franchising businesses, such as KFC, Pizza Hut, and Taco Bell, to focus attention on its core brands, Frito-Lay snacks, Pepsi-Cola beverages, and Tropicana juices. The new millennium saw the company make the biggest strategic decision of its corporate life when, in 2001, it completed a merger with The Quaker Oats Company. This added not only all of the various Quaker food brands to PepsiCo's portfolio but also Gatorade, the pioneer in sports supplement drinks.

The assets section of PepsiCo's consolidated balance sheet pictured here reflects the combined muscle of the company and its new partner, Quaker Oats. Crucial to the future success of the consumer foods giant will be its ability to react quickly to new opportunities to invest valuable resources. The most liquid of these resources are reported on the first two lines of the balance sheet: *cash and cash equivalents* and *short-term investments.* Consumer food companies like PepsiCo also have sizeable amounts tied up in *accounts and notes receivable,* assets resulting from the commonly accepted business practice of extending credit to customers. The ability to collect from those customers on a timely basis and turn those receivables into cash will be a key factor in determining the success of the new and improved PepsiCo.

PepsiCo's 2001 Annual Report

Consolidated Balance Sheet

December 29, 2001 and December 30, 2000

PepsiCo, Inc. and Subsidiaries

(in millions except per share amounts)	2001	2000
ASSETS		
Current Assets		
Cash and cash equivalents	$ 683	$ 1,038
Short-term investments, at cost	966	467
	1,649	1,505
Accounts and notes receivable, net	2,142	2,129
Inventories	1,310	1,192
Prepaid expenses and other current assets	752	791
Total Current Assets	5,853	5,617
Property, Plant and Equipment, net	6,876	6,558
Intangible Assets, net	4,841	4,714
Investments in Unconsolidated Affiliates	2,871	2,979
Other Assets	1,254	889
Total Assets	$21,695	$20,757

Lower cash and cash equivalents

Higher short-term investments

You're in the Driver's Seat

http://www.pepsico.com

PepsiCo, Inc. prides itself on its ability to earn profits for its shareholders. If you owned shares in the company, what questions would you ask about its most liquid resources: cash and cash equivalents, short-term investments, and accounts and notes receivable. Study the chapter to find out how these important assets are related.

LEARNING OBJECTIVES

After studying this chapter, you should be able to:

LO 1 Identify and describe the various forms of cash reported on a balance sheet. (p. 324)

LO 2 Demonstrate an understanding of various techniques that companies use to control cash. (p. 325)

LO 3 Demonstrate an understanding of the accounting for various types of investments companies make. (p. 333)

LO 4 Demonstrate an understanding of how to account for accounts receivable, including bad debts. (p. 343)

LO 5 Demonstrate an understanding of how to account for interest-bearing notes receivable. (p. 351)

LO 6 Demonstrate an understanding of how to account for non-interest-bearing notes receivable. (p. 352)

LO 7 Explain various techniques that companies use to accelerate the inflow of cash from sales. (p. 353)

LO 8 Explain the effects of transactions involving liquid assets on the statement of cash flows. (p. 355)

PepsiCo Inc., like all other businesses, relies on *liquid assets* to function smoothly. *Liquidity* is a relative term. It deals with a company's ability to pay its debts as they fall due. Most obligations must be paid in cash, and therefore cash is considered the most liquid of all assets. Accounts and notes receivable are not as liquid as cash. Their collection does result in an inflow of cash, however. Because cash in its purest form does not earn a return, most businesses invest in various types of securities as a way to use idle cash over the short term. The Current Assets section of PepsiCo's balance sheet, as shown in the chapter opener, indicates three highly liquid assets: cash and cash equivalents, short-term investments, and accounts and notes receivable. Inventories are not considered as liquid as these three assets because they depend on a sale to be realized.

We begin the chapter by considering the various forms cash can take and the importance of cash control to a business. Some companies invest cash in various types of financial instruments, as well as in the stocks and bonds of other companies. The chapter illustrates the accounting for these investments. In many instances the cash available to make these investments comes from the collection of receivables. The chapter concludes with a discussion of the accounting both for accounts receivable and for notes receivable.

WHAT CONSTITUTES CASH?

LO 1 Identify and describe the various forms of cash reported on a balance sheet.

Cash takes many different forms. Coin and currency on hand and cash on deposit in the form of checking, savings, and money market accounts are the most obvious forms of cash. Also included in cash are various forms of checks, including undeposited checks from customers, cashier's checks, and certified checks. The proliferation of different types of financial instruments on the market today makes it very difficult to decide on the appropriate classification of these various items. The key to the classification of an amount as cash is that it be *readily available to pay debts.* Technically, a bank has the legal right to demand that a customer notify it before making withdrawals from savings accounts, or time deposits, as they are often called. Because this right is rarely exercised, however, savings accounts are normally classified as cash. In contrast, a certificate of deposit has a specific maturity date and carries a penalty for early withdrawal and is therefore not included in cash.

Cash Equivalents and the Statement of Cash Flows

Note that the first item on PepsiCo's balance sheet is titled Cash and Cash Equivalents. Examples of items normally classified as cash equivalents are commercial paper issued by corporations, Treasury bills issued by the federal government, and money market funds offered by financial institutions. According to current accounting standards, classification as a **cash equivalent** is limited to those investments that are readily convertible to known amounts of cash and that have an original maturity to the investor of three months or less. Note that according to this definition, a six-month bank certificate of deposit would *not* be classified as a cash equivalent.

Cash equivalent An investment that is readily convertible to a known amount of cash and has an original maturity to the investor of three months or less.

From Concept to Practice 7.1

Reading Winnebago Industries' Notes

Locate in Note 1 of Winnebago Industries' notes a section titled "Statements of Cash Flows." In what types of securities are its cash equivalents invested?

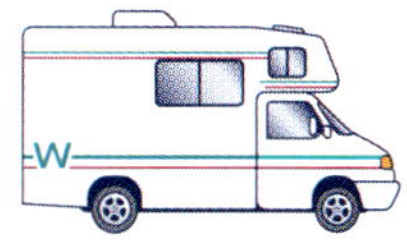

The statement of cash flows that accompanies PepsiCo's balance sheet is shown in Exhibit 7-1. Note the direct tie between this statement and the balance sheet (refer to the Current Assets section of PepsiCo's balance sheet as shown in the chapter opener). The cash and cash equivalents of $683 million at the end of 2001, as shown at the bottom of the statement of cash flows, is the same amount that appears as the first line on the balance sheet. The reason for this is that the statement of cash flows traces the flow of cash from the beginning balance of cash for the year—$1,038 million—to the year's ending balance, $683 million. Cash inflow from operating activities, $4,201 million, minus cash outflow from investing activities, $2,637 million, minus cash outflow from financing activities, $1,919 million, equals a net decrease in cash of $355 million. Deduct $355 million from the beginning cash balance to arrive at $683 million.

Note the fifth category listed under Investing Activities on the statement of cash flows. The changes in short-term investments represent the net purchases or sales of short-term investments during the year. Later in the chapter we will consider the accounting for both short-term and long-term investments. For now, note that any purchases or sales of items classified as short-term investments are considered significant and worthy of reporting on the statement of cash flows. Any purchases or sales of items classified as cash equivalents, however, are not considered significant activities. Instead, they are included with cash on the balance sheet and are considered to be its "equivalent."

CONTROL OVER CASH

In Chapter 5, we discussed the concept of internal control and the critical role it plays for an asset such as cash. Because cash is universally accepted as a medium of exchange, control over it is critical to the smooth functioning of any business, no matter how large or small.

LO 2 Demonstrate an understanding of various techniques that companies use to control cash.

Cash Management

In addition to the need to guard against theft and other abuses related to the physical custody of cash, management of this asset is also important. Cash management is necessary to ensure that at any point in time, a company has neither too little nor too much cash on hand. The need to have enough cash on hand is obvious: suppliers, employees, taxing agencies, banks, and all other creditors must be paid on time if an entity is to remain in business. It is equally important that a company not maintain cash on hand and on deposit in checking accounts beyond a minimal amount that is necessary to support ongoing operations, since cash is essentially a nonearning asset. Granted, some checking accounts pay a very meager rate of interest. However, the superior return that could be earned by investing idle cash in various forms of marketable securities dictates that companies carefully monitor the amount of cash on hand at all times.

An important tool in the management of cash, the cash flows statement, is discussed in detail in Chapter 12. Cash budgets, which are also critical to the management

Exhibit 7-1 PepsiCo's Statement of Cash Flows

Consolidated Statement of Cash Flows

Fiscal years ended December 29, 2001, December 30, 2000, and December 25, 1999

PepsiCo, Inc. and Subsidiaries

(in millions)	2001	2000	1999
Operating Activities			
Net income	**$ 2,662**	$ 2,543	$ 2,505
Adjustments to reconcile net income to net cash provided by operating activities			
Bottling equity income and transaction (gains)/losses, net	**(160)**	(130)	(1,083)
Depreciation and amortization	**1,082**	1,093	1,156
Merger-related costs	**356**	–	–
Other impairment and restructuring charges	**31**	184	73
Cash payments for merger-related costs and other restructuring charges	**(273)**	(38)	(98)
Deferred income taxes	**162**	33	573
Deferred compensation — ESOP	**48**	36	32
Other noncash charges and credits, net	**209**	303	368
Changes in operating working capital, excluding effects of acquisitions and dispositions			
Accounts and notes receivable	**7**	(52)	(141)
Inventories	**(75)**	(51)	(202)
Prepaid expenses and other current assets	**(6)**	(35)	(209)
Accounts payable and other current liabilities	**(236)**	219	357
Income taxes payable	**394**	335	274
Net change in operating working capital	**84**	416	70
Net Cash Provided by Operating Activities	**4,201**	4,440	3,605
Investing Activities			
Capital spending	**(1,324)**	(1,352)	(1,341)
Acquisitions and investments in unconsolidated affiliates	**(432)**	(98)	(430)
Sales of businesses	**–**	33	513
Sales of property, plant and equipment	**–**	57	130
Short-term investments, by original maturity			
More than three months – purchases	**(2,537)**	(4,950)	(2,209)
More than three months – maturities	**2,078**	4,585	2,220
Three months or less, net	**(41)**	(9)	12
Other, net	**(381)**	(262)	(67)
Net Cash Used for Investing Activities	**(2,637)**	(1,996)	(1,172)
Financing Activities			
Proceeds from issuances of long-term debt	**324**	130	3,480
Payments of long-term debt	**(573)**	(879)	(1,216)
Short-term borrowings, by original maturity			
More than three months – proceeds	**788**	198	3,699
More than three months – payments	**(483)**	(155)	(2,758)
Three months or less, net	**(397)**	1	(2,814)
Cash dividends paid	**(994)**	(949)	(935)
Share repurchases – common	**(1,716)**	(1,430)	(1,285)
Share repurchases – preferred	**(10)**	–	–
Quaker share repurchases	**(5)**	(254)	(382)
Proceeds from reissuance of shares	**524**	–	–
Proceeds from exercises of stock options	**623**	690	383
Net Cash Used for Financing Activities	**(1,919)**	(2,648)	(1,828)
Effect of exchange rate changes on cash and cash equivalents	**–**	(4)	3
Net (Decrease)/Increase in Cash and Cash Equivalents	**(355)**	(208)	608
Cash and Cash Equivalents, Beginning of Year	**1,038**	1,246	638
Cash and Cash Equivalents, End of Year	**$ 683**	$ 1,038	$ 1,246
Supplemental Cash Flow Information			
Interest paid	**$ 159**	$ 226	$ 384
Income taxes paid	**$ 857**	$ 876	$ 689
Acquisitions:			
Fair value of assets acquired	**$ 604**	$ 80	$ 717
Cash paid and debt issued	**(432)**	(98)	(438)
Liabilities assumed	**$ 172**	$ (18)	$ 279

This amount appears as the first line on the balance sheet.

See accompanying notes to consolidated financial statements.

of cash, are discussed in management accounting and business finance texts. Cash management is just one important aspect of control over cash. Beyond cash management, companies often use two other cash control features: bank reconciliations and petty cash funds. Before we turn to these control devices, we need to review the basic features of a bank statement.

Reading a Bank Statement

Two fundamental principles of internal control discussed in Chapter 5 are worth repeating: all cash receipts should be deposited daily intact, and all cash payments should be made by check. Checking accounts at banks are critical in this regard. These accounts allow a company to carefully monitor and control cash receipts and cash payments. Control is aided further by the monthly **bank statement.** Most banks mail their customers a monthly bank statement for each account. The statement provides a detailed list of all activity for a particular account during the month. An example of a typical bank statement is shown in Exhibit 7-2. Note that the bank statement indicates the activity in one of the cash accounts maintained by Weber Products Inc. at the Mt. Etna State Bank.

Bank statement A detailed list, provided by the bank, of all the activity for a particular account during the month.

Exhibit 7-2 Bank Statement

MT. ETNA STATE BANK
CHICAGO, ILLINOIS
STATEMENT OF ACCOUNT

Weber Products Inc.
502 Dodge St.
Chicago, IL 66606

FOR THE MONTH ENDING **June 30, 2004**
ACCOUNT **0371-22-514**

Date	Description	Subtractions	Additions	Balance
6-01	Previous balance			3,236.41
6-01	Check 497	723.40		2,513.01
6-02	Check 495	125.60		2,387.41
6-06	Check 491	500.00		1,887.41
6-07	Deposit		1,423.16	3,310.57
6-10	Check 494	185.16		3,125.41
6-13	NSF check	245.72		2,879.69
6-15	Deposit		755.50	3,635.19
6-18	Check 499	623.17		3,012.02
6-20	Check 492	125.00		2,887.02
6-22	Deposit		1,875.62	4,762.64
6-23	Service charge	20.00		4,742.64
6-24	Check 493	875.75		3,866.89
6-24	Check 503	402.10		3,464.79
6-26	Customer note, interest		550.00	4,014.79
6-26	Service fee on note	16.50		3,998.29
6-27	Check 500	1,235.40		2,762.89
6-28	Deposit		947.50	3,710.39
6-30	Check 498	417.25		3,293.14
6-30	Interest earned		15.45	3,308.59
6-30	Statement Totals	5,495.05	5,567.23	

Before we look at the various items that appear on a bank statement, it is important to understand the route a check takes after it is written. Assume that Weber writes a check on its account at the Mt. Etna State Bank. Weber mails the check to one of its suppliers, Keese Corp., which deposits the check in its account at the Second City Bank. At this point, Second City presents the check to Mt. Etna for payment, and Mt. Etna reduces the balance in Weber's account accordingly. The canceled check has now "cleared" the banking system. Either the canceled check itself or a copy of it is returned with Weber's next bank statement.

The following types of items appear on Weber's bank statement:

Canceled checks—Weber's checks that cleared the bank during the month of June are listed with the corresponding check number and the date paid. Keep in mind that some of these checks may have been written by Weber in a previous month but were not presented for payment to the bank until June. You also should realize that during June, Weber may have written some checks that do not yet appear on the bank statement because they have not been presented for payment. A check written by a company but not yet presented to the bank for payment is called an **outstanding check.**

Outstanding check A check written by a company but not yet presented to the bank for payment.

Deposits—In keeping with the internal control principle calling for the deposit of all cash receipts intact, most companies deposit all checks, coin, and currency on a daily basis. For the sake of brevity, we have limited to four the number of deposits that Weber made during the month. Keep in mind that Weber also may have made a deposit on the last day or two of the month and that this deposit may not yet be reflected on the bank statement. This type of deposit is called a **deposit in transit.**

Deposit in transit A deposit recorded on the books but not yet reflected on the bank statement.

NSF check—NSF is an abbreviation for *not sufficient funds*. The NSF check listed on the bank statement on June 13 is a customer's check that Weber recorded on its books, deposited, and thus included in its cash account. When Mt. Etna State Bank learned that the check was not good because the customer did not have sufficient funds on hand in its bank account to cover the check, the bank deducted the amount from Weber's account. Weber needs to contact its customer to collect the amount due; ideally, the customer will issue a new check once it has sufficient funds in its account.

Service charge—Banks charge for various services they provide to customers. Among the most common bank service charges are monthly activity fees, fees charged for new checks, for the rental of a lockbox at the bank in which to store valuable company documents, and for the collection of customer notes by the bank.

Customer note and interest—It is often convenient to have customers pay amounts owed to a company directly to that company's bank. The bank simply acts as a collection agency for the company.

Interest earned—Most checking accounts pay interest on the average daily balance in the account. Rates paid on checking accounts are usually significantly less than could be earned on most other forms of investment.

The Bank Reconciliation

Bank reconciliation A form used by the accountant to reconcile or resolve any differences between the balance shown on the bank statement for a particular account with the balance shown in the accounting records.

A **bank reconciliation** should be prepared for each individual bank account as soon as the bank statement is received. Ideally, the reconciliation should be performed or, at a minimum, thoroughly reviewed by someone independent of custody, record-keeping, and authorization responsibilities relating to cash. As the name implies, the purpose of a bank reconciliation is to *reconcile* or resolve any differences between the balance that the bank shows for an account with the balance that appears on the company's books. Differences between the two amounts are investigated, and if necessary, adjustments are made. The following are the steps in preparing a bank reconciliation:

1. Trace deposits listed on the bank statement to the books. Any deposits recorded on the books but not yet shown on the bank statement are deposits in transit. Prepare a list of the deposits in transit.
2. Arrange the canceled checks in numerical order, and trace each of them to the books. Any checks recorded on the books but not yet listed on the bank statement are outstanding. List the outstanding checks.
3. List all items, other than deposits, shown as additions on the bank statement, such as interest paid by the bank for the month and amounts collected by the bank from one of the company's customers. When the bank pays interest or collects an amount

owed to a company by one of the company's customers, the bank increases or *credits* its liability to the company on its own books. For this reason, these items are called **credit memoranda.**

Credit memoranda Additions on a bank statement for such items as interest paid on the account and notes collected by the bank for the customer.

4. List all amounts, other than canceled checks, shown as subtractions on the bank statement, such as any NSF checks and the various service charges mentioned earlier. When a company deposits money in a bank, a liability is created on the books of the bank. Therefore, when the bank reduces the amount of its liability for these various items, it *debits* the liability on its own books. For this reason, these items are called **debit memoranda.**
5. Identify any errors made by the bank or by the company in recording the various cash transactions.
6. Use the information collected in steps **1** through **5** to prepare a bank reconciliation.

Debit memoranda Deductions on a bank statement for such items as NSF checks and various service charges.

Companies use a number of different *formats* in preparing bank reconciliations. For example, some companies take the balance shown on the bank statement and reconcile this amount to the balance shown on the books. Another approach, which we will illustrate for Weber Products, involves reconciling the bank balance and the book balance to an adjusted balance, rather than one to the other. As we will see, the advantage of this approach is that it yields the correct balance and makes it easy for the company to make any necessary adjustments to its books. A bank reconciliation for Weber Products is shown in Exhibit 7-3.

Exhibit 7-3

Bank Reconciliation

WEBER PRODUCTS
BANK RECONCILIATION
JUNE 30, 2004

Balance per bank statement, June 30			$3,308.59
Add:	Deposit in transit		642.30
Deduct:	Outstanding checks:		
	No. 496	$ 79.89	
	No. 501	213.20	
	No. 502	424.75	(717.84)
Adjusted balance, June 30			$3,233.05
Balance per books, June 30			$2,895.82
Add:	Customer note collected	$500.00	
	Interest on customer note	50.00	
	Interest earned during June	15.45	
	Error in recording check 498	54.00	619.45
Deduct:	NSF check	$245.72	
	Collection fee on note	16.50	
	Service charge for lockbox	20.00	(282.22)
Adjusted balance, June 30			$3,233.05

The following are explanations for the various items on the reconciliation:

1. The balance per bank statement of $3,308.59 is taken from the June statement as shown in Exhibit 7-2.
2. Weber's records showed a deposit for $642.30 made on June 30 that is not reflected on the bank statement. The deposit in transit is listed as an addition to the bank statement balance.
3. The accounting records indicate three checks written but not yet reflected on the bank statement. The three outstanding checks are as follows:

   496 $ 79.89
   501 $213.20
   502 $424.75

Study Tip

Review your own bank statement to see the similarities and differences between it and the one illustrated here. Also, look on the reverse of your statement for the form of a reconciliation the bank provides. It may or may not be the same format as illustrated in Exhibit 7-3.

Outstanding checks are the opposite of deposits in transit and therefore are deducted from the bank statement balance.

4. The adjusted balance of $3,233.05 is found by adding the deposit in transit and deducting the outstanding checks from the bank statement balance.
5. The $2,895.82 book balance on June 30 is taken from the company's records as of that date.
6. According to the bank statement, $550 was added to the account on June 26 for the collection of a note with interest. We assume that the repayment of the note itself accounted for $500 of this amount and that the other $50 was for interest. The bank statement notifies Weber that the note with interest has been collected. Therefore, Weber must add $550 to the book balance.
7. An entry on June 30 on the bank statement shows an increase of $15.45 for interest earned on the bank account during June. This amount is added to the book balance.
8. A review of the canceled checks returned with the bank statement detected an error made by Weber. The company records indicated that check 498 was recorded incorrectly as $471.25; the check was actually written for $417.25 and reflected as such on the bank statement. This error, referred to as a *transposition error,* resulted from transposing the 7 and the 1 in recording the check in the books. The error is the difference between the amount of $471.25 recorded and the amount of $417.25 that should have been recorded, or $54.00. Because Weber recorded the cash payment at too large an amount, $54.00 must be added back to the book balance.
9. In addition to canceled checks, three other deductions appear on the bank statement. Each of these must be deducted from the book balance:
   a. A customer's NSF check for $245.72 (see June 13 entry on bank statement)
   b. A $16.50 fee charged by the bank to collect the customer's note discussed in item **6** (see June 26 entry on bank statement)
   c. A service fee of $20.00 charged by the bank for rental of a lockbox (see June 23 entry on bank statement)
10. The additions of $619.45 and deductions of $282.22 resulted in an adjusted cash balance of $3,233.05. Note that this adjusted balance agrees with the adjusted bank statement balance on the bank reconciliation (see item **4**). Thus, all differences between the two balances have been explained.

The Bank Reconciliation and the Need for Adjustments to the Records

After it completes the bank reconciliation, Weber must prepare a number of adjustments to its records. In fact, all of the information for these adjustments will be from one section of the bank reconciliation. Do you think that the additions and deductions made to the bank balance or the ones made to the book balance are the basis for the adjustments? It is logical that the additions and deductions to the Cash account *on the books* should be the basis for the adjustments because these are items that Weber was unaware of before receiving the bank statement. Conversely, the additions and deductions to the bank's balance, that is, the deposits in transit and the outstanding checks, are items that Weber has already recorded on its books.

The first journal entry recognizes the bank's collection of customer's note, with interest:

		Debit	Credit
June 30	Cash	550.00	
	Notes Receivable		500.00
	Interest Revenue		50.00
	To record the collection of note and interest.		

Assets	=	Liabilities	+	Owners' Equity
+550				+50
−500				

The next entry is needed to record interest earned and paid by the bank on the average daily balance maintained in the checking account during June:

June 30	Cash	15.45	
	Interest Revenue		15.45
	To record interest earned on checking account.		

Assets	=	Liabilities	+	Owners' Equity
+15.45				+15.45

Recall the error in recording check 498: it was actually written for $417.25, the amount paid by the bank. Weber recorded the cash disbursement on its books as $471.25, however. If we assume that the purpose of the cash payment was to buy supplies, the Cash account is understated and the Supplies account is overstated by the amount of the error. The entry needed to correct both accounts is as follows:

June 30	Cash	54.00	
	Supplies		54.00
	To correct for error in recording purchase of supplies.		

Assets	=	Liabilities	+	Owners' Equity
+54				
−54				

The customer's NSF check is handled by reducing the Cash account and reinstating the Account Receivable:

June 30	Accounts Receivable	245.72	
	Cash		245.72
	To record customer's NSF check.		

Assets	=	Liabilities	+	Owners' Equity
+245.72				
−245.72				

Finally, two entries are needed to recognize the expenses incurred in connection with the fees charged by the bank for collecting the customer's note and for renting the lockbox:

June 30	Collection Fee Expense	16.50	
	Cash		16.50
	To record collection fee on note.		

Assets	=	Liabilities	+	Owners' Equity
−16.50				−16.50

June 30	Rent Expense—Lockbox	20.00	
	Cash		20.00
	To record rental charge on lockbox.		

Assets	=	Liabilities	+	Owners' Equity
−20				−20

Note that we made a separate entry to record each of the increases and decreases in the Cash account. Some companies combine all of the increases in Cash in a single journal entry and all of the decreases in a second entry. Finally, we should note that supervisory review and approval should take place before any of these entries are posted.

Establishing a Petty Cash Fund

Petty cash fund Money kept on hand for making minor disbursements in coin and currency rather than by writing checks.

Recall one of the fundamental rules in controlling cash: all disbursements should be made by check. Most businesses make an exception to this rule in the case of minor expenditures, for which they use a **petty cash fund.** This fund consists of coin and currency kept on hand to make minor disbursements. The necessary steps in setting up and maintaining a petty cash fund follow:

1. A check is written for a lump-sum amount, such as $100 or $500. The check is cashed, and the coin and currency are entrusted to a petty cash custodian.
2. A journal entry is made to record the establishment of the fund.
3. Upon presentation of the necessary documentation, employees receive minor disbursements from the fund. In essence, cash is traded from the fund in exchange for a receipt.
4. Periodically, the fund is replenished by writing and cashing a check in the amount necessary to bring the fund back to its original balance.
5. At the time the fund is replenished, an adjustment is made both to record its replenishment and to recognize the various expenses incurred.

The use of this fund is normally warranted on the basis of cost versus benefits. That is, the benefits in time saved in making minor disbursements from cash are thought to outweigh the cost associated with the risk of loss from decreased control over cash disbursements. The fund also serves a practical purpose for certain expenditures such as taxi fares and messengers which often must be paid in cash.

An Example of a Petty Cash Fund

Assume that on March 1, the treasurer of Keese Corporation cashes a check for $200 and remits the cash to the newly appointed petty cash custodian. On this date, the following journal entry is made:

Mar. 1	Petty Cash Fund	200.00	
	Cash		200.00
	To record establishment of petty cash fund.		

Assets	=	Liabilities	+	Owners' Equity
+200				
−200				

During March the custodian disburses coin and currency to various individuals who present receipts to the custodian for the following:

U.S. Post Office	$ 55.00
Overnight Delivery Service	69.50
Office Supply Express	45.30
Total expenditures	$169.80

At the end of March, the custodian counts the coin and currency on hand and determines the balance to be $26.50. Next, the treasurer writes and cashes a check in the amount of $173.50, which is the amount needed to return the balance in the account to $200.00. The treasurer remits the cash to the custodian. The following entry is made:

Mar. 31	Postage Expense	55.00	
	Delivery Expense	69.50	
	Office Expense	45.30	
	Cash Over and Short	3.70	
	Cash		173.50
	To record replenishment of petty cash fund.		

Assets	=	Liabilities	+	Owners' Equity
−173.50				−55.00
				−69.50
				−45.30
				−3.70

The Cash Over and Short account is necessary because the total expenditures for the month were only $169.80 but a check in the amount of $173.50 was necessary to

Accounting for Your Decisions

You Are the Sorority Treasurer

You are in charge of the sorority's checking account and bank reconciliation. Each month, you are responsible for purchasing supplies, paying for parties, and paying rent and utilities on the sorority house. You also have a card for an automatic teller machine, which you use to draw out cash to pay for miscellaneous activities. Recently, the president of the sorority asked to see you because the sorority's expenses were exceeding revenues by a significant margin. After examining the checkbook and bank reconciliation, she wanted to know why you were spending roughly $200 per month in cash from an ATM. You told her that since there was no cancelled check for these expenditures, you had no record and couldn't answer her question. How could you have avoided this situation?

ANS: First, an important principle of internal control is that the person writing checks on an account should not be the same person who performs the bank reconciliation. Second, an ATM card confers special responsibilities on the user. Because there is no cancelled check, the person receiving cash from an ATM must document all expenses, obtaining receipts whenever possible or documenting the expenditures in a diary.

restore the fund balance to $200.00. The discrepancy of $3.70 could be due to any number of factors, such as an error in making change. Any large discrepancies would be investigated, particularly if they recur. Assuming that the discrepancy is immaterial, a debit balance in the Cash Over and Short account is normally closed to Miscellaneous Expense. A credit balance in the account is closed to Other Income.

ACCOUNTING FOR INVESTMENTS

LO 3 Demonstrate an understanding of the accounting for various types of investments companies make.

The investments that companies make take a variety of forms and are made for various reasons. Some corporations find themselves with excess cash during certain times of the year and invest this idle cash in various highly liquid financial instruments, such as certificates of deposit and money market funds. Earlier in the chapter it was pointed out that these investments are included with cash and are called cash equivalents if they have an original maturity to the investor of three months or less. Otherwise they are accounted for as short-term investments.

In addition to investments in highly liquid financial instruments, some companies invest in the stocks and bonds of other corporations, as well as bonds issued by various government agencies. Securities issued by corporations as a form of ownership in the business, such as common stock and preferred stock, are called **equity securities.** Because these securities are a form of ownership, they do not have a maturity date. As we will see later, investments in equity securities can be classified as either current or long term, depending on the company's intent. Alternatively, bonds issued by corporations and governmental bodies as a form of borrowing are called **debt securities.** The term of a bond can be relatively short, such as 5 years, or much longer, such as 20 or 30 years. Regardless of the term, classification as a current or noncurrent asset by the investor depends on whether it plans to sell the debt securities within the next year.

Equity securities Securities issued by corporations as a form of ownership in the business.

Debt securities Bonds issued by corporations and governmental bodies as a form of borrowing.

INVESTMENTS IN HIGHLY LIQUID FINANCIAL INSTRUMENTS

We now turn our attention to the appropriate accounting for these various types of investments. We begin by considering the accounting for highly liquid financial instruments such as certificates of deposit and then turn to the accounting for investments in the stocks and bonds of other companies.

Investing Idle Cash

The seasonal nature of most businesses leads to the potential for a shortage of cash during certain times of the year and an excess of cash during other times. Companies typically deal with *cash shortages* by borrowing on a short-term basis, either from a bank in the form of notes or from other entities in the form of commercial paper. The maturities of the bank notes or the commercial paper generally range anywhere from 30 days to six months. These same companies use various financial instruments as a way to invest excess cash during other times of the year. We will present the accounting for the most common type of highly liquid financial instrument, a certificate of deposit (CD).

Accounting for an Investment in a Certificate of Deposit (CD)

Assume that on October 2, 2004, Creston Corp. invests $100,000 of excess cash in a 120-day certificate of deposit. The CD matures on January 30, 2005, at which time Creston receives the $100,000 invested and interest at an annual rate of 6%. The entry to record the purchase of the CD is as follows:

2004			
Oct. 2	Short-Term Investments—CD	100,000	
	Cash		100,000
	To record purchase of 6%, 120-day CD.		

Assets	=	Liabilities	+	Owners' Equity
+100,000				
−100,000				

Assuming December 31 is the end of Creston's fiscal year, an entry is needed on this date to record interest earned during 2004, even though no cash will be received until the CD matures in 2005:

2004			
Dec. 31	Interest Receivable	1,500	
	Interest Revenue		1,500
	To record interest earned: $100,000 × 0.06 × 90/360.		

Assets	=	Liabilities	+	Owners' Equity
+1,500				+1,500

The basic formula to compute interest is as follows:

$$\text{Interest } (I) = \text{Principal } (P) \times \text{Interest Rate } (R) \times \text{Time } (T)$$

Because interest rates are normally stated on an annual basis, time is interpreted to mean the fraction of a year that the investment is outstanding. The amount of interest is based on the principal or amount invested ($100,000), times the rate of interest (6%), times the fraction of a year the CD was outstanding in 2004 (29 days in October + 30 days in November + 31 days in December = 90 days). To simplify calculations, it is easiest to assume 360 days in a year in computing interest. With the availability of computers to do the work, however, most businesses now use 365 days in a year to calculate interest. Throughout this book, we assume 360 days in a year to allow us to focus on concepts rather than detailed calculations. Thus, in our example, the fraction of a year that the CD is outstanding during 2004 is 90/360.

The entry on January 30 to record the receipt of the principal amount of the CD of $100,000 and interest for 120 days is as follows:

2005			
Jan. 30	Cash	102,000	
	Short-Term Investments—CD		100,000
	Interest Receivable		1,500
	Interest Revenue		500
	To record the maturity of $100,000 CD.		

Assets	=	Liabilities	+	Owners' Equity
+102,000				+500
−100,000				
−1,500				

This combination journal entry results in the removal of both the CD and the interest receivable from the records and the recognition of $500 in interest earned during the first 30 days of 2005: $100,000 × 0.06 × 30/360 = $500.

We now turn to situations in which companies invest in the stocks and bonds of other companies.

INVESTMENTS IN STOCKS AND BONDS

Corporations frequently invest in the securities of other businesses. These investments take two forms: debt securities and equity securities.

Corporations have varying motivations for investing in the stocks and bonds of other companies. We will refer to the company that invests as the *investor* and the company whose stocks or bonds are purchased as the *investee.* In addition to buying certificates of deposit and other financial instruments, companies invest excess funds in stocks and bonds over the short run. The seasonality of certain businesses may result in otherwise idle cash being available during certain times of the year. In other cases, stocks and bonds are purchased as a way to invest cash over the long run. Often these types of investments are made in anticipation of a need for cash at some distant point in the future. For example, a company may invest today in a combination of stocks and bonds because it will need cash 10 years from today to build a new plant. The investor may be primarily interested in periodic income in the form of interest and dividends, in appreciation in the value of the securities, or in some combination of the two.

Sometimes shares of stock in another company are bought with a different purpose in mind. If a company buys a relatively large percentage of the common stock of the investee, it may be able to secure significant influence over the policies of this company. For example, a company may buy 30% of the common stock of a supplier of its raw materials to ensure a steady source of inventory. When an investor is able to secure influence over the investee, the *equity method* of accounting is used. According to current accounting standards, this method is appropriate when an investor owns at least 20% of the common stock of the investee.

Finally, a corporation may buy stock in another company with the purpose of obtaining control over that other entity. Normally, this requires an investment in excess of 50% of the common stock of the investee. When an investor owns more than half the stock of another company, accountants normally prepare a set of *consolidated financial statements.* This involves combining the financial statements of the individual entities into a single set of statements. An investor with an interest of more than 50% in another company is called the *parent,* and the investee in these situations is called the *subsidiary.*

We will limit our discussion to how companies account for investments that do *not* give them any significant influence over the other company. (Accounting for investments in which there is either significant influence or control is covered in advanced accounting textbooks.) The following chart summarizes the accounting by an investor for investments in the common stock of another company:

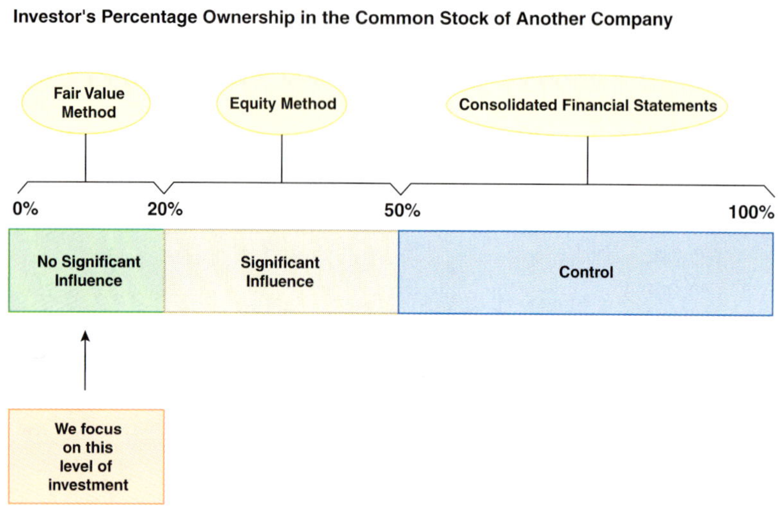

INVESTMENTS WITHOUT SIGNIFICANT INFLUENCE

Companies face a number of major issues in deciding how to account for and report on investments in the stocks and bonds of other companies:

1. What should be the basis for the recognition of periodic income from an investment? That is, what event causes income to be recognized?
2. How should an investment be valued and thus reported at the end of an accounting period? At original cost? At fair value?
3. How should an investment be classified on a balance sheet? As a current asset? As a noncurrent asset?

The answer to each of these questions depends on the type of investment. Accountants classify investments in the securities of other companies into one of three categories.[1]

Held-to-maturity securities Investments in bonds of other companies in which the investor has the positive intent and the ability to hold the securities to maturity.

Trading securities Stock and bonds of other companies bought and held for the purpose of selling them in the near term to generate profits on appreciation in their price.

Available-for-sale securities Stocks and bonds that are not classified as either held-to-maturity or trading securities.

Held-to-maturity securities are investments in the bonds of other companies when the investor has the positive intent and the ability to hold the securities to maturity. *Note that only bonds can qualify as held-to-maturity securities because shares of stock do not have a maturity date.*

Trading securities are stocks and bonds that are bought and held for the purpose of selling them in the near term. These securities are usually held for only a short period of time with the objective of generating profits on short-term appreciation in the market price of the stocks and bonds.

Available-for-sale securities are stocks and bonds that are not classified as either held-to-maturity or trading securities.

Investments in Held-to-Maturity Securities

By their nature, only bonds, not stock, can qualify as held-to-maturity securities. A bond is categorized as a held-to-maturity security if the investor plans to hold it until it matures. An investor may buy the bonds either on the original issuance date or later. If the investor buys them on the date they are originally issued, the purchase is from the issuer. It is also possible, however, for an investor to buy bonds on the *open market* after they have been outstanding for a period of time.

[1] *Statement of Financial Accounting Standards No. 115,* "Accounting for Certain Investments in Debt and Equity Securities" (Stamford, Conn.: Financial Accounting Standards Board, May 1993), pars. 7–12.

Consider the following example. On January 1, 2004, Simpson issues $10,000,000 of bonds that will mature in ten years. Homer buys $100,000 in face value of these bonds at face value, which is the amount that will be repaid to the investor when the bonds mature. In many instances, bonds are purchased at an amount more or less than face value. We will limit our discussion, however, to the simpler case in which bonds are purchased for face value. The bonds pay 10% interest semiannually on June 30 and December 31. This means Homer will receive 5% of $100,000 or $5,000 on each of these dates. The entry on Homer's books to record the purchase is as follows:

2004			
Jan. 1	Investment in Bonds	100,000	
	Cash		100,000
	To record purchase of Simpson bonds.		

Assets	=	Liabilities	+	Owners' Equity
+100,000				
−100,000				

On June 30, Homer must record the receipt of semiannual interest. The entry on this date is as follows:

2004			
June 30	Cash	5,000	
	Interest Income		5,000
	To record interest income on Simpson bonds.		

Assets	=	Liabilities	+	Owners' Equity
+5,000				+5,000

Note that income was recognized when interest was received. If interest is not received at the end of an accounting period, a company should accrue interest earned but not yet received. Also note that an investment in held-to-maturity bonds is normally classified as a *noncurrent asset.* Any held-to-maturity bonds that are one year or less from maturity, however, are classified in the Current Assets section of a balance sheet.

Assume that before the maturity date, Homer needs cash and decides to sell the bonds. Keep in mind that this is a definite change in Homer's plans, since the bonds were initially categorized as held-to-maturity securities. Any difference between the proceeds received from the sale of the bonds and the amount paid for the bonds is recognized as either a gain or a loss.

Assume that on January 1, 2005, Homer sells all its Simpson bonds at 99. This means that the amount of cash received is 0.99 × $100,000, or $99,000. The entry on January 1, 2005, is as follows:

2005			
Jan. 1	Cash	99,000	
	Loss on Sale of Bonds	1,000	
	Investment in Bonds		100,000
	To record sale of Simpson bonds.		

Assets	=	Liabilities	+	Owners' Equity
+99,000				−1,000
−100,000				

The $1,000 loss on the sale of the bonds is the excess of the amount paid for the purchase of the bonds of $100,000 over the cash proceeds from the sale of $99,000. The loss is reported in the Other Income and Expenses section on the 2005 income statement.

Investments in Trading Securities

A company invests in trading securities as a way to profit from increases in the market prices of these securities over the short term. Because the intent is to hold them for the short term, trading securities are classified as current assets. All trading securities are recorded initially at cost, including any brokerage fees, commissions, or other fees paid to acquire the shares. Assume that Dexter Corp. invests in the following securities on November 30, 2004:

SECURITY	COST
Stuart common stock	$50,000
Menlo preferred stock	25,000
Total cost	$75,000

The entry on Dexter's books on the date of purchase is as follows:

2004			
Nov. 30	Investment in Stuart Common Stock	50,000	
	Investment in Menlo Preferred Stock	25,000	
	Cash		75,000
	To record purchase of trading securities for cash.		

Assets	=	Liabilities	+	Owners' Equity
+50,000				
+25,000				
−75,000				

Many companies attempt to pay dividends every year as a signal of overall financial strength and profitability.[2] Assume that on December 10, 2004, Dexter received dividends of $1,000 from Stuart and $600 from Menlo. The dividends received from trading securities are recognized as income as shown in the following entry on Dexter's books:

2004			
Dec. 10	Cash	1,600	
	Dividend Income		1,600
	To record receipt of dividends on trading securities.		

Assets	=	Liabilities	+	Owners' Equity
+1,600				+1,600

Unlike interest on a bond or a note, dividends do not accrue over time. In fact, a company does not have a legal obligation to pay dividends until its board of directors declares them. Up to that point, the investor has no guarantee that dividends will ever be paid.

As noted earlier, trading securities are purchased with the intention of holding them for a short period of time. Assume that Dexter sells the Stuart stock on December 15, 2004, for $53,000. In this case, Dexter recognizes a gain for the excess of the cash proceeds, $53,000, over the amount recorded on the books, $50,000:

2004			
Dec. 15	Cash	53,000	
	Investment in Stuart Common Stock		50,000
	Gain on Sale of Stock		3,000
	To record sale of Stuart common stock.		

Assets	=	Liabilities	+	Owners' Equity
+53,000				+3,000
−50,000				

The gain is considered realized and is classified on the income statement as other income.

Assume that on December 22, 2004, Dexter replaces the Stuart stock in its portfolio by purchasing Canby common stock for $40,000. The entry on this date follows:

[2] IBM's June 2002 dividend of $0.15 per share was the computer company's 349th consecutive quarterly dividend, an uninterrupted string of more than 87 years in which it paid dividends.

2004			
Dec. 22	Investment in Canby Common Stock	40,000	
	Cash		40,000
	To record purchase of trading securities for cash.		

Assets	=	Liabilities	+	Owners' Equity
+40,000				
−40,000				

Now assume that Dexter ends its accounting period on December 31. Should it adjust the carrying value of its investments to reflect their fair values on this date? According to the accounting profession, fair values should be used to report investments in trading securities on a balance sheet. The fair values are thought to be relevant information to the various users of financial statements. Assume the following information for Dexter on December 31, 2004:

SECURITY	TOTAL COST	TOTAL FAIR VALUE ON DECEMBER 31, 2004	GAIN (LOSS)
Menlo preferred stock	$25,000	$27,500	$2,500
Canby common stock	40,000	39,000	(1,000)
Totals	$65,000	$66,500	$1,500

The entry on Dexter's books on this date follows:

2004			
Dec. 31	Investment in Menlo Preferred Stock	2,500	
	Investment in Canby Common Stock		1,000
	Unrealized Gain—Trading Securities (Income Statement)		1,500
	To adjust trading securities to fair value.		

Assets	=	Liabilities	+	Owners' Equity
+2,500				+1,500
−1,000				

Note that this entry results in each security being written up or down so that it will appear on the December 31 balance sheet at its market or fair value. This type of fair value accounting for trading securities is often referred to as a *mark-to-market* approach because at the end of each period, the value of each security is adjusted or marked to its current market value. Also, it is important to realize that for trading securities, the changes in value are recognized on the income statement. The difference of $1,500 between the original cost of the two securities, $65,000, and their fair value, $66,500, is recorded in the account Unrealized Gain—Trading Securities to call attention to the fact that the securities have not been sold. Even though the gain or loss is *unrealized,* it is recognized on the income statement as a form of other income or loss.

Assume one final transaction in our Dexter example. On January 20, 2005, Dexter sells the Menlo stock for $27,000. The entry on Dexter's books on this date follows:

2005			
Jan. 20	Loss on Sale of Stock (Income Statement)	500	
	Cash	27,000	
	Investment in Menlo Preferred Stock		27,500
	To record sale of Menlo preferred stock.		

Assets	=	Liabilities	+	Owners' Equity
+27,000				−500
−27,500				

The important point to note about this entry is that the $500 loss represents the difference between the cash proceeds of $27,000 and the *fair value of the stock at the most recent reporting date,* $27,500. Because the Menlo stock was adjusted to a fair value of $27,500 on December 31, the excess of this amount over the cash proceeds of $27,000 results in a loss of $500. Keep in mind that a gain of $2,500 was recognized last year when the stock was adjusted to its fair value at the end of the year.

Investments in Available-for-Sale Securities

Stocks and bonds that do not qualify as trading securities and bonds that are not intended to be held to maturity are categorized as available-for-sale securities. The accounting for these securities is similar to the accounting for trading securities, with one major exception: *even though fair value accounting is used to report available-for-sale securities at the end of an accounting period, any gains or losses resulting from marking to market are not reported on the income statement but instead are accumulated in a stockholders' equity account.* This inconsistency is justified by the accounting profession on the grounds that the inclusion in income of fluctuations in the value of securities that are available for sale but that are not necessarily being actively traded could lead to volatility in reported earnings. Regardless, reporting gains and losses on the income statement for one class of securities but not for others is a subject of considerable debate. Investments in available-for-sale securities may be classified as either current or noncurrent assets.

To understand the use of fair value accounting for available-for-sale securities, assume that Lenox Corp. purchases two different stocks late in 2004. The costs and fair values at the end of 2004 are as follows:

SECURITY	TOTAL COST	FAIR VALUE ON DECEMBER 31, 2004	GAIN (LOSS)
Adair preferred stock	$15,000	$16,000	$ 1,000
Casey common stock	35,000	32,500	(2,500)
Totals	$50,000	$48,500	$(1,500)

The entry on Lenox's books on this date is as follows:

2004			
Dec. 31	Unrealized Gain/Loss—Available-for-Sale Securities (Stockholders' Equity)	1,500	
	Investment in Adair Preferred Stock	1,000	
	Investment in Casey Common Stock		2,500
	To adjust available-for-sale securities to fair value.		

Assets	=	Liabilities	+	Owners' Equity
+1,000				−1,500
−2,500				

Note the similarity between this entry and the one we made at the end of the period in the example for trading securities. In both instances, the individual investments are adjusted to their fair values for purposes of presenting them on the year-end balance sheet. The unrealized loss of $1,500 does not, however, affect income in this case. Instead, the loss is shown as a reduction of stockholders' equity on the balance sheet.

Now assume that Lenox sells its Casey stock for $34,500 on June 30, 2005. The entry on this date is as follows:

2005			
June 30	Cash	34,500	
	Loss on Sale of Stock (Income Statement)	500	
	Investment in Casey Common Stock		32,500
	Unrealized Gain/Loss—Available-for-Sale Securities (Stockholders' Equity)		2,500
	To record sale of Casey common stock.		

Assets	=	Liabilities	+	Owners' Equity
+34,500				− 500
−32,500				+2,500

Lenox recognizes a loss on the income statement of $500, which represents the excess of the cost of the stock of $35,000 over the cash proceeds of $34,500. Note, however, that the Investment in Casey Common Stock is removed from the books at $32,500, the fair value at the end of the prior period. Thus, it is also necessary to adjust the Unrealized Gain/Loss account for $2,500, the difference between the original cost of $35,000 and the fair value at the end of 2004 of $32,500.

Finally, assume that Lenox does not buy any additional securities during the remainder of 2005 and that the fair value of the one investment it holds, the Adair preferred stock, is $19,000 on December 31, 2005. The entry to adjust the Adair stock to fair value on this date is as follows:

2005			
Dec. 31	Investment in Adair Preferred Stock	3,000	
	Unrealized Gain/Loss—Available-for-Sale Securities (Stockholders' Equity)		3,000
	To adjust available-for-sale securities to fair value.		

Assets	=	Liabilities	+	Owners' Equity
+3,000				+3,000

The increase in the Investment in Adair Preferred Stock account results in a balance of $19,000 in this account, the fair value of the stock. The stockholders' equity account now has a *credit* balance of $4,000, as reflected in the following T account:

UNREALIZED GAIN/LOSS—AVAILABLE-FOR-SALE SECURITIES

	Debit	Credit	
12/31/04 bal.	1,500		
		2,500	6/30/05 entry
		1,000	6/30/05 bal.
		3,000	12/31/05 entry
		4,000	12/31/05 bal.

The balance of $4,000 in this account represents the excess of the $19,000 fair value of the one security now held over its original cost of $15,000.

Summary of Accounting and Reporting Requirements

A summary of the accounting and reporting requirements for each of the three categories of investments is shown in Exhibit 7-4. Periodic income from each of these types of investments is recognized in the form of interest and dividends. Held-to-maturity bonds are reported on the balance sheet at *amortized cost* (see second footnote in Exhibit 7-4 below). Both trading securities and available-for-sale securities are reported on the balance sheet at fair value. Unrealized gains and losses from holding trading

Exhibit 7-4 Accounting for Investments without Significant Influence

CATEGORIES	TYPES	ASSET CLASSIFIED ON BALANCE SHEET AS	RECOGNIZE AS INCOME	REPORT ON BALANCE SHEET AT	REPORT CHANGES IN FAIR VALUE ON
Held-to-maturity	Bonds	Noncurrent*	Interest	Cost**	Not applicable
Trading	Bonds, stock	Current	Interest, dividends	Fair value	Income statement
Available-for-sale	Bonds, stock	Current or noncurrent	Interest, dividends	Fair value	Balance sheet (in stockholders' equity)

*Reclassified as current if they mature within one year of the balance sheet date.
**As mentioned earlier, bonds are often purchased at an amount more or less than face value. When this is the case, the bond account must be adjusted periodically and the asset is reported on the balance sheet at amortized cost.

Business Strategy

Growing Sales and Adding Brands

According to its 2001 annual report, PepsiCo is the world's fourth largest food and beverage company. With annual sales of nearly $27 billion, it trails only Nestle SA, Kraft Foods, and Unilever, and it holds a considerable lead over its traditional chief competitor, The Coca-Cola Company. Brands are naturally the lifeblood of consumer companies, and PepsiCo is no exception, with a portfolio of 15 brands that each generated more than $1 billion in annual retail sales.

How does a company grow to become the fourth largest of its kind? In PepsiCo's case, one need look no further than the most significant transaction in its corporate history. After months of negotiation, in August of 2001, the company completed its merger with The Quaker Oats Company. With this transaction, the new PepsiCo added to its already impressive portfolio such household names as Quaker Oats® and Gatorade®.

The cover of PepsiCo's annual report proclaims that it is a company "Built to Grow," and the shareholders' letter touts "PepsiCo + Quaker: A Recipe for Growth." But while sales growth—or what the company calls "revenue enhancement opportunities"—is certainly part of the equation, cost savings is also seen as crucial to future success. For example, PepsiCo has already found a way to use Quaker's warehouse distribution system to deliver its Tropicana products to stores at a lower cost. Undoubtedly, management has just begun to put to work the combined resources of PepsiCo and Quaker to deliver a superior return to its stockholders. ■

Source: PepsiCo's 2001 annual report.

securities are recognized on the income statement, whereas these same gains and losses for available-for-sale securities are accumulated in a stockholders' equity account.

The Controversy over Fair Value Accounting

Only recently have accounting standards changed to require that certain investments be reported at fair value. Before the change, the lower-of-cost-or-market rule was followed when accounting for these investments. The use of market or fair values is clearly an exception to the cost principle as first introduced in Chapter 1. Whether the exception is justified has been, and will continue to be, a matter of debate.

One concern of financial statement users is the hybrid system now used to report assets on a balance sheet. Consider the following types of assets and how we report them on the balance sheet:

ASSET	REPORTED ON THE BALANCE SHEET AT
Inventories	Lower of cost or market
Investments	Either cost or fair value
Property, plant, and equipment	Original cost, less accumulated depreciation

It is difficult to justify so many different valuation methods to report the assets of a single company. Recall that the lower-of-cost-or-market approach to valuing inventory is based on conservatism. Why should it be used for inventories while fair value is used for investments? Proponents of fair values believe that the information provided to the reader of the statements is more

Which Way to Go?
Fair Value, Significant Influence, or Consolidation?

Taz Industries owns $10 million (40%) of the outstanding bonds and 10% of the voting common stock of the MMartian Corporation. In addition, Theron Ross, the president of Taz, is a member of the board of directors of MMartian. The management of MMartian is very interested in responding positively to the ideas and suggestions of Theron because Taz is MMartian's largest customer.

On its fiscal year-end balance sheet, how should Taz Industries value its investments in the MMartian bonds and common stock? Does Taz have significant influence in the MMartian Corporation? Should Taz use the fair value method, the equity method, or should it prepare consolidated financial statements that include MMartian Corporation's financial information? Why?

relevant, and they argue that the subjectivity inherent in valuing other types of assets is not an issue when dealing with securities that have a ready market. The controversy surrounding the valuation of assets on a balance sheet is likely to continue.

Two-Minute Review

1. *What are the three categories of investments?*
2. *Two of the three categories of investments can contain either stocks or bonds. Which one of the three can only contain bonds? Explain your answer.*
3. *What is the one major distinction between the reporting requirements for trading securities and those for available-for-sale securities?*

Answers on page 358.

ACCOUNTS RECEIVABLE

LO 4 Demonstrate an understanding of how to account for accounts receivable, including bad debts.

http://www.sears.com

To appreciate the significance of credit sales for many businesses, consider the case of Sears, Roebuck & Co. Sears operates retail outlets throughout the United States and around the world. The balance sheet of Sears reported total assets of approximately $44 billion at the end of 2001. Of this total amount, credit card receivables accounted for over $28 billion, or 63.5%, of total assets. Sears or any other company would rather not sell on credit but would prefer to make all sales for cash. Selling on credit causes two problems: it slows down the inflow of cash to the company, and it raises the possibility that the customer may not pay its bill on time or possibly ever. To remain competitive, however, Sears and most other businesses must sell their products and services on credit. Large retailers such as Sears often extend credit through the use of their own credit cards.

http://www.pepsico.com

The types of receivables reported on a corporate balance sheet depend to some extent on a company's business. The "credit card receivables" on the balance sheet of Sears represent the interest-bearing accounts it carries with its retail customers. Alternatively, consider the case of PepsiCo. The beverage and snack-food businesses usually sell their products to distributors. The asset resulting from a sale by Pepsi on credit, with an oral promise that the customer will pay within a specified period of time, is called an account receivable. This type of account does not bear interest and often gives the customer a discount for early payment. For example, the terms of sale might be 2/10, net 30, which means the customer can deduct 2% from the amount due if the bill is paid within 10 days of the date of sale; otherwise, payment in full is required within 30 days. In some instances, PepsiCo requires from a customer at the time of sale a written promise in the form of a promissory note. The asset resulting from a sale on credit, with a written promise that the customer will pay within a specified period of time, is called a note receivable. This type of account usually bears interest.

Delivering such products as Pepsi's Frappuccino drink to retail stores on account creates large receivables for PepsiCo. Indeed, receivables are a large and important part of the asset side of balance sheets of many companies.

The Use of a Subsidiary Ledger

As mentioned earlier, PepsiCo sells its beverages and snack foods through distributors. Assume that it sells $25,000 of Fritos to ABC Distributors on an open account. The journal entry to record the sale would be as follows:

Accounts Receivable	25,000	
Sales Revenue		25,000
To record sale on open account.		

Assets	=	Liabilities	+	Owners' Equity
+25,000				+25,000

It is important for control purposes that PepsiCo keeps a record of *whom* the sale was to and includes this amount on a periodic statement or *bill* sent to the customer.

Subsidiary ledger The detail for a number of individual items that collectively make up a single general ledger account.

Control account The general ledger account that is supported by a subsidiary ledger.

What if a company has a hundred or a thousand different customers? Some mechanism is needed to track the balance owed by each of these customers. The mechanism companies use is called a **subsidiary ledger.**

A subsidiary ledger contains the necessary detail on each of a number of items that collectively make up a single general ledger account, called the **control account.** In theory, any one of the accounts in the general ledger could be supported by a subsidiary ledger. In addition to Accounts Receivable, two other common accounts supported by subsidiary ledgers are Plant and Equipment and Accounts Payable. An accounts payable subsidiary ledger contains a separate account for each of the suppliers or vendors from which a company purchases inventory. A plant and equipment subsidiary ledger consists of individual accounts, along with their balances, for each of the various long-term tangible assets the company owns.

It is important to understand that a subsidiary ledger does *not* take the place of the control account in the general ledger. Instead, at any point in time, the balances of the accounts that make up the subsidiary ledger should total to the single balance in the related control account. In the remainder of this chapter we will illustrate the use of only the control account. Whenever a specific customer's account is increased or decreased we will, however, note the name of the customer next to the control account in the journal entry.

The Valuation of Accounts Receivable

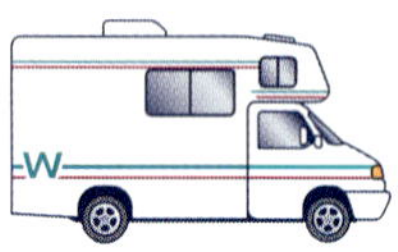

The following presentation of receivables is taken from Winnebago Industries' 2001 annual report:

	2001	2000
Receivables, less allowance for doubtful accounts ($244 and $1,168, respectively)	$20,183	$32,045

As you read this excerpt from the balance sheets, keep two points in mind. First, all amounts are stated in thousands of dollars. Second, these are the balances at the *end* of each of the two years.

Winnebago Industries does not sell its products to distributors under the assumption that any particular customer will *not* pay its bill. In fact, the credit department of a business is responsible for performing a credit check on all potential customers before they are granted credit. Management of Winnebago Industries is not naive enough, however, to believe that all customers will be able to pay their accounts when due. This would be the case only if (1) all customers are completely trustworthy and (2) customers never experience unforeseen financial difficulties that make it impossible to pay on time.

The reduction in Winnebago Industries' receivables for an allowance is the way in which most companies deal with bad debts in their accounting records. Bad debts are unpaid customer accounts that a company gives up trying to collect. Some companies such as Winnebago Industries describe the allowance more fully as the allowance for doubtful accounts, and others call it the allowance for uncollectible accounts. Using the end of 2001 as an example, Winnebago Industries believes that the *net recoverable amount* of its receivables is $20,183 thousand, even though the *gross* amount of receivables is $244 thousand higher than this amount. The company has reduced the gross receivables for an amount that it believes is necessary to reflect the asset on the books at the *net recoverable amount* or *net realizable value.* We now take a closer look at how a company accounts for bad debts.

Two Methods to Account for Bad Debts

Assume that Roberts Corp. makes a $500 sale to Dexter Inc. on November 10, 2004, with credit terms of 2/10, net 60. Roberts makes the following entry on its books on this date:

Accounting for Your Decisions

You Are the Credit Manager

You are the credit manager of USA Department Store, which offers its customers USA Department Store credit cards. An existing customer, Jane Doe, has requested a credit line increase. In processing her request, you must determine the current balance of her account. How would you use the accounting system to find her current balance? What other factors might you consider in granting Jane's request?

ANS: You would find Jane's current balance by looking for her account in the accounts receivable subsidiary ledger. The subsidiary ledger should have a current balance because daily postings are made to each customer's account. Other factors to consider in processing Jane's request can include researching her payment history to see if she paid on time not only for this credit card but for all debts, checking to see if her income is sufficient to cover her existing debt and the new credit line increase, and verifying employment to ensure income stability.

2004			
Nov. 10	Accounts Receivable—Dexter	500	
	Sales Revenue		500
	To record sale on credit, terms of 2/10, net 60.		

Assets	=	Liabilities	+	Owners' Equity
+500				+500

Assume further that Dexter not only misses taking advantage of the discount for early payment but also is unable to pay within 60 days. After pursuing the account for four months into 2005, the credit department of Roberts informs the accounting department that it has given up on collecting the $500 from Dexter and advises that the account should be written off. To do so, the accounting department makes the following entry:

2005			
May 1	Bad Debts Expense	500	
	Accounts Receivable—Dexter		500
	To write off Dexter account.		

Assets	=	Liabilities	+	Owners' Equity
−500				−500

This approach to accounting for bad debts is called the **direct write-off method.** Do you see any problems with its use? What about Roberts's balance sheet at the end of 2004? By ignoring the possibility that not all of its outstanding accounts receivable will be collected, Roberts is overstating the value of this asset at December 31, 2004. Also, what about the income statement for 2004? By ignoring the possibility of bad debts on sales made during 2004, Roberts has violated the *matching principle.* This principle requires that all costs associated with making sales in a period should be matched with the sales of that period. Roberts has overstated net income for 2004 by ignoring bad debts as an expense. The problem is one of *timing:* even though any one particular account may not prove to be uncollectible until a later period (e.g., the Dexter account), the cost associated with making sales on credit (bad debts) should be recognized in the period of sale.

Direct write-off method The recognition of bad debts expense at the point an account is written off as uncollectible.

Accountants use the **allowance method** to overcome the deficiencies of the direct write-off method. They *estimate* the amount of bad debts before these debts actually occur. For example, assume that Roberts's total sales during 2004 amount to $600,000 and that at the end of the year the outstanding accounts receivable total $250,000. Also assume that Roberts estimates that on the basis of past experience, 1% of the sales of the period, or $6,000, eventually will prove to be uncollectible. Under the allowance method, Roberts makes the following adjusting entry at the end of 2004:

Allowance method A method of estimating bad debts on the basis of either the net credit sales of the period or the accounts receivable at the end of the period.

Study Tip

Note the similarities between the Allowance for Doubtful Accounts contra account and another contra account, Accumulated Depreciation. Both are used to reduce an asset account to a lower carrying or book value.

2004			
Dec. 31	Bad Debts Expense	6,000	
	Allowance for Doubtful Accounts		6,000
	To record estimated bad debts for the year.		

Assets	=	Liabilities	+	Owners' Equity
−6,000				−6,000

The debit recognizes the cost associated with the reduction in value of the asset Accounts Receivable. The cost is charged to the income statement, in the form of Bad Debts Expense. A contra-asset account is used to reduce the asset to its net realizable value. This is accomplished by crediting an allowance account, Allowance for Doubtful Accounts. Roberts presents accounts receivable as follows on its December 31, 2004, balance sheet:

Accounts receivable	$250,000
Less: Allowance for doubtful accounts	(6,000)
Net accounts receivable	$244,000

Write-Offs of Uncollectible Accounts with the Allowance Method

Like the direct write-off method, the allowance method reduces Accounts Receivable to write off a specific customer's account. If the account receivable no longer exists, there is no need for the related allowance account and thus this account is reduced as well. For example, assume, as we did earlier, that Dexter's $500 account is written off on May 1, 2005. Under the allowance method, the following entry is recorded:

2005			
May 1	Allowance for Doubtful Accounts	500	
	Accounts Receivable—Dexter		500
	To record the write-off of Dexter account.		

Assets	=	Liabilities	+	Owners' Equity
+500				
−500				

To summarize, whether the direct write-off method or the allowance method is used, the entry to write off a specific customer's account reduces Accounts Receivable. It is the debit that differs between the two methods: under the direct write-off method, an *expense* is increased; under the allowance method, the *allowance* account is reduced.

Two Approaches to the Allowance Method of Accounting for Bad Debts

Because the allowance method results in a better *matching*, accounting standards require the use of this method rather than the direct write-off method unless bad debts are immaterial in amount. Accountants use one of two different variations of the allowance method to estimate bad debts. One approach emphasizes matching bad debts expense with revenue on the income statement and bases bad debts on a percentage of the sales of the period. This was the method we illustrated earlier for Roberts Corp. The other approach emphasizes the net realizable amount (value) of accounts receivable on the balance sheet and bases bad debts on a percentage of the accounts receivable balance at the end of the period.

Percentage of Net Credit Sales Approach If a company has been in business for enough years, it may be able to use the past relationship between bad debts and *net* credit sales to predict bad debt amounts. *Net* means that credit sales have been adjusted for sales discounts and returns and allowances. Assume that the accounting records for Bosco Corp. reveal the following:

YEAR	NET CREDIT SALES	BAD DEBTS
1999	$1,250,000	$ 26,400
2000	1,340,000	29,350
2001	1,200,000	23,100
2002	1,650,000	32,150
2003	2,120,000	42,700
	$7,560,000	$153,700

Although the exact percentage varied slightly over the five-year period, the average percentage of bad debts to net credit sales is very close to 2% ($153,700/$7,560,000 = 0.02033). Bosco needs to determine whether this estimate is realistic for the current period. For example, are current economic conditions considerably different from those in the prior years? Has the company made sales to any new customers with significantly different credit terms? If the answers to these types of questions are yes, Bosco should consider adjusting the 2% experience rate to estimate future bad debts. Otherwise, it should proceed with this estimate. Assuming that it uses the 2% rate and that its net credit sales during 2004 are $2,340,000, Bosco makes the following entry:

2004			
Dec. 31	Bad Debts Expense	46,800	
	Allowance for Doubtful Accounts		46,800
	To record estimated bad debts: 0.02 × $2,340,000.		

Assets	=	Liabilities	+	Owners' Equity
−46,800				−46,800

Thus, Bosco matches bad debt expense of $46,800 with sales revenue of $2,340,000.

Percentage of Accounts Receivable Approach Some companies believe they can more accurately estimate bad debts by relating them to the balance in the Accounts Receivable account at the end of the period rather than to the sales of the period. The objective with both approaches is the same, however: to use past experience with bad debts to predict future amounts. Assume that the records for Cougar Corp. reveal the following:

YEAR	BALANCE IN ACCOUNTS RECEIVABLE DECEMBER 31	BAD DEBTS
1999	$ 650,000	$ 5,250
2000	785,000	6,230
2001	854,000	6,950
2002	824,000	6,450
2003	925,000	7,450
	$4,038,000	$32,330

Accounting for Your Decisions

You Are the Owner

Assume you own a retail business that offers credit sales. To estimate bad debts, your business uses the percentage of net credit sales approach. For the new fiscal year, how would you decide what percentage to use to estimate your bad debts?

ANS: To determine the bad debt percentage for the new fiscal year, you can (1) review historical records to see what the actual percentages of bad debts were, (2) check to see if credit policies have substantially changed, (3) consider current and future economic conditions, and (4) consult with your managers and salespeople to see if they are aware of any changes in customers' paying habits.

The ratio of bad debts to the ending balance in Accounts Receivable over the past five years is \$32,330/\$4,038,000, or approximately 0.008 (0.8%). Assuming balances in Accounts Receivable and the Allowance for Doubtful Accounts on December 31, 2004, of \$865,000 (debit) and \$2,100 (credit), respectively, Cougar records the following entry:

2004				
Dec. 31	Bad Debts Expense		4,820	
	Allowance for Doubtful Accounts			4,820
	To record estimated bad debts:			
	Credit balance required in allowance account after adjustment (\$865,000 × 0.8%)	\$6,920		
	Less: Credit balance in allowance account before adjustment	2,100		
	Amount for bad debt expense entry	\$4,820		

Assets	=	Liabilities	+	Owners' Equity
−4,820				−4,820

Note the one major difference between this approach and the percentage of sales approach: *under the percentage of net credit sales approach, the balance in the allowance account is ignored, and the bad debts expense is simply a percentage of the sales of the period; under the percentage of accounts receivable approach, however, the balance in the allowance account must be considered.* A T account for Allowance for Doubtful Accounts with the balance before and after adjustment appears as follows:

ALLOWANCE FOR DOUBTFUL ACCOUNTS

Debit	Credit	
	2,100	Bal. before adjustment
	4,820	Adjusting entry
	6,920	Bal. after adjustment

In other words, making an adjustment for \$4,820 results in a balance in the account of \$6,920, which is 0.8% of the Accounts Receivable balance of \$865,000. The net realizable value of Accounts Receivable is determined as follows:

Accounts receivable	\$865,000
Less: Allowance for doubtful accounts	(6,920)
Net realizable value	\$858,080

Aging of Accounts Receivable Some companies use a variation of the percentage of accounts receivable approach to estimate bad debts. This variation is actually a refinement of the approach because it considers the length of time that the receivables have been outstanding. It stands to reason that the older an account receivable is, the less likely it is to be collected. An **aging schedule** categorizes the various accounts by length of time outstanding. An example of an aging schedule is shown in Exhibit 7-5. We assume that the company's policy is to allow 30 days for payment of an outstanding account. After that time, the account is past due. An alphabetical list of customers appears in the first column, with the balance in each account shown in the appropriate column to the right. The dotted lines after A. Matt's account indicate that many more accounts appear in the records; we have included just a few to show the format of the schedule. The totals on the aging schedule are used as the basis for estimating bad debts, as shown in Exhibit 7-6.

Aging schedule A form used to categorize the various individual accounts receivable according to the length of time each has been outstanding.

Note that the estimated percentage of uncollectibles increases as the period of time the accounts have been outstanding lengthens. If we assume that the Allowance for Doubtful Accounts has a credit balance of \$1,230 before adjustment, the adjusting entry is as follows:

Exhibit 7-5
Aging Schedule

CUSTOMER	CURRENT	Number of Days Past Due 1–30	31–60	61–90	OVER 90
L. Ash	$ 4,400				
B. Budd	3,200				
C. Cox		$ 6,500			
E. Fudd					$6,300
G. Hoff			$ 900		
A. Matt	5,500				
......					
......					
......					
T. West				$ 3,100	
M. Young				4,200	
Totals*	$85,600	$31,200	$24,500	$18,000	$9,200

*Only a few of the customer accounts are illustrated; thus the column totals are higher than the amounts for the accounts illustrated.

2004				
Dec. 31	Bad Debts Expense		13,324	
	Allowance for Doubtful Accounts			13,324
	To record estimated bad debts:			
	Credit balance required in allowance account after adjustment	$14,554		
	Less: Credit balance in allowance account before adjustment	1,230		
	Amount for bad debt expense entry	$13,324		

Assets = **Liabilities** + **Owners' Equity**
−13,324 **−13,324**

The net realizable value of accounts receivable would be determined as follows:

Accounts receivable	$168,500
Less: Allowance for doubtful accounts	14,554
Net realizable value	$153,946

From Concept to Practice 7.2

Reading Winnebago Industries' Notes

In the Winnebago Industries' annual report, locate the section in Note 1 that is titled "Allowance for Doubtful Accounts." From your reading of this, which method does it appear that Winnebago Industries uses to estimate bad debts? In what line item on the income statement would you expect bad debts expense to be included?

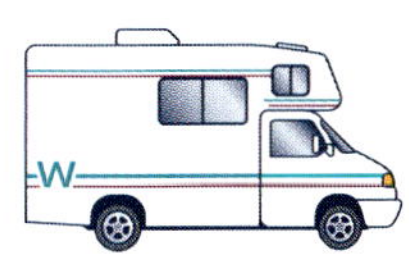

Exhibit 7-6
Use of an Aging Schedule to Estimate Bad Debts

CATEGORY	AMOUNT	ESTIMATED PERCENT UNCOLLECTIBLE	ESTIMATED AMOUNT UNCOLLECTIBLE
Current	$ 85,600	1%	$ 856
Past due:			
1–30 days	31,200	4%	1,248
31–60 days	24,500	10%	2,450
61–90 days	18,000	30%	5,400
Over 90 days	9,200	50%	4,600
Totals	$168,500		$14,554

Two-Minute Review

1. *What is the theoretical justification for recognizing bad debts under the allowance method?*
2. *What account titles are debited and credited at the end of the period to recognize bad debts?*
3. *Two approaches are available to recognize bad debts. What are they? Which one of the two takes into account any existing balance in the Allowance for Doubtful Accounts account when the entry is made to recognize bad debts for the period?*

Answers on page 358.

Analyzing the Accounts Receivable Rate of Collection

Managers, investors, and creditors are keenly interested in how well a company manages its accounts receivable. One simple measure is to compare a company's sales to its accounts receivable. The result is the accounts receivable turnover ratio:

$$\text{Accounts Receivable Turnover} = \frac{\text{Net Credit Sales}}{\text{Average Accounts Receivable}}$$

Typically, the faster the turnover is, the better. For example, if a company has sales of \$10 million and an average accounts receivable of \$1 million, it turns over its accounts receivable 10 times per year. If we assume 360 days in a year, that is once every 36 days. An observer would compare that figure with historical figures to see if the company is experiencing slower or faster collections. A comparison could also be made to other companies in the same industry. If receivables are turning over too slowly, that could mean that the company's credit department is not operating effectively and the company therefore is missing opportunities with the cash that isn't available. On the other hand, a turnover rate that is too fast might mean that the company's credit policies are too stringent and that sales are being lost as a result.

From Concept to Practice 7.3

Reading PepsiCo's Financial Statements

PepsiCo's 2001 net sales were \$26,935 million. Using this information and that given in the chapter opener, compute PepsiCo's accounts and notes receivable turnover for 2001. What is the average length of time it takes to collect a receivable? Does this seem reasonable for the company's type of business?

NOTES RECEIVABLE

Promissory note A written promise to repay a definite sum of money on demand or at a fixed or determinable date in the future.

Maker The party that agrees to repay the money for a promissory note at some future date.

Payee The party that will receive the money from a promissory note at some future date.

A **promissory note** is a written promise to repay a definite sum of money on demand or at a fixed or determinable date in the future. Promissory notes normally require the payment of interest for the use of someone else's money. The party that agrees to repay money is the **maker** of the note, and the party that receives money in the future is the **payee.** A company that holds a promissory note received from another company has an asset, called a **note receivable;** the company that makes or gives a promissory note to another company has a liability, a **note payable.** Over the life of the note, the maker incurs interest expense on its note payable, and the payee earns interest revenue on its note receivable. The following summarizes this relationship:

PARTY	RECOGNIZES ON BALANCE SHEET	RECOGNIZES ON INCOME STATEMENT
Maker	Note payable	Interest expense
Payee	Note receivable	Interest revenue

Promissory notes are used for a variety of purposes. Banks normally require a company to sign a promissory note to borrow money. They are often used in the sale of consumer durables with relatively high purchase prices, such as appliances and automobiles. At times a promissory note is issued to replace an existing overdue account receivable.

Note receivable An asset resulting from the acceptance of a promissory note from another company.

Note payable A liability resulting from the signing of a promissory note.

Important Terms Connected with Promissory Notes

It is important to understand the following terms when dealing with promissory notes:

Principal—the amount of cash received, or the fair value of the products or services received, by the maker when a promissory note is issued.

Maturity date—the date that the promissory note is due.

Term—the length of time a note is outstanding; that is, the period of time between the date it is issued and the date it matures.

Maturity value—the amount of cash the maker is to pay the payee on the maturity date of the note.

Interest—the difference between the principal amount of the note and its maturity value.

Key terms for promissory notes These terms, with their definitions in the text, are important for your understanding.

In some cases, the interest rate on a promissory note is stated explicitly on the face of the note. Even though the note's term may be less than a year, the interest rate is stated on an annual basis. In other cases, an interest rate does not appear on the face of the note. As we will see, however, there is *implicit* interest, because more is to be repaid at maturity than is owed at the time the note is signed. Notes in which an interest rate is explicitly stated are called **interest-bearing notes.** Notes in which interest is implicit in the agreement are called **non-interest-bearing notes.** We now look at the accounting for each of these types of notes.

Interest-bearing note A promissory note in which the interest rate is explicitly stated.

Non-interest-bearing note A promissory note in which interest is not explicitly stated but is implicit in the agreement.

Interest-Bearing Notes

LO 5 Demonstrate an understanding of how to account for interest-bearing notes receivable.

Assume that on December 13, 2004, HighTec sells a computer to Baker Corp. at an invoice price of $15,000. Because Baker is short of cash, it gives HighTec a 90-day, 12% promissory note. The total amount of interest due on the maturity date is determined as follows:

$$\$15{,}000 \times 0.12 \times 90/360 = \underline{\underline{\$450}}$$

The entry to record receipt of the note by HighTec is as follows:

2004			
Dec. 13	Notes Receivable	15,000	
	Sales Revenue		15,000
	To record sale of computer in exchange for promissory note.		

Assets	=	Liabilities	+	Owners' Equity
+15,000				+15,000

If we assume that December 31 is the end of HighTec's accounting year, an adjustment is needed to recognize interest earned but not yet received. It is required when a company uses the accrual basis of accounting. The question is: how many days of interest have been earned during December? *It is normal practice to count the day a note matures, but not the day it is signed, in computing interest.* Thus, in our example, interest would be earned for 18 days (December 14 to December 31) during 2004 and for 72 days in 2005:

MONTH	NUMBER OF DAYS OUTSTANDING
December 2004	18 days
January 2005	31 days
February 2005	28 days
March 2005	13 days (matures on March 13, 2005)
Total days	90 days

An adjusting entry is made on December 31 to record interest earned during 2004:

2004			
Dec. 31	Interest Receivable	90	
	Interest Revenue		90
	To record interest earned: $15,000 × 0.12 × 18/360.		

Assets	=	Liabilities	+	Owners' Equity
+90				+90

On March 13, 2005, HighTec collects the principal amount of the note and interest from Baker and records this entry:

2005			
Mar. 13	Cash	15,450	
	Notes Receivable		15,000
	Interest Revenue		360
	Interest Receivable		90
	To record collection of promissory note.		

Assets	=	Liabilities	+	Owners' Equity
+15,450				+360
−15,000				
−90				

This entry accomplishes a number of purposes. First, it removes the amount of $15,000 originally recorded in the Notes Receivable account. Second, it increases Interest Revenue for the interest earned during the 72 days in 2005 that the note was outstanding. The calculation of interest earned during 2005 is as follows:

$$\$15,000 \times 0.12 \times 72/360 = \underline{\underline{\$360}}$$

Third, the entry decreases Interest Receivable by $90 to remove this account from the records now that the note has been collected. Finally, it increases Cash by $15,450, which represents the principal amount of the note, $15,000, plus interest of $450 for 90 days.

Non-Interest-Bearing Notes

LO 6 Demonstrate an understanding of how to account for non-interest-bearing notes receivable.

Assume that you walk in to an automobile dealership on November 1, 2004, and find the car of your dreams. After extensive negotiation, the dealer agrees to sell you the car outright for $10,000. Because you are short of cash, you give the dealer $1,000 as a down payment and sign a promissory note to pay $9,900 in six months. Even though interest is never mentioned, it is *implicitly* built into the transaction. You owe the car dealer $10,000 − $1,000, or $9,000, today, and you have agreed to pay $9,900 in six months. The $900 excess of the amount to be paid in six months over the amount owed today is *interest*. The note is called a non-interest-bearing note because no interest is *explicitly* stated. Anytime it is necessary to pay more in the future than is owed today, interest is involved. The *effective interest rate* can be found as follows:

1. The amount of interest implicit in the note: $9,900 − $9,000, or $900
2. The length of the note: 6 months
3. The number of 6-month periods in a year: 12/6 = 2
4. The amount of interest that would apply to a full year: $900 × 2, or $1,800
5. The effective annual interest rate: $1,800/$9,000, or 20%

In essence, the car dealer had you sign a promissory note in the amount of $9,900 but gave you credit equivalent to only $9,000 in cash, that is, the difference between the value of the car today, $10,000, and the amount of your down payment, $1,000. The dealer deducted interest of $900 in advance and gave you the equivalent of a $9,000 loan. Another name for this non-interest-bearing note is a **discounted note.** On the date the note is signed, the car dealer makes this entry:

Discounted note An alternative name for a non-interest-bearing promissory note.

2004			
Nov. 1	Cash	1,000	
	Notes Receivable	9,900	
	Discount on Notes Receivable		900
	Sales Revenue		10,000
	To record sale in exchange for note.		

Assets	=	Liabilities	+	Owners' Equity
+1,000				+10,000
+9,900				
−900				

The debit to Cash represents the down payment. The debit to Notes Receivable is for $9,900, the maturity amount of the promissory note. The credit to Sales Revenue represents the amount the car could be sold for today. Discount on Notes Receivable is a contra account to the Notes Receivable account and represents the interest that the dealer will earn over the next six months. As interest is earned, this account will be reduced and Interest Revenue will be recognized. For example, at the end of the year, the dealer will make an adjustment to recognize that two months' interest of the total of six months' interest has been earned:

2004			
Dec. 31	Discount on Notes Receivable	300	
	Interest Revenue		300
	To record interest earned for two months: $900 × 2/6.		

Assets	=	Liabilities	+	Owners' Equity
+300				+300

The Current Assets section of the dealer's balance sheet at December 31, 2004, includes the following:

Notes receivable	$9,900	
Less: Discount on notes receivable	(600)	$9,300

The entry on April 30 to record collection of the maturity amount of the note and to recognize the remaining interest earned is as follows:

2005			
Apr. 30	Cash	9,900	
	Discount on Notes Receivable	600	
	Notes Receivable		9,900
	Interest Revenue		600
	To record collection of note.		

Assets	=	Liabilities	+	Owners' Equity
+9,900				+600
+600				
−9,900				

ACCELERATING THE INFLOW OF CASH FROM SALES

LO 7 Explain various techniques that companies use to accelerate the inflow of cash from sales.

Earlier in the chapter we pointed out why cash sales are preferable to credit sales: credit sales slow down the inflow of cash to the company and create the potential for bad debts. To remain competitive, most businesses find it necessary to grant credit to customers. That is, if one company won't grant credit to a customer, the customer may find another company willing to do so. Companies have found it possible, however, to circumvent the problems inherent in credit sales. In Chapter 5 we discussed the use of sales discounts to motivate timely repayment of accounts receivable. We now consider other approaches that companies use to speed up the flow of cash from sales.

Credit Card Sales

Most retail establishments, as well as many service businesses, accept one or more major credit cards. Among the most common cards are MasterCard®, VISA®, American Express®, Carte Blanche®, Discover Card®, and Diners Club®. Most merchants believe that they must honor at least one or more of these credit cards to remain competitive. In return for a fee, the merchant passes the responsibility for collection on to the credit card company. Thus, the credit card issuer assumes the risk of nonpayment. The basic relationships among the three parties—the customer, the merchant, and the credit card company—are illustrated in Exhibit 7-7. Assume that Joe Smith entertains clients at Club Cafe and charges $100 in meals to his Diners Club credit card. When Joe is presented with his bill at the end of the evening, he is asked to sign a multiple-copy **credit card draft** or invoice. Joe keeps one copy of the draft and leaves the other two copies at Club Cafe. The restaurant keeps one copy as the basis for recording its sales for the day and sends the other copy to Diners Club for payment. Diners Club uses the copy of the draft it gets for two purposes: to reimburse Club Cafe $95 (keeping $5 or 5% of the original sale as a collection fee) and to include Joe Smith's $100 purchase on the monthly bill it mails him.

Credit card draft A multiple-copy document used by a company that accepts a credit card for a sale.

Exhibit 7-7

Basic Relationships among Parties with Credit Card Sales

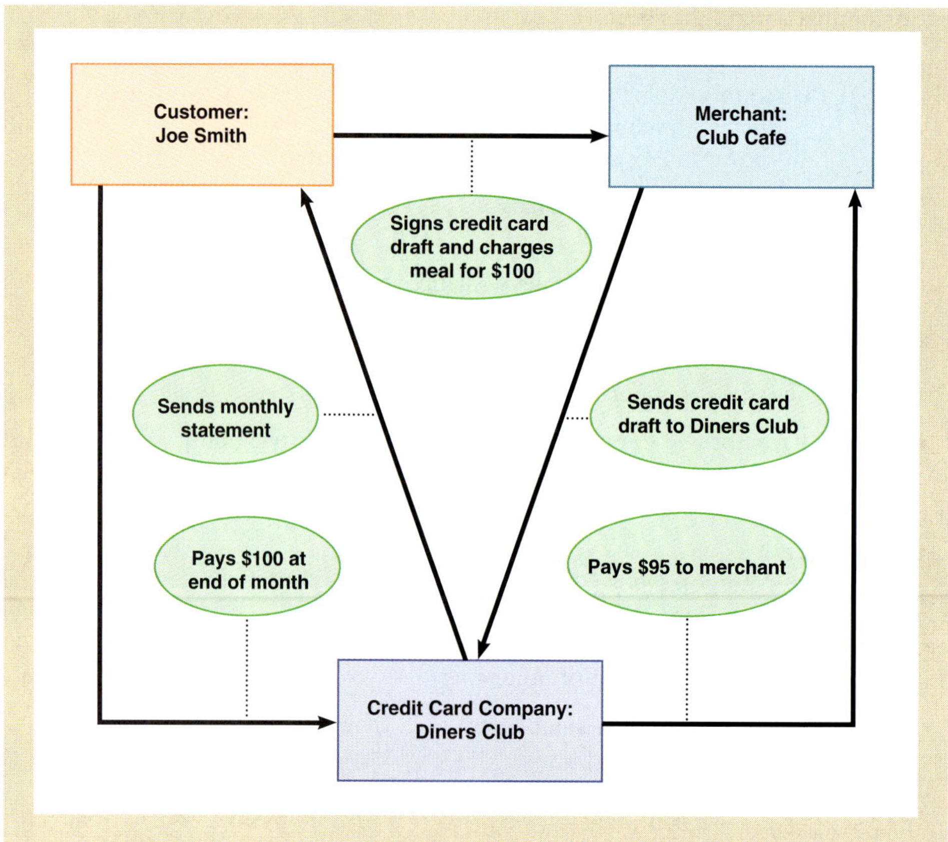

Assume that total credit card sales on June 5 amount to $800. The entry on Club Cafe's books on that day is as follows:

June 5	Accounts Receivable—Diners Club	800	
	Sales Revenue		800
	To record daily credit card sales.		

Assets	=	Liabilities	+	Owners' Equity
+800				+800

Assume that Club Cafe remits the credit card drafts to Diners Club once a week and that the total sales for the week ending June 11 amount to $5,000. Further assume that on June 13 Diners Club pays the amount due to Club Cafe, after deducting a 5% collection fee. The entry on Club Cafe's books is as follows:

June 13	Cash	4,750	
	Collection Fee Expense	250	
	Accounts Receivable—Diners Club		5,000
	To record weekly receipts from credit card company.		

Assets	=	Liabilities	+	Owners' Equity
+4,750				−250
−5,000				

Some credit cards, such as MasterCard and VISA, allow a merchant to present a credit card draft directly for deposit in a bank account, in much the same way the merchant deposits checks, coins, and currency. Obviously, this type of arrangement is even more advantageous for the merchant because the funds are available as soon as the drafts are credited to the bank account. Assume that on July 9 Club Cafe presents VISA credit card drafts to its bank for payment in the amount of $2,000 and that the collection charge is 4%. The entry on its books on the date of deposit is as follows:

July 9	Cash	1,920	
	Collection Fee Expense	80	
	Sales Revenue		2,000
	To record credit card sales.		

Assets	=	Liabilities	+	Owners' Equity
+1,920				−80
				+2,000

Discounting Notes Receivable

Promissory notes are negotiable, which means that they can be endorsed and given to someone else for collection. In other words, a company can sign the back of a note, just as it would a check, sell it to a bank, and receive cash before the note's maturity date. This process is called **discounting** and is another way for companies to speed the collection of cash from receivables. A note can be sold immediately to a bank on the date it is issued, or it can be sold after it has been outstanding but before the due date.

Discounting The process of selling a promissory note.

When a note is discounted at a bank, it is normally done *with recourse.* This means that if the original customer fails to pay the bank the total amount due on the maturity date of the note, the company that transferred the note to the bank is liable for the full amount. Because there is *uncertainty* as to whether the company will have to make good on any particular note that it discounts at the bank, a *contingent liability* exists from the time the note is discounted until its maturity date. The accounting profession has adopted guidelines to decide whether a particular uncertainty requires that the company record a contingent liability on its balance sheet. Under these guidelines, the contingency created by the discounting of a note with recourse is not recorded as a liability. However, a *note* in the financial statements is used to inform the reader of the existing uncertainty.

HOW LIQUID ASSETS AFFECT THE CASH FLOWS STATEMENT

LO 8 Explain the effects of transactions involving liquid assets on the statement of cash flows.

As we discussed earlier in the chapter, cash equivalents are combined with cash on the balance sheet. These items are very near maturity and do not present any significant risk of collectibility. Because of this, any purchases or redemptions of cash equivalents are not considered significant activities to be reported on a statement of cash flows.

The purchase and the sale of investments are considered significant activities and are therefore reported on the statement of cash flows. The classification of these activities on the statement depends on the type of investment. Cash flows from purchases, sales, and maturities of held-to-maturity securities and available-for-sale securities are classified as *investing* activities. On the other hand, these same types of cash flows for trading securities are classified as *operating* activities. We present a complete discussion of the statement of cash flows, including the reporting of investments, in Chapter 12.

The collection of either accounts receivable or notes receivable generates cash for a business and affects the Operating Activities section of the statement of cash flows. Most companies use the indirect method of reporting cash flows and begin the statement of cash flows with the net income of the period. Net income includes the sales revenue of the period. Therefore, a decrease in accounts or notes receivable during the period indicates that the company collected more cash than it recorded in sales revenue. Thus, *a decrease in accounts or notes receivable must be added back to net income because more cash was collected than is reflected in the sales revenue number.* Alternatively, an increase in accounts or notes receivable indicates that the company recorded more sales revenue than cash collected during the period. Therefore, *an increase in accounts or notes receivable requires a deduction from the net income of the period to arrive at cash flow from operating activities.* These adjustments, as well as the cash flows from buying and selling investments, are summarized in Exhibit 7-8. Note that any investments are assumed to be in either held-to-maturity or available-for-sale securities.

Exhibit 7-8

How Investments and Receivables Affect the Statement of Cash Flows

Item	Cash Flow Statement	
	Operating Activities	
	Net income	**xxx**
Increase in accounts receivable		–
Decrease in accounts receivable		+
Increase in notes receivable		–
Decrease in notes receivable		+
	Investing Activities	
Purchases of held-to-maturity and available-for-sale securities		–
Sales/maturities of held-to-maturity and available-for-sale securities		+
	Financing Activities	

http://www.pepsico.com

Refer back to PepsiCo's statement of cash flows in Exhibit 7-1. PepsiCo's purchases and maturities of short-term investments appear in the Investing Activities section of the statement. Purchases of investments with original maturities of more than three months used cash of $2,537 million and maturities of these investments generated cash of $2,078 million.

Ratios for Decision Making

Reporting and analyzing financial statement information related to a company's accounts receivable: The accounts receivable turnover calculation provides information about how well the company is handling its collection of receivables from credit sales. The higher the number, the more frequently cash from credit sales is collected. Comparing the company's turnover rate with its rate in prior years or with the rate of other companies in the same industry can provide an estimate of how well the company is doing with managing its receivables.

Balance Sheet	Income Statement	Statement of Cash Flows	Notes
Accounts Receivable	Net Sales	Cash received from accounts receivable Cash received from cash sales	

$$\text{Accounts Receivable Turnover} = \frac{\text{Net Credit Sales*}}{\text{Average Accounts Receivable**}}$$

*Net credit sales are credit sales minus any sales discounts, returns, and allowances. Net credit sales can be estimated as follows:

Net Sales − cash received from cash sales as reported on the statement of cash flows

**Average accounts receivable can be estimated using the following calculation:

$$\frac{\text{Beginning Accounts Receivable} + \text{Ending Accounts Receivable}}{2}$$

Impact on the Financial Reports

Impact on the Financial Reports

BALANCE SHEET

Current Assets
Cash and cash equivalents[1]
Short-term investments[2]
Accounts receivable[3]
Allowance for doubtful accounts
Notes receivable[4]
Discount on notes receivable
Interest receivable
Supplies
Noncurrent Assets
Current Liabilities
Noncurrent Liabilities
Stockholders' Equity
Unrealized gain (loss)—available-for-sale securities

INCOME STATEMENT

Revenues
Sales revenue
Expenses
Cost of goods sold
Bad debt expense
Rent expense—lockbox
Collection fee expense
Postage expense
Delivery expense
Office expense
Other
Interest revenue
Dividend income
Gain (loss) on sale of investments[5]
Unrealized gain (loss)—trading securities
Miscellaneous income (expense)[6]

STATEMENT OF STOCKHOLDERS' EQUITY

Contributed Capital
Retained Earnings

STATEMENT OF CASH FLOWS

Operating Activities[7]
Cash from sales
Cash received for accounts receivable
Cash received for interest from notes receivable and bond investments
Investing Activities
Cash received from (paid for) debt and equity security investments
Cash dividends received
Financing Activities
Noncash Transactions

NOTES

[1]Includes Petty Cash Fund
[2]May include certificates of deposit, investments in stocks, investments in bonds that mature or are expected to be sold within one year of the balance sheet date.
[3]Accounts receivable less allowance for doubtful accounts = net accounts receivable = net realizable value; accounts receivable includes credit card sales
[4]Notes receivable less discount on notes receivable = net notes receivable = net realizable value
[5]Includes gain (loss) from sale of stocks and bonds
[6]Includes Cash Over or Short
[7]Under the indirect method (explained in detail in Chapter 12), any increase (or decrease) in accounts receivable and in notes receivable and any gain (or loss) from the sale of investments would be shown as a subtraction from (addition to) net income in this section and would replace the items listed above under "Operating Activities."

Answers to the Two-Minute Reviews

Two-Minute Review on Page 343

1. *Held-to-maturity, trading, and available-for-sale.*
2. *Bonds are the only securities that can be held to maturity. Stocks do not have a maturity date.*
3. *Any changes in fair value of trading securities are reported on the income statement. Changes in fair value of available-for-sale securities are reported in stockholders' equity on the balance sheet.*

Two-Minute Review on Page 350

1. *Use of the allowance method is an attempt by accountants to match bad debts as an expense with the revenue of the period in which a sale on credit took place.*
2. *Bad Debts expense is debited, and Allowance for Doubtful Accounts is credited.*
3. *The two approaches are the percentage of net credit sales approach and the percentage of accounts receivable approach. Only the latter takes into account the balance in the Allowance for Doubtful Accounts account.*

Warmup Exercises

Warmup Exercise 7-1 *Composition of Cash* **LO 1**

For the following items, indicate whether each should be included (I) or excluded (E) from the line item titled Cash and Cash Equivalents on the balance sheet.

_______ **1.** Certificate of deposit maturing in 60 days
_______ **2.** Checking account
_______ **3.** Certificate of deposit maturing in six months
_______ **4.** Savings account
_______ **5.** Shares of GM stock
_______ **6.** Petty cash
_______ **7.** Corporate bonds maturing in 30 days
_______ **8.** Certified check

Key to the Solution

Recall the key to classification as part of cash: the amount must be readily available to pay debts and cash equivalents must have an original maturity to the investor of three months or less.

Warmup Exercise 7-2 *Investments* **LO 3**

Indicate whether each of the following events will result in an increase (I), decrease (D), or no effect (NE) on net income for the period.

_______ **1.** Trading securities are sold for more than their carrying value.
_______ **2.** An interest check is received for held-to-maturity securities.
_______ **3.** Available-for-sale securities increase in value during the period.
_______ **4.** Available-for-sale securities are sold for less than their carrying value.
_______ **5.** Trading securities decrease in value during the period.
_______ **6.** Held-to-maturity securities are redeemed on their maturity date at face value.

Key to the Solution

Recall from earlier in the chapter the differences in accounting for the various types of investments.

Warmup Exercise 7-3 *Accounting for Bad Debts* **LO 4**

Brown Corp. ended the year with balances in Accounts Receivable of $60,000 and in Allowance for Doubtful Accounts of $800 (credit balance before adjustment). Net sales for the year amounted to $200,000. Prepare the necessary entry on its books at the end of the year, assuming the following:

1. Estimated percentage of net sales uncollectible is 1%.
2. Estimated percentage of year-end accounts receivable uncollectible is 4%.

Key to the Solution

Recall that the percentage of net sales approach does not take into account any existing balance in the allowance account but the percentage of receivables approach does.

Solutions to Warmup Exercises

Warmup Exercise 7-1

1. I **2.** I **3.** E **4.** I **5.** E **6.** I **7.** E **8.** I

Warmup Exercise 7-2

1. I **2.** I **3.** NE **4.** D **5.** D **6.** NE

Warmup Exercise 7-3

1. Bad Debts Expense	2,000	
Allowance for Doubtful Accounts		2,000
To record estimated bad debts.		

Assets	=	Liabilities	+	Owners' Equity
−2,000				−2,000

2. Bad Debts Expense	1,600	
Allowance for Doubtful Accounts		1,600
To record estimated bad debts.		

Assets	=	Liabilities	+	Owners' Equity
−1,600				−1,600

Review Problem

WebTUTOR™ Advantage

The following items pertain to the Current Assets section of the balance sheet for Jackson Corp. at the end of its accounting year, December 31, 2004. Each item must be considered, and any necessary accounting entry on December 31 must be recorded. Additionally, the accountant for Jackson wants to develop the Current Assets section of the balance sheet as of the end of 2004.

a. Cash in a savings account at the Second State Bank amounts to $13,200.

b. Cash on hand in the petty cash fund amounts to $400.

c. A 9%, 120-day certificate of deposit was purchased on December 1, 2004, for $10,000.

d. The balance on the books for a checking account at the Second State Bank is $4,230. The bank statement indicates that one of Jackson's customers paid a $1,500 promissory note, along with $120 in interest, directly to the bank. The bank deducted a $25 collection fee from the amount it credited to Jackson's account. The statement also indicated that the bank had charged Jackson's account $50 to print new checks.

e. Gross accounts receivable at December 31, 2004, amount to $44,000. Before adjustment, the balance in the Allowance for Doubtful Accounts is $340 (credit). Based on past experience, the accountant estimates that 3% of the gross accounts receivable outstanding at December 31, 2004, will prove to be uncollectible.

f. A customer's 12%, 90-day promissory note in the amount of $6,000 is held at the end of the year. (*Note:* This is a different note than the one in item **d.**) The note has been held for 45 days during 2004.

(continued)

Required

1. Record the accounting entries required in parts **a–f.**
2. Prepare the Current Assets section of Jackson's balance sheet as of December 31, 2004. In addition to items **a–f,** the balances in Inventory and Prepaid Insurance on this date are $65,000 and $4,800, respectively.

Solution to Review Problem

1. The following entries are recorded at December 31, 2004:

   a. & **b.** No entries required.

   c. Jackson needs an adjusting entry to record interest earned on the certificate of deposit at the Second State Bank. The CD has been outstanding for 30 days during 2004, and therefore the amount of interest earned is calculated as follows:

$$\$10{,}000 \times 0.09 \times 30/360 = \$75$$

The adjusting entry follows:

2004			
Dec. 31	Interest Receivable	75	
	Interest Revenue		75
	To record interest earned during 2004.		

Assets	=	Liabilities	+	Owners' Equity
+75				+75

d. Entries are needed to record the bank's collection of the promissory note and interest, the collection charge on the note, and the charge for the new checks:

2004			
Dec. 31	Cash	1,620	
	Notes Receivable		1,500
	Interest Revenue		120
	To record collection of note and interest.		

Assets	=	Liabilities	+	Owners' Equity
+1,620				+120
−1,500				

2004			
Dec. 31	Collection Fee Expense	25	
	Cash		25
	To record deduction from account for collection fee on note.		

Assets	=	Liabilities	+	Owners' Equity
−25				−25

2004			
Dec. 31	Miscellaneous Expense	50	
	Cash		50
	To record deduction from account for new checks.		

Assets	=	Liabilities	+	Owners' Equity
−50				−50

e. Based on gross accounts receivable of $44,000 at year-end and an estimate that 3% of this amount will be uncollectible, the balance in the Allowance for Doubtful Accounts should be $1,320 ($44,000 × 3%). Given a current balance of $340, an adjusting entry for $980 ($1,320 − $340) is needed to bring the balance to the desired amount of $1,320:

2004			
Dec. 31	Bad Debts Expense	980	
	Allowance for Doubtful Accounts		980
	To record estimated bad debts for the year.		

Assets	=	Liabilities	+	Owners' Equity
−980				−980

f. An adjusting entry is needed to accrue interest on the promissory note ($6,000 × 0.12 × 45/360 = $90):

2004			
Dec. 31	Interest Receivable	90	
	Interest Revenue		90
	To record interest earned on promissory note.		

Assets	=	Liabilities	+	Owners' Equity
+90				+90

2. The Current Assets section of Jackson's balance sheet appears as follows:

JACKSON CORP.
PARTIAL BALANCE SHEET
DECEMBER 31, 2004

Current Assets		
Cash		$ 19,375*
Certificate of deposit		10,000
Accounts receivable	$44,000	
Less: Allowance for doubtful accounts	1,320	42,680
Notes receivable		6,000
Interest receivable		165**
Inventory		65,000
Prepaid insurance		4,800
Total current assets		$148,020

*Savings account	$13,200
Petty cash fund	400
Checking account ($4,230 + $1,620 − $25 − $50)	5,775
Total	$19,375

**$75 from CD and $90 from promissory note

Chapter Highlights

1. **LO 1** The amount of cash reported on the balance sheet includes all items that are readily available to satisfy obligations. Items normally included in cash are coin and currency, petty cash funds, customers' undeposited checks, cashier's checks, certified checks, savings accounts, and checking accounts.
2. **LO 1** Cash equivalents include such items as commercial paper, money market funds, certificates of deposit, and Treasury bills. They are included with cash on the balance sheet and are limited to those investments that are readily convertible to known amounts of cash and have original maturities of three months or less.
3. **LO 2** A bank reconciliation is normally prepared monthly for all checking accounts to reconcile the amount of cash recorded on the books with the amount reported on the bank statement. One popular form for the reconciliation, and the one illustrated in the chapter, reconciles the balance on the bank statement and the balance on the books to the correct balance. Adjustments must be made for all items in the balance per books section of the reconciliation.
4. **LO 2** Many companies use a petty cash fund to disburse small amounts of cash that would otherwise require the use of a check and a more lengthy approval process. The fund is established by writing and cashing a check and placing the coin and currency in a secure place controlled by a custodian. At this point, an adjustment is made to record the establishment of the fund. On presentation of a supporting receipt to the custodian, employees receive disbursements from the fund. The fund is replenished periodically, and an adjustment is made to record the replenishment and to recognize the various expenses incurred.
5. **LO 3** At times, companies invest idle cash in highly liquid financial instruments such as certificates of deposit. They also invest in the debt and equity securities of other companies.

(continued)

Some investments are made without the intention of influencing or controlling the other company. Accountants classify these investments as held-to-maturity securities, trading securities, or available-for-sale securities. Other investments are made to exert significant influence over the policies of the other companies. The equity method is used in these instances. Finally, companies may buy enough of the common stock of another company to control it. This situation normally results in the presentation of consolidated financial statements.

6. **LO 3** Held-to-maturity securities are bonds that are purchased with the intention of holding them until they mature. The cost method results in the recognition of periodic interest income and the recognition of a gain or loss if the securities are sold prior to when they mature.
7. **LO 3** Trading securities are stocks and bonds held for the short term with the intention of profiting from appreciation in their trading price. Interest or dividends are recognized as income. Trading securities are adjusted to their fair value at the end of each period, and any increase or decrease in value is reported on the income statement.
8. **LO 3** Available-for-sale securities are investments that are not classified as either held-to-maturity or trading securities. The accounting and reporting requirements for this category are similar to the rules for trading securities. The primary difference is that unrealized gains and losses from holding available-for-sale securities (changes in fair value from one period to the next) are not recognized on the income statement. Instead, these amounts are reported as a separate component of stockholders' equity.
9. **LO 4** The allowance method of accounting for bad debts matches the cost associated with uncollectible accounts to the revenue of the period in which the sale took place. One of two variations is used to estimate bad debts under the allowance method. Some companies base bad debts on a percentage of net credit sales. Others use an aging schedule as a basis for relating the amount of bad debts to the balance in Accounts Receivable at the end of the period.
10. **LO 5** A promissory note is a written promise to repay a definite sum of money on demand or at a fixed or determinable date in the future. Situations in which a promissory note is used include the purchase of consumer durables, the lending of money to another party, and the replacement of an existing account receivable. Interest earned but not yet collected should be accrued at the end of an accounting period.
11. **LO 6** The interest on certain promissory notes is implicitly included in the agreement instead of stated explicitly as a percentage of the principal amount of the note. Any difference between the cash purchase price of an item or, in the case of a loan, the amount borrowed and the amount to be repaid at maturity is interest. As is the case for interest-bearing notes, any interest earned but not yet collected is recognized as income at the end of an accounting period.
12. **LO 7** Many businesses accept credit cards in lieu of cash. In return for a fee, the credit card company assumes responsibility for collecting the customer charges. A credit card draft or invoice is the basis for recording a credit card sale and an account receivable. When the drafts are presented to the credit card company for payment, the excess of accounts receivable for these sales over the amount of cash received represents the expense associated with accepting credit cards. In some instances, companies do not have to wait to collect from the credit card company but can instead present the drafts for deposit to their bank account.
13. **LO 7** Because a promissory note is negotiable, it can be sold to another party, such as a bank. The sale of a note is called *discounting* and is a way for a company to accelerate the inflow of cash. If the note is sold or discounted with recourse, the company selling it is contingently liable until the maturity date of the loan. A footnote is used to report this contingency to financial statement readers.
14. **LO 8** Cash equivalents are included with cash on the balance sheet, and therefore changes in them do not appear as significant activities on a statement of cash flows. Purchases and sales of investments do appear in the statement of cash flows. Under the indirect method of preparing the Operating Activities category of the statement of cash flows, increases in accounts and notes receivable are deducted from net income; decreases are added back to net income.

http://

http://porter.swlearning.com

Technology and other resources for your success

If you need additional help, visit the text's Web site. Also, see pages xv–xvii in this text's preface for a description of available technology and other resources. If your instructor is using PERSONAL Trainer in this course, you may complete, on line, the assignments identified by PT.

Key Terms Quiz

Because of the large number of terms introduced in this chapter, it has two key terms quizzes. Read each definition below and then write the number of the definition in the blank beside the appropriate term it defines. The quiz solutions appear at the end of the chapter.

Quiz 1: Cash and Investments

____ Cash equivalent

____ Petty cash fund

_____ Bank statement
_____ Outstanding check
_____ Deposit in transit
_____ Bank reconciliation
_____ Credit memoranda
_____ Debit memoranda
_____ Equity securities
_____ Debt securities
_____ Held-to-maturity securities
_____ Trading securities
_____ Available-for-sale securities

1. Additions on a bank statement for such items as interest paid on the account and notes collected by the bank for the customer.
2. An investment that is readily convertible to a known amount of cash and has an original maturity to the investor of three months or less.
3. Deductions on a bank statement for such items as NSF checks and various service charges.
4. A deposit recorded on the books but not yet reflected on the bank statement.
5. Securities issued by corporations as a form of ownership in the business.
6. A check written by a company but not yet presented to the bank for payment.
7. Bonds issued by corporations and governmental bodies as a form of borrowing.
8. A detailed list, provided by the bank, of all the activity for a particular account during the month.
9. A form used by the accountant to reconcile the balance shown on the bank statement for a particular account with the balance shown in the accounting records.
10. Money kept on hand for making minor disbursements in coin and currency rather than by writing checks.
11. Stocks and bonds of other companies bought and held for the purpose of selling them in the near term to generate profits on appreciation in their price.
12. Stocks and bonds that are not classified as either held-to-maturity or trading securities.
13. Investments in bonds of other companies in which the investor has the positive intent and the ability to hold the securities to maturity.

Quiz 2: Receivables

_____ Subsidiary ledger
_____ Control account
_____ Direct write-off method
_____ Allowance method
_____ Aging schedule
_____ Promissory note
_____ Maker
_____ Payee
_____ Note receivable
_____ Note payable
_____ Principal
_____ Maturity date
_____ Term
_____ Maturity value
_____ Interest
_____ Interest-bearing note
_____ Non-interest-bearing note
_____ Discounted note
_____ Credit card draft
_____ Discounting

1. A method of estimating bad debts on the basis of either the net credit sales of the period or the amount of accounts receivable at the end of the period.
2. The party that will receive the money from a promissory note at some future date.
3. A written promise to repay a definite sum of money on demand or at a fixed or determinable date in the future.
4. A liability resulting from the signing of a promissory note.
5. A multiple-copy document used by a company that accepts a credit card for a sale.
6. An asset resulting from the acceptance of a promissory note from another company.
7. The process of selling a promissory note.
8. The party that agrees to repay the money for a promissory note at some future date.
9. A promissory note in which the interest rate is explicitly stated.
10. A form used to categorize the various individual accounts receivable according to the length of time each has been outstanding.
11. An alternative name for a non-interest-bearing promissory note.
12. The detail for a number of individual items that collectively make up a single general ledger account.
13. A promissory note in which interest is not explicitly stated but is implicit in the agreement.
14. The recognition of bad debts expense at the point an account is written off as uncollectible.
15. The general ledger account that is supported by a subsidiary ledger.
16. The amount of cash received, or the fair value of the products or services received, by the maker when a promissory note is issued.
17. The date that the promissory note is due.
18. The length of time a note is outstanding; that is, the period of time between the date it is issued and the date it matures.
19. The amount of cash the maker is to pay the payee on the maturity date of the note.
20. The difference between the principal amount of the note and its maturity value.

Answers on p. 381.

Alternate Terms

Allowance for doubtful accounts Allowance for uncollectible accounts

Credit card draft Invoice

Debt securities Bonds

Equity securities Stocks

Net realizable value Net recoverable amount

Non-interest-bearing note Discounted note

Short-term investments Marketable securities

Questions

1. What is a cash equivalent? Why is it included with cash on the balance sheet?
2. Why does the purchase of an item classified as a cash equivalent *not* appear on the statement of cash flows as an investing activity?
3. A friend says to you: "I understand why it is important to deposit all receipts intact and not keep coin and currency sitting around the business. Beyond this control feature, however, I believe that a company should strive to keep the maximum amount possible in checking accounts to always be able to pay bills on time." How would you evaluate your friend's statement?
4. A friends says to you: "I'm confused. I have a memo included with my bank statement indicating a $20 service charge for printing new checks. If the bank is deducting this amount from my account, why do they call it a 'debit memorandum'? I thought a decrease in a cash account would be a credit, not a debit." How can you explain this?
5. Different formats for bank reconciliations are possible. What is the format for a bank reconciliation in which a service charge for a lockbox is *added* to the balance per the bank statement? Explain your answer.
6. Stanzel Corp. purchased 1,000 shares of IBM common stock. What will determine whether the shares are classified as trading securities or available-for-sale securities?
7. On December 31, Stockton Inc. invests idle cash in two different certificates of deposit. The first is an 8%, 90-day CD, and the second has an interest rate of 9% and matures in 120 days. How is each of these CDs classified on the December 31 balance sheet?
8. What is the primary difference in the accounting requirements for trading securities and those for available-for-sale securities? How is the primary difference justified?
9. Why are changes in the fair value of trading securities reported in the account *Unrealized* Gains/Losses—Trading Securities even though the gains and losses are reported on the income statement?
10. What is the theoretical justification for the allowance method of accounting for bad debts?
11. In estimating bad debts, why is the balance in Allowance for Doubtful Accounts considered when the percentage of accounts receivable approach is used but not when the percentage of net credit sales approach is used?
12. When estimating bad debts on the basis of a percentage of accounts receivable, what is the advantage to using an aging schedule?
13. What is the distinction between an account receivable and a note receivable?
14. How would you evaluate the following statement? "Given the choice, it would always be better to require an interest-bearing note from a customer as opposed to a non-interest-bearing note. This is because interest on a note receivable is a form of revenue and it is only in the case of an interest-bearing note that interest will be earned."
15. Why does the discounting of a note receivable with recourse result in a contingent liability? Should the liability be reported on the balance sheet?

Exercises

Exercise 7-1 ***Items on a Bank Reconciliation*** **LO 2**

Assume that a company is preparing a bank reconciliation for the month of June. It reconciles the bank balance and the book balance to the correct balance. For each of the following items, indicate whether the item is an addition to the bank balance (A-Bank), an addition to the book balance (A-Book), a deduction from the bank balance (D-Bank), a deduction from the book balance (D-Book), or would not appear on the June reconciliation (NA).

_______ 1. Check written in June but not yet returned to the bank for payment

_______ 2. Customer's NSF check

_______ 3. Customer's check written in the amount of $54 but recorded on the books in the amount of $45*

_______ 4. Service charge for new checks

_______ 5. Principal and interest on a customer's note collected for the company by the bank

_______ 6. Customer's check deposited on June 30 but not reflected on the bank statement

_______ 7. Check written on the company's account, paid by the bank, and returned with the bank statement

_______ 8. Check written on the company's account for $123 but recorded on the books as $132*

_______ 9. Interest on the checking account for the month of June

*Answer in terms of the adjustment needed to correct for the error.

Exercise 7-2 ***Petty Cash Fund*** **LO 2**

On January 2, 2004, Cleaver Video Stores decided to set up a petty cash fund. The treasurer established the fund by writing and cashing a $300 check and placing the coin and currency in a locked petty cash drawer. Edward Haskell was designated as the custodian for the fund. During January, the following receipts were given to Haskell in exchange for cash from the fund:

U.S. Post Office (stamps)	$76.00
Speedy Delivery Service	45.30
Cake N Cookies (party for retiring employee)	65.40
Office Supply Superstore (paper, pencils)	36.00

A count of the cash in the drawer on January 31 revealed a balance of $74.10. The treasurer wrote and cashed a check on the same day to restore the fund to its original balance of $300. Prepare the necessary journal entries, with explanations, for January. Assume that all stamps and office supplies were used during the month.

Exercise 7-3 ***Certificate of Deposit*** **LO 3**

On May 31, 2004, Elmer Corp. purchased a 120-day, 9% certificate of deposit for $50,000. The CD was redeemed on September 28, 2004. Prepare the journal entries on Elmer's books to account for the CD, including any entry on June 30, the end of the company's fiscal year. Assume 360 days in a year.

Exercise 7-4 ***Classification of Investments*** **LO 3**

Red Oak makes the following investments in the stock of other companies during 2004. For each investment, indicate how it would be accounted for and reported on; use the following designations: trading security (T), available-for-sale security (AS), equity investee (E), or a subsidiary included in consolidated statements (S).

_______ 1. 500 shares of ABC common stock to be held for short-term share appreciation

_______ 2. 20,000 shares of the 50,000 shares of Ace common stock to be held for the long term

_______ 3. 100 shares of Creston preferred stock to be held for an indefinite period of time

_______ 4. 80,000 of the 100,000 shares of Orient common stock

_______ 5. 10,000 of the 40,000 shares of Omaha preferred stock to be held for the long term

Exercise 7-5 ***Classification of Investments*** **LO 3**

Fill in the blanks below to indicate whether each of the following investments should be classified as a held-to-maturity security (HM), a trading security (T), or an available-for-sale security (AS):

_______ 1. Shares of IBM stock to be held indefinitely.

_______ 2. GM bonds due in 10 years. The intent is to hold them until they mature.

_______ 3. Shares of Motorola stock. Plans are to hold the stock until the price goes up by 10% and then sell it.

_______ 4. Ford Motor Company bonds due in 15 years. The bonds are part of a portfolio that turns over on the average of every 60 days.

_______ 5. Chrysler bonds due in 10 years. Plans are to hold them indefinitely.

Exercise 7-6 ***Purchase and Sale of Bonds*** **LO 3**

Starship Enterprises enters into the following transactions during 2004 and 2005:

2004	
Jan. 1	Purchased $100,000 face value of Northern Lights Inc. bonds at face value. The newly issued bonds have an interest rate of 8% paid semiannually on June 30 and December 31. The bonds mature in five years.
June 30	Received interest on the Northern Lights bonds.
Dec. 31	Received interest on the Northern Lights bonds.
2005	
Jan. 1	Sold the Northern Lights Inc. bonds for $102,000.

Assume Starship classifies all bonds as held to maturity.

Required

1. Prepare all necessary journal entries on Starship's records to account for its investment in the Northern Lights bonds.
2. Why was Starship able to sell its Northern Lights bonds for $102,000?

Exercise 7-7 ***Investment in Stock*** **LO 3**

On December 1, 2004, Chicago Corp. purchases 1,000 shares of the preferred stock of Denver Corp. for $40 per share. Chicago expects the price of the stock to increase over the next few months and plans to sell it for a profit. On December 20, 2004, Denver declares a dividend of $1 per share to be paid on January 15, 2005. On December 31, 2004, Chicago's accounting year-end, the Denver stock is trading on the market at $42 per share. Chicago sells the stock on February 12, 2005, at a price of $45 per share.

Required

1. Should Chicago classify its investments as held-to-maturity, trading, or available-for-sale securities? Explain your answer.
2. Prepare all necessary entries on Chicago's books in connection with its investment, beginning with the purchase on December 1, 2004, and ending with the sale on February 12, 2005. Indicate next to each account title in your entries whether the account appears on the balance sheet (BS) or the income statement (IS).
3. In what category of the balance sheet should Chicago classify its investment on its December 31, 2004, balance sheet?

Exercise 7-8 ***Investment in Stock*** **LO 3**

On August 15, 2004, Cubs Corp. purchases 5,000 shares of common stock in Sox Inc. at a market price of $15 per share. In addition, Cubs pays brokerage fees of $1,000. Cubs plans to hold the stock indefinitely rather than as a part of its active trading portfolio. The market value of the stock is $13 per share on December 31, 2004, the end of Cubs' accounting year. On July 8, 2005, Cubs sells the Sox stock for $10 per share.

Required

1. Should Cubs classify its investment as held-to-maturity, trading, or available-for-sale securities? Explain your answer.
2. Prepare all necessary entries on Cubs' books in connection with the investment, beginning with the purchase on August 15, 2004, and ending with the sale on July 8, 2005. Indicate next to each account title in your entries whether the account appears on the balance sheet (BS) or the income statement (IS).
3. In what category of the balance sheet should Cubs classify its investment on its December 31, 2004, balance sheet?

DECISION MAKING

Exercise 7-9 ***Comparison of the Direct Write-Off and Allowance Methods of Accounting for Bad Debts*** **LO 4**

In its first year of business, Rideaway Bikes has net income of $145,000, exclusive of any adjustment for bad debt expense. The president of the company has asked you to calculate net income under each of two alternatives of accounting for bad debts: the direct write-off method and the allowance method. The president would like to use the method that will result in the higher net income. So far, no entries have been made to write off uncollectible accounts or to estimate bad debts. The relevant data are as follows:

Write-offs of uncollectible accounts during the year	$ 10,500
Net credit sales	$650,000
Estimated percentage of net credit sales that will be uncollectible	2%

Required

Compute net income under each of the two alternatives. Does Rideaway have a choice as to which method to use? Should it base its choice on which method will result in the higher net income? (Ignore income taxes.)

Exercise 7-10 ***Allowance Method of Accounting for Bad Debts—Comparison of the Two Approaches*** **LO 4**

Kandel Company had the following data available for 2004 (before making any adjustments):

Accounts receivable, 12/31/04	$320,100 (dr.)
Allowance for doubtful accounts	2,600 (cr.)
Net credit sales, 2004	834,000 (cr.)

Required

1. Prepare the journal entry to recognize bad debts under the following assumptions: (a) bad debt expense is expected to be 2% of net credit sales for the year and (b) Kandel expects it will not be able to collect 6% of the balance in accounts receivable at year-end.
2. Assume instead that the balance in the allowance account is a $2,600 debit. How will this affect your answers to **1**?

Exercise 7-11 ***Accounts Receivable Turnover for General Mills*** **LO 4**

The 2001 annual report of General Mills (the makers of Cheerios and Wheaties) reported the following amounts (in millions of dollars).

http://www.generalmills.com

Sales, for the year ended May 27, 2001	$7,077.7
Receivables, less allowance for doubtful accounts of $5.7, May 27, 2001	664.0
Receivables, less allowance for doubtful accounts of $5.8, May 28, 2000	500.6

Required

1. Compute General Mills' accounts receivable turnover ratio for 2001. (Assume that all sales are on credit.)
2. What is the average collection period, in days, for an account receivable? Explain your answer.
3. Give some examples of the types of customers you would expect General Mills to have. Do you think the average collection period for sales to these customers is reasonable? What other information do you need to fully answer this question?

Exercise 7-12 ***Interest-Bearing Notes Receivable*** **LO 5**

On September 1, 2004, Dougherty Corp. accepted a six-month, 7%, $45,000 interest-bearing note from the Rozelle Company in payment of an accounts receivable. Dougherty's year-end is December 31. Rozelle paid the note and interest on the due date.

Required

1. Who is the maker and who is the payee of the note?
2. What is the maturity date of the note?
3. Prepare all journal entries Dougherty needs to make in connection with this note.

Exercise 7-13 ***Non-Interest-Bearing Note*** **LO 6**

On May 1, Radtke's Music Mart sold an electronic keyboard to Mary Reynolds. Reynolds made a $300 down payment and signed a 10-month note for $1,625. The normal selling price of the keyboard is $1,800 in cash. Radtke's fiscal year ends December 31. Reynolds paid Radtke in full on the maturity date.

Required

1. How much total interest did Radtke receive on this note?
2. Prepare the journal entries on Radtke's books on May 1, December 31, and the maturity date.
3. What is the effective interest rate on the note?

Exercise 7-14 *Credit Card Sales* **LO 7**

Darlene's Diner accepts American Express credit cards from its customers. Darlene's is closed on Sundays and on that day records the weekly sales and remits the credit card drafts to American Express. For the week ending on Sunday, June 12, cash sales totaled $2,430, and credit card sales amounted to $3,500. On June 15, Darlene's received $3,360 from American Express as payment for the credit card drafts. Prepare the necessary journal entries on Darlene's books on June 12 and June 15. As a percentage, what collection fee is American Express charging Darlene?

Exercise 7-15 *Impact of Transactions Involving Receivables on Statement of Cash Flows* **LO 8**

From the following list, identify whether the change in the account balance during the year would be added to or deducted from net income when the indirect method is used to determine cash flows from operating activities.

_______ Increase in accounts receivable
_______ Decrease in accounts receivable
_______ Increase in notes receivable
_______ Decrease in notes receivable

Exercise 7-16 *Cash Collections—Direct Method* **LO 8**

Emily Enterprises' comparative balance sheets included accounts receivable of $224,600 at December 31, 2003, and $205,700 at December 31, 2004. Sales reported on Emily's 2004 income statement amounted to $2,250,000. What is the amount of cash collections that Emily will report in the Operating Activities category of its 2004 statement of cash flows assuming that the direct method is used?

Multi-Concept Exercises

Exercise 7-17 *Composition of Cash* **LO 1, 2, 3**

Using a Y for yes or an N for no, indicate whether each of the following items should be included in cash and cash equivalents on the balance sheet. If an item should not be included in cash and cash equivalents, indicate where it should appear on the balance sheet.

_______ **1.** Checking account at Third County Bank
_______ **2.** Petty cash fund
_______ **3.** Coin and currency
_______ **4.** Postage stamps
_______ **5.** An IOU from an employee
_______ **6.** Savings account at the Ft. Worth Savings & Loan
_______ **7.** A six-month CD
_______ **8.** Undeposited customer checks
_______ **9.** A customer's check returned by the bank and marked NSF
_______ **10.** Sixty-day U.S. Treasury bills
_______ **11.** A cashier's check

Exercise 7-18 *Classification of Cash Equivalents and Investments on a Balance Sheet* **LO 1, 3**

Classify each of the following items as either a cash equivalent (CE), a short-term investment (STI), or a long-term investment (LTI).

_______ **1.** A 120-day certificate of deposit.
_______ **2.** Three hundred shares of GM common stock. The company plans on selling the stock in six months.
_______ **3.** A six-month U.S. Treasury bill.
_______ **4.** A 60-day certificate of deposit.
_______ **5.** Ford Motor Co. bonds maturing in 15 years. The company intends to hold the bonds until maturity.
_______ **6.** Commercial paper issued by ABC Corp., maturing in four months.

_______ **7.** Five hundred shares of Chrysler common stock. The company plans to sell the stock in 60 days to help pay for a note due at that time at the bank.

_______ **8.** Two hundred shares of GE preferred stock. The company intends to hold the stock for 10 years and at that point sell it to help finance construction of a new factory.

_______ **9.** Ten-year U.S. Treasury bonds. The company plans to sell the bonds on the open market in six months.

_______ **10.** A 90-day U.S. Treasury bill.

Exercise 7-19 ***Cash Equivalents*** **LO 1, 3, 8**

Systematic Enterprises invested its excess cash in the following instruments during December 2004:

Certificate of deposit, due January 31, 2007	$ 75,000
Certificate of deposit, due March 30, 2005	150,000
Commercial paper, original maturity date February 28, 2005	125,000
Deposit into a money market fund	25,000
Investment in stock	65,000
90-day Treasury bills	100,000
Treasury note, due December 1, 2034	500,000

Required

Determine the amount of cash equivalents which should be combined with cash on the company's balance sheet at December 31, 2004, and for purposes of preparing a statement of cash flows for the year ended December 31, 2004.

Exercise 7-20 ***Impact of Transactions Involving Cash and Receivables on Statement of Cash Flows*** **LO 1, 8**

From the following list, identify each item as operating (O), investing (I), financing (F), or not separately reported on the statement of cash flows (N). Assume that the indirect method is used to determine the cash flows from operating activities.

_______ Purchase of cash equivalents

_______ Redemption of cash equivalents

_______ Purchase of available-for-sale securities

_______ Sale of available-for-sale securities

_______ Replenishment of the petty cash fund

_______ Write-off of customer account (under the allowance method)

Problems

Problem 7-1 ***Bank Reconciliation and Journal Entries*** **LO 2**

The following information is available to assist you in preparing a bank reconciliation for Calico Corners on May 31, 2004:

a. The balance on the May 31, 2004, bank statement is $8,432.11.

b. Not included on the bank statement is a $1,250.00 deposit made by Calico Corners late on May 31.

c. A comparison between the canceled checks returned with the bank statement and the company records indicated that the following checks are outstanding at May 31:

No. 123	$ 23.40
No. 127	145.00
No. 128	210.80
No. 130	67.32

d. The Cash account on the company's books shows a balance of $9,965.34.

e. The bank acts as a collection agency for interest earned on some municipal bonds held by Calico Corners. The May bank statement indicates interest of $465.00 earned during the month.

(continued)

f. Interest earned on the checking account and added to Calico Corners' account during May was $54.60. Miscellaneous bank service charges amounted to $50.00.

g. A customer's NSF check in the amount of $166.00 was returned with the May bank statement.

h. A comparison between the deposits listed on the bank statement and the company's books revealed that a customer's check in the amount of $123.45 was recorded on the books during May but was never added to the company's account. The bank erroneously added the check to the account of Calico Closet, which has an account at the same bank.

i. The comparison of deposits per the bank statement with those per the books revealed that another customer's check in the amount of $101.10 was correctly added to the company's account. In recording the check on the company's books, however, the accountant erroneously increased the Cash account $1,011.00.

Required

1. Prepare a bank reconciliation in good form.
2. Prepare the necessary journal entries on the books of Calico Corners.
3. A friend says to you: "I don't know why companies bother to prepare bank reconciliations—it seems a waste of time. Why don't they just do like I do and adjust the cash account for any difference between what the bank shows as a balance and what shows up in the books?" Explain to your friend *why* a bank reconciliation should be prepared as soon as a bank statement is received.

Problem 7-2 ***The Effect of Petty Cash on Cash and Income*** **LO 2**

ABC Company established a petty cash fund in the amount of $500. One month later, it replenished the fund based on the following receipts:

a. $40, postage due on computer supplies used in the administrative offices

b. $5.80, postage stamps used by the president when she is on the road and without access to the postage meter

c. $180, advertising fliers to be used by the marketing department and sent COD to the company

d. $95, office supplies purchased at a local store for use in the administrative offices

Required

1. Prepare the journal entry to establish the petty cash fund. Cash on hand at the end of the first month is $174. Do you believe that the $500 amount was an appropriate amount for ABC's petty cash fund? Explain.
2. Prepare the journal entry to replenish the petty cash fund at the end of the month. What is the effect of this entry on the total assets of the company? on income?
3. Explain why a petty cash fund is allowed even though proper accounting control over cash requires that all payments be made by check.

GENERAL LEDGER

Problem 7-3 ***Investments in Bonds and Stock*** **LO 3**

Swartz Inc. enters into the following transactions during 2004:

July 1	Paid $10,000 to acquire on the open market $10,000 face value of Gallatin bonds. The bonds have a stated annual interest rate of 6% with interest paid semiannually on June 30 and December 31. The bonds mature in $5^1/_2$ years.
Oct. 23	Purchased 600 shares of Eagle Rock common stock at $20 per share.
Nov. 21	Purchased 200 shares of Montana preferred stock at $30 per share.
Dec. 10	Received dividends of $1.50 per share on the Eagle Rock stock and $2.00 per share on the Montana stock.
Dec. 28	Sold 400 shares of Eagle Rock common stock at $25 per share.
Dec. 31	Received interest from the Gallatin bonds.
Dec. 31	Noted market price of $29 per share for the Eagle Rock stock and $26 per share for the Montana stock.

Required

1. Prepare all necessary journal entries on Swartz's records to account for its investments during 2004. Swartz classifies the bonds as held-to-maturity securities and all stock investments as trading securities.

2. Prepare a partial balance sheet as of December 31, 2004, to indicate the proper presentation of the investments.
3. Indicate the items, and the amount of each, that will appear on the 2004 income statement relative to the investments.

Problem 7-4 ***Investments in Stock*** **LO 3**

Atlas Superstores occasionally finds itself with excess cash to invest and consequently entered into the following transactions during 2004:

Jan. 15	Purchased 200 shares of Sears common stock at $50 per share, plus $500 in commissions.
May 23	Received dividends of $2 per share on the Sears stock.
June 1	Purchased 100 shares of Ford Motor Co. stock at $74 per share, plus $300 in commissions.
Oct. 20	Sold all the Sears stock at $42 per share, less commissions of $400.
Dec. 15	Received notification from Ford Motor Co. that a $1.50 per share dividend had been declared. The checks will be mailed to stockholders on January 10, 2005.
Dec. 31	Noted that the Ford Motor Co. stock was quoted on the stock exchange at $85 per share.

Required

1. Prepare journal entries on the books of Atlas Superstores during 2004 to record these transactions, including any necessary entry on December 15, when the dividend was declared, and at the end of the year. Assume that Atlas categorizes all investments as available-for-sale securities.
2. What is the total amount that Atlas should report on its income statement from its investments during 2004?
3. Assume all the same facts except that Atlas categorizes all investments as trading securities. How would your answer to part **2** change? Explain why your answer would change.

Problem 7-5 ***Allowance Method for Accounting for Bad Debts*** **LO 4**

At the beginning of 2004, EZ Tech Company's Accounts Receivable balance was $140,000, and the balance in the Allowance for Doubtful Accounts was $2,350 (cr.). EZ Tech's sales in 2004 were $1,050,000, 80% of which were on credit. Collections on account during the year were $670,000. The company wrote off $4,000 of uncollectible accounts during the year.

Required

1. Prepare summary journal entries related to the sale, collections, and write-offs of accounts receivable during 2004.
2. Prepare journal entries to recognize bad debts assuming (a) bad debt expense is 3% of credit sales and (b) amounts expected to be uncollectible are 6% of the year-end accounts receivable.
3. What is the net realizable value of accounts receivable on December 31, 2004, under each assumption (**a** and **b**) in **2**?
4. What effect does the recognition of bad debt expense have on the net realizable value? What effect does the write-off of accounts have on the net realizable value?

Problem 7-6 ***Aging Schedule to Account for Bad Debts*** **LO 4**

SPREADSHEET

Sparkle Jewels distributes fine stones. It sells on credit to retail jewelry stores and extends terms of 2/10, net 60. For accounts that are not overdue, Sparkle has found that there is a 95% probability of collection. For accounts up to one month past due, the likelihood of collection decreases to 80%. If accounts are between one and two months past due, the probability of collection is 60%, and if an account is more than two months past due, Sparkle Jewels estimates that there is only a 40% chance of collecting the receivable.

On December 31, 2004, the credit balance in Allowance for Doubtful Accounts is $12,300. The amounts of gross receivables, by age, on this date are as follows:

(continued)

Category	Amount
Current	$200,000
Past due:	
Less than one month	45,000
One to two months	25,000
More than two months	10,000

Required

1. Prepare a schedule to estimate the amount of uncollectible accounts at December 31, 2004.
2. On the basis of the schedule in part **1,** prepare the journal entry on December 31, 2004, to estimate bad debts.
3. Show how accounts receivable would be presented on the December 31, 2004, balance sheet.

Problem 7-7 ***Accounts Receivable Turnover for Whirlpool and Maytag*** **LO 4**

http://www.whirlpool.com

The following information was summarized from the 2001 annual report of Whirlpool Corporation:

	(in millions)
Trade receivables, less allowances	
(2001: $93; 2000: $103)	
December 31, 2001	$ 1,515
December 31, 2000	1,748
Net sales for the year ended December 31:	
2001	10,343
2000	10,325

http://www.maytag.com

The following information was summarized from the 2001 annual report of Maytag Corporation:

	(in thousands)
Accounts receivable, less allowance for doubtful accounts (2001–$24,121; 2000–$15,583):	
December 31, 2001	$ 618,101
December 31, 2000	476,211
Net sales for the year ended:	
December 31, 2001	4,323,713
December 31, 2000	3,994,918

Required

1. Calculate the accounts receivable turnover ratios for Whirlpool and Maytag for 2001.
2. Calculate the average collection period, in days, for both companies for 2001. Comment on the reasonableness of the collection periods considering the types of companies that you would expect to be customers of Whirlpool and Maytag.
3. Which company appears to be performing better? What other information should you consider to determine how these companies are performing in this regard?

Problem 7-8 ***Non-Interest-Bearing Note Receivable*** **LO 6**

Northern Nursery sells a large stock of trees and shrubs to a landscaping business on May 31, 2004. The landscaper makes a down payment of $5,000 and signs a promissory note agreeing to pay $20,000 on August 29, 2004, the end of its busy season. The cash selling price of the nursery stock on May 31 was $24,000.

Required

1. Prepare the appropriate journal entry on Northern's books on each of the following dates:
   - **a.** May 31, 2004, to record the receipt of the down payment and the promissory note
   - **b.** June 30, 2004, the end of Northern's fiscal year
   - **c.** August 29, 2004, to record collection of the note
2. Compute the effective rate of interest earned by Northern on the note. Explain your answer.

Problem 7-9 ***Credit Card Sales*** **LO 7**

Gas stations sometimes sell gasoline at a lower price to customers who pay cash than to customers who use a charge card. A local gas station owner pays 2% of the sales price to the credit card company when customers pay with a credit card. He pays $0.75 per gallon of gasoline and must earn at least $0.25 per gallon of gross margin to stay competitive.

Required

1. Determine the price the owner must charge credit card customers to maintain his gross margin.
2. How much discount could the owner offer to cash customers and still maintain the same gross margin?

Problem 7-10 ***Effects of Changes in Receivable Balances on Statement of Cash Flows*** **LO 8**

Stegner Inc. reported net income of $130,000 for the year ended December 31, 2004. The following items were included on Stegner's balance sheets at December 31, 2004 and 2003:

	12/31/04	12/31/03
Cash	$105,000	$110,000
Accounts receivable	223,000	83,000
Notes receivable	95,000	100,000

Stegner uses the indirect method to prepare its statement of cash flows. Stegner does not have any other current assets or current liabilities and did not enter into any investing or financing activities during 2004.

Required

1. Prepare Stegner's 2004 statement of cash flows.
2. Draft a brief memo to the owner to explain why cash decreased during a profitable year.

Multi-Concept Problems

Problem 7-11 ***Cash and Liquid Assets on the Balance Sheet*** **LO 1, 3**

The following accounts are listed in a company's general ledger. The accountant wants to place the items in order of liquidity on the balance sheet.

Accounts receivable
Certificates of deposit (six months)
Trading securities
Prepaid rent
Money market fund
Cash in drawers

Required

Rank the accounts in terms of liquidity. Identify items to be included in the total of cash, and explain why the items not included in cash on the balance sheet are not as liquid as cash. Explain how these items should be classified.

Problem 7-12 ***Accounts and Notes Receivable*** **LO 4, 5**

GENERAL LEDGER

Linus Corp. sold merchandise for $5,000 to C. Brown on May 15, 2004, with credit terms of net 30. Subsequent to this, Brown experienced cash flow problems and was unable to pay its debt. On August 10, 2004, Linus stopped trying to collect the outstanding receivable from Brown and wrote the account off as uncollectible. On December 1, 2004, Brown sent Linus a check for $1,000 and offered to sign a two-month, 9%, $4,000 promissory note to satisfy the remaining obligation. Brown paid the entire amount due Linus, with interest, on January 31, 2005. Linus ends its accounting year on December 31 each year, and uses the allowance method to account for bad debts.

Required

1. Prepare all of the necessary journal entries on the books of Linus Corp. from May 15, 2004, to January 31, 2005.

(continued)

2. Why would Brown bother to send Linus a check for $1,000 on December 1 and agree to sign a note for the balance, given that such a long period of time had passed since the original purchase?

Alternate Problems

Problem 7-1A ***Bank Reconciliation*** **LO 2**

The following information is available to assist you in preparing a bank reconciliation for Karen's Catering on March 31, 2004:

a. The balance on the March 31, 2004, bank statement is $6,506.10.

b. Not included on the bank statement is a deposit made by Karen's late on March 31 in the amount of $423.00.

c. A comparison between the canceled checks listed on the bank statement and the company records indicated that the following checks are outstanding at March 31:

No. 112	$ 42.92
No. 117	307.00
No. 120	10.58
No. 122	75.67

d. The bank acts as a collection agency for checks returned for insufficient funds. The March bank statement indicates that one such check in the amount of $45.00 was collected and deposited and a collection fee of $4.50 was charged.

e. Interest earned on the checking account and credited to Karen's account during March was $4.30. Miscellaneous bank service charges amounted to $22.00.

f. A comparison between the deposits listed on the bank statement and the company's books revealed that a customer's check in the amount of $1,250.00 appears on the bank statement in March but was never credited to the customer's account on the company's books.

g. The comparison of checks cleared per the bank statement with those per the books revealed that the wrong amount was charged to the company's account for a check. The amount of the check was $990.00. The proof machine encoded the check in the amount of $909.00, the amount charged against the company's account.

Required

1. Determine the balance on the books before any adjustments as well as the corrected balance to be reported on the balance sheet.
2. What would you recommend Karen do as a result of the bank error in item **g** above? Why?

Problem 7-2A ***The Effect of Petty Cash on Cash and Income*** **LO 2**

Arlington Inc. established a petty cash fund in the amount of $50. One month later, it replenished the fund based on the following receipts:

a. $4, postage due on computer supplies purchased for the administrative offices

b. $5.80, postage stamps used by the receptionist so that he does not need to leave his desk to use the postage meter

c. $18, a cake for the secretary's birthday

d. $20, materials purchased at a local store for use by the sales staff

Required

1. Prepare the journal entry to establish the petty cash fund. Cash on hand at the end of the month is $1.15. Do you believe that the $50 amount was an appropriate amount for Arlington's petty cash fund? Explain.
2. Prepare the journal entry to replenish the petty cash fund at the end of the month. What is the effect of this entry on the total assets of the company? on income?
3. Who should oversee the petty cash fund? Write a short description of how the process should be handled in the company.

Problem 7-3A ***Investments in Bonds and Stock*** **LO 3**

GENERAL LEDGER

Vermont Corp. enters into the following transactions during 2004:

July 1	Paid $10,000 to acquire on the open market $10,000 face value of Maine bonds. The bonds have a stated annual interest rate of 8% with interest paid semiannually on June 30 and December 31. The remaining life of the bonds on the date of purchase is 3½ years.
Oct. 23	Purchased 1,000 shares of Virginia common stock at $15 per share.
Nov. 21	Purchased 600 shares of Carolina preferred stock at $8 per share.
Dec. 10	Received dividends of $.50 per share on the Virginia stock and $1.00 per share on the Carolina stock.
Dec. 28	Sold 700 shares of Virginia common stock at $19 per share.
Dec. 31	Received interest from the Maine bonds.
Dec. 31	The Virginia Stock and the Carolina stock have market prices of $20 per share and $11 per share, respectively.

Required

1. Prepare all necessary journal entries on Vermont's records to account for its investments during 2004. Vermont classifies the bonds as held-to-maturity securities and all stock investments as trading securities.
2. Prepare a partial balance sheet as of December 31, 2004, to indicate the proper presentation of the investments.
3. Indicate the items, and the amount of each, that will appear on the 2004 income statement relative to the investments.

Problem 7-4A ***Investments in Stock*** **LO 3**

Trendy Supercenter occasionally finds itself with excess cash to invest and consequently entered into the following transactions during 2004:

Jan. 15	Purchased 100 shares of IBM common stock at $130 per share, plus $250 in commissions.
May 23	Received dividends of $1 per share on the IBM stock.
June 1	Purchased 200 shares of General Motors stock at $60 per share, plus $300 in commissions.
Oct. 20	Sold all of the IBM stock at $140 per share, less commissions of $400.
Dec. 15	Received notification from General Motors that a $0.75 per share dividend had been declared. The checks will be mailed to stockholders on January 10, 2005.
Dec. 31	Noted that the General Motors stock was quoted on the stock exchange at $45 per share.

Required

1. Prepare journal entries on the books of Trendy Supercenter during 2004 to record these transactions, including any necessary entry on December 15 when the dividend was declared and at the end of the year. Assume that Trendy categorizes all investments as available-for-sale securities.
2. What is the total amount of income that Trendy should recognize from its investments during 2004?
3. Assume all of the same facts except that Trendy categorizes all investments as trading securities. How would your answer to part **2** change? Explain why your answer would change.

Problem 7-5A ***Allowance Method for Accounting for Bad Debts*** **LO 4**

At the beginning of 2004, Miyazaki Company's Accounts Receivable balance was $105,000 and the balance in the Allowance for Doubtful Accounts was $1,950 (cr.). Miyazaki's sales in 2004 were $787,500, 80% of which were on credit. Collections on account during the year were $502,500. The company wrote off $3,000 of uncollectible accounts during the year.

(continued)

Required

1. Prepare summary journal entries related to the sales, collections, and write-offs of accounts receivable during 2004.
2. Prepare journal entries to recognize bad debts assuming (a) bad debt expense is 3% of credit sales or (b) amounts expected to be uncollectible are 6% of the year-end accounts receivable.
3. What is the net realizable value of accounts receivable on December 31, 2004, under each assumption (**a** and **b**) in **2?**
4. What effect does the recognition of bad debt expense have on the net realizable value? What effect does the write-off of accounts have on the net realizable value?

SPREADSHEET

Problem 7-6A ***Aging Schedule to Account for Bad Debts*** **LO 4**

Rough Stuff is a distributor of large rocks. It sells on credit to commercial landscaping companies and extends terms of 2/10, net 60. For accounts that are not overdue, Rough has found that there is a 90% probability of collection. For accounts up to one month past due, the likelihood of collection decreases to 75%. If accounts are between one and two months past due, the probability of collection is 65%, and if an account is more than two months past due, Rough estimates that there is only a 25% chance of collecting the receivable.

On December 31, 2004, the credit balance in Allowance for Doubtful Accounts is $34,590. The amounts of gross receivables, by age, on this date are as follows:

Category	Amount
Current	$135,000
Past due:	
Less than one month	60,300
One to two months	35,000
More than two months	45,000

Required

1. Prepare a schedule to estimate the amount of uncollectible accounts at December 31, 2004.
2. Rough knows that $40,000 of the $45,000 amount that is more than two months overdue is due from one customer that is in severe financial trouble. It is rumored that the customer will be filing for bankruptcy in the near future. As controller for Rough Stuff, how would you handle this situation?
3. Show how accounts receivable would be presented on the December 31, 2004, balance sheet.

Problem 7-7A ***Accounts Receivable Turnover for Boise Cascade and Georgia-Pacific Corporation*** **LO 4**

http://www.boisecascade.com

The following information was summarized from the 2001 annual report of Boise Cascade Corporation and Subsidiaries (receivables are net of allowances):

	(in thousands)
Receivables, December 31:	
2001	$ 424,722
2000	671,793
Sales for the year ended December 31:	
2001	7,422,175
2000	7,806,657

http://www.gp.com

The following information was summarized from the 2001 annual report of Georgia-Pacific Corporation (receivables are net of allowances):

	(in millions)
Receivables:	
December 29, 2001	$ 2,352
December 30, 2000	2,704
Net sales for the year ended:	
December 29, 2001	25,016
December 30, 2000	22,050

Required

1. Calculate the accounts receivable turnover ratios for Boise Cascade and Georgia-Pacific for 2001.
2. Calculate the average collection period, in days, for both companies for 2001. Comment on the reasonableness of the collection periods considering the types of companies that you would expect to be customers of Boise Cascade and Georgia-Pacific.
3. Which company appears to be performing better? What other information should you consider to determine how these companies are performing in this regard?

Problem 7-8A ***Non-Interest-Bearing Note Receivable*** **LO 6**

Midwest Poultry sells a large stock of birds to a processor on May 31, 2004. The processor makes a $12,000 down payment and signs a $36,900 promissory note agreeing to pay the remainder on August 29, 2004, the end of its busy season. The cash selling price of the birds on May 31 was $48,000.

1. Prepare the appropriate journal entry on Midwest's books on August 29, 2004, to record collection of the note. Midwest's accounting year ends on September 30.
2. Compute the effective rate of interest earned by Midwest on the note. Explain your answer.

Problem 7-9A ***Credit Card Sales*** **LO 7**

A local fast-food store is considering the use of major credit cards in its outlets. Current annual sales are $800,000 per outlet. The company can purchase the equipment needed to handle credit cards and have an additional phone line installed in each outlet for approximately $800 per outlet. The equipment will be an expense in the year it is installed. The employee training time is minimal. The credit card company will charge a fee equal to 1.5% of sales for the use of credit cards. The company is unable to determine by how much, if any, sales will increase and whether cash customers will use a credit card rather than cash. No other fast-food stores in the local area accept credit cards for sales payment.

Required

1. Assuming only 5% of existing cash customers will use a credit card, what increase in sales is necessary to pay for the credit card equipment in the first year?
2. What other factors might the company consider in addition to an increase in sales dollars?

Problem 7-10A ***Effects of Changes in Receivable Balances on Statement of Cash Flows*** **LO 8**

St. Charles Antique Market reported a net loss of $6,000 for the year ended December 31, 2004. The following items were included on St. Charles Antique Market's balance sheets at December 31, 2004 and 2003:

	12/31/04	12/31/03
Cash	$ 36,300	$ 3,100
Accounts receivable	79,000	126,000
Notes receivable	112,600	104,800

St. Charles Antique Market uses the indirect method to prepare its statement of cash flows. St. Charles Antique Market does not have any other current assets or current liabilities and did not enter into any investing or financing activities during 2004.

Required

1. Prepare St. Charles Antique Market's 2004 statement of cash flows.
2. Draft a brief memo to the owner to explain why cash increased during such an unprofitable year.

Alternate Multi-Concept Problems

Problem 7-11A ***Cash and Liquid Assets on the Balance Sheet*** **LO 1, 3**

The following accounts are listed in a company's general ledger:

(continued)

	December 31, 2004	December 31, 2003
Accounts receivable	$12,300	$10,000
Certificates of deposit (three months)	10,000	10,000
Marketable securities	4,500	4,000
Prepaid rent	1,200	1,500
Money market fund	25,800	28,000
Cash in checking account	6,000	6,000

Required

1. Which items are cash equivalents?
2. Explain where items that are not cash equivalents should be classified on the balance sheet.
3. What are the amount and the direction of change in cash and cash equivalents for 2004? Is the company as liquid at the end of 2004 as it was at the end of 2003? Explain your answer.

GENERAL LEDGER

Problem 7-12A ***Accounts and Notes Receivable*** **LO 4, 5**

Tweedy Inc. sold merchandise for $6,000 to P.D. Cat on July 31, 2004, with credit terms of net 30. Subsequent to this, Cat experienced cash flow problems and was unable to pay its debt. On December 24, 2004, Tweedy stopped trying to collect the outstanding receivable from Cat and wrote the account off as uncollectible. On January 15, 2005, Cat sent Tweedy a check for $1,500 and offered to sign a two-month, 8%, $4,500 promissory note to satisfy the remaining obligation. Cat paid the entire amount on the note due Tweedy, with interest, on March 15, 2005. Tweedy ends its accounting year on December 31 each year.

Required

1. Prepare all of the necessary journal entries on the books of Tweedy Inc. from July 31, 2004, to March 15, 2005.
2. Why would Cat bother to send Tweedy a check for $1,500 on January 15 and agree to sign a note for the balance, given that such a long period of time had passed since the original purchase?

Cases

Reading and Interpreting Financial Statements

Case 7-1 ***Reading and Interpreting Winnebago Industries' Financial Statements*** **LO 4**

Refer to the financial statements for 2001 included in Winnebago Industries' annual report. Answer each of the following questions by reference to the account titled "Receivables" rather than the one titled "Dealer Financing Receivables."

Required

1. What is the balance in the Allowance for Doubtful Accounts at the end of each of the two years presented? What is the net realizable value at the end of each year?
2. Calculate the ratio of the Allowance for Doubtful Accounts to Gross Accounts Receivable at the end of each of the two years.
3. Why do you think the balance in the Allowance for Doubtful Accounts was decreased at the end of 2001? Does this mean that the company expects a lesser percentage of bad debts?

Case 7-2 ***Comparing Two Companies in the Same Industry: Winnebago Industries and Monaco Coach Corporation*** **LO 4**

http://www.winnebagoind.com
http://www.monacocoach.com

Refer to the financial statement information of Winnebago Industries and Monaco Coach Corporation in Appendices A and B at the end of the text. Answer the questions below with reference to the account titled "Receivables" for Winnebago Industries and the account titled "Trade Receivables" of Monaco Coach.

1. What is the balance of the Allowance for Doubtful Accounts at the end of each of the two years presented for Monaco Coach? What is the net realizable value at the end of each year?
2. Calculate the ratio of the Allowance for Doubtful Accounts to Gross Receivable at the end of each of the two years for Monaco Coach. How do these ratios compare to those for Winnebago Industries? What does the comparison tell you about the receivables of the two

companies? (Refer to your answers to requirement **2** in Case 7-1 for the Winnebago Industries information.)

3. Monaco Coach had an increase in Trade Receivables from 2000 to 2001. What are logical explanations for this increase?
4. Calculate the receivables turnover for Winnebago Industries and Monaco Coach for the year 2001? Compare the two companies on the basis of this ratio.

Case 7-3 *Reading PepsiCo's Notes* LO 4

The following note was included in PepsiCo's 2001 annual report (all amounts are in millions of dollars):

http://www.pepsico.com

Note 6—Accounts and Notes Receivable, net

	2001	2000	1999
Trade receivables	$1,663	$1,613	
Receivables from affiliates	171	190	
Other receivables	429	452	
	2,263	2,255	
Allowance, beginning of year	$ 126	$ 109	$ 148
Charged to expense	41	42	32
Other additions	2	8	5
Deductions	(48)	(33)	(76)
Allowance, end of year	121	126	$ 109
Net receivables	$2,142	$2,129	

Other additions include acquisitions, currency translation effects and reclassifications. Deductions include the impact of the bottling transactions, accounts written off and currency translation effects.

Required:

1. Based on year-end balances for both 2001 and 2000, compute the ratio of the allowance account to the gross receivables. Did this ratio increase or decrease in 2001 compared to 2000?
2. What was the amount of bad debts expense for each of the two years, 2001 and 2000? Which of the lines shown in the note contains the amounts of accounts written off in each of the years?
3. What is the net realizable value of the company's receivables at the end of each of the two years? Where will these amounts appear on the financial statements?
4. Can you tell from the information given in the note which of the two basic methods PepsiCo uses to estimate bad debts?

Making Financial Decisions

Case 7-4 *Liquidity* LO 1, 2

R Montague and J Capulet both distribute films to movie theaters. The following are the current assets for each at the end of the year (all amounts are in millions of dollars):

DECISION MAKING

	R Montague	J Capulet
Cash	$10	$ 5
Six-month certificates of deposit	9	0
Short-term investments in stock	0	6
Accounts receivable	15	23
Allowance for doubtful accounts	(1)	(1)
Total current assets	$33	$33

Required

As a loan officer for the First National Bank of Verona Heights, assume that both companies have come to you asking for a $10 million, six-month loan. If you could lend money to only one of the two, which one would it be? Justify your answer by writing a brief memo to the president of the bank.

DECISION MAKING

Case 7-5 *Notes Receivable* LO 5, 6

Warren Land Development is considering two offers for a lot. Builder A has offered to pay $12,000 down and sign a 10%, $80,000 promissory note, with interest and principal due in one year. Builder B would make a down payment of $20,000 and sign a non-interest-bearing, one-year note for $80,000. The president believes that the deal with Builder A is better because it involves interest and the loan to Builder B does not. The vice president of marketing thinks the offer from Builder B is better because it involves more money "up front." The sales manager is indifferent, reasoning that both builders would eventually pay $100,000 in total and that because the lot was recently appraised at $75,000, both would be paying more than fair market value.

Required

1. Regardless of which offer it accepts, how much revenue should Warren recognize from the sale of the lot? Explain your answer.
2. Which offer do you think Warren should accept? Or is the sales manager correct that it doesn't matter which one is accepted? Explain your answer.

Accounting and Ethics: What Would You Do?

Case 7-6 *Fair Market Values for Investments* LO 3

Kennedy Corp. operates a chain of discount stores. The company regularly holds stock of various companies in a trading securities portfolio. One of these investments is 10,000 shares of Clean Air Inc. stock purchased for $100 per share during December 2004.

Clean Air manufactures highly specialized equipment used to test automobile emissions. Unfortunately, the market price of Clean Air's stock dropped during December 2004 and closed the year trading at $75 per share. Kennedy expects the Clean Air stock to experience a turn around, however, as states pass legislation to require an emissions test on all automobiles.

As controller for Kennedy, you have followed the fortunes of Clean Air with particular interest. You and the company's treasurer are both concerned by the negative impact that a write-down of the stock to fair value would have on Kennedy's earnings for 2004. You have calculated net income for 2004 to be $400,000, exclusive of the recognition of any loss on the stock.

The treasurer comes to you on January 31, 2005, with the following idea:

> Since you haven't closed the books yet for 2004, and we haven't yet released the 2004 financials, let's think carefully about how Clean Air should be classified. I realize that we normally treat these types of investments as trading securities, but if we categorize the Clean Air stock on the balance sheet as available-for-sale rather than a trading security, we won't need to report the adjustment to fair value on the income statement. I don't see anything wrong with this since we would still report the stock at its fair value on the balance sheet.

Required

1. Compute Kennedy's net income for 2004, under two different assumptions: (a) the stock is classified as a trading security and (b) the stock is classified as an available-for-sale security.
2. Which classification do you believe is appropriate, according to accounting standards? Explain your answer.
3. Would you have any ethical concerns in following the treasurer's advice? Explain your answer.

Case 7-7 *Notes Receivable* LO 6

Patterson Company is a large diversified business with a unit that sells commercial real estate. As a company, Patterson has been profitable in recent years with the exception of the real estate business, where economic conditions have resulted in weak sales. The vice president of the real estate division is aware of the poor performance of his group and needs to find ways to "show a profit."

During the current year the division is successful in selling a 100-acre tract of land for a new shopping center. The original cost of the property to Patterson was $4 million. The buyer has agreed to sign a $10 million note with payments of $2 million due at the end of each of the next five years. The property was appraised late last year at a market value of $7.5 million. The vice president has come to you, the controller, and asked that you record the sale as follows:

Notes Receivable	10,000,000	
Sales Revenue		10,000,000
To record sale of 100-acre tract.		

Required

1. Does the entry suggested by the vice president to record the sale violate any accounting principle? If so, explain the principle it violates.
2. What would you do? Write a brief memo to the vice president explaining the proper accounting for the sale.

Internet Research Case

Case 7-8 *PepsiCo*

PepsiCo, the number two soft drink maker in the world with major products in snack foods as well, is undergoing changes that it believes will respond to major changes in the grocery business, its biggest customer.

To answer the following questions, examine the chapter opening text and the financial statements shown in Chapter 7, read the Business Strategy box that details the changes occurring at PepsiCo in 2001, and access its Web site to focus on both the company and its latest financial information.

INTERNET

http://www.pepsico.com

1. What are the cash and cash equivalents for PepsiCo for the latest year available?
2. What reason does the company give for the change in cash and equivalents for the most recent year available?
3. What are the short-term investments for the latest year available?
4. What reasons does the company give for the change in short-term investments for the latest year available?
5. What are accounts and notes receivable for the latest year available? Can you tell from the notes how much was for accounts receivable and how much for notes receivable?
6. Comparing the latest annual report with the financial information from 2001 in the textbook, what are the three most significant changes to the financial statements? What is the most significant change to PepsiCo as a company?

Solutions to Key Terms Quiz

Quiz 1: Cash and Investments

- 2 Cash equivalent (p. 325)
- 8 Bank statement (p. 327)
- 6 Outstanding check (p. 328)
- 4 Deposit in transit (p. 328)
- 9 Bank reconciliation (p. 328)
- 1 Credit memoranda (p. 329)
- 3 Debit memoranda (p. 329)
- 10 Petty cash fund (p. 331)
- 5 Equity securities (p. 333)
- 7 Debt securities (p. 333)
- 13 Held-to-maturity securities (p. 336)
- 11 Trading securities (p. 336)
- 12 Available-for-sale securities (p. 336)

Quiz 2: Receivables

- 12 Subsidiary ledger (p. 344)
- 15 Control account (p. 344)
- 14 Direct write-off method (p. 345)
- 1 Allowance method (p. 345)
- 10 Aging schedule (p. 348)
- 3 Promissory note (p. 350)
- 8 Maker (p. 350)
- 2 Payee (p. 350)
- 6 Note receivable (p. 351)
- 4 Note payable (p. 351)
- 16 Principal (p. 351)
- 17 Maturity date (p. 351)
- 18 Term (p. 351)
- 19 Maturity value (p. 351)
- 20 Interest (p. 351)
- 9 Interest-bearing note (p. 351)
- 13 Non-interest-bearing note (p. 351)
- 11 Discounted note (p. 353)
- 5 Credit card draft (p. 354)
- 7 Discounting (p. 355)

Chapter 8

Operating Assets: Property, Plant, and Equipment, Natural Resources, and Intangibles

Roadmap to Success

Focus on Financial Results

The merger of AOL and Time Warner has produced a media giant that markets information and entertainment in virtually every medium. The strength of such brands as CNN, TNT, the Cartoon Network, HBO, Time-Life, *People, Time,* and *Sports Illustrated;* of recording artists such as Missy Elliot, Sugar Ray, Linkin Park, Enya, Uncle Kracker, Stevie Nicks, and Eden's Crush; and of film and TV hits such as *The Matrix, Lord of the Rings,* and *The West Wing* have made the company influential in almost every media market. In fact, the company reported a total of more than 137 million subscribers to the AOL Time Warner cable division and to its on-line services as of 2001.

The economic slowdown in 2001 and the post-merger time period have proved challenging for the company. The company's reported net loss for the third quarter of 2001 alone was $996 million, or $0.22 per share, including $134 million in merger related expenses and $196 million in pre-tax non-cash charges reflecting the write-down of certain investments in the AOL Time Warner investment portfolio. As a result, its stock price has declined from its highest selling price after the merger. However, the company feels that the diversity of their offerings and their appeal to a wide audience will lead to a profitable future in the long run. For sustainable growth, the firm will leverage its tangible assets of *property, plant,* and *equipment* and natural resources into new profit opportunities. But *intangibles,* like the company's potent brand names, are probably its most important assets. In fact, the AOL brand name is widely recognized as one of the most important brand names in the U.S. economy, and the company has stated that its management has a mastery of what it takes to originate brands that turn into sources of growth and profit. The importance of intangible assets cannot be overstated for a media company, or for many other companies where technology plays an important role.

Investors must be able to read AOL Time Warner's financial statements and understand how their assests influence the value of the company. Those investor decisions have a major impact on the company's stock price. Hopefully, the stock price accurately reflects the value of the company's assets and the company's ability to use those assets wisely. But it is always difficult to gauge the value of intangible assets and to know how long those assets will last. Accountants have had to consider carefully the proper accounting for all long-lived assets, but especially how to account for intangible assets in a company such as AOL Time Warner.

Source: AOL Time Warner's press release and financial statements of third quarter, 2001.

http://www.aoltimewarner.com

Report

AOL Time Warner Inc.
Consolidated Balance Sheet
December 31,
(millions, except per share amounts)

	2001 HISTORICAL	2000 HISTORICAL
ASSETS		
Current assets		
Cash and equivalents	$ 719	$ 2,610
Short-term investments	—	886
Receivables, less allowances of $1.889 billion and $97 million	6,054	464
Inventories	1,791	—
Prepaid expenses and other current assets	1,710	711
Total current assets	10,274	4,671
Noncurrent inventories and film costs	6,853	—
Investments, including available-for-sale securities	6,886	3,824
Property, plant and equipment	12,684	1,041
Music catalogues and copyrights	2,927	—
Cable television and sports franchises	27,109	—
Brands and trademarks	10,684	—
Goodwill and other intangible assets	128,338	713
Other assets	2,804	578
Total assets	$208,559	$10,827

You're in the Driver's Seat

If you were an AOL Time Warner manager, how would you establish the value of intangibles on the balance sheet? How would you determine the life of such assets? How would you evaluate whether the merged company has effectively utilized the intangibles? As you study this chapter, compare the ways organizations report tangible and intangible assets on the balance sheet.

LEARNING OBJECTIVES

After studying this chapter, you should be able to:

LO 1 Understand balance sheet disclosures for operating assets. (p. 384)

LO 2 Determine the acquisition cost of an operating asset. (p. 384)

LO 3 Explain how to calculate the acquisition cost of assets purchased for a lump sum. (p. 385)

LO 4 Describe the impact of capitalizing interest as part of the acquisition cost of an asset. (p. 386)

LO 5 Compare depreciation methods and understand the factors affecting the choice of method. (p. 387)

LO 6 Understand the impact of a change in the estimate of the asset life or residual value. (p. 391)

LO 7 Determine which expenditures should be capitalized as asset costs and which should be treated as expenses. (p. 393)

LO 8 Analyze the effect of the disposal of an asset at a gain or loss. (p. 395)

LO 9 Understand the balance sheet presentation of intangible assets. (p. 399)

LO 10 Describe the proper amortization of intangible assets. (p. 402)

LO 11 Explain the impact that long-term assets have on the statement of cash flows. (p. 405)

OPERATING ASSETS: PROPERTY, PLANT, AND EQUIPMENT

Balance Sheet Presentation

LO 1 Understand balance sheet disclosures for operating assets.

Operating assets constitute the major productive assets of many companies. Current assets are important to a company's short-term liquidity; operating assets are absolutely essential to its long-term future. These assets must be used to produce the goods or services the company sells to customers. The dollar amount invested in operating assets may be very large, as is the case with most manufacturing companies. On the other hand, operating assets on the balance sheet may be insignificant to a company's value, as is the case with a computer software firm or many of the so-called Internet firms. Users of financial statements must assess the operating assets to make important decisions. For example, lenders are interested in the value of the operating assets as collateral when making lending decisions. Investors must evaluate whether the operating assets indicate long-term potential and can provide a return to the stockholders.

The terms used to describe the operating assets and the balance sheet presentation of those assets vary somewhat by company. Some firms refer to this category of assets as *fixed* or *plant assets.* Other firms prefer to present operating assets in two categories: *tangible assets* and *intangible assets.* The balance sheet of **Johnson Controls, Inc.**, uses another way to classify operating assets. The company presents one line item for *property, plant, and equipment* and presents the details in the footnotes. Because the latter term can encompass a variety of items, we will use the more descriptive term *intangible assets* for the second category. We begin by examining the accounting issues concerned with the first category: property, plant, and equipment.

http://www.johnsoncontrols.com

The September 30, 2001, notes of Johnson Controls, Inc., present property, plant, and equipment shown at the top of the following page (in millions). Note that the acquisition costs of the buildings and improvements, machinery and equipment, construction in progress, and land are stated and the amount of accumulated depreciation is deducted to determine the net amount. The accumulated depreciation is related to the first three assets, since land is not a depreciable item.

Acquisition of Property, Plant, and Equipment

LO 2 Determine the acquisition cost of an operating asset.

Assets classified as property, plant, and equipment are initially recorded at acquisition cost (also referred to as *historical cost*). As indicated in Johnson Control's notes, these

Property, Plant, and Equipment

	September 30, 2001 (in millions)
Buildings and improvements	$ 1,242.9
Machinery and equipment	3,191.1
Construction in progress	310.7
	$ 4,744.7
Land	223.8
	$ 4,968.5
Less accumulated depreciation	(2,588.7)
Property, plant, and equipment (net)	$ 2,379.8

assets are normally presented on the balance sheet at original acquisition cost minus accumulated depreciation. It is important, however, to define the term acquisition cost (also known as original cost) in a more exact manner. What items should be included as part of the original acquisition? **Acquisition cost** should include all of the costs that are normal and necessary to acquire the asset and prepare it for its intended use. Items included in acquisition cost would generally include the following:

Acquisition cost The amount that includes all of the cost normally necessary to acquire an asset and prepare it for its intended use.

Purchase price

Taxes paid at time of purchase (for example, sales tax)

Transportation charges

Installation costs

An accountant must exercise careful judgment to determine which costs are "normal" and "necessary" and should be included in the calculation of the acquisition cost of operating assets. Acquisition cost should not include expenditures unrelated to the acquisition (for example, repair costs if an asset is damaged during installation) or costs incurred after the asset was installed and use begun.

Accounting for Your Decisions

You Are an Attorney

You are a newly licensed attorney who just opened a legal firm. As part of your office operations, you have purchased some slightly used computers. Should the cost of repairing the computers be considered as part of the acquistion cost?

ANS: If you were aware that the computers needed to be repaired when purchased, the repair costs are part of the cost of acquisition. If the computers were damaged after they were purchased, the costs should be treated as an expense on the income statement.

Group Purchase Quite often a firm purchases several assets as a group and pays a lump-sum amount. This is most common when a company purchases land and a building situated on it and pays a lump-sum amount for both. It is important to measure separately the acquisition cost of the land and of the building. Land is not a depreciable asset, but the amount allocated to the building is subject to depreciation. In cases such as this, the purchase price should be allocated between land and building on the basis of the proportion of the *fair market values* of each.

LO 3 Explain how to calculate the acquisition cost of assets purchased for a lump sum.

For example, assume that on January 1, Payton Company purchased a building and the land that it is situated on for $100,000. The accountant was able to establish that the fair market values of the two assets on January 1 were as follows:

Land	$ 30,000
Building	90,000
Total	$120,000

On the basis of the estimated market values, the purchase price should be allocated as follows:

To land	$100,000 × $30,000/$120,000 = $25,000
To building	$100,000 × $90,000/$120,000 = $75,000

The journal entry to record the purchase would be as follows:

Jan. 1	Land	25,000	
	Building	75,000	
	Cash		100,000
	To record the purchase of land and building for a lump-sum amount.		

Assets	=	Liabilities	+	Owners' Equity
+25,000				
+75,000				
−100,000				

Market value is best established by an independent appraisal of the property. If such appraisal is not possible, the accountant must rely on the market value of other similar assets, on the value of the assets in tax records, or on other available evidence.

These efforts to allocate dollars between land and buildings will permit the appropriate allocation for depreciation. But when an investor or lender views the balance sheet, he or she is often more interested in the current market value. The best things that can be said about historical cost are that it is a verifiable number and that it is conservative. But it is still up to the lender or the investor to determine the appropriate value for these assets.

LO 4 Describe the impact of capitalizing interest as part of the acquisition cost of an asset.

Capitalization of Interest We have seen that acquisition cost may include several items. But should the acquisition cost of an asset include the interest cost necessary to finance the asset? That is, should interest be treated as an asset, or should it be treated as an expense of the period?

Generally, the interest on borrowed money should be treated as an expense of the period. If a company buys an asset and borrows money to finance the purchase, the interest on the borrowed money is not considered part of the asset's cost. Financial statements generally treat investing and financing as separate decisions. Purchase of an asset, an investing activity, is treated as a business decision that is separate from the decision concerning the financing of the asset. Therefore, interest is treated as a period cost and should appear on the income statement as interest expense in the period incurred.

Capitalization of interest Interest on constructed assets is added to the asset account.

There is one exception to this general guideline, however. If a company constructs an asset over a period of time and borrows money to finance the construction, the amount of interest incurred during the construction period is not treated as interest expense. Instead, the interest must be included as part of the acquisition cost of the asset. This is referred to as **capitalization of interest**. The amount of interest that is capitalized (treated as an asset) is based on the *average accumulated expenditures.* The logic of using the average accumulated expenditure is that this number represents an average amount of money tied up in the project over a year. If it takes $400,000 to construct a building, the interest should not be figured on the full $400,000 because there were times during the year when less than the full amount was being used.

When it costs $400,000 to build an asset and the amount of interest to be capitalized is $10,000, the acquisition cost of the asset is $410,000. The asset should appear on the balance sheet at that amount. Depreciation of the asset should be based on $410,000, less any residual value.

Land Improvements It is important to distinguish between land and other costs associated with it. The acquisition cost of land should be kept in a separate account because land has an unlimited life and is not subject to depreciation. Other costs associated with land should be recorded in an account such as Land Improvements. For example, the costs of paving a parking lot or landscaping costs are properly treated as **land improvements,** which have a limited life. Therefore, the acquisition costs of land improvements should be depreciated over their useful lives.

Study Tip

Land improvements represent a depreciable asset with a limited life. Land itself is not depreciable.

Land improvements Costs that are related to land but that have a limited life.

Use and Depreciation of Property, Plant, and Equipment

LO 5 Compare depreciation methods and understand the factors affecting the choice of method.

All property, plant, and equipment, except land, have a limited life and decline in usefulness over time. The accrual accounting process requires a proper *matching* of expenses and revenue to accurately measure income. Therefore, the accountant must estimate the decline in usefulness of operating assets and allocate the acquisition cost in a manner consistent with the decline in usefulness. This allocation is the process generally referred to as **depreciation.**

Depreciation The allocation of the original cost of an asset to the periods benefited by its use.

Unfortunately, proper matching for operating assets is not easy because of the many factors involved. An asset's decline in usefulness is related to *physical deterioration* factors such as wear and tear. In some cases, the physical deterioration results from heavy use of the asset in the production process, but it may also result from the passage of time or exposure to the elements.

The decline in an asset's usefulness is also related to *obsolescence* factors. Some operating assets, such as computers, decline in usefulness simply because they have been surpassed by a newer model or newer technology. Finally, the decline in an asset's usefulness is related to a company's *repair and maintenance* policy. A company with an aggressive and extensive repair and maintenance program will not experience a decline in usefulness of operating assets as rapidly as one without such a policy.

Because the decline in an asset's usefulness is related to a variety of factors, several depreciation methods have been developed. In theory, a company should use a depreciation method that allocates the original cost of the asset to the periods benefited and that allows the company to accurately match the expense to the revenue generated by the asset. We will present three methods of depreciation: *straight line, units of production,* and *double declining balance.*

From Concept to Practice 8.1

What amount did Winnebago Industries report as depreciation in fiscal year 2001? Where is it disclosed? What depreciation method was used?

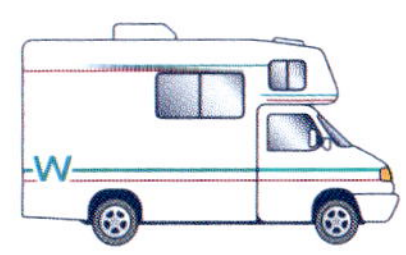

All depreciation methods are based on the asset's original acquisition cost. In addition, all methods require an estimate of two additional factors: the asset's *life* and its *residual value.* The residual value (also referred to as *salvage value*) should represent the amount that could be obtained from selling or disposing of the asset at the end of its useful life. Often, this may be a small amount or even zero.

Straight-Line Method The **straight-line method** of depreciation allocates the cost of the asset evenly over time. This method calculates the annual depreciation as follows:

Straight-line method A method by which the same dollar amount of depreciation is recorded in each year of asset use.

$$\text{Depreciation} = (\text{Acquisition Cost} - \text{Residual Value})/\text{Life}$$

For example, assume that on January 1, 2004, Kemp Company purchased a machine for $20,000. The company estimated that the machine's life would be five years and its residual value at the end of 2008 would be $2,000. The annual depreciation should be calculated as follows:

$$\text{Depreciation} = (\text{Acquisition Cost} - \text{Residual Value})/\text{Life}$$
$$\text{Depreciation} = (\$20{,}000 - \$2{,}000)/5$$
$$= \$3{,}600$$

Book value The original cost of an asset minus the amount of accumulated depreciation.

An asset's **book value** is defined as its acquisition cost minus its total amount of accumulated depreciation. Thus, the book value of the machine in this example is $16,400 at the end of 2004:

$$\textbf{Book Value} = \textbf{Acquisition Cost} - \textbf{Accumulated Depreciation}$$
$$\text{Book Value} = \$20{,}000 - \$3{,}600$$
$$= \$16{,}400$$

The book value at the end of 2005 is $12,800:

$$\text{Book Value} = \text{Acquisition Cost} - \text{Accumulated Depreciation}$$
$$\text{Book Value} = \$20{,}000 - (2 \times \$3{,}600)$$
$$= \$12{,}800$$

The most attractive features of the straight-line method are its ease and its simplicity. It is the most popular method for presenting depreciation in the annual report to stockholders.

Units-of-production method Depreciation is determined as a function of the number of units the asset produces.

Units-of-Production Method In some cases, the decline in an asset's usefulness is directly related to wear and tear as a result of the number of units it produces. In those cases, depreciation should be calculated by the **units-of-production method.** With this method, the asset's life is expressed in terms of the number of units that the asset can produce. The depreciation *per unit* can be calculated as follows:

$$\textbf{Depreciation per Unit} = \textbf{(Acquisition Cost} - \textbf{Residual Value)/ Total Number of Units in Asset's Life}$$

The annual depreciation for a given year can be calculated based on the number of units produced during that year, as follows:

$$\textbf{Annual Depreciation} = \textbf{Depreciation per Unit} \times \textbf{Units Produced in Current Year}$$

For example, assume that Kemp Company in the previous example wanted to use the units-of-production method for 2004. Also assume that Kemp has been able to estimate that the total number of units that will be produced during the asset's five-year life is 18,000. During 2004 Kemp produced 4,000 units. The depreciation per unit for Kemp's machine can be calculated as follows:

$$\text{Depreciation per Unit} = (\text{Acquisition Cost} - \text{Residual Value})/\text{Life in Units}$$
$$\text{Depreciation per Unit} = (\$20{,}000 - \$2{,}000)/18{,}000$$
$$= \$1 \text{ per Unit}$$

The amount of depreciation that should be recorded as an expense for 2004 is $4,000:

$$\text{Annual Depreciation} = \text{Depreciation per Unit} \times \text{Units Produced in 2004}$$
$$\text{Annual Depreciation} = \$1 \text{ per Unit} \times 4{,}000 \text{ Units}$$
$$= \$4{,}000$$

Depreciation will be recorded until the asset produces 18,000 units. The machine cannot be depreciated below its residual value of $2,000.

The units-of-production method is most appropriate when the accountant is able to estimate the total number of units that will be produced over the asset's life. For example, if a factory machine is used to produce a particular item, the life of the asset may be expressed in terms of the number of units produced. Further, the units produced must be related to particular time periods so that depreciation expense can be matched accurately with the related revenue.

Accelerated Depreciation Methods In some cases, more cost should be allocated to the early years of an asset's use and less to the later years. For those assets, an accelerated method of depreciation is appropriate. The term **accelerated depreciation** refers to several depreciation methods by which a higher amount of depreciation is recorded in the early years than in later ones.

Accelerated depreciation A higher amount of depreciation is recorded in the early years and a lower amount in the later years.

Double-declining-balance method Depreciation is recorded at twice the straight-line rate, but the balance is reduced each period.

One form of accelerated depreciation is the **double-declining-balance method.** Under this method, depreciation is calculated at double the straight-line rate but on a declining amount. The first step is to calculate the straight-line rate as a percentage. The straight-line rate for the Kemp asset with a five-year life is

100%/5 Years = 20%

The second step is to double the straight-line rate:

2 × 20% = 40%

This rate will be applied in all years to the asset's book value at the beginning of each year. As depreciation is recorded, the book value declines. Thus, a constant rate is applied to a declining amount. This constant rate is applied to the full cost or initial book value, not to cost minus residual value as in the other methods. However, the machine cannot be depreciated below its residual value.

Study Tip

Residual value is deducted for all depreciation methods except for the declining-balance methods

The amount of depreciation for 2004 would be calculated as follows:

Depreciation = Beginning Book Value × Rate
Depreciation = $20,000 × 40%
= $8,000

The amount of depreciation for 2005 would be calculated as follows:

Depreciation = Beginning Book Value × Rate
Depreciation = ($20,000 − $8,000) × 40%
= $4,800

The complete depreciation schedule for Kemp Company for all five years of the machine's life would be as follows:

YEAR	RATE	BOOK VALUE AT BEGINNING OF YEAR	DEPRECIATION	BOOK VALUE AT END OF YEAR
2004	40%	$20,000	$ 8,000	$12,000
2005	40	12,000	4,800	7,200
2006	40	7,200	2,880	4,320
2007	40	4,320	1,728	2,592
2008	40	2,592	592	2,000
Total			$18,000	

In the Kemp Company example, the depreciation for 2008 cannot be calculated as $2,592 × 40% because this would result in an accumulated depreciation amount of more than $18,000. The total amount of depreciation recorded in Years 1 through 4 is $17,408. The accountant should record only $592 depreciation ($18,000 − $17,408) in 2008 so that the remaining value of the machine is $2,000 at the end of 2008.

The double-declining-balance method of depreciation results in an accelerated depreciation pattern. It is most appropriate for assets subject to a rapid decline in usefulness as a result of technical or obsolescence factors. Double-declining-balance depreciation is not widely used for financial statement purposes but may be appropriate for certain assets. As discussed earlier, most companies use straight-line depreciation for financial statement purposes because it generally produces the highest net income, especially in growing companies that have a stable or expanding base of assets.

Comparison of Depreciation Methods In this section, you have learned about several methods of depreciating operating assets. Exhibit 8-1 presents a comparison of the depreciation and book values of the Kemp Company asset for 2004–2008 using the straight-line and double-declining-balance methods (we have excluded the units-of-production method). Note that both methods result in a depreciation total of $18,000 over the five-year time period. The amount of depreciation per year depends, however, on the method of depreciation chosen.

Exhibit 8-1

Comparison of Depreciation and Book Values of Straight-Line and Double-Declining-Balance Methods

	Straight Line		Double-Declining Balance	
YEAR	DEPRECIATION	BOOK VALUE	DEPRECIATION	BOOK VALUE
2004	$ 3,600	$16,400	$ 8,000	$12,000
2005	3,600	12,800	4,800	7,200
2006	3,600	9,200	2,880	4,320
2007	3,600	5,600	1,728	2,592
2008	3,600	2,000	592	2,000
Totals	$18,000		$18,000	

Nonaccountants often misunderstand the accountant's concept of depreciation. Accountants do not consider depreciation to be a process of *valuing* the asset. That is, depreciation does not describe the increase or decrease in the market value of the asset. Accountants consider depreciation to be a process of *cost allocation.* The purpose is to allocate the original acquisition cost to the periods benefited by the asset. The depreciation method chosen should be based on the decline in the asset's usefulness. A company can choose a different depreciation method for each individual fixed asset or for each class or category of fixed assets.

The choice of depreciation method can have a significant impact on the bottom line. If two companies are essentially identical in every other respect, a different depreciation method for fixed assets can make one company look more profitable than another. Or a company that uses accelerated depreciation for one year can find that its otherwise declining earnings are no longer declining if it switches to straight-line depreciation. Investors should pay some attention to depreciation methods when comparing companies. Statement users must be aware of the different depreciation methods to understand the calculation of income and to compare companies that may not use the same methods.

Some investors ignore depreciation altogether when evaluating a company, not because they do not know that assets depreciate but because they want to focus on cash flow instead of earnings. Depreciation is a "noncash" charge that reduces net income.

Depreciation and Income Taxes Financial accounting involves the presentation of financial statements to external users of accounting information, users such as investors and creditors. When depreciating an asset for financial accounting purposes, the accountant should choose a depreciation method that is consistent with the asset's decline in usefulness and that properly allocates its cost to the periods that benefit from its use.

Depreciation is also deducted for income tax purposes. Sometimes depreciation is referred to as a *tax shield* because it reduces (as do other expenses) the amount of income tax that would otherwise have to be paid. When depreciating an asset for tax purposes, a company should generally choose a depreciation method that reduces the present value of its tax burden to the lowest-possible amount over the life of the asset. Normally, this is best accomplished with an accelerated depreciation method, which allows a company to save more income tax in the early years of the asset. This happens because the higher depreciation charges reduce taxable income more than the straight-line method does. The method allowed for tax purposes is referred to as MACRS, which stands for Modified Accelerated Cost Recovery System. As a form of accelerated depreciation, it results in a larger amount of depreciation in the early years of asset life and a smaller amount in later years.

Choice of Depreciation Method As we have stated, in theory a company should choose the depreciation method that best allocates the original cost of the asset to the periods benefited by the use of the asset. Theory aside, it is important to examine the other factors that affect a company's decision in choosing a depreciation method or methods. Exhibit 8-2 presents the factors that affect this decision and the likely choice that arises from each factor. Usually, the factors that are the most important are whether depreciation is calculated for presentation on the financial statements to stockholders or is calculated for income tax purposes.

Exhibit 8-2

Management's Choice of Depreciation Method

Factor	Likely Choice
Simplicity	The straight-line method is easiest to compute and record.
Reporting to stockholders	Usually firms wish to maximize net income in reporting to stockholders and will use the straight-line method.
Comparability	Usually firms use the same depreciation method as other firms in the same industry or line of business.
Management bonus plans	If management is paid a bonus based on net income, they are likely to use the straight-line method.
Technological competitiveness	If technology is changing rapidly, a firm should consider an accelerated method of depreciation.
Reporting to the Internal Revenue Service	Firms will usually use an accelerated method of depreciation to minimize taxable income in reporting to the IRS.

When depreciation is calculated for financial statement purposes, a company generally wants to present the most favorable impression (the highest income) possible. Therefore, most companies choose the straight-line method of depreciation. In fact, more than 90% of large companies use the straight-line method for financial statement purposes.

If the objective of the company's management is to minimize its income tax liability, then the company will generally not choose the straight-line method for tax purposes. As discussed in the preceding section, accelerated depreciation allows the company to save more on income taxes because depreciation is a tax shield.

Therefore, it is not unusual for a company to use *two* depreciation methods for the same asset, one for financial reporting purposes and another for tax purposes. This may seem somewhat confusing, but it is the direct result of the differing goals of financial and tax accounting. See Chapter 10 for more about this issue.

LO 6 Understand the impact of a change in the estimate of the asset life or residual value.

Change in Depreciation Estimate An asset's acquisition cost is known at the time it is purchased, but its life and its residual value must be estimated. These estimates are then used as the basis for depreciating it. Occasionally, an estimate of the asset's life or residual value must be altered after the depreciation process has begun. This is an example of an accounting change that is referred to as a **change in estimate.**

Change in estimate A change in the life of the asset or in its residual value.

Assume the same facts as in the Kemp Company example. The company purchased a machine on January 1, 2004, for $20,000. Kemp estimated that the machine's life would be five years and its residual value at the end of five years would be $2,000. Assume that Kemp has depreciated the machine using the straight-line method for two years. At the beginning of 2006, Kemp believes that the total machine life will be seven years, or another five years beyond the two years the machine has been used. Thus, depreciation must be adjusted to reflect the new estimate of the asset's life.

A change in estimate should be recorded *prospectively,* meaning that the depreciation recorded in prior years is not corrected or restated. Instead, the new estimate should affect the current year and future years. Kemp Company should depreciate the remaining depreciable amount during 2006 through 2010. The amount to be depreciated over that time period should be calculated as follows:

Acquisition Cost, January 1, 2004	$20,000
Less: Accumulated Depreciation	
(2 years at $3,600 per year)	7,200
Book Value, January 1, 2006	$12,800
Less: Residual Value	2,000
Remaining Depreciable Amount	$10,800

The remaining depreciable amount should be recorded as depreciation over the remaining life of the machine. In the Kemp Company case, the depreciation amount for 2006 and the following four years would be $2,160:

Depreciation = Remaining Depreciable Amount/Remaining Life

Depreciation = $10,800/5 Years

= $2,160

The journal entry to record depreciation for the year 2006 is as follows:

2006			
Dec. 31	Depreciation Expense	2,160	
	Accumulated Depreciation		2,160
	To record depreciation for 2006.		

Assets	=	Liabilities	+	Owners' Equity
−2,160				−2,160

If the change in estimate is a material amount, the company should disclose in the footnotes to the 2006 financial statements that depreciation has changed as a result of a change in estimate. The company's auditors have to be very careful that management's decision to change its estimate of the depreciable life of the asset is not simply an attempt

Accounting for Your Decisions

You Are the Sole Owner

Your accountant has presented you with three sets of financial statements—each with a different depreciation method—and asks you which depreciation method you prefer. You answer that other than for tax purposes, you don't really care. Should you?

ANS: For tax purposes you would prefer to use the accelerated depreciation method, which minimizes your net income so that you can pay the minimum allowable taxes. For financial statement purposes you may use a different method. As a sole owner, you may believe that the depreciation method chosen does not matter because you are more concerned with the cash flow of the firm and depreciation is a noncash item. However, the depreciation method is important if you are going to show your statements to external parties—for example, if you must present your statements to a banker in order to get a loan.

to manipulate earnings. Particularly in capital-intensive manufacturing concerns, lengthening the useful life of equipment can have a material impact on earnings.

A change in estimate of an asset's residual value is treated in a manner similar to a change in an asset's life. There should be no attempt to correct or restate the income statements of past periods that were based on the original estimate. Instead, the accountant should use the new estimate of residual value to calculate depreciation for the current and future years.

A change in estimate is not treated the same way as a *change in principle*. If a company changes its *method* of depreciation, for example, from accelerated depreciation to the straight-line method, this constitutes a change in accounting principle and must be disclosed separately on the income statement.

Two-Minute Review

1. *What items should be included when calculating the acquisition cost of an asset?*
2. *Which will be higher in the early years of an asset's life—straight-line depreciation or accelerated depreciation? Which will be higher in the later years? Which will be higher in total over the entire life of the asset?*

Answers—p. 408

Capital versus Revenue Expenditures

LO 7 Determine which expenditures should be capitalized as asset costs and which should be treated as expenses.

Capital expenditure A cost that improves the asset and is added to the asset account.

Revenue expenditure A cost that keeps an asset in its normal operating condition and is treated as an expense.

Accountants must often decide whether certain expenditures related to operating assets should be treated as an addition to the cost of the asset or as an expense. One of the most common examples involving this decision concerns repairs to an asset. Should the repairs constitute capital expenditures or revenue expenditures? A **capital expenditure** is a cost that is added to the acquisition cost of the asset. A **revenue expenditure** is not treated as part of the cost of the asset but as an expense on the income statement. Thus, the company must decide whether to treat an item as an asset (balance sheet) and depreciate its cost over its life or to treat it as an expense (income statement) of a single period.

The distinction between capital and revenue expenditures is a matter of judgment. Generally, the guideline that should be followed is that if an expenditure increases the life of the asset or its productivity, it should be treated as a capital expenditure and added to the asset account. If an expenditure simply maintains an asset in its normal operating condition, however, it should be treated as an expense. The *materiality* of the expenditure must also be considered. Most companies establish a policy of treating an expenditure smaller than a specified amount as a revenue expenditure (an expense on the income statement).

It is very important that a company not improperly capitalize a material expenditure that should have been written off right away. The capitalization policies of companies are closely watched by Wall Street analysts who try to assess the value of these companies. When a company is capitalizing rather than expensing certain items to artificially boost earnings, that revelation can be very damaging to the stock price.

Expenditures related to operating assets may be classified in several categories. For each type of expenditure, its treatment as capital or revenue should be as follows:

CATEGORY	EXAMPLE	ASSET OR EXPENSE
Normal maintenance	Repainting	Expense
Minor repair	Replace spark plugs	Expense
Major repair	Replace a vehicle's engine	Asset, if life or productivity is enhanced
Addition	Add a wing to a building	Asset

Accounting for Your Decisions

You Are the Owner

You are a realtor whose business car has just had its transmission rebuilt for $400. Would you classify this "repair" as a capital expenditure or a revenue expenditure? Why is it important to properly classify the $400?

ANS: If the business car's life is not extended, then the repair should be treated as a revenue expenditure, in which the cost is expensed on the income statement. It is important to properly classify capital and revenue expenditures because capitalizing rather than expensing costs can artificially boost earnings. The opposite effect would occur if costs are expensed and not capitalized.

An item treated as a capital expenditure affects the amount of depreciation that should be recorded over the asset's remaining life. We return to the Kemp Company example to illustrate. Assume again that Kemp purchased a machine on January 1, 2004, for $20,000. Kemp estimated that its residual value at the end of five years would be $2,000 and has depreciated the machine using the straight-line method for 2004 and 2005. At the beginning of 2006, Kemp made a $3,000 overhaul to the machine, extending its life by three years. Because the expenditure qualifies as a capital expenditure, the cost of overhauling the machine should be added to the asset account. The journal entry to record the overhaul is as follows:

2006			
Jan. 1	Machine	3,000	
	Cash		3,000
	To record the overhaul of an operating asset.		

Assets	=	Liabilities	+	Owners' Equity
+3,000				
−3,000				

For the years 2004 and 2005, Kemp recorded depreciation of $3,600 per year:

Depreciation = (Acquisition Cost − Residual Value)/Life

Depreciation = ($20,000 − $2,000)/5

= $3,600

Beginning in 2006, Kemp should record depreciation of $2,300 per year, computed as follows:

Original Cost, January 1, 2004	$20,000
Less: Accumulated Depreciation (2 years × $3,600)	7,200
Book Value, January 1, 2006	$12,800
Plus: Major Overhaul	3,000
Less: Residual Value	(2,000)
Remaining Depreciable Amount	$13,800

Depreciation = Remaining Depreciable Amount/Remaining Life

Depreciation per year = $13,800/6 Years

= $2,300

The entry to record depreciation for the year 2006 follows:

2006			
Dec. 31	Depreciation Expense	2,300	
	Accumulated Depreciation—Asset		2,300
	To record annual depreciation on operating asset.		

Assets	=	Liabilities	+	Owners' Equity
−2,300				−2,300

Environmental Aspects of Operating Assets

As the number of the government's environmental regulations has increased, businesses have been required to expend more money complying with them. A common example involves costs to comply with federal requirements to clean up contaminated soil surrounding plant facilities. In some cases, the costs are very large and may exceed the value of the property. Should such costs be considered an expense and recorded entirely in one accounting period, or should they be treated as a capital expenditure and added to the cost of the asset? If there is a legal obligation to clean up the property or to restore the property to its original condition, companies are required to record the cost of asset retirement obligations as part of the cost of the asset. For example, if a company owns a factory and has made a binding promise to restore the property that is used by the factory to its original condition, then the costs of restoring the property must be added to the asset account. Of course, it is sometimes difficult to determine whether a legal obligation exists. It is important, however, for companies at least to conduct a thorough investigation to determine the potential environmental considerations that may affect the value of operating assets and to ponder carefully the accounting implications of new environmental regulations.

© PHILLIP SPEARS/GETTY IMAGES/PHOTODISC

Should the costs of cleaning up a contaminated factory be considered an expense of one period or a capital expenditure added to the cost of the plant asset? To make the best decision, management should gather all the facts about the extent of the cleanup and its environmental impact.

Disposal of Property, Plant, and Equipment

LO 8 Analyze the effect of the disposal of an asset at a gain or loss.

An asset may be disposed of in any of several different ways. One common method is to sell the asset for cash. Sale of an asset involves two important considerations. First, depreciation must be recorded up to the date of sale. If the sale does not occur at the fiscal year-end, usually December 31, depreciation must be recorded for a partial period from the beginning of the year to the date of sale. Second, the company selling the asset must calculate and record the gain or loss on its sale.

Refer again to the Kemp Company example. Assume that Kemp purchased a machine on January 1, 2004, for $20,000, estimating its life to be five years and the residual value to be $2,000. Kemp used the straight-line method of depreciation. Assume that Kemp sold the machine on July 1, 2006, for $12,400. Depreciation for the six-month time period from January 1 to July 1, 2006, is $1,800 ($3,600 per year × 1/2 year = $1,800) and should be recorded as follows:

2006			
July 1	Depreciation Expense	1,800	
	Accumulated Depreciation—Machine		1,800
	To record depreciation for a six-month time period.		

Assets	=	Liabilities	+	Owners' Equity
−1,800				−1,800

After the July 1 entry, the balance of the Acumulated Depreciation—Machine account is $9,000, which reflects depreciation for the $2^1/_2$ years from the date of purchase to the date of sale. The entry to record the sale follows:

2006			
July 1	Accumulated Depreciation—Machine	9,000	
	Cash	12,400	
	Machine		20,000
	Gain on Sale of Asset		1,400
	To record the sale of the machine.		

Assets	=	Liabilities	+	Owners' Equity
+9,000				+1,400
+12,400				
−20,000				

Gain on sale of asset The excess of the selling price over the asset's book value.

When an asset is sold, all accounts related to it must be removed. In the preceding entry, the Machine account is reduced (credited) to eliminate the account, and the Accumulated Depreciation—Machine account is reduced (debited) to eliminate it. The **Gain on Sale of Asset** indicates the amount by which the sale price of the machine *exceeds* the book value. Thus, the gain can be calculated as follows:

Asset cost	$20,000
Less: Accumulated depreciation	9,000
Book value	$11,000
Sale price	12,400
Gain on sale of asset	$ 1,400

The account Gain on Sale of Asset is an income statement account and should appear in the Other Income/Expense category of the statement. The Gain on Sale of Asset account is not treated as revenue because it does not constitute the company's ongoing or central activity. Instead, it appears as income but in a separate category to denote its incidental nature.

The calculation of a loss on the sale of an asset is similar to that of a gain. Assume in the above example that Kemp had sold the machine on July 1, 2006, for $10,000 cash. As in the previous example, depreciation must be recorded to the date of sale, July 1. The following is the entry to record the sale of the asset:

2006			
July 1	Accumulated Depreciation—Machine	9,000	
	Cash	10,000	
	Loss on Sale of Asset	1,000	
	Machine		20,000
	To record the sale of the machine.		

Assets	=	Liabilities	+	Owners' Equity
+9,000				−1,000
+10,000				
−20,000				

Loss on sale of asset The amount by which selling price is less than book value.

The **Loss on Sale of Asset** indicates the amount by which the asset's sales price *is less than* its book value. Thus, the loss could be calculated as follows:

Asset cost	$20,000
Less: Accumulated depreciation	9,000
Book value	$11,000
Sale price	10,000
Loss on sale of asset	$ 1,000

The Loss on Sale of Asset account is an income statement account and should appear in the Other Income/Expense category of the income statement.

Business Strategy

Valuing Complex Assets

Five of the nation's seven largest media conglomerates boast broadcast television networks among their many assets. Along with book- and magazine-publishing companies, music publishers, theme parks, cable TV stations, professional sports teams, and movie companies, these five giants own the WB Network (AOL Time Warner), ABC (Walt Disney), CBS (Viacom/CBS), Fox (New Corp.), and NBC (GE).

For most of these firms, broadcasting—whether network or cable—provides several billions of dollars of revenue each year, amounting to approximately a quarter to half their annual revenue. The exception is GE, which earns only 5 percent of its $100 billion yearly from NBC and other TV stations it owns. AOL Time Warner's cable programming business includes ownership of HBO, TNT, TBS, Turner Classic Movies, Cinemax, and CNN. Its cable business is particularly profitable, bringing the firm one-quarter of the cable industry's growing advertising budget.

Cable programming is drawing more and more consumers from network television every year, and in recent years every broadcast network experienced a decline in the number of viewers. AOL Time Warner expects that trend to continue, and from a glance at its cable assets, it appears the firm is well prepared to reap the benefits.

Amid speculation that GE may sell its NBC division, General Electric has adopted the opposite strategy. To remain competitive, the company purchased additional television stations in key markets. Late in 2001, the company announced plans to buy KNTV in the San Francisco area for $230 million. The purchase gave NBC a two-station cluster in the market and provided an important outlet for its Olympic coverage. How should an asset such as a television station be valued, and how will the acquisition affect the business strategy of a prime competitor, AOL Time Warner? ■

Sources: AOL Time Warner 2001 annual report and General Electric press release October 11, 2001.

OPERATING ASSETS: NATURAL RESOURCES

Balance Sheet Presentation

Natural resources Assets that are consumed during their use.

Important operating assets for some companies consists of **natural resources** such as coalfields, oil wells, other mineral deposits, and timberlands. Natural resources share one characteristic: the resource is consumed as it is used. For example, the coal a utility company uses to make electricity is consumed in the process. Most natural resources cannot be replenished in the foreseeable future. Coal and oil, for example, can be replenished only by nature over millions of years. Timberlands may be replenished in a shorter time period, but even trees must grow for many years to be usable for lumber.

Natural resources should be carried in the Property, Plant, and Equipment category of the balance sheet as an operating asset. Like other assets in the category, natural resources should initially be recorded at *acquisition cost.* Acquisition cost should include the cost of acquiring the natural resource and the costs necessary to prepare the asset for use. The preparation costs for natural resources may often be very large; for example, a utility may spend large sums to remove layers of dirt before the coal can be mined. These preparation costs should be added to the cost of the asset.

Depletion of Natural Resources

When a natural resource is used or consumed, it should be treated as an expense. The process of recording the expense is similar to the depreciation or amortization process but is usually referred to as *depletion.* The amount of depletion expense each period should reflect the portion of the natural resource that was used up during the current year.

Assume, for example, that Local Coal Company purchased a coalfield on January 1, 2004, for $1 million. The company employed a team of engineering experts who estimated the total coal in the field to be 200,000 tons and who determined that the field's residual value after removal of the coal would be zero. Local Coal should calculate the depletion per ton as follows:

$$\text{Depletion per Ton} = \text{(Acquisition Cost} - \text{Residual Value)} / \text{Total Number of Tons in Asset's Life}$$
$$= (\$1{,}000{,}000 - 0)/200{,}000 \text{ tons}$$
$$= \$5 \text{ per ton}$$

Depletion expense for each year should be calculated as follows:

$$\text{Depletion Expense} = \text{Depletion per Ton} \times \text{Tons Mined during Year}$$

Assume that Local Coal Company mined 10,000 tons of coal during 2004. The depletion expense for 2004 for Local Coal follows:

$$\$5 \times 10{,}000 \text{ tons} = \$50{,}000$$

Local Coal should record the depletion in an Accumulated Depletion—Coalfield account, which would appear as a contra-asset on the balance sheet. The company should record the following journal entry:

2004			
Dec. 31	Depletion Expense	50,000	
	Accumulated Depletion—Coalfield		50,000
	To record depletion for 2004.		

Assets	=	Liabilities	+	Owners' Equity
−50,000				−50,000

Rather than using an accumulated depletion account, some companies may decrease (credit) the asset account directly.

There is an interesting parallel between depletion of natural resources and depreciation of plant and equipment. That is, depletion is very similar to depreciation using the units-of-production method. Both require an estimate of the useful life of the asset in terms of the total amount that can be produced (for units-of-production method) or consumed (for depletion) over the asset's life.

Natural resources may be important assets for some companies. For example, Exhibit 8-3 highlights the asset portion of the 2001 balance sheet and the accompany-

Exhibit 8-3 Boise Cascade Corporation and Subsidiaries 2001 Assets Section and Natural Resources Note

	December 31	
	2001	2000
Property and equipment (in thousands):		
Land and land improvements	$ 68,482	$ 70,551
Buildings and improvements	675,905	648,256
Machinery and equipment	4,606,102	4,447,628
	$5,350,489	$5,166,435
Accumulated depreciation	(2,742,650)	(2,584,784)
	$2,607,839	$2,581,651
Timber, timberlands, and timber deposits	322,132	291,132
	$2,929,971	$2,872,783

Cost of company timber harvested and amortization of logging roads are determined on the basis of the annual amount of timber cut in relation to the total amount of recoverable timber. Timber and timberlands are stated at cost, less the accumulated cost of timber previously harvested.

ing note of **Boise Cascade Corporation.** Boise Cascade had timber and timberlands, net of depletion, of $322,132,000 as of December 31, 2001. The note indicates that the company records the cost of timber harvested on the basis of annual amount of timber cut in relation to the total amount of recoverable timber.

http://www.boisecascade.com

OPERATING ASSETS: INTANGIBLE ASSETS

Intangible assets are long-term assets with no physical properties. Because one cannot see or touch most intangible assets, it is easy to overlook their importance. Intangibles are recorded as assets, however, because they provide future economic benefits to the company. In fact, an intangible asset may be the most important asset a company owns or controls. For example, a pharmaceutical company may own some property, plant, and equipment, but its most important asset may be its patent for a particular drug or process. Likewise, the company that publishes this textbook may consider the copyrights to textbooks to be among its most important revenue-producing assets.

Intangible assets Assets with no physical properties.

The balance sheet includes the intangible assets that meet the accounting definition of assets. Patents, copyrights, and brand names are included because they are owned by the company and will produce a future benefit that can be identified and measured. The balance sheet, however, would indicate only the acquisition cost of those assets, not the value of the assets to the company or the sales value of the assets.

From Concept to Practice 8.2

Which items on AOL Time Warner's balance sheet should be considered intangible assets? Intangible assets constitute what portion of total assets on AOL Time Warner's balance sheet of December 31, 2001?

Of course, the balance sheet does not include all of the items that may produce future benefit to the company. A company's employees, its management team, its location, or the intellectual capital of a few key researchers may well provide important future benefits and value. They are not recorded on the balance sheet, however, because they do not meet the accountant's definition of *assets* and cannot be easily identified or measured.

Balance Sheet Presentation

Intangible assets are long-term assets and should be shown separately from property, plant, and equipment. Exhibit 8-4 contains a list of the most common intangible assets. Some companies develop a separate category, Intangible Assets, for the various types of intangibles. For example, Exhibit 8-5 presents the Assets section and the accompanying note of the 2001 balance sheet of **Nike, Inc.** Nike presents only one line for intangible assets, but the note indicates that intangibles consist primarily of goodwill (see below), which is amortized on a straight-line basis. The presentation of intangible assets varies widely, however.

LO 9 Understand the balance sheet presentation of intangible assets.

http://nike.com

Exhibit 8-4

Most Common Intangible Assets

INTANGIBLE ASSET	DESCRIPTION
Patent	Right to use, manufacture, or sell a product; granted by the U.S. Patent Office. Patents have a legal life of 20 years.
Copyright	Right to reproduce or sell a published work. Copyrights are granted for 50 years plus the life of the creator.
Trademark	A symbol or name that allows a product or service to be identified; provides legal protection for 20 years plus an indefinite number of renewal periods.
Goodwill	The excess of the purchase price to acquire a business over the value of the individual net assets acquired.

Exhibit 8-5 The Nike, Inc., Consolidated Assets Section and Intangibles Note

Consolidated Balance Sheets

	May 31	
	2001	2000
Assets (in millions)		
Current Assets:		
Cash and equivalents	**$ 304.0**	$ 254.3
Accounts receivable, less allowance for doubtful accounts of $72.1 and $65.4	**1,621.4**	1,569.4
Inventories (Note 2)	**1,424.1**	1,446.0
Deferred income taxes (Notes 1 and 6)	**113.3**	111.5
Prepaid expenses (Note 1)	**162.5**	215.2
Total current assets	**3,625.3**	3,596.4
Property, plant and equipment, net (Note 3)	**1,618.8**	1,583.4
Identifiable intangible assets and goodwill, net (Note 1)*	**397.3**	410.9
Deferred income taxes and other assets (Notes 1 and 6)	**178.2**	266.2
Total assets	**$5,819.6**	$5,856.9

Identifiable intangible assets and goodwill:

At May 31, 2001 and 2000, the Company had patents, trademarks, and other identifiable intangible assets recorded at a cost of $218.6 million and $215.2 million, respectively. The Company's excess of purchase cost over the fair value of net assets of businesses acquired (goodwill) was $322.5 million and $323.5 million at May 31, 2001 and 2000, respectively.

Identifiable intangible assets and goodwill are being amortized over their estimated useful lives on a straight-line basis over five to forty years. Accumulated amortization was $143.8 million and $127.8 million at May 31, 2001 and 2000, respectively.

*Note that the company recorded amortization of goodwill for 2001 and 2000. Beginning in 2002, amortization of goodwill is no longer allowed under GAAP.

http://www.alberto-culver.com

Exhibit 8-6 presents the Assets section and the accompanying note of the 2001 balance sheet of **Alberto-Culver Company.** Alberto-Culver presents the intangible assets of goodwill and trade names immediately after the Property, Plant, and Equipment category. Both accounts are presented net of the accumulated amortization. The note indicates that amortization was computed on the straight-line basis.

Goodwill The excess of the purchase price to acquire a business over the value of the individual net assets acquired.

The nature of many intangibles is fairly evident, but goodwill is not so easily understood. **Goodwill** represents the amount of the purchase price paid in excess of the market value of the individual net assets when a business is purchased. Goodwill is recorded only when a business is purchased. It is not recorded when a company engages in activities that do not involve the purchase of another business entity. For example, customer loyalty or a good management team may represent "goodwill," but neither meets the accountants' criteria to be recorded as an asset on a firm's financial statements.

International accounting standards allow firms *either* to present goodwill separately as an asset or to deduct it from stockholders' equity at the time of purchase. The result is that the presentation of goodwill on the financial statements of non-U.S. companies can look much different from that for U.S. companies. Similarly, some investors in U.S. companies believe that goodwill is not an asset because it is difficult to determine the factors that caused this asset. They prefer to focus their attention on a company's tangible assets. These investors simply reduce the amount shown on the balance sheet by the amount of goodwill, deducting it from total assets and reducing stockholders' equity by the same amount.

Exhibit 8-6 Alberto-Culver Company and Subsidiaries 2001 Consolidated Assets Section and Intangibles Note

CONSOLIDATED BALANCE SHEETS

Alberto-Culver Company and Subsidiaries

(In thousands, except share data)	September 30, 2001	September 30, 2000
Assets		
Current assets:		
Cash and equivalents	$ 201,970	$ 114,637
Short-term investments	869	314
Receivables, less allowance for doubtful accounts of $11,387 in 2001 and $10,135 in 2000	169,657	154,207
Inventories:		
Raw materials	41,521	45,197
Work-in-process	4,782	4,819
Finished goods	432,008	395,241
Total inventories	478,311	445,257
Other current assets	26,142	26,122
Total current assets	876,949	740,537
Property, plant, and equipment:		
Land	13,593	13,640
Buildings and leasehold improvements	151,306	148,911
Machinery and equipment	306,958	288,877
Total property, plant, and equipment	471,857	451,428
Accumulated depreciation	236,035	211,337
Property, plant, and equipment, net	235,822	240,091
Goodwill, net	264,339	263,847
Trade names, net	79,532	83,788
Other assets	59,859	57,335
	$1,516,501	$1,385,598

Goodwill and Trade Names the cost of goodwill and trade names is amortized on a straight-line basis over periods raging from ten to forty years.*

*Note that the company recorded amortization of goodwill for 2001 and 2000. Beginning in 2002, amortization of goodwill is no longer allowed under GAAP.

Acquisition Cost of Intangible Assets

As was the case with property, plant, and equipment, the acquisition cost of an intangible asset includes all of the costs to acquire the asset and prepare it for its intended use. This should include all necessary costs such as legal costs incurred at the time of acquisition. Acquisition cost also should include those costs that are incurred after acquisition and that are necessary to the existence of the asset. For example, if a firm must pay legal fees to protect a patent from infringement, the costs should be considered part of the acquisition cost and should be included in the patent account.

You should also be aware of one item that is similar to intangible assets but is *not* on the balance sheet. **Research and development costs** are expenditures incurred in the discovery of new knowledge and the translation of research into a design or plan for a new product or service or in a significant improvement to an existing product or service. Firms that engage in research and development do so because they believe such activities provide future benefit to the company. In fact, many firms have become leaders in an industry by engaging in research and development and the discovery of new products or technology. It is often very difficult, however, to identify the amount of future benefits of

Research and development costs Costs incurred in the discovery of new knowledge.

research and development and to associate those benefits with specific time periods. Because of the difficulty in predicting future benefits, the FASB has ruled that firms are not allowed to treat research and development costs as assets; all such expenditures must be treated as expenses in the period incurred. Many firms, especially high-technology ones, argue that this accounting rule results in seriously understated balance sheets. In their view, an important "asset" is not portrayed on their balance sheet. They also argue that they are at a competitive disadvantage when compared with foreign companies that are allowed to treat at least a portion of research and development as an asset. Users of financial statements somehow need to be aware of those "hidden assets" when analyzing the balance sheets of companies that must expense research and development costs.

It is important to distinguish between patent costs and research and development costs. Patent costs include legal and filing fees necessary to acquire a patent. Such costs are capitalized as an intangible asset, Patent. However, the Patent account should not include the costs of research and development of a new product. Those costs are not capitalized but are treated as an expense, Research and Development.

Accounting for Your Decisions

You Are the Student Intern

Your colleagues at the investment house where you are doing a summer internship insist that the intangible assets on the Nike and Alberto-Culver balance sheets are worthless and should be removed before any analysis can be completed on the two companies. Would you agree or disagree with their position?

ANS: Intangible assets are not worthless. Just because an asset is "intangible" and difficult to quantify doesn't mean it should be removed. Intangible assets such as goodwill and trademarks are frequently listed on balance sheets. They represent assets from an accounting viewpoint and may indeed be some of the most important assets of the company. The patents and trademarks of Nike and Alberto-Culver are assets because they will provide future benefits in the form of sales of products.

Amortization of Intangibles

LO 10 Describe the proper amortization of intangible assets.

There has been considerable discussion over the past few years about whether intangible assets should be amortized and, if so, over what period of time. The term *amortization* is very similar to depreciation of property, plant, and equipment. Amortization involves allocating the acquistion cost of an intangible asset to the periods benefited by the use of the asset. If an intangible asset is amortized, most companies use the straight-line method of amortization, and we will use that method for illustration purposes. Occasionally, however, you may see instances of an accelerated form of amortization if the decline in usefulness of the intangible asset does not occur evenly over time.

If an intangible asset has a finite life, amortization must be recognized. A finite life exists when an intangible asset is legally valid only for a certain length of time. For example, a patent is granted for a time period of 20 years and gives the patent holder the legal right to exclusive use of the patented design or invention. A copyright is likewise granted for a specified legal life. A finite life also exists when there is no legal life but the management of the company knows for certain that they will only be able to use the intangible asset for a specified period of time. For example, a company may have purchased the right to use a list of names and addresses of customers for a two-year time period. In that case, the intangible asset can only be used for two years and has a finite life.

When an intangible asset with a finite life is amortized, the time period over which amortization should be recorded must be considered carefully. The general guideline that should be followed is that *amortization should be recorded over the legal life or the useful life, whichever is shorter.* For example, patents may have a legal life of 20 years, but many are not useful for that long because new products and technology make the patent obsolete. The patent should be amortized over the number of years in which the firm receives benefits, which may be a period shorter than the legal life.

Assume that ML Company developed a patent for a new product on January 1, 2004. The costs involved with patent approval were $10,000, and the company wants to record amortization on the straight-line basis over a five-year life with no residual value. The accounting entry to record the amortization for 2004 is as follows:

2004			
Dec. 31	Patent Amortization Expense	2,000	
	Accumulated Amortization—Patent		2,000
	To record amortization of patent for one year.		

Assets	=	Liabilities	+	Owners' Equity
−2,000				−2,000

Rather than use an accumulated amortization account, some companies decrease (credit) the intangible asset account directly. In that case, the preceding transaction is recorded as follows:

2004			
Dec. 31	Patent Amortization Expense	2,000	
	Patent		2,000
	To record amortization of patent for one year.		

Assets	=	Liabilities	+	Owners' Equity
−2,000				−2,000

No matter which of the two preceding entries is used, the asset should be reported on the balance sheet at acquisition cost ($10,000) less accumulated amortization ($2,000), or $8,000, as of December 31, 2004.

While intangibles such as patents and copyrights have a finite life, many others do not. *If an intangible asset has an indefinite life, amortization should not be recognized.* For example, a television or radio station may have paid to acquire a broadcast license. A broadcast license is usually for a certain time period but can be renewed at the end of that time period. In that case, the life of the asset is indefinite, and amortization of the intangible asset representing the broadcast rights should not be recognized. A second example would be a trademark. For many companies, such as Coca-Cola or AOL Time Warner, a trademark is a very valuable asset that provides name recognition and enhances sales. But a trademark is not subject to a legal life, and the life may be quite indefinite. The value of some trademarks may continue for a long time. Because the life of an intangible asset represented by trademarks is indefinite, amortization should not be recorded.

Goodwill is an important intangible asset on the balance sheet of many companies. Until 2001, accounting rules had required companies to record amortization of goodwill over a time period not to exceed 40 years. However, in 2001, the FASB ruled that goodwill should be treated as an intangible asset with an *indefinite* life and companies should no longer record amortization expense related to goodwill. Companies have generally favored the new accounting stance. Hopefully, it will allow companies to more accurately inform statement users of their true value.

While companies should not record amortization of intangible assets with an indefinite life, they are required each year to determine whether the asset has been *impaired.* A discussion of asset impairment is beyond the scope of this text, but generally, it means a loss should be recorded when the value of the asset has declined. For example, some trademarks, such as Xerox and Polaroid, that were quite powerful in the past have declined in value over time. By recognizing an impairment of the asset, the loss is recorded in the time period that the value declines rather than when the asset is sold. It requires a great deal of judgment to determine when intangible assets have been impaired because the true value of an intangible asset is often difficult to determine. A rather drastic example of impairment occurs when a company realizes that an intangible asset has become completely worthless and should be written off.

Assume in the ML example that ML learns on January 1, 2005, when accumulated amortization is $2,000 (or the book value of the patent is $8,000), that a competing company has developed a new product that renders ML's patent worthless. ML has a loss of $8,000 and should record an entry to write off the asset as follows:

2005			
Jan. 1	Loss on Patent	8,000	
	Accumulated Amortization—Patent	2,000	
	Patent		10,000
	To record the write-off of patent.		

Assets	=	Liabilities	+	Owners' Equity
+2,000				−8,000
−10,000				

Two-Minute Review

1. *What are some examples of intangible assets?*
2. *Over what time period should intangibles with a finite life be amortized? What method is generally used?*

Answers—p. 408

ANALYZING LONG-TERM ASSETS FOR AVERAGE LIFE AND ASSET TURNOVER

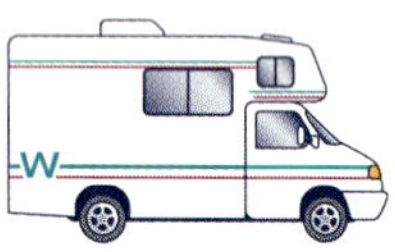

Because long-term assets constitute the major productive assets of most companies, it is important to analyze the age and composition of these assets. We will analyze the assets of Winnebago Industries in the following section. Analysis of the age of the assets can be accomplished fairly easily for those companies that use the straight-line method of depreciation. A rough measure of the *average life* of the assets can be calculated as follows:

Average Life = Property, Plant, and Equipment/Depreciation Expense

The *average age* of the assets can be calculated as follows:

Average Age = Accumulated Depreciation/Depreciation Expense

On August 25, 2001, Winnebago Industries had property and equipment of $134,685,000 and accumulated depreciation of $88,149,000. A careful reading of the annual report also indicates depreciation expense of $7,380,000 for the year ended August 25, 2001. Therefore, the average life of Winnebago Industries' assets is calculated as follows:

Average Life = Property, Plant, and Equipment/Depreciation Expense

Average Life = $134,685,000/$7,380,000

= 18.25 years

This is a rough estimate because it assumes that the company has purchased assets fairly evenly over time. Because it is an average, it indicates that some assets have a life longer than 18.25 years and others shorter lives.[1]

[1]The amount of $7,380,000 used to calculate the age of assets is not technically correct because it includes both depreciation and amortization. Winnebago Industries does not disclose the amount of depreciation by itself. Because the amount of intangible assets is fairly small, we have used the combined amount for our calculations.

The average age of Winnebago Industries' assets is calculated as follows:

Average Age = Accumulated Depreciation/Depreciation Expense

Average Age = $88,149,000/$7,380,000
= 11.9 years

This indicates that Winnebago Industries' assets are, on average, aging, and the company may need to invest fairly heavily in new assets in the future.

The asset category of the balance sheet is also important in analyzing the company's *profitability.* The asset turnover ratio is a measure of the productivity of the assets and is measured as follows:

Asset Turnover = Net Sales/Average Total Assets

This ratio is a measure of how many dollars of assets are necessary for every dollar of sales. If a company is using its assets efficiently, each dollar of assets will create a high amount of sales. Technically, the ratio is based on average *total assets,* but long-term assets often constitute the largest portion of a company's total assets.

HOW LONG-TERM ASSETS AFFECT THE STATEMENT OF CASH FLOWS

LO 11 Explain the impact that long-term assets have on the statement of cash flows.

Determining the impact that acquisition, depreciation, and sale of long-term assets have on the statement of cash flows is important. Each of these business activities influences the statement of cash flows. Exhibit 8-7 illustrates the items discussed in this chapter and their effect on the statement of cash flows.

The acquisition of a long-term asset is an investing activity and should be reflected in the Investing Activities category of the statement of cash flows. The acquisition should appear as a deduction or negative item in that section because it requires the use of cash to purchase the asset. This applies whether the long-term asset is property, plant, and equipment or an intangible asset.

The depreciation or amortization of a long-term asset is not a cash item. It was referred to earlier as a noncash charge to earnings. Nevertheless, it must be presented on the statement of cash flows (if the indirect method is used for the statement). The reason is that it was deducted from earnings in calculating the net income figure. Therefore, it must be eliminated or "added back" if the net income amount is used to indicate the amount of cash generated from operations. Thus, depreciation and amortization should be presented in the Operating Activities category of the statement of cash flows as an addition to net income.

Exhibit 8-7

Long-Term Assets and the Statement of Cash Flows

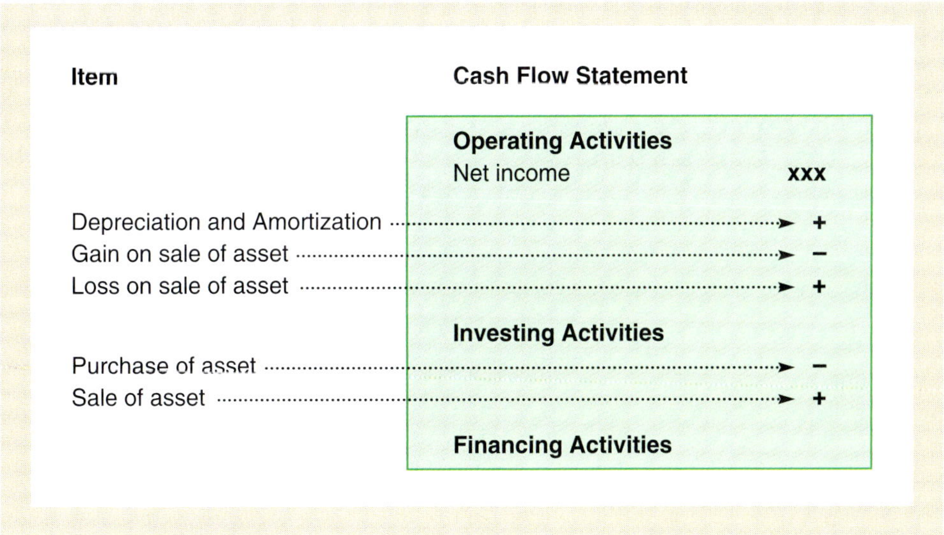

http://www.aoltimewarner.com

The sale or disposition of long-term assets is an investing activity. When an asset is sold, the amount of cash received should be reflected as an addition or plus amount in the Investing Activities category of the statement of cash flows. If the asset was sold at a gain or loss, however, one additional aspect should be reflected. Because the gain or loss was reflected on the income statement, it should be eliminated from the net income amount presented in the Operating Activities category (if the indirect method is used). A sale of an asset is not an activity related to normal, ongoing operations, and all amounts involved with the sale should be removed from the Operating Activities category. Exhibit 8-8 indicates the Operating and Investing categories of the 2001 statement of cash flows of AOL Time Warner. The company had a net loss during 2001; that loss, of $4,921 million, is the first line of the Operations category of the cash flow statement. AOL Time Warner's performance is an excellent example of the difference between the net income on the income statement and actual cash flow. Note that the company generated a positive cash flow from operations of $5,294 million. One of the primary reasons was that depreciation and amortization of $11,583 ($9,203 + $2,380) million affected the income statement but do not involve a cash outflow and are therefore added on the cash flow statement. Also note that the Investing Activities category indicates major outlays of cash for new assets: $4,177 million for investments and acquisitions and $3,634 million for capital expenditures and product development costs, which constitute additions to property, plant, and equipment.

Which Way To Go?

R&D Expense or Long-Term Asset?

For the past six months, Taz Industries has been struggling with a problem in its production line. The number of units produced each day has been steadily dropping. The company believes worn-out equipment is partly the cause. Three months ago, the plant manager put an engineer and the senior machinist to work, full time, to solve the problem. They created a new, electronic tool that, when used in the assembly process, significantly improves production. It is expected that this tool will be useful for at least the next five years.

The total cost of the salaries for the engineer and machinist for three months, plus the cost of materials used in the development process, is $35,000. This includes the cost of time and materials for creating early models that did not solve the problem.

Even though the company plans to use the new tool only for internal production and has no intention of selling it, management believes obtaining a patent is a good idea. The various fees involved in obtaining the patent are expected to total $10,000.

How should the company record the costs? Why should they be recorded in this manner?

Exhibit 8-8 AOL Time Warner Partial Consolidated Statement of Cash Flows

Year ended December 31, (millions)	2001
Operating Activities	
Net income (loss)	$(4,921)
Adjustments for noncash and nonoperating items:	
Depreciation and amortization	9,203
Amortization of film costs	2,380
Loss on writedown of investments	2,537
Net gains on the sale of investments	(34)
Equity in losses of other investee companies after distributions	975
Changes in operating assets and liabilities, net of acquisitions:	
Receivables	(484)
Inventories	(2,801)
Accounts payable and other liabilities	(1,952)
Other balance sheet changes	391
Cash provided by operating activities	5,294
Investing Activities	
Acquisition of AOL Time Warner Inc. cash and equivalents	690
Investments and acquisitions	(4,177)
Capital expenditures and product development costs	(3,634)
Investment proceeds	1,851
Cash used by investing activities	(5,270)

Ratios for Decision Making

Long-term assets are used to produce the products and services that allow a company to operate profitably. Therefore, it is important for investors and creditors to analyze whether the long-term assets are sufficient to support the company's activities. Investors and creditors should analyze the average life of the assets, the average age of the assets, and the asset turnover. The asset turnover is a measure of how many dollars of assets are necessary to generate a dollar of sales. The following ratios can be used to calculate the life, age, and turnover of the long-term assets (assuming the company is using the straight-line method of depreciation):

Balance Sheet

Property, plant, equipment
Less: accumulated depreciation

Total assets

Income Statement

Net sales

Depreciation expense

Statement of cash flows

Operating activities

Depreciation expense

$$\text{Average life} = \frac{\text{Property, plant, and equipment}}{\text{Depreciation expense}}$$

$$\text{Average age} = \frac{\text{Accumulated depreciation}}{\text{Depreciation expense}}$$

$$\text{Asset turnover} = \frac{\text{Net sales}}{\text{Average total assets}}$$

Impact on the Financial Reports

Impact on the Financial Reports

BALANCE SHEET

Current Assets
Noncurrent Assets
Property, plant, and equipment
Less: accumulated depreciation of property, plant, and equipment
Intangible assets, net of accumulated amortization
Current Liabilities
Noncurrent Liabilities
Equity

INCOME STATEMENT

Revenues
Expenses
Depreciation expense
Amortization expense
Other
Losses on sale of assets
Gains on sale of assets

STATEMENT OF STOCKHOLDERS' EQUITY

Contributed Capital
Retained Earnings

STATEMENT OF CASH FLOWS

Operating Activities
Depreciation expense
Amortization expense
Loss on sale of asset
Gain on sale of asset
Investing Activities
Purchase of asset
Sale of asset
Financing Activities
Noncash Transactions

NOTES

The methods used to depreciate long-term assets and the life of the assets should be presented in the accounting policies note.

Answers to the Two-Minute Reviews

Two-Minute Review on Page 393

1. *The general rule for calculating the acquisition cost of an asset is to include all of the costs that were necessary to acquire the asset and prepare it for use. Normally, that would include the purchase price but would also include costs such as freight costs, taxes, and installation costs if they were necessary to prepare the asset for use.*
2. *Accelerated depreciation will be higher in the early years of the asset, and straight-line will be higher in the later years. Over the life of the asset, the total amount of depreciation will be the same under all of the methods, assuming that the same amount of salvage value is estimated for each of the methods.*

Two-Minute Review on Page 404

1. *Intangibles are assets that have no physical properties. Examples are copyrights, trademarks, patents, franchises, and goodwill.*
2. *Intangibles with a finite life should be amortized over the legal life of the asset or the useful life, whichever is shorter. Most companies use the straight-line method of amortization. Accelerated methods of amortization are allowed but are not often used.*

Warmup Exercises

Warmup Exercise 8-1 ***Depreciation Methods*** **LO 5**

Assume that a company purchases a depreciable asset on January 1 for $10,000. The asset has a four-year life and will have zero residual value at the end of the fourth year.

Required

Calculate depreciation expense for each of the four years using the straight-line method and the double-declining-balance method.

Warmup Exercise 8-2 ***Depreciation and Cash Flow*** **LO 5**

Use the information from Exercise 8-1. Assume that the double-declining-balance method will be used for tax purposes and the straight-line method will be used for the financial statement to be given to the stockholders. Also assume that the tax rate is 40%.

Required

How much will the tax savings be in the first year as a result of using the accelerated method of depreciation?

Solutions to Warmup Exercises

Warmup Exercise 8-1

	Straight Line	Double Declining Balance	
Year 1	$2,500*	$10,000 × .50** =	$5,000
2	2,500	($10,000 − $5,000) × .50 =	2,500
3	2,500	($10,000 − $7,500) × .50 =	1,250
4	2,500	($10,000 − $8,750) × .50 =	625

**$10,000/4 years*

***Straight-line rate as a percentage is 1 year/4 year, or 25%. Double the rate is 25% × 2, or 50%.*

Warmup Exercise 8-2

The tax savings is equal to the difference in depreciation between the two methods times the tax rate. Therefore, the tax savings is ($5,000 − $2,500) × .40 = $1,000.

Review Problem

WebTUTOR™ Advantage

The accountant for Becker Company wants to develop a balance sheet as of December 31, 2004. A review of the asset records has revealed the following information:

a. Asset A was purchased on July 1, 2002, for $40,000 and has been depreciated on the straight-line basis using an estimated life of six years and a residual value of $4,000.

b. Asset B was purchased on January 1, 2003, for $66,000. The straight-line method has been used for depreciation purposes. Originally, the estimated life of the asset was projected to be six years with a residual value of $6,000; however, at the beginning of 2004, the accountant learned that the remaining life of the asset was only three years with a residual value of $2,000.

c. Asset C was purchased on January 1, 2003, for $50,000. The double-declining-balance method has been used for depreciation purposes, with a four-year life and a residual value estimate of $5,000.

Required

1. Assume that these assets represent pieces of equipment. Calculate the acquisition cost, accumulated depreciation, and book value of each asset as of December 31, 2004.
2. How would the assets appear on the balance sheet on December 31, 2004?
3. Assume that Becker Company sold Asset B on January 2, 2005, for $25,000. Calculate the amount of the resulting gain or loss, and prepare the journal entry for the sale. Where would the gain or loss appear on the income statement?

Solution to Review Problem

1.

Asset A

2002	Depreciation	($40,000 − $4,000)/6 × 1/2 Year	=	$ 3,000
2003		($40,000 − $4,000)/6	=	6,000
2004		($40,000 − $4,000)/6	=	6,000
Accumulated Depreciation				$15,000

Asset B

2003	Depreciation	($66,000 − $6,000)/6	=	$10,000
2004		($66,000 − $10,000 − $2,000)/3	=	18,000
Accumulated Depreciation				$28,000

Note the impact of the change in estimate on 2004 depreciation.

Asset C

2003	Depreciation	$50,000 × 25% × 2	=	$25,000
2004		($50,000 − $25,000) × (25% × 2)	=	12,500
Accumulated Depreciation				$37,500

BECKER COMPANY
SUMMARY OF ASSET COST AND ACCUMULATED DEPRECIATION
AS OF DECEMBER 31, 2004

Asset	Acquisition Cost	Accumulated Depreciation	Book Value
A	$ 40,000	$15,000	$25,000
B	66,000	28,000	38,000
C	50,000	37,500	12,500
Totals	$156,000	$80,500	$75,500

2. The assets would appear in the Long-Term Assets category of the balance sheet as follows:

Equipment	$156,000	
Less: Accumulated depreciation	80,500	
Equipment (net)		$75,500

3.

Asset B book value	$ 38,000
Selling price	25,000
Loss on sale of asset	$ 13,000

The journal entry to record the sale is as follows:

2005			
Jan. 2	Cash	25,000	
	Accumulated Depreciation	28,000	
	Loss on Sale of Asset	13,000	
	Asset B		66,000
	To record the sale of Asset B.		

Assets	=	Liabilities	+	Owners' Equity
+25,000				−13,000
+28,000				
−66,000				

The Loss on Sale of Asset account should appear in the Other Income/Other Expense category of the income statement. It is similar to an expense but is not the company's major activity.

Chapter Highlights

1. **LO 1** Operating assets are normally presented on the balance sheet in one category for property, plant, and equipment and a second category for intangibles.
2. **LO 1** Operating assets should be presented at original acquisition cost less accumulated depreciation or amortization.
3. **LO 2** Acquisition cost should include all costs necessary to acquire the asset and prepare it for its intended use.
4. **LO 3** When assets are purchased for a lump sum, acquisition cost should be determined as the proportion of the market values of the assets purchased.
5. **LO 4** Interest on assets constructed over time should be capitalized. The amount of interest capitalized should be the average accumulated expenditures times an interest rate.
6. **LO 5** Several depreciation methods are available to describe the decline in usefulness of operating assets. The straight-line method is the most commonly used and assigns the same amount of depreciation to each time period over the asset's life.
7. **LO 5** Accelerated depreciation allocates a greater expense to the earlier years of an asset's life and less to later years. The double-declining-balance method is one form of accelerated depreciation.
8. **LO 6** Depreciation is based on an estimate of the life of the asset and the residual value. When it is necessary to change the estimate, the amount of depreciation expense is adjusted for the current year and future years. Past depreciation amounts are not restated.
9. **LO 7** Capital expenditures are costs that increase an asset's life or its productivity. Capital expenditures should be added to the cost of the asset. Revenue expenditures should be treated as an expense in the period in which they are incurred because they benefit only the current period.
10. **LO 8** The gain or loss on the disposal of an asset is the difference between the asset's book value and its selling price.
11. **LO 9** Intangible assets should be presented on the balance sheet at acquisition cost less accumulated amortization, if any. Acquisition cost should include all costs necessary to acquire the asset.
12. **LO 10** Research and development costs are not treated as an intangible asset. Instead, they are treated as an expense in the year they are incurred.
13. **LO 10** Intangibles with a finite life should be amortized over the shorter of their legal or useful life
14. **LO 11** The acquisition of long-term assets should be reflected in the Investing Activities category of the statement of cash flows.

http://

http://porter.swlearning.com

Technology and other resources for your success

If you need additional help, visit the text's Web site. Also, see pages xv–xvii in this text's preface for a description of available technology and other resources. If your instructor is using PERSONAL Trainer in this course, you may complete, on line, the assignments identified by PT.

Key Terms Quiz

Read each definition below and then write the number of the definition in the blank beside the appropriate term it defines. The quiz solutions appear at the end of the chapter.

_____ Acquisition cost
_____ Capitalization of interest
_____ Land improvements
_____ Depreciation
_____ Straight-line method
_____ Book value
_____ Units-of-production method
_____ Accelerated depreciation
_____ Double-declining-balance method
_____ Change in estimate
_____ Capital expenditure
_____ Revenue expenditure
_____ Gain on Sale of Asset
_____ Loss on Sale of Asset
_____ Natural resources
_____ Intangible assets
_____ Goodwill
_____ Research and development costs

1. This amount includes all of the costs normally necessary to acquire an asset and prepare it for its intended use.
2. Additions made to a piece of property such as paving or landscaping a parking lot. The costs are treated separately from land for purposes of recording depreciation.
3. A method by which the same dollar amount of depreciation is recorded in each year of asset use.
4. A method by which depreciation is determined as a function of the number of units the asset produces.
5. The process of treating the cost of interest on constructed assets as a part of the asset cost rather than as an expense.
6. A change in the life of an asset or in its expected residual value.
7. The allocation of the original acquisition cost of an asset to the periods benefited by its use.
8. A cost that improves an operating asset and is added to the asset account.
9. The original acquisition cost of an asset minus the amount of accumulated depreciation.
10. A cost that keeps an operating asset in its normal operating condition and is treated as an expense of the period.
11. An account whose amount indicates that the selling price received on an asset's disposal exceeds its book value.
12. An account whose amount indicates that the book value of an asset exceeds the selling price received on its disposal.
13. A term that refers to several methods by which a higher amount of depreciation is recorded in the early years of an asset's life and a lower amount is recorded in the later years.
14. Long-term assets that have no physical properties; for example, patents, copyrights, and goodwill.
15. A method by which depreciation is recorded at twice the straight-line rate but the depreciable balance is reduced in each period.
16. The amount indicating that the purchase price of a business exceeded the total fair market value of the identifiable net assets at the time the business was acquired.
17. Expenditures incurred in the discovery of new knowledge and the translation of research into a design or plan for a new product.
18. Assets that are consumed during their use; for example, coal or oil.

Answers on p. 427.

Alternate Terms

Accumulated depreciation Allowance for depreciation

Acquisition cost Historical cost

Capitalize Treat as asset

Construction in progress Construction in process

Goodwill Purchase price in excess of the market value of assets

Hidden assets Unrecorded or off–balance-sheet assets

Property, Plant, and Equipment Fixed assets

Prospective Current and future years

Residual value Salvage value

Revenue expenditure An expense of the period

Questions

1. What are several examples of operating assets? Why are operating assets essential to a company's long-term future?
2. What is the meaning of the term acquisition cost of operating assets? Give some examples of costs that should be included in the acquisition cost.
3. When assets are purchased as a group, how should the acquisition cost of the individual assets be determined?
4. Why is it important to account separately for the cost of land and building, even when the two assets are purchased together?
5. Under what circumstances should interest be capitalized as part of the cost of an asset?
6. What factors may contribute to the decline in usefulness of operating assets? Should the choice of depreciation method be related to these factors? Must a company choose just one method of depreciation for all assets?
7. Why do you think that most companies use the straight-line method of depreciation?
8. How should the residual value of an operating asset be treated when using the straight-line method? How should it be treated when using the double-declining-balance method?
9. Why do many companies use one method to calculate depreciation for the income statement developed for stockholders and another method for income tax purposes?
10. What should a company do if it finds that the original estimate of the life of an asset or the residual value of the asset must be changed?
11. What are the meanings of the terms capital expenditures and revenue expenditures? What determines whether an item is a capital or revenue expenditure?
12. How is the gain or loss on the sale of an operating asset calculated? Where would the Gain on Sale of Asset account appear on the financial statements?
13. What are several examples of items that constitute intangible assets? In what category of the balance sheet should intangible assets appear?
14. What is the meaning of the term goodwill? Give an example of a transaction that would result in the recording of goodwill on the balance sheet.
15. Do you agree with the FASB's ruling that all research and development costs should be treated as an expense on the income statement? Why or why not?
16. Do you agree with some accountants who argue that intangible assets have an indefinite life and therefore should not be subject to amortization?
17. When an intangible asset is amortized, should the asset's amortization occur over its legal life or over its useful life? Give an example in which the legal life exceeds the useful life.
18. Suppose that an intangible asset is being amortized over a 10-year time period but a competitor has just introduced a new product that will have a serious negative impact on the asset's value. Should the company continue to amortize the intangible asset over the 10-year life?

Exercises

Exercise 8-1 ***Acquisition Cost*** **LO 2**

Ruby Company purchased a piece of equipment with a list price of $60,000 on January 1, 2004. The following amounts were related to the equipment purchase:

- Terms of the purchase were 2/10, net 30. Ruby paid for the purchase on January 8.
- Freight costs of $1,000 were incurred.
- A state agency required that a pollution-control device be installed on the equipment at a cost of $2,500.
- During installation, the equipment was damaged and repair costs of $4,000 were incurred.
- Architect's fees of $6,000 were paid to redesign the work space to accommodate the new equipment.
- Ruby purchased liability insurance to cover possible damage to the asset. The three-year policy cost $8,000.
- Ruby financed the purchase with a bank loan. Interest of $3,000 was paid on the loan during 2004.

Required

Determine the acquisition cost of the equipment.

Exercise 8-2 ***Lump-Sum Purchase*** **LO 3**

To add to his growing chain of grocery stores, on January 1, 2004, Danny Marks bought a grocery store of a small competitor for $520,000. An appraiser, hired to assess the value of the assets acquired, determined that the land had a market value of $200,000, the building a market value of $150,000, and the equipment a market value of $250,000.

Required

1. What is the acquisition cost of each asset? Prepare a journal entry to record the acquisition.
2. Danny plans to depreciate the operating assets on a straight-line basis for 20 years. Determine the amount of depreciation expense for 2004 on these newly acquired assets.
3. How would the assets appear on the balance sheet as of December 31, 2004?

Exercise 8-3 *Straight-Line and Units-of-Production Methods* LO 5

DECISION MAKING

Assume that Sample Company purchased factory equipment on January 1, 2004, for $60,000. The equipment has an estimated life of five years and an estimated residual value of $6,000. Sample's accountant is considering whether to use the straight-line or the units-of-production method to depreciate the asset. Because the company is beginning a new production process, the equipment will be used to produce 10,000 units in 2004, but production subsequent to 2004 will increase by 10,000 units each year.

Required

Calculate the depreciation expense, the accumulated depreciation, and the book value of the equipment under both methods for each of the five years of the asset's life. Do you think that the units-of-production method yields reasonable results in this situation?

Exercise 8-4 *Accelerated Depreciation* LO 5

DECISION MAKING

GENERAL LEDGER

Koffman's Warehouse purchased a forklift on January 1, 2004, for $6,000. It is expected to last for five years and have a residual value of $600. Koffman's uses the double-declining-balance method for depreciation.

Required

1. Calculate the depreciation expense, the accumulated depreciation, and the book value for each year of the forklift's life.
2. Prepare the journal entry to record depreciation expense for 2004.
3. Refer to Exhibit 8-2. What factors may have influenced Koffman to use the double-declining-balance method?

Exercise 8-5 *Change in Estimate* LO 6

GENERAL LEDGER

Assume that Bloomer Company purchased a new machine on January 1, 2004, for $80,000. The machine has an estimated useful life of nine years and a residual value of $8,000. Bloomer has chosen to use the straight-line method of depreciation. On January 1, 2006, Bloomer discovered that the machine would not be useful beyond December 31, 2009, and estimated its value at that time to be $2,000.

Required

1. Calculate the depreciation expense, the accumulated depreciation, and the book value of the asset for each year, 2004 to 2009.
2. Was the depreciation recorded in 2004 and 2005 wrong? If so, why was it not corrected?

Exercise 8-6 *Asset Disposal* LO 8

Assume that Gonzalez Company purchased an asset on January 1, 2002, for $60,000. The asset had an estimated life of six years and an estimated residual value of $6,000. The company used the straight-line method to depreciate the asset. On July 1, 2004, the asset was sold for $40,000 cash.

Required

1. Make the journal entry to record depreciation for 2004. Also record all transactions necessary for the sale of the asset.
2. How should the gain or loss on the sale of the asset be presented on the income statement?

Exercise 8-7 *Asset Disposal* LO 8

Refer to Exercise 8-6. Assume that Gonzalez Company sold the asset on July 1, 2004, and received $15,000 cash and a note for an additional $15,000.

(continued)

Required

1. Make the journal entry to record depreciation for 2004. Also record all transactions necessary for the sale of the asset.
2. How should the gain or loss on the sale of the asset be presented on the income statement?

Exercise 8-8 ***Amortization of Intangibles*** **LO 10**

For each of the following intangible assets, indicate the amount of amortization expense that should be recorded for the year 2004 and the amount of accumulated amortization on the balance sheet as of December 31, 2004.

	Trademark	Patent	Copyright
Cost	$40,000	$50,000	$80,000
Date of purchase	1/1/97	1/1/99	1/1/02
Useful life	indefinite	10 yrs.	20 yrs.
Legal life	undefined	20 yrs.	50 yrs.
Method	SL*	SL	SL

**Represents the straight-line method.*

Exercise 8-9 ***Impact of Transactions Involving Operating Assets on Statement of Cash Flows*** **LO 11**

From the following list, identify each item as operating (O), investing (I), financing (F), or not separately reported on the statement of cash flows (N).

_______ Purchase of land
_______ Proceeds from sale of land
_______ Gain on sale of land
_______ Purchase of equipment
_______ Depreciation expense
_______ Proceeds from sale of equipment
_______ Loss on sale of equipment

Exercise 8-10 ***Impact of Transactions Involving Intangible Assets on Statement of Cash Flows*** **LO 11**

From the following list, identify each item as operating (O), investing (I), financing (F), or not separately reported on the statement of cash flows (N).

_______ Cost incurred to acquire copyright
_______ Proceeds from sale of patent
_______ Gain on sale of patent
_______ Research and development costs
_______ Amortization of patent

Multi-Concept Exercises

Exercise 8-11 ***Capital versus Revenue Expenditures*** **LO 1, 7**

On January 1, 2002, Jose Company purchased a building for $200,000 and a delivery truck for $20,000. The following expenditures have been incurred during 2004, related to the building and the truck:

- The building was painted at a cost of $5,000.
- To prevent leaking, new windows were installed in the building at a cost of $10,000.
- To allow an improved flow of production, a new conveyor system was installed at a cost of $40,000.
- The delivery truck was repainted with a new company logo at a cost of $1,000.
- To allow better handling of large loads, a hydraulic lift system was installed on the truck at a cost of $5,000.
- The truck's engine was overhauled at a cost of $4,000.

Required

1. Determine which of these costs should be capitalized. Also record the journal entry for the capitalized costs. Assume that all costs were incurred on January 1, 2004.
2. Determine the amount of depreciation for the year 2004. The company uses the straight-line method and depreciates the building over 25 years and the truck over 6 years. Assume zero residual value for all assets.
3. How would the assets appear on the balance sheet of December 31, 2004?

Exercise 8-12 ***Capitalization of Interest and Depreciation*** **LO 4, 5**

During 2004, Mercator Company borrowed \$80,000 from a local bank and, in addition, used \$120,000 of cash to construct a new corporate office building. Based on average accumulated expenditures, the amount of interest capitalized during 2004 was \$8,000. Construction was completed and the building was occupied on January 1, 2005.

Required

1. Determine the acquisition cost of the new building.
2. The building has an estimated useful life of 20 years and a \$5,000 salvage value. Assuming that Mercator uses the straight-line basis to depreciate its operating assets, determine the amount of depreciation expense for 2004 and 2005.

Exercise 8-13 ***Research and Development and Patents*** **LO 9, 10**

Erin Company incurred the following costs during 2004.

a. Research and development costs of \$20,000 were incurred. The research was conducted to discover a new product to sell to customers in future years. A product was successfully developed, and a patent for the new product was granted during 2004. Erin is unsure of the period benefited by the research but believes the product will result in increased sales over the next five years.

b. Legal costs and application fees of \$10,000 for the patent were incurred on January 1, 2004. The patent was granted for a life of 20 years.

c. A patent infringement suit was successfully defended at a cost of \$8,000. Assume that all costs were incurred on January 1, 2005.

Required

Determine how the costs in parts **a** and **b** should be presented on Erin's financial statements as of December 31, 2004. Also determine the amount of amortization of intangible assets that Erin should record in 2004 and 2005.

Problems

Problem 8-1 ***Balance Sheet and Note Disclosures for Delta Air Lines*** **LO 1**

The June 30, 2000, balance sheet of Delta Air Lines Inc. revealed the following information in the property and equipment category (in millions):

http://www.deltaairlines.com

SPREADSHEET

	2000	1999
Flight equipment	\$15,838	\$13,595
Less: Accumulated depreciation	5,037	4,405
	\$10,801	\$ 9,190
Ground property and equipment	\$ 4,212	\$ 3,862
Less: Accumulated depreciation	2,250	2,123
	\$ 1,962	\$ 1,739

The notes that accompany the financial statements revealed the following:

Depreciation and Amortization—Owned flight equipment is depreciated on a straight-line basis to residual values over its estimated life. Ground property and equipment are depreciated on a straight-line basis over their estimated service lives, which range from 3 years to 30 years.

(continued)

Required

1. Assume that Delta Air Lines did not dispose of any ground property and equipment during the fiscal year 2000. Calculate the amount of depreciation expense for the year.
2. What was the average life of the ground property and equipment as of 2000?
3. What was the average age of the ground property and equipment as of 2000?

Problem 8-2 *Lump-Sum Purchase of Assets and Subsequent Events* LO 3

DECISION MAKING

Carter Development Company purchased, for cash, a large tract of land that was immediately platted and deeded into smaller sections:

Section 1, retail development with highway frontage
Section 2, multifamily apartment development
Section 3, single-family homes in the largest section

Based on recent sales of similar property, the fair market values of the three sections are as follows:

Section 1, $630,000
Section 2, $378,000
Section 3, $252,000

Required

1. What value is assigned to each section of land if the tract was purchased for (a) $1,260,000, (b) $1,560,000, or (c) $1,000,000?
2. How does the purchase of the tract affect the balance sheet?
3. Why would Carter be concerned with the value assigned to each section? Would Carter be more concerned with the values assigned if instead of purchasing three sections of land, it purchased land with buildings? Why or why not?

Problem 8-3 *Depreciation as a Tax Shield* LO 5

The term *tax shield* refers to the amount of income tax saved by deducting depreciation for income tax purposes. Assume that Supreme Company is considering the purchase of an asset as of January 1, 2004. The cost of the asset with a five-year life and zero residual value is $100,000. The company will use the straight-line method of depreciation.

Supreme's income for tax purposes before recording depreciation on the asset will be $50,000 per year for the next five years. The corporation is currently in the 35% tax bracket.

Required

Calculate the amount of income tax that Supreme must pay each year if the asset is not purchased. Calculate the amount of income tax that Supreme must pay each year if the asset is purchased. What is the amount of the depreciation tax shield?

Problem 8-4 *Book versus Tax Depreciation* LO 5

Griffith Delivery Service purchased a delivery truck for $33,600. The truck has an estimated useful life of six years and no salvage value. For the purposes of preparing financial statements, Griffith is planning to use straight-line depreciation. For tax purposes, Griffith follows MACRS. Depreciation expense using MACRS is $6,720 in Year 1, $10,750 in Year 2, $6,450 in Year 3, $3,870 in each of Years 4 and 5, and $1,940 in Year 6.

Required

1. What is the difference between straight-line and MACRS depreciation expense for each of the six years?
2. Griffith's president has asked why you have used one method for the books and another for calculating taxes. "Can you do this? Is it legal? Don't we take the same total depreciation either way?" he asked. Write a brief memo answering his questions and explaining the benefits of using two methods for depreciation.

Problem 8-5 *Depreciation and Cash Flow* LO 11

O'hare Company's only asset as of January 1, 2004, was a limousine. During 2004, only three transactions occurred:

Provided services of $100,000 on account.

Collected all accounts receivable.

Depreciation on the limousine was $15,000.

Required

1. Develop an income statement for O'hare for 2004.
2. Determine the amount of the net cash inflow for O'hare for 2004.
3. Explain in one or more sentences why the amount of the net income on O'hare's income statement does not equal the amount of the net cash inflow.
4. If O'hare developed a cash flow statement for 2004 using the indirect method, what amount would appear in the category titled Cash Flow from Operating Activities?

Problem 8-6 ***Reconstruct Net Book Values Using Statement of Cash Flows*** **LO 11**

Centralia Stores Inc. had property, plant, and equipment, net of accumulated depreciation of $4,459,000; and intangible assets, net of accumulated amortization, of $673,000 at December 31, 2004. The company's 2004 statement of cash flows, prepared using the indirect method, included the following items.

The Cash Flows from Operating Activities section included three additions to net income: (1) depreciation expense in the amount of $672,000, (2) amortization expense in the amount of $33,000, and (3) the loss on the sale of equipment in the amount of $35,000. The Cash Flows from Operating Activities section also included a subtraction from net income for the gain on the sale of a copyright of $55,000. The Cash Flows from Investing Activities section included outflows for the purchase of a building in the amount of $292,000 and $15,000 for the payment of legal fees to protect a patent from infringement. The Cash Flows from Investing Activities section also included inflows from the sale of equipment in the amount of $315,000 and the sale of a copyright in the amount of $75,000.

Required

1. Determine the book values of the assets that were sold during 2004.
2. Reconstruct the amount of property, plant, and equipment, net of accumulated depreciation, that was reported on the company's balance sheet at December 31, 2003.
3. Reconstruct the amount of intangibles, net of accumulated amortization, that was reported on the company's balance sheet at December 31, 2003.

Multi-Concept Problems

Problem 8-7 ***Cost of Assets, Subsequent Book Values, and Balance Sheet Presentation*** **LO 1, 3, 5, 7, 8**

The following events took place at Pete's Painting Company during 2004:

a. On January 1, Pete bought a used truck for $14,000. He added a tool chest and side racks for ladders for $4,800. The truck is expected to last four years and then be sold for $800. Pete uses straight-line depreciation.

b. On January 1, he purchased several items at an auction for $2,400. These items had fair market values as follows:

10 cases of paint trays and roller covers	$ 200
Storage cabinets	600
Ladders & scaffolding	2,400

Pete will use all the paint trays and roller covers this year. The storage cabinets are expected to last nine years, and the ladders and scaffolding for four years.

c. On February 1, Pete paid the city $1,500 for a three-year license to operate the business.

d. On September 1, Pete sold an old truck for $4,800. The truck had cost $12,000 when it was purchased on September 1, 1999. It had been expected to last eight years and have a salvage value of $800.

Required

1. For each situation, explain the value assigned to the asset when it is purchased (or for part **d,** the book value when sold).

(continued)

2. Determine the amount of depreciation or other expense to be recorded for each asset for 2004.
3. How would these assets appear on the balance sheet as of December 31, 2004?

Problem 8-8 ***Cost of Assets and the Effect on Depreciation*** **LO 2, 5**

Early in its first year of business, Toner Company, a fitness and training center, purchased new workout equipment. The acquisition included the following costs:

Purchase price	$150,000
Tax	15,000
Transportation	4,000
Setup*	25,000
Painting*	3,000

**The equipment was adjusted to Toner's specific needs and painted to match the other equipment in the gym.*

The bookkeeper recorded an asset, Equipment, $165,000 (purchase price and tax). The remaining costs were expensed for the year. Toner used straight-line depreciation. The equipment was expected to last 10 years with zero salvage value.

Required

1. How much depreciation did Toner report on its income statement related to this equipment in Year 1? What do you believe is the correct amount of depreciation to report in Year 1 related to this equipment?
2. Income is $100,000, before costs related to the equipment are reported. How much income will Toner report in Year 1? What amount of income should it report? You may ignore income tax.
3. Using the equipment as an example, explain the difference between a cost and an expense.

Problem 8-9 ***Capital Expenditures, Depreciation, and Disposal*** **LO 5, 7, 8**

DECISION MAKING

Merton Company purchased an office building at a cost of $364,000 on January 1, 2003. Merton estimated that the building's life would be 25 years and the residual value at the end of 25 years would be $14,000.

On January 1, 2004, the company made several expenditures related to the building. The entire building was painted and floors were refinished at a cost of $21,000. A federal agency required Merton to install additional pollution-control devices in the building at a cost of $42,000. With the new devices, Merton believed it was possible to extend the life of the building by an additional six years.

In 2005 Merton altered its corporate strategy dramatically. The company sold the factory building on April 1, 2005, for $392,000 in cash and relocated all operations in another state.

Required

1. Determine the amount of depreciation that should be reflected on the income statement for 2003 and 2004.
2. Explain why the cost of the pollution-control equipment was not expensed in 2004. What conditions would have allowed Merton to expense the equipment? If Merton has a choice, would it prefer to expense or capitalize the equipment?
3. What amount of gain or loss did Merton record when it sold the building? What amount of gain or loss would have been reported if the pollution-control equipment had been expensed in 2004?

Problem 8-10 ***Amortization of Intangible, Revision of Rate*** **LO 6, 10**

During 1999, Reynosa Inc.'s R&D department developed a new manufacturing process. R&D costs were $85,000. The process was patented on October 1, 1999. Legal costs to acquire the patent were $11,900. Reynosa decided to expense the patent over a 20-year time period. Reynosa's fiscal year ends on September 30.

On October 1, 2004, Reynosa's competition announced that it had obtained a patent on a new process that would make Reynosa's patent completely worthless.

Required

1. How should Reynosa record the $85,000 and $11,900 costs?

2. How much amortization expense should Reynosa report in each year through the year ended September 30, 2004?
3. What amount of loss should Reynosa report in the year ended September 30, 2005?

Problem 8-11 ***Purchase and Disposal of Operating Asset and Effects on Statement of Cash Flows*** **LO 8, 11**

On January 1, 2004, Castlewood Company purchased some machinery for its production line for $104,000. Using an estimated useful life of eight years and a residual value of $8,000, the annual straight-line depreciation of the machinery was calculated to be $12,000. Castlewood used the machinery during 2004 and 2005 but then decided to automate its production process. On December 31, 2005, Castlewood sold the machinery at a loss of $5,000 and purchased new, fully automated machinery for $205,000.

Required

1. How would the transactions described above be presented on Castlewood's statements of cash flows for the years ended December 31, 2004 and 2005?
2. Why would Castlewood sell at a loss machinery that had a remaining useful life of six years and purchase new machinery with a cost almost twice that of the old?

Problem 8-12 ***Amortization of Intangibles and Effects on Statement of Cash Flows*** **LO 9, 10, 11**

Tableleaf Inc. purchased a patent a number of years ago. The patent is being amortized on a straight-line basis over its estimated useful life. The company's comparative balance sheets as of December 31, 2004 and 2003, included the following line item:

	12/31/04	12/31/03
Patent, less accumulated amortization of $119,000 (2004) and $102,000 (2003)	$170,000	$187,000

Required

1. How much amortization expense was recorded during 2004?
2. What was the patent's acquisition cost? When was it acquired? What is its estimated useful life? How was the acquisition of the patent reported on that year's statement of cash flows?
3. Assume that Tableleaf uses the indirect method to prepare its statement of cash flows. How is the amortization of the patent reported annually on the statement of cash flows?
4. How would the sale of the patent on January 1, 2005, for $200,000 be reported on the 2005 statement of cash flows?

Alternate Problems

Problem 8-1A ***Disclosures of Operating Assets*** **LO 1**

The notes to the December 31, 2004, financial statements of TBW included the following disclosures for the Property, Plant, and Equipment account:

SPREADSHEET

Property, Plant, and Equipment (in millions)	2004	2003
Land and Buildings	$ 963	$ 962
Cable Television Equipment	1,035	941
Furniture, Fixtures, and other Equipment	1,400	1,337
	$3,398	$3,240
Less: Accumulated Depreciation	(1,407)	(1,151)
Total	$1,991	$2,089

Required

Assume that TBW disposed of Property, Plant, and Equipment during 2004 with accumulated depreciation of $600 million.

(continued)

1. Based on the note disclosures, what was the amount of depreciation expense for fiscal year 2004 for Property, Plant, and Equipment?
2. What was the average life of the assets in the Property, Plant, and Equipment categories?
3. What was the average age of the assets in the Property, Plant, and Equipment categories?

Problem 8-2A ***Lump-Sum Purchase of Assets and Subsequent Events*** **LO 3**

Dixon Manufacturing purchased, for cash, three large pieces of equipment. Based on recent sales of similar equipment, the fair market values are as follows:

Piece 1	$200,000
Piece 2	$200,000
Piece 3	$440,000

Required

1. What value is assigned to each piece of equipment if the equipment was purchased for (a) $960,000, (b) $680,000, or (c) $800,000?
2. How does the purchase of the equipment affect total assets?

Problem 8-3A ***Depreciation as a Tax Shield*** **LO 5**

DECISION MAKING

The term *tax shield* refers to the amount of income tax saved by deducting depreciation for income tax purposes. Assume that Rummy Company is considering the purchase of an asset as of January 1, 2004. The cost of the asset with a five-year life and zero residual value is $60,000. The company will use the double-declining-balance method of depreciation.

Rummy's income for tax purposes before recording depreciation on the asset will be $62,000 per year for the next five years. The corporation is currently in the 30% tax bracket.

Required

Calculate the amount of income tax that Rummy must pay each year if the asset is not purchased and then the amount of income tax that Rummy must pay each year if the asset is purchased. What is the amount of tax shield over the life of the asset? What is the amount of tax shield for Rummy if it uses the straight-line method over the life of the asset? Why would Rummy choose to use the accelerated method?

Problem 8-4A ***Book versus Tax Depreciation*** **LO 5**

Payton Delivery Service purchased a delivery truck for $28,200. The truck will have a useful life of six years and zero salvage value. For the purposes of preparing financial statements, Payton is planning to use straight-line depreciation. For tax purposes, Payton follows MACRS. Depreciation expense using MACRS is $5,650 in Year 1, $9,025 in Year 2, $5,400 in Year 3, $3,250 in each of Years 4 and 5, and $1,625 in Year 6.

Required

1. What would be the difference between straight-line and MACRS depreciation expense for each of the six years?
2. Payton's president has asked why you have used one method for the books and another for calculating taxes. "Can you do this? Is it legal? Don't we take the same total depreciation either way?" he asked. Write a brief memo answering his questions and explaining the benefits of using two methods for depreciation.

Problem 8-5A ***Amortization and Cash Flow*** **LO 11**

Book Company's only asset as of January 1, 2004, was a copyright. During 2004, only three transactions occurred:

Royalties earned from copyright use, $500,000 in cash
Cash paid for advertising and salaries, $62,500
Depreciation, $50,000

Required

1. What amount of income will Book report in 2004?

2. What is the amount of cash on hand at December 31, 2004?
3. Explain how the cash balance increased from zero at the beginning of the year to its end-of-year balance. Why does the increase in cash not equal the income?

Problem 8-6A ***Reconstruct Net Book Values Using Statement of Cash Flows*** **LO 11**

E-Gen Enterprises Inc. had property, plant, and equipment, net of accumulated depreciation, of $1,555,000; and intangible assets, net of accumulated amortization, of $34,000 at December 31, 2004. The company's 2004 statement of cash flows, prepared using the indirect method, included the following items.

The Cash Flows from Operating Activities section included three additions to net income: (1) depreciation expense in the amount of $205,000, (2) amortization expense in the amount of $3,000, and (3) the loss on the sale of land in the amount of $17,000. The Cash Flows from Operating Activities section also included a subtraction from net income for the gain on the sale of a trademark of $7,000. The Cash Flows from Investing Activities section included outflows for the purchase of equipment in the amount of $277,000 and $6,000 for the payment of legal fees to protect a copyright from infringement. The Cash Flows from Investing Activities section also included inflows from the sale of land in the amount of $187,000 and the sale of a trademark in the amount of $121,000.

Required

1. Determine the book values of the assets that were sold during 2004.
2. Reconstruct the amount of property, plant, and equipment, net of accumulated depreciation, that was reported on the company's balance sheet at December 31, 2003.
3. Reconstruct the amount of intangibles, net of accumulated amortization, that was reported on the company's balance sheet at December 31, 2003.

Alternate Multi-Concept Problems

Problem 8-7A ***Cost of Assets, Subsequent Book Values, and Balance Sheet Presentation*** **LO 1, 5, 8, 9, 10**

The following events took place at Tasty-Toppins Inc., a pizza shop that specializes in home delivery, during 2004:

a January 1, purchased a truck for $16,000 and added a cab and oven at a cost of $10,900. The truck is expected to last five years and be sold for $300 at the end of that time. The company uses straight-line depreciation for its trucks.

b. January 1, purchased equipment for $2,700 from a competitor who was retiring. The equipment is expected to last three years with zero salvage value. The company uses the double-declining-balance method to depreciate its equipment.

c. April 1, sold a truck for $1,500. The truck had been purchased for $8,000 exactly five years earlier, had an expected salvage value of $1,000, and was depreciated over an eight-year life using the straight-line method.

d. July 1, purchased a $14,000 patent for a unique baking process to produce a new product. The patent is valid for 15 more years; however, the company expects to produce and market the product for only four years. The patent's value at the end of the four years will be zero.

Required

For each situation, explain the amount of depreciation or amortization recorded for each asset in the current year and the book value of each asset at the end of the year. For part **c**, indicate the accumulated depreciation and book value at the time of sale.

Problem 8-8A ***Cost of Assets and the Effect on Depreciation*** **LO 2, 5**

Early in its first year of business, Key Inc., a locksmith and security consultant, purchased new equipment. The acquisition included the following costs:

Purchase price	$168,000
Tax	16,500
Transportation	4,400
Setup*	1,100
Operating Cost for First Year	26,400

**The equipment was adjusted to Key's specific needs.*

(continued)

The bookkeeper recorded the asset, Equipment, at $216,400. Key used straight-line depreciation. The equipment was expected to last 10 years with zero residual value.

Required

1. Was $216,400 the proper amount to record for the acquisition cost? If not, explain how each expenditure should be recorded.
2. How much depreciation did Key report on its income statement related to this equipment in Year 1? How much should have been reported?
3. If Key's income before the costs associated with the equipment is $55,000, what amount of income did Key report? What amount should it have reported? You may ignore income tax.
4. Explain how Key should determine the amount to capitalize when recording an asset. What is the effect on the income statement and balance sheet of Key's error?

Problem 8-9A *Capital Expenditures, Depreciation, and Disposal* LO 7, 8

DECISION MAKING

Wagner Company purchased a retail shopping center at a cost of $612,000 on January 1, 2003. Wagner estimated that the life of the building would be 25 years and the residual value at the end of 25 years would be $12,000.

On January 1, 2004, the company made several expenditures related to the building. The entire building was painted and floors were refinished at a cost of $115,200. A local zoning agency required Wagner to install additional fire-protection equipment, including sprinklers and built-in alarms, at a cost of $87,600. With the new protection, Wagner believed it was possible to increase the residual value of the building to $30,000.

In 2005 Wagner altered its corporate strategy dramatically. The company sold the retail shopping center on January 1, 2005, for $360,000 of cash.

Required

1. Determine the amount of depreciation that should be reflected on the income statement for 2003 and 2004.
2. Explain why the cost of the fire-protection equipment was not expensed in 2004. What conditions would have allowed Wagner to expense it? If Wagner has a choice, would it prefer to expense or capitalize the improvement?
3. What amount of gain or loss did Wagner record when it sold the building? What amount of gain or loss would have been reported if the fire-protection equipment had been expensed in 2004?

Problem 8-10A *Amortization of Intangible, Revision of Rate* LO 6, 10

During 1999, Maciel Inc.'s R&D department developed a new manufacturing process. R&D costs were $350,000. The process was patented on October 1, 1999. Legal costs to acquire the patent were $23,800. Maciel decided to expense the patent over a 20-year time period using the straight-line method. Maciel's fiscal year ends on September 30.

On October 1, 2004, Maciel's competition announced that it had obtained a patent on a new process that would make Maciel's patent completely worthless.

Required

1. How should Maciel record the $350,000 and $23,800 costs?
2. How much amortization expense should Maciel report in each year through the year ended September 30, 2004?
3. What amount of loss should Maciel report in the year ended September 30, 2005?

Problem 8-11A *Purchase and Disposal of Operating Asset and Effects on Statement of Cash Flows* LO 8, 11

On January 1, 2004, Mansfield Inc. purchased a medium-sized delivery truck for $45,000. Using an estimated useful life of five years and a residual value of $5,000, the annual straight-line depreciation of the trucks was calculated to be $8,000. Mansfield used the truck during 2004 and 2005 but then decided to purchase a much larger delivery truck. On December 31, 2005, Mansfield sold the delivery truck at a loss of $12,000 and purchased a new, larger delivery truck for $80,000.

Required

1. How would the transactions described above be presented on Mansfield's statements of cash flows for the years ended December 31, 2004 and 2005?

2. Why would Mansfield sell a truck that had a remaining useful life of three years at a loss and purchase a new truck with a cost almost twice that of the old?

Problem 8-12A ***Amortization of Intangibles and Effects on Statement of Cash Flows*** **LO 9, 10, 11**

Quickster Inc. acquired a patent a number of years ago. The patent is being amortized on a straight-line basis over its estimated useful life. The company's comparative balance sheets as of December 31, 2004 and 2003, included the following line item:

	12/31/04	12/31/03
Patent, less accumulated amortization of $1,661,000 (2004) and $1,510,000 (2003)	$1,357,000	$1,508,000

Required

1. How much amortization expense was recorded during 2004?
2. What was the patent's acquisition cost? When was it acquired? What is its estimated useful life? How was the acquisition of the patent reported on that year's statement of cash flows?
3. Assume that Quickster uses the indirect method to prepare its statement of cash flows. How is the amortization of the patent reported annually on the statement of cash flows?
4. How would the sale of the patent on January 1, 2005, for $1,700,000 be reported on the 2005 statement of cash flows?

Cases

Reading and Interpreting Financial Statements

Case 8-1 ***Winnebago Industries*** **LO 1, 9**

Refer to the financial statements and notes included in the 2001 annual report of Winnebago Industries.

http://www.winnebagoind.com

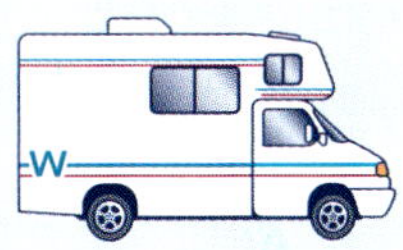

Required

1. What items does Winnebago Industries list in the Property and Equipment category?
2. What method is used to depreciate the operating assets?
3. What is the estimated useful life of the operating assets?
4. What are the accumulated depreciation and book values of property and equipment for the most recent fiscal year?
5. Were any assets purchased or sold during the most recent fiscal year?

Case 8-2 ***Winnebago Industries' Statement of Cash Flows*** **LO 11**

Refer to the statement of cash flows in Winnebago Industries' 2001 annual report and answer the following questions:

http://www.winnebagoind.com

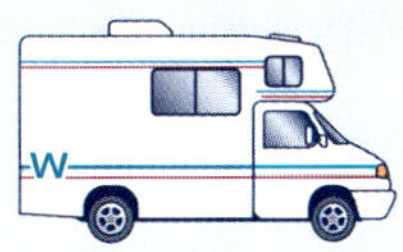

1. What amount of cash was used to purchase property and equipment during 2001?
2. Did Winnebago Industries sell any property and equipment during 2001?
3. What amount was reported for depreciation and amortization during 2001? Does the fact that depreciation and amortization are listed in the Cash Flow from Operating Activities section mean that Winnebago Industries created cash by reporting depreciation?

Case 8-3 ***Comparing Two Companies in the Same Industry: Winnebago Industries and Monaco Coach Corporation*** **LO 1, 9**

The following information was taken from the 2001 annual report of Monaco Coach Corporation, one of Winnebago Industries' competitors in the recreational vehicle industry.

http://www.winnebagoind.com
http://www.monacocoach.com

(continued)

Property, plant, and equipment note:

Property, plant and equipment consist of the following:

	December 30 2000	December 29 2001
	(in thousands)	
Land	$ 6,687	$ 11,999
Buildings	83,564	99,333
Equipment	20,559	22,838
Furniture and fixtures	6,644	9,479
Vehicles	1,232	1,571
Leasehold improvements	854	1,472
Construction in progress	3,504	2,376
	$123,044	$149,068
Less: Accumulated depreciation and amortization	19,454	26,273
Totals	$103,590	$122,795

Accounting policy note excerpt:

DECISION MAKING

The cost of plant and equipment is depreciated using the straight-line method over the estimated useful lives of the related assets. Buildings are generally depreciated over 39 years, and equipment is depreciated over 3 to 10 years. Leasehold improvements are amortized under the straight-line method based on the shorter of the lease periods or the estimated useful lives.

Maintenance and repairs are charged to expense as incurred. Replacements and renewals are capitalized. When assets are sold, retired, or otherwise disposed of, the cost and accumulated depreciation are removed from the accounts, and any resulting gain or loss is reflected in income.

Refer to the annual reports in Appendices A & B at the end of the text for any additional information you might need about Monaco Coach Corporation or Winnebago Industries.

Required

1. Compare the list of property, plant, and equipment represented in the Monaco Coach note to the list on the Winnebago Industries' balance sheet. How are these lists similar? Note the differences between these lists and provide a logical reason for the differences.
2. What method is used by each company to depreciate the assets? Why do you think each company has chosen the method it uses?
3. What are the accumulated depreciation and book values of the property and equipment for each company? What does this information tell you about these competitors?
4. What is the estimated life of the Monaco Coach assets? How does this compare to the estimated life of the Winnebago Industries assets?
5. Refer to the investing activities portion of the cash flow statements of the two companies. Were any assets purchased or sold by either company during the year? This section of the statements does not tell if there was a gain or loss on the sale of long-term assets. Where would you find that information?

Making Financial Decisions

Case 8-4 *Comparing Companies* LO 1, 5

Assume that you are a financial analyst attempting to compare the financial results of two companies. The 2004 income statement of Straight Company is as follows:

DECISION MAKING

Sales		$720,000
Cost of goods sold		360,000
Gross profit		$360,000
Administrative costs	$ 96,000	
Depreciation expense	120,000	216,000
Income before tax		$144,000
Tax expense (40%)		57,600
Net income		$ 86,400

Straight Company depreciates all operating assets using the straight-line method for tax purposes and for the annual report provided to stockholders. All operating assets were purchased on the same date, and all assets had an estimated life of five years when purchased. Straight Company's balance sheet reveals that on December 31, 2004, the balance of the Accumulated Depreciation account was $240,000.

You want to compare the annual report of Straight Company to that of Accelerated Company. Both companies are in the same industry, and both have exactly the same assets, sales, and expenses except that Accelerated uses the double-declining-balance method for depreciation for income tax purposes and for the annual report provided to stockholders.

Required

Develop Accelerated Company's 2004 income statement. As a financial analyst interested in investing in one of the companies, do you find Straight or Accelerated more attractive? Because depreciation is a "noncash" expense, should you be indifferent between the two companies? Explain your answer.

Case 8-5 *Depreciation Alternatives* LO 5

DECISION MAKING

Medsupply Inc. produces supplies used in hospitals and nursing homes. Its sales, production, and costs to produce are expected to remain constant over the next five years. The corporate income tax rate is expected to increase over the next three years. The current rate, 15%, is expected to increase to 20% next year and then to 25% and continue at that rate indefinitely.

Medsupply is considering the purchase of new equipment that is expected to last for five years and to cost $150,000 with zero salvage value. As the controller, you are aware that the company can use one method of depreciation for accounting purposes and another method for tax purposes. You are trying to decide between the straight-line and the double-declining-balance methods.

Required

Recommend which method to use for accounting purposes and which to use for tax purposes. Be able to justify your answer on both a numerical and a theoretical basis. How does a noncash adjustment to income, such as depreciation, affect cash flow?

Accounting and Ethics: What Would You Do?

Case 8-6 *Valuing Assets* LO 3

Denver Company recently hired Terry Davis as an accountant. He was given responsibility for all accounting functions related to fixed asset accounting. Tammy Sharp, Terry's boss, asked him to review all transactions involving the current year's acquisition of fixed assets and to take necessary action to ensure that acquired assets were recorded at proper values. Terry is satisfied that all transactions are proper except for an April 15 purchase of an office building and the land on which it is situated. The purchase price of the acquisition was $200,000. Denver Company has not separately reported the land and building, however.

Terry hired an appraiser to determine the market values of the land and the building. The appraiser reported that his best estimates of the values were $150,000 for the building and $70,000 for the land. When Terry proposed that these values be used to determine the acquisition cost of the assets, Tammy disagreed. She told Terry to request another appraisal of the property and asked him to stress to the appraiser that the land component of the acquisition could not be depreciated for tax purposes. The second appraiser estimated that the values were $180,000 for the building and $40,000 for the land. Terry and Tammy agreed that the second appraisal should be used to determine the acquisition cost of the assets.

Required

Did Terry and Tammy act ethically in this situation? Explain your answer.

Case 8-7 *Depreciation Estimates* LO 5

Langsom's Mfg. is planning for a new project. Usually Langsom's depreciates long-term equipment for 10 years. The equipment for this project is specialized and will have no further use at the end of the project in three years. The manager of the project wants to depreciate the equipment over the usual 10 years and plans on writing off the remaining book value at the end of Year 3 as a loss. You believe that the equipment should be depreciated over the three-year life.

Required

Which method do you think is conceptually better? What should you do if the manager insists on depreciating the equipment over 10 years?

Internet Research Case

Case 8-8 AOL Time Warner

INTERNET

http://www.aoltimewarner.com

Time Warner announced a merger with America Online (AOL) in 1999 that became final in 2000. The union was driven by Time Warner's huge assets in content and media brands, along with its cable systems, and by the potential audience represented by AOL's over 25 million on-line members. The merger resulted in a company with enormous potential for growth and profitability. Unfortunately, the results of the merger were not as positive as planned. Advertising revenue declined because of a tight economy and a downturn in the climate for on-line advertising. The value of the company's intangible assets also declined as did the value of media brand names, copyrights, and cable systems of other technology companies. As a result, the price of AOL Time Warner stock declined drastically and was selling near $13 per share in mid-2002.

Access the AOL Time Warner Web site and review the most current annual report available along with recent news items about the company. Then answer the following questions.

1. The AOL Time Warner annual report referred to a large "impairment" of assets. Explain what is meant by an impairment of assets and how accounting for the impairment has affected the amount of intangible assets on the balance sheet.
2. Has the amount of intangible assets increased or decreased since the 2001 annual report? Which intangible assets have changed the most?
3. What is the current market price of the stock? How has the stock price responded since the $13 price in mid-2002?
4. Determine the number of on-line subscribers of the company. Has this number increased or decreased since the two companies merged?

Solutions to Key Terms Quiz

1	Acquisition cost (p. 385)	6	Change in estimate (p. 391)
5	Capitalization of interest (p. 386)	8	Capital expenditure (p. 393)
2	Land improvements (p. 387)	10	Revenue expenditure (p. 393)
7	Depreciation (p. 387)	11	Gain on Sale of Asset (p. 396)
3	Straight-line method (p. 387)	12	Loss on Sale of Asset (p. 396)
9	Book value (p. 388)	18	Natural resources (p. 397)
4	Units-of-production method (p. 388)	14	Intangible assets (p. 399)
13	Accelerated depreciation (p. 389)	16	Goodwill (p. 400)
15	Double-declining-balance method (p. 389)	17	Research and development costs (p. 401)

Part II

Integrative Problem

SPREADSHEET

Correct an income statement and statement of cash flows and assess the impact of a change in inventory method; compute the effect of a bad-debt recognition.

The following income statement, statement of cash flows, and additional information are available for PEK Company:

PEK COMPANY
INCOME STATEMENT
FOR THE YEAR ENDED DECEMBER 31, 2004

Sales revenue		$1,250,000
Cost of goods sold		636,500
Gross profit		$ 613,500
Depreciation on plant equipment	$58,400	
Depreciation on buildings	12,000	
Interest expense	33,800	
Other expenses	83,800	188,000
Income before taxes		$ 425,500
Income tax expense (30% rate)		127,650
Net income		$ 297,850

PEK COMPANY
STATEMENT OF CASH FLOWS
FOR THE YEAR ENDED DECEMBER 31, 2004

Cash flows from operating activities:	
Net income	$297,850
Adjustments to reconcile net income to net cash provided by operating activities (includes depreciation expense)	83,200
Net cash provided by operating activities	$381,050
Cash flows from financing activities:	
Dividends	(35,000)
Net increase in cash	$346,050

Additional information:

a. Beginning inventory and purchases for the one product the company sells are as follows:

	Units	Unit Cost
Beginning inventory	50,000	$2.00
Purchases:		
February 5	25,000	2.10
March 10	30,000	2.20
April 15	40,000	2.50
June 16	75,000	3.00
September 5	60,000	3.10
October 3	40,000	3.25

b. During the year, the company sold 250,000 units at $5 each.

c. PEK uses the periodic FIFO method to value its inventory and the straight-line method to depreciate all of its long-term assets.

d. During the year-end audit, it was discovered that a January 3, 2004, transaction for the lump-sum purchase of a mixing machine and a boiler was not recorded. The fair market values of the mixing machine and the boiler were $200,000 and $100,000, respectively. Each asset has an estimated useful life of 10 years with no residual value expected. The purchase of the assets was financed by issuing a $270,000 five-year promissory note directly to the seller. Interest of 8% is paid annually on December 31.

Required

1. Prepare a revised income statement and a revised statement of cash flows to take into account the omission of the entry to record the purchase of the two assets. (Hint: You will need to take into account any change in income taxes as a result of changes in any income statement items. Assume that income taxes are paid on December 31 of each year.)
2. Assume the same facts as above, except that the company is considering the use of an accelerated method rather than the straight-line method for the assets purchased on January 3, 2004. All other assets would continue to be depreciated on a straight-line basis. Prepare a revised income statement and a revised statement of cash flows, assuming the company decides to use the accelerated method for these two assets rather than the straight-line method resulting in depreciation of $49,091 for 2004.

Treat the answers in requirements **3** and **4** as independent of the other parts.

3. Assume PEK decides to use the LIFO method rather than the FIFO method to value its inventory and recognize cost of goods sold for 2004. Compute the effect (amount of increase or decrease) this would have on cost of goods sold, income tax expense, and net income.
4. Assume PEK failed to record an estimate of bad debts for 2004 (bad debt expense is normally included in "other expenses"). Before any adjustment, the balance in Allowance for Doubtful Accounts is $8,200. The credit manager estimates that 3% of the $800,000 of sales on account will prove to be uncollectible. Based on this information, compute the effect (amount of increase or decrease) of recognition of the bad-debt estimate on other expenses, income tax expense, and net income.

Part III

Accounting for Liabilities and Owners' Equity

A Word to Students about Part III

By now it's clear that this book is organized along the lines of a balance sheet. That is, Part II covered assets; Part III will cover liabilities and owner's equity. As we'll see, taking on liabilities to pay for assets is one way to provide financing for the future of the company; the other alternative is to issue stock.

Also, the chapters in Part III continue to discuss how the related transactions affect the statement of cash flows, which is key to understanding how companies' statements—and their activities—are interrelated.

Chapter 9

Current Liabilities, Contingencies, and the Time Value of Money

Focus on Financial Results

J. C. Penney has stated that its objective is "to provide our target customers with timely and competitive selections of fashionable, quality merchandise with unquestionable day-in, day-out value."[1] J. C. Penney wants to be the customer's first choice for the products and services they offer. In 2002, the 100-year-old firm was in the No. 5 spot among U.S. retailers.

Through its 1,100 stores located in the 50 U.S. states, Puerto Rico, and Mexico, its well-known catalog, and a Web site, the familiar retailer offers family apparel, jewelry, shoes, accessories, and home furnishings that bear national, as well as exclusive and private, brand names.

Yet, Penney's retail business did not perform well recently and the company admits that its performance was disappointing and that conditions have been "exceptionally challenging."[2] Improving profitability has become a key goal for the firm in future years. Allen Questrom, Penney's CEO, may well continue the short- and long-term strategies that have been in place for several years. These strategies focus on overhauling the department store merchandising process, simplifying pricing, closing underperforming stores, lowering operating costs, and becoming a major e-commerce retailer.

The first two of these objectives have implications for inventory. During 2000 and 2001, the company worked on reacting more quickly to fast- and slow-selling items to reduce inventory, hoping to take fewer markdowns and yield more profit. Suppliers became an integral part of inventory management during the year.

Managing inventory well also means managing *accounts payable,* one of J. C. Penney's *current liabilities.* That, in turn, means having enough current assets on hand to pay current liabilities, such as suppliers' bills, on time. So Penney's realizes that its profitability goals are directly linked to the effective management of inventory and the related current liabilities.

[1]J. C. Penney's annual report, p. 1.
[2]Ibid., p. 1.

J. C. Penney's 2001 Annual Report

Consolidated Balance Sheets

J. C. Penney Company, Inc. and Subsidiaries

($ in millions, except per share data)	January 26 2002	January 27 2001
Assets		
Current assets		
Cash (including short-term investments of $2,834 and $935)	$ 2,840	$ 944
Receivables (net of bad debt reserves of $27 and $30)	698	893
Merchandise inventory (net of LIFO reserves of $377 and $339)	4,930	5,269
Prepaid expenses	209	151
Total current assets	8,677	7,257
Property and equipment		
Land and buildings	2,987	2,949
Furniture and fixtures	4,105	3,919
Leasehold improvements	1,225	1,194
Accumulated depreciation	(3,328)	(2,948)
Property and equipment, net	4,989	5,114
Goodwill and other intangible assets (net of accumulated amortization of $573 and $452)	2,740	2,870
Other assets	1,642	1,474
Assets of discontinued operations (including cash and short-term investments of $0 and $156)	–	3,027
Total assets	$18,048	$19,742
Liabilities and stockholders' equity		
Current liabilities		
Accounts payable and accrued expenses	$ 3,465	$ 3,877
Short-term debt	15	–
Current maturities of long-term debt	920	250
Deferred taxes	99	108
Total current liabilities	4,499	4,235
Long-term debt	5,179	5,448
Deferred taxes	1,231	1,136
Other liabilities	1,010	978
Liabilities of discontinued operations	–	1,686
Total liabilities	11,919	13,483
Stockholders' equity		
Preferred stock, no par value and stated value of $600 per share: authorized, 25 million shares; issued and outstanding, 0.6 million and 0.7 million shares Series B ESOP convertible preferred	363	399
Common stock, par value $0.50 per share: authorized, 1,250 million shares; issued and outstanding 264 million and 263 million shares	3,324	3,294
Deferred stock compensation	6	–
Reinvested earnings	2,573	2,636
Accumulated other comprehensive (loss)	(137)	(70)
Total stockholders' equity	6,129	6,259
Total liabilities and stockholders' equity	$18,048	$19,742

The accompanying notes are an integral part of these Consolidated Financial Statements.

You're in the Driver's Seat

If you were a bank loan officer looking for information about J. C. Penney Company, Inc.'s credit rating, what information would you want about current liabilities? While you study this chapter, consider which accounts on Penney's balance sheet are current liabilities and how they might influence its financial position.

http://www.jcpenney.com

LEARNING OBJECTIVES

After studying this chapter, you should be able to:

LO 1 Identify the components of the current liability category of the balance sheet. (p. 434)

LO 2 Examine how accruals affect the current liability category. (p. 439)

LO 3 Demonstrate an understanding of how changes in current liabilities affect the statement of cash flows. (p. 440)

LO 4 Determine when contingent liabilities should be presented on the balance sheet or disclosed in notes and how to calculate their amounts. (p. 442)

LO 5 Explain the difference between simple and compound interest. (p. 448)

LO 6 Calculate amounts using the future value and present value concepts. (p. 449)

LO 7 Apply the compound interest concepts to some common accounting situations. (p. 457)

LO 8 Demonstrate an understanding of the deductions and expenses for payroll accounting (Appendix A). (p. 469)

LO 9 Determine when compensated absences must be accrued as a liability (Appendix A). (p. 472)

CURRENT LIABILITIES

LO 1 Identify the components of the current liability category of the balance sheet.

A classified balance sheet presents financial statement items by category in order to provide more information to financial statement users. The balance sheet generally presents two categories of liabilities, current and long-term.

Current liabilities finance the working capital of the company. At any given time during the year, current liabilities may fluctuate substantially. It is important that the company generates sufficient cash flow to retire these debts as they come due. As long as the company's ratio of current assets to current liabilities stays fairly constant from quarter to quarter or year to year, financial statement users are not going to be too concerned.

http://www.mcdonalds.com

The current liability portion of the 2001 balance sheet of McDonald's Corporation is highlighted in Exhibit 9-1. Some companies list the accounts in the current liability category in the order of payment due date. That is, the account that requires payment first is listed first, the account requiring payment next is listed second, and so forth. This allows users of the statement to assess the cash flow implications of each account. McDonald's uses a different approach and lists Notes Payable as the first account.

Current liability Accounts that will be satisfied within one year or the current operating cycle.

Current liabilities were first introduced to you in Chapter 2 of this text. In general, a **current liability** is an obligation that will be satisfied within one year. Although current liabilities are not due immediately, they are still recorded at face value; that is, the time until payment is not taken into account. If it were, current liabilities would be recorded at a slight discount to reflect interest that would be earned between now and the due date. The face value amount is generally used for all current liabilities because the time period involved is short enough that it is not necessary to record or calculate an interest factor. In addition, when interest rates are low, one need not worry about the interest that could be earned in this short period of time. In Chapter 10 we will find that many long-term liabilities must be stated at their present value on the balance sheet.

The current liability classification is important because it is closely tied to the concept of *liquidity.* Management of the firm must be prepared to pay current liabilities within a very short time period. Therefore, management must have access to liquid assets, cash, or other assets that can be converted to cash in amounts sufficient to pay the current liabilities. Firms that do not have sufficient resources to pay their current liabilities are often said to have a liquidity problem.

Exhibit 9-1 McDonald's Corporation 2001 Consolidated Balance Sheet

Consolidated Balance Sheet

IN MILLIONS, EXCEPT PER SHARE DATA	December 31, **2001**	2000
Assets		
Current assets		
Cash and equivalents	$ 418.1	$ 421.7
Accounts and notes receivable	881.9	796.5
Inventories, at cost, not in excess of market	105.5	99.3
Prepaid expenses and other current assets	413.8	344.9
Total current assets	1,819.3	1,662.4
Other assets		
Investments in and advances to affiliates	990.2	824.2
Goodwill, net	1,419.8	1,278.2
Miscellaneous	1,015.7	871.1
Total other assets	3,425.7	2,973.5
Property and equipment		
Property and equipment, at cost	24,106.0	23,569.0
Accumulated depreciation and amortization	(6,816.5)	(6,521.4)
Net property and equipment	17,289.5	17,047.6
Total assets	$22,534.5	$21,683.5
Liabilities and shareholders' equity		
Current liabilities		
Notes payable	$ 184.9	$ 275.5
Accounts payable	689.5	684.9
Income taxes	20.4	92.2
Other taxes	180.4	195.5
Accrued interest	170.6	149.9
Other accrued liabilities	824.9	608.4
Current maturities of long-term debt	177.6	354.5
Total current liabilities	2,248.3	2,360.9
Long-term debt	8,555.5	7,843.9
Other long-term liabilities and minority interests	629.3	489.5
Deferred income taxes	1,112.2	1,084.9
Common equity put options and forward contracts	500.8	699.9
Shareholders' equity		
Preferred stock, no par value; authorized–165.0 million shares; issued–none		
Common stock, $.01 par value; authorized–3.5 billion shares; issued–1,660.6 million shares	16.6	16.6
Additional paid-in capital	1,591.2	1,441.8
Unearned ESOP compensation	(106.7)	(115.0)
Retained earnings	18,608.3	17,259.4
Accumulated other comprehensive income	(1,708.8)	(1,287.3)
Common stock in treasury, at cost; 379.9 and 355.7 million shares	(8,912.2)	(8,111.1)
Total shareholders' equity	9,488.4	9,204.4
Total liabilities and shareholders' equity	$22,534.5	$21,683.5

Highlighted items will require payments within one year.

See notes to consolidated financial statements.

From Concept to Practice 9.1

Reading J. C. Penney's Balance Sheet

Refer to J. C. Penney's January 26, 2002 balance sheet in the chapter opener. What accounts are listed as current liabilities? How much did Accounts Payable and Accrued Expenses change from 2001 to 2002?

A handy ratio to help creditors or potential creditors determine a company's liquidity is the current ratio. A current ratio of current assets to current liabilities of 2:1 is usually a very comfortable margin. If the firm has a large amount of inventory, it is sometimes useful to exclude inventory (prepayments are also excluded) when computing the ratio. That provides the "quick" ratio. Usually, one would want a quick ratio of at least 1.5:1 to feel secure that the company could pay its bills on time. Of course, the guidelines given for the current ratio, 2:1, and the quick ratio, 1.5:1, are only rules of thumb. The actual current and quick ratios of companies vary widely and depend on the company, the management policies, and the type of industry. Exhibit 9-2 presents the current and quick ratios for the companies that are used as examples in this chapter. The ratios do vary from company to company, yet all are solid companies without liquidity problems.

Exhibit 9-2

Current and Quick Ratios of Selected Companies for 2001

COMPANY	INDUSTRY	CURRENT RATIO	QUICK RATIO
Georgia-Pacific	building products/lumber	0.94	0.51
J. C. Penney	retailing	1.92	0.79
Johnson Controls	auto	0.99	0.72
McDonald's	fast food	0.81	0.59
Pfizer	drug	1.35	1.04

Accounting for current liabilities is an area in which U.S. accounting standards are very similar to those of most other countries. Nearly all countries encourage firms to provide a breakdown of liabilities into current and long-term in order to allow users to evaluate liquidity.

Accounting for Your Decisions

You Are a Student

What types of current liabilities could you, as a student, have? What makes them liabilities? What makes them current?

ANS: Your current liabilities might include the current payments due from (1) student loans, (2) car loans, (3) loans from family members, (4) rent or mortgage payments, (5) credit card charges, (6) cafeteria charges, and similar charges. These items are current liabilities because they are obligations that will be satisfied within a year.

Accounts Payable

Accounts payable Amounts owed for inventory, goods, or services acquired in the normal course of business.

Accounts payable represent amounts owed for the purchase of inventory, goods, or services acquired in the normal course of business. Often, Accounts Payable is the first account listed in the current liability category because it requires the payment of cash before other current liabilities. McDonald's is different from most other companies because it lists Notes Payable before Accounts Payable.

Normally, a firm has an established relationship with several suppliers, and formal contractual arrangements with those suppliers are unnecessary. Accounts payable usually do not require the payment of interest, but terms may be given to encourage early payment. For example, terms may be stated as 2/10, n30, which means that a 2% discount is available if payment occurs within the first 10 days and that if payment is not made within 10 days, the full amount must be paid within 30 days.

Timely payment of accounts payable is an important aspect of the management of cash flow. Generally, it is to the company's benefit to take advantage of discounts when they are available. After all, if your supplier is going to give you a 2% discount for paying on Day 10 instead of Day 30, that means you are earning 2% on your money over 20/360 of a year. If you took the 2% discount throughout the year, you would be getting a 36% annual return on your money, since there are 18 periods of 20 days each in a year. It is essential, therefore, that the accounts payable system be established in a manner that alerts management to take advantage of offered discounts.

Notes Payable

The first current liability on McDonald's 2001 balance sheet is notes payable of $184.9 million. How is a note payable different from an account payable? The most important difference is that an account payable is not a formal contractual arrangement, whereas a **note payable** is represented by a formal agreement or note signed by the parties to the transaction. Notes payable may arise from dealing with a supplier or from acquiring a cash loan from a bank or creditor. Those notes that are expected to be paid within one year of the balance sheet date should be classified as current liabilities.

Notes payable Amounts owed that are represented by a formal contract.

The accounting for notes payable depends on whether the interest is paid on the note's due date or is deducted before the borrower receives the loan proceeds. With the first type of note, the terms stipulate that the borrower receives a short-term loan and agrees to repay the principal and interest at the note's due date. For example, assume that Lamanski Company receives a one-year loan from First National Bank on January 1. The face amount of the note of $1,000 must be repaid on December 31 along with interest at the rate of 12%. Lamanski would make the following entries to record the loan and its repayment:

		Debit	Credit
Jan. 1	Cash	1,000	
	Notes Payable		1,000
	To record loan of $1,000.		

Assets	=	Liabilities	+	Owners' Equity
+1,000		+1,000		

		Debit	Credit
Dec. 31	Notes Payable	1,000	
	Interest Expense	120	
	Cash		1,120
	To record the repayment of loan with interest.		

Assets	=	Liabilities	+	Owners' Equity
−1,120		−1,000		−120

Banks also use another form of note, one in which the interest is deducted in advance. Suppose that on January 1, 2004, First National Bank granted to Lamanski a $1,000 loan, due on December 31, 2004, but deducted the interest in advance and gave Lamanski the remaining amount of $880 ($1,000 face amount of the note less interest of $120). This is sometimes referred to as *discounting a note* because a Discount on Notes Payable account is established when the loan is recorded. On January 1, Lamanski must make the following entry:

		Debit	Credit
Jan. 1	Cash	880	
	Discount on Notes Payable	120	
	Notes Payable		1,000
	To record loan of $1,000 less interest deducted in advance.		

Assets	=	Liabilities	+	Owners' Equity
+880		−120		
		+1,000		

The **Discount on Notes Payable** account should be treated as a reduction of Notes Payable (and should have a debit balance). If a balance sheet was developed immediately after the January 1 loan, the note would appear in the current liability category as follows:

Discount on notes payable A contra liability that represents interest deducted from a loan in advance.

Study Tip

Discount on Notes Payable is a contra-liability account and will have a debit balance.

Notes Payable	$1,000
Less: Discount on Notes Payable	120
Net Liability	$ 880

The original balance in the Discount on Notes Payable account represents interest that must be transferred to interest expense over the life of the note. Before Lamanski presents its year-end financial statements, it must make an adjustment to transfer the discount to interest expense. The effect of the adjustment on December 31 is as follows:

Dec. 31	Interest Expense	120	
	Discount on Notes Payable		120
	To record interest on note payable.		

Assets	=	Liabilities	+	Owners' Equity
		+120		−120

Thus, the balance of the Discount on Notes Payable account is zero, and $120 has been transferred to interest expense. When the note is repaid on December 31, 2004, Lamanski must repay the full amount of the note as follows:

Dec. 31	Notes Payable	1,000	
	Cash		1,000
	To record payment of the note on its due date.		

Assets	=	Liabilities	+	Owners' Equity
−1,000		−1,000		

It is important to compare the two types of notes payable. In the previous two examples, the stated interest rate on each note was 12%. The dollar amount of interest incurred in each case was $120. However, the interest *rate* on a discounted note, the second example, is always higher than it appears. Lamanski received the use of only $880, yet it was required to repay $1,000. Therefore, the interest rate incurred on the note was actually $120/$880, or approximately 13.6%.

Current Maturities of Long-Term Debt

Current maturities of long-term debt The portion of a long-term liability that will be paid within one year.

Another account that appears in the current liability category of McDonald's balance sheet is **Current Maturities of Long-Term Debt.** On other companies' balance sheets, this item may appear as Long-Term Debt, Current Portion. This account should appear when a firm has a liability and must make periodic payments. For example, assume that on January 1, 2004, your firm obtained a $10,000 loan from the bank. The terms of the loan require you to make payments in the amount of $1,000 per year for 10 years, payable each January 1, beginning January 1, 2005. On December 31, 2004, an entry should be made to classify a portion of the balance as a current liability as follows:

2004			
Dec. 31	Long-Term Liability	1,000	
	Current Portion of Liability		1,000
	To record the current portion of bank loan.		

Assets	=	Liabilities	+	Owners' Equity
		−1,000		
		+1,000		

The December 31, 2004, balance sheet should indicate that the liability for the note payable is classified into two portions: a $1,000 current liability that must be repaid within one year and a $9,000 long-term liability.

On January 1, 2005, the company must pay $1,000, and the entry should be recorded as follows:

2005

Jan. 1	Current Portion of Liability	1,000	
	Cash		1,000
	To record payment of $1,000 on bank loan.		

Assets	=	Liabilities	+	Owners' Equity
−1,000		−1,000		

On December 31, 2005, the company should again record the current portion of the liability. Therefore, the 2005 year-end balance sheet should indicate that the liability is classified into two portions: a $1,000 current liability and an $8,000 long-term liability. The process should be repeated each year until the bank loan has been fully paid. When an investor or creditor reads a balance sheet, he or she wants to distinguish between debt that is long-term and debt that is short-term. Therefore, it is important to segregate that portion of the debt that becomes due within one year.

The balance sheet account labeled Current Maturities of Long-Term Debt should include only the amount of principal to be paid. The amount of interest that has been incurred but is unpaid should be listed separately in an account such as Interest Payable.

Taxes Payable

LO 2 Examine how accruals affect the current liability category.

Corporations pay a variety of taxes, including federal and state income taxes, property taxes, and other taxes. Usually, the largest dollar amount is incurred for state and federal income taxes. Taxes are an expense of the business and should be accrued in the same manner as any other business expense. A company that ends its accounting year on December 31 is not required to calculate the amount of tax owed to the government until the following March 15 or April 15, depending on the type of business. Therefore, the business must make an accounting entry, usually as one of the year-end adjusting entries, to record the amount of tax that has been incurred but is unpaid. Normally, the entry would be recorded as follows:

Dec. 31	Tax Expense	xxx	
	Tax Payable		xxx
	To accrue income tax for the year.		

Assets	=	Liabilities	+	Owners' Equity
		+xxx		−xxx

The calculation of the amount of tax a business owes is very complex. For now, the important point is that taxes are an expense when incurred (not when they are paid) and must be recorded as a liability as incurred.

Some analysts prefer to measure a company's profits before it pays taxes for several reasons. For one thing, tax rates change from year to year. A small change in the tax rate may drastically change a firm's profitability. Also, investors should realize that taxes occur in every year but that tax changes are not a recurring element of a business. Additionally, taxes are somewhat beyond the control of a company's management. For these reasons, it is important to consider a firm's operations *before* taxes to better evaluate management's ability to control operations.

Other Accrued Liabilities

McDonald's 2001 balance sheet listed an amount of $824.9 million as current liability under the category of Other Accrued Liabilities. What items might be included in this category?

In previous chapters, especially Chapter 4, we covered many examples of accrued liabilities. **Accrued liabilities** include any amount that has been incurred due to the passage of time but has not been paid as of the balance sheet date. A common example is salary or wages payable. Suppose that your firm has a payroll of $1,000 per day, Monday through Friday, and that employees are paid at the close of work each Friday. Also suppose that December 31 is the end of your accounting year and falls on a Tuesday. Your firm will then have to record the following entry as of December 31:

Accrued liability A liability that has been incurred but not yet paid.

Dec. 31	Salary Expense	2,000	
	Salary Payable		2,000
	To record two days' salary as expense.		

Assets	=	Liabilities	+	Owners' Equity
		+2,000		−2,000

The amount of the salary payable would be classified as a current liability and could appear in a category such as Other Accrued Liabilities.

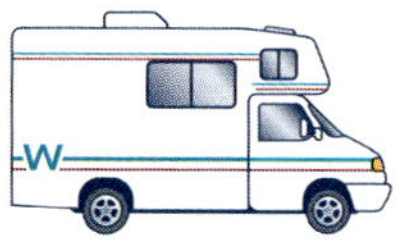

From Concept to Practice 9.2

Reading Winnebago Industries' Balance Sheet

What accounts are listed as Accrued Expenses on Winnebago Industries' balance sheet? Why do you think these items are not included in the Accounts Payable account?

Interest is another item that often must be accrued at year-end. Assume that you received a one-year loan of $10,000 on December 1. The loan carries an interest rate of 12%. On December 31, an accounting entry must be made to record interest, even though the money may not actually be due:

Dec. 31	Interest Expense	100	
	Interest Payable		100
	To record one month's interest as expense.		

Assets	=	Liabilities	+	Owners' Equity
		+100		−100

The Interest Payable account should be classified as a current liability, assuming that it is to be paid within one year of the December 31 date.

Reading the Statement of Cash Flows for Changes in Current Liabilities

LO 3 Demonstrate an understanding of how changes in current liabilities affect the statement of cash flows.

It is important to understand the impact that current liabilities have on a company's cash flows. Exhibit 9-3 illustrates the placement of current liabilities on the statement of cash flows (using the indirect method) and their effect. Most current liabilities are directly related to a firm's ongoing operations. Therefore, the change in the balance of each current liability account should be reflected in the Operating Activities category of the statement of cash flows. A decrease in a current liability account indicates that cash has been used to pay the liability and should appear as a deduction on the cash flow statement. An increase

Exhibit 9-3

Current Liabilities on the Statement of Cash Flows

Item	Cash Flow Statement	
	Operating Activities	
	Net income	xxx
Increase in current liability		+
Decrease in current liability		−
	Investing Activities	
	Financing Activities	
Increase in notes payable		+
Decrease in notes payable		−

Business Strategy

Effectively Expanding into Different Market Segments

Few department stores today focus on a narrow band of customers. Most savvy retailers realize the value of appealing to as many different market segments as possible while still establishing a distinctive identity for the store, to set it apart from its competitors.

http://www.jcpenney.com

J. C. Penney uses a wide array of private and national clothing brands to attract customers from many different demographic groups. National brands like Dockers®, Vanity Fair®, Jockey®, Haggar®, Adidas®, Crazy Horse®, and Joneswear® are all featured in Penney's stores. Private (store) brands such as Arizona Jeans®, Worthington®, Stafford®, and St. John's Bay® have proved successful enough to earn their own store-within-a-store departments, which J. C. Penney plans to expand. Despite this differentiation by brand, accounting information for all brands is added together for financial reporting purposes.

http://www.gap.com

Gap, Inc., on the other hand, sells only its own brand of clothes and accessories in its stores. When the company decided in 1994 to develop a new brand of trendy, budget-priced clothing, it spun off a whole new line of stores to showcase the clothing, and Old Navy® was born. This strategy had already allowed Gap to open the Banana Republic chain of slightly upscale clothing stores and contributed to Old Navy's initial success. Gap has faltered badly in recent years, and many investors are now questioning whether Gap adopted the right strategy. With so many competitors selling the kind of snappy casual clothes that Gap and its Banana Republic and Old Navy offshoots were famous for, the retailer has decided it is time for a new approach. The trendier offerings seem to have turned off mainstream shoppers, store sales have declined, and profits have fallen dramatically. In addition, the past several quarters of fashion misfires have been hard lessons for the company, but Gap appears to have become more disciplined in ways that will carry it through a few more quarters of disappointing sales. "Into the late '90s, Gap didn't have much use for operational controls. But now that product is falling off, they do," says Kindra Devaney, an analyst with Fulcrum Global Partners. Investors hope the company can rekindle some of the old magic and return to profitability.

Sources: *Business Week* online, December 17, 2001, by Amy Tsao and J. C. Penney's 2000 annual report.

in a current liability account indicates a recognized expense that has not yet been paid. Look for it as an increase in the Operating Activities category of the cash flow statement.

The cash flow statement of McDonald's Corporation is presented in Exhibit 9-4. Note that one of the items in the 2001 Operating Activities category is listed as Taxes and Other Liabilities of $160.0 million. This means that the balance of those current liabilities increased by $160.0 million, resulting in an increase of cash.

Almost all current liabilities appear in the Operating Activities category of the statement of cash flows, but there are exceptions. If a current liability is not directly related to operating activities, it should not appear in that category. For example, McDonald's uses some notes payable as a means of financing, distinct from operating activities. Therefore, note borrowings and repayments are reflected in the Financing Activities rather than the Operating Activities category (see Exhibit 9-4).

Two-Minute Review

1. *What is the definition of current liabilities? Give some examples of items that are typically in the current liability category.*
2. *How is the current ratio calculated? What is it intended to measure?*
3. *In which category of the cash flow statement do most current liability items appear?*

Answers on page 460.

Exhibit 9-4 McDonald's Corporation 2001 Consolidated Statement of Cash Flows

Consolidated Statement of Cash Flows

IN MILLIONS Years ended December 31,	**2001**	2000	1999
Operating activities			
Net income	**$ 1,636.6**	$ 1,977.3	$ 1,947.9
Adjustments to reconcile to cash provided by operations			
Depreciation and amortization	**1,086.3**	1,010.7	956.3
Deferred income taxes	**(87.6)**	60.5	52.9
Changes in operating working capital items			
Accounts receivable	**(104.7)**	(67.2)	(81.9)
Inventories, prepaid expenses and other current assets	**(62.9)**	(29.6)	(47.7)
Accounts payable	**10.2**	89.7	(23.9)
Taxes and other liabilities	**160.0**	(45.8)	270.4
Other	**50.4**	(244.1)	(65.1)
Cash provided by operations	**2,688.3**	2,751.5	3,008.9
Investing activities			
Property and equipment expenditures	**(1,906.2)**	(1,945.1)	(1,867.8)
Purchases of restaurant businesses	**(331.6)**	(425.5)	(340.7)
Sales of restaurant businesses and property	**375.9**	302.8	262.4
Other	**(206.3)**	(144.8)	(315.7)
Cash used for investing activities	**(2,068.2)**	(2,212.6)	(2,261.8)
Financing activities			
Net short-term borrowings (repayments)	**(248.0)**	59.1	116.7
Long-term financing issuances	**1,694.7**	2,381.3	902.5
Long-term financing repayments	**(919.4)**	(761.9)	(682.8)
Treasury stock purchases	**(1,068.1)**	(2,023.4)	(891.5)
Common stock dividends	**(287.7)**	(280.7)	(264.7)
Other	**204.8**	88.9	193.0
Cash used for financing activities	**(623.7)**	(536.7)	(626.8)
Cash and equivalents increase (decrease)	**(3.6)**	2.2	120.3
Cash and equivalents at beginning of year	**421.7**	419.5	299.2
Cash and equivalents at end of year	**$ 418.1**	$ 421.7	$ 419.5
Supplemental cash flow disclosures			
Interest paid	**$ 446.9**	$ 469.7	$ 411.5
Income taxes paid	**773.8**	854.2	642.2

See notes to consolidated financial statements.

Note the impact of changes in current liabilities on cash flow

CONTINGENT LIABILITIES

LO 4 Determine when contingent liabilities should be presented on the balance sheet or disclosed in notes and how to calculate their amounts.

Contingent liability An existing condition for which the outcome is not known but depends on some future event.

We have seen that accountants must exercise a great deal of expertise and judgment in deciding what to record and in determining the amount to record. This is certainly true regarding contingent liabilities. A **contingent liability** is an obligation that involves an existing condition for which the outcome is not known with certainty and depends on some event that will occur in the future. The actual amount of the liability must be estimated because we cannot clearly predict the future. The important accounting issues are whether contingent liabilities should be recorded and, if so, in what amounts.

This is a judgment call that is usually resolved through discussions among the company's management and its outside auditors. Management usually would rather not disclose contingent liabilities until they come due. The reason is that investors' and creditors' judgment of management is based on the company's earnings, and the recording of a contingent liability must be accompanied by a charge to (reduction in) earnings. Auditors, on the other hand, want management to disclose as much as possible because the auditors are essentially representing the interests of investors and creditors, who want to have as much information as possible.

Study Tip

Contingent liabilities are recorded only if they are probable and if the amount can be reasonably estimated.

Contingent Liabilities That Are Recorded

A contingent liability should be accrued and presented on the balance sheet if it is probable and if the amount can be reasonably estimated. But when is an event *probable*, and what does *reasonably estimated* mean? The terms must be defined based on the facts of each situation. A financial statement user would want the company to err on the side of full disclosure. On the other hand, the company should not be required to disclose every remote possibility.

A common contingent liability that must be presented as a liability by firms involves product warranties or guarantees. Many firms sell products for which they provide the customer a warranty against defects that may develop in the products. If a product becomes defective within the warranty period, the selling firm ensures that it will repair or replace the item. This is an example of a contingent liability because the expense of fixing a product depends on some of the products becoming defective—an uncertain, although likely, event.

At the end of each period, the selling firm must estimate how many of the products sold in the current year will become defective in the future and the cost of repair or replacement. This type of contingent liability is often referred to as an **estimated liability** to emphasize that the costs are not known at year-end and must be estimated.

Estimated liability A contingent liability that is accrued and reflected on the balance sheet.

As an example, assume that Quickkey Computer sells a computer product for \$5,000. When the customer buys the product, Quickkey provides a one-year warranty in case it must be repaired. Assume that in 2004 Quickkey sold 100 computers for a total sales revenue of \$500,000. At the end of 2004, Quickkey must record an estimate of the warranty costs that will occur on 2004 sales. Using an analysis of past warranty records, Quickkey estimates that repairs will average 2% of total sales. Therefore, Quickkey should record the following transaction at the end of 2004:

Dec. 31	Warranty Expense	10,000	
	Estimated Liability		10,000
	To record estimated liability at 2% of sales.		

Assets	=	Liabilities	+	Owners' Equity
		+10,000		−10,000

The amount of warranty costs that a company presents as an expense is of interest to investors and potential creditors. If the expense as a percentage of sales begins to rise, one might conclude that the product is becoming less reliable.

Warranties are an excellent example of the matching principle. In our Quickkey example, the warranty costs related to 2004 sales were estimated and recorded in 2004. This was done to match the 2004 sales with the expenses related to those sales. If actual repairs of the computers occurred in 2005, they do not result in an expense. The repair costs incurred in 2005 should be treated as a reduction in the liability that had previously been estimated.

Product warranties represent a contingent liability that must be presented on the balance sheet. This is because some amount of warranty work is probable and can be estimated. As the level of warranty expense rises, often so does investors' skepticism toward these retailers.

Because items such as warranties involve estimation, you may wonder what happens if the amount estimated is not accurate. The company must analyze past warranty records carefully and incorporate any changes in customer buying habits, usage, technological changes, and other changes. Still, even with careful analysis, the actual amount of the expense is not likely to equal the estimated amount. Generally, firms do not change the amount of the expense recorded in past periods for such differences. They may adjust the amount recorded in future periods, however.

Warranties provide an example of a contingent liability that must be estimated and recorded. Another example is premium or coupon offers that accompany many products. Cereal boxes are an everyday example of premium offers. The boxes often allow customers to purchase a toy or game at a reduced price if the purchase is accompanied by cereal box tops or proof of purchase. The offer given to cereal customers represents a contingent liability. At the end of each year, the cereal company must estimate the number of premium offers that will be redeemed and the cost involved and must report a contingent liability for that amount.

Legal claims that have been filed against a firm are also examples of contingent liabilities. In today's business environment, lawsuits and legal claims are a fact of life. They represent a contingent liability because an event has occurred but the outcome of that event, the resolution of the lawsuit, is not known. The defendant in the lawsuit must make a judgment about the outcome of the lawsuit in order to decide whether the item should be recorded on the balance sheet or should be disclosed in the notes. If an unfavorable outcome to the legal claim is deemed to be probable, then an amount should be recorded as a contingent liability on the balance sheet. Exhibit 9-5 provides portions of a note disclosure that accompanied the 2001 financial statements of **Georgia-Pacific Corporation.** The note concerned litigation over environmental damage that is alleged to have occurred as a result of the company's activities. Environmental remediation claims are very common for companies in many industries. In this case, Georgia-Pacific believed that an unfavorable outcome had become probable and, as a result, recorded a contingent liability of $121 million as an estimate of the amount that will be owed at the eventual outcome of this claim.

http://www.gp.com

Exhibit 9-5

Note Disclosure for Contingent Liability from Georgia-Pacific's 2001 Financial Statements

Note 18

The Corporation is involved in environmental remediation activities at approximately 170 sites, both owned by the Corporation and owned by others, where it has been notified that it is or may be a potentially responsible party under the Comprehensive Environmental Response, Compensation and Liability Act or similar state "superfund" laws.

The Corporation has established reserves for environmental remediation costs for these sites in amounts that it believes are probable and reasonably estimable. Based on analysis of currently available information and previous experience with respect to the cleanup of hazardous substances, the Corporation believes that it is reasonably possible that costs associated with these sites may exceed current reserves by amounts that may prove insignificant or that could range, in the aggregate, up to approximately $121 million.

As you might imagine, firms are not usually eager to record contingent lawsuits as liabilities because the amount of loss is often difficult to estimate. Also, some may view the accountant's decision as an admission of guilt if a lawsuit is recorded as a liability before the courts have finalized a decision. Accountants must often consult with lawyers or other legal experts to determine the probability of the loss of a lawsuit. In cases involving contingencies, it is especially important that the accountant make an independent judgment based on the facts and not be swayed by the desires of other parties.

Contingent Liabilities That Are Disclosed

Any contingent liability that both is probable and can be reasonably estimated must be reported as a liability. We now must consider contingent liabilities that do not meet the probable criterion or cannot be reasonably estimated. In either case, a contingent liability must be disclosed in the financial statement notes but not reported on the balance sheet if the contingent liability is at least reasonably possible.

Although information in the notes to the financial statements contains very important data on which investors base decisions, some accountants believe that note disclosure does not have the same impact as does recording a contingent liability on the balance sheet. For one thing, note disclosure does not affect the important financial ratios that investors use to make decisions.

In the previous section, we presented a legal claim involving Georgia-Pacific as an example of a contingent liability that was probable and therefore was recorded on the balance sheet as a liability. Most lawsuits, however, are not recorded as liabilities either because the risk of loss is not considered probable or because the amount of the loss cannot be reasonably estimated. If a company does not record a lawsuit as a liability, it must still consider whether the lawsuit should be disclosed in the notes to the financial statements. If the risk of loss is at least *reasonably possible,* then the company should provide note disclosure. This is the course of action taken for most contingent liabilities involving lawsuits.

Exhibit 9-6 contains excerpts from the notes to the 2001 financial statements of Pfizer, a large drug and pharmaceutical company. The first portion of Exhibit 9-6 indicates that Pfizer is subject to a variety of lawsuits and legal actions, which arise from patent, product liability, environmental, tax claims, and other matters. The second portion of the exhibit concerns some of the most common types of lawsuits in our economy—claims concerning asbestos. Note that in this case Pfizer acquired another company with products containing asbestos, and as a result, several hundred lawsuits are now being filed against Pfizer alleging injury as far back as the 1960s.

http://www.pfizer.com

Exhibit 9-6 Note Disclosure for Contingencies from Pfizer's 2001 Annual Report

We are involved in various patent, product liability, consumer, environmental, and tax claims and litigations, and additional matters that arise from time to time in the ordinary course of our business. These include challenges to the coverage and/or validity of patents on products or processes and allegations of injuries caused by drugs or medical devices. In addition, we are subject to national, state, and local environmental laws and regulations. We are also involved in or are the subject of governmental or regulatory agency inquiries or investigations from time to time. Litigation is inherently unpredictable and excessive verdicts that are not justified by the evidence can occur. We believe that we have valid defenses with respect to the legal matters pending against us and, taking into account our insurance and reserves, we believe that the ultimate resolution of these matters will not have a material adverse impact on our financial condition, results of operations, or cash flows. It is possible, however, that cash flows or results of operations could be affected in any particular period by the resolution of one or more of these contingencies.

Among the principal matters pending against us are the following:

Asbestos. In the 1960s, Pfizer acquired two businesses, the Gibsonburg Lime Products Company (GLPC) and Quigley Company, Inc., that had limited sales of minor products that contained small amounts of chrysotile asbestos and that now form the basis for the Company's asbestos litigation. Between 1967 and 1982, Warner-Lambert Company owned American Optical Corporation, which manufactured and sold respiratory protective devices and asbestos safety clothing.

Approximately 168,000 claims naming Pfizer and/or Quigley, and numerous other defendants, are currently pending in state and federal courts seeking damages for alleged asbestos exposure. Because many claimants name both Pfizer and Quigley, despite the fact that their work histories make exposure to both GLPC and Quigley products highly unlikely, the number of claims overstates the number of claimants, which we estimate to be approximately 112,000. In addition, approximately 61,000 claimants have named American Optical as a defendant. Based upon available data and our experience in handling asbestos claims, we believe that the vast majority of plaintiffs do not have any impairing medical condition. For those claimants who do, we believe we have meritorious defenses and are defending these cases vigorously.

Since the inception of this litigation, Pfizer and Quigley have closed, through settlement for varying amounts or through litigation, in excess of 185,000 asbestos suits or claims. In the same period, American Optical has closed in excess of 40,000 such suits or claims.

You should note that the excerpts in Exhibit 9-6 are examples of contingent liabilities that have been disclosed in the notes to the financial statements *but have not been recorded as liabilities on the balance sheet.* Readers of the financial statements, and analysts, must carefully read the notes to determine the impact of such contingent liabilities.

The amount and the timing of the cash outlays associated with contingent liabilities are especially difficult to determine. Lawsuits, for example, may extend several years into the future, and the dollar amount of possible loss may be subject to great uncertainty.

Accounting for Your Decisions

You Are the CEO

You run a high-technology company that grows fast some quarters and disappoints investors in other quarters. As a result, your company's stock price fluctuates widely, and you have attracted the unwanted attention of a law firm that filed a lawsuit on behalf of disgruntled shareholders. How do you reflect this lawsuit on your financial statements?

ANS: Your legal counsel should be consulted to determine whether the plaintiff's case has merit. If a loss is probable and the amount can be estimated, the lawsuit should be recorded as a liability. Unfortunately, lawsuits have become very common for many companies. In some cases, the lawsuits are totally without merit and are frivolous. If your attorneys agree that this case will not result in a loss, then no disclosure would be required.

Contingent Liabilities versus Contingent Assets

Contingent liabilities that are probable and can be reasonably estimated must be presented on the balance sheet before the outcome of the future events is known. This accounting rule applies only to contingent losses or liabilities. It does not apply to contingencies by which the firm may gain. Generally, contingent gains or **contingent assets** are not reported until the gain actually occurs. That is, contingent liabilities may be accrued, but contingent assets are not accrued. Exhibit 9-7 contains a portion of the notes from the 2001 financial statements of Johnson Controls, Inc., a large company that is a supplier to the auto makers. Like many other companies, Johnson Controls has had to accrue rather large amounts for environmental remediation costs. The note indicates that Johnson Controls believes that its insurance policies should cover part of the costs. This is an example of a contingent asset because the company may receive some amounts at a future time. The financial statements reveal that Johnson Controls has recorded liabilities related to the remediation costs but has not recorded any of the potential recoveries from insurance even though it appears quite likely that some amount will be received. This may seem inconsistent—it is. Remember, however, that accounting is a discipline based on a conservative set of principles. It is prudent

Which Way to Go?

Is It Really a Current Liability?

Taz Industries has signed a contract with Wile E. Industrial Builders. It will take Wile E. two years to build a new manufacturing plant behind the existing one. Under the agreement, Wile E. will bill Taz for part of the agreed upon price each time one-fourth of the project has been completed. Taz, therefore, will make four equal payments to Wile E., with the last one being made when the building is completed.

On June 30, 2003, Taz's fiscal year-end, Wile E. began the building process. By the end of July, the accountants at Taz were about to release the year-end balance sheet information. In anticipation of the building being 50% complete before June 30, 2004, and the need to make two payments to Wile E. during the year, the accountants classified half of the contract price as a current liability.

Have the accountants correctly reported the obligation? Why or why not? Would your answer change if, on July 25, 2003, the accountants learned that Wile E. had run into a problem with the building process and there probably would be a six to nine-month delay in construction so the second payment would not be due before January 1, 2005? Why or why not?

NOTE 15

Contingencies

The Company is involved in a number of proceedings and potential proceedings relating to environmental matters. At September 30, 2001, the Company had an accrued liability of approximately $28 million relating to environmental matters. The Company's environmental liabilities are undiscounted and do not take into consideration any possible recoveries of future insurance proceeds. Because of the uncertainties associated with environmental assessment and remediation activities, the Company's future expenses to remediate the currently identified sites could be considerably higher than the accrued liability. Although it is difficult to estimate the liability of the Company related to these environmental matters, the Company believes that these matters will not have a materially adverse effect upon its capital expenditures, earnings or competitive position.

Additionally, the Company is involved in a number of product liability and various other suits incident to the operation of its businesses. Insurance coverages are maintained and estimated costs are recorded for claims and suits of this nature. It is management's opinion that none of these will have a materially adverse effect on the Company's financial position, results of operations or cash flows.

Exhibit 9-7

Note Disclosure for Contingent Asset (Proceeds from Insurance) from Johnson Controls' Financial Statements

and conservative to delay the recording of a gain until an asset is actually received but to record contingent liabilities in advance.

Of course, even though the contingent assets are not reported, the information may still be important to investors. Wall Street analysts make their living trying to place a value on contingent assets that they believe will result in future benefits. By buying stock of a company that has unrecorded assets, or advising their clients to do so, investment analysts hope to make money when those assets become a reality.

Contingent assets An existing condition for which the outcome is not known but by which the company stands to gain.

http://www.johnsoncontrols.com

Two-Minute Review

1. *Under what circumstances should contingent liabilities be reported in the financial statements?*
2. *Under what circumstances should contingent liabilities be disclosed in the notes and not recorded in the financial statements?*
3. *Are contingent assets treated the same as contingent liabilities?*

Answers on page 460.

TIME VALUE OF MONEY CONCEPTS

In this section we will study the impact that interest has on decision making because of the time value of money. The **time value of money** concept means that people prefer a payment at the present time rather than in the future because of the interest factor. If an amount is received at the present time, it can be invested, and the resulting accumulation will be larger than if the same amount is received in the future. Thus, there is a *time value* to cash receipts and payments. This time value concept is important to every student for two reasons: it affects your personal financial decisions, and it affects accounting valuation decisions.

Time value of money An immediate amount should be preferred over an amount in the future.

Exhibit 9-8 indicates some of the personal and accounting decisions affected by the time value of money concept. In your personal life, you make decisions based on the time value of money concept nearly every day. When you invest money, you are interested in how much will be accumulated, and you must determine the *future value* based on the amount of interest that will be compounded. When you borrow money, you must determine the amount of the payments on the loan. You may not always realize it, but the amount of the loan payment is based on the *present value* of the loan, another time value of money concept.

Exhibit 9-8

Importance of the Time Value of Money

DECISION MAKING

Personal Financial Decision	Action
■ How much money will accumulate if you invest in a CD or money market account? →	Calculate the future value based on compound interest.
■ If you take out an auto loan, what will be the monthly loan payments? →	Calculate the payments based on the present value of the loan.
■ If you invest in the bond market, what should you pay for a bond? →	Calculate the present value of the bond based on compound interest.
■ If you win the lottery, should you take an immediate payment or payment over time? →	Calculate the present value of the alternatives based on compound interest.

Valuation Decisions on the Financial Statements	Valuation
■ Long-term assets →	Historical cost, but not higher than present value of the cash flows
■ Notes receivable →	Present value of the cash flows
■ Loan payments →	Based on the present value of the loan
■ Bond issue price →	Present value of the cash flows
■ Leases →	Present value of the cash flows

Time value of money is also important because of its implications for accounting valuations. We will discover in Chapter 10 that the issue price of a bond is based on the present value of the cash flows that the bond will produce. The valuation of the bond and the recording of the bond on the balance sheet are based on this concept. Further, the amount that is considered interest expense on the financial statements is also based on time value of money concepts. The bottom portion of Exhibit 9-8 indicates that the valuations of many other accounts, including Notes Receivable and Leases, are based on compound interest calculations.

The time value of money concept is used in virtually every advanced business course. Investment courses, marketing courses, and many other business courses will use the time value of money concept. *In fact, it is probably the most important decision-making tool to master in preparation for the business world.* This section of the text begins with an explanation of how simple interest and compound interest differ and then proceeds to the concepts of present values and future values.

Simple Interest

LO 5 Explain the difference between simple and compound interest.

Simple interest is interest earned on the principal amount. If the amount of principal is unchanged from year to year, the interest per year will remain the same. Interest can be calculated by the following formula:

$$I = P \times R \times T$$

where

I = Dollar amount of interest per year

P = Principal

R = Interest rate as a percentage

T = Time in years

Simple interest Interest is calculated on the principal amount only.

For example, assume that our firm has signed a two-year note payable for $3,000. Interest and principal are to be paid at the due date with simple interest at the rate of 10% per year. The amount of interest on the note would be $600, calculated as $3,000 × 0.10 × 2. We would be required to pay $3,600 on the due date: $3,000 principal and $600 interest.

Compound Interest

Compound interest Interest calculated on the principal plus previous amounts of interest.

Compound interest means that interest is calculated on the principal plus previous amounts of accumulated interest. Thus, interest is compounded, or we can say that there is interest on interest. For example, assume a $3,000 note payable for which interest and principal are due in two years with interest compounded annually at 10% per year. Interest would be calculated as follows:

YEAR	PRINCIPAL AMOUNT AT BEGINNING OF YEAR	INTEREST AT 10%	ACCUMULATED AT YEAR-END
1	$3,000	$300	$3,300
2	3,300	330	3,630

We would be required to pay $3,630 at the end of two years, $3,000 principal and $630 interest. A comparison of the note payable with 10% simple interest in the first example with the note payable with 10% compound interest in the second example clearly indicates that the amount accumulated with compound interest is always a higher amount because of the interest-on-interest feature.

Interest Compounding

LO 6 Calculate amounts using the future value and present value concepts.

For most accounting problems, we will assume that compound interest is compounded annually. In actual business practice, compounding usually occurs over much shorter intervals. This can be confusing because the interest rate is often stated as an annual rate even though it is compounded over a shorter period. If compounding is not done annually, you must adjust the interest rate by dividing the annual rate by the number of compounding periods per year.

For example, assume that the note payable from the previous example carried a 10% interest rate compounded semiannually for two years. The 10% annual rate should be converted to 5% per period for four semiannual periods. The amount of interest would be compounded, as in the previous example, but for four periods instead of two. The compounding process is as follows:

PERIOD	PRINCIPAL AMOUNT AT BEGINNING OF YEAR	INTEREST AT 5% PER PERIOD	ACCUMULATED AT END OF PERIOD
1	$3,000	$150	$3,150
2	3,150	158	3,308
3	3,308	165	3,473
4	3,473	174	3,647

The example illustrates that compounding more frequently results in a larger amount accumulated. In fact, many banks and financial institutions now compound interest on savings accounts on a daily basis.

Accounting for Your Decisions

You Invest Some Unexpected Cash

You want to invest some extra money you received from a long-lost uncle. You have narrowed your options down to two: (1) invest in a bond that offers 10% interest compounded semiannually, or (2) invest in a certificate of deposit that offers 10% interest compounded quarterly. Both options cover a one-year time period. Using the time value of money concepts you have learned in this accounting course, would you choose Option 1 or 2? Why?

ANS: You should choose Option 2, offering the same interest rate as the first option but compounding on a quarterly basis instead of a semiannual basis. More frequent compounding results in more interest, thus making Option 2's quarterly compounding more appealing than Option 1's semiannual compounding.

In the remainder of this section, we will assume that compound interest is applicable. Four compound interest calculations must be understood:

1. Future value of a single amount
2. Present value of a single amount
3. Future value of an annuity
4. Present value of an annuity

Future Value of a Single Amount

We are often interested in the amount of interest plus principal that will be accumulated at a future time. This is called a *future amount* or *future value.* The future amount

Assume you won the lottery and this check is yours. Which payment option would you take—a lump sum or an amount every year for 10 years? Only by understanding time value of money concepts could you make an intelligent choice.

is always larger than the principal amount (payment) because of the interest that accumulates. The formula to calculate the **future value of a single amount** is as follows:

Future value of a single amount Amount accumulated at a future time from a single payment or investment.

$$FV = p(1 + i)^n,$$

where

$$FV = \text{Future value to be calculated}$$
$$p = \text{Present value or principal amount}$$
$$i = \text{Interest rate}$$
$$n = \text{Number of periods of compounding}$$

Example 1: Your three-year-old son, Robert, just inherited $50,000 in cash and securities from his grandfather. If the funds were left in the bank and in the stock market and received an annual return of 10%, how much would be there in 15 years when Robert starts college?

Solution:

$$\begin{aligned} FV &= \$50{,}000(1 + 0.10)^{15} \\ &= \$50{,}000(4.177) \\ &= \$208{,}850 \end{aligned}$$

In some cases, we will use time diagrams to illustrate the relationships. A time diagram to illustrate a future value would be of the following form:

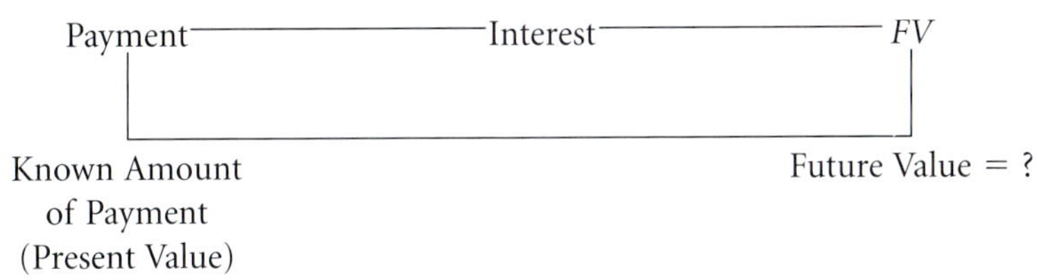

Example 2: Consider a $2,000 note payable that carries interest at the rate of 10% compounded annually. The note is due in two years, and the principal and interest must be paid at that time. The amount that must be paid in two years is the future value. The future value can be calculated in the manner we have used in the previous examples:

YEAR	PRINCIPAL AMOUNT AT BEGINNING OF YEAR	INTEREST AT 10%	ACCUMULATED AT YEAR-END
1	$2,000	$200	$2,200
2	2,200	220	2,420

The future value can also be calculated by using the following formula:

$$\begin{aligned} FV &= \$2{,}000(1 + 0.10)^2 \\ &= \$2{,}000(1.21) \\ &= \$2{,}420 \end{aligned}$$

Rather than using a formula, there are other methods to calculate future value. Tables can be constructed to assist in the calculations. Table 9-1 on page 465 indicates the future value of $1 at various interest rates and for various time periods. To find the future value of a two-year note at 10% compounded annually, you read across the line for two periods and down the 10% column and see an interest rate factor of 1.210. Because the table has been constructed for future values of $1, we would determine the future value of $2,000 as follows:

$$\begin{aligned} FV &= \$2{,}000 \times 1.210 \\ &= \$2{,}420 \end{aligned}$$

Many financial calculators are also available to perform future value calculations. We will illustrate the calculations with a widely used calculator, **Texas Instrument's** Advanced Business Analyst® (BA II). All financial calculators perform the calculations in the same manner, but you should be aware that the methods to enter the data, the keystrokes, might vary somewhat from one calculator to another.[3]

To calculate the future value in our example, you should perform the following steps:

ENTER	DISPLAY
2 N	N = 2
10 I/Y	I/Y = 10
0 PMT	PMT= 0
2000 PV	PV = 2,000
CPT FV	FV = 2,420

A third method used to perform the calculations is to use the built-in functions of a computerized spreadsheet. In Appendix B, we will illustrate how to use a common spreadsheet, Microsoft® Excel, to perform the same calculations. *Note that the numbers produced by each method may differ by a few dollars because of rounding differences. You should ignore those small differences and concentrate on the methods used to perform the interest rate calculations.*

We mentioned that compounding does not always occur annually. How does this affect the calculation of future value amounts?

Example 3: Suppose we want to find the future value of a \$2,000 note payable due in two years. The note payable requires interest to be compounded quarterly at the rate of 12% per year. To calculate the future value, we must adjust the interest rate to a quarterly basis by dividing the 12% rate by the number of compounding periods per year, which in the case of quarterly compounding is four:

$$12\%/4 \text{ quarters} = 3\% \text{ per Quarter}$$

Also, the number of compounding periods is eight—four per year times two years.

The future value of the note can be found in two ways. First, we can insert the proper values into the future value formula:

$$\begin{aligned} FV &= \$2{,}000(1 + 0.03)^8 \\ &= \$2{,}000(1.267) \\ &= \$2{,}534 \end{aligned}$$

We can arrive at the same future value amount with the use of Table 9-1. Refer to the interest factor in the table indicated for 8 periods and 3%. The future value would be calculated as follows:

$$\begin{aligned} FV &= \$2{,}000(\text{interest factor}) \\ &= \$2{,}000(1.267) \\ &= \$2{,}534 \end{aligned}$$

The steps using the calculator are as follows:

ENTER	DISPLAY
8 N	N = 8
3 I/Y	I/Y = 3
0 PMT	PMT= 0
2000 PV	PV = 2,000
CPT FV	FV = 2,534

[3]Some preliminary steps are necessary before using the calculator for the calculations we will illustrate. First, we will assume that your calculator is set to accommodate annual payments, rather than monthly payments. See your calculator instruction manual to set it to annual payments if necessary. Second, when we calculate the present value or future value of an annuity of payments, we will assume that the payments constitute an ordinary annuity, also called an annuity in arrears. That is, we will assume the payments occur at the end of each period. Your calculator should be set to end-of-period payments. Again, refer to your instruction manual to make sure it is set correctly.

Present Value of a Single Amount

In many situations, we do not want to calculate how much will be accumulated at a future time. Rather, we want to determine the present amount that is equivalent to an amount at a future time. This is the present value concept. The **present value of a single amount** represents the value today of a single amount to be received or paid at a future time. This can be portrayed in a time diagram as follows:

Present value of a single amount Amount at a present time that is equivalent to a payment or investment at a future time.

PV ——— Discount ——— Payment

PV = ? Known Amount of Payment (Future Value)

The time diagram portrays discount, rather than interest, because we often speak of "discounting" the future payment back to the present time.

Example 4: Suppose you know that you will receive \$2,000 in two years. You also know that if you had the money now, it could be invested at 10% compounded annually. What is the present value of the \$2,000? Another way to ask the same question is, What amount must be invested today at 10% compounded annually in order to have \$2,000 accumulated in two years?

The formula used to calculate present value is as follows:

$$PV = \text{Future value} \times (1 + i)^{-n}$$

where

$$PV = \text{Present value amount in dollars}$$
$$\text{Future value} = \text{Amount to be received in the future}$$
$$i = \text{Interest rate or discount rate}$$
$$n = \text{Number of periods}$$

We can use the present value formula to solve for the present value of the \$2,000 note as follows:

$$\begin{aligned} PV &= \$2{,}000 \times (1 + 0.10)^{-2} \\ &= \$2{,}000 \times (0.826) \\ &= \$1{,}652 \end{aligned}$$

Example 5: A recent magazine article projects that it will cost \$120,000 to attend a four-year college 10 years from now. If that is true, how much money would you have to put into an account today to fund that education, assuming a 5% rate of return?

Study Tip

When interest rates *increase*, present values *decrease*. This is called an *inverse relationship*.

$$\begin{aligned} PV &= \$120{,}000(1 + 0.05)^{-10} \\ &= \$12{,}000(0.614) \\ &= \$73{,}680 \end{aligned}$$

Tables have also been developed to determine the present value of \$1 at various interest rates and number of periods. Table 9-2 on page 466 presents the present value or discount factors for an amount of \$1 to be received at a future time. To use the table for our two-year note example, you must read across the line for two periods and down the 10% column to the discount factor of 0.826. The present value of \$2,000 would be calculated as follows:

$$\begin{aligned} PV &= \$2{,}000(\text{discount factor}) \\ &= \$2{,}000(0.826) \\ &= \$1{,}652 \end{aligned}$$

The steps using the calculator are as follows:

ENTER	DISPLAY
2 N	N = 2
10 I/Y	I/Y = 10
0 PMT	PMT= 0
2000 FV	FV = 2,000
CPT PV	PV = 1,653

Two other points are important. First, the example illustrates that the present value amount is always less than the future payment. This happens because of the discount factor. In other words, if we had a smaller amount at the present (the present value), we could invest it and earn interest that would accumulate to an amount equal to the larger amount (the future payment). Second, study of the present value and future value formulas indicates that each is the reciprocal of the other. When we want to calculate a present value amount, we normally use Table 9-2 and multiply a discount factor times the payment. However, we could also use Table 9-1 and divide by the interest factor. Thus, the present value of the $2,000 to be received in the future could also be calculated as follows:

$$\begin{aligned} PV &= \$2{,}000/1.210 \\ &= \$1{,}652 \end{aligned}$$

Future Value of an Annuity

Annuity A series of payments of equal amounts.

The present value and future value amounts are useful when a single amount is involved. Many accounting situations involve an annuity, however. **Annuity** means a series of payments of equal amounts. We will now consider the calculation of the future value when a series of payments is involved.

Example 6: Suppose that you are to receive $3,000 per year at the end of each of the next four years. Also assume that each payment could be invested at an interest rate of 10% compounded annually. How much would be accumulated in principal and interest by the end of the fourth year? This is an example of an annuity of payments of equal amounts. A time diagram would portray the payments as follows:

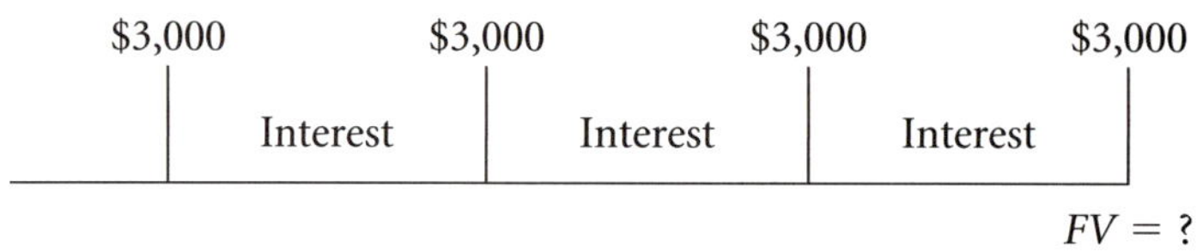

Because we are interested in calculating the future value, we could use the future value of $1 concept and calculate the future value of each $3,000 payment using Table 9-1 as follows:

$3,000 × 1.331 Interest for 3 Periods	$ 3,993
3,000 × 1.210 Interest for 2 Periods	3,630
3,000 × 1.100 Interest for 1 Period	3,300
3,000 × 1.000 Interest for 0 Periods	3,000
Total Future Value	$13,923

It should be noted that four payments would be received but that only three of them would draw interest because the payments are received at the end of each period.

Future value of an annuity Amount accumulated in the future when a series of payments is invested and accrues interest.

Fortunately, there is an easier method to calculate the **future value of an annuity.** Table 9-3 on page 467 has been constructed to indicate the future value of a series of payments of $1 per period at various interest rates and number of periods. The table can be used for the previous example by reading across the four-period line and down the 10% column to a table factor of 4.641. The future value of an annuity of $3,000 per year can be calculated as follows:

$$\begin{aligned} FV &= \$3{,}000(\text{table factor}) \\ &= \$3{,}000(4.641) \\ &= \$13{,}923 \end{aligned}$$

The steps using the calculator are as follows:

ENTER	DISPLAY
4 N	N = 4
10 I/Y	I/Y = 10
3000 PMT	PMT= 3,000
0 PV	PV = 0
CPT FV	FV = 13,923

Example 7: Your cousin just had a baby girl two weeks ago and is already thinking about sending her to college. When the girl is 15, how much money would be in her college account if your cousin deposits $2,000 into it on each of her 15 birthdays? The interest rate is 10%.

$$\begin{aligned} FV &= \$2{,}000(\text{table factor}) \\ &= \$2{,}000(31.772) \\ &= \$63{,}544 \end{aligned}$$

The steps using the calculator are as follows:

ENTER	DISPLAY
15 N	N = 15
10 I/Y	I/Y = 10
2000 PMT	PMT= 2,000
0 PV	PV = 0
CPT FV	FV = 63,545

When compounding occurs more frequently than annually, adjustments must be made to the interest rate and number of periods, adjustments similar to those discussed previously for single amounts.

Example 8: How would the future value be calculated if the previous example was modified so that we deposited $1,000 semiannually and the interest rate was 10% compounded semiannually (or 5% per period) for 15 years? Table 9-3 could be used by reading across the line for 30 periods and down the column for 5% to obtain a table factor of 66.439. The future value would be calculated as follows:

$$\begin{aligned} FV &= \$1{,}000(\text{table factor}) \\ &= \$1{,}000(66.439) \\ &= \$66{,}439 \end{aligned}$$

The steps using the calculator are as follows:

ENTER	DISPLAY
30 N	N = 30
5 I/Y	I/Y = 5
1000 PMT	PMT= 1,000
0 PV	PV = 0
CPT FV	FV = 66,439

Comparing the two examples illustrates once again that more frequent compounding results in larger accumulated amounts.

Present Value of an Annuity

Many accounting applications of the time value of money concept concern situations for which we want to know the present value of a series of payments that will occur in the future. This involves calculating the present value of an annuity. An annuity is a series of payments of equal amounts.

Example 9: Suppose that you will receive an annuity of $4,000 per year for four years, with the first received one year from today. The amounts received can be invested at a rate of 10% compounded annually. What amount would you need at the present time to have an amount equivalent to the series of payments and interest in the future? To answer this question, you must calculate the **present value of an annuity.** A time diagram of the series of payments would appear as follows:

Present value of an annuity The amount at a present time that is equivalent to a series of payments and interest in the future.

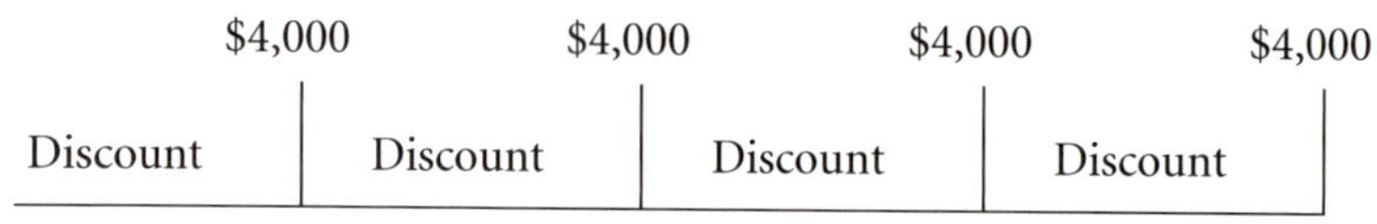

PV = ?

Because you are interested in calculating the present value, you could refer to the present value of $1 concept and discount each of the $4,000 payments individually using table factors from Table 9-2 as follows:

$4,000 × 0.683 Factor for Four Periods	$ 2,732
4,000 × 0.751 Factor for Three Periods	3,004
4,000 × 0.826 Factor for Two Periods	3,304
4,000 × 0.909 Factor for One Period	3,636
Total Present Value	$12,676

For a problem of any size, it is very cumbersome to calculate the present value of each payment individually. Therefore, tables have been constructed to ease the computational burden. Table 9-4 on page 468 provides table factors to calculate the present value of an annuity of $1 per year at various interest rates and number of periods. The previous example can be solved by reading across the four-year line and down the 10% column to obtain a table factor of 3.170. The present value would then be calculated as follows:

$$\begin{aligned} PV &= \$4{,}000(\text{table factor}) \\ &= \$4{,}000(3.170) \\ &= \$12{,}680 \end{aligned}$$

You should note that there is a $4 difference in the present value calculated by the first and second methods. This difference is caused by a small amount of rounding in the table factors that were used.

The steps using the calculator are as follows:

ENTER	DISPLAY
4 N	N = 4
10 I/Y	I/Y = 10
4000 PMT	PMT= 4,000
0 FV	FV = 0
CPT PV	PV = 12,680

Example 10: You just won the lottery. You can take your $1 million in a lump sum today, or you can receive $100,000 per year over the next 12 years. Assuming a 5% interest rate, which would you prefer, ignoring tax considerations?

Solution:

$$PV = \$100{,}000(\text{table factor})$$
$$= \$100{,}000(8.863)$$
$$= \$886{,}300$$

The steps using the calculator are as follows:

ENTER	DISPLAY
12 N	N = 12
5 I/Y	I/Y = 5
100,000 PMT	PMT= 100,000
0 FV	FV = 0
CPT PV	PV = 886,325

Because the present value of the payments over 12 years is less than the $1 million immediate payment, you should prefer the immediate payment.

Solving for Unknowns

LO 7 Apply the compound interest concepts to some common accounting situations.

In some cases, the present value or future value amounts will be known but the interest rate or the number of payments must be calculated. The formulas that have been presented thus far can be used for such calculations, but you must be careful to analyze each problem to be sure that you have chosen the correct relationship. We will use two examples to illustrate the power of the time value of money concepts.

Assume that you have just purchased a new automobile for $14,420 and must decide how to pay for it. Your local bank has graciously granted you a five-year loan. Because you are a good credit risk, the bank will allow you to make annual payments on the loan at the end of each year. The amount of the loan payments, which include principal and interest, is $4,000 per year. You are concerned that your total payments will be $20,000 ($4,000 per year for five years) and want to calculate the interest rate that is being charged on the loan.

Because the market or present value of the car, as well as the loan, is $14,420, a time diagram of our example would appear as follows:

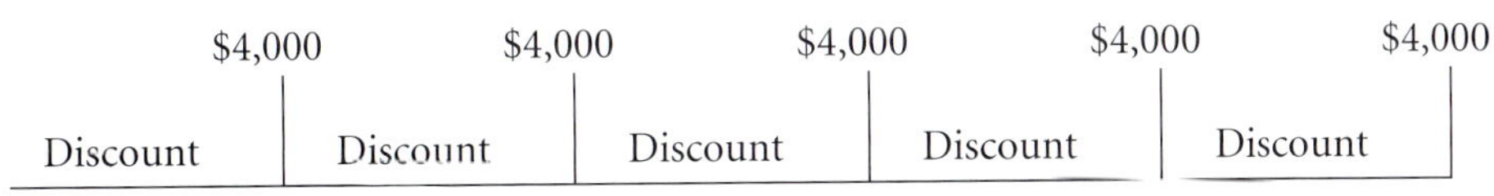

$PV = 14{,}420$

The interest rate that we must solve for represents the discount rate that was applied to the $4,000 payments to result in a present value of $14,420. Therefore, the applicable formula is the following:

$$PV = \$4{,}000(\text{table factor})$$

In this case, PV is known, so the formula can be rearranged as follows:

$$\text{Table factor} = PV/\$4{,}000$$
$$= \$14{,}420/\$4{,}000$$
$$= 3.605$$

The value of 3.605 represents a table factor in Table 9-4. We must read across the five-year line until we find a table factor of 3.605. In this case, that table factor is found in the 12% column. Therefore, the rate of interest being paid on the auto loan is 12%.

The steps using the calculator are as follows:

ENTER	DISPLAY
5 N	N = 5
14420 PV	PV = 14,420
4000 PMT +/−	PMT= −4,000
0 FV	FV = 0
CPT I/Y	I/Y = 11.99

[*Note:* On many calculators, including **Texas Instrument's** BA II, the payment amount (PMT) must be entered as a negative value in order to calculate I/Y.]

The second example involves solving for the number of interest periods. Assume that you want to accumulate $12,000 as a down payment on a home. You believe that you can save $1,000 per semiannual period, and your bank will pay interest of 8% per year, or 4% per semiannual period. How long will it take you to accumulate the desired amount?

The accumulated amount of $12,000 represents the future value of an annuity of $1,000 per semiannual period. Therefore, we can use the interest factors of Table 9-3 to assist in the solution. The applicable formula in this case is the following:

$$FV - \$1{,}000(\text{table factor})$$

The future value is known to be $12,000, and we must solve for the interest factor or table factor. Therefore, we can rearrange the formula as follows:

$$\begin{aligned}\text{Table factor} &= FV/\$1{,}000\\ &= \$12{,}000/\$1{,}000\\ &= 12.00\end{aligned}$$

Using Table 9-3, we must scan down the 4% column until we find a table value that is near 12.00. The closest table value we find is 12.006. That table value corresponds to 10 periods. Therefore, if we deposit $1,000 per semiannual period and invest the money at 4% per semiannual period, it will take 10 semiannual periods (five years) to accumulate $12,000.

The steps using the calculator are as follows:

ENTER	DISPLAY
4 I/Y	I/Y = 4
1000 PMT +/−	PMT= −1,000
12,000 FV	FV = 12,000
CPT N	N = 10

[*Note:* On many calculators, including **Texas Instrument's** BA II, the payment amount (PMT) must be entered as a negative value in order to calculate N.]

Ratios for Decision Making

Checking the working capital information on the balance sheet to make sure there are enough current assets to cover the current liabilities is a simple way to get an idea about a company's liquidity. Then, calculating the current ratio provides decision makers with information about how adequate that coverage is. The quick ratio is a more conservative measure because inventory generally is not as quick to convert to cash as other current assets. The quick ratio also does not include prepaid items or other items that can not be converted to cash quickly. Thus, the quick ratio will be lower than the current ratio for any company that has inventory. The higher the working capital, the current ratio, and the quick ratio, the better the company's position to meet its current obligations as shown as follows.

Ratios for Decision Making

Balance Sheet
Current assets
Current liabilities

Working capital* = Current assets − Current liabilities

$$\textbf{Current ratio*} = \frac{\textbf{Current assets}}{\textbf{Current liabilities}}$$

$$\textbf{Quick ratio} = \frac{\textbf{Quick assets**}}{\textbf{Current liabilities}}$$

*From Chapter 2
**Current assets − Inventory − Prepaids

Impact on the Financial Reports

Impact on the Financial Reports

BALANCE SHEET
Cash
Current Assets
Noncurrent Assets
Current Liabilities
Notes payable
Discount on notes payable
Interest payable
Tax payable
Estimated warranty liability
Current portion of long-term liability
Noncurrent Liabilities
Stockholders' Equity

INCOME STATEMENT
Revenues
Expenses
Warranty expense
Other
Interest expense
Tax expense

STATEMENT OF STOCKHOLDERS' EQUITY
Contributed Capital
Retained Earnings

STATEMENT OF CASH FLOWS
Operating Activities
Interest payments
Tax payments
Investing Activities
Financing Activities
Cash from short-term borrowings
Cash repayments of short-term borrowings
Noncash Transactions

NOTES
Disclosures of contingent liabilities*

*These are contingent liabilities that can not be reasonably estimated or are not probable.

Answers to the Two-Minute Reviews

Two-Minute Review on Page 441

1. *Current liabilities are defined as items that will be paid within one year of the balance sheet date. Examples of current liabilities include accounts payable, notes payable if due within one year, taxes payable, and other accrued liabilities. Also, if a portion of a long-term debt will be paid within one year, that portion should be reported as a current liability.*
2. *The current ratio is calculated as total current assets divided by total current liabilities. It is a measure of the liquidity of the company, or the ability of the company to pay its short-term obligations.*
3. *Most current liabilities are reported in the operating activities category of the cash flow statement. You should note that it is the change in the balance of the current liability that is reported.*

Two-Minute Review on Page 447

1. *Contingent liabilities should be reported in the financial statements if they are probable and the amount of the liability can be reasonably estimated.*
2. *Contingent liabilities should be disclosed in the notes if they are reasonably possible.*
3. *Contingent assets are generally not recorded until the amount is received. They are not treated in the same manner as contingent liabilities. This indicates the conservative nature of accounting.*

Warmup Exercises

Warmup Exercise 9-1 LO 1

A company has the following current assets: Cash, $10,000; Accounts Receivable, $70,000; and Inventory, $20,000. The company also has current liabilities of $40,000. Calculate the company's current ratio and quick ratio.

Warmup Exercise 9-2 LO 3

A company has the following current liabilities at the beginning of the period: Accounts Payable, $30,000; Taxes Payable $10,000. At the end of the period the balances of the account are as follows: Accounts Payable, $20,000; Taxes Payable, $15,000. What amounts will appear in the cash flow statement, and in what category of the statement will they appear?

Warmup Exercise 9-3 LO 6

A. You invest $1,000 at the beginning of the year. How much will be accumulated in five years if you earn 10% interest compounded annually?

B. You invest $1,000 *per year* at the end of each year for five years. How much will be accumulated in five years if you earn 10% interest compounded annually?

C. You will receive $1,000 in five years. What is the present value of that amount if you can earn 10% interest compounded annually?

D. You will receive $1,000 *per year* at the end of each year for five years. What is the present value of that amount if you can earn 10% interest compounded annually?

Solutions to Warmup Exercises

Warmup Exercise 9-1

Current Ratio: Current Assets/Current Liabilities

Cash ($10,000) + Accounts Receivable ($70,000) + Inventory ($20,000) = $100,000

$100,000/$40,000 = 2.5 Current Ratio

Quick Ratio: Quick Assets/Current Liabilities

Cash ($10,000) + Accounts Receivable ($70,000) = $80,000

$80,000/$40,000 = 2.0 Quick Ratio

Warmup Exercise 9-2

The amounts appearing in the cash flow statement should be in the Operating Activities category of the statement. The amounts shown should be the *changes* in the balances of the accounts.

Accounts Payable decreased by $10,000 and should appear as a decrease in the cash flow statement.

Taxes Payable increased by $5,000 and should appear as an increase in the cash flow statement.

Warmup Exercise 9-3

A. $FV = \$1{,}000(\text{table factor})$ using Table 9-1
$= \$1{,}000(1.611)$ where $i = 10\%, n = 5$
$= \$1{,}611$

A.

ENTER	DISPLAY
5 N	N = 5
10 I/Y	I/Y = 10
0 PMT	PMT= 0
1000 PV	PV = 1,000
CPT FV	FV = 1,611

B. $FV = \$1{,}000(\text{table factor})$ using Table 9-3
$= \$1{,}000(6.105)$ where $i = 10\%, n = 5$
$= \$6{,}105$

B.

ENTER	DISPLAY
5 N	N = 5
10 I/Y	I/Y = 10
1000 PMT	PMT= 1,000
0 PV	PV = 0
CPT FV	FV = 6,105

C. $PV = \$1{,}000(\text{table factor})$ using Table 9-2
$= \$1{,}000(0.621)$ where $i = 10\%, n = 5$
$= \$621$

C.

ENTER	DISPLAY
5 N	N = 5
10 I/Y	I/Y = 10
0 PMT	PMT= 0
1000 FV	FV = 1,000
CPT PV	PV = 621

D. $PV = \$1{,}000(\text{table factor})$ using Table 9-4
$= \$1{,}000(3.791)$ where $i = 10\%, n = 5$
$= \$3{,}791$

D.

ENTER	DISPLAY
5 N	N = 5
10 I/Y	I/Y = 10
1000 PMT	PMT= 1,000
0 FV	FV = 0
CPT PV	PV = 3,791

Review Problem

WebTUTOR Advantage

Part A

The accountant for Lunn Express wants to develop a balance sheet as of December 31, 2004. The following items pertain to the liability category and must be considered in order to determine the items that should be reported in the Current Liability section of the balance sheet. You may assume that Lunn began business on January 1, 2004, and therefore the beginning balance of all accounts was zero.

a. During 2004 Lunn purchased $100,000 of inventory on account from suppliers. By year-end, $40,000 of the balance has been eliminated as a result of payments. All items were purchased on terms of 2/10, n/30. Lunn uses the gross method of recording payables.

b. On April 1, 2004, Lunn borrowed $10,000 on a one-year note payable from Philips Bank. Terms of the loan indicate that Lunn must repay the principal and 12% interest at the due date of the note.

c. On October 1, 2004, Lunn also borrowed $8,000 from Dove Bank on a one-year note payable. Dove Bank deducted 10% interest in advance and gave to Lunn the net amount. At the due date, Lunn must repay the principal of $8,000.

d. On January 1, 2004, Lunn borrowed $20,000 from Owens Bank by signing a 10-year note payable. Terms of the note indicate that Lunn must make annual payments of principal each January 1 beginning in 2005 and also must pay interest each January 1 in the amount of 8% of the outstanding balance of the loan.

e. The accountant for Lunn has completed an income statement for 2004 that indicates that income before taxes was $10,000. Lunn must pay tax at the rate of 40% and must remit the tax to the Internal Revenue Service by April 15, 2005.

f. As of December 31, 2004, Lunn owes to employees salaries of $3,000 for work performed in 2004. The employees will be paid on the first payday of 2005.

g. During 2004 two lawsuits were filed against Lunn. In the first lawsuit, a customer sued for damages because of an injury that occurred on Lunn's premises. Lunn's legal counsel advised that it is probable that the lawsuit will be settled in 2005 at an amount of $7,000. The second lawsuit involves a patent infringement suit of $14,000 filed against Lunn by a competitor. The legal counsel has advised that there is some possibility that Lunn may be at fault but that a loss does not appear probable at this time.

Part B

a. What amount will be accumulated by January 1, 2008, if $5,000 is invested on January 1, 2004, at 10% interest compounded semiannually?

b. Assume that we are to receive $5,000 on January 1, 2008. What amount at January 1, 2004, is equivalent to the $5,000 that is to be received in 2008? Assume that interest is compounded annually at 10%.

c. What amount will be accumulated by January 1, 2008, if $5,000 is invested each semiannual period for eight periods beginning with June 30, 2004, and ending December 31, 2007? Interest will accumulate at 10% compounded semiannually.

d. Assume that we are to receive $5,000 each semiannual period for eight periods beginning on June 30, 2004. What amount at January 1, 2004, is equivalent to the future series of payments? Assume that interest will accrue at 10% compounded semiannually.

e. Assume that a new bank has begun a promotional campaign to attract savings accounts. The bank advertisement indicates that customers who invest $1,000 will double their money in 10 years. Assuming annual compounding of interest, what rate of interest is the bank offering?

Required

1. Consider all items in part **A.** Develop the Current Liability section of Lunn's balance sheet as of December 31, 2004. To make investment decisions about this company, what additional data would you need? You do not need to consider the notes that accompany the balance sheet.
2. Answer the five questions in part **B.**

Solution to Part A

The accountant's decisions for items **a** through **g** of part **A** should be as follows:

a. The balance of the Accounts Payable account should be $60,000. The payables should be reported at the gross amount, and discounts would not be reported until the time of payment.

b. The note payable to Philips Bank of $10,000 should be included as a current liability. Also, interest payable of $900 ($10,000 × 12% × 9/12) should be considered a current liability.

c. The note payable to Dove Bank should be considered a current liability and listed at $8,000 minus the contra account Discount on Note Payable of $600 ($8,000 × 10% × 9/12 remaining).

d. The debt to Owens Bank should be split between current liability and long-term liability with the current portion shown as $2,000. Also, interest payable of $1,600 ($20,000 × 8% × 1 year) should be considered a current liability.

e. Income taxes payable of $4,000 ($10,000 × 40%) is a current liability.

f. Salaries payable of $3,000 represent a current liability.

g. The lawsuit involving the customer must be reported as a current liability of $7,000 because the possibility of loss is probable. The second lawsuit should not be reported but should be disclosed as a note to the balance sheet.

LUNN EXPRESS
PARTIAL BALANCE SHEET
AS OF DECEMBER 31, 2004

Current Liabilities		
Accounts payable		$60,000
Interest payable ($900 + $1,600)		2,500
Salaries payable		3,000
Taxes payable		4,000
Note payable to Philips Bank		10,000
Note payable to Dove Bank	$8,000	
Less: Discount on note payable	(600)	7,400
Current maturity of long-term debt		2,000
Contingent liability for pending lawsuit		7,000
Total Current Liabilities		$95,900

Other data necessary to make an investment decision might include current assets, total assets, and current liabilities as of December 31, 2003 and 2004. If current assets are significantly larger than current liabilities, you can be comfortable that the company is capable of paying its short-term debt. The dollar amount of current assets and liabilities must be evaluated with regard to the size of the company. The larger the company, the less significant $95,900 in current liabilities would be. Knowing last year's current liabilities would give you an idea about the trend in current liabilities. If they are rising, you would want to know why.

Solution to Part B

a. $FV = \$5,000(\text{table factor})$ using Table 9-1

$= \$5,000(1.477)$ where $i = 5\%$, $n = 8$

$= \$7,385$

a.

ENTER	DISPLAY
8 N	N = 8
5 I/Y	I/Y = 5
0 PMT	PMT= 0
5000 PV	PV = 5,000
CPT FV	FV = 7,387

b. $PV = \$5,000(\text{table factor})$ using Table 9-2

$= \$5,000(0.683)$ where $i = 10\%$, $n = 4$

$= \$3,415$

b.

ENTER	DISPLAY
4 N	N = 4
10 I/Y	I/Y = 10
0 PMT	PMT= 0
5000 FV	FV = 5,000
CPT PV	PV = 3,415

(continued)

c. FV annuity $= \$5,000$(table factor) using Table 9-3

$= \$5,000(9.549)$ where $i = 5\%$, $n = 8$

$= \$47,745$

c.

ENTER	DISPLAY
8 N	N = 8
5 I/Y	I/Y = 5
5000 PMT	PMT= 5,000
0 PV	PV = 0
CPT FV	FV = 47,746

d. PV annuity $= \$5,000$(table factor) using Table 9-4

$= \$5,000(6.463)$ where $i = 5\%$, $n = 8$

$= \$32,315$

d.

ENTER	DISPLAY
8 N	N = 8
5 I/Y	I/Y = 5
5000 PMT	PMT= 5,000
0 FV	FV = 0
CPT PV	PV = 32,316

e. $FV = \$1,000$(table factor) using Table 9-1

Because the future value is known to be $2,000, the formula can be written as

$\$2,000 = \$1,000$(table factor)

and rearranged as

Table factor $= \$2,000/\$1,000 = 2.0.$

In Table 9-1, the table factor of 2.0 and 10 years corresponds with an interest rate of between 7% and 8%.

e.

ENTER	DISPLAY
10 N	N = 10
0 PMT	PMT= 0
1000 PV +/−	PV = −1,000
2000 FV	FV = 2,000
CPT I/Y	I/Y = 7.177

(*Note:* In this case, the present value must be entered as a negative amount.)

TABLE 9-1 Future Value of $1

(N) PERIODS	Rate of Interest in %											
	2	3	4	5	6	7	8	9	10	11	12	15
1	1.020	1.030	1.040	1.050	1.060	1.070	1.080	1.090	1.100	1.110	1.120	1.150
2	1.040	1.061	1.082	1.103	1.124	1.145	1.166	1.188	1.210	1.232	1.254	1.323
3	1.061	1.093	1.125	1.158	1.191	1.225	1.260	1.295	1.331	1.368	1.405	1.521
4	1.082	1.126	1.170	1.216	1.262	1.311	1.360	1.412	1.464	1.518	1.574	1.749
5	1.104	1.159	1.217	1.276	1.338	1.403	1.469	1.539	1.611	1.685	1.762	2.011
6	1.126	1.194	1.265	1.340	1.419	1.501	1.587	1.677	1.772	1.870	1.974	2.313
7	1.149	1.230	1.316	1.407	1.504	1.606	1.714	1.828	1.949	2.076	2.211	2.660
8	1.172	1.267	1.369	1.477	1.594	1.718	1.851	1.993	2.144	2.305	2.476	3.059
9	1.195	1.305	1.423	1.551	1.689	1.838	1.999	2.172	2.358	2.558	2.773	3.518
10	1.219	1.344	1.480	1.629	1.791	1.967	2.159	2.367	2.594	2.839	3.106	4.046
11	1.243	1.384	1.539	1.710	1.898	2.105	2.332	2.580	2.853	3.152	3.479	4.652
12	1.268	1.426	1.601	1.796	2.012	2.252	2.518	2.813	3.138	3.498	3.896	5.350
13	1.294	1.469	1.665	1.886	2.133	2.410	2.720	3.066	3.452	3.883	4.363	6.153
14	1.319	1.513	1.732	1.980	2.261	2.579	2.937	3.342	3.797	4.310	4.887	7.076
15	1.346	1.558	1.801	2.079	2.397	2.759	3.172	3.642	4.177	4.785	5.474	8.137
16	1.373	1.605	1.873	2.183	2.540	2.952	3.426	3.970	4.595	5.311	6.130	9.358
17	1.400	1.653	1.948	2.292	2.693	3.159	3.700	4.328	5.054	5.895	6.866	10.761
18	1.428	1.702	2.026	2.407	2.854	3.380	3.996	4.717	5.560	6.544	7.690	12.375
19	1.457	1.754	2.107	2.527	3.026	3.617	4.316	5.142	6.116	7.263	8.613	14.232
20	1.486	1.806	2.191	2.653	3.207	3.870	4.661	5.604	6.727	8.062	9.646	16.367
21	1.516	1.860	2.279	2.786	3.400	4.141	5.034	6.109	7.400	8.949	10.804	18.822
22	1.546	1.916	2.370	2.925	3.604	4.430	5.437	6.659	8.140	9.934	12.100	21.645
23	1.577	1.974	2.465	3.072	3.820	4.741	5.871	7.258	8.954	11.026	13.552	24.891
24	1.608	2.033	2.563	3.225	4.049	5.072	6.341	7.911	9.850	12.239	15.179	28.625
25	1.641	2.094	2.666	3.386	4.292	5.427	6.848	8.623	10.835	13.585	17.000	32.919
26	1.673	2.157	2.772	3.556	4.549	5.807	7.396	9.399	11.918	15.080	19.040	37.857
27	1.707	2.221	2.883	3.733	4.822	6.214	7.988	10.245	13.110	16.739	21.325	43.535
28	1.741	2.288	2.999	3.920	5.112	6.649	8.627	11.167	14.421	18.580	23.884	50.066
29	1.776	2.357	3.119	4.116	5.418	7.114	9.317	12.172	15.863	20.624	26.750	57.575
30	1.811	2.427	3.243	4.322	5.743	7.612	10.063	13.268	17.449	22.892	29.960	66.212

TABLE 9-2 Present Value of $1

(N) PERIODS	Rate of Interest in %											
	2	3	4	5	6	7	8	9	10	11	12	15
1	0.980	0.971	0.962	0.952	0.943	0.935	0.926	0.917	0.909	0.901	0.893	0.870
2	0.961	0.943	0.925	0.907	0.890	0.873	0.857	0.842	0.826	0.812	0.797	0.756
3	0.942	0.915	0.889	0.864	0.840	0.816	0.794	0.772	0.751	0.731	0.712	0.658
4	0.924	0.888	0.855	0.823	0.792	0.763	0.735	0.708	0.683	0.659	0.636	0.572
5	0.906	0.863	0.822	0.784	0.747	0.713	0.681	0.650	0.621	0.593	0.567	0.497
6	0.888	0.837	0.790	0.746	0.705	0.666	0.630	0.596	0.564	0.535	0.507	0.432
7	0.871	0.813	0.760	0.711	0.665	0.623	0.583	0.547	0.513	0.482	0.452	0.376
8	0.853	0.789	0.731	0.677	0.627	0.582	0.540	0.502	0.467	0.434	0.404	0.327
9	0.837	0.766	0.703	0.645	0.592	0.544	0.500	0.460	0.424	0.391	0.361	0.284
10	0.820	0.744	0.676	0.614	0.558	0.508	0.463	0.422	0.386	0.352	0.322	0.247
11	0.804	0.722	0.650	0.585	0.527	0.475	0.429	0.388	0.350	0.317	0.287	0.215
12	0.788	0.701	0.625	0.557	0.497	0.444	0.397	0.356	0.319	0.286	0.257	0.187
13	0.773	0.681	0.601	0.530	0.469	0.415	0.368	0.326	0.290	0.258	0.229	0.163
14	0.758	0.661	0.577	0.505	0.442	0.388	0.340	0.299	0.263	0.232	0.205	0.141
15	0.743	0.642	0.555	0.481	0.417	0.362	0.315	0.275	0.239	0.209	0.183	0.123
16	0.728	0.623	0.534	0.458	0.394	0.339	0.292	0.252	0.218	0.188	0.163	0.107
17	0.714	0.605	0.513	0.436	0.371	0.317	0.270	0.231	0.198	0.170	0.146	0.093
18	0.700	0.587	0.494	0.416	0.350	0.296	0.250	0.212	0.180	0.153	0.130	0.081
19	0.686	0.570	0.475	0.396	0.331	0.277	0.232	0.194	0.164	0.138	0.116	0.070
20	0.673	0.554	0.456	0.377	0.312	0.258	0.215	0.178	0.149	0.124	0.104	0.061
21	0.660	0.538	0.439	0.359	0.294	0.242	0.199	0.164	0.135	0.112	0.093	0.053
22	0.647	0.522	0.422	0.342	0.278	0.226	0.184	0.150	0.123	0.101	0.083	0.046
23	0.634	0.507	0.406	0.326	0.262	0.211	0.170	0.138	0.112	0.091	0.074	0.040
24	0.622	0.492	0.390	0.310	0.247	0.197	0.158	0.126	0.102	0.082	0.066	0.035
25	0.610	0.478	0.375	0.295	0.233	0.184	0.146	0.116	0.092	0.074	0.059	0.030
26	0.598	0.464	0.361	0.281	0.220	0.172	0.135	0.106	0.084	0.066	0.053	0.026
27	0.586	0.450	0.347	0.268	0.207	0.161	0.125	0.098	0.076	0.060	0.047	0.023
28	0.574	0.437	0.333	0.255	0.196	0.150	0.116	0.090	0.069	0.054	0.042	0.020
29	0.563	0.424	0.321	0.243	0.185	0.141	0.107	0.082	0.063	0.048	0.037	0.017
30	0.552	0.412	0.308	0.231	0.174	0.131	0.099	0.075	0.057	0.044	0.033	0.015

TABLE 9-3 Future Value of Annuity of $1

(N) PERIODS	Rate of Interest in % 2	3	4	5	6	7	8	9	10	11	12	15
1	1.000	1.000	1.000	1.000	1.000	1.000	1.000	1.000	1.000	1.000	1.000	1.000
2	2.020	2.030	2.040	2.050	2.060	2.070	2.080	2.090	2.100	2.110	2.120	2.150
3	3.060	3.091	3.122	3.153	3.184	3.215	3.246	3.278	3.310	3.342	3.374	3.473
4	4.122	4.184	4.246	4.310	4.375	4.440	4.506	4.573	4.641	4.710	4.779	4.993
5	5.204	5.309	5.416	5.526	5.637	5.751	5.867	5.985	6.105	6.228	6.353	6.742
6	6.308	6.468	6.633	6.802	6.975	7.153	7.336	7.523	7.716	7.913	8.115	8.754
7	7.434	7.662	7.898	8.142	8.394	8.654	8.923	9.200	9.487	9.783	10.089	11.067
8	8.583	8.892	9.214	9.549	9.897	10.260	10.637	11.028	11.436	11.859	12.300	13.727
9	9.755	10.159	10.583	11.027	11.491	11.978	12.488	13.021	13.579	14.164	14.776	16.786
10	10.950	11.464	12.006	12.578	13.181	13.816	14.487	15.193	15.937	16.722	17.549	20.304
11	12.169	12.808	13.486	14.207	14.972	15.784	16.645	17.560	18.531	19.561	20.655	24.349
12	13.412	14.192	15.026	15.917	16.870	17.888	18.977	20.141	21.384	22.713	24.133	29.002
13	14.680	15.618	16.627	17.713	18.882	20.141	21.495	22.953	24.523	26.212	28.029	34.352
14	15.974	17.086	18.292	19.599	21.015	22.550	24.215	26.019	27.975	30.095	32.393	40.505
15	17.293	18.599	20.024	21.579	23.276	25.129	27.152	29.361	31.772	34.405	37.280	47.580
16	18.639	20.157	21.825	23.657	25.673	27.888	30.324	33.003	35.950	39.190	42.753	55.717
17	20.012	21.762	23.698	25.840	28.213	30.840	33.750	36.974	40.545	44.501	48.884	65.075
18	21.412	23.414	25.645	28.132	30.906	33.999	37.450	41.301	45.599	50.396	55.750	75.836
19	22.841	25.117	27.671	30.539	33.760	37.379	41.446	46.018	51.159	56.939	63.440	88.212
20	24.297	26.870	29.778	33.066	36.786	40.995	45.762	51.160	57.275	64.203	72.052	102.444
21	25.783	28.676	31.969	35.719	39.993	44.865	50.423	56.765	64.002	72.265	81.699	118.810
22	27.299	30.537	34.248	38.505	43.392	49.006	55.457	62.873	71.403	81.214	92.503	137.632
23	28.845	32.453	36.618	41.430	46.996	53.436	60.893	69.532	79.543	91.148	104.603	159.276
24	30.422	34.426	39.083	44.502	50.816	58.177	66.765	76.790	88.497	102.174	118.155	184.168
25	32.030	36.459	41.646	47.727	54.865	63.249	73.106	84.701	98.347	114.413	133.334	212.793
26	33.671	38.553	44.312	51.113	59.156	68.676	79.954	93.324	109.182	127.999	150.334	245.712
27	35.344	40.710	47.084	54.669	63.706	74.484	87.351	102.723	121.100	143.079	169.374	283.569
28	37.051	42.931	49.968	58.403	68.528	80.698	95.339	112.968	134.210	159.817	190.699	327.104
29	38.792	45.219	52.966	62.323	73.640	87.347	103.966	124.135	148.631	178.397	214.583	377.170
30	40.568	47.575	56.085	66.439	79.058	94.461	113.283	136.308	164.494	199.021	241.333	434.745

TABLE 9-4 Present Value of Annuity of $1

(N) PERIODS	Rate of Interest in % 2	3	4	5	6	7	8	9	10	11	12	15
1	0.980	0.971	0.962	0.952	0.943	0.935	0.926	0.917	0.909	0.901	0.893	0.870
2	1.942	1.913	1.886	1.859	1.833	1.808	1.783	1.759	1.736	1.713	1.690	1.626
3	2.884	2.829	2.775	2.723	2.673	2.624	2.577	2.531	2.487	2.444	2.402	2.283
4	3.808	3.717	3.630	3.546	3.465	3.387	3.312	3.240	3.170	3.102	3.037	2.855
5	4.713	4.580	4.452	4.329	4.212	4.100	3.993	3.890	3.791	3.696	3.605	3.352
6	5.601	5.417	5.242	5.076	4.917	4.767	4.623	4.486	4.355	4.231	4.111	3.784
7	6.472	6.230	6.002	5.786	5.582	5.389	5.206	5.033	4.868	4.712	4.564	4.160
8	7.325	7.020	6.733	6.463	6.210	5.971	5.747	5.535	5.335	5.146	4.968	4.487
9	8.162	7.786	7.435	7.108	6.802	6.515	6.247	5.995	5.759	5.537	5.328	4.772
10	8.983	8.530	8.111	7.722	7.360	7.024	6.710	6.418	6.145	5.889	5.650	5.019
11	9.787	9.253	8.760	8.306	7.887	7.499	7.139	6.805	6.495	6.207	5.938	5.234
12	10.575	9.954	9.385	8.863	8.384	7.943	7.536	7.161	6.814	6.492	6.194	5.421
13	11.348	10.635	9.986	9.394	8.853	8.358	7.904	7.487	7.103	6.750	6.424	5.583
14	12.106	11.296	10.563	9.899	9.295	8.745	8.244	7.786	7.367	6.982	6.628	5.724
15	12.849	11.938	11.118	10.380	9.712	9.108	8.559	8.061	7.606	7.191	6.811	5.847
16	13.578	12.561	11.652	10.838	10.106	9.447	8.851	8.313	7.824	7.379	6.974	5.954
17	14.292	13.166	12.166	11.274	10.477	9.763	9.122	8.544	8.022	7.549	7.120	6.047
18	14.992	13.754	12.659	11.690	10.828	10.059	9.372	8.756	8.201	7.702	7.250	6.128
19	15.678	14.324	13.134	12.085	11.158	10.336	9.604	8.950	8.365	7.839	7.366	6.198
20	16.351	14.877	13.590	12.462	11.470	10.594	9.818	9.129	8.514	7.963	7.469	6.259
21	17.011	15.415	14.029	12.821	11.764	10.836	10.017	9.292	8.649	8.075	7.562	6.312
22	17.658	15.937	14.451	13.163	12.042	11.061	10.201	9.442	8.772	8.176	7.645	6.359
23	18.292	16.444	14.857	13.489	12.303	11.272	10.371	9.580	8.883	8.266	7.718	6.399
24	18.914	16.936	15.247	13.799	12.550	11.469	10.529	9.707	8.985	8.348	7.784	6.434
25	19.523	17.413	15.622	14.094	12.783	11.654	10.675	9.823	9.077	8.422	7.843	6.464
26	20.121	17.877	15.983	14.375	13.003	11.826	10.810	9.929	9.161	8.488	7.896	6.491
27	20.707	18.327	16.330	14.643	13.211	11.987	10.935	10.027	9.237	8.548	7.943	6.514
28	21.281	18.764	16.663	14.898	13.406	12.137	11.051	10.116	9.307	8.602	7.984	6.534
29	21.844	19.188	16.984	15.141	13.591	12.278	11.158	10.198	9.370	8.650	8.022	6.551
30	22.396	19.600	17.292	15.372	13.765	12.409	11.258	10.274	9.427	8.694	8.055	6.566

Appendix A: Accounting Tools: Payroll Accounting

LO 8 Demonstrate an understanding of the deductions and expenses for payroll accounting.

Salaries payable was one of the current liabilities discussed in Chapter 2. At the end of each accounting period, the accountant must accrue salaries that have been earned by the employees but have not yet been paid. To this point, we have not considered the accounting that must be done for payroll deductions and other payroll expenses.

Payroll deductions and expenses occur not only at year-end but every time, throughout the year, that employees are paid. The amount of cash paid for salaries and wages is the largest cash outflow for many firms. It is imperative that sufficient cash be available not only to meet the weekly or monthly payroll but also to remit the payroll taxes to the appropriate government agencies when required. The purpose of this appendix is to introduce the calculations and the accounting entries that are necessary when payroll is recorded.

The issue of payroll expenses is of great concern to businesses, particularly small entrepreneurial ones. One of the large issues facing companies is how to meet the increasing cost of hiring people. Salary is just one component. How are they going to pay salaries plus benefits such as health insurance, life insurance, disability, unemployment benefits, workers' compensation, and so on? More and more companies are trying to keep their payrolls as small as possible in order to avoid these costs. Unfortunately, this has been a contributing factor in the trends of using more part-time employees and of outsourcing some business functions. Outsourcing, or hiring independent contractors, allows the company to reduce salary expense and the expenses related to fringe benefits. However, it does not necessarily improve the company's profitability. The expenses that are increased as a result of hiring outside contractors must also be considered. A manager must carefully consider all of the costs that are affected before deciding whether to hire more employees or go with an independent contractor.

CALCULATION OF GROSS WAGES

We will cover the payroll process by indicating the basic steps that must be performed. The first step is to calculate the **gross wages** of all employees. The gross wage represents the wage amount before deductions. Companies often have two general classes of employees, hourly and salaried. The gross wage of each hourly employee is calculated by multiplying the number of hours worked times his or her hourly wage rate. Salaried employees are not paid on a per-hour basis but at a flat rate per week, month, or year. For both hourly and salaried employees, the payroll accountant must also consider any overtime, bonus, or other salary supplement that may affect gross wages.

Gross wages The amount of wages before deductions.

CALCULATION OF NET PAY

The second step in the payroll process is to calculate the deductions from each employee's paycheck to determine **net pay.** Deductions from the employees' checks represent a current liability to the employer because the employer must remit the amounts at a future time to the proper agencies or government offices, for example to the U.S. Treasury Service. The deductions that are made depend on the type of company and the employee. The most important deductions are indicated in the following sections.

Net pay The amount of wages after deductions.

Income Tax

The employer must withhold federal income tax from most employees' paychecks. The amount withheld depends on the employee's earnings and the number of *exemptions* claimed by that employee. An exemption reflects the number of dependents a taxpayer can claim. The more exemptions, the lower is the withholding amount required by the government. Tables are available from the Internal Revenue Service to calculate the proper amount that should be withheld. This amount must be remitted to the U.S. Treasury Service periodically; the frequency depends on the company's size and its payroll. Income tax withheld represents a liability to the employer and is normally classified as a current liability.

Many states also have an income tax, and the employer must often withhold additional amounts for the state tax.

FICA—Employees' Share

FICA stands for Federal Insurance Contributions Act; it is commonly called the *social security tax*. The FICA tax is assessed on both the employee and the employer. The employees' portion must be withheld from paychecks at the applicable rate. Currently, the tax is assessed at the rate of 7.65% on the first $84,900 paid to the employee each year. Other rates and special rules apply to certain types of workers and to self-employed individuals. The amounts withheld from the employees' checks must be remitted to the federal government periodically.

FICA taxes withheld from employees' checks represent a liability to the employer until remitted. It is important to remember that the employees' portion of the FICA tax does not represent an expense to the employer.

Voluntary Deductions

If you have ever received a paycheck, you are probably aware that a variety of items was deducted from the amount you earned. Many of these are voluntary deductions chosen by the employee. They may include health insurance, pension or retirement contributions, savings plans, contributions to charities, union dues, and others. Each of these items is deducted from the employees' paychecks, is held by the employer, and is remitted at a future time. Therefore, each represents a current liability to the employer until remitted.

EMPLOYER PAYROLL TAXES

The payroll items discussed thus far do not represent expenses to the employer because they are assessed on the employees and deducted from their paychecks. However, there are taxes that the employer must pay. The two most important are FICA and unemployment taxes.

FICA—Employer's Share

The FICA tax is assessed on both the employee and the employer. The employee amount is withheld from the employees' paychecks and represents a liability but is not an expense to the employer. Normally, an equal amount is assessed on the employer. Therefore, the employer must pay an additional 7.65% of employee wages to the federal government. The employer's portion represents an expense to the employer and should be reflected in a Payroll Tax Expense account or similar type of account. This portion is a liability to the employer until it is remitted.

Unemployment Tax

Most employers must also pay unemployment taxes. The state and federal governments jointly sponsor a program to collect unemployment tax from employers and to pay workers who lose their jobs. The maximum rate of unemployment taxes is 3.4%, of which 2.7% is the state portion and 0.7% the federal, on an employee's first $7,000 of wages earned each year. The rate is adjusted according to a company's employment history, however. If a company has been fairly stable and few of its employees have filed for unemployment benefits, the rate is adjusted downward.

Unemployment taxes are levied against the employer, not the employee. Therefore, the tax represents an expense to the employer and should be reflected in a Payroll Tax Expense account or similar type of account. The tax also represents a liability to the employer until it is remitted.

AN EXAMPLE

Assume that Kori Company has calculated the gross wages of all employees for the month of July to be $100,000. Also assume that the following amounts have been withheld from the employees' paychecks:

Income Tax	$20,000
FICA	7,650
United Way Contributions	5,000
Union Dues	3,000

In addition, assume that Kori's unemployment tax rate is 3%, that no employees have reached the $7,000 limit, and that Kori's portion of FICA matches the employees' share. Kori must make the following entries to record the payroll, to pay the employees, and to record the employer's payroll expenses.

July 31	Salary Expense	100,000	
	Salary Payable		64,350
	Income Tax Payable		20,000
	FICA Payable		7,650
	United Way Payable		5,000
	Union Dues Payable		3,000
	To record July salary and deductions.		

Assets	=	Liabilities	+	Owners' Equity
		+64,350		−100,000
		+20,000		
		+7,650		
		+5,000		
		+3,000		

July 31	Salary Payable	64,350	
	Cash		64,350
	To record payment of employee salaries.		

Assets	=	Liabilities	+	Owners' Equity
−64,350		−64,350		

July 31	Payroll Tax Expense	10,650	
	FICA Payable		7,650
	Unemployment Tax Payable		3,000
	To record employer's payroll taxes.		

Assets	=	Liabilities	+	Owners' Equity
		+7,650		−10,650
		+3,000		

Periodically, Kori must remit amounts to the appropriate government body or agency. The accounting entry to record remittance, assuming remittance at the end of July, is as follows:

		Debit	Credit
July 31	Income Tax Expense	20,000	
	FICA Payable	15,300	
	United Way Payable	5,000	
	Union Dues Payable	3,000	
	Unemployment Tax Payable	3,000	
	Cash		46,300
	To record remittance of withheld amounts.		

Assets	=	Liabilities	+	Owners' Equity
−46,300		−20,000		
		−15,300		
		−5,000		
		−3,000		
		−3,000		

COMPENSATED ABSENCES

LO 9 Determine when compensated absences must be accrued as a liability.

Compensated absences Employee absences for which the employee will be paid.

Most employers allow employees to accumulate a certain number of sick days and to take a certain number of paid vacation days each year. This causes an accounting question when recording payroll amounts. When should the sick days and vacation days be treated as an expense—in the period they are earned or in the period they are taken by the employee?

The FASB has coined the term **compensated absences.** These are absences from employment, such as vacation, illness, and holidays, for which it is expected that employees will be paid. The FASB has ruled that an expense should be accrued if certain conditions are met: the services have been rendered, the rights (days) accumulate, and payment is probable and can be reasonably estimated. The result of the FASB ruling is that most employers are required to record a liability and expense for vacation days when earned but sick days are not recorded until employees are actually absent.

Compensated absence is another example of the matching principle at work, and so it is consistent with good accounting theory. Unfortunately, it has also resulted in some complex calculations and additional work for payroll accountants. Part of the complexity is due to unresolved legal issues about compensated absences.

U.S. accounting standards on this issue are much more detailed and extensive than the standards of many foreign countries. As a result, U.S. companies may believe that they are subject to higher record-keeping costs than their foreign competitors.

Appendix B: Accounting Tools: Using Excel for Problems Involving Interest Calculations

The purpose of Appendix B is to illustrate how the functions built in to the Excel spreadsheet can be used to calculate future value and present value amounts. We will illustrate the use of Excel with the same examples that are used in the body of Chapter 9.

To view the Excel functions, you should click on the PASTE function of the Excel toolbar (the paste function is on the top of the Excel toolbar and is noted by the symbol *fx*) and then choose the FINANCIAL option. Several different calculations are available. We will illustrate two of them: FV and PV.

Example 1: Your three-year-old son, Robert, just inherited $50,000 in cash and securities from his grandfather. If the funds were left in the bank and in the stock market and received an annual return of 10%, how much would be there in 15 years when Robert starts college?

Solution: In Excel, you should use the FV function and enter the values as follows:

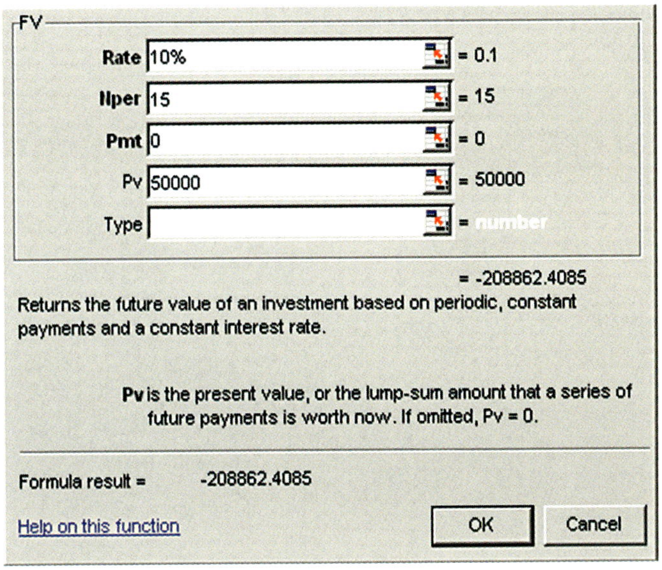

Note that the future value of $208,862 is slightly different than that given in the body of the text because of rounding when using the table factors.

Example 2: Consider a $2,000 note payable that carries interest at the rate of 10% compounded annually. The note is due in two years, and the principal and interest must be paid at that time. What amount must be paid in two years?

Solution: In Excel, you should use the FV function and enter the values as follows:

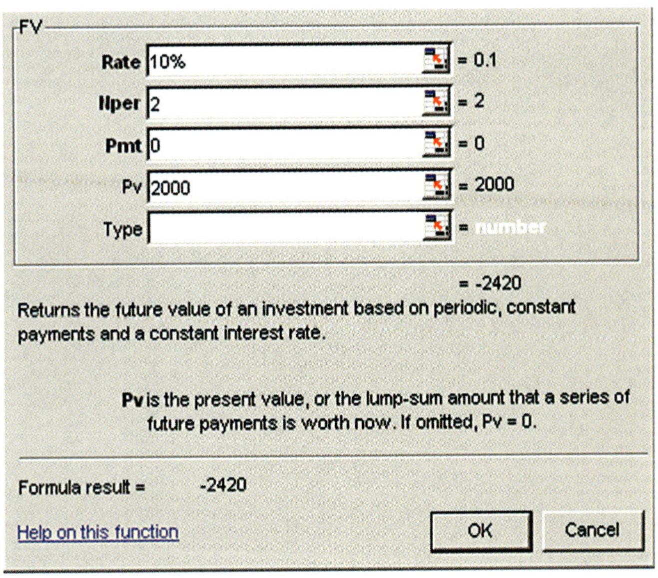

The future value is $2,420.

Example 3: Suppose we want to find the future value of a $2,000 note payable due in two years. The note payable requires interest to be compounded quarterly at the rate of 12% per year. What future amount must be paid in two years?

Solution: In Excel, you should use the FV function and enter the values as follows:

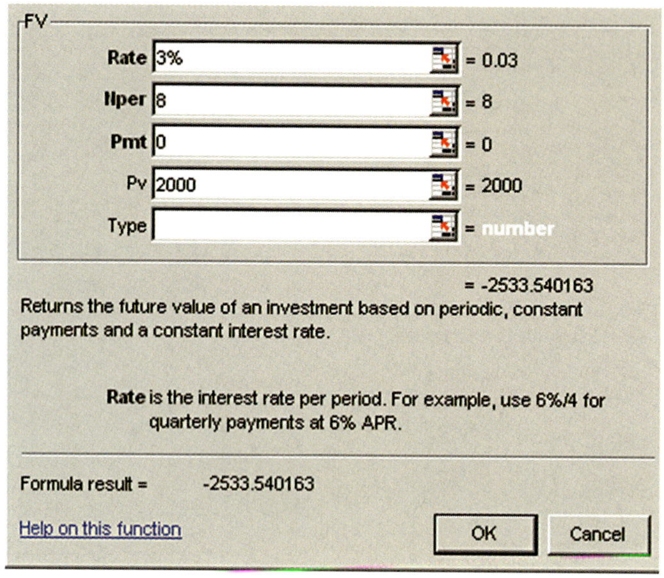

The future value is $2,534 (rounded to the nearest dollar).

Example 4: Suppose you know that you will receive $2,000 in two years. You also know that if you had the money now, it could be invested at 10% compounded annually. What is the present value of the $2,000?

Solution: Since this problem requires the calculation of a present value, the PV function of Excel should be chosen and used as follows:

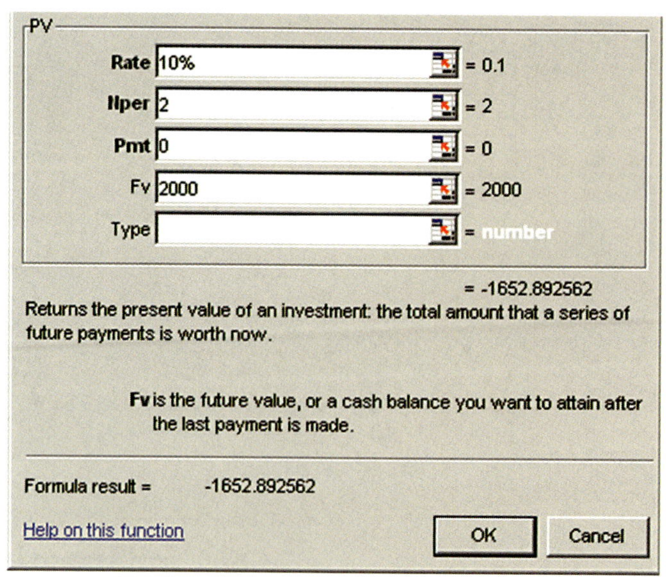

The present value is $1,653 (rounded to the nearest dollar).

Example 5: A recent magazine article projects that it will cost $120,000 to attend a four-year college 10 years from now. If that is true, how much money would you have to put into an account today to fund that education, assuming a 5% rate of return?

Solution: The PV function of Excel should again be used as follows:

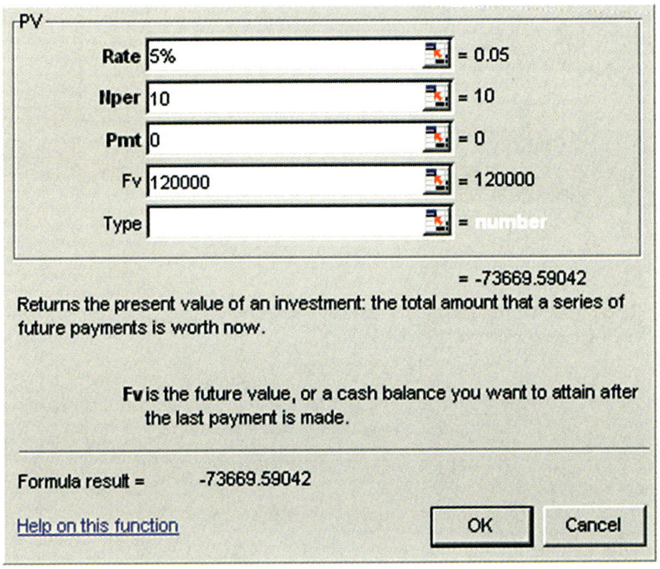

The present value calculated ($73,670—rounded to the nearest dollar) differs slightly from that derived when using the table factors because of rounding in the tables.

Example 6: Suppose that you are to receive $3,000 per year at the end of each of the next four years. Also assume that each payment could be invested at an interest rate of 10% compounded annually. How much would be accumulated in principal and interest by the end of the fourth year?

Solution: This problem involves the calculation of the future value of an annuity, and you should use the FV function of Excel as follows:

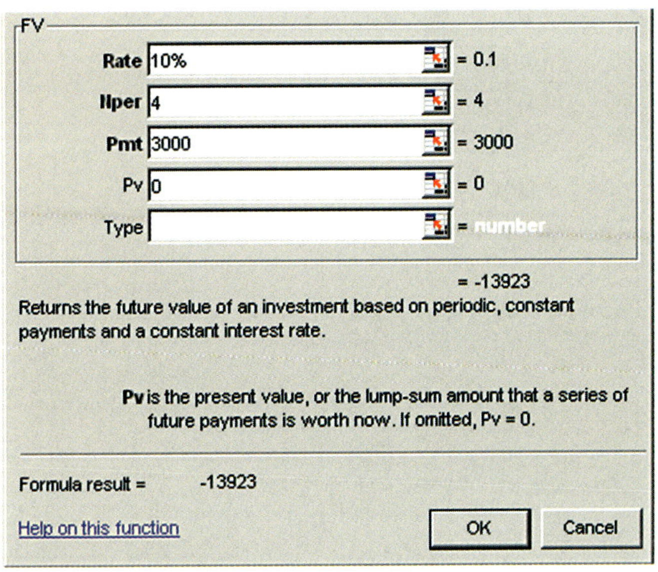

The future value of the series of payments is $13,923. Note that the payments are simply entered as the Pmt variable in the spreadsheet.

Example 7: Your cousin just had a baby girl two weeks ago and is already thinking about sending her to college. When the girl is 15, how much money would be in her college account if your cousin deposits $2,000 into it on each of her 15 birthdays? The interest rate is 10%.

Solution: You should again use the Excel FV function as follows:

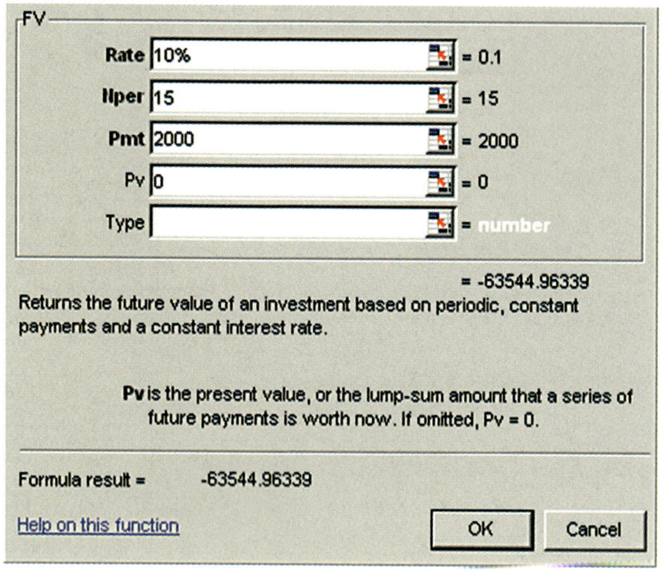

The future value amount is $63,545 (rounded to the nearest dollar).

Example 8: How would the future value be calculated if the previous example was modified so that we deposited $1,000 semiannually and the interest rate was 10% compounded semiannually (or 5% per period) for 15 years?

Solution: Because the compounding is semiannually, you should use the FV function of Excel as follows:

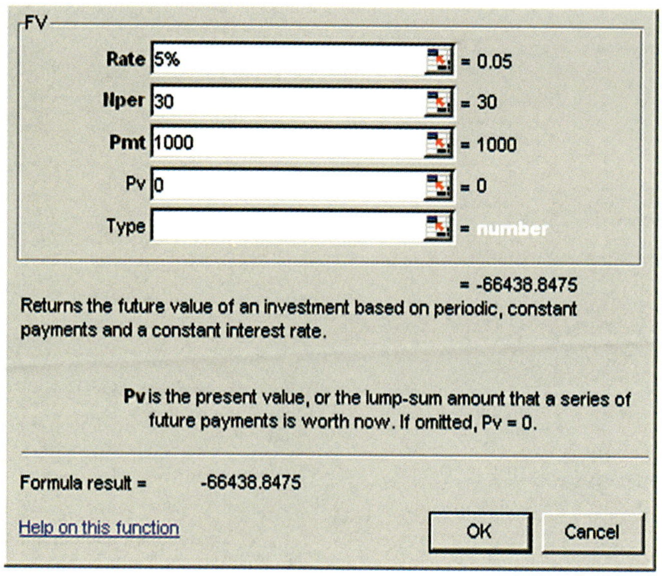

The future value is $66,439 (rounded to the nearest dollar).

Example 9: Suppose that you will receive an annuity of $4,000 per year for four years, with the first received one year from today. The amounts received can be invested at a rate of 10% compounded annually. What amount would you need at the present time to have an amount equivalent to the series of payments and interest in the future?

Solution: This problem involves the calculation of the present value of an annuity, and you should use the PV function of Excel as follows:

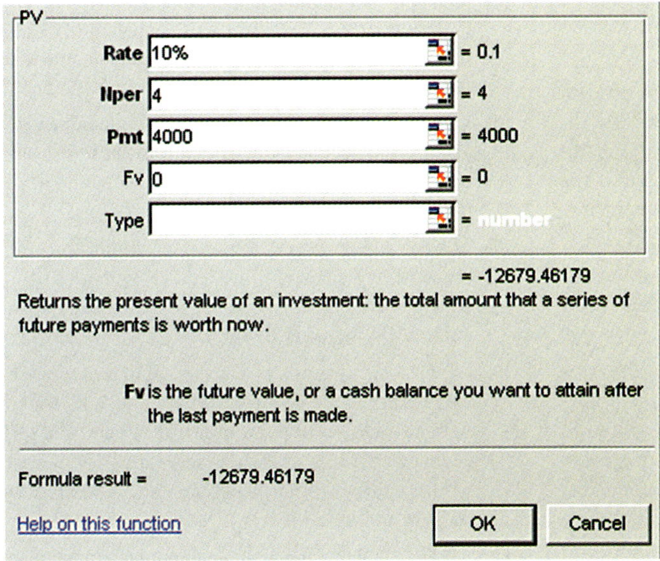

The present value of $12,679 (rounded to the nearest dollar) differs slightly from that derived when using the tables because of rounding in the table factors.

Example 10: You just won the lottery. You can take your $1 million in a lump sum today, or you can receive $100,000 per year over the next 12 years. Assuming a 5% interest rate, which would you prefer, ignoring tax considerations?

Solution: You should use the PV function of Excel as follows:

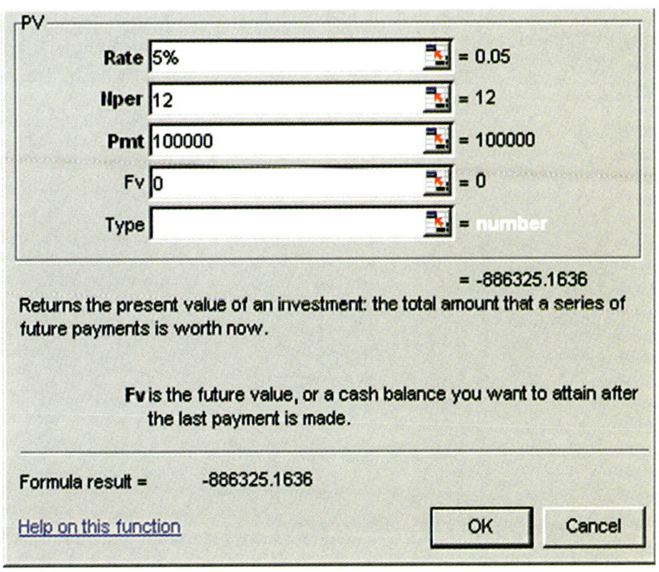

Because the present value of the payments over 12 years is $886,325 (rounded to the nearest dollar) and is less than the $1 million that can be received immediately, you should choose the immediate payment.

Chapter Highlights

1. **LO 1** Balance sheets generally have two categories of liability: current liabilities and long-term liabilities. Current liabilities are obligations that will be satisfied within one year or within the next operating cycle.
2. **LO 2** Accruals are expenses that have been incurred, but not paid, by the balance sheet date. They increase current liabilities and should be valued at the face amount or the amount necessary to settle the obligation. They are not reported at the present value because of the short time span until payment.
3. **LO 2** Accounts payable represent amounts owed for the purchase of inventory, goods, or services. Accounts payable usually do not require the payment of interest, but a discount may be available to encourage prompt payment.
4. **LO 2** The accounting for notes payable depends on the terms of the note. Some notes payable require the payment of interest at the due date. If so, accounting entries must be made to accrue interest expense to the proper periods. Interest is an expense when incurred, not when paid. Alternatively, the terms of the note may require interest to be deducted in advance. The interest deducted should initially be recorded in a Discount on Notes Payable account and transferred to Interest Expense over the life of the note.
5. **LO 2** Accrued liabilities include any amount that is owed but not actually due as of the balance sheet date. These liabilities may be grouped together in an account such as Other Accrued Liabilities.
6. **LO 3** The changes in current liabilities affect the cash flow statement and, for most items, are reflected in the Operating Activities category. Decreases in current liabilities indicate a reduction of cash; increases in current liabilities indicate an increase in cash.
7. **LO 4** Contingent liabilities involve an existing condition whose outcome depends on some future event. If a contingent liability is probable and the amount of loss can be reasonably estimated, it should be reported on the balance sheet. If a contingent liability is reasonably possible, it must be disclosed but not reported.
8. **LO 5** Simple interest is interest earned on the principal amount. It is often calculated by the well-known formula of principal times rate times time. Compound interest is calculated on the principal plus previous amounts of interest accumulated.
9. **LO 6** The future value of a single amount represents the amount of interest plus principal that will be accumulated at a future time. The future value of a single amount can be calculated by formula or by the use of Table 9-1.
10. **LO 6** The present value of a single amount represents the amount at a present time that is equivalent to an amount at a future time. The present value of a single amount can be calculated by formula or by the use of Table 9-2.
11. **LO 6** An annuity is a series of payments of equal amount. The future value of an annuity represents the amount that will be accumulated in principal and interest if a series of payments is invested for a specified time and for a specified rate. The future value of an annuity can be calculated by formula or by the use of Table 9-3.
12. **LO 6** The present value of an annuity represents the amount at a present time that is equivalent to a series of payments in the future that will occur for a specified time and at a specified interest or discount rate. The present value of an annuity can be calculated by formula or by the use of Table 9-4.
13. **LO 7** The compound interest concepts are also useful when solving for unknowns such as the number of interest periods or the interest rate on a series of payments using compound interest techniques.
14. **LO 8** There are two types of payroll deductions and expenses. Deductions from the employee's check are made to determine net pay and represent a current liability to the employer. Employer's payroll taxes are also assessed directly on the employer and represent an expense. (Appendix A)
15. **LO 9** Compensated absences such as sick pay and vacation pay are expenses and must be accrued by the employer if certain conditions are met. (Appendix A)

http://

http://porter.swlearning.com

Technology and other resources for your success

If you need additional help, visit the text's Web site. Also, see pages xv–xvii in this text's preface for a description of available technology and other resources. If your instructor is using PERSONAL *Trainer* in this course, you may complete, on line, the assignments identified by PT.

Key Terms Quiz

Read each definition below, and then write the number of the definition in the blank beside the appropriate term it defines. The quiz solutions appear at the end of the chapter.

_____ Current liability
_____ Accounts payable
_____ Notes payable
_____ Discount on Notes Payable
_____ Current Maturities of Long-Term Debt
_____ Accrued liability
_____ Contingent liability
_____ Estimated liability
_____ Contingent asset
_____ Time value of money
_____ Simple interest
_____ Compound interest
_____ Future value of a single amount
_____ Present value of a single amount
_____ Annuity
_____ Future value of an annuity
_____ Present value of an annuity
_____ Gross wages (Appendix A)
_____ Net pay (Appendix A)
_____ Compensated absences (Appendix A)

1. Accounts that will be satisfied within one year or the next operating cycle.
2. The amount needed at the present time to be equivalent to a series of payments and interest in the future.
3. Amounts owed for the purchase of inventory, goods, or services acquired in the normal course of business.
4. A contra-liability account that represents interest deducted from a loan or note in advance.
5. A series of payments of equal amount.
6. The portion of a long-term liability that will be paid within one year of the balance sheet date.
7. A liability that has been incurred but has not been paid as of the balance sheet date.
8. Amounts owed that are represented by a formal contractual agreement. These amounts usually require the payment of interest.
9. A liability that involves an existing condition for which the outcome is not known with certainty and depends on some future event.
10. Interest that is earned or paid on the principal amount only.
11. A contingent liability that is accrued and is reflected on the balance sheet. Common examples are warranties, guarantees, and premium offers.
12. An amount that involves an existing condition dependent on some future event by which the company stands to gain. These amounts are not normally reported.
13. Interest calculated on the principal plus previous amounts of interest accumulated.
14. The concept that indicates that people should prefer to receive an immediate amount at the present time over an equal amount in the future.
15. The amount that will be accumulated in the future when one amount is invested at the present time and accrues interest until the future time.
16. The amount that will be accumulated in the future when a series of payments is invested and accrues interest until the future time.
17. The present amount that is equivalent to an amount at a future time.
18. The amount of an employee's wages before deductions.
19. Employment absences, such as sick days and vacation days, for which it is expected that employees will be paid.
20. The amount of an employee's paycheck after deductions.

Answers on p. 498.

Alternate Terms

Accrued Interest Interest payable

Compensated Absences Accrued vacation or sick pay

Compound Interest Interest on interest

Contingent Asset Contingent gain

Contingent Liability Contingent loss

Current Liability Short-term liability

Current Maturities of Long-Term Debt Long-term debt, current portion

Discounting a Note Interest in advance

FICA Social Security

Future Value of an Annuity Amount of an annuity

Gross Wages Gross pay

Income Tax Liability Income tax payable

Warranties Guarantees

Questions

1. What is the definition of *current liabilities?* Why is it important to distinguish between current and long-term liabilities?
2. Most firms attempt to pay their accounts payable within the discount period to take advantage of the discount. Why is that normally a sound financial move?
3. Assume that your local bank gives you a $1,000 loan at 10% per year but deducts the interest in advance. Is 10% the "real" rate of interest that you will pay? How could the true interest rate be calculated?
4. Is the account Discount on Notes Payable an income statement or balance sheet account? Does it have a debit or credit balance?
5. A firm's year ends on December 31. Its tax is computed and submitted to the U.S. Treasury on March 15 of the following year. When should the taxes be reported as a liability?
6. What is a contingent liability? Why are contingent liabilities accounted for differently than contingent assets?
7. Many firms believe that it is very difficult to estimate the amount of a possible future contingency. Should a contingent liability be reported even if the dollar amount of the loss is not known? Should it be disclosed in the notes to financial statements?
8. Assume that a lawsuit has been filed against your firm. Your legal counsel has assured you that the likelihood of loss is not probable. How should the lawsuit be disclosed on the financial statements?
9. What is the difference between simple interest and compound interest? Would the amount of interest be higher or lower if the interest is simple rather than compound?
10. What is the effect if interest is compounded quarterly versus annually?
11. What is the meaning of the terms *present value* and *future value?* How can you determine whether to calculate the present value of an amount versus the future value?
12. What is the meaning of the word *annuity?* Could the present value of an annuity be calculated as a series of single amounts? If so, how?
13. Assume that you know the total dollar amount of a loan and the amount of the monthly payments on the loan. How could you determine the interest rate as a percentage of the loan?
14. The present value and future value concepts are applied to measure the amount of several accounts commonly encountered in accounting. What are some accounts that are valued in this manner?
15. Your employer withholds federal income tax from your paycheck and remits it to the U.S. Treasury. How is the federal tax treated on the employer's financial statements? (Appendix A)
16. Unemployment tax is a tax on the employer rather than on the employee. How should unemployment taxes be treated on the employer's financial statements? (Appendix A)
17. What is the meaning of the term *compensated absences?* Give some examples. (Appendix A)
18. Do you agree or disagree with the following statement: "Vacation pay should be reported as an expense when the employee takes the vacation"? (Appendix A)

Exercises

Exercise 9-1 ***Current Liabilities*** **LO 1**

The items listed below are accounts on Smith's balance sheet of December 31, 2004.

Taxes Payable
Accounts Receivable
Notes Payable, 9%, due in 90 days
Investment in Bonds
Capital Stock
Accounts Payable
Estimated Warranty Payable in 2005
Retained Earnings
Trademark
Mortgage Payable ($10,000 due every year until 2021)

Required

Identify which of the above accounts should be classified as a current liability on Smith's balance sheet. For each item that is not a current liability, indicate the category of the balance sheet in which it would be classified.

Exercise 9-2 ***Current Liabilities*** **LO 1**

The following items all represent liabilities on a firm's balance sheet.

a. An amount of money owed to a supplier based on the terms 2/20, net 40, for which *no* note was executed
b. An amount of money owed to a creditor on a note due April 30, 2005
c. An amount of money owed to a creditor on a note due August 15, 2006

d. An amount of money owed to employees for work performed during the last week in December

e. An amount of money owed to a bank for the use of borrowed funds due on March 1, 2005

f. An amount of money owed to a creditor as an annual installment payment on a 10-year note

g. An amount of money owed to the federal government, based on the company's annual income

Required

1. For each lettered item, state whether it should be classified as a current liability on the December 31, 2004, balance sheet. Assume that the operating cycle is shorter than one year. If the item should not be classified as a current liability, indicate where on the balance sheet it should be presented.
2. For each item identified as a current liability in part **1**, state the account title that is normally used to report the item on the balance sheet.
3. Why would an investor or creditor be interested in whether an item is a current or a long-term liability?

Exercise 9-3 *Current Liabilities Section* LO 1

Jackie Company had the following accounts and balances on December 31, 2004:

Income Taxes Payable	$61,250
Allowance for Doubtful Accounts	17,800
Accounts Payable	24,400
Interest Receivable	5,000
Unearned Revenue	4,320
Wages Payable	6,000
Notes Payable, 10%, due June 2, 2005	1,000
Accounts Receivable	67,500
Discount on Notes Payable	150
Current Maturities of Long-Term Debt	6,900
Interest Payable	3,010

Required

Prepare the Current Liabilities section of Jackie Company's balance sheet as of December 31, 2004.

Exercise 9-4 *Transaction Analysis* LO 2

Polly's Cards & Gifts Shop had the following transactions during the year:

GENERAL LEDGER

a. Polly's purchased inventory on account from a supplier for $8,000. Assume that Polly's uses a periodic inventory system.

b. On May 1, land was purchased for $44,500. A 20% down payment was made, and an 18-month, 8% note was signed for the remainder.

c. Polly's returned $450 worth of inventory purchased in item **a**, which was found broken when the inventory was received.

d. Polly's paid the balance due on the purchase of inventory.

e. On June 1, Polly signed a one-year, $15,000 note to 1st State Bank and received $13,800.

f. Polly's sold 200 gift certificates for $25 each for cash. Sales of gift certificates are recorded as a liability. At year-end, 35% of the gift certificates had been redeemed.

g. Sales for the year were $120,000, of which 90% were for cash. State sales tax of 6% applied to all sales and must be remitted to the state by January 31.

Required

1. Record all necessary journal entries relating to these transactions.
2. Assume that Polly's accounting year ends on December 31. Prepare any necessary adjusting journal entries.
3. What is the total of the current liabilities at the end of the year?

Exercise 9-5 ***Current Liabilities and Ratios*** **LO 2**

Listed below are several accounts that appeared on Kruse's 2004 balance sheet.

Accounts Payable	$ 55,000
Marketable Securities	40,000
Accounts Receivable	180,000
Notes Payable, 12%, due in 60 days	20,000
Capital Stock	1,150,000
Salaries Payable	10,000
Cash	15,000
Equipment	950,000
Taxes Payable	15,000
Retained Earnings	250,000
Inventory	85,000
Allowance for Doubtful Accounts	20,000
Land	600,000

Required

1. Prepare the Current Liabilities section of Kruse's 2004 balance sheet.
2. Compute Kruse's working capital.
3. Compute Kruse's current ratio. What does this ratio indicate about Kruse's condition?

Exercise 9-6 ***Discounts*** **LO 2**

Each of the following situations involves the use of discounts.

1. How much discount may Seals Inc. take in each of the following transactions? What was the annualized interest rate?
   a. Seals purchases inventory costing $450, 2/10, n/40.
   b. Seals purchases new office furniture costing $1,500, terms 1/10, n/30.
2. Calculate the discount rate Croft Co. received in each of these transactions.
   a. Croft purchased office supplies costing $200 and paid within the discount period with a check for $196.
   b. Croft purchased merchandise for $2,800. It paid within the discount period with a check for $2,674.

Exercise 9-7 ***Notes Payable and Interest*** **LO 2**

On July 1, 2004, Jo's Flower Shop borrowed $25,000 from the bank. Jo signed a 10-month, 8% promissory note for the entire amount. Jo's uses a calendar year-end.

Required

1. Prepare the journal entry on July 1 to record the issuance of the promissory note.
2. Prepare any adjusting entries needed at year-end.
3. Prepare the journal entry on May 1 to record the payment of principal and interest.

Exercise 9-8 ***Non-Interest-Bearing Notes Payable*** **LO 2**

On October 1, 2004, Ratkowski Inc. borrowed $18,000 from 2nd National Bank by issuing a 12-month note. The bank discounted the note at 9%.

Required

1. Prepare the journal entry needed to record the issuance of the note.
2. Prepare the journal entry needed at December 31, 2004, to accrue interest.
3. Prepare the journal entry to record the payment of the note on October 1, 2005.
4. What effective rate of interest did Ratkowski pay?

Exercise 9-9 ***Impact of Transactions Involving Current Liabilities on Statement of Cash Flows*** **LO 3**

From the following list, identify whether the change in the account balance during the year would be reported as an operating (O), investing (I), or financing (F) activity, or not separately reported on the statement of cash flows (N). Assume that the indirect method is used to determine the cash flows from operating activities.

________ Accounts payable

________ Current maturities of long-term debt

________ Notes payable
________ Other accrued liabilities
________ Salaries and wages payable
________ Taxes payable

Exercise 9-10 *Impact of Transactions Involving Contingent Liabilities on Statement of Cash Flows* **LO 3**

From the following list, identify whether the change in the account balance during the year would be reported as an operating (O), investing (I), or financing (F) activity, or not separately reported on the statement of cash flows (N). Assume that the indirect method is used to determine the cash flows from operating activities.

________ Estimated liability for warranties
________ Estimated liability for product premiums
________ Estimated liability for probable loss relating to litigation

Exercise 9-11 *Impact of Transactions Involving Payroll Liabilities on Statement of Cash Flows (Appendix A)* **LO 3**

From the following list, identify whether the change in the account balance during the year would be reported as an operating (O), investing (I), or financing (F) activity, or not separately reported on the statement of cash flows (N). Assume that the indirect method is used to determine the cash flows from operating activities.

________ Accrued vacation days (compensated absences)
________ Health insurance premiums payable
________ FICA payable
________ Union dues payable
________ Salary payable
________ Unemployment taxes payable

Exercise 9-12 *Warranties* **LO 4**

Clean Corporation manufactures and sells dishwashers. Clean provides all customers with a two-year warranty guaranteeing to repair, free of charge, any defects reported during this time period. During the year, it sold 100,000 dishwashers, for $325 each. Analysis of past warranty records indicates that 12% of all sales will be returned for repair within the warranty period. Clean expects to incur expenditures of $14 to repair each dishwasher. The account Estimated Liability for Warranties had a balance of $120,000 on January 1. Clean incurred $150,000 in actual expenditures during the year.

Required

Prepare all journal entries necessary to record the events related to the warranty transactions during the year. Determine the adjusted ending balance in the Estimated Liability for Warranties account.

Exercise 9-13 *Simple Versus Compound Interest* **LO 5**

Part 1. For each of the following notes, calculate the simple interest due at the end of the term.

Note	Face Value (Principal)	Rate	Term
1	$20,000	4%	6 years
2	20,000	6%	4 years
3	20,000	8%	3 years

Part 2. Now assume that the interest on the notes is compounded annually. Calculate the amount of interest due at the end of the term for each note.

Part 3. Now assume that the interest on the notes is compounded semiannually. Calculate the amount of interest due at the end of the term for each note.

What conclusion can you draw from a comparison of your results in parts **1**, **2**, and **3**?

Exercise 9-14 *Present Value, Future Value* **LO 6**

Brian Inc. estimates it will need $150,000 in 10 years to expand its manufacturing facilities. A bank has agreed to pay Brian 5% interest, compounded annually, if the company deposits the entire amount now needed to accumulate $150,000 in 10 years. How much money does Brian need to deposit now?

Exercise 9-15 *Effect of Compounding Period* **LO 6**

Kern Company deposited $1,000 in the bank on January 1, 2004, earning 8% interest. Kern Company withdraws the deposit plus accumulated interest on January 1, 2006. Compute the amount of money Kern withdraws from the bank, assuming that interest is compounded (a) annually, (b) semiannually, and (c) quarterly.

Exercise 9-16 *Present Value, Future Value* **LO 6**

The following situations involve time value of money calculations.

1. A deposit of $7,000 is made on January 1, 2004. The deposit will earn interest at a rate of 8%. How much will be accumulated on January 1, 2009, assuming that interest is compounded (a) annually, (b) semiannually, and (c) quarterly?
2. A deposit is made on January 1, 2004, to earn interest at an annual rate of 8%. The deposit will accumulate to $15,000 by January 1, 2009. How much money was originally deposited, assuming that interest is compounded (a) annually, (b) semiannually, and (c) quarterly?

Exercise 9-17 *Present Value, Future Value* **LO 6**

The following are situations requiring the application of the time value of money.

1. On January 1, 2004, $16,000 is deposited. Assuming an 8% interest rate, calculate the amount accumulated on January 1, 2009, if interest is compounded (a) annually, (b) semiannually, and (c) quarterly.
2. Assume that a deposit made on January 1, 2004, earns 8% interest. The deposit plus interest accumulated to $20,000 on January 1, 2009. How much was invested on January 1, 2004, if interest was compounded (a) annually, (b) semiannually, and (c) quarterly?

Exercise 9-18 *Annuity* **LO 7**

Steve Jones has decided to start saving for his son's college education by depositing $2,000 at the end of every year for 15 years. A bank has agreed to pay interest at the rate of 4% compounded annually. How much will Steve have in the bank immediately after his 15th deposit?

Exercise 9-19 *Calculation of Years* **LO 7**

Kelly Seaver has decided to start saving for her daughter's college education. She wants to accumulate $41,000. The bank will pay interest at the rate of 4% compounded annually. If Kelly plans to make payments of $1,600 at the end of each year, how long will it take her to accumulate $41,000?

Exercise 9-20 *Value of Payments* **LO 7**

DECISION MAKING

On graduation from college, Susana Lopez signed an agreement to buy a used car. Her annual payments, due at the end of each year for two years, are $1,480. The car dealer used a 12% rate compounded annually to determine the amount of the payments.

Required

1. What should Susana consider the value of the car to be?
2. If she had wanted to make quarterly payments, what would her payments have been, based on the value of the car as determined in part **1**? How much less interest would she have had to pay if she had been making quarterly payments instead of annual payments? What do you think would have happened to the amount of the payment and the interest if she had asked for monthly payments?

Exercise 9-21 *Payroll Entries (Appendix A)* **LO 8**

During the month of January, VanderSalm Company's employees earned $385,000. The following rates apply to VanderSalm's gross payroll:

Federal Income Tax Rate	28%
State Income Tax Rate	5%
FICA Tax Rate	7.65%
Federal Unemployment Tax Rate	0.8%
State Unemployment Tax Rate	3.2%

In addition, employee deductions were $7,000 for health insurance and $980 for union dues.

Required

1. Prepare the journal entry the company made to record the January payroll.

2. Prepare the journal entry the company made to record the employer's portion of payroll taxes for January.
3. If the company paid fringe benefits, such as employees' health insurance coverage, how would these contributions affect the payroll entries?

Exercise 9-22 *Payroll, Employer's Portion (Appendix A)* LO 8

Tasty Bakery Shop has six employees on its payroll. Payroll records include the following information on employee earnings for each employee:

Name	Earnings from 1/1 to 6/30/2004	Earnings for 3rd Quarter, 2004
Dell	$ 23,490	$11,710
Fin	4,240	2,660
Hook	34,100	15,660
Patty	63,300	26,200
Tuss	30,050	19,350
Woo	6,300	3,900
Totals	$161,480	$79,480

FICA taxes are levied at 7.65% on the first $84,900 of each employee's current year's earnings. The unemployment tax rates are 0.8% for federal and 2.6% for state unemployment. Assume that unemployment taxes are levied on the first $7,000 of each employee's current year's earnings.

Required

1. Calculate the employer's portion of payroll taxes incurred by Tasty Bakery for each employee for the third quarter of 2004. Round your answers to the nearest dollar.
2. Prepare the journal entry that Tasty's should make to record the employer's portion of payroll taxes.

Exercise 9-23 *Compensated Absences (Appendix A)* LO 9

Wonder Inc. has a monthly payroll of $72,000 for its 24 employees. In addition to their salary, employees earn one day of vacation and one sick day for each month that they work. There are 20 workdays in a month.

Required

1. Prepare the end-of-the-month journal entry, if necessary, to record (a) vacation benefits and (b) sick days.
2. From the owner's perspective, should the company offer the employees vacation and sick pay that accumulates year to year?

Multi-Concept Exercises

Exercise 9-24 *Compare Alternatives* LO 6, 7

Jane Bauer has won the lottery and has four options for receiving her winnings:

DECISION MAKING

1. Receive $100,000 at the beginning of the current year
2. Receive $108,000 at the end of the year
3. Receive $20,000 at the end of each year for 8 years
4. Receive $10,000 at the end of each year for 30 years

Jane can invest her winnings at an interest rate of 8% compounded annually at a major bank. Which of the payment options should Jane choose?

Exercise 9-25 *Two Situations* LO 6, 7

The following situations involve the application of the time value of money concepts.

1. Sampson Company just purchased a piece of equipment with a value of $53,300. Sampson financed this purchase with a loan from the bank and must make annual loan payments of $13,000 at the end of each year for the next five years. Interest is compounded annually on the loan. What is the interest rate on the bank loan?

(continued)

2. Simon Company needs to accumulate $200,000 to repay bonds due in six years. Simon estimates it can save $13,300 at the end of each semiannual period at a local bank offering an annual interest rate of 8% compounded semiannually. Will Simon have enough money saved at the end of six years to repay the bonds?

Problems

Problem 9-1 *Notes and Interest* LO 2

GENERAL LEDGER

Glencoe Inc. operates with a June 30 year-end. During 2004, the following transactions occurred:

a. January 1: Signed a one-year, 10% loan for $25,000. Interest and principal are to be paid at maturity.

b. January 10: Signed a line of credit with the Little Local Bank to establish a $400,000 line of credit. Interest of 9% will be charged on all borrowed funds.

c. February 1: Issued a $20,000 non-interest-bearing, six-month note to pay for a new machine. Interest on the note, at 12%, was deducted in advance.

d. March 1: Borrowed $150,000 on the line of credit.

e. June 1: Repaid $100,000 on the line of credit, plus accrued interest.

f. June 30: Made all necessary adjusting entries.

g. August 1: Repaid the non-interest-bearing note.

h. September 1: Borrowed $200,000 on the line of credit.

i. November 1: Issued a three-month, 8%, $12,000 note in payment of an overdue open account.

j. December 31: Repaid the one-year loan (from item **a**) plus accrued interest.

Required

1. Record all journal entries necessary to report these transactions.
2. As of December 31, which notes are outstanding, and how much interest is due on each?

Problem 9-2 *Effects of Sara Lee's Current Liabilities on Its Statement of Cash Flows* LO 3

http://www.saralee.com

DECISION MAKING

The following items are classified as current liabilities on Sara Lee Corporation's consolidated balance sheet at June 30, 2001 and July 1, 2000 (in millions):

	2001	2000
Notes payable	$ 101	$2,054
Accounts payable	1,505	1,762
Accrued liabilities:		
Payroll and employee benefits	812	928
Advertising and promotions	343	421
Taxes other than payroll and income	84	104
Income taxes	423	55
Other	1,210	1,054
Current maturities of long-term debt	480	381

Required

1. Sara Lee uses the indirect method to prepare its statement of cash flows. Prepare the Operating Activities section of the cash flow statement, which indicates how each item will be reflected as an adjustment to net income. If you did not include any of the items set forth above, explain why not.
2. How would you decide whether Sara Lee has the ability to pay these liabilities as they become due?

http://www.tommyhilfiger.com

Problem 9-3 *Effects of Tommy Hilfiger's Changes in Current Assets and Liabilities on Statement of Cash Flows* LO 3

SPREADSHEET

The following items, listed in alphabetical order, are included in the Current Assets and Current Liabilities categories on the consolidated balance sheet of Tommy Hilfiger Corporation at March 31, 2001 and 2000 (in thousands):

	2001	2000
Accounts payable	$ 38,628	$ 31,289
Accounts receivable	237,414	221,110
Accrued expenses and other liabilities	171,640	233,430
Short-term borrowings	–0–	523
Inventories	205,446	218,793
Other current assets	90,353	103,707

Required

1. Tommy Hilfiger uses the indirect method to prepare its statement of cash flows. Prepare the Operating Activities section of the cash flow statement, which indicates how each item will be reflected as an adjustment to net income.
2. If you did not include any of the items set forth above in your answer to part **1**, explain how these items would be reported on the statement of cash flows.

Problem 9-4 *Warranties* LO 4

DECISION MAKING

Clearview Company manufactures and sells high-quality television sets. The most popular line sells for $1,000 each and is accompanied by a three-year warranty to repair, free of charge, any defective unit. Average costs to repair each defective unit will be $90 for replacement parts and $60 for labor. Clearview estimates that warranty costs of $12,600 will be incurred during 2004. The company actually sold 600 television sets and incurred replacement part costs of $3,600 and labor costs of $5,400 during the year. The adjusted 2004 ending balance in the Estimated Liability for Warranties account is $10,200.

Required

1. How many defective units from this year's sales does Clearview Company estimate will be returned for repair?
2. What percentage of sales does Clearview Company estimate will be returned for repair?
3. What steps should Clearview take if actual warranty costs incurred during 2005 are significantly higher than the estimated liability recorded at the end of 2004?

Problem 9-5 *Warranties* LO 4

Bombeck Company sells a product for $1,500. When the customer buys it, Bombeck provides a one-year warranty. Bombeck sold 120 products during 2004. Based on analysis of past warranty records, Bombeck estimates that repairs will average 3% of total sales.

Required

1. Prepare the journal entry to record the estimated liability.
2. Assume that products under warranty must be repaired during 2004 using repair parts from inventory costing $4,950. Prepare the journal entry to record the repair of products.

Problem 9-6 *Comparison of Simple and Compound Interest* LO 5

On June 30, 2004, Rolf Inc. borrowed $25,000 from its bank, signing a 8%, two-year note.

Required

1. Assuming that the bank charges simple interest on the note, prepare the journal entry Rolf will record on each of the following dates:

   December 31, 2004
   December 31, 2005
   June 30, 2006

2. Assume instead that the bank charges 8% on the note, which is compounded semiannually. Prepare the necessary journal entries on the dates in part **1**.
3. How much additional interest expense will Rolf have in part **2** over part **1**?

Problem 9-7 *Investment with Varying Interest Rate* LO 6

Shari Thompson invested $1,000 in a financial institution on January 1, 2004. She leaves her investment in the institution until December 31, 2008. How much money does Shari accumulate if she earned interest, compounded annually, at the following rates?

(continued)

2004	4%
2005	5
2006	6
2007	7
2008	8

DECISION MAKING

Problem 9-8 ***Comparison of Alternatives*** **LO 6**

On January 1, 2004, Chen Yu's Office Supply Store plans to remodel the store and install new display cases. Chen has the following options of payment. Chen's interest rate is 8%.

a. Pay $180,000 on January 1, 2004.

b. Pay $196,200 on January 1, 2005.

c. Pay $220,500 on January 1, 2006.

d. Make four annual payments of $55,000 beginning on December 31, 2004.

Required

Which option should he choose? (*Hint:* Calculate the present value of each option as of January 1, 2004.)

GENERAL LEDGER

Problem 9-9 ***Payroll Entries (Appendix A)*** **LO 8**

Vivian Company has calculated the gross wages of all employees for the month of August to be $210,000. The following amounts have been withheld from the employees' paychecks:

Income Tax	$42,500
FICA	16,000
Heart Fund Contributions	5,800
Union Dues	3,150

Vivian's unemployment tax rate is 3%, and its portion of FICA matches the employees' share.

Required

1. Prepare the journal entry to record the payroll as an amount payable to employees.

2. Prepare the journal entry that would be recorded to pay the employees.

3. Prepare the journal entry to record the employer's payroll costs.

4. Prepare the journal entry to remit the withholdings.

Problem 9-10 ***Compensated Absences (Appendix A)*** **LO 9**

Hetzel Inc. pays its employees every Friday. For every four weeks that employees work, they earn one vacation day. For every six weeks that they work without calling in sick, they earn one sick day. If employees quit or retire, they can receive a lump-sum payment for their unused vacation days and unused sick days.

Required

Write a short memo to the bookkeeper to explain how and when he should report vacation and sick days. Explain how the matching principle applies and why you believe that the timing you recommend is appropriate.

Multi-Concept Problems

Problem 9-11 ***Interest in Advance versus Interest Paid When Loan Is Due*** **LO 2, 5**

On July 1, 2004, Leach Company needs exactly $103,200 in cash to pay an existing obligation. Leach has decided to borrow from State Bank, which charges 14% interest on loans. The loan will be due in one year. Leach is unsure, however, whether to ask the bank for (a) an interest-bearing loan with interest and principal payable at the end of the year or (b) a loan due in one year but with interest deducted in advance.

Required

1. What will be the face value of the note assuming that

   a. interest is paid when the loan is due?

   b. interest is deducted in advance?

2. Calculate the effective interest rate on the note assuming that
   a. interest is paid when the loan is due.
   b. interest is deducted in advance.
3. Assume that Leach negotiates and signs the one-year note with the bank on July 1, 2004. Also assume that Leach's accounting year ends December 31. Prepare all the journal entries necessary to record the issuance of the note and the interest on the note, assuming that
   a. interest is paid when the loan is due.
   b. interest is deducted in advance.
4. Prepare the appropriate balance sheet presentation for July 1, 2004, immediately after the note has been issued, assuming that
   a. interest is paid when the loan is due.
   b. interest is deducted in advance.

Problem 9-12 ***Contingent Liabilities*** **LO 1, 4**

Listed below are several items for which the outcome of events is unknown at year-end.

a. A company offers a two-year warranty on sales of new computers. It believes that 4% of the computers will require repairs.
b. The company is involved in a trademark infringement suit. The company's legal experts believe an award of $500,000 in the company's favor will be made.
c. A company is involved in an environmental clean-up lawsuit. The company's legal counsel believes it is possible the outcome will be unfavorable but has not been able to estimate the costs of the possible loss.
d. A soap manufacturer has included a coupon offer in the Sunday newspaper supplements. The manufacturer estimates that 25% of the 50-cent coupons will be redeemed.
e. A company has been sued by the federal government for price fixing. The company's legal counsel believes there will be an unfavorable verdict and has made an estimate of the probable loss.

Required

1. Identify which of the items **a** through **e** should be recorded at year-end.
2. Identify which of the items **a** through **e** should not be recorded but should be disclosed in the year-end financial statements.

Problem 9-13 ***Time Value of Money Concepts*** **LO 6, 7**

The following situations involve the application of the time value of money concept.

1. Janelle Carter deposited $9,750 in the bank on January 1, 1987, at an interest rate of 11% compounded annually. How much has accumulated in the account by January 1, 2004?
2. Mike Smith deposited $21,600 in the bank on January 1, 1994. On January 2, 2004, this deposit has accumulated to $42,487. Interest is compounded annually on the account. What is the rate of interest that Mike earned on the deposit?
3. Lee Spony made a deposit in the bank on January 1, 1997. The bank pays interest at the rate of 8% compounded annually. On January 1, 2004, the deposit has accumulated to $15,000. How much money did Lee originally deposit on January 1, 1997?
4. Nancy Holmes deposited $5,800 in the bank on January 1 a few years ago. The bank pays an interest rate of 10% compounded annually, and the deposit is now worth $15,026. How many years has the deposit been invested?

Problem 9-14 ***Comparison of Alternatives*** **LO 6, 7**

Brian Imhoff's grandparents want to give him some money when he graduates from high school. They have offered Brian three choices:

DECISION MAKING

a. Receive $15,000 immediately. Assume that interest is compounded annually.
b. Receive $2,250 at the end of each six months for four years. The first check will be received in six months.
c. Receive $4,350 at the end of each year for four years. Assume interest is compounded annually.

(continued)

Required

Brian wants to have money for a new car when he graduates from college in four years. Assuming an interest rate of 8%, what option should he choose to have the most money in four years?

Alternate Problems

Problem 9-1A ***Notes and Interest*** **LO 2**

GENERAL LEDGER

McLaughlin Inc. operates with a June 30 year-end. During 2004, the following transactions occurred:

a. January 1: Signed a one-year, 10% loan for $35,000. Interest and principal are to be paid at maturity.

b. January 10: Signed a line of credit with the Little Local Bank to establish a $560,000 line of credit. Interest of 9% will be charged on all borrowed funds.

c. February 1: Issued a $28,000 non-interest-bearing, six-month note to pay for a new machine. Interest on the note, at 12%, was deducted in advance.

d. March 1: Borrowed $210,000 on the line of credit.

e. June 1: Repaid $140,000 on the line of credit, plus accrued interest.

f. June 30: Made all necessary adjusting entries.

g. August 1: Repaid the non-interest-bearing note.

h. September 1: Borrowed $280,000 on the line of credit.

i. November 1: Issued a three-month, 8%, $16,800 note in payment of an overdue open account.

j. December 31: Repaid the one-year loan (from item **a**) plus accrued interest.

Required

1. Record all journal entries necessary to report these transactions.
2. As of December 31, which notes are outstanding, and how much interest is due on each?

Problem 9-2A ***Effects of Boeing's Current Liabilities on Its Statement of Cash Flows*** **LO 3**

http://www.boeing.com

DECISION MAKING

The following items are classified as current liabilities on **Boeing Company's** consolidated statements of financial condition (or balance sheet) at December 31 (in millions):

	2001	2000
Accounts payable and other liabilities	$13,872	$12,312
Advances in excess of related costs	4,306	3,517
Income taxes payable	909	1,866
Short-term debt and current portion of long-term debt	1,399	1,232

Required

1. Boeing uses the indirect method to prepare its statement of cash flows. Prepare the Operating Activities section of the cash flow statement, which indicates how each item will be reflected as an adjustment to net income. If you did not include any of the items set forth above, explain why not.
2. How would you decide whether Boeing has the ability to pay these liabilities as they become due?

SPREADSHEET

http://www.nike.com

Problem 9-3A ***Effects of Nike's Changes in Current Assets and Liabilities on Its Statement of Cash Flows*** **LO 3**

The following items, listed in alphabetical order, are included in the Current Assets and Current Liabilities categories on the consolidated balance sheet of **Nike Inc.** at May 31, 2001 and 2000 (in millions):

	2001	2000
Accounts payable	$ 432.0	$ 543.8
Accounts receivable	1,621.4	1,569.4
Accrued liabilities	472.1	621.9
Current portion of long-term debt	5.4	50.1
Income taxes payable	21.9	–0–
Inventories	1,424.1	1,446.0
Notes payable	855.3	924.2
Prepaid expenses	162.5	215.2
Deferred income tax	113.3	111.5

Required

1. Nike uses the indirect method to prepare its statement of cash flows. Prepare the Operating Activities section of the cash flow statement, which indicates how each item will be reflected as an adjustment to net income.
2. If you did not include any of the items set forth above in your answer to part **1**, explain how these items would be reported on the statement of cash flows.

Problem 9-4A *Warranties* LO 4

Sound Company manufactures and sells high-quality stereo sets. The most popular line sells for $2,000 each and is accompanied by a three-year warranty to repair, free of charge, any defective unit. Average costs to repair each defective unit will be $180 for replacement parts and $120 for labor. Sound estimates that warranty costs of $25,200 will be incurred during 2004. The company actually sold 600 sets and incurred replacement part costs of $7,200 and labor costs of $10,800 during the year. The adjusted 2004 ending balance in the Estimated Liability for Warranties account is $20,400.

Required

1. How many defective units from this year's sales does Sound Company estimate will be returned for repair?
2. What percent of sales does Sound Company estimate will be returned for repair?

Problem 9-5A *Warranties* LO 4

Beck Company sells a product for $3,200. When the customer buys it, Beck provides a one-year warranty. Beck sold 120 products during 2004. Based on analysis of past warranty records, Beck estimates that repairs will average 4% of total sales.

Required

1. Prepare the journal entry to record the estimated liability.
2. Assume that during 2004, products under warranty must be repaired using repair parts from inventory costing $10,200. Prepare the journal entry to record the repair of products.
3. Assume that the balance of the Estimated Liabilities for Warranties account as of the beginning of 2004 was $1,100. Calculate the balance of the account as of the end of 2004.

Problem 9-6A *Comparison of Simple and Compound Interest* LO 5

On June 30, 2004, Rolloff Inc. borrowed $25,000 from its bank, signing a 6% note. Principal and interest are due at the end of two years.

Required

1. Assuming that the note earns simple interest for the bank, calculate the amount of interest accrued on each of the following dates:

    December 31, 2004
    December 31, 2005
    June 30, 2006

2. Assume instead that the note earns 6% for the bank but is compounded semiannually. Calculate the amount of interest accrued on the same dates as in part **1**.
3. How much additional interest expense will Rolloff have to pay with semiannual interest?

Problem 9-7A ***Investment with Varying Interest Rate*** **LO 6**

Trena Thompson invested $2,000 in a financial institution on January 1, 2004. She leaves her investment in the institution until December 31, 2008. How much money did Trena accumulate if she earned interest, compounded annually, at the following rates?

2004	4%
2005	5
2006	6
2007	7
2008	8

Problem 9-8A ***Comparison of Alternatives*** **LO 6**

DECISION MAKING

On January 1, 2004, Li Ping's Office Supply Store plans to remodel the store and install new display cases. Li Ping has the following options of payment. Li's interest rate is 8%.

a. Pay $270,000 on January 1, 2004.
b. Pay $294,300 on January 1, 2005.
c. Pay $334,750 on January 1, 2006.
d. Make four annual payments of $82,500 beginning on December 31, 2004.

Required

Which option should Li choose? (*Hint:* Calculate the present value of each option as of January 1, 2004.)

Problem 9-9A ***Payroll Entries (Appendix A)*** **LO 8**

GENERAL LEDGER

Calvin Company has calculated the gross wages of all employees for the month of August to be $336,000. The following amounts have been withheld from the employees' paychecks:

Income Tax	$68,000
FICA	25,600
Heart Fund Contributions	9,280
Union Dues	5,040

Calvin's unemployment tax rate is 3%, and its portion of FICA matches the employees' share.

Required

1. Prepare the journal entry to record the payroll as an amount payable to employees.
2. Prepare the journal entry that would be recorded to pay the employees.
3. Prepare the journal entry to record the employer's payroll costs.
4. Prepare the journal entry to remit the withholdings, including FICA, and the unemployment tax.

Problem 9-10A ***Compensated Absences (Appendix A)*** **LO 9**

DECISION MAKING

Assume that you are the accountant for a large company with several divisions. The manager of Division B has contacted you with a concern. During 2004, several employees retired from Division B. The company's policy is that employees can be paid for days of sick leave accrued at the time they retire. Payment occurs in the year following retirement. The manager has been told by corporate headquarters that she cannot replace the employees in 2005 because the payment of the accrued sick pay will be deducted from Division B's budget in that year.

Required

In a memo to the manager of Division B, explain the proper accounting for accrued sick pay. Do you think that the policies of corporate headquarters should be revised?

Alternate Multi-Concept Problems

Problem 9-11A ***Interest in Advance versus Interest Paid When Loan Is Due*** **LO 2, 5**

On July 1, 2004, Moton Company needs exactly $206,400 in cash to pay an existing obligation. Moton has decided to borrow from State Bank, which charges 14% interest on loans. The loan will be due in one year. Moton is unsure, however, whether to ask the bank for (a) an interest-bearing loan with interest and principal payable at the end of the year or (b) a non-interest-bearing loan due in one year but with interest deducted in advance.

Required

1. What will be the face value of the note, assuming that
   a. interest is paid when the loan is due?
   b. interest is deducted in advance?
2. Calculate the effective interest rate on the note, assuming that
   a. interest is paid when the loan is due.
   b. interest is deducted in advance.
3. Assume that Moton negotiates and signs the one-year note with the bank on July 1, 2004. Also assume that Moton's accounting year ends December 31. Prepare all the journal entries necessary to record the issuance of the note and the interest on it, assuming that
   a. interest is paid when the loan is due.
   b. interest is deducted in advance.
4. Prepare the appropriate balance sheet presentation for July 1, 2004, immediately after the note has been issued, assuming that
   a. interest is paid when the loan is due.
   b. interest is deducted in advance.

Problem 9-12A *Contingent Liabilities* LO 1, 4

Listed below are several events for which the outcome is unknown at year-end.

a. A company has been sued by the federal government for price fixing. The company's legal counsel believes there will be an unfavorable verdict and has made an estimate of the probable loss.
b. A company is involved in an environmental clean-up lawsuit. The company's legal counsel believes it is possible the outcome will be unfavorable but has not been able to estimate the costs of the possible loss.
c. The company is involved in a trademark infringement suit. The company's legal experts believe an award of $750,000 in the company's favor will be made.
d. A company offers a three-year warranty on sales of new computers. It believes that 6% of the computers will require repairs.
e. A snack food manufacturer has included a coupon offer in the Sunday newspaper supplements. The manufacturer estimates that 30% of the 40-cent coupons will be redeemed.

Required

1. Identify which of the items **a** through **e** should be recorded at year-end.
2. Identify which of the items **a** through **e** should not be recorded but should be disclosed on the year-end financial statements.

Problem 9-13A *Time Value of Money Concepts* LO 6, 7

The following situations involve the application of the time value of money concept.

1. Jan Cain deposited $19,500 in the bank on January 1, 1987, at an interest rate of 11% compounded annually. How much has been accumulated in the account by January 1, 2004?
2. Mark Schultz deposited $43,200 in the bank on January 1, 1994. On January 2, 2004, this deposit has accumulated to $84,974. Interest is compounded annually on the account. What is the rate of interest that Mark earned on the deposit?
3. Les Hinckle made a deposit in the bank on January 1, 1997. The bank pays interest at the rate of 8% compounded annually. On January 1, 2004, the deposit has accumulated to $30,000. How much money did Les originally deposit on January 1, 1997?
4. Val Hooper deposited $11,600 in the bank on January 1 a few years ago. The bank pays an interest rate of 10% compounded annually, and the deposit is now worth $30,052. For how many years has the deposit been invested?

Problem 9-14A *Comparison of Alternatives* LO 6, 7

DECISION MAKING

Darlene Page's grandparents want to give her some money when she graduates from high school. They have offered Darlene three choices.

(continued)

a. Receive $16,000 immediately. Assume that interest is compounded annually.

b. Receive $2,400 at the end of each six months for four years. The first check will be received in six months.

c. Receive $4,640 at the end of each year for four years. Assume interest is compounded annually.

Required

Darlene wants to have money for a new car when she graduates from college in four years. Assuming an interest rate of 8%, what option should she choose to have the most money in four years?

Cases

Reading and Interpreting Financial Statements

Case 9-1 *Winnebago Industries' Current Liability* LO 1, 2

http://www.winnebagoind.com

Refer to **Winnebago Industries'** 2001 annual report. Using the company balance sheet and accompanying notes, write a response to the following questions:

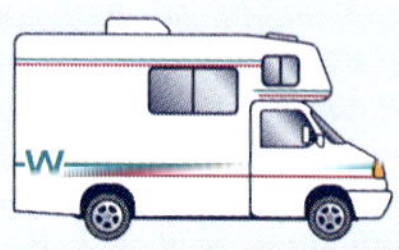

Required

1. Determine the company's current ratio for fiscal years 2001 and 2000. What do the ratios indicate about the liquidity of the company?
2. Explain why accrued compensation and product warranties are considered current liabilities on the company's balance sheet.
3. Refer to the company's notes. Does the company have any contingent liabilities for lawsuits or litigation? If so, how were these contingent liabilities treated on the financial statements?

Case 9-2 *Winnebago Industries' Cash Flow Statement* LO 3

http://www.winnebagoind.com

Refer to **Winnebago Industries'** statement of cash flows in its 2001 annual report to answer the following questions:

Required

1. The net cash provided by operating activities increased significantly in fiscal year 2001. What were the primary reasons for the increase?
2. In fiscal year 2001, receivables, inventories, accounts payable, and accrued expenses all appear as positive amounts on the cash flows statement. Explain whether these accounts actually increased or decreased. What do the changes in these accounts indicate about the company's liquidity and its future performance?

Case 9-3 *Comparing Two Companies in the Same Industry: Winnebago Industries and Monaco Coach Corporation* LO 3

http://www.winnebagoind.com
http://www.monacocoach.com

Refer to the 2001 cash flow statements of **Monaco Coach Corporation** and of Winnebago Industries in Appendices A and B at the end of the text. (*Note:* Monaco presents the most recent statement in the right-hand column.)

Required

1. Monaco Coach's net cash provided by operating activities increased significantly in fiscal year 2001 despite a decline in net income. What were the primary reasons for the increase?
2. Compare the operating activities category of each company's cash flow statement. What company was able to generate more cash from its operating activities? What appears to be the top three reasons for the difference?
3. For each company, look at the following line items listed in the operating section of its 2001 cash flow statement:
   - Monaco Coach: trade receivables, inventories, and accounts payable
   - Winnebago Industries: receivables and other assets, inventories, and accounts payable and accrued expenses.

   Did cash flow increase or decrease for each of these line items? What do the changes in these accounts indicate about each company's liquidity and its future performance?

4. Reach each company's disclosure about warranty claims in its Note 1 to the 2001 financial statements. How are these disclosures similar? How are they different? What information is most helpful for evaluating the company's risk?

Case 9-4 ***Microsoft Corporation's Contingent Liabilities*** **LO 3, 4**

Microsoft Corporation has a fiscal year ending on June 30 and uses the indirect method to prepare its statement of cash flows. The notes to the 2001 financial statements include the following information about contingencies:

http://www.microsoft.com

> On January 23, 2001, Microsoft and Sun Microsystems, Inc. ("Sun") entered into a Settlement Agreement. Under the terms of the public agreement, the parties agreed to a dismissal with prejudice of all pending claims in the suit brought by Sun against Microsoft on October 7, 1997 in the U.S. District Court for the Northern District of California. Sun also granted to Microsoft a non-exclusive license to continue distribution of certain Sun technology for a seven year period. Microsoft further agreed to pay Sun $20 million.
>
> In other ongoing investigations, the DOJ and several state Attorneys General have requested information from Microsoft concerning various issues. In addition, the European Commission has instituted proceedings in which it alleges that Microsoft has failed to disclose information that Microsoft competitors claim they need to interoperate fully with Windows 2000 clients and servers and has engaged in discriminatory licensing of such technology. The remedies sought, though not fully defined, include mandatory disclosure of Microsoft Windows operating system technology and imposition of fines. Microsoft denies the European Commission's allegations and intends to contest the proceedings vigorously.

Required

1. Regarding the first paragraph of the contingency note, is disclosure of the settlement in the notes to the financial statements all that is required of Microsoft, or is accrual required? At what point should accrual occur? If you decide that accrual is required, how would this contingent liability be reported on Microsoft's balance sheet at June 30, 2001?
2. If accrual is required, how would it affect the statement of cash flows for the year ended June 30, 2001?
3. Regarding the second paragraph of the contingency note, is disclosure of the legal dispute in the notes to the financial statements all that is required of Microsoft, or is accrual required? At what point should accrual occur?

Case 9-5 ***Ford Motor Company's Contingent Liability*** **LO 4**

The following is an excerpt from Ford Motor Company's notes that accompanied its financial statements for the year ended December 31, 2000.

http://www.ford.com

> In the United States, the recall of certain Firestone tires, most of which were installed as original equipment on Ford Explorers, has led to a significant number of personal injury and class action lawsuits against Ford and Firestone. Plaintiffs in the personal injury cases typically allege that their injuries were caused by defects in the tire that caused it to lose its tread and/or by defects in the Explorer that caused the vehicle to roll over. For those cases involving Explorer rollovers in which damages have been specified, the damages specified by the plaintiffs, including both actual and punitive damages, aggregated approximately $590 million. However, in most of the actions described above, no dollar amount of damages is specified or the specific amount referred to is only the jurisdictional minimum. It has been our experience that in cases that allege a specific amount of damages in excess of the jurisdictional minimum, such amounts, on average, bear little relation to the actual amounts of damages, if any, paid by Ford in resolving such cases.

Required

1. Based on this excerpt, how should Ford's contingencies be treated on its financial statements for the year ended December 31, 2000?
2. Find more recent financial statements of Ford Motor Company. At what point did the company record amounts related to the Firestone tire legal issues?

Making Financial Decisions

Case 9-6 ***Current Ratio Loan Provision*** **LO 1, 2**

DECISION MAKING

Assume that you are the controller of a small, growing sporting goods company. The prospects for your firm in the future are quite good, but like most other firms, it has been experienc-

(continued)

ing some cash flow difficulties because all available funds have been used to purchase inventory and finance start-up costs associated with a new business. At the beginning of the current year, your local bank advanced a loan to your company. Included in the loan is the following provision:

> The company is obligated to pay interest payments each month for the next five years. Principal is due and must be paid at the end of Year 5. The company is further obligated to maintain a current assets to current liabilities ratio of 2 to 1 as indicated on quarterly statements to be submitted to the bank. If the company fails to meet any loan provisions, all amounts of interest and principal are due immediately upon notification by the bank.

You, as controller, have just gathered the following information as of the end of the first month of the current quarter:

Current liabilities:	
Accounts payable	$400,000
Taxes payable	100,000
Accrued expenses	50,000
Total current liabilities	$550,000

You are concerned about the loan provision that requires a 2:1 ratio of current assets to current liabilities.

Required

1. Indicate what actions could be taken during the next two months to meet the loan provision. Which of the available actions should be recommended?
2. What is the meaning of the term *window-dressing* financial statements? What are the long-run implications of actions taken to window-dress financial statements?

Case 9-7 *Alternative Payment Options* LO 7

DECISION MAKING

Kathy Clark owns a small company that makes ice machines for restaurants and food-service facilities. Kathy knows a lot about producing ice machines but is less familiar with the best terms to extend to her customers. One customer is opening a new business and has asked Kathy to consider any of the following options to pay for his new $20,000 ice machine.

a. Term 1: 10% down, the remainder paid at the end of the year plus 8% simple interest.
b. Term 2: 10% down, the remainder paid at the end of the year plus 8% interest, compounded quarterly.
c. Term 3: $0 down, but $21,600 due at the end of the year.

Required

Make a recommendation to Kathy. She believes that 8% is a fair return on her money at this time. Should she accept option **a, b,** or **c,** or take the $20,000 cash at the time of the sale? Justify your recommendation with calculations. What factors, other than the actual amount of cash received from the sale, should be considered?

Accounting and Ethics: What Would You Do?

Case 9-8 *Warranty Cost Estimate* LO 4

John Walton is an accountant for ABC Auto Dealers, a large auto dealership in a metropolitan area. ABC sells both new and used cars. New cars are sold with a five-year warranty, the cost of which is carried by the manufacturer. For several years, however, ABC has offered a two-year warranty on used cars. The cost of the warranty is an expense to ABC, and John has been asked by his boss, Mr. Sawyer, to review warranty costs and recommend the amount to accrue on the year-end financial statements.

For the past several years, ABC has recorded as warranty expense 5% of used car sales. John has analyzed past repair records and found that repairs, although fluctuating somewhat from year to year, have averaged near the 5% level. John is convinced, however, that 5% is inadequate for the coming year. He bases his judgment on industry reports of increased repair costs and on the fact that several cars that were recently sold on warranty have experienced very high repair costs. John believes that the current-year repair accrual will be at least 10%. He discussed the higher expense amount with Mr. Sawyer, who is the controller of ABC.

Mr. Sawyer was not happy with John's decision concerning warranty expense. He reminded John of the need to control expenses during the recent sales downturn. He also reminded John that ABC is seeking a large loan from the bank and that the bank loan officers may not be happy with recent operating results, especially if ABC begins to accrue larger amounts for future estimated amounts such as warranties. Finally, Mr. Sawyer reminded John that most of the employees of ABC, including Mr. Sawyer, were members of the company's profit-sharing plan and would not be happy with the reduced share of profits. Mr. Sawyer thanked John for his judgment concerning warranty cost but told him that the accrual for the current year would remain at 5%.

John left the meeting with Mr. Sawyer somewhat frustrated. He was convinced that his judgment concerning the warranty costs was correct. He knew that the owner of ABC would be visiting the office next week and wondered whether he should discuss the matter with him personally at that time. John also had met one of the loan officers from the bank several times and considered calling her to discuss his concern about the warranty expense amount on the year-end statements.

Required

Discuss the courses of action available to John. What should John do concerning his judgment of warranty costs?

Case 9-9 ***Retainer Fees As Sales*** **LO 4**

Bunch o' Balloons markets balloon arrangements to companies who want to thank clients and employees. Bunch o' Balloons has a unique style that has put it in high demand. Consequently, Bunch o' Balloons has asked clients to establish an account. Clients are asked to pay a retainer fee equal to about three months of client purchases. The fee will be used to cover the cost of arrangements delivered and will be reevaluated at the end of each month. At the end of the current month Bunch o' Balloons has $43,900 of retainer fees in its possession. The controller is eager to show this amount as sales because "it represents certain sales for the company."

Required

Do you agree with the controller? When should the sales be reported? Why would the controller be eager to report the cash receipts as sales?

Internet Research Case

Case 9-10 ***J. C. Penney***

http://www.jcpenney.com

INTERNET

J. C. Penney hopes a network of retail stores, augmented by catalog sales and a burgeoning e-commerce business, will help the company meet its strategic growth goals and respond to intense competition from other retailers. In recent years, J. C. Penney has established the company as a family of businesses—department stores and catalog, Eckerd drugstores, direct marketing, and international operations. Their mission is to change business processes so as to contain expenses, increase revenue and, especially, raise net income.

JCPenney.com contains a wealth of information about the company. Use this web site to compare the financial numbers presented in this chapter to the latest numbers available; examine management's plans to improve the company's processes; and find news of interest to investors, analysts, and researchers.

1. Based on the latest information available, determine the total current assets and total liabilities for J. C. Penney. How do these compare with the amounts of the previous year?
2. Calculate J. C. Penney's current ratio based on the latest information available.
3. If you were a supplier of merchandise to J. C. Penney, how might its current ratio affect your willingness to extend credit to the company?
4. What major changes in J. C. Penney's operations have been implemented in the latest year available? What do you see as the effect, if any, on the financial statements and notes?

Solutions to Key Terms Quiz

1	Current liability (p. 434)
3	Accounts payable (p. 436)
8	Notes payable (p. 437)
4	Discount on Notes Payable (p. 437)
6	Current Maturities of Long-Term Debt (p. 438)
7	Accrued liability (p. 439)
9	Contingent liability (p. 442)
11	Estimated liability (p. 443)
12	Contingent asset (p. 447)
14	Time value of money (p. 447)
10	Simple interest (p. 449)
13	Compound interest (p. 449)
15	Future value of a single amount (p. 451)
17	Present value of a single amount (p. 453)
5	Annuity (p. 454)
16	Future value of an annuity (p. 454)
2	Present value of an annuity (p. 456)
18	Gross wages (p. 469)
20	Net pay (p. 469)
19	Compensated absences (p. 472)

Chapter 10

Long-Term Liabilities

© TERRI MILLER/E-VISUAL COMMUNICATIONS, INC

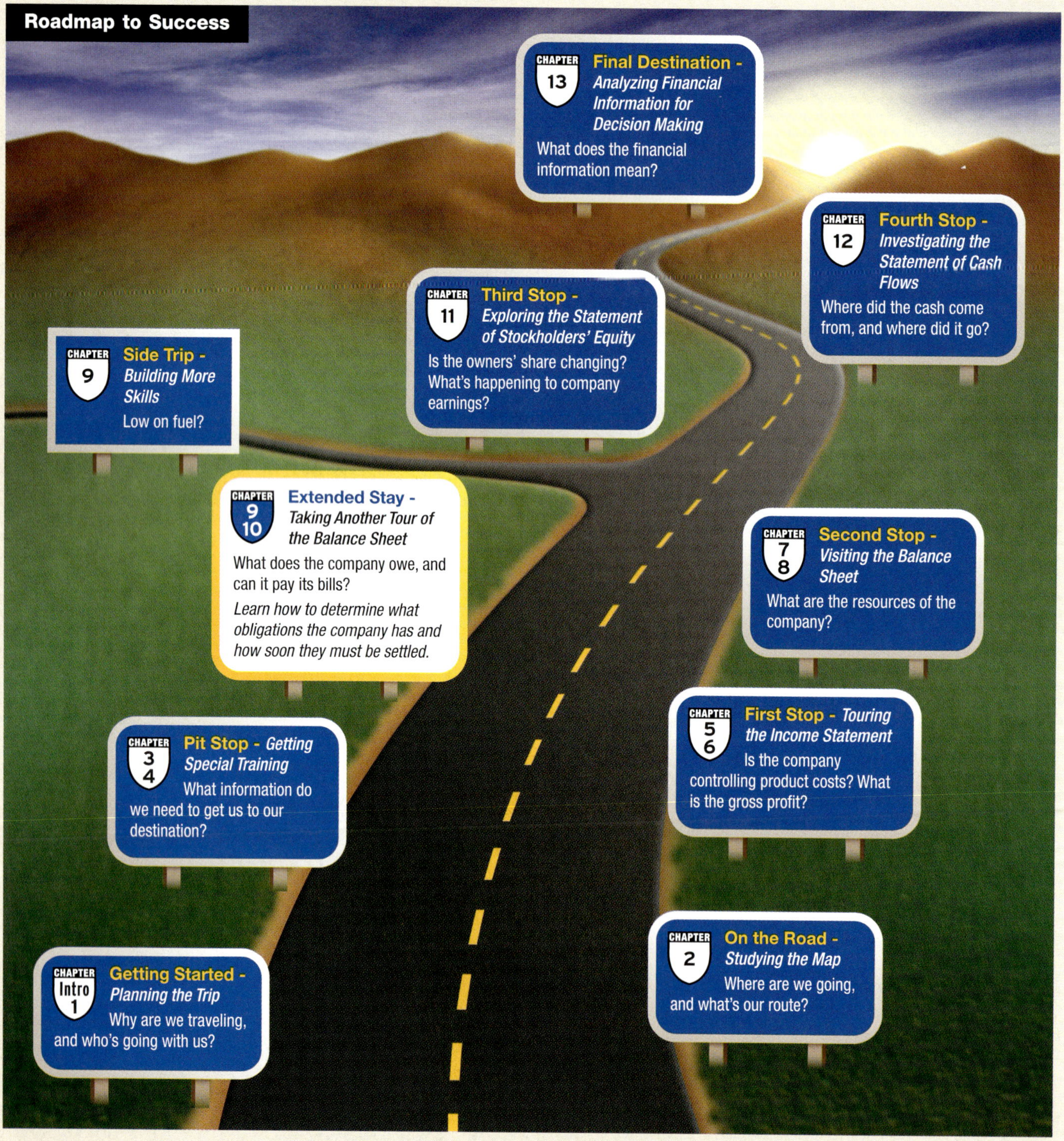

Focus on Financial Results

Coca-Cola® is one of the world's foremost brands with worldwide sales of more than $20 billion in 2001. The company is truly a global corporation with nearly 300 brands in almost 200 countries. While it began many years ago in the United States, now more than 70% of Coca-Cola Company's income comes from business outside the United States. Recently, the growth in company sales has slowed to 3% or less per year, and the company has faced new challenges in the beverage industry. Despite continued turbulence in worldwide markets and challenges from competitors, the firm maintains its focus on growth.

To meet long-term growth objectives, Coca-Cola must make significant investments to support its products. The process also involves investment to develop new global brands and to acquire local or global brands, when appropriate. In addition, the company makes significant marketing investments to encourage consumer loyalty. Coca-Cola has developed relationships with many sports organizations, including the NBA and NASCAR, to enhance consumer awareness and promote sales of its products. Outside the United States, there is a strong push to sell in many other markets, including those in India and Brazil.

To expand profitably, Coca-Cola requires more money than it generates in profits. Therefore, it uses a common financing tool: *long-term debt.* In fact, the balance sheet of December 31, 2001, indicates the company has over $2 billion of long-term debt and other liabilities. The 2001 annual report states, "We use debt financing to lower our overall cost of capital, which increases our return on share-owners equity."[1] The company monitors interest rates conditions carefully and in 2001 retired nearly $4 billion in debt and replaced it with other debt to take advantage of falling interest rates. Because it is a global company, Coca-Cola has access to key financial markets around the world, which allows it to borrow at the lowest possible rates. While most of its loans are in U.S. dollars, management continually adjusts the composition of the debt to accommodate shifting interest rates and currency exchange rates to minimize the overall cost.

http://www.cocacola.com

Coca-Cola 2001 annual report

The Coca-Cola Company and Subsidiaries

December 31,	2001	2000
LIABILITIES AND SHARE-OWNERS' EQUITY		
CURRENT		
Accounts payable and accrued expenses	$ 3,679	$ 3,905
Loans and notes payable	3,743	4,795
Current maturities of long-term debt	156	21
Accrued income taxes	851	600
TOTAL CURRENT LIABILITIES	8,429	9,321
LONG-TERM DEBT	1,219	835
OTHER LIABILITIES	961	1,004
DEFERRED INCOME TAXES	442	358
SHARE-OWNERS' EQUITY		
Common stock, $.25 par value		
Authorized: 5,600,000,000 shares		
Issued: 3,491,465,016 shares in 2001; 3,481,882,834 shares in 2000	873	870
Capital surplus	3,520	3,196
Reinvested earnings	23,443	21,265
Accumulated other comprehensive income and unearned compensation on restricted stock	(2,788)	(2,722)
	25,048	22,609
Less treasury stock, at cost (1,005,237,693 shares in 2001; 997,121,427 shares in 2000)	13,682	13,293
	11,366	9,316
	$ 22,417	$ 20,834

Coca-Cola's long-term debt.

See Notes to Consolidated Financial Statements.

NET OPERATING REVENUES BY OPERATING SEGMENT*

The Coca-Cola Company and Subsidiaries

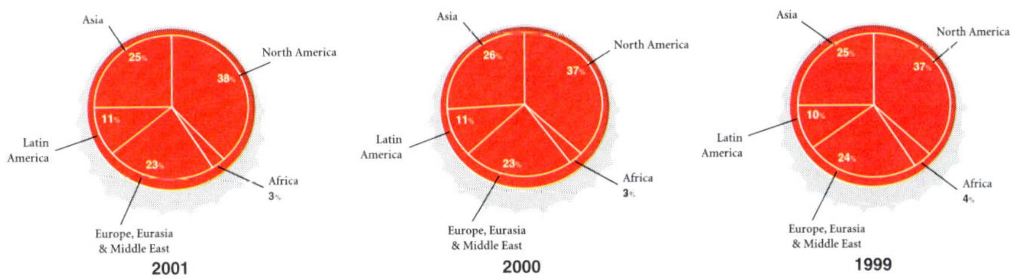

*Charts and percentages are calculated excluding Corporate.

You're in the Driver's Seat

What interest rates does Coca-Cola Company have to pay on long-term debt? How do accountants record the transactions related to long-term debt? Look for the answers as you study this chapter. Check Coca-Cola's most recent annual report to identify any changes in its long-term liabilities.

[1]Coca-Cola's 2001 annual report, p. 44.

LEARNING OBJECTIVES

After studying this chapter, you should be able to:

LO 1 Identify the components of the long-term liability category of the balance sheet. (p. 502)

LO 2 Define the important characteristics of bonds payable. (p. 502)

LO 3 Determine the issue price of a bond using compound interest techniques. (p. 505)

LO 4 Demonstrate an understanding of the effect on the balance sheet of issuance of bonds. (p. 507)

LO 5 Find the amortization of premium or discount using effective interest amortization. (p. 509)

LO 6 Find the gain or loss on retirement of bonds. (p. 514)

LO 7 Determine whether a lease agreement must be reported as a liability on the balance sheet. (p. 516)

LO 8 Explain the effects that transactions involving long-term liabilities have on the statement of cash flows. (p. 521)

LO 9 Explain deferred taxes and calculate the deferred tax liability. (Appendix) (p. 529)

LO 10 Demonstrate an understanding of the meaning of a pension obligation and the effect of pensions on the long-term liability category of the balance sheet. (Appendix) (p. 532)

BALANCE SHEET PRESENTATION

LO 1 Identify the components of the long-term liability category of the balance sheet.

Long-term liability An obligation that will not be satisfied within one year or the current operating cycle.

In general, **long-term liabilities** are obligations that will not be satisfied within one year. Essentially, all liabilities that are not classified as current liabilities are classified as long-term. We will concentrate on the long-term liabilities of bonds or notes, leases, deferred taxes, and pension obligations. On the balance sheet, the items are listed after current liabilities. For example, the Noncurrent Liabilities section of PepsiCo, Inc.'s balance sheet is highlighted in Exhibit 10-1. PepsiCo has acquired financing through a combination of long-term debt, stock issuance, and internal growth or retained earnings. Exhibit 10-1 indicates that long-term debt is one portion of the long-term liability category of the balance sheet. But the balance sheet also reveals two other items that must be considered part of the long-term liability category: deferred income taxes and other liabilities. We begin by looking at a particular type of long-term debt, bonds payable.

From Concept to Practice 10.1

Reading Coca-Cola's Balance Sheet

Coca-Cola lists three items as long-term liabilities on its 2001 balance sheet. What are those items? Did they increase or decrease?

BONDS PAYABLE

Characteristics of Bonds

LO 2 Define the important characteristics of bonds payable.

Face value The principal amount of the bond as stated on the bond certificate.

A bond is a security or financial instrument that allows firms to borrow money and repay the loan over a long period of time. The bonds are sold, or *issued,* to investors who have amounts to invest and want a return on their investment. The *borrower* (issuing firm) promises to pay interest on specified dates, usually annually or semiannually. The borrower also promises to repay the principal on a specified date, the *due date* or maturity date.

A bond certificate, illustrated in Exhibit 10-2, is issued at the time of purchase and indicates the *terms* of the bond. Generally, bonds are issued in denominations of $1,000. The denomination of the bond is usually referred to as the **face value** or par value. This is the amount that the firm must pay at the maturity date of the bond.

Exhibit 10-1 PepsiCo Balance Sheet

Consolidated Balance Sheet

December 29, 2001 and December 30, 2000

PepsiCo, Inc. and Subsidiaries

(In millions except per share amounts)	2001	2000
ASSETS		
Current Assets		
Cash and cash equivalents	$ 683	$ 1,038
Short-term investments, at cost	966	467
	1,649	1,505
Accounts and notes receivable, net	2,142	2,129
Inventories	1,310	1,192
Prepaid expenses and other current assets	752	791
Total Current Assets	5,853	5,617
Property, Plant and Equipment, net	6,876	6,558
Intangible Assets, net	4,841	4,714
Investments in Unconsolidated Affiliates	2,871	2,979
Other Assets	1,254	889
Total Assets	$ 21,695	$ 20,757
LIABILITIES AND SHAREHOLDERS' EQUITY		
Current Liabilities		
Short-term borrowings	$ 354	$ 202
Accounts payable and other current liabilities	4,461	4,529
Income taxes payable	183	64
Total Current Liabilities	4,998	4,795
Long-Term Debt	2,651	3,009
Other Liabilities	3,876	3,960
Deferred Income Taxes	1,496	1,367
Preferred Stock, no par value	26	49
Deferred Compensation—preferred	–	(27)
Common Shareholders' Equity		
Common stock, par value 1²/₃¢ per share (issued 1,782 and 2,029 shares, respectively)	30	34
Capital in excess of par value	13	375
Deferred compensation	–	(21)
Retained earnings	11,519	16,510
Accumulated other comprehensive loss	(1,646)	(1,374)
	9,916	15,524
Less: repurchased common stock, at cost (26 and 280 shares, respectively)	(1,268)	(7,920)
Total Common Shareholders' Equity	8,648	7,604
Total Liabilities and Shareholders' Equity	$21,695	$20,757

PepsiCo's long-term debt

See accompanying notes to consolidated financial statements.

Exhibit 10-2 Bond Certificate

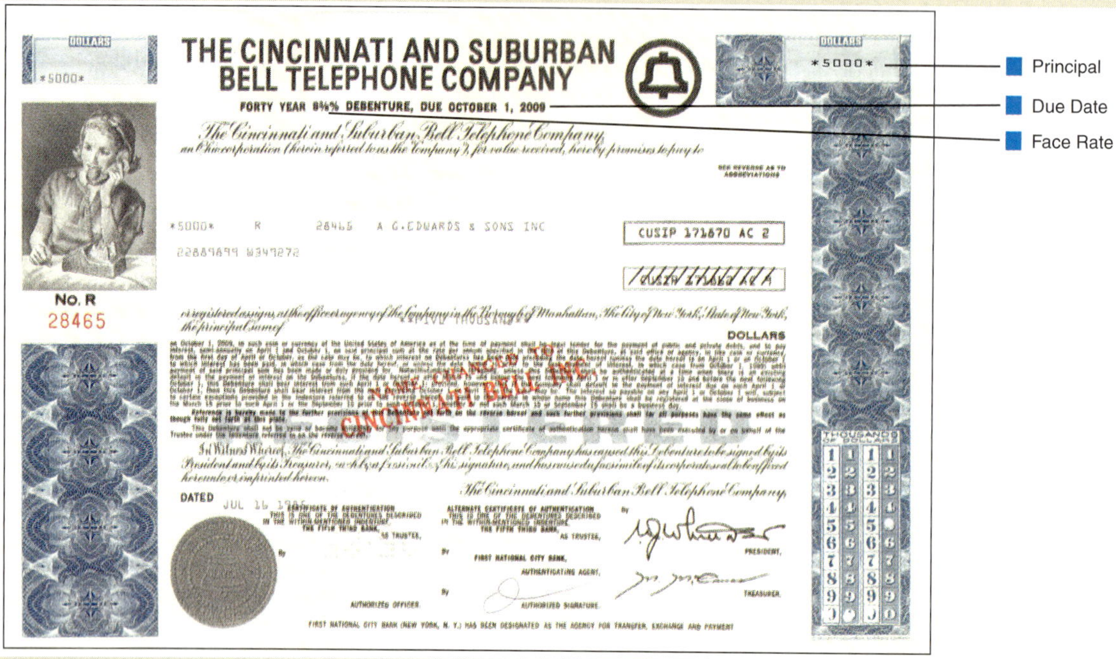

Debenture bonds, like this one from Cincinnati Bell, Inc. (now named Broadwing, Inc.), are backed by the general creditworthiness of the issuing company, not by its assets as collateral. Buyers of such bonds should check the issuer's credit rating, should know how to read the firm's financial statements, and should learn as much as possible about its operations.

Firms issue bonds in very large amounts, often in millions in a single issue. After bonds are issued, they may be traded on a bond exchange in the same way that stocks are sold on the stock exchanges. Therefore, bonds are not always held until maturity by the initial investor but may change hands several times before their eventual due date. Because bond maturities are as long as 30 years, the "secondary" market in bonds—the market for bonds already issued—is a critical factor in a company's ability to raise money. Investors in bonds may want to sell them if interest rates paid by competing investments become more attractive or if the issuer becomes less creditworthy. Buyers of these bonds may be betting that interest rates will reverse course or that the company will get back on its feet. Trading in the secondary market does not affect the financial statements of the issuing company.

We have described the general nature of bonds, but it should not be assumed that all bonds have the same terms and features. Following are some important features that often appear in the bond certificate.

Debenture bonds Bonds that are not backed by specific collateral.

Collateral

The bond certificate should indicate the *collateral* of the loan. Collateral represents the assets that back the bonds in case the issuer cannot make the interest and principal payments and must default on the loan. **Debenture** bonds are not backed by specific collateral of the issuing company. Rather, the investor must examine the general creditworthiness of the issuer. If a bond is a *secured bond,* the certificate indicates specific assets that serve as collateral in case of default.

Serial bonds Bonds that do not all have the same due date; a portion of the bonds comes due each time period.

Due Date

The bond certificate specifies the date that the bond principal must be repaid. Normally, bonds are *term bonds,* meaning that the entire principal amount is due on a single date. Alternatively, bonds may be issued as **serial bonds,** meaning that not all of the principal is due on the same date. For example, a firm may issue serial bonds that have a portion of the principal due each year for the next 10 years. Issuing firms may prefer serial bonds because a firm does not need to accumulate the entire amount for principal repayment at one time.

Other Features Some bonds are issued as convertible or callable bonds. *Convertible bonds* can be converted into common stock at a future time. This feature allows the investor to buy a security that pays a fixed interest rate but that can be converted at a future date into an equity security (stock) if the issuing firm is growing and profitable. The conversion feature is also advantageous to the issuing firm because convertible bonds normally carry a lower rate of interest.

Callable bonds may be retired before their specified due date. *Callable* generally refers to the issuer's right to retire the bonds. If the buyer or investor has the right to retire the bonds, they are referred to as *redeemable bonds.* Usually, callable bonds stipulate the price to be paid at redemption; this price is referred to as the *redemption price* or the *reacquisition price.* The callable feature is like an insurance policy for the company. Say a bond pays 10%, but interest rates plummet to 6%. Rather than continuing to pay 10%, the company is willing to offer a slight premium over face value for the right to retire those 10% bonds so that it can borrow at 6%. Of course, the investor is invariably disappointed when the company invokes its call privilege.

Callable bonds Bonds that may be redeemed or retired before their specified due date.

As you can see, various terms and features are associated with bonds. Each firm seeks to structure the bond agreement in the manner that best meets its financial needs and will attract investors at the most favorable rates.

Bonds are a popular source of financing because of the tax advantages when compared with the issuance of stock. Interest paid on bonds is deductible for tax purposes, but dividends paid on stock are not. This may explain why the amount of debt on many firms' balance sheets has increased in recent years. Debt became popular in the 1980s to finance mergers and again in recent years when interest rates reached 20-year lows. Still, investors and creditors tend to downgrade a company when the amount of debt it has on the balance sheet is deemed to be excessive.

Issuance of Bonds

When bonds are issued, the issuing firm must recognize the incurrence of a liability in exchange for cash. If bonds are issued at their face amount, the accounting entry is straightforward. For example, assume that on April 1 a firm issues bonds with a face amount of $10,000 and receives $10,000. In this case, the asset Cash and the liability Bonds Payable are both increased by $10,000. The accounting entry is as follows:

Apr. 1	Cash	10,000	
	Bonds Payable		10,000
	To record the issuance of bonds at face value.		

Assets	=	Liabilities	+	Owners' Equity
+10,000		+10,000		

Factors Affecting Bond Price

LO 3 Determine the issue price of a bond using compound interest techniques.

With bonds payable, two interest rates are always involved. The **face rate of interest** (also called the *stated rate, nominal rate, contract rate, or coupon rate*) is the rate specified on the bond certificate. It is the amount of interest that will be paid each interest period. For example, if $10,000 worth of bonds is issued with an 8% annual face rate of interest, then interest of $800 ($10,000 × 8% × 1 year) would be paid at the end of each annual period. Alternatively, bonds often require the payment of interest semiannually. If the bonds in our example required the 8% annual face rate to be paid semiannually (at 4%), then interest of $400 ($10,000 × 8% × $^1/_2$ year) would be paid each semiannual period.

Face rate of interest The rate of interest on the bond certificate.

The second important interest rate is the **market rate of interest** (also called the *effective rate* or *bond yield*). The market rate of interest is the rate that bondholders could obtain by investing in other bonds that are similar to the issuing firm's bonds. The issuing firm does not set the market rate of interest. That rate is determined by the bond market on the basis of many transactions for similar bonds. The market rate incor-

Market rate of interest The rate that investors could obtain by investing in other bonds that are similar to the issuing firm's bonds.

Study Tip

Calculating the issue price of a bond always involves a calculation of the present value of the cash flows.

Bond issue price The present value of the annuity of interest payments plus the present value of the principal.

porates all of the "market's" knowledge about economic conditions and all its expectations about future conditions. Normally, issuing firms try to set a face rate that is equal to the market rate. However, because the market rate changes daily, there are almost always small differences between the face rate and the market rate at the time bonds are issued.

In addition to the number of interest payments and the maturity length of the bond, the face rate and the market rate of interest must both be known in order to calculate the issue price of a bond. The **bond issue price** equals the *present value* of the cash flows that the bond will produce. Bonds produce two types of cash flows for the investor: interest receipts and repayment of principal (face value). The interest receipts constitute an annuity of payments each interest period over the life of the bonds. The repayment of principal (face value) is a one-time receipt that occurs at the end of the term of the bonds. We must calculate the present value of the interest receipts (using Table 9-4) and the present value of the principal amount (using Table 9-2). The total of the two present-value calculations represents the issue price of the bond.

An Example Suppose that on January 1, 2004, Discount Firm wants to issue bonds with a face value of $10,000. The face or coupon rate of interest has been set at 8%. The bonds will pay interest annually, and the principal amount is due in four years. Also suppose that the market rate of interest for other similar bonds is currently 10%. Because the market rate of interest exceeds the coupon rate, investors will not be willing to pay $10,000 but something less. We want to calculate the amount that will be obtained from the issuance of Discount Firm's bonds.

Discount's bond will produce two sets of cash flows for the investor: an annual interest payment of $800 ($10,000 × 8%) per year for four years and repayment of the principal of $10,000 at the end of the fourth year. To calculate the issue price, we must calculate the present value of the two sets of cash flows. A time diagram portrays the cash flows as follows:

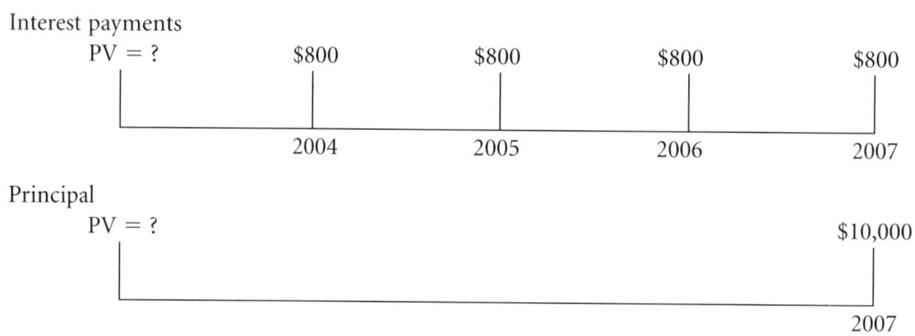

We can calculate the issue price by using the compound-interest tables found in Chapter 9, as follows:

$800 × 3.170 (factor from Table 9-4 for 4 periods, 10%)	$2,536
$10,000 × 0.683 (factor from Table 9-2 for 4 periods, 10%)	6,830
Issue price	$9,366

You should perform the following steps when using a calculator to determine the present value in our example:

ENTER	DISPLAY
4 N	N = 4
10 I/Y	I/Y = 10
800 PMT	PMT = 800
10000 FV	FV = 10,000
CPT PV	PV = 9,366

Accounting for Your Decisions

You Rate the Bonds

One of the factors that determine the rate of interest on a bond is a rating by a rating agency such as Standard & Poor's or Moody's Investor Service. Bonds with a higher rating are considered less risky and can be issued for a lower rate of interest. You have been given an assignment to rate the bonds issued by PepsiCo. What factors would you consider in your rating?

ANS: There are many factors that affect your evaluation of the riskiness of the company's bonds. One factor would be the amount of debt on PepsiCo's books, which can be found by examining the liability section of the balance sheet. It is important to relate the amount of debt to the total equity of the company; this is often done by computing the debt-to-equity ratio. Another important factor is the company's competitive position within its industry. If PepsiCo can operate profitably, it will generate cash that can be used to pay the interest and principal on the bonds.

The factors used to calculate the present value represent four periods and 10% interest. This is a key point. The issue price of a bond is always calculated using the market rate of interest. The face rate of interest determines the amount of the interest payments, but the market rate determines the present value of the payments and the present value of the principal (and therefore the issue price).

Our example of Discount Firm reveals that the bonds with a $10,000 face value amount would be issued for $9,366. The bond markets and the financial press often state the issue price as a percentage of the face amount. The percentage for Discount's bonds can be calculated as ($9,366/$10,000) × 100, or 93.66%.

Exhibit 10-3 illustrates how bonds are actually listed in the reporting of the bond markets. The exhibit lists two types of IBM bonds that were traded on a particular day. The portion immediately after the company name, for example "6⅜ 06," indicates that the face rate of interest is 6⅜% and the due date of the bonds is the year 2006. The next column, for example "6.5," indicates that the bond investor who purchased the bonds on that day will receive a yield of 6.5%. The column labeled "vol" indicates the number of bonds, in thousands, that were bought and sold during the day. The column labeled "close" indicates the market price of the bonds at the end of the day. For example, the first issue of IBM bonds closed at 98¾, which means that the price was 98¾% of the face value of the bonds. These bonds are trading at a discount because the face rate (6⅜%) is less than the market rate of 6.5%. The bonds in the second issue—"7¼ 08"—have a face rate of 7¼%, will become due in the year 2008, and closed at 101½, or at a premium. The net change column indicates the change in the bond price that occurred for the day's trading.

http://www.ibm.com

BONDS	CUR YLD	VOL	CLOSE	NET CHG
IBM 6⅜06	6.5	280	98¾	−¼
IBM 7¼08	7.1	68	101½	+¼

Exhibit 10-3
Listing of Bonds on the Bond Market

Premium or Discount on Bonds

LO 4 Demonstrate an understanding of the effect on the balance sheet of issuance of bonds.

Premium or **discount** represents the difference between the face value and the issue price of a bond. We may state the relationship as follows:

Premium = Issue Price − Face Value
Discount = Face Value − Issue Price

Premium The excess of the issue price over the face value of the bonds.

Discount The excess of the face value of bonds over the issue price.

In other words, when issue price exceeds face value, the bonds have sold at a premium, and when the face value exceeds the issue price, the bonds have sold at a discount.

We will continue with the Discount Firm example to illustrate the accounting for bonds sold at a discount. Discount Firm's bonds sold at a discount calculated as follows:

$$\text{Discount} = \$10{,}000 - \$9{,}366$$
$$= \$634$$

Discount Firm would record both the discount and the issuance of the bonds in the following journal entry:

Jan. 1	Cash	9,366	
	Discount on Bonds Payable	634	
	Bonds Payable		10,000
	To record the issuance of bonds payable.		

Assets	=	Liabilities	+	Owners' Equity
+9,366		−634		
		+10,000		

The Discount on Bonds Payable account is shown as a contra liability on the balance sheet in conjunction with the Bonds Payable account and is a deduction from that account. If Discount Firm prepared a balance sheet immediately after the bond issuance, the following would appear in the Long-Term Liabilities category of the balance sheet:

Long-term liabilities:	
Bonds payable	$10,000
Less: Discount on bonds payable	634
	$ 9,366

The Discount Firm example has illustrated a situation in which the market rate of a bond issue is higher than the face rate. Now we will examine the opposite situation, when the face rate exceeds the market rate. Again, we are interested in calculating the issue price of the bonds.

Issuing at a Premium Suppose that on January 1, 2004, Premium Firm wants to issue the same bonds as in the previous example: $10,000 face value bonds, with an 8% face rate of interest and with interest paid annually each year for four years. Assume, however, that the market rate of interest is 6% for similar bonds. The issue price is calculated as the present value of the annuity of interest payments plus the present value of the principal at the market rate of interest. The calculations are as follows:

$800 × 3.465 (factor from Table 9-4 for 4 periods, 6%)	$ 2,772
$10,000 × 0.792 (factor from Table 9-2 for 4 periods, 6%)	7,920
Issue price	$10,692

You should perform the following steps when using a calculator to determine the present value in our example:

ENTER	DISPLAY
4 N	N = 4
6 I/Y	I/Y = 6
800 PMT	PMT = 800
10000 FV	FV = 10,000
CPT PV	PV = 10,693*
*(rounded)	

We have calculated that the bonds would be issued for $10,692. Because the bonds would be issued at an amount that is higher than the face value amount, they would be issued at a premium. The amount of the premium is calculated as follows:

$$\text{Premium} = \$10{,}692 - \$10{,}000 = \$692$$

The premium is recorded at the time of bond issuance in the following entry:

Jan. 1	Cash	10,692	
	Bonds Payable		10,000
	Premium on Bonds Payable		692
	To record the issuance of bonds payable.		

Assets	=	Liabilities	+	Owners' Equity
+10,692		+10,000		
		+692		

The account Premium on Bonds Payable is an addition to the Bonds Payable account. If Premium Firm presented a balance sheet immediately after the bond issuance, the Long-Term Liabilities category of the balance sheet would appear as follows:

Long-term liabilities:	
Bonds payable	$10,000
Plus: Premium on bonds payable	692
	$10,692

Study Tip

When interest rates increase, present values decrease. This is called an *inverse relationship.*

You should learn two important points from the Discount Firm and Premium Firm examples. First, you should be able to determine whether a bond will sell at a premium or discount by the relationship that exists between the face rate and the market rate of interest. *Premium* and *discount* do not mean "good" and "bad." Premium or discount arises solely because of the difference that exists between the face rate and the market rate of interest for a bond issue. The same relationship always exists, so that the following statements hold true:

If Market Rate = Face Rate, THEN bonds are issued at face value amount.
If Market Rate > Face Rate, THEN bonds are issued at a discount.
If Market Rate < Face Rate, THEN bonds are issued at a premium.

The examples also illustrate a second important point. The relationship between interest rates and bond prices is always inverse. To understand the term *inverse relationship,* refer to the Discount Firm and Premium Firm examples. The bonds of the two firms are identical in all respects except for the market rate of interest. When the market rate was 10%, the bond issue price was $9,366 (the Discount Firm example). When the market rate was 6%, the bond issue price increased to $10,692 (the Premium Firm example). The examples illustrate that as interest rates decrease, prices on the bond markets increase and that as interest rates increase, bond prices decrease.

Many investors in the stock market perceive that they are taking a great deal of risk with their capital. In truth, bond investors are taking substantial risks too. The most obvious risk is that the company will fail and not be able to pay its debts. But another risk is that interest rates on comparable investments will rise. Interest rate risk can have a devastating impact on the current market value of bonds. One way to minimize interest rate risk is to hold the bond to maturity, at which point the company must pay the face amount.

Bond Amortization

Purpose of Amortization The amount of interest expense that should be reflected on a firm's income statement for bonds payable is the true, or effective, interest. The effective interest should reflect the face rate of interest as well as inter-

LO 5 Find the amortization of premium or discount using effective interest amortization.

est that results from issuing the bond at a premium or discount. To reflect that interest component, the amount initially recorded in the Premium on Bonds Payable or the Discount on Bonds Payable account must be amortized or spread over the life of the bond.

Amortization refers to the process of transferring an amount from the discount or premium account to interest expense each time period to adjust interest expense. One commonly used method of amortization is the effective interest method. We will illustrate how to amortize a discount amount and then how to amortize a premium amount.

To illustrate amortization of a discount, we need to return to our Discount Firm example introduced earlier. We have seen that the issue price of the bond could be calculated as $9,366, resulting in a contra-liability (debit) balance of $634 in the Discount on Bonds Payable account (see the entry on page 10). But what does the initial balance of the Discount account really represent? The discount should be thought of as additional interest that Discount Firm must pay over and above the 8% face rate. Remember that Discount received only $9,366 but must repay the full principal of $10,000 at the bond due date. For that reason, the $634 discount is an additional interest cost that must be reflected as interest expense. It is reflected as interest expense by the process of amortization. In other words, interest expense is made up of two components: cash interest and amortization. We will now consider how to amortize premium or discount.

Effective interest method of amortization The process of transferring a portion of the premium or discount to interest expense; this method results in a constant effective interest rate.

Carrying value The face value of a bond plus the amount of unamortized premium or minus the amount of unamortized discount.

Effective Interest Method: Impact on Expense The **effective interest method of amortization** amortizes discount or premium in a manner that produces a constant effective interest rate from period to period. The *dollar amount* of interest expense will vary from period to period, but the rate of interest will be constant. This interest rate is referred to as the *effective interest rate* and is equal to the market rate of interest at the time the bonds are issued.

To illustrate this point, we introduce two new terms. The **carrying value** of bonds is represented by the following:

Carrying Value = Face Value − Unamortized Discount

For example, the carrying value of the bonds for our Discount Firm example, as of the date of issuance of January 1, 2004, could be calculated as follows:

$10,000 − $634 = $9,366

In those situations in which there is a premium instead of a discount, carrying value is represented by the following:

Carrying Value = Face Value + Unamortized Premium

For example, the carrying value of the bonds for our Premium Firm example, as of the date of issuance of January 1, 2004, could be calculated as follows:

$10,000 + $692 = $10,692

The second term has been suggested earlier. The *effective rate of interest* is represented by the following:

Effective Rate = Annual Interest Expense/Carrying Value

Effective Interest Method: An Example The amortization table in Exhibit 10-4 illustrates effective interest amortization of the bond discount for our Discount Firm example.

As illustrated in Exhibit 10-4, the effective interest method of amortization is based on several important concepts. The relationships can be stated in equation form as follows:

Cash Interest (in Column 1) = Bond Face Value × Face Rate
Interest Expense (in Column 2) = Carrying Value × Effective Rate
Discount Amortized (in Column 3) = Interest Expense − Cash Interest

DATE	COLUMN 1 CASH INTEREST	COLUMN 2 INTEREST EXPENSE	COLUMN 3 DISCOUNT AMORTIZED	COLUMN 4 CARRYING VALUE
	8%	10%	Col. 2 − Col. 1	
1/1/2004	—	—	—	$ 9,366
12/31/2004	$800	$937	$137	9,503
12/31/2005	800	950	150	9,653
12/31/2006	800	965	165	9,818
12/31/2007	800	982	182	10,000

Exhibit 10-4

Discount Amortization: Effective Interest Method of Amortization

The first column of the exhibit indicates that the cash interest to be paid is $800 ($10,000 × 8%). The second column indicates the annual interest expense at the effective rate of interest (market rate at the time of issuance). This is a constant rate of interest (10% in our example) and is calculated by multiplying the carrying value *as of the beginning of the period* by the market rate of interest. In 2004, the interest expense is $937 ($9,366 × 10%). Note that the amount of interest expense changes each year because the carrying value changes as discount is amortized. The amount of discount amortized each year in Column 3 is the difference between the cash interest in Column 1 and the interest expense in Column 2. Again, note that the amount of discount amortized changes in each of the four years. Finally, the carrying value in Column 4 is the previous year's carrying value plus the discount amortized in Column 3. When bonds are issued at a discount, the carrying value starts at an amount less than face value and increases each period until it reaches the face value amount.

The amortization table in Exhibit 10-4 is the basis for the accounting entries that must be recorded. Discount Firm may record two entries for each period. The first entry at the end of 2004 is recorded to reflect the cash interest payment:

Dec. 31	Interest Expense	800	
	Cash		800
	To record annual interest payment on bonds payable.		

Assets	=	Liabilities	+	Owners' Equity
−800				−800

The second entry is recorded to amortize a portion of the discount and to reflect that amount as an adjustment of interest expense:

Dec. 31	Interest Expense	137	
	Discount on Bonds Payable		137
	To amortize annual portion of discount on bonds payable.		

Assets	=	Liabilities	+	Owners' Equity
		+137		−137

Instead of making two entries, firms often make one entry that combines the two. Thus, the entry for 2004 could also be recorded in the following manner:

Dec. 31	Interest Expense	937	
	Cash		800
	Discount on Bonds Payable		137
	To record annual interest payment and to amortize annual portion of discount on bonds payable.		

Assets	=	Liabilities	+	Owners' Equity
−800		+137		−937

The T accounts of the issuing firm as of December 31, 2004, would appear as follows:

BONDS PAYABLE		
	10,000	1/1/04

DISCOUNT ON BONDS PAYABLE			
1/1/04	634	137	12/31/04
Bal.	497		

INTEREST EXPENSE		
12/31/04	800	
12/31/04	137	
Bal.	937	

The balance of the Discount on Bonds Payable account as of December 31, 2004, would be calculated as follows:

Beginning balance, January 1, 2004	$634
Less: Amount amortized	137
Ending balance, December 31, 2004	$497

The December 31, 2004, balance represents the amount *unamortized*, or the amount that will be amortized in future time periods. On the balance sheet presented as of December 31, 2004, the unamortized portion of the discount appears as the balance of the Discount on Bonds Payable account as follows:

Long-term liabilities	
Bonds payable	$10,000
Less: Discount on bonds payable	497
	$ 9,503

The process of amortization would continue for four years, until the balance of the Discount on Bonds Payable account has been reduced to zero. By the end of 2007, all of the balance of the Discount on Bonds Payable account will have been transferred to the Interest Expense account and represents an increase in interest expense each period.

The amortization of a premium has an impact opposite that of the amortization of a discount. We will use our Premium Firm example to illustrate. Recall that on January 1, 2004, Premium Firm issued $10,000 face value bonds with a face rate of interest of 8%. At the time the bonds were issued, the market rate was 6%, resulting in an issue price of $10,692 and a credit balance in the Premium on Bonds Payable account of $692.

The amortization table in Exhibit 10-5 illustrates effective interest amortization of the bond premium for Premium Firm. As the exhibit illustrates, effective interest amortization of a premium is based on the same concepts as amortization of a discount. The following relationships still hold true:

Cash Interest (in Column 1) = Bond Face Value × Face Rate
Interest Expense (in Column 2) = Carrying Value × Effective Rate

The first column of the exhibit indicates that the cash interest to be paid is $800 ($10,000 × 8%). The second column indicates the annual interest expense at the effective rate.

Exhibit 10-5

Premium Amortization: Effective Interest Method of Amortization

DATE	COLUMN 1 CASH INTEREST	COLUMN 2 INTEREST EXPENSE	COLUMN 3 PREMIUM AMORTIZED	COLUMN 4 CARRYING VALUE
	8%	**6%**	**Col. 1 − Col. 2**	
1/1/2004	—	—	—	$10,692
12/31/2004	$800	$642	$158	10,534
12/31/2005	800	632	168	10,366
12/31/2006	800	622	178	10,188
12/31/2007	800	612	188	10,000

In 2004 the interest expense is \$642 (\$10,692 × 6%). Note, however, two differences between Exhibit 10-4 and Exhibit 10-5. In the amortization of a premium, the cash interest in Column 1 exceeds the interest expense in Column 2. Therefore, the premium amortized is defined as follows:

Premium Amortized (in Column 3) = Cash Interest − Interest Expense

Also note that the carrying value in Column 4 starts at an amount higher than the face value of \$10,000 (\$10,692) and is amortized downward until it reaches face value. Therefore, the carrying value at the end of each year is the carrying value at the beginning of the period minus the premium amortized for that year. For example, the carrying value in Exhibit 10-5 at the end of 2004 (\$10,534) was calculated by subtracting the premium amortized for 2004 (\$158 in Column 3) from the carrying value at the beginning of 2004 (\$10,692).

The amortization table in Exhibit 10-5 again serves as the basis for the accounting entries that must be recorded. Premium Firm may record two entries for each period. The first entry at the end of 2004 is recorded to reflect the cash interest payment:

Dec. 31	Interest Expense	800	
	Cash		800
	To record annual interest payment on bonds payable.		

Assets	=	Liabilities	+	Owners' Equity
−800				−800

The second entry is recorded to amortize a portion of the premium and to reflect that amount as an adjustment of interest expense:

Dec. 31	Premium on Bonds Payable	158	
	Interest Expense		158
	To amortize annual portion of premium on bonds payable.		

Assets	=	Liabilities	+	Owners' Equity
		−158		+158

Of course, Premium Firm could combine the preceding two entries into one entry as follows:

Dec. 31	Interest Expense	642	
	Premium on Bonds Payable	158	
	Cash		800
	To record annual interest payment and to amortize annual portion of premium on bonds payable.		

Assets	=	Liabilities	+	Owners' Equity
−800		−158		−642

The balance of the Premium on Bonds payable account as of December 31, 2004, would be calculated as follows:

Beginning balance, January 1, 2004	\$692
Less: Amount amortized	158
Ending balance, December 31, 2004	\$534

The December 31, 2004, balance represents the amount *unamortized*, or the amount that will be amortized in future time periods. On the balance sheet presented as of December 31, 2004, the unamortized portion of the premium appears as the balance of the Premium on Bonds payable account as follows:

Long-term liabilities:	
Bonds payable	\$10,000
Plus: Premium on bonds payable	534
	\$10,534

Study Tip

Amortization of a discount increases interest expense. Amortization of a premium reduces interest expense.

The process of amortization would continue for four years, until the balance of the Premium on Bonds Payable account has been reduced to zero. By the end of 2007, all of the balance of the Premium on Bonds Payable account will have been transferred to the Interest Expense account and represents a reduction of interest expense each period.

Two-Minute Review

1. *How do you calculate the issue price of a bond?*
2. *What effect does amortizing a premium have on the amount of interest expense for the bond? What effect does amortizing a discount have?*

Answers on p. 524

Redemption of Bonds

Redemption at Maturity The term *redemption* refers to retirement of bonds by repayment of the principal. If bonds are retired on their due date, the accounting entry is not difficult. Refer again to the Discount Firm example. If Discount Firm retires its bonds on the due date of December 31, 2007, it must repay the principal of $10,000, and Cash is reduced by $10,000. The following entry is recorded:

Dec. 31	Bonds Payable	10,000	
	Cash		10,000
	To record the retirement of bonds payable.		

Assets	=	Liabilities	+	Owners' Equity
−10,000		−10,000		

This assumes that the interest payment that was paid on December 31, 2007, and the discount amortization on that date have already been recorded. The balance of the Discount on Bonds Payable account is zero, since it has been fully amortized.

Notice that no gain or loss is incurred because the carrying value of the bond at that point is $10,000.

LO 6 Find the gain or loss on retirement of bonds.

Retired Early at a Gain A firm may want to retire bonds before their due date for several reasons. A firm may simply have excess cash and may determine that the best use of those funds is to repay outstanding bond obligations. Bonds may also be retired early because of changing interest rate conditions. If interest rates in the economy decline, firms may find it advantageous to retire bonds that have been issued at higher rates. Of course, what is advantageous to the issuer is not necessarily so for the investor. Early retirement of callable bonds is always a possibility that must be anticipated. Large institutional investors expect such a development and merely reinvest the money elsewhere. Many individual investors are more seriously inconvenienced when a bond issue is called.

Bond terms generally specify that if bonds are retired before their due date, they are not retired at the face value amount but at a call price or redemption price indicated on the bond certificate. Also, the amount of unamortized premium or discount on the bonds must be considered when bonds are retired early. The retirement results in a **gain or loss on redemption** that must be calculated as follows:

Gain or loss on redemption The difference between the carrying value and the redemption price at the time bonds are redeemed.

Gain = Carrying Value − Redemption Price
Loss = Redemption Price − Carrying Value

In other words, the issuing firm must calculate the carrying value of the bonds at the time of redemption and compare it with the total redemption price. If the carrying value is higher than the redemption price, the issuing firm must record a gain. If the carrying value is lower than the redemption price, the issuing firm must record a loss.

We will use the Premium Firm example to illustrate the calculation of gain or loss. Assume that on December 31, 2004, Premium Firm wants to retire its bonds due in 2007. Assume, as in the previous section, that the bonds were issued at a premium of \$692 at the beginning of 2004. Premium Firm has used the effective interest method of amortization and has recorded the interest and amortization entries for the year (see page 15). This has resulted in a balance of \$534 in the Premium on Bonds Payable account as of December 31, 2004. Assume also that Premium Firm's bond certificates indicate that the bonds may be retired early at a call price of 102 (meaning 102% of face value). Thus, the redemption price is 102% of \$10,000, or \$10,200.

Premium Firm's retirement of bonds would result in a gain. The gain can be calculated using two steps. First, we must calculate the carrying value of the bonds as of the date they are retired. The carrying value of Premium Firm's bonds at that date is calculated as follows:

Carrying Value = Face Value + Unamortized Premium
= \$10,000 + \$534
= \$10,534

Note that the carrying value we have calculated is the same amount indicated for December 31, 2004, in Column 4 of the effective interest amortization table of Exhibit 10-5.

The second step is to calculate the gain:

Gain = Carrying Value − Redemption Price
= \$10,534 − (\$10,000 × 1.02)
= \$10,534 − \$10,200
= \$334

It is important to remember that when bonds are retired, the balance of the Bonds Payable account and the remaining balance of the Premium on Bonds Payable account must be eliminated from the balance sheet.

Retired Early at a Loss To illustrate retirement of bonds at a loss, assume that Premium Firm retires bonds at December 31, 2004, as in the previous section. However, assume that the call price for the bonds is 107 (or 107% of face value).

We can again perform the calculations in two steps. The first step is to calculate the carrying value:

Carrying Value = Face Value + Unamortized Premium
= \$10,000 + \$534
= \$10,534

The second step is to compare the carrying value with the redemption price to calculate the amount of the loss:

Loss = Redemption Price − Carrying Value
= (\$10,000 × 1.07) − \$10,534
= \$10,700 − \$10,534
= \$166

In this case, a loss of \$166 has resulted from the retirement of Premium Firm bonds. A loss means that the company paid more to retire the bonds than the amount at which the bonds were recorded on the balance sheet.

Financial Statement Presentation of Gain or Loss The accounts Gain on Bond Redemption and Loss on Bond Redemption are income statement accounts. A gain on bond redemption increases Premium Firm's income; a loss decreases its income. In most cases, a gain or loss should not be considered "unusual" or "infrequent" and therefore should not be placed in the section of the income statement where extraordinary items are presented. While gains and losses should be treated as part of the company's operating income, some statement users may consider them as "one-time" events and wish to exclude them when predicting a company's future income. For that reason, it would be very helpful if companies would present their gains and losses separately on the income statement so that readers could determine whether such amounts will affect future periods.

Business Strategy

http://www.cocacola.com
http://www.pepsico.com

Product Strategy to Meet Competition

Competition in the beverage industry is fierce, and Coca-Cola must constantly adjust its strategy to match its competitors. Coca-Cola continues to be the world's No. 1 soft drink company, but it has recently been losing market share to PepsiCo and to other companies. In early 2001, PepsiCo announced that United Airlines would serve only Pepsi soft drinks on its flights; thus, it would no longer serve Coca-Cola Company products. In addition, PepsiCo's Gatorade sports drink has been outselling Coca-Cola's Powerade drink. Other companies have begun to make inroads into the market with noncarbonated drinks and even drinking water, such as Evian's.

Coca-Cola has countered by stepping up the marketing campaigns of its existing products, including Cherry Coke and Diet Coke with lemon, and reintroducing its popular fruit-flavored Fanta brand. It also unveiled a new vanilla-flavored version of its flagship Coke brand. "It has a broad range of appeal all the way from teens to young adults and adults," said Chris Lowe, Coca-Cola's senior vice president for worldwide brands and advertising. "Vanilla seems to cross the generational gap the same way that Coca-Cola does." Analysts have said the product launches highlight the intense see-saw battle for soft drink supremacy in the U.S. market. Although both companies have scored successes, Coca-Cola believes its management and marketing strategies will allow it to continue to be in the No. 1 spot around the world.

Source: Elizabeth S. Armbuster, "Stocks on the Move: Pepsi Bumps Coke off United Planes," March 25, 2002, Morningstar.com.

LIABILITY FOR LEASES

Long-term bonds and notes payable are important sources of financing for many large corporations and are quite prominent in the long-term liability category of the balance sheet for many firms. But other important elements of that category of the balance sheet also represent long-term obligations. We will introduce you to leases because they are a major source of financing for many companies. We will introduce two other liabilities, deferred taxes and pensions, in the appendix at the end of this chapter. In some cases, these liabilities are required to be reported on the financial statements and are important components of the Long-Term Liabilities section of the balance sheet. In other cases, the items are not required to be presented in the financial statements and can be discerned only by a careful reading of the notes to the financial statements.

Leases

LO 7 Determine whether a lease agreement must be reported as a liability on the balance sheet.

A *lease,* a contractual arrangement between two parties, allows one party, the *lessee,* the right to use an asset in exchange for making payments to its owner, the *lessor.* A common example of a lease arrangement is the rental of an apartment. The tenant is the lessee and the landlord is the lessor.

Lease agreements are a form of financing. In some cases, it is more advantageous to lease an asset than to borrow money to purchase it. The lessee can conserve cash because a lease does not require a large initial cash outlay. A wide variety of lease arrangements exists, ranging from simple agreements to complex ones that span a long time period. Lease arrangements are popular because of their flexibility. The terms of a lease can be structured in many ways to meet the needs of the lessee and lessor. This results in difficult accounting questions:

1. Should the right to use property be reported as an asset by the lessee?
2. Should the obligation to make payments be reported as a liability by the lessee?
3. Should all leases be accounted for in the same manner regardless of the terms of the lease agreement?

The answers are that some leases should be reported as an asset and a liability by the lessee and some should not. The accountant must examine the terms of the lease agreement and compare those terms with an established set of criteria.

Accounting for Your Decisions

Should You Lease or Buy?

You want to acquire a new car and are considering leasing instead of buying. What factors should you consider to determine whether leasing is the better alternative?

ANS: To make this decision, answer the following questions: Do you have the cash to buy the car? If not, what is the cost of borrowing? How long will the car be used? Will another car be needed in the near future? What is the purpose of the car? How will the lease payments compare with the purchase payments? Will you own the car at the end of the lease?

Lease Criteria From the viewpoint of the lessee, there are two types of lease agreements: operating and capital leases. In an **operating lease,** the lessee acquires the right to use an asset for a limited period of time. The lessee is *not* required to record the right to use the property as an asset or to record the obligation for payments as a liability. Therefore, the lessee is able to attain a form of *off–balance-sheet financing.* That is, the lessee has attained the right to use property but has not recorded that right, or the accompanying obligation, on the balance sheet. By escaping the balance sheet, the lease does not add to debt or impair the debt-to-equity ratio that investors usually calculate. Management has a responsibility to make sure that such off–balance-sheet financing is not in fact a long-term obligation. The company's auditors are supposed to analyze the terms of the lease carefully to make sure that management has exercised its responsibility.

Operating lease A lease that does not meet any of the four criteria and is not recorded as an asset by the lessee.

The second type of lease agreement is a **capital lease.** In this type of lease, the lessee has acquired sufficient rights of ownership and control of the property to be considered its owner. The lease is called a *capital lease* because it is capitalized (recorded) on the balance sheet by the lessee.

Capital lease A lease that is recorded as an asset by the lessee.

A lease should be considered a capital lease by the lessee if one or more of the following criteria are met:[2]

1. The lease transfers ownership of the property to the lessee at the end of the lease term.
2. The lease contains a bargain-purchase option to purchase the asset at an amount lower than its fair market value.
3. The lease term is 75% or more of the property's economic life.
4. The present value of the minimum lease payments is 90% or more of the fair market value of the property at the inception of the lease.

If none of the criteria are met, the lease agreement is accounted for as an operating lease. This is an area in which it is important for the accountant to exercise professional judg-

[2]*Statement of Financial Accounting Standards No. 13,* "Accounting for Leases" (Stamford, Conn.: FASB, 1976).

ment. In some cases, firms may take elaborate measures to evade or manipulate the criteria that would require lease capitalization. The accountant should determine what is full and fair disclosure based on an unbiased evaluation of the substance of the transaction.

Operating Leases You have already accounted for operating leases in previous chapters when recording rent expense and prepaid rent. A rental agreement for a limited time period is also a lease agreement.

Suppose, for example, that Lessee Firm wants to lease a car for a new salesperson. A lease agreement is signed with Lessor Dealer on January 1, 2004, to lease a car for the year for $4,000, payable on December 31, 2004. Typically, a car lease does not transfer title at the end of the term, does not include a bargain-purchase price, and does not last for more than 75% of the car's life. In addition, the present value of the lease payments is not 90% of the car's value. Because the lease does not meet any of the specified criteria, it should be presented as an operating lease. Lessee Firm would simply record lease expense, or rent expense, of $4,000 for the year.

http://www.fasb.org

http://www.tommy.com

Although operating leases are not recorded on the balance sheet by the lessee, they are mentioned in financial statement notes. The FASB requires note disclosure of the amount of future lease obligations for leases that are considered operating leases. Exhibit 10-6 provides a portion of the note from Tommy Hilfiger Corporation's 2001 annual report. The note reveals that Tommy Hilfiger has used operating leases as an important source of financing and has significant off–balance-sheet commitments in future periods as a result. An investor might want to add this off–balance-sheet item to the debt on the balance sheet to get a conservative view of the company's obligations.

Exhibit 10-6 Tommy Hilfiger Corporation 2001 Note Disclosure of Leases

Operating leases can be used as an important source of financing.

Commitments and Contingencies

Leases (in millions)

The Company leases office, warehouse and showroom space, retail stores and office equipment under operating leases, which expire not later than 2023. The Company normalizes fixed escalations in rental expense under its operating leases. Minimum annual rentals under non-cancelable operating leases, excluding operating cost escalations and contingent rental amounts based upon retail sales, are payable as follows:

Fiscal Year Ending March 31,	
2002	$31,479
2003	29,608
2004	24,326
2005	20,220
2006	15,106
Thereafter	75,092

Rent expense was $22,561, $20,092, and $16,362 for the years ended March 31, 2001, 2000, and 1999, respectively.

Capital Leases Capital leases are presented as assets and liabilities by the lessee because they meet one or more of the lease criteria. Suppose that Lessee Firm in the previous example wanted to lease a car for a longer period of time. Assume that on January 1, 2004, Lessee signs a lease agreement with Lessor Dealer to lease a car. The terms of the agreement specify that Lessee will make annual lease payments of $4,000 per year for five years, payable each December 31. Assume also that the lease specifies that at the end of the lease agreement, the title to the car is transferred to Lessee Firm. Lessee must decide how to account for the lease agreement.

The contractual arrangement between Lessee Firm and Lessor Dealer is called a lease agreement, but clearly the agreement is much different from a year-to-year lease arrangement. Essentially, Lessee Firm has acquired the right to use the asset for its entire life and does not need to return it to Lessor Dealer. You may call this agreement a lease, but it actually represents a purchase of the asset by Lessee with payments made over time.

The lease should be treated as a capital lease by Lessee because it meets at least one of the four criteria (it meets the first criteria concerning transfer of title). A capital lease must be recorded at its present value by Lessee as an asset and as an obligation. As of January 1, 2004, we must calculate the present value of the annual payments. If we assume an interest rate of 8%, the present value of the payments is $15,972 ($4,000 × an annuity factor of 3.993 from Table 9-4).

You should perform the following steps when using a calculator to determine the present value in our example:

ENTER	DISPLAY
5 N	N = 5
8 I/Y	I/Y = 8
4000 PMT	PMT = 4,000
0 FV	FV = 0
CPT PV	PV = 15,971*
*(rounded)	

Study Tip

It is called a *capital lease* because the lease is capitalized, or put on the books of the lessee as an asset.

The first entry is made on the basis of the present value as follows:

Jan. 1	Leased Asset	15,972	
	Lease Obligation		15,972
	To record a capital lease agreement.		

Assets	=	Liabilities	+	Owners' Equity
+15,972		+15,972		

The Leased Asset account is a long-term asset similar to plant and equipment and represents the fact that Lessee has acquired the right to use and retain the asset. Because the leased asset represents depreciable property, depreciation must be reported for each of the five years of asset use. On December 31, 2004, Lessee records depreciation of $3,194 ($15,972/5 years) as follows, assuming that the straight-line method is adopted:

Dec. 31	Depreciation Expense	3,194	
	Accumulated Depreciation—Leased Assets		3,194
	To record depreciation of leased assets.		

Assets	=	Liabilities	+	Owners' Equity
−3,194				−3,194

Depreciation of leased assets is referred to as *amortization* by some firms.

On December 31, Lessee Firm also must make a payment of $4,000 to Lessor Dealer. A portion of each payment represents interest on the obligation (loan), and the remainder represents a reduction of the principal amount. Each payment must be separated into its principal and interest components. Generally, the effective interest method is used for that purpose. An effective interest table can be established using the same concepts as were used to amortize a premium or discount on bonds payable.

Exhibit 10-7 illustrates the effective interest method applied to the Lessee Firm example. Note that the table begins with an obligation amount equal to the present value of the payments of $15,972. Each payment is separated into principal and interest amounts so that the amount of the loan obligation at the end of the lease agreement equals zero. The amortization table is the basis for the amounts that are reflected on the financial statement. Exhibit 10-7 indicates that the $4,000 payment in 2004 should be considered as interest of $1,278 (8% of $15,972) and reduction of principal

Exhibit 10-7

Lease Amortization: Effective Interest Method of Amortization

DATE	COLUMN 1 LEASE PAYMENT	COLUMN 2 INTEREST EXPENSE	COLUMN 3 REDUCTION OF OBLIGATION	COLUMN 4 LEASE OBLIGATION
		8%	Col. 1 − Col. 2	
1/1/2004	—	—	—	$15,972
12/31/2004	$4,000	$1,278	$2,722	13,250
12/31/2005	4,000	1,060	2,940	10,310
12/31/2006	4,000	825	3,175	7,135
12/31/2007	4,000	571	3,429	3,706
12/31/2008	4,000	294	3,706	–0–

of $2,722. On December 31, 2004, Lessee Firm records the following entry for the annual payment:

Dec. 31	Interest Expense	1,278	
	Lease Obligation	2,722	
	Cash		4,000
	To record annual lease payment.		

Assets	=	Liabilities	+	Owners' Equity
−4,000		−2,722		−1,278

Therefore, for a capital lease, Lessee Firm must record both an asset and a liability. The asset is reduced by the process of depreciation. The liability is reduced by reductions of principal using the effective interest method. According to Exhibit 10-7, the total lease obligation as of December 31, 2004, is $13,250. This amount must be separated into current and long-term categories. The portion of the liability that will be paid within one year of the balance sheet should be considered a current liability. Reference to Exhibit 10-7 indicates that the liability will be reduced by $2,940 in 2005, and that amount should be considered a current liability. The remaining amount of the liability, $10,310 ($13,250 − $2,940), should be considered long-term. On the balance sheet as of December 31, 2004, Lessee Firm reports the following balances related to the lease obligation:

Assets:		
Leased assets	$15,972	
Less: Accumulated depreciation	3,194	
		$12,778
Current liabilities:		
Lease obligation		$ 2,940
Long-term liabilities:		
Lease obligation		$10,310

Notice that the depreciated asset does not equal the present value of the lease obligation. This is not unusual. For example, an automobile often may be completely depreciated but still have payments due on it.

The criteria used to determine whether a lease is an operating or a capital lease have provided a standard accounting treatment for all leases. The accounting for leases in foreign countries generally follows guidelines similar to those used in the United States. The criteria used in foreign countries to determine whether a lease is a capital lease are usually less detailed and less specific, however. As a result, capitalization of leases occurs less frequently in foreign countries than in the United States because of the increased use of judgment necessary in applying the accounting rules.

Two-Minute Review

1. *When a lease is considered a capital lease to the lessee, what entry is made to initially record the lease agreement?*
2. *When the lessee makes a lease payment on a capital lease, how is the payment recorded?*

Answers on p. 524

ANALYZING DEBT TO ASSESS A FIRM'S ABILITY TO PAY ITS LIABILITIES

Long-term liabilities are a component of the "capital structure" of the company and are included in the calculation of the debt-to-equity ratio:

$$\textbf{Debt-to-Equity Ratio} = \frac{\textbf{Total Liabilities}}{\textbf{Total Stockholders' Equity}}$$

For example, refer to the liability category of PepsiCo's balance sheet given in Exhibit 10-1. PepsiCo's total liabilities are $13,021 million (current liabilities of $4,998, long-term debt of $2,651, other liabilities of $3,876, and deferred income taxes of $1,496). Its total shareholders' equity is $8,674 million (including the preferred stock). (See Chapter 11 for more discussion of preferred stock.) Therefore, the debt-to-equity ratio is $13,021/$8,674, or 1.5, which means that PepsiCo has 1.5 times as much debt as equity, a situation that is not uncommon for companies in the beverage industry.

Most investors would prefer to see equity rather than debt on the balance sheet. Debt, and its interest charges, make up a fixed obligation that must be repaid in a finite period of time. In contrast, equity never has to be repaid, and the dividends that are declared on it are optional. Stock investors view debt as a claim against the company that must be satisfied before they get a return on their money.

Other ratios used to measure the degree of debt obligation include the times interest earned ratio and the debt service coverage ratio:

$$\textbf{Times Interest Earned Ratio} = \frac{\textbf{Income before Interest and Tax}}{\textbf{Interest Expense}}$$

$$\textbf{Debt Service Coverage Ratio} = \frac{\textbf{Cash Flow from Operations before Interest and Tax}}{\textbf{Interest and Principal Payments}}$$

Lenders want to be sure that borrowers can pay the interest and repay the principal on a loan. Both of the preceding ratios, which will be explored in more detail in Chapter 13, reflect the degree to which a company can make its debt payments out of current cash flow.

From Concept to Practice 10.2

Reading Winnebago Industries' Balance Sheet

Calculate the 2000 and 2001 debt-to-equity ratios for Winnebago Industries. Did the 2001 ratio go up or down from the previous year?

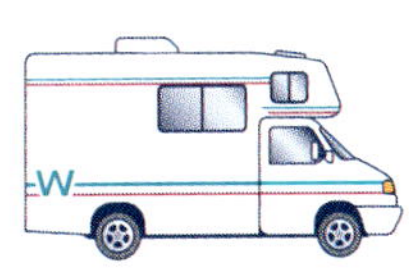

HOW LONG-TERM LIABILITIES AFFECT THE STATEMENT OF CASH FLOWS

LO 8 Explain the effects that transactions involving long-term liabilities have on the statement of cash flows.

Exhibit 10-8 indicates the impact that long-term liabilities have on a company's cash flow and their placement on the cash flow statement.

Most long-term liabilities are related to a firm's financing activities. Therefore, the change in the balance of each long-term liability account should be reflected in the

Exhibit 10-8

Long-Term Liabilities on the Statement of Cash Flows

Item	Statement of Cash Flows	
	Operating Activities	
	Net income	xxx
Increase in current liability	→	+
Decrease in current liability	→	−
	Investing Activities	
	Financing Activities	
Increase in long-term liability	→	+
Decrease in long-term liability	→	−

Financing Activities category of the statement of cash flows. The decrease in a long-term liability account indicates that cash has been used to pay the liability. Therefore, in the cash flow statement, a decrease in a long-term liability account should appear as a subtraction or reduction. The increase in a long-term liability account indicates that the firm has obtained additional cash via a long-term obligation. Therefore, an increase in a long-term liability account should appear in the cash flow statement as an addition.

The cash flow statement of Coca-Cola Company is presented in Exhibit 10-9. Note that the Financing Activities category contains two items related to long-term liabilities. In 2001, long-term debt was issued for $3,011 million and is an addition to cash. This indicates that Coca-Cola increased its cash position by borrowings. Second, the payment of debt is listed as a deduction of $3,937 million. This indicates that Coca-Cola paid long-term liabilities resulting in a reduction of cash.

Although most long-term liabilities are reflected in the Financing Activities category of the statement of cash flows, there are exceptions. The most notable exception involves the Deferred Tax account (discussed in the appendix at the end of this chapter). The change in this account is reflected in the Operating Activities category of the statement of cash flows. This presentation is necessary because the Deferred Tax account is related to an operating item, income tax expense. For example, in Exhibit 10-9, Coca-Cola listed $56 million in the Operating Activities category of the 2001 statement of cash flows. This indicates that $56 million more was recorded as expense than was paid out in cash. Therefore, the amount is a positive amount in, or an addition to, the Operating Activities category.

http://www.cocacola.com

Which Way to Go?

Does the Debt Really Have to Be Reported on the Balance Sheet?

The fiscal year-end for Taz Industries is June 30. To improve the price of the company's common stock in the market, management has been working hard to pay off the company's long-term debt. On July 15 of the current year, a large payment was made to buy back from the market 25% of the outstanding Taz Industry bonds, which were immediately retired. As a result of this transaction, the debt-to-equity ratio dropped from 2.0 to 1.5; the times interest earned ratio will also drop significantly over this new fiscal year.

Generally, it takes six weeks after the fiscal year-end for Taz Industries' annual report information to be prepared, submitted to the SEC, and posted on the company's Web site. Because the significant debt retirement occurred so soon after June 30, the president of Taz wants the June 30 balance sheet to show the lower debt amount. Certainly, there will be disclosure of the transaction in the notes, but why not show the company's balance sheet in the best position possible? After all, people will be reading the annual report information after July 15. Wouldn't it be more accurate to show the debt on the balance sheet at its more current, lower amount?

What debt amount should be shown on the June 30 balance sheet and why?

Exhibit 10-9 Coca-Cola Company and Subsidiaries 2001 Consolidated Statements of Cash Flows

CONSOLIDATED STATEMENTS OF CASH FLOWS

The Coca-Cola Company and Subsidiaries

Year Ended December 31, (In millions)	2001	2000	1999
OPERATING ACTIVITIES			
Net income	$ 3,969	$ 2,177	$ 2,431
Depreciation and amortization	803	773	792
Deferred income taxes	56	3	97
Equity income or loss, net of dividends	(54)	380	292
Foreign currency adjustments	(60)	196	(41)
Gains on issuances of stock by equity investees	(91)	—	—
Gains on sales of assets, including bottling interests	(85)	(127)	(49)
Other operating charges	—	916	799
Other items	34	119	119
Net change in operating assets and liabilities	(462)	(852)	(557)
Net cash provided by operating activities	4,110	3,585	3,883
INVESTING ACTIVITIES			
Acquisitions and investments, principally trademarks and bottling companies	(651)	(397)	(1,876)
Purchases of investments and other assets	(456)	(508)	(518)
Proceeds from disposals of investments and other assets	455	290	176
Purchases of property, plant and equipment	(769)	(733)	(1,069)
Proceeds from disposals of property, plant and equipment	91	45	45
Other investing activities	142	138	(179)
Net cash used in investing activities	(1,188)	(1,165)	(3,421)
FINANCING ACTIVITIES			
Issuances of debt	3,011	3,671	3,411
Payments of debt	(3,937)	(4,256)	(2,455)
Issuances of stock	164	331	168
Purchases of stock for treasury	(277)	(133)	(15)
Dividends	(1,791)	(1,685)	(1,580)
Net cash used in financing activities	(2,830)	(2,072)	(471)
EFFECT OF EXCHANGE RATE CHANGES ON CASH AND CASH EQUIVALENTS	(45)	(140)	(28)
CASH AND CASH EQUIVALENTS			
Net increase (decrease) during the year	47	208	(37)
Balance at beginning of year	1,819	1,611	1,648
Balance at end of year	$ 1,866	$ 1,819	$ 1,611

Changes in long-term debt generally affect the financing activities category.

See Notes to Consolidated Financial Statements.

Ratios for Decision Making

Reporting and analyzing financial statement information related to a company's long-term debt:
The impact of debt in investment and credit decisions can be significant. Because the company must meet its debt obligations in order to remain in business, investors and creditors carefully review its financial information. The following ratios are key to determining whether the company is likely to have resources to pay its liabilities: (a) the proportion of current earnings, before interest and tax expenses, to the current interest expense and (b) the amount of net cash, before interest and taxes have been paid, currently created by company operations when compared to the amount of interest and principal payments that have been paid in the current period. In addition, the ratio of total debt to total equity indicates how heavily the company is burdened by its liabilities.

In this chapter, you learned about three new ratios used for decision making. These ratios and the sources of the information needed for the analysis are presented below:

Balance Sheet

Total Liabilities
Total Stockholders' Equity

Income Statement

Income before Interest and Tax
Interest Expense

Statement of Cash Flows*

Operating Activities
Net Cash Flow from Operations

Financing Activities
Principal Payments

Notes*

Times Interest Earned Ratio = Income before Interest and Tax / Interest Expense

Debt Service Coverage Ratio = Cash Flow from Operations (with Interest and Tax Payments added back) / Interest and Principal Payments

Debt-to-Equity Ratio = Total Liabilities / Total Stockholders' Equity

*When the statement of cash flows is prepared under the indirect method, the interest payment amount is disclosed in the notes to the financial statements. Under the direct method, explained in detail in Chapter 12, the interest amount appears on the statement of cah flows in the operating activities section.

Answers to the Two-Minute Reviews

Two-Minute Review on Page 514

1. *To calculate the issue price of a bond, you must calculate the present value of the annuity of interest payments and add to it the present value of the principal to be repaid, using the market rate of interest as the rate in the calculations.*
2. *When a premium is amortized, it decreases the amount of interest on the bond, and when a discount is amortized, it increases the amount of interest expense on the bond.*

Two-Minute Review on Page 521

1. *A capital lease is recorded as an asset, in an account such as Leased Asset, and as a liability, in an account such as Lease Obligation. The lease is recorded at the amount of the present value of the lease payments.*
2. *When a lease payment is made, the portion of the payment that is interest would be recorded to the Interest Expense account, and the portion of the payment that is principal is considered a reduction in the Lease Obligation account.*

Impact on the Financial Reports

Impact on the Financial Reports

BALANCE SHEET

Current Assets

Noncurrent Assets

Leased Assets, net of accumulated depreciation, obtained under capital lease agreements

Current Liabilities

Current liabilities, such as Accounts Payable and Wages Payable, that will require payment within the next fiscal year

Current portion of long-term debt, both interest and principal, that will require payment within the next fiscal year

Noncurrent Liabilities

Obligations, such as Bonds Payable and Lease Obligations, that will not require asset resources within the next fiscal year

Equity

INCOME STATEMENT

Revenues

Expenses

Rent expense under operating lease agreements

Current-period depreciation expense on assets under capital lease agreements

Other

Current-period interest expense on current and long-term obligations

Gain or loss on early retirement of debt

STATEMENT OF STOCKHOLDERS' EQUITY

Contributed Capital

Retained Earnings

STATEMENT OF CASH FLOWS

*Operating Activities***

Depreciation expense for a leased asset is added back, which increases the cash amount from operating activities

Investing Activities

Financing Activities

Decrease due to principal payments on capital leases

Increase/decrease due to borrowing/paying off long-term debt (notes, bonds)

Noncash Transactions

NOTES

Disclosure includes basic information about lease obligations and bonds, such as the scheduled repayments of the debt.

**When the direct method, explained in Chapter 12, is used to prepare the statement of cash flows, the operating section would show a decrease due to payments for operating leases and would not show any depreciation amount since depreciation expense does not use cash.

Warmup Exercises

Warmup Exercise 10-1

A bond due in 10 years, with face value of $1,000 and face rate of interest of 8%, is issued when the market rate of interest is 6%.

Required

1. What is the issue price of the bond?
2. What is the amount of premium or discount on the bond at the time of issuance?
3. What amount of interest expense will be shown on the income statement for the first year of the bond?
4. What amount of the premium or discount will be amortized during the first year of the bond?

Warmup Exercise 10-2

You have signed an agreement to lease a car for four years and will make annual payments of \$4,000 at the end of each year. (Assume that the lease meets the criteria for a capital lease.)

Required

1. Calculate the present value of the lease payments, assuming an 8% interest rate.
2. What is the journal entry to record the leased asset?
3. When the first lease payment is made, what portion of the payment will be considered interest?

Solutions to Warmup Exercises

Warmup Exercise 10-1

1. The issue price of the bond would be calculated at the present value:

\$80 (7.360) =	\$ 588.80	using Table 9-4, where i = 6% and n = 10
\$1,000 (0.558) =	558.00	using Table 9-2, where i = 6% and n = 10
Issue price	\$1,146.80	

You should perform the following steps when using a calculator to determine the present value:

ENTER	DISPLAY
10 N	N = 10
6 I/Y	I/Y = 8
80 PMT	PMT = 80
1000 FV	FV = 1000
CPT PV	PV = 1,147*
*(rounded)	

2. The amount of the premium is the difference between the issue price and the face value:

Premium = \$1,146.80 − \$1,000
= \$146.80

3. The amount of interest expense can be calculated as follows:

Interest Expense = \$1,146.80 × 0.06
= \$68.81

4. The amount that will be amortized can be calculated as follows:

Amortized = Cash Interest − Interest Expense
= (\$1,000 × 0.08) − (\$1,146.80 × 0.06)
= \$80.00 − \$68.81
= \$11.19

Warmup Exercise 10-2

1. The present value of the lease payments can be calculated as follows:

Present Value = \$4,000 (3.312) using Table 9-4, where i = 8%, n = 4
= \$13,248

You should perform the following steps when using a calculator to determine the present value:

ENTER	DISPLAY
4 N	N = 4
8 I/Y	I/Y = 8
4000 PMT	PMT = 4,000
0 FV	FV = 0
CPT PV	PV = 13,248*
*(rounded)	

2. The journal entry to record the lease agreement:

Leased Asset	13,248	
Lease Obligation		13,248

3. The amount of interest can be calculated as follows:

$$\text{Interest} = \$13{,}248 \times 0.08 = \$1{,}059.84$$

Review Problem

WebTUTOR™ Advantage

The following items pertain to the liabilities of Brent Foods. You may assume that Brent Foods began business on January 1, 2004, and therefore the beginning balance of all accounts was zero.

a. On January 1, 2004, Brent Foods issued bonds with a face value of $50,000. The bonds are due in five years and have a face interest rate of 10%. The market rate on January 1 for similar bonds was 12%. The bonds pay interest annually each December 31. Brent has chosen to use the effective interest method of amortization for any premium or discount on the bonds.

b. On December 31, Brent Foods signed a lease agreement with Cordova Leasing. The agreement requires Brent to make annual lease payments of $3,000 per year for four years, with the first payment due on December 31, 2005. The agreement stipulates that ownership of the property is transferred to Brent at the end of the four-year lease. Assume that an 8% interest rate is used for the leasing transaction.

c. On January 1, 2005, Brent redeems its bonds payable at the specified redemption price of 101. Because this item occurs in 2005, it does not affect the balance sheet prepared for year-end 2004.

Required

1. Make the accounting entries necessary on December 31, 2004, to record the interest adjustment in item **a** and the signing of the lease in item **b.**
2. Develop the Long-Term Liabilities section of Brent Foods' balance sheet as of December 31, 2004, based on items **a** and **b.** You do not need to consider the notes that accompany the balance sheet.
3. Would the company prefer to treat the lease in item **b** as an operating lease? Why or why not?
4. Calculate the gain or loss on the bond redemption for item **c.**

Solution to Review Problem

1. **a.** The issue price of the bonds on January 1 must be calculated at the present value of the interest payments and the present value of the principal, as follows:

$5,000 × 3.605	$18,025
$50,000 × 0.567	28,350
Issue price	$46,375

You should perform the following steps when using a calculator to determine the present value:

ENTER	DISPLAY
5 N	N = 5
12 I/Y	I/Y = 12
5000 PMT	PMT = 5,000
50000 FV	FV = 50,000
CPT PV	PV = 46,395

Note: The difference is caused by rounding that occurs when using the factors from Tables 9-2 and 9-4.

The amount of the discount is calculated as follows:

$$\$50{,}000 - \$46{,}375 = \$3{,}625$$

The following is the entry on December 31, 2004, to record interest and to amortize discount:

Dec. 31	Interest Expense	5,565	
	Cash		5,000
	Discount on Bonds Payable		565
	To record interest and amortize discount.		

Assets	=	Liabilities	+	Owners' Equity
−5,000		+565		−5,565

The interest expense is calculated using the effective interest method by multiplying the carrying value of the bonds times the market rate of interest ($46,375 × 12%).

Brent must show two accounts in the Long-Term Liabilities section of the balance sheet: Bonds Payable of $50,000 and Discount on Bonds Payable of $3,060 ($3,625 less $565 amortized).

b. The lease meets the criteria to be a capital lease. Brent must report the lease as an asset and report the obligation for lease payments as a liability. The transaction should be reported at the present value of the lease payments, $9,936 (computed by multiplying $3,000 by the annuity factor of 3.312). The accounting entry should be as follows:

Dec. 31	Leased Asset	9,936	
	Lease Obligation		9,936
	To record lease as a capital lease.		

Assets	=	Liabilities	+	Owners' Equity
+9,936		+9,936		

Because the lease agreement was signed on December 31, 2004, it is not necessary to amortize the Lease Obligation account in 2004. The account should be stated in the Long-Term Liabilities section of Brent's balance sheet at $9,936.

2. The Long-Term Liabilities section of Brent's balance sheet for December 31, 2004, on the basis of items **a** and **b** is as follows:

BRENT FOODS
PARTIAL BALANCE SHEET
AS OF DECEMBER 31, 2004

Long-term liabilities:		
Bonds payable	$50,000	
Less: Unamortized discount on bonds payable	3,060	$46,940
Lease obligation		9,936
Total long-term liabilities		$56,876

3. The company would prefer that the lease be an operating lease because it would not have to report the asset or liability on the balance sheet. This off–balance-sheet financing may give a more favorable impression of the company.

4. Brent must calculate the loss on the bond redemption as the difference between the carrying value of the bonds ($46,940) and the redemption price ($50,000 × 1.01). The amount of the loss is calculated as follows:

$50,500 − $46,940 = $3,560 loss on redemption

Appendix: Accounting Tools: Other Liabilities

In this appendix we will discuss two additional items that are found in the long-term liabilities category of many companies: deferred taxes and pensions. Both items are complex financial arrangements, and our primary purpose is to make you aware of their existence when reading financial statements.

Deferred Tax

LO 9 Explain deferred taxes and calculate the deferred tax liability.

http://www.pepsico.com
http://www.cocacola.com

The financial statements of most major firms include an item titled Deferred Income Taxes or Deferred Tax (see PepsiCo's deferred taxes in Exhibit 10-1 and Coca-Cola's in the chapter opening). In most cases, the account appears in the Long-Term Liabilities section of the balance sheet, and the dollar amount may be large enough to catch the user's attention. For another example, Exhibit 10-10 illustrates the presentation of deferred tax in the 2001 comparative balance sheets of **Tribune Company and Subsidiaries.** The Deferred Income Taxes account is listed immediately after Long-Term Debt and for Tribune Company should be considered a long-term liability. At the end of 2001, the firm had more than $2,143 million of deferred tax. The size of that account relative to the other liabilities should raise questions concerning its exact meaning. In fact, deferred income taxes represent one of the most misunderstood aspects of financial statements. In this section, we will attempt to address some of the questions concerning deferred taxes.

http://www.tribune.com

Deferred tax The account used to reconcile the difference between the amount recorded as income tax expense and the amount that is payable as income tax.

Deferred tax is an amount that reconciles the differences between the accounting done for purposes of financial reporting to stockholders ("book" purposes) and the accounting done for tax purposes. It may surprise you that U.S. firms are allowed to use accounting methods for financial reporting that differ from those used for tax calculations. The reason is that the Internal Revenue Service defines income and expense differently than does the Financial Accounting Standards Board. As a result, companies tend to use accounting methods that minimize income for tax purposes but maximize income in the annual report to stockholders. This is not true in some foreign countries where financial accounting and tax accounting are more closely aligned. Firms in those countries do not report deferred tax, because the difference between methods is not significant.

http://www.irs.gov
http://www.fasb.org

When differences between financial and tax reporting do occur, we can classify them into two types: permanent and temporary. **Permanent differences** occur when an item is included in the tax calculation and is never included for book purposes—or vice versa, when an item is included for book purposes but not for tax purposes.

Permanent difference A difference that affects the tax records but not the accounting records, or vice versa.

For example, the tax laws allow taxpayers to exclude interest on certain investments, usually state and municipal bonds, from their income. These are generally called *tax-exempt bonds.* If a corporation buys tax-exempt bonds, it does not have to declare the interest as income for tax purposes. When the corporation develops its income statement for stockholders (book purposes), however, the interest is included and appears in the Interest Income account. Therefore, tax-exempt interest represents a permanent difference between tax and book calculations.

Temporary differences occur when an item affects both the book and the tax calculations but not in the same time period. A difference caused by depreciation methods is the most common type of temporary difference. In previous chapters you have learned that depreciation may be calculated using a straight-line method or an accelerated method such as the double-declining-balance method. Most firms do not use the same depreciation method for book and tax purposes, however. Generally, straight-line depreciation is used for book purposes and an accelerated method is used for tax purposes because accelerated depreciation lowers taxable income—at least in early years—and therefore reduces the tax due. The IRS refers to this accelerated method as the *Modified Accelerated Cost Recovery System (MACRS).* It is similar to other accelerated depreciation methods in that it allows the firm to take larger depreciation deductions for tax purposes in the early years of the asset and smaller deductions in the later years. Over the life of the depreciable asset, the total depreciation using straight-line is equal to that using MACRS. Therefore, this difference is an example of a temporary difference between book and tax reporting.

Temporary difference A difference that affects both book and tax records but not in the same time period.

The Deferred Tax account is used to reconcile the differences between the accounting for book purposes and for tax purposes. It is important to distinguish between permanent and temporary differences because the FASB has ruled that not all differences should affect the Deferred Tax account. The Deferred Tax account should reflect temporary differences but not items that are permanent differences between book accounting and tax reporting.[3]

[3] *Statement of Financial Accounting Standards No. 109,* "Accounting for Income Taxes" (Stamford, Conn.: FASB, 1992).

Exhibit 10-10 Tribune Company and Subsidiaries 2001 Liabilities and Shareholders' Equity

TRIBUNE COMPANY AND SUBSIDIARIES
CONSOLIDATED BALANCE SHEETS

(In thousands of dollars, except share data)

	Dec. 30, 2001	Dec. 31, 2000
Liabilities and Shareholders' Equity		
Current Liabilities		
Long-term debt due within one year	$ 410,890	$ 141,404
Accounts payable	223,563	249,186
Employee compensation and benefits	159,979	231,684
Contracts payable for broadcast rights	298,165	271,510
Deferred income	104,368	90,421
Income taxes	8,147	129,954
Other	328,080	327,565
Total current liabilities	1,533,192	1,441,724
Long-Term Debt		
PHONES debt related to AOL Time Warner stock	684,000	700,000
Other long-term debt (less portions due within one year)	3,000,692	3,307,041
Other Non-Current Liabilities		
Deferred income taxes	2,143,205	2,146,416
Contracts payable for broadcast rights	522,854	390,657
Deferred compensation and benefits	372,204	348,662
Other obligations	597,381	448,296
Total other non-current liabilities	3,635,644	3,334,031
Commitment and Contingent Liabilities (Note 13)	—	—
Shareholders' Equity		
Series B convertible preferred stock (without par value) Authorized: 1,600,000 shares; Issued and outstanding: 1,141,450 shares in 2001 and 1,212,834 shares in 2000 (liquidation value $220 per share)	250,146	265,790
Series C convertible preferred stock Authorized: 900,000 shares; Issued and outstanding: 88,519 shares (net of 354,077 treasury shares) (liquidation value $500 per share)	44,260	44,260
Series D-1 convertible preferred stock Authorized: 400,000 shares; Issued and outstanding: 76,194 shares (net of 304,778 treasury shares) (liquidation value $500 per share)	38,097	38,097
Series D-2 convertible preferred stock Authorized: 300,000 shares; Issued and outstanding: 49,020 shares (net of 196,080 treasury shares) (liquidation value $500 per share)	24,510	24,510
Common stock ($0.01 par value) Authorized: 1,400,000 shares; 536,886,513 shares issued	3,116	3,116
Additional paid-in capital	8,180,291	8,190,835
Retained earnings	4,231,467	4,278,464
Treasury common stock (at cost) 238,680,840 shares in 2001 and 236,727,470 shares in 2000	(7,118,509)	(6,970,703)
Treasury common stock held by Tribune Stock Compensation Fund (at cost) 202,431 shares in 2001 and 641,094 shares in 2000	(8,313)	(26,707)
Unearned compensation related to ESOP	(66,255)	(97,517)
Accumulated other comprehensive income	72,358	135,771
Total shareholders' equity	5,651,168	5,885,916
Total liabilities and shareholders' equity	$14,504,696	$14,668,712

See Notes to Consolidated Financial Statements.

Deferred tax is a liability for Tribune Company and Subsidiaries

Example of Deferred Tax Assume that Startup Firm begins business on January 1, 2004. During 2004 the firm has sales of $6,000 and has no expenses other than depreciation and income tax at the rate of 40%. Startup has depreciation on only one asset. That asset was purchased on January 1, 2004, for $10,000 and has a four-year life. Startup has decided to use the straight-line depreciation method for financial reporting purposes. Startup's accountants have chosen to use MACRS for tax purposes, however, resulting in $4,000 depreciation in 2004 and a decline of $1,000 per year thereafter.

The depreciation amounts for each of the four years for Startup's asset are as follows:

Year	Tax Depreciation	Book Depreciation	Difference
2004	$ 4,000	$ 2,500	$1,500
2005	3,000	2,500	500
2006	2,000	2,500	(500)
2007	1,000	2,500	(1,500)
Totals	$10,000	$10,000	$ 0

Startup's tax calculation for 2004 is based on the accelerated depreciation of $4,000, as follows:

Sales	$6,000
Depreciation Expense	4,000
Taxable Income	$2,000
× Tax Rate	40%
Tax Payable to IRS	$ 800

For the year 2004, Startup owes $800 of tax to the Internal Revenue Service. This amount is ordinarily recorded as tax payable until the time it is remitted.

Startup wants also to develop an income statement to send to the stockholders. What amount should be shown as tax expense on the income statement? You may guess that the Tax Expense account on the income statement should reflect $800 because that is the amount to be paid to the IRS. That is not true in this case, however. Remember that the tax payable amount was calculated using the depreciation method that Startup chose for tax purposes. The income statement must be calculated using the straight-line method, which Startup uses for book purposes. Therefore, Startup's income statement for 2004 appears as follows:

Sales	$6,000
Depreciation Expense	2,500
Income before Tax	$3,500
Tax Expense (40%)	1,400
Net Income	$2,100

Startup must make the following accounting entry to record the amount of tax expense and tax payable for 2004:

Dec. 31	Tax Expense	1,400	
	Tax Payable		800
	Deferred Tax		600
	To record income tax for the year 2004.		

Assets	=	Liabilities	+	Owners' Equity
		+800		−1,400
		+600		

The Deferred Tax account is a balance sheet account. A balance in it reflects the fact that Startup has received a tax benefit by recording accelerated depreciation, in effect delaying the ultimate obligation to the IRS. To be sure, the amount of deferred tax still represents a liability of Startup. The Deferred Tax account balance of $600 represents the amount of the 2004 temporary difference of $1,500 times the tax rate of 40% ($1,500 × 40% = $600).

What can we learn from the Startup example? First, when you see a firm's income statement, the amount listed as tax expense does not represent the amount of cash paid to the government for taxes. Accrual accounting procedures require that the tax expense amount be calculated using the accounting methods chosen for book purposes.

Second, when you see a firm's balance sheet, the amount in the Deferred Tax account reflects all of the temporary differences between the accounting methods chosen for tax and book purposes. The accounting and financial communities are severely divided on whether the Deferred Tax account represents a "true" liability. For one thing, many investment analysts do not view it as a real liability because they have noticed that it continues to grow year after year. Others look at it as a bookkeeping item that is simply there to balance the books. The FASB has taken the stance that deferred tax is an amount that results in a future obligation and meets the definition of a liability. The controversy concerning deferred taxes is likely to continue for many years.

Pensions

LO 10 Demonstrate an understanding of the meaning of a pension obligation and the effect of pensions on the long-term liability category of the balance sheet.

Pension An obligation to pay employees for service rendered while employed.

Many large firms establish pension plans to provide income to employees after their retirement. These pension plans often cover a large number of employees and involve millions of dollars. The large amounts in pension funds have become a major force in our economy, representing billions of dollars in stocks and bonds. In fact, pension funds are among the major "institutional investors" that have an enormous economic impact on our stock and bond exchanges.

Pensions are complex financial arrangements that involve difficult estimates and projections developed by specialists and actuaries. Pension plans also involve very difficult accounting issues requiring a wide range of estimates and assumptions about future cash flows.

We will concern ourselves with two accounting questions related to pensions. First, the employer must report the cost of the pension plan as an expense over some time period. How should that expense be reported? Second, the employer's financial statements should reflect a measure of the liability associated with a pension plan. What is the liability for future pension amounts, and how should it be recorded or disclosed? Our discussion will begin with the recording of pension expense.

Pensions on the Income Statement

Most pension plans are of the following form:

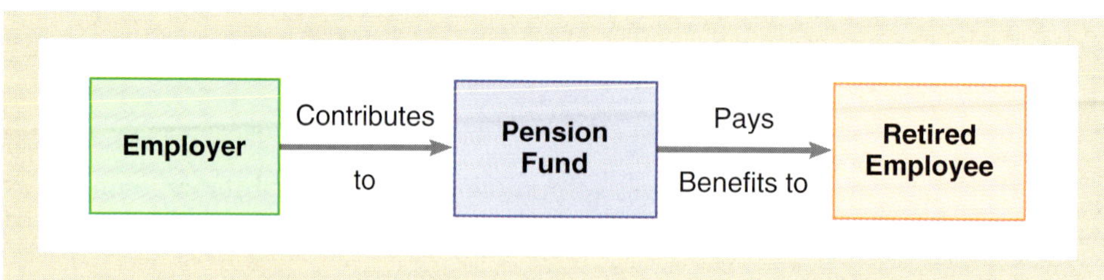

Funding payment A payment made by the employer to the pension fund or its trustee.

Normally, the employer must make payments to the pension fund at least annually, perhaps more frequently. This is often referred to as *funding the pension* or as the **funding payment.** *Funding* simply means that the employer has contributed cash to the pension fund. The pension fund is usually administered by a trustee, often a bank or other financial institution. The trustee must invest the employer's funds so that they earn interest and dividends sufficient to pay the amounts owed to retired employees.

Our first accounting question concerns the amount that should be shown by the employer as pension expense. This is another example of the difference between cash-basis accounting and accrual accounting. The cash paid as the funding payment is not the same as the expense. When using the accrual basis of accounting, we must consider the amount of pension cost incurred, not the amount paid. Pension expense should be accrued in the period that the employee earns the benefits, regardless of the amount paid to the pension trustee. The amount expensed and the amount paid involve two separate decisions.

The FASB has specified the methods that should be used to calculate the amount of annual pension expense to record on the employer's income statement.[4] The accountant must determine the costs of the separate components of the pension and total them to arrive at the amount of pension expense. The components include the employee's service during the current year, the interest cost, the earnings on pension investments, and other factors. The details of those calculations are beyond our discussion.

To illustrate, suppose that Employer Firm has calculated its annual pension expense to be $80,000 for 2004. Also suppose that Employer has determined that it will make a funding payment of $60,000 to the pension fund. On the basis of those decisions, Employer should make the following accounting entry for the year:

Dec. 31	Pension Expense	80,000	
	Cash		60,000
	Accrued Pension Cost		20,000
	To record annual pension expense and funding payment.		

Assets	=	Liabilities	+	Owners' Equity
−60,000		+20,000		−80,000

The Pension Expense account is an income statement account and is reflected on Employer's 2004 income statement.

Pensions on the Balance Sheet The **Accrued Pension Cost** account in the preceding example is a balance sheet account. The account could represent an asset or a liability, depending on whether the amount expensed is more or less than the amount of the funding payment. If the amount expensed is less than the amount paid, it is reported by Employer Firm as an asset and labeled as Prepaid Pension Cost. Normally, the amount expensed is greater than the amount paid, as in the example here. In that case, the Accrued Pension Cost is reported by Employer Firm as a long-term liability.

Accrued pension cost The difference between the amount of pension recorded as an expense and the amount of the funding payment.

But what is the meaning of the Accrued Pension Cost account? Is it really a liability? It certainly is not a measure of the amount that is owed to employees at the time of retirement. In fact, the only true meaning that can be given to the account is to say that it is the difference between the amount expensed and the amount funded.[5] In that regard, the Accrued Pension Cost account is inadequate in determining a firm's liability to its employees for future retirement benefits. The FASB requires a great deal of note information for pension plans. This note section can be used to develop a clearer picture of the status of a firm's pension obligation.

Pension Note Information Readers of financial statements are often interested in the *funding status* of pension plans. This indicates whether sufficient assets are available in the pension fund to cover the amounts to be paid to employees as retirement benefits. We will use the note disclosures of an actual firm to illustrate the use of pension information.

Exhibit 10-11 presents portions of the 2001 pension footnote for PepsiCo Company. PepsiCo is a large company with thousands of employees who are covered by the company's pension plans. Analysts who follow the industry must assess whether PepsiCo's pension is adequate for its employees. The amounts on the balance sheet give some indication about the status of the plan, but a more complete picture is provided in the company's notes. Fortunately, the notes can assist us as we determine whether the pension plans could be considered underfunded. Several items in the note need to be defined.

[4]*Statement of Financial Accounting Standards No. 87*, "Employers' Accounting for Pension Plans" (Stamford, Conn.: FASB, 1985).

[5]Some pension plans that are underfunded may be required to report an additional amount as a liability. This is referred to as the *minimum liability provision*.

Exhibit 10-11

PepsiCo Company's Pension Note for 2001

	Pension (in millions)	
	2001	2000
Fair value of plan assets	$3,129	$3,251
Obligation at end of year	3,556	3,170
Selected information for plans with accumulated benefit obligation in excess of plan assets:		
Projected benefit obligation	(419)	(307)
Accumulated benefit obligation	(252)	(193)
Fair value of plan assets	51	36

http://www.pepsico.com

First, PepsiCo has disclosed the amount of *plan assets* at fair value. This is a measure of the total dollar amount of assets that has been accumulated in the pension fund. The footnote indicates that as of year-end 2001, PepsiCo had assets of $3,129 million. Second, PepsiCo disclosed a $3,556 million obligation to retirees at the end of 2001. When the obligation is larger than the amount of assets available in the pension fund, the fund is referred to as *underfunded.* At December 29, 2001, PepsiCo's pension funds were slightly underfunded, but the difference between assets and obligation was small enough that it should not be cause for concern. Because PepsiCo has several different pension plans, the company is required to disclose amounts separately for the plans that are underfunded. There are two measures of the amount owed to employees at the time of retirement. One measure is referred to as the **accumulated benefit obligation (ABO).** This is a measure of the amount of pension benefits that would be payable to employees if they were to retire at their existing salary levels. The note indicates that for the plans that were underfunded as of the end of 2001, PepsiCo had an accumulated benefit obligation of $252 million.

Accumulated benefit obligation (ABO) A measure of the amount owed to employees for pensions if they retire at their existing salary levels.

Projected benefit obligation (PBO) A measure of the amount owed to employees for pensions if estimates of future salary increases are considered.

Another measure provides a higher estimate of that obligation. The **projected benefit obligation (PBO)** is a measure of the amount of pension benefits payable to employees if an assumption is made concerning the future salary increases that will be earned by the employees. This is probably a more realistic view of the amount of the obligation to employees, but it is a less objective number because of the difficulty in estimating future salary increases for employees. The note indicates that for the plans that were underfunded as of year-end 2001, PepsiCo had a projected benefit obligation of $419 million.

PepsiCo's pension plans may be slightly underfunded but overall their pension plans certainly appear to be quite healthy. Not all firms are as fortunate. There have been many press reports of firms whose pension plans are seriously underfunded and for which it is quite questionable whether sufficient assets are available to pay impending retirement benefits. Such underfunded plans must be considered an off–balance-sheet liability by investors or creditors in assessing the company's health.

Users of the financial statements of U.S. firms are somewhat fortunate because the disclosure of pensions on the balance sheet and in the notes is quite extensive. The accounting for pensions by firms outside the United States varies considerably. Many countries do not require firms to accrue pension costs, and the expense is reported only when paid to retirees. Furthermore, within the statements and notes, there is much less disclosure, making an assessment of the funding status of pensions much more difficult.

Postretirement Benefits

Pensions represent a benefit paid to employees after their retirement. In addition to pensions, other benefits may be paid to employees after their retirement. For example, many firms promise to pay a portion of retirees' health care costs. The accounting question is whether postretirement benefits should be considered an expense when paid or during the period that the employee worked for the firm.

A few years ago, most firms treated postretirement benefits as an expense when they were paid to the retiree. It was widely believed that costs such as those for health care after retirement were too uncertain to be accrued as an expense and that such costs did not meet the definition of a liability and thus did not merit recording. The result of this expense-as-you-pay accounting was that firms had an obligation that was not recorded as a liability. As health care costs began to escalate, this unrecorded—and often undisclosed—cost became a concern for many firms as well as for stockholders, analysts, and employees.

The FASB has modified the accounting for other postemployment benefits to be consistent with pension costs. Under the matching principle, postretirement costs must now be accrued as an expense during the period that the employee helps the firm generate revenues and thus *earns* the benefits. The accountant must determine the costs of the separate components of postretirement benefits and total them to calculate the amount of the expense. The amount of the expense is reflected on the income statement in the Postretirement Expense account. The balance sheet should normally reflect the Accrued Postretirement Cost account. That account should be classified as a liability in the long-term liability category; it indicates the employer's obligation to present and future retirees.

The dollar amount of the liability represented by postretirement obligations is very large for many companies. For example, in 2001 PepsiCo's notes to the financial statement reveal the obligation to its employees for these retirement costs was $911 million (in addition to its pension plan amounts, disclosed in Exhibit 10-11).

There is still much controversy concerning the accounting for postretirement costs. Many firms object to the accounting requirements because of the uncertainty involved in measuring an obligation that extends far into the future. They also object because the requirements result in reduced profits on the income statement and huge liabilities on the balance sheet. Interestingly, this accounting rule had little impact on the stock market because the investment community already knew the magnitude of the postretirement obligations.

Chapter Highlights

1. **LO 1** Balance sheets generally have two categories of liabilities: current liabilities and long-term liabilities. Long-term liabilities are obligations that will not be satisfied within one year.
2. **LO 2** The terms of a bond payable are given in the bond certificate. The denomination of a bond is its face value. The interest rate stated in the bond certificate is referred to as the *face rate* or *stated rate of interest.* Term bonds all have the same due date. Serial bonds are not all due on the same date. Convertible bonds can be converted into common stock by the bondholders. Callable bonds may be redeemed or retired before their due date.
3. **LO 3** The issue price of a bond is the present value of the cash flows that the bond will provide to the investor. To determine the price, you must calculate the present values of the annuity of interest payments and of the principal amount. The present values must be calculated at the market rate of interest.
4. **LO 4** A bond sells at a discount or premium, depending on the relationship of the face rate to the market rate of interest. If the face rate exceeds the market rate, a bond is issued at a premium. If the face rate is less than the market rate, it will be issued at a discount.
5. **LO 5** Premiums or discounts must be amortized by transferring a portion of the premium or the discount each period to interest expense. The effective interest method of amortization reduces the balance of the premium or discount such that the effective interest rate on the bond is constant over its life.
6. **LO 5** The carrying value of the bond equals the face value plus unamortized premium or minus unamortized discount.
7. **LO 6** When bonds are redeemed before their due date, a gain or loss on redemption results. The gain or loss is the difference between the bond carrying value at the date of redemption and the redemption price.
8. **LO 7** A lease, a contractual arrangement between two parties, allows the lessee the right to use property in exchange for making payments to the lessor.
9. **LO 7** There are two major categories of lease agreements: operating and capital. The lessee does not report an operating lease as an asset and does not present the obligation to make payments as a liability. Capital leases are reported as assets and liabilities by the lessee. Leases are reported as capital leases if they meet one or more of four criteria.
10. **LO 7** Capital lease assets must be depreciated by the lessee over the life of the lease agreement. Capital lease payments must be separated into interest expense and reduction of principal using the effective interest method.

11. **LO 8** Long-term liabilities represent methods of financing. Therefore, changes in the balances of long-term liability accounts should be reflected in the Financing Activities category of the statement of cash flows.

12. **LO 9** There are many differences between the accounting for tax purposes and the accounting for financial reporting purposes. Permanent differences occur when an item affects one calculation but never affects the other. Temporary differences affect both book and tax calculations but not in the same time period. (Appendix)

13. **LO 9** The amount of tax payable is calculated using the accounting method chosen for tax purposes. The amount of tax expense is calculated using the accounting method chosen for financial reporting purposes. The Deferred Tax account reconciles the differences between tax expense and tax payable. It reflects all of the temporary differences times the tax rate. Deferred taxes is a controversial item on the balance sheet, raising questions as to whether it is a true liability. (Appendix)

14. **LO 10** Pensions represent an obligation to compensate retired employees for service performed while employed. (Appendix)

15. **LO 10** Pension expense is represented on the income statement and is calculated on the basis of several complex components that have been specified by the FASB. (Appendix)

16. **LO 10** Pension expense does not represent the amount of cash paid by the employer to the pension fund. The cash payment is referred to as the *funding payment.* The Accrued Pension account is recorded as the difference between the amount of pension expense and the amount of the funding. (Appendix)

17. **LO 10** The required note information on pensions can be used to evaluate the funding status of a firm's pension plan. If the amount of assets in the pension fund exceeds the pension obligation, the fund is considered to be overfunded, generally indicating that it is healthy and well managed. An overfunded plan is an example of an "off–balance-sheet" asset that an investor can count toward the value of the company's stock. (Appendix)

http://

http://porter.swlearning.com

Technology and other resources for your success

If you need additional help, visit the text's Web site. Also, see pages xv–xvii in this text's preface for a description of available technology and other resources. If your instructor is using PERSONAL Trainer in this course, you may complete, on line, the assignments identified by PT.

Key Terms Quiz

Read each definition below and then write the number of that definition in the blank beside the appropriate term it defines. The quiz solutions appear at the end of the chapter.

_____ Long-term liability
_____ Face value
_____ Debenture bonds
_____ Serial bonds
_____ Callable bonds
_____ Face rate of interest
_____ Market rate of interest
_____ Bond issue price
_____ Premium
_____ Discount
_____ Effective interest method of amortization
_____ Carrying value
_____ Gain or loss on redemption
_____ Operating lease
_____ Capital lease
_____ Deferred tax (Appendix)
_____ Permanent difference (Appendix)
_____ Temporary difference (Appendix)
_____ Pension (Appendix)
_____ Funding payment (Appendix)
_____ Accrued pension cost (Appendix)
_____ Accumulated benefit obligation (ABO) (Appendix)
_____ Projected benefit obligation (PBO) (Appendix)

1. The principal amount of the bond as stated on the bond certificate.
2. Bonds that do not all have the same due date. A portion of the bonds comes due each time period.
3. The interest rate stated on the bond certificate. It is also called the *nominal or coupon rate.*
4. The total of the present value of the cash flows produced by a bond. It is calculated as the present value of the annuity of interest payments plus the present value of the principal.
5. An obligation that will not be satisfied within one year.
6. The excess of the issue price over the face value of bonds. It occurs when the face rate on the bonds exceeds the market rate.
7. Bonds that are backed by the general creditworthiness of the issuer and are not backed by specific collateral.
8. The excess of the face value of bonds over the issue price. It occurs when the market rate on the bonds exceeds the face rate.

9. Bonds that may be redeemed or retired before their specified due date.
10. The process of transferring a portion of premium or discount to interest expense. This method transfers an amount resulting in a constant effective interest rate.
11. The face value of a bond plus the amount of unamortized premium or minus the amount of unamortized discount.
12. The interest rate that bondholders could obtain by investing in other bonds that are similar to the issuing firm's bonds.
13. The difference between the carrying value and the redemption price at the time bonds are redeemed. This amount is presented as an income statement account.
14. A measure of the amount owed to employees for pensions if estimates of future salary increases are incorporated.
15. A lease that does not meet any of four criteria and is not recorded by the lessee.
16. A payment made by the employer to the pension fund or its trustee.
17. A lease that meets one or more of four criteria and is recorded as an asset by the lessee.
18. A difference between the accounting for tax purposes and the accounting for financial reporting purposes. This type of difference affects both book and tax calculations but not in the same time period.
19. The account used to reconcile the difference between the amount recorded as income tax expense and the amount that is payable as income tax.
20. A difference between the accounting for tax purposes and the accounting for financial reporting purposes. This type of difference occurs when an item affects one set of calculations but never affects the other set.
21. An obligation to pay retired employees as compensation for service performed while employed.
22. An account that represents the difference between the amount of pension recorded as an expense and the amount of the funding payment made to the pension fund.
23. A measure of the amount owed to employees for pensions if the employees retire at their existing salary levels.

Answers on p. 551.

Alternate Terms

Accumulated Benefit Obligation ABO

Bond Face Value Bond par value

Bonds Payable Notes payable

Bond Retirement Extinguishment of bonds

Carrying Value of Bond Book value of bond

Effective Interest Amortization Interest method of amortization

Face Rate of Interest Stated rate or nominal rate or coupon rate of interest

Long-Term Liabilities Noncurrent liabilities

Market Rate of Interest Yield or effective rate of interest

Postretirement Costs Other postemployment benefits

Projected Benefit Obligation PBO

Redemption Price Reacquisition price

Temporary Difference Timing difference

Questions

1. Which interest rate, the face rate or the market rate, should be used when calculating the issue price of a bond? Why?
2. What is the tax advantage that companies experience when bonds are issued instead of stock?
3. Does the issuance of bonds at a premium indicate that the face rate is higher or lower than the market rate of interest?
4. How does the effective interest method of amortization result in a constant rate of interest?
5. What is the meaning of the following sentence: "Amortization affects the amount of interest expense"? How does amortization of premium affect the amount of interest expense? How does amortization of discount affect the amount of interest expense?
6. Does amortization of a premium increase or decrease the bond carrying value? Does amortization of a discount increase or decrease the bond carrying value?
7. Is there always a gain or loss when bonds are redeemed? How is the gain or loss calculated?
8. What are the reasons that not all leases are accounted for in the same manner? Do you think it would be possible to develop a new accounting rule that would treat all leases in the same manner?
9. What is the meaning of the term *off–balance-sheet financing?* Why do some firms want to engage in off–balance-sheet transactions?
10. What are the effects on the financial statements if a lease is considered an operating rather than a capital lease?
11. Should depreciation be reported on leased assets? If so, over what period of time should depreciation occur?
12. Why do firms have a Deferred Tax account? Where should that account be shown on the financial statements? (Appendix)
13. How can you determine whether an item should reflect a permanent or a temporary difference when calculating the deferred tax amount? (Appendix)
14. Does the amount of income tax expense presented on the income statement represent the amount of tax actually paid? Why or why not? (Appendix)

15. When an employer has a pension plan for employees, what information is shown on the financial statements concerning the pension plan? (Appendix)

16. How can you determine whether a pension plan is overfunded or underfunded? (Appendix)

17. What is the difference between the two measures of a pension plan's obligation, the projected benefit obligation and the accumulated benefit obligation? (Appendix)

18. Do you agree with this statement: "All liabilities could be legally enforced in a court of law"? (Appendix)

Exercises

Exercise 10-1 *Relationships* LO 2

The following components are computed annually when a bond is issued for other than its face value:

- Cash interest payment
- Interest expense
- Amortization of discount/premium
- Carrying value of bond

Required

State whether each component will increase (I), decrease (D), or remain constant (C) as the bond approaches maturity, given the following situations:

1. Issued at a discount.
2. Issued at a premium.

Exercise 10-2 *Issue Price* LO 3

Youngblood Inc. plans to issue $500,000 face value bonds with a stated interest rate of 8%. They will mature in 10 years. Interest will be paid semiannually. At the date of issuance, assume the market rate is (a) 8%, (b) 6%, and (c) 10%.

Required

For each market interest rate, answer the following questions:

1. What is the amount due at maturity?
2. How much cash interest will be paid every six months?
3. At what price will the bond be issued?

Exercise 10-3 *Issue Price* LO 3

The following terms relate to independent bond issues:

a. 500 bonds; $1,000 face value; 8% stated rate; 5 years; annual interest payments
b. 500 bonds; $1,000 face value; 8% stated rate; 5 years; semiannual interest payments
c. 800 bonds; $1,000 face value; 8% stated rate; 10 years; semiannual interest payments
d. 2,000 bonds; $500 face value; 12% stated rate; 15 years; semiannual interest payments

Required

Assuming the market rate of interest is 10%, calculate the selling price for each bond issue.

Exercise 10-4 *Impact of Two Bond Alternatives* LO 4

DECISION MAKING

Yung Chong Company wants to issue 100 bonds, $1,000 face value, in January. The bonds will have a 10-year life and pay interest annually. The market rate of interest on January 1 will be 9%. Yung Chong is considering two alternative bond issues: (a) bonds with a face rate of 8% and (b) bonds with a face rate of 10%.

Required

1. Could the company save money by issuing bonds with an 8% face rate? If it chooses alternative (a), what would be the interest cost as a percentage?
2. Could the company benefit by issuing bonds with a 10% face rate? If it chooses alternative (b), what would be the interest cost as a percentage?

Exercise 10-5 *Redemption of Bonds* LO 6

Reynolds Corporation issued $75,000 face value bonds at a discount of $2,500. The bonds contain a call price of 103. Reynolds decides to redeem the bonds early when the unamortized discount is $1,750.

Required

1. Calculate Reynolds Corporation's gain or loss on the early redemption of the bonds.
2. Describe how the gain or loss would be reported on the income statement and in the notes to the financial statements.

Exercise 10-6 *Redemption of a Bond at Maturity* LO 6

On March 31, 2004, Sammonds Inc. issued $250,000 face value bonds at a discount of $7,000. The bonds were retired at their maturity date, March 31, 2014.

Required

Assuming the last interest payment and the amortization of discount have already been recorded, calculate the gain or loss on the redemption of the bonds on March 31, 2014. Prepare the journal entry to record the redemption of the bonds.

Exercise 10-7 *Leased Asset* LO 7

Hopper Corporation signed a 10-year capital lease on January 1, 2004. The lease requires annual payments of $8,000 every December 31.

Required

1. Assuming an interest rate of 9%, calculate the present value of the minimum lease payments.
2. Explain why the value of the leased asset and the accompanying lease obligation are not initially reported on the balance sheet at $80,000.

Exercise 10-8 *Financial Statement Impact of a Lease* LO 7

Benjamin's Warehouse signed a six-year capital lease on January 1, 2004, with payments due every December 31. Interest is calculated annually at 10%, and the present value of the minimum lease payments is $13,065.

Required

1. Calculate the amount of the annual payment that Benjamin's must make every December 31.
2. Calculate the amount of the lease obligation that would be presented on the December 31, 2005, balance sheet (after two lease payments have been made).

Exercise 10-9 *Leased Assets* LO 7

Koffman and Sons signed a four-year lease for a forklift on January 1, 2004. Annual lease payments of $1,510, based on an interest rate of 8%, are to be made every December 31, beginning with December 31, 2004.

Required

1. Assume the lease is treated as an operating lease.
   - a. Will the value of the forklift appear on Koffman's balance sheet?
   - b. What account will indicate lease payments have been made?
2. Assume the lease is treated as a capital lease.
   - a. Prepare any journal entries needed when the lease is signed. Explain why the value of the leased asset is not recorded at $6,040 ($1,510 × 4).
   - b. Prepare the journal entry to record the first lease payment on December 31, 2004.
   - c. Prepare the adjusting entry to record depreciation expense on December 31, 2004.
   - d. At what amount would the lease obligation be presented on the balance sheet as of December 31, 2004?

Exercise 10-10 ***Impact of Transactions Involving Bonds on Statement of Cash Flows*** **LO 8**

From the following list, identify each item as operating (O), investing (I), financing (F), or not separately reported on the statement of cash flows (N).

_______ Proceeds from issuance of bonds payable
_______ Interest expense
_______ Redemption of bonds payable at maturity

Exercise 10-11 ***Impact of Transactions Involving Capital Leases on Statement of Cash Flows*** **LO 8**

Assume that Garnett Corporation signs a lease agreement with Duncan Company to lease a piece of equipment and determines that the lease should be treated as a capital lease. Garnett records a leased asset in the amount of $53,400 and a lease obligation in the same amount on its balance sheet.

Required

1. Indicate how this transaction would be reported on Garnett's statement of cash flows.
2. From the following list of transactions relating to this lease, identify each item as operating (O), investing (I), financing (F), or not separately reported on the statement of cash flows (N).

_______ Reduction of lease obligation (principal portion of lease payment)
_______ Interest expense
_______ Depreciation expense—leased assets

Exercise 10-12 ***Impact of Transactions Involving Tax Liabilities on Statement of Cash Flows*** **LO 8**

From the following list, identify each item as operating (O), investing (I), financing (F), or not separately reported on the statement of cash flows (N). For items identified as operating, indicate whether the related amount would be added to or deducted from net income in determining the cash flows from operating activities.

_______ Decrease in taxes payable
_______ Increase in deferred taxes

Exercise 10-13 ***Temporary and Permanent Differences (Appendix)*** **LO 9**

Madden Corporation wants to determine the amount of deferred tax that should be reported on its 2004 financial statements. It has compiled a list of differences between the accounting conducted for tax purposes and the accounting used for financial reporting (book) purposes.

Required

For each of the following items, indicate whether the difference should be classified as a permanent or a temporary difference.

1. During 2004, Madden received interest on state bonds purchased as an investment. The interest can be treated as tax-exempt interest for tax purposes.
2. During 2004, Madden paid for a life insurance premium on two key executives. Madden's accountant has indicated that the amount of the premium cannot be deducted for income tax purposes.
3. During December 2004, Madden received money for renting a building to a tenant. Madden must report the rent as income on its 2004 tax form. For book purposes, however, the rent will be considered income on the 2005 income statement.
4. Madden owns several pieces of equipment that it depreciates using the straight-line method for book purposes. An accelerated method of depreciation is used for tax purposes, however.
5. Madden offers a warranty on the product it sells. The corporation records the expense of the warranty repair costs in the year the product is sold (the accrual method) for book purposes. For tax purposes, however, Madden is not allowed to deduct the expense until the period when the product is repaired.

6. During 2004, Madden was assessed a large fine by the federal government for polluting the environment. Madden's accountant has indicated that the fine cannot be deducted as an expense for income tax purposes.

Exercise 10-14 ***Deferred Tax (Appendix)*** **LO 9**

On January 1, 2004, Kunkel Corporation purchased an asset for $32,000. Assume this is the only asset owned by the corporation. Kunkel has decided to use the straight-line method to depreciate it. For tax purposes, it will be depreciated over three years. It will be depreciated over five years, however, for the financial statements provided to stockholders. Assume that Kunkel Corporation is subject to a 40% tax rate.

Required

Calculate the balance that should be reflected in the Deferred Tax account for Kunkel Corporation for each year 2004 through 2008.

Exercise 10-15 ***Pension Analysis (Appendix)*** **LO 10**

The following information was extracted from a note found in the 2004 annual report of a company.

Plan Assets	$2.6 billion
Accumulated Benefit Obligation	$1.7 billion
Projected Benefit Obligation	$2.1 billion

Required

1. Determine whether the pension plan is overfunded or underfunded.
2. Explain what your response to part **1** implies about the ability of the plan to provide benefits to future retirees.

Multi-Concept Exercises

Exercise 10-16 ***Issuance of a Bond at Face Value*** **LO 4, 5**

On January 1, 2004, Whitefeather Industries issued 300, $1,000 face value bonds. The bonds have a five-year life and pay interest at the rate of 10%. Interest is paid semiannually on July 1 and January 1. The market rate of interest on January 1 was 10%.

Required

1. Calculate the issue price of the bonds and record the issuance of the bonds on January 1, 2004.
2. Explain how the issue price would have been affected if the market rate of interest had been higher than 10%.
3. Prepare the journal entry to record the payment of interest on July 1, 2004.
4. Prepare the journal to record the accrual of interest on December 31, 2004.

Exercise 10-17 ***Impact of a Discount*** **LO 4, 5**

Berol Corporation sold 20-year bonds on January 1, 2004. The face value of the bonds was $100,000, and they carry a 9% stated rate of interest, which is paid on December 31 of every year. Berol received $91,526 in return for the issuance of the bonds when the market rate was 10%. Any premium or discount is amortized using the effective interest method.

Required

1. Prepare the journal entry to record the sale of the bonds on January 1, 2004, and the proper balance sheet presentation on this date.
2. Prepare the journal entry to record interest expense on December 31, 2004, and the proper balance sheet presentation on this date.
3. Explain why it was necessary for Berol to issue the bonds for only $91,526 rather than $100,000.

Exercise 10-18 ***Impact of a Premium*** **LO 4, 5**

Assume the same set of facts for Berol Corporation as in Exercise 10-17 except that it received $109,862 in return for the issuance of the bonds when the market rate was 8%.

Required

1. Prepare the journal entry to record the sale of the bonds on January 1, 2004, and the proper balance sheet presentation on this date.
2. Prepare the journal entry to record interest expense on December 31, 2004, and the proper balance sheet presentation on this date.
3. Explain why the company was able to issue the bonds for $109,862 rather than for the face amount.

Problems

Problem 10-1 ***Factors That Affect the Bond Issue Price*** **LO 3**

Becca Company is considering the issue of $100,000 face value, 10-year term bonds. The bonds will pay 6% interest each December 31. The current market rate is 6%; therefore, the bonds will be issued at face value.

Required

1. For each of the following independent situations, indicate whether you believe that the company will receive a premium on the bonds or will issue them at a discount or at face value. Without using numbers, explain your position.
   a. Interest is paid semiannually instead of annually.
   b. Assume instead that the market rate of interest is 7%; the nominal rate is still 6%.
2. For each situation in part **1**, prove your statement by determining the issue price of the bonds given the changes in parts **a** and **b**.

Problem 10-2 ***Amortization of Discount*** **LO 5**

SPREADSHEET

Stacy Company issued five-year, 10% bonds with face value of $10,000 on January 1, 2004. Interest is paid annually on December 31. The market rate of interest on this date is 12%, and Stacy Company receives proceeds of $9,275 on the bond issuance.

Required

1. Prepare a five-year table (similar to Exhibit 10-4) to amortize the discount using the effective interest method.
2. What is the total interest expense over the life of the bonds? cash interest payment? discount amortization?
3. Prepare the journal entry for the payment of interest and the amortization of discount on December 31, 2006 (the third year), and determine the balance sheet presentation of the bonds on that date.

Problem 10-3 ***Amortization of Premium*** **LO 5**

Assume the same set of facts for Stacy Company as in Problem 10-2 except that the market rate of interest of January 1, 2004, is 8% and the proceeds from the bond issuance equal $10,803.

Required

1. Prepare a five-year table (similar to Exhibit 10-5) to amortize the premium using the effective interest method.
2. What is the total interest expense over the life of the bonds? cash interest payment? premium amortization?
3. Prepare the journal entry for the payment of interest and the amortization of premium on December 31, 2006 (the third year), and determine the balance sheet presentation of the bonds on that date.

Problem 10-4 ***Redemption of Bonds*** **LO 6**

McGee Company issued $200,000 face value bonds at a premium of $4,500. The bonds contain a call provision of 101. McGee decides to redeem the bonds, due to a significant decline in interest rates. On that date, McGee had amortized only $1,000 of the premium.

Required

1. Calculate the gain or loss on the early redemption of the bonds.
2. Calculate the gain or loss on the redemption, assuming that the call provision is 103 instead of 101.
3. Indicate where the gain or loss should be presented on the financial statements.
4. Why do you suppose the call price is normally higher than 100?

Problem 10-5 ***Financial Statement Impact of a Lease*** **LO 7**

On January 1, 2004, Muske Trucking Company leased a semitractor and trailer for five years. Annual payments of $28,300 are to be made every December 31, beginning December 31, 2004. Interest expense is based on a rate of 8%. The present value of the minimum lease payments is $113,000 and has been determined to be greater than 90% of the fair market value of the asset on January 1, 2004. Muske uses straight-line depreciation on all assets.

Required

1. Prepare a table similar to Exhibit 10-7 to show the five-year amortization of the lease obligation.
2. Prepare the journal entry for the lease transaction on January 1, 2004.
3. Prepare all necessary journal entries on December 31, 2005 (the second year of the lease).
4. Prepare the balance sheet presentation as of December 31, 2005, for the leased asset and the lease obligation.

Problem 10-6 ***Deferred Tax (Appendix)*** **LO 9**

Erinn Corporation has compiled its 2004 financial statements. Included in the Long-Term Liabilities category of the balance sheet are the following amounts:

	2004	2003
Deferred tax	$180	$100

Included in the income statement are the following amounts related to income taxes:

	2004	2003
Income before tax	$500	$400
Tax expense	200	160
Net income	$300	$240

In the notes that accompany the 2004 statement are the following amounts:

	2004
Current provision for tax	$120
Deferred portion	80

Required

1. Prepare the journal entry in 2004 for income tax expense, deferred tax, and income tax payable.
2. Assume that a stockholder has inquired about the meaning of the numbers recorded and disclosed about deferred tax. Explain why the Deferred Tax liability account exists. Also, what do the terms *current provision* and *deferred portion* mean? Why is the deferred amount in the note $80 when the deferred amount on the 2004 balance sheet is $180?

Problem 10-7 ***Deferred Tax Calculations (Appendix)*** **LO 9**

Wyhowski Inc. reported income from operations, before taxes, for 2002–2004 as follows:

2002	$210,000
2003	240,000
2004	280,000

(continued)

When calculating income, Wyhowski deducted depreciation on plant equipment. The equipment was purchased January 1, 2002, at a cost of $88,000. The equipment is expected to last three years and have $8,000 salvage value. Wyhowski uses straight-line depreciation for book purposes. For tax purposes, depreciation on the equipment is $50,000 in 2002, $20,000 in 2003, and $10,000 in 2004. Wyhowski's tax rate is 35%.

Required

1. How much did Wyhowski pay in income tax each year?
2. How much income tax expense did Wyhowski record each year?
3. What is the balance in the Deferred Income Tax account at the end of 2002, 2003, and 2004?

Problem 10-8 *Financial Statement Impact of a Pension (Appendix)* LO 10

Smith Financial Corporation prepared the following schedule relating to its pension expense and pension-funding payment for the years 2002 through 2004.

Year	Expense	Payment
2002	$100,000	$ 90,000
2003	85,000	105,000
2004	112,000	100,000

At the beginning of 2002, the Prepaid/Accrued Pension Cost account was reported on the balance sheet as an asset with a balance of $4,000.

Required

1. Prepare the journal entries to record Smith Financial Corporation's pension expense for 2002, 2003, and 2004.
2. Calculate the balance in the Prepaid/Accrued Pension Cost account at the end of 2004. Does this represent an asset or a liability?
3. Explain the effects that pension expense, the funding payment, and the balance in the Prepaid/Accrued Pension Cost account have on the 2004 income statement and balance sheet.

Multi-Concept Problems

Problem 10-9 *Bond Transactions* LO 4, 5

Brand Company issued $1,000,000 face value, eight-year, 12% bonds on April 1, 2004, when the market rate of interest was 12%. Interest payments are due every October 1 and April 1. Brand uses a calendar year-end.

Required

1. Prepare the journal entry to record the issuance of the bonds on April 1, 2004.
2. Prepare the journal entry to record the interest payment on October 1, 2004.
3. Explain why additional interest must be recorded on December 31, 2004. What impact does this have on the amounts paid on April 1, 2005?
4. Determine the total cash inflows and outflows that occurred on the bonds over the eight-year life.

Problem 10-10 *Partial Classified Balance Sheet for Walgreens* LO 1, 9, 10

http://www.walgreens.com

The following items, listed alphabetically, appear on Walgreens' consolidated balance sheet at August 31, 2001 (in millions).

Accrued expenses and other liabilities	$ 937.5
Deferred income tax (long-term)	137.0
Income taxes payable	86.6
Other noncurrent liabilities	478.0
Short-term borrowings	440.7
Trade accounts payable	1,546.8

Required

1. Prepare the Current Liabilities and Long-Term Liabilities sections of Walgreens' classified balance sheet at August 31, 2001.
2. Walgreens' had total liabilities of $2,869.7 million and total shareholders' equity of $4,234.0 at August 31, 2000. Total shareholders' equity at August 31, 2001, amounted to $5,207.2. Compute the company's debt-to-equity ratio at August 31, 2001 and 2000, respectively. As an investor, how would you react to the changes in this ratio?
3. What other related ratios would the company's lenders use to assess the company? What do these ratios measure?

Alternate Problems

Problem 10-1A *Factors that Affect the Bond Issue Price* **LO 3**

Rivera Inc. is considering the issuance of $500,000 face value, 10-year term bonds. The bonds will pay 5% interest each December 31. The current market rate is 5%; therefore, the bonds will be issued at face value.

Required

1. For each of the following independent situations, indicate whether you believe that the company will receive a premium on the bonds or will issue them at a discount or at face value. Without using numbers, explain your position.
   a. Interest is paid semiannually instead of annually.
   b. Assume instead that the market rate of interest is 4%; the nominal rate is still 5%.
2. For each situation in part **1**, prove your statement by determining the issue price of the bonds given the changes in parts **a** and **b.**

Problem 10-2A *Amortization of Discount* **LO 5**

Ortega Company issued five-year, 5% bonds with face value of $50,000 on January 1, 2004. Interest is paid annually on December 31. The market rate of interest on this date is 8%, and Ortega Company receives proceeds of $44,011 on the bond issuance.

SPREADSHEET

Required

1. Prepare a five-year table (similar to Exhibit 10-4) to amortize the discount using the effective interest method.
2. What is the total interest expense over the life of the bonds? cash interest payment? discount amortization?
3. Prepare the journal entry to record interest expense on December 31, 2006 (the third year), and the balance sheet presentation of the bonds on that date.

Problem 10-3A *Amortization of Premium* **LO 5**

Assume the same set of facts for Ortega Company as in Problem 10-2A except that the market rate of interest of January 1, 2004, is 4% and the proceeds from the bond issuance equal $52,230.

Required

1. Prepare a five-year table (similar to Exhibit 10-5) to amortize the premium using the effective interest method.
2. What is the total interest expense over the life of the bonds? cash interest payment? premium amortization?
3. Prepare the journal entry to record interest expense on December 31, 2006 (the third year), and the balance sheet presentation of the bonds on that date.

Problem 10-4A *Redemption of Bonds* **LO 6**

Elliot Company issued $100,000 face value bonds at a premium of $5,500. The bonds contain a call provision of 101. Elliot decides to redeem the bonds, due to a significant decline in interest rates. On that date, Elliot has amortized only $2,000 of the premium.

(continued)

Required

1. Calculate the gain or loss on the early redemption of the bonds.
2. Calculate the gain or loss on the redemption, assuming that the call provision is 104 instead of 101.
3. Indicate how the gain or loss would be reported on the income statement and in the notes to the financial statements.
4. Why do you suppose that the call price of the bonds is normally an amount higher than 100?

Problem 10-5A *Financial Statement Impact of a Lease* LO 7

On January 1, 2004, Kiger Manufacturing Company leased a factory machine for six years. Annual payments of $21,980 are to be made every December 31, beginning December 31, 2004. Interest expense is based on a rate of 9%. The present value of the minimum lease payments is $98,600 and has been determined to be greater than 90% of the fair market value of the machine on January 1, 2004. Kiger uses straight-line depreciation on all assets.

Required

1. Prepare a table similar to Exhibit 10-7 to show the six-year amortization of the lease obligation.
2. Prepare the journal entry to record the signing of the lease on January 1, 2004.
3. Prepare all journal entries necessary on December 31, 2005 (the second year of the lease).
4. Prepare the balance sheet presentation as of December 31, 2005, for the leased asset and the lease obligation.

Problem 10-6A *Deferred Tax (Appendix)* LO 9

Thad Corporation has compiled its 2004 financial statements. Included in the Long-Term Liabilities category of the balance sheet are the following amounts:

	2004	2003
Deferred tax	$180	$200

Included in the income statement are the following amounts related to income taxes:

	2004	2003
Income before tax	$500	$400
Tax expense	100	150
Net income	$400	$250

Required

1. Prepare the journal entry recorded in 2004 for income tax expense, deferred tax, and income tax payable.
2. Assume that a stockholder has inquired about the meaning of the numbers recorded. Explain why the Deferred Tax liability account exists.

Problem 10-7A *Deferred Tax Calculations (Appendix)* LO 9

Clemente Inc. has reported income for book purposes as follows for the past three years:

(in Thousands)	Year 1	Year 2	Year 3
Income before taxes	$120	$120	$120

Clemente has identified two items that are treated differently in the financial records and in the tax records. The first one is interest income on municipal bonds, which is recognized on the financial reports to the extent of $5,000 each year but does not show up as a revenue item on the company's tax return. The other item is equipment that is depreciated using the straight-line method, at the rate of $20,000 each year, for financial accounting but is depreciated for tax purposes at the rate of $30,000 in Year 1, $20,000 in Year 2, and $10,000 in Year 3.

Required

1. Determine the amount of cash paid for income taxes each year by Clemente. Assume that a 40% tax rate applies to all three years.

2. Calculate the balance in the Deferred Tax account at the end of Years 1, 2, and 3. How does this account appear on the balance sheet?

Problem 10-8A *Financial Statement Impact of a Pension (Appendix)* LO 10

Premier Consulting Corporation prepared the following schedule relating to its pension expense and pension-funding payment for the years 2002 through 2004:

Year	Expense	Payment
2002	$100,000	$110,000
2003	85,000	80,000
2004	112,000	100,000

At the beginning of 2002, the Prepaid/Accrued Pension Cost account was reported on the balance sheet as an asset with a balance of $5,000.

Required

1. Prepare the journal entries to record Premier Consulting Corporation's pension expense for 2002, 2003, and 2004.
2. Calculate the balance in the Prepaid/Accrued Pension Cost account at the end of 2004.
3. Explain the effects that pension expense, the funding payment, and the balance in the Prepaid/Accrued Pension Cost account have on the 2004 income statement and balance sheet.

Alternate Multi-Concept Problems

Problem 10-9A *Financial Statement Impact of a Bond* LO 4, 6

Worthington Company issued $1,000,000 face value, six-year, 10% bonds on July 1, 2004, when the market rate of interest was 12%. Interest payments are due every July 1 and January 1. Worthington uses a calendar year-end.

Required

1. Prepare the journal entry to record the issuance of the bonds on July 1, 2004.
2. Prepare the adjusting journal entry on December 31, 2004, to accrue interest expense.
3. Prepare the journal entry to record the interest payment on January 1, 2005.
4. Prepare the journal entry to record the retirement of the bonds on the maturity date.

Problem 10-10A *Partial Classified Balance Sheet for Boeing* LO 1, 9, 10

The following items appear on the consolidated balance sheet of **Boeing Inc.** at December 31, 2001 (in millions). The information in parentheses was added to aid in your understanding.

http://www.boeing.com

Accounts payable and other liabilities	$13,872
Accrued retiree healthcare	5,367
Advances in excess of related costs	1,251
Short-term debt and current portion of long-term debt	1,399
Income tax payable	909
Long-term debt	10,866
Deferred income taxes	177
Deferred lease income (long-term)	622

Required

1. Prepare the Current Liabilities and Long-Term Liabilities sections of Boeing's classified balance sheet at December 31, 2001.
2. Boeing had total liabilities of $36,896 and total shareholders' equity of $11,020 at December 31, 2000. Total stockholders' equity amounted to $10,825 at December 31, 2001. (All amounts are in millions.) Compute Boeing's debt-to-equity ratio at December 31, 2001 and 2000. As an investor, how would you react to the change in this ratio?
3. What other related ratios would the company's lenders use to assess the company? What do these ratios measure?

Cases

Reading and Interpreting Financial Statements

http://www.winnebagoind.com
http://www.monacocoach.com

Case 10-1 ***Comparing Two Companies in the Same Industry: Winnebago Industries and Monaco Coach Corporation*** **LO 1, 7**

The Current Liabilities and Long-Term Liabilities sections of Monaco Coach Corporation's balance sheet as of December 29, 2001 and March 30, 2002, are as follows (in thousands):

	December 29, 2001	March 30, 2002
LIABILITIES		
Current liabilities:		
Book overdraft	$ 5,889	$ 12,534
Line of credit	26,004	11,004
Current portion of long-term note payable	10,000	10,000
Accounts payable	66,859	91,369
Income taxes payable		545
Accrued expenses and other liabilities	66,904	70,073
Total current liabilities	$175,656	$195,525
Long-term note payable	30,000	27,500
Deferred income taxes	8,312	12,209
Total liabilities	$213,968	$235,234

Refer to the annual reports in Appendices A and B at the end of the text for any additional information you might need about Monaco Coach Corporation or Winnebago Industries.

Required

1. Calculate the debt-to-equity ratio on December 29, 2001 for Monaco Coach and on August 25, 2001 for Winnebago Industries. How do the two ratios compare? What does that tell you about the two companies?
2. Comment on the reasons for the change in Monaco Coach's total liabilities from December 29, 2001, to March 30, 2002. What are the most important changes? What impact do these changes have on the company's cash flow?
3. A note to Monaco Coach's 2001 financial statements indicates:

   The company has a long-term note payable of $40 million outstanding at December 29, 2001. The term note bears interest at varying rates that fluctuate based on the Prime rate or LIBOR, and are determined based on the Company's leverage ratio. The term note requires monthly interest payments and quarterly principal payments and is collateralized by all the assets of the Company. The term note is due and payable in full on September 28, 2005. As of December 29, 2001, the interest rate on the term debt was 3.94%.

   What does the term "collateralized by all of the assets" mean? If you were a lender to the company, what factors should you have considered before lending money to the company?
4. Look at Note 4 to Winnebago Industries' 2001 financial statements. How does the disclosed information in that note compare with Monaco Coach's disclosure above? Does one company appear to have more restrictions with its notes than the other? Explain your answer.

http://www.coachmen.com

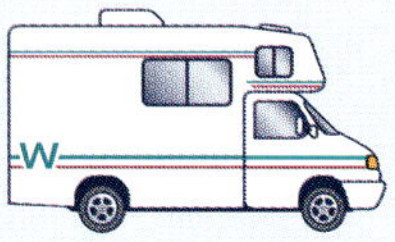

Case 10-2 ***Evaluating Winnebago Industries' Competitor*** **LO 1**

The Current Liabilities and Long-Term Liabilities sections of Coachmen Industries' balance sheet as of December 31, 2001, are as follows (in thousands):

	2001	2000
CURRENT LIABILITIES		
Accounts payable, trade	$18,944	$24,015
Accrued income taxes	494	845
Accrued expenses and other liabilities	38,846	31,988
Current maturities of long-term debt	917	865
Total current liabilities	$59,201	$57,713

Long-term debt	11,001	11,795
Deferred income taxes	1,257	3,370
Other	8,461	8,619
Total liabilities	$79,920	$81,497

Required

1. Explain why current maturities of long-term debt is shown as a current liability for the company.
2. The notes to the balance sheet provide the following information:

   The Company maintains an Amended and Restated Revolving Credit Facility that provides a secured line of credit aggregating $30 million through June 30, 2003. This agreement was amended on November 5, 2001, to modify available borrowings to $30 million from $50 million, to provide certain collateral to the bank, and to modify certain financial covenants to reflect current business conditions.

   What is meant by a "line of credit?" Explain what is meant by "financial covenants." Why would a lender specify financial covenants when extending a loan?
3. If you were a lender, what measures or ratios would you calculate to determine whether a loan should be extended to the company?

Case 10-3 *Reading PepsiCo's Statement of Cash Flows (Appendix)* LO 8, 9

A portion of the financing activities section of PepsiCo's statement of cash flows for the year ended December 29, 2001, follows (in millions):

http://www.pepsico.com

Financing Activities:	
Proceeds from the issuance of long-term debt	$ 324
Payment of long-term debt	(573)
Short-term borrowings by original maturity:	
More than three months—proceeds	788
More than three months—payments	(483)
Three months or less, net	(397)

Required

1. Explain why proceeds from debt is shown as a positive amount and payment of debt is shown as a negative amount.
2. During 2001, interest rates had declined to low levels. Explain why the company paid off debt during such conditions.
3. PepsiCo has a Deferred Income Tax account listed in the asset category of its balance sheet. Would an increase in that account result in an addition or a subtraction on the statement of cash flows? In which category?

Making Financial Decisions

Case 10-4 *Making a Loan Decision* LO 1

DECISION MAKING

Assume that you are a loan officer in charge of reviewing loan applications from potential new clients at a major bank. You are considering an application from Molitor Corporation, which is a fairly new company with a limited credit history. It has provided a balance sheet for its most recent fiscal year as follows:

MOLITOR CORPORATION
BALANCE SHEET
DECEMBER 31, 2004

Assets		Liabilities	
Cash	$ 10,000	Accounts payable	$100,000
Receivables	50,000	Notes payable	200,000
Inventory	100,000		
Equipment	500,000	**Stockholders' Equity**	
		Common stock	80,000
		Retained earnings	280,000
Total assets	$660,000	Total liabilities and stockholders' equity	$660,000

(continued)

Your bank has established certain guidelines that must be met before making a favorable loan recommendation. These include minimum levels for several financial ratios. You are particularly concerned about the bank's policy that loan applicants must have a total-assets-to-debt ratio of at least 2-to-1 to be acceptable. Your initial analysis of Molitor's balance sheet has indicated that the firm has met the minimum total-assets-to-debt ratio requirement. On reading the notes that accompany the financial statements, however, you discover the following statement:

> Molitor has engaged in a variety of innovative financial techniques resulting in the acquisition of $200,000 of assets at very favorable rates. The company is obligated to make a series of payments over the next five years to fulfill its commitments in conjunction with these financial instruments. Current generally accepted accounting principles do not require the assets acquired or the related obligations to be reflected on the financial statements.

Required

1. How should this note affect your evaluation of Molitor's loan application? Calculate a revised total-assets-to-debt ratio for Molitor.
2. Do you believe that the bank's policy concerning a minimum total-assets-to-debt ratio can be modified to consider financing techniques that are not reflected on the financial statements? Write a statement that expresses your position on this issue.

Case 10-5 ***Bond Redemption Decision*** **LO 6**

DECISION MAKING

Armstrong Areo Ace, a flight training school, issued $100,000 of 20-year bonds at face value when the market rate was 10%. The bonds have been outstanding for 10 years. The company pays annual interest on January 1. The current rate for similar bonds is 4%. On January 1, the controller would like to purchase the bonds on the open market, retire the bonds, then issue $100,000 of 10-year bonds to pay 4% annual interest.

Required

Draft a memo to the controller advising him to retire the outstanding bonds and issue new debt. Ignore taxes. (*Hint:* Find the selling price of bonds that pay 10% when the market rate is 4%.)

Accounting and Ethics: What Would You Do?

Case 10-6 ***Determination of Asset Life*** **LO 7**

Jen Latke is an accountant for Hale's Manufacturing Company. Hale's has entered into an agreement to lease a piece of equipment from EZ Leasing. Jen must decide how to report the lease agreement on Hale's financial statements.

Jen has reviewed the lease contract carefully. She has also reviewed the four lease criteria specified in the accounting rules. She has been able to determine that the lease does not meet three of the criteria. However, she is concerned about the criterion that indicates that if the term of the lease is 75% or more of the life of the property, the lease should be classified as a capital lease. Jen is fully aware that Hale's does not want to record the lease agreement as a capital lease but prefers to show it as a type of off–balance-sheet financing.

Jen's reading of the lease contract indicates that the asset has been leased for seven years. She is unsure of the life of such assets, however, and has consulted two sources to determine it. One of them states that equipment similar to that owned by Hale's is depreciated over nine years. The other, a trade publication of the equipment industry, indicates that equipment of this type will usually last for 12 years.

Required

1. How should Jen report the lease agreement in the financial statements?
2. If Jen decides to present the lease as an off–balance-sheet arrangement, has she acted ethically?

Case 10-7 ***Overfunded Pension Plan (Appendix)*** **LO 10**

Witty Company has sponsored a pension plan for employees for several years. Each year Witty has paid cash to the pension fund, and the pension trustee has used that cash to invest in stocks and bonds. Because the trustee has invested wisely, the amount of the pension assets exceeds the accumulated benefit obligation as of December 31, 2004.

The president of Witty Company wants to pay a dividend to the stockholders at the end of 2004. The president believes that it is important to maintain a stable dividend pattern. Unfortunately, the company, though profitable, does not have enough cash on hand to pay a dividend and must find a way to raise the necessary cash if the dividend is declared. Several executives of the company have recommended that assets be withdrawn from the pension fund. They have pointed out that the fund is currently "overfunded." Further, they have stated that a withdrawal of assets will not have an impact on the financial statements because the overfunding is an "off–balance-sheet item."

Required

Comment on the proposal to withdraw assets from the pension fund to pay a dividend to stockholders. Do you believe it is unethical?

Internet Research Case

Case 10-8 Coca-Cola

Sold in over 200 countries, Coca-Cola is the most recognized brand name in the world. Sales of Classic Coke, diet Coke, and Sprite provide the company with the cash necessary to pay off debts.

Conduct a search of the World Wide Web, obtain Coca-Cola's most recent annual report, or use library resources to obtain company information to answer the following:

INTERNET

http://www.coca-cola.com

1. Based on the latest information available, what is the amount of Coca-Cola's long-term debt? How does this compare with the long-term debt in the "Focus on Financial Results" in the opening vignette shown at the start of this chapter?
2. What is the face rate on a Coca-Cola bond currently trading on the bond market? How does that rate compare with the current yield for the same bond?
3. During the past three to six months, has the yield for Coca-Cola's bonds increased or decreased?

Optional Research. Obtain information from the company's Web site to determine recent business activities and international expansion that may have affected the amount of long-term debt used by the company.

Solutions to Key Terms Quiz

5 Long-term liability (p. 502)
1 Face value (p. 502)
7 Debenture bonds (p. 504)
2 Serial bonds (p. 504)
9 Callable bonds (p. 505)
3 Face rate of interest (p. 505)
12 Market rate of interest (p. 505)
4 Bond issue price (p. 506)
6 Premium (p. 507)
8 Discount (p. 507)
10 Effective interest method of amortization (p. 510)
11 Carrying value (p. 510)
13 Gain or loss on redemption (p. 514)
15 Operating lease (p. 517)
17 Capital lease (p. 517)
19 Deferred tax (p. 529)
20 Permanent difference (p. 529)
18 Temporary difference (p. 529)
21 Pension (p. 532)
16 Funding payment (p. 532)
22 Accrued pension cost (p. 533)
23 Accumulated benefit obligation (ABO) (p. 534)
14 Projected benefit obligation (PBO) (p. 534)

Chapter 11

Stockholders' Equity

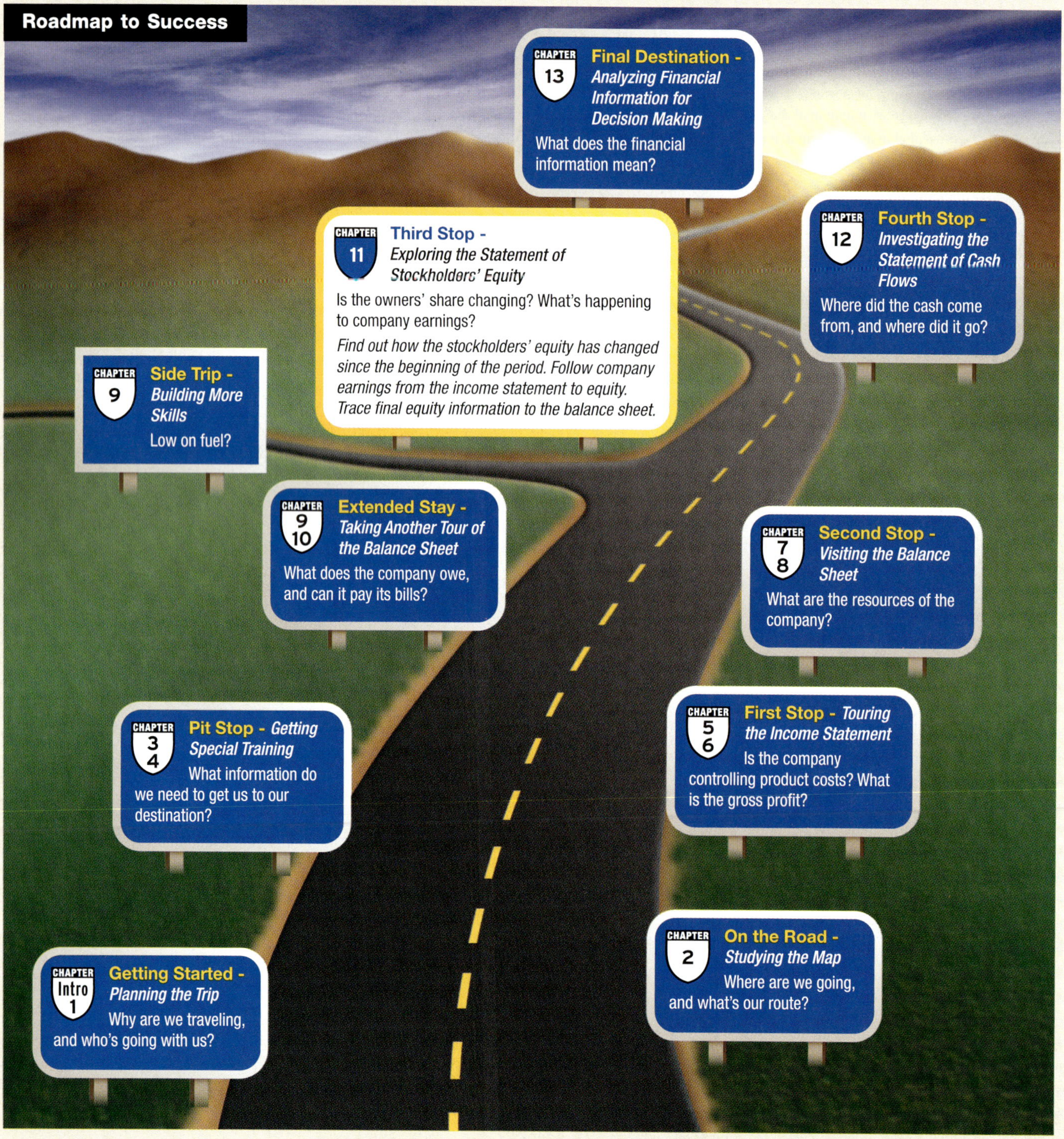

Focus on Financial Results

The airline industry is volatile, and Delta Air Lines has certainly experienced its share of ups and downs. The period of the late 1990s was a period of growth and profitability for the company. In fact, diluted earnings per share had grown over 150% from 1995 to 1999. However, the events surrounding the tragedy of September 11, 2001, had a dramatic effect on the travel industry. Delta reported a net loss of $1.2 billion for 2001 and has struggled to respond to safety concerns, customer expectations, and the need to make cuts in service and in the number of employees. With reduced revenues, weak demand, high fixed costs, and increasing expenses for security and insurance, the outlook for the airline industry remained grim for the remainder of 2001 and into 2002.

Throughout the struggle, Delta has been committed to keeping focused on its long-term strategic goal of building shareholder value, which contributes to the *stockholders' equity* portion of the balance sheet shown here. For one of the world's busiest airlines, that goal is paramount and even more important than the need to find capital resources to reinvest in the business. How is stockholders' equity built?

For Delta, building value means adopting innovative technology to speed check-in and boarding; developing a customer-service initiative to ensure reliable and courteous service; continually refurbishing and renovating its fleet of planes and ground facilities; and entering into business alliances with Aeormexico, Air France, CSA Czech Airlines, and Korean Air.

Delta believes it has responded quickly and decisively to challenges resulting from the tragedy. The company remains focused on its long-term strategy and feels that it has established a foundation of disciplined cost control and expanded growth potential. The company made a commitment to its stockholders by continuing to pay dividends even in the face of the difficult financial picture. If the company returns to profitability, it will be the stockholders who will benefit.

Delta Air Lines 2001 Annual Report

Delta Air Lines Partial Balance Sheet

	2001	2000
Employee Stock Ownership Plan Preferred Stock:		
Series B ESOP Convertible Preferred Stock, $1.00 par value, $72.00 stated and liquidation value; 6,278,210 shares issued and outstanding at December 31, 2001, and 6,405,563 shares issued and outstanding at December 31, 2000	**452**	460
Unearned compensation under employee stock ownership plan	**(197)**	(226)
Total Employee Stock Ownership Plan Preferred Stock	**255**	234
Shareowners' Equity:		
Common stock, $1.50 par value; 450,000,000 shares authorized; 180,890,356 shares issued at December 31, 2001 and 180,764,057 shares issued at December 31, 2000	**271**	271
Additional paid-in capital	**3,267**	3,264
Retained earnings	**2,930**	4,176
Accumulated other comprehensive income	**25**	360
Treasury stock at cost, 57,644,690 shares at December 31, 2001 and 57,750,685 shares at December 31, 2000	**(2,724)**	(2,728)
Total shareowners' equity	**3,769**	5,343
Total liabilities and shareowners' equity	**$23,605**	$21,931

The accompanying notes are an integral part of these Consolidated Balance Sheets.

You're in the Driver's Seat

http://www.delta.com

If you were a Delta Air Lines stockholder, what information about the stock would you want to learn from Delta's balance sheet? What additional information would you want about the company's plans? Use this chapter to develop your answers, and look at Delta's most recent annual report to see whether the stock has responded to the company's attempts to build shareholder value.

LEARNING OBJECTIVES

After studying this chapter, you should be able to:

LO 1 Identify the components of the Stockholders' Equity category of the balance sheet and the accounts found in each component. (p. 557)

LO 2 Demonstrate an understanding of the characteristics of common and preferred stock and the differences between the classes of stock. (p. 560)

LO 3 Determine the financial statement impact when stock is issued for cash or for other consideration. (p. 561)

LO 4 Describe the financial statement impact of stock treated as treasury stock. (p. 563)

LO 5 Compute the amount of cash dividends when a firm has issued both preferred and common stock. (p. 566)

LO 6 Demonstrate an understanding of the difference between cash and stock dividends and the effect of stock dividends. (p. 567)

LO 7 Determine the difference between stock dividends and stock splits. (p. 569)

LO 8 Demonstrate an understanding of the statement of stockholders' equity and comprehensive income. (p. 570)

LO 9 Understand how investors use ratios to evaluate owners' equity. (p. 573)

LO 10 Explain the effects that transactions involving stockholders' equity have on the statement of cash flows. (p. 575)

LO 11 Describe the important differences between the sole proprietorship and partnership forms of organization versus the corporate form (Appendix). (p. 582)

AN OVERVIEW OF STOCKHOLDERS' EQUITY

Equity as a Source of Financing

Whenever a company needs to raise money, it must choose from the alternative financing sources that are available. Financing can be divided into two general categories: debt (borrowing from banks or other creditors) and equity (issuing stock). The company's management must consider the advantages and disadvantages of each alternative. Exhibit 11-1 indicates a few of the factors that must be considered.

Issuing stock is a very popular method of financing because of its flexibility. It provides advantages for the issuing company and the investors (stockholders). Investors are

Accounting for Your Decisions

You Are the Investor

You have the opportunity to buy a company's bonds that pay 8% interest or the same company's stock. The stock has paid an 8% dividend rate for the last few years. The company is a large, reputable firm and has been profitable during recent times. Should you be indifferent between the two alternatives?

ANS: Interest on bonds is a fixed obligation. Unless the company goes out of business, you can count on receiving the 8% interest if you invest in the bonds. Dividends on stock are not fixed. There is no guarantee that the company will continue to pay 8% as the dividend on your investment. If the company is not profitable, it may decrease the size of the dividend. On the other hand, if the company becomes more profitable, it may pay a larger dividend.

Exhibit 11-1

Advantages and Disadvantages of Stock versus Debt Financing

DECISION MAKING

Advantages of Financing with Stock

1. Flexibility → Dividends on stock can be increased in profitable years, reduced when the company is less profitable. Debt interest is fixed. (An advantage for issuing company)

2. Exchanges facilitate trading → Large companies have ready markets for stock through the stock exchanges. (An advantage for issuing company and investors) Sometimes debt is not as widely traded.

3. Return on investment → Stock generally provides a higher return in dividends and in growth than interest on debt. (An advantage for investors)

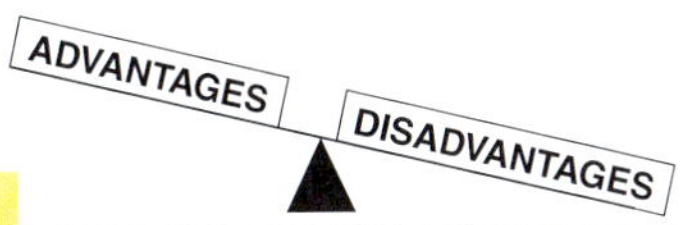

Disadvantages of Financing with Stock

1. Control → Issuing stock involves giving voting rights to new investors, less control of the company for existing stockholders. (A disadvantage for issuing company)

2. Tax consequences → Interest on debt is tax deductible for the issuing company, dividends on stock are not. (A disadvantage for issuing company)

3. Impact on ratios → Issuing stock decreases several important financial ratios, including earnings per share. (A disadvantage for issuing company)

primarily concerned with the return on their investment. With stock, the return may be in the form of dividends paid to the investors but may also be the price appreciation of the stock. Stock is popular because it generally provides a higher rate of return (but also a higher degree of risk) than can be obtained by creditors who receive interest from lending money. Stock is popular with issuing companies because dividends on stock can be adjusted according to the company's profitability; higher dividends can be paid when the firm is profitable and lower dividends when it is not. Interest on debt financing, on the other hand, is generally fixed and is a legal liability that cannot be adjusted when a company experiences lower profitability.

There are several disadvantages in issuing stock. Stock usually has voting rights, and issuing stock allows new investors to vote. Existing investors may not want to share the control of the company with new stockholders. From the issuing company's viewpoint, there is also a serious tax disadvantage to stock versus debt. As indicated in Chapter 10, interest on debt is tax deductible and results in lower taxes. Dividends on stock, on the other hand, are not tax deductible and do not result in tax savings to the issuing company. Finally, the following sections of this chapter indicate the impact that issuing stock has on the company's financial statements. Issuing stock decreases several important financial ratios, such as earnings per share. Issuing debt does not have a similar effect on the earnings per share ratio.

Management should consider many other factors in deciding between debt and equity financing. The company's goal should be financing the company in a manner that results in the lowest overall cost of capital to the firm. Usually, companies attain that goal by having a reasonable balance of both debt and equity financing.

Stockholders' Equity on the Balance Sheet

The basic accounting equation is often stated as follows:

Assets = Liabilities + Owners' Equity

Owners' equity is viewed as a residual amount. That is, the owners of a corporation have a claim to all assets after the claims represented by liabilities to creditors have been satisfied.

In this chapter, we concentrate on the corporate form of organization and refer to the owners' equity as *stockholders' equity*. Therefore, the basic accounting equation for a corporation can be restated as follows:

Assets = Liabilities + Stockholders' Equity

The stockholders are the owners of a corporation. They have a residual interest in its assets after the claims of all creditors have been satisfied.

The stockholders' equity category of all corporations has two major components or subcategories:

Total Stockholders' Equity = Contributed Capital + Retained Earnings

Contributed capital represents the amount the corporation has received from the sale of stock to stockholders. Retained earnings is the amount of net income that the corporation has earned but not paid as dividends. Instead, the corporation retains and reinvests the income.

Although all corporations maintain the two primary categories of contributed capital and retained earnings, within these categories they use a variety of accounts that have several alternative titles. The next section examines two important items: income and dividends, and their impact on the Retained Earnings account.

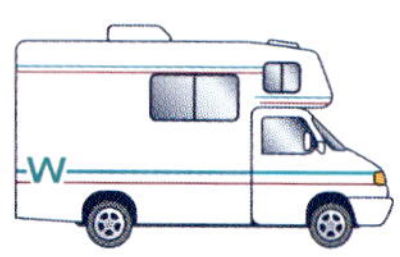

From Concept to Practice 11.1

Reading Winnebago Industries' Annual Report

Winnebago Industries' retained earnings is titled Reinvested Earnings. What was the balance of the reinvested earnings at the end of 2001? Did the balance increase from the end of 2000?

How Income and Dividends Affect Retained Earnings

The Retained Earnings account plays an important role because it serves as a link between the income statement and the balance sheet. The term *articulated statements* refers to the fact that the information on the income statement is related to the information on the balance sheet. The bridge (or link) between the two statements is the Retained Earnings account. Exhibit 11-2 presents this relationship graphically. As the exhibit indicates, the income statement is used to calculate a company's net income for a given period of time. The amount of the net income is transferred to the statement of retained earnings and is added to the beginning balance of retained earnings (with dividends deducted) to calculate the ending balance of retained earnings. The ending balance of retained earnings is the amount that is portrayed on the balance sheet in the stockholders' equity category. That is why you must always prepare the income statement before you prepare the balance sheet, as you have discovered when developing financial statements in previous chapters of the text.

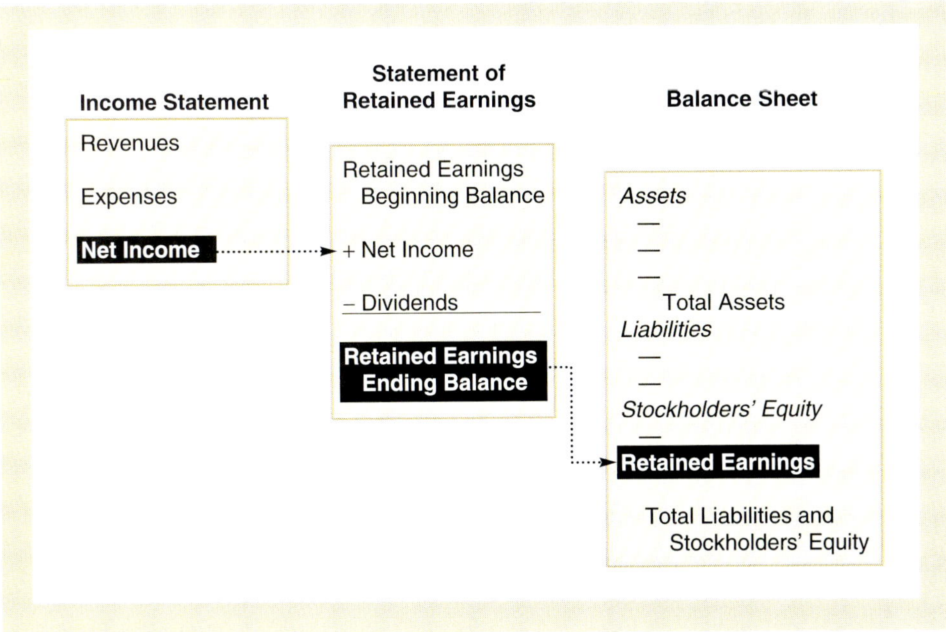

Exhibit 11-2

Retained Earnings Connects the Income Statement and the Balance Sheet

Identifying the Components of the Stockholders' Equity Section of the Balance Sheet

LO 1 Identify the components of the Stockholders' Equity category of the balance sheet and the accounts found in each component.

The liabilities and stockholders' equity portion of the balance sheet of AMR Corporation (American Airlines) is provided in Exhibit 11-3. We will focus on the Stockholders' (Shareholders') Equity category of the balance sheet. All corporations, including AMR, begin the Stockholders' Equity category with a list of the firm's contributed capital. In some cases, there are two categories of stock: common stock and preferred stock (the latter is discussed later in this chapter). Common stock normally carries voting rights. The common stockholders elect the officers of the corporation and establish its by-laws and governing rules. It is not unusual for corporations to have more than one type of common stock, each with different rights or terms. For example, Continental Airlines, Inc., one of AMR's competitors, has two classes of common stock listed on its 2001 balance sheet.

http://www.amrcorp.com

http://www.continental.com

Number of Shares It is important to determine the number of shares of stock for each stock account. Corporate balance sheets report the number of shares in three categories: **authorized, issued,** and **outstanding shares.**

To become incorporated, a business must develop articles of incorporation and apply to the proper state authorities for a corporate charter. The corporation must specify the maximum number of shares that it will be allowed to issue. This maximum number of shares is called the *authorized stock.* A corporation applies for authorization to issue many more shares than it will issue immediately, to allow for future growth and other events that may occur over its long life. For example, AMR Corporation indicates that it has 750,000,000 shares of common stock authorized but that only 182,278,766 shares had been issued as of December 31, 2001.

The number of shares *issued* indicates the number of shares that have been sold or transferred to stockholders. The number of shares issued does not necessarily mean, however, that those shares are currently outstanding. The term *outstanding* indicates shares actually in the hands of the stockholders. Shares that have been issued by the corporation and then repurchased are counted as shares issued but not as shares outstanding. Quite often corporations repurchase their own stock as treasury stock (explained in more detail later in this chapter). Treasury stock reduces the number of shares outstanding. The number of AMR's shares of common stock outstanding at December 31, 2001, could be calculated as follows:

Authorized shares The maximum number of shares a corporation may issue as indicated in the corporate charter.

Issued shares The number of shares sold or distributed to stockholders.

Outstanding shares The number of shares issued less the number of shares held as treasury stock.

Exhibit 11-3 AMR Corporation's Partial Balance Sheet

(in millions, except shares and par value)	December 31, 2001	2000
Liabilities and Stockholders' Equity		
Current Liabilities		
Accounts payable	$ 1,785	$ 1,267
Accrued salaries and wages	721	955
Accrued liabilities	1,471	1,276
Air traffic liability	2,763	2,696
Current maturities of long-term debt	556	569
Current obligations under capital leases	216	227
Total current liabilities	7,512	6,990
Long-Term Debt, Less Current Maturities	8,310	4,151
Obligations Under Capital Leases, Less Current Obligations	1,524	1,323
Other Liabilities and Credits		
Deferred income taxes	1,627	2,385
Deferred gains	520	508
Postretirement benefits	2,538	1,706
Other liabilities and deferred credits	5,437	1,974
	10,122	6,573
Commitments and Contingencies	—	—
Stockholders' Equity		
Preferred stock—20,000,000 shares authorized; None issued		
Common stock—$1 par value; 750,000,000 shares authorized; 182,278,766 shares issued	182	182
Additional paid-in capital	2,865	2,911
Treasury shares at cost: 2001—27,794,380; 2000—30,216,218	(1,716)	(1,865)
Accumulated other comprehensive loss	(146)	(2)
Retained earnings	4,188	5,950
	5,373	7,176
Total Liabilities and Stockholders' Equity	$ 32,841	$ 26,213

AMR's contributed capital

Study Tip

Treasury stock is included in the number of shares issued. It is not part of the number of shares outstanding.

Number of shares issued	182,278,766
Less: Treasury stock	27,794,380
Number of shares outstanding	154,484,386

Par value An arbitrary amount that represents the legal capital of the firm.

Par Value: The Firm's "Legal Capital" The Stockholders' Equity category of many balance sheets refers to an amount as the *par value* of the stock. For example, AMR's common stock has a par value of $1 per share. **Par value** is an arbitrary amount stated on the face of the stock certificate and represents the legal capital of the corporation. Most corporations set the par value of the stock at very low amounts because there are legal difficulties if stock is sold at less than par. Therefore, par value does not indicate the stock's value or the amount that is obtained when it is sold on the stock exchange; it is simply an arbitrary amount that exists to fulfill legal requirements. A company's legal requirement depends on its state of incorporation. Some states do not require corporations to indicate a par value; others require them to designate the *stated value* of the stock. A stated value is accounted for in the same manner as a par value and appears in the Stockholders' Equity category in the same manner as a par value.

The amount of the par value is the amount that is presented in the stock account. That is, the dollar amount in a firm's stock account can be calculated as its par value per share times number of shares issued. For AMR, the dollar amount appearing in the common stock account can be calculated as follows:

$1 Par Value per Share × 182,278,766 Shares Issued =
$182 million (rounded to millions) Balance in the Common Stock Account

Additional Paid-in Capital The dollar amounts of the stock accounts in the Stockholders' Equity category do not indicate the amount that was received when the stock was sold to stockholders. The Common Stock and Preferred Stock accounts indicate only the par value of the stock. When stock is issued for an amount higher than the par value, the excess is reported as **additional paid-in capital.** Several alternative titles are used for this account, including Paid-in Capital in Excess of Par, Capital Surplus (an old term that should no longer be used), and Premium on Stock. Regardless of the title, the account represents the amount received in excess of par when stock was issued.

Additional paid-in capital The amount received for the issuance of stock in excess of the par value of the stock.

AMR's balance sheet indicates additional paid-in capital of $2,865 million at December 31, 2001. AMR, as well as many other corporations, presents only one amount for additional paid-in capital for all stock transactions. Therefore, we are unable to determine whether the amount resulted from the issuance of common stock or other stock transactions. As a result, it is often impossible to determine the issue price of each category of stock even with a careful analysis of the balance sheet and the accompanying notes.

Retained Earnings: The Amount *Not* Paid as Dividends **Retained earnings** represents net income that the firm has earned but has *not* paid as dividends. Remember that retained earnings is an amount that is accumulated over the entire life of the corporation and does not represent the income or dividends for a specific year. For example, the balance of the Retained Earnings account on AMR's balance sheet at December 31, 2001, is $4,188 million. That does not mean that AMR

Retained earnings Net income that has been made by the corporation but not paid out as dividends.

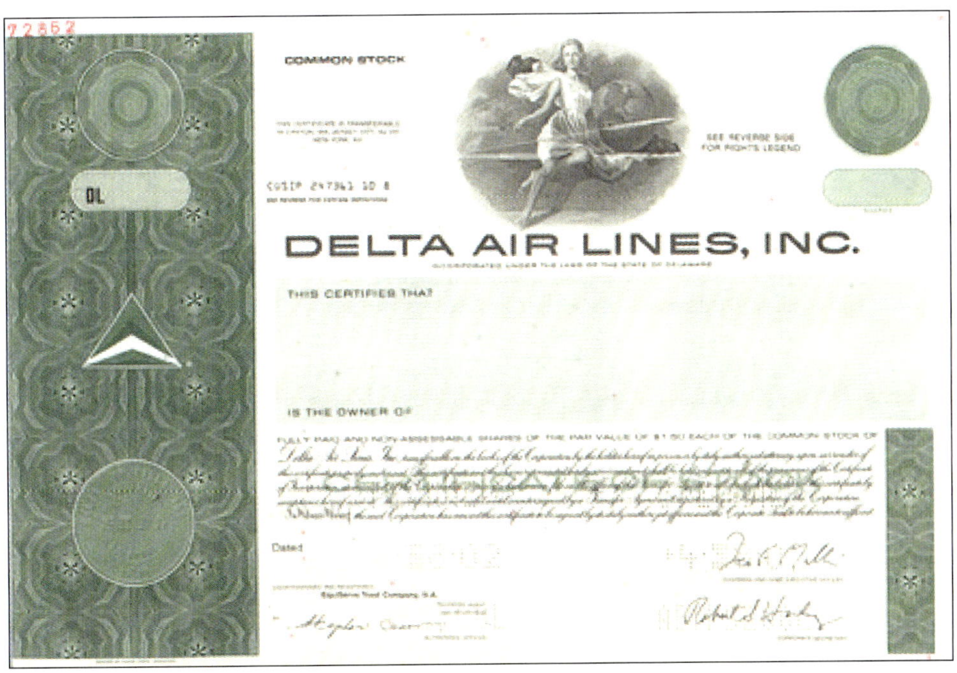

A prospective stockholder may purchase shares and receive certificates, like this one, either directly from the company or through a stockbroker. Usually, a broker purchases shares in its own name for the investor's account—and the investor never sees a certificate.

Business Strategy

Strategic Handling for Value Creation

Delta Air Lines has always had a long-term strategy for increasing the value of the company to its shareholders, but it had to adjust its short-term strategy drastically and quickly in response to the tragedy of September 11, 2001. It was forced to cut its flight schedule, remove many of its aircraft from active service, reduce staff, and request personnel to retire early. Contracts for facilities were modified or canceled, and technology projects were delayed.

All of these actions had an impact on the financial results of 2001. The company recorded a loss of $1.1 billion related to asset write-downs and other "nonrecurring costs" such as severance pay and early retirement incentives. However, this loss was partially offset by a payment received from the federal government. The Stabilization Act of 2001 provided payments to the airlines to compensate for their losses and to benefit the travel industry. Delta received a payment of $634 million as its share, but the payment presented an interesting accounting issue. How should it have been presented on the financial statements? Delta chose to report the amount as a "gain" on its 2001 income statement and provided an extensive note to explain the amount received. ■

Source: Delta Air Lines Management Discussion and Analysis in 2001 Annual Report.

had a net income of this amount in 2001; it simply means that over the life of the corporation, AMR has retained $4,188 million more net income than it paid out as dividends to stockholders.

It is also important to remember that the balance of the Retained Earnings account does not mean that liquid assets of that amount are available to the stockholders. Corporations decide to retain income because they have needs other than paying dividends to stockholders. The needs may include the purchase of assets, the retirement of debt, or other financial needs. Money spent for those needs usually benefits the stockholders in the long run, but liquid assets equal to the balance of the Retained Earnings account are not necessarily available to stockholders. In theory, income should be retained whenever the company can reinvest the money and get a better return within the business than the shareholders can get on their own. In summary, retained earnings is a stockholders' equity account. Although the company's assets have increased, retained earnings does not represent a pool of liquid assets.

WHAT IS PREFERRED STOCK?

LO 2 Demonstrate an understanding of the characteristics of common and preferred stock and the differences between the classes of stock.

Many companies have a class of stock called *preferred stock*. One of the advantages of preferred stock is the flexibility it provides because its terms and provisions can be tailored to meet the firm's needs. These terms and provisions are detailed in the stock certificate. Generally, preferred stock offers holders a preference to dividends declared by the corporation. That is, if dividends are declared, the preferred stockholders must receive dividends first, before the holders of common stock.

The dividend rate on preferred stock may be stated in two ways. First, it may be stated as a percentage of the stock's par value. For example, if a stock is presented on the balance sheet as $100 par, 7% preferred stock, its dividend rate is $7 per share ($100 times 7%). Second, the dividend may be stated as a per-share amount. For example, a stock may appear on the balance sheet as $100 par, $7 preferred stock, meaning that the dividend rate is $7 per share. Investors in common stock should note the dividend requirements of the preferred shareholder. The greater the obligation to the preferred shareholder, the less desirable the common stock becomes.

From Concept to Practice 11.2

Reading Delta's Annual Report

Which financial statements could you look at to identify the different classes of stock issued by Delta? Which classes of stock are issued? How many shares have been issued?

Several important provisions of preferred stock relate to the payment of dividends. Some preferred stock issues have a **cumulative feature,** which means that if a dividend is not declared to the preferred stockholders in one year, dividends are considered to be *in arrears.* Before a dividend can be declared to common stockholders in a subsequent period, the preferred stockholders must be paid all dividends in arrears as well as the current year's dividend. The cumulative feature ensures that the preferred stockholders will receive a dividend before one is paid to common stockholders. It does not guarantee a dividend to preferred stockholders, however. There is no legal requirement mandating that a corporation declare a dividend, and preferred stockholders have a legal right to receive a dividend only when it has been declared.

Cumulative feature The right to dividends in arrears before the current-year dividend is distributed.

Some preferred stocks have a **participating feature.** Its purpose is to allow the preferred stockholders to receive a dividend in excess of the regular rate when a firm has been particularly profitable and declares an abnormally large dividend. When the participating feature is present and a firm declares a dividend, the preferred stockholders first have a right to the current year's dividend, and then the common stockholders must receive an equal portion (usually based on the par or stated value of the stocks) of the dividend. The participating feature then applies to any dividend declared in excess of the amounts in the first two steps. The preferred stockholders are allowed to share in the excess, normally on the basis of the total par value of the preferred and common stock. The participating feature is explained in more detail in the section of this chapter concerning dividends.

Participating feature Allows preferred stockholders to share on a percentage basis in the distribution of an abnormally large dividend.

Preferred stock may also be convertible or callable. The **convertible feature** allows the preferred stockholders to convert their stockholdings to common stock. Convertible preferred stock offers stockholders the advantages of the low risk generally associated with preferred stock and the possibility of the higher return that is associated with common stock. The **callable feature** allows the issuing firm to retire the stock after it has been issued. Normally, the call price is specified as a fixed dollar amount. Firms may exercise the call option to eliminate a certain class of preferred stock so that control of the corporation is maintained in the hands of fewer stockholders. The call option also may be exercised when the dividend rate on the preferred stock is too high and other, more cost-effective financing alternatives are available.

Convertible feature Allows preferred stock to be exchanged for common stock.

Callable feature Allows the firm to eliminate a class of stock by paying the stockholders a specified amount.

Preferred stock is attractive to many investors because it offers a return in the form of a dividend at a level of risk that is lower than that of most common stocks. Usually, the dividend available on preferred stock is more stable from year to year, and as a result, the market price of the stock is also more stable. In fact, if preferred stock carries certain provisions, the stock is very similar to bonds or notes payable. Management must evaluate whether such securities really represent debt and should be presented in the liability category of the balance sheet or whether they represent equity and should be presented in the equity category. Such a decision involves the concept of *substance over form.* That is, a company must look not only at the legal form but also at the economic substance of the security to decide whether it is debt or equity.

ISSUANCE OF STOCK

Stock Issued for Cash

Stock may be issued in several different ways. It may be issued for cash or for noncash assets. When stock is issued for cash, the amount of its par value should be reported in the stock account and the amount in excess of par should be reported in

LO 3 Determine the financial statement impact when stock is issued for cash or for other consideration.

an additional paid-in capital account. For example, assume that on July 1 a firm issued 1,000 shares of $10 par common stock for $15 per share. The transaction is recorded as follows:

July 1	Cash	15,000	
	Common Stock		10,000
	Additional Paid-in Capital—Common		5,000
	To record the issuance of 1,000 shares of $10 common stock at $15 per share.		

Assets	=	Liabilities	+	Owners' Equity
+15,000				+10,000
				+5,000

As noted earlier, the Common Stock account and the Additional Paid-in Capital account are both presented in the Stockholders' Equity category of the balance sheet and represent the contributed capital component of the corporation.

If no-par stock is issued, the corporation does not distinguish between common stock and additional paid-in capital. If the firm in the previous example had issued no-par stock on July 1 for $15 per share, the entire amount of $15,000 would be presented in the Common Stock account and would be recorded as follows:

July 1	Cash	15,000	
	Common Stock		15,000
	To record the issuance of 1,000 shares of no-par common stock at $15 per share.		

Assets	=	Liabilities	+	Owners' Equity
+15,000				+15,000

Stock Issued for Noncash Consideration

Occasionally, stock is issued in return for something other than cash. For example, a corporation may issue stock to obtain land or buildings. When such a transaction occurs, the company faces the difficult task of deciding what value to place on the transaction. This is especially difficult when the market values of the elements of the transaction are not known with complete certainty. According to the general guideline, the transaction should be reported at fair market value. Market value may be indicated by the value of the consideration given (stock) or the value of the consideration received (property), whichever can be most readily determined.

Assume that on July 1 a firm issued 500 shares of $10 par preferred stock to acquire a building. The stock is not widely traded, and the current market value of the stock is not evident. The building has recently been appraised by an independent firm as having a market value of $12,000. In this case, the issuance of the stock should be recorded as follows:

July 1	Building	12,000	
	Preferred Stock		5,000
	Additional Paid-in Capital—Preferred		7,000
	To record the issuance of preferred stock for building.		

Assets	=	Liabilities	+	Owners' Equity
+12,000				+5,000
				+7,000

In other situations, the market value of the stock may be more readily determined and should be used as the best measure of the value of the transaction. Market value may be represented by the current stock-market quotation or by a recent cash sale of the stock. The company should attempt to develop the best estimate of the market value of the noncash transaction and should neither intentionally overstate nor intentionally understate the assets received by the issuance of stock.

WHAT IS TREASURY STOCK?

LO 4 Describe the financial statement impact of stock treated as treasury stock.

Treasury stock Stock issued by the firm and then repurchased but not retired.

The Stockholders' Equity category of AMR's balance sheet in Exhibit 11-3 includes **treasury stock** in the amount of $1,716 million. The Treasury Stock account is created when a corporation buys its own stock sometime after issuing it. For an amount to be treated as treasury stock, (1) it must be the corporation's own stock, (2) it must have been issued to the stockholders at some point, (3) it must have been repurchased from the stockholders, and (4) it must not be retired but must be held for some purpose. Treasury stock is not considered outstanding stock and does not have voting rights.

A corporation may repurchase stock as treasury stock for several reasons. The most common is to have stock available to distribute to employees for bonuses or as part of an employee-benefit plan. Firms also may buy treasury stock to maintain a favorable market price for the stock or to improve the appearance of the firm's financial ratios. More recently, firms have purchased their stock to maintain control of the ownership and to prevent unwanted takeover or buyout attempts. Of course, the lower the stock price, the more likely a company is to buy back its own stock and wait for the shares to rise in value before reissuing them.

The two methods to account for treasury stock transactions are the cost method and the par value method. We will present the more commonly used cost method. Assume that the Stockholders' Equity section of Rezin Company's balance sheet on December 31, 2003, appears as follows:

Common stock, $10 par value,	
1,000 shares issued and outstanding	$10,000
Additional paid-in capital—Common	12,000
Retained earnings	15,000
Total stockholders' equity	$37,000

Assume that on February 1, 2004, Rezin buys 100 of its shares as treasury stock at $25 per share. Rezin records the following transaction at that time:

Feb. 1	Treasury Stock	2,500	
	Cash		2,500
	To record the purchase of 100 shares of treasury stock.		

Assets	=	Liabilities	+	Owners' Equity
−2,500				−2,500

The purchase of treasury stock does not directly affect the Common Stock account itself. The Treasury Stock account is considered to be a contra account and is subtracted from the total of contributed capital and retained earnings in the Stockholders' Equity section. Treasury Stock is *not* an asset account. When a company buys its own stock, it is contracting its size and reducing the equity of stockholders. Therefore, Treasury Stock is a contra-equity account, not an asset.

The Stockholders' Equity section of Rezin's balance sheet on February 1, 2004, after the purchase of the treasury stock, appears as follows:

Common stock, $10 par value,	
1,000 shares issued, 900 outstanding	$10,000
Additional paid-in capital—Common	12,000
Retained earnings	15,000
Total contributed capital and retained earnings	$37,000
Less: Treasury stock, 100 shares at cost	2,500
Total stockholders' equity	$34,500

Corporations may choose to reissue stock to investors after it has been held as treasury stock. When treasury stock is resold for more than it cost, the difference between the sales price and the cost appears in the Additional Paid-in Capital—Treasury Stock account. For example, if Rezin resold 100 shares of treasury stock on May 1, 2004, for $30 per share, the Treasury Stock account would be reduced by $2,500 (100 shares times $25 per share), and the Additional Paid-in Capital—Treasury Stock account would be increased by $500 (100 shares times the difference between the purchase price of $25 and the reissue price of $30).

When treasury stock is resold for an amount less than its cost, the difference between the sales price and the cost is deducted from the Additional Paid-in Capital—Treasury Stock account. If that account does not exist, the difference should be deducted from the Retained Earnings account. For example, assume that Rezin Company had resold 100 shares of treasury stock on May 1, 2004, for $20 per share, instead of $30 in the previous example. In this example, Rezin has had no other treasury stock transactions, and therefore, no balance existed in the Additional Paid-in Capital—Treasury Stock account. Rezin would then reduce the Treasury Stock account by $2,500 (100 shares times $25 per share) and would reduce Retained Earnings by $500 (100 shares times the difference between the purchase price of $25 and the reissue price of $20 per share). Thus, the Additional Paid-in Capital—Treasury Stock account may have a positive balance, but entries that result in a negative balance in the account should not be made.

Note that *income statement accounts are never involved* in treasury stock transactions. Regardless of whether treasury stock is reissued for more or less than its cost, the effect is reflected in the stockholders' equity accounts. It is simply not possible for a firm to engage in transactions involving its own stock and have the result affect the performance of the firm as reflected on the income statement.

Two-Minute Review

1. *Where does the Treasury Stock account appear on the balance sheet?*
2. *What is the effect on stockholders' equity when stock is purchased as treasury stock?*
3. *How does treasury stock affect the number of shares issued and outstanding?*

Answers on page 578.

RETIREMENT OF STOCK

Retirement of stock When the stock is repurchased with no intention to reissue at a later date.

Retirement of stock occurs when a corporation buys back stock after it has been issued to investors and does not intend to reissue the stock. Retirement often occurs because the corporation wants to eliminate a particular class of stock or a particular group of stockholders. When stock is repurchased and retired, the balances of the stock account and the paid-in capital account that were created when the stock was issued must be eliminated. When the original issue price is higher than the repurchase price of the stock, the difference is reflected in the Paid-in Capital from Stock Retirement account. When the repurchase price of the stock is more than the original issue price, the difference reduces the Retained Earnings account. The general principle for retirement of stock is the same as for treasury stock transactions. No income statement accounts are affected by the retirement. The effect is reflected in the Cash account and the stockholders' equity accounts.

DIVIDENDS: DISTRIBUTION OF INCOME TO SHAREHOLDERS

Cash Dividends

Corporations may declare and issue several different types of dividends, the most common of which is a cash dividend to stockholders. Cash dividends may be declared quarterly, annually, or at other intervals. Normally, cash dividends are declared on one date, referred to as the *date of declaration,* and are paid out on a later date, referred to as the *payment date.* The dividend is paid to the stockholders that own the stock as of a particular date, the *date of record.*

Generally, two requirements must be met before the board of directors can declare a cash dividend. First, sufficient cash must be available by the payment date to pay to the stockholders. Second, the Retained Earnings account must have a sufficient positive balance. Dividends reduce the balance of the account, and therefore Retained Earnings must have a balance before the dividend declaration. Most firms have an established policy concerning the portion of income that will be declared as dividends. The **dividend payout ratio** is calculated as the annual dividend amount divided by the annual net income. The dividend payout ratios of three members of the retail industry are given in Exhibit 11-4. The dividend payout ratio for many firms is 50% or 60% and seldom exceeds 70%. Typically, utilities pay a high proportion of their earnings. In contrast, fast-growing companies in technology often pay nothing to shareholders. Some investors want and need the current income of a high-dividend payout, but others would rather not receive dividend income and prefer to gamble that the stock price will appreciate.

Dividend payout ratio The annual dividend amount divided by the annual net income.

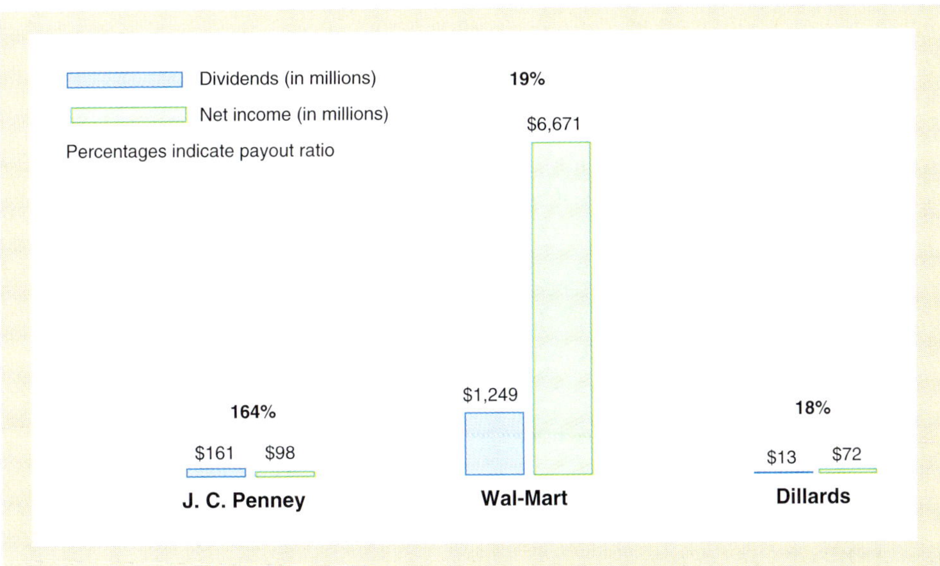

Exhibit 11-4

2001 Dividend Payout Ratios to Common Stockholders in the Retail Industry

http://www.jcpenney.com
http://www.walmart.com
http://www.dillards.com

Cash dividends become a liability on the date they are declared. An accounting entry should be recorded on that date to acknowledge the liability and reduce the balance of the Retained Earnings account. For example, assume that on July 1 the board of directors of Grant Company declared a cash dividend of $7,000 to be paid on September 1. Grant reflects the declaration as a reduction of Retained Earnings and an increase in Cash Dividend Payable as follows:

July 1	Retained Earnings	7,000	
	Cash Dividend Payable		7,000
	To record the declaration of a cash dividend.		

Assets	=	Liabilities	+	Owners' Equity
		+7,000		−7,000

Study Tip

A dividend is not an expense on the income statement. It is a reduction of retained earnings and appears on the retained earnings statement. If it is a cash dividend, it also reduces the cash balance when paid.

The Cash Dividend Payable account is a liability and is normally shown in the Current Liabilities section of the balance sheet.

Grant records the following accounting transaction on September 1 when the cash dividend is paid:

Sept. 1	Cash Dividend Payable	7,000	
	Cash		7,000
	To record the payment of a cash dividend.		

Assets	=	Liabilities	+	Owners' Equity
−7,000		−7,000		

The important point to remember is that dividends reduce the amount of retained earnings *when declared.* When dividends are paid, the company reduces the liability to stockholders reflected in the Cash Dividend Payable account.

Cash Dividends for Preferred and Common Stock

LO 5 Compute the amount of cash dividends when a firm has issued both preferred and common stock.

When cash dividends involving more than one class of stock are declared, the corporation must determine the proper amount to allocate to each class of stock. As indicated earlier, the amount of dividends that preferred stockholders have rights to depends on the terms and provisions of the preferred stock. We will illustrate the proper allocation of cash dividends with an example of a firm that has two classes of stock, preferred and common.

Assume that on December 31, 2004, Stricker Company has outstanding 10,000 shares of $10 par, 8% preferred stock and 40,000 shares of $5 par common stock. Stricker was unable to declare a dividend in 2002 or 2003 but wants to declare a $70,000 dividend for 2004. The dividend is to be allocated to preferred and common stockholders in accordance with the terms of the stock agreements.

Noncumulative Preferred Stock If the terms of the stock agreement indicate that the preferred stock is not cumulative, the preferred stockholders do not have a right to dividends in arrears. The dividends that were not declared in 2002 and 2003 are simply lost and do not affect the distribution of the dividend in 2004. Therefore, the cash dividend declared in 2004 is allocated between preferred and common stockholders as follows:

	TO PREFERRED	TO COMMON
Step 1: Distribute current year dividend to preferred (10,000 shares × $10 par × 8% × 1 year)	$8,000	
Step 2: Distribute remaining dividend to common ($70,000 − $8,000)		$62,000
Total allocated	$8,000	$62,000
Dividend per share		
Preferred: $8,000/10,000 shares	$0.80	
Common: $62,000/40,000 shares		$1.55

Cumulative Preferred Stock If the terms of the stock agreement indicate that the preferred stock is cumulative, the preferred stockholders have a right to dividends in arrears before the current year's dividend is distributed. Therefore, Stricker performs the following steps:

	TO PREFERRED	TO COMMON
Step 1: Distribute dividends in arrears to preferred (10,000 shares × $10 par × 8% × 2 years)	$16,000	
Step 2: Distribute current-year dividend to preferred (10,000 shares × $10 par × 8% × 1 year)	8,000	
Step 3: Distribute remainder to common ($70,000 − $24,000)		$46,000
Total allocated	$24,000	$46,000
Dividend per share		
Preferred: $24,000/10,000 shares	$2.40	
Common: $46,000/40,000 shares		$1.15

Cumulative and Participating Preferred Stock If the terms of the stock agreement indicate that the preferred stock is both cumulative and participating, the preferred stockholders have a right to dividends in arrears (the cumulative feature) and to a portion of the current year's dividend that exceeds a specified amount (the participating feature). Assume that Stricker Company preferred stockholders participate in any dividend in excess of 8% of total par value and that the participation is based on the proportion of the total par value of the preferred and common stock. The 2004 dividend is distributed as follows:

	TO PREFERRED	TO COMMON
Step 1: Distribute dividend in arrears to preferred		
(10,000 shares × \$10 par × 8% × 2 years)	\$16,000	
Step 2: Distribute current-year dividend to preferred		
(10,000 shares × \$10 par × 8% × 1 year)	8,000	
Step 3: Distribute equal percentage to common		
(40,000 shares × \$5 par × 8%)		\$16,000
Step 4: Remainder to preferred and common on basis of total par value		
Preferred:		
(\$70,000 − \$40,000) × \$100,000[a]/\$300,000	10,000	
Common:		
(\$70,000 − \$40,000) × \$200,000[b]/\$300,000		20,000
Total allocated	\$34,000	\$36,000
Dividend per share		
Preferred: \$34,000/10,000 shares	\$3.40	
Common: \$36,000/40,000 shares		\$0.90

[a]10,000 shares × \$10 par
[b]40,000 shares × \$5 par

The Stricker Company example illustrates the flexibility available with preferred stock. The provisions and terms of the preferred stock can be established to make the stock attractive to investors and to provide an effective form of financing for the corporation. The cumulative and participating features make the preferred stock more attractive. However, these features may make the *common stock* less attractive because more dividends for the preferred stockholders may mean less dividends for the common stockholders.

Stock Dividends

LO 6 Demonstrate an understanding of the difference between cash and stock dividends and the effect of stock dividends.

Stock dividend The issuance of additional shares of stock to existing stockholders.

Cash dividends are the most popular and widely used form of dividend, but corporations may at times use stock dividends instead of, or in addition to, cash dividends. A **stock dividend** occurs when a corporation declares and issues additional shares of its own stock to its existing stockholders. Firms use stock dividends for several reasons. First, a corporation may simply not have sufficient cash available to declare a cash dividend. Stock dividends do not require the use of the corporation's resources and allow cash to be retained for other purposes. Second, stock dividends result in additional shares of stock outstanding and may decrease the market price per share of stock if the dividend is large (small stock dividends tend to have little effect on market price). The lower price may make the stock more attractive to a wider range of investors and allow enhanced financing opportunities. Finally, stock dividends normally do not represent taxable income to the recipients and may be attractive to some wealthy stockholders.

Similar to cash dividends, stock dividends are normally declared by the board of directors on a specific date, and the stock is distributed to the stockholders at a later date. The corporation recognizes the stock dividend on the date of declaration. Assume that Shah Company's Stockholders' Equity category of the balance sheet appears as follows as of January 1, 2004:

Common stock, $10 par,	
5,000 shares issued and outstanding	$ 50,000
Additional paid-in capital—Common	30,000
Retained earnings	70,000
Total stockholders' equity	$150,000

Assume that on January 2, 2004, Shah declares a 10% stock dividend to common stockholders to be distributed on April 1, 2004. Small stock dividends (usually those of 20 to 25% or less) normally are recorded at the *market value* of the stock as of the date of declaration. Assume that Shah's common stock is selling at $40 per share on that date. Therefore, the total market value of the stock dividend is $20,000 (10% of 5,000 shares outstanding, or 500 shares, times $40 per share). Shah records the transaction on the date of declaration as follows, with the par value per share recorded in the Common Stock Dividend Distributable account:

Jan. 2	Retained Earnings	20,000	
	Additional Paid-in Capital—Common		15,000
	Common Stock Dividend Distributable		5,000
	To record the declaration of a stock dividend.		

Assets	=	Liabilities	+	Owners' Equity
				−20,000
				+15,000
				+5,000

The Common Stock Dividend Distributable account represents shares of stock to be issued; it is not a liability account because no cash or assets are to be distributed to the stockholders. Thus, it should be treated as an account in the Stockholders' Equity section of the balance sheet and is a part of the contributed capital component of equity.

Note that the declaration of a stock dividend does not affect the total stockholders' equity of the corporation, although the retained earnings are reduced. That is, the Stockholders' Equity section of Shah's balance sheet on January 2, 2004, is as follows after the declaration of the dividend:

Common stock, $10 par,	
5,000 shares issued and outstanding	$ 50,000
Common stock dividend distributable, 500 shares	5,000
Additional paid-in capital—Common	45,000
Retained earnings	50,000
Total stockholders' equity	$150,000

The account balances are different, but total stockholders' equity is $150,000 both before and after the declaration of the stock dividend. In effect, retained earnings has been capitalized (transferred permanently to the contributed capital accounts). When a corporation actually issues a stock dividend, it is necessary to transfer an amount from the Stock Dividend Distributable account to the appropriate stock account.

Our stock dividend example has illustrated the general rule that stock dividends should be reported at fair market value. That is, in the transaction to reflect the stock dividend, retained earnings is decreased in the amount of the fair market value per share of the stock times the number of shares to be distributed. When a large stock dividend is declared, however, accountants do not follow the general rule we have illustrated. A large stock dividend is a stock dividend of more than 20% to 25% of the number of shares of stock outstanding. In that case, the stock dividend is reported at *par value* rather than at fair market value. That is, Retained Earnings is decreased in the amount of the par value per share times the number of shares to be distributed.

Refer again to the Shah Company example. Assume that instead of a 10% dividend, on January 2, 2004, Shah declares and distributes a 100% stock dividend to be distributed on April 1, 2004. The stock dividend results in 5,000 additional shares being issued and certainly meets the definition of a large stock dividend. Shah records the following transaction on January 2, the date of declaration:

Jan. 2	Retained Earnings	50,000	
	Common Stock Dividend Distributable		50,000
	To record the declaration of a large stock dividend.		

Assets	=	Liabilities	+	Owners' Equity
				−50,000
				+50,000

The accounting transaction to be recorded when the stock is actually distributed is as follows:

Apr. 1	Common Stock Dividend Distributable	50,000	
	Common Stock		50,000
	To record the distribution of a stock dividend.		

Assets	=	Liabilities	+	Owners' Equity
				−50,000
				+50,000

The Stockholders' Equity category of Shah's balance sheet as of April 1 after the stock dividend is as follows:

Common stock, $10 par,	
10,000 shares issued and outstanding	$100,000
Additional paid-in capital—Common	30,000
Retained earnings	20,000
Total stockholders' equity	$150,000

Again, you should note that the stock dividend has not affected total stockholders' equity. Shah has $150,000 of stockholders' equity both before and after the stock dividend. The difference between large and small stock dividends is the amount transferred from retained earnings to the contributed capital portion of equity.

Stock Splits

LO 7 Determine the difference between stock dividends and stock splits.

Stock split The creation of additional shares of stock with a reduction of the par value of the stock.

A **stock split** is similar to a stock dividend in that it results in additional shares of stock outstanding and is nontaxable. In fact, firms may use a stock split for nearly the same reasons as a stock dividend: to increase the number of shares, reduce the market price per share, and make the stock more accessible to a wider range of investors. There is an important legal difference, however. Stock dividends do not affect the par value per share of the stock, whereas stock splits reduce the par value per share. There also is an important accounting difference. An accounting transaction is *not recorded* when a corporation declares and executes a stock split. None of the stockholders' equity accounts are affected by the split. Rather, the note information accompanying the balance sheet must disclose the additional shares and the reduction of the par value per share.

Return to the Shah Company example. Assume that on January 2, 2004, Shah issued a 2-for-1 stock split instead of a stock dividend. The split results in an additional 5,000 shares of stock outstanding but should not be recorded in a formal accounting transaction. Therefore, the Stockholders' Equity section of Shah Company immediately after the stock split on January 2, 2004, is as follows:

Common stock, $5 par,	
10,000 shares issued and outstanding	$ 50,000
Additional paid-in capital—Common	30,000
Retained earnings	70,000
Total stockholders' equity	$150,000

You should note that the par value per share has been reduced from $10 to $5 per share of stock as a result of the split. Like a stock dividend, the split does not affect total stockholders' equity because no assets have been transferred. Therefore, the split simply results in more shares of stock with claims to the same net assets of the firm.

http://www.bestbuy.com

Exhibit 11-5 presents the stockholders' equity category of **Best Buy Co. Inc.'s** balance sheets as of March 3, 2001. At that time, the company had 208,138,000 shares of common stock outstanding. During 2002, the company declared a 3-for-2 stock split. That means that every stockholder that was holding two shares of stock before the stock split had three shares of stock after the split. The effect of the stock split was to increase the number of shares of stock by 3/2. Thus, if there were 208,138,000 shares of stock at the time of the split (the number could have changed slightly after the balance sheet date in the exhibit), the number of shares after the split would have been 208,138,000 × 3/2, or 312,207,000. However, each stockholder still had the same *proportional* ownership of the company. When a company has a stock split, it restates the number of shares for all previous years also. Although a stock split does not increase the wealth of the shareholder, it is usually a good sign. Companies with rising stock prices declare a stock split to make the stock more marketable to the small investor, who would be more likely to buy a stock at $50 per share than at $100.

Exhibit 11-5 Best Buy's Stockholders' Equity Section

CONSOLIDATED BALANCE SHEETS

(in thousands, except per share amounts)	March 3, 2001	Feb. 26, 2000
Shareholders' equity:		
Preferred stock, $1.00 par value: Authorized—400,000 shares; issued and outstanding—none	—	—
Common stock, $.10 par value: Authorized—1,000,000,000 shares; issued and outstanding—208,138,000 and 200,379,000 shares, respectively	20,814	20,038
Additional paid-in capital	576,818	247,490
Retained earnings	1,224,296	828,457
Total shareholders' equity	1,821,928	1,095,985

Shares outstanding before stock split

STATEMENT OF STOCKHOLDERS' EQUITY

LO 8 Demonstrate an understanding of the statement of stockholders' equity and comprehensive income.

In addition to a balance sheet, an income statement, and a cash flow statement, many annual reports contain a **statement of stockholders' equity.** The purpose of this statement is to explain all the reasons for the difference between the beginning and the ending balance of each of the accounts in the Stockholders' Equity category of the balance sheet. Of course, if the only changes are the result of income and dividends, a statement of retained earnings is sufficient. When other changes have occurred in stockholders' equity accounts, this more complete statement is necessary.

The statement of stockholders' equity of **Walgreens** is presented in Exhibit 11-6 for the year 2001. The statement starts with the beginning balances of each of the accounts as of August 31, 2000. Walgreens stockholders' equity is presented in four categories (the columns on the statement) as of August 31, 2000, as follows (in millions):

Statement of stockholders' equity Reflects the differences between beginning and ending balances for all accounts in the Stockholders' Equity category of the balance sheet.

http://www.walgreens.com

Number of shares	1,010,818,890
Common stock	$79.0
Paid-in capital	$367.2
Retained earnings	$3,787.8

Exhibit 11-6 Walgreens' Statement of Stockholders' Equity, 2001

Walgreens Co. and Subsidiaries
For the Year Ended August 31, 2001

(Dollars in millions, except per share data)

	Shareholders' Equity	Common Stock Shares	Common Stock Amount	Paid-In Capital*	Retained Earnings
	Balance, August 31, 2000	1,010,818,890	$79.0	$367.2	$3,787.8
1	Net earnings	—	—	—	885.6
2	Cash dividends declared ($0.14 per share)	—	—	—	(142.5)
3	Employee stock purchase and option plans	8,606,162	0.6	229.5	—
	Balance, August 31, 2001	1,019,425,052	$79.6	$596.7	$4,530.9

*This represents additional paid-in capital and is a good example of how terminology varies from company to company.

The statement of stockholders' equity indicates the items or events that affected stockholders' equity during 2001. The items or events were as follows:

ITEM OR EVENT	EFFECT ON STOCKHOLDERS' EQUITY
Net earnings →	Increased retained earnings by $885.6 million
Dividends →	Decreased retained earnings by $142.5 million
Shares issued →	Increased common stock by $0.6 million and Increased paid-in capital by $229.5 million

The last line of the statement of stockholders' equity indicates the ending balances of the stockholders' equity accounts as of the balance sheet date, August 31, 2001. You should note that each of the stockholders' equity accounts increased during 2001. The statement of stockholders' equity is useful in explaining the reasons for the changes that occurred.

WHAT IS COMPREHENSIVE INCOME?

There has always been some question about which items or transactions should be shown on the income statement and should be included in the calculation of net income. Generally, the accounting rule-making bodies have held that the income statement should reflect an *all-inclusive* approach. That is, all events and transactions that affect income should be shown on the income statement. This approach prevents the manipulation of the income figure by those who would like to show "good news" on the income statement and "bad news" directly on the retained earnings statement or the statement of stockholders' equity. The result of the all-inclusive approach is that the income statement includes items that are not necessarily under management's control, such as losses from natural disasters, and thus the income statement may not be a true reflection of a company's future potential.

The FASB has accepted certain exceptions to the all-inclusive approach and has allowed items to be recorded directly to the stockholders' equity category. This text has discussed one such item: unrealized gains and losses on investment securities. Exhibit 11-7 presents several additional items that are beyond the scope of this text. Items such as these have been excluded from the income statement for various reasons. Quite often, the justification is a concern for the volatility of the net income number. The items we have cited are often large dollar amounts; if included in the income statement, they would cause income to fluctuate widely from period to period. Therefore, the income statement is deemed to be more useful if the items are excluded.

Exhibit 11-7 The Relationship of the Income Statement and Statement of Comprehensive Income

Income Statement For Year Ended December 31, 20XX	
Revenues	xxx
Expenses	xxx
Other gains and losses	xxx
Income before tax	xxx
Income tax expense	xxx
Net income	xxx

All Inclusive Earnings
These items, *excluded* from the income statement, are included on a statement of comprehensive income.

Statement of Comprehensive Income For Year Ended December 31, 20XX	
Net income	xxx
Foreign currency translation adjustment	xxx
Unrealized holding gains/losses	xxx
Minimum pension liability adjustment	xxx
Other comprehensive income	xxx
Comprehensive income	xxx

Comprehensive income The total change in net assets from all sources except investments by or distributions to the owners.

A new term has been coined to incorporate the "income-type" items that escape the income statement. **Comprehensive income** is the net assets increase resulting from all transactions during a time period (except for investments by owners and distributions to owners). Exhibit 11-7 presents the statement of comprehensive income and its relationship to the traditional income statement. It illustrates that comprehensive income encompasses all the revenues and expenses that are presented on the income statement to calculate net income and also includes items that are not presented on the income statement but affect total stockholders' equity.[1] The comprehensive income measure is truly all-inclusive because it includes such transactions as unrealized gains and prior period adjustments that affect stockholders' equity. Firms are required to disclose comprehensive income because it provides a more complete measure of performance.

[1]The format of Exhibit 11-7 is suggested by the FASB. The FASB also allows other possible formats of the statement of comprehensive income.

WHAT ANALYZING OWNERS' EQUITY REVEALS ABOUT A FIRM'S VALUE

Book Value per Share

LO 9 Understand how investors use ratios to evaluate owners' equity.

Book value per share Total stockholders' equity divided by the number of shares of common stock outstanding.

Users of financial statements are often interested in computing the value of a corporation's stock. This is a difficult task because *value* is not a well-defined term and means different things to different users. One measure of value is the book value of the stock. **Book value per share** of common stock represents the rights that each share of common stock has to the net assets of the corporation. The term *net assets* refers to the total assets of the firm minus total liabilities. In other words, net assets equal the total stockholders' equity of the corporation. Therefore, when only common stock is present, book value per share is measured as follows:

$$\text{Book Value per Share} = \frac{\text{Total Stockholders' Equity}}{\text{Number of Shares of Stock Outstanding}}$$

Refer again to the statement of stockholders' equity of Walgreens that appears in Exhibit 11-6. As of August 31, 2001, the total stockholders' equity is $5,207.2 million ($79.6 + $596.7 + $4,530.9), and the number of outstanding shares of common stock is 1,019.4 million. Therefore, the book value per share for Walgreens is $5.11, calculated as follows:

$$\$5{,}207.2/1{,}019.4 = \$5.11$$

This means that the company's common stockholders have the right to $5.11 per share of net assets in the corporation.

The book value per share indicates the recorded minimum value per share of the stock. In a sense, it indicates the rights of the common stockholders in the event that the company is liquidated. It does not indicate the market value of the common stock. That is, book value per share does not indicate the price that should be paid by those who want to buy or sell the stock on the stock exchange. Book value is also an incomplete measure of value because the corporation's net assets are normally measured on the balance sheet at the original historical cost, not at the current value of the assets. Thus, book value per share does not provide a very accurate measure of the price that a stockholder would be willing to pay for a share of stock. The book value of a stock is often thought to be the "floor" of a stock price. An investor's decision to pay less than book value for a share of stock suggests that he or she thinks that the company is going to continue to lose money, thus shrinking book value.

Calculating Book Value When Preferred Stock Is Present

The focus of the computation of book value per share is always on the value per share of the *common* stock. Therefore, the computation must be adjusted for corporations that have both preferred and common stock. The numerator of the fraction, total stockholders' equity, should be reduced by the rights that preferred stockholders have to the corporation's net assets. Normally, this can be accomplished by deducting the redemption value or liquidation value of the preferred stock along with any dividends in arrears on cumulative preferred stock. The denominator should not include the number of shares of preferred stock.

To illustrate the computation of book value per share when both common and preferred stock are present, we will refer to the stockholders' equity category of Delta Air Lines, presented in Exhibit 11-8. When calculating book value per share, we want to consider only the *common* stockholders' equity. Exhibit 11-8 indicates **1** that Delta's total stockholders' equity in 2001 was $3,769 million but also **2** that preferred stockholders had a right to $452 million in the event of liquidation. Therefore, $452 million must be deducted to calculate the rights of the common stockholders:

http://www.delta.com

$$\$3{,}769 - \$452 = \$3{,}317 \text{ million common stockholders' equity}$$

Exhibit 11-8 Delta Air Lines Stockholders' Equity Section

SHAREOWNERS' EQUITY (In Millions, Except Share Data)	2001	2000
Employee Stock Ownership Plan Preferred Stock:		
2 Series B ESOP Convertible Preferred Stock, $1.00 par value, $72.00 stated and liquidation value; 6,278,210 shares issued and outstanding at December 31, 2001, and 6,405,563 shares issued and outstanding at December 31, 2000	452	460
Unearned compensation under employee stock ownership plan	(197)	(226)
Total Employee Stock Ownership Plan Preferred Stock	255	234
Shareowners' Equity:		
Common stock, $1.50 par value; 450,000,000 shares authorized; 180,890,356 shares issued at December 31, 2001 and 180,764,057 shares issued at December 31, 2000	271	271
Additional paid-in capital	3,267	3,264
Retained earnings	2,930	4,176
Accumulated other comprehensive income	25	360
Treasury stock at cost, 57,644,690 shares at December 31, 2001 and 57,750,685 shares at December 31, 2000	(2,724)	(2,728)
1 Total shareowners' equity	3,769	5,343

Deduct preferred stock before calculating book value per share.

The number of shares of common stock *outstanding* can be calculated from Exhibit 11-8 as follows:

180,890,356	shares issued
− 57,644,690	treasury shares
123,245,666	shares outstanding

Therefore, the computation of book value per share is as follows:

$$\$3{,}317{,}000{,}000/123{,}245{,}666 = \$26.91 \text{ Book Value per Share}$$

This indicates that if the company was liquidated and the assets sold at their recorded values, the common stockholders would receive $26.91 per share. Of course, if the company went bankrupt and had to liquidate assets at distressed values, stockholders would receive something less than book value.

Two-Minute Review

1. *What effect does a stock dividend have on a firm's stockholders' equity?*
2. *What effect does a stock split have on a firm's stockholders' equity?*
3. *How is book value per share calculated?*

Answers on page 579.

Market Value per Share

Market value per share The selling price of the stock as indicated by the most recent transactions.

http://www.gm.com

The market value of the stock is a more meaningful measure of the value of the stock to those financial statement users interested in buying or selling shares of stock. The **market value per share** is the price at which stock is currently selling. When stock is sold on a stock exchange, the price can be determined by its most recent selling price. For example, the listing for General Motors stock on the Internet may indicate the following[2]:

[2]On-line at http://www.gm.com, Investor Relations—Stock Performance, September 20, 2002.

52-Week			Daily			
HIGH	LOW	SYM	HIGH	LOW	LAST	CHANGE
68.17	39.17	GM	43.3	42.01	42.93	+0.48 (1.13%)

The two left-hand columns indicate the stock price for the last 52-week period. General Motors sold as high as $68.17 and as low as $39.17 during that time period. The right-hand portion indicates the high and low for the previous day's trading and the closing price. General Motors sold as high as $43.30 per share and as low as $42.01 per share and closed at $42.93. For the day, the stock increased by 1.13% or $0.48 per share.

The market value of the stock depends on many factors. Stockholders must evaluate a corporation's earnings and liquidity as indicated in the financial statements. They must also consider a variety of economic factors and project all of the factors into the future to determine the proper market value per share of the stock. Many investors use sophisticated investment techniques, including large databases, to identify factors that affect a company's stock price.

Which Way to Go?

Is It Better to Issue Stocks or Bonds?

Taz Industries' president has asked Fleming LaRue, the controller, and Clarissa Ping, the treasurer, to determine the best way for the company to raise cash to pay for expanding operations. Fleming feels strongly that it is in the best interest of the company to issue bonds. Clarissa does not agree and wants the company to issue more shares of common stock. They have decided to compromise and recommend issuing cumulative, convertible preferred stock. Currently, Taz has only common stock outstanding.

The president is very concerned about how the board of directors and the current stockholders will react to the recommendation. Should she be concerned? Why might the board and stockholders be unhappy with issuing the new stock? What can the president say to convince them that this would be a good solution?

HOW CHANGES IN STOCKHOLDERS' EQUITY AFFECT THE STATEMENT OF CASH FLOWS

LO 10 Explain the effects that transactions involving stockholders' equity have on the statement of cash flows.

It is important to determine the effect that the issuance of stock, the repurchase of stock, and the payment of dividends have on the statement of cash flows. Each of these business activities' impact on cash must be reflected on the statement. Exhibit 11-9 indicates how these stockholders' equity transactions affect cash flow and where the items should be placed on the statement of cash flows.

Exhibit 11-9

The Effect of Stockholders' Equity Items on the Statement of Cash Flows

Item	Statement of Cash Flows	
	Operating Activities	
	Net income	**XXX**
	Investing Activities	
	Financing Activities	
Issuance of stock →		+
Retirement or repurchase of stock →		−
Payment of dividends →		−

The issuance of stock is a method to finance business. Therefore, the cash *inflow* from the sale of stock to stockholders should be reflected as an inflow in the Financing Activities section of the statement of cash flows. Generally, companies do not disclose

Study Tip

Transactions affecting the Stockholders' Equity category of the balance sheet will appear in the Financing Activities category of the cash flow statement. Dividends are included in the cash flow statement when actually paid rather than when they are declared.

http://www.delta.com

separately the amount received for the par value of the stock and the amount received in excess of par. Rather, one amount is listed to indicate the total inflow of cash.

The repurchase or retirement of stock also represents a financing activity. Therefore, the cash *outflow* should be reflected as a reduction of cash in the Financing Activities section of the statement of cash flows. Again, companies do not distinguish between the amount paid for the par of the stock and the amount paid in excess of par. One amount is generally listed to indicate the total cash outflow to retire stock.

Dividends paid to stockholders represent a cost of financing the business with stock. Therefore, dividends paid should be reflected as a cash *outflow* in the Financing Activities section of the statement of cash flows. It is important to distinguish between the declaration of dividends and the payment of dividends. The cash outflow occurs at the time the dividend is paid and should be reflected on the statement of cash flows in that period.

The 2001 statement of cash flows for Delta Air Lines is given in Exhibit 11-10. Note in particular three lines in the Financing Activities category of the cash flow statement. First, the cash dividends line indicates cash payments of $40 million for the payment of dividends. Also, a line for the issuance of stock indicates the company had cash inflows during 2001 of $2 million from such transactions. Finally, Delta did not repurchase stock during the year, but that line indicates that cash payments of $502 million were made to repurchase the stock during the previous year.

Ratios for Decision Making

Reporting and analyzing financial statement information related to a company's stockholders' equity:

The book value per share represents the *right* each share of common stock has to the net assets of the company. This is an estimate since, should the company be sold, the amount received by shareholders for each share of stock owned may be more or less than the book value per share.

Balance Sheet	Income Statement	Statement of Cash Flows	Notes
Preferred Stock**			
Common Stock (number of shares authorized, issued, and outstanding)*			
Total Stockholders' Equity			

$$\textbf{Book Value per Share} = \frac{\textbf{Total Stockholders' Equity**}}{\textbf{Number of Common Shares Outstanding}}$$

*If the number of shares of common stock outstanding is not stated on the common stock line, it can be determined by subtracting the total number of treasury stock shares from the total number of common stock shares issued.

**When there is preferred stock outstanding, the redemption value or liquidation value (disclosed on the preferred stock line or in the notes) of the preferred stock must be subtracted from total stockholders' equity.

Exhibit 11-10 Delta Air Lines 2001 Statement of Cash Flows

CONSOLIDATED STATEMENTS OF CASH FLOWS

For the Years Ended December 31, 2001, 2000 and 1999

(in millions)	2001	2000	1999
Cash Flows From Operating Activities:			
Net income (loss)	$ (1,216)	$ 828	$ 1,208
Adjustments to reconcile net income (loss) to cash provided by operating activities:			
Cumulative effect of change in accounting principle	—	100	54
Asset writedowns	339	0	453
Depreciation and amortization	1,283	1,187	1,057
Deferred income taxes	(648)	396	321
Fair value adjustments of SFAS 133 derivatives	(68)	159	—
Pension, postretirement and postemployment expense in excess of (less than) payments	419	(17)	33
Dividends in excess of (less than) equity income	51	(28)	48
Net gain from sale of investments	(127)	(301)	(927)
Income tax benefit from exercise of stock options	—	5	21
Changes in certain current assets and liabilities:			
Decrease in accounts receivable	47	86	310
Decrease (increase) in prepaid expenses and other current assets	60	92	(186)
(Decrease) increase in air traffic liability	(215)	(49)	73
Increase in other payables and accrued expenses	274	395	169
Other, net	37	45	13
Net cash provided by operating activities	236	2,898	2,647
Cash Flows From Investing Activities:			
Property and equipment additions:			
Flight equipment, including advance payments	(2,321)	(3,426)	(2,497)
Ground property and equipment	(472)	(634)	(558)
Increase in restricted investments related to the Boston airport terminal project	(485)	—	—
Decrease (increase) in short-term investments, net	238	456	(367)
Proceeds from sale of flight equipment	66	384	215
Proceeds from sale of investments	286	73	1,167
Acquisitions of companies, net of cash acquired	—	(232)	(1,922)
Other, net	(8)	(17)	—
Net cash used in investing activities	(2,696)	(3,396)	(3,962)
Cash Flows From Financing Activities:			
Payments on long-term debt and capital lease obligations	(173)	(853)	(1,927)
Prepayment of long-term lease obligations	—	(215)	—
Cash dividends	(40)	(40)	(43)
Issuance of long-term obligations	2,335	1,867	4,496
Issuance of long-term debt by Massachusetts Port Authority	498	—	—
Proceeds from (payments on) short-term obligations and notes payable, net	701	(51)	265
Issuance of common stock	2	33	104
Repurchase of common stock	—	(502)	(625)
Other, net	(17)	—	—
Net cash provided by financing activities	3,306	239	2,270
Net Increase (Decrease) in Cash and Cash Equivalents	846	(259)	955
Cash and cash equivalents at beginning of year	1,364	1,623	668
Cash and cash equivalents at end of year	$ 2,210	$ 1,364	$ 1,623

Changes in stockholders' equity are shown in the Financing Activities category.

Impact on the Financial Reports

Impact on the Financial Reports

BALANCE SHEET

Current Assets
Cash
Noncurrent Assets
Current Liabilities
Cash dividend payable
Noncurrent Liabilities
Stockholders' Equity
Contributed Capital[1]
Preferred stock[2]
Additional paid-in capital—preferred
Common stock
Additional paid-in capital—common (or Paid-in capital in excess of par)
Paid-in capital from stock retirement
Common stock dividend distributable
Total Contributed Capital
Retained earnings
Treasury stock[3]
Total Stockholders' Equity

INCOME STATEMENT

Revenues
Expenses
Other

[1]The number of shares in each of the following categories is disclosed for each class of stock: (a) authorized, (b) issued, and (c) outstanding.

[2]The most common features for preferred stock are (a) cumulative, (b) participating, (c) convertible, and (d) callable.

[3]This reduces stockholders' equity.

STATEMENT OF STOCKHOLDERS' EQUITY

Contributed Capital
Number of shares issued
Number of shares repurchased
Paid-in capital (par and excess) from shares issued
Amount paid for repurchase of stock (for treasury or retirement)
Retained Earnings
Current period net income (net loss)
Cash dividends declared

STATEMENT OF CASH FLOWS

Operating Activities
Investing Activities
Financing Activities
Cash received from issuance of stock
Cash paid for treasury shares
Cash received from sale of treasury shares
Cash paid to retire stock
Cash paid for dividends
Noncash Transactions

NOTES

Answers to the Two-Minute Reviews

Two-Minute Review on Page 564

1. *Treasury Stock is a contra-equity account, and the balance should appear as a reduction in the Stockholders' Equity category of the balance sheet.*
2. *When treasury stock is purchased, it reduces total stockholders' equity.*
3. *Treasury stock is still stock that has been issued and so does not affect the number of shares issued. But it is stock that is held by the company, rather than the stockholders, and the purchase of treasury stock reduces the number of shares of stock outstanding.*

Answers to the Two-Minute Reviews (*Continued*)

Two-Minute Review on Page 574

1. *A stock dividend does not change a firm's total stockholders' equity but does affect the balances of accounts within that category of the balance sheet. Generally, a stock dividend will reduce the retained earnings account and will increase the capital stock account.*
2. *A stock split does not affect total stockholders' equity or the accounts within stockholders' equity. No accounting entry is made for a stock split.*
3. *Book value per share is determined by dividing total stockholders' equity (less an amount representing the rights of preferred shareholders) by the number of shares of common stock outstanding.*

Warmup Exercises

Warmup Exercise 11-1

A company has a retained earnings account with a January 1 balance of $500,000. The accountant has reviewed the following information for the current year:

Increase in cash balance	$50,000
Net income	80,000
Dividends declared	30,000
Dividends paid	20,000
Decrease in accounts receivable balance	10,000

Required

Calculate the ending balance of the Retained Earnings account.

Key to the Solution

Cash and accounts receivable do not affect retained earnings. Also note that dividends are deducted from retained earnings at the time they are declared rather than when they are paid.

Warmup Exercise 11-2

A company begins business on January 1 and issues 100,000 shares of common stock. On July 1, the company declares and issues a 2-for-1 stock split. On October 15, the company purchases 20,000 shares of stock as treasury stock and reissues 5,000 shares by the end of the month.

Required

Calculate the number of shares issued and the number of shares outstanding as of the end of the first year of operations.

Warmup Exercise 11-3

A. Company A has total stockholders' equity at year-end of $500,000 and has 10,000 shares of stock.

B. Company B has total stockholders' equity at year-end of $500,000 and has 10,000 shares of stock. The company also has 50,000 shares of preferred stock, which has a $1 par value and a liquidation value of $3 per share.

Required

Calculate the book value per share for Company A and Company B.

Key to the Solution

Book value per share is calculated for the common stockholder. If preferred stock is present, an amount must be deducted that represents the amount the preferred stockholder would receive at liquidation.

Solution to Warmup Exercises

Warmup Exercise 11-1

The ending balance of the Retained Earnings account should be calculated as follows:

Beginning balance	$500,000
Plus: Net income	80,000
Less: Dividends declared	(30,000)
Ending balance	$550,000

Warmup Exercise 11-2

The number of shares of stock issued is 200,000, or 100,000 times 2 because of the stock split. The number of shares outstanding is 185,000, calculated as follows:

Number of shares after split	100,000 × 2 =	200,000
Less purchase of treasury stock		(20,000)
Plus stock reissued		5,000
Total outstanding		185,000 shares

Warmup Exercise 11-3

A. Book value per share is $50, or $500,000/10,000.

B. Book value per share is $35, or ($500,000 − $150,000)/10,000.

Review Problem

WebTUTOR™ Advantage

Andrew Company was incorporated on January 1, 2004, under a corporate charter that authorized the issuance of 50,000 shares of $5 par common stock and 20,000 shares of $100 par, 8% preferred stock. The following events occurred during 2004. Andrew wants to record the events and develop financial statements on December 31, 2004.

a. Issued for cash 10,000 shares of common stock at $25 per share and 1,000 shares of preferred stock at $110 per share on January 15, 2004.

b. Acquired a patent on April 1 in exchange for 2,000 shares of common stock. At the time of the exchange, the common stock was selling on the local stock exchange for $30 per share.

c. Repurchased 500 shares of common stock on May 1 at $20 per share. The corporation is holding the stock to be used for an employee bonus plan.

d. Declared a cash dividend of $1 per share to common stockholders and an 8% dividend to preferred stockholders on July 1. The preferred stock is noncumulative, nonparticipating. The dividend will be distributed on August 1.

e. Distributed the cash dividend on August 1.

f. Declared and distributed to preferred stockholders a 10% stock dividend on September 1. At the time of the dividend declaration, preferred stock was valued at $130 per share.

g. On December 31, calculated the annual net income for the year to be $200,000.

Required

1. Record the accounting entries for items **a** through **g.**
2. Develop the Stockholders' Equity section of Andrew Company's balance sheet at December 31, 2004. You do not need to consider the notes that accompany the balance sheet.
3. Determine the book value per share of the common stock. Assume that the preferred stock can be redeemed at par.

Solution to Review Problem

1. The following entries should be recorded:

   a. The entry to record the issuance of stock:

Jan. 15	Cash	360,000	
	Common Stock		50,000
	Additional Paid-In Capital—Common		200,000
	Preferred Stock		100,000
	Additional Paid-In Capital—Preferred		10,000
	To record the issuance of stock for cash.		

Assets	=	Liabilities	+	Owners' Equity
+360,000				+50,000
				+200,000
				+100,000
				+10,000

   b. The patent received for stock should be recorded at the value of the stock:

Apr. 1	Patent	60,000	
	Common Stock		10,000
	Additional Paid-In Capital—Common		50,000
	To record the issuance of stock for patent.		

Assets	=	Liabilities	+	Owners' Equity
+60,000				+10,000
				+50,000

   c. Stock reacquired constitutes treasury stock and should be recorded as follows:

May 1	Treasury Stock	10,000	
	Cash		10,000
	To record the purchase of treasury stock.		

Assets	=	Liabilities	+	Owners' Equity
−10,000				−10,000

   d. A cash dividend should be declared on the number of shares of stock outstanding as of July 1. The dividend is recorded as follows:

July 1	Retained Earnings	19,500	
	Dividends Payable—Common		11,500
	Dividends Payable—Preferred		8,000
	To record the declaration of a cash dividend.		

Assets	=	Liabilities	+	Owners' Equity
		+11,500		−19,500
		+8,000		

   The number of shares of common stock outstanding should be calculated as the number of shares issued (12,000) less the number of shares of treasury stock (500). The preferred stock dividend should be calculated as 1,000 shares times $100 par times 8%.

   e. The entry to record the distribution of a cash dividend is as follows:

Aug. 1	Dividends Payable—Common	11,500	
	Dividends Payable—Preferred	8,000	
	Cash		19,500
	To record the payment of cash dividend.		

Assets	=	Liabilities	+	Owners' Equity
−19,500		−11,500		
		−8,000		

(continued)

f. A stock dividend should be based on the number of shares of stock outstanding and should be declared and recorded at the market value of the stock as follows:

Sept. 1	Retained Earnings	13,000	
	Preferred Stock		10,000
	Additional Paid-In Capital—Preferred		3,000
	To record the declaration of a stock dividend.		

Assets	=	Liabilities	+	Owners' Equity
				−13,000
				+10,000
				+3,000

The amount of the debit to retained earnings should be calculated as the number of shares outstanding (1,000) times 10% times $130 per share.

g. The entry to close the Income Summary account to stockholders' equity should be recorded as follows:

Dec. 31	Income Summary	200,000	
	Retained Earnings		200,000
	To record the annual net income.		

Assets	=	Liabilities	+	Owners' Equity
				−200,000
				+200,000

2. The Stockholders' Equity for Andrew Company after completing these transactions appears as follows:

Preferred stock, $100 par, 8%, 20,000 shares authorized, 1,100 issued	$110,000
Common stock, $5 par, 50,000 shares authorized, 12,000 issued	60,000
Additional paid-in capital—Preferred	13,000
Additional paid-in capital—Common	250,000
Retained earnings	167,500*
Total contributed capital and retained earnings	$600,500
Less: Treasury stock, 500 shares, common	(10,000)
Total stockholders' equity	$590,500

*$200,000 − $19,500 − $13,000 = $167,500

3. The book value per share of the common stock is calculated as follows:

($590,500 − $110,000)/11,500 shares = $41.78

Appendix: Accounting Tools: Unincorporated Businesses

LO 11 Describe the important differences between the sole proprietorship and partnership forms of organization versus the corporate form.

The focus of Chapter 11 has been on the corporate form of organization. Most of the large, influential companies in the United States are organized as corporations. They have a legal and economic existence that is separate from that of the owners of the business, the stockholders. Yet many other companies in the economy are organized as sole proprietorships or partnerships. The purpose of this appendix is to show briefly how the characteristics of such organizations affect the accounting, particularly the accounting for the Owners' Equity category of the balance sheet.

Sole Proprietorships

A **sole proprietorship** is a business owned by one person. Most sole proprietorships are small in size, with the owner serving as the operator or manager of the company. The primary advantage of the sole proprietorship form of organization is its simplicity. The Owner's Equity category of the balance sheet consists of one account, the owner's capital account. The owner answers to no one but himself or herself. A disadvantage of the sole proprietorship is that all the responsibility for the success or failure of the venture attaches to the owner, who often has limited resources.

Sole proprietorship A business with a single owner.

There are three important points to remember about this form of organization. First, a sole proprietorship is not a separate entity for legal purposes. This means that the law does not distinguish between the assets of the business and those of its owner. If an owner loses a lawsuit, for example, the law does not limit an owner's liability to the amount of assets of the business but extends liability to the owner's personal assets. Thus, the owner is said to have *unlimited liability.*

Second, accountants adhere to the *entity principle* and maintain a distinction between the owner's personal assets and the assets of the sole proprietorship. The balance sheet of a sole proprietorship should reflect only the "business" assets and liabilities, with the difference reflected as owner's capital.

Third, a sole proprietorship is not treated as a separate entity for federal income tax purposes. That is, the sole proprietorship does not pay tax on its income. Rather, the business income must be declared as income on the owner's personal tax return, and income tax is assessed at the personal tax rate rather than the rate that applies to companies organized as corporations. This may or may not be advantageous, depending on the amount of income involved and the owner's tax situation.

Typical Transactions

When the owners of a corporation, the stockholders, invest in the corporation, they normally do so by purchasing stock. When investing in a sole proprietorship, the owner simply contributes cash, or other assets, into the business. For example, assume that on January 1, 2004, Peter Tom began a new business by investing $10,000 cash. Peter Tom Company records the transaction as follows:

Jan. 1	Cash	10,000	
	Peter Tom, Capital		10,000
	To record the investment of cash in the business.		

Assets	=	Liabilities	+	Owner's Equity
+10,000				+10,000

The Peter Tom, Capital account is an owner's equity account and reflects the rights of the owner to the business assets.

An owner's withdrawal of assets from the business is recorded as a reduction of owner's equity. Assume that on July 1, 2004, Peter Tom took an auto valued at $6,000 from the business to use as his personal auto. The transaction is recorded as follows:

July 1	Peter Tom, Drawing	6,000	
	Equipment		6,000
	To record the withdrawal of an auto from the business.		

Assets	=	Liabilities	+	Owner's Equity
−6,000				−6,000

The Peter Tom, Drawing account is a contra-equity account. Sometimes a drawing account is referred to as a *withdrawals account,* as in Peter Tom, Withdrawals. An increase (debit) in the account reduces the owner's equity. At the end of the fiscal year, the drawing account should be closed to the capital account as follows:

Dec. 31	Peter Tom, Capital	6,000	
	Peter Tom, Drawing		6,000
	To close the drawing account to capital.		

Assets	=	Liabilities	+	Owner's Equity
				−6,000
				+6,000

The amount of the net income of the business should also be reflected in the capital account. Assume that all revenue and expense accounts of Peter Tom Company have been closed to the Income Summary account, resulting in a credit balance of $4,000, the net income for the year. The Income Summary account is closed to capital as follows:

Dec. 31	Income Summary	4,000	
	Peter Tom, Capital		4,000
	To close income summary to the capital account.		

Assets	=	Liabilities	+	Owner's Equity
				−4,000
				+4,000

The Owner's Equity section of the balance sheet for Peter Tom Company consists of one account, the capital account, calculated as follows:

Beginning balance, Jan. 1, 2004	$ 0
Plus: Investments	10,000
Net income	4,000
Less: Withdrawals	(6,000)
Ending balance, Dec. 31, 2004	$ 8,000

Partnerships

Partnership A business owned by two or more individuals and with the characteristic of unlimited liability.

A **partnership** is a company owned by two or more persons. Like sole proprietorships, most partnerships are fairly small businesses formed when individuals combine their capital and managerial talents for a common business purpose. Other partnerships are large, national organizations. For example, the major public accounting firms are very large, national companies but are organized in most states as partnerships.

Partnerships have characteristics similar to those of sole proprietorships. The following are the most important characteristics of partnerships:

1. *Unlimited liability.* Legally, the assets of the business are not separate from the partners' personal assets. Each partner is personally liable for the debts of the partnership. Creditors have a legal claim first to the assets of the partnership and then to the assets of the individual partners.
2. *Limited life.* Corporations have a separate legal existence and an unlimited life; partnerships do not. The life of a partnership is limited; it exists as long as the contract between the partners is valid. The partnership ends when a partner withdraws or a new partner is added. A new partnership must be created for the business to continue.
3. *Not taxed as a separate entity.* Partnerships are subject to the same tax features as sole proprietorships. The partnership itself does not pay federal income tax. Rather, the income of the partnership is treated as personal income on each of the partners' individual tax returns and is taxed as personal income. All partnership income is subject to federal income tax on the individual partners' returns even if it is not distributed to the partners. A variety of other factors affects the tax consequences of partnerships versus the corporate form of organization. These aspects are quite complex and beyond the scope of this text.

Partnership agreement Specifies how much the owners will invest, their salaries, and how profits will be shared.

A partnership is based on a **partnership agreement.** It is very important that the partners agree, in writing, about all aspects of the partnership. The agreement should detail items such as how much capital each partner is to invest, the time each is expected to devote to the business, the salary of each, and how income of the partnership is to be divided. If a partnership agreement is not present, the courts may be forced to settle disputes among partners. Therefore, the partners should develop a partnership agreement when the firm is first established and should review the agreement periodically to determine whether changes are necessary.

Investments and Withdrawals In a partnership, it is important to account separately for the capital of each of the partners. A capital account should be established in the Owners' Equity section of the balance sheet for each partner of the company. Investments into the company should be credited to the partner making the investment. For example, assume that on January 1, 2004, Page Thoms and Amy Rebec begin a partnership named AP Company. Page contributes $10,000 cash, and Amy contributes equipment valued at $5,000. The accounting transaction recorded by AP Company follows:

Jan. 1	Cash	10,000	
	Equipment	5,000	
	Page Thoms, Capital		10,000
	Amy Rebec, Capital		5,000
	To record the contribution of assets to the business.		

Assets	=	Liabilities	+	Owners' Equity
+10,000				+10,000
+5,000				+5,000

A drawing account also should be established for each owner of the company to account for withdrawals of assets. Assume that on April 1, 2004, each owner withdraws $2,000 of cash from AP Company. The accounting entry is recorded:

Apr. 1	Page Thoms, Drawing	2,000	
	Amy Rebec, Drawing	2,000	
	Cash		4,000
	To record the withdrawal of assets from the business.		

Assets	=	Liabilities	+	Owners' Equity
−4,000				−2,000
				−2,000

Distribution of Income The partnership agreement governs the manner in which income should be allocated to partners. The distribution may recognize the partners' relative investment in the business, their time and effort, their expertise and talents, or other factors. We will illustrate three methods of income allocation, but you should be aware that partnerships use many other allocation methods. Although these allocation methods are straightforward, partnerships dissolve often because one or more of the partners believes that the allocation is unfair. It is very difficult to devise a method that will make all partners happy.

One way to allocate income is to divide it evenly between or among the partners. In fact, when a partnership agreement is not present, the courts specify that an equal allocation must be applied, regardless of the relative contributions or efforts of the partners. For example, assume that AP Company has $30,000 of net income for the period and has established an agreement that income should be allocated evenly between the two partners, Page and Amy. The accounting entry that AP Company records during the closing entry process is as follows:

Dec. 31	Income Summary	30,000	
	Page Thoms, Capital		15,000
	Amy Rebec, Capital		15,000
	To record the allocation of income between partners.		

Assets	=	Liabilities	+	Owners' Equity
				−30,000
				+15,000
				+15,000

An equal distribution of income to all partners is easy to apply but is not fair to those partners who have contributed more in money or time to the partnership.

Another way to allocate income is to specify in the partnership agreement that income be allocated according to a *stated ratio.* For example, Page and Amy may specify that all income of AP Company should be allocated on a 2-to-1 ratio, with Page receiving the larger portion. If that allocation method is applied to the preceding example, AP Company records the following transaction at year-end:

Dec. 31	Income Summary	30,000	
	Page Thoms, Capital		20,000
	Amy Rebec, Capital		10,000
	To record the allocation of income between partners.		

Assets	=	Liabilities	+	Owners' Equity
				−30,000
				+20,000
				+10,000

Finally, we illustrate an allocation method that more accurately reflects the partners' input. It is based on salaries, interest on invested capital, and a stated ratio. Assume that the partnership agreement of AP Company specifies that Page and Amy be allowed a salary of $6,000 and $4,000 respectively, that each partner receive 10% on her capital balance, and that any remaining income be allocated equally. Assume that AP Company has been in operation for several years and the capital balances of the owners at the end of 2004, before the income distribution, are as follows:

Page Thoms, Capital	$40,000
Amy Rebec, Capital	50,000

If AP Company calculated that its 2004 net income (before partner salaries) was $30,000, income would be allocated between the partners as follows:

	PAGE	AMY
Distributed for salaries:	$ 6,000	$ 4,000
Distributed for interest:		
Page: ($40,000 × 10%)	4,000	
Amy: ($50,000 × 10%)		5,000
Remainder = $30,000 − $10,000 − $9,000 = $11,000		
Remainder distributed equally:		
Page: ($11,000/2)	5,500	
Amy: ($11,000/2)		5,500
Total distributed	$15,500	$14,500

The accounting transaction to transfer the income to the capital accounts is as follows:

Dec. 31	Income Summary	30,000	
	Page Thoms, Capital		15,500
	Amy Rebec, Capital		14,500
	To record the allocation of income to partners.		

Assets	=	Liabilities	+	Owners' Equity
				−30,000
				+15,500
				+14,500

This indicates that the amounts of $15,500 and $14,500 were allocated to Page and Amy respectively. It does not indicate the amount actually paid to (or withdrawn by) the partners. However, for tax purposes, the income of the partnership is treated as personal income on the partners' individual tax returns regardless of whether the income is actually paid in cash to the partners. This aspect often encourages partners to withdraw income from the business and makes it difficult to retain sufficient capital for the business to operate profitably.

Chapter Highlights

1. **LO 1** The Stockholders' Equity category is composed of two parts. Contributed capital is the amount derived from stockholders and other external parties. Retained earnings is the amount of net income not paid as dividends.
2. **LO 1** The Stockholders' Equity category reveals the number of shares authorized, issued, and outstanding. Treasury stock is stock that the firm has issued and repurchased but not retired.
3. **LO 2** *Preferred stock* refers to a stock that has preference to dividends declared. If a dividend is declared, the preferred stockholders must receive a dividend before the common stockholders.
4. **LO 3** When stock is issued for cash, the par value of the stock should be reported in the stock account and the amount in excess of par should be reported in an additional paid-in capital account.
5. **LO 3** When stock is issued for a noncash asset, the transaction should reflect the value of the stock given or the value of the property received, whichever is more evident.
6. **LO 4** Treasury stock is accounted for as a reduction of stockholders' equity. When treasury stock is reissued and the cost is less than reissue price, the difference is added to additional paid-in capital. When cost exceeds reissue price, additional paid-in capital or retained earnings is reduced for the difference.
7. **LO 5** The amount of cash dividends to be paid to common and preferred stockholders depends on the terms of the preferred stock. If the stock is cumulative, preferred stockholders have the right to dividends in arrears before current-year dividends are paid. Participating preferred stock indicates that preferred stockholders can share in the dividend amount that exceeds a specified amount.
8. **LO 6** Stock dividends involve the issuance of additional shares of stock. The dividend should normally reflect the fair market value of the additional shares.
9. **LO 7** Stock splits are similar to stock dividends except that splits reduce the par value per share of the stock. No accounting transaction is necessary for splits.
10. **LO 8** The statement of stockholders' equity reflects the changes in the balances of all stockholder equity accounts.
11. **LO 9** Book value per share is calculated as net assets divided by the number of shares of common stock outstanding. It indicates the rights that stockholders have, based on recorded values, to the net assets in the event of liquidation and is therefore not a measure of the market value of the stock.
12. **LO 9** When a corporation has both common and preferred stock, the net assets attributed to the rights of the preferred stockholders must be deducted from the amount of net assets to determine the book value per share of the common stock.
13. **LO 10** Transactions involving stockholders' equity accounts should be reflected in the Financing Activities category of the statement of cash flows.
14. **LO 11** A sole proprietorship is a business owned by one person. It is not a separate entity for legal purposes and does not pay taxes on its income. However, a balance sheet should present the assets and liabilities of the business separate from those of the owner. (Appendix)
15. **LO 11** A partnership is a company owned by two or more persons. Like sole proprietorships, partnerships are not a separate legal or tax entity. The balance sheet of the partnership should present the assets and liabilities of the business separate from those of the owners. (Appendix)

http://

Technology and other resources for your success

http://porter.swlearning.com

If you need additional help, visit the text's Web site. Also, see pages xv–xvii in this text's preface for a description of available technology and other resources. If your instructor is using PERSONAL Trainer in this course, you may complete, on line, the assignments identified by PT.

Key Terms Quiz

Read each definition below and then write the number of the definition in the blank beside the appropriate term it defines. The quiz solutions appear at the end of the chapter.

_____ Authorized shares
_____ Issued shares
_____ Outstanding shares
_____ Par value
_____ Additional paid-in capital
_____ Retained earnings
_____ Cumulative feature
_____ Participating feature
_____ Convertible feature
_____ Callable feature

(continued)

______ Treasury stock
______ Retirement of stock
______ Dividend payout ratio
______ Stock dividend
______ Stock split
______ Statement of stockholders' equity
______ Comprehensive income
______ Book value per share
______ Market value per share
______ Sole proprietorship (Appendix)
______ Partnership (Appendix)
______ Partnership agreement (Appendix)

1. The number of shares sold or distributed to stockholders.
2. An arbitrary amount that is stated on the face of the stock certificate and that represents the legal capital of the firm.
3. Net income that has been made by the corporation but not paid out as dividends.
4. The right to dividends in arrears before the current-year dividend is distributed.
5. Allows preferred stock to be returned to the corporation in exchange for common stock.
6. Stock issued by the firm and then repurchased but not retired.
7. The annual dividend amount divided by the annual net income.
8. A statement that reflects the differences between beginning and ending balances for all accounts in the Stockholders' Equity category.
9. Creation of additional shares of stock and reduction of the par value of the stock.
10. Total stockholders' equity divided by the number of shares of common stock outstanding.
11. The total change in net assets from all sources except investments by or distributions to the owners.
12. The selling price of the stock as indicated by the most recent stock transactions on, for example, the stock exchange.
13. The maximum number of shares a corporation may issue as indicated in the corporate charter.
14. The number of shares issued less the number of shares held as treasury stock.
15. The amount received for the issuance of stock in excess of the par value of the stock.
16. A provision allowing the preferred stockholders to share, on a percentage basis, in the distribution of an abnormally large dividend.
17. Allows the issuing firm to eliminate a class of stock by paying the stockholders a fixed amount.
18. When the stock of a corporation is repurchased with no intention to reissue at a later date.
19. A corporation's declaration and issuance of additional shares of its own stock to existing stockholders.
20. A business owned by two or more individuals and with the characteristic of unlimited liability.
21. A document that specifies how much each owner should invest, the salary of each owner, and how profits are to be shared.
22. A business with a single owner.

Answers on p. 606.

Alternate Terms

Additional paid-in capital Paid-in capital in excess of par value

Additional paid-in capital—treasury stock Paid-in capital from treasury stock transactions

Callable Redeemable

Capital account Owners' equity account

Contributed capital Paid-in capital

Retained earnings Retained income

Small stock dividend Stock dividend less than 20%

Stockholders' equity Owners' equity

Questions

1. What are the two major components of stockholders' equity? Which accounts generally appear in each component?
2. Corporations disclose the number of shares authorized, issued, and outstanding. What is the meaning of these terms? What causes a difference between the number of shares issued and the number outstanding?
3. Why do firms designate an amount as the par value of stock? Does par value indicate the selling price or market value of the stock?
4. If a firm has a net income for the year, will the balance in the Retained Earnings account equal the net income? What is the meaning of the balance of the account?
5. What is the meaning of the statement that preferred stock has a preference to dividends declared by the corporation? Do preferred stockholders have the right to dividends in arrears on preferred stock?
6. Why might some stockholders be inclined to buy preferred stock rather than common stock? What are the advantages of investing in preferred stock?
7. Why are common shareholders sometimes called *residual owners* when a company has both common and preferred stock outstanding?
8. When stock is issued in exchange for an asset, at what amount should the asset be reported? How could the fair market value be determined?

9. What is treasury stock? Why do firms use it? Where does it appear on a corporation's financial statements?
10. When treasury stock is bought and sold, the transactions do not result in gains or losses reported on the income statement. What account or accounts are used instead? Why are no income statement amounts recorded?
11. Many firms operate at a dividend payout ratio of less than 50%. Why do firms not pay a larger percentage of income as dividends?
12. What is a *stock dividend?* How should it be recorded?
13. Would you rather receive a cash dividend or a stock dividend from a company? Explain.
14. What is the difference between stock dividends and stock splits? How should stock splits be recorded?
15. How is the book value per share calculated? Does the amount calculated as book value per share mean that stockholders will receive a dividend equal to the book value?
16. Can the market value per share of stock be determined by the information on the income statement?
17. What is the difference between a statement of stockholders' equity and a retained earnings statement?
18. What is an advantage of organizing a company as a corporation rather than a partnership? Why don't all companies incorporate? (Appendix)
19. What are some ways that partnerships could share income among the partners? (Appendix)

Exercises

Exercise 11-1 *Stockholders' Equity Accounts* LO 1

MJ Company has identified the following items. Indicate whether each item is included in an account in the Stockholders' Equity category of the balance sheet and identify the account title. Also indicate whether the item would increase or decrease stockholders' equity.

1. Preferred stock issued by MJ
2. Amount received by MJ in excess of par value when preferred stock was issued
3. Dividends in arrears on MJ preferred stock
4. Cash dividend declared but unpaid on MJ stock
5. Stock dividend declared but unissued by MJ
6. Treasury stock
7. Amount received in excess of cost when treasury stock is reissued by MJ
8. Retained earnings

Exercise 11-2 *Solve for Unknowns* LO 1

The Stockholders' Equity category of Zache Company's balance sheet appears below.

Common stock, $10 par, 10,000 shares issued, 9,200 outstanding	$??
Additional paid-in capital	??
Total contributed capital	$350,000
Retained earnings	100,000
Treasury stock, ?? shares at cost	10,000
Total stockholders' equity	$??

Required

1. Determine the missing values that are indicated by question marks.
2. What was the cost per share of the treasury stock?

Exercise 11-3 *Stock Issuance* LO 3

Horace Company had the following transactions during 2004, its first year of business.

a. Issued 5,000 shares of $5 par common stock for cash at $15 per share.
b. Issued 7,000 shares of common stock on May 1 to acquire a factory building from Barkley Company. Barkley had acquired the building in 2000 at a price of $150,000. Horace estimated that the building was worth $175,000 on May 1, 2004.
c. Issued 2,000 shares of stock on June 1 to acquire a patent. The accountant has been unable to estimate the value of the patent but has determined that Horace's common stock was selling at $25 per share on June 1.

(continued)

Required

1. Record an entry for each of the transactions.
2. Determine the balance sheet amounts for common stock and additional paid-in capital.

Exercise 11-4 *Stock Issuances* LO 3

The following transactions are for Weber Corporation in 2004:

a. On March 1, the corporation was organized and received authorization to issue 5,000 shares of 8%, $100 par value preferred stock and 2,000,000 shares of $10 par value common stock.
b. On March 10, Weber issued 5,000 shares of common stock at $35 per share.
c. On March 18, Weber issued 100 shares of preferred stock at $120 per share.
d. On April 12, Weber issued another 10,000 shares of common stock at $45 per share.

Required

1. Determine the effect on the accounting equation of each of the events. Prepare journal entries when they are appropriate.
2. Prepare the Stockholders' Equity section of the balance sheet as of December 31, 2004.
3. Does the balance sheet indicate the market value of the stock at year-end? Explain.

Exercise 11-5 *Treasury Stock* LO 4

The Stockholders' Equity category of Bradford Company's balance sheet on January 1, 2004, appeared as follows:

Common stock, $10 par, 10,000 shares issued and outstanding	$100,000
Additional paid-in capital	50,000
Retained earnings	80,000
Total stockholders' equity	$230,000

The following transactions occurred during 2004:

a. Reacquired 2,000 shares of common stock at $20 per share on July 1.
b. Reacquired 400 shares of common stock at $18 per share on August 1.

Required

1. Record the entries in journal form.
2. Assume the company resold the shares of treasury stock at $28 per share on October 1. Did the company benefit from the treasury stock transaction? If so, where is the "gain" presented on the balance sheet?

Exercise 11-6 *Treasury Stock Transactions* LO 4

The stockholders' equity category of Little Joe's balance sheet on January 1, 2004, appeared as follows:

Common stock, $5 par, 40,000 shares issued and outstanding	$200,000
Additional paid-in capital	90,000
Retained earnings	100,000
Total stockholders' equity	$390,000

The following transactions occurred during 2004:

a. Reacquired 5,000 shares of common stock at $20 per share on February 1.
b. Reacquired 1,200 shares of common stock at $13 per share on March 1.

Required

1. Record the entries in journal form.
2. Assume that the treasury stock was reissued on October 1 at $12 per share. Did the company benefit from the treasury stock reissuance? Where is the "gain" or "loss" presented on the financial statements?
3. What effect did the two transactions to purchase treasury stock and the later reissuance of that stock have on the Stockholders' Equity section of the balance sheet?

Exercise 11-7 *Cash Dividends* LO 5

Kerry Company has 1,000 shares of $100 par value, 9% preferred stock and 10,000 shares of $10 par value common stock outstanding. The preferred stock is cumulative and nonparticipating. Dividends were paid in 2000. Since 2000, Kerry has declared and paid dividends as follows:

2001	$ 0
2002	10,000
2003	20,000
2004	25,000

Required

1. Determine the amount of the dividends to be allocated to preferred and common stockholders for each year, 2002 to 2004.
2. If the preferred stock had been noncumulative, how much would have been allocated to the preferred and common stockholders each year?

Exercise 11-8 *Cash Dividends* LO 5

The Stockholders' Equity category of Jackson Company's balance sheet as of January 1, 2004, appeared as follows:

Preferred stock, $100 par, 8%, 2,000 shares issued and outstanding	$200,000
Common stock, $10 par, 5,000 shares issued and outstanding	50,000
Additional paid-in capital	300,000
Total contributed capital	$550,000
Retained earnings	400,000
Total stockholders' equity	$950,000

The notes that accompany the financial statements indicate that Jackson has not paid dividends for the two years prior to 2004. On July 1, 2004, Jackson declares a dividend of $100,000 to be paid to preferred and common stockholders on August 1.

Required

1. Determine the amounts of the dividend to be allocated to preferred and common stockholders, assuming that the preferred stock is noncumulative, nonparticipating stock.
2. Record the appropriate journal entries on July 1 and August 1, 2004.
3. Determine the amounts of the dividend to be allocated to preferred and common stockholders, assuming instead that the preferred stock is cumulative, nonparticipating stock.

Exercise 11-9 *Cash Dividends—Participating Feature* LO 5

Refer to Jackson Company's Stockholders' Equity category in Exercise 11-8. Assume that the notes to the financial statements indicate that Jackson has not paid dividends for the two years prior to 2004. On July 1, 2004, Jackson declares a dividend of $100,000 to be paid to preferred and common stockholders on August 1.

Required

1. Determine the amounts of the dividend to be allocated to preferred and common stock, assuming that the preferred stock is cumulative and participates in dividends in proportion to the total par value of preferred and common stock.
2. Record the appropriate journal entries on July 1 and August 1, 2004.

Exercise 11-10 *Stock Dividends* LO 6

The Stockholders' Equity category of Worthy Company's balance sheet as of January 1, 2004, appeared as follows:

Common stock, $10 par, 40,000 shares issued and outstanding	$400,000
Additional paid-in capital	100,000
Retained earnings	400,000
Total stockholders' equity	$900,000

(continued)

The following transactions occurred during 2004:

a. Declared a 10% stock dividend to common stockholders on January 15. At the time of the dividend, the common stock was selling for $30 per share. The stock dividend was to be issued to stockholders on January 30, 2004.

b. Distributed the stock dividend to the stockholders on January 30, 2004.

Required

1. Record the 2004 transactions in journal form.
2. Develop the Stockholders' Equity category of Worthy Company's balance sheet as of January 31, 2004, after the stock dividend was issued. What effect did these transactions have on total stockholders' equity?

Exercise 11-11 ***Stock Dividends versus Stock Splits*** **LO 7**

Campbell Company wants to increase the number of shares of its common stock outstanding and is considering a stock dividend versus a stock split. The Stockholders' Equity of the firm on its most recent balance sheet appeared as follows:

Common stock, $10 par,	
50,000 shares issued and outstanding	$ 500,000
Additional paid-in capital	750,000
Retained earnings	880,000
Total stockholders' equity	$2,130,000

If a stock dividend is chosen, the firm wants to declare a 100% stock dividend. Because the stock dividend qualifies as a "large stock dividend," it must be recorded at par value. If a stock split is chosen, Campbell will declare a 2-for-1 split.

Required

1. Compare the effects of the stock dividends and stock splits on the accounting equation.
2. Develop the Stockholders' Equity category of Campbell's balance sheet (a) after the stock dividend and (b) after the stock split.

Exercise 11-12 ***Stock Dividends and Stock Splits*** **LO 7**

Whitacre Company's Stockholders' Equity section of the balance sheet on December 31, 2003, was as follows:

Common stock, $10 par value,	
60,000 shares issued and outstanding	$ 600,000
Additional paid-in capital	480,000
Retained earnings	1,240,000
Total stockholders' equity	$2,320,000

On May 1, 2004, Whitacre declared and issued a 15% stock dividend, when the stock was selling for $20 per share. Then on November 1, it declared and issued a 2-for-1 stock split.

Required

1. How many shares of stock are outstanding at year-end?
2. What is the par value per share of these shares?
3. Develop the Stockholders' Equity category of Whitacre's balance sheet as of December 31, 2004.

Exercise 11-13 ***Reporting Changes in Stockholders' Equity Items*** **LO 8**

On May 1, 2003, Ryde Inc. had common stock of $345,000, additional paid-in capital of $1,298,000 and retained earnings of $3,013,000. Ryde did not purchase or sell any common stock during the year. The company reported net income of $556,000 and declared dividends in the amount of $78,000 during the year ended April 30, 2004.

Required

Prepare a financial statement that explains all the reasons for the differences between the beginning and ending balances for the accounts in the Stockholders' Equity category of the balance sheet.

Exercise 11-14 ***Comprehensive Income*** **LO 8**

Assume that you are the accountant for Ellis Corporation, which has issued its 2004 annual report. You have received an inquiry from a stockholder who has questions about several items in the annual report, including why Ellis has not shown certain transactions on the income statement. In particular, Ellis's 2004 balance sheet revealed two accounts in Stockholders' Equity (Unrealized Gain/Loss—Available-for-Sale Securities and Loss on Foreign Currency Translation Adjustments) for which the dollar amounts involved were not reported on the income statement.

Required

Draft a written response to the stockholder's inquiry that explains the nature of the two accounts and the reason that the amounts involved were not recorded on the 2004 income statement. Do you think the concept of comprehensive income would be useful to explain the impact of all events for Ellis Corporation?

Exercise 11-15 ***Payout Ratio and Book Value per Share*** **LO 9**

Divac Company has developed a statement of stockholders' equity for the year 2004 as follows:

	Preferred Stock	Paid-In Capital—Preferred	Common Stock	Paid-In Capital—Common	Retained Earnings
Balance Jan. 1	$100,000	$50,000	$400,000	$40,000	$200,000
Stock issued			100,000	10,000	
Net income					80,000
Cash dividend					− 45,000
Stock dividend	10,000	5,000			− 15,000
Balance Dec. 31	$110,000	$55,000	$500,000	$50,000	$220,000

Divac's preferred stock is $100 par, 8% stock. If the stock is liquidated or redeemed, stockholders are entitled to $120 per share. There are no dividends in arrears on the stock. The common stock has a par value of $5 per share.

Required

1. Determine the dividend payout ratio for the common stock.
2. Determine the book value per share of Divac's common stock.

Exercise 11-16 ***Impact of Transactions Involving Issuance of Stock on Statement of Cash Flows*** **LO 10**

From the following list, identify each item as operating (O), investing (I), financing (F), or not separately reported on the statement of cash flows (N).

_______ Issuance of common stock for cash
_______ Issuance of preferred stock for cash
_______ Issuance of common stock for equipment
_______ Issuance of preferred stock for land and building
_______ Conversion of preferred stock into common stock

Exercise 11-17 ***Impact of Transactions Involving Treasury Stock on Statement of Cash Flows*** **LO 10**

From the following list, identify each item as operating (O), investing (I), financing (F), or not separately reported on the statement of cash flows (N).

_______ Repurchase common stock as treasury stock
_______ Reissuance of common stock (held as treasury stock)
_______ Retirement of treasury stock

Exercise 11-18 ***Impact of Transactions Involving Dividends on Statement of Cash Flows*** **LO 10**

From the following list, identify each item as operating (O), investing (I), financing (F), or not separately reported on the statement of cash flows (N).

(continued)

________ Payment of cash dividend on common stock
________ Payment of cash dividend on preferred stock
________ Distribution of stock dividend
________ Declaration of stock split

Exercise 11-19 ***Determining Dividends Paid on Statement of Cash Flows*** **LO 10**

Clifford Company's comparative balance sheet included dividends payable of $80,000 at December 31, 2003, and $100,000 at December 31, 2004. Dividends declared by Clifford during 2004 amounted to $400,000.

Required

1. Calculate the amount of dividends actually paid to stockholders during 2004.
2. How will Clifford report the dividend payments on its 2004 statement of cash flows?

Exercise 11-20 ***Sole Proprietorship (Appendix)*** **LO 11**

Terry Woods opened Par Golf as a sole proprietor by investing $50,000 cash on January 1, 2004. Because the business was new, it operated at a net loss of $10,000 for 2004. During the year, Terry withdrew $20,000 from the business for living expenses. Terry also had $4,000 of interest income from sources unrelated to the business.

Required

1. Record all the necessary entries for 2004 on the books of Par Golf.
2. Present the Owner's Equity category of Par Golf's balance sheet as of December 31, 2004.

Exercise 11-21 ***Partnerships (Appendix)*** **LO 11**

Sports Central is a sporting goods store owned by Lewis, Jamal, and Lapin in partnership. On January 1, 2004, their capital balances were as follows:

Lewis, Capital	$20,000
Jamal, Capital	50,000
Lapin, Capital	30,000

During 2004, Lewis withdrew $5,000; Jamal, $12,000; and Lapin, $9,000. Income for the partnership for 2004 was $50,000.

Required

If the partners agreed to allocate income equally, what was the ending balance in each of their capital accounts on December 31, 2004?

Problems

Problem 11-1 ***Stockholders' Equity Category*** **LO 1**

Peeler Company was incorporated as a new business on January 1, 2004. The corporate charter approved on that date authorized the issuance of 1,000 shares of $100 par, 7% cumulative, nonparticipating preferred stock and 10,000 shares of $5 par common stock. On January 10, Peeler issued for cash 500 shares of preferred stock at $120 per share and 4,000 shares of common at $80 per share. On January 20, it issued 1,000 shares of common stock to acquire a building site, at a time when the stock was selling for $70 per share.

During 2004, Peeler established an employee benefit plan and acquired 500 shares of common stock at $60 per share as treasury stock for that purpose. Later in 2004, it resold 100 shares of the stock at $65 per share.

On December 31, 2004, Peeler determined its net income for the year to be $40,000. The firm declared the annual cash dividend to preferred stockholders and a cash dividend of $5 per share to the common stockholders. The dividends will be paid in 2005.

Required

Develop the Stockholders' Equity category of Peeler's balance sheet as of December 31, 2004. Indicate on the statement the number of shares authorized, issued, and outstanding for both preferred and common stock.

Problem 11-2 ***Evaluating Alternative Investments*** **LO 2**

DECISION MAKING

Ellen Hays received a windfall from one of her investments. She would like to invest $100,000 of the money in Linwood Inc., which is offering common stock, preferred stock, and bonds on the open market. The common stock has paid $8 per share in dividends for the past three years and the company expects to be able to perform as well in the current year. The current market price of the common stock is $100 per share. The preferred stock has an 8% dividend rate, cumulative and nonparticipating. The bonds are selling at par with an 8% stated rate.

1. What are the advantages and disadvantages of each type of investment?
2. Recommend one type of investment over the others to Ellen, and justify your reason.

Problem 11-3 ***Dividends for Preferred and Common Stock*** **LO 5**

The Stockholders' Equity category of Greenbaum Company's balance sheet as of December 31, 2004, appeared as follows:

Preferred stock, $100 par, 8%,	
1,000 shares issued and outstanding	$ 100,000
Common stock, $10 par,	
20,000 shares issued and outstanding	200,000
Additional paid-in capital	250,000
Total contributed capital	$ 550,000
Retained earnings	450,000
Total stockholders' equity	$1,000,000

The notes to the financial statements indicate that dividends were not declared or paid for 2002 or 2003. Greenbaum wants to declare a dividend of $59,000 for 2004.

Required

Determine the total and the per-share amounts that should be declared to the preferred and common stockholders under the following assumptions:

1. The preferred stock is noncumulative, nonparticipating.
2. The preferred stock is cumulative, nonparticipating.
3. The preferred stock is cumulative and participating on the basis of the proportion of the total par values of the preferred and common stock.

Problem 11-4 ***Effect of Stock Dividend*** **LO 6**

Favre Company has a history of paying cash dividends on its common stock. The firm did not have a particularly profitable year, however, in 2004. At the end of the year, Favre found itself without the necessary cash for a dividend and therefore declared a stock dividend to its common stockholders. A 50% stock dividend was declared to stockholders on December 31, 2004. The board of directors is unclear about a stock dividend's effect on Favre's balance sheet and has requested your assistance.

Required

1. Write a statement to indicate the effect that the stock dividend has on the financial statements of Favre Company.
2. A group of common stockholders has contacted the firm to express its concern about the effect of the stock dividend and to question the effect the stock dividend may have on the market price of the stock. Write a statement to address the stockholders' concerns.

Problem 11-5 ***Dividends and Stock Splits*** **LO 7**

On January 1, 2004, Frederiksen's Inc.'s Stockholders' Equity category appeared as follows:

Preferred stock, $80 par value, 7%,	
3,000 shares issued and outstanding	$ 240,000
Common stock, $10 par value,	
15,000 shares issued and outstanding	150,000
Additional paid-in capital—Preferred	60,000
Additional paid-in capital—Common	225,000
Total contributed capital	$ 675,000
Retained earnings	2,100,000
Total stockholders' equity	$2,775,000

(continued)

The preferred stock is noncumulative and nonparticipating. During 2004, the following transactions occurred:

a. On March 1, declared a cash dividend of $16,800 on preferred stock. Paid the dividend on April 1.

b. On June 1, declared a 5% stock dividend on common stock. The current market price of the common stock was $18. The stock was issued on July 1.

c. On September 1, declared a cash dividend of $0.50 per share on the common stock; paid the dividend on October 1.

d. On December 1, issued a 2-for-1 stock split of common stock, when the stock was selling for $50 per share.

Required

1. Explain each transaction's effect on the stockholders' equity accounts and the total stockholders' equity.
2. Develop the Stockholders' Equity category of the December 31, 2004, balance sheet. Assume the net income for the year was $650,000.
3. Write a paragraph that explains the difference between a stock dividend and a stock split.

Problem 11-6 *Statement of Stockholders' Equity* LO 8

Refer to all the facts in Problem 11-1.

Required

Develop a statement of stockholders' equity for Peeler Company for 2004. The statement should start with the beginning balance of each stockholders' equity account and explain the changes that occurred in each account to arrive at the 2004 ending balances.

Problem 11-7 *Wal-Mart's Comprehensive Income* LO 8

http://www.walmart.com

The consolidated statement of shareholders' equity of Wal-Mart Stores, Inc. for the year ended December 31, 2001, appears below:

Consolidated Statement of Shareholders' Equity (Amounts in millions)

	Number of Shares	Common Stock	Capital in Excess of Par Value	Retained Earnings	Accumulated Comprehensive Income	Total
Balance, January 31, 2001	4,470	$447	$1,411	$30,169	$(684)	$31,343
Comprehensive Income						
Net income				6,671		6,671
Other accumulated comprehensive income						
Foreign currency translation adjustment					(472)	(472)
Hedge accounting adjustment					(112)	(112)
Total Comprehensive Income						$ 6,087
Cash dividends ($0.28 per share)				(1,249)		$(1,249)
Purchase of Company stock	(24)	(2)	(62)	(1,150)		(1,214)
Stock options exercised and other	7		135			$ 135
Balance, January 31, 2002	4,453	$445	$1,484	$34,441	$(1,268)	$35,102

Required

1. Which items were included in comprehensive income? If these items had been included on the income statement as part of net income, what would have been the effect?
2. Do you think that the concept of comprehensive income would be useful to explain the impact of all the events that took place during 2001 to the stockholders of Wal-Mart?

Problem 11-8 ***Effects of Stockholders' Equity Transactions on Statement of Cash Flows*** **LO 10**

Refer to all the facts in Problem 11-1.

Required

Indicate how each of the transactions affects the cash flows of Peeler Company, by preparing the Financing Activities section of the 2004 statement of cash flows. Provide an explanation for the exclusion of any of these transactions from the Financing Activities section of the statement.

Problem 11-9 ***Income Distribution of a Partnership (Appendix)*** **LO 11**

Louise Abbott and Buddie Costello are partners in a comedy club business. The partnership agreement specifies the manner in which income of the business is to be distributed. Louise is to receive a salary of $20,000 for managing the club, and Buddie is to receive interest at the rate of 10% on her capital balance of $300,000. Remaining income is to be distributed on a 2-to-1 ratio.

Required

Determine the amount that should be distributed to each partner, assuming the following business net incomes:

1. $15,000
2. $50,000
3. $80,000

Problem 11-10 ***Sole Proprietorships (Appendix)*** **LO 11**

On May 1, Chong Yu deposited $120,000 of his own savings in a separate bank account to start a printing business. He purchased copy machines for $42,000. Expenses for the year, including depreciation on the copy machines, were $84,000. Sales for the year, all in cash, were $108,000. Chong withdrew $12,000 during the year.

Required

1. Prepare the journal entries for the following transactions: the May 1 initial investment, Chong's withdrawal of cash, and the December 31 closing entries. Chong closes revenues and expenses to an Income Summary account.
2. What is the balance in Chong's capital account at the end of the year?
3. Explain why the balance in Chong's capital account is different from the amount of cash on hand.

Problem 11-11 ***Partnerships (Appendix)*** **LO 11**

Kirin Nerise and Milt O'Brien agreed to form a partnership to operate a sandwich shop. Kirin contributed $25,000 cash and will manage the store. Milt contributed computer equipment worth $8,000 and $92,000 cash. Milt will keep the financial records. During the year, sales were $90,000 and expenses were $76,000. Kirin withdrew $500 per month. Milt withdrew $4,000 (total). Their partnership agreement specified that Kirin would receive a salary of $7,200 for the year. Milt would receive 6% interest on his initial capital investment. All remaining income or loss would be equally divided.

Required

Calculate the ending balance in the equity account of each of the partners.

Multi-Concept Problems

Problem 11-12 ***Analysis of Stockholders' Equity*** **LO 1, 4**

The Stockholders' Equity section of the December 31, 2004, balance sheet of Eldon Company appeared as follows:

Preferred stock, $30 par value, 5,000 shares authorized, ? shares issued	$120,000
Common stock, ? par, 10,000 shares authorized, 7,000 shares issued	70,000
Additional paid-in capital—Preferred	6,000
Additional paid-in capital—Common	560,000
Additional paid-in capital—Treasury stock	1,000

(continued)

Total contributed capital	$757,000
Retained earnings	40,000
Less: Treasury stock, preferred, 100 shares	(3,200)
Total stockholders' equity	$??

Required

Determine the following items, based on Eldon's balance sheet:

1. The number of shares of preferred stock issued
2. The number of shares of preferred stock outstanding
3. The average per-share sales price of the preferred stock when issued
4. The par value of the common stock
5. The average per-share sales price of the common stock when issued
6. The cost of the treasury stock per share
7. The total stockholders' equity
8. The per-share book value of the common stock, assuming that there are no dividends in arrears and that the preferred stock can be redeemed at its par value

Problem 11-13 ***Effects of Stockholders' Equity Transactions on the Balance Sheet*** **LO 3, 4, 7**

The following transactions occurred at Horton Inc. during its first year of operation:

a. Issued 100,000 shares of common stock at $5 each; 1,000,000 shares are authorized at $1 par value.

b. Issued 10,000 shares of common stock for a building and land. The building was appraised for $20,000, but the value of the land is undeterminable. The stock is selling for $10 on the open market.

c. Purchased 1,000 shares of its own common stock on the open market for $16 per share.

d. Declared a dividend of $0.10 per share on outstanding common stock. The dividend is to be paid after the end of the first year of operations. Market value of the stock is $26.

e. Declared a 2-for-1 stock split. The market value of the stock was $37 before the stock split.

f. Reported $180,000 of income for the year.

Required

1. Indicate each transaction's effect on the assets, liabilities, and owners' equity of Horton Inc.
2. Prepare the Stockholders' Equity section of the balance sheet.
3. Write a paragraph that explains the number of shares of stock issued and outstanding at the end of the year.

Problem 11-14 ***Stockholders' Equity Section of the Balance Sheet*** **LO 1, 4**

The newly hired accountant at Ives Inc. prepared the following balance sheet:

Assets	
Cash	$ 3,500
Accounts receivable	5,000
Treasury stock	500
Plant, property, and equipment	108,000
Retained earnings	1,000
Total assets	$118,000
Liabilities	
Accounts payable	$ 5,500
Dividends payable	1,500
Owners' Equity	
Common stock, $1 par, 100,000 shares issued	100,000
Additional paid-in capital	11,000
Total liabilities and owners' equity	$118,000

Required

1. Prepare a corrected balance sheet. Write a short explanation for each correction.
2. Why does the Retained Earnings account have a negative balance?

Alternate Problems

Problem 11-1A ***Stockholders' Equity Category*** **LO 1**

Kebler Company was incorporated as a new business on January 1, 2004. The corporate charter approved on that date authorized the issuance of 2,000 shares of $100 par 7% cumulative, nonparticipating preferred stock and 20,000 shares of $5 par common stock. On January 10, Kebler issued for cash 1,000 shares of preferred stock at $120 per share and 8,000 shares of common at $80 per share. On January 20, it issued 2,000 shares of common stock to acquire a building site, at a time when the stock was selling for $70 per share.

During 2004 Kebler established an employee benefit plan and acquired 1,000 shares of common stock at $60 per share as treasury stock for that purpose. Later in 2004, it resold 100 shares of the stock at $65 per share.

On December 31, 2004, Kebler determined its net income for the year to be $80,000. The firm declared the annual cash dividend to preferred stockholders and a cash dividend of $5 per share to the common stockholders. The dividend will be paid in 2005.

Required

Develop the Stockholders' Equity category of Kebler's balance sheet as of December 31, 2004. Indicate on the statement the number of shares authorized, issued, and outstanding for both preferred and common stock.

Problem 11-2A ***Evaluating Alternative Investments*** **LO 2**

DECISION MAKING

Rob Lowe would like to invest $100,000 in Franklin Inc., which is offering common stock, preferred stock, and bonds on the open market. The common stock has paid $1 per share in dividends for the past three years, and the company expects to be able to double the dividend in the current year. The current market price of the common stock is $10 per share. The preferred stock has an 8% dividend rate. The bonds are selling at par with a 5% stated rate.

Required

1. Explain Franklin's obligation to pay dividends or interest on each instrument.
2. Recommend one type of investment over the others to Rob, and justify your reason.

Problem 11-3A ***Dividends for Preferred and Common Stock*** **LO 5**

The Stockholders' Equity category of Rausch Company's balance sheet as of December 31, 2004, appeared as follows:

Preferred stock, $100 par, 8%,	
2,000 shares issued and outstanding	$ 200,000
Common stock, $10 par,	
40,000 shares issued and outstanding	400,000
Additional paid-in capital	500,000
Total contributed capital	$1,100,000
Retained earnings	900,000
Total stockholders' equity	$2,000,000

The notes to the financial statements indicate that dividends were not declared or paid for 2002 or 2003. Rausch wants to declare a dividend of $118,000 for 2004.

Required

Determine the total and the per-share amounts that should be declared to the preferred and common stockholders under the following assumptions:

1. The preferred stock is noncumulative, nonparticipating.
2. The preferred stock is cumulative, nonparticipating.
3. The preferred stock is cumulative and participating on the basis of the proportion of the total par values of the preferred and common stock.

Problem 11-4A *Effect of Stock Dividend* LO 6

Travanti Company has a history of paying cash dividends on its common stock. Although the firm has been profitable this year, the board of directors has been planning construction of a second manufacturing plant. To reduce the amount that they must borrow to finance the expansion, the directors are contemplating replacing their usual cash dividend with a 40% stock dividend. The board is unsure what the effect of a stock dividend will be on the company's balance sheet and has requested your assistance.

Required

1. Write a statement to indicate the effect that the stock dividend has on the financial statements of Travanti Company.
2. A group of common stockholders has contacted the firm to express its concern about the effect of the stock dividend and to question the effect that the stock dividend may have on the market price of the stock. Write a statement to address the stockholders' concerns.

Problem 11-5A *Dividends and Stock Splits* LO 7

On January 1, 2004, Svenberg Inc.'s Stockholders' Equity category appeared as follows:

Preferred stock, $80 par value, 8%, 1,000 shares issued and outstanding	$ 80,000
Common stock, $10 par value, 10,000 shares issued and outstanding	100,000
Additional paid-in capital— Preferred	60,000
Additional paid-in capital— Common	225,000
Total contributed capital	$ 465,000
Retained earnings	1,980,000
Total stockholders' equity	$2,445,000

The preferred stock is noncumulative and nonparticipating. During 2004, the following transactions occurred:

a. On March 1, declared a cash dividend of $6,400 on preferred stock. Paid the dividend on April 1.

b. On June 1, declared an 8% stock dividend on common stock. The current market price of the common stock was $26. The stock was issued on July 1.

c. On September 1, declared a cash dividend of $0.70 per share on the common stock; paid the dividend on October 1.

d. On December 1, issued a 3-for-1 stock split of common stock, when the stock was selling for $30 per share.

Required

1. Explain each transaction's effect on the stockholders' equity accounts and the total stockholders' equity.
2. Develop the Stockholders' Equity category of the balance sheet. Assume the net income for the year was $720,000.
3. Write a paragraph that explains the difference between a stock dividend and a stock split.

Problem 11-6A *Statement of Stockholders' Equity* LO 8

Refer to all the facts in Problem 11-1A.

Required

Develop a statement of stockholders' equity for Kebler Company for 2004. The statement should start with the beginning balance of each stockholders' equity account and explain the changes that occurred in each account to arrive at the 2004 ending balances.

Problem 11-7A *AMR's Comprehensive Income* LO 8

http://www.amrcorp.com

The consolidated statement of stockholders' equity of AMR Corporation for the year ended December 31, 2001, appears on the following page.

Consolidated Statement of Stockholders' Equity

AMR CORPORATION
CONSOLIDATED STATEMENT OF STOCKHOLDERS' EQUITY
(IN MILLIONS, EXCEPT SHARE AMOUNTS)

	Common Stock	Additional Paid-In Capital	Treasury Stock	Accumulated Other Comprehensive Loss	Retained Earnings	Total
Balance at December 31, 2000	$182	$2,911	$(1,865)	$ (2)	$5,950	$7,176
Net loss	—	—	—	—	(1,762)	(1,762)
Adjustment for minimum pension liability, net of tax of $60	—	—	—	(101)	—	(101)
Changes in fair value of derivative financial instruments, net of tax of $29	—	—	—	(46)	—	(46)
Unrealized gain on investments, net of tax of $2	—	—	—	3	—	3
Total comprehensive loss				(1,906)		
Issuance of 2,421,838 shares from Treasury pursuant to stock option, deferred stock and restricted stock incentive plans, net of tax of $58	—	(46)	149	—	—	103
Balance at December 31, 2001	$182	$2,865	$(1,716)	$(146)	$4,188	$5,373

Required

1. Explain the item that caused AMR's net income to be different from its comprehensive income. What does the term *unrealized gain* mean? What does a positive amount of $3 for unrealized gain on investments mean?
2. Do you think that AMR's stockholders would find the concept of comprehensive income useful to evaluate the performance of the company?

Problem 11-8A ***Effects of Stockholders' Equity Transactions on the Statement of Cash Flows*** **LO 10** PT

Refer to all the facts in Problem 11-1A.

Required

Indicate how each of the transactions affects the cash flows of Kebler Company, by preparing the Financing Activities section of the 2004 statement of cash flows. Provide an explanation for the exclusion of any of these transactions from the Financing Activities section of the statement.

Problem 11-9A ***Income Distribution of a Partnership (Appendix)*** **LO 11** PT

Kay Katz and Doris Kan are partners in a dry-cleaning business. The partnership agreement specifies the manner in which income of the business is to be distributed. Kay is to receive a salary of $40,000 for managing the business. Doris is to receive interest at the rate of 10% on her capital balance of $600,000. Remaining income is to be distributed on a 2-to-1 ratio.

Required

Determine the amount that should be distributed to each partner, assuming the following business net incomes:

1. $30,000
2. $100,000
3. $160,000

Problem 11-10A ***Sole Proprietorships (Appendix)*** **LO 11** PT

On May 1, Chen Chien Lao deposited $150,000 of her own savings in a separate bank account to start a printing business. She purchased copy machines for $52,500. Expenses for the year, including depreciation on the copy machines, were $105,000. Sales for the year, all in cash, were $135,000. Chen withdrew $15,000 during the year.

(continued)

Required

1. Prepare the journal entries for the following transactions: the May 1 initial investment, Chen's withdrawal of cash, and the December 31 closing entries. Chen closes revenues and expenses to an Income Summary account.
2. What is the balance in Chen's capital account at the end of the year?
3. Explain why the balance in Chen's capital account is different from the amount of cash on hand.

Problem 11-11A *Partnerships (Appendix)* LO 11

Karen Locke and Gina Keyes agreed to form a partnership to operate a sandwich shop. Karen contributed $35,000 cash and will manage the store. Gina contributed computer equipment worth $11,200 and $128,800 cash. Gina will keep the financial records. During the year, sales were $126,000 and expenses were $106,400. Karen withdrew $700 per month. Gina withdrew $5,600 (total). Their partnership agreement specified that Karen would receive a salary of $10,800 for the year. Gina would receive 6% interest on her initial capital investment. All remaining income or loss would be equally divided.

Required

Calculate the ending balance in the equity account of each of the partners.

Alternate Multi-Concept Problems

Problem 11-12A *Analysis of Stockholders' Equity* LO 1, 4

The Stockholders' Equity section of the December 31, 2004, balance sheet of Carter Company appeared as follows:

Preferred stock, $50 par value, 10,000 shares authorized, ? shares issued	$ 400,000
Common stock, ? par value, 20,000 shares authorized, 14,000 shares issued	280,000
Additional paid-in capital—Preferred	12,000
Additional paid-in capital—Common	980,000
Additional paid-in capital—Treasury stock	2,000
Total contributed capital	$1,674,000
Retained earnings	80,000
Less: Treasury stock, preferred, 200 shares	(12,800)
Total stockholders' equity	$??

Determine the following items, based on Carter's balance sheet.

1. The number of shares of preferred stock issued
2. The number of shares of preferred stock outstanding
3. The average per-share sales price of the preferred stock when issued
4. The par value of the common stock
5. The average per-share sales price of the common stock when issued
6. The cost of the treasury stock per share
7. The total stockholders' equity
8. The per-share book value of the common stock, assuming that there are no dividends in arrears and that the preferred stock can be redeemed at its par value

Problem 11-13A *Effects of Stockholders' Equity Transactions on Balance Sheet* LO 3, 4, 7

The following transactions occurred at Hilton Inc. during its first year of operation:

a. Issued 10,000 shares of common stock at $10 each; 100,000 shares are authorized at $1 par value.

b. Issued 10,000 shares of common stock for a patent, which is expected to be effective for the next 15 years. The value of the patent is undeterminable. The stock is selling for $10 on the open market.

c. Purchased 1,000 shares of its own common stock on the open market for $10 per share.

d. Declared a dividend of $0.50 per share of outstanding common stock. The dividend is to be paid after the end of the first year of operations. Market value of the stock is $10.

e. Income for the year is reported as $340,000.

Required

1. Indicate each transaction's effect on the assets, liabilities, and owners' equity of Hilton Inc.
2. Hilton's president has asked you to explain the difference between contributed capital and retained earnings. Discuss these terms as they relate to Hilton.
3. Determine the book value per share of the stock at the end of the year.

Problem 11-14A ***Stockholders' Equity Section of the Balance Sheet*** **LO 1, 4**

The newly hired accountant at Grainfield Inc. is considering the following list of accounts as he prepares the balance sheet. All of the accounts have positive balances. The company is authorized to issue 1,000,000 shares of common stock and 10,000 shares of preferred stock. The treasury stock was purchased at $5 per share.

Treasury stock (common)	$ 15,000
Retained earnings	54,900
Dividends payable	1,500
Common stock, $1 par	100,000
Additional paid-in capital	68,400
Preferred stock, $10 par, 5%	50,000

Required

1. Prepare the Stockholders' Equity section of the balance sheet for Grainfield.
2. Explain why some of the listed accounts are not shown in the Stockholders' Equity section.

Cases

Reading and Interpreting Financial Statements

Case 11-1 ***Winnebago Industries' Stockholders' Equity Category*** **LO 1, 2**

Refer to Winnebago Industries' 2001 annual report.

http://www.winnebagoind.com

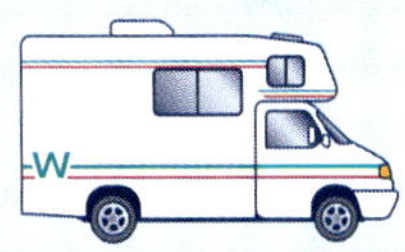

Required

1. What are the numbers of shares of common stock authorized, issued, and outstanding as of the balance sheet date?
2. Calculate the book value per share of the common stock.
3. The balance of the Reinvested Earnings account increased during the year. What are the possible factors that affect its balance?
4. The total stockholders' equity as of August 25, 2001, is $207,464,000. Does that mean that stockholders will receive that amount if the company is liquidated?

Case 11-2 ***Comparing Two Companies in the Same Industry: Winnebago Industries and Monaco Coach Corporation*** **LO 1, 8**

Refer to the stockholders' equity section of the balance sheets of Monaco Coach Corporation as of December 29, 2001 and of Winnebago Industries as of August 25, 2001 that are provided in Appendices A and B at the end of the text.

http://www.winnebagoind.com
http://www.monacocoach.com

Required

1. For each company, what are the numbers of shares of common stock authorized, issued, and outstanding as of the balance sheet date?
2. Calculate the book value per share for each company on its balance sheet date. What does this information tell you?
3. Did the balance of the Retained Earnings account of each company increase or decrease during the year? What are the possible factors that affect the Retained Earnings balance?

(continued)

4. How does the total stockholders' equity of each company compare to the other company? Does the difference mean that one company's stock is more valuable than the others? Explain your answer.

Case 11-3 *Reading Winnebago Industries' Statement of Cash Flows* LO 10

http://www.winnebagoind.com

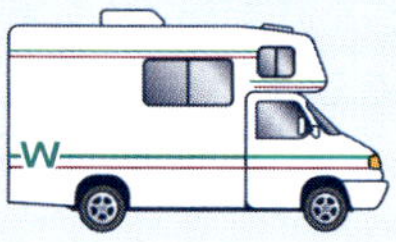

A portion of the cash flow statement of Winnebago Industries for the year ended August 25, 2001, is as follows:

	Year Ended		
(In thousands)	**August 25, 2001**	**August 26, 2000**	**August 28, 1999**
Cash flows from financing activities and capital transactions:			
Payments for purchase of common stock	(10,686)	(19,726)	(8,975)
Payments of cash dividends	(4,121)	(4,324)	(4,443)
Proceeds from issuance of common and treasury stock	3,449	1,176	2,019
Net cash used by financing activities and capital transactions	(11,358)	(22,874)	(11,399)

Required

1. Explain how each of the items in the Financing Activities category affected the amount of the company's cash.
2. Winnebago Industries generated cash by selling treasury stock during the year. What are possible reasons for buying stock as treasury stock? Why would a company resell treasury stock after it has been purchased?
3. The cash flow statement indicates a use of cash for dividends paid. How do dividends affect the Stockholders' Equity category of the balance sheet?

Making Financial Decisions

DECISION MAKING

Case 11-4 *Debt versus Preferred Stock* LO 1, 2

Assume that you are an analyst attempting to compare the financial structures of two companies. In particular, you must analyze the debt and equity categories of the two firms and calculate a debt-to-equity ratio for each firm. The liability and equity categories of First Company at year-end appeared as follows:

Liabilities	
Accounts payable	$ 500,000
Loan payable	800,000
Stockholders' Equity	
Common stock	300,000
Retained earnings	600,000
Total liabilities and equity	$2,200,000

First Company's loan payable bears interest at 8%, which is paid annually. The principal is due in five years.

The liability and equity categories of Second Company at year-end appeared as follows:

Liabilities	
Accounts payable	$ 500,000
Stockholders' Equity	
Common stock	300,000
Preferred stock	800,000
Retained earnings	600,000
Total liabilities and equity	$2,200,000

Second Company's preferred stock is 8%, cumulative stock. A provision of the stock agreement specifies that the stock must be redeemed at face value in five years.

Required

1. It appears that the loan payable of First Company and the preferred stock of Second Company are very similar. What are the differences between the two securities?
2. When calculating the debt-to-equity ratio, do you believe that the Second Company preferred stock should be treated as debt or as stockholders' equity? Write a statement expressing your position on this issue.

Case 11-5 *Preferred versus Common Stock* LO 2

DECISION MAKING

Rohnan Inc. needs to raise $500,000. It is considering two options:

a. Issue preferred stock, $100 par, 8%, cumulative, nonparticipating, callable at $110. The stock could be issued at par.

b. Issue common stock, $1 par, market $10. Currently, the company has 400,000 shares outstanding equally in the hands of five owners. The company has never paid a dividend.

Required

Rohnan has asked you to consider both options and make a recommendation. It is equally concerned with cash flow and company control. Write your recommendations.

Accounting and Ethics: What Would You Do?

Case 11-6 *Inside Information* LO 9

Jim Brock was an accountant with Hubbard Inc., a large corporation with stock that was publicly traded on the New York Stock Exchange. One of Jim's duties was to manage the corporate reporting department, which was responsible for developing and issuing Hubbard's annual report. At the end of 2004, Hubbard closed its accounting records, and initial calculations indicated a very profitable year. In fact, the net income exceeded the amount that had been projected during the year by the financial analysts who followed Hubbard's stock.

Jim was very pleased with the company's financial performance. In January 2005, he suggested that his father buy Hubbard's stock because he was sure the stock price would increase when the company announced its 2004 results. Jim's father followed the advice and bought a block of stock at $25 per share.

On February 15, 2005, Hubbard announced its 2004 results and issued the annual report. The company received favorable press coverage about its performance, and the stock price on the stock exchange increased to $32 per share.

Required

What was Jim's professional responsibility to Hubbard Inc. concerning the issuance of the 2004 annual report? Did Jim act ethically in this situation?

Case 11-7 *Dividend Policy* LO 5

Hancock Inc. is owned by nearly 100 shareholders. Judith Stitch owns 48% of the stock. She needs cash to fulfill her commitment to donate the funds to construct a new art gallery. Some of her friends have agreed to vote for Hancock to pay a larger-than-normal dividend to shareholders. Judith has asked you to vote for the large dividend because she knows that you also support the arts. When informed that the dividend may create a working capital hardship on Hancock, Judith responded: "There is plenty of money in Retained Earnings. The dividend will not affect the cash of the company." Respond to her comment. What ethical questions do you and Judith face? How would you vote?

Internet Research Case

Case 11-8 *Delta Air Lines*

INTERNET

http://www.delta.com

Delta Air Lines operates in the highly volatile airline industry. It must respond to competition and to innovative technology, and it must do so in ways that continue to build shareholder value. Conduct a search of the World Wide Web, obtain Delta's most recent annual report, or use library resources to obtain company information to answer the following:

1. Based on the latest information available, what is Delta's (a) authorized number of common stock shares, (b) issued number of shares, (c) outstanding number of shares, and (d) the average issue price for those shares?
2. For the most recent year available, what dividend per common share did Delta pay its stockholders?
3. Locate the past 52-week high and low and the most current market price for Delta Air Lines common stock. What financial factors may have affected the company's stock price over the past three to six months? Would you buy Delta stock at this time? Explain your response.

http://www.travelocity.com
http://www.expedia.com

Optional Research. Use an online reservation system to investigate how the prices of Delta Air Lines plane tickets compare with those of the other airlines. Are they higher or lower? Are there some routes where Delta has a competitive advantage?

Solutions to Key Terms Quiz

Answer	Term	Answer	Term
13	Authorized shares (p. 557)	7	Dividend payout ratio (p. 565)
1	Issued shares (p. 557)	19	Stock dividend (p. 567)
14	Outstanding shares (p. 557)	9	Stock split (p. 569)
2	Par value (p. 558)	8	Statement of stockholders' equity (p. 571)
15	Additional paid-in capital (p. 559)	11	Comprehensive income (p. 572)
3	Retained earnings (p. 559)	10	Book value per share (p. 573)
4	Cumulative feature (p. 561)	12	Market value per share (p. 574)
16	Participating feature (p. 561)	22	Sole proprietorship (p. 583)
5	Convertible feature (p. 561)	20	Partnership (p. 584)
17	Callable feature (p. 561)	21	Partnership agreement (p. 584)
6	Treasury stock (p. 563)		
18	Retirement of stock (p. 564)		

Part III

Integrative Problem

Evaluating financing options for asset acquisition and their impact on financial statements

Following are the financial statements for Griffin Inc. for the year 2004.

GRIFFIN INC.
BALANCE SHEET
DECEMBER 31, 2004
(IN MILLIONS)

Assets		**Liabilities**	
Cash	$ 1.6	Current portion of lease obligation	$ 1.0
Other current assets	6.4	Other current liabilities	3.0
Leased assets (net of accumulated depreciation)	7.0	Lease obligation—Long-term	6.0
Other long-term assets	45.0	Other long-term liabilities	6.0
		Total liabilities	$16.0
		Stockholders' Equity	
		Preferred stock	$ 1.0
		Additional paid-in capital on preferred stock	2.0
		Common stock	4.0
		Additional paid-in capital on common stock	16.0
		Retained earnings	21.0
		Total stockholders' equity	$44.0
Total assets	$60.0	Total liabilities and stockholders' equity	$60.0

GRIFFIN INC.
INCOME STATEMENT
FOR THE YEAR ENDED DECEMBER 31, 2004
(IN MILLIONS)

Revenues		$50.0
Expenses:		
Depreciation of leased asset	$ 1.0	
Depreciation—Other assets	3.2	
Interest on leased asset	0.5	
Other expenses	27.4	
Income tax (30% rate)	5.4	
Total expenses		(37.5)
Income before extraordinary loss		$12.5
Extraordinary loss (net of $0.9 taxcs)		(2.1)
Net income		$10.4
EPS before extraordinary loss		$3.10
EPS extraordinary loss		(0.53)
EPS—Net income		$2.57

Additional Information:

Griffin Inc. has authorized 500,000 shares of 10%, $10 par value cumulative preferred stock. There were 100,000 shares issued and outstanding at all times during 2004. The firm has also authorized 5 million shares of $1 par common stock, with 4 million shares issued and outstanding.

On January 1, 2004, Griffin Inc. acquired an asset, a piece of specialized heavy equipment, for $8 million with a capital lease. The lease contract indicates that the term of the lease is eight years. Payments of $1.5 million are to be made each December 31. The first lease payment was made December 31, 2004 and consisted of $1 million principal and $0.5 million of interest expense. The capital lease is depreciated using the straight-line method over eight years with zero salvage value.

Required

1. Assuming the equipment was acquired using a capital lease, provide the entries for the acquisition, depreciation, and lease payment.
2. The management of Griffin Inc. is considering the financial statement impact of methods of financing, other than the capital lease, that could have been used to acquire the equipment. For each alternative **a**, **b**, and **c**, provide all necessary entries, each entry's impact on the accounting equation, and revised 2004 financial statements and calculate, as revised, the following amounts or ratios:

   Current ratio
   Debt-to-equity ratio
   Net income
   EPS—Net income

Assume that the following alternative actions would have taken place on January 1, 2004.

a. Instead of acquiring the equipment with a capital lease, the company negotiated an operating lease to use the asset. The lease requires annual year-end payments of $1.5 million and results in "off-balance sheet" financing. (*Hint:* The $1.5 million should be treated as rental expense.)

b. Instead of acquiring the equipment with a capital lease, Griffin Inc. issued bonds for $8 million and purchased the equipment with the proceeds of the bond issue. Assume the bond interest of $0.5 million was accrued and paid on December 31, 2004. A portion of the principal also is paid each year for eight years. On December 31, 2004, the company paid $1 million of principal and anticipated another $1 million of principal to be paid in 2005. Assume the equipment would have an eight-year life and would be depreciated on a straight-line basis with zero salvage value.

c. Instead of acquiring the equipment with a capital lease, Griffin Inc. issued 200,000 additional shares of 10% preferred stock to raise $8 million and purchased the equipment for $8 million with the proceeds from the stock issue. Dividends on the stock are declared and paid annually. Assume that a dividend payment was made on December 31, 2004. Assume the equipment would have an eight-year life and would be depreciated on a straight-line basis with zero salvage value.

Part IV

Additional Topics in Financial Reporting

A Word to Students about Part IV

Part IV will be fascinating and even fun—as long as you *keep practicing the concepts and reading the links from chapter to chapter.* **How does the corporation report cash flows?** See Chapter 12 to learn how to evaluate a company based on its cash flows. **Can you find the trends in a company's performance?** Use any set of financial statements you can find to practice the analysis concepts and skills presented in Chapter 13.

Chapter 12

The Statement of Cash Flows

© TERRI MILLER/E-VISUAL COMMUNICATIONS, INC.

Focus on Financial Results

Cash, and the steady flow of it, is the lifeblood of any business, and IBM is no exception. As shown on the accompanying consolidated statement of cash flows, IBM ended 2001 with over $6.3 billion of cash and cash equivalents, an amount nearly double what it reported only a year earlier. Cash flow from operating activities topped $14 billion in 2001, which is significantly higher than the $9 billion and $10 billion generated in 2000 and 1999, respectively.

What a company does with the cash it generates from its operations is crucial to its future success. For example, how much of the cash is used to pay for new plant and equipment? IBM reports that it used $5.660 billion of its cash for "payments for plant, rental machines and other property" during 2001. To be successful in the highly competitive information technology industry requires that a company continually add to its asset base, as attested to by the nearly $6 billion IBM has spent in each of the last three years on capital additions.

How much cash generated from buying and selling products and services remains after investing in new plant and equipment? For IBM, this amounted to over $8 billion in 2001, and nearly $3 billion of this was added to the ending cash balance. The remaining $5 billion was used in a variety of financing activities, including the settlement of existing debts, the repurchase of its own stock on the market, and the payment of dividends to stockholders.

Source: 2001 IBM annual report.

IBM's 2001 Annual Report

Consolidated Statement of Cash Flows
INTERNATIONAL BUSINESS MACHINES CORPORATION
and Subsidiary Companies

(dollars in millions)

FOR THE YEAR ENDED DECEMBER 31:	2001	2000*	1999*
CASH FLOW FROM OPERATING ACTIVITIES:			
Net income	$7,723	$8,093	$7,712
Adjustments to reconcile net income to net cash provided from operating activities:			
Depreciation	4,195	4,513	6,159
Amortization of software	625	482	426
Deferred income taxes	658	29	(713)
Gain on asset sales	(317)	(792)	(4,791)
Write-down of impaired investment assets	405	—	—
Other changes that provided/(used) cash:			
Receivables	3,284	(4,720)	(1,677)
Inventories	337	(55)	301
Other assets	(545)	(643)	(130)
Accounts payable	(969)	2,245	(3)
Other liabilities	(1,131)	122	2,827
NET CASH PROVIDED FROM OPERATING ACTIVITIES	14,265	9,274	10,111
CASH FLOW FROM INVESTING ACTIVITIES:			
Payments for plant, rental machines and other property	(5,660)	(5,616)	(5,959)
Proceeds from disposition of plant, rental machines and other property	1,165	1,619	1,207
Investment in software	(655)	(565)	(464)
Purchases of marketable sercurities and other investments	(778)	(750)	(2,628)
Proceeds from marketable sercurities and other investments	738	1,393	2,616
Proceeds from sale of the Global Network	—	—	4,880
Acquisitions	(916)	(329)	(1,321)
NET CASH USED IN INVESTING ACTIVITIES	(6,106)	(4,248)	(1,669)
CASH FLOW FROM FINANCING ACTIVITIES:			
Proceeds from new debt	4,535	9,604	6,133
Short-term borrowings/(repayments) less than 90 days –net	2,926	(1,400)	276
Payments to settle debt	(7,898)	(7,561)	(7,510)
Preferred stock transactions–net	(254)	—	—
Common stock transactions–net	(3,652)	(6,073)	(6,645)
Cash dividends paid	(966)	(929)	(879)
NET CASH USED IN FINANCING ACTIVITIES	(5,309)	(6,359)	(8,625)
Effect of exchange rate changes on cash and cash equivalents	(83)	(147)	(149)
Net change in cash and cash equivalents	2,767	(1,480)	(332)
Cash and cash equivalents at January 1	3,563	5,043	5,375
CASH AND CASH EQUIVALENTS AT DECEMBER 31	$6,330	$3,563	$5,043
SUPPLEMENTAL DATA:			
Cash paid during the year for:			
Income taxes	$2,279	$2,697	$1,904
Interest	$1,247	$1,447	$1,574

*Reclassified to conform with 2001 presentation.
The accompanying notes on pages 75 through 105 are an integral part of the financial statements.

You're in the Driver's Seat

IBM's 2001 statement of cash flows portrays a company ready to take advantage of its strong cash position and use this strength to create new opportunities in the highly competitive and constantly changing technology industry. Look up IBM's most recent annual report. Has the company continued to generate healthy profits and at the same time maintained a strong cash position? If you owned shares of IBM stock, would you be satisfied with the amount of dividends it is currently paying? Has the amount of dividends paid gone up, gone down, or remained relatively steady since 2001?

http://www.ibm.com

LEARNING OBJECTIVES

After studying this chapter, you should be able to:

LO 1 Explain the purpose of a statement of cash flows. (p. 613)

LO 2 Explain what cash equivalents are and how they are treated on the statement of cash flows. (p. 615)

LO 3 Describe operating, investing, and financing activities, and give examples of each. (p. 616)

LO 4 Describe the difference between the direct and the indirect methods of computing cash flow from operating activities. (p. 620)

LO 5 Use T accounts to prepare a statement of cash flows, using the direct method to determine cash flow from operating activities. (p. 625)

LO 6 Use T accounts to prepare a statement of cash flows, using the indirect method to determine cash flow from operating activities. (p. 638)

LO 7 Use a work sheet to prepare a statement of cash flows, using the indirect method to determine cash flow from operating activities (Appendix). (p. 648)

CASH FLOWS AND ACCRUAL ACCOUNTING

The *bottom line* is a phrase used in many different ways in today's society. "I wish politicians would cut out all of the rhetoric and get to the bottom line." "The bottom line is that the manager was fired because the team wasn't winning." "Our company's bottom line is twice what it was last year." This last use of the phrase, in reference to a company's net income, is probably the way in which *bottom line* was first used. In recent years, managers, stockholders, creditors, analysts, and other users of financial statements have become more and more wary of focusing on any one number as an indicator of a company's overall performance. Most experts now agree that there has been a tendency to rely far too heavily on net income and its companion, earnings per share, and in many cases to ignore a company's cash flows. As you know by now from your study of accounting, you can't pay bills with net income; you need cash!

http://www.ibm.com

To understand the difference between a company's bottom line and its cash flow, consider the case of IBM Corporation in 2001. IBM reported net earnings (income) of \$7.723 billion in 2001. However, as shown in the chapter opener, during this same time period its cash increased by only \$2.767 billion. How is this possible? First, net income is computed on an accrual basis, not a cash basis. Second, the income statement primarily reflects events related to the operating activities of a business, that is, selling products or providing services.

If you think about it, any one of four combinations is possible. That is, a company's cash position can increase or decrease during a period, and it can report a net profit or a net loss. Exhibit 12-1 illustrates this point by showing the performance of four well-known computer companies, including IBM, during 2001. IBM is the only one of the

Exhibit 12-1

Cash Flows and Net Income for Four Computer Companies in 2001 (all amounts in millions of dollars)

COMPANY	BEGINNING BALANCE IN CASH	ENDING BALANCE IN CASH	INCREASE (DECREASE) IN CASH	NET INCOME (LOSS)
IBM	\$3,563	\$6,330	\$2,767	\$7,723
Sun Microsystems (fiscal year ended June 30, 2001)	1,849	1,472	(377)	927
Gateway, Inc.	484	731	247	(1,034)
Western Digital (fiscal year ended June 29, 2001)	184	168	(16)	(99)

four companies that both improved its cash position in 2001 and reported a net profit. Sun Microsystems reported a net profit but saw its cash decline in 2001. Gateway reported a net loss in 2001 but improved its cash position. Finally, Western Digital both experienced a net loss in 2001 and saw its cash decline. To summarize, a company with a profitable year does not necessarily increase its cash position, nor does a company with an unprofitable year always experience a decrease in cash.

http://www.sun.com
http://www.gateway.com
http://www.wdc.com

PURPOSE OF THE STATEMENT OF CASH FLOWS

LO 1 Explain the purpose of a statement of cash flows.

The **statement of cash flows** is an important complement to the other major financial statements. It summarizes the operating, investing, and financing activities of a business over a period of time. The balance sheet summarizes the cash on hand and the balances in other assets, liabilities, and owners' equity accounts, providing a snapshot at a specific point in time. The statement of cash flows reports the changes in cash over a period of time and, most important, *explains these changes.*

Statement of cash flows The financial statement that summarizes an entity's cash receipts and cash payments during the period from operating, investing, and financing activities.

The income statement summarizes performance on an accrual basis. As you have learned in your study of accrual accounting, income on this basis is considered a better indicator of *future* cash inflows and outflows than is a statement limited to current cash flows. The statement of cash flows complements the accrual-based income statement by allowing users to assess a company's performance on a cash basis. As we will see in the following simple example, however, it also goes beyond presenting data related to operating performance and looks at other activities that affect a company's cash position.

An Example

Consider the following discussion between the owner of Fox River Realty and the company accountant. After a successful first year in business in 2003, in which it earned a profit of $100,000, the owner reviews the income statement for the second year, as presented in Exhibit 12-2.

Exhibit 12-2

Income Statement for Fox River Realty

FOX RIVER REALTY
INCOME STATEMENT
FOR THE YEAR ENDED DECEMBER 31, 2004

Revenues	$400,000
Depreciation expense	$ 50,000
All other expenses	100,000
Total expenses	$150,000
Net income	$250,000

The owner is pleased with the results and asks to see the balance sheet. Comparative balance sheets for the first two years are presented in Exhibit 12-3.

Where Did the Cash Go? At first glance, the owner is surprised to see the significant decline in the Cash account. She immediately presses the accountant for answers. With such a profitable year, where has the cash gone? Specifically, why has cash decreased from $150,000 to $50,000, even though income rose from $100,000 in the first year to $250,000 in the second year?

The accountant begins his explanation to the owner by pointing out that income on a cash basis is even *higher* than the reported $250,000. Because depreciation expense is an expense that does not use cash (cash is used when the plant and equipment are purchased, not when they are depreciated), cash provided from operating activities is calculated as follows:

Exhibit 12-3

Comparative Balance Sheets for Fox River Realty

FOX RIVER REALTY
COMPARATIVE BALANCE SHEETS
DECEMBER 31

	2004	2003
Cash	$ 50,000	$150,000
Plant and equipment	600,000	350,000
Accumulated depreciation	(150,000)	(100,000)
Total assets	$500,000	$400,000
Notes payable	$100,000	$150,000
Common stock	250,000	200,000
Retained earnings	150,000	50,000
Total equities	$500,000	$400,000

Net income	$250,000
Add back: Depreciation expense	50,000
Cash provided by operating activities	$300,000

Further, the accountant reminds the owner of the additional $50,000 that she invested in the business during the year. Now the owner is even more bewildered: with cash from operations of $300,000 and her own infusion of $50,000, why did cash *decrease* by $100,000? The accountant refreshes the owner's memory on three major outflows of cash during the year. First, even though the business earned $250,000, she withdrew $150,000 in dividends during the year. Second, the comparative balance sheets indicate that notes payable with the bank were reduced from $150,000 to $100,000, requiring the use of $50,000 in cash. Finally, the comparative balance sheets show an increase in plant and equipment for the year from $350,000 to $600,000—a sizable investment of $250,000 in new long-term assets.

Statement of Cash Flows To summarize what happened to the cash, the accountant prepares a statement of cash flows as shown in Exhibit 12-4. Although the owner is not particularly happy with the decrease in cash for the year, she is at least satisfied with the statement as an explanation of where the cash came from and how it was used. The statement summarizes the important cash activities for the year and fills a void created with the presentation of just an income statement and a balance sheet.

Exhibit 12-4

Statement of Cash Flows for Fox River Realty

FOX RIVER REALTY
STATEMENT OF CASH FLOWS
FOR THE YEAR ENDED DECEMBER 31, 2004

Cash provided (used) by operating activities:	
Net income	$ 250,000
Add back: Depreciation expense	50,000
Net cash provided (used) by operating activities	$ 300,000
Cash provided (used) by investing activities:	
Purchase of new plant and equipment	$(250,000)
Cash provided (used) by financing activities:	
Additional investment by owner	$ 50,000
Cash dividends paid to owner	(150,000)
Repayment of notes payable to bank	(50,000)
Net cash provided (used) by financing activities	$(150,000)
Net increase (decrease) in cash	$(100,000)
Cash balance at beginning of year	150,000
Cash balance at end of year	$ 50,000

REPORTING REQUIREMENTS FOR A STATEMENT OF CASH FLOWS

Accounting standards specify both the basis for preparing the statement of cash flows and the classification of items on the statement.[1] First, the statement must be prepared on a cash basis. Second, the cash flows must be classified into three categories:

- Operating activities
- Investing activities
- Financing activities

We now take a closer look at each of these important requirements in preparing a statement of cash flows.

The Definition of Cash: Cash and Cash Equivalents

LO 2 Explain what cash equivalents are and how they are treated on the statement of cash flows.

The purpose of the statement of cash flows is to provide information about a company's cash inflows and outflows. Thus, it is essential to have a clear understanding of what the definition of *cash* includes. According to accounting standards, certain items are recognized as being equivalent to cash and are combined with cash on the balance sheet and the statement of cash flows.

Commercial paper (short-term notes issued by corporations), money market funds, and Treasury bills are examples of cash equivalents. To be classified as a **cash equivalent,** an item must be readily convertible to a known amount of cash and have a maturity *to the investor* of three months or less. For example, a three-year Treasury note purchased two months before its maturity is classified as a cash equivalent. The same note purchased two years before maturity would be classified as an investment instead.

Cash equivalent An item readily convertible to a known amount of cash and with a maturity to the investor of three months or less.

To understand why cash equivalents are combined with cash when preparing a statement of cash flows, assume that a company has a cash balance of $10,000 and no assets that qualify as cash equivalents. Further assume that the $10,000 is used to purchase 90-day Treasury bills and is recorded by the following entry:

Investment in Treasury Bills	10,000	
Cash		10,000
To record the purchase of 90-day Treasury bills.		

Assets	=	Liabilities	+	Owners' Equity
+10,000				
−10,000				

For record-keeping purposes, it is important to recognize this transaction as a transfer between cash in the bank and an investment in a government security. In the strictest sense, the investment represents an outflow of cash. The purchase of a security with such a short maturity does not, however, involve any significant degree of risk in terms of price changes and thus is not reported on the statement of cash flows as an outflow. Instead, for purposes of classification on the balance sheet and the statement of cash flows, this is merely a transfer *within* the cash and cash equivalents category. The point is that before the purchase of the Treasury bills the company had $10,000 in cash and cash equivalents, and after the purchase it still had $10,000 in cash and cash equivalents. *Because nothing changed, the transaction is not reported on the statement of cash flows.*

Consider a different transaction involving the $10,000 and the following entry:

Investment in GM Common Stock	10,000	
Cash		10,000
To record the purchase of GM common stock.		

Assets	=	Liabilities	+	Owners' Equity
+10,000				
−10,000				

[1] *Statement of Financial Accounting Standards No. 95,* "Statement of Cash Flows" (Stamford, Conn.: Financial Accounting Standards Board, November 1987).

This purchase involves a certain amount of risk for the company making the investment. The GM stock is not convertible to a known amount of cash because its market value is subject to change. Thus, for balance sheet purposes, the investment is not considered a cash equivalent and is not therefore combined with cash but is classified as either a trading security or an available-for-sale security, depending on the company's intent in holding the stock (the distinction between these two types was discussed in Chapter 7). In the preparation of a statement of cash flows, the *investment in stock of another company is considered a significant activity and thus is reported on the statement of cash flows.*

Classification of Cash Flows

LO 3 Describe operating, investing, and financing activities, and give examples of each.

For the statement of cash flows, companies are required to classify activities into three categories: operating, investing, or financing. These categories represent the major functions of an entity, and classifying activities in this way allows users to look at important relationships. For example, one important financing activity for many businesses is borrowing money. Grouping the cash inflows from borrowing money during the period with the cash outflows from repayments of loans during the period makes it easier for analysts and other users of the statements to evaluate the company.

Each of the three types of activities can result both in cash inflows and in cash outflows to the company. Thus, the general format for the statement is as shown in Exhibit 12-5. Note the direct tie between the bottom portion of this statement and the balance sheet. The beginning and ending balances in cash and cash equivalents, shown as the last two lines on the statement of cash flows, are taken directly from the comparative balance sheets. Some companies end their statement of cash flows with the figure for the net increase or decrease in cash and cash equivalents and do not report the beginning and ending balances in cash and cash equivalents directly on the statement of cash flows. Instead, the reader must turn to the balance sheet for these amounts. We now take a closer look at the types of activities that appear in each of the three categories on the statement of cash flows.

Exhibit 12-5

Format for the Statement of Cash Flows

THE SMITH CORPORATION STATEMENT OF CASH FLOWS FOR THE YEAR ENDED DECEMBER 31, 2004		
Cash flows from operating activities:		
Inflows	$ xxx	
Outflows	(xxx)	
Net cash provided (used) by operating activities		$xxx
Cash flows from investing activities:		
Inflows	$ xxx	
Outflows	(xxx)	
Net cash provided (used) by investing activities		xxx
Cash flows from financing activities:		
Inflows	$ xxx	
Outflows	(xxx)	
Net cash provided (used) by financing activities		xxx
Net increase (decrease) in cash and cash equivalents		$xxx
Cash and cash equivalents at beginning of year		xxx
Cash and cash equivalents at end of year		$xxx

Operating Activities **Operating activities** involve acquiring and selling products and services. The specific activities of a business depend on its type. For example, the purchase of raw materials is an important operating activity for a manufacturer. For a retailer, the purchase of inventory from a distributor constitutes an operating activity. For a realty company, the payment of a commission to a salesperson is an operating activity. All three types of businesses sell either products or services, and their sales are important operating activities.

Operating activities Activities concerned with the acquisition and sale of products and services.

A statement of cash flows reflects the cash effects, either inflows or outflows, associated with each of these activities. For example, the manufacturer's payment for purchases of raw materials results in a cash outflow. The receipt of cash from collecting an account receivable results in a cash inflow. The income statement reports operating activities on an accrual basis. The statement of cash flows reflects a company's operating activities on a cash basis.

Investing Activities **Investing activities** involve acquiring and disposing of long-term assets. Replacing worn-out plant and equipment and expanding the existing base of long-term assets are essential to all businesses. In fact, cash paid for these acquisitions, often called *capital expenditures,* is usually the largest single item in the Investing Activities section of the statement. The following excerpt from IBM's 2001 statement of cash flows (also shown in the chapter opener) indicates that the company spent $5,660 million for 1 plant, rental machines, and other property during 2001 (all amounts are in millions of dollars):

Investing activities Activities concerned with the acquisition and disposal of long-term assets.

	Cash flow from investing activities:	
1	Payments for plant, rental machines and other property	(5,660)
2	Proceeds from disposition of plant, rental machines and other property	1,165
	Investment in software	(655)
3	Acquisitions	(916)
4	Purchases of marketable securities and other investments	(778)
5	Proceeds from marketable securities and other investments	738
	Net cash used in investing activities	(6,106)

Sales of long-term assets, such as plant and equipment, are not generally a significant source of cash. These assets are acquired to be used in producing goods and services, or to support this function, rather than to be resold, as is true for inventory. Occasionally, however, plant and equipment may wear out or no longer be needed and are offered for sale. In fact, the excerpt from IBM's report indicates that it generated $1,165 million of cash in 2001 from 2 disposals of plant, rental machines and other property.

In Chapter 7, we explained why companies sometimes invest in the stocks and bonds of other companies. The classification of these investments on the statement of cash flows depends on the type of investment. The acquisition of one company by another, whether in the form of a merger or a stock acquisition, is an important *investing* activity to bring to the attention of statement readers. IBM spent $916 million to 3 acquire other companies during 2001. Note also that in 2001 IBM spent $778 million to 4 buy marketable securities and other investments and 5 generated $738 million from selling these investments. According to a note to IBM's statements, the company classifies marketable securities as available for sale.

Cash flows from purchases, sales, and maturities of held-to-maturity securities (bonds) and available for sale securities (stocks and bonds) are classified as *investing* activities. On the other hand, these same types of cash flows for trading securities are classified as *operating* activities. This apparent inconsistency in the accounting rules is based on the idea that trading securities are held for the express purpose of generating short-term profits and thus are operating in nature.

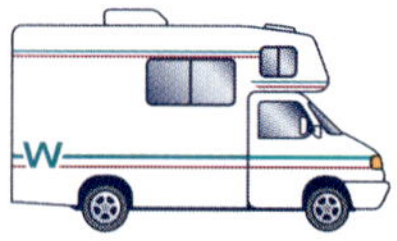

From Concept to Practice 12.1

Reading Winnebago Industries' Statement of Cash Flows

According to Winnebago Industries' Investing Activities section of its statement of cash flows, how much did the company spend in 2001 to acquire property and equipment? What types of expenditures would you expect to find in this category?

Financing activities Activities concerned with the raising and repayment of funds in the form of debt and equity.

Financing Activities

All businesses rely on internal financing, external financing, or a combination of the two in meeting their needs for cash. Initially, a new business must have a certain amount of investment by the owners to begin operations. After this, many companies use notes, bonds, and other forms of debt to provide financing.[2] Issuing stock and various forms of debt results in cash inflows that appear as **financing activities** on the statement of cash flows. On the other side, the repurchase of a company's own stock and the repayment of borrowings are important cash outflows to be reported in the Financing Activities section of the statement. Another important activity listed in the Financing Activities section of the statement is the payment of dividends to stockholders. IBM's 2001 statement of cash flows lists most of the common cash inflows and outflows from financing activities (amounts in millions of dollars):

	Cash flow from financing activities:	
1	Proceeds from new debt	4,535
	Short-term borrowings less than 90 days—net	2,926
2	Payments to settle debt	(7,898)
	Preferred stock transactions—net	(254)
	Common stock transactions—net	(3,652)
	Cash dividends paid	(966)
	Net cash used in financing activities	(5,309)

In 2001, IBM 1 received $4,535 million from issuing new debt and 2 paid $7,898 million to retire old debt. In analyzing IBM, you would probably next read the long-term debt note to see whether the company essentially refinanced the old debt with new debt at a lower interest rate and, if it did, what the interest saving is, because this will continue to be a benefit for many years.

Summary of the Three Types of Activities

To summarize the categorization of the activities of a business as operating, investing, and financing, refer to Exhibit 12-6. The exhibit lists examples of each of the three activities along with the related accounts on the balance sheet and the account classifications on the balance sheet.

In the exhibit, operating activities center on the acquisition and sale of products and services and related costs, such as wages and taxes. Two important observations can be made about the cash flow effects from the operating activities of a business. *First, the cash flows from these activities are the cash effects of transactions that enter into the determination of net income.* For example, the sale of a product enters into the calculation of net income. The cash effect of this transaction—that is, the collection of the account receivable—results in a cash inflow from operating activities. *Second, cash flows from operating activities usually relate to an increase or decrease in either a current asset or a current liability.* For example, the payment of taxes to the government results in a decrease in taxes payable, which is a current liability on the balance sheet.

Study Tip

Later in the chapter, you will learn a technique to use in preparing the statement of cash flows. Recall the observations made here regarding what types of accounts affect each of the three activities when you get to that section of the chapter.

Note that investing activities normally relate to long-term assets on the balance sheet. For example, the purchase of new plant and equipment increases long-term assets, and the sale of these same assets reduces long-term assets on the balance sheet.

[2]Wm. Wrigley Jr. Company is unusual in this regard in that it relies almost solely on funds generated from stockholders, in the form of common stock, for financing. The company had no short-term notes payable at December 31, 2001, and total long-term liabilities accounted for less than 9% of the total liabilities and stockholders' equity on the balance sheet on that date.

Exhibit 12-6 Classification of Items on the Statement of Cash Flows

ACTIVITY	EXAMPLES	EFFECT ON CASH	RELATED BALANCE SHEET ACCOUNT	CLASSIFICATION ON BALANCE SHEET
Operating	Collection of customer accounts	Inflow	Accounts receivable	Current asset
	Payment to suppliers for inventory	Outflow	Accounts payable	Current liability
			Inventory	Current asset
	Payment of wages	Outflow	Wages payable	Current liability
	Payment of taxes	Outflow	Taxes payable	Current liability
Investing	Capital expenditures	Outflow	Plant and equipment	Long-term asset
	Purchase of another company	Outflow	Long-term investment	Long-term asset
	Sale of plant and equipment	Inflow	Plant and equipment	Long-term asset
	Sale of another company	Inflow	Long-term investment	Long-term asset
Financing	Issuance of capital stock	Inflow	Capital stock	Stockholders' equity
	Issuance of bonds	Inflow	Bonds payable	Long-term liability
	Issuance of bank note	Inflow	Notes payable	Long-term liability
	Repurchase of stock	Outflow	Treasury stock	Stockholders' equity
	Retirement of bonds	Outflow	Bonds payable	Long-term liability
	Repayment of notes	Outflow	Notes payable	Long-term liability
	Payment of dividends	Outflow	Retained earnings	Stockholders' equity

Finally, *note that financing activities usually relate to either long-term liabilities or stockholders' equity accounts.* There are exceptions to these observations about the type of balance sheet account involved with each of the three types of activities, but these rules of thumb are useful as we begin to analyze transactions and attempt to determine their classification on the statement of cash flows.

Business Strategy

Listening to Customers

The year 2001 was significant in the life of **IBM**. It was the last of nine years in which Lou Gerstner Jr. led Big Blue. He turned over the CEO title in early 2002 to Sam Palmisano. It would be hard to imagine a decade in the life of the IT powerhouse that saw more changes than the one during which Mr. Gerstner was at the helm. Certainly, the swings in the company's performance are a testimony to this claim. The company reported a net loss of over $8 billion in 1993 and rebounded to report profits of approximately the same amount in both 2000 and 2001!

As Gerstner explains in his farewell letter in the 2001 annual report, the past decade has witnessed "a tale of two revolutions," both of which he views as good news for IBM. Innovations in both business and technology have created challenges as well as opportunities for the industry, one that IBM has led from the beginning. As the retiring CEO sees it, the guiding light for IBM came down to a simple notion: focusing on the customer. Rather than inventing new technology and then hoping a customer could use it, the company decided to listen to its customers and work with them to address their needs.

In the same 2001 annual report, Sam Palmisano gives high praise to Lou Gerstner, saying that he was "the man who recreated IBM." The new CEO believes the company has the right strategic vision—one that involves seizing new opportunities and leading change. The next 10 years will prove whether that vision will allow IBM to remain the leader of the IT industry. ■

Source: 2001 IBM annual report.

Two Methods of Reporting Cash Flow from Operating Activities

LO 4 Describe the difference between the direct and the indirect methods of computing cash flow from operating activities.

Direct method For preparing the Operating Activities section of the statement of cash flows, the approach in which cash receipts and cash payments are reported.

Indirect method For preparing the Operating Activities section of the statement of cash flows, the approach in which net income is reconciled to net cash flow from operations.

Companies use one of two different methods to report the amount of cash flow from operating activities. The first approach, called the **direct method,** involves reporting major classes of gross cash receipts and cash payments. For example, cash collected from customers is reported separately from any interest and dividends received. Each of the major types of cash payments related to the company's operations follows, such as cash paid for inventory, for salaries and wages, for interest, and for taxes. An acceptable alternative to this approach is the **indirect method.** Under the indirect method, net cash flow from operating activities is computed by adjusting net income to remove the effect of all deferrals of past operating cash receipts and payments and all accruals of future operating cash receipts and payments.

Although the direct method is preferred by the Financial Accounting Standards Board, it is used much less frequently than the indirect method in practice. In fact, an annual survey of 600 companies reported that 593 companies used the indirect method and only 7 companies used the direct method.[3]

To compare and contrast the two methods, assume that Boulder Company begins operations as a corporation on January 1, 2004, with the owners' investment of $10,000 in cash. An income statement for 2004 and a balance sheet as of December 31, 2004, are presented in Exhibits 12-7 and 12-8, respectively.

Exhibit 12-7

Boulder Company Income Statement

BOULDER COMPANY INCOME STATEMENT FOR THE YEAR ENDED DECEMBER 31, 2004	
Revenues	$80,000
Operating expenses	(64,000)
Income before tax	$16,000
Income tax expense	(4,000)
Net income	$12,000

Exhibit 12-8

Boulder Company Balance Sheet

BOULDER COMPANY
BALANCE SHEET
AS OF DECEMBER 31, 2004

Assets		Liabilities and Stockholders' Equity	
Cash	$15,000	Accounts payable	$ 6,000
Accounts receivable	13,000	Capital stock	10,000
		Retained earnings	12,000
Total	$28,000	Total	$28,000

Direct Method To report cash flow from operating activities under the direct method, we look at each of the items on the income statement and determine how much cash each of these activities either generated or used. For example, revenues for the period were $80,000. Since the balance sheet at the end of the period shows a balance in Accounts Receivable of $13,000, however, Boulder collected only $80,000 − $13,000, or $67,000, from its sales of the period. Thus, the first line on the statement of cash flows in Exhibit 12-9 reports $67,000 in cash collected from customers. Remember that the *net increase* in Accounts Receivable must be deducted from sales to find cash collected. For a new company, this is the same as the ending balance because the company starts the year without a balance in Accounts Receivable.

[3] *Accounting Trends & Techniques,* 55th ed. (New York: American Institute of Certified Public Accountants, 2001).

Exhibit 12-9

Statement of Cash Flows Using the Direct Method

BOULDER COMPANY STATEMENT OF CASH FLOWS FOR THE YEAR ENDED DECEMBER 31, 2004	
Cash flows from operating activities	
Cash collected from customers	$ 67,000
Cash payments for operating purposes	(58,000)
Cash payments for taxes	(4,000)
Net cash inflow from operating activities	$ 5,000
Cash flows from financing activities	
Issuance of capital stock	$ 10,000
Net increase in cash	$ 15,000
Cash balance, beginning of period	–0–
Cash balance, end of period	$ 15,000

The same logic can be applied to determine the amount of cash expended for operating purposes. Operating expenses on the income statement are reported at $64,000. According to the balance sheet, however, $6,000 of the expense is unpaid at the end of the period as evidenced by the balance in Accounts Payable. Thus, the amount of cash expended for operating purposes as reported on the statement of cash flows in Exhibit 12-9 is $64,000 − $6,000, or $58,000. The other cash payment in the Operating Activities section of the statement is $4,000 for income taxes. Because no liability for income taxes is reported on the balance sheet, we know that $4,000 represents both the income tax expense of the period and the amount paid to the government. The only other item on the statement of cash flows in Exhibit 12-9 is the cash inflow from financing activities for the amount of cash invested by the owner in return for capital stock.

Indirect Method When the indirect method is used, the first line in the Operating Activities section of the statement of cash flows as shown in Exhibit 12-10 is the net income of the period. Net income is then *adjusted* to reconcile it to the amount of cash provided by operating activities. As reported on the income statement, this net income figure includes the sales of $80,000 for the period. As we know, however, the amount of cash collected was $13,000 less than this because not all customers paid Boulder the amount due. *The increase in Accounts Receivable for the period is deducted from net income on the statement because the increase indicates that the company sold more during the period than it collected in cash.*

The logic for the addition of the increase in Accounts Payable is similar, although the effect is the opposite. The amount of operating expenses deducted on the income

Exhibit 12-10

Statement of Cash Flows Using the Indirect Method

BOULDER COMPANY STATEMENT OF CASH FLOWS FOR THE YEAR ENDED DECEMBER 31, 2004	
Cash flows from operating activities	
Net income	$ 12,000
Adjustments to reconcile net income to net cash from operating activities:	
Increase in accounts receivable	(13,000)
Increase in accounts payable	6,000
Net cash inflow from operating activities	$ 5,000
Cash flows from financing activities	
Issuance of capital stock	$ 10,000
Net increase in cash	$ 15,000
Cash balance, beginning of period	–0–
Cash balance, end of period	$ 15,000

statement was $64,000. We know, however, that the amount of cash paid was $6,000 less than this, as the balance in Accounts Payable indicates. *The increase in Accounts Payable for the period is added back to net income on the statement because the increase indicates that the company paid less during the period than it recognized in expense on the income statement.* One observation can be noted about this example. Because this is the first year of operations for Boulder, we wouldn't be too concerned that accounts receivable is increasing faster than accounts payable. If this becomes a trend, however, we would try to improve the accounts receivable collections process.

Two important observations should be made in comparing the two methods illustrated in Exhibits 12-9 and 12-10. First, the amount of cash provided by operating activities is the same under the two methods: $5,000; the two methods are simply different computational approaches to arrive at the cash generated from operations. Second, the remainder of the statement of cash flows is the same, regardless of which method is used. The only difference between the two methods is in the Operating Activities section of the statement.

From Concept to Practice 12.2

Reading IBM's Statement of Cash Flows

Does IBM use the direct or the indirect method in the Operating Activities section of its statement of cash flows? How can you tell which it is?

Noncash Investing and Financing Activities

Occasionally, companies engage in important investing and financing activities that do not affect cash. For example, assume that at the end of the year Wolk Corp. issues capital stock to an inventor in return for the exclusive rights to a patent. Although the patent has no ready market value, the stock could have been sold on the open market for $25,000. Thus, the following entry is made on Wolk's books:

Patent	25,000	
Capital Stock		25,000
To record issuance of stock in exchange for patent.		

Assets	=	Liabilities	+	Owners' Equity
+25,000				+25,000

This transaction does not involve cash and is therefore not reported on the statement of cash flows. However, what if we changed the scenario slightly? Assume that Wolk wants the patent but the inventor is not willing to accept stock in return for it. So instead Wolk sells stock on the open market for $25,000 and then pays this amount in cash to the inventor for the rights to the patent. Now Wolk records two journal entries. The first is as follows:

Cash	25,000	
Capital Stock		25,000
To record issuance of capital stock for cash.		

Assets	=	Liabilities	+	Owners' Equity
+25,000				+25,000

It next records this entry:

Patent	25,000	
Cash		25,000
To record acquisition of patent for cash.		

Assets	=	Liabilities	+	Owners' Equity
+25,000				
−25,000				

How would each of these two transactions be reported on a statement of cash flows? The first transaction appears as a cash inflow in the Financing Activities section of the statement; the second is reported as a cash outflow in the Investing Activities section. The point is that even though the *form* of this arrangement (with stock sold for cash and then the cash paid to the inventor) differs from the form of the first arrangement (with stock exchanged directly for the patent), the *substance* of the two arrangements is the same. That is, both involve a significant financing activity, the issuance of stock, and an important investing activity, the acquisition of a patent. Because the substance is what matters, accounting standards require that any significant noncash transactions be reported either in a separate schedule or in a note to the financial statements. For our transaction in which stock was issued directly to the inventor, presentation in a schedule is as follows:

Supplemental schedule of noncash investing and financing activities	
Acquisition of patent in exchange for capital stock	$25,000

To this point, we have concentrated on the purpose of a statement of cash flows and the major reporting requirements related to it. We turn our attention next to a methodology to use in actually preparing the statement.

Two-Minute Review

1. *What are cash equivalents, and why are any increases or decreases in them not reported on a statement of cash flows?*
2. *What are the three types of activities reported on a statement of cash flows?*
3. *What are the two methods of reporting cash flow from operating activities, and how do they differ?*

Answers on page 645.

HOW THE STATEMENT OF CASH FLOWS IS PUT TOGETHER

Two interesting observations can be made about the statement of cash flows. First, the "answer" to a statement of cash flows is known before we start to prepare it. That is, the change in cash for the period is known by comparing two successive balance sheets. Thus, it is not the change in cash itself that is emphasized on the statement of cash flows but the *explanations* for the change in cash. That is, each item on a statement of cash flows helps to explain why cash changed by the amount it did during the period. The second important observation about the statement of cash flows relates even more specifically to how we prepare it. Both an income statement and a balance sheet are prepared simply by taking the balances in each of the various accounts in the general ledger and putting them in the right place on the right statement. This is not true for the statement of cash flows, however. Instead, it is necessary to analyze the transactions during the period and attempt to (1) determine which of these affected cash and (2) classify each of the cash effects into one of the three categories.

In the simple examples presented so far in the chapter, we prepared the statement of cash flows without the use of any special tools. In more complex situations, however, some type of methodology is needed. We first will review the basic accounting equation and then illustrate a T-account approach for preparing the statement. The chapter appendix presents a work-sheet approach to the preparation of the statement of cash flows.

The Accounting Equation and the Statement of Cash Flows

The basic accounting equation is as follows:

Assets = Liabilities + Owners' Equity

Next, consider this refinement of the equation:

Assets	=	**Liabilities and Owners' Equity**
Cash + Noncash current assets + Long-term assets	=	Current liabilities + Long-term liabilities + Capital stock + Retained earnings

The equation can be rearranged so that only cash is on the left side and all other items are on the right side:

Cash	=	Current liabilities + Long-term liabilities + Capital stock + Retained earnings − **Noncash current assets** − **Long-term assets**

Therefore, any changes in cash must be accompanied by a corresponding change in the right side of the equation. For example, an increase or inflow of cash could result from an *increase* in long-term liabilities in the form of issuing bonds payable, an important financing activity for many companies. Or an increase in cash could come from a *decrease* in long-term assets in the form of a sale of fixed assets. The various possibilities for inflows (+) and outflows (−) of cash can be summarized by activity as follows:

ACTIVITY	LEFT SIDE	RIGHT SIDE	EXAMPLE
Operating			
	+ Cash	− Noncash current assets	Collect accounts receivable
	− Cash	+ Noncash current assets	Prepay insurance
	+ Cash	+ Current liabilities	Collect customer's deposit
	− Cash	− Current liabilities	Pay suppliers
	+ Cash	+ Retained earnings	Make a cash sale
Investing			
	+ Cash	− Long-term assets	Sell equipment
	− Cash	+ Long-term assets	Buy equipment
Financing			
	+ Cash	+ Long-term liabilities	Issue bonds
	− Cash	− Long-term liabilities	Retire bonds
	+ Cash	+ Capital stock	Issue capital stock
	− Cash	− Capital stock	Buy capital stock
	− Cash	− Retained earnings	Pay dividends

By considering these examples we see that inflows and outflows of cash relate to increases and decreases in the various balance sheet accounts. We now turn to analyzing these accounts as a way to assemble a statement of cash flows.

A Master T-Account Approach to Preparing the Statement of Cash Flows: Direct Method

LO 5 Use T accounts to prepare a statement of cash flows, using the direct method to determine cash flow from operating activities.

The following steps can be used to prepare a statement of cash flows:

1. **Set up three master T accounts with the following headings:**
   a. Cash Flows from Operating Activities
   b. Cash Flows from Investing Activities
   c. Cash Flows from Financing Activities

   These master T accounts take the place of the Cash account. As we analyze the transactions that affect each of the noncash balance sheet accounts, any cash effects are entered on the appropriate master account. When completed, the three master accounts contain all of the information needed to prepare a statement of cash flows.
2. **Determine the cash flows from operating activities.** Generally, this requires analyzing each item on the *income statement* and the *current asset* and *current liability* accounts. Draft journal entries for each transaction, using a lettering system for identification purposes, and post them to the appropriate balance sheet accounts. In many instances, these will be summary entries for the entire period. For example, we make one entry for all credit sales for the period, one entry for all collections on account, and so on. Enter any increases in cash on the left side of the Cash Flow from Operating Activities master T account and any decreases on the right side.
3. **Determine the cash flows from investing activities.** Generally, this requires analyzing the *long-term asset* accounts and any additional information provided. Draft journal entries for each transaction, and post them to the appropriate balance sheet accounts. Enter any increases in cash on the left side of the Cash Flow from Investing Activities master T account and any decreases on the right side. Enter any significant noncash activities on a supplemental schedule.
4. **Determine the cash flows from financing activities.** Generally, this requires analyzing the *long-term liability* and *stockholders' equity* accounts and any additional information provided. Draft journal entries for each transaction. Enter any increases in cash on the left side of the Cash Flow from Financing Activities master T account and any decreases on the right side of the T account. Enter any significant noncash activities on a supplemental schedule.

Remember that these are general rules that the cash effects of changes in current accounts are reported in the operating section, those relating to long-term asset accounts in the investing section, and those relating to long-term liabilities and stockholders' equity in the financing section. The general rules for classification of activities have a few exceptions, but we will not concern ourselves with them.

To illustrate this approach, we will refer to the income statement in Exhibit 12-11 and to the comparative balance sheets and the additional information provided for Julian Corp. in Exhibit 12-12.

Determine the Cash Flows from Operating Activities To do this, we need to consider each of the items on the income statement and any related current assets or liabilities from the balance sheet.

Sales Revenue and Accounts Receivable Sales as reported on the income statement in Exhibit 12-11 amounted to $670,000. The journal entry was as follows:

		Debit	Credit
(a)	Accounts Receivable	670,000	
	Sales Revenue		670,000
	To record sales on account.		

Assets	=	Liabilities	+	Owners' Equity
+670,000				+670,000

Exhibit 12-11

Julian Corp. Income Statement

JULIAN CORP. INCOME STATEMENT FOR THE YEAR ENDED DECEMBER 31, 2004		
Revenues and gains:		
Sales revenue	$670,000	
Interest revenue	15,000	
Gain on sale of machine	5,000	
Total revenues and gains		$690,000
Expenses and losses:		
Cost of goods sold	$390,000	
Salaries and wages	60,000	
Depreciation	40,000	
Insurance	12,000	
Interest	15,000	
Income taxes	50,000	
Loss on retirement of bonds	3,000	
Total expenses and losses		570,000
Net income		$120,000

Based on the beginning and ending balances in Exhibit 12-12, a T account for Accounts Receivable appears as follows after posting the debit for the sales of the period:

ACCOUNTS RECEIVABLE

Bal. Jan. 1	57,000		
(a) Sales on account	670,000	?	Cash collections (b)
Bal. Dec. 31	63,000		

Accounts Receivable increased by $6,000 for the period. *This indicates that Julian had $6,000 more in sales to its customers than it collected in cash from them* (assuming that all sales are on credit). Thus, cash collections must have been $670,000 − $6,000, or $664,000. Another way to look at this is as follows:

Beginning accounts receivable	$ 57,000
+ Sales revenue	670,000
− Cash collections	(*X*)
= Ending accounts receivable	$ 63,000

Solving for *X*, we can find cash collections:

$$57{,}000 + 670{,}000 - X = 63{,}000$$
$$X = 664{,}000$$

The journal entry to record cash collections was as follows:

(b) Cash	664,000	
Accounts Receivable		664,000
To record cash collected on account.		

Assets	=	Liabilities	+	Owners' Equity
+664,000				
−664,000				

At this point, note the debit to Cash for $664,000 as shown in the master T account Cash Flows from Operating Activities, in Exhibit 12-13.

Exhibit 12-12

Julian Corp. Comparative Balance Sheets

JULIAN CORP. COMPARATIVE BALANCE SHEETS	December 31	
	2004	2003
Cash	$ 35,000	$ 46,000
Accounts receivable	63,000	57,000
Inventory	84,000	92,000
Prepaid insurance	12,000	18,000
Total current assets	$194,000	$213,000
Long-term investments	$120,000	$ 90,000
Land	150,000	100,000
Property and equipment	320,000	280,000
Accumulated depreciation	(100,000)	(75,000)
Total long-term assets	$490,000	$395,000
Total assets	$684,000	$608,000
Accounts payable	$ 38,000	$ 31,000
Salaries and wages payable	7,000	9,000
Income taxes payable	8,000	5,000
Total current liabilities	$ 53,000	$ 45,000
Notes payable	$ 85,000	$ 35,000
Bonds payable	200,000	260,000
Total long-term liabilities	$285,000	$295,000
Capital stock	$100,000	$ 75,000
Retained earnings	246,000	193,000
Total stockholders' equity	$346,000	$268,000
Total liabilities and stockholders' equity	$684,000	$608,000

Additional Information

1. Long-term investments were purchased for $30,000. The securities are classified as available for sale.
2. Land was purchased by issuing a $50,000 note payable.
3. Equipment was purchased for $75,000.
4. A machine with an original cost of $35,000 and a book value of $20,000 was sold for $25,000.
5. Bonds with a face value of $60,000 were retired by paying $63,000 in cash.
6. Capital stock was issued in exchange for $25,000 in cash.

Exhibit 12-13

Master T Account for Cash Flows from Operating Activities

Cash Flows from Operating Activities			
Cash receipts from:		Cash payments for:	
(b) Sales on account	664,000	(f) Inventory purchases	375,000
(c) Interest	15,000	(h) Salaries and wages	62,000
		(k) Insurance	6,000
		(l) Interest	15,000
		(n) Taxes	47,000

Interest Revenue Julian reported interest revenue on the income statement of $15,000. Did the company actually receive this amount of cash, or was it merely an accrual of revenue earned but not yet received? The answer can be found by examining the Current Assets section of the balance sheet. *Because there is no Interest Receivable account, the amount of interest earned was the amount of cash received:*

		Debit	Credit
(c)	Cash	15,000	
	Interest Revenue		15,000
	To record interest earned and received.		

Assets	=	Liabilities	+	Owners' Equity
+15,000				+15,000

The debit should be entered in the master T account Cash Flows from Operating Activities, as shown in Exhibit 12-13.

Gain on Sale of Machine A gain on the sale of machine of $5,000 is reported as the next line on the income statement. Any cash received from the sale of a long-term asset is reported in the Investing Activities section of the statement of cash flows. Thus, we ignore the gain when reporting cash flows from operating activities under the direct method.

Cost of Goods Sold, Inventory, and Accounts Payable Cost of goods sold, as reported on the income statement, amounts to $390,000 and was recorded with this entry:

		Debit	Credit
(d)	Cost of Goods Sold	390,000	
	Inventory		390,000
	To record cost of goods sold.		

Assets	=	Liabilities	+	Owners' Equity
−390,000				−390,000

We see that $390,000 is not the amount of cash expended to pay suppliers of inventory. First, cost of goods sold represents the cost of the inventory sold during the period, not the amount purchased. Thus, we must analyze the Inventory account to determine the purchases of the period. Second, the amount of purchases is not the same as the cash paid to suppliers, because purchases are normally on account. Thus, we must analyze the Accounts Payable account to determine the cash payments.

Based on the beginning and ending balances from Exhibit 12-12, a T account for Inventory appears as follows after posting the reduction in the account for cost of goods sold:

INVENTORY

Bal. Jan. 1	92,000		
(e) Purchases on account	?	390,000	Cost of goods sold (d)
Bal. Dec. 31	84,000		

Note the $8,000 net decrease in Inventory. *This means that the cost of inventory sold was $8,000 more than the purchases of the period.* Thus, purchases must have been $390,000 − $8,000, or $382,000. Another way to look at this is as follows:

	Beginning inventory	$ 92,000
+	Purchases	*X*
−	Cost of goods sold	(390,000)
=	Ending inventory	$ 84,000

Solving for *X*, we can find purchases:

$$92{,}000 + X - 390{,}000 = 84{,}000$$

$$X = \underline{\underline{382{,}000}}$$

The journal entry to record purchases was as follows:

(e)	Inventory	382,000	
	Accounts Payable		382,000
	To record purchases on account.		

Assets	=	Liabilities	+	Owners' Equity
+382,000		+382,000		

From Exhibit 12-12, a T account for Accounts Payable, after posting the credit for purchases of the period, is as follows:

ACCOUNTS PAYABLE

		31,000	Bal. Jan. 1
(f) Cash payments	?	382,000	Purchases (e)
		38,000	Bal. Dec. 31

Note the $7,000 net increase in Accounts Payable. *This means that Julian's purchases were $7,000 more during the period than its cash payments.* Thus, cash payments must have been $382,000 − $7,000, or $375,000. Another way to look at this is as follows:

	Beginning accounts payable	$ 31,000
+	Purchases	382,000
−	Cash payments	(X)
=	Ending accounts payable	$ 38,000

Solving for X, we can find cash payments:

$$31{,}000 + 382{,}000 - X = 38{,}000$$
$$X = \underline{\underline{375{,}000}}$$

The journal entry to record payments on account was as follows:

(f)	Accounts Payable	375,000	
	Cash		375,000
	To record cash payments on account.		

Assets	=	Liabilities	+	Owners' Equity
−375,000		−375,000		

At this point, the credit to cash should be entered in the master T account Cash Flows from Operating Activities, as shown in Exhibit 12-13.

Salaries and Wages Expense and Salaries and Wages Payable The entry to record salaries and wages expense was as follows:

(g)	Salaries and Wages Expense	60,000	
	Salaries and Wages Payable		60,000
	To record salaries and wages.		

Assets	=	Liabilities	+	Owners' Equity
		+60,000		−60,000

After this entry is posted to Salaries and Wages Payable, note the $2,000 net decrease in the account for the period:

SALARIES AND WAGES PAYABLE

		9,000	Bal. Jan. 1
(h) Cash payments	?	60,000	Expense (g)
		7,000	Bal. Dec. 31

This means that the amount of cash paid to employees was $2,000 more than the amount of expense accrued. Another way to look at the cash payments of $60,000 + $2,000, or $62,000, is as follows:

	Beginning salaries and wages payable	$ 9,000
+	Salaries and wages expense	60,000
−	Cash payments to employees	(X)
=	Ending salaries and wages payable	$ 7,000

Solving for X, we can find cash payments:

$$9{,}000 + 60{,}000 - X = 7{,}000$$
$$X = 62{,}000$$

The journal entry to record the cash paid was as follows:

		Debit	Credit
(h)	Salaries and Wages Payable	62,000	
	Cash		62,000
	To record cash paid to employees.		

Assets	=	Liabilities	+	Owners' Equity
−62,000		−62,000		

As you see in Exhibit 12-13, the credit of $62,000 in this entry appears in the T account for Cash Flows from Operating Activities.

Depreciation Expense The next item on the income statement is depreciation of $40,000. The entry to record depreciation was as follows:

		Debit	Credit
(i)	Depreciation Expense	40,000	
	Accumulated Depreciation		40,000
	To record depreciation.		

Assets	=	Liabilities	+	Owners' Equity
−40,000				−40,000

Depreciation of tangible long-term assets, amortization of intangible assets, and depletion of natural resources are different from most other expenses in that they have no effect on cash flow. The only related cash flows are from the purchase and the sale of these long-term assets, and these are reported in the Investing Activities section of the statement of cash flows.

Accounting for Your Decisions

You Are an Entrepreneur

You operate a coffee cart in the lobby of an office building. You started the business this year by investing $5,000 of your own money to buy the coffee cart. Even though you think the cart will last for five years, a friend who has studied accounting has advised you to recognize the entire cost of the cart as an expense the first year. He reasons that "the first year is very crucial to any business and since depreciation is added back in the Operating Activities section of the statement of cash flows, why not add back the maximum amount so that you will maximize the cash flow from operations?" Is your friend's reasoning sound?

ANS: Your friend is correct in stating that depreciation is added back in the Operating Activities section, assuming use of the indirect method. The only reason that depreciation is added back, however, is because it was deducted as an expense on the income statement but does not use any cash. Depreciation is not a cash flow, and any manipulation of the amount of depreciation expensed in any one year will not affect the amount of cash generated from operations.

Insurance Expense and Prepaid Insurance According to the income statement in Exhibit 12-11, Julian recorded Insurance Expense of $12,000 during 2004. This amount is not the cash payments for insurance, however, because Julian has a Prepaid Insurance account on the balance sheet. The entry to record expense involves a reduction in the Prepaid Insurance account as follows:

(j) Insurance Expense	12,000	
Prepaid Insurance		12,000
To record expiration of insurance.		

Assets	=	Liabilities	+	Owners' Equity
−12,000				−12,000

When the credit to Prepaid Insurance is posted, note the $6,000 net decrease in the account for the period:

PREPAID INSURANCE

Bal. Jan. 1	18,000		
(k) Cash payments	?	12,000	Expense (j)
Bal. Dec. 31	12,000		

This means that the amount of cash paid for insurance was $6,000 less than the amount of expense recognized. Thus, the cash payments must have been $12,000 − $6,000, or $6,000. Another way to look at the cash payments is as follows:

Beginning prepaid insurance	$18,000
+Cash payments for insurance	*X*
−Insurance expense	(12,000)
=Ending prepaid insurance	$12,000

Solving for *X*, we can find the amount of cash paid:

$$18{,}000 + X - 12{,}000 = 12{,}000$$
$$X = \underline{\underline{6{,}000}}$$

The journal entry to record the cash paid was as follows:

(k) Prepaid Insurance	6,000	
Cash		6,000
To record cash paid for insurance.		

Assets	=	Liabilities	+	Owners' Equity
+6,000				
−6,000				

Note that the credit to Cash is entered in Exhibit 12-13 in the T account for Cash Flows from Operating Activities.

Interest Expense The amount of interest expense reported on the income statement is $15,000. Because the balance sheet does not report an accrual of interest owed but not yet paid (an Interest Payable account), we know that $15,000 is also the amount of cash paid:

(l) Interest Expense	15,000	
Cash		15,000
To record interest expense.		

Assets	=	Liabilities	+	Owners' Equity
−15,000				−15,000

The entry is recorded as a cash outflow in Exhibit 12-13. Whether interest paid is properly classified as an operating activity is subject to considerable debate. The Financial Accounting Standards Board decided in favor of classification of *interest* as an *operating* activity because, unlike dividends, it appears on the income statement. This, it was argued, provides a direct link between the statement of cash flows and the income statement. Many argue, however, that it is inconsistent to classify dividends paid as a financing activity but interest paid as an operating activity. After all, both represent returns paid to providers of capital: interest to creditors and dividends to stockholders.

Income Tax Expense and Income Taxes Payable The entry to record Income Tax Expense was as follows:

(m)	Income Taxes Expense	50,000	
	Income Taxes Payable		50,000
	To record income taxes.		

Assets	=	Liabilities	+	Owners' Equity
		+50,000		−50,000

When the credit to Income Taxes Payable is posted, note the $3,000 net increase in the account for the period:

INCOME TAXES PAYABLE

		5,000	Bal. Jan. 1
(n) Cash payments	?	50,000	Expense (m)
		8,000	Bal. Dec. 31

This means that the amount of cash paid to the government in taxes was $3,000 less than the amount of expense accrued. Another way to look at the cash payments of $50,000 − $3,000, or $47,000, is as follows:

Beginning income taxes payable	$ 5,000
+Income tax expense	50,000
−Cash payments for taxes	(X)
=Ending income taxes payable	$ 8,000

Solving for X, we can find the amount of cash paid:

$$5{,}000 + 50{,}000 - X = 8{,}000$$
$$X = \underline{\underline{47{,}000}}$$

The journal entry to record cash paid was as follows:

(n)	Income Taxes Payable	47,000	
	Cash		47,000
	To record cash paid in taxes.		

Assets	=	Liabilities	+	Owners' Equity
−47,000		−47,000		

As you see by examining Exhibit 12-13, the cash payments for taxes is the last item in the T account for Cash Flows from Operating Activities.

Loss on Retirement of Bonds A $3,000 loss on the retirement of bonds is reported as the last item under expenses and losses on the income statement in Exhibit 12-11. Any cash paid to retire a long-term liability is reported in the Financing Activities section of the statement of cash flows. Thus, we ignore the loss when reporting cash flows from operating activities under the direct method.

Compare Net Income with Net Cash Flow from Operating Activities

At this point, all of the items on the income statement have been analyzed, as have all of the current asset and current liability accounts. All of the information needed to prepare the Operating Activities section of your statement of cash flows has been gathered.

To summarize, the preparation of the Operating Activities section of the statement of cash flows requires the conversion of each item on the income statement to a cash basis.

The current asset and current liability accounts are analyzed to discover the cash effects of each item on the income statement. Exhibit 12-14 summarizes this conversion process.

Note in the exhibit the various adjustments made to put each income statement item on a cash basis. For example, the $6,000 increase in accounts receivable for the period is deducted from sales revenue of $670,000 to arrive at cash collected from customers. Similar adjustments are made to each of the other income statement items with the exception of depreciation, the gain, and the loss. Depreciation is ignored because it does not have an effect on cash flow. The gain relates to the sale of a long-term asset, and any cash effect is reflected in the Investing Activities section of the statement of cash flows. Similarly, the loss resulted from the retirement of bonds, and any cash flow effect is reported in the Financing Activities section. The bottom of the exhibit highlights an important point: Julian reported net income of $120,000 but actually generated $174,000 in cash from operations.

Exhibit 12-14 Conversion of Income Statement Items to Cash Basis

INCOME STATEMENT	AMOUNT	ADJUSTMENTS	CASH FLOWS
Sales revenue	$670,000		$670,000
		+ Decreases in accounts receivable	–0–
		– Increases in accounts receivable	(6,000)
		Cash collected from customers	$664,000
Interest revenue	15,000		$ 15,000
		+ Decreases in interest receivable	–0–
		– Increases in interest receivable	–0–
		Cash collected in interest	$ 15,000
Gain on sale of machine	5,000	*Not an operating activity*	$ –0–
Cost of goods sold	390,000		$390,000
		+ Increases in inventory	–0–
		– Decreases in inventory	(8,000)
		+ Decreases in accounts payable	–0–
		– Increases in accounts payable	(7,000)
		Cash paid to suppliers	$375,000
Salaries and wages	60,000		$ 60,000
		+ Decreases in salaries/wages payable	2,000
		– Increases in salaries/wages payable	–0–
		Cash paid to employees	$ 62,000
Depreciation	40,000	*No cash flow effect*	$ –0–
Insurance	12,000		$ 12,000
		+ Increases in prepaid insurance	–0–
		– Decreases in prepaid insurance	(6,000)
		Cash paid for insurance	$ 6,000
Interest	15,000		$ 15,000
		+ Decreases in interest payable	–0–
		– Increases in interest payable	–0–
		Cash paid for interest	$ 15,000
Income taxes	50,000		$ 50,000
		+ Decreases in income taxes payable	–0–
		– Increases in income taxes payable	(3,000)
		Cash paid for taxes	$ 47,000
Loss on retirement of bonds	3,000	*Not an operating activity*	$ –0–
Net income	$120,000	Net cash flow from operating activities	$174,000

Determine the Cash Flows from Investing Activities At this point, we turn our attention to the long-term asset accounts and any additional information available about these accounts. Julian has three long-term assets on its balance sheet: Long-Term Investments, Land, and Property and Equipment.

Long-Term Investments Item 1 in the additional information in Exhibit 12-12 indicates that Julian purchased $30,000 of investments during the year. The $30,000 net increase in the Long-Term Investments account confirms this (no mention is made of the sale of any investments during 2004):

LONG-TERM INVESTMENTS

Bal. Jan. 1	90,000	
(o) Purchases	?	
Bal. Dec. 31	120,000	

The entry to record the purchase was as follows:

(o) Long-Term Investments	30,000	
Cash		30,000
To record purchase of investments.		

Assets	=	Liabilities	+	Owners' Equity
+30,000				
−30,000				

The credit in this entry is the first cash outflow in the master T account Cash Flows from Investing Activities, as shown in Exhibit 12-15.

Exhibit 12-15

Master T Account for Cash Flows from Investing Activities

Cash Flows from Investing Activities

Cash inflows from:		Cash outflows for:	
(r) Sale of machine	25,000	(o) Purchase of investments	30,000
		(q) Purchase of property and equipment	75,000

Land Note the $50,000 net increase in land:

LAND

Bal. Jan. 1	100,000	
(p) Acquisitions	?	
Bal. Dec. 31	150,000	

Item 2 in the additional information indicates that Julian purchased land by issuing a $50,000 note payable. The entry to record the purchase was as follows:

(p) Land	50,000	
Notes Payable		50,000
To record acquisition of land in exchange for note.		

Assets	=	Liabilities	+	Owners' Equity
+50,000		+50,000		

This entry obviously does not involve cash. The transaction has both an important financing element and an investing component, however. The issuance of the note is a financing activity, and the acquisition of land is an investing activity. Because no cash was involved, the transaction is reported in a separate schedule instead of directly on the statement of cash flows:

Supplemental schedule of noncash investing and financing activities	
Acquisition of land in exchange for note payable	$50,000

Property and Equipment Property and equipment increased by $40,000 during 2004. However, Julian both acquired equipment and sold a machine (items 3 and 4 in the additional information). The acquisition of the equipment for $75,000 resulted in this journal entry:

(q)	Property and Equipment	75,000	
	Cash		75,000
	To record acquisition of equipment for cash.		

Assets	=	Liabilities	+	Owners' Equity
+75,000				
−75,000				

As we discussed earlier in the chapter, acquisitions of new plant and equipment are important investing activities for most businesses. Thus, the credit to Cash appears in the master T account Cash Flows from Investing Activities in Exhibit 12-15.

After this entry is posted to the Property and Equipment account, it appears as follows:

PROPERTY AND EQUIPMENT

Bal. Jan. 1	280,000		
(q) Acquisitions	75,000	?	Disposals (r)
Bal. Dec. 31	320,000		

Julian obviously disposed of fixed assets during the period. In fact, item 4 in the additional information in Exhibit 12-12 reports the sale of a machine with an original cost of $35,000. An analysis of the Property and Equipment account at this point confirms this amount:

Beginning property and equipment	$280,000
+ Acquisitions	75,000
− Disposals	(*X*)
= Ending property and equipment	$320,000

Solving for *X*, we can find the *cost* of the fixed assets sold during the year:

$$280{,}000 + 75{,}000 - X = 320{,}000$$
$$X = \underline{\underline{\$35{,}000}}$$

A T account for Accumulated Depreciation appears as follows after posting Depreciation Expense in entry (i):

ACCUMULATED DEPRECIATION

		75,000	Bal. Jan. 1
(r) Disposals	?	40,000	Depreciation expense (i)
		100,000	Bal. Dec. 31

The additional information also indicates that the book value of the machine sold was $20,000. This means that if the original cost was $35,000 and the book value was $20,000, the Accumulated Depreciation on the machine sold must have been $35,000 − $20,000, or $15,000. An analysis similar to the one we just looked at for Property and Equipment confirms this amount:

Beginning accumulated depreciation	$ 75,000
+ Depreciation expense (entry i)	40,000
− Accumulated depreciation on assets sold	(*X*)
= Ending accumulated depreciation	$100,000

Solving for X, we can find the accumulated depreciation on the assets disposed of during the year:

$$75{,}000 + 40{,}000 - X = 100{,}000$$
$$X = \underline{\underline{\$15{,}000}}$$

Finally, we are told in the additional information that the machine was sold for $25,000. *If the selling price was $25,000 and the book value was $20,000, Julian reports a gain on sale of $5,000, an amount that is confirmed on the income statement in Exhibit 12-11.* The journal entry to record the sale of the machine was as follows:

		Debit	Credit
(r)	Cash	25,000	
	Accumulated Depreciation	15,000	
	Property and Equipment		35,000
	Gain on Sale of Machine (Retained Earnings)		5,000
	To record sale of machine.		

Assets	=	Liabilities	+	Owners' Equity
+25,000				+5,000
+15,000				
−35,000				

To summarize, the machine was sold for $25,000, an amount that exceeded its book value of $20,000, thus generating a gain of $5,000. The debit to Cash is entered in the master T account for Cash Flows from Investing Activities in Exhibit 12-15.

Determine the Cash Flows from Financing Activities These activities generally involve long-term liabilities and stockholders' equity. We first consider Julian's two long-term liabilities, Notes Payable and Bonds Payable, and then the two stockholders' equity accounts: Capital Stock and Retained Earnings.

Notes Payable Recall that item 2 in the additional information reported that Julian purchased land in exchange for a $50,000 note payable. The T account for Notes Payable confirms this amount:

NOTES PAYABLE

Debit		Credit	
		35,000	Bal. Jan. 1
		?	Additional issuances (p)
		85,000	Bal. Dec. 31

In our discussion of investing activities, we recorded entry (p) to account for this exchange and entered the transaction on a supplemental schedule of noncash activities because it was a significant financing activity but did not involve cash.

Bonds Payable A T account for Bonds Payable appears as follows:

BONDS PAYABLE

Debit		Credit	
		260,000	Bal. Jan. 1
(s) Retirement	?		
		200,000	Bal. Dec. 31

Item 5 in the additional information in Exhibit 12-12 indicates that bonds with a face value of $60,000 were retired by paying $63,000 in cash. The book value of the bonds retired is the same as the face value of $60,000 because there is no unamortized discount or premium on the records. *When a company has to pay more in cash ($63,000) to settle a debt than the book value of the debt ($60,000), it reports a loss.* Recall the $3,000 loss reported on the income statement in Exhibit 12-11. The entry to record the retirement of the bonds was as follows:

(s)	Loss on Retirement of Bonds (Retained Earnings)	3,000	
	Bonds Payable	60,000	
	Cash		63,000
	To record retirement of bonds.		

Assets	=	**Liabilities**	+	**Owners' Equity**
−63,000		**−60,000**		**−3,000**

The credit to Cash in this entry is presented in the master T account Cash Flows from Financing Activities, as shown in Exhibit 12-16.

Exhibit 12-16

Master T Account for Cash Flows from Financing Activities

Cash Flows from Financing Activities

Cash inflows from:		Cash outflows for:	
(t) Issuance of stock	25,000	(s) Retirement of bonds	63,000
		(u) Payment of cash dividends	67,000

Capital Stock The Capital Stock account indicates a $25,000 net increase during 2004:

CAPITAL STOCK

	75,000	Bal. Jan. 1
	?	Stock issued (t)
	100,000	Bal. Dec. 31

Julian issued capital stock in exchange for $25,000 in cash, according to item 6 in the additional information in Exhibit 12-12. Some companies issue additional stock after the initial formation of a corporation to raise needed capital. The entry was as follows:

(t)	Cash	25,000	
	Capital Stock		25,000
	To record issuance of stock in exchange for cash.		

Assets	=	**Liabilities**	+	**Owners' Equity**
+25,000				**+25,000**

The debit to Cash in this entry is presented as a cash inflow in the master T account Cash Flows from Financing Activities, as shown in Exhibit 12-16.

Accounting for Your Decisions

You Decide for Your Investment Club

You are a member of an investment club and have been given the assignment of analyzing the statements of cash flows for the Norfolk Corp. for the last three years. The company has neither issued nor retired any stock during this time period. You notice that the company's cash balance has increased steadily during this period but that a majority of the increase is due to a large net inflow of cash from financing activities in each of the three years. Should you be concerned?

ANS: The net inflow of cash from financing activities indicates that the company is borrowing more than it is repaying. Certainly borrowing can be an attractive means of financing the purchase of new plant and equipment. At some point, however, the debt, along with interest, will need to be repaid. The company must be able to generate sufficient cash from its operations to make these payments.

Retained Earnings An analysis of the Retained Earnings account indicates the following:

RETAINED EARNINGS

		193,000	Bal. Jan. 1
(u) Cash dividends	?	120,000	Net income for 2004
		246,000	Bal. Dec. 31

We can determine the amount of cash dividends for 2004 in the following manner:

	Beginning retained earnings	$193,000
+	Net income	120,000
−	Cash dividends	(X)
=	Ending retained earnings	$246,000

Solving for X, we can find the amount of cash dividends paid during the year:[4]

$$193{,}000 + 120{,}000 - X = 246{,}000$$
$$X = \$67{,}000$$

Item 7 in the additional information confirms that this was in fact the amount of dividends paid during the year. The final entry was as follows:

(u)	Retained Earnings	67,000	
	Cash		67,000
	To record cash dividends paid.		

Assets	=	Liabilities	+	Owners' Equity
−67,000				−67,000

The credit to Cash in this entry appears in the master T account Cash Flows from Financing Activities, as presented in Exhibit 12-16.

Using the Master T Accounts to Prepare a Statement of Cash Flows

All of the information needed to prepare a statement of cash flows is now available in the three master T accounts, along with the supplemental schedule prepared earlier. From the information gathered in Exhibits 12-13, 12-15, and 12-16, a completed statement of cash flows appears in Exhibit 12-17.

What does Julian's statement of cash flows tell us? Cash flow from operations totaled $174,000. Cash used to acquire investments and equipment amounted to $80,000, after receiving $25,000 from the sale of a machine. A net amount of $105,000 was used for financing activities. Thus, Julian used more cash than it generated, and that's why the cash balance declined. That's okay for a year or two, but if this continues, the company won't be able to pay its bills.

A Master T-Account Approach to Preparing the Statement of Cash Flows: Indirect Method

LO 6 Use T accounts to prepare a statement of cash flows, using the indirect method to determine cash flow from operating activities.

The purpose of the Operating Activities section of the statement changes when we use the indirect method. Instead of reporting cash receipts and cash payments, *the objective is to reconcile net income to net cash flow from operating activities.* The other two sections of the completed statement in Exhibit 12-17, the investing and financing sections, are unchanged. The use of the indirect or the direct method for presenting cash flow from operating activities does not affect these two sections.

[4]Any decrease in Retained Earnings represents the dividends *declared* during the period rather than the amount paid. If there had been a Dividends Payable account, we would analyze it to find the amount of dividends paid. The lack of a balance in such an account at either the beginning or the end of the period tells us that Julian paid the same amount of dividends that it declared during the period.

Exhibit 12-17

Completed Statement of Cash Flows for Julian Corp.

JULIAN CORP. STATEMENT OF CASH FLOWS FOR THE YEAR ENDED DECEMBER 31, 2004	
Cash flows from operating activities	
Cash receipts from:	
Sales on account	$ 664,000
Interest	15,000
Total cash receipts	$ 679,000
Cash payments for:	
Inventory purchases	$(375,000)
Salaries and wages	(62,000)
Insurance	(6,000)
Interest	(15,000)
Taxes	(47,000)
Total cash payments	$(505,000)
Net cash provided by operating activities	$ 174,000
Cash flows from investing activities	
Purchase of investments	$ (30,000)
Purchase of property and equipment	(75,000)
Sale of machine	25,000
Net cash used by investing activities	$ (80,000)
Cash flows from financing activities	
Retirement of bonds	$ (63,000)
Issuance of stock	25,000
Payment of cash dividends	(67,000)
Net cash used by financing activities	$(105,000)
Net decrease in cash	$ (11,000)
Cash balance, December 31, 2003	46,000
Cash balance, December 31, 2004	$ 35,000
Supplemental schedule of noncash investing and financing activities	
Acquisition of land in exchange for note payable	$ 50,000

A T-account methodology, similar to that used for the direct method can be used to prepare the Operating Activities section of the statement of cash flows under the indirect method.

Net Income Recall that the first line in the Operating Activities section of the statement under the indirect method is net income. That is, we start with the assumptions that all revenues and gains reported on the income statement increase cash flow and that all expenses and losses decrease cash flow. Julian's net income of $120,000, as reported on its income statement in Exhibit 12-11, is reported as the first item in the Operating Activities section of the statement of cash flows as shown in Exhibit 12-18.

Accounts Receivable The net increase in Accounts Receivable, as shown below in T-account form, indicates that Julian recorded more sales than cash collections during the period:

ACCOUNTS RECEIVABLE		
Bal. Jan. 1	57,000	
Net increase	6,000	
Bal. Dec. 31	63,000	

Because net income includes sales, as opposed to cash collections, the $6,000 *net increase* must be *deducted* to adjust net income to cash from operations. To help remem-

Exhibit 12-18

Indirect Method for Reporting Cash Flows from Operating Activities

JULIAN CORP.
PARTIAL STATEMENT OF CASH FLOWS
FOR THE YEAR ENDED DECEMBER 31, 2004

Net cash flows from operating activities	
Net income	$120,000
Adjustments to reconcile net income to net cash provided by operating activities:	
Increase in accounts receivable	(6,000)
Gain on sale of machine	(5,000)
Decrease in inventory	8,000
Increase in accounts payable	7,000
Decrease in salaries and wages payable	(2,000)
Depreciation expense	40,000
Decrease in prepaid insurance	6,000
Increase in income taxes payable	3,000
Loss on retirement of bonds	3,000
Net cash provided by operating activities	$174,000

ber to deduct the net increase in accounts receivable in the Operating Activities section of the statement, consider the following. The $6,000 net increase appears in the preceding T account as a *debit.* Think of the deduction on the statement of cash flows as the equivalent of a *credit.* That is, the debit is to Accounts Receivable, and the credit is recorded as a bracketed amount (i.e., as a deduction) on the statement of cash flows.

From Concept to Practice 12.3

Reading IBM's Statement of Cash Flows

Did IBM's Receivables increase or decrease during 2001? Why is the change in this account added on the statement of cash flows?

Gain on Sale of Machine The gain itself did not generate any cash, but the *sale* of the machine did. And as we found earlier, the cash generated by selling the machine was reported in the Investing Activities section of the statement. The cash proceeds included the gain. Because the gain is included in the net income figure, it must be *deducted* to determine cash from operations. Also note that the gain is included twice in cash inflows if it is not deducted from the net income figure in the Operating Activities section. Note the deduction of $5,000 in Exhibit 12-18.

Inventory As the $8,000 net decrease in the Inventory account indicates, Julian liquidated a portion of its stock of inventory during the year:

INVENTORY

Bal. Jan. 1	92,000		
		8,000	Net decrease
Bal. Dec. 31	84,000		

A net decrease in this account indicates that the company sold more products than it purchased during the year. As shown in Exhibit 12-18, the *net decrease* of $8,000 is *added back* to net income. As discussed for Accounts Receivable, note the debit and credit logic for this adjustment. Because Inventory is credited in the T account for the decrease, the statement of cash flows shows an increase, which is equivalent to a debit to Cash.

Accounts Payable Julian owed suppliers $31,000 at the start of the year. By the end of the year, the balance had grown to $38,000. A T account for Accounts Payable follows:

ACCOUNTS PAYABLE

		31,000	Bal. Jan. 1
		7,000	Net increase
		38,000	Bal. Dec. 31

Effectively, the company saved cash by delaying the payment of some of its outstanding accounts payable. The *net increase* of $7,000 in this account is *added back* to net income, as shown in Exhibit 12-18.

Salaries and Wages Payable A T account for Salaries and Wages Payable indicates a net decrease of $2,000:

SALARIES AND WAGES PAYABLE

		9,000	Bal. Jan. 1
Net decrease	2,000		
		7,000	Bal. Dec. 31

The rationale for *deducting* the $2,000 *net decrease* in this liability in Exhibit 12-18 follows from what we just said about an increase in Accounts Payable. The payment to employees of $2,000 more than the amount included in expense on the income statement requires an additional deduction under the indirect method.

Depreciation Expense Depreciation is a noncash expense. Because it was deducted to arrive at net income, we must *add back* $40,000, the amount of depreciation, to find cash from operations. The same holds true for amortization of intangible assets and depletion of natural resources.

Prepaid Insurance This account decreased by $6,000, according to the T account:

PREPAID INSURANCE

Bal. Jan. 1	18,000		
		6,000	Net decrease
Bal. Dec. 31	12,000		

A decrease in this account indicates that Julian deducted more on the income statement for the insurance expense of the period than it paid in cash for new policies. That is, the cash outlay for insurance protection was not as large as the amount of expense reported on the income statement. Thus, the *net decrease* in the account is *added back* to net income in Exhibit 12-18.

Income Taxes Payable A T account for Income Taxes Payable indicates a net increase of $3,000:

INCOME TAXES PAYABLE

		5,000	Bal. Jan. 1
		3,000	Net increase
		8,000	Bal. Dec. 31

The *net increase* of $3,000 in this liability is *added back* to net income in Exhibit 12-18 because the payments to the government were $3,000 less than the amount included on the income statement.

Loss on Retirement of Bonds The $3,000 loss from retiring bonds was reported on the income statement as a deduction. There are two parts to the explanation for *adding back* the loss to net income to eliminate its effect in the Operating Activities section of the statement. First, any cash outflow from retiring bonds is properly classified as a financing activity, not an operating activity. The entire cash outflow should be reported in one classification rather than being allocated between two classifications. Second, the amount of the cash outflow is $63,000, not $3,000. To summarize, to convert net income to a cash basis, we add the loss back in the Operating Activities section to eliminate its effect. The actual use of cash to retire the bonds is shown in the financing section of the statement.

Study Tip

Note from this list how changes in current assets and current liabilities are treated on the statement. For example, because accounts receivable and accounts payable are on opposite sides of the balance sheet, increases in each of them are handled in opposite ways. But an increase in one and a decrease in the other are treated in the same way.

Summary of Adjustments to Net Income under the Indirect Method

The following is a list of the most common adjustments to net income when the indirect method is used to prepare the Operating Activities section of the statement of cash flows:

ADDITIONS TO NET INCOME	DEDUCTIONS FROM NET INCOME
Decrease in accounts receivable	Increase in accounts receivable
Decrease in inventory	Increase in inventory
Decrease in prepayments	Increase in prepayments
Increase in accounts payable	Decrease in accounts payable
Increase in accrued liabilities	Decrease in accrued liabilities
Losses on sales of long-term assets	Gains on sales of long-term assets
Losses on retirements of bonds	Gains on retirements of bonds
Depreciation, amortization, and depletion	

Comparison of the Indirect and Direct Methods

Earlier in the chapter we pointed out that the amount of cash provided by operating activities is the same under the direct and the indirect methods. The relative merits of the two methods, however, have stirred considerable debate in the accounting profession. The Financial Accounting Standards Board has expressed a strong preference for the direct method but allows companies to use the indirect method.

If a company uses the indirect method, it must separately disclose two important cash payments: income taxes paid and interest paid. Thus, if Julian uses the indirect method, it reports the following either at the bottom of the statement of cash flows or in a note to the financial statements:

Income taxes paid	$47,000
Interest paid	$15,000

Advocates of the direct method believe that the information provided with this approach is valuable in evaluating a company's operating efficiency. For example, the use of the direct method allows the analyst to follow any trends in cash receipts from customers and compare them with cash payments to suppliers. The information presented in the Operating Activities section of the statement under the direct method is certainly user-friendly. Someone without a technical background in accounting can easily tell where cash came from and where it went during the period.

Advocates of the indirect method argue two major points. Many companies believe that the use of the direct method reveals too much about their business by telling readers exactly the amount of cash receipts and cash payments from operations. Whether the use of the direct method tells the competition too much about a company is subject to debate. The other argument made for the indirect method is that it focuses attention on the differences between income on an accrual basis and a cash basis. In fact, this reconciliation of net income and cash provided by operating activities is considered to be important enough that *if a company uses the direct method, it must present a separate schedule to reconcile net income to net cash from operating activities.* This schedule, in effect, is the same as the Operating Activities section for the indirect method.

THE USE OF CASH FLOW INFORMATION

The statement of cash flows is a critical disclosure to a company's investors and creditors. Many investors focus on cash flow from operations, rather than net income, as their key statistic. Similarly, many bankers are as concerned with cash flow from operations as they are with net income because they care about a company's ability to pay its bills. There is the concern that accrual accounting can mask cash flow problems. For example, a company with smooth earnings could be building up accounts receivable and inventory. This may not become evident until the company is in deep trouble.

The statement of cash flows provides investors, analysts, bankers, and other users with a valuable starting point as they attempt to evaluate a company's financial health. From this point, these groups must decide *how* to use the information presented on the statement. They pay particular attention to the *relationships* among various items on the statement, as well as to other financial statement items. In fact, many large banks have their own cash flow models, which typically involve a rearrangement of the items on the statement of cash flows to suit their needs. We now turn our attention to two examples of how various groups use cash flow information.

© AP/WIDE WORLD PHOTOS

Managers, investors, and brokers gauge the relative strengths of retailers by observing which stores are the most popular. But they also study the financial statements, particularly the statement of cash flows and its indicators of cash flow adequacy, as the most fundamental way to measure a firm's strength.

http://www.sec.gov

http://www.ibm.com

Creditors and Cash Flow Adequacy

Bankers and other creditors are especially concerned with a company's ability to meet its principal and interest obligations. *Cash flow adequacy* is a measure intended to help in this regard.[5] It gauges the cash available to meet future debt obligations after paying taxes and interest costs and making capital expenditures. Because capital expenditures on new plant and equipment are a necessity for most companies, analysts are concerned with the cash available to repay debt *after* the company has replaced and updated its existing base of long-term assets.

Cash flow adequacy can be computed as follows:

$$\text{Cash Flow Adequacy} = \frac{\text{Cash Flow from Operating Activities} - \text{Capital Expenditures}}{\text{Average Amount of Debt Maturing over Next Five Years}}$$

How could you use the information in an annual report to measure a company's cash flow adequacy? First, whether a company uses the direct or indirect method to report cash flow from operating activities, this number represents cash flow *after* paying interest and taxes. The numerator of the ratio is determined by deducting capital expenditures, as they appear in the Investing Activities section of the statement, from cash flow from operating activities. A disclosure required by the **Securities and Exchange Commission** provides the information needed to calculate the denominator of the ratio. This regulatory body requires companies to report the annual amount of long-term debt maturing over each of the next five years.

IBM's Cash Flow Adequacy As an example of the calculation of this ratio, consider the following amounts from IBM's statement of cash flows for the year ended December 31, 2001 (amounts in millions of dollars):

Net cash provided from operating activities	$14,265
Payments for plant, rental machines and other property	$ 5,660

Note j in IBM's 2001 annual report provides the following information:

> Annual maturities in millions of dollars on long-term debt outstanding at December 31, 2001, are as follows: 2002, $5,186; 2003, $3,106; 2004, $1,501; 2005, $1,904; 2006, $2,261; 2007 and beyond, $6,471.

[5]An article appearing in the January 10, 1994, edition of *The Wall Street Journal* reported that Fitch Investors Service Inc. has published a rating system to compare the cash flow adequacy of companies that it rates single-A in its credit ratings. The rating system is intended to help corporate bond investors assess the ability of these companies to meet their maturing debt obligations. Lee Berton, "Investors Have a New Tool for Judging Issuers' Health: 'Cash-Flow Adequacy,'" p. C1.

We can now compute IBM's cash flow adequacy for the year ended December 31, 2001, as follows:

$$\text{Cash Flow Adequacy} = \frac{\$14{,}265 - \$5{,}660}{(\$5{,}186 + \$3{,}106 + \$1{,}501 + \$1{,}904 + \$2{,}261)/5}$$

$$= \frac{\$8{,}605}{\$2{,}791.6} = 3.08$$

Would you feel comfortable lending to IBM if you knew that its ratio of cash flow from operations, after making necessary capital expenditures, to average maturities of debt over the next five years was over 3 to 1? Before answering this question, you would want to compare the ratio with the ratios for prior years as well as with the ratio for companies of similar size and in lines of business similar to those of IBM. As a starting point, however, IBM's ratio of 3 to 1 indicates that its 2001 cash flow was more than sufficient to repay its average annual debt over the next five years.

Stockholders and Cash Flow per Share

As we will see in Chapter 13, one measure of the relative worth of an investment in a company is the ratio of the stock's market price per share to the company's earnings per share (that is, the price/earnings ratio). But many stockholders and Wall Street analysts are even more interested in the price of the stock in relation to the company's cash flow per share. Cash flow for purposes of this ratio is normally limited to cash flow from operating activities. This ratio has been used by these groups to evaluate investments—even though the accounting profession has expressly forbidden the reporting of cash flow per share information in the financial statements. The accounting profession's belief is that this type of information is not an acceptable alternative to earnings per share as an indicator of company performance.

Accounting for Your Decisions

You Are the Banker

You and your old college roommate are having an argument. You say that cash flow is all that matters when looking at a company's prospects. Your roommate says that the most important number is earnings per share. Who's right?

ANS: You're both wrong. True, bankers are interested in cash flow to make sure that a company can pay back its loans. But earnings per share is important also because it is less easily manipulated. After all, companies can decide when they want to finance expansion, pay down debt, or invest in new businesses. A company with strong earnings can appear weak from a cash flow perspective if it invests too much in new operating assets or other businesses. On the other hand, a company that wants to appear cash-rich can avoid making all of the investments that it ought to be making. Although companies can manipulate earnings to some extent, the matching principle ensures that revenues and expenses relating to those revenues take place during the same period.

Ratios for Decision Making

Reporting and analyzing financial statement information related to a company's cash flows: Of critical importance to companies, their creditors, and their investors is the company's ability to pay its debts when required. For long-term debts, the statement of cash flows and the disclosure in the notes of the upcoming maturities of those debts are very helpful to project whether or not the company will be able to meet its obligations in the future. The cash flow adequacy ratio tells how many times the current amount of net cash inflows from operating activities, after deducting capital expenditures, could pay for the upcoming maturities of long-term debts. The higher the number, the better the company's position. The ratio assumes the current net cash inflow from operating activities and the expenditures for capital assets are typical of the company over time.

Balance Sheet	Income Statement	Statement of Cash Flows	Notes
		Operating Activities Net Cash from Operating Activities Investing Activities Net Cash Paid for Capital Expenditures	Information about Upcoming Debt Maturities*

$$\text{Cash Flow Adequacy} = \frac{\text{Cash Flow from Operating Activities} - \text{Capital Expenditures}}{\text{Average Amount of Debt Maturing over Next Five Years*}}$$

*Total debt that will be paid off over the next five years ÷ 5

Answers to the Two-Minute Review

Two-Minute Review on Page 623

1. *A cash equivalent is an item readily convertible to a known amount of cash and with an original maturity to the investor of three months or less. Because the maturity date of these items, such as a 60-day certificate of deposit, is so near, they are not considered to carry any significant risks in terms of price changes. Thus, any changes in cash equivalents are not reported on the statement of cash flows.*
2. *Operating, investing, and financing activities.*
3. *Direct and indirect methods. The direct method involves reporting major classes of gross cash receipts and cash payments. Under the indirect method, net cash flow from operating activities is computed by adjusting net income to remove the effect of all deferrals of past operating cash receipts and payments and all accruals of future operating cash receipts and payments.*

Warmup Exercises

Warmup Exercise 12-1 *Purpose of the Statement of Cash Flows* **LO 1**

Most companies begin the statement of cash flows by indicating the amount of net income and ending it with the beginning and ending cash balances. Why is the statement necessary if net income already appears on the income statement and the cash balances can be found on the balance sheet?

Key to the Solution

Recall the *purpose* of the statement of cash flows as described in the beginning of the chapter.

Warmup Exercise 12-2 *Classification of Activities* **LO 3**

For each of the following activities, indicate whether it should appear on the statement of cash flows as an operating (O), investing (I), or financing (F) activity. Assume the company uses the direct method of reporting in the Operating Activities section.

_______ **1.** New equipment is acquired for cash.
_______ **2.** Thirty-year bonds are issued.
_______ **3.** Cash receipts from the cash register are recorded.
_______ **4.** The bi-weekly payroll is paid.
_______ **5.** Common stock is issued for cash.
_______ **6.** Land that was being held for future expansion is sold at book value.

Key to the Solution

Recall the general rules for each of the categories: operating activities involve acquiring and selling products and services; investing activities deal with acquiring and disposing of long-term assets; and financing activities are concerned with the raising and repayment of funds in the form of debt and equity.

Warmup Exercise 12-3 *Adjustments to Net Income with the Indirect Method* **LO 6**

Assume that a company uses the indirect method to prepare the Operating Activities section of the statement of cash flows. For each of the following items, indicate whether it would be added to net income (A), deducted from net income (D), or not reported in this section of the statement under the indirect method (NR).

_______ **1.** Decrease in accounts payable
_______ **2.** Increase in accounts receivable
_______ **3.** Decrease in prepaid insurance
_______ **4.** Purchase of new factory equipment
_______ **5.** Depreciation expense
_______ **6.** Gain on retirement of bonds

Key to the Solution

Refer to the summary of adjustments to net income under the indirect method on page 642.

Solutions to Warmup Exercises

Warmup Exercise 12-1

The statement of cash flows is a complement to the other statements in that it summarizes the operating, investing, and financing activities over a period of time. Even though the net income and cash balances are available on other statements, the statement of cash flows explains to the reader *why* net income is different than cash flow from operations and *why* cash changed by the amount it did during the period.

Warmup Exercise 12-2

1. I **2.** F **3.** O **4.** O **5.** F **6.** I

Warmup Exercise 12-3

1. D **2.** D **3.** A **4.** NR **5.** A **6.** D

Review Problem

An income statement and comparative balance sheets for Dexter Company are shown below:

WebTUTOR™ Advantage

DEXTER COMPANY
INCOME STATEMENT
FOR THE YEAR ENDED DECEMBER 31, 2004

Sales revenue	$89,000
Cost of goods sold	57,000
Gross margin	$32,000
Depreciation expense	6,500
Advertising expense	3,200
Salaries expense	12,000
Total operating expenses	$21,700
Operating income	$10,300
Loss on sale of land	2,500
Income before tax	$ 7,800
Income tax expense	2,600
Net income	$ 5,200

DEXTER COMPANY
COMPARATIVE BALANCE SHEETS

	December 31	
	2004	**2003**
Cash	$ 12,000	$ 9,500
Accounts receivable	22,000	18,400
Inventory	25,400	20,500
Prepaid advertising	10,000	8,600
Total current assets	$ 69,400	$ 57,000
Land	$120,000	$ 80,000
Equipment	190,000	130,000
Accumulated depreciation	(70,000)	(63,500)
Total long-term assets	$240,000	$146,500
Total assets	$309,400	$203,500
Accounts payable	$ 15,300	$ 12,100
Salaries payable	14,000	16,400
Income taxes payable	1,200	700
Total current liabilities	$ 30,500	$ 29,200
Capital stock	$200,000	$100,000
Retained earnings	78,900	74,300
Total stockholders' equity	$278,900	$174,300
Total liabilities and stockholders' equity	$309,400	$203,500

Additional Information

1. Land was acquired during the year for $70,000.
2. An unimproved parcel of land was sold during the year for $27,500. Its original cost to Dexter was $30,000.
3. A specialized piece of equipment was acquired in exchange for capital stock in the company. The value of the capital stock was $60,000.
4. In addition to the capital stock issued in item **3**, stock was sold for $40,000.
5. Dividends of $600 were paid.

Required

Prepare a statement of cash flows for 2004 using the direct method in the Operating Activities section of the statement. Include supplemental schedules to report any noncash investing and financing activities and to reconcile net income to net cash provided by operating activities.

(continued)

Solution to Review Problem

DEXTER COMPANY
STATEMENT OF CASH FLOWS
FOR THE YEAR ENDED DECEMBER 31, 2004

Cash flows from operating activities	
Cash collections from customers	$ 85,400
Cash payments:	
To suppliers	$(58,700)
For advertising	(4,600)
To employees	(14,400)
For income taxes	(2,100)
Total cash payments	$(79,800)
Net cash provided by operating activities	$ 5,600
Cash flows from investing activities	
Purchase of land	$(70,000)
Sale of land	27,500
Net cash used by investing activities	$(42,500)
Cash flows from financing activities	
Issuance of capital stock	$ 40,000
Payment of cash dividends	(600)
Net cash provided by financing activities	$ 39,400
Net increase in cash	$ 2,500
Cash balance, December 31, 2003	9,500
Cash balance, December 31, 2004	$ 12,000
Supplemental schedule of noncash investing and financing activities	
Acquisition of specialized equipment in exchange for capital stock	$ 60,000
Reconciliation of net income to net cash provided by operating activities	
Net income	$ 5,200
Adjustments to reconcile net income to net cash provided by operating activities:	
Increase in accounts receivable	(3,600)
Increase in inventory	(4,900)
Increase in prepaid advertising	(1,400)
Increase in accounts payable	3,200
Decrease in salaries payable	(2,400)
Increase in income taxes payable	500
Depreciation expense	6,500
Loss on sale of land	2,500
Net cash provided by operating activities	$ 5,600

Appendix: Accounting Tools: A Work-Sheet Approach to the Statement of Cash Flows

LO 7 Use a work sheet to prepare a statement of cash flows, using the indirect method to determine cash flow from operating activities.

In the chapter, we illustrated the use of T accounts to aid in the preparation of a statement of cash flows. We pointed out that T accounts are simply tools to help in analyzing the transactions of the period. We now consider the use of a work sheet as an alternative tool to organize the information needed to prepare the statement. We will use the information given in the chapter for Julian Corp. (refer to Exhibits 12-11 and

12-12 for the income statements and comparative balance sheets). Although it is possible to use a work sheet to prepare the statement when the Operating Activities section is prepared under the direct method, we illustrate the use of a work sheet using the more popular *indirect* method.

A work sheet for Julian Corp. is presented in Exhibit 12-19. The following steps were followed in preparing the work sheet:

Exhibit 12-19 Julian Corp. Statement of Cash Flows Work Sheet

JULIAN CORP.
STATEMENT OF CASH FLOWS WORK SHEET (INDIRECT METHOD)
(ALL AMOUNTS IN THOUSANDS OF DOLLARS)

	Balances			Cash Inflows (Outflows)			
ACCOUNTS	12/31/04	12/31/03	CHANGES	OPERATING	INVESTING	FINANCING	NONCASH ACTIVITIES
Cash	35	46	(11)[16]				
Accounts Receivable	63	57	6[10]	(6)[10]			
Inventory	84	92	(8)[11]	8[11]			
Prepaid Insurance	12	18	(6)[12]	6[12]			
Long-Term Investments	120	90	30[1]		(30)[1]		
Land	150	100	50[2]				(50)[2]
Property and Equipment	320	280	75[3]		(75)[3]		
			(35)[4]		25[4]		
Accumulated Depreciation	(100)	(75)	15[4]				
			(40)[9]	40[9]			
Accounts Payable	(38)	(31)	(7)[13]	7[13]			
Salaries and Wages Payable	(7)	(9)	2[14]	(2)[14]			
Income Taxes Payable	(8)	(5)	(3)[15]	3[15]			
Notes Payable	(85)	(35)	(50)[2]				50[2]
Bonds Payable	(200)	(260)	60[5]			(63)[5]	
Capital Stock	(100)	(75)	(25)[6]			25[6]	
Retained Earnings	(246)	(193)	67[7]	(5)[4]		(67)[7]	
				3[5]			
			(120)[8]	120[8]	—	—	—
Totals	-0-	-0-	-0-	174	(80)	(105)	-0-
Net decrease in cash				(11)[16]			

SOURCE: The authors are grateful to Jeannie Folk for the development of this work sheet.

Step 1: The balances in each account at the end and at the beginning of the period are entered in the first two columns of the work sheet. For Julian, these balances can be found in its comparative balance sheets in Exhibit 12 12. Note that credit balances are bracketed on the work sheet. Because the work sheet lists all balance sheet accounts, the total of the debit balances must equal the total of the credit balances, and thus, the totals at the bottom for these first two columns equal $0.

Step 2: The additional information listed at the bottom of Exhibit 12-12 is used to record the various investing and financing activities on the work sheet (the item numbers discussed below correspond to the superscript numbers on the work sheet in Exhibit 12-19):

1. Long-term investments were purchased for $30,000. Because this transaction required the use of cash, it is entered as a bracketed amount in the Investing column and as an addition to the Long-Term Investments account in the Changes column.
2. Land was acquired by issuing a $50,000 note payable. This transaction is entered on two lines on the work sheet. First, $50,000 is added to the Changes column for Land and as a corresponding deduction in the Noncash column (the last column on the work sheet). Likewise, $50,000 is added for Notes Payable to the Changes column and to the Noncash column.
3. Item 3 in the additional information indicates the acquisition of equipment for $75,000. This amount appears on the work sheet as an addition to Property and Equipment in the Changes column and as a deduction (cash outflow) in the Investing column.
4. A machine with an original cost of $35,000 and a book value of $20,000 was sold for $25,000, resulting in four entries on the work sheet. First, the amount of cash received, $25,000, is entered as an addition in the Investing column on the line for property and equipment. On the same line, the cost of the machine, $35,000, is entered as a deduction in the Changes column. The difference between the cost of the machine, $35,000, and its book value, $20,000, is its accumulated depreciation of $15,000. This amount is shown as a deduction from this account in the Changes column. Because the gain of $5,000 is included in net income, it is deducted in the Operating column (on the Retained Earnings line).
5. Bonds with a face value of $60,000 were retired by paying $63,000 in cash, resulting in the entry of three amounts on the work sheet. The face value of the bonds, $60,000, is entered as a reduction of Bonds Payable in the Changes column. The amount paid to retire the bonds, $63,000, is entered on the same line in the Financing column. The loss of $3,000 is added in the Operating column because it was a deduction to arrive at net income.
6. Capital stock was issued for $25,000. This amount is entered on the Capital Stock line under the Changes column (as an increase in the account) and under the Financing column as an inflow.
7. Dividends of $67,000 were paid. This amount is entered as a reduction in Retained Earnings in the Changes column and as a cash outflow in the Financing Activities column.

Step 3: Because the indirect method is being used, net income of $120,000 for the period is entered as an addition to Retained Earnings in the Operating column of the work sheet (entry 8). The amount is also entered as an increase (bracketed) in the Changes column.

Step 4: Any noncash revenues or expenses are entered on the work sheet on the appropriate lines. For Julian, depreciation expense of $40,000 is added (bracketed) to Accumulated Depreciation in the Changes column and in the Operating column. This entry is identified on the work sheet as entry 9.

Step 5: Each of the changes in the noncash current asset and current liability accounts is entered in the Changes column and in the Operating column. These entries are identified on the work sheet as entries 10 through 15.

Step 6: Totals are determined for the Operating, Investing, and Financing columns and entered at the bottom of the work sheet. The total for the final column, Noncash Activities, of $0, is also entered.

Step 7: The net cash inflow (outflow) for the period is determined by adding the totals of the operating, investing, and financing columns. For Julian, the net cash *outflow* is $11,000, shown as entry 16 at the bottom of the statement. This same amount is then transferred to the line for Cash in the Changes column. Finally, the total of the Changes column at this point should net to $0.

Chapter Highlights

1. **LO 1** The purpose of a statement of cash flows is to summarize the cash flows of an entity during a period of time. The cash inflows and outflows are categorized into three activities: operating, investing, and financing.
2. **LO 2** Cash equivalents are convertible to a known amount of cash and are therefore included with cash on the balance sheet. Because such items as commercial paper, money market funds, and Treasury bills do not involve any significant risk, neither their purchase nor their sale is shown as an investing activity on the statement of cash flows.
3. **LO 3** Operating activities are generally the effects of items that enter into the determination of net income, such as the effects of buying and selling products and services. Other operating activities include payments of compensation to employees, taxes to the government, and interest to creditors. Preparation of the Operating Activities section of the statement of cash flows requires an analysis of the current assets and current liabilities.
4. **LO 3** Investing activities are critical to the success of a business because they involve the replacement of existing productive assets and the addition of new ones. Capital expenditures are normally the single largest cash outflow for most businesses. Occasionally, companies generate cash from the sale of existing plant and equipment. The information needed to prepare the Investing Activities section of the statement of cash flows is found by analyzing the long-term asset accounts.
5. **LO 3** All businesses rely on financing in one form or another. At least initially, all corporations sell stock to raise funds. Many turn to external sources as well, generating cash from the issuance of promissory notes and bonds. The repayment of debt and the reacquisition of capital stock are important uses of cash for some companies. Given the nature of financing activities, long-term liability and stockholders' equity accounts must be examined in preparing this section of the statement of cash flows.
6. **LO 4** Two different methods are acceptable to report cash flow from operating activities. Under the direct method, cash receipts and cash payments related to operations are reported. Under the indirect method, net income is reconciled to net cash flow from operating activities. Regardless of which method is used, the amount of cash generated from operations is the same.
7. **LO 5** Preparation of the Operating Activities section under the direct method requires the conversion of income statement items from an accrual basis to a cash basis. Certain items, such as depreciation, do not have a cash effect and are not included on the statement. Gains and losses typically relate to either investing or financing activities and are not included in the Operating Activities section of the statement. When the direct method is used to present cash flow from operating activities, a separate schedule is required to reconcile net income to net cash flow from operating activities. This schedule is the same as the Operating Activities section under the indirect method. Some type of methodology, such as a T-account approach, can be helpful in preparing the statement for more complex situations.
8. **LO 6** When the indirect method is used, the reconciliation of net income to net cash flow from operating activities appears on the face of the statement. Adjustments are made for the changes in each of the operating-related current asset and current liability accounts, as well as adjustments for noncash items, such as depreciation. The effects of gains and losses on net income must also be removed to convert to a cash basis. If the indirect method is used, a company must separately disclose the amount of cash paid for taxes and for interest.
9. **LO 7** A work sheet is sometimes used in preparing a statement of cash flows. Similar to T accounts, the work sheet acts as a tool to aid in the preparation of the statement. (Appendix)

http://

http://porter.swlearning.com

Technology and other resources for your success

If you need additional help, visit the text's Web site. Also, see pages xv–xvii in this text's preface for a description of available technology and other resources. If your instructor is using PERSONAL*Trainer* in this course, you may complete, on line, the assignments identified by PT.

Key Terms Quiz

Read each definition below and then write the number of that definition in the blank beside the appropriate term it defines. The quiz solutions appear at the end of the chapter.

_____ Statement of cash flows
_____ Cash equivalent
_____ Operating activities
_____ Investing activities
_____ Financing activities
_____ Direct method
_____ Indirect method

1. Activities concerned with the acquisition and sale of products and services.
2. For preparing the Operating Activities section of the statement of cash flows, the approach in which net income is reconciled to net cash flow from operations.

(continued)

3. The financial statement that summarizes an entity's cash receipts and cash payments during the period from operating, investing, and financing activities.
4. An item readily convertible to a known amount of cash and with a maturity to the investor of three months or less.
5. Activities concerned with the acquisition and disposal of long-term assets.
6. For preparing the Operating Activities section of the statement of cash flows, the approach in which cash receipts and cash payments are reported.
7. Activities concerned with the raising and repayment of funds in the form of debt and equity.

Answers on p. 676.

Alternate Terms

Bottom line Net income

Cash flow from operating activities Cash flow from operations

Statement of cash flows Cash flows statement

Questions

1. What is the purpose of the statement of cash flows? As a flows statement, explain how it differs from the income statement.
2. What is a cash equivalent? Why is it included with cash for purposes of preparing a statement of cash flows?
3. Preston Corp. acquires a piece of land by signing a $60,000 promissory note and making a down payment of $20,000. How should this transaction be reported on the statement of cash flows?
4. Hansen Inc. made two purchases during December. One was a $10,000 Treasury bill that matures in 60 days from the date of purchase. The other was a $20,000 investment in Motorola common stock that will be held indefinitely. How should each of these be treated for purposes of preparing a statement of cash flows?
5. Companies are required to classify cash flows as operating, investing, or financing. Which of these three categories do you think will most likely have a net cash *outflow* over a number of years? Explain your answer.
6. A fellow student says to you: "The statement of cash flows is the easiest of the basic financial statements to prepare because you know the answer before you start. You compare the beginning and ending balances in cash on the balance sheet and compute the net inflow or outflow of cash. What could be easier?" Do you agree? Explain your answer.
7. What is your evaluation of the following statement? "Depreciation is responsible for providing some of the highest amounts of cash for capital-intensive businesses. This is obvious by examining the Operating Activities section of the statement of cash flows. Other than the net income of the period, depreciation is often the largest amount reported in this section of the statement."
8. Which method for preparing the Operating Activities section of the statement of cash flows, the direct or the indirect method, do you believe provides more information to users of the statement? Explain your answer.
9. Assume that a company uses the indirect method to prepare the Operating Activities section of the statement of cash flows. Why would a decrease in accounts receivable during the period be added back to net income?
10. Why is it necessary to analyze both inventory and accounts payable in trying to determine cash payments to suppliers when the direct method is used?
11. A company has a very profitable year. What explanations might there be for a decrease in cash?
12. A company reports a net loss for the year. Is it possible that cash could increase during the year? Explain your answer.
13. What effect does a decrease in income taxes payable for the period have on cash generated from operating activities? Does it matter whether the direct or the indirect method is used?
14. Why do accounting standards require a company to separately disclose income taxes paid and interest paid if it uses the indirect method?
15. Is it logical that interest paid is classified as a cash outflow in the *Operating* Activities section of the statement of cash flows but that dividends paid are included in the *Financing* Activities section? Explain your answer.
16. Jackson Company prepays the rent on various office facilities. The beginning balance in Prepaid Rent was $9,600, and the ending balance was $7,300. The income statement reports Rent Expense of $45,900. Under the direct method, what amount would appear for cash paid in rent in the Operating Activities section of the statement of cash flows?
17. Baxter Inc. buys 2,000 shares of its own common stock at $20 per share as treasury stock. How is this transaction reported on the statement of cash flows?
18. Duke Corp. sold a delivery truck for $9,000. Its original cost was $25,000, and the book value at the time of the sale was $11,000. How does the transaction to record the sale appear on a statement of cash flows prepared under the indirect method?
19. Billings Company has a patent on its books with a balance at the beginning of the year of $24,000. The ending balance for the asset was $20,000. The company neither bought nor sold any patents during the year, nor does it use an Accumulated Amortization account. Assuming that the company uses the indirect method in preparing a statement of cash flows, how is the decrease in the Patents account reported on the statement?
20. Ace Inc. declared and distributed a 10% stock dividend during the year. Explain how, if at all, you think this transaction should be reported on a statement of cash flows.

Exercises

Exercise 12-1 ***Cash Equivalents*** **LO 2**

Metropolis Industries invested its excess cash in the following instruments during December 2004:

Certificate of deposit, due January 31, 2005	$ 35,000
Certificate of deposit, due June 30, 2005	95,000
Investment in City of Elgin bonds, due May 1, 2006	15,000
Investment in Quantum Data stock	66,000
Money Market Fund	105,000
90-day Treasury bills	75,000
Treasury note, due December 1, 2005	200,000

Required

Determine the amount of cash equivalents that should be combined with cash on the company's balance sheet at December 31, 2004, and for purposes of preparing a statement of cash flows for the year ended December 31, 2004.

Exercise 12-2 ***Classification of Activities*** **LO 3**

For each of the following transactions reported on a statement of cash flows, fill in the blank to indicate if it would appear in the Operating Activities section (O), in the Investing Activities section (I), or in the Financing Activities section (F). Put an *S* in the blank if the transaction does not affect cash but is reported in a supplemental schedule of noncash activities. Assume the company uses the direct method in the Operating Activities section.

_______ **1.** A company purchases its own common stock in the open market and immediately retires it.

_______ **2.** A company issues preferred stock in exchange for land.

_______ **3.** A six-month bank loan is obtained.

_______ **4.** Twenty-year bonds are issued.

_______ **5.** A customer's open account is collected.

_______ **6.** Income taxes are paid.

_______ **7.** Cash sales for the day are recorded.

_______ **8.** Cash dividends are declared and paid.

_______ **9.** A creditor is given shares of common stock in the company in return for cancellation of a long-term loan.

_______ **10.** A new piece of machinery is acquired for cash.

_______ **11.** Stock of another company is acquired as an investment.

_______ **12.** Interest is paid on a bank loan.

_______ **13.** Factory workers are paid.

Exercise 12-3 ***Retirement of Bonds Payable on the Statement of Cash Flows—Indirect Method*** **LO 3**

Redstone Inc. has the following debt outstanding on December 31, 2004:

10% bonds payable, due 12/31/08	$500,000	
Discount on bonds payable	(40,000)	$460,000

On this date, Redstone retired the entire bond issue by paying cash of $510,000.

Required

1. Prepare the journal entry to record the bond retirement.
2. Describe how the bond retirement would be reported on the statement of cash flows, assuming that Redstone uses the indirect method.

Exercise 12-4 ***Cash Collections—Direct Method*** **LO 5**

Stanley Company's comparative balance sheets included accounts receivable of $80,800 at December 31, 2003, and $101,100 at December 31, 2004. Sales reported by Stanley on its 2004 income statement amounted to $1,450,000. What is the amount of cash collections that Stanley

(continued)

will report in the Operating Activities section of its 2004 statement of cash flows assuming that the direct method is used?

Exercise 12-5 ***Cash Payments—Direct Method*** **LO 5**

Lester Enterprises' comparative balance sheets included inventory of $90,200 at December 31, 2003, and $70,600 at December 31, 2004. Lester's comparative balance sheets also included accounts payable of $57,700 at December 31, 2003, and $39,200 at December 31, 2004. Lester's accounts payable balances are composed solely of amounts due to suppliers for purchases of inventory on account. Cost of goods sold, as reported by Lester on its 2004 income statement, amounted to $770,900. What is the amount of cash payments for inventory that Lester will report in the Operating Activities section of its 2004 statement of cash flows assuming that the direct method is used?

Exercise 12-6 ***Operating Activities Section—Direct Method*** **LO 5**

The following account balances for the noncash current assets and current liabilities of Labrador Company are available:

	December 31	
	2004	**2003**
Accounts receivable	$ 4,000	$ 6,000
Inventory	32,000	25,000
Office supplies	7,000	10,000
Accounts payable	7,500	4,500
Salaries and wages payable	1,500	2,500
Interest payable	500	1,000
Income taxes payable	4,500	3,000

In addition, the income statement for 2004 is as follows:

	2004
Sales revenue	$100,000
Cost of goods sold	75,000
Gross profit	$ 25,000
General and administrative expense	$ 8,000
Depreciation expense	3,000
Total operating expenses	$ 11,000
Income before interest and taxes	$ 14,000
Interest expense	3,000
Income before tax	$ 11,000
Income tax expense	5,000
Net income	$ 6,000

Required

1. Prepare the Operating Activities section of the statement of cash flows using the direct method.
2. What does the use of the direct method reveal about a company that the indirect method does not?

Exercise 12-7 ***Determination of Missing Amounts—Cash Flow from Operating Activities*** **LO 5**

The computation of cash provided by operating activities requires analysis of the noncash current asset and current liability accounts. Using T accounts, determine the missing amounts for each of the following independent cases:

Case 1	
Accounts receivable, beginning of year	$150,000
Accounts receivable, end of year	100,000
Credit sales for the year	175,000
Cash sales for the year	60,000
Write-offs of uncollectible accounts	35,000
Total cash collections for the year (from cash sales and collections on account)	?

Case 2	
Inventory, beginning of year	$ 80,000
Inventory, end of year	55,000
Accounts payable, beginning of year	25,000
Accounts payable, end of year	15,000
Cost of goods sold	175,000
Cash payments for inventory (assume all purchases of inventory are on account)	?

Case 3	
Prepaid insurance, beginning of year	$ 17,000
Prepaid insurance, end of year	20,000
Insurance expense	15,000
Cash paid for new insurance policies	?

Case 4	
Income taxes payable, beginning of year	$ 95,000
Income taxes payable, end of year	115,000
Income tax expense	300,000
Cash payments for taxes	?

Exercise 12-8 *Dividends on the Statement of Cash Flows* LO 5

The following selected account balances are available from the records of Lewistown Company:

	December 31	
	2004	**2003**
Dividends payable	$ 30,000	$ 20,000
Retained earnings	375,000	250,000

Other information available for 2004 follows:

a. Lewistown reported $285,000 net income for the year.

b. It declared and distributed a stock dividend of $50,000 during the year.

c. It declared cash dividends at the end of each quarter and paid them within the next 30 days of the following quarter.

Required

1. With the use of T accounts, determine the amount of cash dividends *paid* during the year for presentation in the Financing Activities section of the statement of cash flows.
2. Should the stock dividend described in part **b** appear on a statement of cash flows? Explain your answer.

Exercise 12-9 *Adjustments to Net Income with the Indirect Method* LO 6

Assume that a company uses the indirect method to prepare the Operating Activities section of the statement of cash flows. For each of the following items, fill in the blank to indicate whether it would be added to net income (A), deducted from net income (D), or not reported in this section of the statement under the indirect method (NR).

________ **1.** Depreciation expense
________ **2.** Gain on sale of used delivery truck
________ **3.** Bad debts expense
________ **4.** Increase in accounts payable
________ **5.** Purchase of new delivery truck
________ **6.** Loss on retirement of bonds
________ **7.** Increase in prepaid rent
________ **8.** Decrease in inventory
________ **9.** Increase in short-term investments (classified as available-for-sale securities)
________ **10.** Amortization of patents

Exercise 12-10 *Operating Activities Section—Indirect Method* LO 6

The following account balances for the noncash current assets and current liabilities of Suffolk Company are available:

	December 31	
	2004	2003
Accounts receivable	$43,000	$35,000
Inventory	30,000	40,000
Prepaid rent	17,000	15,000
Totals	$90,000	$90,000
Accounts payable	$26,000	$19,000
Income taxes payable	6,000	10,000
Interest payable	15,000	12,000
Totals	$47,000	$41,000

Net income for 2004 is $40,000. Depreciation expense is $20,000. Assume that all sales and all purchases are on account.

Required

1. Prepare the Operating Activities section of the statement of cash flows using the indirect method.
2. Provide a brief explanation as to why cash flow from operating activities is more or less than the net income of the period.

Multi-Concept Exercises

Exercise 12-11 *Classification of Activities* LO 2, 3

Use the following legend to indicate how each of the following transactions would be reported on the statement of cash flows (assume that the stocks and bonds of other companies are classified as available-for-sale securities):

II = Inflow from investing activities
OI = Outflow from investing activities
IF = Inflow from financing activities
OF = Outflow from financing activities
CE = Classified as a cash equivalent and included with cash for purposes of preparing the statement of cash flows

_______ 1. Purchased a six-month certificate of deposit.
_______ 2. Purchased a 60-day Treasury bill.
_______ 3. Issued 1,000 shares of common stock.
_______ 4. Purchased 1,000 shares of stock in another company.
_______ 5. Purchased 1,000 shares of its own stock to be held in the treasury.
_______ 6. Invested $1,000 in a money market fund.
_______ 7. Sold 500 shares of stock of another company.
_______ 8. Purchased 20-year bonds of another company.
_______ 9. Issued 30-year bonds.
_______ 10. Repaid a six-month bank loan.

Exercise 12-12 *Classification of Activities* LO 3, 5

Use the following legend to indicate how each of the following transactions would be reported on the statement of cash flows (assume that the company uses the direct method in the Operating Activities section):

IO = Inflow from operating activities
OO = Outflow from operating activities
II = Inflow from investing activities
OI = Outflow from investing activities
IF = Inflow from financing activities
OF = Outflow from financing activities
NR = Not reported in the body of the statement of cash flows but included in a supplemental schedule

_______ 1. Collected $10,000 in cash from customers' open accounts for the period.

_______ 2. Paid one of the company's inventory suppliers $500 in settlement of an open account.

_______ 3. Purchased a new copier for $6,000; signed a 90-day note payable.

_______ 4. Issued bonds at face value of $100,000.

_______ 5. Made $23,200 in cash sales for the week.

_______ 6. Purchased an empty lot adjacent to the factory for $50,000. The seller of the land agrees to accept a five-year promissory note as consideration.

_______ 7. Renewed the property insurance policy for another six months. Cash of $1,000 is paid for the renewal.

_______ 8. Purchased a machine for $10,000.

_______ 9. Paid cash dividends of $2,500.

_______ 10. Reclassified as short-term a long-term note payable of $5,000 that is due within the next year.

_______ 11. Purchased 500 shares of the company's own stock on the open market for $4,000.

_______ 12. Sold 500 shares of Nike stock for book value of $10,000 (they had been classified as available-for-sale securities).

Exercise 12-13 *Long-Term Assets on the Statement of Cash Flows—Indirect Method* LO 3, 6

The following account balances are taken from the records of Martin Corp. for the past two years (credit balances are in parentheses):

	December 31	
	2004	2003
Plant and equipment	$ 750,000	$ 500,000
Accumulated depreciation	(160,000)	(200,000)
Patents	92,000	80,000
Retained earnings	(825,000)	(675,000)

Other information available for 2004 follows:

a. Net income for the year was $200,000.
b. Depreciation expense on plant and equipment was $50,000.
c. Plant and equipment with an original cost of $150,000 were sold for $64,000 (you will need to determine the book value of the assets sold).
d. Amortization expense on patents was $8,000.
e. Both new plant and equipment and patents were purchased for cash during the year.

Required

Indicate, with amounts, how all items related to these long-term assets would be reported in the 2004 statement of cash flows, including any adjustments in the Operating Activities section of the statement. Assume that Martin uses the indirect method.

Exercise 12-14 *Income Statement, Statement of Cash Flows (Direct Method), and Balance Sheet* LO 1, 5

The following events occurred at Handsome Hounds Grooming Company during its first year of business:

a. To establish the company, the two owners contributed a total of $50,000 in exchange for common stock.
b. Grooming service revenue for the first year amounted to $150,000, of which $40,000 was on account.
c. Customers owe $10,000 at the end of the year from the services provided on account.
d. At the beginning of the year a storage building was rented. The company was required to sign a three-year lease for $12,000 per year and make a $2,000 refundable security deposit. The first year's lease payment and the security deposit were paid at the beginning of the year.

(continued)

e. At the beginning of the year the company purchased a patent at a cost of $100,000 for a revolutionary system to be used for dog grooming. The patent is expected to be useful for 10 years. The company paid 20% down in cash and signed a four-year note at the bank for the remainder.

f. Operating expenses, including amortization of the patent and rent on the storage building, totaled $80,000 for the first year. No expenses were accrued or unpaid at the end of the year.

g. The company declared and paid a $20,000 cash dividend at the end of the first year.

Required

1. Prepare an income statement for the first year.
2. Prepare a statement of cash flows for the first year, using the direct method in the Operating Activities section.
3. Did the company generate more or less cash flow from operations than it earned in net income? Explain why there is a difference.
4. Prepare a balance sheet as of the end of the first year.

Problems

Problem 12-1 *Statement of Cash Flows—Indirect Method* LO 6

The following balances are available for Chrisman Company:

	December 31	
	2004	**2003**
Cash	$ 8,000	$ 10,000
Accounts receivable	20,000	15,000
Inventory	15,000	25,000
Prepaid rent	9,000	6,000
Land	75,000	75,000
Plant and equipment	400,000	300,000
Accumulated depreciation	(65,000)	(30,000)
Totals	$462,000	$401,000
Accounts payable	$ 12,000	$ 10,000
Income taxes payable	3,000	5,000
Short-term notes payable	35,000	25,000
Bonds payable	75,000	100,000
Common stock	200,000	150,000
Retained earnings	137,000	111,000
Totals	$462,000	$401,000

Bonds were retired during 2004 at face value, plant and equipment were acquired for cash, and common stock was issued for cash. Depreciation expense for the year was $35,000. Net income was reported at $26,000.

Required

1. Prepare a statement of cash flows for 2004, using the indirect method in the Operating Activities section.
2. Did Chrisman generate sufficient cash from operations to pay for its investing activities? How did it generate cash other than from operations? Explain your answers.

Problem 12-2 *Statement of Cash Flows Using a Work Sheet—Indirect Method (Appendix)* LO 7

Refer to all of the facts in Problem 12-1.

Required

1. Using the format in the chapter's appendix, prepare a statement of cash flows work sheet.
2. Prepare a statement of cash flows for 2004, using the indirect method in the Operating Activities section.

3. Did Chrisman generate sufficient cash from operations to pay for its investing activities? How did it generate cash other than from operations? Explain your answers.

Problem 12-3 *Statement of Cash Flows—Direct Method* **LO 5**

DECISION MAKING

Peoria Corp. has just completed another very successful year, as indicated by the following income statement:

	For the Year Ended December 31, 2004
Sales revenue	$1,250,000
Cost of goods sold	700,000
Gross profit	$ 550,000
Operating expenses	150,000
Income before interest and taxes	$ 400,000
Interest expense	25,000
Income before taxes	$ 375,000
Income tax expense	150,000
Net income	$ 225,000

Presented below are comparative balance sheets:

	December 31	
	2004	2003
Cash	$ 52,000	$ 90,000
Accounts receivable	180,000	130,000
Inventory	230,000	200,000
Prepayments	15,000	25,000
Total current assets	$ 477,000	$ 445,000
Land	$ 750,000	$ 600,000
Plant and equipment	700,000	500,000
Accumulated depreciation	(250,000)	(200,000)
Total long-term assets	$1,200,000	$ 900,000
Total assets	$1,677,000	$1,345,000
Accounts payable	$ 130,000	$ 148,000
Other accrued liabilities	68,000	63,000
Income taxes payable	90,000	110,000
Total current liabilities	$ 288,000	$ 321,000
Long-term bank loan payable	$ 350,000	$ 300,000
Common stock	$ 550,000	$ 400,000
Retained earnings	489,000	324,000
Total stockholders' equity	$1,039,000	$ 724,000
Total liabilities and stockholders' equity	$1,677,000	$1,345,000

Other information follows:

a. Dividends of $60,000 were declared and paid during the year.

b. Operating expenses include $50,000 of depreciation.

c. Land and plant and equipment were acquired for cash, and additional stock was issued for cash. Cash was also received from additional bank loans.

The president has asked you some questions about the year's results. She is very impressed with the profit margin of 18% (net income divided by sales revenue). She is bothered, however, by the decline in the cash balance during the year. One of the conditions of the existing bank loan is that the company maintain a minimum cash balance of $50,000.

Required

1. Prepare a statement of cash flows for 2004, using the direct method in the Operating Activities section.

2. On the basis of your statement in requirement **1**, draft a brief memo to the president to explain why cash decreased during such a profitable year. Include in your explanation any recommendations for improving the company's cash flow in future years.

Problem 12-4 ***Statement of Cash Flows—Indirect Method*** **LO 6**

Refer to all of the facts in Problem 12-3.

DECISION MAKING

Required

1. Prepare a statement of cash flows for 2004, using the indirect method in the Operating Activities section.
2. On the basis of your statement in requirement **1**, draft a brief memo to the president to explain why cash decreased during such a profitable year. Include in your explanation any recommendations for improving the company's cash flow in future years.

Problem 12-5 ***Statement of Cash Flows Using a Work Sheet—Indirect Method (Appendix)*** **LO 7**

Refer to all of the facts in Problem 12-3.

DECISION MAKING

Required

1. Using the format in the chapter's appendix, prepare a statement of cash flows work sheet.
2. Prepare a statement of cash flows for 2004, using the indirect method in the Operating Activities section.
3. On the basis of your statement in requirement **2**, draft a brief memo to the president to explain why cash decreased during such a profitable year. Include in your explanation any recommendations for improving the company's cash flow in future years.

Problem 12-6 ***Statement of Cash Flows—Direct Method*** **LO 5**

The income statement for Astro Inc. for 2004 follows:

DECISION MAKING

	For the Year Ended December 31, 2004
Sales revenue	$ 500,000
Cost of goods sold	400,000
Gross profit	$ 100,000
Operating expenses	180,000
Loss before interest and taxes	$ (80,000)
Interest expense	20,000
Net loss	$(100,000)

Presented below are comparative balance sheets:

	December 31	
	2004	**2003**
Cash	$ 95,000	$ 80,000
Accounts receivable	50,000	75,000
Inventory	100,000	150,000
Prepayments	55,000	45,000
Total current assets	$ 300,000	$ 350,000
Land	$ 475,000	$ 400,000
Plant and equipment	870,000	800,000
Accumulated depreciation	(370,000)	(300,000)
Total long-term assets	$ 975,000	$ 900,000
Total assets	$1,275,000	$1,250,000
Accounts payable	$ 125,000	$ 100,000
Other accrued liabilities	35,000	45,000
Interest payable	15,000	10,000
Total current liabilities	$ 175,000	$ 155,000
Long-term bank loan payable	$ 340,000	$ 250,000
Common stock	$ 450,000	$ 400,000
Retained earnings	310,000	445,000
Total stockholders' equity	$ 760,000	$ 845,000
Total liabilities and stockholders' equity	$1,275,000	$1,250,000

Other information follows:

a. Dividends of $35,000 were declared and paid during the year.

b. Operating expenses include $70,000 of depreciation.

c. Land and plant and equipment were acquired for cash, and additional stock was issued for cash. Cash was also received from additional bank loans.

The president has asked you some questions about the year's results. He is disturbed with the $100,000 net loss for the year. He notes, however, that the cash position at the end of the year is improved. He is confused about what appear to be conflicting signals: "How could we have possibly added to our bank accounts during such a terrible year of operations?"

Required

1. Prepare a statement of cash flows for 2004, using the direct method in the Operating Activities section.
2. On the basis of your statement in requirement **1**, draft a brief memo to the president to explain why cash increased during such an unprofitable year. Include in your memo your recommendations for improving the company's bottom line.

Problem 12-7 *Statement of Cash Flows—Indirect Method* **LO 6**

Refer to all of the facts in Problem 12-6.

DECISION MAKING

Required

1. Prepare a statement of cash flows for 2004, using the indirect method in the Operating Activities section.
2. On the basis of your statement in requirement **1**, draft a brief memo to the president to explain why cash increased during such an unprofitable year. Include in your memo your recommendations for improving the company's bottom line.

Problem 12-8 *Statement of Cash Flows Using a Work Sheet—Indirect Method (Appendix)* **LO 7**

Refer to all of the facts in Problem 12-6.

DECISION MAKING

Required

1. Using the format in the chapter's appendix, prepare a statement of cash flows work sheet.
2. Prepare a statement of cash flows for 2004, using the indirect method in the Operating Activities section.
3. On the basis of your statement in requirement **2**, draft a brief memo to the president to explain why cash increased during such an unprofitable year. Include in your memo your recommendations for improving the company's bottom line.

Problem 12-9 *Year-End Balance Sheet and Statement of Cash Flows—Indirect Method* **LO 6**

The balance sheet of Terrier Company at the end of 2003 is presented below, along with certain other information for 2004:

	December 31, 2003
Cash	$ 140,000
Accounts receivable	155,000
Total current assets	$ 295,000
Land	$ 300,000
Plant and equipment	500,000
Accumulated depreciation	(150,000)
Investments	100,000
Total long-term assets	$ 750,000
Total assets	$1,045,000
Current liabilities	$ 205,000
Bonds payable	$ 300,000
Common stock	$ 400,000
Retained earnings	140,000
Total stockholders' equity	$ 540,000
Total liabilities and stockholders' equity	$1,045,000

(continued)

Other information follows:

a. Net income for 2004 was $70,000.
b. Included in operating expenses was $20,000 in depreciation.
c. Cash dividends of $25,000 were declared and paid.
d. An additional $150,000 of bonds was issued for cash.
e. Common stock of $50,000 was purchased for cash and retired.
f. Cash purchases of plant and equipment during the year were $200,000.
g. An additional $100,000 of bonds was issued in exchange for land.
h. Sales exceeded cash collections on account during the year by $10,000. All sales are on account.
i. The amount of current liabilities remained unchanged during the year.

Required

1. Prepare a statement of cash flows for 2004, using the indirect method in the Operating Activities section. Include a supplemental schedule for noncash activities.
2. Prepare a balance sheet at December 31, 2004.
3. Provide a possible explanation as to why Terrier decided to issue additional bonds for cash during 2004.

Problem 12-10 ***Statement of Cash Flows Using a Work Sheet—Indirect Method (Appendix)*** **LO 7**

Refer to all of the facts in Problem 12-9.

Required

1. Prepare a balance sheet at December 31, 2004.
2. Using the format in the chapter's appendix, prepare a statement of cash flows work sheet.
3. Prepare a statement of cash flows for 2004, using the indirect method in the Operating Activities section.
4. Provide a possible explanation as to why Terrier decided to issue additional bonds for cash during 2004.

Multi-Concept Problems

Problem 12-11 ***Statement of Cash Flows—Direct Method*** **LO 4, 5**

SPREADSHEET

Glendive Corp. is in the process of preparing its statement of cash flows for the year ended June 30, 2004. An income statement for the year and comparative balance sheets follow:

	For the Year Ended June 30, 2004
Sales revenue	$550,000
Cost of goods sold	350,000
Gross profit	$200,000
General and administrative expenses	$ 55,000
Depreciation expense	75,000
Loss on sale of plant assets	5,000
Total expenses and losses	$135,000
Income before interest and taxes	$ 65,000
Interest expense	15,000
Income before taxes	$ 50,000
Income tax expense	17,000
Net income	$ 33,000

	June 30 2004	2003
Cash	$ 31,000	$ 40,000
Accounts receivable	90,000	75,000
Inventory	80,000	95,000
Prepaid rent	12,000	16,000
Total current assets	$213,000	$226,000

	June 30	
	2004	2003
Land	$250,000	$170,000
Plant and equipment	750,000	600,000
Accumulated depreciation	(310,000)	(250,000)
Total long-term assets	$690,000	$520,000
Total assets	$903,000	$746,000
Accounts payable	$155,000	$148,000
Other accrued liabilities	32,000	26,000
Income taxes payable	8,000	10,000
Total current liabilities	$195,000	$184,000
Long-term bank loan payable	$100,000	$130,000
Common stock	$350,000	$200,000
Retained earnings	258,000	232,000
Total stockholders' equity	$608,000	$432,000
Total liabilities and stockholders' equity	$903,000	$746,000

Dividends of $7,000 were declared and paid during the year. New plant assets were purchased for $195,000 in cash during the year. Also, land was purchased for cash. Plant assets were sold during 2004 for $25,000 in cash. The original cost of the assets sold was $45,000, and their book value was $30,000. Additional stock was issued for cash, and a portion of the bank loan was repaid.

Required

1. Prepare a statement of cash flows, using the direct method in the Operating Activities section.
2. Evaluate the following statement: "Whether a company uses the direct or the indirect method to report cash flows from operations is irrelevant because the amount of cash flow from operating activities is the same regardless of which method is used."

Problem 12-12 *Statement of Cash Flows—Indirect Method* LO 4, 6

Refer to all of the facts in Problem 12-11.

SPREADSHEET

Required

1. Prepare a statement of cash flows for 2004, using the indirect method in the Operating Activities section.
2. Evaluate the following statement: "Whether a company uses the direct or indirect method to report cash flows from operations is irrelevant because the amount of cash flow from operating activities is the same regardless of which method is used."

Problem 12-13 *Statement of Cash Flows—Direct Method* LO 2, 5

Lang Company has not yet prepared a formal statement of cash flows for 2004. Comparative balance sheets (thousands omitted) as of December 31, 2004 and 2003, and a statement of income and retained earnings for the year ended December 31, 2004, follow:

LANG COMPANY
BALANCE SHEET
DECEMBER 31

Assets	2004	2003
Current assets:		
Cash	$ 60	$ 100
U.S. Treasury bills (six-month)	–0–	50
Accounts receivable	610	500
Inventory	720	600
Total current assets	$1,390	$1,250
Long-term assets:		
Land	$ 80	$ 70
Buildings and equipment	710	600
Accumulated depreciation	(180)	(120)
Patents (less amortization)	105	130
Total long-term assets	$ 715	$ 680
Total assets	$2,105	$1,930

Liabilities and Owners' Equity	2004	2003
Current liabilities:		
Accounts payable	$ 360	$ 300
Taxes payable	25	20
Notes payable	400	400
Total current liabilities	$ 785	$ 720
Term notes payable—due 2008	200	200
Total liabilities	$ 985	$ 920
Owners' equity:		
Common stock outstanding	$ 830	$ 700
Retained earnings	290	310
Total owners' equity	$1,120	$1,010
Total liabilities and owners' equity	$2,105	$1,930

LANG COMPANY
STATEMENT OF INCOME AND RETAINED EARNINGS
FOR THE YEAR ENDED DECEMBER 31, 2004
(THOUSANDS OMITTED)

Sales		$2,408
Less expenses and interest:		
Cost of goods sold	$1,100	
Salaries and benefits	850	
Heat, light, and power	75	
Depreciation	60	
Property taxes	18	
Patent amortization	25	
Miscellaneous expense	10	
Interest	55	2,193
Net income before income taxes		$ 215
Income taxes		105
Net income		$ 110
Retained earnings—January 1, 2004		310
		$ 420
Stock dividend distributed		130
Retained earnings—December 31, 2004		$ 290

Required

1. For purposes of a statement of cash flows, are the U.S. Treasury bills cash equivalents? If not, how should they be classified? Explain your answers.
2. Prepare a statement of cash flows for 2004, using the direct method in the Operating Activities section. (CMA adapted)

Alternate Problems

Problem 12-1A *Statement of Cash Flows—Indirect Method* LO 6

The following balances are available for Madison Company:

	December 31	
	2004	**2003**
Cash	$ 12,000	$ 10,000
Accounts receivable	10,000	12,000
Inventory	8,000	7,000
Prepaid rent	1,200	1,000
Land	75,000	75,000
Plant and equipment	200,000	150,000
Accumulated depreciation	(75,000)	(25,000)
Totals	$231,200	$230,000

	December 31	
	2004	2003
Accounts payable	$ 15,000	$ 15,000
Income taxes payable	2,500	2,000
Short-term notes payable	20,000	22,500
Bonds payable	75,000	50,000
Common stock	100,000	100,000
Retained earnings	18,700	40,500
Totals	$231,200	$230,000

Bonds were issued during 2004 at face value, and plant and equipment were acquired for cash. Depreciation expense for the year was $50,000. A net loss of $21,800 was reported.

Required

1. Prepare a statement of cash flows for 2004, using the indirect method in the Operating Activities section.
2. Explain briefly how Madison was able to increase its cash balance during a year in which it incurred a net loss.

Problem 12-2A ***Statement of Cash Flows Using a Work Sheet—Indirect Method (Appendix)*** **LO 7**

Refer to all of the facts in Problem 12-1A.

Required

1. Using the format in the chapter's appendix, prepare a statement of cash flows work sheet.
2. Prepare a statement of cash flows for 2004, using the indirect method in the Operating Activities section.
3. Explain briefly how Madison was able to increase its cash balance during a year in which it incurred a net loss.

Problem 12-3A ***Statement of Cash Flows—Direct Method*** **LO 5**

DECISION MAKING

Wabash Corp. has just completed another very successful year, as indicated by the following income statement:

	For the Year Ended December 31, 2004
Sales revenue	$2,460,000
Cost of goods sold	1,400,000
Gross profit	$1,060,000
Operating expenses	460,000
Income before interest and taxes	$ 600,000
Interest expense	100,000
Income before taxes	$ 500,000
Income tax expense	150,000
Net income	$ 350,000

The following are comparative balance sheets:

	December 31	
	2004	2003
Cash	$ 140,000	$ 210,000
Accounts receivable	60,000	145,000
Inventory	200,000	180,000
Prepayments	15,000	25,000
Total current assets	$ 415,000	$ 560,000
Land	$ 600,000	$ 700,000
Plant and equipment	850,000	600,000
Accumulated depreciation	(225,000)	(200,000)
Total long-term assets	$1,225,000	$1,100,000
Total assets	$1,640,000	$1,660,000

(continued)

	December 31	
	2004	2003
Accounts payable	$ 140,000	$ 120,000
Other accrued liabilities	50,000	55,000
Income taxes payable	80,000	115,000
Total current liabilities	$ 270,000	$ 290,000
Long-term bank loan payable	$ 200,000	$ 250,000
Common stock	$ 450,000	$ 400,000
Retained earnings	720,000	720,000
Total stockholders' equity	$1,170,000	$1,120,000
Total liabilities and stockholders' equity	$1,640,000	$1,660,000

Other information follows:

a. Dividends of $350,000 were declared and paid during the year.

b. Operating expenses include $25,000 of depreciation.

c. Land was sold for its book value, and new plant and equipment was acquired for cash.

d. Part of the bank loan was repaid, and additional common stock was issued for cash.

The president has asked you some questions about the year's results. She is very impressed with the profit margin of 14% (net income divided by sales revenue). She is bothered, however, by the decline in the company's cash balance during the year. One of the conditions of the existing bank loan is that the company maintain a minimum cash balance of $100,000.

Required

1. Prepare a statement of cash flows for 2004, using the direct method in the Operating Activities section.
2. On the basis of your statement in requirement **1**, draft a brief memo to the president to explain why cash decreased during such a profitable year. Include in your explanation any recommendations for improving the company's cash flow in future years.

Problem 12-4A ***Statement of Cash Flows—Indirect Method*** **LO 6**

DECISION MAKING

Refer to all of the facts in Problem 12-3A.

Required

1. Prepare a statement of cash flows for 2004, using the indirect method in the Operating Activities section.
2. On the basis of your statement in requirement **1**, draft a brief memo to the president to explain why cash decreased during such a profitable year. Include in your explanation any recommendations for improving the company's cash flow in future years.

Problem 12-5A ***Statement of Cash Flows Using a Work Sheet—Indirect Method (Appendix)*** **LO 7**

DECISION MAKING

Refer to all of the facts in Problem 12-3A.

Required

1. Using the format in the chapter's appendix, prepare a statement of cash flows work sheet.
2. Prepare a statement of cash flows for 2004, using the indirect method in the Operating Activities section.
3. On the basis of your statement in requirement **2**, draft a brief memo to the president to explain why cash decreased during such a profitable year. Include in your explanation any recommendations for improving the company's cash flow in future years.

Problem 12-6A ***Statement of Cash Flows—Direct Method*** **LO 5**

DECISION MAKING

The income statement for Pluto Inc. for 2004 follows:

	For the Year Ended December 31, 2004
Sales revenue	$350,000
Cost of goods sold	150,000
Gross profit	$200,000
Operating expenses	250,000
Loss before interest and taxes	$(50,000)
Interest expense	10,000
Net loss	$(60,000)

Presented below are comparative balance sheets:

	December 31	
	2004	2003
Cash	$ 25,000	$ 10,000
Accounts receivable	30,000	80,000
Inventory	100,000	100,000
Prepayments	36,000	35,000
Total current assets	$191,000	$225,000
Land	$300,000	$200,000
Plant and equipment	500,000	250,000
Accumulated depreciation	(90,000)	(50,000)
Total long-term assets	$710,000	$400,000
Total assets	$901,000	$625,000
Accounts payable	$ 50,000	$ 10,000
Other accrued liabilities	40,000	20,000
Interest payable	22,000	12,000
Total current liabilities	$112,000	$ 42,000
Long-term bank loan payable	$450,000	$100,000
Common stock	$300,000	$300,000
Retained earnings	39,000	183,000
Total stockholders' equity	$339,000	$483,000
Total liabilities and stockholders' equity	$901,000	$625,000

Other information follows:

a. Dividends of $84,000 were declared and paid during the year.

b. Operating expenses include $40,000 of depreciation.

c. Land and plant and equipment were acquired for cash. Cash was received from additional bank loans.

The president has asked you some questions about the year's results. He is disturbed with the net loss of $60,000 for the year. He notes, however, that the cash position at the end of the year is improved. He is confused about what appear to be conflicting signals: "How could we have possibly added to our bank accounts during such a terrible year of operations?"

Required

1. Prepare a statement of cash flows for 2004, using the direct method in the Operating Activities section.
2. On the basis of your statement in requirement 1, draft a brief memo to the president to explain why cash increased during such an unprofitable year. Include in your memo your recommendations for improving the company's bottom line.

Problem 12-7A ***Statement of Cash Flows—Indirect Method*** **LO 6**

Refer to all of the facts in Problem 12-6A.

Required

1. Prepare a statement of cash flows for 2004, using the indirect method in the Operating Activities section.

(continued)

2. On the basis of your statement in requirement **1**, draft a brief memo to the president to explain why cash increased during such an unprofitable year. Include in your memo your recommendations for improving the company's bottom line.

Problem 12-8A *Statement of Cash Flows Using a Work Sheet—Indirect Method (Appendix)* LO 7

Refer to all of the facts in Problem 12-6A.

Required

1. Using the format in the chapter's appendix, prepare a statement of cash flows work sheet.
2. Prepare a statement of cash flows for 2004, using the indirect method in the Operating Activities section.
3. On the basis of your statement in requirement **2**, draft a brief memo to the president to explain why cash increased during such an unprofitable year. Include in your memo your recommendations for improving the company's bottom line.

Problem 12-9A *Year-End Balance Sheet and Statement of Cash Flows—Indirect Method* LO 6

The balance sheet of Poodle Company at the end of 2003 is presented below along with certain other information for 2004:

	December 31, 2003
Cash	$ 155,000
Accounts receivable	140,000
Total current assets	$ 295,000
Land	$ 100,000
Plant and equipment	700,000
Accumulated depreciation	(175,000)
Investments	125,000
Total long-term assets	$ 750,000
Total assets	$1,045,000
Current liabilities	$ 325,000
Bonds payable	$ 100,000
Common stock	$ 500,000
Retained earnings	120,000
Total stockholders' equity	$ 620,000
Total liabilities and stockholders' equity	$1,045,000

Other information follows:

a. Net income for 2004 was $50,000.
b. Included in operating expenses was $25,000 in depreciation.
c. Cash dividends of $40,000 were declared and paid.
d. An additional $50,000 of common stock was issued for cash.
e. Bonds payable of $100,000 were purchased for cash and retired at no gain or loss.
f. Cash purchases of plant and equipment during the year were $60,000.
g. An additional $200,000 of land was acquired in exchange for a long-term note payable.
h. Sales exceeded cash collections on account during the year by $15,000. All sales are on account.
i. The amount of current liabilities decreased by $20,000 during the year.

Required

1. Prepare a statement of cash flows for 2004, using the indirect method in the Operating Activities section. Include a supplemental schedule for noncash activities.
2. Prepare a balance sheet at December 31, 2004.
3. What primary uses did Poodle make of the cash it generated from operating activities?

Problem 12-10A *Statement of Cash Flows Using a Work Sheet—Indirect Method (Appendix)* LO 7

Refer to all of the facts in Problem 12-9A.

Required

1. Prepare a balance sheet at December 31, 2004.
2. Using the format in the chapter's appendix, prepare a statement of cash flows work sheet.
3. Prepare a statement of cash flows for 2004, using the indirect method in the Operating Activities section.
4. Provide a possible explanation as to why Poodle decided to purchase and retire bonds during 2004.

Alternate Multi-Concept Problems

Problem 12-11A ***Statement of Cash Flows—Direct Method*** **LO 4, 5**

Bannack Corp. is in the process of preparing its statement of cash flows for the year ended June 30, 2004. An income statement for the year and comparative balance sheets follow:

	For the Year Ended June 30, 2004
Sales revenue	$400,000
Cost of goods sold	240,000
Gross profit	$160,000
General and administrative expenses	$ 40,000
Depreciation expense	80,000
Loss on sale of plant assets	10,000
Total expenses and losses	$130,000
Income before interest and taxes	$ 30,000
Interest expense	15,000
Income before taxes	$ 15,000
Income tax expense	5,000
Net income	$ 10,000

	June 30	
	2004	**2003**
Cash	$ 25,000	$ 40,000
Accounts receivable	80,000	69,000
Inventory	75,000	50,000
Prepaid rent	2,000	18,000
Total current assets	$ 182,000	$ 177,000
Land	$ 60,000	$ 150,000
Plant and equipment	575,000	500,000
Accumulated depreciation	(310,000)	(250,000)
Total long-term assets	$ 325,000	$ 400,000
Total assets	$ 507,000	$ 577,000
Accounts payable	$ 145,000	$ 140,000
Other accrued liabilities	50,000	45,000
Income taxes payable	5,000	15,000
Total current liabilities	$ 200,000	$ 200,000
Long-term bank loan payable	$ 75,000	$ 150,000
Common stock	$ 100,000	$ 100,000
Retained earnings	132,000	127,000
Total stockholders' equity	$ 232,000	$ 227,000
Total liabilities and stockholders' equity	$ 507,000	$ 577,000

Dividends of $5,000 were declared and paid during the year. New plant assets were purchased for $125,000 in cash during the year. Also, land was sold for cash at its book value. Plant assets were sold during 2004 for $20,000 in cash. The original cost of the assets sold was $50,000, and their book value was $30,000. A portion of the bank loan was repaid.

Required

1. Prepare a statement of cash flows for 2004, using the direct method in the Operating Activities section.

(continued)

2. Evaluate the following statement: "Whether a company uses the direct or the indirect method to report cash flows from operations is irrelevant because the amount of cash flow from operating activities is the same regardless of which method is used."

Problem 12-12A ***Statement of Cash Flows—Indirect Method*** **LO 4, 6**

Refer to all of the facts in Problem 12-11A.

Required

1. Prepare a statement of cash flows for 2004, using the indirect method in the Operating Activities section.
2. Evaluate the following statement: "Whether a company uses the direct or the indirect method to report cash flows from operations is irrelevant because the amount of cash flow from operating activities is the same regardless of which method is used."

Problem 12-13A ***Statement of Cash Flows—Direct Method*** **LO 2, 5**

Shepard Company has not yet prepared a formal statement of cash flows for 2004. Comparative balance sheets as of December 31, 2004 and 2003, and a statement of income and retained earnings for the year ended December 31, 2004, follow:

SHEPARD COMPANY
BALANCE SHEET
DECEMBER 31
(THOUSANDS OMITTED)

Assets	**2004**	**2003**
Current assets:		
Cash	$ 50	$ 75
U.S. Treasury bills (six-month)	25	0
Accounts receivable	125	200
Inventory	525	500
Total current assets	$ 725	$ 775
Long-term assets:		
Land	$ 100	$ 80
Buildings and equipment	510	450
Accumulated depreciation	(190)	(150)
Patents (less amortization)	90	110
Total long-term assets	$ 510	$ 490
Total assets	$1,235	$1,265
Liabilities and Owners' Equity		
Current liabilities:		
Accounts payable	$ 370	$ 330
Taxes payable	10	20
Notes payable	300	400
Total current liabilities	$ 680	$ 750
Term notes payable—due 2008	200	200
Total liabilities	$ 880	$ 950
Owners' equity:		
Common stock outstanding	$ 220	$ 200
Retained earnings	135	115
Total owners' equity	$ 355	$ 315
Total liabilities and owners' equity	$1,235	$1,265

SHEPARD COMPANY
STATEMENT OF INCOME AND RETAINED EARNINGS
YEAR ENDED DECEMBER 31, 2004
(THOUSANDS OMITTED)

Sales		$1,416
Less expenses and interest:		
Cost of goods sold	$990	
Salaries and benefits	195	
Heat, light, and power	70	
Depreciation	40	

Property taxes	2	
Patent amortization	20	
Miscellaneous expense	2	
Interest	45	1,364
Net income before income taxes		$ 52
Income taxes		12
Net income		$ 40
Retained earnings—January 1, 2004		115
		$ 155
Stock dividend distributed		20
Retained earnings—December 31, 2004		$ 135

Required

1. For purposes of a statement of cash flows, are the U.S. Treasury bills cash equivalents? If not, how should they be classified? Explain your answers.
2. Prepare a statement of cash flows for 2004, using the direct method in the Operating Activities section. (CMA adapted)

Cases

Reading and Interpreting Financial Statements

Case 12-1 *Reading and Interpreting Winnebago Industries' Statement of Cash Flows* LO 2, 3

Refer to **Winnebago Industries'** statement of cash flows for 2001 and any other pertinent information in its annual report.

http://www.winnebagoind.com

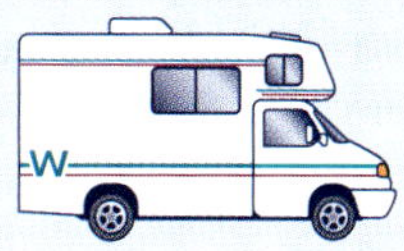

Required

1. According to a note in the annual report, how does the company define cash equivalents?
2. According to the statement of cash flows, did inventories increase or decrease during the most recent year? Explain your answer.
3. What are the major reasons for the difference between net income and net cash provided by operating activities?
4. Excluding operations, what was Winnebago Industries' largest source of cash during the most recent year? the largest use of cash?
5. In the Financing Activities section of its statement of cash flows, Winnebago Industries reports an amount used for the purchase of common stock. Locate this same amount on the statement of changes in stockholders' equity and explain why this amount appears on both statements.

Case 12-2 *Comparing Two Companies in the Same Industry: Winnebago Industries and Monaco Coach Corporation* LO 2, 3

http://www.winnebagoind.com
http://www.monacocoach.com

Refer to the financial statement information of **Winnebago Industries** and **Monaco Coach Corporation** in Appendices A and B at the end of the text. Use the cash flow statements in the annual reports for 2001 to answer the following questions:

Required

1. Did inventory increase or decrease for Monaco Coach during 2001? How does that compare to the change in inventory levels of Winnebago Industries? What are logical reasons for those changes in inventory levels?
2. The cash flow generated from operating activities increased significantly for Monaco Coach from 2000 to 2001. What was the most important reason for the improved performance? How does the cash flow from operating activities compare for the two companies?
3. In 2001, Monaco Coach expanded through an acquisition of another company. What impact did this have on the investing activities and financing activities portion of the cash flows statement? Was there similar activity reported by Winnebago Industries in its 2001 cash flow statement?

(continued)

4. What is the primary source of cash for financing activities for each of the two companies? Why do you think the companies did not use stock more extensively in 2001 as a way to acquire cash? Do you think this was a good strategic move? Why or why not?

Case 12-3 *Reading and Interpreting Gateway's Statement of Cash Flows* LO 4

http://www.gateway.com

Presented below is the Operating Activities section of Gateway, Inc.'s 2001 statement of cash flows (amounts are in thousands of dollars):

Cash flows from operating activities:	
Net income (loss)	$(1,033,915)
Adjustments to reconcile net income (loss) to net cash provided by (used in) operating activities:	
Depreciation and amortization	199,976
Provision for uncollectible accounts receivable	23,151
Deferred income taxes	(29,831)
Loss on investments	186,745
Write-down of long-lived assets	418,304
Cumulative effect of change in accounting principle	23,851
Extraordinary gain on extinguishment of debt	(4,341)
Other, net	(1,707)
Changes in operating assets and liabilities:	
Accounts receivable	301,630
Inventory	194,799
Other assets	21,729
Accounts payable	(442,312)
Accrued liabilities	(87,714)
Accrued royalties	(2,747)
Other liabilities	(37,957)
Net cash provided by (used in) operating activities	$ (270,339)

Required

1. Which method, direct or indirect, does Gateway use in preparing the Operating Activities section of its statement of cash flows? Explain.
2. According to the statement of cash flows, did Accounts Receivable increase or decrease during the year? Explain your answer.
3. According to the statement of cash flows, did Accounts Payable increase or decrease during the year? Explain your answer.
4. Based on your review of this section of Gateway's 2001 statement of cash flows, what is the largest adjustment (other than changes in operating assets and liabilities) to reconcile the net loss of over $1 billion to the much smaller net cash used in operating activities of approximately $270 million? Explain the meaning of this adjustment and tell why it is either added or deducted from the net loss to arrive at net cash provided by operating activities.

Making Financial Decisions

Case 12-4 *Dividend Decision and the Statement of Cash Flows—Direct Method* LO 1, 5

DECISION MAKING

Bailey Corp. just completed the most profitable year in its 25-year history. Reported earnings of $1,020,000 on sales of $8,000,000 resulted in a very healthy profit margin of 12.75%. Each year before releasing the financial statements, the board of directors meets to decide on the amount of dividends to declare for the year. For each of the past nine years, the company has declared a dividend of $1 per share of common stock, which has been paid on January 15 of the following year.

Presented below are the income statement for the year and comparative balance sheets as of the end of the last two years.

	For the Year Ended December 31, 2004
Sales revenue	$8,000,000
Cost of goods sold	4,500,000
Gross profit	$3,500,000

	For the Year Ended December 31, 2004
Operating expenses	1,450,000
Income before interest and taxes	$2,050,000
Interest expense	350,000
Income before taxes	$1,700,000
Income tax expense 40%	680,000
Net income	$1,020,000

	December 31	
	2004	2003
Cash	$ 480,000	$ 450,000
Accounts receivable	250,000	200,000
Inventory	750,000	600,000
Prepayments	60,000	75,000
Total current assets	$1,540,000	$1,325,000
Land	$3,255,000	$2,200,000
Plant and equipment	4,200,000	2,500,000
Accumulated depreciation	(1,250,000)	(1,000,000)
Long-term investments	500,000	900,000
Patents	650,000	750,000
Total long-term assets	$7,355,000	$5,350,000
Total assets	$8,895,000	$6,675,000
Accounts payable	$ 350,000	$ 280,000
Other accrued liabilities	285,000	225,000
Income taxes payable	170,000	100,000
Dividends payable	0	200,000
Notes payable due within next year	200,000	0
Total current liabilities	$1,005,000	$ 805,000
Long-term notes payable	$ 300,000	$ 500,000
Bonds payable	2,200,000	1,500,000
Total long-term liabilities	$2,500,000	$2,000,000
Common stock, $10 par	$2,500,000	$2,000,000
Retained earnings	2,890,000	1,870,000
Total stockholders' equity	$5,390,000	$3,870,000
Total liabilities and stockholders' equity	$8,895,000	$6,675,000

Additional information follows:

a. All sales are on account, as are all purchases.

b. Land was purchased through the issuance of bonds. Additional land (beyond the amount purchased through the issuance of bonds) was purchased for cash.

c. New plant and equipment were acquired during the year for cash. No plant assets were retired during the year. Depreciation expense is included in operating expenses.

d. Long-term investments were sold for cash during the year.

e. No new patents were acquired, and none were disposed of during the year. Amortization expense is included in operating expenses.

f. Notes payable due within next year represents the amount reclassified from long-term to short-term.

g. Fifty thousand shares of common stock were issued during the year at par value.

As Bailey's controller, you have been asked to recommend to the board whether to declare a dividend this year and, if so, whether the precedent of paying a $1 per share dividend can be maintained. The president is eager to keep the dividend at $1 in view of the successful year just completed. He is also concerned, however, about the effect of a dividend on the company's cash position. He is particularly concerned about the large amount of notes payable that comes due next year. He further notes the aggressive growth pattern in recent years, as evidenced this year by large increases in land and plant and equipment.

(continued)

Required

1. Using the format in Exhibit 12-14, convert the income statement from an accrual basis to a cash basis.
2. Prepare a statement of cash flows, using the direct method in the Operating Activities section.
3. What do you recommend to the board of directors concerning the declaration of a cash dividend? Should the $1 per share dividend be declared? Should a smaller amount be declared? Should no dividend be declared? Support your answer with any necessary computations. Include in your response your concerns, from a cash flow perspective, about the following year.

Case 12-5 ***Equipment Replacement Decision and Cash Flows from Operations*** **LO 1, 6**

DECISION MAKING

Conrad Company has been in operation for four years. The company is pleased with the continued improvement in net income but is concerned about a lack of cash available to replace existing equipment. Land, buildings, and equipment were purchased at the beginning of Year 1. No subsequent fixed asset purchases have been made, but the president believes that equipment will need to be replaced in the near future. The following information is available (all amounts are in millions of dollars):

	Year of Operation			
	Year 1	Year 2	Year 3	Year 4
Net income (loss)	$(10)	$ (2)	$15	$20
Depreciation expense	30	25	15	14
Increase (decrease) in:				
Accounts receivable	32	5	12	20
Inventories	26	8	5	9
Prepayments	0	0	10	5
Accounts payable	15	3	(5)	(4)

Required

1. Compute the cash flow from operations for each of Conrad's first four years of operation.
2. Write a memo to the president explaining why the company is not generating sufficient cash from operations to pay for the replacement of equipment.

Accounting and Ethics: What Would You Do?

Case 12-6 ***Loan Decision and the Statement of Cash Flows—Indirect Method*** **LO 1, 6**

Mega Enterprises is in the process of negotiating an extension of its existing loan agreements with a major bank. The bank is particularly concerned with Mega's ability to generate sufficient cash flow from operating activities to meet the periodic principal and interest payments. In conjunction with the negotiations, the controller prepared the following statement of cash flows to present to the bank:

MEGA ENTERPRISES
STATEMENT OF CASH FLOWS
FOR THE YEAR ENDED DECEMBER 31, 2004
(ALL AMOUNTS IN MILLIONS OF DOLLARS)

Cash flows from operating activities	
Net income	$ 65
Adjustments to reconcile net income to net cash provided by operating activities:	
Depreciation and amortization	56
Increase in accounts receivable	(19)
Decrease in inventory	27
Decrease in accounts payable	(42)
Increase in other accrued liabilities	18
Net cash provided by operating activities	$ 105
Cash flows from investing activities	
Acquisitions of other businesses	$ (234)
Acquisitions of plant and equipment	(125)
Sale of other businesses	300
Net cash used by investing activities	$ (59)

Cash flows from financing activities	
Additional borrowings	$ 150
Repayments of borrowings	(180)
Cash dividends paid	(50)
Net cash used by financing activities	$ (80)
Net decrease in cash	$ (34)
Cash balance, January 1, 2004	42
Cash balance, December 31, 2004	$ 8

During 2004, Mega sold one of its businesses in California. A gain of $150 million was included in 2004 income as the difference between the proceeds from the sale of $450 million and the book value of the business of $300 million. The entry to record the sale is as follows:

Cash	450	
California Properties		300
Gain on Sale of Business		150
To record sale of a business.		

Required

1. Comment on the presentation of the sale of the California business on the statement of cash flows. Does the way in which the sale was reported violate generally accepted accounting principles? Regardless of whether it violates GAAP, does the way in which the transaction was reported on the statement result in a misstatement of the net decrease in cash for the period? Explain your answers.
2. Prepare a revised statement of cash flows for 2004, with the proper presentation of the sale of the California business.
3. Has the controller acted in an unethical manner in the way the sale was reported on the statement of cash flows? Explain your answer.

Case 12-7 *Cash Equivalents and the Statement of Cash Flows* LO 2, 3

In December 2004, Rangers Inc. invested $100,000 of idle cash in U.S. Treasury notes. The notes mature on October 1, 2005, at which time Rangers expects to redeem them at face value of $100,000. The treasurer believes that the notes should be classified as cash equivalents because of the plans to hold them to maturity and receive face value. He would also like to avoid presentation of the purchase as an investing activity because the company has made sizable capital expenditures during the year. The treasurer realizes that the decision about classification of the Treasury notes rests with you, as controller.

Required

1. According to generally accepted accounting principles, how should the investment in U.S. Treasury notes be classified for purposes of preparing a statement of cash flows for the year ended December 31, 2004? Explain your answer.
2. As controller for Rangers, what would you do in this situation? What would you tell the treasurer?

Internet Research Case

Case 12-8 *IBM*

INTERNET

http://www.ibm.com

As all companies are required to do, IBM reports in its notes to financial statements information on the various segments in which it does business. Although the company operates primarily in a single industry, information technology, it breaks down its financial results into a total of seven identifiable segments: global services, three different hardware segments, software, global financing, and enterprise investments. With over $37 billion in total revenues in 2001, the first of these, global services, accounted for approximately 40% of the total revenues of the segments.

Required

1. Based on the latest information available, how many segments does IBM now report on, and what are the names of each of them? Which of these segments generated the most revenue for IBM, and what amount did it earn?

2. Based on the latest financial information, what is the amount of IBM's (a) cash flows from operating activities; (b) cash flows from investing activities; and (c) cash flows from financing activities? How do these compare to the corresponding numbers from 2001 in the "Focus on Financial Results" vignette at the start of the chapter? What is the trend?
3. What are three major changes in line items you see in the latest year's statement of cash flows? Using information available in the annual report, and in business news services, what changes do they represent within the company?

Solutions to Key Terms Quiz

3	Statement of cash flows (p. 613)	7	Financing activities (p. 618)
4	Cash equivalent (p. 615)	6	Direct method (p. 620)
1	Operating activities (p. 617)	2	Indirect method (p. 620)
5	Investing activities (p. 617)		

Chapter 13

Financial Statement Analysis

Focus on Financial Results

Although its products are variations on a single theme of chewing gum, the 111-year-old **Wm. Wrigley Jr. Company** has enjoyed a long and highly successful run. In the best year of its first decade, the firm had sales of about $40,000 each month. Now, it takes less than 10 minutes to reach that number! Wrigley has customers in more than 140 countries, and it garners about half of all chewing gum profits in Europe alone. What accounts for this success?

Basic data for assessing the results of Wrigley's steady investments in marketing and new product innovations appear in the Financial Highlights section of the company's annual report, pictured here. Both net sales and net earnings reached record levels in 2001. Note that nearly half of those earnings ($168 million) were paid out to stockholders in dividends. However, the company has to make some tradeoffs. The more earnings that it pays in dividends, the less it has available to invest in future growth in such markets as China and Russia, where it has made inroads that it plans to broaden. (At present, China represents Wrigley's second largest volume country in the world.) Regardless, most companies and their stockholders would be envious of the robust return on average equity of over 30% that Wrigley achieved in 2001.

Sources: 2001 Wrigley annual report and Web site.

Wrigley's 2001 Annual Report

FINANCIAL HIGHLIGHTS

in thousands of dollars except per share amounts

	2001
Net Sales	$2,429,646
Net Earnings	**$ 362,986**
Per Share of Common Stock (basic and diluted)	$ 1.61
Dividends Paid	**$ 167,922**
Per Share of Common Stock	$ 0.745
Additions to Property, Plant and Equipment	$ 181,760
Stockholders' Equity	$1,276,197
Return on Average Equity	30.1%
Stockholders of Record at Close of Year	38,701
Average Shares Outstanding (000)	225,349

About half of the earnings was paid out to owners as dividends.

You're in the Driver's Seat

http://www.wrigley.com

If you were considering buying shares of stock in the Wm. Wrigley Jr. Company, you would want to compare Wrigley with alternative investments and assess its ability to generate income and pay dividends. What measures of financial performance would be most important to you? Find the company's most recent annual report and determine whether those measures have improved since 2001.

LEARNING OBJECTIVES

After studying this chapter, you should be able to:

LO 1 Explain the various limitations and considerations in financial statement analysis. (p. 680)

LO 2 Use comparative financial statements to analyze a company over time (horizontal analysis). (p. 682)

LO 3 Use common-size financial statements to compare various financial statement items (vertical analysis). (p. 687)

LO 4 Compute and use various ratios to assess liquidity. (p. 690)

LO 5 Compute and use various ratios to assess solvency. (p. 695)

LO 6 Compute and use various ratios to assess profitability. (p. 698)

LO 7 Explain how to report on and analyze other income statement items (Appendix). (p. 712)

PRECAUTIONS IN STATEMENT ANALYSIS

Various groups have different purposes for analyzing a company's financial statements. For example, a banker is primarily interested in the likelihood that a loan will be repaid. Certain ratios, as we will see, indicate the ability to repay principal and interest. A stockholder, on the other hand, is concerned with a fair return on the amount invested in the company. Again, certain ratios are helpful in assessing the return to the stockholder. The managers of a business are also interested in the tools of financial statement analysis because various outside groups judge managers by using certain key ratios. Fortunately, most financial statements provide information about financial performance. Publicly held corporations are required to include in their annual reports a section that reviews the past year, with management's comments on its performance as measured by selected ratios and other forms of analysis.

Before we turn to various techniques commonly used in the financial analysis of a company, it is important to understand some of the limitations and other considerations in statement analysis.

Watch for Alternative Accounting Principles

LO 1 Explain the various limitations and considerations in financial statement analysis.

Every set of financial statements is based on various assumptions. For example, a cost-flow method must be assumed in valuing inventory and recognizing cost of goods sold. The accountant chooses FIFO, LIFO, or one of the other acceptable methods. The analyst or other user finds this type of information in the notes to the financial statements. The selection of a particular inventory valuation method has a significant effect on certain key ratios. Recognition of the acceptable alternatives is especially important in comparing two or more companies. *Changes* in accounting methods, such as a change in the depreciation method, also make comparing results for a given company over time more difficult. Again, the reader must turn to the notes for information regarding these changes.

Take Care When Making Comparisons

Users of financial statements often place too much emphasis on summary indicators and key ratios, such as the current ratio and the earnings per share amount. No single ratio is capable of telling the user everything there is to know about a particular company. The calculation of various ratios for a company is only a starting point. One technique we discuss is the comparison of ratios for different periods of time. Has the ratio gone up or down from last year? What is the percentage of increase or decrease in the ratio over the last five years? Recognizing trends in ratios is important in analyzing any company.

The potential investor must also recognize the need to compare one company with others in the same industry. For example, a particular measure of performance may cause an investor to conclude that the company is not operating efficiently. Comparison with an industry standard, however, might indicate that the ratio is normal for companies in that industry. Various organizations publish summaries of selected ratios for a sample of companies in the United States. The ratios are usually organized by industry. Dun & Bradstreet's *Industry Norms and Key Business Ratios,* for example, is an annual review that organizes companies into major industries segments and approximately 800 specific lines of business.

Although industry comparisons are useful, caution is necessary in interpreting the results of such analyses. Few companies in today's economy operate in a single industry. Exceptions exist (Wrigley is almost exclusively in the business of making and selling chewing gum), but most companies cross the boundaries of a single industry. *Conglomerates,* companies operating in more than one industry, present a special challenge to the analyst. Keep in mind also the point made earlier about alternative accounting methods. It is not unusual to find companies in the same industry using different inventory valuation techniques or depreciation methods.

Finally, many corporate income statements contain nonoperating items, such as extraordinary items, cumulative effects from accounting changes, and gains and losses from discontinued operations. When these items exist, the reader must exercise extra caution in making comparisons. To assess the future prospects of a group of companies, you may want to compare income statements *before* taking into account the effects these items have on income.

Understand the Possible Effects of Inflation

Inflation, or an increase in the level of prices, is another important consideration in analyzing financial statements. The statements, to be used by outsiders, are based on historical costs and are not adjusted for the effects of increasing prices. For example, consider the following trend in a company's sales for the past three years:

	2004	2003	2002
Net sales	$121,000	$110,000	$100,000

Business Strategy

Focusing on New Products

How does a company grow its sales for 10 consecutive years without merging or greatly diversifying its core business of making and selling chewing gum? For Wm. Wrigley Jr. Company, the secret to success is relatively simple: generate a continuous wave of new product activity.

Internationally, the Chicago-based gum manufacturer has already begun its initial shipments to the United Kingdom and Australia of XCite®, an innovative combination chewing gum and mint. In the United States, the company was preparing for another new product launch and two other re-launches during the first quarter of 2002. First, Eclipse Flash Strips®, described as high-intensity, dissolvable breath films, were scheduled for roll-out in early 2002. And in May 2002, Wrigley planned to begin shipments of improved versions of Spearmint® and Doublemint®, two of the most recognizable brands in the world, with lives of 109 and 88 years, respectively.

Bill Wrigley, Jr., president and CEO, fully realizes the patience needed to launch new products. He acknowledges the negative effect that investment in new products can have on short-term earnings. However, Wrigley stockholders should be among the most patient and understanding investors in the world. Not too many companies regularly pay dividends of nearly 50% of earnings and provide a return on equity of over 30%, as Wrigley did for its stockholders in 2001. ■

http://www.wrigley.com

Sources: 2001 Wrigley annual report and Web site.

As measured by the actual dollars of sales, sales have increased by 10% each year. Caution is necessary in concluding that the company is better off in each succeeding year because of the increase in sales *dollars.* Assume, for example, that 2002 sales of $100,000 are the result of selling 100,000 units at $1 each. Are 2003 sales of $110,000 the result of selling 110,000 units at $1 each or of selling 100,000 units at $1.10 each? Although on the surface it may seem unimportant which result accounts for the sales increase, the answer can have significant ramifications. If the company found it necessary to increase selling price to $1.10 in the face of increasing *costs,* it may be no better off than it was in 2002 in terms of gross profit. On the other hand, if the company is able to increase sales revenue by 10% primarily based on growth in unit sales, then its performance would be considered stronger than if the increase is merely due to a price increase. The point to be made is one of caution: published financial statements are stated in historical costs and therefore have not been adjusted for the effects of inflation.

Fortunately, inflation has been relatively subdued in the past several years. During the late 1970s, the FASB actually required a separate note in the financial statements to calculate the effects of inflation. The requirement was abandoned in the mid-1980s when inflation had subsided and the profession decided that the cost of providing inflation-adjusted information exceeded the benefits to the users.

ANALYSIS OF COMPARATIVE AND COMMON-SIZE STATEMENTS

Horizontal analysis A comparison of financial statement items over a period of time.

Vertical analysis A comparison of various financial statement items within a single period with the use of common-size statements.

We are now ready to analyze a set of financial statements. We will begin by looking at the comparative statements of a company for a two-year period. The analysis of the statements over a series of years is often called **horizontal analysis.** We will then see how the statements can be recast in what are referred to as *common-size statements.* The analysis of common-size statements is called **vertical analysis.** Finally, we will consider the use of a variety of ratios to analyze a company.

Horizontal Analysis

LO 2 Use comparative financial statements to analyze a company over time (horizontal analysis).

Comparative balance sheets for a hypothetical entity, Henderson Company, are presented in Exhibit 13-1. The increase or decrease in each of the major accounts on the balance sheet is shown in both absolute dollars and as a percentage. The base year for computing the percentage increase or decrease in each account is the first year, 2003, and is normally shown on the right side. By reading across from right to left (thus the term *horizontal analysis*), the analyst can quickly spot any unusual changes in accounts from the previous year. Three accounts stand out: **1** Cash decreased by 76%, **2** Inventory increased by 73%, and **3** Accounts Payable increased by 70%. (These lines are also boldfaced for convenience.) Individually, each of these large changes is a red flag. Taken together, these changes send the financial statement user the warning that the business may be deteriorating. Each of these large changes should be investigated further.

Exhibit 13-2 shows comparative statements of income and retained earnings for Henderson for 2004 and 2003. At first glance, **1** the 20% increase in sales to $24 million appears promising, but management was not able to limit the increase in either **2** cost of goods sold or **3** selling, general, and administrative expense to 20%. The analysis indicates that cost of goods sold increased by 29% and selling, general, and administrative expense increased by 50%. The increases in these two expenses more than offset the increase in sales and resulted in a **4** decrease in operating income of 25%.

Companies that experience sales growth often become lax about controlling expenses. Their managements sometimes forget that it is the bottom line that counts, not the top line. Perhaps the salespeople are given incentives to increase sales without considering the costs of the sales. Maybe management is spending too much on overhead, including its own salaries. The owners of the business will have to address these concerns if they want to get a reasonable return on their investment.

Exhibit 13-1 Comparative Balance Sheets—Horizontal Analysis

Read from earlier year to later year. Usually this is from right to left.

HENDERSON COMPANY
COMPARATIVE BALANCE SHEETS
DECEMBER 31, 2004 AND 2003
(ALL AMOUNTS IN THOUSANDS OF DOLLARS)

	December 31		Increase (Decrease)	
	2004	**2003**	**Dollars**	**Percent**
Cash	**$ 320**	**$ 1,350**	**$ (1,030)**	[1] **(76)%**
Accounts receivable	5,500	4,500	1,000	22
Inventory	**4,750**	**2,750**	**2,000**	[2] **73**
Prepaid insurance	150	200	(50)	(25)
Total current assets	$10,720	$ 8,800	$ 1,920	22
Land	2,000	2,000	–0–	–0–
Buildings and equipment	6,000	4,500	1,500	33
Accumulated depreciation	(1,850)	(1,500)	(350)	(23)
Total long-term assets	$ 6,150	$ 5,000	$ 1,150	23
Total assets	$16,870	$13,800	$ 3,070	22
Accounts payable	**$ 4,250**	**$ 2,500**	**$ 1,750**	[3] **70**
Taxes payable	2,300	2,100	200	10
Notes payable	600	800	(200)	(25)
Current portion of bonds	100	100	–0–	–0–
Total current liabilities	$ 7,250	$ 5,500	$ 1,750	32
Bonds payable	700	800	(100)	(13)
Total liabilities	$ 7,950	$ 6,300	$ 1,650	26
Preferred stock, $5 par	500	500	–0–	–0–
Common stock, $1 par	1,000	1,000	–0–	–0–
Retained earnings	7,420	6,000	1,420	24
Total stockholders' equity	$ 8,920	$ 7,500	$ 1,420	19
Total liabilities and stockholders' equity	$16,870	$13,800	$ 3,070	22

NOTE: Referenced amounts boldfaced for convenience.

The base year is normally on the right.

Dollar change from year to year.

Percentage change from one year to the next year.

In **horizontal analysis**, read right to left to compare one year's results with the next as a dollar amount of change and as a percentage of change from year to year.

From Concept to Practice 13.1

Reading Winnebago Industries' Annual Report

Where does Winnebago Industries' annual report provide a financial summary? How many years does it include? In terms of a trend over time, which item on the summary do you think is the most significant?

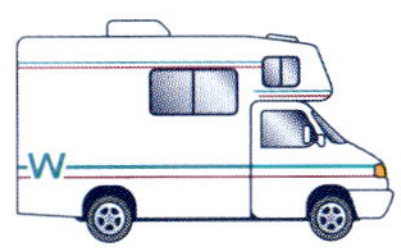

Horizontal analysis can be extended to include more than two years of results. At a minimum, publicly held companies are required to include income statements and statements of cash flows for the three most recent years and balance sheets as of the end of the two most recent years. Many annual reports include, as supplementary information, financial summaries of operations for extended periods of time. As illustrated in Exhibit 13-3, for example, Wrigley includes an 11-year summary of selected financial data, such as net sales, dividends paid, return on average equity, and total assets. Note the increase in net sales in every year over the 11-year period. Also note, however, that Wrigley does not include in the summary the gross profit ratio (gross profit divided by net sales). A

Exhibit 13-2 Comparative Statements of Income and Retained Earnings—Horizontal Analysis

HENDERSON COMPANY
COMPARATIVE STATEMENTS OF INCOME AND RETAINED EARNINGS
FOR THE YEARS ENDED DECEMBER 31, 2004 AND 2003
(ALL AMOUNTS IN THOUSANDS OF DOLLARS)

	December 31		Increase (Decrease)	
	2004	2003	Dollars	Percent
Net sales	**$24,000**	**$20,000**	**$ 4,000**	1 **20%**
Cost of goods sold	**18,000**	**14,000**	**4,000**	2 **29**
Gross profit	$ 6,000	$ 6,000	$ –0–	–0–
Selling, general, and administrative expense	**3,000**	**2,000**	**1,000**	3 **50**
Operating income	**$ 3,000**	**$ 4,000**	**$(1,000)**	4 **(25)**
Interest expense	140	160	(20)	(13)
Income before tax	$ 2,860	$ 3,840	$ (980)	(26)
Income tax expense	1,140	1,540	(400)	(26)
Net income	$ 1,720	$ 2,300	$ (580)	(25)
Preferred dividends	50	50		
Income available to common	$ 1,670	$ 2,250		
Common dividends	250	250		
To retained earnings	$ 1,420	$ 2,000		
Retained earnings, 1/1	6,000	4,000		
Retained earnings, 12/31	$ 7,420	$ 6,000		

These three increases in revenue and expenses resulted in an operating income *decrease* of 25%.

NOTE: Referenced amounts boldfaced for convenience.

comparison of the trend in this ratio would help to determine whether the company has effectively controlled the cost to manufacture its products. The summary does show that Wrigley has reported an increase in net earnings before any nonrecurring gains and accounting changes for 10 consecutive years, an enviable record for any company.

Tracking items over a series of years, a practice called *trend analysis,* can be a very powerful tool for the analyst. Advanced statistical techniques are available for analyzing trends in financial data and, most important, for projecting those trends to future periods. Some of the techniques, such as time series analysis, have been used extensively in forecasting sales trends.

From Concept to Practice 13.2

Reading Wrigley's Annual Report

Refer to Wrigley's financial highlights in Exhibit 13-3 on pages 686–687. Compute the company's gross profit ratio for each of the 11 years. Is there a noticeable upward or downward trend in the ratio over this time period?

Historically, attention has focused on the balance sheet and income statement in analyzing a company's position and results of operation. Only recently have analysts and other users begun to appreciate the value in incorporating the statement of cash flows into their analyses.

Comparative statements of cash flows for Henderson appear in Exhibit 13-4. Henderson's financing activities remained constant over the two-year period, as indicated in that section of the statements. Each year the company paid $200,000 on notes, another $100,000 to retire bonds, and $300,000 to stockholders in dividends. Cash outflow from investing activities slowed down somewhat in 2004, with the purchase of $1,500,000 in new buildings, compared with $2,000,000 the year before.

Exhibit 13-4 Comparative Statements of Cash Flow—Horizontal Analysis

HENDERSON COMPANY
COMPARATIVE STATEMENTS OF CASH FLOWS
FOR THE YEARS ENDED DECEMBER 31, 2004 AND 2003
(ALL AMOUNTS IN THOUSANDS OF DOLLARS)

	2004	2003	Increase (Decrease) Dollars	Increase (Decrease) Percent
Net Cash Flows from Operating Activities				
2 Net income	**$1,720**	**$2,300**	**$ (580)**	**(25)%**
Adjustments:				
Depreciation expense	350	300		
Changes in:				
3 Accounts receivable	**(1,000)**	**500**		
4 Inventory	**(2,000)**	**(300)**		
Prepaid insurance	50	50		
Accounts payable	1,750	(200)		
Taxes payable	200	300		
Net cash provided by operating activities 1 Unfavorable	**$1,070**	**$2,950**	**$(1,880)**	**(64)%**
Net Cash Flows from Investing Activities				
Purchase of buildings	**$(1,500)**	**$(2,000)**	**$ (500)**	**(25)%**
Net Cash Flows from Financing Activities				
Repayment of notes	**$ (200)**	**$ (200)**	–0–	–0–
Retirement of bonds	**(100)**	**(100)**	–0–	–0–
Cash dividends—preferred	**(50)**	**(50)**	–0–	–0–
Cash dividends—common	**(250)**	**(250)**	–0–	–0–
Net cash used by financing activities	$ (600)	$ (600)	–0–	–0–
Net increase (decrease) in cash	$(1,030)	$ 350		
Beginning cash balance	1,350	1,000		
Ending cash balance	$ 320	$ 1,350		
Supplemental Information				
Interest paid	$ 140	$ 160		
Income taxes paid	$ 940	$ 1,440		

NOTE: Referenced amounts boldfaced for convenience.

The most noticeable difference between Henderson's statements of cash flows for the two years is in the Operating Activities section. Operations 1 generated almost $2 million less in cash in 2004 than in 2003 ($1.07 million in 2004 versus $2.95 million in 2003). The decrease in net income 2 was partially responsible for this reduction in cash from operations. However, the increases in 3 accounts receivable and 4 inventories in 2004 had a significant impact on the decrease in cash generated from operating activities.

Vertical Analysis

LO 3 Use common-size financial statements to compare various financial statement items (vertical analysis).

Often it is easier to examine comparative financial statements if they have been standardized. *Common-size statements* recast all items on the statement as a percentage of a selected item on the statement. This excludes size as a relevant variable in the analysis. One could use this type of analysis to compare Wal-Mart with the smaller KMart or to compare IBM with the much smaller Apple Computer. It is also a convenient way to compare the same company from year to year.

Selected Financial Data

In thousands of dollars and shares except per share amounts

Net sales has increased each year in the 11-year period.

	2001	2000	1999	1998
OPERATING DATA				
Net Sales	**$2,429,646**	2,145,706	2,061,602	2,004,719
Cost of Sales	**997,054**	904,266	904,183	894,988
Income Taxes	**164,380**	150,370	136,247	136,378
Earnings before factory closure and sale in 1998-96, nonrecurring gain on sale of Singapore property in 1994, and cumulative effect of accounting changes in 1992	**362,986**	328,942	308,183	297,738
Per Share of Common Stock (basic and diluted)	**1.61**	1.45	1.33	1.28
Net Earnings	**362,986**	328,942	308,183	304,501
Per Share of Common Stock (basic and diluted)	**1.61**	1.45	1.33	1.31
Dividends Paid	**167,922**	159,138	153,812	150,835
Per Share of Common Stock	**.745**	.70	.66	.65
As a Percent of Net Earnings	**46%**	48%	50%	50%
Dividends Declared				
Per Share of Common Stock	**.76**	.70	.74	.66
Average Shares Outstanding	**225,349**	227,037	231,722	231,928
OTHER FINANCIAL DATA				
Net Property, Plant and Equipment	**684,379**	607,034	559,140	520,090
Total Assets	**1,765,648**	1,574,740	1,547,745	1,520,855
Working Capital	**581,519**	540,505	551,921	624,546
Stockholders' Equity	**1,276,197**	1,132,897	1,138,775	1,157,032
Return on Average Equity	**30.1%**	29.0%	26.8%	28.4%
Stockholders of Record at Close of Year	**38,701**	37,781	38,626	38,052
Employees at Close of Year	**10,800**	9,800	9,300	9,200
Market Price of Stock				
High	**53.297**	48.313	50.313	52.156
Low	**42.938**	29.938	33.250	35.469

Exhibit 13-3 Wrigley Financial Summary (continued)

1997	1996	1995	1994	1993	1992	1991
1,937,021	1,835,987	1,754,931	1,596,551	1,428,504	1,286,921	1,148,875
892,751	859,414	820,478	737,239	653,687	606,263	540,591
122,614	128,840	126,492	122,746	103,944	83,730	79,362
273,771	243,262	223,739	205,767	174,891	148,573	128,652
1.18	1.05	.96	.88	.75	.63	.55
271,626	230,272	223,739	230,533	174,891	141,295	128,652
1.17	.99	.96	.99	.75	.60	.55
135,680	118,308	111,401	104,694	87,344	72,511	64,609
.59	.51	.48	.45	.37	.31	.27
50%	51%	50%	45%	50%	51%	50%
.60	.51	.50	.47	.38	.32	.28
231,928	231,966	232,132	232,716	233,022	234,110	235,034
430,474	388,149	347,491	289,420	239,868	222,137	201,386
1,343,126	1,233,543	1,099,219	978,834	815,324	711,372	625,074
571,857	511,272	458,683	413,414	343,132	299,149	276,047
985,379	897,431	796,852	688,470	575,182	498,935	463,399
28.9%	27.2%	30.1%	36.5%	32.6%	29.4%	29.8%
36,587	34,951	28,959	24,078	18,567	14,546	11,086
8,200	7,800	7,300	7,000	6,700	6,400	6,250
41.031	31.438	27.000	26.938	23.063	19.938	13.500
27.281	24.188	21.438	19.063	14.750	11.063	8.188

Vertical analysis involves looking at the relative size and composition of various items on a particular financial statement. Common-size comparative balance sheets for Henderson Company are presented in Exhibit 13-5. Note that all asset accounts are stated as a percentage of total assets. Similarly, all liability and stockholders' equity accounts are stated as a percentage of total liabilities and stockholders' equity. The combination of the comparative balance sheets for the two years and the common-size feature allows the analyst to spot critical changes in the composition of the assets. We noted in Exhibit 13-1 that cash had decreased by 76% over the two years. The decrease of cash from 9.8% of total assets to only 1.9% **1** is highlighted in Exhibit 13-5.

Exhibit 13-5 Common-Size Comparative Balance Sheets—Vertical Analysis

HENDERSON COMPANY
COMMON-SIZE COMPARATIVE BALANCE SHEETS
DECEMBER 31, 2004 AND 2003
(ALL AMOUNTS IN THOUSANDS OF DOLLARS)

	December 31, 2004		December 31, 2003	
	Dollars	Percent	Dollars	Percent
Cash	$ 320	**1.9%**	$ 1,350 **1**	**9.8%**
Accounts receivable	5,500	32.6	4,500	32.6
Inventory	**4,750**	**28.1**	**2,750** **3**	**19.9**
Prepaid insurance	150	0.9	200	1.5
Total current assets	**$10,720**	**2** **63.5%**	**$ 8,800**	**63.8%**
Land	2,000	11.9%	2,000	14.5%
Buildings and equipment, net	4,150	24.6	3,000	21.7
Total long-term assets	$ 6,150	36.5%	$ 5,000	36.2%
Total assets	$16,870	100.0%	$13,800	100.0%
Accounts payable	$ 4,250	25.2%	$ 2,500	18.1%
Taxes payable	2,300	13.6	2,100	15.2
Notes payable	600	3.6	800	5.8
Current portion of bonds	100	0.6	100	0.7
Total current liabilities	**$ 7,250**	**4** **43.0%**	**$ 5,500**	**39.8%**
Bonds payable	700	**5** 4.1	800	5.8
Total liabilities	$ 7,950	47.1%	$ 6,300	45.6%
Preferred stock, $5 par	500	3.0%	500	3.6%
Common stock, $1 par	1,000	5.9	1,000	7.3
Retained earnings	7,420	44.0	6,000	43.5
Total stockholders' equity	**$ 8,920**	**6** **52.9%**	**$ 7,500**	**54.4%**
Total liabilities and stockholders' equity	$16,870	100.0%	$13,800	100.0%

NOTE: Referenced amounts boldfaced for convenience.

Compare percentages across years to spot year-to-year trends.

In **vertical analysis,** compare each line item as a percentage of total (100%) to highlight a company's overall condition.

One can also observe in the exhibit that **2** total current assets have continued to represent just under two-thirds (63.5%) of total assets. If cash has decreased significantly in terms of the percentage of total assets, what accounts have increased to maintain current assets at two-thirds of total assets? We can quickly determine from the data in Exhibit 13-5 that **3** although inventory represented 19.9% of total assets at the end of 2003, the percentage is up to 28.1% at the end of 2004. This change in the relative composition of current assets between cash and inventory may have important implications. The change, for instance, may signal that the company is having trouble selling inventory.

Total current liabilities **4** represent a slightly higher percentage of total liabilities and stockholders' equity at the end of 2004 than at the end of 2003. The increase is balanced by a slight decrease in the relative percentages of 5 long-term debt (the bonds) and of 6 stockholders' equity. We will return later to further analysis of the composition of both the current and the noncurrent accounts.

Common-size comparative income statements for Henderson are presented in Exhibit 13-6. The *base*, or benchmark, on which all other items in the income statement are compared is 1 net sales. Again, observations from the comparative statements alone are further confirmed by examining the common-size statements. Although the **gross profit ratio**—*gross profit as a percentage of net sales*—was 30% in 2003, the same ratio for 2004 is only 25% 2. Recall the earlier observation that although sales increased by 20% from one year to the next, 3 cost of goods sold increased by 29%.

Gross profit ratio Gross profit to net sales.

Exhibit 13-6 Common-Size Comparative Income Statements—Vertical Analysis

HENDERSON COMPANY
COMMON-SIZE COMPARATIVE INCOME STATEMENTS
FOR THE YEARS ENDED DECEMBER 31, 2004 AND 2003
(ALL AMOUNTS IN THOUSANDS OF DOLLARS)

	2004		2003	
	Dollars	Percent	Dollars	Percent
Net sales	**$24,000**	1 **100.0%**	**$20,000**	**100.0%**
Cost of goods sold	3 18,000	75.0	14,000	70.0
Gross profit	**$ 6,000**	2 **25.0%**	**$ 6,000**	**30.0%**
Selling, general, and administrative expense	3,000	12.5	2,000	10.0
Operating income	$ 3,000	12.5%	$ 4,000	20.0%
Interest expense	140	0.6	160	0.8
Income before tax	**$ 2,860**	**11.9%**	**$ 3,840**	**19.2%**
Income tax expense	1,140	4.8	1,540	7.7
Net income	**$ 1,720**	4 **7.1%**	**$ 2,300**	**11.5%**

NOTE: Referenced amounts boldfaced for convenience.

Gross profit as a percentage of sales is the **gross profit ratio.**

The ratio of net income to net sales is the **profit margin ratio.**

In addition to the gross profit ratio, an important relationship from Exhibit 13-6 is the *ratio of net income to net sales*, or **profit margin ratio.** The ratio, an overall indicator of management's ability to control expenses, reflects the amount of income for each dollar of sales. Some analysts prefer to look at income before tax, rather than final net income, because taxes are not typically an expense that can be controlled. Further, if the company does not earn a profit before tax, it will incur no tax expense. Note 4 the decrease in Henderson's profit margin: from 11.5% in 2003 to 7.1% in 2004 (or from 19.2% to 11.9% on a before-tax basis).

Profit margin ratio Net income to net sales.

Two-Minute Review

1. *Explain the basic difference between horizontal and vertical analysis.*
2. *Assume that you are concerned about whether accounts receivable has been increasing over the last few years. Which type of analysis, horizontal or vertical, would you perform to help address your concern?*
3. *Assume that you are concerned about whether selling and administrative expenses were unreasonable this past year given the level of sales. Which type of analysis, horizontal or vertical, would you perform to help address your concern?*

Answers on page 706.

LIQUIDITY ANALYSIS AND THE MANAGEMENT OF WORKING CAPITAL

LO 4 Compute and use various ratios to assess liquidity.

Two ratios were discussed in the last section: the *gross profit ratio* and the *profit margin ratio.* A ratio is simply the relationship, normally stated as a percentage, between two financial statement amounts. In this section, we consider a wide range of ratios used by management, analysts, and others for a variety of purposes. We classify the ratios in three main categories according to their use in performing (1) liquidity analysis, (2) solvency analysis, and (3) profitability analysis.

Liquidity The nearness to cash of the assets and liabilities.

Liquidity is a relative measure of the nearness to cash of the assets and liabilities of a company. Nearness to cash deals with the length of time before cash is realized. Various ratios are used to measure liquidity, and they basically concern the company's ability to pay its debts as they come due. Recall the distinction between the current and long-term classifications on the balance sheet. Current assets are assets that will be either converted into cash or consumed within one year or the operating cycle, if the cycle is longer than one year. The operating cycle for a manufacturing company is the length of time between the purchase of raw materials and the eventual collection of any outstanding account receivable from the sale of the product. Current liabilities are a company's obligations that require the use of current assets or the creation of other current liabilities to satisfy them.

The nearness to cash of the current assets is indicated by their placement on the balance sheet. Current assets are listed on the balance sheet in descending order of their nearness to cash. Liquidity is, of course, a matter of degree, with cash being the most liquid of all assets. With few exceptions, such as prepaid insurance, most current assets are convertible into cash. However, accounts receivable is closer to being converted into cash than is inventory. An account receivable need only be collected to be converted to cash. An item of inventory must first be sold, and then, assuming that sales of inventory are on account, the account must be collected before cash is realized.

Working Capital

Working capital Current assets minus current liabilities.

Working capital is the excess of current assets over current liabilities at a point in time:

Working Capital = Current Assets − Current Liabilities

Reference to Henderson's comparative balance sheets in Exhibit 13-1 indicates the following:

	December 31	
	2004	2003
Current assets	$10,720,000	$8,800,000
Current liabilities	7,250,000	5,500,000
Working capital	$ 3,470,000	$3,300,000

The management of working capital is an extremely important task for any business. A comparison of Henderson's working capital at the end of each of the two years indicates a slight increase in the degree of protection for short-term creditors of the company. Management must always strive for the ideal balance of current assets and current liabilities. The amount of working capital is limited in its informational value, however. For example, it tells us nothing about the composition of the current accounts. Also, the dollar amount of working capital may not be useful for comparison with other companies of different sizes in the same industry. Working capital of $3,470,000 may be adequate for Henderson Company, but it might signal impending bankruptcy for a company much larger than Henderson.

Current Ratio

Current ratio The ratio of current assets to current liabilities.

The **current ratio** is one of the most widely used of all financial statement ratios and is calculated as follows:

$$\text{Current Ratio} = \frac{\text{Current Assets}}{\text{Current Liabilities}}$$

For Henderson Company, the ratio at each year-end is as follows:

December 31	
2004	2003
$\frac{\$10,720,000}{\$7,250,000} = 1.48 \text{ to } 1$	$\frac{\$8,800,000}{\$5,500,000} = 1.60 \text{ to } 1$

At the end of 2004, Henderson had $1.48 of current assets for every $1 of current liabilities. Is this current ratio adequate? Or is it a sign of impending financial difficulties? There is no definitive answer to either of these questions. Some analysts use a general rule of thumb of 2:1 for the current ratio as a sign of short-term financial health. The answer depends first on the industry. Companies in certain industries have historically operated with current ratios much less than 2:1.

A second concern in interpreting the current ratio involves the composition of the current assets. Cash is usually the only acceptable means of payment for most liabilities. Therefore, it is important to consider the makeup, or *composition,* of the current assets. Refer to Exhibit 13-5 and Henderson's common-size balance sheets. Not only did the current ratio decline during 2004 but also the proportion of the total current assets made up by inventory increased whereas the proportion made up by accounts receivable remained the same. Recall that accounts receivable is only one step removed from cash, whereas inventory requires both sale and collection of the subsequent account.

Study Tip

Some of the ratios discussed in this chapter, such as the current ratio, were introduced in earlier chapters. Use the information here as a review of those earlier introductions.

Acid-Test Ratio

The **acid-test** or **quick ratio** is a stricter test of a company's ability to pay its current debts as they are due. Specifically, it is intended to deal with the composition problem because it *excludes* inventories and prepaid assets from the numerator of the fraction:

Acid-test or quick ratio A stricter test of liquidity than the current ratio; excludes inventory and prepayments from the numerator.

$$\text{Acid-Test or Quick Ratio} = \frac{\text{Quick Assets}}{\text{Current Liabilities}}$$

where

$$\text{Quick Assets} = \text{Cash} + \text{Marketable Securities} + \text{Current Receivables}$$

Henderson's quick assets consist of only cash and accounts receivable, and its quick ratios are as follows:

December 31	
2004	2003
$\frac{\$320,000 + \$5,500,000}{\$7,250,000} = 0.80 \text{ to } 1$	$\frac{\$1,350,000 + \$4,500,000}{\$5,500,000} = 1.06 \text{ to } 1$

Does the quick ratio of less than 1:1 at the end of 2004 mean that Henderson will be unable to pay creditors on time? *For many companies, an acid-test ratio below 1 is not desirable because it may signal the need to liquidate marketable securities to pay bills, regardless of the current trading price of the securities.* Although the quick ratio is a better indication of short-term debt-paying ability than the current ratio, it is still not perfect. For example, we would want to know the normal credit terms that Henderson extends to its customers, as well as the credit terms that the company receives from its suppliers.

Assume that Henderson requires its customers to pay their accounts within 30 days and that the normal credit terms extended by Henderson's suppliers allow payment anytime within 60 days. The relatively longer credit terms extended by Henderson's suppliers give it some cushion in meeting its obligations. The due date of the $2,300,000 in taxes payable could also have a significant effect on the company's ability to remain in business.

Cash Flow from Operations to Current Liabilities

Cash flow from operations to current liabilities ratio A measure of the ability to pay current debts from operating cash flows.

Two limitations exist with either the current ratio or the quick ratio as a measure of liquidity. First, almost all debts require the payment of cash. Thus, a ratio that focuses on cash is more useful. Second, both ratios focus on liquid assets at a *point in time.* Cash flow from operating activities, as reported on the statement of cash flows, can be used to indicate the flow of cash during the year to cover the debts due.[1] The **cash flow from operations to current liabilities ratio** is computed as follows:

$$\text{Cash Flow from Operations to Current Liabilities Ratio} = \frac{\text{Net Cash Provided by Operating Activities}}{\text{Average Current Liabilities}}$$

Note the use of *average* current liabilities in the denominator. This results in a denominator that is consistent with the numerator, which reports the cash flow over a period of time. Because we need to calculate the *average* current liabilities for both years, it is necessary to add the ending balance sheet for 2002 for use in the analysis. The balance sheet for Henderson on December 31, 2002, is given in Exhibit 13-7. The ratio for Henderson for each year is as follows:

2004	2003
$\frac{\$1{,}070{,}000}{(\$7{,}250{,}000 + \$5{,}500{,}000)/2} = 16.8\%$	$\frac{\$2{,}950{,}000}{(\$5{,}500{,}000 + \$5{,}600{,}000)/2} = 53.2\%$

Two factors are responsible for the large decrease in this ratio from 2003 to 2004. First, cash generated from operations during 2004 was less than half what it was during 2003 (the numerator). Second, average current liabilities were smaller in 2003 than

Exhibit 13-7

Henderson's Balance Sheet, End of 2002

HENDERSON COMPANY
BALANCE SHEET
DECEMBER 31, 2002
(ALL AMOUNTS IN THOUSANDS OF DOLLARS)

Cash	$ 1,000
Accounts receivable	5,000
Inventory	2,450
Prepaid insurance	250
Total current assets	$ 8,700
Land	$ 2,000
Buildings and equipment, net	1,300
Total long-term assets	$ 3,300
Total assets	$12,000
Accounts payable	$ 2,700
Taxes payable	1,800
Notes payable	1,000
Current portion of bonds	100
Total current liabilities	$ 5,600
Bonds payable	900
Total liabilities	$ 6,500
Preferred stock, $5 par	$ 500
Common stock, $1 par	1,000
Retained earnings	4,000
Total stockholders' equity	$ 5,500
Total liabilities and stockholders' equity	$12,000

[1]For a detailed discussion on the use of information contained in the statement of cash flows in performing ratio analysis, see Charles A. Carslaw and John R. Mills, "Developing Ratios for Effective Cash Flow Statement Analysis," *Journal of Accountancy* (November 1991), pp. 63–70.

in 2004 (the denominator). In examining the health of the company in terms of its liquidity, an analyst would concentrate on the reason for these decreases.

Accounts Receivable Analysis

The analysis of accounts receivable is an important component in the management of working capital. A company must be willing to extend credit terms that are liberal enough to attract and maintain customers, but at the same time, management must continually monitor the accounts to ensure collection on a timely basis. One measure of the efficiency of the collection process is the **accounts receivable turnover ratio:**

Accounts receivable turnover ratio A measure of the number of times accounts receivable are collected in a period.

$$\text{Accounts Receivable Turnover Ratio} = \frac{\text{Net Credit Sales}}{\text{Average Accounts Receivable}}$$

Note an important distinction between this ratio and either the current or the quick ratio. Although both of those ratios measure liquidity at a point in time and all numbers come from the balance sheet, a turnover ratio is an *activity* ratio and consists of an activity (sales, in this case) divided by a base to which it is naturally related (accounts receivable). Because an activity such as sales is for a period of time (a year, in this case), the base should be stated as an average for that same period of time.

The accounts receivable turnover ratios for both years can now be calculated (we assume that all sales are on account):

2004	2003
$\frac{\$24{,}000{,}000}{(\$5{,}500{,}000 + \$4{,}500{,}000)/2} = 4.8$ times	$\frac{\$20{,}000{,}000}{(\$4{,}500{,}000 + \$5{,}000{,}000)/2} = 4.2$ times

Accounts turned over, on average, 4.2 times in 2003, compared with 4.8 times in 2004. This means that the average number of times accounts were collected during each year was between four and five times. What does this mean about the average length of time that an account was outstanding? Another way to measure efficiency in the collection process is to calculate the **number of days' sales in receivables:**

Number of days' sales in receivables A measure of the average age of accounts receivable.

$$\text{Number of Days' Sales in Receivables} = \frac{\text{Number of Days in the Period}}{\text{Accounts Receivable Turnover}}$$

For simplicity, we assume 360 days in a year:

2004	2003
$\frac{360 \text{ days}}{4.8 \text{ times}} = 75$ days	$\frac{360 \text{ days}}{4.2 \text{ times}} = 86$ days

The average number of days an account is outstanding, or the average collection period, is 75 days in 2004, down from 86 days in 2003. Is this acceptable? The answer depends on the company's credit policy. If Henderson's normal credit terms require payment within 60 days, further investigation is needed, even though the number of days outstanding has decreased from the previous year.

Management needs to be concerned with both the collectibility of an account as it ages and the cost of funds tied up in receivables. For example, a $1 million average receivable balance that requires an additional month to collect suggests that the company is forgoing $10,000 in lost profits if we assume that the money could be reinvested in the business to earn 1% per month, or 12% per year.

Inventory Analysis

A similar set of ratios can be calculated to analyze the efficiency in managing inventory. The **inventory turnover ratio** is as follows:

Inventory turnover ratio A measure of the number of times inventory is sold during a period.

$$\text{Inventory Turnover Ratio} = \frac{\text{Cost of Goods Sold}}{\text{Average Inventory}}$$

Accounting for Your Decisions

You Examine Your Business's Trends

You are a small business owner and have noticed that over the past two years, sales have increased but the accounts receivable turnover ratio has decreased. Should you be concerned?

ANS: You should certainly be pleased with an increase in sales, but a decrease in accounts receivable turnover should concern you. A decline in this ratio indicates that the average time to collect an open account is increasing. Regardless of the specific reason for this change (e.g., more liberal credit terms, change in creditworthiness of customers, lack of follow-up on overdue accounts), the increase in the time to collect may result in cash flow problems for you.

The ratio for each of the two years follows:

2004	2003
$\frac{\$18{,}000{,}000}{(\$4{,}750{,}000 + \$2{,}750{,}000)/2} = 4.8 \text{ times}$	$\frac{\$14{,}000{,}000}{(\$2{,}750{,}000 + \$2{,}450{,}000)/2} = 5.4 \text{ times}$

Henderson was slightly more efficient in 2003 in moving its inventory. The number of "turns" each year varies widely for different industries. For example, a wholesaler of perishable fruits and vegetables may turn over inventory at least 50 times per year. An airplane manufacturer, however, may turn over its inventory once or twice a year. What does the number of turns per year tell us about the average length of time it takes to sell an item of inventory? The **number of days' sales in inventory** is an alternative measure of the company's efficiency in managing inventory. It is the number of days between the date an item of inventory is purchased and the date it is sold:

Number of days' sales in inventory A measure of how long it takes to sell inventory.

$$\textbf{Number of Days' Sales in Inventory} = \frac{\textbf{Number of Days in the Period}}{\textbf{Inventory Turnover}}$$

The number of days' sales in inventory for Henderson is as follows:

2004	2003
$\frac{360 \text{ days}}{4.8 \text{ times}} = 75 \text{ days}$	$\frac{360 \text{ days}}{5.4 \text{ times}} = 67 \text{ days}$

This measure can reveal a great deal about inventory management. For example, an unusually low turnover (and, of course, high number of days in inventory) may sig-

Accounting for Your Decisions

You Are the Analyst

http://www.boeing.com
http://www.safeway.com

You have been presented with two companies—Boeing and Safeway. Boeing, a commercial aircraft company, has a very slow inventory turnover, while Safeway, a grocery chain, has a very fast inventory turnover. Would it be correct to conclude that Safeway is a better investment because its inventory turns over faster?

http://www.albertsons.com

ANS: Not at all. These industries are completely different and not comparable. On the contrary, comparing Safeway's inventory turnover with Albertson's, another grocery chain, might be useful, just as comparing Boeing with Lockheed Martin Marietta might make sense. Ratios can be used when comparing companies in the same industry, but not companies in different industries.

nal a large amount of obsolete inventory or problems in the sales department. Or, it may indicate that the company is pricing its products too high and the market is reacting by reducing demand for the company's products.

Cash Operating Cycle

The **cash to cash operating cycle** is the length of time between the purchase of merchandise for sale, assuming a retailer or wholesaler, and the eventual collection of the cash from the sale. One method to approximate the number of days in a company's operating cycle involves combining two measures:

Cash to cash operating cycle The length of time from the purchase of inventory to the collection of any receivable from the sale.

Cash to Cash Operating Cycle = Number of Days' Sales in Inventory + Number of Days' Sales in Receivables

Henderson's operating cycles for 2004 and 2003 are as follows:

2004	2003
75 days + 75 days = 150 days	67 days + 86 days = 153 days

The average length of time between the purchase of inventory and the collection of cash from sale of the inventory was 150 days in 2004. Note that although the length of the operating cycle did not change significantly from 2003 to 2004, the composition did change: the increase in the average number of days in inventory was offset by the decrease in the average number of days in receivables.

SOLVENCY ANALYSIS

LO 5 Compute and use various ratios to assess solvency.

Solvency refers to a company's ability to remain in business over the long term. It is related to liquidity but differs in time. Although liquidity relates to the firm's ability to pay next year's debts as they come due, solvency concerns the ability of the firm to stay financially healthy over the period of time that existing debt (short- and long-term) will be outstanding.

Solvency The ability of a company to remain in business over the long term.

© TERRI MILLER/E-VISUAL COMMUNICATIONS, INC.

Due to the perishable nature of their products, grocery chains have high inventory turnovers and short cash to cash operating cycles. Firms in other segments have relatively longer cycles.

Debt-to-Equity Ratio

Capital structure is the focal point in solvency analysis. This refers to the composition of the right side of the balance sheet and the mix between debt and stockholders' equity. The composition of debt and equity in the capital structure is an important determinant of the cost of capital to a company. We will have more to say later about the effects that the mix of debt and equity has on profitability. For now, consider the **debt-to-equity ratio:**

Debt-to-equity ratio The ratio of total liabilities to total stockholders' equity.

$$\textbf{Debt-to-Equity Ratio} = \frac{\textbf{Total Liabilities}}{\textbf{Total Stockholders' Equity}}$$

Henderson's debt-to-equity ratio at each year-end is as follows:

December 31	
2004	**2003**
$\frac{\$7,950,000}{\$8,920,000} = 0.89 \text{ to } 1$	$\frac{\$6,300,000}{\$7,500,000} = 0.84 \text{ to } 1$

The 2004 ratio indicates that for every $1 of capital that stockholders provided, creditors provided $0.89. Variations of the debt-to-equity ratio are sometimes used to assess solvency. For example, an analyst might calculate the ratio of total liabilities to the sum of total liabilities and stockholders' equity. This results in a ratio that differs from the debt-to-equity ratio, but the objective of the measure is the same—to determine the degree to which the company relies on outsiders for funds.

What is an *acceptable* ratio of debt to equity? As with all ratios, the answer depends on the company, the industry, and many other factors. You should not assume that a lower debt-to-equity ratio is better. Certainly taking on additional debt is risky. Many companies are able to benefit from borrowing money, however, by putting the cash raised to good uses in their businesses. Later in the chapter we discuss the concept of leverage: using borrowed money to benefit the company and its stockholders.

Study Tip

The elements in many ratios are intuitive and should not require memorization to remember. For example, it is logical that the debt-to-equity ratio is computed by dividing total liabilities by total stockholders' equity.

In the 1980s, investors and creditors tolerated a much higher debt-to-equity ratio than is considered prudent today. The savings and loan crisis in the 1980s prompted the federal government to enact regulations requiring financial institutions to have a lower proportion of debt-to-equity. By the mid-1990s, investors and creditors were demanding that all types of companies display lower debt-to-equity ratios.

Times Interest Earned

The debt-to-equity ratio is a measure of the company's overall long-term financial health. Management must also be aware of its ability to meet current interest payments to creditors. The **times interest earned ratio** indicates the company's ability to meet current-year interest payments out of current-year earnings:

Times interest earned ratio An income statement measure of the ability of a company to meet its interest payments.

$$\textbf{Times Interest Earned Ratio} = \frac{\textbf{Net Income + Interest Expense + Income Tax Expense}}{\textbf{Interest Expense}}$$

Both interest expense and income tax expense are added back to net income in the numerator because interest is a deduction in arriving at the amount of income subject to tax. Stated slightly differently, if a company had just enough income to cover the payment of interest, tax expense would be zero. The greater the interest coverage is, the better, as far as lenders are concerned. Bankers often place more importance on the times interest earned ratio than even on earnings per share. The ratio for Henderson for each of the two years indicates a great deal of protection in this regard:

2004	2003
$\frac{\$1,720,000 + \$140,000 + \$1,140,000}{\$140,000}$	$\frac{\$2,300,000 + \$160,000 + \$1,540,000}{\$160,000}$
= 21.4 to 1	= 25 to 1

Debt Service Coverage

Two problems exist with the times interest earned ratio as a measure of the ability to pay creditors. First, the denominator of the fraction considers only *interest*. Management must also be concerned with the *principal* amount of loans maturing in the next year. The second problem deals with the difference between the cash and the accrual bases of accounting. The numerator of the times interest earned ratio is not a measure of the *cash* available to repay loans. Keep in mind the various noncash adjustments, such as depreciation, that enter into the determination of net income. Also, recall that the denominator of the times interest earned ratio is a measure of interest expense, not interest payments. The **debt service coverage ratio** is a measure of the amount of cash that is generated from operating activities during the year and that is available to repay interest due and any maturing principal amounts (that is, the amount available to "service" the debt):

Debt service coverage ratio A statement of cash flows measure of the ability of a company to meet its interest and principal payments.

$$\text{Debt Service Coverage Ratio} = \frac{\text{Cash Flow from Operations before Interest and Tax Payments}}{\text{Interest and Principal Payments}}$$

Some analysts use an alternative measure in the numerator of this ratio, as well as for other purposes. The alternative is referred to as EBITDA, which stands for earnings before interest, taxes, depreciation, and amortization. Whether EBITDA is a good substitute for cash flow from operations before interest and tax payments depends on whether there were significant changes in current assets and current liabilities during the period. If significant changes in these accounts occurred during the period, cash flow from operations before interest and tax payments is a better measure of a company's ability to cover interest and debt payments.

Cash flow from operations is available on the comparative statement of cash flows in Exhibit 13-4. As was the case with the times interest earned ratio, the net cash provided by operating activities is adjusted to reflect the amount available *before* paying interest and taxes.

Keep in mind that the income statement in Exhibit 13-2 reflects the *expense* for interest and taxes each year. The amounts of interest and taxes *paid* each year are shown as supplemental information at the bottom of the statement of cash flows in Exhibit 13-4 and are relevant in computing the debt service coverage ratio.

We must include any principal payments with interest paid in the denominator of the debt service coverage ratio. According to the Financing Activities section of the statements of cash flows in Exhibit 13-4, Henderson repaid $200,000 each year on the notes payable and $100,000 each year on the bonds. The debt service coverage ratios for the two years are calculated as follows:

2004

$$\frac{\$1{,}070{,}000 + \$140{,}000 + \$940{,}000}{\$140{,}000 + \$200{,}000 + \$100{,}000} = 4.89 \text{ times}$$

2003

$$\frac{\$2{,}950{,}000 + \$160{,}000 + \$1{,}440{,}000}{\$160{,}000 + \$200{,}000 + \$100{,}000} = 9.89 \text{ times}$$

Like Henderson's times interest earned ratio, its debt service coverage ratio decreased during 2004. According to the calculations, however, Henderson still generated almost $5 of cash from operations during 2004 to "cover" every $1 of required interest and principal payments.

Cash Flow from Operations to Capital Expenditures Ratio

Cash flow from operations to capital expenditures ratio A measure of the ability of a company to finance long-term asset acquisitions with cash from operations.

One final measure is useful in assessing the solvency of a business. The **cash flow from operations to capital expenditures ratio** measures a company's ability to use operations to finance its acquisitions of productive assets. To the extent that a company is able to do this, it should rely less on external financing or additional contributions by the owners to replace and add to the existing capital base. The ratio is computed as follows:

$$\text{Cash Flow from Operations to Capital Expenditures Ratio} = \frac{\text{Cash Flow from Operations} - \text{Total Dividends Paid}}{\text{Cash Paid for Acquisitions}}$$

Note that the numerator of the ratio measures the cash flow *after* meeting all dividend payments.[2] The calculation of the ratios for Henderson follows:

2004	2003
$\frac{\$1{,}070{,}000 - \$300{,}000}{\$1{,}500{,}000} = 51.3\%$	$\frac{\$2{,}950{,}000 - \$300{,}000}{\$2{,}000{,}000} = 132.5\%$

Although the amount of capital expenditures was less in 2004 than in 2003, the company generated considerably less cash from operations in 2004 to cover these acquisitions. In fact, the ratio of less than 100% in 2004 indicates that Henderson was not able to finance all of its capital expenditures from operations *and* cover its dividend payments.

Two-Minute Review

1. *Explain the difference between liquidity and solvency as it relates to a company's financial position.*
2. *Assume that you are a supplier and are considering whether to sell to a company on account. Which of the two, liquidity or solvency, are you more concerned with?*

Answers on page 706.

PROFITABILITY ANALYSIS

LO 6 Compute and use various ratios to assess profitability.

Profitability How well management is using company resources to earn a return on the funds invested by various groups.

Liquidity analysis and solvency analysis deal with management's ability to repay short- and long-term creditors. Creditors are concerned with a company's profitability because a profitable company is more likely to be able to make principal and interest payments. Of course, stockholders care about a company's profitability because it affects the market price of the stock and the ability of the company to pay dividends. Various measures of **profitability** indicate how well management is using the resources at its disposal to earn a return on the funds invested by various groups. Two frequently used profitability measures, the gross profit ratio and the profit margin ratio, were discussed earlier in the chapter. We now turn to other measures of profitability.

Rate of Return on Assets

Return on assets ratio A measure of a company's success in earning a return for all providers of capital.

Before computing the rate of return, we must answer an important question: *return to whom? Every return ratio is a measure of the relationship between the income earned by the company and the investment made in the company by various groups.* The broadest rate of return ratio is the **return on assets ratio** because it considers the investment made by *all* providers of capital, from short-term creditors to bondholders to stockholders. Therefore, the denominator, or base, for the return on assets ratio is average total liabilities and stockholders' equity—which of course is the same as average total assets.

[2]Dividends paid are reported on the statement of cash flows in the Financing Activities section. The amount *paid* should be used for this calculation rather than the amount declared, which appears on the statement of retained earnings.

The numerator of a return ratio will be some measure of the company's income for the period. The income selected for the numerator must match the investment or base in the denominator. For example, if average total assets is the base in the denominator, it is necessary to use an income number that is applicable to all providers of capital. Therefore, the income number used in the rate of return on assets is income *after* adding back interest expense. This adjustment considers creditors as one of the groups that have provided funds to the company. In other words, we want the amount of income before either creditors or stockholders have been given any distributions (that is, interest to creditors or dividends to stockholders). Interest expense must be added back on a net-of-tax basis. Because net income is on an after-tax basis, for consistency purposes interest must also be placed on a net, or after-tax, basis.

The return on assets ratio is as follows:

$$\textbf{Return on Assets Ratio} = \frac{\textbf{Net Income + Interest Expense, Net of Tax}}{\textbf{Average Total Assets}}$$

If we assume a 40% tax rate (which *is* the actual ratio of income tax expense to income before tax for Henderson), its return on assets ratios are as follows:

		2004		2003
Net income		$ 1,720,000		$ 2,300,000
Add back:				
Interest expense	$140,000		$160,000	
× (1 − tax rate)	× 0.6	84,000	× 0.6	96,000
Numerator		$ 1,804,000		$ 2,396,000
Assets, beginning of year		$13,800,000		$12,000,000
Assets, end of year		16,870,000		13,800,000
Total		$30,670,000		$25,800,000
Denominator:				
Average total assets (total above divided by 2)		$15,335,000		$12,900,000
		$ 1,804,000 / $15,335,000		$ 2,396,000 / $12,900,000
Return on assets ratio		= 11.76%		= 18.57%

Components of Return on Assets

What caused Henderson's return on assets to decrease so dramatically from the previous year? The answer can be found by considering the two individual components that make up the return on assets ratio. The first of these components is the **return on sales ratio** and is calculated as follows:

Return on sales ratio A variation of the profit margin ratio; measures earnings before payments to creditors.

$$\textbf{Return on Sales Ratio} = \frac{\textbf{Net Income + Interest Expense, Net of Tax}}{\textbf{Net Sales}}$$

The return on sales ratios for Henderson for the two years follow:

2004	2003
$\frac{\$1,720,000 + \$84,000}{\$24,000,000} = 7.52\%$	$\frac{\$2,300,000 + \$96,000}{\$20,000,000} = 11.98\%$

The ratio for 2004 indicates that for every $1 of sales, the company was able to earn a profit, before the payment of interest, of between 7 and 8 cents, as compared with a return of almost 12 cents on the dollar in 2003.

The other component of the rate of return on assets is the **asset turnover ratio.** The ratio is similar to both the inventory turnover and the accounts receivable turnover

Asset turnover ratio The relationship between net sales and average total assets.

ratios because it is a measure of the relationship between some activity (net sales, in this case) and some investment base (average total assets):

$$\text{Asset Turnover Ratio} = \frac{\text{Net Sales}}{\text{Average Total Assets}}$$

For Henderson, the ratio for each of the two years follows:

2004	2003
$\frac{\$24,000,000}{\$15,335,000} = 1.57$ times	$\frac{\$20,000,000}{\$12,900,000} = 1.55$ times

It now becomes evident that the explanation for the decrease in Henderson's return on assets lies in the drop in the return on sales, since the asset turnover ratio was almost the same. To summarize, note the relationship among the three ratios:

$$\text{Return on Assets} = \text{Return on Sales} \times \text{Asset Turnover}$$

For 2004, Henderson's return on assets consists of the following:

$$\frac{\$1,804,000}{\$24,000,000} \times \frac{\$24,000,000}{\$15,335,000} = 7.52\% \times 1.57 = 11.8\%$$

Finally, notice that net sales cancels out of both ratios, leaving the net income adjusted for interest divided by average assets as the return on assets ratio.

Return on Common Stockholders' Equity

Reasoning similar to that used to calculate return on assets can be used to calculate the return on capital provided by the common stockholder. Because we are interested in the return to the common stockholder, our base is no longer average total assets but average common stockholders' equity. Similarly, the appropriate income figure for the numerator is net income less preferred dividends because we are interested in the return to the common stockholder after all claims have been settled. Income taxes and interest expense have already been deducted in arriving at net income, but preferred dividends have not been because dividends are a distribution of profits, not an expense.

Return on common stockholders' equity ratio A measure of a company's success in earning a return for the common stockholders.

The **return on common stockholders' equity ratio** is computed as follows:

$$\text{Return on Common Stockholders' Equity Ratio} = \frac{\text{Net Income} - \text{Preferred Dividends}}{\text{Average Common Stockholders' Equity}}$$

The average common stockholders' equity for Henderson is calculated using information from Exhibits 13-1 and 13-7:

	Account Balances at December 31		
	2004	2003	2002
Common stock, $1 par	$1,000,000	$1,000,000	$1,000,000
Retained earnings	7,420,000	6,000,000	4,000,000
Total common equity	$8,420,000	$7,000,000	$5,000,000

Average common equity:
2003: ($7,000,000 + $5,000,000)/2 = $6,000,000
2004: ($8,420,000 + $7,000,000)/2 = $7,710,000

Net income less preferred dividends—or "income available to common," as it is called—can be found by referring to net income on the income statement and to preferred dividends on the statement of retained earnings. The combined statement of income and retained earnings in Exhibit 13-2 gives the relevant amounts for the numerator. Henderson's return on equity for the two years is as follows:

2004		2003	
$\frac{\$1,720,000 - \$50,000}{}$	= 21.66%	$\frac{\$2,300,000 - \$50,000}{}$	= 37.50%

Even though Henderson's return on stockholders' equity ratio decreased significantly from one year to the next, most stockholders would be very happy to achieve these returns on their money. Very few investments offer much more than 10% return unless substantial risk is involved.

Return on Assets, Return on Equity, and Leverage

The return on assets for 2004 was 11.8%. But the return to the common stockholders was much higher: 21.7%. How do you explain this phenomenon? Why are the stockholders receiving a higher return on their money than all of the providers of money combined are getting? A partial answer to these questions can be found by reviewing the cost to Henderson of the various sources of capital.

Exhibit 13-1 indicates that notes, bonds, and preferred stock are the primary sources of capital other than common stock (accounts payable and taxes payable are *not* included because they represent interest-free loans to the company from suppliers and the government). These sources and the average amount of each outstanding during 2004 follow:

	Account Balances at December 31		
	2004	2003	AVERAGE
Notes payable	$ 600,000	$ 800,000	$ 700,000
Current portion of bonds	100,000	100,000	100,000
Bonds payable—Long-term	700,000	800,000	750,000
Total liabilities	$1,400,000	$1,700,000	$1,550,000
Preferred stock	$ 500,000	$ 500,000	$ 500,000

What was the cost to Henderson of each of these sources? The cost of the money provided by the preferred stockholders is clearly the amount of dividends of $50,000. The cost as a percentage is $50,000/$500,000, or 10%. The average cost of the borrowed money can be approximated by dividing the 2004 interest expense of $140,000 by the average of the notes payable and bonds payable of $1,550,000. The result is an average cost of these two sources of $140,000/$1,550,000, or approximately 9%.

The concept of **leverage** refers to the practice of using borrowed funds and amounts received from preferred stockholders in an attempt to earn an overall return that is higher than the cost of these funds. Recall the rate of return on assets for 2004: 11.8%. Because this return is on an after-tax basis, it is necessary, for comparative purposes, to convert the average cost of borrowed funds to an after-tax basis. Although we computed an average cost for borrowed money of 9%, the actual cost of the borrowed money is 5.4% [9% × (100% − 40%)] after taxes. Because dividends are *not* tax-deductible, the cost of the money provided by preferred stockholders is 10%, as calculated earlier.

Leverage The use of borrowed funds and amounts contributed by preferred stockholders to earn an overall return higher than the cost of these funds.

Has Henderson successfully employed favorable leverage? That is, has it been able to earn an overall rate of return on assets that is higher than the amounts that it must pay creditors and preferred stockholders? Henderson has been successful in using outside money: neither of the sources must be paid a rate in excess of the 11.8% overall rate on assets used. Also keep in mind that Henderson has been able to borrow some amounts on an interest-free basis. As mentioned earlier, the accounts payable and taxes payable represent interest-free loans from suppliers and the government, although the loans are typically for a short period of time, such as 30 days.

In summary, the excess of the 21.7% return on equity over the 11.8% return on assets indicates that the Henderson management has been successful in employing leverage; that is, there is favorable leverage. Is it possible to be unsuccessful in this pursuit; that is, can there be unfavorable leverage? If the company must pay more for the amounts provided by creditors and preferred stockholders than it can earn overall, as indicated by the return on assets, there will, in fact, be unfavorable leverage. This may occur when interest requirements are high and net income is low. A company would likely have a high debt-to-equity ratio as well when there is unfavorable leverage.

Earnings per Share

Earnings per share A company's bottom line stated on a per-share basis.

Earnings per share is one of the most quoted statistics for publicly traded companies. Stockholders and potential investors want to know what their share of profits is, not just the total dollar amount. Presentation of profits on a per-share basis also allows the stockholder to relate earnings to what he or she paid for a share of stock or to the current trading price of a share of stock.

In simple situations, such as our Henderson Company example, earnings per share (EPS) is calculated as follows:

$$\text{Earnings per Share} = \frac{\text{Net Income} - \text{Preferred Dividends}}{\text{Weighted Average Number of Common Shares Outstanding}}$$

Because Henderson had 1,000,000 shares of common stock outstanding throughout both 2003 and 2004, its EPS for each of the two years is as follows:

2004	2003
$\frac{\$1,720,000 - \$50,000}{1,000,000 \text{ shares}} = \$1.67$ per share	$\frac{\$2,300,000 - \$50,000}{1,000,000 \text{ shares}} = \$2.25$ per share

A number of complications can arise in the computation of EPS, and the calculations can become exceedingly complex for a company with many different types of securities in its capital structure. These complications are beyond the scope of this book and are discussed in more advanced accounting courses.

Price/Earnings Ratio

Earnings per share is an important ratio for an investor because of its relationship to dividends and market price. Stockholders hope to earn a return by receiving periodic dividends or eventually selling the stock for more than they paid for it, or both. Although earnings are related to dividends and market price, the latter two are of primary interest to the stockholder.

Price/earnings (P/E) ratio The relationship between a company's performance according to the income statement and its performance in the stock market.

We mentioned earlier the desire of investors to relate the earnings of the company to the market price of the stock. Now that we have stated Henderson's earnings on a per-share basis, we can calculate the **price/earnings (P/E) ratio.** What market price is relevant? Should we use the market price that the investor paid for a share of stock, or should we use the current market price? Because earnings are based on the most recent evaluation of the company for accounting purposes, it seems logical to use current market price, which is based on the stock market's current assessment of the company. Therefore, the ratio is computed as follows:

$$\text{Price/Earnings Ratio} = \frac{\text{Current Market Price}}{\text{Earnings per Share}}$$

Assume that the current market price for Henderson's common stock is $15 per share at the end of 2004 and $18 per share at the end of 2003. The price/earnings ratio for each of the two years is as follows:

2004	2003
$\frac{\$15 \text{ per share}}{\$1.67 \text{ per share}} = 9$ to 1	$\frac{\$18 \text{ per share}}{\$2.25 \text{ per share}} = 8$ to 1

What is normal for a P/E ratio? As is the case for all other ratios, it is difficult to generalize as to what is good or bad. The P/E ratio compares the stock market's assessment of a company's performance with its success as reflected on the income statement.

A relatively high P/E ratio may indicate that a stock is overpriced by the market; one that is relatively low could indicate that it is underpriced.

The P/E ratio is often thought to indicate the "quality" of a company's earnings. For example, assume that two companies have identical EPS ratios of $2 per share. Why should investors be willing to pay $20 per share (or 10 times earnings) for the stock of one company but only $14 per share (or 7 times earnings) for the stock of the other company? First, we must realize that many factors in addition to the reported earnings of the company affect market prices. General economic conditions, the outlook for the particular industry, and pending lawsuits are just three examples of the various factors that can affect the trading price of a company's stock. The difference in P/E ratios for the two companies may reflect the market's assessment of the accounting practices of the companies, however. Assume that the company with a market price of $20 per share uses LIFO in valuing inventory and that the company trading at $14 per share uses FIFO. The difference in prices may indicate that investors believe that even though the companies have the same EPS, the LIFO company is "better off" because it will have a lower amount of taxes to pay. (Recall that in a period of inflation, the use of LIFO results in more cost of goods sold, less income, and therefore less income taxes.) Finally, aside from the way investors view the accounting practices of different companies, they also consider the fact that, to a large extent, earnings reflect the use of historical costs, as opposed to fair market values, in assigning values to assets. Investors must consider the extent to which a company's assets are worth more than what was paid for them.

Accounting for Your Decisions

You Are the CEO

You have just been promoted to the chief executive officer position at Orange Computer, a company that has recently fallen on hard times. Sales and earnings have been sluggish. Part of the reason that the prior CEO was dismissed by the board was the lagging stock price. Although the typical computer company stock price is roughly 25 times earnings, Orange Computer is languishing at just 8 times earnings. What can you do to restore the company's stock price?

ANS: The best way to boost your company's stock price is to restore earnings to levels comparable to that of other companies in the industry. If investors see that you are cutting costs, boosting sales, and restoring earnings, they may see a future earnings and dividends stream from Orange Computer that matches other competing investments. Investors' optimism may well translate to an improved stock price.

Dividend Ratios

Two ratios are used to evaluate a company's dividend policies: the **dividend payout ratio** and the **dividend yield ratio.** The dividend payout ratio is the ratio of the common dividends per share to the earnings per share:

Dividend payout ratio The percentage of earnings paid out as dividends.

Dividend yield ratio The relationship between dividends and the market price of a company's stock.

$$\text{Dividend Payout Ratio} = \frac{\text{Common Dividends per Share}}{\text{Earnings per Share}}$$

Exhibit 13-2 indicates that Henderson paid $250,000 in common dividends each year, or with 1 million shares outstanding, $0.25 per share. The two payout ratios are as follows:

2004	2003
$\frac{\$0.25}{\$1.67} = 15.0\%$	$\frac{\$0.25}{\$2.25} = 11.1\%$

Henderson management was faced with an important financial policy decision in 2004. Should the company maintain the same dividend of $0.25 per share, even though EPS dropped significantly? Many companies prefer to maintain a level dividend pattern, hoping that a drop in earnings is only temporary.

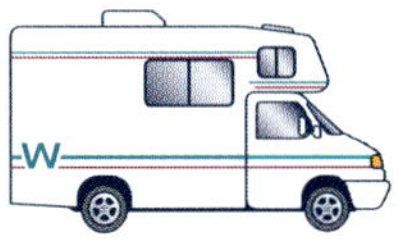

From Concept to Practice 13.3

Reading Winnebago Industries' 10 Annual Report

Refer to Winnebago Industries' statement of income and statement of changes in stockholders' equity. Compute the company's dividend payout ratio for both 2001 and 2000. Did the ratio in 2001 go up or down from the prior year?

The second dividend ratio of interest to stockholders is the dividend yield ratio:

$$\textbf{Dividend Yield Ratio} = \frac{\textbf{Common Dividends per Share}}{\textbf{Market Price per Share}}$$

The yield to Henderson's stockholders would be calculated as follows:

2004	2003
$\frac{\$0.25}{\$15} = 1.7\%$	$\frac{\$0.25}{\$18} = 1.4\%$

As we see, Henderson common stock does not provide a high yield to its investors. The relationship between the dividends and the market price indicates that investors buy the stock for reasons other than the periodic dividend return.

The dividend yield is very important to investors who depend on dividend checks to pay their living expenses. Utility stocks are popular among retirees because these shares have dividend yields as high as 5%. That is considered a good investment with relatively low risk and some opportunity for gains in the stock price. On the other hand, investors who want to put money into growing companies are willing to forgo dividends if it means the potential for greater price appreciation.

Summary of Selected Financial Ratios

We have now completed our review of the various ratios used to assess a company's liquidity, solvency, and profitability. For ease of reference, Exhibit 13-8 summarizes the ratios discussed in this chapter. Keep in mind that this list is not all-inclusive and that certain ratios used by analysts and others may be specific to a particular industry or type of business.

Exhibit 13-8 Summary of Selected Financial Ratios

Liquidity Analysis	
Working capital	Current Assets − Current Liabilities
Current ratio	$\frac{\text{Current Assets}}{\text{Current Liabilities}}$
Acid-test ratio (quick ratio)	Cash + Marketable Securities + Current Receivables
Cash flow from operations to current liabilities ratio	$\frac{\text{Net Cash Provided by Operating Activities}}{\text{Average Current Liabilities}}$
Accounts receivable turnover ratio	$\frac{\text{Net Credit Sales}}{\text{Average Accounts Receivable}}$

Exhibit 13-8 Summary of Selected Financial Ratios (*continued*)

Liquidity Analysis (continued)	
Number of days' sales in receivables	$\frac{\text{Number of Days in the Period}}{\text{Accounts Receivable Turnover}}$
Inventory turnover ratio	$\frac{\text{Cost of Goods Sold}}{\text{Average Inventory}}$
Number of days' sales in inventory	$\frac{\text{Number of Days in the Period}}{\text{Inventory Turnover}}$
Cash to cash operating cycle	Number of Days' Sales in Inventory + Number of Days' Sales in Receivables
Solvency Analysis	
Debt-to-equity ratio	$\frac{\text{Total Liabilities}}{\text{Total Stockholders' Equity}}$
Times interest earned ratio	$\frac{\text{Net Income + Interest Expense + Income Tax Expense}}{\text{Interest Expense}}$
Debt service coverage ratio	$\frac{\text{Cash Flow from Operations before Interest and Tax Payments}}{\text{Interest and Principal Payments}}$
Cash flow from operations to capital expenditures ratio	$\frac{\text{Cash Flow from Operations} - \text{Total Dividends Paid}}{\text{Cash Paid for Acquisitions}}$
Profitability Analysis	
Gross profit ratio	$\frac{\text{Gross Profit}}{\text{Net Sales}}$
Profit margin ratio	$\frac{\text{Net Income}}{\text{Net Sales}}$
Return on assets ratio	$\frac{\text{Net Income + Interest Expense, Net of Tax}}{\text{Average Total Assets}}$
Return on sales ratio	$\frac{\text{Net Income + Interest Expense, Net of Tax}}{\text{Net Sales}}$
Asset turnover ratio	$\frac{\text{Net Sales}}{\text{Average Total Assets}}$
Return on common stockholders' equity ratio	$\frac{\text{Net Income} - \text{Preferred Dividends}}{\text{Average Common Stockholders' Equity}}$
Earnings per share	$\frac{\text{Net Income} - \text{Preferred Dividends}}{\text{Weighted Average Number of Common Shares Outstanding}}$
Price/earnings ratio	$\frac{\text{Current Market Price}}{\text{Earnings per Share}}$
Dividend payout ratio	$\frac{\text{Common Dividends per Share}}{\text{Earnings per Share}}$
Dividend yield ratio	$\frac{\text{Common Dividends per Share}}{\text{Market Price per Share}}$

Accounting for Your Decisions

You Decide on a Stock Purchase

You are starting college and your parents have agreed to help pay your tuition. They will put money into a stock fund for four years and allow you to use the dividends from the fund to pay your quarterly tuition. Should you advise your parents to find a stock with a relatively low dividend yield ratio if it has an above-average return on stockholders' equity?

ANS: Regardless of how attractive a company's return on equity ratio might be, you need cash on a regular basis to pay tuition. You should advise your parents to find a stock with a relatively high dividend yield ratio.

Answers to the Two-Minute Reviews

Two-Minute Review on Page 689

1. *Horizontal analysis is used to compare a particular financial statement item over a period of time, whereas vertical analysis allows someone to compare various financial statement items within a single period. With vertical analysis, all of the items are stated as a percentage of a specific item on that statement, such as sales on the income statement or total assets on the balance sheet.*
2. *Horizontal analysis could be used to examine the trend in accounts receivable over recent years.*
3. *Vertical analysis could be used to examine the relationship between selling and administrative expenses and sales. However, you may also want to compare this percentage with the ratio in prior years (thus, you would be performing horizontal analysis as well).*

Two-Minute Review on Page 698

1. Liquidity *is a relative measure of the nearness to cash of the assets and liabilities of a company. Measures of liquidity are intended to determine the company's ability to pay its debts as they come due.* Solvency *refers to a company's ability to remain in business over the long term. Liquidity and solvency are certainly related, but the latter takes a much more long-term view of the financial health of the company.*
2. *Because you need to assess the ability of the company to pay its account on a timely basis, you would be more concerned with the liquidity of the company over the short term.*

Warmup Exercises

Warmup Exercise 13-1 *Types of Ratios* **LO 4, 5, 6**

Fill in the blanks that follow to indicate whether each of the following ratios is concerned with a company's liquidity (L), its solvency (S), or its profitability (P).

_______ 1. Return on assets ratio
_______ 2. Current ratio
_______ 3. Debt-to-equity ratio

________ 4. Earnings per share
________ 5. Inventory turnover ratio
________ 6. Gross profit ratio

Key to the Solution

Review the summary of selected ratios in Exhibit 13-8.

Warmup Exercise 13-2 ***Accounts Receivable Turnover*** **LO 4**

Company A reported sales during the year of $1,000,000. Its average accounts receivable balance during the year was $250,000. Company B reported sales during the same year of $400,000 and had an average accounts receivable balance of $40,000.

Required

1. Compute the accounts receivable turnover for both companies.
2. What is the average length of time each company takes to collect its receivables?

Key to the Solution

Review the summary of selected ratios in Exhibit 13-8.

Warmup Exercise 13-3 ***Earnings Per Share*** **LO 6**

A company reported net income during the year of $90,000 and paid dividends of $15,000 to its common stockholders and $10,000 to its preferred stockholders. During the year, 20,000 shares of common stock were outstanding and 10,000 shares of preferred stock were outstanding.

Required

Compute earnings per share for the year.

Key to the Solution

Recall that earnings per share only has relevance to the common stockholders and therefore it is a measure of the earnings per common share outstanding, after taking into account any claims of preferred stockholders.

Solutions to Warmup Exercises

Warmup Exercise 13-1

1. P **2.** L **3.** S **4.** P **5.** L **6.** P

Warmup Exercise 13-2

1. Company A turns over its accounts receivable, on the average, 4 times during the year ($1,000,000/$250,000) and Company B 10 times during the year ($400,000/$40,000).
2. Assuming 360 days in a year, Company A takes, on the average, 90 days to collect its accounts receivable, and Company B takes, on the average, 36 days.

Warmup Exercise 13-3

Earnings per share: ($90,000 − $10,000)/20,000 shares = $4 per share.

Review Problem

On pages 708–711 are the comparative financial statements for Wm. Wrigley Jr. Company, the chewing gum manufacturer, as shown in its 2001 annual report.

WebTUTOR™ Advantage

Required

1. Compute the following ratios for the two years 2001 and 2000, either for each year or as of the end of each of the years, as appropriate. Beginning balances for 2000 are not available; that is, you do not have a balance sheet as of the end of 1999. Therefore, to be consistent,

(continued)

Consolidated Statement of Earnings

In thousands of dollars except for per share amounts

	2001	2000	1999
EARNINGS			
Net sales	$ 2,429,646	2,145,706	2,061,602
Cost of sales	997,054	904,266	904,183
Gross profit	1,432,592	1,241,440	1,157,419
Selling and general administrative expense	919,236	778,197	721,813
Operating income	513,356	463,243	435,606
Investment income	18,553	19,185	17,636
Other expense	(4,543)	(3,116)	(8,812)
Earnings before income taxes	527,366	479,312	444,430
Income taxes	164,380	150,370	136,247
Net earnings	$ 362,986	328,942	308,183
PER SHARE AMOUNTS			
Net earnings per share of Common Stock (basic and diluted)	$ 1.61	1.45	1.33
Dividends paid per share of Common Stock	$ 0.745	0.70	0.66

See accompanying accounting policies and notes.

use year-end balances for both years where you would normally use average amounts for the year. To compute the return on assets ratio, you will need to find the tax rate. Use the relationship between income taxes and earnings before taxes to find the rate for each year.

a. Current ratio
b. Quick ratio
c. Cash flow from operations to current liabilities ratio
d. Number of days' sales in receivables
e. Number of days' sales in inventory
f. Debt-to-equity ratio
g. Debt service coverage ratio
h. Cash flow from operations to capital expenditures ratio
i. Return on assets ratio
j. Return on common stockholders' equity ratio

2. Comment on Wrigley's liquidity. Has it improved or declined over the two-year period?
3. Does Wrigley appear to be solvent to you? Does there appear to be anything unusual about its capital structure?
4. Comment on Wrigley's profitability. Would you buy stock in the company?

Consolidated Statement of Cash Flows

In thousands of dollars	2001	2000	1999
OPERATING ACTIVITIES			
Net earnings	$ 362,986	328,942	308,183
Adjustments to reconcile net earnings to net cash provided by operating activities:			
Depreciation	68,326	57,880	61,225
Loss on sales of property, plant and equipment	2,910	778	390
(Increase) Decrease in:			
Accounts receivable	(53,162)	(18,483)	(21,174)
Inventories	(29,487)	(2,812)	(9,894)
Other current assets	(8,079)	199	2,807
Deferred charges and other assets	(6,931)	30,408	(22,277)
Increase in:			
Accounts payable	20,365	12,988	4,670
Accrued expenses	16,532	18,015	18,583
Income and other taxes payable	9,565	14,670	2,649
Deferred income taxes	5,570	2,546	2,024
Other noncurrent liabilities	1,896	3,152	10,850
Net cash provided by operating activities	390,491	448,283	358,036
INVESTING ACTIVITIES			
Additions to property, plant and equipment	(181,760)	(125,068)	(127,733)
Proceeds from property retirements	2,376	1,128	7,909
Purchases of short-term investments	(24,448)	(125,728)	(32,078)
Maturities of short-term investments	26,835	115,007	150,300
Net cash used in investing activities	(176,997)	(134,661)	(1,602)
FINANCING ACTIVITIES			
Dividends paid	(167,922)	(159,138)	(153,812)
Common Stock purchased, net	(34,173)	(131,765)	(121,268)
Net cash used in financing activities	(202,095)	(290,903)	(275,080)
Effect of exchange rate changes on cash and cash equivalents	(4,213)	(10,506)	(7,540)
Net increase in cash and cash equivalents	7,186	12,213	73,814
Cash and cash equivalents at beginning of year	300,599	288,386	214,572
Cash and cash equivalents at end of year	$ 307,785	300,599	288,386
SUPPLEMENTAL CASH FLOW INFORMATION			
Income taxes paid	$ 146,858	136,311	130,562
Interest paid	$ 1,101	749	709
Interest and dividends received	$ 18,570	19,243	17,579

See accompanying accounting policies and notes.

(continued)

Consolidated Balance Sheet

In thousands of dollars	2001	2000
ASSETS		
Current assets:		
Cash and cash equivalents	$ 307,785	300,599
Short-term investments, at amortized cost	25,450	29,301
Accounts receivable		
(less allowance for doubtful accounts: 2001—$7,712; 2000—$7,065)	239,885	191,570
Inventories		
Finished goods	75,693	64,676
Raw materials and supplies	203,288	188,615
	278,981	253,291
Other current assets	46,896	39,728
Deferred income taxes—current	14,846	14,226
Total current assets	913,843	828,715
Marketable equity securities, at fair value	25,300	28,535
Deferred charges and other assets	115,745	83,713
Deferred income taxes—noncurrent	26,381	26,743
Property, plant and equipment, at cost:		
Land	39,933	39,125
Buildings and building equipment	359,109	344,457
Machinery and equipment	857,054	756,050
	1,256,096	1,139,632
Less accumulated depreciation	571,717	532,598
Net property, plant and equipment	684,379	607,034
TOTAL ASSETS	$1,765,648	1,574,740

Solution to Review Problem

1. Ratios:
   a. 2001: \$913,843/\$332,324 = 2.75
      2000: \$828,715/\$288,210 = 2.88
   b. 2001: (\$307,785 + \$25,450 + \$239,885)/\$332,324 = 1.72
      2000: (\$300,599 + \$29,301 + \$191,570)/\$288,210 = 1.81
   c. 2001: \$390,491/\$332,324 = 1.18
      2000: \$448,283/\$288,210 = 1.56

Consolidated Balance Sheet (continued)

In thousands of dollars and shares	2001	2000
LIABILITIES AND STOCKHOLDERS' EQUITY		
Current liabilities:		
Accounts payable	$ 91,225	73,129
Accrued expenses	128,436	113,779
Dividends payable	42,741	39,467
Income and other taxes payable	68,467	60,976
Deferred income taxes—current	1,455	859
Total current liabilities	332,324	288,210
Deferred income taxes—noncurrent	43,206	40,144
Other noncurrent liabilities	113,921	113,489
Stockholders' equity:		
Preferred Stock—no par value		
Authorized: 20,000 shares		
Issued: None		
Common Stock—no par value		
Common Stock		
Authorized: 400,000 shares		
Issued: 2001—189,800 shares; 2000—188,368 shares	12,646	12,558
Class B Common Stock—convertible		
Authorized: 80,000 shares		
Issued and outstanding:		
2001—42,641 shares; 2000—44,073 shares	2,850	2,938
Additional paid-in capital	1,153	346
Retained earnings	1,684,337	1,492,547
Common Stock in treasury, at cost (2001—7,491 shares; 2000—6,917 shares)	(289,799)	(256,478)
Accumulated other comprehensive income		
Foreign currency translation adjustment	(149,310)	(136,365)
Gain on derivative contracts	46	—
Unrealized holding gains on marketable equity securities	14,274	17,351
	(134,990)	(119,014)
Total stockholders' equity	1,276,197	1,132,897
TOTAL LIABILITIES AND STOCKHOLDERS' EQUITY	$1,765,648	1,574,740

See accompanying accounting policies and notes.

(continued)

d. 2001: 360 days/[($2,429,646/$239,885)] = 360/10.13 = 36 days

2000: 360 days/[($2,145,706/$191,570)] = 360/11.20 = 32 days

e. 2001: 360 days/[($997,054/$278,981)] = 360/3.57 = 101 days

2000: 360 days/[($904,266/$253,291)] = 360/3.57 = 101 days

f. 2001: ($332,324 + $43,206 + $113,921)/$1,276,197 = 0.38

2000: ($288,210 + $40,144 + $113,489)/$1,132,897 = 0.39

g. 2001: ($390,491 + $146,858 + $1,101)/$1,101 = 489

2000: ($448,283 + $136,311 + $749)/$749 = 781

h. 2001: ($390,491 − $167,922)/$181,760 = 1.22

2000: ($448,283 − $159,138)/$125,068 = 2.31

i. 2001: $362,986 + [$1,101[a](1 − 0.31[b])]/$1,765,648 = 20.6%

2000: $328,942 + [$749[a](1 − 0.31[b])]/$1,574,740 = 20.9%

j. 2001: $362,986/$1,276,197[c] = 28.4%

2000: $328,942/$1,132,897[c] = 29.0%

2. Although both the current ratio and the quick ratio declined during 2001, neither was a very significant decrease. Cash flow from operations to current liabilities declined more significantly, although the ratio at the end of 2001 was still greater than 1 to 1 overall. Wrigley appears to be quite liquid and should have no problems meeting its short-term obligations.
3. Wrigley is extremely solvent. Its capital structure reveals that it does not rely in any significant way on long-term debt to finance its business. The amount of noncurrent liabilities is less than 10% of total liabilities and stockholders' equity at the end of each year. In fact, a majority of Wrigley's debt is in the form of interest-free current liabilities. Most revealing is the debt service coverage ratio of 489 times in 2001 and 781 times in 2000. The total interest expense each year is insignificant.
4. The return on assets for 2001 is 20.6%, and the return on common stockholders' equity is 28.4%. Although these return ratios are down slightly from the prior year, they indicate a very profitable company. It should be noted that the company paid nearly half of its 2001 earnings in dividends. Wrigley appears to be a very sound investment, but many other factors, including information on the current market price of the stock, should be considered before making a decision.

---

[a]Wrigley does not separately disclose interest expense on its income statement; the amounts of interest paid that are reported at bottom of statements of cash flows have been used for the calculations.

[b]Tax rate for each of the two years:

2001: $164,380/$527,366 = 0.31

2000: $150,370/$479,312 = 0.31

[c]In addition to its common stock, Wrigley has outstanding Class B common stock. Because this is a second class of stock (similar in many respects to preferred stock), the contributed capital attributable to it should be deducted from total stockholders' equity in the denominator. Similarly, any dividends paid on the Class B common stock should be deducted from net income in the numerator to find the return to the regular common stockholders. We have ignored the difficulties involved in determining these adjustments in our calculations of return on equity.

Appendix: Accounting Tools: Reporting and Analyzing Other Income Statement Items

LO 7 Explain how to report on and analyze other income statement items.

Not all companies have income statements that are as easy to understand and interpret as **Wrigley's** statement. Some companies report any one or some combination of the following three items on their income statements: discontinued operations, extraordinary items, and cumulative effect of a change in accounting principle. Although the nature of each of these items is very distinct, the three do share some common characteristics. First, they are all reported near the end of the income statement, after income from continuing operations. Second, they are reported separately on the income statement to call the reader's attention to their unique nature and to the fact that any additions to, or deductions from, income that they give rise to may not necessarily reoccur in future periods. Finally, each of these items is shown net of their tax effects. This means that any additional taxes due because of them, or any tax benefits from them, are deducted from the items themselves. Following is a brief description of each item.

Discontinued Operations

When a company decides to either sell or otherwise dispose of one of its operations, it must separately report on that division or segment of the business on its income statement. This includes any gain or loss from the disposal of the business as well as any net income or loss from operating the business until the date of disposal. Because the discontinued segment of the business will not be part of the company's operations in the future, **discontinued operations** are separately disclosed on the income statement. Analysts and other users would normally only consider income from continuing operations in making their decisions.

Discontinued operations A line item on the income statement to reflect any gains or losses from the disposal of a segment of the business as well as any net income or loss from operating that segment.

Extraordinary Items

According to accounting standards, certain events that give rise to gains or losses are deemed to be extraordinary and are thus separately disclosed on the income statement. To qualify for extraordinary treatment, the gain or loss must be due to an event that is both unusual in nature and infrequent in occurrence.[3] Under current accounting standards, an **extraordinary item** is relatively rare, such as when a natural catastrophe like a tornado destroys a plant in an area not known for tornadoes. As is the case for discontinued operations, analysts and others often ignore the amount of such gains and losses in reaching their decisions since they are aware that these items are not likely to reoccur in the future.

Extraordinary item A line item on the income statement to reflect any gains or losses that arise from an event that is both unusual in nature and infrequent in occurrence.

Cumulative Effect of a Change in Accounting Principle

This line item on the income statement arises when a company makes a change in one of its accounting principles, practices, or methods. For example, when a company changes its depreciation from straight-line to accelerated or its method of valuing inventory from FIFO to average cost, it must report a separate line item on its income statement called **cumulative effect of a change in accounting principle.** The amount of this line item represents the difference in income in all prior years between the old method and the new method.

Cumulative effect of a change in accounting principle A line item on the income statement to reflect the effect on prior years' income from a change in accounting principle.

Sometimes, a change in accounting principle is dictated by a new accounting standard. For example, in response to a pronouncement from the Securities and Exchange Commission, Winnebago Industries changed the timing of when it recognizes revenue. Under the new standard, revenue is reported when the company's products are delivered to dealers, which is when title passes, rather than when the RVs are shipped by Winnebago Industries. The 2001 income statement reflected the cumulative effect from this change in the timing of revenue recognition as follows (all amounts are in thousands of dollars):

http://www.sec.gov
http://www.winnebagoind.com

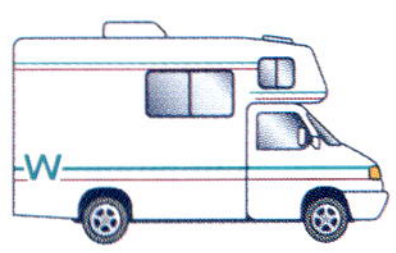

Income before cumulative effect of change in accounting principle	$43,754
Cumulative effect of change in accounting principle, net of taxes	(1,050)
Net income	$42,704

An analyst trying to predict the future profitability of Winnebago Industries might very well ignore the cumulative effect reported as part of 2001 net income knowing that this item will not likely reoccur in the future.

[3] *APB Opinion No. 30,* "Reporting the Results of Operations," Accounting Principles Board, 1973.

Chapter Highlights

1. **LO 1** Various parties, including management, creditors, stockholders, and others, perform financial statement analysis. Care must be exercised, however, in all types of financial analysis. For example, the existence of alternative accounting principles can make comparing different companies difficult. Published financial statements are not adjusted for the effects of inflation, and thus comparisons over time must be made with caution.
2. **LO 2** Horizontal analysis uses comparative financial statements to examine the increases and decreases in items from one period to the next. The analysis can look at the change in items over an extended period of time. Many companies present a summary of selected financial items for a 5- or 10-year period.
3. **LO 3** Vertical analysis involves stating all items on a particular financial statement as a percentage of one item on the statement. For example, all expenses on a common-size income statement are stated as a percentage of net sales. This technique, along with horizontal analysis, can be useful in spotting problem areas within a company.
4. **LO 4** Ratios can be categorized according to their primary purpose. Liquidity ratios indicate the company's ability to pay its debts as they are due. The focus of liquidity analysis is on a company's current assets and current liabilities.
5. **LO 5** Solvency ratios deal with a company's long-term financial health, that is, its ability to repay long-term creditors. The right side of the balance sheet is informative in this respect because it reports on the various sources of capital to the business.
6. **LO 6** Profitability ratios measure how well management has used the assets at its disposal to earn a return for the various providers of capital. Return on assets indicates the return to all providers; return on common stockholders' equity measures the return to the residual owners of the business. Certain other ratios are used to relate a company's performance according to the financial statements with its performance in the stock market.
7. **LO 7** Certain items must be reported separately at the bottom of the income statement. These include discontinued operations, extraordinary gains and losses, and the cumulative effect of a change in accounting principle. By reporting these items separately, the company allows users of the income statement to determine whether or not to consider them in trying to predict future income.

http://

http://porter.swlearning.com

Technology and other resources for your success

If you need additional help, visit the text's Web site. Also, see pages xv–xvii in this text's preface for a description of available technology and other resources. If your instructor is using PERSONAL *Trainer* in this course, you may complete, on line, the assignments identified by PT.

Key Terms Quiz

Because of the number of terms introduced in this chapter, there are two key terms quizzes. For each quiz, read each definition below and then write the number of that definition in the blank beside the appropriate term it defines. The quiz solutions appear at the end of the chapter.

Quiz 1:

_____ Horizontal analysis
_____ Vertical analysis
_____ Gross profit ratio
_____ Profit margin ratio
_____ Liquidity
_____ Working capital
_____ Current ratio
_____ Acid-test or quick ratio
_____ Cash flow from operations to current liabilities ratio
_____ Accounts receivable turnover ratio
_____ Number of days' sales in receivables
_____ Inventory turnover ratio
_____ Number of days' sales in inventory
_____ Cash to cash operating cycle

1. A stricter test of liquidity than the current ratio; excludes inventory and prepayments from the numerator.
2. Current assets minus current liabilities.
3. The ratio of current assets to current liabilities.
4. A measure of the average age of accounts receivable.
5. A measure of the ability to pay current debts from operating cash flows.
6. A measure of the number of times accounts receivable are collected in a period.
7. A measure of how long it takes to sell inventory.

8. The length of time from the purchase of inventory to the collection of any receivable from the sale.
9. A measure of the number of times inventory is sold during a period.
10. Gross profit to net sales.
11. A comparison of various financial statement items within a single period with the use of common-size statements.
12. Net income to net sales.
13. The nearness to cash of the assets and liabilities.
14. A comparison of financial statement items over a period of time.

Quiz 2:

_____ Solvency
_____ Debt-to-equity ratio
_____ Times interest earned ratio
_____ Debt service coverage ratio
_____ Cash flow from operations to capital expenditures ratio
_____ Profitability
_____ Return on assets ratio
_____ Return on sales ratio
_____ Asset turnover ratio
_____ Return on common stockholders' equity ratio
_____ Leverage
_____ Earnings per share
_____ Price/earnings (P/E) ratio
_____ Dividend payout ratio
_____ Dividend yield ratio
_____ Discontinued operations (Appendix)
_____ Extraordinary item (Appendix)
_____ Cumulative effect of a change in accounting principle (Appendix)

1. A measure of a company's success in earning a return for the common stockholders.
2. The relationship between a company's performance according to the income statement and its performance in the stock market.
3. The ability of a company to remain in business over the long term.
4. A variation of the profit margin ratio; measures earnings before payments to creditors.
5. A company's bottom line stated on a per-share basis.
6. The percentage of earnings paid out as dividends.
7. The ratio of total liabilities to total stockholders' equity.
8. A measure of the ability of a company to finance long-term asset acquisitions with cash from operations.
9. A measure of a company's success in earning a return for all providers of capital.
10. The relationship between net sales and total assets.
11. The relationship between dividends and the market price of a company's stock.
12. The use of borrowed funds and amounts contributed by preferred stockholders to earn an overall return higher than the cost of these funds.
13. An income statement measure of the ability of a company to meet its interest payments.
14. A statement of cash flows measure of the ability of a company to meet its interest and principal payments.
15. How well management is using company resources to earn a return on the funds invested by various groups.
16. A line item on the income statement to reflect any gains or losses that arise from an event that is both unusual in nature and infrequent in occurrence.
17. A line item on the income statement to reflect the effect on prior years' income from a change in accounting principle.
18. A line item on the income statement to reflect any gains or losses from the disposal of a segment of the business as well as any net income or loss from operating that segment.

Answers on p. 741.

Alternate Terms

Acid-test ratio Quick ratio

Horizontal analysis Trend analysis

Number of days' sales in receivables Average collection period

Price/earnings ratio P/E ratio

Questions

1. Two companies are in the same industry. Company A uses the LIFO method of inventory valuation, and Company B uses FIFO. What difficulties does this present when comparing the two companies?
2. You are told to compare the company's results for the year, as measured by various ratios, with one of the published surveys that arranges information by industry classification. What are some of the difficulties you may encounter when making comparisons using industry standards?

(continued)

3. What types of problems does inflation cause in analyzing financial statements?

4. Distinguish between horizontal and vertical analysis. Why is the analysis of common-size statements called *vertical* analysis? Why is horizontal analysis sometimes called *trend* analysis?

5. A company experiences a 15% increase in sales over the previous year. However, gross profit actually decreased by 5% from the previous year. What are some of the possible causes for an increase in sales but a decline in gross profit?

6. A company's total current assets have increased by 5% over the prior year. Management is concerned, however, about the composition of the current assets. Why is the composition of current assets important?

7. Ratios were categorized in the chapter according to their use in performing three different types of analysis. What are the three types of ratios?

8. Describe the operating cycle for a manufacturing company. How would the cycle differ for a retailer?

9. What accounts for the order in which current assets are presented on a balance sheet?

10. A company has a current ratio of 1.25 but an acid test or quick ratio of only 0.65. How can this difference in the two ratios be explained? What are some concerns that you would have about this company?

11. Explain the basic concept underlying all turnover ratios. Why is it advisable in computing a turnover ratio to use an average in the denominator (for example, average inventory)?

12. Sanders Company's accounts receivable turned over nine times during the year. The credit department extends terms of 2/10, net 30. Does the turnover ratio indicate any problems that management should investigate?

13. The turnover of inventory for Ace Company has slowed from 6.0 times per year to 4.5 times. What are some of the possible explanations for this decrease?

14. How does the operating cycle for a manufacturer differ from the operating cycle for a service company, for example, an airline?

15. What is the difference between liquidity analysis and solvency analysis?

16. Why is the debt service coverage ratio a better measure of solvency than the times interest earned ratio?

17. A friend tells you that the best way to assess solvency is by comparing total debt to total assets. Another friend says that solvency is measured by comparing total debt to total stockholders' equity. Which one is right?

18. A company is in the process of negotiating with a bank for an additional loan. Why will the bank be very interested in the company's debt service coverage ratio?

19. What is the rationale for deducting dividends when computing the ratio of cash flow from operations to capital expenditures?

20. The rate of return on assets ratio is computed by dividing net income and interest expense, net of tax, by average total assets. Why is the numerator net income and interest expense, net of tax, rather than just net income?

21. A company has a return on assets of 14% and a return on common stockholders' equity of 11%. The president of the company has asked you to explain the reason for this difference. What causes the difference? How is the concept of financial leverage involved?

22. What is meant by the "quality" of a company's earnings? Explain why the price/earnings ratio for a company may indicate the quality of earnings.

23. Some ratios are more useful for management, whereas others are better suited to the needs of outsiders, such as stockholders and bankers. What is an example of a ratio that is primarily suited to management use? What is one that is more suited to use by outsiders?

24. The needs of service-oriented companies in analyzing financial statements differ from those of product-oriented companies. Why is this true? Give an example of a ratio that is meaningless to a service business.

25. What is the reason for reporting discontinued operations, extraordinary items, and the cumulative effect of a change in accounting principle separately on an income statement? (Appendix)

Exercises

Exercise 13-1 ***Accounts Receivable Analysis*** **LO 4**

The following account balances are taken from the records of the Faraway Travel Agency:

	December 31		
	2004	**2003**	**2002**
Accounts receivable	$150,000	$100,000	$80,000

	2004	**2003**
Net credit sales	$600,000	$540,000

Faraway extends credit terms requiring full payment in 60 days, with no discount for early payment.

Required

1. Compute Faraway's accounts receivable turnover ratio for 2004 and 2003.

2. Compute the number of days' sales in receivables for 2004 and 2003. Assume 360 days in a year.
3. Comment on the efficiency of Faraway's collection efforts over the two-year period.

Exercise 13-2 *Inventory Analysis* LO 4

The following account balances are taken from the records of Lewis Inc., a wholesaler of fresh fruits and vegetables:

	December 31		
	2004	**2003**	**2002**
Merchandise inventory	$ 200,000	$ 150,000	$120,000
	2004	**2003**	
Cost of goods sold	$7,100,000	$8,100,000	

Required

1. Compute Lewis's inventory turnover ratio for 2004 and 2003.
2. Compute the number of days' sales in inventory for 2004 and 2003. Assume 360 days in a year.
3. Comment on your answers in parts **1** and **2** relative to the company's management of inventory over the two years. What problems do you see in its inventory management?

Exercise 13-3 *Accounts Receivable and Inventory Analyses for Coca-Cola and Pepsi* LO 4

The following information was obtained from the 2001 and 2000 financial statements of Coca-Cola Company and Subsidiaries and PepsiCo Inc. and Subsidiaries (year ends for PepsiCo are December 29, 2001 and December 30, 2000):

http://www.cocacola.com
http://www.pepsico.com

(in millions)		Coca-Cola	PepsiCo
Accounts and notes receivable, net[a]	12/31/01	$ 1,882	$ 2,142
	12/31/00	1,757	2,129
Inventories	12/31/01	1,055	1,310
	12/31/00	1,066	1,192
Net sales[b]	2001	20,092	26,935
	2000	19,889	25,479
Cost of goods sold[c]	2001	6,044	10,754
	2000	6,204	10,226

[a]Described as "trade accounts receivable" by Coca-Cola.
[b]Described as "net operating revenues" by Coca-Cola.
[c]Described as "cost of sales" by PepsiCo.

Required

1. Using the information provided above, compute the following for each company for 2001:
   a. Accounts receivable turnover ratio
   b. Number of days' sales in receivables
   c. Inventory turnover ratio
   d. Number of days' sales in inventory
   e. Cash to cash operating cycle
2. Comment briefly on the liquidity of each of these two companies.

Exercise 13-4 *Liquidity Analyses for Coca-Cola and Pepsi* LO 4

The following information was summarized from the balance sheets of the Coca-Cola Company and Subsidiaries at December 31, 2001 and PepsiCo Inc. and Subsidiaries at December 29, 2001:

(continued)

(in millions)	Coca-Cola	PepsiCo
Cash and cash equivalents	$ 1,866	$ 683
Short-term investments/marketable securities	68	966
Accounts and notes receivables, net	1,882	2,142
Inventories	1,055	1,310
Prepaid expenses and other current assets	2,300	752
Total current assets	$ 7,171	$5,853
Current liabilities	$ 8,429	$4,998
Other liabilities	2,622	8,023
Stockholders' equity	11,366	8,674

Required

1. Using the information provided above, compute the following for each company at the end of 2001:
   a. Current ratio
   b. Quick ratio
2. Comment briefly on the liquidity of each of these two companies. Which appears to be more liquid?
3. What other ratios would help you to more fully assess the liquidity of these companies?

Exercise 13-5 ***Liquidity Analyses for McDonald's and Wendy's*** **LO 4**

http://www.mcdonalds.com
http://www.wendys.com

DECISION MAKING

The following information was summarized from the balance sheets of McDonald's Corporation and Wendy's International Inc. at December 31, 2001, and December 30, 2001, respectively:

	McDonald's (in millions)	Wendy's (in thousands)
Current Assets:		
Cash and cash equivalents	$ 418.1	$ 111,121
Accounts receivable, net*	881.9	83,603
Notes receivable, net	—	11,295
Inventories	105.5	45,334
Other current assets	413.8	15,000
Total current assets	$ 1,819.3	$ 266,353
Current liabilities	$ 2,248.3	$ 296,687
Other liabilities	$10,797.8	$ 749,577
Stockholders' equity	$ 9,488.4	$1,029,779

*McDonald's combines accounts and notes receivable.

Required

1. Using the information provided above, compute the following for each company at year end:
   a. Working capital
   b. Current ratio
   c. Quick ratio
2. Comment briefly on the liquidity of each of these two companies. Which appears to be more liquid?
3. McDonald's reported cash flows from operations of $2,688.3 million during 2001. Wendy's reported cash flows from operations of $305,196 thousand. Current liabilities reported by McDonald's at December 31, 2000, and Wendy's at December 30, 2000, were $2,360.9 million and $296,416 thousand, respectively. Calculate the cash flow from operations to current liabilities ratio for each company. Does the information provided by this ratio change your opinion as to the relative liquidity of each of these two companies?
4. What steps might be taken by McDonald's to cover its short-term cash requirements?

Exercise 13-6 ***Solvency Analyses for Tommy Hilfiger*** **LO 5**

http://www.tommy.com

The following information was obtained from the comparative financial statements included in Tommy Hilfiger Corporation's 2001 annual report (all amounts are in thousands of dollars):

	March 31, 2001	March 31, 2000
Total liabilities	$ 993,963	$1,103,807
Total shareholders' equity	1,348,593	1,277,714

	For the Fiscal Years Ended March 31	
	2001	2000
Interest expense	$ 41,412	$ 41,024
Provision for income taxes	42,497	55,173
Net income	130,961	172,358
Net cash provided by operating activities	190,968	231,209
Total dividends paid	—	—
Cash used to purchase property and equipment	73,890	151,984
Payments on long-term debt	50,000	40,000

Required

1. Using the information provided above, compute the following for 2001 and 2000:
   a. Debt-to-equity ratio (at each year-end)
   b. Times interest earned ratio
   c. Debt service coverage ratio
   d. Cash flow from operations to capital expenditures ratio
2. Comment briefly on the company's solvency.

Exercise 13-7 ***Solvency Analysis*** **LO 5**

The following information is available from the balance sheets at the ends of the two most recent years and the income statement for the most recent year of Impact Company:

	December 31	
	2004	2003
Accounts payable	$ 65,000	$ 50,000
Accrued liabilities	25,000	35,000
Taxes payable	60,000	45,000
Short-term notes payable	0	75,000
Bonds payable due within next year	200,000	200,000
Total current liabilities	$ 350,000	$ 405,000
Bonds payable	$ 600,000	$ 800,000
Common stock, $10 par	$1,000,000	$1,000,000
Retained earnings	650,000	500,000
Total stockholders' equity	$1,650,000	$1,500,000
Total liabilities and stockholders' equity	$2,600,000	$2,705,000

	2004
Sales revenue	$1,600,000
Cost of goods sold	950,000
Gross profit	$ 650,000
Selling and administrative expense	300,000
Operating income	$ 350,000
Interest expense	89,000
Income before tax	$ 261,000
Income tax expense	111,000
Net income	$ 150,000

Other Information

a. Short-term notes payable represents a 12-month loan that matured in November 2004. Interest of 12% was paid at maturity.

b. One million dollars of serial bonds had been issued 10 years earlier. The first series of $200,000 matured at the end of 2004, with interest of 8% payable annually.

c. Cash flow from operations was $185,000 in 2004. The amounts of interest and taxes paid during 2004 were $89,000 and $96,000, respectively.

Required

1. Compute the following for Impact Company:
   a. The debt-to-equity ratio at December 31, 2004, and December 31, 2003
   b. The times interest earned ratio for 2004
   c. The debt service coverage ratio for 2004
2. Comment on Impact's solvency at the end of 2004. Do the times interest earned ratio and the debt service coverage ratio differ in their indication of Impact's ability to pay its debts?

Exercise 13-8 ***Return Ratios and Leverage*** **LO 6**

The following selected data are taken from the financial statements of Evergreen Company:

Sales revenue	$ 650,000
Cost of goods sold	400,000
Gross profit	$ 250,000
Selling and administrative expense	100,000
Operating income	$ 150,000
Interest expense	50,000
Income before tax	$ 100,000
Income tax expense (40%)	40,000
Net income	$ 60,000
Accounts payable	$ 45,000
Accrued liabilities	70,000
Income taxes payable	10,000
Interest payable	25,000
Short-term loans payable	150,000
Total current liabilities	$ 300,000
Long-term bonds payable	$ 500,000
Preferred stock, 10%, $100 par	$ 250,000
Common stock, no par	600,000
Retained earnings	350,000
Total stockholders' equity	$1,200,000
Total liabilities and stockholders' equity	$2,000,000

Required

1. Compute the following ratios for Evergreen Company:
   a. Return on sales
   b. Asset turnover (assume that total assets at the beginning of the year were $1,600,000)
   c. Return on assets
   d. Return on common stockholders' equity (assume that the only changes in stockholders' equity during the year were from the net income for the year and dividends on the preferred stock)
2. Comment on Evergreen's use of leverage. Has it successfully employed leverage? Explain.

Exercise 13-9 ***Relationships among Return on Assets, Return on Sales, and Asset Turnover*** **LO 6**

A company's return on assets is a function of its ability to turn over its investment (asset turnover) and earn a profit on each dollar of sales (return on sales). For each of the *independent* cases below, determine the missing amounts. (*Note:* Assume in each case that the company has no interest expense; that is, net income is used as the definition of income in all calculations.)

Case 1	
Net income	$ 10,000
Net sales	$ 80,000
Average total assets	$ 60,000
Return on assets	?

Case 2	
Net income	$ 25,000
Average total assets	$250,000
Return on sales	2%
Net sales	?

Case 3	
Average total assets	$ 80,000
Asset turnover	1.5 times
Return on sales	6%
Return on assets	?

Case 4	
Return on assets	10%
Net sales	$ 50,000
Asset turnover	1.25 times
Net income	?

Case 5	
Return on assets	15%
Net income	$ 20,000
Return on sales	5%
Average total assets	?

Exercise 13-10 *EPS, P/E Ratio, and Dividend Ratios* LO 6

DECISION MAKING

The stockholders' equity section of the balance sheet for Cooperstown Corp. at the end of 2004 appears as follows:

8%, $100 par, cumulative preferred stock, 200,000 shares authorized, 50,000 shares issued and outstanding	$ 5,000,000
Additional paid-in capital on preferred	2,500,000
Common stock, $5 par, 500,000 shares authorized, 400,000 shares issued and outstanding	2,000,000
Additional paid-in capital on common	18,000,000
Retained earnings	37,500,000
Total stockholders' equity	$65,000,000

Net income for the year was $1,300,000. Dividends were declared and paid on the preferred shares during the year, and a quarterly dividend of $0.40 per share was declared and paid each quarter on the common shares. The closing market price for the common shares on December 31, 2004, was $24.75 per share.

Required

1. Compute the following ratios for the common stock:
   a. Earnings per share
   b. Price/earnings ratio
   c. Dividend payout ratio
   d. Dividend yield ratio
2. Assume that you are an investment adviser. What other information would you want to have before advising a client regarding the purchase of Cooperstown stock?

Exercise 13-11 *Earnings Per Share and Extraordinary Items* LO 6

The stockholders' equity section of the balance sheet for Lahey Construction Company at the end of 2004 follows:

9%, $10 par, cumulative preferred stock, 500,000 shares authorized, 200,000 shares issued and outstanding	$ 2,000,000
Additional paid-in capital on preferred	7,500,000
Common stock, $1 par, 2,500,000 shares authorized, 1,500,000 shares issued and outstanding	1,500,000
Additional paid-in capital on common	21,000,000
Retained earnings	25,500,000
Total stockholders' equity	$57,500,000

(continued)

The lower portion of the 2004 income statement indicates the following:

Net income before tax		$ 9,750,000
Income tax expense (40%)		(3,900,000)
Income before extraordinary items		$ 5,850,000
Extraordinary loss from flood	$(6,200,000)	
Less related tax effect (40%)	2,480,000	(3,720,000)
Net income		$ 2,130,000

Assume the number of shares outstanding did not change during the year.

Required

1. Compute earnings per share *before* extraordinary items.
2. Compute earnings per share *after* the extraordinary loss.
3. Which of the two EPS ratios is more useful to management? Explain your answer. Would your answer be different if the ratios were to be used by an outsider, for example, by a potential stockholder? Why?

Multi-Concept Exercises

Exercise 13-12 ***Common-Size Balance Sheets and Horizontal Analysis*** **LO 2, 3**

Comparative balance sheets for Farinet Company for the past two years are as follows:

	December 31	
	2004	**2003**
Cash	$ 16,000	$ 20,000
Accounts receivable	40,000	30,000
Inventory	30,000	50,000
Prepaid rent	18,000	12,000
Total current assets	$104,000	$112,000
Land	$150,000	$150,000
Plant and equipment	800,000	600,000
Accumulated depreciation	(130,000)	(60,000)
Total long-term assets	$820,000	$690,000
Total assets	$924,000	$802,000
Accounts payable	$ 24,000	$ 20,000
Income taxes payable	6,000	10,000
Short-term notes payable	70,000	50,000
Total current liabilities	$100,000	$ 80,000
Bonds payable	$150,000	$200,000
Common stock	$400,000	$300,000
Retained earnings	274,000	222,000
Total stockholders' equity	$674,000	$522,000
Total liabilities and stockholders' equity	$924,000	$802,000

Required

1. Using the format in Exhibit 13-5, prepare common-size comparative balance sheets for the two years for Farinet Company.
2. What observations can you make about the changes in the relative composition of Farinet's accounts from the common-size balance sheets? List at least five observations.
3. Using the format in Exhibit 13-1, prepare comparative balance sheets for Farinet Company, including columns both for the dollars and for the percentage increase or decrease in each item on the statement.
4. Identify the four items on the balance sheet that experienced the largest change from one year to the next. For each of these, explain where you would look to find additional information about the change.

Exercise 13-13 *Common-Size Income Statements and Horizontal Analysis* **LO 2, 3**

Income statements for Mariners Corp. for the past two years follow:

	(Amounts in Thousands of Dollars)	
	2004	**2003**
Sales revenue	$60,000	$50,000
Cost of goods sold	42,000	30,000
Gross profit	$18,000	$20,000
Selling and administrative expense	9,000	5,000
Operating income	$ 9,000	$15,000
Interest expense	2,000	2,000
Income before tax	$ 7,000	$13,000
Income tax expense	2,000	4,000
Net income	$ 5,000	$ 9,000

Required

1. Using the format in Exhibit 13-6, prepare common-size comparative income statements for the two years for Mariners Corp.
2. What observations can you make about the common-size statements? List at least four observations.
3. Using the format in Exhibit 13-2, prepare comparative income statements for Mariners Corp., including columns both for the dollars and for the percentage increase or decrease in each item on the statement.
4. Identify the two items on the income statement that experienced the largest change from one year to the next. For each of these, explain where you would look to find additional information about the change.

Problems

Problem 13-1 *Effect of Transactions on Working Capital, Current Ratio, and Quick Ratio* **LO 4**

(*Note:* Consider completing Problem 13-2 after this problem to ensure that you obtain a clear understanding of the effect of various transactions on these measures of liquidity.)

The following account balances are taken from the records of Liquiform Inc.:

Cash	$ 70,000
Trading securities (short-term)	60,000
Accounts receivable	80,000
Inventory	100,000
Prepaid insurance	10,000
Accounts payable	75,000
Taxes payable	25,000
Salaries and wages payable	40,000
Short-term loans payable	60,000

Required

1. Use the information provided above to compute the amount of working capital and Liquiform's current and quick ratios (round to three decimal points).
2. Determine the effect that each of the following transactions will have on Liquiform's working capital, current ratio, and quick ratio by recalculating each and then indicating whether the measure is increased, decreased, or not affected by the transaction. (For the ratios, round to three decimal points.) Consider each transaction independently; that is, assume that it is the *only* transaction that takes place.

(continued)

Transaction	Effect of Transaction on Working Capital	Current Ratio	Quick Ratio
a. Purchased inventory on account for $20,000.			
b. Purchased inventory for cash, $15,000.			
c. Paid suppliers on account, $30,000.			
d. Received cash on account, $40,000.			
e. Paid insurance for next year, $20,000.			
f. Made sales on account, $60,000.			
g. Repaid short-term loans at bank, $25,000.			
h. Borrowed $40,000 at bank for 90 days.			
i. Declared and paid $45,000 cash dividend.			
j. Purchased $20,000 of trading securities (classified as current assets).			
k. Paid $30,000 in salaries.			
l. Accrued additional $15,000 in taxes.			

Problem 13-2 *Effect of Transactions on Working Capital, Current Ratio, and Quick Ratio*
LO 4

(*Note:* Consider completing this problem after Problem 13-1 to ensure that you obtain a clear understanding of the effect of various transactions on these measures of liquidity.)

The following account balances are taken from the records of Veriform Inc.:

Cash	$ 70,000
Trading securities (short-term)	60,000
Accounts receivable	80,000
Inventory	100,000
Prepaid insurance	10,000
Accounts payable	75,000
Taxes payable	25,000
Salaries and wages payable	40,000
Short-term loans payable	210,000

Required

1. Use the information provided above to compute the amount of working capital and Veriform's current and quick ratios (round to three decimal points).
2. Determine the effect that each of the following transactions will have on Veriform's working capital, current ratio, and quick ratio by recalculating each and then indicating whether the measure is increased, decreased, or not affected by the transaction. (For the ratios, round to three decimal points.) Consider each transaction independently; that is, assume that it is the *only* transaction that takes place.

Transaction	Effect of Transaction on Working Capital	Current Ratio	Quick Ratio
a. Purchased inventory on account for $20,000.			
b. Purchased inventory for cash, $15,000.			
c. Paid suppliers on account, $30,000.			
d. Received cash on account, $40,000.			
e. Paid insurance for next year, $20,000.			
f. Made sales on account, $60,000.			
g. Repaid short-term loans at bank, $25,000.			
h. Borrowed $40,000 at bank for 90 days.			
i. Declared and paid $45,000 cash dividend.			
j. Purchased $20,000 of trading securities (classified as current assets).			
k. Paid $30,000 in salaries.			
l. Accrued additional $15,000 in taxes.			

Problem 13-3 ***Goals for Sales and Return on Assets*** **LO 6**

DECISION MAKING

The president of Blue Skies Corp. is reviewing with his vice presidents the operating results of the year just completed. Sales increased by 15% from the previous year to $60,000,000. Average total assets for the year were $40,000,000. Net income, after adding back interest expense, net of tax, was $5,000,000.

The president is happy with the performance over the past year but is never satisfied with the status quo. He has set two specific goals for next year: (1) a 20% growth in sales and (2) a return on assets of 15%.

To achieve the second goal, the president has stated his intention to increase the total asset base by 12.5% over the base for the year just completed.

Required

1. For the year just completed, compute the following ratios:
   a. Return on sales
   b. Asset turnover
   c. Return on assets
2. Compute the necessary asset turnover for next year to achieve the president's goal of a 20% increase in sales.
3. Calculate the income needed next year to achieve the goal of a 15% return on total assets. (*Note:* Assume that *income* is defined as net income plus interest, net of tax.)
4. Based on your answers to parts **2** and **3**, comment on the reasonableness of the president's goals. What must the company focus on to attain these goals?

Problem 13-4 ***Goals for Sales and Income Growth*** **LO 6**

DECISION MAKING

SPREADSHEET

Sunrise Corp. is a major regional retailer. The chief executive officer (CEO) is concerned with the slow growth both of sales and of net income and the subsequent effect on the trading price of the common stock. Selected financial data for the past three years follow.

SUNRISE CORP.
(IN MILLIONS)

	2004	2003	2002
1. Sales	$200.0	$192.5	$187.0
2. Net income	6.0	5.8	5.6
3. Dividends declared and paid	2.5	2.5	2.5
December 31 balances:			
4. Owners' equity	70.0	66.5	63.2
5. Debt	30.0	29.8	30.3
Selected year-end financial ratios			
Net income to sales	3.0%	3.0%	3.0%
Asset turnover	2 times	2 times	2 times
6. Return on owners' equity*	8.6%	8.7%	8.9%
7. Debt to total assets	30.0%	30.9%	32.4%

*Based on year-end balances in owners' equity.

The CEO believes that the price of the stock has been adversely affected by the downward trend of the return on equity, the relatively low dividend payout ratio, and the lack of dividend increases. To improve the price of the stock, she wants to improve the return on equity and dividends. She believes that the company should be able to meet these objectives by (1) increasing sales and net income at an annual rate of 10% a year and (2) establishing a new dividend policy that calls for a dividend payout of 50% of earnings or $3,000,000, whichever is larger.

The 10% annual sales increase will be accomplished through a new promotional program. The president believes that the present net income to sales ratio of 3% will be unchanged by the cost of this new program and any interest paid on new debt. She expects that the company can accomplish this sales and income growth while maintaining the current relationship of total assets to sales. Any capital that is needed to maintain this relationship and that is not generated internally would be acquired through long-term debt financing. The CEO hopes that debt would not exceed 35% of total liabilities and owners' equity.

(continued)

Required

1. Using the CEO's program, prepare a schedule that shows the appropriate data for the years 2005, 2006, and 2007 for the items numbered 1 through 7 on the preceding schedule.
2. Can the CEO meet all of her requirements if a 10% per year growth in income and sales is achieved? Explain your answer.
3. What alternative actions should the CEO consider to improve the return on equity and to support increased dividend payments?
4. Explain the reasons that the CEO might have for wanting to limit debt to 35% of total liabilities and owners' equity. (CMA adapted)

Multi-Concept Problems

Problem 13-5 ***Basic Financial Ratios*** **LO 4, 5, 6**

The accounting staff of CCB Enterprises has completed the financial statements for the 2004 calendar year. The statement of income for the current year and the comparative statements of financial position for 2004 and 2003 follow.

CCB ENTERPRISES
STATEMENT OF INCOME
FOR THE YEAR ENDED DECEMBER 31, 2004
(THOUSANDS OMITTED)

Revenue:	
Net sales	$800,000
Other	60,000
Total revenue	$860,000
Expenses:	
Cost of goods sold	$540,000
Research and development	25,000
Selling and administrative	155,000
Interest	20,000
Total expenses	$740,000
Income before income taxes	$120,000
Income taxes	48,000
Net income	$ 72,000

CCB ENTERPRISES
COMPARATIVE STATEMENTS OF FINANCIAL POSITION
DECEMBER 31, 2004 AND 2003
(THOUSANDS OMITTED)

	2004	2003
Assets		
Current assets:		
Cash and short-term investments	$ 26,000	$ 21,000
Receivables, less allowance for doubtful accounts ($1,100 in 2004 and $1,400 in 2003)	48,000	50,000
Inventories, at lower of FIFO cost or market	65,000	62,000
Prepaid items and other current assets	5,000	3,000
Total current assets	$144,000	$136,000
Other assets:		
Investments, at cost	$106,000	$106,000
Deposits	10,000	8,000
Total other assets	$116,000	$114,000
Property, plant, and equipment:		
Land	$ 12,000	$ 12,000
Buildings and equipment, less accumulated depreciation ($126,000 in 2004 and $122,000 in 2003)	268,000	248,000
Total property, plant, and equipment	$280,000	$260,000
Total assets	$540,000	$510,000

Liabilities and Stockholders' Equity		
Current liabilities:		
Short term loans	$ 22,000	$ 24,000
Accounts payable	72,000	71,000
Salaries, wages, and other	26,000	27,000
Total current liabilities	$120,000	$122,000
Long-term debt	$160,000	$171,000
Total liabilities	$280,000	$293,000
Stockholders' equity:		
Common stock, at par	$ 44,000	$ 42,000
Paid-in capital in excess of par	64,000	61,000
Total paid-in capital	$108,000	$103,000
Retained earnings	152,000	114,000
Total stockholders' equity	$260,000	$217,000
Total liabilities and stockholders' equity	$540,000	$510,000

Required:

1. Calculate the following financial ratios for 2004 for CCB Enterprises:
   - **a.** Times interest earned
   - **b.** Return on total assets
   - **c.** Return on common stockholders' equity
   - **d.** Debt-equity ratio (at December 31, 2004)
   - **e.** Current ratio (at December 31, 2004)
   - **f.** Quick (acid-test) ratio (at December 31, 2004)
   - **g.** Accounts receivable turnover ratio (assume that all sales are on credit)
   - **h.** Number of days' sales in receivables
   - **i.** Inventory turnover ratio (assume that all purchases are on credit)
   - **j.** Number of days' sales in inventory
   - **k.** Number of days in cash operating cycle
2. Prepare a few brief comments on the overall financial health of CCB Enterprises. For each comment, indicate any information that is not provided in the problem and that you would need to fully evaluate the company's financial health. (CMA adapted)

Problem 13-6 ***Projected Results to Meet Corporate Objectives*** **LO 5, 6**

Tablon Inc. is a wholly owned subsidiary of Marbel Co. The philosophy of Marbel's management is to allow the subsidiaries to operate as independent units. Corporate control is exercised through the establishment of minimum objectives for each subsidiary, accompanied by substantial rewards for success and penalties for failure. The time period for performance review is long enough for competent managers to display their abilities.

Each quarter the subsidiary is required to submit financial statements. The statements are accompanied by a letter from the subsidiary president explaining the results to date, a forecast for the remainder of the year, and the actions to be taken to achieve the objectives if the forecast indicates that the objectives will not be met.

Marbel management, in conjunction with Tablon management, had set the objectives listed below for the year ending May 31, 2005. These objectives are similar to those set in previous years.

- Sales growth of 20%
- Return on stockholders' equity of 15%
- A long-term debt-to-equity ratio of not more than 1.0
- Payment of a cash dividend of 50% of net income, with a minimum payment of at least $400,000

Tablon's controller has just completed the financial statements for the six months ended November 30, 2004, and the forecast for the year ending May 31, 2005. The statements are presented below.

(continued)

After a cursory glance at the financial statements, Tablon's president concluded that not all objectives would be met. At a staff meeting of the Tablon management, the president asked the controller to review the projected results and recommend possible actions that could be taken during the remainder of the year so that Tablon would be more likely to meet the objectives.

TABLON INC.
INCOME STATEMENT
(THOUSANDS OMITTED)

	Year Ended May 31, 2004	Six Months Ended November 30, 2004	Forecast for Year Ending May 31, 2005
Sales	$25,000	$15,000	$30,000
Cost of goods sold	$13,000	$ 8,000	$16,000
Selling expenses	5,000	3,500	7,000
Administrative expenses and interest	4,000	2,500	5,000
Income taxes (40%)	1,200	400	800
Total expenses and taxes	$23,200	$14,400	$28,800
Net income	$ 1,800	$ 600	$ 1,200
Dividends declared and paid	600	0	600
Income retained	$ 1,200	$ 600	$ 600

TABLON INC.
STATEMENT OF FINANCIAL POSITION
(THOUSANDS OMITTED)

	May 31, 2004	November 30, 2004	Forecast for May 31, 2005
Assets			
Cash	$ 400	$ 500	$ 500
Accounts receivable (net)	4,100	6,500	7,100
Inventory	7,000	8,500	8,600
Plant and equipment (net)	6,500	7,000	7,300
Total assets	$18,000	$22,500	$23,500
Liabilities and Equities			
Accounts payable	$ 3,000	$ 4,000	$ 4,000
Accrued taxes	300	200	200
Long-term borrowing	6,000	9,000	10,000
Common stock	5,000	5,000	5,000
Retained earnings	3,700	4,300	4,300
Total liabilities and equities	$18,000	$22,500	$23,500

Required

1. Calculate the projected results for each of the four objectives established for Tablon Inc. State which results will not meet the objectives by year-end.
2. From the data presented, identify the factors that seem to contribute to the failure of Tablon Inc. to meet all of its objectives.
3. Explain the possible actions that the controller could recommend in response to the president's request.

(CMA adapted)

Problem 13-7 ***Comparison with Industry Averages*** **LO 4, 5, 6**

Heartland Inc. is a medium-size company that has been in business for 20 years. The industry has become very competitive in the last few years, and Heartland has decided that it must grow if it is going to survive. It has approached the bank for a sizable five-year loan, and the bank has requested its most recent financial statements as part of the loan package.

The industry in which Heartland operates consists of approximately 20 companies relatively equal in size. The trade association to which all of the competitors belong publishes an annual survey of the industry, including industry averages for selected ratios for the competitors. All companies voluntarily submit their statements to the association for this purpose.

Heartland's controller is aware that the bank has access to this survey and is very concerned about how the company fared this past year compared with the rest of the industry. The ratios included in the publication, and the averages for the past year, are as follows:

Ratio	Industry Average
Current ratio	1.23
Acid-test (quick) ratio	0.75
Accounts receivable turnover	33 times
Inventory turnover	29 times
Debt-to-equity ratio	0.53
Times interest earned	8.65 times
Return on sales	6.57%
Asset turnover	1.95 times
Return on assets	12.81%
Return on common stockholders' equity	17.67%

The financial statements to be submitted to the bank in connection with the loan follow:

HEARTLAND INC.
STATEMENT OF INCOME AND RETAINED EARNINGS
FOR THE YEAR ENDED DECEMBER 31, 2004
(THOUSANDS OMITTED)

Sales revenue	$542,750
Cost of goods sold	(435,650)
Gross margin	$107,100
Selling, general, and administrative expenses	$ (65,780)
Loss on sales of securities	(220)
Income before interest and taxes	$ 41,100
Interest expense	(9,275)
Income before taxes	$ 31,825
Income tax expense	(12,730)
Net income	$ 19,095
Retained earnings, January 1, 2004	58,485
	$ 77,580
Dividends paid on common stock	(12,000)
Retained earnings, December 31, 2004	$ 65,580

HEARTLAND INC.
COMPARATIVE STATEMENTS OF FINANCIAL POSITION
(THOUSANDS OMITTED)

	December 31, 2004	December 31, 2003
Assets		
Current assets:		
Cash	$ 1,135	$ 750
Marketable securities	1,250	2,250
Accounts receivable, net of allowances	15,650	12,380
Inventories	12,680	15,870
Prepaid items	385	420
Total current assets	$ 31,100	$ 31,670
Long-term investments	$ 425	$ 425
Property, plant, and equipment:		
Land	$ 32,000	$ 32,000
Buildings and equipment, net of accumulated depreciation	216,000	206,000
Total property, plant, and equipment	$248,000	$238,000
Total assets	$279,525	$270,095

(continued)

	December 31, 2004	December 31, 2003
Liabilities and Stockholders' Equity		
Current liabilities:		
Short-term notes	$ 8,750	$ 12,750
Accounts payable	20,090	14,380
Salaries and wages payable	1,975	2,430
Income taxes payable	3,130	2,050
Total current liabilities	$ 33,945	$ 31,610
Long-term bonds payable	$ 80,000	$ 80,000
Stockholders' equity:		
Common stock, no par	$100,000	$100,000
Retained earnings	65,580	58,485
Total stockholders' equity	$165,580	$158,485
Total liabilities and stockholders' equity	$279,525	$270,095

Required

1. Prepare a columnar report for the controller of Heartland Inc., comparing the industry averages for the ratios published by the trade association with the comparable ratios for Heartland. For Heartland, compute the ratios as of December 31, 2004, or for the year ending December 31, 2004, whichever is appropriate.
2. Briefly evaluate Heartland's ratios relative to the industry averages.
3. Do you think that the bank will approve the loan? Explain your answer.

Alternate Problems

Problem 13-1A ***Effect of Transactions on Debt-to-Equity Ratio*** **LO 5**

(*Note:* Consider completing Problem 13-2A after this problem to ensure that you obtain a clear understanding of the effect of various transactions on this measure of solvency.)

The following account balances are taken from the records of Monet's Garden Inc.:

Current liabilities	$150,000
Long-term liabilities	375,000
Stockholders' equity	400,000

Required

1. Use the information provided above to compute Monet's debt-to-equity ratio (round to three decimal points).
2. Determine the effect that each of the following transactions will have on Monet's debt-to-equity ratio by recalculating the ratio and then indicating whether the ratio is increased, decreased, or not affected by the transaction. (Round to three decimal points.) Consider each transaction independently; that is, assume that it is the *only* transaction that takes place.

Transaction	Effect of Transaction on Debt-To-Equity Ratio
a. Purchased inventory on account for $20,000.	
b. Purchased inventory for cash, $15,000.	
c. Paid suppliers on account, $30,000.	
d. Received cash on account, $40,000.	
e. Paid insurance for next year, $20,000.	
f. Made sales on account, $60,000.	
g. Repaid short-term loans at bank, $25,000.	
h. Borrowed $40,000 at bank for 90 days.	
i. Declared and paid $45,000 cash dividend.	
j. Purchased $20,000 of trading securities (classified as current assets).	
k. Paid $30,000 in salaries.	
l. Accrued additional $15,000 in taxes.	

Problem 13-2A ***Effect of Transactions on Debt-to-Equity Ratio*** **LO 5**

(*Note:* Consider completing this problem after Problem 13-1A to ensure that you obtain a clear understanding of the effect of various transactions on this measure of solvency.)

The following account balances are taken from the records of Degas Inc.:

Current liabilities	$ 25,000
Long-term liabilities	125,000
Stockholders' equity	400,000

Required

1. Use the information provided above to compute Degas' debt-to-equity ratio (round to three decimal points).
2. Determine the effect that each of the following transactions will have on Degas' debt-to-equity ratio by recalculating the ratio and then indicating whether the ratio is increased, decreased, or not affected by the transaction. (Round to three decimal points.) Consider each transaction independently; that is, assume that it is the *only* transaction that takes place.

Transaction	Effect of Transaction on Debt-To-Equity Ratio
a. Purchased inventory on account for $20,000.	
b. Purchased inventory for cash, $15,000.	
c. Paid suppliers on account, $30,000.	
d. Received cash on account, $40,000.	
e. Paid insurance for next year, $20,000.	
f. Made sales on account, $60,000.	
g. Repaid short-term loans at bank, $25,000.	
h. Borrowed $40,000 at bank for 90 days.	
i. Declared and paid $45,000 cash dividend.	
j. Purchased $20,000 of trading securities (classified as current assets).	
k. Paid $30,000 in salaries.	
l. Accrued additional $15,000 in taxes.	

Problem 13-3A *Goals for Sales and Return on Assets* LO 6

DECISION MAKING

The president of Blue Moon Corp. is reviewing with her department managers the operating results of the year just completed. Sales increased by 12% from the previous year to $750,000. Average total assets for the year were $400,000. Net income, after adding back interest expense, net of tax, was $60,000.

The president is happy with the performance over the past year but is never satisfied with the status quo. She has set two specific goals for next year: (1) a 15% growth in sales and (2) a return on assets of 20%.

To achieve the second goal, the president has stated her intention to increase the total asset base by 10% over the base for the year just completed.

Required

1. For the year just completed, compute the following ratios:
   a. Return on sales
   b. Asset turnover
   c. Return on assets
2. Compute the necessary asset turnover for next year to achieve the president's goal of a 15% increase in sales.
3. Calculate the income needed next year to achieve the goal of a 20% return on total assets. (*Note:* Assume that *income* is defined as net income plus interest, net of tax.)
4. Based on your answers to parts **2** and **3**, comment on the reasonableness of the president's goals. What must the company focus on to attain these goals?

Problem 13-4A *Goals for Sales and Income Growth* LO 6

DECISION MAKING

Sunset Corp. is a major regional retailer. The chief executive officer (CEO) is concerned with the slow growth both of sales and of net income and the subsequent effect on the trading price of the common stock. Selected financial data for the past three years follow.

(continued)

SPREADSHEET

SUNSET CORP.
(IN MILLIONS)

	2004	2003	2002
1. Sales	$100.0	$96.7	$93.3
2. Net income	3.0	2.9	2.8
3. Dividends declared and paid	1.2	1.2	1.2
December 31 balances:			
4. Owners' equity	40.0	38.2	36.5
5. Debt	10.0	10.2	10.2
Selected year-end financial ratios			
Net income to sales	3.0%	3.0%	3.0%
Asset turnover	2 times	2 times	2 times
6. Return on owners' equity*	7.5%	7.6%	7.7%
7. Debt to total assets	20.0%	21.1%	21.8%

*Based on year-end balances in owners' equity.

The CEO believes that the price of the stock has been adversely affected by the downward trend of the return on equity, the relatively low dividend payout ratio, and the lack of dividend increases. To improve the price of the stock, he wants to improve the return on equity and dividends.

He believes that the company should be able to meet these objectives by (1) increasing sales and net income at an annual rate of 10% a year and (2) establishing a new dividend policy that calls for a dividend payout of 60% of earnings or $2,000,000, whichever is larger.

The 10% annual sales increase will be accomplished through a product enhancement program. The president believes that the present net income to sales ratio of 3% will be unchanged by the cost of this new program and any interest paid on new debt. He expects that the company can accomplish this sales and income growth while maintaining the current relationship of total assets to sales. Any capital that is needed to maintain this relationship and that is not generated internally would be acquired through long-term debt financing. The CEO hopes that debt would not exceed 25% of total liabilities and owners' equity.

Required

1. Using the CEO's program, prepare a schedule that shows the appropriate data for the years 2005, 2006, and 2007 for the items numbered 1 through 7 on the preceding schedule.
2. Can the CEO meet all of his requirements if a 10% per-year growth in income and sales is achieved? Explain your answers.
3. What alternative actions should the CEO consider to improve the return on equity and to support increased dividend payments? (CMA adapted)

Alternate Multi-Concept Problems

Problem 13-5A ***Basic Financial Ratios*** **LO 4, 5, 6**

The accounting staff of SST Enterprises has completed the financial statements for the 2004 calendar year. The statement of income for the current year and the comparative statements of financial position for 2004 and 2003 follow.

SST ENTERPRISES
STATEMENT OF INCOME
YEAR ENDED DECEMBER 31, 2004
(THOUSANDS OMITTED)

Revenue:	
Net sales	$600,000
Other	45,000
Total revenue	$645,000
Expenses:	
Cost of goods sold	$405,000
Research and development	18,000
Selling and administrative	120,000
Interest	15,000
Total expenses	$558,000
Income before income taxes	$ 87,000
Income taxes	27,000
Net income	$ 60,000

SST ENTERPRISES
COMPARATIVE STATEMENTS OF FINANCIAL POSITION
DECEMBER 31, 2004 AND 2003
(THOUSANDS OMITTED)

	2004	2003
Assets		
Current assets:		
Cash and short-term investments	$ 27,000	$ 20,000
Receivables, less allowance for doubtful accounts ($1,100 in 2004 and $1,400 in 2003)	36,000	37,000
Inventories, at lower of FIFO cost or market	35,000	42,000
Prepaid items and other current assets	2,000	1,000
Total current assets	$100,000	$100,000
Property, plant, and equipment:		
Land	$ 9,000	$ 9,000
Buildings and equipment, less accumulated depreciation ($74,000 in 2004 and $62,000 in 2003)	191,000	186,000
Total property, plant, and equipment	$200,000	$195,000
Total assets	$300,000	$295,000
Liabilities and Stockholders' Equity		
Current liabilities:		
Short-term loans	$ 20,000	$ 15,000
Accounts payable	80,000	68,000
Salaries, wages, and other	5,000	7,000
Total current liabilities	$105,000	$ 90,000
Long-term debt	15,000	40,000
Total liabilities	$120,000	$130,000
Stockholders' equity:		
Common stock, at par	$ 50,000	$ 50,000
Paid-in capital in excess of par	25,000	25,000
Total paid-in capital	$ 75,000	$ 75,000
Retained earnings	105,000	90,000
Total stockholders' equity	$180,000	$165,000
Total liabilities and stockholders' equity	$300,000	$295,000

Required

1. Calculate the following financial ratios for 2004 for SST Enterprises:
   - **a.** Times interest earned
   - **b.** Return on total assets
   - **c.** Return on common stockholders' equity
   - **d.** Debt-equity ratio (at December 31, 2004)
   - **e.** Current ratio (at December 31, 2004)
   - **f.** Quick (acid-test) ratio (at December 31, 2004)
   - **g.** Accounts receivable turnover ratio (assume that all sales are on credit)
   - **h.** Number of days' sales in receivables
   - **i.** Inventory turnover ratio (assume that all purchases are on credit)
   - **j.** Number of days' sales in inventory
   - **k.** Number of days in cash operating cycle
2. Prepare a few brief comments on the overall financial health of SST Enterprises. For each comment, indicate any information that is not provided in the problem and that you would need to fully evaluate the company's financial health.

(CMA adapted)

Problem 13-6A ***Projected Results to Meet Corporate Objectives*** **LO 5, 6**

Grout Inc. is a wholly owned subsidiary of Slait Co. The philosophy of Slait's management is to allow the subsidiaries to operate as independent units. Corporate control is exercised through

(continued)

the establishment of minimum objectives for each subsidiary, accompanied by substantial rewards for success and penalties for failure. The time period for performance review is long enough for competent managers to display their abilities.

Each quarter the subsidiary is required to submit financial statements. The statements are accompanied by a letter from the subsidiary president explaining the results to date, a forecast for the remainder of the year, and the actions to be taken to achieve the objectives if the forecast indicates that the objectives will not be met.

Slait management, in conjunction with Grout management, had set the objectives listed below for the year ending September 30, 2005. These objectives are similar to those set in previous years.

- Sales growth of 10%
- Return on stockholders' equity of 20%
- A long-term debt-to-equity ratio of not more than 1.0
- Payment of a cash dividend of 50% of net income, with a minimum payment of at least $500,000

Grout's controller has just completed preparing the financial statements for the six months ended March 31, 2005, and the forecast for the year ending September 30, 2005. The statements are presented below.

After a cursory glance at the financial statements, Grout's president concluded that not all objectives would be met. At a staff meeting of the Grout management, the president asked the controller to review the projected results and recommend possible actions that could be taken during the remainder of the year so that Grout would be more likely to meet the objectives.

GROUT INC.
INCOME STATEMENT
(THOUSANDS OMITTED)

	Year Ended September 30, 2004	Six Months Ended March 31, 2005	Forecast for Year Ending September 30, 2005
Sales	$10,000	$6,000	$12,000
Cost of goods sold	$ 6,000	$4,000	$ 8,000
Selling expenses	1,500	900	1,800
Administrative expenses and interest	1,000	600	1,200
Income taxes	500	300	600
Total expenses and taxes	$ 9,000	$5,800	$11,600
Net income	$ 1,000	$ 200	$ 400
Dividends declared and paid	500	0	400
Income retained	$ 500	$ 200	$ 0

GROUT INC.
STATEMENT OF FINANCIAL POSITION
(THOUSANDS OMITTED)

	September 30, 2004	March 31, 2005	Forecast for September 30, 2005
Assets			
Cash	$ 400	$ 500	$ 500
Accounts receivable (net)	2,100	3,400	2,600
Inventory	7,000	8,500	8,400
Plant and equipment (net)	2,800	2,500	3,200
Total assets	$12,300	$14,900	$14,700
Liabilities and Equities			
Accounts payable	$ 3,000	$ 4,000	$ 4,000
Accrued taxes	300	200	200
Long-term borrowing	4,000	5,500	5,500
Common stock	4,000	4,000	4,000
Retained earnings	1,000	1,200	1,000
Total liabilities and equities	$12,300	$14,900	$14,700

Required

1. Calculate the projected results for each of the four objectives established for Grout Inc. State which results will not meet the objectives by year-end.
2. From the data presented, identify the factors that seem to contribute to the failure of Grout Inc. to meet all of its objectives.
3. Explain the possible actions that the controller could recommend in response to the president's request. (CMA adapted)

Problem 13-7A ***A Comparison with Industry Averages*** **LO 4, 5, 6**

Midwest Inc. is a medium-size company that has been in business for 20 years. The industry has become very competitive in the last few years, and Midwest has decided that it must grow if it is going to survive. It has approached the bank for a sizable five-year loan, and the bank has requested its most recent financial statements as part of the loan package.

The industry in which Midwest operates consists of approximately 20 companies relatively equal in size. The trade association to which all of the competitors belong publishes an annual survey of the industry, including industry averages for selected ratios for the competitors. All companies voluntarily submit their statements to the association for this purpose.

Midwest's controller is aware that the bank has access to this survey and is very concerned about how the company fared this past year compared with the rest of the industry. The ratios included in the publication, and the averages for the past year, are as follows:

Ratio	Industry Average
Current ratio	1.20
Acid-test (quick) ratio	0.50
Inventory turnover	35 times
Debt-to-equity ratio	0.50
Times interest earned	25 times
Return on sales	3%
Asset turnover	3.5 times
Return on common stockholders' equity	20%

The financial statements to be submitted to the bank in connection with the loan follow:

MIDWEST INC.
STATEMENT OF INCOME AND RETAINED EARNINGS
FOR THE YEAR ENDED DECEMBER 31, 2004
(THOUSANDS OMITTED)

Sales revenue	$420,500
Cost of goods sold	(300,000)
Gross margin	$120,500
Selling, general, and administrative expenses	(85,000)
Income before interest and taxes	$ 35,500
Interest expense	(8,600)
Income before taxes	$ 26,900
Income tax expense	(12,000)
Net income	$ 14,900
Retained earnings, January 1, 2004	12,400
	$ 27,300
Dividends paid on common stock	(11,200)
Retained earnings, December 31, 2004	$ 16,100

(continued)

MIDWEST INC.
COMPARATIVE STATEMENTS OF FINANCIAL POSITION
(THOUSANDS OMITTED)

	December 31, 2004	December 31, 2003
Assets		
Current assets:		
Cash	$ 1,790	$ 2,600
Marketable securities	1,200	1,700
Accounts receivable, net of allowances	400	600
Inventories	8,700	7,400
Prepaid items	350	400
Total current assets	$ 12,440	$ 12,700
Long-term investments	$ 560	$ 400
Property, plant, and equipment:		
Land	$ 12,000	$ 12,000
Buildings and equipment, net of accumulated depreciation	87,000	82,900
Total property, plant, and equipment	$ 99,000	$ 94,900
Total assets	$112,000	$108,000
Liabilities and Stockholders' Equity		
Current liabilities:		
Short-term notes	$ 800	$ 600
Accounts payable	6,040	6,775
Salaries and wages payable	1,500	1,200
Income taxes payable	1,560	1,025
Total current liabilities	$ 9,900	$ 9,600
Long-term bonds payable	$ 36,000	$ 36,000
Stockholders' equity:		
Common stock, no par	$ 50,000	$ 50,000
Retained earnings	16,100	12,400
Total stockholders' equity	$ 66,100	$ 62,400
Total liabilities and stockholders' equity	$112,000	$108,000

Required

1. Prepare a columnar report for the controller of Midwest Inc., comparing the industry averages for the ratios published by the trade association with the comparable ratios for Midwest. For Midwest, compute the ratios as of December 31, 2004, or for the year ending December 31, 2004, whichever is appropriate.
2. Briefly evaluate Midwest's ratios relative to the industry.
3. Do you think that the bank will approve the loan? Explain your answer.

Cases

Reading and Interpreting Financial Statements

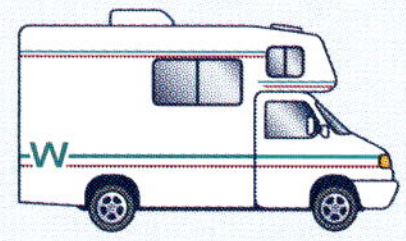

Case 13-1 ***Horizontal Analysis for Winnebago Industries*** **LO 2**

Refer to Winnebago Industries' comparative income statements included in its annual report.

Required

1. Prepare a work sheet with the following headings:

	Increase (Decrease) from			
	2000 to 2001		1999 to 2000	
Income Statement Accounts	**Dollars**	**Percent**	**Dollars**	**Percent**

2. Complete the work sheet using each of the account titles on Winnebago Industries' income statement. Round dollar amounts to the nearest one-tenth of $1 million and percentages to the nearest one-tenth of a percent.

3. What observations can you make from this horizontal analysis? What is your overall analysis of operations? Have the company's operations improved over the three-year period?

Case 13-2 *Vertical Analysis for Winnebago Industries* **LO 3**

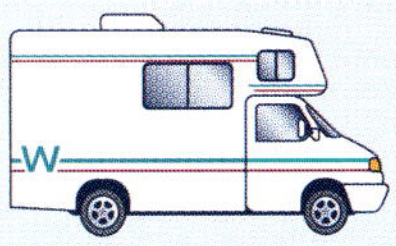

Refer to Winnebago Industries' financial statements included in its annual report.

Required

1. Using the format in Exhibit 13-6, prepare common-size comparative income statements for 2001 and 2000. Round dollar amounts to the nearest one-tenth of $1 million and percentages to the nearest one-tenth of a percent.
2. What changes do you detect in the income statement relationships from 2000 to 2001?
3. Using the format in Exhibit 13-5, prepare common-size comparative balance sheets at the end of 2001 and 2000. Round dollar amounts to the nearest one-tenth of $1 million and percentages to the nearest one-tenth of a percent.
4. What observations can you make about the relative composition of Winnebago Industries' assets from the common-size statements? What observations can be made about the changes in the relative composition of liabilities and owners' equity accounts?

Case 13-3 *Comparing Two Companies in the Same Industry: Winnebago Industries and Monaco Coach Corporation* **LO 3**

http://www.winnebagoind.com
http://www.monacocoach.com

This case should be completed after responding to the requirements in Case 13-2. Refer to the financial statement information of Winnebago Industries and Monaco Coach Corporation in Appendices A and B at the end of the text.

Required:

1. Using the format in Exhibit 13-6, prepare common size comparative income statements for 2001 and 2000 for Monaco Coach. Round dollar amounts to the nearest one-tenth of $1 million and percentages to the nearest one-tenth of a percent.
2. The common size comparative income statements indicates the relative importance of items on the statement. Compare the common size income statements of Monaco Coach and Winnebago Industries. What are the most important differences between the two companies' income statements?
3. Using the format in Exhibit 13-5, prepare common size balance sheets at the end of 2001 and 2000 Monaco Coach. Round the dollar amounts to the nearest one-tenth of $1 million and percentages to the nearest one-tenth of a percent.
4. The common size comparative balance sheets indicates the relative importance of items on the statement. Compare the common size balance sheets of Monaco Coach and Winnebago Industries. What are the most important differences between the two companies' balance sheets?

Case 13-4 *Ratio Analysis for Winnebago Industries* **LO 4, 5, 6**

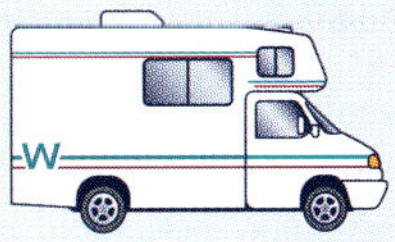

Refer to Winnebago Industries' financial statements included in its annual report.

Required

1. Compute the following ratios and other amounts for each of the two years, 2001 and 2000. Because only two years of data are given on the balance sheets, to be consistent you should use year-end balances for each year in lieu of average balances. Assume a 40% tax rate and 360 days to a year. State any other necessary assumptions in making the calculations. Round all ratios to the nearest one-tenth of a percent.
   a. Working capital
   b. Current ratio
   c. Acid-test ratio
   d. Cash flow from operations to current liabilities
   e. Number of days' sales in receivables
   f. Number of days' sales in inventory
   g. Debt-to-equity ratio
   h. Cash flow from operations to capital expenditures
   i. Asset turnover

(continued)

j. Return on sales
k. Return on assets
l. Return on common stockholders' equity

2. What is your overall analysis of the financial health of Winnebago Industries? What do you believe are the company's strengths and weaknesses?

Making Financial Decisions

DECISION MAKING

Case 13-5 *Acquisition Decision* LO 4, 5, 6

Diversified Industries is a large conglomerate and is continually in the market for new acquisitions. The company has grown rapidly over the last 10 years through buyouts of medium-size companies. Diversified does not limit itself to companies in any one industry but looks for firms with a sound financial base and the ability to stand on their own financially.

The president of Diversified recently told a meeting of the company's officers: "I want to impress two points on all of you. First, we are not in the business of looking for bargains. Diversified has achieved success in the past by acquiring companies with the ability to be a permanent member of the corporate family. We don't want companies that may appear to be a bargain on paper but can't survive in the long run. Second, a new member of our family must be able to come in and make it on its own—the parent is not organized to be a funding agency for struggling subsidiaries."

Ron Dixon is the vice president of acquisitions for Diversified, a position he has held for five years. He is responsible for making recommendations to the board of directors on potential acquisitions. Because you are one of his assistants, he recently brought you a set of financials for a manufacturer, Heavy Duty Tractors. Dixon believes that Heavy Duty is a "can't-miss" opportunity for Diversified and asks you to confirm his hunch by performing basic financial statement analysis on the company. The most recent income statement and comparative balance sheets for the company follow:

HEAVY DUTY TRACTORS INC.
STATEMENT OF INCOME AND RETAINED EARNINGS
FOR THE YEAR ENDED DECEMBER 31, 2004
(THOUSANDS OMITTED)

Sales Revenue	$875,250
Cost of goods sold	542,750
Gross margin	$332,500
Selling, general, and administrative expenses	264,360
Operating income	$ 68,140
Interest expense	45,000
Net income before taxes and extraordinary items	$ 23,140
Income tax expense	9,250
Income before extraordinary items	$ 13,890
Extraordinary gain, less taxes of $6,000	9,000
Net income	$ 22,890
Retained earnings, January 1, 2004	169,820
	$192,710
Dividends paid on common stock	10,000
Retained earnings, December 31, 2004	$182,710

HEAVY DUTY TRACTORS INC.
COMPARATIVE STATEMENTS OF FINANCIAL POSITION
(THOUSANDS OMITTED)

	December 31, 2004	December 31, 2003
Assets		
Current assets:		
Cash	$ 48,500	$ 24,980
Marketable securities	3,750	0
Accounts receivable, net of allowances	128,420	84,120
Inventories	135,850	96,780
Prepaid items	7,600	9,300
Total current assets	$324,120	$215,180
Long-term investments	$ 55,890	$ 55,890

	December 31, 2004	December 31, 2003
Property, plant, and equipment:		
Land	$ 45,000	$ 45,000
Buildings and equipment, less accumulated depreciation of $385,000 in 2004 and $325,000 in 2003	545,000	605,000
Total property, plant, and equipment	$590,000	$650,000
Total assets	$970,010	$921,070
Liabilities and Stockholders' Equity		
Current liabilities:		
Short-term notes	$ 80,000	$ 60,000
Accounts payable	65,350	48,760
Salaries and wages payable	14,360	13,840
Income taxes payable	2,590	3,650
Total current liabilities	$162,300	$126,250
Long-term bonds payable, due 2011	$275,000	$275,000
Stockholders' equity:		
Common stock, no par	$350,000	$350,000
Retained earnings	182,710	169,820
Total stockholders' equity	$532,710	$519,820
Total liabilities and stockholders' equity	$970,010	$921,070

Required

1. How liquid is Heavy Duty Tractors? Support your answer with any ratios that you believe are necessary to justify your conclusion. Also indicate any other information that you would want to have in making a final determination on its liquidity.
2. In light of the president's comments, should you be concerned about the solvency of Heavy Duty Tractors? Support your answer with the necessary ratios. How does the maturity date of the outstanding debt affect your answer?
3. Has Heavy Duty demonstrated the ability to be a profitable member of the Diversified family? Support your answer with the necessary ratios.
4. What will you tell your boss? Should he recommend to the board of directors that Diversified put in a bid for Heavy Duty Tractors?

Case 13-6 *Pricing Decision* LO 3

DECISION MAKING

BPO's management believes that the company has been successful at increasing sales because it has not increased the selling price of the products, even though its competition has increased prices and costs have increased. Price and cost relationships in Year 1 were established because they represented industry averages. The following income statements are available for BPO's first three years of operation:

	Year 3	Year 2	Year 1
Sales	$125,000	$110,000	$100,000
Cost of goods sold	62,000	49,000	40,000
Gross profit	$ 63,000	$ 61,000	$ 60,000
Operating expenses	53,000	49,000	45,000
Net income	$ 10,000	$ 12,000	$ 15,000

Required

1. Using the format in Exhibit 13-6, prepare common-size comparative income statements for the three years.
2. Explain why net income has decreased while sales have increased.
3. Prepare an income statement for Year 4. Sales volume in units is expected to increase by 10%, and costs are expected to increase by 8%.
4. Do you think BPO should raise its prices or maintain the same selling prices? Explain your answer.

Accounting and Ethics: What Would You Do?

Case 13-7 *Provisions in a Loan Agreement* LO 4, 5

As controller of Midwest Construction Company, you are reviewing with your assistant, Dave Jackson, the financial statements for the year just ended. During the review, Jackson reminds you of an existing loan agreement with Southern National Bank. Midwest has agreed to the following conditions:

- The current ratio will be maintained at a minimum level of 1.5 to 1.0 at all times.
- The debt-to-equity ratio will not exceed 0.5 to 1.0 at any time.

Jackson has drawn up the following preliminary, condensed balance sheet for the year just ended:

MIDWEST CONSTRUCTION COMPANY
BALANCE SHEET
DECEMBER 31
(IN MILLIONS OF DOLLARS)

Current assets	$16	Current liabilities	$10
Long-term assets	64	Long-term debt	15
		Stockholders' equity	55
Total	$80	Total	$80

Jackson wants to discuss two items with you. First, long-term debt currently includes a $5 million note payable, to Eastern State Bank, that is due in six months. The plan is to go to Eastern before the note is due and ask it to extend the maturity date of the note for five years. Jackson doesn't believe that Midwest needs to include the $5 million in current liabilities because the plan is to roll over the note.

Second, in December of this year, Midwest received a $2 million deposit from the state for a major road project. The contract calls for the work to be performed over the next 18 months. Jackson recorded the $2 million as revenue this year because the contract is with the state; there shouldn't be any question about being able to collect.

Required

1. Based on the balance sheet Jackson prepared, is Midwest in compliance with its loan agreement with Southern? Support your answer with any necessary computations.
2. What would you do with the two items in question? Do you see anything wrong with the way Jackson has handled each of them? Explain your answer.
3. Prepare a revised balance sheet based on your answer to part **2.** Also, compute a revised current ratio and debt-to-equity ratio. Based on the revised ratios, is Midwest in compliance with its loan agreement?

Case 13-8 *Inventory Turnover* LO 4

Garden Fresh Inc. is a wholesaler of fresh fruits and vegetables. Each year it submits a set of financial ratios to a trade association. Even though the association doesn't publish the individual ratios for each company, the president of Garden Fresh thinks it is important for public relations that his company look as good as possible. Due to the nature of the fresh fruits and vegetables business, one of the major ratios tracked by the association is inventory turnover. Garden Fresh's inventory stated at FIFO cost was as follows:

	Year Ending December 31	
	2004	**2003**
Fruits	$10,000	$ 9,000
Vegetables	30,000	33,000
Totals	$40,000	$42,000

Sales revenue for the year ending December 31, 2004, is $3,690,000. The company's gross profit ratio is normally 40%.

Based on these data, the president thinks the company should report an inventory turnover ratio of 90 times per year.

Required

1. Explain, using the necessary calculations, how the president came up with an inventory turnover ratio of 90 times.
2. Do you think the company should report a turnover ratio of 90 times? If not, explain why you disagree and explain, with calculations, what you think the ratio should be.
3. Assume you are the controller for Garden Fresh. What will you tell the president?

Internet Research Case

Case 13-9 *Wm. Wrigley Jr. Company*

INTERNET

http://www.wrigley.com

To many, the names **Wrigley** and chewing gum are synonymous. Not surprisingly, since it is the number one maker of chewing gum in the world and can claim some of the world's best-known brands such as Juicy Fruit® and Doublemint.®

By reading Wrigley's financial statements and notes and using them to calculate selected financial ratios, as in the review problem, you can develop a current picture of Wrigley's performance that can help you interpret how Wrigley has performed most recently.

1. Based on the financial information for the last two years available, compute the 10 ratios required in the Review Problem on page 707.
2. Comment on Wrigley's liquidity. Has it improved or declined over the two-year period?
3. Comment on Wrigley's solvency and Wrigley's capital structure.
4. Comment on Wrigley's profitability.
5. By looking at various sources such as the financial news and Wrigley's Financial Data pages, what management plans and initiatives, such as announced increases in building of plants or increases in hiring, are likely to change your analysis of Wrigley's performance the most in future years?

Solutions to Key Terms Quiz

Quiz 1:

14 Horizontal analysis (p. 682)
11 Vertical analysis (p. 682)
10 Gross profit ratio (p. 689)
12 Profit margin ratio (p. 689)
13 Liquidity (p. 690)
2 Working capital (p. 690)
3 Current ratio (p. 690)
1 Acid-test or quick ratio (p. 691)
5 Cash flow from operations to current liabilities ratio (p. 692)
6 Accounts receivable turnover ratio (p. 693)
4 Number of days' sales in receivables (p. 693)
9 Inventory turnover ratio (p. 693)
7 Number of days' sales in inventory (p. 694)
8 Cash to cash operating cycle (p. 695)

Quiz 2:

3 Solvency (p. 695)
7 Debt-to-equity ratio (p. 696)
13 Times interest earned ratio (p. 696)
14 Debt service coverage ratio (p. 697)
8 Cash flow from operations to capital expenditures ratio (p. 697)
15 Profitability (p. 698)
9 Return on assets ratio (p. 698)
4 Return on sales ratio (p. 699)
10 Asset turnover ratio (p. 699)
1 Return on common stockholders' equity ratio (p. 700)
12 Leverage (p. 701)
5 Earnings per share (p. 702)
2 Price/earnings (P/E) ratio (p. 702)
6 Dividend payout ratio (p. 703)
11 Dividend yield ratio (p. 703)
18 Discontinued operations (p. 713)
16 Extraordinary item (p. 713)
17 Cumulative effect of a change in accounting principle (p. 713)

Part IV

Integrative Problem

Presented below are comparative balance sheets and a statement of income and retained earnings for Gallagher, Inc., which operates a national chain of sporting goods stores:

GALLAGHER, INC.
COMPARATIVE BALANCE SHEETS
DECEMBER 31, 2004 AND 2003
(ALL AMOUNTS IN THOUSANDS OF DOLLARS)

	December 31	
	2004	**2003**
Cash	$ 840	$ 2,700
Accounts receivable	12,500	9,000
Inventory	8,000	5,500
Prepaid insurance	100	400
Total current assets	$21,440	$17,600
Land	$ 4,000	$ 4,000
Buildings and equipment	12,000	9,000
Accumulated depreciation	(3,700)	(3,000)
Total long-term assets	$12,300	$10,000
Total assets	$33,740	$27,600
Accounts payable	$ 7,300	$ 5,000
Taxes payable	4,600	4,200
Notes payable	2,400	1,600
Current portion of bonds	200	200
Total current liabilities	$14,500	$11,000
Bonds payable	1,400	1,600
Total liabilities	$15,900	$12,600
Preferred stock, $5 par	$ 1,000	$ 1,000
Common stock, $1 par	2,000	2,000
Retained earnings	14,840	12,000
Total stockholders' equity	$17,840	$15,000
Total liabilities and stockholders' equity	$33,740	$27,600

GALLAGHER, INC.
STATEMENT OF INCOME AND RETAINED EARNINGS
FOR THE YEAR ENDED DECEMBER 31, 2004
(ALL AMOUNTS IN THOUSANDS OF DOLLARS)

Net sales	$48,000
Cost of goods sold	36,000
Gross profit	$12,000
Selling, general and administrative expense	6,000
Operating income	$ 6,000
Interest expense	280
Income before tax	$ 5,720
Income tax expense	2,280
Net income	$ 3,440
Preferred dividends	100
Income available to common	$ 3,340
Common dividends	500
To retained earnings	$ 2,840
Retained earnings, 1/1	12,000
Retained earnings, 12/31	$14,840

Required

1. Prepare a statement of cash flows for Gallagher, Inc. for the year ended December 31, 2004, using the **indirect** method in the Operating Activities section of the statement.
2. Gallagher's management is concerned with both its short-term liquidity and its solvency over the long run. To help it evaluate these, compute the following ratios, rounding all answers to the nearest one-tenth of a percent:
   a. Current ratio
   b. Acid-test ratio
   c. Cash flow from operations to current liabilities ratio
   d. Accounts receivable turnover ratio
   e. Number of days' sales in receivables
   f. Inventory turnover ratio
   g. Number of days' sales in inventory
   h. Debt-to-equity ratio
   i. Debt service coverage ratio
   j. Cash flow from operations to capital expenditures ratio
3. Comment on Gallagher's liquidity and its solvency. What additional information do you need to fully evaluate the company?

2001 ANNUAL REPORT

Table of Contents

Corporate Profile

Winnebago Industries, Inc., headquartered in Forest City, Iowa, is a leading United States manufacturer of motor homes, self-contained recreation vehicles used primarily in leisure travel and outdoor recreation activities. The Company builds quality motor homes with state-of-the-art computer-aided design and manufacturing systems on automotive-styled assembly lines. The Company's products are subjected to what the Company believes is the most rigorous testing in the RV industry. These vehicles are sold through dealer organizations primarily under the Winnebago®, Itasca®, Rialta® and Ultimate® brand names. The Company markets its recreation vehicles on a wholesale basis to a broadly diversified dealer organization located throughout the United States, and to a limited extent, in Canada. As of August 25, 2001, the motor home dealer organization in the United States and Canada included approximately 305 dealer locations. Motor home sales by Winnebago Industries represented at least 86 percent of its revenues in each of the past five fiscal years. In addition, the Company's subsidiary, Winnebago Acceptance Corporation, engages in floor plan financing for a limited number of the Company's dealers. Other products manufactured by the Company consist principally of a variety of component parts for other manufacturers.

Winnebago Industries was incorporated under the laws of the state of Iowa on February 12, 1958, and adopted its present name on February 28, 1961.

Recent Financial Performance

(In thousands, except per share data)

	Fiscal 2001	Fiscal 2000	Fiscal 1999
Net Revenues	$ 681,834	$ 753,382	$ 677,011
Gross Profit	$ 94,504	$ 112,894	$ 102,408
Operating Income	$ 55,474	$ 70,654	$ 63,982
Net Income	$ 42,704	$ 48,399	$ 44,260
Diluted Income Per Share	$ 2.03	$ 2.20	$ 1.96
Diluted Weighted Average Shares	21,040	22,011	22,537

Selected Financial Data

(dollars in thousands, except per share data)	Aug. 25, 2001(1)	Aug. 26, 2000	Aug. 28, 1999	Aug. 29, 1998	Aug. 30, 1997
For the Year:					
Net revenues (2)	$681,834	$753,382	$677,011	$533,385	$445,621
Income before taxes	59,228	73,992	66,609	35,927	6,992
Pretax profit % of revenue	8.7%	9.8%	9.8%	6.7%	1.6%
Provision for income taxes	$ 15,474	$ 25,593	$ 22,349	$ 11,543	$ 416
Income tax rate	26.1%	34.6%	33.6%	32.1%	5.9%
Income from continuing operations	$ 42,704	$ 48,399	$ 44,260	$ 24,384	$ 6,576
Gain on sale of Cycle-Sat subsidiary	---	---	---	---	16,472
Net income	$ 42,704	$ 48,399	$ 44,260	$ 24,384	$ 23,048
Income per share:					
Continuing operations:					
Basic	$ 2.06	$ 2.23	$ 1.99	$ 1.01	$ .26
Diluted	2.03	2.20	1.96	1.00	.26
Discontinued operations:					
Basic	---	---	---	---	.65
Diluted	---	---	---	---	.64
Net income per share:					
Basic	$ 2.06	$ 2.23	$ 1.99	$ 1.01	$ .91
Diluted	2.03	2.20	1.96	1.00	.90
Weighted average common shares outstanding (in thousands):					
Basic	20,735	21,680	22,209	24,106	25,435
Diluted	21,040	22,011	22,537	24,314	25,550
Cash dividends per share	$ .20	$ .20	$ .20	$ .20	$ .20
Book value	9.99	8.22	6.70	5.11	4.86
Return on assets (ROA)	12.5%	15.7%	15.5%	10.6%	10.8%
Return on equity (ROE)	20.6%	27.7%	29.6%	20.9%	18.6%
Unit Sales:					
Class A	5,666	6,819	6,054	5,381	4,834
Class C	3,410	3,697	4,222	3,390	2,724
Total Class A & C Motor Homes	9,076	10,516	10,276	8,771	7,558
Class B Conversions (EuroVan Campers)	703	854	600	978	1,205
At Year End:					
Total assets	$342,033	$307,095	$285,889	$230,612	$213,475
Stockholders' equity	207,464	174,909	149,384	116,523	123,882
Working capital	174,248	143,274	123,720	92,800	100,772
Long-term debt	---	---	---	---	---
Current ratio	3.5 to 1	3.0 to 1	2.5 to 1	2.5 to 1	3.4 to 1
Number of employees	3,325	3,300	3,400	3,010	2,830

(1) Includes a noncash after tax cumulative effect of change in accounting principle of $1.1 million expense or $.05 per share due to the adoption of SAB No. 101.
(2) Net revenues have been restated for the adoption of a new accounting principle related to shipping and handling fees and costs.

Net Revenues
(Dollars in Millions)

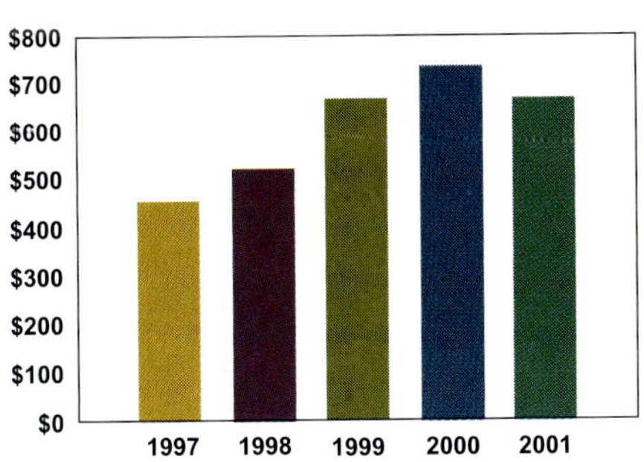

Net Income Per Diluted Share
(Dollars)

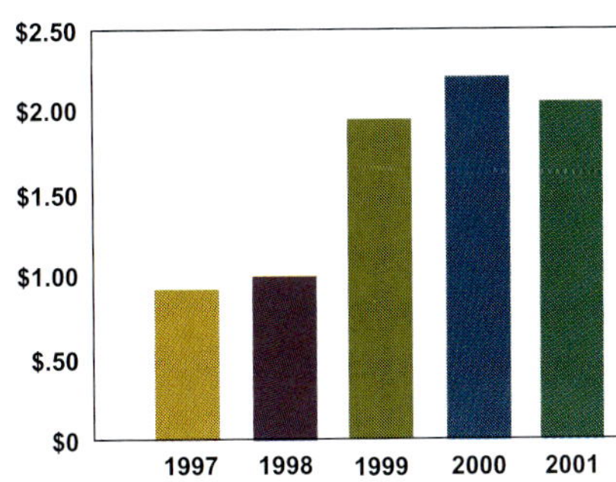

Shareholders' Equity
(Dollars In Millions)

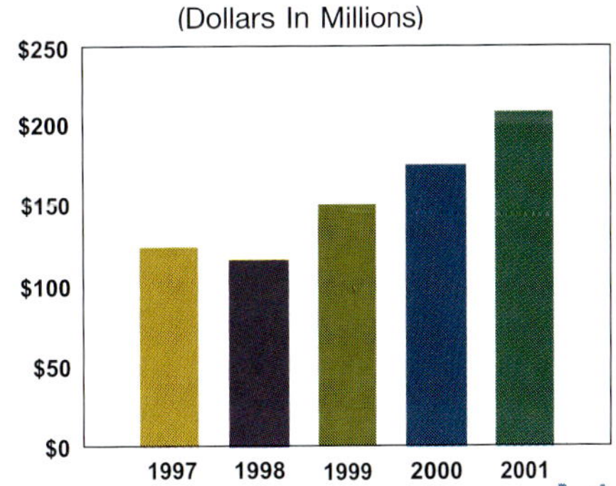

WINNEBAGO INDUSTRIES, INC.

Mission Statement

Winnebago Industries, Inc. is a leading United States manufacturer of recreation vehicles (RVs) and related products and services. Our mission is to continually improve our products and services to meet or exceed the expectations of our customers. We emphasize employee teamwork and involvement in identifying and implementing programs to save time and lower production costs while maintaining the highest quality products. These strategies allow us to prosper as a business with a high degree of integrity and to provide a reasonable return for our shareholders, the ultimate owners of our business.

Values

How we accomplish our mission is as important as the mission itself. Fundamental to the success of the Company are these basic values we describe as the four P's:

People -- Our employees are the source of our vast strength. They provide our corporate intelligence and determine our reputation and vitality. Involvement and teamwork are our core corporate values.

Products -- Our products are the end result of our teamwork's combined efforts, and they should be the best in meeting or exceeding our customers' expectations. As our products are viewed, so are we viewed.

Plant -- Our facilities are believed to be the most technologically advanced in the RV industry. We continue to review facility improvements that will increase the utilization of our plant capacity and enable us to build the best quality product for the investment.

Profitability -- Profitability is the ultimate measure of how efficiently we provide our customers with the best products for their needs. Profitability is required to survive and grow. As our respect and position within the marketplace grows, so will our profit.

Guiding Principles

Quality comes first -- To achieve customer satisfaction, the quality of our products and services must be our number one priority.

Customers are central to our existence -- Our work must be done with our customers in mind, providing products and services that meet or exceed the expectations of our customers. We must not only satisfy our customers, we must also surprise and delight them.

Continuous improvement is essential to our success -- We must strive for excellence in everything we do: in our products, in their safety and value, as well as in our services, our human relations, our competitiveness, and our profitability.

Employee involvement is our way of life -- We are a team. We must treat each other with trust and respect.

Dealers and suppliers are our partners -- The Company must maintain mutually beneficial relationships with dealers, suppliers and our other business associates.

Integrity is never compromised -- The Company must pursue conduct in a manner that is socially responsible and that commands respect for its integrity and for its positive contributions to society.

To My Fellow Shareholders:

Winnebago Industries, Inc. completed fiscal 2001 with its third highest net revenues and net income in its history, in spite of the economic challenges we faced as a nation. We believe the Company's performance in fiscal 2001 is a result of the excellent acceptance of our new products, the solid performance of our dealer partners, our brand name recognition and strong quality reputation - all of which are competitive advantages in the marketplace.

On the following pages, we will detail many advantages that have contributed to Winnebago Industries' success during fiscal 2001, and which we believe will continue to have a positive impact on our future.

Financial measurements show that Winnebago Industries is leading the RV industry in:

- Return on Shareholders' Equity
- Return on Assets
- Operating Margin
- Net Profit Margin

Class A & C Retail Market Share

(As reported by Statistical Surveys, Inc. CYTD Through September 2001)

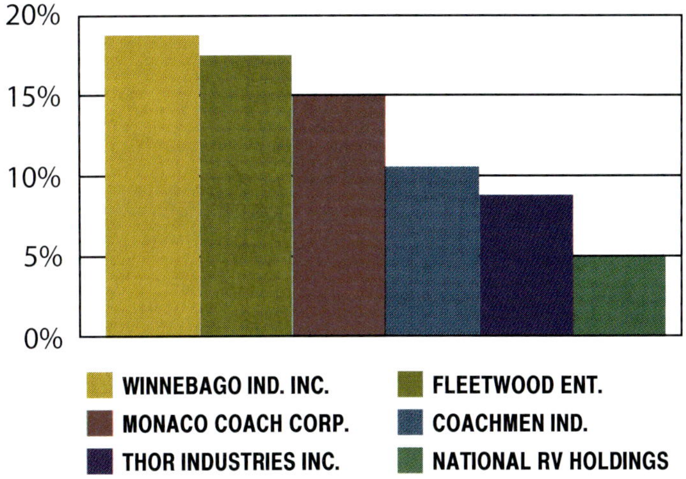

Since fiscal 1997 we have chosen to refocus on our core motor home business with an emphasis on new product development. Through this product development process, over 65% of our 2002 motor homes were introduced as brand new products with innovative new features. We have also emphasized additional and improved sales and service programs, and the manufacturing of high quality products.

2002 Winnebago Sightseer and Itasca Sunova

Competitive Comparison

(Information obtained from last 12 months public filings.)

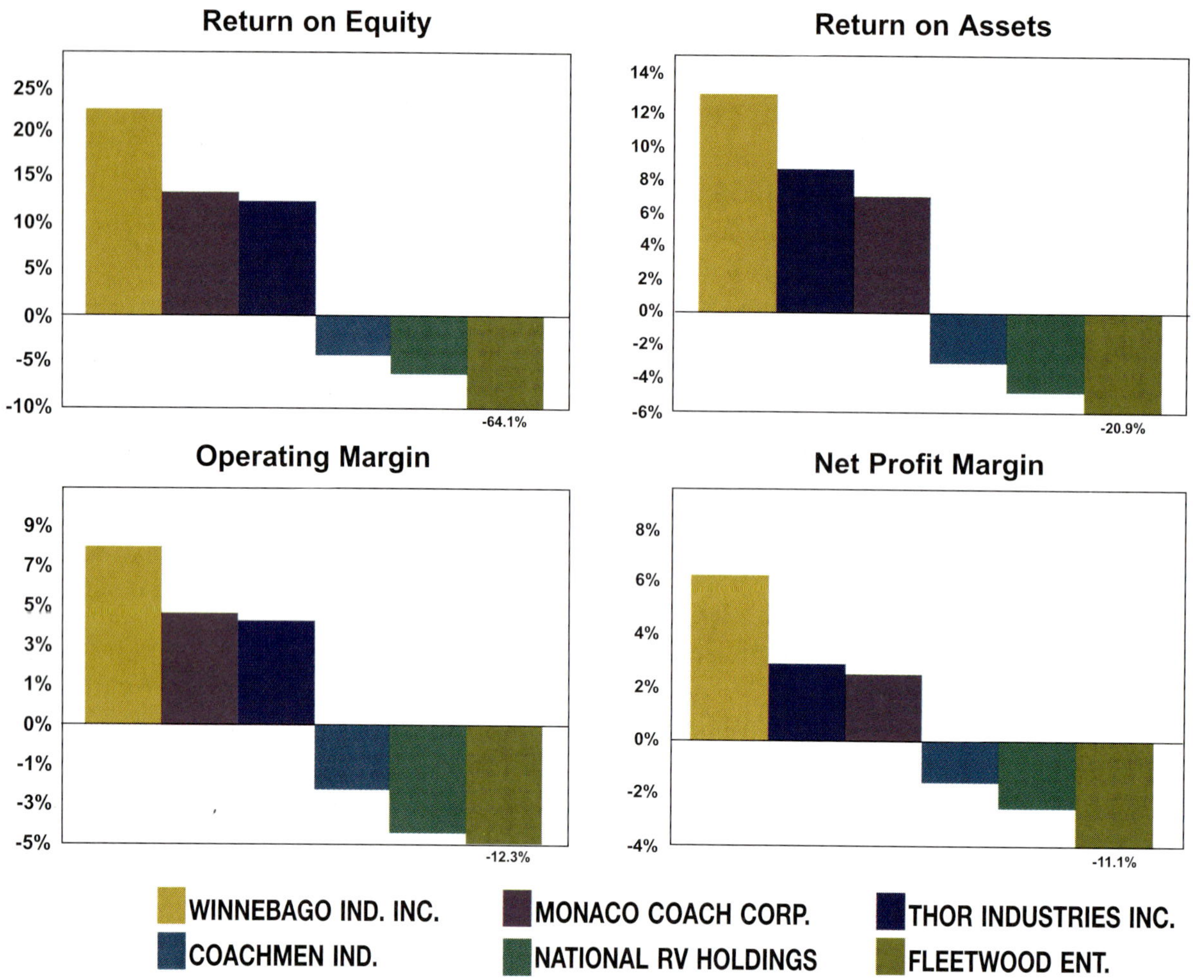

As a result of this change in focus, we've experienced healthy market share gains. Winnebago Industries' market share is up 10 percent calendar year to date through September 2001 versus one year ago, placing us in the number one position in combined Class A and C retail sales for the first time in 20 years. Certainly, this is a very significant achievement for the Company.

According to Statistical Surveys, Inc., the recreation vehicle (RV) retail reporting firm, Winnebago Industries achieved 18.9 percent of the combined Class A and C retail market nationally calendar year to date through September 2001 versus 17.2 percent for the same period last year.

Winnebago Industries believes that it also leads the industry in RV manufacturing technology. We continue to refine our systems and processes to enhance our ability to increase quality, while maximizing the productivity of our workforce and facilities.

To further enhance shareholder value, in March 2001, Winnebago Industries' Board of Directors authorized the repurchase of up to $15 million of the Company' s common stock. Since November 1997 through November 12, 2001, Winnebago Industries has had five repurchase programs, repurchasing approximately 5.9 million shares, or 23 percent, of the Company's outstanding stock as of November 1997.

We are encouraged by the continued reduction in interest rates, and the acceptance of our new products, however, the economic environment since the September 11 tragedy leads us to be cautious about the next couple of quarters. Long-term, however, demographics are still in our favor as our target market of consumers age 50 and older is expected to increase for the next 30 years.

Winnebago Industries was pleased to have received six consecutive Quality Circle Awards from the Recreation Vehicle Dealers Association. These awards are testaments to the Company's emphasis on quality in its total operation. By providing our customers with the highest quality motor homes with industry-leading sales and service programs, while creating solid working relationships with our dealer partners and our dedicated employees, we are ultimately delivering the best value for the owners of our corporation -- you, our shareholders. Winnebago Industries is the leading motor home manufacturer and believes that it has the competitive advantages necessary to continue to grow our market share and enhance our shareholder value well into the future.

Bruce D. Hertzke
Chairman of the Board,
Chief Executive Officer and President

November 28, 2001

Land of the Free
Home of the Brave
A Tribute to our Heroes

Winnebago Industries wishes to honor those killed and injured in the September 11 attacks and those who fight to protect our many freedoms on a daily basis.

The following timely message has been displayed in Winnebago Industries' Visitors Center since 1986.

"One of our most precious freedoms is the freedom to travel...to see and experience the ever-changing tapestry of life throughout the land. American enthusiasm for travel is rooted deep in our pioneer heritage.

"Motor homes are a uniquely American way to enjoy that freedom..."

Luise V. and John K. Hanson, Founders
Winnebago Industries, Inc.

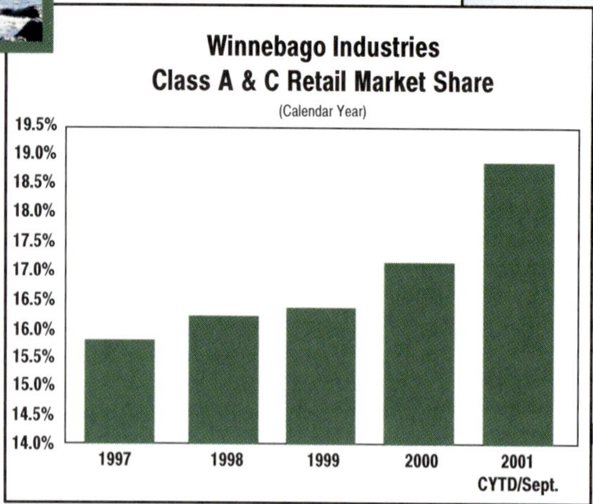

2002 Itasca Sunstar

Operations Review

Market Leadership

Winnebago Industries strengthened its market leadership role in fiscal 2001. In fact, Winnebago Industries ended its fiscal year in the number one motor home retail sales position for the first time in 20 years. Obviously, the Company's competitive advantages have had an effect in the marketplace. As stated in the Report to Shareholders, the Company has grown its retail market share of combined Class A and C motor homes from 15.8 percent in calendar 1997 to 18.9 percent year to date through September 2001. Also, Winnebago Industries improved its market share by 10 percent when compared to the same period last year.

New Product Advantages

Competitive advantage was gained through the continued introduction of new product offerings with consistent high quality. New product lines are important for several reasons. Expanded product offerings create broader exposure of Winnebago Industries' products at the Company's dealerships and allow the Company to be able to reach more customers. New product lines also create additional opportunities for current owners of Winnebago Industries' products or other brands in the RV industry to trade up or down. Consumers often want the latest and greatest offerings available in the marketplace.

Winnebago Industries' innovative motor home lineup for 2002 consists of Winnebago, Itasca, Rialta and Ultimate motor homes. In total, 65 percent of Winnebago Industries model lineup is new for 2002, including four brand new product lines: the Class A Winnebago Sightseer™ and Itasca Sunova™ and the Class C Winnebago Vista™ and Itasca Sunstar™. In addition to the four models mentioned above, the new 2002 model lineup also includes the redesigned Winnebago Chieftain® and Itasca Sunflyer®. These high-line gas motor homes feature luxurious offerings in each of their four floorplans, and spaciousness with a dual slideout design.

Along with the expansion of product offerings, Winnebago Industries has provided more features as standard equipment, as well as a continued emphasis on increasing usable interior space through greater utilization of slideouts on the Company's 2002 product offerings. Slideouts are now included in 82 percent of the Company's Class A & C product floorplans and all of Winnebago Industries Class A products. Also, all of Winnebago Industries' Class A diesel lineup and 83 percent of the Company's total Class A products feature two slideouts, while 24 percent of the Company's Class C models are now dual slides as well.

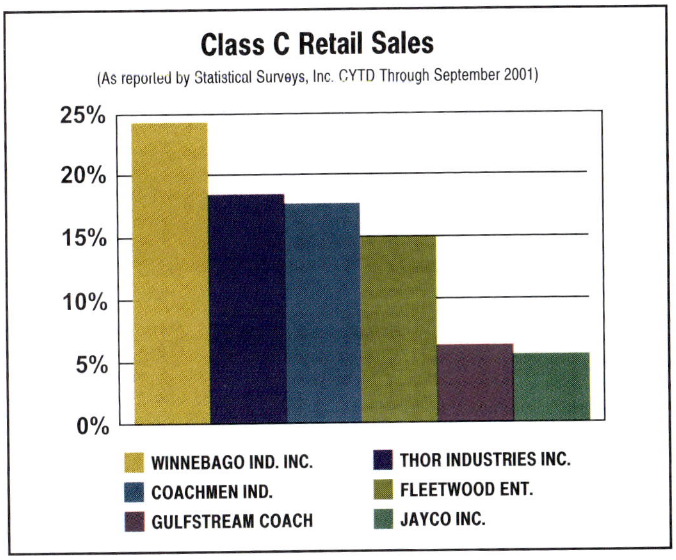

Class C Advantages

Winnebago Industries, the top selling Class C manufacturer since 1998, continues to expand its Class C model lineup for 2002.

The aerodynamic 2002 Rialta is built on the highly-maneuverable, front-wheel-drive Volkswagen chassis. The new 2.8L VR6+ engine featured in 2002 increases the Rialta's horsepower to 201hp, a 44 percent increase from the VR6 previously offered, while maintaining excellent fuel efficiency of approximately 16.3 miles per gallon combined city and highway using the Environmental Protection Agency testing guidelines. The Rialta is available in three models with four 22-foot floorplan options, each maximizing space without sacrificing comfort.

2002 Winnebago Vista

The brand new Winnebago Vista and Itasca Sunstar Class C motor homes are unique, fuel-efficient motor homes that are also built on the front-wheel-drive 7,275-lb. gross vehicle weight rating (GVWR) Volkswagen chassis. Offering great maneuverability, the Vista and Sunstar provide a multitude of sleeping areas, a full galley and a bathroom area with wardrobe in a compact 21-foot size.

Multiple sleeping areas, slideout availability for expanded living areas and basement storage are all key ingredients to making the Winnebago Minnie® and Itasca Spirit® motor homes a must for great family trips. The Minnie and Spirit are excellent value-priced motor homes, each with seven models to choose from ranging from 22- to 31-feet in length. Two new models join the lineup for 2002, the 24F with a front slideout and the 29B with both a front lounge and rear bedroom slideout.

2002 Itasca Spirit 24F

The Winnebago Minnie Winnie® and Itasca Sundancer® lines each feature three, widebody models for 2002. Featuring below floor construction, box-fold style valance doors and a curved fiberglass roof, the Minnie Winnie and Sundancer are designed with Class A features, yet have the conveniences of a Class C. Ranging from 27- to 31-feet in length, the 27P and the new 30V each offer two slideout rooms. The 27P features a refrigerator/dinette slideout, while the 30V features a galley/dinette slideout and the 31C features a dinette/couch slideout. The 27P and 30V models also feature a rear bed slideout, large bedroom wardrobe with drawers and a convenient desk/vanity area.

Class A Advantages

Winnebago Industries also continues to expand its offerings of Class A motor homes, all of which feature slideouts in 2002.

Brand new for 2002, the Winnebago Sightseer and Itasca Sunova offer outstanding value, quality construction and comfort at an affordable price. These wide-body, basement-style Class A models are available in 27- and 30-foot models and feature many standard features typically found as options on competitive coaches in this price class. The Sightseer and Sunova 27C models feature a unique dinette/refrigerator and pantry slideout, while the 30B models have a dinette/couch slideout. The 27C model utilizes the 14,800-lb. GVWR Workhorse® chassis, while the 30B model is available with the standard 18,000-lb. GVWR Ford® chassis, or the optional 18,000 lb. GVWR Workhorse chassis. The striking exterior features a durable fiberglass skin, attractive graphics and large storage compartments with painted, box-fold one-piece doors like those typically found on more expensive motor homes.

The Winnebago Brave® and Itasca Sunrise® have been repositioned to a higher appointment and feature level in 2002. Ranging from 30- to 36-feet in length, three of the four models (32V, 34D and 36M) are brand new for 2002 and feature both a dinette/couch slideout and a 30-inch bedroom slideout room for increased living space, while the 30W model features a functional L-shaped galley/dinette slideout.

The Winnebago Adventurer® motor home is the bes selling Class A motor home on the market. Winnebag Industries also believes the Adventurer and the compa rable Itasca Suncruiser® are the most user-friendl motor homes on the market today. Ranging in size fron 30- to 37-feet in length, three of the four models in eacl line are new for 2002 and feature dual slideouts.

2002 Winnebago Adventurer

2002 Itasca Sunova

The newly redesigned Winnebago Chieftain and asca Sunflyer also make their mark in 2002. Filling niche for motor home consumers who want top-of-e-line elegance in front-engine gas-powered motor omes, the Chieftain and Sunflyer feature exclusive nenities and upgrades with the convenience, per-ırmance and floorplan flexibility only front-engine as-powered motor homes can provide. Thanks to the ew heavier 22,000 lb. GVWR Workhorse chassis with andard 22.5-inch aluminum wheels, Winnebago ıdustries was able to offer four spacious and luxuri-us floorplans ranging from 36- to 39-feet in length. ffering a front, flat floor slideout as well as a rear ideout in the bedroom, each model offers floorplan exibility with innovative galley designs and a beau-ful new entertainment center with expansive 32-inch olor TV on most floorplans.

Winnebago Industries continued its growth in the iesel pusher market as well. Since calendar 1998 ırough the most recent reported period ending calen-ar year to date through September, Winnebago ndustries' percentage of the diesel retail market has rown by 111 percent from 4.5 percent in calendar 1998) 9.5 percent year to date through September 2001.

The Winnebago Journey® series is Winnebago ndustries' entry-level diesel pusher product. Three of he four Journey models are new for 2002 and all fea-ure dual slideouts. Ranging in length from 32- to 36-feet, the Journey is built on the 26,850-lb. GVWR Freightliner chassis with 275 hp Cummins engine and 5-speed MH 1000 Allison transmission.

Available in five models (four are new for 2002) ranging in length from 32- to 39-feet in length, the Journey DL® is built on the 26,850-lb. GVWR Freightliner chassis with 330 hp Caterpillar diesel engine, 6-speed Allison transmission, rear radiator and Jacobs Extarder exhaust brake. The 32TD model offers a 300 hp Cummins engine and 6-speed transmission.

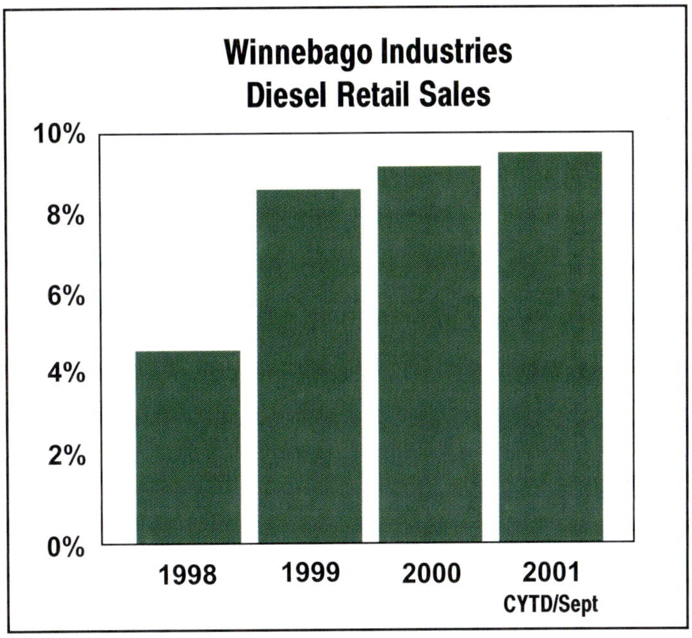

2002 Winnebago Chieftain

The Itasca Horizon™ features four models in 32-foot and 39-foot lengths, three of which are new for 2002. All of the Horizon models feature both front slideout room extensions as well as rear bedroom slides. The Itasca Horizon models are also built on the Freightliner 26,850 lb. GVWR chassis with a 330 hp Caterpillar engine and 6-speed transmission. The 32TD model offers a 300 hp Cummins engine and 6-speed transmission.

2002 Itasca Horizon

Offering increased horsepower and GVWR in 2002, Winnebago Industries' premium diesel pusher Ultimate Advantage® line is now based on the 32,000-lb. GVWR Spartan chassis with a 350 hp Cummins diesel engine. The Ultimate Advantage is available in four models, three of which are new for 2002. The Ultimate Advantage features dual slides, a side radiator, independent front suspension, hydraulic leveling jacks and a Bi-Directional Isolator Relay Delay™, which charges either battery when needed. Also in 2002, the trailer hitch was increased in towing capacity from 5,000 to 10,000 pounds.

Winnebago Industries' top-of-the-line Ultimate Freedom® is built on the 32,000 lb. GVWR Spartan Mountain Master GT chassis. Increased from 350 hp to 370 hp the Ultimate Freedom features a Cummins diesel engine, independent front suspension, side radiator and 6-speed Allison transmission. The Freedom also features the Bi-Directional Isolator Relay Delay. The Ultimate Freedom has two luxurious new floorplans for 2002, the 40JD and new 40WD. Both of these models feature a galley/sofa slideout in the front lounge area and unique rear chest of drawer slide in the bedroom with a 19-inch color TV with remo mounted above for optimal viewing.

The 2002 Ultimate Advantage and Ultima Freedom offer numerous new conveniences such as remote doorbell, global positioning system, and t new SmartWheel™ steering wheel. This innovati steering wheel includes controls for the windshie wipers, ICC courtesy blink and cruise control.

Working with Spartan Custom Chassis, Winneba Industries' designers utilize the Company's Ulti-Bay chassis design for the Ultimate Advantage and Ultima Freedom, providing major efficiencies in terms material use and storage space utilization.

Spartan provides the front and rear sections of t chassis, while Winnebago Industries completes t mid-section structure of the chassis and body with ta extremely spacious storage compartments in the are normally claimed by chassis rails. The Ulti-Bay desig centralizes exterior storage and provides a tremendo increase in storage space - up to 203 cubic feet of ext rior storage space is available. The Ulti-Bay design als provides a consistent location for important comp nents such as the electrical and water service center generator, etc.

New Feature Advantages

Most 2002 models feature the new RV Radio™ Designed by Winnebago Industries' engineers and th radio manufacturer exclusively for RV usage, the cus tomized RV Radio features an AM/FM radio, cassett and CD, as well as weatherband so you can check th weather whenever and wherever you're traveling. Th large knobs and easy to read display make this inno vative cassette/CD/radio the first of its kind in th industry.

2002 Itasca Horizon with new dining table/computer desk.

A unique new dining table/computer desk is available for 2002 in the Winnebago Journey DL, Itasca Horizon, Ultimate Advantage and Ultimate Freedom models. The dining table easily extends to seat four people comfortably, while an adjacent cabinet provides additional storage for computer equipment or supplies.

Finally, there's an electric slideout that meets Winnebago Industries high quality standards. The DigiSync® dual-arm slide system from Kwikee® is new to select Company products for 2002. Designed exclusively for the Company with the help of Winnebago Industries' engineers, this revolutionary new concept in slideout room design is a dual arm slide system that digitally synchronizes both slideout arms as they smoothly extend and retract to automatically square up the slideout room. The Kwikee DigiSync Electric Slide is featured in the Winnebago Minnie and Itasca Spirit Class C motor homes and the new Winnebago Sightseer and Itasca Sunova Class A motor homes.

A rave success when introduced last year, the Rest Easy™ Multi-Position Lounge is now available on many of Winnebago Industries motor homes. Designed exclusively by Winnebago Industries, Rest Easy looks like a normal couch, but after pressing the electric switch, it turns into a cozy lounger with ottoman. Press the switch again, and presto - it's a comfortable bed. Variations of the Rest Easy are available in most Winnebago, Itasca and Ultimate models.

Corporate Hospitality Vehicle

Commercial and Specialty Vehicle Advantages

Winnebago Industries maintains a competitive advantage with over 30 years experience in the commercial and specialty vehicle business, manufacturing a broad range of offerings. Products sold by the Commercial Vehicle Division continue to be an important source of incremental sales for Winnebago Industries. Several models are offered that can be custom designed for a wide variety of applications including medical, dental, law enforcement, and computer training. An upscale, 40-foot "corporate hospitality" vehicle based on the Ultimate Freedom platform was also developed in fiscal 2001. This versatile unit was created to meet the hospitality needs of race teams, corporate sponsors or vendors. The floor plan design provides a conference room in the rear and a spacious lounge environment in the forward area. The Specialty Vehicle Department is responsible for the sale of ability-equipped motor homes that are custom built for individuals with special mobility needs. Ability-equipped motor homes can be outfitted with wider entrance doors, wheelchair lifts, roll-in showers, hand driving controls, and other equipment needed to make them wheel chair accessible.

OEM Advantages

Another competitive advantage, Winnebago Industries manufactures the majority of the parts used in its motor homes. This allows the Company to maintain strict quality standards, design parts to unique motor home needs and easily facilitate parts replacement for years to come. In addition, Winnebago

Industries is able to maximize its production capacity through the sale of original equipment manufacturing (OEM) components, while providing the added benefit of low cost component parts. Winnebago Industries generated revenues of $24.3 million from the sale of original equipment manufacturing (OEM) components in fiscal 2001.

The largest portion of OEM revenues were generated by Winnebago Industries Creative Aluminum Products Company (CAPCO), which produces aluminum extrusion products, primarily for the RV and home building industries.

Marketing Advantages

Winnebago Industries also realizes a competitive advantage due to its strong brand name recognition. Winnebago Industries participated in several outstanding marketing opportunities in fiscal 2001. These opportunities continued to maximize our brand strength while further positioning us as the industry leader.

Winnebago Industries participated in two media tours sponsored by the Recreation Vehicle Industry Association (RVIA) during fiscal 2001. For their second season touring as RVIA spokespersons, Brad and Amy Herzog used a 2001 Winnebago Adventurer for their "Baby Makes Three...in an RV" tour. The tour capitalized on Brad's recent national TV appearances and best-selling book *States of Mind,* which describes Brad and Amy's 11-month Steinbeck-like journey across America in their motor home. The addition of Luke, their 8-month old son, has also helped reinforce the ease and flexibility of RV travel for the whole family.

In his 10th consecutive year as RVIA spokesperson, David Woodworth used a 2001 Winnebago Journey DL for his "National RV History Tour." As a noted RV historian, David also towed an antique "Mae West" motor home behind the Journey DL to relate the long history of RV travel benefits.

Winnebago Industries also provided several motor homes during fiscal 2001 for "Biff Henderson's America" segments that appeared on the CBS "Late Show with David Letterman" TV show. We worked closely with RVIA, CBS and Letterman's staff to support these humorous Charles Kuralt-style segments.

"Jeopardy" and "The Wheel of Fortune" TV shows also utilize Winnebago Braves as their contestant search vehicles. In addition, Winnebago Industries motor homes continued to be offered as grand prizes for "The Wheel of Fortune".

In a spring promotion, some 1.8 million packages of Nabisco Mini Oreo bite size cookies appeared in grocery and convenience stores across the United States.

RV Historian David Woodworth with 2001 Winnebago Journey DL and 1931Mae West HouseCar.

vith a Winnebago Minnie 31C featured on both the ront and back of the package. The 2001 Minnie was he Grand Prize for the motorsports theme promotion.

Also in fiscal 2001, the Nevada Commission on ourism launched a campaign that will award up to five Vinnebago Industries motor homes as grand prizes hroughout the duration of the sweepstakes to the year 003. The $1 million campaign also prominently feaures a 2001 Adventurer in the promotional material.

This continued exposure in the media is a compettive advantage that is immeasurable in terms of coninued brand recognition.

ales and Service Support Advantages

Further competitive advantage is realized by Vinnebago Industries' comprehensive sales and servce support for our dealers and retail customers. The Company believes that providing quality product and ervice support to our dealers through hands-on training and support materials, such as our on-line WIN NET information system, will ensure that our retail cusomers are more satisfied; thus promoting long-term growth and profitability.

Winnebago Industries started its new "Peak Performer" product knowledge program in fiscal 2000 to encourage dealer sales staff to continue to build on their product knowledge. An additional "Best Product Knowledge" award program linked to this training program was started in fiscal 2001. The Best Product Knowledge awards honor the salespersons who have the best product knowledge of the features and benefits of the Company's Winnebago, Itasca, Rialta and Ultimate motor homes. From the over one thousand individuals in the Peak Performer program, one sales professional from each of the Company's 15 sales districts achieved the "Best Product Knowledge" status. These individuals were selected by their district sales managers based upon test results, training participation and application of product knowledge in their sales presentations. From the district winners, four ultimate "survivors" were then selected to compete in the final "Survivor" competition at Winnebago Industries' Dealer Days event in August, 2001.

Winnebago Industries also prides itself on providing what it believes to be the highest level of warranty, parts and service programs in the industry and conducts extensive service training. In the past few years, Winnebago Industries has implemented additional industry-leading programs like the 40 percent warranty parts mark up, TripSaver Emergency Warranty Parts Shipments, and the enhanced WIN NET data entry system.

To ensure that our sales and service programs are effective, we continually monitor our customer's satisfaction levels through surveys. From this data, Winnebago Industries has developed a Customer Satisfaction Index (CSI) that is used to shape our sales and service programs and to reward our most effective dealers. In 1986, Winnebago Industries initiated the first dealer recognition program within the RV industry. This "Circle of Excellence" Award recognized 139 dealers with this top honor for the 2001 model year, including six dealers who have achieved this exclusive status each year since the program was initiated 15 years ago, as well as 15 first-time winners.

Discussion of steel cab advantages during dealer product training session.

Winnebago Industries' service department personnel provide technical assistance to owners of the Company's motor homes during the annual WIT Grand National Rally held in Forest City, Iowa.

WIT Advantages

The Winnebago-Itasca Travelers (WIT) Club is very important to Winnebago Industries, particularly as club members have proven themselves to be extremely loyal, repeat buyers of the Company's products. The WIT Club enables the Company to stay connected with our motor home owners and provides added benefits to our owners as well. Caravans, rallies and tours held frequently throughout the year provide WIT Club members with a way to use their motor homes, remain active and keep in touch with their club-member friends. Winnebago Industries encourages its dealers to actively participate in local chapters by offering complimentary memberships to new purchasers and to host "Show & Tell" events on the dealership lots. The WIT Club also provides member benefits such as a monthly magazine, professional trip routing, purchasing and service discounts, mail forwarding and various types of insurance.

Quality Advantages

Quality is also a competitive advantage for Winnebago Industries. The Company was pleased to again receive the Quality Circle Award from the Recreation Vehicle Dealers' Association (RVDA). Quality Circle status is the result of outstanding ratings on the RVDA's annual Dealer Satisfaction Index survey. Winnebago Industries was one of the two motor home manufacturers and the only company among th six largest motor home manufacturers to receive th Quality Circle Award. Winnebago Industries was als the only major motor home manufacturer to have wo this award each year since it was instituted six year ago.

Quality Circle Award

Winnebago Industries Chairman, CEO and Presiden Bruce Hertzke (second from right) and Winnebago Industries Vice President of Sales and Marketing Jim Jaskoviak (right) proudly accept the Quality Circle Award from RVDA President Mike Molino (left) and former RVDA Chairman of the Board Ernie Frieser (second from left) at the Company's display during the 2000 National RV Trade Show in Louisville, KY.

Additional programs continue to be a tremendous benefit to Winnebago Industries and the quality of our products as well. The Cost Savings Suggestion Program rewards employees for suggesting improvements to the Company's motor homes or internal processes that result in cost and/or time savings. Also, Action Teams have been developed to maximize efficiencies in our manufacturing system. The continued implementation of new technology is also allowing Winnebago Industries to continually improve quality, while increasing its production capacities.

Technology Advantages

Winnebago Industries believes that it is the most technologically advanced RV manufacturer in the industry and remains on the cutting edge in terms of computerized equipment at all of its facilities. An addional $9.1 million was spent on capital expenditures n fiscal 2001 to upgrade manufacturing equipment and xpand manufacturing capabilities in order to increase roductivity and improve the quality of Winnebago ndustries products. The new manufacturing technology installed in fiscal 2001 includes:

Slideout room lowered for installation from new mezzanine.

• A new mezzanine was constructed over the assembly lines at the end of our main motor home manufacturing facility in order to expand the manufacturing capacity of slideout rooms.

• A new material handling system was installed in Winnebago Industries' main motor home manufacturing facility in order to facilitate the transfer of components by conveyer to drop points on each assembly line.

• A welding robot was installed for the welding of components for parts assemblies.

Welding Robot

• A windshield manipulator was installed to assist with windshield placement.

• A fourth laser cutting system was installed in the Company's Metal Stamping Division.

• A new CNC router was installed in the Company's Charles City Hardwoods Division.

• The Plastics Division installed their first CNC router to route several different sizes, shapes and types of plastic components. (Winnebago Industries now has a total of 14 CNC routers and mills throughout the corporation.)

Compartment door production in Hampton facility.

• A compartment door manufacturing cell was added to the Company's Hampton facility, now building approximately 80 percent of the Company's compartment doors.

• A new heat plenum roll former was installed to form aluminum heat runs for the Company's motor homes.

• A new low pressure RTM (resin transfer molding) device was installed in the Company's Hampton facility. This new device allows Winnebago Industries to manufacture fiberglass in a closed mold environment for improved surface quality and material thickness, as well as lower air emissions.

• The ceramic floor installation area was expanded, enabling Winnebago Industries' capacity for installation in the Company's most luxurious motor homes to increase from two to 10 motor homes per day.

• The sidewall laser projection system was replaced in the Company's main motor home complex. This system is used for placement of steel within the motor homes' sidewalls to enable secure installation of cabinets and appliances.

Winnebago Industries' employees have worked extremely hard to successfully develop the Company's many competitive advantages. With the country's positive demographics trends and in spite of the current economic slowdown, Winnebago Industries believes it has the competitive advantages necessary to deliver the best results for its shareholders and continue to lead the RV industry as the industry faces demographic growth for the next 30 years.

Motor Home Product Classification

Class A Motor Homes

These are conventional motor homes constructed directly on medium-duty truc chassis which include the engine and drivetrain components. The living area an the driver's compartment are designed and produced by Winnebago Industrie Class A motor homes from Winnebago Industries include: Winnebago Sightsee Brave, Adventurer, Chieftain, Journey and Journey DL; Itasca Sunova, Sunris Suncruiser, Sunflyer and Horizon; and Ultimate Advantage and Ultimat Freedom.

Class B Van Campers

These are panel-type trucks to which sleeping, kitchen, and/or toilet facilities ar added. These models also have a top extension to provide more headroom Winnebago Industries converts the EuroVan Camper, which is distributed b Volkswagen of America and Volkswagen of Canada.

Class C Motor Homes (Mini)

These are mini motor homes built on a van-type chassis onto which manufac turers construct a living area with access to the driver's compartment. Class C motor homes from Winnebago Industries include: Winnebago Vista, Minnie an Minnie Winnie; Itasca Sunstar, Spirit and Sundancer; and Rialta.

WINNEBAGO INDUSTRIES

Motor Home Family Tree

Winnebago Industries manufactures four brands of Class A and C motor homes. Listed below are the brand names and model designations of the Company's 2002 product line.

WINNEBAGO

- Vista
- Minnie
- Minnie Winnie
- Sightseer
- Brave
- Adventurer
- Chieftain
- Journey/Journey DL

ITASCA

- Sunstar
- Spirit
- Sundancer
- Sunova
- Sunrise
- Suncruiser
- Sunflyer
- Horizon

Rialta

- Rialta

ULTIMATE

- Ultimate Advantage
- Ultimate Freedom

Management's Discussion and Analysis of Financial Condition and Results of Operations

FORWARD LOOKING INFORMATION

Certain of the matters discussed in this Annual Report are "forward looking statements" as defined in the Private Securities Litigation Reform Act of 1995, which involve risks and uncertainties, including, but not limited to, reactions to actual or threatened terrorist attacks, availability and price of fuel, a significant increase in interest rates, a further slowdown in the economy, availability of chassis, slower than anticipated sales of new or existing products, new product introductions by competitors, collections of dealer receivables and other factors which may be disclosed throughout this Annual Report. Any forecasts and projections in this report are "forward looking statements," and are based on management's current expectations of the Company's near-term results, based on current information available pertaining to the Company, including the aforementioned risk factors; actual results could differ materially.

GENERAL

The primary use of recreation vehicles (RVs) for leisure travel and outdoor recreation has historically led to a peak retail selling season concentrated in the spring and summer months. The Company's sales of RVs are generally influenced by this pattern in retail sales, but can also be affected by the level of dealer inventory. The Company's products are generally manufactured against orders from the Company's dealers and from time to time to build inventory to satisfy the peak selling season.

RESULTS OF OPERATIONS

Fiscal 2001 Compared to Fiscal 2000

Net revenues for recreation vehicles and other manufactured products were $677,593,000 for fiscal 2001, a decrease of $71,881,000, or 9.6 percent, from fiscal 2000. Motor home shipments (Class A and C) during fiscal 2001 were 9,076 units, a decrease of 1,440 units, or 13.7 percent, compared to fiscal 2000. The percentage decrease in net revenues was less than the percentage decrease in motor home unit sales because the Company's fiscal 2001 sales, as a percentage of total units sales, contained relatively more higher-priced units with slideout features as well as diesel powered Class A vehicles. The Company's net revenues during fiscal 2001 continued to reflect the decline in consumer confidence levels and a slowdown in the economy. The Company's performance within the RV industry in fiscal 2001 is a result of the excellent acceptance of its new products, solid performance of its dealer partners, brand recognition and strong quality reputation.

Net revenues for dealer financing at Winnebago Acceptance Corporation (WAC) were $4,241,000 for fiscal 2001, an increase of $333,000 or 8.5 percent from fiscal 2000. Increased revenues for dealer financing reflect an increase in dealer receivable balances and to a lesser extent, an increase in interest rates charged when comparing fiscal 2001 to fiscal 2000.

Cost of manufactured products, as a percent of manufactured product revenues, was 86.7 percent for fiscal 2001, compared to 85.5 percent for fiscal 2000. The Company's lower volume of production and sales of motor homes contributed to the reduced margins for fiscal 2001.

Selling expenses increased by $305,000 to $25,423,000 comparing fiscal 2001 to fiscal 2000 and increased as a percentage of net revenues to 3.7 percent from 3.3 percent. The increases in dollars and percentage can be attributed primarily to increases in the Company's promotional programs. Decreased sales volume, during fiscal 2001 also contributed to the increase in percentage.

General and administrative expenses decreased by $3,515,000 to $13,607,000 and to 2.0 percent of net revenues from 2.3 percent when comparing fiscal 2001 to fiscal 2000. Lower payments for employee incentive programs and reduced product liability costs were the primary reasons for the decreases in both dollars and percentages.

For fiscal 2001, the Company had net financial income of $3,754,000 compared to net financial income of $3,338,000 during fiscal 2000. During 2001, the Company recorded $3,731,000 of net interest and dividend income and gains of $23,000 in foreign currency transactions. During fiscal 2000, the Company recorded $3,280,000 of net interest and dividend income and gains of $58,000 in foreign currency transactions. The increase in interest and dividend income when comparing the two periods was due primarily to larger cash balances available for investing during fiscal 2001.

The effective income tax rate decreased from 34.6 percent in fiscal 2000 to 26.1 percent in fiscal 2001. The primary reason for the decrease was due to the Company realizing certain tax benefits during fiscal 2001 which had not been recorded previously due to the uncertainty of realization.

For fiscal 2001, the Company had income before cumulative effect of a change in accounting principle (Staff Accounting Bulletin [SAB] No. 101) of $43,754,000, or $2.08 per diluted share. The comparable results for fiscal 2000 was net income of $48,399,000, or $2.20 per diluted share.

The Company adopted SAB No. 101 at the beginning of fiscal 2001. SAB No. 101 which was issued by the Securities and Exchange Commission (SEC) in December 1999 sets forth the views of the SEC concerning revenue recognition. As a result of SAB No. 101, the Company began recording revenue upon the dealers' receipt of products rather than upon shipment by the Company. Adoption of SAB No. 101 during fiscal 2001 resulted in a decrease in the Company's net income of $1,050,000, or $.05 per diluted share.

For fiscal 2001, the Company had net income of $42,704,000, or $2.03 per diluted share compared to fiscal 2000's net income of $48,399,000, or $2.20 per diluted share.

Fiscal 2000 Compared to Fiscal 1999

Net revenues for manufactured products were $749,474,000 for fiscal 2000, an increase of $75,458,000, or 11.2 percent, from fiscal 1999. Motor home shipments (Class A and C) during fiscal 2000 were 10,516 units, an increase of 240 units, or 2.3 percent, compared to fiscal 1999. Increased revenues reflected the Company's efforts to provide the market with more higher-priced units with slideout features as

well as diesel-powered Class A vehicles.

Net revenues for dealer financing at WAC were $3,908,000 for fiscal 2000, an increase of $913,000 or 30.5 percent from fiscal 1999. Increased revenues for dealer financing reflected an increase in dealer receivable balances and to a lesser extent, an increase in interest rates charged when comparing fiscal 2000 to fiscal 1999.

Cost of manufactured products, as a percent of manufactured product revenues, was 85.5 percent for fiscal 2000, compared to 85.3 percent for fiscal 1999. Increases in the Company's discount programs during fiscal 2000 contributed to the reduced margins.

Selling expenses increased by $797,000 to $25,118,000 comparing fiscal 2000 to fiscal 1999 but decreased as a percentage of net revenues to 3.3 percent from 3.6 percent. The increase in dollars can be attributed primarily to increases in advertising costs and in the Company's promotional programs. Increased sales volume, during fiscal 2000 contributed to the decrease in percentage.

General and administrative expenses increased by $3,017,000 to $17,122,000 and to 2.3 percent of net revenues from 2.1 percent when comparing fiscal 2000 to fiscal 1999. Increases in insurance and legal costs during fiscal 2000 were the primary reasons for the increases in both dollars and percentages. A portion of the increase between the two periods was the result of expenses for fiscal 1999 being reduced due to monies the Company received and recorded on a previously fully reserved receivable.

For fiscal 2000, the Company had net financial income of $3,338,000 compared to net financial income of $2,627,000 during fiscal 1999. During fiscal 2000, the Company recorded $3,280,000 of net interest and dividend income and gains of $58,000 in foreign currency transactions. During fiscal 1999, the Company recorded $2,615,000 of net interest and dividend income and gains of $12,000 in foreign currency transactions. The increase in interest and dividend income when comparing the two periods was due primarily to higher rates of returns earned on available invested cash and larger cash balances during fiscal 2000.

The effective income tax rate increased from 33.6 percent in fiscal 1999 to 34.6 percent in fiscal 2000. The primary reason for the increase was due to increased state income taxes.

For fiscal 2000, the Company had net income of $48,399,000, or $2.20 per diluted share, compared to fiscal 1999's net income of $44,260,000, or $1.96 per diluted share.

ANALYSIS OF FINANCIAL CONDITION, LIQUIDITY AND RESOURCES

The Company generally meets its working capital, capital equipment and cash requirements with funds generated from operations.

At August 25, 2001, working capital was $174,248,000, an increase of $30,974,000 from the amount at August 26, 2000. Cash provided by operations was $73,411,000, $51,412,000 and $25,004,000 during fiscal years ended August 25, 2001, August 26, 2000 and August 28, 1999, respectively. Operating cash flows were provided in fiscal 2001 primarily by income generated from operations as well as a decrease in working capital components. Cash flows used by investing activities were $19,717,000, $25,255,000 and

$20,185,000 in fiscal 2001, 2000 and 1999, respectively. Cash flows used by investing activities primarily include increases in dealer receivables and investments in capital expenditures. Capital expenditures were $9,089,000 in fiscal 2001, $14,548,000 in fiscal 2000 and $11,577,000 in fiscal 1999. Net cash used by financing activities was $11,358,000 in fiscal 2001, $22,874,000 in fiscal 2000 and $11,399,000 in fiscal 1999. Cash used by financing activities in fiscal 2001, 2000 and 1999 was primarily to repurchase shares of the Company's common stock at a cost of $10,686,000, $19,726,000 and $8,975,000, respectively. (See Consolidated Statements of Cash Flows.)

The Company's sources of liquidity consisted principally of cash and cash equivalents in the amount of $93,779,000 at August 25, 2001 compared to $51,443,000 at August 26, 2000.

On October 19, 2000, the Company entered into an unsecured Credit Agreement with Wells Fargo Bank Iowa, National Association. The Credit Agreement provides the Company with a line of credit of $20,000,000 until January 31, 2002. The Company did not borrow under the line of credit with Wells Fargo Bank during fiscal 2001. (See Note 4 to the Company's 2001 Consolidated Financial Statements).

Principal expected demands at August 25, 2001 on the Company's liquid assets for fiscal 2002 include capital expenditures of approximately $14,800,000 and payments of cash dividends. On March 14, 2001, the Board of Directors authorized the repurchase of outstanding shares of the Company's common stock, depending on market conditions, for an aggregate purchase price of up to $15,000,000. As of October 3, 2001, 218,000 shares had been repurchased for an aggregate consideration of approximately $4,491,000 under this authorization.

Management currently expects its cash on hand and funds from operations to be sufficient to cover both short-term and long-term operating requirements.

NEW ACCOUNTING STANDARDS

On August 27, 2000, the Company adopted Statement of Financial Accounting Standard (SFAS) No. 133, "Accounting for Derivative Instruments and Hedging Activities," as amended by SFAS No. 138, "Accounting for Certain Derivative Instruments and Certain Hedging Activities." SFAS No. 133 establishes accounting and reporting standards for derivative instruments and for hedging activities. It requires that all derivatives, including those embedded in other contracts, be recognized as either assets or liabilities and that those financial instruments be measured at fair value. The accounting for changes in the fair value of derivatives depends on their intended use and designation.

All contracts that contain provisions meeting the definition of a derivative also meet the requirements of, and have been designated as, normal purchases or sales. The Company's policy is not to enter into contracts with terms that cannot be designated as normal purchases or sales. The adoption of SFAS No. 133 on August 27, 2000, resulted in no transition adjustment.

On August 27, 2000, the Company adopted the SEC's SAB No. 101, "Revenue Recognition in Financial Statements," which the SEC staff issued in December 1999. SAB No. 101 sets forth the SEC's

views concerning revenue recognition. As a result of SAB No. 101 the Company began recording revenue upon receipt of products by Winnebago Industries dealers rather than upon shipment by the Company. This change in revenue recognition required a non-cash charge to income in the Company's first quarter 2001 results, which reflects the cumulative effect of the prior year's results due to the application of SAB No. 101.

IMPACT OF INFLATION

Historically, the impact of inflation on the Company's operations has not been significantly detrimental, as the Company has usually been able to adjust its prices to reflect the inflationary impact on the cost of manufacturing its products. The inability of the Company to successfully offset increases in manufacturing costs could have a material adverse effect on the Company's results of operations.

COMPANY OUTLOOK

Due to the September 11 tragedy and the current economic environment, the Company is cautious about the next few quarters. Long-term, demographics are in the Company's favor as its target market of consumers age 50 and older is expected to increase for the next 30 years. Order backlog for the Company's Class A and Class C motor homes was approximately 1,600 orders at August 25, 2001, approximately 1,300 orders at August 26, 2000 and approximately 2,700 orders at August 28, 1999. The Company includes in its backlog all accepted purchase orders from dealers shippable within the next six months. Orders in backlog can be canceled or postponed at the option of the purchaser at any time without penalty and, therefore, backlog may not necessarily be a measure of future sales.

Consolidated Balance Sheets

(dollars in thousands)	August 25, 2001	August 26, 2000
Assets		
Current assets:		
Cash and cash equivalents	$ 93,779	$ 51,443
Receivables, less allowance for doubtful accounts ($244 and $1,168, respectively)	20,183	32,045
Dealer financing receivables, less allowance for doubtful accounts ($117 and $27, respectively)	40,263	32,696
Inventories	79,815	85,707
Prepaid expenses	3,604	3,952
Deferred income taxes	6,723	7,675
Total current assets	244,367	213,518
Property and equipment, at cost:		
Land	1,029	1,138
Buildings	45,992	45,219
Machinery and equipment	82,182	78,099
Transportation equipment	5,482	5,414
	134,685	129,870
Less accumulated depreciation	88,149	84,415
Total property and equipment, net	46,536	45,455
Investment in life insurance	22,223	21,028
Deferred income taxes	21,495	19,044
Other assets	7,412	8,050
Total assets	$ 342,033	$ 307,095

See notes to consolidated financial statements.

(dollars in thousands)	August 25, 2001	August 26, 2000
Liabilities and Stockholders' Equity		
Current liabilities:		
Accounts payable, trade	$ 30,789	$ 26,212
Income taxes payable	4,938	8,790
Accrued expenses:		
Accrued compensation	13,730	13,924
Product warranties	8,072	8,114
Insurance	4,567	5,384
Promotional	3,181	3,145
Other	4,842	4,675
Total current liabilities	70,119	70,244
Postretirement health care and deferred compensation benefits	64,450	61,942
Contingent liabilities and commitments		
Stockholders' equity:		
Capital stock common, par value $.50; authorized 60,000,000 shares, issued 25,886,000 and 25,878,000 shares, respectively	12,943	12,939
Additional paid-in capital	22,261	21,994
Reinvested earnings	234,139	195,556
	269,343	230,489
Less treasury stock, at cost	61,879	55,580
Total stockholders' equity	207,464	174,909
Total liabilities and stockholders' equity	$ 342,033	$
307,095		

Consolidated Statements of Income

(in thousands, except per share data)	August 25, 2001	Year Ended August 26, 2000	August 28, 1999
Revenues:			
Manufactured products	$ 677,593	$ 749,474	$ 674,016
Dealer financing	4,241	3,908	2,995
Total net revenues	681,834	753,382	677,011
Costs and expenses:			
Cost of manufactured products	587,330	640,488	574,603
Selling	25,423	25,118	24,321
General and administrative	13,607	17,122	14,105
Total costs and expenses	626,360	682,728	613,029
Operating income	55,474	70,654	63,982
Financial income	3,754	3,338	2,627
Income before income taxes	59,228	73,992	66,609
Provision for taxes	15,474	25,593	22,349
Income before cumulative effect of change in accounting principle	43,754	48,399	44,260
Cumulative effect of change in accounting principle, net of taxes	(1,050)	- - -	- - -
Net income	$ 42,704	$ 48,399	$ 44,260
Earnings per common share (basic):			
Income before cumulative effect of change in accounting principle	$ 2.11	$ 2.23	$ 1.99
Cumulative effect of change in accounting principle	(.05)	- - -	- - -
Income per share (basic)	$ 2.06	$ 2.23	$ 1.99
Earnings per common share (diluted):			
Income before cumulative effect of change in accounting principle	$ 2.08	$ 2.20	$ 1.96
Cumulative effect of change in accounting principle	(.05)	- - -	- - -
Income per share (diluted)	$ 2.03	$ 2.20	$ 1.96
Weighted average shares of common stock outstanding:			
Basic	20,735	21,680	22,209
Diluted	21,040	22,011	22,537

See notes to consolidated financial statements

Consolidated Statements of Cash Flows

(in thousands)	August 25, 2001	Year Ended August 26, 2000	August 28, 1999
Cash flows from operating activities			
Net income	$ 42,704	$ 48,399	$ 44,260
Adjustments to reconcile net income to net cash from operating activities:			
Depreciation and amortization	7,380	6,622	5,748
Loss on disposal of property, leases and other assets	325	350	82
Provision (credit) for doubtful receivables	34	203	(1,049)
Tax benefit of stock options	1,209	- - -	- - -
Change in assets and liabilities:			
Decrease (increase) in receivables and other assets	12,344	702	(11,740)
Decrease (increase) in inventories	5,892	1,324	(31,598)
Increase (decrease) in accounts payable and accrued expenses	3,727	(8,306)	19,781
(Decrease) increase in income taxes payable	(3,852)	180	(2,422)
Increase in deferred income taxes	(1,499)	(2,674)	(2,659)
Increase in postretirement benefit	5,147	4,612	4,601
Net cash provided by operating activities	73,411	51,412	25,004
Cash flows from investing activities:			
Purchases of property and equipment	(9,089)	(14,548)	(11,577)
Proceeds from sale of property and equipment	338	531	355
Investments in dealer receivables	(114,907)	(103,125)	(91,386)
Collections of dealer receivables	107,261	95,061	79,611
Investments in other assets	(3,320)	(3,724)	(2,962)
Proceeds from other assets	- - -	550	5,774
Net cash used by investing activities	(19,717)	(25,255)	(20,185)
Cash flows from financing activities and capital transactions:			
Payments for purchase of common stock	(10,686)	(19,726)	(8,975)
Payments of cash dividends	(4,121)	(4,324)	(4,443)
Proceeds from issuance of common and treasury stock	3,449	1,176	2,019
Net cash used by financing activities and capital transactions	(11,358)	(22,874)	(11,399)
Net increase (decrease) in cash and cash equivalents	42,336	3,283	(6,580)
Cash and cash equivalents at beginning of year	51,443	48,160	54,740
Cash and cash equivalents at end of year	$ 93,779	$ 51,443	$ 48,160

See notes to consolidated financial statements.

Consolidated Statements of Changes in Stockholders' Equity

(amounts in thousands except per share data)	Common Shares Number	Common Shares Amount	Additional Paid-In Capital	Reinvested Income	Treasury Stock Number	Treasury Stock Amount
Balance, August 29, 1998	25,865	$ 12,932	$ 22,507	$ 111,665	3,052	$ 30,581
Proceeds from the sale of common stock to employees	9	5	(600)	---	(254)	(2,614)
Payments for purchase of common stock	---	---	---	---	777	8,975
Cash dividends on common stock - $.20 per share	---	---	---	(4,443)	---	---
Net income	---	---	---	44,260	---	---
Balance, August 28, 1999	25,874	12,937	21,907	151,482	3,575	36,942
Proceeds from the sale of common stock to employees	4	2	87	---	(98)	(1,088)
Payments for purchase of common stock	---	---	---	---	1,127	19,726
Cash dividends on common stock - $.20 per share	---	---	---	(4,325)	---	---
Net income	---	---	---	48,399	---	---
Balance, August 26, 2000	25,878	12,939	21,994	195,556	4,604	55,580
Proceeds from the sale of common stock to employees	8	4	267	- - -	(364)	(4,387)
Payments for purchase of common stock	- - -	- - -	- - -	- - -	883	10,686
Cash dividends on common stock - $.20 per share	- - -	- - -	- - -	(4,121)	- - -	- - -
Net income	- - -	- - -	- - -	42,704	- - -	- - -
Balance, August 25, 2001	25,886	$12,943	$22,261	$234,139	5,123	$61,879

See notes to consolidated financial statements.

Notes to Consolidated Financial Statements

Note 1: Nature of Business and Significant Accounting Policies

The Company's operations are conducted predominantly in two industry segments: the manufacture and sale of recreation vehicles and other manufactured products, and floor plan financing for selected Winnebago, Itasca, Rialta, and Ultimate dealers. The recreation vehicle market is highly competitive, both as to price and quality of the product. The Company believes its principal marketing advantages are its brand name recognition, the quality of its products, its dealer organization, its warranty and service capability and its marketing techniques. The Company also believes that its prices are competitive with the competitions' units of comparable size and quality.

Principles of Consolidation. The consolidated financial statements include the parent company and subsidiary companies. All material intercompany balances and transactions with subsidiaries have been eliminated.

Statements of Cash Flows. For purposes of these statements, cash equivalents primarily consisted of commercial paper, tax exempt money market preferreds and variable rate auction preferred stock with an original maturity of three months or less. For cash equivalents, the carrying amount is a reasonable estimate of fair value.

Fiscal Period. The Company follows a 52/53 week fiscal year period. The financial statements presented are all 52 week periods.

Revenue Recognition. The Company adopted SAB 101, "Revenue Recognition," as of the beginning of fiscal 2001. This new accounting principle requires the Company to recognize revenue upon delivery of products to the dealer, which is when title passes, instead of when shipped by the Company. Interest income from dealer floor plan receivables is recorded on the accrual basis in accordance with the terms of the loan agreements.

Shipping Revenues and Expenses. Shipping revenues for products shipped are included within sales, while shipping expenses are included within cost of goods sold, in accordance with Emerging Issues Task Force No. 00-10, Accounting for Shipping and Handling Fees and Costs (EITF 00-10). Shipping revenue and expense was previously reported as a net amount within selling expenses. Prior period revenues and expenses have been reclassified to revenues and cost of goods sold, which had no effect on previously reported net income.

Inventories. Inventories are valued at the lower of cost or market, with cost being determined by using the last-in, first-out (LIFO) method and market defined as net realizable value.

Property and Equipment. Depreciation of property and equipment is computed using the straight-line method on the cost of the assets, less allowance for salvage value where appropriate, at rates based upon their estimated service lives as follows:

Asset Class	Asset Life
Buildings	10-30 yrs.
Machinery and Equipment	3-10 yrs.
Transportation Equipment	3-6 yrs.

Management periodically reviews the carrying values of long-lived assets for impairment whenever events or

changes in circumstances indicate that the carrying value may not be recoverable. In performing the review for recoverability, management estimates the nondiscounted future cash flows expected to result from the use of the asset and its eventual disposition.

Provision for Warranty Claims. Estimated warranty costs are provided at the time of sale of the warranted products. Estimates of future warranty costs are based on prior experience and known current events.

Income Taxes. The Company accounts for income taxes under SFAS No. 109, "Accounting for Income Taxes." This Statement requires recognition of deferred assets and liabilities for the expected future tax consequences of events that have been included in the financial statements or tax returns. Under this method, deferred tax assets and liabilities are determined based on the differences between the financial statement and tax basis of assets and liabilities using enacted tax rates in effect for the years in which the differences are expected to reverse.

Derivative Instruments and Hedging Activities. All contracts that contain provisions meeting the definition of a derivative also meet the requirements of, and have been designated as, normal purchases or sales. The Company's policy is to not enter into contracts with terms that cannot be designated as normal purchases or sales.

Allowance for Doubtful Accounts. The allowance for doubtful accounts is based on previous loss experience. Additional amounts are provided through charges to income as management believes necessary after evaluation of receivables and current economic conditions. Amounts which are considered to be uncollectible are charged off and recoveries of amounts previously charged off are credited to the allowance upon recovery.

Research and Development. Research and development expenditures are expensed as incurred. Development activities generally relate to creating new products and improving or creating variations of existing products, to meet new applications. During fiscal 2001, 2000 and 1999, the Company spent approximately $2,121,000, $2,293,000 and $1,978,000, respectively, on research and development activities.

Income Per Common Share. Basic income per common share is computed by dividing net income by the weighted average common shares outstanding during the period.

Diluted income per common share is computed by dividing net income by the weighted average common shares outstanding plus the incremental shares that would have been outstanding upon the assumed exercise of dilutive stock options (See Note 13).

Fair Value Disclosures of Financial Instruments. All financial instruments are carried at amounts believed to approximate fair value.

Use of Estimates. The preparation of financial statements in conformity with accounting principles generally accepted in the United States of America requires management to make estimates and assumptions that affect the reported amounts of assets and liabilities and disclosure of contingent assets and liabilities at the date of the financial statements and the reported amounts of revenues and expenses during the reporting period. Actual results could differ from those estimates.

Reclassifications. Certain prior year information has been reclassified to conform to the current year presentation. This reclassification had no affect on net income or stockholders' equity as previously reported.

Note 2: Dealer Financing Receivables
Dealer floor plan receivables are collateralized by recreation vehicles and are due upon the dealer's sale of the vehicle, with the entire balance generally due at the end of one year. At August 25, 2001 and August 26, 2000, the Company had a concentration of credit risks whereby $39,243,000 and $32,565,000, respectively, of dealer financing receivables were due from one dealer.

Note 3: Inventories
Inventories consist of the following:

(dollars in thousands)	August 25, 2001	August 26, 2000
Finished goods	$ 36,930	$ 28,286
Work-in-process	21,725	19,577
Raw materials	44,232	59,674
	102,887	107,537
LIFO reserve	23,072	21,830
	$ 79,815	$ 85,707

The above value of inventories, before reduction for the LIFO reserve, approximates replacement cost at the respective dates.

Note 4: Notes Payable
Short-term lines of credit and related borrowings outstanding at fiscal year-end are as follows:

(dollars in thousands)	August 25, 2001	August 26, 2000
Available Credit Lines	$ 20,000	$ 30,000
Outstanding	- - -	- - -
Interest Rate	4.52%	10.0%

During the first quarter of fiscal 2001, the Company terminated a financing and security agreement with Bank of America Specialty Group (formerly Nations Bank Specialty Lending Unit). On October 19, 2000, the Company entered into an unsecured Credit Agreement with Wells Fargo Bank Iowa, National Association. The Credit Agreement provides the Company with a line of credit of $20,000,000 until January 31, 2002, at an interest rate of either (1) a variable rate per annum of one percent below the Bank's prime rate in effect from time to time or (2) a fixed rate per annum determined by the Bank to be one percent above LIBOR, as selected by the Company in accordance with the Credit Agreement. The Credit Agreement contains covenants that, among other matters, impose certain limitations on mergers, transfers of assets and encumbering or otherwise pledging the Company's assets. In addition, the Company is required to satisfy certain financial covenants and tests relating to tangible net worth, total liabilities and current ratio which the Company was in compliance with at August 25, 2001. There were no outstanding borrowings under the Financing and Security Agreement and/or the Credit Agreement during fiscal 2001 or fiscal 2000.

Note 5: Employee Retirement Plans
The Company has a qualified profit sharing and contributory 401(k) plan for eligible employees. The plan provides for contributions by the Company in such amounts as the Board of Directors may determine. Contributions to the plan in cash for fiscal 2001, 2000 and 1999 were $2,283,000, $2,685,000 and $2,391,000, respectively.

The Company also has a non-qualified deferred compensation program which permits key employees to annually elect (via individual contracts) to defer a portion of their compensation until their retirement. The retirement benefit to be provided is based upon the amount of compensation deferred and the age of the individual at the time of the contracted deferral. An individual generally vests at the later of age 55 and five years of service since the deferral was made. For defer-

rals prior to December 1992, vesting occurs at the later of age 55 and five years of service from first deferral or 20 years of service. Deferred compensation expense was $1,659,000, $1,645,000 and $1,923,000, in fiscal 2001, 2000 and 1999, respectively. Total deferred compensation liabilities were $24,646,000 and $26,192,000 at August 25, 2001 and August 26, 2000, respectively.

To assist in funding the deferred compensation liability, the Company has invested in corporate-owned life insurance policies. The cash surrender value of these policies (net of borrowings of $13,637,000 and $11,640,000 at August 25, 2001 and August 26, 2000, respectively) are presented as assets of the Company in the accompanying balance sheets.

The Company provides certain health care and other benefits for retired employees who have fulfilled eligibility requirements at age 55 with 15 years of continuous service. Retirees are required to pay a monthly premium for medical coverage based on years of service at retirement and then current age. The Company's postretirement health care plan currently is not funded. The status of the plan is as follows:

(dollars in thousands)	**August 25, 2001**	**August 26, 2000**
Change in benefit obligation:		
Benefit obligation, beginning of year	$ 36,925	$ 28,045
Service cost	1,955	1,714
Interest cost	2,750	1,953
Net benefits paid	(587)	(475)
Plan amendment	(1,089)	- - -
Actuarial loss	1,225	5,688
Benefit obligation, end of year	$ 41,179	$ 36,925
Funded status - benefit obligation	$ 41,179	$ 36,925
Unrecognized net actuarial loss	(2,777)	(1,537)
Unrecognized prior service cost	1,402	362
Accrued benefit cost	$ 39,804	$ 35,750

The discount rate used in determining the accumulated postretirement benefit obligation was 7.0 percent at August 25, 2001 and 7.5 percent at August 26, 2000. The average assumed health care cost trend rate used in measuring the accumulated postretirement benefit obligations as of August 25, 2001 was 9.6 percent, decreasing each successive year until it reaches 5.3 percent in 2022 after which it remains constant.

Net postretirement benefit expense for the fiscal years ended August 25, 2001, August 26, 2000 and August 28, 1999 consisted of the following components:

(dollars in thousands)	Aug. 25, 2001	Aug. 26, 2000	Aug. 28, 1999
Components of net periodic benefit cost:			
Service cost	$ 1,955	$ 1,714	$ 1,880
Interest cost	2,750	1,953	1,834
Net amortization and deferral	(65)	(129)	(48)
Net periodic benefit cost	$ 4,640	$ 3,538	$ 3,666

Assumed health care cost trend rates have a significant effect on the amounts reported for the health care plans. A one percentage point change in assumed health care cost trend rates would have the following effects:

(dollars in thousands)	One Percentage Point Increase	One Percentage Point Decrease
Effect on total of service and interest cost components	$ 1,325	$ (979)
Effect on postretirement benefit obligation	$ 10,034	$ (7,576)

Note 6: Contingent Liabilities and Commitments

It is customary practice for companies in the recreation vehicle industry to enter into repurchase agreements with lending institutions which have provided wholesale floor plan financing to dealers. Most dealers are financed on a "floor plan" basis under which a bank or finance company lends the dealer all, or substantially all, of the purchase price, collateralized by a lien upon, or title to, the merchandise purchased. Upon request of a lending institution financing a dealer's purchases of the Company's products, and after completion of a credit investigation of the dealer involved, the Company will execute a repurchase agreement. These agreements provide that, in the event of default by the dealer on the agreement to pay the lending institution, the Company will repurchase the financed merchandise. The agreements provide that the Company's liability will not exceed 100 percent of the dealer invoice and provide for periodic liability reductions based on the time since the date of the original invoice. The Company's contingent obligations under these repurchase agreements are reduced by the proceeds received upon the sale of any repurchased unit. The Company's contingent liability on all repurchase agreements was approximately $216,784,000 and $219,873,000 at August 25, 2001 and August 26, 2000. The Company's losses under repurchase agreements were approximately $197,000, $282,000, and $55,000 during fiscal 2001, 2000 and 1999, respectively.

Included in these contingent liabilities are certain dealer receivables subject to full recourse to the Company with Bank of America Specialty Group (formerly NationsBank Specialty Lending Unit) and Conseco Financing Servicing Group (formerly Green Tree Financial Servicing Corporation). Contingent liabilities under these recourse agreements were $3,276,000 and $6,846,000 at August 25, 2001 and August 26, 2000, respectively. The Company did not incur any actual losses under these recourse agreements during fiscal 2001, 2000 and 1999.

The Company self-insures for a portion of product liability claims. Self-insurance retention liability varies annually based on market conditions and for the past four fiscal years was at $2,500,000 per occurrence and $6,000,000 in aggregate per policy year. Liabilities in excess of these amounts are the responsibility of the insurer.

The Company is involved in various legal proceedings which are ordinary routine litigation incident to its business, many of which are covered in whole or in part

by insurance. While it is impossible to estimate with certainty the ultimate legal and financial liability with respect to this litigation, management is of the opinion that while the final resolution of any such litigation may have an impact on the Company's consolidated results for a particular reporting period, the ultimate disposition of such litigation will not have any material adverse effect on the Company's financial position, results of operations or liquidity.

Note 7: Income Taxes

The components of the provision for income taxes are as follows:

	Year Ended		
(dollars in thousands)	**Aug. 25, 2001**	**Aug. 26, 2000**	**Aug. 28, 1999**
Current:			
Federal	$ 16,448	$ 27,162	$ 24,693
State	524	1,105	315
	$ 16,972	$ 28,267	$ 25,008
Deferred: (Principally federal)	(1,498)	(2,674)	(2,659)
Total provision	$ 15,474	$ 25,593	$ 22,349

The following is a reconciliation of the U.S. statutory tax rate to the effective income tax rates (benefit) provided:

	Year Ended		
	August 25, 2001	**August 26, 2000**	**August 28, 1999**
U.S. federal statutory rate	35.0%	35.0%	35.0%
Cash surrender value	(0.7)	(0.6)	(0.6)
Life insurance premiums	0.1	0.1	0.1
Tax credits	(0.5)	(0.3)	(0.7)
State taxes, net of federal benefit	0.6	0.8	0.5
Foreign sales corporation commissions	(0.2)	(0.2)	(0.2)
Previously unrecorded tax benefits	(7.7)	- - -	- - -
Other	(0.5)	(0.2)	(0.5)
Total	26.1%	34.6%	33.6%

The tax effect of significant items comprising the Company's net deferred tax assets are as follows:

(dollars in thousands)	August 25, 2001 Assets	August 25, 2001 Liabilities	August 25, 2001 Total	August 26, 2000 Total
Current:				
Accrued vacation	$ 1,404	$ - - -	$ 1,404	$ 1,394
Legal reserves	365	- - -	365	498
Warranty reserves	2,825	- - -	2,825	2,840
Bad debt reserves	126	- - -	126	418
Self-insurance reserve	1,598	- - -	1,598	2,055
Miscellaneous reserves	624	(219)	405	470
Subtotal	6,942	(219)	6,723	7,675
Noncurrent:				
Postretirement health care benefits	13,931	- - -	13,931	12,512
Deferred compensation	10,788	- - -	10,788	9,507
Property and equipment	- - -	(3,224)	(3,224)	(2,975)
Subtotal	24,719	(3,224)	21,495	19,044
Total	$ 31,661	$ (3,443)	$ 28,218	$ 26,719

Note 8: Financial Income and Expense

The following is a reconciliation of financial income (expense):

(dollars in thousands)	Year Ended August 25, 2001	Year Ended August 26, 2000	Year Ended August 28, 1999
Interest income from investments and receivables	$ 1,332	$ 1,478	$ 1,085
Dividend income	2,488	2,076	1,621
Interest expense	(89)	(274)	(91)
Gains on foreign currency transactions	23	58	12
	$ 3,754	$ 3,338	$ 2,627

Note 9: Dividend Declared

On October 17, 2001, the Board of Directors declared a cash dividend of $.10 per common share payable January 7, 2002, to shareholders of record on December 7, 2001.

Note 10: Stock Option Plans

The Company's 1987 stock option plan allowed the granting of non-qualified and incentive stock options to key employees at prices not less than 100 percent of fair market value, determined by the mean of the high and low prices, on the date of grant. The plan expired in fiscal 1997; however, exercisable options representing 81,418 shares remain outstanding at August 25, 2001.

The Company's stock option plan for outside directors provided that each director who was not a current or former full-time employee of the Company received an option to purchase 10,000 shares of the Company's common stock at prices equal to 100 percent of the fair market value, determined by the mean of the high and low prices on the date of grant. The Board of Directors has terminated this plan as to future grants. Future grants of options to outside directors will be made under the Company's 1997 stock option plan described as follows.

The Company's 1997 stock option plan provides additional incentives to those officers, employees, directors, advisors and consultants of the Company whose substantial contributions are essential to the continued growth and success of the Company's business. A total of 2,000,000 shares of the Company's common stock may be issued or transferred or used as the basis of stock appreciation rights under the 1997 stock option plan. The plan allows the granting of non-qualified and incentive stock options as well as stock appreciation rights. The plan is administered by a committee appointed by the Company's Board of Directors. The option prices for these shares shall not be less than 85 percent of the fair market value of a share at the time of option granting for non-qualified stock options or less than 100 percent for incentive stock options. The term of each option expires and all rights to purchase shares thereunder cease ten years after the date such option is granted or on such date prior thereto as may be fixed by the Committee. Options granted under this plan become exercisable six months after the date the option is granted unless otherwise set forth in the agreement. Outstanding options granted to employees generally vest in three equal annual installments provided that all options granted under the 1997 stock option plan shall become vested in full and immediately upon the occurrence of a change in control of the Company.

A summary of stock option activity for fiscal 2001, 2000 and 1999 is as follows:

	2001			2000			1999		
	Shares	Price per Share	Wtd. Avg. Exercise Price/Sh	Shares	Price per Share	Wtd. Avg. Exercise Price/Sh	Shares	Price per Share	Wtd. Avg. Exercise Price/Sh
Outstanding at beginning of year	795,514	$4 - $20	$ 10.88	680,176	$4 - $15	$ 8.56	650,695	$4 - $9	$ 7.34
Options granted	312,000	12 - 18	12.83	180,800	19 - 20	18.59	259,250	10 - 15	10.47
Options exercised	(312,944)	4 - 19	8.64	(65,462)	6 - 10	8.15	(227,098)	6 - 10	7.24
Options canceled	(6,402)	9 - 19	13.84	---	---	---	(2,671)	8	7.75
Outstanding at end of year	788,168	$7 - $20	$ 12.51	795,514	$4 - $20	$10.88	680,176	$4 - $15	$8.56
Exercisable at end of year	352,018	$7 - $20	$ 11.33	469,214	$4 - $20	$8.40	309,593	$4 - $15	$7.47

The following table summarizes information about stock options outstanding at August 25, 2001:

Range of Exercise Prices	Number Outstanding at August 25, 2001	Weighted Remaining Contractual Life	Weighted Average Exercise Price	Number Exercisable at August 25, 2001	Weighted Average Exercise Price
$ 7.19 - $ 7.75	49,418	5	$ 7.58	49,418	$ 7.58
8.56 - 9.00	113,336	5	8.65	113,336	8.65
10.19 - 15.38	452,114	8	11.71	116,364	10.99
18.00 - 19.72	173,300	8	18.53	72,900	18.58
	788,168	8	$ 12.51	352,018	$ 11.33

In 1997, the Company adopted SFAS No. 123, "Accounting for Stock Based Compensation." The Company has elected to continue following the accounting guidance of Accounting Principles Board Opinion No. 25, "Accounting for Stock Issued to Employees" for measurement and recognition of stock-based transactions with employees. No compensation cost has been recognized for options issued under the stock option plans because the exercise price of all options granted was not less than 100 percent of fair market value of the common stock on the date of grant. Had compensation cost for the stock options issued been determined based on the fair value at the grant date, consistent with provisions of SFAS No. 123, the Company's 2001, 2000 and 1999 income and income per share would have been changed to the pro forma amounts indicated as follows:

(dollars in thousands, except per share data)	2001	2000	1999
Net income			
As reported	$ 42,704	$ 48,399	$ 44,260
Pro forma	41,006	47,143	43,508
Income per sharc (basic)			
As reported	$ 2.06	$ 2.23	$ 1.99
Pro forma	1.98	2.17	1.96
Income per share (diluted)			
As reported	$ 2.03	$ 2.20	$ 1.96
Pro forma	1.95	2.14	1.93

The fair value of each option grant is estimated on the date of grant using the Black-Scholes option pricing model with the following assumptions:

	2001	2000	1999
Dividend yield	1.13%	1.21%	1.54%
Risk-free interest rate	4.55%	6.92%	6.05%
Expected life	5 years	5 years	7 years
Expected volatility	49.92%	49.64%	44.36%
Estimated fair value of options granted per share	$5.29	$8.30	$5.06

Note 11: Supplemental Cash Flow Disclosure

Cash paid during the year for:

(dollars in thousands)		Year Ended	
	August 25, 2001	August 26, 2000	August 28, 1999
Interest	$ 3	$ 249	$ 96
Income taxes	18,205	28,305	27,430

Note 12: Business Segment Information

The Company defines its operations into two business segments: Recreation Vehicles and Other Manufactured Products and Dealer Financing. Recreation Vehicles and Other Manufactured Products includes all data relative to the manufacturing and selling of the Company's Class A, B and C motor home products as well as sales of component products for other manufacturers and recreation vehicle related parts and service revenue. Dealer Financing includes floorplan financing for a limited number of the Company's dealers. Management focuses on operating income as a segment's measure of profit or loss when evaluating a segment's financial performance. Operating income is before interest expense, interest income, and income taxes. A variety of balance sheet ratios are used by management to measure the business. Maximizing the return from each segment's assets excluding cash and cash equivalents is the primary focus. The accounting policies of the segments are the same as those described in the Summary of Significant Accounting Policies (Note 1). Identifiable assets are those assets used in the operations of each industry segment. General Corporate assets consist of cash and cash equivalents, deferred income taxes and other corporate assets not related to the two business segments. General Corporate income and expenses include administrative costs. Inter-segment sales and expenses are not significant.

For the years ended August 25, 2001, August 26, 2000 and August 28, 1999, the Company's segment information is as follows:

(dollars in thousands)	Recreation Vehicles & Other Manufactured Products	Dealer Financing	General Corporate	Total
2001				
Net revenues	$ 677,593	$ 4,241	$ - - -	$ 681,834
Operating income (loss)	52,120	4,102	(748)	55,474
Identifiable assets	175,343	40,856	125,834	342,033
Depreciation and amortization	7,158	5	217	7,380
Capital expenditures	8,974	19	96	9,089
2000				
Net revenues	$ 749,474	$ 3,908	$ ---	$ 753,382
Operating income (loss)	67,252	3,892	(490)	70,654
Identifiable assets	191,501	33,508	82,086	307,095
Depreciation and amortization	6,375	4	243	6,622
Capital expenditures	14,412	---	136	14,548
1999				
Net revenues	$ 674,016	$ 2,995	$ --	$ 677,011
Operating income (loss)	60,435	4,085	(538)	63,982
Identifiable assets	181,951	25,439	78,499	285,889
Depreciation and amortization	5,507	4	237	5,748
Capital expenditures	11,463	18	96	11,577

Operating income of the dealer financing segment reflects a $1,100,000 repayment of a previously fully reserved receivable.

Note 13: Income Per Share

The following table reflects the calculation of basic and diluted income per share for the past three fiscal years.

(in thousands, except per share data)	August 25, 2001	August 26, 2000	August 28, 1999
Income per share - basic:			
Net income	$ 42,704	$ 48,399	$ 44,260
Weighted average shares outstanding	20,735	21,680	22,209
Net income per share - basic	$ 2.06	$ 2.23	$ 1.99
Income per share - assuming dilution:			
Net income	$ 42,704	$ 48,399	$ 44,260
Weighted average shares outstanding	20,735	21,680	22,209
Dilutive impact of options outstanding	305	331	328
Weighted average shares and potential dilutive shares outstanding	21,040	22,011	22,537
Net income per share - assuming dilution	$ 2.03	$ 2.20	$ 1.96

Note 14: Preferred Stock and Shareholders Rights Plan

The Board of Directors may authorize the issuance from time to time of preferred stock in one or more series with such designations, preferences, qualifications, limitations, restrictions, and optional or other special rights as the Board may fix by resolution. In connection with the Rights Plan discussed below, the Board of Directors has reserved, but not issued, 300,000 shares of preferred stock.

In May 2000, the Company adopted a shareholder rights plan providing for a dividend distribution of one preferred share purchase right for each share of common stock outstanding on and after May 26, 2000. The rights can be exercised only if an individual or group acquires or announces a tender offer for 15 percent or more of the Company's common stock. Certain members of the Hanson family (including trusts and estates established by such Hanson family members and the John K. and Luise V. Hanson Foundation) are exempt from the applicability of the Rights Plan as it relates to the acquisition of 15 percent or more of the Company's outstanding common stock. If the rights first become exercisable as a result of an announced tender offer, each right would entitle the holder (other than the individual or group acquiring or announcing a tender offer for 15 percent or more of the Company's common stock) to buy 1/100th of a share of a new series of preferred stock at an exercise price of $67.25. The preferred shares will be entitled to 100 times the per share dividend payable on the Company's common stock and to 100 votes on all matters submitted to a vote of the shareowners. Once an individual or group acquires 15 percent or more of the Company's common stock, each right held by such individual or group becomes void and the remaining rights will then entitle the holder to purchase the number of common shares having a market value of twice the exercise price of the right. In the event the Company is acquired in a merger or 50 percent or more of its consolidated assets or earnings power are sold, each right will then entitle the holder to purchase a number of the acquiring company's common shares having a market value of twice the exercise price of the right. After an individual or group acquires 15 percent of the Company's common stock and before they acquire 50 percent, the Company's Board of Directors may exchange the rights in whole or in part, at an exchange ratio of one share of common stock per right. Before an individual or group acquires 15 percent of the Company's common stock, the rights are redeemable for $.01 per right at the option of the Company's Board of Directors. The Company's Board of Directors is authorized to reduce the 15 percent threshold to no less than 10 percent. Each right will expire on May 3, 2010, unless earlier redeemed by the Company.

REPORT OF INDEPENDENT AUDITORS

To the Board of Directors and Shareholders
Winnebago Industries, Inc.
Forest City, Iowa

We have audited the consolidated balance sheets of Winnebago Industries, Inc. and subsidiaries (the Company) as of August 25, 2001 and August 26, 2000 and the related consolidated statements of income, cash flows and changes in stockholders' equity for each of the three years in the period ended August 25, 2001. These consolidated financial statements are the responsibility of the Company's management. Our responsibility is to express an opinion on these consolidated financial statements based on our audits.

We conducted our audits in accordance with auditing standards generally accepted in the United States of America. Those standards require that we plan and perform the audit to obtain reasonable assurance about whether the consolidated financial statements are free of material misstatement. An audit includes examining, on a test basis, evidence supporting the amounts and disclosures in the consolidated financial statements. An audit also includes assessing the accounting principles used and significant estimates made by management, as well as evaluating the overall financial statement presentation. We believe that our audits provide a reasonable basis for our opinion.

In our opinion, the consolidated financial statements present fairly, in all material respects, the financial position of the Company as of August 25, 2001 and August 26, 2000, and the results of their operations and their cash flows for each of the three years in the period ended August 25, 2001 in conformity with accounting principles generally accepted in the United States of America.

Deloitte & Touche LLP
Minneapolis, Minnesota

October 3, 2001

Net Revenues By Major Product Class (Unaudited)

(dollars in thousands)	Fiscal Year Ended (1) Aug. 25, 2001	Aug. 26, 2000	Aug. 28, 1999	Aug. 29, 1998	Aug. 30, 1997
Motor homes (Class A & C)	$630,017	$695,767	$619,171	$474,954	$387,161
	92.4%	92.4%	91.5%	89.0%	86.9%
Other recreation vehicle revenues (2)	17,808	18,813	16,620	19,222	21,159
	2.6%	2.5%	2.5%	3.6%	4.7%
Other manufactured products revenues (3)	29,768	34,894	38,225	37,133	35,881
	4.4%	4.6%	5.6%	7.0%	8.1%
Total manufactured products revenues	677,593	749,474	674,016	531,309	444,201
	99.4%	99.5%	99.6%	99.6%	99.7%
Finance revenues (4)	4,241	3,908	2,995	2,076	1,420
	.6%	.5%	.4%	.4%	.3%
Total net revenues	$681,834	$753,382	$677,011	$533,385	$445,621
	100.0%	100.0%	100.0%	100.0%	100.0%

(1) All fiscal years in the table contained 52 weeks.
(2) Primarily recreation vehicle related parts, EuroVan Campers (Class B motor homes), and recreation vehicle service revenue.
(3) Primarily sales of extruded aluminum, commercial vehicles, and component products for other manufacturers.
(4) WAC revenues from dealer financing.

Interim Financial Information (Unaudited)

(dollars in thousands, except per share data)

Fiscal 2001	Quarter Ended November 25, 2000	February 24, 2001	May 26, 2001	August 25, 2001
Net revenues	$164,167	$142,531	$197,005	$178,131
Gross profit	22,483	17,166	27,986	26,869
Operating income	13,380	8,550	18,098	15,446
Net income	8,546	6,184	12,444	15,530
Net income per share (basic)	.40	.30	.61	.75
Net income per share (diluted)	.40	.30	.60	.74

Net revenues for the quarter ended November 25, 2000 reflect the impact of the adoption of SAB 101.

Fiscal 2000 as reported	Quarter Ended November 27, 1999	February 26, 2000	May 27, 2000	August 26, 2000
Net revenues	$184,946	$189,568	$214,070	$164,798
Gross profit	29,149	28,571	34,577	20,597
Operating income	18,060	17,003	23,713	11,878
Net income	12,381	11,851	16,257	7,910
Net income per share (basic)	.56	.54	.76	.37
Net income per share (diluted)	.55	.54	.74	.37

Certain prior periods' information has been reclassified to conform to the current year end presentation. This reclassification has no impact on net income as previously reported.

Fiscal 2000 Pro Forma	Quarter Ended November 27, 1999	February 26, 2000	May 27, 2000	August 26, 2000
Net revenues	$187,096	$183,004	$217,511	$165,239
Net income	12,436	11,216	16,633	8,159
Earnings per share - basic	.56	.52	.77	.38
Earnings per share - diluted	.55	.51	.76	.38

The above pro forma quarterly financial information reflects the impact of the adoption of SAB 101 on August 27, 2000.

Common Stock Data

The Company's common stock is listed on the New York, Chicago and Pacific Stock Exchanges. Ticker symbol: WGO
Shareholders of record as of November 19, 2001 : 5,513
Below are the New York Stock Exchange high, low and closing prices of Winnebago Industries, Inc. stock for each quarter of fiscal 2001 and fiscal 2000.

Fiscal 2001	High	Low	Close	Fiscal 2000	High	Low	Close
First Quarter	$13.63	$10.75	$11.50	First Quarter	$28.25	$15.56	$19.00
Second Quarter	19.00	11.56	17.10	Second Quarter	21.50	18.63	21.38
Third Quarter	19.60	15.60	18.77	Third Quarter	21.75	14.25	14.56
Fourth Quarter	30.75	18.44	28.02	Fourth Quarter	14.69	12.06	12.81

Cash Dividends Per Share

Fiscal 2001 Amount	Date Paid	Fiscal 2000 Amount	Date Paid
$ .10	January 8, 2001	$ .10	January 10, 2000
.10	July 9, 2001	.10	July 10, 2000

Shareholder Information

Publications
A notice of Annual Meeting of Shareholders and Proxy Statement is furnished to shareholders in advance of the annual meeting.

Copies of the Company's quarterly financial news releases and the annual report on Form 10-K (without exhibits), required to be filed by the Company with the Securities and Exchange Commission, may be obtained without charge from the corporate offices as follows:

Investor Relations Department
Winnebago Industries, Inc.
605 W. Crystal Lake Road
P.O. Box 152
Forest City, Iowa 50436-0152
Telephone: (641) 585-3535
Fax: (641) 585-6966
E-Mail: ir@winnebagoind.com

This annual report as well as corporate news releases may also be viewed online in the Investor Relations section of Winnebago Industries website: http://www.winnebagoind.com

Shareholder Account Assistance
Transfer Agent to contact for address changes, account certificates and stock holdings:
Wells Fargo Bank Minnesota, N.A.
P.O. Box 64854
St. Paul, Minnesota 55164-0854
or
161 North Concord Exchange
South St. Paul, Minnesota 55075-1139
Telephone: (800) 468-9716 or (651) 450-4064
E-Mail: stocktransfer@wellsfargo.com

Annual Meeting
The Annual Meeting of Shareholders will be held on Tuesday, January 15, 2002, at 7:30 p.m. (CST) in Friendship Hall, Highway 69 South, Forest City, Iowa.

Auditor
Deloitte & Touche LLP
400 One Financial Plaza
120 South Sixth Street
Minneapolis, Minnesota 55402-1844

Purchase of Common Stock
Winnebago Industries stock may be purchased from Netstock through the Company's website at http://www.winnebagoind.com/ investor_relations.htm. Winnebago Industries is not affiliated with Netstock and has no involvement in the relationship between Netstock and any of its customers.

Directors and Officers

Directors

Bruce D. Hertzke (50)
Chairman of the Board,
Chief Executive Officer
and President
Winnebago Industries, Inc.

Gerald E. Boman (66)
Former Senior Vice President
Winnebago Industries, Inc.

Jerry N. Currie (56)
President and
Chief Executive Officer
CURRIES Company and
GRAHAM Manufacturing

Joseph W. England (61)
Former Senior Vice President
Deere and Company

John V. Hanson (59)
Former Deputy Chairman
of the Board
Winnebago Industries, Inc.

Gerald C. Kitch (63)
Former Executive
Vice President
Pentair, Inc.

Richard C. Scott (67)
Vice President,
University Development
Baylor University

Frederick M. Zimmerman (65)
Professor of Manufacturing Systems
Engineering
The University of St. Thomas

Luise V. Hanson (88)
Director Emeritus

Officers

Bruce D. Hertzke (50)
Chairman of the Board,
Chief Executive Officer
and President

Robert L. Gossett (50)
Vice President, Administration

William J. O'Leary(52)
Vice President, Product Development

Edwin F. Barker (54)
Vice President, Chief Financial
Officer

Brian J. Hrubes (50)
Controller

Robert J. Olson (50)
Vice President, Manufacturing

Raymond M. Beebe (59)
Vice President, General Counsel
and Secretary

James P. Jaskoviak (49)
Vice President, Sales and Marketing

Joseph L. Soczek, Jr. (58)
Treasurer

MONACO COACH CORPORATION

2001 ANNUAL REPORT
NYSE: MNC

The year 2001 was highlighted by MNC's acquisition of industry rival and Oregon neighbor SMC Corporation.

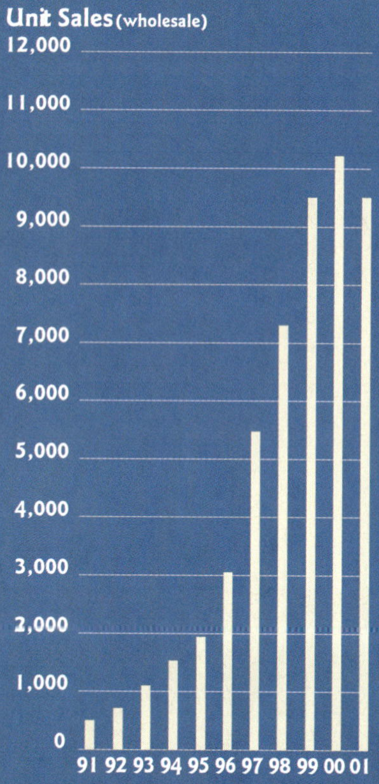

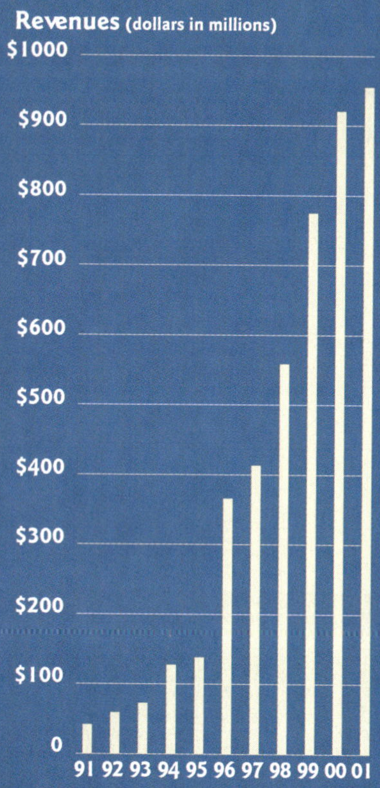

Financial Highlights

Dollars in thousands, except earnings per share and shares outstanding data.

	1999	2000	2001*
Sales	$780,815	$901,890	$937,073
Gross Profit	$122,279	$ 129,650	$113,990
Operating Income	$72,843	$69,830	$42,658
Pretax Income	$71,842	$69,380	$40,635
Net Income	$43,761	$42,521	$24,919
Earnings Per Share	$1.51	$1.47	$0.85
Average Common Shares Outstanding	29,050,454	28,978,265	$29,288,688

* Includes results from Safari and Beaver divisions acquired on August 6, 2001.

Our Foundation

As Monaco Coach Corporation continues to broaden its product line, expand its customer base, add more dealerships and attract new stockholders, the company is committed to maintaining those standards which make the Monaco Difference so important to every member of the MNC "family."

To do this, the company continues to follow our six corporate goals:

To operate the business on the basis of honesty, integrity and superior service.

To produce the highest-quality recreational vehicles at the most competitive prices.

To create and nurture a lifestyle for RV owners that exceeds their dreams.

To offer a working environment in which all employees have the opportunity to realize their personal and professional goals.

To create a bond with our suppliers and retail dealers that ensures our mutual success.

To provide our shareholders with a positive return on their investment.

These are not lofty goals or idealistic statements; rather, a continuation of the basic guidelines and principles which have been an integral part of the company's success.

Maintaining these guidelines and principles throughout the company's current and future growth will enable MNC to retain the outstanding loyalty of its present customers, employees and dealers; and forge an equally strong link with new customers, employees, dealers and stockholders who are now-or soon will be-part of the MNC family.

Monaco Coach Corporation moved into their Coburg, Oregon facility in 1995 and expanded at that location in 1999.

Corporate Profile

Monaco Coach Corporation is the world's leading manufacturer of luxury motorcoaches and one of the most prominent companies in the overall recreational vehicle field.

The corporation's broad product line includes 39 different models of motorcoaches and towables sold under the Monaco, Holiday Rambler, Safari, Beaver, Royale Coach and McKenzie brand names. This highly-diversified line, ranging in price from $20,000 travel trailers to prestigious coaches costing $1,000,000 or more, is represented through an expanding network of independent retail dealerships.

The year 2001 was highlighted by Monaco Coach Corporation's acquisition of industry rival and Oregon neighbor SMC Corporation. This acquisition further broadens the company's product offerings, expands its retail dealer representation and results in manufacturing efficiencies that are an important component of the company's growth strategy.

Headquartered in Coburg, Oregon and traded on the NYSE under the symbol MNC, Monaco Coach Corporation has grown sales revenues from $46 million in 1991 to more than $937 million in 2001. Unit sales have increased from 370 in 1991 to over 9,400 in 2001. The company's growth rate over that period of time is unmatched by any publicly traded company in the recreational vehicle industry.

In the past year, Monaco Coach Corporation increased its share of the Class A diesel market by 39% and became the premier manufacturer in the overall Class A motorhome field.

Total Unit Sales
(wholesale)

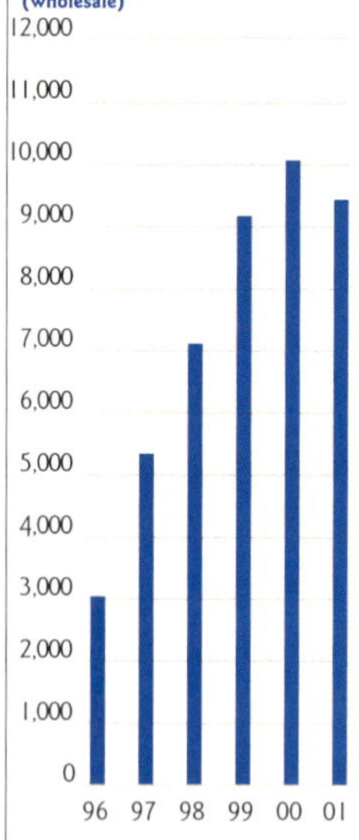

Motorhome Sales
(wholesale)

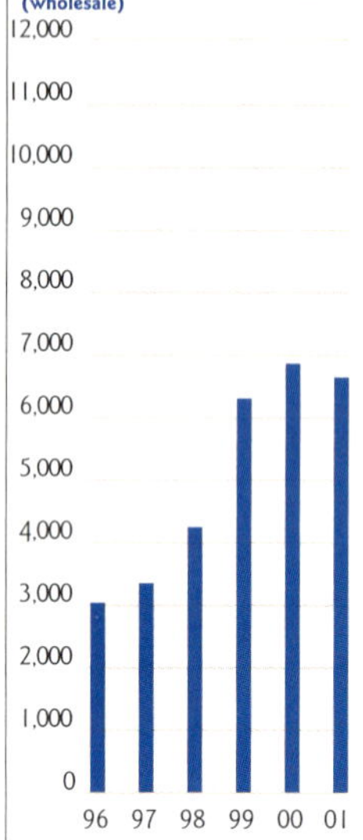

Towable Sales
(wholesale)

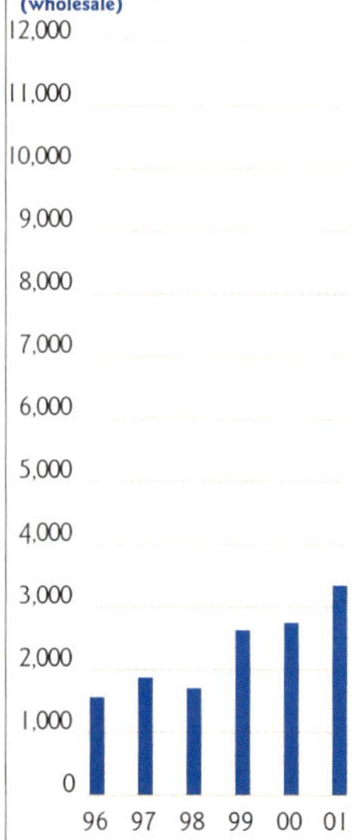

The year 2001 will long live in our memories.

It was a year that was really two years in one; the period before September 11 and the days after. In retrospect, it was a somber year for our country, but an accomplished year for your company.

I am happy to report that we recorded another year of growth in sales revenue, and our market share gains were unmatched in our industry. Our overall revenues reached $937 million with earnings-per-share (adjusted for our 3-for-2 stock split) of 85 cents. At the end of the year, our Class A motorhome market share grew to 20.5%, while our share of the diesel-powered motorhome market rose to 37.1%.

For as long as I can remember, the performance of our industry has been a leading indicator of the overall economy. We typically see the bulls or the bears about six months before the general economy. In fact, we began to see economic challenges developing in early 2000.

As we neared the second half of 2000, higher interest rates impacted our retail dealers' ability to finance their inventory. In order to control these costs, our dealers began shrinking their inventory, which set in motion a chain reaction of wholesale discounts by our competitors.

Since we share dealer lot space with our competition, we responded with price concessions of our own, which reduced our gross margin and increased our sales expenses. However, we approached it differently. Instead of only offering deep discounts to our dealers, we created retail incentive programs, such as our "Free Fuel for a Year," that assisted our dealers in clearing their existing inventory and paved the way for new orders.

Business conditions were tough in the latter half of 2000 and the first half of 2001. But as the year progressed, we began to enjoy the benefits of falling interest rates and rising consumer confidence. Dealers began to restock their depleted inventories. As anticipated, our discounting and concessions to dealers nearly disappeared.

While the events of September 11 dampened our sales and temporarily limited some of our new-found momentum, it wasn't long before retail buyers were back. We began to experience an increase in wholesale activity as 2001 neared an end. The reasons are easy to explain. As the retail customer returned, our dealers' low inventory levels, combined with lower inventory finance rates, put them in an excellent position to order additional units.

"Within weeks following the (SMC) acquisition, we added new Safari and Beaver products targeted at the most attractive price segments within our market."

Looking ahead, our powerful market presence and customer-driven approach to product development will allow us to capitalize on the rebound our industry is experiencing as we enter 2002. We're seeing the strengthening of our market reflected in our order backlog, which has reached near-record levels.

I still can't forget the images of September 11. The pictures are ingrained in our collective memories, much like memories of the JFK assassination. While I don't want to over-dramatize, I'd like to relate a story that happened to six of us in the days following September 11.

Monaco Coach Corporation Chairman and CEO Kay Toolson (right) pictured with VP and CFO Marty Daley (middle) and President John Nepute (left).

As you recall, the skies were closed following the attacks. Several members of management, including me, were working in our Indiana offices, far away from our Oregon homes. For the next few anxious days, rumors kept us waiting for our flight home to be released. Frustration, uncertainty and a strong desire to see our families in Oregon motivated us to take a 2,400 mile joyride in one of our motorhomes. For the next 2 days, we enjoyed every minute and every mile. It seemed like each bridge and overpass we came upon was draped in red, white and blue. Every town between Indiana and Oregon was decorated in support of freedom. We experienced America as it was meant to be and it was a journey that none of us will ever forget.

While much of 2001 was framed by the tragic events of September 11, one of the highlights of our year was our August acquisition of SMC Corporation, manufacturer of the Beaver and Safari brand motorhomes. We were very familiar with SMC, as their headquarters was just a few miles from our corporate home in Coburg, Oregon.

"We're seeing the strengthening of our market reflected in our order backlog, which has reached near-record levels."

Immediately after the acquisition was finalized, we transferred the production of selected SMC motorhomes to our production facility in Coburg, which will allow us to take advantage of higher production run rates and improved efficiencies at that location. Within weeks following the acquisition, we added new Safari and Beaver products targeted at the most attractive price segments within our market. We also identified opportunities to develop additional Safari and Beaver retail distribution points in order to bolster market representation. Although these post-acquisition steps were necessary to improve ongoing manufacturing efficiency and brand positioning, they created understandable challenges for our sales, product development and production teams that resulted in gross margin pressure during the fourth quarter of 2001.

As you read this annual report to shareholders, you'll find detailed information pertaining to the past year's business events, including the market and industry trends that our company experienced and those issues we are addressing as we move forward. We'll also discuss how the new Monaco Coach Corporation, with the addition of SMC, fits into the RV industry and we'll share our outlook and expectations for the coming year. There's no doubt that we're focused on 2002 with optimism and a sound plan to grow our company into an even more powerful force within our industry.

We couldn't do it without our valued shareholders, Board of Directors, vendors and suppliers, retail dealer partners, dedicated employees and especially our great customers. Your support and confidence has been instrumental in our success and will play a significant role in our future. I am proud and blessed to be a part of this wonderful family, and on behalf of everyone associated with Monaco Coach Corporation, I thank you.

Kay L. Toolson, Chairman and CEO
Monaco Coach Corporation

Gross Margin

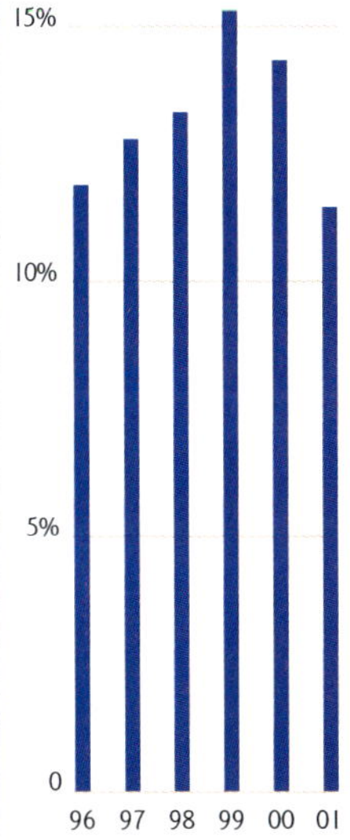

Operating Margin

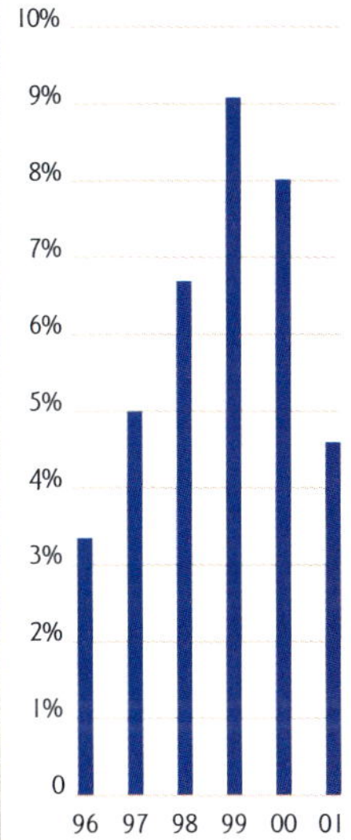

S,G & A
(as a % of Revenue)

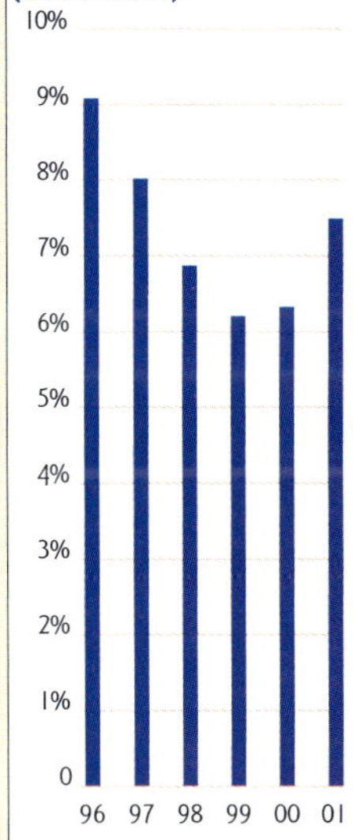

In August 2001, Monaco Coach Corporation's Board of Directors approved a 3 for 2 split of the company's common stock. The split was effected as a stock dividend, and all stockholders of record as of August 20 were issued a certificate representing one additional share for every two shares held.

The stock split increased the number of shares of MNC common stock outstanding from approximately 19 million to 28.5 million.

The stock split was the company's fourth since 1995. According to Monaco Coach Corporation President John Nepute, the purpose of the latest split was to "maintain a high liquidity for the stock and keep it attractive to smaller investors."

Nepute also noted that stock splits have historically been good for MNC shareholders, citing the performance of the stock following the three previous splits.

Nepute added, "The perceived value of MNC stock is strong as more and more investors discover our company's outstanding growth record, our well-established market and our solid manufacturing base."

RV Business Magazine Again Names MNC's Kay Toolson as a "Newsmaker of the Year"

In its January 2002 issue, RV Business magazine selected Monaco Chairman Kay Toolson as a 2001 "Newsmaker of the Year". The selection marked the second time in three years that Mr. Toolson was so honored.

According to RV Business, the award acknowledges individuals for their "sheer impact" on the recreational vehicle industry in 2001.

From RV Business Magazine, January 2002

"If there was a lifetime achievement award for Newsmakers, Monaco Coach Corp.'s Kay Toolson would probably be in the running because he or his company have rarely failed to make the Newsmaker roster over the past few years.

This time, Toolson and the Coburg, Ore.-based company of which he is chairman and CEO made headlines by assuming the No. 1 slot in Class A motorhome sales, the first time anyone new has held that position since the mid-1980s.

Publicly held Monaco had been positioning itself to assume the top Class A slot earlier in the year.

But it was Monaco's acquisition of its competitive Oregon neighbor, SMC Corp.--another event that generated headlines in 2001--that propelled Monaco over the top.

Given past performances and his company's history with acquisitions, it won't be too surprising to see Toolson, a Utah native, making headlines again in 2002.

To assimilate SMC, for instance, Toolson is reportedly using the same formula that made Monaco's buyout of Holiday Rambler so successful several years ago.

That formula basically involves maximizing and reorganizing production space and welcoming the best employees of the acquired firm into the Monaco fold so their talents can be fully utilized and so the transition can be that much more seamless.

The Holiday Rambler acquisition was a defining moment for Monaco because it led the company into the industry's mainstream and proved that Monaco could operate Holiday Rambler successfully and profitably--something Harley-Davidson's management was unable to do in 10 years of ownership. And the SMC buyout may prove to be yet another defining moment."

MNC Stock Splits (3 for 2) and Price per Share: 1997-2001

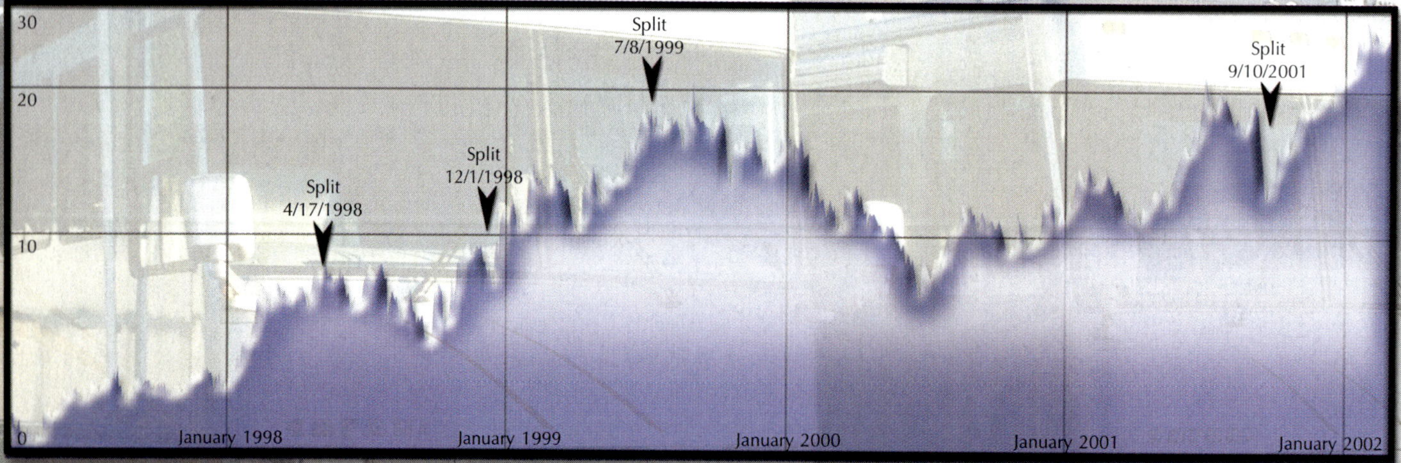

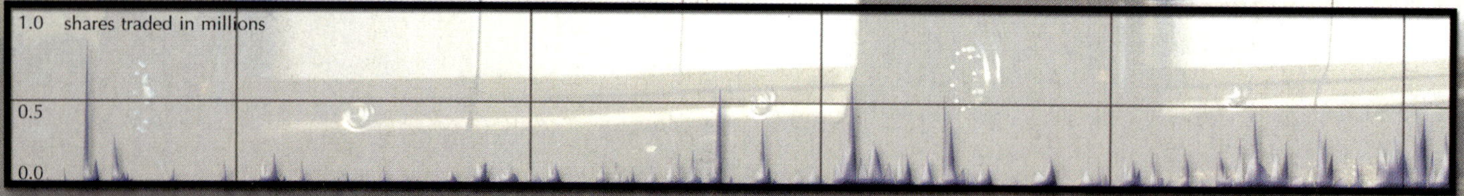

Beaver and Safari Brands Join Lineup

On August 2, 2001, Monaco Coach Corporation acquired SMC Corporation, America's tenth-largest manufacturer of Class A motorhomes, for a total of $36 million in cash and refinanced debt. The acquisition brings SMC's Beaver and Safari brands into the Monaco Coach Corporation family.

Beaver, founded in 1979, is best known for its highline diesel motorhomes and, like Monaco, is one of the companies which helped define the current luxury RV market.

The Safari brand has created a specialized niche in the mid-range Class A market with a line of unique motorhomes positioned as an alternative to more traditional Class A models. Safari's recognizable design and innovative features have attracted a loyal following to the brand.

According to MNC chairman Kay Toolson, the SMC brands are "a perfect fit into both our product lineup and marketing strategy. Like Monaco and Holiday Rambler, Beaver and Safari have a strong brand equity in the Class A market. This will allow us to further diversify our line of quality products with well-established names. And it further reinforces our lead in the diesel Class A market, since about 90% of the current Safari and Beaver products are diesel-powered."

At the time of the acquisition, SMC motorhomes accounted for 3.9% of the Class A market. As a result, Monaco Coach Corporation's overall Class A market share rose to more than 20% after the purchase. The acquisition also brought about 40 additional retail dealers into the MNC dealer network.

In a message to shareholders, MNC Vice President and CFO Marty Daley said, "We believe that this acquisition will result in greater shareholder value in the long run. The acquisition provides our company with an opportunity to further grow market share, expand our strong dealer network and maximize return on our facilities investment."

The SMC purchase is MNC's second major acquisition in the past six years. In 1996, the company purchased Holiday Rambler from Harley-Davidson for approximately $50 million. That acquisition is generally considered the pivotal point in MNC's transformation from a specialty highline builder to an industry force.

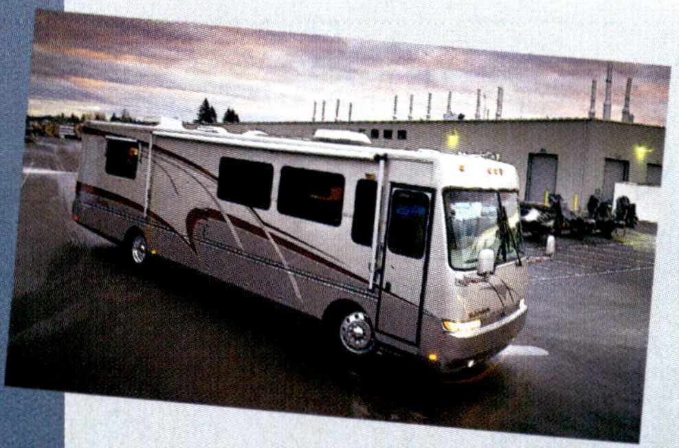

Production of Safari motorhomes is underway at MNC's Coburg, Oregon facility. Safari Zanzibar pictured here.

MNC Introduces New Beaver and Safari Motorhomes.

On November 30, 2001, Monaco Coach Corporation introduced the first new Beaver and Safari models designed and built following the acquisition.

The Beaver Santiam and Safari Sahara are diesel-powered motorhomes developed to compete in the popular $150,000-$200,000 price range, a highly-competitive market segment in which neither brand was previously represented.

The new models were a top priority after the SMC acquisition, according to Vice President of Sales, Mike Snell, who added that "the $150,000 - $200,000 price range is by far the hottest part of today's Class A diesel market, so these new models fill a major gap in the Beaver and Safari lines. They also underline our strong commitment to both the Beaver and Safari brands and their dealers."

Snell also noted how the Santiam and Sahara illustrate MNC's design and production capabilities, since the new products went from the concept stage to a marketable product in less than 4 months after the SMC acquisition.

Both new models are built on MNC's Roadmaster chassis and assembled in MNC's manufacturing plants in Coburg, Oregon and Wakarusa, Indiana.

MNC's leadership position in the Class A market caps a decade of growth which has taken the entire RV industry by surprise.

Monaco Coach Corporation became the world's leading manufacturer of Class A motorhomes in 2001, sparking a change at the top of the industry for the first time in nearly 20 years.

At year end 2001, MNC held a 20.5% share of the overall Class A market--a 38% increase in market share over the previous year. MNC officials attribute this gain to the outstanding growth in the diesel market and the company's popular diesel-powered products, its expanded presence in the gasoline market segment and the acquisition of SMC Corp.

MNC's leadership position in the Class A market caps a decade of growth which has taken the entire industry by surprise. In 1991, the company built only 370 units and had under 2% of the market.

The acquisition of Holiday Rambler in 1996, a continuous broadening of the product line, a significant investment in manufacturing facilities and the recent SMC acquisition have all played a major role in the company's growth, says MNC President John Nepute.

"While Monaco had always been highly respected in the industry for its quality and innovation, we weren't really considered a major player until the Holiday Rambler acquisition," said Nepute. "That move propelled us closer to the top of our industry and we've worked hard to build upon that foundation."

Class A Market Share - 1992-2001

In addition to reaching the top spot in Class A sales, MNC also recorded the highest average price-per-unit ever achieved by a leading RV manufacturer. The company's highline origins and continued strength in luxury diesel models resulted in an average retail sales price near $165,000.

This high price-per-unit is more typical of a specialty company than a major manufacturer. According to one industry analyst, "Monaco outselling its competitors is like Mercedes-Benz outselling General Motors."

What are Class A motorhomes? Class A motorhomes are the large bus-shaped units that most of us think of when we hear the term "motorhome." These RVs are built on chassis specifically designed for motorhome use. Other classes of motorized recreational vehicles include converted vans (Class B) or units built on an existing van or light truck chassis, typically retaining the original factory cab (Class C). There are two primary types of Class A motorhomes--those powered by gasoline engines (usually front-mounted) and those powered by diesel engines mounted in the rear of the unit. These are often referred to as "diesel pushers."

Class A Market Share
MNC 20.5%

Diesel Market Share
MNC 37.1%

Gas Market Share
MNC 8.4%

What makes a diesel motorhome so special, and why is the diesel market growing? The diesel engines utilized by recreational vehicle manufacturers offer far more power and torque than comparable gasoline engines, allowing more carrying capacity and a higher vehicle weight. Diesel engines are also known for longer powertrain life and extended service intervals. In fact, the diesel engines used in motorhomes are essentially the same as those used in tractor trailers, commercial busses and large yachts. In addition to the advantages of the diesel engine itself, the engine's rear placement allows greater floorplan flexibility, less engine noise in the cockpit and better overall balance and handling. Due to the higher cost of a diesel engine and the more sophisticated chassis needed to optimize its advantages, diesel pushers have traditionally been limited to the luxury segment of the motorhome market. The diesel market has been growing, however, as diesel powertrain suppliers are working hard to develop lower cost alternatives that have allowed companies with excellent product development, like MNC, to market lower priced diesel motorhomes.

If diesel motorhomes are so great, why are most motorhomes still gasoline-powered? In one word, affordability. Although the entry price in the diesel-powered market is trending down, gasoline-powered Class A motorhomes are still typically lower-priced than their diesel counterparts. Gasoline-powered motorhomes range from about $45,000 to $120,000, while the lowest-priced diesel models have only recently dropped into the $110,000 range.

MNC introduced the Monaco Cayman and Holiday Rambler Neptune models in 2001. These well-appointed diesel motorhomes are leading the market into a new area that may further the trend toward diesel-powered units. With models ranging from $110,000 - $130,000, the Cayman and Neptune offer excellent value and performance at a retail price more commonly associated with a gasoline-powered motorhome.

MNC's proprietary Roadmaster Chassis

Monaco Coach Corporation's share of the Class-A diesel motorhome market rose to 37.1% in 2001, according to industry statistics. This represents a 38% increase in market share over the previous year for the world's leading manufacturer of diesel-powered motorhomes.

While some of this growth was the result of the SMC acquisition, MNC Chairman Kay Toolson noted that most of the market share increase occurred within the company's existing product lines. He attributed this to the company's unique position in the burgeoning diesel market.

"Monaco's highline reputation and recognized leadership in the diesel market sets us well apart from our competition in the buyer's eye. Having diesel products in a broad spectrum of price ranges makes our highline quality accessible to a greater number of prospective buyers. That's a pretty good combination for sales in the fastest-growing segment of the RV market."

Toolson continued, "Although our strength in the diesel market is a big part of our recent success, our gasoline coaches continue to gain share. We're excited about the growth of the diesel market, but we'll continue to invest in our gasoline product lines and we've identified opportunities in that market."

According to industry statistics, approximately 40% of all Class-A motorhomes sold in 2001 were diesel units--the highest percentage in industry history. In the past 5 years, the diesel segment of the Class A market has grown by 67%.

This dramatic shift toward the diesel segment is expected to continue as more affordable diesel models, such as the Monaco Cayman and Holiday Rambler Neptune, further expand the boundaries of the market.

MNC's revenue breakdown by product category.

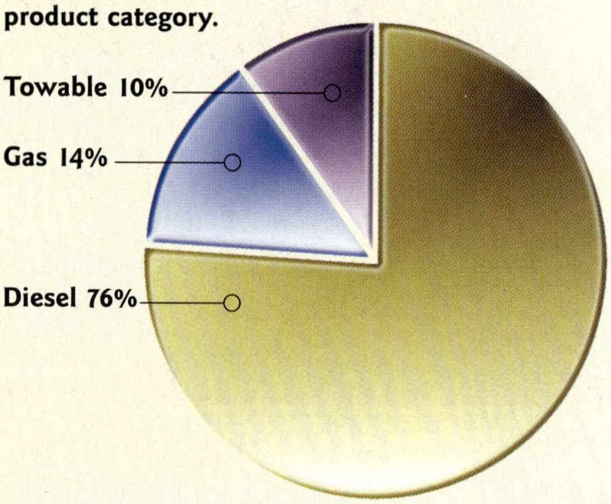

The Class A diesel market (gold) has grown at a faster rate than the overall Class A motorhome market (blue).

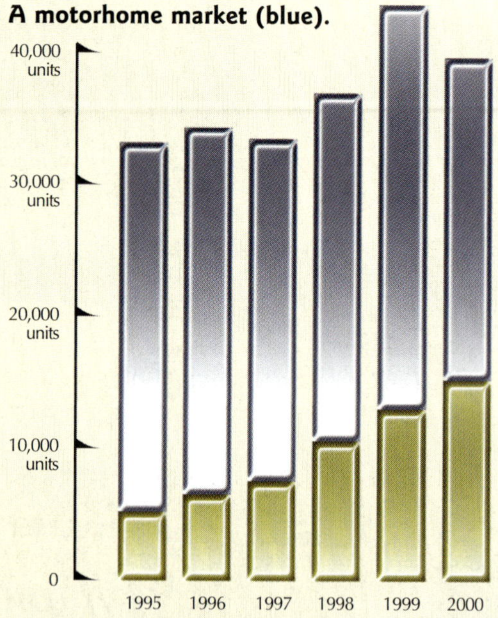

MNC Expands Product Line To 39 Models

Through the acquisition of SMC Corporation and the introduction of several new motorhomes, MNC added 15 more models to its product line in 2001. The company now offers a total of 39 different models under 6 different brand names.

The 39 models range from $20,000 travel trailers to $1.2 million luxury coaches. Most models are available in a variety of sizes, floorplans and decor options, resulting in a total of about 2,000 individual products.

The company's expanded product line for 2001 is part of an overall "steppingstone" marketing strategy, said Monaco Chairman Kay Toolson, noting that "offering a wide range of quality RVs not only attracts a broader spectrum of new buyers to our brands, but also makes it possible for current owners of an MNC-built unit to move up within our own product lines."

As an illustration of how new products and innovations affect the marketplace, Toolson noted that nearly one third of the company's Class A units sold in 2001 featured the triple-slideout option pioneered by MNC.

Toolson also cited the company's exclusive 2-bath option and designer interior fabrics by Ralph Lauren and Martha Stewart as examples of MNC's continuing efforts to stay ahead of the market and position its products apart from the competition.

MNC remains focused on providing the most innovative vehicles.

Cayman and Neptune Models Create a New Class A Market.

In 2001, MNC introduced two motorhomes which redefined the Class A diesel market by redefining "affordable" diesel motorhomes.

The Monaco Cayman and Holiday Rambler Neptune are the first Class-A diesel motorhomes offered in the $110,000-$135,000 price range. In addition to being the lowest-priced motorhomes in the diesel market, the Cayman and Neptune are the first diesel units which are directly price-competitive with highline gasoline-powered models.

According to Vice President of Sales Mike Snell, "The Cayman/Neptune models are among the most important products we've ever introduced. They create a new market unique to MNC and they allow gasoline coach owners to trade up to a diesel model. They don't compete with other MNC products and they give our dealers something unique in the market."

Despite their low cost, the models should be very profitable for MNC, according to President John Nepute, who noted that "Our state-of-the-art facilities make these models easy to build and our manufacturing efficiencies allow us to keep the costs down while still producing a high quality product."

Production of the Monaco Cayman at MNC's Coburg, Oregon facility.

Why does MNC build similar RVs under different brand names?

Monaco Coach Corporation now builds several products under different brand names. Examples of this in 2001 were the Monaco Cayman/Holiday Rambler Neptune and the Beaver Santiam/Safari Sahara.

The reason for this multi-brand approach is that very few dealers carry more than one MNC brand. Monaco dealers generally carry only the Monaco line, Holiday Rambler dealers carry only the Holiday Rambler line and so on.

By producing multiple products under different brands MNC can increase the number of dealerships carrying a specific model with a comparable difference in sales.

This multiple-branding is a logical extension of MNC's proven "steppingstone" approach, expanding that philosophy to each individual brand. This allows every Monaco, Holiday Rambler, Beaver and Safari dealer to carry the widest possible selection of MNC-built units and eliminates product line gaps which might otherwise be filled by competing brands.

Towable RVs continue to play an important roll in MNC's market strategy.

Monaco Coach Corporation's production capacity increased in 2001 as SMC's plants and subassembly facilities were added to the company's manufacturing infrastructure.

The Beaver plant in Bend, Oregon is a 140,000 square-foot complex which currently builds more than 500 luxury diesel motorhomes a year. The facility, which also includes an in-house woodworking operation known for its outstanding cabinetry, will continue to build Beaver units.

MNC also acquired two SMC subassembly facilities specializing in electronics/wiring harnesses and fiberglass/lamination. These operations now service all MNC divisions, increasing the efficiency of each facility and lowering the component cost for many MNC products.

The SMC facilities are the latest additions to a dynamic expansion program which began with MNC's new Coburg facility in 1995. In 1997, the company opened a new 670,000 square foot motorhome plant in Indiana. In 1999, 650,000 square feet were added to the Coburg complex. In 2000, the company opened a new 250,000 square foot Roadmaster chassis plant in Indiana.

This investment in facilities allows the company greater flexibility in each of its plants. The new Beaver Santiam and Safari Sahara models, which are built in MNC's Oregon and Indiana plants, are a shining example. According to President John Nepute, "These important new models went from conception to production in less than four months. Although this presented challenges for our production teams that resulted in gross margin pressure, our investment in facilities allows us to work through these issues quickly. The increased production rates as a result of these new model introductions will help us reach higher efficiency levels in the long run."

After the SMC acquisition, why did MNC keep one SMC plant in operation and not the other?
The decision in each case was based on maximizing the company's overall efficiency and capacity while retaining the skilled workforce of each plant.

The Beaver plant in Bend, Oregon was a fairly efficient self-contained operation at the time of the acquisition. While Beaver production could have been moved to MNC's Coburg complex, the 120 mile distance between the plants would have made it impossible to retain loyal Beaver employees.

Since the workforce is a key asset of the SMC acquisition, the company decided to continue operation of the Bend plant and focus on increasing the plant's profitability through shared corporate efficiencies. The results are enhanced manufacturing capabilities for the company, a solid base for Beaver production and the retention of highly-experienced and highly-trained personnel.

The same factors were involved in the company's decision to close the Safari plant in Harrisburg, Oregon and convert the facility to a service center.

Since the Safari plant did not have the production efficiency or capacity needed for future growth of the brand, integrating Safari production into MNC's Coburg complex made sense from a corporate standpoint.The Safari facility is now the home for Monaco Coach Corporation's Oregon factory service center, enhancing the company's service capabilities. The decision to move Safari production was an easy one since the Safari plant was only 8 miles from Coburg.

MNC Expands Dealer and Customer Service Network

The acquisition of SMC Corporation and MNC's continued success in attracting new dealers expanded the company's dealer network to nearly 400 dealerships in 2001, a substantial increase over the prior year.

In addition to the 40 Beaver and Safari dealers brought into the MNC network, the company's established market presence drew more dealers into the Monaco and Holiday Rambler networks as well, according to Vice President of Sales Mike Snell.

"We continue to devote tremendous resources to supporting our dealers, resulting in a unique 'partnership' that's a model for the industry" Snell said. "When you combine that with the reputation of our products and our outstanding market share growth, our appeal to prospective dealers becomes very obvious."

These same factors, combined with the company's broad line in attractive product categories, have also encouraged current dealers to devote more "floor space" to MNC products than ever before, Snell noted, adding that "from a competitive standpoint, floor space is critical. Since dealers can only stock a finite number of units, any increase in MNC inventory generally comes at the expense of a competitor's product."

To support this growing dealer network and increasing customer base, MNC significantly expanded its service capabilities in 2001. The former SMC manufacturing plant in Harrisburg, Oregon was converted into a 40-bay service center similar to existing facilities in Florida and Indiana. The company's three factory service centers now have a combined total of 96 service bays.

The company also opened a new dealer and customer call center which more effectively routes all parts, service and warranty calls to the right person in far less time. The call center is staffed by nearly 100 employees, each of whom is a specialist in a particular product or service area.

Why don't most dealers carry the entire lineup of a particular MNC brand? Unlike automotive dealerships, where a dealer sells and services an entire line of vehicles from one manufacturer, the typical RV dealer sells and services a specific type or class of vehicle from several different manufacturers.

This focus may be on type (towables, Class A gasoline, Class A diesel, Class C, etc.) or price range ($75,000-$200,000, for example).

This product specialization and multi-brand inventory allows the dealer to offer a broader range of products in a specific category, increasing the opportunity for sales. It also allows the dealer to develop greater product knowledge in a particular market segment, establish a precise understanding of a specific customer's needs and offer a more efficient and effective service operation.

MONACO MOTORHOMES

Roya

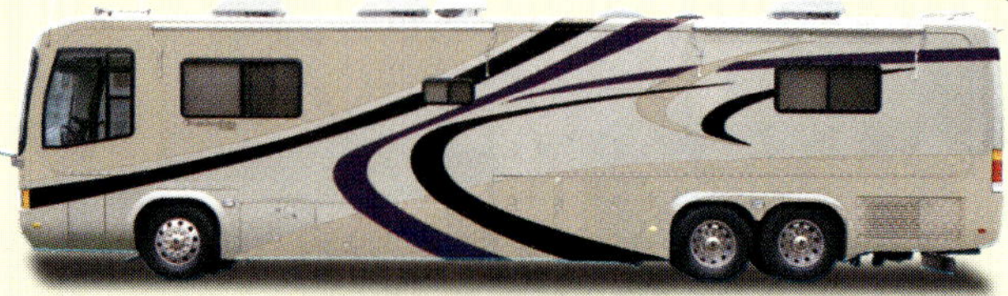

Signature Series
$400,000-$500,000

Executive
$340,000-$400,000

Dynasty
$250,000-$325,000

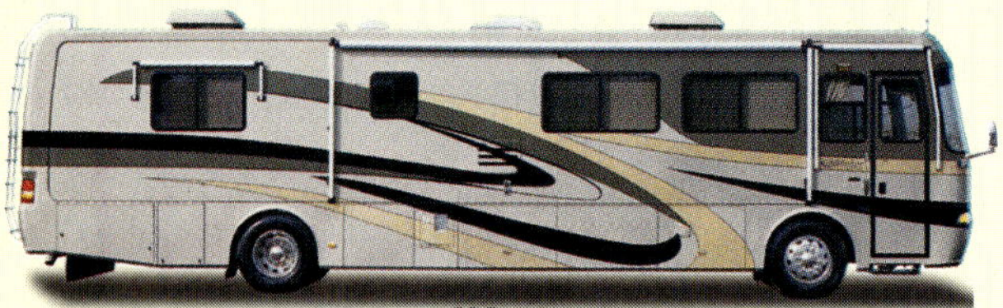

Windsor
$215,000-$270,000

Diesel Products

Camelot
$185,000-$225,000

Gas Products

Socialite
Available in Gas or Diesel Models $120,000-$185,000

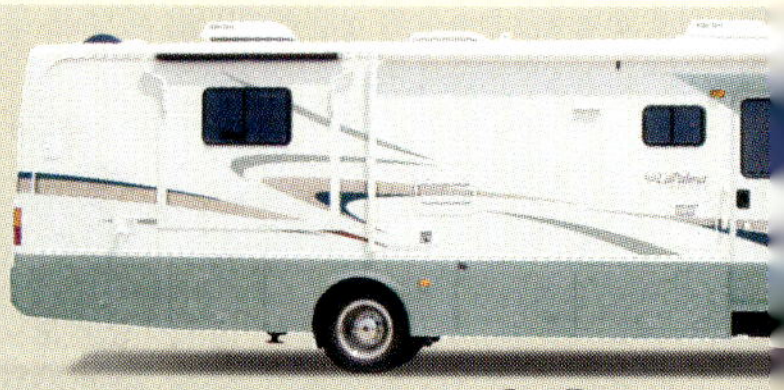

La Palma
$90,000-$120,000

Class C

Towables

McKENZIE

ch

Royale Coach Luxury Bus Conversions
$600,000-$1,000,000

Zanzibar
$185,000-$220,000

Sahara
$165,000-$185,000

Cheetah
$140,000-$160,000

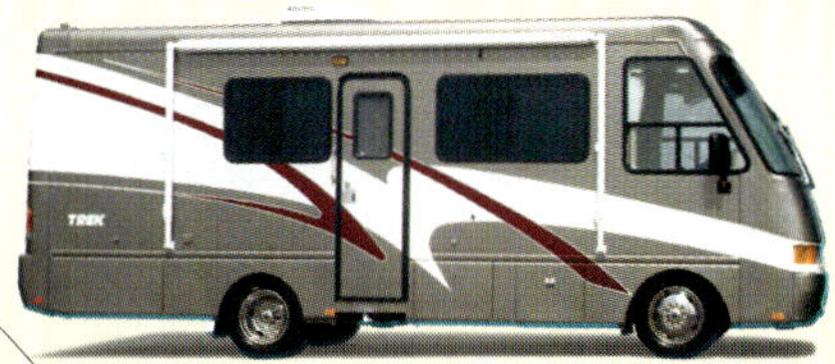

Trek (Gas Product Only)
$85,000-$110,000

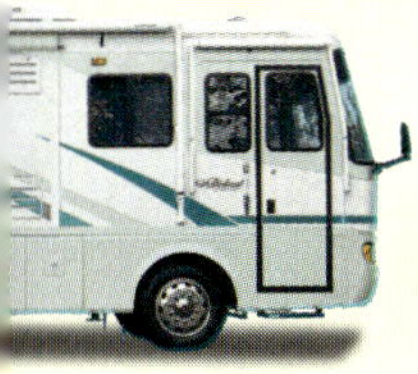

000

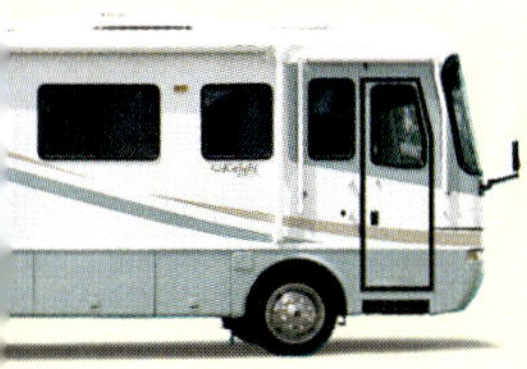

000

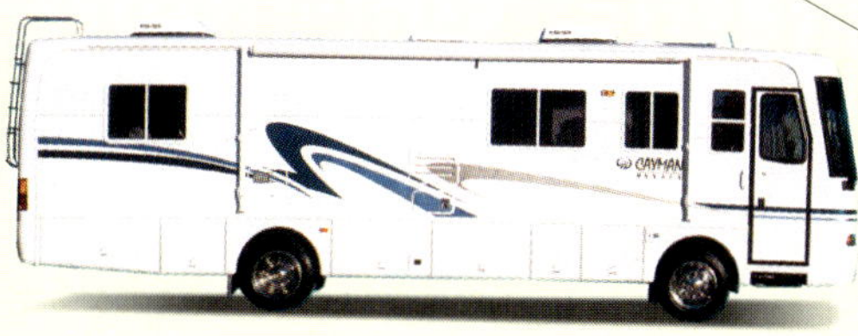

Cayman
$110,000-$130,000

Monaco Coach

Monarch
$75,000-$110,500

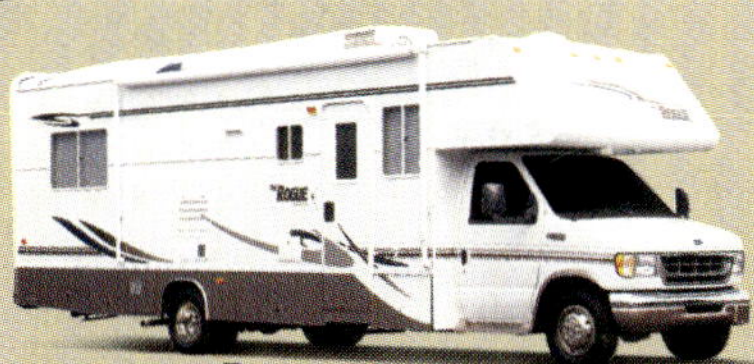

Rogue
$60,000-$70,000

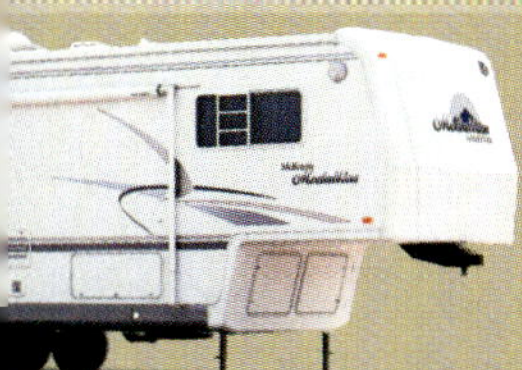

allion Fifth Wheel
$40,000-$65,000

Lakota Fifth Wheel
$30,000-$50,000

Lakota Travel Trailer
$20,000-$30,000

Monaco Coach

Marquis
$450,000-$515,000

Patriot
$255,000-$355,000

Monterey
$185,000-$200,000

Contessa
$220,000-$245,000

Santiam
$155,000-$180,000

$

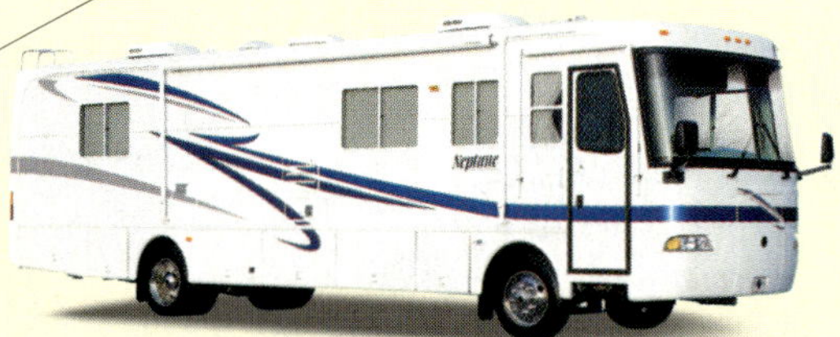

Neptune
$110,000-$130,000

$

Admiral
$75,000-$100,000

VA
$90,

Alumascape Travel Trailer
$20,000-$30,000

Alumascape Fifth Wheel
$30,000-$35,000

Beaver

HOLIDAY RAMBLER®

NAVIGATOR
$315,000-$395,000

IMPERIAL
$230,000-$275,000

Diesel Products

ENDEAVOR DIESEL
$155,000-$195,000

Gas Products

ENDEAVOR GAS
$105,000-$120,000

Class C

ATLANTIS
$60,000-$75,000

Towables

AL TRAVEL TRAILER
000-$45,000

PRESIDENTIAL FIFTH WHEEL
$40,000-$50,000

Monaco Coach Corporation's growth in recent years is a prelude to the company's plans for the future, according to Chairman Kay Toolson, who noted that the next ten years should be a decade of expansion for the RV industry as the "baby boom generation" –born between 1945 and 1955–comes of RV age.

"The 55-64 year-old segment of the population has always been RVing's primary target market," said Toolson, "and in the the next decade, this primary market will explode in size."

According to U.S. Census Bureau data, the 55-64 age group will grow 65.5% between 2000 and 2010. This compounded growth rate of 5.2% a year is several times the projected growth of the population as a whole.

Combined with this demographic bulge are other factors which indicate a higher propensity for RVs than any previous generation. The baby boom generation is by far the most affluent ever to enter the RV market and also the most travel-oriented. It all adds up to a market potential never before seen in this industry.

With the baby boom generation now starting to arrive, Monaco Coach Corporation is uniquely positioned to take advantage of this influx of new buyers, said Toolson.

"With modern plants and 5,000 dedicated employees, we already have the manufacturing capacity to match tomorrow's demands, a broad product line encompassing many price points from $20,000 up, a reputation that sets our products apart, a network of nearly 400 dealers to market those products and the service capabilities to back up every additional sale we make."

"Our current leadership in the Class A market also gives us a definite advantage in attracting more dealers and gaining more floor space for our products as the market expands."

Toolson also emphasized that while MNC's position as the world's largest Class A manufacturer was gratifying, the reasons behind that success are far more important in the company's long-range plans.

"Everything we've done in the past has simply been a spring-board for the future. That's why none of us here consider the company's current market position to be an end in itself."

"But, as the RV industry enters a new era, we consider it a pretty good place to start."

The Company's Common Stock is traded on the New York Stock Exchange under the symbol "MNC." The following table sets forth for the periods indicated the high and low closing sale prices for the Common Stock (rounded to the nearest $.01 per share).

2001	**High**	**Low**
First Quarter	$ 14.49	$ 10.89
Second Quarter	$ 22.13	$ 10.77
Third Quarter	$ 20.73	$ 12.10
Fourth Quarter	$ 22.65	$ 13.91
2000		
First Quarter	$ 16.67	$ 10.46
Second Quarter	$ 12.92	$ 7.38
Third Quarter	$ 12.08	$ 8.17
Fourth Quarter	$ 12.25	$ 9.29

Monaco Coach Corporation remains dedicated to providing innovative recreational vehicles, tremendous value and world-class customer support.

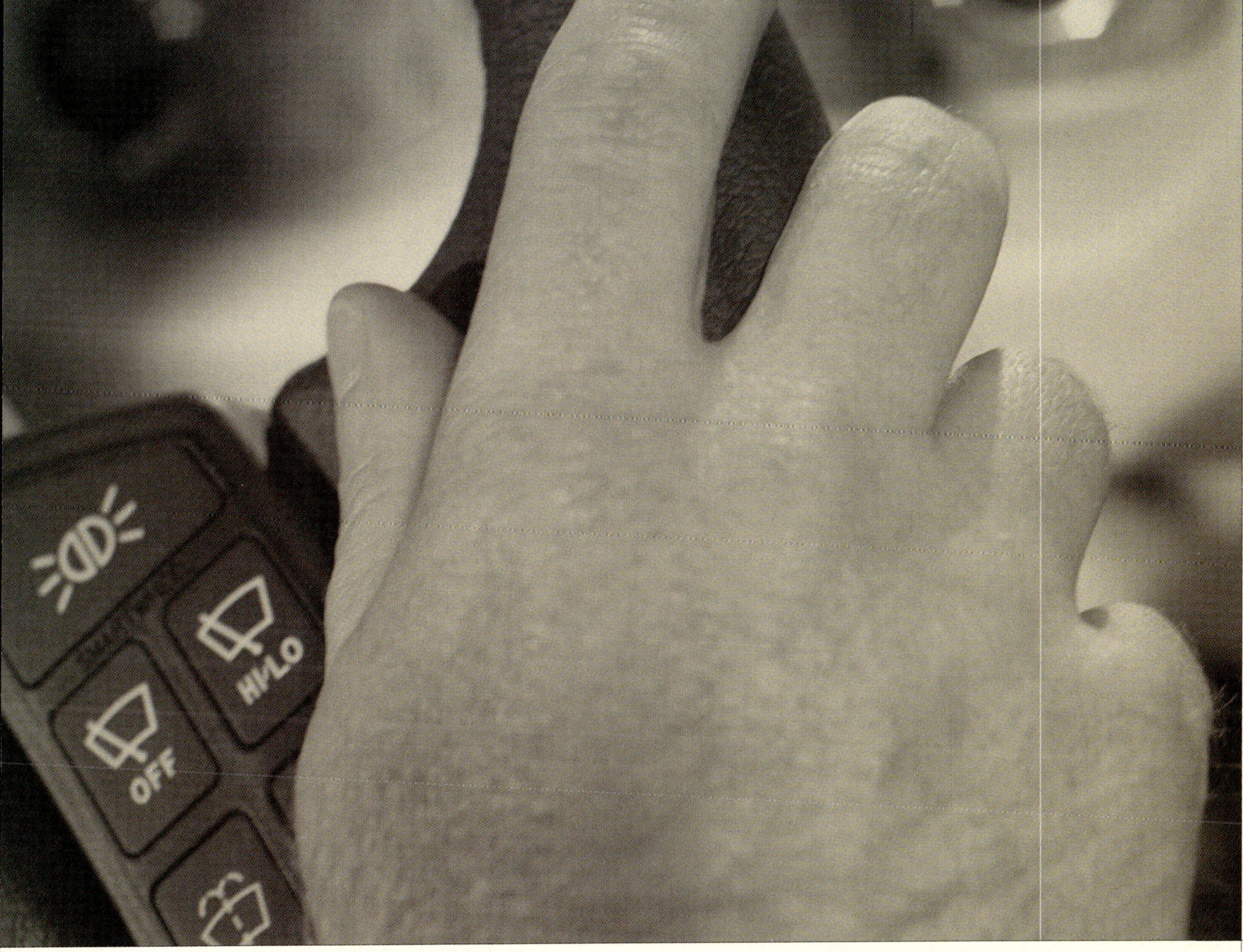

MANAGEMENT DISCUSSION AND ANALYSIS OF FINANCIAL CONDITION AND RESULTS OF OPERATIONS

This Annual Report contains forward-looking statements within the meaning of section 27A of the Securities Act of 1933, as amended, and Section 21E of the Securities Exchange Act of 1934, as amended. These statements include without limitation those below marked with an asterisk (*). In addition, the Company may from time to time make oral forward-looking statements through statements that include the words "believes", "expects", "anticipates" or similar expressions. Such forward-looking statements involve known and unknown risks, uncertainties and other factors that may cause actual results, performance or achievements of the Company to differ materially from those expressed or implied by such forward-looking statements, including those set forth below under "Factors That May Affect Future Operating Results." The following discussions entitled "Results of Operations" and "Liquidity and Capital Resources" should be read in conjunction with the consolidated financial statements and related notes included elsewhere herein, the Company's annual report on form 10-K, as well as the section below entitled "Factors that may Affect Future Operating Results." The Company cautions the reader, however, that these factors may not be exhaustive.

OVERVIEW

The Company is the successor to a company formed in 1968 (the "Predecessor") and commenced operations on March 5, 1993 by acquiring substantially all of the assets and liabilities of the Predecessor. The Predecessor's management and the manufacturing of its High-Line Class A motor coaches were largely unaffected by the Predecessor Acquisition. However, the Company's consolidated financial statements for fiscal years 1999, 2000 and 2001 all contain Predecessor Acquisition-related expenses, consisting primarily of the amortization of goodwill.

On March 4, 1996, the Company acquired from Harley-Davidson certain assets of Holiday Rambler (the "Holiday Acquisition") in exchange for $21.5 million in cash, 65,217 shares of the Company's Redeemable Preferred Stock (which was subsequently converted into 230,767 shares of the Company's Common Stock), and the assumption of most of the liabilities of Holiday Rambler. Concurrently, the Company acquired ten Holiday World Dealerships for $13.0 million, including a $12.0 million subordinated promissory note, and the assumption of certain liabilities. The Company sold seven Holiday World Dealerships in 1996, retired the $12.0 million note from the proceeds of these sales, and sold the remaining three dealerships in 1997. The Holiday Acquisition was accounted for using the purchase method of accounting.

Beginning on March 4, 1996, the acquired operations were incorporated into the Company's consolidated financial statements. The Company's consolidated financial statements for the fiscal years 1999, 2000 and 2001 contain expenses related to the Holiday Acquisition, consisting of interest expense, the amortization of debt issuance costs and Holiday Acquisition goodwill.

On August 2, 2001, the Company acquired Safari Motor Coach (the "SMC Acquisition") in exchange for $24.3 million in cash including transaction expenses. The purchase was accounted for using the purchase method of accounting. The purchase was effected through a tender offer on August 2, 2001, and completed through a back end merger on August 6, 2001, at which time all shares of SMC Corporation (SMC) were retired.

Beginning on August 2, 2001, the acquired SMC operations were incorporated into the Company's consolidated financial statements. The Company's consolidated financial statements for the fiscal year 2001 contain expenses related to the SMC Acquisition, consisting of interest expense and amortization of debt issuance costs.

RESULTS OF OPERATIONS
2001 COMPARED WITH 2000

Net sales increased 3.9% from $901.9 million in 2000 to $937.1 million in 2001. The Company's overall unit sales were down 5.2% from 10,009 in 2000 to 9,489 units in 2001. The Company's units sales were down 6.1% on the motorized side reflecting lower sales during the first half of 2001 which were nearly offset by increases in the latter part of 2001, mostly from the addition of the Safari and Beaver line of products. Motorized gross sales were up 2.7% reflecting the higher mix of diesel unit sales in 2001. The Company's unit sales of towable products in 2001 were down only 3.4% while gross sales were up 8.2% as sales from the towable operations had a shift in the mix from the prior year of fewer travel trailers and more higher priced fifth wheel units. The Company's overall average unit selling price increased from $91,800 in 2000 to $99,900 in 2001 reflecting the continuing increases in sales of diesel motor coaches. The Company's broad range of product offerings which include several in the less expensive gasoline motor coach market as well as the towable market is expected to keep the overall average selling price under $120,000.*

Gross profit decreased by $15.7 million from $129.7 million in 2000 to $114.0 million in 2001 and gross margin decreased from 14.4% in 2000 to 12.2% in 2001. The decrease in gross margin in 2001 was due to a combination of factors resulting from competitive pressures in the market. Through the first half of 2001, the Company found it necessary to offer above normal discounts to maintain sales to dealers. In addition, throughout 2001, the Company's efforts to match production with the models that were selling well in the market resulted in production inefficiencies caused by shifting volume among production lines and changing the mix of models produced on those lines, as well as integrating the Safari production into the Coburg facility. The Company's overall gross margin may fluctuate in future periods if the mix of products shifts from higher to lower gross margin units or if the Company encounters unexpected manufacturing difficulties or competitive pressures.

Selling, general and administrative expenses increased by $11.5 million from $59.2 million in 2000 to $70.7 million in 2001 and increased as a percentage of sales from 6.6% in 2000 to 7.5% in 2001. Approximately 42% of the increase was due to retail sales and dealer promotions, as well as show and rally expenses. The remainder of the increase was from administrative and sales wages and commissions, mostly due to the combining of SMC operations which have historically run higher selling, general and administraive costs as a percentage of sales than the Company.

Operating income decreased $27.1 million from $69.8 million in 2000 to $42.7 million in 2001. The Company's higher level of selling, general, and administrative expense as a percentage of sales combined with the reduction in the Company's gross margin, resulted in a decrease in operating margin from 7.7% in 2000 to 4.6% in 2001.

Net interest expense increased $1.7 million from $632 thousand in 2000 to $2.4 million in 2001. This increase was related to increased debt due to higher levels of inventory during the first half of 2001, combined with cash requirements to complete the SMC Acquisition in the third quarter of 2001. The Company capitalized $192,000 of interest expense in 2000 relating to the construction in Indiana and Florida, and no interest was capitalized in 2001. The Company's interest expense included $61,300 in 2000 and $14,000 in 2001 related to the amortization of debt issuance costs recorded in conjunction with the Company's credit facilities. Additionally, interest expense in 2000 included $52,700, from accelerated amortization of debt issuance costs related to the credit facilities. The Company also paid off its revolving credit facility in the third quarter of 2001 and obtained financing from a consortium of lenders. See "Liquidity and Capital Resources."

The Company reported a provision for income taxes of $15.7 million, or an effective tax rate of 38.7%, for 2001, compared to $26.9 million, or an effective tax rate of 38.7% for 2000.

Net income decreased by $17.6 million from $42.5 million in 2000 to $24.9 million in 2001, due to the increase in net sales being offset with a lower operating margin.

2000 COMPARED WITH 1999

Net sales increased 15.5% from $780.8 million in 1999 to $901.9 million in 2000. The Company's overall unit sales were up 5.3% from 9,502 in 1999 to 10,009 units in 2000. The Company's units sales were up 6.4% on the motorized side reflecting a full year of production in the facilities expanded in third quarter of 1999 in Coburg, Oregon, combined with slightly higher production rates in the other existing motorized facilities in both Coburg, Oregon and Wakarusa, Indiana. Motorized gross sales were up 17.6% reflecting the shift in sales from the Company's gas units to diesel unit sales. The Company's fiscal year 2000 sales of motorized units were helped by the introduction in late 1999 of one new gas and two new diesel motorized products which accounted for 1,344 of the 6,632 motorized units sold in 2000. The Company's 1999 sales of motorized units were helped by the introduction of two new motorized products introduced in 1998 which accounted for 1,643 of the 6,233 motorized units sold in 1999. The Company's unit sales of towable products were up 3.3% from 1999 to 2000 as McKenzie towable operations reported strong increases. The Company's overall average unit selling price increased from $82,900 in 1999 to $91,800 in 2000 reflecting the strong sales growth of the Company's higher priced diesel motorized products.

Gross profit increased by $7.4 million from $122.3 million in 1999 to $129.7 million in 2000 and gross margin decreased from 15.7% in 1999 to 14.4% in 2000. The decrease in gross margin in 2000 was due to a combination of factors resulting from competitive pressures in the market. In the second half of 2000, the Company found it necessary to offer above normal discounts to maintain sales to dealers. In addition, in efforts to match production to the models that were selling well in the market, the Company experienced some production inefficiencies resulting from shifting volume among production lines as well as changing the mix of models produced on those lines.

Selling, general, and administrative expenses increased by $10.4 million from $48.8 million in 1999 to $59.2 million in 2000 and increased as a percentage of sales from 6.2% in 1999 to 6.6% in 2000. Selling, general, and administrative expenses benefited in 1999 from a $1.75 million reduction in the estimated accrual for 1998 incentive based compensation. Without this benefit, selling, general, and administrative expenses in 1999 would have been $50.5 million or 6.5% of sales, only slightly lower than the 6.6% of sales in 2000.

Operating income decreased $3.0 million from $72.8 million in 1999 to $69.8 million in 2000. The Company's static level of selling, general, and administrative expense as a percentage of sales combined with the reduction in the Company's gross margin, resulted in a decrease in operating margin to 7.7% in 2000 compared to 9.3% in 1999. The Company's operating margin in 1999 was positively affected by the $1.75 million reduction of incentive based compensation accrued for 1998. Without this benefit, the Company's operating margin in 1999 would have been 9.1%.

Net interest expense decreased $511,000 from $1.1 million in 1999 to $632,000 in 2000. The Company capitalized $195,000 of interest expense in 1999 relating to the construction in Oregon and $192,000 in 2000 relating to the construction in Indiana. The Company's interest expense included $176,000 in 1999 and $61,300 in 2000 related to the amortization of debt issuance costs recorded in conjunction with the Company's credit facilities. Additionally, interest expense in 1999 and 2000 included $639,000 and $52,700, respectively, from accelerated amortization of debt issuance costs related to the credit facilities. The Company paid off its long term debt of approximately $10 million at the end of the first quarter of 1999 and also reduced the amount of availability on its revolving line of credit. The Company also paid off its revolving credit facility in the third quarter of 2000 and obtained financing from another lender.

The Company reported a provision for income taxes of $28.1 million, or an effective tax rate of 39.1%, for 1999, compared to $26.9 million, or an effective tax rate of 38.7% for 2000. Net income decreased by $1.3 million from $43.8 million in 1999 to $42.5 million in 2000, due to the increase in net sales being offset with a lower operating margin.

INFLATION

The Company does not believe that inflation has had a material impact on its results of operations for the periods presented.

CRITICAL ACCOUNTING POLICIES

The discussion and analysis of our financial condition and results of operations are based upon our consolidated financial statements, which have been prepared in accordance with accounting principles generally accepted in the United States of America. The preparation of these financial statements requires us to make estimates and judgments that affect the reported amounts of assets, liabilities, revenues and expenses, and related disclosure of contingent assets and liabilities. On an on-going basis, we evaluate our estimates, including those related to warranty costs, product liability, and impairment of goodwill. We base our estimates on historical experience and on various other assumptions that are believed to be reasonable under the circumstances. Actual results may differ from these estimates under different assumptions or conditions. We believe the following critical accounting policies and related judgments and estimates affect the preparation of our consolidated financial statements.

WARRANTY COSTS The Company provides an estimate for accrued warranty costs at the time a product is sold. This estimate is based on historical average repair costs, as well as other reasonable assumptions as have been deemed appropriate by management.

PRODUCT LIABILITY The Company provides an estimate for accrued product liability based on current pending cases, as well as for those cases which are incurred but not reported. This estimate is developed by legal counsel based on professional judgment, as well as historical experience.

IMPARMENT OF GOODWILL The Company assesses the potential impairment of goodwill in accordance with Financial Accounting Standards Board (FASB) statement No. 121. This estimate involves management comparing historical cash flows from operations to projected future cash flows to determine if goodwill has been impaired.

FACTORS THAT MAY AFFECT FUTURE OPERATING RESULTS

ACQUISITION OF SMC CORPORATION The Company announced on June 25, 2001 that it had agreed with Oregon based motor home manufacturer SMC Corporation ("SMC") to acquire all of the outstanding shares of SMC pursuant to a cash tender offer at a price of $3.70 per share. On August 6, the Company had completed it's purchase of all SMC Corporation shares. The anticipated benefits of this acquisition may not be achieved unless Monaco successfully integrates SMC into Monaco's operations. SMC incurred a net loss from operations of $5.4 million for 2000 and $1.9 million for the first quarter of 2001. Unless Monaco is able to increase sales or reduce the operating expenses of SMC substantially from historical expense levels, the acquisition could have a material adverse affect on the financial condition and results of operations of Monaco. The process of integration may result in unforeseen operating difficulties and expenditures and may absorb significant management attention that would otherwise be available for the ongoing development of Monaco's business. This may cause an interruption or a loss of momentum in the operating activities of Monaco which in turn would have a material adverse affect on Monaco's operating results and financial condition. Moreover, the acquisition involves a number of additional risks, such as the assimilation of the operations and personnel of the acquired business, the incorporation of acquired products into Monaco's existing product line, adverse short-term effects of reported operating results, the amortization of debt issuance costs, the loss of key employees of SMC as a result of the acquisition, and the difficulty of integrating disparate corporate cultures and presenting a unified corporate image. Accordingly, the anticipated benefits may not be realized or the acquisition may have a material adverse affect on Monaco's operating results and financial condition.

CARRYING VALUES OF INTANGIBLE ASSETS MAY BE SUBJECT TO PERIODIC WRITE-DOWN, ADVERSELY AFFECTING OUR OPERATIONS Goodwill and other intangible assets are reviewed for impairment whenever an event or change in circumstances indicates that the carrying amount may not be recoverable. If the carrying value of our intangible assets exceeds the expected undiscounted future cash flows, a loss would be recog-nized to the extent the carrying amount of assets exceeds their fair values. This loss may negatively impact our results of operation.

POTENTIAL FLUCTUATIONS IN OPERATING RESULTS The Company's net sales, gross margin and operating results may fluctuate significantly from period to period due to factors such as the mix of products sold, the ability to utilize and expand manufacturing resources efficiently, material shortages, the introduction and consumer acceptance of new models offered by the Company, competition, the addition or loss of dealers, the timing of trade shows and rallies, and factors affecting the recreational vehicle industry as a whole. In addition, the Company's overall gross margin on its products may decline in future periods to the extent the Company increases its sales of lower gross margin towable products or if the mix of motor coaches sold shifts to lower gross margin units. Due to the relatively high selling prices of the Company's products (in particular, its High-Line Class A motor coaches), a relatively small variation in the number of recreational vehicles sold in any quarter can have a significant effect on sales and operating results for that quarter. Demand in the overall recreational vehicle industry generally declines during the winter months, while sales and revenues are generally higher during the spring and summer months. With the broader range of recreational vehicles now offered by the Company, seasonal factors could have a significant impact on the Company's operating results in the future. In addition, unusually severe weather conditions in certain markets could delay the timing of shipments from one quarter to another.

CYCLICALITY AND ECONOMIC SLOWDOWN The recreational vehicle industry has been characterized by cycles of growth and contraction in consumer demand, reflecting prevailing economic, demographic and political conditions that affect disposable income for leisure-time activities. Unit sales of recreational vehicles (excluding conversion vehicles) reached a peak of approximately 259,000 units in 1994 and declined to approximately 247,000 units in 1996. The industry peaked again in 1999 at approximately 321,000 units and began declining thereafter as unit sales in 2000 and 2001 were approximately 300,000 and 257,000, respectively. Furthermore, the Company offers a broad range of recreational vehicle products and is susceptible to the cyclicality inherent in the recreational vehicle industry. Factors affecting cyclicality in the recreational vehicle industry include fuel availability and fuel prices, prevailing interest rates, the level of discretionary spending, the availability of credit and overall consumer confidence. In particular, the decline in consumer confidence and/or a slowing of the overall economy has had a material adverse effect on the recreational vehicle market. An extended continuance of these conditions could have a material adverse effect on the Company's business, results of operations and financial condition.

MANAGEMENT OF GROWTH Over the past several years the Company has experienced significant growth in the number of its employees and the scope of its business. This growth has resulted in the addition of new management personnel and increased responsibilities for existing management personnel, and has placed added pressure on the Company's operating, financial and management information systems. While management believes it has been successful in managing this expansion, there can be no assurance that the Company will not encounter problems in the future associated with the continued growth of the Company. Failure to adequately support and manage the growth of its business could have a material adverse effect on the Company's business, results of operations and financial condition.

MANUFACTURING EXPANSION The Company has significantly increased its manufacturing capacity over the last few years. The integration of the Company's facilities and the expansion of the Company's manufacturing operations involve a number of risks including unexpected building and production difficulties. In the past, the Company experienced startup inefficiencies in manufacturing a new model and also has experienced difficulty in increasing production rates at a plant. There can be no assurance that the Company will successfully integrate its manufacturing facilities or that it will achieve the anticipated benefits and efficiencies from its expanded manufacturing operations. In addition, the Company's operating results could be materially and adversely affected if sales of the Company's products do not increase at a rate sufficient to offset the Company's increased expense levels resulting from this expansion.

The setup of new models and scale-up of production facilities involve various risks and uncertainties, including timely performance of a large number of contractors, subcontractors, suppliers and various government agencies that regulate and license construction, each of which is beyond the control of the Company. The setup of production for new models involves risks and costs associated with the development and acquisition of new production lines, molds and other machinery, the training of employees, and compliance with environmental, health and safety and other regulatory requirements. The inability of the Company to complete the scale-up of its facilities and to commence full-scale commercial production in a timely manner could have a material adverse effect on the Company's business, results of operations and financial condition. In addition, the Company may from time to time experience lower than anticipated yields or production constraints that may adversely affect its ability to satisfy customer orders. Any prolonged inability to satisfy customer demand could have a material adverse effect on the Company's business, results of operations and financial condition.

CONCENTRATION OF SALES TO CERTAIN DEALERS Although the Company's products were offered by 385 dealerships located primarily in the United States and Canada at the end of 2001, a significant percentage of the Company's sales have been and will continue to be concentrated among a relatively small number of independent dealers. Sales to Lazy Days RV Center, Inc. accounted for 12.1% of the Company's sales in 2000 and 11.7% in 2001. The Company's 10 largest dealers, including Lazy Days RV Center, Inc., accounted for a combined 36.0% of sales in 2000 and 39.0% in 2001. The loss of a significant dealer or a substantial decrease in sales by such a dealer could have a material adverse effect on the Company's business, results of operations and financial condition. See "Business--Sales and Marketing."

POTENTIAL LIABILITY UNDER REPURCHASE AGREEMENTS As is common in the recreational vehicle industry, the Company enters into repurchase agreements with the financing institutions used by its dealers to finance their purchases. These agreements obligate the Company to repurchase a dealer's inventory under certain circumstances in the event of a default by the dealer to its lender. If the Company were obligated to repurchase a significant number of its products in the future, it could have a material adverse effect on the Company's financial condition, business and results of operations. The Company's contingent obligations under repurchase agreements vary from period to period and totaled approximately $366.8 million as of December 29, 2001, with approximately 7.44% concentrated with one dealer. See "Liquidity and Capital Resources" and Note 16 of Notes to the Company's Consolidated Financial Statements.

AVAILABILITY AND COST OF FUEL An interruption in the supply, or a significant increase in the price or tax on the sale, of diesel fuel or gasoline on a regional or national basis could have a material adverse effect on the Company's business, results of operations and financial condition. Diesel fuel and gasoline have, at various times in the past, been difficult to obtain, and there can be no assurance that the supply of diesel fuel or gasoline will continue uninterrupted, that rationing will not be imposed, or that the price of or tax on diesel fuel or gasoline, will not significantly increase in the future, any of which could have a material adverse effect on the Company's business, results of operations and financial condition.

DEPENDENCE ON CERTAIN SUPPLIERS A number of important components for certain of the Company's products are purchased from single or limited sources, including its turbo diesel engines (Cummins and Caterpillar), substantially all of its transmissions (Allison), axles (Dana) for all diesel motor coaches and chassis (Workhorse and Ford) for certain of its motor home products. The Company has no long term supply contracts with these suppliers or their distributors, and there can be no assurance that these suppliers will be able to meet the Company's future requirements for these components. In 1997, Allison put all chassis manufacturers on allocation with respect to one of the transmissions the Company uses, and in 1999 Ford put one of its gasoline powered chassis on allocation. The Company presently believes that its allocation by suppliers of all components is sufficient to meet planned production volumes, and the Company does not foresee any operating difficulties as a result of vendor supply issues.* Nevertheless, there can be no assurance that Allison, Ford, or any of the Company's other suppliers will be able to meet the Company's future requirements for transmissions, chassis or other key components. An extended delay or interruption in the supply of any components obtained from a single or limited source supplier could have a material adverse effect on the Company's business, results of operations and financial condition. See "Business -- Changes."

NEW PRODUCT INTRODUCTIONS The Company believes that the introduction of new features and new models will be critical to its future success. Delays in the introduction of new models or product features or a lack of market acceptance of new models or features and/or quality problems with new models or features could have a material adverse effect on the Company's business, results of operations and financial condition. For example, unexpected costs associated with model changes have adversely affected the Company's gross margin in the past. Future product introductions could divert revenues from existing models and adversely affect the Company's business, results of operations and financial condition.

COMPETITION The market for the Company's products is highly competitive. The Company currently competes with a number of other manufacturers of motor coaches, fifth wheel trailers and travel trailers, many of which have significant financial resources and extensive distribution capabilities. There can be no assurance that either existing or new competitors will not develop products that are superior to, or that achieve better consumer acceptance than, the Company's products, or that the Company will continue to remain competitive.

RISKS OF LITIGATION The Company is subject to litigation arising in the ordinary course of its business, including a variety of product liability and warranty claims typical in the recreational vehicle industry. Although the Company does not believe that the outcome of any pending litigation, net of insurance coverage, will have a material adverse effect on the business, results of operations or financial condition of the Company, due to the inherent uncertainties associated with litigation there can be no assurance in this regard.*

To date, the Company has been successful in obtaining product liability insurance on terms the Company considers acceptable. The Company's current policies jointly provide coverage against claims based on occurrences within the policy periods up to a maximum of $100.1 million for each occurrence and $102.0 million in the aggregate. There can be no assurance that the Company will be able to obtain insurance coverage in the future at acceptable levels or that the costs of insurance will be reasonable. Furthermore, successful assertion against the Company of one or a series of large uninsured claims, or of one or a series of claims exceeding any insurance coverage, could have a material adverse effect on the Company's business, results of operations and financial condition.

WE MAY BE UNABLE TO ATTRACT AND RETAIN KEY EMPLOYEES, DELAYING PRODUCT DEVELOPMENT AND MANUFACTURING
Our success depends upon attracting and retaining highly skilled professionals. A number of our employees are highly skilled engineers and other technical professionals, and our failure to continue to attract and retain such individuals could adversely affect our ability to compete in the industry.

FLUCTUATIONS IN QUARTERLY PERFORMANCE CAN RESULT IN INCREASES IN OUR INVENTORY AND RELATED CARRYING COSTS, CAN DIMINISH OUR OPERATING RESULTS AND CASH FLOW AND CAN RESULT IN A LOWER STOCK PRICE In the past three fiscal years, our sales volumes have not fluctuated more than 10% quarter to quarter. This quarter to quarter variation is not seasonal or predictable. We attempt to accurately forecast orders for our products and commence purchasing and manufacturing prior to the receipt of such orders. However, it is highly unlikely that we will consistently accurately forecast the timing and rate of orders. This aspect of our business makes our planning inexact and, in turn, affects our shipments, costs, inventories, operating results and cash flow for any given quarter. In addition, our quarterly operating results are affected by competitive pricing, announcements regarding new product developments and cyclical conditions in the industry. Accordingly, we may experience wide quarterly fluctuations in our operating performance and profitability, which may adversely affect our stock price even if our year to year performance is more stable, which it also may not be. In addition, many of our products require significant manufacturing time, making it difficult to increase production on short notice. If we are unable to satisfy unexpected customer orders, our business and customer relationships could suffer.

CARRYING VALUES OF INVENTORIES OF OUR PRODUCTS AND COMPONENTS THEREFORE MAY BE SUBJECT TO PERIODIC WRITE-DOWN, ADVERSELY AFFECTING OUR OPERATIONS To be competitive in some of our markets, we will occasionally be required to build up invento-ries of certain products in anticipation of future orders. There can be no assurance that we will not experience problems of obsolete, excess or slow-moving inventory if we are not able to properly balance inventories against the prospect of future orders, and our operations may be adversely affected by inventory write-downs.

OUR PRODUCTS COULD FAIL TO PERFORM ACCORDING TO SPECIFICATION OR PROVE TO BE UNRELIABLE, CAUSING DAMAGE TO OUR CUSTOMER RELATIONSHIPS AND INDUSTRY REPUTATION AND RESULTING IN LOSS OF SALES Our customers require demanding specifications for product performance and reliability. Because our products are complex and often use state-of-the-art components, processes and techniques, undetected errors and design flaws may occur. Product defects result in higher product service and warranty and replacement costs and may cause serious damage to our customer relationships and industry reputation, all of which will negatively impact our sales and business.

LIQUIDITY AND CAPITAL RESOURCES

The Company's primary sources of liquidity are internally generated cash from operations and available borrowings under its credit facilities. During 2001, the Company had cash flows of $21.0 million from operating activities. The Company generated $32.5 million from net income and non-cash expenses such as depreciation and amortization, which was partially offset by a net increase in the Company's working capital accounts, as adjusted by the working capital accounts from the SMC Acquisition, excluding the Company's current bank debt. Accounts receivable, adjusted for $1.7 million from SMC, increased $13.2 million due to a higher number of shipments of product the final week of the quarter. Inventories, adjusted for $25.4 million related to SMC, decreased by $12.7 million, reflecting the results of the Company's plan to reduce finished goods levels from the prior year. Accounts payable, adjusted for $24.1 million from SMC, decreased by $10.3 million. Accrued liabilities, after adding $34.1 million from SMC, decreased by $5.7 million. While current demand for the Company's products remains strong, a significant decrease could result in negative cash flows from operations.

During the third quarter of 2001, the Company paid off its revolving line of credit and obtained a new line of credit with a consortium of lenders. The Company's new permanent credit facility consists of a revolving line of credit of up to $70.0 million (the "Revolving Loan") and a term note of $40.0 million (the "Term Loan"). At the election of the Company, the Revolving Loan and Term Loan bear interest at varying rates that fluctuate based on the Prime rate or LIBOR, and are determined based on the Company's leverage ratio. The Company also pays interest monthly on the unused available portion of the Revolving Loan at varying rates, determined by the Company's leverage ratio. The Revolving loan is due and payable in full on September 30, 2004, while the Term Loan is due and payable in full on September 28, 2005 and both require monthly interest payments. The balance outstanding under the Revolving Loan at December 29, 2001 was $26.0 million and the balance on the Term Loan was $40.0 million. The Revolving Loan and Term Loan are collateralized by all the assets of the Company and include various restrictions and financial covenants. The Company was in compliance with the debt covenants at December 29, 2001. The Company utilizes "zero balance" bank disbursement accounts in which an advance on the line of credit is automatically made for checks clearing each day. Since the balance of the disbursement account at the bank returns to zero at the end of each day, the outstanding checks of the Company are reflected as a liability. The outstanding check liability is combined with the Company's positive cash balance accounts to reflect a net book overdraft or a net cash balance for financial reporting.

The Company's principal working capital requirements are for purchases of inventory and financing of trade receivables. The Company's dealers typically finance product purchases under wholesale floor plan arrangements with third parties as described below. At December 29, 2001, the Company had working capital of approximately $63.7 million, a decrease of $5.6 million from working capital of $69.3 million at December 30, 2000. The Company has been using short-term credit facilities and cash flow to finance its construction of facilities and other capital expenditures.

The Company believes that cash flow from operations and funds available under its credit facilities will be sufficient to meet the Company's liquidity requirements for the next 12 months.* The Company's capital expenditures were $10.2 million in 2001, primarily for completing the Company's warranty and service center projects. In the fiscal year 2001, the Company also spent about $4 to $5 million on routine capital expenditures for computer system upgrades and additions, smaller scale plant remodeling projects and normal replacement of outdated or worn-out equipment. The Company is expecting capital expenditures in 2002 to be approximately $12 to $15 million, which includes minor modifications to existing manufacturing facilities.* The Company may require additional equity or debt financing to address working capital and facilities expansion needs, particularly if the Company significantly increases the level of working capital assets such as inventory and accounts receivable. The Company may also from time to time seek to acquire businesses that would complement the Company's current business, and any such acquisition could require additional financing. There can be no assurance that additional financing will be available if required or on terms deemed favorable by the Company.

As is typical in the recreational vehicle industry, many of the Company's retail dealers utilize wholesale floor plan financing arrangements with third party lending institutions to finance their purchases of the Company's products. Under the terms of these floor plan arrangements, institutional lenders customarily require the recreational vehicle manufacturer to agree to repurchase any unsold units if the dealer fails to meet its commitments to the lender, subject to certain conditions. The Company has agreements with several institutional lenders under which the Company currently has repurchase obligations. The Company's contingent obligations under these repurchase agreements are reduced by the proceeds received upon the sale of any repurchased units. The Company's obligations under these repurchase agreements vary from period to period. At December 29, 2001, approximately $366.8 million of products sold by the Company to independent dealers were subject to potential repurchase under existing floor plan financing agreements with approximately 7.44% concentrated with one dealer. If the Company were obligated to repurchase a significant number of units under any repurchase agreement, its business, operating results and financial condition could be adversely affected.

As part of the normal course of business, the Company incurs certain contractual obligations and commitments which will require future cash payments. The following tables summarize the significant obligations and commitments.

PAYMENTS DUE BY PERIOD

Contractual Obligations (in thousands)	1 year or less	1 to 3 years	4 to 5 years	Thereafter	Total
Long-term debt (1)	$ 10,000	$ 30,000	$ 0	$ 0	$ 40,000
Operating Leases (2)	2,938	3,539	1,350	4,333	12,160
Total Contractual Cash Obligations	**$12,938**	**$33,539**	**$1,350**	**$4,333**	**$52,160**

AMOUNT OF COMMITMENT EXPIRATION BY PERIOD

Other Commitments (in thousands)	1 year or less	1 to 3 years	4 to 5 years	Thereafter	Total
Lines of Credit (3)	$ 0	$ 70,000	0	0	$ 70,000
Guarantees	11,200 (4)	16,039 (2)	0	0	27,239
Repurchase Obligations (5)	0	366,800	0	0	366,800
Total Commitments	**$11,200**	**$452,839**	**0**	**0**	**$464,039**

(1) See Note 7 to the Company's Consolidated Financial Statements.
(2) See Note 11 to the Company's Consolidated Financial Statements.
(3) See Note 6 to the Company's Consolidated Financial Statements. The amount listed represents available borrowings on the line of credit at Decmeber 29, 2001.
(4) See Note 16 to the Company's Consolidated Financial Statements.
(5) Reflects obligations under manufacturer repurchase committments. See Note 16 to the Company's Consolidated Financial Statements.

NEWLY ISSUED FINANCIAL REPORTING PRONOUNCEMENTS

See "New Accounting Pronouncements" in Note 1 of Notes to the Company's Consolidated Financial Statements.

MONACO COACH CORPORATION
CONSOLIDATED BALANCE SHEETS

(in thousands of dollars, except share and per share data)

	December 30, 2000	December 29, 2001
ASSETS		
Current assets:		
Trade receivables, net of $164 and $541, respectively	$67,998	$82,885
Inventories	114,397	127,075
Prepaid expenses	1,046	2,063
Deferred income taxes	13,197	27,327
Total current assets	**196,638**	**239,350**
Notes receivable	2,800	8,157
Property, plant and equipment, net	103,590	122,795
Debt issuance costs, net of accumulated amortization of $75		940
Goodwill, net of accumulated amortization of $4,675 and $5,320, respectively	18,582	55,856
Total assets	**$321,610**	**$427,098**
LIABILITIES		
Current liabilities:		
Book overdraft	$15,178	$5,889
Line of credit	20,585	26,004
Current portion of long-term note payable		10,000
Accounts payable	53,098	66,859
Accrued expenses and other liabilities	38,478	66,904
Total current liabilities	**127,339**	**175,656**
Long-term note payable		30,000
Deferred income taxes	7,646	8,312
	134,985	**213,968**
Commitments and contingencies (Note 16)		
STOCKHOLDERS' EQUITY		
Common stock, $.01 par value; 50,000,000 shares authorized, 18,952,107 and 28,632,774 issued and outstanding respectively	190	286
Additional paid-in capital	47,032	48,522
Retained earnings	139,403	164,322
Total stockholders' equity	**186,625**	**213,130**
Total liabilities and stockholders' equity	**$321,610**	**$427,098**

The accompanying notes are an integral part of these consolidated financial statements.

MONACO COACH CORPORATION
CONSOLIDATED STATEMENTS OF INCOME
for the years ended January 1, 2000, December 30, 2000 and December 29, 2001

(in thousands of dollars, except share and per share data)

	1999	2000	2001
Net sales	$780,815	$901,890	$937,073
Cost of sales	658,536	772,240	823,083
Gross profit	**122,279**	**129,650**	**113,990**
Selling, general and administrative expenses	48,791	59,175	70,687
Amortization of goodwill	645	645	645
Operating income	**72,843**	**69,830**	**42,658**
Other income, net	142	182	334
Interest expense	(1,143)	(632)	(2,357)
Income before income taxes	**71,842**	**69,380**	**40,635**
Provision for income taxes	28,081	26,859	15,716
Net income	**$43,761**	**$42,521**	**$24,919**
Earnings per common share:			
Basic	$ 1.55	$ 1.50	$ .87
Diluted	$ 1.51	$ 1.47	$ .85
Weighted average common shares outstanding:			
Basic	28,213,445	28,377,123	28,531,593
Diluted	29,050,454	28,978,265	29,288,688

The accompanying notes are an integral part of these consolidated financial statements.

MONACO COACH CORPORATION
CONSOLIDATED STATEMENTS OF STOCKHOLDERS' EQUITY
for the years ended January 1, 2000, December 30, 2000 and December 29, 2001

(in thousands of dollars, except share data)

	Common Stock		Additional	Retained	
	Shares	Amount	Paid-in Capital	Earnings	Total
Balances, January 2, 1999	12,481,095	$125	$44,947	$53,121	$98,193
Issuance of common stock	116,311	1	956		957
Tax benefit of stock options exercised			428		428
Stock splits	6,273,678	63	(63)		0
Net income				43,761	43,761
Balances, January 1, 2000	**18,871,084**	**189**	**46,268**	**96,882**	**143,339**
Issuance of common stock	81,023	1	727		728
Tax benefit of stock options exercised			37		37
Net income				42,521	42,521
Balances, December 30, 2000	**18,952,107**	**190**	**47,032**	**139,403**	**186,625**
Issuance of common stock	161,848	1	1,115		1,116
Tax benefit of stock options exercised			470		470
Stock splits	9,518,819	95	(95)		0
Net income				24,919	24,919
Balances, December 29, 2001	**28,632,774**	**$286**	**$48,522**	**$164,322**	**$213,130**

The accompanying notes are an integral part of these consolidated financial statements.

MONACO COACH CORPORATION
CONSOLIDATED STATEMENTS OF CASH FLOWS
for the years ended January 1, 2000, December 30, 2000 and December 29, 2001
(in thousands of dollars)

	1999	2000	2001
Increase (Decrease) in Cash:			
Cash flows from operating activities:			
Net income	$43,761	$42,521	$24,919
Adjustments to reconcile net income to net cash provided by operating activities:			
Depreciation and amortization	5,904	6,359	7,543
Gain on disposal of equipment			(74)
Deferred income taxes	(1,491)	3,609	6,005
Change in assets and liabilities:			
Trade receivables, net	(465)	(31,460)	(13,154)
Inventories	(28,030)	(26,801)	12,682
Prepaid expenses	(179)	(724)	(903)
Accounts payable	8,414	16,186	(10,318)
Income taxes payable	(2,743)	(1,406)	0
Accrued expenses and other liabilities	6,990	(1,931)	(5,720)
Net cash provided by operating activities	**32,161**	**6,353**	**20,980**
Cash flows from investing activities:			
Additions to property, plant and equipment	(32,228)	(19,750)	(10,210)
Proceeds from sale of assets			106
Collections on notes receivable	910		
Payment for business acquisition			(24,320)
Issuance of notes receivable		(2,800)	(5,357)
Net cash used in investing activities	**(31,318)**	**(22,550)**	**(39,781)**
Cash flows from financing activities:			
Book overdraft	1,959	2,700	(10,840)
Borrowings (payments) on line of credit, net	6,213	12,732	(10,930)
(Payments) borrowings on long-term notes payable	(10,400)		40,000
Issuance of common stock	1,385	765	1,586
Debt issuance costs			(1,015)
Net cash (used in) provided by financing activities	**(843)**	**16,197**	**18,801**
Net change in cash	0	0	0
Cash at beginning of period	0	0	0
Cash at end of period	**$0**	**$0**	**$0**

The accompanying notes are an integral part of these consolidated financial statements.

MONACO COACH CORPORATION
NOTES TO CONSOLIDATED FINANCIAL STATEMENTS

1. BUSINESS AND SIGNIFICANT ACCOUNTING POLICIES:

Business

Monaco Coach Corporation and its subsidiaries (the "Company") manufacture premium motor coaches, bus conversions and towable recreational vehicles at manufacturing facilities in Oregon and Indiana. These products are sold primarily to independent dealers throughout the United States and Canada.

Pursuant to Statement of Financial Accounting Standards (SFAS) No. 131, "Disclosures about Segments of an Enterprise and Related Information," effective for fiscal years beginning after December 31, 1997, the Company has determined that it has a single reportable operating segment consisting of the design, manufacture, and sale (wholesale) of recreational vehicles including motor coaches and towable fifth wheel and travel trailers. These product lines have similar economic characteristics and are similar in the nature of products, manufacturing processes, customer characteristics, and distribution methods.

Consolidation Policy

The accompanying consolidated financial statements include the accounts of the Company and its wholly-owned subsidiaries. All material intercompany transactions and balances have been eliminated.

Fiscal Period

The Company follows a 52/53 week fiscal year period ending on the Saturday closest to December 31. Interim periods also end on the Saturday closest to the calendar quarter end. For 1999, 2000, and 2001, all fiscal periods were 52 weeks long. All references to years in the consolidated financial statements relate to fiscal years rather than calendar years.

Stock Splits

On August 6, 2001 the Board of Directors declared a three-for-two stock split in the form of a 50% stock dividend on the Company's Common stock. Accordingly, all historical weighted average share and per share amounts have been restated to reflect the stock split. Share amounts presented in the Consolidated Statement of Stockholders' Equity reflect the actual share amounts outstanding for each period presented.

Estimates and Industry Factors

Estimates - The preparation of financial statements in conformity with accounting principles generally accepted in the United States of America, requires management to make estimates and assumptions that affect the reported amounts of assets and liabilities and disclosure of contingent assets and liabilities at the date of the financial statements and the reported amounts of revenues and expenses during the reporting period. Actual results could differ from those estimates.

Concentration of Credit Risk - The Company distributes its products through an independent dealer network for recreational vehicles. Sales to one customer were approximately 10%, 12%, and 12% of net revenues for the fiscal years ended January 1, 2000, December 30, 2000, and December 29, 2001, respectively. No other individual dealers represented over 10% of net revenues in 1999, 2000, or 2001. The loss of a significant dealer or a substantial decrease in sales by such a dealer could have a material adverse effect on the Company's business, results of operations and financial results.

Concentrations of credit risk exist for accounts receivable and repurchase agreements (see Note 16), primarily for the Company's largest dealers. The Company generally sells to dealers throughout the United States and there is no geographic concentration of credit risk.

Reliance on Key Suppliers - The Company's production strategy relies on certain key suppliers' ability to deliver subassemblies and component parts in time to meet manufacturing schedules. The Company has a variety of key suppliers, including Allison, Workhorse, Cummins, Dana, and Ford. The Company does not have any long-term contracts with these suppliers or their distributors. In 1997, Allison put all chassis manufacturers on allocation with respect to one of the transmissions the Company uses, and in 1999 Ford put one of its gasoline powered chassis on allocation. In light of these dependencies, it is possible that failure of Allison, Ford or any of the other suppliers to meet the Company's future requirements for transmissions, chassis or other key components could have a material near-term impact on the Company's business, results of operations and financial condition.

Warranty Claims - Estimated warranty costs are provided for at the time of sale of products with warranties covering the products for up to one year from the date of retail sale (five years for the front and sidewall frame structure, and three years on Magnum chassis). These estimates are based on historical average repair costs, as well as other reasonable assumptions as have been deemed appropriate by management.

Litigation Claims - Estimated litigation costs are provided for at the time of sale of products, or at the time a determination is made that an estimable loss has occurred. These estimates are developed by legal counsel based on professional judgment, as well as historical experience.

Inventories

Inventories consist of raw materials, work-in-process and finished recreational vehicles and are stated at the lower of cost (first-in, first-out) or market. Cost of work-in-process and finished recreational vehicles includes material, labor and manufacturing overhead costs.

Property, Plant and Equipment

Property, plant and equipment, including significant improvements thereto, are stated at cost less accumulated depreciation and amortization. Cost includes expenditures for major improvements, replacements and renewals and the net amount of interest cost associated with significant capital additions during periods of construction. Capitalized interest was $195,000 in 1999, $192,000 in 2000, and zero in 2001. Maintenance and repairs are charged to expense as incurred. Replacements and renewals are capitalized. When assets are sold, retired or otherwise disposed of, the cost and accumulated depreciation are removed from the accounts and any resulting gain or loss is reflected in income.

The cost of plant and equipment is depreciated using the straight-line method over the estimated useful lives of the related assets. Buildings are generally depreciated over 39 years and equipment is depreciated over 3 to 10 years. Leasehold improvements are amortized under the straight-line method based on the shorter of the lease periods or the estimated useful lives.

At each balance sheet date, management assesses whether there has been permanent impairment in the value of long-lived assets. The amount of any such impairment is determined by comparing anticipated undiscounted future cash flows from operating activities with the associated carrying value. The factors considered by management in performing this assessment include current operating results, trends and prospects, as well as the effects of obsolescence, demand, competition and other economic factors.

Goodwill and Debt Issuance Costs

Goodwill represents the excess of the cost of acquisition over the fair value of net assets acquired. The Company is the successor to a company formed in 1968 (the "Predecessor") and commenced operations on March 5, 1993 by acquiring substantially all of the assets and liabilities of the Predecessor. The goodwill arising from the acquisition of the assets and operations of the Company's Predecessor in March 1993 has been amortized on a straight-line basis over 40 years and, at December 29, 2001, the unamortized amount was $16.1 million. In March 1996, the Company acquired the Holiday Rambler Division of Harley-Davidson, Inc. ("Holiday Rambler"). The goodwill arising from the acquisition of Holiday Rambler has been amortized on a straight-line basis over 20 years and, at December 29, 2001, the unamortized amount was $1.8 million. The Company also recorded $37.9 million of goodwill associated with the August 2, 2001 acquisition of SMC Corporation (SMC). For the fiscal year ended December 29, 2001, in accordance with the Financial Accounting Standards Board (FASB) statement No. 142, "Accounting for Goodwill and Other Intangible Assets," no amortization of goodwill associated with the acquisition of SMC has been recorded.

At each balance sheet date, management assesses whether there has been permanent impairment in the value of goodwill. The amount of any such impairment is determined by comparing anticipated undiscounted future cash flows from operating activities with the associated carrying value. The factors considered by management in performing this assessment include current operating results, trends and prospects, as well as the effects of obsolescence, demand, competition and other economic factors. As of December 29, 2001, in accordance with FASB statement No. 121, management has determined that there has been no impairment of goodwill requiring a write down.

Income Taxes

Deferred taxes are recognized based on the difference between the financial statement and tax bases of assets and liabilities at enacted tax rates in effect in the years in which the differences are expected to reverse. Deferred tax expense or benefit represents the change in deferred tax asset/liability balances. A valuation allowance is established for deferred tax assets when it is more likely than not that the deferred tax asset will not be realized.

Revenue Recognition

The Company recognizes revenue from the sale of recreational vehicles upon shipment.

In December 1999, the Securities and Exchange Commission issued Staff Accounting Bulletin (SAB) No. 101, Revenue Recognition in Financial Statements. SAB No. 101 provides guidance for revenue recognition under certain circumstances. The Company has complied with the guidance provided by SAB No. 101 for the fiscal years 1999, 2000 and 2001.

Advertising Costs

The Company expenses advertising costs as incurred, except for prepaid show costs which are expensed when the event takes place. During 2001, approximately $10.1 million ($6.4 million in 1999 and $7.8 million in 2000) of advertising costs were expensed.

Research and Development Costs

Research and development costs are charged to expense as incurred and were $6.2 million for 2001 ($4.7 million in 1999 and $5.1 million for 2000).

New Accounting Pronouncements

In June 2001, the Financial Accounting Standards Board (FASB or the "Board") issued Statement of Financial Accounting Standards No. 141 (SFAS 141), Business Combinations, and No. 142 (SFAS 142), Goodwill and Other Intangible Assets, collectively referred to as the "Standards." The provisions of SFAS 141 (1) require that the purchase method of accounting be used for all business combinations initiated after June 30, 2001, (2) provide specific criteria for the initial recognition and measurement of intangible assets apart from goodwill, and (3) require that unamortized negative goodwill be written off immediately as an extraordinary gain instead of being deferred and amortized. SFAS 141 also requires that upon adoption of SFAS 142 the Company reclassify the carrying amounts of certain intangible assets into or out of goodwill, based on certain criteria. SFAS 142 primarily addresses the accounting for goodwill and intangible assets subsequent to their initial recognition. The provisions of SFAS 142 (1) prohibit the amortization of goodwill and indefinite-lived intangible assets, (2) require that goodwill and indefinite-lived intangibles assets be tested annually for impairment (and in interim periods if certain events occur indicating that the carrying value of goodwill and/or indefinite-lived intangible assets may be impaired), (3) require that reporting units be identified for the purpose of assessing potential future impairments of goodwill, and (4) remove the forty-year limitation on the amortization period of intangible assets that have finite lives.

The Company will adopt the provisions of SFAS 142 in its first quarter of 2002. The Company is preparing for its adoption of SFAS 142 and is making the determinations as to what its reporting units are and what amounts of goodwill, intangible assets, other assets, and liabilities should be allocated to those reporting units. The Company expects that it will no longer record $645,000 of annual amortization expense relating to its existing goodwill and indefinite-lived intangibles, as adjusted for the reclassifications just mentioned.

SFAS 142 requires that goodwill be tested annually for impairment using a two-step process. The first step is to identify a potential impairment and, in transition, this step must be measured as of the beginning of the fiscal year. However, a company has six months from the date of adoption to complete the first step. The Company expects to complete that first step of the goodwill impairment test during the first quarter of 2002. The second step of the goodwill impairment test measures the amount of the impairment loss (measured as of the beginning of the year of adoption), if any, and must be completed by the end of the Company's fiscal year. Intangible assets deemed to have an indefinite life will be tested for impairment using a one-step process which compares the fair value to the carrying amount of the asset as of the beginning of the fiscal year, and pursuant to the requirements of SFAS 142 will be completed during the first quarter of 2002. Any impairment loss resulting from the transitional impairment tests will be reflected as the cumulative effect of a change in accounting principle in the first quarter of 2002. The Company is in the process of assessing the impact of SFAS 142 on the financial statements.

In June 2001, FASB issued Statement No. 143, Accounting for Asset Retirement Obligations. FASB Statement No. 143 is effective for the fiscal years beginning after June 15, 2002. FASB Statement No. 143, addresses financial accounting and reporting for obligations associated with the retirement of tangible long-lived assets and the associated asset retirement costs. FASB Statement No. 143 requires that the fair value of a liability for an asset retirement obligation be recognized in the period in which it is incurred if a reasonable estimate of fair value can be made. The associated asset retirement costs are capitalized as part of the carrying amount of the long-lived asset. The impact of this pronouncement on the Company's financial statements is not expected to be material.

In August 2001, FASB issued statement No. 144, Accounting for the Impairment or Disposal of Long-Lived Assets. FASB Statement No. 144 is effective for the fiscal years beginning after December 15, 2001. This statement supersedes FASB Statement No. 121, Accounting for the Impairment of Long-Lived Assets and for Long-Lived Assets to Be Disposed Of, and the accounting and reporting provisions of APB Opinion No. 30, Reporting the Results of Operations -- Reporting the Effects of Disposal of a Segment of a Business, and Extraordinary, Unusual and Infrequently Occurring Events and Transactions, for the disposal of a segment of a business. FASB Statement No. 121 did not address the accounting for a segment of a business accounted for as a discontinued operation under APB Opinion No. 30, accordingly two accounting models existed for long-lived assets to be disposed of. FASB Statement No. 144, establishes a single accounting model, based on the framework established in Statement No. 121, for long-lived assets to be disposed of by sale. In addition, FASB Statement No. 144 resolves significant implementation issues related to Statement No. 121. The Company is in the process of assessing the impact of SFAS 144 on the financial statements.

Supplemental Cash Flow Disclosures:

	1999	2000	2001
		(in thousands)	
Cash paid during the period for:			
Interest, net of amount capitalized of $195 in 1999, $192 in 2000 and $0 in 2001	$1,131	$632	$2,206
Income taxes	30,823	28,226	16,231

2. ACQUISITION OF SMC CORPORATION

The Company announced on June 25, 2001 that it had reached an agreeement with Oregon based motor home manufacturer SMC Corporation ("SMC") to acquire all of the outstanding shares of SMC pursuant to a cash tender offer at a price of $3.70 per share. On August 6, 2001, the Company completed the back-end merger, and owned 100% of the shares.

The cash paid for SMC, including transaction costs of $3,062,000, totaled $24,320,000. The total assets acquired and liabilities assumed of SMC based on estimated fair values at August 6, 2001, is as follows:

	(in thousands)
Receivables	$1,733
Inventories	25,360
Deferred tax asset	19,469
Property and equipment	15,850
Prepaids and other assets	114
Goodwill	37,919
Total assets acquired	**100,445**
Book overdraft	(1,551)
Notes payable	(16,349)
Accounts payable	(24,079)
Accrued liabilities	(34,146)
Total liabilities assumed	**(76,125)**
Total assets acquired and liabilities assumed	**$24,320**

The allocation of the purchase price and the related goodwill is subject to adjustment upon resolution of pre-SMC Acquisition contingencies. The effects of resolution of pre-SMC Acquisition contingencies occurring: (i) within one year of the acquisition date will be reflected as an adjustment of the allocation of the purchase price and of goodwill, and (ii) after one year they will be recognized in the determination of net income.

The following unaudited pro forma information presents the consolidated results as if the acquisition had occurred at the beginning of the period and giving effect to the adjustments for the related interest on financing the purchase price, goodwill and depreciation. The pro forma information does not necessarily reflect results that would have occurred or is it necessarily indicative of future operating results.

	(in thousands, except per share data)	
	2000	2001
Net sales	$1,093,000	$1,015,000
Net income	36,000	14,000
Diluted earnings per common share	$1.25	$0.48

3. INVENTORIES:

Inventories consist of the following:

	December 30, 2000	December 29, 2001
	(in thousands)	
Raw materials	$45,187	$53,160
Work-in-process	31,739	44,436
Finished units	37,471	29,479
	$114,397	**$127,075**

4. PROPERTY, PLANT AND EQUIPMENT:

Property, plant and equipment consist of the following:

	December 30, 2000	December 29, 2001
	(in thousands)	
Land	$6,687	$11,999
Buildings	83,564	99,333
Equipment	20,559	22,838
Furniture and fixtures	6,644	9,479
Vehicles	1,232	1,571
Leasehold improvements	854	1,472
Construction in progress	3,504	2,376
	123,044	**149,068**
Less accumulated depreciation and amortization	19,454	26,273
	$103,590	**$122,795**

5. ACCRUED EXPENSES AND OTHER LIABILITIES:

	December 30, 2000	December 29, 2001
	(in thousands)	
Payroll, vacation and related accruals	$11,371	$12,580
Payroll and property taxes	1,491	1,172
Reserve for warranty claims	15,479	29,721
Reserve for product liability claims	6,391	17,597
Promotional and advertising	1,271	1,345
Other	2,475	4,489
	$38,478	**$66,904**

6. LINE OF CREDIT:

During the third quarter of 2001, the Company obtained a new credit facility from a consortium of lenders. The Company's new permanent credit facility consists of a revolving line of credit of up to $70.0 million (the "Revolving Loan"). At the election of the Company, the Revolving Loan bears interest at variable rates based on the Prime Rate or LIBOR. The Revolving Loan is due and payable in full on September 30, 2004, and requires monthly interest payments. The balance outstanding under the Revolving Loan at December 29, 2001 was $26.0 million. The Revolving Loan is collateralized by all of the assets of the Company, and include various restrictions and financial covenants.

The weighted average interest rate on the outstanding borrowings under the revolving line of credit was 8.9% and 5.8% for 2000 and 2001, respectively. Interest expense on the unused available portion of the line was $44,000 or 0.4% and $85,000 or 0.2% of weighted average outstanding borrowings for 2000 and 2001, respectively. The revolving line of credit is collateralized by all the assets of the Company. The agreement contains restrictive covenants as to the Company's leverage ratio, current ratio, fixed charge coverage ratio and tangible net worth. As of December 29, 2001, the Company was in compliance with these covenants.

7. LONG-TERM NOTE PAYABLE:

The Company has a long-term note payable of $40 million outstanding at December 29, 2001. The term note bears interest at varying rates that fluctuate based on the Prime rate or LIBOR, and are determined based on the Company's leverage ratio. The term note requires monthly interest payments and quarterly principal payments and is collateralized by all the assets of the Company. The term note is due and payable in full on September 28, 2005. As of December 29, 2001, the interest rate on the term debt was 3.94%

The following table displays the scheduled principal payments by year that will be due on the term loan.

Year	Amount of payment due
	(in thousands)
2002	$10,000
2003	$12,500
2004	$10,000
2005	$ 7,500
	$40,000

8. PREFERRED STOCK:

The Company has authorized "blank check" preferred stock (1,934,783 shares authorized, $.01 par value) ("Preferred Stock"), which may be issued from time to time in one or more series upon authorization by the Company's Board of Directors. The Board of Directors, without further approval of the stockholders, is authorized to fix the dividend rights and terms, conversion rights, voting rights, redemption rights and terms, liquidation preferences, and any other rights, preferences, privileges and restrictions applicable to each series of the Preferred Stock. There were no shares of Preferred Stock outstanding as of December 30, 2000 or December 29, 2001.

9. INCOME TAXES:

The provision for income taxes is as follows:

	1999	2000	2001
		(in thousands)	
Current:			
Federal	$24,439	$19,120	$8,262
State	5,133	4,130	1,606
	29,572	**23,250**	**9,868**
Deferred:			
Federal	(1,222)	2,945	4,880
State	(269)	664	968
Provision for income taxes	**$28,081**	**$26,859**	**$15,716**

The reconciliation of the provision for income taxes at the U.S. federal statutory rate to the Company's effective income tax rate is as follows:

	1999	2000	2001
		(in thousands)	
Expected U.S. federal income taxes at statutory rates	$25,145	$24,283	$14,222
State and local income taxes, net of federal benefit	3,162	3,116	1,673
Other	(226)	(540)	(179)
	$28,081	**$26,859**	**$15,716**

The components of the current net deferred tax asset and long-term net deferred tax liability are:

	December 30, 2000	December 29, 2001
	(in thousands)	
Current deferred income tax assets:		
Warranty liability	$6,121	$11,909
Product liability	2,527	6,376
Inventory reserves	1,853	3,144
Payroll and related accruals	958	1,911
Other accruals	1,738	3,987
	$13,197	**$27,327**
Long-term deferred income tax liabilities:		
Depreciation	$5,197	$8,741
Amortization	2,449	2,846
Net operating loss (NOL) carryforward	0	(6,070)
Valuation allowance on NOL carryforward	0	2,795
	$7,646	**$8,312**

Management believes that the temporary differences which gave rise to the deferred income tax assets will be realized in the foreseeable future, except for benefits arising from the NOL carryforward associated with the SMC Acquisition. Accordingly, management has provided a valuation allowance for the portion of the NOL carryforward that may not be fully recognized.

10. EARNINGS PER SHARE:

Basic earnings per common share is based on the weighted average number of shares outstanding during the period using net income attributable to common stock as the numerator. Diluted earnings per common share is based on the weighted average number of shares outstanding during the period, after consideration of the dilutive effect of stock options and convertible preferred stock, using net income as the numerator. The weighted average number of common shares used in the computation of earnings per common share for the years ended January 1, 2000, December 30, 2000, and December 29, 2001 are as follows:

	1999	2000	2001
Basic			
Issued and outstanding shares (weighted average)	28,213,445	28,377,123	28,531,593
Effect of Dilutive Securities			
Stock options	837,009	601,142	757,095
Diluted	**29,050,454**	**28,978,265**	**29,288,688**

11. LEASES:

The Company has commitments under certain noncancelable operating leases. Total rental expense for the fiscal years ended January 1, 2000, December 30, 2000, and December 29, 2001 related to operating leases amounted to approximately $1.0 million, $2.4 million and $2.8 million, respectively. The Company's most significant lease is a two-year operating lease for an aircraft with annual renewals for up to three additional years. The future minimum rental commitments under the initial term of this lease are $1.4 million in both 2002 and 2003. In addition, if the Company chooses the return option at the end of the initial lease term in February of 2004, the Company has guaranteed up to $16 million of any deficiency in the event that the Lessor's net sales proceeds of the aircraft are less than $18.5 million.

Approximate future minimum rental commitments under these leases at December 29, 2001 are summarized as follows:

Fiscal Year	(in thousands)
2002	2,938
2003	2,182
2004	682
2005	675
2006	675
2007 and thereafter	5,008

12. BONUS PLAN:

The Company has a discretionary bonus plan for certain key employees. Bonus expense included in selling, general and administrative expenses for the years ended January 1, 2000, December 30, 2000, and December 29, 2001 was $8.0 million, $9.0 million and $6.1 million, respectively.

13. STOCK OPTION PLANS:

The Company has an Employee Stock Purchase Plan (the "Purchase Plan") - 1993, a Non-employee Director Stock Option Plan (the "Director Plan") - 1993, and an Incentive Stock Option Plan (the "Option Plan") - 1993:

Stock Purchase Plan

The Company's Purchase Plan qualifies under Section 423 of the Internal Revenue Code. The Company has reserved 683,087 shares of Common Stock for issuance under the Purchase Plan. During the years ended December 30, 2000 and December 29, 2001, 52,725 shares and 64,643 shares, respectively, were purchased under the Purchase Plan. The weighted-average fair value of purchase rights granted in 2000 and 2001 was $9.57 and $8.74, respectively. Under the Purchase Plan, an eligible employee may purchase shares of common stock from the Company through payroll deductions of up to 10% of base compensation, at a price per share equal to 85% of the lesser of the fair market value of the Company's Common Stock as of the first day (grant date) or the last day (purchase date) of each six-month offering period under the Purchase Plan.

The Purchase Plan is administered by a committee appointed by the Board. Any employee who is customarily employed for at least 20 hours per week and more than five months in a calendar year by the Company, or by any majority-owned subsidiary designated from time to time by the Board, and who does not own 5% or more of the total combined voting power or value of all classes of the Company's outstanding capital stock, is eligible to participate in the Purchase Plan.

Directors' Option Plan

Each non-employee director of the Company is entitled to participate in the Company's "Director Plan." The Board of Directors and the stockholders have authorized a total of 352,500 shares of Common Stock for issuance pursuant to the Director Plan. Under the terms of the Director Plan, each eligible non-employee director is automatically granted an option to purchase 8,000 shares of Common Stock (the "Initial Option") on the latter of the effective date of the Company's initial public offering or the date on which the optionee first becomes a director of the Company. Thereafter, each optionee is automatically granted an additional option to purchase 3,500 shares of Common Stock (a "Subsequent Option") on September 30 of each year if, on such date, the optionee has served as a director of the Company for at least six months. Each Initial Option vests over five years at the rate of 20% of the shares subject to the Initial Option at the end of each anniversary following the date of grant. Each Subsequent Option vests in full on the fifth anniversary of its date of grant. The exercise price of each option is the fair market value of the Common Stock as determined by the closing price reported by the New York Stock Exchange on the date of grant. As of December 29, 2001, 24,300 options had been exercised, and options to purchase 135,750 shares of common stock were outstanding.

Option Plan

The Option Plan provides for the grant to employees of incentive stock options within the meaning of Section 422 of the Internal Revenue Code of 1986, as amended (the "Code"), and for the grant to employees and consultants of the Company of nonstatutory stock options. A total of 2,657,813 shares of Common Stock have been reserved for issuance under the Option Plan. As of December 29, 2001, options to purchase 1,235,023 shares of Common Stock were outstanding. These options vest ratably over five years commencing with the date of grant.

The exercise price of all incentive stock options granted under the Option Plan must be at least equal to the fair market value of a share of the Company's Common Stock on the date of grant. With respect to any participant possessing more than 10% of the voting power of the Company's outstanding capital stock, the exercise price of any option granted must equal at least 110% of the fair market value on the grant date, and the maximum term of the option must not exceed five years. The terms of all other options granted under the Option Plan may not exceed ten years.

Transactions involving the Director Plan and the Option Plan are summarized with corresponding weighted-average exercise prices as follows:

	Shares	Price
Outstanding at January 2, 1999	1,172,317	$ 3.99
Granted	232,727	10.44
Exercised	(186,398)	3.48
Forfeited	(4,458)	5.62
Outstanding at January 1, 2000	**1,214,188**	**5.99**
Granted	206,851	12.43
Exercised	(68,810)	3.25
Forfeited	(14,661)	7.93
Outstanding at December 30, 2000	**1,337,568**	**6.48**
Granted	218,401	12.42
Exercised	(140,163)	3.95
Forfeited	(45,033)	8.21
Outstanding at December 29, 2001	**1,370,773**	**$ 7.62**

For various price ranges, weighted average characteristics of all outstanding stock options at December 29, 2001 were as follows:

	Options Outstanding			Options Exercisable	
Range of Exercise Prices	Shares	Remaining Life (years)	Weighted-Average Price	Shares	Weighted-Average Price
$ 1.62	94,786	1.2	$ 0.65	94,786	$ 0.65
$ 1.63 - 3.25	268,286	3.3	2.81	268,286	2.81
$ 3.26 - 4.88	155,909	5.1	3.59	102,236	3.52
$ 6.50 - 8.13	230,263	6.3	7.73	123,729	7.74
$ 9.75- 11.38	228,827	7.4	10.32	77,521	10.25
$11.39 - 13.00	358,952	8.8	12.30	32,790	12.66
$13.01 - 14.63	14,000	9.8	14.25	---	---
$14.64 - 16.25	19,750	9.4	16.19	---	---
	1,370,773			**699,348**	

The Company complies with the disclosure-only provisions of SFAS No. 123, "Accounting for Stock-Based Compensation," and thus no compensation cost has been recognized for the Director Plan, the Option Plan or the Purchase Plan. Had compensation cost for the three stock-based compensation plans been determined based on the fair value of options at the date of grant consistent with the provisions of SFAS No. 123, the Company's pro forma net income and pro forma earnings per share would have been as follows:

	1999	2000	2001
	(In thousands, except per share data)		
Net income - as reported	$43,761	$42,521	$24,919
Net income - pro forma	43,067	41,743	23,880
Diluted earnings per share - as reported	$ 1.51	$1.47	$0.85
Diluted earnings per share - pro forma	1.48	1.44	0.82

The pro forma effect on net income for 1999, 2000 and 2001 is not representative of the pro forma effect in future years because compensation expense related to grants made in prior years is not considered. For purposes of the above pro forma information, the fair value of each option grant was estimated at the date of grant using the Black-Scholes option pricing model with the following weighted average assumptions:

	1999	2000	2001
Risk-free interest rate	5.29%	6.27%	4.42%
Expected life (in years)	6.65	5.68	6.23
Expected volatility	55.65%	54.63%	55.02%
Expected dividend yield	0.00%	0.00%	0.00%

14. FAIR VALUE OF FINANCIAL INSTRUMENTS:

The fair value of the Company's financial instruments are presented below. The estimates require subjective judgments and are approximate. Changes in methodologies and assumptions could significantly affect estimates.

Line of Credit - The carrying amount outstanding on the revolving line of credit is $20.6 million and $26.0 million at December 30, 2000 and December 29, 2001, respectively, which approximates the estimated fair value as this instrument requires interest payments at a market rate of interest plus a margin.

Long-term Note Payable - The carrying amount outstanding on the long-term note payable is $40.0 million (including $10.0 million of current payable) at December 29, 2001, which approximates the estimated fair value as this instrument requires interest payments at a market rate of interest plus a margin.

15. 401(K) DEFINED CONTRIBUTION PLAN:

The Company sponsors a 401(k) defined contribution plan covering substantially all full-time employees. Company contributions to the plan totaled $571,000 in 1999, $593,000 in 2000 and $629,000 in 2001.

16. COMMITMENTS AND CONTINGENCIES:

Repurchase Agreements

Substantially all of the Company's sales to independent dealers are made on terms requiring cash on delivery. The Company does not finance dealer purchases. However, most purchases are financed on a "floor plan" basis by a bank or finance company which lends the dealer all or substantially all of the wholesale purchase price and retains a security interest in the vehicles. Upon request of a lending institution financing a dealer's purchases of the Company's product, the Company will execute a repurchase agreement. These agreements provide that, for up to 18 months after a unit is shipped, the Company will repurchase a dealer's inventory in the event of a default by a dealer to its lender.

The Company's liability under repurchase agreements is limited to the unpaid balance owed to the lending institution by reason of its extending credit to the dealer to purchase its vehicles, reduced by the resale value of vehicles which may be repurchased. The risk of loss is spread over numerous dealers and financial institutions.

No significant net losses were incurred during the years ended January 1, 2000, December 30, 2000 or December 29, 2001. The approximate amount subject to contingent repurchase obligations arising from these agreements at December 29, 2001 is $366.8 million, with approximately 7.44% concentrated with one dealer. If the Company were obligated to repurchase a significant number of recreational vehicles in the future, losses and reduction in new recreational vehicle sales could result.

Product Liability

The Company is subject to regulations which may require the Company to recall products with design or safety defects, and such recall could have a material adverse effect on the Company's business, results of operations and financial condition.

The Company has from time to time been subject to product liability claims. To date, the Company has been successful in obtaining product liability insurance on terms the Company considers acceptable. The terms of the policy contain a self-insured retention amount of $100,000 per occurrence, with a maximum annual aggregate self-insured retention of $1.0 million. Overall product liability insurance, including umbrella coverage, is available to a maximum amount of $100.1 million for each occurrence and an annual aggregate of $102.0 million. There can be no assurance that the Company will be able to obtain insurance coverage in the future at acceptable levels or that the cost of insurance will be reasonable. Furthermore, successful assertion against the Company of one or a series of large uninsured claims, or of one or a series of claims exceeding any insurance coverage, could have a material adverse effect on the Company's business, results of operations and financial condition.

Litigation

The Company is involved in various legal proceedings which are incidental to the industry and for which certain matters are covered in whole or in part by insurance or, otherwise, the Company has recorded accruals for estimated settlements. Management believes that any liability which may result from these proceedings will not have a material adverse effect on the Company's consolidated financial statements.

Debt Guarantee

In 2000, the Company loaned $2.8 million to Outdoor Resorts of Las Vegas ("ORLV") for the purpose of constructing a luxury motor coach resort in Las Vegas, Nevada, and an additional amount of $5.3 million in 2001 for resorts in Naples, Florida and Indio, California. Accrued interest receivable from the loans was $639,000 at December 29, 2001, of which approximately $200,000 was in arrears due to delays in development of the project in Las Vegas, Nevada.

As part of the financing structure for the new resorts, the Company also agreed to act as co-guarantor with ORLV's parent company, Outdoor Resorts of America ("ORA"), on a $12.0 million construction loan. In return for the Company's loan and guarantee commitment, ORLV has agreed to pay interest and income participation to the Company. At December 29, 2001 ORLV had drawn $9.7 million on the construction loan.

17. QUARTERLY RESULTS (UNAUDITED):

Year ended January 1, 2000	1st Quarter	2nd Quarter	3rd Quarter	4th Quarter
(In thousands, except per share data)				
Net sales	$193,201	$199,178	$196,694	$191,742
Gross profit	29,164	31,347	30,998	30,770
Operating income	17,300	18,919	18,373	18,251
Net income	9,878	11,457	11,227	11,199
Earnings per common share:				
Basic	$0.35	$0.41	$0.40	$0.40
Diluted	$0.34	$0.39	$0.39	$0.38

Year ended December 30, 2000	1st Quarter	2nd Quarter	3rd Quarter	4th Quarter
(In thousands, except per share data)				
Net sales	$237,983	$226,091	$226,393	$211,423
Gross profit	37,314	32,117	30,908	29,311
Operating income	21,375	18,217	16,143	14,095
Net income	12,918	11,148	9,807	8,648
Earnings per common share:				
Basic	$0.46	$0.39	$0.35	$0.30
Diluted	$0.44	$0.39	$0.34	$0.30

Year ended December 29, 2001	1st Quarter	2nd Quarter	3rd Quarter	4th Quarter
(In thousands, except per share data)				
Net sales	$211,228	$223,424	$240,831	$261,590
Gross profit	25,488	25,804	30,548	32,150
Operating income	9,088	9,153	11,438	12,979
Net income	5,197	5,480	6,623	7,619
Earnings per common share:				
Basic	$0.18	$0.19	$0.23	$0.27
Diluted	$0.18	$0.19	$0.23	$0.26

Report of Independent Accountants

To the Stockholders and Board of Directors of Monaco Coach Corporation:

In our opinion, the accompanying consolidated balance sheets and the related consolidated statements of income, of stockholders' equity, and of cash flows listed in the accompanying index present fairly, in all material respects, the financial position of Monaco Coach Corporation and Subsidiaries (the Company) at December 30, 2000 and December 29, 2001, and the results of their operations and their cash flows for each of the three years in the period ended December 29, 2001, in conformity with accounting principles generally accepted in the United States of America. These financial statements are the responsibility of the Company's management; our responsibility is to express an opinion on these financial statements based on our audits. We conducted our audits of these financial statements in accordance with auditing standards generally accepted in the United States of America, which require that we plan and perform the audit to obtain reasonable assurance about whether the financial statements are free of material misstatement. An audit includes examining, on a test basis, evidence supporting the amounts and disclosures in the financial statements, assessing the accounting principles used and significant estimates made by management, and evaluating the overall financial statement presentation. We believe that our audits provide a reasonable basis for our opinion.

PricewaterhouseCoopers LLP

PricewaterhouseCoopers LLP

Portland, Oregon

January 26, 2002

Five-Year Selected Financial Data

The following table sets forth financial data of Monaco Coach Corporation for the years indicated (in thousands of dollars, except share and per share data and consolidated operating data).

Fiscal Year	1997 (1)	1998	1999	2000	2001
Consolidated Statements of Income Data:					
Net sales	$441,895	$594,802	$780,815	$901,890	$937,073
Cost of sales	382,367	512,570	658,536	772,240	823,083
Gross profit	**59,528**	**82,232**	**122,279**	**129,650**	**113,990**
Selling, general and administrative expenses	36,307	41,571	48,791	59,175	70,687
Amortization of goodwill	594	645	645	645	645
Operating income	**22,627**	**40,016**	**72,843**	**69,830**	**42,658**
Other income, net	(468)	(607)	(142)	(182)	(334)
Interest expense	2,379	1,861	1,143	632	2,357
Gain on sale of dealership assets	539	---	---	---	---
Income before provision for income taxes	**21,255**	**38,762**	**71,842**	**69,380**	**40,635**
Provision for income taxes	8,819	16,093	28,081	26,859	15,716
Net income	**12,436**	**22,669**	**43,761**	**42,521**	**24,919**
Redeemable preferred stock dividends	---	---	---	---	---
Accretion of redeemable preferred stock	(317)	---	---	---	---
Net income attributable to common stock	**$ 12,119**	**$ 22,669**	**$43,761**	**$42,521**	**$24,919**
Earnings per common share:					
Basic	$0.48	$0.81	$1.55	$1.50	$0.87
Diluted	$0.47	$0.79	$1.51	$1.47	$0.85
Weighted average shares outstanding:					
Basic	25,298,763	27,987,004	28,213,444	28,377,123	28,531,593
Diluted	26,318,196	28,622,976	29,050,453	28,978,264	29,288,688
Consolidated Operating Data:					
Units sold: (2)					
Motor coaches	3,347	4,768	6,233	6,632	6,228
Towables	2,397	2,217	3,269	3,377	3,261
Dealerships at end of period	208	263	294	338	385
Consolidated Balance Sheet Data:					
Working capital	$10,412	$23,676	$38,888	$69,299	$63,694
Total assets	159,832	190,127	246,727	321,610	427,098
Long-term borrowings, less current portion	11,500	5,400	---	---	30,000
Redeemable preferred stock	---	---	---	---	---
Total stockholders' equity	74,748	98,193	143,339	186,625	213,130

(1) Includes the operations of Holiday Rambler and the Holiday World Dealerships from March 4, 1996. The Holiday World Dealerships generated $6.8 million in net sales in 1997, which included the sale of 211 units in 1997, that were either previously owned or not Holiday Rambler units, as well as service revenues. The Company sold seven Holiday World Dealerships in 1996 and the remaining three dealerships in 1997.

(2) Excludes units sold by the Holiday World Dealerships that were either previously owned or not Holiday Rambler units.

MONACO COACH CORPORATION BOARD OF DIRECTORS

Kay L. Toolson
Chairman and Chief Executive Officer, Monaco Coach Corporation

Robert P. Hanafee, Jr.
Private Investor

Michael J. Kluger
Partner, ML Healthcare Partners (Financial Services)

L. Ben Lytle
Chairman, Anthem, Inc. (Healthcare Services)

Carl E. Ring, Jr.
Partner, Liberty Partners (Financial Services)

Richard A. Rouse
Private Investor

Roger A. Vandenberg
President, Cariad Capital (Financial Services)

COMPANY OFFICERS

Kay L. Toolson
Chairman and Chief Executive Officer

John W. Nepute
President

Marty Daley
Vice President and Chief Financial Officer

Richard E. Bond
Senior Vice President, Chief Administrative Officer and Secretary

Irv Yoder
Vice President and Director of Indiana Manufacturing

Marty Garriott
Vice President and Director of Oregon Manufacturing

Mike Snell
Vice President of Sales

Patrick Carroll
Vice President and Director of Product Development

John Healey
Vice President of Purchasing

OTHER OFFICERS AND DIRECTORS

Kurt W. Anderson, Terri Archambault, Chris A. Ballinger, Joni S. Beachy, Michael R. Becker, Steve Bettis, Mikeal D. Blomme, Elise A. Burkart, Marvin P. Burns, Jeffrey P. Butler, Russell Cobb, Lee G. Covey, John Cunningham, Arthur N. Deeds, Mike Dodson, Michael Duncan, Darryl F. Emery, Ron L. Ericson, Gordon C. Foster, James A. Fox, Paul E. Freet, Dennis E. Girod, Peter J. Hanes, Garth R. Herring, Scott Hicks, Dale D. Hoogenboom, Chris G. Hundt, Enoch R. Hutchcraft, Sandra J. Kadash, Mark P. Kealoha, Charles J. Kimball, Edgar F. Kinney, April A. Klein, Donald J. Lance, Scott A. Lilly, Philip R. Lord, Jim Mac, Richard K. Mackin, Melanie Hoover Marsh, Jack R. Mason, Daryl L. Maurer, John Mayger, B. Ray Mehaffey, Gary W. Mehaffey, Ty Meier, Arnold P. Morosky, Wes Murphy, Deanna R. Ota, T. Michael Pangburn, D. Page Robertson, T. Alan L. Schmucker, Rick A. Schraw, Defoe A. Shook, Jr., Michael A. Spencer, Lyle D. Stutzman, Charles Tillery, Don Turner, Mike Warren, Dale D. Weins, Terry L. Welles, Carter Yoder, Scott E. Zimmer, Tom Zoll, Joe Zurbuch

CORPORATE INFORMATION

Corporate Headquarters/Oregon Manufacturing Facilities
91320 Industrial Way, Coburg, OR 97408, Telephone (574) 686-8011

INDIANA FACILITIES

606 Nelson's Parkway, Wakarusa, IN 46573, Telephone (574) 862-7211

ON THE WORLD WIDE WEB

www.monaco-online.com

STOCK TRANSFER AGENT

Wells Fargo Bank Minnesota, N.A.
St. Paul, MN

COMMON STOCK

The company's common stock is listed on the New York Stock Exchange. Its trading symbol is MNC.

EMPLOYEES

5,169 total employees.

SERVICE AND WARRANTY CENTERS

30725 Diamond Hill Road, Harrisburg, OR 97446, Telephone (800) 283-0869
1809 West Hively Avenue, Elkhart, IN 46517, Telephone (574) 295-8060
3701 West Main Street, Leesburg, FL 34748, Telephone (352) 326-2907

INDEPENDENT AUDITORS

PricewaterhouseCoopers LLP, Portland, Oregon

ANNUAL MEETING

The 2002 annual meeting will be held on May 16, 2002 in Coburg, Oregon.

FORM 10-K AND INVESTOR INFORMATION

Copies of the Annual Report on Form 10-K filed with the Securities and Exchange Commission and other investor information may be obtained without charge from the Company upon written request to its Coburg, Oregon office, attention Investor Relations.

CORPORATE COUNSEL

Wilson, Sonsini, Goodrich and Rosati, Professional Corporation, Palo Alto, California

INVESTOR RELATIONS INQUIRIES SHOULD BE DIRECTED TO:

Monaco Coach Corporation
91320 Industrial Way, Coburg, OR 97408
Attention: Investor Relations
Telephone (800) 634-0855 or on the World Wide Web at www.monaco-online.com

Design by Kaufman/Kane; Photography by Mark Clifford; Contributing Writer John Schug; Illustration and Layout by Mark Comstock

Printed in USA.

Glossary

Accelerated depreciation A higher amount of depreciation is recorded in the early years and a lower amount in the later years. (p. 389)

Account Record used to accumulate amounts for each individual asset, liability, revenue, expense, and component of owners' equity. (p. 111)

Accounting The process of identifying, measuring, and communicating economic information to various users. (p. 14)

Accounting controls Procedures concerned with safeguarding the assets or the reliability of the financial statements. (p. 237)

Accounting cycle A series of steps performed each period and culminating with the preparation of a set of financial statements. (p. 173)

Accounting system Methods and records used to accurately report an entity's transactions and to maintain accountability for its assets and liabilities. (p. 237)

Accounts payable Amounts owed for inventory, goods, or services acquired in the normal course of business. (p. 436)

Accounts receivable turnover ratio A measure of the number of times accounts receivable are collected in a period. (p. 693)

Accrual Cash has not yet been paid or received, but expense has been incurred or revenue earned. (p. 168)

Accrual basis A system of accounting in which revenues are recognized when earned and expenses when incurred. (p. 153)

Accrued asset An asset resulting from the recognition of a revenue before the receipt of cash. (p. 168)

Accrued liability A liability resulting from the recognition of an expense before the payment of cash. (pp. 168, 439)

Accrued pension cost The difference between the amount of pension recorded as an expense and the amount of the funding payment. (p. 533)

Accumulated benefit obligation (ABO) A measure of the amount owed to employees for pensions if they retire at their existing salary levels. (p. 534)

Acid-test or quick ratio A stricter test of liquidity than the current ratio; excludes inventory and prepayments from the numerator. (p. 691)

Acquisition cost The amount that includes all of the cost normally necessary to acquire an asset and prepare it for its intended use. (p. 385)

Additional paid-in capital The amount received for the issuance of stock in excess of the par value of the stock. (p. 559)

Adjusting entries Journal entries made at the end of a period by a company using the accrual basis of accounting. (p. 160)

Administrative controls Procedures concerned with efficient operation of the business and adherence to managerial policies. (p. 237)

Aging schedule A form used to categorize the various individual accounts receivable according to the length of time each has been outstanding. (p. 348)

Allowance method A method of estimating bad debts on the basis of either the net credit sales of the period or the accounts receivable at the end of the period. (p. 345)

American Accounting Association The professional organization for accounting educators. (p. 28)

American Institute of Certified Public Accountants (AICPA) The professional organization for certified public accountants. (p. 24)

Annuity A series of payments of equal amounts. (p. 454)

Asset A future economic benefit. (p.8)

Asset turnover ratio The relationship between net sales and average total assets. (p. 699)

Audit committee Board of directors subset that acts as a direct contact between stockholders and the independent accounting firm. (p. 236)

Auditing The process of examining the financial statements and the underlying records of a company in order to render an opinion as to whether the statements are fairly represented. (p. 26)

Auditors' report The opinion rendered by a public accounting firm concerning the fairness of the presentation of the financial statements. (p. 26)

Authorized shares The maximum number of shares a corporation may issue as indicated in the corporate charter. (p. 557)

Available-for-sale securities Stocks and bonds that are not classified as either held-to-maturity or trading securities. (p. 336)

Balance sheet The financial statement that summarizes the assets, liabilities, and owners' equity at a specific point in time. (p. 17)

Bank reconciliation A form used by the accountant to reconcile the balance shown on the bank statement for a particular account with the balance shown in the accounting records. (p. 328)

Bank statement A detailed list, provided by the bank, of all the activity for a particular account during the month. (p. 327)

Blind receiving report Form used by the receiving department to account for the quantity and condition of merchandise received from a supplier. (p. 236)

Board of directors Group composed of key officers of a corporation and outside members responsible for general oversight of the affairs of the entity. (p. 236)

Bond A certificate that represents a corporation's promise to repay a certain amount of money and interest in the future. (p. 6)

Bond issue price The present value of the annuity of interest payments plus the present value of the principal. (p. 506)

Book value The original cost of an asset minus the amount of accumulated depreciation. (p. 388)

Book value per share Total stockholders equity divided by the number of shares of common stock outstanding. (p. 573)

Business All the activities necessary to provide the members of an economic system with goods and services. (p. 4)

Business entity An organization operated to earn a profit. (p. 6)

Callable bonds Bonds that may be redeemed or retired before their specified due date. (p. 505)

Callable feature Allows the firm to eliminate a class of stock by paying the stockholders a specified amount. (p. 561)

Capital expenditure A cost that improves the asset and is added to the asset account. (p. 393)

Capital lease A lease that is recorded as an asset by the lessee. (p. 517)

Capital stock Indicates the owners' contributions to a corporation. (p. 8)

Capitalization of interest Interest on constructed assets is added to the asset account. (p. 386)

Carrying value The face value of a bond plus the amount of unamortized premium or minus the amount of unamortized discount. (p. 510)

Cash basis A system of accounting in which revenues are recognized when cash is received and expenses when cash is paid. (p. 153)

Cash equivalent An investment that is

readily convertible to a known amount of cash and a maturity to the investor of three months or less. (pp. 325, 615)

Cash flow from operations to capital expenditures ratio A measure of the ability of a company to finance long-term asset acquisitions with cash from operations. (p. 697)

Cash flow from operations to current liabilities ratio A measure of the ability to pay current debts from operating cash flows. (p. 692)

Cash to cash operating cycle The length of time from the purchase of inventory to the collection of any receivable from the sale. (p. 695)

Change in estimate A change in the life of the asset or in its residual value. (p. 391)

Chart of accounts A numerical list of all the accounts used by a company. (p. 111)

Closing entries Journal entries made at the end of the period to return the balance in all nominal accounts to zero and transfer the net income or loss and the dividends to Retained Earnings. (p. 174)

Comparability For accounting information, the quality that allows a user to analyze two or more companies and look for similarities and differences. (p. 57)

Compensated absences Employee absences for which the employee will be paid. (p. 472)

Compound interest Interest calculated on the principal plus previous amounts of interest. (p. 449)

Comprehensive income The total change in net assets from all sources except investments by or distributions to the owners. (p. 572)

Conservatism The practice of using the least optimistic estimate when two estimates of amounts are about equally likely. (p. 59)

Consistency For accounting information, the quality that allows a user to compare two or more accounting periods for a single company. (p. 58)

Contingent assets An existing condition for which the outcome is not known but by which the company stands to gain. (pp. 446, 447)

Contingent liability An existing condition for which the outcome is not known but depends on some future event. (p. 442)

Contra account An account with a balance that is opposite that of a related account. (p. 162)

Control account The general ledger account that is supported by a subsidiary ledger. (p. 344)

Controller The chief accounting officer for a company. (p. 24)

Convertible feature Allows preferred stock to be exchanged for common stock. (p. 561)

Corporation A form of entity organized under the laws of a particular state; ownership evidenced by shares of stock. (p. 6)

Cost of goods available for sale Beginning inventory plus cost of goods purchased. (p. 227)

Cost of goods sold Cost of goods available for sale minus ending inventory. (p. 228)

Cost principle Assets recorded at the cost to acquire them. (p. 22)

Credit An entry on the right side of an account. (p. 113)

Credit card draft A multiple-copy document used by a company that accepts a credit card for a sale. (p. 354)

Credit memoranda Additions on a bank statement for such items as interest paid on the account and notes collected by the bank for the customer. (p. 329)

Creditor Someone to whom a company or person has a debt. (p. 8)

Cumulative effect of a change in accounting principle A line item on the income statement to reflect the effect on prior years' income from a change in accounting principle. (p. 713)

Cumulative feature The right to dividends in arrears before the current-year dividend is distributed. (p. 561)

Current asset An asset that is expected to be realized in cash or sold or consumed during the operating cycle or within one year if the cycle is shorter than one year. (p. 63)

Current liability An obligation that will be satisfied within the next operating cycle or within one year if the cycle is shorter than one year. (pp. 64, 434)

Current maturities of long-term debt The portion of a long-term liability that will be paid within one year. (p. 438)

Current ratio Current assets divided by current liabilities. (pp. 66, 690)

Current value The amount of cash, or its equivalent, that could be received by selling an asset currently. (p. 151)

Debenture bonds Bonds that are not backed by specific collateral. (p. 504)

Debit An entry on the left side of an account. (p. 113)

Debit memoranda Deductions on a bank statement for such items as NSF checks and various service charges. (p. 329)

Debt securities Bonds issued by corporations and governmental bodies as a form of borrowing. (p. 333)

Debt service coverage ratio A statement of cash flow measure of the ability of a company to meet its interest and principal payments. (p. 697)

Debt-to-equity ratio The ratio of total liabilities to total stockholders' equity. (p. 696)

Deferral Cash has either been paid or received, but expense or revenue has not yet been recognized. (p. 168)

Deferred expense An asset resulting from the payment of cash before the incurrence of expense. (p. 168)

Deferred revenue A liability resulting from the receipt of cash before the recognition of revenue. (p. 168)

Deferred tax The account used to reconcile the difference between the amount recorded as income tax expense and the amount that is payable as income tax. (p. 529)

Deposit in transit A deposit recorded on the books but not yet reflected on the bank statement. (p. 328)

Depreciation The process of allocating the cost of a long-term tangible asset over its useful life. (pp. 57, 387)

Direct method For preparing the Operating Activities section of the statement of cash flows, the approach in which cash receipts and cash payments are reported. (p. 620)

Direct write-off method The recognition of bad debts expense at the point an account is written off as uncollectible. (p. 345)

Discontinued operations A line item on the income statement to reflect any gains or losses from the disposal of a segment of the business as well as any net income or loss from operating that segment. (p. 713)

Discount The excess of the face value of bonds over the issue price. (p. 508)

Discount on notes payable A contra liability that represents interest deducted from a loan in advance. (p. 437)

Discounted note An alternative name for a non-interest-bearing promissory note. (p. 353)

Discounting The process of selling a promissory note. (p. 355)

Dividend payout ratio The annual dividend amount divided by the annual net income. (pp. 565, 703)

Dividend yield ratio The relationship between dividends and the market price of a company's stock. (p. 703)

Dividends A distribution of the net income of a business to its owners. (p. 19)

Double declining-balance method Depreciation is recorded at twice the straight-line rate, but the balance is reduced each period. (p. 389)

Double-entry system A system of accounting in which every transaction is recorded with equal debits and credits and the accounting equation is kept in balance. (p. 116)

Earnings per share A company's bottom line stated on a per-share basis. (p. 702)

Economic entity concept The assumption that a single, identifiable unit must be accounted for in all situations. (p. 6)

Effective interest method of amortization The process of transferring a portion of the premium or discount to interest expense; this method results in a constant effective interest rate. (p. 510)

Equity securities Securities issued by corporations as a form of ownership in the business. (p. 333)

Estimated liability A contingent liability that is accrued and reflected on the balance sheet. (p. 443)

Event A happening of consequence to an entity. (p. 104)

Expenses Outflows of assets or incurrences of liabilities resulting from delivering goods, rendering services, or carrying out other activities. (pp. 9, 160)

External event An event involving interaction between an entity and its environment. (p. 104)

Extraordinary item A line item on the income statement to reflect any gains or losses that arise from an event that is both unusual in nature and infrequent in occurrence. (p. 713)

Face rate of interest The rate of interest on the bond certificate. (p. 505)

Face value The principal amount of the bond as stated on the bond certificate. (p. 502)

FIFO method An inventory costing method that assigns the most recent costs to ending inventory. (p. 278)

Financial Accounting Standards Board (FASB) The group in the private sector with authority to set accounting standards. (p. 24)

Financial accounting The branch of accounting concerned with the preparation of financial statements for outsider use. (p. 15)

Financing activities Activities concerned with the raising and repayment of funds in the form of debt and equity. (p. 618)

Finished goods A manufacturer's inventory that is complete and ready for sale. (p. 273)

FOB destination point Terms that require the seller to pay for the cost of shipping the merchandise to the buyer. (p. 232)

FOB shipping point Terms that require the buyer to pay for the shipping costs. (p. 232)

Foreign Corrupt Practices Act Legislation intended to increase the accountability of management for accurate records and reliable financial statements. (p. 236)

Funding payment A payment made by the employer to the pension fund or its trustee. (p. 532)

Future value of a single amount Amount accumulated at a future time from a single payment or investment. (p. 451)

Future value of an annuity Amount accumulated in the future when a series of payments is invested and accrues interest. (p. 454)

Gain on sale of asset The excess of the selling price over the asset's book value. (p. 396)

Gain or loss on redemption The difference between the carrying value and the redemption price at the time bonds are redeemed. (p. 514)

General journal The journal used in place of a specialized journal. (p. 119)

General ledger A book, file, hard drive, or other device containing all the accounts. (p. 112)

Generally accepted accounting principles (GAAP) The various methods, rules, practices, and other procedures that have evolved over time in response to the need to regulate the preparation of financial statements. (p. 23)

Going concern The assumption that an entity is not in the process of liquidation and that it will continue indefinitely. (p. 22)

Goodwill The excess of the purchase price of a business over the total market value of identifiable assets. (p. 400)

Gross profit Sales less cost of goods sold. (p. 68)

Gross profit method A technique used to establish an estimate of the cost of inventory stolen, destroyed, or otherwise damaged or of the amount of inventory on hand at an interim date. (p. 290)

Gross profit ratio Gross profit to net sales. (pp. 69, 689)

Gross wages The amount of wages before deductions. (p. 469)

Held-to-maturity securities Investments in bonds of other companies in which the investor has the positive intent and the ability to hold the securities to maturity. (p. 336)

Historical cost The amount paid for an asset and used as a basis for recognizing it on the balance sheet and carrying it on later balance sheets. (p. 151)

Horizontal analysis A comparison of financial statement items over a period of time. (p. 682)

Income statement A statement that summarizes revenues and expenses. (p. 19)

Indirect method For preparing the Operating Activities section of the statement of cash flows, the approach in which net income is reconciled to net cash flow from operations. (p. 620)

Installment method The method in which revenue is recognized at the time cash is collected. (p. 158)

Intangible assets Assets with no physical properties. (p. 399)

Interest The difference between the principal amount of the note and its maturity value. (p. 351)

Interest-bearing note A promissory note in which the interest rate is explicitly stated. (p. 351)

Interim statements Financial statements prepared monthly, quarterly, or at other intervals less than a year in duration. (p. 176)

Internal audit staff Department responsible for monitoring and evaluating the internal control system. (p. 236)

Internal auditing The department responsible in a company for the review and appraisal of its accounting and administrative controls. (p. 25)

Internal control system Policies and procedures necessary to ensure the safeguarding of an entity's assets, the reliability of its accounting records, and the accomplishment of overall company objectives. (p. 234)

Internal event An event occurring entirely within an entity. (p. 104)

International Accounting Standards Board (IASB) The organization formed to develop worldwide accounting standards. (p. 24)

Inventory profit The portion of the gross profit that results from holding inventory during a period of rising prices. (p. 282)

Inventory turnover ratio A measure of the number of times inventory is sold during a period. (pp. 292, 693)

Investing activities Activities concerned with the acquisition and disposal of long-term assets. (p. 617)

Invoice Form sent by the seller to the buyer as evidence of a sale. (p. 249)

Invoice approval form Form the accounting department uses before making payment to document the accuracy of all the information about a purchase. (p. 249)

Issued shares The number of shares sold or distributed to stockholders. (p. 557)

Journal A chronological record of transactions, also known as the book of original entry. (p. 118)

Journalizing The act of recording journal entries. (p. 119)

Land improvements Costs that are related to land but that have a limited life. (p. 387)

Leverage The use of borrowed funds and amounts contributed by preferred stockholders to earn an overall return higher than the cost of these funds. (p. 701)

Liability An obligation of a business. (p. 8)

LIFO conformity rule The IRS requirement that if LIFO is used on the tax return, it must also be used in reporting income to stockholders. (p. 281)

LIFO liquidation The result of selling more units than are purchased during the period, which can have negative tax consequences if a company is using LIFO. (p. 281)

LIFO method An inventory method that assigns the most recent costs to cost of goods sold. (p. 279)

LIFO reserve The excess of the value of a company's inventory stated at FIFO over the value stated at LIFO. (p. 282)

Liquidity The nearness to cash of the assets and liabilities. (pp. 65, 690)

Long-term liability An obligation that will be settled within one year or the current operating cycle. (p. 502)

Loss on sale of asset The amount by which selling price is less than book value. (p. 396)

Lower-of-cost-or-market (LCM) rule A conservative inventory valuation approach that is an attempt to anticipate declines in the value of inventory before its actual sale. (p. 287)

Maker The party that agrees to repay the money for a promissory note at some future date. (p. 350)

Management accounting The branch of accounting concerned with providing management with information to facilitate planning and control. (p. 14)

Market rate of interest The rate that investors could obtain by investing in other bonds that are similar to the issuing firm's bonds. (p. 505)

Market value per share The selling price of the stock as indicated by the most recent transactions. (p. 574)

Matching principle The association of revenue of a period with all of the costs necessary to generate that revenue. (p. 159)

Materiality The magnitude of an accounting information omission or misstatement that will affect the judgment of someone relying on the information. (p. 59)

Maturity date The date that the promissory note is due. (p. 351)

Maturity value The amount of cash the maker is to pay the payee on the maturity date of the note. (p. 351)

Merchandise inventory The account wholesalers and retailers use to report inventory held for resale. (p. 272)

Monetary unit The yardstick used to measure amounts in financial statements; the dollar in the United States. (p. 23)

Moving average The name given to an average cost method when it is used with a perpetual inventory system. (p. 301)

Multiple-step income statement An income statement that shows classifications of revenues and expenses as well as important subtotals. (p. 68)

Natural resources Assets that are consumed during their use. (p. 397)

Net pay The amount of wages after deductions. (p. 469)

Net sales Sales revenue less sales returns and allowances and sales discounts. (p. 223)

Nominal accounts The name given to revenue, expense, and dividend accounts because they are temporary and are closed at the end of the period. (p. 174)

Nonbusiness entity Organization operated for some purpose other than to earn a profit. (p. 7)

Non-interest-bearing note A promissory note in which interest is not explicitly stated but is implicit in the agreement. (p. 351)

Note payable A liability resulting from the signing of a promissory note. (pp. 351, 437)

Note receivable An asset resulting from the acceptance of a promissory note from another company. (p. 351)

Number of days' sales in inventory A measure of how long it takes to sell inventory. (pp. 292, 694)

Number of days' sales in receivables A measure of the average age of accounts receivable. (p. 693)

Operating activities Activities concerned with the acquisition and sale of products and services. (p. 617)

Operating cycle The period of time between the purchase of inventory and the collection of any receivable from the sale of the inventory. (p. 61)

Operating lease A lease that does not meet any of the four criteria and is not recorded as an asset by the lessee. (p. 517)

Outstanding check A check written by a company but not yet presented to the bank for payment. (p. 328)

Outstanding shares The number of shares issued less the number of shares held as treasury stock. (p. 557)

Owners' equity The owners' claim on the assets of an entity. (p. 17)

Par value An arbitrary amount that represents the legal capital of the firm. (p. 558)

Participating feature Allows preferred stockholders to share on a percentage basis in the distribution of an abnormally large dividend. (p. 561)

Partnership A business owned by two or more individuals and with the characteristic of unlimited liability. (pp. 6, 584)

Partnership agreement Specifies how much the owners will invest, their salaries, and how profits will be shared. (p. 584)

Payee The party that will receive the money from a promissory note at some future date. (p. 350)

Pension An obligation to pay employees for service rendered while employed. (p. 532)

Percentage-of-completion method The method used by contractors to recognize revenue before the completion of a long-term contract. (p. 157)

Periodic system System in which the Inventory account is updated only at the end of the period. (p. 228)

Permanent difference A difference that affects the tax records but not the accounting records, or vice versa. (p. 529)

Perpetual system System in which the inventory account is increased at the time of each purchase and decreased at the time of each sale. (p. 228)

Petty cash fund Money kept on hand for making minor disbursements in coin and currency rather than by writing checks. (p. 331)

Posting The process of transferring amounts from a journal to the ledger accounts. (p. 118)

Premium The excess of the issue price over the face value of the bonds. (p. 508)

Present value of a single amount Amount at a present time that is equivalent to a payment or investment at a future time. (p. 453)

Present value of an annuity The amount at a present time that is equivalent to a series of payments and interest in the future. (p. 456)

Price/earnings (P/E) ratio The relationship between a company's performance according to the income statement and its performance in the stock market. (p. 702)

Principal The amount of cash received, or the fair value of the products or services received, by the maker when a promissory note is issued. (p. 351)

Production method The method in which revenue is recognized when a commodity is produced rather than when it is sold. (p. 158)

Profit margin Net income divided by sales. (p. 69)

Profit margin ratio Net income to net sales. (p. 689)

Profitability How well management is using company resources to earn a return on the funds invested by various groups. (p. 698)

Projected benefit obligation (PBO) A measure of the amount owed to employees for pensions if estimates of future salary increases are considered. (p. 534)

Promissory note A written promise to repay a definite sum of money on demand or at a fixed or determinable date in the future. (p. 350)

Purchase Discounts Contra-purchases account used to record reductions in purchase price for early payment to a supplier. (p. 232)

Purchase order Form sent by the purchasing department to the supplier. (p. 248)

Purchase requisition form Form a department uses to initiate a request to order merchandise. (p. 248)

Purchase Returns and Allowances Contra-purchases account used in a periodic inventory system when a refund is received from a supplier or a reduction given in the balance owed to a supplier. (p. 231)

Purchases Account used in a periodic inventory system to record acquisitions of merchandise. (p. 231)

Quantity discount Reduction in selling price for buying a large number of units of a product. (p. 225)

Quick ratio A stricter test of liquidity than the current ratio; excludes inventory and prepayments from the numerator. (p. 691)

Raw materials The inventory of a manufacturer before the addition of any direct labor or manufacturing overhead. (p. 272)

Real accounts The name given to balance sheet accounts because they are permanent and are not closed at the end of the period. (p. 174)

Recognition The process of recording an item in the financial statements as an asset, liability, revenue, expense, or the like. (p. 150)

Relevance The capacity of information to make a difference in a decision. (p. 56)

Reliability The quality that makes accounting information dependable in representing the events that it purports to represent. (p. 57)

Replacement cost The current cost of a unit of inventory. (p. 252)

Report of management Written statement in the annual report indicating the responsibility of management for the financial statements. (p. 235)

Research and development costs Costs incurred in the discovery of new knowledge. (p. 401)

Retail inventory method A technique used by retailers to convert the retail value of inventory to a cost basis. (p. 292)

Retained earnings The part of owners' equity that represents the income earned less dividends paid over the life of an entity. (pp. 17, 559)

Retirement of stock When the stock is repurchased with no intention to reissue at a later date. (p. 564)

Return on assets ratio A measure of a company's success in earning a return for all providers of capital. (p. 698)

Return on common stockholders' equity ratio A measure of a company's success in earning a return for the common stockholders. (p. 700)

Return on sales ratio A variation of the profit margin ratio; measures earnings before payments to creditors. (p. 699)

Revenue Inflow of assets resulting from the sale of goods and services. (p. 9)

Revenue expenditure A cost that keeps an asset in its normal operating condition and is treated as an expense. (p. 393)

Revenue recognition principle Revenues are recognized in the income statement when they are realized, or realizable, and earned. (p. 156)

Revenues Inflows of assets or settlements of liabilities from delivering or producing goods, rendering services, or conducting other activities. (p. 156)

Sales Discounts Contra-revenue account used to record discounts given customers for early payment of their accounts. (p. 226)

Sales Returns and Allowances Contra-revenue account used to record both refunds to customers and reductions of their accounts. (p. 224)

Securities and Exchange Commission (SEC) The federal agency with ultimate authority to determine the rules in preparing statements for companies whose stock is sold to the public. (p. 24)

Serial bonds Bonds that do not all have the same due date; a portion of the bonds comes due each time period. (p. 504)

Share of stock A certificate that acts as ownership in a corporation. (p. 6)

Simple interest Interest is calculated on the principal amount only. (pp. 448, 449)

Single-step income statement An income statement in which all expenses are added together and subtracted from all revenues. (p. 67)

Sole proprietorship A business with a single owner. (pp. 6, 583)

Solvency The ability of a company to remain in business over the long term. (p. 695)

Source document A piece of paper that is used as evidence to record a transaction. (p. 105)

Specific identification method An inventory costing method that relies on matching unit costs with the actual units sold. (p. 276)

Statement of cash flows The financial statement that summarizes an entity's cash receipts and cash payments during the period from operating, investing, and financing activities. (p. 613)

Statement of retained earnings The statement that summarizes the income earned and dividends paid over the life of a business. (p. 20)

Statement of stockholders' equity Reflects the differences between beginning and ending balances for all accounts in the Stockholders' Equity category of the balance sheet. (p. 571)

Stock dividend The issuance of additional shares of stock to existing stockholders. (p. 567)

Stock split The creation of additional shares of stock with a reduction of the par value of the stock. (p. 569)

Stockholder One of the owners of a corporation. Also called a shareholder. (p. 8)

Stockholders' equity The owners' equity in a corporation. (p. 17)

Straight-line method A method by which the same dollar amount of depreciation is recorded in each year of asset use. (pp. 162, 387)

Subsidiary ledger The detail for a number of individual items that collectively make up a single general ledger account. (p. 344)

Temporary difference A difference that affects both book and tax records but not in the same time period. (p. 529)

Term The length of time a note is outstanding; that is, the period of time between the date it is issued and the date it matures. (p. 351)

Time period Artificial segment on the calendar, used as the basis for preparing financial statements. (p. 23)

Time value of money An immediate amount should be preferred over an amount in the future. (p. 447)

Times interest earned ratio An income statement measure of the ability of a company to meet its interest payments. (p. 696)

Trade discount Selling price reduction offered to a special class of customers. (p. 224)

Trading securities Stock and bonds of other companies bought and held for the purpose of selling them in the near term to generate profits on appreciation in their price. (p. 336)

Transaction Any event that is recognized in a set of financial statements. (p. 104)

Transportation-in Adjunct account used to record freight costs paid by the buyer. (p. 230)

Treasurer The officer responsible in an organization for the safeguarding and efficient use of a company's liquid assets. (p. 24)

Treasury stock Stock issued by the firm and then repurchased but not retired. (p. 563)

Trial balance A list of each account and its balance; used to prove equality of debits and credits. (p. 121)

Understandability The quality of accounting information that makes it comprehensible to those willing to spend the necessary time. (p. 56)

Units-of-production method Depreciation is determined as a function of the number of units the asset produces. (p. 388)

Vertical analysis A comparison of various financial statement items within a single period with the use of common-size statements. (p. 682)

Weighted average cost method An inventory costing method that assigns the same unit cost to all units available for sale during the period. (p. 277)

Work in process The cost of unfinished products in a manufacturing company. (p. 273)

Work sheet A device used at the end of the period to gather the information needed to prepare financial statements without actually recording and posting adjusting entries. (p. 173)

Working capital Current assets minus current liabilities. (pp. 65, 690)

Company Index

Subject Index

Managerial Accounting
A Focus on Decision Making

Second Edition

Steve Jackson
The University of Tennessee at Martin

Roby Sawyers
North Carolina State University

SOUTH-WESTERN
THOMSON LEARNING™

Brief Contents

CONTENTS

PART V OTHER TOPICS 449

About the Authors

Steve Jackson, C.P.A., an Associate Professor at the University of Tennessee at Martin, holds the Hardy-Graham Distinguished Professorship. He earned a Ph.D. from Arizona State University and a B.S. from the University of Montana. He has published articles in such refereed journals as *The Journal of Accounting and Finance Research, The Journal of Economic and Social Measurement, The Accounting Educators Journal,* and *The Journal of Accountancy.* His major research interest is in the accounting education area. He also works in behavioral accounting research.

Dr. Jackson's professional activities include membership in the American Institute of Certified Public Accountants, the American Accounting Association, and the Institute of Management Accountants. He is a former staff accountant with Touche Ross & Co. in Seattle and has more than 12 years of public accounting experience. He has been a faculty member at Northern Arizona University, Western New England College, the University of Southern Mississippi, and the University of Southern Maine, as well as the University of Tennessee at Martin. He has more than 17 years of teaching experience and has taught courses in managerial and cost accounting, auditing, and financial accounting.

While a doctoral student at Arizona State University, he was awarded three excellence-in-teaching awards, and while at the University of Southern Mississippi also received three teaching awards, one of which was the outstanding-faculty award given by the USM Gulf Coast Accounting Society. He has previously published two managerial accounting study guides and an instructor's manual/test bank for a major managerial accounting textbook. He also was the recipient of the University of Southern Maine Faculty Senate Intellectual Contributions award for the School of Business in 1999.

He lives with his wife in Martin, Tennessee, where he enjoys fly-fishing, golf, and all UTM Skyhawk sports. He has three grown children and a dog named Boots.

Roby Sawyers, C.M.A., C.P.A., is Associate Professor of Accounting at North Carolina State University. He earned a Ph.D. from Arizona State University, a master's in accounting from the University of South Florida, and a B.S.B.A. from the University of North Carolina at Chapel Hill. He has published articles in a variety of journals, including the *Journal of Accountancy*, the *Journal of Business Ethics*, the *Journal of the American Taxation Association, Advances in Taxation, The Tax Adviser*, and *Auditing: A Journal of Practice and Theory.* His research interests include individual behavior and decision making in a variety of contexts, as well as corporate ethics. He has more than 10 years of teaching experience and has taught courses in managerial and cost accounting, individual and business taxation, and the taxation of estates, gifts, and trusts. He has also taught a variety of continuing education and review courses for the American Institute of CPAs, the Institute of Management Accountants, and McGladrey and Pullen, LLP.

Dr. Sawyers's professional activities include membership in the American Accounting Association, the Institute of Management Accountants, and the American Taxation Association. He has served as an appointed member of the American Institute of CPAs tax division and is a member of the North Carolina Association of CPAs. He has worked in public accounting and provides tax and consulting services to a variety of individual and business clients.

He lives with his wife and daughter in Raleigh, North Carolina, where he enjoys hiking, camping, singing in the church choir, managing his farm, and attending college basketball games.

Chapter 1

Accounting Information and Managerial Decisions

Study Tools

A Preview of This Chapter

In Chapter 1, we begin the study of managerial accounting by discussing what is meant by accounting information and how accounting information is used by both internal and external users to make decisions. The chapter also describes the decision-making role of managers in organizations, provides a decision framework for assessing those decisions, and discusses the role of relevant factors, risk, and ethics in decision making.

Key concepts include:

- Accounting information includes both financial (quantitative) and nonfinancial (qualitative) information used by decision makers.
- Managerial accountants facilitate management decision making.
- Accounting information systems are continually evolving to meet the changing demands of their users.
- Never make decisions with just the numbers! Always consider nonnumerical (qualitative) information.
- Sunk costs are not relevant.
- Future costs that do not differ between alternatives are not relevant.
- Opportunity costs are relevant.

A Preview of Upcoming Chapters

Chapters 2 through 4 provide an introduction into the basics of production processes used by manufacturing companies, cost flows in manufacturing, merchandising and service companies, and basic product and service costing methods used in various types of organizations.

Learning Objectives

After studying the material in this chapter, you should be able to:

LO1 Understand the uses and users of accounting information

LO2 Understand the decision-making role of managers

LO3 Apply a basic four-step decision-making model

LO4 Evaluate the role of relevant factors and decision making

LO5 Understand and evaluate the role of risk in decision making

LO6 Understand and evaluate the role of ethics in decision making

The main focus of accounting is decision making. In fact, the American Accounting Association defines accounting as "the process of identifying, measuring and communicating economic information to permit informed judgments and decisions by users of information" (A Statement of Basic Accounting Theory, *1966, 1). All organizations—large and small; manufacturing, merchandising, or service; profit or nonprofit—have a need for accounting information. The primary role of accounting is to provide useful information for the decision-making needs of investors, lenders, owners, managers, and others both inside and outside the company. However, the needs of internal users and external users often differ. This chapter defines accounting information and its application by both external and internal users. The chapter then describes the decision-making role of management in planning, operating, and controlling and provides a framework for assessing decisions that commonly face managers of organizations. The chapter also provides a discussion of the role of relevant factors, risk, and ethics as they pertain to decision making.*

Introduction

All types of organizations, from large multinational manufacturing companies like Ford Motor Company to small custom-furniture manufacturers, have a need for accounting information. Retailers, such as Wal-Mart and locally owned hardware stores; large service companies, such as FedEx and local CPA and law firms; and even nonprofit organizations, such as the American Red Cross and small local museums and homeless shelters, need accounting information. This information is used by internal managers in their day-to-day decision making and also by external users, such as investors, creditors, donors, and even the Internal Revenue Service.

Accounting Information

LO1
Understand the uses and users of accounting information

Accounting information is provided by a company's **accounting information system (AIS).** Traditionally, the AIS was simply a transaction processing system that captured financial data resulting from accounting transactions. For example, the AIS would document a transaction to purchase materials by recording a journal entry showing the date of purchase, a debit to raw materials inventory, and a credit to accounts payable or cash.

Under this view of AIS, accounting information was simply financial information (sales, net income, total assets, costs of products, etc.) expressed in terms of dollars or other monetary units (e.g., yen, francs, pesos). Other nonmonetary information—such as (1) the number of units of materials or inventory on hand, (2) the number of budgeted labor hours to produce a product, (3) the number of units necessary to break even, and (4) the time it takes to manufacture a product—were likely collected and processed outside the traditional accounting information system. The use of multiple information systems within a company causes a number of problems. It is costly to support multiple systems. Perhaps more important, it is difficult to integrate information coming from various systems and to make decisions for a company with multiple sources of information. In addition, other useful information concerning transactions—such as the quality of the material purchased, the timeliness of its delivery, or customer satisfaction with an order—might not be captured at all and therefore not evaluated by management.

Over the past few years, **enterprise resource planning (ERP) systems** have been developed in an attempt to address these shortcomings. ERP systems integrate the traditional AIS with other information systems to capture both quantitative and qualitative data, to collect and organize that data into useful information, and to transform that information into knowledge that can be communicated throughout an organization (see Exhibit 1-1). These systems can be customized to provide specific and relevant information to various types of users. For example, information for tax-reporting purposes must conform to the requirements of federal, state, and local taxing authorities, whereas information used in preparing financial statements and annual reports for shareholders and creditors must meet the requirements of generally accepted accounting principles (GAAP) and the Securities and Exchange Commission (SEC). On the other hand, information provided to internal users (managers) is thoroughly integrated across the organization and yet is customized to the needs and desires of the particular user.

http://www.sec.gov

With an ERP system, the sale of a product not only generates financial information by updating the cost of goods sold and profits but also updates inventory records, adjusts production schedules if necessary, and orders raw materials. In addition, delivery time, warranty claims, and service calls can be tracked and are available to managers across the organization. Therefore, production managers would know when to expect shipments of materials. Sales representatives could access information about expected delivery times to their customers, and customer service representatives could see records of previous service calls. All this information contributes to the cost-effective management of a company and to better decision making.

Throughout our study of managerial accounting information and its use in decision making, the importance of considering both quantitative and qualitative information is

EXHIBIT 1-1 A Contemporary View of Accounting Information

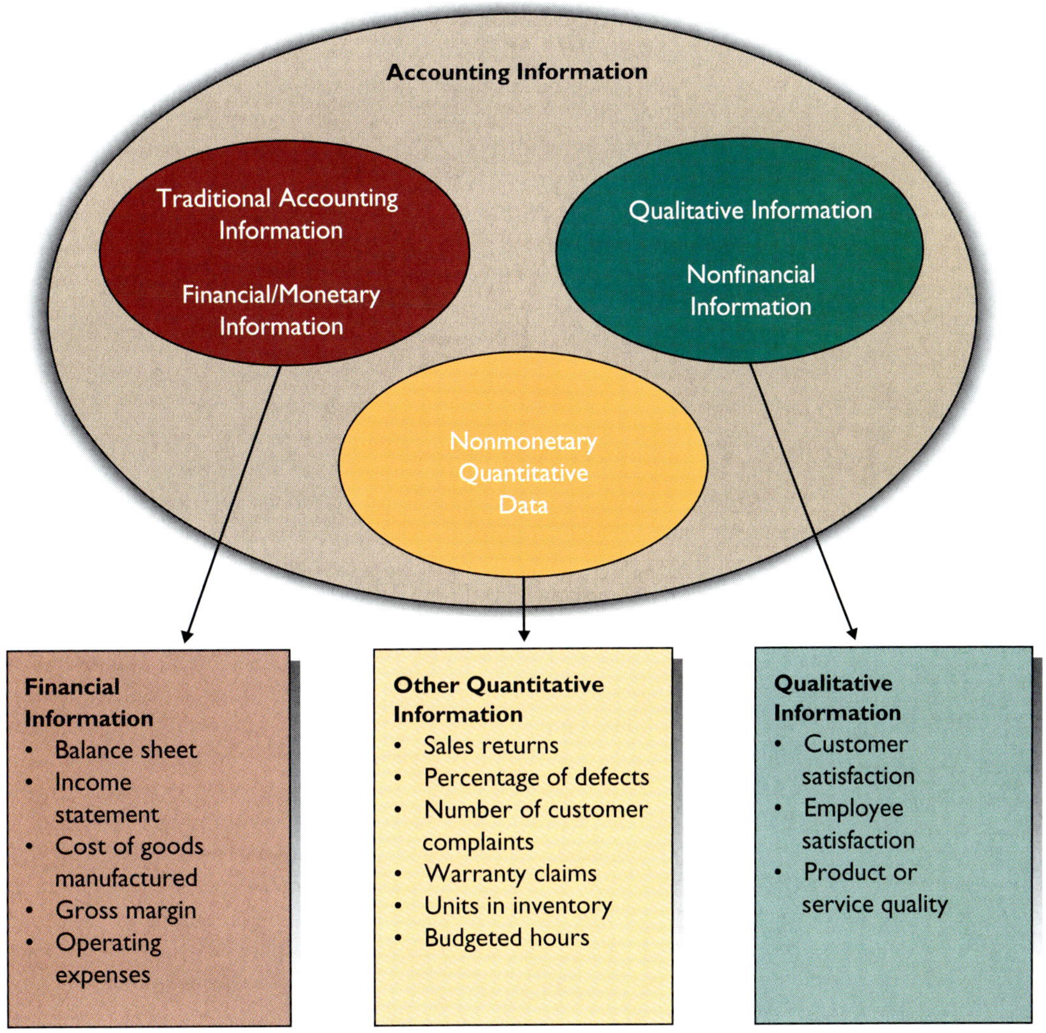

emphasized. The uses of ERP systems as decision-making tools are discussed more fully in Chapter 13. At this point, it is important simply to understand that in order to provide managers with the information they need to effectively plan, operate, and control their businesses, financial data must be linked to nonfinancial (qualitative) data, transformed into useful information and knowledge, and communicated throughout an organization.

Key Concept: *Accounting information includes both financial (quantitative) and nonfinancial (qualitative) information used by decision makers.*

THE USERS OF ACCOUNTING INFORMATION

EXTERNAL USERS

There are many different users of accounting information both external and internal to the organization. Stockholders, potential investors, creditors, government taxing agencies and regulators, suppliers, and customers are all external users. What type of information do external users need? Stockholders and potential investors want information to help them analyze the current and future profitability of an organization. Companies that have issued stock to the public (or those that plan to) provide this information in the form of annual reports, registration statements, prospectuses, and other reports issued to shareholders, prospective investors, and the SEC. The information required in these reports and the accounting methods used to prepare them are governed by the SEC and GAAP. Although this information is primarily quantitative and monetary (sales and net income), it also may include nonmonetary information, such as units shipped and market share. It also may include qualitative information, such as "management's discussion and analysis of financial condition and results of operations," which is found in annual reports.

http://www.redcross.org

What about smaller companies that are owned by just a few members of a family (closely held) or nonprofit organizations, such as the Red Cross? External users of financial information, such as banks or potential donors to nonprofit organizations, still need accounting information to make the proper decision about lending or donating money. However, their needs may differ from those of stockholders and potential investors. Creditors generally want to assess a company's overall financial health and may be particularly interested in a company's cash flow or ability to repay their loans. Potential contributors to nonprofit organizations may have a need for both monetary information, such as how much of the Red Cross's budget is spent for charitable purposes, and nonmonetary information, such as how many women with children are served by the local homeless shelter.

TECHNOLOGY FOCUS

Wal-Mart Stores Inc., which pioneered the idea of retailer and supplier sharing sales data, recently expanded the amount of data available to suppliers from five quarters to two years. Wal-Mart shares data on sales, profit margin, and inventory levels with more than 7,000 suppliers that access Wal-Mart's database 120,000 times per week ("Wal-Mart Expands Access to Product Sales History," *Wall Street Journal*, August 18, 1999, B8).

Government agencies (federal, state, and local) have very specific information needs, including the measurement of income, payroll, and assets for purposes of assessing taxes. This accounting information is typically provided on income tax returns, payroll reports, and other forms designed specifically to meet the requirements of each agency.[1]

Generally, accounting information provided to shareholders, creditors, and government agencies is characterized by a lack of flexibility (its content is often dictated by the user), the reporting of past events using historical costs (financial statements for the previous three years), and an emphasis on the organization as a whole.

Suppliers and customers are also external users. However, their accounting information needs are likely to be very different from those of other external users and may be more clearly aligned with the needs of internal users. For example, suppliers of car parts to General Motors need detailed information on inventory levels of specific parts in order to know when to manufacture and ship parts. Bank customers may want to check on their account or loan balances before making a major purchase. Someone buying a new computer may want to check on the expected delivery date or whether a product is back-ordered before placing an order. This type of information needs to be much more detailed and timely than that provided to most other external users.

© ANDY SACKS/STONE

Automobile manufacturers must provide suppliers with detailed inventory records so that parts, such as these engine blocks, can be provided on a timely basis.

[1]It should be noted that many nonprofit organizations that do not pay income taxes are still required to provide the Internal Revenue Service with information that is available for use by donors and other interested parties.

INTERNAL USERS

Internal users of accounting information include individual employees as well as teams, departments, regions, and top management of an organization. For convenience, these internal users are often just referred to as managers. Managers are involved in a variety of activities, including planning, operating, and controlling. These activities all involve making decisions both on an individual basis and in teams (see Exhibit 1-2).

THE DECISION-MAKING ROLE OF MANAGERS

PLANNING

LO2
Understand the decision-making role of managers

Planning involves the development of both the short-term (operational) and the long-term (strategic) objectives and goals of an organization and an identification of the resources needed to achieve them. Operational planning involves the development of short-term objectives and goals (typically, those to be achieved in less than one year). Examples of operational planning for Ben & Jerry's include planning the raw material and production needs for each type of ice cream for the next four quarters or determining the company's short-term cash needs. Operational planning for a hospital would include budgeting for the number of physicians, nurses, and other staff that are needed for the upcoming month or determining the appropriate level of medical supplies to have in inventory. Operational planning also involves the determination of short-term performance goals and objectives, including meeting customer service expectations, sales quotas, time budgets, and so on.

http://www.benjerry.com

Strategic planning addresses long-term questions of how an organization positions and distinguishes itself from competitors. For example, Ben & Jerry's strategy for producing high-quality ice cream is very different from that used for producing a store brand of lower-priced ice cream. Long-term decisions about where to locate plants and other facilities, whether to invest in new state-of-the-art production equipment, and whether to introduce new products or services and enter new markets are strategic planning decisions. Strategic planning also involves the determination of long-term performance and profitability measures, such as market share, sales growth, and stock price.

PAUSE & Reflect

Identify some potential strategic planning decisions that would be made by a nonprofit organization whose mission is to provide medical services to the poor.

EXHIBIT 1-2 Percentage of IMA Survey Respondents Who Work on Cross-Functional Teams

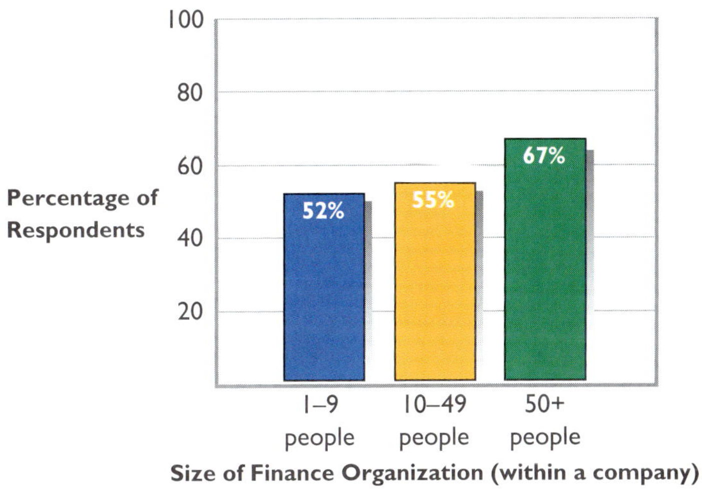

SOURCE: "Counting More, Counting Less: The 1999 Practice Analysis of Management Accounting," Institute of Management Accountants, 10.

Operating

Operating activities encompass what managers must do to run the business on a day-to-day basis. Operating decisions for manufacturing companies include whether to accept special orders, how many parts or other raw materials to buy (or whether to make the parts internally), whether to sell a product or process it further, whether to schedule overtime, which products to produce, and what price to charge. Other operating decisions affecting all organizations include assigning tasks to individual employees, whether to advertise (and the corresponding impact of advertising on sales and profits), and whether to hire full-time employees or to outsource.

Controlling

Controlling activities involve the motivation and monitoring of employees and the evaluation of people and other resources used in the organization's operations. The purpose of control is to make sure that the goals of the organization are being attained. It includes using incentives and other rewards to motivate employees to accomplish an organization's goals and mechanisms to detect and correct deviations from those goals. Control often involves the comparison of actual outcomes (cost of products, sales, etc.) with desired outcomes as stated in the organization's operating and strategic plans. Control decisions include questions of how to evaluate performance, what measures to use, and what types of incentives to implement. For example, a company that emphasizes high-quality products and excellent customer service may evaluate and reward production workers who have exceeded goals based on these virtues (such goals, for example, may involve specifying the percentage of allowable defective units or scrap, monitoring customer complaints, or a myriad of other factors).

The Role of the Managerial Accountant

http://www.imanet.org

In 1996, the Institute of Management Accountants (IMA) commissioned a "Practice Analysis of Management Accounting." Through surveys of 4,000 accountants working in organizations and detailed interviews of accountants at nine corporations, the IMA Practice Analysis provides a detailed view of what managerial accountants do and are expected to do in the future. This study was updated in 1999.

So what do they do? Managerial accountants have traditionally been thought of as the bean counters or number crunchers in an organization. However, the Practice Analysis found that advances in accounting information systems and other changes in the past five or ten years have resulted in the automation of traditional accounting functions involving data collection, data entry, and data reporting and a corresponding shifting of those functions from management accounting to clerical staff. The study found that

> management accountants in many companies have been liberated from the mechanical tasks of their work. Instead of collecting information, management accountants are expected to use that freed-up time to analyze it. Instead of preparing financial statements, they interpret the financial information and explain the business implications to managers. They are doing more financial planning and more financial modeling. They work with managers to make informed business decisions. (Siegel and Kulesza, 1996, 21)

Management accountants have become decision-support specialists who "see their role as distilling diverse information, putting it into a useful format, and facilitating management decision making" (Siegel and Kulesza, 1996, 22) (see Exhibit 1-3).

Key Concept: *Managerial accountants facilitate management decision making.*

EXHIBIT 1-3 Change in Nature of Work of Management Accountants, 1995–1999

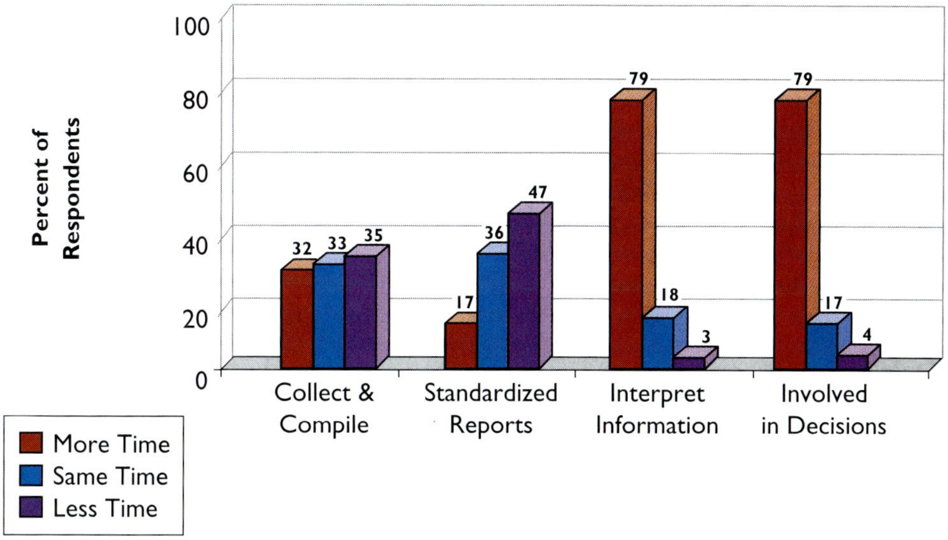

SOURCE: "Counting More, Counting Less: The 1999 Practice Analysis of Management Accounting," Institute of Management Accountants, 7.

MANAGEMENT ACTIONS AND DECISIONS

http://www.merckcapitalventures.com

GARY LUBIN
Merck Capital Ventures, LLC

Effective decision making is critical in today's business environment. According to Gary Lubin of Merck Capital Ventures (MCV), "business is about making decisions; the better the decision, the better the result."

MCV is a subsidiary of Merck & Co. Its focus is to invest in technologies (e.g., the Internet) that accelerate innovation related to the pharmaceutical business, the pharmacy benefit management industry, and many other sectors of health care delivery.

In his current position at MCV, Lubin (a licensed CPA with an accounting degree from Washington University and an M.B.A. from Harvard) is responsible for the identification and review of investment opportunities for MCV and for coordinating work between MCV and other Merck business units. His previous assignments at Merck include serving as vice president of Merck-Medco's E-Business Department and as vice president of sales, planning, and operations for Merck-Medco Managed Care, LLC.

At MCV, "when evaluating whether to invest in a company, we use accounting techniques to frame our alternatives, understand the tradeoffs, identify risks and value the business. Accounting information becomes the common denominator and an important way to evaluate different options."

The Role of Other Managers

Managers are found in all functional areas of an organization, including marketing, operations/production, human resources, and finance. What kind of accounting information does this diverse group of managers need, and what is the role of the managerial accountant in providing it? Although managers rely on the same information provided to external users, they have other needs as well. In addition, information flow is a two-way street. Whereas managers in other functional areas rely on accounting information to make decisions, managerial accountants also rely on information provided by marketing, operations/production, human resources, and finance.

Marketing Managers

Marketing is the "process of planning and executing the conception, pricing, promotion, and distribution of ideas, goods, services, organizations, and events to create and maintain relationships that satisfy individual and organizational objectives" (Boone and Kurtz, 1998, 9). Marketing managers need to know how much a product costs in order to help establish a reasonable selling price. They need to know how a given advertising campaign and its resulting impact on the number of units sold is expected to affect income. They need to know how enhancing a product's features or changing its packaging will influence its cost. Commissions paid to sales representatives may be based on a company's profits. All these marketing decisions require accounting information. Note that information also flows from marketing to accounting. For example, marketing will provide sales forecasts and estimates to managerial accountants for purposes of budgeting.

Operations/Production Managers

The operations and production function produces the products or services that an organization provides to its customers. Production and operations managers are concerned with providing quality products and services that can compete in a global marketplace. They need accounting information to make planning decisions affecting how and when products and services are produced. They need to know the costs of producing and storing products in order to decide how much inventory should be kept on hand. They need to know the costs of labor when making decisions to schedule overtime to complete a production run or when deciding how many physicians are needed in the emergency room. These decisions are also influenced by information provided by the marketing managers, including the expected customer reaction if products are not available when orders are placed or if doctors are not available when patients need them.

Operations and production managers have been forced by a global economy and increasing customer demands to change the methods used to produce products and services. As a consequence, they have placed demands on accounting information systems to provide even more timely and accurate information for decision making as well. The information provided by accounting information systems is continually evolving to meet the demands of its users.

Key Concept: *Accounting information systems are continually evolving to meet the changing demands of their users.*

Finance Managers

The finance function is responsible for managing the financial resources of the organization. Finance managers make decisions about how to raise capital as well as where and how it is invested. Finance managers need accounting information to answer such questions as whether money should be raised through borrowing (issuing bonds) or selling stock. Finance managers make decisions concerning whether a new piece of manufacturing equipment should be purchased or leased and whether a plant expansion should be paid for in cash or by borrowing money from the bank.

HUMAN RESOURCE MANAGERS

Although all managers who supervise, motivate, and evaluate other employees are human resource managers, the human resource function is concerned with the utilization of human resources to help an organization reach its goals. More specifically, human resource managers support other functions and managers by recruiting and staffing, designing compensation and benefit packages, ensuring the safety and overall health of personnel, and providing training and development opportunities for employees. These decisions require input from all other functional areas. What kind of accounting information do human resource managers need? Human resource decisions, such as hiring new employees, are often made under budget constraints. Ensuring safe workplaces for employees may involve the redesign of manufacturing processes. Accountants can provide information regarding the cost of the redesign. The decision to train employees to use new equipment may require an analysis of the costs and benefits of the new program.

A SUMMARY OF ACCOUNTING INFORMATION USED BY INTERNAL AND EXTERNAL USERS

In general, accounting information needed by internal users differs from that needed by external users in the following ways:

- It is more flexible.
- It is geared to the specific company and user and does not have to meet the requirements of the SEC, GAAP, or government taxing agencies.
- It is more forward looking, often emphasizing the future rather than the past.
- It is more timely, sometimes sacrificing accuracy in the process.
- It emphasizes segments of an organization more than the company as a whole.

Exhibit 1-4 summarizes the external and internal users of accounting information, the type of information typically needed by these users, and the source of the information.

AN INTRODUCTION TO DECISION MAKING

© DAVID YOUNG-WOLFF/STONE

Although the problems and questions facing marketing, production, finance, and human resource managers of organizations are all different, the decision-making process that they follow is remarkably uniform. In fact, it is the same decision-making model that you are likely to use when making nonbusiness decisions. Do you remember the decision-making process you went through the last time you made a major decision? It could have been a decision to purchase or sell a car, a computer, or a stereo system. It could have been a decision to attend a particular college, accept a summer job, or perhaps even get married.

Decisions such as these have many variables or factors that must be considered. If you were making a decision to purchase a car, you would consider such variables as its cost, features, color, and financing options. If you were making a decision about what college to attend, factors might include the cost, proximity to your home, and academic reputation. Different decision makers might even consider different factors for the same decision situation. For example, the color of a car may not be important to one buyer but critical to another. The number and type of variables considered might be different for each individual and for each decision the individual makes.

Decisions may have to be made under time, budget, or other constraints. Your choice of a car may be limited to those that cost under $10,000. Your decision to accept a summer job may be limited to those that are within 30 miles of your home. Your decision to

EXHIBIT 1-4 External and Internal Users of Accounting Information

Users	Type of Accounting Information Needed	Provided in
Shareholders and creditors	Sales, gross profit, net income, cash flow, assets and liabilities, earnings per share, etc. Although this information is primarily monetary, it may also include nonmonetary information (units in inventory). This information is often provided in summary form (for the company as a whole) and typically is historical in nature.	Annual reports, financial statements, and other available documents
Government agencies	Varies by agency but includes taxable income, sales, assets, comparisons of actual expenditures to budgets, etc. This information is usually provided for the company as a whole and is historical in nature. It can include both monetary and nonmonetary information.	Tax returns and other reports
Customers and suppliers	Order status, shipping dates, inventory levels, etc. This information must be very detailed and timely to be useful.	Limited-access databases available to specific customers and suppliers
Marketing, operations and production, finance, and human resource managers	Timely and detailed information on sales and expenses, product costs, budget information, and measures of performance. Often includes nonmonetary data (direct labor hours, units to break even, etc.). Accounting information is often needed for segments of an organization and is more likely future oriented than historical.	Cost reports, budgets, and other internal documents

attend a college may have to be made by a certain date. In addition, many decisions are made with missing information or at least with imperfect information. In deciding which car to buy, you would probably want to consider the cost of future repairs for various models. Although you might estimate these costs by using such sources as *Consumer Reports,* you will not know with certainty. Decisions may not be perfect, but they should be the best you can make given the information that is available to you at the time. The process you go through is to gather all the information you can to reduce the risk of an incorrect or less than optimal decision.

Decisions often lead to other decisions. Once you have decided to buy a car or a stereo, you need to make other decisions, such as whether to pay cash or to finance the purchase or whether to buy an extended warranty. It does seem as though life is a never-ending string of decisions.

In this chapter, we discuss decision problems in general and how to gather as much relevant information as possible to reduce the risk of incorrect decisions. The decision-making model presented here will allow you to approach complex decisions in an orderly fashion.

Decision making is the process of identifying different courses of action and selecting one appropriate to a given situation. All decisions require using judgment. The quality of the decision often depends on how good that judgment is. Judgment refers to the cognitive aspects of the decision-making process. By cognitive, we mean taking a logical, thinking approach to making decisions rather than just making decisions on the spur of the moment. In this section of the chapter, we learn how to structure a decision problem so that we will use better judgment when making decisions.

Using a basic decision-making model does not guarantee that all our decisions will be correct, but it will allow us to increase the odds of making a good decision. A lot of decisions have more than one acceptable solution, as do a lot of the problems and cases in this textbook. The trick is to pick the *best* solution for each particular decision-making situation.

PAUSE & Reflect

Outline as best you can the process you went through in selecting the last major item you purchased.

A Decision-Making Model

Step 1: Define the Problem

LO3
Apply a basic four-step decision-making model

When faced with a problem, the first step is to define it accurately. Managers (and students) often act without a clear understanding of the real problem. In fact, many bad decisions are made simply because the decision maker is trying to solve the wrong problem. For example, a company experiencing a reduction in sales might erroneously define the problem as low sales volume (and attempt to solve the problem by providing increased sales incentives) when the real problem is poor quality of the product sold. Problem definition requires the cooperation of managers in all functional areas of an organization. Whereas a single manager might focus on the reduction in sales, input by accounting, operations, marketing, and sales managers will most likely result in a clearer picture of the underlying problem (poor quality) causing the reduction in sales. This may lead to even further refinements, such as identifying the specific type of material that is causing the quality problem. Accurately defining a problem requires a willingness to listen to others, good judgment, and lots of practice.

Step 1 DEFINE THE PROBLEM

PAUSE & Reflect

In retrospect, should you have considered other options and variables when making your most recent big purchase?

Step 2: Identify Objectives

The second step in the decision-making process is to identify the objectives in finding a solution to the problem. Objectives may be **quantitative** (to buy at the best price or to increase net income), **qualitative** (to buy the highest-quality component or to increase customer satisfaction), or a combination of the two.

Step 2 IDENTIFY OBJECTIVES

Step 3: Identify and Analyze Available Options

The third step in the decision-making process is to identify the options available to achieve your objectives and analyze those options. This step requires the consideration of relevant variables affecting the problem and of alternative courses of action. Most decisions require the decision maker to consider more than one option and multiple variables.

Step 3 IDENTIFY AND ANALYZE AVAILABLE OPTIONS

DILBERT BY SCOTT ADAMS

DILBERT reprinted by permission of United Media Inc.

These variables should include both quantitative and qualitative factors. The key here is to identify only the variables that are relevant to a particular decision. The concept of relevant factors is discussed in more detail on page 15.

IN THE NEWS http://www.consumerreports.org

Every year, *Consumer Reports* publishes an issue called a "Buyers Guide." This guide provides a variety of qualitative information to aid your decision in purchasing products evaluated by this organization.

STEP 4: SELECT THE BEST OPTION

Step 4 SELECT THE BEST OPTION

The fourth and last step is to select the best option. We need to answer the question of how well each of our options will achieve our objective or objectives. This is sometimes the most difficult step in the process. Just as our options and variables included both quantitative and qualitative factors, our solution should consider both as well. As a general rule, you should never make decisions based only on quantitative information. Often, qualitative information is at least as important as or more important than quantitative information.

Key Concept: *Never make decisions with just the numbers! Always consider nonnumerical (qualitative) information.*

MANAGEMENT ACTIONS AND DECISIONS http://www.merckcapitalventures.com

To be successful in a business like Merck, Lubin says that "employees need to possess a broad array of skills and must be able to think through and look beyond the numbers." When hiring new employees for entry-level positions, Merck looks for students who have an appreciation for the breadth of tools and techniques that can be applied to understand a business situation as opposed to the depth of any one technical tool.

COURTESY OF GARY LUBIN, MERCK CAPITAL VENTURES

GARY LUBIN
Merck Capital Ventures, LLC

PAUSE & Reflect

What were the risks in your decision to purchase a particular product?

At this stage, the decision maker must also recognize that decisions are often made in the face of uncertainty. This step in the decision process will involve our preference for risk and our estimate of what chance the future events have of happening. The impact of risk on decision making is discussed more completely on page 16.

To summarize, we follow these four steps in the process of making decisions (see Exhibit 1-5):

1. Define the problem.
2. Identify objectives.
3. Identify and analyze available options.
4. Select the best option.

PAUSE & Reflect

Evaluate your decision to purchase a product. Was your decision a good one?

Once we have completed the preceding process and chosen the best option, we must then implement our decision and evaluate the results. We may have to go back to Step 1 and repeat the process if the decision turns out to be less than optimal.

EXHIBIT 1-5 The Decision-Making Model

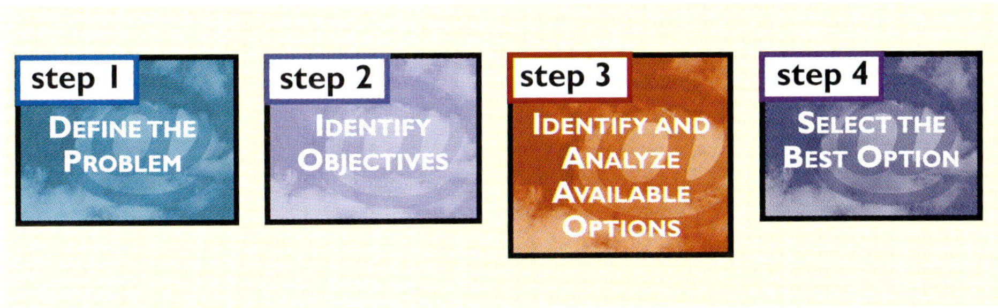

RELEVANT FACTORS AND DECISION MAKING

Step 3 — IDENTIFY AND ANALYZE AVAILABLE OPTIONS

LO4
Evaluate the role of relevant factors and decision making

Step 3 in our decision-making model is to identify and analyze relevant factors affecting the decision. How do decision makers determine whether a factor is relevant? Relevant factors are those that affect a particular decision. Therefore, they must be factors that differ between alternatives. In deciding between automobiles, if they all have the same options at the same cost (air conditioning, AM/FM stereo, etc.), those options are not relevant to the decision. Very often, costs are key factors that must be considered in decisions. As with other factors, **relevant costs** are those that differ between alternatives. Another way to view relevant costs is to identify those that are avoidable or can be eliminated by choosing one alternative over another. In choosing between automobiles, if one car has air conditioning and another does not, the cost of air conditioning is relevant because choosing one of the alternatives could eliminate that cost.

Sunk costs are costs that have already been incurred. Because sunk costs cannot be avoided, they are not relevant in decisions. In your decision to trade in your old vehicle, the amount that you paid for it may appear to be important. However, because that cost is sunk, it cannot be avoided, is not relevant, and should not be considered in your decision.

Key Concept: *Sunk costs are not relevant.*

Concept Question: *As a production manager of a manufacturing company, you have become aware of a new machine that can reduce the cost of making a product by 30 percent. However, your boss says that you can't buy the new equipment until the old equipment is fully depreciated in two more years. Is the depreciation on the old machine a relevant cost? What factors are relevant?*

Concept Answer: Depreciation on the old machine is sunk and therefore is not relevant. ■

If sunk costs are not relevant, what about other costs that will be incurred in the future? Are all costs that are not sunk relevant? Again, the key is that relevant costs are avoidable costs. If future costs do not differ between alternatives, they are not avoidable (they will be incurred regardless of the alternative chosen) and therefore are not relevant. In your choice of an automobile, if the cost of an option is the same, that cost is not relevant in your decision.

Key Concept: *Future costs that do not differ between alternatives are not relevant.*

Opportunity costs are the benefits forgone by choosing one alternative over another and are relevant costs for decision-making purposes as well. For example, in choosing to go to college, you are forgoing the salary you could receive by working full time. Almost all alternatives have opportunity costs. In choosing to work instead of going to school, the

PAUSE & *Reflect*

Making a decision to stop producing a product is a difficult one that depends on an analysis of both quantitative costs and qualitative factors. For example, assume that you are the manager of a consumer electronics manufacturing company that makes televisions and videocassette recorders (VCRs). What quantitative costs would be relevant in making the decision to stop making VCRs? Remember, relevant costs are those that can be avoided by choosing one alternative over another. What qualitative factors should be considered?

PAUSE & *Reflect*

In making the decision to stop producing VCRs, what opportunity costs might be involved? Consider, for example, alternative uses of the facilities and other products that might be manufactured instead of VCRs.

opportunity cost is the higher salary that you might earn if you choose to go to school. Opportunity costs are sometimes difficult to quantify but nevertheless should be considered in making decisions.

Key Concept: *Opportunity costs are relevant.*

Risk and Decision Making

LO5
Understand and evaluate the role of risk in decision making

As mentioned earlier, most decisions involve **risk.** A decision maker's goal is to consider (and possibly to minimize) the risk of decisions. One of the factors that come into play when selecting the best option (Step 4) is the attitude toward risk. If the decision makers are risk seekers, they will rate the alternatives one way. If they are risk averse, they will probably rate the alternatives differently. For example, risk-averse decision makers may rate more highly an automobile that has been in production a couple of years and has a history of being reliable than a brand new model with no track record.

A quantitative method of considering the risk of decision factors is by adjusting the discount rate used in time value of money calculations (see Chapter 8 for a more detailed discussion of this important concept). Cash flows occurring farther in the future might be discounted at a higher interest rate than cash flows occurring in the next year or two. Increasing the interest rate in present-value calculations has the impact of decreasing the present value of those cash flows.

A second way of adjusting for risk is by considering the probability that certain events will occur. For example, in the choice of an automobile, the interest rate on the loan may be an important factor. However, a particular dealer may not guarantee the interest rate before the loan is approved. Knowing that the probability of the rate's changing is 50 percent, you can adjust the rating accordingly to take this risk into account.

A third method of considering risk is through **sensitivity analysis.** Sensitivity analysis is the process of changing the values of key variables considered in the analysis to determine how sensitive decisions are to those changes. For example, if the purchaser of an automobile is not 100 percent sure of qualifying for the best possible loan package at all the dealers, he or she may want to consider the cost of that automobile, taking into account all possible finance packages. If this adjustment changes the decision, the decision is sensitive to changes in that variable. If it does not change the decision, the decision is not sensitive to that variable.

Ethics and Decision Making

LO6
Understand and evaluate the role of ethics in decision making

Ethical issues frequently arise in the course of personal decision making. Sometimes the ethical issues are clear (should you keep the money in the wallet you found or return it to its owner) but at other times they may be a little cloudy. For example, what ethical responsibilities does the owner of a used car have in telling a prospective buyer about potential problems?

Likewise, ethical issues in business decisions may be fuzzy. Although most of us would agree that it would be unethical for businesses to sell products that are known to be unsafe to customers, cigarette manufacturers do just that every day. Is the use of inexpensive foreign labor by shoe and apparel manufacturers an acceptable business practice or a serious lapse of ethical responsibility? Is the release of chemicals into the environment as a by-product of an electric utility or a paper mill an acceptable cost of providing products to a demanding customer or an unacceptable and unethical practice?

Regardless of how you feel about these and other ethical issues, companies must consider the implications of such decisions. As special-interest groups grow more vocal about environmental issues and working conditions, consumers boycott products and switch brands, and investors consider ethical and social criteria in making investments, ethical

MANAGEMENT ACTIONS AND DECISIONS

http://www.merckcapitalventures.com

The importance of high ethical standards in business cannot be overstated. At Merck, Gary Lubin notes that employees "must understand the importance of quality and completeness, appreciate the process as well as the result, exhibit self-confidence, work well both independently and in teams, and, above all, demonstrate high ethical behavior."

COURTESY OF GARY LUBIN, MERCK CAPITAL VENTURES

GARY LUBIN
Merck Capital Ventures, LLC

PAUSE & Reflect

Pricing decisions are an important consideration for companies attempting to maximize their profitability. However, pricing decisions are likely to influence other factors (such as the volume of products sold) and cannot be made in isolation. The impact of changing prices on the number of units sold is usually not known with certainty. How might you as a manager take this risk into account in determining the selling price of your products?

decisions become crucial business decisions. In a study of the 500 largest publicly held companies in the United States, the 126 companies that specifically mentioned a code of conduct or ethics system in their annual reports had a significantly higher average financial performance than did companies with no mention of ethics in their annual reports (Verschoor, "Principles Build Profits," *Management Accounting,* October 1997).

Ethical problems arise in organizations for a number of reasons. Sometimes, pressure to reach unrealistic short-run goals may lead to unethical behavior, such as padding budgets or using poor-quality materials in production to save money. Strictly adhering to an organizational hierarchy can be problematic when subordinates blindly follow orders. In the past, managers often viewed their goals in strictly monetary terms—to earn a profit and to increase shareholder wealth. More recently, there has been a call for a return to the view of business as a moral practice in which managers are concerned about the ethical consequences of what they do. In this view, decisions must be made in an environment that encourages the evaluation of a multitude of values, not only dollars and cents.

© DAVID YOUNG-WOLFF/PHOTOEDIT

Do companies have responsibilities to other stakeholders?

Concept Question: *What ethical responsibilities does a company have to its shareholders, employees, customers, and the communities in which it is located?*

Concept Answer: Although companies take various approaches to ethical responsibility, they often provide guidance to their employees through the use of a formal code of ethics concerning what is acceptable ethical behavior.[2] Codes may be very specific and mention acceptable and unacceptable behavior or just provide a general framework and value system that employees can use in their day-to-day decision making. For example, Ben & Jerry's mission statement consists of three interrelated parts:

> Product—to make, distribute and sell the finest quality all natural ice cream and related products in a wide variety of innovative flavors made from Vermont dairy products.
>
> Economic—to operate the Company on a sound financial basis of profitable growth, increasing value for our shareholders, and creating career opportunities and financial rewards for our employees.
>
> Social—to operate the Company in a way that actively recognizes the central role that business plays in the structure of society by initiating innovative ways to improve the quality of life of a broad community—local, national, and international (http://www.benjerry.com). ■

PAUSE & Reflect

Is adhering to laws and regulations sufficient to ensure ethical behavior in organizations?

A variety of professional organizations also have ethical codes of conduct that apply to their members. In 1997, the Institute of Management Accountants issued a revised code

[2]Berenebeim reports that 84 percent of U.S. companies surveyed had an ethics code and that 45 percent have enacted them since 1987 ("The Corporate Ethics Test," *Business and Society Review,* 1992).

PAUSE & Reflect

A supplier offers to sell you at a sizable discount aluminum used in the manufacture of aluminum baseball bats. After inspecting the aluminum, you find that although it meets your technical qualifications, it shatters under extreme use in some cases. What objectives might you consider to explicitly take into account your company's ethical responsibilities in this situation? What relevant factors should be considered?

of ethics for management accountants, stating that "practitioners of management accounting and financial management have an obligation to the public, their profession, the organizations they serve, and themselves, to maintain the highest standards of ethical conduct." The full text of the code is provided in the appendix to this chapter.

With a little elaboration, our four-step decision model is sufficient to handle the consideration of ethical issues. In Step 2, objectives should include the consideration of a company's ethical responsibilities. This might include such statements as, "the decision should result in a higher-quality product or a safer product for customers." It might require explicit acknowledgment that the well-being of employees will be considered in the decision or that the decision must not harm the environment. Ethical decision making requires managers to consider who will be affected by the decision and how.

If a company's objectives include the consideration of ethical responsibilities, it is important to identify the major principles, laws, and values that have a bearing on the decision in Step 3. Principles include such qualities as integrity, honesty, and respect for others. Laws affecting business decisions include the Internal Revenue Code and the Foreign Corrupt Practices Act of 1977, which makes it illegal for U.S. corporations to make improper payments or bribes to help in the acquisition of sales. Values include not only such things as the importance of the quality and safety of products but also the desire to earn a profit or protect one's job. If a company's ethical responsibilities are adequately and explicitly acknowledged in Step 2 and Step 3 of the decision model, selecting the best option in Step 4 will consider ethical objectives as well as the monetary impact of a particular decision.

IN THE NEWS http://www.anheuser-busch.com

In the mid 1990s, Anheuser-Busch launched a campaign to discourage beer distributors from carrying microbrews. The company offered discounts and subsidized advertising and limited distributors' ability to bring rival brews to bars and retailers. When the distributors began to abandon the microbrews, the microbrews brought suit against Anheuser-Busch. Anheuser-Busch maintains that the actions are legitimate and legal.

APPENDIX

STANDARDS OF ETHICAL CONDUCT FOR PRACTITIONERS OF MANAGEMENT ACCOUNTING AND FINANCIAL MANAGEMENT

Practitioners of management accounting and financial management have an obligation to the public, their profession, the organizations they serve, and themselves, to maintain the highest standards of ethical conduct. In recognition of this obligation, the Institute of Management Accountants has promulgated the following standards of ethical conduct for practitioners of management accounting and financial management. Adherence to these standards, both domestically and internationally, is integral to achieving the Objectives of Management Accounting. Practitioners of management accounting and financial management shall not commit acts contrary to these standards nor shall they condone the commission of such acts by others within their organizations.

COMPETENCE

Practitioners of management accounting and financial management have a responsibility to:

- Maintain an appropriate level of professional competence by ongoing development of their knowledge and skills.
- Perform their professional duties in accordance with relevant laws, regulations, and technical standards.
- Prepare complete and clear reports and recommendations after appropriate analyses of relevant and reliable information.

CONFIDENTIALITY

Practitioners of management accounting and financial management have a responsibility to:

- Refrain from disclosing confidential information acquired in the course of their work except when authorized, unless legally obligated to do so.
- Inform subordinates as appropriate regarding the confidentiality of information acquired in the course of their work and monitor their activities to assure the maintenance of that confidentiality.
- Refrain from using or appearing to use confidential information acquired in the course of their work for unethical or illegal advantage either personally or through third parties.

INTEGRITY

Practitioners of management accounting and financial management have a responsibility to:

- Avoid actual or apparent conflicts of interest and advise all appropriate parties of any potential conflict.
- Refrain from engaging in any activity that would prejudice their ability to carry out their duties ethically.
- Refuse any gift, favor, or hospitality that would influence or would appear to influence their actions.
- Refrain from either actively or passively subverting the attainment of the organization's legitimate and ethical objectives.
- Recognize and communicate professional limitations or other constraints that would preclude responsible judgment or successful performance of an activity.

- Communicate unfavorable as well as favorable information and professional judgments or opinions.
- Refrain from engaging in or supporting any activity that would discredit the profession.

Objectivity

Practitioners of management accounting and financial management have a responsibility to:

- Communicate information fairly and objectively.
- Disclose fully all relevant information that could reasonably be expected to influence an intended user's understanding of the reports, comments, and recommendations presented.

Resolution of Ethical Conflict

In applying the standards of ethical conduct, practitioners of management accounting and financial management may encounter problems in identifying unethical behavior or in resolving an ethical conflict. When faced with significant ethical issues, practitioners of management accounting and financial management should follow the established policies of the organization bearing on the resolution of such conflict. If these policies do not resolve the ethical conflict, such practitioners should consider the following courses of action:

- Discuss such problems with the immediate superior except when it appears that the superior is involved, in which case the problem should be presented initially to the next higher managerial level. If satisfactory resolution cannot be achieved when the problem is initially presented, submit the issues to the next higher managerial level. If the immediate superior is the chief executive officer, or equivalent, the acceptable reviewing authority may be a group such as the audit committee, executive committee, board of directors, board of trustees, or owners. Contact with levels above the immediate superior should be initiated only with the superior's knowledge, assuming the superior is not involved. Except where legally prescribed, communication of such problems to authorities or individuals not employed or engaged by the organization is not considered appropriate.
- Clarify relevant ethical issues by confidential discussion with an objective advisor (e.g., IMA Ethics Counseling Service) to obtain a better understanding of possible courses of action.
- Consult your own attorney as to legal obligations and rights concerning the ethical conflict.
- If the ethical conflict still exists after exhausting all levels of internal review, there may be no other recourse on significant matters than to resign from the organization and to submit an informative memorandum to an appropriate representative of the organization. After resignation, depending on the nature of the ethical conflict, it may also be appropriate to notify other parties.

Summary of Key Concepts

- Accounting information includes both financial (quantitative) and nonfinancial (qualitative) information used by decision makers. (p. 5)
- Managerial accountants facilitate management decision making. (p. 8)
- Accounting information systems are continually evolving to meet the changing demands of their users. (p. 10)

- Never make decisions with just the numbers! Always consider nonnumerical (qualitative) information. (p. 14)
- Sunk costs are not relevant. (p. 15)
- Future costs that do not differ between alternatives are not relevant. (p. 15)
- Opportunity costs are relevant. (p. 16)

KEY DEFINITIONS

Accounting information system (AIS) A transaction processing system that captures financial data resulting from accounting transactions within a company (p. 4)

Enterprise resource planning (ERP) systems Systems used to collect, organize, report, and distribute organizational data and transform that data into critical information and knowledge (p. 4)

Planning The development of both the short-term (operational) and the long-term (strategic) objectives and goals of an organization and an identification of the resources needed to achieve them (p. 7)

Operating activities The day-to-day operations of a business (p. 8)

Controlling activities The motivation and monitoring of employees and the evaluation of people and other resources used in the operations of the organization (p. 8)

Decision making The process of identifying alternative courses of action and selecting an appropriate alternative in a given decision-making situation (p. 12)

Quantitative Can be expressed in terms of dollars or other quantities (units, pounds, etc.) (p. 13)

Qualitative Deals with nonnumerical attributes or characteristics (p. 13)

Relevant costs Those costs that differ between alternatives (p. 15)

Sunk costs Costs that have already been incurred (p. 15)

Opportunity costs The benefits forgone by choosing one alternative over another (p. 15)

Risk The likelihood that an option chosen in a decision situation will yield unsatisfactory results (p. 16)

Sensitivity analysis The process of changing the values of key variables to determine how sensitive decisions are to those changes (p. 16)

COMPUTER SIMULATION

You can now turn to **Appendix A** of your text to start the portion of the Big Al's simulation covering the decision to expand an existing pizza restaurant to include wholesale production and sales.

MULTIPLE CHOICE

1. Operational planning might address:
   a. long-term investment decisions
   b. measuring relative market share
   c. quarterly production needs
   d. all of the above

2. Which of the following statements is true?
   a. Production managers find managerial accounting information useful.
   b. Marketing managers would not find managerial accounting information useful.
   c. Corporate managers rarely consider managerial accounting information in their decision-making process.
   d. The costs of managerial accounting information often exceed the benefits.

3. In the past 10–20 years, the role of the management accountant has:
   a. not changed much
   b. been eliminated
   c. adapted to changes in the environment of business
   d. replaced the role of the financial accountant
4. __________ managers need to know how a given advertising campaign and its resulting impact on the number of units sold is expected to affect income.
   a. Marketing
   b. Operations/production
   c. Finance
   d. Human resource
5. Which of the following sequences of steps in the decision-making process is correct?
   a. define the problem, identify objectives, identify and analyze available options, select the best option
   b. identify objectives, define the problem, identify and analyze available options, select the best option
   c. select the best option, identify objectives, define the problem, identify and analyze available options
   d. define the problem, identify and analyze available options, select the best option
6. Sunk costs:
   a. have already been incurred
   b. can not be avoided
   c. are not relevant
   d. all of the above
7. Which of the following statements about the IMA's Standards of Ethical Conduct is true?
   a. Answers to all ethical questions can be found in the IMA Standards of Ethical Conduct.
   b. Management accountants who do not follow the IMA Standards of Ethical Conduct will be prosecuted by the IMA's disciplinary board.
   c. The IMA's Standards of Ethical Conduct provide guidelines for acceptable behavior.
   d. All accountants are required by law to comply with the IMA's Standards of Ethical Conduct.
8. Which of the following statements about ethics is true?
   a. Managerial accountants do not face ethical issues.
   b. Ethical issues frequently arise in the course of personal decision making.
   c. Research has found no link between ethics and the financial performance of large companies.
   d. Most managers within a company are likely to agree on ethical issues.
9. The four categories of responsibility in the IMA Standards of Ethical Conduct include all of the following *except:*
   a. compliance
   b. confidentiality
   c. integrity
   d. objectivity
10. In the IMA Standards of Ethical Conduct, *avoiding actual or apparent conflicts of interest and advising all appropriate parties of any potential conflict* is an example of:
   a. competence
   b. confidentiality
   c. integrity
   d. objectivity

CONCEPT REVIEW

11. Accounting information systems generate both monetary and nonmonetary accounting information. List two examples of each.

12. Is information produced by an accounting information system all quantitative? Why or why not? Give examples.

13. Define quantitative and qualitative information. Include in your definition some examples.

14. Give examples of quantitative and qualitative information for purchasing a new car. Would a car-purchase decision include both types of information?

15. List the most common external users of accounting information and what type of information they might need.

16. List the most common internal users of accounting information and what type of information they might need.

17. Discuss how a financial report for an internal user might differ from a financial report prepared for an external user.

18. Define strategic and operational planning.

19. Define control from a management perspective.

20. Assume that you have a 16-year-old son who has just received his driver's license. Your son does not do all the assigned work in his high school classes. What could you do to "control" his behavior regarding doing the assigned work in school? In other words, what sort of rewards or incentives would be appropriate to motivate him?

21. How has the role of the managerial accountant changed over time? What do managerial accountants do?

22. What type of accounting information do marketing managers need to make better decisions?

23. What type of accounting information do operations/production managers need to make better decisions?

24. What type of accounting information do finance managers need to make better decisions?

25. What type of accounting information do human resource managers need to make better decisions?

26. List and describe the four steps of the decision-making model.

27. How can risk be addressed in the decision-making model?

28. Define sunk costs and opportunity costs, and discuss their importance in decision making.

APPLICATION OF CONCEPTS

29. You are faced with the decision of choosing a new car. You have narrowed your options to four types of automobiles that fit your needs.

	Automobile 1	Automobile 2	Automobile 3	Automobile 4
Price	$12,000	$13,000	$14,000	$15,000
Options	Radio, $250	Cassette, $350	CD player, $500	CD/Cassette player, $750
Air	None	$1,200	$1,250	$1,200
Automatic Transmission	$1,000	$1,200	$1,250	$1,500
Power Package	None	$850	$1,250	$500

Required

A. Define as best you can the decision problem that you face in choosing the best automobile for you.

B. What would be your objectives in choosing an automobile? Separate the objectives into qualitative and quantitative areas. In your specific situation, what would be your most important objective and why?

C. As you will recall, Step 3 of the decision-making model requires you to identify all available options. Discuss what you consider to be the available options in your decision to choose a new automobile. Discuss all relevant quantitative and qualitative variables affecting these options.

D. Which of the four automobiles is the best quantitative choice? Why?

E. List and discuss qualitative factors that may cause you or any other decision maker to choose an automobile that is not the best quantitative choice.

30. Kent Jackson, an English major, has to decide which course to enroll in during the summer session. A science course he wants to take is being offered at a cost of $800 plus laboratory fees of $10 per class (25 classes total). His other choice is a writing workshop with tuition of $950. In addition to selecting a course, Kent needs a place to stay during the summer. Although he already paid $500 for a dormitory room, Kent has decided that he can no longer live on campus. There are two rooms available: a private residence that would cost him $900 and a semiprivate room that would cost $600. Kent could sublet his dormitory but feels that he should keep it empty in case he changes his mind and returns to campus in the fall.

Required

A. What other costs should Kent consider in making his decision?

B. What are some qualitative factors Kent might want to consider before he makes his decision? Why?

C. Discuss all relevant variables pertaining to this decision.

D. If Kent has a fixed amount of $2,000 to live on during the summer, how would this fact affect his decision?

31. A friend has informed you of an opportunity for a part-time job that you are considering accepting during your last semester before graduation. It would start at the beginning of your last semester and require working 20 hours per week at a rate of $15 per hour. It would also provide some good experience that could lead to a full-time job after you graduate. However, it would require a 2-hour round-trip commute four days a week. In addition, you currently receive a monthly scholarship of $1,000 that stipulates that you cannot work off campus. Consequently, if you accept the job, you will have to give up the scholarship. You expect to register for 15 credit hours (five classes) during your last semester and have been told that each of the courses is very demanding. In addition to class time, you expect to study about 30 hours each week.

Required

Using the decision-making model introduced in the chapter:

A. Define the problem you face in deciding whether to accept the job.

B. Using your own personal situation, define your objectives related to the problem identified in part A.

C. What are your options, and what factors are likely to be relevant in making your decision?

D. What opportunity costs are associated with the decision?

E. Is the decision risky? How would you take risk into account when making your decision?

32. Many airlines offer special low rates to certain destinations, but these rates are available only to customers who can fly on short notice. Sometimes, low hotel rates are also available at the last minute. How can this behavior be explained in terms of relevant costs?

33. Bob would like to impress Jessica on their first date and is wondering whether he should make dinner or whether they should go to a nice restaurant. What factors are relevant in the decision?

34. It's final exam time for Janet, and she is panicking because she doesn't have enough time to study for her last two exams. She currently has the same average in both calculus and history. She estimates that, with sufficient study time, she could increase her grade in calculus by 15 points and her grade in history by 10 points. However, she has only six hours of study time available. Janet estimates that she can increase her final grade in calculus by 2 points for each one hour studied and increase her final grade in history by 3 points for every hour of study. To maximize her additional points, how much time should Janet study for each exam?

35. Is it ethical for a U.S. company operating in a foreign country to offer bribes to suppliers or government officials if it is an acceptable business practice in the foreign country?

36. A story on *60 Minutes* highlighted the widespread practice of automotive service businesses attempting to sell customers unneeded parts and services. What are the ethical issues involved? Who are the stakeholders?

37. As an engineer with a multinational aerospace firm, you become aware of a potential defect in an airplane engine part. Your tests indicate that at low temperatures, a seal may leak, allowing hot gases from the engine to ignite. Although the risks of such a leak are very low, the consequences are potentially disastrous. What ethical issues are involved? Who are the stakeholders? What should the manager do?

38. Veda Inc. produces batteries for riding lawn mowers. The company provides the batteries to some of the largest manufacturers of riding lawn mowers in the United States. In the last few months, the company has received reports of batteries exploding from high heat. The incidents have all been in southern states and have occurred with only one particular brand and model of lawn mower. In these models, the batteries are installed beneath the seats of the mower. In more than one case, the exploding batteries have resulted in serious injuries to operators of the lawn mowers. Company officials are aware of the potential danger but have been unable to pinpoint the problem. Some company officials think that the problem may be with the lawn mower and not with the batteries. Internal testing has been inconclusive.

Required

A. Comment on the responsibility the company should take for the potential danger of the battery exploding.

B. Should company management try to shift blame to the manufacturer of the lawn mower, as the problems are only with one particular brand of mower?

C. Discuss the ethical considerations involved with this situation.

Part I

The Costing of Products and Services

Chapter 2

THE PRODUCTION PROCESS AND PRODUCT (SERVICE) COSTING

Study Tools

A Review of the Previous Chapter
Chapter 1 provided an overview of accounting information, its users, and the types of decisions that are made by both external and internal users of accounting information.

A Preview of This Chapter
In this chapter, we learn about basic production processes manufacturing companies use, cost terminology, the flow of costs in manufacturing, merchandising and service companies, and the impact of product costs and period costs on a company's income statement and balance sheet.

Key concepts include:
- Costs flow in the same way that products flow through a production facility.
- Product costs attach to the product and are expensed only when the product is sold, whereas period costs are expensed in the period in which they are incurred.

A Preview of Upcoming Chapters
Chapter 3 provides an introduction to the cost systems used to accumulate, track, and assign costs to products and services and to the particular difficulties and problems the allocation of overhead causes. Chapter 4 discusses the allocation of overhead to products using activity-based costing (ABC) and how activity information is used to help managers control and manage costs.

LEARNING OBJECTIVES

After studying the material in this chapter, you should be able to:

LO1 Understand basic production processes traditional manufacturing companies use with and without inventory

LO2 Apply the concepts of product costs for manufacturing, merchandising, and service companies

LO3 Understand basic cost flows applicable to manufacturing, merchandising, and service companies

LO4 Evaluate the impact of product costs and period costs on a company's income statement and balance sheet

Product (and service) costing is important for both external users and managerial decision making. Externally, the cost of products and services must be known to value inventory (for products) and to determine the gross profit on sales. Internally, managers must know the costs of products and services for a variety of reasons, including making pricing decisions and budgeting for expected cash disbursements. The costing of products and services is described in Chapters 2, 3, and 4. Chapter 2 begins with a description of the production process for both traditional manufacturing companies with inventory and manufacturing companies with little or no inventory. The chapter also provides an introduction to basic cost terminology applicable to manufacturing companies, merchandising companies, and service providers and concludes with a description of cost flows in each type of company. In Chapter 3, we discuss systems that companies use to accumulate, track, and assign costs to specific products and services and some of the issues related to measuring and allocating overhead and other product costs. In Chapter 4, we discuss some of the problems inherent in traditional methods of overhead allocation and describe a contemporary costing system, called activity-based costing, that may be more appropriate for internal decision making. ■

INTRODUCTION

Regardless of the type of company involved, costs are associated with the products and services produced and sold. Although it might appear simple to determine the cost of a product or service, the process can be quite complicated, as you will see in the next few chapters. How should companies determine the costs of producing products and providing services? What costs should be included? Before we can answer these questions, we should also ask why companies want to determine their product costs. For example, a company might be preparing financial statements for a bank to use in determining whether to make a loan to the company or may be filing its income tax return for the year. Generally accepted accounting principles (GAAP) and tax laws govern costing for financial statement purposes and for tax purposes, respectively. On the other hand, a company might want to determine the cost of a particular product in order to determine its sales price or to estimate a product's profitability. Cost information is also helpful for budgeting and evaluation purposes. Costing for internal decision making is the focus of Chapters 2, 3, and 4.[1]

MANUFACTURING, MERCHANDISING, AND SERVICE ORGANIZATIONS

LO1
Understand basic production processes traditional manufacturing companies use with and without inventory

Every company provides a product or a service to customers and clients. **Manufacturing companies** (such as Intel, Toyota, mom-and-pop bakeries, or custom-furniture makers) take raw materials and produce new products from them. Retail and wholesale merchandising companies sell products that someone else has manufactured. Examples are large department stores, such as Sears and Target, as well as the independent record shop or clothing store on the corner. In contrast to manufacturing and merchandising companies, service companies do not sell a tangible product as their primary business. Service providers are the fastest-growing segment of the U.S. economy, employing roughly 75 percent of the workforce. Service providers include such diverse companies and industries as airlines, hospitals, automobile repair shops, brokerage firms, law firms, and CPA firms.

THE PRODUCTION PROCESS

PAUSE & *Reflect*

Grocery stores sell products that other companies have manufactured but may also have their own bakeries in which they transform raw materials into new products. Should grocery stores be classified as manufacturing or merchandising companies? Brokerage firms sell information to clients. Is information a product or a service?

Manufacturing companies purchase raw materials from other companies and transform them into a finished product. This transformation typically requires labor and the incurring of other costs, such as utilities, the depreciation of factory equipment, or supplies. Manufacturing companies may produce a single product or many products. Likewise, companies may have only a few customers or many thousands. The process used to manufacture these products depends on the specific product or products made, the customers who buy the product(s), and the company itself. Some companies are very labor intensive, whereas others rely heavily on automation. Some companies choose to make very high quality products, whereas other companies emphasize low cost. Some companies choose to carry large amounts of inventory, whereas others manufacture their products in small batches and make their products just in time to meet customer demand.

MANUFACTURING IN A TRADITIONAL ENVIRONMENT

Traditionally, the factory of a manufacturing company is organized so that similar machines are grouped together. For example, a furniture manufacturer might have areas de-

[1]It should be noted that companies might want to cost other objects in addition to products. For example, a company might want to know the costs of a particular department or division or even the costs of servicing a particular customer.

© PETE SOUZA/LIAISON

Traditional furniture manufacturers, such as this one, may have significant amounts of work-in-process inventory.

voted to cutting and rough sanding, shaping the cut lumber into furniture pieces (such as chair legs), using lathes and routers, drilling holes and dovetailing joints, assembling the furniture pieces, and finishing. As raw material (in this case, lumber) is processed in each area, it is "pushed" to the next area for further processing. Lumber is brought into the factory from the warehouse and is cut and rough sanded according to specifications for specific products. It is then moved to another area in the factory for shaping the rough lumber into chair legs, bed posts, and tabletops. Next, the lumber might move to an area containing drill presses and machines to make dovetail joints. After drilling and jointing, it would be moved to still another area for assembly. In this area, workers glue or screw the various parts together and attach necessary hardware and glass. After assembly, the furniture is moved to an area where it is sanded again and varnish or paint finishes applied. It would not be unusual for one or more of these areas to be in different buildings or sometimes in entirely different plants. After leaving the finishing department, the furniture is ready for packing and selling to customers.

In this traditional system, it was normal (and perhaps even desirable) to accumulate **raw materials inventory** and finished-products inventory (called **finished-goods inventory**) to serve as buffers in case of unexpected demand for products or unexpected problems in production. It was also normal to accumulate inventories of partially completed products (called **work-in-process inventory,** or WIP). WIP might result, for example, when furniture pieces that have been drilled and jointed are pushed to the assembly area before the workers in that area are ready for them.

PAUSE & Reflect

Can you think of other reasons that it may be desirable to have buffers of inventory on hand?

MANUFACTURING IN A JIT ENVIRONMENT

One of the big changes affecting manufacturing companies in the past 20 years or so has been the adoption of **just-in-time (JIT) production systems.** In an effort to reduce costs and become more efficient producers, companies began to focus on the costs and problems associated with the traditional manufacturing facility and the practice of carrying large amounts of inventory.

Concept Question: *In addition to costs of storage and insurance, what are some of the other costs of holding large amounts of inventory?*

Concept Answer: In addition to the obvious costs of storage and insuring inventory, traditional manufacturing systems may result in other, not-so-obvious costs, including the production of lower-quality products with more defects. The buffers that seem so desirable may in fact lead workers to pay less attention to detail and work less efficiently. In addition, the organization of factories in which similar machines are grouped together greatly increases the time necessary to manufacture products and makes it more difficult to meet special orders or unexpected increases in demand without having large amounts of inventory on hand. ■

In a just-in-time system, materials are purchased and products are made "just in time" to meet customer demand. Unlike traditional production, the process begins with a customer order, and products are "pulled" through the manufacturing process. Under ideal conditions, companies operating in a JIT environment would reduce inventories of raw materials, work-in-process, and finished goods to very low levels or even zero.

Without a buffer of extra finished goods and raw materials, it is imperative that companies employing JIT be able to manufacture products very quickly. This typically entails restructuring the factory itself. In the traditional factory, similar machines were often grouped together, resulting in raw materials and unfinished products being handled and moved a great deal from area to area. In the traditional factory, it also was difficult and time consuming to switch production from one product to another (from tables to chairs, for example) because the same machines were used for both. In contrast, factories in a JIT environment are typically organized so that all the machinery and equipment needed to make a product is available in one area. These groupings of machines are called manufacturing cells. The use of cells minimizes the handling and moving of products. It also reduces or eliminates setup time (the time needed to switch production from tables to chairs) because we now have one cell devoted just to the manufacture of tables and one cell devoted just to the manufacture of chairs. Sometimes, workers are trained to operate all the machinery in a manufacturing cell, increasing speed and efficiency even more. Dell Computer uses just-in-time manufacturing techniques to assemble build-to-order personal computers. As you can see in Exhibit 2-1, Dell can ship a computer to a customer within 12 hours of receiving an order. The actual assembly takes under 2 hours.

http://www.dell.com

IN THE NEWS

Disruptions in shipments of air freight and heightened security at border crossings following the World Trade Center terrorist attacks exposed one of the risks facing companies operating just-in-time factories. Without needed parts, several auto makers were forced to temporarily shut down assembly lines ("Flight Ban Slows 'Just in Time' Factories," *Wall Street Journal,* September 13, 2001, B3).

Concept Question: *Using the decision-making model introduced in Chapter 1, discuss the problem, objectives, and options facing a company like GM in deciding to employ JIT techniques in its manufacturing operations. What factors and variables are relevant in its decision?*

Step 1 DEFINE THE PROBLEM

Concept Answer: The problem facing GM and other automobile manufacturers is that traditional manufacturing practices, in which cars are manufactured and delivered to dealers before the car is sold, are costly and can be inefficient. When consumer demand changes (i.e., consumers demand more sport utility vehicles than estimated), manufacturers and their dealers are sometimes left with large numbers of unsold cars. In addition, when consumers can't get the cars they desire, they may get angry and decide to purchase from another manufacturer, resulting in lost sales and customer ill-will.

Step 2 IDENTIFY OBJECTIVES

GM likely has multiple objectives, including reducing the costs associated with holding large amounts of inventory, decreasing the time it takes to deliver a vehicle to a customer, increasing the flexibility of the manufacturing facilities, and increasing the quality of automobiles produced.

EXHIBIT 2-1 JIT Business in Action at Dell Computer Corp.

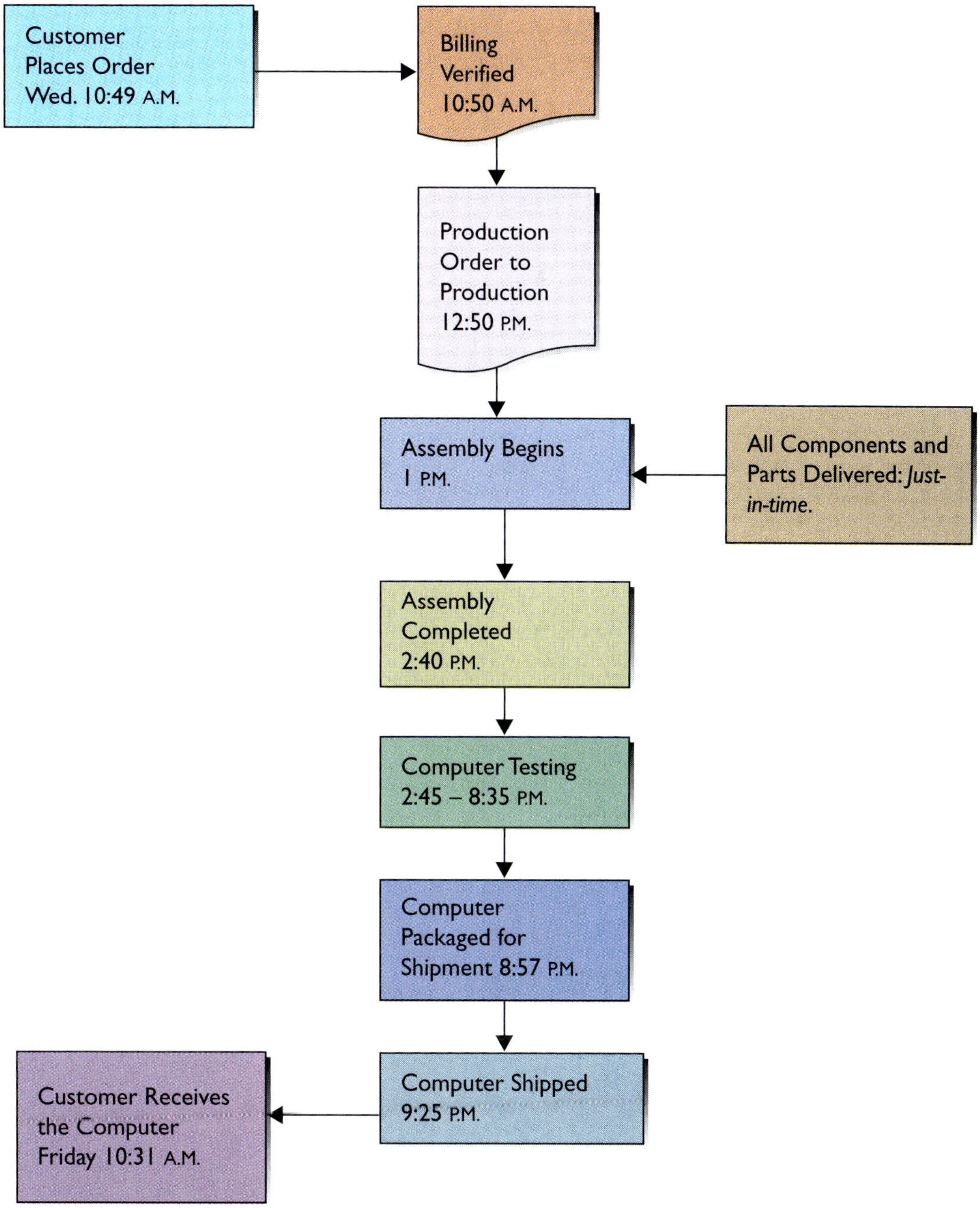

SOURCE: Adapted from Stephanie Losee, "Mr. Cozzette Buys a Computer," *Fortune* (1997).

Step 3 IDENTIFY AND ANALYZE AVAILABLE OPTIONS

GM's objectives might be met in a number of ways. Among the options it may consider are more (or less) automation of manufacturing facilities (without adopting JIT practices), doing away with the dealer network by requiring customers to order cars directly from GM, reducing the number and variety of car and truck models offered to customers, and adopting JIT techniques in its manufacturing processes. GM should consider the impact of each of these options on its objectives of reducing the costs of holding inventory, decreasing delivery time, increasing flexibility, and increasing quality. GM should also consider the impact on the existing workforce, suppliers, dealers, customers, shareholders, and other stakeholders. ■

Regardless of the size of the company involved, the number or products made, or the type of manufacturing system used, manufacturing companies must know how much their products cost.

> **IN THE NEWS**
>
> When U.S. car manufacturers began to make small cars to compete with foreign imports in the 1970s, foreign manufacturers routinely priced their small cars lower than did U.S. companies. Although foreign manufacturers were probably more efficient and had lower costs than their U.S. counterparts, U.S. manufacturers found that they really did not have a good idea how much their various lines of automobiles really cost! They routinely overcost the high-volume small cars they manufactured and undercost the lower-volume large cars. This bias in costing high-volume and low-volume products is discussed more in Chapter 4.

PRODUCT COSTS IN A MANUFACTURING COMPANY

LO2
Apply the concepts of product costs for manufacturing, merchandising, and service companies

It is convenient to distinguish costs incurred directly in the manufacture of a product (manufacturing costs) from those incurred elsewhere in the company (nonmanufacturing costs). **Manufacturing costs** are costs incurred in the factory or plant and typically consist of three components: *direct materials, direct labor,* and *manufacturing overhead.*

DIRECT MATERIALS

Direct materials are defined as materials that can be directly and conveniently traced to a particular product or other cost object *and* that become an integral part of the finished product. At Ford Motor Company, sheet metal and tires are direct materials. At Dell Computer, the computer chips made by Intel and used in Dell computers are direct materials.

Companies often will not make the effort to count every screw, tack, or nail in a product and would rather elect to classify these items as indirect materials.

© PETER DAZELY/IMAGEBANK

Direct materials typically cause few problems in the costing of products. The amount of direct material used in making products can usually be accurately measured by using engineering studies, and the accounting systems of most companies are capable of tracing the materials used and the costs of those materials to specific products. However, questions do arise and judgment is often needed to correctly classify materials as direct or indirect.

Materials that we know are used in the manufacture of products but cannot be measured with reasonable accuracy and easily and conveniently traced to a particular product are indirect costs **(indirect materials).** For example, the rivets and welding materials Ford Motor Company uses and the screws and solder Dell Computer uses would probably be classified as indirect materials.

DIRECT LABOR

Direct labor is the labor cost (including fringe benefits) of all production employees who work directly on the product being made or service being provided. Sometimes, direct labor is called touch labor to reflect the hands-on relationship between the employee and the product or service. Assembly-line workers are the clearest example of direct labor. As with direct material, identifying direct labor cost is usually straightforward and accurate. Time sheets may be used to keep track of the work employees perform on different products and the wages they are paid. Other labor cost incurred in the manufacture of a product (such as the cost of work performed by janitors, maintenance workers, and even supervisors who do not work on the products directly) is classified as an indirect cost **(indirect labor).**

MANUFACTURING OVERHEAD

All costs incurred that are not properly classified as direct material or direct labor in the factory are called **manufacturing overhead.** These costs may include utilities, depreciation of factory equipment and buildings, rent, repairs and maintenance, insurance, and so on. Manufacturing overhead also includes indirect materials and indirect labor and may include overtime and idle-time costs for direct labor workers. In a traditional manufacturing environment, the costs included in manufacturing overhead are most often indirect in nature and cannot be conveniently and accurately traced and assigned to a specific product. Remember, our machinery and equipment was typically used to make multiple products, making it difficult to trace the cost of a machine to a specific product. Although many overhead costs in a JIT environment will also be indirect in nature (rent and utilities, for example), more of the costs are likely to be direct in nature. For example, in a JIT environment, the cost of machinery in a manufacturing cell can be traced to a specific product (tables) if it is used only to make tables.

Because of the indirect nature of most overhead costs and the inability of companies to directly measure the amount of overhead included in products or to trace manufacturing overhead to products, accountants have come up with various methods of allocating manufacturing overhead to products. Traditional methods of allocating overhead using job and process costing are discussed in Chapter 3. A contemporary method, called activity-based costing, is discussed in Chapter 4.

NONMANUFACTURING COSTS

Nonmanufacturing costs consist of those costs that are incurred outside the plant or factory and typically are categorized as selling and administrative costs. Although nonmanufacturing costs are necessarily incurred in running a business, they are not directly incurred in the production of products. A general rule of thumb is to imagine the product not being produced. If a particular cost would still occur, it is generally a nonmanufacturing cost. Common examples of nonmanufacturing costs include advertising costs, commissions paid to salespersons, administrative and accounting salaries, and office supplies. Nonmanufacturing costs also include rent, insurance, taxes, utilities, and depreciation of equipment when used in selling and administrative activities.

Concept Question: *Classify the following costs as manufacturing or nonmanufacturing costs:*

1. *Depreciation of factory machinery*
2. *Depreciation of vehicles used by salespersons*
3. *Lease expense on factory equipment*
4. *Lubricants used for maintenance on factory machinery*
5. *Factory supervisors' salaries*
6. *Heat, water, and power used in the factory building*
7. *Material used to construct the product*
8. *Materials used in packaging the finished product for shipment*
9. *Fringe benefits paid to assembly-line workers*
10. *Depreciation of furniture used in the employee cafeteria*
11. *Overtime paid to assembly-line workers*

Concept Answer: The key to identifying costs as manufacturing or nonmanufacturing is to think about where in the process the cost occurs. If the cost occurs in the factory while the product is being produced, it is a manufacturing cost. If the cost occurs after the product is produced or outside the manufacturing area, it is a nonmanufacturing cost. In the preceding Concept Question, items 1, 3, 4, 5, 6, 7, 9, and 11 are manufacturing costs; the remainder are not. ■

PAUSE & Reflect

A manufacturing firm buys computers that are used to control the production process and to process accounting information for management. Are the costs of the computers (depreciation) classified as manufacturing or nonmanufacturing costs?

Concept Question: *Which of the items in the previous Concept Question would be considered manufacturing overhead?*

Concept Answer: Items 1, 3, 4, 5, and 6 would be considered manufacturing overhead. In addition, overtime paid to assembly-line workers (item 11) may be considered overhead. This is discussed more fully in Chapter 3. ■

LIFE-CYCLE COSTS AND THE VALUE CHAIN

This simple classification of costs as manufacturing or nonmanufacturing leaves a lot to be desired. How should costs associated with research and development be classified? What about costs that are incurred in the engineering and design of products or costs that are incurred after the sale, owing to warranty work or other customer service? **Life-cycle costing** takes into account all the activities in an organization's **value chain.** The value chain of an organization is simply the set of activities that increase the value of an organization's products and services. A typical value chain includes research and development, design, production, marketing, distribution, and customer service activities (see Exhibit 2-2). Life-cycle costing therefore includes all the costs incurred throughout a product's life, not just in the manufacturing and selling of the product.

COST FLOWS IN A MANUFACTURING COMPANY—TRADITIONAL ENVIRONMENT WITH INVENTORY

If companies simply used all the materials they purchased to make one product, finished making all the units of that product that they started, and sold everything they finished,

EXHIBIT 2-2 Life-Cycle Costs and the Value Chain

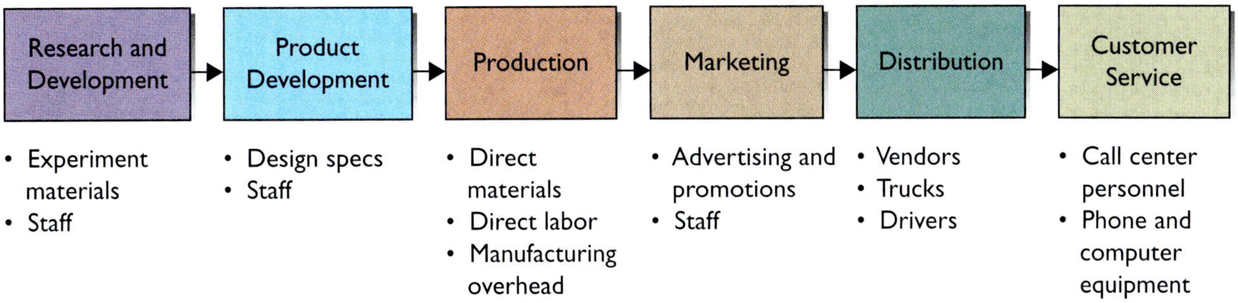

calculating the income or loss from selling the product would be relatively easy. However, when multiple products are made or when materials are not all used, goods are not all finished, or products are not all sold, the process becomes more difficult.

LO3
Understand basic cost flows applicable to manufacturing, merchandising, and service companies

To accurately cost products of manufacturing companies, you must somehow trace or allocate manufacturing costs to each individual product as it is being produced and then move through various inventory accounts as the product progresses toward eventual completion and sale. At the point of sale, the cost of producing the product (the cost of goods sold) must be matched with the sales price to compute a profit or loss on the sale (called gross margin, or gross profit). Subtracting nonmanufacturing costs from the gross margin provides a measure of profitability for the company as a whole. When materials are not all used in production, goods are not finished, or finished goods are not all sold, costs must be accounted for in the appropriate raw material, work-in-process, or finished-goods inventory accounts.

Manufacturing costs include direct material, direct labor, and manufacturing overhead. These costs are also called product costs because they attach to the product as it goes through the production process. Picture a product moving down an assembly line. As labor, material, and overhead costs are incurred, they attach to the product being produced and remain with that product until it is sold. Costs flow in the same way that products flow through a production facility.

Key Concept: Costs flow in the same way that products flow through a production facility.

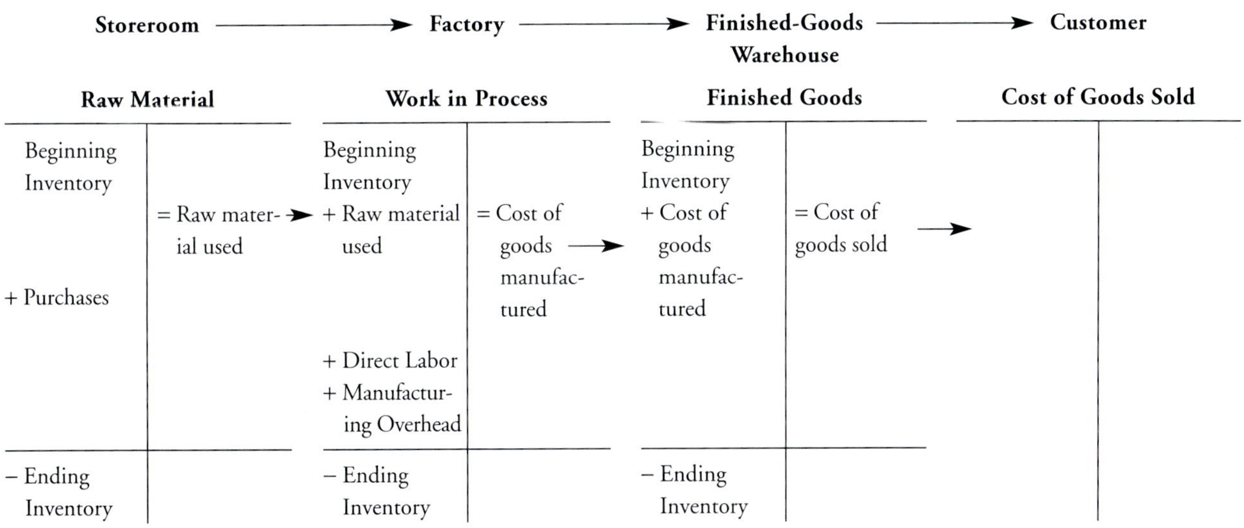

This basic cost flow model is appropriate (with slight variations) for companies using either job-costing or process-costing systems. The differences between job-costing and process-costing systems are discussed more fully in Chapter 3.

THE COST-OF-GOODS-SOLD MODEL FOR A TRADITIONAL MANUFACTURING COMPANY WITH INVENTORY

To illustrate the production process and some of the associated problems with costing products, we will use a fictional company called Northern Lights Custom Cabinets. Northern Lights Custom Cabinets manufactures and sells custom-ordered kitchen and bathroom cabinets. The company sells primarily to building contractors but occasionally deals directly with homeowners. Northern Lights is located in Anchorage, Alaska, and has been in business only a few years, so management is still learning the business and how to properly determine the cost of each cabinet.

Northern Lights has an engineering and design division, which is involved in all custom-cabinet jobs. Quality control dictates that the engineering and design division must design all cabinets. Northern Lights strives to minimize the costs of production without sacrificing quality. Once the design phase of each cabinet job is complete, the material must be ordered. The material is stored in the raw materials warehouse until needed for each job and is then moved to the production area.

The production factory is separated into three distinct areas: (1) cutting, (2) assembly, and (3) finishing. In the cutting area, all wood is cut into the required pieces, based on the plans from the engineering and design division. The pieces are all numbered and bundled for each particular section of the cabinet job. After cutting is completed, the bundles are moved to the assembly area, where the cabinets are constructed using glue and wood dowels. The assembled cabinets are moved to the finish area, where they are finished and stored for delivery to the home. This process can take up to one month to complete and is very labor intensive. After the cabinets have been completed, they are delivered to the home. Because each job is custom, Northern Lights also provides installation services for an extra charge.

Northern Lights purchases raw materials and stores the materials in a warehouse that is separate from the production facility or factory. While these materials are in the warehouse, the costs of the raw materials are included in a raw material inventory account. Northern Lights began 2001 with raw materials costing \$10,000 on hand and purchased an additional \$40,000 of raw materials during the year. Therefore, the company had \$50,000 of raw materials available for use during the year.

Description	Item	Amount
Raw materials on hand to start the period	Beginning inventory of raw materials	\$10,000
Acquisitions of raw materials during the period	+ Cost of raw materials purchased	+ 40,000
The pool of raw materials available for use during the period	= Raw materials available for use	= \$50,000

When the raw material is moved to the factory, the raw material costs move with the material to a work-in-process inventory account. Any raw materials not used during the year remain in the raw materials inventory account. Northern Lights moves \$45,000 of raw materials to the factory for use in manufacturing cabinets; \$5,000 of raw materials remains in raw materials inventory.

Description	Item	Amount
The pool of raw materials available for use during the period	Raw materials available for use	$50,000
The amount of raw materials used in production (and moved to a WIP account)	− Raw materials used in production	− 45,000
Raw materials on hand at the end of the period	= Ending inventory of raw materials	= $ 5,000

Raw Materials

Debit	Credit
$10,000 + 40,000	$45,000 →
$ 5,000	

Work in Process

Debit	Credit

As direct labor costs of $65,000 are incurred (factory workers work on the cabinets), the cost of the workers is added to the raw material cost in the work-in-process inventory account. Likewise, as manufacturing overhead costs ($85,000 of machine costs, rent, depreciation, utilities, indirect material, etc.) are incurred, they are added to the work-in-process account. As long as each set of cabinets remains in the factory, the costs associated with them are recorded in the work-in-process account.

If there is no beginning inventory of work in process and everything that is started in 2001 is finished (there is no ending inventory of WIP), the cost of goods manufactured is simply the sum of raw materials used, direct labor, and manufacturing overhead. When beginning or ending inventories exist, the cost of goods manufactured must be adjusted accordingly. At the beginning of 2001, Northern Lights had $15,000 of unfinished cabinets (started in 2000) in the factory. These cabinets were completed in early 2001. However, the company got even further behind in 2001, resulting in $20,000 of cabinets being partially finished at the end of 2001. Therefore, the cost of goods (cabinets) manufactured in 2001 and transferred to finished goods was $190,000.

Description	Item	Amount
Work in process on hand at the beginning of the period	Beginning inventory of WIP	$ 15,000
The amount of raw materials used in production	+ Raw materials used	+ 45,000
The amount of direct labor cost incurred	+ Direct labor	+ 65,000
The amount of manufacturing overhead incurred	+ Manufacturing overhead	+ 85,000
Work in process at the end of the period	− Ending inventory of WIP	− 20,000
The cost of goods manufactured during the period	= Cost of goods manufactured	= $190,000

Work in Process

Debit	Credit
$15,000 + 45,000 + 65,000 + 85,000	$190,000 →
$20,000	

Finished Goods

Debit	Credit

When a cabinet is sold, the accumulated costs in the finished-goods inventory account are moved to the cost-of-goods-sold account. If there is no beginning inventory of finished goods and all the goods finished in the current year are sold (there is no ending inventory), the cost of goods sold is equal to the cost of goods manufactured. However, when beginning and ending inventories exist, the cost of goods sold must be adjusted accordingly. Northern Lights had one order (costing $30,000) that was not delivered to customers by the end of 2000. Likewise, at the end of 2001, the company had $5,000 of cabinets that were finished but not sold. Therefore, the cost of goods (cabinets) sold during 2001 was $215,000.

Description	Item	Amount
Finished goods on hand at the beginning of the period	Beginning inventory of finished goods	$ 30,000
The cost of goods manufactured during the period	+ Cost of goods manufactured	+ 190,000
Finished goods on hand at the end of the period	− Ending inventory of finished goods	− 5,000
The cost of goods sold during the period	= Cost of goods sold	=$215,000

Finished Goods		Cost of Goods Sold	
$ 30,000	$215,000 →		
+ 190,000			
$ 5,000			

COST FLOWS IN A MANUFACTURING COMPANY—JIT ENVIRONMENT

How do cost flows differ in a manufacturing company utilizing JIT? Remember, in a JIT environment, the physical flow of goods is streamlined by the use of manufacturing cells that largely eliminate inventories of raw materials, WIP, and finished goods. Cost flows are streamlined as well. Although the mechanics of an accounting system for companies utilizing JIT are covered more fully in the appendix to Chapter 3, direct material, direct labor, and overhead costs can essentially be accumulated directly in a cost-of-goods-sold account. Because raw materials are immediately placed into production when purchased, there is no need to record their purchase in a separate raw materials inventory account. Likewise, because all goods are typically finished and shipped out immediately to customers, there is no reason to keep track of WIP or finished-goods inventories.

Description	Item	Amount
The amount of raw materials purchased and used in production	Raw materials purchased and used	$ 50,000
The amount of direct labor costs incurred	+ Direct labor	+ 65,000
The amount of overhead cost incurred	+ Manufacturing overhead	+ 85,000
The cost of goods sold during the period	= Cost of goods sold	=$200,000

MERCHANDISING COMPANIES AND THE COST OF PRODUCTS

Wholesalers and retailers purchase merchandise in finished form from other companies. With the exception of packaging and other minor changes, they simply offer the products for resale to other companies (wholesalers) or to the ultimate consumer (retailers). Therefore, the product cost of a wholesaler or a retailer is simply the purchase price of the merchandise the wholesaler or retailer sells.

Because merchandising companies simply purchase goods for resale, the flow of costs in a retail or a wholesale establishment is fairly simple. On the balance sheet, merchandising companies use a single account for inventory, called merchandise inventory. The costs incurred in inventory are simply the costs to purchase the inventory.

How are the costs incurred in purchasing inventory for resale expensed? You may recall from financial accounting that the principle of matching revenue from sales with the costs associated with that revenue means that the cost of purchasing merchandise is expensed as cost of goods sold as the merchandise is sold. However, the cost of goods sold is not necessarily equal to the cost of merchandise purchased during the period. If merchandise is purchased and not sold or if merchandise that was purchased in another period is sold in the current period, cost of goods sold must be adjusted accordingly.

The Cost-of-Goods-Sold Model for a Merchandising Company

Description	Item	Amount
Merchandise on hand to start the period	Beginning inventory	$15,000
Acquisitions of merchandise during the period	+ Cost of goods purchased	+ 63,000
The pool of merchandise available for sale during the period	= Cost of goods available for sale	= $78,000
Merchandise on hand at the end of the period	− Ending inventory	− (18,000)
The expense recognized on the income statement	= Cost of goods sold	= $60,000

COST FLOWS IN A SERVICE COMPANY

© DENNIS O'CLAIR/STONE

Many similarities exist between the costing of products in a manufacturing company and the costing of services. Like product costs, the cost of services includes three components: direct material, direct labor, and overhead. However, the proportions of each may vary dramatically. Service companies typically have few direct materials (or indirect materials, for that matter) and large amounts of direct labor and overhead.

In a movie studio, costumes and props are direct material and the salaries of actors and directors are direct labor. Overhead would include the costs of the studio itself and all the recording and production equipment. Camera operators and other support people would more than likely be classified as indirect labor because they would likely work on more than one film at a time. In a CPA firm or a law firm, direct material costs would likely be very small, whereas direct labor costs for CPAs and attorneys would be very large.

Concept Question: *In a CPA firm, paper is used in the preparation of tax returns. Is the paper likely to be considered direct or indirect material? Secretarial staff may be used to enter* *data into a computer for tax return preparation or for making copies of returns. Is the secretarial labor properly classified as direct labor or indirect labor?*

Concept Answer: The paper would likely be considered indirect material because it is probably immaterial in amount, and accounting for the paper used in each return would be difficult and inconvenient. On the other hand, if a significant amount of secretarial time is spent inputting data, it is likely that the CPA firm would keep track of those hours and trace them directly to a tax return as direct labor. Secretarial time spent on copying would most likely be considered indirect labor. Note that indirect material and indirect labor are still treated as costs of providing services by the CPA firm.

Although service companies have both direct and indirect costs, in general they have larger proportions of indirect overhead costs. For example, in a hospital, although the costs of specific drugs and special tests or X-rays can be traced to a specific patient, the costs of operating rooms and equipment and the salaries of administrators, discharge personnel, orderlies, and maintenance workers would all be indirect. ■

Concept Question: *Would a service company ever have the need for a WIP account?*

Concept Answer: Work-in-process (WIP) accounts could be used on projects that were incomplete at month end, such as audits by CPA firms, lengthy legal cases by law firms, and consulting engagements that are long term. In fact, this is a very common way to account for the accumulation of costs on these types of engagements. ■

PRODUCT COSTS AND PERIOD COSTS

LO4
Evaluate the impact of product costs and period costs on a company's income statement and balance sheet

Manufacturing costs are called **product costs,** or inventoriable costs, because they attach to products as they go through the manufacturing process. Direct material, direct labor, and overhead costs remain with the product until the product is sold. Only when it is sold are product costs expensed as cost of goods sold on the income statement. Until the sale of the product, the costs of manufacturing are included in one of three inventory accounts: raw material, work in process, and finished goods. These inventory accounts appear on the balance sheet along with other assets and liabilities. On the other hand, nonmanufacturing costs are called **period costs** because they are expensed in the period incurred. Selling and administrative costs are expensed immediately on the income statement in the period in which they are incurred (see Exhibit 2-3).

EXHIBIT 2-3 The Path to the Income Statement—Product and Period Costs

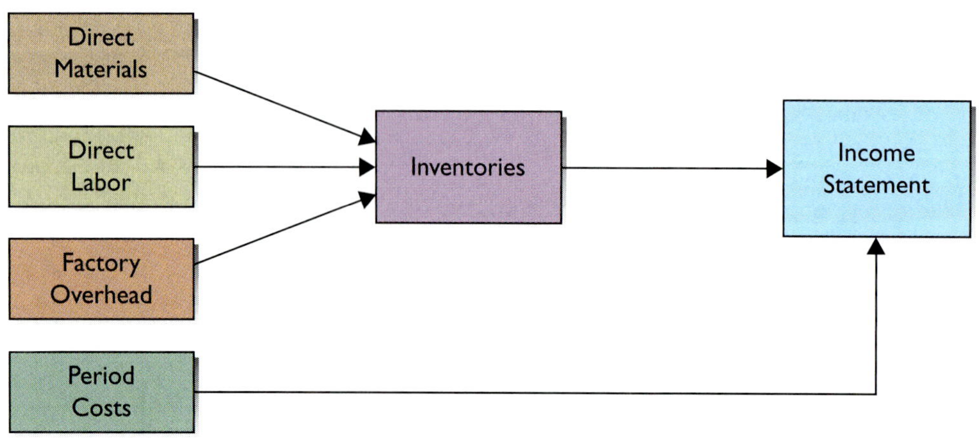

Key Concept: *Product costs attach to the product and are expensed only when the product is sold, whereas period costs are expensed in the period in which they are incurred.*

Balance sheets of a traditional manufacturing company (Ben & Jerry's) and a merchandising company (Circuit City) are shown in Exhibit 2-4. Note that merchandise inventory makes up about half of Circuit City's total assets but a much smaller portion of Ben & Jerry's total assets.

http://www.benjerry.com
http://www.circuitcity.com

Income statements (called a statement of operations by Ben & Jerry's and a statement of earnings by Circuit City) are shown in Exhibit 2-5. Income statements show the expensing of product costs as goods are sold (called cost of sales and buying and warehousing by Ben & Jerry's and Circuit City, respectively) and period costs (selling, general, and administrative expenses).

Note that the information provided in the balance sheets and income statements of Ben & Jerry's and Circuit City is historical in nature, is in summary form, and is provided for the company as a whole. This is typical of financial information provided to external users (stockholders, investors, and creditors).

EXHIBIT 2-4 Consolidated Balance Sheets (Partial) (in thousands)

BEN & JERRY'S 1998 ANNUAL REPORT CONSOLIDATED FINANCIAL STATEMENTS

CONSOLIDATED BALANCE SHEETS

(In thousands except share amounts)	December 26, 1998	December 27, 1997
ASSETS		
CURRENT ASSETS:		
Cash and cash equivalents	$ 25,111	$ 47,318
Short term investments	22,118	481
Trade accounts receivable: (less allowance of $979 in 1998 and $1,066 in 1997 for doubtful accounts)	11,338	12,710
Inventories	13,090	11,122
Deferred income taxes	7,547	6,071
Prepaid expenses and other current assets	3,105	2,378
TOTAL CURRENT ASSETS	82,309	80,080
Property, plant, and equipment, net	63,451	62,724
Investments	303	1,061
Other assets	3,438	2,606
TOTAL ASSETS	$149,501	$146,471

continued on next page

EXHIBIT 2-4 Consolidated Balance Sheets (Partial) (in thousands)

CONSOLIDATED BALANCE SHEETS

(Amounts in thousands except share data)	At February 28 1999	At February 28 1998
ASSETS		
CURRENT ASSETS:		
Cash and cash equivalents	**$ 265,880**	$ 116,612
Net accounts receivable [NOTE 12]	**574,316**	598,035
Inventory	**1,517,675**	1,410,545
Prepaid expenses and other current assets	**36,644**	21,157
TOTAL CURRENT ASSETS	**2,394,515**	2,146,349
Property and equipment, net [NOTES 4 AND 5]	**1,005,773**	1,048,434
Other assets	**44,978**	36,918
TOTAL ASSETS	**$3,445,266**	$3,231,701

EXHIBIT 2-5 Income Statements (Partial) (in thousands)

BEN & JERRY'S 1998 ANNUAL REPORT CONSOLIDATED STATEMENTS OF OPERATIONS

	Fiscal Year Ended		
(In thousands except share amounts)	**December 26, 1998**	**December 27, 1997**	**December 28, 1996**
Net sales	$209,203	$174,206	$167,155
Cost of sales	136,225	114,284	115,212
Gross profit	72,978	59,922	51,943
Selling, general, and administrative expenses	63,895	53,520	45,531
OTHER INCOME (EXPENSE):			
Interest income	2,248	1,938	1,676
Interest expense	(1,888)	(1,992)	(1,996)
Other income (expense), net	333	(64)	243
	693	(118)	(77)
Income before income taxes	9,776	6,284	6,335
Income taxes	3,534	2,388	2,409
Net Income	**$ 6,242**	**$ 3,896**	**$ 3,926**

continued on next page

CONSOLIDATED STATEMENTS OF EARNINGS

	Years Ended February 28					
(Amounts in thousands except share data)	**1999**	**%**	**1998**	**%**	**1997**	**%**
NET SALES AND OPERATING REVENUES	**$10,804,447**	100.0	$8,870,797	100.0	$7,663,811	100.0
Cost of sales, buying and warehousing	**8,359,428**	77.4	6,827,133	77.0	5,902,711	77.0
GROSS PROFIT...............................	**2,445,019**	22.6	2,043,664	23.0	1,761,100	23.0
Selling, general and administrative expenses [NOTE 11]...........................	**2,186,177**	20.2	1,848,559	20.8	1,511,294	19.7
Interest expense [NOTE 5]	**28,319**	0.3	26,861	0.3	29,782	0.4
TOTAL EXPENSES	**2,214,496**	20.5	1,875,420	21.1	1,541,076	20.1

In contrast, companies provide very detailed financial statements for use by internal managers. A manager of a Circuit City store would want to know detailed information on sales of specific merchandise (televisions, VCRs, stereo components) and accessories. A divisional manager would want sales information for each store in his or her region. Marketing and production managers at Ben & Jerry's need to know the gross margin for each product, not just the overall gross margin. Managers also need detailed information on the balance sheet. For example, managers at Circuit City would want to know exactly how many of various products are in inventory and how long they have been there.

© LIAISON

IN THE NEWS http://www.paramount.com

Actors, writers, and directors sometimes contract with movie studios to receive a percentage of a movie's profits in lieu of a set salary. However, misunderstandings concerning how profits are defined have led to problems. As an example, although *Forrest Gump* is one of the highest grossing movies ever produced, with domestic ticket sales of $330 million, a year after its release, Paramount Studios reported a $63 million loss. At that time, ticket sales amounted to $191 million but expenses were reported to be $254 million. Among the expenses were $50 million in production costs, $74 million in marketing costs, $62 million in distribution costs, $62 million in payments to actors and producers, and $6 million in interest. Apparently, Paramount expensed all the product costs associated with the movie as soon as it was released rather than matching costs with revenues earned over time.

SUMMARY OF KEY CONCEPTS

- Costs flow in the same way that products flow through a production facility. (p. 37)
- Product costs attach to the product and are expensed only when the product is sold, whereas period costs are expensed in the period in which they are incurred. (p. 43)

KEY DEFINITIONS

Manufacturing companies Companies that purchase raw materials from other companies and transform those raw materials into a finished product (p. 30)

Raw materials inventory Inventory of materials needed in the production process but not yet moved to the production area (p. 31)

Finished-goods inventory Inventory of finished product waiting for sale and shipment to customers (p. 31)

Work-in-process inventory Inventory of unfinished product (in other words, what is left in the factory at the end of the period) (p. 31)

Just-in-time (JIT) production systems The philosophy of having raw materials arrive just in time to be used in production and for finished-goods inventory to be completed just in time to be shipped to customers (p. 31)

Manufacturing costs Costs incurred in the factory or plant to produce a product; typically consists of three elements: direct materials, direct labor, and manufacturing overhead (p. 34)

Direct materials Materials that can easily and conveniently be traced to the final product (p. 34)

Indirect materials Materials used in the production of products but not directly traceable to the specific product (p. 35)

Direct labor Labor that can easily and conveniently be traced to particular products (p. 35)

Indirect labor Labor used in the production of products but not directly traceable to the specific product (p. 35)

Manufacturing overhead Indirect material and labor and any other expenses related to the production of products but not directly traceable to the specific product (p. 35)

Nonmanufacturing costs Costs that include selling and administrative costs (p. 35)

Life-cycle costing Includes all the costs incurred throughout a product's life, not just in the manufacturing and selling of the product (p. 36)

Value chain The set of activities that increase the value of an organization's products and services: research and development, design, production, marketing, distribution, and customer service activities (p. 36)

Product costs Costs that attach to the products as they go through the manufacturing process; also called inventoriable costs (p. 42)

Period costs Costs that are expensed in the period incurred; attached to the period as opposed to the product (p. 42)

COMPUTER SIMULATION

You can now turn to Appendix A of your text to complete the portion of the Big Al's simulation covering product costs, setting a sales price, and the impact of changes to costs.

MULTIPLE CHOICE

1. Which of the following statements regarding the traditional manufacturing environment is *not* true?
   a. Factories were organized so that similar machines were grouped together.
   b. Finished-goods inventories were accumulated in case of unanticipated demand.
   c. Raw materials were purchased "just-in-time" to meet customer demand.
   d. Products were "pushed" through the production process to maximize output.

2. Danielle's Dresses manufactures women's clothing. In 2001, wage and salary expenses included the following:

Machine operators	$ 200,000
Quality control supervisors	100,000
Fabric cutters	75,000
Factory janitor	18,000
Company president	150,000

What was the amount of indirect labor incurred in 2001?
   a. $75,000
   b. $118,000
   c. $250,000
   d. $543,000

Use the following information to answer questions 3 and 4.

Coed Novelties manufactures key chains for college bookstores. During 2002, the company incurred the following costs:

Direct materials used	$31,000
Direct labor	18,000
Factory rent	12,000
Equipment depreciation—factory	2,000
Equipment depreciation—office	750
Marketing expenses	2,500
Administrative expenses	40,000

35,000 units were produced in 2002.

3. What is the product cost per unit?
   a. $1.24
   b. $1.80
   c. $3.04
   d. $2.85

4. What is Coed Novelties' net income for 2002 if 30,000 units are sold for $3.50 each?
   a. $122,000
   b. $105,000
   c. $7,750
   d. $(1,250)

5. Pottery Works, which produces pottery bowls, had the following summary cost information:

Direct materials used	$14,000
Direct labor	$12,000
Factory rent	$ 4,000
Equipment depreciation	$ 7,500
Units produced	15,000
Marketing expenses	$15,000
Administrative expenses	$13,000
Shipping charges	$ 5,000

If 14,500 of the 15,000 units are sold, what is the cost of goods sold?

a. $68,150
b. $25,085
c. $36,250
d. $37,500

Use the following information to answer questions 6, 7, and 8.

Christopher's Creations had the following information available for the month of January:

	Beginning	Ending
Raw materials inventory	$110,000	$115,000
Work-in-process inventory	55,000	58,000
Finished-goods inventory	41,000	37,000
Raw materials purchased		121,000
Direct labor (2,500 hours at $12.00)		30,000
Overhead		53,000

6. Raw materials used in January are:

a. $5,000
b. $116,000
c. $121,000
d. $126,000

7. Christopher's cost of goods manufactured in January is:

a. $196,000
b. $199,000
c. $254,000
d. $364,000

8. Christopher's cost of goods sold for January is:

a. $4,000
b. $37,000
c. $196,000
d. $200,000

9. Cost of goods manufactured equals:

a. beginning direct materials inventory plus all production costs incurred less ending direct materials inventory
b. beginning direct materials inventory plus all production costs incurred less ending work-in-process inventory
c. beginning work-in-process inventory plus direct materials used plus direct labor used plus manufacturing overhead used less ending work-in-process inventory
d. beginning work-in-process inventory plus direct materials used plus direct labor used plus manufacturing overhead used plus beginning finished-goods inventory

10. The production cost flow model is best described as:

a. raw materials storeroom, work-in-process, finished-goods inventory
b. raw materials storeroom, partially finished goods, finished-goods inventory
c. work-in-process, raw materials storeroom, finished-goods inventory
d. all of the above

CONCEPT REVIEW

11. Are the terms *cost* and *expense* synonymous? Why or why not?

12. Compare the terms *direct* and *indirect* cost.

13. In 1990, a study found that overhead of U.S. manufacturers was 50 percent greater than that of Japanese manufacturers and 20 percent greater than that of European manufacturers. What impact might this have on the U.S. companies? Why might U.S. companies have higher overhead?

14. What are some of the reasons that companies want or need to determine accurate product costs?

15. Discuss the differences between costing a product (such as building an airliner) and costing a service (such as flying passengers on an airline).

16. What has changed in the manufacturing environment in the past 20 years or so that has caused some companies to reevaluate their product costs?

17. Describe what a JIT environment means. What are some of the pluses and minuses of making a product or producing a service just in time to be sold?

18. Define the three components of manufacturing costs.

19. Define nonmanufacturing costs.

20. Define life-cycle costs.

21. Compare product and period costs. Why is the designation important?

22. Why is manufacturing overhead considered an indirect cost of a product?

APPLICATION OF CONCEPTS

23. Tom's Thimbles, a manufacturing company, began the month with raw materials costing $7,000 on hand; purchases during the month totaled $15,000. If $6,000 of raw materials were remaining at the end of the month, what was the amount used for production during the current month?

24. The Quilt Shop manufactures decorative quilts. In 2001 wage and salary expenses included the following:

Machine operators	$100,000
Quality control supervisors	50,000
Fabric cutters	25,000
Factory janitor	8,000
Company president	100,000

Required

A. What was the amount of direct labor incurred in 2001?

25. The Smiling Place manufactures extra-whitening toothpaste. During 2002, the company had the following costs:

Direct materials used	$41,000
Direct labor	28,000
Factory rent	12,000
Equipment depreciation—factory	4,000
Equipment depreciation—office	750
Marketing expense	3,500
Administrative expenses	50,000

45,000 units were produced in 2002.

Required

A. What are the total product costs for 2002?

B. What is the product cost per unit?

C. What are the total nonmanufacturing costs for 2002?

D. What is the net income for 2002 if 40,000 units are sold for $4 each?

26. Deskmakers is a new company that manufactures desks. In its first month of operation, it began and completed 500 desks. The following production information has been provided:

Direct material cost per unit	$ 18
Estimated indirect material costs	$ 220
Direct labor hours per unit	4
Cost per direct labor hour	$ 15
Estimated indirect labor costs	$ 400
Factory rent	$2,000
Marketing expenses	$ 750
Administrative expenses	$1,600

Required

A. What is the cost of direct labor per desk?

B. What were the total overhead costs for the first month's production?

C. What were the total product costs for the first month's production?

D. What are the total period (nonmanufacturing) costs for the first month's production?

E. What would the net income for the first month be if 500 of the desks were sold at a price of $85 each?

27. Becca's Bakery had the following information available for the month of January:

	Beginning	**Ending**
Raw materials inventory	$110,000	$115,000
Work-in-process inventory	55,000	58,000
Finished goods inventory	41,000	37,000
Raw materials purchased		121,000
Direct labor (2,500 hrs@$12)		30,000
Overhead		53,000

Required

A. How much raw material was used in January?

B. What is the cost of goods manufactured in January?

C. What is the cost of goods sold in January?

28. Perfect Pictures, which produces specialty picture frames, had the following summary cost information:

Direct materials used	$24,000
Direct labor	$22,000
Factory rent	$ 6,000
Equipment depreciation	$ 7,500
Units produced	25,000
Marketing expense	$15,000
Administrative expense	$13,000
Shipping charges	$ 5,000

Required

A. Based on the above information, what is the manufacturing cost per unit?

B. If 24,000 of the 25,000 units are sold, what is the cost of goods sold?

C. If 24,000 of the 25,000 units are sold, what is the value of ending inventory?

29. The following payroll records for Signmakers reflect amounts paid in March.

Assembly line workers	$15,000
Janitorial staff	2,000
Maintenance workers	5,000
Production supervisors	22,000

Required

A. What is the amount of indirect labor costs for March?

B. What is the amount of direct labor costs for March?

30. The following direct labor information pertains to the manufacture of stone hinges:

Direct labor hours to make one hinge	6
Number of hours per week, per worker	40
Weekly wages per worker	$700

Required

A. What is the direct labor cost per unit?

31. Fred's Furniture manufactures modern furniture. In 2001, wage and salary expenses included the following:

Machine operators	$250,000
Quality control supervisors	150,000
Fabric cutters	125,000
Factory janitor	28,000
Company president	150,000

Required

A. What was the amount of direct labor incurred in 2001?

B. What was the amount of indirect labor incurred in 2001?

32. Campus Coolers manufactures portable coolers with college logos. During 2002, the company had the following costs (in thousands):

Direct materials used	$41,000
Direct labor	28,000
Factory rent	22,000
Equipment depreciation—factory	12,000
Equipment depreciation—office	750
Marketing expenses	5,500
Administrative expenses	30,000

4,500 units were produced in 2002.

Required

A. What are the total product costs for 2002?

B. What is the product cost per unit?

C. What are the total period costs for 2002?

D. What is the net income for 2002 if 3,000 units are sold for $25 each?

33. Doormakers is a new company that manufactures doors. In its first month of operation, it began and completed 1,500 doors. The following production information has been provided:

Direct materials cost per unit	$ 35
Estimated indirect material costs	$1,100
Direct labor hours per unit	4
Cost per direct labor hour	$ 12
Estimated indirect labor costs	$4,000
Factory rent	$5,000
Marketing expenses	$ 750
Administrative expenses	$1,500

Required

A. What is the cost of direct labor per door?

B. What were the total overhead costs for the first month's production?

C. What were the total product costs for the first month's production?

D. What is the unit product cost?

E. What are the total period (nonmanufacturing) costs for the first month's production?

F. What would the net income for the first month be if 1,250 of the doors were sold at a price of $95 each?

34. Purple Pants, Inc., had the following information available for the month of January:

	Beginning	**Ending**
Raw materials inventory	$315,000	$310,000
Work-in-process inventory	65,000	58,000
Finished-goods inventory	32,000	25,000
Raw materials purchased		227,000
Direct labor (2,500 hrs@$12)		30,000
Overhead		155,000

Required

A. Determine the raw materials used in January.

B. Determine Purple's cost of goods manufactured in January.

C. Determine Purple's cost of goods sold for January.

35. You are the president of Box Creations. Your new accountant, who had recently graduated from Not-So-Good University, presented you with the following income statement for the month of January:

Sales Revenues	$660,000
Total January Expenses	595,000
Net Income	$ 65,000

By talking to the production departments, you learn that 60,000 units were produced in January at a cost of $420,000 (total product costs). The sales department notes that 55,000 units were sold for $11 each. Monthly administrative and marketing costs total $75,000.

Required

A. Based on this information, prepare a corrected income statement for January.

B. Explain what was wrong with the new accountant's income statement.

36. Urns Unlimited, which produces decorative urns, had the following summary cost information:

Direct materials used	$22,000
Direct labor	$10,000
Factory rent	$ 5,000
Marketing expenses	$ 3,000
Administrative expenses	$11,000
Shipping charges	$ 5,000
Equipment depreciation	$ 3,500
Units produced	15,000

Required

A. Based on this information, what is the manufacturing cost per unit?

B. If 14,500 of the 15,000 units are sold, what is the cost of goods sold?

C. If 14,500 of the 15,000 units are sold, what is the value of ending inventory?

37. Leacy's Department Store features women's fashions. At the beginning of 2002, the store had $514,000 in merchandise. Annual purchases totaled $463,000.

Required

A. If the year-end inventory revealed $488,000 on hand, what was the cost of goods sold for 2002?

B. What was the pool of merchandise available for sale during the period?

C. If sales were $675,000 and other costs were $115,000, what was net income for the year?

38. Jack's Slacks is a local men's clothing store. Jack buys clothing and accessories from manufacturers and marks them up by 55 percent. Jack began the year with $155,000 ($240,250 retail value) and bought $350,000 (retail value $542,500) more items during the year. Ending inventory is $95,000 (retail value $147,250).

Required

A. What were Jack's sales for the year?

B. What was Jack's cost of goods sold for the year?

C. What was Jack's gross margin for the year?

39. Following are some costs incurred in 2003.

Material Costs	
Aluminum	$271,000
Oil and grease for production machinery	3,000
Screws and nails	5,000
Labor Costs	
Equipment operators	$ 80,000
Equipment mechanics	54,000
Factory supervisors	90,000

Required

A. What is the total direct material cost for 2003?

B. What is the total direct labor cost for 2003?

C. What are the total indirect costs for 2003?

D. Explain why you considered some costs indirect.

40. Dunn Computer Company began manufacturing personal computers for small businesses at the beginning of 2001. During the year, Dunn purchased 30,000 mouse pads with the company's name and logo at a cost of $2.50 each. The marketing manager used 2,500 of the pads as an advertising gimmick at a local trade show, and 25,000 of the pads were packaged with computers that were manufactured during 2001. Eighty percent of the computers were finished during the year; of that amount, 90 percent were sold.

Determine the cost of the mouse pads that would be included in the following accounts as of December 31, 2001, and specify whether the account would appear on the balance sheet or the income statement:

a. Raw materials

b. Work in process

c. Finished goods

d. Cost of goods sold

e. Advertising expense

41. Ehmke Technologies manufactures storage devices for personal computers. Although most of the company's sales are to computer manufacturers, about 30 percent of sales are made directly to individuals via mail order. Ehmke Technologies recently hired you as a sales manager. Your duties include dealing directly with the computer manufacturers that buy your company's products and supervising the employees who take phone orders from individual customers. Because most of your time is spent dealing with the manufacturing companies, the company's vice president for marketing says that your $45,000 salary should be classified as a manufacturing cost. The company's controller says that it should be classified as a selling expense.

Required

A. Which viewpoint is correct? Why?

B. The company's president doesn't understand what all the fuss is about and says that the company's income will be the same regardless, so who cares! Is she right? Explain your answer.

42. Eldred Inc., a manufacturing company, prepays its insurance coverage for a three-year period. The premium for the three years is $19,000 and is paid at the beginning of the first year. Three-fourths of the premium applies to factory operations and one-fourth applies to selling and administration activities.

Required

Answer the following questions for the first year of coverage:

A. What amount of the cost should be considered product costs?

B. What amount of the cost should be considered period costs?

43. Erdmann Inc. manufactures area rugs. Among Erdmann's 2001 manufacturing costs were the following salaries and wages:

Rug weaving machine operators	$155,000
Factory foreman	65,000
Machine mechanics	50,000
Factory maintenance workers	45,000

Required

A. What was the amount of direct labor incurred in 2001?

B. What was the amount of indirect labor incurred in 2001?

44. Ertz Inc. recently changed to a just-in-time philosophy from a traditional costing philosophy. How will this new philosophy affect the work-in-process inventory balance in the future? Can management expect to see a change in the finished-goods inventory balance? Explain your answer.

45. The following direct labor cost information pertains to the manufacture of televisions at Estes TV:

Time required to manufacture one television	6 direct labor hours
Number of workers	45
Number of hours per week each employee worked on manufacturing televisions	38
Weekly wages per worker	$1,200
Workers' benefits as a percentage of wages	35%

Required

A. What is the cost of direct labor per television?

B. What is the cost of indirect labor per television?

C. Explain the difference between direct and indirect labor.

46. Favre Co. produces complete sets of football pads and has prepared the following summary of cost information:

Direct materials used	$4,000
Direct labor	$2,000
Factory rent	$4,000
Factory equipment depreciation	$3,500
Units produced	7,000
Marketing expenses	$5,000
Administrative expenses	$3,000

Required

A. Based on the preceding data, calculate the manufacturing cost per set of pads.

B. Explain why you included or did not include each cost item.

47. The books of Evans Co. show the following cost and inventory data for the year 2001.

Costs Incurred

Raw material purchased	$125,000
Direct labor	75,000
Indirect labor	40,000
Equipment maintenance	10,000
Insurance on factory	12,000
Rent on factory	30,000
Depreciation on factory	20,000
Factory supplies	11,000
Advertising expenses	15,000
Selling and administrative expenses	21,000

Inventory Balances	1/1/01	12/31/01
Raw materials	$10,000	$17,000
Work in process	20,000	31,000
Finished goods	30,000	25,000

Required

A. Calculate the cost of goods manufactured.

B. Calculate the cost of goods sold.

C. List the costs not included in the preceding requirements, and discuss why you elected to exclude them.

D. If raw material and work-in-process inventories had decreased during the year, would the financial statements be different? How?

48. Fausel Company manufactures wooden rocking chairs. Fausel purchased the following materials in June:

1,500 springs (part of the rocking mechanism) at a cost of $15,000; each chair uses two springs

Glue at a cost of $1,500 (enough to manufacture 500 chairs)

Stain at a cost of $500 (enough to manufacture 500 chairs)

Wood at a cost of $5,000 (enough to build 1,000 chair frames)

Fausel produces 500 chairs during June and has no beginning balances of raw materials, WIP, or finished-goods inventory

Required

A. Which of these material costs should be classified as direct? Which as indirect?

B. If Fausel finishes only 400 of the 500 chairs on which production was started, what is the balance in the finished-goods inventory account?

C. If 380 of the finished chairs are sold, what is the cost of goods sold?

D. What is the June 30 balance in the work-in-process inventory account?

49. Cape Fear Inc. is a clothing store located in a major shopping mall. The company buys clothing and accessories from a number of manufacturers and generally marks them up 60 percent over cost. At the end of 2001, Cape Fear Inc. had clothing and accessories in the store with a cost of $60,000 (retail value of $96,000). During 2002, the company bought an additional $220,000 of clothing. Cape Fear Inc. had sales during 2002 of $420,000.

Required

A. What was the cost of goods sold for 2002?

B. What was the ending inventory of merchandise at December 31, 2002?

50. Fletcher & Fuller LLP is a local CPA firm that prepares approximately 1,000 tax returns each year for its clients. The managing partner of the firm has asked for information concerning the costs of preparing tax returns from the accounting department. He has been provided with the following report:

Average wage per hour of tax preparation staff	$35
Average wage per hour of clerical staff	$12
Average number of hours per return (preparation)	10
Average number of hours per return (clerical)	2

Required

A. What is the average direct labor cost of preparing a tax return at Fletcher & Fuller?

B. What are the options available for reducing the cost of preparing tax returns? What are the implications of these options?

C. Fletcher & Fuller has the option of purchasing tax preparation software for $5,000 per year. If the software is used, the hours needed to prepare the return would decrease to three hours per return and the clerical time would increase to four hours because of additional computer operator time. How would the purchase affect the cost of labor per tax return?

D. Does it appear to be a good business decision to purchase the software? What other costs must be considered?

E. What are the qualitative aspects of the preceding decision?

51. Gagstetter Manufacturing was organized on January 1 of the current year. Independent investors financed the business totally. These investors have stipulated that the company must show a profit by the sixth month or the financing would be stopped. Gagstetter has shown losses for the first four months but was expecting to show a profit in the fifth and current month. After reviewing the income statement for the fifth month (May), the president, Craig, was disappointed with the performance and called an employee meeting. At the meeting, Craig informed the employees that based on the performance for the first five months and in particular the month of May, he saw very little hope of a profit by the sixth month. He also informed the employees that they should prepare to close the business. Promptly after the employee meeting, the controller quit, leaving you in charge of the accounting function. The latest financial information is as follows:

Gagstetter Manufacturing Income Statement for the Month Ended May 31, 2002

Sales		$325,000
Less:		
Raw material purchased	$140,000	
Direct labor	75,000	
Indirect labor	10,000	
Utilities	25,000	
Depreciation	30,000	
Insurance	15,000	
Rent	12,000	
SG&A expenses	30,000	
Advertising	25,000	
		362,000
Net loss		$ (37,000)

Other Information

Inventory Balances	**4/30/02**	**5/31/02**
Raw material	$10,000	$30,000
Work in process	15,000	22,000
Finished goods	50,000	70,000

Seventy-five percent of utilities, depreciation, insurance, and rent are related to the factory, whereas 25 percent of those costs are related to selling and administrative activities.

Required

A. Redo the income statement for May. (Include a statement of cost of goods manufactured and a statement of cost of goods sold.)

B. Do you agree with the president's assessment of the situation? Why or why not?

C. How will you explain to the investors why your income statement is different from the one the controller presented earlier?

52. Barcourt Inc. manufactures baseball bats and has recently had a fire that destroyed most of the inventory and almost all the accounting records. The controller at Barcourt Inc., Dana Genzel-Diaz, has approached you to reconstruct the records. She gives you a box of charred accounting records with which you are to reconstruct the income statement for the month of the fire. The following is the reconstruction of the accounting records:

Direct materials used	$ 9,000
Direct labor	4,000
Manufacturing overhead	11,000
Total manufacturing costs	?
Beginning work in process	?
Ending work in process	6,000
Cost of goods manufactured	21,000

Sales	35,000
Beginning finished-goods inventory	7,000
Cost of goods manufactured	?
Goods available for sale	?
Ending finished-goods inventory	10,000
Cost of goods sold	?
Gross margin	?
Selling and administrative expenses	7,000
Net income	?

Required

A. Supply the missing data.

B. Prepare a new complete income statement.

53. Hemphill Inc. manufactures soccer balls. A recent earthquake destroyed most of the inventory and almost all the accounting records. The controller at Hemphill Inc., Chip Gillikin, has approached you to reconstruct the records. He gives you a box of partially destroyed accounting records with which you are to reconstruct the income statement for the month of the earthquake. The following is the reconstruction of the accounting records:

Direct materials used	$19,000
Direct labor	14,000
Manufacturing overhead	?
Total manufacturing costs	35,000
Beginning work in process	11,000
Ending work in process	13,500
Cost of goods manufactured	?
Sales	50,000
Beginning finished-goods inventory	?
Cost of goods manufactured	?
Goods available for sale	?
Ending finished-goods inventory	14,000
Cost of goods sold	25,500
Gross margin	?
Selling and administrative expenses	?
Net income	15,500

Required

A. Supply the missing data.

B. Prepare a new complete income statement.

54. Hardball Inc. manufactures baseballs. A recent flood destroyed most of the inventory and almost all the accounting records. The controller at Hardball Inc., Mary Goodwin, has approached you to reconstruct the records. She gives you a box of partially destroyed, wet accounting records with which you are to reconstruct the income statement for the month of the flood. The following is the reconstruction of the accounting records:

Direct materials used	$16,000
Direct labor	?
Manufacturing overhead	17,000
Total manufacturing costs	48,000
Beginning work in process	12,000
Ending work in process	?
Cost of goods manufactured	46,000
Sales	50,000
Beginning finished-goods inventory	7,000
Cost of goods manufactured	?

Goods available for sale	?
Ending finished-goods inventory	?
Cost of goods sold	8,000
Gross margin	?
Selling and administrative expenses	?
Net income	13,000

Required

A. Supply the missing data.

B. Prepare a new complete income statement.

55. Slots R Us owns a gambling boat on the Gulf Coast and has recently experienced Hurricane Jennifer, which severely damaged the boat and almost all the accounting records. The controller at Slots R Us, Tim Guglielmo, has approached you to reconstruct the records. He gives you a box of partially destroyed, wet, windblown accounting records with which you are to reconstruct the income statement for the month of the hurricane. The following is the reconstruction of the accounting records:

Direct materials used	$18,000
Direct labor	13,000
Manufacturing overhead	31,000
Total manufacturing costs	?
Beginning work in process	?
Ending work in process	12,000
Cost of goods manufactured	?
Sales	90,000
Beginning finished-goods inventory	19,000
Cost of goods manufactured	60,000
Goods available for sale	?
Ending finished-goods inventory	17,000
Cost of goods sold	?
Gross margin	?
Selling and administrative expenses	20,000
Net income	?

Required

A. Supply the missing data.

B. Prepare a new complete income statement.

56. Northern Lights Custom Cabinets manufactures and sells custom-ordered kitchen and bathroom cabinets. The company sells primarily to building contractors but occasionally deals directly with homeowners. Following is a summary of inventory and cost information for 2001:

	Balance 1/1/01	Balance 12/31/01
Raw material inventory	$10,000	$15,000
Work-in-process inventory	15,000	12,000
Finished goods inventory	30,000	32,000

During the year, raw material used in the production of cabinets was purchased for $350,000. Northern Lights also incurred $200,000 for labor cost in the factory and had $175,000 in manufacturing overhead for the year.

Required

A. Determine the amount of direct material transferred to work in process in 2001.

B. Calculate total manufacturing costs for 2001.

C. Calculate total cost of goods manufactured for 2001.

D. Calculate cost of goods sold for 2001

57. As controller, you have been asked to prepare and to submit financial statements to your company's bank as part of a loan application. From previous conversations with bank loan personnel, you know that your company's cost of goods sold as a percent of sales is unusually high. Your supervisor has asked you to reclassify some product costs as period costs, thereby decreasing the cost of goods sold to an acceptable amount. Because your total costs would be the same (just classified differently), your supervisor says that there is nothing wrong with making the reclassification. Discuss the ethical issues involved in this decision.

58. Business Games Inc. (BGI) has designed the ultimate business board game. The game has been on the market for 10 years and the company has sold more than 20 million games. The games sell for \$9 to stores and the suggested retail price is \$15. BGI has computed the cost of producing the games to be \$5.40. The cost includes direct material, direct labor, and overhead. Management of BGI has decided that the time is right to produce a special edition of the game in a mahogany collector's box. BGI will also design a special game board and new game pieces. Your job is to set a new sales price and decide whether the special game should be produced. You receive the following report from the accounting department to help you with your decision:

	Present Game	**Special Game (estimated)**
Direct material	\$1.25	\$30.50
Direct labor	2.00	3.50
Overhead	2.15	2.15
	\$5.40	\$36.15

Required

A. Is the cost information provided sufficient to determine a sales price for each game? Why or why not?

B. What qualitative factors should be considered in deciding whether to produce and sell the special game?

59. Finding ways to decrease product costs is an area of increasing concern for many manufacturers. Conduct an Internet search of the *Wall Street Journal* and other business publications to find recent articles dealing with product costing. Summarize the cost-cutting efforts of three manufacturers discussed in the articles.

http://www.intel.com
http://www.circuitcity.com

60. Arrange a visit to a locally owned restaurant or coffeehouse and ask the manager how the establishment determines the cost of its products. What is included in the cost of a cup of coffee or a meal?

61. Examine the financial statements of a manufacturing company (e.g., Intel) and a merchandising company (e.g., Circuit City). Compare their balance sheets and the percentage of total assets in inventory. What similarities and differences do you see?

62. Big Al's Pizza Inc. (a new subsidiary of Big Al's Pizza Emporium) has been established to produce fresh, packaged 16-inch pizzas to be sold wholesale to grocery stores, convenience stores, and school cafeterias. Big Al's will have 10 production lines with five workers on each line. Each worker is responsible for one of the five stages of production: dough, sauce, cheese, toppings, or packaging. The following flowchart of the production lines shows the time needed at each workstation. These time estimates include normal downtime, breaks, and so on.

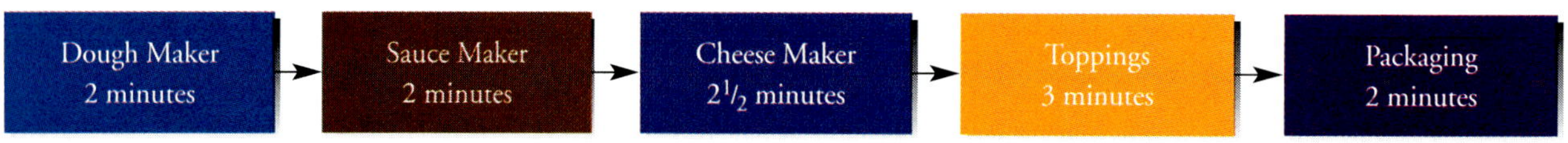

Moving products between stations takes approximately 30 seconds. So the total time to produce one pizza is the total of all the time needed at each step plus 2 minutes for product movement (4 at ½ minute), or 13½ minutes per pizza.

Big Al's production facility is organized in a very traditional fashion. Dough preparation, sauce preparation, cheese preparation, topping preparation, and packaging are all done in separate areas of the factory. In addition, employees on the production lines are responsible for only one task.

Required

A. Can you think of other, more efficient ways to organize the production facility?

B. If Big Al's adopted JIT inventory practices, what changes would have to be made in manufacturing procedures?

C. Prepare a sketch of how the pizza product line would be arranged to be more efficient and use JIT inventory practices.

Chapter 3

Product-Costing Measurement Decisions

Study Tools

A Review of the Previous Chapter

Chapter 2 gave us an overview of the production process and the costing of products and services in an organization.

A Preview of This Chapter

In this chapter, we learn about the specifics of costing products and services, using job costing, process costing, and operations costing, and the particular problems caused by the allocation of overhead to products. The chapter introduces the concept of applying overhead to products, using cost drivers, and the issues that managers must consider in choosing a suitable cost driver.

Key concepts include:

- Overhead cannot be directly tracked to products and services but must instead be allocated using cost drivers.
- Understanding what causes overhead costs to be incurred (what drives them) is the key to allocating overhead.
- Accuracy in overhead application has become much more important as overhead costs have increased and make up a larger portion of the total costs of products.
- In order to provide relevant information for decision making, overhead must often be estimated.

A Preview of Upcoming Chapters

Chapter 4 extends the discussion of overhead application and provides an introduction to the use of activity-based costing and activity-based management.

Learning Objectives

After studying the material in this chapter, you should be able to:

LO1 Understand the differences among job, process, and operations costing and how they are used to accumulate, track, and assign product costs

LO2 Understand the basics of job costing

LO3 Analyze issues related to the measurement of direct materials, direct labor, and overhead costs in job costing

LO4 Analyze problems related to the application of overhead costs to products

LO5 Analyze the role of cost pools and cost drivers in overhead application

LO6 Evaluate the advantages and disadvantages of using plantwide versus departmental overhead rates

LO7 Evaluate topics related to the choice of cost driver and the use of estimates in overhead application

LO8 Understand the basics of backflush and process costing

In Chapter 2, we defined product costs and discussed the flow of costs in manufacturing, merchandising, and service companies. Chapter 3 begins with a discussion of the basic systems that companies use to accumulate, track, and assign costs to products and services. These systems are called job costing, process costing, and operations costing. Job, process, and operations costing have the same goals—to accumulate, track, and assign direct material, direct labor, and overhead costs to the products and services a company produces. Direct material and direct labor can usually be traced directly to products and services. But because of their indirect nature, overhead costs must be allocated to the products or services a company provides. Chapter 3 introduces the concept of cost pools and cost drivers and explains how they are used to allocate overhead, using plantwide and departmental overhead rates. The chapter includes a discussion of the use of overhead estimates (predetermined overhead rates) in product costing and the treatment of over- or underapplied overhead. The appendix of the chapter introduces backflush costing (a costing system that is appropriate for companies employing just-in-time manufacturing techniques) and discusses process costing in more detail. ■

INTRODUCTION

LO1
Understand the differences among job, process, and operations costing and how they are used to accumulate, track, and assign product costs

One of the most important roles of managerial accountants is to help determine the cost of the products or services being produced and sold by a company. Cost information is equally important for manufacturing and service businesses and is used by managers across the organization. Pricing decisions made by marketing managers, manufacturing decisions made by production managers, and finance decisions made by finance managers are all influenced by the cost of products.

In today's competitive environment, managers must be aware of the impact of financial decisions on the overall success of their business. For example, marketing managers need to set a competitive price that will capture the needed market share and provide a fair profit. If the price of the product is set too low, a larger market share may be captured but the business may not earn a satisfactory profit. On the other hand, if the price of the product is too high, the business may not capture sufficient market share to remain competitive. These pricing decisions require product cost information in order for an optimal price to be set. Pricing decisions are discussed more fully in Chapter 7.

PAUSE & Reflect

As a reaction to decreasing sales in its restaurants, McDonald's proposed a radical price reduction on its Big Mac in early 1997. The sandwich (usually priced around $1.90) would be offered for 55 cents with the purchase of fries and a drink. The proposal required the approval of a majority of franchisees. As an owner of a local McDonald's, you estimate that the cost of making a Big Mac is 63 cents. Would you vote for the proposal?

http://www.mcdonalds.com

APPLICATION IN BUSINESS

http://www.gm.com

After a labor strike in 1998, General Motors instituted an aggressive marketing campaign including large price rebates in order to gain back market share.

Production managers make decisions concerning whether to buy components used in manufacturing a product or to make them internally. For example, an automobile manufacturer could choose to make batteries used in its cars or to buy them from an outside supplier. The cost to make the battery compared to the cost of buying it would be important in this decision. The company would also consider qualitative factors, such as the reliability of the supplier and the quality of the battery. This and other production decisions are also discussed in Chapter 7.

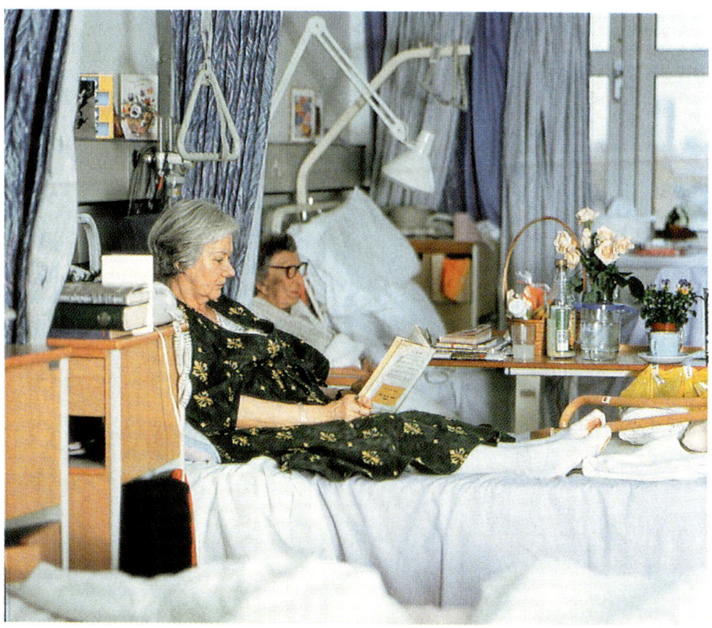

In this hospital, each patient would be considered a "job."

PRODUCT-COSTING SYSTEMS

LO2
Understand the basics of job costing

Just as various companies use various techniques to manufacture products or to provide services, companies also use various product-costing systems to accumulate, track, and assign the costs of production to the goods and services produced. Companies that manufacture customized products or provide customized services to clients use a costing system called **job costing,** which accumulates, tracks, and assigns costs for each job. Jobs are simply the individual units of a product. For a builder of custom homes, each house is a job. For a CPA firm, a job might be an individual tax return, an audit engagement, or a consulting engagement for a particular client. For a print shop, each order for wedding invitations, graduation announcements, or custom letterhead is a job. For a hospital, each patient is a job.

On the other hand, companies that produce a homogeneous product on a continuous basis (oil refineries, breweries, paint and paper manufacturers, for example) use **process costing** to accumulate, track, and assign costs to products. Rather than accumulating the costs for each unit produced and directly tracking and assigning costs to each unique unit, process costing accumulates and tracks costs for each process as products pass through the process and then assigns costs equally to the units that come out of each process. A process is simply the work that is performed on a product. For a paint manufacturer, blending and pouring are processes. For a bread baker, mixing, baking, and slicing are processes. The details of process costing are demonstrated in the appendix to this chapter.

Operations costing is a hybrid of job and process costing and is used by companies, such as clothing or automobile manufacturers, that make products in batches—large numbers of products that are standardized within a batch. For example, a clothing manufacturer might make 5,000 identical shirts in one batch. Each batch is costed like a job in job costing, but each shirt in the batch is costed like a homogeneous product in process costing. The table summarizes the types of products that would most likely be costed using job, operations, and process costing.

In this clothing manufacturer, each batch of T-shirts is costed using operations costing.

	Costing System		
System	**Job Costing**	**Operations Costing**	**Process Costing**
Type of Product	Custom	Standardized within batches	Homogeneous
Examples	Construction, movie studios, hospitals, print shops, CPA and law firms	Automobile and clothing manufacturers	Beverages, oil refineries, paint, paper, rolled steel

BASIC JOB-ORDER COSTING FOR MANUFACTURING AND SERVICE COMPANIES

LO3
Analyze issues related to the measurement of direct materials, direct labor, and overhead costs in job costing

Northern Lights Custom Cabinets uses job costing to accumulate, track, and assign costs to the cabinets it produces. The direct material, direct labor, and overhead costs for a specific job are accumulated on a job cost report. This report may be kept manually or be totally automated. Regardless, its role is to keep track of the material, labor, and overhead costs that are incurred for a particular job. A job cost report for Northern Lights is shown in Exhibit 3-1.

MEASURING AND TRACKING DIRECT MATERIAL

Measuring direct material cost should be a relatively easy task for Northern Lights. The company has to identify only the amount of material actually used in each job and attach the proper cost to it. Northern Lights uses a variety of material, including wood, Formica,

EXHIBIT 3-1 Cost Sheet for Job 101

Northern Lights Custom Cabinets

Job Number: 101
Date Started: March 6
Description: Smith house

Customer: Robyn Gray
Date Finished: March 9

Direct Materials		Direct Labor			Manufacturing Overhead		
Type	**Cost**	**Employee**	**Hours**	**Amount**	**Hours**	**Rate**	**Amount**
Oak	$875	Staley	12.6	$255.15	22.4	$16.67	$373.41
Marble	600	Chen	4.5	91.13			
Particle-board	78	Kent	5.3	107.33			
Brass Pulls	330						

Cost Summary		
	Direct Materials	$1,883.00
	Direct Labor	453.61
	Manufacturing Overhead	373.41
	Total	$2,710.02

and marble for countertops and stained glass, glue, screws, dowels, and stain in constructing a finished set of custom cabinets. Although some of the more common materials are stored in inventory, exotic and more expensive woods and marbles and hardware items, such as handles and pulls, are typically purchased just in time for their use in a particular job. As it is needed for a particular cabinet job, raw material is recorded on the job cost record. In Exhibit 3-1, you can see that Northern Lights used oak and marble in the manufacture of Job 101 (for the Smith house), as well as particleboard. These materials can all be traced directly to Job 101 and are treated as direct materials. Also included as direct material are various pieces of hardware, such as handles and drawer pulls. The amount and type of direct materials used in a job depend on the specific set of cabinets built. Because they will differ with each job, they must be accumulated, tracked, and assigned by job.

Some of the materials are stocked in inventory, whereas others are purchased just in time for use in a job. It would not make good business sense for Northern Lights to stock a large amount of expensive hardware items for cabinets when some of the special hardware items may be used only once a year. On the other hand, because oak is used in over 50 percent of cabinets, Northern Lights chooses to keep enough on hand to meet two to three months of expected demand.

In the Smith house (Job 101), the customer has requested that the countertop be made of a synthetic marble, a material that is very durable but has a tendency to crack while being cut. Sure enough, as the material is being cut, it cracks and has to be discarded. How should the cost of the cracked material (spoilage) be treated? If the spoilage is considered normal, the cost is included in the determination of product costs. **Normal spoilage** results from the regular operation of the production process and includes the discarded ends of a sheet of wood or marble. If the broken marble is considered normal spoilage, its cost is treated as part of the direct material cost for the job being produced. On the other hand, other reasons, perhaps improper handling, poorly trained craftspeople, or equipment that is in poor condition, cause **abnormal spoilage.** If the marble was broken because a saw blade has not been properly sharpened, it would probably be considered abnormal spoilage.

Concept Question: *How would you treat the cost of abnormal spoilage? Would it be fair to treat it as part of the direct material cost for the job being produced? Should the cost of abnormal waste be passed on to the customer as an increase in the sales price?*

Step 1 DEFINE THE PROBLEM

Concept Answer: Abnormal spoilage should probably be expensed as a period cost or included in manufacturing overhead, where the cost is spread across all jobs completed during the period. Abnormal spoilage should probably not be treated as direct material, where it would be considered in the cost of a specific job. ■

Concept Question: *Northern Lights also uses a variety of wooden dowels, screws, glues, and finishing nails in the construction of cabinets. However, you should note that these are not listed as direct materials on the job cost report in Exhibit 3-1. Why? How is Northern Lights accounting for the cost of these materials?*

Step 2 IDENTIFY OBJECTIVES

Concept Answer: Although it may be physically possible to track the specific screws, glue, and nails to a particular cabinet, the cost of doing so is great and the benefits are few. Northern Lights has chosen to treat these materials as indirect material that will be allocated to the Smith job as part of overhead. ■

Companies that primarily provide services to clients or have minimal material costs may not treat any materials as direct. For example, a law firm that primarily prepares wills and other paper documents may choose to treat the costs of paper as an indirect material (part of overhead). Likewise, although CPA firms may use a lot of paper and other materials processing tax returns for clients, they may not track the paper to specific jobs on a job cost report. On the other hand, a hospital might choose to itemize every pill (even aspirin) and other medication given to a patient and every bandage used in an operation on a patient's job cost report (the patient's case file).

Concept Question: *Why might a hospital keep track of every aspirin given to a patient?*

Concept Answer: Tracking the use of pills and other medications to a patient provides other valuable benefits to doctors and the hospital. Doctors need to know exactly what medications have been given and when. Although it may also provide a way to charge patients for the cost of medications they consume during a hospital stay, the costing of the medications is probably not as important as the tracking itself. ■

MEASURING AND TRACKING DIRECT LABOR

The measurement of direct labor cost also should be a relatively easy task. Direct labor cost refers to labor that is directly related to the manufacture of a product or the provision of a service. Assembly-line workers in a manufacturing setting and CPAs working on tax returns are examples of direct labor. On the other hand, manufacturing supervisors, janitorial staff, and maintenance personnel in a manufacturing company and secretarial staff in a CPA firm are considered indirect labor and are included in overhead. The costs of direct labor for a specific job are accumulated on a job cost report, but most companies keep track of each employee's time by requiring the completion of time sheets. Time sheets may be prepared by hand or be totally automated and integrated with the job cost system. Regardless of the form used, employees must keep track of how much time they spend on specific jobs. For assembly-line workers, management needs to know how much time is spent manufacturing a specific product. For CPAs and attorneys, the managing partner needs to know how many hours are spent servicing a particular client.

The cost of direct labor is simply calculated by multiplying a wage rate for each employee by the number of hours that each employee works on each product. However, in addition to the hourly cost of labor, wage rates must also include the cost of **fringe benefits.** These fringe benefits include the employer's cost for health, dental, and other insurance; retirement plans; and so on. The employer portion of social security tax and state and federal unemployment taxes would also be included. Studies have shown that fringe benefits typically cost a company 30 to 35 percent of the base wage of each full-time employee. The job cost report in Exhibit 3-1 shows that three employees of Northern Lights Custom Cabinets worked 22.4 hours on Job 101 at a cost of $20.25 per hour. This cost includes a $15 hourly wage rate plus benefits of $5.25 per hour.

Northern Lights custom cabinets

Concept Question: *Owing to a power outage, Northern Lights incurred idle time while working on Job 101. Would Northern Lights most likely treat this idle time as overhead or an additional cost of direct labor assigned directly to Job 101?*

Concept Answer: Not all the time that direct labor workers are paid for is spent productively. For example, if machinery and equipment break down or if materials are not available when needed, **idle time** results. How should idle time of direct labor workers be treated? Although idle time could be traced to a specific job (the job that is being worked on when the idle time occurs), most companies choose to treat idle time as an overhead cost rather than a cost of a specific job. ■

Overtime premiums paid to direct labor workers cause similar classification problems. Overtime is typically paid at 150 percent of the normal wage rate (sometimes called "time and a half") for hours worked in excess of 40 per week. For example, let's assume that the hourly pay for an assembly-line worker is $15. An overtime premium for this worker would be $7.50 per hour, increasing the total hourly wage to $22.50. With fringe benefits at 35 percent, the cost of labor rises to $30.38 per hour. Overtime may be incurred for a number of reasons. Sometimes, production problems cause a company to get behind on a job. When this happens, the company may choose to incur overtime costs (work over the weekend) to finish up a job on time. In other situations, a company might accept an order, knowing that it will require the scheduling of overtime.

Concept Question: *On Friday morning, the building contractor who had ordered Job 101 called Northern Lights and said he needed the cabinets next Monday instead of next Wednes-*

day. The Northern Lights staff worked eight hours on Saturday, and the company incurred overtime premiums in order to finish the job by the new due date. How should Northern Lights treat the overtime premium—as part of direct labor or as overhead? Should this overtime increase the selling price to the customer?

Concept Answer: In practice, the treatment of overtime costs depends on the reason the overhead is incurred. If overtime is incurred as a result of production problems, most companies treat the cost as overhead. On the other hand, if the overtime results from the acceptance of a rush order, most companies would treat the overhead as a direct labor cost that would be assigned directly to the specific job (and would most likely be included in determining its price). ■

In highly automated manufacturing environments, the cost of direct labor has been reduced significantly as automated machinery and robotics have replaced direct labor workers. This shift in product costs from labor to overhead has had important implications for product costing. Whereas the cost of direct labor is relatively easy to accumulate, track, and assign to products, overhead costs are a different matter.

MANUFACTURING OVERHEAD

LO4
Analyze problems related to the application of overhead costs to products

Overhead is the most difficult product cost to accumulate, track, and assign to products. Unlike direct materials and direct labor, overhead is made up of lots of seemingly unrelated costs—rent, depreciation, insurance, repairs and maintenance, utilities, indirect labor, indirect material, and so on. In addition, in traditional manufacturing environments, most overhead is indirect in nature. As a result, it cannot be directly tracked to products and services but must instead be allocated. Although many overhead costs in a just-in-time (JIT) environment will also be indirect in nature (rent and utilities, for example), more of the costs are likely to be direct in nature. For example, in a JIT environment, the cost of machinery in a manufacturing cell can be traced to a specific product (tables) if it is used only to make tables.

Key Concept: *Overhead cannot be directly tracked to products and services but must instead be allocated using cost drivers.*

Allocation involves finding a logical method of assigning overhead costs to the products or services a company produces. If a company produces only one product, the allocation would be simple. We could simply divide the total overhead cost by the total number of units produced. If our total overhead costs incurred during the year were \$100,000 and we produced 20,000 identical tables during the year, it would be logical to assign \$5 of overhead to each table (\$100,000/20,000 tables). However, what if we make 10,000 tables and 10,000 chairs? Does it still make sense to allocate overhead based on the number of units produced? Probably not. A more logical approach might be to allocate the overhead to the tables and chairs based on the number of direct labor hours or machine hours consumed in the manufacture of each. If chairs take twice as long to manufacture as tables, twice as much overhead would be allocated to them. The choice of allocation base requires a thorough understanding of what causes overhead costs to be incurred.

THE ROLE OF COST POOLS AND COST DRIVERS

LO5
Analyze the role of cost pools and cost drivers in overhead application

Understanding what causes overhead costs to be incurred is the key to allocating overhead. The choice of a logical base on which to allocate overhead depends on finding a cause-and-effect relationship between the base and the overhead. A good allocation base is one that drives the incurrence of the overhead cost. Therefore, allocation bases are often referred to as **cost drivers.** A cost driver causes a cost to be incurred.

Key Concept: *Understanding what causes overhead costs to be incurred (what drives them) is the key to allocating overhead.*

One way to think about cost drivers is to imagine something causing something else to happen. A cost driver for overhead is an activity that causes overhead to be incurred. If we wanted to allocate the cost of utilities incurred to run machines in the factory to products, we would want to find a cost driver that causes the utility costs to be incurred. In this case, the time the machines were in use (machine hours) might be an appropriate allocation base. In our previous example, if it takes twice as many machine hours to make chairs than it does to make tables, chairs would correspondingly be allocated twice as much utility cost.

Other overhead costs associated with machines, such as depreciation and repairs and maintenance, could be allocated using the same cost driver. In companies that are more labor intensive, the cost of utilities might be allocated using direct labor hours as the cost driver. In that case, if it takes three labor hours to make a table and only one labor hour to make a chair, a table would be allocated three times as much overhead as a chair. The choice of cost driver depends on the specific company and the production processes it utilizes in providing products and services to customers, but as you can see, it definitely has an impact on the cost of products and services.

Northern Lights
custom cabinets

Concept Question: *Northern Lights incurs utility costs of $1,000 during the month and starts and finishes 12 cabinet jobs. Each job requires machine time but the time varies greatly, depending on the materials used and the difficulty of the job. Job 101 required 22.4 labor hours, whereas Job 104 required 60 hours. The total labor hours during the month totaled 500. If Northern Lights allocates utility cost using labor hours as the cost driver, how much of the utility cost should be allocated to Job 101? How much to Job 104?*

Concept Answer: Utility costs are $2 per direct labor hour ($1,000/500 direct labor hours). Therefore, $44.80 of utility costs (22.4 × $2 per hour) should be allocated to Job 101, whereas $120 of utility costs (60 hours × $2 per hour) should be allocated to Job 104.

PAUSE & *Reflect*

In a law firm, overhead costs consist of the cost of office space for attorneys, the salaries of secretaries, the cost of research material, and so on. What allocation base might be used as a cost driver for overhead in a law firm?

Overhead consists of a variety of costs with potentially different drivers for each. For example, the salaries of janitors and supervisors in the factory are overhead costs. The costs of rent and insurance for the factory building are overhead costs. The costs of indirect materials are overhead costs. Instead of identifying cost drivers for each component of overhead, companies have traditionally lumped overhead into similar **cost pools** to simplify the task. In the most extreme case, companies lump all overhead into one cost pool for the entire factory. Other companies have separate pools of overhead for each department. Still others use cost pools for each activity performed in making a product. Regardless of the number of cost pools and method of overhead allocation used, overhead rates are calculated using the same basic formula:

Manufacturing overhead / Cost driver

DEPARTMENTAL OVERHEAD RATES

LO6
Evaluate the advantages and disadvantages of using plantwide versus departmental overhead rates

In traditional manufacturing companies and service industries, direct labor hours, or direct labor cost, have often served as cost drivers. As recently as 1991, a survey of U.S. manufacturing companies found that 62 percent used direct labor hours or dollars as their overhead cost driver (Cohen and Paquette, "Management Accounting Practices: Perceptions of Controllers," *Journal of Cost Management,* Fall 1991). Another 13 percent used machine hours as the cost driver. Allocating overhead based on direct labor or machine time worked well (and still does) when companies make only a few products, when they incur relatively small overhead costs compared to labor and material costs, and when that overhead is related to the volume of products produced.

EXHIBIT 3-2 Applying Overhead Using a Plantwide Rate

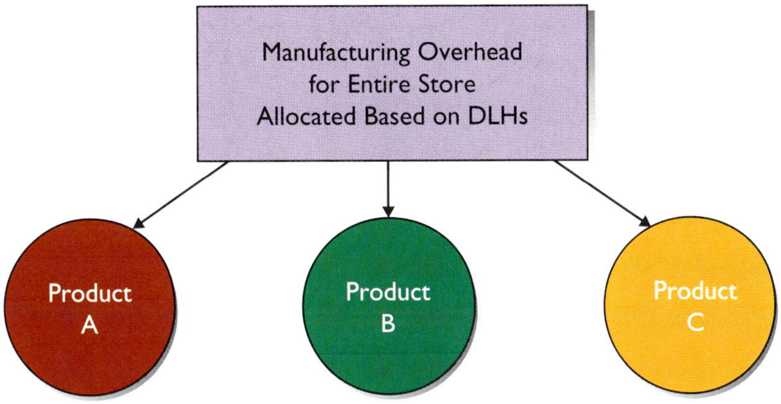

For example, as demonstrated in Exhibit 3-2, a take-out pizza restaurant with a single location and no delivery might apply overhead by using a single plantwide (storewide) predetermined overhead rate. The costs of pizza ovens, rent, utilities, and other overhead costs would be lumped into one storewide cost pool and allocated to products (pizzas), based on the amount of labor time (direct labor hours, or DLHs) it takes to make each pizza. In this case, the cost of overhead is relatively small and is likely to be related to the number of pizzas made. In other words, it is volume based.

However, as companies make more diverse products and become more heavily automated, the use of plantwide cost pools and single cost drivers may provide less than accurate cost information. Companies using departmental overhead rates form separate cost pools for each department. The overhead in each cost pool can then be applied to products based on different cost drivers. Consider the pizza restaurant again. To expand its market to wholesale customers (grocery stores), the restaurant buys a new automated pizza oven, new mixers, and new packaging machinery, and it expands its facility. The new oven, mixers, and packaging machinery are used entirely to make pizzas for the wholesale market, whereas the take-out market is served with the existing oven and mixer. In this scenario, it would probably make sense for the restaurant to accumulate overhead costs into two cost pools—one for the take-out department and one for the wholesale department. Although the overhead costs associated with the take-out activities might still be allocated based on direct labor hours incurred, a better driver of the costs associated with the wholesale activities (which is more heavily automated) might be machine hours, or MHs (see Exhibit 3-3). Although the use of departmental rates in this example is probably not significantly more difficult or time consuming than the use of a plantwide rate, that is not always the case.

Concept Question: *Using the decision-making model introduced in Chapter 1, the management team of RGS Inc. has identified a problem (Step 1) caused by its current method of allocating overhead to products, using a plantwide rate based on direct labor hours. Although its new product requires substantial machine time to manufacture, it requires very little direct labor, resulting in an allocation of only a small amount of overhead. As a result, the company's management accountant feels that the new product is being undercosted and underpriced. Management's objective (Step 2) is to develop a method of allocating overhead to products that will provide accurate costs for both their traditional labor-intensive product and their new product. The team is considering using multiple overhead rates as one option (Step 3). What factors are likely to be relevant in its decision?*

Step 1 DEFINE THE PROBLEM

Step 2 IDENTIFY OBJECTIVES

Step 3 IDENTIFY AND ANALYZE AVAILABLE OPTIONS

Concept Answer: The choice of a single plantwide overhead rate or multiple overhead rates depends on a variety of factors and an analysis of the costs and benefits of each approach. The use of a single plantwide rate is easier, less time consuming, and cheaper than the use of multiple departmental overhead rates. But departmental rates can provide more accurate cost information.

EXHIBIT 3-3 Applying Overhead Using Departmental Rates

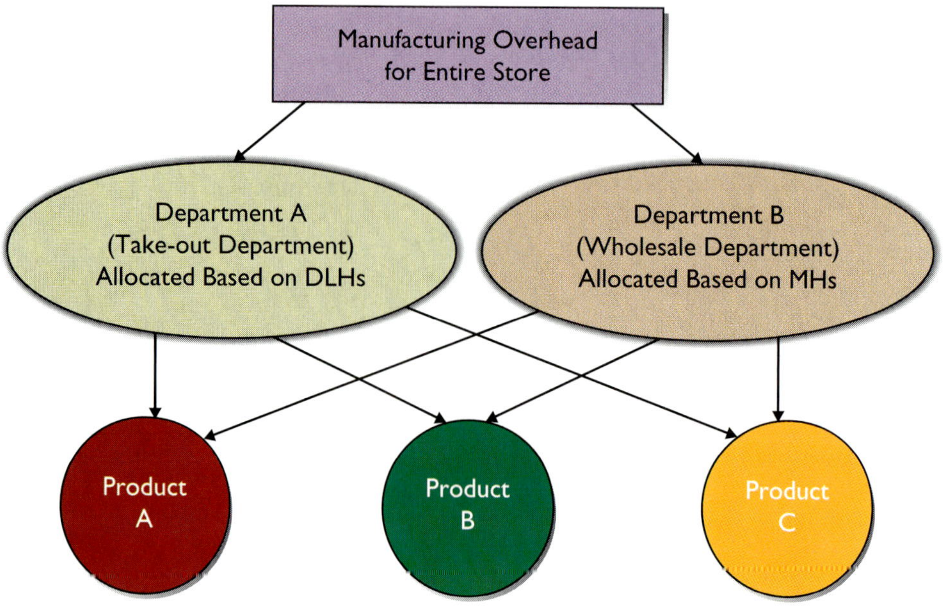

This is particularly true when multiple products are produced, the products consume resources differently, and departments perform very different activities. Regardless of whether a single rate or multiple rates are used, choosing an appropriate cost driver is an important factor.

In heavily automated manufacturing environments, direct labor costs have shrunk to as little as 5 percent of total production costs, whereas overhead costs have soared to 60 percent or more of total product costs. It's not hard to see why. Consider a modern automobile manufacturing plant. High-tech computers control robots that weld, paint, and perform other jobs that were previously done by humans. These machines are very expensive and are treated as part of overhead cost. As overhead costs have increased and make up a much larger portion of the total costs of products, accuracy in overhead application has become much more important as well. Overhead allocation using multiple cost pools and overhead rates based on the activities performed in a company is discussed in Chapter 4.

Key Concept: *Accuracy in overhead application has become much more important as overhead costs have increased and make up a larger portion of the total costs of products.*

THE USE OF ESTIMATES

LO7
Evaluate topics related to the choice of cost driver and the use of estimates in overhead application

It is not unusual for managers to want to estimate the cost of a product before it is actually produced. Having timely cost information is useful for pricing decisions as well as for production decisions. However, because the actual amount of many overhead items will not be known until the end of a period (perhaps when an invoice is received), companies often estimate the amount of overhead that will be incurred in the coming period. For example, a manufacturer of computers that are custom made to meet customer requirements needs to know the cost of producing each computer so it can establish a sales price. Customers place orders 24 hours per day, and the company's policy is to ship computers to customers within 48 hours of the order. Although the company has records of each component and other material used in the assembly of the computer and knows the exact amount of time workers spend putting the computer together (remember the job cost report discussed earlier), calculating the actual amount of overhead cost incurred is virtually impossible to do in a timely manner. Why? Because the amount of most overhead items, such as utilities expense, maintenance expense, supplies, and so forth, will not be known until after the computer is assembled and shipped. The only alternative, short of requiring the customer to wait until the end of the period to know the actual price of the computer, is to estimate the amount of overhead on each computer and to set the sales price accordingly. Using estimates has another advantage as well. It is not unusual for overhead to fluctuate during the year. For example, the utilities costs incurred by Ben & Jerry's (whose factory is located in Vermont) during the winter are likely to be higher than those incurred in the summer. If Ben & Jerry's used actual overhead costs to cost products, the ice cream the company makes in February would cost more than the ice cream it makes in May. Using estimates smoothes out, or normalizes, seasonal and random fluctuations in overhead costs. Thus, this method of costing is often called normal costing.

http://www.benjerry.com

Key Concept: *In order to provide relevant information for decision making, overhead must often be estimated.*

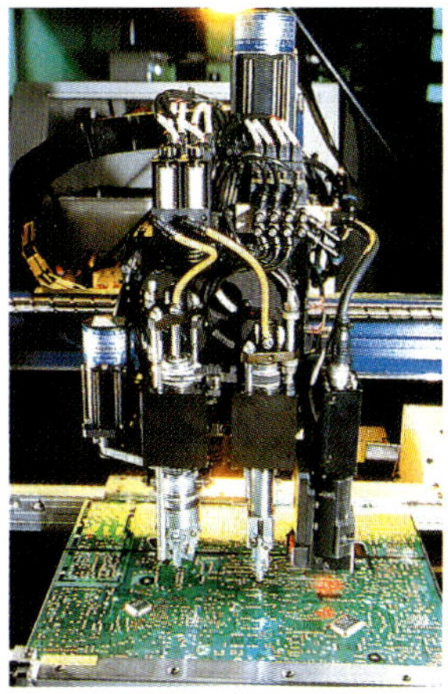

© MARK SEGAL/STONE

Overhead costs may account for 60 percent of total production costs in heavily automated companies utilizing robotics in their manufacturing processes.

PREDETERMINED OVERHEAD RATES

Companies that estimate the amount of overhead cost incurred in costing products allocate overhead by using predetermined overhead rates. **Predetermined overhead rates** are calculated using a slight modification of the basic overhead rate formula:

$$\frac{\text{Estimated overhead for the cost pool}}{\text{Estimated units of the cost driver}} = \text{Predetermined overhead rate (for a cost pool)}$$

Predetermined overhead rates are typically calculated using annual estimates of overhead and cost drivers, although some companies do more frequent calculations. The allocation of overhead using predetermined overhead rates is called an application of overhead. The amount of overhead applied to a product is calculated by multiplying the predetermined overhead rate by the actual units of the cost driver incurred in producing the product or service. The cost of a product or a service for a company utilizing normal costing therefore includes an actual amount of direct material, an actual amount of direct labor, and an applied amount of manufacturing overhead based on estimates.

Calculating predetermined overhead rates is a three-step process. Step 1 involves the identification and estimation of the indirect overhead costs included in the plantwide or departmental cost pool. Step 2 involves the identification and estimation of the appropriate allocation base (the cost driver). Step 3 is the actual computation of the predetermined overhead rate.

Northern Lights custom cabinets

As an example, let's assume that Northern Lights has chosen to lump all overhead into one cost pool for the entire factory (a plantwide cost pool). The company identifies overhead costs as including the cost of utilities, insurance, and rent for the factory building; depreciation and repairs and maintenance of manufacturing equipment; supplies used in the factory; and the salaries of a production supervisor and janitor in the factory. The company further estimates that these costs should total about $100,000 in the next year. As Northern Lights is very labor intensive, it has chosen labor hours as the cost driver and estimates using 6,000 labor hours during the next year. Dividing the estimated overhead of $100,000 by the estimated allocation base of 6,000 labor hours results in a predetermined overhead rate of $16.67 per labor hour.

$$\frac{\$100{,}000}{6{,}000} = \$16.67 \text{ per labor hour}$$

In other words, for every labor hour worked on a product, the company should apply $16.67 in overhead cost. As you can see in Exhibit 3-1, since Job 101 required 22.4 labor hours, it was allocated $373.41 of overhead.

THE PROBLEM OF OVER- AND UNDERAPPLIED OVERHEAD

Northern Lights custom cabinets

Because overhead is applied to products by using predetermined overhead rates based on estimates, it is likely that actual overhead costs (when they become known) will differ from that applied. If applied overhead is greater than actual overhead, the company **overapplied overhead.** If the applied overhead is less than actual overhead, the company **underapplied overhead** for the period. Over- and underapplied overhead can occur for a couple of reasons—estimating the overhead incorrectly or estimating the cost driver incorrectly. For example, Northern Lights had a predetermined overhead rate of $16.67 per direct labor hour ($100,000 estimated overhead/6,000 estimated direct labor hours). If during the year, 6,000 direct labor hours are actually incurred in making cabinets, our total applied overhead will total $100,000. But what if our actual overhead costs total $101,000? Northern Lights will have underapplied overhead by $1,000. What impact does the underapplication have on the cost of cabinets produced by Northern Lights?

Because applied overhead is accumulated in work in process (WIP) and then transferred to finished goods as units are completed and then to cost of goods sold as units are sold, if everything is sold, adjusting for over- or underapplied overhead simply involves adjusting the balance of the cost-of-goods-sold account. If Northern Lights sells all the cabinets it produces, its cost of goods sold would be understated by $1,000. But what if some of the cabinets were not sold or perhaps not even finished? Then the $1,000 should be allocated in some fashion to work in process, finished goods, and cost of goods sold to recognize that all three accounts are too low. This allocation is usually based on the amount of overhead in each account. As an alternative, if the amount of the adjustment is small, companies may choose to adjust only the cost of goods sold account.

BASIC PROCESS COSTING

LO8
Understand the basics of backflush and process costing

Companies that produce beverages and other products (paint, paper, oil, and textiles) in a continuous flow production process typically use process costing. As mentioned previously, instead of accumulating, tracking, and assigning direct material and direct labor costs directly to each job, process costing systems accumulate and track direct material and direct labor costs by department and then assign the costs evenly to the products that pass through each department. Likewise, instead of applying overhead to each specific job, overhead is applied to each department and then assigned evenly to each product that passes through. Although the application to job or department differs, the amount of overhead applied is calculated in exactly the same way. After predetermined overhead rates are developed, overhead is applied by multiplying the predetermined overhead rate by the actual units of cost driver incurred in each department. A comparison of the cost flows in job costing and process costing is shown in Exhibit 3-4.

In companies with no beginning or ending inventories (all units are finished), the mechanics of process costing are very simple. Because all the units produced are identical, costs accumulated and tracked in each department can simply be averaged across all the units that are produced. If $30,000 of direct material costs and $70,000 of direct labor and overhead costs are incurred in the blending department, and 10,000 gallons of product are produced, the cost of blending each gallon is obviously $10 per gallon and the 10,000 finished units cost $100,000 to produce.

However, problems quickly arise when companies have inventories. Let's assume that the blending department finishes blending only 8,000 gallons and that 2,000 gallons are left in ending work in process at the end of the year. These 2,000 gallons are 50 percent complete and will require additional materials, labor, and overhead during the next period before they are finished. Should each gallon (finished or unfinished) still cost $10 in this case? That would mean that our 8,000 finished units cost $80,000, whereas our 2,000 unfinished units cost $20,000. Of course, that would not make sense, because we would expect our finished units to cost more per gallon than those that are only half finished!

EXHIBIT 3-4 A Comparison of Cost Flows

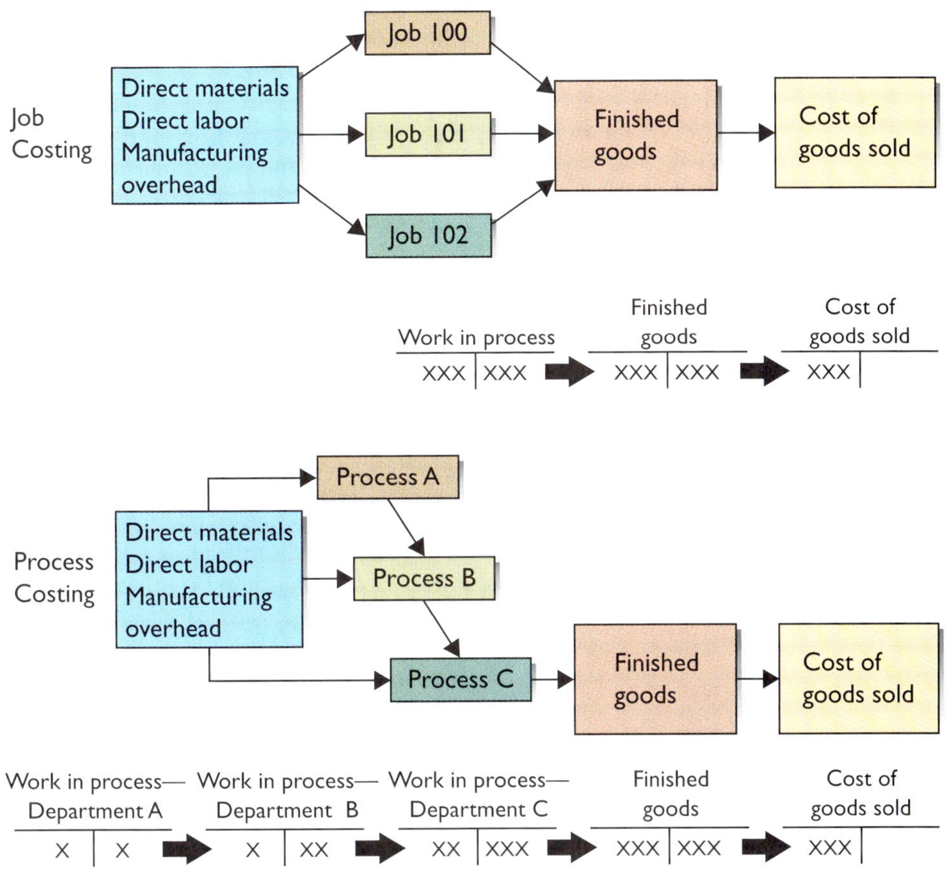

To get around this problem, we need to calculate the number of **equivalent units** completed during the period. If two units are uniformly 50 percent finished at the end of a period, we have finished the equivalent of one complete unit. In the previous example, we partially finished 2,000 units with each unit uniformly 50 percent complete. How many finished units could we have completed using the same amount of direct materials, labor, and overhead? The 2,000 units that are 50 percent finished are the equivalent of 1,000 finished units. Therefore, our total equivalent units finished during the period are equal to 9,000—the 8,000 units we actually finished plus another 1,000 equivalent finished units in ending inventory.

Our cost per equivalent unit is therefore $11.11 ($100,000/9,000 equivalent units) and the 8,000 finished units cost $88,880, whereas the 2,000 units in ending inventory (1,000 equivalent units) cost $11,120 ($100,000 – $88,880). Process costing and the calculation of equivalent units are substantially more complicated when companies have both beginning and ending inventories of work in process.

Another difference between job costing and process costing is that process-cost systems often require multiple WIP accounts—one for every process. As products are moved from one process to another, the costs of the previous process are simply transferred to the next process. For example, a paint manufacturer accumulates and tracks direct material, direct labor, and overhead costs to a WIP account for each process (blending and pouring). The total costs for each process are then assigned to the paint by dividing by the number of gallons of paint that come out of each process. The total cost of each gallon is therefore the sum of the costs assigned from each process and an average of the costs incurred in each process. For a more detailed discussion of process costing, see the appendix to this chapter on page 77.

BACKFLUSH COSTING

Companies utilizing just-in-time manufacturing techniques generally have little or no inventory of raw material, WIP, or finished goods. Remember that products are typically produced only after an order has been placed, so theoretically all units produced will be sold. Although managers still need to know the cost of goods produced using JIT techniques, the costing process used is greatly simplified by recording all manufacturing costs directly into cost of goods sold. As can be seen in Exhibit 3-5, instead of sequentially tracking manufacturing costs through raw materials inventory, WIP, finished goods, and cost of goods sold, manufacturing costs are flushed directly into cost of goods sold. At the end of the period, if the company has small amounts of inventory on hand, manufacturing costs are backflushed into the appropriate inventory account. This is the exception rather than the rule. In most cases, we would expect all costs to remain in cost of goods sold.

A chief attraction of **backflush costing** is its simplicity. Simple systems, however, generally do not yield as much information as do more complex systems. Criticisms of backflush costing focus mainly on the inability of the accounting system to pinpoint the uses of resources at each step of the production process. Managers, however, keep track of operations by personal observations, computer monitoring, and nonfinancial measures. In a backflush costing system, control shifts away from accounting numbers toward critical physical measures observable by management in the factory.

EXHIBIT 3-5 A Comparison of Cost Flows

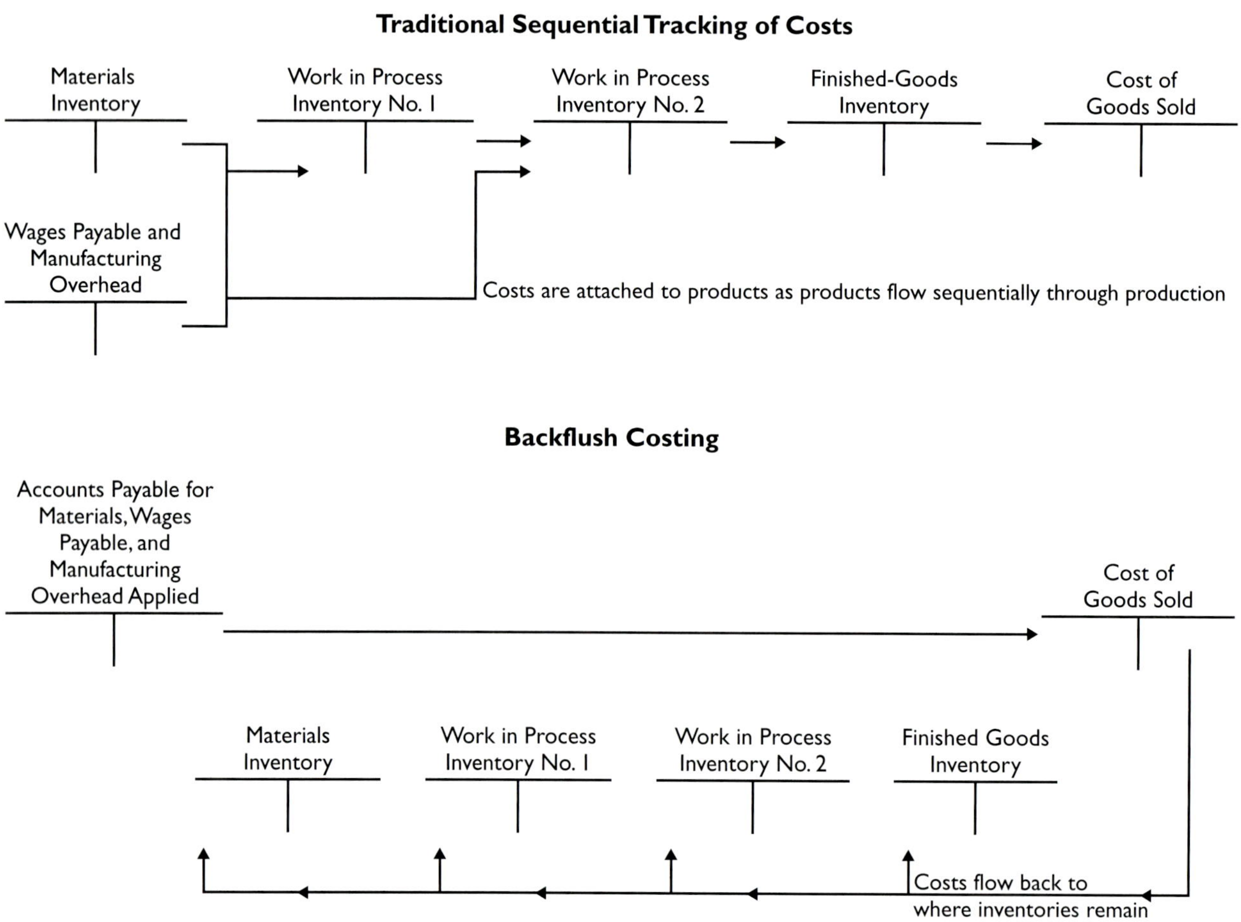

APPENDIX

ADDITIONAL TOPICS IN PROCESS COSTING

When a company has both beginning and ending inventories of work in process (WIP), process costing becomes more complicated. In addition, partially completed inventory may not be uniformly finished. That is, the inventory may be 100 percent complete with respect to direct materials (all materials were added early in the process) but partially finished with respect to conversion costs (the cost of direct labor and overhead incurred to convert the direct materials to a finished product).

In these situations, it is useful to view process costing in four steps. In Step 1, the physical flow of units and their associated costs are analyzed. In this step, it is essential to note the percentage of completion of both the beginning and ending inventories of WIP. For example, let's assume that the blending department of a paint manufacturer has 2,000 gallons of paint in its beginning inventory of WIP. This paint-blending process was started last period but was not completed by the end of the period and will be finished this period. In addition, let's assume that $2,000 of direct material costs (DM) and $1,000 of conversion costs (CC) have already been incurred in blending these 2,000 gallons of paint and that they are 100 percent finished with respect to direct materials and 80 percent finished with respect to conversion costs (Exhibit 3-6).

EXHIBIT 3-6 Step 1: WIP, Beginning Inventory

WIP—Blending Department		
Beginning Inventory	2,000 gallons ↙ ↘ 100% DM 80% CC $2,000 DM $1,000 CC	

During the current period, another 12,000 gallons of paint are started in the blending department, so 14,000 gallons are now in process. The company incurs another $20,000 of direct material costs and $7,000 of conversion costs working on these 14,000 gallons. The total costs incurred in the blending department now include $22,000 for direct material ($2,000 incurred last period and $20,000 incurred this period) and $8,000 for conversion costs ($1,000 incurred last period and $7,000 incurred this period) (Exhibit 3-7).

EXHIBIT 3-7 Step 1: WIP, Current Period

WIP—Blending Department		
Beginning Inventory	2,000 gallons $2,000 DM $1,000 CC	
Units Started	12,000 gallons $20,000 DM $ 7,000 CC	

Of the 14,000 gallons of paint now in process in the blending department, 13,000 gallons are finished by the end of the period. Consequently, 1,000 gallons remain in ending inventory (Exhibit 3-8). Let's assume that these 1,000 gallons are 100 percent complete with respect to direct materials (remember that materials are added at the very beginning of the process) and 50 percent complete with respect to conversion costs.

EXHIBIT 3-8 Step 1: WIP, Ending Inventory

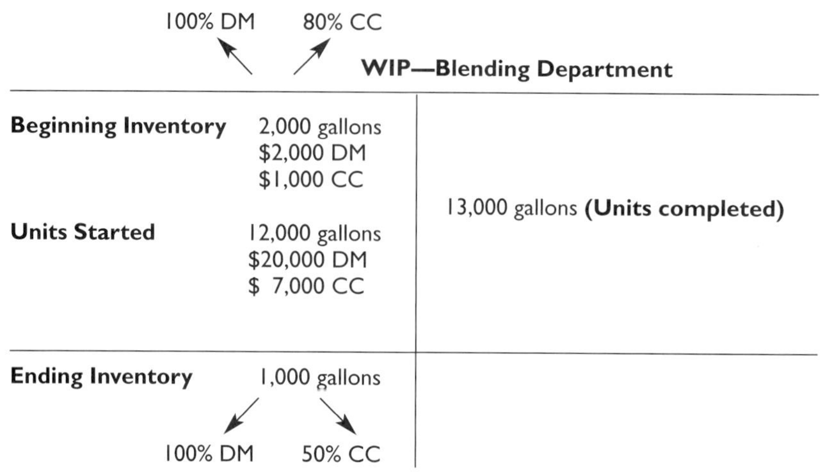

The goal of a process-costing system is to allocate the $30,000 of manufacturing costs that have been incurred in the blending department ($22,000 of DM and $8,000 of CC) to the 13,000 gallons of paint that are finished and transferred out (in this case, to the next processing department) and to the 1,000 gallons of paint that remain in the blending department's ending inventory.

In Step 2, equivalent units of production (EU) are calculated. This calculation can be made by either of two methods: FIFO (first-in-first-out) or weighted average. With the FIFO method, the 2,000 gallons in beginning WIP are assumed to be the first units finished. Consequently, of the 12,000 gallons started this period, 11,000 are finished whereas 1,000 gallons are partially completed and remain in ending WIP (Exhibit 3-9).

EXHIBIT 3-9 Step 2: Calculation

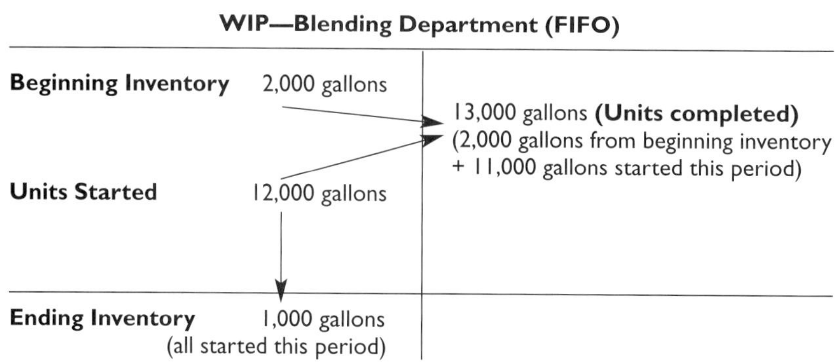

With the FIFO method, the equivalent units in beginning WIP (the units considered already complete at the beginning of the period) are correctly excluded from the calculation of equivalent units of production for the current period. Basically, we want to know the number of equivalent units completed *this* period. If the completion percentage differs for direct materials and conversion costs, as in our example, this calculation must be done separately for direct materials and for conversion costs.

EU Calculation under FIFO

	Direct Materials	Conversion Costs
Equivalent units of beginning WIP completed this period	2,000 × 0%* = **0**	2,000 × 20%† = **400**
Equivalent units started and completed this period	**11,000**	**11,000**
Equivalent units of ending WIP completed this period	1,000 × 100% = **1,000**	1,000 × 50% = **500**
Total equivalent units	**12,000**	**11,900**

*The beginning inventory was 100 percent complete with respect to direct material, so nothing is left to complete this period.
†The beginning inventory was 80 percent complete with respect to conversion costs, so 20 percent is left to complete this period.

In contrast to the FIFO method, the weighted-average method treats the units in beginning inventory as if they were started in the current period. That is, we combine the units we know were partially completed last period with the units started this period. Consequently, the 13,000 gallons of completed units and the 1,000 gallons of paint in ending WIP are both assumed to come from the 14,000 units we treat as having been started in the current period (Exhibit 3-10).

EXHIBIT 3-10 Weighted Average, Beginning Inventory

WIP—Blending Department (Weighted Average)

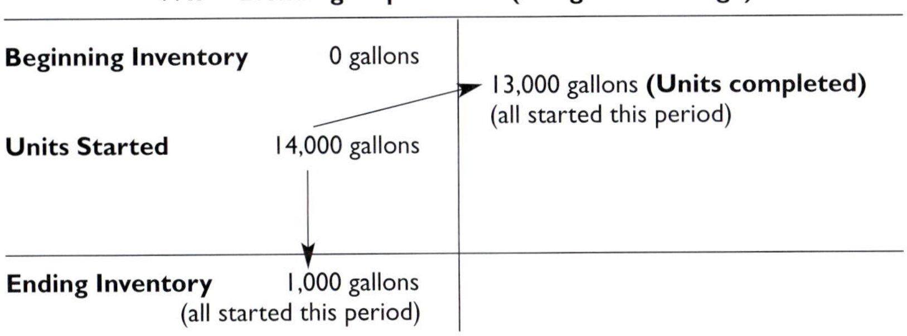

This simplifies the calculation of equivalent units, as follows:

EU Calculation under Weighted-Average Method

	Direct Materials	Conversion Costs
Equivalent units started and completed this period:		
Units completely finished	**13,000**	**13,000**
Equivalent units of ending WIP completed this period	1,000 × 100% = **1,000**	1,000 × 50% = **500**
Total equivalent units	**14,000**	**13,500**

In Step 3, manufacturing costs per equivalent unit are calculated. With the FIFO method, only the current period costs ($20,000 of DM and $7,000 of CC) are included in the calculation. Last period's costs of $3,000 ($2,000 of DM and $1,000 of CC) are correctly segregated from the costs incurred this period. This is consistent with including only the percentage of beginning inventory completed this period in the calculation of equivalent units.

Cost per Equivalent Unit under FIFO

	Direct Materials	Conversion Costs
Current period costs ÷ Equivalent units of production	\$20,000÷12,000	\$7,000÷11,900
= Cost per equivalent unit	**\$1.667**	**\$0.588**

With the weighted-average method, last period's costs are combined with the current period's costs in the calculation of cost per equivalent unit. This is consistent with treating the units in beginning inventory as if they were started this period in the calculation of equivalent units.

Cost per Equivalent Unit under Weighted Average

	Direct Materials	Conversion Costs
Total costs ÷ Equivalent units of production	\$22,000÷14,000	\$8,000÷13,500
= Cost per equivalent unit	**\$1.571**	**\$0.593**

In Step 4, the \$30,000 of costs incurred (\$3,000 from last period associated with the beginning inventory and \$27,000 incurred this period) are allocated to the 13,000 gallons of finished paint and the 1,000 gallons of partially finished paint.

FIFO METHOD

With the FIFO method, you will recall, the 2,000 gallons in beginning inventory are assumed to be finished first (first-in-first-out). Consequently, of the 12,000 units started in the current period, 11,000 are assumed to be finished, and 1,000 are assumed to still be in ending inventory.

Because all 2,000 units in beginning inventory are assumed to be completed this period, the \$3,000 of costs associated with those units will be allocated to the costs of the 13,000 finished units. Of course, we must incur additional costs this period to finish those 2,000 units and to start and finish another 11,000 units. How much are these additional costs? According to our earlier calculations of the cost per equivalent unit under FIFO, it costs \$1.667 per equivalent unit for direct material and \$0.588 per equivalent unit for conversion costs to blend paint this period (Exhibit 3-11). The following calculation shows that the 13,000 gallons of finished paint cost \$28,040 (consisting of \$20,337 of DM and \$7,703 of CC):

Cost of the 13,000 Finished Units under FIFO

	Direct Materials	Conversion Costs
Cost of the 2,000 units from beginning inventory:		
Cost incurred last period	\$ 2,000	\$ 1,000
Cost to finish the units this period:		
DM (\$1.667 per EU × 0 EUs)	\$ 0	
CC (\$0.588 per EU × 400 EUs)		\$ 235
Cost of the 11,000 units started and finished this period:		
DM (\$1.667 per EU × 11,000 EUs)	\$18,337	
CC (\$0.588 per EU × 11,000 EUs)		\$6,468
Total cost	**\$20,337**	**\$7,703**

EXHIBIT 3-11 FIFO, Calculation of Additional Costs

WIP—Blending Department (FIFO)

Beginning Inventory	2,000 gallons $2,000 DM $1,000 CC	13,000 gallons **(Units completed)**
Units Started	12,000 gallons $1.667 per EU for DM $0.588 per EU for CC	(to complete the 2,000 gallons in beginning inventory and 11,000 gallons of the 12,000 units started this period)
Ending Inventory	1,000 gallons	

The 1,000 units in ending inventory are easier to cost. All are considered to come from the 12,000 units started this period and cost $1.667 per equivalent unit for direct material and $0.588 per equivalent unit for conversion costs (Exhibit 3-12). The following calculation shows that the cost of the 1,000 units in ending inventory is $1,960 (consisting of $1,667 of DM and $293 of CC):

Cost of the 1,000 Units in Ending Inventory under FIFO

	Direct Materials	**Conversion Costs**
Cost of the 1,000 units in ending WIP:		
DM ($1.667 per EU × 1,000 EUs)	$1,667	
CC ($0.588 per EU × 500 EUs)		$293 (rounded)
Total Cost	**$1,667**	**$293**

EXHIBIT 3-12 FIFO, Cost of Ending Inventory

WIP—Blending Department (FIFO)

Beginning Inventory	2,000 gallons	13,000 gallons **(Units completed)** **(Cost of finished units = $28,040)**
Units Started	12,000 gallons $1.667 per EU for DM $0.588 per EU for CC	
Ending Inventory	1,000 gallons	

Concept Question: *Is there an easier way to calculate the cost of the ending work in process?*

Concept Answer: You should note that the total cost allocated to the 13,000 finished units and the 1,000 units of ending WIP must total $30,000. Consequently, if the finished units cost $28,040, the ending inventory must cost $1,960.

WEIGHTED-AVERAGE METHOD

Under the weighted-average method, the 2,000 gallons in beginning inventory are combined with the 12,000 units started this period. Consequently, of the 14,000 units assumed to have been started in the current period, 13,000 are finished, and 1,000 are still in ending inventory.

As all 2,000 units in beginning inventory were assumed to have been started this period, the $3,000 of costs associated with those units were combined with the $27,000 of current-period costs in calculating the cost per equivalent unit for direct material and conversion costs, using the weighted-average method. According to our earlier calculations of the cost per equivalent unit under the weighted-average method, each of the 13,000 gallons of paint completed in the current period costs $1.571 per equivalent unit for DM and $0.593 per equivalent unit for CC (Exhibit 3-13). The following calculation shows that the 13,000 gallons of completely finished paint cost $28,132 (consisting of $20,423 of DM and $7,709 of CC):

Cost of the 13,000 Finished Units under Weighted Average

	Direct Materials	**Conversion Costs**
Cost of the 13,000 units started and completely finished:		
DM ($1.571 per EU × 13,000 EUs)	$20,423	
CC ($0.593 per EU × 13,000 EUs)		$7,709
Total cost	**$20,423**	**$7,709**

EXHIBIT 3-13 Weighted-Average Method, Calculation of Costs

WIP—Blending Department (Weighted Average)

Beginning Inventory 0 gallons	
Units Started 14,000 gallons $1.571 per EU for DM $0.593 per EU for CC	→ 13,000 gallons **(Units completed)**
Ending Inventory 1,000 gallons	

The 1,000 units in ending inventory must also have come from the 14,000 units assumed to be started this period (Exhibit 3-14). Consequently, the cost of the 1,000 units in ending inventory is $1,868 (consisting of $1,571 of DM and $297 of CC):

Cost of the 1,000 Units in Ending Inventory under Weighted Average

	Direct Materials	**Conversion Costs**
Cost of the 1,000 units in ending WIP:		
DM ($1.571 per EU × 1,000 EUs)	$1,571	
CC ($0.592 per EU × 500 EUs)		$297 (rounded)
Total cost	**$1,571**	**$297**

Once again, note that regardless of whether FIFO or the weighted-average method is used, the costs allocated to the finished units and ending WIP total $30,000.

EXHIBIT 3-14 Weighted-Average Method, Cost of Ending Inventory

WIP—Blending Department (Weighted Average)

Beginning Inventory	0 gallons	13,000 gallons **(Units completed)**
Units Started	14,000 gallons	**Cost of finished units = $28,132**
	$1.571 per EU for DM $0.593 per EU for CC	
Ending Inventory	1,000 gallons	

Concept Question: *In a JIT environment, which method is likely to be preferable?*

Concept Answer: Although the FIFO method is conceptually superior, the weighted-average method will provide similar cost calculations when inventory levels are small, as in a JIT environment, or when costs are relatively stable from period to period.

SUMMARY OF KEY CONCEPTS

- Overhead cannot be directly tracked to products and services but must instead be allocated using cost drivers. (p. 69)
- Understanding what causes overhead costs to be incurred (what drives them) is the key to allocating overhead. (p. 70)
- Accuracy in overhead application has become much more important as overhead costs have increased and make up a larger portion of the total costs of products. (p. 72)
- In order to provide relevant information for decision making, overhead must often be estimated. (p. 73)

KEY DEFINITIONS

Job costing A costing system that accumulates, tracks, and assigns costs for each job produced by a company (p. 65)

Process costing A costing system that accumulates and tracks costs for each process performed and then assigns those costs equally to each unit produced (p. 65)

Operations costing A hybrid of job and process costing; used by companies that make products in batches (p. 65)

Normal spoilage Spoilage resulting from the regular operations of the production process (p. 67)

Abnormal spoilage Spoilage resulting from unusual circumstances, including improper handling, poorly trained employees, faulty equipment, and so on (p. 67)

Fringe benefits Payroll costs in addition to the basic hourly wage (68)

Idle time Worker time that is not used in the production of the finished product (p. 68)

Overtime premiums An additional amount added to the basic hourly wage owing to overtime worked by the workers (p. 68)

Allocation The process of finding a logical method of assigning overhead costs to the products or services a company produces (p. 69)

Cost drivers Factors that cause, or drive, the incurrence of costs (p. 69)

Cost pools Groups of overhead costs that are similar; used to simplify the task of assigning costs to products using ABC costing (p. 70)

Predetermined overhead rates Used to apply overhead to products; calculated by dividing the estimated overhead for a cost pool by the estimated units of the cost driver (p. 73)

Overapplied overhead The amount of applied overhead in excess of actual overhead (p. 74)

Underapplied overhead The amount of actual overhead in excess of applied overhead (p. 74)

Equivalent units The number of finished units that can be made from the materials, labor, and overhead included in partially completed units (p. 75)

Backflush costing A costing system in which manufacturing costs are directly flushed into cost of goods sold instead of flowing through inventory (p. 76)

COMPUTER SIMULATION

You can now turn to Appendix A of your text to complete the portion of the Big Al's simulation covering overhead allocation problems and the impact of adding an additional product.

MULTIPLE CHOICE

1. Which of the following costing systems often require multiple WIP accounts?
a. process **c.** backflush
b. job **d.** all of the above

2. Which of the following organizations would be most likely to adopt a job-cost system?
a. custom-home builder **c.** paint manufacturer
b. beverage maker **d.** all of the above

3. Abnormal spoilage:
a. results from the regular operation of the production process
b. is treated as a period cost
c. is treated as a product cost
d. all of the above

4. Which of the following costs is *not* considered a product cost?
a. employee benefits **c.** indirect labor
b. idle time **d.** advertising

5. Cost allocation:
a. is quite useful for direct material and direct labor costs
b. involves the logical assignment of overhead costs to products and services
c. is not allowed when a process-costing system is selected
d. requires the approval of the Institute of Management Accountants

6. A good allocation base:
a. involves the logical assignment of overhead costs to products and services
b. is one that is related to direct costs
c. refers to direct labor hours or direct labor dollars
d. depends on finding a cause-and-effect relationship between the base and overhead

7. At Lamply and Associates LLP, overhead is assigned to clients based on direct labor hours. At the beginning of 2002, estimated overhead costs were $156,000, and estimated direct labor hours were 20,800. Actual overhead costs amounted to $166,400, and 20,904 direct labor hours were worked. How much overhead should be applied to a client whose file notes 120 direct labor hours in 2002? (Round to the nearest cent.)
a. $895.20 **c.** $955.20
b. $900.00 **d.** $960.00

8. In a traditional manufacturing environment, ________ have often served as the primary cost driver for overhead allocation.
a. units of production
b. number of purchase orders
c. direct labor hours
d. number of production shifts

9. All the following statements regarding a plantwide allocation rate are true, *except:*
a. The use of a plantwide rate is easy.
b. A plantwide rate provides less accurate cost information than does a departmental rate.

c. A plantwide rate is less time consuming to prepare than is a departmental rate.
d. A plantwide rate is more costly to prepare than is a departmental rate.

10. In its initial year of operation, Computertren completed 1,000 computer screens and had a batch of 200 more computer screens that were 50 percent done. Production costs for the year totaled $220,000. How many equivalent units were completed during the year?

a. 100
b. 1,000
c. 1,100
d. 1,200

Appendix

11. Under which of the following conditions will the FIFO method produce the same cost of goods manufactured as the weighted-average method?
   a. There is no work-in-process ending inventory.
   b. There is no work-in-process beginning inventory.
   c. The beginning and ending work-in-process inventories are equal.
   d. The beginning and ending work-in-process inventories are both 50 percent complete.
   e. Both **a** and **b** are required.

12. ABC Company has a beginning work-in-process inventory of 25,000 units, 40 percent complete. During the period, 100,000 units were transferred in from a preceding process. The ending work-in-process inventory was 20,000 units, 80 percent complete. What are the equivalent units for the conversion costs, assuming that ABC uses the weighted-average method?

a. 106,000
b. 115,000
c. 121,000
d. 131,000

13. The costs included in the cost per equivalent unit using the weighted-average method are:
   a. current costs
   b. beginning work in process
   c. ending work in process
   d. all of the above
   e. both **a** and **b**

CONCEPT REVIEW

14. What type of organization might use a job-order costing system? Explain why.
15. Job costing is most appropriate for what type of product?
16. Describe a situation in which backflush costing would be appropriate.
17. What type of costing system would a service organization, such as public accounting firms, be most likely to use?
18. The concept of equivalent whole or completed units is necessary in what type of costing system?
19. If Clinton Company uses normal costing, when would an adjustment to the applied overhead account increase product costs?
20. When should a normalized overhead rate be used?
21. What is a predetermined overhead rate? Why is it needed? How is it computed?
22. Why would a company decide to use a predetermined overhead rate instead of the actual overhead cost incurred?
23. What are some of the variables that must be considered in selecting a base to be used in computing the predetermined overhead rate?
24. What is overapplied overhead? What is underapplied overhead?
25. List two reasons why overhead might be overapplied.
26. List two reasons why overhead might be underapplied.
27. Explain the importance of product cost information in the context of management decision making.
28. Distinguish between job-order and process costing.
29. Why is it easier to accumulate costs using a process-costing system?
30. How are work-in-process accounts maintained in a company using process costing?
31. Define the term *equivalent units of production.*

APPLICATION OF CONCEPTS

32. George is a typical employee who works 40 hours per week. Last week, George spent 4 hours talking football with his supervisor and had only 36 productive hours, although he was paid for all 40 hours. He is paid $6 per hour. In a job-costing system, how should his labor costs be classified?

33. BN Rabbit Enterprises calculates predetermined overhead rates for each department. In the feeding department, total overhead costs were $3,400 in 2001, and are expected to total $4,000 in 2002. There were 325 pens in 2001 and plans for 400 pens in 2002.

Required

A. The number of pens is used as the cost driver. Calculate the 2002 predetermined overhead rate (rounded to the nearest cent).

B. The number of pens is used as the cost driver. Calculate the amount of overhead applied in 2002 if there were 390 pens in operation.

C. Based on the rate computed in B, what was the amount of under- or overapplied overhead in 2002 if actual overhead was $5,000?

34. At Donegan and Donegan LLP, overhead is assigned to clients based upon direct labor hours. At the beginning of 2002, estimated overhead costs were $106,000 and estimated direct labor hours were 10,800. Actual overhead costs amounted to $116,400, and 10,904 direct labor hours were worked.

Required

A. Compute the predetermined overhead rate used to apply overhead to clients. (Round to the nearest cent.)

B. How much overhead should be applied to a client whose file notes 120 direct labor hours in 2002? (Round to the nearest cent.)

35. Carl's Pottery Barn had no beginning or ending WIP inventory balance. Costs transferred to WIP during the month included $400 for direct labor and $375 for indirect costs. If the month's cost of goods manufactured totaled $1,050, how much direct material was used during the month?

36. Carl's Pottery Barn uses number of minutes in the firing oven to allocate overhead costs to items. In a typical month, 5,000 firing minutes are expected, and average monthly overhead expenses are $350. During January, 5,000 firing minutes were used, and total overhead costs were $275. Compute Carl's predetermined overhead rate, applied overhead for January, and the amount of over- or underapplied overhead for the month.

37. During March, TAL Productions purchased $30,000 of direct materials. Total manufacturing costs were $115,000. Indirect labor costs were $20,000, and direct labor costs were $25,000. There was no beginning direct materials inventory, but ending direct materials inventory was $10,000. Total manufacturing overhead costs must have been how much?

38. Lowen Enterprises applies overhead using direct labor hours. The following information is available for the year:

Expected direct labor hours	600,000
Actual direct labor hours	540,000
Overhead applied	$2,950,000
Actual overhead	$2,800,000

Required

What was the overhead application rate?

39. Grandma R knits made-to-order blankets. The following is an incomplete job-cost report for job 314.

DIRECT MATERIALS			DIRECT LABOR		OVERHEAD
Type of Yarn	Cost	Date	Knitting Hours	Total Cost	Total Applied
Blue—4 skeins	$14	1/23	5	$40	$4.50
Brown—2 skeins	11	1/24	7	?	?
Green—2 skeins	13	1/25	3	24	2.70

Required

A. What is the direct labor cost per hour?
B. What is the direct labor cost for January 24?
C. Based on this job-cost report, how is overhead being assigned to each blanket?
D. How much overhead should be applied for the January 24 knitting?
E. What is the total manufacturing cost for this blanket?
F. Which yarn is the most expensive?

40. Jenny's Jingles manufactures holiday decorations. Overhead to products is applied based on direct labor hours. Last year, total overhead costs were expected to be $85,000, based on an estimated 8,500 direct labor hours. Actual expenses totaled $88,750 for 8,400 actual hours.

Required

A. Compute the predetermined overhead rate.
B. How much overhead should be applied to a job that was completed in 3 direct labor hours?
C. What is the amount of over- or underapplied overhead at the end of the year?

41. The following events took place during the year for the Billy Joelle Company:

Purchased $100,000 of raw materials
Incurred 4,500 direct labor hours
Paid indirect labor costs of $25,000
Incurred utilities, rent, and depreciation totaling $45,000
Direct materials used in production amounted to $70,000
Applied overhead at 125 percent of direct labor costs
Direct labor averaged $11 per hour
$180,000 of products were transferred to finished goods
Products costing $160,000 were sold

All beginning inventory balances were zero.

Required

A. Calculate the direct materials ending inventory.
B. Calculate the work-in-process ending inventory.
C. Calculate the finished-goods ending inventory.
D. Calculate the over- or underapplied overhead for the period.

42. Martha's Magnets creates special-order magnets for its customers. The company's estimated overhead cost for the year is $11,000, and the number of direct labor hours is typically 2,100. In the first month, the following jobs were completed:

	Job 101	Job 102
Direct materials used	$1,100	$1,450
Direct labor cost	$1,500	$1,250
Direct labor hours	150	125

Required

A. What was the company's predetermined overhead rate, using direct labor hours as a base?

B. How much overhead was applied to each job?

C. What were the total manufacturing costs for each job?

43. Tripp Sound Works Inc. estimated its overhead costs for 2002 to be $1,750,000. Tripp expected to produce 350,000 units during the year. During 2002, the company incurred overhead costs of $1,600,000 and produced 400,000 units. What rate would be used to apply manufacturing-overhead costs to products? Calculate the amount of manufacturing-overhead costs applied to units produced. Calculate the amount of under- or overapplied manufacturing overhead for the year.

44. The following events took place during the current year for Moody Blues Company.

1. Purchased direct materials	$100,000
2. Incurred direct labor costs	60,000
3. Incurred indirect labor costs	30,000
4. Incurred utilities, rent, and depreciation	50,000
5. Direct materials issued to production	85,000
6. Overhead is applied at $9 per machine hour	
7. Machine hours used	10,000
8. Transferred to finished goods	$210,000
9. Cost of goods sold during period	190,000

Required

A. Calculate the direct materials ending inventory.

B. Calculate the work-in-process ending inventory.

C. Calculate the finished-goods ending inventory.

D. Calculate the over- or underapplied overhead for the period.

45. Clapton Company applies overhead costs to products at a rate of $2.50 per direct labor hour. The company uses a separate overhead account. The following data relate to the manufacturing activities of Clapton Company during October:

	October 1	October 30
Direct materials inventory	$ 60,250	$61,750
Work-in-process inventory	44,000	43,500
Finished-goods inventory	24,150	23,000

Factory Costs Incurred during the Month

Direct materials purchased	$155,000
Direct labor costs incurred	270,000 (27,000 direct labor hours)
Factory utilities	35,000
Factory rent	52,000
Factory supervisor	43,000
Depreciation on factory equipment	25,000

Required

A. Calculate the cost of direct materials used during October.

B. Using normal costing, calculate the cost of units completed during October and sent to the finished-goods storeroom.

C. Using normal costing, calculate the cost of goods sold during October. Assume that the company waits until the end of the year to adjust cost of goods sold for the over- or underapplied overhead.

46. For May, Guess Who CPAs worked 280 hours for Albert Flasher and 390 hours for Glamor Boy. Guess Who bills clients at the rate of $150 per hour. The accounting staff is paid $55 per hour. The accounting staff is estimated to work a total of 800 hours during the month, but 100 of these hours are not expected to be billed to clients. The estimated amount of service-overhead costs to be paid during the month is $9,600. Service overhead is assigned proportionally to clients, based on direct labor hours. The company also spent $5,000 in marketing and administrative costs.

Required

A. Calculate the predetermined overhead rate and the amounts applied to Albert Flasher and Glamor Boy.

B. If actual overhead costs incurred were $10,000, would overhead be over- or underapplied?

C. In a CPA firm, would this appear to be the best way to apply overhead? Why?

47. The Beatle Products Company uses a job-costing system. The company estimated its annual overhead to be $100,000 and the number of direct labor hours for the year to be 20,000 hours. In the first month, the following jobs were completed:

	Honey Pie	Savoy Truffle
Direct materials used	$11,000	$14,500
Direct labor cost	$23,000	$12,500
Direct labor hours	1,500	1,250

Required

A. What is the company's predetermined overhead rate, using direct labor hours as the base?

B. What is the overhead assigned to Honey Pie?

C. What is the overhead assigned to Savoy Truffle?

D. What is the total manufacturing cost of Honey Pie?

E. What is the total manufacturing cost of Savoy Truffle?

48. KENCOR Brewery uses the latest in modern brewing technology to produce a prize-winning beer. In both 2001 and 2002, KENCOR produced and sold 100,000 cases of beer and had no raw material, work-in-process, or finished-goods inventory at the beginning or end of either year. At the end of 2001, the company installed machines to perform some of the repetitive tasks previously performed with direct labor. At the beginning of 2002, KENCOR's bookkeeper estimated that net income would increase from $530,000 in 2001 to $706,000 in 2002.

	2001 (Actual)	2002 (Estimated)
Beer sales (100,000 cases)	$1,000,000	$1,000,000
Less: Cost of goods sold		
Direct material	150,000	150,000
Direct labor	125,000	25,000
Applied overhead*	95,000	19,000
Gross profit	$ 630,000	$ 806,000
Less: Selling and administrative costs	100,000	100,000
Net income	$ 530,000	$ 706,000

*For 2002, overhead was applied at the 2001 rate of $9.50 per direct labor hour for an estimated 2,000 hours of direct labor. A total of 10,000 direct labor hours were worked in 2001. KENCOR's bookkeeper estimates that 5,000 machine hours will be worked in 2002.

However, when actual overhead is used to calculate net income at the end of the year, net income decreased from $530,000 in 2001 to $435,000 in 2002.

	2001 (Actual)	2002 (Actual)
Beer sales (100,000 cases)	$1,000,000	$1,000,000
Less: Cost of goods sold		
Direct material	150,000	150,000
Direct labor	125,000	25,000
Actual overhead:		
Lease expense	25,000	25,000
Utilities expense	15,000	30,000
Depreciation (equipment)	50,000	200,000
Equipment maintenance	5,000	35,000
Gross profit	$ 630,000	$ 535,000
Less: Selling and administrative costs	100,000	100,000
Net income	$ 530,000	$ 435,000

Required

Step 1 DEFINE THE PROBLEM

Step 2 IDENTIFY OBJECTIVES

Step 3 IDENTIFY AND ANALYZE AVAILABLE OPTIONS

Step 4 SELECT THE BEST OPTION

A. What potential problems do you see in the bookkeeper's estimate of income for 2002?

B. Based on the information given, would you change the cost driver or predetermined overhead rate for 2002? What cost driver would you suggest?

C. Using the cost driver and predetermined overhead rate you suggested in B, and assuming that 5,000 machine hours will be incurred, recalculate KENCOR's estimated net income for 2002.

D. KENCOR has set a goal of increasing net income in 2003 to $550,000. However, sales are expected to be flat. Using the decision model from Chapter 1, identify some options for KENCOR. How might it reach its goal of increasing income to $550,000? What qualitative factors should be considered in its decision?

49. Boots R Us manufactures hunting boots. The company is currently trying to choose the best method of allocating manufacturing overhead to boots produced. Following is information from the accounting department of Boots R Us:

Estimated Income Statement	
Sales	$1,000,000 (10,000 pairs of boots)
Direct materials	300,000
Direct labor	150,000 (10,000 hrs)
Estimated overhead	100,000
Net profit on boots	$ 450,000
Estimated machine hours	15,000

Required

A. Compute the predetermined overhead rate for Boots R Us, using (1) direct labor hours, (2) direct labor dollars, and (3) machine hours.

B. If actual labor cost was $170,000 for 10,500 direct labor hours and actual machine hours used were 18,500, what would be the applied overhead, using the three predetermined overhead rates computed in A?

C. If actual overhead is $115,000, compute over/underapplied overhead for all three allocation bases used in A and B.

Step 3 IDENTIFY AND ANALYZE AVAILABLE OPTIONS

D. Compare the over- and underapplied overhead calculated with the three drivers in C. Why do different drivers result in different amounts of applied overhead? Which cost driver appears to be best?

E. What other factors must Boots R Us consider in choosing a cost driver?

50. Scott Herring Hammocks has two departments: assembly and packaging. The company uses a job-order cost system and computes a predetermined overhead rate in each department. The assembly department bases its rate on machine hours, and the packaging department bases its rate on direct labor hours. At the beginning of the year, the company made the following estimates:

	DEPARTMENT	
	Assembly	**Packaging**
Direct labor hours	10,000	50,000
Machine hours	40,000	2,000
Manufacturing overhead	$600,000	$250,000
Direct labor cost	$100,000	$500,000

Required

A. Compute the predetermined overhead rate for each department.

B. The job-cost sheet for job 8260 (50 hammocks), which was started and completed during the year, showed the following:

	DEPARTMENT	
	Assembly	**Packaging**
Direct labor hours	5	20
Machine hours	50	20
Materials	$725	$225
Direct labor cost	$ 50	$200

Compute the total applied overhead for job 8260.

C. If the company uses a plantwide rate (based on direct labor hours) to apply overhead, what is the total applied overhead for job 8260?

D. What problems could using a plantwide rate cause for managerial decision making?

51. Northern Lights Custom Cabinets is a very labor-intensive operation, so it has elected to apply overhead costs to products, using direct labor hours as the cost driver. The following data relate to the manufacturing activities of Northern Lights Custom Cabinets during January 2002:

	January 1	**January 31**
Direct materials inventory	$ 50,250	$51,750
Work-in-process inventory	34,000	33,500
Finished-goods inventory	14,000	13,000

Estimated

Factory overhead costs	$157,500
Direct labor hours	$ 17,500

Actual Factory Costs Incurred during the Month

Direct materials purchased	$ 75,000
Direct labor costs incurred	170,000 (17,000 direct labor hours)
Factory utilities	35,000
Factory rent	50,000
Factory supervisor	50,000
Depreciation on factory equipment	25,000

Required

A. Calculate the cost of direct materials used during January.

B. Using normal costing, calculate the cost of units completed during January and transferred to the finished-goods showroom.

C. Using normal costing, calculate the cost of goods sold during January. Assume that the company waits until the end of the year to adjust cost of goods sold for the over- or underapplied overhead.

52. Tom Payne is employed by Dunagan Auto Parts and assembles a component for one of the company's auto parts. He is paid $20 per hour for regular time and time and a half for all work in excess of 40 hours per week.

Required

A. Assume that during the week, Tom is idle for 6 hours because of machine repairs and is idle for 3 more hours because of a shortage of raw material. He works 40 hours during the week. Allocate Tom's wages between direct labor cost and manufacturing-overhead cost for the week.

B. Assume that during the following week, Tom works a total of 50 hours and has no idle time. Allocate Tom's wages between direct labor cost and manufacturing-overhead cost for the week.

53. Your son called from college last night to explain that he took his mountain bike into the local bike repair shop for some repairs and its annual tune-up. When he returned to pick up the bike, the bill showed a $140 charge for 3 hours of labor—2 hours at $40 and 1 hour at $60—plus a charge of $200 for parts. He tells you that when he questioned the manager about the increased rate for the third hour, he was told that the third hour was after the worker's normal 8-hour day, so he was paid overtime at time and one half. This is common practice to pass on the "overtime premium" to the customer. The manager also explained that they were behind all day but did catch up in time to finish the job on your son's bike.

Required:

A. Do you agree with the computation on your son's repair bill?

B. Assume that the shop pays its mechanics $20 per hour for the first 8 hours worked each day and $30 for any additional hours worked in a day. How should the employees' time be allocated between direct labor and overhead?

C. Give an example of a situation in which the shop would be justified in charging an overtime premium to the customer.

54. Martha's Magnets creates special-order magnets for its customers. The company's estimated overhead costs average $10,000, and the number of direct labor hours is typically 2,000, whereas machine hours are typically 1,500. Martha's Magnets has two departments. The assembly department uses 1,800 of the labor hours, and the finishing department uses 1,200 of the machine hours. The $10,000 in overhead is allocated with $7,500 of the total traced to the assembly department and $2,500 to the finishing department. During the first month, the following jobs were completed:

	Job 101	Job 102
Direct materials used	$1,100	$1,450
Direct labor cost	$2,300	$1,250
Direct labor hours	150	25
Machine hours	25	230

Required

A. What is the company's plantwide predetermined overhead rate using direct labor hours as the base?

B. What is the company's plantwide predetermined overhead rate using machine hours as the base?

C. How much overhead would be applied to each job if direct labor hours were used as the cost driver for overhead?

D. How much overhead would be applied to each job if machine hours were used as the cost driver for overhead?

E. If Martha's Magnets decides to use department overhead rates, what would the overhead rates be for each department?

F. Assume that 80 percent of the labor hours on each job are from the assembly department and that 75 percent of the machine hours on each job are from the finishing department. What would be the overhead allocation to each job?

55. Products at Granty Enterprises go through two departments: assembly and finishing. The following information was available for Granty Enterprises last month:

Direct material used	2,500 pounds @ $0.75 per pound
Direct labor	200 hours (Wage rate: $7.50 per hour, Benefits: $1.50 per hour)
Estimated monthly overhead per department	$5,000
Estimated monthly direct labor hours	250 (200 assembly + 50 finishing)
Estimated monthly machine hours	200 (25 assembly + 175 finishing)
Actual Expenses	
Factory rent	$3,000
Factory utilities	3,700
Advertising	2,500
Factory equipment depreciation	3,000
Sales commissions	2,500

Required

A. Calculate a plantwide predetermined overhead rate using direct labor hours as the cost driver.

B. Calculate a plantwide predetermined overhead rate using machine hours as the cost driver.

C. Using the plantwide rate calculated in A, how much overhead would be applied to a job using 225 actual direct labor hours?

D. Using the plantwide rate calculated in B, how much overhead would be applied to a job using 210 actual machine hours?

E. Granty is considering the use of departmental overhead rates. Assuming that the cost driver for the assembly department is direct labor hours and that the cost driver for the finishing department is machine hours, how much overhead would be applied to a job using 180 direct labor hours and 30 machine hours in the assembly department and 45 direct labor hours and 180 machine hours in the finishing department?

F. Which method of allocating overhead results in the smaller over- or underapplied overhead?

56. Ernie's Pizzeria has been in business for three months selling a very good three-cheese pizza. Because of customer demand, it has decided to introduce a meat pizza and a veggie pizza next month to complement the cheese pizza. Since the start of the business, Ernie's has allocated overhead to each pizza by dividing the total overhead by the number of pizzas. Now the meat and veggie pizzas will require more preparation time and more time in the oven. Ernie's doesn't expect the total volume of pizzas to change; people who now order cheese will simply switch to one of the other options.

Required

A. Does it make sense to still allocate overhead by number of pizzas if the total number of pizzas remains the same? Why or why not?

B. What are the alternatives for Ernie's Pizzeria in allocating overhead to pizzas?

57. Doheny and Nesbitt manufactures computer desks. The company currently allocates overhead to each desk by dividing the total overhead for each period by the number of desks produced. Currently, 1,000 desks are produced and sold. Because demand for the desks is declining, the company has decided to start producing an ergonomic chair to complement the desks. The company plans to produce 500 desks and 500 chairs in the coming period.

Required

A. Does it make sense to still allocate overhead based on the total volume of desks and chairs if the number of total items produced is the same? Why or why not?

B. Give an example of a situation in which it does make sense to continue to allocate overhead based on numbers of items produced.

C. What are the alternatives for Doheny and Nesbitt in allocating overhead to desks and chairs?

Appendix

58. The Aqua Water Corporation manufactures flavored bottled water and uses process costing to account for the cost of the products manufactured. Raw materials are added to production at the beginning of the process. Data for the bottling department for March 2002 are as follows:

		Costs	
	Units	**Materials**	**Conversion**
Work in process, March 1	5,000	$68,750	$167,650
Started during March	100,000	300,000	903,350
Work in process, March 31	10,000		

Beginning inventory was 70 percent complete with respect to conversion costs. Ending inventory was 40 percent complete with respect to conversion costs.

Required

A. How many units were completed in March?

B. How many equivalent units were completed in March with respect to conversion costs, assuming that Aqua Water uses the FIFO method?

C. How many equivalent units were completed in March with respect to direct materials, assuming that Aqua Water uses the FIFO method?

D. What is the cost per equivalent unit for direct materials under FIFO?

E. What is the cost per equivalent unit for conversion costs under FIFO?

F. What is the cost of the ending WIP under FIFO?

G. What is the cost of the units transferred out of the bottling department?

59. Using the same information as provided in the preceding problem, answer A through G assuming that Aqua Water uses the weighted-average method.

60. The production manager at Aqua Water estimated that the ending inventory in WIP was 40 percent complete with respect to conversion costs. However, after reviewing the month-end financial information, Aqua Water's controller calls in the production manager and asks him to increase the estimate of percentage of completion to 60 percent.

Required

A. What is the likely motive of the controller?

B. What impact will increasing the percentage of completion have on Aqua Water's financial statements?

C. Should the production manager agree with the request?

61. The Kent Company adds raw materials to production at the beginning of the process in the production department. It uses a single-step process. Data on material for this department for October 2001 are as follows:

Production Data (units)	
In process, beginning of October	10,000
Started during October	60,000
Completed and transferred out during October	55,000
Manufacturing Cost (direct materials only)	
Work in process, beginning	$ 39,000
Raw materials used in October	186,000

Required

A. Assuming that the Kent Company uses the weighted-average method, what is the cost of the raw materials in WIP on October 31?

B. Assuming that the Kent Company uses the FIFO method, what is the cost of the raw materials in the units finished and transferred out?

62. Champ Inc. manufactures a product that passes through two processes: mixing and molding. All manufacturing costs are added uniformly in the mixing department. Information for the mixing department for October follows:

Work in Process, October 1	
Units (35 percent complete)	7,500
Direct materials	$36,000
Direct labor	$45,000
Overhead	$15,000

During October 26,750 units were completed and transferred to the molding department. The following costs were incurred by the mixing department during October:

Direct materials	$135,000
Direct labor	180,000
Overhead (applied)	45,000

On October 31, 3,750 units that were 80 percent complete remained in the mixing department.

Required

A. Using the FIFO method, what is the cost of goods transferred to the molding department during October?

B. Using the weighted-average method, what is the cost of goods transferred to the molding department during October?

Chapter 4

Product Costing for Management Decisions: Activity-Based Costing and Activity-Based Management

Study Tools

A Review of the Previous Chapter

Chapter 3 provided an introduction into product costing in various types of production environments and various types of companies and the difficulties of allocating overhead to products.

A Preview of This Chapter

In this chapter, we learn about the benefits of applying overhead to products by using activity-based costing (ABC) and the use of activity-based management (ABM) to aid in controlling costs and making better decisions.

Key concepts include:

- Unit-level costs are incurred each time a unit is produced. Batch-level costs are incurred each time a batch of goods is produced. Product-level costs are incurred as needed to support the production of each type of product. Facility-level costs simply sustain a facility's general manufacturing process.
- The key feature of an ABC system is allocating overhead costs based on activities that drive costs rather than on the volume or number of units produced.
- Volume-based costing systems often result in overcosting high-volume products and undercosting low-volume products. This cross subsidy is eliminated by the use of ABC.
- Activity-based management focuses on managing activities to reduce costs and to make better decisions.
- The successful implementation of ABC and ABM requires a long-term commitment by top management and the cooperation of all functional areas of a business organization.

Learning Objectives

After studying the material in this chapter, you should be able to:

LO1 Discuss activity-based costing (ABC) systems

LO2 Apply ABC systems to cost products and services

LO3 Analyze the use of cost drivers in ABC systems

LO4 Compare traditional volume-based costing to activity-based costing

LO5 Apply ABC systems to selling and administrative activities

LO6 Understand the application of ABC in a JIT environment

LO7 Evaluate the benefits and limitations of ABC systems

LO8 Understand activity-based management (ABM) and the value chain

A Preview of Upcoming Chapters

Chapters 5 through 8 build on the concepts of product costing introduced in Chapters 2 through 4. In Chapter 5, the nature of costs is discussed, and students are introduced to concepts of cost behavior, relevant costs, the impact of income taxes, and the time value of money on costs and decision making.

In this chapter, we revisit the problems of overhead application and discuss the use of an alternative product-costing system called activity-based costing (ABC). Assigning overhead to products and services using traditional allocation methods and volume-based cost drivers may not provide adequate information to managers to make good decisions. Activity-based costing (ABC) provides more accurate cost information by focusing on the activities or work that is performed in the manufacturing of a product or provision of a service and the cost drivers associated with those activities. The benefits and limitations of ABC are discussed, as is the application of ABC to selling and administrative activities and in a just-in-time (JIT) environment. The last part of the chapter discusses the use of activity information in controlling and managing costs (activity-based management). ■

INTRODUCTION

The previous chapter examined a number of problems associated with the application of overhead to products and services. Owing to the indirect nature of overhead and the fact that overhead consists of a variety of seemingly unrelated costs, it is often difficult to determine how much overhead should be included when costing specific products and services. To complicate matters further, overhead costs must often be estimated in order to provide timely cost information to managers.

In the past, overhead typically made up a smaller portion of the total cost of a product or service. The environment was one of "labor-intensive" manufacturing. With labor as the dominant activity and therefore the cost driver, direct labor hours worked was a logical activity base with which to allocate overhead to products. As the manufacturing environment has matured and the use of machines or robotics in production has increased, overhead cost has become a larger percentage of the total manufacturing cost. In heavily automated manufacturing environments, direct labor costs have shrunk to as little as 5 percent of total production costs, whereas overhead costs have soared to 60 percent or more of total product costs (see Exhibit 4-1). It's not difficult to see why. Consider a modern automobile manufacturing plant. High-tech computers control robots that weld, paint, and perform other jobs that used to be done by human labor. High-tech computer-operated equipment, such as robots, is very expensive and is treated as part of overhead cost. As overhead costs increase and make up a larger portion of the total costs of products, accuracy in overhead application has become much more important. At the same time, advances in information technology have allowed even the smallest businesses to take advantage of computers. These advances have provided more and more timely information to managers than ever before.

ACTIVITY-BASED COSTING

LO1
Discuss activity-based costing (ABC) systems

Traditional overhead allocation methods, which use one or two volume-based cost drivers to assign overhead costs to products, can provide misleading product-cost information in heavily automated manufacturing environments in which companies make a variety of diverse products. Volume-based allocation methods work best if the manufacturing environment includes mostly unit-level costs (costs that vary with every unit produced or the volume of production).

However, costs incurred in setting up machinery to make different products, costs incurred in designing a new model, and costs incurred in providing manufacturing facilities

EXHIBIT 4-1 Percentage Change in Manufacturing Costs

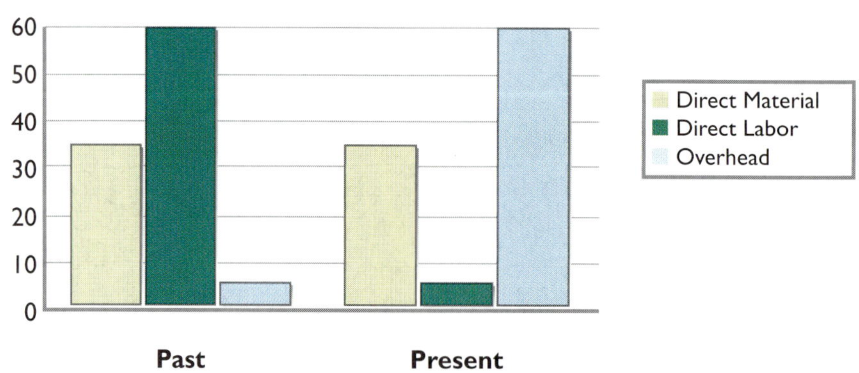

are not incurred every time an individual unit (a table) is produced. Rather, batch-level costs, such as machine setups, are incurred only when a batch of products (100 tables) is produced. Likewise, product-level costs (designing a new model) are incurred only when a new product is introduced. Finally, facility-level costs, such as the rent on the factory building, are incurred to sustain the overall manufacturing processes and don't vary with the number or type of products produced.[1]

Examples of unit-, batch-, product- and facility-level overhead costs are provided in the following table.

Overhead Costs and Cooper's Hierarchy

Unit-Level Costs	**Product-Level Costs**
Supplies for factory	Salaries of engineers
Depreciation on factory machinery	Depreciation of engineering equipment
Energy costs for factory machinery	Product development costs (testing)
Repairs and maintenance of factory machinery	Quality control costs
Batch-Level Costs	**Facility-Level Costs**
Salaries related to purchasing and receiving	Depreciation of factory building or rent
Salaries related to moving material	Salary of plant manager
Quality control costs	Insurance, taxes, etc.
Depreciation of setup equipment	Training

Key Concept: *Unit-level costs are incurred each time a unit is produced. Batch-level costs are incurred each time a batch of goods is produced. Product-level costs are incurred as needed to support the production of each type of product. Facility-level costs simply sustain a facility's general manufacturing process.*

LO2
Apply ABC systems to cost products and services

When concentrated at the unit level, it makes sense that the number of units produced should be correlated with the amount of overhead costs allocated to each unit. However, as companies incur more and more batch-, product-, and facility-level costs, the correlation between the volume of product produced and the allocation of overhead becomes very fuzzy. **Activity-based costing (ABC),** which is based on the concept of assigning costs based on activities that drive costs rather than on the volume or number of units produced, provides more accurate costing in these situations. **Activities** are procedures or processes that cause work to be accomplished. Activities consume resources, and products consume activities.

Key Concept: *The key feature of an ABC system is allocating overhead costs based on activities that drive costs rather than on the volume or number of units produced.*

Overhead costs are assigned to products in an ABC system in two stages. In Stage 1, activities are identified, and overhead costs are traced to each activity. Examples of typical activities of a company are shown in the first column of the following table. It should be noted that overhead costs can be traced to more than one activity. For example, utilities may be related to purchasing, engineering, and machining activities. An employee who provides maintenance services and runs machines in the factory might have his salary split between machining and maintenance activities. Likewise, whereas depreciation of factory equipment is related to machining, depreciation of other equipment might be related to maintenance or quality control activities.

---

[1]This classification of unit-level, batch-level, product-level, and facility-level costs is commonly referred to as Cooper's hierarchy.

Activities and Cost Drivers

Activity (level)	Potential Cost Drivers
Purchasing (batch)	Number of purchase orders or number of parts
Receiving (batch)	Amount of material or number of receipts
Product testing (product)	Number of change orders, number of tests, hours of testing time
Machine setups (batch)	Number of setups
Machining (unit)	Machine hours, labor hours, or number of units
Customer orders (batch)	Number of orders, number of customers
Maintenance of machines (unit)	Machine hours
Quality control inspections (unit, batch, or product)	Number of inspections, number of parts
Supervision (batch or product)	Number of supervision hours
Plant occupancy (facility)	Square footage, number of employees, labor hours, machine hours
Product movements (batch)	Pounds of material handled

COST DRIVERS

LO3
Analyze the use of cost drivers in ABC systems

In Stage 2, cost drivers for activities are chosen. As discussed in Chapter 2, cost drivers should cause, or drive, the incurrence of costs. For example, costs of purchasing might be driven by the number of purchase orders processed, whereas engineering costs might be driven by the number of parts in a product. Typical cost drivers for the activities identified in the preceding table are provided in the second column of the table.

Unit-, batch-, and product-level activities are assigned to products by using cost drivers that capture the underlying behavior of the costs that are being assigned. Facility-level costs, however, are usually not allocated to products or allocated to products in an arbitrary manner. For example, in the previous table, plant occupancy is a facility-level activity that would include such costs as plant managers' salaries, depreciation of the factory building, rent, taxes, and insurance. Allocation of these costs would require the use of arbitrary cost drivers, such as square footage, number of employees, labor hours, or machine hours.

CHOOSING COST DRIVERS TO MOTIVATE BEHAVIOR

Cost drivers should generally be chosen based on a cause-and-effect relationship between the driver and the specific cost being considered. However, cost drivers may have motivational effects that must be considered as well. As an example, consider an activity like taking customer orders by telephone. Although there might be a causal relationship between the time spent on each call and the various costs of the customer order activity, if objectives of the customer order department include increasing sales per customer and improving customer service, using the time spent on each call as a cost driver might give employees a mixed message. If time on the phone relates to the assignment of cost, employees will be encouraged to spend as little time on the phone as possible, to minimize the cost and also possibly answer more calls. As an alternative, if the number of sales is used as a cost driver, employees will be less likely to cut a call short, risking a lost sale or a dissatisfied customer.

Concept Question: *Overhead costs incurred in purchasing materials and supplies used in production are often related to the number of purchase orders processed by a company (the more purchase orders processed, the higher the purchasing costs). Using the decision-making model introduced in Chapter 1, what objectives might a company have in choosing a cost driver for these overhead costs (Step 2)? What other cost drivers might be considered as options in Step 3? What factors should be considered in deciding whether to use the number of purchase orders as the cost driver for purchasing costs?*

Concept Answer: Step 2: Objectives might include reducing overhead costs related to purchasing, ensuring high-quality supplies and materials, ensuring timely delivery of materials and supplies, etc. The particular objectives of a company determine the options to be considered in Step 3.

Step 2 IDENTIFY OBJECTIVES

Step 3 IDENTIFY AND ANALYZE AVAILABLE OPTIONS

Step 3: Other possible cost drivers include the number of different parts needed in production, the number of suppliers, or even the proximity of suppliers to your business. Factors to be considered in making a decision concerning a cost driver include the out-of-pocket costs of purchasing materials and supplies, the costs of storing materials and supplies, the reliability of suppliers, the quality of materials and supplies purchased, etc. ■

It should be recognized that because of different types of production processes and products, every business would have a different set of activities and costs drivers. In addition, the more complex the business or the production process, the more complex the ABC system is likely to be. Management must work together to design an appropriate cost system for the business.

TRADITIONAL OVERHEAD ALLOCATION AND ABC—AN EXAMPLE

As an example, let's consider TopSail Construction, a fictional beach-housing contractor. TopSail Construction usually builds about 30 houses per year. On average, it takes about 5 months (20 weeks) to build each house. As in all manufactured products, the cost of a house consists of three main components: direct material, direct labor, and overhead.

TopSail Construction

Many types of materials are used in the construction of a house. Raw materials needed in home construction range from lumber and roofing to insulation, sheet rock, brick, siding, and more. These types of raw materials can usually be accumulated, tracked, and assigned to specific homes with relative ease and thus are classified as direct materials. Indirect materials would include such things as nails, screws, and glue, which are not worth the effort to try and measure with complete accuracy.

Direct labor is also fairly straightforward in the construction business. Like many building contractors, TopSail does not employ brick masons, electricians, plumbers, sheet rock installers, and painters but rather uses subcontractors to perform this work. Because subcontractor labor can be traced directly to each house built, these costs are classified as direct. TopSail has only six full-time employees. Two are carpenters who work directly on houses; they are also classified as direct labor costs. Two are construction supervisors whose primary job is to supervise the subcontractors and inspect the work done on each house. The construction supervisors typically spend their days going from house to house. TopSail consequently classifies their salaries as indirect labor. TopSail also employs a full-time administrative assistant and a secretary in the office to handle the ordering of materials and processing of change orders for each house as well as payroll, billing, accounts payable, and other accounting and administrative tasks related to the business. Because about one half of the time of the office staff is spent directly on manufacturing duties, one half of the cost of their salaries (indirect labor) and other office expenses, such as rent, insurance, utilities, and supplies (overhead), is treated as a product cost. The other half is related to administrative duties and is treated as a period cost. In addition, TopSail has two part-time employees who deliver materials every morning and clear construction debris after work is complete each day. The salary of these workers is classified as indirect labor.

LO4
Compare traditional volume-based costing to activity-based costing

TopSail Construction incurs other overhead costs, including the cost of tools (saws, drills, etc.) used on the job, trucks used for material delivery and cleanup, trucks used by the construction supervisors, rent of construction trailers used as temporary offices at large construction sites, and so on. TopSail estimates that its overhead costs will total $485,000 in 2002. The following table provides a breakdown of this estimate.

Estimated Overhead Costs for 2002

Overhead Item	Estimated Cost
Indirect materials	$180,000
Indirect labor:	
Construction supervisors	130,000
Office staff	30,000
Part-time workers	30,000
Other overhead:	
Office expenses	48,000
Tools	15,000
Trucks and other equipment	40,000
Rent on construction trailers	12,000
Total	$485,000

TopSail Construction

If TopSail produced only one type of house, the overhead-allocation process would be very simple. As discussed in Chapter 3, all the company would have to do is divide the total overhead of $485,000 by the number of houses constructed. If TopSail constructed 30 houses in 2002, each house would be allocated $16,167 of overhead costs. However, to meet the specific needs of customers, TopSail builds both standard homes in large subdivisions and custom homes (on the beach) of different design, size, and features. The construction of custom homes requires TopSail to give more attention to the proper allocation of overhead costs to each house.

Using a traditional volume-based overhead allocation method would result in TopSail Construction using only one predetermined overhead rate, such as direct labor hours, to allocate overhead to houses. If TopSail estimates that the total direct labor hours used in 2002 in building homes will be 88,000, it would have a predetermined overhead rate of $5.51 per hour of direct labor used to construct each house ($485,000/88,000 direct labor hours). If a standard house takes 2,400 hours of labor to build, it would be allocated $13,224 of overhead costs. Likewise, a custom home requiring 4,000 direct labor hours would be allocated $22,040 of overhead costs. The following table illustrates the total cost of a standard house and a custom house, using traditional volume-based costing.

Traditional Volume-Based Allocation Method Using Direct Labor Hours

Cost	Standard House	Custom House
Direct material	$ 75,000	$112,500
Direct labor	60,000	100,000
	(2,400 hours at $25 per hour)	(4,000 hours at $25 per hour)
Overhead	13,224	22,040
	(2,400 hours at $5.51 per hour)	(4,000 hours at $5.51 per hour)
Total costs	$148,224	$234,540
Sales price	178,000	281,500

TopSail typically establishes a sales price equal to about 120 percent of total manufacturing costs. Remember, this is not all profit, as TopSail must still cover all selling and administrative costs (half of its office expenses, advertising, commissions on sales made by real estate agents, etc.). If all the overhead costs were related to the amount of labor hours needed to build the house, a volume-based overhead-allocation system would provide management with the information needed to make good decisions.

However, because TopSail builds two types of houses, a standard beach house with very few options and a custom home designed for beach property that will have many different options, the traditional volume-based overhead-allocation method may not provide the best information to management. The custom house requires much more inspection activity and typically has many more change orders than the standard house. In addition, the materials used in a custom house are more varied, resulting in more frequent purchases and deliveries. The use of an activity-based costing system might be more appropriate. In the next section, we explore TopSail's use of ABC.

STAGE 1: IDENTIFICATION OF ACTIVITIES

The first step in the implementation of an ABC system is the identification of production activities and the tracing of overhead costs to each activity. Remember that activities are processes or procedures that cause work to be accomplished. TopSail Construction identifies five primary activities that consume the resources of the company:

1. Inspections
2. Purchasing

3. Supervision
4. Material delivery and handling
5. Processing of change orders

The following table provides the overhead costs associated with each activity. Note that the total overhead is $485,000 regardless of whether it is allocated using volume-based drivers or using ABC.

Estimated Overhead Costs for 2002

Activity	Estimated Cost
Inspections	$ 50,000
Purchasing	30,000
Supervision	100,000
Material delivery and handling	225,000
Processing change orders	80,000
Total	$485,000

An example of "standard" beach houses.

An example of a "custom" beach house.

STAGE 2: IDENTIFICATION OF COST DRIVERS AND ALLOCATION OF COSTS

TopSail Construction

Once the activities have been identified and overhead costs traced to each activity, cost drivers must be identified for each activity. The cost drivers chosen are as follows:

1. Inspections: Cost driver = Number of inspections
2. Purchasing: Cost driver = Number of purchase orders
3. Supervision: Cost driver = Hours of supervisor time
4. Material delivery and handling: Cost driver = Number of deliveries
5. Change orders: Cost driver = Number of change orders

As you can see from the cost drivers chosen, they are more closely related to the activity than to direct labor hours. It simply makes more sense to allocate the cost of processing change orders based on the number of change orders processed rather than on the number of labor hours to build each house.

TopSail estimates that it will make 20 standard houses and 10 custom houses during the next year. TopSail further estimates that each standard house will require weekly inspections over the estimated 20-week construction period (20 per house), whereas the custom homes will require daily inspections (100 per house). Custom homes built on the beach must meet specific state and local building codes to withstand hurricane-force winds and tidal surges. They require more detailed inspections at more frequent time intervals than do TopSail's standard homes.

Standard houses also require less supervision time (125 hours) than does a custom house (150 hours). Custom homes require different and more varied materials than does the standard house. Thus, TopSail expects that material will be ordered and delivered about 30 times over the five-month construction period for a standard house (1.5 times per week on average), whereas the custom house will require about three orders and deliveries per week. Finally, TopSail expects to process considerably more change orders with the custom house (30 per house) compared to only 10 for the standard house. The following table summarizes the total number of inspections, purchase orders, supervision hours, deliveries, and change orders TopSail expects next year.

Estimated Cost Driver Activity

Cost Driver	Standard Houses (each)	Standard Houses (total for 20 houses)	Custom Houses (each)	Custom Houses (total for 10 houses)	Total
Number of inspections	20	400	100	1,000	1,400
Number of purchase orders	30	600	60	600	1,200
Supervision hours	125	2,500	150	1,500	4,000
Number of deliveries	30	600	60	600	1,200
Number of change orders	10	200	30	300	500

In the following table, predetermined overhead rates are calculated for each activity and cost driver, just as we did using a plantwide or departmental overhead rate with volume-based cost drivers.

TopSail Construction: Activity-Based Costing

Activity	Total Estimated Cost	Cost Driver and Estimated Amount	Predetermined Overhead Rate
Inspections	$ 50,000	Number of inspections (1,400)	$35.71 per hour of inspection time
Purchasing	30,000	Number of purchase orders (1,200)	$25 per purchase order
Supervision	100,000	Hours of supervisor time (4,000)	$25 per supervisor hour
Material delivery and handling	225,000	Number of deliveries (1,200)	$187.50 per delivery
Processing change orders	80,000	Number of change orders (500)	$160 per change order
Total overhead	$485,000		

The following table illustrates the total cost of a standard house and a custom house using an activity-based costing system.

Activity-Based Costing System

Cost	Standard House	Custom House
Direct materials	$ 75,000	$112,500
Direct labor	60,000	100,000
Inspections	714	3,571
Purchasing	750	1,500
Supervision	3,125	3,750
Material handling and delivery	5,625	11,250
Processing change orders	1,600	4,800
Total costs	$146,814	$237,371

TopSail Construction

If we compare the two methods of allocating overhead costs to standard and custom houses, we can see why volume-based allocation and activity-based costing resulted in different amounts of overhead being applied to each house, and we can see the impact these differences could have on sales price decisions for management. Allocating overhead costs using an activity-based costing system results in greater allocations of overhead to the custom house because it consumes more of the purchasing, inspection, supervision, material-handling, and processing change order activities than does the standard house. Although the custom house was also allocated more overhead under the volume-based costing system, the amount is different (as is our rationale for the allocation). Under a traditional volume-based costing system, the custom house was allocated more overhead than the standard house simply because it consumed more direct labor hours. Remember that the custom house required 4,000 direct labor hours, whereas the standard house required only 2,400 direct labor hours. Notice that using volume-based costing resulted in overcosting the standard house and undercosting the custom house compared to costing under ABC.

One important aspect of ABC systems is the elimination of cross subsidies between products. Cross subsidies occur when high-volume products, such as the standard house, are assigned more than their fair share of overhead costs. At the same time, more complicated low-volume products, such as the custom house, are allocated too little overhead.

This cross subsidy may make high-volume products appear unprofitable when they may not be, or it may make them appear to show less profit than they actually do. Activity-based costing systems eliminate the cross subsidy between high- and low-volume products.

Key Concept: *Volume-based costing systems often result in overcosting high-volume products and undercosting low-volume products. This cross subsidy is eliminated by the use of ABC.*

Concept Question: *Under what circumstances would volume-based costing and activity-based costing result in exactly the same overhead allocation?*

Concept Answer: Volume-based costing and activity-based costing result in different allocations of overhead when products consume activities in different proportions. On the other hand, volume-based costing and activity-based costing result in the same allocations of overhead when products consume resources in the same proportions. For example, producing a standard house consumed 2,400 direct labor hours, whereas producing a custom house consumed 4,000 direct labor hours (see the table on page 103). Based on this consumption of resources, the standard house was allocated 37.5 percent, or $13,224 of overhead, whereas the custom house was allocated 62.5 percent, or $22,040 of overhead. If the standard house and the custom house had consumed all resources related to inspections, purchase orders, supervision, deliveries, and processing change orders in the same proportion as they consumed direct labor (37.5 percent for the standard house and 62.5 percent for the custom house), the total overhead allocated to each house using volume-based costing and ABC would be exactly the same. ■

Although the differences may seem slight, consider the impact of the cost differences on TopSail's pricing policy. Under ABC, TopSail would price the standard house at $176,000 instead of $178,000 and the custom house at $285,000 instead of $281,500. In the very price-conscious standard-housing market, overpricing the standard house by $2,000 could result in a loss of sales, which could impact TopSail Construction's profit margin. Likewise, in the more flexible custom-home market, TopSail could have likely priced its custom house at a higher price than that indicated by traditional costing methods.

As this example illustrates, the allocation of costs using activity-based costing is more accurate and reflects the consumption of costs based on the activities that drive them rather than on one volume-based cost driver. In addition to providing management with more accurate cost information for pricing decisions, it also affects a variety of other decisions discussed in Part II of this book.

ABC SYSTEMS IN SERVICE INDUSTRIES

Service providers currently make up the fastest-growing segment of the U.S. economy, employing almost 75 percent of the workforce. As service companies expand the scope and quality of services offered, the need for fast, accurate costing information becomes more important. Can ABC be used to cost services as well as products? Do the same principles that we learned for manufacturing companies apply to service businesses? The answer is yes! In fact, ABC is every bit as important for service providers as it is for manufacturing companies. Although ABC was developed for use primarily by manufacturing companies, it has gained widespread acceptance in the service sector.

IN THE NEWS

In a recent survey, 61 percent of nonmanufacturing companies (financial, nonprofit, utilities, and service organizations) reported adopting ABC compared to 45 percent of manufacturing companies (Krumwiede, "ABC: Why It's Tried and How It Succeeds," *Management Accounting,* April 1998).

However, implementing ABC in service companies is not without its problems. One common problem is that the type of work done in service companies tends to be nonrepetitive. Unlike highly automated manufacturing companies, analyzing the activities of a service provider can be difficult when the activities differ greatly for each customer or service. In addition, service-oriented companies are likely to have proportionately more facility-level costs than do manufacturing companies. Remember from our earlier discussion that facility-level costs are allocated arbitrarily to goods and services (if at all).

ABC and Selling and Administrative Activities

LO5
Apply ABC systems to selling and administrative activities

The principles of ABC can be applied to selling and administrative activities as well. Instead of computing the cost of a product or a service, the goal is to determine the cost of providing a selling or administrative service. For example, a company might use ABC to determine the cost of providing payroll services. This information can be used to help management determine whether to continue processing payroll in-house or whether to outsource.

In the News http://www.usps.gov

The U.S. Post Office recently used activity-based costing to help determine the costs and benefits of allowing customers to pay with debit and credit cards. In this case, the Post Office focused on the impact of using debit and credit cards on customer satisfaction even though cost savings were also likely to be seen (Carter, Sedaghat, and Williams, "How ABC Changed the Post Office," *Management Accounting*, February 1998).

ABC and Just in Time (JIT)

LO6
Understand the application of ABC in a JIT environment

ABC can be used by companies employing traditional manufacturing techniques with inventory and by those utilizing just-in-time (JIT) production systems. JIT systems were described in Chapter 2 as production systems in which materials are purchased and products are produced just in time to be used in production or sold to customers. Because factories are typically redesigned in a JIT environment so that all machinery and equipment needed to make a product is available in one area (a manufacturing cell), overhead costs are more likely to be traced to products as unit-, batch-, or product-level costs. Fewer overhead costs are likely to be considered facility-level costs requiring arbitrary allocation. Although utilizing JIT production techniques does not eliminate all facility-level costs, combining ABC and JIT should result in even more accurate product costing.

Cost Flows and ABC

The flow of costs from raw materials to work in process to finished goods and cost of goods sold is not affected by the implementation of activity-based costing. Although the existence of multiple overhead rates (rather than plantwide or departmental rates) may make the application of overhead more complex, the cost flows remain the same as that described in Chapter 2 for manufacturing companies with inventory, manufacturing companies operating in a JIT environment, service companies, and merchandising companies.

BENEFITS AND LIMITATIONS OF ABC

LO7
Evaluate the benefits and limitations of ABC systems

Because of the increase in global competition, companies must strive to achieve and to sustain a competitive advantage. This requires organizations to continually improve performance in all aspects of their business operations. By focusing on continuous improvement, organizations can minimize scrap in the manufacturing process, reduce lead times for customer deliveries or vendor shipments, increase the quality of products and services produced, and control manufacturing and nonmanufacturing costs.

Activity-based costing systems provide more and more accurate cost information that focuses managers on opportunities for continuous improvement. Throughout their planning, operating, and control activities, managers use the information provided by ABC systems. In Chapter 1, planning was defined as the development of short- and long-term objectives and goals of an organization and an identification of the resources needed to achieve them. Using ABC in the budgeting process provides more accurate estimates of these resources.

One of the biggest advantages of ABC is the increased accuracy of cost information it provides for day-to-day decision making by managers (operating decisions). Managers use ABC information to make better decisions related to adding or dropping products, making or buying components used in the manufacturing process, marketing and pricing strategies, and so forth.

ABC also provides benefits related to the control function of managers. Costs that appear to be indirect using volume-based costing systems now are traced to specific activities using cost drivers. This allows managers to better see what causes costs to be incurred, leading to better control.

However, ABC is not for everyone, and the benefits of increased accuracy don't come without costs. Accumulating, tracking, and assigning costs to products and services using ABC requires the use of multiple activity pools and cost drivers. High measurement costs associated with ABC systems are a significant limitation. Companies may decide that the measurement costs associated with implementing ABC systems are greater than the expected benefit from having more accurate cost information. For example, if the market dictates prices, such as with commodity products, and companies have little control over pricing their products, highly reliable product costs may not be necessary for pricing. However, ABC may still prove valuable for planning and cost-reduction efforts.

IN THE NEWS

It has been reported that 54 percent of companies using ABC are using it for decision making outside the accounting function and that 89 percent of companies using ABC say it was worth the implementation costs (Krumwiede, "ABC: Why It's Tried and How It Succeeds," *Management Accounting*, April 1998).

In general, companies that have a high potential for cost distortions are more likely to benefit from ABC. Cost distortions are likely when companies make **diverse products** that consume resources differently. Products that vary a great deal in complexity are typically diverse, but differences in color or other seemingly minor differences in products can lead to product diversity when these differences materially change the products and affect the resources they consume.

PAUSE & Reflect

Are the standard houses and custom houses built by TopSail Construction diverse products?

Concept Question: *A furniture manufacturer makes hand-made custom dining room tables and chairs. Both products are very labor intensive and are made using the same saws, drills, lathes, sanders, and other equipment. Are the tables and chairs diverse products?*

Concept Answer: Although the products are certainly different, they are probably not diverse. They probably consume overhead resources in similar proportions. However, if they were made using different equipment and manufacturing processes, they probably would be considered diverse. ■

Companies that have a large proportion of non-unit-level costs are also likely to benefit from ABC. Remember, unit-level costs vary with the number of units produced and can be allocated with reasonable accuracy using volume-based cost systems and drivers. On the other hand, volume-based costing systems can result in distortions when allocating batch-, product-, and facility-level costs.

Companies that have relatively high proportions of overhead compared to direct materials and direct labor are likely to benefit from ABC as well. This is often the case with highly automated manufacturing companies or companies that have adopted JIT techniques. Note that service companies, such as law or CPA firms, may also have high overhead costs compared to direct material and direct labor and likewise may benefit from the implementation of ABC.

ACTIVITY-BASED MANAGEMENT AND ABC

Although activity-based costing focuses on allocating overhead costs to products based on activities, **activity-based management (ABM)** focuses on managing activities to reduce costs and make better decisions. As mentioned in the previous section, one of the benefits of ABC is that it makes managers more aware of exactly what causes costs to be incurred. For example, the number of different parts and supplies used might drive costs incurred in ordering parts and supplies. This knowledge allows managers to take steps to reduce those costs by redesigning products to use similar or fewer parts.

Key Concept: *Activity-based management focuses on managing activities to reduce costs and to make better decisions.*

IN THE NEWS **http://www.daimlerchrysler.com**

Since implementing ABC in 1991, Chrysler estimates that it has saved hundreds of millions of dollars by simplifying product designs (Ness and Cucuzza, "Tapping the Full Potential of ABC," *Harvard Business Review,* July 1995).

ABM AND THE VALUE CHAIN

LO8
Understand activity-based management (ABM) and the value chain

One of the goals of ABM is to identify and to eliminate activities and costs that don't add value to goods and services. In today's competitive business environment, customers demand high-quality products and services, and organizations that supply these products and services must strive to make sure that each step in the production process adds value to the product or service. The value chain (see Chapter 2) is the term used to describe this linked set of value-creating activities. These activities include everything from research and development to customer service after the sale (see Exhibit 4-2) and include the following:

1. *Research and development.* The creation and development of ideas that lead to new products and services.
2. *Product development.* The detailed development of the research and development ideas that results in new products and services.

COURTESY OF DAIMLER/CHRYSLER

3. *Production.* The use of resources to produce a product or to provide a service.
4. *Marketing.* Providing potential customers with information about the attributes of products or services available that results in customers purchasing the products or services.
5. *Distribution.* The delivery of products or services to customers.
6. *Customer service.* Providing customers with needed support or service during and after the sale.

VALUE-ADDED AND NON-VALUE-ADDED ACTIVITIES

However, not all activities create value. **Non-value-added activities** don't add value to the finished product or service. Non-value-added activities are those that can be eliminated without affecting the quality or performance of a product. Examples of non-value-added activities include storage of materials, work in process and finished goods, moving of materials and parts from storage to the factory in a manufacturing company, idle time of employees while waiting for work, and so on. Likewise, packaging products (unless done for health/safety reasons or to make a product more appealing to a consumer) might be considered a non-value-added activity. Companies that have successfully implemented quality improvement programs resulting in extremely low numbers of defective products may

EXHIBIT 4-2 The Value Chain

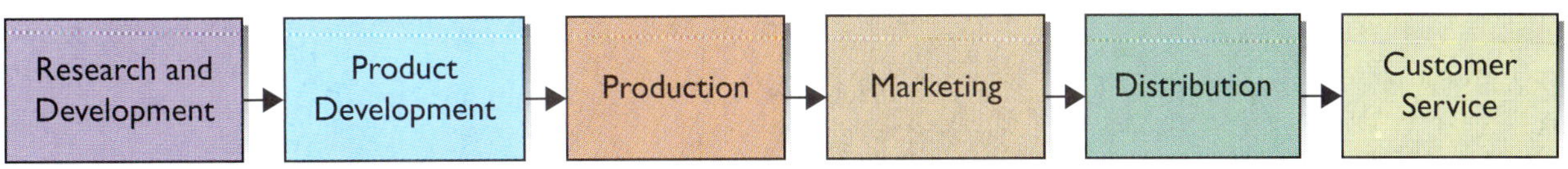

consider quality inspections as a non-value-added activity. These companies would argue that if products are designed correctly and production processes are monitored and controlled effectively, quality of products will be ensured throughout the process. Consequently, inspections of finished products are redundant and don't add value to the product.

PAUSE & Reflect

Can you think of a situation in which you would consider quality inspections to increase the value of a product or a service?

To be competitive, companies must strive to eliminate or to minimize non-value-added activities. Remember that activities cause costs. So reducing or eliminating non-value-added activities would correspondingly reduce costs. The use of JIT production techniques can eliminate (or at least minimize) non-value-added costs associated with inventory storage, product movements, and other activities involved with ordering, receiving, and handling inventory. Likewise, the implementation of total quality management (TQM) programs can significantly reduce non-value-added costs associated with quality inspections, resolving customer complaints owing to defective or poor-quality products and services, recalls, warranties, and so on. TQM is discussed more fully in Chapter 12.

SUCCESSFUL IMPLEMENTATION OF ABC AND ABM

Utilizing activity-based costing information to reduce costs, eliminate non-value-added activities, and manage more effectively requires the cooperation of all functional areas of a business organization and top management.

CROSS-FUNCTIONAL APPLICATIONS

Perhaps nowhere else is cooperation among accountants, marketing managers, production managers, human resource managers, and finance managers more critical than in the implementation of activity-based costing and management systems.

Without active involvement in the process, marketing managers may balk when price changes are thrust upon them, production managers may be hesitant to change a production process used successfully for many years, and human resource managers may criticize the motivational and behavioral implications of suggested changes. Successful implementation also requires a strong commitment from upper management in terms of vocal support, resources provided, and prioritization among the company's other initiatives, such as TQM and JIT.

The full benefits of ABC and ABM require a long-term commitment by management. The benefits of ABC and ABM are simply not realized overnight, and management must be willing to focus on the long-term benefits that are possible through their implementation.

Key Concept: *The successful implementation of ABC and ABM requires a long-term commitment by top management and the cooperation of all functional areas of a business organization.*

MANAGEMENT ACTIONS AND DECISIONS

http://www.accenture.com

COURTESY OF MIKE RIGGINS, ACCENTURE INC.

MIKE RIGGINS
Accenture

According to Mike Riggins, an associate partner with Accenture in its Utilities and Energy Practice Division, companies believe that ABC and ABM give them a competitive advantage in their market space. Companies in the service sector have been embracing ABC/ABM in record numbers over the past decade. This trend is especially true of companies whose industry groups have encountered great changes owing to deregulation (i.e., airlines, telecommunications, utilities, etc.).

In working with various large electric utilities across the United States, Riggins has seen many different levels of ABC/ABM

(continued)

implementations and utilization. Companies that have been the most effective at maximizing their investment in ABC/ABM have usually followed a life cycle that involves three distinct focus areas, as shown in Exhibit 4-3.

ABM is not a "flavor of the month" approach to cost management, and as such it requires lasting lifestyle changes for the organization. Implemented properly, significant benefits (cost reductions as well as revenue enhancements) can be recognized in each phase of the ABM life cycle. Put simply, ABM becomes a way of life for an organization, is ingrained as a part of the organization's day-to-day operations, and becomes a catalyst helping move companies toward continuous improvement and market leadership.

EXHIBIT 4-3 The ABM Life Cycle

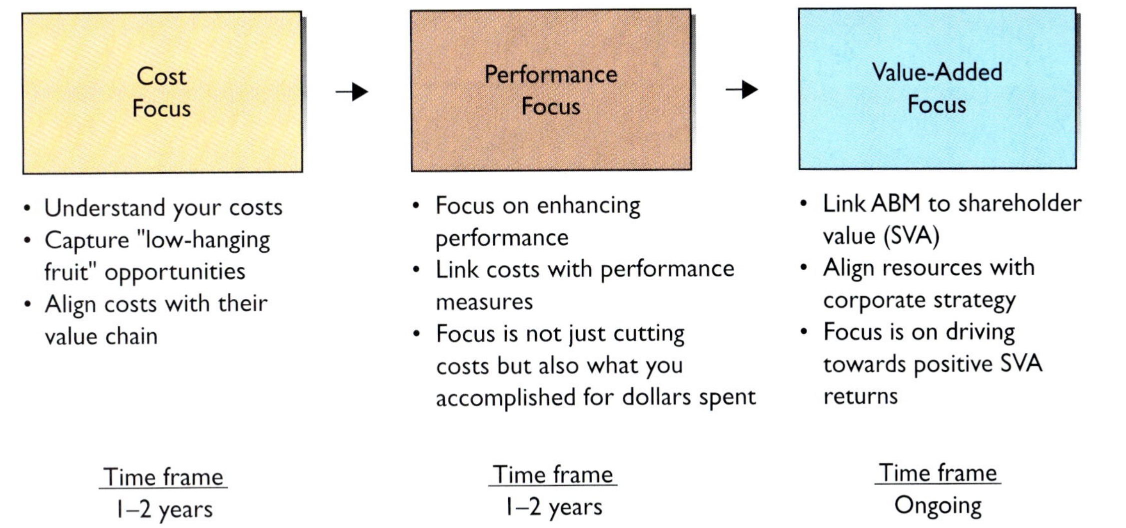

SUMMARY OF KEY CONCEPTS

- Unit-level costs are incurred each time a unit is produced. Batch-level costs are incurred each time a batch of goods is produced. Product-level costs are incurred as needed to support the production of each type of product. Facility-level costs simply sustain a facility's general manufacturing process. (p. 99)
- The key feature of an ABC system is allocating overhead costs based on activities that drive costs rather than on the volume or number of units produced. (p. 99)
- Volume-based costing systems often result in overcosting high-volume products and undercosting low-volume products. This cross subsidy is eliminated by the use of ABC. (p. 107)
- Activity-based management focuses on managing activities to reduce costs and to make better decisions. (p. 110)
- The successful implementation of ABC and ABM requires a long-term commitment by top management and the cooperation of all functional areas of a business organization. (p. 112)

KEY DEFINITIONS

Activity-based costing (ABC) A system of allocating overhead costs that assumes that activities, not volume of production, cause overhead costs to be incurred (p. 99)

Activities Procedures or processes that cause work to be accomplished (p. 99)

Diverse products Products that consume resources in different proportions (p. 109)

Activity-based management (ABM) A system that focuses on managing activities to reduce costs and to make better decisions (p. 110)

Non-value-added activities Activities that can be eliminated without affecting the quality or performance of a product (p. 111)

COMPUTER SIMULATION

You can now turn to **Appendix A** of your text to complete the portion of the Big Al's simulation covering conversion to an activity-based costing (ABC) system.

MULTIPLE CHOICE

1. Which of the following statements comparing traditional and activity-based costing (ABC) systems is true?
   a. Traditional systems are generally more accurate than ABC systems.
   b. ABC systems are generally more accurate than traditional systems.
   c. ABC and traditional systems often produce similar product-cost information.
   d. all of the above

2. Implementing an activity-based costing (ABC) system in a service company:
   a. is exactly the same as implementing an ABC system in a manufacturing company
   b. can be more difficult than implementing an ABC system in a manufacturing company, owing to a general lack of repetitive activities
   c. differs from implementing an ABC system in a manufacturing company because service companies generally have more batch-level costs than do manufacturing companies
   d. is not possible, owing to the nature of service companies

3. Inground Sprinkler Supply sells sprinkler systems suited for large or small yards. The company has decided to adopt an activity-based costing system. Last year, the company incurred $1,000,000 in overhead costs related to the following activities:

Activity	Allocation Base	Overhead Cost
Purchasing	Number of purchase orders	$350,000
Material handling	Number of shipments received	200,000
Quality inspection	Number of inspections	450,000

The activities for large- and small-yard systems were as follows:

	Large	Small
Purchase orders	15,000	20,000
Shipments received	7,500	12,500
Inspections	11,500	11,000

What is the overhead rate for purchasing?
a. $10
b. $20
c. $0.10
d. $0.05

4. The Fancy Drapery Company sells draperies suited for large or small windows. The company has decided to adopt an activity-based costing system. Last year, the company incurred $800,000 in overhead costs related to the following activities:

Activity	Allocation Base	Overhead Cost
Purchasing	Number of purchase orders	$300,000
Receiving	Number of shipments received	200,000
Sales	Number of sales orders	300,000

The activities for large- and small-window draperies were as follows:

	Large	Small
Purchase orders	5,000	10,000
Shipments received	7,500	12,500
Sales orders	6,500	8,500

If a customer requested a bid on a specially designed drapery that would probably require five purchase orders, how much purchasing overhead would you include in the bid?
a. $0
b. $50
c. $100
d. $200

5. Which of the following statements comparing traditional and activity-based costing (ABC) is true?
a. ABC systems eliminate cross subsidies.
b. Traditional systems eliminate cross subsidies.
c. ABC and traditional systems often produce similar product-cost information.
d. all of the above

6. Cross subsidies:
a. occur when high-volume products are assigned less than their fair share of overhead costs
b. occur when high-volume products are assigned more than their fair share of overhead costs
c. occur regularly with both traditional and activity-based costing systems
d. all of the above

7. Activity-based costing (ABC):
a. can be applied to selling and administrative activities
b. cannot be applied to selling and administrative activities, as they are nonmanufacturing costs
c. cannot be applied to service companies
d. can be applied only to manufacturing companies

8. Which of the following statements regarding activity-based costing (ABC) systems in a JIT environment is true?
a. ABC should not be utilized in a JIT environment.
b. ABC can be very successful in a JIT environment because most overhead costs in such a setting are typically facility-level costs.
c. Combining ABC and JIT should result in very accurate product costing.
d. both **b** and **c**

9. Which of the following types of companies would be most likely to benefit from ABC?
   a. companies with a low potential for cost distortions
   b. companies that have a large proportion of unit-level costs
   c. companies that have a relatively high proportion of overhead compared to direct materials and direct labor
   d. all of the above
10. Which of the following statements regarding value-added and non-value-added activities is *false?*
   a. To be competitive, companies must strive to eliminate non-value-added activities.
   b. Companies that have successfully implemented JIT programs are able to minimize controlling non-value-added costs.
   c. Companies that have successfully implemented TQM programs often can significantly reduce non-value-added costs by performing quality inspections.
   d. Non-value-added costs do not add value to the finished product or service.

CONCEPT REVIEW

11. Discuss the impact of robotics on today's manufacturing environment.
12. Is product-cost information absolutely accurate? Why or why not?
13. Discuss the impact of information technology on accounting systems.
14. Discuss the importance of choosing the right cost driver and the potential impact of choosing the wrong cost driver.
15. What are the four categories of overhead costs in Cooper's hierarchy? Briefly define each.
16. Define activity-based costing.
17. Will activity-based costing benefit every business? Why or why not?
18. What are the two stages of cost allocation in an activity-based costing system? Briefly define each.
19. Define the term *activities* as used in activity-based costing systems.
20. What exactly are cross subsidies between products? How can they be controlled?
21. How do activity-based costing systems provide better information for continuous improvement in manufacturing?
22. Discuss the differences in activity-based costing systems for selling and administration activities.
23. Discuss activity-based costing systems in service businesses. How are they different from those used in manufacturing businesses?
24. Why is it important for management to distinguish between value-added and non-value-added activities?
25. Give examples of some common non-value-added activities.
26. The decision process to choose a cost driver can be very important. Use the decision model introduced in Chapter 1 to discuss the process one might go through to choose a cost driver.

APPLICATION OF CONCEPTS

27. The Tip Top Company sells umbrellas suited for large or small picnic tables. The company has decided to adopt an activity-based costing system. Last year, the company incurred $650,000 in overhead costs related to the following activities:

Activity	Allocation Base	Overhead Cost
Purchasing	Number of purchase orders	$250,000
Receiving	Number of shipments received	150,000
Sales	Number of sales orders	250,000

The activities for large and small umbrellas were as follows:

	Large	Small
Purchase orders	5,000	10,000
Shipments received	7,500	12,500
Sales orders	6,500	8,500

Required

A. What is the overhead rate for purchasing?

B. What is the overhead rate for receiving?

C. What is the overhead rate for sales?

D. How much of the purchasing overhead should be assigned to the large umbrellas?

E. How much of the purchasing overhead should be assigned to the small umbrellas?

F. How much of the receiving overhead should be assigned to the large umbrellas?

G. How much of the receiving overhead should be assigned to the small umbrellas?

H. How much of the sales overhead should be assigned to the large umbrellas?

I. How much of the sales overhead should be assigned to the small umbrellas?

J. If a customer requested a bid on a specially designed umbrella that would probably require five purchase orders, how much purchasing overhead would you include in the bid?

28. The Bouncy Baby Crib Mattress Company sells large and small mattresses and is considering the adoption of an activity-based costing system. Last year, the company incurred $800,000 in overhead costs related to the following activities:

Activity	Allocation Base	Overhead Cost
Purchasing	Number of purchase orders	$400,000
Receiving	Number of shipments received	300,000
Sales	Number of sales orders	100,000

During the year, 15,000 purchase orders were issued (7,500 each for large and small mattresses), 20,000 shipments were received (12,500 for large and 7,500 for small), and 25,000 sales orders (15,000 for large and 10,000 for small) were processed.

Required

Determine the amount of overhead that should be assigned to each product, using activity-based costing.

29. The following overhead cost information is available for the Christopher Corporation for the year ended June 30, 2002:

Activity	Allocation Base	Overhead Cost
Purchasing	Number of purchase orders	$400,000
Receiving	Number of shipments received	100,000
Machine setups	Number of setups	400,000
Quality control	Number of inspections	150,000

During the year, 30,000 purchase orders were issued, 25,000 shipments were received, machine setups numbered 2,700, and 22,000 inspections were conducted. A total of 11,000 direct labor hours were charged to various products. The corporate managers are trying to decide whether they should stick with a traditional allocation method, with overhead allocated based upon direct labor hours, or switch to an activity-based costing system.

Required

A. Determine the overhead rate based upon direct labor hours.

B. Determine the overhead rate for each of the activities.

C. A job card for one particular batch of products had the following specifications:

Direct labor hours	7
Purchase orders	7
Shipments received	10
Setups	3
Inspections	3

Compute the estimated overhead allocated to this batch under traditional allocation and activity-based costing.

D. Are there any differences in your two answers from C? If so, why? Which method do you think is better? Why?

30. The following cost information is available for the Brenda and Steve Corporation for the year ended June 30, 2004:

Activity	Allocation Base	Overhead Cost
Purchasing	Number of purchase orders	$125,000
Receiving	Number of shipments received	60,000
Machine setups	Number of setups	200,000
Quality control	Number of inspections	105,000
Direct material	$15 per unit for deluxe items; $11 per unit for regular items	
Direct labor	$18 per hour (including benefits)	

During the year, 30,000 purchase orders were issued, 20,000 shipments were received, machine setups numbered 2,500 and 25,000 inspections were conducted. 11,500 direct labor hours were charged to various products.

Required

A. The corporate managers are trying to decide whether they should stick with a traditional allocation method, where overhead is allocated based upon direct labor hours, or switch to an activity based costing system. Determine the overhead rate based upon direct labor hours and the overhead rate for each of the activities.

B. A job card for one particular batch of 100 deluxe units had the following specifications:

Direct labor hours	7
Purchase orders	7
Shipments received	10
Setups	3
Inspections	3

Compute the estimated overhead allocated to this batch under traditional allocation and activity-based costing.

C. Which costing method do you think is better? Why?

31. The following cost information is available for the Brenda and Steve Corporation for the year ended June 30, 2004:

Activity	Allocation Base	Overhead Cost
Purchasing	Number of purchase orders	$150,000
Receiving	Number of shipments received	50,000
Machine setups	Number of setups	250,000
Quality control	Number of inspections	125,000
Direct material	$14 per unit for deluxe items; $10 per unit for regular items	
Direct labor	$20 per hour (including benefits)	

During the year, 30,000 purchase orders were issued, 20,000 shipments were received, machine setups numbered 2,500, and 25,000 inspections were conducted.

Required

A customer has contacted Brenda and Steve Corporation, requesting comparative bids for an order of 100 deluxe units and 100 regular units. Brenda and Steve estimate the following activities related to the bids:

	Regular	Deluxe
Direct labor hours	7	10
Purchase orders	7	7
Shipments received	10	10
Setups	3	4
Inspections	3	4

Compute the bids for deluxe and regular units.

32. Surfs Up manufactures surfboards. The company produces two models of boards: the small kahuna and the big kahuna. Data regarding the two products follow:

Product	Direct Labor Hours per Unit	Annual Production	Total Direct Labor Hours
Big	1.875	8,000 boards	15,000
Small	0.875	40,000 boards	35,000

The big board requires $75 in direct materials per unit, whereas the small board requires $40. The direct labor rate for the company is $13 per hour. The company has always used direct labor hours as the activity base for applying overhead to product. Manufacturing overhead is estimated to be $1,575,000 per year. The big board is more complex to manufacture than the small board because it requires more machine time.

Because of the big board's requirement for the additional machine work, the company controller, Tim Guglielmo, is considering the use of activity-based costing to apply overhead to product. Tim has identified four separate activity centers in the manufacture of the boards.

			Annual Transactions		
Activity Center	Cost Driver	Traceable Costs	Big	Small	Total
Machine setups	Number of setups	$100,000	100	125	225
Special design	Design hours	225,000	900	100	1,000
Production	Direct labor hours	900,000	15,000	35,000	50,000
Machining	Machine hours	350,000	10,000	1,000	11,000

Required

Assume that Surfs Up continues to use direct labor hours as the base for applying overhead cost to product.

A. Compute the predetermined overhead rate.

B. Determine the cost to produce one unit of each product.

Assume that the company decides to use activity-based costing to apply overhead cost to product.

C. Classify the activity centers into the four levels defined by Cooper: unit, batch, products, and facility.

D. Compute the overhead rate for each activity center. Also compute the amount of overhead cost that would be applied to each product.

E. Determine the cost to produce one unit of each product.

F. Explain why overhead cost shifted from the high-volume product to the low-volume product under activity-based costing.

G. Discuss the concept of cross subsidies between products as it applies in this case.

33. David Hall Inc. manufactures plastic and ceramic outdoor eating dishes. The company's western plant has changed from a labor-intensive operation to a robotics environment. As a result, management is considering changing from a direct-labor-based overhead rate to an activity-based costing system. The controller has chosen the following activity cost pools and cost drivers for factory overhead:

Overhead Cost		Cost Driver	Number
Purchase orders	$200,000	Number of orders	25,000
Setup costs	300,000	Number of setups	15,000
Testing costs	420,000	Number of tests	18,000
Machine maintenance	800,000	Machine hours	50,000

Required

A. Compute the overhead rate for each cost driver.

B. An order for 50 ceramic dish sets had the following requirements:

Number of purchase orders	3
Number of setups	20
Number of product tests	7
Machine hours	150

How much overhead would be assigned to this order?

C. Would you expect the new ABC system to allocate a different amount of overhead per set?

D. Discuss why using an ABC system could provide better information to decision makers regarding the setting of a sales price. What other advantages might David Hall Inc. realize from the new ABC system?

34. Tom Hall Inc. manufactures sailboats and has two major categories of overhead: material handling and quality inspection. The costs expected for these categories for the coming year are as follows:

Material handling	$100,000
Quality inspection	$300,000
Total number of material moves	500
Total number of inspections	200

The plant currently applies overhead using direct labor hours as an activity base. The estimated amount of direct labor hours is 50,000.

Chris Hamilton, the plant manager, has been asked to submit a bid and has assembled the following data on the proposed job:

Direct materials	$3,700
Direct labor (1,000 hours)	$7,000
Overhead	?
Number of material moves	10
Number of inspections	5

Chris has been told that many similar companies use an activity-based approach to assign overhead to jobs. Before submitting a bid, Chris wants to assess the effects of this alternative approach.

Required

A. Compute the total cost of the potential job using traditional overhead application (i.e., direct labor hours to assign overhead).

B. Compute the total cost of the job using activity-based costing with the new cost drivers to allocate overhead (i.e., the number of material moves to allocate material handling costs and the number of inspections to allocate the quality inspection costs).

C. Discuss the difference and what impact the change might have on the decision regarding the bid price.

D. Using the decision model presented in Chapter 1, complete the following tasks:

(1) Define the decision problem Chris faces.

(2) Identify the key objectives in the decision problem.

(3) Identify the different options that Chris has in solving this decision problem.

Step 1 DEFINE THE PROBLEM

Step 2 IDENTIFY OBJECTIVES

Step 3 IDENTIFY AND ANALYZE AVAILABLE OPTIONS

35. Jon Haufe Inc. manufactures TVs that are specifically designed for use in sports bars. The company has budgeted manufacturing overhead costs for the year as follows:

Type of Cost	Cost Pools
Electric power	$2,500,000
Inspection	1,500,000
Budgeted overhead costs	4,000,000

Under a traditional cost system, the company estimated the budgeted capacity for machine hours to be 40,000 hours. Jon Haufe Inc. is considering changing to an activity-based cost system. Thus, the following estimates were provided:

Type of Cost	Activity-Based Cost Drivers
Electric power	50,000 kilowatt hours
Inspection	10,000 inspections

The following information was provided concerning the production of 2,000 units of model #1003:

Direct materials cost	$50,000
Direct labor costs	$75,000
Machine hours	10,000
Direct labor hours	5,000
Electric power—kilowatt hours	20,000
Number of inspections	1,000

The accounting department has provided management with the following report:

Traditional Costing System

Overhead rate per machine hour	$ 100
Manufacturing costs for 2,000 units of #1003:	
Direct materials	50,000
Direct labor	75,000
Applied overhead	1,000,000
Total	$1,125,000
Cost per unit	562.50

Activity-Based Costing System

Electric power overhead rate	$50/kilowatt hour
Inspection cost overhead rate	$150/per inspection
Manufacturing costs for 2,000 units of #1003:	
Direct materials	$ 50,000
Direct labor	75,000
Applied overhead	1,150,000
Total	$1,275,000
Cost per unit	637.50

Required

A. Explain the difference between activity-based costing and conventional costing methods and how ABC might enhance the financial reporting of Jon Haufe Inc.

B. If Jon Haufe Inc. were setting a sales price based on a 20 percent markup, how would profit be affected if the company *did not* change to an ABC system?

36. Grandma's Rocking Chair Company produces 1,000 units of Rocking Chair A and 1,000 units of Rocking Chair B. Currently, the company uses a traditional cost system, but it is considering an activity-based cost system. It wants to know what the cost of inspection would be for both products, assuming the following:

	Product A	**Product B**	**Total**
Number of inspections	2	10	12
Cost per inspection	$1,000	$1,000	$12,000
Direct labor hours per unit	3,000	2,000	5,000

Required

A. Under traditional costing, how much of the $12,000 inspection cost would be allocated to Product A and Product B, respectively?

B. Using activity-based costing, how much of the $12,000 inspection cost would be allocated to Product A and Product B, respectively?

C. Discuss what caused the difference. Would this difference affect management decisions? How? What method is more accurate? Why?

37. Worth Hawes Manufacturing has just completed a major change in its quality control (QC) process. Previously, QC inspectors had reviewed products at the end of each major process, and the company's 10 QC inspectors were charged as direct labor to the operation or job. In an effort to improve efficiency and quality, Worth Hawes Manufacturing purchased a computer video QC system for $250,000. The system consists of a minicomputer, 15 video cameras, other peripheral hardware, and software.

The new system uses cameras stationed by QC engineers at key points in the production process. Each time an operation changes or there is a new operation, the cameras are moved, and a QC engineer loads a new master picture into the computer. The camera takes pictures of the unit in process, and the computer compares them to the picture of a "good" unit. Any differences are sent to a QC engineer, who removes the bad units and discusses the flaws with the production supervisors. The new system has replaced the 10 QC inspectors with 2 QC engineers.

The operating costs of the new QC system, including the salaries of the QC engineers, have been included as overhead in calculating the company's plantwide factory overhead rate, which is based on direct labor dollars.

The company's president is confused. The vice president of production has said how efficient the new system is, yet there is a large increase in the factory overhead rate. The computation of the rate before and after is as follows:

	Before	After
Budgeted overhead	$1,900,000	$2,100,000
Budgeted direct labor	$1,000,000	$ 700,000
Budgeted overhead rate	190%	300%

"Three hundred percent," lamented the president. "How can we compete with such a high factory overhead rate?"

Required

A. Discuss the development of factory overhead rates. Why do we need factory overhead rates, and how are they computed? Discuss the accuracy of the computation of a factory overhead rate.

B. Explain why the increase in the overhead rate should not have a negative impact on Worth Hawes Manufacturing.

C. Explain, in the greatest detail possible, how Worth Hawes Manufacturing could change its overhead accounting system to eliminate confusion over product costs.

D. Discuss how an activity-based costing system might benefit Worth Hawes Manufacturing.

E. Use the decision model presented in Chapter 1 to answer the following questions.

(1) Present a description of the decision problem facing the company in choosing a new costing system.

(2) What are the key objectives involved in the decision problem as defined here?

(3) What option does the company have in this decision problem?

Step 1 DEFINE THE PROBLEM

Step 2 IDENTIFY OBJECTIVES

Step 3 IDENTIFY AND ANALYZE AVAILABLE OPTIONS

38. The Teresa Heine Company manufactures multimedia equipment designed to be sold to universities. The company's southeastern plant has changed from a labor-intensive operation to a robotics environment. As a result, management is considering changing from a direct labor–based overhead rate to an activity-based cost method. The controller has chosen the following activity cost pools and cost drivers for the factory overhead:

	Overhead Cost	Cost Driver	Annual Cost Driver
Purchase orders	$200,000	Number of orders	10,000
Setup costs	25,000	Number of setups	5,000
Testing costs	48,000	Number of tests	6,000
Machine maintenance	350,000	Machine hours	10,000

Required

A. Compute the overhead rate for each cost driver.

B. An order for 1,000 video projectors had the following requirements:

Number of purchase orders	3
Number of setups	5
Number of product tests	20
Machine hours	1,500

How much overhead would be assigned to this order?

C. What could management do to reduce the overhead costs assigned to these video projectors? What would be the impact on company net income of reducing overhead assigned to the video projectors?

D. Use the decision model presented in Chapter 1 to answer the following questions:

(1) Define the decision problem faced by Teresa Heine Company in C.

(2) What are the company's key objectives in solving this decision problem?

Step 1 DEFINE THE PROBLEM

Step 2 IDENTIFY OBJECTIVES

Step 3 IDENTIFY AND ANALYZE AVAILABLE OPTIONS

Step 4 SELECT THE BEST OPTION

(3) What options are available to the company in solving this decision problem?

(4) What options do you think are best and why?

39. The law firm of Duffy and Rowe provides legal services for clients. During the year, corporate clients required 5,000 hours of legal services, whereas individuals required 3,000 hours. The firm has traditionally used direct labor hours to assign overhead. However, Duffy believes that services to businesses cost more than services to individuals and wishes to adopt activity-based costing. The firm's revenues and costs for the year are as follows:

	Corporate	Individual	Total
Revenue	$150,000	$150,000	$300,000
Expenses			
Lawyers' salaries	100,000	50,000	150,000
Overhead			
Filing	$ 10,000		
Quality control	5,000		
Data entry	25,000		
Total overhead	$ 40,000		

Rowe has kept records of the following data for use in the new activity-based costing system:

		ACTIVITY LEVEL	
Overhead Cost	**Cost Driver**	**Corporate**	**Individual**
Filing	Number of clients	5	5
Quality control	Number of hours spent	75	25
Data entry	Number of pages entered	1,000	1,500

Accounting has prepared the following pro forma income statements:

Income Statement Using Traditional Costing

	Corporate	Individual	Total
Revenue	$150,000	$150,000	$300,000
Expenses			
Salaries	100,000	50,000	150,000
Overhead	25,000	15,000	40,000
Total costs	$125,000	$ 65,000	$190,000
Operating profit	25,000	85,000	110,000

Income Statement Using Activity-Based Costing

	Corporate	Individual	Total
Revenue	$150,000	$150,000	$300,000
Expenses			
Salaries	100,000	50,000	150,000
Overhead			
Filing			
($1,000 × 5)	5,000	5,000	10,000
Quality costs			
$50 × 75	3,750		
$50 × 25		1,250	

Data entry			
($10 × 1,000)	10,000		
($10 × 1,500)		15,000	
Total overhead	$ 18,750	$ 21,250	$ 40,000
Total costs	118,750	71,250	190,000
Profit	$ 31,250	$ 78,750	$110,000

Required

Recalculate the computation of overhead in the two income statements. Include the calculation of the individual overhead rates. Discuss the best way to allocate costs in this example, and include the approximate difference in profits between corporate and individual clients. Why would activity-based costing be preferred as a cost allocation method?

40. Baron and Griffin CPAs is a full-service CPA firm that provides accounting, tax, and consulting services to its clients. The firm is considering changing to an activity-based costing system and has asked for your input regarding the design of the system. The firm has identified certain activities that are integral to the practice and would like your suggestions regarding potential cost drivers. The following list of activities and potential cost drivers should be matched. You may not need to use all cost drivers and could use some more than once.

Activity	**Cost Driver**
a. Client interview	a. Professional staff hours
b. Tax return preparation	b. Transactions
c. Tax return review	c. Number of pages
d. Data input	d. Number of employees
e. Report assembly	e. Machine hours
f. Research	f. Clerical staff hours
g. Report writing	
h. Site visits	

41. The University of Tennessee has asked you to help with an activity-based costing system for the admissions office. Identify the most likely cost driver for each activity listed.

Activity	**Cost Driver**
a. Receiving applications	a. number of students
b. Processing applications	b. number of acceptances
c. Receiving student inquiries	c. number of applications
d. Responding to student inquiries	d. labor hours
e. Accepting students	e. number of inquiries
f. Enrolling students	

42. Bob Figgins is the manager of Prather Industries, which provides services to both state government agencies and private organizations. Both types of contracts are awarded on the basis of competitive bids. The government agencies require that the cost of the services be calculated using a specific methodology. In the past, Prather has used this methodology for costing both government and private contracts. Bob's contracts with government agencies provide for reimbursement of costs plus a predetermined markup of 30 percent. Bob's contracts with private organizations are based on negotiated fees and are not directly a function of the estimated costs of the service. The relative profitability of the two types of contracts, based on average-cost information, is as follows:

Costs and Revenues	Government Contract	Private Contract	Total
Costs	$20,000	$20,000	$40,000
Cost + 30%	26,000		
Negotiated fee		30,000	
Profit	$ 6,000	$10,000	$16,000

Bob's recently completed ABC analysis shows that government contracts are much less costly than estimated previously and that the private contracts are more costly. If Bob uses the ABC analysis for contracting and does not renegotiate the fee for the private contract, overall profitability will decrease. Bob would like to use the old method to cost (and price) the government contracts and to use the ABC information to renegotiate the fee for the private contracts. Is this strategy ethical?

Costs and Revenues	Government Contract	Private Contract	Total
ABC costs	$10,000	$30,000	$40,000
Cost + 30%	13,000		
Negotiated fee		30,000	
Profit	$ 3,000	$ 0	$ 3,000

43. Tennessee Welding and Supply's controller, Tina Bynum, developed new-product costs for the standard-, deluxe-, and heavy-duty-model welders using activity-based costing. It was apparent that the firm's traditional product-costing system had been undercosting the deluxe-model welder by a significant amount, largely because of its low volume. Before she could report back to the president, Bynum received a phone call from her friend, Sheryl Breeden, the production manager for the deluxe-model welder. Breeden was upset and let Bynum know it. "Tina, I've seen your new cost analysis report. There's no way the deluxe model costs anywhere near what your numbers say. For years and years, this line has been highly profitable, and its reported product cost was low. Now you're telling us it costs more than twice what we thought. I just don't buy it." Bynum briefly explained to her friend about activity-based costing and why it resulted in more accurate product costs. "Sheryl, the deluxe model is really losing money. It simply has too low a volume to be manufactured efficiently." Breeden was even more upset now. "Tina, if you report these new product costs to the president, he's going to discontinue the deluxe model. My job's on the line, Tina! How about massaging those numbers a little bit. Who's going to know?" "I'll know, Sheryl. And you'll know," responded Bynum. "Look, I'll go over my analysis again to make sure I haven't made an error."

Required

A. Is the controller, Tina Bynum, acting ethically?

B. Is the production manager, Sheryl Breeden, acting ethically?

C. What are Bynum's ethical obligations? To the president? To her friend?

44. Is activity-based costing likely to be advantageous in a company that utilizes just-in-time inventory management techniques?

45. What characteristics of JIT companies may make activity-based costing particularly useful?

46. Pritchett Enterprises manufactures multimedia equipment designed to be sold to theaters. The company's plant in west Tennessee has recently changed from a labor-intensive operation to a robotics environment. As a result, management changed the cost-accounting system to an activity-based costing system. The system has the following activities and cost drivers for factory overhead:

Activity	Overhead Cost Pool	Cost Driver	Cost Driver Volume
Purchase orders	$200,000	Number of orders	10,000
Receiving orders	25,000	Number of orders	10,000
Setup costs	25,000	Number of setups	5,000
Testing costs	48,000	Number of tests	6,000
Machine maintenance	350,000	Machine hours	10,000

The company has now decided to use just-in-time inventory management. Using JIT will reduce the amount of inventory on hand at any time and save $50,000 annually on inventory storage costs. It will also result in 70 percent fewer purchase orders for inventory but twice as many setups for production runs. The company will also be able to receive a 2 percent discount on raw material purchased, because of the long-term nature of the orders.

Required

A. If raw material purchases are $1,000,000 per year, what quantitative impact will the change to JIT have on the overall costs for the company?

B. What qualitative factors will be impacted by the change to JIT?

C. Does it appear that the move to JIT will be positive or negative for the company? Why or why not?

47. ABC Technologies is a consulting and software company specializing in activity-based costing and activity-based management. Access the Web site at http://www.abctech.com and look under "success stories." You will find four categories: (1) process manufacturing, (2) discrete manufacturing, (3) services, and (4) public sector. Choose one or more of these categories and write a short report about at least four of the organizations featured and why ABC or ABM benefited the organization.

Part II

The Nature of Costs in Decision Making

Chapter 5

THE NATURE OF COSTS

Study Tools

A Review of the Previous Chapter

Chapter 4 completed the first part of the book, dealing with the costing of products and services. Up to this point, we have focused our attention on methods used to cost products and services, the difficulties that arise in product costing, and the decisions managers face in reacting to those difficulties.

A Preview of This Chapter

In this chapter, we examine the nature of costs. We introduce the concepts of cost behavior, relevant costs, and the impact of income taxes and the time value of money on costs and decision making.

Key concepts include:

- Costs behave in predictable ways.
- Within the relevant range, fixed costs are constant in total and vary per unit, variable costs vary in total and are constant per unit, and mixed costs vary in total and vary per unit.
- It can be misleading to always view variable costs as relevant and fixed costs as not relevant.
- Managers must consider the impact of taxes on decisions.
- Managers must consider the time value of money when making long-term decisions.

A Preview of Upcoming Chapters

In Chapter 6, the concept of cost behavior is developed further, and a variety of tools (contribution margin ratio, operating leverage, break-even) used in CVP analysis are introduced. Chapter 7 extends the discussion of relevant costs and examines a number of decisions made by managers in their day-to-day activities. Chapter 8 examines the use of time value of money tools in long-term (capital budgeting) decisions.

LEARNING OBJECTIVES

After studying the material in this chapter, you should be able to:

LO1 Understand the nature and behavior of fixed, variable, and mixed costs

LO2 Analyze mixed costs using regression analysis and the high/low method

LO3 Understand the concept of relevant costs and apply the concept to decision making

LO4 Understand the impact of income taxes on costs and decision making

LO5 Understand the time value of money and its impact on costs and decision making

Understanding the nature of costs is of vital importance to managers. Understanding how costs behave, whether costs are relevant to specific decisions, how costs are affected by income taxes, and how to adjust costs incurred in different periods for the time value of money allows managers to determine the impact of changing costs and other factors on a variety of decisions. This chapter introduces concepts and tools that will be used in Chapters 6 through 8. Chapter 5 begins with a definition of cost behavior and illustrates the concepts of fixed costs, variable costs, and mixed costs. Next, the chapter revisits the concept of relevant costs (introduced in Chapter 1) as they apply to variable and fixed costs. The chapter also describes the impact of income taxes on costs and examines the effect of the time value of money on costs incurred in different time periods. ■

INTRODUCTION

In Part I, we defined and determined the cost of a product or a service. We now focus our attention on the nature of those costs and how they are used in decision making. As production volume changes, some costs may increase or decrease and other costs may remain stable, but specific costs behave in predictable ways as volume changes. This concept of predictable **cost behavior** based on volume is very important to the effective use of accounting information for managerial decision making.

Key Concept: *Costs behave in predictable ways.*

THE BEHAVIOR OF FIXED AND VARIABLE COSTS

LO1
Understand the nature and behavior of fixed, variable, and mixed costs

Fixed costs are costs that remain the same in total but vary per unit when production volume changes. Facility-level costs, such as rent, depreciation of a factory building, the salary of a plant manager, insurance, and property taxes, are likely to be fixed costs. Summarizing this cost behavior, fixed costs stay the same in total but vary when expressed on a per unit basis.

Rent is a good example. If the cost to rent a factory building is $10,000 per year and 5,000 units of product are produced, the rent per unit is $2.00 ($10,000/5,000). If production volume decreases to 2,500 units per year, the cost per unit will increase to $4.00 ($10,000/2,500). If production volume increases to 7,500 units, the cost per unit decreases to $1.33 ($10,000/7,500) per unit. However, the total rent remains $10,000 per year.

On the other hand, **variable costs** vary in direct proportion to changes in production volume but are fixed when expressed as per unit amounts. As production increases, variable costs increase in direct proportion to the change in volume; as production decreases, variable costs decrease in direct proportion to the change in volume. Examples include

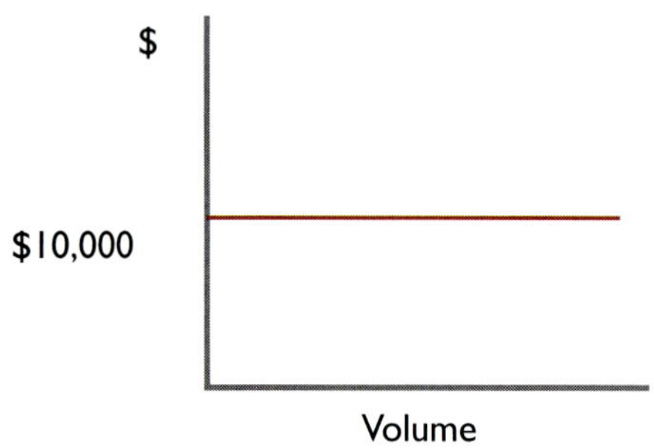

Fixed Cost in Total

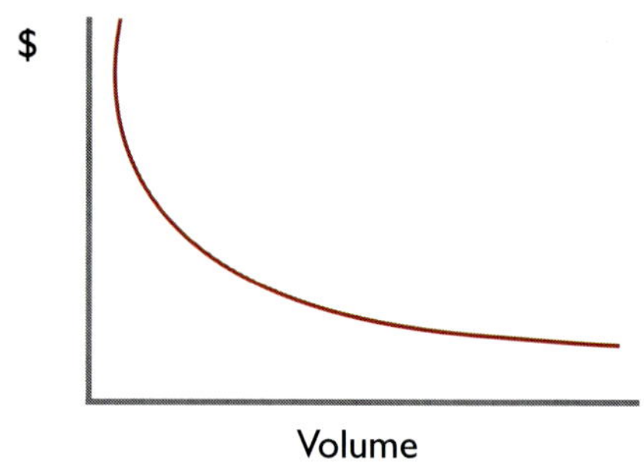

Fixed Cost per Unit

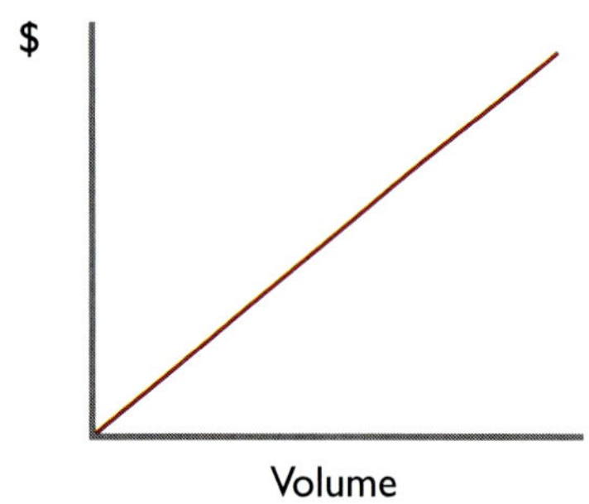

Variable Cost in Total

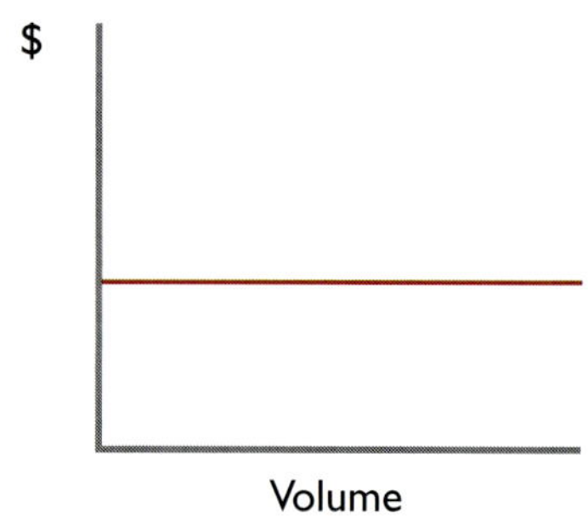

Variable Cost per Unit

direct material, direct labor (if paid per unit of output), and other unit-level costs, such as factory supplies, energy costs to run factory machinery, and so on.

Strictly speaking, a cost that varies in direct proportion to changes in volume requires a linear (straight-line) relationship between the cost and volume. However, in reality costs may behave in a curvilinear fashion. Average costs or cost per unit may increase or decrease as production increases. For example, utility costs per kilowatt-hour may decrease at higher levels of electricity use (and production). Managerial accountants typically get around this problem by assuming that the relationship between the cost and volume is linear within the relevant range of production. In other words, the cost per unit is assumed to remain constant over the relevant range. The **relevant range** is the normal range of production that can be expected for a particular product and company. The relevant range can also be viewed as the volume of production for which the fixed and variable cost relationship holds true. As you can see in Exhibit 5-1, within this narrower range of production, a curvilinear cost can be approximated by a linear relationship between the cost and volume.

APPLICATION IN BUSINESS

Although direct labor is often treated as a variable cost, in reality it may behave more like a fixed cost in many companies, owing to the negotiation of employment contracts with unions. For example, airlines may agree to employment contracts that guarantee a minimum number of hours each week for pilots and flight attendants. This means that even if they are not working (flying), the costs are still there. If they were paid only for actual hours worked and not guaranteed a minimum salary, the cost would be considered a variable cost.

© NAJLAH FEANNY/STOCK, BOSTON

Consider the behavior of direct material costs as production increases and decreases. If the manufacture of a standard classroom desk requires $20 of direct material (wood, hardware, etc.), the total direct material costs incurred will increase or decrease proportionately with increases and decreases in production volume. If 5,000 desks are produced, the total direct material cost will be $100,000 (5,000 × $20). If production volume is increased to 7,500 units (a 50 percent increase), direct material costs will also increase 50

EXHIBIT 5-1 Curvilinear Costs and the Relevant Range

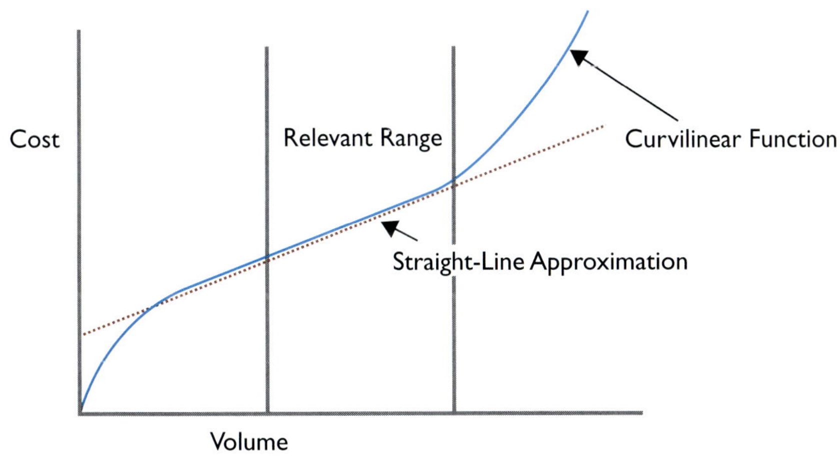

percent to \$150,000 (7,500 × \$20). However the cost per unit is still \$20. Likewise, if production volume is decreased to 2,500 desks, direct material costs will decrease by 50 percent to \$50,000. But once again, the cost per unit remains \$20.

A graphical representation of fixed and variable costs is presented in Exhibit 5-2. Note that rent remains \$10,000 per year regardless of the level of production and that variable costs vary in total as production increases. Also note that variable costs can be represented by a straight line starting at the origin and continuing through each data point and that total variable costs are zero when production is equal to zero.

THE COST EQUATION

Expressing the link between costs and production volume as an algebraic equation is useful. The equation for a straight line is:

$$Y = a + bx$$

The *a* in the equation is the point where the line intersects the vertical (*y*) axis and *b* is the slope of the line. In Exhibit 5-2, if y = total direct material costs and x = units produced, $y = \$0 + \$20x$. The *y* intercept is zero and the slope of the line is \$20. For every one unit increase (decrease) in production (x), direct material costs increase (decrease) by \$20. You can see that direct material costs are variable because they stay the same on a per unit basis but increase in total as production increases. Likewise, we can express the fixed-cost line as an equation. If y = rent cost and x = units produced, $y = \$10,000 + \$0x$. In this case, the *y* intercept is \$10,000 and the slope is zero. In other words, fixed costs are \$10,000 at any level of production within the relevant range.

EXHIBIT 5-2 Fixed and Variable Costs

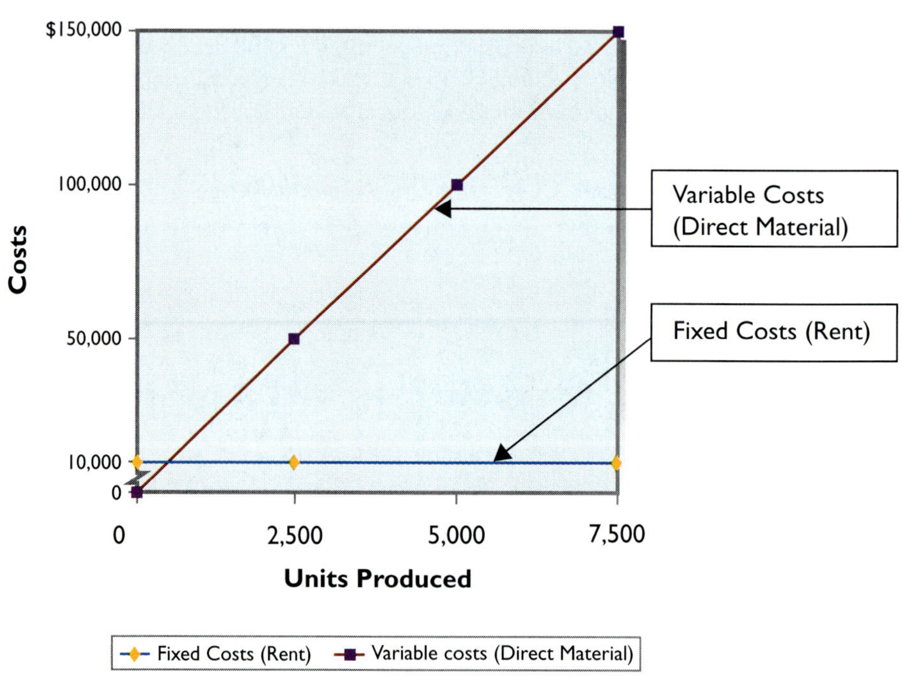

COST BEHAVIOR AND DECISION MAKING

Understanding how costs behave is vitally important when making production decisions, preparing budgets, and so on. To further explore this, let's consider Big Al's Pizza. After operating for one month, the owner of Big Al's Pizza Emporium asked his accountant how much it cost to make 2,100 pizzas last month. Big Al's incurred $4,200 for direct materials (pizza dough, cheese, and other ingredients), $3,150 for direct labor, and $8,400 for overhead (rent, utilities, insurance, depreciation of pizza ovens, supervisor salary, etc.). As shown in the following table, Al calculated the cost of a pizza (the cost of goods sold) as $7.50 ($15,750 total costs/2,100 pizzas).

Cost	Amount	Per Unit
Direct materials	$ 4,200	$2.00
Direct labor	3,150	1.50
Overhead	8,400	4.00
Total	$15,750	$7.50

He then estimated that because production was expected to increase to 2,600 pizzas next month, his total cost of goods sold should be $19,500 (2,600 pizzas × $7.50 each).

Concept Question: *Do you agree with Al's calculation of cost of goods sold? Why or why not?*

Concept Answer: It depends! Although Al did calculate the cost of 2,100 pizzas to be $7.50, this per unit amount is going to change as the volume of pizzas changes if any of the costs of making pizzas are fixed. Remember, fixed costs stay constant in total but vary on a per unit basis. ■

Concept Question: *Assume that direct materials and direct labor are variable costs and that $6,300 of overhead is fixed. The remainder of the overhead cost is a variable utility cost of $1.00 per pizza. With this new information, how much total costs should Al expect to incur next month if 2,600 pizzas are produced?*

Concept Answer: As you can see in the following table, the total cost of making 2,600 pizzas is expected to be $18,000, or $6.92 per pizza. The cost per pizza has decreased from $7.50 to $6.92 as production volume increased from 2,100 to 2,600 pizzas. ■

Cost	Amount		Per Unit
Direct materials	$ 5,200	($2 × 2,600)	$2.00
Direct labor	3,900	($1.50 × 2,600)	1.50
Variable overhead	2,600	($1 × 2,600)	1.00
Fixed overhead	6,300		2.42
Total	$18,000		$6.92

Although the traditional income statement introduced in Chapter 2 is good at separating product and period costs, it commingles fixed and variable costs. Therefore, cost of goods sold consists of both fixed and variable costs and will differ at different levels of production. Even though the traditional income statement's focus on cost of goods sold and gross margin is useful for external reporting purposes, an income statement focusing on

> **APPLICATION IN BUSINESS**
>
> A trend in manufacturing today is to automate, or to replace direct factory labor with robotics and other automated machinery. This trend has the effect of increasing fixed costs (depreciation) and decreasing variable costs (direct labor). Even without automation, labor costs in many industries behave more like fixed costs than variable costs. Companies may be reluctant to lay off highly skilled workers for a short period of time, and labor unions are increasingly successful in negotiating long-term contracts for their members, making it difficult to adjust workforce size as sales (and production) increase or decrease.

cost behavior is more useful for internal decision making. A contribution margin-based income statement focusing on cost behavior is discussed more fully in Chapter 6.

Although there are many advantages to automation and a stable workforce, the impact of increasing fixed costs on the day-to-day decisions made by managers must not be ignored. The impact of cost structure on decision making is discussed in more detail in Chapter 6.

STEP COSTS

BIG AL'S

Classification of costs is not always a simple process. Some costs vary but only with relatively large changes in production. Batch-level costs related to moving materials may vary with the number of batches of product produced but not with every unit of product. Product-level costs associated with quality control inspections may vary when new products are introduced. Costs like these are sometimes referred to as **step costs.** In practice, step costs may look like and be treated as either variable costs or fixed costs. Although step costs are technically not fixed costs, they may be treated as such if they remain constant within a relevant range of production. Consider the costs of janitorial services within a company. As long as production is below 7,500 desks, the company will hire one janitor with salary and fringe benefits totaling $25,000. The cost is fixed as long as production remains below 7,500 units. However, if desk production exceeds 7,500, which increases the amount of waste and cleanup needed, it may be necessary to hire a second janitor at a cost of another $25,000. However, within a relevant range of production between 7,501 and 15,000 units, the cost is essentially fixed ($50,000). A graphical representation of a step (fixed) cost is shown in Exhibit 5-3.

Step costs may look like variable costs in other cases in which the steps are relatively small. Consider the cost of electricity used in baking pizzas at Big Al's Pizza Emporium. Al generally bakes five pizzas at a time in one of two pizza ovens. The electricity costs of the oven are the same whether one pizza or five pizzas are being cooked. Technically, the costs vary with batches of five pizzas. However, within a relevant range of production, the costs per pizza are likely to be stable (a variable cost).

MIXED COSTS

LO2
Analyze mixed costs using regression analysis and the high/low method

Mixed costs present a unique challenge because they include both a fixed and a variable component. Consequently, it is difficult to predict the behavior of a mixed cost as production changes unless the cost is first separated into its fixed and variable components. A good example of a mixed cost is the cost of a delivery vehicle for Big Al's Pizza Emporium. Let's assume that Al enters into a lease agreement that calls for a lease payment of $400 per month for a new delivery van. Every month, Al is required to make

EXHIBIT 5-3 Step Costs

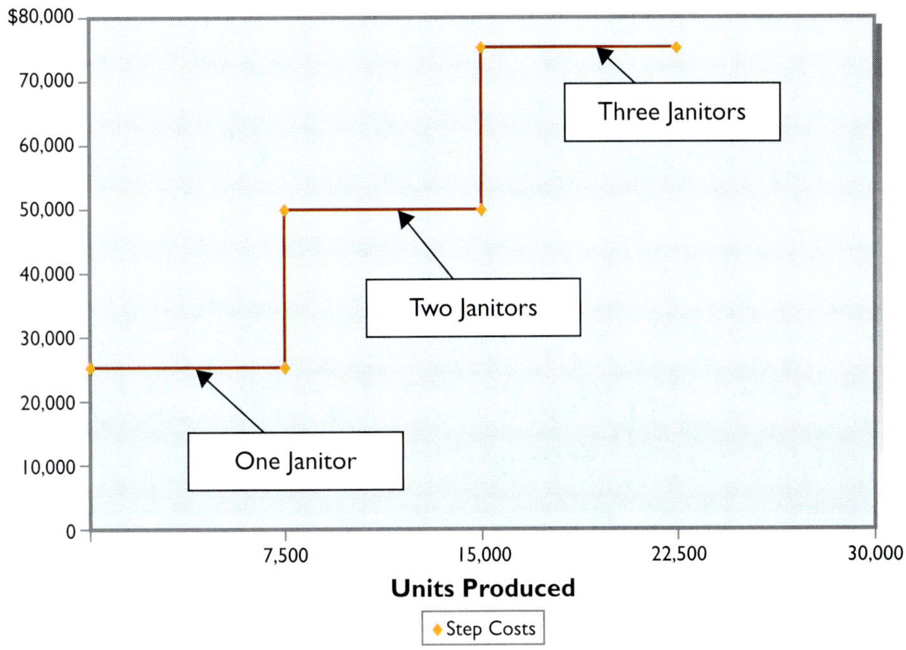

the $400 payment, regardless of whether any deliveries are made; hence, $400 of the cost is fixed. However, Big Al's also incurs costs related to driving the vehicle (gasoline, oil, maintenance costs, etc.) that vary with the number of deliveries made (and miles driven). If these costs average $1.50 per delivery and 200 deliveries are made during the month, Al will incur an additional $300 of variable costs for a total cost of $700. If 100 deliveries are made, the additional cost will be $150. Although the variable portion of the cost of the delivery van varies in total as the number of deliveries increases or decreases, it remains fixed when expressed per unit ($1.50 per delivery). On the other hand, the fixed portion of the cost remains constant in total ($400) but varies when expressed per unit.

Although the fixed and variable components of the delivery van cost are obvious, in many cases they may be difficult to identify. As shown in the following table, Big Al's has incurred the followed overhead costs over the last seven weeks:

PAUSE & Reflect

Can you think of other common examples of mixed costs?

Week	Pizzas	Total Overhead Costs	Cost per Unit
1 (Start-up)	0	$ 679	N/A
2	423	1,842	$4.35
3	601	2,350	3.91
4	347	1,546	4.46
5	559	2,250	4.03
6	398	1,769	4.44
7	251	1,288	5.13

Is the overhead cost a fixed, variable, or mixed cost? Clearly, the cost is not fixed, because it changes each week. However, is it a variable cost? Although the cost changes each week, it does not vary in direct proportion to changes in production. In addition, remember

EXHIBIT 5-4 Mixed Costs

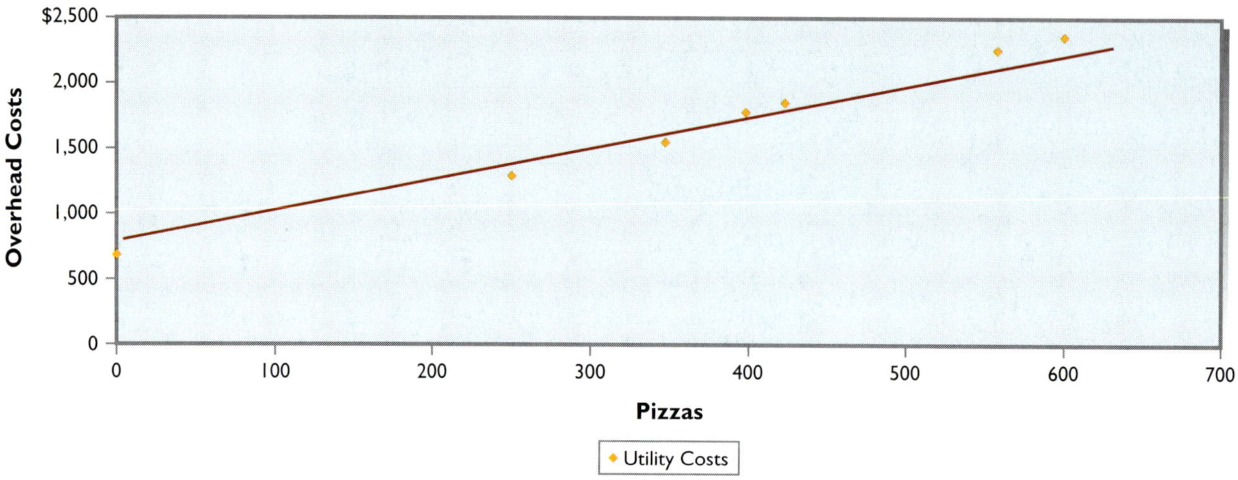

that variable costs remain constant when expressed per unit. In this case, the amount of overhead cost per pizza changes from week to week. A cost that changes in total and also changes per unit is a mixed cost. As you can see in Exhibit 5-4, a mixed cost looks somewhat like a variable cost. However, the cost does not vary in direct proportion to changes in the level of production (you can't draw a straight line through all the data points) and if a line were drawn through the data points back to the *y*-axis, we would still incur overhead cost at a production volume of zero. Like a fixed cost, a mixed cost has a component that is constant regardless of production volume.

Once we know that a cost is mixed, we are left with the task of separating the mixed cost into its fixed and variable components. However, unlike the lease example, it is not clear how much of the overhead cost is fixed and how much is variable. In the next section, we demonstrate the use of a statistical tool called regression analysis to estimate the fixed and variable components of a mixed cost.

SEPARATING MIXED COSTS INTO THEIR FIXED AND VARIABLE COMPONENTS

A variety of tools can be used to estimate the fixed and variable components of a mixed cost. When we separate a mixed cost into its variable and fixed components, what we are really doing is generating the equation for a straight line, with the *y* intercept estimating the fixed cost and the slope estimating the variable cost per unit.

Key Concept: *Within the relevant range, fixed costs are constant in total and vary per unit, variable costs vary in total and are constant per unit, and mixed costs vary in total and vary per unit.*

Continuing our example of Big Al's Pizza Emporium, after the initial seven-week start-up period, Al compiles data regarding the total overhead cost and the number of pizzas produced in the next 12 months. As you can see in the following table, because the overhead cost varies in total and on a per unit basis, it must be a mixed cost. A graph of the data is shown in Exhibit 5-5.

Month	Pizzas	Overhead	Per Pizza
1	2,100	$ 8,400	$4.00
2	2,600	10,100	3.88
3	2,300	8,800	3.83
4	2,450	9,250	3.78
5	2,100	8,050	3.83
6	2,175	8,200	3.77
7	1,450	6,950	4.79
8	1,200	6,750	5.63
9	1,350	7,250	5.37
10	1,750	7,300	4.17
11	1,550	7,250	4.68
12	2,050	7,950	3.88

REGRESSION ANALYSIS

A statistical technique used to estimate the fixed and variable components of a mixed cost is called least squares regression. **Regression analysis** uses statistical methods to fit a cost line (called a regression line) through a number of data points. Note that although the data points in our example do not lie along a straight line, regression analysis statistically finds the line that minimizes the sum of the squared distance from each data point to the line (hence the name least squares regression).

EXHIBIT 5-5 Overhead Costs

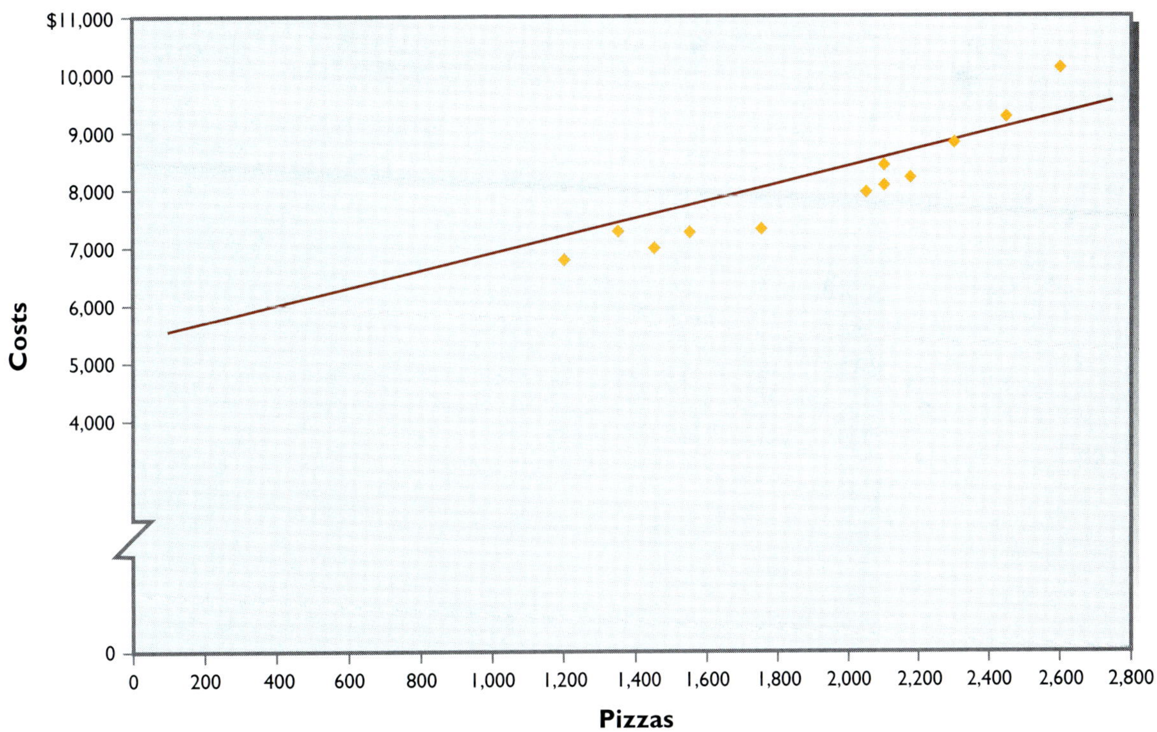

USING A SPREADSHEET PROGRAM TO PERFORM REGRESSION ANALYSIS

Using a spreadsheet program to estimate regression models is a relatively simple process. We are going to use Excel in this example, but all spreadsheet programs are very similar. The first step is to enter the actual values for our mixed cost (called the **dependent variable** in regression analysis because the amount of cost is dependent on production) and the related volume of production (called the **independent variable** because it drives the cost of the dependent variable) into a spreadsheet using one column for each variable. Using data from Big Al's Pizza Emporium for overhead costs incurred and pizzas produced for the first 12 months of operations, the results are shown in the Excel spreadsheet (see Exhibit 5-6).

The next step in Excel (see Exhibit 5-7) is to click on the tools option from the toolbar and choose data analysis from the pull-down menu. From the data analysis screen, scroll down, highlight regression, and either double-click or choose OK.

The regression screen will prompt you to choose a number of options. The first is to input the *y* range. The *y* range will be used to identify the dependent variable (overhead costs) found in column C of your spreadsheet. You can either type in the range of cells or simply highlight the cells in the spreadsheet (be sure not to include the column heading), and click on the icon in the *y*-range box. The next step is to select the *x* range for the independent variable (volume of pizzas). Once again, you can enter the cells directly or highlight the cells in the second column of your spreadsheet.

After inputting the appropriate *y* and *x* ranges, your Excel spreadsheet should look like the example shown in Exhibit 5-8. Click on OK, and the regression model summary output appears as shown in Exhibit 5-9.

EXHIBIT 5-6

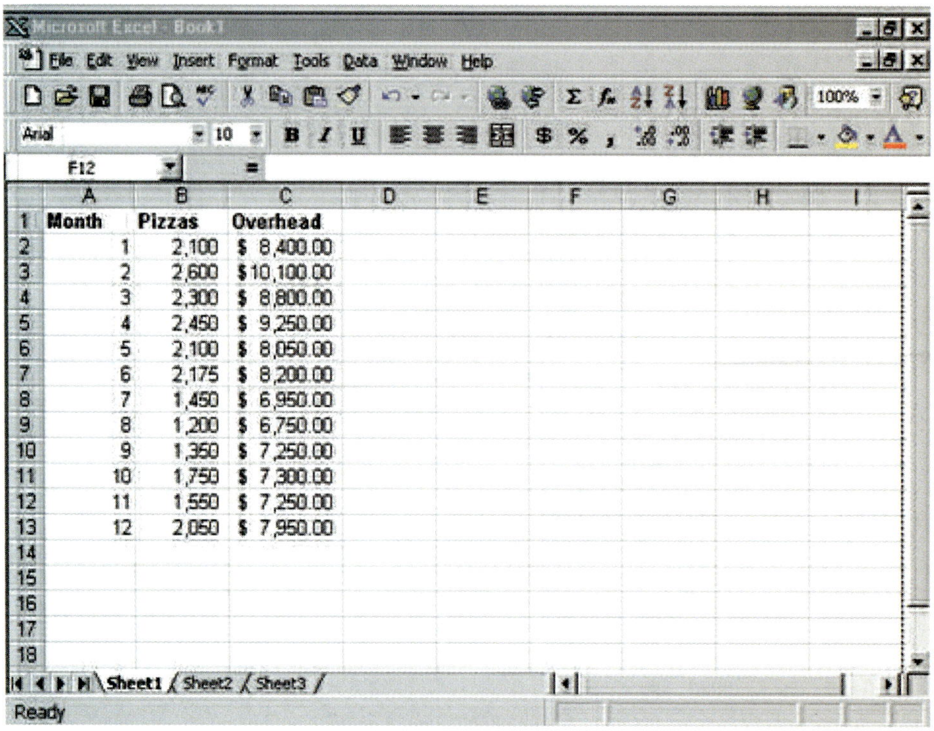

Month	Pizzas	Overhead
1	2,100	$ 8,400.00
2	2,600	$10,100.00
3	2,300	$ 8,800.00
4	2,450	$ 9,250.00
5	2,100	$ 8,050.00
6	2,175	$ 8,200.00
7	1,450	$ 6,950.00
8	1,200	$ 6,750.00
9	1,350	$ 7,250.00
10	1,750	$ 7,300.00
11	1,550	$ 7,250.00
12	2,050	$ 7,950.00

EXHIBIT 5-7

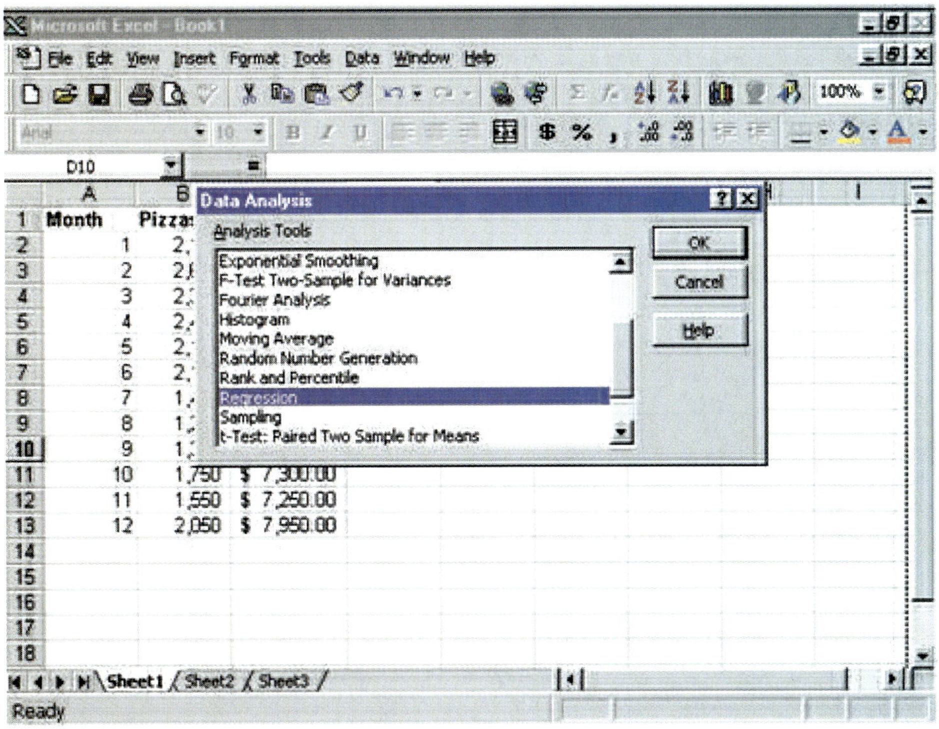

EXHIBIT 5-8

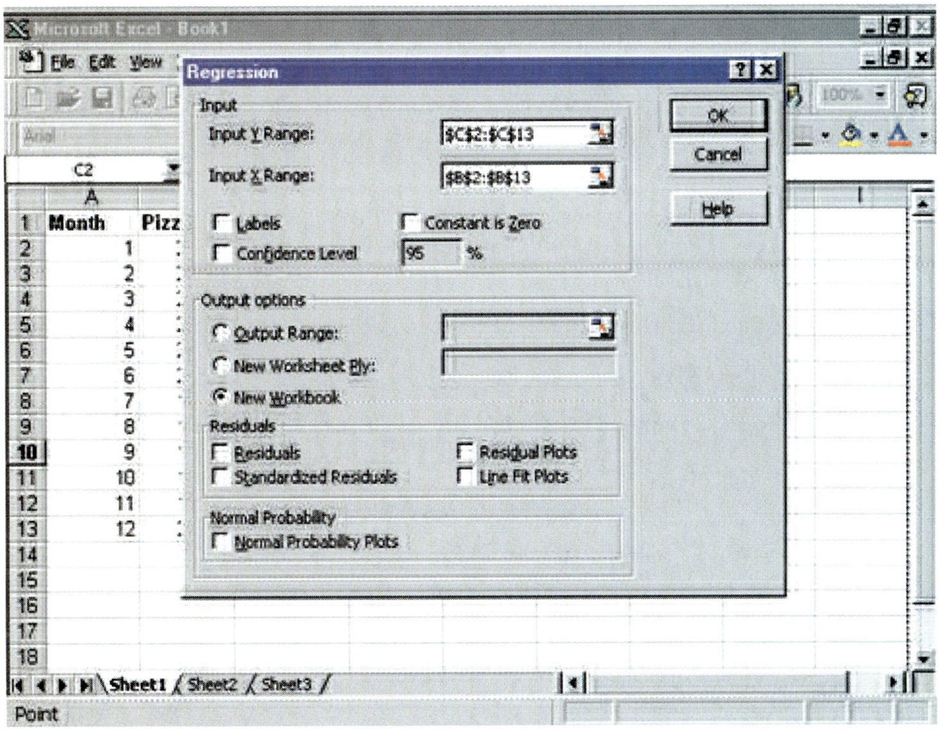

EXHIBIT 5-9

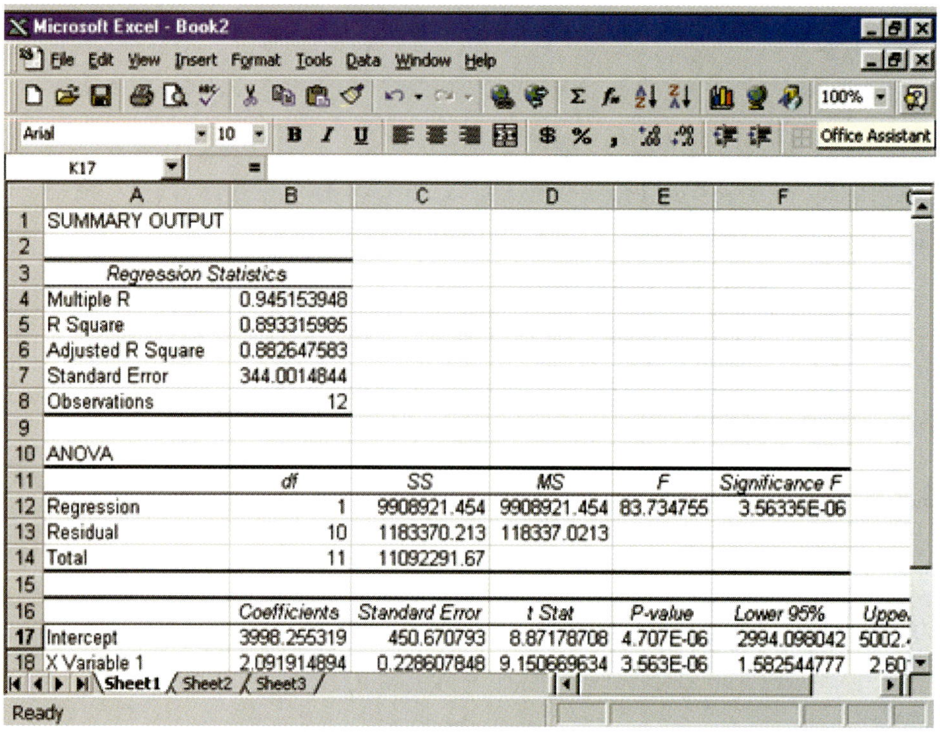

	A	B	C	D	E	F	G
1	SUMMARY OUTPUT						
2							
3	*Regression Statistics*						
4	Multiple R	0.945153948					
5	R Square	0.893315985					
6	Adjusted R Square	0.882647583					
7	Standard Error	344.0014844					
8	Observations	12					
9							
10	ANOVA						
11		*df*	*SS*	*MS*	*F*	*Significance F*	
12	Regression	1	9908921.454	9908921.454	83.734755	3.56335E-06	
13	Residual	10	1183370.213	118337.0213			
14	Total	11	11092291.67				
15							
16		*Coefficients*	*Standard Error*	*t Stat*	*P-value*	*Lower 95%*	*Uppe*
17	Intercept	3998.255319	450.670793	8.87178708	4.707E-06	2994.098042	5002.
18	X Variable 1	2.091914894	0.228607848	9.150669634	3.563E-06	1.582544777	2.60

How is the summary output interpreted? First, note toward the bottom of Exhibit 5-9 that the estimated coefficient (value) of the intercept (the *y* intercept) is 3,998.25 and the estimated coefficient (value) of the *x* variable (the slope) is 2.09. So, the fixed-cost component of our mixed overhead cost is estimated to be $3,998.25, and the variable cost component is estimated to be $2.09 per pizza.

Using the least squares regression results, we can compute the regression line for overhead costs at Big Al's Pizza Emporium:

Total overhead cost = Fixed cost + (Variable cost per unit × Volume)
Total overhead cost = $3,998.25 + (2.09 × Volume)

Graphically, the line for the total overhead costs can be expressed as seen in the following illustration.

Total Overhead Costs for Big Al's Pizza Emporium

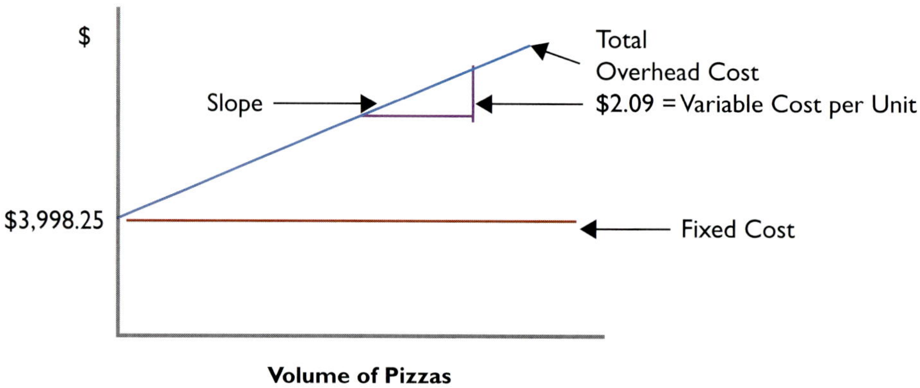

We can use this equation to help predict the amount of overhead costs that will be incurred for any number of pizzas within the relevant range. The relevant range is that range of activity within which management expects to operate, or the range in which this equation is useful or meaningful. Our predictions should be limited to those activity levels within the relevant range. Based on last year's data, Big Al's expects to produce between 1,200 and 2,600 pizzas each month. Next month, Big Al's expects to produce 1,750 pizzas. Based on the regression equation, Big Al's estimates total overhead costs to be \$7,655.75 (\$3,998.25 + (\$2.09 × 1,750 pizzas)).

REGRESSION STATISTICS

The regression statistics section at the top of Exhibit 5-9 provides useful diagnostic tools. The multiple *R* (called the correlation coefficient) is a measure of the proximity of the data points to the regression line. In addition, the sign of the statistic (+ or –) tells us the direction of the correlation between the independent and dependent variables. In this case, there is a positive correlation between the number of pizzas produced and total overhead costs. The ***R* square** (often represented as R^2 and called the coefficient of determination) is a measure of goodness of fit (how well the regression line "fits" the data). An R^2 of 1.0 indicates a perfect correlation between the independent and dependent variables in the regression equation; in other words, 100 percent of the data points are on the regression line. R^2 can be interpreted as the proportion of dependent-variable variation that is explained by changes in the independent variable. In this case, the R^2 of 0.8933 indicates that over 89 percent of the variation in overhead costs are explained by increasing or decreasing pizza production.

Concept Question: *Based on the regression results, we previously estimated that overhead costs should be \$7,655.75 when 1,750 pizzas are produced. However, looking back at month 10, you will note that actual overhead costs were \$7,300 when 1,750 pizzas were produced. Why aren't we able to compute the actual overhead costs in previous months using the regression results?*

Concept Answer: Because the R^2 is less than 1.0. There is not a perfect correlation between the number of pizzas produced and overhead costs incurred. Another way to look at it is that all the data points used to compute the regression equation are not on the computed regression line. ■

An R^2 of less than 1.0 implies that other independent variables might have an impact on the dependent variable. For example, outside temperature and other environmental factors might impact overhead costs incurred by Big Al's. Multiple regression is a technique in which additional independent variables are used to help predict changes in a dependent variable. If we added variables to our regression model, we would probably get a better predictive model. However, it is unlikely that we will ever identify all the relevant variables that cause the total cost to change. Nor is it necessary. The goal of separating a mixed cost into its fixed and variable components is to help managers predict costs in the future, not to compute an exact breakdown.

PAUSE & Reflect

Can you think of other variables that might have an impact on total overhead costs?

OTHER USES OF REGRESSION ANALYSIS

Regression analysis can be used in a variety of ways in managerial decision making. For example, marketing managers may be interested in predicting changes in sales based on changes in advertising expenditures and other variables. Production managers interested in quality control might collect data on overtime worked in a factory and compare that to the number of defective items produced to see whether increases in overtime affect the amount of defective goods produced. This could lead management to hire additional workers rather than working existing workers excessive amounts of overtime.

However, regression analysis must be used with caution. The precision of a computerized statistical technique like regression analysis can be misleading. Regression results, after all, are only estimates. First and foremost, high correlations between independent variables and dependent variables and "good" models do not necessarily indicate a cause-and-effect relationship. It is important that managers use common sense and their intimate knowledge of what activities really drive costs before attempting to model cost equations.

ESTIMATING REGRESSION RESULTS USING THE HIGH/LOW METHOD

If we didn't have access to a computer regression program or for some reason didn't want to use this tool, we could estimate the regression equation using a simpler technique called the high/low method. The high/low method uses only two data points (related to the high and low levels of activity) and mathematically derives an equation for a straight line intersecting those two data points. Though technically inferior to regression analysis (which uses all the data points), from a practical perspective, the high/low method can often provide a reasonable estimate of the regression equation.

In the table on page 139, the high level of activity occurred in month 2, when 2,600 pizzas were produced and \$10,100 of overhead cost was incurred. The low level of activity occurred in month 8, when only 1,200 pizzas were produced and overhead costs totaled \$6,750. The slope of the line connecting those two points can be calculated by dividing the difference between the costs incurred at the high and low levels of activity by the difference in volume (number of pizzas at those levels). Remember, the slope of a line is calculated as the change in cost over the change in volume, in this case the difference in cost to produce pizzas over the difference in volume of pizzas made. As with the regression equation, the slope of the line is interpreted as the variable-cost component of the mixed cost:

$$\frac{\text{Change in cost}}{\text{Change in volume}} = \text{Variable cost per unit}$$

Inserting the data for Big Al's Pizza Emporium, the variable cost is \$2.39 per unit (\$10,100 − \$6,750)/(2,600 − 1,200). This compares with our regression estimate of \$2.09. We then solve for the fixed-cost component by calculating the total variable cost incurred at either the high or the low level of activity and subtracting the variable costs from the total overhead cost incurred at that level. Mathematically, if

$$\text{Total overhead costs} = \text{Fixed costs} + [\text{Variable cost per unit (number of pizzas)}]$$

then

$$\text{Total overhead costs} - \text{Variable costs} = \text{Fixed costs}$$

At the high level of activity, total overhead costs are \$10,100 and variable costs equal \$6,214 (2,600 pizzas × \$2.39 per pizza). Therefore, the fixed-cost component of overhead costs is estimated to be \$3,886 (total overhead costs of \$10,100 less variable costs of \$6,214), and the total overhead cost is estimated to be \$3,886 + \$2.39 (number of pizzas produced).

Why is this equation different from the least squares regression equation? Regression is a statistical tool that fits the "best" line through all 12 data points, whereas the high/low method mathematically derives a straight line between just 2 of the data points. By using the 2 points at the highest and lowest levels of activity, we are forcing a line between those points without regard to the remaining data points. If one or both of these points is unusual (an outlier), the result will be a cost line that is skewed and therefore may not be a good measure of the fixed and variable components of the mixed cost.[1] Therefore, less than optimal decisions could be made owing to the skewed data.

In the case of Big Al's Pizza Emporium, let's see how the high/low estimate would impact our prediction of total overhead costs next month, when 1,750 pizzas are produced. Using the high/low estimate of the cost equation, we would predict total overhead costs of \$8,068.50 (\$3,886 + (\$2.39 × 1,750 pizzas)). This compares with our estimate of \$7,655.75 using the cost equation generated from the regression analysis.

Given the simplicity of generating regression equations using spreadsheet packages and hand-held calculators, the need for computing cost equations in practice using the high/low method is questionable. However, it remains an easy-to-use tool for estimating cost behavior.

Cost Behavior, Activity-Based Costing, and Activity-Based Management

So far, we have examined the behavior of unit-level costs related to changes in production volume (number of pizzas and number of deliveries), but costs are affected by changes in other cost drivers as well. In Chapters 3 and 4, we introduced the concept of activities as procedures or processes that cause work to be accomplished (purchasing, receiving, production, plant occupancy, etc.) and cost drivers as allocation bases that cause, or drive, the incurrence of costs. Some of these drivers are related to volume (machine hours and labor hours), but drivers of batch- and product-level costs are more likely related to the complexity of a product (number of parts, number of inspections) or product diversity (number of setups, number of purchase orders). Although these costs may not vary in direct proportion to volume, they may vary in direct proportion to other cost drivers.

Regression analysis can be used to help managers identify the "best" cost drivers of activities for use in activity-based costing (ABC) and activity-based management (ABM). For example, the activity of processing customer orders might vary with the number of orders or the number of customers. Regression analysis can be used to identify which of the two possible independent variables better explains the variation in the dependent variable (costs of placing customer orders).

Cost Behavior in Merchandising and Service Companies

In merchandising firms, sales revenue is a common cost driver. The cost of merchandise purchased is a variable cost (it varies in direct proportion to changes in sales revenue). The cost of labor is often fixed (although seasonal hires may behave more like variable costs), and many other costs of facilities are fixed. Service-oriented companies have a variety of cost drivers, depending on the industry. For example, a mortgage loan department might classify costs according to how they behave with respect to the number of loan applications processed, whereas an airline might look at number of passengers, passenger miles, and so on.

Relevant Costs and Cost Behavior

LO3
Understand the concept of relevant costs and apply the concept to decision making

As mentioned in Chapter 1, relevant costs are those that are avoidable or can be eliminated by choosing one alternative over another. Relevant costs are also known as differential, or incremental, costs. In general, variable costs are relevant in production decisions because they vary with the level of production. Likewise, fixed costs are generally not relevant, because they typically don't change as production changes. However, variable costs can remain the

[1] It should be noted that the presence of outliers is a problem in regression analysis as well.

same between two alternatives, and fixed costs can vary between alternatives. For example, if the direct material cost of a product is the same for two competing designs, the material cost is not a relevant factor in choosing a design. However, other qualitative factors, such as durability, relating to the material may still be relevant. Likewise, fixed costs can be relevant if they vary between alternatives. Consider rent paid for a facility to store inventory. Although the rent is a fixed cost, it is relevant to a decision to reduce inventory storage costs through just-in-time (JIT) production techniques if the cost of the rent can be avoided (by subleasing the space, for example) by choosing one alternative over another.

Key Concept: *It can be misleading to always view variable costs as relevant and fixed costs as not relevant.*

THE IMPACT OF INCOME TAXES ON COSTS AND DECISION MAKING

LO4
Understand the impact of income taxes on costs and decision making

TAXES AND DECISION MAKING

We always need to consider tax laws and the impact income and other taxes have on costs, revenues, and decision making. Just as an individual should consider the impact of income taxes on a decision to hold or to sell a stock, managers must consider the impact of taxes in a variety of decisions. The first key to understanding the impact of taxes on costs and revenues is the recognition that many costs of operating businesses are deductible for income tax purposes and that most business revenues are taxable. Second, the form of a transaction may impact the amount of tax that is paid or whether a cost is tax deductible. For example, structuring a purchase of a building as a lease with a corresponding payment of rent has different tax implications than a purchase of the same building. Third, the payment of taxes requires a cash outflow and reduces the amount of cash available for other purposes in a business organization. Therefore, the impact of taxes must be considered in a variety of managerial decisions, including production decisions, cost-volume-profit analysis, the purchase of property and equipment, and budgeting.

Key Concept: *Managers must consider the impact of taxes on decisions.*

AFTER-TAX COSTS AND REVENUES

The computation of after-tax costs and after-tax revenues is really very simple. Consider an example in which your current taxable cash revenue is \$100 and tax-deductible cash expenses equal \$60. Taxable income is therefore equal to \$40. If the tax rate is 40 percent, \$16 of income taxes will be paid, leaving you with \$24 cash after tax. Now consider the impact of spending an additional \$20 on tax-deductible expenditures. This reduces your taxable income to \$20. With a 40 percent tax rate, \$8 of income taxes will be paid instead of \$16 (you saved \$8 of income tax) and you will be left with \$12 after tax. Even though you spent an additional \$20, your cash flow decreased by only \$12 (\$24 less \$12).

		Increase Spending by \$20	Increase Revenue by \$20
Revenue	\$100	\$100	\$120
Expense	– 60	– 80	– 60
Taxable income	\$ 40	\$ 20	\$ 60
Tax (rate = 40%)	– 16	– 8	– 24
After-tax cash flow	\$ 24	\$ 12	\$ 36

Mathematically, the after-tax cost of a tax-deductible cash expenditure can be found by subtracting the tax savings from the before-tax cost or by simply multiplying the before-tax amount by (1 – tax rate):

After-tax cost = Pretax cost × (1 – Tax rate)

So if the before-tax cost is \$20 and the tax rate is 40 percent, the after-tax cost is \$12 (\$12 = \$20 × (1 – 0.40)). In this case, the impact of income taxes is to reduce the "real" cost of a tax-deductible expense to the business and to increase cash flow.

Income taxes also have an impact on cash revenues received by a business. Continuing our original example, if taxable cash revenue increases by \$20, taxable income will increase to \$60 (\$120 minus \$60). After payment of \$24 of income taxes, you will be left with \$36 of cash. An increase in revenue of \$20 increases your cash flow by only \$12 (\$36 minus \$24). Why? Because the \$20 is taxable and results in the payment of an additional \$8 of income tax (\$20 × 0.40). Mathematically, the formula to find the after-tax benefit associated with a taxable cash revenue is analogous to the formula for after-tax cost. The after-tax benefit of a taxable cash receipt can be found by subtracting the additional tax to be paid from the before-tax receipt or by simply multiplying the pretax receipt by (1 – tax rate):

After-tax benefit = Pretax receipts × (1 – Tax rate)

So if the before-tax receipt is \$20 and the tax rate is 40 percent, the after-tax benefit is \$12 (\$12 = \$20 × (1 – 0.40)). In this case, the impact of income taxes is to increase the "real" cost to the business and to decrease cash flow.

BEFORE- AND AFTER-TAX NET INCOME

In a similar fashion, managers can calculate the impact of taxes on net income. If we have a tax rate of 40 percent and net income of \$1,000,000, we will have a tax liability of \$400,000 (40 percent of the \$1,000,000) and be left with \$600,000 after tax. This is exactly the same thing that happens to our paychecks as individuals. If an individual earns \$1,000 per week and faces a 30 percent income tax rate, the individual's take-home pay (after considering income tax withholding) is only \$700. Mathematically,

After-tax income = Pretax income × (1 – Tax rate)

Although tax laws are very complex and computing tax due is rarely as simple as applying one rate to net income, estimating the income tax impact on cash receipts and disbursements is important in managerial decision making.

APPLICATION IN BUSINESS

http://www.irs.gov

In the past decade, there have been thousands of changes to the Internal Revenue Code, making tax planning a nightmare for many small businesses. Major tax bills during that time include The Omnibus Budget Reconciliation Act of 1993, The Taxpayer Relief Act of 1997, and The Economic Growth and Tax Relief Reconciliation Act of 2001. Particularly problematic is Congress's habit of making temporary tax changes that expire every few years. Although the changes are made on a temporary basis owing to budget considerations, they are almost always extended at the last minute. Making decisions in an environment characterized by continually changing tax rules is challenging, to say the least.

THE TIME VALUE OF MONEY AND DECISION MAKING

LO5
Understand the time value of money and its impact on costs and decision making

When decisions are affected by cash flows that are paid or received in different time periods, it is also necessary to adjust those cash flows for the time value of money (TVM). Because of our ability to earn interest on money invested, we would prefer to receive $1 today rather than a year from now. Likewise, we would rather pay $1 a year from now than today. A common technique used to adjust cash flows received or paid in different time periods is to discount those cash flows by finding their present value.

***Key Concept:** Managers must consider the time value of money when making long-term decisions.*

To fully understand the calculations involved in finding the present value of future cash flows, it is necessary to step back and examine the nature of interest and the calculation of interest received and paid. The concepts of time value of money are developed more completely in Chapter 8.

SUMMARY OF KEY CONCEPTS

- Costs behave in predictable ways. (p. 132)
- Within the relevant range, fixed costs are constant in total and vary per unit, variable costs vary in total and are constant per unit, and mixed costs vary in total and vary per unit. (p. 138)
- It can be misleading to always view variable costs as relevant and fixed costs as not relevant. (p. 146)
- Managers must consider the impact of taxes on decisions. (p. 146)
- Managers must consider the time value of money when making long-term decisions. (p. 148)

KEY DEFINITIONS

Cost behavior How costs react to changes in production volume or other levels of activity (p. 132)

Fixed costs Costs that remain the same in total when production volume increases or decreases but vary per unit (p. 132)

Variable costs Costs that stay the same per unit but change in total as production volume increases or decreases (p. 132)

Relevant range The normal range of production that can be expected for a particular product and company (p. 133)

Step costs Costs that vary with activity in steps and may look like and be treated as either variable costs or fixed costs; step costs are technically not fixed costs but may be treated as such if they remain constant within a relevant range of production (p. 136)

Mixed costs Costs that include both a fixed and a variable component, making it difficult to predict the behavior of a mixed cost as production changes unless the cost is first separated into its fixed and variable components (p. 136)

Regression analysis The procedure that uses statistical methods (least squares regression) to fit a cost line (called a regression line) through a number of data points (p. 139)

Dependent variable The variable in regression analysis that is dependent on changes in the independent variable (p. 140)

Independent variable The variable in regression analysis that drives changes in the dependent variable (p. 140)

***R* square (R^2)** A measure of goodness of fit (how well the regression line "fits" the data) (p. 143)

COMPUTER SIMULATION

You can now turn to **Appendix A** of your text to complete the portion of the Big Al's simulation covering estimating overhead using the high/low and regression methods.

MULTIPLE CHOICE

1. You are given the following cost and volume information:

Volume	Cost
1 unit	$ 15
10	150
100	1,500

What type of a cost is given?

a. fixed cost
b. variable cost
c. step cost
d. The answer cannot be determined.

2. You are given the following cost and volume information:

Volume	Cost
1 unit	$150
10	150
100	150

What type of a cost is given?

a. fixed cost
b. variable cost
c. step cost
d. The answer cannot be determined.

3. Arrow Company plans to double its advertising budget next year, which will increase its fixed costs by 20 percent. Variable costs will remain the same. The current year costs are as follows:

Variable costs per unit	$ 5
Fixed costs	4,000

If next year's production is 5,000 units, estimated total costs would be:

a. $4,005
b. $29,005
c. $29,800
d. Another number: ____________ .

4. Cash Company plans to double its advertising budget next year, which will increase its fixed costs by 10 percent. Variable costs will remain the same. The current year costs are as follows:

Variable costs per unit	$ 5
Fixed costs	5,000

If next year's production is 25,000 units, estimated total costs would be:

a. $125,000
b. $125,005
c. $130,000
d. Another number: ____________ .

5. You run a regression analysis and receive the following results:

Multiple *R*	0.71196
R square	0.50688
Adjusted *R* square	0.50438
Standard error	1.43764

Analysis of Variance

	DF	Sum of Squares	Mean Square
Regression	1	418.52992	418.52992
Residual	197	407.16375	2.06682

F = 202.49935 Signif. *F* = 0.0000

VARIABLES IN THE EQUATION

Variable	Coefficients	Standard Error	t-Stat	P-value
X variable 1	7.93958	0.055794	14.230	0.0000
Intercept	204.070	0.261513	–0.780	0.4361

If the preceding regression was for production costs and 200 units of X are produced, what are the total production costs?

a. $7.94
b. $204.07
c. $1,588
d. $1,792.07

6. Fancy Shoe Manufacturers documented its production levels and overhead costs for the past five months as follows:

	Production	Overhead Cost
January	10,500 pairs	$40,250
February	10,675	41,000
March	11,500	44,250
April	12,500	45,250
May	11,000	43,750

Using the high/low method, what is the overhead cost equation?

a. $Y = \$0 + \$3.83X$
b. $Y = \$14{,}000 + \$2.50X$
c. $Y = \$29{,}750 + \$3.62$
d. none of the above

7. Generally speaking, variable costs are relevant to production decisions, except when:
   a. the variable costs are part of a mixed cost
   b. the variable costs are unavoidable
   c. the variable costs do not differ between alternatives
   d. none of the above; variable costs are always relevant to production decisions

8. Generally speaking, fixed costs are not relevant to production decisions, except when:
   a. the fixed costs are part of a mixed cost
   b. the fixed costs are unavoidable
   c. the fixed costs differ between alternatives
   d. none of the above; fixed costs are always relevant to production decisions

9. The after-tax cost of a tax-deductible cash expenditure can be calculated as follows:
   a. After-tax cost = Before-tax cost × (1 – Tax rate)
   b. After-tax cost = (Before-tax cost × Tax rate) – 1
   c. After-tax cost = Before-tax cost × Tax rate
   d. After-tax cost = Before-tax cost × (Tax rate – 1)

10. A manager is considering a project that will increase sales revenue by $120 without affecting expenses. What would be the after-tax revenue given a 30 percent tax rate?
    a. $36
    b. $84
    c. $120
    d. $150

CONCEPT REVIEW

11. Discuss the importance of understanding cost behavior in decision making.
12. Define fixed costs.
13. Define variable costs.
14. Describe the behavior of direct material cost in total and per unit as production volume changes.
15. Describe the relevant range and how it relates to cost behavior.
16. How will fixed costs expressed on a per unit basis react to a change in the level of activity?
17. When production increases, how do fixed manufacturing costs react on a per unit basis and in total?
18. Give the equation that best describes the fundamental relationship among total costs (TC), fixed costs (FC), and variable costs per unit (V).
19. Describe the behavior of mixed costs when production volume changes.
20. Discuss the meaning of dependent and independent variables in regression analysis.
21. Discuss the trend toward more fixed costs in a manufacturing environment and how that trend affects the cost per unit when production volume changes.
22. Describe step costs and give an example.
23. Describe a situation in which the normal expected behavior of direct labor cost may change.
24. Discuss the impact of taxes on costs and how that affects decision making.
25. Discuss the meaning of R square in regression analysis. What does an R square of 1 mean?
26. Discuss situations in which the high/low method may provide inaccurate estimates of fixed and variable costs.
27. What makes a cost relevant for decision making?
28. Why aren't fixed costs relevant for most short-term decisions?
29. Compare and contrast the terms *relevant* and *nonrelevant* costs as they pertain to decision making.
30. Why is a dollar received today worth more than a dollar received one year from now?
31. Why would we prefer to pay one dollar a year from now rather than today?

APPLICATION OF CONCEPTS

32. You run a regression analysis and receive the following results:

Multiple *R*	0.71196
R Square	0.50688
Adjusted *R* Square	0.50438
Standard Error	1.43764

Analysis of Variance

	DF	**Sum of Squares**	**Mean Square**
Regression	1	418.52992	418.52992
Residual	197	407.16375	2.06682

F = 202.49935 Signif. *F* = 0.0000

VARIABLES IN THE EQUATION

Variable	**Coefficients**	**Standard Error**	**t-Stat**	**P-Value**
X variable 1	7.93958	0.055794	14.230	0.0000
Intercept	204.070	0.261513	–0.780	0.4361

Required

A. What is the fixed cost?

B. What is the variable cost per unit?

C. What is the cost equation?

D. How much variance in the *Y* variable (cost) is explained by the *X* variable?

E. If the above regression was for production costs and 250 units of *X* are produced, what are total fixed costs?

F. If the above regression was for production costs and 300 units of *X* are produced, what are total variable costs?

G. If the above regression was for production costs and 350 units of *X* are produced, what are total production costs?

33. Smithfield Silver documented their production levels and overhead costs for the past five months.

	Production	**Overhead Cost**
January	10,600 candlesticks	$40,250
February	10,575	41,000
March	11,500	44,250
April	12,500	45,250
May	11,000	43,750

Required

A. Using the high/low method, what is the variable cost per unit?

B. Using the high/low method, what is the fixed cost?

C. Using the high/low method, what would you expect the total cost of producing 12,000 candlesticks to be?

34. You run a regression analysis and receive the following results:

Multiple *R*	0.39429
R Square	0.15547
Adjusted *R* Square	0.14964
Standard Error	0.44416

Analysis of Variance

	DF	Sum of Squares	Mean Square
Regression	1	5.26588	5.26588
Residual	145	28.60536	0.19728

$F = 26.69262$ Signif. $F = 0.0000$

VARIABLES IN THE EQUATION

Variable	Coefficients	Standard Error	t-Stat	P-Value
X Variable 1	11.0323	0.021353	5.166	0.0000
Intercept	8833.07	0.090586	9.751	0.0000

Required

A. What is the fixed cost in this regression analysis?

B. What is the variable cost per unit?

C. Prepare the cost equation based upon these results.

D. Does this regression equation "fit" the data well? What information did you examine to answer this question?

35. Minor Corporation anticipates net income of $1,200,000 this year. It is considering an equipment lease that would result in a $175,000 deductible expense this year. The tax rate is 35 percent.

Required

A. What would be the tax expense and net income after taxes for the anticipated net income without the lease of the equipment?

B. What would be the tax expense and net income after taxes if the equipment is leased?

C. What would be the after-tax effect of the lease expense?

36. Christopher Corporation documented its production levels and utility costs for the past six months, as follows:

	Production	Utility Cost
January	113,000 units	$1,712
February	114,000	1,716
March	90,000	1,469
April	115,000	1,619
May	112,000	1,698
June	101,000	1,691

Required

A. Using the high/low method, what is its utility cost equation?

B. What would be the expected utility cost of producing 120,000 units?

C. Using the data shown and a spreadsheet program, run a regression analysis. Discuss any differences in the results and the potential impact on decision making.

37. Collins Company has the following current-year costs:

Variable costs	$ 6 per unit
Fixed costs	7,000

The company and supplier plan to enter into an arrangement that will result in a per unit decrease of $0.50 in variable costs next year. The company will also reduce its rental space, which will decrease fixed costs by 10 percent.

Required

A. If current year production is 12,000 units, what are total fixed costs?

B. If the company makes these changes, what will be the new cost equation?

C. Given the new cost equation, determine estimated total costs if production remains at 12,000 units.

38. Hester Company incurred a total cost of $10,000 to produce 500 units of output. A total of 550 hours was incurred for this effort. If the variable cost was $10 per direct labor hour, how much was the fixed cost?

39. Hickman Company produces two products: Bert and Ernie; Hickman has provided you with the following data. Production and cost data for the two products are as follows:

Number of Units (Bert)	Total Cost
1	$ 10
10	100
100	1,000

Number of Units (Ernie)	Unit Cost
1	$5,000
10	500
100	50

How would you describe the behavior of costs for Bert and Ernie?

40. Simon Company operates in a relevant range from 1,000 to 1,500 units and incurs the following overhead costs:

Units Produced	Utilities	Lease Costs	Indirect Labor Costs
1,000	$10,000	$15,000	$13,000
1,500	12,500	15,000	15,600

Required

A. Classify the preceding costs as fixed, variable, or mixed.

B. At a production volume of 1,300 units, what are Simon Company's total estimated overhead costs?

41. Garfunkel Company incurs the following overhead costs at a production volume of 2,000 and 8,000 units:

Units Produced	Maintenance Expense	Rent	Indirect Labor
2,000	$24,250	$21,000	$22,000
8,000	67,000	21,000	88,000

Required

A. Describe the cost behavior of each element of overhead cost listed.

B. At a production volume of 9,000 units, what are Garfunkel's expected overhead costs?

42. The controller of Sawyer College has determined that a janitor can clean an average of 20 dorm rooms each day. Bay View Dorm has 100 rooms and is projected to be 80 percent full for the spring semester (January to May). In the summer (June to August), the dorm is used only for summer camps and so is projected to be only 50 percent full. In the fall semester (September to December), the dorm is projected to be 100 percent full. Each occupied room is cleaned daily. Sawyer College outsources its maintenance and housekeeping services from a company that charges Sawyer College $2,000 per month for each janitor hired.

Required

A. Compute the cost for janitorial service for Bay View Dorm for each of the three periods of time.

B. What cost behavior pattern best describes janitorial costs for Bay View Dorm?

C. How would you predict the costs of janitorial services for the dorm in the future?

43. Chris Gaines has leased a new automobile, using a special lease plan. If the auto is driven 1,000 miles or less during a one-month period, the lease payment is $250. If the mileage ranges between 1,001 and 1,500 miles, the lease payment becomes $300. For 1,501 to 2,000 miles, the lease payment rises to $350.

Required

A. How would you describe the lease cost?

B. If Chris always drives between 1,200 and 1,400 miles per month, how would you classify the lease cost for planning purposes?

C. If Chris's monthly mileage ranges from 0 miles to 1,800 miles, how would you classify the lease cost for planning purposes?

44. Data from the duplicating department of Hope Services for the previous six months are as follows:

	Number of Copies Made	Duplicating Department's Costs
January	20,000	$17,000
February	25,000	19,500
March	27,000	21,000
April	22,000	18,000
May	24,000	19,000
June	30,000	24,000

Regression output from the previous data is as follows:

Coefficient of intercept	2807.895
R square	0.967696
Number of observations	6
X coefficient (independent variable)	0.686842

Required

A. What is the variable rate per copy for Hope Services?

B. What is the fixed cost for Hope Services?

C. Based on the regression output for Hope Services, what equation should be used to compute an estimate of future total costs?

D. If 26,000 copies are made next month, what total cost should be incurred?

E. Based on the information given, how good will the equation described in C be at predicting the total cost each month for Hope Services?

45. Regression results for Robyn's Flower Shop Inc. are as follows:

Dependent variable—overhead costs	
Independent variable—direct labor costs	
Coefficient of intercept	$4,000
Coefficient of independent variable	3.00
Correlation coefficient	0.67
R square	0.45

The company is planning on operating at a level that would call for direct labor costs of $10,000 per month for the coming year.

Required

A. Using the regression output for Robyn's Flower Shop Inc., give the equation that best represents the overhead-cost equation.

B. What percentage of variation in overhead costs is explained by the independent variable in the regression output for Robyn's Flower Shop Inc.? How good will the equation be at predicting total cost?

C. Discuss how the prediction ability could be improved.

46. Calculate the after tax impact of the following situations.

Before-Tax Cost	Tax Rate	After-Tax Cost
(1) $25,000	40%	?
(2) 50,000	20	?
(3) 35,000	35	?
(4) 75,000	25	?
(5) 85,000	45	?

47. Calculate the after-tax impact of the following situations.

Before-Tax Revenue	Tax Rate	After-Tax Revenue
(1) $100,000	40%	?
(2) 200,000	20	?
(3) 135,000	35	?
(4) 175,000	25	?
(5) 185,000	45	?

48. Mandy Lifeboats Cruise Co. is in need of better information for planning new cruises. You have been retained as a consultant to provide a planning model. You are provided with the following information regarding last year's average costs for 12 cruises on the MS *Robyn,* a cruise ship that has a maximum capacity of 525 passengers and has a crew of 250. All cruises on the MS *Robyn* are for either seven or ten days.

Cruise	Days	Passengers	Total Cost
1	7	455	$315,010
2	7	420	297,525
3	7	473	317,595
4	7	510	326,615
5	7	447	314,510
6	7	435	310,015
7	10	445	365,015
8	10	495	370,015
9	10	480	367,035
10	10	505	375,000
11	10	471	367,500
12	10	439	365,090

The total cost of a cruise includes all costs of running the ship (fuel, maintenance, depreciation etc.) and meals, entertainment, and crew costs.

Required

A. Using the number of passengers as the independent variable, run a regression analysis (or use the high/low method) to arrive at the total-cost formula for a cruise.

B. How accurate is the planning model calculated in A?

C. What are the total fixed costs per cruise?

D. What are the variable costs per passenger?

E. What other independent variables might Mandy use to predict total cruise costs? Using regression analysis or the high/low method, calculate the cost equation, using this new independent variable.

F. Using the decision-making model described in Chapter 1, define the problem facing Mandy (Step 1), its likely objectives in choosing a planning model (Step 2), and options and factors it would likely consider (Step 3).

G. Using the best planning model you can develop using the data presented, what is the estimated cost of a 10-day cruise at full capacity of 525 passengers?

Step 1 DEFINE THE PROBLEM

Step 2 IDENTIFY OBJECTIVES

Step 3 IDENTIFY AND ANALYZE AVAILABLE OPTIONS

49. B.B. Lean, a major retailing and mail-order operation, has been in business for the past 10 years. During that time, the mail-order operations have grown from a sideline to more than 80 percent of the company's annual sales. Of course, the company has suffered growing pains. There were times when overloaded or faulty computer programs resulted in lost sales, and the scheduling of temporary workers to augment the permanent staff during peak periods has always been a problem.

Ann Humes, manager of mail-order operations, has developed procedures for handling most problems. However, she is still trying to improve the scheduling of temporary workers to take telephone orders from customers. Under the current system, Humes keeps a permanent staff of 60 employees who handle the basic workload. Based on her estimate of the upcoming telephone volume each week, she determines the number of temporary workers needed for the next week. The permanent workers are paid an average of $10 per hour plus 30 percent fringe benefits. The temporary workers are paid $7 per hour with no fringe benefits. The full-time workers are very seldom sent home when volume is light but are not paid for hours missed. Temporary workers are paid only for the hours worked. Ann normally keeps three supervisors at $1,000 per month but adds one additional supervisor when the temporary workers are used.

Humes has decided to try regression analysis as a way to improve the prediction of total costs of processing telephone orders. By summarizing the daily labor hours into monthly totals for the past year, she was able to determine the number of labor hours incurred each month. In addition, she summarized the number of orders that had been processed each month. After entering the data into a spreadsheet, Ann ran two regressions. Regression 1 related the total hours worked (permanent staff plus temporary workers) to the total cost to run the phone center. Regression 2 related the number of orders taken to the total cost. The output of these regressions is as follows:

Month	Total Cost	Total Hours	Number of Orders
January	$134,000	9,600	10,560
February	133,350	9,550	10,450
March	132,700	9,500	10,200
April	134,000	9,600	10,700
May	133,675	9,575	10,400
June	139,900	10,100	10,700
July	143,820	10,500	11,100
August	140,880	10,200	10,450
September	137,940	9,900	10,200

October	153,620	11,500	12,200
November	163,420	12,500	12,900
December	150,680	11,200	11,490

Regression equation: $TC = FC + VC$ (orders), or $TC = FC + VC$ (hours), where $TC =$ total cost; $FC =$ fixed cost, and $VC =$ variable cost per hour or order.

	Regression 1	Regression 2
Intercept (*FC*)	36,180.42	21,595.15
X Variable (*VC*)	10.21475	10.95427
R-square	0.997958	0.890802

Required:

A. What are the equations (planning models) for each of the two regressions?

B. Ann Humes estimates that 12,470 orders will be received and 12,000 hours worked during January. Predict the total cost of running the phone center, using both cost equations. Round your answer to the nearest whole number.

C. Ann needs to choose one of the models to use to predict total costs for next year's monthly budget. Using the decision model presented in Chapter 1:

Step 1 DEFINE THE PROBLEM

Step 2 IDENTIFY OBJECTIVES

Step 3 IDENTIFY AND ANALYZE AVAILABLE OPTIONS

(1) Define the problem Ann faces (Step 1).

(2) What are the objectives of the decision problem (Step 2)?

(3) What are Ann's options (Step 3)? Can you think of other independent variables that might be used to predict the costs of the phone center?

(4) What other factors should Ann consider?

50. Hunziker Rapid Delivery Service wants to determine the cost behavior pattern of maintenance costs to its delivery vehicles. The company has decided to use linear regression by employing the equation $y = a + bx$ for maintenance costs. The prior year's data regarding maintenance hours and costs and the results of the regression analysis are as follows:

	Hours of Activity	Maintenance Costs
January	480	$4,200
February	320	3,000
March	400	3,600
April	300	2,820
May	500	4,350
June	310	2,960
July	320	3,030
August	520	4,470
September	490	4,260
October	470	4,050
November	350	3,300
December	340	3,160

Regression Output

Coefficient of intercept	684.65
X coefficient	7.2884
R square	0.99448

Required

A. Based on the data derived from the regression analysis, what maintenance costs should be budgeted for a month in which 420 maintenance hours will be worked?

B. What is the percentage of the total variance that can be explained by the regression equation?

51. Data from the duplicating department of Kool Kopy Company for the previous nine months are as follows:

	Number of Copies Made	Duplicating Department's Costs
January	20,000	$17,000
February	25,000	11,000
March	27,000	27,000
April	22,000	18,000
May	24,000	30,000
June	30,000	24,000
July	22,000	18,000
August	23,000	18,500
September	34,000	26,000

Regression Output

Coefficient of intercept	4,104.372
R square	0.244367
X coefficient	0.672073

Required

Review the preceding actual data and the regression output.

A. Do you think the data could be improved by removing any outliers? If so, identify likely outliers from the data given and state reasons why you would remove them.

B. Would removing these data points change the regression output? How?

C. Give reasons for the change and direction the values may move. Give reasons why you might want to leave the data as is.

52. Data from the duplicating department of Hope Services for the previous six months are as follows:

	Number of Copies Made	Duplicating Department's Costs
January	20,000	$17,000
February	25,000	19,500
March	27,000	21,000
April	22,000	18,000
May	24,000	19,000
June	30,000	24,000

Required

A. Using the high/low method, separate the fixed and variable expenses and give the resulting equation.

B. Compare the equation generated in A to the equation generated by the regression output in problem 44. Explain the difference. Discuss why one method may be better than the other for identifying fixed- and variable-cost components.

C. If Hope Services estimates that it will make 23,000 copies in July, what will be the total duplicating costs? What will be the total fixed and variable costs for July?

D. If Hope wanted to predict total duplicating costs for 50,000 copies, would either the model in problem 44 or the model calculated here do a good job of estimating total cost at the level of production? Include a discussion of the relevant range.

53. Hunziker Rapid Delivery Service wants to determine the cost behavior pattern of maintenance costs to its delivery vehicles. The prior year's data regarding maintenance hours and costs are as follows:

	Hours of Activity	Maintenance Costs
January	480	$ 4,200
February	320	3,000
March	400	3,600
April	300	2,820
May	500	4,350
June	310	2,960
July	320	3,030
August	520	4,470
September	490	4,260
October	470	4,050
November	350	3,300
December	340	3,160
Total	4,800	$43,200

Required

A. Using the high/low method, compute the fixed costs and the variable rate, and give the resulting equation.

B. Compare the equation in A to the regression results in problem 50. Compare the equations and comment on the difference.

C. Explain what the best method is for management to use in cost analysis at Hunziker Rapid Delivery Service.

54. Data from the duplicating department of Kool Kopy Company for the previous nine months are as follows:

	Number of Copies Made	Duplicating Deptartment's Costs
January	20,000	$17,000
February	25,000	11,000
March	27,000	27,000
April	22,000	18,000
May	24,000	30,000
June	30,000	24,000
July	22,000	18,000
August	23,000	18,500
September	34,000	26,000

Required

A. Using the high/low method, identify the fixed costs and the variable cost per unit, and show the resulting equation.

B. Compare the equation generated in problem 51 using regression analysis, to the equation in A. Comment on the differences. Why do you think this model using the high/low method is different? What, if anything, could be done to improve the accuracy of the high/low model in this problem?

55. Mack has just returned from his annual one-week trip to Montana to fly-fish for trophy rainbow trout. Dee, his wife, is trying to convince him that the trip is too expensive and presents him with the following cost estimate per fish. Mack practices "catch and release" fishing, so he brings home only one fish, which he has mounted to display in his den. He caught and released 35 fish per day while on his seven-day trip. He goes fishing almost every weekend at home.

Airfare to Montana	$ 350
Resort expenses (room, board)	1,000
Fishing equipment (three rods and reels) 20-year life	2,500
Flies (50 per trip, enough for five fish)	150
Other equipment	350
Montana fishing license	50
Tennessee fishing license	35
Money lost playing backgammon (every weekend)	100
A fifth of Jack Daniels (for warmth while playing backgammon)	25
Total cost	$ 4,560
Cost per fish ($4,560÷245)	$18.61

Required

A. Assuming that the fishing trip is typical of the costs every year, what costs are relevant to a decision to go or not go on the Montana trip every year?

B. If Mack were to catch 300 fish on his next trip to Montana, what would be the additional cost for the additional 55 fish?

C. Which costs are relevant to a decision to give up fishing altogether?

56. ABC Enterprises has five stores, three of which are very profitable and two of which are losing money. Management is trying to decide whether to close one or both of the stores. The following income statements are presented for the two stores:

Store One (in local mall)		**Store Two (in strip mall)**	
Sales	$1,250,000	Sales	$1,000,000
Cost of sales	800,000	Cost of sales	700,000
Gross margin	$ 450,000	Gross margin	$ 300,000
Rent	250,000	Rent	200,000
Advertising	50,000	Advertising	50,000
Corporate expense	75,000	Corporate Expense	75,000
Salaries	125,000	Salaries	90,000
Net income	$ (50,000)	Net income	$ (115,000)

If the two stores are closed, the corporate expense will be allocated to the other three stores, and the salaries, for the store managers, will be eliminated. The advertising expense is specific to each store, so that expense would be eliminated. The rent for Store One is $125,000 per year plus 10 percent of the sales dollars. The lease is for five years and cannot be canceled. The rent for Store Two is monthly; with 30-days notice, the lease can be canceled.

Required

A. What items on each income statement are relevant to the decision to close each store?

B. What would you recommend that management do? Why?

Chapter 6

COST BEHAVIOR AND DECISION MAKING: COST-VOLUME-PROFIT ANALYSIS

Study Tools

A Review of the Previous Chapter

In Chapter 5, we examined the nature of costs. We introduced concepts of cost behavior, relevant costs, and the impact of income taxes and the time value of money on costs and decision making.

A Preview of This Chapter

In this chapter, the concept of cost behavior is developed further, and we introduce a variety of tools (contribution margin ratio, operating leverage, break-even) used in cost-volume-profit (CVP) analysis.

Key concepts include:

- The contribution margin income statement is structured to emphasize cost behavior as opposed to cost function.
- For every unit change in sales, contribution margin will increase or decrease by the contribution margin per unit multiplied by the increase or decrease in sales volume.
- The contribution margin per unit and the contribution margin ratio will remain constant as long as sales vary in direct proportion to volume.
- For every dollar change in sales, contribution margin will increase or decrease by the contribution margin ratio multiplied by the increase or decrease in sales dollars.
- The payment of income taxes is an important variable in target profit and other CVP decisions.
- A company operating near the break-even point will have a high level of operating leverage, and income will be very sensitive to changes in sales volume.
- Variable costing is consistent with CVP's focus on differentiating fixed from variable costs and provides useful decision-making information that is often not apparent when using absorption costing.

LEARNING OBJECTIVES

After studying the material in this chapter, you should be able to:

LO1 Determine the format and use of the contribution margin income statement

LO2 Use the contribution margin per unit and the contribution margin ratio to determine the impact of changes in sales on income

LO3 Use the decision-making model in CVP analysis

LO4 Analyze what-if decisions, using contribution margin per unit, contribution margin ratio, and operating leverage

LO5 Compute a company's break-even point in a single and a multiproduct environment

LO6 Use break-even analysis in an activity-based costing environment

LO7 Analyze target profit before and after the impact of income tax

LO8 Identify the assumptions inherent in CVP analysis

LO9 Identify the differences between variable costing and absorption costing and the use of variable costing for decision making

A Preview of Upcoming Chapters

Chapter 7 extends the discussion of relevant costs and examines a variety of decisions made by managers in their day-to-day activities.

In Chapter 5, we emphasized the importance of understanding the nature of costs. In this chapter, we focus on one aspect of the nature of costs (cost behavior) and develop a set of tools that focus on the distinction between fixed and variable costs. These tools include measures of a company's contribution margin, contribution margin ratio, and operating leverage—the cornerstones of cost-volume-profit (CVP) analysis. CVP analysis provides marketing and operations managers with useful information concerning sales necessary in order to break even or to earn a target profit and how profit is affected when the costs, volume, or prices of products or services are changed. The effect of income taxes on CVP analysis is also discussed. ■

INTRODUCTION

Some of the more important decisions managers make involve the analysis of the relationship among the cost, volume, and profitability of products produced and services provided by a company. **Cost-volume-profit (CVP) analysis** focuses on the relationship among the following five factors and the overall profitability of a company:

1. The prices of products or services
2. The volume of products or services produced and sold
3. The per unit variable costs
4. The total fixed costs
5. The mix of products or services produced

THE CONTRIBUTION MARGIN INCOME STATEMENT

LO1
Determine the format and use of the contribution margin income statement

As mentioned in Chapter 5, the traditional income statement required for external financial reporting focuses on function (product costs versus period costs) in calculating the cost of goods sold and a company's gross profit. **Gross profit** is the difference between sales and cost of goods sold. However, because cost of goods sold includes both fixed costs (facility-level costs) and variable costs (unit-level costs, such as direct material), the behavior of cost of goods sold and gross profit is difficult to predict when production increases or decreases.

APPLICATION IN BUSINESS

Gross profit (usually as a percentage of sales) is used by investment analysts as a measure of cost control and efficiency in the manufacturing process and thus is useful in assessing the value of a company.

In contrast, the contribution margin income statement is structured by behavior rather than by function. Following are a traditional income statement and a contribution margin income statement shown side by side so you can see the difference.

Comparison of Income Statements

Traditional			Contribution Margin		
Sales		$1,000	Sales		$1,000
Less: Cost of goods sold			Less: Variable costs		
Variable costs	$350		Manuf. costs	$350	
Fixed costs	150		S & A costs	50	
Total cost of goods sold		500	Total variable costs		400
Gross profit		$ 500	Contribution margin		$ 600
Less: S & A costs			Less: Fixed costs		
Variable costs	$ 50		Manuf. costs	$150	
Fixed costs	250		S & A costs	250	
Total S & A costs		300	Total fixed costs		400
Net income		$ 200	Net income		$ 200

As you can see, although the net income is the same for both statements, the traditional statement focuses on the function of the costs, whereas the contribution margin income statement focuses on the behavior of the costs. In the traditional income statement, cost of goods sold and selling and administrative (S&A) costs include both variable and fixed costs. In the contribution margin income statement, costs are separated by behavior (variable versus fixed) rather than by function. Note, however, that the contribution margin income statement combines product and period costs. Variable costs include both variable product costs (direct materials) and variable selling and administrative costs (commissions on sales), whereas fixed costs likewise include both product and period costs.

Key Concept: *The contribution margin income statement is structured to emphasize cost behavior as opposed to cost function.*

Because of the focus on cost behavior, the information in the contribution margin income statement is very useful for managerial decision making. For example, a contribution margin income statement for HD Inc. (a manufacturer of floppy disk drives for computers) follows. Note that per unit cost information is also shown in the statement. This information is helpful in understanding the usefulness of the contribution margin income statement.

	Total	Per Unit
Sales (100,000 units)	$200,000	$2.00
Less: Variable costs	80,000	0.80
Contribution margin	$120,000	$1.20
Less: Fixed costs	40,000	
Net income	$ 80,000	

CONTRIBUTION MARGIN PER UNIT

As you can see in the preceding income statement, the contribution margin is $1.20 per unit. What exactly does that tell us? It tells us that every floppy disk HD Inc. sells contributes $1.20 toward the payment of fixed costs. Once fixed costs are covered, each unit sold will contribute $1.20 toward net income. Remember that variable costs vary in total with production and remain constant when expressed as a per unit amount. As long as total sales vary in direct proportion to the number of units sold, **contribution margin per unit** will also remain constant.

Note what happens to HD's contribution margin if one additional unit is produced and sold. Increasing sales by one unit increases contribution margin by $1.20. Assuming that fixed costs don't change, net income increases by the same $1.20.

	Total	Per Unit
Sales (100,001 units)	$200,002.00	$2.00
Less: Variable costs	80,000.80	0.80
Contribution margin	$120,001.20	$1.20
Less: Fixed costs	40,000.00	
Net income	$ 80,001.20	

What happens if HD Inc. increases sales by 100 units (from 100,000 to 100,100)? As you can see, contribution margin and net income increase by $120 (100 units × $1.20 per unit) to $120,120 and $80,120, respectively. You can also analyze this as a 99-unit change from 100,001 units. Contribution margin and net income increase by $118.80 (99 units × $1.20 per unit) to $120,120 and $80,120, respectively.

	Total	Per Unit
Sales (100,100 units)	$200,200.00	$2.00
Less: Variable costs	80,080.00	0.80
Contribution margin	$120,120.00	$1.20
Less: Fixed costs	40,000.00	
Net income	$ 80,120.00	

What happens if sales decrease from the original 100,000 units to 99,000 units (a decrease of 1,000 units)? Contribution margin and net income will decrease by $1,200 (1,000 units × $1.20 per unit). This can also be viewed as a 1,100-unit decrease from sales of 100,100 units. As you can see, contribution margin and net income will decrease by $1,320 (1,100 units × $1.20 per unit).

	Total	Per Unit
Sales (99,000 units)	$198,000.00	$2.00
Less: Variable costs	79,200.00	0.80
Contribution margin	$118,800.00	$1.20
Less: Fixed costs	40,000.00	
Net income	$ 78,800.00	

As you can see, the use of contribution margin per unit makes it very easy to predict how both increases and decreases in sales volume impact contribution margin and net income.

***Key Concept:** For every unit change in sales, contribution margin will increase or decrease by the contribution margin per unit multiplied by the increase or decrease in sales volume.*

***Concept Question:** How much net income will HD Inc. earn if sales decrease to 90,000 units?*

Concept Answer: Note that you can calculate the change in net income from any starting point. From 99,000 units, net income will decrease by $10,800 (9,000 units × $1.20 per unit) to $68,000. You can get the same answer starting at 100,000 units. A 10,000-unit reduction in sales will reduce income by $12,000 (10,000 × $1.20 per unit) to $68,000. ■

Note what happens when sales volume decreases to 33,334 units. At this point, HD Inc.'s net income is zero. The company is at the break-even point when the contribution margin just covers fixed expenses and net income is zero. The calculation of a firm's break-even point is discussed in more detail later in the chapter.

	Total	Per Unit
Sales (33,334 units)	$66,668	$2.00
Less: Variable costs	26,668	0.80
Contribution margin	$40,000	$1.20
Less: Fixed costs	40,000	
Net income	$ 0	

CONTRIBUTION MARGIN RATIO

The contribution margin income statement can also be presented using percentages, as shown in the following income statement. The **contribution margin ratio** is calculated by dividing the contribution margin in dollars by sales dollars:

$$\text{Contribution margin ratio} = \frac{\text{Contribution margin (in \$)}}{\text{Sales (in \$)}}$$

The contribution margin ratio can be viewed as the amount of each sales dollar contributing to the payment of fixed costs and increasing net profit—that is, 60 cents of each sales dollar contributes to the payment of fixed costs or increases net income. Like the contribution margin per unit, the contribution margin ratio will remain constant as long as sales vary in direct proportion to volume.

	Total	**Percentage**
Sales (100,000 units)	$200,000	100%
Less: Variable costs	80,000	40
Contribution margin	$120,000	60% (120,000/200,000)
Less: Fixed costs	40,000	
Net income	$ 80,000	

Key Concept: *The contribution margin per unit and the contribution margin ratio will remain constant as long as sales vary in direct proportion to volume.*

Like contribution margin per unit, the contribution margin ratio allows us to very quickly see the impact of a change in sales on contribution margin and net income. As you saw in the income statement on page 166, a $200 increase in sales (100 units) will increase contribution margin by $120 ($200 × 60%). Assuming that fixed costs don't change, this $120 increase in contribution margin increases net income by the same amount. On page 166, we decreased sales by 1,000 units ($2,000), resulting in a decrease in contribution margin and net income of $1,200 ($2,000 × 60%).

PAUSE & *Reflect*

Go back and calculate the contribution margin ratio in the HD Inc. income statements presented on the last few pages. Make sure you understand the calculations. You will see that it is always 60 percent.

Key Concept: *For every dollar change in sales, contribution margin will increase or decrease by the contribution margin ratio multiplied by the increase or decrease in sales dollars.*

Concept Question: *Using either contribution margin per unit or contribution margin ratio, calculate HD Inc.'s net income (loss) when sales are as follows:*

1. *25,000 units, or $50,000*
2. *50,000 units, or $100,000*

Concept Answer: Using the contribution margin per unit of $1.20, if sales are 25,000 units, the contribution margin will be $30,000 (25,000 × $1.20 per unit). Subtracting fixed costs of $40,000 leaves a net loss of $10,000. The contribution margin can also be calculated by multiplying sales of $50,000 by the contribution margin ratio of 60%. In a similar fashion, when sales are equal to 50,000 units ($100,000), contribution margin is equal to $60,000 and net income is equal to $20,000. ■

THE CONTRIBUTION MARGIN AND ITS USES

To illustrate the many uses of the contribution margin income statement in managerial decision making, let's look at the income statement of Happy Daze Game Company. Happy Daze produces just one game but plans to increase its product line to include more games in the near future. The latest income statement for Happy Daze is as follows:

Happy Daze Game Company

	Total	Per Unit	Percentage
Sales (8,000 units)	$100,000	$12.50	100%
Less: Variable costs	72,000	9.00	72
Contribution margin	$ 28,000	$ 3.50	28%
Less: Fixed costs	35,000		
Net income (loss)	$ (7,000)		

LO2
Use the contribution margin per unit and the contribution margin ratio to determine the impact of changes in sales on income

In this case, Happy Daze is losing $7,000 on sales of $100,000. What would happen if sales were to increase by 3,000 units? Using what we know about the contribution margin income statement, we can see that every unit sold contributes $3.50, or 28 percent of every sales dollar, toward fixed costs. If Happy Daze sells 3,000 more units, contribution margin and net income will increase by $10,500 (3,000 × $3.50). We can use the contribution margin ratio to arrive at the same solution. Increasing sales by 3,000 units at $12.50 per unit will increase sales dollars by $37,500. With a contribution margin ratio of 28 percent and no changes in fixed costs, a $37,500 increase in sales will increase net income by $10,500 ($37,500 × 28%). What does this mean for Happy Daze? If the company can increase sales volume by 3,000 units (without changing anything else), it will show a profit of $3,500 instead of a loss of $7,000.

However, increases in sales may not happen in isolation. In order for Happy Daze to increase sales by 3,000 units, management might choose to lower the sales price, increase incentives to the sales staff, improve the quality of the product, or perhaps increase the advertising budget. As you will see in the next section, CVP analysis helps managers determine the impact on net income when these and other "what-if" decisions are made.

WHAT-IF DECISIONS USING CVP

LO3
Use the decision-making model in CVP analysis

In Chapter 1, we introduced a decision-making model. This model is summarized in Exhibit 6-1. The first step in the decision-making model is to accurately define the problem. Although it might be convenient to identify Happy Daze's problem as its net loss, the real problem is that contribution margin is not sufficient to cover fixed costs. Defining the problem in this way allows a more complete identification of objectives and options in Steps 2 and 3.

EXHIBIT 6-1 The Decision-Making Model

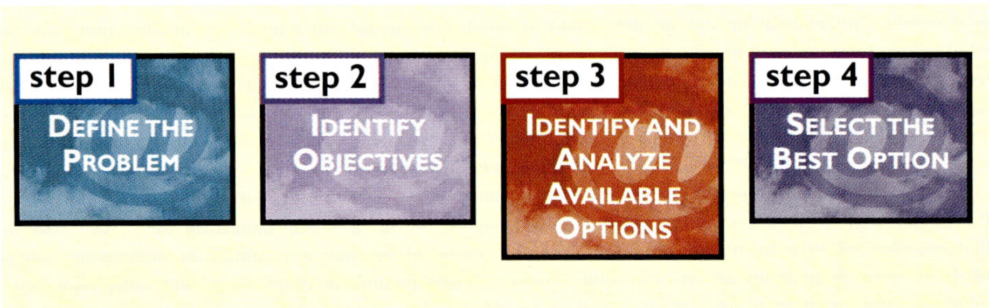

Step 2 IDENTIFY OBJECTIVES

Step 2 in our decision process is to identify objectives. In this case, Happy Daze has two primary objectives—to increase net income and to maintain high-quality products.

Step 3 IDENTIFY AND ANALYZE AVAILABLE OPTIONS

Step 3 is to identify Happy Daze's options. Our identification of the problem—that contribution margin is not sufficient to cover fixed costs—is helpful in fully exploring options in this step. For example, contribution margin can be increased in one of two ways: by increasing sales without a corresponding increase in variable costs (or by a greater percentage than variable costs) or by decreasing variable costs without a corresponding decrease in sales (or by a greater percentage than sales). As an alternative, Happy Daze could focus on decreasing fixed costs while holding contribution margin steady or some combination of the two. Within each of these general options, Happy Daze has a multitude of specific alternatives available that require an analysis of relevant variables.

After consultation with marketing, operations, and accounting managers, the CEO of Happy Daze identifies three options that she would like to consider in more depth:

1. Reducing the variable costs of manufacturing the product
2. Increasing sales through a change in the sales incentive structure or commissions (which would also increase variable costs)
3. Increasing sales through increasing advertising (a fixed cost)

OPTION 1

LO4
Analyze what-if decisions using contribution margin per unit, contribution margin ratio, and operating leverage

When variable costs are reduced, contribution margin will increase. So the question becomes: what can be done to reduce the variable costs of manufacturing? Happy Daze could find a less expensive supplier of raw material. The company could also investigate the possibility of reducing the amount of labor used in the production process or of using lower-wage employees in the production process.

In either case, qualitative factors must be considered. If Happy Daze finds a less expensive supplier of raw materials, the reliability (shipments may be late, causing down time) of the supplier and the quality (paper products are not as good, adhesive is not bonding) of the material must be considered. Reducing labor costs also has both quantitative and qualitative implications. If less labor is involved in the production process, more machine time may be needed. Although this option certainly lowers variable costs, it also raises

Happy Daze Game Co.

fixed costs. Using lower-skilled workers to save money could result in more defective products owing to mistakes made by lack of experience on the part of the workers. Another possible result of using fewer workers is that it can adversely affect employee morale. Being short-staffed can cause stress on workers, owing to the likelihood that they will be overworked.

A key point in Step 3 is that a decision maker should consider only those costs and other factors that are relevant to the decision. In other words, only those costs and other factors that vary between each of the options should be considered.

Happy Daze decides to decrease variable costs by reducing the costs of direct labor. This reduces variable costs by 10 percent and, as shown in the following analysis, results in an overall increase in net income of $7,200.

Happy Daze Game Company Impact of Reducing Variable Costs by 10 Percent

	Current	Option 1
Sales	$100,000	$100,000
Less: Variable costs	72,000	64,800
Contribution margin	$ 28,000	$ 35,200
Less: Fixed costs	35,000	35,000
Net income (loss)	$ (7,000)	$ 200

OPTION 2

The CEO of Happy Daze would also like to consider providing additional sales incentives in an effort to increase sales volume. For example, the marketing manager estimates that if Happy Daze raises the sales commission by 10 percent on all sales above the present level, sales will increase by $30,000, or 2,400 games. (The additional sales commission will be $3,000.) The results of Option 2 are as follows:

Happy Daze Game Company Impact of Increasing Sales Incentives (sales increase to $130,000)

	Current	Option 2
Sales	$100,000	$130,000
Less: Variable costs	72,000	96,600
Contribution margin	$ 28,000	$ 33,400
Less: Fixed costs	35,000	35,000
Net income (loss)	$ (7,000)	$ (1,600)

Happy Daze can increase net income by $5,400 by increasing the sales commission by 10 percent on all sales of more than $100,000. The new variable costs are calculated by using a variable-cost percentage of 72 percent on sales up to $100,000 and 82 percent on all sales of more than $100,000. However, note that Happy Daze still has a net loss under this option. In addition, it is important to remember that the increase in sales is an estimate, and actual sales may be higher or lower than $130,000. As you can see in the following income statement, if sales increase by $40,000 instead of $30,000, income will increase by $7,200, and Happy Daze will report net income of $200.

Happy Daze Game Company Impact of Increasing Sales Incentives (sales increase to $140,000)

	Current	Option 2A
Sales	$100,000	$140,000
Less: Variable costs	72,000	104,800
Contribution margin	$ 28,000	$ 35,200
Less: Fixed costs	35,000	35,000
Net income (loss)	$ (7,000)	$ 200

In Option 1 and Option 2, the ultimate change in net income can be determined by focusing solely on the change in contribution margin. Fixed costs are not relevant in either analysis, because they do not vary. However, as you will see in Option 3, that is not always the case.

OPTION 3

The marketing manager estimates that spending an additional $10,000 on advertising will increase sales by $40,000, or 3,200 games. Contribution margin is again relevant because it differs between options. In addition, fixed costs are relevant in analyzing Option 3 because the increase in sales will occur only with an increase in advertising (a fixed cost).

What is the impact of Option 3 on the contribution margin and net income of Happy Daze? As shown next, increasing sales by $40,000 (3,200 games) will increase contribution margin by $11,200 [($12.50 – $9) × 3,200], or [$40,000 × 0.28]. However, because fixed costs will also increase by $10,000, net income will increase (the net loss will decrease) by only $1,200.

Happy Daze Game Company Impact of Increasing Advertising

	Current (8,000 units)	Option 3 (11,200 units)
Sales	$100,000	$140,000
Less: Variable cost	72,000	100,800
Contribution margin	$ 28,000	$ 39,200
Less: Fixed cost	35,000	45,000
Net income (loss)	$ (7,000)	$ (5,800)

Step 4 SELECT THE BEST OPTION

Step 4 requires the CEO of Happy Daze to select the best of the three options. How well does each option meet the stated objectives of increasing net income while maintaining a high-quality product? The CEO of Happy Daze should analyze each alternative solution in the same manner and choose the best course of action based on both quantitative and qualitative factors.

From a quantitative perspective, Option 1 results in an increase in net income of $7,200, Option 2 increases net income by $5,400, and Option 3 increases net income by $1,200. However, remember that if sales increase to $140,000 in Option 2A, net income will increase by $7,200. The increase in sales predicted in Option 3 is also not known with certainty. Step 4 requires an assessment of the risk inherent in each option and the sensitivity of a decision to changes in key assumptions. For example, in Option 3, the marketing

http://www.dell.com

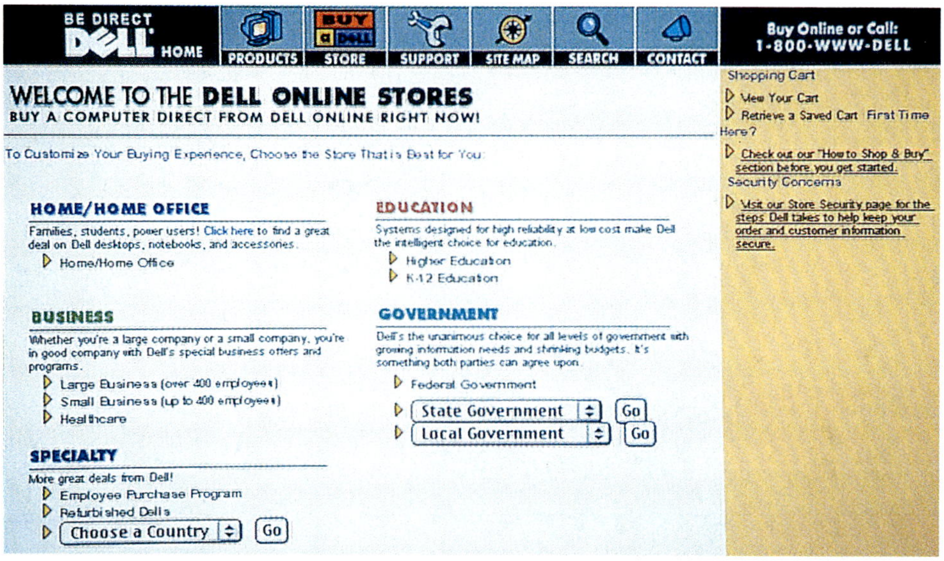

COURTESY OF DELL COMPUTER CORP.

IN THE NEWS

Dell Computer continually adjusts its incentives on computer systems, offering special promotions that are available to various customer groups: business users, home users, educators, and government agencies. In addition, in order to increase sales of a particular model of computer, Dell might offer free shipping or free peripherals, such as printers, free memory upgrades, etc. By continually adjusting these incentives (and the prices charged for a particular system), Dell is essentially using the basics of CVP analysis to increase profit.

manager thinks that increased advertising could increase sales by as much as $60,000. This would result in an increase in income of $6,800. Option 1 has little quantitative risk because the decrease in costs is known with certainty, no increase in sales is projected, and it is generally easier to lower costs than it is to raise sales. Based only on a quantitative analysis, Option 1 appears to be Happy Daze's best choice. However, Happy Daze must also consider the impact of the three options on the quality of its product. Of particular concern, Happy Daze should consider whether reducing labor costs in Option 1 will have a negative impact on the quality of its product. If the reduction in labor costs results from using lower-paid but inadequately skilled workers, quality may be adversely affected.

CHANGES IN PRICE AND VOLUME

Managers in almost all companies frequently make decisions using CVP analysis. One decision concerns how a price change (and the resulting change in sales volume) will impact net income. Changes in sales price can have a significant impact on sales volume. Raising the sales price may result in a decrease in sales volume. However, the impact on total sales revenue may be offset by the increase in sales price. Likewise, a decrease in sales price may result in an increase in sales volume without a corresponding increase in total sales revenue.

The change in volume is a projection based on the best information available at the time. Changes in sales price can be difficult to reverse. After a sales price is lowered, customers may react unfavorably to a later unexpected increase. Consequently, risk analysis is very important in these decisions.

CROSS-FUNCTIONAL APPLICATIONS *These business strategy decisions involve individuals in many areas of an organization, such as marketing, sales, production management, and even human resources personnel for hiring decisions. The implications of a bad decision in this area can affect the firm's bottom line.*

CHANGES IN COST, PRICE, AND VOLUME

Changes can be made to cost, price, and volume at the same time. In fact, changes in cost, price, and volume are never made in a vacuum and almost always impact one or both of the other variables. As an example, let's look at ZIA Motors, a manufacturer of automobiles. ZIA sells only one type of automobile (the Zoomer) at the low end of the price range. The car provides good, basic transportation but has experienced a significant drop in demand (and therefore profitability) in the past year. As a result, ZIA has decided to improve the quality of the Zoomer and to market the car as a higher-quality but still economical alternative to its better-known American-made competitors. The cost of direct material and other variable costs in the redesigned model will increase by 20 percent (from $6,000 to $7,200), owing to higher labor costs and the use of higher-quality engine materials and insulation to provide a quieter ride. Fixed costs will also increase, owing to the additional machinery needed. ZIA will need to invest $100 million in new equipment and robotics, resulting in annual depreciation of $20 million. ZIA also plans a $10 million advertising and public relations campaign to let the buying public know about the enhancements to the car. ZIA also plans to increase the sales price of the redesigned Zoomer from $8,000 to $10,000. The marketing department estimates that these changes will increase demand by somewhere between 2,000 and 10,000 cars per year. (Current demand is 30,000 cars.) When pressed for its best forecast, the marketing department estimates new sales at 35,000 automobiles. Current and projected income statements for ZIA follow:

ZIA MOTORS

Current and Projected Income Statements for ZIA Motors

	Current	After Proposed Changes
Sales	$240,000,000	$350,000,000
Less: Variable costs	180,000,000	252,000,000
Contribution margin	$ 60,000,000	$ 98,000,000
Less: Fixed costs	75,000,000	105,000,000
Net income	$ (15,000,000)	$ (7,000,000)

As you can see, although net income increases with the proposed changes, ZIA is still losing money on the Zoomer. Even though contribution margin increases by $38 million, fixed costs increase by $30 million, resulting in an overall increase in net income of $8 million.

IN THE NEWS **http://www.hyundai.com**

For years, Hyundai has been dealing with the public perception of the quality of its automobiles. In the past, it had a reputation for building inexpensive, lower-quality cars and has struggled to raise the selling prices of its newer cars to reflect their higher quality.

***Concept Question:** If sales increase by only 2,000 cars, how much will income increase (decrease)? What if sales increase by 10,000 cars?*

Concept Answer: These types of what-if questions can be answered most easily by using concepts of CVP analysis already at your disposal. In the previous example, if the proposed changes are made, the sale of each car will contribute \$2,800 toward fixed costs and ultimately net income. In other words, the contribution margin of each car sold is \$2,800 (\$10,000 sales price less \$7,200 variable costs). If 32,000 cars are sold, total contribution margin will be \$89,600,000 (32,000 × \$2,800). Although this is an increase of \$29,600,000, the change in fixed costs must also be considered. Because fixed costs increase by \$30,000,000, income will actually decrease by \$400,000 if only 32,000 cars are sold. On the other hand, if 40,000 cars are sold, contribution margin will be \$112 million, an increase of \$52 million (40,000 × \$2,800). This more than offsets the \$30 million increase in fixed costs and income will increase by \$22 million. ■

Step 4 SELECT THE BEST OPTION

Step 4 of the decision model explicitly recognizes the uncertainty inherent in many decisions. In this case, our decision is sensitive to assumptions made concerning the demand for the remodeled car. If demand for redesigned Zoomers is only 32,000 cars, net income will actually decrease, and ZIA will choose not to make the changes. If sales increase to 35,000 or 40,000 cars, income will increase under the proposed changes.

***Concept Question:** At what level of sales will ZIA be indifferent to making the proposed change? In other words, at what level of sales will ZIA Motors' current loss of \$15 million remain the same?*

Concept Answer: Because fixed costs increase by \$30 million under the new proposal, contribution margin must also increase by \$30 million for ZIA Motors to be equally well off under the proposed changes. A \$30 million increase in contribution margin requires a new contribution margin of \$90 million and sales of 32,143 cars (32,143 cars × \$2,800 contribution margin per car = \$90 million (rounded)). ■

BREAK-EVEN ANALYSIS

In addition to what-if analysis, it is useful for a company to know how many units or the dollar amount of sales that are necessary for it to break even. The **break-even point** is the level of sales at which contribution margin just covers fixed costs and consequently net income is equal to zero. Break-even analysis is really just a variation of CVP analysis in which volume is increased or decreased in an effort to find the point at which net income is equal to zero.

Break-even analysis is facilitated through the use of a mathematical equation derived directly from the contribution margin income statement. Another way to look at these relationships is to put the income statement into equation form:

$$\text{Sales} - \text{Variable costs} - \text{Fixed costs} = \text{Net income}$$

or

$$\text{Net income} = (\text{Sales price per unit} \times \text{Volume}) - (\text{Variable cost per unit} \times \text{Volume}) - \text{Fixed costs}$$

Substituting symbols, we have the following:

$$NI = SP\,(x) - VC(x) - FC$$

where x = sales volume. Because $SP - VC$ = contribution margin, the formula is simplified to

$$NI = CM(x) - FC$$

Because $NI = 0$ at the break-even point, total CM must equal FC:

$$CM(x) = FC$$

and the volume of sales in order to break even (x) can be calculated by dividing FC by CM:

$$\text{Break-even (units)} = \frac{\text{Fixed costs}}{\text{Contribution margin per unit}}$$

By dividing the contribution margin of each product into the fixed cost, we are calculating the number of units that must be sold to cover the fixed costs. At that point, the total contribution margin will be equal to fixed costs, and net income will be zero. For example, if Happy Daze has fixed costs of \$35,000 and the contribution margin per unit is \$3.50, as shown earlier, the break-even point is computed as follows:

$$\begin{aligned}\text{Break-even (units)} &= \frac{\text{Fixed costs}}{\text{Contribution margin per unit}}\\ &= \frac{\$35{,}000}{\$3.50}\\ &= 10{,}000 \text{ units}\end{aligned}$$

We can use a similar formula to compute the amount of sales dollars needed to break even:

$$\text{Break-even (\$)} = \frac{\text{Fixed costs}}{\text{Contribution margin ratio}}$$

Using the amounts from the previous example,

$$\text{Break-even (\$)} = \frac{\$35{,}000}{28\%\ \text{(see page 168)}}$$
$$= \$125{,}000$$

Concept Question: *Refer to the income statement on page 173 for ZIA Motors. How many Zoomers does ZIA have to sell under the proposed changes in order to break even?*

Concept Answer:

$$\text{Break-even (units)} = \frac{\text{Fixed costs}}{\text{Contribution margin per unit}}$$
$$= \frac{\$105{,}000{,}000}{\$2{,}800}$$
$$= 37{,}500\ \text{units}$$

Graphically, the break-even point can be found by comparing a company's total revenue with its total costs (both fixed and variable). As seen in Exhibit 6-2, the break-even point is the volume at which total revenue is equal to total cost.

EXHIBIT 6-2 Break-Even Graph

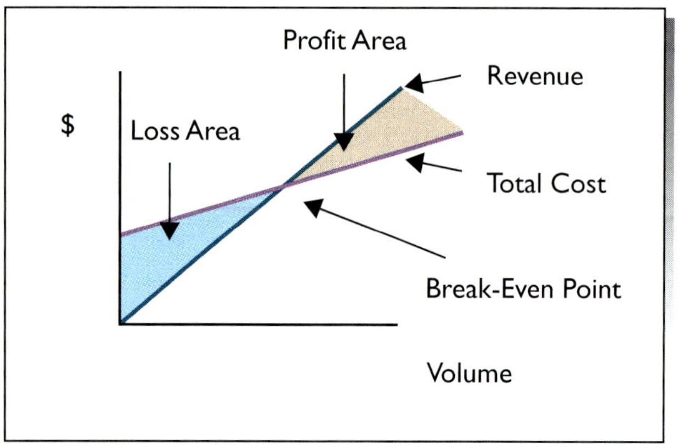

BREAK-EVEN CALCULATIONS WITH MULTIPLE PRODUCTS

Break-even calculations become more difficult when more than one product is produced and sold. In a multiproduct environment, a manager calculating the break-even point is

LO5
Compute a company's break-even point in a single and a multi-product environment

concerned not so much with the unit sales or the dollar sales of a single product but with the amount of total sales necessary to break even. This requires the calculation of an "average" contribution margin for all the products produced and sold. This in turn requires an estimate of the sales mix—the relative percentage of total units or total sales dollars expected from each product.[1] However, customers (and sales volume) will not always behave in the manner that we predict. For example, although the expected sales product mix may be 600 units of Product A and 400 units of Product B, we can estimate our customers' buying habits only from past experience. If the sales product mix ends up being 700 units of A and 300 units of B, the break-even analysis will change accordingly.

Assume that Happy Daze adds another game to its product line. The company estimates that the new game will achieve sales of approximately 50 percent of the old game. So if 8,000 units of the old game were sold, Happy Daze would expect to sell about 4,000 units of the new game. The expected sales product mix (in units) is therefore two-thirds $\left(\frac{8,000}{12,000}\right)$ old game and one-third $\left(\frac{4,000}{12,000}\right)$ new game. The new game will be priced at $15 per unit and requires $11 of variable production, selling, and administrative costs, so the contribution margin per unit is $4. The game will also require an investment of $15,000 in additional fixed costs. A summary of the price and cost of the old and new games follows:

Happy Daze Game Company

	Old Game (8,000 units)	Per Unit	New Game (4,000 units)	Per Unit
Sales	$100,000	$12.50	$60,000	$15.00
Less: Variable costs	72,000	9.00	44,000	11.00
Contribution margin	$ 28,000	$ 3.50	$16,000	$ 4.00
Less: Fixed costs	35,000		15,000	
Net income (loss)	$ (7,000)		$ 1,000	

The calculation of "average" contribution margin is *really* a weighted average. Although the simple-average contribution margin of the old game ($3.50) and the new game ($4.00) is $3.75, the weighted average is $3.67 (rounded). This can be seen most easily by examining the Total column of the income statement.

Happy Daze Game Company

	Old Game (8,000)	Per Unit	New Game (4,000)	Per Unit	Total (12,000)	Per Unit
Sales	$100,000	$12.50	$60,000	$15.00	$160,000	$13.33
Less: Variable costs	72,000	9.00	44,000	11.00	116,000	9.67
Contribution margin	$ 28,000	$ 3.50	$16,000	$ 4.00	$ 44,000	$ 3.67
Less: Fixed costs	35,000		15,000		50,000	
Net income (loss)	$ (7,000)		$ 1,000		$ (6,000)	

[1] Calculating the optimum mix of products to produce given limited resources and demand constraints is addressed in Chapter 7. The optimum mix will result in the highest overall contribution margin and also the highest overall profit for a company.

Dividing the total contribution margin of \$44,000 by 12,000 units sold gives us a total contribution margin of \$3.67 (rounded) per unit. The weighted-average contribution margin can be calculated more directly by multiplying the unit contribution margin for each game by the proportion of each game in the sales mix and adding the resulting numbers. This effectively weights each product's contribution margin by the relative sales mix for that product.

$$\text{Old game} = \frac{2}{3} \times \$3.50 = \$2.333$$

$$\text{New game} = \frac{1}{3} \times \$4.00 = \$1.333$$

$$\text{Weighted-average contribution margin} = \$3.67 \text{ (rounded)}$$

The weighted-average contribution margin for Happy Daze Game Company is therefore \$3.67 per game (rounded).

Concept Question: *Assuming a sales mix of 50 percent old games and 50 percent new games, calculate the new weighted-average contribution margin for Happy Daze. Does it increase or decrease? What if the sales mix changes to 40 percent old games and 60 percent new games? Why does the weighted-average contribution margin continue to increase as Happy Daze sells more new games and fewer old games?*

Concept Answer: With the sales mix at 50 percent old and 50 percent new, the weighted-average contribution margin becomes \$3.75 [(0.50 × 3.50)+(0.50 × 4.00)]. When the mix changes to 40 percent old and 60 percent new, the weighted-average contribution margin changes to \$3.80 [(0.40 × 3.50) + (0.60 × 4.00)]. Notice that when the volume shifts toward selling more of the product with the highest contribution margin, the weighted-average contribution margin increases. ■

The break-even formula for a company with multiple products is therefore as follows:

$$\text{Break-even (units)} = \frac{\text{Fixed costs}}{\text{Weighted-average contribution margin per unit}}$$

Happy Daze's break-even point is therefore: $\left(\frac{\$50{,}000}{3.67}\right)$, or 13,624 units (rounded). How is this number interpreted? Remember that the weighted-average contribution margin is dependent on the sales mix. Likewise, the break-even point is dependent on the sales mix (two-thirds old games and one-third new games). Assuming a sales mix of two-thirds to one-third, Happy Daze must sell 9,083 old games and 4,541 new games (rounded) to break even.

$$\text{Old game: } 13{,}624 \times \frac{2}{3} = 9{,}083$$

$$\text{New game: } 13{,}624 \times \frac{1}{3} = 4{,}541$$

Concept Question: *Refer to the previous concept question. If the sales mix changes to 50 percent old games and 50 percent new games, what will be the impact on the break-even point? What if the sales mix changes to 40 percent old games and 60 percent new games?*

© CHUCK KEELER/STONE

PAUSE & Reflect

Imagine how difficult it is for large retail stores, such as Wal-Mart or REI, to compute a break-even point for the entire store or company.

http://www.walmart.com
http://www.rei.com

Concept Answer: As the sales mix changes and Happy Daze sells more new games with a higher contribution margin, the break-even point will decrease. ■

The break-even point calculated using a weighted-average contribution margin for multiple products is valid only for the sales mix used in the calculation. If the sales mix changes, the break-even point will also change. Obviously, the more products involved in the sales mix, the more sensitive the calculation becomes to changes in sales mix.

BREAK-EVEN CALCULATIONS USING ACTIVITY-BASED COSTING

LO6
Use break-even analysis in an activity-based costing environment

Computing break-even when using activity-based costing (ABC) requires some slight modifications to the general formulas presented thus far. Conventional CVP analysis assumes that all costs are either variable or fixed. In ABC, costs are classified as unit, batch, product, or facility level, and CVP analysis must be modified accordingly. Whereas unit-level costs behave like true variable costs and vary directly with volume, and facility-level costs behave like fixed costs, batch- and product-level costs are likely to vary with drivers related to the complexity of a product or product diversity. Along with fixed costs, batch- and product-level costs are included in the numerator of the break-even formula. However, unlike traditional break-even analysis, they are allowed to vary with changes in their appropriate cost drivers. Although it may appear that the value of CVP would diminish when using ABC, in fact CVP analysis may be even more useful in decision making because the cost behavior information in an ABC system is more accurate.

The break-even equation when using ABC is modified as follows:

$$\text{Break-even (units)} = \frac{\text{(Fixed costs + Batch-level costs + Product-level costs)}}{\text{Contribution margin per unit}}$$

In the formula, batch-level costs are equal to the cost per unit multiplied by the appropriate batch-level driver(s), and product-level costs are equal to the cost per unit multiplied by the appropriate product-level driver(s). The contribution margin per unit is calculated by subtracting unit-level variable costs from the sales price. The main differences between the two calculations are as follows:

1. The fixed costs differ. Some costs that were previously identified as being fixed may actually vary with nonunit cost drivers (batch- and product-level costs).
2. These nonunit-level variable costs are included in the numerator along with fixed costs.

An ABC analysis of Happy Daze's product costs follows:

Sales price	$ 12.50 per unit
Variable costs:	
Direct material	$ 3.00 per unit
Direct labor	2.00 per unit
Variable overhead	4.00 per unit
Total variable costs	$ 9.00 per unit
Setup costs (batch)	$10,000 (10 setups @ $1,000 per setup)
Testing costs (product)	$ 5,000 (200 testing hours @ $25 per testing hour)
Facility-level fixed costs	$20,000

Putting these numbers into the ABC break-even formula results in the following:

$$\text{Break-even (units)} = \frac{(\$20{,}000 + \$10{,}000 + \$5{,}000)}{\$3.50}$$
$$= 10{,}000 \text{ units}$$

Concept Question: *Why is the break-even point using the ABC break-even formula the same as that computed using the conventional break-even formula?*

Concept Answer: Using the conventional break-even formula, fixed costs are $35,000 and consist of true fixed costs and nonunit-level variable costs associated with setups and testing. As long as the number of setups and inspection hours remain constant, the break-even will be the same under conventional break-even analysis and ABC. ■

However, if setups or the number of inspection or testing hours change, break-even will be different. Conventional break-even calculations ignore the changes in batch- and product-level costs. (Remember that they are treated as fixed under a conventional break-even analysis.) But these activity levels can change. For example, if Happy Daze discovers that it can reduce the direct labor involved with production of games from $2.00 to $1.85 per unit, its contribution margin will increase to $3.65, and the break-even point will decrease to 9,589 units (rounded). Using the conventional break-even formula would lead one to believe that the reduction in direct labor does in fact reduce the break-even point. However, what if Happy Daze has to increase the amount of time spent inspecting or testing the product as a result of the reduction in direct labor? Because the ABC system treats inspection or testing time as a nonunit-level variable cost, the additional hours of inspection time will impact the break-even point. If the reduction in direct labor adds 70 inspection hours, total costs will increase to \$6,750 (270 hours × \$25 per hour), and the break-even point will be as follows:

$$\text{Break-even (units)} = \frac{\$20{,}000 + \$10{,}000 + \$6{,}750}{\$3.65}$$
$$= 10{,}069 \text{ units (rounded)}$$

As can be seen from this computation of the break-even point using the ABC formula, the break-even point actually is higher than before the reduction in direct labor. Why is that? At a sales volume of 10,000 units (the old break-even point), the reduction in direct labor is \$1,500 (10,000 × 0.15), but the increased inspection expense is \$1,750 (70 hours × \$25). So what appears to be a cost reduction really isn't. Break-even analysis using ABC allows managers to more clearly see these tradeoffs, often leading to better decisions.

TARGET PROFIT ANALYSIS (BEFORE AND AFTER TAX)

LO7
Analyze target profit before and after the impact of income tax

The goal of most businesses is not to break even but to earn a profit. Luckily, we can easily modify the break-even formula to compute the amount of sales (units or dollars) needed to earn a target profit (before tax). Instead of solving for the sales necessary to earn a net income of zero, we simply solve for the sales necessary to reach a target profit.

$$\text{Sales} - \text{Variable costs} - \text{Fixed costs} = \text{Target profit (before tax)}$$

or

$$\text{Target profit} = (\text{Sales price per unit} \times \text{Volume}) - (\text{Variable cost per unit} \times \text{Volume}) - \text{Fixed costs}$$

Substituting symbols, we have

$$TP \text{ (before tax)} = SP\,(x) - VC(x) - FC$$

where x = sales volume. Because $SP - VC$ = contribution margin, the formula is simplified to

$$TP \text{ (before tax)} = CM(x) - FC$$

or

$$CM(x) = FC + TP \text{ (before tax)}$$

To solve for x, divide each side by CM:

$$\text{Sales volume (to reach a target profit before tax)} = \frac{[FC + TP \text{ (before tax)}]}{CM}$$

Happy Daze Game Co.

Happy Daze has decided that it must earn a target profit of $100,000 or the owners/stockholders will not want to continue their investment in the business. The question is, How many games does the company have to sell to earn that amount of profit? Using the target profit formula presented earlier and the data for the old game from page 168, consider the following equation:

$$\text{Sales volume (to reach a target profit before tax)} = \frac{(\$35,000 + \$100,000)}{\$3.50}$$
$$= 38,572 \text{ units (rounded)}$$

Although Happy Daze must sell only 10,000 games to break even, the company must sell 38,572 games to reach a before-tax target profit of $100,000. In fact, once we know that Happy Daze's break-even point is 10,000 units, we can directly calculate the sales necessary to reach a target profit of $100,000, using the CM per unit. Because each additional unit sold (above the break-even point) will contribute $3.50 toward net income, Happy Daze must sell an additional 28,572 units $\left(\frac{\$100,000}{3.50}\right)$ to earn a profit of $100,000.

Concept Question: *Using your knowledge of CVP analysis, how many units must Happy Daze sell in order to earn a target profit of $50,000?*

Concept Answer: To reach a before-tax target profit of $50,000, Happy Daze must sell 24,286 units calculated as follows:

$$\text{Sales volume (to reach a target profit before tax)} = (\$35,000 + \$50,000)/\$3.50$$
$$= 24,286 \text{ units (rounded)}$$

The multiple-product break-even and ABC break-even formulas can be modified in a similar fashion to solve for the sales necessary to reach a target profit. In a multiple-product environment:

$$\text{Sales volume (to reach target profit)} = \frac{(\text{Fixed costs} + \text{Target profit})}{\text{Weighted-average contribution margin per unit}}$$

Using ABC, we modify the formula as follows:

$$\text{Sales volume (to reach target profit)} = \frac{(\text{Fixed costs} + \text{Batch-level costs} + \text{Product-level costs} + \text{Target profit})}{\text{Contribution margin per unit}}$$

THE IMPACT OF TAXES

The payment of income taxes also needs to be considered in the target profit formula. If Happy Daze sells 38,572 games and earns the projected $100,000 in target profit, the company still won't have $100,000 cash flow to distribute to the owners as dividends, because it must pay income tax on the profit. If we assume that the income tax rate for Happy Daze is 35 percent, the company will have to pay \$35,000 in income tax (\$100,000 × 35%) and will be left with after-tax profit of \$65,000. The after-tax profit can be found by multiplying the before-tax profit by (1 – tax rate). Correspondingly, the before-tax profit is equal to the after-tax profit divided by (1 – tax rate):

$$\text{Before-tax profit} = \text{After-tax profit}/(1 - \text{tax rate})$$

If Happy Daze desires to earn an after-tax profit of \$100,000, the company must earn a before-tax profit of \$153,846 (rounded).

$$\text{Before-tax profit} = \$100{,}000/(1 - .35) = \$153{,}846$$

Modifying the before-tax target profit equation accordingly, we have

$$\text{Sales volume (to reach an after-tax target profit)} = \frac{[\text{FC} + \text{After-tax profit}/(1 - \text{tax rate})]}{\text{CM}}$$

Consequently, Happy Daze must sell 53,956 units in order to reach a before-tax profit of \$153,846 and an after-tax profit of \$100,000.

$$\text{Sales volume (to reach an after-tax target profit)} = \frac{(\$35{,}000 + \$153{,}846)}{\$3.50}$$
$$= 53{,}956 \text{ units}$$

This is confirmed in the following income statement for Happy Daze:

Happy Daze Game Company

Sales (53,956 units)	\$674,450
Less: Variable costs	485,604
Contribution margin	\$188,846
Less: Fixed costs	35,000
Net income	\$153,846
Less: Income tax @ 35%	53,846
Net income after tax	\$100,000

Key Concept: *The payment of income taxes is an important variable in target profit and other CVP decisions.*

Not accounting for the impact of income taxes in profit planning and break-even decisions can be a costly error.

APPLICATION IN BUSINESS http://www.irs.gov

The top federal income tax rate applicable to corporations is currently 35 percent. The top federal income tax rate applicable to individuals and small businesses operated as sole proprietorships is approximately 39 percent. Most states also levy some kind of tax on the earnings of businesses. It is not unusual for a business to face total income tax rates of 40 percent or higher.

PAUSE & Reflect

What impact do income taxes have on the calculation of the break-even point?

ASSUMPTIONS OF CVP ANALYSIS

LO8
Identify the assumptions inherent in CVP analysis

As in any form of analysis involving projections of the future, there are certain assumptions that must be taken into consideration. The major assumptions are as follows:

1. The selling price is constant throughout the entire relevant range. In other words, we assume that the sales price of the product will not change as volume changes.
2. Costs are linear throughout the relevant range. As discussed in Chapter 5, although costs may behave in a curvilinear fashion, they can often be approximated by a linear relationship between cost and volume within the relevant range.
3. The sales mix used to calculate the weighted-average contribution margin is constant.
4. The amount of inventory is constant. In other words, the number of units produced is equal to the number of units sold.

Although some of these assumptions appear to be violated often in real business settings, the violations are usually minor and have little or no impact on management decisions. CVP analysis can still be considered valid and very useful in decision making.

COST STRUCTURE AND OPERATING LEVERAGE

As mentioned in Chapter 5, cost structure refers to the relative proportion of fixed and variable costs in a company. Highly automated manufacturing companies with large investments in property, plant, and equipment are likely to have cost structures dominated by fixed costs. On the other hand, labor-intensive companies, such as home builders, are likely to have cost structures dominated by variable costs. Even companies in the same industry can have very different cost structures. A company's cost structure is important because it directly affects the sensitivity of a company's profits to changes in sales volume. Consider, for example, two companies that make the same product (furniture), with the same sales and same income. Company A is highly automated and uses state-of-the-art machinery to design, cut, and assemble its products. On the other hand, Company B is highly labor intensive and uses skilled craftspeople to cut and assemble its products. Contribution margin income statements for both companies are provided in Exhibit 6-3.

Concept Question: *Which company would you prefer to be?*

Concept Answer: Although you might opt for Company A with its high level of automation and correspondingly higher contribution margin ratio relative to Company B, consider the impact of changes in sales volume on the net income of each company. Although *increasing* sales will benefit Company A more than Company B, what happens when sales *decline*? If sales decline by 10 percent ($20,000), the income of Company A will decline by $16,000 ($20,000 × 80%), whereas the income of Company B will decline by $12,000 ($20,000 × 60%).

EXHIBIT 6-3 Contribution Margin Ratio and Operating Leverage

	Company A	Company B
Sales	$200,000	$200,000
Less: Variable costs	40,000	80,000
Contribution margin	$160,000	$120,000
Less: Fixed costs	80,000	40,000
Net income	$ 80,000	$ 80,000
Contribution margin ratio	80%	60%
Operating leverage	2.0	1.5

A company with a cost structure characterized by a large proportion of fixed costs relative to variable costs will see wider fluctuations in income as sales increase and decrease than a company with more variable costs in its cost structure.

OPERATING LEVERAGE

Operating leverage is a measure of the proportion of fixed costs in a company's cost structure and is used as an indicator of how sensitive profit is to changes in sales volume. A company with high fixed costs in relation to variable costs will have a high level of operating leverage. In this case, net income will be very sensitive to changes in sales volume. In other words, a small percentage increase in sales dollars will result in a large percentage increase in net income. On the other hand, a company with high variable costs in relation to fixed costs will have a low level of operating leverage, and income will not be as sensitive to changes in sales volume. Operating leverage is computed using the following formula:

$$\text{Operating leverage} = \frac{\text{Contribution margin}}{\text{Net income}}$$

In Exhibit 6-3, Company A has an operating leverage of 2.0 $\left(\frac{\$160,000}{\$80,000}\right)$, whereas Company B has an operating leverage of 1.5 $\left(\frac{\$120,000}{\$80,000}\right)$. What does this mean? When sales increase (decrease) by a given percentage, the income of Company A will increase (decrease) by 2 times that percentage increase (decrease), whereas the income of Company B will increase (decrease) by 1.5 times the percentage change in sales. When sales increase by 10 percent, the income of Company A will increase by 20 percent, or $16,000 ($80,000 × 20%). In other words, when sales of Company A increase to $220,000, income will increase to $96,000. The income of Company B will increase by 15 percent, or $12,000 ($80,000 × 15%), to a new income of $92,000. Likewise, when sales decrease by 10 percent, the income of Company A will decrease by 20 percent, whereas the income of Company B will decrease by 15 percent.

***Concept Question:** Using operating leverage and the income statements in Exhibit 6-3, calculate the net income of Company A and Company B when sales increase (decrease) by 50 percent, or $100,000.*

Concept Answer: When sales increase by 50 percent, the income of Company A will increase by 100 percent (2 × 50%) to $160,000 ($80,000 + $80,000). The income of Company B will increase by 75 percent (1.5 × 50%) to $140,000 ($80,000 + $60,000). When sales decrease by 50 percent, the income of Company A will decrease by 100 percent to $0 ($80,000 – $80,000), and the income of Company B will decrease by 75 percent to $20,000 ($80,000 – $60,000). ■

PAUSE & Reflect

You should note that the same answers can be found using the contribution margin per unit or the contribution margin ratio.

Unlike measures of contribution margin, operating leverage changes as sales change. Consider the following table, which provides contribution margin income statements for Company B at various levels of sales.

Company B

	500 Units	1,000 Units	2,000 Units
Sales	$100,000	$200,000	$400,000
Less: Variable costs	40,000	80,000	160,000
Contribution margin	$ 60,000	$120,000	$240,000
Less: Fixed costs	40,000	40,000	40,000
Net income	$ 20,000	$ 80,000	$200,000
Operating leverage	$\frac{\$60,000}{\$20,000} = 3.0$	$\frac{\$120,000}{\$80,000} = 1.5$	$\frac{\$240,000}{\$200,000} = 1.2$

At a sales level of 1,000 units ($200,000), Company B's operating leverage is 1.5. A 10 percent increase in sales increases net income by 15 percent. At a sales level of 500 units, operating leverage increases to 3.0, and a 10 percent increase in sales will increase net income by 30 percent (3 × 10%). At a sales level of 2,000 units, operating leverage is reduced to 1.2, and a 10 percent increase in sales will increase income by 12 percent.

As a company gets closer and closer to the break-even point, operating leverage will continue to increase, and income will be very sensitive to changes in sales. Company B's break-even point is 334 units (rounded). At this level of sales, contribution margin is equal to $40,080, income is equal to $80, and operating leverage is equal to 501 $\left(\frac{\$40,080}{\$80}\right)$. A 10 percent increase in sales at this point will increase net income by 5,010 percent!

Company B

Sales (334 units)	$66,800
Less: Variable costs	26,720
Contribution margin	$40,080
Less: Fixed costs	40,000
Net income	$ 80

Key Concept: *A company operating near the break-even point will have a high level of operating leverage, and income will be very sensitive to changes in sales volume.*

Understanding the concepts of contribution margin and operating leverage and how they are used in CVP analysis are very important in managerial decision making. Using these tools, managers can quickly estimate the impact on net income of changes in cost, sales volume, and price.

VARIABLE COSTING FOR DECISION MAKING

LO9
Identify the differences between variable costing and absorption costing and the use of variable costing for decision making

In Chapter 2, a system of product costing was introduced in which all manufacturing costs, fixed and variable, were treated as product costs. Product costs included direct materials, direct labor, and all manufacturing overhead (both fixed and variable). You will recall that product costs attach to the product and are expensed only when the product is sold. On the other hand, selling and administrative costs (period costs) are expensed immediately in the period in which they are incurred. Commonly called **absorption costing, or full costing,** this method is required for both external financial statements prepared under generally accepted accounting principles (GAAP) and for income tax reporting.

On the other hand, **variable costing, or direct costing,** treats only variable production costs (direct material, direct labor, and variable manufacturing overhead) as product costs, whereas fixed manufacturing overhead is treated as a period cost (along with selling and administrative costs). Variable costing is more consistent with CVP's focus on differentiating fixed from variable costs and provides useful information for internal decision making that is often not apparent when using absorption costing.

Exhibit 6-4 provides a summary of the two costing methods. As you can see, *the only difference between absorption and variable costing is the treatment of fixed overhead.* Under absorption costing, fixed overhead is treated as a product cost, added to the cost of the product and expensed only when the product is sold (as cost of goods sold). Under variable costing, fixed overhead is treated as a period cost and is expensed as incurred. The impact of this difference on reported income becomes evident when a company's production and sales are different (units produced are greater than units sold or units sold are greater than units produced).

Because absorption costing treats fixed overhead as a product cost, if units of production remain unsold at year-end, fixed overhead remains attached to those units and is included on the balance sheet as an asset (the cost of inventory). Using variable costing, all fixed manufacturing overhead is expensed each period, regardless of the level of production or sales. Consequently, when production is greater than sales and inventories increase, absorption costing will result in higher net income than will variable costing.

Let's look at a simple example in which HD Inc. produces 100,000 units each year. The cost of each unit includes direct material of \$0.30, direct labor of \$0.35, and variable overhead of \$0.10 per unit. In addition, fixed manufacturing overhead costs of \$30,000 are incurred. Variable selling and administrative costs are \$0.05 per unit sold, and fixed selling and administrative costs are equal to \$10,000. The selling price of one

Happy Daze Game Co.

EXHIBIT 6-4 Absorption and Variable Costing

ABSORPTION COSTING		VARIABLE COSTING	
Product Costs	**Period Costs**	**Product Costs**	**Period Costs**
Direct materials		Direct materials	
Direct labor		Direct labor	
Variable overhead		Variable overhead	
Fixed overhead			**Fixed overhead**
	Selling & admin.		Selling & admin.

unit is $2. The cost of one unit of product under absorption and variable costing is calculated as follows:

Product Costs

Absorption Costing		Variable Costing	
Direct material	$0.30	Direct material	$0.30
Direct labor	0.35	Direct labor	0.35
Variable overhead	0.10	Variable overhead	0.10
Fixed overhead	0.30		
Total per unit	$1.05	Total per unit	$0.75

The only difference between the two methods is $0.30 of fixed overhead $\left(\frac{\$30{,}000}{\$100{,}000 \text{ units}}\right)$, which is treated as a product cost under absorption costing and a period cost under variable costing. If all 100,000 units are sold in year 1, how much income is reported under each method?

Under absorption costing, fixed manufacturing costs are expensed as part of cost of goods sold. Under variable costing, fixed manufacturing overhead costs are deducted as a fixed period cost. Regardless, when all units produced are sold, the net income reported under each method would be the same.

Year I Comparison of Absorption and Variable Costing

Absorption Costing		Variable Costing	
Sales	$200,000	Sales	$200,000
Less: Cost of goods sold	105,000	Less: Variable costs	80,000
Gross profit	$ 95,000	Contribution margin	$120,000
Less: Selling & admin. costs	15,000	Less: Fixed costs	40,000
Net income	$ 80,000	Net income	$ 80,000

Assume that in year 2, 100,000 units are produced but only 80,000 units are sold. In this case, the variable-costing method would expense the entire $30,000 of fixed manufacturing overhead as a period cost, whereas the absorption method would expense only $24,000 (80,000 units sold × $0.30 per unit). When production exceeds sales, absorption costing will report higher net income than will variable costing. Part of the $30,000 of fixed overhead (20,000 units × $0.30 per unit, or $6,000) remains in inventory until those units are sold.

Year 2 (80,000 units sold)

Absorption Costing		Variable Costing	
Sales	$160,000	Sales	$160,000
Less: Cost of goods sold*	84,000	Less: Variable costs	64,000
Gross profit	$ 76,000	Contribution margin	$ 96,000
Less: Selling & admin. costs	14,000	Less: Fixed costs†	40,000
Net income	$ 62,000	Net income	$ 56,000

*Cost of goods sold includes $24,000 (80,000 × $0.30) of fixed manufacturing overhead.

†Fixed costs include $30,000 of fixed manufacturing overhead.

Assume that in year 3, 100,000 units are produced and 120,000 units are sold. (The 20,000 remaining units from year 2 are sold.) In this case, under variable costing, $30,000 of fixed manufacturing overhead would continue to be expensed as a period cost. Under absorption costing, the $30,000 would get expensed plus an extra $6,000 related to the 20,000 units produced last year and sold this year (20,000 units × $0.30 per unit = $6,000). When units sold exceed units produced, variable costing will report higher net income than will absorption costing.

Year 3 (120,000 units sold)

Absorption Costing		Variable Costing	
Sales	$240,000	Sales	$240,000
Less: Cost of goods sold*	126,000	Less: Variable costs	96,000
Gross profit	$114,000	Contribution margin	$144,000
Less: Selling & admin. costs	16,000	Less: Fixed costs†	40,000
Net income	$ 98,000	Net income	$104,000

*Cost of goods sold includes $36,000 (120,000 × $0.30) of fixed manufacturing overhead.

†Fixed costs include $30,000 of fixed manufacturing overhead.

To summarize the three rules:

1. When units sold equal units produced, net income is the same under both costing methods.
2. When units produced exceed units sold, absorption costing will report higher net income than will variable costing.
3. When units sold exceed units produced, variable costing will report higher net income than will absorption costing.

The use of absorption costing for internal decision making can result in less than optimal decisions. For example, consider the case of the unemployed executive who offered his services to a manufacturing company for only $1 per year in salary and a bonus equal to 50 percent of any increase in net income generated for the year. Reviewing the absorption costing income statement for the previous year, he learned that although 10,000 units of product were produced and sold, the company had the capacity to produce 20,000 units. In addition, variable production costs were $40 per unit, variable selling and administrative costs were $10 per unit sold, fixed manufacturing overhead costs were equal to $300,000 ($30 per unit produced), and fixed selling and administrative costs were equal to $100,000. As shown here, last year's net income was $100,000.

Absorption Costing Income (10,000 units produced)

Sales (10,000 units)	$1,000,000
Less: Cost of goods sold*	700,000
Gross profit	$ 300,000
Less: Selling & admin. costs	200,000
Net income	$ 100,000

*Includes $300,000 (10,000 units × $30) of fixed manufacturing overhead.

Happy Daze Game Co.

By increasing production to 20,000 units, the per unit allocation of fixed manufacturing overhead is reduced to \$15 $\left(\frac{\$300{,}000}{20{,}000 \text{ units}} = \$15\right)$. Remember that under absorption costing, fixed overhead is a product cost and is expensed only when the product is sold. Therefore, only \$150,000 of fixed overhead costs will be expensed. The remaining \$150,000 of fixed manufacturing overhead costs is included in inventory and is reported as an asset on the balance sheet. The cost of goods sold is reduced to \$550,000, and net income is increased by \$150,000, to \$250,000. The manager is entitled to a bonus of \$75,000, whereas the company is saddled with 10,000 units of unsold inventory and the attendant costs of storing and insuring it.

Absorption Costing Income (20,000 units produced)

Sales (10,000 units)	\$1,000,000
Less: Cost of goods sold*	550,000
Gross profit	\$ 450,000
Less: Selling & admin. costs	200,000
Net income	\$ 250,000

*Includes \$150,000 (10,000 units × \$15) of fixed costs.

If income had been measured using a variable-costing approach, net income would be the same each year, and the manager would not be able to pull off this scheme.

Key Concept: *Variable costing is consistent with CVP's focus on differentiating fixed from variable costs and provides useful decision-making information that is often not apparent when using absorption costing.*

Many other decisions, such as whether to accept special orders, to make or to buy component parts, and to add or to drop product lines, are influenced by the costing approach a company uses. These decisions are discussed in more detail in Chapter 7. In addition, you should note that problems like these are minimized in a just-in-time (JIT) environment, in which inventory levels are minimized and companies strive to produce only enough product to meet demand.

SUMMARY OF KEY CONCEPTS

- The contribution margin income statement is structured to emphasize cost behavior as opposed to cost function. (p. 165)
- For every unit change in sales, contribution margin will increase or decrease by the contribution margin per unit multiplied by the increase or decrease in sales volume. (p. 166)
- The contribution margin per unit and the contribution margin ratio will remain constant as long as sales vary in direct proportion to volume. (p. 167)
- For every dollar change in sales, contribution margin will increase or decrease by the contribution margin ratio multiplied by the increase or decrease in sales dollars. (p. 167)
- The payment of income taxes is an important variable in target profit and other CVP decisions. (p. 183)
- A company operating near the break-even point will have a high level of operating leverage, and income will be very sensitive to changes in sales volume. (p. 186)
- Variable costing is consistent with CVP's focus on differentiating fixed from variable costs and provides useful decision-making information that is often not apparent when using absorption costing. (p. 190)

KEY DEFINITIONS

Cost-volume-profit (CVP) analysis A tool that focuses on the relationship between a company's profits and (1) the prices of products or services, (2) the volume of products or services, (3) the per unit variable costs, (4) the total fixed costs, and (5) the mix of products or services produced (p. 164)

Gross profit The difference between sales and cost of goods sold (p. 164)

Contribution margin per unit The sales price per unit of product less all variable costs to produce and to sell the unit of product; used to calculate the change in contribution margin resulting from a change in unit sales (p. 165)

Contribution margin ratio The contribution margin divided by sales; used to calculate the change in contribution margin resulting from a dollar change in sales (p. 166)

Break-even point The level of sales at which contribution margin just covers fixed costs and net income is equal to zero (p. 174)

Operating leverage The contribution margin divided by net income; used as an indicator of how sensitive net income is to the change in sales (p. 185)

Absorption (full) costing A method of costing in which product costs include direct material, direct labor, and fixed and variable overhead; required for external financial statements and for income tax reporting (p. 187)

Variable (direct) costing A method of costing in which product costs include direct material, direct labor, and variable overhead; fixed overhead is treated as a period cost; consistent with CVP's focus on cost behavior (p. 187)

COMPUTER SIMULATION

You can now turn to **Appendix A** of your text to complete the portion of the Big Al's simulation covering cost-volume-profit (CVP), break-even, and target profit analysis.

MULTIPLE CHOICE

1. Sales of Quickie Computers are down, and management has planned to increase salespersons' commissions on the sales of this product by 10 percent in hopes of raising sales volume by 10 percent. What effect should this change have?
- **a.** Sales price will increase.
- **b.** Sales price will decrease.
- **c.** Variable costs will increase.
- **d.** Variable costs will decrease.

2. If a company has a positive contribution margin but net income is low or negative, what are some ways of increasing net income?
- **a.** Increase sales price.
- **b.** Increase sales volume.
- **c.** Decrease variable costs.
- **d.** All of the above.

3. Decision makers should consider:
- **a.** quantitative factors
- **b.** qualitative factors
- **c.** both quantitative and qualitative factors
- **d.** none of the above

4. Gorham Gaslight Inc. has the following product information:

Sales price	$ 4.50 per unit
Variable costs	$ 3.25 per unit
Fixed costs	$5,000
Units sold	20,000

If one more unit is sold, net income will:

a. increase by $4.50
b. increase by $1.25
c. decrease by $3.25
d. decrease by $3.50

5. The Alexander Grant Company has the following information available regarding last year's operations:

Sales (150,000 units)	$300,000
Variable costs	100,000
Contribution margin	200,000
Fixed costs	80,000
Net income	120,000

The company's operating leverage is:

a. 1.25
b. 2.5
c. 0.50
d. 1.67

6. In a multiproduct environment,

a. CVP analysis cannot be used
b. contribution margin is based on sales mix
c. CVP analysis is much easier to use
d. break-even point remains the same even if sales mix changes

7. Heathcliff Company has the following product information:

Sales price	$ 6.00 per unit
Variable costs	$ 2.25 per unit
Fixed costs	$10,000
Units sold	20,000

What is the break-even point in sales dollars?

a. $120,000
b. $16,000
c. $2,667
d. $1,667

8. Scuffy Company has the following product information:

Sales price	$ 7.50 per unit
Variable costs	$ 2.25 per unit
Fixed costs	$10,000
Units sold	20,000

What is the break-even point in units?

a. 1,333
b. 1,905
c. 20,000
d. 4,444

9. Howard Enterprises has a contribution margin ratio of 65 percent and fixed costs of $15,000. What would sales have to be for an after-tax net income of $50,000? The company is in the 40 percent tax bracket.

a. $23,077
b. $100,000
c. $151,282
d. $69,231

10. Butterfly Murals, Inc., has the following cost information:

Variable selling & admin. costs	$	2.00 per unit
Direct materials	$	7.50 per unit
Variable overhead	$	2.25 per unit
Direct labor	$	1.25 per unit
Fixed selling & admin. costs	$50,000	
Fixed overhead	$75,000	
Units sold	25,000	

If 25,000 units are produced and sold at a price of $20, what is the net income under variable costing and absorption costing, respectively?

a. $0; $0
b. $125,000; $50,000
c. $50,000; $50,000
d. $125,000; $125,000

CONCEPT REVIEW

11. Discuss why cost-volume-profit analysis could be useful to managers.

12. The cost-volume-profit model is consistent with what type of costing?

13. Describe decisions that use the cost-volume-profit model.

14. If the total contribution margin is decreased by a given amount, what will be the effect on operating profit?

15. Define the term *contribution margin.*

16. Describe the formula for computing the break-even point.

17. Give the formula to calculate the contribution margin ratio, and describe what it represents.

18. If a firm has a negative contribution margin, what options are available to management to reach the break-even point?

19. Describe various options to increase the break-even point.

20. Discuss the meaning of the term *break even.* Why would a manager be concerned with the break-even point? Does a break-even calculation provide absolute accuracy? Why or why not? Discuss the impact of multiple products on the calculation of the break-even point.

21. How does cost-volume-profit analysis allow management to determine the relative profitability of a product?

22. At the break-even point, fixed cost is always what amount?

23. A company's break-even point in sales dollars may be affected by equal percentage increases in both selling price and variable cost per unit (assume all other factors are equal within the relevant range). The equal percentage changes in selling price and variable cost per unit will cause the break-even point in sales dollars to behave in what manner?

24. If fixed expenses decrease and the variable expenses (as a percentage of sales) decrease, what will be the effect on the contribution margin ratio (CMR) and the break-even point (BEP)?

25. If fixed expenses decrease while variable cost per unit remain constant, what will happen to the contribution margin?

26. In using cost-volume-profit analysis to calculate the expected sales level expressed in units, how would a predicted operating loss be included?

27. What are the major assumptions as to cost and revenue behavior underlying conventional cost-volume-profit calculations?

28. What is the basic difference between absorption costing and variable costing?

29. Under variable costing, are selling and administration considered product or period costs?

30. Describe how fixed manufacturing costs can be shifted between periods, using absorption costing.

31. Discuss why variable costing might be preferred over absorption costing.

32. Discuss why absorption costing might be preferred over variable costing.

33. If units sold exceed units produced, which method, variable or absorption, would show the higher net income? Why?

34. If units produced exceed units sold, which method, variable or absorption, would show the higher net income? Why?

35. If a company is using absorption costing, is it possible to increase net income without increasing sales? How?

36. Discuss how the use of JIT inventory systems could reduce the difference between net income reported between variable and absorption costing.

APPLICATION OF CONCEPTS

37. MacAulay Company produces one type of machine with the following costs and revenues for the year:

Total revenues	$4,200,000
Total fixed costs	$1,400,000
Total variable costs	$2,800,000
Total units produced and sold	700,000

Required

A. What is the selling price per unit?

B. What is the variable cost per unit?

C. What is the contribution margin per unit?

D. What is the break-even point in units?

E. How many units must be sold to make an operating profit of $1 million for the year?

38. Johnston Plumbing Company's sales price per house call is $100; variable costs per call are $60, and fixed costs for the year are $200,000. How many house calls must the company make to break even?

39. Krygowski Company has variable costs of $20 per unit and sells its product for $50. Fixed costs are $3,000 per month. How many units must it sell to earn a profit of $6,000?

40. If Lannefeld Company's selling price per unit is $10, variable costs per unit are $4, and fixed costs for the year are $105,000, how many units must it sell to earn a 10 percent return on sales?

41. Lause's Family Restaurant currently breaks even at 1,000 meals. Its fixed costs are $25,000, and its variable costs are $10 per meal. What is Lause's average selling price per meal?

42. Leake Fishing Rod Company's selling price is $12 per fishing rod, variable cost is $3 per rod, and fixed costs are $36,000. If fixed costs increased by $3,000, how many additional fishing rods must be sold to break even?

43. Lincoln Company's selling price is $18 per unit, variable cost is $6 per unit, and fixed costs are $36,000. If fixed costs increased by $3,000, how many additional units must be sold to break even?

44. Lockwood Company currently sells its deadbolt locks for $30. The variable costs are $10, and the annual fixed costs are $150,000. The company's tax rate is 40 percent. Calculate the number of units needed to earn an after-tax profit of $24,000.

45. Long Company produces two products, A and B, and sells 60 percent product A and 40 percent product B. A sells for $16 and has variable costs of $8; B sells for $12 and has variable costs of $9. Fixed costs for the period are $36,000. What is the break-even point in total units?

46. Lubin Company produces two products, A and B. A sells for $16 and has variable costs of $10; B sells for $12 and has variable costs of $8. Fixed costs for the period are $35,000. An equal number of A and B units are sold. At the break-even volume, how many units of A will be sold?

47. Lutz Company produces two products, widgets and gizmos. Widgets sell for $16 and have variable costs of $6. Gizmos sell for $12 and have variable costs of $8. Fixed costs for the period are $40,000. Normally, four units of widgets are sold for every two units of gizmos. How many units of gizmos must be sold if the company expects profits of $50,000?

48. Martinez Company has a break-even of 200 units with variable expenses of $200 and fixed expense of $100. What would one more unit sold contribute to net income before tax?

49. If Massey Company increased the selling price of a widget from $0.50 to $0.55 and fixed expenses increased from $200,000 to $240,000 while variable expense per unit remained stable, what would be the effect on the break-even point?

50. Matthews Lawn Service sells lawn mowing for $35 per yard with variable expenses of $21 per yard. If the company raises its selling price 40 percent, how much can unit sales decline before total net income declines?

51. Last year, Mayes Company had a contribution margin of 30 percent. This year, fixed expenses are expected to remain at $120,000, and sales are expected to be $550,000, which is 10 percent higher than last year. For the company to increase income by $15,000 in the coming year, the contribution margin ratio must be what level?

52. McGarity Company plans to sell 200,000 special Rose Bowl footballs with fixed costs of $400,000 and variable expenses at 60 percent of sales. To have a net income of $100,000, McGarity's management must set the sales price at what?

53. MacMaster Inc. is considering the introduction of a new custom neon signage product with the following price and costs:

Sales price	$ 75 each
Variable cost	25 each
Fixed cost	300,000 per year

It expects to sell 7,000 units for the year.

Required

A. How many signs must be sold to break even?

B. How many signs must be sold to make an operating profit of $15,000?

C. If 7,000 signs are sold, what operating profit is expected?

D. What would be the break-even point if the sales price decreased by 20 percent?

E. What would be the break-even point if variable costs per sign decreased by 40 percent?

F. What would be the break-even point if fixed costs were increased by $50,000?

54. In planning its operations for next year based on a sales forecast of $3,000,000, ZIA Motors prepared the following estimated costs and expenses:

	Variable	**Fixed**
Direct material	$ 800,000	
Direct labor	700,000	
Factory overhead	300,000	$450,000
Selling expense	120,000	180,000
General admin. expense	30,000	70,000
	$1,950,000	$700,000

Required

Step 3 IDENTIFY AND ANALYZE AVAILABLE OPTIONS

A. What would be the amount of sales dollars at the break-even point?

B. If ZIA must show a net income of $700,000, what options does it have to achieve its goal?

C. What qualitative factors should be considered for each option in B?

55. Marshall Advertising Company is contemplating an expansion program based on the following budget data:

Projected sales	$300,000
Variable expenses	210,000
Fixed expense	60,000

Required

A. Based on this projection, what would be the budgeted break-even point in sales dollars?

B. What would sales have to be to make a net income of $100,000?

56. Martin's Rock Company has provided the following information:

Sales (25,000 units)	$500,000
Direct materials	100,000
Direct labor	50,000
Variable factory overhead	20,000
Fixed factory overhead	35,000
Selling & admin. expense:	
Variable	5,000
Fixed	30,000

Required

A. Compute the break-even point in units for Martin's Rock Company.

B. Compute the contribution margin ratio for Martin's Rock Company.

C. If Martin Rock Company were to spend $10,000 on advertising, it projects that sales would increase by $20,000. Should the company increase the advertising? Why?

57. HD Inc. produces CD burners. The following information concerning last year is provided:

Units produced	100,000
Units sold	95,000
Direct material per unit	$ 55
Direct labor per unit	25
Variable manufacturing overhead per unit	15
Fixed manufacturing overhead	300,000

Required

A. Compute the cost per unit using absorption costing.

B. Compute the cost per unit using variable costing.

C. Compute the difference in net income between the two methods. Which costing method results in a higher net income?

D. Assume that production was 90,000 units and sales were 100,000 units. What would be the difference in net income between the two methods? Which costing method shows the greater net income?

E. Assume that production was 100,000 units and sales were 100,000 units. What would be the difference in net income between the two methods?

F. Which method is required by GAAP?

58. Parker Company produces watches. The following information concerning last year is provided:

Beginning inventory (units)	25,000
Units produced	90,000
Units sold	95,000
Direct material per unit	$ 15
Direct labor per unit	5
Variable manufacturing overhead per unit	10
Fixed manufacturing overhead	100,000

Required

A. Gail, the owner of Parker Company, is going to the bank to negotiate a line of credit and wants to show the maximum amount of income without changing last year's results. What costing method of inventory (variable or absorption) should she choose? Why?

B. If the bank requires GAAP financial statements, what method would she choose?

C. The bank sends her off with the comment, "We need more net income for a couple of months before we can grant you the line of credit." Because Gail projects no increase in demand for her watches in the next few months, what options are available to her?

Step 3 IDENTIFY AND ANALYZE AVAILABLE OPTIONS

D. Which option should she choose and why? Are the options legal? Are they ethical?

Step 4 SELECT THE BEST OPTION

59. Oliver Inc. produces an oak rocking chair that is designed to ease back problems. The chairs sell for $200 each. The results of last year's operations are as follows:

Units in beginning inventory	0
Units produced during the year	20,000
Units sold during the year	18,000
Units left in ending inventory	2,000
Variable manufacturing costs per unit:	
Direct materials	$ 70
Direct labor	20
Variable manufacturing overhead	15
Variable selling and administrative	10
Total variable cost per unit	$ 115
Fixed costs:	
Fixed manufacturing overhead	$ 500,000
Fixed selling & admin.	530,000
Total fixed costs	$1,030,000

Required

A. Assume that the company uses variable costing. Compute the unit product cost to produce one rocking chair.

B. Prepare an income statement based on variable costing.

C. Assume that the company uses absorption costing. Compute the unit product cost to produce one rocking chair.

D. Prepare an income statement based on absorption costing.

E. Compare the two and analyze the difference. What causes the net incomes to differ?

F. If production was 18,000 chairs and sales were 20,000 chairs (assume 2,000 chairs in beginning inventory), what would be the impact on the two income statements?

G. If the manager of the business was paid a bonus based on net income and had a choice of methods to use to report income, what method would he choose using the original income statement? If the situation described in F were to occur, would that change his decision? Why?

60. McGuinness Company produces two beers, Light and Stout, with the following characteristics:

	Light	**Stout**
Selling price per case	$10	$15
Variable cost per case	$ 8	$10
Expected sales (cases)	20,000	5,000

Total fixed costs for the company are $39,000.

Required

A. What is the anticipated level of profits for the expected sales volume?

B. Assuming that the product mix would be the same at the break-even point, compute the break-even point in terms of each of the products.

C. If only Stout were sold, how many units would be needed to break even?

D. If only Light were sold, how many units would be needed to break even?

E. If the product mix changed so that equal units of Light and Stout were sold, what would be the new break-even point in total units?

F. Discuss the accuracy of these calculations with regards to planning. What types of occurrences could affect the accuracy of the calculations? What assumptions must be made to use the calculations in planning and decision making?

61. Mebust Company sells three products, X, Y, and Z. The company has fixed costs in the amount of $2,600. The following information is presented to you:

	X	**Y**	**Z**
Price per unit	$11	$15	$17
Variable costs per unit	$ 6	$12	$16
Number of units sold	1,000	2,000	2,000

Required

A. Assuming that the product mix will be the same at the break-even point, compute the break-even in total units.

B. What are the break-even units for each product line?

C. What options are available to change the break-even point?

Step 3 IDENTIFY AND ANALYZE AVAILABLE OPTIONS

62. Meng Delivery Corporation wishes to earn a 30 percent return on its $100,000 investment in bicycles and cars used to make deliveries. Based on estimated sales of 10,000 delivery jobs, the cost per job would be as follows:

Variable manufacturing costs	$5
Fixed selling and administrative costs	2
Fixed costs	1

Required

A. What sales price should be set for each delivery?

B. What is the break-even point?

C. What options does Meng have to increase return to 35 percent?

D. What qualitative factors must be considered in this decision?

Step 3 IDENTIFY AND ANALYZE AVAILABLE OPTIONS

63. Miller Company has the following revenue and cost budgets for the two types of eyeglasses it sells:

	Plastic Frames	Metal Frames
Sales price	$10	$15
Direct materials	$ (2)	$ (3)
Direct labor	$ (3)	$ (5)
Variable overhead	$ (3)	$ (4)
Net income per unit	$ 2	$ 3
Budgeted unit sales	100,000	300,000

The budgeted unit sales equal the current unit demand, and total fixed overhead for the year is budgeted at $975,000. Assume that the company plans to maintain the same proportional mix. In numerical calculations, Miller rounds to the nearest cent and unit.

Required

A. What is the total number of units Miller needs to produce and to sell to break even?

B. What is the total number of units needed to break even if the budgeted direct labor costs were $2 for plastic frames instead of $3?

C. What is the total number of units needed to break even if sales were budgeted at 150,000 units of plastic frames and 300,000 units of metal frames, with all other costs remaining constant?

64. Mistry Company produces two products, Alfa and Beta. Alfa sells for $16 and has variable costs of $10. Beta sells for $12 and has variable costs of $8. Fixed costs for the period are $35,000. Normally, two units of Alfa are sold for every one unit of Beta.

Required

A. What is the break-even point?

B. How many units of Beta must be sold if the company expects profits of $50,000?

65. Moore Inc. invented a secret process to double the growth rate of hatchery trout and manufactures a variety of products related to this process. Each product is independent of the others and is treated as a separate profit/loss division. Product managers have a great deal of freedom to manage their divisions as they think best. Failure to produce target division income is dealt with severely; however, rewards for exceeding one's profit objective are, as one division manager described them, lavish.

The Morey Division sells an additive that is added to the pond water. Morey has had a new manager in each of the three previous years because the predecessor manager failed to reach Moore's target profit. Kassy Morgan has just been promoted to manager and is studying ways to meet the current target profit for Morey.

The target profit for Morey for the coming year is $800,000 (20 percent return on the investment in the annual fixed costs of the division). Other constraints on division operations are as follows:

- Production cannot exceed sales, because Moore's corporate advertising stresses completely new additives each year, even though the "newness" of the models may be only cosmetic.
- The Morey selling price may not vary above the current selling price of $200 per gallon, but it may vary as much as 10 percent below $200 ($180).

Morgan is now examining data gathered by her staff to determine whether Morey can achieve its target profit of $800,000.

- Last year's sales were 30,000 units at $200 per gallon.
- The present capacity of Morey's manufacturing facility is 40,000 gallons per year, but capacity can be increased to 80,000 gallons per year with an additional investment of $1,000,000 per year in fixed costs.
- Present variable costs amount to $80 per unit, but if commitments are made for more than 60,000 gallons, Morey's vendors are willing to offer raw material discounts amounting to $20 per gallon, beginning with gallon 60,001.

Morgan believes that these projections are reliable, and she is now trying to determine what Morey must do to meet the profit objectives assigned by Moore's board of directors.

Required

A. Calculate the dollar value of Morey's current annual fixed costs.

B. Determine the number of gallons that Morey must sell at $200 in order to achieve the profit objective. Be sure to consider any relevant constraints. What if the selling price is $180?

C. Without prejudice to your previous answers, assume that Kassy Morgan decides to sell 40,000 gallons at $200 per gallon and 24,000 gallons at $180 per gallon. Prepare a pro forma income statement for Morey, showing whether Kassy Morgan's decision will achieve Morey's profit objectives.

66. Happy Daze Game Company expects its sales during the next two months, July and August, to be $250,000 and $210,000, respectively. Variable costs at these levels will be $150,000 and $126,000, respectively, and fixed costs will be $100,000. July sales are expected to be 5,000 units and August sales are expected to be 4,200 units.

Happy Daze Game Co.

Required

A. What is the expected break-even point in July and August?

B. If the selling price is increased by 20 percent, what is the new variable cost ratio?

C. If the selling price is increased by 20 percent, what is the new break-even point?

D. Independent of your answer to C, if fixed costs decrease by 20 percent and variable costs increase by 20 percent per unit, what is the new break-even point?

67. Peter Nasta, cost accountant for Southeast Construction, has just finished his break-even analysis for each product line within the company. The analysis reveals a deficiency with three product lines: Townhouses, Basic houses, and Customhouses. A different division manufactures each of these houses. Based on current sales forecasts, the company as a whole will not reach the sales volume needed to break even. If two of the three product lines (Townhouses, Basic houses, and Customhouses) are dropped, the company will be able to remain profitable. Peter recommended that Townhouses and Customhouses be dropped.

When Peter started with the company, he worked for the division that manufactures Basic houses. In fact, his wife, Mary, still works for that division. What are the ethical issues involved in this decision?

68. David Nurkiewicz assisted in developing break-even points for various products within his company. He was hired by another company to determine selling prices of the company's products. David feels it is unacceptable to use the information he gathered for his previous employer, but he is being pressured by his new supervisor to divulge this information. What should David do?

69. McDonnell Douglas Aircraft Corporation (MacDac) manufactures the C-17, the newest jet transport used by the U.S. Air Force. MacDac sells the C-17 for a "flyaway cost" of $175,000,000 per jet. The variable production cost of each C-17 was estimated to be approximately $165,000,000. When the C-17 was first proposed, the Air Force expected to eventually purchase 400 of the jets. Later, following the collapse of the former Soviet Union, the projected total purchase volume dropped to 300 jets, then 200, then 150, and finally 120 jets.

Production began, and at one point MacDac was faced with the following situation. With 20 jets finished, a block of 20 more in production, and funding approved for purchase of a third block of 20 jets, the U.S. Congress began indicating that it would approve funding for the order and purchase of only 20 more jets (for a total of 80). This was a problem for MacDac because company officials had indicated previously that the break-even point for the C-17 was around 100 aircraft.

Because MacDac is headquartered in St. Louis, all the members of Congress from Missouri rushed to the company's aid, and now at least 120 C-17s will be ordered.

Required

A. Compute the actual break-even point for the C-17, assuming fixed costs of $1,000,000,000.

B. If MacDac sold only 80 C-17s, calculate the income or loss on the project.

C. Assume that MacDac had been told up front that the Air Force would buy only 80 jets. Calculate the selling price per jet that MacDac would have to charge to achieve a target profit (before tax) of $10,000,000 per jet.

70. Happy Daze Game Co. provides you with the following product costs:

Sales price per unit	$ 13.00
Variable costs per unit:	
Direct material	3.50
Direct labor	2.50
Variable overhead	3.50
Total variable cost	9.50 per unit
Setup cost (batch)	11,000 (10 setups @ $1,100 per setup)
Testing cost (product)	5,000 (200 testing hours @ $25 per testing hour)
Facility-level fixed costs	25,000

Required

A. Compute break-even, using the conventional break-even formula.

B. Compute break-even, using the ABC break-even formula.

C. Explain the difference.

D. Assume that the cost per setup is reduced to $1,000 and that testing hours are reduced to 150. What is the impact on the break-even point?

Chapter 7

Accounting Information, Relevant Costs, and Decision Making

Study Tools

A Review of the Previous Chapter

Chapter 6 provided a set of tools, including contribution margin, contribution margin ratio, and operating leverage, that are the cornerstones of cost-volume-profit analysis and that managers use to make a number of day-to-day decisions.

A Preview of This Chapter

In this chapter, we analyze a variety of decisions affecting managers. Each of these decisions is dependent on an analysis of relevant costs and relevant qualitative factors.

Key concepts include:

- The price of a product must be sufficient to cover all the costs of the product and to provide a profit.
- The price of a special order must be higher than the additional variable costs incurred in accepting the special order plus any opportunity costs incurred.
- A product should continue to be made internally and labor incurred internally if the avoidable costs are less than the additional costs that will be incurred by buying or outsourcing.
- A product should be dropped when the fixed costs avoided are greater than the contribution margin lost.
- Resource utilization decisions hinge on an analysis of the contribution margin earned per unit of the limited resource.
- A product should be processed further if the additional revenue is greater than the additional cost.

Learning Objectives

After studying the material in this chapter, you should be able to:

LO1 Identify factors and issues affecting the pricing of goods and services

LO2 Analyze the pricing of a special order

LO3 Analyze a decision involving the outsourcing of labor or making or buying a component

LO4 Analyze a decision dealing with adding or dropping a product, product line, or service

LO5 Analyze a decision dealing with scarce or limited resources

LO6 Analyze a decision dealing with selling a product or processing it further

LO7 Evaluate the impact of ABC on relevant costs and decision making

A Preview of Upcoming Chapters

Chapter 8 completes our study of the nature of costs in decision making and develops a set of tools that allow managers to consider the time value of money in making long-term capital investment decisions.

In Chapter 5, we emphasized that only relevant costs and factors should be considered by managers when making decisions. Following the decision-making framework developed in Chapter 1 and building on what we know about the nature of costs from Chapter 5, in Chapter 7 we analyze a variety of decisions affecting managers. These decisions include an examination of general pricing issues and the pricing of special orders; whether to outsource labor; whether to make or buy a component used to manufacture a product; whether to add or drop a product, product line, or service; and how to utilize limited resources to maximize profit. We also consider the impact of ABC on these decisions. ■

INTRODUCTION

As we discussed in Chapter 1, operating activities include a wide range of decisions that managers make on a day-to-day basis. The manager of a local florist shop must determine the selling prices of its floral arrangements. Managers of a company that makes t-shirts must determine the price for a special one-time order. The manager of a restaurant must continually assess the status of its menu items, just as managers of a large manufacturer of stereo components must consider whether to add new products or to drop unprofitable ones. Managers of a company that makes bicycles must decide whether to buy tires from another manufacturer or to make them internally. The manager of a local video store must determine whether to hire employees to repair VCRs or to outsource that service to someone else. The manager of a hardware store must determine which products to put on the shelves, and a book publisher must determine which books to publish. All these decisions require relevant, timely accounting information to aid in the decision-making process. In this chapter, we discuss the tools that managers use to make these and other business decisions.

PRICING OF PRODUCTS AND SERVICES

LO1
Identify factors and issues affecting the pricing of goods and services

In a competitive marketplace, consumers will seek out the best product at the most favorable price. Determining the selling price of products is one of the most important decisions that management will be required to make. If the price of the product is too high, market demand for that product may be less than is needed to earn a fair profit. On the other hand, if the price of the product is too low, the demand may be very high but the product may produce minimal profit or even show a negative contribution margin.

IN THE NEWS http://www.omnihotels.com

Many hotel chains and airlines use sophisticated yield management computer software that continuously monitors and adjusts rates based on a variety of factors, including historical trends and expected occupancy. This can result in continually changing prices for rooms and airfares. At the Omni Park West in Dallas, Texas, rooms are priced as high as \$199 on strong-demand nights and as low as \$59 on low-demand nights. The Omni Park West estimates that the software has increased revenues by 4 percent to 6 percent (Templin, "Your Room Costs \$250. . . No! \$200. . . No. . . ," *Wall Street Journal*, May 5, 1999, B1).

In some business situations, the cost of the product or the service does not affect the sales price. In these circumstances, the market determines the selling price, and the company will produce the product as efficiently as possible and sell it for a predetermined market price. Many agricultural products fall into this category, in which the market determines the selling price. However, in most instances, the cost of a product or a service is very important in establishing price. Consider, for example, the manufacture of furniture or automobiles. In these situations, higher-cost items are typically priced higher than are lower cost items. In other words, if the car costs more to produce, the price to the consumer will be higher because the extra costs usually mean higher quality or more options.

The demand for products at different stages in their life cycles also affects pricing. For example, when VCRs were introduced in the 1980s, they sold for up to \$1,000 but now sell for less than \$100.

© ZEPHYR PICTURE/INDEX STOCK IMAGERY

IN THE NEWS

Even when cost is used to help establish the price of products or services, other factors may be equally or more important. Although the price of lumber has risen over the past couple of years, furniture manufacturers have been reluctant to pass on those price increases to retailers. For example, furniture manufacturers may try to help retailers maintain key "price points," knowing that consumers may be reluctant to spend above a threshold dollar amount on a new dresser or bed (Buggs, "Furniture Prices to Sit Still," *Raleigh News and Observer,* October 17, 1998, 1D).

In the long run, the selling price of a product or service must be sufficient to cover the "cost" of the product plus provide a profit. The question then becomes, What is the cost of the product? As we have discussed throughout the book, there are a number of ways to compute the cost of a product. In Chapter 6, we learned that absorption, or full costing, includes fixed manufacturing overhead as a product cost, whereas variable costing includes only direct material, direct labor, and variable manufacturing costs. Chapters 3 and 4 stated that some companies assign overhead to products by using traditional volume-based cost drivers, whereas other companies use activity-based costing. In Chapter 4, we saw that the use of ABC can have a tremendous impact on the calculation of cost. Using conventional volume-based cost drivers has the general effect of overcosting simple products and undercosting complex products. The use of multiple cost drivers in ABC generally results in more accurate product costs. **Life-cycle cost** refers to the costs accumulated over the entire life cycle of a product. As was discussed in Chapter 2, the product life cycle refers to the entire life span of a product from initial research and development to the time when customer support of the product is finished.

Regardless of the way companies compute the cost of their product or service, it should be obvious that in the long run, the price of a product must be sufficient to cover all the costs incurred in developing, designing, manufacturing, marketing, distributing, and servicing the product. In practice, companies use a variety of approaches to determine prices.

Key Concept: *The price of a product must be sufficient to cover all the costs of the product and to provide a profit.*

TARGET PRICING

Target pricing is used when a price is preset by market conditions or when a company wishes to set a price in order to capture a predetermined market share or to meet other marketing goals. In situations in which the price is preset by market conditions (as with agricultural products), the product manufacturer or service provider has little control over sales price. In these cases, the decision is really not one of establishing a price at all but rather deciding whether a product can be developed and manufactured at a cost low enough to provide an acceptable profit. In other situations, a company has control over setting prices but sets a price based on the marketing goals (to enter a new market, establish a predetermined market share, etc.) rather than the cost of the product or service. Surveys indicate that almost 20 percent of U.S. companies routinely use some sort of market-based target pricing.

Target pricing is used to determine the maximum cost that can be incurred in order to earn a desired profit (the target profit). This maximum cost is often called the target cost and is calculated by subtracting the target profit from the target selling price:

$$\text{Target cost} = \text{Target price} - \text{Target profit}$$

Target pricing (and target costing) are prevalent in the computer industry, in which the goal may be to produce a computer that can be marketed for under \$500. After determining an acceptable profit on the computer (\$100, for example), the goal is to determine how to design, develop, manufacture, sell, and service the computer for a cost no higher than \$400. If the target cost is within the range of acceptable estimates, the computer can be manufactured. In reality, most production costs are determined during the early stages of the value chain (research and development and design), and very little can be done to control these costs once the product is in production. This means that estimating costs accurately and at an early stage in the value chain is crucial in deciding whether a product can ultimately be sold at a profit.

CROSS-FUNCTIONAL APPLICATIONS *Target pricing requires the cooperation of marketing, engineering, production, accounting, and finance managers in multidisciplinary teams.*

APPLICATION IN BUSINESS

Determining a target cost is more difficult when the target price is not known with certainty. For example, in the agricultural market, coffee bean prices are set by auction and are not known until after the beans are grown and harvested.

COST-PLUS PRICING

When the market allows some flexibility in setting prices, companies often use some sort of **cost-plus pricing** to determine the selling price of products or services.

The general formula for determining a target selling price using a cost-plus approach is

$$\text{Target selling price} = \text{Cost} + (\text{Markup \%} \times \text{Cost})$$

In cost-plus pricing, managers determine the cost of the product or service and then add a markup percentage to that cost to arrive at the sales price. In some cases, costs are estimated and selling prices are set based on those estimates. In other cases, companies can wait until they know their actual costs before setting the selling price in a cost-plus contract. For example, a builder of custom homes would probably use cost-plus pricing. In Chapter 4, TopSail Construction used full costing and ABC to determine the total manufacturing costs of a custom house to be $237,371 (see page 106). The selling price of $285,000 was determined by adding a predetermined markup of 20 percent on the total manufacturing costs (and rounding up to the nearest thousand). If TopSail uses estimated costs to determine a selling price (and enters a contract to build a house for a predetermined price), it becomes critically important for TopSail to accurately estimate those costs. If costs are estimated too high and the selling price is too high, TopSail will not be awarded the construction job; if costs are estimated too low (and the price is too low), the company may lose money or make less profit than desired.

Some companies use only variable costs to price their products; other companies use absorption costs, or life-cycle costs. There are advantages and disadvantages to each. Using variable costs is consistent with the economic model of maximizing profit by setting prices in which marginal cost is equal to marginal revenue. However, it can be misleading to managers focusing on long-run decisions. Using full costs has the benefit of motivating managers to control fixed costs. ABC has also made the practice of allocating fixed costs to products more accurate. In practice, full costs are used by almost 70 percent of U.S. companies, whereas variable costs are used by only 12 percent (Shim and Sudit, "How Manufacturers Price Products," *Management Accounting*, February 1995). Although the use of life-cycle costs is appealing, as a practical matter, they are also difficult to estimate.

The **markup percentage** is a very important component of the preceding formula. The markup must be sufficient to cover any costs not included in the company's definition of product cost, as well as produce an acceptable profit. For a company using variable costing as the starting point in cost-plus pricing, the markup must cover fixed manufacturing costs; all selling and administrative costs; other life-cycle costs incurred in the design, development, and servicing of the product; and a profit. At the other extreme, the markup for a company using life-cycle costing will include only a desired profit. The amount used can be a simple rule of thumb or an industry standard. Whatever method is used, the markup percentage should be reviewed often.

Some companies use a combination of target pricing and cost-plus pricing. For example, Parker Brothers (a division of Hasbro) manufactures and sells board games, such as Monopoly and Scrabble. The company's approach to pricing is to first have the marketing department estimate the probable retail-selling price of a prototype game—the target price. Parker Brothers then backs into the maximum cost (the target cost) that can be incurred in manufacturing the game by applying predetermined profit margins at the retail and wholesale levels. If the target cost is too low (the company cannot manufacture the game at or below the target cost), Parker Brothers then takes a cost-plus approach to pricing and goes back to the marketing department with a higher suggested wholesale price. It is then up to the marketing department to decide whether the game can be successfully marketed at this higher price.

http://www.hasbro.com

TIME AND MATERIAL PRICING

In service industries, in which labor is the primary cost incurred, prices are often set based on time and material used. For example, CPA firms that provide audit services must provide a client with an estimate of an audit fee prior to starting the work. This fee usually will not vary unless additional work is needed that was unanticipated before the engagement began. Also, extreme problems can arise that cause the firm to spend much more time on the engagement, which could cause the fee to increase. The price is based on the estimated number of hours needed to complete the audit. Obviously, more complex audit engagements will require more time and will be priced at a higher rate. As another example of **time and material pricing,** an auto shop bills customers based on mechanic labor hours plus any parts used in the repair.

MANAGEMENT ACTIONS AND DECISIONS

http://www.hasbro.com

COURTESY OF GARY BERGMANN

GARY BERGMANN

One of the questions that comes up when we discuss pricing in the classroom is, How are prices determined in the real world? Gary Bergmann, a former vice president of product acquisition and product design for Hasbro Games, shares some opinions on how Hasbro viewed pricing. Mr. Bergmann, who worked with Hasbro for more than 20 years, met with game inventors throughout the world to review their game concepts as candidates for the Milton Bradley and Parker Brothers game lines, collectively known as Hasbro Games. Out of 3,000 game concepts per year, only 15 to 20 actually reach the retail marketplace.

"When a game was considered to be marketable, we first asked the marketing team what the suggested retail price on the game might be (target pricing). We then reduced that amount by the required markups to arrive at the target cost to manufacture (target costing). If the calculated cost to manufacture was too low to allow for a properly designed game, we reversed the process by asking the manufacturing team to calculate the cost to produce the game as we would design it, then added the needed markups to arrive at the new suggested retail price. This new price was delivered to the marketing team for a sales projection using the new parameters. This procedure allowed us to approach the project from two different angles and in some cases gave a candidate game a second chance at being manufactured and sold."

VALUE PRICING

PAUSE & Reflect

Do you think value pricing is ethical?

In special circumstances, the price of services is based on the perceived or actual value of the service provided to a customer. A good example of **value pricing** occurs in the consulting business. Consulting firms may charge clients based on a percentage of cost savings that result from an engagement. Large CPA firms often enter into these types of arrangements. For example, a CPA firm may contract with a client to evaluate its property tax assessments and to negotiate reductions in those taxes based on faulty valuations of property. Rather than establishing a fixed price for the services (or working on a cost-plus contract), the firm may set a price equal to 30 percent of the cost savings.

LEGAL AND ETHICAL ISSUES IN PRICING

A variety of laws at the local, state, and national levels prevent companies from using predatory pricing to prevent or eliminate competition. Many types of price discrimination are illegal unless the differences in price are based on cost differences in servicing and selling to different customers. Price gouging, or setting the price higher for unusual situations, such as doubling the price of plywood when a hurricane is approaching, may also be illegal in some cases. In addition to the legal implications of pricing decisions, companies must consider the ethical issues involved in pricing products and services. For example, pharmaceutical companies may choose to sell a drug below cost and doctors may treat some patients at little or no cost. However, examples also abound of companies' taking advantage of customers by increasing the prices of products and services that are in high demand.

IN THE NEWS http://www.merck.com

The pharmaceutical company Merck sells two prescription drugs containing the same active ingredient—finasteride. The two drugs are identical except for dose. One drug, Propecia, is used to treat male-pattern baldness and sells for $45 to $50 per 1 mg dose of finasteride. The other drug, Proscar, is a prostate medication and sells for $13 to $16 per 1 mg dose; a 5 mg tablet sells for about $65. Do you think the pricing scheme Merck uses is ethical? How do you think Merck set the price for Propecia? (*Wall Street Journal,* April 13, 1999, B1).

SPECIAL ORDERS

LO2
Analyze the pricing of a special order

Deciding whether to accept a special order is really just a pricing decision. However, unlike the pricing decisions discussed earlier, **special-order decisions** are short-run decisions. Management must decide what sales price is appropriate when customers place orders that are different from those placed in the regular course of business (larger quantity, one-time sale to a foreign customer, etc.).[1] These decisions are affected by whether the company has excess production capacity (can produce additional units with existing machinery, labor, and facilities). Qualitative factors, such as the reaction of regular customers, must also be considered when establishing the price of a special order. As with other decisions discussed in this chapter, managers must consider the relevant costs associated with each specific special order.

Sunset Airlines

Consider the case of Sunset Airlines. A major corporation has asked the company to provide 150 seats to San Diego for corporate executives attending a convention. The corporation offers the airline $150 per ticket, although the normal fare for this route is $275. The tickets can be used on only one day, but the executives need to be able to fly one of the five flights offered that day. The aircraft that Sunset Airlines flies on this route carries 180 passengers, and Sunset has five scheduled flights each day, resulting in a seat capacity of 900 seats. The normal passenger load on the day requested is between 77 percent and 78 percent of available capacity (700 passengers), so Sunset should have plenty of excess capacity (40 seats per plane, or 200 seats total). However, should Sunset accept the special order at the discounted price of $150 per ticket? Referring back to the decision model presented in Chapter 1, recall that the first step in any decision is to accurately define the problem.

Step 1 DEFINE THE PROBLEM

In this case, the problem is clear—should Sunset Airlines sell 150 tickets at a reduced price of $150 per ticket? Step 2 in the decision process is identifying the objectives.

Step 2 IDENTIFY OBJECTIVES

The objective of Sunset Airlines is to maximize income in the short run without reducing income in the long run. The third step is to identify and analyze the available options.

Step 3 IDENTIFY AND ANALYZE AVAILABLE OPTIONS

The options in this case include selling the tickets for $150 (accepting the special order), letting the marketplace determine the level of sales at a predetermined price of $275, or selling the tickets at another price. The risk in this situation is that the airline will have to turn away full-fare passengers if it accepts the special order. An analysis of the options requires that the relevant costs and other factors be identified. The accounting department of Sunset Airlines has provided the following information:

	Per Passenger	Per Flight
Cost of meals and drinks	$ 3.25	$ 585
Cost of fuel	138.89	25,000
Cost of cabin crew (four flight attendants)	9.38	1,688
Cost of flight crew	13.89	2,500
Depreciation of aircraft	5.56	1,000
Aircraft maintenance	4.17	750
Total	$175.14	$31,523

[1]Although rush orders and orders requiring special handling, packaging, or different manufacturing specifications might be considered "special orders," these types of decisions are not discussed here.

Step 4 SELECT THE BEST OPTION

This decision appears to be an easy one, as the special-order price of $150 is less than the total cost per passenger of $175.14. Based on the full cost reported by the accounting department, Sunset Airlines would be losing $25.14 on each passenger purchasing a ticket for $150. But would it? To analyze the options in this decision problem correctly, only the relevant costs should be considered. In this decision, the only costs that are relevant are those that will differ depending on whether the special order is accepted. Another way to look at the problem is by determining which costs can be avoided by choosing one alternative over the other.

In this case, almost all the costs are fixed with respect to the number of passengers on the plane. In fact, owing to the unique nature of the airline business, most operating costs are fixed. For example, the aircraft will require the same maintenance and flight crew costs regardless of how many passengers are on board. Although the costs of the cabin crew may vary, let us assume that in this situation, regulations require four flight attendants for any flight with more than 125 passengers. In this case, four flight attendants are required regardless of whether the plane carries 125 passengers or 180 passengers, and acceptance of the special order will not change the cost of the cabin crew. In essence, the cost of the flight crew is fixed. Likewise, depreciation is a fixed cost. Even fuel costs would not be expected to vary much with the addition of 30 to 40 passengers. In fact, the only cost that would vary with the number of passengers on the plane is likely to be the small additional cost of meals and drinks. Because Sunset Airlines appears to have plenty of excess capacity (empty seats), any sales price above the variable costs of providing the seats will increase the income of the company. If the cost of meals and drinks is the only variable cost, Sunset should be willing to accept the special order at any price over $3.25. In situations in which excess capacity exists, the general rule is that in order to maximize income, the special-order price must simply be higher than the additional variable costs incurred in accepting the special order.

Sunset Airlines

What if Sunset does not have any excess capacity? If the airline expects to sell out all its tickets at the regular price of $275, accepting the special order involves an opportunity cost. Remember from Chapter 1 that an opportunity cost is the benefit forgone from choosing one alternative over another. If Sunset Airlines accepts the special order, it will forgo the receipt of $271.75 of contribution margin on each ticket ($275 selling price less the $3.25 variable cost of meals and drinks). Therefore, it would not be willing to accept a special order for any price below the $275 market price. The relevant costs in this case are the variable costs of $3.25 and the opportunity cost of $271.75.

Fixed costs can be relevant to a special-order decision when they change depending on the option chosen. For example, let's consider the case of flight attendants again. Instead of requiring four flight attendants for any flight with more than 125 passengers, let's assume that regulations require one flight attendant for every 35 passengers. Whereas four attendants are sufficient for a flight of 140 passengers, adding 30 additional passengers will require the addition of an extra flight attendant at a cost of $422, or $14 per additional passenger. Assuming that excess capacity exists, the special-order price would need to exceed $17.25 to be acceptable to Sunset Airlines.

Key Concept: *The price of a special order must be higher than the additional variable costs incurred in accepting the special order plus any opportunity costs incurred.*

Concept Question: *Instead of 150 extra passengers flying on the five regularly scheduled flights, assume that Sunset Airlines has an additional airplane that is currently idle but can be chartered for the flight. In this case, what costs are likely to be relevant in the decision to accept the special order?*

Concept Answer: In this case, fuel costs, the cost of the flight and cabin crews, and maintenance are likely to be relevant. Depreciation is still not a relevant cost, but the other costs probably are. It is important to note that determining what is relevant and what is not depends on the specific situation.

A number of qualitative factors must also be considered in special-order decisions. First, if it accepts the special order and its passenger-load predictions are wrong, Sunset Airlines may have to turn away passengers that would otherwise pay full fare. If that happens and these passengers turn to competing airlines, Sunset Airlines faces the potential of losing long-term customers. Second, the impact of selling seats at a discount on those customers paying regular fares must be considered.

IN THE NEWS **http://www.aa.com, http://www.delta.com**

Sometimes, the most important qualitative factor in business decisions is the potential effect on customers. In the last few years, pilots at both American Airlines and Delta have gone on strike to protest the low pay received by pilots flying for a subsidiary airline. These strikes stranded thousands of passengers all over the country and may very well hurt the long-term customer loyalty of both airlines.

Concept Question: *Historically, airlines charge much higher fares to last-minute travelers when the relevant costs associated with these additional passengers are very small. Ironically, business travelers, who are the airline's most frequent flyers, often pay these higher fares. Why haven't airlines been willing to offer special pricing to customers in these situations?*

Concept Answer: Many airlines are beginning to do just that. Faced with added competition from discount airlines that offer cheaper fares with no advance-purchase requirements, many of the major airlines also offer last-minute flyers fares at deep discounts. However, these fares are often restricted to flights on certain days and may not be convenient for business travelers. In addition, although these fares are discounted, they are still much higher than the true relevant costs of flying the additional passengers.

http://www.delta.com

OUTSOURCING AND OTHER MAKE-OR-BUY DECISIONS

LO3
Analyze a decision involving the outsourcing of labor or making or buying a component

A decision to outsource labor or to purchase components used in manufacturing from another company rather than to provide the services or to produce the components internally is an important decision. This **outsourcing or make-or-buy decision** affects a wide range of manufacturing, merchandising, and service organizations. For example, a university can contract with an outside company to provide janitorial and repair services for on-campus dormitories, or it can provide those services by using university employees. A local florist can provide payroll processing internally, or it can hire a CPA to provide those services. Hewlett-Packard can make carrying cases for its calculators internally, or it can buy them from an outside supplier.

STRATEGIC ASPECTS OF OUTSOURCING AND MAKE-OR-BUY DECISIONS

Although these decisions might appear to be simple on the surface, they require an in-depth analysis of relevant quantitative and qualitative factors and a consideration of the costs and benefits of outsourcing and vertical integration. The decision to outsource labor requires a consideration of a variety of factors, including the impact of taxes, the payment of fringe benefits to salaried employees, and the impact on the remaining workforce. Advantages to outsourcing include reduced costs. Although hourly rates paid to independent contractors may be higher than hourly wages paid to salaried employees, a company may benefit from cost reductions as a result of not being required to pay payroll taxes and fringe benefits (medical insurance, retirement plan contributions, etc.). However, outsourcing can have disadvantages, such as a perceived lack of stability in the company and a resulting lack of loyalty in the workforce (as well as other negative impacts outsourcing may have on the remaining workforce). For example, if a company decided to outsource maintenance and laid off all the maintenance workers, other workers in the company, such as the cafeteria personnel, may perceive that move as meaning that the company is going to outsource more of the service functions. Workers who feel that they are just "treading water" and waiting for their area to be eliminated will be less motivated to do the best job possible and may very well leave the company if and when a better opportunity presents itself.

Universities, such as the University of California–Davis, can choose to outsource their food service to national restaurant chains in an effort to focus costs on institutional core competencies, such as faculty.

http://www.subway.com

Vertical integration is accomplished when a company is involved in multiple steps of the value chain. In an extreme example, the same company might own a gold mine, a manufacturing facility to produce gold jewelry, and a retail jewelry store. Most companies operate with some form of vertical integration (they market the products they produce, or they develop the products that they manufacture), but the extent of integration varies greatly from company to company and indeed from product to product within a company. All elements of the value chain—from initial research and development through design, manufacture of the product, marketing, distribution, and customer service—must be considered for making or buying components needed for production of the final product.

There are advantages to making components internally instead of buying them from an outside supplier. Vertically integrated companies are not dependent on suppliers for timely delivery of services or components needed in the production process or for the quality of those services and components. However, vertically integrated companies have disadvantages as well.

IN THE NEWS **http://www.gm.com**

In the summer of 1998, General Motors (GM) found it difficult to restart production in its vehicle plants because of strikes in two of its *own* plants that supplied body stampings and other parts used in GM cars. In this case, the lack of alternative suppliers forced GM to shut down plants that were not directly affected by the strike (*Wall Street Journal,* July 8, 1998, A3).

There are other disadvantages to making parts internally. The supplier may be able to provide a higher-quality part for less cost. For this reason, computer manufacturers do not produce their own computer chips. The producers of those chips produce in such large quantities that they can provide the chips more cheaply than the company could produce them internally. Chip manufacturers also spend billions of dollars on research and development to ensure high-quality and high-performance chips.

THE MAKE-OR-BUY DECISION

Birdie Maker Golf Company produces custom sets of golf clubs that are advertised to be far superior to other golf clubs on the market. These golf clubs sell for $1,000 per set, and Birdie currently sells about 1,000 sets each year. Birdie Maker currently manufactures all the golf clubs in the set but is considering acquiring the putter from Flutter Putter Inc., a manufacturer of custom putters. The purchased putter would be customized for Birdie and matched to the other clubs, so customers should not be able to distinguish it from the rest of the clubs in the set. The costs incurred in the manufacture of the putter are as follows:

Birdie Maker

	Total (1,000 sets of clubs)	Per Unit
Direct materials	$ 5,000	$ 5.00
Direct labor	9,000	9.00
Variable manufacturing overhead	3,000	3.00
Fixed manufacturing overhead	9,500	9.50
Total cost	$26,500	$26.50

flutter putter

CASE I

Birdie Maker

The expected production for the year is 1,000 sets of clubs, so the full cost of each putter is $26.50 ($26,500/1,000). Flutter Putter Inc. is offering to sell the putters to Birdie Maker for $25 per putter. Although this decision seems to be a very easy one ($25 is less than $26.50), the decision is more complex than it appears. If we refer back to the decision-making model presented in Chapter 1 and repeated in Exhibit 7-1, we can once again structure our decision using that framework.

Step 1 DEFINE THE PROBLEM

Step 1 in our decision-making model is to accurately define the problem. In this case, Birdie Maker must decide whether to continue making the putter or to purchase it from Flutter Putter Inc. Step 2 requires Birdie Maker to consider its objectives in making the decision.

Step 2 IDENTIFY OBJECTIVES

Although Birdie Maker would like to maximize income by producing or buying the putter at the lowest possible cost, the company is also very concerned about the quality of the putter and the potential impact of the putter on sales of other clubs. Step 3 requires an identification of options and an analysis of the costs and other factors that are relevant in the decision.

Step 3 IDENTIFY AND ANALYZE AVAILABLE OPTIONS

Relevant costs and factors are those that differ between alternatives. As we discussed in Chapter 5, relevant costs are those that can be avoided by choosing one alternative over another. The key, then, is to analyze the costs of manufacturing the putter with an eye toward identifying those costs that can be *avoided* or eliminated if the putter is purchased from Flutter Putter. If Birdie Maker continues to manufacture the putter internally, it will incur costs of $26,500. If Birdie Maker decides to purchase the putters from Flutter Putter Inc., it will incur costs of $25,000 ($25 × 1,000 putters) *plus* any manufacturing costs that are not avoidable. Although the costs related to direct material, direct labor, and variable manufacturing overhead are variable (and thus avoidable), fixed manufacturing overhead is not.

Step 4 SELECT THE BEST OPTION

So although it appears on the surface that Birdie Maker can save $1,500 ($26,500 – $25,000) by buying the putters from Flutter Putter Inc., as you can see in the following table, buying the club from Flutter Putter will in reality cost Birdie an additional $8 per club, or $8,000. What is the best solution? From a purely quantitative perspective, Birdie Maker would maximize its income by choosing to continue making putters. However, before making this decision, the company must be convinced that it can manufacture a putter of acceptable quality and that it will be able to keep up with any technological changes affecting the manufacture of the putter in the future.

	Cost to Make (per unit)	Cost to Buy (per unit)
Direct materials	$ 5.00	
Direct labor	9.00	
Variable manufacturing overhead	3.00	
Fixed manufacturing overhead	9.50	$ 9.50
Purchase price from Flutter Putter Inc.		25.00
	$26.50	$34.50

CASE II

flutter putter

Sometimes, fixed costs are relevant to the analysis. For example, assume that $5,500 of the fixed manufacturing cost is for specialized machinery that is currently being leased under a month-to-month contract. If the putters are purchased from Flutter Putter Inc., the equipment will be returned to the lessor. That means that $5.50 of the fixed manufacturing costs ($5,500/1,000 putters) is avoidable if the putter is bought from Flutter Putter and that only $4.00 of fixed overhead will be incurred if the putter is purchased from Flutter Putter. The resulting analysis is shown in the following table:

EXHIBIT 7-1 The Decision-Making Model

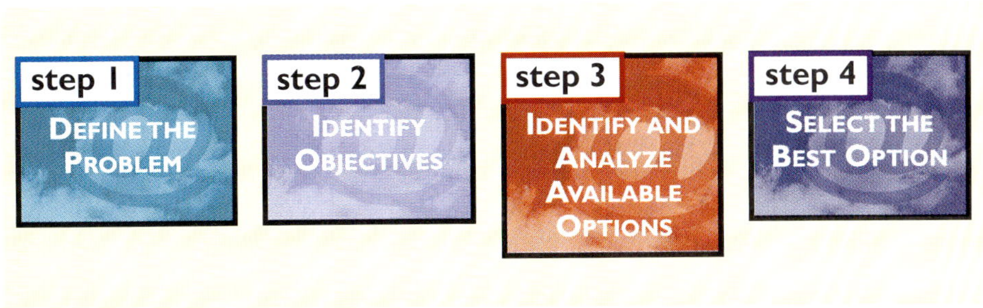

	Cost to Make	Cost to Buy
Direct materials	$ 5.00	
Direct labor	9.00	
Variable manufacturing overhead	3.00	
Fixed manufacturing overhead	9.50	$ 4.00
Purchase price from Flutter Putter Inc.		25.00
	$26.50	$29.00

Step 4 SELECT THE BEST OPTION

Although it still remains preferable to make the putters internally, the cost difference shrinks to $2.50 per putter instead of $8.00. In this situation, Birdie Maker must carefully consider the qualitative factors relevant to the decision, including the quality of the putters, the importance of keeping up with changing technology, and the dependability of the supplier.

Another way to look at this analysis is to compare the total avoidable costs to the purchase price. In this case, if the putter is purchased from Flutter Putter, the avoidable costs include direct materials ($5.00), direct labor ($9.00), variable manufacturing overhead ($3.00), and $5.50 per putter for fixed manufacturing overhead. The $22.50 of total avoidable costs should then be compared to the $25.00 purchase price. Regardless of how you choose to look at the problem, Birdie Maker is better off by $2.50 per putter if it continues making the putter.

CASE III

Make-or-buy decisions can be volume dependent. Assuming the same facts as in Case II, the full cost to make each putter will increase to $36 if Birdie Maker has a decrease in production volume to 500 sets of golf clubs. The increase results from the behavior of fixed costs.

Step 4 SELECT THE BEST OPTION

Remember that fixed costs stay the same in total but vary on a per unit basis as volume changes. In this example, if volume decreases to 500 putters, the unavoidable fixed costs of $4,000 increase to $8 per putter from $4 in Case II. This increase in per unit production cost will change the decision and make it advantageous for the company to purchase the putter rather than to continue making it ($33 compared to $36).

	Cost to Make	Cost to Buy
Direct materials	$ 5.00	
Direct labor	9.00	
Variable manufacturing overhead	3.00	
Fixed manufacturing overhead	19.00	$ 8.00
Purchase price from Flutter Putter Inc.		25.00
	$36.00	$33.00

CASE IV

The last case to be considered is one involving an opportunity cost. Using the same facts as in Case I, consider the impact of renting out the factory space that is now used to manufacture putters for $10,000.

Step 4 SELECT THE BEST OPTION

By effectively reducing the cost to purchase the putters by $10,000, or $10 per putter, we find that the effective cost to purchase the putter from Flutter Putter is reduced to $24.50, so Birdie Maker would be better off by $2.00 per putter by purchasing the putters.

	Cost to Make	Cost to Buy
Direct materials	$ 5.00	
Direct labor	9.00	
Variable manufacturing overhead	3.00	
Fixed manufacturing overhead	9.50	$ 9.50
Purchase price from Flutter Putter Inc.		25.00
Rental of unused factory space		(10.00)
	$26.50	$24.50

Once again, as an alternative, we could treat the $10 opportunity cost as a relevant cost of making the putter internally. In that case, the total relevant costs of making the putter increase to $36.50 compared to the purchase price of $34.50. In addition to quality and reliability considerations, other factors to consider in this case include the long-term potential for renting out the unused space, potential other uses of the space, and so on.

Key Concept: *A product should continue to be made internally and labor incurred internally if the avoidable costs are less than the additional costs that will be incurred by buying or outsourcing.*

IN THE NEWS **http://www.llbean.com**

Rol Fessenden, the vice president of product acquisition for L.L. Bean, selects the factories to supply Bean with the multitude of products available in its catalogs. Rather than focusing on price, his first criterion in choosing a supplier is product quality, the second is delivery reliability, and the third is price. All these factors are captured in Mr. Fessenden's view of cost as a concept that includes the entire spectrum of value—price, quality, reliability, and the ultimate success of the product in the marketplace (*Wall Street Journal,* April 16, 1999, B1).

THE DECISION TO DROP A PRODUCT OR A SERVICE

LO4
Analyze a decision dealing with adding or dropping a product, product line, or service

The decision to drop a product or a service is among the most difficult that a manager can make. Like other decisions discussed in this chapter, deciding whether to drop an old product or product line hinges on an analysis of the relevant costs and qualitative factors affecting the decision. Qualitative factors are sometimes more important than focusing solely on income.

© SUSAN VAN ETTEN

IN THE NEWS http://www.pg.com

In a recent news story, Procter & Gamble said that it was weighing the sale of its Prell hair-care brand *even though it was profitable.* The company stated that it wanted to focus on brands with global potential, such as Pantene Pro-V and Head and Shoulders, while cutting its smallest brands. In 1998, Prell posted U.S. sales of about $10 million, less than 1 percent of P&G's total beauty-care sales (*Wall Street Journal,* May 16, 1999, B13).

Clayton Herring Tire Co. is considering dropping one of the ten models of tires that it manufactures and sells. Sales of a special mud and snow tire have been disappointing, and based on the latest financial information (shown in the following table), the tires appear to be losing money.

Clayton Herring Tire Co.

Clayton Herring Tire Co.

	Mud and Snow	All Other Tires	Total
Sales	$25,500	$150,000	$175,500
Less: Direct material	12,000	50,600	62,600
Direct labor	5,000	30,000	35,000
Variable overhead	2,000	12,000	14,000
Contribution margin	$ 6,500	$ 57,400	$ 63,900
Less: Fixed overhead	7,000	21,000	28,000
Net income	$ (500)	$ 36,400	$ 35,900

Chris (the CEO of Clayton Herring Tire) asked Karen (the controller) why the mud and snow tires were losing money. Karen explained that the tires required more machine time than other tires. Consequently, they were allocated a greater portion of fixed overhead. Chris then asked Karen whether she would recommend that production of the mud and snow tires be discontinued. Karen explained that although it appears that net income for the company would increase to $36,400 if the mud and snow tires were dropped from the product line, further analysis revealed that a large portion of the fixed overhead allocated to the tires resulted from the rental of machines used to make the tires. On further inspection, Karen determined that these machines were used to make several models of tires and could not be disposed of if the mud and snow tires were dropped. Consequently, $5,000 of the fixed costs allocated to mud and snow tires would have to be reallocated to other product lines. These costs would remain even if the mud and snow tires were discontinued. Based on this new information, Karen prepared another report for Chris, showing the effect of dropping the mud and snow tires:

Clayton Herring Tire Co.

Clayton Herring Tire Co.

	With Snow Tires	Without Snow Tires
Tire sales	$175,500	$150,000
Less: Direct material	62,600	50,600
Direct labor	35,000	30,000
Variable overhead	14,000	12,000
Contribution margin	$ 63,900	$ 57,400
Less: Fixed overhead	28,000	26,000
Net income	$ 35,900	$ 31,400

Why did the net income for the company decrease by $4,500 (from $35,900 to $31,400) when the mud and snow tires were dropped, even though they appeared to be losing money? The answer is that contribution margin decreased by $6,500, whereas fixed costs decreased by only $2,000 when the tires were dropped. Only $2,000 of the fixed costs were avoidable and relevant to this decision. The other $5,000 of fixed costs originally allocated to the mud and snow tires would simply be reallocated to one or more of the other models of tires. A simple way to analyze this problem is to compare the contribution margin lost when the product line is dropped to the fixed costs that are avoided. In this case, Clayton Herring Tire Company loses $6,500 of contribution margin while saving (avoiding) only $2,000 of fixed overhead.

Key Concept: *A product should be dropped when the fixed costs avoided are greater than the contribution margin lost.*

Concept Question: *If the machine used to produce the tires was unique and could be disposed of resulting in a savings of $5,000, how much would income increase (decrease) if the mud and snow tires were discontinued? (Assume that the other $2,000 of fixed overhead could still be avoided.)*

Concept Answer: Although contribution margin would still be reduced by \$6,500, the entire \$7,000 of fixed costs would be avoided, resulting in an overall increase in net income of \$500. But what about qualitative factors in this decision? As we discussed earlier, qualitative factors are sometimes more important than quantitative factors in these decisions. For example, what impact will discontinuing the sale of mud and snow tires have on sales of the remaining product lines? Tire retailers are likely to prefer purchasing tires from a company offering a full line of tires. Retailers that cannot offer mud and snow tires may have difficulty selling tires to individuals in the winter. On the other hand, like Procter & Gamble with its Prell brand, Clayton Herring Tire may choose to discontinue the tires even if they are profitable. ■

RESOURCE UTILIZATION DECISIONS

LO5
Analyze a decision dealing with scarce or limited resources

A company faces a **constraint** when the capacity to manufacture a product or to provide a service is limited in some manner. A **resource utilization decision** requires an analysis of how best to use a resource that is available in limited supply. The limited resource may be a rare material or component used in manufacturing a product but more likely is related to the time required to make a product or to provide a service or the space required to store a product. For example, building custom furniture requires skilled craftspeople, who may be in short supply. Deciding how best to utilize the limited labor time available is a resource utilization decision. The manufacture of golf clubs requires special machinery. If a company has only one machine that can be used to manufacture shafts for putters and other clubs, machine time may be a limited resource.

Concept Question: *What is likely to be a limited resource in a grocery store?*

Concept Answer: Grocery stores and other retail stores have limited shelf space. The resource utilization decision involves an analysis of how best to use this limited resource. Which products should be carried? How many? Although it may seem easy to conclude that stores should carry those products that are most profitable, decisions like this are complicated by the fact that the multitudes of products carried in large stores require different amounts of shelf space. Multipacks of paper towels take up several times the shelf space required for a box of macaroni and cheese. Although the multipack of paper towels may be more profitable per unit, this has to be balanced with the requirement of more shelf space. A decision concerning how much of each product to have on hand must also consider the impact of qualitative factors, such as customer reaction if a product is not carried, the impact on sales of other products, and so on. ■

Resource utilization decisions are typically short-term decisions. In the short run, such resources as machine time, labor hours, and shelf space are fixed and cannot be increased. However, in the long run, new machines can be purchased, additional skilled laborers can be hired, and stores can be expanded. When faced with short-run constraints, managers must focus on the contribution margin provided by each product per unit of limited resource rather than on the profitability of each product.[2]

Sun Devil Golf Balls produces two types of golf balls: the pro model and the tour model. The balls are sold to retailers in cartons containing 360 balls (30 boxes containing 4 sleeves per box, with each sleeve holding 3 balls). Both models are made using the same machines. The constraint, or limited resource, is the number of hours that the machines can run. The pro-model golf ball takes 30 minutes of machine time to produce 360 balls, whereas the tour ball takes 45 minutes to produce the same number. The difference in production time results mainly from the different materials used in construction. Although

SUN DEVIL GOLF BALLS

[2]Decisions involving limited resources or constraints often include multiple constraints, such as storage space, machine time, labor hours, and even dollars available to invest. When we have more than one constraining factor, the decision-making process becomes more complicated and is facilitated by the use of computerized linear programming models. A discussion of linear programming is beyond the scope of this text.

weekend golfers purchase both models, professionals on the PGA Tour use the tour model. The relevant data concerning the two models follows:

	Pro Model	Tour Model
Sales price (per carton)	$450	$540
Less: Direct material	200	265
Direct labor	50	50
Variable overhead	50	75
Contribution margin	$150	$150

In this case, the contribution margin per carton is the same for both the pro model and the tour model. Other things being equal, each model is equally profitable. However, if we compute contribution margin per unit of the constrained, or limited, resource, we see that each carton of pro-model balls has a contribution margin of $300 per hour of machine time, whereas each carton of tour-model balls has a contribution margin of $200 per hour of machine time:

	Pro Model	Tour Model
Sales price (per carton)	$450	$540
Less: Direct material	200	265
Direct labor	50	50
Variable overhead	50	75
Contribution margin	$150	$150
Required machine time	0.50 hours	0.75 hours
Contribution margin per machine hour	$300	$200
	($150/0.50)	($150/0.75)

If demand is not a factor and qualitative considerations are not important, Sun Devil Golf Balls will maximize profit by producing and selling only pro-model golf balls. However, if demand for either product is limited, Sun Devil must decide on the optimal product mix. For example, if machine time is limited to 300 hours per month, the demand for the pro model is 400 cartons per month, and the demand for the tour model is 150 cartons, how much of each product should Sun Devil produce? Although Sun Devil has the capacity to produce 600 cartons (300 hours/0.5 hours) of pro-model balls, it can sell only 400 cartons. Producing 400 cartons requires 200 machine hours, leaving 100 additional machine hours per month for the production of tour balls. Sun Devil can maximize income by producing 400 cartons of pro balls and 133 cartons of tour balls each month.

Qualitative factors, including the impact of discontinuing the sale of the tour ball, must also be considered. Visibility of the tour ball on the professional tour may be a valuable source of advertising contributing to sales of the pro model.

Other options include adding machines to increase the amount of available machine hours or reducing the machine time needed to produce a carton of balls. Maximizing profits by focusing on the constraint itself in order to loosen the constraint is the focus of the theory of constraints.

***Key Concept:** Resource utilization decisions hinge on an analysis of the contribution margin earned per unit of the limited resource.*

THE THEORY OF CONSTRAINTS

The **theory of constraints** is a management tool for dealing with constraints. The theory of constraints identifies **bottlenecks** in the production process. Bottlenecks limit throughput, which can be thought of as the amount of finished goods that result from the production

EXHIBIT 7-2 An Example of a Production Bottleneck

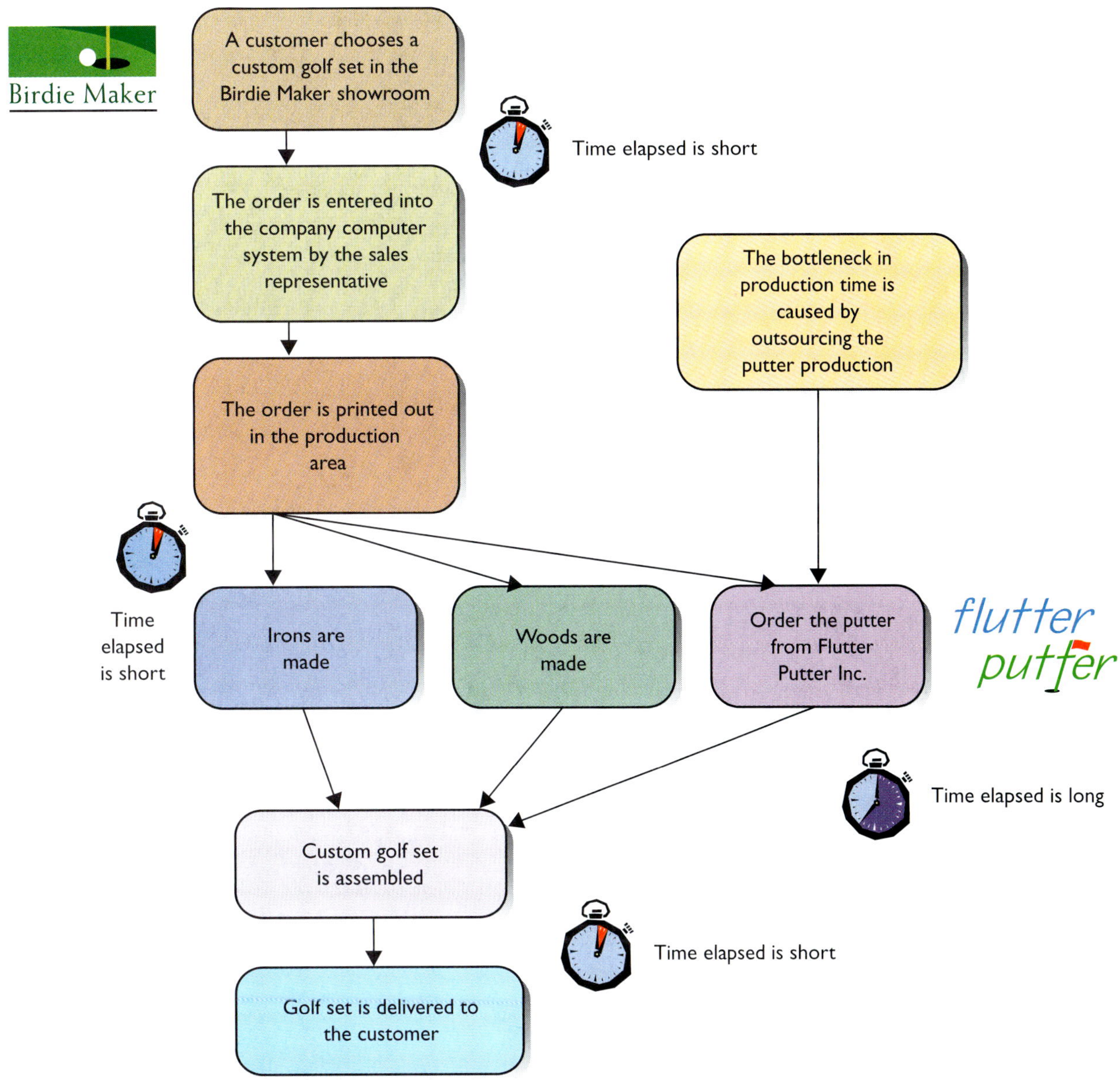

process. In the previous example, machine time is a bottleneck that limits the amount of throughput. Another example is the airline industry, in which certain tasks performed while the aircraft is on the ground delay departure and increase the turnaround time for the plane.

The key to the theory of constraints is identifying and managing bottlenecks. Once a bottleneck is identified, management must focus its time and resources on relieving the bottleneck. Utilizing resources to increase the efficiency of a non-bottleneck operation will rarely increase throughput. For example, increasing the efficiency of machines with excess capacity in a factory or reducing flight time for an airline will result in very limited increases in throughput (if any) until bottlenecks are relieved.

In Exhibit 7-2, Birdie Maker has discovered that delays in delivery of golf clubs to customers are a result of the extra time it takes to order and receive putters from Flutter Putter Inc. Reducing the time spent manufacturing irons or woods would not reduce overall delivery time until the bottleneck with the putters is relieved.

Decisions to Sell or Process Further

LO6
Analyze a decision dealing with selling a product or processing it further

The decision to sell a product as is or to process it further to generate additional revenue is another common management decision. For example, furniture manufacturers may sell furniture unassembled and unfinished, assembled and unfinished, or assembled and finished. Pizza parlors may sell ready-to-bake pizzas or fully cooked pizzas. The key in deciding to sell or process further is that all costs that are incurred up to the point where the decision is made are sunk costs and therefore not relevant.

The relevant costs are the incremental or additional processing costs. Managers should compare the additional sales revenue that can be earned from processing the product further to the additional processing costs. If the additional revenue is greater than the additional costs, the product should be processed further. If the additional costs exceed the revenues, the product should be sold as is. For example, the cost to finish a piece of furniture must be less than the additional revenue that can be expected from selling finished furniture. As with limited-resource problems, demand for the products must also be considered.

Key Concept: *A product should be processed further if the additional revenue is greater than the additional cost.*

In the News http://www.wsj.com

Sometimes, further processing of an undesirable by-product can even be profitable. Since 1970, electric utilities have been scrubbing the smoke emitted from their smokestacks to remove sulfur and ash from the atmosphere. They do this by spraying a mixture of water and ground limestone into the smoke. Until recently, the utilities collected the toothpastelike mixture that collected at the bottom of the stacks and buried it in landfills. However, adding oxygen turns the mixture into calcium sulfate, which has the same chemical composition as gypsum. The gypsum can be sold to farmers as a soil enhancer or to wallboard manufacturers as a raw material (*Wall Street Journal,* October 5, 1998, B1).

ABC and Relevant-Cost Analysis

LO7
Evaluate the impact of ABC on relevant costs and decision making

As described in Chapter 4, activity-based costing (ABC) uses multiple cost drivers to trace overhead costs directly to products. ABC's focus on activities that cause costs to be incurred sheds new light on the concept of relevant costs. Whereas traditional cost analysis focuses on changes in costs associated with volume, ABC focuses on changes in costs associated with a variety of activities, including material handling, inspection, purchasing, and machine setups. Although fixed costs may not appear to be avoidable (and therefore relevant) under traditional costing because they do not vary with changes in volume, these same costs may be avoidable when the amount of material, inspections, purchase orders, or setups is changed. ABC helps managers to identify what costs are really avoidable in a relevant-cost analysis.

However, it is important to remember that not all traceable costs are relevant costs. For example, ABC may trace depreciation of a machine directly to a product. However, if the depreciation relates to an existing piece of equipment, the depreciation is a sunk cost and is still not relevant.

SUMMARY OF KEY CONCEPTS

- The price of a product must be sufficient to cover all the costs of the product and to provide a profit. (p. 206)
- The price of a special order must be higher than the additional variable costs incurred in accepting the special order plus any opportunity costs incurred. (p. 210)
- A product should continue to be made internally and labor incurred internally if the avoidable costs are less than the additional costs that will be incurred by buying or outsourcing. (p. 216)
- A product should be dropped when the fixed costs avoided are greater than the contribution margin lost. (p. 218)
- Resource utilization decisions hinge on an analysis of the contribution margin earned per unit of the limited resource. (p. 220)
- A product should be processed further if the additional revenue is greater than the additional cost. (p. 222)

KEY DEFINITIONS

Life-cycle cost The costs accumulated over the entire life cycle of a product (p. 205)

Target pricing A pricing method used when a price is preset by market conditions or when a company wishes to set a price in order to capture a predetermined market share or to meet other marketing goals (p. 206)

Cost-plus pricing A method of pricing in which managers determine the cost of the product or service and then add a markup percentage to that cost to arrive at the sales price (p. 206)

Markup percentage The amount added to cost to determine the sales price in cost-plus pricing; must be sufficient to cover any costs not included in the company's definition of product cost plus produce an acceptable profit (p. 207)

Time and material pricing A pricing method often used in service industries, in which labor is the primary cost incurred (p. 207)

Value pricing A pricing method that bases the price of services on the perceived or actual value of the service provided to a customer (p. 208)

Special-order decisions Short-run pricing decisions in which management must decide what sales price is appropriate when customers place orders that are different from those placed in the regular course of business (larger quantity, one-time sale to a foreign customer, etc.) (p. 209)

Outsourcing or make-or-buy decision A short-term decision to outsource labor or purchase components used in manufacturing from another company rather than to provide services or to produce components internally (p. 212)

Vertical integration Accomplished when a company is involved in multiple steps of the value chain (p. 213)

Constraint A restriction that occurs when the capacity to manufacture a product or to provide a service is limited in some manner (p. 219)

Resource utilization decision A decision requiring an analysis of how best to use a resource that is available in limited supply (p. 219)

Theory of constraints A management tool for dealing with constraints; identifies and focuses on bottlenecks in the production process (p. 220)

Bottlenecks Production-process steps that limit throughput or the number of finished products that go through the production process (p. 220)

BIG AL'S

COMPUTER SIMULATION

You can now turn to **Appendix A** of your text to complete the portion of the Big Al's simulation covering pricing strategy, special orders, make versus buy decisions, and the theory of constraints.

MULTIPLE CHOICE

1. Under cost-plus pricing, the markup percentage:
   a. is determined by market conditions
   b. must be sufficient to cover costs and to earn a profit in the long run
   c. is usually set by the board of directors and stated in the company's articles of incorporation
   d. all of the above
2. The Beach Hut sells hotdogs for $2 each. The costs associated with each hot dog are estimated at $1 of variable costs and $0.35 of fixed-overhead costs. A summer camp, whose campers will be visiting the beach once during the summer, wishes to buy 100 hotdogs for $1.25 each. If the special order were accepted, net income would:
   a. increase by $125
   b. increase by $25
   c. decrease by $75
   d. decrease by $10
3. Shoeworks produces and sells athletic shoes for children. The costs associated with each pair of shoes are estimated as $12 of variable costs and $4 of fixed-overhead costs. The shoes typically sell for $20 per pair. A local children's football league has contacted Shoeworks and wishes to purchase 50 pairs of sneakers for $15 each. The league's normal supplier of shoes was unable to provide shoes, owing to a labor strike. Which of the following factors should be considered before making this special-order decision?
   a. Does Shoeworks have the available capacity to produce these 50 pairs of shoes in addition to its usual sales?
   b. Will regular customers become angry if they learn that the football players have paid less for their shoes?
   c. Will the relevant costs of providing these 50 pairs of shoes be covered?
   d. all of the above
4. Book Publishing, Inc., operates a bookbinding division. Management is considering whether the binding should be done internally or outsourced at a cost of $25 per book. The current internal binding costs average $26.50, including fixed costs of $4,000 for the 1000 books bound annually; however, 75 percent of the fixed costs can be avoided if the binding is outsourced. What would you recommend Book Publishing do in this situation, and what is the effect on net income?
   a. make internally; increases net income by $500
   b. make internally; increases net income by $1,500
   c. outsource; increases net income by $500
   d. outsource; increases net income by $1,500
5. Bubblemania has three product lines: A, B, and C.

	A	B	C	Total
Sales	$10,000	$9,000	$12,000	$31,000
Variable costs	4,500	7,000	6,000	17,500
Contribution margin	5,500	2,000	6,000	13,500
Fixed costs	3,500	6,000	3,000	12,500
Net income	2,000	(4,000)	3,000	1,000

   Product line B appears unprofitable, and management is considering discontinuing the line. If it is discontinued, $1,000 of the line's fixed costs can be avoided. The discontinuation of product line B would:
   a. increase net income by $3,000
   b. decrease net income by $3,000
   c. increase net income by $1,000
   d. decrease net income by $1,000
6. Soft Mattress Inc. produces both a queen- and a king-size soft bed. Selected data related to each product follow:

	Queen	King
Sales price	$525	$635
Direct material	$350	$365
Direct labor	$ 75	$ 85
Variable Overhead	$ 25	$ 35
Stuffing hours	1	3

The two employees who are trained to stuff the secret soft ingredient into the mattresses have a maximum of 4,000 stuffing hours per year. If demand is strong for both types of bed and the company could sell an unlimited amount of units produced for either style, which beds should be produced?

a. 4,000 queen-size beds **b.** 4,000 king-size beds **c.** 1,333 king-size beds
d. 2,000 queen-size beds and 667 king-size beds

7. Zoney Products produces both a standard- and a deluxe-model TV. Selected data related to each product follow:

	Standard	Deluxe
Sales price	$725	$935
Direct material	$325	$400
Direct labor	$200	$210
Variable overhead	$ 75	$125
Tuning hours	2	4

TV tuning is performed on one of four expensive tuning machines that can operate a maximum of 8,000 tuning hours per year. What is the contribution margin per limited resource for each type of TV?

Standard	Deluxe
a. 125	200
b. 200	125
c. 62.5	50
d. 50	62.5

8. Canned Foods Unlimited is trying to decide whether to sell its canned corn in whole kernels or to process it further into creamed corn. The cost of producing whole-kernel corn is $0.20 per can, and the can sells for $0.40. Additional processing costs to produce creamed corn are $0.06 per can, and each can sells for $0.45. Which of the following costs are relevant in this decision to sell or process further?

a. $0.20 production cost **c.** both **a** and **b**
b. $0.06 processing cost **d.** none of the above

9. Bakery Creations has three pastries that can be sold after baking or decorated and then sold. All pastries sell whether presented as baked or as decorated. The following sales and cost information is provided:

	Pastry A	Pastry B	Pastry C
Initial sales price	$1.25	$1.50	$1.75
Initial cost	$0.75	$0.75	$0.75
Sales price after decorating	$1.60	$2.00	$2.25
Cost of decorating	$0.30	$0.60	$0.40
Number sold per day	100	50	30

What is the maximum amount that net income could increase with further processing?

a. $85 **b.** $8 **c.** $3
d. No increase is possible, as all pastries will be sold either way.

10. When activity-based costing is used for relevant-cost analysis:

a. All traceable costs are relevant costs.
b. All traceable costs are not necessarily relevant costs.
c. Fixed costs are not avoidable and therefore are not relevant.
d. all of the above

CONCEPT REVIEW

11. What term is used to describe the pricing approach that adds a markup to the firm's cost?
12. What is target pricing, and when would it be appropriate to use it?
13. Production of a special order will increase income when the additional revenue from the special order is greater than what?
14. In considering a special order that will enable a company to make use of presently idle capacity, list the costs that would more than likely be relevant in the decision-making process.
15. What costs are usually relevant in a make-or-buy decision?
16. Name some qualitative factors that would cause a decision maker to favor the buy choice in a make-or-buy decision.
17. In deciding whether to manufacture a part or to buy it from an outside supplier, name a cost that would not be relevant to that short-run decision.
18. The decision to drop a product line should be based on what factors?
19. In the short run, which element is most critical to limited-resource decisions?
20. What steps should be taken when dealing with a production bottleneck?
21. How does ABC affect relevant-cost analysis?
22. Explain why an activity-based costing system might provide better information for a make-or-buy decision.
23. Explain why an activity-based costing system might provide better information for a decision to sell or to process further.
24. Explain why an activity-based costing system might provide better information for a decision to drop a product or a segment.

APPLICATION OF CONCEPTS

25. The variable production costs of a product are $15. Fixed costs are $4 per unit, based on 8,000 units produced during this period. The company has adequate capacity to accept a special order of 500 units. What is the minimum price that could be charged for this special order?
26. Old Balance Company manufactures lacrosse sticks. The company's capacity is 4,500 sticks per month; however, it currently is selling only 3,000 sticks per month. Long-Meadow Sports has asked Old Balance to sell 700 lacrosse sticks at $50 each. Normally, Old Balance sells its sticks for $65. The company records report the cost of each stick to be $40, which includes fixed costs of $20. If Old Balance were to accept Long-Meadow's offer, what would be the impact on Old Balance's operating income?
27. Scott Inc. sells a product for $25 per unit. It incurs the following costs for the product: direct materials, $11; direct labor, $7; variable overhead, $2; fixed overhead, $1; total, $21. Scott Inc. received a special order for 75 units of the product. The order would require rental of a special tool that rents for $300 for the period needed. What is the minimum price per unit that Scott Inc. could charge for this special order if management requires a $500 minimum profit on any special order? Scott Inc. has sufficient idle capacity to produce the needed product for this order.
28. Husky Sports manufactures footballs. The forecasted income statement for the year before any special orders is as follows:

	Amount	Per Unit
Sales	$4,000,000	$10.00
Manufacturing cost of goods sold	3,200,000	8.00
Gross profit	$ 800,000	$ 2.00
Selling expenses	300,000	0.75
Operating income	$ 500,000	$ 1.25

Required

A. Fixed costs included in the preceding forecasted income statement are $1,200,000 in manufacturing cost of goods sold and $100,000 in selling expenses. Husky

Sports received a special order for 50,000 footballs at $7.50 each. Assume that Husky Sports has sufficient capacity to manufacture 50,000 more footballs. What is the relevant unit cost?

B. By what amount would operating income of Husky Sports be increased or decreased as a result of accepting the special order?

29. Great Falls Brewery's regular selling price for a case of product is $15. Variable costs are $8 per case. Fixed costs total $2 per case based on 250,000 cases and remain unchanged within the relevant range of 50,000 cases to total capacity of 300,000 cases. After sales of 180,000 cases were projected for the year, a special order was received for an additional 30,000 cases. What is Great Falls Brewery's minimum acceptable selling price for this special order?

30. Violette Inc. uses 10,000 pounds of a certain product in the production of life preservers each year. Presently, this product is purchased from an outside supplier at $11 per pound. For some time now, the factory has had idle capacity that could be utilized to make this product. The costs associated with manufacturing the product internally rather than buying it from the outside supplier are as follows:

Direct materials per unit	$3
Direct labor per unit	$3
Variable overhead per unit	$2
Fixed overhead per unit (based on production of 10,000 pounds per year)	$2
Annual salary of new supervisor	$32,000

Required

A. At what price per pound from the outside supplier would the company be indifferent (on economic grounds) to buying or making the product internally?

B. If Violette Inc. chooses to make the product instead of buying it from the outside vendor, what would be the change, if any, in the company's net income per year?

31. Langer Company has three products (A, B, and C) that use common facilities. The relevant data concerning these three products follow:

	A	B	C	Total
Sales	$10,000	$30,000	$ 40,000	$ 80,000
Variable costs	5,000	20,000	25,000	50,000
Contribution margin	$ 5,000	$10,000	$ 15,000	$ 30,000
Fixed costs	5,000	15,000	30,000	50,000
Operating loss	$ 0	$ (5,000)	$(15,000)	$(20,000)

Required

A. If fixed costs allocated to product line C are not avoidable and if product line C is dropped, what will be the impact on operating profits?

B. If $15,000 of the fixed costs allocated to product line C are avoidable and product line C is dropped, what will be the impact on operating profits?

C. What other qualitative factors should Langer Company consider before it makes the decision to drop product line C?

32. Paul Allyn Productions produces music videos. They are produced in two lengths on separate videocassettes. The company can sell its entire production of either product. The relevant data for these two products follow:

	Video 1	Video 2
Machine time per unit	5 hours	2 hours
Selling price per unit	$10	$20
Variable costs per unit	$ 2	$ 4

Total fixed overhead is $240,000. The company has only 100,000 machine hours available for production. Because of the constraint on the maximum number of machine hours, Paul Allyn Productions must decide which cassette to produce to maximize its return. Which product should the company select to maximize operating profits?

33. Grace Sullivan & Company has two sales offices: one located in Portland and one in Portsmouth. The company's records report the following information:

	Portland	**Portsmouth**
Sales	$40,000	$50,000
Direct costs:		
Variable	15,000	25,000
Fixed	10,000	10,000

Management is considering dropping the Portland office. What will be the resulting operating income if Portland is eliminated and half of its fixed costs are avoidable?

34. Kenny Washburn Toys manufactured 500 stuffed lobsters that were defective. The manufacturing costs of the lobsters follow:

Direct materials	$30
Direct labor	24
Variable overhead	10
Fixed overhead	12

The lobsters normally sell for $100. The company can rework the lobsters, which will cost $20 for direct materials, $20 for direct labor, and $2 for variable overhead. In addition, fixed overhead will be applied at the rate of 75 percent of direct labor cost. Alternatively, the company could sell the lobsters "as is" for a selling price of $70. What should management do to maximize profits?

35. Foley Corporation makes motorcycle engines. The company's records show the following costs to manufacture part #61645:

Direct materials	$12
Direct labor	15
Variable overhead	20
Fixed overhead	10

Another manufacturer has offered to supply Foley Corporation with part #61645 for a cost of $50 per unit. Foley Corporation uses 1,000 units annually. If Foley Corporation accepts the offer, what will be the short-run impact on operating income?

Birdie Maker

36. If Birdie Maker Golf Company needs to mark up all costs by 30 percent to earn the desired profit, what would the selling price be if the costs of a set of golf clubs were (a) cost of clubs = $500; (b) cost of clubs = $700? Recalculate the selling price if the markup percentage drops to 25 percent.

37. If Pryor Construction marks up the cost of construction by 24 percent, what would the selling price be on a house that cost $225,000 to build? What if the markup percentage increased to 30 percent?

Birdie Maker

38. If Birdie Maker Golf Company is limited to a selling price of $700 for a set of golf clubs because of market constraints but still must maintain a 30 percent markup on cost, what is the target cost for a set of golf clubs? What if the market price is $800 and the markup is 35 percent?

39. Clayton Herring Tire Co. is considering adding a special tire for sports cars. The market research indicates that the maximum price for this type of tire is $75. If the company must have at least a 40 percent markup on all tires, what is the maximum cost to produce the new tire? If the production department estimates the cost to be $50, what options are available at this point?

Clayton Herring Tire Co.

40. Old Balance Company would like to introduce a new high-tech lacrosse stick. The new stick would sell for $75. If Old Balance marks up the cost of all products by 20 percent, what is the maximum cost it can incur to produce the new stick? What if the company decides to raise the price of the stick to $80?

41. Potts Sports is considering outsourcing its maintenance work. The total labor cost for the maintenance department is $150,000 and the company has an offer from Robyn Maintenance to provide the service for $125,000. The maintenance equipment currently used cannot be sold and has annual depreciation of $10,000. The overhead allocated to the maintenance department is $20,000 per year and would not be avoidable. Based on the information given, what should be done? What if the equipment could not be sold but the overhead allocation decreased to $10,000? What other nonquantitative factors should be considered?

42. Mandy Lifeboats produces life preservers with a cost of $10 per unit. The cost is broken down as follows:

Direct materials	$3
Direct labor	3
Variable overhead	2
Fixed overhead	2 (based on 20,000 units)

Mandy Lifeboats can outsource the service function on the manufacturing equipment to U. R. Saved Service Co. for $12,000 per year. Currently, the service function is included in variable overhead at $0.50 per unit. If the service function is outsourced, the fixed overhead would also decrease by $0.50 per unit. Based on these amounts, what should be done? Suppose that fixed costs remain the same. Would that change the decision? What other non-quantitative factors should be considered?

43. Watson Company uses a special compound to manufacture two models of beach balls: the bouncer and the floater. The floater uses 10 ounces of the compound and the bouncer uses 7 ounces. The maximum amount of special compound available each month is 200 pounds. Watson Company can sell up to 225 floaters and up to 300 bouncers. The compound costs $5 per pound. The floater sells for $7 and the bouncer sells for $6.50. Each ball takes ½ hour to produce, and the average wage rate is $7 per hour. Overhead amounts to $0.50 per ball. Which ball should the company make first?

44. Porker Enterprises produces hams from locally raised pigs. The cost of getting the meat ready for market is $1 per pound. Hams weigh an average of 12 pounds and sell for $1.50 per pound. Porker can smoke the hams for an additional $0.50 per pound. The smoked hams would sell for $2.25 per pound. Should Porker smoke the hams? What if the selling price for smoked hams were $1.75 per pound?

45. For the past 10 years, Gutmann Company has produced the small gas motors that fit into its main product line of weed-cutting machines. As material costs have steadily increased, the controller of Gutmann Company is reviewing the decision to continue to make the small motors and has identified the following facts:

a. The equipment used to manufacture the gas motors has a book value of $350,000.

b. The space now occupied by the gas motor manufacturing department could be used to eliminate the need for storage space now being rented.

c. Comparable units can be purchased from an outside supplier for $89.95.

d. Five of the people who work in the gas motor manufacturing department would be terminated and given eight weeks' severance pay.

e. A $25,000 unsecured note is still outstanding on the equipment used in the manufacturing process.

f. Some communities in which Gutmann operates have a noise-reduction law.

Required

A. Which of the preceding items are relevant to the decision that the controller has to make? Give a reason or reasons why each item is or is not relevant.

B. Suppose that the motor supplied by the outside supplier has a muffler that exceeds the noise level allowed in some communities in which you sell. Would that change your decision? Suppose that the outside supplier could provide the motors with a quieter muffler for $95. What other factors should be considered?

Step 2 IDENTIFY OBJECTIVES

46. Jain Simmons Company needs 10,000 units of a certain part to be used in production. If Jain Simmons Company buys the part from Sullivan Company instead of making it, Jain Simmons Company could not use the present facilities for another manufacturing activity. Sixty percent of the fixed overhead applied will continue regardless of what decision is made.

The following quantitative information is available regarding the situation presented:

Cost to Jain Simmons Company to make the part:

Direct materials	$ 6
Direct labor	24
Variable overhead	12
Fixed overhead applied	15
	$57

Cost to buy the part from Sullivan Company: $53

Required

A. In deciding whether to make or to buy the part, how much are Jain Simmons's total relevant costs to make the part?

B. Which alternative is more desirable for Jain Simmons and by what amount?

C. Suppose that Jain Simmons Company is in an area of the country with a high unemployment rate and that it is unlikely that displaced direct-labor employees will be able to find alternative employment. How might that impact your decision?

47. The Hemp Division of West Company produces rope. One-third of the Hemp Division's output is sold to the Hammock Products Division of West; the remainder is sold to outside customers. The Hemp Division's estimated sales and cost data for the fiscal year ending Sept. 30 are as follows:

	Hammock Products	Outsiders
Sales	$15,000	$40,000
Variable costs	(10,000)	(20,000)
Fixed costs	(3,000)	(6,000)
Gross margin	2,000	14,000
Unit sales	10,000	20,000

The Hemp Division has an opportunity to purchase 10,000 feet of identical-quality rope from an outside supplier at a cost of $1.25 per unit on a continuing basis. Assume that the Hemp Division cannot sell any additional product to outside customers.

Required

A. Should West allow its Hemp Division to purchase the rope from the outside supplier? Why or why not?

B. Assume that the Hemp Division is now at full capacity and that sufficient demand exists to sell all production to outsiders at present prices. What is the differential cost (benefit) of producing the rope internally?

C. Assume that the quality of the rope is found to be of a lesser, but still satisfactory, quality. What factors should be considered?

D. Assume that the quality of the rope is found to be of questionable quality but that the price is $1.00 per unit. What factors should be considered in the decision?

48. Patterson Manufacturing Company manufactures part #52749 for use in its production cycle. The costs per unit for 10,000 units of part #52749 are as follows:

Direct materials	$ 3
Direct labor	15
Variable overhead	6
Fixed overhead	8

Blundell Company has offered to sell Patterson 10,000 units of part #52749 for $30 per unit. If Patterson accepts Blundell's offer, the released facilities could be used to save $45,000 in relevant costs in the manufacture of part #60657. In addition, $5 per unit of the fixed overhead applied to part #52749 would be totally eliminated.

Required

A. What are the total relevant costs to manufacture part #52749?

B. What are the total relevant costs to buy part #52749?

C. What alternative is more desirable and by what amount?

D. Suppose that the purchased part is of lower quality than the part being produced internally. How would that influence your decision? What if the price of the part is reduced to $25 per unit?

49. The Schoof Manufacturing Co. manufactures part #81199 for use in producing a mountain bike. The costs per unit for 20,000 units of part #81199 are as follows:

Direct material	$ 6
Direct labor	30
Variable overhead	12
Fixed overhead	16
	$64

Kelley Manufacturing has offered to sell Schoof 20,000 units of part #81199 for $60 per unit. The company will decide to buy the part from Kelley if the savings total $250,000. If the part is purchased from the outside supplier, Schoof will realize savings of $9 per part for fixed overhead. Furthermore, the released facilities could be leased for additional revenue. What amount of lease payment must be charged to reach the required $250,000 savings? What qualitative factors should be considered before making a final decision? Why?

50. Foggy Mountain Company manufactures several styles of banjos. Management estimates that during the second quarter of the current year, the company will be operating at 80 percent of normal capacity. Because Foggy Mountain wants to increase utilization of the plant, the company has decided to consider special orders for its products.

Foggy Mountain has just received inquiries from a number of companies concerning the possibility of a special order and has narrowed the possibilities down to two companies. The first is from CCR Company, which would like to market a banjo very similar to one of Foggy Mountain's. The CCR banjo would be marketed under CCR's own label. CCR has offered Foggy Mountain $57.50 per banjo for

20,000 banjos to be shipped by June 1. The cost data for the Foggy Mountain banjo are as follows:

Regular selling price per banjo	$90
Costs per unit:	
Raw material	$25
Direct labor (5 hours @ $6)	30
Overhead (2.5 machine hours @ $4)	10
Total costs	$65

According to the specifications provided by CCR, the banjo that the company wants would require less-expensive raw material. Consequently, the raw material would cost only $22 per banjo. Management has also estimated that the remaining costs would stay the same.

The second special order was submitted by Seager & Buffet Company for 7,500 banjos at $75 per banjo. These banjos would be marketed under the Seager & Buffet label and also should be shipped by June 1. However, the Seager & Buffet model is different from any banjo in the Foggy Mountain product line. The estimated per unit costs are as follows:

Raw materials	$32.50
Direct labor (5 hours @ $6)	30.00
Overhead (5 machine hours @ $4)	20.00
Total costs	$82.50

In addition, Foggy Mountain will incur $15,000 in additional setup costs and will have to purchase a $25,000 special machine to manufacture these banjos; this machine will be discarded once the special order is completed.

The Foggy Mountain manufacturing capabilities are limited in the total machine hours available. The plant capacity under normal operations is 900,000 machine hours per year, or 75,000 machine hours per month. The budgeted fixed overhead for the year is $2,160,000. All manufacturing overhead costs are applied to production on the basis of machine hours at $4 per hour.

Foggy Mountain will have the entire second quarter to work on the special orders. Management does not expect any repeat sales to be generated from either special order. Company practice precludes Foggy Mountain from subcontracting any portion of an order when special orders are not expected to generate repeat sales.

Required

A. What is the excess capacity of machine hours available in the second quarter?

B. What is the variable overhead rate per machine hour?

C. Based on the preceding information and your analysis, would you accept CCR's offer?

D. What is the unit contribution margin per banjo for the Seager & Buffet order?

E. What is the actual gain (loss) incurred by accepting Seager & Buffet's offer?

51. Cecilia Louse Inc. has the following cost structure for the upcoming year:

Sales (20,000 units @ $25)	$500,000	
Manufacturing costs:		
Variable		$10 per unit
Fixed	180,000	
Marketing and administrative costs:		
Variable		$5 per unit
Fixed	20,000	

Required

A. What is the expected level of operating profits?

B. Should the company accept a special order for 1,000 units at a selling price of $20 if variable marketing expenses associated with this special order would be $2 per unit? Calculate the incremental profits if the order is accepted.

C. Suppose that the company received a special order for 3,000 units at a selling price of $19 with no variable marketing expenses. Calculate the impact on operating profits.

D. Assume that if the special order is accepted, all the regular customers would be aware of the price paid for the special order. Would that influence your decision? Why?

52. The Belik Company has the capacity to produce 5,000 units per year. Its predicted operations for the year are as follows:

Sales (4,000 units @ $20 each)	$80,000
Manufacturing costs:	
Variable	$5 per unit
Fixed	10,000
Marketing and administrative costs:	
Variable	$1 per unit
Fixed	8,000

The accounting department has prepared the following projected income statement for the coming year for your use in making decisions:

Sales		$80,000
Variable costs:		
Manufacturing ($5 × 4,000)	$20,000	
Marketing ($1 × 4,000)	4,000	24,000
Contribution margin		$56,000
Fixed costs:		
Manufacturing	$10,000	
Marketing	8,000	18,000
Operating profit		$38,000

Required

A. Should the company accept a special order for 500 units at a selling price of $8? Assuming that there are no variable marketing and administrative costs for this order and that regular sales will not be affected, what is the impact of this decision on company profits?

B. Suppose that the preceding order has a one-time setup fee of $1,000. Should the special order be accepted? Why?

C. What other factors should be considered, and how would they impact your decision to accept the special order?

D. Suppose that regular sales would be reduced by 200 units if the special order were accepted. What impact would this have on the company's decision?

53. Avery Inc. is a wholesale distributor supplying a wide range of moderately priced sporting equipment to large chain stores. About 60 percent of Avery's products are purchased from other companies, and the remainder of the products are manufactured by Avery. The company has a plastics department that is currently manufacturing molded fishing tackle boxes. Avery is able to manufacture and sell 8,000 tackle boxes annually, making full use of its direct-labor capacity at available workstations.

The following table presents the selling price and costs associated with Avery's tackle boxes:

Selling price		$86.00
Costs per box:		
Molded plastic	$ 8.00	
Hinges, latches, handle	9.00	
Direct labor ($15/hour)	18.75	
Manufacturing overhead	12.50	
Selling and administrative cost	17.00*	65.25
Profit per box		$20.75

*Includes $6 per unit of fixed distribution costs.

Because Avery believes that it could sell 12,000 tackle boxes, the company has looked into the possibility of purchasing the tackle boxes for distribution. Craig Products, a steady supplier of quality products, would be able to provide up to 9,000 tackle boxes per year at a price of $68 per box delivered to Avery's facility. Four dollars of variable selling and administrative costs will be incurred if the tackle boxes are purchased.

Bart Johnson, Avery's product manager, has suggested that the company could make better use of its plastics department by purchasing the tackle boxes and manufacturing skateboards. To support his position, Johnson has a market study that indicates an expanding market for skateboards and a need for additional suppliers. Johnson believes that Avery could expect to sell 17,500 skateboards annually at a price of $45.00 per skateboard. Johnson's estimate of the costs to manufacture the skateboards is presented here:

Selling price per skateboard	$45.00
Costs per skateboard:	
Molded plastic	$ 5.50
Wheels, plastic	7.00
Direct labor ($15/hour)	7.50
Manufacturing overhead	5.00
Selling and administrative cost	9.00*
Total cost per skateboard	$34.00
Profit per skateboard	$11.00

*Includes $6 per unit of fixed distribution costs.

In the plastics department, Avery uses direct labor hours as the application base for manufacturing overhead. Included in the manufacturing overhead for the current year is $50,000 factorywide, fixed manufacturing overhead that has been allocated to the plastic department.

Required

Step 1 DEFINE THE PROBLEM

Step 2 IDENTIFY OBJECTIVES

Step 3 IDENTIFY AND ANALYZE AVAILABLE OPTIONS

Step 4 SELECT THE BEST OPTION

A. Define the problem faced by Avery Inc., based on the facts as presented.

B. What are the relevant objectives in this problem?

C. What options are available to Avery Inc. in solving the problem?

D. Rank the options in order of preference.

E. What qualitative factors should Avery consider in the decision?

F. Should Avery consider the potential liability that comes with selling skateboards? It has been shown that skateboards are responsible for 25 deaths per year and more than 500 serious accidents. Would that change your decision to make skateboards?

54. Big Ben Tours Inc. operates a large number of tours throughout the southwestern United States. A careful study has indicated that some of the tours are not profitable, and the management of Big Ben Tours is considering dropping these tours in order to improve the company's overall operating performance.

One such tour is a two-day bus trip to the world-famous London Bridge on the Colorado River. An income statement from one of these tours is given in the following table:

Ticket revenue (100 seats × 45% occupancy × $80 ticket price)		$3,600	100%
Less: Variable expenses ($24 per person)		1,080	30%
Contribution margin		$2,520	70%
Less tour expenses:			
Tour promotion	$620		
Salary of bus driver	400		
Tour guide fee	825		
Fuel for bus	100		
Depreciation for bus	400		
Liability insurance, bus	250		
Overnight parking fee, bus	50		
Room and meals, bus driver, and tour guide	75		
Bus maintenance and preparation	325		
Total tour expenses		$3,045	
Net loss		$ (525)	

The following additional information is available about the tour:

a. Bus drivers are paid fixed annual salaries; tour guides are paid for each tour conducted.

b. The "bus maintenance and preparation" cost is an allocation of the salaries of mechanics and other service personnel who are responsible for keeping the company's fleet of buses in good operating condition.

c. This particular tour is very important to Ben, the founder and owner, who often takes the tour himself as driver or tour guide. He would like to see the tour retained.

Required

A. Prepare an analysis showing what the impact will be on company profits if this tour is discontinued.

B. Ben has criticized the company's tour director, Amy, because only about 50 percent of the seats on the London Bridge tours are being filled as compared to an average of 60 percent for the industry. The tour director has explained that the company's average seat occupancy could be improved considerably by eliminating about 10 percent of the tours, but doing so would reduce profits. Do you agree with the tour director's conclusion? Explain your response.

C. What other options are available to Big Ben Tours Inc.?

Step 3 IDENTIFY AND ANALYZE AVAILABLE OPTIONS

D. List qualitative factors that you think should be considered in this decision, and discuss the potential impact of each factor on the decision.

55. Smoluk Mining Company currently is operating at less than 50 percent of capacity. The management of the company expects sales to drop below the present level of 10,000 tons of ore per month very soon. The sales price per ton is $3 and the variable cost per ton is $2. Fixed costs per month total $10,000.

Management is concerned that a further drop in sales volume will generate a loss and, accordingly, is considering the temporary suspension of operations until demand in the metals markets rebounds and prices once again rise. Over the past year, management has implemented a cost-reduction program that has been successful in reducing costs to the point that suspending operations appears to be the only viable alternative. Management estimates that suspending operations would reduce fixed costs from $10,000 to $4,000 per month.

Required

A. Why does management estimate that the fixed costs will persist at $4,000 even though the mine is temporarily closed?

B. At what sales volume will the loss be greater or less than the shutdown cost of $4,000 per month?

C. List any qualitative factors that you think management should consider in this decision, and discuss the potential impact of each factor on the decision.

56. Jagolinzer Company is currently operating at 80 percent capacity. Worried about the company's performance, Phil, the general manager, reviewed the company's operating performance.

	SEGMENT			
	North	South	East	West
Sales	$30	$40	$20	$10
Less variable costs	12	8	21	8
Contribution margin	$18	$32	$ (1)	$ 2
Less fixed costs	9	12	6	3
Operating profit (loss)	$ 9	$20	$ (7)	$ (1)

Required

A. What is the current operating profit for the company as a whole?

B. If Phil eliminated the unprofitable segments, what would be the new operating profit for the company as a whole?

C. What options does management have to maximize profits?

Step 3 IDENTIFY AND ANALYZE AVAILABLE OPTIONS

D. What qualitative factors do you think management should consider before making this decision? What impact could these qualitative factors have on the decision?

57. Sanders Manufacturing uses 10 hours of labor to produce one piece of radar equipment. The unit cost to manufacture this unit is as follows:

Direct materials	$1,000
Materials handling (20 percent of direct material cost)	200
Direct labor	150
Manufacturing overhead (150 percent of direct labor)	225
Total manufacturing cost	$1,575

Material handling represents the direct variable costs of the receiving department and is applied to direct materials and purchased components on the basis of their cost. This is a separate charge in addition to manufacturing overhead. Sanders's annual manufacturing overhead budget is one-third variable and two-thirds fixed. John's Supply, one of Sanders's reliable vendors, has offered to provide the labor to produce the radar equipment for $175 per unit.

Required

A. If the labor is outsourced to John's Supply, Sanders will avoid all direct labor costs. If Sanders decides to outsource the labor, by what amount would the unit cost increase or decrease? Be sure to consider the impact of overhead on your answer.

B. Assume that Sanders must pay six months' severance pay to all employees laid off as a result of this decision. Sanders has 10 employees who are paid $1,200 per month and would be affected by this decision. If Sanders produces 160 radar units per month, what is the time needed to recapture the severance pay?

C. What qualitative factors should Sanders consider before making this decision? What impact would each have on the decision?

58. Voyer Company manufactures plugs used in its manufacturing cycle. The cost is $36 per unit, including $8 of fixed overhead. Voyer needs 30,000 of these plugs annually, and John Company has offered to sell these units to Voyer at $33 per unit. If Voyer decides to purchase the plugs, $60,000 of the annual fixed overhead applied will be eliminated, and the company may be able to rent the facility previously used for manufacturing the plugs.

Required

A. If Voyer Company purchases the plugs but does not rent the unused facility, what is the per unit impact on the company?

B. If the plugs are purchased and the facility rented, Voyer Company wishes to realize $100,000 in savings annually. To achieve this goal, what must be the minimum annual rent on the facility?

59. John Carey Company produces computer games that have a maximum market price of $50. The company is considering introducing some new games to be used with an enhanced game machine manufactured by another company and just released. The company must realize a profit of 30 percent of cost in order to remain profitable with this division of the company.

Required

A. What is the target cost for these games given the constraints presented?

B. Suppose that the production department has projected the production costs of the game to be $40. What is the problem facing the company?

C. What are the relevant costs in this problem?

D. What additional information do you need to make the optimal decision?

E. Under what circumstances might the company consider producing the games?

Step 1 DEFINE THE PROBLEM

Step 2 IDENTIFY OBJECTIVES

Step 3 IDENTIFY AND ANALYZE AVAILABLE OPTIONS

60. Regina Johnson Company produces children's books that must sell for $10 or less. The company is considering a proposal to introduce a series of books. The company has always tried to realize a profit of 50 percent on the cost of all new projects undertaken.

Required

A. What is the target cost for producing these books?

B. Part of the cost of producing the books is the royalties paid to the author. The company has typically paid 10 percent royalties on the cost of the book. In other words, 10 percent of the cost to produce the book will be allocated to royalties. The author of these new books wants a 12 percent royalty on the entire series. If the market will not allow an increase in sales price, what are the options available to the company? Show calculations of the impact on company profits.

61. Vincent Martinez Company is considering taking over a hot dog vending booth at the local AA Minor League baseball stadium. Because of limitations on the retail price that may be charged for hot dogs in the stadium and a limitation on the profit percentage that may be earned, the company has very limited options. The stadium owner has set a limit on the price of a hot dog at $1.75 and limits all vendors to no more than 30 percent profit on any food sold.

Required

A. Given the limits imposed by the stadium owner, what is the maximum price that Vincent Martinez Company can pay for all ingredients needed?

B. After computing the maximum cost of the ingredients, the company finds that to purchase all ingredients at the quality level expected, the cost is $1.50.

C. Accurately define the problem faced by Vincent Martinez Company.

Step 1	DEFINE THE PROBLEM
Step 2	IDENTIFY OBJECTIVES
Step 3	IDENTIFY AND ANALYZE AVAILABLE OPTIONS
Step 4	SELECT THE BEST OPTION

D. What are the key variables in this decision problem?

E. What are the available options, within the limits imposed, to solve the problem?

F. What is the best option? Why?

62. Janie Pierce-Bratcher Company wants to provide lawn maintenance services to a condo association. The company has typically priced services by adding a 60 percent markup to the costs of providing the service. The costs of providing the lawn maintenance service are as follows:

Direct labor (5 workers @ 2 hours each @ $10/hour)	$100
Gas and oil for mowers @ $2.50 per hour	25
Maintenance on mowers @ $2.00 per hour	20
Total costs	$145

Required

A. What price should Janie Pierce-Bratcher Company bid for the condo association lawn maintenance service?

B. What additional costs, if any, should the company consider?

C. Based on your answer in A and any estimated costs you considered in B, how profitable will this venture be?

63. Refer to the information in problem 62. The condo association also has asked Janie Pierce-Bratcher Company to bid on additional services needed. The association would like the company to trim along all sidewalks and driveways and to fertilize the lawns three times per year.

Required

A. What additional information does the company need to accurately bid on the preceding services?

B. If the costs of the additional services are $50 per edging and $250 for each fertilization, what would the bid price be?

64. Carrillo Snow Plowing has been asked to bid on the snow-plowing needs of a large private subdivision. Assume that if the bid is successful, the company will have to acquire equipment and new employees to provide the service. Carrillo has a number of these types of contracts and always marks up the estimated costs by 70 percent, owing to the unpredictable nature of winter storms. All labor hired has to be for the entire winter, so the snowplow operators are paid even if there is no snow to plow.

Required

A. What types of information must be gathered for the bid to be completed? Be specific, but do not estimate amounts.

B. If the total cost of all labor, equipment, and supplies is $5,000 for the five-month winter period, how much should the bid price be?

C. If the bid is not accepted and Carrillo stills wants to try and get the business, what can the company do?

D. If we assume that Carrillo decides to mark up the costs by only 50 percent, what potential risks will the company face by underbidding the normal markup?

65. Cheney, Christiansen, and Clements CPAs has decided to bid on the audit of Comeau Inc., a local manufacturing firm. After learning all they can about the potential new client, the partners have estimated the following:

Staff accountant hours	1,500
Manager hours	200
Partner hours	100
Other out-of-pocket costs (est.)	$10,000

All staff, managers, and partners are paid on average 30 percent of the desired client billing rate ($75, $125, $250). Fringe benefits average 30 percent of the pay rate. Other out-of-pocket costs include supplies, travel, and clerical costs and are usually fairly accurate.

Required

A. If the firm normally marks up nonlabor costs by 20 percent to arrive at the client fee, what should the bid price be?

B. Using the information available to you, compute the actual out-of-pocket cost to the CPA firm to complete this audit. Out-of-pocket costs do not include any profit built into the client billing rate.

C. Using your answer in B, what is the lowest price the CPA firm could charge and not lose money?

D. If Comeau Inc. rejects the bid and states that it will pay no more than $100,000 for the audit, what are the options open to the CPA firm?

66. Sunset Airlines is considering a frequent-flyer program. The airline would offer a free round-trip ticket for every 10,000 miles of travel. The average round-trip ticket on Sunset Airlines is 1,000 miles, so the airline would be giving a free ticket for every 10 tickets purchased. The cost structure for Sunset Airlines is as follows:

	Per Passenger	Per Flight
Cost of meals and drinks	$ 3.25	$ 585
Cost of fuel	138.89	25,000
Cost of cabin crew (four flight attendants)	9.38	1,688
Cost of flight crew	13.89	2,500
Depreciation of aircraft	5.56	1,000
Aircraft maintenance	4.17	750
Total	$175.14	$31,523

The maximum capacity of the airplanes used by Sunset Airlines is 180 seats with an average load of 140 passengers per flight.

Required

A. What is the cost to Sunset Airlines to provide a free ticket to passengers under the proposed frequent-flyer program?

B. What are the risks to Sunset Airlines of providing free tickets with the frequent-flyer program?

C. What qualitative factors should management consider before deciding to implement the frequent-flyer program, and how would they affect the decision?

D. If Sunset Airlines was already flying at 95 percent capacity, or filling up 171 seats on every flight, would the airline still be as motivated to start the frequent-flyer program? Why or why not?

67. Birdie Maker Golf Company produces custom sets of golf clubs that are advertised to be far superior to other golf clubs on the market. These golf clubs sell for $1,000 per set, and Birdie currently sells about 1,000 sets each year. Birdie Maker currently manufactures all the golf clubs in the set but is considering acquiring the putter from Flutter Putter Inc., a manufacturer of custom putters. The purchased putter would be customized for Birdie and matched to the other clubs, so customers should not be able to distinguish it from the rest of the clubs in the set. The costs incurred in the manufacture of the putter are as follows:

	Total (1,000 sets of clubs)	Per Unit
Direct materials	$ 5,000	$ 5.00
Direct labor	9,000	9.00
Variable manufacturing overhead	3,000	3.00
Fixed manufacturing overhead	9,500	9.50
Total cost	$26,500	$26.50

The expected production for the year is 1,000 sets of clubs, so the full cost of each putter is $26.50 ($26,500/1,000). Flutter Putter Inc. is offering to sell the putters to Birdie Maker for $20 per putter.

Required

A. Compute the cost to make the putters, and compare that to the cost to buy. What is the better choice for Birdie Maker?

B. What qualitative factors should Birdie Maker consider before making a final decision?

flutter putter

68. Refer to the facts in problem 67. Now assume that $5,500 of the fixed manufacturing cost is for specialized machinery that is currently being leased under a month-to-month contract. If the putters are purchased from Flutter Putter Inc., the equipment will be returned to the lessor.

Required

A. Compute the cost to make the putters, and compare that to the cost to buy. What is the better choice for Birdie Maker?

B. What qualitative factors should Birdie Maker consider before making a final decision?

Birdie Maker

69. Refer to the facts in problem 67. Now assume that Birdie Maker has a decrease in production volume to 600 sets of golf clubs and that all other costs stay the same as presented in problem 67.

Required

A. Compute the cost to make the putters, and compare that to the cost to buy. What is the better choice for Birdie Maker?

B. What qualitative factors should Birdie Maker consider before making a final decision?

70. Refer to the facts in problem 67. Birdie Maker can rent out the factory space that is now used to manufacture putters for $10,000. All other costs stay the same as presented in problem 67.

Required

A. Compute the cost to make the putters, and compare that to the cost to buy. What is the better choice for Birdie Maker?

B. What qualitative factors should Birdie Maker consider before making a final decision?

Clayton Herring Tire Co.

71. Clayton Herring Tire Co. is considering dropping one of the 10 models of tires that it manufactures and sells. Sales of a special raised-white-letter truck tire have been disappointing. Based on the latest financial information, the tires appear to be losing money.

Clayton Herring Tire Co.

	Truck Tires	**All Other Tires**	**Total**
Sales	$15,500	$150,000	$165,500
Less: Direct material	8,000	50,600	58,600
Direct labor	2,000	30,000	32,000
Variable overhead	1,000	12,000	13,000
Contribution margin	$ 4,500	$ 57,400	$ 61,900
Less: Fixed overhead	7,000	21,000	28,000
Net income	$ (2,500)	$ 36,400	$ 33,900

If the truck tires are dropped from the product line, $5,000 of the fixed costs allocated to truck tires would have to be reallocated to other product lines.

Required

A. What would be the effect on net income if the truck tires are dropped from the product line?

B. If the total fixed costs of $7,000 could be eliminated by discontinuing the truck tires, what would be the effect on net income?

C. If the result in B leads to dropping the product line, what qualitative factors should be considered before making a final decision? How would those factors impact the decision?

72. Cooney Grocery Store is a small corner grocery store in rural Montana, and shelf space is very limited. Management must decide how to allocate shelf space for salsa. Cooney's has been given an opportunity to sell a very popular brand of salsa produced by Bob DeLucia, a popular rock star. The unique bottle is taller and thinner than the other popular brands on the market, to give it visibility on the shelf. The sales and cost data for the new salsa and the three other brands presently sold are as follows:

	Salsa #1	**Salsa #2**	**Salsa #3**	**New Salsa**
Sales price per jar	$2.50	$2.75	$3.00	$4.00
Cost to purchase	$1.25	$1.35	$1.50	$3.20
Contribution margin	$1.25	$1.40	$1.50	$0.80
Bottles per foot of shelf space	10	9	7	12

Required

A. Rank the salsas based on expected revenue if each is given 10 feet of shelf space and all bottles are expected to be sold.

B. Based on the information given, which salsa should get the most shelf space? Why?

C. What qualitative factors should be considered in this decision? How would these factors impact the decision?

73. Sun Devil Golf Balls produces two types of golf balls: the pro model and the tour model. The balls are sold to retailers in cartons containing 360 balls (30 boxes containing 4 sleeves per box, with each sleeve holding 3 balls). Both models are made using the same machines. It takes 30 minutes of machine time to produce 360 pro-model golf balls, whereas it takes 45 minutes to produce the same number of the tour-model balls. The difference in production time results mainly from the different materials used in construction. The relevant data concerning the two models are as follows:

	Pro Model	Tour Model
Sales price (per carton)	$450	$540
Less: Direct material	200	265
Direct labor	50	50
Variable overhead	50	75
Contribution margin	$150	$150
Required machine time	0.50 hours	0.75 hours

Required

A. If the amount of machine time available to Sun Devil Golf Balls is limited, which golf ball should be produced in the larger quantity?

B. If the total machine time available is 200 hours per month and the demand for each model of golf ball is 100,000 balls per month, how many of each model should be produced to maximize profit?

C. What other factors should be considered in this decision, and how would they impact the decision?

74. DePaulis Furniture Manufacturers makes unfinished furniture for sale to customers from its own stores. Recently, the company has been considering taking the production one additional step and finishing some of the furniture for sale as finished furniture. To analyze the problem, DePaulis is going to look at only one product, a very popular dining room chair. The chair can be produced now for $65 and sells for $85 unfinished. If DePaulis were to finish the chair, the cost would increase to $90, but the company could sell the finished chairs for $125.

Required

A. Should DePaulis finish the chairs or continue to sell them unfinished? Show computations to support your decision.

B. What other information should be considered in this decision?

C. What if DePaulis decided it needed a new store to sell the finished furniture and the cost of the new store would add $20 to the cost of each chair? Would that change the decision? Why or why not?

75. DeVito's Fish House buys fish from local fishermen and sells the fish to the public from its booth at the public market. Lately, the fish house has had a number of requests for smoked salmon and has decided to investigate whether that would be a profitable item. The salmon DeVito's buys now costs the company $2 per pound. DeVito's would have to take the fish to a smoke house to have it smoked, which would increase the total cost to $3.25 for each pound of salmon. The salmon sells now for $5.50 per pound but would sell for $6.50 per pound if it were smoked.

Required

A. Based on the facts given, would it be profitable to smoke the salmon? Why or why not?

B. The owner of DeVito's feels strongly that the company will lose customers if smoked salmon is not available for purchase. Based on your analysis in A and considering this information, should the company reconsider its decision?

C. If the cost of the smoking process could be reduced by $0.50 per pound, would that change the decision?

D. What qualitative factors should be considered before making the final decision?

76. The Toledo Turnpin Co. manufactures screws for use in producing a grill. The costs per unit for 10,000 units of each screw are as follows:

Direct material	$ 6
Direct labor	30
Variable overhead	12
Fixed overhead	16
	$64

Thompson Manufacturing has offered to sell Toledo Turnpin 10,000 units of screws for $60 per unit. The company will decide to buy the part from Thompson if the savings total $250,000. If the part is purchased from the outside supplier, Toledo Turnpin will realize savings of $6 per part for fixed overhead. Furthermore, the released facilities could be leased for additional revenue.

Prior to making a decision, the company's CEO commissioned a special study to see whether there would be any further decrease in the fixed-overhead costs. The results of the study revealed that the remaining overhead is related to costs incurred in setting up equipment, inspecting the parts, and handling material, as well as engineering costs. An activity analysis of these costs has indicated that purchasing the part from Thompson Manufacturing will result in the following additional savings:

Three setups—$2,000 each (the setups would be avoided and total spending could be reduced by $2,000 per setup)
One less inspector needed—$35,000
One less material handler needed—$24,500

Required

A. Ignore the special study and determine whether the part should be produced internally or purchased from the supplier.

B. Now, using the special study data, repeat the analysis.

C. Discuss the qualitative factors that would affect the decision.

D. After reviewing the special study, the controller remarked, "This study ignores the additional activity demands that purchasing would cause. For example, although the demand for inspecting the part on the production floor decreases, will we not have a need to inspect the incoming parts in the receiving area? Will we save any inspection costs?" Is the controller right? Would this problem be avoided if Schoof had an activity-based costing system?

Chapter 8

Long-Term (Capital Investment) Decisions

Study Tools

A Review of the Previous Chapter

In Chapter 7, we analyzed pricing decisions and special orders, make-or-buy decisions, decisions to drop a product or a service, resource utilization decisions, and decisions to sell or to process further. Each of these decisions is dependent on an analysis of relevant costs and qualitative factors.

A Preview of This Chapter

In this chapter, we provide a set of tools that allow managers to consider the time value of money in making long-term capital investment decisions.

Key concepts include:

- Long-term investment decisions require a consideration of the time value of money. The time value of money is based on the concept that a dollar received today is worth more than a dollar received in the future.
- The time value of money is considered in capital investment decisions by using one of two techniques: the net present value (NPV) method or the internal rate of return (IRR) method.
- If the present value of cash inflows is greater than or equal to the present value of cash outflows (the NPV is greater than or equal to zero), the investment provides a return at least equal to the discount rate (the minimum required rate of return), and the investment is acceptable.
- The internal rate of return (IRR) is the actual yield, or return, earned by an investment.
- Taxes are a major source of cash outflows for many companies and must be taken into consideration in calculations of the time value of money.
- Analyzing the costs and benefits of investments in automated and computerized design and manufacturing equipment and robotics requires careful consideration of both quantitative and qualitative factors.

Learning Objectives

After studying the material in this chapter, you should be able to:

LO1 Discuss the importance of focusing on cash flow in capital investment decisions

LO2 Apply the decision-making model to capital investment decisions

LO3 Evaluate capital investment decisions by using discounted cash flow analysis (NPV and IRR)

LO4 Discuss key assumptions of the NPV and IRR methods

LO5 Evaluate the impact of taxes on capital investment decisions

LO6 Discuss the impact of the new manufacturing environment on capital investment decisions

LO7 Discuss appropriate applications of nondiscounting methods (the payback method) in capital investment decisions

- The payback method can be useful as a quick approximation of the discounted-cash-flow methods when the cash flows follow similar patterns.

A Preview of Upcoming Chapters

In Chapter 9, we introduce the concept of budgeting and discuss how budgets assist managers in planning and decision making. In Chapter 10, we expand the discussion of flexible budgeting and introduce the concept of standard costs and variance analysis as tools to help managers "manage by exception" and evaluate performance in their control function.

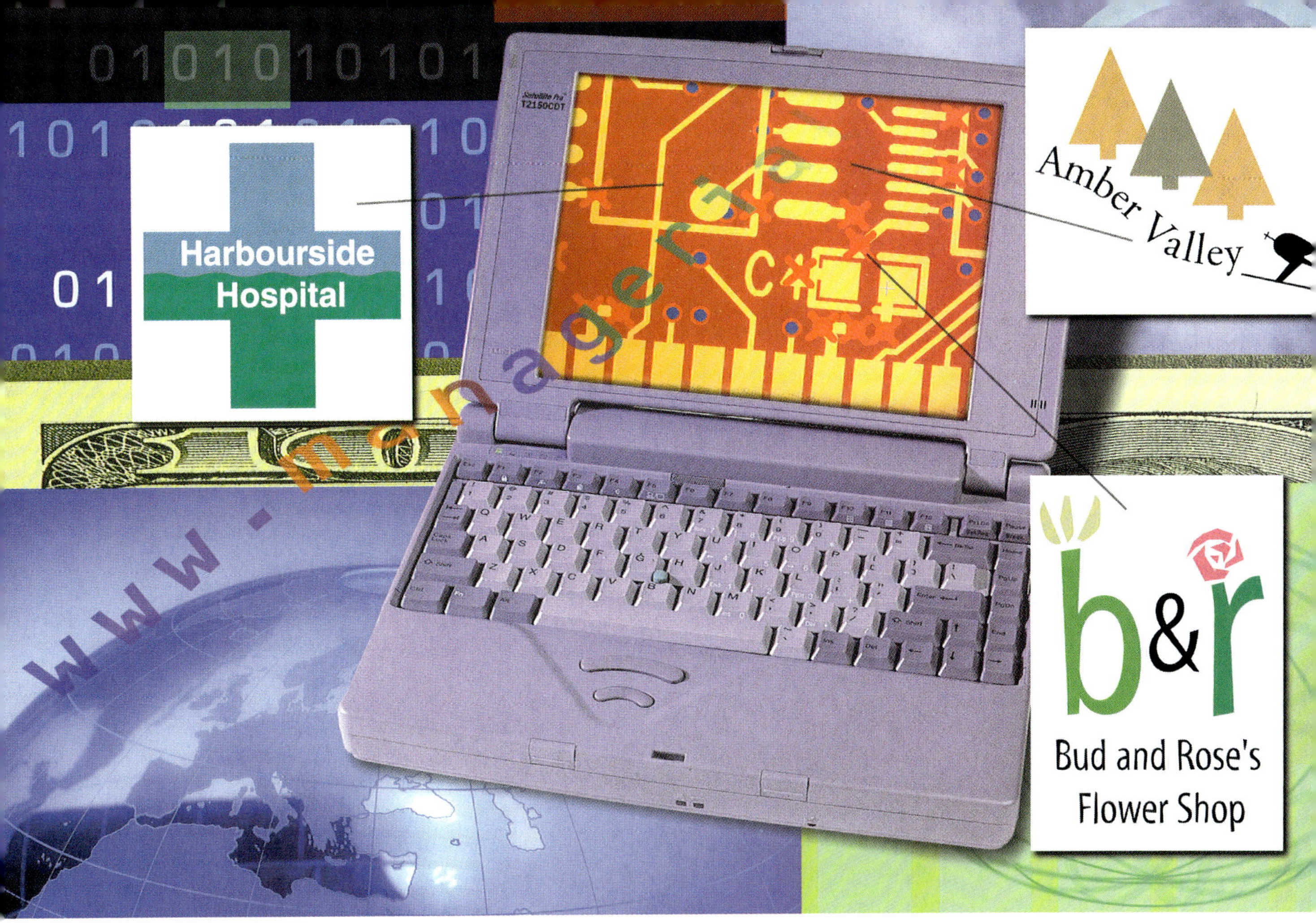

Long-term decisions require a consideration of the time value of money in addition to cost behavior and the relevance of costs. In this chapter, we develop tools that aid managers in making long-term decisions to purchase new property, plant, and equipment (capital investment decisions). These tools help managers quantify the impact of paying or receiving cash flows in different time periods.

Net present value and internal rate of return are two methods that allow for the explicit consideration of the time value of money. The use of these tools in both screening decisions and preference decisions is discussed, as is the impact of income taxes on the analysis. The impact of new manufacturing techniques on capital investment decisions and the importance of qualitative factors in the analysis are also discussed. An approach to long-term purchasing decisions that does not take into consideration the time value of money, the payback method, is also mentioned. ■

INTRODUCTION

Capital investment decisions are made by all types and sizes of organizations and involve the purchase (or lease) of new machinery and equipment and the acquisition or expansion of facilities used in a business. A decision by a local florist to purchase or to lease a new delivery van is a capital investment decision, as is the decision to upgrade the computer system at a law firm. A decision by Wal-Mart to build and open a new store and a decision by Ford to invest in new automated production equipment are capital investment decisions. Long-term purchasing decisions such as these often involve large sums of money and considerable risk because they commit companies to a chosen course of action for many years.

One of the key factors to be considered in a long-term purchasing decision is the return of the investment and also the return on the investment—in other words, whether the benefits of the investment exceed its cost. The costs and benefits include both qualitative and quantitative factors. Qualitative costs and benefits include employee, customer, and community reaction to changes in location, the impact of automation on displaced employees, quality improvements that result from new equipment, and so forth. Quantitative costs and benefits include large initial outlays of cash and the need for future repairs and maintenance, the potential for increased sales, and reductions in production and other costs.

FOCUS ON CASH FLOW

LO1
Discuss the importance of focusing on cash flow in capital investment decisions

Because capital investments involve large sums of money and last for many years, a quantitative analysis of the costs and benefits of capital investment decisions must consider the **time value of money.** In addition, the focus of the time value of money is on cash flow, not accounting net income. Accounting net income and cash flow are often not the same. Accounting net income is calculated based on the accrual of income and expenses rather than on the receipt and payment of cash. Whereas measurements of both income and cash flow are useful to managers, investors, and creditors, time-value-of-money calculations are based on the concept that a dollar received (paid) today is worth more (less) than a dollar received (paid) in the future and thus focus on the cash flow of an organization.

Key Concept: *Long-term investment decisions require a consideration of the time value of money. The time value of money is based on the concept that a dollar received today is worth more than a dollar received in the future.*

IN THE NEWS

Although stock analysts and investors have traditionally focused on current and expected earnings of a company in assessing its potential as an investment, analysts increasingly favor the use of cash flow. Analysts like focusing on cash flow because, they say, it "ignores accounting tricks and shows the true economic health of companies" (MacDonald, "Analysts Increasingly Favor Using Cash Flows over Reported Earnings in Stock Valuations," *Wall Street Journal,* April 1, 1999, C2).

Typical cash outflows include the original investment in the project, any additional working capital needed during the life of the investment, repairs and maintenance needed for machinery and equipment, and additional operating costs that may be incurred.

Concept Question: *Working capital is the excess of current assets over current liabilities. In making a decision to open a new store, what kind of increases in working capital might be expected by a large retail store like Wal-Mart?*

http://www.walmart.com

Concept Answer: In addition to the construction costs of the new store, Wal-Mart would incur additional costs related to stocking the store with inventory, putting cash in the cash registers, and so on. ■

Typical cash inflows include projected incremental revenues from the project, cost reductions in operating expenses, the salvage value (if any) of the investment at the end of its useful life, and the release of working capital at the end of a project's useful life.

With the exception of the initial cash outflow associated with the investment, other cash inflows and outflows are likely to be estimates. The extended time period involved in long-term purchasing decisions makes the projection of these cash inflows and outflows difficult at best. The impact of uncertainty on capital investment decisions and the use of sensitivity analysis are discussed in more detail later in the chapter.

SCREENING AND PREFERENCE DECISIONS

LO2
Apply the decision-making model to capital investment decisions

Capital investment decisions typically fall into one of two categories: screening decisions or preference decisions. **Screening decisions** involve deciding whether an investment meets a predetermined company standard, whereas **preference decisions** involve choosing between alternatives. The decision-making model introduced in Chapter 1 (and presented here as Exhibit 8-1) is especially useful in analyzing preference decisions.

Typical problems addressed in capital investment decisions are as follows:

1. Should old equipment be replaced with new equipment that promises to be more cost efficient?
2. Should a new delivery vehicle be purchased or leased?
3. Should a manufacturing plant be expanded?
4. Should a new retail store be opened?

Once the problem is defined, the next step is to identify objectives. Objectives include both quantitative factors (increase production, increase sales, reduce costs) and qualitative factors (make a higher-quality product, provide better customer service). Step 3 involves both a quantitative analysis of the options, using tools that recognize the time value of money, and a qualitative analysis. Once the potential investments are screened and analyzed in Step 3, the best option is chosen in Step 4.

Step 3 IDENTIFY AND ANALYZE AVAILABLE OPTIONS

Step 4 SELECT THE BEST OPTION

EXHIBIT 8-1 The Decision-Making Model

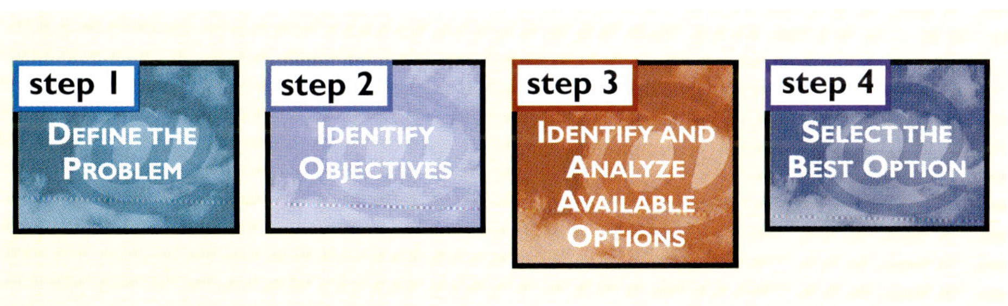

DISCOUNTED CASH FLOW ANALYSIS

LO3
Evaluate capital investment decisions by using discounted cash flow analysis (NPV and IRR)

LO4
Discuss key assumptions of the NPV and IRR methods

The time value of money is considered in capital investment decisions by using one of two techniques: the **net present value (NPV)** method or the **internal rate of return (IRR)** method.[1] In both methods, two simplifying assumptions are made when discounting cash flows to their present value. The first is that all cash flows are assumed to occur at the end of each period (typically at the end of a year). Although most cost reductions and cash inflows resulting from increased sales are likely to occur uniformly throughout the year, this assumption greatly simplifies present-value calculations. The second is that all cash inflows are immediately reinvested in another project or investment. This is analogous to the immediate reinvesting of dividends in a stock investment. The rate of return assumed earned on the reinvested amounts depends on whether the net present value or the internal rate of return method is used. Under the NPV method, cash inflows are assumed to be reinvested at the discount rate used in the analysis. Under the IRR method, cash inflows are assumed to be reinvested at the internal rate of return of the original investment.

Key Concept: *The time value of money is considered in capital investment decisions by using one of two techniques: the net present value (NPV) method or the internal rate of return (IRR) method.*

NET PRESENT VALUE

The net present value (NPV) method requires the choice of a discount rate to be used in the analysis. Many companies choose to use the cost of capital. The **cost of capital** represents what the firm would have to pay to borrow (issue bonds) or to raise funds through equity (issue stock) in the financial marketplace. In NPV analysis, the discount rate serves as a hurdle rate, or a minimum required rate of return—the return that the company feels must be earned in order for any potential investment to be profitable. The **discount rate** is often adjusted to reflect the risk and the uncertainty of cash flows expected to occur many years in the future. Adjusting the rate for uncertainty is discussed in more detail later in the chapter.

Computing net present value requires comparing the present value of all cash inflows associated with a project with the present value of all cash outflows. If the present value of the inflows is greater than or equal to the present value of the outflows (the NPV is greater than or equal to zero), the investment provides a return at least equal to the discount rate (the minimum required rate of return), and the investment is acceptable. If the present value of the outflows is greater than the present value of the inflows, the NPV will be negative, and the investment will not be acceptable, because it provides a return less than the discount rate.

Key Concept: *If the present value of cash inflows is greater than or equal to the present value of cash outflows (the NPV is greater than or equal to zero), the investment provides a return at least equal to the discount rate (the minimum required rate of return), and the investment is acceptable.*

b&r
Bud and Rose's Flower Shop

To illustrate NPV decisions, let's discuss Bud and Rose's Flower Shop, which is considering the purchase of a new refrigerated delivery van that will cost $50,000. It will allow the company to accept large flower orders for weddings, receptions, and so on and is expected to increase cash income from sales (net of increased expenses) by $14,000 per year for six years. The van is not expected to have any salvage value at the end of the six years. Bud

[1]The following discussion assumes that readers are already familiar with the basic concepts of discounting and the calculation of present value for single sums and annuities. If not, you should study the appendix at the end of this chapter.

and Rose have a minimum required rate of return of 12 percent and use that as their discount rate.

The only cash outflow in this case is the initial purchase price of $50,000. The annual cash inflow of $14,000 can most easily be viewed as an ordinary annuity for purposes of calculating present value. NPV calculations using present-value factors from Table 8-2 on page 277 are as follows:

Cash Flow	Year	Amount	12% Factor	Present Value
Initial investment	Now	$(50,000)	1.0000	$(50,000.00)
Annual cash income	1–6	14,000	4.1114	57,559.60
Net present value				$ 7,559.60

Using the built-in function in Microsoft Excel, =PV(12%,6,–14000) returns a present value for the cash inflows equal to $57,559.70 (see Exhibit 8-2). The $0.10 difference results from rounding.

Because the NPV is positive, the delivery van should be purchased. Although the positive NPV tells us that the return on the investment is at least 12 percent, it does not tell us exactly what the return is. Is it 14 percent, 16 percent, or an even higher number? We could find the actual return by trial and error. Remember, an NPV of zero means that an investment is earning exactly the discount rate used in the analysis. Increasing the discount rate to 14 percent reduces the NPV to $4,446.[2] Going up to 16 percent reduces the NPV to $1,590, but going up to 18 percent results in a negative NPV of $1,028. The true yield of the investment must be somewhere between 16 percent and 18 percent and would be closer to 18 percent. The present value of an annuity table can also be used to find the true rate of return for the delivery van.

As discussed in the appendix, the present value of an annuity (PVA) can be found using the following formula:

$$PVA = R(DFA_{n,r})$$

In this case, we know the *PVA*, the annual cash inflow (R), and the number of periods (n) and can solve indirectly for the interest rate (r).

EXHIBIT 8-2 Finding the Present Value Using the PV Function in Excel

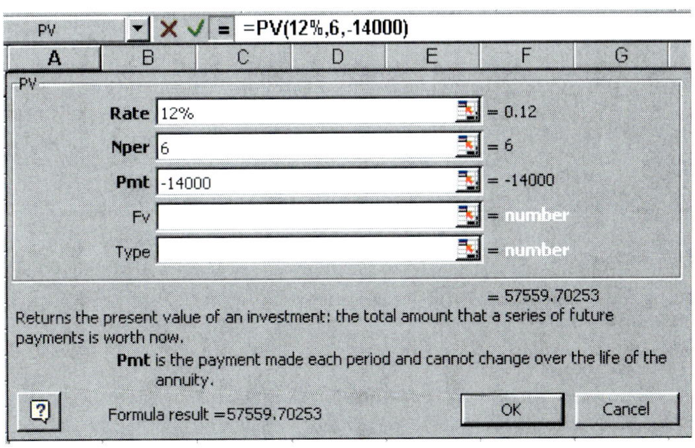

[2]Extended present-value tables can be found in Tables 8-1 and 8-2 on pages 276 and 277.

$$PVA_{6,??} = \$14{,}000(DFA_{6,??})$$
$$\$50{,}000 = \$14{,}000(DFA_{6,,??})$$
$$DFA_{6,,??} = 3.5714$$

From Table 8-2 on page 277 and looking at the row for an *n* of 6, we see that a *DFA* of 3.5714 is about halfway between an *r* of 16 percent and an *r* of 18 percent.

INTERNAL RATE OF RETURN

The internal rate of return (IRR) is the actual yield, or return, earned by an investment. We can find the yield of an investment in a number of ways. One way of looking at the IRR is that it is the discount rate that equates the present value of all cash inflows to the present value of all cash outflows. In other words, IRR is the discount rate that makes the NPV = 0.

Key Concept: *The internal rate of return (IRR) is the actual yield, or return, earned by an investment.*

Although a present-value table *can* be used to calculate IRR, it is inconvenient in this case because the true yield lies between the rates provided on the table. However, IRR can easily be calculated using a financial calculator or Microsoft Excel (see appendix). In Excel, =RATE (6,–14000,50000,0,0) generates an annual yield of 17.191 percent (see Exhibit 8-3).

Calculations of net present value and internal rate of return get significantly more difficult when cash inflows and outflows are more numerous and when the cash flows are uneven. Consider an example in which Harbourside Hospital is considering the purchase of a new X-ray machine for cardiac catheterizations. Harbourside is a nonprofit hospital and has a slightly lower hurdle rate of 10 percent. In addition, one of the hospital's objectives is to improve the quality of care provided to cardiac patients in the area. Currently, patients have to travel as far as 100 miles to a hospital equipped with this type of X-ray machine. The machine will cost $1,200,000 plus installation costs of another $50,000 and will have a useful life of approximately six years. Owing to frequent changes in tech-

EXHIBIT 8-3 Finding the Internal Rate of Return Using the RATE Function in Excel

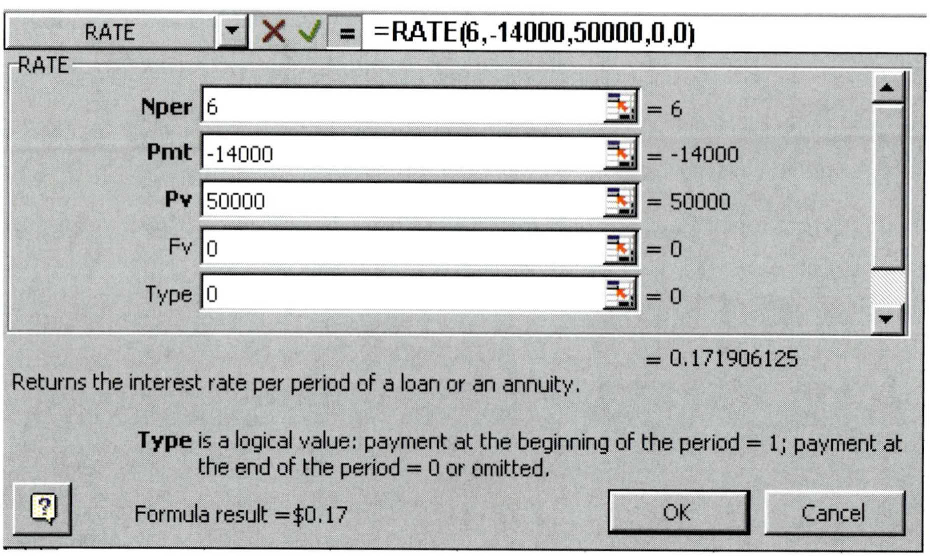

EXHIBIT 8-5 C

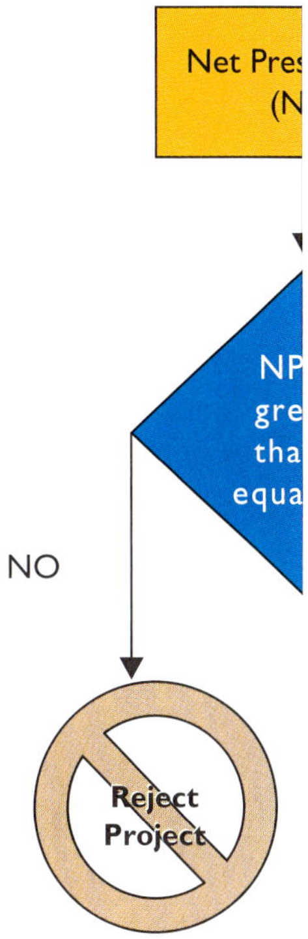

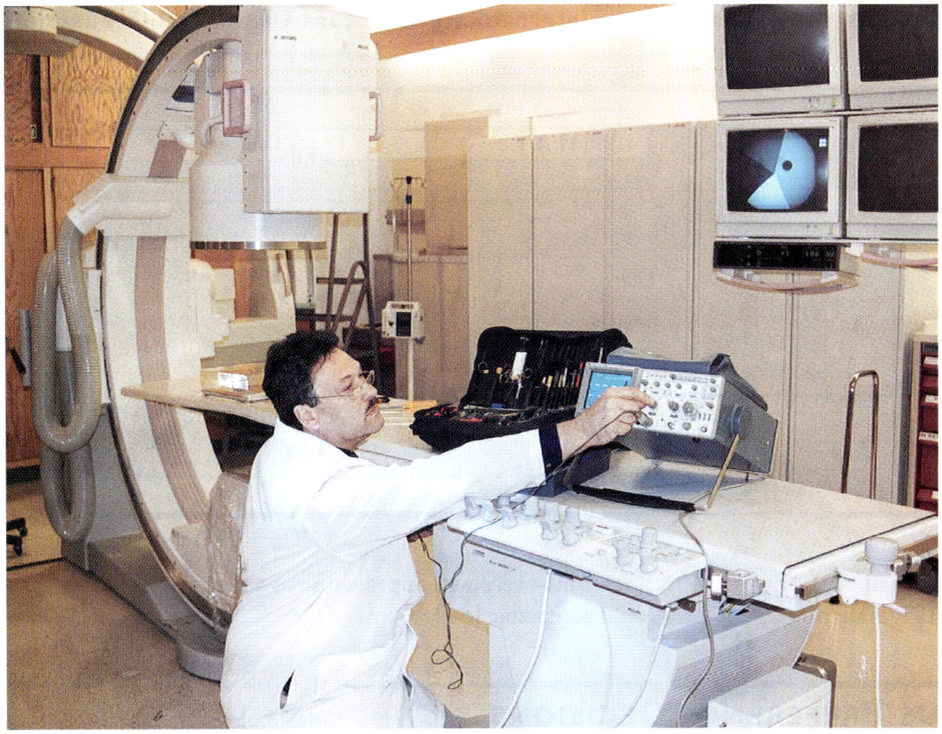
COURTESY OF ROBY SAWYERS

nology, the machine would have little salvage value at the end of its useful life. Harbourside expects that it can sell the machine to a hospital in a developing country for $20,000. It is expected to increase revenues by $400,000 per year but will require the hiring of two new technicians at $40,000 per year for each technician, and it will require maintenance and repairs averaging $20,000 per year, which results in a net annual cash flow of $300,000 ($400,000 – $80,000 – $20,000). In addition, it is expected to require the installation of a new X-ray tube at the end of years 3 and 5 at a cost of $50,000 each. The following provides a detailed NPV analysis using discount factors from Table 8-1 on page 276 and Table 8-2 on page 277.

Cash Flow	Year	Amount	10% Factor	Present Value
Initial investment	Now	$(1,250,000)	1.0000	$(1,250,000)
Net annual cash inflow	1–6	300,000	4.3553	1,306,590
New X-ray tube	3	(50,000)	0.7513	(37,565)
New X-ray tube	5	(50,000)	0.6209	(31,045)
Salvage value	6	20,000	0.5645	11,290
Net present value				$ (730)

In this case, the NPV is negative, indicating that this investment would earn Harbourside less than its minimum required rate of return of 10 percent. Using Microsoft Excel's IRR function, the internal rate of return of the X-ray machine is calculated as 9.9796 percent (see Exhibit 8-4).

Although the quantitative analysis performed in Step 3 of our decision model would indicate that the investment is not acceptable, Harbourside should also consider qualitative factors in its decision.[3] In this case, because improving the quality of patient care is

Step 3 IDENTIFY AND ANALYZE AVAILABLE OPTIONS

[3]Harbourside must also consider the impact of uncertainty on the decision. In this case, the only cash flow known with certainty is likely to be the initial purchase price. Changes in assumptions about future revenue and costs are likely to affect the decision. Adjusting the discounted cash flow analysis for the impact of uncertainty is discussed in more depth later in the chapter.

Which is preferre
$20,000 investment.
and generate cash in
from one $20,000 in
calculation of a profi
ferent size. The **prof**
the cash inflows by t
that the NPV is posi
and the project is ac
projects, the project
calculated as follows:

Present value of cash
Initial investment
Profitability index

The $10,000 investment has a higher PI of 1.20 and is preferred over the $20,000 investment with a PI of 1.10.

Concept Question: *What is the IRR of investments 1 and 2?*

Concept Answer: Using Microsoft Excel's RATE function, the IRR of investment 1 is 17.55 percent [=RATE (5, 3165.56, −10000,0,0) = 17.55%], whereas the IRR of investment 2 is only 13.84 percent [=RATE (5, 5803.52, −20000,0,0) = 13.84%].

In cases like this, in which the investment lives are equal and the cash flows follow similar patterns (annual cash flows for five years), IRR can be used to make preference decisions. However, when asset lives are unequal and cash flows follow different patterns, the use of IRR can result in incorrect decisions even when the initial investment is the same.

Consider the following example, in which two $20,000 projects are being considered. Project A reduces cash operating costs (increases cash flow) by $12,500 per year for the next two years, whereas project B reduces operating costs by $5,000 per year for six years. Assuming a discount rate of 10 percent, the NPV, PI, and IRR of each investment are calculated as follows:

SCREENING

	Project A	Project B
Initial investment	$(20,000.00)	$(20,000.00)
PV of cash inflows	21,693.75	21,776.50
NPV	1,693.75	1,776.50
PI	1.085	1.089
IRR	16.26%	12.98%

Although IRR would indicate that project A is preferable to project B, NPV and PI indicate that project B is better. Which is right? Well, it depends. As we discussed earlier in the chapter, the IRR method assumes that cash inflows are immediately reinvested at the IRR earned on the original investment—in this case, over 16 percent. In contrast, the NPV method assumes that cash inflows are reinvested at the cost of capital or other discount rate used in the analysis—10 percent in our analysis. If you can reinvest the large cash inflows received in project A at the end of years 1 and 2 at a high rate of return, project A would indeed be preferred. If not, project B, offering a return of almost 13 percent for six years, would be preferred. The use of IRR generally favors short-term investments with high yields, whereas NPV favors longer-term investments even if the return is lower.

THE IMPACT OF TAXES ON CAPITAL INVESTMENT DECISIONS

LO5
Evaluate the impact of taxes on capital investment decisions

Nonprofit organizations, such as Harbourside Hospital, don't pay income taxes and don't need to consider the impact of income taxes on capital investment decisions (or other decisions, for that matter).[4] However, profit-making companies must pay income taxes on any taxable income earned (just like individuals must) and must therefore consider the impact of income taxes on capital investment and other management decisions. With

[4]Hospitals, museums, churches, and a multitude of other organizations are often structured as organizations exempt from federal and state income taxes. In order to qualify, they must meet certain requirements as specified by Congress and the Internal Revenue Service. These organizations may also be exempt from local property taxes.

federal income tax rates on corporations ranging from 15 percent to 35 percent of taxable income (and state income taxes typically adding another 5 to 10 percent), taxes are a major source of cash outflows for many companies and must be taken into consideration for any long-term investment decision.

As demonstrated in Chapter 5, the after-tax benefit or cost of a taxable cash inflow or a tax-deductible cash outflow is found by multiplying the before-tax cash inflow or before-tax cash outflow by (1 – tax rate). For a company with a combined federal and state income tax rate of 40 percent, a taxable cash inflow of $100,000 results in a $60,000 after-tax cash inflow [$100,000 × (1 –0.40)]. Likewise, a $20,000 tax-deductible cash outflow for repairs results in an after-tax outflow of only $12,000.

The disposal of assets may also have tax consequences. When an asset is sold or otherwise disposed of, gain or loss is calculated on the difference between the sales price and book value. Because current tax law rules do not consider salvage value in the computation of depreciation (assets are depreciated to zero even if they have a salvage value), the book value of an asset at the end of its useful life will be zero, and any salvage value realized will be taxed as gain. The after-tax cash flow associated with the sale of an asset for its salvage value is therefore found by multiplying the salvage value by (1 – tax rate).[5] For simplicity, we will assume that a gain on disposal of an asset is taxed at the same rate as operating income of a company. In practice, the tax calculation on the sale of depreciable assets can be quite complicated.

Not all tax-deductible expenses involve cash outflows. Depreciation is a tax-deductible expense that does not involve a direct payment of cash. Although depreciation does not result in a direct cash outflow, it does result in an indirect cash *inflow* owing to the impact of depreciation on income taxes paid. Depreciation expense reduces a company's taxable income and thus its income tax, resulting in an increase in cash flow.

Key Concept: *Taxes are a major source of cash outflows for many companies and must be taken into consideration in calculations of the time value of money.*

As an example, let's go back to Bud and Rose's Flower Shop and consider the purchase of a delivery van. The van cost $50,000 and will be depreciated using the straight-line method over six years for federal income tax purposes.[6] Depreciation expense is equal to $5,000 for years 1 and 6 and $10,000 for years 2 through 5. Assuming an income tax rate

Bud and Rose's Flower Shop

The Impact of Depreciation on Cash Flow

Year	Depreciation	Tax Savings from Depreciation
1	$ 5,000	$2,000
2	10,000	4,000
3	10,000	4,000
4	10,000	4,000
5	10,000	4,000
6	5,000	2,000

[5] When assets are sold during their useful life, it is possible to generate tax-deductible losses as well as taxable gains. When assets are sold at a loss, their after-tax cash flow is more difficult to compute. It consists of the cash received from the sale *plus* the tax savings generated from the deductible loss.

[6] Although the van would be depreciated over a useful life of five years, tax law generally requires the use of a convention whereby a half year of depreciation is deducted in the year of acquisition (regardless of when the asset is purchased) and a half year's depreciation is deducted in the sixth year. In addition, the tax law currently allows the use of an accelerated method of depreciation for machinery and equipment. The intricacies of tax depreciation rules are beyond the scope of this book.

of 40 percent, the depreciation deduction results in tax savings of \$2,000 for years 1 and 6 (\$5,000 × 40%) and \$4,000 for years 2 through 5 (\$10,000 × 40%).

Concept Question: *Refer to the NPV calculation of the delivery van on page 249. What other adjustments need to be made in order to calculate the NPV after taxes?*

Concept Answer: In the following table, the annual cash inflow of \$14,000 has been adjusted to the equivalent after-tax amount (\$14,000 × 0.6 = \$8,400). In addition, the discount rate has been changed to its equivalent after-tax rate (12% × 0.6 = 7.2%). Note that the discount factors in the table can be calculated using the mathematical formulas in the appendix. ■

Cash Flow	Year	After-Tax Amount	7.2% Factor	Present Value
Initial investment	Now	(\$50,000)	1.0000	(\$50,000.00)
Annual cash income	1–6	8,400	4.7375	39,795.00
Tax savings from				
depreciation	1	2,000	0.9328	1,865.60
	2	4,000	0.8702	3,480.80
	3	4,000	0.8118	3,247.20
	4	4,000	0.7572	3,028.80
	5	4,000	0.7064	2,825.60
	6	2,000	0.6589	1,317.80
Net present value				\$5,560.80

PAUSE & *Reflect*

Why isn't the original purchase price of \$50,000 adjusted for the impact of income tax?

The NPV of the new delivery van is still positive, indicating that it will provide a return greater than the company's 7.2 percent after-tax cost of capital. Using Excel's IRR function, the after-tax return of the investment is 10.715 percent (see Exhibit 8-6).

AN EXTENDED EXAMPLE

Amber Valley

Amber Valley Ski Resort is considering installing a chair lift for a new undeveloped area that would expand the area available for skiing. The options are to put in a double, triple, or quadruple chair lift to carry two, three, or four skiers on each chair. The costs of the chair lifts are \$3,000,000, \$5,000,000, and \$7,000,000, respectively. The chair lifts all have a 25-year life and will be depreciated using the straight-line method. The operating costs (includ-

EXHIBIT 8-6 The IRR Function in Excel

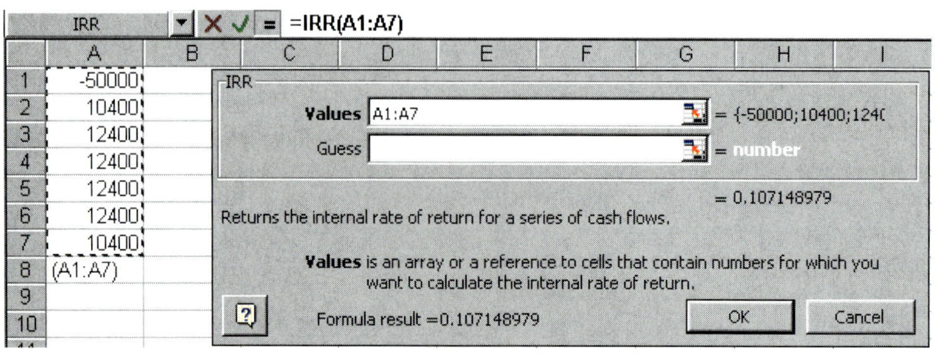

© A. RAMEY/PHOTOEDIT

ing routine maintenance) of the new lifts are $250,000, $300,000, and $350,000 per year. In addition, the chair lifts require major repairs every five years (at the end of years 5, 10, 15, and 20) of $100,000, $125,000, and $150,000, respectively. The lifts are difficult to resell and are assumed to have no salvage value at the end of their 25-year useful life.

Lift tickets are $49 per day and allow the skiers to ride any of the lifts at the resort. Any increase in revenue from the new chair lift will have to come from increasing the number of skiers who visit the resort. The management of Amber Valley believes that with the addition of a new lift and the new slopes, they can attract more skiers to the resort. Right now, the lift lines at the existing chair lifts are considered too long by most skiers. The overall use of the resort is down, and part of the blame is attributed to the crowded conditions. Amber Valley averages 5,000 skiers per day at the present time. The projections used for the new lifts assume that the average number of skiers per day will increase by 100, 200, and 260 skiers, respectively. Assuming 120 ski days per year, this will increase revenue by $588,000, $1,176,000, and $1,528,800, respectively.

The managers of Amber Valley are confident that the new lift will increase the number of skiers sufficiently to justify its addition. However, they have asked the controller to analyze the proposed acquisition and to provide a recommendation concerning the purchase of the double, triple, or quadruple lift. Amber Valley's combined federal and state income tax rate is 40 percent, and it has an after-tax cost of capital of 8 percent.

Before-tax cash inflows and outflows associated with the purchase of each chair lift are summarized as follows:

Before-Tax Cash Inflows and Outflows

Cash Flows	Double Chair Lift	Triple Chair Lift	Quad. Chair Lift
Purchase price	$3,000,000	$5,000,000	$7,000,000
Additional revenue	588,000	1,176,000	1,528,800
Annual operating costs	(250,000)	(300,000)	(350,000)
Major repairs (every five years)	(100,000)	(125,000)	(150,000)

After-tax cash flows as adjusted are shown as follows:

After-Tax Cash Inflows and Outflows

Cash Flows	Double Chair Lift	Triple Chair Lift	Quad. Chair Lift
Purchase price	$3,000,000	$5,000,000	$7,000,000
Additional revenue	352,800	705,600	917,280
Annual operating costs	(150,000)	(180,000)	(210,000)
Major repairs (every 5 years)	(60,000)	(75,000)	(90,000)
Annual tax savings from depreciation*	80,000	133,333	186,667

*Although the lifts have a useful life of 25 years, they would likely be depreciated over 15 years for tax purposes. To simplify calculations, depreciation was calculated using the straight-line method, ignoring the half-year convention (a full year's depreciation was assumed for each of the 15 years). Once again, the intricacies of the tax rules for depreciation are beyond the scope of this book.

Concept Question: *Is this a screening or a preference decision? What discounted cash flow method(s) would be appropriate to analyze this decision?*

Concept Answer: The problem is a preference decision. In addition, because it involves investments of different sizes, NPV should not be used without calculating a profitability index. Because the investments have similar useful lives and patterns of cash flow, IRR can also be used to provide the quantitative analysis for the problem.

PAUSE & *Reflect*

What qualitative factors should Amber Valley consider in its decision?

As you can see in Exhibit 8-7, the NPV of the double lift is negative (and the PI is less than 1.0), indicating that the investment is not acceptable. The IRR of 6.93 percent confirms the fact that the project provides a return below the minimum acceptable rate of return of 8 percent. Both the triple lift and the quadruple lift are acceptable investments with positive NPVs, PIs greater than 1.0, and IRRs exceeding the cost of capital. Note, however, when comparing the triple lift with the quadruple lift, the quadruple lift has the higher NPV but the triple lift has the higher PI and IRR. Given the different-size investments required, management should focus on the PI or the IRR and choose to purchase the triple lift.

EXHIBIT 8-7

		DOUBLE LIFT	
	Years	**Cash Flow**	**Present Value**
Cost to purchase	now	$(3,000,000.00)	$(3,000,000.00)
After-tax cash flow	1 through 25	202,800.00	2,164,844.61
Tax savings from depreciation	1 through 15	80,000.00	684,758.30
Major repairs	5, 10, 15, 20	(60,000.00)	(100,414.00)
Discount rate	8%		
Net present value			$ (250,811.09)
Profitability index			0.916
Internal rate of return			6.93%

EXHIBIT 8-7 Continued

TRIPLE LIFT

	Years	Cash Flow	Present Value
Cost to purchase	now	$(5,000,000.00)	$(5,000,000.00)
After-tax cash flow	1 through 25	525,600.00	5,610,662.36
Tax Savings from depreciation	1 through 15	133,333.00	1,141,260.97
Major repairs	5, 10, 15, 20	(75,000.00)	(125,517.49)
Discount rate	8%		
Net present value			$ 1,626,405.84
Profitability index			1.325
Internal rate of return			11.83%

QUADRUPLE LIFT

	Years	Cash Flow	Present Value
Cost to purchase	now	$(7,000,000.00)	$(7,000,000.00)
After-tax cash flow	1 through 25	707,280.00	7,550,055.70
Tax Savings from depreciation	1 through 15	186,667.00	1,597,772.21
Major repairs	5, 10, 15, 20	(90,000.00)	(150,620.99)
Discount rate	8%		
Net present value			$ 1,997,206.92
Profitability index			1.285
Internal rate of return			11.38%

THE IMPACT OF UNCERTAINTY ON CAPITAL INVESTMENT DECISIONS

As discussed previously, all long-term purchasing decisions involve some uncertainty. Whenever decisions involve long periods of time, there is uncertainty. In fact, the longer the projected time frame of the project, the more the uncertainty. As has been discussed, one way to adjust for risk is to increase the cost of capital used in the NPV calculation. Raising the discount rate has the effect of reducing the present value of future cash inflows, thus reducing the NPV of an investment.

Concept Question: *If Amber Valley increases the discount rate used in its NPV and PI analyses to 10 percent, is the triple lift still an acceptable investment? Exhibit 8-7 is provided as an Excel template on the CD that came with your textbook. Using the template, compute the NPV and PI for each lift if the discount rate is 10 percent instead of 8 percent.*

Concept Answer: The triple lift is still acceptable and the best choice. Its NPV is positive, and it has the highest PI of the three lifts. In fact, had we simply focused on the IRR of the triple and quadruple lifts in Exhibit 8-7, we could have surmised that both the triple and the quadruple lifts would be acceptable at a discount rate of 10 percent because the internal rate of return of both exceeded 10 percent.

SENSITIVITY ANALYSIS

Amber Valley estimates an increase in skiers of 100, 200, or 260 per day for each of the lifts. What if the number of skiers increases by only 150 per day for the triple lift? Will the acquisition of the new lift still result in a sufficient return of and on investment? **Sensitivity analysis** is used to highlight decisions that may be affected by changes in expected cash flows. We can use what-if analysis to determine how sensitive capital investment decisions are to these changes.

Concept Question: *Exhibit 8-7 is provided as an Excel template on the CD that came with your textbook. Using the template, compute the NPV, PI, and IRR for the triple lift if the number of skiers increases by only 150 per day. Hint: The after-tax cash flow (additional revenues less annual operating costs) will be $349,200.*

Concept Answer: With an increase of only 150 skiers, the NPV of the triple lift will be negative, and the PI will be slightly less than 1.0. The IRR of 7.35 percent is a little less than the cost of capital of 8 percent. Based on a quantitative analysis, the triple lift will not be an acceptable investment with an increase of 150 skiers per day.

Concept Question: *How many more skiers would be required in order for the triple lift to be acceptable? Hint: Using the template, compute the number of skiers necessary in order to provide a PI of 1.0 or an IRR of 8 percent.*

Concept Answer: Increasing the number of skiers to 157 per day would result in additional after-tax cash flows of $373,896. This would result in a PI of 1.001 and an IRR of 8.02 percent.

All decisions should be evaluated after they are implemented in order to see whether they accomplished their objectives. However, in this example, as in most long-term purchasing decisions, the project is very difficult to reverse. Once a ski lift is installed, it must be used even if the projected skier volume is not reached. At that point, other decisions would be made regarding how to increase the numbers of skiers. Thus, short-term decisions may become critical in making long-term capital investment decisions successful.

THE IMPACT OF THE NEW MANUFACTURING ENVIRONMENT ON CAPITAL INVESTMENT DECISIONS

LO6
Discuss the impact of the new manufacturing environment on capital investment decisions

Investments in automated and computerized design and manufacturing equipment and robotics tend to be very large, although many of the benefits may be indirect and intangible or at the very least difficult to quantify (increased quality resulting in fewer warranty expenses). These types of investments may be difficult to evaluate using purely quantitative data. For this reason, it is critically important to consider the impact of qualitative factors in these decisions.

Automating a process in a manufacturing environment is much more extensive and expensive than just purchasing a piece of equipment. The total cost of automating a process can be as much as 30 or 40 times that of installing a single machine, owing to additional software needs, additional training of personnel, and the development of new processes. The benefits of automating production processes include the following:

1. Decreased labor costs
2. An increase in the quality of the finished product or a reduction in defects, resulting in fewer inspections, less waste in the production process, less rework of defective goods, and less warranty work on defective goods
3. Increased speed of the production process
4. Increased reliability of the finished product
5. An overall reduction in the amount of inventory

These improvements will not only save costs but may also allow the company to increase market share. When the competition has automated production systems, companies must often follow suit or risk loss of business. Although some of the preceding benefits are difficult to measure, they must nevertheless be considered when making capital investment decisions in the new manufacturing environment.

Key Concept: *Analyzing the costs and benefits of investments in automated and computerized design and manufacturing equipment and robotics requires careful consideration of both quantitative and qualitative factors.*

THE PAYBACK METHOD

LO7
Discuss appropriate applications of nondiscounting methods (the payback method) in capital investment decisions

Capital investment tools that recognize the time value of money and use discounted cash flow techniques are preferred by most decision makers when dealing with capital investment decisions. In practice, however, some managers still use nondiscounting methods. Although these methods are declining in popularity, the payback method can still be useful in some cases as a fast, easy approximation of the more complicated, discounted cash flow methods.

The **payback period** is defined as the length of time needed for a long-term project to recapture, or pay back, the initial investment. In other words, how long does it take for a project to pay for itself? Obviously, the quicker the payback, the more desirable the investment. The formula used to compute the payback period is as follows:

$$\text{Payback period} = \frac{\text{Original investment}}{\text{Net annual cash inflows}}$$

Because the payback method ignores the time value of money, it must be used with caution. Consider an example in which we are considering investing in project A or project B, each requiring an initial investment of $20,000. (This is the same example as used earlier, on page 254.) Project A promises cash inflows of $12,500 per year for two years, whereas project B promises cash inflows of $5,000 per year for six years.

	Project A	**Project B**
Initial investment	$(20,000.00)	$(20,000.00)
Annual cash inflows	12,500.00	5,000.00
PV of cash inflows	21,693.75	21,776.50
NPV	1,693.75	1,776.50
PI	1.085	1.089
IRR	16.26%	12.98%
Payback	1.6 years (20,000/12,500)	4 years (20,000/5,000)

Although a manager using the payback method would prefer project A, the method ignores the time value of money and ignores any cash flow received after the initial investment is paid for. Even when NPV and IRR give the same signal, payback can provide managers with misleading information.

Payback calculations are slightly more complicated with uneven cash flows. Using Amber Valley Ski Resort as an example, we can calculate the payback period for the three chair lifts being considered. In Exhibit 8-8, the first column for each ski lift shows the

EXHIBIT 8-8

	DOUBLE LIFT		TRIPLE LIFT		QUADRUPLE LIFT	
Year	**Cash Flow**	**Unrecovered**	**Cash Flow**	**Unrecovered**	**Cash Flow**	**Unrecovered**
0	$(3,000,000.00)		$(5,000,000.00)		$(7,000,000.00)	
1	282,800.00	$(2,717,200.00)	658,933.00	$(4,341,067.00)	893,947.00	$(6,106,053.00)
2	282,800.00	(2,434,400.00)	658,933.00	(3,682,134.00)	893,947.00	(5,212,106.00)
3	282,800.00	(2,151,600.00)	658,933.00	(3,023,201.00)	893,947.00	(4,318,159.00)
4	282,800.00	(1,868,800.00)	658,933.00	(2,364,268.00)	893,947.00	(3,424,212.00)
5	222,800.00	(1,646,000.00)	583,933.00	(1,780,335.00)	803,947.00	(2,620,265.00)
6	282,800.00	(1,363,200.00)	658,933.00	(1,121,402.00)	893,947.00	(1,726,318.00)
7	282,800.00	(1,080,400.00)	658,933.00	(462,469.00)	893,947.00	(832,371.00)
8	282,800.00	(797,600.00)	658,933.00		893,947.00	
9	282,800.00	(514,800.00)	658,933.00		893,947.00	
10	222,800.00	(292,000.00)	583,933.00		803,947.00	
11	282,800.00	(9,200.00)	658,933.00		893,947.00	
12	282,800.00		658,933.00		893,947.00	
13	282,800.00		658,933.00		893,947.00	
14	282,800.00		658,933.00		893,947.00	
15	222,800.00		583,933.00		803,947.00	
16	202,800.00		525,600.00		707,280.00	
17	202,800.00		525,600.00		707,280.00	
18	202,800.00		525,600.00		707,280.00	
19	202,800.00		525,600.00		707,280.00	
20	142,800.00		450,600.00		617,280.00	
21	202,800.00		525,600.00		707,280.00	
22	202,800.00		525,600.00		707,280.00	
23	202,800.00		525,600.00		707,280.00	
24	202,800.00		525,600.00		707,280.00	
25	202,800.00		525,600.00		707,280.00	
Payback		11.033 years		7.702 years		7.931 years

cash flow each year. The second column shows the amount of original investment that still must be recovered at the end of each year. For the double lift, the investment is almost fully recovered after the eleventh year. At the end of year 11, only $9,200 of the original $3,000,000 investment has not been paid back. In year 12, another $282,800 of cash inflows are received. Thus, it takes an additional 0.033 of a year $\left(\frac{9,200}{282,800}\right)$ to fully recover the investment. The calculations for the triple and quadruple lifts are similar.

If we use payback period to evaluate the desirability of these options, the triple lift is preferable. It has a payback of 7.7 years versus a payback of 7.9 years for the quadruple lift and slightly more than 11 years for the double lift. In this case, this is the same preference ordering that we got using the profitability index and IRR to evaluate the lifts. The payback method can be useful as a quick approximation of the discounted cash flow methods when the cash flows follow similar patterns. It can also be useful in screening decisions if cash flow is a serious concern and management wants to eliminate projects that would have adverse cash flow consequences. For example, smaller businesses, such as Bud and Rose's Flower Shop, may be very concerned about cash flow in the short run even if the long-term profitability of a project is lower than with alternative projects. In these situations, the amount of time needed to recover cash outlays may be a very important criterion when evaluating capital investment decisions.

Key Concept: *The payback method can be useful as a quick approximation of the discounted-cash-flow methods when the cash flows follow similar patterns.*

APPENDIX

TIME VALUE OF MONEY AND DECISION MAKING

When decisions are affected by cash flows that are paid or received in different time periods, it is necessary to adjust those cash flows for the time value of money (TVM). Because of our ability to earn interest on money invested, we would prefer to receive $1 today rather than a year from now. Likewise, we would prefer to pay $1 a year from now rather than today. A common technique used to adjust cash flows received or paid in different time periods is to discount those cash flows by finding their present value. The **present value (PV)** of cash flows is the amount of future cash flows discounted to their equivalent worth today. To fully understand the calculations involved in finding the present value of future cash flows, it is necessary to step back and examine the nature of interest and the calculation of interest received and paid. Interest is simply a payment made to use someone else's money. When you invest money in a bank account, the bank pays you interest for the use of your money for a period of time. If you invest $100 and the bank pays you $106 at the end of the year, it is clear that you earned $6 of interest on your money (and 6 percent interest for the year).

PAUSE & Reflect

What interest rate do you earn on your checking and savings account at the local bank? How is the interest compounded?

FUTURE VALUE

Mathematically, the relationship between your initial investment (present value), the amount in the bank at the end of the year (future value), and the interest rate (r) is as follows:

$$FV_{(\text{year } 1)} = PV(1 + r)$$

In our example, $FV_{(\text{year } 1)} = 100(1 + 0.06) = \$106$. If you leave your money in the bank for a second year, what happens? Will you earn an additional $6 of interest? It depends on whether the bank pays you simple interest or compound interest. **Simple interest** is interest on the invested amount only, whereas **compound interest** is interest on the invested amount plus interest on previous interest earned but not withdrawn. Simple interest is sometimes computed on short-term investments and debts (i.e., those that are shorter than six months to a year). Compound interest is typically computed for financial arrangements longer than one year. We will assume that interest is compounded in all examples in this book. Extending the future-value formula to find the amount we have in the bank in two years gives us the following formula:

$$FV_{(\text{year } 2)} = PV(1 + r)(1 + r) \text{ or}$$
$$FV_{(\text{year } 2)} = PV(1 + r)^2$$

In our example, $FV_{(\text{year } 2)} = 100(1 + 0.06)^2$, or \$112.36. We earned \$6.36 of interest in year 2—\$6 on our original \$100 investment and \$0.36 on the \$6 of interest earned but not withdrawn in year 1 (\$6 × 0.06).

In this example, we have assumed that compounding is on an annual basis. Compounding can also be calculated semiannually, quarterly, monthly, daily, or even continually. Go back to our original \$100 investment in the bank. If the bank pays 6 percent interest compounded semiannually instead of annually, we would have \$106.09 after one year. Note that the interest rate is typically expressed as a percentage rate per year. We are really earning 3 percent for each semiannual period, not 6 percent. It is usually easier to visualize the concept of interest rate compounding graphically, with the help of time lines. Exhibit 8A-1 graphically demonstrates the impact of annual, semiannual, and monthly compounding of the 6 percent annual rate on our original \$100 investment.

EXHIBIT 8A-1

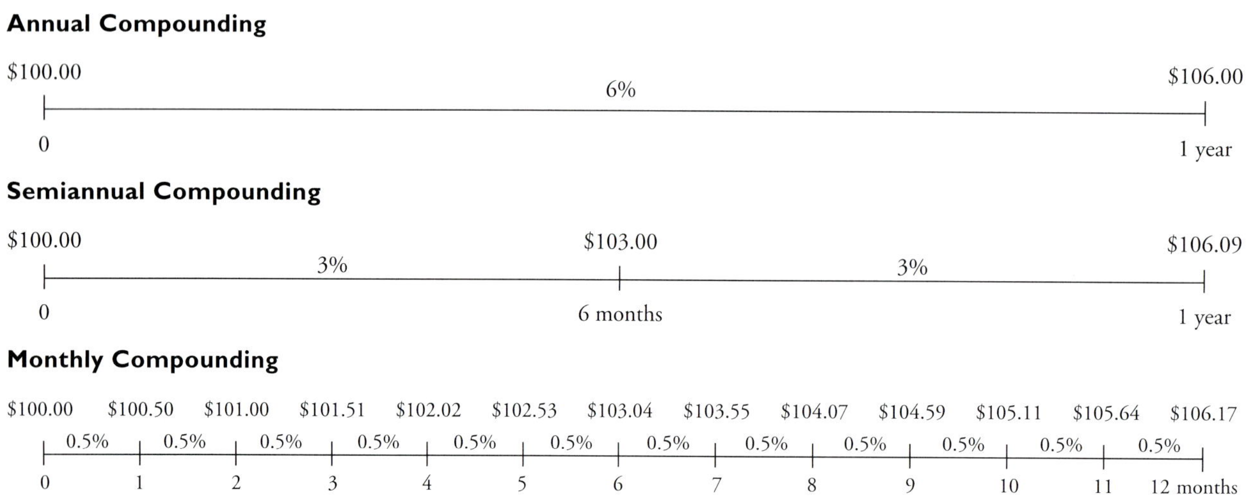

Mathematically, our formula for future value can once again be modified slightly to account for interest rates compounded at different intervals. $FV_{(n \text{ periods in the future})} = PV(1 + r)^n$, where n is the number of compounding periods per year multiplied by the number of years, and r is the annual interest rate divided by the number of compounding periods per year. Before the advent of hand-held calculators and computers, tables were developed to simplify the calculation of FV by providing values for $(1 + r)^n$ for several combinations of n and r. These tables are still commonly used, and an example is provided in Table 8A-1. The factors in Table 8A-1 are commonly referred to as cumulative factors (CF) and are simply calculations of $(1 + r)^n$ for various values of n and r.

TABLE 8A-1 Future Value of $1

n/r	0.5%	1%	2%	3%	4%	5%	6%	7%	8%	10%	12%
1	1.0050	1.0100	1.0200	1.0300	1.0400	1.0500	1.0600	1.0700	1.0800	1.1000	1.1200
2	1.0100	1.0201	1.0404	1.0609	1.0816	1.1025	1.1236	1.1449	1.1664	1.2100	1.2544
3	1.0151	1.0303	1.0612	1.0927	1.1249	1.1576	1.1910	1.2250	1.2597	1.3310	1.4049
4	1.0202	1.0406	1.0824	1.1255	1.1699	1.2155	1.2625	1.3108	1.3605	1.4641	1.5735
5	1.0253	1.0510	1.1041	1.1593	1.2167	1.2763	1.3382	1.4026	1.4693	1.6105	1.7623
6	1.0304	1.0615	1.1262	1.1941	1.2653	1.3401	1.4185	1.5007	1.5869	1.7716	1.9738
7	1.0355	1.0721	1.1487	1.2299	1.3159	1.4071	1.5036	1.6058	1.7138	1.9487	2.2107
8	1.0407	1.0829	1.1717	1.2668	1.3686	1.4775	1.5938	1.7182	1.8509	2.1436	2.4760
9	1.0459	1.0937	1.1951	1.3048	1.4233	1.5513	1.6895	1.8385	1.9990	2.3579	2.7731
10	1.0511	1.1046	1.2190	1.3439	1.4802	1.6289	1.7908	1.9672	2.1589	2.5937	3.1058
11	1.0564	1.1157	1.2434	1.3842	1.5395	1.7103	1.8983	2.1049	2.3316	2.8531	3.4785
12	1.0617	1.1268	1.2682	1.4258	1.6010	1.7959	2.0122	2.2522	2.5182	3.1384	3.8960
24	1.1272	1.2697	1.6084	2.0328	2.5633	3.2251	4.0489	5.0724	6.3412	9.8497	15.1786
36	1.1967	1.4308	2.0399	2.8983	4.1039	5.7918	8.1473	11.4239	15.9682	30.9127	59.1356
48	1.2705	1.6122	2.5871	4.1323	6.5705	10.4013	16.3939	25.7289	40.2106	97.0172	230.3908

Using this new terminology, the future value formula is simply

$$FV_{(n\text{ periods in the future})} = PV(CF_{n,r})$$

With 6 percent annual compounding, our $100 investment grows to

$$\$100(CF_{1,6\,\%}) = \$100(1.060) = \$106.00$$

With 6 percent semiannual compounding,

$$\$100(CF_{2,3\,\%}) = \$100(1.0609) = \$106.09$$

With 6 percent monthly compounding,

$$\$100(CF_{12,.5\,\%}) = \$100(1.0617) = \$106.17$$

Most financial calculators will compute future value after the user inputs data for present value, the annual interest rate, the number of compounding periods per year, and the number of years. For example, using a business calculator to compute the future value of $100.00 with 6 percent annual compounding requires the following steps:

Keys	Display	Description
1 [P/YR]	1.00	Sets compounding periods per year to 1 because interest is compounded annually
100 [±] [PV]	−100.00	Stores the present value as a negative number
6.0 [I/YR]	6.0	Stores the annual interest rate
1 [N]	1	Sets the number of years or compounding periods to 1
[FV]	106.00	Calculates the future value

Calculating the future value of $100 with 6 percent monthly compounding simply requires changing both the compounding periods per year (*P/YR*) and number of compounding periods (N) to 12.

Keys	Display	Description
12 [P/YR]	12	Sets the compounding periods per year to 12
12 [N]	12	Sets the number of compounding periods to 12
[FV]	106.17	Calculates the future value

Likewise, many spreadsheet programs (Microsoft Excel, Lotus 1-2-3, etc.) have built-in functions (formulas) that calculate future value. The Excel function called FV simply requires input of an interest rate (Rate), number of compounding periods (Nper), and present value (Pv) in the following format =FV(Rate, Nper, Pmt, Pv, Type).[7] Entries for Pmt and Type are not applicable to simple future-value problems. To calculate the future value of $100 in one year at 6 percent interest compounded monthly, enter =FV(.5%, 12, , −100). Excel returns a value of $106.17.

PRESENT VALUE

A present-value formula can be derived directly from the future-value formula. If

$$FV_{(n \text{ periods in the future})} = PV(1+r)^n$$

EXHIBIT 8A-2 Finding the Future Value Using the FV Function in Excel

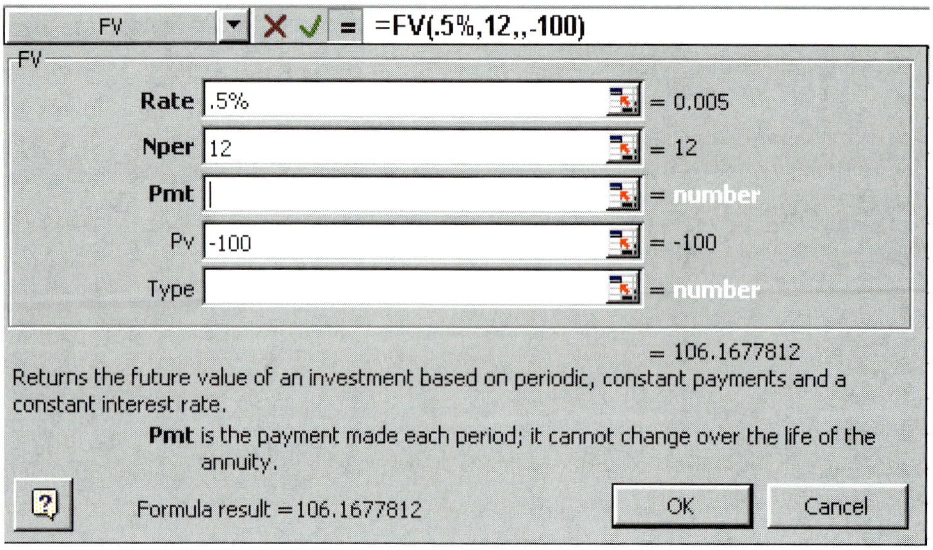

[7]Built-in functions can be accessed in Microsoft Excel by clicking on the paste function icon, clicking on financial, and then scrolling down to the desired function.

then

$$PV = FV \div (1 + r)^n \text{ or } PV = FV[1 \div (1 + r)^n]$$

Just as a cumulative factor table was developed to calculate $(1 + r)^n$, present-value tables calculate $1 \div (1 + r)^n$ for various combinations of n and r. These factors are called discount factors, or DFs. An example of a DF table is provided in Table 8A-2. Our PV formula can now be rewritten as follows:

$$PV = FV(DF_{n,r})$$

TABLE 8A-2 Present Value of $1

n/r	0.5%	1%	2%	3%	4%	5%	6%	7%	8%	10%	12%
1	0.9950	0.9901	0.9804	0.9709	0.9615	0.9524	0.9434	0.9346	0.9259	0.9091	0.8929
2	0.9901	0.9803	0.9612	0.9426	0.9246	0.9070	0.8900	0.8734	0.8573	0.8264	0.7972
3	0.9851	0.9706	0.9423	0.9151	0.8890	0.8638	0.8396	0.8163	0.7938	0.7513	0.7118
4	0.9802	0.9610	0.9238	0.8885	0.8548	0.8227	0.7921	0.7629	0.7350	0.6830	0.6355
5	0.9754	0.9515	0.9057	0.8626	0.8219	0.7835	0.7473	0.7130	0.6806	0.6209	0.5674
6	0.9705	0.9420	0.8880	0.8375	0.7903	0.7462	0.7050	0.6663	0.6302	0.5645	0.5066
7	0.9657	0.9327	0.8706	0.8131	0.7599	0.7107	0.6651	0.6227	0.5835	0.5132	0.4523
8	0.9609	0.9235	0.8535	0.7894	0.7307	0.6768	0.6274	0.5820	0.5403	0.4665	0.4039
9	0.9561	0.9143	0.8368	0.7664	0.7026	0.6446	0.5919	0.5439	0.5002	0.4241	0.3606
10	0.9513	0.9053	0.8203	0.7441	0.6756	0.6139	0.5584	0.5083	0.4632	0.3855	0.3220
11	0.9466	0.8963	0.8043	0.7224	0.6496	0.5847	0.5268	0.4751	0.4289	0.3505	0.2875
12	0.9419	0.8874	0.7885	0.7014	0.6246	0.5568	0.4970	0.4440	0.3971	0.3186	0.2567
24	0.8872	0.7876	0.6217	0.4919	0.3901	0.3101	0.2470	0.1971	0.1577	0.1015	0.0659
36	0.8356	0.6989	0.4902	0.3450	0.2437	0.1727	0.1227	0.0875	0.0626	0.0323	0.0169
48	0.7871	0.6203	0.3865	0.2420	0.1522	0.0961	0.0610	0.0389	0.0249	0.0103	0.0043

Now we are ready to calculate the present value of a future cash flow. For example, how much must be invested today at 8 percent compounded annually to have $1,000 in two years? Mathematically,

$$PV = \$1{,}000[1 \div (1 + 0.08)^2] = \$857.34$$

or using the DF table,

$$PV = \$1{,}000(DF_{2,.08}) = \$1{,}000(0.8573) = \$857.30 \text{ (rounded)}$$

Once again, the frequency of compounding affects our calculation. Just as more frequent compounding *increases* future values, increasing the frequency of compounding decreases present values. This is demonstrated in Exhibit 8A-3 for annual, semiannual, and quarterly compounding.

EXHIBIT 8A-3

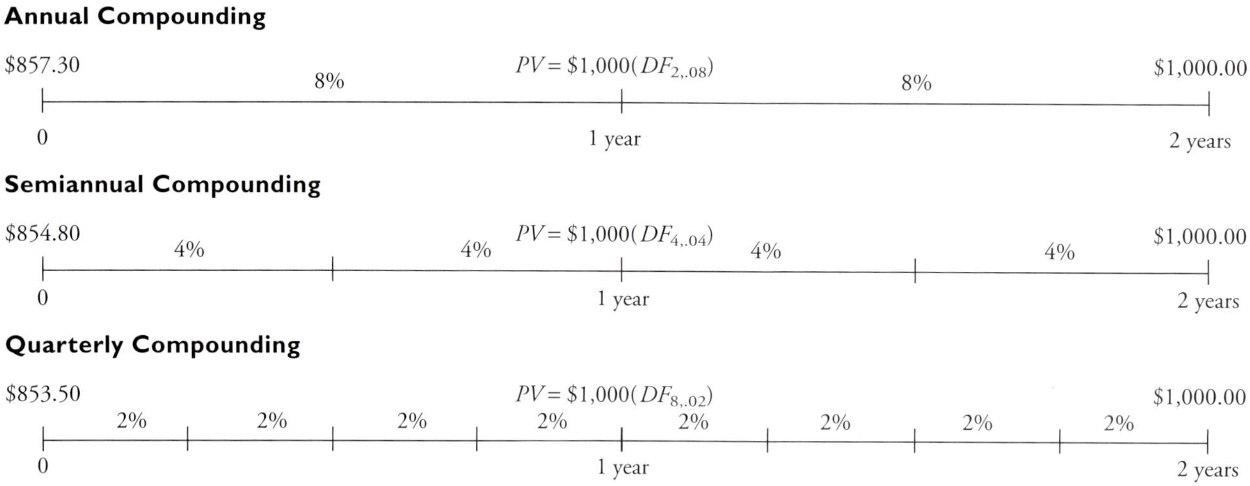

PAUSE & Reflect

Why does more frequent compounding increase future values and decrease present values?

Using a business calculator to compute present value is similar to computing future value. For example, the present value of $1,000 received or paid in two years at 8 percent compounded quarterly requires the following steps:

Keys	Display	Description
4 [P/YR]	4.00	Sets the compounding periods per year to 4
1,000 [FV]	1000.00	Stores the future value as a positive number
8.0 [I/YR]	8.0	Stores the annual interest rate
8 [N]	8.0	Sets the number of compounding periods to 8
[PV]	−853.49	Calculates the present value

In Microsoft Excel, the built-in function is called PV and requires input of the applicable interest rate (Rate), number of compounding periods (Nper), and future value (Fv) in the following format [=PV(Rate, Nper, Pmt, Fv, Type)]. In the previous example, entering =PV(2%, 8, , −1000) returns a value of $853.49. Note once again that Pmt and Type are left blank in simple present-value problems, as they were in future-value calculations (see Exhibit 8A-4).

PAUSE & Reflect

Why does a 50 percent increase in return from 8 percent to 12 percent result in almost a 100 percent increase in future value (from $20,000 to $40,000)?

Concept Question: *Eighteen years from now, the cost of one year of education at a state university is expected to cost more than $20,000, and the cost of a year at a private institution is expected to exceed $40,000. How much would parents of a newborn baby have to invest today in order to accumulate the $20,000 (or $40,000) in 18 years? Assume that you can earn an 8 percent return on your money. What if you earn 12 percent?*

Concept Answer: Using the built-in functions in Microsoft Excel, the present value of $20,000 ($40,000) in 18 years at a discount rate of 8 percent is $5,004.98 and $10,009.96, respectively. At 12 percent, the present value decreases to $2,600.79 and $5,201.58, respectively. In other words, a $5,000 investment that earns 8 percent a year for 18 years will be worth almost $20,000. If you can earn 12 percent on your investment, a $5,200 investment will grow to almost $40,000. ■

EXHIBIT 8A-4 Finding the Present Value Using the PV Function in Excel

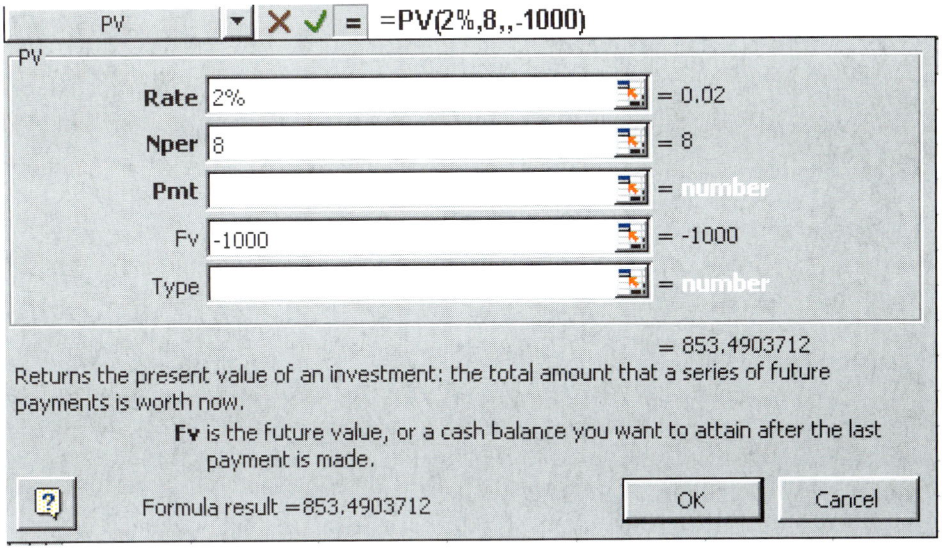

IN THE NEWS

Many states now offer students and their parents prepaid tuition plans. Some of these plans allow parents to prepay a fixed amount today that is guaranteed to cover tuition when their child enters college. For example, in Ohio, a $3,600 investment for a newborn child will cover a year of tuition at any public university in the state when the child enters college 18 years later. Note, however, that admission is not guaranteed and although refunds are typically made if a child does not choose to go to college or drops out, penalties may apply.

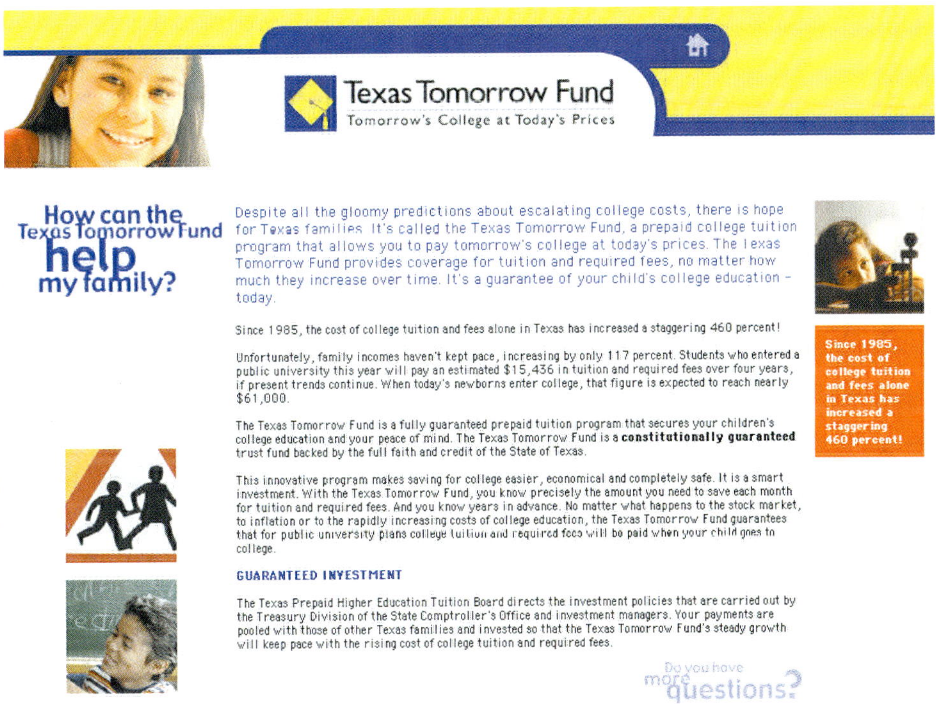

http://www.texastomorrowfund.org

When FV and PV are known, either formula can be used to calculate one of the other variables in the equations (n or r). For example, if you know that your \$100 bank deposit is worth \$200 in six years, what rate of interest compounded annually did you earn? Using the mathematical present-value formula,

$$PV = FV[1 \div (1 + r)^n]$$

or

$$\$100 = \$200[1 \div (1 + r)^6]$$

Simplifying by dividing each side by \$100, $1 = 2 \div (1 + r)^6$ and multiplying each side by $(1 + r)^6$, the equation is simplified to $(1 + r)^6 = 2$. The value of r can be calculated by using a financial calculator or mathematically by using logarithmic functions.[8] When using a business calculator, the following steps are typical:

Keys	Display	Description
1 [P/YR]	1.00	Sets compounding periods per year to 1
200 [FV]	200	Stores the future value
100 [±] [PV]	−100	Stores the present value as a negative number
2 [N]	2.0	Sets the number of compounding periods to 2
[I/YR]	0.122462	Calculates the annual interest rate

The tables can also be used to solve for n and r. Using our table formula, $PV = FV(DF_{n,r})$, if $PV = 100$ and $FV = 200$, DF must be equal to 0.5. If we know that n is equal to 6, we can simply move across the table until we find a factor close to 0.5. The factor at 12 percent is 0.5066. If we examine the factors at both 10 percent (0.5645) and 14 percent (0.456), we can infer that the actual interest rate will be slightly higher than 12 percent. Our logarithmic calculation is 12.2462 percent. In Microsoft Excel, the RATE function requires input of Nper, Pv, and Fv in the following format: =RATE(Nper, Pmt, Pv, Fv, Type, Guess). Because Excel uses an iterative trial-and-error method to calculate the interest rate, Guess provides a starting point. It is generally not necessary but may be required in complicated problems. Entering =RATE(6, ,–100, 200) returns an interest rate of 12.2462 percent (see Exhibit 8A-5).

The calculation of n is done in a similar fashion. If we know that our investment earns 12 percent but do not know how long it will take for our \$100 to grow to \$200, mathematically, we have the following:

$$PV = FV[1 \div (1 + r)^n]$$

or

$$\$100 = \$200[1 \div (1 + 0.12)^n]$$

[8]In logarithmic form, $(1+r)^6 = 2$ can be rewritten as $\log(1+r)^6 = \log 2$, or $6 \log(1+r) = \log 2$. Therefore, $\log(1+r) = \log 2 \div 6$, which simplifies to $\log(1+r) = 0.1155245$. Switching back to the equivalent exponential form, $e^{0.1155245} = (1+r)$, $(1+r) = 1.122462$, and $r = 0.122462$ (12.2462%).

EXHIBIT 8A-5 Finding the Interest Rate Using the RATE Function in Excel

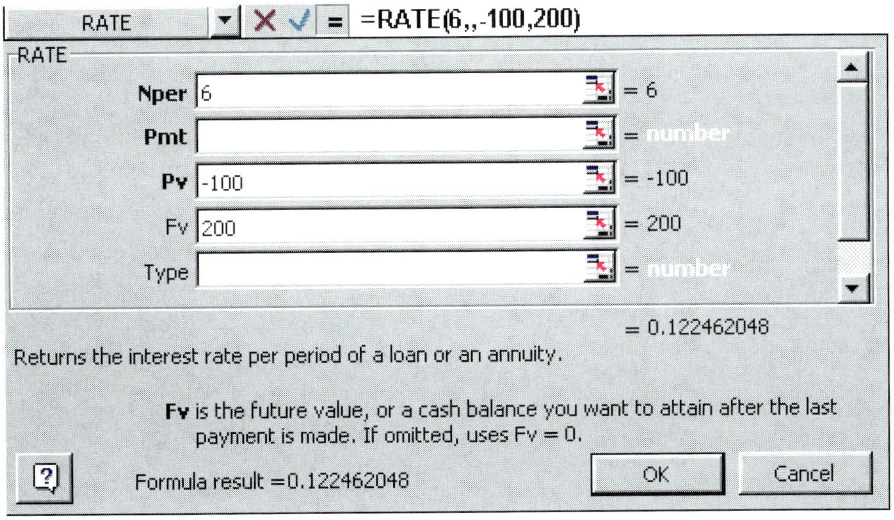

Solving the equation by using logarithms or a financial calculator gives us an n of 6.116 years.[9] Using the DF formula, *DF* must again be equal to 0.5. If r is known to be 12 percent, we simply move down the 12 percent column until we find a DF close to 0.5. Not surprisingly, we find a factor of 0.5066 for an n of 6. Examining the factors for an n of 5(0.5674) and 7(0.4523), we can infer that the actual time will be something slightly greater than 6 years. The NPER function in Microsoft Excel requires input of Rate, Pmt, Pv, Fv, and Type in the following format: [=NPER(12%, , –100, 200)] and returns a value of 6.116 years. Note that Pv is entered as a negative amount and that Pmt and Type are not necessary, as this is essentially a present-value problem (see Exhibit 8A-6).

EXHIBIT 8A-6 Finding the Number of Periods Using the NPER Function in Excel

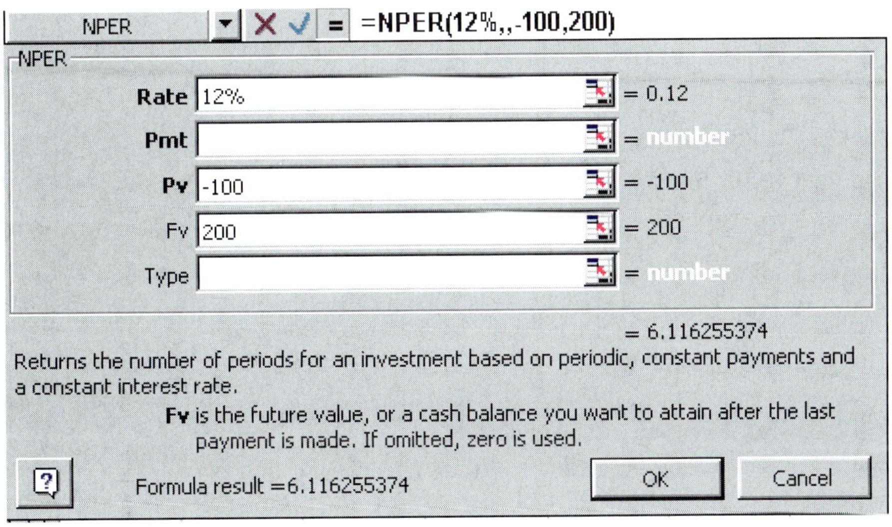

[9]Using a business calculator, simply input 1 P/YR, 200 FV, 100 PV, and 12 I/YR and solve for n. In logarithmic form, $(1+0.12)^n = 2$ can be rewritten as $\log(1+0.12)^n = \log 2$, or $n \log 1.12 = \log 2$. Therefore, $n = (\log 2)/(\log 1.12) = 6.116$.

ANNUITIES

An **annuity** is a series of cash flows of equal amount paid or received at regular intervals.[10] Common examples include mortgage and loan payments. The present value of an ordinary annuity (PVA) is the amount invested or borrowed today that will provide for a series of withdrawals or payments of equal amount for a set number of periods. Conceptually, the present value of an annuity is simply the sum of the present values of each withdrawal or payment. For example, the present value of an annuity of $100 paid at the end of each of the next four years at an interest rate of 10 percent looks like this:

PVA		$100		$100		$100		$100
	10%		10%		10%		10%	
0		1 year		2 years		3 years		4 years

Although cumbersome, the present value of an annuity can be calculated by finding the present value of each $100 payment, using the present-value table on page 267.

$$\begin{aligned} PVA &= \$100(DF_{1,.10}) + \$100(DF_{2,.10}) + \$100(DF_{3,.10}) + \$100(DF_{4,.10}) \\ &= \$100(0.9091) + \$100(0.8264) + \$100(0.7513) + \$100(0.6830) \\ &= \$316.98 \end{aligned}$$

The mathematical formula for PVA can be derived from the formula for PV and is equal to:

$$PVAn,r = R\left(\frac{1 - \dfrac{1}{(1+r)^n}}{r}\right)$$

where R refers to the periodic payment or withdrawal (commonly called a rent). Calculated values for various combinations of n and r are provided in Table 8A-3.

TABLE 8A-3 Present Value of an Ordinary Annuity

n/r	0.50%	1%	2%	3%	4%	5%	6%	7%	8%	10%	12%
1	0.9950	0.9901	0.9804	0.9709	0.9615	0.9524	0.9434	0.9346	0.9259	0.9091	0.8929
2	1.9851	1.9704	1.9416	1.9135	1.8861	1.8594	1.8334	1.8080	1.7833	1.7355	1.6901
3	2.9702	2.9410	2.8839	2.8286	2.7751	2.7232	2.6730	2.6243	2.5771	2.4869	2.4018
4	3.9505	3.9020	3.8077	3.7171	3.6299	3.5460	3.4651	3.3872	3.3121	3.1699	3.0373
5	4.9259	4.8534	4.7135	4.5797	4.4518	4.3295	4.2124	4.1002	3.9927	3.7908	3.6048
6	5.8964	5.7955	5.6014	5.4172	5.2421	5.0757	4.9173	4.7665	4.6229	4.3553	4.1114
7	6.8621	6.7282	6.4720	6.2303	6.0021	5.7864	5.5824	5.3893	5.2064	4.8684	4.5638
8	7.8230	7.6517	7.3255	7.0197	6.7327	6.4632	6.2098	5.9713	5.7466	5.3349	4.9676
9	8.7791	8.5660	8.1622	7.7861	7.4353	7.1078	6.8017	6.5152	6.2469	5.7590	5.3282
10	9.7304	9.4713	8.9826	8.5302	8.1109	7.7217	7.3601	7.0236	6.7101	6.1446	5.6502
11	10.6770	10.3676	9.7868	9.2526	8.7605	8.3064	7.8869	7.4987	7.1390	6.4951	5.9377
12	11.6189	11.2551	10.5753	9.9540	9.3851	8.8633	8.3838	7.9427	7.5361	6.8137	6.1944
24	22.5629	21.2434	18.9139	16.9355	15.2470	13.7986	12.5504	11.4693	10.5288	8.9847	7.7843
36	32.8710	30.1075	25.4888	21.8323	18.9083	16.5469	14.6210	13.0352	11.7172	9.6765	8.1924
48	42.5803	37.9740	30.6731	25.2667	21.1951	18.0772	15.6500	13.7305	12.1891	9.8969	8.2972

[10] An ordinary annuity is paid or received at the end of each period, whereas an annuity due is paid or received at the beginning of each period. In examples throughout this book, we will assume the annuity is ordinary.

The PVA formula can therefore be rewritten as follows:

$$PVA = R(DFA_{n,r})$$

As previously discussed, common examples of annuities are mortgages and loans. For example, say you are thinking about buying a new car. Your bank offers to loan you money at a special 6 percent rate compounded monthly for a 24-month term. If the maximum monthly payment you can afford is $399, how large a car loan can you get? In other words, what is the present value of a $399 annuity paid at the end of each of the next 24 months, assuming an interest rate of 6 percent compounded monthly? Using a time line, the problem looks like this:

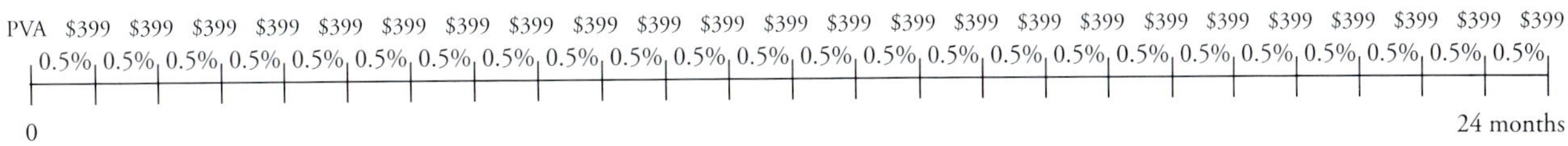

Mathematically,

$$PVA_{24,.005} = 399\left(\frac{1-\dfrac{1}{(1+0.005)^{24}}}{0.005}\right)$$

Using the DFA table,

$$PVA_{24,.005} = \$399(DFA_{24,.005}) = \$399(22.5629) = \$9{,}002.60 \text{ (rounded)}$$

The following steps are common when using a business calculator:

Keys	Display	Description
12 [P/YR]	12.00	Sets periods per year
2 × 12 [N]	24.00	Stores numer of periods in loan
0 [FV]	0	Stores the amount left to pay after 2 years
6 [I/YR]	6	Stores interest rate
399 [±] [PMT]	−399.00	Stores desired payment as a negative number
12 [P/YR]	12.00	Sets periods per year
[PV]	9,002.58	Calculates the loan you can afford with a $399 per month payment

In Microsoft Excel, the PV function is used to calculate the present value of an annuity, with additional entries for the payment amount (Pmt) and type of annuity (Type). The payment is entered as a negative number, and the annuity type is 0 for ordinary and 1 for an annuity due. The format is therefore PV(Rate, Nper, Pmt, Fv, Type). Entering =PV(.5%, 24, −399, 0, 0) returns a value of $9,002.58 (see Exhibit 8A-7).

The PVA formula can also be used to calculate R, r, and n if the other variables are known. This is most easily accomplished using the DFA table or using a financial calculator. If the car you want to buy costs $20,000 and you can afford a $3,000 down payment

EXHIBIT 8A-7 Finding the Present Value of an Annuity Using the PV Function in Excel

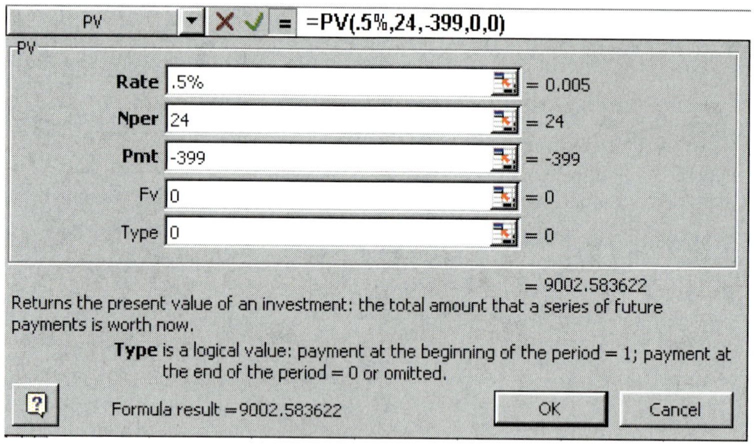

(your loan balance is $17,000), how much will your 36 monthly payments be, assuming that the bank charges you 6 percent interest compounded monthly?

Using the DFA table,

$$PVA_{36,.005} = R(DFA_{36,.005})$$
$$\$17{,}000 = R(32.871)$$
$$R = \$517.17$$

The following steps are common when using a business calculator:

Keys	Display	Description
12 [P/YR]	12.00	Sets periods per year
3 × 12 [N]	36.00	Stores numer of periods in loan
0 [FV]	0	Stores the amount left to pay after 3 years
12 [P/YR]	12.00	Sets periods per year
6 [I/YR]	6	Stores interest rate
17,000 [PV]	17,000	Stores amount borrowed
[PMT]	–517.17	Calculates the monthly payment

In Microsoft Excel, the calculation is simply =PMT (.005, 36, –17000, 0, 0) (see Exhibit 8A-8).

In a similar fashion, assume that a used-car dealer offers you a "special deal" in which you can borrow $12,000 with low monthly payments of $350 per month for 48 months. What rate of interest are you being charged in this case? Using the DFA table,

$$PVA_{48,.??} = \$350(DFA_{48,.??})$$
$$\$12{,}000 = 350(DFA_{48,.??})$$
$$DFA_{48,.??} = 34.2857$$

Looking at the row for an n of 48, we see that a DFA of 34.2857 is about halfway between an r of 1 percent and r of 2 percent (closer to 1 percent), which means that you are being

EXHIBIT 8A-8 Finding the Payment Using the PMT Function in Excel

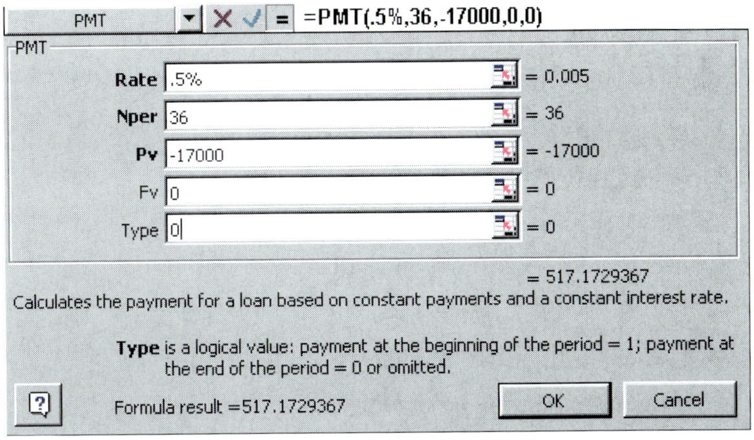

charged an annual rate of almost 18 percent (1.5% × 12)—not such a good deal after all! Using a business calculator, observe the following:

Keys	Display	Description
12 [P/YR]	12.00	Sets periods per year
4 × 12 [N]	48.00	Stores numer of periods in loan
0 [FV]	0	Stores the amount left to pay after 4 years
12,000 [PV]	12,000	Stores amount borrowed
350 [±] [PMT]	−350	Stores the monthly payment
[I/YR]	17.60	Calculates the annual interest rate

In Excel, =RATE(48, −350, 12,000, 0) generates a monthly rate of 1.4667 percent and an annual rate of 17.60 percent.

The use of the RATE function requires that the payments are the same each period. Excel's IRR function is more flexible, allowing different payments. However, each payment has to be entered separately. For example, if the car is purchased for $17,000 with annual payments of $4,000, $5,000, $6,000, and $7,000 at the end of each of the next four years, the interest rate charged on the car loan can be calculated by using the IRR function (see Exhibit 8A-9).

EXHIBIT 8A-9 Finding the Interest Rate Using the IRR Function in Excel

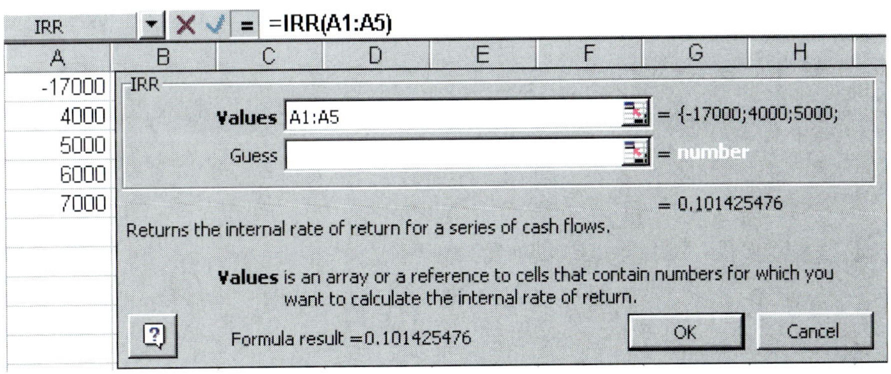

TABLE 8-1 Present Value of $1 Due in n Periods

$$\text{Factor} = \frac{1}{(1+r)^n}$$

\(n) Period	1%	2%	3%	4%	5%	6%	7%	8%	9%	10%	12%	14%	15%	16%	18%	20%	24%
1	0.9901	0.9804	0.9709	0.9615	0.9524	0.9434	0.9346	0.9259	0.9174	0.9091	0.8929	0.8772	0.8696	0.8621	0.8475	0.8333	0.8065
2	0.9803	0.9612	0.9426	0.9426	0.9070	0.8900	0.8734	0.8573	0.8417	0.8264	0.7972	0.7695	0.7561	0.7432	0.7182	0.6944	0.6504
3	0.9706	0.9423	0.9151	0.8890	0.8638	0.83%	0.8163	0.7938	0.7722	0.7513	0.7118	0.6750	0.6575	0.6407	0.6086	0.5787	0.5245
4	0.9610	0.9238	0.8885	0.8548	0.8227	0.7921	0.7629	0.7350	0.7084	0.6830	0.6355	0.5921	0.5718	0.5523	0.5158	0.4823	0.4230
5	0.9515	0.9057	0.8626	0.8219	0.7835	0.7473	0.7130	0.6806	0.6499	0.6209	0.5574	0.5194	0.4972	0.4761	0.43731	0.4019	0.3411
6	0.9420	0.8880	0.8375	0.7903	0.7462	0.7050	0.6663	0.6302	0.5963	0.5645	0.5066	0.4556	0.4323	0.4104	0.3704	0.3349	0.2751
7	0.9327	0.8706	0.8131	0.7599	0.7107	0.6651	0.6227	0.5835	0.5470	0.5132	0.4523	0.3996	0.3759	0.3538	0.3139	0.2791	0.2218
8	0.9235	0.8535	0.7894	0.7307	0.6768	0.6274	0.5820	0.5403	0.5019	0.4665	0.4039	0.3506	0.3269	0.3050	0.2660	0.2326	0.1789
9	0.9143	0.8368	0.7664	0.7026	0.6446	0.5919	0.5439	0.5002	0.4604	0.4241	0.3606	0.3075	0.2843	0.2630	0.2255	0.1938	0.1443
10	0.9053	0.8203	0.7441	0.6756	0.6139	0.5584	0.5083	0.4632	0.4224	0.3855	0.3220	0.2697	0.2472	0.2267	0.1911	0.1615	0.1164
11	0.8963	0.8043	0.7224	0.6496	0.5847	0.5268	0.4751	0.4289	0.3875	0.3505	0.2875	0.2366	0.2149	0.1954	0.1619	0.1346	0.0938
12	0.8874	0.7885	0.7014	0.6246	0.5568	0.4970	0.4440	0.3971	0.3555	0.3186	0.2567	0.2076	0.1869	0.1685	0.1372	0.1122	0.0757
13	0.8787	0.7730	0.6810	0.6006	0.5303	0.4688	0.4150	0.3677	0.3262	0.2897	0.2292	0.1821	0.1625	0.1452	0.1163	0.0935	0.0610
14	0.8700	0.7579	0.6611	0.5775	0.5051	0.4423	0.3878	0.3405	0.2992	0.2633	0.2046	0.1597	0.1413	0.1252	0.0985	0.0779	0.0492
15	0.8613	0.7430	0.6419	0.5553	0.4810	0.4173	0.3624	0.3152	0.2745	0.2394	0.1827	0.1401	0.1229	0.1079	0.0835	0.0649	0.0397
16	0.8528	0.7284	0.6232	0.5339	0.4581	0.3936	0.3387	0.2919	0.2519	0.2176	0.1631	0.1229	0.1069	0.0930	0.0708	0.0541	0.0320
17	0.8444	0.7142	0.6050	0.5134	0.4363	0.3714	0.3166	0.2703	0.2311	0.1978	0.1456	0.1078	0.0929	0.0802	0.0600	0.0451	0.0258
18	0.8360	0.7002	0.5874	0.4936	0.4155	0.3503	0.2959	0.2502	0.2120	0.1799	0.1300	0.0946	0.0808	0.0691	0.0508	0.0376	0.0208
19	0.8277	0.6864	0.5703	0.4746	0.3957	0.3305	0.2765	0.2317	0.1945	0.1635	0.1161	0.0829	0.0703	0.0596	0.0431	0.0313	0.0168
20	0.8195	0.6730	0.5537	0.4564	0.3769	0.3118	0.2584	0.2145	0.1784	0.1486	0.1037	0.0728	0.0611	0.0514	0.0365	0.0261	0.0135
21	0.8114	0.6598	0.5375	0.4388	0.3589	0.2942	0.2415	0.1987	0.1637	0.1351	0.0926	0.0638	0.0531	0.0443	0.0309	0.0217	0.0109
22	0.8034	0.6468	0.5219	0.4220	0.3418	0.2775	0.2257	0.1839	0.1502	0.1228	0.0826	0.0560	0.0462	0.0382	0.0262	0.0181	0.0088
23	0.7954	0.6342	0.5067	0.4057	0.3256	0.2618	0.2109	0.1703	0.1378	0.1117	0.0738	0.0491	0.0402	0.0329	0.0222	0.0151	0.0071
24	0.7876	0.6217	0.4919	0.3901	0.3101	0.2470	0.1971	0.1577	0.1264	0.1015	0.0659	0.0431	0.0349	0.0284	0.0188	0.0126	0.0057
25	0.7798	0.6095	0.4776	0.3751	0.2953	0.2330	0.1842	0.1460	0.1160	0.0923	0.0588	0.0378	0.0304	0.0245	0.0160	0.0105	0.0046
26	0.7720	0.5976	0.4637	0.3607	0.2812	0.2198	0.1722	0.1352	0.1064	0.0839	0.0525	0.0331	0.0264	0.0211	0.0135	0.0087	0.0037
27	0.7644	0.5859	0.4502	0.3468	0.2678	0.2074	0.1609	0.1252	0.0976	0.0763	0.0469	0.0291	0.0230	0.0182	0.0115	0.0073	0.0030
28	0.7568	0.5744	0.4371	0.3335	0.2551	0.1956	0.1504	0.1159	0.0895	0.0693	0.0419	0.0255	0.0200	0.0157	0.0097	0.0061	0.0024
29	0.7493	0.5631	0.4243	0.3207	0.2429	0.1846	0.1406	0.1073	0.0822	0.0630	0.0374	0.0224	0.0174	0.0135	0.0082	0.0051	0.0020
30	0.7419	0.5521	0.4120	0.3083	0.2314	0.1741	0.1314	0.0994	0.0754	0.0573	0.0334	0.0196	0.0151	0.0116	0.0070	0.0042	0.0016

TABLE 8-2 Present Value of an Annuity of $1 per Period

$$\text{Factor} = \frac{1 - \dfrac{1}{(1+r)^n}}{r}$$

(n) Period	1%	2%	3%	4%	5%	6%	7%	8%	9%	10%	12%	14%	15%	16%	18%	20%	24%
1	0.9901	0.9804	0.9709	0.9615	0.9524	0.9434	0.9346	0.9259	0.9174	0.9091	0.8929	0.8772	0.8696	0.8621	0.8475	0.8333	0.8065
2	1.9704	1.9416	1.9135	1.8861	1.8594	1.8334	1.8080	1.7833	1.7591	1.7355	1.6901	1.6467	1.6257	1.6052	1.5656	1.5278	1.4568
3	2.9410	2.8839	2.8286	2.7751	2.7232	2.6730	2.6243	2.5771	2.5313	2.4869	2.4018	2.3216	2.2832	2.2459	2.1743	2.1065	1.9813
4	3.9020	3.8077	3.7171	3.6299	3.5460	3.4651	3.3872	3.3121	3.2397	3.1699	3.0373	2.9137	2.8550	2.7982	2.6901	2.5887	2.4043
5	4.8534	4.7135	4.5797	4.4518	4.3295	4.2124	4.1002	3.9927	3.8897	3.7908	3.6048	3.4331	3.3522	3.2743	3.1272	2.9906	2.7454
6	5.7955	5.6014	5.4172	5.2421	5.0757	4.9173	4.7665	4.6229	4.4859	4.3553	4.1114	3.8887	3.7845	3.6847	3.4976	3.3255	3.0205
7	6.7282	6.4720	6.2303	6.0021	5.7864	5.5824	5.3893	5.2064	5.0330	4.8684	4.5638	4.2883	4.1604	4.0386	3.8115	3.6046	3.2423
8	7.6517	7.3255	7.0197	6.7327	6.4632	6.2098	5.9713	5.7466	5.5348	5.3349	4.9676	4.6389	4.4873	4.3436	4.0776	3.8372	3.4212
9	8.5660	8.1622	7.7861	7.4353	7.1078	6.8017	6.5152	6.2469	5.9952	5.7590	5.3282	4.9464	4.7716	4.6065	4.3030	4.0310	3.5655
10	9.4713	8.9826	8.5302	8.1109	7.7217	7.3601	7.0236	6.7101	6.4177	6.1446	5.6502	5.2161	5.0188	4.8332	4.4941	4.1925	3.6819
11	10.3676	9.7868	9.2526	8.7605	8.3064	7.8869	7.4987	7.1390	6.8052	6.4951	5.9377	5.4527	5.2337	5.0286	4.6560	4.3271	3.7757
12	11.2551	10.5753	9.9540	9.3851	8.8633	8.3838	7.9427	7.5361	7.1607	6.8137	6.1944	5.6603	5.4206	5.1971	4.7932	4.4392	3.8514
13	12.1337	11.3484	10.6350	9.9856	9.3936	8.8527	8.3577	7.9038	7.4869	7.1034	6.4235	5.8424	5.5831	5.3423	4.9095	4.5327	3.9124
14	13.0037	12.1062	11.2961	10.5631	9.8986	9.2950	8.7455	8.244	7.7862	7.3667	6.6283	6.0021	5.7245	5.4675	5.0081	4.6106	3.9616
15	13.8651	12.8493	11.9379	11.1184	10.3797	9.7122	9.1079	8.5595	8.0607	7.6061	6.8109	6.1422	5.8474	5.5755	5.0916	4.6755	4.0013
16	14.7179	13.5777	12.5611	11.6523	10.8378	10.1059	9.4466	8.8514	8.3126	7.8237	6.9740	6.2651	5.9542	5.6685	5.1624	4.7296	4.0333
17	15.5623	14.2919	13.1661	12.1657	11.2741	10.4773	9.7632	9.1216	8.5436	8.0216	7.1196	6.3729	6.0472	5.7487	5.2223	4.7746	4.0591
18	16.3983	14.9920	13.7535	12.6593	11.6896	10.8276	10.0591	9.3719	8.7556	8.2014	7.2497	6.4674	6.1280	5.8178	5.2732	4.8122	4.0799
19	17.2260	15.6785	14.3238	13.1339	12.0853	11.1581	10.3356	9.6036	8.9501	8.3649	7.3658	6.5504	6.1982	5.8775	5.3162	4.8435	4.0967
20	18.0456	16.3514	14.8775	13.5903	12.4622	11.4699	10.5940	9.8181	9.1285	8.5136	7.4694	6.6231	6.2593	5.9288	5.3527	4.8696	4.1103
21	18.8570	17.0112	15.4150	14.0292	12.8212	11.7641	10.8355	10.0168	9.2922	8.6487	7.5620	6.6870	6.3125	5.9731	5.3837	4.8913	4.1212
22	19.6604	17.6580	15.9369	14.4511	13.1630	12.0416	11.0612	10.2007	9.4424	8.7715	7.6446	6.7429	6.3587	6.0113	5.4099	4.9094	4.1300
23	20.4558	18.2922	16.4436	14.8568	13.4886	12.3034	11.2722	10.3711	9.5802	8.8832	7.7184	6.7921	6.3988	6.0422	5.4321	4.9245	4.1371
24	21.2434	18.9139	16.9355	15.2470	13.7986	12.5504	11.4693	10.5288	9.7066	8.9847	7.7843	6.8351	6.4338	6.0726	5.4509	4.9371	4.1428
25	22.0232	19.5235	17.4131	15.6221	14.0939	12.7834	11.6536	10.6748	9.8226	9.0770	7.8431	6.8729	6.4641	6.0971	5.4669	4.9476	4.1474
26	22.7952	20.1210	17.8768	15.9828	14.3752	13.0332	11.8258	10.8100	9.9290	9.1609	7.8957	6.9061	6.4906	6.1182	5.4804	4.9563	4.1511
27	23.5596	20.7069	18.3270	16.3296	14.6430	13.2105	11.9867	10.9352	10.0266	9.2372	7.9426	6.9352	6.5135	6.1364	5.4919	4.9636	4.1542
28	24.3164	21.2813	18.7641	16.6631	14.8981	13.4062	12.1371	11.0511	10.1161	9.3066	7.9844	6.9607	6.5335	6.1520	5.5016	4.9697	4.1566
29	25.0658	21.8444	19.1885	16.9837	15.1411	13.5907	12.2777	11.1584	10.1983	9.3696	8.0218	6.9830	6.5509	6.1656	5.5098	4.9747	4.1585
30	25.8077	22.3965	19.6004	17.2920	15.3725	13.7648	12.4090	11.2578	10.2737	9.4269	8.0552	7.0027	6.5660	6.1772	5.5168	4.9789	4.1601

SUMMARY OF KEY CONCEPTS

- Long-term investment decisions require a consideration of the time value of money. The time value of money is based on the concept that a dollar received today is worth more than a dollar received in the future. (p. 246)
- The time value of money is considered in capital investment decisions by using one of two techniques: the net present value (NPV) method or the internal rate of return (IRR) method. (p. 248)
- If the present value of cash inflows is greater than or equal to the present value of cash outflows (the NPV is greater than or equal to zero), the investment provides a return at least equal to the discount rate (the minimum required rate of return), and the investment is acceptable. (p. 248)
- The internal rate of return (IRR) is the actual yield, or return, earned by an investment. (p. 250)
- Taxes are a major source of cash outflows for many companies and must be taken into consideration in calculations of the time value of money. (p. 255)
- Analyzing the costs and benefits of investments in automated and computerized design and manufacturing equipment and robotics requires careful consideration of both quantitative and qualitative factors. (p. 261)
- The payback method can be useful as a quick approximation of the discounted-cash-flow methods when the cash flows follow similar patterns. (p. 262)

KEY DEFINITIONS

Capital investment decisions Long-term decisions involving the purchase (or lease) of new machinery and equipment and the acquisition or expansion of facilities used in a business (p. 246)

Time value of money The concept that a dollar received (paid) today is worth more (less) than a dollar received (paid) in the future (p. 246)

Screening decisions Decisions about whether an investment meets a predetermined company standard (p. 247)

Preference decisions Decisions that involve choosing between alternatives (p. 247)

Net present value (NPV) A technique for considering the time value of money whereby the present value of all cash inflows associated with a project is compared with the present value of all cash outflows (p. 248)

Internal rate of return (IRR) The actual yield, or return, earned by an investment (p. 248)

Cost of capital What the firm would have to pay to borrow (issue bonds) or raise funds through equity (issue stock) in the financial marketplace (p. 248)

Discount rate Used as a hurdle rate, or minimum rate of return in calculations of the time value of money; adjusted to reflect risk and uncertainty (p. 248)

Profitability index (PI) Calculated by dividing the present value of cash inflows by the initial investment (p. 253)

Sensitivity analysis Used to highlight decisions that may be affected by changes in expected cash flows (p. 260)

Payback period The length of time needed for a long-term project to recapture, or pay back, the initial investment (p. 261)

Present value (PV) The amount of future cash flows discounted to their equivalent worth today (p. 263)

Simple interest Interest on the invested amount only (p. 263)

Compound interest Interest on the invested amount plus interest on previous interest earned but not withdrawn (p. 263)

Annuity A series of cash flows of equal amount paid or received at regular intervals (p. 272)

COMPUTER SIMULATION

You can now turn to **Appendix A** of your text to complete the portion of the Big Al's simulation covering long-term capital budgeting decisions.

MULTIPLE CHOICE

1. Calculations of the time value of money are based on the premise that:
   a. a dollar received today is worth more than a dollar received in the future
   b. a dollar received today is worth less than a dollar received in the future
   c. a dollar of net income in the future is equal to cash flows paid today
   d. large cash outlays require cash flow projections to be successful

2. Screening decisions involve:
   a. choosing between alternatives
   b. identifying objectives
   c. defining a problem
   d. deciding whether an investment meets a predetermined criterion

3. You are considering the following two projects:

	Project A	**Project B**
Initial investment	$(2,000)	$(4,000)
PV of cash inflows	2,600	3,400
Net present value	600	(600)

   Based on profitability index, which of the projects is acceptable?
   a. A only
   b. B only
   c. A and B
   d. neither A nor B

4. GCL Co. is considering an investment with a cost of $55,000. Annual cash savings of $10,000, with a present value at 12 percent of $53,282, are expected for the next nine years.

   Based on this information, which of the following statements is true?
   a. This investment offers a 12 percent rate of return.
   b. This investment offers more than a 12 percent rate of return.
   c. This investment offers less than a 12 percent rate of return.
   d. Not enough information is available to answer this question.

5. Which of the following have tax consequences that should be considered when making capital investment decisions?
   a. positive net income
   b. disposal of an asset
   c. depreciation
   d. all of the above

6. If LH Enterprises is in the 40 percent tax bracket and has a 10 percent rate of return, its after-tax benefit should be calculated by using a rate of return of:
   a. 6 percent
   b. 10 percent
   c. 40 percent
   d. 60 percent

7. The benefits of automating production processes include:
   a. decreased labor costs
   b. increased speed of the production process
   c. increased reliability of the finished good
   d. all of the above
8. With the compounding of interest, you:
   a. will earn more interest on an investment than with simple interest over the same time period
   b. will earn less interest on an investment than with simple interest over the same time period
   c. will earn the same amount of interest on an investment as with simple interest over the same time period
   d. cannot compare amounts of interest earned without more information
9. Your company has a policy of accepting projects with a payback period of seven years or less. Which of the following projects would be acceptable?

	Project A	Project B
Initial investment	$40,000	$50,000
Annual cash flows	7,000	5,000

   a. A only
   b. B only
   c. A and B
   d. neither A nor B
10. The Unique Bookshelf Company is considering the purchase of a custom delivery van costing approximately $50,000. Using a discount rate of 20 percent, you estimate the present value of future cost savings at $51,200. To yield the 20 percent return, the actual cost of the van should not exceed the $50,000 estimate by more than:
   a. $50,000
   b. $51,200
   c. $1,200
   d. The answer cannot be determined with the information given.

CONCEPT REVIEW

11. Define capital investment decisions.
12. Define what is meant by the term *time value of money.*
13. Compare screening decisions with preference decisions.
14. Compare net present value (NPV) with internal rate of return (IRR). What are the principal differences in the two methods?
15. Define the term *cost of capital.* How would cost of capital be used in an investment decision?
16. Which method of project selection ignores the time value of money?
17. Define profitability index and discuss how it is used in capital investment decisions.
18. Define payback period.
19. Describe how internal rate of return equates to net present value.
20. Describe the process by which projects are accepted using the internal rate of return.
21. For the internal rate of return to rank projects the same way as the present value, which condition must exist?
22. The calculation of the net present value of a proposed project requires estimates of what?
23. If the net present value of a proposed project is negative, then the actual rate of return is what?
24. Competing investment projects where accepting one project eliminates the possibility of taking the remaining projects is referred to as what?

APPLICATION OF CONCEPTS

25. A planned factory expansion project has an estimated initial cost of $800,000. With a discount rate of 20 percent, the present value of the future cost savings from the expansion is $843,000. To yield exactly a 20 percent return on investment, the actual investment expenditure should not exceed the $800,000 estimate by more than what amount?

26. If the present value of future cash flows is $17,000 and the initial investment is $10,000, what is the profitability index?

27. If the future cash flows are expected to be $4,000 for year 1 and $3,000 for years 2 through 5 and the initial investment is $10,000, the payback period is how many years?

28. The Orr Golf Club is considering an investment into golf carts that requires $20,000 and promises to return $28,090 in three years. The company's income tax rate is 40 percent. What is the internal rate of return?

29. The Nassy Day Care Center is considering an investment that will require an initial cash outlay of $300,000 to purchase nondepreciable assets that have a ten-year life. The organization requires a minimum four-year payback. What must the annual cash flows generated by the project be in order for the company to make the investment?

30. The Pearce Club Inc. is considering investing in an exercise machine that would increase revenues by $2,000 a year for five years. The machine would be depreciated using the straight-line method over its useful life (with no half-year convention). The company's marginal tax rate is 30 percent. If the company pays $5,000 for the machine, what is the internal rate of return on the equipment?

31. Powers Inc. has a project that requires an initial investment of $43,000 and has the following expected stream of cash flows:

Year 1	$20,000
Year 2	30,000

What is the project's internal rate of return?

32. Rechtin Company has a project that requires an initial investment of $35,000 and has the following expected stream of cash flows:

Year 1	$25,000
Year 2	20,000
Year 3	10,000

The company's cost of capital is 12 percent. What is the profitability index for the project?

33. Relue Inc. has a project with an expected cash inflow of $1 million at the end of year 5. Relue has a second project with an expected cash inflow of $200,000 to be received at the end of each year for the next five years. If both projects have the same expected cash outflows, what can be said of the net present value of the first project compared to the second project?

34. Rupp Inc. purchased an asset at a cost of $80,000. Annual operating cash flows are expected to be $30,000 each year for four years. At the end of the asset life, there will be no residual (salvage) value. What is the net present value if the cost of capital is 12 percent (ignore income taxes)?

35. Schaefer Organic Farms purchased a new tractor at a cost of $80,000. Annual operating cash flows are expected to be $30,000 each year for four years. At the end of the asset life, the salvage value of the tractor is expected to be $5,000. What is the net present value if the cost of capital is 12 percent (ignore income taxes)?

36. Schaller Company purchased an asset at a cost of $40,000. Annual operating cash flows are expected to be $20,000 each year for four years. At the end of the asset life, there will be no residual (salvage) value. The income tax rate is 30 percent, and the company uses straight-line depreciation with no half-year convention. What is the net present value if the cost of capital is 10 percent?

37. Schanz Quick Photo Company purchased a new photo developing machine at a cost of $80,000. Annual operating cash flows are expected to be $25,000 each year for four years. At the end of the asset life, the salvage value is expected to be $5,000. The income tax rate is 30 percent, and the company uses straight-line depreciation with no half-year convention. What is the net present value if the cost of capital is 12 percent?

38. Schlue Company invested $180,000 in a new machine. The machine will generate cash flows before taxes at year-end of $90,000, $80,000, and $70,000 for the next three years. The company uses a 15 percent cost of capital. What is the net present value of purchasing the machine?

39. Seeger Company recently invested in a computerized manufacturing system. The project required an initial investment of $100,000 and is expected to provide equal cost savings over the next eight years. Based on an 8 percent discount rate, the project generated a net present value of zero. The investment is not expected to have any salvage value at the end of its life. Ignoring income taxes, what are the expected annual cost savings of the project? What other factors should be considered?

40. Simmons Trucking is considering replacing its moving truck. The truck is expected to cost $60,000 and is expected to last 10 years with no salvage value. The truck is expected to generate additional net cash flows of $15,000 a year. Based on Simmons's analysis, the project has a net present value of $39,450. What rate of cost of capital did the company use to compute the net present value?

41. Speakman Company will dispose of an asset for $6,000 at the end of its five-year life. If the asset is fully depreciated and Speakman's tax rate is 40 percent, what is the present value of the future cash flow? Assume that Speakman's cost of capital is 12 percent.

42. Stamenkovich Law Associates is evaluating a capital investment proposal for new computers for this current year. The initial investment would be $50,000. It would be depreciated on a straight-line basis over five years with no salvage value. The before-tax annual cash inflow from this investment is $15,000, and the income tax rate is 40 percent paid in the same year as incurred. The desired after-tax rate of return is 15 percent. All cash flows occur at year-end. What is the net present value of the capital investment proposal? Should the proposal be accepted? Why or why not?

43. Each of two projects being considered by Stein Company require an investment of $1,000 in equipment. The firm's cost of capital is 12 percent. The cash flow patterns are as follows:

	Cash Flows	
Year	**Project C**	**Project D**
1	$600	$300
2	600	600
3	600	800
4	600	700

Calculate the present value of each project at each of the following costs of capital: (1) 8 percent, (2) 10 percent, (3) 12 percent. Indicate which project should be accepted at each of these costs of capital.

44. Stembridge Medical Associates is planning to acquire a $250,000 X-ray machine that will provide increased efficiencies, thereby reducing annual patient operating costs by $80,000. The machine will be depreciated by the straight-line method over five years (no half-year convention), with no salvage value at the end of five years. Assuming a 40 percent income tax rate, compute the machine's after-tax payback period.

45. Stephens Industries is contemplating four projects: Project P, Project Q, Project R, and Project S. The capital costs and estimated after-tax net cash flows of each mutually exclusive project follow. Stephens's desired after-tax cost of capital is 12 percent, and the company has a capital budget for the year of $450,000. Idle funds cannot be reinvested at greater than 12 percent.

	Project P	Project Q	Project R	Project S
Initial cost	$200,000	$235,000	$190,000	$210,000
Annual cash flows:				
Year 1	93,000	90,000	45,000	40,000
Year 2	93,000	85,000	55,000	50,000
Year 3	93,000	75,000	65,000	60,000
Year 4	0	55,000	70,000	65,000
Year 5	0	50,000	75,000	75,000
Net present value	23,370	29,827	27,233	(7,854)
Internal rate of return	18.7%	17.6%	17.2%	10.6%
Profitability index	1.12	1.13	1.14	0.95

Required

A. Which project will the company choose?

B. If only one project can be accepted, which one should the company choose?

46. Stewart Corporation is reviewing an investment proposal. The initial cost and other related data for each year are presented in the following schedule. The cash flows are all assumed to take place at the end of the year. All salvage value of the investment at the end of each year is equal to its net book value, and there will be no salvage value at the end of the investment's life.

Investment Proposal

Year	Initial Cost and Book Value	Annual Net After-Tax Cash Flows	Annual Net Income
0	$105,000	$ 0	$ 0
1	70,000	50,000	15,000
2	42,000	45,000	17,000
3	21,000	40,000	19,000
4	7,000	35,000	21,000
5	0	30,000	23,000

Stewart uses a 24 percent after-tax target rate of return for new investment proposals.

Required

A. What is the traditional payback period for the investment proposal?

B. What is the net present value of the investment proposal?

47. Stoehr Company manufactures three models of paper shredders, including the waste container, which serves as the base. Whereas the shredder heads are different for all three models, the waste container is the same. The number of waste containers that Stoehr will need during the next five years is estimated as follows:

Year	Number of Containers
2002	50,000
2003	50,000
2004	52,000
2005	55,000
2006	55,000

The equipment used to manufacture the waste container must be replaced because it has broken and cannot be repaired. The new equipment would have a purchase price of $945,000. The equipment is expected to have a salvage value of $12,000 at the end of its economic life, in 2006. The new equipment would be more efficient than the old equipment, resulting in a 25 percent reduction in direct material and a one-time decrease in working capital requirements of $2,500 resulting from a reduction in direct material inventories. This working capital reduction would be recognized at the time of equipment acquisition.

The old equipment is fully depreciated and is not included in the fixed overhead. The old equipment from the plant can be sold for a salvage amount of $1,500. Stoehr has no alternative use for the manufacturing space at this time, so if the waste containers were purchased, the old equipment would be left in place.

Rather than replace the equipment, one of Stoehr's production managers has suggested that the waste containers be purchased. One supplier has quoted a price of $27 per container. This price is $8 less than the current manufacturing cost, which is as follows:

Direct materials	$10.00	
Direct labor	8.00	
Variable overhead	6.00	$24.00
Fixed overhead:		
Supervision	$ 2.00	
Facilities	5.00	
General	4.00	$11.00
Total manufacturing cost per unit		$35.00

Stoehr employs a plantwide fixed overhead rate in its operations. If the waste containers were purchased outside, the salary and benefits of one supervisor, included in the fixed overhead at $45,000, would be eliminated. There would be no other changes in the other cash and noncash items included in fixed overhead.

Stoehr is subject to a 40 percent income tax rate. Management assumes that all annual cash flows and tax payments occur at the end of the year and uses a 12 percent after-tax discount rate.

Required

Step I **DEFINE THE PROBLEM**

A. Define the problem that Stoehr faces.

B. Calculate the net present value of the estimated after-tax cash flows for each option you identify.

48. The Strength Corporation sells computer services to its clients. The firm is contemplating the acquisition of a computer but is undecided as to whether it should be leased or purchased. Information regarding the computer follows:

Cash purchase price	$275,000
Maintenance taxes per year	25,000
Rental price (includes maintenance and taxes)	75,000 plus 10 percent of billings
Salvage value at the end of three years	120,000
Estimated billings:	
Year 1	230,000
Year 2	250,000
Year 3	240,000
Operating expenses per year	75,000
Setup expense charge to year 1	20,000
Income tax rate	40%
Depreciation method	Straight-line
Minimum desired rate of return	12%

Step 1 DEFINE THE PROBLEM

Step 2 IDENTIFY OBJECTIVES

Step 3 IDENTIFY AND ANALYZE AVAILABLE OPTIONS

Step 4 SELECT THE BEST OPTION

Prepare an analysis using the decision model that will indicate which alternative should be selected. Identify that alternative.

49. Stutesman Enterprises has three possible projects. Each project requires the same initial investment of $1,000,000. The cash flows are as follows:

Year	Project X	Project Y	Project Z
1	$1,250,000	$ 0	$ 500,000
2	1,250,000	0	2,000,000
3	1,250,000	0	2,000,000
4	1,250,000	5,000,000	500,000

Ignoring taxes, compute the net present value of each project at a 15 percent cost of capital. Which project should be chosen? Be sure to show supporting calculations.

50. Sullivan Company will acquire a new asset that costs $400,000 and is anticipated to have a salvage value of $30,000 at the end of four years. The new asset (1) will replace an old asset that currently has a tax basis of $80,000 and can be sold for $60,000 now, and (2) will continue to generate the same operating revenues as the old asset ($200,000 per year). However, savings in operating costs will be experienced as follows: a total of $120,000 in each of the first three years and $90,000 in the fourth year. Sullivan is subject to a 40 percent tax rate and has a cost of capital of 10 percent.

Required

A. What is the present value of the depreciation tax shield for the new asset for year 1?

B. What are the cash flows (net of tax) associated with the disposal of the old asset?

C. What is the investment's net present value (after tax)?

51. Sutherlin Corporation has agreed to sell some used computer equipment to Brett Sullivan, one of the company's employees.

Required

A. Assume a 6 percent discount rate. If Sutherlin sells the computers to Sullivan for a $1,000 down payment paid immediately, followed by $1,000 payments at the end of each of the next four years, what value is Sutherlin placing on the computer equipment?

B. Sullivan agrees to the immediate down payment of $1,000 but would like the note for $4,000 to be payable in full at the end of the fourth year. What impact does this change have on Sutherlin?

C. How much would the payment need to be at the end of four years to make Sutherlin indifferent to receiving $1,000 at the end of each of the next four years or one payment at the end of year 4?

52. Vaida Miller, president of CLJ Products, is considering the purchase of a computer-aided manufacturing system that requires an initial investment of $4,000,000 and will have a life of 10 years. The company's cost of capital is 12 percent. The annual after-tax cash benefits/savings associated with the system are as follows:

Decrease in defective products	$100,000
Increased revenue from better quality	150,000
Decrease in operating costs	300,000

Required

A. Calculate the payback period for the system. Assume that the company has a policy of accepting only projects with a payback of five years or less. Would the system be acquired?

B. Calculate the NPV and the IRR for the project. Should the system be purchased? What if it doesn't meet the payback criterion?

C. The project manager reviewed the projected cash flows and pointed out that two items had been missed. First, the system would have a salvage value, net of any tax effects, of $500,000 at the end of 10 years. Second, the increased quality and delivery performance would allow the company to increase its market share by 30 percent. This would produce an additional annual after-tax benefit of $180,000. Given this new information, recalculate the payback period, NPV, and IRR. Does the decision change? Why?

53. Tate Enterprises is a nonprofit organization that has a cost of capital of 10 percent. The organization is considering the replacement of its computer system. The old computer has a book value of $3,000 and a remaining estimated life of five years, with no salvage value at that time. The salvage value of the old computer is currently $1,500. The new computer will cost $10,000. It has an estimated life of five years, with no salvage value. Annual cash operating costs are $4,000 for the old computer and $2,000 for the new computer.

Required

A. What is the present value of the operating cash outflows for the old machine?

B. What is the present value of the operating cash outflows for the new machine?

Step 3 IDENTIFY AND ANALYZE AVAILABLE OPTIONS

C. What is the present value of the salvage value of the old machine if it is replaced now?

Step 4 SELECT THE BEST OPTION

D. Would you advise the organization to replace the machine?

54. Taylor Company is considering opening a new sales territory. Management expects the initial investment to be $150,000 and subsequent investments of $100,000 and $50,000 at the end of the first and second years. Net cash flow from the sales territory is expected to yield an after-tax cash inflow for five more years: $75,000 for the first two years and $60,000 for the remaining years. The company's cost of capital is 12 percent. Calculate the net present value of this project.

55. Rob Thorton is a member of the planning and analysis staff for Thurston Inc., an established manufacturer of frozen foods. Rick Ungerman, chief financial officer of Thurston Inc., has asked him to prepare an analysis of net present value for a proposed capital equipment expenditure that should improve the profitability of the southwestern plant. This analysis will be given to the board of directors for expenditure approval.

Several years ago, as director of planning and analysis, Ungerman was instrumental in convincing the board to open the southwestern plant. However, recent competitive pressures have forced all Thurston's manufacturing divisions to consider alternatives to improve their market position. To Ungerman's dismay, the southwestern plant may be sold in the near future unless significant improvements in cost control and production efficiency are achieved.

Southwestern's production manager, an old friend of Ungerman's, has submitted a proposal for the acquisition of an automated materials-movement system. Ungerman is eager to have this proposal approved, as it will ensure the continuance of the southwestern plant and preserve his friend's position. The plan calls for the replacement of a number of forklift trucks and operators with a computer-controlled conveyor belt system that feeds directly into the refrigeration units. This automation would eliminate the need for a number of materials handlers and increase the output capacity of the plant.

Ungerman has given this proposal to Thorton and instructed him to use the following information to prepare his analysis:

Materials Movement System Projections

Projected useful life	10 years
Purchase/installation of equipment	$4,500,000
Increased working capital needed*	1,000,000
Increased annual operating costs	
(exclusive of depreciation)	200,000
Equipment repairs to maintain production efficiency (end of year 5)	800,000
Increase in annual sales revenue	700,000
Reduction in annual manufacturing costs	500,000
Reduction in annual maintenance costs	300,000
Estimated salvage value of conveyor belt system	850,000

*The working capital will be released at the end of the 10-year useful life of the conveyor belt system.

The forklift trucks have a net book value of $500,000, with a remaining useful life of five years and no salvage value for depreciation purposes. If the conveyor belt system is purchased now, these trucks will be sold for $100,000. Thurston has a 40 percent effective tax rate, has chosen the straight-line depreciation method, and uses a 12 percent discount rate. For the purpose of analysis, all tax effects and cash flows from the equipment acquisition and disposal are considered to occur at the time of the transactions, whereas those from operations are considered to occur at the end of each year.

When Thorton completed his initial analysis, the proposed project appeared quite healthy. However, after investigating equipment similar to that proposed, he discovered that the estimated residual value of $850,000 was very optimistic; information several vendors previously provided estimates this value to be $100,000. He also discovered that industry trade publications considered eight years to be the maximum life of similar conveyor belt systems. As a result, he prepared a second analysis, based on this new information. When Ungerman saw the second analysis, he told Thorton to discard this revised material, warned him not to discuss the new estimates with anyone, and ordered him not to present any of this information to the board of directors.

Required

A. Prepare an analysis of the net present value of the purchase and installation of the materials-movement system, using the revised estimates obtained by Thorton. Be sure to present supporting calculations.

B. Accurately describe the decision problem facing Thorton. — **Step 1** DEFINE THE PROBLEM

C. What alternatives does he have? — **Step 3** IDENTIFY AND ANALYZE AVAILABLE OPTIONS

D. What is the best alternative from a quantitative analysis?

E. What other qualitative factors should be considered and why? — **Step 4** SELECT THE BEST OPTION

Part III

Planning, Performance Evaluation, and Control

Chapter 9

The Use of Budgets in Planning and Decision Making

Study Tools

A Review of the Previous Chapter

Chapter 8 completed our study of the nature of costs in decision making and provided a set of tools that allow managers to consider the time value of money in making long-term capital investment decisions.

A Preview of This Chapter

In this chapter, we introduce the concept of budgeting and discuss how budgets assist managers in planning and decision making.

Key concepts include:

- Budgets must start with a top-down strategic plan that guides and integrates the whole company and its individual budgets.
- Budgeting is a management task, not a bookkeeping task.
- Budgets are used throughout managers' planning, operating, and control activities.
- Budgets are future oriented and make extensive use of estimates and forecasts.
- Flexible budgets are based on the actual number of units produced rather than on the budgeted units of production.

A Preview of Upcoming Chapters

In Chapter 10, we expand the discussion of flexible budgeting and introduce the concept of standard costs and variance analysis as tools to help managers "manage by exception" and evaluate performance in their control function. The chapter ends with a discussion of budgeting culture and the various behavioral issues involved in the budgeting process.

Learning Objectives

After studying the material in this chapter, you should be able to:

LO1 Understand the concept and purpose of budgets

LO2 Understand the use of financial budgets in operational planning and decision making

LO3 Prepare the sales budget and apply it to decision problems

LO4 Prepare production and purchases budgets and apply them to decision problems

LO5 Prepare direct labor and overhead budgets and apply them to decision problems

LO6 Prepare cash receipts and disbursements budgets

LO7 Prepare the summary cash budget and apply it to decision problems

LO8 Prepare budgeted income statements and balance sheets and evaluate the importance of budgeted financial statements for decision making

LO9 Understand the importance of financial budgets for merchandising and service companies

LO10 Understand the use and importance of nonfinancial budgets

LO11 Prepare flexible budgets and understand how they are used in activity-based costing environments

In this chapter, we introduce the concept of budgeting and discuss how budgets assist managers in planning and decision making. As discussed in Chapter 1, planning involves the development of both short-term (operational) and long-term (strategic) goals and objectives. Budgeting helps managers determine the resources needed to meet their goals and objectives and thus is a key ingredient in good decision making. In this chapter, we discuss and demonstrate the preparation of operational budgets for a traditional manufacturing company with inventory, as well as for a company operating in a JIT environment. We also discuss the use of operational budgets in merchandising and service companies.

The focus of budgeting is planning—planning for production requirements, planning for purchases of raw materials, planning for the use of direct labor and other resources, and, most important, planning for cash needs. In this chapter, we pay special attention to the preparation and use of the cash budget for managerial decision making and tie it into the preparation of the statement of cash flows used extensively by external users.

In the last section of the chapter, static and flexible budgets are discussed, with particular emphasis on the impact of ABC on flexible budgets. Nonfinancial budgets are also introduced. ■

INTRODUCTION

Budgets are plans dealing with the acquisition and use of resources over a specified time period. Everyone budgets, from the college student to the large multinational corporation. Although budgets are often thought of in terms of dollars (monetary or financial budgets), budgets are used for other purposes as well. For example, a college student carrying 15 credit hours, working 20 hours a week in a part-time job, and volunteering 10 hours per week at the local hospital might need to prepare a time budget to plan his or her use of time throughout the week. A monetary budget for a college student can be as simple as jotting down expected cash inflows from loans, parents, and maybe a part-time job and expected outflows for school and living expenses.

At the other end of the budgeting spectrum, multinational companies may have very sophisticated budgets, used to plan for the acquisition and use of thousands of different materials, the manufacture of hundreds of products, and the sale of those products.

PAUSE & Reflect

Have you ever prepared a budget? Was it a monetary or a nonmonetary budget? How did you use it?

© MICHAEL NEWMAN/PHOTOEDIT

Budgets for entertainment business are based on projected attendance figures. How flexible must the master budget be for the Portland Seadogs minor league franchise? How might this compare to the budget of a blockbuster movie that just opened for the summer season? **http://www.portlandseadogs.com**

COURTESY OF PORTLAND SEADOGS

IN THE NEWS

http://www.whitesox.com

Budgeting for a professional baseball team may seem easy, but according to Tim Buzard, VP of Finance for the Chicago White Sox, "it's a challenge to predict anything." "Attendance is the greatest variable in the budget and attendance is dependent on winning. Parking, concessions and souvenir sales, and even the number of security people hired all depend on attendance. A losing season can totally change the projections of revenue. The budgeting process must be very flexible and is sometimes changed on a daily basis to account for changes in attendance" ("Budgeting for Curve Balls," *Journal of Accountancy,* September 1998, 89–92).

THE BUDGET DEVELOPMENT PROCESS

LO1
Understand the concept and purpose of budgets

Traditionally, budgeting is a bottom-up process dependent on departmental managers providing a detailed plan for the upcoming month, quarter, or year. Some companies start their budget process based on last year's numbers, whereas others employ **zero-based budgeting.** Zero-based budgets require managers to build budgets from the ground up each year rather than just add a percentage increase to last year's numbers. Although we typically think of budgets as being prepared annually, as discussed in the preceding "In the News" feature, changing expectations often require that budgets be revised frequently.

APPLICATION IN BUSINESS

Many state governments prepare budgets biannually (every two years). This can cause major problems when unexpected costs are incurred because of natural disasters or when tax revenue falls because of unexpected downturns in the economy.

TECHNOLOGY FOCUS

In recent years, spreadsheets have given way to enterprise resource planning (ERP) software as a key budgeting tool. ERP systems link data from across all areas of a business—a key for effective budgeting and planning. ERP systems are discussed in more depth in Chapter 13.

Regardless of the specific process used, budgets, to be successful, must start with a top-down strategic plan that guides and integrates the whole company and its individual budgets. In addition, in order to motivate managers and other employees to meet the objectives and goals provided in budgets, companies must structure bonuses, merit pay, and other tangible and intangible rewards in ways that link these rewards to measurable goals outlined in the budgets.

***Key Concept:** Budgets must start with a top-down strategic plan that guides and integrates the whole company and its individual budgets.*

DILBERT BY SCOTT ADAMS

One of the misconceptions about budgeting is that the budgeting process is just a mechanical number-crunching task for bookkeepers. Although the preparation of budgets is often very mechanical (and can be a little tricky), the use of spreadsheets, such as Lotus 1-2-3 and Microsoft Excel, make their preparation much simpler. In reality, budgeting is a management task, not a mechanical bookkeeping task, and it requires a great deal of planning and thoughtful input from a broad range of managers in a company. This concept of budgeting as a management task will focus our discussion of the budgeting process in this chapter.

Key Concept: *Budgeting is a management task, not a bookkeeping task.*

BUDGETS FOR PLANNING, OPERATING, AND CONTROL

LO2
Understand the use of financial budgets in operational planning and decision making

Managers use budgeting as they go about their **planning, operating,** and **control** activities (see Exhibit 9-1). Planning is the cornerstone of good management. Planning involves developing objectives and goals for the organization, as well as the actual preparation of budgets. Operating involves day-to-day decision making by managers, which is facilitated by budgets. Control involves ensuring that the objectives and goals developed by the organization are being attained. Control often involves a comparison of budgets to actual performance and the use of budgets for performance evaluation purposes. The use of budgets for cost control and performance evaluation is discussed in more depth in Chapter 10.

Key Concept: *Budgets are used throughout managers' planning, operating, and control activities.*

EXHIBIT 9-1 Budgeting Is an Integral Part of Managers' Planning, Operating, and Control Activities

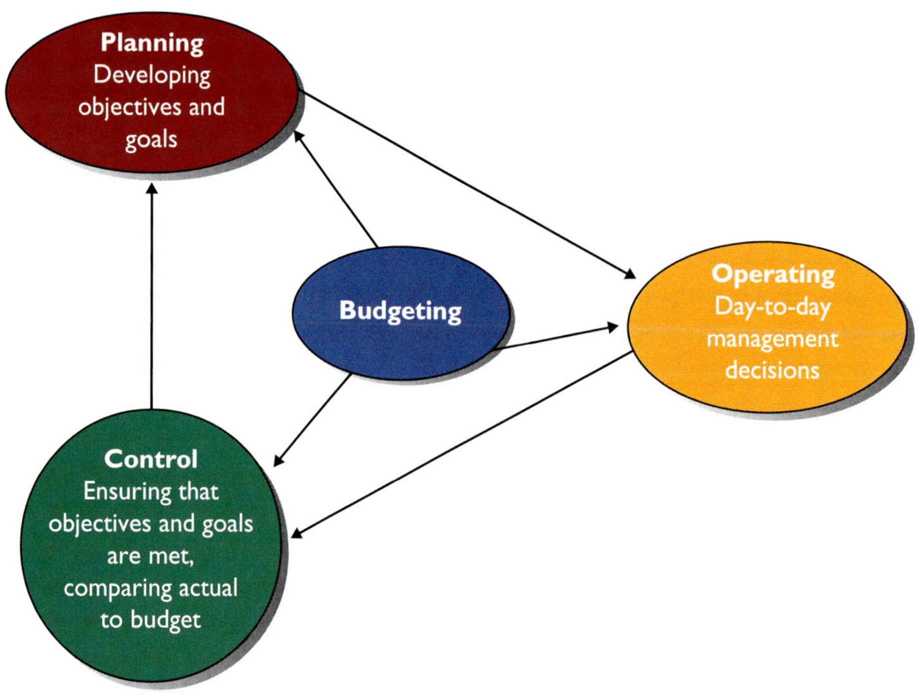

EXHIBIT 9-2 The Operating Cycle

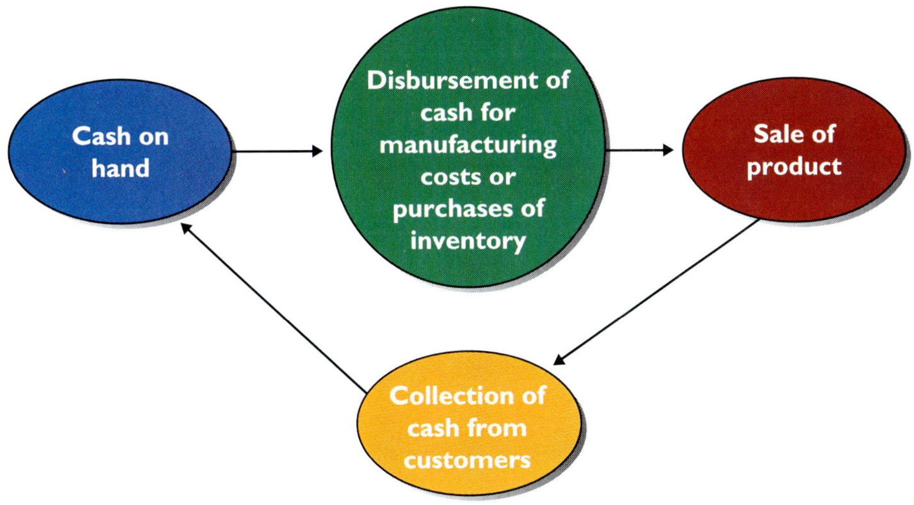

In this chapter, we emphasize the use of budgets in planning and operating activities, including decisions concerning how much of a product to produce, how much material to buy, how much labor to hire, and the borrowing and investment of cash. The concept of budgeting for cash is tied back to the operating cycle discussed in your financial accounting course. The operating cycle focuses on cash flow, beginning with the investment of cash in inventory or the use of cash to manufacture products, continuing with the sale of those products to customers, and ending with the collection of cash from those customers (see Exhibit 9-2).

One of the main reasons small businesses fail is the lack of adequate planning for cash needs. A small business that views budgeting for cash as too time consuming or expensive is destined for failure. With the availability and affordability of computers in today's business environment, even the smallest business can very easily perform the analysis necessary to successfully plan and budget for the future.

ADVANTAGES OF BUDGETING

Although the previous introduction pointed out the clear need for budgeting as a planning, operating, and control tool requiring managers to think about organizational goals and objectives, budgeting has other advantages as well.

1. The budgeting process forces communication throughout the organization.
2. The budgeting process forces management to focus on the future and not be distracted by daily crisis in the organization.
3. The budgeting process can help management identify and deal with potential bottlenecks or constraints before they become major problems.
4. The budgeting process can increase the coordination of organizational activities and help facilitate goal congruence. Goal congruence refers to making sure that the personal goals of the managers are closely aligned with the goals of the organization.
5. The budgeting process can define specific goals and objectives that can become benchmarks, or standards of performance, for evaluating future performance.

BUDGETING FOR SALES

LO3
Prepare the sales budget and apply it to decision problems

All organizations require the forecasting of future sales volume and the preparation of a sales budget. A professional baseball team needs to forecast the number of fans that attend home games each season. Airlines need to forecast the number of passengers who fly on each route, and hotels need to forecast occupancy rates for various days and months. Retail stores, such as Wal-Mart and J. C. Penney, must forecast retail sales of many different products at many different locations. Manufacturing firms, such as Ford, Chrysler, and General Motors, must forecast consumer demand for each model of car or truck that they sell.

The **sales forecast** and **sales budget** are the starting points in the preparation of production budgets for manufacturing companies, purchases budgets for merchandising companies, and labor budgets for service companies. The sales budget is also used in planning the cash needs for manufacturing, merchandising, and service companies.

CROSS-FUNCTIONAL APPLICATIONS

In large companies, preparation of the sales forecast is usually accomplished by the marketing department and requires significant effort in the area of market research to arrive at an accurate forecast of expected sales. In smaller companies, the sales forecast may be made by an individual or a small group of managers.

There are many different ways to forecast sales. Most forecasting will combine information from many different sources either informally or through the use of computer programs. Regardless of the size of the company or the sophistication of the forecasting methods used, the usual starting point in sales forecasting is last year's level of sales. Other factors and information sources typically used in sales forecasting are as follows:

1. Historical data, such as sales trends for the company, competitors, and the industry (if available).
2. General economic trends or factors, such as inflation rates, interest rates, population growth, and personal spending.
3. Regional and local factors expected to affect sales.
4. Anticipated price changes in both purchasing costs and sales prices.
5. Anticipated marketing or advertising plans.
6. The impact of new products or changes in product mix on the entire product line.
7. Other factors, such as political and legal events and weather changes.

This list is not meant to be all-inclusive, and every organization will have unique factors that it needs to consider. Each organization will also attach a different level of importance to each factor.

IN THE NEWS

Sometimes, weather can affect your business in ways that cannot be easily predicted. In the winter of 1999, New England ski areas had plenty of snow, but the communities at lower elevations (from which most of their customers came) did not. Even though the ski resorts used extensive advertising to promote the good ski conditions, skiers stayed away from the slopes because of the warm weather and lack of snow at home.

The size and complexity of the organization will often determine the complexity of the sales forecasting system. Some companies will use elaborate econometric planning models

© MIRO VINTONIV/STOCK, BOSTON

and regression analysis to forecast sales volume. Others may use very informal models and rely heavily on the intuition and opinions of managers. Regardless of the level of sophistication used in forecasting models, it is important to remember that sales forecasting is still just that—a forecast.

As you will see in the rest of this chapter, all the remaining budgets and the decisions that are made based on their forecasts are dependent on this estimate of sales. For that reason, it is important to estimate sales with as much accuracy as possible. A small error in a sales forecast can cause larger errors in other budgets that depend on the sales forecast.

PAUSE & Reflect

What unique factors might a CPA firm specializing in tax planning and the preparation of tax returns consider in forecasting sales?

Key Concept: *Budgets are future oriented and make extensive use of estimates and forecasts.*

OPERATING BUDGETS—AN EXAMPLE

Operating budgets are used by companies to plan for the short term—usually one year or less. As an example of the budgeting process, let's consider the case of Tina's Fine Juices, a bottler of orange juice located in the Northeast. Tina's produces bottled orange juice from fruit concentrate purchased from suppliers in Florida, Arizona, and California. The only ingredients in the juice are water and concentrate. The juice is blended, pasteurized, and bottled for sale in 12-ounce plastic bottles. The process is heavily automated and is centered on five machines that control the mixing and bottling of the juice. Each machine is run by one employee and can process 10 bottles of juice per minute, or 600 bottles per hour. The amount of labor required is very small per bottle of juice. The average worker can process 10 bottles of juice per minute, or 600 bottles per hour.

TINA'S Fine Juices

The juice is sold by a number of grocery stores under their store brand name and in smaller restaurants, delis, and bagel shops under the name of Tina's Fine Juices. Tina's has been in business for several years and uses a sophisticated sales forecasting model based on prior sales, expected changes in demand, and economic factors affecting the industry.

PAUSE & Reflect

What kind of costing system is Tina's likely to use?

TINA'S Fine Juices

Sales of juice are highly seasonal, peaking in the first quarter of the year. Forecasted sales for the first quarter of 2003 are as follows:

Sales Forecast

January	250,000 bottles
February	325,000 bottles
March	450,000 bottles

Tina's sells the juice for $1.05 per 12-ounce bottle, in cartons of 50 bottles. A sales budget for the first quarter of the year is as follows.[1] A sales budget is the projected volume of product to be sold times the expected sales price per unit.

Sales Budget

	January	February	March	First Quarter
Projected sales (bottles)	250,000	325,000	450,000	1,025,000
Price per bottle	$1.05	$1.05	$1.05	$1.05
Total projected sales	$262,500	$341,250	$472,500	$1,076,250

BUDGETING FOR A TRADITIONAL MANUFACTURING COMPANY WITH INVENTORY

LO4
Prepare production and purchases budgets and apply them to decision problems

PRODUCTION BUDGET

For manufacturing companies, the next step in the budgeting process is to complete the **production budget.** Once the sales volume has been projected, companies must forecast how many units of product to produce in order to meet the sales projections. Although this might seem to be an easy task—just manufacture what you plan to sell—traditional manufacturing companies, as you will recall from Chapter 2, often choose to hold a minimum level of finished-goods inventory (as well as direct material inventory) to serve as buffers in case of unexpected demand for products or unexpected problems in production.

In this case, the sales forecast must be adjusted to account for any expected increase or decrease in finished-goods inventory. A basic production budget is as follows:

Basic Production Budget

Sales forecast (in units)
\+ Projected ending inventory
= Total projected production needs
− Beginning inventory
= Projected production volume

[1]The sales budget and the remaining operating budgets and budgeted financial statements for Tina's Fine Juices were prepared using Microsoft Excel (see the Chapter 9 template on the CD accompanying the textbook). All dollar amounts on the spreadsheets are rounded to the nearest dollar, resulting in some math "errors" in the budgets. As you will see, the use of spreadsheets greatly simplifies the mechanical budget process, particularly when changes are made to the sales or production budgets.

In the basic production budget, the key term is *projected*. The overriding concept in budgeting is that *budgets are estimates*.

Tina's Fine Juices tries to maintain at least 10 percent of the next month's sales forecast in inventory at the end of each month. Because sales have been projected to increase very rapidly, the company does not want to run the risk of running out of juice to ship to customers, so Tina's Fine Juices keeps a minimum amount on hand at all times. Other problems, such as shipping delays or weather, could also affect the amount of desired ending inventory. Based on these requirements Tina's would want to have 32,500 bottles of juice on hand at the end of January (10 percent of February's forecasted sales of 325,000). A production budget for Tina's Fine Juices is as follows:

Production Budget

	January	February	March	First Quarter
Projected sales (bottles)	250,000	325,000	450,000	1,025,000
+ Projected ending inventory	32,500	45,000	50,000	50,000
= Total projected needs	282,500	370,000	500,000	1,075,000
– Beginning inventory	25,000 (given)	32,500	45,000	25,000
= Projected production (bottles)	257,500	337,500	455,000	1,050,000

You should note that to complete the production budget for the first quarter, we need to have some additional information. We need to know the forecasted sales for April in order to determine the projected ending inventory for the end of March. April sales are projected to be 500,000 units, so the projected ending inventory is 50,000 units.[2] The beginning inventory for January is 25,000 bottles. (This amount is also the ending inventory for December.) Closer examination of the production budget model will show that projected production needs are just the projected sales, plus or minus any projected change in inventory during the month. In January, the projected sales are 250,000 units, and inventories are projected to increase by 7,500 units (from 25,000 to 32,500). If we add the projected inventory increase to the sales projection, we have a projected production level of 257,500 (250,000 + 7,500). You should also note that the arrows in the exhibit point out that the projected ending inventory for any month is the projected beginning inventory for the next month.

Projected production = Projected sales + Change in finished-goods inventory

One other important concept in the production budget model is that the projected ending inventory for the quarter is the ending inventory on the last day of the quarter, in this case March 31, and that the projected beginning inventory is the beginning inventory on the first day of the quarter, or January 1.

MATERIAL PURCHASES BUDGET

Once the production budget is completed, the next budget to be prepared is the **material purchases budget.** Once again, because many traditional companies desire to keep materials on hand at all times in order to plan for unforeseen changes in demand, the desired ending inventory for materials must be added to the projected production needs for materials

[2]The Microsoft Excel template shows both December and April sales and the links between those months and the first-quarter production budget.

to arrive at the total expected needs for materials. Then an adjustment is made for any inventory on hand at the beginning of the month.

Tina's Fine Juices needs to prepare two purchases budgets—one for the concentrate used in its orange juice and one for the bottles that are purchased from an outside supplier. Tina's has determined that it takes one gallon of orange concentrate for every 32 bottles of finished product. Each gallon of concentrate costs \$4.80. Tina's also requires 20 percent of next month's direct material needs to be on hand at the end of the budget period. The material purchases budget for orange concentrate follows. Note that the starting point for this budget is the production budget. The next step in the preparation of the direct materials purchases budget is to compute the raw material needed based on the projected production. In this case, we take the number of bottles to be produced and divide by 32, which is the number of bottles that can be produced with one gallon of concentrate. The ending inventory needs are then added to that figure to arrive at the projected direct materials needed to fulfill the production and ending inventory needs. Beginning inventory is then subtracted from the projected needs to arrive at the projected purchases in gallons, and the last step is to convert that amount to dollars by taking the number of gallons times the price per gallon.

To calculate the projected ending inventory in March, Tina's must estimate sales for May. (April sales were already estimated to be 500,000 bottles.) If May sales are estimated at 400,000 bottles, April ending inventory will be estimated to be 40,000 (0.10 × 400,000), and April production will be 490,000 bottles (April sales of 500,000 + ending inventory of 40,000 − beginning inventory of 50,000). The production of 490,000 bottles in April requires 15,313 gallons of concentrate $\left(\frac{490{,}000 \text{ bottles}}{32 \text{ bottles per gallon}}\right)$. Accordingly, Tina's will plan on holding 3,063 gallons of concentrate in inventory at the end of March (20 percent of the material usage for April).

Materials Purchases Budget—Orange Concentrate

	January	February	March	First Quarter
Projected production (bottles)	257,500	337,500	455,000	1,050,000
Orange concentrate needed (gallons) for production*	8,047	10,547	14,219	32,813
+ Projected ending inventory	2,109	2,844	3,063†	3,063
= Projected needs	10,156	13,391	17,281	35,875
− Projected beginning inventory	1,609‡	2,109	2,844	1,609
= Gallons to be purchased	8,547	11,281	14,438	34,266
Projected purchases§	\$41,027	\$54,150	\$69,300	\$164,477

* Projected production divided by 32 bottles per gallon.

† May sales are projected to be 400,000 bottles, so April ending inventory is 40,000 bottles and production for April is projected to be 490,000 bottles. The production of 490,000 bottles requires 15,313 gallons of concentrate. Twenty percent of 15,313 gallons is 3,063 gallons.

‡ This is the actual beginning inventory (given).

§ Projected gallons times \$4.80 per gallon.

Note: Table may not foot, owing to rounding on the accompanying Excel spreadsheet.

Tina's will prepare a similar budget for bottles. The bottles are purchased from an outside supplier for \$0.10 per bottle. The supplier provides labels and caps for the bottles as

Materials Purchases Budget—Bottles

	January	February	March	First Quarter
Projected production (bottles)	257,500	337,500	455,000	1,050,000
+ Projected ending inventory	67,500	91,000	98,000*	98,000
= Projected needs	325,000	428,500	553,000	1,148,000
− Projected beginning inventory	51,500†	67,500	91,000	51,500
= Bottles to be purchased	273,500	361,000	462,000	1,096,500
Projected purchases ($)‡	$27,350	$36,100	$46,200	$109,650

* May sales are projected to be 400,000 bottles, so April ending inventory is 40,000 bottles and production for April is projected to be 490,000 bottles. Twenty percent of 490,000 bottles is 98,000.

† This is the actual beginning inventory of bottles (given).

‡ Projected bottles times $0.10 per bottle.

part of the purchase price. Tina's has the same inventory policy for bottles and orange concentrate. A material purchases budget for bottles is as follows:

DIRECT LABOR BUDGET

The **direct labor budget** is one of the easiest budgets to prepare. As with the material purchases budget, the direct labor budget starts with the production budget. However, unlike the material budget, no adjustments need to be made for beginning and ending inventory.

The direct labor budget is prepared by simply multiplying the units to be produced by the number of direct labor hours required to produce each unit. As was discussed earlier, the production process utilizes a worker assigned to each of the five mixing and bottling machines. Each machine (and thus each worker) can process 600 bottles of orange juice per hour. At Tina's Fine Juices, factory workers are paid an average of $15 per hour, including fringe benefits and payroll taxes. If the production schedule doesn't allow for full utilization of the workers and machines, the worker is temporarily moved to another department. Dividing the labor rate of $15 by the time required per bottle shows that the amount of direct labor cost per bottle of juice is $0.025 ($\frac{\$15}{600 \text{ bottles}}$). A direct labor budget for the first quarter is as follows:

PAUSE & *Reflect*

Why are we not concerned with inventories in the direct labor budget?

LO5
Prepare direct labor and overhead budgets and apply them to decision problems

Direct Labor Budget

	January	February	March	First Quarter
Projected production (bottles)	257,500	337,500	455,000	1,050,000
Direct labor time per 600 bottles	1 hour	1 hour	1 hour	1 hour
Direct labor hours needed for production	429.17 (257,500/600)	562.5 (337,500/600)	758.33 (455,000/600)	1,750 (1,050,000/600)
Direct labor rate per hour	$15	$15	$15	$15
Projected direct labor cost	$6,438	$8,438	$11,375	$26,250

Tina's Fine Juices

MANUFACTURING-OVERHEAD BUDGET

Preparation of the **manufacturing-overhead budget** involves estimating overhead costs. As was discussed in detail in Part I of this book, estimating overhead can be accomplished in a number of ways using plantwide or departmental predetermined overhead rates, or activity-based costing. At Tina's Fine Juices, most of the production process is automated, the juice is mixed by machine, and machines do the bottling and packaging. Overhead costs are incurred almost entirely in the mixing and bottling process. Consequently, Tina's has chosen to use a plantwide cost driver (machine hours) to apply manufacturing overhead to products.

However, as you will recall from Chapter 5, not all overhead is expected to behave in the same fashion, as production increases and decreases each month. Although variable overhead costs will vary in direct proportion to the number of bottles of juice produced, fixed overhead costs will remain constant regardless of production. For budgeting purposes, Tina's separates variable overhead from fixed overhead and calculates a predetermined overhead rate for variable manufacturing-overhead costs.

Tina's Fine Juices has estimated that variable overhead will total $438,000 for the year and that the machines will run approximately 8,000 hours at the projected production volume for the year (4,775,000 bottles). The estimated machine hours are 80 percent of capacity for the five machines. Therefore, Tina's predetermined overhead rate for variable overhead is $54.75 per machine hour ($\frac{\$438{,}000}{8{,}000 \text{ machine hours}}$). Tina's has also estimated fixed overhead to be $1,480,000 per year ($123,333 per month), of which $1,240,000 per year ($103,333 per month) is depreciation on existing property, plant, and equipment.

The manufacturing-overhead budget is presented next. Note that variable overhead is budgeted based on the predetermined overhead rate and varies with production each month, whereas fixed manufacturing overhead is budgeted at a constant $123,333 per month.

Manufacturing Overhead Budget

	January	February	March	First Quarter
Budgeted machine hours*	429.17	562.5	758.33	1,750
Variable overhead rate	$ 54.75	$ 54.75	$ 54.75	$ 54.75
Projected variable overhead	$ 23,497	$ 30,797	$ 41,519	$ 95,813
Budgeted fixed overhead	$123,333	$123,333	$123,333	$370,000
Total projected manufacturing overhead	$146,830	$154,130	$164,852	$465,813

*Budgeted machine hours are the same as budgeted labor hours. Each machine can process 600 bottles of orange juice per hour.

The material purchases budget, the direct labor budget, and the manufacturing-overhead budget are summarized in a total manufacturing-cost budget. This budget provides Tina's Fine Juices with an estimate of the total manufacturing costs expected to be incurred in the first quarter of 2003.

Total Manufacturing Cost Budget

	January	February	March	First Quarter
Projected material cost—concentrate	$41,027	$54,150	$69,300	$164,477
Projected material cost—bottles	27,350	36,100	46,200	109,650
Projected direct labor cost	6,438	8,438	11,375	26,250
Projected manufacturing-overhead cost	146,830	154,130	164,852	465,813
Total projected manufacturing costs	221,645	252,818	291,727	766,189

Note: Table may not foot, owing to rounding on the accompanying Excel spreadsheet.

CASH BUDGETS

WHY FOCUS ON CASH?

LO6
Prepare cash receipts and disbursements budgets

Many managers consider managing cash flow to be the single most important consideration in running a successful business. After all, cash, *not* income, pays the bills. Whereas income (earnings per share) is often important to external investors, cash flow often takes center stage for managers.

IN THE NEWS

In fact, external investors sometimes focus on cash flow as well. Cash flow valuations are now in vogue in the cable, high-tech, Internet, pharmaceutical, and financial-services sectors. Stock analysts sometimes use cash flow to help value companies because it "ignores accounting tricks and thus shows the true economic health of companies" ("Analysts Increasingly Favor Using Cash Flow over Reported Earnings in Stock Valuations," by Elizabeth MacDonald, *Wall Street Journal,* April 1, 1999, C2).

The timing of cash inflows and outflows is critical to the overall planning process. When cash inflows are delayed because of the extension of credit to buyers, there may not be sufficient cash to pay suppliers, creditors, and employee wages. Timely payment is necessary to maintain good business relationships with suppliers (and to keep employees happy) and to take the maximum discounts that may be available on purchases. Cash budgeting forces managers to focus on cash flow and to plan for the purchase of materials, the payment of creditors, and the payment of salaries. Sufficient cash must be available to pay dividends to stockholders and to acquire new fixed assets. As can be seen in the following example, cash budgets also point out the need for borrowing cash or when excess cash can be invested or used to repay debt.

THE CASH RECEIPTS BUDGET

The first cash budget that must be prepared is the **cash receipts budget.** The cash receipts budget shows cash receipts that are generated from operating activities—cash sales of inventory or services and customer payments on account. Other cash receipts (from the sale of property, investment income, etc.) are included in the summary cash budget.

TINA'S Fine Juices

All the sales of Tina's Fine Juices are on account. Based on experience in previous years, Tina's estimates that 50 percent of the sales each month will be paid for in the month of sale. Tina's also estimates that 35 percent of the month's sales will be collected in the month following sale and that 15 percent of each month's sales will be collected in the second month following sale.[3] A cash receipts budget for cash received from operating activities is presented in the following table. As you will recall from the sales budget, sales for January, February, and March were projected to be $262,500, $341,250, and $472,500, respectively. Because collections lag sales by up to two months (some of November's sales will not be collected until January, and some of December's sales will not be collected until February), completing the cash receipts budget also requires that we include sales for November and December. November's sales were $200,000, whereas December's sales were $250,000.

Cash Receipts Budget—Operating Activities

	Cash Receipts			
	January	**February**	**March**	**First Quarter**
50% of January sales ($262,500)	$131,250			$131,250
35% of December sales ($250,000)	87,500			87,500
15% of November sales($200,000)	30,000			30,000
50% of February sales ($341,250)		$170,625		170,625
35% of January sales ($262,500)		91,875		91,875
15% of December sales ($250,000)		37,500		37,500
50% of March sales ($472,500)			$236,250	236,250
35% of February sales ($341,250)			119,438	119,438
15% of January sales ($262,500)			39,375	39,375
Totals	$248,750	$300,000	$395,063	$943,812

Note: Table may not foot, owing to rounding on the accompanying Excel spreadsheet.

The preparation of the cash receipts budget is straightforward once the payment scheme is set. In each month, we collect 50 percent of that month's sales (50 percent of January's sales are collected in January), 35 percent of the previous month's sales (35 percent of December's sales are collected in January), and 15 percent of the second previous month's sales (15 percent of November's sales are collected in January). And then the payment scheme is repeated for the remainder of the months in the budget.

An alternative way to look at the cash receipts budget is as follows:

Cash Receipts Budget—Operating Activities

	Cash Receipts			
Sales	**January**	**February**	**March**	**First Quarter**
November ($200,000)	$ 30,000 (15%)			$ 30,000
December ($250,000)	87,500 (35%)	$ 37,500 (15%)		125,000
January ($262,500)	131,250 (50%)	91,875 (35%)	$ 39,375 (15%)	262,500
February ($341,250)		170,625 (50%)	119,438 (35%)	290,063
March ($472,500)			236,250 (50%)	236,250
Totals	$248,750	$300,000	$395,063	$943,812

Note: Table may not foot, owing to rounding on the accompanying Excel spreadsheet.

[3]It would not be unusual for some of the sales to never be collected. If Tina's thinks that some of the accounts receivable are uncollectible, the cash receipts budget should be adjusted accordingly.

A closer look at the cash receipts budget shows that budgeted cash receipts are significantly different from budgeted sales revenue. In February and March, cash receipts are expected to be less than sales revenue. When sales are increasing, and there is a lag between sales and the collection of cash, this is usually the case. It seems ironic, but businesses that are growing rapidly will often be short of cash. The next component in the cash budgeting process is the **cash disbursements budget.** The cash disbursements budget includes cash outflows resulting from operating activities—payments to suppliers for materials, cash outflows for salaries and other labor costs, and cash outflows for overhead expenditures. Cash disbursements for selling and administrative costs are also included, although other cash outflows (for equipment purchases, payment of dividends, etc.) are usually not included.[4] These nonoperating disbursements will be included in the summary cash budget but not in the cash disbursements budget for operating activities.

Budgeting for the cash disbursements related to materials, labor, and overhead is not as easy as just looking at the material, labor, and overhead budgets. Purchases of material are often made on account, resulting in lags between the date items are purchased and the date cash actually changes hands. The manufacturing-overhead budget often includes noncash items, such as depreciation, that must be adjusted as well.

A cash disbursements budget for Tina's Fine Juices follows. Tina's has a policy of paying 50 percent of the direct materials purchases in the month of purchase and the balance in

Cash Disbursements Budget—Operating Activities

	CASH DISBURSEMENTS			
	January	**February**	**March**	**First Quarter**
Material purchases: concentrate				
December	$ 18,220			$ 18,220
January	20,513	$ 20,513		41,025
February		27,075	$ 27,075	54,150
March			34,650	34,650
Material purchases: bottles				
December	12,146			12,146
January	13,675	13,675		27,350
February		18,050	18,050	36,100
March			23,100	23,100
Total disbursements for material	64,554	79,313	102,875	246,741
Total disbursements for direct labor	6,438	8,438	11,375	26,250
Manufacturing overhead: December	20,917			20,917
Manufacturing overhead: January	21,748	21,748		43,497
Manufacturing overhead: February		25,398	25,398	50,797
Manufacturing overhead: March			30,759	30,759
Total disbursements for overhead	42,666	47,147	56,158	145,971
Total disbursements for selling and administrative costs	100,000 (given)	100,000 (given)	100,000 (given)	300,000
Total cash disbursements	$213,657	$234,897	$270,408	$718,962

Note: Table may not foot, owing to rounding on the accompanying Excel spreadsheet.

[4]A separate budget for selling and administrative expenses (period costs) would likely be prepared by Tina's Fine Juices. It would include both variable selling and administrative expenses, such as commissions and shipping costs, as well as fixed selling and administrative expenses related to advertising, salaries, insurance, rent, depreciation of equipment used in selling and administrative activities, etc. An example of a selling and administrative expense budget for a merchandising company is shown later in the chapter.

the month after purchase. This policy offsets to a certain extent the lag in cash receipts from sales. Purchases of direct material are taken directly off the material purchases budgets (adjusted for the payment lag). All direct labor costs are paid in the month incurred and come directly from the direct labor budget. Manufacturing-overhead costs are paid on a lag, with 50 percent paid for in the month incurred and 50 percent in the following month. However, the manufacturing-overhead budget must be adjusted for depreciation of property, plant, and equipment, which does not have a direct impact on cash flow.[5] As was discussed earlier, of the total budgeted fixed overhead included in the manufacturing-overhead budget ($123,333 per month), $103,333 per month pertains to depreciation and will not be included in the cash disbursements budget. Cash disbursements for selling and administrative costs are expected to be $100,000 per month.

PAUSE & *Reflect*

Can you trace each of the amounts in the cash disbursements budget back to the original budget in which it appears?

A **summary cash budget** consists of three sections: (1) cash flows from operating activities, (2) cash flows from investing activities, and (3) cash flows from financing activities. These three sections are the same as used in the cash flow statement prepared under generally accepted accounting principles. Preparation and use of the statement of cash flows is covered in detail in Chapter 15.

LO7
Prepare the summary cash budget and apply it to decision problems

Cash flows from operating activities have already been discussed. Cash flows from investing activities include purchases and sales of property, plant, equipment and other investments, and interest and dividends earned on investment assets. Cash flows from financing activities include payments for the retirement of any debt issued by the company, sales or repurchases of stock, payment of dividends, and any borrowing or repayments of other long-term liabilities.

Summary Cash Budget

	January	February	March	First Quarter
Beginning cash balance	$ 50,000	$ 50,000	$ 50,000	$ 50,000
Cash Flows from Operating Activities:				
Cash receipts	248,750	300,000	395,063	943,812
Cash disbursements	(213,657)	(234,898)	(270,408)	(718,962)
Income taxes			(3,190)[*]	(3,190)
Cash Flows from Investing Activities				
Equipment purchases		(75,000)		(75,000)
Cash Flows from Financing Activities				
Payment of dividends	(50,000)			(50,000)
Interest on long-term debt			(30,000)[†]	(30,000)
Cash balance before borrowing/repayment	35,093	40,102	141,464	116,659
Borrowing from line of credit	14,907[‡]	9,898[§]		24,805
Repayments of line of credit			(24,805)[‖]	(24,805)
Interest on line of credit			(538)[#]	(538)
Final cash balance	$ 50,000	$ 50,000	$ 116,122	$ 116,122

*See the Pro Forma Income Statement on page 308.

†Long-term liabilities (see the Pro Forma Balance Sheet on page 309) are $1,500,000. Interest is paid quarterly at an annual rate of 8%. $1,500,000 × 8% × 3/12 = $30,000.

‡The minimum cash balance at the end of each month is $50,000: $50,000 − $35,093 = $14,907.

§The minimum cash balance at the end of each month is $50,000: $50,000 − $40,102 = $9,898.

‖Because there is excess cash at the end of March, the draws on the line of credit ($14,907 and $9,898) are repaid at the end of March.

#The line of credit is borrowed against in January and February and repaid in March. Interest on the line of credit is calculated as $14,907 × 10% × 3/12 + $9,898 × 10% × 2/12.

Note: interest on the repaid amounts is also paid in March.

---

[5]You will recall from Chapter 8 that depreciation can have an indirect impact on cash flow through its impact on income taxes. The impact of income tax is taken into account in the summary cash budget.

Summary cash budgets can be fairly straightforward or very complex, depending on the size and complexity of the company. Tina's Fine Juices has a fairly simple summary cash budget (see page 306).

Cash receipts and disbursements from operating activities have already been summarized in the cash receipts and disbursements budgets. Tina's plans to buy some new machinery in February at a cost of $75,000. The company also plans on paying a dividend of $50,000 in January. Tina's also desires to keep a cash balance of at least $50,000 on hand at the end of any month. If the projected cash balance is less than that, a line of credit at Tina's local bank will be used to make up the shortage. If Tina's draws on the line of credit, the company is charged an interest rate of 10 percent annually. If the line of credit is used, money is borrowed at the beginning of the month. Repayments are made at the end of months in which there is sufficient excess cash (over $50,000) to pay back the entire line of credit. Last, but not least, Tina's pays estimated income taxes on a quarterly basis (in March, June, September, and December) on the income earned during the respective quarter. Tina's estimates that its total tax liability (federal and state) is around 35 percent of taxable income.

BUDGETED FINANCIAL STATEMENTS

LO8
Prepare budgeted income statements and balance sheets and evaluate the importance of budgeted financial statements for decision making

Companies may also desire to prepare budgeted financial statements. These are used both for internal planning purposes and to provide information to external users. For example, a bank might want to examine a budgeted income statement and balance sheet before lending money to a company. The budgeted financial statements are often called **pro forma financial statements.**

A pro forma statement of cost of goods manufactured and cost of goods sold is as follows:

Pro Forma Cost of Goods Manufactured (Absorption Costing)

	Amount	Where Information Obtained
Beginning inventory—raw materials	$ 12,873	Material purchases budgets (pp. 300, 301) (1,609 gallons of concentrate × $4.80 per gallon + 51,500 bottles × $0.10 per bottle)
Purchases of raw material	274,127	Material purchases budgets (pp. 300, 301)($164,477 + $109,650)
Raw materials available for use	287,000	
Ending inventory—raw materials	(24,500)	Material purchases budgets (pp. 300, 301) (3,063 gallons × $4.80 per gallon + 98,000 bottles × $0.10 per bottle)
Raw material used	262,500	
Direct labor cost	26,250	Direct labor budget (p. 301)
Manufacturing overhead	465,813	Manufacturing-overhead budget (p. 302)
Total manufacturing costs	754,563	
Beginning inventory—WIP	—	Assumed to be $0
Ending inventory—WIP	—	Assumed to be $0
Cost of goods manufactured	754,563	
Beginning inventory—finished goods	17,966	Production budget (p. 299) (25,000 bottles × $0.71864 per bottle [given])
Cost of goods manufactured	754,563	Pro forma cost of goods manufactured (p. 307)

(continued)

Pro Forma Cost of Goods Sold (Absorption Costing)

Description	Amount	Where Information Obtained
Beginning inventory—finished goods	$ 17,966	Production budget (p. 299) (25,000 bottles × $0.71864 per bottle (given))
Cost of goods manufactured	754,563	Pro forma cost of goods manufactured (p. 307)
Less: Ending inventory—finished goods	35,932	Production budget (p. 299) and the pro forma cost of goods manufactured (50,000 bottles of juice × $754,563 cost of goods manufactured / 1,050,000 bottles produced)
Cost of goods sold	$736,597	

Note that the cost of goods manufactured and the cost of goods sold are calculated using absorption costing. Likewise, the following pro forma income statement is prepared using the traditional format:

Pro Forma Income Statement (Traditional Format)

Description	Amount	Where Information Obtained
Sales revenue	$1,076,250	Sales budget (p. 298)
Cost of goods sold	736,597	Pro forma cost of goods sold (p. 308)
Gross margin	$ 339,653	
Selling, general, and administrative expenses	300,000	Cash disbursements budget (p. 305)
Operating income	$ 39,653	
Interest expense	30,538	Summary cash budget (pp. 306)
Income (before taxes)	$ 9,116	
Income taxes	3,191	(Income × 35%)
Net Income	5,925	

Note: Table may not foot, owing to rounding on the accompanying Excel spreadsheet.

Variable costing statements of cost of goods manufactured and cost of goods sold and a contribution format income statement are provided as part of the Chapter 9 template on the CD accompanying the textbook.

Concept Question: *The operating income on the contribution margin format income statement (on the template) is $30,844. Why is the income reported under the two methods different?*

Concept Answer: As you will recall from Chapter 6, variable costing and absorption costing will result in different levels of operating income when a company's production and sales are different (units produced are greater than units sold or vice versa). In this case, Tina's Fine Juices produces 1,050,000 bottles during the quarter but sells only 1,025,000 bottles. Because production is greater than sales, absorption costing will report higher income than variable costing. Further, the difference in the amount of operating income reported under the two methods ($8,809) is solely a result of treating fixed overhead differently and can be found by multiplying the fixed overhead per unit of production—$\frac{\$370{,}000}{1{,}050{,}000 \text{ bottles}} = \$0.35238$ per bottle—by the difference between units produced and units sold (25,000 bottles): 25,000 × $0.35238 = $8,809.

The pro forma balance sheet is as follows:

Pro Forma Balance Sheet

Description	Amount	Where Information Obtained
Current Assets		
Cash	$ 116,122	Summary cash budget (p. 306)
Accounts receivable	287,438	Sales budget (p. 298) ($341,250 × 0.15 + $472,500 × 0.50)
Inventory: Direct materials	24,500	Pro forma cost of goods manufactured (p. 307)
Inventory: Finished goods	35,932	Pro forma cost of goods sold (p. 308)
Total current assets	$ 463,991	
Fixed assets	5,075,000	$5,000,000 beginning balance (given) and summary cash budget (p. 306)
Total assets	$5,538,991	
Current Liabilities		
Accounts payable	88,509	Material purchases budgets (pp. 300, 301) and manufacturing-overhead budget (p. 302) ($69,300 × .5 + $46,200 × 0.5 + ($164,852 – $103,333 × 0.5))
Line of credit	—	Summary cash budget (p. 306)
Total current liabilities	$ 88,509	
Long-term liabilities	1,500,000	Beginning balance (given)
Total liabilities	$1,588,509	
Stockholders Equity		
Common stock	3,500,000	Beginning balance (given)
Retained earnings	450,481	Beginning balance of $494,556 (given) + income of $5,925 (pro forma income statement) – dividends paid of $50,000 (summary cash budget)
Total liabilities and stockholders equity	$5,538,991	

Note: Table may not foot, owing to rounding on the accompanying Excel spreadsheet.

As you can see, the set of operating budgets (sometimes called the master budget) form an interrelated set of planning tools that are vital for managers' decisions affecting the number of units to produce, the amount of materials to purchase, how many employees to schedule for a particular time period (and when to schedule training, for example), the timing of major acquisitions and sales of equipment, and the overall management of cash. However, what happens when key assumptions change? For example, in mid-February, Tina's receives a large new order for juice, increasing its budgeted sales to 350,000 bottles. Changing the sales budget changes all the budgets following it. If prepared by hand, changing such assumptions as sales or the price of materials or desired inventory levels would involve a long and tedious revision of each and every succeeding budget. However, when prepared as a template using spreadsheet software, the changes can be made in just a few seconds.

TINA'S Fine Juices

Concept Question: *Using the Chapter 9 template on the CD accompanying the textbook, what is the impact on ending cash and income of changing February sales to 350,000 bottles?*

Concept Answer: Ending cash increases to $123,511, and income (after-tax) is increased to $16,843. ■

Concept Question: *What happens to the amounts borrowed and repaid on the summary cash budget if February sales change to 375,000 bottles?*

Concept Answer: Interestingly, the amount borrowed in January increases when February sales increase. Why? Because more materials must be purchased and other costs must be incurred in January to meet the increased production schedule for February. Note that the repayment of the line of credit still occurs in March, as the cash balance at the end of February is not sufficient to repay the entire loan balance (without reducing the cash balance below $50,000). ■

BUDGETS FOR A MANUFACTURING COMPANY IN A JIT ENVIRONMENT

As we discussed more fully in Chapter 2, the physical flow of goods is streamlined in companies adopting just-in-time (JIT) techniques. Raw materials are immediately placed into production, and all goods are typically finished and shipped out immediately to customers, resulting in little raw material, work in process, or finished-goods inventory. Just as this process simplified cost flows, budgeting is simplified as well. In JIT companies, production is typically equal to sales, so the production budget and sales budget are essentially the same. Materials are purchased for current production, eliminating the need to account for beginning and ending inventories of raw materials. With no beginning or ending inventories of work in process (WIP) or finished goods, the cost of goods manufactured and the cost of goods sold are the same and are simply budgeted as the sum of raw materials used in production, direct labor costs incurred, and overhead costs incurred.

BUDGETS FOR MERCHANDISING COMPANIES AND SERVICE COMPANIES

LO9
Understand the importance of financial budgets for merchandising and service companies

The budgeting process for merchandising companies is similar to that of manufacturing companies, with a few important differences. Merchandising companies are not involved in manufacturing the goods they sell. A merchandising company buys finished goods from manufacturing companies and sells them to other companies for resale (wholesalers) or to final customers (retailers). Merchandising companies will still produce a sales budget but will not prepare budgets for production, direct material purchases, direct labor, or manufacturing overhead. However, merchandising companies will prepare a purchases budget (for finished goods) based on the projections in the sales budget. In addition, many merchandising companies hold some level of finished-goods inventory and will need to estimate desired inventory balances and to adjust sales projections accordingly.

In addition, selling and administrative expenses are often carefully budgeted in merchandising companies. A selling and administrative expense budget will include variable expenses, such as commissions, shipping costs, and some clerical expenses related to order taking and filling. The budget will also include fixed costs, such as rent, utilities, insurance, advertising, salaries of clerical workers and administrators, depreciation of property, plant and equipment, and so on. An example of a selling and administrative expense budget for a merchandising company is as follows:

Selling and Administrative Expense Budget

	January	February	March	First Quarter
Commissions	$ 50,000	$ 55,000	$ 45,000	$150,000
Shipping costs	10,000	12,000	8,000	30,000
Clerical salaries	15,000	16,000	13,000	44,000
Supplies	2,000	2,100	1,900	6,000
Rent	10,000	10,000	10,000	30,000
Utilities	2,500	2,500	2,500	7,500
Insurance	3,500	3,500	3,500	10,500
Advertising	5,000	5,000	5,000	15,000
Depreciation	20,000	20,000	20,000	60,000
Total	$118,000	$126,100	$108,900	$353,000

The preparation of cash budgets and budgeted financial statements in merchandising companies is similar to that in manufacturing companies. Although the budgeting process for merchandising is a little less complex than in manufacturing companies, it is just as important to effective decision making.

Service companies have the same need to budget for effective decision making, but once again, the budgets needed will differ slightly from those used in manufacturing companies. Service companies will prepare sales budgets and may prepare modified "production" budgets as well. For example, a CPA firm may budget for not only total revenues but also the amount of revenue expected to be generated by each type of engagement (tax, audit, etc.), the number of those engagements expected (how many tax returns will be prepared), and the number of labor hours expected to be incurred in each. As a result, the main focus of budgeting for service companies will often be the labor budget. The use of time budgets by service companies is discussed in more detail in a later section, on nonmonetary budgets.

Overhead is another important area of concern for service companies. A detailed budget of expected overhead expenditures (rent, utilities, insurance, etc.) is extremely useful in planning for cash outflows.

LIFE-CYCLE COSTS, THE VALUE CHAIN, AND BUDGETING

As discussed earlier in the book, a company must consider all the costs incurred throughout a product's life cycle (the value chain) in making production and pricing decisions. This includes costs incurred in product planning (research and development), product design, product testing, actual production, the distribution (sale) of the product, and customer service provided both during and after the sale.

EXHIBIT 9-3 Life-Cycle Costing

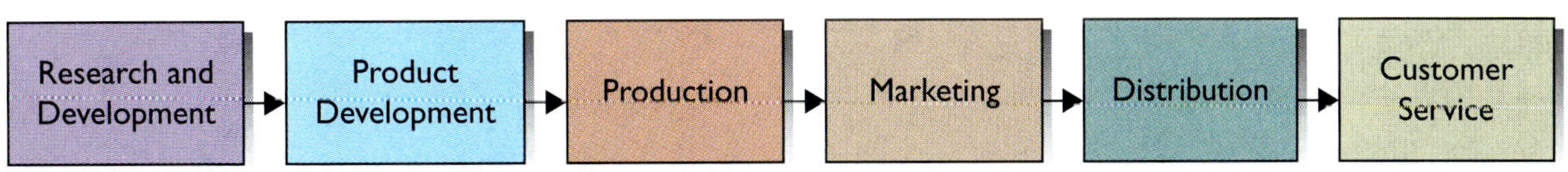

In making decisions to introduce new products, the forecasted sales over the life of the product must exceed its life-cycle costs. The product life cycle can be very short (a year or less) in some industries, such as electronics and computers, whereas in other industries and with other products, it can exceed several years. Given that a significant percentage of total costs are incurred before a new product is actually produced and sold, early and accurate budgeting is critically important in making good decisions regarding the introduction of new products.

Budgeting in an International Environment

PAUSE & Reflect

What type of issues might Tina's Fine Juices face if it builds a new bottling plant in Brazil?

In today's environment, many companies operate across national borders. Companies may make sales to foreign countries, purchase supplies internationally, manufacture products in other countries, or have foreign branches and subsidiaries. In budgeting, companies with international operations must consider such things as the following:

1. Translating foreign currency into U.S. dollars (and vice versa). Because of continual fluctuations in exchange rates, this can be challenging.
2. Predicting inflation rates (and prices) in countries with unstable economics. This can add a great deal of complexity and uncertainty to the budgeting process.
3. Predicting sales in countries with different consumer preferences.
4. Dealing with different labor laws, social customs, and norms affecting wage rates and the productivity of workers.

Company budgets must allow for volatile currency fluctuations around the globe.

© AFP/CORBIS

Nonmonetary Budgets

LO10
Understand the use and importance of nonfinancial budgets

Companies may also prepare nonmonetary budgets to help in the planning, operating, and control functions of managers. These budgets are just as important and in some cases may be more important than financial budgets focusing on costs and cash flows.

Examples of nonfinancial budgets are the following:

1. *Time budgets.* In service firms, such as CPA firms and law offices, time budgets are used to plan the number of hours expected to be incurred in each engagement (tax return preparation, audit, etc.). This allows firms to better plan the timing of engagements and to utilize employees as efficiently as possible. For example, if a time budget shows that professional staff will not be fully utilized in the summer, continuing education and other training courses might be planned at that time.
2. *Customer-satisfaction measures.* Customer satisfaction is an important measure of success for many companies. Consequently, many companies prepare budgets and measure key indicators of customer satisfaction. Although businesses may have many different measures of customer satisfaction, common indicators include the number of returned or defective items, the number of customer complaints, time waiting to be served, and so on.

PAUSE & *Reflect*

Can you think of any measures of customer satisfaction that are not mentioned here? How are you affected when you are not satisfied with a purchasing experience?

APPLICATION IN BUSINESS

As the manager of a local restaurant, you have been considering the use of a time budget to focus your staff's attention on "table turns." Table turns are the number of meals served at each table over a specified time period. Some restaurants see this as a very important measure of profitability—the higher number of table turns, the higher the profit. However, you are also concerned about the impact of increasing table turns on customer satisfaction. If you rush people from their tables, they are likely to not come back again. How might you balance these conflicting concerns?

STATIC VERSUS FLEXIBLE BUDGETS

LO11
Prepare flexible budgets and understand how they are used in activity-based costing environments

Static budgets are budgets that are set at the beginning of the period and remain constant throughout the budget period. The budgets that are presented for Tina's Fine Juices are static budgets. Although static budgets are useful for planning and operating purposes, they can be problematic when used for control. As we discussed in Chapter 1, control involves motivating and monitoring employees and evaluating people and other resources used in the operations of an organization. The purpose of control is to make sure that the goals of the organization are being attained. Control requires the comparison of actual outcomes (cost of products, sales, etc.) with desired outcomes as stated in the organization's operating and strategic plans (including budgets). The idea is to compare budgeted amounts to actual results and then to analyze any differences for likely causes. However, when static budgets are used and actual sales are different from budgeted sales, such a comparison is like comparing apples to oranges. If actual sales differ from projected sales, differences in production, material purchases, labor costs, and variable overhead should be expected. If actual sales are lower than budgeted sales, actual costs of materials, labor, and variable overhead *should* be lower than budgeted costs. The fact that a company's actual costs are lower than those budgeted under static conditions does not necessarily mean that the company (or its employees) spent less or was more efficient than budgeted.

TINA'S Fine Juices

For example, assume that Tina's Fine Juices produces 250,000 bottles of juice in January instead of the budgeted amount of 257,500 bottles. The projected direct labor cost (see direct labor budget on page 301) based on a static budget of 257,500 bottles was

$6,438. At the end of January, Tina's had actual direct labor costs of $6,300. So Tina's spent $138 *less* than provided for in the static budget.

	Static Budget	Actual	Difference
Projected production (bottles)	257,500	250,000	
Direct labor time per 600 bottles	1 hour		
Direct labor hours needed for production	429		
Direct labor rate per hour	$ 15		
Projected direct labor cost	$6,438	$6,300	$138

However, the comparison of actual labor costs to make 250,000 bottles with the budgeted labor costs to produce 257,500 bottles really does not make sense. Tina's ought to spend less for labor because fewer bottles were produced. The question becomes, How much less? What we would really like to know is how much the labor costs should have been had we known that production was going to be 250,000 bottles instead of 257,500.

Flexible budgets do just that. Flexible budgets take differences in cost owing to volume differences out of the analysis by budgeting for labor (and other costs) based on the *actual* number of units produced.

***Key Concept:** Flexible budgets are based on the* actual *number of units produced rather than on the budgeted units of production.*

A flexible direct labor budget for Tina's Fine Juices would budget labor costs based on the actual January production of 250,000 bottles. Based on the labor time needed to produce 600 bottles and the direct labor rate per hour of $15, Tina's projected labor costs would be $6,250, or $\frac{250{,}000 \text{ bottles}}{600 \text{ bottles per hour}} = 416.666 \text{ hours} \times \$15$ per hour, instead of $6,438. If we now compare the actual direct labor cost of $6,300 to the flexible budget amount of $6,250, we see that Tina's actually spent $50 *more* than expected instead of $138 *less* than expected.

	Flexible Budget	Actual	Difference
Projected production (bottles)	250,000	250,000	
Direct labor time per 600 bottles	1 hour		
Direct labor hours needed for production	417		
Direct labor rate per hour	$ 15		
Projected direct labor cost	$6,250	$6,300	$(50)

Why the turnaround? By using flexible budgeting, Tina's removes any differences in cost caused by differences in volume of production and focuses only on differences arising from other factors.

What are those other factors? Perhaps Tina's paid more than $15 per hour for labor. However, another explanation is that Tina's used more than 417 labor hours or even some combination of the two. Without further analysis, we simply don't know. In Chapter 10, the use of flexible budgets is expanded to allow managers to break down these differences into variances resulting from either spending too much (or too little) or using too much (or too little). This process is called variance analysis.

ABC AND FLEXIBLE BUDGETS

The use of activity-based costing (ABC) makes flexible budgets even more useful (although a bit more complicated). As we discussed in Chapter 4, companies utilizing ABC to assign costs to products and services identify activities (the procedures and processes that cause work to be accomplished) and the cost drivers associated with those activities. For example, Tina's Fine Juices might identify the movement of materials (orange juice concentrate and bottles) as an activity that consumes resources, and the number of times the material is moved as the driver of the costs incurred. In preparing a flexible budget for manufacturing overhead costs, Tina's would budget costs for moving materials based on the budgeted cost per move and the actual number of moves made during the month. Likewise, Tina's would compute the per unit budget amounts for other batch-level and product-level costs and include those in the flexible budget, along with the regular variable (unit-level) costs and fixed costs. A detailed example of a flexible budget for a company utilizing ABC is provided in Chapter 10 as well.

SUMMARY OF KEY CONCEPTS

- Budgets must start with a top-down strategic plan that guides and integrates the whole company and its individual budgets. (p. 293)
- Budgeting is a management task, not a bookkeeping task. (p. 294)
- Budgets are used throughout managers' planning, operating, and control activities. (p. 294)
- Budgets are future oriented and make extensive use of estimates and forecasts. (p. 297)
- Flexible budgets are based on the *actual* number of units produced rather than on the budgeted units of production. (p. 314)

KEY DEFINITIONS

Budgets Plans dealing with the acquisition and use of resources over a specified time period (p. 292)

Zero-based budgeting Requires managers to build budgets from the ground up each year (p. 293)

Planning The cornerstone of good management; involves developing objectives and goals for the organization, as well as the actual preparation of budgets (p. 294)

Operating Involves day-to-day decision making by managers, which is often facilitated by budgeting (p. 294)

Control Involves ensuring that the objectives and goals developed by the organization are being attained; often involves a comparison of budgets to actual performance and the use of budgets for performance-evaluation purposes (p. 294)

Sales forecast Combines with the sales budget to form the starting points in the preparation of production budgets for manufacturing companies, purchases budgets for merchandising companies, and labor budgets for service companies (p. 296)

Sales budget Used in planning the cash needs for manufacturing, merchandising, and service companies (p. 296)

Operating budgets Used to plan for the short term (typically one year or less) (p. 297)

Production budget Used to forecast how many units of product to produce in order to meet the sales projections (p. 298)

Material purchases budget Used to project the dollar amount of raw material purchased for production (p. 299)

Direct labor budget Used to project the dollar amount of direct labor cost needed for production (p. 301)

Manufacturing-overhead budget Used to project the dollar amount of manufacturing overhead needed for production (p. 302)

Cash receipts budget Used to project the amount of cash expected to be received from sales and cash collections from customers (p. 303)

Cash disbursements budget Used to project the amount of cash to be disbursed during the budget period (p. 305)

Summary cash budget Consists of three sections: (1) cash flows from operating activities, (2) cash flows from investing activities, and (3) cash flows from financing activities; these three sections are the same as used in the cash flow statement prepared under generally accepted accounting principles (GAAP) (p. 306)

Pro forma financial statements Budgeted financial statements that are sometimes used for internal planning purposes but more often are used by external users (p. 307)

Static budgets Budgets that are set at the beginning of the period and remain constant throughout the budget period (p. 313)

Flexible budgets Take differences in spending owing to volume differences out of the analysis by budgeting for labor (and other costs) based on the *actual* number of units produced (p. 314)

COMPUTER SIMULATION

You can now turn to **Appendix A** of your text to complete the portion of the Big Al's simulation covering cash receipts and disbursements budgets, summary cash budgets, and the impact of borrowing and repayment on cash flows.

MULTIPLE CHOICE

1. Budgets are:
  a. future oriented
  b. for managers only
  c. required by GAAP
  d. typically not used by small businesses

2. One advantage of the budgeting process is that it:
  a. reduces communication throughout the organization
  b. forces management to focus on the past and not be distracted by daily crisis in the organization
  c. can help management identify and deal with potential bottlenecks or constraints before they become major problems
  d. can decrease the coordination of organizational activities

3. Last year, Berra Toys sold 100,000 sets of baseball cards at \$1.50 each. If sales volume is expected to increase by 30 percent and the price of each deck of cards is expected to decrease 20 percent, what is the expected sales revenue for the coming year?
  a. \$120,000
  b. \$150,000
  c. \$156,000
  d. It cannot be determined from the information provided.

4. Tea Leaves, Inc., had 10,000 boxes for packaging tea bags on hand at the end of 2001. The company plans to sell 120,000 boxes in 2002 and 2003 and has a policy of maintaining 10 percent of the boxes needed for next year's expected sales in the ending inventory. During 2001, the company produced and sold 125,000 boxes. How many boxes were purchased during the year?
  a. 125,000
  b. 127,000
  c. 137,000
  d. It cannot be determined from the information provided.

5. Broihan Corp. had the following purchases budget for the last half of 2002:

July	$100,000
August	80,000
September	110,000
October	90,000
November	100,000
December	94,000

Historically, the company pays one half at the time of purchase and the remainder in the month following purchase. What are the expected cash disbursements in November?
 a. $95,000
 b. $97,000
 c. $100,000
 d. $147,000

6. Cash flows from ____________ activities include payments for the retirement of any debt issued by the company, sales or repurchases of stock, payment of dividends, and any borrowing or repayments of other long-term liabilities.
 a. operating
 b. investing
 c. financing
 d. all of the above

7. Budgeted financial statements:
 a. are required by GAAP
 b. are included in the set of audited financial statements
 c. are used by both internal and external users
 d. all of the above

8. Which of the following statements regarding budgeting by merchandisers and manufacturers is true?
 a. Merchandising companies will produce a sales budget.
 b. Manufacturing companies will not prepare budgets for production, direct material purchases, direct labor, or overhead.
 c. Merchandising companies will prepare a direct material purchases budget.
 d. All of the above.

9. Which of the following statements is true regarding nonmonetary budgets?
 a. There is no such thing as a nonmonetary budget.
 b. A nonmonetary budget may be more important than a financial (monetary) budget.
 c. A nonmonetary budget is useful for the control function only.
 d. Even nonmonetary budgets contain some monetary items.

10. In 2002, Tara Company budgeted sales of 45,000 units, produced 44,600 units, and sold 44,500 units. Tara's 2002 sales flexible budget was based upon ____________ units.
 a. 45,000
 b. 44,600
 c. 44,500
 d. It cannot be determined from the information provided.

CONCEPT REVIEW

11. Discuss why budgeting is a management task as opposed to a bookkeeping task.

12. Define the term *budgets* and discuss how budgets are used in decision making.

13. Discuss how budgets relate to the operating cycle.

14. Outline, using no amounts, a budget that you might use in budgeting your personal finances.

15. What is the main cause of business failure today? What is one potential safeguard against business failure?

16. Define planning as used in management decision making.

17. Define control as used in management decision making.

18. Compare and contrast planning and control in decision making.

19. What are some advantages of budgeting?

20. What are some of the characteristics of a typical budget?

21. Why is the sales budget the most important piece of the budgeting process?

22. List and describe some of the major factors and information sources typically used in sales forecasting.

23. If you were forecasting revenue for a ski area, what factors might you consider in your decision?

24. If you were forecasting revenues for a CPA firm, what factors might you consider in your decision?

25. If you were forecasting revenues for an airline, what factors might you consider in your decision?

26. Discuss ways that regression analysis might be used to aid the revenue-forecasting task.

27. What type of decisions could management address using the cash receipts budget?

28. What type of decisions could management address using the cash disbursements budget?

29. Why are budgets focused on cash flow?

30. Discuss why financial budgets for merchandising companies are different from those for manufacturing companies.

31. Discuss why financial budgets for service companies are different from those for manufacturing and merchandising companies.

32. Discuss the difference between static and flexible budgets.

33. Discuss how activity-based costing (ABC) impacts the preparation and use of flexible budgets.

34. Give some examples of nonfinancial budgets and how management uses them.

35. Discuss life-cycle budgeting. What are the five distinct phases in the life of a product, and how does budgeting change over those phases?

36. What types of problems must be considered when budgeting in an international environment?

APPLICATION OF CONCEPTS

37. Ringle Brothers sells pretzels for $1.50 per bag. The marketing department prepared the following first-quarter sales forecast:

January	25,000 bags
February	22,000
March	26,000
Total	73,000 bags

Required

A. What is the sales budget for January?

B. What is the sales budget for the first quarter?

C. If the brothers try to maintain 10 percent of the next month's forecasted sales in inventory, what is the projected production for February?

38. Pat's Pacifiers sells pacifiers for $1.25 each. The marketing department prepared the following first-quarter sales forecast:

January	$125,000
February	135,000
March	170,000
Total	$430,000

Pat tries to maintain 10 percent of the next month's forecasted sales in inventory. January's beginning inventory was 14,000. April sales are expected to be 195,000.

Required

Prepare a sales budget and a production budget for each month of the quarter.

39. Babs' Bicycles produces and sells bicycles. The production manager prepared the following second-quarter production forecast:

April	$ 60,000
May	35,000
June	80,000
Total	$175,000

Each bicycle requires two identical tires. Babs tries to maintain 10 percent of the next month's forecasted production needs in inventory. April's beginning inventory was 6,000. July production is expected to be 75,000.

Required

Prepare a purchases budget for each month of the quarter.

40. Greybar Inc. sells plastic baby bottles for $1.25 each. The marketing department prepared the following semiannual sales forecast:

January	$150,000
February	125,000
March	180,000
April	165,000
May	165,000
June	155,000
Total	$940,000

Historically, the cash collection of sales has been as follows: 55 percent of sales collected in month of sale, 35 percent of sales collected in month following sale, and 9 percent of sales collected in second month following sale.

Required

Prepare a sales budget for each month and a cash receipts budget for each month of the second quarter (April, May, and June).

41. Granny sells homemade cookies locally for $2.50 per box. Grandpop prepared the following first-quarter sales forecast:

January	1,500 boxes
February	1,200
March	1,600
Total	4,300 boxes

For scheduling purposes, Granny and Grandpop try to maintain 10 percent of the next month's forecasted sales in inventory.

Granny and Grandpop expect cash collection of sales to be as follows:

55 percent of sales collected in month of sale
35 percent of sales collected in month following sale
8 percent of sales collected in second month following sale

Required

A. Prepare a sales budget for the first quarter.

B. Prepare a schedule of cash collections, beginning with January sales.

C. Prepare a production budget for the first quarter. Beginning inventory in January is 150 boxes; April sales are expected to equal 1,100.

42. Clapton Company's sales budget shows the following projections for the year ending December 31, 2002:

Quarter	Guitars
First, 2002	30,000
Second, 2002	40,000
Third, 2002	22,500
Fourth, 2002	27,500
Total	120,000
First, 2003	34,500

Inventory at December 31 of the prior year was budgeted at 6,000 guitars. The quantity of finished-goods inventory at the end of each quarter is to equal 20 percent of the next quarter's budgeted unit sales. How much should the production budget show for units to be produced for each quarter in 2002?

43. Abraham Company's sales budget shows the following projections for the year ending December 31, 2002:

Month	Units
January	25,000
February	27,000
March	32,000
April	28,500
May	31,400
June	34,500
July	36,700

Inventory at December 31 of the prior year was budgeted at 6,250 units. The desired quantity of finished-goods inventory at the end of each month in 2002 is to be equal to 25 percent of the next month's budgeted unit sales. Prepare a production budget for January through June of 2002.

44. Allen Company's sales budget shows the following projections for the year ending December 31, 2002:

Month	Units
January	10,000
February	17,000
March	13,000
April	18,500
May	22,100
June	24,300
July	26,200

Inventory at December 31 of the prior year was budgeted at 1,500 units. The desired quantity of finished goods inventory at the end of each month in 2002 is to be equal to 15 percent of the next month's budgeted unit sales.

Required

A. Prepare a production budget for January through June of 2002.

45. Alvarez Company's sales budget shows the following projections for the year ending December 31, 2002:

Month	Units
January	25,000
February	27,000
March	32,000
April	28,500
May	31,400
June	34,500
July	36,700
August	35,000

Inventory at December 31 of the prior year was budgeted at 6,250 units. The desired quantity of finished-goods inventory at the end of each month in 2002 is to be equal to 25 percent of the next month's budgeted unit sales. Each unit of finished product requires three pounds of raw material. The company wants to have 30 percent of next month's required raw material on hand at the end of each month. Prepare production and purchases budgets for January through June of 2002, assuming that each pound of raw material costs $22.

46. Anderson Company's sales budget shows the following projections for the year ending December 31, 2002:

Month	Units
January	10,000
February	17,000
March	13,000
April	18,500
May	22,100
June	24,300
July	26,200
August	27,000

Inventory at December 31 of the prior year was budgeted at 1,500 units. The desired quantity of finished-goods inventory at the end of each month in 2002 is to be equal to 15 percent of the next month's budgeted unit sales. Each completed unit of finished product requires 1.5 gallons of raw material. The company has determined that it needs 20 percent of next month's raw material needs on hand at the end of each month. Prepare production and purchases budgets for January through June of 2002, assuming that raw material costs are $10 per gallon.

47. Ash Company's production budget shows the following projections for the period ending June 30:

Month	Units
January	25,000
February	27,000
March	32,000
April	28,500
May	31,400
June	34,500

Each unit of finished product requires 2.5 hours of direct labor. The company applies overhead at the rate of $7 per direct labor hour. Prepare direct labor and overhead budgets for January through June of 2002, assuming that the direct labor rate is $15 per hour.

48. Babcock Builder's production budget shows the following projections for the year ending December 31, 2002:

Month	Units
January	10,000
February	17,000
March	13,000
April	18,500
May	22,100
June	24,300
July	26,200

Each completed unit of finished product requires 3.5 hours of direct labor. Each hour of direct labor is $25. The company applies overhead at the rate of $3 per direct labor hour. Prepare direct labor and overhead budgets for January through June of 2002.

49. Barrera's Outdoor Outfitters' sales budget shows the following projections for the period ending July 31, 2002:

Month	Scarfs
January	25,000
February	27,000
March	32,000
April	28,500
May	31,400
June	34,500
July	36,700

The sales price per scarf is $12. The company estimates that it collects 70 percent of each month's sales in the month of sale and 20 percent the following month. The remaining outstanding sales are collected in the next month. The balance of accounts receivable at December 31, 2001, was $141,600. Of the accounts receivable balance, $33,600 represents uncollected November sales. Prepare a cash receipts budget for January through June of 2002.

50. Baum Company's sales budget shows the following projections for the period ending July 31, 2002:

Month	Units
January	10,000
February	17,000
March	13,000
April	18,500
May	22,100
June	24,300
July	26,200

The average sales price of each unit is $15. The company estimates that it collects 50 percent of each month's sales in the month of sale, with 30 percent being collected in the second month and 15 percent being collected in the third month after sale. The remaining 5 percent is estimated to be bad-debt expense. The balance in accounts receivable at December 31, 2001, is $180,000, with $135,000 of that balance being from December sales. All of the December 31 accounts receivable balance is expected to be collected in full. Prepare a cash receipts budget for January through June of 2002.

51. Barley's Breakfast has requested that you prepare a cash budget for the month of June. The following information has been provided:

a. The beginning cash balance is $10,000

b. The actual sales for April and May and the budgeted sales for June are as follows:

	April	May	June
Cash sales	$16,500	$15,500	$17,500
Sales on account	30,000	40,000	50,000
Total sales	$46,500	$55,500	$67,500

Sales on account are collected over a two-month period, with 70 percent being collected in the first month and the remainder being collected in the second month.

c. Inventory purchases will be $35,000 in June. The company pays for inventory purchases in the month following purchase. The balance of May's purchases is $22,000.

d. Selling and administrative expenses are budgeted to be $14,000 for June. Of that amount, 50 percent is depreciation.

e. Equipment costing $14,000 will be purchased in June for cash, and dividends will be paid in the amount of $2,500.

f. The company wants to maintain a minimum cash balance of $10,000 and has set up a line of credit to cover any shortage. If the company must borrow, the loan will be made at the beginning of the month, and any repayment will be made at the end of the month of repayment.

Required

A. Prepare a cash receipts budget for June.

B. Prepare a cash disbursements budget for June.

C. Using the preceding budgets, prepare a schedule of any financing needed.

52. Baxter Bagels has requested that you prepare a cash budget for the month of June. The following information has been provided:

The beginning cash balance is $10,000. The budgeted sales for March, April, May, and June are as follows:

	March	April	May	June
Cash sales	$14,000	$16,500	$15,500	$17,500
Sales on account	29,000	30,000	40,000	50,000
Total sales	$43,000	$46,500	$55,500	$67,500

Sales on account are collected over a two-month period, with 70 percent being collected in the first month and the remainder being collected in the second month.

Inventory purchases are budgeted to be 60 percent of budgeted sales each month. The company pays for inventory purchases in the month following purchase.

Selling and administrative expenses are budgeted to be 30 percent of each month's sales. Of that amount, 50 percent is depreciation.

Equipment costing $24,000 will be purchased in April for cash, and dividends will be paid in the amount of $12,500 in the same month.

The company wants to maintain a minimum cash balance of $10,000 and has set up a line of credit to cover any shortage. If the company must borrow, the loan will be made at the beginning of the month, and any repayment will be made at the end of the month of repayment.

Required

A. Prepare a cash receipts budget for April, May, and June.

B. Prepare a cash disbursements budget for April, May, and June.

C. Using the preceding budgets, prepare a schedule of any financing needed for the months of April, May, and June.

53. The following records from Benson Inc. are provided. Benson Inc. requires a minimum cash balance of $7,000 to start each quarter.

	QUARTER			
	1	2	3	4
Beginning cash balance	$ 10	$?	$?	$?
Cash collections	?	?	126	80
Total cash available	$ 86	$?	$?	$?
Inventory purchases	41	59	?	33
Operating expenses	?	43	55	?
Equipment purchases	11	9	8	5
Dividends	3	3	3	3
Total disbursements	$?	$114	$?	$?
Excess (deficiency) of cash	(4)	?	30	?
Financing:				
Borrowings	?	21	—	—
Repayments*	—	—	(?)	(8)
Total	$?	$?	$?	$?
Ending cash balance	$?	$?	$?	$?

* Includes interest.

Fill in the missing amounts.

54. Benzinger Motors is preparing a sales budget for the service department, based on last year's actual amounts. Last year's sales amounts are as follows:

	Mechanic Hours	Total Revenues
January	1,174	$11,681
February	1,057	10,538
March	1,125	11,261
April	1,516	15,008
May	1,724	16,981
June	2,515	25,014
July	2,746	27,185
August	3,107	30,604
September	2,421	23,823
October	2,211	22,154
November	1,709	17,090
December	1,524	15,164
January	1,495	15,050

Required

A. Compute the average revenue per mechanic hour for the current year.

B. Assuming that sales volume will grow by an average of 10 percent in the current year, prepare a monthly sales budget for the current year.

C. Assume that the average sales price increased by 5 percent; prepare a monthly sales budget for the current year.

D. For the year in total, is it more advantageous to increase sales volume by 10 percent or sales price by 5 percent? Remember the impact of variable and fixed cost on these projections.

55. Dip Em Donuts Inc. had 20,000 pounds of flour on hand at the beginning of the year. The company plans to produce 200,000 boxes of 12 donuts each during the year. Each box of donuts takes half a pound of flour. The company would like to have 10,000 pounds of flour on hand at the end of each year. How many pounds of flour must be purchased during the year to have enough for production needs and the desired ending inventory?

56. Clayton's FunLand Inc. had 14,000 games on hand at the end of the previous year. The company has a policy of maintaining 10 percent of the current year's requirements in ending inventory of any year. During the current year, the company sold 150,000 games. How many games did Clayton's FunLand purchase during the current year?

57. Berger Inc. sold 100,000 video games at $10 each last year. The company anticipates that volume will increase by 25 percent. In addition, the new price for a video game will increase by 20 percent. What are the expected sales revenues for the coming year?

58. Bernys Modems Inc. forecasts sales of 420,000 modems during the coming year. Each modem requires three internal memory chips. The inventory of memory chips at the beginning of the year was 20,000 chips. There was no beginning inventory of modems. Management desires to maintain an ending inventory of modems equal to 10 percent of the current year's sales and an ending inventory of chips equal to 10 percent of the current year's usage. How many memory chips must Bernys Modems purchase during the year?

59. Martinez's Ointments is a chemical company that manufactures a very popular ointment used in a variety of cosmetic products. Forecasted sales for the next year are 100,000 pounds of ointment. The beginning finished-goods inventory consists of 20,000 pounds. The desired amount for each year's ending inventory is 15,000 units. How many units should be scheduled for production this year?

60. Blanchard Company budgets on an annual basis for its fiscal year. The following beginning and ending inventory levels (in units) are planned for the fiscal year of July 1, 2002, through June 30, 2003:

	July 1, 2002	June 30, 2003
Raw material*	40,000	50,000
Work in process	10,000	10,000
Finished goods	80,000	50,000

*Two (2) units of raw material are needed to produce each unit of finished product.

Required

A. If Blanchard Company plans to sell 480,000 units during the 2002–2003 fiscal year, how many units would it have to manufacture during the year?

B. If Blanchard Company were to manufacture 500,000 finished units during the 2002–2003 fiscal year, how many units of raw material would it need to purchase?

61. Bochet Company expects to begin the coming year with 12,000 units of product X in the inventory of finished goods. It expects to sell 130,000 units of the product and end the year with 15,800 units in finished-goods inventory. Five pounds of material A go into each unit of product X. The company expects to have 2,000 pounds of material A on hand at the beginning of the coming year and wishes to end the year with 3,400 pounds in inventory.

Required

A. Calculate the number of units of product X that the company must manufacture in carrying out these plans.

B. Calculate the number of pounds of material A the company must purchase during the year.

TINA'S
Fine Juices

62. Tina's Fine Juices is a bottler of orange juice located in the Northeast. Tina's produces bottled orange juice from fruit concentrate purchased from suppliers in Florida, Arizona, and California. The only ingredients in the juice are water and concentrate. The juice is blended, pasteurized, and bottled for sale in 12-ounce plastic bottles. The process is heavily automated and is centered on five machines that control the mixing and bottling of the juice. Each machine is run by one employee and can process 10 bottles of juice per minute or 600 bottles per hour. The amount of labor required is very small per bottle of juice. The average worker can process 10 bottles of juice per minute or 600 bottles per hour. The juice is sold by a number of grocery stores under their store brand name and in smaller restaurants, delis, and bagel shops under the name of Tina's Fine Juices. Tina's has been in business for several years and uses a sophisticated sales forecasting model based on prior sales, expected changes in demand, and economic factors affecting the industry. Sales of juice are highly seasonal, peaking in the first quarter of the year.

Forecasted sales for 2003 are as follows:

Sales Forecast

November, 2002	375,000 bottles
December, 2002	370,000
January	350,000
February	425,000
March	400,000
April	395,000
May	375,000
June	350,000
July	375,000
August	385,000
September	395,000
October	405,000
November	400,000
December	365,000

Other information:

a. Tina's sells the juice for \$1.05 per 12-ounce bottle, in cartons of 50 bottles.

b. Tina's Fine Juices tries to maintain at least 10 percent of the next month's sales forecast in inventory at the end of each month.

c. Tina's Fine Juices needs to prepare two purchases budgets—one for the concentrate used in its orange juice and one for the bottles that are purchased from an outside supplier. Tina's has determined that it takes one gallon of orange concentrate for every 32 bottles of finished product. Each gallon of concentrate costs \$4.80. Tina's also requires 20 percent of next month's direct material needs to be on hand at the end of the budget period. Bottles can be purchased from an outside supplier for \$0.10 each.

d. At Tina's Fine Juices, factory workers are paid an average of \$15 per hour, including fringe benefits and payroll taxes. If the production schedule doesn't allow for full utilization of the workers and machines, the worker is temporarily moved to another department.

e. At Tina's Fine Juices most of the production process is automated, the juice is mixed by machine, and machines do the bottling and packaging. Overhead costs are incurred almost entirely in the mixing and bottling process. Consequently, Tina's has chosen to use a plantwide cost driver (machine hours) to apply manufacturing overhead to products.

f. Variable overhead costs will be in direct proportion to the number of bottles of juice produced, but fixed overhead costs will remain constant, regardless of production. For budgeting purposes, Tina's separates variable overhead from fixed overhead and calculates a predetermined overhead rate for variable manufacturing overhead costs.

g. Tina's Fine Juices has estimated that variable overhead will total $438,000 for the year and that the machines will run approximately 8,000 hours at the projected production volume for the year (4,775,000 bottles). The estimated machine hours are 80 percent of capacity for the five machines. Therefore, Tina's predetermined overhead rate for variable overhead is $54.75 per machine hour ($\frac{\$438{,}000}{8{,}000 \text{ machine hours}}$). Tina's has also estimated fixed overhead to be $1,480,000 per year ($123,333 per month), of which $1,240,000 per year ($103,333 per month) is depreciation on existing property, plant, and equipment.

h. All the sales of Tina's Fine Juices are on account. Based on the company's experience in previous years, Tina's estimates that 50 percent of the sales each month will be paid for in the month of sale. The company also estimates that 35 percent of the month's sales will be collected in the month following sale and that 15 percent of each month's sales will be collected in the second month following sale.

i. Tina's has a policy of paying 50 percent of the direct materials purchases in the month of purchase and the balance in the month after purchase.

j. Tina's plans to buy some new machinery in February at a cost of $75,000. The equipment will have a useful life of 10 years and uses straight-line depreciation. The company also plans on paying a dividend of $50,000 in January. Tina's also desires to keep a cash balance of at least $50,000 on hand at the end of any month. If the projected cash balance is less than that, a line of credit at First National Bank will be used to make up the shortage. If the company draws on the line of credit, Tina's is charged an interest rate of 10 percent annually. If the line of credit is used, money is borrowed at the beginning of the month. Repayments are made at the end of months in which there is sufficient excess cash (over $50,000) to pay back the entire line of credit. Last, but not least, Tina's pays estimated income taxes on a quarterly basis (in March, June, September, and December) on the income earned during the respective quarter. Tina's estimates that its total tax liability (federal and state) is around 35 percent of taxable income.

Required

Using the Excel template provided on the CD accompanying the textbook:

A. Prepare a sales budget for the first quarter of 2003.

B. Prepare a production budget for the first quarter of 2003.

C. Prepare a purchases budget for the first quarter of 2003.

D. Prepare a direct labor budget for the first quarter of 2003.

E. Prepare an overhead budget for the first quarter of 2003.

F. Preparc cash rcccipts and disbursements budgets for the first quarter of 2003.

G. Prepare a summary cash budget for the first quarter of 2003.

H. Prepare a pro forma income statement for the first quarter of 2003.

I. Prepare a pro forma balance sheet as of March 31, 2003.

Chapter 10

The Use of Budgets for Cost Control and Performance Evaluation

Study Tools

A Review of the Previous Chapter

In Chapter 9, we introduced the concept of budgeting and discussed how budgets assist managers in planning and decision making.

A Preview of This Chapter

In this chapter, we expand the discussion of flexible budgeting and introduce the concept of standard costs and variance analysis as tools to help managers "manage by exception" and evaluate performance in their control function.

Key concepts include:

- The purpose of the control function in management is to make sure that the goals of the organization are being attained.
- Management by exception is the key to effective variance analysis and involves taking action only when actual and planned results differ significantly.
- The flexible budgeting process removes any differences, or variances, owing only to variations in volume.
- "Favorable" and "unfavorable" designations for variances do not always refer to "good" and "bad."
- The variable-overhead efficiency variance does not measure the efficient use of overhead but rather the efficient use of the cost driver, or overhead allocation base, used in the flexible budget.
- Total over- or underapplied overhead is the sum of the four overhead variances.
- The fixed-overhead volume variance should not be interpreted as favorable or unfavorable or as a measure of the efficient utilization of facilities.
- The advantages of variance analysis for overhead costs are enhanced in companies using activity-based costing (ABC).
- Variance analysis is most effective in stable companies with mature production environments and has a number of drawbacks when used in many modern manufacturing environments.

Learning Objectives

After studying the material in this chapter, you should be able to:

LO1 Apply and use standard costing in variance analysis

LO2 Understand how managers use flexible budgets to help control operations and evaluate performance

LO3 Compute and analyze the flexible budget variance

LO4 Analyze the flexible budget variance, using the sales price variance, cost variances related to direct material, direct labor, variable and fixed overhead, and selling and administrative variances

LO5 Compute and interpret price and usage variances for material and labor

LO6 Compute and interpret variable and fixed manufacturing overhead variances

LO7 Evaluate the impact of activity-based costing systems on flexible budgets

LO8 Analyze important considerations in using and interpreting variances, including the concept of management by exception

LO9 Evaluate behavioral considerations in using standard costing and variance analysis

A Preview of Upcoming Chapters

In Chapter 11, we discuss financial measures of performance and other tools for cost control and performance evaluation in a decentralized environment. Nonfinancial performance measures are discussed in more detail in Chapter 12.

In Chapter 9, we discussed the use of budgets for planning and decision making. We focused on the preparation of operating budgets, beginning with the sales budget and ending with budgeted financial statements. Special emphasis was placed on the use of budgeting in cash planning and the use of operating budgets to plan production, material purchases and use, and labor requirements. We also introduced the concept of flexible budgets and their use as a mechanism for control and evaluation. In this chapter, we expand the discussion of flexible budgeting and introduce the concept of standard costs and variance analysis as tools to help managers "manage by exception" and evaluate performance in their control function. We also demonstrate the calculation of variances for direct material, direct labor, variable overhead, and fixed overhead and discuss the use of variance analysis for selling and administrative costs. The chapter ends with a discussion of variance analysis in an ABC environment, the limitations of standard costing and variance analysis, and behavioral considerations. ■

INTRODUCTION

As discussed in the previous chapter, budgeting is a tool that managers use to plan and make decisions. In this chapter, we expand our discussion of budgeting to include its use as a control tool. **Control** involves the motivation and monitoring of employees and the evaluation of people and other resources used in the operations of the organization. The purpose of control is to make sure that the goals of the organization are being attained. It includes the use of incentives and other rewards to motivate employees to accomplish an organization's goals as well as mechanisms to detect and correct deviations from those goals.

Key Concept: *The purpose of the control function in management is to make sure that the goals of the organization are being attained.*

A control mechanism is a little like a thermostat in your house. If you desire to keep your house at 70 degrees (the budgeted temperature), the thermostat continually measures the actual temperature in the room and compares the actual temperature to the budgeted temperature. If the actual temperature deviates from 70 degrees, the thermostat will signal the heating system to come on (if the actual temperature is less than 70 degrees) or will turn on the air conditioning (if the temperature is above 70 degrees). Managers need a similar type of control system to control budgetary differences.

In business, control often involves the comparison of actual outcomes (cost of products, units sold, sales prices, etc.) with desired outcomes as stated in an organization's operating and strategic plans. Control decisions include questions of how to evaluate performance, what measures to use, and what types of incentives to use. At the end of an accounting period (month, quarter, year, etc.), managers can use the budget as a control tool by comparing budgeted sales, budgeted production, and budgeted manufacturing costs with actual sales, production, and manufacturing costs. These comparisons are typically made through a process called **variance analysis.** Variance analysis allows managers to see whether sales, production, and manufacturing costs are higher or lower than planned and, more important, *why* actual sales, production, and costs differ from those budgeted.

The key to effective variance analysis is **management by exception.** Management by exception is the process of taking action only when actual results deviate significantly from planned. The key term in this definition is *significant.* Managers typically don't have the time to investigate every deviation from budget (nor would such investigations likely add value to the organization), so they tend to focus on material, or significant, differences. This allows managers to focus their energy where they are needed and where they are likely to make a difference. The concept of materiality and its use in variance analysis is discussed in more depth later in the chapter.

Key Concept: *Management by exception is the key to effective variance analysis and involves taking action only when actual and planned results differ significantly.*

STANDARD COSTING

LO1
Apply and use standard costing in variance analysis

To facilitate the use of flexible budgeting for control purposes, it is useful to examine the budget at a micro level rather than a macro level—that is, to develop a budget for a single unit of a product or a service rather than for the company as a whole. A budget for a single unit of a product or a service is known as its **standard cost.** Just as the cost of a product consists of three components—direct materials, direct labor, and manufacturing overhead—a standard cost will be developed for each component. In addition, each component consists of two separate standards—a standard quantity and a standard price. The **standard quantity** tells us the budgeted *amount* of material, labor, and overhead in a product, whereas the **standard price** tells us the budgeted *price* of the material, labor, or overhead for each unit (gallon, hour, etc.).

Standards can be determined in a couple of ways. Management can analyze historical cost and production data to determine how much material and labor was used in each unit of product and how much the material and labor cost. Likewise, management can look at historical data to determine the amount of overhead costs incurred in the past in producing a certain number of units. For companies with a long history of producing the same product, historical data can be very useful in forecasting future prices and quantities. However, historical data must be used with caution and adjusted when necessary. For example, changes in product design or manufacturing processes can dramatically change both the amounts and the prices of materials, labor, and overhead.

Another method of setting standards is called **task analysis.** Task analysis examines the production process in detail, with an emphasis on determining what it *should* cost to produce a product, not what it cost last year. Task analysis typically involves the use of engineers who perform time-and-motion studies to determine how much material should be used in a product, how long it takes to perform certain labor tasks in manufacturing the product, how much electricity is consumed, and so on. Typically, some combination of task analysis and historical cost analysis will be used in determining standard costs.

IN THE NEWS http://www.ups.com

In the mid 1980s, United Parcel Service (UPS) went so far as to develop standards for how fast drivers should walk to a customer's door (three feet per second) and how long it should take to handle a customer's package (Machalaba, "Up to Speed: United Parcel Service Gets Deliveries Done by Driving Its Workers," *Wall Street Journal,* April 22, 1986).

IDEAL VERSUS PRACTICAL STANDARDS

Because standard costs are used to evaluate performance, human behavior can influence how the standards are determined. Should standards be set so they are easy to attain or set so they can rarely be attained? An **ideal standard** is one that is attained only when near-perfect conditions are present. An ideal standard assumes that every aspect of the production process, from purchasing through shipment, is at peak efficiency. Some managers like ideal standards because they believe that employees will be motivated to achieve more when the goals are set very high. Others would argue that employees are discouraged by standards that are not attainable. Employees may be motivated to cut corners, use less than optimum material, or skimp on labor to achieve the standards. This type of behavior can lead to poor quality and an increase in defective units produced, which may cost the company more in the long run.

A **practical standard** should be attainable under normal, efficient operating conditions. Practical standards take into consideration that machines break down occasionally, that employees are not always perfect, that waste in materials does occur. Most managers would agree that practical standards would encourage employees to be more positive and productive.

PAUSE & *Reflect*

How do you think you would react to being evaluated using ideal standards? Practical standards?

USE OF STANDARDS BY NONMANUFACTURING ORGANIZATIONS

http://www.panasonic.com

The use of standard costing applies to merchandising and service organizations as well. Just as Panasonic needs to determine how much it should cost to make a telephone, an automobile dealership needs to know how much it should cost to sell a car, the city of Atlanta needs to know how much it should cost to provide garbage pickup to a residence,

PAUSE & Reflect

The estimated cost of providing an education to a student at a typical state university has been estimated to exceed $30,000 per year. However, in-state tuition at most public universities rarely exceeds $3,000 to $5,000 per year. Who is paying the rest of the cost?

and North Carolina State University needs to determine how much it should cost to provide an education to an incoming student. CPA firms have standards for the amount of time needed to prepare certain types of tax forms or returns, auto repair shops have standards for the time needed to make each repair, and airlines have standards for on-time departures. The use of standards is very common in all types of businesses.[1]

APPLICATION IN BUSINESS

Some managed health care companies have gone so far as to develop a standard amount of time for doctors seeing patients for particular ailments. For example, an initial office visit might have a standard time of 20 minutes, whereas a full physical for a patient might have a standard time of 45 minutes.

FLEXIBLE BUDGETING WITH STANDARD COSTS

LO2
Understand how managers use flexible budgets to help control operations and evaluate performance

In Chapter 9, we introduced the concept of flexible budgeting, based on the actual volume of production rather than on the planned level of production. Flexible budgets based on standard costs are the centerpiece of effective variance analysis.

To illustrate the concept of flexible budgets, consider the case of Corinne's Country Rockers. Corinne's builds a high-quality rocking chair with a reputation for lasting a lifetime and also uses a unique (and patented) rocking mechanism not found on other rockers. The chairs are sold directly by Corinne's through mail order and the Internet and have a retail price of $250 each. Corinne's produces each chair to order and has the capacity to produce 600 chairs per month. The standard quantity, standard price, and standard cost of direct material, direct labor, and variable overhead in each chair is summarized as follows. Estimated variable selling and administrative costs (per unit) and total fixed overhead and fixed selling and administrative costs are also provided.

Standard Costs for Corinne's Country Rockers

	Standard Quantity	Standard Price	Standard Cost
Direct material	20 linear feet of oak	$ 2 per foot	$ 40
Direct labor	5 labor hours	12 per hour	60
Variable overhead	5 labor hours	3 per hour	15
Total variable production costs			$ 115
Variable selling and administrative costs			25
Total variable costs			$ 140
Fixed overhead ($5,000 per month, or $15,000 per quarter)			$15,000
Fixed selling and administrative costs ($6,000 per month, or $18,000 per quarter)			18,000
Total fixed costs			$33,000

[1]Companies also use standard costs to price products and services. For example, a CPA firm may use its budget for the time normally needed to prepare a variety of schedules on a tax return to compute the price of the tax return. Likewise, auto repair shops may use the amount of time budgeted for each type of repair to determine a price for the repair service.

A static budget based on estimated production and sales of 1,500 chairs is provided in the following table. In addition, a flexible budget based on the actual production and sale of 1,600 rockers is provided.

Corinne's Country Rockers
Comparison of Budget to Actual (Quarter 1)

	Static Budget	Flexible Budget	Actual Results
Units sold	1,500	1,600	1,600
Units produced	1,500	1,600	1,600
Sales revenue	$375,000	$400,000	$396,800
– Variable manufacturing costs	172,500	184,000	189,200
– Variable selling and administrative	37,500	40,000	40,800
= Contribution margin	$165,000	$176,000	$166,800
– Fixed manufacturing costs	15,000	15,000	16,000
– Fixed selling and administrative costs	18,000	18,000	16,000
= Operating income	$132,000	$143,000	$134,800

As you can see, the actual operating income for Corinne's is somewhere in the middle of that predicted by the static budget and the flexible budget. What does that mean? Unfortunately, not much! It means that Corinne's earned more than budgeted at the beginning of the year. But remember, the static budget was based on expected production and sales of 1,500 units. Corinne's ended up producing and selling 1,600 units. Comparing the static budget to the actual results is like comparing apples with oranges. It just does not make sense!

It can be useful to compare the static budget to the flexible budget. Differences in the static budget and the flexible budget are solely a result of differences in budgeted production and sales and actual production and sales. The sales volume variance is the difference between the operating income of $132,000 (based on the static budget) and the operating income of $143,000 (based on the flexible budget). Note that this $11,000 difference in operating income is the same as the $11,000 difference in contribution margin.

Concept Question: *Why is the difference between the static budget and the flexible budget contribution margin the same as the difference between the static budget and flexible budget operating income?*

Concept Answer: Because budgeted fixed costs are the same in a static and a flexible budget, differences in contribution margin are directly reflected as differences in income.

SALES VOLUME VARIANCE

The **sales volume variance** is computed by taking the difference between the actual sales volume used in the flexible budget and the budgeted sales volume and multiplying that difference by the budgeted contribution margin per unit.

LO3
Compute and analyze the flexible budget variance

Sales volume variance =
(Actual – Budgeted sales volume) × (Budgeted contribution margin per unit)

The sales volume variance for Corinne's is as follows:

(Actual − Budgeted sales volume) × (Budgeted contribution margin per unit)
(1,600 − 1,500) × $110 = $11,000

This variance is obviously a result of actual sales used for the flexible budget exceeding the budgeted sales used for the static budget. However, beyond that it is not particularly informative. We don't know *why* actual sales were greater than budgeted. A reduction in sales price, a change in advertising strategy, or simply an increase in demand may have caused it.

Corinne's Country Rockers
The Sales Volume (Activity) Variance (Quarter 1)

	Static Budget	Sales Volume (Activity) Variance	Flexible Budget
Units sold	1,500		1,600
Units produced	1,500		1,600
Sales revenue	$375,000	$25,000	$400,000
− Variable manufacturing costs	172,500	11,500	184,000
− Variable selling and administrative	37,500	2,500	40,000
= Contribution margin	$165,000	$11,000	$176,000
− Fixed manufacturing costs	15,000		15,000
− Fixed selling and administrative costs	18,000		18,000
= Operating income	$132,000	$11,000	$143,000

Comparing the flexible budget amounts with the actual results is more meaningful. Remember that the flexible budget was calculated based on the actual production and sales

Corinne's Country Rockers
The Flexible Budget Variance (Quarter 1)

	Flexible Budget	Flexible Budget Variance	Actual Results
Units sold	1,600		1,600
Average sales price per unit	$ 250		$ 248
Units produced	1,600		1,600
Sales revenue	$400,000	$3,200 under	$396,800
− Variable manufacturing costs	184,000	5,200 over	189,200
− Variable selling and administrative	40,000	800 over	40,800
= Contribution margin	$176,000	9,200 under	$166,800
− Fixed manufacturing costs	15,000	1,000 over	16,000
− Fixed selling and administrative costs	18,000	2,000 under	16,000
= Operating income	$143,000	**$8,200 under**	$134,800

of 1,600 units. It represents the amount of revenue and cost that Corinne's expected to incur during the first quarter for the actual number of units produced and sold. The difference between the flexible budget operating income and actual operating income is called the **flexible budget variance.** As shown in the preceding table, the flexible budget variance for Corinne's is $8,200.

As we mentioned in Chapter 9, the flexible budget removes any differences owing to volume. However, we still don't have much information concerning exactly *why* operating income is $8,200 below budget. It appears to be caused by a combination of factors—sales are $3,200 below budget and variable manufacturing and selling and administrative costs are $6,000 over budget (resulting in contribution margin that is $9,200 below budget). Fixed manufacturing costs are $1,000 over budget and fixed selling and administrative costs are $2,000 under budget.

Key Concept: *The flexible budgeting process removes any differences, or variances, owing only to variations in volume.*

Now the question becomes, Why didn't Corinne's reach the sales dollar budget? Once we have eliminated the volume component of the variance, the only explanation is that the average sales price of $248 $\left(\frac{\$396{,}800}{1{,}600 \text{ units}}\right)$ was lower than budgeted sales price of $250 $\left(\frac{\$400{,}000}{1{,}600 \text{ units}}\right)$.

SALES PRICE VARIANCE

LO4
Analyze the flexible budget variance, using the sales price variance, cost variances related to direct material, direct labor, variable and fixed overhead, and selling and administrative variances

The **sales price variance** is computed by comparing the actual sales price to the flexible budget sales price and multiplying that amount by the actual sales volume.

$$\text{Sales price variance} = (\text{Actual} - \text{Expected sales price}) \times \text{Actual volume}$$

Plugging in the numbers for Corinne's, the sales price variance is as follows:

$$(\$248 - \$250) \times 1{,}600 = -\$3{,}200$$

The sales price variance can direct management's attention to a potential problem area. However, at this point, it is difficult to tell whether the unfavorable variance is the result of reducing the sales price of all rockers by $2 or perhaps the result of accepting a special order of 100 rockers at a price of $218 per chair. The variance simply points out that the actual sales price is different from the budgeted sales price. Management should investigate it further to determine its cause.

VARIABLE MANUFACTURING COST VARIANCES

The flexible budget variance shows us that actual variable manufacturing costs were $5,200 higher than budgeted, but determining the true cause of that variance is a little more difficult. Did Corinne's spend too much on material or use too much? Did the company incur more labor costs than usual, owing to paying a higher wage, or did it spend more time making each chair than budgeted? Did Corinne's spend more than budgeted on electricity, supplies, and other variable overhead or use more than budgeted? We simply don't know. In fact, the real reason may be a combination of any or all of the preceding.

To analyze the variable cost variances based on a flexible budget, we must step back and examine the flexible budget in more detail. Based on the standard cost information provided on page 332, the flexible budget for variable manufacturing costs is as shown in the following table. More detail concerning the actual variable overhead costs of $189,200 is also provided.

Corinne's Country Rockers
Variable Manufacturing Cost Budget

	Flexible Budget	Actual Costs	Flexible Budget Variance
Direct material	$ 64,000*	$ 63,840§	$ 160 F
Direct labor	96,000†	101,640‖	5,640 U
Variable overhead	24,000‡	23,720#	280 F
Total variable manufacturing costs	$184,000	$189,200	$5,200 U

*Flexible budget for direct materials = (20 feet per unit × 1,600 units) × $2 per unit = $64,000.
†Flexible budget for direct labor = (5 hours per unit × 1,600 units) × $12 per hour = $96,000.
‡Flexible budget for variable overhead = (5 hours per unit × 1,600 units) × $3 per hour = $24,000
§33,600 feet × $1.90 per foot = $63,840.
‖8,400 hours × $12.10 per hour = $101,640.
#Actual variable overhead costs consist of the variable portion of utilities ($16,390), shop supplies and indirect materials ($4,140), and repairs and maintenance ($3,190).

The total variance for variable manufacturing costs is $5,200. Note that this is the same as the flexible budget variance for variable manufacturing costs shown on page 334. Because actual costs are greater than budgeted, this variance is treated as "unfavorable" (indicated by a "U" following the amount in the last column of the table). Even though Corinne's actual expenditures for total variable production costs were greater than budgeted, Corinne's spent slightly less than the amount budgeted for direct materials and variable overhead but much more for direct labor.

Because actual costs for direct materials are less than the flexible budget amount, the $160 difference is "favorable." As you will see later in the chapter, "favorable" should not necessarily be confused with "good." Although it is useful to know that we spent less than budgeted for direct material, this type of analysis still does not tell us *why* Corinne's spent less. Did the company use less lumber than budgeted or pay less for each foot? To fully utilize the available information, we need to break down the total direct material variance presented earlier into its components and calculate both price and usage (quantity) variances.

Key Concept: *"Favorable" and "unfavorable" designations for variances do not always refer to "good" and "bad."*

We can examine the direct labor variance in the same way. Because actual labor costs are greater than the flexible budget amount, the variance is unfavorable. However, once again we don't really know *why* Corinne's spent more than budgeted. It could be because the company used more labor hours than budgeted or paid more for each hour of labor or some combination of the two. In addition, as with favorable variances, unfavorable variances are not necessarily "bad." Further analysis is necessary to break down the total labor variance into its price and usage components and to fully understand the cause of the variances.

Analyzing variable overhead is much like analyzing direct material and direct labor. Of course, direct material and direct labor are also variable costs. Although we know that Corinne's spent less on variable overhead than budgeted (the variance is favorable), we do not know whether the price paid for electricity, supplies, and other variable overhead was less than budgeted or whether Corinne's used less.

As you will recall, rather than budget each individual item, we prepared the flexible budget in Chapter 9 by combining all variable overhead costs and budgeting these separately from fixed overhead costs. The flexible budget for variable overhead for Corinne's was prepared by multiplying the predetermined overhead rate of $3 per direct labor hour by the number of direct labor hours expected to be incurred in producing 1,600 units (8,000 hours).

Unfortunately, although traditional variance analysis of variable overhead can help provide answers to questions about whether a company spent more or less or used more or less in total, it does not provide us with information concerning the components of overhead. In other words, traditional analysis does not tell us whether we spent more than budgeted on electricity or supplies, just that the overall amount of spending was higher than budgeted. Companies adopting activity-based costing to allocate overhead to products can extend variance analysis to look at the overhead costs associated with each activity and its associated cost driver. This provides much more detailed information than provided by traditional variance analysis. The analysis of overhead variances for companies using ABC is discussed in more detail later in the chapter.

A Model for Variance Analysis

The next step in variance analysis is to break down the direct material, direct labor, and variable overhead variances into their components (a price variance and a usage or quantity variance), using the basic variance model shown here:

Basic Variance Analysis Model

AQ* × *AP **(Actual Cost)**	***AQ* × *SP***	***SQ* × *SP*** **(Flexible Budget Amount)**
***AQ*(*AP* – *SP*)** **Price Variance**		***SP*(*AQ* – *SQ*)** **Usage Variance**

AQ **= Actual Quantity or Actual Hours;** ***AP*** **= Actual Price or Actual Rate**
SP **= Standard Price or Standard Rate;** ***SQ*** **= Standard Quantity or Standard Hours**

$$\text{Usage variance} = \text{Standard price } (SP) \times [\text{Actual quantity } (AQ) - \text{Standard quantity } (SQ)]$$
$$\text{Price variance} = \text{Actual quantity } (AQ) \times [\text{Actual price } (AP) - \text{Standard price } (SP)]$$

Whereas *AQ*, *AP*, and *SP* are self-explanatory, the calculation of *SQ* needs to be elaborated a little. In Chapter 9, the flexible budget was prepared based on the cost that should have been incurred to manufacture the actual number of units produced. *SQ* is a similar concept. It is the standard (budgeted) quantity of material or number of hours that should be incurred for the actual level of production. As you can see, the **material price variance** is the difference between the actual quantity multiplied by the actual price ($AQ \times AP$) and the actual quantity multiplied by the standard price ($AQ \times SP$). Simplifying, $(AQ \times AP) - (AQ \times SP) = AQ(AP - SP)$. The price variance is simply the difference in price multiplied by the actual quantity. Likewise, the **usage variance** is the difference between the actual quantity multiplied by the standard price ($AQ \times SP$) and the standard quantity multiplied by the standard price ($SQ \times SP$). Simplifying, $(AQ \times SP) - (SQ \times SP) = SP(AQ - SQ)$. The usage variance is simply the difference in quantity multiplied by the standard price. The variance model separates the overall flexible budget variance $(AQ \times AP) - (SQ \times SP)$ into two components—one the result of paying more or less than budgeted and the other the result of using more or less than budgeted.

DIRECT MATERIAL VARIANCES

LO5
Compute and interpret price and usage variances for material and labor

Using the standard cost data for Corinne's Country Rockers provided on page 332 and the breakdown of actual direct material costs shown on page 336, direct material variances are calculated as shown here:

Analysis of Direct Material Variances

$AQ \times AP$	$AQ \times SP$	$SQ \times SP$
33,600 × $1.90	33,600 × $2.00	32,000 × $2.00
		(20 ft./unit x 1,600 units) × $2.00
= $63,840	= $67,200	= $64,000

33,600($1.90 – $2.00)	$2.00(33,600 – 32,000)
$AQ(AP - SP)$	$SP(AQ - SQ)$
Price Variance	**Usage Variance**
$3,360 F	**$3,200 U**

Total Direct Material Variance = $3,360 F + $3,200 U = $160 F

AQ = Actual Quantity **AP = Actual Price**
SP = Standard Price **SQ = Standard Quantity**

The price variance is calculated by multiplying the actual amount of material purchased (33,600 feet) by the difference in the actual price paid per foot ($1.90) and the standard, or budgeted, price per foot ($2.00). This variance of $3,360 is considered favorable because the actual price was less than the budgeted price.

The usage variance for direct materials is found by multiplying the standard price by the difference in the actual quantity used and standard quantity allowed. Remember that the standard quantity allowed is the amount of direct material that *should* have been used to produce the actual output (the flexible budget amount). In this case, the budget for materials is 20 feet of lumber per chair. Corinne's actually produced 1,600 chairs during the quarter and should have used 32,000 feet of lumber (1,600 chairs × 20 feet per chair = 32,000 feet). The variance of $3,200 is considered unfavorable because the actual quantity of material used (33,600 feet) was greater than the flexible budget amount (32,000 feet).

The total favorable variance of $160 for direct materials can now be examined in more detail. It is the sum of a favorable price variance of $3,360 and an unfavorable usage variance of $3,200. Although the overall direct material variance was quite small, you can see that both the price variance and the usage variance are quite large and just happen to offset each other. Possible reasons for a favorable price variance include taking advantage of unexpected quantity discounts or negotiating reduced prices with suppliers. However, favorable direct material price variances can also result from the purchase of low-quality materials. Unfavorable material usage variances can likewise be caused by a number of reasons—poorly trained workers, machine breakdowns, or perhaps even the use of low-quality materials if they result in more defective units, machine downtime, rework, and so on.

Concept Question: *What are some possible reasons for an unfavorable direct material price variance and a favorable material usage variance?*

Concept Answer: Unfavorable material price variances might result from rush orders (requiring faster delivery and higher prices), purchasing in small lot sizes (and not taking advantage of quantity discounts), and purchasing higher-quality materials than budgeted. Favorable material usage variances are likely a result of highly efficient workers and well-maintained machinery and equipment. However, a favorable variance should not *necessarily* be considered "good." For example, the highly trained, efficient worker might require a higher salary than budgeted.

The investigation of variances and their causes using the decision-model framework is discussed in more detail later in the chapter.

If the amount of material purchased is not the same as the amount of material used in production, the variance model for materials must be slightly modified. To isolate the variances as soon as possible, the price variance should be calculated using the total amount of material purchased, whereas the usage variance should be calculated based on the amount of material actually used in production. For example, if Corinne's purchases 35,000 feet of lumber but uses only 33,600 feet, the price variance would be calculated as follows:

$$AQ_{\text{purchased}}\,(AP - SP)$$

or

$$35{,}000\,(\$1.90 - \$2.00) = \$3{,}500\text{ F}$$

The usage variance is calculated as before, that is

$$SP\,(AQ_{\text{used}} - SQ)$$

or

$$\$2.00\,(33{,}600 - 32{,}000) = \$3{,}200\text{ U}$$

Analysis of Direct Material Variances When Quantity Purchased Is Different from Quantity Used

$AQ_{purchased} \times AP$	$AQ_{purchased} \times SP$	$AQ_{used} \times SP$	$SQ \times SP$
35,000 × $1.90	**35,000 × $2.00**	**33,600 × $2.00**	**32,000 × $2.00**
= $66,500	**= $70,000**	**= $67,200**	**= $64,000**

35,000($1.90 – $2.00)	**$2.00(33,600 – 32,000)**
$AQ_{purchased}\ (AP - SP)$	$SP(AQ_{used} - SQ)$
Price Variance	**Usage Variance**
$3,500 F	**$3,200 U**

$AQ_{purchased}$ = Actual Quantity Purchased
SP = Standard Price
AQ_{used} = Actual Quantity Used
AP = Actual Price
SQ = Standard Quantity

You should note that when the amount of material purchased is not equal to the amount of material used, the price and usage variances cannot be added together to calculate the total direct material variance.

DIRECT LABOR VARIANCES

Direct labor variances are calculated using the same basic variance model used to calculate direct material variances. Because we are talking about labor instead of material, we substitute rates for price (*AR* and *SR* instead of *AP* and *SP*) and hours for quantity (*AH* and *SH* instead of *AQ* and *SQ*). In addition, the direct labor usage variance is often referred to as an efficiency variance. Using the standard cost data for Corinne's Country Rockers provided on page 332 and the breakdown of actual direct labor costs on page 336, direct labor variances are calculated as follows:

Direct Labor Variances

$AH \times AR$	$AH \times SR$	$SH \times SR$
8,400 × $12.10	8,400 × $12.00	8,000 × $12.00
= $101,640	= $100,800	= $96,000

8,400($12.10 – $12.00)	$12(8,400 – 8,000)
AH(*AR* – *SR*)	*SR*(*AH* – *SH*)
Rate Variance	Efficiency Variance
$ 840 U	$4,800 U

Total Direct Labor Variance = $840 U + $4,800 U = $5,640 U

***AH* = Actual Hours** | ***AR* = Actual Rate**
***SH* = Standard Hours** | ***SR* = Standard Rate**

If we evaluate the two components of the direct labor variance, we see that most of the variance results from inefficiencies in the use of labor. Potential causes of an unfavorable direct labor efficiency variance include poorly trained workers, machine breakdowns, the use of poor-quality raw materials (resulting in more time spent in production), or just general employee inefficiencies resulting from poor supervision. In this case, the unfavorable direct labor rate variance is small but still may be important. Potential causes of unfavorable direct labor rate variances include the use of higher-paid workers than budgeted, unexpected increases in wages owing to union negotiations, and so on.

Concept Question: *What are some possible reasons for* favorable *direct labor rate and efficiency variances?*

Concept Answer: Hiring workers at a lower wage rate is one obvious reason for a favorable direct labor rate variance. However, that may be problematic if the workers are less skilled than required. On the other hand, favorable labor efficiency variances most often result from using highly skilled workers. Obviously, there are tradeoffs here. Paying higher wage rates can result in unfavorable labor rate variances and favorable labor efficiency variances, whereas paying lower wage rates can result in favorable labor rate variances and unfavorable labor efficiency variances. ■

VARIABLE-OVERHEAD VARIANCES

With slight modifications, we can calculate variable overhead variances using the same variance model as for direct material and direct labor variances. As with direct material and direct labor, ($AQ \times AP$) is simply the actual cost incurred—in this case, the actual

LO6
Compute and interpret variable and fixed manufacturing overhead variances

variable overhead costs. *SR* is the variable predetermined overhead rate (sometimes called *SVR*). Because variable overhead was estimated using direct labor as the cost driver, *AH* is simply the actual number of labor hours incurred. Likewise, *SH* is the standard number of labor hours allowed for actual production. Consequently, $SH \times SVR$ is the amount of applied variable overhead.[2] The price variance is often called a variable-overhead spending variance and like the labor usage variance, the usage variance for variable overhead is called an efficiency variance.

The variable overhead spending and efficiency variances are calculated as follows:

Variable Overhead Variances

Actual Variable Overhead Expense	***AH* × *SVR*** **8,400 × \$3.00**	***SH* × *SVR*** **8,000 × \$3.00**
= \$23,720	**= \$25,200**	**= \$24,000**

Actual − (*AH* × *SVR*) **\$23,720 − (8,400 × \$3.00)** **Spending Variance**	***SVR* (*AH* − *SH*)** **\$3.00(8,400 − 8,000)** **Efficiency Variance**
\$1,480 F	**\$1,200 U**

Total Variable Overhead Variance = \$1,480 F + 1,200 U = \$280 F

AH **= Actual Hours**   ***SH*** **= Standard Hours**
SVR **= Standard Variable Rate**   ***SR*** **= Standard Rate**

What do these variances tell us? Whereas the price variance for materials and the rate variance for labor tell us whether the price of materials and the rate for labor are more or less than budgeted, the interpretation of the variable-overhead spending variance is a little different. Whereas a spending variance for variable overhead indicates that the actual price of variable overhead items, such as supplies, utilities, repairs, and maintenance, was more or less than the flexible budget amount, it is also affected by excessive *usage* of overhead caused by inefficient operations or waste. For example, although the rates for electricity usage (charged by the utility) might be exactly as budgeted, excessive usage might result from poorly maintained equipment. Likewise, even if the price of supplies was lower than budgeted, excessive use of the supplies owing to waste could still result in an unfavorable variable-overhead spending variance.

The variable-overhead efficiency variance is also interpreted differently from the direct material and direct labor usage variances. It does not measure the efficient use of overhead at all but rather the efficient use of the cost driver, or overhead allocation base, used in the flexible budget. The efficiency variance has nothing to do with the efficient use of utilities, maintenance, and supplies. The efficiency variance shows only how efficiently the organization used the base chosen to apply overhead to the cost of product produced.

Key Concept: *The variable-overhead efficiency variance does not measure the efficient use of overhead but rather the efficient use of the cost driver, or overhead allocation base, used in the flexible budget.*

In the case of Corinne's Country Rockers, the favorable variable-overhead spending variance tells us that Corinne's spent less than budgeted on the items included in the variable-overhead portion of its flexible budget. Although this might have resulted from paying

[2] Of course, overhead can be applied using cost drivers other than direct labor. If overhead is applied based on machine hours, *AH* is simply the actual number of machine hours used, and *SH* is the budgeted number of machine hours allowed for actual production.

less per kilowatt-hour for electricity, it might also have resulted from using less electricity than expected. A detailed analysis of each line item would provide more information. The unfavorable variable-overhead efficiency variance tells us simply that more *direct labor hours* were used than budgeted. It does not tell us anything about the efficient use of electricity, supplies, or repairs and maintenance.

The interpretation of variable-overhead spending and efficiency variances is made difficult by the use of a single cost driver to apply variable overhead to products and services. The use of multiple cost drivers and ABC makes the interpretation of these variances much more useful. This is illustrated in more detail later in the chapter.

FIXED-OVERHEAD VARIANCES

Corinne's Country Rockers

Corinne's fixed manufacturing overhead variance (see page 334) is $1,000 over budget ($16,000 actual costs compared to the flexible budget amount of $15,000). Unlike variable overhead, fixed overhead (and other fixed costs) should not be affected when production increases or decreases. Consequently, the variance model used in analyzing variable costs (direct material, direct labor, and variable overhead) is not appropriate for analyzing the fixed-overhead variance.

Fixed-overhead variances consist of a budget variance and a volume variance. The **budget variance** (or spending variance) is simply the difference between the amount of fixed overhead actually incurred and the flexible budget amount. Because fixed overhead is not dependent on production volume, no activity levels are used in its calculation.

Fixed overhead budget (spending) variance
= Actual fixed overhead − Budgeted fixed overhead

The **volume variance** is the difference between the flexible budget amount and the amount of fixed overhead *applied* to products. Overhead is applied by multiplying the predetermined overhead rate (for fixed overhead) by the standard hours (or budgeted hours) allowed to complete the actual units produced.

Fixed-overhead volume variance = Budgeted fixed overhead − Applied fixed overhead

APPLICATION IN BUSINESS

A company using variable (direct) costing rather than absorption (full) costing treats fixed overhead as a period cost and expenses it immediately (see Chapter 6). In these companies, there won't be a fixed-overhead volume variance, because fixed overhead is not "applied" to products. It is simply expensed in the period incurred.

Fixed-overhead variances for Corinne's Country Rockers are calculated in the following table. The predetermined fixed-overhead rate is $2 per labor hour ($15,000 budgeted fixed overhead divided by 7,500 budgeted labor hours (1,500 budgeted units × 5 hours per unit)). Applied fixed overhead is $16,000 ($2 predetermined overhead rate × 8,000 hours (1,600 actual units × 5 hours per unit)).

Fixed Overhead Variances

Actual Fixed-Overhead Expense	Budgeted Fixed Overhead	Applied Fixed Overhead
	(7,500 labor hours × $2.00/hour)	(8,000 labor hours × $2.00)
	(1,500 chairs × 5 hours)	(1,600 chairs × 5 hours)
= $16,000	= $15,000	= $16,000

Actual – Budget	Budget – Applied
Spending Variance	Volume Variance
$1,000 U	$1,000 F

The spending variance is unfavorable because Corinne's spent more on fixed-overhead items than the company had budgeted. As you can see, the volume variance is simply a result of Corinne's manufacturing more chairs than budgeted (1,600 instead of 1,500). Everything else in the comparison of budgeted and applied overhead is the same. The fixed-overhead volume variance is calculated primarily as a method of reconciling the amount of overhead applied to products under an absorption costing system with the amount of overhead actually incurred—and, consequently, the over- or underapplied overhead. The total amount of the variable-overhead spending variance, variable-overhead efficiency variance, fixed-overhead spending variance, and fixed-overhead volume variance will equal the company's over- or underapplied overhead for a period.

Key Concept: *Total over- or underapplied overhead is the sum of the four overhead variances.*

For Corinne's, manufacturing overhead was overapplied by $280 for the quarter. This is the sum of Corinne's $1,480 favorable variable-overhead spending variance, $1,200 unfavorable variable-overhead efficiency variance, $1,000 unfavorable fixed-overhead spending variance, and $1,000 favorable fixed-overhead volume variance.[3]

Concept Question: *What was Corinne's actual overhead for variable and fixed costs? What was Corinne's applied overhead for variable and fixed costs?*

Concept Answer: Actual variable-overhead cost was $23,720 (see page 341) and the actual fixed-overhead cost was $16,000 (see chart this page), resulting in actual total overhead of $39,720. The applied variable overhead was $24,000 (8,000 labor hours × the variable predetermined overhead rate of $3 per hour), and the applied fixed overhead was $16,000 (8,000 labor hours × the fixed predetermined overhead rate of $2 per hour), resulting in total applied overhead of $40,000. The difference between actual and applied overhead? $280!

The fixed-overhead volume variance generally should not be interpreted as favorable or unfavorable and should not be interpreted as a measure of over- or underutilization of facilities. This can be particularly problematic when the applied overhead is smaller than the budgeted amount (when a company produces fewer products than budgeted). Companies may reduce production for a number of reasons, including reduced demand for products, temporary material or labor shortages, and so on.

[3] The fixed-overhead volume variance is considered favorable for this purpose because actual production was greater than budgeted production.

Key Concept: *The fixed-overhead volume variance should not be interpreted as favorable or unfavorable or as a measure of the efficient utilization of facilities.*

ACTIVITY-BASED COSTING AND VARIANCE ANALYSIS

LO7
Evaluate the impact of activity-based costing systems on flexible budgets

The advantages of variance analysis for overhead costs are enhanced in companies using activity-based costing. Because ABC systems break down overhead into multiple cost pools associated with activities (with a cost driver for each), companies that employ ABC can analyze price and usage variances for each activity making up the total overhead variance. Just as the use of ABC systems enhances the quality of information available for decision making, analyzing variances by activity has a similar effect.

Key Concept: *The advantages of variance analysis for overhead costs are enhanced in companies using activity-based costing (ABC).*

Corinne's flexible budget for variable overhead was $24,000, whereas the flexible budget for fixed overhead was $15,000. When Corinne's analyzes this overhead using ABC, the $39,000 of budgeted overhead is traced to six activities—material handling, setting up machinery, assembly, finishing, maintenance, and inspections. The costs associated with each activity and their respective cost drivers are as follows:

Corinne's Country Rockers
Activity-Based Costing Flexible Budget

Activity	Flexible Budget Amount	Cost Driver	Budgeted Volume	Cost Formula
Material handling	$ 6,000	Number of moves	200	$30 per move
Setting up machinery	4,000	Number of setups	80	50 per setup
Assembly	14,000	Number of assembly (labor) hours	6,000	2.33 per assembly hour
Finishing	4,800	Number of finishing (labor) hours	2,000	2.40 per finishing hour
Maintenance	4,800	Number of maintenance hours	160	30 per maintenance hour
Inspections	5,400	Number of inspections	2,400	2.25 per inspection
Total	**$39,000**			

The cost formula is simply the predetermined overhead rate for each activity. It is found by dividing the estimated overhead for each activity by the estimated activity level of the cost driver. Once the actual cost associated with each activity and the actual volume of cost driver associated with each activity are known, a spending variance and efficiency variance can be computed. The detailed calculations of variances for each of the six activities identified at Corinne's Country Rockers are on page 345.

Although the preceding example is very simple, the ABC flexible overhead budget with variance analysis provides a wealth of information for managerial decision making. Although the total overhead variance is only $720, the detailed analysis shows us that the efficiency variances are almost all unfavorable. In all cases (except maintenance), Corinne's used more of the relevant cost driver than budgeted. On the other hand, the spending variances include an even number of favorable and unfavorable variances. Spending on machine setups, assembly, and finishing was favorable, whereas spending related to material handling, maintenance, and inspections was unfavorable. As always, Corinne's should pay special attention to any possible interactions between the variances.

Spending Variances and Efficiency Variances by Activity

Activity	Actual Cost	Spending Variance	Actual Base × Std Rate	Efficiency Variance	Standard Base × Std Rate	Total Variance
Material handling	$ 6,200	$ 50 U	205 × $30 = $6,150	$150 U	200 × $30 = $6,000	$200 U
Setting up machinery	4,150	350 F	90 × $50 = $4,500	500 U	80 × $50 = $4,000	150 U
Assembly	13,925	754 F	6,300 × $2.33 = $14,679	679 U	6,000 × $2.33 = $14,000	75 F
Finishing	4,775	265 F	2,100 × $2.40 = $5,040	240 U	2,000 × $2.40 = $4,800	25 F
Maintenance	5,120	620 U	150 × $30 = $4,500	300 F	160 × $30 = $4,800	320 U
Inspections	5,550	60 U	2,440 × $2.25 = $5,490	90 U	2,400 × $2.25 = $5,400	150 U
Totals	**$39,720**	**$639 F**	**$40,359**	**$1,359 U**	**$39,000**	**$720 U**

SELLING AND ADMINISTRATIVE-EXPENSE VARIANCE

As shown in the flexible budget variance calculation on page 334, Corinne's had an $800 unfavorable variance for variable selling and administrative costs and a $2,000 favorable variance for fixed selling and administrative costs. Variable selling and administrative costs include such things as commissions on sales, advertising brochures that are sent out with each chair purchased, administrative time to process each sale, and so on. Fixed selling and administrative costs include the salaries of the sales manager and personnel manager and such facility costs as rent and insurance. Like overhead variances, selling and administrative variances are difficult to analyze and to interpret. However, companies utilizing

Selling and administrative-expense variances are vitally important to home shopping companies and others that sell products via mail order.

ABC systems may have sufficient detail to analyze portions of this variance in more detail. For example, Corinne's is interested in reducing the costs associated with processing mail-order sales made by telephone and has established a quantity standard for the time spent to process each call (6 minutes). Likewise, it has established a price standard for this activity, consisting of the salary costs incurred by sales representatives handling the call ($1 per call based on a salary of $10 per hour) plus the direct costs of the toll-free line ($0.60 at $0.10 per minute). The actual costs incurred in handling sales calls can then be compared to the flexible budget amount, and price and usage variances can be calculated.

INTERPRETING AND USING VARIANCE ANALYSIS

LO8
Analyze important considerations in using and interpreting variances, including the concept of management by exception

Although standard costs and variance analysis can be useful to managers attempting to diagnose organizational performance, they are most effective in stable companies with mature production environments characterized by a heavy reliance on direct labor. On the other hand, they may not be much help in rapidly changing companies, companies with flexible manufacturing systems (in which more than one product is manufactured on an assembly line), companies with heavily automated manufacturing processes, or companies that emphasize continuous improvement and reducing non-value-added activities in the production process. Although variance analysis may still be of value as a summary report for top management, it has a number of drawbacks when used in many modern manufacturing environments:

1. The information from variance analysis is likely to be too aggregated for operating managers to use. To be useful, material variances may need to be broken down into detail by specific product lines and even batches of product, whereas labor variances may need to be calculated for specific manufacturing cells.
2. The information from variance analysis is not timely enough to be useful to managers. As product life cycles are reduced, timely reporting is even more critical than in the past.
3. Traditional variance analysis of variable and fixed overhead provides little useful information for managers. As the relative proportion and importance of overhead grows in comparison to direct material and direct labor, the usefulness of traditional overhead variance analysis has declined.
4. Traditional variance analysis focuses on cost control instead of product quality, customer service, delivery time, and other nonfinancial measures of performance. These measures are discussed in more detail in Chapter 12.

Key Concept: *Variance analysis is most effective in stable companies with mature production environments and has a number of drawbacks when used in many modern manufacturing environments.*

Even in traditional and stable manufacturing environments, the effective use of variance analysis for control and performance purposes requires the proper application of "management by exception" and careful interpretation of variances (including understanding their causes).

The proper application of "management by exception" requires an understanding that it is neither necessary nor desirable to investigate all variances. If you think about it, it is likely that actual costs will always deviate from budgeted costs to some extent. Utility prices are affected by the weather, and prices of raw materials can change suddenly owing to shortages, surpluses, and new sources of competing products. Unexpected machine breakdowns affect the amount of time workers spend manufacturing products. Even fixed costs can differ from budgeted costs when rent is unexpectedly increased, new equipment is purchased, or insurance rates go up. Because of these random fluctuations, managers should generally investigate only those variances that are material in amount and outside a normal acceptable range. Traditionally, materiality thresholds were often based on absolute size (investigate everything over $1,000) or relative size (investigate everything over 10 percent of the budgeted amount) or some combination of the two. Today, companies are more likely to use statistical techniques and to investigate variances that fall outside a "normal" range of fluctuations. For example, companies may investigate variances that are more than two standard deviations from the mean. Regardless of materiality, trends in variances might also warrant investigation. For example, continually occurring and increasing material price variances might be vitally important to a restaurant regardless of their absolute size.

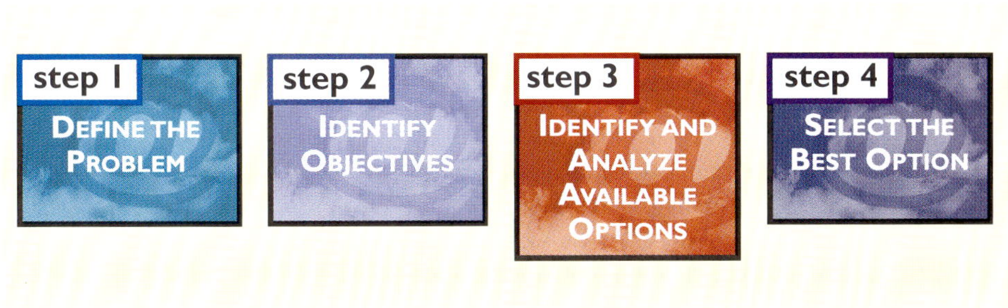

Step 1 DEFINE THE PROBLEM

The preceding decision-making model, introduced in Chapter 1, aids in the proper use and interpretation of variances and their causes. Step 1 of the decision model requires an accurate definition of the problem. This requires input from managers across all functional areas of a company. For example, consider a company investigating an unfavorable direct labor efficiency variance. Although on the surface, the unfavorable variance would seem to indicate a "problem" in worker efficiency, the real problem may be the combination of a workforce that is "fixed" in the short run and a lack of sufficient orders to keep workers busy.[4]

PAUSE & Reflect

Even though the purchasing manager caused the "problem," the material price variance would be favorable. As we discussed earlier, favorable variances are not necessarily "good."

Likewise, an unfavorable direct material usage variance generally points to a problem in production. However, further analysis might reveal that usage was high because of an unusual number of defective parts and that the large number of defective parts was a result of the purchasing manager's buying materials of inferior quality. The problem becomes one of the purchasing manager's buying inferior materials, not the production manager's using excessive amounts of material.

Step 2 IDENTIFY OBJECTIVES

Identifying management's objectives (Step 2) is vitally important in deciding how to use and interpret variances. If the problem is one of insufficient orders and management is truly concerned about controlling costs, management must be careful *not* to use the direct labor efficiency variance for purposes of motivating and controlling the production supervisor. Although this may seem counterintuitive, put yourself in the shoes of the production manager. The production supervisor really has two options—either continue producing products to keep workers busy or have an unfavorable labor efficiency variance. But keeping workers busy has definite drawbacks. Building inventory levels is costly. Holding high levels of inventory results in additional costs of storage and insurance and can result in increased waste owing to theft and obsolescence.

In other situations, understanding whether the primary objective of management is cost control or producing a high-quality product is important. If cost control is paramount, an unfavorable direct material price variance might well be considered "bad"; however, if management's objective is to provide a high-quality product, an unfavorable material price variance might be acceptable if the higher price is necessary to obtain high-quality materials.

[4] Companies may be reluctant to lay off workers for short periods of time when demand is unexpectedly reduced or other problems make it difficult to keep them fully employed. It may be costly to rehire workers or they may find other jobs. As discussed elsewhere, this often makes direct labor a fixed cost in the short run.

Step 3 IDENTIFY AND ANALYZE AVAILABLE OPTIONS

Step 3 in the decision model involves the identification and analysis of available options. With respect to variance analysis, options can be considered at two points in the process. The first involves deciding how the variances should be used and interpreted and who should be held responsible (if anyone). As we have already discussed, assigning responsibility for variances can be problematic when managers use the information without understanding the root causes of problems. Options may include controlling costs and evaluating performance using other measures along with variance analysis. Some of these other measures are discussed in more detail in Chapters 11 and 12.

Step 4 SELECT THE BEST OPTION

Once managers are sure of the root cause(s) of a variance, they can intelligently consider options available to deal with the problem. This step in the decision process includes a careful consideration of the relevant factors affecting the problem. For example, if management finds that an unfavorable direct labor efficiency variance is caused by a lack of customer orders and a workforce that is "fixed" in the short run, options may include accepting special orders, utilizing the workers in other areas, utilizing the time to train workers or to repair machinery, and so on.

The last step in the decision model involves choosing the best option. This involves paying special attention to management's objectives as discussed in Step 2. If the primary objective is cost control, managers are likely to choose an option different from one they would choose if their primary objectives were qualitative.

BEHAVIORAL CONSIDERATIONS

LO9
Evaluate behavioral considerations in using standard costing and variance analysis

As you have seen throughout this chapter, the use of standard costs and variance analysis, although useful for control and performance evaluation, can also cause dysfunctional behavior among employees and management. The use of ideal standards can cause resentment among managers when continually faced with "unfavorable" variances. Some companies tie compensation to performance that is at least partly measured by variances. Even though this is likely to make managers aware of costs, it may have undesirable side effects. Too much emphasis on the direct material usage variance can cause production managers to increase production so as to appear efficient, causing inventories to rise above acceptable levels. By focusing on variances, a purchasing manager may be encouraged to purchase inferior products to make his or her performance appear better, even though the manager knows that the poor-quality material will cause problems in the production area. It is important to understand the root causes of variances and to assign responsibility accordingly. It is also important to remember that variance analysis provides just one measure of performance. The uses of other financial and nonfinancial measures of performance are discussed in Chapters 11 and 12.

© STEPHEN DERR/IMAGEBANK

Book store managers may face "unfavorable variances" for ordering too many books from publishers. However, too much emphasis on controlling purchases and inventory may result in students' not being able to obtain the books they need for class.

SUMMARY OF KEY CONCEPTS

- The purpose of the control function in management is to make sure that the goals of the organization are being attained. (p. 330)
- Management by exception is the key to effective variance analysis and involves taking action only when actual and planned results differ significantly. (p. 330)
- The flexible budgeting process removes any differences, or variances, owing only to variations in volume. (p. 335)
- "Favorable" and "unfavorable" designations for variances do not always refer to "good" and "bad." (p. 336)
- The variable overhead efficiency variance does not measure the efficient use of overhead but rather the efficient use of the cost driver, or overhead allocation base, used in the flexible budget. (p. 341)
- Total over- or underapplied overhead is the sum of the four overhead variances. (p. 343)
- The fixed-overhead volume variance should not be interpreted as favorable or unfavorable or as a measure of the efficient utilization of facilities. (p. 344)
- The advantages of variance analysis for overhead costs are enhanced in companies using activity-based costing (ABC). (p. 344)
- Variance analysis is most effective in stable companies with mature production environments and has a number of drawbacks when used in many modern manufacturing environments. (p. 346)

KEY DEFINITIONS

Control Involves the motivation and monitoring of employees and the evaluation of people and other resources used in the operations of the organization (p. 330)

Variance analysis Allows managers to see whether sales, production, and manufacturing costs are higher or lower than planned and, more important, *why* actual sales, production, and costs differ from budget (p. 330)

Management by exception The process of taking action only when actual results deviate significantly from planned (p. 330)

Standard cost A budget for a single unit of product or service (p. 330)

Standard quantity The budgeted amount of material, labor, or overhead for each product (p. 330)

Standard price The budgeted price of the material, labor, or overhead for each unit (p. 331)

Task analysis A method of setting standards that also examines the production process in detail to determine what it should cost to produce a product (p. 331)

Ideal standard A standard that is attained only when near-perfect conditions are present (p. 331)

Practical standard A standard that should be attained under normal, efficient operating conditions (p. 331)

Sales volume variance The difference between the actual sales volume and the budgeted sales volume times the budgeted contribution margin (p. 333)

Flexible budget variance The difference between the flexible budget operating income and actual operating income (p. 335)

Sales price variance Computed by comparing the actual sales price to the flexible budget sales price times the actual sales volume (p. 335)

Material price variance The difference between the actual price and the standard price times the actual volume purchased (p. 337)

Usage variance The difference between the actual quantity and the standard quantity times the standard price (p. 337)

Budget variance The difference between the amount of fixed overhead actually incurred and the flexible budget amount; also known as the spending variance (p. 342)

Volume variance The difference between the flexible budget and the fixed overhead applied to a product (p. 342)

COMPUTER SIMULATION

You can now turn to Appendix A of your text to complete the portion of the Big Al's simulation covering sales price and volume variances, direct material and labor variances, and overhead variances.

MULTIPLE CHOICE

1. Alex's Angling Shop had the following budget for the production and sale of 500 homemade lures during 2001:

Sales revenue	$575
Cost of goods sold	500
Other expenses (fixed)	25
Income from lures	50

If only 400 lures were sold, budgeted net income would be:

a. $35
b. $50
c. $60
d. The answer cannot be determined from the information given.

2. Last year, Banana Corporation budgeted for production and sales of 7,000 banana products. The company actually produced and sold 6,000 products. Each product has a standard requiring 1.4 pounds of material at a budgeted cost of $1.50 per pound and 3 hours of assembly time at a cost of $10.50 per hour. The products sell for $30. Actual costs for the production of 6,000 products were $12,900 for materials (8,600 pounds at $1.50 per pound) and $178,300 for labor (17,400 hours at $10.25 per hour).

What was Banana's flexible budget variance?

a. $10,350 U
b. $10,950 F
c. $10,350 F
d. $10,950 U

Use the following information to answer questions 3–6.

Last year, Bandana Corporation budgeted for production and sales of 11,000 bandanas. The company produced and sold 10,500 bandanas. Each bandana has a standard requiring 2 feet of material at a budgeted cost of $1.50 per foot and 30 minutes of sewing time at a cost of $0.30 per minute. The bandanas sell for $14.75. Actual costs for the production of 10,500 bandanas were $33,880 for materials (22,000 feet at $1.54 per foot) and $92,800 for labor (320,000 minutes at $0.29 per minute).

3. What was the actual contribution margin per unit?

a. $3.39
b. $2.69
c. $2.75
d. $3.19

4. What was Bandana's sales volume variance?
   a. $1,695
   b. $1,345
   c. $1,375
   d. $1,595
5. What were Bandana's direct materials price and usage variances?
   a. $1,500 F, $880 F
   b. $1,500 U, $800 U
   c. $880 F, $1,500 F
   d. $880 U, $1,500 U
6. What were Bandana's labor rate and efficiency variances?
   a. $1,500 F, $3,200 U
   b. $1,500 U, $3,200 F
   c. $3,200 F, $1,500 U
   d. $3,200 U, $1,500 F
7. Konrad Enterprises had actual variable-overhead expenses totaling $33,750 last year for production of 6,000 units. Variable overhead is applied at a rate of $3.00 per direct labor hour, and 2 direct labor hours are budgeted for each unit; 11,990 direct labor hours were incurred.
   The total variable overhead variance is:
   a. $2,250 F
   b. $2,220 F
   c. $2,250 U
   d. $2,220 U
8. Which of the following statements about activity-based costing and variance analysis is true?
   a. The advantages of variance analysis for overhead costs are enhanced in companies using activity-based costing.
   b. Because ABC systems break down overhead into multiple cost pools associated with activities (with a cost driver for each), companies that use ABC can analyze price and usage variances for each activity making up the total overhead variance.
   c. Just as the use of ABC systems enhances the quality of information available for decision making, analyzing variances by activity has a similar effect.
   d. all of the above
9. The proper application of "management by exception":
   a. requires managers to investigate all variances
   b. suggests that managers should generally investigate only those variances that are material in amount and outside a normal acceptable range
   c. prohibits the use of materiality thresholds to trigger investigations of variances
   d. is effective only for direct material and labor variances
10. The use of standard costs:
   a. is mandatory when using "management by exception"
   b. can cause dysfunctional behavior among employees and management
   c. is effective only for direct material standards
   d. none of the above

CONCEPT REVIEW

11. Discuss the purpose of the planning and control process.
12. Discuss ideal versus practical standards and how they might affect employee behavior.
13. Discuss the pros and cons of management by exception.
14. Discuss the value of a flexible budget to management decision making.
15. What is the primary difference between a static budget and a flexible budget?
16. Which area of management would normally be responsible for sales price variances? Why?
17. What factors are considered when measuring the sales volume variance?
18. Give the formula for computing the generic price variance, and explain each term.
19. Give the formula for computing the generic usage variance, and explain each term.
20. Discuss the impact on fixed and variable cost per unit when production volume decreases when using a flexible budget.
21. Usage variances focus on what?
22. The predetermined fixed-overhead application rate is a function of a predetermined "normal" activity level. If standard hours allowed for good output equal this predetermined activity level for a given period, what will the volume variance be?
23. Husky Manufacturing relies on unfavorable material variances to signal quality problems that require excessive rework and materials use. Discuss the pros and cons of this practice.
24. Incentive-compatible compensation schemes often create many opportunities as well as problems. Identify two negative outcomes of incentive-compensation systems, and suggest how companies can overcome them.
25. Discuss the meaning of the terms *favorable* and *unfavorable* with regard to variances. How does each type of variance affect operating profits? Do the terms refer to good or bad variances? Give an example of each, with the effect on profits and the interpretation of the meaning of the term.

APPLICATION OF CONCEPTS

26. Total production costs for Sun Devil Advertising Agency are budgeted at $330,000 for 60,000 hours of budgeted output and $380,000 for 70,000 hours of budgeted output. How much is Sun Devil's budgeted variable costs per hour of output?
27. Grizzly Manufacturing uses the following flexible budget formula for annual maintenance cost:

    Total cost = $9,200 + 0.80 per machine hour

    The current month's budget is based upon 30,000 hours of planned machine time. What is the maintenance cost included in this flexible budget?
28. The budget formula for manufacturing costs is $13,500 + $5.00 per unit produced. The budget formula for marketing and administrative costs is $10,000 + $7.50 per unit sold. If 10,000 units are expected to be produced but only 8,000 units are expected to be sold, what are the total budgeted operating expenses for the period?
29. A direct marketing company expects to incur fixed expenses of $50,000 per month and variable costs of $4 per sales call and $2 per telephone call in generating sales of $75,000. During the month, the sales force made 100 sales calls and 500 telephone calls and generated sales of $70,000. Actual costs incurred included $52,000 for fixed costs and $1,200 for variable costs. Compute the flexible budget variance.
30. The Brisick Quick Copy Shop had an unfavorable sales price variance of $150. The budgeted selling price was $10 per unit, and the number of units sold was 50. What was the actual selling price?

31. Burke Long Distance Company expects to sell 100 phone card units at a selling price of $15 each. Variable costs are expected to be $10 each. What is the sales volume variance if the company actually sells 110 phone card units at $16 and its variable costs are $12?

32. Simpson Company's budget shows straight-line depreciation on factory equipment of $258,000. The budget was prepared at an annual production volume of 103,200 units of product. This production volume is expected to occur uniformly throughout the year. During September, Simpson produced 8,170 units of product, and the accounts reflected actual depreciation on factory machinery of $20,500. Simpson controls manufacturing costs with a flexible budget. What would the flexible budget amount for depreciation on factory machinery for September be?

33. Morgan Corporation's budget calls for the production of 5,000 units of product monthly. The budget includes indirect labor of $144,000 annually; Morgan considers indirect labor to be a variable cost. During April, 4,500 units of product were produced, and indirect labor costs of $10,100 were incurred. What would be the budget variance for indirect labor utilizing flexible budgeting?

34. Fort Worth Company prepared a budget last period that called for sales of 10,000 units at a price of $10 each. The costs per unit were estimated to amount to $5 variable and $2 fixed. During the period, production was exactly equal to actual sales of 12,000 units. The selling price was $9.50 per unit. Variable costs were $6 per unit. Fixed costs actually incurred were $21,000. Prepare a report to show the difference between the actual contribution margin and the budgeted contribution margin per the static budget. Now compare the actual contribution margin with the budgeted contribution margin per the flexible budget.

35. As a hobby, Janie makes knitted caps for sale at ski resorts. Her budget for the production and sale of 150 caps is as follows:

Sales revenue	$1,500.00
Variable costs:	
Direct material (yarn)	375.00
Direct labor	750.00
Commission to resort	112.50
Fixed costs	75.00
Net income	$ 187.50

Janie came down with a bad case of the flu and was able to make and sell only 125 caps.

Required

Prepare a flexible budget for the production and sale of 125 caps.

36. As a hobby, Jim makes souvenir wood sculptures for sale at ski resorts. His budgeted revenue and expenses are as follows:

Sales revenue per sculpture	$100
Variable costs per sculpture:	
Direct material	25
Direct labor	15
Commission to resort	10
Fixed costs	$ 50 for the production of up to 75 sculptures

Required

Prepare a flexible budget for the production and sale of 50 sculptures.

37. Last year, Wheeler Corporation budgeted for production and sales of 1,200 items. The company produced and sold 1,100 items. Each item has a standard requiring

1 foot of material at a budgeted cost of $1.50 per foot and 2 hours of assembly time at a cost of $12 per hour. The items sell for $30. Actual costs for the production of 1,100 items were $1435.50 for materials (990 feet at $1.45 per foot) and $29,161.10 for labor (2,420 hours at $12.05 per hour).

Required

A. Calculate the budgeted contribution margin per unit.

B. Calculate the actual contribution margin per unit.

C. Calculate the sales volume variance.

D. Calculate the flexible budget variance.

E. Calculate the direct materials price variance.

F. Calculate the direct materials usage variance.

G. Calculate the labor rate variance.

H. Calculate the labor efficiency variance.

38. Last year, Boring Corporation budgeted for production and sales of 1,000 items. The company produced and sold 1,100 items. Each item has a standard requiring 1 pound of material at a budgeted cost of $5.00 per pound and 2 hours of assembly time at a cost of $12 per hour. The items sell for $40. Actual costs for the production of 1,100 items included 1,150 pounds of material at $4.75 per pound and 2,220 labor hours at $12.05 per hour.

Required

A. Calculate the direct materials price variance.

B. Calculate the direct materials usage variance.

C. Calculate the labor rate variance.

D. Calculate the labor efficiency variance.

39. Simon Enterprises applies variable overhead at a rate of $1.50 per direct labor hour and fixed overhead at a rate of $1.75 per direct labor hour. Two direct labor hours are budgeted for each of the 5,900 units expected to be produced. Simon incurred actual variable-overhead expenses totaling $18,750 and actual fixed-overhead expenses totaling $21,500 last year in the production of 6,000 units; 11,800 direct labor hours were actually incurred. Compute the variable-overhead efficiency variance, the variable-overhead spending variance, the fixed-overhead volume variance, and the fixed-overhead spending variance.

40. Garfunkel Company, which uses standard costing, shows the following overhead information for the current period:

Actual overhead incurred:	
Fixed	$10,500
Variable	$66,810
Budgeted fixed overhead	$11,000
Variable-overhead rate per direct labor hour	$ 5
Standard hours allowed for actual production	13,100
Actual labor hours used	13,000

Required

A. What is the variable-overhead spending variance?

B. What is the variable-overhead efficiency variance?

41. Last year, Bachman Corporation budgeted for production and sales of 5,000 units of its product. The company actually produced and sold 6,000 units. Each unit has a standard requiring 1.5 pounds of material at a budgeted cost of $1.52 per pound and 2 hours of assembly time at a cost of $12.50 per hour. The product sells for $32. Actual costs for the production of 6,000 units were $12,900 for materials (8,600 pounds at $1.50 per pound) and $161,700 for labor (13,200 at $12.25 per hour).

Required

A. What was the budgeted contribution margin per unit?

B. What was the actual contribution margin per unit?

C. What was Bachman's sales volume variance?

D. What was Bachman's flexible budget variance?

E. What was Bachman's direct materials price variance?

F. What was Bachman's direct materials usage variance?

G. What was Bachman's labor rate variance?

H. What was Bachman's labor efficiency variance?

I. If each Bachman product sold for $33, what would the sales price variance be?

42. Last year, Turner Corporation budgeted for production and sales of 12,000 overdrive transmission parts. The company produced and sold 11,000 parts. Each part has a standard requiring 1 pound of material at a budgeted cost of $1.50 per pound and 20 minutes of assembly time at a cost of $0.25 per minute. The parts sell for $8. Actual costs for the production of 11,000 parts were $17,094 for materials (11,100 pounds purchased and used at $1.54 per pound) and $58,080 for labor (242,000 minutes at $0.24 per minute).

Required

A. What was the budgeted contribution margin per unit?

B. What was the actual contribution margin per unit?

C. What was Turner's sales volume variance?

D. What was Turner's flexible budget variance?

E. What was Turner's direct materials price variance?

F. What was Turner's direct materials usage variance?

G. What was Turner's labor rate variance?

H. What was Turner's labor efficiency variance?

43. Pooh Enterprises had the following standard costs for the production of one bear:

Direct materials	1.5 pounds of stuffing @ $2 per lb
Direct labor	2 hours of assembly @ $15 per hr

Actual production costs for the production of 1,000 bears included 1,750 pounds of stuffing @ $1.95 per pound and 1,950 labor hours at $15.25 per hour.

Required

A. What is the direct materials price variance?

B. What is the direct materials usage variance?

C. What is the labor rate variance?

D. What is the labor efficiency variance?

44. Byrd Company's actual results with a sales volume of 400,000 units are as follows:

Sales Revenues		$2,440,000
Variable Costs		
Manufacturing	$1,060,000	
Marketing and administrative	748,000	1,808,000
Contribution margin		$ 632,000
Fixed Costs		
Manufacturing	$ 400,000	
Marketing and administrative	200,000	600,000
Operating profit		$ 32,000

The company planned to produce and sell 375,000 at $6 each. At that volume, variable manufacturing costs were budgeted at $2.50, and variable marketing and administrative costs were budgeted at $2.00 each. In addition, the company expected an operating profit of $62,500.

Required

A. Re create the static budget.

B. Prepare the flexible budget.

C. Calculate the sales price variance.

D. Calculate the sales volume variance.

E. Calculate the variable manufacturing variances.

F. Calculate the fixed-cost variances.

G. Reconcile the budgeted operating profits of $62,500 to the actual operating profits of $32,000 by fully explaining all variances.

45. Each year, the Patterson Company begins its budgeting process in September. Managers are asked to provide sales forecasts by product line. Wishing to provide an incentive to improve performance, the president, Jim Sr., always increases the forecast by 25 percent. Discuss the impact of the president's actions on the sales force as well as on the production personnel.

46. The Short Sheets Company established standard costs as follows:

Materials	5 pieces of fabric @ $1 per piece
Labor	2 hours @ $7 per hour

In October, 1,000 units were completed. During the month, 5,400 pieces of fabric were purchased at $1.08 per piece. Labor costs were $13,650 for 2,100 hours.

Required

A. What is the material price variance?

B. What is the material efficiency variance?

C. What is the labor price variance?

D. What is the labor efficiency variance?

47. The following information pertains to the assembly department of MacPage Manufacturing for February:

Units produced	5,500
Materials purchased	$26,400 ($2.20 per pound)
Materials used	13,000 pounds
Labor costs incurred	$ 9,187.50
Labor hours worked	2,450
Standard price/pound for materials	$ 2.10 per pound

Standard labor time/finished unit	30 minutes
Material usage variance	$ 1,575 F
Total labor variance	$ 712.50 F

Required

A. What is the standard usage of material per finished unit?

B. What is the labor efficiency variance?

C. The given information remains unchanged except for the number of units produced. If the standard wage rate per hour were $3.30, how many units would have been produced during February?

D. The given information remains unchanged except for the number of units produced and the standard time per finished unit. If the number of units produced were 825 units and the standard wage rate per hour were $4, the standard time per finished unit would have been how much?

48. The flexible budget level for the assembly department of Guice Manufacturing during the month of December was 10,000 direct labor hours. The actual number of direct labor hours worked during December was 9,000. Overhead is applied on the basis of direct labor hours. What kind of variance occurred?

49. The Comet Company's budget contains these standards for materials and direct labor for a unit:

Material	5 pounds @ $1 per pound	$ 5
Labor	2 hours @ $5 per hour	$10

Although 2,500 units were budgeted, 3,000 were actually produced. Materials weighing 16,000 pounds were purchased for $18,400. Materials weighing 15,500 were issued to production. Direct labor costs were $33,075 for 6,750 hours.

Required

A. Compute the materials purchase price variance.

B. Compute the materials efficiency variance.

C. Compute the labor price variance.

D. Compute the labor efficiency variance.

50. Surfs Up Company, which uses standard costing, shows the following overhead information for the current period:

Actual overhead incurred:	
Fixed	$10,500
Variable	$66,810
Budgeted fixed overhead	$11,000
Variable-overhead rate per direct labor hour	$ 5
Standard hours allowed for actual production	13,100
Actual labor hours used	13,000

Required

A. What is the variable-overhead spending variance?

B. What is the variable-overhead efficiency variance?

C. What is the fixed-overhead budget variance?

51. The Small Tykes World Company mass produces wooden chairs. The standard costs follow:

Plastic	10 pounds at $4.50 per pound
Molding	3 feet at $3.00 per foot
Direct labor	4 hours at $6.00 per hour
Variable overhead	$3 per direct labor hour
Fixed overhead	$55,000 per period

Transactions during June follow:

a. Small Tykes purchased plastic at $4.45 per pound and issued 185,000 pounds to production.

b. Small Tykes purchased molding at $3.10 per foot and issued 50,000 feet to production.

c. The direct labor payroll was 72,500 hours at $6.00.

d. Overhead costs were $275,000, of which $221,125 was variable.

e. Small Tykes produced 18,000 chairs during the month.

Required

A. Calculate all variances to the extent permitted by the data.

Step 2 IDENTIFY OBJECTIVES

B. Interpret the variances (in other words, tell the story of the variances). What do they tell us about the performance of the company?

Step 3 IDENTIFY AND ANALYZE AVAILABLE OPTIONS

C. Suggest what areas need to be investigated as a result of your analysis of the variances.

D. What options are available?

Step 4 SELECT THE BEST OPTION

E. In your opinion, what are the best options? Why?

52. Seats R Us manufactures office chairs. Recently, it established standard costs as follows:

Material	4 pieces per unit at $2 per piece
Labor	1½ hours per unit at $8 per hour

In April, 6,000 pieces of material were purchased for $2.25 per piece. Of that number, 5,500 pieces of material were used to produce 1,325 units. Labor costs were $16,300 for 2,000 hours.

Required

A. Compute the materials price variance.

B. Compute the material usage variance.

C. Compute the labor price variance.

D. Compute the labor efficiency variance.

53. The following overhead data of the Simon Travel Company are presented for analysis of the variances from standard:

Forecast Data (expected capacity)	
Direct labor hours	40,000
Estimated overhead:	
Fixed	$16,000
Variable	$30,000
Actual Results	
Direct labor hours	37,200
Overhead:	
Fixed	$16,120
Variable	$28,060

Allowed or standard hours for actual production was 37,000 hours.

Required

A. Calculate the variable-overhead spending variance.

B. Calculate the variable-overhead efficiency variance.

C. Calculate the fixed-overhead budget variance.

54. Oil Inc. uses from one to three chemicals to manufacture oil products. Variance data for the month follow (F indicates a favorable variance; U indicates an unfavorable variance):

	Chemical X	Chemical Y	Chemical Z
Materials price variance	$ 84,000 F	$ 50,000 F	$ 42,000 U
Material usage variance	$ 80,000 U	$ 60,000 U	$ 96,000 U
Total materials variance	$ 4,000 F	$ 10,000 U	$138,000 U
Oil products requiring this chemical	200,000	220,000	250,000

The budget allowed one pound for each kind of chemical for each oil product requiring that kind of chemical. For chemical X, the average price paid was $0.40 per pound less than standard; for chemical Y, it was $0.20 less; for chemical Z, it was $0.14 greater. The company purchased and used all chemicals in a given period.

Required

A. For chemical X, calculate the following:
  (1) The number of pounds of material purchased
  (2) The standard cost per pound of material
  (3) The total standard material cost

B. For chemical Y, calculate the following:
  (1) The number of pounds of material purchased
  (2) The standard cost per pound of material
  (3) The total standard material cost

C. For chemical Z, calculate the following:
  (1) The number of pounds of material purchased
  (2) The standard cost per pound of material
  (3) The total standard material cost

55. Sparky Electric produces a single product: outlets. The standard costs per unit for direct materials and direct labor are as follows:

	Cost Standards	
Material A	2 pounds at $6.00 per pound	$12.00
Material B	3 gallons at $3.00 per gallon	9.00
Labor	4 hours at $3.20 per hour	12.80
Total standard unit cost		$33.80

The performance report for February appears as follows (F denotes favorable; U denotes unfavorable):

Comparison of Actual and Standard

	Actual	Standard	Total Variance
Material A	$37,515	$38,400	$ 885 F
Material B	30,195	28,800	1,395 U
Direct labor	39,525	40,960	1,435 F

Analysis of Total Variance

	Total	Price	Usage
Material A	$ 885 F	$ 615 U	$1,500 F
Material B	1,395 U	495 U	900 U
Direct labor	1,435 F	1,275 F	160 F

There were no beginning or ending inventories of material A or material B.

Required

A. How many units were produced during February?

B. What was the actual price paid per pound for material A during February?

C. How many pounds of material A were used during February?

D. What was the actual price paid per gallon for material B during February?

E. How many gallons of material B were purchased during February?

F. What was the actual wage rate per hour during February?

G. How many actual labor hours were used during February?

56. Ben Inc. manufactures video games. Market saturation and technological innovations have caused pricing pressures, which have resulted in declining profits. To stem the slide in profits until new products can be introduced, top management has turned its attention to both manufacturing economics and increased production. To realize these objectives, an incentive program has been developed to reward production managers who contribute to an increase in the number of units produced and effect cost reductions.

The production managers have responded to the pressure of improving manufacturing in several ways that have resulted in increased completed units over normal production levels. The video game machines are put together by the programming group (PG) and the graphics group (GG). To attain increased production levels, PG and GG groups commenced rejecting games that previously would have been tested and modified to meet manufacturing standards. Preventive maintenance on machines used in the production of these games has been postponed, with only emergency repair work being performed to keep production lines moving. The maintenance department is concerned that there will be serious breakdowns and unsafe operating conditions.

The more aggressive assembly group production supervisors have pressured maintenance personnel to attend to their machines at the expense of other groups. This has resulted in machine downtime in the PG and GG groups, which, when coupled with demands for accelerated delivery by the assembly group, has led to more frequent rejections and increased friction among departments.

Ben Inc. operates under a standard cost system. The standard costs for video games are as follows:

Cost Item	Quantity	Cost	Total
Direct Materials			
CD	1	$20	$20
Package	1	15	15
Labels	2	1	2
Direct Labor			
Assembly group	2 hours	8	16
PG group	1 hour	9	9
GG group	1.5 hours	10	15
Variable overhead	4.5 hours	2	9
Total standard cost per unit			$ 86

Ben's prepares monthly performance reports based on standard costs. Presented in the following table is the contribution report for May, when production and sales both reached 2,200 units:

Ben Inc. Contribution Report for May

	Budget	Actual	Variance
Units	2,000	2,200	200 F
Revenue	$200,000	$220,000	$20,000 F
Variable Costs			
Direct material	74,000	85,600	11,600 U
Direct labor	80,000	93,460	13,460 U
Variable overhead	18,000	18,800	800 U
Total variable costs	$172,000	$197,860	$25,860 U
Contribution margin	$ 28,000	$ 22,140	$ 5,860 U

Ben's top management was surprised by the unfavorable contribution to overall corporate profits in spite of the increased sales in May. Al Miller, the cost accountant, was assigned to identify and report on the reasons for the unfavorable contribution results as well as the individuals or groups responsible. After review, Miller prepared the following usage report:

Ben Inc. Usage Report for May

Direct Materials	Quantity	Actual Cost
CDs	2,200 units	$ 44,000
Package	2,200 units	35,000
Labels	4,400 units	6,600
Direct Labor		
Assembly	3,900 hours	31,200
CDs	2,400 hours	23,760
Packages/labels	3,500 hours	38,500
Variable overhead	9,800 hours	18,800
Total variable cost		$197,860

Miller reported that the PG and GG groups supported the increased production levels but experienced abnormal machine downtime, causing idle labor, which required the use of overtime to keep up with the accelerated demand for parts. The idle time was charged to direct labor. Miller also reported that the production managers of these two groups resorted to parts rejection as opposed to testing and modification procedures formerly applied. Miller determined that the assembly group met management's objectives by increasing production while using lower than standard hours.

Required

A. For May, Ben Inc.'s labor rate variance was $5,660 unfavorable, and the labor efficiency variance was $200 favorable. By using these two variances and calculating the following five variances, prepare an explanation of the $5,860 unfavorable variance between budgeted and actual contribution margin during May.

(1) Materials price variance

(2) Materials quantity variance

(3) Variable overhead efficiency variance

(4) Variable overhead spending variance

(5) Sales volume variance

B. Tell the story of the variances.

Step 2 IDENTIFY OBJECTIVES

C. Identify and briefly explain the behavioral factors that may promote friction among the production managers and between the production managers and the maintenance manager.

Step 3 IDENTIFY AND ANALYZE AVAILABLE OPTIONS

D. Evaluate Al Miller's analysis of the unfavorable contribution results in terms of its completeness and its effect on the behavior of the production groups. What decisions need to be made about increasing the contribution margin?

57. Franklin Glass Works' production budget for the year ended November 30, 2002, was based on 200,000 units. Each unit requires two standard hours of labor for completion. Total overhead was budgeted at $900,000 for the year, and the fixed-overhead rate was estimated to be $3 per unit. Both fixed and variable overhead are assigned to the product on the basis of direct labor hours. The actual data for the year ended November 30, 2002, are as follows:

Actual production in units	198,000
Actual direct labor hours	440,000
Actual variable overhead	$352,000
Actual fixed overhead	$575,000

Required

A. What are the standard hours allowed for actual production for the year ended November 30, 2002?

B. What is Franklin's variable-overhead efficiency variance for the year?

C. What is Franklin's variable-overhead spending variance for the year?

D. What is Franklin's fixed-overhead spending variance for the year?

E. What is the fixed overhead applied to Franklin's production for the year?

58. JanDan Inc. (JDI) is a specialty frozen food processor located in the southeastern states. Since its founding in 1992, JDI has enjoyed a loyal local clientele that is willing to pay premium prices for the high-quality frozen foods it prepares from specialized recipes. In the past two years, the company has experienced rapid sales growth in its operating region and has had many inquiries about supplying its products on a national basis. To meet this growth, JDI expanded its processing capabilities, which resulted in increased production and distribution costs. Furthermore, JDI has been encountering pricing pressure from competitors outside its normal marketing region.

As JDI desires to continue its expansion, Nick Guice, CEO, has engaged a consulting firm to assist JDI in determining its best course of action. The consulting firm concluded that premium pricing is sustainable in some areas, but if sales growth is to be achieved, JDI must make some price concessions. Also, in order to maintain profit margins, costs must be reduced and controlled. The consulting firm recommended the institution of a standard cost system that would also facilitate a flexible budgeting system to better accommodate the changes in demand that can be expected when serving an expanding market area.

Guice met with his management team and explained the recommendations of the consulting firm. Guice then assigned the task of establishing standard costs to his management team. After discussing the situation with their respective staffs, the management team met to review the matter.

Janie Morgan, purchasing manager, advised that meeting expanded production would necessitate obtaining basic food supplies from other than JDI's traditional sources. This would entail increased raw material and shipping costs and might result in lower-quality supplies. Consequently, these increased costs would need to be made up by the processing department if current cost levels are to be maintained or reduced.

Dan Walters, processing manager, countered that the need to accelerate processing cycles to increase production, coupled with the possibility of receiving lower-grade supplies, can be expected to result in a slip in quality and a greater product rejection rate. Under these circumstances, per unit labor utilization cannot be maintained or reduced, and forecasting future unit labor content becomes very difficult.

Corinne Kelly, production engineer, advised that if the equipment is not properly maintained and thoroughly cleaned at prescribed daily intervals, it can be anticipated that the quality and unique taste of the frozen food product will be affected. Kent Jackson, vice president of sales, stated that if quality cannot be maintained, JDI cannot expect to increase sales to the levels projected.

When Guice was apprised of the problems encountered by his management team, he advised them that if agreement could not be reached on appropriate standards he would arrange to have them set by the consulting firm, and everyone would have to live with the results.

Required

A. List the major advantages of using a standard cost system.

B. List disadvantages that can result from using a standard cost system.

C. Identify those who should participate in setting standards, and describe the benefits of their participation in the standard-setting process.

D. Explain the general features and characteristics associated with the introduction and operation of a standard cost system that make it an effective tool for cost control.

E. What could be the consequences if Nick Guice, CEO of JanDan Inc., has the standards set by an outside consulting firm?

F. Explain what is meant by variance and variance analysis.

G. Discuss the materials variances and why they would occur.

H. Explain the overhead variances. Include a discussion of variable and fixed-overhead variances.

59. Corinne's Country Rockers' flexible budget for variable overhead is $24,000, and the flexible budget for fixed overhead is $15,000. When Corinne's analyzes this overhead using activity-based costing, the $39,000 of budgeted overhead is traced to six activities: material handling, setting up machinery, assembly, finishing, maintenance, and inspections. The costs associated with each activity and their respective cost drivers are as follows:

Activity	Flexible Budget Amount	Cost Driver	Budgeted Volume
Material handling	$ 6,000	Number of moves	200
Setting up machinery	4,000	Number of setups	80
Assembly	14,000	Number of labor hours	6,000
Finishing	4,800	Number of labor hours	2,000
Maintenance	4,800	Number of maintenance hours	160
Inspections	5,400	Number of inspections	2,400

The actual cost and volume for each activity are as follows:

Activity	Cost	Volume
Material handling	$ 6,200	205 moves
Setting up machinery	4,150	90 setups
Assembly	13,925	6,300 labor hours
Finishing	4,775	2,100 labor hours
Maintenance	5,120	150 maintenance hours
Inspections	5,400	2,440 inspections

Required

A. Compute the overhead application rate for each activity. Put your answer in the format of an activity-based costing flexible budget.

B. Using the actual volume and cost, compute the spending and efficiency variances for each activity. Compute the total variance for each activity and the overall variance.

Chapter 11

Other Tools for Cost Control and Performance Evaluation

Study Tools

A Review of the Previous Chapter

In Chapter 10, we discussed flexible budgeting and introduced the concept of standard costs and variance analysis as tools to help managers "manage by exception" and evaluate performance in their control function. The chapter also included a discussion of the use of variance analysis in an ABC environment, the limitations of standard costing, and variance analysis and behavioral considerations.

A Preview of This Chapter

In this chapter, we discuss cost control and performance evaluation in a decentralized environment and the impact of responsibility accounting and segment reporting on decision making in decentralized organizations. We discuss performance evaluation in cost, profit, and investment centers, utilizing variance analysis and other financial measures of performance, including the segmented income statement, return on investment (ROI), residual income, and economic value added (EVA).

Key concepts include:

- There are advantages and disadvantages to decentralized companies.
- Decentralized organizations require well-developed and well-integrated information systems.
- The key to effective decision making in a decentralized organization is responsibility accounting—holding managers responsible for only those things under their control.
- Evaluating investment centers requires focusing on the level of investment required in generating a segment's profit.
- The transfer price that provides the most benefit to the company as a whole is the one that should be chosen.

A Preview of Upcoming Chapters

In Chapter 12, we discuss a variety of nonfinancial and qualitative measures used in a "balanced-scorecard" approach to measuring performance.

Learning Objectives

After studying the material in this chapter, you should be able to:

LO1 Understand the structure and organization of decentralized operations

LO2 Evaluate how responsibility accounting is used to help manage in decentralized operations

LO3 Understand the concept of cost, profit, and investment centers and how managers of each must be evaluated differently

LO4 Compute segment margin to evaluate the performance of managers and the segments under their control

LO5 Compute and interpret return on investment (ROI), residual income, and economic value added (EVA) as measures of financial performance for investment centers

LO6 Evaluate the impact of transfer pricing on segment performance and decision making

In this chapter, we discuss organizations with an emphasis on cost control and performance evaluation in a decentralized environment. We also discuss the impact of responsibility accounting and segment reporting on decision making in decentralized organizations. We discuss performance evaluation in cost, profit, and investment centers utilizing variance analysis and other financial measures of performance, including the segmented income statement, return on investment (ROI), residual income, and economic value added (EVA). Nonfinancial performance measures are discussed in more detail in Chapter 12. We conclude the chapter with a discussion of transfer pricing issues with respect to cost control and performance evaluation. ■

INTRODUCTION

As the owner and CEO of a chain of local retail shoe stores, you would be responsible for all aspects of your company's performance—from purchasing shoes to setting prices to investing in new fixtures or even to expanding operations by opening new stores. Consequently, your performance should be evaluated based on all these factors—the costs incurred, the revenue generated, and the investment made in the company. Contrast the responsibilities of the CEO of the company to the responsibilities of a manager of a specific store. As the store manager, you are likely to have some authority over setting prices of shoes, but purchasing decisions are made for the entire chain. Likewise, although you are likely to have some responsibility over making improvements to your store, major renovations and expansions can be made only with the approval of the CEO. Obviously, it would not be fair to the store manager to evaluate his or her performance based on the profit earned by the entire chain. In addition, it would probably not be appropriate to evaluate the store manager's performance based on the profit of his or her store, as a major component of the costs (the costs of shoes sold) is out of the store manager's control. In general, managers should be held responsible for only those things over which they have control. The dilemma for companies is to find tools that allow the evaluation of managers at all levels in the organization—from a plant manager in a factory to the manager of a retail store to the regional sales manager to the CEO.

MANAGEMENT OF DECENTRALIZED ORGANIZATIONS

LO1
Understand the structure and organization of decentralized operations

A **decentralized organization** is one in which decision-making authority is spread throughout the organization as opposed to being confined to top-level management. When a few individuals at the top of an organization retain decision-making authority, the organization is referred to as centralized. In a decentralized environment, managers at various levels throughout the organization make key decisions about operations relating to their specific areas of responsibility. These areas are called segments. Segments can be branches and divisions or individual products. Any activity or part of the business for which a manager needs cost, revenue, or profit data can be considered a segment. Reporting financial and other information by segments is called segment reporting. This chapter discusses segment reporting and cost control and performance evaluation issues in segments of decentralized organizations.

Decentralization varies from organization to organization. Most organizations are decentralized to some degree. At one end of the spectrum, managers are given complete authority to make decisions at their level of operations. At the other extreme, managers have little, if any, authority to make decisions. Most firms will fall somewhere in the middle. However, the tendency is to move toward more, rather than less, decentralization.

IN THE NEWS

http://www.ford.com

In 1999, Ford Motor Company reorganized its senior management by shifting authority to its regional operations in an effort to react more quickly to changing market conditions and to boost sales. Under the new structure, Ford's regional and brand executives have more authority in deciding what kinds of cars and trucks to make and how to market them ("Ford's Wallace Gets Top Financial Post, and Some Management Is Decentralized," *Wall Street Journal,* October 18, 1999, B4).

There are many benefits to decentralization. Generally, those closest to a problem are most familiar with the problem and its root causes. In the past, decentralization has been key in improving customer service. By pushing decision-making authority down to lower levels, managers most familiar with a problem have the opportunity to solve it. At the same time, top management is left with more time to devote to long-range strategic planning, as decentralization removes the responsibility for much of the day-to-day decision making. Third, studies have shown that managers allowed to make decisions in a decentralized environment have higher job satisfaction than do managers in centralized organizations. Finally, managers who are given increased responsibility for decision making early in their careers generally become better managers because of the on-the-job training they receive. In other words, experience is the best teacher. Ford's decentralization was designed in part to help develop new talent by giving more executives responsibilities for entire businesses (see the previous "In the News").

However, there can be drawbacks. When decision-making authority is spread among too many managers, a lack of company focus can occur. Managers may become so concerned with their own areas of responsibility that they lose sight of the big picture. Because of this lack of focus on the company as a whole, managers may tend to make decisions benefiting their own segments, which may not always be in the best interest of the company. In addition, managers may not be adequately trained in decision making at the early stages of their careers. The costs of training managers can be high, and the potential costs of bad decisions while new managers are being trained should be considered.

Key Concept: *There are advantages and disadvantages to decentralized companies.*

Accounting Information Systems and Decentralized Organizations

Decentralized organizations require well-developed and well-integrated information systems. The flow of information and open communication between divisions and upper and lower management is critical. This can be a problem for companies whose systems simply don't provide the kind of quantitative and qualitative information needed at the segment level. For this reason, the use of enterprise resource planning (ERP) systems has been particularly helpful in decentralized organizations. ERP systems (which are discussed in more detail in Chapter 13) integrate and provide information to managers throughout an organization. Information on individual segments and business lines is more readily available than ever before.

Key Concept: *Decentralized organizations require well-developed and well-integrated information systems.*

Responsibility Accounting and Segment Reporting

LO2
Evaluate how responsibility accounting is used to help manage in decentralized operations

The key to effective decision making in a decentralized organization is **responsibility accounting**—holding managers responsible for only those things under their control. In reality, the amount of control a manager has can vary greatly from situation to situation. For example, 75 percent of the shoes offered for sale at the shoe department of your local J. C. Penney store may be purchased regionally or nationally to obtain quantity-purchase discounts from suppliers, whereas 25 percent are purchased at the discretion of the individual store manager. Should the manager of the shoe department of the local J. C. Penney's be held responsible for the cost of shoes purchased and the profit earned on shoe sales?

In the previous chapter, variance analysis was used to help evaluate the performance of managers by focusing on who had responsibility for a variance. Usage variances were typically the responsibility of production managers, and price variances were typically the responsibility of purchasing managers. However, as you will recall, general rules like this must be used with caution. For example, the purchasing manager might be responsible for a usage variance if low-quality materials contributed to excessive waste.

In decentralized organizations, detailed information is needed to evaluate the effectiveness of managerial decision making. Companywide budgets, cost standards, income statements, and so on are not sufficient to evaluate the performance of each of a company's segments. For example, overall financial statements generated for external reporting purposes would be of limited use in evaluating the performance of the myriad of managers at General Motors. The manager of the Chevy truck division would be evaluated just on the results of the Chevy truck division, whereas the manager of the GM car division would be evaluated just on the results of that division. Going down a step further, a production manager dealing only with the manufacture of the Chevy S-10 pickup and a production manager who works only with the C/K Silverado series of full-size trucks would be evaluated using different information. Even within a product line, managers should be held responsible only for those things under their control. A manager on an engine assembly line should not be evaluated and held responsible for a production problem dealing with the vehicle body. Plant managers would be evaluated based on activities in their plant, regional sales managers would be held responsible for sales in their region, and so on.

http://www.gm.com

Key Concept: *The key to effective decision making in a decentralized organization is responsibility accounting—holding managers responsible for only those things under their control.*

COST, PROFIT, AND INVESTMENT CENTERS

To enhance the use of responsibility accounting for decision making, organizations typically identify the different segments, or levels of responsibility, as cost, revenue, profit, or investment centers and attach different levels of responsibility to each segment. A **cost center** manager has control over costs but not over revenue or capital investment (purchasing) decisions. The purchasing manager of a store, the production manager for a particular type of CD player, the maintenance manager in a hotel, and the human resources manager of a CPA firm would likely be considered managers of cost centers. The manager of a cost center should be evaluated on how well he or she controls costs in the respective segment. Consequently, performance reports typically focus on differences between budgeted and actual costs using variance analysis. A **performance report** provides key financial and nonfinancial measures of performance appropriate for a particular segment.

A **revenue center** manager has control over the generation of revenue but not costs. Examples include the sales manager of a retail store, the sales department of a production facility, and the reservation department of an airline. Performance reports of a revenue center often focus on sales volume and sales price variances (discussed in Chapter 10).

A **profit center** manager has control over both cost and revenue but not capital investment decisions. Whereas the purchasing manager of a retail store was a manager of a cost center, the overall manager of the store would probably be a profit center manager. Likewise, the manager of an entire product line in a factory, the manager of a particular hotel location, and the partner in charge of the tax department at a CPA firm would be considered profit center managers. It is important to understand that profit center managers still don't have control over making investment decisions. For example, the profit center managers described here could not make decisions to remodel a store, buy new manufacturing equipment, add a swimming pool to a hotel, or open a new office.

The manager of a profit center should be evaluated on both revenue generation and cost control. Consequently, performance reports typically focus on income measures,

© AMY C. ETRA/PHOTOEDIT

© AMY C. ETRA/PHOTOEDIT

such as the overall flexible budget variance (discussed in Chapter 10). The flexible budget variance is the difference between the actual and budgeted operating income. However, this can be a problem when uncontrollable fixed costs are included in the analysis. Segment managers should be held responsible for only those costs under their control. Consequently, other measures of profit center performance, such as segment margin, are also commonly used.

In addition to being responsible for a segment's revenue and expenses, an **investment center** manager is responsible for the amount of capital invested in generating its income. An investment center (also called a **strategic business unit or SBU**) is in essence a separate business with its own value chains. An investment center manager is involved in decisions ranging from research and development to production to marketing and sales and customer service.

Although the manager of an investment center can be evaluated using some of the same tools as profit centers, the amount of assets or investment under the manager's control must also be considered. Measures of performance for investment centers are discussed later in the chapter.

PAUSE & Reflect

The J. C. Penney store in your local shopping mall is likely treated as a profit center. What about a small independently owned and operated store like the one pictured?

http://www.jcpenney.com

PROFIT CENTER PERFORMANCE AND SEGMENTED INCOME STATEMENTS

Segmented income statements calculate income for each major segment of an organization in addition to the company as a whole. Although it is usually easy to keep records of sales by segment, tracing costs to a particular segment and deciding how to treat costs that are incurred for more than one segment can be very difficult.

Variable costs (unit-level costs) are generally traced directly to a segment. Remember, variable costs vary in direct proportion to sales volume. Therefore, they can be allocated to a segment based on sales volume.

Deciding which fixed costs to assign, or allocate, to a segment requires an analysis of the overall company and the individual areas of responsibility (segments) within an organization. **Segment costs** should include *all* costs attributable to that segment but *only* those costs that are actually caused by the segment. Fixed costs that can be easily and conveniently traced to a segment should obviously be assigned to that segment. The problem is that many fixed costs are indirect in nature. Should indirect fixed costs be allocated to segments? A good test for deciding whether to allocate indirect fixed costs is to determine whether the cost would be reduced or eliminated if the segment were eliminated. If

LO3
Understand the concept of cost, profit, and investment centers and how managers of each must be evaluated differently

the cost cannot be reduced or eliminated, it is referred to as a common cost. **Common costs** are indirect costs that are incurred to benefit more than one segment and cannot be directly traced to a particular segment or allocated in a reasonable manner based on what causes the cost to be incurred. In general, common costs should not be allocated to segments.

CAMELBACK MOUNTAIN COMMUNITY BANK

For example, Camelback Mountain Community Bank (headquartered in Phoenix, Arizona) has six branches located in and around the Phoenix metropolitan area. One of those branches is located in Tempe. The Tempe branch incurs fixed lease expense to rent the building in which the bank is located. Obviously, this lease expense is directly traceable to the individual branch (a segment) and should be allocated to that segment. However, if the lease expense is for the corporate headquarters building in Phoenix, the cost is an indirect one and probably should not be allocated to the Tempe branch. In this case, it is doubtful that the lease expense for the headquarters building would be reduced or eliminated if the Tempe branch were eliminated. Therefore, it is probably best treated as a common cost and not allocated to the segment.[1]

Other indirect costs can be allocated to segments if there is a sufficient causal relationship between the cost and the segment. For example, all loan processing for Camelback Mountain Community Bank is done in the headquarters building in Phoenix. Although these costs (for credit checks, loan processing, staff salaries, etc.) may be difficult to directly trace to the Tempe branch, they can be allocated in a manner that reflects the cause of the costs (the number of loans processed, the dollar amount of loans processed, etc.). In addition, it is reasonable to assume that at least some of the loan-processing costs would be reduced or eliminated if the branch were closed.

To allocate indirect costs, there should be a causal relationship between the allocation base and a segment's use of the common cost. Allocating costs using an arbitrary allocation base is inappropriate. Although Camelback Mountain Community Bank could allocate the lease cost of the headquarters building to its branches based on an allocation base, such as square footage or total deposits, such a base would be completely arbitrary. There is no causal relationship between the square footage or total deposits in a branch and the lease expense in the headquarters building. Arbitrary allocations like this may result in a profitable segment appearing unprofitable and may lead to less than optimal decisions concerning that segment.

PAUSE & *Reflect*

Do you think the allocation base is still appropriate or should J. C. Penney treat the auditing, legal, and personnel costs as common costs?

IN THE NEWS **http://www.jcpenney.com**

In the early 1980s, J. C. Penney began allocating the corporate costs of auditing, legal, and personnel services to its subsidiaries based on the time spent providing the services to each subsidiary. Before that time, the allocation was made based on the revenue earned by each subsidiary ("Teamwork Pays Off at Penney's," *Business Week,* April 12, 1982, 107–108).

THE SEGMENTED INCOME STATEMENT

GARCIA&BUFFET CPAs

Garcia and Buffett is a full-service local CPA firm offering services in three departments: tax, audit, and consulting. The tax department is further broken down into individual and business divisions. Garcia and Buffett has annual client billings of $1,000,000, with 50 percent generated from the tax department, 40 percent from the audit department, and the remaining 10 percent from the consulting department. The following table shows

[1] In practice, companies sometimes allocate common costs from headquarters to segments without using them for evaluation purposes. This practice has the advantage of making the segment manager aware that the cost is being incurred and that the cost must ultimately be paid for by revenue generated by the segment.

a segmented income statement broken down into three segments based on the three practice departments:

LO4
Compute segment margin to evaluate the performance of managers and the segments under their control

Segmented Income Statement Using Contribution Format
Segments Defined as Departments

	Total Firm	Tax Department	Audit Department	Consulting Department
Client billings	$1,000,000	$500,000	$400,000	$100,000
Less: Variable expenses	400,000	200,000	160,000	40,000
Contribution margin	$ 600,000	$300,000	$240,000	$ 60,000
Less: Traceable fixed	200,000	100,000	75,000	25,000
Segment margin	$ 400,000	$200,000	$165,000	$ 35,000
Less: Common fixed	200,000			
Net income	$ 200,000			

The $100,000 of fixed costs traceable to the tax department include advertising specifically geared to the tax department, the salary of the tax manager, the costs of research material used in the tax library, and computer software used for tax preparation. Common fixed costs (for the firm as a whole) include salaries of the managing partner of the firm, the human resources manager, and the receptionist and depreciation of the office building.

In the following table, Garcia and Buffett goes a step further and provides a segmented income statement for the two divisions within the tax department. Note that the statements are based on the contribution margin format introduced in Chapter 6. The primary difference is the separation of fixed costs into traceable fixed costs and common fixed costs and the interim calculation of segment margin.

Segmented Income Statement Using Contribution Format
Segments Defined as Divisions

	Tax Department	Individual Tax Division	Business Tax Division
Client billings	$500,000	$100,000	$400,000
Less: Variable expenses	200,000	80,000	120,000
Contribution margin	$300,000	$ 20,000	$280,000
Less: Traceable fixed	80,000	30,000	50,000
Divisional segment margin	$220,000	$ (10,000)	$230,000
Less: Common fixed	20,000		
Departmental segment margin	$200,000		

Note that although $100,000 of fixed costs were traced to the tax department in the first table (when segments were defined as departments), only $80,000 are subsequently traced to the individual and business divisions; $20,000 of traceable costs have become common costs. In this case, the advertising costs for the tax division and the cost of research materials in the tax library cannot be traced directly to either the individual or the business division.

PAUSE & Reflect

Garcia and Buffett has considered allocating the advertising costs to each division based on the revenue generated in each division. Comment on whether this is appropriate allocation base.

As discussed in Chapter 6, contribution margin is primarily a measure of short-run profitability, as it ignores fixed costs. It is used extensively in short-run decisions, such as CVP analysis and evaluation of special orders. On the other hand, **segment margin** is a measure of long-term profitability and is more appropriate in addressing long-term decisions, such as whether to drop product lines.

In the case of Garcia and Buffett, the segment margin of the tax department is positive, but the segment margin of the individual tax division is negative. In the long run, the individual tax division is not profitable. However, before the firm decides to eliminate the individual tax division, it should consider other factors (both quantitative and qualitative), including the impact on its highly profitable business tax division.

For example, it may be important for the firm to be perceived as a full-service firm where owners of small businesses can come for help with all their tax and business problems. In addition, planning for a small business must often be integrated with planning for the individual owner of the business. For these reasons, the firm may decide to retain the division even if it has not been profitable. Instead of eliminating the division, Garcia and Buffett may decide to focus on ways to make the division profitable through expanding the array of services offered to clients. For example, the firm may begin offering personal financial planning services to its clients to help them meet their overall financial goals.

Segment Performance and the Value Chain

When segment margin is used to evaluate performance and to make such decisions as whether a segment should be discontinued, it is important to remember that costs are incurred throughout the value chain, not just in the manufacturing process. The value chain includes costs associated with research and development, product design, manufacturing, marketing, distribution, and customer service (see Exhibit 11-1). When making long-run decisions regarding the profitability of a segment (for example, whether to stop manufacturing a product or providing a service), it is imperative that managers consider all costs incurred in the value chain.

Exhibit 11-1 The Value Chain

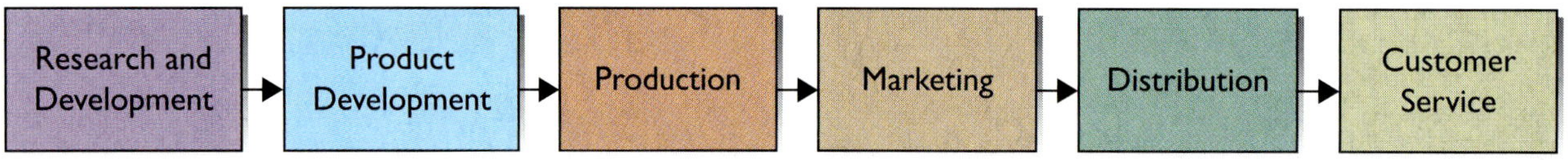

Segment Performance and Activity-Based Costing

The use of activity-based costing (ABC) can affect the classification of costs as traceable or common. As you will recall from the discussion in Chapter 4, when ABC is used, many costs that were previously considered "fixed" are found to vary with respect to batch- or product-level cost drivers. In manufacturing firms, batch-level and product-level activities and costs are often driven by such factors as the number of setups, the number of parts, the number of customer orders, the number of supervision hours, and so on. In service-oriented companies, these costs may vary with the number of customers serviced, the size of the client, or the number of hours spent reviewing files. For example, the "fixed" costs of a research aid in the tax research library at Garcia and Buffett might be driven by the number of research hours provided to each division.

Application in Business

CPA firms incur a variety of costs related to auditing and providing other services to large clients that are publicly held (have stock owned by the general public). These costs (additional training for employees, peer reviews, and other quality reviews mandated by regulators, etc.) might traditionally be considered fixed because they don't vary with revenue or other measures of volume. However, they are in fact driven by the size of clients serviced. If a firm has only a few large publicly held clients, it may choose to stop servicing those clients in order to eliminate a variety of these product-level costs.

INVESTMENT CENTERS AND MEASURES OF PERFORMANCE

LO5
Compute and interpret return on investment (ROI), residual income, and economic value added (EVA) as measures of financial performance for investment centers

In addition to being responsible for a segment's revenue and expenses, an investment center manager is responsible for the amount of capital invested in generating its income. Investment center managers can make capital purchasing decisions, including decisions to remodel facilities, purchase new equipment, expand facilities, or add new locations. Investment centers are typically major divisions or branch operations of a company involved in all aspects of the value chain. In addition to being evaluated using the approaches discussed earlier for cost and profit centers, evaluating investment centers requires focusing on the level of investment required in generating a segment's profit. For this reason, performance reports focus on measures specifically developed for this purpose—return on investment, residual income, and economic value added.

Key Concept: *Evaluating investment centers requires focusing on the level of investment required in generating a segment's profit.*

Concept Question: *Does the manager of a local branch of a national bank likely manage a profit or an investment center? What about the manager of the local Pizza Hut? What about the manager-owner of an independent pizza restaurant or clothing store?*

http://www.pizzahut.com

Concept Answer: Although the answer depends on exactly what the manager of each segment controls, the managers of the local branch of the bank and the Pizza Hut franchise are likely to be evaluated as the managers of profit centers, whereas the owners of the independent stores would likely be treated as managers of investment centers. ■

Managers of investment centers are given complete control over all activities in their respective segments. In fact, an investment center is often treated like a separate business—hence the name *strategic business units.* Managers want to be associated with well-run, profitable divisions. Competition between investment center managers within an organization is sometimes intense. Because of compensation issues, such as year-end bonuses based on performance, managers of investment centers must also be evaluated. Although all the financial measures of performance used in evaluating the managers of cost, revenue, and profit centers apply to investment center managers, they are not sufficient. To some extent, controlling costs and generating revenue (and income) is a function of the investment assets under a manager's control. For example, if a manager had unlimited resources, production costs could be reduced by buying the most efficient equipment available, regardless of the cost. Likewise, sales might be maximized by additional spending on advertising. Income is often larger in big companies than in small companies. However, an investment center manager with low costs, high revenues, and high income cannot really be evaluated without reference to the size of the investment center being managed and the assets under the manager's control.

RETURN ON INVESTMENT (ROI)

http://www.dupont.com

DuPont was the first major company in the United States to recognize that the performance of an investment center must consider the level of investment along with the income generated from that investment. **Return on investment (ROI)** measures the rate of return generated by an investment center's assets.

ROI can be a very simple concept. For example, if you invest $1,000 in a bank certificate of deposit for one year and receive $50 at the end of the year, your return on that investment is 5 percent ($50/$1,000). However, the calculation of return gets a little more complicated when the income is reinvested in another certificate, the amount of assets change, and costs are incurred to manage the money.

In business, the calculation of ROI is generally broken down into two components—a measure of operating performance (called margin) and a measure of how effectively assets are used during a period (called asset turnover). **Margin** is found by dividing an investment center's net operating income by its sales. As such, it can be viewed as the profit that is earned on each dollar of sales. A margin of 10 percent indicates that 10 cents of every sales dollar is profit. **Asset turnover** is calculated by dividing an investment center's sales by its average operating assets during a period. It measures the sales that are generated for a given level of assets.

The formula for return on investment (ROI) is as follows:

$$\text{ROI} = \text{Margin} \times \text{Turnover}$$
$$\text{Margin} = \text{Net operating income/Sales}$$
$$\text{Turnover} = \text{Sales/Average operating assets}$$
$$\text{ROI} = \frac{\text{Net operating income}}{\text{Sales}} \times \frac{\text{Sales}}{\text{Average operating assets}}$$

or

$$\text{ROI} = \frac{\text{Net operating income}}{\text{Average operating assets}}$$

The elements comprising ROI are shown in graphical form in Exhibit 11-2.

Although various investment centers (including companies) may have similar ROIs, their margin and turnover may be very different. For example, a grocery store and a furniture store both have an ROI of 20 percent. However, the grocery store's ROI may be made up of a profit margin of $0.02 per dollar of product sold and a turnover of 10, whereas the furniture store may have a margin of $0.10 per dollar of product sold and a turnover of 2. In this case, the grocery store does not make much from each dollar of sales but generates a lot of sales for the amount of its assets. On the other hand, the furniture store makes more from each sale but does not generate as many sales for the amount of assets under its control.

Net operating income is most frequently used as the measure of income in the ROI formula. Net operating income is defined as income before interest and taxes.

Likewise, the most common measure of investment is average operating assets. **Operating assets** typically include cash, accounts receivable, inventory, and property, plant, and equipment needed to operate a business. Land and other assets held for resale or assets that are idle (a plant that is not being used) are typically not included in operating assets. Because income is measured over time, assets are also generally measured as an av-

Inventory turnover in a grocery store is likely to be much higher than turnover in a furniture store.

© STEVE PETERS/STONE

© MICHAEL NEWMAN/PHOTOEDIT

EXHIBIT 11-2 Elements of Return on Investment (ROI)

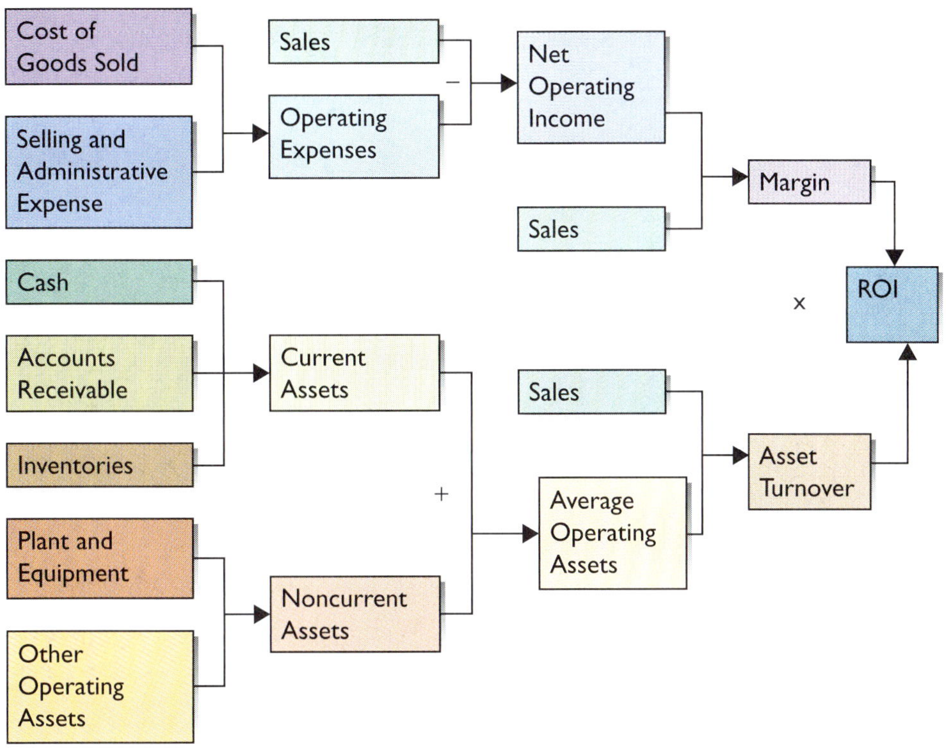

erage of beginning and end-of-period numbers. By focusing on operating income and average operating assets, ROI attempts to isolate the financial performance of a company's core operations.

Whereas cash, accounts receivable, and inventory are generally easy to measure, the measurement of depreciable property, plant, and equipment for purposes of determining ROI poses some interesting questions. The use of net book value (the cost of the assets less accumulated depreciation) is consistent with the calculation of operating income (which includes depreciation expense) but can have some undesirable consequences. For example, as an asset ages, the net book value of the asset decreases. Using net book value can cause ROI to increase over time simply because of the reduction in book value of assets used in the calculation. Choice of depreciation method can also affect ROI calculations. By choosing an accelerated method over straight-line, the book value of the asset decreases more rapidly, increasing ROI. Both of these factors may discourage managers from replacing old assets, such as manufacturing equipment. If managers are evaluated based on ROI, they may be very reluctant to replace aging machinery with a very low book value with an expensive but more efficient piece of equipment.

PAUSE & Reflect

Why might investing in new assets decrease ROI? Will ROI always go down when new equipment is purchased?

The use of gross book value to measure operating assets eliminates age of an asset as a factor in the ROI calculation and any distortions that can be caused by the depreciation method chosen. To illustrate the use of ROI, consider the financial results of Big Al's Pizza Emporium (see page 376). During 2001, Big Al's had average operating assets of \$100,000, consisting of cash, accounts receivable, inventory, and furniture and equipment at book value. All are considered operating assets. Big Al's sales for the year were \$350,000 (consisting of \$275,000 for 23,000 pizzas and \$75,000 for drinks and other side orders). Operating income was \$17,500. The ROI for Big Al's, using the net book value method, would be 17.5 percent, consisting of margin of 0.05 $\left(\frac{\$17,500}{\$350,000}\right)$ and asset turnover of 3.5 $\left(\frac{\$350,000}{\$100,000}\right)$.

A contribution-format income statement for Big Al's is provided in the following table:

Big Al's Pizza Emporium
Contribution-Format Income Statement

Sales Revenue		$350,000	100%
Variable Costs			
Production	$175,000		
Selling, General, and Administrative (S G & A)	75,000	250,000	
Contribution margin		$100,000	28.57
Fixed Costs			
Production	50,000		
S G & A	32,500	82,500	
Net operating income		$ 17,500	

If Big Al would like to increase ROI, what are his options? In general, sales can be increased, operating expenses can be reduced, or the investment in operating assets can be reduced. The first two alternatives increase operating income, and the last option decreases net operating assets.

INCREASE SALES VOLUME OR SALES PRICE

Sales revenue can be raised by either increasing sales volume without changing the sales price or by increasing the sales price without affecting volume. Remember that when sales volume increases, variable costs increase by the same proportional amount because variable costs stay the same per unit but increase in total as more units are sold. In addition, fixed costs remain the same. Thus, if sales volume increases by 5 percent (resulting in sales revenue of $367,500), income will increase by $5,000, to $22,500. ROI will correspondingly increase to 22.5 percent $\left(\frac{\$22,500}{\$100,000}\right)$.

Big Al's Pizza Emporium
Contribution-Format Income Statement

Sales Revenue		$367,500	100%
Variable Costs			
Production	$183,750		
S G & A	78,750	262,500	
Contribution margin		$105,000	28.57
Fixed Costs			
Production	50,000		
S G & A	32,500	82,500	
Net operating income		$ 22,500	

Remember that the contribution margin ratio can be used to quickly calculate the impact on income of a change in sales. If sales increase by $17,500, income will increase by 28.57 percent × $17,500, or $5,000.

Concept Question: *How much would sales volume have to increase to increase Big Al's ROI to 20 percent?*

Concept Answer: Net operating income of $20,000 would generate an ROI of 20 percent ($20,000/$100,000). Using the contribution margin ratio of 28.57 percent, increasing income by $2,500 would require a $8,750 increase in sales revenue to $358,750.

If Big Al just changes the price of his products, the analysis is a little different. Increasing sales prices (without a corresponding change in volume) does *not* affect variable costs or fixed costs. Thus, if revenue were increased by $17,500 because of a 5 percent increase in sales price, income would increase by the same $17,500. ROI would increase to 35 percent $\left(\frac{\$35,000}{\$100,000}\right)$.

Concept Question: *How might Big Al increase sales volume without decreasing sales prices or increasing other costs, such as advertising, or increase sales prices without affecting volume?*

Concept Answer: Neither is likely. As a practical matter, changing sales volume or sales price is likely to impact other variables as well. For this reason, Big Al might try to increase ROI by using other options.

DECREASE OPERATING COSTS

ROI can also be increased by decreasing operating costs. The decrease in costs can be concentrated in variable or fixed costs or both. The key is that any decrease in operating costs will increase operating income and have a positive impact on ROI. In the following income statement, variable production costs are reduced by 5 percent by using a different supplier for direct materials. Income increases by $8,750, resulting in an ROI of 26.25 percent $\left(\frac{\$26,250}{\$100,000}\right)$.

Big Al's Pizza Emporium
Contribution-Format Income Statement

Sales Revenue		$350,000	100%
Variable Costs			
Production	$166,250		
S G & A	75,000	241,250	
Contribution margin		$108,750	31.07
Fixed Costs			
Production	50,000		
S G & A	32,500	82,500	
Net operating income		$ 26,250	

Concept Question: *Why did the contribution margin percentage increase when the variable costs were lowered? Would it change if fixed costs were lowered?*

Concept Answer: Remember the structure of the contribution-format income statement. Contribution margin is equal to sales minus all the variable costs, so when the variable costs are lowered, the contribution margin will increase, as will the percentage. Because fixed costs are deducted from contribution margin, a change in fixed cost would not affect contribution margin.

DECREASE THE AMOUNT OF OPERATING ASSETS

The third way to increase ROI is to decrease the amount invested in operating assets. Although this may be difficult to do in the short run with property, plant, and equipment, the amount of average operating assets can be decreased through better management of accounts receivable, a reduction in inventory levels, and so on. For example, let's assume that Big Al's reduces operating assets by 10 percent by lowering the amount of materials kept in inventory and more prudently collecting accounts receivable. Reducing average operating assets to $90,000 will increase ROI to 19.44 percent.

In some cases, evaluating the performance of an investment center and its manager using ROI can cause problems. For example, Big Al is thinking about opening a second location and bringing in a new manager to run the business at the existing location. (Because the new location will be substantially larger than the existing location, he wants to devote his full attention to the successful start-up of the new location.) Before leaving, Big Al worked diligently to reduce operating costs and increased the location's net operating income to $22,500. He also reduced the location's average operating assets to $90,000 through actively managing his inventory. ROI was therefore 25 percent. His goal and minimum acceptable return for both locations is to maintain an ROI of 20 percent. However, the new manager may reject potential projects or investments that are profitable (and earn a return greater than 20 percent) but would lower the location's overall ROI. For example, the new manager is considering purchasing a new automated pizza oven that will reduce the time it takes to make a pizza and the electricity consumed. The equipment costs $15,000 and is expected to result in increased income of $3,200. Although the return on investment for this particular piece of equipment is over 21 percent, the manager is likely to reject the purchase because it will reduce his overall ROI.

Using ROI to compare segments within a company can also be a problem. For example, a consulting division of a company operated as an investment center is likely to have few tangible assets compared to an asset-intensive manufacturing division operated as an investment center. If both generate an ROI of 15 percent, which appears to be doing better? Rather than comparing the ROI of divisions with different assets, costs, and revenue streams, it is often preferable to compare the ROI of a segment to a budget or a goal for that segment.

RESIDUAL INCOME

As an alternative to ROI, the manager of an investment center can be evaluated based on the residual income generated by the strategic business unit (SBU). **Residual income** is the amount of income earned in excess of a predetermined minimum level of return on assets. All other things being equal, the higher the residual income of an investment center, the better.

$$\text{Residual income} = \text{Net operating income} - (\text{Average operating assets} \times \text{Minimum required rate of return})$$

In the case of Big Al's (discussed earlier) at the time the new location is opened, the residual income at the existing location would be as follows:

$$\$22,500 - (\$90,000 \times 20\%) = \$4,500$$

If the new manager has the opportunity to purchase a new pizza oven at a cost of $15,000 and expects that profits will increase by $3,200, evaluating the new manager using residual income will result in the manager's purchasing the new oven. The residual income of the existing location will increase from $4,500, to $4,700, as follows:

$$\$25{,}700 - (\$105{,}000 \times 20\%) = \$4{,}700$$

Concept Question: *If Big Al's has a minimum required rate of return equal to 20 percent and generates a residual income of zero on sales of $350,000 and average operating assets of $90,000, what is its ROI?*

Concept Answer: Big Al's income must be equal to $18,000, resulting in an ROI of 20 percent $\left(\frac{\$18{,}000}{\$90{,}000}\right)$. ■

Residual income has its problems as well. It should not be used to compare the performance of investment centers of different sizes. For example, Big Al's new location will be considerably larger than the existing location. As shown here, average operating assets in the new location total $300,000, compared to $105,000 in the existing location.

Return on Investment and Residual Income

	Existing Location	**New Location**
Average operating assets	$105,000	$300,000
Minimum required return	20%	20%
Net operating income	$ 25,700	$ 70,000
Residual income	$ 4,700	$ 10,000
ROI	24.5%	23.3%

In this case, the residual income of the new location (run by Big Al) is higher than the residual income of the existing location (run by the new manager). However, Big Al did not necessarily manage the new location better; it's just bigger. As you can see, the ROI of the new division is actually lower than the ROI of the existing location. Which measure is better? Both are useful but often for different purposes. Residual income is more useful as a performance measure for a single investment center, whereas ROI is better suited as a comparative measure. However, as mentioned earlier, ROI must be used cautiously when comparing investment centers with different core businesses or those with markedly different revenue and cost structures.

TECHNOLOGY FOCUS

E-business and Internet companies often have very few tangible assets. On the other hand, they may have large investments in employee resources and intellectual capital. How might traditional measures, such as ROI and residual income, be adjusted to reflect these new types of businesses?

APPLICATION IN BUSINESS

http://www.daimlerchrysler.com

Large international companies may have several core businesses. For example, DaimlerChrysler has more than a half dozen major business components operating as strategic business units. The revenue generated from the SBUs ranges from under $1 billion annually in the diesel engine and automotive electronic divisions, to more than $64 billion in the Chrysler automobile division. The company also has a financial services division with revenue of more than $16 billion.

ECONOMIC VALUE ADDED (EVA)

The most contemporary measure of investment center performance is **economic value added (EVA).**[2] In a nutshell, by focusing on whether after-tax profits are greater than the cost of capital, EVA tells management whether shareholder wealth is being created. Although EVA is primarily a measure of shareholder wealth, companies may use it internally as part of incentive compensation plans or to encourage managers to undertake desired behavior.

Economic value added = After-tax operating profit − [(Total assets − Current liabilities) × Weighted average cost of capital]

As you can see, the calculation of EVA is very similar to that for residual income. However, EVA does have several important differences. First, EVA is based on after-tax operating profit, not before-tax operating profit. Second, assets are often shown net of current liabilities. In addition, companies may modify income and asset measurements based on generally accepted accounting principles (GAAP) to better reflect the changing nature of business today. For example, to encourage investments in research and development, employee training, and customer development, expenditures in these areas may be capitalized as an asset for EVA purposes rather than expensed against income. Inventories may be restated to their replacement cost, and the value of assets may be restated to reflect their true economic value.

Finally, EVA considers the actual cost of capital, both debt and equity, as compared to a minimum required rate of return. The calculation of the cost of debt is straightforward and is equal to the interest paid on that debt. However, the cost of equity is more complex and is basically assumed to be the amount that an investor could earn on an investment with similar risk.

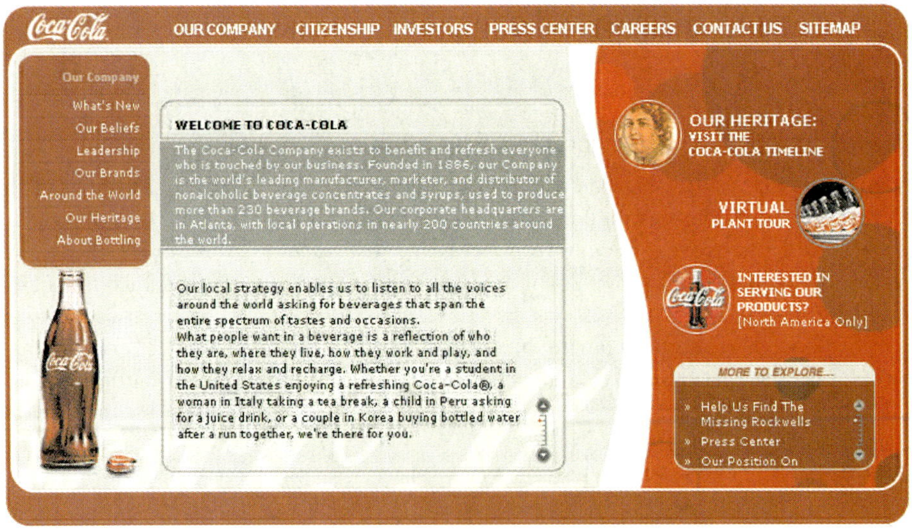

COURTESY OF COCA-COLA

IN THE NEWS **http://www.coca-cola.com**

Roberto Goizueeta, the past CEO of Coca-Cola, explains EVA this way: "We raise capital to make concentrate, and sell it and make operating profit. Then we pay the cost of capital. Shareholders pocket the difference" ("The Real Key to Creating Wealth," by Shawn Tully, *Fortune*, September 20, 1993, 38).

[2]EVA is a registered trademark used with permission of Stern Stewart & Company.

MANAGEMENT ACTIONS AND DECISIONS

http://www.sprint.com

At Sprint, managers are given recommendations on how to incorporate EVA into their everyday decisions.

Commit new capital to value-creating projects. For example:

- What equipment should we buy to provide new and better products and services to our customers?
- What new marketing efforts will improve customer satisfaction and result in increased sales and profits?
- What new business opportunities should we pursue?

Increase profits without using additional capital. For example:

- How can we reduce customer churn or sell more products without spending more?
- What costs can be reduced through Business Process Improvement efforts?
- How can we change government regulation to make our business operate more efficiently?

Withdraw capital from activities that produce inadequate returns compared to other uses for that capital. For example:

- What products and customers are not as profitable as we expect?
- How can accounts receivable or inventories be reduced to free up cash?
- What assets should be sold or redeployed?

EVA is used in a variety of business management processes to align our actions with creating value.

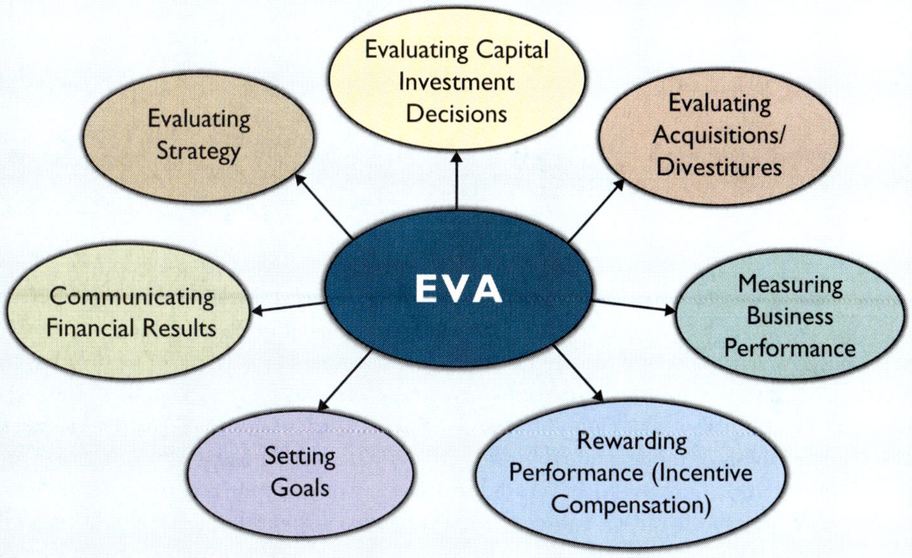

As an example, assume that a division operating as an SBU has the following results:

Operating income (before tax) per GAAP financial statements	$1,000,000
Total assets per GAAP financial statements	4,000,000
Expenditures related to employee training, research and development, and customer development*	1,000,000
Fair market value of property, plant, and equipment†	2,500,000
Current liabilities	500,000
Tax rate	40%
Weighted average cost of capital	10%

*These expenditures were expensed on the GAAP financial statements. Management chooses to capitalize them for purposes of calculating EVA.

†Included on the balance sheet at cost of $2,000,000. Management chooses to use the fair market value of assets in calculating EVA.

After adjusting for the impact of capitalizing expenditures related to employee training, research and development, and customer development, operating income is equal to $2,000,000, and after-tax operating income is $1,200,000 [($2,000,000 × (1 – 0.40)]. Total assets of $4,000,000 (per GAAP) are increased by $1,500,000 to reflect the impact of the capitalized expenses of $1,000,000 and to increase property, plant, and equipment to fair market value. After adjusting for current liabilities, assets used in the EVA calculation are equal to $5,000,000.

$$\begin{aligned} \text{EVA} &= \$1{,}200{,}000 - [\$5{,}000{,}000 \times 10\%] \\ &= \$1{,}200{,}000 - \$500{,}000 \\ &= \$700{,}000 \end{aligned}$$

SEGMENT PERFORMANCE AND TRANSFER PRICING

LO6
Evaluate the impact of transfer pricing on segment performance and decision making

When segments within the same company sell products or services to one another, special problems arise when evaluating performance of the segments. For example, when an automobile manufacturer also manufactures car batteries, what price does the battery division charge the auto division for the battery? This may seem like an easy or unimportant question because the transfer is made within the same company. After all, if I am the owner of the company, what comes out of one pocket simply goes in the other. However, when the managers of the separate divisions are evaluated based on profit or other performance measures, such as ROI or EVA, the **transfer price** becomes very important.

Let's refer back to Chapter 7 and use Birdie-Maker Golf Inc. as an example. As you will recall, Birdie-Maker manufactures and sells golf clubs. Birdie-Maker is organized into two divisions—a club division that manufactures the shafts and heads for its clubs and a grip division that manufactures grips for its clubs. Because Birdie-Maker evaluates division managers based on the profit generated in their respective profit centers, the manager of the grip division will want to charge the highest possible price for its product, and the manager of the club division will want to buy grips at the lowest possible price. Therein lies the problem in transfer pricing. The amount to set for the transfer price is a complex problem with no easy solution.

There are basically three approaches to establishing transfer prices. The first is to use a market price if available. The second is to base the transfer price on the cost of the product transferred. The third is to let the buyer and the seller negotiate the price.

TRANSFER PRICE AT MARKET

If there is an outside market for the product being transferred between divisions, the transfer price should be based on the market price of the product. However, in order to be effective, the manager of the buying division must have the authority to purchase from an outside supplier if the selling division does not want to meet the market price, and the manager of the selling division must have the authority to sell to outside buyers if he or she can earn a higher profit. The use of a market price thus provides an incentive for both the selling division and the buying division to maximize their profits. In reality, few transfers take place at exactly the market price. For example, the grip division of Birdie-Maker can sell grips to another club manufacturer for $10 per grip. However, if the grip division sells internally to the Birdie-Maker club division, it will realize some cost savings from reduced storage and shipping costs. This may lead to negotiations between the manager of the grip division and the manger of the club division and a transfer at a price somewhat under $10.

Birdie Maker

If the selling division is not at full capacity, the transfer price will often be adjusted as well. For example, if the grip division has the capacity to make 20,000 grips but can sell only 10,000 to outside buyers, it is likely that the two divisions will set transfer prices based on cost or negotiate a transfer price below the full market price of the grips.

TRANSFER PRICE AT COST

When no outside market exists or when the selling division has excess capacity, transfer prices are often established based on the cost of the product being transferred.

No Outside Market Let's assume that Birdie-Maker's grip is unique and therefore cannot be sold to other club manufacturers. Birdie-Maker's grip division manufactures grips for $6, which consists of $4 of direct material, direct labor, and variable overhead and $40,000 of fixed manufacturing costs (based on a capacity of 20,000 grips). Administrative costs include $1 of variable costs and $20,000 of fixed costs.

If Birdie-Maker chooses to set the transfer price using product cost as the basis, the question becomes, at what cost? Variable manufacturing costs are $4 per grip, and total variable costs are $5 per grip, whereas the full absorption cost of making a grip is $6. Total costs, including the fixed administrative costs, are $7. In order for the grip division to truly operate as a profit center (and to be evaluated as such), it must be able to earn a profit. However, the club division may be reluctant to "buy" at whatever price is established by the grip division. What price is fair?

When we use our decision model to address this problem (see Exhibit 11-3), we first define the decision to be made. The decision to be made is to establish a transfer price for grips that are to be sold to the club division. The objectives of the decision are to set a price that does not adversely affect either manager or the firm and to maximize Birdie-Maker's overall profit. The options in this situation are to establish the transfer price at the variable manufacturing costs of making the grips, the full cost of making the grips, or even to set the price so that the grip division earns an acceptable profit.

EXHIBIT 11-3 The Decision-Making Model

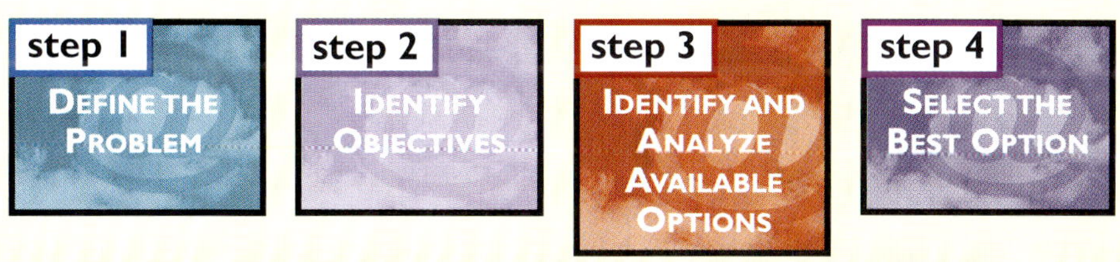

If the transfer is made at cost (either variable or full), the grip division cannot be evaluated as a profit center. Rather, it should be evaluated as a cost center and be held responsible only for the costs incurred in manufacturing grips. Transfers based on costs also can result in some problems from the buying division's perspective. If the selling division is simply allowed to pass along all costs to the buying division, inefficiencies in cost control in the selling division will be passed along to the buying division in the form of a higher "price."

Birdie Maker

Outside Market and Excess Capacity When an outside market exists for the product and Birdie-Maker can sell grips to other club manufacturers, the transfer price hinges on whether the manufacturing facility has excess capacity. As we already discussed, if the grip division has no excess capacity and can sell all its grips to an outside buyer, the transfer price should be based on the market price (potentially adjusted for cost savings). If the grip division has excess capacity, the problem gets more difficult. As in the case of accepting special orders, the grip division will benefit in the short run, as long as the transfer price exceeds all the variable costs associated with the product. Thus, the grip division should be willing to sell grips to the club division at any price over $5. The actual price is likely to be negotiated between the grip division and the club division.

NEGOTIATED TRANSFER PRICES

In many cases, transfer prices are negotiated between buyer and seller and end up somewhere between cost and the market price. Negotiated prices work best when there is no reliable market price or in situations in which the general transfer pricing formula (discussed in the next section) provides different minimum and maximum transfer prices.

A GENERAL MODEL FOR COMPUTING TRANSFER PRICES

Regardless of the method chosen, a general formula for computing transfer prices can be developed in which the minimum transfer price is the variable cost of making and selling the product plus any contribution margin that may be lost to the selling division as a result of giving up sales to outside customers.

Minimum transfer price = Variable costs of producing and selling
+ Contribution margin lost on outside sales

The contribution margin lost on outside sales is an opportunity cost—the benefit the selling division would forgo by not selling to an outside buyer. The maximum price of the transfer should be the market price (if available).

Continuing our example, if the grip division has no outside market for grips, the minimum transfer price will be $5 + 0 = $5. Because there is no outside market, there is no lost contribution margin. It is likely that the actual transfer price would be negotiated up from this $5 minimum. If the grip division is at full capacity and can sell all its grips to an outside buyer for $10, the minimum transfer price will be $5 + $5 = $10. For every grip that is sold internally, the grip division will lose $5 of contribution margin on outside sales. Note that the maximum price will also be $10 (the market price). If the grip division is not at full capacity but still has an outside market for its product, the pricing gets more interesting. For example, let's assume that the grip division has a capacity of 12,000 clubs and can sell only 8,000 to outside buyers. If the club division needs all 12,000 clubs, the transfer price on the first 8,000 should be set at the market price of $10. The other 4,000 can be sold at any price greater than the $5 of variable costs. If all 12,000 grips are sold internally, the general pricing formula in this case gives us a minimum price of $8.33. The variable costs of making the grips equal $5, whereas the contribution margin lost on outside sales equals $3.33 per club (8,000 clubs sold at market price of $10 − variable costs of $5 = a lost contribution margin of $40,000; spread over the entire 12,000 clubs, the lost contribution margin per club is $3.33).

Note that if all 12,000 clubs are sold at an internal price of $8.33, the total revenue to the grip division is equal to $100,000. This is the same as the revenue earned if the grip division sells 8,000 clubs at $10 each to outside buyers while selling 4,000 clubs internally at the minimum transfer price of $5.

A key concept in transfer pricing is that no matter what the desires of the division managers, the transfer price that provides the most benefit to the company as a whole is the one that should be chosen. Forcing a transfer when the best course of action for the company is to buy outside or preventing a transfer when the best choice is to transfer the product internally results in inefficient use of a company's resources.

Key Concept: *The transfer price that provides the most benefit to the company as a whole is the one that should be chosen.*

INTERNATIONAL ASPECTS OF TRANSFER PRICING

When an organization has international divisions, the same type of problems arise, but the focus of transfer pricing changes.[3] The focus of transfer pricing when international divisions are involved centers on minimizing taxes, duties, and foreign exchange risks. By artificially setting high transfer prices, selling divisions in low-tax countries can show high levels of income while correspondingly reducing the income of a buying division located in a high-tax country. If the selling division is in a high-tax country, the transfer price can likewise be set at an artificially low price to reduce income in the high-tax country and to increase income in the low-tax country.

© IAN MURPHY/STONE

Selling and shipping goods internationally introduces many opportunities for manipulating transfer prices.

[3]This discussion also applies to divisions located in different states if they have different income tax rates.

In the News

A recent study estimates that multinational companies avoided paying $44.5 billion in income taxes in 2000 by artificially manipulating transfer prices. Examples of underpriced exported items include ice cream exported to the Cayman Islands for 20 cents per kilogram, laser printers exported to Mexico at $50 per printer, and missile and rocket launchers exported to Turkey at $12.44 each. By lowering the price, the U.S. operations show no profit and pay no or little taxes. U.S. companies also buy products from related companies at artificially high prices, including razor blades from Panama for $24.98, toothbrushes from India for $171.80, and molasses from Lebanon for $103.70 per liter (Simon Pak and John Zdanowicz, "An Estimate of 2000 Lost U.S. Federal Income Tax Revenues Due to Over-Invoiced Imports and Under-Invoiced Exports," Trade Research Institute, Inc., Miami, Florida).

Issues of international competition and foreign government relations are also important components of any transfer pricing decision. Managers must be aware and sensitive to geographic, political, and economic circumstances in the environment in which they operate. The goal of transfer pricing in any environment is to optimize the performance of the total company, not just the individual divisions.

Summary of Key Concepts

- There are advantages and disadvantages to decentralized companies. (p. 367)
- Decentralized organizations require well-developed and well-integrated information systems. (p. 367)
- The key to effective decision making in a decentralized organization is responsibility accounting—holding managers responsible for only those things under their control. (p. 368)
- Evaluating investment centers requires focusing on the level of investment required in generating a segment's profit. (p. 373)
- The transfer price that provides the most benefit to the company as a whole is the one that should be chosen. (p. 385)

Key Definitions

Decentralized organization An organization in which decision-making authority is spread throughout the organization (p. 366)

Responsibility accounting An accounting system that assigns responsibility to a manager for those areas that are under that manager's control (p. 367)

Cost center An organizational segment, or division, in which the manager has control over costs but not over revenue or investment decisions (p. 368)

Performance report Provides key financial and nonfinancial measures of performance for a particular segment (p. 368)

Revenue center An organizational segment, or division, in which the manager has control over revenue but not costs or investment decisions (p. 368)

Profit center An organizational segment, or division, in which the manager has control over both costs and revenue but not investment decisions (p. 368)

Investment center An organizational segment, or division, in which the manager has control over costs, revenue, and investment decisions (p. 369)

Strategic business unit (SBU) Another term for investment center (p. 369)

Segmented income statements Calculate income for each major segment of an organization in addition to the company as a whole (p. 369)

Segment costs All costs attributable to a particular segment of an organization but only those costs that are actually caused by the segment (p. 369)

Common costs Indirect costs that are incurred to benefit more than one segment and cannot be directly traced to a particular segment or allocated in a reasonable manner (p. 370)

Segment margin The profit margin of a particular segment of an organization, typically the best measure of long-run profitability (p. 371)

Return on investment (ROI) Measures the rate of return generated by an investment center's assets (p. 373)

Margin For each sales dollar, the percentage that is recognized as net profit (p. 374)

Asset turnover The measure of activity used in the ROI calculation; it measures the sales that are generated for a given level of assets (p. 374)

Net operating income Net income from operations before interest and taxes (p. 374)

Operating assets Typically include cash, accounts receivable, inventory, and property, plant, and equipment needed to operate a business (p. 374)

Residual income The amount of income earned in excess of a predetermined minimum level of return on assets (p. 378)

Economic value added (EVA) A contemporary measure of performance focusing on shareholder wealth (p. 380)

Transfer price The price charged by one segment, or division, to another segment, or division, within the same organization for the transfer of goods or services (p. 382)

COMPUTER SIMULATION

You can now turn to **Appendix A** of your text to complete the portion of the Big Al's simulation covering transfer pricing problems.

MULTIPLE CHOICE

1. When a few individuals at the top of an organization retain decision-making authority, the organization is referred to as a(n):
   a. centralized organization
   b. decentralized organization
   c. profit center
   d. investment center

2. Which of the following statements about responsibility accounting is true?
   a. With responsibility accounting, managers are held responsible for both usage and price variances.
   b. Companywide budgets and cost standards are useful in evaluating the performance of company segments.
   c. The theme of responsibility accounting is that managers are held responsible for only those things under their control.
   d. all of the above

3. Which of the following statements about segment costs is *not* true?
   a. Common costs are indirect costs that are incurred to benefit more than one segment and cannot be directly traced to a particular segment.
   b. Segment costs should include *all* costs attributable to that segment but *only* those costs that are actually caused by the segment.
   c. A good test for deciding whether to allocate indirect fixed costs is to determine whether the cost would be reduced or eliminated if the segment were eliminated.
   d. In general, all common costs should be allocated to segments.

4. If the segment margin of a division is positive but the segment margin of an individual branch within the division is negative:
   a. the individual branch should be closed immediately
   b. in the long run, the individual branch is not profitable
   c. before deciding to eliminate the individual division, the firm should consider a number of quantitative and qualitative factors
   d. both **b** and **c**
5. Kids Place offers day care for two-, three-, and four-year-old children. Monthly data for each division within the facility are as follows:

	Two-Year Olds	Three-Year Olds	Four-Year Olds
Revenues	$15,000	$15,000	$20,000
Variable costs	12,000	10,000	8,000
Contribution margin	$ 3,000	$ 5,000	$12,000
Traceable fixed costs	2,000	2,000	8,000

   Common fixed costs of $6,000 are divided equally among the divisions. Segment margin for four-year olds is:
   a. $4,000
   b. $2,000
   c. $ 0
   d. ($2,000)
6. Candy Creations had sales of $950,000 and net operating income of $575,000. Operating assets during the year averaged $450,000. The manager of Candy Creations is considering the acquisition of a new machine, which would increase average operating assets by 10 percent. The new ROI would be:
   a. 60.5 percent
   b. 116.2 percent
   c. 127.7 percent
   d. 211.1 percent
7. Residual income:
   a. is an alternative to ROI for manager performance evaluation
   b. is the amount of income earned in excess of a predetermined minimum level of return on assets
   c. is equal to ROI – (Average operating assets × Minimum required rate of return)
   d. both **a** and **b**
8. Economic value added (EVA) is equal to:
   a. Before-tax operating profit – [(Total Assets – Current liabilities) × Weighted-average cost of capital]
   b. After-tax operating profit – [(Total Assets – Current liabilities) × Weighted-average cost of capital]
   c. Before-tax operating profit – [(Current Assets – Current liabilities) × Weighted-average cost of capital]
   d. After-tax operating profit – [(Current Assets – Current liabilities) × Weighted-average cost of capital]
9. Creative Child Learning Company manufactures and sells children's CD-ROMs. The costs per unit for "Kid Fun" CD-ROMs are as follows:

Direct materials	$2.50
Direct labor	4.50
Variable overhead	2.00
Fixed overhead	0.80
Total cost	$9.80

The company sells CD-ROMs to retail outlets for full cost plus a 25 percent markup. Each "Kid Fun" CD can also be sold to another corporate division to be upgraded and packaged with other CD-ROMs.

The minimum transfer price for "Kid Fun" CD-ROMs, assuming that no contribution margin loss on outside sales exists, is:

a. $7.00
b. $9.00
c. $9.80
d. less than $7.00

10. Silly Slippers Company manufactures and sells children's slippers. The costs for each pair of infant slippers are as follows:

Direct materials	$0.75
Direct labor	1.00
Variable overhead	0.50
Fixed overhead	0.75
Total cost	$3.00

The company sells slippers to retail outlets for full cost plus a 20 percent markup. Slippers can also be sold to another corporate division to be packaged with a bib and a rattle as a gift set.

Because an outside market exists for the product, the appropriate transfer price would be:

a. $2.25
b. $3.00
c. $3.60
d. It cannot be determined from the information provided.

CONCEPT REVIEW

11. What is a decentralized organization?

12. Why might firms choose to decentralize?

13. Identify the benefits and disadvantages of decentralization.

14. Discuss the impact of accounting information systems (AIS) on decentralization.

15. What is responsibility accounting, and what is its impact on decision making?

16. How is the philosophy of "management by exception" employed in a decentralized organization to control operations?

17. What type of information should the accounting information system provide for effective decision making in decentralized organizations?

18. Define a cost center.

19. Define a profit center.

20. Define an investment center.

21. Describe the function of segmented income statements in performance evaluation.

22. Describe segment costs and compare them to common costs.

23. Discuss the impact of the value chain on segment margin reporting.

24. Discuss the impact of ABC on segment margin reporting.

25. How does the number of turns impact margin in the ROI calculation?

26. Define residual income and discuss how it compares to ROI.

27. Define EVA and discuss how it compares to ROI and residual income.

28. Other factors remaining the same, how could the rate of return on investment be improved?

29. Define transfer pricing and why it is necessary.

30. Discuss some of the disadvantages of transfer prices when using actual cost.

31. What is the general rule in establishing transfer prices consistent with economic decision making?

32. What would be the appropriate transfer price for a firm operating at full capacity?

33. When is it appropriate to negotiate transfer prices?

34. Explain how transfer pricing relates to decentralization.

35. Explain return on investment (ROI).

36. Describe alternative ways transfer prices are established.

37. What benefits can arise from using transfer prices for service organizations?

38. Discuss the following statement: "The complexity of the transfer-pricing problem is a function of the size and growth rate of a company."

39. Discuss transfer pricing rules, issues, and methods.

40. Each divisional manager at Lakewood Inc. is evaluated based on ROI. A downturn in sales leaves cost as the only factor managers can control to maintain an adequate ROI. Cost can be cut in each division if it fails to implement pollution control devices recommended by local authorities. Discuss the ethical considerations.

APPLICATION OF CONCEPTS

41. Bachman Inc. produces and sells two main products. Revenue and cost information relating to the products are as follows:

	PRODUCT	
	Turner	**Overdrive**
Selling price per unit	$ 10.00	$ 27.00
Variable expenses per unit	4.30	19.00
Traceable fixed expenses per year	$142,000	$54,000

Common fixed expenses in the company total $125,000 per year. Last year, Bachman Inc. produced and sold 42,500 units of Turner and 19,000 units of Overdrive.

Required

Prepare a report showing the profit for each product.

42. Simon Company operates two divisions: Garfunkel and Robinson. A segmented income statement for the company's most recent year is as follows:

	Total Company	**Garfunkel Division**	**Robinson Division**
Sales	$850,000	$250,000	$600,000
Less variable expenses	505,000	145,000	360,000
Contribution margin	$345,000	$105,000	$240,000
Less traceable fixed costs	145,000	45,000	100,000
Division segment margin	$200,000	$ 60,000	$140,000
Less common fixed costs	130,000		
Net income	$ 70,000		

Required

A. If Garfunkel Division increased its sales by $85,000 per year, how much would the company's net income change? Assume that all cost behavior patterns remained constant.

B. Assume that Robinson Division increased sales by $100,000, Garfunkel Division sales remained the same, and there was no change in fixed costs.

(1) Compute the net income amounts for each division and the total company.

(2) Compute the segment margin ratios before and after these changes and comment on the results. Explain the changes.

43. Paradise Company makes two products in separate divisions: Cheese and Burger. Segmented income statements for the most recent year follow:

	Total Company	Cheese Division	Burger Division
Sales	$850,000	$250,000	$600,000
Less variable expenses	545,000	185,000	360,000
Contribution margin	$305,000	$ 65,000	$240,000
Less traceable fixed costs	145,000	45,000	100,000
Division segment margin	$160,000	$ 20,000	$140,000
Less common fixed costs	130,000		
Net income	$ 30,000		

Paradise Company would like to initiate a special advertising campaign on the Super Bowl television show. The company can feature only one product because of the expense and needs to decide which product to feature. The campaign will cost $28,000. Marketing studies have indicated that such a campaign could increase sales of the Cheese Division by $100,000 or increase sales of the Burger Division by $75,000.

Required

Which product should be featured in the campaign? Why? Show computations.

44. The ABC Division reported sales of $150,000, an asset turnover ratio of 3.0, and a rate of return on average assets of 18 percent. The percentage of net income to sales is how much?

45. The VCR division of Allied Electronics has sales of $400,000, operating profit of $40,000, and investment of $1,000,000. What is the ROI for the division?

46. The Tea Division of A Cup of Joe's Coffee has sales of $600,000, operating profit of $15,000, and investment of $1,200,000. What is the asset turnover for the Tea Division?

47. Watson Investments generates sales of $2,500,000 and operating profits of $75,000 on $1,500,000 of assets under its control. What is the profit margin?

48. A division has $3,000,000 in sales, operating profit of $250,000, and investment of $1,250,000. Assuming a 10 percent cost of capital, what is the division's residual income?

49. An advertising company spent $400,000 to purchase computer equipment that will be depreciated over four years, with no salvage value. The company started the year with nondepreciable assets of $100,000. Annual cash profits are expected to be $150,000. The company uses end-of-year asset values in determining ROI.

Required

A. What is the ROI for year 1 using net book value?

B. What is the ROI for year 1 using gross book value?

C. If sales for year 1 totaled $700,000, what was the profit margin?

50. The Upstart Shoe Company has two divisions: Stitching and Soles. The Soles division has a total cost of $15 per unit for its product, rubber soles, of which $10 is fixed. The Soles division also has idle capacity for up to 25,000 units per month. The Stitching division would like to purchase 20,000 units from the Soles division but feels that the $15 price is too high. What is the lowest price the Soles division can sell at in order to suffer no additional losses?

51. The Newton Company has two divisions: X and Y. Division X has a total cost of $30 per unit for its product, of which $20 is fixed. Division X is at full capacity. Division Y would like to purchase 20,000 units from Division X but thinks that the $35 price Division X normally charges on the outside is too high. At what price should Division X sell to Division Y in order to suffer no additional losses?

52. A division can sell externally for $60 per unit. Its variable manufacturing costs are $26 per unit, and its fixed manufacturing cost per unit is $10. What is the opportunity cost of transferring internally if the division is operating at capacity?

53. Miller company has two divisions, B and S, each operated as a profit center. Division B charges Division S $35 per unit for each unit transferred to Division S. Other data are as follows:

B's variable cost per unit	$ 30
B's fixed costs	$10,000
B's annual sales to S	5,000 units
B's sales to outsiders	50,000 units

Division B is planning to raise its transfer price to $50 per unit. Division S can purchase units at $40 each from outside vendors, but doing so would idle Division B's facilities now committed to producing units for Division S. Division B cannot increase its sales to outsiders. From the perspective of the company as a whole, from whom should Division S acquire the units, assuming Division S's market is unaffected?

54. Eat More Food Company began business in January 2001. It produces various food products that pass through two divisions. Division A processes the food, and Division B packages it. During 2001, Division A processed 100,000 pounds of food at a cost of $250,000. Its administration and other expenses amounted to $50,000. Division B incurred $100,000 of additional manufacturing costs in completing the 100,000 pounds. Division B sold the 100,000 pounds of completed units for $450,000. Division B's selling and administrative expenses for the year were $30,000.

Required

A. Prepare divisional income statements for 2001 for each of these two divisions, assuming that the transfer price is equal to Division A's total cost.

B. Prepare divisional income statements for 2001 for each of these two divisions, assuming that the transfer price is based on the external market price of $3.50 per pound.

C. Which statement presents a better measure of each division's performance? Why?

55. The following information summarizes the operations of one division of Goods Enterprises for 2002:

Sales	$2,500,000
Variable expenses	(1,000,000)
Fixed expenses	(1,000,000)
Income before taxes	$ 500,000
Average total assets	4,000,000
Company cost of capital	10%

Required

A. Compute the return on investment (ROI).

B. Compute the residual income (RI).

56. You are the manager of a franchise operating division of a "Kwik-Copies" Company. Your division has $9,000,000 in assets, and your budgeted income statement for the fiscal year is as follows:

Revenue	$16,500,000
Costs	
Variable	3,000,000
Fixed	7,750,000
Depreciation	2,375,000
Division profit	$ 3,375,500

Your company evaluates your division using ROI, computed with end-of-year gross asset balances. Your bonus is based on the percentage increase in ROI over the prior year.

During the year, you consider buying a new copy machine for $4,000,000, which will enable you to expand the output of your division and to save costs. The copy machine would have no salvage value and would be depreciated over five years using straight-line depreciation. It will increase output by 10 percent while reducing fixed costs by $4,000,000. If you accept the copy machine, it will be installed in late December but will not be placed in use until the following year. As a result, no depreciation will be taken on it this year.

If you do buy the copy machine, you will have to dispose of the copy machine you are now using, which you just purchased during the current year. The old copy machine cost you $4,000,000 but has no salvage value. Of the depreciation in the income statement, $1,000,000 is for this machine.

In the ROI calculations, the company includes any gains or losses from copy equipment disposal as part of the numerator.

Required

A. What is your division's ROI this year if you do not acquire the new machine?

B. What is your division's ROI this year if you do acquire the new copy machine?

C. What is your division's expected ROI for next year if the copy machine is acquired and meets expectations? Assume that unit costs and prices do not change.

D. As the manager, what action will you take and why?

Step 3 IDENTIFY AND ANALYZE AVAILABLE OPTIONS

Step 4 SELECT THE BEST OPTION

57. Top management is trying to determine a consistent but fair valuation system to use to evaluate each of its four divisions. This year's performance data is summarized as follows:

	DIVISION			
	1	2	3	4
Income	$1,000	$1,200	$ 1,600	$1,600
Operating assets	4,000	6,000	15,000	8,000
Current liabilities	400	2,000	2,400	200

Required

A. Which division would earn a bonus if top management used return on investment based on operating assets?

B. Which division would earn a bonus if top management used return on investment based on operating assets minus current liabilities?

C. Which division would earn a bonus if top management used return on investment based on operating assets assuming a minimum desired ROI of 12 percent?

D. Which division would earn a bonus if top management used return on investment based on operating assets minus current liabilities assuming a minimum desired ROI of 12 percent?

58. A manufacturing company is presented with the following report on its two divisions:

	Division A	Division B
Sales	$100,000	$200,000
Cost of goods sold	(50,000)	(160,000)
Gross profit	$ 50,000	$ 40,000
Marketing and administrative	(20,000)	(10,000)
Operating profit	$ 30,000	$30,000

Top management plans to award equal bonuses to the divisions based on their identical operating profits.

Required

Step 1 DEFINE THE PROBLEM

Step 3 IDENTIFY AND ANALYZE AVAILABLE OPTIONS

Step 4 SELECT THE BEST OPTION

A. What problems do you see in the bonus plan suggested by top management?

B. What questions should be addressed by top management before concluding that the operating performance of Division A and Division B are identical?

C. What alternatives would you suggest to top management?

59. Adler Industries is a vertically integrated firm with several divisions that operate as decentralized profit centers. Adler's Systems Division manufactures scientific instruments and uses the products of two of Adler's other divisions. The Board Division manufactures printed circuit boards (PCBs). One PCB model is made exclusively for the Systems Division, using proprietary designs, whereas less complex models are sold in outside markets. The products of the Transistor Division are sold in a well-developed competitive market; however, one transistor model is also used by the Systems Division.

The costs per unit of the products used by the Systems Division are as follows:

	PCB	Transistor
Direct materials	$2.50	$0.80
Direct labor	4.50	1.00
Variable overhead	2.00	0.50
Fixed overhead	0.80	0.75
Total cost	$9.80	$3.05

The Board Division sells its commercial products at full cost plus a 25 percent markup and believes that the proprietary board made for the Systems Division would sell for $12.25 per unit on the open market. The market price of the transistor used by the Systems Division is $3.70 per unit.

Required

A. What would be the impact on the Transistor Division if the per unit transfer price from the Transistor Division to the Systems Division were the full cost of $3.05?

B. Assume that the Systems Division is able to purchase a large quantity of transistors from an outside source at $2.90 per unit. The Transistor Division, having excess capacity, agrees to lower its transfer price to $2.90 per unit. What would be the result of this action for the company as a whole?

C. The Board and Systems Divisions have negotiated a transfer price of $11.00 per printed circuit board. What is the likely response from each division if this negotiated price is used?

60. Raddington Industries produces tool and die machinery for manufacturers. The company expanded vertically in 1999 by acquiring one of its suppliers of alloy steel plates, Regis Steel Company. In order to manage the two separate businesses, the operations of Regis Steel are reported separately as an investment center.

Raddington monitors its divisions on the basis of both unit contribution and return on average investment (ROI), with investment defined as average operating assets employed. Management bonuses are determined on ROI. All investments in operating assets are expected to earn a minimum return of 11 percent before income taxes.

Regis's cost of goods sold is considered to be entirely variable, whereas the division's administrative expenses are not dependent on volume. Selling expenses are a mixed cost with 40 percent attributed to sales volume. Regis's ROI has ranged from 11.8 percent to 14.7 percent since 1999. During the fiscal year ended November 30, 2001, Regis contemplated a capital acquisition with an estimated ROI of 11.5 percent; however, division management decided against the investment because it believed that the investment would decrease Regis's overall ROI.

The 2001 operating statement for Regis is presented here. The division's operating assets employed were $15,750,000 at November 30, 2001, a 5 percent increase over the 2000 year-end balance.

Regis Steel Division Operating Statement for the Year Ended November 30, 2001 ($000 omitted)

Sales revenue		$25,000
Less: Cost of goods sold	$16,500	
Administrative expenses	3,955	
Selling expenses	2,700	23,155
Income from operations before income taxes		$ 1,845

Required

A. Calculate the unit contribution for Regis Steel Division if 1,484,000 units were produced and sold during the year ended November 30, 2001.

B. Calculate the return on investment (ROI) for Regis Steel Division for 2001.

C. Calculate the residual income using the average operating assets employed for 2001 for the Regis Steel Division.

D. Explain why the management of Regis Steel Division would have been more likely to accept the contemplated acquisition if residual income rather than ROI were used as a performance measure.

E. The Regis Steel Division is a separate investment center within Raddington Industries. Identify several items that Regis Steel should control if it is to be evaluated fairly by either the ROI or residual income performance measure.

Chapter 12

Nonfinancial Measures of Performance

Study Tools

A Review of the Previous Chapter

In Chapter 11, we discussed the impact of responsibility accounting and segment reporting on decision making in decentralized organizations. We also discussed performance evaluation in cost, revenue profit, and investment centers, utilizing variance analysis and other financial measures of performance, including the segmented income statement, return on investment (ROI), residual income, and economic value added (EVA).

A Preview of This Chapter

In this chapter, we expand the discussion of performance evaluation to include a variety of nonfinancial and qualitative measures used in a "balanced-scorecard" approach.

Key concepts include:

- The balanced-scorecard approach integrates financial and nonfinancial performance measures.
- The balanced-scorecard approach requires looking at performance from four different but related perspectives: financial, customer, internal business, and learning and growth.
- The four perspectives of the balanced scorecard revolve around measures of quality, productivity, efficiency and timeliness, and marketing success.

A Preview of Upcoming Chapters

Part IV of the textbook introduces two contemporary topics in management decision making: dealing with information and knowledge management, in Chapter 13, and management fraud and internal control, in Chapter 14.

Learning Objectives

After studying the material in this chapter, you should be able to:

LO1 Apply the concept of the balanced-scorecard approach to performance measurement

LO2 Understand key dimensions of the financial, customer, internal business, and learning and growth perspectives of the balanced scorecard

LO3 Apply key measures of performance based on quality

LO4 Interpret the costs of quality and the tradeoffs among prevention costs, appraisal costs, internal failure costs, and external failure costs

LO5 Apply key measures of performance based on productivity

LO6 Apply key measures of performance based on efficiency and timeliness

LO7 Apply key measures of performance based on marketing effectiveness

LO8 Understand the use of quality, productivity, efficiency and timeliness, and marketing-effectiveness measures within the four perspectives of the balanced scorecard

In the previous two chapters, we discussed cost control and performance evaluation in cost, revenue, profit, and investment centers, using such financial measures as variance analysis, segmented income statements, return on investment, residual income, and economic value added. In this chapter, we expand that analysis to include a variety of nonfinancial and qualitative measures used in a "balanced-scorecard" approach to measuring performance. Because of changing technology, global competition, and an increased awareness of the need to focus on customer needs, these nonfinancial and qualitative performance measures have become an integral component of effective managerial decision making.

The balanced scorecard looks at performance from four unique but related perspectives: financial, customer, internal business, and learning and growth. The chapter concludes with a discussion of key measures of quality, productivity, efficiency and timeliness, and marketing effectiveness within the four perspectives of the balanced scorecard. ■

INTRODUCTION

© STEWART COHEN/STONE

When customers choose a restaurant for a meal, they are probably *not* concerned with how well the restaurant meets its cost goals, whether its segment margin is positive, or the level of its return on investment (ROI). Customers probably *are* concerned with the price of the meal, how long they have to wait to be seated and waited on, and the quality of the food that is served.

Customers who have a bad experience may choose to not return to the restaurant. Those customers also have a tendency to inform friends or relatives about the bad experience. These factors are difficult to measure but are critically important to the success of the restaurant. The manager of the restaurant can be very competent at controlling costs, but if customers go elsewhere, the restaurant will not be financially successful and will eventually fail.[1]

In today's competitive business environment, characterized by rapidly changing technology, global competition, and a focus on meeting and exceeding customer's expectations, managers, in order to be successful, must focus on factors other than financial performance. Traditional measures of financial performance are simply not adequate to fully assess the performance of companies and their segments in this environment. Quality may be important than cost, timeliness more important than meeting budget, and customer service more important than ROI.[2]

THE BALANCED SCORECARD

LO1
Apply the concept of the balanced-scorecard approach to performance measurement

Traditional accounting measures of performance dealing with historical financial data are of little use in making decisions concerning customer satisfaction, quality issues, productivity, efficiency, and employee satisfaction. Managers also need information concerning the success or failure of new products or marketing campaigns and the success of programs designed to enhance customer value. The **balanced-scorecard approach** to performance measurement uses a set of financial and nonfinancial measures that relate to the critical success factors of the organization. By integrating financial and nonfinancial performance measures, the balanced-scorecard approach helps to keep management focused on all of a company's critical success factors, not just its financial ones. The balanced scorecard also helps to keep short-term operating performance in line with long-term strategy.

PAUSE & *Reflect*

Nonfinancial measures must be used with caution. For example, table turns may be an important nonfinancial measure of performance for restaurants. However, if too much emphasis is placed on the quick turnover of tables, customers may feel that they are being rushed and choose to go elsewhere. Can you identify restaurants that emphasize table turns? How about restaurants that do not emphasize table turns? What was your overall opinion of each type?

Key Concept: *The balanced-scorecard approach integrates financial and nonfinancial performance measures.*

As shown in Exhibit 12-1, utilizing a balanced-scorecard approach requires looking at performance from four different but related perspectives: financial, customer, internal business, and learning and growth.

---

[1]It should be noted that financial measures of performance would eventually capture customer service problems when they impact income. A decrease in customer satisfaction will eventually lead to reduced sales, which will reduce income and have a negative impact on ROI. However, these measures are not timely enough or detailed enough to help management correct any customer service problems.

[2]Although quality, timeliness, customer service, and other nonfinancial measures may be more important than their financial counterparts, it should be noted that traditional transaction-based accounting information systems may not even capture this type of information.

LO2
Understand key dimensions of the financial, customer, internal business, and learning and growth perspectives of the balanced scorecard

EXHIBIT 12-1 The Balanced-Scorecard Strategy

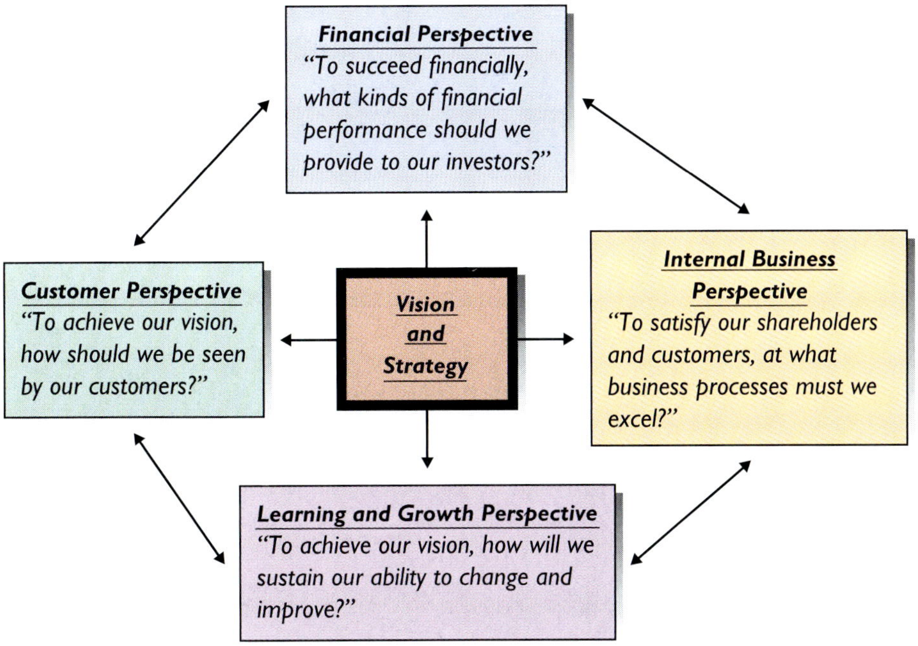

FINANCIAL PERSPECTIVE

The primary goal of every profit-making enterprise is to show a profit. Profit allows the enterprise to provide a return on investment to investors, to repay creditors, and to adequately compensate management and employees. Financial measures of success (costs, variances, earnings, segment margin, ROI, EVA) have been discussed in the earlier chapters in this book. Increasing sales, reducing costs, and increasing profits are critical success factors in many companies. However, under the balanced-scorecard approach, financial performance is seen in the larger context of the company's overall goals and objectives relating to its customers and suppliers, internal processes, and employees.

CUSTOMER PERSPECTIVE

Many successful businesses have found that focusing on customers and meeting or exceeding their needs is more important in the long run than simply focusing on financial measures of performance. After all, it is the customer who ultimately incurs the costs of producing products and contributes to a company's profits. Considering the customer perspective is therefore critical in attaining the financial goals of a company. Critical success factors under this perspective are likely to include increasing the quality of products and services, reducing delivery time, and increasing customer satisfaction. Measures of performance appropriate under this perspective include the number of warranty claims and returned products (for quality), customer response time and the percentage of on-time deliveries (for reducing delivery time), and customer complaints and repeat business (for customer satisfaction). A second dimension of the customer perspective deals with increasing market share and penetrating new markets. Measures of performance appropriate for this dimension include market share, market saturation, and new products introduced into the marketplace.

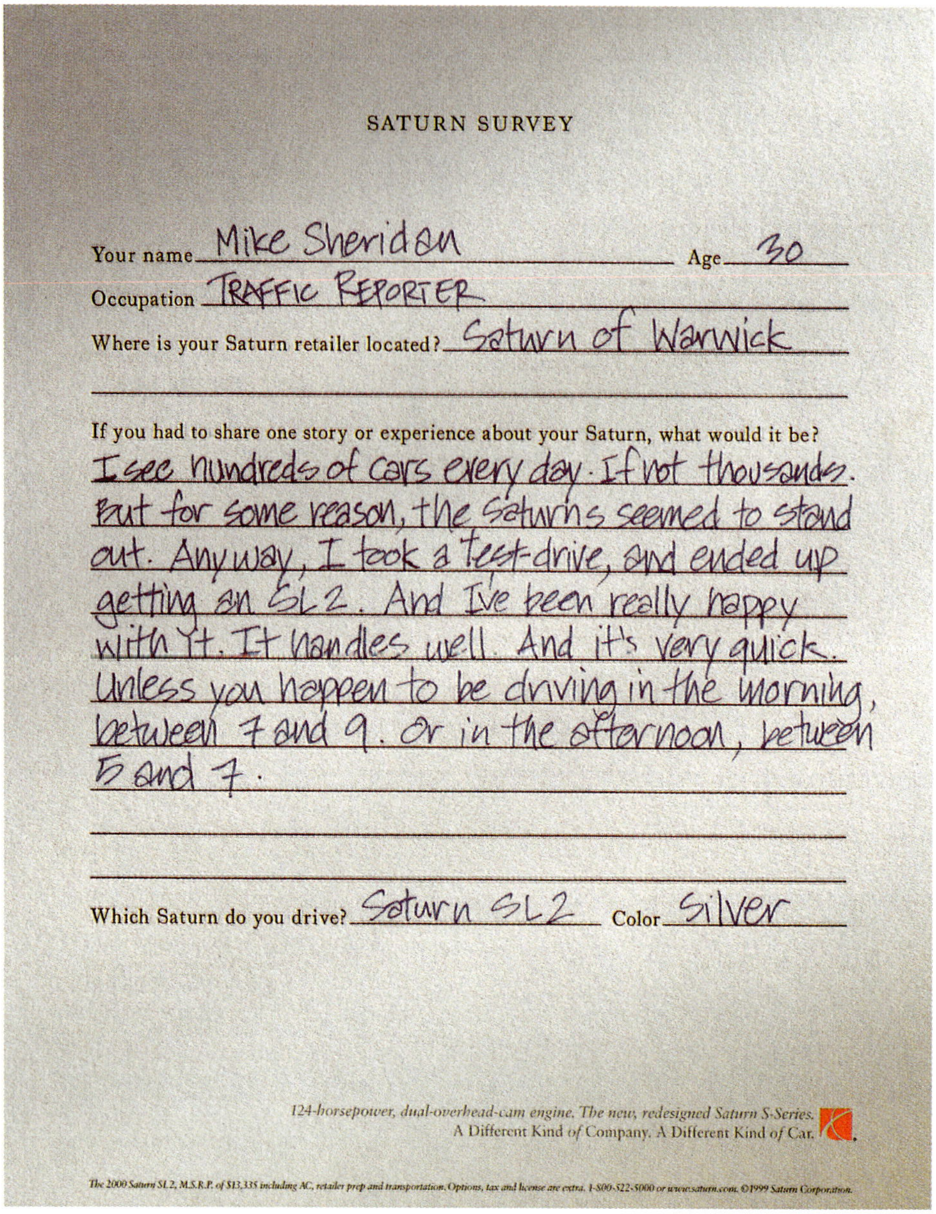

COURTESY OF SATURN CORPORATION

http://www.saturn.com

Saturn relies on customer surveys and other measures in evaluating the customer perspective of the balanced scorecard.

INTERNAL BUSINESS PERSPECTIVE

The internal business process perspective deals with objectives across the company's entire value chain: from research and development to postsale customer service. It is linked to the financial perspective through its emphasis on improving the efficiency of manufacturing processes and with the customer perspective through its focus on improving processes and products to better meet customer needs. Every company will approach this perspective differently, as the processes that add value to products and services are likely to differ by company. However, critical success factors are likely to include improving quality throughout the production process, increasing productivity, and increasing efficiency and timeliness.

LEARNING AND GROWTH PERSPECTIVE

The learning and growth perspective links the critical success factors in the other perspectives and ensures an environment that supports and allows the objectives of the other three perspectives to be achieved. Critical success factors center on three areas. The first is the efficient and effective use of employees (employee empowerment). Measures include improving employee morale, increasing skill development, increasing employee satisfaction, reducing employee turnover, and increasing the participation of employees in the decision process. The second critical success factor is increasing information systems capabilities through improving the availability and timeliness of information. The third critical success factor involves measures of product innovation, such as increasing the number of new products, new patents, and so on.

Key Concept: *The balanced-scorecard approach requires looking at performance from four different but related perspectives: financial, customer, internal business, and learning and growth.*

IN THE NEWS **http://www.llbean.com**

Rol Fessenden, the head of global procurement for L.L. Bean, says that "good working conditions go hand in hand with high quality, high reliability, and, in the broad view, lower costs." When L.L. Bean replaced a supplier for keeping poor wage records, the new supplier not only had better administrative practices but better products as well ("A Humanist Executive Leads by Thinking in Broader Terms," *Wall Street Journal,* April 16, 1999, B1).

A FOCUS ON QUALITY

LO3
Apply key measures of performance based on quality

Over the past 20 years or so, the demand by customers for quality products and services at an affordable price has drastically changed the way companies do business. Quality is no longer just a buzzword but a way of life. Managers have come to realize that improving quality increases sales through higher customer satisfaction and demand, reduces costs, and increases the long-term profitability of companies. However, before we go any further, just what is meant by quality? Although you may "know it when you see it," most businesses describe **quality** as "meeting or exceeding customers' expectations." Of course, this requires that a product perform as it is intended but also requires that a product be reliable and durable and that these features be provided at a competitive price.

Companies have focused on improving the quality of the products or services they sell through a variety of initiatives, such as total quality management (TQM), market-driven quality, and strategic quality management. Although the details of these methods may differ, all focus on meeting or exceeding customer expectations, continuous improvement, and employee empowerment. Continuous improvement, an idea pioneered by Toyota in Japan, refers to a system of improvement based on a series of gradual and often small improvements rather than major changes requiring very large investments.[3] Called **kaizen** in Japan, it requires active participation by all of a company's employees—from the CEO to the worker on the assembly line. Kaizen takes the view that everyone is responsible for continuous improvement. Employee empowerment refers to companies' providing appropriate opportunities for training, skill development, and advancement so those employees can become active participants and active decision makers in an organization. As discussed earlier, empowering employees is a key dimension of the innovation and growth perspective of the balanced scorecard.

http://www.toyota.com

[3]In addition to quality improvements, kaizen techniques are used to continually reduce the cost of products and services.

Along with their quality improvement initiatives, many companies seek ISO 9000 certification. **ISO 9000** is a set of guidelines for quality management focusing on the design, production, inspection, testing, installing, and servicing of products, processes, and services. Although originally developed by the International Standards Organization (ISO) to control the quality of products sold in Europe, it has been widely adopted in the United States and in other countries worldwide. U.S. companies may also compete for the Malcolm Baldrige National Quality Award. This award was created in 1987 to recognize quality excellence in manufacturing, small business, service, education, and health care.

IN THE NEWS http://www.fedex.com

Total quality management (TQM) pays off handsomely. The results of a study published in *Business Week* found that quality award winners did two to three times as well in growth of operating income, sales, assets, and employment and 50 percent better in stock appreciation, compared with a corporate control group ("Rewards of Quality Rewards," *Business Week,* September 21, 1998, 26).

Improving the quality of products and services is an important component in both the customer perspective and the internal business perspective of the balanced scorecard. From a customer perspective, one of the most important measures of quality is customer satisfaction and the number of customer complaints. If the number of meals returned to the kitchen is increasing, management should probably infer that customers are unhappy with the quality of the meal. The number of warranty claims can also serve as a measure of quality. The increase in warranty work performed on a certain model of automobile indicates a potential problem with the production process and the quality of the car produced. If customer complaints and warranty claims are increasing, they provide a signal to management that quality may be a problem. However, poor quality is not the only explanation for increasing customer complaints. In addition, these measures are not perfect in that customers do not always complain or return products when quality problems are evident. For example, restaurant patrons may not complain about subpar meals, and customers may simply discard defective merchandise instead of returning it. Therefore, management must be careful to provide a mechanism to make it easy for customers to complain, easy to return defective products, and so on.

From the internal business perspective, quality measures center on improving output yields, reducing defects in raw materials and finished products, and reducing downtime owing to quality problems. Ideally, defects are detected before they leave the factory and the manufacturing process adapted accordingly. The amount of scrap can also indicate potential quality problems in the production process. Although a certain amount of scrap is acceptable and even necessary in most manufacturing environments, an excessive amount should raise a red flag indicating possible problems that are causing an increase in the number of defective units in the process.

THE COSTS OF QUALITY

LO4
Interpret the costs of quality and the tradeoffs among prevention costs, appraisal costs, internal failure costs, and external failure costs

Improving quality can be costly. On average, U.S. companies spend 20 to 30 percent of every sales dollar on quality costs.[4] However, improving quality can also prove very prof-

[4]Michael R. Ostrega, "Return on Investment Through the Costs of Quality," *Journal of Cost Management* (Summer 1991): p. 37.

itable. Xerox estimates that it saved more than $200 million over a four-year period by improving quality.[5]

http://www.xerox.com

In evaluating managers based on quality concerns, it is useful to have a framework for comparing the benefits of providing a high-quality product or service with the costs that result from poor quality. To facilitate this comparison, quality costs are typically classified into four general categories: (1) prevention costs, (2) appraisal costs, (3) internal failure costs, and (4) external failure costs.

Prevention costs are incurred to prevent product failure from occurring. These costs are typically incurred early in the value chain and include design and engineering costs, as well as training, supervision, and the costs of quality improvement projects. If parts are purchased from an outside supplier, these costs may include providing training and technical support to the supplier in order to increase the quality of purchased materials. Prevention costs are incurred to eliminate quality problems before they occur. Most companies find that incurring prevention costs up front is less expensive in the long run than product failure costs.

Appraisal (detection) costs are incurred in inspecting, identifying, and isolating defective products and services before they reach the customer. These include the costs of inspecting raw materials, testing goods throughout the manufacturing process, and final product testing and inspection. In practice, it is very difficult to ensure quality through inspection. It is time consuming and costly to inspect every unit of product. Therefore, sampling is usually used to identify the problems with the production process. However, sampling is certainly not foolproof and is not likely to catch all quality problems. In general, it is more effective to design quality into a product through prevention activities rather than to inspect quality into a product using appraisal activities.

If a product or a service is defective in any way or does not meet customer expectations, failure costs are incurred. **Internal failure costs** are incurred once the product is produced and then determined to be defective (through the appraisal process) but before it is sold to customers. Internal failure costs include the material, labor, and other manufacturing costs incurred in reworking defective products and the costs of scrap and spoilage. Internal failure costs also include downtime caused by quality problems, design changes, and the costs of reinspections and retesting. If no defects exist, internal failure costs will be zero. On the other hand, a high level of internal failure costs should be an indication to management that more attention needs to be spent in preventing quality problems to eliminate or to reduce the number of defective products during the production process.

Inspecting raw materials and finished goods is classified as an appraisal, or detection, cost of quality.

External failure costs are incurred after a defective product is delivered to a customer. External failure costs include the cost of repairs made under warranty or the replacement of defective parts, product recalls (such as in the automobile industry), liability costs arising from legal actions against the seller, and eventually lost sales. Although the cost of potential lawsuits and lost sales may be difficult to measure, the cost of external failures is likely to exceed other quality costs. Failure costs, both internal and external, are like bandages; they address only symptoms rather than fix the underlying problem. When unhappy customers decide not to purchase products from a company because of quality problems, the domino effect can be devastating—particularly when safety is a concern.

Although quality costs in many U.S. companies may reach 20 to 30 percent of sales, experts suggest that the total costs of quality should not exceed 2 to 4 percent of sales. The problem faced by management is to reduce the costs of quality while maintaining a high-quality product or service. The goal, of course, is to minimize all the quality costs. However, it may be prudent to increase expenditures in one or more areas in order to decrease other costs. For example, as you have seen, external failure costs are serious and potentially devastating to companies. Both external and internal failure costs can be reduced (theoretically to zero) by paying more attention to quality issues early in the value chain. Products can be designed to emphasize quality and durability, suppliers can be certified,

[5]Lawrence P. Carr, "How Xerox Sustains the Costs of Quality," *Management Accounting* (August 1995): pp. 26–32.

IN THE NEWS http://www.coca-cola.com

© AP/WIDE WORLD PHOTOS

In the summer of 1999, Coca-Cola faced one of the most serious crises in its history. The problem? A Coke bottling plant in Antwerp, Belgium, failed to follow crucial quality control procedures, including receiving quality assurances from its suppliers and simply making sure that the carbon dioxide used to give Coke its fizz tasted and smelled fresh. As a result, contaminated carbon dioxide was pumped into the holding tanks at the bottling plant, resulting in bad-smelling Coca-Cola and hundreds of sick consumers. In the aftermath, Coke products were recalled all over Europe. Coca-Cola Enterprises Inc. (the bottling company owned 40 percent by Coca-Cola) estimates that the problems resulted in a charge against earnings of more than $100 million (Deogun, Hagerty, Stecklow, Johannes, and Barrett, "Anatomy of a Recall: How Coke's Controls Fizzled Out in Europe," *Wall Street Journal,* June 29, 1999, A1, and McKay, "Coca Cola Enterprises Raises Estimate of Cost of Big Recall in Europe," *Wall Street Journal,* July 13, 1999, A4).

employees can be trained, and the manufacturing process can be improved to increase quality throughout the value chain. Increasing expenditures related to prevention and appraisal can result in significant overall cost savings in the long run. As you can see in Exhibit 12-2, the traditional view of managing total quality costs suggests that increasing prevention and appraisal costs will reduce defective units (and failure costs) but that there are tradeoffs in doing so. The traditional view suggests that total quality costs are minimized at a level of product quality below 100 percent.

Exhibit 12-2 implies that total quality costs are minimized at a point less than that associated with zero defects. However, additional prevention and appraisal activities are likely to reduce defects even further. Should companies continue to incur prevention and appraisal costs beyond this point?

A more contemporary view of quality costs recognizes that a number of failure costs are difficult to measure. For example, poor quality can lead to lost sales. This tends to increase the costs of external failures as the percentage of defective units increases. In addition, rather than continually increasing as quality improves (as in Exhibit 12-2), prevention and appraisal costs may actually decrease as a company nears a level of zero defects. As you can see in Exhibit 12-3, this implies that total quality costs are minimized at a level of zero defects.

PRODUCTIVITY MEASURES

LO5
Apply key measures of performance based on productivity

In a company's effort to continually improve products and processes, improvements in productivity are often emphasized. **Productivity** is simply a measure of the relationship between outputs and inputs. How many cars are produced per labor hour, how many loaves of bread are baked per bag of flour, how many calculators are produced per machine hour, how many customers are serviced per shift, and how many sales dollars are generated per full-time sales clerk are all measures of productivity. Measures of output per unit of input, such as labor or machine hours, can be very important when evaluating the efficiency of a production process. These measures are similar to the traditional financial measures used in variance analysis (direct material and direct labor efficiency variances). However, the focus when using productivity measures is on continually improving productivity rather than simply using less material or incurring fewer labor hours than budgeted.

EXHIBIT 12-2 Traditional View of the Costs of Quality

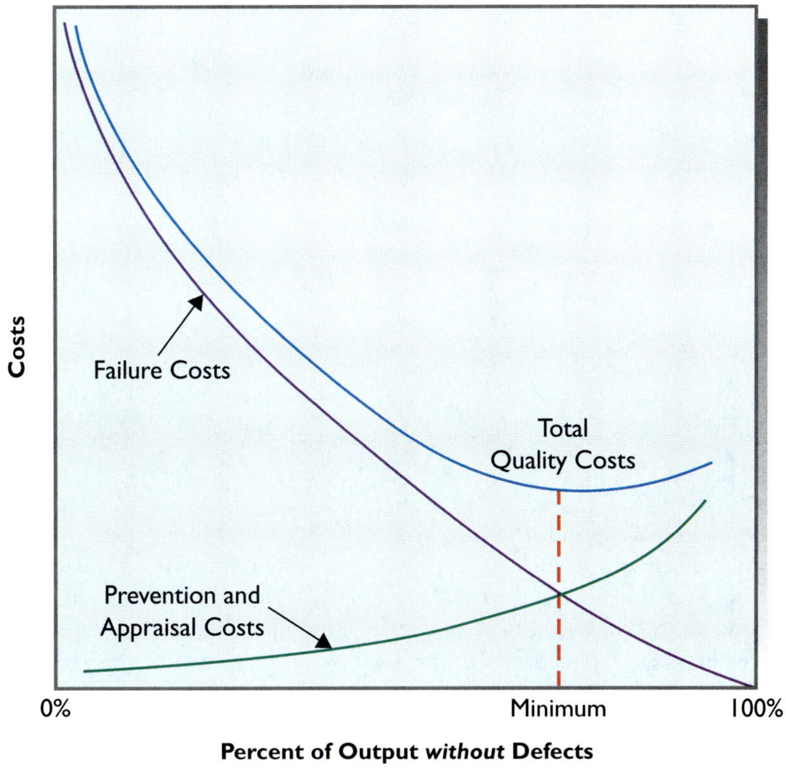

EXHIBIT 12-3 Contemporary View of the Costs of Quality

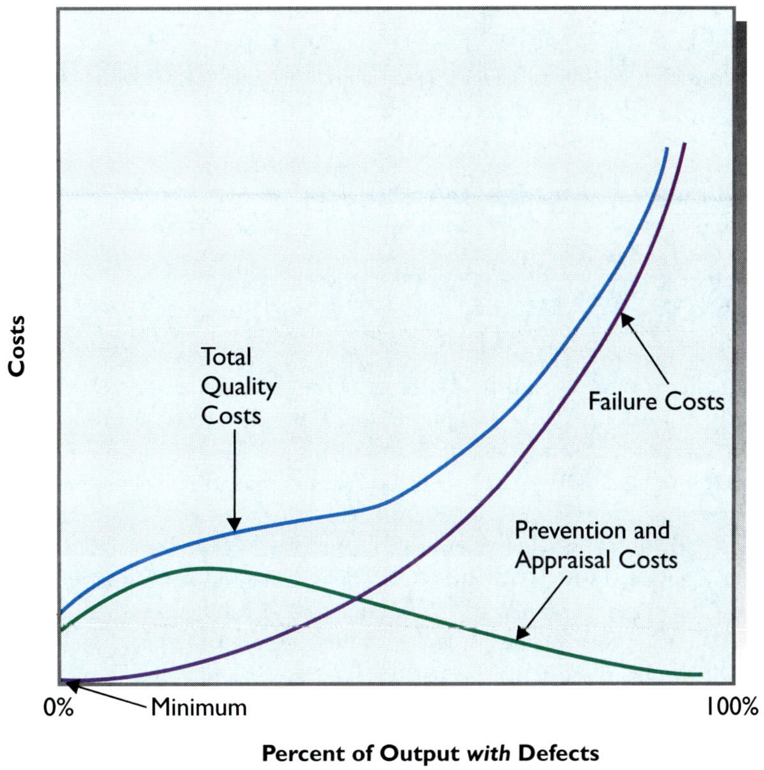

IN THE NEWS http://www.gm.com, http://www.daimlerchrysler.com, http://www.ford.com, http://www.honda.com, http://www.nissandriven.com, http://www.toyota.com

The average labor hours and labor costs per vehicle for U.S. automakers is much higher than for Japanese automakers. Labor costs per GM vehicle were almost double those of Toyota. The labor productivity of General Motors, DaimlerChrysler, and Ford was less than that of Honda, Nissan, or Toyota ("Productivity Improves among U.S. Auto Makers," *Wall Street Journal,* June 18, 1999, A2).

Auto Company	Labor Hours per Vehicle	Total Labor Cost per Vehicle	Annual Volume
General Motors	45.60	$2,052	4,946,000
DaimlerChrysler	44.25	1,991	2,906,000
Ford	34.79	1,566	4,299,000
Honda	30.84	1,079	695,000
Nissan	30.76	1,077	309,000
Toyota	30.38	1,063	647,000

PAUSE & Reflect

What type of productivity measures might be appropriate for a nonprofit organization, such as Motheread Inc., whose mission is to educate mothers and fathers of the benefits of reading and to provide hands-on literacy training for parents and their children?

In service organizations, productivity measures are important when evaluating the efficiency of personnel. In HMOs, the number of patients seen per physician in a given time period can be an important measure of profitability. Likewise, advertising agencies and CPA and law firms are very concerned with the revenue generated per partner.

To be useful, productivity measures must be used in conjunction with quality measures. A company that uses fewer workers, machines, materials, and other resources to generate the same amount of goods and services as its competitors will realize a competitive advantage only if the quality of products and services is not compromised in the process.

IN THE NEWS http://www.toyota.com

In 1999, Toyota announced that it would begin custom producing the Camry Solara coupe according to customer specifications in just five days. This was a radical departure from the norm in the auto industry where customers typically had to choose a car from those available at a dealer or wait 30 to 60 days for a custom order ("An Automaker Tries the Dell Way," *Wall Street Journal,* August 30, 1999, A26).

EFFICIENCY AND TIMELINESS MEASURES

LO6
Apply key measures of performance based on efficiency and timeliness

Although quality is certainly a primary focus of the customer perspective, products and services must also be provided on a timely basis. **Customer response time** is the time it takes to deliver a product or a service after an order is placed. As shown in Exhibit 12-4, it includes such non-value-added time as order receipt time (time from when the order is placed to when the order is ready for setup) and order wait time (time from when the order is ready for setup to when the setup is complete). Order receipt time can occur when orders are mailed or when there is a delay between the placing of an order and its production. This can occur when products are made in batches or when an order is too small to initiate a production run. Total customer response time also includes the time that the order spends in the actual manufacturing process and any delivery time required to get the product into the customer's hands.

Obviously, the standard customer response time will vary with the type of product or service provided. In a restaurant, the response time should be relatively short. On the

EXHIBIT 12-4 Elements of Customer Response Time

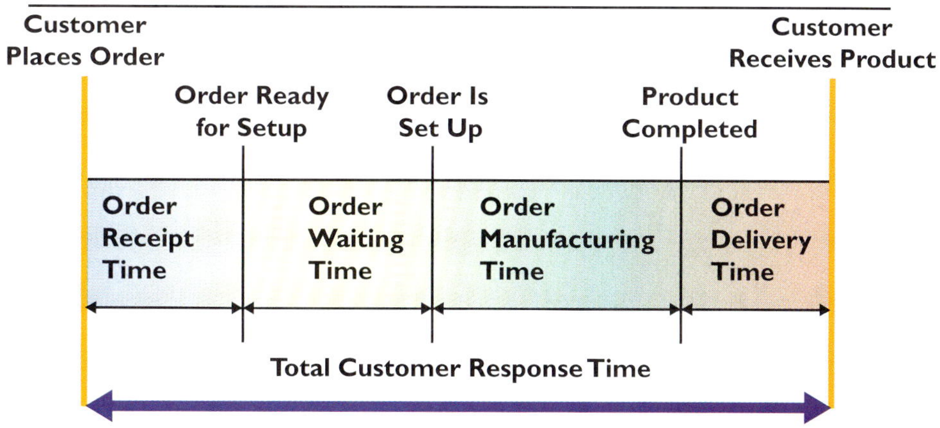

other hand, when ordering an automobile with special options or a custom piece of furniture, the customer response time can be considerably longer. Another measure of timeliness applicable to the customer service perspective is the number of on-time deliveries.

From an internal business perspective, efficiency and timeliness are often measured using manufacturing cycle time, velocity, throughput, and manufacturing-cycle efficiency. **Manufacturing-cycle time** is the amount of time it takes to produce a good unit of product from the time raw material is received until the product is ready to deliver to customers. As such, it is one element in the customer response time (see Exhibit 12-4). In addition to actual processing time, cycle time includes time spent moving materials and products from one place to the next, time spent waiting for machine availability, and time spent inspecting materials and finished goods. The concept of manufacturing-cycle time is directly related to velocity, or **throughput.** Whereas manufacturing-cycle time is the time required to produce a unit of product, throughput refers to the number of good units that can be made in a given period of time. The shorter the manufacturing-cycle time, the greater the throughput. Because manufacturing-cycle time and throughput focus on the production of good units, they are directly influenced by quality. As such, you can view throughput and manufacturing-cycle time as directly related to quality and productivity measures:

PAUSE & *Reflect*

Are any of the activities in the order manufacturing time likely to be non-value-added activities? What about the delivery time?

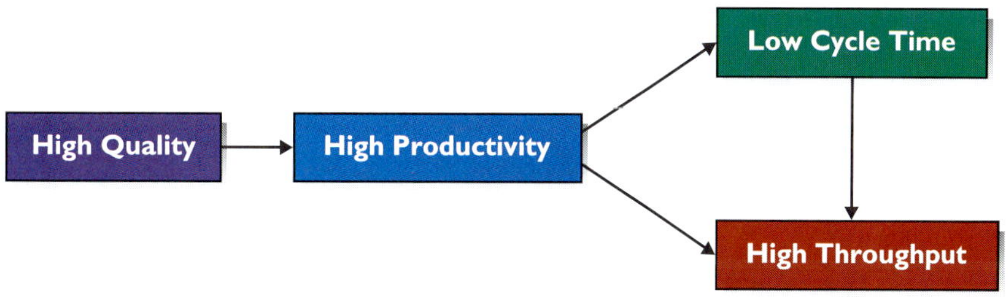

Manufacturing-cycle efficiency (MCE) is the value-added time in the production process divided by the total manufacturing-cycle time:

$$MCE = \frac{\text{Value-added time}}{\text{Manufacturing-cycle time}}$$

Value-added time includes time spent in the actual manufacturing of a product (machining, assembly, painting, etc.). Non-value-added time includes the time a product is waiting to move to the next step in the production process or time spent moving the product to the next step. Manufacturing-cycle efficiency is a key measure of performance directly related to the customer service perspective as well as to the internal operations perspective. By increasing MCE, customer response time is reduced, and non-value-added activities are reduced.

As an example, consider Northern Lights Custom Cabinets (introduced in Chapter 2). Northern Lights manufactures approximately 30 custom cabinets each year and maintains records related to wait time, inspection time, processing time, and move time of its cabinets as follows:

Wait time	12 hours
Inspection time	2 hours
Processing time	48 hours
Move time	2 hours

The cabinets are shipped to the job site as soon as they are complete. Northern Lights used these amounts to compute the following values:

Manufacturing Cycle Time

= Wait time + Processing time + Inspection time + Move time
= 12 + 48 + 2 + 2 = 64 hours
= 8 days

Throughput

$$= \frac{250 \text{ work days}}{8 \text{ days}} = 31.25 \text{ units}$$

Value-Added Time

= Processing time
= 48 hours, or 6 days

Non-Value-Added Time

= Wait time + Inspection time + Move time
= 12 hours + 2 hours + 2 hours
= 2 days

Manufacturing-Cycle Efficiency (MCE)

= Value-added time / Manufacturing-cycle time
= 6 days/8 days
= 75 percent

So what do these values mean? Once raw materials are received by Northern Lights, it takes an average of eight days to manufacture a set of custom cabinets. Seventy-five percent of the manufacturing cycle time is value added (related to actual processing of the cabinets), whereas only 25 percent is non-value-added, resulting in an MCE of 75 percent.

Although an MCE of 75 percent would likely be considered very good, these numbers can really be analyzed only by comparison to previous months or to industry standards for this type of business. Regardless, the MCE of 75 percent highlights the non-value-added waiting time, which Northern Lights may be able to reduce.

PAUSE & *Reflect*

Can you think of other examples in which wait time would be considered value added?

***Concept Question:** In a brewery, beer must sit in storage vats for a period of time while waiting to be bottled or packaged for delivery. Is this value-added or non-value-added "wait time"?*

Concept Answer: Although wait and storage times are normally considered non-value-added activities, the real question is whether the wait time adds value to the finished product. In the case of the brewery, the wait time is a necessary, value-added activity, as the beer must age to be of better quality.

MARKETING MEASURES

LO7
Apply key measures of performance based on marketing effectiveness

Marketing measures are linked to the financial, customer, and learning and growth perspectives of the balanced scorecard. Market share is directly associated with financial performance and is indirectly linked to customer satisfaction. As an example, a large supermarket chain in the Northeast started giving customers double credit for manufacturer coupons in order to increase market share by enticing customers away from competing stores. The chain stated that each 1 percent increase in market share in New England was worth $50 million dollars in annual sales.

Other measures of marketing effectiveness include the success of new products. The number of new products introduced by a toy company, the number of new patents applied for by a drug company, and the number of new services offered and used by customers of a bank are market measures linked to both the customer service and innovation and growth perspectives of a business.

To illustrate how nonfinancial measures of performance might be used in a variety of companies, let's go back and look at some of the companies featured throughout the book. As previously discussed, Northern Lights Custom Cabinets manufactures custom kitchen and bathroom cabinets. The following table shows a variety of performance measures Northern Lights might use to assess the customer, internal business, and learning and growth perspectives of the balanced scorecard, using measures of quality, productivity, efficiency and timeliness, and marketing success.

Northern Lights Custom Cabinets
Nonfinancial Measures of Performance

Quality Measures	***Method of Measuring***
Customer satisfaction	Customer complaints/Warranty claims
Defects per unit	Hours of time to rework defective cabinets
Percentage of external failures	Warranty claims/Returns
Percentage of scrap	Pounds of scrap lumber compared to raw material put into production
Efficiency and Timeliness Measures	
Customer response time	Time between customer order and delivery
Service time	Time spent servicing cabinets already installed
Delivery performance	Time from completion to installation of cabinets
Manufacturing cycle time	Total production time
Manufacturing cycle efficiency	Value-added time divided by cycle time
Marketing Measures	
Growth in market share	Percentage of remodeling jobs and new homes installing Northern Lights cabinets
Product innovation	The number of new features and designs offered
New-market saturation	Percentage of new homes installing Northern Lights cabinets
Productivity Measures	
Output per unit of input	Output per hour of labor, machine time, and board foot of lumber

Likewise, the following table provides similar measures for Big Al's Pizza Emporium. Although Big Al's is also in the business of providing a product to customers, the specific measures used by Big Al's are likely to differ substantially from those used by Northern Lights.

Big Al's Pizza Emporium
Nonfinancial Measures of Performance

Quality Measures	***Method of Measuring***
Customer satisfaction	Customer complaints/Returned meals/Amount of leftover food
Inspections of raw material	Amount of food not meeting quality criteria
Percentage of scrap	Food discarded in kitchen
Efficiency and Timeliness Measures	
Customer response time	Time from customer order to delivery of meal
Manufacturing-cycle time	Meals served per hour
Marketing Measures	
Growth in market share	Percentage change in sales compared to industry standards
Product innovation	Sales of new menu items
Productivity Measures	
Output per unit of input	Finished meals per measure of key ingredients, meals per table per hour (table turns), sales dollars per table, etc.
Machine availability and utilization	Output per hour of pizza oven use

LO8
Understand the use of quality, productivity, efficiency and timeliness, and marketing-effectiveness measures within the four perspectives of the balanced scorecard

The next table illustrates potential nonfinancial measures of performance for Garcia and Buffett CPAs, a service firm discussed in Chapter 11. Once again, we see differences in the specific measures of performance owing to differences in the business itself. For example, the number of billable hours per professional employee is very important to a professional-services firm.

GARCIA&BUFFET CPAS

Garcia and Buffett CPAs
Nonfinancial Measures of Performance

Quality Measures	***Method of Measuring***
Customer satisfaction	Client complaints/Number of lost clients/Number of new clients referred by current clients
Percentage of external failures	IRS audits/Mistakes on client financial statements
Efficiency and Timeliness Measures	
Customer response time	Total time between client's delivering tax information and completion of tax return
Delivery performance	Number of extended tax returns
Marketing Measures	
Growth in market share	Percentage change in sales compared to industry standards
Product innovation	Sales of new services to existing clients
New-market saturation	Percentage of new businesses that become clients
Productivity Measures	
Output per unit of input	Revenue per dollar of payroll, revenue per partner, billable hours per professional staff member

Although specific measures used in companies will differ, virtually every organization has a need to measure performance using nonfinancial measures of quality, productivity, efficiency and timeliness, and marketing success. Combined with traditional financial measures of performance, such as cost variances, segment margin, ROI, and EVA, these measures allow companies to integrate the financial, customer, internal business, and learning and growth perspectives of the balanced scorecard.

Key Concept: *The four perspectives of the balanced scorecard revolve around measures of quality, productivity, efficiency and timeliness, and marketing success.*

SUMMARY OF KEY CONCEPTS

- The balanced-scorecard approach integrates financial and nonfinancial performance measures. (p. 398)
- The balanced-scorecard approach requires looking at performance from four different but related perspectives: financial, customer, internal business, and learning and growth. (p. 401)
- The four perspectives of the balanced scorecard revolve around measures of quality, productivity, efficiency and timeliness, and marketing success. (p. 411)

KEY DEFINITIONS

Balanced-scorecard approach Uses a set of financial and nonfinancial measures that relate to the critical success factors of any organization (p. 398)

Quality Usually defined as meeting or exceeding customers' expectations (p. 401)

Kaizen A system of improvement based on a series of gradual and often small improvements (p. 401)

ISO 9000 A set of guidelines for quality management focusing on the design, production, inspection, testing, installing, and servicing of products, processes, and services (p. 402)

Prevention costs Costs incurred to prevent product failures from occurring, typically related to design and engineering (p. 403)

Appraisal (detection) costs Costs incurred to inspect finished products or products in the process of production (p. 403)

Internal failure costs Costs incurred once the product is produced and then determined to be defective (p. 403)

External failure costs Costs incurred when a defective product is delivered to a customer (p. 403)

Productivity A measure of the relationship between outputs and inputs (p. 404)

Customer response time The time it takes to deliver the product or service after the order is received (p. 406)

Manufacturing-cycle time The total time a product is in production, which includes process time, inspection time, wait time, and move time; cycle time will include both value-added and non-value-added time (p. 407)

Throughput The amount of product produced in a given amount of time, such as a day, week, or month (p. 407)

Manufacturing-cycle efficiency (MCE) The value-added time in the production process divided by the throughput, or cycle, time (p. 407)

MULTIPLE CHOICE

1. Which of the following statements about the balanced scorecard is true?

a. The four perspectives of the balanced scorecard revolve around measures of quality, productivity, efficiency and timeliness, and marketing success.

b. The balanced-scorecard approach requires looking at performance from four different but related perspectives: financial, customer, internal business, and learning and growth.

c. The balanced-scorecard approach integrates financial and nonfinancial performance measures.

d. all of the above

2. The number of warranty claims and returned products are measures of performance under the ____________ perspective of the balanced scorecard.
   a. financial
   b. customer
   c. internal business
   d. learning and growth
3. The efficient and effective use of employees is a measure of performance under the ____________ perspective of the balanced scorecard.
   a. financial
   b. customer
   c. internal business
   d. learning and growth
4. The ____________ perspective deals with objectives across the company's entire value chain: from research and development to postsale customer service.
   a. financial
   b. customer
   c. internal business
   d. learning and growth
5. Improving quality throughout the production process, increasing productivity, and increasing efficiency and timeliness are critical success factors under the ____________ perspective.
   a. financial
   b. customer
   c. internal business
   d. learning and growth
6. Which of the following statements regarding quality is true?
   a. Over the past 20 years or so, the demand by customers for quality products and services at an affordable price has drastically changed the way companies do business.
   b. Improving quality increases sales through higher customer satisfaction and demand, reduces costs, and increases the long-term profitability of companies.
   c. Companies have focused on improving the quality of the products or the services they sell through a variety of initiatives, such as total quality management (TQM), market-driven quality, and strategic quality management.
   d. all of the above
7. Which of the following statements about quality costs is true?
   a. Both external and internal failure costs can be reduced (theoretically to zero) by paying more attention to quality issues early in the value chain.
   b. Increasing expenditures related to prevention and appraisal can result in significant overall cost savings in the long run.
   c. It may be prudent to increase expenditures in one or more areas in order to decrease other costs.
   d. all of the above
8. Which of the following statements about productivity measures is true?
   a. In order to be useful, productivity measures must be used in conjunction with activity-based costing.
   b. In service organizations, productivity measures are important when evaluating the efficiency of personnel.
   c. When using productivity measures, the focus is on reducing manufacturing-cycle efficiency.
   d. all of the above

9. From an internal business perspective, efficiency and timeliness is often measured using:
   a. manufacturing-cycle time
   b. velocity
   c. throughput
   d. all of the above
10. Which of the following are examples of marketing efficiency?
   a. growth in market share
   b. product innovation
   c. new-market saturation
   d. all of the above

CONCEPT REVIEW

11. Based on the material covered in this chapter, why do you think a firm should be aware of its customers' needs?
12. Describe a balanced scorecard, and explain how it helps an organization meet its goals.
13. Discuss the financial perspective of the balanced scorecard. How does this perspective differ from financial measures of performance discussed earlier in this textbook? How does this perspective relate to the other balanced-scorecard perspectives?
14. Discuss the customer perspective of the balanced scorecard. How does this perspective relate to the other balanced-scorecard perspectives?
15. Discuss the internal operations perspective of the balanced scorecard. How does this perspective relate to the value chain? How does it relate to the other balanced-scorecard perspectives?
16. Discuss the innovation and learning perspective of the balanced scorecard. How does this perspective relate to the other three perspectives of the balanced scorecard?
17. Discuss the need for both financial and nonfinancial measures of performance and how they relate to the balanced scorecard.
18. Comment on the phrase "Managers will devote most of their time to activities that can be measured."
19. Discuss the use of performance measurement and the impact on improvement of performance.
20. Discuss why managers could be tempted to manipulate performance measures and how the design of performance measures should take that possibility into consideration.
21. Discuss the use of throughput. What does it measure?
22. Discuss what is meant by quality in today's manufacturing environment.
23. Describe continuous improvement and how it might impact decision making in today's business environment.
24. Discuss kaizen costing, and relate it to continuous improvement.
25. How does "employee empowerment" relate to continuous improvement?
26. Describe in detail the three critical success factors that relate to meeting customer quality requirements.
27. Describe the two costs of *controlling quality* and the two costs of *failing to control quality*.
28. Although the "cost of quality" concept is prevalent among companies throughout the world, a current theme in business today is that "quality is free." Discuss what that statement means.
29. Operational measures of time indicate the speed and reliability with which organizations supply products and services to customers. Companies generally use which two measures of time? Describe each of these measures.
30. What are the four quality costing categories? Include in your answer at least three examples for each category.
31. Describe ISO 9000 and comment on its importance. Research and compare other quality certification programs.
32. Describe value-added time. Give examples.
33. Describe non-value-added time. Give examples.
34. Describe how each element of manufacturing-cycle efficiency impacts the overall measurement.
35. Discuss marketing measures of performance and the impact of these measures on the balanced scorecard.

APPLICATION OF CONCEPTS

36. The following information has been gathered from Three Dog Nite Company:

Warranty claims	$ 60,000
Product liability lawsuits	0
Rework costs	200,000
Quality training	305,000
Inspection of incoming materials	900,000
Statistical process control	400,000
Waste	100,000
Product quality audits	250,000
Total yearly sales	50,000,000

Required

A. What are total prevention costs?

B. What are total appraisal costs?

C. What are total internal failure costs?

D. What are total external failure costs?

E. Compare prevention and appraisal costs to internal and external failure costs.

37. The following information was received from Two Black Cats Restaurant Chain:

Warranty claims	$ 120,000
Food poisoning liability lawsuits	200,000
Remaking entrees	600,000
Quality training	305,000
Inspection of incoming ingredients	900,000
Statistical process control	650,000
Spoilage and waste	300,000
Product quality audits	475,000
Total sales	50,000,000

Required

A. Compute the total prevention costs.

B. Compute the total appraisal costs.

C. Compute the total internal failure costs.

D. Compute the total external failure costs.

E. Compare prevention and appraisal costs to internal and external failure costs.

F. Two Black Cats Restaurant Chain is considering spending more on inspections. What is the likely impact on other failure costs? What do you recommend?

38. The following information was received from Down East Coffee Company:

Warranty claims	$ 60,000
Product liability lawsuits	100,000
Rework costs	300,000
Quality training	152,500
Inspection of incoming material	450,000
Statistical process control	325,000
Waste	150,000
Product quality audits	237,500
Total sales	25,000,000

Required

Prepare a report for Down East Coffee Company, showing total prevention, appraisal, internal failure, and external failure costs as a percentage of sales. Based on the report, what recommendations would you make?

39. Rebecca's Pottery Loft makes a variety of handmade pottery items. She has asked for your advice on one of the items manufactured—a clay pelican. The following information is provided:

Defective pelicans	1,100
Number of pelicans returned	150
Pelicans reworked	200
Profit per good pelican	$ 10
Profit per defective pelican	$ 5
Cost to rework defective pelican	$ 4
Processing cost of a returned pelican	$ 20
Appraisal costs	$3,400
Prevention costs	$6,000

Required

A. Calculate the total profits lost because Rebecca sold some defective pelicans.

B. Calculate the rework cost.

C. Calculate the cost of processing customer returns.

D. Calculate total failure cost.

E. Calculate total quality cost.

40. Cheryl's Country Creations is a chain of craft stores. The company evaluates its managers on the basis of both financial and nonfinancial performance measures. One of the nonfinancial measures used is throughput to measure performance in the manufacturing divisions. The following data pertain to the company's branch in Biloxi, Mississippi. The unit of measurement is units.

Units started into production	180,000
Total good units completed	135,000
Total hours of value-added production time	90,000
Total production hours	120,000

Required

A. Compute the manufacturing-cycle efficiency.

B. What was the total throughput per hour?

41. Dan Foley's Pubs is a chain of brewpubs in the Pacific Northwest. The company evaluates its managers on the basis of both financial and nonfinancial performance measures. One of the nonfinancial measures used is throughput to measure performance in the brewing divisions. The following data pertain to the company's brewpub in Federal Way, Washington. The unit of measurement is gallons:

Units started into production	280,000
Total good units completed	235,000
Total hours of value-added production time	190,000
Total production hours	220,000

Required

A. Compute the manufacturing-cycle efficiency.

B. What was the total throughput per hour?

42. Mandy Lifeboats Yacht Company has always measured divisional performance using only financial measures. Top management has started to question this approach to evaluating performance and is evaluating alternative measures. The managers are specifically interested in focusing on activities that generate value for their customers and so are considering using throughput. They have gathered the following data and have asked for your opinion.

Units started into production	3,000
Total good units completed	2,900
Total hours of value-added production time	180,000
Total hours of division production time	210,000

Required

A. What is the manufacturing-cycle efficiency?

B. What is the total throughput per hour?

C. Is there evidence of potentially poor quality in the production process as measured by the number of defective units? (Remember the type of business.)

Part IV

The Impact of Management Decisions

Chapter 13

The Management of Information and Knowledge for Better Decisions

Study Tools

A Review of the Previous Chapter

In Chapter 12, we discussed a variety of nonfinancial and qualitative measures used in a "balanced-scorecard" approach to measuring performance.

A Preview of This Chapter

In this chapter, we introduce the concept of knowledge management—the process of formally managing information and knowledge resources in order to facilitate access and reuse of that information and knowledge. Knowledge management tools facilitate human resource management, supply-chain management, and customer relationship management, ultimately leading to better and faster decision making.

Key concepts include:

- Data become information when organized, processed, and summarized, and information becomes knowledge when it is shared and exploited to add value to an organization.
- E-business can be used to support an organization's entire value chain. One of the key benefits of e-business is the ability to quickly access and share knowledge inside and outside an organization.
- The combination of enterprise resource planning (ERP), electronic data interchange (EDI), and e-business via the Internet has vastly changed the traditional supply chain, allowing organizations to link employees, suppliers, and customers into a communications network whose benefits extend well beyond simple exchanges of data.
- The use of the Internet facilitates customer relationship management (CRM) by allowing data to be gathered, stored, accessed, and shared more easily and by providing a feedback loop from customers to companies.

Learning Objectives

After studying the material in this chapter, you should be able to:

LO1 Understand changes that require more effective information and knowledge management in the business environment

LO2 Evaluate the impact of technological innovations like the Internet and electronic business on information and knowledge management

LO3 Identify key tools for effective knowledge management

LO4 Explain the use and benefits of knowledge warehouses and enterprise resource planning (ERP) systems as knowledge management tools

LO5 Analyze the impact of ERP, EDI, and e-business on supply-chain management and customer relationship management

A Preview of Upcoming Chapters

In Chapter 14, we discuss management fraud and the importance of good internal control systems on the reliability of accounting information in decision making. The chapter describes common types of management and employee fraud and looks at the role of the internal auditor and external auditor in ensuring that financial information is presented fairly and reliably.

In this chapter, we introduce the concept of knowledge management—the process of formally managing information and knowledge resources in order to facilitate access and reuse of that information and knowledge. Information and knowledge resources may vary for each company but include traditional sources of data provided by the accounting information system, as well as such things as internal memos, training manuals, and information supplied by customers and suppliers.

Just as information and knowledge resources vary among companies, knowledge management tools may vary as well. Typical knowledge management tools include knowledge warehouses and enterprise resource planning (ERP) systems. Knowledge management tools facilitate human resource management, supply-chain management, and customer relationship management, ultimately leading to better and faster decision making. ■

INTRODUCTION

LO1
Understand changes that require more effective information and knowledge management in the business environment

Business environments have changed dramatically in the past few decades. Companies of all sizes can now compete in a dynamic global marketplace through electronic commerce (e-business) and other emerging technologies. Downsizing, combined with a more mobile workforce, has placed a premium on retaining talented, knowledgeable employees. Customers demand specialized products and services and real-time information concerning product availability, order status, and delivery times. Suppliers need information on their buyers' sales and inventory levels in order to tailor their production schedules and delivery times to meet the buyers' demands. Shareholders demand greater value from their investments. Although these changes have provided opportunities for companies able to adapt and take advantage of them, they have also resulted in challenges. Above all else, these changes require more effective management of knowledge within an organization. In today's business environment, knowledge is power and must be managed for companies to remain competitive.

Although sometimes used interchangeably, the term knowledge should not be confused with data or information. Companies generate literally tons of **data**—financial statements, customer lists, inventory records, and the number and type of products and services sold. However, getting that data into an accessible and usable form is another matter. When data are organized, processed, and summarized, they become **information.** When that information is shared and exploited so that it adds value to an organization, it becomes **knowledge.**

Key Concept: *Data become information when organized, processed, and summarized and information becomes knowledge when it is shared and exploited to add value to an organization.*

THE EVOLUTION OF DATA, INFORMATION, AND KNOWLEDGE MANAGEMENT

Many of us take for granted that a computer will be available to assist us in the completion of our everyday business and personal tasks (letter writing, note taking, basic word processing, accounting/bookkeeping, presentations, etc.). But those of us who are old enough remember when the entire process of running an organization—from human resources (hiring, firing, and employee benefits) to accounting (source documents, cost sheets, financial statements, etc.) to production (machine specifications, product output, and inventory records)—was manually accounted for and documented without the benefit of computers. Business data were recorded on reams of paper, information was stored in file cabinets, and knowledge resided in people's minds.

Data and information management evolved with the introduction and availability of mainframe computers in the 1960s and 1970s and personal computers in the 1980s. Accounting information systems were often computerized, and training manuals, internal memos, and customer records could all be stored electronically. However, the problems of knowledge management did not go away. The stored data were not easily organized, accessed, or searched. Although information was arguably available, just how did one find it and use it? Until the widespread adoption of relational databases in the 1980s, it was still difficult to access and retrieve data. Sales staff still did not always know what was going on in production, and customer service representatives had no way of knowing that a customer's problem had already been addressed by another representative dealing with a different customer in a different city. In addition, key employees still left for other jobs, taking with them all their knowledge that was not written down or otherwise shared. Although the widespread use of intranets (networks of linked computers inside a company) made access to information faster and easier, exploiting that information as usable knowledge was and still is difficult.

THE INTERNET AND ELECTRONIC COMMERCE

LO2
Evaluate the impact of technological innovations like the Internet and electronic business on information and knowledge management

Yet another transformation in data and information management was made possible with the wide-scale use of the Internet and electronic commerce in the 1990s. Electronic business, or **e-business,** includes a vast array of business activities conducted electronically. The first widespread application of e-business involved direct sales of products to customers over the Internet. A wide variety of products and services are sold on-line via electronic catalogs. Examples of companies that offer customers the opportunity to shop on-line include computer manufacturers, such as Dell Computer and Gateway; resellers, such as Amazon.com and wine sellers; and food sellers, such as PeaPod, an on-line grocery. Consumer sites, such as eBay.com and Amazon.com attract millions of visitors each year and account for billions of dollars of revenue.

http://www.dell.com
http://www.gateway.com
http://www.amazon.com
http://www.wine.com
http://www.peapod.com
http://www.ebay.com

From a purely operational perspective, on-line business has the ability to increase sales, reduce customer response time, increase efficiency, and quicken new products' time to market while decreasing transaction costs. Sales via the Internet allow a raw material producer to sell directly to the end consumer, eliminating costs of the intermediary without reducing value to the consumer. From the consumer's perspective, 24-hour access to products, as well as the company's ability to help develop and tailor products, should increase customer satisfaction and thus increase customer retention rates. In summary, online sales allow companies to reach new markets, remain open for business 24 hours a day, 7 days a week, and, potentially, enhance customer service.

IN THE NEWS

http://www.hancockgourmetlobster.com

Taking orders through its Web site, Hancock Gourmet Lobster Company in Cundy's Harbor, Maine, ships lobster stew, lobster tails, and other fresh and frozen lobster products anywhere in the United States. According to the owner, Cal Hancock, the company's Web site attracts new customers and makes it more convenient for current customers to place orders 24 hours a day, 7 days a week. It also allows customers to be contacted directly via e-mail with special promotions.

In addition to the benefits of on-line sales, e-business can be used to support an organization's entire value chain. As introduced in Chapter 2, the value chain describes the linked set of value-creating activities required by today's competitive business environment (Exhibit 13-1).

Although we often think of e-business as consumer-related purchases of goods and services, e-business covers the entire spectrum of business activities. In fact, business-to-business (B2B) sales are expected to exceed $2.5 trillion by 2004 ("The Next Phase," *Wall Street Journal,* May 21, 2001, R8).

IN THE NEWS **http://www.intel.com**

One of the largest B2B sellers, Intel, averages almost $2 billion in on-line orders each month from customers (other companies) in 46 countries. These companies can use the Internet to check product specifications, pricing, availability, order status, and delivery dates in real time. Data are personalized for every company and for every type of user ("By the Numbers," *Wall Street Journal,* May 21, 2001, R6, and September 20, 1999, B11).

http://www.ge.com
http://www.target.com

Although other B2B activities may be smaller in scope, they often result in significant cost savings. For example, according to General Electric, 25 percent of its total sales of plastic resins is conducted on-line via GEPolymerland.com. Ninety-five percent of these sales require no human intervention, resulting in savings in transaction costs, inventory costs, and customer service costs. GE estimates that its on-line ventures contributed $1 billion in productivity savings in 2001 ("Just One Word: Plastics," *Wall Street Journal,* May 21, 2001, R20).

B2B activities also include on-line purchasing networks in which large corporations band together to create their own marketplaces for on-line buying and selling. For example, Target and more than 50 other large retailers formed Worldwide Retail Exchange in March 2000. Target uses the on-line exchange to purchase office products, fax paper, and cleaning products, as well as plastic coat hangers and merchandise for resale. In five years, Target expects all of its purchasing to be conducted over the Internet ("The Next Phase," *Wall Street Journal,* May 21, 2001, R8).

Finally, B2B activities include private networks in which companies are linked directly to suppliers in order to better track and manage inventory levels. These activities are discussed more fully in the Supply-Chain Management section (page 427).

Key Concept: *E-business can be used to support an organization's entire value chain. One of the key benefits of e-business is the ability to quickly access and share knowledge inside and outside an organization.*

http://www.ey.com

Even with these technological innovations in data and information management occurring in the past 30 to 40 years, Ernst & Young estimates that up to 80 percent of a company's accumulated knowledge is not utilized in business decisions ("Knowledge Based

EXHIBIT 13-1 The Value Chain

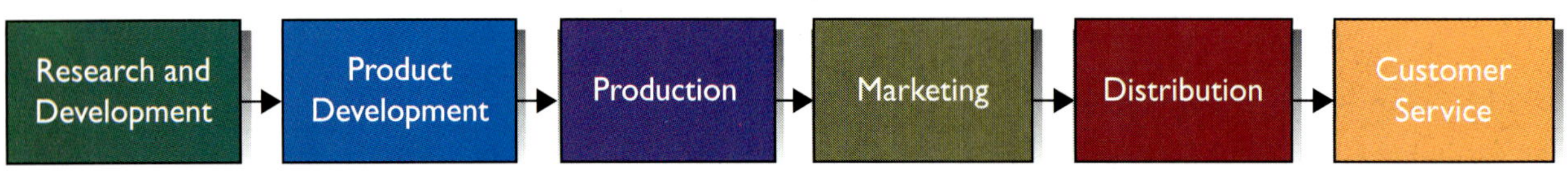

Businesses, Overview: Knowledge is Power," Ernst and Young (http://www.ey.com), 1999). The reasons are varied. One possible explanation is that accounting information systems still may not provide timely information that is easily accessible and easily shared.

As discussed in Chapter 1, the accounting information system (AIS) was traditionally simply a transaction processing system that captured financial data resulting from accounting transactions. Other nonmonetary information was likely collected and processed outside the traditional AIS, if collected at all. Useful information concerning transactions, such as the quality of the material purchased and the timeliness of its delivery or customer satisfaction with an order, might not be captured at all and therefore not evaluated by management. Although the contemporary view of accounting information has been broadened to include both nonmonetary quantitative data and qualitative data (see Exhibit 13-2), this information was not readily accessible and readily shared until the advent of enterprise resource planning (ERP) systems in the past few years.

Other potential reasons that knowledge is not effectively used and managed in businesses may include geographic and cultural barriers resulting from international expansion and the continued workforce mobility, with key employees and managers leaving for other jobs and taking critical knowledge with them.

EXHIBIT 13-2 A Contemporary View of Accounting Information

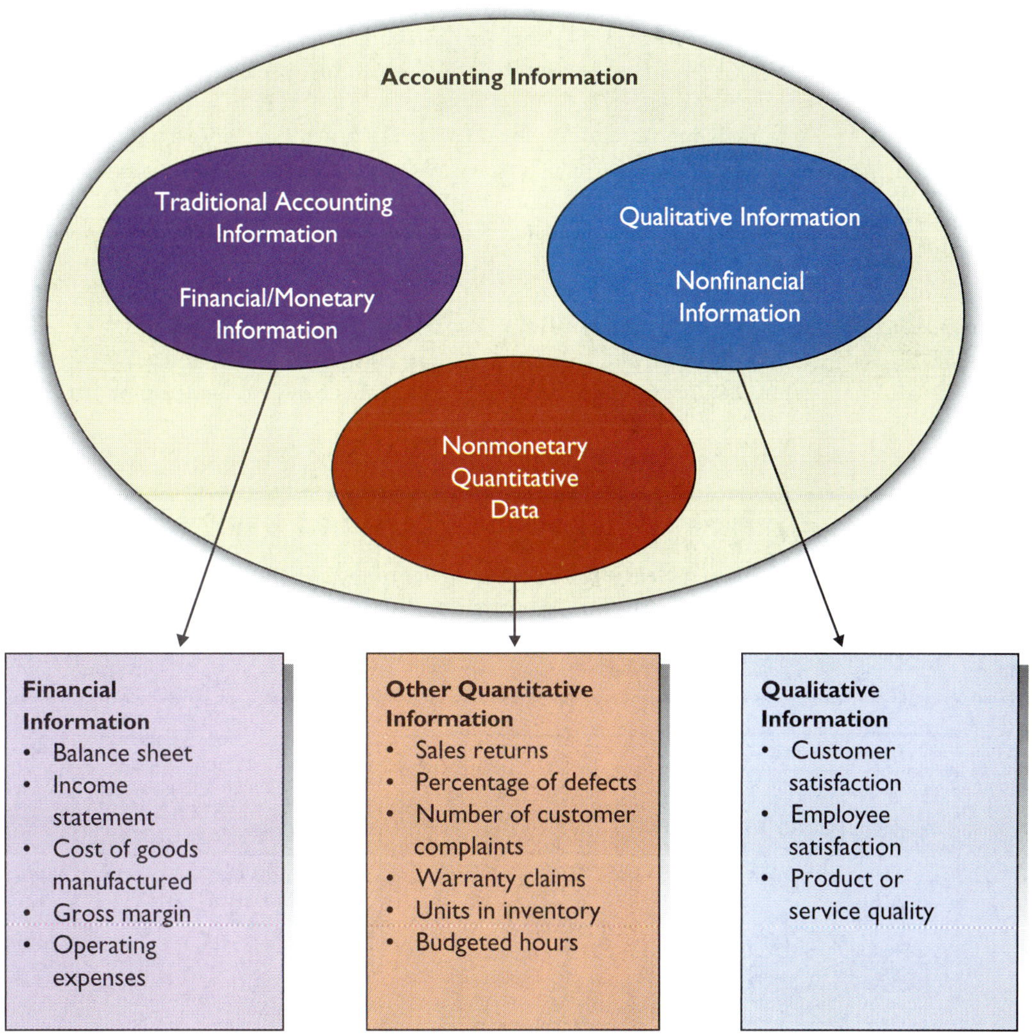

KNOWLEDGE MANAGEMENT TOOLS

LO3
Identify key tools for effective knowledge management

Effective knowledge management can result in faster and better business decisions, leading ultimately to increased profitability through better strategic planning, more timely development of products and completion of projects, improved customer service, and cost savings. A variety of knowledge management tools, including data and knowledge warehouses and ERP systems, facilitate effective knowledge management.

DATA AND KNOWLEDGE WAREHOUSES

Data warehouses are simply central depositories for electronic data. Data warehouses often contain many years of transactions, which can be accessed and browsed electronically. Although data warehouses contain the ingredients for good business decisions, turning that data into information and knowledge requires other tools. A variety of technological tools are available to help managers dig out the information they need to make business decisions. The term **data mining** was coined as a way to express, in modern-day technical terms, how a manager can search for and extract information from the corporate computer system, much like a coal miner searches for and extracts coal from a mine. Data mining software, such as Enterprise Miner from SAS Institute, is used to help find business opportunities in large amounts of data. For example, every time you make a purchase using a value card at a grocery store, the grocery store collects data on what you purchase, how much you purchase, whether you use coupons, and whether you pay with cash, check, or credit card. Data-mining software looks for data patterns that can be used to help managers make decisions concerning product placement, product pricing, inventory management, and advertising campaigns.

Knowledge warehouses are organized to provide access to a wide variety of qualitative data. Memos, news articles, client and customer notes, product specifications, documentation of problem resolution, employee information (education, skills, and specialty areas), and competitor intelligence may all be part of a searchable knowledge warehouse. Data-mining techniques can be used to determine the available skill set of employees, identify untapped expertise and opportunities for growth, and identify needs for additional skills and training. Technological tools, such as Lotus Notes, were traditionally used to store this type of data and to facilitate its access and use. Today, Web-based tools, such as Internet newsgroups, are often used to collect and to share knowledge. As discussed in the next section, ERP systems are another tool enabling organizations to gather information and to disseminate knowledge to their employees.

PAUSE & *Reflect*

Think of other ways that data can be collected on your buying habits to help marketing efforts.

ENTERPRISE RESOURCE PLANNING SYSTEMS

Companies use **enterprise resource planning (ERP) systems** to collect, organize, report, and distribute data throughout an organization and to transform that data into usable

DILBERT BY SCOTT ADAMS

DILBERT reprinted by permission of United Media Inc.

knowledge necessary for managers to make proper business decisions. These systems typically integrate payroll, purchasing, sales, manufacturing, inventory, product costing, and billing, providing a more comprehensive view of the organization.

An ERP system digitally records every business transaction a company makes, regardless of whether it is input through accounting, purchasing, sales, or manufacturing, and automatically updates all connected systems to reflect each transaction. This approach provides real-time information to decision makers throughout a company. When a sales associate on the road places an order for a product, the information is automatically conveyed to purchasing, accounts receivable, and production so that materials can be ordered, invoices can be processed, and production can be scheduled.

ERP systems help businesses evolve from data generators to information gatherers to knowledge creators and sharers. The ultimate goal of the ERP system is to get the right information to the right people at the right time. With better knowledge management, an organization can better identify its strengths, pinpoint its weaknesses, uncover new opportunities, capitalize on trends, and make better business decisions.

When used effectively, ERP systems can allow an organization to achieve higher levels of profitability. They can provide more accurate and complete information, resulting in reduced purchasing and manufacturing costs, reduced customer response time, increased quality of products and services, increased customer satisfaction, and better business decisions. After the installation of an ERP system at Belvedere (a $30 million manufacturer and distributor of beauty salon furnishings), customer response time was reduced from five days to two days, inventory was reduced by 30 percent, order-processing capacity was increased by 15 percent, and customer complaints dropped (Piturro, "How Midsize Companies are Buying ERP," *Journal of Accountancy,* September 1999, 41).

The benefits of ERP are not limited to manufacturing companies. Service organizations have also come to realize the increased benefits of ERP systems. Organizational efficiencies, such as improved customer service and better communication, provide benefits to all types of companies.

TECHNOLOGY FOCUS

ERP system providers include such companies as Great Plains Software (http://www.greatplains.com), SAP AG (http://www.sap.com), Oracle Systems (http://www.oracle.com), PeopleSoft (http://www.peoplesoft.com), Baan (http://www.baan.com), and J. D. Edwards (http://www.jdedwards.com).

http://www.belvedere.com

LO4

Explain the use and benefits of knowledge warehouses and enterprise resource planning (ERP) systems as knowledge management tools

IN THE NEWS **http://www.computereconomics.com**

According to Computer Economics, ERP software systems were being utilized by over 50 percent of discrete manufacturing organizations and almost 40 percent of process manufacturing organizations and transportation organizations in the period from 1998 to 2000. In contrast, less than 15 percent of healthcare, insurance, utility, and government organizations had operational ERP systems during this time ("Technology Implementation Status TriMark—1998 to 2000," *2001 Information Systems and E-Business Spending,* Computer Economics, February 2001).

Although ERP systems have provided benefits to many companies, they are not without their costs. ERP systems tend to involve large-scale financial, human resource, time, and information technology costs. When there are glitches in the systems, the results can be disastrous.

IN THE NEWS **http://www.hersheys.com**

In July 1999, Hershey Foods (the nation's largest candy producer) went on-line with its $112 million ERP system designed to do everything: track raw ingredients, schedule production, set prices, measure the effectiveness of promotional campaigns, schedule delivery, and decide how to stack products inside trucks. However, glitches in the system left many distributors and retailers with empty candy shelves in the season leading to Halloween. At one point, Hershey could not even tell what had been shipped or who it had been shipped to ("Hershey's Biggest Dud Has Turned Out to Be New Computer System," *Wall Street Journal,* October 29, 1999, A1).

© AP/WIDE WORLD PHOTOS

Great Plains Software focuses on providing integrated e-business solutions for small- to midsize companies.

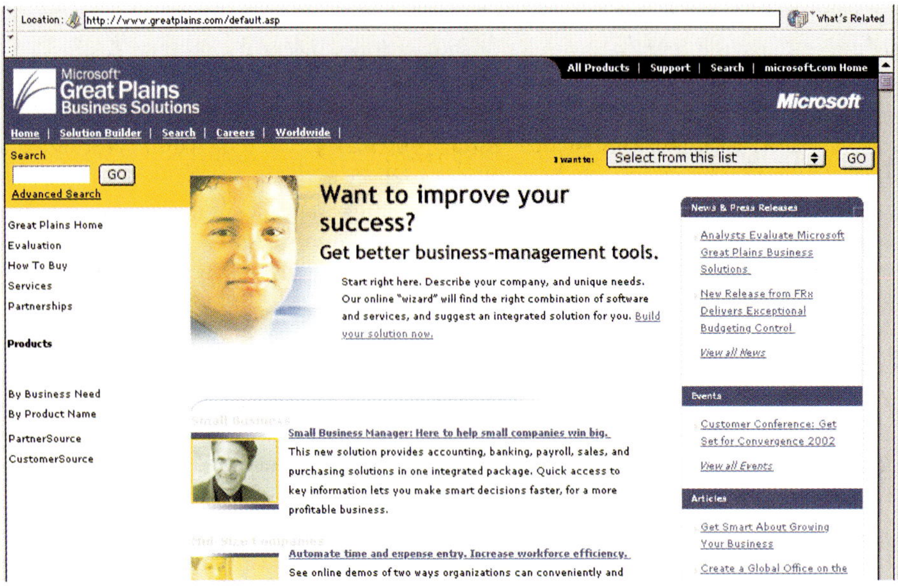

COURTESY OF MICROSOFT GREAT PLAINS BUSINESS SOLUTIONS

ERP systems are generally not meant to *solve* business inefficiencies. Rather, they can point to where inefficiencies exist within an organization and allow corporate decision makers to take appropriate corrective measures. A number of companies have reengineered their business processes through involvement with ERP systems, resulting in substantial returns from their ERP investments.

The success of an ERP system usually depends on how quickly it can provide useful information for managerial decision making. This need favors rapid implementation, which shortens the time needed to recapture the investment. However, the average implementation time of a system is 23 months. In addition, it can take up to two years after implementation for a company to achieve a quantifiable return on investment.

Many small corporations have been reluctant to invest in ERP systems, owing to the high cost and the implementation time involved. However, several of the larger ERP system vendors have begun to market scaled-down versions of their ERP packages in order to tap the small- to medium-sized-company market. Companies that either could not afford ERP systems in the past or were merely too small to integrate the applications can now compete with their larger counterparts.

ERP, EDI, AND E-BUSINESS

LO5
Analyze the impact of ERP, EDI, and e-business on supply-chain management and customer relationship management

http://www.nabisco.com

Electronic data interchange (EDI) and e-business via the Internet allow suppliers and customers to be brought into the ERP network so that on-line orders from customers initiate a series of highly integrated transactions that ultimately fulfill the request—from materials acquisition to manufacturing to shipping. EDI is simply the electronic transmission of data, such as purchase orders and invoices. Although originally limited to large companies with a direct data connection or companies on the same network, the Internet has made EDI technology available to a wide range of medium and small businesses. EDI has several benefits. It increases the speed and quality of information exchange, reduces lead times, and reduces processing costs. Nabisco estimates that the cost of processing a paper-based purchase order is $70, whereas the same transaction performed through EDI costs less than $1 (Millman, "A Brief History of EDI," *Infoworld,* April 6, 1998, 83). Government agencies and a variety of service organizations also use EDI. Wisconsin's Worker's Compensation Division uses EDI to allow electronic reporting of injury claims. Reporting electronically saves time and money for the division and for insurance carriers, employers, and injured workers. It also increases the accuracy of claims and enhances data flexibility by providing a rich database for future use (Greenstein and Feinman, *Electronic Commerce: Security Risk Management and Control,* McGraw-Hill, 2000).

SUPPLY-CHAIN MANAGEMENT

Supply-chain management includes a variety of activities centered on making the purchase of materials and inventory more efficient and less costly. When coupled with ERP systems, EDI allows a company to place a great deal of the burden of inventory management and raw materials ordering in the hands of its suppliers, resulting in an evolution of supply-chain management from "loosely coupled relationships into virtual organizations" (O'Leary, "Supply Chain Processes and Relationships for Electronic Commerce," *Handbook of Electronic Commerce,* Springer Verlag, 2000, 431–444). In these organizations, suppliers monitor sales in real time and determine order quantities and order times for buyers. Wal-Mart shares data on sales, profit margin, and inventory levels with more than 7,000 suppliers that access Wal-Mart's database 120,000 times per week. This allows suppliers to more closely match their production schedules to Wal-Mart's peak selling seasons and to deliver products when Wal-Mart needs them ("Wal-Mart Expands Access to Product Sales History," *Wall Street Journal,* August 18, 1999, B8).

http://www.walmart.com

In other companies, e-business, ERP, and EDI are changing the supply chain in other ways. When Coca-Cola rolled out its ERP system, it included 11 of its major worldwide bottling partners, including Coca-Cola Enterprises. This allowed Coca-Cola and the bottlers to pool requisitions for raw materials, such as corn syrup and aluminum, and to coordinate shipping, resulting in volume discounts and other cost savings ("ERP: Extending the Enterprise," *Discount Store News,* May 24, 1999, 7).

http://www.coca-cola.com

TECHNOLOGY FOCUS

Participating in supply-chain management systems can benefit suppliers as well as buyers. For example, Manco (http://manco.com), a manufacturer of adhesive products, participates in a private network with Ace Hardware (http://www.acehardware.com) to manage the inventory of such products as duct tape and shelf liners. The system helps to highlight trends in product demand (such as red duct tape during the Christmas season), allowing Manco to reduce its distribution costs by 28 percent and its freight costs by 18 percent ("Private Exchanges May Allow B-to-B commerce to Thrive After All," *Wall Street Journal,* March 16,2001, B1).

Key Concept: *The combination of ERP, EDI, and e-business via the Internet has vastly changed the traditional supply chain, allowing organizations to link employees, suppliers, and customers into a communications network whose benefits extend well beyond simple exchanges of data.*

CUSTOMER RELATIONSHIP MANAGEMENT

The goal of **customer relationship management (CRM)** is to bring a company closer to its customers in order to serve them better. Whether customers are served by in-store representatives, outside sales associates, or call-center operators, the use of ERP and the Internet facilitates CRM by allowing information to be gathered, stored, and most important, easily accessed and shared. CRM utilizing the ERP and the Internet allows organizations to focus sales efforts on what the customer values and to anticipate and react to customer needs.

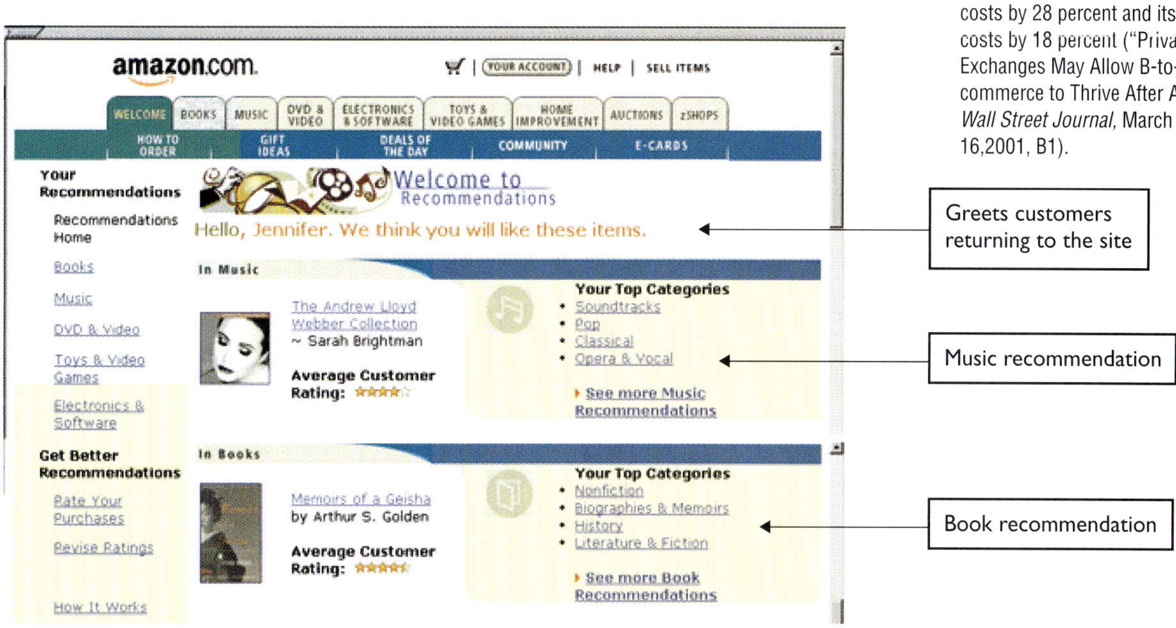

COURTESY OF AMAZON.COM

IN THE NEWS http://www.amazon.com

Amazon.com collects data on each customer and anticipates the customer's preferences and buying habits. This allows Amazon to e-mail the customer with the latest products that fit the particular customer and to greet each customer accessing its Web site with personalized suggestions based on previous purchases.

PAUSE & Reflect

Who owns customer information? Is collecting customer information without the customer's knowledge and sharing that information with other parties ethical?

The use of the Internet creates an interactive feedback "loop" from customers to companies, making it possible to more accurately and consistently forecast, manage, and meet customer expectations. Through the Internet, an organization can manage the entire life cycle of its customer relationships, including marketing analysis and planning, customer acquisition and retention, order management, and customer service and support. A variety of car manufacturers, including Toyota and GM, are using the Web to enhance their CRM efforts. Up to now, car manufacturers tried to forecast consumer demand for different models and delivered vehicles to dealers based on those forecasts. However, if consumer tastes changed, dealers (and the manufacturer) were often left with a large inventory of cars that were difficult to sell. Both Toyota and GM have announced goals of manufacturing and delivering a custom vehicle within 10 to 12 days of receiving an on-line order from a customer. This benefits all stakeholders by reducing inventory carrying costs for the manufacturer and dealer, allowing manufacturers to quickly identify and react to changes in customer demand, and providing built-to-order products in a timely fashion to consumers ("General Motors Looks to the Future with Internet Unit," *Wall Street Journal,* August 11, 1999, B4; see also http://www.gm.com and http://www.toyota.com).

***Key Concept:** The use of the Internet facilitates CRM by allowing data to be gathered, stored, accessed, and shared more easily and by providing a feedback loop from customers to companies.*

SUMMARY OF KEY CONCEPTS

- Data become information when organized, processed, and summarized, and information becomes knowledge when it is shared and exploited to add value to an organization. (p. 420)
- E-business can be used to support an organization's entire value chain. One of the key benefits of e-business is the ability to quickly access and share knowledge inside and outside an organization. (p. 422)
- The combination of ERP, EDI, and e-business via the Internet has vastly changed the traditional supply chain, allowing organizations to link employees, suppliers, and customers into a communications network whose benefits extend well beyond simple exchanges of data. (p. 427)
- The use of the Internet facilitates CRM by allowing data to be gathered, stored, accessed, and shared more easily and by providing a feedback loop from customers to companies. (p. 428)

KEY DEFINITIONS

Data Reports, such as financial statements, customer lists, inventory records, and so on (p. 420)

Information Data that have been organized, processed, and summarized (p. 420)

Knowledge Information that is shared and exploited so that it adds value to an organization (p. 420)

E-business Business activities conducted electronically (p. 421)

Data warehouses Central depositories for electronic data (p. 424)

Data mining A process of searching and extracting information from data (p. 424)

Knowledge warehouses Used to store and provide access to a wide variety of qualitative data (p. 424)

Enterprise resource planning (ERP) systems Used to collect, organize, report, and distribute data from all aspects of a company's business and to transform that data into useful knowledge (p. 424)

Electronic data interchange (EDI) The electronic transmission of data, such as purchase orders and invoices (p. 426)

Supply-chain management Includes a variety of activities centered on making the purchase of materials and inventory more efficient and less costly (p. 427)

Customer relationship management (CRM) Designed to bring a company closer to its customers in order to serve them better (p. 427)

MULTIPLE CHOICE

1. Customers in today's competitive marketplace demand information about:
   a. product availability
   b. order status
   c. delivery times
   d. all of the above

2. Which of the following statements is true?
   a. Information becomes knowledge when it is shared and exploited to add value to an organization.
   b. Information becomes data when organized, processed, and summarized.
   c. Information and knowledge are synonymous terms.
   d. all of the above

3. Which of the following statements about information and knowledge management is true?
   a. Information and knowledge resources replace the traditional sources of data provided by the accounting information system, as well as such things as internal memos and training manuals.
   b. Knowledge management is the process of formally managing information and knowledge resources in order to facilitate access and reuse of that information and knowledge.
   c. Typical knowledge management tools include e-mail and the Internet.
   d. all of the above

4. Which of the following is *not* a benefit of e-business?
   a. E-business has the ability to increase customer response time.
   b. E-business can be used to support an organization's entire value chain.
   c. E-business enhances a company's ability to quickly access and share knowledge in and outside an organization.
   d. none of the above

5. An example of *monetary,* or *financial,* information in an accounting information system is:
   a. gross margin
   b. operating expenses
   c. net income
   d. all of the above

6. Data and knowledge warehouses and ERP systems are examples of:
   a. e-business
   b. knowledge management tools
   c. accounting information systems
   d. Internet facilities

7. Which of the following statements about data warehouses is true?
   a. Data warehouses often contain many years of transactions, which can be accessed and browsed electronically.
   b. Data warehouses contain the ingredients for good business decisions, and turning that data into information is quite simple.
   c. Data warehousing can be used to collect, organize, report, and distribute data throughout an organization and to transform that data into useable knowledge.
   d. Data warehousing is too costly in most cases to be practical.
8. Which of the following statements regarding ERP systems is *not* true?
   a. ERP systems provide real-time information to decision makers throughout a company.
   b. The ultimate goal of the ERP system is to reduce production costs.
   c. ERP systems are costly to implement.
   d. The benefits of ERP are not limited to manufacturing companies.
9. Which of the following statements about EDI is *not* true?
   a. EDI increases lead times and reduces processing costs.
   b. The Internet has made EDI technology available to a wide range of small- and medium-size businesses.
   c. EDI increases the speed and quality of information exchange.
   d. EDI and e-business via the Internet allow suppliers and customers to be brought into the ERP network so that on-line orders from customers initiate a series of highly integrated transactions.
10. Which of the following statements about the Internet and customer relationship management (CRM) is *not* true?
   a. The Internet facilitates CRM by allowing information to be gathered and stored.
   b. The Internet facilitates CRM by allowing information to be easily accessed and shared.
   c. CRM utilizing ERP and the Internet allows organizations to influence the purchasing patterns of customers with Web-based advertising.
   d. CRM utilizing ERP and the Internet allows organizations to focus sales efforts on what the customer values and to anticipate and react to customer needs.

CONCEPT REVIEW

11. Explain how e-business has impacted the business environment today. How has e-business changed your life specifically?
12. Discuss the relationship among data, information, and knowledge.
13. Visit http://www.internetindicators.com and go to the case studies section. Choose any company and write a short (1–2 page) report on the success or failure of the case study chosen. Print out the case study as a reference for your paper.
14. Go to http://www.dell.com and visit the higher education, faculty, staff, and student area. Price the latest special computer offered for purchase. Print out the material.
15. Go to http://www.gateway.com and price a remanufactured computer of your choice. Print out the material.
16. Go to http://www.llbean.com and research and write a short report on discovery schools. Print out the material to support your paper.
17. Go to http://www.landsend.com and research what luggage is offered. Print out the material.
18. Go to http://www.intel.com and research employment opportunities. Print out the material.
19. Go to http://www.gmc.com and research any current special offers for automobiles. Print out the material.
20. Go to http://www.sap.com and write a short paper about what the company provides in the way of ERP systems. What is the company's competitive advantage?
21. Go to http://www.oracle.com and write a short paper about what the company provides in the way of ERP systems. What is the company's competitive advantage?

22. Go to http://www.peoplesoft.com and write a short paper about what the company provides in the way of ERP systems. What is the company's competitive advantage?
23. Go to http://www.baan.com and write a short paper about what the company provides in the way of ERP systems. What is the company's competitive advantage?
24. Go to http://www.jdedwards.com and write a short paper about what the company provide in the way of ERP systems. What is the company's competitive advantage?
25. Visit all the sites of software vendors offering ERP systems that were mentioned in the chapter, and contrast and compare them. What company would you choose to provide an ERP system to your business? Why?
26. Discuss on-line sales and the impact they can have on business today.
27. Do you think that on-line sales can reduce the price to the consumer? Why or why not?
28. Discuss why traditional accounting information systems may not provide all the information needed for effective decision making.
29. Discuss what is meant by "effective knowledge management."
30. Discuss how ERP systems can enhance effective knowledge management.
31. Discuss the impact of data and knowledge warehouses on decision making.
32. Discuss the benefits and limitations of ERP systems.
33. Discuss the impact of electronic data interchange (EDI) technology on decision making in business.
34. Discuss the impact of the Internet on customer relationship management (CRM).
35. Using the *Wall Street Journal* and other business resources, research how companies are using on-line supply networks to facilitate their business operations. What problems are companies facing?

Chapter 14

Internal Control and the Prevention of Fraud

Study Tools

A Review of the Previous Chapter

In Chapter 13, we introduced the concept of knowledge management—the process of formally managing information and knowledge resources in order to facilitate access and reuse of that information and knowledge. Typical knowledge management tools include knowledge warehouses and enterprise resource planning (ERP) systems. Knowledge management tools facilitate supply-chain management and customer relationship management, ultimately leading to better and faster decision making.

A Preview of This Chapter

In this chapter, we discuss the importance of internal control systems in detecting fraud. We also discuss key characteristics of an internal control system, common internal control procedures, and the impact of e-business on fraud and internal control.

Key concepts include:

- Fraud is more narrowly defined in a business context than in common law.
- Management fraud can be very difficult to detect.
- Good internal control systems can usually detect and prevent most types of employee fraud.
- Individuals engage in fraudulent activity as a result of situational pressures, opportunity, and personal characteristics.
- The internal control system's impact on promoting effective and efficient operations is perhaps even more important than detecting fraudulent activity.
- Upper-level management sets the tone of ethical behavior and the overall atmosphere of the organization.
- To be effective, internal control systems must be communicated throughout an organization and modified as new risks are identified.
- E-business activities entail new risks and require new internal control procedures.

A Preview of Upcoming Chapters

In Chapter 15 and Chapter 16, we discuss the preparation and use of the statement of cash flows and the analysis of financial statement information.

Learning Objectives

After studying the material in this chapter, you should be able to:

LO1 Distinguish management fraud from employee fraud

LO2 Understand ethical issues surrounding earnings management

LO3 Explain the typical causes of fraudulent activities

LO4 Understand the roles of the internal audit department and the external auditor

LO5 Explain the objectives, design, and characteristics of good internal control systems

LO6 Understand common internal control procedures

LO7 Understand the behavioral implications of internal control systems

LO8 Understand the impact of e-business on internal control

This chapter examines the importance of internal control systems in detecting and controlling management and employee fraud. The chapter explores common types of fraud and the role of internal managers and external auditors in detecting and preventing fraud. The chapter also introduces characteristics of an internal control system (including the key internal control procedures that are used to prevent and detect fraudulent activities). The chapter concludes with a discussion of the impact of e-business on internal control systems and risk. ■

INTRODUCTION

http://www.kpmg.com

A 1998 survey of executives at more than 5,000 corporations, universities, and federal, state, and local governments and agencies found that 59 percent of respondents believed that fraud will become more of a problem in the future (1998 Fraud Survey, KPMG LLP). Although fraud has been a problem as long as businesses have been in existence, organizations may face increased risks in today's business environment for a number of reasons. The sheer size of many corporations makes it difficult to monitor thousands of employees. In some cases, globalization has increased opportunities for fraud as companies expand internationally without a firm understanding of the culture of the country. Reduced stability in the workforce and a resulting reduction in corporate loyalty may increase fraud, as may increasing pressure to meet earnings expectations of shareholders or the expectations of other stakeholders. Most recently, the increased computerization of accounting systems and growing reliance on the Internet as a sales tool and as a way to share information and knowledge with customers and suppliers has led to new concerns about the security of data and the manipulation of data by hackers and disgruntled employees.

FRAUD

LO1
Distinguish management fraud from employee fraud

What exactly is **fraud**? Common-law requirements for fraud include a false representation of a material fact made by one party with the intent to deceive and induce another party to justifiably rely on the fact, to his or her detriment.

In a business context, the meaning of fraud is narrower than the common-law definition. Fraud may include internal deceptions by management, a manipulation of financial data, or a misappropriation of the organization's assets. Misappropriation of assets can include embezzling funds, stealing assets, or causing the organization to pay for goods or services it did not receive. Fraudulent acts may involve falsifying documents or accounting records and can involve one or more individuals at any level in the organization.

Key Concept: *Fraud is more narrowly defined in a business context than in common law.*

MANAGEMENT FRAUD

Management fraud typically involves misstating financial statements in order to mislead readers of those statements or to take advantage of incentives or other benefits tied to earnings. The most common types of management fraud involve improper revenue recognition, overstating assets, or understating liabilities. These types of frauds typically are the result of pressure on management to report good operating results. This pressure may come from stockholders to meet earnings expectations but may also be a result of unrealistic sales goals or other budgets set internally or compensation plans that are tied directly to the financial results of the organization. For example, sales managers may record sales in the wrong period to meet sales quotas. If a large order is received on January 2, 2002, the paperwork might be altered to record the sale in 2001. This type of fraud increases sales and earnings for 2001 but will correct itself by the end of 2002. In other words, the combined sales for 2001 and 2002 will be correct, although one year will be overstated and the other year understated.

Revenues can also be inflated by recording false sales or not recording returned merchandise. This has the impact of falsely inflating revenues and overstating accounts receivable. Other examples of financial statement manipulation include inflating inventory values by leaving obsolete inventory on the books or creating fake documents to show purchases of inventory.

IN THE NEWS

One of the most famous examples of fraudulent manipulation of revenue involved ZZZZ Best Company. Founded by Barry Minkow in 1982 as a carpet-cleaning business run out of his parents' garage, the company's reported net income grew from $200,000 in 1984 to $5 million in 1987 on revenues of $50 million. In 1987, the stock market valued the company at over $200 million. However, by 1989 Barry Minkow was serving a 25-year sentence for 57 counts of securities fraud. ZZZZ Best recorded revenues from restoration of damaged buildings, when in fact it did no actual restoration work at all. When the company was liquidated in July 1987, the assets brought in only $62,000 (Domanick, *Faking It in America: Barry Minkow and the Great ZZZZ Best Scam*, Contemporary Books, 1989).

© BENNO FRIEDMAN/CORBIS OUTLINE

Management fraud can be difficult to detect and can cause irreparable damage to the financial position of a company. This type of fraud is often called **performance fraud** because the manipulation of the financial information is often designed to inflate earnings or to cover up a decline in financial position.

PAUSE & Reflect

How might companies reduce the risk of management fraud?

Key Concept: *Management fraud can be very difficult to detect.*

Although the examples of financial statement manipulation discussed here are clearly fraudulent, earnings "management" is another story entirely.

EARNINGS MANAGEMENT

LO2
Understand ethical issues surrounding earnings management

Generally accepted accounting principles (GAAP) are the principles that guide the preparation of financial statements for external users. However, the very same financial statements may be used by internal decision makers for a variety of purposes, including promotion decisions, compensation levels, and year-end bonuses to management. In addition, GAAP leaves considerable leeway to managers to make choices that can impact earnings. For example, management has control over depreciation methods and determining the useful lives of assets. Management also has control over when to write off obsolete inventory or bad debts and increases or decreases in the allowance for bad-debts account. These and other choices provide management with ample opportunities to manage earnings. **Earnings management** may be used to "smooth" earnings from quarter to quarter or to otherwise manipulate financial results for a variety of reasons. Is earnings management fraudulent behavior? Probably not. However, the press and others are increasingly questioning it as inappropriate.

IN THE NEWS http://www.microsoft.com

In 1999, Microsoft came under fire for earnings management related to a memo from the company's CFO to Bill Gates, urging that the company "do all we can do" to smooth its profits and keep a "steady state earnings model." Microsoft was accused of setting aside revenue not needed to make current sales and profit targets as a "reserve" that could be used to increase revenue and earnings in the future. The Security and Exchange Commission (SEC) strongly objects to this practice and considers it a manipulation of financial statements.

© REUTERS NEWMEDIA INC./CORBIS

PAUSE & Reflect

How do you feel about "earnings management"? Which stakeholders should management consider in making decisions to smooth earnings? Is earnings management ethical?

Employee Fraud

In contrast to the financial statement manipulation common in management fraud, **employee fraud** typically involves the theft of cash or other assets of the organization. Employee fraud is almost always carried out for the personal benefit of the employee or employees involved in the scheme. However, thefts must be concealed in order to avoid detection. As discussed later, good internal control systems can usually detect and prevent most types of employee fraud.

Key Concept: *Good internal control systems can usually detect and prevent most types of employee fraud.*

Causes of Fraud

LO3
Explain the typical causes of fraudulent activities

Fraudulent activity results from an interaction of forces both within an individual's personality and the external environment. These forces include situational pressures, opportunity, and personal characteristics (Romney, Albrecht, and Cherrington, "Auditors and the Detection of Fraud," *Journal of Accountancy,* May 1980, 63). Situational pressures include such things as real or imagined grievances against the company or management and management pressure to meet budgets. They may also include such societal factors as the inadequate punishment of convicted criminals and the overall weakening of society's values. Opportunity can arise as a result of ongoing transactions with related parties or as a result of insufficient internal controls. Personal characteristics that may serve as warning signals, or "red flags," include such things as high levels of stress and economic pressure resulting from large amounts of personal financial debt, an extravagant lifestyle, or drug, alcohol, and gambling addictions. Ethical standards are also very important personal characteristics.

Combinations of high situational pressures, high opportunity, and low ethical standards are more likely to lead to fraud than situations characterized by low situational pressure, low opportunity, and high ethical standards. Ethical standards and behavior typically have more impact on the scale than the other factors. Even when situational pressures and opportunity are high, high ethical values will sometimes tip the scale back toward nonfraudulent behavior.

Key Concept: *Individuals engage in fraudulent activity as a result of situational pressures, opportunity, and personal characteristics.*

Concept Question: *Just as fraudulent activities have increased in business, fraudulent activities, such as cheating and plagiarism, are rampant in many colleges and universities. What are some possible causes of fraudulent activities in an academic setting?*

Concept Answer: Even though specific causes vary, the same forces impacting the behavior of managers in business are likely to influence students and professors at a college or university—situational pressures, opportunity, and personal characteristics.

Although personal characteristics of employees and managers are difficult to control, situational pressures and opportunities for fraudulent behavior can be controlled. One role of the internal audit department of a company is to develop internal control systems that reduce situational pressures and opportunities for fraudulent behavior.

Role of the Internal Audit Department

An **internal auditor** is responsible for improving the ability of an organization to meet its operational and strategic goals. Internal auditing also deals with the quality and reliability of the accounting information supplied to management for decision making. As such, the internal audit department is responsible for the design and maintenance of an internal control system. Internal auditors also conduct periodic audit procedures to ensure that errors and irregularities in financial information are detected. However, an internal audit department is responsible for not only the integrity of the financial information but also evaluating the effectiveness and efficiency of operations of the various departments and divisions of the company. These evaluations are often called *operational audits.* Although internal auditors must become very familiar with the operations of the divisions or departments being audited, they must also be independent of all department and divisions and should report directly to the board of directors.

ROLE OF THE EXTERNAL AUDITOR

LO4
Understand the roles of the internal audit department and the external auditor

The main objective of the financial statement audit conducted by the independent **external auditor** is to attest to the fairness of a company's financial statements and to report any discovered fraud or irregularities to shareholders. Although external auditors are required to design their audit tests to minimize the risk of financial statement misstatements, their role is not to prevent fraud but rather to plan for and to perform an audit to obtain reasonable assurance that material misstatements owing to fraud will be detected. Fraud prevention is left to the internal auditor and the internal control system.

INTERNAL CONTROL SYSTEMS AND THE PREVENTION OF FRAUD

LO5
Explain the objectives, design, and characteristics of good internal control systems

Internal control is defined as follows:

> A process, effected by an entity's board of directors, management, and other personnel, designed to provide reasonable assurance regarding the achievement of objectives in the following categories: (1) reliability of financial reporting, (2) compliance with applicable laws and regulations, and (3) effectiveness and efficiency of operations (Rittenberg and Schwieger, *Auditing: Concepts for a Changing Environment,* 3d ed., Harcourt, 2001, 171).

Internal control involves the methods used by an organization to make sure that financial reporting is accurate and reliable, that applicable laws and regulations are followed, and that assets are protected and used to promote effective and efficient use in the operation of the business. Internal control is the key ingredient in preventing losses from management and employee fraud. However, internal control is more than just a fraud-prevention measure. Good internal controls promote quality decision making by providing reliable information to internal managers. Good internal control can also help ensure that policies and strategic plans are being followed and can help prevent costly legal action by preventing violation of applicable laws and regulations. Although an effective system of internal controls is a must for preventing fraudulent activities, the internal control system's impact on promoting effective and efficient operations is perhaps even more important.

Key Concept: *The internal control system's impact on promoting effective and efficient operations is perhaps even more important than detecting fraudulent activity.*

DESIGN OF INTERNAL CONTROL SYSTEMS

PAUSE & Reflect

What types of fraudulent activities might the employees of Amber Valley undertake?

The need for internal control systems is predicated on the assumption that managers and employees of a company will not always exhibit behavior that is in the best interest of the owners or shareholders of the company. If we consider a very small business in which the owners/shareholders and managers/employees are one and the same, internal control concerns are negligible. On the other hand, the internal control system of Amber Valley Ski Resort, which has dozens of managers and hundreds of employees, is likely to be quite complex. Fraud by managers and employees is a real concern, and the internal control system must be designed to minimize opportunities for fraudulent activity and to detect it if it occurs.

CHARACTERISTICS OF AN INTERNAL CONTROL SYSTEM

Although internal control systems will vary from company to company, a good internal control system must consider the following:[1]

- The organizational environment in which the system exists
- The risks that affect the ability of a company to meet its objectives and the activities a company uses to control its risks (risk assessment and risk control)
- The methods and procedures a company uses to communicate and to monitor its internal control system to make sure it is functioning properly (communication and monitoring procedures)

Organizational Environment Upper-level management sets the tone for ethical behavior in an organization. If upper management has high ethical standards and shares those standards with the rest of the organization, other managers and employees are likely to exhibit similar high standards. As an example, if upper management of Top-Sail Construction behaves ethically in its dealings with customers, employees who are actually constructing the homes will have a tendency to act in a similar manner. On the other hand, if management makes a practice of inflating costs or using low-quality materials in construction, employees will receive a signal that this type of behavior is acceptable, and the risk of employee theft or other types of less than desirable behavior increases.

TopSail Construction

***Key Concept:** Upper-level management sets the tone of ethical behavior and the overall atmosphere of the organization.*

The organizational environment can also be influenced through the adoption and use of a formal code of ethical conduct. For example, partners and employees of Garcia and Buffett CPAs are governed by a code of ethical conduct that spells out ethical responsibilities to their clients. Among other things, Garcia and Buffett does not allow partners or other employees to own stock or have any financial interest in an audit client of the firm. Owning stock in a company that is audited by the firm raises questions of independence on the part of the CPA firm.

G&B GARCIA&BUFFET CPAS

PAUSE & Reflect

Why would owning stock in an audit client raise concerns about independence?

IN THE NEWS **http://www.pwcglobal.com**

In 1999, partners and employees of PricewaterhouseCoopers (the largest CPA firm in the world) were ordered to dump their investments in companies the firm audits. The charges centered on the firm's Tampa office, where 11 employees owned stock in 70 publicly held companies that the firm audited and the companywide retirement plan that owned stock in 45 audit clients. Five PricewaterhouseCoopers partners and an undisclosed number of associates were fired for not selling their stocks in a timely manner (MacDonald and Agins, "Price Waterhouse Curbs Investing by Managers," *Wall Street Journal*, June 29, 1999, A2).

Risk Assessment and Risk Control **Risk assessment and control** involves identifying potential risks to the organization and ways to minimize or manage those

[1]The content of this section was adapted from: The Committee of Sponsoring Organizations of the Treadway Commission, "Internal Control—Integrated Framework," 1992.

risks. All companies face risks. These risks can come from internal or external sources. Internal risks can be minimized with the cooperation of upper management and affected employees. Minimizing external risks requires understanding competitive pressures facing a company and its managers and the impact of new products, technology changes, and changes in laws and regulations on a company. When a company introduces new products, places new equipment on-line, makes management changes, or enters new markets, the corresponding level of risk must be assessed.

The manner in which an organization manages and controls risk is very important. After specific risks are identified, the likelihood of occurrence must be established. An identified risk with a low probability of occurrence should be given low priority. If a risk has a high probability of occurrence, the potential loss from that occurrence should be determined. If the risk has a high likelihood of occurring and the amount of potential loss is material, an organization must design internal controls to manage and control the risk. For example, Zia Motors has determined that it faces risks from the theft of automobile parts held in inventory. If the likelihood of theft is high and the potential losses are material, ZIA must develop specific controls to manage and control the risk. Potential controls might involve installing more lighting, hiring security guards, and so forth.

ZIA MOTORS

Communication and Monitoring Procedures Internal control procedures are also impacted by the methods, records, and reports a company uses to communicate with employees and external decision makers and the procedures a company uses to monitor its internal control system to make sure it is functioning properly. As discussed in more detail later in the chapter, internal control systems must be continually monitored and modified as new risks are identified.

INTERNAL CONTROL PROCEDURES

LO6
Understand common internal control procedures

Companies use **internal control procedures** to address areas of risk identified during the risk assessment process. Most internal control procedures are designed to prevent specific events (such as the theft of assets) from occurring. Typical types of internal control procedures are shown in Exhibit 14-1.

Internal control procedures are designed to focus on activities that are determined to increase the risk of management or employee fraud. These activities typically involve transactions affecting cash, accounts receivable, inventory, and payroll.

REVIEWING FINANCIAL REPORTS THAT COMPARE ACTUAL RESULTS TO BUDGETED AMOUNTS

This internal control procedure is very easy to implement and is effective in detecting large errors or irregularities. Every month when financial statements are prepared, they

EXHIBIT 14-1 Internal Control Procedures

1. Reviewing financial reports that compare actual results to budgeted amounts
2. Checking the accuracy of recorded transactions
3. Segregating of duties among employees so that people who authorize transactions do not also record them and have access to related assets
4. Securing assets, such as cash, inventory, and property, plant, and equipment
5. Comparing financial data with other supporting data, such as sales and shipping documents

should be compared to budgeted amounts for the same month. For example, if Big Al's projects selling 2,000 pizzas per week but actually sells 3,000 pizzas per week, internal auditors should expect variable costs to be 50 percent higher than budgeted in the static budget at the beginning of the year. Comparing actual amounts to flexible budget estimates using variance analysis can provide information about the possible theft of materials and products and the efficient (or inefficient) use of corporate resources.

CHECKING THE ACCURACY OF RECORDED TRANSACTIONS

Checking the accuracy of recorded transactions is especially important in businesses that have a high volume of cash transactions. For example, Big Al's Pizza Emporium and Amber Valley Ski Resort have a high volume of small cash transactions. On the other hand, Northern Lights Custom Cabinets and TopSail Construction have a smaller volume of mostly larger dollar transactions. Most large transactions will involve checks that are deposited directly into the bank. Not only are smaller amounts easier to steal, but also they are more likely to go unnoticed. If Big Al's sells $10,000 of pizzas a night, a few missing $10 receipts may be explained by errors, whereas large checks would be difficult to hide.

Internal control procedures at Big Al's might include the use of sequentially numbered sales tickets and detailed deposit information. In most retail businesses, bar coding and automatic scanners are used to control inventory and to check the accuracy of sales transactions. Timely bank reconciliations are a common control technique used to check the accuracy of sales and purchase transactions.

SEGREGATING DUTIES

Segregation of duties is a crucial internal control procedure. Separation of duties in the cash area is of particular importance. Employees who collect cash should not be responsible for recording its collection. Likewise, employees who prepare deposits should not have duties related to cash collection or recording. In a clothing store, the clerk who handles customer returns of merchandise should not be responsible for recording the returned merchandise in inventory. Segregation of duties can be difficult in small companies with only a few employees. In these cases, other internal control procedures become even more important.

SECURING ASSETS

Securing assets is a common internal control procedure. Cash can be physically isolated in vaults and safes, and access to it can be limited. Inventory is often susceptible to theft by customers and employees. Although a number of tools (clothing tags, for example) can be used to reduce theft by customers, controlling theft by employees can be more difficult. Good internal control procedures can include restricting access to merchandise or requiring employees to "check out" each night with a security guard. Periodic inventory counts can also be used to combat this problem.

COMPARING FINANCIAL DATA WITH OTHER SUPPORTING DATA

Another useful internal control procedure—comparing financial data with supporting physical documents—can take many shapes and forms. At Amber Valley, using two-part lift tickets is likely to be an effective internal control tool. The part of the lift ticket retained can be compared to the cash collected to ensure that all sales are recorded and that cash is collected. At Big Al's, matching invoices for food purchases to receiving reports is a useful tool for ensuring that inventory is properly recorded in the company's financial records.

© DEAN CONGER/CORBIS

Casinos use security cameras to identify illegal activities and to secure assets.

COMMON FRAUDS AND EFFECTIVE INTERNAL CONTROLS

Companies with large amounts of sales on account are especially susceptible to theft through a scheme called lapping. CableOne, a cable TV company, bills all customers monthly. The customer then mails a check to CableOne or pays the bill with a check or cash at the office. The employee collecting the cash can steal payments and cover the theft by using a technique called lapping. Lapping involves using a subsequent payment to cover the payment that was taken. When payments are typically of the same amount, lapping can be difficult to detect. For example, assume that the cashier at CableOne collects all payments made at the office. The employee takes a cash payment for the normal monthly fee of $25 and keeps it rather than crediting it to a customer's account. The customer, Susan Schumaker, gets a receipt and then leaves. The next customer, Sheri Armstrong, pays her bill for $25, and the cashier uses Sheri's payment to record the missing payment on Susan's account. Then the next payment for $25 can be used to cover Sheri's missing payment, and so on.

CableOne can minimize the likelihood of lapping through segregation of duties and by simply requiring that employees take two weeks of vacation at least once per year. The lapping scheme just described would likely be discovered very quickly when the cashier couldn't continue applying the collected amounts to the accounts previously shorted. External auditors use confirmations sent directly to customers and returned to the auditors to verify the accuracy of amounts that are owed. These confirmations can detect a lapping scheme when the time lag between collection and posting increases. In other words, if the cashier continues lapping for an extended period of time, it may be days or weeks before payments can be applied to amounts owed by customers.

Requiring vacations can be a useful internal control tool in other types of fraud as well. CherLee Financial is a loan company that approves personal loans up to $2,500 over the phone. Because of a unique state law, CherLee can make these loans without a customer's signature. Loan papers are simply signed by a loan officer and mailed to the customer along with a check for the loan proceeds. This procedure led to an interesting fraud case when an employee, whose duties included keeping track of delinquent loans, processed loan applications for herself. Loan officers signed and disbursed funds without paying attention to the payee on the checks, and the employee simply never reported the delinquent loans to her supervisors. However, during a required two-week vacation, the scheme was uncovered by another employee.

Payroll is another area that is susceptible to theft by mangers and other employees. Schemes include simple plans involving the fraudulent reporting of overtime and requesting reimbursement of fictitious travel expenses to complex schemes involving fictitious employees. Computer systems may also be susceptible to manipulation. For example, a computer programmer may change a payroll program to round down all payroll checks to an even dollar amount while adding the difference to his or her check. However, internal control procedures, such as segregation of duties and timely bank reconciliations, should be effective in detecting these frauds.

Northern Lights custom cabinets

Employee theft can also occur by employees' setting up fictitious companies to sell merchandise to the employee's company. For example, working in the accounts payable area, an employee at Northern Lights Custom Cabinets could set up a fake company and sell Northern Lights material for cabinet construction. When invoices are submitted by the fake company, the employee simply authorizes payment, even though the materials are never received. These types of schemes can also be controlled through periodic inventory counts and adequate segregation of duties.

BEHAVIORAL IMPLICATIONS OF INTERNAL CONTROL SYSTEMS

LO7
Understand the behavioral implications of internal control systems

Well-designed internal control systems can detect many types of fraudulent activity. However, the real goal of an internal control system is to prevent the fraudulent activity in the first place. To prevent fraudulent activity from occurring, internal controls must be communicated throughout an organization. If adequate internal controls are in place and employees and managers are aware of the controls, fraudulent activity is much less likely to take place. However, in order for an internal control system to continue to be effective, the procedures must be monitored and modified as the environment changes and new risks are identified.

Key Concept: *To be effective, internal control systems must be communicated throughout an organization and modified as new risks are identified.*

INTERNAL CONTROL IN AN E-BUSINESS ENVIRONMENT

http://www.irs.gov

As discussed in Chapter 13, e-business involves direct sales to customers (B2C) as well as business-to-business applications (B2B). The government is also using the Internet to conduct business with citizens. The Internal Revenue Service now accepts electronic tax returns, and some state and local governments are allowing vehicle registration to be done on-line.

LO8
Understand the impact of e-business on internal control

Although e-business has provided new opportunities to companies, it also entails new risks. Because it is conducted on a public network (the World Wide Web), the information is susceptible to being viewed, copied, or altered by nonusers who gain access to the data. Although much work is being done to raise the level of comfort with the security and reliability of information being transmitted over the Internet, risks remain that data can be stolen, corrupted, misused, altered, or falsely generated when transmitted over a public network. As shown in Exhibit 14-2, threats can come from a variety of directions and sources.

EXHIBIT 14-2 Threats in an E-Business Environment

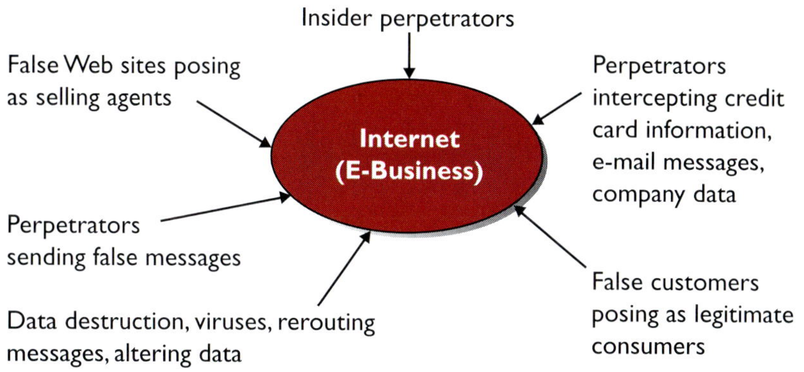

SOURCE: Adapted from Greenstein and Geinman, *Electronic Commerce: Security, Risk Management, and Control,* McGraw-Hill, 2000, 132.

IN THE NEWS

In a recent survey, more than one-third of information technology professionals said that their company's information systems had been compromised in the past year. Financial losses from these break-ins exceeded more than $120 million (Earp, Ingraham, and Jenkins, "The Newest Technology Tools: (Un)Limited Access?" *CPA Journal,* January 2000, 58–59).

Specific risks to e-business providers include the following:

- *Customer impersonation.* False customers can enter a seller's computer system and corrupt data or place false orders, using the assumed customer's identification.
- *Denial-of-service attacks.* These are used to destroy, shut down, or degrade a system. The goal of this type of attack is to flood the site with information so that legitimate messages or orders cannot be received.
- *Unauthorized access to data.* Data are particularly vulnerable at intermediate network junctions that handle the transfer of information from one site to another.
- *Sabotage by former employers.* Former employees who are laid off, fired, or leave under unpleasant circumstances are a threat because of their knowledge of the systems and the organization.
- *Threats by current employees.* These types of threats include stealing trade secrets to sell to competitors and embezzling assets from the company.

How does an organization reduce the risks associated with e-business activities? Overall, the same types of internal controls that we have discussed previously will serve to reduce the risks. However, specific internal controls associated with e-business activities are also useful. These include the following:

- Passwords to limit access to computer systems
- Firewalls to limit access to computer networks by screening all network traffic and controlling access to critical information
- Encryption of sensitive data to be readable only by persons holding the decryption key
- Moving critical data to a separate server that is not connected to the outside world
- Shutting off computers during nonbusiness hours
- Staying up-to-date with technology

Key Concept: *E-business activities entail new risks and require new internal control procedures.*

External auditors also need to consider the impact of e-business activities on the reliability of financial reports. Data that are created and stored electronically may be more vulnerable to manipulation. As a result, auditors should pay particular attention to a company's policies and procedures regarding computer security (Earp, Ingraham, and Jenkins, "The Newest Technology Tools: (Un)Limited Access?" *CPA Journal,* January 2000, 58–59).

Summary of Key Concepts

- Fraud is more narrowly defined in a business context than in common law. (p. 434)
- Management fraud can be very difficult to detect. (p. 435)
- Good internal control systems can usually detect and prevent most types of employee fraud. (p. 436)
- Individuals engage in fraudulent activity as a result of situational pressures, opportunity, and personal characteristics. (p. 436)
- The internal control system's impact on promoting effective and efficient operations is perhaps even more important than detecting fraudulent activity. (p. 437)
- Upper-level management sets the tone of ethical behavior and the overall atmosphere of the organization. (p. 438)
- To be effective, internal control systems must be communicated throughout an organization and modified as new risks are identified. (p. 442)
- E-business activities entail new risks and require new internal control procedures. (p. 444)

Key Definitions

Fraud A false representation of a material fact made by one party with the intent to deceive and induce another party to justifiably rely on the fact to his or her detriment (p. 434)

Management fraud Typically involves misstating the financial statements in order to mislead readers of the financial statements, such as stockholders and creditors (p. 434)

Performance fraud Another term for management fraud, used because the manipulation of the financial information is often designed to inflate earnings or to cover up a decline in financial position (p. 435)

Earnings management A method of recording used to "smooth" earnings from quarter to quarter or to otherwise manipulate financial results for a steady income stream (p. 435)

Employee fraud The main focus of employee fraud is taking possession of assets or cash of the organization (p. 436)

Internal auditor An auditor employed by the organization being audited (p. 436)

External auditor Usually a CPA independent of the organization being audited (p. 437)

Internal control A process, effected by an entity's board of directors, management, and other personnel, designed to provide reasonable assurance regarding the achievement of objectives in the following categories: (1) reliability of financial reporting, (2) compliance with applicable laws and regulations, and (3) effectiveness and efficiency of operations (p. 437)

Risk assessment and control Involves identifying potential risks of the organization and also ways to minimize or manage those risks (p. 438)

Internal control procedures Used to address areas of risk that were identified during the risk-assessment process (p. 439)

MULTIPLE CHOICE

1. Which of the following statements regarding fraud is *not* true?
- **a.** Fraud is more narrowly defined in a business context than in common law.
- **b.** Management fraud is very easy to detect.
- **c.** Adequate internal control systems can usually detect and prevent most types of employee fraud.
- **d.** Individuals engage in fraudulent activity as a result of situational pressures, opportunity, and personal characteristics.

2. Management fraud can be perpetrated by:
- **a.** improper revenue recognition
- **b.** overstating assets
- **c.** both **a** and **b**
- **d.** neither **a** nor **b**

3. Which of the following are used by management to perpetrate "earnings management"?
- **a.** discretion about the useful lives of assets
- **b.** timing of bad-debt write-offs
- **c.** increases and decreases to the allowance for bad debts
- **d.** all of the above

4. Which of the following characterizes the optimal corporate situation?

	Situational Pressures	Opportunity	Ethical Standards
a.	Low	Low	Low
b.	High	Low	Low
c.	Low	High	Low
d.	Low	Low	High

5. Which of the following statements about internal and external auditors is true?
- **a.** Internal auditors are not required to be independent, as they work for the company they audit.
- **b.** Internal auditors are responsible for the integrity of a company's financial information and the effectiveness and efficiency of operations.
- **c.** External auditors are responsible for conducting operational audits.
- **d.** External auditors are concerned primarily with fraud prevention.

6. Why are internal control systems necessary?
- **a.** They are required by generally accepted accounting principles.
- **b.** They are predicated on the assumption that managers and employees of a company will not always exhibit behavior that is in the best interest of the owners or the shareholders of the company.
- **c.** They are needed to ensure that fraud cannot occur within an organization.
- **d.** all of the above

7. Which of the following controls would reduce the incidence of reporting false hours on employee time cards?
- **a.** securing assets
- **b.** timely bank reconciliations
- **c.** supervisor review of time cards
- **d.** both **b** and **c**

8. Which of the following statements about internal control systems is *not* true?
- **a.** To be effective, internal control systems must be communicated throughout an organization and modified as new risks are identified.
- **b.** Well-designed internal control systems detect all types of fraudulent activity.
- **c.** If adequate internal controls are in place and employees and managers are aware of the controls, fraudulent activity is much less likely to take place.
- **d.** The goal of an internal control system is to prevent the fraudulent activity.

9. The risks associated with e-business include all the following *except:*
   a. customer impersonation
   b. earnings management
   c. unauthorized access to data
   d. sabotage by former employers
10. Which of the following controls would reduce the incidence of unauthorized data access in an e-business?
   a. required vacation time
   b. timely bank reconciliations
   c. password controls
   d. both **a** and **c**

CONCEPT REVIEW

11. What is the formal definition of fraud?
12. Discuss the common-law requirements for a fraudulent act.
13. Discuss the meaning of fraud in a business context. How does that differ from the common-law definition?
14. What is the formal definition of management fraud?
15. What are the most common types of management fraud?
16. What is performance fraud?
17. Discuss various ways to "manage earnings."
18. Discuss various ways to misstate revenue.
19. Discuss employee fraud. How does it differ from management fraud?
20. What are the three forces that increase the chances an individual will commit a fraudulent act?
21. The 1998 Fraud Survey conducted by KPMG LLP identifies three factors contributing to fraud. Read the survey, which can be accessed through the KPMG Web site (http://www.us.kpmg.com) under Forensic and Litigation Services, and briefly discuss these factors.
22. The 1998 Fraud Survey conducted by KPMG LLP identifies several warning signals, or "red flags," that employees may exhibit prior to the discovery of internal fraud. Read the survey, which can be accessed through the KPMG Web site (http://www.us.kpmg.com) under Forensic and Litigation Services, and briefly discuss these warning signals.
23. Why do organizations employ internal auditors? What is the function of an internal audit department?
24. What are the main objectives of an internal audit department?
25. What is meant by an operational audit?
26. What is the role of the external auditor in detecting fraud?
27. Discuss the main difference between the internal and external audit functions.
28. What is the formal definition of internal control?
29. What are the goals of an internal control system?
30. What are the characteristics of a good internal control system?
31. What is meant by risk assessment?
32. Discuss various ways of reducing risk.
33. Discuss the tradeoff between cost and benefit of controls for theft.
34. Discuss typical internal control procedures.
35. Discuss control procedures that are based on human behavior patterns.
36. Discuss why e-business has increased the risk of error or fraudulent behavior.
37. What are the specific added risks to e-business providers?
38. What additional security measures are needed for good internal control with e-business?
39. Explain why risk assessment is important to the overall design of internal control systems.

APPLICATION OF CONCEPTS

Northern Lights custom cabinets

40. Warren Abraham is the controller of Northern Lights Custom Cabinets. Warren stated, "Northern Lights has a very strong internal control system. The ledger must always balance, and this ensures that all transactions are properly transferred to our general ledger." What do you think of Warren's comment? Do the balanced books ensure good internal controls?

41. Upper management at TopSail Construction has been advised that the present system of internal control needs to be improved. It has recently come to management's attention that the controller, who has almost complete control over cash and the accounting records, is experiencing financial difficulties as the result of a personal tragedy in the family. Is this a potential "red flag" for management to be concerned with? If so, what steps should upper management take with respect to this problem?

42. Cindy is the vice president of research and development for Big Al's Pizza Inc. She submits a request for expense reimbursement each month, and Lori, the controller, has noticed that Cindy's requests are always higher than those of anyone else in the company. What should the controller do? Is this a potential internal control problem?

43. Terry is an accountant at Happy Daze Game Company. Her main function is to prepare production-cost reports for distribution to upper management. Her good friend Tracy is the production supervisor on one of the production lines. While preparing this month's cost report, Terry noticed a substantial increase in production costs on Tracy's production line. To make her friend look better, Terry shifted some of the costs to other lines, thinking that there must be an accounting error somewhere. The shift in costs was never noticed. Did Terry act appropriately? Discuss the alternative courses of action that Terry could have taken. Would this be considered a fraudulent act?

44. Mark is a sales clerk at a clothing store in the local mall. Mark has been short of cash in the past and has prepared fake sales-return forms and taken money from the cash register equal to those forms. The scheme has not been caught, and now Mark is preparing to take even more money, as the managers seem unaware of the scheme. What internal controls would you suggest to assist management in eliminating this opportunity?

45. LaRue's Machine Shop takes custom orders for metal parts. In order to machine some of the parts, the shop uses various solvents that must be disposed of in compliance with local hazardous-waste rules. For years before the new laws went into effect, LaRue's routinely dumped the solvents in a pit behind the shop. The new law has been in effect for three years, and LaRue's has yet to comply with it. What risks do you think the company faces by not properly disposing of the solvents?

46. The local credit union has a written policy that states in part: "All employees are strictly prohibited from accepting any gratuities, gifts, donations, or any other remuneration from credit union members for which the fair market value of such gift, gratuity, or donation exceeds $5." How does such a policy strengthen the credit union's system of internal control?

47. Heather Hogan, the vice president of the local credit union mentioned in the preceding problem, has always accepted invitations to join credit union members who own skyboxes at the local ball park. She has never paid for the tickets and, in fact, accepts free food and drink provided in the skybox. What effect will her actions have on the internal control environment at the credit union?

48. Irene's Greeting Cards sells custom greeting cards to drugstores across the country. All sales are on credit, and payment is expected within 30 days of the order. The company provides an invoice with each delivery but does not send subsequent statements. The salespeople who call on the customers are allowed to collect any outstanding invoices. If the company started sending statements, would that have an effect on the internal control over accounts receivable?

49. Bonnie's Beautiful Lights is a wholesale lighting contractor selling to residential building contractors. The company has very few staff members, so the bookkeeper collects all payments on account, makes the bank deposits, writes checks to pay all accounts payable, and reconciles the bank statement at the end of the month. The company also does not count inventory on a regular basis. Discuss any internal control weaknesses you see, and suggest possible solutions.

50. At the drive-through window of your local fast-food outlet, you notice a sign that reads, "If the amount you pay is not the same as your sales receipt, your meal is free." What is the restaurant trying to accomplish with the receipts?

51. Chip's Crazy Pies, the local pizza parlor, has a cash register that randomly prints a red star on the sales receipts. If you get a red star, you get a free meal on your next visit. Your friend says that the red stars are for marketing and promotion, nothing else. You have just completed studying this chapter on internal control and think there may be more to this than just promotion. Give reasons for the red stars other than promotion. Can this be a method of increasing control? How?

52. Ben's Cinema, a new 10-plex movie house, is so busy that management has decided to forgo collecting ticket stubs at the entrance to each movie and tear the stub at the register. Do you see any control problems with this practice? If so, what controls could be put in place to correct any weaknesses? If Ben's hires only high school and college students to work the theater, does that introduce any other potential weaknesses? What if they are paid only minimum wage? What solution to these problems do you suggest? Ben's is hiring a new manager, and a background check shows that the new manager has a lot of credit card debt, drives a new car, and is known to like to bet on local sporting events. Does this manager present any internal control risk? If so, what should Ben's do to reduce or eliminate this risk? What other red flags should the company look for?

53. Dolly's Antiques has decided to add a Web page and go on-line to sell merchandise, and the company has come to you for advice. What potential control problems might Dolly's face with this type of business? What controls can reduce or eliminate the risks faced by e-business providers?

54. Discuss why middle managers might be particularly prone to fraudulent activity. What specific internal controls could reduce this risk?

Part V

OTHER TOPICS

Chapter 15

The Statement of Cash Flows: Reporting and Analyzing

Study Tools

A Review of the Previous Chapter

In Chapter 14, we discussed fraud and the importance of internal control systems in detecting and controlling management and employee fraud. We discussed the primary forces impacting fraudulent behavior and the role of the internal auditor and the external auditor in preventing fraud. We also discussed characteristics of an internal control system and key internal control procedures that are used to prevent and to detect fraudulent activities and the impact of e-business on fraud and internal control.

A Preview of This Chapter

In this chapter, we discuss the preparation and use of the statement of cash flows and its use in decision making.

Key concepts include:

- The only difference between the direct and indirect methods is in the presentation of the cash flows from operating activities. Cash flows from investing activities and cash flows from financing activities are calculated in exactly the same way.
- When using the indirect method, increases (decreases) in asset (liability) accounts during the year must be deducted from net income. When asset (liability) accounts decrease (increase) during the year, the amount of decrease or increase must be added to net income in arriving at net cash provided by operating activities.

A Preview of Upcoming Chapters

In Chapter 16, we discuss the analysis of financial statement information by investors, creditors, and managers, using ratio analysis and other techniques.

Learning Objectives

After studying the material in this chapter, you should be able to:

LO1 Understand the purpose of a statement of cash flows and why accrual accounting creates a need for the statement of cash flows

LO2 Discuss the types of transactions that result from operating, investing, and financing activities and how they are presented on the statement of cash flows

LO3 Discuss the difference between the direct and the indirect methods of computing cash flow from operating activities

LO4 Prepare a statement of cash flows

LO5 Analyze the statement of cash flows and use the information in decision making

In the previous 14 chapters of this textbook, we have concentrated on using internally generated accounting information for managerial decision making. In this chapter, we present an in-depth discussion of the preparation and use of the statement of cash flows. Although this statement is used primarily by those external to the organization, the statement of cash flows and the related cash budget (discussed in Chapter 9) are also useful tools for managerial decision making. ■

INTRODUCTION

http://www.boston market.com
http://www.upi.com
http://www.wards.com
http://www.filenes basement.com

During the 1990s, there were numerous business failures of companies that appeared financially healthy and profitable in the years immediately preceding the failures. Among those businesses are some very well known companies, such as Boston Market, United Press International, Montgomery Ward, and Filene's Basement. However, each of these companies filed for bankruptcy protection owing to the company's inability to generate sufficient cash flow to cover operating costs, capital expansion, and debt repayment. Investors and others sometimes learn too late that to be successful, companies must generate sufficient cash to pay their bills!

This chapter discusses the statement of cash flows. The statement of cash flows reports the impact of a firm's operating, investing, and financing activities on cash flows during the accounting period. Along with the balance sheet, income statement, and the statement of changes in stockholders' equity, this statement is a required component of a company's external financial statements.

Users of financial statements have made the statement of cash flows one of the most important of the four required financial statements. In today's highly competitive global environment, users of financial accounting information have learned that cash flows may be a better indicator of financial performance than net income or earnings per share.

IN THE NEWS

Although stock analysts typically have focused on earnings in valuing companies, a *Wall Street Journal* article reported that stock analysts are increasingly using cash flow rather than earnings to value companies. Among other things, "it ignores accounting tricks and shows the true health of companies" (MacDonald, "Analysts Increasingly Favor Using Cash Flow over Reported Earnings in Stock Valuations," *Wall Street Journal,* April 1, 1999, C2).

PURPOSE OF THE STATEMENT OF CASH FLOWS

LO1
Understand the purpose of a statement of cash flows and why accrual accounting creates a need for the statement of cash flows

The main purpose of the statement of cash flows is to provide information to decision makers about a company's cash inflows and outflows during the period. The statement of cash flows provides information relating to the change in cash balances between two balance sheet dates. Balance sheets provide a "snapshot" of the financial position of a company at a particular point in time, whereas the statement of cash flows reports changes over time. The statement of cash flows should be viewed as an explanation of the changes to the cash balance reported on the balance sheet. The statement of cash flows also discloses items that affect how the balance sheet changed but that don't show up in the income statement, such as issuance of stock or acquisitions of property, plant, and equipment.

THE COMPOSITION OF THE STATEMENT OF CASH FLOWS

The statement of cash flows summarizes and explains all major cash receipts (inflows) and cash payments (outflows) during the period and categorizes the changes as resulting from operating, investing, or financing activities.

OPERATING ACTIVITIES

Operating activities include acquiring and selling products in the normal course of business. Different types of businesses will have different transactions that are included in cash flows from operating activities. Typical types of items reported in this section of the statement of cash flows as inflows are cash from sales to customers, collection of cash from past sales that were made on credit, and interest and dividends received. Typical outflows of cash from operating activities are purchases of merchandise for sale or materials to manufacture products, payments for operating expenses, interest on debt, payments for services, and payments of taxes.

INVESTING ACTIVITIES

Cash flows from **investing activities** include cash inflows from the sale of property, plant, and equipment; the sale of securities (stocks and bonds) of other companies; and the receipt of loan payments. Cash outflows include the purchase of property, plant, and equipment; the purchase of securities; and making loans as investments. Loans directly related to the sale of products or services are likely classified as operating activities. The interest on loans included as an investing activity is also classified as a cash flow from operating activities.

FINANCING ACTIVITIES

Cash flows from **financing activities** include cash inflows from selling stock or from issuing bonds (see Exhibit 15-1). Cash inflows from financing activities also include contributions from owners and borrowing from banks on a long-term basis. Cash outflows from financing activities include repayment of notes and bonds, cash payments to repurchase stock (Treasury stock), and the payment of dividends. Once again, all interest payments are included in cash flows from operating activities.

As an example, consider Hasbro, whose Consolidated Statements of Cash Flows are presented in Exhibit 15-2. Note than even though Hasbro's 1999 earnings were almost $189 million, cash and cash equivalents increased by only $102.4 million. Likewise, between 1999 and 2000, when the company experienced a loss of $144.6 million, cash decreased by $153 million.

http://www.hasbro.com

Concept Question: *Review the Hasbro Consolidated Statements of Cash Flows and identify reasons that cash and cash equivalents increased in 1999.*

Concept Answer: The increase in cash in 1999 appears to have resulted from a combination of things. Net cash provided by operating activities was much higher in 1999 ($391.5 million) than in 1998 ($126.5 million). Likewise, net cash utilized by investing activities was lower in 1999 ($429 million) than in 1998 ($792.7 million). These increases in cash more than offset the lower amount of cash provided by financing activities in 1999 ($145.6 million) than in 1998 ($491.6 million). ■

LO2
Discuss the types of transactions that result from operating, investing, and financing activities and how they are presented on the statement of cash flows

EXHIBIT 15-1 A Summary of Activities Making Up a Cash Flow Statement

Cash Flows from ***Operating Activities***	=	Cash received from the sale of goods or services	–	Cash paid for operating expenses
Cash Flows from ***Investing Activities***	=	Cash received from the sale of investments and from the sale of property, plant, and equipment	–	Cash paid for investments and purchases of property, plant, and equipment
Cash Flows from ***Financing Activities***	=	Cash received from the sale of capital stock or the borrowing of funds	–	Cash paid for dividends on stock or repayments of debt or reacquiring capital stock

EXHIBIT 15-2 Consolidated Statements of Cash Flows

Hasbro, Inc.

CONSOLIDATED STATEMENTS OF CASH FLOWS

Fiscal Years Ended in December (Thousands of Dollars)	2000	1999	1998
Cash flows from operating activities			
Net earnings (loss)	$(144,631)	188,953	206,365
Adjustments to reconcile net earnings (loss) to net cash provided by operating activities:			
Depreciation and amortization of plant and equipment	106,458	103,791	96,991
Other amortization	157,763	173,533	72,208
Deferred income taxes	(67,690)	(38,675)	1,679
Compensation earned under restricted stock programs	2,754	—	—
Loss on sale of business units	43,965	—	—
Acquired in-process research and development	—	—	20,000
Change in operating assets and liabilities (other than cash and cash equivalents):			
Decrease (increase) in accounts receivable	395,682	(11,248)	(126,842)
Decrease (increase) in inventories	69,657	(44,212)	(44,606)
Increase in prepaid expenses and other current assets	(84,006)	(26,527)	(113,451)
(Decrease) increase in trade payables and other current liabilities	(292,313)	193,626	17,668
Long-term advances and other	(25,083)	(147,729)	(3,425)
Net cash provided by operating activities	162,556	391,512	126,587
Cash flows from investing activities			
Additions to property, plant and equipment	(125,055)	(107,468)	(141,950)
Investments and acquisitions, net of cash acquired	(138,518)	(352,417)	(667,736)
Other	82,863	30,793	16,986
Net cash utilized by investing activities	(180,710)	(429,092)	(792,700)
Cash flows from financing activities			
Proceeds from borrowings with original maturities of more than three months	912,979	460,333	407,377
Repayments of borrowings with original maturities of more than three months	(291,779)	(308,128)	(24,925)
Net (repayments) proceeds of other short-term borrowings	(341,522)	226,103	271,895
Purchase of common stock	(367,548)	(237,532)	(178,917)
Stock option and warrant transactions	2,523	50,358	58,493
Dividends paid	(42,494)	(45,526)	(42,277)
Net cash (utilized) provided by financing activities	(127,841)	145,608	491,646
Effect of exchange rate changes on cash	(7,049)	(5,617)	(9,570)
(Decrease) increase in cash and cash equivalents	(153,044)	102,411	(184,037)
Cash and cash equivalents at beginning of year	280,159	177,748	361,785
Cash and cash equivalents at end of year	$ 127,115	280,159	177,748
Supplemental information			
Cash paid during the year for			
Interest	$ 91,180	64,861	25,135
Income taxes	$ 95,975	108,342	128,436

See accompanying notes to consolidated financial statements.

THE DEFINITION OF CASH: CASH AND CASH EQUIVALENTS

Before we begin our discussion of the preparation of the statement of cash flows, it is important to be specific about exactly what is meant by cash. Accounting standards define certain items as equivalent to cash, which are combined with cash on the balance sheet and the statement of cash flows.

Cash outflows for operating expenses = Operating expenses + Beginning accounts payable – Ending accounts payable

Therefore, the cash outflow from operating expenses is $580,000 ($640,000 + $0 – $60,000). Assuming that the company's tax payments are made in cash (note that there is no liability for taxes payable), cash flows from operating activities are as follows:

Cash Flows from Operating Activities (Direct Method)

Cash collected from customers	$670,000
Cash payments for operating activities	(580,000)
Cash payments for taxes	(40,000)
Net cash inflow from operating activities	$ 50,000

INDIRECT METHOD

The indirect method of preparing the cash flows from operating activities starts with the net income for the period, which is $120,000. This amount is then adjusted to arrive at the amount of cash provided by operating activities. The first adjustment to net income will be the change in accounts receivable. In this case, the increase of $130,000 will be subtracted from revenue. The next adjustment will be for the decrease in accounts payable ($60,000). The increase in accounts receivable means that some of the sales were not collected so did not result in cash flows. The decrease in accounts payable means that cash in excess of current period expenses (shown on the income statement) was used to pay expenses from prior periods. Using the indirect method, cash flows from operations are presented as follows:

Cash Flows from Operating Activities (Indirect Method)

Net income	$120,000
Adjustments to Reconcile Net Income to Net Cash	
Increase in accounts receivable	(130,000)
Increase in accounts payable	60,000
Net cash inflow from operating activities	$ 50,000

Key Concept: *The only difference between the direct and indirect methods is in the presentation of the cash flows from operating activities. Cash flows from investing activities and cash flows from financing activities are calculated in exactly the same way.*

Proponents of the direct method point to the straightforward presentation of the cash flows from operating activities and point out that anyone, even someone with no training in accounting, can very easily use this information in decision making. Proponents of the direct method also argue that this method provides more useful information for evaluating operating efficiency.

Supporters of the indirect method argue that it focuses attention on differences between the cash and accrual basis of accounting, which is very important for decision making. They also point out that if the direct method is used, the indirect schedule must still be prepared. Consequently, more companies choose to report using the indirect method.

THE STATEMENT OF CASH FLOWS AND THE ACCOUNTING EQUATION

The basic accounting equation as presented in your financial accounting course is

$$\text{Assets} = \text{Liabilities} + \text{Owners' equity}$$

In more detail,

$$\text{Cash} + \text{NCCA} + \text{LTA} = \text{CL} + \text{LTL} + \text{CS} + \text{RE}$$

where

$$\begin{aligned} \text{NCCA} &= \text{noncash current assets} \\ \text{LTA} &= \text{long-term assets} \\ \text{CL} &= \text{current liabilities} \\ \text{LTL} &= \text{long-term liabilities} \\ \text{CS} &= \text{capital stock} \\ \text{RE} &= \text{retained earnings} \end{aligned}$$

We can rearrange the equation so that cash is on the left side and all other items are on the right side:

$$\text{Cash} = \text{CL} + \text{LTL} + \text{CS} + \text{RE} - \text{NCCA} - \text{LTA}$$

Using this equation, we see that any changes in cash (the left side of the equation) must be accompanied by a corresponding change on the right side of the equation. For example:

Transaction	Activity	Left Side	Right Side
Collect accounts receivable	Operating	+ Cash	– NCCA
Prepay insurance	Operating	– Cash	+ NCCA
Collect customer's deposit	Operating	+ Cash	+ CL
Pay suppliers	Operating	– Cash	– CL
Make a cash sale	Operating	+ Cash	+ RE
Sell equipment	Investing	+ Cash	– LTA
Buy equipment	Investing	– Cash	+ LTA
Issue bonds	Financing	+ Cash	+ LTL
Retire bonds	Financing	– Cash	– LTL
Issue capital stock	Financing	+ Cash	+ CS
Buy treasury stock	Financing	– Cash	– CS
Pay dividends	Financing	– Cash	– RE

PREPARING THE STATEMENT OF CASH FLOWS

LO4
Prepare a statement of cash flows

To prepare the statement of cash flows, we must gather appropriate information, which includes comparative balance sheets (last year's and this year's), the current income statement, and additional information needed to analyze noncash transactions. After gathering the preceding information, we must complete six steps in preparing the statement of cash flows.

1. Compute the net change in cash (increase or decrease)
2. Compute net cash provided or used by operating activities
3. Compute net cash provided or used by investing activities
4. Compute net cash provided or used by financing activities
5. Compute net cash flow by combining the results from operating, investing, and financing activities
6. Report any significant noncash investing and/or financing activities in a separate schedule or a footnote

As an example, consider the financial statements for Robyn's Boutique, a retail store specializing in children's clothes.

ROBYN'S BOUTIQUE

Robyn's Boutique
Income Statement
For the Year Ended December 31, 2002

Revenues and Gains	
Sales revenue	$700,000
Interest income	75,000
Gain on sale of vehicle	25,000
Total revenues and gains	$800,000

ROBYN'S BOUTIQUE

Expenses and Losses	
Cost of goods sold	$500,000
Payroll expense	50,000
Insurance expense	30,000
Interest expense	7,000
Rent expense	18,000
Depreciation	35,000
Loss on sale of long-term investments	25,000
Income tax expense	40,000
Total expenses and losses	$705,000
Net income	$ 95,000

Robyn's Boutique
Comparative Balance Sheets

	12/31/2002	12/31/2001
Cash	$130,000	$110,000
Accounts receivable	130,000	120,000
Inventory	225,000	215,000
Prepaid insurance	25,000	30,000
Total current assets	$510,000	$475,000
Long-term investments	$110,000	$ 75,000
Land	200,000	175,000
Property and equipment	215,000	95,000
Accumulated depreciation	(105,000)	(80,000)
Total long-term assets	$420,000	$265,000
Total assets	930,000	740,000
Accounts payable	$ 60,000	$ 50,000
Payroll payable	10,000	8,000
Income tax payable	10,000	9,000
Total current liabilities	$ 80,000	$ 67,000
Notes payable	$400,000	$380,000
Total long-term liabilities	$400,000	$380,000
Capital stock	$200,000	$100,000
Retained earnings	250,000	193,000
Total	$930,000	$740,000

Additional Information

1. Long-term investments were purchased for $85,000.
2. Long-term investments were sold for $25,000, with a book value of $50,000, resulting in a loss of $25,000.
3. Land was purchased for $25,000 by issuing a $20,000 note and a cash payment of $5,000.
4. Equipment was purchased for $180,000.
5. A vehicle with an original cost of $60,000 and a book value of $50,000 was sold for $75,000, resulting in a gain of $25,000.
6. Capital stock was issued for cash of $100,000.
7. Dividends of $38,000 were paid.

Step 1: Compute the Net Change in Cash The net change in cash as shown on the balance sheet is $20,000.

Step 2: Compute Net Cash Provided or Used by Operating Activities

DIRECT METHOD

Operating activities generating cash inflows for Robyn's Boutique include selling goods and services and collecting interest income. Sales revenue was reported as $700,000. However, we must consider the change in accounts receivable to determine how much cash was actually collected from sales. Using the formula on page 456, cash collections are equal to $690,000 ($700,000 sales + $120,000 beginning accounts receivable − $130,000 ending accounts receivable). Interest income reported on the income statement is $75,000. How can we tell whether the entire $75,000 was collected in cash? In this case, because there is no "interest receivable" account on the balance sheet, the entire amount must have been collected in cash.

Operating activities generating cash outflows include buying merchandise for resale to customers, making payments to employees, and making payments for other operating expenses, such as insurance, interest, rent, and taxes. Cost of goods sold is reported at $500,000. However, cash outflows for purchases of inventory may be different. To determine the amount of cash expended to purchase inventory, we must analyze changes in the inventory account as well as changes in accounts payable because inventory purchases are normally made on credit. Using the cost-of-goods-sold model for a merchandising company developed in Chapter 2 (see page 41):

$$\text{Beginning inventory} + \text{Cost of goods purchased} - \text{Ending inventory} = \text{Cost of goods sold}$$

Consequently, the cost of goods purchased equals the following:

$$\text{Cost of goods purchased} = \text{Cost of goods sold} - \text{Beginning inventory} + \text{Ending inventory}$$

Therefore, the cost of goods purchased by Robyn's is $510,000 ($500,000 − $215,000 + $225,000). However, we still don't know whether all these purchases were for cash. Using the formula developed earlier for analyzing cash expenditures for operating expenses:

$$\text{Cash outflows for purchases} = \text{Cost of goods purchased} + \text{Beginning accounts payable} - \text{Ending accounts payable}$$

Robyn's cash outflows for purchases equals $500,000 ($510,000 + $50,000 − $60,000).

Next, consider payroll expense of $50,000. Once again, if any payroll expense is accrued at the end of the year for employees who are owed wages but not paid by year-end, the payroll expense must be adjusted by changes in payroll liabilities to determine the cash outflows for payroll. The formula is as follows:

$$\text{Cash outflows for payroll} = \text{Payroll expense} + \text{Beginning payroll payable} - \text{Ending payroll payable}$$

Cash outflows for payroll are therefore $48,000 ($50,000 + $8,000 − $10,000).

Another way to look at the cash outflow for payroll is to assume that Robyn's paid the amount owed from last year ($8,000) plus all this year's expense ($50,000) except the amount owed at the end of the current year ($10,000)—in other words, $8,000 + $50,000 − $10,000 = $48,000.

ROBYN'S BOUTIQUE

The next item on the income statement is insurance expense. Although there are no liabilities for insurance at the end of 2001 or 2002, you will note that the balance sheet does include an asset called prepaid insurance with a beginning-of-year balance of $30,000 and an end-of-year balance of $25,000. The $30,000 beginning balance represents prepayments that were made in 2001 for insurance coverage provided in 2002. This $30,000 was expensed on the income statement in 2002 as insurance coverage was provided for Robyn's Boutique. Likewise, the $25,000 prepaid balance at the end of 2002 represents cash outflows for insurance that occurred in 2002. This amount will be expensed on the income statement for the year ended December 31, 2003.

Cash outflows for interest expense and rent expense are equal to $7,000 and $18,000, respectively. Note that Robyn's must have paid for these items in cash because no related liabilities or assets appear on the balance sheet. Although Robyn's also reports depreciation expense of $35,000, depreciation does not result in a cash outflow. The cash outflow occurs at the time the depreciable property is purchased and is shown in the investing activities section of the cash flow statement. Finally, income tax expense is equal to $40,000. Adjusting for related increases in income tax liabilities on the balance sheet, cash outflows for income taxes during the year must have been $39,000 ($40,000 income tax expense + Beginning income tax payable balance of $9,000 – Ending income tax payable balance of $10,000).

Net Cash Flows from Operating Activities (Direct Method)

Cash Receipts From	
Sales on account	$690,000
Interest	75,000
Cash Payments For	
Inventory purchases	(500,000)
Payroll	(48,000)
Insurance	(25,000)
Interest	(7,000)
Rent expense	(18,000)
Taxes	(39,000)
Net cash provided (used) by operating activities	$128,000

INDIRECT METHOD

The indirect method reconciles net income to net cash flow from operating activities by taking the income statement amounts of revenues and expenses and adjusting for changes in related noncash assets and liabilities:

Income statement amount
\+ Increases in related liabilities
\+ Decreases in related noncash assets
– Increases in related noncash assets
– Decreases in related liabilities
= Cash flow amount

Additions to Net Income	**Deductions from Net Income**
Decrease in accounts receivable	Increase in accounts receivable
Decrease in inventory	Increase in inventory
Decrease in prepaid assets	Increase in prepaid assets
Increase in accounts payable	Decrease in accounts payable
Increase in accrued liabilities	Decrease in accrued liabilities

***Key Concept:** When using the indirect method, increases (decreases) in asset (liability) accounts during the year must be deducted from net income. When asset (liability) accounts decrease (increase) during the year, the amount of decrease or increase must be added to net income in arriving at net cash provided by operating activities.*

In addition, gains (losses) on sales of assets and securities must be deducted (added) to net income because these amounts are not operating cash flows. Although the cash received from the sale will affect cash flow, it will be reported in the investing activities section of the cash flow statement rather than in the operating activities section. Likewise, because depreciation expense does not affect cash flow, it must be added back to net income, using the indirect method.

With the indirect method, the net cash provided by the operating activities section of the cash flow statement for Robyn's Boutique would appear as follows:

Robyn's Boutique
Net Cash Flows from Operating Activities (Indirect Method)

Net income	$ 95,000
Adjustments to Reconcile Net Income to Net Cash Provided (Used) by Operating Activities	
Increase in accounts receivable	(10,000)
Increase in inventory	(10,000)
Decrease in prepaid insurance	5,000
Increase in accounts payable	10,000
Increase in payroll payable	2,000
Increase in income taxes payable	1,000
Gain on sale of vehicle	(25,000)
Loss on the sale of securities	25,000
Depreciation expense	35,000
Net cash provided (used) by operating activities	$128,000

Step 3: Compute Net Cash Provided or Used by Investing Activities Investing activities for Robyn's Boutique include cash inflows from the sale of a vehicle and the sale of long-term investments and cash outflows for purchases of land, equipment, and long-term investments. As shown on the income statement, the sale of the car (shown on the balance sheet as property and equipment) generated a gain of $25,000. However, the actual cash generated from the sale was the sales price of $75,000.

The vehicle that was sold had a book value of $50,000 and originally cost $60,000, which means that accumulated depreciation was $10,000 ($60,000 – $50,000).

***Concept Question:** Can you calculate the ending accumulated depreciation amount of $105,000 shown on the balance sheet?*

Concept Answer: The beginning balance in accumulated depreciation ($80,000) is increased by the current year's depreciation expense of $35,000 and decreased by $10,000 of accumulated depreciation written off at the time the vehicle is sold, leaving an ending balance of $105,000.

Likewise, the sale of securities generates cash inflows equal to the amount of cash that was received ($25,000), not the loss on securities sold.

Long-term investments increased by $35,000 during the year (from $75,000 to $110,000). However, just looking at the net change in the accounts does not really tell the

ROBYN'S BOUTIQUE

complete story of what happened during the year. During the year, long-term investments were purchased for $85,000 cash (increasing the asset account by $85,000), and investments with a book value of $50,000 were sold.

Equipment was purchased for $180,000. Land was also purchased for $25,000. However, paying only $5,000 in cash made the purchase.

Concept Question: *Reconcile the beginning and ending balance of the property and equipment asset account.*

Concept Answer: The beginning balance of $95,000 was increased by $180,000 for purchases of equipment and decreased by $60,000 (the original cost of the car sold).

Net Cash Flows from Investing Activities	
Cash Inflows From	
Sale of note	$ 25,000
Sale of vehicle	75,000
Cash Outflows For	
Purchase of long-term investments	(85,000)
Purchase of equipment	(180,000)
Purchase of land	(5,000)
Net cash provided (used) by investing activities	$(170,000)

Because the acquisition of land also included the issuance of a note payable for $20,000 rather than the payment of cash currently, this information is disclosed on a supplemental schedule of noncash investing and financing activities as follows:

Supplemental Schedule of Noncash Investing and Financing Activities	
Acquisition of land in exchange for note payable	$20,000

Step 4: Compute Net Cash Provided or Used by Financing Activities Activities reported in this section include a $100,000 increase in capital stock and payment of dividends of $38,000.

Net Cash Flows from Financing Activities	
Cash Inflows For	
Issuance of stock	$100,000
Cash Outflows From	
Payment of cash dividends	(38,000)
Net cash provided (used) by financing activities	$ 62,000

Step 5: Compute Net Cash Flow by Combining the Results from Operating, Investing, and Financing Activities Combining all the information contained in the three schedules of operating, investing, and financing activities and adding the supplemental schedule, we can easily prepare the completed statement of cash flows for Robyn's Boutique for the year ended December 31, 2002.

Robyn's Boutique
Statement of Cash Flows (Direct Method)
for the Year Ended December 31, 2002

Cash Flows from Operating Activities	
Cash Receipts From	
Sales	$690,000
Interest	75,000
Total cash receipts	$765,000
Cash Payments For	
Inventory purchases	$500,000
Payroll	48,000
Insurance	25,000
Interest	7,000
Rent expense	18,000
Taxes	39,000
Total cash payments	$(637,000)
Net cash provided (used) by operating activities	$128,000
Cash Flows from Investing Activities	
Sale of securities	$ 25,000
Sale of vehicle	75,000
Purchase of equipment	(180,000)
Purchase of long-term investments	(85,000)
Purchase of land	(5,000)
Net cash provided (used) by investing activities	$(170,000)
Cash Flows from Financing Activities	
Issuance of stock	$100,000
Payment of cash dividends	(38,000)
Net cash provided (used) by financing activities	$ 62,000
Net increase in cash	$ 20,000
Cash balance 12/31/01	110,000
Cash balance 12/31/02	$130,000

Step 6: Report Any Significant Noncash Investing or Financing Activities in a Separate Schedule or a Footnote

Supplemental Schedule of Noncash Investing and Financing Activities	
Acquisition of land in exchange for note payable	$20,000

USING THE CASH FLOW STATEMENT IN DECISION MAKING

LO5
Analyze the statement of cash flows and use the information in decision making

The statement of cash flows is a major source of information to investors and creditors. Many users view the statement of cash flows as the most important of the three main financial statements. Many investors and bankers focus on cash flows as opposed to net income because they are concerned about the ability of the company to meet its short-term obligations. Accrual accounting is felt to mask cash flow problems. Sophisticated users of financial statements may determine the cash flows of a business by using only the income statement and balance sheet through such details as purchases of property, plant, and equipment, and details of financing and investing activities may not be evident without the separate statement of cash flows.

CASH FLOW ADEQUACY

Creditors are concerned about the ability of the organization to repay its debts and meet its interest payments. **Cash flow adequacy** is a measure designed to help users of the financial statements make better lending decisions. Cash flow adequacy measures the cash available to meet future debt obligations after payment of interest and taxes and any long-term expenditures. Analysts are concerned about the amount of cash available to repay debt after the company has replaced or updated its existing property, plant, and equipment. Cash flow adequacy is computed as follows:

$$\text{Cash flow adequacy} = \frac{\text{Cash flow from operating activities} - \text{Interest} - \text{Taxes} - \text{Capital expenditure}}{\text{Average amount of debt maturing over the next five years}}$$

http://www.walmart.com
http://www.carnivalcorp.com

How is this measure used in decision making? Looking at annual reports for Wal-Mart, Carnival Cruise Lines, and Hasbro and gathering cash flow statement data and information from the required footnote on long-term debt, we calculate cash flow adequacy ratios as follows:

Wal-Mart: (all amounts in millions)

$$\text{Cash flow adequacy (1999)} = \frac{\$7{,}580 - 3{,}734}{\$3{,}828}, \text{ or } 1.0047$$

Carnival Cruise Lines: (all amounts in thousands)

$$\text{Cash flow adequacy (1998)} = \frac{\$1{,}091{,}840 - 1{,}150{,}413}{\$169{,}212}, \text{ or } -0.3462$$

Hasbro: (all amounts in thousands)

$$\text{Cash flow adequacy (1998)} = \frac{\$126{,}587 - \$141{,}950}{305{,}800}, \text{ or } -0.0502$$

What do these ratios mean? In general, if the ratio is less than 1, it indicates that cash flow is insufficient to repay average annual long-term debt over the next five years. Any ratio above 1 would indicate sufficient cash flow to repay long-term debt. However, as with any ratio, the results should not be used without looking at the previous year's ratios to determine trends and also to compare with industry standards. Short-term fluctuations from positive to negative are common.

Some investment analysts prefer using cash flow per share as a measure of financial health as opposed to earnings per share. The accounting profession has expressly forbidden reporting information on cash flow per share in external financial statements. The profession believes that this type of information is not an acceptable alternative to earnings per share as an indicator of company performance. As is the case in a lot of areas of accounting disclosure, there is disagreement on what is the most useful information to disclose. Individuals will use the information that best serves their needs for each specific decision situation.

© JAMES MARSHALL/CORBIS

© AP/WIDE WORLD PHOTOS

© HASBRO/GETTY IMAGES

PAUSE & *Reflect*

Visit Web sites for Wal-Mart (http://www.walmart.com), Carnival Cruise Lines (http://www.carnivalcorp.com), and Hasbro (http://www.hasbro.com) and examine their cash flow statements. How do these three companies compare?

SUMMARY OF KEY CONCEPTS

- The only difference between the direct and indirect methods is in the presentation of the cash flows from operating activities. Cash flows from investing activities and cash flows from financing activities are calculated in exactly the same way. (p. 457)
- When using the indirect method, increases (decreases) in asset (liability) accounts during the year must be deducted from net income. When asset (liability) accounts decrease (increase) during the year, the amount of decrease or increase must be added to net income in arriving at net cash provided by operating activities. (p. 463)

KEY DEFINITIONS

Operating activities Include acquiring and selling products in the normal course of business (p. 452)

Investing activities Include the purchase and sale of property, plant, and equipment; the purchases and sales of securities; and loans made as investments (p. 453)

Financing activities Include cash flows from selling or repurchasing capital stock, long-term borrowing, and contributions from owners (p. 453)

Cash equivalent An item that can be readily converted to a known amount of cash and has an original maturity to the investor of three months or less (p. 455)

Direct method Reports cash collected from customers and cash paid for inventory, salaries, wages, and so on (p. 455)

Indirect method Starts with net income and removes the impact of noncash items and accruals (p. 455)

Cash flow adequacy A measure of cash available to meet future debt obligations (p. 466)

MULTIPLE CHOICE

1. Which of the following statements is *not* true?
   - **a.** Even companies that appear financially healthy and profitable can become business failures owing to an inability to generate sufficient cash flow.
   - **b.** The statement of cash flows provides information relating to the change in cash and receivable balances between two balance sheet dates.
   - **c.** The statement of cash flows reports the impact of a firm's operating, investing, and financing activities on cash flows during the accounting period.
   - **d.** Along with the balance sheet, income statement, and the statement of changes in stockholders' equity, the statement of cash flows is a required component of a company's external financial statements.

2. Which of the following statements regarding financial statements is *not* true?
   - **a.** Balance sheets report the financial position of a company at a particular time.
   - **b.** The income statement discloses items that affect how the balance sheet changed but that don't show up on the statement of cash flows.
   - **c.** The statement of cash flows discloses items that affect how the balance sheet changed but that don't show up in the income statement.
   - **d.** Along with the balance sheet, income statement, and the statement of changes in stockholders' equity, the statement of cash flows is a required component of a company's external financial statements.

3. Cash flows from financing activities are equal to:
   - **a.** cash received from the sale of goods and services less cash paid for operating expenses
   - **b.** cash received from the sale of investments and property, plant, and equipment less cash paid for investments and purchases of property, plant, and equipment

c. cash received from the sale of property, plant, and equipment less cash paid for operating expenses
d. cash received from the sale of capital stock or the borrowing of funds less cash paid for dividends on stock or repayments of debt or reacquiring capital stock

4. Cash flows from investing activities are equal to:
a. cash received from the sale of goods and services less cash paid for operating expenses
b. cash received from the sale of investments and property, plant, and equipment less cash paid for investments and purchases of property, plant, and equipment
c. cash received from the sale of property, plant, and equipment less cash paid for operating expenses
d. cash received from the sale of capital stock or the borrowing of funds less cash paid for dividends on stock or repayments of debt or reacquiring capital stock

5. Carlton Company had the following information related to sales last year:

Cash sales	$125,000
Credit sales	120,000
Accounts receivable, beginning	145,000
Accounts receivable, ending	135,000

What amount would be recorded as "cash collections from customers" on the direct statement of cash flows?
a. $125,000
b. $120,000
c. $245,000
d. $255,000

6. Which of the following statements about the direct and indirect methods of reporting cash flows is *not* true?
a. Proponents of the direct method point to the straightforward presentation of the cash flows from operating activities.
b. Proponents of the direct method argue that this method provides more useful information for evaluating operating efficiency.
c. Supporters of the indirect method argue that it focuses attention on differences between the cash and accrual basis of accounting, which is very important for decision making.
d. Supporters of the indirect method point out that if the indirect method is used, the direct schedule must still be prepared.

7. Cane Company had the following information related to purchases last year:

Cost of goods purchased	$250,000
Accounts payable, beginning	175,000
Accounts payable, ending	185,000

What amount would be recorded as "cash outflows for purchases" on the direct statement of cash flows?
a. $250,000
b. $240,000
c. $260,000
d. It cannot be determined from the information provided.

8. Webster Company has no liabilities for insurance at the end of 2001 or 2002, but you note that the 12/31/00 balance sheet does include an asset called prepaid insurance with a balance of $30,000 and a 12/31/01 balance of $25,000. The $30,000 balance represents prepayments that were made in 2001 for insurance coverage provided in 2002. The $25,000 prepaid balance at the end of 2002 represents cash paid in 2002 for insurance that will be used in 2003.

What are cash outflows in 2001 for insurance?

a. $25,000
b. $30,000
c. $50,000
d. $55,000

9. Cable Car Company had the following information available from its 2002 financial statements:

Cash flow from operating activities	$175,000
Cash flow from financing activities	75,000
Cash flow from investing activities	25,000
Interest	10,000
Taxes	8,000
Capital expenditure	15,000
Average amount of debt maturing over the next five years	150,000

Cable Car Company's cash flow adequacy ratio is:

a. 0.50
b. 0.947
c. 1.056
d. 1.613

10. Capitol Company had the following information available from its 2002 financial statements:

Cash flow from operating activities	$197000
Cash flow from financing activities	125,000
Cash flow from investing activities	75,000
Interest	15,000
Taxes	0
Capital expenditures	25,000
Average amount of debt maturing over the next five years	175,000

Capitol Company's cash flow adequacy ratio is:

a. 0.20
b. 0.947
c. 0.897
d. 0.486

Concept Review

11. What is the purpose of the statement of cash flows?

12. Discuss how the statement of cash flows differs from an income statement.

13. What is a cash equivalent? How is it used in preparation of the statement of cash flows?

14. "The statement of cash flows is the easiest of the basic financial statements to prepare because you know the answer before you start." Do you agree with this statement? Why or why not?

15. "To prepare a statement of cash flows, all you have to do is compare the beginning and ending balances in cash on the balance sheet and compute the net inflow or outflow of cash." Do you agree with this statement? Why or why not?

16. How is depreciation expense handled on the statement of cash flows?

17. Which method for preparing the operating activities section of the statement of cash flows—the direct or the indirect method—provides the most information to users of the statement? Explain your answer.

18. Explain why, when a company uses the indirect method to prepare the operating activities section of the statement of cash flows, a decrease in a current asset is added back to net income.

19. Can a company show a decrease in cash even if reporting net income? Why?

20. Can a company show an increase in cash even if reporting a net loss? Why?

21. Why do you think accounting standards require a company to separately disclose income taxes paid and interest paid if it uses the indirect method?

APPLICATION OF CONCEPTS

22. Van Buren Inc. acquires a piece of land by signing a $100,000 promissory note and making a $30,000 down payment. How should this transaction be reported on the statement of cash flows?

23. Van Patten Inc. made two purchases during September. One was a $25,000 certificate of deposit that matures in 90 days. The other was a $50,000 investment in Microsoft common stock that will be held indefinitely. How should each of these transactions be treated on the statement of cash flows?

24. Vardy Toys Inc. prepays insurance in January of each year on various policies. The beginning balance in prepaid insurance was $12,500, and the ending balance was $10,000. The income statement reports insurance expense of $65,000. Under the direct method, what amount would appear for cash paid for insurance in the operating section of the statement of cash flows?

25. Walden Book Buyers Inc. buys 5,000 shares of its own common stock at $25 per share. The company purchases the shares as Treasury stock. How is this transaction reported on the statement of cash flows?

26. Washburn Delivery Company sold a company car for $12,000. Its original cost was $35,000, and the accumulated depreciation at the time of sale was $20,000. How does the transaction to record the sale appear on a statement of cash flows prepared using the indirect method?

27. Whitney R.V.'s Inc. declared and distributed a 10 percent stock dividend during the year. Explain how, if at all, you would report this transaction on the statement of cash flows.

28. Whitney R.V.'s Inc. has invested its excess cash in the following instruments during December 2001:

Certificate of deposit, due Jan. 31, 2002	$100,000
Certificate of deposit, due May 31, 2002	150,000
Investment in City of Portland bonds, due June 30, 2002	110,000
Investment in Sheetz Inc. stock	125,000
A money market fund	225,000
90-day Treasury bills	125,000
Treasury note, due December 2002	200,000

Required

A. What should be included in cash equivalents at year-end 2001?

B. Where should the amount of cash equivalents be disclosed?

29. For each of the following transactions reported on a statement of cash flows, fill in the blank to indicate whether it would appear in the Operating Activities section (O), in the Investing Activities section (I), or in the Financing Activities section (F). Put an (S) in the blank if the transaction does not affect cash but is reported in a supplemental schedule of noncash activities. Assume that the company uses the direct method in the Operating Activities section.

a. ____________ A company purchases its own common stock in the open market and immediately retires it.

b. ____________ A company issues common stock in exchange for land.

c. ____________ A six-month bank loan is obtained.

d. ____________ Thirty-year bonds are issued.

e. ____________ A customer pays the balance in an open account.

f. ____________ Income taxes are paid.

g. ____________ Cash sales are recorded.

h. ______________ Cash dividends are declared and paid.

i. ______________ A creditor is given common stock in exchange for a long-term note.

j. ______________ A new piece of machinery is acquired for cash.

k. ______________ Stock of another company is acquired as an investment.

l. ______________ Interest is paid on a bank loan.

m. ______________ Workers are paid for one week's wages.

30. Williams Media Inc.'s comparative balance sheets included accounts receivable of $100,000 at December 31, 2001, and $125,000 at December 31, 2002. Sales of consulting services reported by Williams Media Inc. on its 2002 income statement amounted to $2,000,000. What is the amount of cash collections that Williams Media Inc. should report in the Operating section of its 2002 statement of cash flows, assuming that the direct method is used?

31. Workman-Smith Co.'s comparative balance sheets included inventory of $120,000 at December 31, 2001, and $110,000 at December 31, 2002. Workman-Smith's comparative balance sheets also included accounts payable of $60,000 at December 31, 2001, and $55,000 at December 31, 2002. Workman-Smith's accounts payable balances are composed solely of amounts due to suppliers for purchases on inventory. Cost of goods sold, as reported by Workman-Smith on its 2002 income statement, amounted to $850,000. What is the amount of cash payments for inventory that Workman-Smith should report in the Operating Activities section of its 2002 statement of cash flows assuming that the direct method is used?

32. The following account balances are for the noncash current assets and current liabilities of Wynn Bicycle Company for 2001 and 2002:

	DECEMBER 31	
	2001	**2002**
Accounts receivable	$ 4,000	$ 6,000
Inventory	30,000	20,000
Office supplies	5,000	8,000
Accounts payable	10,000	7,000
Salaries and wages payable	2,500	4,000
Interest payable	1,500	2,500
Income taxes payable	5,500	2,500

In addition, the income statement for 2002 is as follows:

	2002
Sales revenue	$110,000
Cost of goods sold	85,000
Gross profit	$ 25,000
General and administrative expense	$ 9,000
Depreciation expense	2,000
Total operating expenses	$ 11,000
Income before interest and taxes	$ 14,000
Interest expense	2,000
Income before tax	$ 12,000
Income tax expense	4,800
Net income	$ 7,200

Required

A. Prepare the Operating Activities section of the statement of cash flows, using the indirect method.

B. What does the use of the direct method reveal about a company that the indirect method does not?

33. Determine the missing amounts in the following cases:

Case 1

Accounts receivable, beginning balance	$250,000
Accounts receivable, ending balance	200,000
Credit sales for the year	275,000
Cash sales for the year	160,000
Uncollectible accounts written off	135,000
Total cash collections for the year	?

Case 2

Inventory, beginning balance	$180,000
Inventory, ending balance	155,000
Accounts payable, beginning balance	125,000
Accounts payable, ending balance	115,000
Cost of goods sold	275,000
Cash payments for inventory (assume that all purchases are on account)	?

Case 3

Prepaid insurance, beginning balance	$ 27,000
Prepaid insurance, ending balance	30,000
Insurance expense	25,000
Cash paid for new insurance	?

Case 4

Interest payable, beginning balance	$105,000
Interest payable, ending balance	125,000
Interest expense	300,000
Cash payments for interest	?

Case 5

Income taxes payable, beginning balance	$ 55,000
Income taxes payable, ending balance	75,000
Income tax expense	100,000
Cash payments for income taxes	?

34. The following selected account balances are available from the records of Yuen Seafood Specialty Company:

	December 31	
	2001	**2002**
Dividends payable	$130,000	$120,000
Retained earnings	475,000	350,000

Other information is as follows:

a. Yuen reported $385,000 in net income for 2002.

b. The company declared and distributed a stock dividend of $150,000 during the year.

c. It declared cash dividends at the end of each quarter and paid them within the next 30 days of the following quarter.

Required

A. Determine the amount of cash dividends paid during the year for presentation in the Financing Activities section of the statement of cash flows.

B. Should the stock dividend appear on the statement of cash flows? Explain your answer.

35. Assume that a company uses the indirect method to prepare the Operating Activities section of the statement of cash flows.

Required

For each of the following items, fill in the blank to indicate whether it would be added to net income (A), deducted from net income (D), or not reported in this section of the statement under the indirect method (NR).

A. Depreciation expense ____________

B. Gain on the sale of used delivery truck ____________

C. Bad-debt expense ____________

D. Increase in accounts payable ____________

E. Purchase of a new delivery truck ____________

F. Loss on retirement of bonds ____________

G. Increase in prepaid rent ____________

H. Decrease in inventory ____________

I. Increase in short-term investments (classified as available-for-sale securities) ____________

J. Amortization of patents ____________

36. The account balances for the noncash current assets and current liabilities of Abraham Music Company are as follows:

	DECEMBER 31	
	2001	**2002**
Dividends payable	$ 50,000	$ 40,000
Retained earnings	545,000	375,000

Other information for 2002:

a. Abraham reported $375,000 in net income for 2002.

b. The company declared and distributed a stock dividend of $85,000 during the year.

c. The company declared cash dividends at the end of each quarter and paid them within the first 30 days of the next quarter.

Required

A. Determine the amount of cash dividends paid during the year for presentation in the Financing Activities section of the statement of cash flows.

B. Should the stock dividend appear on a statement of cash flows? Explain your answer.

37. The account balances for the noncash current assets of Allen Company are as follows:

	DECEMBER 31	
	2001	**2002**
Accounts receivable	$ 45,000	$ 38,000
Inventory	40,000	50,000
Prepaid insurance	21,000	17,000
Total current assets	$106,000	$105,000

Net income for 2002 is $35,000. Depreciation expense is $22,000. Assume that all sales and all purchases are on account.

Required

A. Prepare the Operating Activities section of the statement of cash flows, using the indirect method. Explain why cash flow from operating activities is more or less than the net income for the period.

B. What additional information do you need to prepare the Operating Activities section of the statement of cash flows using the direct method?

C. Explain the usefulness of each method for managerial decision making.

38. For each of the following transactions, indicate how they would be reported on the statement of cash flows. Use the following legend, and assume that the stocks and bonds of other companies are classified as available-for-sale securities.

II = inflow from investing activities
OI = outflow from investing activities
IF = inflow from financing activities
OF = outflow from financing activities
CE = classified as a cash equivalent and included with cash for purposes of preparing the statement of cash flows.

A. Purchased a six-month certificate of deposit

B. Purchased a 90-day Treasury bill

C. Issued 10,000 shares of common stock

D. Purchased 5,000 shares of stock of another company

E. Purchased 10,000 shares of its own stock to be held in the treasury

F. Invested $10,000 in a money market fund

G. Sold 1,500 shares of stock of another company

H. Purchased 10-year bonds of another company

I. Issued 20-year bonds

J. Repaid a nine-month bank note

39. The following account balances are taken from the records of Roadhouse Corp. for the past two years:

	DECEMBER 31	
	2002	**2001**
Plant and equipment	$750,000	$500,000
Accumulated depreciation	160,000	200,000
Patents	92,000	80,000
Retained earnings	825,000	675,000

Other information available for 2002 follows:

a. Net income for the year was $200,000.

b. Depreciation expense on plant and equipment was $50,000.

c. Plant and equipment with an original cost of $150,000 were sold for $64,000 (you will need to determine the book value of the assets sold).

d. Amortization expense on patents was $8,000.

e. Both new plant and equipment and patents were purchased for cash during the year.

Required

Indicate, with amounts, how all items related to these long-term assets would be reported in the 2002 statement of cash flows, including any adjustments in the Operating Activities section of the statement. Assume that Roadhouse Corp. uses the indirect method.

Chapter 16

Financial Statement Analysis

Study Tools

A Review of the Previous Chapter

In the first 14 chapters of this textbook, we discussed uses of accounting information in decision making by managers. In Chapter 15, we discussed the preparation and use of the statement of cash flows and its use in decision making.

A Preview of This Chapter

In this chapter, we discuss ratio analysis and other techniques used by investors, creditors, analysts, and managers in decision making.

Key concepts include:

- Ratio analysis provides additional information necessary to enhance the decision-making ability of the users of the information.
- Rather than focus on a single ratio, decision makers need to evaluate a company by comparing ratios to those of previous years, budgeted amounts, and industry standards.
- Horizontal analysis is used to analyze changes in accounts occurring between years.
- Vertical analysis uses common-size financial statements to remove size as a relevant variable in ratio analysis.
- Ratio analysis is useful in assessing the impact of transactions on ROI, residual income, EVA, and other key measures of performance.

Learning Objectives

After studying the material in this chapter, you should be able to:

LO1 Understand why decision makers analyze financial statements

LO2 Understand the limitations of financial statement analysis

LO3 Use comparative financial statements to analyze the performance of a company over time (horizontal analysis)

LO4 Prepare and use common-size financial statements to compare various financial statement items (vertical analysis)

LO5 Prepare and use liquidity ratios to analyze a company

LO6 Prepare and use solvency ratios to analyze a company

LO7 Prepare and use profitability ratios to analyze a company

F*inancial statement analysis involves the application of analytical tools to financial statements and supplemental data included with the financial statements to enhance the ability of decision makers to make optimal decisions. Investors and creditors need to make decisions to provide a company with loans or other capital. The primary source of information provided to external users is financial statements. The management team also makes decisions using financial statement information. For both groups, the use of financial statement analysis techniques enhances the usefulness of the information contained in the financial statements.* ■

INTRODUCTION

Decision makers need a variety of information in the decision-making process. Bankers and other lenders are interested in the ability of an organization to repay loans. Stockholders or potential stockholders are interested in earning a fair return on their investment. The management team of a company is concerned about these issues and more—the adequacy of cash flow to pay operating expenses, the efficient use of company resources, and how to improve the overall performance of the company. Financial statement analysis is a useful tool for both external and internal users as they make decisions about a company or for a company.

WHY ANALYZE FINANCIAL STATEMENTS?

LO1
Understand why decision makers analyze financial statements

The most compelling reason to analyze financial statements is simply that it provides useful information to supplement information directly provided in financial statements. Ratio analysis provides additional information necessary to enhance the decision-making ability of the users of the information. Although we will spend some time on the computation of the ratios, the most important aspect of the discussion is what the ratios mean and how to improve performance of the organization by analyzing trends and changes in these ratios. In addition to showing how the company has done in the past, financial ratios are very useful in predicting the future direction and financial position of organizations.

Key Concept: *Ratio analysis provides additional information necessary to enhance the decision-making ability of the users of the information.*

LIMITATIONS OF FINANCIAL STATEMENT ANALYSIS

LO2
Understand the limitations of financial statement analysis

Financial statements are prepared using generally accepted accounting principles (GAAP). However, GAAP allows financial statement preparers to use a variety of methods, estimates, and assumptions in their preparation. To properly prepare and interpret financial statement ratios, these methods, estimates, and assumptions must be taken into consideration. For example, inventory valuation methods include FIFO, LIFO, and other accepted cost flow assumptions. These methods impact the cost of inventory shown on the balance sheet. For example, a company using the LIFO method of inventory costing in a period of rising prices is always selling the most costly inventory purchased (the last inventory purchased is the first to be sold), whereas the inventory shown on the balance sheet is the oldest and least costly. As a result, inventory balances on the balance sheet may be very low and "undercosted" based on today's prices. When comparing companies, differences in accounting methods and cost flow assumptions need to be taken into consideration. If accounting methods or assumptions are changed from year to year, comparisons between years can be difficult.

Decision makers using financial statements and the resulting ratios should not place too much emphasis on any single ratio. Ratios must be looked at as a story that cannot be told without all the pieces. Ratios should be compared with prior years' results, with the budget for the current year, and with industry standards. These industry standards can be found in publications by Moody's and Standard & Poor's. These services provide up-to-date information on most industries and regions. Regional differences are very important factors in evaluating performance. In addition, owing to the size and complexity of many companies, industry standards are sometimes useful in evaluating only divisions of a business. For example, hotels that are affiliated with a casino are operated differently from hotels that are only in the hotel business. Rates for rooms are different, as are

http://www.moodys.com
http://www.standardpoor.com

expectations, and the analysis of the financial ratios must be interpreted in light of these differences.

Key Concept: *Rather than focus on a single ratio, decision makers need to evaluate a company by comparing ratios to those of previous years, budgeted amounts, and industry standards.*

The Impact of Inflation on Financial Statement Analysis

Financial statements are prepared using historical costs and are not adjusted for the effects of increasing prices. For example, although sales may have increased by 5 percent each year for the past five years, the impact of inflation on changing prices needs to be considered. If inflation averaged 3 percent annually over that same period of time, the real increase in sales dollars is only 2 percent. The impact of changing prices on long-term assets can be even more dramatic. Consider a building purchased 30 years ago for \$100,000. If inflation averages 3 percent per year over the life of the building, the market value of the building today will be more than double the historical cost used to record the building when purchased. To compound the problem, the building is likely to be almost fully depreciated, so the book value of the building may be very small.

Horizontal Analysis

LO3
Use comparative financial statements to analyze the performance of a company over time (horizontal analysis)

Analyzing financial statements over time is called **horizontal analysis.** To demonstrate the concept of horizontal analysis, the financial statements for Robyn's Boutique are presented on page 480. The idea behind horizontal analysis is to analyze changes in accounts occurring between years. To facilitate this analysis, dollar changes and percentage changes in each item on the balance sheet are often provided. The percentage changes are the amount of change from the previous year. In the following example, cash increased by \$20,000, which is 18.2 percent of the 2001 balance $\left(\frac{\$20,000}{\$110,000}\right)$.

ROBYN'S BOUTIQUE

Key Concept: *Horizontal analysis is used to analyze changes in accounts occurring between years.*

Robyn's Boutique
Comparative Balance Sheets
Increase (Decrease)

	2002	2001	$ Change	% Change
Cash	$130,000	$110,000	$ 20,000	18.2%
Accounts receivable	130,000	120,000	10,000	8.3
Inventory	225,000	215,000	10,000	4.7
Prepaid insurance	25,000	30,000	(5,000)	(16.7)
Total current assets	$510,000	$475,000	$ 35,000	7.4
Long-term investments	$110,000	$ 75,000	$ 35,000	46.7
Land	200,000	175,000	25,000	14.3
Property and equipment	215,000	95,000	120,000	126.3
Accum. depr.	(105,000)	(80,000)	(25,000)	(31.3)
Total assets	$930,000	$740,000	$190,000	25.7
Accounts payable	$ 60,000	$ 50,000	$ 10,000	20.0
Payroll payable	10,000	8,000	2,000	25.0
Taxes payable	10,000	9,000	1,000	11.1
Total current liabilities	$ 80,000	$ 67,000	$ 13,000	19.4
Notes payable	$100,000	$ 80,000	$ 20,000	25.0
Capital stock	500,000	400,000	100,000	25.0
Retained earnings	250,000	193,000	57,000	29.5
Total liabilities and stockholders' equity	$930,000	$740,000	$190,000	25.7

Looking closely at the balance sheet for Robyn's Boutique, we see two accounts with large percentage changes between 2001 and 2002. Long-term investments have increased by 46.7 percent $\left(\frac{\$35,000}{\$75,000}\right)$, and property and equipment has increased by 126.3 percent $\left(\frac{\$120,000}{\$95,000}\right)$. Although increases like these are common in growing companies, analysts and others will likely be interested in how Robyn's paid for the acquisitions.

Concept Question: *Where can analysts find information on the source of funds used to acquire the additional long-term investments and property and equipment?*

Concept Answer: As you will recall from Chapter 15, the statement of cash flows provides that information.

Changes in the income statement for Robyn's Boutique can be analyzed in a similar fashion:

Robyn's Boutique
Comparative Statements of Income and Retained Earnings
Increase (Decrease)

	2002	2001	$ Change	% Change
Sales revenue	$700,000	$650,000	$50,000	7.7%
Cost of goods sold	500,000	455,000	45,000	9.9
Gross profit	$200,000	$195,000	$ 5,000	2.6
Payroll expense	$ 50,000	$ 42,250	$ 7,750	18.3
Insurance expense	30,000	29,000	1,000	3.4

Rent expense	18,000	18,000	—	—
Depreciation	35,000	15,000	20,000	133.3
Total expenses	$133,000	$104,250	$ 28,750	27.6
Operating Income	67,000	90,750	(23,750)	(26.2)
Interest expense	$ (7,000)	$ (5,000)	$ (2,000)	40.0
Gain on vehicle sale	25,000	—	25,000	—
Loss on sale of securities	(25,000)	—	(25,000)	—
Interest revenue	75,000	50,000	25,000	50.0
Net income before interest and taxes	$135,000	$135,750	$ (750)	(0.06)
Tax	(40,000)	(40,250)	250	(0.06)
Net income	$ 95,000	$ 95,500	$ (500)	(0.05)
Dividends	(38,000)	(38,000)		
To retained earnings	$ 57,000	$ 57,500		
Retained earnings 1/1	193,000	136,000		
Retained earnings 12/31	$250,000	$193,500		

Sales increased by $50,000 (7.7 percent) from 2001 to 2002. On the surface, this would appear to be a positive sign. However, further analysis shows that the cost of goods sold increased by $45,000, or 9.9 percent, whereas total operating expenses increased by $28,750, or 27.6 percent. Although sales increased, expenses appear to be rising much faster than sales! This information is likely to be important for both external users and internal managers. A large decrease in operating income can indicate serious problems with cost management.

Horizontal analysis of financial statements can and should include more than just two years of data. Many annual reports include, as supplemental information, up to 10 years of financial data. Using these supplemental reports, readers of financial statements can perform **trend analysis.** Decision makers can use trend analysis to build prediction models to forecast financial performance in the future. Trend analysis can also be used to identify problem areas by looking for sudden or abnormal changes in accounts.

Horizontal analysis can also include the statement of cash flows:

PAUSE & *Reflect*

Note that focusing on net income without looking at other changes in income statement items would definitely be a mistake in this case. Although net income was virtually unchanged from 2001 to 2002, operating income decreased by more than 26 percent.

Comparative Statements of Cash Flow
For the Years Ended December 31, 2002 and 2001

	2002	2001	$Change	% Change
Cash Flows from Operating Activities				
Cash Receipts From				
Sales on account	$690,000	$640,000	$50,000	7.8%
Interest	75,000	50,000	25,000	50.0
Total cash receipts	$765,000	$690,000	$75,000	
Cash Payments For				
Inventory purchases	$500,000	$470,000	$30,000	6.4
Payroll	48,000	42,250	5,750	13.6
Insurance	25,000	29,000	(4,000)	(13.8)
Interest	7,000	5,000	2,000	40.0
Rent expense	18,000	18,000	—	—
Taxes	39,000	40,250	(1,250)	(3.1)
Total cash payments	$(637,000)	$(604,500)	$32,500	5.4
Net cash provided (used) by operating activities	$128,000	$ 85,500	$42,500	49.7

Cash Flows from Investing Activities				
Sale of note	$ 25,000	—	$ 25,000	—
Sale of vehicle	75,000	—	75,000	—
Purchase of equipment	(180,000)	$(20,000)	(160,000)	800
Purchase of long-term investments	(85,000)	—	(85,000)	—
Purchase of land	(5,000)	—	(5,000)	—
Net cash provided (used) by investing activities	$(170,000)	$(20,000)	$(150,000)	750
Cash Flows from Financing Activities				
Issuance of stock	$ 100,000	—	$ 100,000	—
Payment of cash dividends	(38,000)	$(38,000)	—	—
Net cash provided (used) by financing activities	$ 62,000	$(38,000)	100,000	263.2
Net increase in cash	$ 20,000	$ 27,500	$ (7,500)	(27.3)
Cash balance 1/1	110,000	82,500		
Cash balance 12/31	$ 130,000	$110,000		
Supplemental Schedule of Noncash Investing and Financing Activities				
Acquisition of land in exchange for note payable	$ 20,000	(2,000)		

Robyn's Boutique shows consistent and increasing cash flows from operations: $765,000 in 2002 and $690,000 in 2001. The boutique also shows an increase in net cash provided by operating activities of $42,500, or 49.7 percent. These two changes indicate a good trend in cash flows from operating activities. Although the net increase in cash for 2002 was less than the increase in 2001, the decrease can be easily explained by the additional cash used for investing activities in 2002.

VERTICAL ANALYSIS

LO4
Prepare and use common-size financial statements to compare various financial statement items (vertical analysis)

Vertical analysis compares financial statements of different companies and financial statements of the same company across time after controlling for differences in size. When comparing companies of different sizes, it is useful to standardize the statements. **Common-size financial statements** are statements in which all items have been restated as a percentage of a selected item on the statements. Common-size financial statements remove size as a relevant variable in ratio analysis and can be used to compare companies that make similar products and that are different in size (such as Boeing and Cessna, both aircraft manufacturers). They also can be used to compare the same company across years.

http://www.boeing.com
http://www.cessna.com

Key Concept: *Vertical analysis uses common-size financial statements to remove size as a relevant variable in ratio analysis.*

ROBYN'S BOUTIQUE

Common-size comparative balance sheets for Robyn's Boutique follow. Note that all asset accounts are stated as a percentage of total assets. Similarly, all liability and stockholders' equity accounts are stated as a percentage of total liabilities and stockholders' equity.

Robyn's Boutique
Comparative Balance Sheets
Increase (Decrease)

	2002	Percent	2001	% Change
Cash	$130,000	14%	$110,000	14.9%
Accounts receivable	130,000	14	120,000	16.2
Inventory	225,000	24.2	215,000	29.1

Prepaid insurance	25,000	2.7	30,000	4.1
Total current assets	$510,000	54.8	$475,000	64.2
Long-term investments	110,000	11.8	75,000	10.1
Land	200,000	21.5	175,000	23.6
Property and equipment	215,000	23.1	95,000	12.8
Accum. Depr.	(105,000)	(11.3)	(80,000)	(10.8)
Total assets	$930,000	100%	$740,000	100%
Accounts payable	$ 60,000	6.5	$ 50,000	6.8
Payroll payable	10,000	1.1	8,000	1.1
Taxes payable	10,000	1.1	9,000	1.2
Total current liabilities	$ 80,000	8.7	$ 67,000	9.1
Notes payable	$100,000	10.8	$ 80,000	10.8
Capital stock	500,000	53.8	400,000	54.1
Retained earnings	250,000	26.9	193,000	26.1
Total liabilities and stockholders' equity	$930,000	100 %	$740,000	100 %

As mentioned earlier, there are two ways to use common-size financial statements. The first is a comparison between years or over a number of years. The second is a comparison of similar companies of different sizes.

When comparing across years, analysts and other decision makers look for critical changes in the composition of accounts. One important measure from the balance sheet is working capital. **Working capital** is defined as the excess of current assets over current liabilities and is a measure of an entity's **liquidity,** or its ability to meet its immediate financial obligations. Robyn's Boutique had current assets and current liabilities in 2002 and 2001 as follows:

	2002	2001
Current assets	$510,000	$475,000
Current liabilities	(80,000)	(67,000)
Working capital	$430,000	$408,000

The amount of working capital has increased by $22,000 from 2001 to 2002, indicating that Robyn's has increased the amount of current assets available to pay current liabilities. However, without information concerning the makeup of working capital, the information is of limited use. If current assets consist primarily of inventory, the company's liquidity could still be in jeopardy. In such a case, a slower conversion to cash would result than it would if current assets consisted primarily of accounts receivable.

Common-size comparative income statements for Robyn's Boutique are presented here. The base on which all income statement accounts are compared is net sales, presented simply as sales revenues in our demonstration.

Robyn's Boutique
Common-Size Comparative Income Statements

	2002	Percent	2001	Percent
Sales revenue	$700,000	100.0%	$650,000	100.0%
Cost of goods sold	500,000	71.4	455,000	70.0
Gross profit	$200,000	28.6	$195,000	30.0
Payroll expense	50,000	7.1	42,250	6.0
Insurance expense	30,000	4.3	29,000	4.5

ROBYN'S BOUTIQUE

Rent expense	18,000	—	18,000	—
Depreciation	35,000	5.0	15,000	2.3
Total expenses	$133,000	19.0	$104,250	16.0
Operating Income	$ 67,000	9.6	$ 90,750	14.0
Interest expense	(7,000)	(1.0)	(5,000)	(0.8)
Gain on vehicle sale	25,000	3.6	0	—
Loss on sale of securities	(25,000)	(3.6)	0	—
Interest revenue	75,000	10.7	50,000	7.7
Net Income before interest and taxes	$135,000	19.3	$135,750	20.9
Tax	(40,000)	(5.7)	(40,250)	(6.2)
Net income	$ 95,000	13.6%	$ 95,500	14.7%

LO5
Prepare and use liquidity ratios to analyze a company

The common-size income statement points out some interesting but small changes between the two years presented. The gross profit percentage decreased from 30 percent to 28.6 percent. This is a closely watched ratio in many companies and industries.

COMPARISON OF ROBYN'S TO THE GAP

http://www.gap.com

An important use of common-size financial statements is to compare companies that are in similar lines of business but are of different sizes. For example, in a recent year, the GAP had working capital of $839 million, representing 25.15 percent of total assets. Robyn's working capital is 46.24 percent of total assets. Other financial statement amounts from Robyn's and the GAP are as follows:

Comparison of Robyn's Boutique and the GAP

ACCOUNT	ROBYN'S (2002)	GAP
	Percentage of Total Assets	**Percentage of Total Assets**
Cash	14 .0	27.0
Inventory	24.0	22.0
Prepaids	2.7	5.5
Property and equipment (net)	33.3	40.9
Long-term investments	11.8	0
	Percentage of Liabilities and Equity	**Percentage of Liabilities and Equity**
Accounts payable	6.5	12.5
Income tax	1.1	2.5
Long-term debt	10.8	14.8
Cost of goods sold	71.4	61.8
Operating expense	19.0	25.1
Net income after tax	13.6	8.2

PAUSE & *Reflect*

Spend some time looking at the preceding comparison, and speculate on what would cause the differences between the two companies.

RATIO ANALYSIS

Financial statement ratios simply refer to a relationship between two financial statement amounts stated as a percentage.

© GAIL MOONEY/CORBIS

RATIO ANALYSIS AND RETURN ON INVESTMENT

As discussed in Chapter 11, managers and the investment centers under their control are often evaluated using a measure of return on invested assets. These measures include return on investment (ROI), residual income, and economic value added (EVA). The measures are similar in that they look at performance in relation to the amount of assets or investment under a manager's control. As you will recall from Chapter 11,

$$\text{ROI} = \text{Profit margin} \times \text{Asset turnover}$$

where

$$\text{Profit margin} = \frac{\text{Net operating income}}{\text{Sales}}$$

$$\text{Asset turnover} = \frac{\text{Sales}}{\text{Average operating assets}}$$

$$\text{ROI} = \frac{\text{Net operating income}}{\text{Sales}} \times \frac{\text{Sales}}{\text{Average operating assets}}$$

The elements of ROI are shown in more detail in Exhibit 16-1.

Key Concept: *Ratio analysis is useful in assessing the impact of transactions on ROI, residual income, EVA, and other key measures of performance.*

CURRENT RATIO

The **current ratio,** or working capital ratio, is a measure of an entity's liquidity. The formula for the current ratio is as follows:

$$\text{Current ratio} = \frac{\text{Current assets}}{\text{Current liabilities}}$$

EXHIBIT 16-1 Elements of Return on Investment

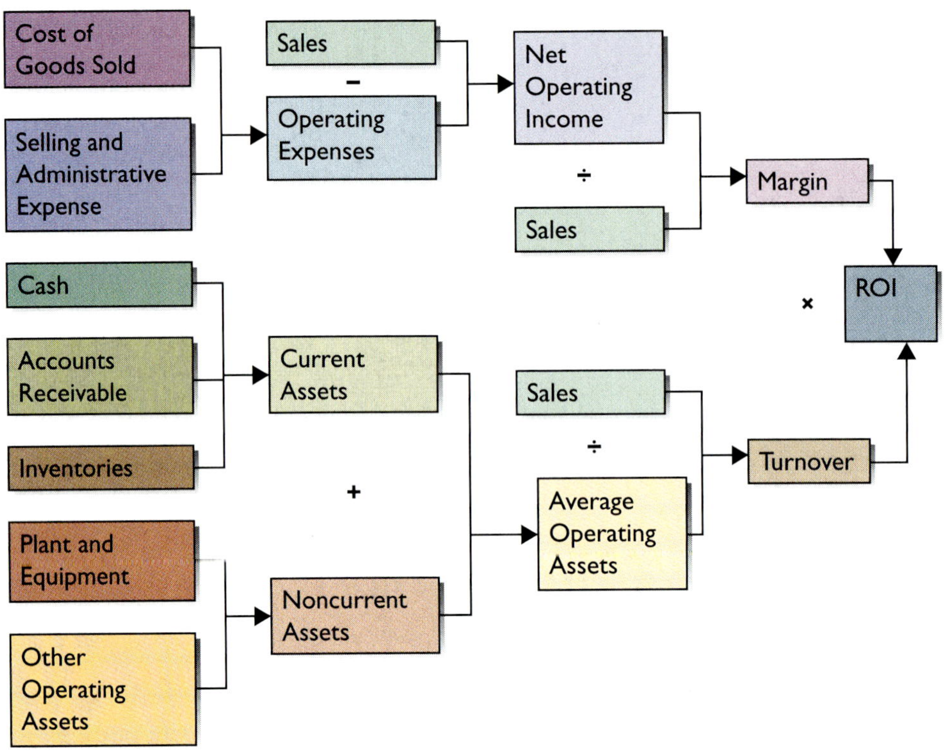

ROBYN'S BOUTIQUE

The current ratios for Robyn's Boutique for the past two years are as follows:

2002	2001
$\frac{\$510,000}{\$80,000} = \mathbf{6.375}$	$\frac{\$475,000}{\$67,000} = \mathbf{7.090}$

What does this ratio tell us? In 2002, Robyn's Boutique has $6.38 of current assets for every dollar of current liabilities, and in 2001 the boutique had $7.09 for every dollar of current liabilities. Although high current ratios would appear to be good (if you are a creditor of a company, a high current ratio indicates that you are more likely to be paid), a ratio that is very high may indicate that a company holds too much cash, accounts receivable, or inventory. Historically, a current ratio of 2.0 was considered good. However, many companies strive to maintain current ratios that are closer to 1.0. Internal managers look closely at the current ratio and its composition so that they can better control levels of current assets. As we have discussed elsewhere, holding inventory can be very costly for companies. High levels of accounts receivable may indicate problems collecting cash from customers, and cash held in non-interest-bearing accounts might be more productively used elsewhere.

What is the impact of the current ratio on ROI, residual income, and EVA? The only way to increase the current ratio is to increase current assets or to decrease current liabilities. Although decreasing liabilities has no direct impact on measures of return on investment, increasing current assets with no change in current liabilities will decrease ROI, residual income, and EVA.

ACID-TEST RATIO

One way to reduce the concern of the composition of the current accounts when computing the current ratio is to use the quick ratio, or acid-test ratio. The **quick ratio** is a stricter test of a company's ability to pay its current debts with highly liquid current assets. The quick ratio removes inventories and prepaid assets from the current-asset amount used in the calculation of the current ratio. These current assets are considered the least liquid. The quick-ratio formula is as follows:

$$\text{Quick ratio} = \frac{\text{Quick assets}}{\text{Current liabilities}}$$

Using the amounts from Robyn's Boutique, we can calculate the quick ratio as follows:

2002	2001
$\frac{\$260{,}000}{\$80{,}000} = \mathbf{3.25}$	$\frac{\$230{,}000}{\$67{,}000} = \mathbf{3.433}$

A quick ratio less than 1.0 should be of concern to both creditors and internal managers, as it indicates that liquid current assets are not sufficient to meet current obligations. On the other hand, Robyn's has unusually high quick ratios. High quick ratios may indicate other problems to management. Unless there are good reasons for holding excess cash (large purchases of property, plant, and equipment; future expansion; etc.), Robyn's should probably try to convert its excess cash into assets generating higher returns.

CASH FLOW FROM OPERATIONS TO CURRENT-LIABILITIES RATIO

The current ratio and the quick ratio have two major weaknesses. The first is that all debt payments are made with cash, whereas current assets include noncash assets. The second is that both ratios focus on liquid and current assets at one point in time (the balance sheet date). However, cash, inventories, accounts receivable, and other current assets change over the course of the year. For these reasons, the amount of cash flow from operations (from the statement of cash flows) is sometimes used as the numerator in a ratio with an average balance of current liabilities in the denominator:

$$\text{Cash flow from operations to current liabilities ratio} = \frac{\text{Net cash provided by operating activities}}{\text{Average current liabilities}}$$

The computation of the 2001 ratio requires the 2000 end-of-year current-liability balance. The December 31, 2000, balance sheet for Robyn's Boutique is as follows:

Robyn's Boutique
Balance Sheet
December 31, 2000

Cash	$ 95,000
Accounts receivable	105,000
Inventory	175,000
Prepaid insurance	25,000
Total current assets	$400,000
Long-term investments	$ 45,000
Land	175,000
Property and equipment	85,000
Accumulated depreciation	(60,000)
Total long-term assets	$245,000
Total assets	$645,000
Accounts payable	$ 35,000
Payroll payable	6,500
Income tax payable	7,000
Total current liabilities	$ 48,500
Notes payable	$ 70,000
Total long-term liabilities	$ 70,000
Capital stock	$400,000
Retained earnings	126,500
Total liabilities and stockholders' equity	$645,000

The ratios for Robyn's Boutique are as follows:

2002	**2001**
$\frac{\$128{,}000}{\left[\frac{(\$80{,}000 + \$67{,}000)}{2}\right]} = \mathbf{1.74}$	$\frac{\$85{,}500}{\left[\frac{(\$67{,}000 + \$48{,}500)}{2}\right]} = \mathbf{1.48}$

Robyn's is generating sufficient cash from operations to pay current obligations.

Accounts Receivable Analysis

The **accounts receivable turnover ratio** is one of the best measures of the efficiency of the collection process. Management's analysis of accounts receivable is very important in monitoring collection and credit-granting policies. The accounts receivable turnover ratio is

$$\text{Accounts receivable turnover ratio} = \frac{\text{Net credit sales}}{\text{Average accounts receivable}}$$

This ratio is known as an activity ratio, which means that it consists of an activity (sales) divided by a related base (accounts receivable). Using the accounts receivable balances in the 2000, 2001, and 2002 balance sheets, we calculate the ratios for Robyn's Boutique as follows:

2002	2001
$\dfrac{\$700{,}000}{\left[\dfrac{(\$120{,}000 + \$130{,}000)}{2}\right]} = \mathbf{5.60}$	$\dfrac{\$650{,}000}{\left[\dfrac{(\$105{,}000 + \$120{,}000)}{2}\right]} = \mathbf{5.78}$

These ratios tell us that on average, Robyn's Boutique sold on account and subsequently collected accounts receivable almost six times during the year. To convert this to a more understandable measure, consider this question: If you can do something almost six times in a year, how many days did it take you to do it once? The average number of days to collect a credit sale, computed as follows, measures this concept:

$$\text{Number of days sales are in receivables} = \frac{\text{Number of days in the period}}{\text{Accounts receivable turnover}}$$

The calculations for Robyn's for 2001 and 2002 are as follows:

2002	2001
$\dfrac{360}{5.6} = \mathbf{64.29\ days}$	$\dfrac{360}{5.78} = \mathbf{62.28\ days}$

This ratio tells us that the average time to collect sales on account was 62.28 days in 2001 and 64.29 days in 2002. Is this amount of time to collect sales acceptable? That depends on the credit policy of the particular business and on industry standards. If the accounts are due in 30 days, a collection period in excess of 60 is not good. If the credit policy allows for 60 days, the collection period is in line with existing policy.

The accounts receivable turnover ratio will have an impact on ROI and other measures of return on invested assets. One of the key components of ROI is turnover of assets. When turnover is increased, ROI and related measures will also increase.

INVENTORY ANALYSIS

Analysis of inventory is very similar to the analysis of accounts receivable. The first ratio is the inventory turnover ratio:

$$\text{Inventory turnover ratio} = \frac{\text{Cost of goods sold}}{\text{Average inventory}}$$

The ratios for Robyn's for 2001 and 2002 are as follows:

2002	2001
$\dfrac{\$500{,}000}{\left[\dfrac{(\$215{,}000 + \$225{,}000)}{2}\right]} = \mathbf{2.27}$	$\dfrac{\$455{,}000}{\left[\dfrac{(\$175{,}000 + \$215{,}000)}{2}\right]} = \mathbf{2.33}$

These ratios tell us that on average, Robyn's Boutique bought inventory and then subsequently sold it 2.33 and 2.27 times per year in 2001 and 2002. This ratio does not mean that every item in inventory is sold 2.33 times but that the value of inventory was sold 2.33 times. Determining whether inventory turns are good is totally dependent on industry and company standards. Some businesses expect higher inventory turns than others do. For example, a grocery store would expect inventory turns of 50 or even 100 times per year. A bakery may expect inventory turns as high as 200 because it would expect to sell all fresh baked goods the same day they are produced. At the other extreme, furniture stores may expect inventory turns of only 1 or 2 per year. Retail clothing stores should expect to turn over inventory much more frequently than 2 times per year. This is a serious concern for management. Another way to look at inventory turnover is to calculate the number of days inventory is held before it is sold:

$$\text{Number of days inventory is held before sale} = \frac{\text{Number of days in the period}}{\text{Inventory turnover}}$$

On average, Robyn's is holding inventory for more than 150 days in both 2001 and 2002, calculated as follows:

2002	2001
$\frac{360}{2.27} = \mathbf{158.59\ days}$	$\frac{360}{2.33} = \mathbf{154.51\ days}$

Low turnover ratios and a correspondingly high number of days in which inventory is held for sale can direct management's attention toward a variety of problems. A large amount of obsolete inventory that is not being written off can adversely impact these ratios. These ratios can also indicate problems in the sales department or problems with the product, both of which can cause decreases in sales. As with accounts receivable turnover, if inventory turnover increases, ROI and other measures of return on invested assets will also increase.

CASH-TO-CASH OPERATING CYCLE RATIO

This ratio measures the length of time between the purchase of inventory and the eventual collection of cash from sales. To calculate this ratio, we combine two measures:

$$\text{Cash-to-cash operating cycle ratio} = \text{Number of days in inventory} + \text{Number of days in receivables}$$

The cash-to-cash operating cycle ratios for Robyn's Boutique are as follows:

2002	2001
158.59 + 64.29 = **222.88 days**	154.51 + 62.28 = **216.79 days**

On average, it took Robyn's 216.79 days in 2001 and 222.88 days in 2002 to turn purchased inventory into cash.

LO6
Prepare and use solvency ratios to analyze a company

Solvency refers to a company's ability to remain in business over the long term. Solvency is related to liquidity but differs with respect to time frame. Liquidity measures the ability to pay short-term debt, whereas solvency measures the ability to stay financially healthy over the long run.

DEBT-TO-EQUITY RATIO

The main focus of solvency analysis is capital structure. Capital structure refers to the relationship between debt and stockholders' equity. The debt-to-equity ratio is as follows:

$$\text{Debt-to-equity ratio} = \frac{\text{Total liabilities}}{\text{Total stockholders' equity}}$$

Robyn's debt-to-equity ratio at 2001 and 2002 is as follows:

2002	2001
$\frac{\$180{,}000}{\$750{,}000} = \mathbf{0.24\ to\ 1}$	$\frac{\$147{,}000}{\$593{,}000} = \mathbf{0.25\ to\ 1}$

These ratios tell us that for every $1 of capital (capital stock and retained earnings), creditors provided 25 cents in 2001 and 24 cents in 2002. Low debt-to-equity ratios indicate a preference to raise funds through equity financing and a tendency to avoid the higher risk of debt financing. What is considered a good debt-to-equity ratio? As with all other ratios, this is dependent on the business, the industry, and other factors. Although a high debt-to-equity ratio may be of concern to creditors, it may be desirable and necessary for a new business to borrow money. The decision to capitalize a company with debt or equity involves many variables, including the income tax impact of debt versus equity to both a corporation and its shareholders. If management borrows funds at 8 percent and earns a return on investment of 10 percent, the use of debt (leverage) is desirable. But it adds some risk, owing to the obligation to repay the debt and the interest on the debt. This level of risk can be measured by the next ratio, times interest earned.

TIMES-INTEREST-EARNED RATIO

Times interest earned measures a company's ability to meet current interest payments to creditors by specifically measuring its ability to meet current-year interest payments out of current-year earnings:

$$\text{Times interest earned} = \frac{\text{Net income} + \text{Interest expense} + \text{Income tax}}{\text{Interest expense}}$$

Both interest expense and income tax expense are added back to net income because interest is deducted from net income to arrive at taxable income. This adjustment gives us a "purer" measure of income available to pay interest. This ratio is especially important to bankers and other lenders. The ratios for times interest earned for Robyn's are as follows:

2002	2001
$\frac{\$135{,}000 + \$7{,}000 + \$40{,}000}{\$7{,}000} = \mathbf{26.0\ to\ 1}$	$\frac{\$135{,}750 + \$5{,}000 + \$40{,}250}{\$5{,}000} = \mathbf{36.2\ to\ 1}$

The ratios for Robyn's Boutique are very good. Robyn's could pay (from current earnings) the interest on debt 36 times in 2001 and 26 times in 2002.

DEBT SERVICE COVERAGE RATIO

Two major weaknesses are associated with the use of the times-interest-earned ratio as a measure of the ability to pay creditors. First, the ratio considers only interest expense. Management and other decision makers must also be concerned about the amount of principal that must be repaid on the currently maturing debt. Second, the ratio does not take into account any noncash adjustments to net income that arise because of accrual accounting. The debt service coverage ratio is used to measure the amount of cash generated from operating activities that is available to repay principal and interest in the upcoming year. That ratio is as follows:

$$\text{Debt service coverage ratio} = \frac{\text{Cash flow from operations before interest and taxes}}{\text{Interest and principal payments}}$$

Referring back to the comparative statement of cash flows, we can compute the ratios for Robyn's:

2002	2001
$\frac{(\$128{,}000 - \$7{,}000 - \$39{,}000)}{\$25{,}000} = \mathbf{3.28}$	$\frac{(\$85{,}500 - \$5{,}000 - \$40{,}250)}{\$25{,}000} = \mathbf{1.61}$

These ratios indicate that Robyn's generated \$1.61 in cash for every \$1 of interest and principal paid in 2001 and \$3.28 for every \$1 of interest and principal paid in 2002. The 2001 ratio is weak, but the improvement is dramatic.

CASH FLOW FROM OPERATIONS TO CAPITAL EXPENDITURES RATIO

This ratio measures a company's ability to use cash flow from operations to finance its acquisitions of property, plant, and equipment. The ability to use cash from operations diminishes the need to acquire outside financing, such as debt. The ratio is computed as follows:

$$\text{Cash flow from operations to capital expenditures ratio} = \frac{\text{Cash flow from operations} - \text{Total dividends paid}}{\text{Cash paid for acquisitions}}$$

The calculation of these ratios for Robyn's is as follows:

2002	2001
$\frac{\$128{,}000 - \$38{,}000}{\$105{,}000} = \mathbf{86\%}$	$\frac{\$85{,}500 - \$38{,}000}{\$20{,}000} = \mathbf{238\%}$

These ratios tell us that in 2001, Robyn's generated cash from operations approximately 2.4 times greater than what was needed for acquisition of capital assets. In 2002, the ratio shows that Robyn's generated cash from operations to cover only 86 percent of the capital asset needs. Note that the amount used in 2002 to compute the ratio was net assets acquired. Robyn's had acquired \$180,000 of new assets but sold a vehicle for \$75,000.

Another group of ratios of importance to decision makers are those concerned with profitability analysis. Creditors are concerned with profitability because it indicates an ability to make required principal and interest payments. Stockholders are very interested in profitability because of related increases in stock prices or dividends paid to shareholders. Managers are also concerned with profitability, as it is often related to performance evaluations and tangible rewards from bonus payments and other incentive compensation plans.

LO7
Prepare and use profitability ratios to analyze a company

RETURN ON ASSETS

Return ratios measure the relationship between a return and a specific investment made in the company by various groups of investors, creditors, and owners. Return on assets (ROA) considers the return to investors on all assets invested in the company. Because we are measuring a return to investors, net income is often adjusted by interest expense paid to creditors. The formula for computation of return on assets is as follows:

$$\text{ROA} = \frac{\text{Net income} + \text{Interest expense (net of tax)}}{\text{Average total assets}}$$

Assuming a 30 percent tax rate, we calculate ROA as follows:

	2002		2001	
Net income		$95,000		$95,500
Add back				
Interest expense	7,000		5,000	
× (1 – Tax rate)	× 0.70	4,900	× 0.70	3,500
Numerator:		99,900		99,000
Assets, beginning of year		$740,000		$645,000
Assets, end of year		930,000		740,000
Total		$1,670,000		$1,385,000
Denominator:				
Average total assets	$\left(\frac{1{,}670{,}000}{2}\right)$	= $835,000	$\left(\frac{1{,}385{,}000}{2}\right)$	= $692,500
ROA	$\frac{\$99{,}900}{\$835{,}000}$	= **11.96%**	$\frac{\$99{,}000}{\$692{,}500}$	= **14.30%**

© LEE SNIDER/CORBIS

Which ratios might investors have focused on to predict Woolworth's financial difficulties?

Interpretation of this ratio is based on the company's required return on assets, industry standards, and trends. In this case, the decline in ROA is likely to be of concern to the owners of Robyn's Boutique.

Like return on investment, ROA can be broken down into margin and turnover components: return on sales and asset turnover. The two ratios are computed as follows:

$$\text{Return on sales} = \frac{\text{Net income} + \text{Interest expense (net of tax)}}{\text{Net sales}}$$

$$\text{Asset turnover ratio} = \frac{\text{Net sales}}{\text{Average total assets}}$$

ROBYN'S BOUTIQUE

The ratios for Robyn's are as follows:

	2002	2001
Return on sales =	$\frac{\$99{,}900}{\$700{,}000} = \mathbf{14.27\%}$	$\frac{\$99{,}000}{\$650{,}000} = \mathbf{15.23}$
Asset turnover ratio =	$\frac{\$700{,}000}{\$835{,}000} = \mathbf{0.84\ times}$	$\frac{\$650{,}000}{\$692{,}500} = \mathbf{0.94\ times}$

Both the return on sales (income generated as a percentage of sales) and the asset turnover ratio (sales generated as a percentage of assets) declined from 2001 to 2002. Of particular concern to management is the low asset turnover ratio.

Return on Common Stockholders' Equity

Return on common stockholders' equity (ROCSE) measures the return to common stockholders (net income reduced by preferred dividends) as a percentage of stockholders' equity:

$$\text{ROCSE} = \frac{\text{Net income} - \text{Preferred dividends}}{\text{Average common stockholders' equity}}$$

The ROCSE ratios for Robyn's are as follows:

2002	2001
$\frac{\$95{,}000}{\left[\frac{(\$593{,}000 + \$750{,}000)}{2}\right]} = \mathbf{14.15\%}$	$\frac{\$95{,}500}{\left[\frac{(\$526{,}500 + \$593{,}000)}{2}\right]} = \mathbf{17.06\%}$

The ratios indicate that the common stockholders are earning a 17 percent return in 2001 and a 14 percent return in 2002. Adequacy of return on stockholders' equity is dependent on a number of factors, including the risk of the investment.

Earnings per Share

Current stockholders and potential investors use earnings per share (EPS) as a key measure of performance. In contrast to measures of net income, EPS can be used to compare the performance of companies of different sizes. However, it should be used with caution in comparing companies across different industries. EPS is calculated as follows:

$$\text{EPS} = \frac{\text{Net income} - \text{Preferred dividends}}{\text{Average number of common shares outstanding}}$$

The EPS for Robyn's is as follows:

2002	2001
$\text{EPS} = \frac{\$95{,}000}{45{,}000} = \mathbf{\$2.11}$	$\text{EPS} = \frac{\$95{,}500}{40{,}000} = \mathbf{\$2.39}$

Robyn's Boutique has a $10 per share par value, resulting in 40,000 shares outstanding in 2001. In 2002, the boutique sold another 10,000 shares for $100,000, so 50,000 shares were outstanding at the end of 2002. The average number of shares outstanding in 2002 was 45,000 $\left(\frac{40{,}000 + 50{,}000}{2}\right)$.

© AP/WIDE WORLD PHOTOS

PRICE EARNINGS RATIO

Earnings per share is a very important ratio for investors because of the relationship of earnings to dividends and the market price of a company's stock. Investors are also interested in the current price of a company's stock in comparison to its earnings. The price/earnings (P/E) ratio is computed as follows:

$$\text{Price earnings ratio} = \frac{\text{Current market price}}{\text{EPS}}$$

Assuming that the current market price for Robyn's Boutique stock is $13 per share, we can compute the P/E ratio as follows:

2002	2001
$\frac{\$13}{\$2.11} = \mathbf{6.16\ to\ 1}$	$\frac{\$13}{\$2.39} = \mathbf{5.44\ to\ 1}$

P/E ratios are highly dependent on industry. A high P/E ratio can indicate that a stock is overpriced, and a low P/E ratio can indicate that a stock is underpriced.

PAUSE & Reflect

In the past, Internet companies often reflected high share prices with no historical earnings and minimal projected earnings. What do you think the prices of Internet stocks were based on? Reference current and past values of such companies as Amazon.com, eBay.com, and priceline.com.

http://www.amazon.com
http://www.ebay.com
http://www.priceline.com

IN THE NEWS

The common stock of publicly held companies has generally been considered to be priced at a market value tied to historical earnings. However, many growth stocks appear to be priced based on *projected earnings,* not historical earnings.

Summary of Key Concepts

- Ratio analysis provides additional information necessary to enhance the decision-making ability of the users of the information. (p. 478)
- Rather than focus on a single ratio, decision makers need to evaluate a company by comparing ratios to those of previous years, budgeted amounts, and industry standards. (p. 479)
- Horizontal analysis is used to analyze changes in accounts occurring between years. (p. 480)
- Vertical analysis uses common-size financial statements to remove size as a relevant variable in ratio analysis. (p. 482)
- Ratio analysis is useful in assessing the impact of transactions on ROI, residual income, EVA, and other key measures of performance. (p. 485)

Key Definitions

Horizontal analysis When financial statements are analyzed over time (p. 479)

Trend analysis Horizontal analysis of multiple years of data (p. 481)

Common-size financial statements Statements in which all items have been restated as a percentage of a selected item on the statements (p. 482)

Working capital The excess of current assets over current liabilities, which is a measure of an entity's liquidity (p. 483)

Liquidity A measure of the ability of a company to meet its immediate financial obligations (p. 483)

Current ratio A measure of an entity's liquidity; also known as working capital ratio (p. 485)

Quick ratio A strict test of a company's ability to pay its current debts with highly liquid current assets (p. 487)

Accounts receivable turnover ratio One of the best measures of the efficiency of the collection process (p. 488)

Multiple Choice

1. Which of the following statements about ratio analysis is *not* true?

a. Financial ratios can show how a company has done in the past but is not very useful in predicting its future direction and financial position.

b. The most compelling reason to analyze financial statements is simply that it provides useful information to supplement information directly provided in financial statements.

c. Financial statement analysis involves the application of analytical tools to financial statements and supplemental data included with the financial statements to enhance the ability of decision makers to make optimal decisions.

d. For both internal and external users, financial statement analysis enhances the usefulness of the information contained in the financial statements.

2. Which of the following is *not* a limitation of financial statement analysis?

a. When comparing companies, you need to take into consideration differences in accounting methods and cost flow assumptions.

b. Financial statement analysis involves the application of analytical tools to financial statements and supplemental data included with the financial statements to enhance the ability of decision makers to make optimal decisions.

c. In order to properly prepare and interpret financial statement ratios, these methods, estimates, and assumptions must be taken into consideration.

d. Ratios must be looked at as a story that can't be told without all the pieces.

3. To perform horizontal analysis:
   a. dollar changes and percentage changes in each item on the balance sheet are often provided
   b. common-size financial statements are prepared
   c. return on investment (ROI), residual income, and economic value added (EVA) are computed
   d. all of the above
4. Which of the following statements regarding trend analysis is *not* true?
   a. Many annual reports include, as supplemental information, up to 10 years of financial data that can be used to perform trend analysis.
   b. Decision makers can use trend analysis to build prediction models to forecast financial performance.
   c. Trend analysis is also known as vertical analysis.
   d. Trend analysis can be used to identify problem areas by looking for sudden or abnormal changes in accounts.
5. Achmed's Animations had current assets and current liabilities in 2002 and 2001 as follows:

	2002	2001
Current assets	$500,000	$475,000
Current liabilities	60,000	67,000

   The amount of working capital from 2001 to 2002 has:
   a. increased by $25,000
   b. decreased by $7,000
   c. increased by $32,000
   d. decreased by $32,000
6. Carla's Creations had sales of $950,000 and net operating income of $575,000. If operating assets during the year average $450,000, Carla's Creations' asset turnover is:
   a. 0.605
   b. 0.783
   c. 1.277
   d. 2.111

Use the following information from Paddington's 12/31/02 financial statements to answer questions 7 and 8:

Cash	$150,000	Accounts payable	$ 60,000
Accounts receivable	130,000	Payroll payable	10,000
Inventory	125,000	Taxes payable	10,000
Prepaid insurance	25,000	Total current liabilities	$ 80,000
Total current assets	$430,000	Notes payable	50,000
Long-term investments	110,000	Capital stock	500,000
Land	200,000	Retained earnings	220,000
Property and equipment	215,000	Total	$850,000
Accum. depr.	(105,000)		
Total	$420,000		
Total assets	$850,000		

Current liabilities (12/31/01)	$ 70,000
Net cash provided by operating activities	120,000
Accounts receivable (12/31/01)	120,000
Net cash provided by investing activities	100,000
Inventory (12/31/01)	100,000
Net cash provided by financing activities	80,000
Net credit sales	500,000
Cost of goods sold	380,000

7. Paddington's current ratio is:
  a. 5.375
  b. 3.81
  c. 3.50
  d. It cannot be determined from the information provided.

8. Paddington's debt-to-equity ratio is:
  a. 0.10
  b. 0.11
  c. 0.18
  d. It cannot be determined from the information provided.

9. The following information was obtained from Chandler's 12/31/02 financial statements:

Cash	$250,000	Accounts payable	$160,000
Accounts receivable	110,000	Payroll payable	110,000
Inventory	125,000	Taxes payable	110,000
Prepaid assets	25,000	Total current liab.	$380,000
Total current assets	$510,000	Notes payable	50,000
Long-term investments	$110,000	Capital stock	400,000
Land	200,000	Retained earnings	90,000
Property and equipment	205,000	Total	$920,000
Accum. depr.	(105,000)		
Total	$410,000		
Total assets	$920,000		

Current liabilities (12/31/01)	$270,000
Net cash provided by operating activities	120,000
Accounts receivable (12/31/01)	120,000
Net cash provided by investing activities	100,000
Inventory (12/31/01)	100,000
Net cash provided by financing activities	80,000
Net credit sales	450,000
Cost of goods sold	380,000

Chandler's return on common stockholders' equity is:
  a. 0.18
  b. 0.14
  c. 1.25
  d. It cannot be determined from the information provided.

10. Brown's Breads had the following financial statement information for 2002:

Net sales	$1,500,000
Gross profit margin	$1,250,000
Interest expense (net of tax)	240,000
Net income	$900,000

Total assets, 12/31/01	$1,010,000
Total assets, 12/31/02	$1,200,000
Total liabilities, 12/31/02	$ 260,000
Stockholders' equity, 12/31/01	$ 650,000
Stockholders' equity, 12/31/02	$ 750,000
Preferred dividends	100,000
Average number of shares outstanding	1,000,000

The return on common stockholders' equity for Brown's Breads is:

a. 1.14
b. 1.20
c. 1.38
d. It cannot be determined from the information provided.

CONCEPT REVIEW

11. The rate of return on assets can be separated into what two components?
12. Discuss ways to increase the rate of return on assets.
13. Give the formula to compute accounts receivable turnover.
14. Give the formula to compute inventory turnover.
15. Give the formula to compute asset turnover.
16. If sales are $475, beginning assets are $420, and ending assets are $480, what is the asset turnover ratio?
17. If the cost of goods sold was $500, beginning inventory was $50, and ending inventory was $80, what is the inventory turnover ratio?
18. If a company's sales (all on account) equal $600, beginning accounts receivable were $68, and ending accounts receivable were $54, what is the accounts receivable turnover?
19. A company has a current ratio of 3 to 1 but would like to decrease the ratio. What types of options does it have to accomplish this?
20. At the beginning of 2002, the Golden Eagle Company had a current ratio of 2 to 1. What could Golden Eagle do to increase this ratio?
21. If current assets exceed current liabilities, what will a payment to short-term creditors do to the ratio?
22. Spendthrift Inc. has ordered goods on credit from Prudence Co. Before Prudence ships the goods, however, it would like to be sure that Spendthrift is likely to be able to pay the bill when due. Assuming that Prudence has access to Spendthrift's financial statements, which ratios will Prudence find most useful? Why?
23. Explain the purpose of financial statement analysis.
24. Explain the limitations of ratio analysis.

APPLICATION OF CONCEPTS

25. Using the following financial statements for Eagle Company, compute the required ratios:

Eagle Company Statement of Financial Position as of December 31 (in millions)

	2000	2001	2002
Assets			
Cash	$ 2.6	$ 1.8	$ 1.6
Government securities	0.4	0.2	0.0
Accounts and notes receivable	8.0	8.5	8.5
Inventories	2.8	3.2	2.8
Prepaid assets	0.7	0.6	0.6
Total current assets	$14.5	$14.3	$13.5
Property, plant, and equipment (net)	4.3	5.4	5.9
Total assets	$18.8	$19.7	$19.4
Liabilities and Equity			
Notes payable	$ 3.2	$ 3.7	$ 4.2
Accounts payable	2.8	3.7	4.1
Accrued expenses	0.9	1.1	1.0
Total current liabilities	$ 6.9	$ 8.5	$ 9.3
Long-term debt, 6 % interest	3.0	2.0	1.0
Total liabilities	$ 9.9	$10.5	$10.3
Shareholders' equity	8.9	9.2	9.1
Total liabilities and equity	$18.8	$19.7	$19.4

Income Statement for the Year Ended December 31 (in millions)

	2000	2001	2002
Net sales	$24.2	$24.5	$24.9
Cost of goods sold	(16.9)	(17.2)	(18.0)
Gross margin	$ 7.3	$ 7.3	$ 6.9
Selling and administrative	(6.6)	(6.8)	(7.3)
Earnings (Loss) before taxes	$ 0.7	$ 0.5	$(0.4)
Income taxes	(0.3)	(0.2)	0.2
Net income	$ 0.4	$ 0.3	$(0.2)

Required

A. What is the rate of return on total assets for 2002?

B. What is the current ratio for 2002?

C. What is the quick (acid test) ratio for 2002?

D. What is the profit margin for 2001?

E. What is the profit margin for 2002?

F. What is the inventory turnover for 2001?

G. What is the inventory turnover for 2002?

H. What is the rate of return on stockholders' equity for 2001?

I. What is the rate of return on stockholders' equity for 2002?

J. What is the debt-equity ratio for 2002?

http://www.coca-cola.com
http://www.pepsico.com

26. Recent annual reports of Coca-Cola and PepsiCo reveal the following for year 3 (in millions):

	Coca-Cola	PepsiCo
Revenues	$8,338	$13,007
Interest expense	199	345
Net income	1,045	762
Average total assets	8,028	10,079

The income tax rate for year 3 is 34 percent.

Required

A. Calculate the rate of return on assets for each company.

B. Break the rate of return on assets into return on sales and total asset turnover.

C. Comment on the relative profitability of the two companies for year 3.

27. Information taken from recent annual reports of two retailers follows (amounts in millions). Dan's Duds and Handsome Hal's both sell men's clothing. The income tax rate is 34 percent. Indicate which of these companies is the discount store and which is the specialty retailer. Explain your answer.

	Dan's Duds	Handsome Hal's
Sales	$4,071	$20,649
Interest expense	64	136
Net income	245	837
Average total assets	2,061	5,746

28. Annual reports of Kellogg's and Quaker Oats reveal the following for a recent year (amounts in millions): **http://www.kelloggs.com http://www.quakeroats.com**

	Kellogg's	Quaker Oats
Sales	$3,793	$3,671
Accounts receivable, January 1	219	505
Accounts receivable, December 31	275	537

Required

A. Compute the accounts receivable for each company.

B. Compute the average number of days that accounts receivable are outstanding for each company.

C. Which of these two companies is managing its accounts receivable more efficiently?

29. The following relates to the activities of Eli Lilly, a pharmaceutical company (amounts in millions): **http://www.elililly.com**

	Year 5	Year 6	Year 7	Year 8
Sales	$3,271	$3,720	$3,644	$4,070
Cost of goods sold	1,175	1,346	1,303	1,337
Average inventory	662	694	655	645

Required

A. Compute the inventory turnover for each year.

B. Compute the average number of days that inventories are held each year.

C. Compute the cost of goods sold to sales percentage for each year.

D. How well has the company managed its inventories over the four years?

30. The following information relates to a manufacturer of CD players (amounts in millions):

	Year 2	Year 3	Year 4
Sales	$210	$538	$1,051
Average total assets	70	145	256
Net income	36	87	137

Required

A. Compute the asset turnover ratio for each year.

B. How well has the company managed its investment in plant assets over the three years?

31. Information taken from the annual reports of National Medical Enterprises for three recent years is as follows (amounts in millions):

	Year 4	Year 5	Year 6
Revenues	$2,962	$2,881	$3,202
Net income	118	140	170
Average total assets	3,069	3,365	3,471
Average common stockholders' equity	974	968	944

Required

A. Compute the rate of return on common stockholders' equity for each year.

B. Break the rate of return on assets into the return on sales and the asset turnover ratio.

C. How has the profitability of the company changed over the three years?

32. The following data show five items from the financial statements of three companies for a recent year (amounts in millions):

	Company A	Company B	Company C
For the Year			
Revenues	$8,824	$9,000	$11,742
Income before interest and related taxes[a]	615	1,043	611
Net income to common shareholders[b]	477	974	503
Average during the Year			
Total assets	9,073	6,833	7,163
Common shareholders' equity	2,915	3,494	2,888

[a]Net income + Interest expense × (1 − tax rate)
[b]Net income − Preferred stock dividends

Required

A. Compute the rate of return on assets for each company. Separate the rate of return on assets into the return on sales and the asset turnover ratio.

B. The three companies are American Airlines, Johnson & Johnson, and May Department Stores. Which of the companies corresponds to A, B, and C? What clues did you use in reaching your conclusions?

http://www.aa.com
http://www.johnsonandjohnson.com
http://www.mayco.com

33. The 2001 financial statements for the Griffin Company are as follows:

Griffin Company
Statement of Financial Position

	12/31/01	12/31/00
Assets		
Cash	$ 40,000	$ 10,000
Accounts receivable	30,000	55,000
Inventory	110,000	70,000
Property, plant, and equipment	250,000	257,000
Total assets	$430,000	$392,000
Liabilities and Stockholders' Equity		
Current liabilities	$ 60,000	$ 50,000
5 percent mortgage payable	120,000	162,000
Common stock (30,000 shares)	150,000	150,000
Retained earnings	100,000	30,000
Total liabilities and equity	$430,000	$392,000

Griffin Company
Income Statement for the Year Ended December 31, 2001

Sales on Account	$420,000
Less Expenses	
Cost of goods sold	$214,000
Salary expense	50,000
Depreciation expense	7,000
Interest expense	9,000
Total expenses	$280,000
Income before taxes	140,000
Income tax expense (50 percent)	$ 70,000
Net income	$ 70,000

Required

Compute the following ratios for the Griffin Company for the year ending December 31, 2001:

A. Profit margin ratio (before interest and taxes)

B. Total asset turnover

C. Rate of return on total assets

D. Rate of return on common stockholders' equity

E. Earnings per share of stock

F. Inventory turnover

G. Current ratio

H. Quick ratio

I. Accounts receivable turnover

J. Debt-to-equity ratio

K. Times Interest Earned

34. Avantronics is a manufacturer of electronic components and accessories with total assets of $20,000,000. Selected financial ratios for Avantronics and the industry averages for firms of similar size are as follows:

	AVANTRONICS			INDUSTRY AVERAGE
	1999	2000	2001	
Current ratio	2.09	2.27	2.51	2.24
Quick ratio	1.15	1.12	1.19	1.22
Inventory turnover	2.40	2.18	2.02	3.50
Profit margin	0.14	0.15	0.17	0.11
Debt-to-equity ratio	0.24	0.37	0.44	0.35

Avantronics is being reviewed by several entities whose interests vary, and the company's financial ratios are a part of the data being considered. Each of the following parties must recommend an action based on its evaluation of Avantronics' financial position.

MidCoastal Bank. The bank is processing Avantronics' application for a new five-year term note. MidCoastal has been the banker for Avantronics for several years but must reevaluate the company's financial position for each major transaction.

Ozawa Company. Ozawa is a new supplier to Avantronics and must decide on the appropriate credit terms to extend to the company.

Drucker & Denon. A brokerage firm specializing in the stock of electronics firms that are sold over the counter, Drucker & Denon must decide whether it will include Avantronics in a new fund being established for sale to Drucker & Denon's clients.

Working Capital Management Committee. This is a committee of Avantronics' management personnel chaired by the chief operating officer. The committee is responsible for periodically reviewing the company's working capital position, comparing actual data against budgets, and recommending changes in strategy as needed.

Required

A. Describe the analytical use of each of the five ratios just presented.

B. For each of the four entities described, identify the financial ratios, from those ratios presented, that would be most valuable as a basis for its decision regarding Avantronics.

C. Discuss what the financial ratios presented in the question reveal about Avantronics. Support your answer by citing specific ratio levels and trends as well as the interrelationships among these ratios.

35. Following are the income statements for Martha's Miscellaneous for 2001 and 2002.

Martha's Miscellaneous Comparative Statements of Income and Retained Earnings

	2002	2001	$ Change	% Change
Sales revenue	$700,000	$650,000		
Cost of goods sold	500,000	455,000		
Gross profit	$200,000	$195,000		
Payroll expense	50,000	42,250		
Insurance expense	30,000	29,000		
Rent expense	18,000	18,000		
Depreciation	35,000	15,000		
Total expenses	$133,000	$104,250		
Operating income	$ 67,000	$ 90,750		
Interest expense	(7,000)	(5,000)		
Gain on vehicle sale	25,000	—		
Loss on sale of securities	(25,000)	—		
Interest revenue	75,000	50,000		
Net income before interest & taxes	$135,000	$135,750		
Tax	40,000	40,250		
Net income	$95,000	$95,500		
Dividends	38,000	38,000		
Total retained earnings	$57,000	$57,500		
Retained earnings 1/1	193,000	136,000		
Retained earnings 12/31	$250,000	$193,000		

Required

Complete the comparative income statement by computing dollar change ($ change) and percentage change (% change).

36. Following are the balance sheets for Howard's Hammocks for December 31, 2002, and 2001.

Howard's Hammocks Comparative Balance Sheets

	2002	2001
Cash	$130,000	$110,000
Accounts receivable	130,000	120,000
Inventory	225,000	215,000
Prepaid insurance	25,000	30,000
Total current assets	$510,000	$475,000
Long-term investments	110,000	75,000
Land	200,000	175,000
Property & equipment	215,000	95,000
Accum. depr.	(105,000)	(80,000)
Total	$420,000	$265,000
Total assets	$930,000	$740,000
Accounts payable	$ 60,000	$ 50,000
Payroll payable	10,000	8,000
Taxes payable	10,000	9,000
Total current liabilities	$ 80,000	$ 67,000
Notes payable	100,000	80,000
Capital stock	500,000	400,000
Retained earnings	250,000	193,000
Total	$930,000	$740,000

Required

Using the preceding income statement figures, prepare common-size statements for 2002 and 2001.

Appendix A

Big Al's Pizza: Business Simulation

CHAPTER 1: THE DECISION TO EXPAND

Big Al's Pizza Emporium is a pizza restaurant in Tempe, Arizona. Big Al's has been very successful because it is located close to a major university, and most of the restaurant's business is from college-age customers. Big Al's would like to expand the business and sell pizzas to grocery and convenience stores and to school cafeterias. The restaurant staff would prepare and freeze the pizza for wholesale distribution. In order to expand, the business must acquire new kitchen space and equipment. The pizza restaurant is not capable of handling any additional volume. Big Al's has hired you to evaluate the proposed expansion and to lead the company through the first year of operations.

Required

A. What information do you think Big Al's should gather in order to analyze the feasibility of the expansion?

B. What do you think it costs to produce a 16-inch pizza? Make sure that you include all ingredients and some labor time, but don't worry about the equipment needed.

C. What equipment do you think the restaurant needs to acquire?

D. Using the decision-making model presented in this chapter, determine the problem definition.

E. What variables should be considered?

F. What qualitative factors should be considered in the decision?

CHAPTER 2: PRODUCT COSTS, SALES PRICE, AND CHANGES TO COSTS

Big Al's Pizza Inc., a new subsidiary of Big Al's Pizza Emporium, has been established to produce fresh, packaged 16-inch meat pizzas to be sold wholesale to grocery and convenience stores and school cafeterias. The marketing department has finished its market research and has determined that the current total market demand for fresh, packaged 16-inch pizzas is 150,000 units per month. As a new entrant to the market, the company's goal is to sell 25,000 pizzas in the first month and 325,000 pizzas in the first year. Following the first quarter, the goal is to increase sales by about 10 percent each year.

Big Al's deals exclusively with Pizza Products Inc. to purchase material and equipment. Pizza Products Inc. offers a full range of pizza supplies, from raw materials to semifinished products. It offers three levels of products: gold, its best-quality, most expensive brand; bronze, its most basic, cost-effective brand; and silver, its mainstream, midpriced brand.

Big Al's Pizza Inc. will have 10 production lines. Each of the five workers on each line will be responsible for one of the five stages of production: dough, sauce, cheese, toppings, and packaging. The time needed at each workstation on a production line follows. These time estimates include normal downtime, breaks, and so on.

Dough maker	2 minutes
Sauce maker	2 minutes
Cheese maker	2.5 minutes
Toppings	3 minutes
Packaging	2 minutes

Moving products between stations takes approximately 30 seconds. Therefore, the time required to produce one pizza is the total of all the time needed at each stage plus 2 minutes for product movement (four at 0.5 minute), or 13.5 minutes per pizza. The slowest stage in the process is applying the toppings—3 minutes—so the production process is limited to 20 pizzas per hour (60 minutes divided by 3 minutes). All production-line workers work 8 hours per day. Because it has 10 production lines, Big Al's can produce 200 pizzas per hour, or 1,600 pizzas per 8-hour shift. Assuming 20 workdays per month, Big Al's has the capacity to produce 32,000 pizzas per month, or 384,000 pizzas per year. However, as mentioned earlier, Big Al's goal is production of 325,000 pizzas during the first year.

Pizzas are produced in batches of up to 1,600, based on the orders received from grocery stores, convenience stores, and school cafeterias. All pizzas are shipped daily.

Following are the projected costs for Big Al's Inc.

Material Costs (per unit)

Complete dough shells	\$0.15 (gold)
	0.12 (silver)
	0.10 (bronze)
Complete sauce package	\$0.25 (gold)
	0.20 (silver)
	0.15 (bronze)
Complete cheese package	\$0.10 (gold)
	0.08 (silver)
	0.05 (bronze)
Complete meat package	\$0.40 (gold)
	0.30 (silver)
	0.25 (bronze)
Complete assembly package	\$0.05 (gold)
	0.04 (silver)
	0.03 (bronze)

The main difference in the three levels of product purchased from Pizza Products Inc. is the spoilage level and the quality of each ingredient. The normal spoilage is 0–2% for the gold level, 1–4% for the silver level, and 2–6% for the bronze level.

Direct labor employees are paid on an hourly basis according to hours worked. Once production-line workers finish a day's scheduled production, they are sent home. They can work a maximum of 8 hours each day without incurring overtime costs. The overtime premium is an additional 50 percent of the basic hourly rate of \$7.50. Assume 20 workdays per month. Supervisors and other indirect labor employees are salaried.

Labor Costs

Rate for direct labor	\$ 7.50 per hour (plus 30% fringe benefits)
Indirect labor:	
Supervisor (including fringe benefits)	3,500 per month
Other indirect labor (including fringe benefits)	2,000 per month

Overhead Costs (per month)

Rent on production facility	\$1,000
Utilities	1,500
Other overhead:	
Indirect material	2,500
Maintenance costs	1,500
Quality inspection costs	2,000
Equipment (lease cost)*	2,500

*The lease, for a term of 5 years, can be terminated at any time with a penalty of \$10,000.

Selling and Administrative Costs (per month)

Administrative salaries	$4,000 (including fringe benefits)
Salaries of sales staff	5,000 (including fringe benefits)
Product promotion and advertising	2,000
Rent on office space for administrative and sales staff	2,000
Utilities, insurance, etc.	500
Lease of office furniture and equipment	800

Required

Use the cost information given to answer the following questions.

A. What are the estimated direct material costs per pizza at each cost level?

B. What are the estimated direct labor costs per pizza?

C. What are the estimated manufacturing overhead costs per pizza?

D. What is the estimated total manufacturing cost per pizza at each cost level?

E. Big Al's production facility is organized in a very traditional fashion. The five production stages are all done in separate areas of the factory. In addition, employees on the production lines are responsible for only one task. Can you think of other, more efficient, ways to organize the production facility?

F. If you had to set a sales price for each type of pizza, what would it be? In addition to product costs, what other costs must the sales price cover?

G. Identify all period costs for Big Al's Pizza Inc. How much are they per month?

H. What if material costs increased 5 percent? What does that do to the sales price if the current markup is maintained? What factors should be considered if a decision must be made to raise the sales price or to leave it as is?

I. Discuss ways to lower costs and what impact each option could have on the business.

CHAPTER 3: OVERHEAD ALLOCATION AND ADDING A PRODUCT

As discussed in Chapter 2, Big Al's Pizza Inc. produces fresh, packaged 16-inch meat pizzas for sale to grocery stores, convenience stores, and school cafeterias. Big Al's deals exclusively with Pizza Products Inc. to purchase ingredients and equipment. The cost of material, labor, overhead, and selling and administrative costs is provided in Chapter 2.

During the first year of operations, Big Al's determined the cost of overhead to be allocated to each of its pizzas by dividing the total amount of overhead expected to be incurred for the year by the expected annual production. The predetermined overhead rate for its first year of operation was therefore:

Predetermined overhead rate =
$198,000/325,000 pizzas = $.609 per pizza.

During the first month of operation (January), Big Al's produced 25,784 pizzas. Direct material costs were $19,854 (materials were purchased at the silver-quality level) and direct labor costs were $55,950 for 5,960 hours worked. Overhead during January was equal to $17,200.

In its second year of operations, Big Al's has decided to expand the product line by producing a veggie pizza. This new pizza will require the purchase of a veggie package from Pizza Products Inc. at a cost of $0.20, $0.18, or $0.15, respectively for gold-, silver-, and bronze-quality levels. Of course, the meat package will not be required. All other ingredients and prices remain the same

The veggie toppings require additional processing time (cutting and dicing) of approximately 1 minute per pizza. Therefore, the total time to apply toppings for a veggie pizza is 4 minutes, compared to 3 minutes for a meat pizza. The remaining processing time for dough, sauce, cheese, and packaging is the same for the new veggie pizza and the meat pizza. Total processing time for the veggie pizza is therefore 14.5 minutes, compared to 13.5 minutes for the meat pizza.

The new veggie pizza is not expected to affect sales of the meat pizza. In the second year of operations, Big Al's expects to produce and to sell about 350,000 meat pizzas and 25,000 veggie pizzas.

Increasing production is expected to increase overhead costs by 5 percent in year 2. Direct labor costs are not expected to change. The costs of product promotion and advertising are expected to increase to $3,000 per month. All other selling and administrative costs are expected to remain the same as in year 1.

Production during January of year 2 was 28,761 meat pizzas and 2,118 veggie pizzas. Direct material costs were $21,858 for the meat pizzas and $1,165 for the veggie pizzas. Direct labor costs were $43,605 for the meat pizzas and $3,037.50 for the veggie pizzas, representing 6,460 and 450 direct labor hours, respectively. Overhead costs during January were $19,825.

Required

Use the information given to answer the following questions.

- **A.** Comment on Big Al's allocation of overhead based on the estimated number of pizzas to be produced in year 1. Was it appropriate when Big Al's produced only one type of pizza?
- **B.** Using normal costing, what was the cost of the 25,784 meat pizzas produced in January of year 1?
- **C.** Was overhead over- or underapplied in January of year 1?
- **D.** Can Big Al's still allocate overhead based on the number of pizzas produced in year 2?
- **E.** What appears to be the most logical cost driver for allocating overhead in year 2?
- **F.** Compute a predetermined overhead rate for Big Al's in year 2, using the cost driver you identified in E.
- **G.** Using normal costing and the predetermined overhead rate calculated in F, compute the total manufacturing cost for the 28,761 meat pizzas and the 2,118 veggie pizzas made in January of year 2.
- **H.** Assuming that in year 2, Big Al's applies overhead based on the number of units expected to be produced, compute the total manufacturing costs for the meat pizzas and the veggie pizzas made in January. Compare the two methods and comment on the differences.
- **I.** The marketing manager of Big Al's estimates year 3 sales of 385,000 meat pizzas and 30,000 veggie pizzas. The production manager is concerned about being able to produce that number of pizzas without incurring significant overtime or making changes in the production process. In terms of the four-step decision-making model, outline the problem, potential objectives, and options that the management team of Big Al's should consider.

CHAPTER 4: CONVERSION TO AN ABC SYSTEM

As you will recall from Chapter 2, Big Al's expects to incur the following overhead costs in year 1. Costs are expected to increase by 5 percent in year 2.

Estimated Year 1 Overhead Costs (per month)

Rent on production facility	$1,000
Utilities	1,500
Indirect labor:	
Supervisors (including fringe benefits)	3,500
Other indirect labor (including fringe benefits)	$2,000

Other overhead:	
Indirect material	2,500
Maintenance costs	1,500
Miscellaneous factory costs	2,000
Equipment (lease cost)	2,500

Lee Dworsky, the accounting manager at Big Al's, has just returned from a conference on activity-based costing and thinks that Big Al's should consider implementing an ABC system at the beginning of year 2. Lee has identified five primary activities taking place in the production facility at Big Al's, has traced overhead costs to each activity, and has identified a cost driver for each activity as follows:

Estimated Year 2 Overhead Costs

Activity	Monthly Overhead Cost	Cost Driver
Material delivery and handling	$4,410	Number of shipments
Assembly of pizzas	5,670	Direct labor hours
Packaging	1,260	Number of pizzas
Storage of materials	3,150	Refrigerator space
Quality inspections	2,835	Number of inspections

The estimated activity for each cost driver follows.

Cost Driver	Meat Pizza (350,000 pizzas)	Veggie Pizza (25,000 pizzas)	Total
Number of material shipments	52	104	156
Direct labor hours	?	?	?
Number of pizzas	350,000	25,000	375,000
Refrigerator space (cubic feet)	2,500	700	3,200
Number of inspections	75,000	3,000	78,000

Required

A. Using the overhead categories identified previously for year 1, classify Big Al's overhead costs as unit level, batch level, product level, or facility level.

B. Based on information provided in Chapters 2 and 3, calculate the number of direct labor hours expected to be incurred in manufacturing 350,000 meat pizzas and 25,000 veggie pizzas.

C. Using the preceding activities and drivers, calculate a predetermined overhead rate for each activity.

D. Using ABC, how much estimated overhead would be allocated to a meat pizza and a veggie pizza?

E. Compare the estimated overhead allocation using ABC to the estimated overhead allocation using direct labor hours or number of pizzas.

F. What are some of the advantages and disadvantages of using ABC in this case?

G. Would you suggest that Big Al's adopt an ABC system?

H. Does the information provided by the ABC system give you some insight into areas of cost reduction? What areas have the greatest potential for cost reduction, and what are the potential impacts on the business from these cost reductions?

CHAPTER 5: ESTIMATING OVERHEAD

During the first two years of operations, Big Al's overhead costs have fluctuated from month to month. Although overhead appears to go up and down according to the number of pizzas produced each month, the accounting manager has noticed that that is not always the case. For example, in the fourteenth month of operations, the manufacturing facility was closed for almost 10 days because of severe weather, and production for the month was very low. However, overhead costs were only about 25 percent lower than those incurred in the previous month. In an effort to estimate overhead costs in year 3, the manager has collected the following information for the past 24 months of operation and has asked for your assistance in analyzing the data.

Month	Pizzas Produced	Total Overhead Costs
1	25,784	$17,200
2	25,897	17,300
3	25,750	17,450
4	26,352	17,600
5	27,567	17,950
6	28,492	18,125
7	27,398	17,900
8	28,112	17,955
9	29,499	18,507
10	28,879	18,295
11	29,344	18,325
12	29,399	18,550
13	30,879	19,825
14	15,167	14,800
15	28,379	18,732
16	29,765	19,832
17	30,334	19,965
18	30,761	19,786
19	31,300	20,359
20	31,804	20,149
21	31,795	20,508
22	32,016	20,489
23	32,379	21,166
24	32,675	20,852

Required

A. Do the data present any special problems that might impact the accuracy of using either the high/low method or regression analysis to predict overhead costs? What suggestions would you make to company accountant Lee Dworsky before analyzing the data?

B. Use the high/low method to estimate the fixed and variable components of total overhead costs.

C. What if the accountant takes your advice and considers month 14 an outlier? Redo the calculation in B to reflect this change.

D. Use regression analysis to estimate the fixed and variable components of total overhead costs.

E. Should the accounting manager consider using an independent variable other than pizzas produced to predict overhead costs?

F. During year 3, Big Al's estimates January production of 33,000 pizzas. Based on this estimate of production, how much overhead would you estimate for Big Al's?

G. How else might Lee Dworsky estimate overhead costs in year 3?

CHAPTER 6: CVP, BREAK-EVEN, AND TARGET PROFIT ANALYSIS

During the third year of operations, Big Al's estimates that 415,000 pizzas (385,000 meat pizzas and 30,000 veggie pizzas) will be produced. Direct materials are purchased at the silver level for each pizza. Direct labor costs per unit are estimated to be the same as in year 2, as are selling and administrative costs.

Required

A. Compute the break-even point in year 3 for Big Al's Pizza. Use the regression results without the outlier from Chapter 5 to estimate variable- and fixed-overhead costs. Assume a 30 percent markup on cost to arrive at the sales price for each pizza.

B. What options does Big Al's have to reduce the break-even point? Discuss both the quantitative and the qualitative factors that must be considered with each option.

C. How many meat and veggie pizzas, respectively, would Big Al's need to sell in year 3 to earn a before-tax profit of $150,000?

D. If its tax rate is 30 percent, how many pizzas does Big Al's need to sell in year 3 to earn an after-tax profit of $150,000?

E. How will the break-even point change if the sales mix changes to 80 percent meat pizzas and 20 percent veggie pizzas?

F. Should Big Al's lower the markup percentage to try and increase market share? What are the consequences of this decision on the long-term health of the business?

G. What would happen to the break-even point if labor costs increased by 10 percent?

H. What would happen to the break-even point if Big Al's decided to change to gold-level ingredients? Bronze level? What are potential impacts on the business from those two actions?

I. What would happen to the break-even point if Big Al's decided to mark up production costs by 10 percent—to 40 percent—to arrive at the sales price? What are potential impacts on the business from that action?

CHAPTER 7: PRICING STRATEGY, SPECIAL ORDERS, MAKE VERSUS BUY, AND THEORY OF CONSTRAINTS

Currently, Big Al's uses cost-plus pricing, adding a markup of 30 percent on total manufacturing costs. However, competitors are offering similar meat pizzas and veggie pizzas for $6 each.

Required

A. Comment on Big Al's current pricing strategy. What recommendations would you make?

B. In year 3, Big Al's receives a special offer from an athletic arena to purchase 5,000 meat pizzas and 3,000 veggie pizzas for a special event. Assuming sufficient excess capacity, what is the minimum price that Big Al's would be willing to accept for this special order? Without excess capacity, what minimum price would be acceptable? What qualitative factors should Big Al's consider?

C. Big Al's is considering purchasing all ingredients separately rather than buying them prepackaged from Pizza Products Inc. This will reduce direct material costs by 5 percent but will require the hiring of five new employees, at a cost of $2,000 each per month, to prepare dough, sauce, cheese, and meat. This will raise the cost of labor by $0.16 per pizza. Should Big Al's continue to buy the prepackaged ingredients from the outside supplier or buy them separately and assemble them in-house? What qualitative factors should Big Al's consider in making this decision?

D. Big Al's is nearing its manufacturing capacity and needs to consider ways to increase throughput. What options does Big Al's have to increase capacity? What bottlenecks does it face? What recommendations would you make?

CHAPTER 8: LONG-TERM CAPITAL BUDGETING

As discussed in earlier chapters, Big Al's currently leases its equipment from Pizza Products Inc. for $2,500 per month. Two years of the 5-year lease term remain. Big Al's can terminate the lease at any time by paying a penalty of $10,000. Big Al's is considering purchasing equipment to replace the equipment being leased. Big Al's can purchase equipment at the following prices:

Equipment	Price (per unit)
Dough ball press	$5,450
Assembly table	2,100
Cardboard cutter	4,100
Plastic sealer	2,695
Label installer	1,000

One unit of each piece of equipment is used on each of Big Al's 10 assembly lines. (Big Al's must purchase 10 units of each piece of equipment.) If purchased, all equipment will be depreciated over 5 years, using straight-line depreciation, and will have no salvage value. Big Al's tax rate is 40 percent.

Required

A. Using NPV analysis, compare the present value of the lease payments with the cost of buying the equipment. Assuming a discount rate of 10 percent, which option is preferable?

B. Big Al's has the option of purchasing equipment from another supplier at a cost of $190,000. The supplier promises that the new equipment will reduce operating costs by $1,000 per month over the life of the equipment. Assuming a 10 percent discount rate, which option is preferable?

C. Calculate the after-tax NPV for each option discussed previously. Is your decision still the same?

D. What factors other than cost savings should Big Al's consider in these decision problems?

CHAPTER 9: BUDGETS AND CASH FLOWS

Big Al's Pizza Inc. needs a cash budget for year 3 and has provided you with the following information. Sales are all on account and are estimated to be collected over a three-month period, with 70 percent collected in the month of sale, 25 percent collected the next month, and 4 percent collected the third month. The remaining 1 percent is estimated to be uncollectible. December and November sales from the previous year were $201,638 and $185,000, respectively.

Because of the lag in collecting cash from sales on account, Big Al's delays payment on some of its purchases of materials. Big Al's estimates that 60 percent of each month's material purchases are paid in the month of purchase and 40 percent in the following month. The accounts payable balance for materials at the end of the previous year was $20,000.

Big Al's also requires a minimum balance of $40,000 in cash at the end of each month. The company will use its line of credit when needed to bring the balance up to that minimum level. For any money borrowed, the interest rate is 6 percent compounded annually. For simplicity, you can assume that cash is borrowed on the first day of the month and that loan repayments are made at the end of the month.

Big Al's plans to exercise the option on the leased production equipment in March (as described in Chapter 2). The purchase price on the equipment will be $153,450, with payments of $3,260.36 per month. Big Al's also plans on expanding the existing production space in May at a cost of $200,000. Big Al's would like to finance the expansion out of current earnings and so will use the line of credit, if necessary, in May. The expansion will cause fixed manufacturing overhead to increase by $10,000 per month, starting in May.

Required

A. Prepare a cash receipts budget for year 3, assuming estimated sales of 385,000 meat pizzas and 30,000 veggie pizzas and the following monthly distribution of sales. Assume cost and sales prices from Chapter 6.

January	8.3%	July	8.5%
February	9.2	August	9.8
March	10.3	September	7.5
April	7.6	October	9.1
May	8.0	November	7.2
June	6.9	December	7.6

B. Prepare a cash disbursements budget for the year.

C. Prepare a summary cash budget for the year, showing any borrowing and repayment of debt with interest. Discuss Big Al's ability to repay the expansion loan. Include a discussion of the feasibility of the project. Include qualitative factors to be considered.

D. What if the sales forecast was increased by 50 percent? What impact does that have on the budget, and what is the potential impact on the company?

CHAPTER 10: SALES PRICE AND VARIANCES

In December (month 24) of year 2 of operations, Big Al's produced and sold 32,675 pizzas, consisting of 30,570 meat pizzas and 2,105 veggie pizzas. The budgeted sales price for meat pizzas was $4.52; for veggie pizzas, $4.59. The estimated production and sales during December was 31,678 meat pizzas and 2,595 veggie pizzas.

Required

A. Compute the price and volume variances for sales, assuming that Big Al's sold all pizzas produced for $137,565 (meat) and $9,051 (veggie). What might explain these variances?

B. Compute the price and quantity variances for direct materials for each type of pizza, assuming that Big Al's paid $29,093 for 32,325 units of raw material for meat pizzas and $1,453 for 2,401 units of raw material for veggie pizzas. (A unit consists of dough shell, sauce, cheese, meat or veggies, and assembly materials). In addition, 30,955 units were used to produce meat pizzas, and 2,149 units were used to produce veggie pizzas. The budgeted (standard) costs of materials were based on the purchase of silver-level ingredients. How would these variances be interpreted? What might explain these variances? Would you consider them to be material?

C. Compute the labor rate and efficiency variances, assuming that Big Al's paid $71,350 in labor costs for 7,150 hours of labor for meat pizzas and $6,425 in labor costs for 650 hours of labor for veggie pizzas. How would these variances be interpreted? What might explain them? Would you consider them to be material?

D. Compute the variable-overhead rate and efficiency variances, assuming that Big Al's paid \$20,852 in total overhead costs consisting of \$17,002 of variable overhead and \$3,850 of fixed overhead. Use the predetermined overhead rate, using direct labor hours as a base from Chapter 3. How would these variances be interpreted? What might explain these variances? Would you consider them to be material?

E. How might Big Al's extend its variance analysis to be compatible with its use of activity-based costing as discussed in Chapter 4?

CHAPTER 11: TRANSFER PRICING

Big Al's Pizza Emporium, a subsidiary of Big Al's Pizza Inc., has decided to sell frozen pizzas in its restaurants. Restaurant customers will take these pizzas home and cook them. The restaurants will sell frozen meat pizzas for \$10 and frozen veggie pizzas for \$11.50.

Although the restaurants would like to purchase the pizzas from Big Al's Pizza Inc., Big Al's Pizza Emporium has found an unrelated supplier that will provide the meat pizzas for \$4.55 and veggie pizzas for \$5.75. Assume that Big Al's Pizza Inc. has excess capacity and can supply the frozen pizzas to Big Al's Pizza Emporium without affecting sales.

Required

A. Using estimated cost data for year 3, at what minimum price should Big Al's Pizza Inc. agree to transfer meat and veggie pizzas to Big Al's Pizza Emporium?

B. What is the maximum price that Big Al's Pizza Emporium should pay Big Al's Pizza Inc. for the pizzas?

C. If Big Al's Pizza Emporium purchases pizzas from Big Al's Pizza Inc., what is the ideal transfer price? Why?

D. Should Big Al's Pizza Emporium buy pizzas from Big Al's Pizza Inc.? What qualitative factors should be considered in making this decision?

E. What should the transfer price be if Big Al's Pizza Inc. is at full capacity?

GLOSSARY

Abnormal spoilage Spoilage resulting from unusual circumstances, including improper handling, poorly trained employees, faulty equipment, and so on (p. 67)

Absorption (full) costing A method of costing in which product costs include direct material, direct labor, and fixed and variable overhead; required for external financial statements and for income tax reporting (p. 187)

Accounting information system (AIS) A transaction processing system that captures financial data resulting from accounting transactions within a company (p. 4)

Accounts receivable turnover ratio One of the best measures of the efficiency of the collection process (p. 488)

Activities Procedures or processes that cause work to be accomplished (p. 99)

Activity-based costing (ABC) A system of allocating overhead costs that assumes that activities, not volume of production, cause overhead costs to be incurred (p. 99)

Activity-based management (ABM) A system that focuses on managing activities to reduce costs and to make better decisions (p. 110)

Allocation The process of finding a logical method of assigning overhead costs to the products or services a company produces (p. 69)

Annuity A series of cash flows of equal amount paid or received at regular intervals (p. 272)

Appraisal (detection) costs Costs incurred to inspect finished products or products in the process of production (p. 403)

Asset turnover The measure of activity used in the ROI calculation; it measures the sales that are generated for a given level of assets (p. 374)

Backflush costing A costing system in which manufacturing costs are directly flushed into cost of goods sold instead of flowing through inventory (p. 76)

Balanced-scorecard approach Uses a set of financial and nonfinancial measures that relate to the critical success factors of any organization (p. 398)

Bottlenecks Production-process steps that limit throughput or the number of finished products that go through the production process (p. 220)

Break-even point The level of sales at which contribution margin just covers fixed costs and net income is equal to zero (p. 174)

Budget variance The difference between the amount of fixed overhead actually incurred and the flexible budget amount; also known as the spending variance (p. 342)

Budgets Plans dealing with the acquisition and use of resources over a specified time period (p. 292)

Capital investment decisions Long term decisions involving the purchase (or lease) of new machinery and equipment and the acquisition or expansion of facilities used in a business (p. 246)

Cash disbursements budget Used to project the amount of cash to be disbursed during the budget period (p. 305)

Cash equivalent An item that can be readily converted to a known amount of cash and has an original maturity to the investor of three months or less (p. 455)

Cash flow adequacy A measure of cash available to meet future debt obligations (p. 466)

Cash receipts budget Used to project the amount of cash expected to be received from sales and cash collections from customers (p. 303)

Common costs Indirect costs that are incurred to benefit more than one segment and cannot be directly traced to a particular segment or allocated in a reasonable manner (p. 370)

Common-size financial statements Statements in which all items have been restated as a percentage of a selected item on the statements (p. 482)

Compound interest Interest on the invested amount plus interest on previous interest earned but not withdrawn (p. 263)

Constraint A restriction that occurs when the capacity to manufacture a product or provide a service is limited in some manner (p. 219)

Contribution margin per unit The sales price per unit of product less all variable costs to produce and to sell the unit of product; used to calculate the change in contribution margin resulting from a change in unit sales (p. 165)

Contribution margin ratio The contribution margin divided by sales; used to calculate the change in contribution margin resulting from a dollar change in sales (p. 166)

Control Involves ensuring that the objectives and goals developed by the organization are being attained; often involves a comparison of budgets to actual performance and the use of budgets for performance evaluation purposes (p. 294). Involves the motivation and monitoring of employees and the evaluation of people and other resources used in the operations of the organization (p. 330)

Controlling activities The motivation and monitoring of employees and the evaluation of people and other resources used in the operations of the organization (p. 8)

Cost behavior How costs react to changes in production volume or other levels of activity (p. 132)

Cost center An organizational segment, or division, in which the manager has control over costs but not over revenue or investment decisions (p. 368)

Cost drivers Factors that cause, or drive, the incurrence of costs (p. 69)

Cost of capital What the firm would have to pay to borrow (issue bonds) or raise funds through equity (issue stock) in the financial marketplace (p. 248)

Cost pools Groups of overhead costs that are similar; used to simplify the task of assigning costs to products using ABC costing (p. 70)

Cost-plus pricing A method of pricing in which managers determine the cost of the product or service and then add a markup percentage to that cost to arrive at the sales price (p. 206)

Cost-volume-profit (CVP) analysis A tool that focuses on the relationship between a company's profits and (1) the prices of products or services, (2) the volume of products or services, (3) the per unit variable costs, (4) the total fixed costs, and (5) the mix of products or services produced (p. 164)

Current ratio A measure of an entity's liquidity; also known as working capital ratio (p. 485)

Customer relationship management (CRM) Designed to bring a company closer to its customers in order to serve them better (p. 427)

Customer response time The time it takes to deliver the product or service after the order is received (p. 406)

Data Reports, such as financial statements, customer lists, inventory records, and so on (p. 420)

Data mining A process of searching and extracting information from data (p. 424)

Data warehouses Central depositories for electronic data (p. 424)

Decentralized organization An organization in which decision-making authority is spread throughout the organization (p. 366)

Decision making The process of identifying alternative courses of action and selecting an appropriate alternative in a given decision-making situation (p. 12)

Dependent variable The variable in regression analysis that is dependent on changes in the independent variable (p. 140)

Direct labor Labor that can easily and conveniently be traced to particular products (p. 35)

Direct labor budget Used to project the dollar amount of direct labor cost needed for production (p. 301)

Direct materials Materials that can easily and conveniently be traced to the final product (p. 34)

Direct method Reports cash collected from customers and cash paid for inventory, salaries, wages, and so on (p. 455)

Discount rate Used as a hurdle rate, or minimum rate of return in calculations of the time value of money; adjusted to reflect risk and uncertainty (p. 248)

Diverse Products Products that consume resources in different proportions (p. 109)

E-business Business activities conducted electronically (p. 421)

Earnings management A method of recording used to "smooth" earnings from quarter to quarter or to otherwise manipulate financial results for a steady income stream (p. 435)

Economic value added (EVA) A contemporary measure of performance focusing on shareholder wealth (p. 380)

Electronic data interchange (EDI) The electronic transmission of data, such as purchase orders and invoices (p. 426)

Employee fraud The main focus of employee fraud is taking possession of assets or cash of the organization (p. 436)

Enterprise resource planning (ERP) systems Systems used to collect, organize, report, and distribute organizational data and transform that data into critical information and knowledge (p. 4). Used to collect, organize, report, and distribute data from all aspects of a company's business and to transform that data into useful knowledge (p. 424)

Equivalent units The number of finished units that can be made from the materials, labor, and overhead included in partially completed units (p. 75)

External auditor Usually a CPA independent of the organization being audited (p. 437)

External failure costs Costs incurred when a defective product is delivered to a customer (p. 403)

Financing activities Include cash flows from selling or repurchasing capital stock, long-term borrowing, and contributions from owners (p. 453)

Finished-goods inventory Inventory of finished product waiting for sale and shipment to customers (p. 31)

Fixed costs Costs that remain the same in total when production volume increases or decreases but vary per unit (p. 132)

Flexible budget variance The difference between the flexible budget operating income and actual operating income (p. 335)

Flexible budgets Take differences in spending owing to volume differences out of the analysis by budgeting for labor (and other costs) based on the *actual* number of units produced (p. 314)

Fraud A false representation of a material fact made by one party with the intent to deceive and induce another party to justifiably rely on the fact to his or her detriment (p. 434)

Fringe benefits Payroll costs in addition to the basic hourly wage (p. 68)

Gross profit The difference between sales and cost of goods sold (p. 164)

Horizontal analysis When financial statements are analyzed over time (p. 479)

Ideal standard A standard that is attained only when near-perfect conditions are present (p. 331)

Idle time Worker time that is not used in the production of the finished product (p. 68)

Independent variable The variable in regression analysis that drives changes in the dependent variable (p. 140)

Indirect labor Labor used in the production of products but not directly traceable to the specific product (p. 35)

Indirect materials Materials used in the production of products but not directly traceable to the specific product (p. 35)

Indirect method Starts with net income and removes the impact of noncash items and accruals (p. 455)

Information Data that have been organized, processed, and summarized (p. 420)

Internal auditor An auditor employed by the organization being audited (p. 436)

Internal control A process, effected by an entity's board of directors, management, and other personnel, designed to provide reasonable assurance regarding the achievement of objectives in the following categories: (1) reliability of financial reporting, (2) compliance with applicable laws and regulations, and (3) effectiveness and efficiency of operations (p. 437)

Internal control procedures Used to address areas of risk that were identified during the risk-assessment process (p. 439)

Internal failure costs Costs incurred once the product is produced and then determined to be defective (p. 403)

Internal rate of return (IRR) The actual yield, or return, earned by an investment (p. 248)

Investing activities Include the purchase and sale of property, plant, and equipment; the purchases and sales of securities; and loans made as investments (p. 453)

Investment center An organizational segment, or division, in which the manager has control over costs, revenue, and investment decisions (p. 369)

ISO 9000 A set of guidelines for quality management focusing on the design, production, inspection, testing, installing, and servicing of products, processes, and services (p. 402)

Just-in-time (JIT) production systems The philosophy of having raw materials arrive just in time to be used in production and for finished-goods inventory to be completed just in time to be shipped to customers (p. 31)

Job costing A costing system that accumulates, tracks, and assigns costs for each job produced by a company (p. 65)

Kaizen A system of improvement based on a series of gradual and often small improvements (p. 401)

Knowledge Information that is shared and exploited so that it adds value to an organization (p. 420)

Knowledge warehouses Used to store and provide access to a wide variety of qualitative data (p. 424)

Life-cycle cost The costs accumulated over the entire life cycle of a product (p. 205)

Life-cycle costing Includes all the costs incurred throughout a product's life, not just in the manufacturing and selling of the product (p. 36)

Liquidity A measure of the ability of a company to meet its immediate financial obligations (p. 483)

Management by exception The process of taking action only when actual results deviate significantly from planned (p. 330)

Management fraud Typically involves misstating the financial statements in order to mislead readers of the financial statements, such as stockholders and creditors (p. 434)

Manufacturing companies Companies that purchase raw materials from other companies and transform those raw materials into a finished product (p. 30)

Manufacturing costs Costs incurred in the factory or plant to produce a product; typically consists of three elements: direct materials, direct labor, and manufacturing overhead (p. 34)

Manufacturing overhead Indirect material and labor and any other expenses related to the production of products but not directly traceable to the specific product (p. 35)

Manufacturing-cycle efficiency (MCE) The value-added time in the production process divided by the throughput, or cycle, time (p. 407)

Manufacturing-cycle time The total time a product is in production, which includes process time, inspection time, wait time, and move time; cycle time will include both value-added and non-value-added time (p. 407)

Manufacturing-overhead budget Used to project the dollar amount of manufacturing overhead needed for production (p. 302)

Margin For each sales dollar, the percentage that is recognized as net profit (p. 374)

Markup percentage The amount added to cost to determine the sales price in cost-plus pricing; must be sufficient to cover any costs not included in the company's definition of product cost plus produce an acceptable profit (p. 207)

Material price variance The difference between the actual price and the standard price times the actual volume purchased (p. 337)

Material purchases budget Used to project the dollar amount of raw material purchased for production (p. 299)

Mixed costs Costs that include both a fixed and a variable component, making it difficult to predict the behavior of a mixed cost as production changes unless the cost is first separated into its fixed and variable components (p. 136)

Net operating income Net income from operations before interest and taxes (p. 374)

Net present value (NPV) A technique for considering the time value of money whereby the present value of all cash inflows associated with a project is compared with the present value of all cash outflows (p. 248)

Nonmanufacturing costs Costs that include selling and administrative costs (p. 35)

Non-value-added activities Activities that can be eliminated without affecting the quality or performance of a product (p. 111)

Normal spoilage Spoilage resulting from the regular operations of the production process (p. 67)

Operating Involves day-to-day decision making by managers, which is often facilitated by budgeting (p. 294)

Operating activities The day-to-day operations of a business (p. 8). Include acquiring and selling products in the normal course of business (p. 452)

Operating assets Typically include cash, accounts receivable, inventory, and property, plant, and equipment needed to operate a business (p. 374)

Operating budgets Used to plan for the short term (typically one year or less) (p. 297)

Operating leverage The contribution margin divided by net income; used as an indicator of how sensitive net income is to the change in sales (p. 185)

Operations costing A hybrid of job and process costing; used by companies that make products in batches (p. 65)

Opportunity costs The benefits forgone by choosing one alternative over another (p. 15)

Outsourcing or make-or-buy decision A short-term decision to outsource labor or purchase components used in manufacturing from another company rather than to provide services or to produce components internally (p. 212)

Overapplied overhead The amount of applied overhead in excess of actual overhead (p. 74)

Overtime premiums An additional amount added to the basic hourly wage owing to overtime worked by the workers (p. 68)

Payback period The length of time needed for a long-term project to recapture, or pay back, the initial investment (p. 261)

Performance fraud Another term for management fraud, used because the manipulation of the financial information is often designed to inflate earnings or to cover up a decline in financial position (p. 435)

Performance report Provides key financial and nonfinancial measures of performance for a particular segment (p. 368)

Period costs Costs that are expensed in the period incurred; attached to the period as opposed to the product (p. 42)

Planning The development of both the short-term (operational) and the long-term (strategic) objectives and goals of an organization and an identification of the resources needed to achieve them (p. 7). The cornerstone of good management; involves developing objectives and goals for the organization, as well as the actual preparation of budgets (p. 294)

Practical standard A standard that should be attained under normal, efficient operating conditions (p. 331)

Predetermined overhead rates Used to apply overhead to products; calculated by dividing the estimated overhead for a cost pool by the estimated units of the cost driver (p. 73)

Preference decisions Decisions that involve choosing between alternatives (p. 247)

Present value (PV) The amount of future cash flows discounted to their equivalent worth today (p. 263)

Prevention costs Costs incurred to prevent product failures from occurring, typically related to design and engineering (p. 403)

Pro forma financial statements Budgeted financial statements that are sometimes used for internal planning purposes but more often are used by external users (p. 307)

Process costing A costing system that accumulates and tracks costs for each process performed and then assigns those costs equally to each unit produced (p. 65)

Product costs Costs that attach to the products as they go through the manufacturing process; also called inventoriable costs (p. 42)

Production budget Used to forecast how many units of product to produce in order to meet the sales projections (p. 298)

Productivity A measure of the relationship between outputs and inputs (p. 404)

Profit center An organizational segment, or division, in which the manager has control over both costs and revenue but not investment decisions (p. 368)

Profitability index (PI) Calculated by dividing the present value of cash inflows by the initial investment (p. 253)

Qualitative Deals with nonnumerical attributes or characteristics (p. 13)

Quality Usually defined as meeting or exceeding customers' expectations (p. 401)

Quantitative Can be expressed in terms of dollars or other quantities (units, pounds, etc.) (p. 13)

Quick ratio A strict test of a company's ability to pay its current debts with highly liquid current assets (p. 487)

R square (R^2) A measure of goodness of fit (how well the regression line "fits" the data) (p. 143)

Raw materials inventory Inventory of materials needed in the production process but not yet moved to the production area (p. 31)

Regression analysis The procedure that uses statistical methods (least squares regression) to fit a cost line (called a regression line) through a number of data points (p. 139)

Relevant costs Those costs that differ between alternatives (p. 15)

Relevant range The normal range of production that can be expected for a particular product and company (p. 133)

Residual income The amount of income earned in excess of a predetermined minimum level of return on assets (p. 378)

Resource utilization decision A decision requiring an analysis of how best to use a resource that is available in limited supply (p. 219)

Responsibility accounting An accounting system that assigns responsibility to a manager for those areas that are under that manager's control (p. 367)

Return on investment (ROI) Measures the rate of return generated by an investment center's assets (p. 373)

Revenue center An organizational segment, or division, in which the manager has control over revenue but not costs or investment decisions (p. 368)

Risk The likelihood that an option chosen in a decision situation will yield unsatisfactory results (p. 16)

Risk assessment and control Involves identifying potential risks of the organization and also ways to minimize or manage those risks (p. 438)

Sales budget Used in planning the cash needs for manufacturing, merchandising, and service companies (p. 296)

Sales forecast Combines with the sales budget to form the starting points in the preparation of production budgets for manufacturing companies, purchases budgets for merchandising companies, and labor budgets for service companies (p. 296)

Sales price variance Computed by comparing the actual sales price to the flexible budget sales price times the actual sales volume (p. 335)

Sales volume variance The difference between the actual sales volume and the budgeted sales volume times the budgeted contribution margin (p. 333)

Screening decisions Decisions about whether an investment meets a predetermined company standard (p. 247)

Segment costs All costs attributable to a particular segment of an organization but only those costs that are actually caused by the segment (p. 369)

Segment margin The profit margin of a particular segment of an organization, typically the best measure of long-run profitability (p. 371)

Segmented income statements Calculate income for each major segment of an organization in addition to the company as a whole (p. 369)

Sensitivity analysis The process of changing the values of key variables to determine how sensitive decisions are to those changes (p. 16). Used to highlight decisions that may be affected by changes in expected cash flows (p. 260)

Simple interest Interest on the invested amount only (p. 263)

Special-order decisions Short-run pricing decisions in which management must decide what sales price is appropriate when customers place orders that are different from those placed in the regular course of business (larger quantity, one-time sale to a foreign customer, etc.) (p. 209)

Standard cost A budget for a single unit of product or service (p. 330)

Standard price The budgeted price of the material, labor, or overhead for each unit (p. 331)

Standard quantity The budgeted amount of material, labor, or overhead for each product (p. 330)

Static budgets Budgets that are set at the beginning of the period and remain constant throughout the budget period (p. 313)

Step costs Costs that vary with activity in steps and may look like and be treated as either variable costs or fixed costs; step costs are technically not fixed costs but may be treated as such if they remain constant within a relevant range of production (p. 136)

Strategic business unit (SBU) Another term for investment center (p. 369)

Summary cash budget Consists of three sections: (1) cash flows from operating activities, (2) cash flows from investing activities, and (3) cash flows from financing activities; these three sections are the same as used in the cash flow statement prepared under generally accepted accounting principles (GAAP) (p. 306)

Sunk costs Costs that have already been incurred (p. 15)

Supply-chain management Includes a variety of activities centered on making the purchase of materials and inventory more efficient and less costly (p. 427)

Target pricing A pricing method used when a price is preset by market conditions or when a company wishes to set a price in order to capture a predetermined market share or to meet other marketing goals (p. 206)

Task analysis A method of setting standards that also examines the production process in detail to determine what it should cost to produce a product (p. 331)

Theory of constraints A management tool for dealing with constraints; identifies and focuses on bottlenecks in the production process (p. 220)

Throughput The amount of product produced in a given amount of time, such as a day, week, or month (p. 407)

Time and material pricing A pricing method often used in service industries, in which labor is the primary cost incurred (p. 207)

Time value of money The concept that a dollar received (paid) today is worth more (less) than a dollar received (paid) in the future (p. 246)

Transfer price The price charged by one segment, or division, to another segment, or division, within the same organization for the transfer of goods or services (p. 382)

Trend analysis Horizontal analysis of multiple years of data (p. 481)

Underapplied overhead The amount of actual overhead in excess of applied overhead (p. 74)

Usage variance The difference between the actual quantity and the standard quantity times the standard price (p. 337)

Value chain The set of activities that increase the value of an organization's products and services: research and development, design, production, marketing, distribution, and customer service activities (p. 36)

Value pricing A pricing method that bases the price of services on the perceived or actual value of the service provided to a customer (p. 208)

Variable costs Costs that stay the same per unit but change in total as production volume increases or decreases (p. 132)

Variable (direct) costing A method of costing in which product costs include direct material, direct labor, and variable overhead; fixed overhead is treated as a period cost; consistent with CVP's focus on cost behavior (p. 187)

Variance analysis Allows managers to see whether sales, production, and manufacturing costs are higher or lower than planned and, more important, *why* actual sales, production, and costs differ from budget (p. 330)

Vertical integration Accomplished when a company is involved in multiple steps of the value chain (p. 213)

Volume variance The difference between the flexible budget and the fixed overhead applied to a product (p. 342)

Working capital The excess of current assets over current liabilities, which is a measure of an entity's liquidity (p. 483)

Work-in-process inventory Inventory of unfinished product (in other words, what is left in the factory at the end of the period) (p. 31)

Zero-based budgeting Requires managers to build budgets from the ground up each year (p. 293)

Company Index

Subject Index